KERLY'S

LAW OF

TRADE MARKS

AND TRADE NAMES

THIRTEENTH EDITION

By

DAVID KITCHIN
One of Her Majesty's Counsel, 8 New Square

DAVID LLEWELYN
Solicitor, Partner, White & Case, London

JAMES MELLOR
Barrister, 8 New Square

RICHARD MEADE
Barrister, 8 New Square

THOMAS MOODY-STUART
Barrister, 8 New Square

Consulting Editor
The Hon. Sir Robin Jacob

LONDON
SWEET & MAXWELL
2001

First Edition	(1894)	By D. M. Kerly
Second Edition	(1901)	By D. M. Kerly
Third Edition	(1908)	By D. M. Kerly
Fourth Edition	(1913)	By F. G. Underhay
Fifth Edition	(1923)	By F. G. Underhay
Sixth Edition	(1927)	By F. G. Underhay
Seventh Edition	(1951)	By R. G. Loyd and F. E. Bray
Eighth Edition	(1960)	By R. G. Loyd
Ninth Edition	(1966)	By T. A. Blanco White
Tenth Edition	(1972)	By T. A. Blanco White and Robin Jacob
Eleventh Edition	(1983)	By T. A. Blanco White and Robin Jacob
Twelth Edition	(1986)	By T. A. Blanco White and Robin Jacob
Thirteenth Edition	(2001)	By D. Kitchin, D. Llewelyn, J. Mellor, R. Meade and T. Moody-Stuart

Published in 2001 by
Sweet & Maxwell Limited of
100 Avenue Road
London NW3 3PF

Typeset by LBJ Typesetting Ltd of Kingsclere
Printed and Bound in Great Britain
By Clays Ltd, St Ives Plc.

No natural forests were destroyed
to make this product, only farmed
timber was used and replanted.

ISBN 0421—45610—8

A CIP catalogue record for this book
is available from the British Library.

FOREWORD

It is a pleasure to welcome this new edition of one of the classic textbooks of English law. Kerly, first published in 1894, has been for generations a mainstay of trade mark practitioners.

Here, however, is not merely a classic, but a classic completely modernised. The new edition, the first since 1986, takes full account of the Trade Marks Act 1994, itself a wholesale modernisation of the law.

Above all, the new Act and the new law are now in many fundamental respects not only English law but European law. The new edition thus introduces the European dimension of trade mark law. The Act implements the 1988 Trade Marks Directive, which harmonises the laws of the Member States on many of the basic features of trade mark law. The Directive lays down, among many other things, the essential provisions governing the nature of a trade mark; the grounds for refusal or invalidity; the rights conferred by a trade mark; and the conditions governing the exhaustion of rights.

Moreover, national trade marks—all of them subject in these and other ways to the Directive—now coexist with the Community trade mark (introduced by the Community Trade Mark Regulation of 1993, Regulation 40/94). Since the Community trade mark is valid, and has identical effects, throughout the Community, the Trade Marks Act also makes provision for the Community trade mark.

Thus, while the Directive harmonises the national laws governing national trade marks, the Regulation creates the conditions for the constitution of a Community trade mark. The distinction between the Directive and the Regulation as sources of law is also of some importance; the Directive is implemented in the United Kingdom, as it has to be, by U.K. legislation, while the Regulation, like all E.C. regulations, is directly applicable in all Members States, although legislation may be necessary to give it full effect. The whole of U.K. law, however, has to be understood and interpreted in the light of the Community instruments—and indeed the Treaties.

Throughout this book, the authors show how the subject is affected by European law: both by the Community legislation (the Trade Marks Directive and the Community Trade Mark Regulation) and by the case law of the European Court of Justice, which is binding on the courts and tribunals of all Member States—the binding effect of the Court's case law being spelt out, for the United Kingdom, in section 3(1) of the European Communities Act 1972.

The Community legislation is broadly framed, and so too, therefore, is the U.K. Act. Many of the provisions call for interpretation, and it is this task which is given not only to the national courts, but also to the Court of Justice. Under Article 234 (formerly 177) of the E.C. Treaty, wherever a decision on a question of Community law is necessary to enable the national court to give judgment, the national court may, and courts of last instance must, refer the question to the Court of Justice.

The Court applies principles of interpretation which may differ from those of national law and from those traditionally followed by English courts. It will have regard to the purposes of the legislation, to the preamble (which may be lost sight of when the substantive provisions are transposed into national legislation) and if necessary to the different language versions of the Community texts: no fewer than eleven languages are now equally authentic. As national courts have recognised, the Court of Justice is best placed to resolve points of principle in the interpretation of Community texts. Moreover, its rulings, since they are binding on all national courts, will have the effect of maintaining the unity of the law.

Already the Court has ruled on numerous fundamental aspects of the Community legislation. Full account is given in this book of the Court's case law—rightly, in view of its binding character—and the authors are willing to examine the implications of the case law and how it might develop.

Some aspects of the Court's case law have been criticised—not least by English practitioners, and occasionally even by English judges. This is hardly surprising (have the decisions of any court on any important topic ever escaped criticism?), and I do not seek here to defend the case law "globally"—although I must record that in many encounters with practitioners across Europe, I have four d a high level of appreciation for the main lines of the case law.

From a European perspective, one of the great virtues of this book is that it recognises the European dimension. It thus recognises that the Act cannot be taken at face value: the Act must be understood in the light, in particular, of the Directive and, as the Court held in the *Marleasing* case, national courts must give effect to a directive by interpreting all national legislation, so far as possible, in the light of its wording and purpose in order to achieve the result it pursues.

Thus, the authors recognise that the approach to statutory interpretation customarily taken by English courts is not appropriate to the Act where effect has to be given to the Directive. Even where the Act directly transposes the Directive's provisions, it will be necessary to have regard, for example, to the preamble to the Directive; otherwise the provisions may mislead.

Because Kerly in this edition treats English Law in its European context, it can also be regarded as, in embryo, a European textbook: where it draws attention to points of Community law, and where it records the views of the English courts on questions of interpretation, it will be of interest not only to English practitioners but throughout the United Kingdom and the European Union.

The new edition of Kerly is therefore assured a wide as well as a warm welcome.

Francis G. Jacobs
Advocate General
Court of Justice of the European Communities.

PREFACE

Continue the following series: 7, 7, 5, 10, 4, 23, 9, 6, 6, 11, 3 . . . If someone had been asked that over the last few years, he would have been stumped for an answer. We now know the next number, though none after. That next is 14. I am, of course, talking about the number of years between successive editions of *Kerly*. Looked at "globally"—the "in" word from the ECJ—the answer is not too bad. *Kerly* has come out within six years of the new Trade Marks Act 1994. That is a lot better than the time it took for a new edition after the 1938 Act. Even the war was no excuse for it was not until 1951 that *Kerly* resurfaced. And the period from 1927 up to the Act had been wholly unproductive.

The current authors have a substantial achievement to their credit. After all, the entire law of registered trade marks has not only been re-written but has become ever so complicated. And there is already a mass of case law following upon the Trade Marks Directive. It is that case law which justifies the delay of *Kerly* until now. Of course, in theory, there might have been an edition hard upon the 1994 Act. But the book would have been of little use in the way of providing firm guidance, which is what *Kerly* is really for. A 1994 or 1995 *Kerly* would have included the Act, the Directive and the Community Trade Marks Regulation in the Appendices. But the text would have consisted merely of recitations of the important bits of these coupled with guesses as to what the courts would make of them. That would have been the best that could be done. Actually it *was* done. David Kitchin and James Mellor's 1995 commentary consisted of just that. It is instructive to compare what they wrote then with what has happened since. I will just go over some examples.

First, there was the thicket of potential problems caused by the United Kingdom's slightly late implementation of the Directive. Were there cases where a party could sue the State, could there be horizontal effects, etc.? A worry at the time, but in the event a non-problem.

Next, the authors wondered whether, for infringement, a sign had to be used as a trade mark. Was that implicit in the whole scheme of things even if the Directive, rather typically, abstained from dealing with such a basic concept? The Court of Appeal in *Philips*, and I in *Treat*, said no. I am still wondering whether that is right. We shall have to see what the ECJ says.

Another concept of the Directive, "similar goods", was bound to turn up in the courts soon. Kitchin and Mellor considered it but failed to predict the answer given by the ECJ in *Canon*. The concept is woolly—as long as a piece of string. I tried to give the string some sort of defined length in *Treat*. I was disappointed to find the ECJ take a different view in *Canon*—the concept is as long as a piece of elastic. To say, as the court did, that whether or not the goods of the infringer are "similar" to the goods of the registered mark depends in part on the degree of distinctiveness of the registered mark, means that one can never be quite sure where one stands. Goods may be "similar" one day and not the next or for one pair of marks but not another. I understand from practitioners that, in advising clients about infringement or registration, just what I feared would happen is indeed happening—pages of advice with significant uncertainty. I console myself with the thought that my working rule at the Bar is perhaps even truer now than it was then. I used to say that, by and large, the whole system of registered trade marks, save in the case of unused marks, was nearly unnecessary—if there was passing off the court stopped it, if not, not. The reader is invited to test the rule for him/herself.

Incidentally, the court, in *Canon*, made an assertion that I think is difficult to understand. It said that the more distinctive a mark, the more likely is it that a similar mark is likely to confuse. I think that observation is peculiar: the more famous a mark, the more likely is it that the public will recognise a difference between it and an alleged infringement. Take an example. Years ago I was in court when a consent copyright order was made stopping someone from selling shirts labelled "Horrids" with the familiar lettering of Harrods. In real life no one would be confused—if they were, the whole point of the offensive spoof would be missed. What is the legal status of a wrong statement of fact by the ECJ?

Moving on, the whole *Wagamama/Puma* saga has taken place. Kitchin and Mellor foresaw the problem but not the ferocity of the debate. That such a problem was left to the ECJ was evident from the Directive. I am glad of the resolution—a Rorschach inkblot rule for determining infringement would have been overprotective and of uncertain scope. Following on from that debate, it seems likely that the court is setting a standard for "confusion" which is not overprotective. The "nanny" view, that people must be protected even from their own silly careless-ness, does not look to be part of the future of trade marks.

Next I come to shape, a matter touched upon lightly by Kitchin and Mellor. It was entirely predictable that owners of well-known designs would seize upon the possibility of obtaining perpetual protection via the law of trade marks. *Philips* and *Lego* are obvious examples in the limelight now. But there are plenty of other people having a go at getting monopolies in designs, engineering artefacts and containers. The Official Journals of the United Kingdom and Alicante offices, as well as to OHIM Boards of Appeal decisions, show this clearly. This edition of *Kerly* can only report on the state of play. We shall have to see what the court makes of the difficult problems thrown up by this type of mark. The relevant part of the next edition will surely look different from what you find here.

Finally, I should mention a point to watch for the future. Trade marks are about signs used in trade. It is apparent from the specifications of goods being allowed by OHIM that owners are being allowed to register for ranges of goods or services far wider than their use, actual or intended. This causes the Office massive unnecessary work—hours are spent ploughing through long specifications to find out whether, buried in there, are goods or services of which the mark is descriptive. Even more seriously these overbroad registrations are likely to hamper trade. And of course they may put up costs for anyone seeking registration of a mark or contemplating using it. The problem needs resolution. Sooner, rather than later, rules will have to be developed to stop this nonsense. It is not good enough to say that there can be later part-cancellation of wide specifications for non-use. Who would bother with the expense and time involved when they want to get on with their business? An OHIM Board of Appeal missed a chance to deal with the problem in *Trillium TM* (March 28, 2000) by holding that the doctrine of bad faith cannot be used to deal with it. That may or may not be right. If it is not then another way ought to be found.

This edition has involved a mass of work by the authors. I admit to using the pressure of my office as an excuse for not actually writing anything for *Kerly*—the first time since 1972. I feel guilty at leaving it all to the authors. They have not only had to cope with all the new legislation, but with other things too. The new procedural rules, the Brussels Convention and the problems arising from the Internet are just obvious examples. On top of that there has been the regular accretion of case law in fields, such as passing off, E.U. and competition law. In truth, this edition of *Kerly* is a new start. It is the foundation for a line of editions stretching into the far future. It does not read like a first draft. But it is just that—of the next and successive editions. With so much spadework now done, one can confidently expect that the next number in the series will be a lot less than 14.

Robin Jacob
The Royal Courts of Justice
August 2000

ACKNOWLEDGMENTS

If the original team (DK, JM, RM) had appreciated the amount of work involved in producing this edition of *Kerly*, the process might never have been started. We were very grateful to be joined by TMS and particularly by DL, without whose work the process might never have been finished. As we anticipated in the Supplement to the 12th Edition, virtually the entire book has been re-written. Special thanks go to Shereagh Dunphy and Ben Muir, whose analysis of all passing-off cases decided since the last edition significantly reduced the amount of time required on Chapter 14. We are indebted also to Mark Chacksfield for his work on Chapter 16. All involved at Sweet & Maxwell have been very patient with us in guiding this edition to publication.

We have attempted to state the law as at June 1, 2000, but have included as many decisions as possible which were given after that date and before the proofs were finalised. Responsibility for all errors and omissions lies with us alone. Please address any comments on editorial matters to *kerly@8newsquare.co.uk.*

DK, DL, JM, RM, TMS
October 2000

CONTENTS

CONTENTS

APPENDICES

TABLE OF CASES

TABLE OF STATUTES

[References in bold type indicate the text of the provisions concerned]

TABLE OF STATUTORY INSTRUMENTS

[References in bold type indicate the text of the provisions concerned]

TABLE OF EUROPEAN LEGISLATION

[References in bold type indicate the text of the provisions concerned]

TABLE OF INTERNATIONAL CONVENTIONS AND TREATIES

[References in bold type indicate the text of the provisions concerned]

PART 1

CHAPTER 1

INTRODUCTION

Since the last edition of this work, registered trade mark law in the **1–01**
United Kingdom has undergone fundamental changes and to a large
extent has started from scratch. The trade marks regime begun by the
Trade Marks Act, 1875, which was itself founded upon earlier equitable
principles, has been replaced exactly a century after the first edition of
Kerly by a system much of the detail of which is dictated by developments at the European Community and international level.

The principal basis for the Trade Marks Act 1994 (the Act) is the 1988 **1–02**
Council Directive relating to trade marks, which required important
changes in two main areas: the conditions for validly registering a trade
mark and the rights conferred by registration. The detail of these
changes is set out and explained in Chapters 5 and 13: basically, it is
now easier to obtain registered trade marks and the rights conferred by
registration are broader than under previous Acts. Secondly, the Act
makes provision in connection with the Community Trade Mark introduced by Council Regulation 40/94 of December 20, 1993. Thirdly, effect
is given to the Madrid Protocol which provides a mechanism for so-
called "international registration of trade marks". Fourthly, the Act
gives long overdue effect to certain provisions of the Paris Convention
of 1883. Overall, the effect is to bring about "a general modernisation of
the law of trade marks".

1. The origins of the trade marks directive

The Trade Marks Directive is "The First Council Directive of 21 **1–03**
December 1988 to approximate the laws of the Member States relating to
trade marks"; "The First" indicating that approximation is not complete.
The third recital to the Directive says:

> ". . . it does not appear to be necessary at present to undertake full-
> scale approximation of the trade marks laws of the Member States
> and it will be sufficient if approximation is limited to those national
> provisions of law which most directly affect the functioning of the
> internal market".

The first proposal for "a first Council Directive to approximate the law **1–04**
of the Member States relating to trade marks" was published in

November 1980.[1] It coincided with a proposal for the Community Trade Mark. The proposed Directive was seen as a necessary step to pave the way for the establishment of a Community Trade Mark system. The proposal was submitted to the Economic and Social Committee for its opinion[2] which resulted in a revised proposal being submitted to the Council in December 1985.[3] This revised text was submitted to the Working Group and a new text was published in December 1987.

The Council approved the new text[4] in June 1988, the advice of the Economic and Social Committee was received in October 1988, the European Parliament gave its opinion in December 1988;[5] and the Directive was finally adopted by the Council on December 21, 1988.[6]

1–05 At the meeting of the Council at which the Directive was adopted, certain statements were made by the Council and the Commission which were entered into the Minutes of the Council. The Minutes have subsequently become available and are accessible on the website of the Office for the Harmonisation of the Internal Market (OHIM). Although of historical interest, it is now relatively clear that the Minutes (which consist of various comments on a number of the Articles in the Directive) are of no legal significance and cannot be used for the purpose of interpreting legislation as no reference is made to them in the wording of the Directive.[7] The Minutes have been referred to on a number of occasions by the Appeal Boards at OHIM,[8] but the better view is that such reference has been made only when the Minutes support a position adopted by the relevant Board and not because they are in any way binding or of legal significance.

2. Statutory interpretation and *Pepper (Inspector of Taxes) v. Hart*

1–06 Quite apart from matters European, the standard rules in *Pepper (Inspector of Taxes) v. Hart*[9] apply to the Parliamentary debates during passage of the Trade Marks Bill. It should be noted that the rule in *Pepper (Inspector of Taxes) v. Hart* operates by way of an exception to the general rule that excludes reference to Parliamentary material as an aid to statutory construction. Reference is permitted under *Pepper (Inspector of Taxes) v. Hart* if: (1) legislation was ambiguous or obscure or led to absurdity; (2) the material relied upon consisted of one or more

---

[1] See the Explanatory Memorandum, COM (80) 635 final, and the first draft of the Directive, December 31, 1980: [1980] O.J. C351/1.

[2] [1981] O.J. C310/22.

[3] [1985] O.J. C251/4.

[4] In E.U. parlance "adopted a common position".

[5] [1988] O.J. C309.

[6] [1989] O.J. L40/1. See Appendix 7.

[7] *R. v. Immigration Appeal Tribunal, ex p. Antonissen* [1991] 2 C.M.L.R. 373, ECJ.

[8] See, *e.g. Giacomelli*, at 2–84 *et seq.*

[9] [1993] A.C. 593.

statements by a Minister or other promoter of the Bill together, if necessary, with such other Parliamentary material that is necessary to understand such statements and their effect; and (3) the statements relied upon were clear.

However, the Parliamentary debates on the Bill are unlikely to **1–07** provide much fruit to aid interpretation of provisions in Part I of the Act, for the simple reason that the Government resisted and secured the defeat or withdrawal of all amendments which altered wording derived from the Trade Marks Directive, by saying that they were obliged to implement the Directive. Thus:

"in the case of a provision intended to implement a Directive I cannot think that the *Pepper* principle can apply. The intention of Parliament is to implement whatever the Directive means. Views expressed in Parliament about the meaning, even by a Minister, cannot assist in resolving any ambiguity which stems from the Directive itself. Neither the courts of any other country whose trade mark laws are supposed to implement the Directive, or the European Court of Justice in interpreting it, would refer to what a British Minister said in Parliament in the course of implementation here. It would be irrelevant. What matters is the language of the Directive",

per Jacob J. in the *"Treat"* case.[10]

The learned judge also declined to refer to *Hansard* for the same reason, although this may still be possible in relation to provisions contained in the remainder of the Act, particularly the criminal provisions contained in section 92.

3. Community trade mark

The 1993 Council Regulation introducing the Community Trade Mark **1–08** (CTM) means that it is now possible to obtain a registered trade mark with effect in the United Kingdom by two different routes. The first is the traditional route to the Trade Marks Registry in Newport[11] (which may now be made via Geneva—see below); the second is via an application to the Office for the Harmonisation of the Internal Market (OHIM) in Alicante, Spain. If satisfied that the mark complies with the conditions for registrability set out in the Regulation, OHIM will grant a E.U.-wide right with effect in the United Kingdom as well as all other Member States. Thus, the two systems run in parallel and the details of the CTM system are set out in Chapter 6.

---

[10] [1996] R.P.C. 281 at 292.
[11] Or through the branch offices.

4. Madrid Protocol

1–09 A United Kingdom registered trade mark may now be obtained via the mechanism provided in the Madrid Protocol.[12] Under the Protocol an applicant for a so-called "international registration" must file through the national trade marks office in which a base national application or registration has been made. That office then transmits the application to WIPO in Geneva and thereafter the mark is sent to and treated by the individual national offices specified as if it is a normal domestic application. Effectively, the Protocol provides a means of obtaining registrations in a large number of signatory countries at less cost and inconvenience than if applications were filed in each country separately. The details are set out in Chapter 6.

5. Paris Convention

1–10 For the first time, the 1994 Act provides specific protection for "well-known marks" within the meaning of Article 6*bis* of the Paris Convention. The protection conferred is independent of the rights conferred by registration and applies to marks falling within Article 6*bis* regardless of whether they are registered in the United Kingdom or not. Other provisions specifically implementing parts of the Paris Convention include the injunctive remedy, based on Article 6*septies*, for a proprietor of a mark against unauthorised use in the United Kingdom by his agent.

The details of how the Act gives effect to certain provisions of the Paris Convention are set out in the relevant sections of this work.

6. Old authorities

1–11 Whilst it is true that the 1994 Act provides a fresh start for the law of registered trade marks in the United Kingdom, every system for the registration of trade marks has to deal with the underlying concepts forming the foundation of such a system: concepts such as distinctiveness; what is required for registration; descriptiveness; what degree will prevent registration; similarity between a registered mark and an allegedly infringing sign; what degree of similarity is required for infringement. What a coherent trade mark system has to do when dealing with these (and other) concepts is to decide where the line is drawn: for example, what degree of distinctiveness or descriptiveness or similarity or confusion/risk of confusion is required? It is in these areas, as well as many others, that reference to cases decided under previous Acts is frequently of assistance. But assistance only: it should not be

---

[12] This is a Protocol to the Madrid Agreement 1891, which in turn is a specialised agreement under the Paris Convention 1883. The U.K. is not a party to the Madrid Agreement.

forgotten at any point that the system is fundamentally different and frequently demands a fresh look.

On the other hand, the forensic nature of the legal process in the **1–12** United Kingdom requires a deep analysis of both the purpose and coherence of the new system. It is the words of the Act (and behind it the TM Directive) which must be interpreted and applied: as was noted by Laddie J. in *Wagamama*[13] if a fundamental change is intended it should be made clear, in extent and scope. The law remains a law of registered trade marks, it is not a law against unfair competition and in applying and interpreting the provisions of the Act (and the TM Directive and the CTM Regulation, when relevant) the practitioner must always bear this in mind.

7. Common law

Other aspects of the legal treatment of unfair trading have changed **1–13** significantly in the years since the last edition and developments in areas such as passing off and trade libel are described and commented upon. In addition, to a large extent the chapters on passing off and trade libel have been re-written in a more modern format.

8. Procedure

In recent years there has been a marked shift in the attitude of the courts **1–14** away from the use of the interim injunction as the main tool for curtailing alleged trade mark infringements or passing off. This has been coupled with a streamlining of procedure and more pro-active judicial involvement to ensure a shortening of the time taken to litigate intellectual property disputes. In addition, in April 1999, the new Civil Procedure Rules (CPR) became operative, with the overriding objective of "enabling the courts to deal with cases justly".[14] The CPR apply both to High Court proceedings involving trade marks and to proceedings in the Registry. They move procedure in the English courts in the direction of the civil law tradition, at least to the extent of making judges the managers of litigation through its various stages.

Where relevant, changes in procedure are identified and commented upon.

---

[13] See para. 8–59.
[14] CPR, r. 1.1.

CHAPTER 2

THE DEFINITION OF A TRADE MARK

1. Introduction

2–01 "Section 1

> (1) In this Act a "trade mark" means any sign capable of being represented graphically which is capable of distinguishing goods or services of one undertaking from those of other undertakings.
>
> A trade mark may, in particular, consist of words (including personal names), designs, letters, numerals or the shape of goods or their packaging.
>
> (2) References in this Act to a trade mark include, unless the context otherwise requires, references to a collective mark (see section 49) or certification mark (see section 50)."

2–02 The Trade Marks Act 1994 starts with this fundamental definition of "trade mark", which applies to every type of mark. This chapter is concerned with signs or marks of individual undertakings. Collective and certification marks perform a somewhat different function and are dealt with in Chapter 11.

2–03 The definition contains four requirements. To qualify as a trade mark, the candidate must be (1) a sign which (2) is capable of being represented graphically and which (3) is capable of distinguishing the goods or services of one undertaking from those of other undertakings. The fourth requirement is subsumed in the third: it is that the sign in question must be used in relation to goods or services. For most marks, this fourth requirement passes without notice. However, it achieves significance in the debate over whether registrations for "retail services" and the like should be permitted, a topic discussed at the end of this chapter.

2–04 The three principal requirements will be discussed in turn. The first two are self-contained and are dealt with in this chapter, as is the interpretation of the third requirement—"capable of distinguishing". It will be seen that there is a good deal of interplay between section 1(1) and section 3(1), particularly as regards this third requirement. It is part of the key issue of distinctiveness, which is discussed further in the context of the absolute grounds for refusal of a mark—see Chapter 7. The first of those grounds, in section 3(1)(a), cross-refers to this

8

definition in section 1(1), and prohibits registration of a sign which does not meet the requirements of section 1(1).

Derivation[1]

Section 1(1) of the 1994 Act is derived from Article 2 of the Trade Marks **2–05** Directive. There is some change in language: Article 2 appears to be permissive: "A trade mark may consist of. . ." whereas section 1(1) is definitive: "In this Act a trade mark means. . .", with the result that the Act does not expand upon the definition in the TM Directive. The definition of a Community trade mark[2] is substantially identical to the definition in the TM Directive.

2. Sign

The word "sign" is used in the 1994 Act and TM Directive as a general **2–06** term to include all candidates which may constitute a "trade mark" and all candidates for allegations of infringement.[3] It is clear that a "sign" must signify something or convey a message. There is an argument that the message conveyed by a "sign" must be something to do with the goods or services, so that a mere decoration would not even constitute a sign. The sign may be a badge of origin, in which case the sign will qualify as a trade mark. A sign may convey a message which is descriptive or laudatory of the goods, but it is still conveying a message concerning the goods or services in question.

In terms of what types of sign may qualify as trade marks, the use of **2–07** the word "sign" makes the definition of "trade mark" flexible and open-ended, subject only to the other requirements. Section 1(1) includes a list of examples of what types of sign are included. The list is obviously not exhaustive.

The passing of the 1994 Act gave rise to debate about the types of mark which became registrable for the first time. "Sign" is an expression wide enough to include a wide range of unusual marks, such as marks consisting of a single colour, a smell, a sound or a moving image. The challenge for such unusual signs is in satisfying the other requirements for registration, subjects which are discussed in further detail below.

---

[1] Derivation is discussed in more detail below at 2–62 *et seq.*
[2] See the CTM Regulation, Art. 4.
[3] The 1994 Act, s.10, uses the neutral word "sign" (as opposed to "trade mark", used in s.9) to describe what infringes a registered trade mark. Section 11 uses both "sign" and "indication" in defining some of the defences to infringement.

3. Capable of being represented graphically

2–08 In order to be the subject of a valid application or registration, the sign must be represented graphically. In this part of section 1(1) of the 1994 Act, the capability must be realised.[4]

Selecting the graphic representation

2–09 The selection of the graphic representation is an important step for any applicant because the trade mark is defined by the graphic representation which is filed on or with the application form. The graphic representation provides a fixed point of reference showing what the mark is. During the application process, the ability to amend the graphic representation is extremely limited, since it is only possible to correct errors of wording or copying or obvious mistakes and even those corrections must not substantially affect the identity of the trade mark.

2–10 Almost every applicant has some degree of manoeuvre when selecting the graphic representation for his application. Even conventional word marks are likely to be used or proposed to be used in a particular script and/or in conjunction with other distinctive matter. In such a case, the applicant may have to choose between representing his sign (1) with all accompanying distinctive matter; (2) as the word in the particular script; or (3) as the word in any script. In making the choice, the applicant has to consider the particular circumstances of his sign and balance the desire to secure wider rights for his sign against the risk that the graphic representation he selects may increase the force of any absolute or relative grounds for refusal. At least for conventional marks, this type of selection process is not new, being a familiar process under the 1938 Act.

2–11 Under the open-ended definition contained in section 1(1) of the 1994 Act, it is possible to characterise as a "sign" virtually any feature used in trade. The more unconventional the feature or sign, the greater the problems for the applicant in meeting the requirements of graphic representation and capability of distinguishing. The remainder of this discussion is largely directed at the sorts of problems which arise for unconventional signs.

Reasons for this requirement

2–12 This requirement arises from important practical considerations concerned with certainty. First, the relevant trade mark office must know with certainty what is comprised in the sign in question, so that it can

---

[4] Until the applicant files a graphic representation which is acceptable, the U.K. Registry treats the application as incomplete, with the result that the application is not afforded a filing date until it is complete: see *Ty Nant Spring Water Ltd's Application* [1999] E.T.M.R. 981 (apptd person, G. Hobbs Q.C.). The Registry issues a "filing deficiency notice" under r. 11, which gives the applicant two months within which to present an acceptable representation. See PAC 2/00, paras 6–8.

maintain an accessible Register of Trade Marks and fulfil its functions of examination and publication of applications. Secondly, and of greater importance, other traders must be able to ascertain with certainty exactly what their competitors (actual or potential) have registered or have applied to register. These considerations have been explained as follows:

"It is . . . essential for traders to be able to identify with clarity what the registered trade mark is. . . . This is a fundamental aspect of the law and it is for this reason that the graphical representation, being the means by which the trade mark is defined, must be adequate to enable the public to determine precisely what the sign is that is the subject of the registration."[5]

"The degree of precision with which the sign is represented must **2-13** be sufficient to permit full and effective implementation of the provisions of the Act relating to absolute unregistrability (section 3), relative unregistrability (section 5), infringement (section 10) and public inspection of the Register (section 63). These provisions call for a fixed point of reference: a graphic representation in which the identity of the relevant sign is clearly and unambiguously recorded. There may be more than one way of representing a sign graphically with that degree of precision. It seems clear that a sign (such as a sound or aroma) can be taken to have been represented graphically with the required degree of precision when figuratively represented, even though interpretation or analysis may then be required in order to detect or demonstrate use of it."[6]

For those dealing with more unconventional trade marks, there may be **2-14** more than one way in which to represent the sign graphically, in which case the applicant may have to balance competing considerations. On the one hand, the scope of the rights obtained through registration of one form of graphic representation may be wider because the sign is defined in a less precise manner than is dictated by another form of graphic representation. On the other hand, the applicant will be concerned to ensure that his choice of representation is acceptable to the Registry, not least so that he maintains the priority of his filing date. The general scheme of the 1994 Act is that rights are secured by the first to file, rather than the first to use (which was broadly the position under the 1938 Act). In practice, wealthy traders can avoid any dilemma by filing a number of applications, each one featuring a more ambitious graphic representation.[7] In that way, the trader avoids any priority concerns but at the same time presses the boundaries of graphic

---

[5] Simon Thorley Q.C. as the appointed person in *Swizzels Matlow Ltd's Application (No. 2)* [2000] E.T.M.R. 58.
[6] Geoffrey Hobbs Q.C. as the appointed person in *Ty Nant Spring Water Ltd's Trade Mark Application* [2000] R.P.C. 55.
[7] Although they might not want to signal their intentions so clearly.

representation so as to secure the widest possible protection for the signs he considers to be distinctive of his goods or services. For less wealthy traders, it may be important to get the graphic representation right first time.

Approach taken by the United Kingdom Trade Marks Registry

2–15 The Trade Mark Registry is wise to the fact that the graphic representation is one respect in which applicants may attempt to widen the scope of their rights. When deciding whether a sign is properly and adequately graphically represented, the Registry apply three criteria, which have been approved as "highly relevant considerations".[8] The criteria are set out in the Registry Work Manual,[9] as follows:

> "In the Registrar's view, a sign is graphically represented when:
>
> (a) it is possible to determine from the graphical representation precisely what the sign is that the applicant uses or proposes to use without the need for supporting samples etc;
>
> (b) the graphical representation can stand in place of the sign used or proposed to be used by the applicant because it represents that sign and no other;
>
> (c) it is reasonably practicable for persons inspecting the register, or reading the Trade Marks Journal, to understand from the graphical representation what the trade mark is."

These criteria have been reinforced by Practice Amendment Circular 2/00, which addresses the subject of acceptable forms of graphical representation.

2–16 The first criterion confirms that the sign is defined by the graphic representation on the form of application. Provided that the observer has first been equipped with any skills necessary to interpret the graphic representation (as to which, see below at 2–19), the representation should stand on its own to identify the trade mark. It is not permissible to refer to extraneous matter, either explicitly or implicitly. The idea of an implicit reference may seem odd, but an applicant may, deliberately or otherwise, choose to file a graphic representation which does not precisely define the sign he actually uses.[10] It is a natural tendency for anyone looking at a graphic representation to try to understand and make sense of it. Unconsciously, the observer may be filling in the gaps

---

[8] By Simon Thorley Q.C. as the appointed person in *Swizzels Matlow Ltd's Application (No. 2)* [2000] E.T.M.R. 58.

[9] Chap. 6, para. 2.3 (August 1998 edition).

[10] See, *e.g.* the written description in *Swizzels Matlow Ltd's Application (No. 2)* [2000] E.T.M.R. 58: "The trade mark consists of a circular compressed tablet bearing a raised heart outline on both flat surfaces and containing within the heart outline on one side any of several different words or phrases.", which some will recognise as *a* description of "Lovehearts".

by drawing on his knowledge of the sign which the trader actually uses in practice. This must be resisted. Any prior knowledge of the way in which a sign may be used in practice must be put out of mind when examining the graphic representation.[11]

The second criterion refers to the degree of precision with which the **2–17** trade mark should represent the sign which the applicant either uses or proposes to use in trade. The required degree of precision is given in the passages set out above: "a fixed point of reference: a graphic representation in which the identity of the sign is clearly and unambiguously recorded". The sign which is either used or proposed to be used in trade must obviously be the guide, together with the public perception, actual or anticipated, of the sign. It is suggested that the representation should be a faithful one, particularly if the sign has not yet been used. If the sign has been used and the applicant wishes to register a less than faithful representation of it, there must be a heavy onus on him to justify that his alternative representation should be registered.[12] Of course, lack of precision in the representation which is sought to be registered may create greater problems for the applicant in showing that the representation possesses sufficient distinctive character to warrant registration. In exceptional circumstances, it may be possible to justify an alternative representation by showing that it coincides with the public perception of the trade mark.

The third criterion is concerned with the ease with which the graphic **2–18** representation can be understood. There can be no uniform standard, it must be a question of degree depending largely on the type of mark involved. However, it is suggested that once the observer has been equipped with the necessary interpretative skills, understanding what the mark comprises should be an immediate[13] consequence. If undue effort is required to understand the graphic representation, or if the observer is left in a state of uncertainty, it is likely to be an indication that the representation as filed does not adequately represent the sign which lies behind the application. More effort is likely to be required to understand representations of less conventional types of mark.

How much interpretation is permissible

The remaining issue concerns the range of interpretative skills with **2–19** which the notional observer from the relevant trade comes equipped. It is obvious that understanding what a trade mark is should be easy.

---

[11] PAC 2/00 says "The representation put forward should not assume that the reader has prior knowledge of the actual sign used by the applicant", but if the reader does have prior knowledge, it must be put out of mind.

[12] PAC 2/00 says: "Attempts to define signs more broadly in terms of perceived infringement rights inevitably lead to ambiguity and rejection."

[13] PAC 2/00 says this: "Any colour standards, musical notation or scientific measurements put forward to represent marks must be precise and (a) make it reasonably practical for users of the system to be able to obtain a clear understanding of the mark, and (b) be able to accurately compare the sign the applicant uses or proposes to use with other similar signs."

After all, for a trade mark to carry out its function in the market, recognition of it by the relevant public has to be almost instantaneous. It is suggested that the notional observer cannot be expected to have anything more than familiarity with everyday skills and modes of expression. Some examples should illustrate the point.

2–20   (1) Signs which contain words, designs, letters or numerals are considered conventional. The only skills required to understand the graphic representation of such marks are a familiarity with our alphabet, our systems of numerals and a degree of literacy, all of which are taken for granted.

(2) The same skills are required to understand a written description of a sign. However, written descriptions alone raise particular problems which are considered below at 2–24.

2–21   (3) Three-dimensional signs (shapes, etc.) are normally expected to be graphically represented by a line drawing or photograph. Line drawings are likely to be easier to understand, being clearer and more precise than photographs.

(4) A sound mark may be graphically represented in conventional musical notation: notes on a stave.[14] It seems to be accepted that the notional observer can understand musical notation, even though only a musician may be able to understand the representation immediately, whereas others less familiar with musical notation may either require some help or more time to work out what the sound is. Other non-musical sound marks may be represented using onomatopoeic words,[15] where no special skills are required.

2–22   (5) So far as colour marks are concerned, the United Kingdom Registry appears to accept colours being defined by reference to well-known colour standards such as Pantone. The alternative is simply to file a representation showing the actual colour which is claimed. Attempts to define colours by reference to anything more complicated than Pantone colours are likely to be rejected.[16] For example, a mark defined as "a blue bottle of optical characteristics such that if the wall thickness is 3 mm the bottle has, in air, a dominant wavelength of 472 to 474 nanometres, a purity of 44 to 48%, an optical brightness of 28 to

---

[14] A Dutch company providing IP and marketing advice managed to register in the Benelux marks using nine different ways of representing what was essentially a sound mark consisting of the first nine notes of "Fur Elise", and three different ways of representing another sound mark of the crowing of a cock. A number of the representations were word marks, probably because there are difficulties in registering sound marks in Benelux. Claims for infringement of all these marks were rejected: *Shield Mark BV v. B.Kist* [2000] E.T.M.R. 147.

[15] An example from America is the mark "Clop, clop, clop, moo" for restaurant services. A CTM application for the sound mark "click" was rejected because the representation was insufficiently clear and precise: Case R1/1998–2, OHIM BoA, noted as *Qlicksmart Pty Ltd's Application* [1999] E.T.M.R. 335.

[16] Further guidelines on colours are contained in PAC 2/00.

32%." required the use of a spectrophotometer to translate those optical characteristics into the colour known as cobalt blue or to test any other colour to see if it fell within the definition. The precision in the definition served to veil the identity of the sign.[17]

(6) The same point applies to marks consisting of an aroma: **2–23** precision could be achieved using gas or high performance liquid chromatography, but it would conceal the identity of the sign. There are accepted standards of classification for odorants such as Zwaardemaker (1985), with 30 sub-classes, or Linnaeus (1756) with seven classes, but any graphical representation for a smell mark is likely to be rejected unless phrased using everyday terms, for example, "the smell of fresh cut grass" for tennis balls.[18]

Descriptions in words alone

In general terms, a graphic representation which consists only of a **2–24** description in words requires careful scrutiny. In particular circumstances, a description in words alone may be acceptable: perhaps the best example to date is the sign consisting of "the smell of fresh cut grass" for tennis balls.[19] That description was held to give clear enough information to those reading it to be able to walk away with an immediate and unambiguous idea of what the mark is. Generally, however, trade mark examiners are right to be suspicious where the applicant has chosen a verbal description of his sign. This is particularly so where the description concerns a three-dimensional shape mark, where one would normally expect to see the mark defined in a line drawing or photograph showing the shape itself. In those circumstances, the conclusion is almost irresistible that the applicant is trying to avoid defining his sign with any degree of precision, hoping that he will obtain wider rights using a description. It has been rightly observed that it is unlikely that a mere description of a three-dimensional article would, in practice, ever be sufficiently precise to meet the needs of the Act,[20] and there are already numerous examples where a description was held not to be an acceptable representation of the mark. They did not provide the necessary "fixed point of reference":

---

[17] *Ty Nant Spring Water Ltd's Trade Mark Application* [2000] R.P.C. 55 (apptd person).
[18] *Venootschap Onder Firma Senta Aromatic Marketing's Application* [1999] E.T.M.R. 429, OHIM BoA. An example from America is "The mark is a high impact, fresh, floral fragrance reminiscent of Plumeria blossoms" registered for sewing thread and embroidery yarn.
[19] See n. 18, above.
[20] By the appointed person, Simon Thorley Q.C., in *Swizzels Matlow Ltd's Application (No. 2)* [2000] E.T.M.R. 58 ("Lovehearts"). Prompted by that observation, PAC 2/00 states: "The Registrar will normally refuse to accord a filing date to applications describing three-dimensional marks in words until a pictorial representation of the shape is filed."

2-25   (1) A sign described as "a chewy sweet on a stick" was held to be incapable of being represented graphically.[21]

(2) The application for a three-dimensional mark contained the following representation: "the trade mark consists of a circular compressed tablet bearing a raised heart outline on both flat surfaces and containing within the heart outline on one side any of several different words or phrases." That description was held to be inadequate to constitute a graphical representation.[22] It was also said that "the description pre-supposes a knowledge on the part of the trader of the Lovehearts product as sold over the years and as is shown in [the] declaration. This cannot be a correct approach."

2-26   (3) The graphic representation was a hologram. The applicant admitted that it was "very unlikely that a relatively low number of photographic views would suffice for a complete description of the mark". Accordingly, the mark was not graphically represented and the application rejected under section 3(1)(a) of the 1994 Act.[23]

(4) "The marks consist of a set of forty nine coloured lottery balls, each marked with a number. . . nine white balls. . . ten blue balls. . . ten pink balls . . ." etc. The application was rejected under section 3(1)(a).[24]

2-27 Examples from OHIM are:

(a) A sign described as "the vacuum packing of an article of clothing in an envelope of plastic" was held by the Second Board of Appeal at OHIM not to convey a clear and precise appearance of the mark itself. The description could not be considered to be a *reproduction* of the mark[25] (emphasis added). The issue concerning the requirement to file a reproduction of the mark is discussed further below at 2–28.

(b) The applicant specified the type of mark as a colour mark and stated that the mark consisted of the colour "orange". Objection was taken that this description was too vague, since the wide generic term "orange" encompassed a wide range of different colour shades, from dark to light and from yellowish to reddish orange.[26]

(c) By contrast, an application for the colour mark LIGHT GREEN included a specimen of the precise colour claimed together with

[21] *Swizzels Matlow Ltd's Application (No.1)* [1998] R.P.C. 244, (Regy).
[22] *Swizzels Matlow Ltd's Application (No.2)* [2000] E.T.M.R. 58. Simon Thorley Q.C. as the appointed person.
[23] *Checkpoint Security Services Ltd's Application*, June 7, 1999. (Regy).
[24] *Camelot Group Plc's Application* SRIS O/125/99, April 8, 1999 (Regy). "The description filed gives rise to an infinite variety of marks."
[25] *Antoni and Alison's Application* [1998] E.T.M.R. 460, OHIM BoA.
[26] *Orange Ltd's Application* [1998] E.T.M.R. 337, OHIM BoA.

the following description "the colour light-green itself in the specific hue as is shown on the enclosed specimen of the colour". This was an acceptable graphic representation, although the application was refused on other grounds.[27]

Descriptions of three-dimensional signs

There has been a slight divergence in practice between OHIM and the United Kingdom Registry as to what is required for a three-dimensional sign to be graphically represented. The United Kingdom Registry allows for the possibility, in exceptional cases, of a three-dimensional mark being registered on the basis of a description only, whereas OHIM appears not to do so, at least for the moment. The OHIM position is probably the result of a combination of an ill-drafted rule 3 (representation of the mark) of the Implementing Regulation, and muddled interpretation. Rule 3 adopts the following scheme: if the applicant does not claim any special graphic feature or colour, the mark should be reproduced in normal script on the application form; otherwise, rule 3(2) says that the mark must be *reproduced* on a sheet accompanying the application form; in those cases covered by rule 3(2), rule 3(3) provides that the application may contain a *description* of the mark if a three-dimensional mark is applied for, then rule 3(4) requires the representation to consist of either a photographic or a graphic representation of the mark (emphasis added).

2-28

In *Antoni and Alison's Application*[28] the Board of Appeal decided that these provisions required a reproduction or visual image of the sign to be filed. The Board held that a mere description of the sign was not enough, even if it conveyed the clear and precise appearance of the mark itself, because a description could not be considered to be a reproduction. This cannot have been intended to be the position, as was explained by the appointed person in *Swizzels Matlow's Application*[29]: one can have a representation of the sign in question which is not a visual image or reproduction of it, perhaps the best example being the use of musical notation to represent a sound mark, and there are other means of figurative representation of signs which constitute graphic representations yet which are not visual images or reproductions of the sign. The Board of Appeal may have failed to appreciate the distinction between the sign and the mark. The mark is the graphic representation (whether it is a description or something else). Rule 3(2) requires nothing more than a reproduction of the mark, *i.e.* a reproduction of the graphic representation.

2-29

---

[27] *Wm Wrigley Jr Company's Application* [1999] E.T.M.R. 214, OHIM BoA.
[28] [1998] E.T.M.R. 460. The sign was described as "the vacuum packing of an article of clothing in an envelope of plastic". The application was rightly rejected as not being graphically represented, but for the wrong reasons. The real point was that the description was too vague and imprecise.
[29] *Swizzels Matlow Ltd's Application (No. 2)* [2000] E.T.M.R. 58, Mr Simon Thorley Q.C. (Lovehearts).

Consequence of deficiency in graphic representation

2–30 If it is concluded that the graphic representation is inadequate, it does not follow that the application concerns a sign which is not "capable of being represented graphically". An applicant may then be given an opportunity to file a proper graphic representation, which he must do within two months.[30] The consequence is a loss of priority, because an application is only accorded a filing date once everything required is furnished by the applicant either to the United Kingdom Registry[31] or to OHIM.[32]

4. Capable of distinguishing the goods or services of one undertaking from those of other undertakings

Summary

2–31 For those who do not need or desire to know the detail, this is a summary of the United Kingdom interpretation of this expression and in particular the words "capable of distinguishing". Necessarily, reference must be made to section 3(1) of the 1994 Act because section 3(1)(a) incorporates this requirement by reference: "signs which do not satisfy the requirements of section 1(1)" shall not be registered.

> (1) To satisfy this requirement in section 1(1) a sign need only be "capable" to the limited extent of being "not incapable" of distinguishing goods or services of one undertaking from those of other undertakings: *AD2000*.[33]
>
> (2) This requirement is the first stage of three in the test for distinctiveness:
>
> > (a) first, a sign must comply with this requirement before it is elevated to the status of a "trade mark";
> >
> > (b) secondly, the "trade mark" is considered against section 3(1)(b),(c) or (d) (devoid of distinctive character, descriptive or generic);
> >
> > (c) thirdly, and only if one or more of subsections (1)(b), (c) or (d) of section 3 apply, the proviso to section 3(1) is applied to see if the trade mark has acquired a distinctive character through use: *AD2000; Philips v. Remington*[34]*; Bach Flower Remedies*[35]*; Maasland N.V.'s Application.*[36]

---

[30] Trade Mark Rules, r. 11, which gives a period of two months to remedy any deficiencies. For CTM applications, the Implementing Regulation, r. 9(2) is to the same effect.
[31] 1994 Act, s.33(1).
[32] Implementing Regulation, r. 9(1).
[33] [1997] R.P.C. 168, G Hobbs Q.C. as the appointed person.
[34] [1999] R.P.C. 809, CA.
[35] [2000] R.P.C. 513, CA.
[36] August 3, 1999, G. Hobbs Q.C. as the appointed person.

(3) In considering whether a sign is "capable of distinguishing", it **2–32** is permissible to take into account the use which has been made of the sign *in so far as the prior use affects the meaning of the sign,* even though it is not permissible to apply the proviso to section 3(1) to section 3(1)(a). In other words, use can affect meaning but any distinctive character acquired by use must be ignored: *Bach Flower Remedies; Maasland N.V.'s Application.*

(4) It may be permissible to take a short cut (by-passing this requirement) and simply ask whether the sign possesses "a distinctive character",[37] because that is what subsections (1)(a) to (d) of section 3 require: *Maasland N.V.'s Application.*

At this point, three observations will be made. First, if the position **2–33** appears confusing, it is. Secondly, according to this interpretation the Trade Marks Act 1994 appears to contain, in section 1(1), a definition of "trade mark" which happens to include a large category of signs which do not perform the essential function of a trade mark, which is to act as a badge of origin, to distinguish the goods or services of one undertaking from those of other undertakings. Thirdly, the debate over the interpretation of "capable of distinguishing" does not really matter to properly registrable trade marks. It only matters in the case of applications at the very border-line of distinctiveness and registrability.

It is suggested that the correct interpretation of "capable of dis- **2–34** tinguishing" is much less complicated than that summarised above. "Capable" is used not in the negative senses of "not incapable" or "unrealised capacity". It is used in the positive sense of "able to" or "serves to distinguish". It expresses a positive requirement that a sign must possess a capacity or ability to distinguish before it is elevated to the status of "trade mark". In other words, before a sign can be registered as a "trade mark", it must possess a distinctive character. Section 1(1) imposes the positive requirement that a trade mark must possess a distinctive character.[38]

If this conclusion is correct, the 1994 Act, the TM Directive and the **2–35** Community Trade Marks Regulation contain a sensible definition of "trade mark". It does mean that there is considerable overlap between section 3(1)(a) and (b),(c) and (d), just as there is between (b) and (c) and (d). There is nothing wrong with overlap, it makes the position clear.

The remainder of this long section contains a much more detailed discussion of the position and further reasoning as to why our suggested interpretation is to be preferred.

---

[37] The test for "distinctive character" is dealt with in Chap. 3.
[38] This appears to be the view of the Court of First Instance in *OPTIONS* (Case T–91/99), March 30, 2000, at para. 24: "Consequently, in order to be accepted for registration, a sign must possess a distinctive character throughout the Community. That requirement, enabling consumers to distinguish the goods or services of one undertaking from those of other undertakings in accordance with Article 4 of Regulation No 40/94, is essential for that sign to be able to exercise the function of a Community trade mark in economic life." The CTM Regulation, Art. 4 corresponds to the TM Directive, Art. 2, and the 1994 Act, s.1(1).

Development of the United Kingdom interpretation of "capable of distinguishing"

2–36 In the United Kingdom, the interpretation of this requirement has been dominated by words used in section 3(1)(a) and (b) of the 1994 Act. In *AD2000*[39] the appointed person, G. Hobbs Q.C. explained the interplay as follows:

> "Section 3(1)(a) prohibits the registration of 'signs' which do not satisfy the requirements of section 1(1) (because they are incapable of being represented graphically and/or incapable of distinguishing the goods or services of one undertaking from those of other undertakings) whereas the prohibitions in sections 3(1)(b), 3(1)(c) and 3(1)(d) are applicable to *'trade marks'*, *i.e.* signs which satisfy the requirements of section 1(1), but nonetheless lack a distinctive character in the absence of appropriate use. This implies that the requirements of section 1(1) are satisfied even in cases where a sign represented graphically is only 'capable' to the limited extent of being 'not incapable' of distinguishing goods or services of one undertaking from those of other undertakings. Such signs are not excluded from registration by section 3(1)(a). Section 3(1)(a) has the more limited effect envisaged by article 3(1)(a) of the Directive of preventing the registration of *'signs which cannot constitute a trade mark'* at the time when they are put forward for registration. It is clear that signs which are not objectionable under section 3(1)(a) may nevertheless be objectionable under other provisions of section 3 including sections 3(1)(b), 3(1)(c) and 3(1)(d)."

and in one further short passage:

2–37 "The proviso to section 3(1) indicates that the essence of the objection to registration under section 3(1)(b) is immaturity: the sign in question is not incapable of distinguishing goods or services of one undertaking from those of other undertakings, but it is not distinctive by nature and has not become distinctive by nurture."

2–38 One advantage of this reasoning is that it probably makes the best sense of the words used in sections 1(1) and 3(1), and at the same time incorporates the apparent meaning of Article 3(1)(a) of the TM Directive. The reasoning also skilfully avoids touching upon any of the problems with this interpretation, which are discussed later. For a time, this interpretation was generally, but perhaps not universally, accepted in the United Kingdom. Hence, a sign which is "capable of distinguishing" in section 1(1) is to be interpreted in the limited sense of a sign which is "not incapable of distinguishing".

[39] [1997] R.P.C. 168, G. Hobbs Q.C. as the appointed person.

Philips v. Remington

It is somewhat surprising that when the Court of Appeal gave their **2–39**
provisional judgment in *Philips v. Remington*,[40] pending a reference to the
European Court, there was no mention of the reasoning in *AD2000*. In
the context of section 3(1)(a) of the 1994 Act, Aldous L.J. said this:

"I do not believe that the fact that a trade mark has by use become
such as to denote the goods of a particular trader necessarily means
that it is capable of distinguishing as required by section 1 (Article
2). I have already pointed out that use is relevant when deciding
registrability under section 3(1)(b), (c) and (d), but not under section
3(1)(a) (see Articles 3(1)(a), (b), (c) and 3(3)). That suggests that the
capability of distinguishing depends upon the features of the trade
mark itself, not on the result of its use. Thus a person who has had
monopoly use of a trade mark for many years may be able to
establish that it does in fact denote his goods exclusively, but that
does not mean that it has a feature which will distinguish his goods
from those of a rival who comes into the market. The more the
trade mark describes the goods, whether it consists of a word or
shape, the less likely it will be capable of distinguishing those goods
from similar goods of another trader. An example of a trade mark
which is capable of distinguishing is WELDMESH, whereas
WELDED MESH would not be. The former, despite its primary
descriptive meaning, has sufficient capricious addition to enable it
to acquire a secondary meaning, thereby demonstrating that it is
capable of distinguishing. The latter has no such alteration. Whatever the extent of the use, whether or not it be monopoly use and
whether or not there is evidence that the trade and the public
associate it with one person, it retains its primary meaning, namely
mesh that is welded. It does not have any feature which renders it
capable of distinguishing one trader's welded mesh from other
traders' welded mesh."

And, later:

"The scheme of the Act and Directive appears to require that signs
which are not capable of distinguishing are excluded from registration at the initial stage. Those which are capable of distinguishing
will be excluded unless they have or have acquired some distinctive
character. An example is the trade mark WELDMESH to which I
have referred. It is capable of distinguishing, but without use would
retain its primary meaning of, welded mesh. It would therefore be
devoid of any character that was distinctive. However use could
provide a secondary meaning, namely that the welded mesh to

[40] [1999] R.P.C. 809.

21

which the trade mark was applied came from a particular trader. Upon that being established it would become registrable as it would pass the dual test laid down by section (Article) 3(1)(a) and (b)."

2–40 The references in these passages to "capable of distinguishing" may be consistent with the "not incapable" interpretation. However, the expression appears to have been used more in the sense of "able to distinguish". No doubt guidance will be forthcoming from the European Court on this issue. This provisional judgment of the Court of Appeal is not easy to follow and raises a number of other important issues, which are discussed later.

2–41 Shortly after the provisional judgment was given, the appointed person (S. Thorley Q.C.) gave further explanation of the approach taken by Aldous L.J.:

"In his judgment in the *Philips* appeal, Aldous L.J. makes it plain that section 3(1)(a) is an overriding provision which prevents registration of a mark which is so descriptive or so lacking in content capable of performing the function of a trade mark that it cannot be registered. Section 3(1)(b) prevents from registration, without proof of distinctiveness, trade marks which are not so wholly lacking in trade mark content as to be registrable at all but which, without evidence of use, do not display a sufficiently distinctive content."[41]

2–42 This passage shows the lengths to which United Kingdom tribunals have gone to try to make sense of section 3(1)(a) and (b). On this reasoning, the absolute standard suggested by the words "devoid of any distinctive character" has been elevated so that it only prevents registration of marks which "do not display a sufficiently distinctive content". This attempt at reconciliation raises more problems than it seeks to solve. First, the words in section 3(1)(b) are given an unnatural meaning. Secondly, we are now presented with three standards of distinctiveness: not incapable/so descriptive; lacking a sufficiently distinctive content; and thirdly, under the proviso, a distinctive character. There is no guidance anywhere in the 1994 Act or the TM Directive as to what is or is not "a sufficiently distinctive content", other than the fact that the standard falls somewhere between the other two. Of the three suggested standards, only the requirement for "a distinctive character" under the proviso has real relevance to the function of a trade mark.

2–43 At first instance in the *Philips* case, Jacob J. pointed out that if you write this requirement for a sign to be a trade mark into Article 3(1)(b) you have "a sign which is capable of distinguishing which is devoid of any distinctive character". As he said[42]: "This seems (and indeed is)

---

[41] "Messiah from Scratch" [2000] R.P.C. 44 at 47, para. 13.
[42] *Philips v. Remington* [1998] R.P.C. 283 at 299.

confusing". Lloyd J. has said[43]: "That puzzle may be resolved by construing s. 1(1) and 3(1)(a) as setting up a low minimum standard and as meaning no more than "not incapable" of distinguishing. . . see *AD2000*. . . .".

The consistent theme in these authorities is that section 3(1)(a) and (b) set a dual test concerning distinctiveness, to which one can add, without controversy, a third stage from the proviso to section 3(1).

Chadwick L.J. in *Bach Flower Remedies*,[44] put the point slightly **2–44** differently:

> "The interrelationship of paragraphs (a) and (b) in section 3(1)— read with the proviso—serves to identify three categories of sign:
>
> (i) those which are not capable of distinguishing the goods of one undertaking from those of other undertakings;"
>
> [which] "subsumes two sub-categories (i) (A) those signs which have never been capable of distinguishing the goods of one undertaking from those of other undertakings and (i)(B) those which once had the capacity to distinguish but have, through use, ceased to be capable of doing so."
>
> "(ii) those that have the capacity to distinguish, but which do not do so—section 3(1)(b); and
>
> (iii) those that have the capacity to distinguish and (whether from the outset or through use) actually do so."

In this passage, "capable of distinguishing" appears to have been interpreted in the sense of an unrealised capacity to distinguish, apparently a concept which is separate and distinct from distinctive character, either inherent or acquired.

Summary of the English approach so far

The English approach (whether "not incapable" or unrealised capacity) **2–45** suggests that the structure of the relevant provisions in the 1994 Act and the TM Directive require distinctiveness to be addressed logically in the following three stages:

(1) Does the sign satisfy the requirements of section 1(1): is it capable of distinguishing in the sense of being "not incapable" or having an unrealised capacity to distinguish? If it is incapable, the application fails. If yes:

(2) Is the mark devoid of any distinctive character, descriptive or generic, contrary to one or more of section 3(1)(b), (c) or (d)? If no, then subject to any other objections, the mark proceeds. If yes:

---

[43] *Dualit Ltd's (Toaster Shapes) Trade Mark Applications* [1999] R.P.C. 890.
[44] [2000] R.P.C. 513 at 533, CA.

(3) Has the mark, through the use which has been made of it, acquired a distinctive character?

Is there a dual test for distinctiveness?

2–46 For many marks which are presented for registration, the assessment of distinctive character is a straightforward process. If the mark can be seen to possess distinctive character, whether inherent or acquired, then the three stages are bypassed.[45] However, such is the desire of traders to attempt to monopolise all types of sign used on or as part of their goods or services that cases of difficulty will continue to arise: cases where the distinctiveness of the sign in question needs to be assessed carefully against the requirements of the 1994 Act and the TM Directive. It is important that these requirements are clearly understood and uniformly applied throughout the E.U. This is no doubt why the Court of Appeal in *Philips* has asked the European Court the fundamental question as to whether there is a dual test (in section 3(1)(a) to (d)) at all:

> "Is there a category of marks which is not excluded from registration by Articles 3(1)(b)–(d) and Article 3(3) of the Council Directive 89/104/EEC, which is nonetheless excluded from registration by Article 3(1)(a) of the Directive (as being incapable of distinguishing the goods of the proprietor from those [of] other undertakings)?"

Issues raised by the English interpretation

2–47 Before discussing the possible answers to the *Philips* question, it is helpful to be aware of two problems with the United Kingdom interpretation of "capable of distinguishing". Perhaps the most serious problem is that the Trade Marks Act 1994 now contains, at its heart, a definition of "trade mark" which is distinctly odd. Bearing in mind that the essential function of a trade mark is to distinguish, one might expect that before a sign graduated to the status of "trade mark" the sign had to be "capable of distinguishing" in the sense that, if put to use, it would actually distinguish the goods or services of one undertaking from those of other undertakings. This interpretation of "capable of distinguishing" would have the benefit that the definition of "trade mark" in section 1(1) would include only those signs which, if put to use, would perform the essential function of a trade mark. Instead, the interpretations adopted by United Kingdom tribunals, as set out above, leaves the 1994 Act with a definition of "trade mark" which includes not just those signs which

---

[45] *cf.* the summary of the position in *Maasland N.V.'s Application* August 3, 1999, G. Hobbs Q.C. as the appointed person.

are properly called and function as "trade marks", but a much larger class of signs which might or might not be able to perform the essential function of a trade mark at some indeterminate point in the future depending on whether and/or how they are used over the intervening period of years. This is a nonsense.

The second problem is the puzzle presented by the wording of section **2–48** 3(1)(b)—a sign which is capable of distinguishing which is devoid of any distinctive character. Similar puzzles are presented by section 3(1)(c) and (d): a sign which is capable of distinguishing which is exclusively descriptive/generic. These puzzles are not satisfactorily resolved by either the "not incapable" or the unrealised capacity interpretations. The words "devoid of any distinctive character" appear to indicate a fairly absolute standard. If distinctive character were assessed on a scale from 0 to 100, those words set a standard of zero or near zero. A sign which is incapable of distinguishing would also score zero. But why have two expressions which mean or amount to the same thing? There is no point. However, consideration of the concept of a sign which is "capable of distinguishing" would suggest that the sign must have some distinctive character in order to be capable of distinguishing or to have some capacity to distinguish. Therefore the puzzle remains.

Further questions arise. For example: section 3(1) appears to contain a **2–49** perfectly logical and simple test of distinctiveness. Before something can be registered as a trade mark, it must possess distinctive character, whether by nature or by nurture. Why have a second and much lower test for distinctiveness, when no other test is necessary?

Also, section 3(1)(b), (c) and (d) appear to set absolute standards: **2–50** "*devoid* of *any* distinctive character", a trade mark which consists *exclusively* of something which is descriptive or generic. They appear to leave no room for any other prior and lower distinctiveness requirement.

Also, the legislative purpose of Articles 3(1)(b),(c),(d) and 3(3) is readily understandable. If there is another prior and lower distinctiveness requirement contained in "capable of distinguishing", what is the purpose of it? What is the policy which lies behind it? There is nothing in the TM Directive or the CTM Regulation which provides any answers to these points.

Possible answers to the *Philips* question

The range of likely answers to the question posed in the *Philips* case by **2–51** the Court of Appeal may be summarised as follows:

(1) Yes, there is another category of marks prohibited from registration because they are incapable of distinguishing, *i.e.* there is
a dual test of distinctiveness. This answer might involve adopting the "not incapable" or unrealised capacity interpretation of

"capable of distinguishing" or, possibly, some other interpretation.[46]

(2) Yes, there are categories of "signs" which are excluded from registration, not for any reason concerned with distinctiveness or lack of it, but because there are still some categories of signs which cannot constitute trade marks. Article 3(1)(a),(b),(c) and (d) and Article 3(3) combine to present a single distinctiveness requirement. To achieve registration, a sign must possess a distinctive character, whether by nature or by nurture. (For the purposes of this argument, any problem with graphical representation or other grounds of objection is left on one side).

(3) No. There are no categories of sign which cannot constitute trade marks, and Article 3(1)(a),(b),(c) and (d) and Article 3(3) combine to present a single distinctiveness requirement.

2-52 In order to explain why the first answer would be very unsatisfactory and why either the second or third answer should be the correct one, it is necessary to consider the structure and derivation of the relevant provisions of the TM Directive. They, in turn, require consideration of the relevant provisions of the CTM Regulation and their derivation. As an aside, it may be helpful to explain why the apparently fundamental issue posed in the *Philips* question is one which either does not arise at all in other Member States or does not arise in such a stark manner.

Essential function of a trade mark and the TM Directive

2-53 Over a number of years, the European Court of Justice has made it clear that the essential function of a trade mark is to distinguish. For example, in Case C-39/97 *Canon Kabushiki Kaisha v. Metro-Goldwyn-Mayer Inc.*,[47] it stated:

> ". . . according to the settled case-law of the court, the essential function of the trade mark is to guarantee the identity of the origin of the marked product to the consumer or end user by enabling him, without any possibility of confusion, to distinguish the product or service from others which have another origin. For the trade mark to be able to fulfil its essential role in the system of undistorted competition which the Treaty seeks to establish, it must offer a guarantee that all goods bearing it have originated under the control of a single undertaking which is responsible for their quality (see, in particular, Case C–10/89 *HAG GF (HAG II)* [1990] E.C.R. I–3711, paragraphs 14 and 13)."

---

[46] One commentator has suggested what he characterises as the German approach. "Capable of distinguishing" is an abstract test of the mark alone, apparently for any goods or services, whereas "devoid of distinctive character" is the concrete test for distinctiveness.

[47] [1999] R.P.C. 117.

In short, the essential function of a trade mark is to distinguish, by **2–54** origin. Against that background, one moves to the relevant provisions of the TM Directive, which are as follows:

Recital (7):
"Whereas attainment of the objectives at which this approximation of laws is aiming requires that the conditions for obtaining and continuing to hold a registered trade mark are, in general, identical in all Member States; whereas, to this end, it is necessary to list examples of signs which may constitute a trade mark, provided that such signs are capable of distinguishing the goods or services of one undertaking from those of other undertakings; whereas the grounds for refusal or invalidity concerning the trade mark itself, for example, the absence of any distinctive character, ... are to be listed in an exhaustive manner."

Recital (10): **2–55**
". . . the function of [the registered trade mark] is in particular to guarantee the trade mark as an indication of origin. . . ."

Article 2: *Signs of which a trade mark may consist*
"A trade mark may consist of any sign capable of being represented graphically, particularly words, including personal names, designs, letters, numerals, the shape of goods or their packaging, provided that such signs are capable of distinguishing the goods or services of one undertaking from those of other undertakings."

Article 3: *Grounds for refusal or invalidity*
"1. The following shall not be registered or if registered shall be liable to be declared invalid:

(a) signs which cannot constitute a trade mark;
(b) trade marks which are devoid of any distinctive character;" *etc.*

The process of partial harmonisation of the trade mark laws of **2–56** Member States meant that new types of sign would become registrable in many Member States. Therefore, as Recital 7 said, it was necessary to list examples of signs which may constitute a trade mark and this was done in Article 2. It lists "signs of which a trade mark may consist". Article 2 does not expressly define "trade mark" for the purposes of the TM Directive, although it does so implicitly by defining a class of those signs which may constitute a trade mark *provided that such signs are capable of distinguishing.*

The expression "capable of distinguishing" is one which can bear a **2–57** range of possible meanings. However, consideration of the essential function of a trade mark—something which distinguishes—indicates that before a sign can constitute a trade mark, its capability must be realised. At this point, it is necessary to have regard to the fact that some signs which are presented for registration have not yet been used and may not be used until registration has been secured. Article 2 does not require use but contemplates use: if used, would this sign distinguish?: if so, it constitutes a "trade mark". If "capable of distinguishing" is interpreted in this sense, it has the advantage that Article 2 implicitly defines a "trade mark" as something which would, as soon as it is used, perform the essential function of a trade mark. Such a sign should properly be afforded the privilege of registration as a trade mark, upon application.

2–58   At the other end of the scale of possible meanings, "capable of distinguishing" has the much more limited meaning of being "not incapable". This has the disadvantage that the definition implicit in Article 2 is then much wider. It includes not just those signs which do or are able (if used) to perform the essential function of a trade mark but all those signs which may be able to perform that function in the future, but which do not do so at present. Such a wide definition is unnecessary. It would mean that the only difference between "sign" and "trade mark" was the requirement for a graphic representation. However, in the vast majority of cases, there is no difference between the sign which is used and a graphical representation of it, so that for the vast majority of marks, "sign" would equal "trade mark". Such a wide definition would also debase the very concept of a "trade mark".

Implementation in the United Kingdom

2–59 The United Kingdom sought to implement Articles 2 and 3(1) of the TM Directive in sections 1(1) and 3 of the 1994 Act. Section 1(1) defines as "trade marks" all those signs which were listed in Article 2 as possible candidates for that status—*signs of which a trade mark may consist.* In this altered context, the true force of *provided that such signs are capable of distinguishing* is now more likely to be misunderstood, particularly since *provided that* has been replaced by *which.*

2–60   In addition, the absolute ground in Article 3(1)(a) *signs which cannot constitute a trade mark,* has also been subtly altered, so that section 3(1)(a) reads *signs which do not satisfy the requirements of section 1(1).* This alteration was largely ignored in *AD2000* and attention was focussed on the wording in the TM Directive. It was also pointed out in *AD2000* that the wording used in section 3(1)(a) is much closer to the wording used in Article 7(1)(a) of the CTM Regulation.

2–61   Presented with these provisions in the 1994 Act, it is to the credit of the United Kingdom tribunals that they have managed to achieve an interpretation which is at least consistent with a possible interpretation of the TM Directive, even though it leaves the United Kingdom with an odd definition of "trade mark". The remaining issue is whether this possible interpretation of the Directive is correct.

Derivation of the relevant provisions of the TM Directive

Some care is required when looking at the derivation of particular **2–62** provisions in the TM Directive, because there are several layers of information and only some of them are publicly available. At the highest level, the drafting history of the Directive may be traced through the various documents published in the Official Journal—the original proposal, the opinion of the Economic and Social Committee, the amendments suggested by the European Parliament, the amended proposal, the advice of the Economic and Social Committee, the opinion of the Parliament and the Directive adopted by the Council. The references to all these documents are included in the TM Directive itself. At a second level, there are the explanatory memoranda which accompanied the original and the amended proposals. These are available in particular libraries. It is debatable whether it is permissible to go further than the explanatory memoranda. Participants in the process are no doubt able to proffer opinions as to how and why a particular change was made. No doubt these opinions are honestly held, but there is no guarantee that everyone involved would share exactly the same opinion. This type of information can hardly be a legitimate aid to interpretation. Therefore, in what follows, we have restricted consideration to the documents published in the Official Journal together with the explanatory memoranda which accompanied the original and amended proposals.

The proposals which led to the Directive were closely intertwined with proposals which led to the CTM Regulation. Set out in the Annex to this chapter are relevant extracts from the various proposals for the TM Directive and the CTM Regulation.

Conclusions to be drawn from the proposals leading to the TM Directive

The following points emerge from the extracts from the various **2–63** proposals:

(1) The expression "capable of distinguishing" first appeared in the 1980 proposal for the CTM Regulation. The accompanying commentary said that the definition of signs of which a Community trade mark may consist "is geared particularly to the question whether the relevant sign is capable of performing the basic function of a trade mark. That function, in economic and legal terms, is to indicate the origin of goods or services and to distinguish them from those of other undertakings." This commentary indicates clearly that "capable of distinguishing" in what was then the proposed Article 3 was used in the sense of "able to" or "serves to distinguish" and not in the much more limited sense of being "not incapable" of distinguishing.

29

2–64   (2) In the 1980 proposal for the CTM Regulation, the first absolute ground of refusal prohibited the registration of "trade marks which do not conform to the requirements of Article 3. . .". In other words, this prohibited registration of signs which, if put into use, did not serve to distinguish.

    (3) In 1980 and 1985, the proposals for the TM Directive did not contain the expression "capable of distinguishing". Instead, these proposals left Member States to decide those "signs which, under the law of the Member State concerned, *cannot constitute a trade mark*" (emphasis added, because those are the words used in Article 3(1)(a) of the Directive). As far as the Commission was concerned, at that stage, "the definition of registrable signs . . . can . . . wait until a later Directive." This view evidently changed later.

2–65   (4) Hence, the first absolute ground of refusal in the 1980 and 1985 proposals for the TM Directive provided that "Trade marks shall be refused registration . . . if they consist of signs, which under the law of the Member State concerned, cannot constitute a trade mark. . .".

    (5) As far as the second and subsequent absolute grounds were concerned, the proposals for both the TM Directive and the CTM Regulation were consistent in presenting grounds which resulted in sub-paragraphs (b), (c) and (d) of Article 3(1) of the Directive and Article 7(1) of the Regulation. These three grounds were clearly based throughout on Article 6 *quinquies* B.2. of the Paris Convention, which contain the provisions in the Convention concerned with distinctiveness (or lack of it). It was only in the final stages of both the Directive and the Regulation that the exact words used in the Paris Convention were adopted. Throughout, each of the three grounds applied to "trade marks".

2–66   (6) One consequence of the two preceding points is as follows. Member States were being left with the decision as to what types of sign could constitute trade marks in their individual jurisdictions. In view of the stated aims of this first stage of approximation of laws, it seems unlikely that Member States were also being left to decide upon whether to adopt a second test for distinctiveness and if so, the nature of that test.

    (7) At a relatively late stage in the process which led to the TM Directive, it was decided that this first stage of harmonisation should include the definition of registrable signs. The consequence of this decision was that the first absolute ground of refusal changed from "signs, which under the law of the Member State concerned, cannot constitute a trade mark" to, simply, "signs which cannot constitute a trade mark". At the same time, it was necessary to introduce a definition of registrable signs which, naturally enough, was taken from the proposed CTM Regulation with the addition of the requirement

that the sign be "capable of graphical representation". The same addition was made to the definition in the Regulation.

(8) If "capable of distinguishing" means "able to" or "serves to distinguish", then the legislative intent of this requirement is clear. To constitute a registrable trade mark, the sign in question must, if put to use, distinguish. In other words, the sign must possess a distinctive character, whether by nature or by nurture. **2–67**

(9) If, on the other hand, "capable of distinguishing" means something else, such as "not incapable of distinguishing", then nowhere, in any of the proposals for the TM Directive or CTM Regulation, is there any indication of the legislative purpose of this requirement or how it is to be applied in practice. If the meaning is "not incapable", then it would seem clear that a sign which was incapable of distinguishing would be devoid of any distinctive character, but there is no point in legislating the same requirement twice over, particularly if it resulted in an absurd definition of "trade mark" in the Directive and the Regulation.

To which may be added the following observations: **2–68**

(a) The Paris Convention contains no definition of "trade mark", nor any provision which specifies the "signs of which a trade mark may consist" and does not feature the expression "capable of distinguishing".

(b) The published *travaux preparatoires* for the TM Directive do not indicate the derivation of the definition of "trade mark" which first appeared in the 1980 proposal for the CTM Regulation. However, the wording of that proposed definition bears a striking resemblance to the wording of Article 1 of the Uniform Benelux Law on Marks:

"The following shall be considered individual marks: designations, designs, prints, seals, letters, numbers, shapes of goods or their get-up, and any other symbols which serve to distinguish the goods or services of an enterprise.

However, shapes determined by the very nature of the goods or which affect their actual value or produce industrial results cannot be considered marks."

Even though amendments were made to the Uniform Benelux Law on Marks in 1992 in order to implement the terms of the Directive, the wording of Article 1 was left unchanged. It should be noted that Article 6*bis* (1) was added: "The Benelux Trade mark Office shall refuse to register a filing when it considers that: (a) the sign as filed does not constitute a mark within the meaning of Article 1, particularly due to lack of any distinctive character as provided in Article 6*quinquies* B(2) of the Paris Convention;". **2–69**

Implementation in other Member States

2–70 The ways in which the terms of a Directive have been implemented in other Member States may not be a particularly reliable aid to construction. However, it is likely that the European Court of Justice would be interested in the extent to which an issue of construction referred by a United Kingdom court would affect other Member States, and particularly so if the construction was concerned with something as fundamental as the very concept of a "trade mark".

2–71 At first sight, the implementation by the United Kingdom appears to have been reasonably faithful, in the sense that there is a high degree of correlation between the words used in the TM Directive and the 1994 Act. More analysis reveals the subtle alterations mentioned above at 2–59 *et seq*. Ireland has followed the United Kingdom wording. Other countries have followed the wording of Articles 2 and 3(1)(a) much less closely, but nonetheless may have interpreted the underlying concepts more accurately. There are wide variations but in summary, Austria, Benelux, France and Spain define "trade mark" by reference to the concept of a sign which *serves to distinguish*. Finland refers to "a trade mark as a special symbol to distinguish goods . . .", as something "by means of which goods . . . can be distinguished" and "To be eligible for registration a trade mark must be likely to distinguish. . .". Denmark, Sweden, Germany, Italy and Portugal use the words *capable of distinguishing* but in the context of *signs of which a trade mark may consist* (Denmark has an additional provision "trade marks mean distinctive signs" and Sweden also refers to a trade mark "as a special symbol for the purpose of distinguishing"). Only the United Kingdom, Ireland and Greece have fixed the definition of "trade mark" by reference to *capable of distinguishing*. Even making due allowance for variations in translation, it is a sobering thought that there is such wide variation in the fundamental concept of "trade mark".

2–72 At the same time, it may be noted that only the United Kingdom, Germany, Ireland and Greece use the words "devoid of any distinctive character" when implementing Article 3(1)(b). Benelux refers to "lack of any distinctive character". Sweden says "a trade mark may be registered only if it is distinctive . . .". The other countries have provisions to exclude descriptive and generic trade marks, yet have no explicit provision equating to "devoid of any distinctive character". All countries have implemented Article 3(3)—what we understand as the proviso to section 3(1).

Leaving those in the United Kingdom camp aside, the variations amongst other countries may have little consequence because they have implemented the two basic concepts: a trade mark is something which serves to distinguish and that before a sign can be registered as a trade mark it must possess a distinctive character.

Interpretation of the equivalent CTM provision at OHIM

OHIM appears to have avoided any issue concerning the interpretation 2–73 of "capable of distinguishing". To the end of 1999, some 3,150 applications had been refused under the absolute grounds for refusal in Article 7.1 of the CTM Regulation. In only five cases was Article 7.1(a) (the equivalent of section 3(1)(a)) cited as a ground for refusal. None of those five cases went to the Boards of Appeal. At least some of them involved problems with the graphical representation. For virtually every refused mark, Article 7.1 (b) was cited. Thus, any problems over distinctiveness appear to have been dealt with under Article 7.1 (b) and, occasionally, (c).

Where the Boards of Appeal deal with an Article 7.1(b) ground, 2–74 reference is sometimes made to the fact that a sign must be capable of distinguishing. The expression is used in the sense that the sign must have the ability to distinguish in order to be registered, *i.e.* the capability must be realised. To the same effect, the Boards of Appeal describe a sign as not capable of distinguishing because it was devoid of distinctive character. The two requirements are treated as equivalent[48] or, rather, opposites.

There could be two possible reasons why OHIM has avoided the 2–75 issues which have troubled the English tribunals. The first is that the issues were identified and avoided by invariable reliance on "devoid of distinctive character". The second and more likely explanation is that OHIM did not identify any problem. Identification of the issue as to whether there is a dual test for distinctiveness requires an overly literal approach to interpretation. A more European, more purposive approach to construction avoids the issue.

Is there a dual test?

We return to this question. Earlier in this section, we suggested three 2–76 possible answers to the first question asked of the European Court by the Court of Appeal in *Philips*. For the reasons set out at length above, it is most unlikely that the European Court will approve the interpretation of "capable of distinguishing" adopted in the English cases quoted above. It is suggested that the European Court should state clearly that Article 3(1)(a),(b),(c) and (d) and Article 3(3) combine to present a single distinctiveness requirement. To achieve registration, a sign must possess a distinctive character, whether by nature or by nurture. To be a little more precise "capable of distinguishing" means the sign must possess an ability to distinguish—a distinctive character. The sign, if used, must serve to distinguish the goods or services of one undertaking from the goods or services of other undertakings.

---

[48] For examples, see *LIGHT GREEN* [1999] E.T.M.R. 214, paras 20, 21; and *Ty Nant Spring Water Limited's Application* [1999] E.T.M.R. 974, para. 13, both OHIM BoA.

2–77   We cannot rule out the possibility that the European Court might try to ascribe a separate and different meaning to "capable of distinguishing" because of the approach taken in one or more other E.U. States. It has only been practical to scratch the surface of the approach taken in other countries in the analysis set out above. However, as explained above, there appears to be no need for a dual test. A single test for distinctiveness has the added advantage that we are left with a proper definition of "trade mark" in the E.U.

2–78   Resolution in that way would only leave the issue whether there are categories of "signs" which are excluded from registration, not for any reason concerned with distinctiveness or lack of it, but because there are still some categories of signs which cannot constitute trade marks. When the CTM Regulation was passed, it is evident that the Council and the Commission held the view that there were some categories of sign which could not constitute "trade marks" and they expressed their view in the Minutes.[49] Whether the Commission still adheres to that view remains to be seen. It is suggested that it is unnecessary to exclude some categories of "sign". The requirements in the Directive and CTM Regulation provide sufficient safeguards for other traders. Therefore, it is suggested that the European Court should adopt the third answer, set out above at 2–51.

Remaining difficulties with the "serves to distinguish" interpretation

2–79 This interpretation does not solve all the problems and puzzles posed by the drafting of the TM Directive and the 1994 Act, but it does resolve the most important and fundamental problem which was inherent in the alternative interpretation.

The "serves to distinguish" interpretation requires acceptance of the following:

(1) That there is considerable overlap between section 3(1)(a) and (b)(c) and (d). This is hardly surprising bearing in mind the overlap between subsections (b) and (c) and (d).

(2) The "puzzle" posed by the use of "trade mark" at the beginning of each of subsection (b), (c) and (d). It is likely that this puzzle arises simply because the definition of "trade mark" in the 1994 Act, the TM Directive and the CTM Regulation was grafted onto the group of provisions in subsection (b),(c) and (d) which were taken, *en bloc*, from the Paris Convention. A more rigorous drafting technique might well have resulted in the word "sign" being used instead.

If the English interpretation is correct

2–80 If the English interpretation is correct, the European Court would still have to explain the following issues.

---

[49] Which, of course, are not a legitimate aid to construction: *Antonissen* [1991] E.C.R. I–745, para. 18.

Is the standard of distinctiveness imposed by "capable of distinguishing" the same as "devoid of any distinctive character" or is it different? Certainly a sign which is devoid of any distinctive character can properly be said to be incapable of distinguishing, but that does not necessarily mean the standards are the same.

If the standard imposed by "capable of distinguishing" is different, by what criteria is a sign to be judged against this requirement? As indicated above, there is no guidance anywhere in the TM Directive, the CTM Regulation or the 1994 Act as to the standard to be applied. Without guidance from the European Court, it may be that this standard continues to be applied much more vigorously in the United Kingdom than elsewhere in the E.U.

5. Retail services and equivalents

Background

For some years after the introduction of the 1994 Act and the CTM **2–81** system, both the United Kingdom Registry and OHIM operated a policy of rejecting applications in so far as they covered "retail services" and the like,[50] such as mail order services and the internet equivalent of "electronic trading in goods". The OHIM Examination Guidelines simply stated that the "activity of retail trading in goods is not as such a service".[51] The United Kingdom Registry took a similar line, but provided more reasoning in the Work Manual[52] as to how this objection arose. The objection was taken under section 3(1)(a) on the basis that it is implicit in section 1(1) that the undertakings are *trading* in goods or services. Therefore, it was said "marks in respect of such services provided by retailers which are merely ancillary to trading in goods would not appear to be registrable under the 1994 Act because such services cannot either constitute a business in the provision of services or be services in respect of which a trade mark may be registered."

In the context of section 1(1), this reasoning appeared artificial and **2–82** overly reminiscent of the position under the 1938 Act.[53] It seems reasonable to assume that for many years, members of the public have thought or would think (if asked) that they were being provided with a distinct service in some large department stores or specialist retailers, over and above simply being provided with goods available for pur-

---

[50] Just as test cases were brought under the 1938 Act (*Re Boots Co. sub nom. Dee Corp.* [1990] R.P.C. 159, CA), test cases were brought under the 1994 Act. These eventually caused the U.K. Registry to change its practice on "retail services". See PAC 13/00, September 27, 2000. The outcome is likely to be the same.

[51] OHIM Examination Guidelines 4.3(j).

[52] Chap. 6, paras 2.3.10–12 and 6.5.5.

[53] Established in *Dee's Application* [1990] R.P.C. 159 CA. Of course, the old requirement that the services had to be provided for money or money's worth had to be dropped for the purposes of the 1994 Act.

chase. However luxurious the additional service may be, it is true to say it can only be ancillary to the trade in the goods themselves.

Policy considerations

2–83 There is no express basis for an objection to registrations for "retail services" in the 1994 Act, the TM Directive or the CTM Regulation, and it would be very difficult to formulate an objection to exclude registration for these ancillary "looking after customers" services. The objection appeared to be based on policy grounds concerned with administrative burden, despite the fact that there are other trade mark systems which have accommodated registrations for "retail services" and the like without apparent problem. Here, retailers could already obtain registrations covering the goods that they sold. If every retailer was also entitled to protection covering "retail services" provided in selling those goods, the thinking was that this would place a considerable additional and unnecessary burden on trade mark systems. In fact, this problem (if it be a problem) is not confined to applications from retailers. If registrations were permitted for retail services, in theory every trader would be entitled to a registration to cover the services provided in "looking after customers", whatever the trade and whatever the goods or services. Thus, one would expect every applicant to apply automatically to cover the goods or services in which he traded and for ancillary services under the general rubric of "looking after customers".

Giacomelli[54]

2–84 The prevailing thinking was being challenged in a number of test cases. The first to be decided was an application by Giacomelli Sport SpA for a CTM for the following services:

> "Bringing together, for the benefit of others, of a variety of goods (excluding transport thereof), enabling customers to conveniently view and purchase those goods"

Due to the importance of the issue, the OHIM Board of Appeal invited the President of OHIM to make comment on the appeal. His principal objection against registrations for retail services was that they would amount to "cover-all" registrations, which would be uncertain in scope, leading to difficulties in classification and in the comparison of marks for the purposes of registration and infringement. He also drew attention to the Joint Statement contained in the Minutes of the Council Meeting at which the CTM Regulation was adopted, which expressed the view that a CTM would not be available for retail services.[55]

---

[54] [2000] E.T.M.R. 277, Second BoA.
[55] "The Council and the Commission consider that the activity of retail trading in goods is not as such a service for which a Community trade mark may be registered under this Regulation."

The Board of Appeal rejected any reliance on the statement in the **2–85** Minutes[56] and observed that the President's comments were really concerned with administrative matters and did not impact on the legal position. As to the legal position, the Board observed that "service" was not defined in the CTM Regulation and decided that the concept should be construed widely. The Board then made some observations on the common experience of retailing, observing correctly that the goodwill of a retail business is, by and large, built on the service it provides.[57]

In principle, the Board was prepared to allow a registration for this **2–86** type of service, but remitted the application to the examiner to allow the applicant to specify the services with greater clarity. The services had to be linked to the goods concerned, in this case "sports goods".

This is a sensible decision, reflecting the reality of consumer's experience with retailers. By contrast, the opposing arguments—that retail services are merely ancillary to the trade in goods and benefit only the retailer—look increasingly artificial.

At the time of writing, the status of the *Giacomelli* decision is **2–87** somewhat uncertain.[58] If it is upheld, then registrations covering sales activities are likely to be allowed throughout the E.U. It is already clear that an application simply for "retail services" or at that level of generality will be rejected. The services in question will have to be linked to the goods in which the retailer trades, or to specific services.

The development will not be restricted to traditional retailers. It obviously extends to all modern forms of retailing—mail order, telephone and internet. It is no exaggeration to say that it is applicable to every owner of or applicant for a registered trade mark—it concerns not just business organisations, but every organisation and entity which is capable of securing trade mark protection. All these organisations deal with people and, to a greater or lesser extent, provide services to those people which may be equated with a retailer looking after its customers.

6. Annex

The derivation of the relevant provisions of the TM Directive

As mentioned in the main text, the proposals which led to the TM **2–88** Directive were closely intertwined with proposals which led to the CTM Regulation. Accordingly, it is necessary to track the progress of the

---

[56] Following established ECJ authority in *Antonissen* [1991] E.C.R. I–745, para. 18: ". . .such a declaration cannot be used for the purpose of interpreting a provision of secondary legislation where, as in this case, no reference is made to the content of the declaration in the wording of the provision in question."

[57] There are some web-sites which do nothing except bring together advertisements for goods. They do not even sell the goods, simply taking a commission from the actual seller of the goods. The commission may not even be based on sales of goods, but on hits on the web-site.

[58] There is apparently disagreement within OHIM as to whether *Giacomelli* should be applied. This emphasises the political rather than legal objections to registrations of this type. In the U.K. the Registry has indicated that it will accept applications in respect of "certain aspects" of retail services. It appears the service needs to be something "over and above a normal trade in the proprietor's own goods." See PAC 13/00, September 27, 2000.

relevant provisions chronologically through the various proposals for the TM Directive and the CTM Regulation. Words in italics have been added for clarification. For ease of reference, we start by setting out again the end result, the relevant provisions of the TM Directive:

2–89   Recital (7):
"Whereas attainment of the objectives at which this approximation of laws is aiming requires that the conditions for obtaining and continuing to hold a registered trade mark are, in general, identical in all Member States; whereas, to this end, it is necessary to list examples of signs which may constitute a trade mark, provided that such signs are capable of distinguishing the goods or services of one undertaking from those of other undertakings; whereas the grounds for refusal or invalidity concerning the trade mark itself, for example, the absence of any distinctive character, . . . are to be listed in an exhaustive manner."

2–90   Recital (10):
". . . the function of [the registered trade mark] is in particular to guarantee the trade mark as an indication of origin . . .".

Article 2: *Signs of which a trade mark may consist*
"A trade mark may consist of any sign capable of being represented graphically, particularly words, including personal names, designs, letters, numerals, the shape of goods or their packaging, provided that such signs are capable of distinguishing the goods or services of one undertaking from those of other undertakings."

Article 3 *Grounds for refusal or invalidity*
"1. The following shall not be registered or if registered shall be liable to be declared invalid:

(a) signs which cannot constitute a trade mark;

(b) trade marks which are devoid of any distinctive character;" *etc.*

Proposal for a first Council Directive to approximate the laws of the Member States relating to trade marks[59]—1980

Extracts from the explanatory memorandum

2–91   "Introduction
Initially it is proposed to approximate those provisions of trade mark law which currently have the strongest and most direct influence on the establishment and functioning of the common market in marked goods. These are the rules governing the scope of

---

[59] COM(80) 635 final, dated November 19, 1980.

the protection afforded to trade marks, use of trade marks, amicable settlement of conflicts and the relative and absolute grounds for the refusal of registration or invalidation of trade marks.

The widely advocated approximation of further major areas of national trade mark law, such as the definition of registrable signs . . . can in the Commission's opinion wait until a later Directive.

Another important reason for starting with this limited measure of approximation is the fact that, along with the Directive, a proposal is being submitted to establish a Community trade mark. The proposal for a Regulation seeks the same ends as the Directive but by a different route. . . The two proposals are complementary and must therefore be looked at and judged together."

"Article 2: *commentary*   2–92
"The absolute grounds for refusing registration listed in paragraphs (1) and (2) are similar to those laid down in Article 6 of the proposal for a Regulation. Reference is therefore made to the commentary on that Article in the Explanatory Memorandum to the Regulation.

The list of absolute grounds for refusal is exhaustive. . . ."

Extracts from the recitals

[Whereas]   2–93
"it does not appear to be necessary at present to undertake full-scale harmonisation of the trade mark laws of Member States. It will be sufficient if approximation is limited to those national provisions of law which most directly affect free movement of goods and services . . . It is, further, important not to disregard the solutions and advantages which the Community trade mark system affords to undertakings wishing to acquire trade marks. Under this system, there is no point in requiring the Member States, inter alia, to authorise the registration of additional categories of signs or to recognise service marks. . . . attainment of the objectives at which this approximation of laws is aiming requires that the conditions for obtaining and continuing to hold a trade mark are, in general, identical in all Member States;

The purpose of protection is to guarantee the trade mark's function as an indicator of origin."

Article 2: *text*

"(1) Trade marks shall be refused registration or shall be invali- 2–94
dated if, on the date of application therefor, they consist of signs which, under the law of the Member State concerned, cannot constitute a trade mark or be held as such by the applicant, or if, on that date, are devoid of distinctive character in a Member State, and in particular:

(a) those which consist solely of signs or indications which in trade may be requisite for the purpose of showing the kind, quality . . . *etc.* or other characteristics of the goods or service, unless those marks have acquired distinctive character in consequence of the use made of them;
(b) those which consist solely of signs or indications which are customarily used to designate the goods or service in the current language of the trade or in the bona fide and established practices thereof."

Proposal for a Council Regulation on Community trade marks[60]— 1980

Section 1: Definition of a Community trade mark, obtaining a Community Trade Mark
Article 3: *commentary*

2–95 "This provision defines the types of signs of which Community trade marks may consist. It is geared particularly to the question whether the relevant sign is capable of performing the basic function of a trade mark. That function, in economic and legal terms, is to indicate the origin of goods or services and to distinguish them from those of other undertakings.

No type of sign is automatically excluded from registration as a Community trade mark. Article 3 lists the types of signs used most frequently by undertakings to identify their goods or services, but it is not an exhaustive list. It is designed to simplify the adaptation of administrative practices and court judgments to business requirements and to encourage undertakings to apply for Community trade marks.

Depending on the circumstances, therefore, the Trade Marks Office, the national courts or, in the last resort, the Court of Justice will be responsible for determining whether, for example, solid colours or shades of colours, and signs denoting sound, smell or taste may constitute Community trade marks."

Recitals: *short extracts*

2–96 "The rights in a Community trade mark are not to be capable of being obtained otherwise than by registration, and registration is to be refused if the trade mark is not distinctive, is unlawful or is not available. . . .

The purpose of protection is to guarantee the trade mark's function as an indicator of origin. . .".

---

[60] Contained in the same document as the Proposal for the Directive. See n. 59, above.

Article 1: Community trade marks

"(1) A trade mark for goods or services which conforms with the 2–97
conditions contained in this regulation and is registered in manner
herein provided is hereinafter referred to as a 'Community trade
mark'".

Article 3: Signs of which a Community trade mark may consist

"A Community trade mark may consist of words (including sur- 2–98
names), designs, letters, numerals, combinations of colours, the
shape of goods or of their packaging, or of any other signs which
are capable of distinguishing the goods or services of one undertaking from those of other undertakings."

Article 6: Absolute grounds for refusal

"(1) Trade marks which do not conform to the requirements of 2–99
Article 3 . . . and trade marks which are not distinctive, shall not be
registered; in particular the following trade marks shall not be
registered:

(a) those which consist solely of signs or indications which in
    trade may be requisite for the purpose of showing the kind,
    quality . . . *etc.* . . . or other characteristics of the goods or
    service;
(b) those which consist solely of signs or indications which are
    customarily used to designate the goods or service in the
    current language of the trade or in the bona fide and estab-
    lished practices thereof.

(4) Paragraph 1(a) shall not apply if the trade mark has become
distinctive in consequence of the use which has been made of it.

Amended proposal for a Council Regulation on the Community trade mark[61]—1984

Commentary on the Articles

"Title II: The law relating to trade marks   2–100

Section 1: Definition of a Community trade mark, Obtaining a
Community trade mark

Articles 3 and 4
The amendments to these two articles are purely a matter of
drafting.

[61] COM (84) 470 final, dated July 31, 1984.

Article 6
The wording of paragraph 2(b) was brought into line with that of Article 6 *quinquies* B3 of the Paris Convention. . . ."

Recitals: relevant extracts

2–101   "The rights in a Community trade mark are not to be capable of being obtained otherwise than by registration, and registration is to be refused if the trade mark is not distinctive, is unlawful or is not available. . . .

The purpose of protection is to guarantee the trade mark's function as an indicator of origin . . ."

Text—amendments indicated by underlining

2–102   Article 1: Community trade marks
(1) A trade mark for goods or services which conforms with the conditions contained in this regulation and is registered in manner herein provided is hereinafter referred to as a "Community trade mark".

2–103   Article 3: Signs of which a Community trade mark may consist
A Community trade mark may consist of any signs, particularly words, including personal names, designs, letters, numerals, combinations of colours, the shape of goods or of their packaging, or of any other signs which are capable of distinguishing the goods or services of one undertaking from those of other undertakings.

2–104   Article 6: Absolute grounds for refusal
(1) Trade marks which do not conform to the requirements of Article 3 . . . and trade marks which are not distinctive, shall not be registered; in particular the following trade marks shall not be registered:

    (a) those which consist solely of signs or indications which in trade may be requisite for the purpose of showing the kind, quality . . . *etc.* . . . or other characteristics of the goods or service;

    (b) those which consist solely of signs or indications which are customarily used to designate the goods or service in the current language of the trade or in the bona fide and established practices thereof.

(4) Paragraph 1(a) shall not apply if the trade mark has become distinctive in relation to the goods or services for which registration is requested in consequence of the use which has been made of it."

Amended proposal for a First Council Directive to approximate the laws of the Member States relating to trade marks[62]—1985

Article 2: *text—amendments indicated by underlining*

"(1) Trade marks shall be refused registration or shall be invali- **2–105** dated if, on the date of application therefor, they consist of signs which, under the law of the Member State concerned, cannot constitute a trade mark or be held as such by the applicant, or if, on that date, are devoid of distinctive character in that Member State, and in particular:

(a) those which consist solely of signs or indications which in trade may be requisite for the purpose of showing the kind, quality . . . *etc.* or other characteristics of the goods or service, unless those marks have acquired distinctive character in consequence of the use made of them;

(b) those which consist solely of signs or indications which are customarily used to designate the goods or service in the current language of the trade or in the bona fide and established practices thereof.

(4)Paragraph 1(a) shall not apply if the trade mark has become distinctive in relation to the goods or services for which registration is requested in consequence of the use which has been made of it."

Before the Directive was adopted on December 21, 1988, there was an intermediate text of December 15, 1987, which was not published. The changes made between the 1985 Proposal and the TM Directive are apparent.

[62] COM (85) 793 final, dated December 17, 1985.

CHAPTER 3

THE REGISTER OF TRADE MARKS AND THE TRADE MARKS BRANCH OF THE PATENT OFFICE

1. The Register

The Register

3–01 The Register of Trade Marks was established by the Trade Marks Registration Act 1875[1] and it is now continued under section 63 of the Trade Marks Act 1994, which provides that it is to be maintained by the Registrar. In fact, it has been kept on computer for some years now.

Rule-making power

3–02 By section 78 of the 1994 Act, the Secretary of State has a broad power to make rules under specific sections of the Act authorising the making of rules, to make rules prescribing things which the Act permits or requires to be prescribed, and "generally for regulating practice and procedure" under the Act.[2]

3–03 Particular instances of the rule-making powers include the making of provisions for filing applications and other documents, for making and filing translations, for service, for rectifying irregularities, and for setting and extending time limits.[3]

The current rules are the Trade Marks Rules 2000.[4]

2. The Comptroller or Registrar

Control of the Register

3–04 The Register is maintained by the Comptroller-General of Patents, Designs and Trade Marks, who is referred to in the 1994 Act as "the Registrar".[5]

---

[1] ss.1 and 7.
[2] s.78(1).
[3] s.78(2).
[4] S.I. 2000 No. 136. For the current rules see App. 3, *post*. The Rules made under the 1938 Act may be found in previous editions of this work.
[5] s.62.

One of the duties of the Comptroller-General is to include in her annual report under section 121 of the Patents Act 1977, a report on the execution of the 1994 Act, including the discharge of her functions under the Madrid Protocol. The report also has to include an account of the money received and paid by her in connection with her execution of the Act.[6]

Exclusion of liability of the Registrar

By section 70 of the 1994 Act, the Registrar is not to be taken to warrant **3–05** the validity of any registration of a trade mark under the Act or under any treaty to which the United Kingdom is a party, and her liability in relation to connected examinations, examination reports and proceedings consequent on examinations is also excluded.

It does not seem that the exclusions provided for cover all aspects of **3–06** the Registrar's duties. For example, they would not appear to exclude liability for a failure to maintain the Register accurately, or to provide accurate information about an application.[7]

The exclusion of the Registrar's liability extends to her officers.[8]

3. Division of the Register

Under the Trade Marks Act 1938 Act, and since the Trade Marks Act **3–07** 1919, the Register was divided into two parts, A and B. The distinction, in general terms, was that registration in Part B could be obtained for marks which lacked sufficient distinctiveness to be included in Part A. However, Part B marks conferred more limited rights.

Under the 1994 Act, this distinction has been abolished. In the **3–08** transitional provisions of the 1994 Act, it was provided that existing registered marks at the date of commencement should all be transferred to the new Register kept under the 1994 Act without regard to whether they had previously been in Part A or Part B.[9]

The old distinction potentially has some continuing significance, **3–09** however, in relation to acts alleged to infringe under the 1994 Act but which began before its commencement and have continued since. Under the transitional provisions of the 1994 Act, it is not an infringement to continue use of a mark after commencement if it did not amount to infringement beforehand.[10] Since the test for infringement under the

---

[6] s.71.
[7] Of course, the fact that s.70 does not exclude liability does not mean that the Registrar would be liable if such a failure did take place. A person aggrieved by such a failure would still have to prove the existence of a duty of care, negligence and damage in order to bring a successful action.
[8] s.70(3).
[9] Sched. 3, para. 2(1).
[10] Sched. 3 para 4(2). See Chap. 13 for a more detailed consideration of the defences available under the transitional provisions.

1938 Act depended to some extent on whether the mark in question was registered in Part A or Part B,[11] it may even now, in relation to acts which have been continuing since before commencement of the 1994 Act, be necessary to consider whether, historically, the mark in question was registered in Part A or Part B.

4. Entries on the Register

Introduction

3–10 Both registered trade marks and registrable transactions are to be recorded on the Register.

Details of registered marks to be entered on the Register

3–11 Details of registered trade marks are required to be entered on the Register by section 63(2)(a) of the 1994 Act, and the matters to be entered in respect of them are stipulated by the 2000 Rules.[12] The matters are:

(1) the effective date of registration (*i.e.* the date of filing of the application for registration[13]);
(2) the actual date of registration (*i.e.* the date of entry in the Register);
(3) the priority date (if any);
(4) the name and address of the proprietor;
(5) the address for service (if any)[14];
(6) any disclaimer or limitation;
(7) any memorandum or statement of the effect of any memorandum relating to a trade mark of which the Registrar has been informed;
(8) the goods or services in respect of which the mark is registered;
(9) where the mark is a collective or certification mark, that fact;
(10) where the mark has been registered pursuant to section 5(5) on the basis of consent of the proprietor of an earlier trade mark or other earlier right, that fact;
(11) where the mark is registered pursuant to a transformation application, the number of the international registration and either (a) the date accorded to the international registration under Article 3(4) of the Madrid Protocol, or (b) the date of

---

[11] The law of infringement under the 1938 Act is not considered in any detail in this edition of this work, but is covered in depth in earlier ones.
[12] r. 39.
[13] In accordance with s.40(3).
[14] Under r. 10, an address for service in the U.K. is required for many purposes under the Act. In particular, all applicants for registration must provide one.

recordal of the request for extension to the United Kingdom of the international registration under Article 3*ter* of the Madrid Protocol, as the case may be;

(12) where the mark arises from the conversion of a Community trade mark or an application for a Community trade mark, the number of any other registered trade mark from which the Community trade mark or the application for a Community trade mark claimed seniority and the earliest seniority date.

Entry of registrable transactions on the Register

The general requirement for details of registrable transactions to be **3–12** entered on the Register is contained in section 63(2)(b) of the 1994 Act. In addition, section 25 requires particulars of registrable transactions to be entered on application by a person claiming to be entitled to an interest in or under a registered mark by virtue of a registrable transaction, or any other person claiming to be affected by such a transaction.

The types of dealing which are registrable transactions under the Act[15] **3–13** are as follows:

(1) an assignment of a trade mark or any right in it;
(2) the grant of a licence under a trade mark;
(3) the granting of any security interest (whether fixed or floating) over a registered trade mark or any right in or under it;
(4) the making by personal representatives of an assent in relation to a registered trade mark or any right in or under it;
(5) an order of a court or other competent authority transferring a registered mark or any right in or under it.

Details of registrable transactions to be entered on the Register

The matter to be entered in the Register in respect of a registrable **3–14** transaction is set out in the 2000 Rules[16] and depends on the nature of the transaction, save that in all cases the date on which the entry was made in the Register must be entered.

In relation to assignments, the matters to be entered on the Register **3–15** are (1) the name and address of the assignee, (2) the date of the assignment, and (3) where the assignment is in respect of any right in the mark, a description of the right assigned.

In relation to licences, the matters to be entered on the Register are (1) **3–16** the name and address of the licensee; (2) where the licence is an

---

[15] s.25(2). Further information about the various types of registrable transaction under the Act, and the consequences of registration and non-registration may be found in Chap. 12.

[16] r. 40.

exclusive licence, that fact[17]; (3) where the licence is limited, a description of the limitation; and (4) the duration of the licence if the same is or is ascertainable as a definite period.[18]

3–17   For security interests, the following are to be entered on the Register: (1) the name and address of the grantee; (2) the nature of the interest (whether fixed or floating); (3) the extent of the security and the right in or under the mark secured.

3–18   In the case of the making by personal representatives of an assent, the following matters are to be entered on the Register: (1) the name and address of the person in whom the mark or any right in or under it vests by virtue of the assent; and (2) the date of the assent.

3–19   Finally, where the registrable transaction is an order of a court or other competent authority transferring a mark or any right in or under it, the matters to be entered on the Register are: (1) the name and address of the transferee; (2) the date of the order[19]; and (3) where the transfer is in respect of a right in the mark, a description of the right transferred.

Trusts and equities are specifically excluded from being entered on the Register, and the Registrar is not affected by any notice of them.[20]

Procedure for giving notice of a registrable transaction

3–20   The following forms are to be used for making an application to register a registrable transaction.[21]

For the grant of a licence, Form TM50; for an amendment to, or termination of a licence, Form TM51; for a transaction relating to the grant, amendment or termination of any security interest, or relating to an assent by personal representatives, or an order of a court or competent authority, Form TM24; for an assignment or any other transaction not already mentioned, Form TM16.

3–21   Applications to register assignments must be signed by or on behalf of the parties. Other applications of the types referred to above must be signed by or on behalf of the grantor of the licence or security interest, or be accompanied by sufficient documentary evidence to establish the transaction.[22]

3–22   If a transaction is sought to be registered which has been effected by an instrument chargeable with duty, the application for its registration is

---

[17] Hence if the Register is silent, it seems that it may be taken that the licence is non-exclusive.

[18] It appears that if the licence is not of a definite or definitely ascertainable period, nothing will be entered on the Register, and a person who may be affected by the licence will be unable to find out the likely duration. This is unsatisfactory.

[19] It seems strange that there is no express requirement that the court or other competent authority be named. Usually it will be the Chancery Division of the High Court, but that is not the only possibility.

[20] s.26.

[21] r. 41(1).

[22] r. 41(2).

subject to the Registrar being satisfied that the instrument has been duly stamped.[23]

Transactions concerning applications for registration

Section 27(1) of the Act provides that the provisions of sections 22 to 26, **3–23** which relate to registered trade marks as objects of property, assignments, and registrable transactions, also apply to applications for registration.

However, applications for registration and transactions concerning them are not registered as such. Instead, where an application for registration has been made and is the subject of a transaction which would have been registrable were the mark already registered, notice is given to the Registrar of the details of the transaction.[24]

The procedure and forms used to apply to give notice to the Registrar **3–24** of transactions concerning an application for registration are the same as for transactions concerning a registration.[25]

Where notice has been given to the Registrar of particulars of a **3–25** transaction concerning an application for registration, and the mark concerned is subsequently registered, the Registrar is to enter the particulars on the Register.[26]

Transitional provisions

The transitional provisions concerning registration of transactions affect- **3–26** ing registered trade marks are contained in Schedule 3, paragraph 8 of the 1994 Act. Applications under the 1938 Act (for the registration of a registered user) pending on commencement fall to be dealt with under the 1994 Act.[27] A person who has become entitled to an existing registered trade mark (*i.e.* a 1938 Act mark) before commencement of the 1994 Act but has not registered the transaction is required to do so under section 25 of the 1994 Act.[28] In either such case, the consequences of failure to register the transaction are provided for by section 25 of the 1938 Act, and not by the 1994 Act.[29] Applications determined under the 1938 Act, but not finally determined at commencement fall under the old law,[30] but the resulting registration would then automatically be converted to one under the 1994 Act.[31]

---

[23] r. 41(3). See Chap. 12. Stamp duty is not in fact now chargeable on most assignments concerning trade marks.
[24] s.27(3).
[25] r. 41(1).
[26] r. 41(4).
[27] Sched. 3, para. 8(3).
[28] *ibid.*, para. 8(5).
[29] *ibid.*, para. 8(6).
[30] *ibid.*, para. 8(4).
[31] *ibid*, para. 8(2).

5. Alteration of entries on the Register

Rectification or correction of the Register

3–27 The powers to amend the Register considered here are distinct from the powers to revoke or invalidate a registered trade mark under sections 46 and 47 of the 1994 Act.[32]

3–28 Errors or omissions in the Register may be rectified on the application of "any person having a sufficient interest", except in relation to matters affecting the validity of the registration of a trade mark,[33] and such an application may be made either to the Registrar or to the court. The application must be made to the court if proceedings concerning the trade mark in question are pending in the court, and the Registrar has power to refer the application to the court in any event.[34]

Errors affecting validity

3–29 Presumably, errors which could affect the validity of the registration of a trade mark, and which accordingly could not be corrected under section 64(1), would include such matters as mistakes concerning the identity of its proprietor,[35] or the specification of goods, which affected its liability to revocation for non-use.

3–30 A question which arises under section 64 is the standard to be applied in determining whether the matter in question is one "affecting the validity" of the registration concerned and hence not capable of being addressed under the section. One reading of the section is that the powers conferred may be exercised unless the matter concerned is such that, if not addressed, the mark would actually be wholly or partially invalid. Another possible meaning is that correction under section 64 may not be performed if the matter is of such a nature and/or degree of seriousness that there is a reasonable prospect of the registration being wholly or partially invalid as a result of it.

3–31 It is suggested that the latter meaning is to be preferred. Otherwise, it may be necessary to decide whether and how the validity of the registration concerned would be affected by the correction sought, merely in order to determine the threshold question of whether there is power under the section to deal with the application for correction.

3–32 On the other hand, however, if the proviso under section 64(1) is interpreted too broadly, so that an excessively wide range of matters are treated as "affecting the validity" of the mark in question, the effect will be that proprietors are unfairly precluded from making inoffensive

---

[32] As to which, see Chap. 9, *post*.
[33] s.64(1) of the Act.
[34] s.64(2).
[35] Rather than just an error in describing the correct person, perhaps by a misspelling or by using a trading name instead of the correct corporate name.

corrections. It should be recalled that if section 64 cannot be invoked, the only procedural alternatives are sections 45, 46 and 47, and under those provisions the only possible results which alter the Register are the complete or partial surrender, revocation or invalidity of the mark.

"Person having a sufficient interest"

There is no definition in the Act of a "person having a sufficient **3–33** interest", but clearly it would at least include the proprietor or a party to any registrable transaction incorrectly recorded. Most rectification proceedings under the 1938 Act, which could be brought by persons other than the Registrar or proprietor required that the applicant be a "person aggrieved".[36] The requirement was interpreted very broadly, and in general, anyone in the trade concerned had sufficient *locus* to apply,[37] while anyone alleged to infringe a mark was always a person aggrieved by its registration. The effect of the requirement was therefore to exclude only busybodies or persons with only a fanciful interest.

It seems likely that a similar standard will be applied under section **3–34** 64, although since the provision applies only to errors and omissions and not to matters affecting validity, there will plainly be less interest in its use from persons who are concerned that they are to be sued; they will generally apply under sections 46 and 47 instead.

Procedure for seeking rectification or correction

Rectification or correction under section 64(1) is to be sought on Form **3–35** TM26(R) together with a statement of the grounds on which the application is made and any evidence to support those grounds.[38]

Unless the proprietor himself has applied for rectification or correc- **3–36** tion, the Registrar must send a copy of the application and statement of grounds, and any evidence filed, to the proprietor.[39] The Registrar may, at that time, give directions for the filing of subsequent evidence.[40]

Upon completion of the evidence, the Registrar is to hold a hearing if **3–37** either of the parties requires it. Having made a decision, notice of it is to be sent to the parties, and the time for appeal runs from the date of sending.[41]

A person (other than the proprietor) who claims to have an interest in **3–38** an application under section 64 may apply for leave to intervene. Such an application must be made on Form TM27 stating the nature of the applicant's interest. The Registrar may refuse leave, or grant it on such

---

[36] See the 1938 Act, ss.32, 26, 27(4), 33 and 37 with Sched. 1.
[37] See previous editions of this work for details.
[38] 2000 Rules, r. 34(1).
[39] r. 34(2)(a).
[40] r. 34(2)(b).
[41] r. 34(3) and (4).

terms and conditions (including an undertaking as to costs) as she thinks fit, and there is power to hold a hearing to determine whether intervention should be allowed.[42] If intervention is allowed, the intervener is thereafter treated as a party for the purposes of the proceedings.[43]

Corrections date back

3–39 Errors and omissions corrected under section 64(1) and (2) of the 1994 Act are deemed never to have been made,[44] unless the Registrar or court otherwise directs.

Change of name and address

3–40 Changes of the name and address of the proprietor or a licensee are permitted under section 64(4), and can be made by the Registrar upon request. A request should be made on Form TM21.[45] Applications to change an address for service are to be made on Form TM33.[46]

Removal of matter which has ceased to have effect

3–41 The Registrar can remove from the Register matter which appears to her to have ceased to have effect.[47] An example might be an expired exclusive licence.

The procedure to be followed is provided for by rule 45 of the 2000 Rules. The Registrar may publish her intention to remove the matter, and is obliged to notify her intention to any person whom she considers to be affected by the removal.

3–42 Any person wishing to object to the intended removal must file a notice of opposition on Form TM7. A person whom the Registrar considered to be affected and notified accordingly, may file his objections in writing or may request that his objections be heard orally. If there is an objection, rule 54 applies, and the Registrar must hold a hearing if requested to do so before making a finding adverse to the person objecting.

3–43 If there are no objections, the Registrar may remove the matter (and presumably will do so); if there are objections and the Registrar is still of the view that the matter has wholly or partially ceased to have effect, she may remove it, or, if appropriate, part of it.[48]

---

[42] r. 35(1).
[43] r. 35(2).
[44] s.64(3).
[45] 2000 Rules, r. 48(1). Curiously, the rule allows changes by the proprietor or a licensee or any person having an interest in or charge on a registered mark which has been registered under r. 40, while s.64(4) only allows changes by the proprietor or licensee.
[46] r. 44(2).
[47] 1994 Act s.64(5).
[48] r. 45(3) and (4).

Falsification of the Register

It is an offence to cause a false entry to be made on the Register, **3–44** knowing or believing it to be false. It is also an offence to make anything falsely purporting to be a copy of the Register or to cause such a thing to be tendered in evidence; in either case knowing or having reason to believe in its falsity.[49]

These offences are explained in more detail in Chapter 19.

6. Inspection of the Register, and obtaining information

Inspection and provision of copies of the Register

By section 63(3) of the 1994 Act, the Register is to be open to public **3–45** inspection, and copies of extracts and entries are to be made available. The entry on the Register relating to a registered trade mark may be accessed online at the Trade Mark Registry website.[50]

Rules 42 and 43 of the 2000 Rules implement the requirements of **3–46** section 63(3). Under rule 42(2) the right of inspection extends to any part of the Register kept otherwise than in documentary form.

The Registrar is required to provide a certified copy or extract, or an uncertified copy or extract of any entry in the Register, as requested on Form TM31R.[51]

Requests for information and inspection of documents

In addition to rights to inspect the Register and to obtain copies, section **3–47** 67 of the 1994 Act allows requests for information about applications for registration and registered trade marks to be made. The information which will be made available following such a request depends on whether or not the application for registration of the mark in question has been published.

Before publication, and in the absence of consent from the applicant **3–48** for registration, a person seeking information can only obtain inspection of the application, any amendments to it, and any particulars of a registrable transaction which have been provided to the Registrar under rule 41 of the 2000 Rules.[52] There is a limited exception where a person seeking information has been told of an application and that proceedings are to be brought against him in respect of it following publication. In that case, he may obtain the same information as if the application had already been published.[53]

---

[49] s.94(1) and (2) of the Act.
[50] The website is at *www.patent.gov.uk*. It contains a link to the Trade Mark Enquiry Service, the address of which is presently http://webdb.patent.gov.uk/tm/number.
[51] r. 43.
[52] s.67(2) and r. 49.
[53] s.67(3).

3-49   After publication of an application, the general position is that inspection is to be permitted of all documents filed at the Registry in relation to a registered mark or application for registration.[54] However, there are a number of exceptions to this rule. The Registrar is not required to allow inspection of any document until after she has finished using it for any procedure to which it is relevant.[55] Further, the right of inspection does not extend to:

(1) any document until 14 days after its filing;
(2) purely internal Registry documents;
(3) documents sent to the Registry for inspection and then return to the sender;
(4) requests for information under rule 48;
(5) documents issued by the Registry which the Registrar considers should be treated as confidential;
(6) any document in relation to which the Registrar issues directions under rule 51 that it be treated as confidential.

3-50 In addition, the right of inspection is not retrospective. It does not apply to documents sent to the Registry before commencement of the Act, or documents sent after commencement but relating to applications under the 1938 Act.[56] It also does not apply to documents which disparage any person in a way likely to damage him.[57] There is no right of appeal from a decision of the Registrar to refuse inspection of 1938 Act documents, or disparaging documents.[58]

Confidential documents

3-51 Rule 51 of the 2000 Rules gives the Registrar power to order that any document other than a form required by her be treated as confidential. Documents which might contain confidential information could include financial information in agreements required to be registered, or confidential aspects of evidence submitted to the Registry.

3-52   In relation to a document filed with the Registry, a request that it, or part of it, be treated as confidential must be made when it is filed, or within 14 days thereafter. While the Registrar is considering the request, the document is not open to public inspection.[59]

3-53   Once the Registrar has directed that a document be treated as confidential, it is not open to public inspection except with the leave of

---

[54] r. 50(1).
[55] r. 50(2).
[56] r. 40(4)(b) and (c).
[57] r. 50(4)(a).
[58] r. 50(5). It is hard in any event to see in what sense the Registrar has to make a "decision" in connection with this rule. Other than perhaps in relation to disparaging documents there will be no room for debate as to whether documents should be open for inspection.
[59] r. 51(1).

the Registrar.[60] Such a direction may be withdrawn, but prior consultation with the person who sought confidentiality is required unless it is not reasonably practical.[61]

The Registrar may also direct that a document issued by the Registry **3–54** be treated as confidential. If she gives such a direction, the document is not open to public inspection except by her leave.[62] Such instances are likely to be rare, but could include a situation where written reasons for a Registry decision include extracts from confidential evidence filed by the parties.

Searches

It is generally advisable before offering a mark for registration to cause a **3–55** search to be made through the Register to discover whether any of its essential features have been anticipated in such manner as to be a bar to the application[63]; and it is often necessary or advisable for other purposes. Searches by the public are greatly facilitated by indexes maintained by the Registry and computerised searching facilities which are available.

An effective search against a trade mark will need to take into account both relevant registrations (and applications) for goods and for services.

Caveats

A party wishing to be informed in case some action is taken in respect of **3–56** a registered trade mark may file a caveat with the Trade Mark Registry on Form 31C. Matters of which such a party may ask to be informed include the publication of an application, the filing of an opposition, and the receipt of an application to register an assignment. Once such an event takes place, the Registry will inform the person entering the caveat, and it will be removed.

The *Trade Marks Journal*

The Patent Office publishes a weekly *Trade Marks Journal*. It contains **3–57** details of all trade marks applications accepted that week, registrations, renewals, assignments, licences, other applications which affect the status and scope of registered trade marks as well as news and notices of interest to the trade mark world.

---

[60] r. 51(2).
[61] r. 51(3).
[62] r. 51(4).
[63] See Chap. 8; below

7. Procedural matters concerning the Registry

Agency

3–58 Subject to very limited exceptions, anything required or authorised by the Act to be done by or to a person in connection with the registration of a trade mark, or any procedure relating to a registered trade mark, may be done by an agent.[64]

Requirement for a Hearing before an Adverse Decision

3–59 Rule 53 requires that the Registrar must give a party an opportunity to be heard before taking any decision which is or may be adverse to him.

---

[64] s.82 and rr. 52 and 53. For further details see Chap. 22, below.

CHAPTER 4

CLASSIFICATION OF GOODS AND SERVICES; MARKS FORMERLY ASSOCIATED

1. The classes

Classes

The significance of classification under the Trade Marks Act 1994 is **4–01** markedly different from that under the Trade Marks Act 1938. Under the 1938 Act, the rights conferred by registration were strictly limited to the particular goods (or services) for which the mark was registered.[1] This is no longer so under the 1994 Act, which provides protection in relation to goods or services similar to those for which the mark in question is registered, as well as identical goods or services, provided that a likelihood of confusion on the part of the public can be shown.[2]

This change will no doubt reduce the practical importance of the **4–02** classification of goods and services. In addition, under the 1994 Act, it is now possible to make a single application for a trade mark with a specification of goods and services covering more than one class.[3] As a result, classification is now very largely a matter of administrative convenience.

The scheme of classification used under the 1994 Act now forms **4–03** Schedule 3 to the Rules,[4] which sets out the current version of the classes of the International Classification of Goods and Services drawn up under the Nice Agreement. Subject to amendments which have taken place from time to time, it was also used under the 1938 Act. It provides for 34 classes of goods and eight classes of services.

---

[1] 1938 Act, ss.4–6.
[2] s.5(2) in relation to relative grounds for refusal of registration and s.10(2) in relation to infringement, and see Chaps 8 and 13, *post*.
[3] This was not possible under the 1938 Act and the Rules made under it, which required a separate application for each class: Trade Marks and Service Marks Rules 1986, rr. 21(2) and 23.
[4] The Trade Marks Rules 2000, S.I. 2000 No. 136. See App. 3, *post*. The 1994 Act, s.34, provides for classification, and also that any question as to which class goods fall into is to be decided by the Registrar, whose decision is final.

Registration by reference to the classification

4–04 There has long been a practice for applicants for registration to seek and the Registrar to grant registration for all (or part) of the goods within a particular class by reference to the class, usually with the words "all included in class . . ." in the specification of goods. There are many such marks on the Register. Where this has been done, and the question arises as to whether any particular goods do or do not fall within the registration, the approach adopted under the 1938 Act was to look to the Registrar's practice at the date of registration,[5] rather than simply construing the words defining the class. The same approach has now been applied under the 1994 Act.[6] However, since the rights conferred by registration now extend beyond the particular goods or services specified, this question may not be of such importance in future.

4–05 There has also been a practice in the past of applicants for registration seeking a specification for an entire class, or for a large range of goods or services in a class. In some cases this was acceptable, although the Rules made under the 1938 Act[7] gave the Registrar a discretion to refuse registration for such broad specifications unless she was satisfied that the breadth was merited by the applicant's actual or intended use. It is likely that a different approach is called for under the 1994 Act, particularly in view of the infringement provisions. A specification covering even a single description of goods may be too broad if there are many different and distinct varieties of such goods and the applicant only trades or intends to trade in some of them.[8] This topic is covered in further detail in Chapter 9.

2. Conversion

Conversion to the new classification

4–06 There remain on the Register a number of marks which were originally registered before the commencement of the 1938 Act, and for which the specification of goods was determined in accordance with an earlier classification providing for 50 classes of goods.[9] The 1938 Act[10] contained provisions allowing for the conversion to the new classification, but it was a voluntary scheme under which a proprietor could seek conversion if he wanted it, without giving the Registrar or the Board of Trade any power to require it.

---

[5] *Cal-U-Test* [1967] F.S.R. 39. See also *"GE"* at first instance, [1969] R.P.C. 418 at 458–459. This issue was not addressed by the Court of Appeal.
[6] *Isoact v. Avnet* [1998] F.S.R. 16.
[7] Trade Marks and Service Marks Rules 1986, r. 21(5).
[8] *Mercury Communications Ltd v. Mercury Inter-Active (UK) Ltd.* [1995] F.S.R. 850, where it was held that registration for "computer software" would normally be too wide.
[9] The classification was preserved in Sched. 3 of the Rules under the 1938 Act.
[10] s.36.

The 1994 Act[11] now provides for rules to be made empowering the **4–07** Registrar compulsorily to convert registrations under the old classification to the new one. The Act[12] envisaged that rules might be made empowering the Registrar to require proprietors of marks with old classifications to propose a new form of registration on pain of losing the registration if they did not comply. In the event this approach was not implemented, and the 2000 Rules which have been made[13] leave it to the Registrar to determine in the first instance how the specification of a registered mark should be reclassified.

Procedure for conversion

If the Registrar intends to convert a mark to the new classification, she **4–08** must give the proprietor written notice of her proposals. The proprietor then has three months to make written objections. If he makes no written objections then he loses the right to object any further and the Registrar will publish the proposals.[14] If the proprietor does make objections, then the Registrar will consider them, and thereafter either publish her original proposals, or proposals amended in the light of the objections. The Registrar's decision about the proposals to be published is final and not subject to appeal.[15]

Following publication of the Registrar's proposals under rule 40, there **4–09** is an opportunity to oppose. Any opposition must be filed on Form TM7 within three months of publication of the proposals. The grounds of opposition must be stated, and in particular they must set out how the proposed amendments would be contrary to section 65(3).[16] Evidence is admissible for the determination of the opposition, and the opponent is entitled to a hearing before a decision is made.[17]

If there is no opposition, or following the determination of any **4–10** opposition which is entered, the Registrar is to enter the amendments decided upon. Her decision is final and not subject to appeal.[18]

Conversion cannot generally increase scope of registration

Since the old and new classifications do not exactly correspond, there is **4–11** obviously potential for the scope of a registration to change in the course of conversion. This may in particular be the case where the specification of goods in an old registration is by reference to the classification itself.

---

[11] s.65 and Sched. 3, para. 12 of the transitional provisions to the 1994 Act giving the Registrar power to convert existing registered marks.
[12] s.65(4).
[13] rr. 46 and 47.
[14] r. 46(2) and (3).
[15] r. 46(4).
[16] r. 47(1). As to s.65(3), see below.
[17] r. 47(2).
[18] r. 47(3).

4-12   The 1994 Act recognises that it would in general not be right to extend the scope of the proprietor's monopoly as a side-effect of reclassification. On the other hand, a complete bar to extending the scope of registration could make phrasing the new specification of goods unnecessarily complex and result in specifications which were wordy and unclear.

4-13   Accordingly, section 65(3) provides that the power to reclassify shall not be exercised so as to extend the rights conferred by a registration, except where it appears to the Registrar that avoiding such extension "would involve undue complexity" and that any extension would not be substantial and would not adversely affect the rights of any person. This provision allows the Registrar to form his own view of the significance of a reclassification which extends a registration, even in the absence of observations by the proprietor or anyone else who might be affected. It surely also must mean that if reclassification is opposed by a person whose activities do not infringe the existing registration, but would (or might arguably) infringe the registration as proposed to be amended, the reclassification should not take place in that manner. In any event, even if the extension of the proprietor's rights would not affect anyone else, it can only be permitted if it is not substantial.

3. Marks formerly associated

Associated trade marks—the old law

4-14   Under section 23 of the 1938 Act, the Registrar had the power to require that marks be associated. The Registrar's power to require association arose if a proprietor held or applied for marks which were identical to one another or closely resembled one another, in respect of the same goods or goods of the same description.[19]

4-15   The effect of association was that the proprietor could only assign the marks together. Assignment separately was not permitted unless the Registrar could be persuaded to dissolve the association, and only had power to do so if the Registrar was satisfied that there was no likelihood of deception or confusion if the associated marks were in use by different persons. This requirement reflected the whole purpose of association, which was to avoid the same or similar marks being used on the same or similar goods by different people.

Association did offer some benefits for proprietors, though: under section 30 of the 1938 Act, use of one associated mark could count as use of the others.

Abolition of association

4-16   Association of marks has been abolished by the transitional provisions of the 1994 Act, Schedule 3 paragraph 2(3).[20] Associations entered on the Register ceased to have effect on commencement.

---

[19] The same power existed where identical or similar marks were registered or applied for in respect of goods and associated services: Trade Marks Act 1938, s.23(2A).
[20] Save in the case of marks registered as a series under the 1938 Act: Sched. 3, para. 2(2).

Effect on Marks formerly Associated

The result of associations ceasing to have effect is that associated marks **4–17** may now be assigned separately without any procedural hindrance and without any involvement of the Registrar. However, there may still be difficulties following such an assignment if the result is to mislead consumers. There are a numbers of types of assignment which are permitted under the 1994 Act but which would not have been allowed under the 1938 Act because of their tendency to deceive, and the issues which they present are considered in Chapters 9 and 12.

CHAPTER 5

NATIONAL REGISTRATION OF TRADE MARKS

1. Preliminary

5–01 The Trade Marks Act 1994 makes provision in respect of the registration of trade marks of various types. First, it makes provision in respect of the national registration of trade marks. This chapter is concerned with the process of registration of such marks.

5–02   Secondly, the 1994 Act makes provision in respect of applications under the Madrid Protocol. This came into effect in the United Kingdom on April 1, 1996[1] and is considered in Chapter 6. For the purposes of this chapter it is important to note the following matters. Protection may now be sought in the United Kingdom for an international registration originating in another contracting state. Such an international registration is entitled to become protected in the United Kingdom (and so become a protected international trade mark (UK)) where it satisfies the requirements of a national application for registration. Accordingly, the discussion below of the requirements of a national application is relevant also to an international registration designating the United Kingdom. It is also important to note that an international application may originate in the United Kingdom and be founded on an application for registration of a national mark. If the national application is refused or restricted, for example after opposition, then the Registrar must notify the International Bureau and request that the international registration be cancelled or amended accordingly. It is, however, possible to transform the international application into national applications and hold the original priority date. All these matters and other aspects of the Madrid Protocol are discussed further in Chapter 6.

5–03   Finally, the 1994 Act makes provision in respect of Community trade marks. Applications for Community trade marks are dealt with substantively by the Office for the Harmonisation of the Internal Market (OHIM) located in Alicante, Spain and accordingly are not discussed further here. However, and as in the case of international registrations, the 1994 Act provides for the transformation of applications for such Community trade marks into applications for national registrations. The Community trade mark system is explained in Chapter 6.

5–04   There is a further general matter which should be mentioned at the outset. National applications are prosecuted through the Registry. Here

[1] The Trade Marks (International Registration) Order 1996, S.I. 1996 No. 714.

the practice has been amended to reflect the changes recommended in the Reports by Lord Woolf, "Access to Justice". In general it may be assumed that in so far as the Registrar has a discretion it will be exercised in accordance with the overriding objective set out in rule 1.1 of the Civil Procedure Rules 1998. This includes, so far as is practicable:

(1) ensuring that the parties are on an equal footing;
(2) saving expense;
(3) dealing with the case in ways which are proportionate:

    (a) to the amount of money involved;
    (b) to the importance of the case;
    (c) to the complexity of the issues; and
    (d) to the financial position of each party;

(4) ensuring that it is dealt with expeditiously and fairly; and
(5) allotting to it an appropriate share of the court's resources, while taking into account the need to allot resources to other cases.

2. Procedure on national application to register

Who may apply to register a mark

Any person may apply to register a trade mark provided the statutory **5–05** requirements of an application are met. These are discussed below. The application will proceed and the mark will duly be registered provided that the mark satisfies the definition of a trade mark and is not objectionable by reason of any of the absolute or relative grounds for refusal.[2] The absolute grounds of refusal are discussed in Chapter 7, and the relative grounds for refusal in Chapter 8.

Essential particulars of an application

An application for registration of a trade mark is made to the Registrar. **5–06** Section 32(2) of the 1994 Act requires an application to contain:

(1) a request for registration of a trade mark;
(2) the name and address of the applicant;

---

[2] The Registrar has no residual power to refuse an application if the statutory requirements of an application are met and the mark is not objectionable by reason of any of the absolute or relative grounds for refusal: *Eurolamb* [1997] R.P.C. 279; *Procter & Gamble (bottle shapes)* [1999] R.P.C. 673 at 675, CA. This is in contrast to the position under the Trade Marks Act 1938. Section 17(2) of that Act conferred on the Registrar a discretion to refuse an application for registration even though the requirements for registration were satisfied.

(3) a statement of the goods or services in relation to which it is sought to register the trade mark; and

(4) a representation of the mark.

In addition the application must state that the trade mark is being used, by the applicant or with his consent, in relation to the goods or services specified, or that he has a bona fide intention that it should be so used.[3]

All applications are subject to the payment of the appropriate application and class fees.[4]

Form of the application

General requirements

5–07 The application must be filed on Form TM3.[5] The nature of the mark should be made clear on the application.

The Trade Marks Rules 2000 lay down certain further specific requirements. Applications for three dimensional marks must contain a statement to that effect. Where colour is claimed as an element of the trade mark then the application must contain a statement to that effect and the colour must also be specified. If an application contains a word shown in a particular graphical form on the application then it will be treated as an application to register the word in that form unless the applicant includes a statement that the application is for registration of the word without regard to its graphical form.[6]

Graphical representation must be precise

5–08 The graphical representation must record the identity of the sign clearly and unambiguously.[7]

Date of filing

5–09 The date of filing is the date upon which documents containing everything required by section 32(2) are furnished to the Registrar. If documents are furnished on different days then the date of filing is the

---

[3] s.32(3).

[4] s.32(4) and r. 5(1). The appropriate fees are set out in a schedule published by the Registry and are regularly reviewed. The current schedule is reproduced in App. 4. The fees must be paid within two months of the date of notice to the applicant.

[5] r. 5(1).

[6] r. 5(2), (3) and (4).

[7] *Ty Nant Spring Water's Appln* [1999] R.P.C. 392; [2000] R.P.C. 55 (a colour should have been specified by hue and included a graphic example) and the cases there cited; *Creola* [1997] R.P.C. 507 (application must be sufficiently clear and distinct to allow all the essential features to be identified); *Antoni & Allison's Appln* [1998] E.T.M.R. 460 (a mere description not conveying the clear and precise appearance of a 3D mark not adequate); *Orange Personal Communications Ltd's Appln* [1998] E.T.M.R. 460 (the word "orange" not sufficiently precise); *Swizzels Matlow Ltd's Appln* [1999] R.P.C. 879 (unlikely that a mere description of 3D mark would, in practice, ever be sufficiently precise); *Venootschap onder Firma Senta Aromatic Marketing's Appln* [1999] E.T.M.R. 429 ("the smell of fresh cut grass", for tennis balls, was sufficiently precise, in fact).

last of those days.[8] The filing date is important because, subject to a claim to priority, this is the date from which, once granted, the rights of the proprietor have effect.[9]

Claim to priority

Where a right to priority is claimed then particulars of the claim should **5–10** be included in the application. The requirements are specified in rule 6 of the 2000 Rules. A certificate by the registering or other competent authority of the country of the priority application must be filed within three months of the application.

Application may relate to more than one class

The classification of goods and services is addressed in Chapter 4. An **5–11** application may be made for registration of a trade mark in respect of goods and services in more than one class.[10]

Every application must specify the class to which it relates and list the goods or services appropriate to that class.[11] This aspect of the specification has an important role to play in determining the boundaries of the registration. The scope of the registration will be determined by reference to the specified goods or services and the class. If the application relates to more than one class, then the specification must set out the classes in consecutive numerical order. Where an application covers more than one class then additional fees are payable for each further class.

If the specification contained in the application lists items by reference **5–12** to a class in which they do not fall then the applicant may request that the application be amended to include the appropriate class.[12] But this will only be allowed where it does not offend against section 39(2). Accordingly, amendment will be allowed only in limited circumstances, such as where the specification explicitly lists goods or services which are in a different class and have been included only because of an error of wording or an obvious mistake. Similarly, if there is a contradiction between the whole list of goods or services and the class number then this would likely be regarded as an obvious mistake.[13]

Address for service

Every applicant for registration of a trade mark must file an address for **5–13** service in the United Kingdom.[14] The address for service of an applicant for registration of a trade mark is, on registration, deemed to be the

---

[8] s.33.
[9] s.9(3) provides that the rights of the proprietor have effect from the date of registration which, in accordance with s.40(3), is the date of filing of the application for registration.
[10] r. 8 and Form TM3A.
[11] r. 8(2).
[12] r. 8(3).
[13] Practice Amendment Circular (PAC) 2/99.
[14] r. 10. Any person opposing an application must also file such an address for service.

address for service on the registered proprietor, subject to a filing to the contrary.[15] Anything sent to the applicant (or opponent) at his address for service is deemed to have been properly sent. The Registrar may, where no address for service is filed, treat as the address for service of the person concerned his trade or business address in the United Kingdom, if any. Where an address for service is not filed, the Registrar will send the person concerned notice to file an address for service within two months of the date of the notice, and if that person fails to do so the application will be treated as abandoned (or, in the case of an opposition, withdrawn).

Use or bona fide intention to use

5–14 This statement is a requirement of the 1994 Act. To this end the Form TM3 contains the statement "The Trade Mark is being used by the applicant or with his or her consent, in relation to the goods or services stated, or there is a bona fide intention that it will be so used". The applicant must sign the statement. If he fails to do so it will be treated as a deficiency.[16]

5–15 A number of points arise from this requirement. First, it seems that the requirement extends to all the goods and services the subject of the application. Under the 1938 Act it was common to register the mark for goods of the same description as those in relation to which it was actually intended to use the mark.[17]

5–16 Secondly, it is not at all clear what is meant by the words "or that he has a bona fide intention that it should be so used". These words do not appear in the Directive and it seems likely that they are derived from section 26(1) of the 1938 Act. The authorities under the 1938 Act may accordingly provide some assistance. There it was tolerably clear that bona fide meant genuine, judged by commercial standards, even if carried out for an ulterior motive.[18] It was also a requirement of the 1938

---

[15] A filing to the contrary can be made under r. 10(1) or r. 44(2).

[16] The position may be contrasted with that under the 1938 Act. There it was part of the definition of a trade mark that the mark was used or proposed to be used (s.68). Exceptions were provided by s.29 where either a corporation was about to be established and the applicant intended to assign the mark to the corporation or where the application was accompanied by an application for registration of a person as registered user. This created some anomalies. For example it was held not to cover the situation where the applicant had not yet selected his registered users: *Pussy Galore* [1967] R.P.C. 265.

[17] The proviso to s.26 of the 1938 Act stated that, except where the applicant had been permitted under s.12(2) to register an identical or nearly resembling mark in respect of the goods in question or where the tribunal was of the opinion that he might properly be permitted to register such a mark, the tribunal might refuse an application to remove a mark for non-use if it was shown that any proprietor had in fact made bona fide use of the trade mark in relation to goods of the same description or services associated with the goods or goods of the same description. A similar proviso existed in relation to services.

[18] *Electrolux v. Electrix (No. 2)* (1954) 71 R.P.C. 23, CA; *Imperial v. Philip Morris, "Nerit"* [1982] F.S.R. 72, CA, a ghost mark case; *"Huggars"* [1979] F.S.R. 310, another ghost mark case; *Levi Strauss v. Shah* [1985] R.P.C. 371 at 378; *"Concord"* [1987] F.S.R. 209; *"Kodiak"* [1990] F.S.R. 49; *1–800 Flowers* [2000] E.T.M.R. 369.

Act, although introduced as part of the definition of a trade mark, that the intention to use be a "definite and present intention".[19]

Thirdly, there is as yet no clear authority as to the consequences of **5-17** making such a declaration which is not correct. Certainly there is no express sanction provided by the 1994 Act. It seems that it would render the application vulnerable to an attack under section 3(6) as one made in bad faith. This is a subject addressed in Chapter 7.[20]

Deficiencies in the application

Where an application fails to satisfy the requirements of section 32(2), (3) **5-18** or (4) of the 1994 Act or rule 5(1) or 8(2) or 10 of the 2000 Rules, then the Registrar will notify the applicant of the deficiency or, in the case of section 32(4), the failure to make payment.[21] The applicant then has two months from the date of the notice to remedy the deficiency or default.

If the applicant fails to remedy the deficiency (or make the necessary **5-19** payment) within the two months of the notice then the application will be deemed never to have been made in the case of a failure under section 32(2) and shall be treated as abandoned in the case of a failure under section 32(3) or (4) or rules 5(1), 8(2) or 10.

The time limit of two months is not extendible.[22]

Transitional arrangements

There are still some applications pending which were made under the **5-20** 1938 Act. These are provided for in Schedule 3 of the 1994 Act. As a general rule all such applications are dealt with under the old law (Schedule 3, paragraphs 1 and 10 of the 1994 Act).[23] But that is subject to the following.

In the case of pending applications for registration not advertised **5-21** under section 18 of the 1938 Act prior to commencement, the applicant could give notice to the Registrar claiming to have registrability determined in accordance with the 1994 Act (Schedule 3, paragraph 11 of the 1994 Act and rule 68 of the 2000 Rules). The notice had to be in the prescribed form, accompanied by the appropriate fee and given no later

---

[19] *Imperial v. Philip Morris, supra.*
[20] The courts have not attempted to explain the scope of the provision and it may require a reference to the ECJ: *Road Tech Computer Systems v. Unison Software* [1996] F.S.R. 805. In *Gromax Plasticulture v. Don & Low Nonwovens* [1999] R.P.C. 367, Lindsay J. considered that it includes dishonesty and also some dealings which fall short of the standards of acceptable commercial behaviour observed by reasonable and experienced men in the particular area being examined; *Demon Ale* [2000] R.P.C. 345 (appointed person); *Sheimer ("Visa")* [2000] R.P.C. 484; [1999] E.T.M.R. 519 (appointed person).
[21] rr. 10(6) and 11. See, *e.g. Ty Nant Spring Water Ltd's Appln* [2000] R.P.C. 55.
[22] r. 68.
[23] In the case of applications being dealt with under the 1938 Act the appointed person accordingly has no power to hear appeals from the Registrar on opposition: *"Taboo"* [2000] R.P.C. 360.

than six months after the date of commencement. Any such notice properly given was irrevocable.

5–22   Where an application for registration made under the 1938 Act has been advertised after commencement, the period within which notice of opposition may be filed is three months from the date of advertisement and that period is not extendible (Schedule 3, paragraph 10(2) of the 1994 Act and rule 67 of the 2000 Rules). Section 23 of the 1938 Act (relating to associated marks) is to be disregarded in dealing after commencement with old applications for registration (Schedule 3, paragraph 10(3) of the 1994 Act).

Examination of the application

5–23 Once it has been determined that the application satisfies the basic requirements of the 1994 Act, it proceeds to examination. In particular the Registrar will consider whether the application appears to meet the requirements of section 1, whether any of the absolute grounds of refusal of section 3 apply or whether the application offends against the provisions of section 4 relating to specially protected emblems. In addition, applications which have satisfied the formalities requirements of the Act can be and are entered onto the Optics and Trims database systems. These permit the Registrar to carry out a search of earlier trade marks, as defined in section 6 of the Act, to consider the application for conflict with any such marks and whether any objection should be raised under section 5 of the Act. These objections are discussed further below.

5–24   If it appears to the Registrar that the requirements for registration are not satisfied then the applicant is informed and given an opportunity to make representations or to amend the application.[24] This is done by means of the examination report. If there are significant objections then the applicant will generally be given six months to respond. If the applicant fails to respond to this or a subsequent letter then the Registrar will refuse the application.[25] Generally any objections raised in relation to an application will lead to discussion with the Registry as to the possibilities for resolving the objection by, for example, amending the application or filing evidence. These are discussed further below.

Is the mark a trade mark?

5–25 The Registrar must consider whether the mark applied for is a trade mark within the meaning of section 1 of the 1994 Act. Particular consideration is given to shapes, colours, sounds and smells. To satisfy the requirements of section 1, these must be capable of being represented graphically and capable of distinguishing the goods or services of

---

[24] s.37(3).
[25] s.37(4).

one undertaking from those of other undertakings. Care should be taken in the case of shapes that they do accurately represent the mark sought to be protected. In the case of colours it must be expected that the Registry will take a conservative line in respect of single colours, and much may depend upon the choice of colours and the way they are used.[26] As to sounds and smells, these pose particular problems when it comes to graphical representation and it must also be expected that the Registry will require convincing evidence that they are capable of distinguishing the goods or services of the applicant. (See Chapter 2, para. 2–08 et seq.)

The absolute grounds of refusal

The absolute grounds for refusal are set out in sections 3 and 4 of the **5–26** 1994 Act. The Registrar will raise these grounds as objections where it appears they are applicable. Each of the objections raised will be specified and the basis for it given. To overcome any such objection the applicant should consider lodging evidence of use, restricting the goods or services the subject of the application, limitations and disclaimers and obtaining consents. These are all considered further below.

The relative grounds of objection

The Registrar must search for conflicting marks to determine if any of **5–27** the relative grounds of objection specified in section 5 of the 1994 Act appears to be applicable. This is done using the Optics and Trims systems. The Registrar attempts to search all classes which contain the same or similar goods or services to those the subject of the application. If any marks are found which have an earlier filing date or an earlier priority date, then they will be considered. If the owner of a later filed mark claims earlier use, then the conflicting rights will usually have to be resolved by opposition. The Registrar will determine whether the similarity between the marks and the goods or services is such that there is a likelihood of confusion. If it is considered that there is then the objection will be raised and the basis for it given.[27]

The Registry has issued guidance as to how it deals with pending **5–28** earlier citations.[28] Such earlier citations are earlier trade marks within the meaning of section 6, subject to their being registered. The Registry has indicated they will be dealt with as follows. Where there are other absolute grounds for refusal the Registry will expect applicants to overcome them, and if they should fail to do so then refusal will be

---

[26] See, e.g. Ty Nant Spring Water Ltd's Appln [1999] R.P.C. 392; [2000] R.P.C. 55.
[27] Where the only component of the earlier mark which could be regarded as creating a similarity with a later trade mark is the subject of a disclaimer to any exclusive right, the examiner will not consider the marks to be similar enough to create a likelihood of confusion following Paco Holdings v. Paco Rabanne Parfums [2000] R.P.C. 451; PAC 3/00; cf. "Fountain" [1999] R.P.C. 490.
[28] PAC 1/99.

based upon them, subject to the caveat that there are other potential grounds for refusal which may have to be dealt with on appeal. Where there are other relative grounds for refusal based upon registered trade marks, then again applicants will be expected to progress matters. However, a request for suspension will be considered. Where there are no other grounds for refusal then the Registry will suggest suspending the application. But because suspension is undesirable, objections based upon pending marks will only be maintained by the Registry if they would be clearly fatal to the application should they mature to registration.

5–29   In seeking to overcome any such objection applicants should consider filing evidence of use; restricting the goods or services the subject of the application; honest concurrent use; obtaining consents; removal or limitation of the earlier mark; disclaimers; and division of the application. These are discussed further below.

Evidence of use

5–30   Where an objection is raised under section 3 or 5 of the 1994 Act it may be possible to overcome that objection by filing evidence of use. Indeed, in the case of certain objections under section 3, this is specifically contemplated by the Act which provides that an application shall not be refused registration by virtue of section 3(1)(b), (c) or (d) if, before the application for registration, it has acquired a distinctive character as a result of the use made of it.[29] Evidence of use may also overcome an objection under section 3(3)(b). Such evidence commonly details sales (value and quantity) under the mark on an annual basis, the territory in which sales have occurred, details of advertising and promotion, again on an annual basis, providing illustrative samples and details of how the mark has appeared on the goods or in relation to the services, again providing samples or photographs.

5–31   The extent and duration of use required will vary depending on the nature of the mark objected to. The Registry has given a general indication that it would usually expect a mark, the subject of an objection under section 3(1), to have been used on a reasonable scale for five years. But less use may suffice in cases where the objection is not very strong. Conversely evidence of more use, coupled with trade and possibly survey evidence, may be required where the mark is inherently very descriptive or otherwise lacking a distinctive character.

5–32   It must be remembered that proceedings before the Registrar are proceedings to which the strict rules of evidence apply.[30] Although the

---

[29] s.3(1), proviso.
[30] "St Trudo" [1995] R.P.C. 370; Practice Notice of 4 January 1999 [1999] R.P.C. 294; this supersedes the Practice Direction of 12 July 1995 [1995] R.P.C. 381. In proceedings which began on or after January 31, 1997 evidence is not to be excluded on the basis it is hearsay. The weight to be given to any such evidence is a matter for the Registrar to consider in accordance with the Civil Evidence Act 1995, s.4. See further paras 5–97 to 5–103, below.

Registrar has had a practice of considering informal evidence, such evidence should thereafter be made the subject of a statutory declaration or affidavit because otherwise the task of any appellant tribunal will be made difficult, if not impossible.[31]

The courts have expressed some scepticism that distinctiveness of **5–33** some marks can ever be established by evidence of use alone. In the case of highly descriptive or laudatory words it will be necessary to show that the public recognise the mark applied for as a trade mark distinctive of the goods or services of the applicant.[32]

Restriction of the goods or services

Restriction of the goods or services the subject of the application is one **5–34** of the few amendments of an application permissible under the 1994 Act.[33] This may serve to avoid an objection under section 3 or section 5.

Restriction of the specification can be achieved in a number of ways. **5–35** Particular goods or services which have given rise to the objection can simply be deleted. But often there is a general description which requires amendment. In such cases restriction can be achieved either by excluding particular goods or services by use of the expression ". . . but not including . . ." or by introducing a limitation such as ". . . all for . . ." or ". . . all made from . . .".

Limitation and disclaimer

An applicant may voluntarily disclaim any right to the use of any **5–36** specified element of a trade mark or agree that the rights conferred by the registration shall be subject to a specified or other territorial limitation.[34]

Unlike the position under the 1938 Act, the Registrar has no power to **5–37** impose a condition or limitation or to require a disclaimer.[35] If it is considered that the mark is objectionable and no suitable limitation or disclaimer is offered, then the Registrar has no alternative but to refuse the application.

---

[31] "*Fresh Banking*" [1998] R.P.C. 605.
[32] See *British Sugar v. Robertson* [1996] R.P.C. 281 at 286; *Philips v. Remington* [1998] R.P.C. 283 (Jacob J.) and [1999] R.P.C. 809, CA.
[33] s.39(1). Amendment of an application is only permitted to a limited degree, see paras 5–63 to 5–65, below.
[34] s.13.
[35] Conditions are not permitted under the 1994 Act. Any condition entered on the register under the old law ceased to have effect on commencement of the 1994 Act: Sched. 3, para. 3(1).

5–38   Disclaimers provide a useful way of dealing with objections raised by the Registrar or during opposition and where a disclaimer is necessary to preserve the essential validity of the trade mark.[36] But an applicant's offer to disclaim part of his mark will not often assist in overcoming a section 5 objection because the Registry considers that an admission made by the applicant cannot of itself be deemed to affect the scope of protection of the earlier mark.[37]

5–39   Limitations are also a valuable way of overcoming objections raised by the Registrar or under opposition. So, for example, a limitation may be offered where the specification of goods or services is too wide or where, absent a limitation, such as to colour, the mark would not be distinctive.

5–40   Rule 24 of the 2000 Rules provides that where the applicant for registration of a trade mark or the proprietor by notice in writing sent to the Registrar disclaims any right to the exclusive use of any specified element of a trade mark or agrees that the rights conferred by the registration shall be subject to a specified territorial or other limitation, then the Registrar shall make the appropriate entry in the Register and publish the disclaimer or limitation.

It is notable that conditions are not permissible under the 1994 Act.

Consents

5–41 This is a potentially important way of overcoming objections under section 5. It is provided by section 5(5) that nothing in section 5 prevents the registration of a trade mark where the proprietor of the earlier trade mark or other earlier right consents to the registration. So if the applicant obtains the consent of the proprietor of the cited mark to the registration the Registrar cannot maintain the objection. The Registrar has no discretion in this regard.

5–42   This position is in marked contrast to the position under the 1938 Act. There the consent did not remove the statutory objection and the Registrar could only consider the consent as evidence in relation to the issue of the likelihood of confusion.

5–43   An interesting issue may arise if the consent is only provided on condition that the new mark is used in a particular way.[38] The issue

---

[36] Under the old law the Registrar might require a disclaimer of, for example, a part of the mark which was descriptive even in the case where the mark was prima facie registrable. So, in the case of word marks being variations of ordinary words, he might require a disclaimer of the ordinary word. In the case of devices, he might require a disclaimer of letters or numerals comprised within the device. The assumption behind the requirement of the disclaimer was that no rights could in fact be claimed in the part disclaimed. However, it served to prevent uncertainty in the minds of rival traders as to the scope of the registration. Where on the other hand it was obvious that no rights could be claimed in only part of the mark the Registrar would not require a disclaimer. This valuable role of disclaimers appears to have no place under the new law.

[37] PAC 3/00.

[38] As in *Peck v. Zelcker ("Polly Peck")* [1963] R.P.C. 85.

might turn on the way the transaction is construed. If the consent itself is conditional, then this would not appear to satisfy the requirements of the Act. On the other hand, if the consent is unconditional but is provided as part of an agreement which includes a term specifying the manner of use then, it is suggested, the provision would be satisfied and, in the event of breach, the earlier proprietor would have to sue for breach of contract.

Honest concurrent use

Section 7 of the 1994 Act provides that where the applicant can establish **5–44** by evidence that there has been honest concurrent use, then the Registrar shall not refuse the application under section 5 unless the objection is raised in opposition proceedings. Honest concurrent use means such use that would have constituted honest concurrent use under the 1938 Act. What use satisfies this requirement is explained in Chapter 8. If the Registrar believes it to be established, then she must allow the application to proceed to publication where the proprietor of the earlier right may or may not oppose. There is no requirement in the 1994 Act that the proprietor of the earlier right be notified of the application, although the advertisement will include an indication of the basis upon which it has been allowed to proceed.

If an application for a trade mark is opposed by the proprietor of an **5–45** earlier trade mark or earlier right, then honest concurrent use will not of itself overcome the objection under section 5. But the fact that the two marks have been concurrently used without confusion or without the later mark taking unfair advantage of the earlier mark's reputation may be relevant in reaching a conclusion as to the validity of the objection.[39]

Removal or limitation, transfer or surrender of the earlier mark

In appropriate circumstances an application can be made to remove or **5–46** limit the earlier mark. Such proceedings may be brought under section 46 of the 1994 Act to revoke the earlier mark or under section 47 to seek a declaration of invalidity. In general such an application may be made to the Registrar or the court and the procedure and requirements are discussed in detail in Chapters 9 and 18.

It should be noted that if a trade mark is revoked under section 46 **5–47** then the rights of the proprietor are deemed to have ceased as from the date of the application for revocation unless the court or the Registrar is satisfied that the grounds for revocation existed at an earlier date. Since the merits of an application for registration are considered as at the date of that application, it will be necessary to secure a finding that the mark revoked was invalid as of that date.

---

[39] *"React"* [1999] R.P.C. 529.

5–48   In appropriate cases it may be expected the Registrar will stay an application for registration until such an application for revocation or declaration has been resolved.

An alternative course is to reach an agreement with the earlier proprietor that he surrenders the earlier mark in respect of the relevant or all of the goods or services for which it is registered under section 45, or that he transfers it to the applicant by assignment under section 24. It is notable that pending applications can be assigned under the 1994 Act.[40]

Division

5–49 Division is a useful option where objection is taken to the application on the basis of only some of the goods or services the subject of that application. Rather than holding up or risking refusal of the whole application, an applicant can divide the application into two or more parts.[41] In this way the acceptable part can proceed to publication leaving the applicant to address with the Registrar the goods or services in relation to which objection has been taken.

5–50   Where an application is divided each divisional application will retain the original filing date and is then treated as a separate application. In so far as opposition may have been lodged or third party observations made, they will be treated as having been lodged or raised in relation to each divisional application. Of course, in so far as they related to some only of the goods or services of the original application (which is not unlikely in the case of multi-class applications) they may fall away in relation to one or more of the divisional applications. Upon division of an original application any licence or other interest will be deemed to apply in relation to each of the divisional applications.

An applicant for a series of marks may not divide his application into separate applications of each of the marks, at least at the stage of opposition.[42]

Earlier registrations of the applicant

5–51 Sometimes the Registry will accept an application which it would otherwise deem to be prima facie objectionable on the basis of a prior registration of the applicant where the marks and the goods or services are either the same or very similar.

Acceptance or refusal of the application

5–52 If the Registrar is duly satisfied that the requirements of the Act are met, then she must accept the application and allow it to proceed to publication (advertisement under the 1938 Act).[43] If she is not then she

---

[40] See ss.34 and 37 and Chap. 12.
[41] See 1994 Act, s.41; 2000 Rules, r. 19 and Form TM12.
[42] *Dualit Ltd's Trade Mark Applns* [1999] R.P.C. 304; [1999] R.P.C. 890.
[43] s.37(5); *Proctor & Gamble* [1999] R.P.C. 673, CA. There is no residual discretion to refuse to allow the application to proceed.

must refuse the application. If the Registrar is minded to refuse an application then before making her decision she must give the applicant an opportunity to be heard and she must give the applicant at least 14 days notice of the time when he may be heard, unless the applicant consents to shorter notice.[44] The applicant may attend himself or by an agent or may make submissions in writing.

Where the Registrar makes a decision following a hearing or after **5–53** considering any submission in writing, then she must send a notice of her decision to the applicant. If the notice does not contain reasons then the applicant can request the Registrar to send him a statement of the reasons for the decision.[45] Such a request must be made within one month of the date on which the notice was sent.[46] If the notice contains reasons then, for the purpose of any appeal, the date of the decision is the date upon which the notice is sent. If it does not, then the date upon which the statement of reasons is sent is deemed to be the date of the decision for the purposes of any appeal against it.[47]

As before, it seems that an *ex parte* decision of the Registrar prior to advertisement would not bind her if opposition is entered.[48]

Onus before the Registrar

The Registry has taken the view that the overall effect of section 37 of **5–54** the 1994 Act is that the Registrar is required to make a judgment about whether registration should be allowed, but that there is no overall onus to be discharged, one way or the other.[49]

Appeal from an *ex parte* decision of the Registrar

An appeal lies from a decision of the Registrar to refuse an application **5–55** and such an appeal may be brought either to an appointed person or to the court.[50] Appeals are discussed generally below at 5–125 *et seq.*

Second application for the same mark

Where a mark has already been rejected for registration, a second **5–56** application to register it, raising essentially the same issues, may properly be rejected on that ground alone.[51] Where however the

---

[44] r. 54.
[45] r. 62 and Form TM5.
[46] r. 62(2).
[47] r. 62.
[48] "*Solibrisa*" (1948) 65 R.P.C. 17 at 23 (Regy).
[49] "*Eurolamb*" [1997] R.P.C. 279; *Procter & Gamble (soap tablet shape)* [1998] R.P.C. 710; *Procter & Gamble (bottle shape)* [1999] R.P.C. 673, CA; but note should be taken of s.37(4) which provides that if the applicant fails to satisfy the Registrar that the requirements of the 1994 Act are met, then the Registrar must refuse to accept the application. See also the comments on onus in the course of opposition, in para. 5–109, below.
[50] s.76.
[51] *Massachusetts Saw* (1918) 35 R.P.C. 137. See also *Hunt* (1911) 28 R.P.C. 392, where an opponent waived his right to plead *res judicata* and consented to registration.

application is one calling for evidence of distinctiveness of the mark, it by no means follows that a second application will raise the same issues as the first; the further period of use between the dates of the two applications may well so increase the reputation of the mark as to enable the applicant to produce evidence convincing to the Registrar whereas previously she was unable to do so.[52] Indeed the mere fact that the applications concern different dates may be enough to prevent the identity of issue required for an actual estoppel.[53]

Publication

5-57 When an application has been accepted the Registrar causes it to be published[54] in the Trade Marks Journal. Thereafter third parties may oppose the application and observations may be made to the Registrar in writing.

The published representation must clearly depict the essential features which are sought to be the subject of the rights granted by the registration. If it does not then the advertisement is a nullity.[55]

Observations

5-58 Where an application has been published, any person may at any time before the registration of the trade mark, make observations in writing to the Registrar as to whether the trade mark should be registered. The Registrar will inform the applicant of any such observations.[56] Any person who makes observations does not become a party to the proceedings. This is a new provision, introduced at the request of interests consulted by the Government, and is consistent with the practice of the OHIM and that adopted under the Patents Act 1977.[57]

5-59 Such observations could, for example, suggest that a section 3 objection should have been raised or that a third party has an earlier trade mark which raises a section 5 objection. On receipt of such observations they will be considered by the Registrar and she will issue a preliminary opinion to the person who submitted the observations and to the applicant. If the Registrar considers that the application was accepted in error, the applicant will be invited to respond. If, after

---

[52] Thus the application to register "Daimler" which was successful in 1916 (*Daimler* (1916) 33 R.P.C. 337) must have failed if it had been made in 1901: see *Daimler v. British Motor Traction* (1901) 18 R.P.C. 465. Indeed, in earlier editions of this work it was suggested to be normal practice, where an application was rejected on the ground of insufficient user to establish distinctiveness, to abandon the application and file a fresh one rather than to attempt to appeal.

[53] *Unilever* [1987] R.P.C. 13 at 20.

[54] s.38(1).

[55] *"Creola"* [1997] R.P.C. 507.

[56] s.38(3).

[57] The provision was so explained by Lord Strathclyde, Minister of State, Department of Trade (Public Bill Committee, Third Sitting, January 19, 1994 at col. 81).

considering the applicant's response, the Registrar still considers the application was accepted in error, the applicant will be given the opportunity to amend the application, file evidence and, in due course, attend a hearing before the Registrar reaches a final decision that the application should be rejected.

The Registrar can only reject an application upon the basis of matter **5–60** raised in observations if it appears to her, having regard to matters coming to her notice since she accepted the application, that it was accepted in error.[58] Accordingly, if the observations only raise matter which has previously been considered then it appears the Registrar cannot reject the application.

The weight to be attached to any observations will depend upon all the circumstances of the case.[59]

It should be noted that the time for opposition is not suspended **5–61** whilst observations are being considered.[60] For this reason and that mentioned in the preceding paragraph any potential opponent should be wary of relying on observations rather than filing an opposition.

Further power to refuse

Where an application has been accepted, and there is no opposition or **5–62** any opposition has failed or been withdrawn, then the Registrar must register the mark (provided the proper fee is paid), unless it appears to her having regard to matters coming to her notice since she accepted the application that it was accepted in error.[61] Accordingly, where new facts come to the attention of the Registrar after acceptance which justify refusal of the application, then the original acceptance can be regarded as an error. The Registrar should give the applicant the opportunity to be heard before deciding that the application should not proceed.

Amendment of the application

Amendment of an application is only permitted in limited circumstances **5–63** under the 1994 Act. An applicant may at any time withdraw his application or restrict the goods or services covered by the application.[62] If the application has been published then the Registrar will publish the withdrawal or restriction.

---

[58] s.40(1).

[59] "Messiah from Scratch" [2000] R.P.C. 44.

[60] Although if the application is amended there will be an opportunity to oppose the amendment under r. 18.

[61] s.40(1) and "Creola" [1997] R.P.C. 507. Under the 1938 Act the Board of Trade could also direct the application be refused (s.19(1)); no such power lies in the appointed person under the 1994 Act.

[62] s.39(1). This is a valuable tool for overcoming objections and is referred to in para. 5–34, above.

5–64   In other respects, an application may be amended only by correcting (1) the name or address of the applicant; (2) errors of wording or copying; or (3) obvious mistakes; and then only where the correction does not substantially affect the identity of the trade mark or extend the goods or services covered by the application.[63]

5–65   A request for an amendment of an application to correct an error or to change the name or address of the applicant and, after publication, a request for any amendment must be made on Form TM21.[64] If the application to amend is made under section 39 of the 1994 Act after publication and the amendment would affect the representation of the mark, then the amendment or a statement of the effect of the amendment will be published and thereafter opposition can be lodged by any third party and will be dealt with as a substantive opposition.[65]

Non-completion within the prescribed period

5–66 A trade mark cannot be registered unless the prescribed fee is paid in the prescribed period.[66] If the fee is not paid then the application is deemed to be withdrawn.

Merger of applications

5–67 An applicant for a number of trade marks may apply to have them merged at any time before preparations for their publication have been completed by the Office.[67] The application is made on Form TM17. The Registrar will allow merger if the applications are in respect of the same mark, bear the same date of application and are, at the time of the request, in the name of the same person.

5–68   After registration an application may also be made by a proprietor for merger and, if the registrations to be merged relate to the same mark, merger will be allowed. The application is again made on Form TM17 and must be accompanied by the appropriate fee. Any limitations or disclaimers will apply to the merged mark and if the original applications had different filing dates then the date of the merged registration will be treated as the latest of them. Any particulars of licences or interests in the original registrations will be entered in relation to the merged mark.

---

[63] s.39(2). Under the 1938 Act the discretion was much wider (s.19(1) and r. 121). Accordingly any cases under the old law must be treated with caution. Nevertheless the following cases provide interesting illustrations: in *Baker* [1908] 2 Ch. 86 at 109, 25 R.P.C. 513 at 524, the court allowed a correction to be made to the name of the applicants. In *Mann* (1919) 36 R.P.C. 189, Sargant J., on appeal from the Registrar, allowed the applicant to correct an amendment made by a slip on his part in the statement of his trading name. An application to amend the specification of goods in an opposition was refused as widening in *Crowther* (1948) 65 R.P.C. 369 (Regy).

[64] 2000 Rules, r. 17.

[65] rr. 13 and 18.

[66] s.40(2).

[67] s.41 and r. 20.

Application for a series of marks

An applicant may apply to register a number of marks as a series.[68] The **5–69**
marks must all resemble each other as to their material particulars and
differ only as to matters of a non-distinctive character not substantially
affecting their identity. The advantage of such an application is the
saving in fees and avoidance of separate applications in each case.

Under rule 21 of the 2000 Rules, the application may be divided into **5–70**
separate applications in respect of one or more of the marks in the series
at any time before the preparations for the publication of the series have
been completed by the Office (subject to the Registrar being satisfied
that the division requested conforms with section 41(2) of the 1994 Act
and the payment of the appropriate fees). An application or registration
may be amended at any time to delete a mark in the series. An
application for a series may not be divided under rule 19, at least at the
stage of opposition.[69]

Certificate of registration

On registration the Registrar publishes the registration, specifying the **5–71**
date upon which the registration was entered upon the Register and
she issues to the applicant a certificate of registration (section 40(4) and
rule 16).

Registration has effect as of the date of filing,[70] a provision particularly
important for the purposes of infringement.

Applications to register collective marks

An application may be made to register a collective mark under the **5–72**
provisions of section 49 and Schedule 1 of the 1994 Act. The substantive
topic of collective marks is addressed in Chapter 11. Such a mark is used
to distinguish the goods or services of members of an association which
is the proprietor of the mark from those of other undertakings.

An application is made for a collective trade mark in the same way as **5–73**
for an ordinary trade mark. The formalities of it are checked as for an
ordinary mark and, if they are satisfied, it will be examined.

Within nine months of the date of the application the applicant must **5–74**
file with the Registrar the regulations governing the use of the mark.[71]
These must specify the persons authorised to use the mark, the
conditions of membership of the association and, where they exist, the
conditions of the use of the mark, including any sanctions against
misuse.

---

[68] s.41 and r. 21.
[69] *Dualit Ltd's Trade Mark Applns* [1999] R.P.C. 304; [1999] R.P.C. 980.
[70] s.9(3).
[71] 1994 Act, Sched. 1, para. 5, and 2000 Rules, r. 22.

5–75 The regulations will be considered by the Registrar and, if she is satisfied that they comply with the requirements, are not contrary to public policy and morality (and the prescribed fees are paid) she will duly notify the applicant and allow the application to proceed to publication, as in the case of ordinary applications. The application may be opposed and observations filed. If any opposition is dealt with, then the mark will be registered, just as in the case of an ordinary mark, and the regulations made available for inspection by the public.

The regulations associated with a collective mark may be amended.[72] The Registrar may cause the amendments to be published, in which case they may be opposed.

Applications to register certification trade marks

5–76 An application may be made for a certification mark under the provisions of section 50 and Schedule 2 of the 1994 Act. The substantive topic of certification marks is addressed in Chapter 11.

As in the case of a collective mark, an application is made for a certification trade mark in the same way as for an ordinary trade mark. The formalities of it are checked as for an ordinary mark and, if they are satisfied, it will be examined.

5–77 Within nine months of the date of the application the applicant must file with the Registrar regulations governing the use of the mark.[73] These must indicate who is authorised to use the mark, the characteristics to be certified by the mark, how the certifying body is to test those characteristics and to supervise the use of the mark, the fees (if any) to be paid in connection with the operation of the mark and the procedures for resolving disputes.

5–78 As in the case of a collective mark, the regulations will be considered by the Registrar and, if she is satisfied that they comply with the requirements, are not contrary to public policy and morality, and that the applicant is in a position and competent to certify the goods or services the subject of the application (and the prescribed fees are paid), she will duly notify the applicant and allow the application to proceed to publication. The application may be opposed and observations filed. If any opposition is dealt with, then the mark will be registered, just as in the case of an ordinary mark, and the regulations made available for inspection by the public.

The regulations associated with a certification mark may be amended.[74] The Registrar may cause the amendments to be published, in which case they may be opposed.

Irregularities and extensions of time

5–79 This topic is addressed generally under the heading of "Opposition to Registration."[75]

---

[72] Sched. 1, para. 10 and r. 23.
[73] Sched. 2, para. 6 and r. 22.
[74] Sched. 2, para. 11 and r. 23.
[75] See paras 5–117 to 5–124, below.

3. Opposition to registration

Once an application has been published any person may, within the **5-80** prescribed time, give notice to the Registrar of opposition to the registration.

Procedure on opposition

The procedure relating to opposition proceedings is governed by section **5-81** 38 of the 1994 Act and rule 13 of the 2000 Rules.[76] The rule is clear in its directions and is reproduced in Appendix 3.

In outline the procedure is as follows. Within three months of the date of publication of the application, notice of opposition must be sent to the Registrar in the prescribed form (TM7). The notice of opposition must include a statement of the grounds of opposition. Where the opposition is based on an earlier trade mark, then the notice must include a representation of the earlier trade mark; and if it is registered, the classes in respect of which it is registered; and the goods and services in respect of which it is registered, or if not registered, used; and where the earlier mark is defined in section 6(1)(a) and (b), the application and/or registration number of the mark and, except in the case of a mark the subject of an application not yet published, the number of the publication in which it was published.[77] No extension of this time can be allowed.[78] A copy of the notice will be sent by the Registrar to the applicant.

Subject to the "cooling-off period", within three months of the date **5-82** upon which the Registrar sends to the applicant a copy of the statement, the applicant may file a counter-statement, in conjunction with a notice of the same, on Form TM8.[79] No extension of this time can be allowed (again, subject to the cooling-off period).[80] A copy will be sent by the Registrar to the opponent.

The Rules now provide for a cooling-off period at the start of **5-83** opposition proceedings and when sought by both parties. At any time before the expiry of the three-month period for filing the counter-statement, the Registrar may, on request, grant an extension of three months where the request is filed on Form TM9c and with the consent of both the applicant and the opponent. This is extendible by a further period of three months with the consent of both the parties.[81] Within one

---

[76] As substituted for the original rule 13 by rule 6 of the Trade Mark (Amendment) Rules 1998.

[77] r. 13(2). These are the requirements prescribed by the Rules. In addition, the requirements as to the content and presentation of the statement are discussed in paras 5-88 to 5-92, below.

[78] r. 68(3).

[79] The requirements as to the content and presentation of this document are discussed in paras 5-88 to 5-92, below.

[80] r. 62(3).

[81] r. 13(4) and (5).

month after the expiry of the cooling-off period the applicant may file a counter-statement, in conjunction with notice of the same on Form TM8 and it will be sent, by the Registrar, to the opponent.

5–84   The counter-statement should set out which aspects of the grounds of opposition are admitted and which are denied and any positive grounds relied upon in support of the application.

Where a notice and counter-statement are not filed by the applicant within the prescribed period, then he is deemed to have withdrawn his application for registration.[82]

5–85   Thereafter evidence is filed. The opponent files evidence first, within three months of the sending to him by the Registrar of a copy of the counter-statement. He must also send a copy of the evidence to the applicant. If no evidence is filed by the opponent then, unless the Registrar otherwise directs, the opposition is deemed to have been withdrawn. The Registrar will usually allow the opposition to continue if the opponent wishes to rely on oral submissions and has based his opposition, at least in part, upon an earlier registration. Thereafter the applicant must file evidence within three months and again send a copy to the opponent. Any reply evidence, and it must be reply evidence, must be filed by the opponent within three months of the sending to him of the evidence of the applicant and a copy sent to the applicant. No further evidence may be filed except with the leave of the Registrar.[83] Once the evidence is completed the Registrar will set a date for the hearing, if requested to do so.

Where two rival applicants file cross-oppositions, it is customary to decide the course of proceedings at a preliminary hearing.

Who may oppose

5–86   Any person may oppose a trade mark application, and opposition may be lodged by joint opponents if this is made clear. In general it appears the objections may be taken by any person.[84] But by way of exception, it appears a section 60 objection (application by an agent or representative) may only be taken by the proprietor of the mark in a Convention country.[85]

Grounds of opposition

5–87   The grounds of opposition relied on by an opponent are likely to be drawn from the following:

(1) The sign the subject of the application is not a trade mark within the meaning of the 1994 Act because it is not capable of

---

[82] r. 13(6).
[83] r. 13(11).
[84] See the mandatory words of ss.3, 4 and 5 and s.38(2). *"Wild Child"* [1998] R.P.C. 455.
[85] This includes countries party to the WTO Agreement (TRIPS): S.I. 1999 No. 1899.

being represented graphically or because it is not capable of distinguishing.

(2) The mark is devoid of any distinctive character such that registration would be contrary to section 3(1)(b).

(3) The mark consists exclusively of descriptive matter prohibited by section 3(1)(c) or (d).

(4) The mark consists exclusively of a shape prohibited by section 3(2).

(5) The mark is of such a nature as to deceive the public (for example as to nature, quality, or geographical origin of the goods or service) or is contrary to public policy or to accepted principles of morality.

(6) Use of the mark is prohibited in the United Kingdom by an enactment or rule of law or by a provision of Community law.

(7) The application was made in bad faith, for example with a false statement as to use or intention to use the mark or because the applicant is not properly entitled to the mark (sections 3(6) and 32).

(8) The mark conflicts with an earlier trade mark and registration would be contrary to section 5(1) to (3).

(9) Use of the mark is liable to be prevented by virtue of a rule of law, such as passing off, or by the proprietor of another earlier right such as copyright, design right or a registered design.

(10) Registration would be contrary to the provisions of sections 56 to 60 (relating to the Paris Convention).

(11) The mark consists of a specially protected emblem (sections 3(5) and 4).

Statement of grounds of opposition and counter-statement—content and presentation

The Registry has emphasised that the statements filed before the **5–88** Registry must include all of the grounds which the party responsible for the filing intends to pursue and which are to be supported by evidence. Mere recitation of the relevant sections of the 1994 Act (or the provisions of a rule) will not be sufficient. There must be a sufficient degree of particularisation for the other side (and the Registry) to have a clear view of the nature of the dispute and have sufficient detail of, for example, the earlier trade marks or earlier rights and their use, on which the litigant intends to proceed.[86]

---

[86] TPN 1/2000; reproduced in Appendix 6. This Notice advises of changes in practice effective from April 26, 2000. The changes have been introduced to give effect to the Woolf Recommendations and bring together observations in a number of cases including *"Wild Child"* [1998] R.P.C. 455; *"Coffee Mix"* [1998] R.P.C. 717 and *"Demon Ale"* [2000] R.P.C. 345, all decisions of the appointed person. See also *Julian Higgins' Appln* [2000] R.P.C. 321; and *Club Europe* [2000] R.P.C. 329 (both decisions of the Vice-Chancellor); *"Geobank"* [1999] R.P.C. 682 (Regy).

5–89 If a party fails to provide in the statement of case sufficient information as to the nature or extent of the grounds upon which the proceedings rely, then further particulars should be sought or may be required by the Registrar of her own motion.[87] Until the statement of case is in order the proceedings will not be progressed and the subsequent delay may be a factor which will be taken into account in the award of costs.

5–90 The Registry has issued broad guidelines as how the statements should be set out.[88] In general the person initiating the proceedings should set out the matter in issue, the facts to be relied upon and the relief sought. The facts to be relied upon (as distinct from the evidence that will be adduced to support them) should be set out concisely but fully. Costs need not be claimed specifically, but frequently they are.

5–91 In the counter-statement the applicant should state which of the allegations in the statement of opposition are denied and why (and if it is intended to put forward an alternative version of events, what that version is); which of the allegations in the statement it is unable to admit or deny (because, for example, it has no knowledge of them) but requires the opponent to prove; which of the allegations in the statement it admits. The Registry has also explained that the purpose of the counter-statement is to narrow down the field of dispute. Whilst in the past counter-statements have sometimes been very sketchy, that is no longer acceptable. If a counter-statement leaves uncertainty about what is in dispute, then it is unacceptable; it must deal specifically with every allegation in the statement. Costs need not be claimed specifically, though they usually are.

5–92 If the presentation of the statement or counter-statement is clearly inadequate the Registrar will refuse to serve it.

Statements should contain a declaration confirming the accuracy and truth of the matters contained in them.[89]

Amending grounds of opposition

5–93 The Registrar can, before the opposition is determined, give leave to amend a notice of opposition by, for example, the introduction of a further ground of objection.[90] A counter-statement can also be amended, with leave.

The Registrar does have the power, in an appropriate case, to allow one opponent to be substituted for another.[91]

---

[87] Under Rule 57 and as suggested in *"Wild Child"*, *supra*; see also TPN 1/2000.

[88] We set out below what we perceive to be the essential aspects of the guidance given for the purposes of opposition, but reference should be made to TPN 1/2000 for the whole.

[89] TPN 1/2000, paras 27 to 29.

[90] This was expressly permitted by the Rules under the 1938 Act (r. 121). Under the 1994 Act there is no equivalent rule but such amendments could presumably be treated as irregularities rectifiable with leave under the 2000 Rules, r. 66. For a recent illustration of amendment being allowed where it was considered it would cause no injustice, see *C (Device Trade Mark)* [1998] R.P.C. 439.

[91] *Pharmedica's Appln* [2000] R.P.C. 536; *cf. Kirkbi AG's Applications* [1999] R.P.C. 733.

On appeal in a registration case, whether before publication or in **5–94**
opposition, there is no statutory restriction on the objections which may
be taken.[92] But it is suggested that such an objection could not be taken
without leave and that leave would not be given unless the parties
would suffer no prejudice, for example because it had already been
addressed fully in evidence.[93]

Disclosure

The Registrar has the powers of an official referee of the Supreme Court **5–95**
in relation to disclosure and the production of documents.[94] In addition,
she has the power at any stage of the proceedings to direct that such
documents, information or evidence as she shall reasonably require shall
be filed.[95]

The Registrar accordingly has power to order general or specific **5–96**
disclosure. The Registry has, however, indicated that it is unlikely that
standard disclosure would ever be ordered but that specific disclosure
may be ordered in accordance with the principles set out in the CPR.[96] In
particular the Registrar will take into account all the circumstances of
the case and the overriding objective described in Part 1 of the CPR.[97] In
practice it seems likely that in most cases disclosure will only be ordered
if it relates to matters in question in the proceedings and disclosure is
necessary to dispose fairly of the proceedings or to reduce costs.[98] The
Registry has suggested disclosure would only be ordered after evidence
has been filed.[99] But this must now be regarded with some doubt in the
light of the more recently stated requirements as to the adequacy of
statements of case.[1]

Evidence

General

Evidence is generally filed in the form of statutory declaration or **5–97**
affidavit.[2] But a witness statement verified by a statement of truth[3] may
be used as an alternative although the Registrar may give a direction, as

[92] Such a restriction was provided by the 1938 Act, ss.17(6) and 18(9).
[93] Contrast *Kenrick and Jefferson* (1909) 26 R.P.C. 641, where leave was refused, with *Brown
Shoe* [1959] R.P.C. 641, where it was given, the objection being dismissed as a
technicality, the point having been clearly raised in the evidence.
[94] 2000 Rules, r. 58.
[95] r. 57.
[96] TPN 1/2000.
[97] See para. 5–04, above.
[98] *Merrell Dow Pharmaceuticals Inc's (Terfenadine) Patent* [1991] R.P.C. 221. The value of the
material to be disclosed may be weighed against the burden disclosure would impose:
Molnlycke v. Proctor & Gamble (No. 3) [1990] R.P.C. 498. "Fishing discovery" is unlikely to
be ordered: *British Leyland Motor Corporation v. Wyatt Interpart* [1979] F.S.R. 39; TPN
1/2000.
[99] *"Lifesavers"* [1997] R.P.C. 563.
[1] TPN 1/2000.
[2] 2000 Rules, rr. 13 and 55(1). The formalities for making and subscribing a statutory
declaration or affidavit are set out in r. 56.
[3] TPN 1/2000.

she thinks fit in any particular case, that the evidence must be given by affidavit or statutory declaration instead of or in addition to the witness statement.[4]

5–98 Where a party adduces evidence of a statement made by a person otherwise than while giving oral evidence in proceedings and does not call that person as a witness, then the Registrar may permit the other party to call that person as a witness and cross-examine them on that statement.[5]

Generally the Registrar has the powers of an official referee in relation to the examination of witnesses on oath.[6]

Cross-examination

5–99 In addition to these general powers the 2000 Rules do make further specific provision in relation to the giving of evidence. In any case the Registrar has a discretion to take oral evidence in addition to or in lieu of written evidence and she shall, unless she otherwise directs, allow any witness to be cross examined on that evidence.[7] In practice the Registrar requires notice of any wish to have a witness give oral evidence.[8] Cross-examination before the Registrar is relatively infrequent but more common than it was under the old law. Under the 1938 Act cross-examination of deponents was allowed where the case called for it and there were grounds for thinking it would be positively helpful in coming to a just decision,[9] and it seems likely this practice will continue.[10] Where cross-examination does not take place, the Registrar will nevertheless consider and form her own view as to the evidential value of the evidence before her.[11]

Registrar may require evidence

5–100 The Registrar is not required to rely solely on the evidence the parties wish to place before her. At any stage of the proceedings she may direct that such documents, information or evidence as she may reasonable require shall be filed within such period as she may specify.[12]

Hearsay evidence

5–101 In proceedings which began on or after January 31, 1997 hearsay evidence of matters of fact or opinion will not be excluded. But the weight to be given to any such evidence is a matter for the Registrar, in

---

[4] r. 55(3).
[5] r. 55(5).
[6] r. 58.
[7] r. 55(2).
[8] *Practice Notice of 4 January 1999* [1999] R.P.C. 294.
[9] *"Permo"* [1985] R.P.C. 597 (Regy: the case depended upon evidence of use by the registered proprietor, and the documents relating to such use were produced very late.) This approach was recently referred to, apparently with approval, in *"Wild Child"* [1998] R.P.C. 455, a decision of the appointed person. See also *"Kidax"* [1959] R.P.C. 167 at 176, CA; *Sainsbury* [1981] F.S.R. 406; *"Neutrogena"* [1984] R.P.C. 563.
[10] *"Genius"* [1999] R.P.C. 741, a decision involving a request for an extension of time.
[11] *"Wild Child"* [1998] R.P.C. 455.
[12] 2000 Rules, r. 57.

accordance with section 4 of the Civil Evidence Act 1995.[13] The following points are particularly notable. If the formal evidence contains hearsay, it should be filed in sufficient time and it should contain sufficient particulars to enable the other parties to deal with it. If the provision of further particulars of or relating to it is reasonable and practicable, they should be given on request. Under section 4 of the 1995 Act the weight to be given to the evidence is a matter for the Registrar and regard may be had, in particular, to the following:

(1) whether it would have been reasonable and practicable for the party by whom the evidence was adduced to have produced the maker of the original statement as a witness;

(2) whether the original statement was made contemporaneously with the occurrence or existence of the matters stated;

(3) whether the evidence involves multiple hearsay;

(4) whether any person involved had any motive to conceal or misrepresent matters;

(5) whether the original statement was an edited account, or was made in collaboration with another or for a particular purpose;

(6) whether the circumstances in which the evidence is adduced as hearsay are such as to suggest an attempt to prevent proper evaluation of its weight.

Importance of evidence

The Registrar is unwilling to regard assertions without any real substan- **5–102** tiation as sufficient to sustain an objection under section 5(4) of the 1994 Act.[14]

The question of evidence relating to the deceptive resemblance of marks is discussed in Chapter 16.

Evidence not in proper form

The Registry has the practice of requiring receipt of formally correct **5–103** affidavits, statutory declarations or witness statements to trigger subsequent evidence stages. The Registry will not normally accept the receipt of unsigned witness statements or unsworn affidavits or statutory declarations as meeting time deadlines, but exceptionally may do so provided a proper version of the evidence is filed within a specified period.[15]

---

[13] *Practice Notice of 4 January 1999* [1999] R.P.C. 294. In proceedings which began before the January 31, 1997, the Registrar continues to apply the *Patent Office Practice Direction of 20 June 1995* [1995] R.P.C. 381. See also *"St Trudo"* [1995] R.P.C. 370; *Oasis Stores* [1998] R.P.C. 631.

[14] *"Wild Child"* [1998] R.P.C. 455 at 465. The same ought to be the case for any objection which the Registrar cannot assess for herself, such as an objection under s.5(3) which is supported by a contention that the earlier trade mark is particularly distinctive through use or an objection under s.60. See also under "Onus", below at para. 5–109.

[15] TPN 1/2000.

Case Management, Pre-Hearing Reviews and Alternative Dispute Resolution (ADR)

5–104 At any stage of the proceedings the Registrar may direct that the parties attend at a case management conference where they will have the opportunity to be heard with regard to the conduct of the proceedings.[16] At such a conference the Registrar may give such directions as to the conduct of the hearing as she thinks fit. At least 14 days notice will be given. The purpose of this provision is to allow the Registrar to take a more proactive role in the conduct of the hearing and to consider such matters as the need to clarify the issues, the degree of complexity of the matter, any related actions between the parties and any wider public interest issues.[17]

5–105 Similarly, before any hearing the Registrar may direct the parties to attend a pre hearing review at which directions may be given as to the conduct of the hearing.[18] Again, at least 14 days notice will be given. This gives the Registrar a similar opportunity to consider making directions in relation to the matters referred to above.

The Registrar may ask the parties whether they have considered ADR and, where appropriate, will provide information about ADR.

Stay of Proceedings

5–106 In an appropriate case the Registrar will stay proceedings, for example pending the resolution of High Court proceedings where the same or practically the same questions or issues are being determined.[19]

The Opposition Hearing

Skeleton arguments

5–107 Hearing officers generally expect parties, particularly those represented by professional practitioners, to supply skeleton arguments, together with authorities, at least two days prior to the hearing.[20]

Presentation

5–108 Upon the completion of the evidence the Registrar will fix a date for the hearing, if requested by any party. At the hearing it is now customary for the opponent to begin, the applicant answers and finally the opponent replies to any new points raised by the applicant.

---

[16] 2000 Rules, r. 36.

[17] TPN 1/2000. The same Notice mentions that the Office intends issuing questionnaires on a selective basis, prior to the evidence rounds, which should help the parties and the hearing officer to gain a clearer appreciation of the issues.

[18] r. 37.

[19] *Airport Restaurants v. Southend-on-Sea Corporation* [1960] 2 All E.R. 888; *Thames Launches v. Trinity House Corp.* [1961] Ch. 197; *Sears v. Sears Roebuck* [1993] R.P.C. 370; *"Genius"* [1999] R.P.C. 741. Similarly it may be appropriate to grant a stay pending an appeal where relevant issues of principle are likely to be determined: *Philips Electronics v. Remington (No. 2)* [1999] E.T.M.R. 835.

[20] TPN 1/2000.

The Registrar will encourage the parties to hold hearings, case management conferences and pre-hearing reviews using telephone conferencing arrangements and video links, where this can reasonably be achieved and will save costs.[21]

Onus

There is no overall onus on the applicant in opposition proceedings. **5–109** Accordingly, where the opponent raises objections under section 5(3) or (4) of the 1994 Act, he must make them out.[22]

Time spent on hearing and cross examination

It has been indicated that it is generally the intention of the Registrar not **5–110** to impose time limits on the length of the hearing or cross-examination, but there remains a discretion to do otherwise.[23]

Presentation of new evidence at the hearing

The practice of introducing new evidence at hearings is to be dis- **5–111** couraged and, it must be assumed, such evidence will only rarely be allowed and where it is unlikely to prejudice the other party. Documents may, however, be introduced in cross examination where designed to test the honesty or reliability of a witness.[24]

Hearing in public

Unless the Registrar otherwise directs, the hearing before the Registrar **5–112** of any dispute between two or more parties relating to any matter in connection with an application for the registration of a mark or a registered mark will be held in public.[25]

The decision

When the Registrar has made a decision on the acceptability of an **5–113** opposed mark she will send to the applicant and the opponent written notice of it, stating the reasons for her decision.

Where grounds for refusal of registration exist in respect of only some of the goods or services the subject of the application, then refusal of registration shall cover those goods or services only.[26]

---

[21] TPN 1/2000.
[22] *"Audi-Med"* [1998] R.P.C. 859; *Oasis Stores* [1998] R.P.C. 631. But where an application was accepted on the basis of evidence subsequently shown to be misleading, the applicant ought not to be in a more favourable position in opposition than prior to acceptance and consequently the opposition should be decided on the balance of the evidence and without assuming a burden of proof one way or the other: *Dualit* [1999] R.P.C. 304.
[23] TPN 1/2000.
[24] TPN 1/2000.
[25] 2000 Rules, r. 59.
[26] Art. 13 of the Directive. See also *"Mister Long"* [1998] R.P.C. 401; *"Wild Child"* [1998] R.P.C. 455; *"Naturelle"* [1999] R.P.C. 326; *"QS by S Oliver"* [1999] R.P.C. 520.

Decisions of the Registrar to refuse registration should be based upon grounds of objection which the applicant has been given the opportunity to address in representations to the Registrar, made orally if so desired.[27]

Costs

General

5–115 Under section 68 of the 1994 Act and rule 60 of the 2000 Rules the Registrar may, in any proceedings before her, by order award to any party such costs as she may consider reasonable, and direct how and by what parties they are to be paid. In a contested opposition costs usually follow the event. By tradition costs have been awarded in accordance with published scales which were not intended to cover all expenses actually incurred. A more realistic contribution is to be awarded in proceedings commenced on or after May 22, 2000 and it is intended, far more frequently than in the past, to make costs orders as the cause for them arises and to attach a deadline for payment.[28] The current scales are reproduced in Appendix 6.

Security for costs

5–116 The Registrar may require any person who is a party to any proceedings before her to give security for costs in relation to those proceedings and she may require security for the costs of any appeal from her decision.[29] Security will only be awarded on application and not on the Registry's own initiative. The amount of the award is determined on a case-by-case basis and proportionately to the estimated costs likely to be awarded at the conclusion of the proceedings.[30]

Irregularities

5–117 Subject to the specific provisions of rule 68 of the 2000 Rules relating to time limits, the Registrar has a general power to allow the rectification of any irregularities in procedure in or before the Office or the Registrar on such terms as she may direct.[31]

5–118 Where there has been an interruption or dislocation in the postal services or an interruption in the normal operation of the Office then, by certification, particular days may be disregarded. So also the Registrar may extend any period for the giving, making or filing of any notice, application or other document where failure to meet that time limit was attributable to a failure or undue delay in the United Kingdom postal services.[32]

---

[27] *"Xe"* [2000] R.P.C. 405.
[28] TPN 2/2000; reproduced in Appendix 6.
[29] s.68 and r. 61.
[30] TPN 2/2000.
[31] r. 66.
[32] r. 67.

Alteration of time limits by the Registrar

The Registrar has a general power to extend time limits, with certain **5–119** important exceptions.[33] The exceptions set out in the 2000 Rules are rule 10(6) (failure to file address for service), rule 11 (deficiencies in the application), rule 13(1) (time for filing opposition), rule 13(3) and (5) (time for filing the counter-statement), rule 13(4) (cooling-off period) save as provided by that rule, rule 23(4) (time for filing opposition), rule 25(3) (time for filing opposition), rule 29 (delayed renewal) and rule 30 (restoration of registration), rule 31(2) (time for filing counter-statement), rule 32(2) (time for filing counter-statement), rule 33(2) (time for filing counter-statement) and rule 47 (time for filing opposition). In the case of these exceptions there is no power to extend the time limits at all.

Where the Registrar does have power, then the party seeking an **5–120** extension should apply for the extension before the time limit has expired. The Registrar may grant such extension and on such terms as she thinks fit. If the request is not made until after the time has expired, then the Registrar may nevertheless grant an extension if she is satisfied with the explanation for the delay in requesting the extension and it appears to her just and equitable so to do.[34]

It appears that the Registrar has a general discretion save as expressly **5–121** confined as above. It is for the party in default to satisfy her that, despite the default, the discretion to extend time should be exercised in his favour. All relevant matters should be taken into account including the explanation for any delay, the public interest in ensuring that valid applications for registration should succeed and valid objections to registrations should be upheld without undue delay and whether refusal is likely to lead to another action between the same parties covering essentially the same subject-matter by way of an application to have the registration declared invalid.[35] But it is to be noted that if the request is not made until after the time has expired then the further requirements set out above must be satisfied.[36]

Where a time period for the filing of evidence is due to begin upon **5–122** the expiry of a period in which another party may file evidence and that other party notifies the Registrar that he does not wish to file any, or any further, evidence, then the Registrar may direct that the time period in which the first-mentioned party may file evidence shall begin on the date specified in the direction.[37]

Where there is an irregularity or prospective irregularity relating to a **5–123** failure to comply with a time limit and which is attributable to an error, default or omission on the part of the Office or Registrar then the

---

[33] r. 68.
[34] r. 68(4) and (5).
[35] *"Liquid Force"* [1999] R.P.C. 429. This potentially marks a softening of the approach adopted in *"SAW"* [1996] R.P.C. 507, a decision under the particular words of r. 114 of the 1938 Act to the effect that good reasons must be provided for any extension and the total time allowed should not exceed six months.
[36] *"Genius"* [1999] R.P.C. 741.
[37] 2000 Rules, r. 68(6).

Registrar may alter the time or period in question upon such terms as she may direct.[38]

Regulation of procedure

5–124   The Registrar has a the power to regulate the procedure before her in such a way that she neither creates a substantial jurisdiction where none existed, nor exercises that power in a manner inconsistent with the express provisions conferring jurisdiction upon her.[39]

4. Appeal from the Registrar

The tribunal of appeal

5–125   An appeal lies from any decision by the Registrar, except as otherwise provided by the 2000 Rules. For this purpose "decision" includes any act of the Registrar in the exercise of a discretion vested in her by or under the 1994 Act.[40] Any appeal may be brought to an appointed person or to the court.

5–126   Accordingly, an appeal from the refusal by the Registrar to register a trade mark otherwise than in opposition may be brought to the court or to the appointed person. So also may an appeal be brought to the court or the appointed person from the decision of the Registrar in an opposition. It also appears that an appeal lies against any other decision by the Registrar in the exercise of her discretion, including any interlocutory decision, subject to the exceptions referred to below.

5–127   There are two exceptions where the 2000 Rules expressly provide there shall be no right of appeal. First, a decision of the Registrar under rule 46 to publish proposals for such amendment of entries on the register as she considers necessary for the purpose of reclassifying the specification of a registered trade mark is final and not subject to appeal. So also is her decision on the substantive issue under rule 47. Secondly, no appeal lies from a decision of the Registrar under rule 50(4) not to make any document or part of a document available for public inspection.

   Where an appeal is made to the court, there may be further appeals to the Court of Appeal and to the House of Lords, subject in each case to the appropriate leave.

The nature of the appeal

5–128   An appeal from a decision of the Registrar is to be approached as would an appeal to the Court of Appeal from the High Court. Accordingly it is not a complete rehearing, the decision of the Registrar should not be

---

[38] r. 68(7).
[39] *Pharmedica's Appln, supra; Langley v. North West Water Authority* [1991] 3 All E.R. 610.
[40] s.76.

ignored and it should be affirmed unless it is wrong or unjust because of a serious procedural or other irregularity in the proceedings below.[41]

Time runs from the decision

For the purpose of any appeal, time runs from the decision of the **5–129** Registrar. When the Registrar has made a decision then she must send a notice of her decision in writing to each of the parties to the proceedings. Subject to the following, the date of her decision is deemed to be the date the notice was sent. If a statement of reasons is not included with the notice, then any party may, within one month of the date on which the notice was sent to him, request the Registrar, on the appropriate form, to send him a statement of reasons for the decision and upon such a request the Registrar will send a statement. The date on which the statement is sent is then deemed to be the date of the Registrar's decision for the purposes of any appeal.[42]

Appeal to the appointed person

Any appeal may be brought to an appointed person.[43] There are **5–130** currently three appointed persons, two based in London and one in Scotland. Each is one of Her Majesty's counsel with experience in trade mark matters.

Notice of Appeal must be sent to the Registrar within 28 days of the date of the Registrar's decision which is the subject of the appeal, accompanied by a statement in writing of the appellant's grounds of appeal and his case in support of the appeal.[44] The Registrar will send a copy of the notice and statement to the appointed person and to any other party to the proceedings.[45]

If the appointed person hears and determines the appeal then his **5–131** decision is final. There is no further right of appeal.

An appeal to the appointed person against a decision by the Registrar involving the exercise of discretion is not a rehearing.[46]

Where an appeal is brought to an appointed person he may refer the **5–132** appeal to the court if it appears to him that a point of general legal importance is involved or if the Registrar or any party to the proceed-

---

[41] CPR, r. 52.11; see generally, *Tanfern v. Cameron MacDonald* [2000] 2 All E.R. 801, CA and, in relation to appeals against the exercise of a discretion, *G v. G* [1985] 2 All E.R. 225 at 229; [1985] 1 W.L.R. 647 at 652, HL; *"Magic Ball"* [2000] R.P.C. 439; *Re Procter and Gamble's Appln* [1999] R.P.C. 673 at 677, CA. But if it is not clear that the Registrar has approached the matter in the correct way, then the matter should be considered afresh: *"Open Country"* [1998] R.P.C. 408 at 409; [2000] R.P.C. 477 at 481, CA.
[42] 2000 Rules, r. 62.
[43] 1994 Act, ss.76 and 77.
[44] r. 63(1).
[45] r. 63(2) and (3).
[46] See generally para. 5–128, above, and *A.J. and M.A. Levy's T.M.* [1999] R.P.C. 291.

ings before the Registrar requests that it be so referred.[47] Before referring the appeal the appointed person must give the appellant and any other party an opportunity to make representations as to whether he should adopt that course. One of the factors he will take into account will be that there can be no further appeal from his decision.

The appointed person may remit the matter to the Registrar for further consideration, in an appropriate case.[48]

Practice before the appointed person

5–133 The appointed person has the same powers as the Registrar as to costs, security for costs and evidence. He, like the Registrar, has the powers of an official referee of the Supreme Court.[49]

The statement of the grounds of appeal and the statement of case in support of appeal form an important part of the appeal procedure. They must outline each of the grounds of appeal relied upon and state the case relied upon in support of those grounds. There is an inherent power to amend the documents in an appropriate case.[50]

5–134 If the appeal is to be determined by the appointed person and not referred to the court, then he will send out notice of the time and place of the hearing. After the hearing he will send a copy of his decision, with a statement of his reasons, to the Registrar and to each person who was a party to the proceedings before him.

5–135 The appointed person has an inherent power to regulate the procedure before him in a manner conducive to the just and fair determination of the appeal. The discretionary powers of the appointed person and the High Court are the same[51] and they include a power to hear a representative of the Registrar.[52]

Appeal to the court

5–136 The appeal is brought by appeal notice.[53] The notice should set out the grounds of appeal and why the decision appealed against was wrong or unjust.

---

[47] See s.76(3) and, for the relevant procedure, r. 64. This power should be used sparingly, otherwise the clear object of the legislation to provide a relatively inexpensive, quick and final resolution of appeals by a specialist tribunal would be defeated: *A.J. and M.A. Levy's T.M. (No. 2)* [1999] R.P.C. 358; *"Academy"* [2000] R.P.C. 35. See also *Jimmy Nicks Appln* [1999] E.T.M.R. 445.

[48] *Ty Nant Spring Water Ltd's Appln* [2000] R.P.C. 55; *"Xe"* [2000] R.P.C. 405, where the decision of the Registrar relied on matters not in issue at the hearing and on which the applicant had had no opportunity to respond.

[49] s.76(5).

[50] *"Coffeemix"* [1998] R.P.C. 717.

[51] *"Academy"* [2000] R.P.C. 35.

[52] *"Corgi"* [1999] R.P.C. 549. See also *"Coffeemix"* [1998] R.P.C. 717: the appointed person has an inherent power to allow amendments to the notice of appeal and supporting documents.

[53] CPR, r. 52 and the Practice Direction supplementing Part 52, which set out all the requirements to be met by the appellant and respondent.

The appeal notice must be issued within 28 days of the decision appealed from. Within 21 days of issue the notice of appeal must be served on the Registrar and any respondents and lodged with the clerk or other person in charge of the Chancery List.[54] Thereafter a respondent may file and serve a respondent's notice.[55]

The court may make any decision which ought to have been made by the Registrar or any further or other order as the case may require or may remit the matter for rehearing and determination.[56]   **5–137**

Evidence on appeal

On appeal before the court or the appointed person new evidence may be admitted only with leave.[57] The onus is on the party applying for leave to admit the evidence to justify the exercise of discretion in his favour but there are no express limits placed upon the discretion or criteria set for its exercise, save that the discretion should be exercised in accordance with the overriding objective and the concept of proportionality.[58] Relevant factors are likely to include the following[59]:   **5–138**

(1) Whether the evidence could have been filed earlier and, if so, how much earlier.
(2) If it could have been, what explanation for the late filing has been offered to explain the delay.
(3) The nature of the mark.
(4) The nature of the objections to it.
(5) The potential significance of the new evidence.
(6) Whether the other side will be significantly prejudiced by the admission of the evidence in a way which cannot be compensated, for example by an order for costs.
(7) The desirability of avoiding multiplicity of proceedings.
(8) The public interest in not admitting onto the Register invalid marks.

Modification of the application on appeal

The opportunity to make amendments to an application is strictly limited by the Act and is the subject of earlier discussion. In general an application may be made to amend an application under section 13 of   **5–139**

---

[54] See Practice Direction supplementing CPR Part 49, reproduced in Appendix 32.
[55] CPR, r. 52.5.
[56] CPR, r. 52.10. And see, *e.g. Swiss Miss* [1998] R.P.C. 889, CA.
[57] CPR, r. 52.11, previously RSC, Ord. 55, r. 7(2).
[58] *Club Europe* [2000] R.P.C. 329; *Julian Higgins' Appln* [2000] R.P.C. 321, both decisions of the Vice-Chancellor; *Hunt Wesson ("Swiss Miss")* [1996] R.P.C. 233. In his judgment in *Swiss Miss* Laddie J. reviews the earlier authorities; *Dualit v. Rowlett Catering Appliances* [1999] F.S.R. 865.
[59] *Per* Laddie J., in *Swiss Miss, supra,* at 241–242; although these matters will, in most cases, be the important ones, the Vice-Chancellor has cautioned against any attempt to confine the statutory discretion within a straightjacket: *Club Europe, supra,* at 338.

the 1994 Act by disclaimer or limitation or under section 39 by way of restricting the goods or services the subject of the application. It would seem undesirable that this should be raised on appeal if it has not been the subject of consideration by the Registrar.[60] It is suggested that in such circumstances the appointed person and the court have a discretion to allow it to be raised, assuming the statutory requirements are satisfied, although they would be very reluctant to do so, save in a very clear case. The court and the appointed person certainly have a discretion to remit the matter to the Registrar where appropriate.

Costs on appeal and further appeal

5–140 The appointed person has the power to award to any party such costs as he may consider reasonable, and to direct how and by what parties they are to be paid.[61] In the case of oppositions the appointed person usually awards costs in accordance with the scale of costs which applies in Registry proceedings.[62] In the case of unsuccessful appeals to the appointed person against refusals by the Registrar (*ex parte* proceedings), there will normally be no order for costs.[63]

5–141 In the High Court costs will be awarded in accordance with the High Court practice and will usually follow the event.[64]

The Registrar has indicated that in the case of appeals in "without notice" (*ex parte*) proceedings to the High Court, she would expect costs to be awarded against her should she lose on appeal. So also she should seek costs if successful unless the party paying is likely to suffer some form of hardship or where a significant point of general legal interest is involved.[65]

---

[60] Practical difficulties are also presented in that where the amendment affects the representation of the trade mark or the goods or services the subject of the application, the Registrar is required by the 2000 Rules, r. 18 to publish the amendment for opposition purposes. On the other hand, where an application is amended under s.13, the Registrar is required by r. 24 to publish the amendment, but it is not then open to opposition.

[61] rr. 54 and 59.

[62] See, *e.g*, "*Wild Child*" [1998] R.P.C. 455; "*Academy*" [2000] R.P.C. 35.

[63] "*AD 2000*" [1997] R.P.C. 168. TPN 2/2000. If a party has acted unreasonably then an order for costs may be sought: *Jaleel (S.M.) & Co Ltd's Appln* [2000] R.P.C. 471.

[64] The court must have regard to all the circumstances, including the conduct of the parties and whether a party has succeeded on part of his case, even if he has not been wholly successful. The court will make a summary assessment in cases which have not lasted for more than a day unless there is a good reason not to do so.

[65] TPN 2/2000.

CHAPTER 6

COMMUNITY TRADE MARK PROCEDURE AND INTERNATIONAL TRADE MARKS

The purpose of this chapter is to address the aspects of procedure **6–01** specific to Community trade mark law, both domestic and international, and to provide a guide to the international registration of trade marks under the Madrid Protocol. A Community trade mark ("CTM") is a unitary trade mark providing the same rights and protection, and having equal effect, throughout the European Community. It can only be registered, transferred, revoked or surrendered in respect of the whole Community. Apart from this important "Community wide" aspect and from procedural matters relating the administration of the Community Trade Mark system, many of the provisions of Regulation (EC) No. 40/94 on the Community Trade Mark ("the CTM Regulation") are extremely similar to those of the 1994 Act, unsurprisingly, given the wording of the CTM Regulation is in many places identical to that of the TM Directive in order to give effect to which the 1994 Act was drafted.[1] Where such similarities exist, the reader will be cross-referred to the section in this work addressing the analogous United Kingdom law as well as to those chapters which address the substantive law of CTMs. This chapter deals first with general provisions relating to CTM procedure, then the procedure on application for a CTM, opposition, registration and renewal of a CTM, dealings with CTMs, the jurisdiction of Community trade mark courts, applications for revocation or declarations of invalidity and the conversion of CTMs and CTM applications to national registrations. The final section of the chapter addresses the registration of international marks under the Madrid Protocol.

1. Community trade mark procedure

Source legislation

On December 20, 1993, as part of the European Union's drive towards **6–02** harmonisation of economic activities in the internal market, the Council of the European Union adopted the CTM Regulation, implemented by Commission Regulation (EC) No. 2868/95 ("the Implementing Regu-

---

[1] 89/104/EEC.

lation"). The CTM Regulation is of direct effect, establishing the CTM and providing a complete code determining who is entitled to apply for a CTM, what marks can be registered and the rights conferred on registration, without need for further national legislation.[2] Following the establishment of the World Trade Organisation the CTM Regulation was amended by Council Regulation (EC) No. 3288/94 in order to take account of the provisions of the TRIPs Agreement.[3] The CTM Regulation established the Office for the Harmonisation in the Internal Market (Trade Marks and Designs) ("OHIM") to administer the CTM Register. The formalities of proceedings in OHIM and applications for a CTM are governed by the Implementing Regulation. Further procedural rules governing appeals to the Boards of Appeal in OHIM are provided by Commission Regulation (EC) No. 216/96 ("the Appeals Regulation"). The fees payable in respect of CTM proceedings are set out in Commission Regulation (EC) No 2869/95 of December 13, 1995 on the fees payable to the Office for Harmonisation in the Internal Market (Trade Marks and Designs) ("the Fees Regulation")

Nature of a Community trade mark

6–03 The essential particulars of a CTM are similar to those set out in Article 2 of the TM Directive and given effect in section 1(1) of the 1994 Act. It must be capable of being represented graphically and be capable of distinguishing the goods or services of one undertaking from those of other undertakings. Article 7 of the CTM Regulation sets out the absolute grounds for refusal of a CTM, which to a great extent mirror the provisions of Article 3 of the TM Directive and section 3 of the 1994 Act[4] with the following fundamental differences. First, the absolute grounds of refusal set out in Article 7(1) prevent registration of a mark even if the grounds for non-registrability obtain in only part of the Community.[5] This is a logical consequence of the unitary nature of the CTM set out in Article 1; unregistrability in part of the Community must necessarily lead to rejection of the application if the mark is not to be divided geographically. Note that this provision is not restricted to grounds obtaining in an entire Member State.

6–04 Secondly, there is no "bad faith" provision in Article 7 of the CTM Regulation corresponding to section 3(6) of the 1994 Act. Thus no objection based on an application being too broad may be raised in opposition proceedings. Bad faith can however be relied on as the basis

---

[2] Art. 91 of the CTM Regulation requires Member States to take steps to designate Community trade mark courts to enforce the rights conferred by a CTM and adjudicate declarations of non-infringement, counterclaims for declarations of invalidity/ revocation. The Community Trade Mark Regulations, S.I. 1996 No. 1908, designated the High Court in England and Wales and Northern Ireland and the Court of Session in Scotland as the U.K. Community trade mark courts.
[3] Agreement on Trade Related Aspects of Intellectual Property Rights.
[4] See Chap. 7.
[5] CTM Regulation, Art. 7(2).

for a declaration of invalidity of a registered CTM on application to OHIM or by way of a counterclaim in infringement proceedings.[6]

The relative grounds for refusal of a CTM are to be found at Article 8 **6–05** of the CTM Regulation. Again, the provisions of the Regulation closely mirror those of the TM Directive (Article 4), and consequently, those of the 1994 Act (section 5). The differences between the relative grounds for refusal in national and Community applications arising as a result of differences in the nature of the earlier registered[7] and non-registered rights[8] to be taken into account in each are addressed in detail in Chapter 8.

General OHIM procedure

OHIM, which is situated in Alicante in Spain, was established by Article **6–06** 1 of the Implementing Regulation. It is a legal entity under the laws of each Member State, capable of acquiring and disposing of movable and immovable property and may be a party to legal proceedings. Five bodies within OHIM are competent to decide matters concerning the operation of the CTM system.[9]

(1) Opposition Division: as the name suggests, the Opposition Division is responsible for taking decisions on matters arising in oppositions to applications for a CTM.

(2) Cancellation Division: this is responsible for decisions relating to applications for revocation or a declaration of invalidity of a CTM.

(3) Examination Division: has jurisdiction over matters concerning applications for registration of a CTM not falling within the ambit of the Opposition Division.

(4) Administration of Trade Marks and Legal Division: this division is responsible for all decisions not falling within the competence of the examiners, Opposition Division or Cancellation Division. In general it administers the CTM register and regulates the list of professional representatives (see para. 6–15, below).

(5) Boards of Appeal: hear first instance appeals from decisions of the above four bodies. For commentary on the CTM appeals process (see paras 6–24 *et seq.*, below).

Capacity

In general, if an organisation has legal capacity under the law by which **6–07** it is governed, it is regarded as a legal person for the purposes of the CTM Regulations and related regulations. The rules as to who may be a

---

[6] CTM Regulation, Art. 51.
[7] Art 8(1), (2) and (5).
[8] Art. 8(4).
[9] Arts 125–130.

proprietor of a CTM are set out in Article 5 of the CTM Regulation. An applicant must qualify on one of the following four grounds:

(1) as a national of a Member State; or

(2) as a national of a state party to the Paris Convention or to the Agreement establishing the World Trade Organisation; or

(3) as an entity domiciled in or with a "real and effective" industrial or commercial establishments within the European Community or within a state party to the Paris Convention. Note that such establishments within a state party to the WTO Agreement do not qualify as a party; or

(4) finally, as a national of a state not party to the Paris Convention or to the WTO Agreement but providing the same trade mark protection to nationals of Member States as it does to its own nationals and recognising the registration of a CTM as proof of ownership of a trade mark registration by a national of a Member State. Such applicants must provide proof that the mark in question is already registered in their state of origin (except in the event that their state of origin registers the trade marks of nationals of Member States without proof that such marks have already been registered either as CTMs or as national trade marks of Member States.)

6–08 Article 5(2) of the CTM Regulation sets out detailed provisions relating to the proprietorship of CTMs by stateless persons or refugees, allowing applicants who have formally been granted such status to be regarded as nationals of their host country. These provisions are by their nature of limited application and interested readers are referred to the source materials.

Language of proceedings

6–09 The official languages of OHIM are English, French, German, Italian or Spanish ("the OHIM languages"). However, the provisions of the CTM Regulation and Implementing Regulations which address the languages in which proceedings are to be carried out are baroque to say the least. In the course of an application it is perfectly possible for an applicant and OHIM to communicate with each other in writing in different languages, and during oral hearings at which more than one party is represented different languages may be spoken by various witnesses. The following is a brief summary of the provisions governing the language(s) in which proceedings before OHIM are to be conducted. It is not possible in the space for all possible combinations of languages available to be addressed here, and readers with questions regarding particular circumstances not directly dealt with below are advised to consult the source materials.[10]

---

[10] CTM Regulation, Art. 115; Implementing Regulation, Part N (rr. 95 to 99).

Applications for CTMs may be made in any of the official languages **6–10** of the European Community. Each application must stipulate a second language which is one of the OHIM languages, and in the event that the original language is not one of the OHIM languages OHIM will arrange for the application to be translated into the stipulated second language. If the applicant is the only party to proceedings before OHIM, the language of proceedings will be the language in which the application was made, although OHIM may send written communications to the applicant in the second stipulated language if the original language of the application is not one of the OHIM languages.

Notices of opposition or applications for revocation or for declarations **6–11** of invalidity must be filed in one of the OHIM languages. If the language in which such a notice or application is filed is the language of the original application or the second stipulated language, then that language is designated the language of proceedings. If not, the party filing the notice of opposition or application for revocation must within one month arrange for it to be translated into either the original language of the trade mark application (if it is an OHIM language) or into the stipulated second language at his own expense. The language into which the application is translated is then designated the language of proceedings.

In written proceedings before OHIM any party may use any of the **6–12** OHIM languages. However, if the language used is not the designated language of proceedings, then within one month of the date of submission of the document in question the party must supply a translation thereof into the designated language of proceedings.

Oral proceedings concerning the application for registration of a CTM **6–13** may be carried out in either the original language of the CTM application or the stipulated second language. In all other oral proceedings, the staff of OHIM may use one of the other OHIM languages in place of the designated language of proceedings if all other parties agree. A party to oral proceedings may use one of the official languages of the Community rather than the language of proceedings, but must arrange for it to interpreted into the designated language of proceedings.

Representation

Natural or legal persons domiciled in or having either their principal **6–14** place of business or a real and effective industrial or commercial establishment in the European Union are entitled to represent themselves in proceedings before OHIM.[11] If they wish, such parties may instead be represented by an employee. The employee of a legal person entitled to be represented in this way may also represent other legal persons economically connected with his employer, even if they themselves have no industrial or commercial establishment within the E.U. Other than in respect of filing an application for a CTM, natural or legal

---

[11] CTM Regulation, Art. 88.

persons not domiciled or having either their principal place of business or a real and effective industrial or commercial establishment in the European Union must be professionally represented before OHIM. Representatives acting before OHIM must file a written notice of authorisation signed by the party who appointed them. Authorisations may be filed covering more than one application or CTM registration.[12] Any notification or other communication by OHIM to an authorised representative has the same effect as if it had been addressed to the person represented, and vice versa.

6–15   Only the following people may act as professional representatives before OHIM[13]:

    (1) legal practitioners qualified in a Member State and having their place of business in the E.U., to the extent that they are entitled to act as representatives in trade mark matters in that Member State, or

    (2) those on the list of professional representatives maintained by OHIM.

In order to obtain entry on the the the list of professional representatives, a representative must be a national of a Member State (unless exempt from this requirement by the President of OHIM), must have a place of business or employment in the E.U. and must be entitled to represent natural or legal persons before the central industrial property office of the Member State in which he has his place of business.[14] Entry is obtained on receipt of a request accompanied by a certificate from the central industrial property office of the Member State concerned.

Fees

6–16   The fees payable in respect of a CTM or Community collective mark are set out in the Fees Regulation.[15] All fees are in Euros, and payment must be made by payment or transfer into a bank account held by OHIM,[16] by delivery to OHIM or remittance of cheques made payable to OHIM or in cash at OHIM.

Failure to comply with time limits "restitutio in integrum"

6–17   Article 78 of the CTM Regulation provides that a party to proceedings before OHIM who, in spite of taking all due care required by the circumstances, was unable to observe a time limit (i.e. having failed to

---

[12] Implementing Regulation, r. 76.
[13] CTM Regulation, Art. 89.
[14] Art. 89(2).
[15] Commission Regulation (EC) No. 2869/95 of December 13, 1995, on the fees payable to the Office for Harmonization in the Internal Market (Trade Marks and Designs).
[16] Applicants or their representatives may also set up accounts with OHIM for this purpose. Fees Regulation, Art. 5.

comply with a time limit as a result of the impact of some factor beyond the party's control), is entitled in some circumstances to apply to OHIM for restoration of any right or means of redress lost by way of their non-compliance. The following conditions must be met;

(1) the party must have taken all due care required by the circumstances; and

(2) the failure to comply with the time limit must have had the direct consequence by virtue of provisions of the CTM Regulation of causing the loss to the party of a right or means of redress; and

(3) the time limit must be "*vis a vis*" OHIM. Presumably failure to respond to an observation by another party to proceedings within a stated time limit cannot give rise to this relief; and

(4) the time limits for claiming priority (Article 29(1) of the CTM Regulation) and for filing an opposition to an application for registration of a CTM (Article 32(1)) are excluded from this provision.

The application must be filed in writing within two months of the removal of the cause of non-compliance with the time limit and in any event within a year of the expiry of the time limit in question (note that Article 78(5) expressly excludes these time limits from the scope of the doctrine). The application is not deemed to have been filed until the fee for the re-establishment of the rights sought is paid (the fee for *restitutio in integrum* is set at 200 Euro). The application must state the grounds upon which it is based and set out the facts upon which it relies.

Rights restored under this Article cannot be relied upon by the **6–18** applicant for or proprietor of a CTM against a third party who, in good faith, has put goods on the market or supplied services under a mark which would otherwise infringe the CTM in the period between the loss of the rights in question and the publication of re-establishment of those rights (Article 78 (6)). A third party who can rely on Article 78(6) is entitled to bring third party proceedings against the decision re-establishing the rights in question. Such proceedings must be brought within two months of the date of publication thereof.

Oral proceedings

If OHIM considers that oral proceedings would be "expedient", they **6–19** can be held either at OHIM's own instigation or at the request of any party to proceedings.[17] If OHIM does not consider that an oral hearing is expedient, then no such hearing will take place, notwithstanding any request by the parties. Parties summoned to oral proceedings are given at least one month notice before the hearing.[18] If any party summoned

---

[17] Art. 75, CTM Regulation.
[18] Implementing Regulation, r. 56.

fails to attend, proceedings may continue in their absence. Oral proceedings before the examiners, Opposition Division and Administration of Trade Marks and Legal Divisions are not held in public. Proceedings before the Cancellation Division and the Boards of Appeal are held in public, unless the Division or Board decides that admission of the public could have serious and unjustified disadvantages, in particular for a party to proceedings.

Taking of evidence

6–20 If OHIM considers it necessary for a party, witness or expert to give oral evidence or to make an inspection, it will take a formal decision to that end, stating the means by which it intends to obtain the evidence, the relevant facts to be proved and the date, time and place of the hearing or inspection. If oral evidence was requested by a party, a decision of OHIM will specify a period of time in which the party filing the request has to inform OHIM of the names and addresses of the witnesses to be heard.[19]

6–21 OHIM will then issue a summons for a person to give oral evidence to appear before it, containing an extract from the decision stating the evidence on which the party is to be heard and the date, time and place of the hearing. All parties are informed of the appearance of a witness or expert and have the right to put questions to them.[20]

6–22 If it considers that such evidence is necessary, OHIM has the power to commission expert evidence on its own behalf, deciding the form of the report and appointing the expert. OHIM will provide the appointed expert with[21]:

(1) a precise description of his task;
(2) the time limit laid down for the submission of the expert report;
(3) the names of the parties to the proceedings.

A copy of any written report is then submitted to the parties. The parties can object to an expert on grounds of incompetence, partiality or conflict of interest and OHIM will rule on the objection raised.

Decisions

6–23 All decisions of OHIM must state, in writing, the reasons upon which they are based. In oral proceedings the decision may be given orally, but reasons in writing must be provided subsequently to the parties. Decisions can only be based on evidence and reasons in respect of which all parties concerned have had an opportunity to present their comments (whether in writing or orally).[22] OHIM is generally entitled to

---

[19] Implementing Regulation, r. 57.
[20] CTM Regulation, Art. 76.
[21] Implementing Regulation, r. 58.
[22] CTM Regulation, Art. 75.

examine the facts relating to proceedings before it of its own motion. Opposition proceedings under the relative grounds for refusal[23] provide the exception to this general rule. Such proceedings can only be brought by the proprietor of the earlier right relied upon, and OHIM is restricted to the facts, evidence and arguments adduced by the parties to the proceedings, and may grant only the relief sought.[24] OHIM has a discretion to disregard evidence submitted out of time.[25]

Appeals

Appeals from decisions of examiners, the Opposition Division, the **6–24** Administration of Trade Marks and Legal Division and the Cancellation Division lie at first instance to the Boards of Appeal.[26] Any party to proceedings who is adversely affected by a decision has the right to lodge an appeal, and all other parties to the proceedings may also be parties to the appeal as of right. Decisions which do not terminate proceedings for a party can only be appealed together with the final decision, unless such a decision itself expressly allows for a separate appeal.

Written notice of appeal must be filed with OHIM within two months **6–25** of notification of the decision.[27] Time starts to run from notification of the written, reasoned decisions rather than any oral decision.[28] Decisions which are open to appeal are accompanied by a written notification of the time limit for filing a notice of appeal. The notice must state the name and address of the applicant (and the name and business address of any appointed legal representative) and identify the contested decision and set out the extent to which amendment or cancellation of the decision is sought.[29] The notice must be filed in the language of the proceedings in which the decision was taken. Notice of appeal is only deemed to have been filed on payment of the appeal fee. If the appeal fee is paid after expiration of the time limit, the appeal is deemed not to have been filed and the fee refunded. Detailed written grounds of appeal must be filed within four months of notification of the decision.[30]

Appeals made by parties not entitled to appeal, made in respect of **6–26** decisions not susceptible to appeal or made out of time, are not admissible. Notices of appeal not filed in the relevant language of proceedings or not identifying the contested decision or not setting out the extent to which amendment or cancellation of the decision is sought are also inadmissible, and will be rejected unless the deficiencies in the notice of appeal are remedied before expiration of the time limit for

---

[23] Art. 8.
[24] Art. 74.
[25] Art. 74(2).
[26] Art. 57.
[27] Form for notice of appeal is available from the OHIM web site, at http://oami.eu.int
[28] Implementing Regulation, r. 52.
[29] Implementing Regulation, r. 48.
[30] CTM Regulation, Art. 59.

filing the notice. If the notice of appeal does not properly identify the applicant or his legal representative, the appellant will be notified and requested to remedy the deficiency within a stated time limit. If the appeal is not corrected in good time, it will be rejected.[31]

6–27   In the case of appeals which are not opposed by other interested parties, notices of appeal are initially considered by the department that made the decision complained of. If it considers the appeal to be admissible and well founded, it will rectify its decision. Absent such rectification within one month after receipt of the statement of grounds (for whatever reason), the appeal is remitted to the Board of Appeal without comment as to its merit.

6–28   If an appeal is admissible, the Board of Appeal examines whether or not it is allowable, and will invite parties to file written observations on statements made by other parties and on its own comments. If several appeals are filed against the same decision, they must be considered in the same proceedings. The procedure for filing such observations and for any hearing is governed by the procedural rules of the OHIM division in which the decision being appealed was made.[32]

6–29   Decisions of the Boards of Appeal may be appealed by way of bringing an action before the Court of Justice.[33] Such actions may only be brought on the following grounds:

(1) lack of competence;
(2) infringement of an essential procedural requirement; and
(3) infringement of the Treaty of Rome, the CTM Regulation or any rule of law relating to their application or misuse of this power.

Such actions must be brought before the Court of Justice within two months of notification of the decision of the Board of Appeal. The Court of Justice can annul or alter the contested decision.

Communications with OHIM

6–30 Rules 79 to 82 of the Implementing Regulation provide that written communications with OHIM may be made by submitting a signed original of the document to OHIM (whether by post, personal delivery or other means), by submitting a signed original by telecopier, by telex or telegram or by electronic means.

6–31   Where an application for a CTM is made by telecopier, telex or telegram or electronic means, the required original reproductions of the mark applied for[34] must be submitted directly to OHIM if there is a graphic image in colour or if a device mark might not transmit clearly by fax. If such hard copies are received by OHIM within one month of

---

[31] Implementing Regulation, r. 49.
[32] Implementing Regulation, r. 50.
[33] CTM Regulation, Art. 63.
[34] See para. 6–40, below.

the telecopy, the application is deemed to have been filed on the earlier date. Otherwise, the date of receipt is taken to be that on which the hard copies arrived. OHIM operates a paperless office system, scanning all correspondence (including representations of marks) on receipt. This has the unfortunate effect that images of device marks often get distorted through no fault of the applicant.

If a transmission by telecopier, telex or telegram or electronic means is **6–32** illegible, or OHIM has doubts about the accuracy of the transmission, OHIM will contact the sender and request that a further copy be sent within a stated period of not less than one day. If the request is complied with, the transmission is deemed either to have been received on reception of the retransmission or of the original. If the request is not complied with, the transmission is deemed not to have been received.

Costs in proceedings before OHIM

The unsuccessful party in any proceedings for a declaration of invalidity **6–33** or opposition, revocation or appeal proceedings bears the "essential" costs of the successful party as well as his own costs.[35] However, the tribunal in such cases has the discretion to apportion costs when each party is partly successful. Similarly, a party who withdraws from such contested proceedings bears the costs of the other party. If a case does not proceed to judgment, the costs are in the discretion of the relevant division of OHIM. OHIM will take notice of any settlement on costs reached by the parties to proceedings. A party to such proceedings may apply to the registry of the Opposition Division, Cancellation Division or Boards of Appeal to fix the quantum of costs to be paid.[36]

The level of costs "essential" to the proceedings and so recoverable by **6–34** the successful party are fixed according to an exhaustive tariff addressing transport, subsistence, representation and taking of evidence.[37] Where a successful party is represented by more than one representative, the costs of only one representative are recoverable.

Costs decisions of OHIM are enforceable throughout the E.U. by the **6–35** rules of civil procedure in the state in which enforcement is to be carried out. The order for such enforcement is appended to the decision and is enforceable without other authority than the verification of the decision by the designated authority in each Member State.[38] A party seeking to enforce such an order should use the usual national channels. Enforcement of such costs orders are regulated by the courts of the Member State and may only be suspended by a decision of the Court of Justice.[39]

---

[35] CTM Regulation, Art. 81.
[36] Art. 81(6).
[37] Implementing Regulation, r. 94.
[38] Governed in the U.K. by the European Communities (Enforcement of Community Judgments) Order 1972, S.I. 1972 No. 1590, as amended by S.I. 1998 No. 1259; S.I. 1998 No. 1259.
[39] CTM Regulation, Art. 82.

2. Procedure on application for a community trade mark

Formalities

6–36 The application for a CTM can be filed either at OHIM or at "the central industrial property office of a Member State or at the Benelux Trade Mark Office".[40] In the United Kingdom applications may be filed at the Trade Marks Registry. An application filed at a national office has the same effect as if it had been filed on the same day at OHIM. The general rule is that the filing date of an application is the date on which an application form complying with the formal requirements of Articles 25 and 26 of the CTM Regulation is received. The national offices are obliged to forward all applications to OHIM within two weeks of the filing date. If such national applications do not reach OHIM within one month of being filed, they are deemed to have been withdrawn by virtue of Article 25(3) of the CTM Regulation.

6–37 All applications must contain a representation of the trade mark, a list of the goods and services in respect of which the registration is requested (grouped according to Nice Classification) and a statement of the identity of the applicant setting out its name, address and nationality.[41] It is sufficient to identify natural persons by name. Legal entities must be identified by their official designation and the law of the state governing them must be set out. If priority is claimed from an earlier mark or application, or under the provisions concerning exhibition priority, a declaration to that effect must either be included with the application or made within two months of the filing date.[42]

Examination of the conditions of filing

6–38 On receipt OHIM investigates whether an application for a CTM complies with the formalities prescribed by the CTM Regulation and the Implementing Regulation and whether the prescribed fees have been paid. These requirements are addressed in detail below and the consequences of failure to meet them set out in the relevant place.[43]

Fees on application

6–39 A basic fee (to be paid within one month of filing of the application) is payable on each application. If the basic fee is not paid within that time limit OHIM will notify the applicant of its default.[44] If the fee is received within a further two months, the application can be awarded the date

---

[40] CTM Regulation, Art. 25.
[41] Art. 26.
[42] See para. 6–42 et seq., below.
[43] CTM Regulation, Art. 36; Implementing Regulation, r. 10.
[44] Implementing Regulation, r. 9.

upon which the fee is received as a filing date if all other formalities are complied with. If the basic fee is not received within those two months. the application will lapse. A further fee is payable for each class exceeding three to which the goods and services applied for belong (see the Fees Regulation).[45] An applicant who fails to pay the class fees in full will be notified by OHIM with a request for payment within a specified time limit. If payment is not made within the time limit the application will be deemed to have been withdrawn for the classes not covered by the class fees or basic fee paid. Unless it is clear which class or classes the fees already paid were intended to cover OHIM will take the classes to have been covered in order of classification.[46]

Representation of the mark

If an applicant does not wish to claim any special graphic feature, font **6–40** or colour, the mark should be reproduced in normal script. The case in which a mark is typed in the application will be followed in publications and through to registration. Applications for device marks or marks in fancy script should include a representation of the mark on a separate sheet of paper (no larger than A4) bearing the name and address of the applicant and should be capable of being clearly reproduced in a space 8cm wide by 15cm high.[47] Applications for three-dimensional marks must state this fact, and must depict the mark graphically or photo-graphically, with no more than six different perspectives.[48] An application for a registration in colour should indicate this and must identify the colours making up the mark. The reproduction of the mark should be in the colours claimed. If an application is made for a colour *per se*, then a code number for the colour or a graphical reproduction of the colour must be included. An application to register the colour orange using only the word "orange" to describe the mark did not comply with the necessary formalities.[49]

Failure to comply with formalities

If an application does not comply with the above formalities or the basic **6–41** filing fee is not paid within one month of the filing date, it will be denied that filing date. OHIM will notify the applicant of the deficiencies and if they are remedied within two months of the receipt of such notification the date of filing slips to the date upon which the formalities are complied with. Failing that, the application will lapse and the filing fee will be refunded (if paid, of course).

[45] Commission Regulation (EC) No. 2869/95.
[46] Implementing Regulation, r. 19.
[47] Implementing Regulation, r. 3.
[48] Implementing Regulation, r. 3(4). This is the maximum number of perspective representations allowable. Unfortunately many CTMs are registered on the basis of far poorer graphical representation.
[49] *Orange* [1998] E.T.M.R. 337.

Priority and seniority

6–42 There are three bases upon which priority or seniority can be claimed for an application earlier than the filing date for the purposes of establishing precedence over third party rights. These are priority arising from an earlier application in a Paris Convention/WTO state, priority arising from display of the mark in question at a qualifying exhibition and the more limited seniority rights arising from an earlier national trade mark registration.[50] Priority or seniority can only be claimed in relation to CTM applications for marks identical to the prior mark and in respect of goods or services identical with or contained within those for which the earlier mark has been applied for, registered or exhibited.

6–43 A person who has filed an application for a trade mark in a state party to the Paris Convention or the WTO Agreement (or a state not party to Paris Convention or to the WTO Agreement but providing priority rights to applications for CTMs) obtains a right of priority during the six months following the first application. If a subsequent application is made for the same mark in respect of the same goods and services, it can only be used to determine priority if the first application has been abandoned or refused without being open to public inspection or being used as the basis for another priority claim at the date of the subsequent application. The right to priority arises from any national filing sufficient to establish a filing date, irrespective of the outcome of the application. Thus a United Kingdom application which complied with the requirements of section 32 of the 1994 Act and so was granted a filing date, but was later abandoned, would suffice to provide an earlier priority date. On the other hand, failure to comply with the requirements of section 32(2) of the 1994 Act leads to an application being deemed never to have been made. This would clearly not give rise to a claim to priority. The right to priority is determined by the acquisition of a filing date under national law.

6–44 A party wishing to rely on such a claim to priority must make a declaration of priority either with his application or within two months of the filing date. Such a declaration must state the file number of the prior application relied on and the applicant must supply a certified copy or good quality photocopy[51] of the priority application, together with a certificate stating the filing date thereof, within three months of the date of receipt of the declaration of priority.

6–45 Exhibition priority (which cannot be used to extend the right to priority from an earlier application discussed above[52]) may be claimed by an applicant who has displayed goods or services under the mark applied for at an official or officially recognised international exhibition[53]

---

[50] CTM Regulation, Arts 29–35, as amended by Council Regulation (EC) No. 3288/94.
[51] OHIM President's Practice Direction EX96–3
[52] CTM Regulation, Art. 33.
[53] Falling within the terms of the Convention on International Exhibitions signed at Paris in 1928, as revised.

if the application is filed within six months of the date of first display of the goods or services. A party wishing to claim exhibition priority must make a declaration of priority either with his application or within two months of the filing date.

Such a declaration must state the name of the exhibition and the date **6–46** of first display of the goods or services.[54] Within three months of the date of receipt of the declaration of priority, the applicant must file at OHIM a certificate issued at the exhibition by the authority responsible for the protection of industrial property at the exhibition in question. The certificate must state the opening date of the exhibition, confirm that the mark was in fact used for the goods or services claimed by the applicant and, where the first use of the mark was not the opening day of the exhibition, set out the date of that use.

The proprietor of an earlier trade mark registered in a Member State **6–47** (or registered under international arrangements having effect in a Member State) may claim for the CTM the seniority of the earlier trade mark in the Member State or States in which it was registered. The only effect of such seniority under the CTM Regulation is to grant to the proprietor of an earlier national registration who allows that registration to lapse on acquiring a CTM the same rights as he would have had if the earlier mark had continued to be registered. The right to claim seniority is lost if the national trade mark lapses or is abandoned prior to registration of the CTM. Seniority can be claimed either on application for a CTM or after registration.[55]

If seniority is to be claimed on application for a CTM under Article 34 **6–48** of the CTM Regulation, the applicant must make a declaration of seniority either with his application or within two months of the filing date.[56] Such a declaration must indicate the Member States in which the mark is registered, the date from which the registration was effective, the number of the registration and the goods and services in respect of which it was registered. The applicant must supply a certified copy or good quality photocopy[57] of the relevant registration (together with a statement that the earlier national mark is valid and subsisting) within three months of the date of receipt of the declaration of seniority.

Failure to comply with the requirements of the CTM Regulation and **6–49** Implementing Regulation concerning priority or seniority result in the loss of the priority or seniority claimed. In the case of lost seniority, the loss of seniority claimed on application can presumably be remedied (under Article 35 of the CTM Regulation) once the CTM has proceeded to registration. However, the protection afforded by seniority is no longer available over the application period.

---

[54] Implementing Regulation, r. 7.
[55] CTM Regulation, Art. 35.
[56] Implementing Regulations, r. 8.
[57] OHIM President's practice direction EX96–3.

Examination of entitlement to be proprietor.

6–50 On receipt of an application OHIM will consider whether the applicant is entitled to be a proprietor under the provisions of Article 5 of the CTM Regulation (see para. 6–07, above). If it appears that the applicant does not qualify, OHIM will notify him and specify a period within which he can either withdraw his application or submit observations. If the applicant's observations fail to meet the concerns of OHIM, the application is refused. If the applicant is entitled to be the proprietor of a CTM the application is accorded a filing date.

Equivalence of CTM filing with national filing

6–51 A CTM application that has been accorded a filing date is equivalent to a regular national filing in the Member States and can in certain circumstances (on withdrawal of the CTM application) be converted into an application for a national trade mark.[58] The "national filing" in the Member State resulting from the CTM filing will be accorded the CTM priority date.[59]

Search

6–52 Once an application has been accorded a filing date and OHIM is satisfied that the applicant is entitled to be the proprietor of a CTM, a search will be undertaken of the registers of CTMs (by OHIM) and national trade marks (by national trade mark offices[60]) for the purposes of establishing whether earlier national or CTM registrations or applications provide relative grounds for refusing the application pursuant to Article 8 of the CTM Regulation. Within three months of the search being undertaken the applicant should be provided with a copy of the search report, which will either cite the (CTM) applications and registrations which may be invoked under the relative grounds for refusal or state that no such rights have been found. Unhelpfully, the search report only sets out the class numbers, rather than details specifications, for which cited marks are registered. Upon publication of the application (which cannot occur within less than one month of the results of the search being supplied to the applicant), the proprietors of any marks or applications cited against the application will also be sent a copy of the search report. No further steps can be taken by OHIM in respect of any rights cited against the application without application by the proprietor of those rights. Under Article 8 of the CTM Regulation the relative grounds for refusal can only be exercised by the proprietor of an earlier trade mark.

---

[58] CTM Regulation, Art. 108, and section 11, below.
[59] Art. 32.
[60] France, Germany and Italy currently do not provide search data to OHIM on earlier national marks.

Examination as to absolute grounds for refusal

The absolute grounds for refusal of an application for a CTM are set out **6–25** in Article 7 of the CTM Regulation. The substantive nature of those provisions is addressed in Chapter 7. On receipt OHIM will examine an application for compliance with Article 7, and to the extent that the mark applied for may not be registered for any or all of the goods and services applied for it, will notify the applicant of the grounds for refusing registration.[61] If discussion with the applicant does not remove the grounds for refusal, the examiner will give the applicant two months within which to withdraw or amend the application or submit observations. If no response is received meeting the concerns of the examiner, the application will be refused in whole or in part. Grounds for the refusal will be given in writing.

The applicant may be requested to disclaim any exclusive right to an **6–54** element of the mark applied for as a precondition to registration. Written reasons for the requirement for a disclaimer will be given, and the applicant will be allowed two months in which to amend or withdraw the application or to submit written observations. If such observations do not overcome the examiner's objections the application will be refused to the extent necessary.

Publication

If the application fulfils all the conditions required for acceptance it will **6–55** be published no earlier than one month after the search report has been provided to the applicant. The application will be published in the Community Trade Marks Bulletin.[62] The published application will set out the name and address of the applicant and his legal representative (if applicable), a representation of the mark, indicating whether it is three dimensional and any colours claimed, a classified list of the goods and services applied for, the allocated filing date, particulars of any claim to priority or seniority, any statement that the mark has become distinctive as a consequence of the use made of it, any disclaimer and an indication of the language of the application and the second language nominated by the applicant.

Observations by third parties

Following publication of the CTM application, any natural or legal **6–56** person, and any group or body representing manufacturers, producers, suppliers of services, traders or consumers is entitled to submit written observations to OHIM as to why the mark should not be registered.[63]

[61] Implementing Regulation, r. 11.
[62] Implementing Regulation, r. 12.
[63] CTM Regulation, Art. 41.

Observations by third parties generally relate to the absolute grounds for refusal set out in Article 7 of the CTM Regulation (The relative grounds for refusal[64] only take effect on opposition by the proprietor of the earlier right relied upon). Third parties making observations do not become parties to proceedings before the Office. As such they have no right of appeal if the observation has no effect.

6–57   The examiner will copy any such observations to the applicant and invite it to submit comments if it wishes. If the examiner considers the observations to raise serious doubts as to the validity of the application, this will be stated in the notification. If, as a result of such observations or otherwise, the examiner has serious doubts as to the acceptability of the application at any time prior to registration, the examination will be reopened.

Community collective marks

6–58   The rules in the Implementing Regulation apply to proceedings concerning Community collective marks (see generally Chapter 11) as they do to CTMs, with the following additional requirement on filing an application.[65]

Under Article 65 of the CTM Regulation an applicant for a Community collective mark is obliged to submit regulations governing its use. If such regulations are not contained in the application when filed, the regulations must be submitted in writing to OHIM within a period of two months after the date of filing. Such regulations must specify:

(1) the name of the applicant and his office address;
(2) the object of the association or the object for which the legal person governed by public law is constituted;
(3) the bodies authorised to represent the association or the said legal person;
(4) the conditions for membership;
(5) the persons authorised to use the mark;
(6) and where appropriate, the conditions governing use of the mark, including sanctions for improper use.

6–59   An application for a Community collective mark will also be refused if the regulations governing use are contrary to public policy or to accepted principles of morality,[66] or if the public is liable to be misled as to the character or significance of the mark.[67] Observations on the grounds upon which a collective mark should be refused may be submitted by third parties if the above requirements are not complied with.

---

[64] Art. 8.
[65] Implementing Regulation, rr. 42, 43.
[66] CTM Regulation, Art. 66(1).
[67] Art. 66(2). As to collective marks, see Chap. 11, below.

3. Opposition to applications

In the period of three months following publication of an application[68] **6–60** the application may be opposed on the relative grounds for refusal given by Article 8 of the CTM Regulation. Upon publication of the application the proprietors of any marks or applications cited against the application will also be sent a copy of the search report by OHIM. Oppositions may only be filed by the proprietors of the earlier rights set out in Article 8, or in the case of rights under Article 8(1) and (5) their authorised licensees. Relative grounds for refusal of a CTM are dealt with in Chapter 8. An opposition is not treated as duly entered until the opposition fee has been paid.

The notice of opposition must be in writing and contain the following **6–61** information[69]:

(1) the file number of the application against which opposition is entered;

(2) an indication of the goods and services listed in the CTM application against which opposition is entered;

(3) the name of the applicant for the CTM; the identity and address of the opponent;

(4) state the basis upon which the opponent claims to be entitled to bring the opposition[70];

(5) the identity of any legal representative appointed by the opposing party;

(6) a full statement of the grounds on which the opposition is based;

(7) a representation and, where appropriate, a description of the earlier mark or earlier right relied upon by the opponent, and a statement of the goods and services in respect of which any earlier mark relied upon has been registered or applied for, or in respect of which the earlier mark is well-known within the meaning of Article 8(2)(c) or has a reputation within the meaning of Article 8(5). The notice of opposition should not only set out the goods and services for which the earlier mark relied upon is protected but also identify the goods and services relied upon in the opposition.

A form for the notice of opposition is available from the OHIM web site.[71]

If the opposition is based on an earlier mark, the notice of opposition **6–62** must provide a statement to that effect and identify whether the earlier

---

[68] Also upon re-publication of an amended application pursuant to CTM Regulation, Art. 44. See para. 6–73, below
[69] Implementing Regulation, r. 15.
[70] The precise form of the information to be provided on the identity of the opponent is set out in the Implementing Regulation, r. 15.
[71] http://oami.eu.int

mark is a Community mark or a national registration, identifying the Member State or Member States in which it is registered or, where the earlier mark is an internationally registered mark, an indication of the Member State or Member States to which protection of that earlier mark has been extended. Where available the opposition notice should set out the file number or the registration number and the filing date, including the priority date of the earlier mark or marks relied upon.

6–63   Where the opposition is based on an earlier mark which is a well-known mark within the meaning of the Paris Convention as extended by the WTO Agreement (*i.e.* the opposition is based on an earlier mark as defined in Article 8(2)(c) of the CTM Regulation), it should contain a statement to that effect and set out the Member State or States in which the earlier mark is relied upon as being well-known.

6–64   Where the opposition is based on Article 8(5) of the CTM Regulation, relying on an earlier mark registered in respect of goods or services not similar to those for which the mark is applied for that has a reputation in the Community (in the case of a CTM) or in a Member State (in the case of a national registration), the notice of opposition must provide a statement to that effect and identify where that earlier mark is registered or applied for.

Where the opposition is based on an earlier right under Article 8(4) of the CTM Regulation, the notice must say so and identify the Member State or States where that earlier right exists.

Inadmissible oppositions

6–65   Notices of opposition lodged by parties not entitled to oppose under Article 42 of the CTM Regulation or out of time are not admissible.[72] Notices of opposition which do not clearly identify the application against which opposition is entered or the earlier right or earlier mark relied upon in opposition are also inadmissible and will be rejected unless the deficiencies in the notice are remedied before expiration of the time limit for filing the notice of opposition. If the opposition fee is not paid within the opposition period the notice of opposition is deemed not to have been entered. If the opposition fee is paid after the expiration of the opposition period, it is refunded.

6–66   If the notice of opposition does not comply with other provisions of the CTM Regulation or the rules under the Implementing Regulation, the opponent will be notified and requested to remedy the deficiency within a stated time limit. If the notice is not corrected in good time, it will be rejected.[73] The applicant is notified of any decision to reject a notice of opposition as inadmissible.

[72] Implementing Regulation, r. 18(1).
[73] Implementing Regulation, r. 18(2).

Particulars in support of opposition

The opponent may include particulars of the facts, evidence and **6–67**
arguments presented in support of the opposition, accompanied by the
relevant supporting documents, in the opposition notice.[74] If such
particulars are not filed with the notice, OHIM will request them on
commencement of the opposition proceedings

If the opposition is based on an earlier mark which is not a CTM, the **6–68**
particulars should contain evidence of the registration or filing of that
earlier mark, such as a certificate of registration. If the opposition is
based on a well-known mark (as referred to in Article 8(2)(c) of the CTM
Regulation) or on a mark having a reputation (as referred to in Article
8(5)), the particulars should contain evidence demonstrating that it is
well-known or that it has such a reputation. Similarly, if the opposition
is entered on the basis of any other earlier right, particulars and
evidence should be provided of the acquisition and scope of protection
of that right.

Opposition proceedings

If the notice of opposition is not rejected as inadmissible, OHIM notifies **6–69**
the applicant of the opposition to the application and invites him to file
any observations on the opposition within a specified period.[75] At this
stage OHIM informs the applicant that unless the application is withdrawn or restricted to goods and services against which the opposition
is not directed, the opposition proceedings are deemed to commence
two months after the applicant is informed of the opposition.

If the applicant withdraws or restricts the application within the two **6–70**
month period, OHIM informs the opponent and refunds the opposition
fee. If the application is not withdrawn or restricted, the applicant must
file any observations on the opposition within the period specified by
OHIM.

Article 43(1) of the CTM Regulation obliges OHIM to invite the parties
to opposition proceedings to file observations on submissions by other
parties or communications from OHIM as often as is necessary.

If the opponent elects not to file particulars of the facts, evidence and **6–71**
arguments relied on in support of the opposition with the opposition
notice, OHIM will specify a period within which such particulars must
be filed on commencement of the examination process.[76] Any submission by the opposing party is communicated to the applicant who is
then given an opportunity to reply within a further period specified by
the Office.

---

[74] Implementing Regulation, r. 16.
[75] Implementing Regulation, rr. 19, 20.
[76] Implementing Regulation, r. 20.

6–72   If the applicant files no observations on the opponent's notice and particulars, the Opposition Division is entitled to decide the opposition on the basis of the evidence before it. Any further observations filed by the applicant are copied to the opponent, who is then called upon by OHIM to reply within a specified period.

6–73   An applicant is entitled at any time to restrict the list of goods and services in respect of which a mark is applied for.[77] If the application has already been published, it is republished in its restricted form. If an application is restricted in the course of opposition proceedings, OHIM will inform the opponent and call for observations stating whether the opposition is still maintained and, if so, against which of the remaining goods and services.

6–74   The applicant is entitled to require the opponent to prove that any earlier mark relied upon in the opposition has been put to genuine use in the Community (if a CTM) or the relevant Member State (if a national trade mark) over the period of five years prior to publication of the application, or that there are proper reasons for non-use.[78] This provision only applies if the mark relied upon has at that date been registered for not less than five years. Evidence of use should provide details of the place, time, extent and nature of use of the opposing trade mark for the goods and services in respect of which it is registered and on which the opposition is based, and should consist of sworn evidence supported by documents and items such as packages, labels, price lists, catalogues, invoices and photographs.[79]

6–75   If the opponent fails to provide such proof, the opposition will be rejected. If the opponent only provides proof of use in respect of some of the goods and services for which the mark relied on is registered, then for the purposes of the opposition the mark is treated as being registered only in respect of those goods and services. No provision is made in Article 43(2) as to the effect of only providing proof of proper reasons for non-use in relation to some of the goods and services for which a mark is registered. It is submitted that such partial proof has the same effect as partial proof of use.

6–76   If an opposition is based on a pending application, OHIM may stay proceedings pending determination of that application, or if there are any other circumstances which make a stay appropriate.[80]

Once OHIM has given the parties the opportunity to submit such observations the Opposition Division will examine and decide on the opposition. If examination reveals that the trade mark is not registrable in respect of some or all of the goods and services for which the application was made, it will be refused in respect of those goods and services. Otherwise, the opposition is rejected. Upon becoming final, opposition decisions are published.

[77] CTM Regulation, Art. 44(1).
[78] Art. 43(2).
[79] Implementing Regulation, r. 22.
[80] Implementing Regulation, r. 20(b).

4. Registration

If no opposition is lodged within the three months following publication **6–77** of the application, or all oppositions have been rejected, the application will proceed to registration[81] on payment of a registration fee consisting of a basic fee and an additional class fee for each class exceeding three in respect of which the mark is to be registered.[82] If the applicant (or their agent) has a deposit account with OHIM (see para. 6–16, above) the registration fee is deducted automatically unless instructions to the contrary are received. The registration fee must be paid within two months of it being requested by OHIM. Failure to pay the fee will result in a notification of late payment, after which another two months is allowed to make the payment on condition that an additional fee is also paid. If the fee is not paid within the later period the application is deemed to have been withdrawn.

5. Renewal

The basic duration of a CTM registration is 10 years from the date of **6–78** filing of the application. The registration can be renewed for an unlimited number of further 10-year periods. At least six months prior to the expiry date of the registration, OHIM should notify the proprietor and all parties with a registered right in a CTM of the approaching expiry date (failure by OHIM to provide notification of pending expiry does not affect the expiry date of a mark).[83]

The request for renewal of a CTM registration must be made by the **6–79** proprietor or an expressly authorised representative thereof (such as a trade mark agent). The request must be submitted within the period of six months leading up to the end of the existing registration period. Failing this, requests may be submitted in the six months following expiry of the mark on payment of an additional fee.

An application for renewal of a CTM registration must contain[84]: **6–80**

(1) where the application is filed by the proprietor of the trade mark, his name and address;

(2) where the application is filed by a person expressly authorised to do so by the proprietor of the mark, the name and address of that person and evidence that he is authorised to file the application;

(3) where the applicant has appointed a representative, the name and business address of the representative;

(4) the registration number;

---

[81] Implementing Regulation, r. 23.
[82] Fees Regulation, Art. 2.
[83] CTM Regulation, Art. 47; Implementing Regulation, r. 29.
[84] Implementing Regulation, r. 30.

(5) a statement that renewal is requested for all the goods and services covered by the registration or, if not, a statement of those classes or those goods and services for which renewal is requested and those classes or those goods and services for which renewal is not requested, grouped according to the classes of the Nice Classification, each group being preceded by the number of the class of that classification to which that group of goods or services belongs and presented in the order of the classes of that classification.

6–81 On application for renewal, a renewal fee consisting of a basic fee and an additional class fee for each class exceeding three in respect of which the mark is to be renewed. If a request is submitted or fees paid only in respect of some of the goods and services for which the mark was originally registered, it will be renewed only for those goods and services. If the application does not make clear which class or classes of goods and services are to be covered, OHIM will take the classes into account in order of classification. The renewal of a mark is recorded in the Register.

6–82 If an application for renewal is filed within the six-month time period prior to expiry but the other formalities governing renewal set out above are not complied with, OHIM will inform the applicant of the deficiencies found. If the application is filed by a person whom the proprietor of the trade mark has expressly authorised to do so, the proprietor of the trade mark will also be sent a copy of the notification. If the deficiencies are not remedied within the six month period following expiry of the registration, OHIM will determine that the registration has expired and will notify the proprietor, the applicant for renewal and any person recorded in the Register as having rights in the mark to that effect.

6–83 Where the determination of expiry of a mark has become final, OHIM will cancel the mark from the Register. The cancellation shall take effect from the day after the day on which the existing registration expired.

6. Surrender

6–84 A CTM may be surrendered in respect of some or all of the goods and services in respect of which it is registered.[85] To surrender a registered mark the proprietor must declare his intention to OHIM in writing. Such a declaration must contain[86]:

(1) the registration number of the CTM;
(2) the name and address of the proprietor;
(3) where a representative has been appointed, the name and business address of the representative;

---

[85] CTM Regulation, Art. 49.
[86] Implementing Regulation, r. 36.

(4) where surrender is declared only for some of the goods and services for which the mark is registered, the declaration must specify the goods and services for which the surrender is declared or the goods and services for which the mark is to remain registered.

The surrender does not have effect until entered in the Register, and it **6–85** can only be entered into the register with the agreement of the proprietor of any registered right in the mark, and on notice to any registered licensee. The signature of declaration of surrender by or on behalf of the proprietor of a registered right is sufficient to prove such consent.

If a licence has been registered, then the mark will only be removed **6–86** from the Register on surrender if the proprietor of the trade mark proves both that he has informed his licensee of his intention to surrender. If the proprietor can show that the licensee has consented to the surrender, the surrender is registered forthwith. Otherwise, the surrender is registered three months after the proprietor has satisfied OHIM that the licensee has been informed.

7. Dealings with Community trade marks

The general rule is that a CTM or trade mark application is to be dealt **6–87** with in its entirety and for the whole area of the Community as a national trade mark registered in the Member State in which, according to the Register, the proprietor has his seat or domicile, or failing that, has an establishment (Article 16(1) of the CTM Regulation). If two or more joint proprietors are mentioned in the Register, Article 16(1) is applied to the first named proprietor. If the first named proprietor does not have a domicile, seat or establishment in a Member State then Article 16(1) is applied in turn to each of the subsequent named joint proprietors in the order in which they are mentioned. If no proprietor satisfying the provisions of Article 16(1) is listed, then the CTM or application is dealt with as a Spanish national trade mark (Spain being the Member State in which OHIM is situated).

Notwithstanding the general rule, Articles 17 to 24 of the CTM Regulation set out the substantive law and necessary formalities relating to certain specific dealings with CTMs.

Assignment/transfer

A CTM or application can be assigned in respect of some or all of the **6–88** goods or services in respect of which it is registered or applied for[87] but cannot be transferred or assigned or revoked other than in respect of the

---

[87] CTM Regulation, Art. 17(1).

entire Community.[88] With two exceptions all assignments of CTMs are void unless made in writing and signed by all parties to the assignment. The first exception is that any transfer of the ownership of a whole undertaking which is the proprietor of a CTM or application is deemed to include the transfer of that trade mark or application[89] (except where there is an agreement to the contrary or "circumstances clearly dictate otherwise"). The second exception is that assignments made as a result of judgments need not comply with the usual formalities.

6–89   An application for registration of a transfer or assignment must contain[90]:

(1) the registration number of the CTM or application;

(2) particulars of the new proprietor;

(3) where not all the registered goods or services are included in the transfer, particulars of the registered goods or services to which the transfer relates. On such a partial transfer of a CTM or application OHIM will establish a new file for the new registration, containing a complete copy of the old file prior to the transfer and the application for registration of the partial transfer;

(4) documents proving the transfer or assignment. This requirement is met if the application for registration of the transfer is signed by the registered proprietor or his representative and by the successor in title or his representative or if the application, if submitted by the successor in title, is accompanied by a declaration, signed by the registered proprietor or his representative, that he agrees to the registration of the successor in title or if the application is accompanied by a completed transfer form or document signed by the registered proprietor or his representative and by the successor in title or his representative;

(5) where applicable, the name and business address of the representative of the new proprietor.

Transfers to parties who cannot be proprietors of CTMs will not be registered. The application is not deemed to have been filed until the required fee has been paid.

6–90   If it is clear to OHIM from the transfer documents that as a result of the transfer the CTM is likely to mislead the public concerning the nature, quality or geographical origin of the goods and services in respect of which the mark is registered, OHIM will not register the transfer unless the assignee agrees to limit the registration to goods and services which avoid the risk of the public being misled.[91] This provision

---

[88] Art. 1(2).
[89] Art. 17(2).
[90] Implementing Regulation, r. 31.
[91] CTM Regulation, Art. 17(4).

is somewhat confusing, in that unless a mark is bought along with the business under which it was originally provided or some form of contractual term is imposed on the assignee to maintain the nature and quality of goods or services provided under the mark, it is a natural consequence of the assignment of a CTM that the nature or quality of such goods or services will change, if only to the extent that they are now to be made or provided by a different party. As such, if the CTM had any reputation prior to the assignment, it is difficult to see how an assignment can fail to be likely to mislead the public unless the transfer agreement on its face provides for the nature, quality and geographical origin of the goods and services under the mark to be maintained.

Licensing

A CTM may be licensed in respect of some or all of the goods or services for which it is registered, and in relation to the whole or part of the Community.[92] It may be exclusive or non-exclusive. No formalities are prescribed for the grant of a licence. **6–91**

The proprietor of a CTM may institute infringement proceedings against a licensee who contravenes any provision in the licence concerning duration, form of the mark to be used, scope of goods and services in respect of which the mark may be used, the territory of the licence or the quality of goods or services provided by the licensee under the mark.[93]

An application for registration of a licence or other rights must contain[94]: **6–92**

(1) the registration number of the CTM or application in respect of which the licence or right is to be registered;
(2) particulars of the licensee or proprietor of the right;
(3) where not all the registered goods or services are subject to the licence or other right, particulars of the registered goods or services to which the licence or other right relates;
(4) where applicable, the name and business address of the representative of the licensee or proprietor of the right.

The registration of licence or other rights can be cancelled or modified on application in writing by one of the persons concerned. The application should set out the registration number of the CTM and provide particulars of the right whose registration is to be cancelled and be accompanied by documents showing that the registered right no longer exists or a statement by the licensee or the holder of the right in question that he consents to cancellation or modification of the registration.

---

[92] Art. 22.
[93] Art. 22(2).
[94] Implementing Regulation, r. 33.

Effect of registration of transactions[95]

6–93 Until an assignment has been registered, the assignee is not entitled to rely on his rights arising from registration of a CTM against a third party.[96] Thus an unregistered proprietor cannot issue infringement proceedings or rely on the mark or application for the purposes of opposition.

6–94 Any assignment, licence or grant of a right *in rem* concerning a CTM or trade mark application is only effective either against third parties after entry in the Register or against third parties who had notice of the unregistered transaction before acquiring any right in the trade mark or application themselves.[97] The formalities relating to applications for registration of assignments and licenses are addressed above.

8. Jurisdiction of Community trade mark courts

6–95 Article 91 of the CTM Regulation imposes an obligation on Member States to designate Community trade mark courts of first and second instance within three years of the entry into force of the CTM Regulation (which time limit has now elapsed). The High Court in England and Wales and Northern Ireland and the Court of Session in Scotland were designated Community trade mark courts in the United Kingdom by the Community Trade Marks Regulations 1996 (S.I. 1996 No. 1908), which came into force on August 14, 1996. The United Kingdom has not yet designated Community trade mark courts of second instance to which appeals from the Community trade mark courts lie.[98] Pending designation of such courts of second instance, their role is presumably to be undertaken by the Court of Appeal, pursuant to Article 91(5), which provides that so long as a Member State has not complied with its obligation to designate Community trade mark courts jurisdiction shall lie with those national courts which have jurisdiction in respect of national trade marks. The conditions under which appeals may be made to a Community trade mark court of second instance and the procedure for such appeals are governed by national law.[99]

6–96 Applications for declarations of invalidity or for revocation of a CTM can only be made in the Community trade mark courts by way of counterclaim. They cannot be made by way of an application for a declaration of non-infringement.[1]

The Community trade mark courts have exclusive jurisdiction over CTM infringement actions (and counterclaims for revocation), including *quia timet* actions if permitted under national law, and over actions for declarations of non-infringement in respect of CTMs.

---

[95] See paras 6–89 and 6–92.
[96] CTM Regulation, Art. 17(b).
[97] Art. 23(1).
[98] Art. 101.
[99] Art. 101(2), (3).
[1] Arts 95, 50 and 51.

The jurisdiction of the particular national Community trade mark **6–97** courts is addressed in Articles 93, 94 and 100 of the CTM Regulation. The general rule is that proceedings should be brought in the Community trade mark court of the Member State in which the defendant is domiciled or, if not domiciled in any Member State, has an establishment (Article 93(1)). If the defendant has no such domicile or establishment, proceedings should be brought in the Member State where the claimant is domiciled, or failing that has an establishment. If none of the above conditions can be fulfilled, proceedings must be brought in Spain (the Member State where OHIM has its seat). With the exception of proceedings for a declaration of non-infringement, proceedings may also be brought in the courts of the Member State in which the act of infringement complained of took place or was threatened.[2]

Notwithstanding the above, Article 17 of the Brussels Convention **6–98** applies if the parties agree that a different Community trade mark court should have jurisdiction, and Article 18 of the Brussels Convention applies if the defendant enters an appearance before a different Community trade mark court.[3] (See Chapter 18.)

In any action other than an application for a declaration of non-infringement, a Community trade mark court is obliged by Article 100(1) of the CTM Regulation to stay any proceedings in which the validity of the Community trade mark in question has already been put in issue before another Community trade mark court (*i.e.* by way of counterclaim for revocation or for a declaration of invalidity) or where an application for such relief has already been filed at OHIM, unless there are "special grounds for continuing the hearing". The court in question has the power to grant interim relief for the duration of the stay.

OHIM is itself under a similar obligation to stay proceedings by which **6–100** either revocation or a declaration of invalidity of a Community trade mark is sought if the validity of the mark is already in issue before a Community trade mark court.[4] However, each of the parties to the proceedings before the Community trade mark court may apply to that court for a stay of proceedings pending the determination of the OHIM application. If a stay is granted in the Community trade mark court, the OHIM proceedings continue.[5]

The Community trade mark courts apply the provisions of the CTMR **6–101** with direct effect. In all matters not covered by the CTMR (such as criminal sanctions for misuse of CTMs, remedies for unjustified threats and the powers of the Commissioners of Customs and Excise in respect of importation of infringing goods in the United Kingdom), a Com-

---

[2] Art. 93(5).
[3] CTM Regulation, Art. 94(4).
[4] Art. 100(2).
[5] The provisions of Art. 100 should be read in conjunction with Art. 96, which provides that the proprietor of a Community trade mark being challenged in a Community trade mark court may apply for a stay pending an application by the defendant for revocation and/or a declaration of invalidity of the mark. If no such application is made within a stated time limit, the counterclaim is deemed to have been abandoned.

munity trade mark court applies its national law, including its private international law.[6] The Community Trade Marks Regulations 1996 (S.I. 1996 No. 1908) extended the following sections of the 1994 Act to apply to CTMs: Section 21 (groundless threats), sections 89 to 91 (powers of Customs and Excise in respect of the importation of infringing goods), sections 92, 93 and 97 (criminal offences and forfeiture) and further introduced a criminal offence prohibiting the making of false representations that a mark is a CTM or as to the goods or services for which it is registered.

Effect of actions based on equivalent national and Community trade marks

6–102   Where infringement actions are brought in the courts of different Member States involving the same cause of action and between the same parties, one court seized on the basis of a national trade mark and the other on the basis of a CTM, there would clearly be scope for conflicting decisions if both actions were to proceed to trial concurrently.

6–103   Article 105(1) of the CTM Regulation provides that if the two marks in question are identical and are registered in respect of identical goods or services, the court not seized first must decline jurisdiction (unless the jurisdiction of the court first seized is challenged, in which case the court not first seized may instead stay its proceedings pending resolution of the challenge). If the two marks in question are identical but are registered in respect of similar goods or services, or are similar but are registered in respect of similar or identical goods or services, the court not first seized may stay its proceedings.[7]

6–104   A court hearing an infringement action based on a CTM must dismiss the action if a final judgment on the merits has previously been given on the same cause of action and between the same parties on the basis of an identical national trade mark valid for identical goods or services. Similarly, a court must reject an infringement action based on a national trade mark if final judgment has been given on the same cause of action and between the same parties on the basis of an identical CTM.

The provisions relating to stays and jurisdiction set out in Article 105 do not apply in respect of interim or protective measures.[8]

9.   Applications for revocation/declarations of invalidity

6–105   The substantive law on invalidity and revocation of CTMs is set out in Articles 50 to 53 of the CTM Regulation and addressed in detail in Chapter 9. Applications for revocation and/or a declaration of invalidity of a CTM may either be submitted to OHIM or made by way of

[6] Art. 97.
[7] Art. 105(1)(b).
[8] Art. 105(4).

counterclaim in the designated Community trade mark court of a Member State. Note that the validity of a CTM may not be put in issue in proceedings for a declaration of non-infringement in a Community trade mark court.[9] A plea of invalidity on relative grounds (*i.e.* on the grounds that a defendant owns an earlier right) or that a mark should be revoked for non-use may, however, be made as a defence rather than as a counterclaim in a Community trade mark court.[10] Any claim of invalidity or for revocation on other grounds must be made by way of a counterclaim in the Community trade mark courts or by way of application to OHIM.

Application to OHIM

Any natural or legal person or group having the capacity to sue in its **6–106** own name under the law governing it set up for the purposes of representing the interest of traders or consumers may apply for revocation or a declaration of invalidity under the provisions of Articles 50 or 51 (grounds for revocation and absolute grounds for invalidity, respectively). Note that the precise wording of Article 55(1)(a) provides that such parties may apply to OHIM when Articles 50 *and* 51 apply. It is submitted that this must be read disjunctively.

Where the relative grounds for invalidity are relied upon (Article 52 **6–107** of the CTM Regulation) then applications may only be made to OHIM by the proprietors or licensees of the earlier trade marks relied upon or by the owner of any right to a name, personal portrayal, copyright or other industrial property right relied on under Article 52 (2).[11]

Applications must be made in writing and filed with a reasoned **6–108** statement of grounds: stating the name and address of the applicant and, if the applicant has appointed one, the name and the business address of any representative. The application must also identify the registration number of the CTM under attack, the name and address of the proprietor and specify the registered goods and services in respect of which revocation or a declaration of invalidity is sought.

The statement of grounds must contain an indication of the facts, **6–109** evidence and arguments presented in support of the application, and in particular the following information, depending on the basis upon which the relief is sought[12]:

(1) in the case of an application for revocation or based on the absolute grounds for invalidity (pursuant to Article 50 or Article 51 of the CTM Regulation) a statement of the grounds on which the application for revocation or a declaration of invalidity is based;

[9] Art. 95.
[10] Art. 95(3).
[11] See Chap. 8.
[12] Implementing Regulation, r. 37.

(2) in the case of an application for a declaration of invalidity based on the relative grounds for invalidity pursuant to Article 52(1), particulars of the right on which the application for a declaration of invalidity is based and if necessary particulars showing that the applicant is entitled to adduce the earlier right as grounds for invalidity;

(3) in the case of an application pursuant to Article 52(2), particulars of the right on which the application for a declaration of invalidity is based together with details demonstrating that the applicant is the proprietor of an earlier right as defined by Article 52(2) or is entitled under the national law applicable to lay claim to that right.

6–110 The application is not deemed to have been filed until the application fee stipulated by the Fees Regulation has been paid. If the application does not comply with the above rules or any other provision of the CTMR or the Implementing Regulation, or the fee has not been paid, OHIM will inform the applicant and provide a specified time period in which the deficiencies must be made good.[13] If the deficiencies are not remedied before expiry of the time limit, the OHIM will reject the application as inadmissible. If the required fees are paid after expiry of the period specified by the OHIM, they are refunded.

6–111 If it is not rejected as inadmissible, a copy of the application is forwarded by OHIM to the proprietor of the CTM together with a request to file any observations within such period as it may specify. If the proprietor declines to file any observations, OHIM can decide on the revocation or invalidity on the basis of the evidence before it.[14]

6–112 Any observations filed by the proprietor are communicated to the applicant, who is in turn requested by OHIM, if it sees fit, to reply within a stated period. As can be seen, the procedure is very similar to that on examination of an OHIM opposition. Copies of all observations from the parties and all communications from OHIM are provided to each of the parties.

6–113 The proprietor may require the applicant to prove that any earlier mark relied upon in support of the application has been put to genuine use in the Community (if a CTM) or the relevant Member State (if a national trade mark) over the period of five years prior to the application for a declaration of invalidity, or that there were proper reasons for non-use.[15] This provision is very similar to that under Article 43(2) of the CTM Regulation relating to opposition proceeding.[16] Both only apply if the mark relied upon as an earlier mark had at the relevant date been registered for not less than five years.

6–114 Furthermore, if at the date on which the CTM under attack was published the earlier mark had been registered for not less than five

[13] Implementing Regulation, r. 39.
[14] Implementing Regulation, r. 40.
[15] CTM Regulation, Art. 56(2).
[16] See para. 6–74, above.

years (that is to say the relevant date under Article 43(2)), the applicant must also provide the proof required under Article 43(2). Evidence of use to discharge the burden on the applicant under Article 56(2) should be provided in the same form as that required by Article 43(2) and rule 22 of the Implementing Regulation.[17]

If the applicant fails to provide such proof, the application for a **6–115** declaration of invalidity will be rejected. If the applicant only provides proof of use in respect of some of the goods and services for which the mark relied on is registered, then for the purposes of the opposition the mark is treated as being registered only in respect of those goods and service.[18]

If examination of the application for revocation or for a declaration of **6–116** invalidity reveals that the CTM should not have been registered in respect of some or all of the goods and services for which it was registered, the rights of the proprietor are revoked and/or the mark declared invalid in respect of those goods and services. Otherwise, the application is rejected.

No application is admissible if an earlier application relating to the same subject matter and cause of action and involving the same parties has been previously adjudicated on in the courts of a Member State and has acquired the status of a final decision.

Counterclaims

The validity of CTMs may be challenged by way of counterclaim in the **6–117** Community trade mark courts only in the circumstances set out in Articles 2, 95 and 96 of the CTM Regulation, as set out in paragraph 6–105, above.

On application by the proprietor of a CTM, a Community trade mark **6–118** court may stay proceedings in which a counterclaim for revocation or a declaration of invalidity is being made and request the defendant to submit an application for revocation or the declaration of invalidity sought to OHIM within a stated time limit. If no such application is made, the counterclaim is deemed withdrawn. If the defendant makes such an application, the provisions of Article 100 on related actions apply.[19]

A Community trade mark court will reject a counterclaim for revocation or a declaration of invalidity if an earlier decision by OHIM relating to the same subject matter and cause of action and involving the same parties has already become final.[20]

10. Rights conferred by CTM

The rights conferred on the proprietor of a CTM are addressed in detail **6–119** in Chapter 13, and are to a great extent analogous to those of the proprietor of a national trade mark under section 10 of the 1994 Act (see

---

[17] See para. 6-74, above.
[18] CTM Regulation, Art. 56(5).
[19] See para. 6–99, above.
[20] CTM Regulation, Art. 97.

Article 9 of the CTM Regulation). It is not proposed to address these rights in detail here.

11. Conversion of CTM to national registration

6–120 If and to the extent that a CTM application is withdrawn, deemed to be withdrawn or refused, or that a CTM ceases to have effect, the applicant for or proprietor of a CTM may request that it be converted into a national trade mark application.[21] Conversion cannot occur if:

(1) the rights of the CTM proprietor have been revoked for non-use, unless the mark has been put to use which would be considered genuine use under the national law of the Member State for which conversion has been requested within that Member State; or

(2) grounds for refusal of registration or for revocation or invalidity apply to the CTM or application in the Member State in question.

The national trade mark application resulting from such conversion of a CTM enjoys the same filing date, and if applicable priority and/or seniority as the parent CTM.

6–121 When a CTM ceases to have effect as a result of a decision of OHIM that has become final, or the surrender of the mark has been registered, or a CTM application is deemed withdrawn or refused by a decision of OHIM that has become final, OHIM will notify the proprietor of the right to apply for conversion. The proprietor then has a period of three months in which to file any such request.

6–122 Similarly, the proprietor of a CTM application or CTM has three months in which to apply for conversion following:

(1) the date of withdrawal of a CTM application;

(2) the expiry date on failure to renew a CTM;

(3) the date on which a final decision of a national CTM court cancelling the effect of a CTM acquires the status of a final decision.

6–123 An application for conversion must set out[22]:

(a) the name and the address of the applicant for conversion;

(b) where the applicant for conversion has appointed a representative, the name and the business address of that representative;

(c) the filing number of the CTM application or the registration number of the CTM;

---

[21] Art. 108, CTM Regulation.
[22] Implementing Regulation, r. 44.

(d) the date of filing of the CTM application or the CTM and, where applicable, particulars of any claim to priority or seniority.

(e) a representation of the mark as contained in the application or as registered;

(f) a list of the Member State or the Member States in respect of which conversion is requested;

(g) where the request does not relate to all of the goods and services for which the application has been filed or for which the trade mark has been registered, an indication of the goods and services for which conversion is requested for each Member State (if different);

(h) details of the basis upon which conversion is requested, setting out the date from which the three-month period began to run, and in the case of a CTM that ceased to have effect following a final decision of a Community trade mark court, a copy of that decision.

If an application for conversion does not comply with Article 108(1) **6–124** (that is to say, the CTM application or CTM is still extant in some way which overlaps with the conversion application) or was not filed within the three-month period, it is rejected.[23] Unless the conversion fee set down by the Fees Regulation is paid within the three-month conversion notice period, the application is deemed withdrawn. Where the other requirements governing an application for conversion set out above are not met, OHIM informs the applicant of such deficiencies and asks for them to be remedied within a specified period. If they are not remedied in good time, the application is rejected.

If the application for conversion complies with the requirements of the **6–125** CTMR and the Implementing Regulation it is transmitted to the central industrial property offices of the specified Member States. OHIM informs the applicant of the date of transmission. If the application for conversion relates to a CTM or a CTM application that has previously been published in the Community Trade Mark Bulletin, the application for conversion is itself published in the Community Trade Mark Bulletin.

Once transmitted to a national central industrial property office, those **6–126** offices decide as to the admissibility of the application[24] in accordance with national law. However, Article 110(2) of the CTM Regulation provides that a converted CTM or CTM application "shall not be subjected to formal requirements of national law which are different from or additional to those provided for" in the CTM Regulation and Implementing Regulation. The meaning of this provision is not entirely clear. The national offices are to apply national law in determining the

---

[23] Implementing Regulation, r. 45(1).
[24] CTM Regulation, Art. 110.

application.[25] However the procedural formalities of national application proceedings and renewal process would, on their face, seem to be "formal requirements additional to those provided for" in the CTM Regulation. It is submitted that the restriction on further formal requirements does not apply to formal requirements that come into being after conversion to a national registration or application. This is consistent with Article 110(3) which allows the national office to require that the applicant pay the national application fee, file a translation in one of the official languages of the State in question of the request and of the documents accompanying it, indicate an address for service in the State in question and supply a representation of the trade mark in the number of copies specified by the State in question, all of which are formalities that would otherwise have had to have been complied with at an earlier stage of the application.

12. International registration of trade marks

Introduction

6–127 The Madrid Protocol[26] provides a system for the international registration of trade marks. Rather than creating a unified supranational trade mark (like the CTM) it provides for a centralised register of marks and allows for marks applied for through the national trade mark system to be extended to and registered in other signatory states. The United Kingdom is a signatory to the Madrid Protocol and its provisions were implemented within the United Kingdom by way of the Trade Marks (International Registration) Order 1996[27] ("the 1996 Order") as amended by the Trade Marks (International Registration) (Amendment) Order 2000 (S.I. 2000 No. 138). The basic principle of the international trade mark registration system is that international registrations are protected as national marks in signatory states. International marks obtaining registration in the United Kingdom are entered into a supplemental register maintained by the Trade Marks Registrar, established by article 26 of the 1996 Order as well as the international register maintained by the International Bureau of the World Intellectual Property Organisation ("the International Bureau"). An international mark registered outside of the United Kingdom but designating the United Kingdom as a state within which protection is sought is subject to examination by the Trade Marks Registry, and on registration in the United Kingdom obtains essentially the same protection as is accorded to a United Kingdom

---

[25] At the time of writing the Republic of Ireland had not yet implemented secondary legislation governing the conversion of CTMs to national applications. The application to be converted is given a national file number and then suspended pending enactment (at a time as yet unspecified) of the relevant legislation.

[26] The Protocol Relating to the Madrid Agreement Concerning the International Registration of Marks.

[27] S.I. 1996 No. 714.

registration. Similarly, an application for international registration originating within the United Kingdom is subject to scrutiny by the
authorities of the other states designated before obtaining registration in
the supplemental registers and protection under their trade mark law.
Unless the 1996 Order specifies otherwise,[28] international trade marks
(UK) are dealt with by the Trade Marks Registry in accordance with the
current Trade Marks Rules.[29]

International trade mark registrations are valid for 10 years, and **6–128**
subsequently renewable for further periods of 10 years. Once a mark has
remained on the international register for a period of five or more years,
it becomes independent of the original national mark or application
upon which it is based.

Effect of international registration

The proprietor of an international registration is entitled to the same **6–129**
protection as would have been provided if the application or registration on which the international registration is based had been deposited
directly at the relevant national trade mark office. The proprietor of a
protected international trade mark (UK) is entitled to the rights and
remedies set out in sections 9 to 12 and 14 to 20 of the Trade Marks Act
1994[30] in respect of the goods and services for which the mark has been
designated in the United Kingdom, subject to any relevant disclaimers
or limitations to the international mark from the date on which the mark
is treated as registered in the United Kingdom.[31] Dealings with and the
licensing of an international trade mark (UK) are subject to the provisions of national law.[32] As under national law, such dealings must be
registered to be of full effect (see para. 6–145 *et seq.*, below). The
proprietor of the international registration is subject to the threats
provisions of section 21 of the 1994 Act. The national provisions relating
to criminal offences and forfeiture of infringing goods set out in sections
89 to 93 and 97 of the 1994 Act are applied to international trade marks
(UK) by the 1996 Order.[33] Article 18 of the 1996 Order makes it an
offence to falsely represent that a mark is protected as an international
trade mark (UK).

International registrations designating the United Kingdom

International trade marks are entitled to protection in the United **6–130**
Kingdom if they would have been registrable under the provisions of
the 1994 Act and the Trade Mark Rules if applied for as a national

---

[28] 1996 Order, Art. 32.
[29] Trade Mark Rules 2000.
[30] 1996 Order, Art. 4.
[31] 1996 Order, Arts 12, 21.
[32] 1994 Act, ss.22 to 24 (assignment and co-ownership) and ss.28 to 31 (licensing).
[33] 1996 Order, Arts 16, 17.

registration in the United Kingdom.[34] If the application for an international registration designated the United Kingdom, or an application is made to extend an international trade mark to the United Kingdom after registration, the International Bureau will notify the Registry. Unless within 18 months of the notification,

(1) notification of refusal of the international trade mark is given to the International Bureau by the Registry; or

(2) the International Bureau is notified that the mark has been opposed, and the opposition is ongoing in the Registry; or

(3) the International Bureau is informed by the Registry that oppositions may be filed after the expiry of the 18-month period (this is the usual case) and notification of such oppositions is given in the U.K. unless the application for protection is examined and published within 14 months of the original notification,

the trade mark is registered and protected in the United Kingdom.

6–131 The international mark is examined by the Registrar under essentially the same procedure as a national application.[35] If the requirements for registration are not met, or are only met in relation to some of the goods or services for which the mark has been applied, the International Bureau is informed of the refusal. The International Bureau immediately provides a copy of the notice of refusal to the holder of the mark. The refusal specifies a period within which the holder can make representations in respect of the refusal. If no representations are made, the refusal stands. If representations are filed, when a final decision is reached by the Registry in respect of the refusal, the International Bureau is notified.

6–132 If the application is not refused on examination, it is published by the Registrar. In the 12 months following publication, observations as to whether the mark should be registered may be made in writing to the Registrar by any person.[36] A person filing such observations does not become a party to the proceedings.

6–133 Any person may oppose the application within three months of publication.[37] Notice of opposition must be given in writing and must comply with the provisions of rule 13 of the Trade Mark Rules. On receipt of notice of opposition, the Registrar must send a notification refusing the mark to the International Bureau, identifying any earlier trade mark relied upon and the goods and services in respect of which the opposition is based. The International Bureau provides a copy of the notice to the holder of the mark.

6–134 Within three months of the date on which notice of refusal based on the opposition is given to the International Bureau the holder may file a

[34] 1996 Order, Art. 3.
[35] 1996 Order, Art. 9.
[36] 1996 Order, Art. 10(b).
[37] 1996 Order, Art. 10.

counter-statement (as in national procedure) on Form TM8 (unless a cooling off period has been granted with the agreement of the holder and the opposing party.[38]) The holder must provide an address for service within the United Kingdom. Opposition proceedings then continue as in a national application, governed by rules 13 and 14 of the Trade Mark Rules.

Following a final decision in any opposition proceedings, the Registry **6–135** provides notice to the International Bureau. If and to the extent that the opposition failed, the mark proceeds to registration (recorded both in the United Kingdom supplementary register and the International Register). Otherwise it does not receive protection in the United Kingdom.

If the United Kingdom was designated as a state in which protection **6–136** was sought in the original international application, or the application for protection in the United Kingdom was made subsequently but before the registration date of the international registration, then the trade mark is treated as being registered under the 1994 Act as of the date of that international registration. On the other hand, if the application for protection in the United Kingdom was made after the registration date of the international registration, the international trade mark (UK) is treated as registered as of the date the request for protection in the United Kingdom was recorded in the International Register.

International registrations originating in the United Kingdom

An applicant for a national trade mark, or the proprietor of a national **6–137** registration, may apply for international registration of the mark through the Registrar if the applicant is:

(1) a British citizen, British dependant territories citizen, a British overseas citizen, a British subject or a British protected person;
(2) a body or corporation sole incorporated or constituted under the law of any part of the United Kingdom;
(3) a person domiciled in the United Kingdom; or
(4) a person who has a real and effective industrial or commercial establishment in the United Kingdom.

The applicant may be required by the Registrar to provide evidence to **6–138** establish eligibility on one of the above grounds to apply for international registration.

The application should set out the same particulars as those required in a United Kingdom national application or contained in a United Kingdom registration at the time of application. It should set out the goods or services in respect of which protection is claimed, classified

---

[38] See Chap. 5, para. 5–41 *et seq.*

according to the Nice Classification. If the application complies with the above requirements the Registrar submits it to the International Bureau. On receipt, the International Bureau registers the mark applied for. If the application was received within two months of the filing date at the national office, the mark receives as a registration date the date of application to the national office. If not, the registration is accorded the date of receipt by the International Bureau. The International Bureau notifies the national offices of the states to which the application for international registration extends and those states then process the application under their national law, notifying the International Bureau if or to the extent that the mark is refused in that state. As in the case of United Kingdom registrations of international marks applied for elsewhere, unless notification of refusal is given to the International Bureau the mark will remain on the Register.

Revocation and invalidity

6–139 If the national application or registration upon which an international trade mark is based is revoked, declared invalid, cancelled, lapses or is withdrawn or renounced within five years of the date of the international registration (or if any of the above occur as a result of proceedings or applications started before the expiry of the five year period) then the international mark ceases to be protected. The national trade mark office in the country of origin is under a duty to notify the International Bureau of any such occurrence and request the cancellation of the international registration.[39]

6–140 Applications for revocation or for a declaration of invalidity of an international trade mark must otherwise be made in the national office or courts of the nation in question. In the United Kingdom the provisions of sections 46 and 47 of the 1994 Act apply with the following changes:

(1) The reference in section 46(1) to the date of completion of the registration procedure is taken to refer to the date on which the international trade mark (UK) became protected in the United Kingdom. The references to the goods and services for which a mark is registered (in sections 46(5) and 47(5)) and the form in which the mark is registered (in section 46(2)) are taken as references to the goods and services and form for which the mark is protected.

(2) The references to invalidity and revocation of a trade mark registration are construed as having that effect on an international trade mark (UK) being invalid or revoked.

The provisions of rules 31 to 37 of the Trade Mark Rules 2000, with consequential modifications, apply in relation to the procedure for

[39] Madrid Protocol, Art. 6.

application for revocation or for a declaration of invalidity of an international trade mark (UK).

If or to the extent that an international trade mark (UK) is revoked or declared invalid the Registrar notifies the International Bureau and in the case of a declaration of invalidity, the trade mark is deemed (to that extent) to have never been protected in the United Kingdom and in the case of a revocation, is deemed to have ceased to exist from the date on which the revocation is recorded in the International Register. Moreover, the invalidity or revocation does not affect transactions "past and closed" as at the date when the invalidity is recorded in the International Register.

Transformation into national mark

Where an international registration is cancelled or otherwise removed **6–142** from the Register, it is in certain circumstances open to the proprietor to apply to convert the international mark into a national registration.[40]

In the United Kingdom, when

(1) an international trade mark registration designating the United Kingdom is cancelled in respect of some or all of the goods or services for which it was registered at the request of the country of origin, and

(2) an application is made (on Form TM3) within the three months following the date of cancellation for registration in the United Kingdom of a trade mark identical to that cancelled in respect of some or all of the cancelled goods or services, by the holder of the international registration immediately before its cancellation, then

the trade mark is transformed into a United Kingdom trade mark registration as if it had been registered in the United Kingdom as of the date of application for the international trade mark, unless the application to extend protection to the United Kingdom was made after the original international registration, in which case the United Kingdom date of registration is taken to be the date on which the request to extend was recorded by the International Bureau.

If the international mark had completed the examination and opposi- **6–143** tion procedure in the United Kingdom (see para. 131, above) prior to transformation, then it is registered as a United Kingdom registered trade mark. If not, it continues to undergo the examination and opposition procedure, being treated as a national application.[41]

Effect of concurrent international and national registrations

If a trade mark proprietor owns a United Kingdom registered trade **6–144** mark that is also a protected international trade mark (UK) and,

---

[40] Madrid Protocol, Art. 4bis.
[41] 1996 Order, Art. 20.

(1) all of the goods and services for which the national registration is registered are covered by the international registration, and

(2) the United Kingdom registration has an earlier registration date than that of the international registration,

then the proprietor is entitled to claim seniority for the international mark as a result of the earlier national registration.[42] That is to say, the international trade mark (UK) is treated for the purposes of the 1994 Act as having been registered as of the date of registration of the national mark in respect of all of the goods and services shared by the two marks. Further, for the purposes of determining whether the international mark is an earlier trade mark under the 1994 Act, it is treated as having the date of application of the national mark, taking account of any earlier priority date claimed by the national mark. The holder of the international trade mark (UK) may apply on Form TM28 for the international registration to be noted in the national Register against the United Kingdom registered trade mark.

Notification of dealings with international trade marks

6–145 There are two classes of dealings with international trade marks which must be recorded in the International Register[43]:

(1) "Notifiable Transactions": the grant of a licence under an international trade mark (UK) or the grant of any security interest (fixed or floating) over such a mark or any right in or under it.

(2) "Relevant Transactions": notifiable transactions, assignments of international trade marks (UK) and transfer by assent of a personal representative or by court order of such a mark or any right under or in it.

6–146 On application by a person claiming an interest in or under a notifiable transaction, or any other person claiming to be affected thereby, particulars (as set out in rule 40 of the Trade Mark Rules 2000) of the transaction are entered into the Supplementary Register. Relevant transactions are recorded by the International Bureau at the request of an interested person.

6–147 Until, in the case of a notifiable transaction, such an application has been made for registration, or in the case of any other relevant transaction, the transaction has been recorded in the International Register, the transaction is ineffective as against any person acquiring an interest in or under the international trade mark (UK) without notice. Further, a person claiming to be a licensee by virtue of the transaction does not have the protection of sections 31 and 32 of the 1994 Act.

[42] 1996 Order, Art. 21.
[43] 1996 Order, Art. 6.

Finally, unless a new proprietor or licensee of an international trade **6–148** mark:

(a) applies for registration or recording of the transaction by which the right to the mark was obtained within six months, or

(b) the court is satisfied that it was not practicable for the application to be made within six months and that it was made as soon as possible thereafter,

he is not entitled to an inquiry as to damages or an account of profits in respect of any infringement of the mark occurring between the date of the transaction in question and its registration or recording in the International Register.[44]

---

[44] c.f. 1994 Act, s.25.

ABSOLUTE GROUNDS FOR REFUSAL OF REGISTRATION

Structure of this chapter

7–01 Section 3 of the Trade Marks Act 1994 gathers together the absolute grounds for refusal. For ease of reference, a variety of topics are dealt with in the following sections:

1. Overview
2. Construction and general points
3. Section 3(1): the individual grounds
4. Assessment of distinctive character
5. Shapes—section 3(2).
6. Public policy, deceptive marks—section 3(3).
7. Illegal marks—section 3(4).
8. Specially protected emblems—sections 3(5), 4, 57 and 58.
9. Bad faith—section 3(6)

1. Overview

7–02 Section 3 of the 1994 Act contains the absolute grounds for refusal of a trade mark. The grounds are absolute by contrast with the relative grounds set out in section 5. The relative grounds are concerned with conflict between the trade mark applied for and individual rights held by other traders. Section 3 operates at a more fundamental level, looking at the nature of the mark itself, its distinctiveness, both inherent and acquired, and tests the mark against various public policy matters.

The influence of the Trade Marks Directive

7–03 One of the recitals to the Trade Marks Directive explains that the absolute grounds of refusal "are to be listed in an exhaustive manner" (even though some are optional) in order to ensure that "the conditions for obtaining and continuing to hold a registered trade mark are, in general, identical in all Member States" so as to achieve the Directive's stated aim of approximation of trade mark laws in Member States.

The United Kingdom has elected to implement most, but not all, of the optional grounds for refusal contained in the TM Directive. Section 3 manages to provide an exhaustive list of all the absolute grounds for refusal through cross-references to sections 1(1) and 4, and section 4 (as amended) itself cross-refers to sections 57 and 58 of the 1994 Act.

For the most part, section 3 follows the wording of Article 3 of the TM **7–04** Directive. Where attempts were made to try to improve the wording, the changes either made no difference (in section 3(1)(a)) or introduced obscurity (in section 3(4)). Similarly, Article 3(1) of the Directive is largely identical to Article 7(1) of the CTM Regulation.

The grounds are applicable to all registered Trade Marks

On its face, section 3 of the 1994 Act is directed at applications for trade **7–05** marks under the 1994 Act. In relation to such applications, any of the grounds may be raised by the Registry at the examination stage and/or by a rival trader in opposition proceedings. However, all registered trade marks remain subject to possible scrutiny under the grounds listed in section 3, even those registered long before the 1994 Act came into force. A trade mark may be revoked under section 47 because it was registered in breach of any of the grounds set out in section 3. In theory, section 3 has effect back to the time when the earliest existing registration was put on the Register.

The objections in outline

The absolute grounds for refusal fall into two categories. The grounds in **7–06** sections 3(1) and (2) of the 1994 Act are all concerned with aspects of the key issue of distinctiveness, whereas the remaining subsections are concerned with various policy considerations other than distinctiveness. By way of an overview, the effect of each of the grounds is as follows.

Section 3(1)(a)—the cross-reference to section 1(1) means a sign must **7–07** qualify as a "trade mark" before it can be registered. The sign must be represented graphically and must be capable of distinguishing the goods or services in question from those of other undertakings.

Section 3(1)(b), (c) and (d) are directly concerned with aspects of **7–08** distinctiveness. This is confirmed by the fact that if one of these grounds is established, it can be overcome under the proviso by showing that the mark has, through use, become distinctive. Although section 3(1)(b) ("devoid of distinctive character") comes first, it has the broadest scope and is the sweeping up provision.[1] Section 3(1)(c) is designed to prevent registration of marks which are descriptive, *i.e.* signs which honest traders may legitimately wish to use. There is considerable overlap with section 3(1)(d) ("customary in the trade"), designed to prevent registration of signs which traders actually use to the extent they have become customary. As shorthand, these three grounds prevent registration of

---

[1] See *Procter & Gamble's Application* [1999] R.P.C. 673 at 679, CA.

marks which are non-distinctive, descriptive or generic, unless the mark can be shown to have become distinctive through use.

7–09   Section 3(2) is concerned with shapes. The shapes in question are not the two-dimensional shapes used in device or logo marks, but three-dimensional shapes and two-dimensional representations of them. There are three separate provisions, each dealing with a particular aspect of the distinctiveness of shapes. In essence, these provisions are designed to prevent attempts by traders to monopolise shapes which: (1) are wholly descriptive of the goods themselves or (2) are functional or (3) have "eye appeal". If established, these grounds preclude registration even if the shape in question can in fact be shown to be distinctive of a particular trader's goods. However, if the sign can be proved to be distinctive, it is an indication that the sign consists of more than exclusively the forbidden shape.

7–10   Section 3(3) is concerned with marks which are deceptive or contrary to public policy.

Section 3(4) is concerned with marks the use of which is prohibited by United Kingdom or Community legislation other than trade mark law.

Section 3(5) cross-refers to section 4, which places restrictions on the registration of marks which comprise or contain "official" signs.

Section 3(6) precludes the registration of a trade mark if or to the extent the application is made in bad faith. This ground appears to provide the only mechanism by which proprietorship can be challenged.

2. Construction and general points

7–11   In this section, we deal with a number of general matters, notably construction, the relevant background against which the absolute grounds should be applied, the application of the absolute grounds to different types of mark, the use of disclaimers and limitations and then with a number of arguments of last resort, which are frequently and consistently raised.

Construction

7–12   In some respects, section 3 of the 1994 Act contains a rather disparate list of objections. Some stand on their own, sections 3(5) and 3(6) in particular. Others are the more obvious result of policy considerations and are designed to ensure that, to the extent that trade mark laws in Europe are harmonised, the privilege of registration is secured only for those signs which properly function as trade marks. The legislative intent and therefore the scope of a number of the grounds are not always immediately obvious, which is one reason why it is necessary to construe individual grounds in the context both of section 3 as a whole and as part of the overall scheme of trade mark protection set out in the 1994 Act and the TM Directive.[2]

---

[2] See the approach of Aldous L.J. in *Philips v. Remington* [1999] R.P.C. 809 at 816–817, C.A.

Relevant background

Although these grounds are "absolute", this does not mean that the sign **7–13** in question is considered in a vacuum. Far from it. The tribunal must ensure that it is sufficiently educated about the relevant trade so that it is able properly to assess applicable grounds. This is obvious in the case of section 3(1)(d) of the 1994 Act, but no less important in assessing the grounds in subsections (1)(c), (b), (2) and (3). In the initial stages of examination of an application in the United Kingdom, the Registry has the power to order the provision to it of such further information as it may require.[3]

Application of the absolute grounds

Apart from section 3(2) of the 1994 Act, whose provisions apply only to **7–14** shapes, the grounds apply to all types of sign and trade mark. Under each ground for refusal, the same test must be applied whether the sign consists of a shape, words, numerals or one of the more exotic types of sign.

Each applicable ground must be applied to the sign or trade mark as a whole. Where necessary the effect of the sign or trade mark must be gauged by considering notional and fair use of it across the entire specification of goods or services.

Disclaimers and limitations

A disclaimer serves the same purpose as under the old law—the **7–15** disclaimed matter forms no part of the mark and must be left out of account. Limitations may be territorial or related to some aspect of the goods or services, or the use of colour in the mark. There is a divergence of practice between the Registry and OHIM on disclaimers and limitations.

Section 13(1) of the 1994 Act appears to contemplate only disclaimers and limitations which are volunteered by the applicant: "An applicant. . . may disclaim etc.". By contrasting this with the position under the 1938 Act where there was express power[4] to require a disclaimer of, for example, non-distinctive matter, the Registry has taken the view that it has no power to require an applicant to make a disclaimer or limitation[5] and can only take a passive role. This is an odd position to take and can only lead to shadow boxing between applicant and Registry. It cannot be contrary to section 13 for an examiner to state his view that a mark cannot be registered without non-distinctive matter

---

[3] Rule 57. Note also the use of information gathered from the Internet: PAC 11/00, August 2000.
[4] In s.14.
[5] Work Manual, Chap. 6, para. 14.

being disclaimed. In practice, the application of disclaimers should be uniform so that traders inspecting the Register are not left in doubt over the scope of registrations.

7–16 So far as OHIM is concerned, Article 38(2) of the CTM Regulation provides:

> "Where the trade mark contains an element which is not distinctive, and where the inclusion of said element in the trade mark could give rise to doubts as to the scope of protection for the trade mark, the Office may request, as a condition for registration of the said trade mark, that the applicant state that he disclaims any exclusive right to such element."

The Examination Guidelines[6] indicate how this provision is to be operated in practice. Thus, descriptive and other common non-distinctive elements such as borders and commonplace shapes of containers need not be disclaimed.

Reliance on other trade marks which have achieved registration

7–17 When one or more grounds have been raised, applicants frequently argue the ground cannot apply by relying on other trade marks which have achieved registration. There are essentially three situations, each raising different considerations: (1) same or similar mark, same office; (2) same mark, different offices; (3) similar marks. These are discussed in turn.

The first is where the applicant has existing registration(s) granted by the same office for the same or similar marks. In those circumstances, the existence of the other registrations is likely to provide powerful support for the application in question and to overcome objections.[7]

7–18 The second situation arises most often in connection with applications for CTMs. The examiner raises one of the absolute grounds of objection, to which the applicant responds by citing its registration for the same mark in one or more countries in the E.U. The Examination Guidelines[8] take a sensible approach, suggesting that weight may be given to

---

[6] See para. 8.13.

[7] In *Burst Advisor* [2000] E.T.M.R. 89 (note), the OHIM BoA was influenced by the fact that two other very similar applications had been accepted for almost identical goods: BURSTAID and BURSTWARE. The Examiner's objection under Article 7(1)(b) was overruled because the mark did not convey a direct and precise indication of the nature or intended purpose of the goods applied for "computer software for use in monitoring the rate of data flow"!

[8] See para. 8.1.4: "If a trade mark is already registered in many or all the Member States of the Community this will be an indication to the examiner that absolute grounds for refusal are unlikely to exist. Examiners should take particular account of registrations of trade marks under examination systems in Member States which apply standards of absolute grounds of refusal similar to those in the Regulation. In neither case will existing registrations be decisive for the examiner but he will have to take them into account."

registrations in countries which are known to operate reasonably rigorous examination of applications, such as the United Kingdom, and this does occur in practice.[9] More often than not, the existence of registrations in other countries is treated as insufficient to overcome the reasoning already expressed, particularly where no information is supplied concerning the circumstances or criteria taken into account which lead to the registrations in question.[10] Even if a national trade mark office has held a mark to be sufficiently distinctive to warrant registration, the Boards of Appeal have stated that the same finding does not necessarily have to be reached by the examiner "who must in each case make his own assessment as to the existence of absolute grounds of refusal."[11] The Boards of Appeal have also pointed out that the CTM system runs in parallel with national systems and is not subordinate or ancillary to them, and that, despite harmonisation, one cannot expect that every trade mark office will invariably take the same view.[12] Where national registrations are relied upon by the Boards of Appeal, it is to support the conclusion already reached. Certainly, other registrations are treated as irrelevant where it appears that the sign has a particular meaning in a foreign language which appears not to have been appreciated when granting the other registrations.

In the third situation, applicants rely on the state of the register: they **7–19** cite the existence of registrations for the same type of mark in support of their own application. For example, the objection raised is that the mark is descriptive, contrary to section 3(1)(c). The applicant responds by citing registrations of marks which it believes are as or more descriptive. In these circumstances, the other registrations are rightly regarded as irrelevant. The principal reason is because one has no idea of the circumstances in which the other marks achieved registration— extensive evidence may have been required to achieve registration, alternatively the relevant examiner may have made a mistake.[13]

In this regard there is a slight divergence in practice between the **7–20** United Kingdom Registry and OHIM. In the United Kingdom, it is customary to cite Jacob J. in *British Sugar*[14]:

> "It has long been held under the old Act that comparison with other marks on the register is in principle irrelevant when considering a

---

[9] "The registration of a trade mark for a particular item of goods [in issue] in a Member State . . ., particularly under the harmonised trade mark law . . . has a certain presumptive effect for the registration procedure of a Community trade mark." Case R34/1998–3 *Lasting Performance*, July 27, 1998, para. 17.

[10] See, *e.g.* Case R 94/1998–1 *Optima*, OHIM BoA, where the mark was rejected under the equivalent of s.3(1)(b) and (c) since it means "the very best" in Portugese. The applicant relied on a number of registrations which it had obtained for the mark in Portugal, but it did not explain how those registrations had been achieved.

[11] Case R34/1998–3 *Lasting Performance*, July 27, 1998, para. 17.

[12] See Case R 66/1998 1, *Comfort Plus* [1999] E.T.M.R. 575, para. 18, OHIM BoA.

[13] "That follows from the principle of legality, according to which no person may rely, in support of his claim, on an unlawful act committed in favour of another (see, for example, judgment of the Court of Justice in . . . *Williams v. Court of Auditors* [1985] E.C.R. 2225, paragraph 14 and . . . *Easi-Cash* Case R 96/1998–1, paragraph 17)": Case R 161/1998–1, *100% Pure Goodness*, OHIM First BoA.

[14] [1996] R.P.C. 281 at 305.

particular mark tendered for registration, see *e.g. MADAME Trade Mark* ([1966] R.P.C. 541) and the same must be true under the 1994 Act."

Certain Boards of Appeal have expressed the view that the examiner may be under a duty to consider whether the cases are so similar as to require identical treatment, in particular where the goods or services of the application and the cited registrations are competing.[15] Others have stated that each mark has to be assessed on its own circumstances: any irregularity which might have occurred in relation to some other marks should not be compounded.[16]

Reliance on decisions of tribunals/courts in other member States

7–21 Decisions of the European Court of Justice and the European Court of First Instance (the court of appeal from the OHIM Boards of Appeal) are binding throughout the E.U. Decisions on matters of law of other national tribunals or courts within the E.U. on equivalent provisions are persuasive but not binding. Laddie J. has stated[17]:

"It would not be right for an English Court, if it is firmly of a different view, to follow the route adopted by the courts of another Member State simply because the other courts expressed a view first. The scope of European legislation is too important to be decided on a "first past the post" basis."

Reliance on the available defences

7–22 In cases of marks which are more or less descriptive, the argument is over whether the sign *may* serve, in trade, to designate some characteristic of the goods or services. In this type of case, the applicant is often the first to use the sign in question and says, because of his use, that no other trader could legitimately use the sign. Of course, this argument begs the question as to whether the sign has become distinctive. However, in support of this argument, the applicant places emphasis on the fact that no-one else uses the sign, to which the frequent response is: other traders may wish to use the sign in a descriptive manner. If this view cannot be overcome, then the argument of last resort from the applicant is effectively this: allow my mark to be registered because it is

---

[15] *Xtra* [1998] E.T.M.R. 562, and *Foodsaver* [1999] E.T.M.R. 191 (note).
[16] *Telepaella* [1998] E.T.M.R. 708 (note), OHIM BoA.
[17] *Wagamama* [1995] F.S.R. 713 at 728. In the "three headed rotary shaver" litigation, there was a divergence of view between the majority in the Swedish Court of Appeal on the one hand and Jacob J. and the English Court of Appeal on the other as to the meaning of "shape necessary to achieve a technical result" in s.3(2)(b). The reference to the ECJ should result in further guidance.

distinctive, and any concerns you have about the rights of other traders to use descriptive signs are met by the defence in section 11(2)(b) of the 1994 Act. This type of argument is not confined to section 11(2)(b) and covers any reason which may be put forward as to why another trader would not infringe the registration sought.

The existence of possible reasons for non-infringement is irrelevant to **7–23** the requirements of section 3, as explained by G. Hobbs Q.C. as the appointed person in *AD2000*[18]:

> "Although section 11 of the Act contains various provisions designed to protect the legitimate interests of honest traders, the first line of protection is to refuse the registration of signs which are excluded from registration by the provisions of section 3. In this regard, I consider that the approach to be adopted with regard to registrability under the 1994 Act is the same as the approach adopted under the old Act. This was summarised by Robin Jacob Q.C. in his decision on behalf of the Secretary of State in *Colorcoat TM* [1990] RPC 511 at 517 in the following terms: 'That possible defences (and in particular that the use is merely as a bona fide description) should not be taken into account when considering registration is well settled, see eg. *Yorkshire TM* (1954) RPC 150 at 154 lines 20–25 per Viscount Simonds LC: Essentially the reason for this is that the privilege of a monopoly should not be conferred where it might require honest men to look for a defence'."

This approach recognises the fact that even a registration which is liable to be declared invalid can be a powerful weapon against those who do not have the will or the means to fight.

Reliance on the Examination Guidelines of OHIM or the Work Manual of the Registry

These and other statements of practice which are issued from time to **7–24** time by both OHIM and the United Kingdom Registry are for guidance only. They cannot bind any person charged with applying the 1994 Act or the CTM Regulation. The Boards of Appeal have expressly confirmed that the Guidelines cannot add to or subtract from the legal content of the CTM Regulation or the Implementing Rules. They are no more than "useful aids".[19]

3. The individual grounds—section 3(1)

Introduction

Section 3(1) of the 1994 Act is concerned with the fundamental issue of **7–25** distinctiveness—the essential function of a trade mark. Notwithstanding the structure and wording of section 3(1), it is suggested that it sets out a

[18] [1997] R.P.C. 168.
[19] See, *e.g. Foodsaver* [1999] E.T.M.R. 191 (note) and *IX* [1998] E.T.M.R. 343.

simple and fundamental requirement which any sign must fulfil before it can properly be registered as a trade mark. The requirement is that the sign must possess a distinctive character, inherent or acquired, so that it can carry out the essential function of a trade mark which is to distinguish the goods or services of one undertaking from those of other undertakings. However, the structure and wording of section 3(1) serve to obscure this point in two ways. First, the individual grounds are not mutually exclusive with the result there is much overlap.[20] Secondly, each of the grounds is expressed negatively, the only positive requirements being contained in the proviso, a provision which applies only in limited circumstances, and (via section 3(1)) in section 1(1). These may also be reasons why the interpretation of section 3(1)(a) and (b)/Article 3(1)(a) and (b) has proved to be less than straightforward, certainly in the United Kingdom.

7–26   There can be no dispute that section 3(1) contains a positive requirement that, to be eligible for registration, a sign must possess a distinctive character, inherent or acquired. The issue is where that positive requirement is to be found in the statutory provisions.

It is clear that if a mark possesses inherent distinctive character, it will avoid subsections (1)(b), (c) and (d) of section 3. Accordingly, it is possible to say that those provisions impose a positive requirement for an inherent distinctive character, even though this is normally done purely by reference to section 3(1)(b) and its equivalents.[21] If section 3(1)(b) is the only source of this positive requirement, it is strange that this vital characteristic of any trade mark is left to be implied from negative prohibition(s), particularly when one of the Recitals to the TM Directive draws particular attention to the requirement that a mark is "capable of distinguishing".

7–27   In Chapter 2 (Definition of a trade mark), it was suggested that the "capable of distinguishing" requirement in section 1(1) imposes the positive requirement for registrability that a trade mark must possess a distinctive character. If the trade mark possesses inherent distinctive character, then it does not fall foul of section 3(1)(b), (c) or (d). Signs which are not inherently distinctive may be caught by one or more of those exclusions. Such signs may yet be eligible for registration under the proviso to section 3(1) if it can be shown they have acquired distinctive character through the use which has been made of them.

7–28   The alternative is that "capable of distinguishing" sets a different, initial standard of distinctiveness and therefore, the positive requirement for a distinctive character can only be derived from the negative

[20] See Morritt L.J. in *Bach Flower Remedies* [2000] R.P.C. 513 at 525, para. 33.
[21] See, *e.g. Windsurfing* [1999] E.T.M.R. 585, para. 46; *Philips v. Remington* [1999] R.P.C. 809 at 819.

objection in section 3(1)(b).[22] Although this is an argument,[23] it is suggested that the view offered above makes better sense of all parts of section 3(1) and 1(1), and leaves no or fewer oddities.

Under this general heading of section 3(1), we address the individual subsections in turn, each of which is exclusionary. The proviso to section 3(1) provides a special exception to some of the exclusions but prompts a more general discussion of the positive requirement of distinctive character. (See the next section.)

It should, perhaps, be emphasised that the assessment of distinctive **7–29** character of most trade marks is a straightforward process. One can see they have a degree of inherent distinctive character which is the foundation for additional distinctive character acquired through use. Most of this discussion is concerned with signs which have problems qualifying as trade marks. There are a number of reasons why it will continue to be necessary to examine these problem signs with care:

(1) the enduring reason: "Wealthy traders are habitually eager to enclose part of the great common of the English language and to exclude the general public of the present day and of the future from access to the enclosure."[24];

(2) with the open-ended concept of "sign", the enclosure sought is not confined to matters of language but extends to all features of goods or their packaging;

(3) the advent of the (partially) harmonised law of trade marks represented by the 1994 Act and the TM Directive generated the perception that it is easier to secure registration than previously. Early experience of OHIM strongly contributed to this perception, but there are signs that practice at OHIM is becoming more consistent;

(4) the pressure to employ relatively descriptive marks is probably increasing. The consumer is bombarded with marks. In this environment, the trader wants to get his message across quickly, which means that the characteristic of the goods or

---

[22] See below, and in particular Aldous L.J. in *Philips v. Remington* [1999] R.P.C. 809, CA. This appears to be one consequence of the conclusion that there is a dual test for distinctiveness, with "capable of distinguishing" setting an initial test which is lower than the requirement for a distinctive character. Those familiar with German law appear to be content with a dual test for distinctiveness: abstract and concrete distinctiveness. Note how those terms were used by the First Cancellation Division at OHIM, without explanation as to what they mean: see Case C000090019/1 *KING* (device), para. 11, OHIM First Cancellation Division.

[23] Not least because section/Article 3(1)(b), (c) and (d) were derived from Article 6quinquies B.2 of the Paris Convention. The Paris Convention contains no definition of trade mark equivalent to section 1(1)/Article 2. Therefore, one has to imply into Article 6quinquies B.2, a positive requirement for a distinctive character. The derivation of Article 3(1)(b), (c) and (d) does not necessitate the same approach, simply because of the addition of Article 2. For the reasons set out in the text, it is suggested that construction of Articles 2 and 3 together require a different result.

[24] "Perfection": *Joseph Crosfield & Sons Appln.* (1909) 26 R.P.C. 837 at 854, CA, *per* Cozens-Hardy M.R.

services which the trader wishes to emphasise is often more or less directly described in a mark. At the same time, the trader must distance his product or service from those of his competitors, so he wishes to prevent others using the same or similar mark, no matter how descriptive it is. This is not something confined to wealthy traders.

7–30 Section 3(1)(a):

"s.3(1) The following shall not be registered:

(a) signs which do not satisfy the requirements of section 1(1)"

Derivation

7–31 Article 3(1)(a) of the TM Directive uses the words "signs which cannot constitute a trade mark". Despite the difference in wording, section 3(1)(a) clearly can be and should be interpreted to have the same meaning as the provision in the Directive. Hence, it is suggested there is no difference in meaning. Either way, a sign which does not qualify as a "trade mark" shall not be registered.

The requirements of section 1(1)

7–32 Section 1(1) of the 1994 Act contains the definition of "trade mark" and it appears to contain three (or possibly four) requirements. The candidate must be:

(1) a sign;
(2) which is capable of being represented graphically; and
(3) which is capable of distinguishing goods or services of one undertaking from those of other undertakings.

These requirements are discussed in detail in Chapter 2 (Definition of a trade mark), although the third requirement also enters the discussion in this Chapter under the key topic of distinctiveness. The possibility that there is a fourth requirement (the distinguishing function must be operable in relation to goods or services), implicit in section 1(1), is also discussed in Chapter 2 in the context of marks for "retail services" and the like.

Section 3(1)(b)/Article 3(1)(b), Article 7(1)(b) CTMR: non-distinctive marks

7–33   "s.3(1) The following shall not be registered:

(b) trade marks which are devoid of any distinctive character"

Derivation

7–34 The words used in section 3(1)(b) are identical to those used in Article 3(1)(b) of the TM Directive and Article 7(1)(b) of the CTM Regulation. In fact, the trio of provisions in (b), (c) and (d) derive from Article 6*quinquies* B.2 of the Paris Convention.

Application

The concept is clear enough: devoid of any distinctive character: but **7–35** how does one gauge this in practice? The following dicta, in chronological order, are applicable:

"What does devoid of any distinctive character mean? I think the phrase requires consideration of the mark on its own, assuming no use. Is it the sort of word (or other sign) which cannot do the job of distinguishing without first educating the public that it is a trade mark? A meaningless word or a word inappropriate for the goods concerned (North Pole for bananas) can clearly do. But a common laudatory word such as 'Treat' is, absent use and recognition as a trade mark in itself (I hesitate to use the word from the old Act but the idea is much the same) devoid of any *inherently* distinctive character.":—*per* Jacob J. in *British Sugar v. James Robertson & Sons*.[25]

"The proviso to section 3(1) indicates that the essence of the objection to registration under section 3(1)(b) is immaturity: the sign in question is . . . not distinctive by nature and has not become distinctive by nurture":—*per* Geoffrey Hobbs Q.C. as the appointed person in AD2000.[26]

"As regards Article 7(1)(b) of the CTMR, a trade mark which is **7–36** devoid of any distinctive character, namely one that is not capable of distinguishing the goods of one undertaking from those of another, cannot be registered. The essential function of a trade mark is to guarantee the identity of the origin of the marked product to the consumer or end user, *i.e.* that all the goods and services bearing it have originated from under the control of a single undertaking responsible for its quality (see *inter alia* the judgment of the Court of Justice . . . in . . . *Canon*[27]. . . paragraph 28). A trade mark must, therefore, be distinctive and be capable of serving as an indication of origin (see the seventh recital of the CTMR). It must have the inherent property of distinguishing the goods claimed by their origin from an undertaking. In assessing those properties, both the customary use of trade marks as indications of origin in the industry concerned and the view of the relevant consumer must be taken into consideration.": *LIGHT GREEN*, OHIM Third Board of Appeal.[28]

". . . the context in which the meaning of 'distinctive character' has to be determined: that is, of traders who are in competition with each other in the marketplace, and to whom Parliament wishes to accord proper protection but not any exorbitant monopoly." . . .

[25] [1996] R.P.C. 281 at 306, the words "distinctive" and "inherently" appear to have been mistakenly transposed in the report.
[26] [1997] R.P.C. 168 at 174.
[27] *Canon Kabushiki Kaisha v. Metro-Goldwyn-Mayer Inc.* [1998] E.C.R. I–5507; [1999] R.P.C. 117. ECJ.
[28] [1999] E.T.M.R. 214, para. 20.

7-37   "Despite the fairly strong language of section 3(1)(b), 'devoid of any distinctive character'—and Mr Morcom emphasised the word 'any'—that provision must in my judgment be directed to a visible sign or combination of signs which can by itself readily distinguish one trader's product . . . from that of another competing trader. . . . An objection on those grounds cannot in my judgment be treated (in the words of Younger J. in the *Standard Woven Fabric* case (1918) 35 R.P.C. 53 at 58) as being on 'grounds which were fanciful and which, in a business sense, were insubstantial'. On the contrary, any objection on those grounds would be a practical and businesslike objection.": *per* Robert Walker L.J. in *Procter & Gamble's Trade Mark Application*.[29]

    "The requirement under section (Article) 3(1)(b) is that the mark must have a distinctive character to be registrable. Thus it must have a character which enables it to be distinctive of one trader's goods in the sense that it has a meaning denoting the origin of the goods.": *per* Aldous L.J. in *Philips v. Remington*.[30]

Influence of section 3(1)(b) and section 1(1)

7-38 The attempts in the United Kingdom to interpret "capable of distinguishing" in section 1(1) have had effects on the interpretation of section 3(1)(b). The result has been that the objection in section 3(1)(b) is interpreted as the source for the positive requirement for a trade mark to have a distinctive character. It cannot be disputed that the possession of a distinctive character (whether inherent or acquired) is or should be the positive requirement for a registrable trade mark, but (for the reasons set out in Chapter 2 and above) it is suggested that the primary source of this positive requirement is in section 1(1). The exclusionary provisions in section 3(1)(b), (c) and (d) approach the issue of distinctiveness or lack of it from the negative side. However, avoidance of section/Article 3(1)(b) in practice necessitates a finding of distinctive character.

Interpretation

7-39 As the Court of Appeal has held, this is the sweeping up provision and there is considerable overlap between section 3(1)(c) and (d) and this provision.[31] In appropriate cases, it is easier to apply this provision by asking whether the mark in question is wholly descriptive or wholly generic. If so, then it is easy to conclude that the mark is also devoid of any distinctive character. However, there may be cases where one can only make the general inquiry: is this mark devoid of any distinctive character?

[29] [1999] R.P.C. 673 at 679 and 680–681.
[30] [1999] R.P.C. 809 at 819.
[31] *Re Procter & Gamble Ltd's Trade Mark Application* [1999] R.P.C. 673 at 679, *per* Robert Walker L.J.

What should be considered

Although the passage from the judgment of Jacob J. in *British Sugar* has **7–40** been referred to and applied a number of times, the approach he suggested may be slightly too restrictive. It is important to decide upon the correct approach, because it applies to all three of subsection (1)(b), (c) and (d) of section (3).

The juxtaposition of these provisions and the proviso indicates that Jacob J. was right to indicate that the inquiry is directed to the inherent characteristics of the mark. Any claim to acquired distinctiveness is put on one side if or until it is necessary to consider the proviso. However, the question remains as to what one should take into account when considering the inherent characteristics of the mark. There are two choices: either one considers the mark entirely on its own (albeit not in a vacuum but against the background of the particular trade and the goods or services in question), alternatively one considers what the mark means[32] as at the relevant date of application. For newly coined marks, there is no difference between these two alternatives, so an example will help to explain the distinction.

> When the mark *Jeryl Lynn* was first coined, it had inherent distinc- **7–41** tive character. If use of the mark had been correctly controlled, the registration of it after some 25 years would have been valid. However, the mark was used and allowed to be used so that it acquired an overwhelmingly descriptive/generic meaning. If, having acquired that meaning, application was then made to register the mark, would it be correct to consider (1) the words *Jeryl Lynn* on their own, assuming no use or (2) what the words *Jeryl Lynn* meant as at the date of application? If the former, then the mark would not be devoid of any distinctive character. If the latter, it would be.

It could be said that this issue does not matter, because a registration of **7–42** such a mark would be liable to revocation under section 46(1)(c). However, section 46(1)(c) only applies to a mark which has become the common *name* for the goods, whereas this point could arise for marks other than word marks. In addition, even if the mark was liable to immediate revocation under section 46, that cannot excuse a proper determination of whether a section 3(1)(b) objection exists or not. It is suggested therefore that the tribunal must consider what the mark means as at the relevant date of application, leaving aside any claim to or evidence of acquired distinctiveness. This is the conclusion reached by the Court of Appeal in *Bach Flower Remedies*.[33]

In the vast majority of cases, this approach is identical to that suggested by Jacob J., simply because the ordinary meaning of the mark

---

[32] As Laddie J. pointed out in *Jeryl Lynn*, words are malleable and capable of taking on more than one meaning: [1999] F.S.R. 491 at 498, para. 12.

[33] [2000] R.P.C. 513 at 526, para. 34, *per* Morritt L.J., although there is a very fine line between "meaning" and "acquired distinctiveness".

has never changed. Rather special facts are required before one reaches a situation where the meaning of the mark has changed.

Practice

7–43 Here we list a few examples from the United Kingdom and from OHIM where this ground has been found established and not established, together with some observations which illustrate the types of reasoning employed in these cases. In many OHIM cases, in particular, the reasoning employed under Article 7(1)(b) is more redolent of Article 7(1)(c), but there is nothing objectionable in that.

The United Kingdom Registry has a series of working rules by which it assesses marks consisting of a few letters or numerals, surnames or full names.[34] Likewise, the OHIM Examination Guidelines contain some (much shorter) guidance. Of course, in each case, the test is whether or not the mark is devoid of distinctive character.

United Kingdom decisions
Objection established

7–44　　AD2000 for all goods in classes 29, 30, 32 and 33.
　　　　Bottles with "ghosted" labels for cleaning products.[35]
　　　　COFFEE HOUSE AROMA for coffee.[36]
　　　　EASY FLOSSING for "toothpick with floss holder".[37]
　　　　FORWOMEN for erotic magazines.[38]
　　　　JERYL LYNN for medicinal and pharmaceutical preparations.[39]
　　　　MESSIAH FROM SCRATCH for organisation of musical entertainment services.[40]
　　　　MINI CLAW for gardening implements.[41]
　　　　MINILITE for lightweight wheels for motor cars.[42]
7–45　　PZD for screwdrivers and bits, but allowed for other goods.[43]
　　　　TCS for sheet metal for use in the building industry, on evidence that TCS was in common use for terne coated steel.[44]

---

[34] See Part 3 of Chap. 6 of the Work Manual for the details.
[35] [1999] E.T.M.R. 375. CA. The shapes of the bottles were "typical of the containers in which household cleaning products were commonly sold".
[36] O/110/00, Regy, March 21, 2000. An example of a case where the mark passed s.(1)(a) but failed s.3(1)(b), the hearing officer applying *Philips v. Remington* [1999] R.P.C. 809, CA, and *Maasland N.V.'s TM*, SRIS O/397/99, G. Hobbs Q.C. as the appointed person.
[37] O/031/00, Regy, February 9, 2000. Using the mark with "TM" did not help.
[38] O/046/00, Regy, February 16, 2000.
[39] [1999] F.S.R. 491. Laddie J. actually found that the mark was not capable of distinguishing.
[40] [2000] R.P.C. 44, S. Thorley, Q.C. as the appointed person.
[41] November 26, 1998, Regy. [1999] E.T.M.R. 505 (note).
[42] [2000] E.T.M.R. 256, Regy. On the evidence the mark had become distinctive through use since registration.
[43] O/054/00, Regy, February 17, 2000.
[44] O/351/99, Regy, October 8, 1999, a case where the combination of *AD2000* and *Messiah from Scratch* led the hearing officer to conclude that "the requirements for registration under Section 3(1)(b) of the 1994 Trade Marks Act can be approximated to the threshold for registration under Section 10 of the 1938 Act". This must be entirely the wrong approach.

THE PERFECTIONISTS for women's underwear.[45]
TREAT for dessert sauces and syrups.[46]
WEB LINK (in a device) for computer software.[47]
XpressLink for telecommunications devices.[48]
The shape (and picture) of the head of a three-headed rotary shaver for electric shavers.[49]
The shape of a particular style of toaster for toasters.[50]
A device containing SHOP! and THE HOME SHOPPING CHANNEL.[51]
A device of an inhaler, the mouthpiece cap coloured pink and the remainder maroon for pharmaceutical preparations.[52]

Objection not established

ABERCROMBIE for clothing, there being fewer than 100 entries of **7–46**
that surname in the phone book for any major city.[53]
MISTER LONG for ice creams, etc, provided they were conspicuously long.[54]

OHIM

The degree of inherent distinctiveness required to avoid this ground **7–47**
at OHIM appears to be very low, at least in some decisions. Certainly, it appears that OHIM applies a lower standard than the United Kingdom Registry. Part of this is probably attributable to the start-up phase of the Community trade mark system. Part may also be due to the focus in the United Kingdom on the requirement that a mark display a distinctive character (whether inherent or acquired), as opposed to the focus at OHIM, which is principally on the words of the provision. These differences are a matter of degree, and are slight. For the applicant at OHIM, avoiding an Article 7(1)(b) (or (c)) objection is a huge advantage, because the onus of proving acquired distinctiveness under Article 7(3) is substantial.

Objection established

100% PURE GOODNESS for cosmetics, etc.[55]   **7–48**

---

[45] [1997] E.T.M.R. 505, Regy.
[46] [1996] R.P.C. 281, a case of s.3(1)(b),(c) and (d).
[47] [1997] E.T.M.R. 500, Regy: "the words 'WEB LINK' even as represented in this application cannot distinguish and would at the very least need evidence that shows that through use, it has come to be recognised by the public as a trade mark."
[48] [1999] E.T.M.R. 146, G. Hobbs Q.C. as the appointed person.
[49] *Philips v. Remington* [1999] R.P.C. 809, CA.
[50] *Dualit Limited's Trade Mark Applications* [1999] R.P.C. 890, Lloyd J.
[51] The presence of the descriptive phrase did not elevate SHOP! so that it would be seen as having trade mark significance: O/051/00. S. Thorley Q.C. as the appointed person January 10, 2000.
[52] O/159/00, Regy, May 4, 2000.
[53] O/040/00, Regy, February 14, 2000.
[54] [1999] E.T.M.R. 406, G. Hobbs Q.C. as the appointed person.
[55] Case R 161/1998–1, OHIM First BoA.

7 for two-seater sports cars.[56]

CHEMFINDER for software for use in chemical searching.[57]

COMPLETE for soaps, cosmetics, etc.[58]

EASI-CASH for various goods and services relating to finance and financial services.[59]

GLOBAL CHILLER for cooling apparatus.[60]

GREENFILTER for filters.[61]

INSTANT INTERNET for internet and communications products.[62]

IX for photographic materials and processing.[63]

LANDSCAPE for furniture, office and kitchen fittings and installation services.[64]

7–49 LASTING PERFORMANCE for perfumery, essential oils, cosmetics.[65]

LEND LEASE for provision of housing, hotel, construction, etc., services.[66]

MULTI 2'N'1 for electric power tools.[67]

NATURAL BEAUTY for toilet soaps, perfumery, etc.[68]

OPTIMA for patient membrane oxygenator.[69]

---

[56] [2000] E.T.M.R. 14, OHIM BoA. An example of a case where the BoA found expressly that the mark did not fall foul of Art. 7(1)(a), but did fall foul of Art. 7(1)(b) because it was "not capable of distinguishing" and cannot serve the basic function of a trade mark.

[57] [2000] E.T.M.R. 250, OHIM Second BoA. The fact that the mark would be meaningless if overheard was held not to be the test for distinctiveness: "The example leaves out a vital factor, namely, knowledge of what the goods are. The determination of whether the mark is distinctive or otherwise must not be made by guessing or in the abstract, but in relation to the goods and services for which registration is sought."

[58] [1999] E.T.M.R. 664, OHIM Third BoA: "The trade mark COMPLETE is, therefore, not capable of distinguishing products claimed by the appellant from those of other undertakings and is devoid of distinctive character under Article 7(1)(b)."

[59] [1999] E.T.M.R. 887, OHIM BoA. Remarkably the mark seems to have been allowed for goods which did not expressly relate to financial matters such as "computers, peripherals, printed matter, diaries, calendars etc." An Art. 7(1)(c)/s.3(1)(c) case as well.

[60] [1999] E.T.M.R. 234, OHIM Third BoA.

[61] [1999] E.T.M.R. 426 (note), OHIM Second BoA.

[62] [2000] E.T.M.R. 270 (note), OHIM First BoA: "The alliteration is mild, consisting only of the repetition of the letters IN at the beginning of the two words. That does not soften the impact of the statement, embodied in the words INSTANT INTERNET, to the effect that someone is offering exceptionally swift access to the internet."

[63] [1998] E.T.M.R. 343, OHIM BoA.

[64] Case R 473/1999–1, OHIM First BoA, March 22, 2000.

[65] Case R 34/1998–3, OHIM BoA, but allowed for "toilet soaps". "In accordance with Article 7(1)(b) CTMR, it is not possible to register trade marks which are devoid of distinctive character, that is to say, which are unsuited for distinguishing the goods of one undertaking from those of other undertakings. In particular, a trade mark must be apt to fulfil its function as an indicator of origin. It must render the goods distinguishable according to their origin, not their quality."

[66] Case R 126/1999–3, OHIM BoA, but allowed for other services. See below.

[67] [1999] E.T.M.R. 846 (note), OHIM First BoA. There was nothing fanciful or capricious in the way that "multi" had been combined with "2'n1".

[68] Case R 40/1998–3, OHIM BoA: "The meaning of that word combination is, immediately and without further thought, intelligible not only in English-speaking countries but to all consumers who have a certain knowledge of the English language."

[69] Case R 94/1998–2, OHIM BoA. Optima means "the very best" in Portuguese. A s.3(1)(c) case as well.

PETIT BEBE for clothing, footwear and headgear.[70]
PORTFOLIO held descriptive and therefore devoid of distinctive character for books and other printed matter but not for magnetic data carriers, CD-ROMs, computer software for planning, etc.[71]
PRIMA for clothing, luggage, etc.[72]
SO SOFT for milk, butter, margarine, etc.[73]
SUPREME for photography products.[74]
THE ADVANTAGE OF INFORMATION for access software.[75]
THE WORLD'S BEST WAY TO PAY AND BE PAID for financial services.[76]
ULTRA MOIST for cosmetics, soaps, etc.[77]
WebRecord for computer programmes.[78]
WWW.PRIMEBROKER.COM for software tools for information on publicly traded companies.[79]
The mark comprised "only a marginally stylised and generally true-to-life graphical depiction of an oil container viewed from a slightly elevated angle" for oils, fuels, lubricants, etc.[80]
A 3–D mark described as "a telephone untangler device as shown" for rotary electrical connections for use with telephone handset cords to prevent the telephone cords from becoming tangled.[81]

7–50

---

[70] Case R 95/1998–3, OHIM BoA: "Such words belong in the public domain and form part of the store of words available to all traders of baby products for positioning or marketing their products for babies." However, the case was remitted for consideration of evidence of use.
[71] Case R71/1998–3, OHIM BoA.
[72] Case R 83/1999–2, OHIM Second BoA.
[73] Case R 157/1999–1. OHIM BoA. The Board said that TORQ-SET, which was cited, "is of questionable relevance as a tool for interpreting the legislation governing the" CTM, "the test laid down in that case . . . is transposable to the context of Article 7 CTMR." ". . . if "SO SOFT" were registered . . . it would indeed trespass upon the legitimate freedom of other traders."
[74] [1999] E.T.M.R. 505 (note), OHIM Third BoA: "The word SUPREME *per se* is a common term, without any originality or distinctiveness, and therefore is not eligible for registration. Accordingly, any competitor or non-competitor is free to use that sign."
[75] Case R 614/1999–3, OHIM Third BoA, April 3, 2000.
[76] [2000] E.T.M.R. 263, OHIM First BoA. The Board recognised that advertising slogans may be capable of performing the essential function of a trade mark, but indicated that it is unlikely they are registrable without evidence of distinctiveness.
[77] [1999] E.T.M.R. 896, OHIM First BoA. An Art. 7(1)(c) case as well: "A trade mark which merely describes the nature or quality of the goods in question is not capable of distinguishing the goods of one undertaking from those of another."
[78] [1999] E.T.M.R. 845 (note), OHIM First BoA.
[79] [2000] E.T.M.R. 245, OHIM Second BoA.
[80] [1999] E.T.M.R. 282, OHIM Second BoA: "Where a mark shows no elements beyond the technical or functional features of the product then it lacks the vital capacity to attribute the product to a particular company of origin." "The mere inclusion of arbitrary features is not. . . sufficient to render distinctive something which would otherwise appear primarily functional. There must be something conspicuously different about the shape, that distinguishes it from the shape of other oil containers and results in it being regarded by consumers of such oil products and the like as serving primarily as an indication of origin."
[81] Case R 179/1999–1, OHIM First BoA. The Board declined to make a finding under Art. 7(1)(e)(i) or (ii).

The colour cobalt blue when applied to the entire visible surface of a bottle containing water.[82]
The colour LIGHT GREEN for chewing gum.[83] Likewise, the colour YELLOW for chewing gum.[84]

Not established

7–51 BEAUTY ISN'T ABOUT LOOKING YOUNG BUT LOOKING GOOD for toiletries, soaps, cosmetics, etc.[85]
ENVIRO-CHEM for instruments and installations relating to pollution, its control and abatement.[86]
IMAGESTREAM for computer software.[87]
LASTING PERFORMANCE for toilet soaps.[88]
LEND LEASE for architectural, engineering, landscape gardening, industrial design services, etc.[89]
MAXIMA for surgical and medical apparatus.[90]
NETMEETING for computer programs for providing real-time . . . communications over computer networks.[91]
RENOWN for clothing, luggage, etc.[92]
SIECLE 21 for services concerning real estate.[93]

[82] [1999] E.T.M.R. 974, OHIM Third BoA.
[83] [1999] E.T.M.R. 214, OHIM Third BoA.
[84] Case R 169/1988–3.
[85] [1999] E.T.M.R. 750, OHIM Second BoA. The examiner was of the view that the mark was a banal slogan, containing an unremarkable twist on a venerable stereotyped theme, and would be seen as a promotional text. The BoA overruled him, expressing the view that it had the capacity to distinguish and that a sign viewed as a promotional text serves not only to identify the origin of the goods or services, but also serves a marketing function, drawing attention to them. On appeal, the applicant cited other slogans which had been registered as CTMs, including: E-MAIL WAS MEANT TO BE FREE for computer software; WE MAKE THE ROOMS THAT MAKE A HOME for furniture; WE TEACH ENGLISH TO THE WORLD for educational textbooks; and GO FLY A KITE for toys, games and playthings.
[86] [1999] E.T.M.R. 845 (note), OHIM BoA. The rights of other traders would not be unfairly affected.
[87] Case R 55/1999–1, OHIM First BoA. The combination sufficiently novel to endow the mark with a limited degree of distinctiveness: "Moreover, it does not appear that the rights of other traders would be unfairly affected if trade mark protection were granted."
[88] Case R 34/1998–3, OHIM BoA: "For such products, the claimed word combination cannot be an indication of quality to be reserved for general use and is, albeit lacking somewhat in imaginativeness, also distinctive, though only to a small extent."
[89] Case R 126/1999–3, OHIM Third BoA: "The claimed mark is merely allusive in respect of those services since there is not the direct and immediate link between those services and the activities of lending and leasing of property."
[90] Case R 51/1998–1, OHIM BoA.
[91] Case R 26/1998–3 [1999] E.T.M.R. 386, OHIM BoA: "the trade mark . . . contains, through a skilful but covert allusion, a minimum distinctive character."
[92] Case R 123/98–1, OHIM First BoA: "The word 'renown' does not, by itself, have any particular meaning when applied to the goods in question; it does not amount to a direct statement that the goods on which it is used enjoy a high reputation. Nor would the registration of 'renown' as a trade mark prevent the appellant's competitors from claiming that their goods are 'renowned'."
[93] [1999] E.T.M.R. 781, OHIM Second BoA. The notions that the services in question were futuristic or "state of the art" would have been of concern for goods which were constantly and rapidly changing as a result of technological progress, but not for real estate services.

SmartOS for computer software, interfaces between smartcards and personal computers[94]: ". . . the combination of those two elements is sufficiently novel to endow the term 'SmartOS' with a limited degree of distinctiveness."

SWEDISH FORMULA for cosmetics, soaps, shampoo, etc. The examiner's objection was annulled because he did not point to any Swedish formula applicable to any of the goods.[95]

It is perhaps worth contrasting OPTIMA (ground established) with MAXIMA (not established). In the latter case, the reasoning of the OHIM Board of Appeal was as follows: **7–52**

"The assessment as to whether a trade mark is descriptive or devoid of distinctive character is a complex exercise which involves a combination of objective and subjective elements. The examiner must have regard to the general impression created by the mark as a whole, taking into account the nature of the goods or services, the level of awareness of the likely consumers of those goods or services, and any other relevant factors. The examiner must in particular have regard to the consequences flowing from the registration of a Community trade mark."[96]

"As a general rule, there are compelling reasons for not allowing an individual trader to monopolize the use of ordinary words, or obvious adaptations of ordinary words, which imply that a product possesses exceptional characteristics as regards quality, power, performance, size, fitness for purpose and so forth." **7–53**

"In the present case, however, regard must be had to the sophisticated nature of the relevant market. The products in question will normally be purchased by highly trained professionals who are unlikely to be influenced by any subliminal message, contained in a trade mark, to the effect that the products are in some way superior to competing products. The need to keep available to all traders words that convey such a message is correspondingly smaller than in the case of products intended for

---

[94] Case R 459/1999–3, OHIM Third BoA: "In determining the distinctive character, it is necessary to make a global assessment of the capacity of the mark to identify the goods or services in the application as coming from a particular undertaking, and thus to distinguish those goods and services from those of other undertakings. In making that assessment, account should be taken of all relevant factors and, in particular, of the inherent characteristics of the claimed mark, of the goods or services with which it is to be used, including whether it contains an element descriptive of those goods or services.

Furthermore, the assessment of whether a trade mark should be refused on absolute grounds necessarily involves taking into account the presumed expectations of the average consumer who is reasonably well informed and reasonably observant and circumspect."

". . . undertakings have a legitimate interest in using suggestive or allusive trade marks as opposed to purely descriptive marks"—see *Oilgear*.

[95] [1999] E.T.M.R. 559, OHIM BoA.

[96] This is a standard paragraph for OHIM BoA decisions on this ground.

mass consumption. Since the trade mark MAXIMA, when used in relation to goods such as surgical and medical apparatus, will not in fact be perceived as descriptive of the quality of the goods by the relevant group of consumers, there are no grounds for holding it descriptive . . .. or devoid of any distinctive character . . ."[97]

7–54 Thus, heavy reliance was placed on the fact that the relevant public for the goods were highly trained professionals who would not be influenced by a laudatory mark. This rather misses the point that other traders selling similar goods might wish to use the same or similar laudatory expression in relation to their goods.

The other point to note about OHIM decisions is that the combination of objections under the equivalent of section 3(1)(b) and (c) arise very frequently. Sometimes, CTM examiners appear to be somewhat confused between the two, rightly rejecting an application on one of the equivalent grounds, only to find that the Board of Appeal upholds the rejection on the other, either alone or in addition. This will no doubt reduce with time.

Colours

7–55 In LIGHT GREEN, the OHIM Third Board of Appeal explained the position as regards claims to colours *per se*. Having referred to the properties required to be displayed by a trade mark,[98] the Board stated:

> "A colour *per se* normally lacks those properties. Consumers are not accustomed to making an assumption about the origin of goods on the basis of their colour or the colour of their packaging, in the absence of a graphic or textual element, because a colour *per se* is not normally used as a means of identification in practice. That rule may not apply in the case of, firstly, very specific goods for very specific clientele and, secondly, a colour exhibiting a shade which is extremely unusual and peculiar in the relevant trade (see. . . ORANGE,[99] para 16)."
>
> "Taking as the basis the presumed expectations of the average consumer who is reasonably well informed and reasonably observant and circumspect (see . . . *Gut Springenheide* . . .) the Board considers that neither consumers in general nor the narrower circle of relevant consumers will be accustomed to identifying the origin of the goods from a colour *per se* in the absence of a delimiting shape or figure."[1]

7–56 And, in *Ty Nant*:

---

[97] Case R 51/1998–1, OHIM BoA.
[98] quoted at para. 7–36 above.
[99] [1998] E.T.M.R. 337.
[1] *Light Green* [1999] E.T.M.R. 214, OHIM Third BoA.

"A colour *per se*, however, without any unusual or fanciful features is, according to Article 7(1)(b) . . . devoid of any distinctive character, since it belongs in the public domain and forms part of the store of signs available to all traders. It is not capable of distinguishing the goods and services applied for amongst those of other undertakings and cannot serve the basic function of a trade mark, unless it has become distinctive in consequence of the use which has been made of it pursuant to Article 7(3) (see *LIGHT GREEN*, paras 20 and 21)."[2]

Internet domain names

Internet domain names usually contain various non-distinctive elements **7–57** such as "www" or "http:/" and the various suffices which comprise the top and second level domains, such as ".com", ".org"; ".net"; ".co.uk". The approach of the United Kingdom Registry is to strip away these non-distinctive elements and to see if the remainder has distinctive character.[3] If it has, then the name may be registered.

OHIM has the same approach. For the application to register "WWW.PRIMEBROKER.COM", the Board of Appeal decided whether PRIMEBROKER was registrable, the other elements adding nothing by way of distinctiveness.[4]

Section 3(1)(c)/Article 3(1)(c), Article 7(1)(c) CTMR: descriptive marks

"s.3(1) The following shall not be registered: **7–58**

(c) trade marks which consist exclusively of signs or indications which may serve, in trade, to designate the kind, quality, quantity, intended purpose, value, geographical origin, the time of production of goods or of rendering of services, or other characteristics of goods or services"

Derivation

The wording in sub-section (c) is identical to that used in Article 3(1)(c) **7–59** of the Directive and Article 7(1)(c) of the CTM Regulation. Ultimately, it derives from Article 6*quinquies* B.2 of the Paris Convention.

Purpose

The purpose of this ground of objection is to prevent the registration of **7–60** signs which are descriptive of the goods or services or some characteristic of them. These descriptive marks are excluded from registration

---

[2] *Ty Nant* [1999] E.T.M.R. 974, OHIM Third BoA.
[3] See the Work Manual, Chap. 6, Part 6.5. See also PAC 12/00, September 2000, concerning the approach to Marks with the prefix "e–" or "M–".
[4] [2000] E.T.M.R. 245, OHIM Second BoA.

because they consist of signs or indications which honest traders either use or may wish to use without any improper motive.[5] "They must remain available for general use, since competitors have a legitimate interest in employing, without hindrance, in a descriptive manner such indications relating to the very nature of the claimed goods."[6]

> "Article 3(1)(c) of the Directive pursues an aim which is in the public interest, namely that descriptive signs or indications relating to the categories of goods or services in respect of which registration is applied for may be freely used by all, including as collective marks or as part of complex or graphic marks. Article 3(1)(c) therefore prevents such signs and indications from being reserved to one undertaking alone because they have been registered as trade marks.

7–61
> As regards, more particularly, signs or indications which may serve to designate the geographical origin of the categories of goods in relation to which registration of the mark is applied for, especially geographical names, it is in the public interest that they remain available, not least because they may be an indication of the quality and other characteristics of the categories of goods concerned, and may also, in various ways, influence consumer tastes by, for instance, associating the goods with a place that may give rise to a favourable response."[7]

7-62 The rationale was explained in *AD2000*[8] in a little more detail as follows. The provision is concerned with indications which may serve in trade to designate some characteristic of goods or services. The tenth recital to the TM Directive states that the protection afforded to registered trade marks "is in particular to guarantee the trade mark as an indication of origin". There is nothing for such protection to attach to or bite upon when a sign only serves to designate characteristics other than origin. Signs and indications of that kind can be used with equal truth by traders whose goods or services are possessed of the relevant characteristic. Hence such signs and indications are excluded from registration by this provision.

In relation to this ground, the Court of First Instance has stated:

> "It was thus the intention of the legislature that such signs should, by their very nature, be regarded as incapable of distinguishing the goods of one undertaking from those of another."[9]

Interpretation

7–63 In the majority of cases, the only issue is one of fact: does the mark consist exclusively of one of the relevant characteristics? The tribunal should answer this question taking into account the presumed expecta-

---

[5] *cf.* the test applied under the 1938 Act. See "W + 6", Du Cros (W + 6) Ltd's Application [1913] A.C. 624; 30 R.P.C. 660.
[6] *Global Chiller* [2000] E.T.M.R. 234, OHIM Third BoA, para. 11, as an example.
[7] *Windsurfing* [1999] E.T.M.R. 585, para. 25, ECJ.
[8] [1997] R.P.C. 168 at 174, G. Hobbs, Q.C. as the appointed person.
[9] *Baby-Dry* [1999] E.C.R. II—40, Court of First Instance.

tions of the average consumer who is reasonably well informed and reasonably observant and circumspect.[10] Examples of the relevant characteristics are listed but not exhaustively. Further examples may be gleaned from decided cases (see below). In practice, the decisions involving this ground often state simply that the mark is descriptive without spelling out any particular characteristic of the goods or services. Often it is unnecessary to do so. Since the policy underlying this ground is familiar, so too is the reasoning used in the cases.

The issues on interpretation which have arisen concern the meaning of "exclusively" and "may serve".

Exclusively

The word "exclusively" refers to the content of the mark. It does not **7–64** mean that this ground only applies when the only meaning that can be given to the mark is the descriptive one.[11] Equally, it is not necessary to show that the sign or indication may serve to designate each and every intended purpose of the goods in question, it is sufficient if it describes one of the intended purposes of the goods.[12]

The degree of distinctive character which is required to avoid this objection is discussed in the next section of this chapter.[13]

May serve

In the context of Article 3(1)(c) of the TM Directive and geographical **7–65** names, these words were the subject of elaborate argument in *Windsurfing*.[14] The case concerned various marks for clothing consisting of graphic designs which included the word CHIEMSEE, being the name of the largest lake in Bavaria. The defendants were sued for infringement because they had been selling sports clothing in the area of the lake using the designation Chiemsee. The defendants argued that the trade marks had been registered contrary to Article 3(1)(c) of the TM Directive. The court was presented with essentially two issues: whether Article 3(1)(c) required there to be a real, current or serious need to leave the sign or indication free; and what connection there must be

---

[10] see, *e.g. Complete* [1999] E.T.M.R. 664, OHIM Third BoA; Case R 459/1999–3, "*SmartOS*", OHIM Third BoA.

[11] *cf.* the observations made by H. Laddie Q.C. (as he then was) in *Profitmaker* [1994] R.P.C. 613 at 616: "The fact that honest traders have a number of alternative ways of describing the product is no answer to criticism of the marks. If it were, then all of these alternative ways could, on the same argument, also be the subject of registered trade marks. The honest trader should not need to consult the Register to ensure that common descriptions or laudatory words or not unusual combinations of them, have been monopolised by others", applied in *One Touch View*, see below. To similar effect: *Complete* [1999] E.T.M.R. 664, OHIM Third BoA. ". . . it would be sufficient that any one meaning of the word 'complete' is understood by the average consumer, who is reasonably well-informed and reasonably observant and circumspect (see . . . *Gut Springenheide* . . .) to describe the intended purpose of the appellant's goods."

[12] Case R 57/1998–1 *Foodsaver* [1999] E.T.M.R. 191 (note), OHIM BoA. See further, below.

[13] See paras 7–86 *et seq.* below.

[14] *Windsurfing* [1999] E.T.M.R. 585, ECJ.

between the geographical location and the goods in question. On the first issue, a variety of possibilities were suggested in argument:

> The plaintiff argued that registration was precluded only where the indication designated a specific place, several undertakings manufacture the relevant goods in that place and the name of the place was habitually used to designate the geographical origin of the goods.
>
> The defendants argued that registration was precluded if there was a serious possibility that the name would be used in future to designate geographical origin of the goods.
>
> The Italian Government argued that the mere fact that the indication could be used to designate geographical origin was sufficient.
>
> The Commission argued that the provision should not depend on the existence or otherwise of a real or serious need to leave a sign or indication free for the benefit of third parties.

7–66 The relevant paragraphs of the judgment appear to apply not merely to geographical names. With appropriate allowances, the observations seem to apply to all marks of a descriptive nature:

> "[Article 3(1)(c)] does not prohibit the registration of geographical names as trade marks solely where the names designate places which are, in the mind of the relevant class of persons, currently associated with the category of goods in question; it also applies to geographical names which are liable to be used in future by the undertakings concerned as an indication of the geographical origin of that category of goods;
>
> —where there is currently no association in the mind of the relevant class of persons between the geographical name and the category of goods in question, the competent authority must assess whether it is reasonable to assume that such a name is, in the mind of the relevant class of persons, capable of designating the geographical origin of that category of goods;
>
> —in making that assessment, particular consideration should be given to the degree of familiarity amongst the relevant class of persons with the geographical name in question, with the characteristics of the place designated by that name, and with the category of goods concerned;
>
> —it is not necessary for the goods to be manufactured in the geographical location in order for them to be associated with it."[15]

7–67 The ECJ also concluded that the application of Article 3(1)(c) "does not depend on there being a real, current or serious need to leave a sign or indication free ('Freihaltsbedürfnis') under German case-law . . ."

[15] *Windsurfing, ibid.*, para. 37. For further details of the reasoning, see paras 29–36.

Thus, "may serve" means "it does or is liable to serve". The OHIM Boards of Appeal take a straightforward approach. For example:

". . . the formulation 'may serve' in Article 7(1)(c) CTMR shows that a sign or indication must be refused registration if it may serve in trade to designate the characteristics of the goods, without its being necessary to show that the sign or indication is actually used or needed by the trade in question."[16]

Practice

Here we list a few examples from the United Kingdom and from OHIM **7–68** where this ground has been found established and not established, together with some observations which illustrate the types of reasoning employed in these cases. For convenience the examples are divided into categories of laudatory words, geographical indications, and descriptive.

The United Kingdom Registry has a series of working rules by which it assesses marks indicating geographical origin.[17] Of course, in each case the test to be applied is that contained in section 3(1)(c).

Laudatory words
Objection established:

100% PURE GOODNESS for cosmetics, shampoos, etc.[18]   **7–69**
COMPLETE for soaps, etc.[19]
LASTING   PERFORMANCE   for   perfumery,   essential   oils, cosmetics.[20]
OPTIMA for patient membrane oxygenator.[21]
SUPREME for photography products.[22]
THE PERFECTIONISTS for women's underwear.[23]
TREAT for dessert sauces and syrups.[24]

Not established

MAXIMA for surgical and medical apparatus.[25]

---

[16] Case R 216/1998–1 *Doublemint*, OHIM BoA.
[17] See Part 4 of Chap. 6 of the Work Manual for further details.
[18] Case R 161–1998–1, OHIM BoA.
[19] [1999] E.T.M.R. 664, OHIM BoA: ". . . it contained no additional element that could be regarded as arbitrary, fanciful, imaginative or inventive."
[20] Case R 34/1998–3, OHIM BoA, but allowed for "toilet soaps": "indications of quality describe, inter alia, the mode of action and other essential features of goods. These must be kept available for general use, since competitors have a legitimate interest in employing, without hindrance, in a descriptive manner such indications relating to the very nature of the claimed goods."
[21] Case R 94/1998–2, OHIM BoA. Optima means "the very best" in Portuguese: "the message it imparts is immediate and not subliminal."
[22] [1999] E.T.M.R. 505 (note), OHIM Third BoA: "The word SUPREME *per se* is a common term, without any originality or distinctiveness, and therefore is not eligible for registration. Accordingly, any competitor or non-competitor is free to use that sign."
[23] [1997] E.T.M.R. 505, Regy.
[24] *British Sugar Plc v. James Robertson & Sons Ltd* [1996] R.P.C. 281, Jacob J.
[25] [1999] E.T.M.R. 504 (note), OHIM First BoA. *cf. Optima*, above

LASTING PERFORMANCE for toilet soaps.[26]

Geographical indications
Ground established:

7–70   ISLE OF SKYE for spirits, wines and liqueurs.[27]

Not established:

VAL D'ISERE for ladies lingerie, there being no evidence that ladies underwear is or was likely to be made in the ski resort.[28]

7–71 *Descriptive*
United Kingdom examples
Objection established:

COFFEEMIX for coffee preparations.[29]
EUROLAMB for lamb.[30]
FROOT LOOPS for cereals.[31]
JERYL LYNN for medicinal and pharmaceutical preparations, etc.[32]
MINI CLAW for gardening implements.[33]
ONE TOUCH VIEW for telephone apparatus, especially mobile radio telephones.[34]
XpressLink for telecommunications devices.[35]
The shape of Dualit toasters.[36]
A picture of a Philips three-headed rotary shaver.[37]

---

[26] Case R 34/1998–3, OHIM BoA: "... whether or not afterwards the effects of the cleansing are long-lasting, does not depend on the soap used, but on the user's subsequent behaviour. For such products, the claimed word combination cannot be an indication of quality to be reserved for general use and is, albeit lacking somewhat in imaginativeness, also distinctive, though only to a small extent."

[27] Case R 102/1998–1, OHIM First BoA.

[28] O/085/00, Regy, March 7, 2000.

[29] [1998] R.P.C. 717, S. Thorley, Q.C. as the appointed person, applying the sentiments expressed in "*I Can't Believe It's Yoghurt*" [1992] R.P.C. 533 at 539 (R. Jacob Q.C.) with those in *Profitmaker* [1994] R.P.C. 613 at 616 (H. Laddie Q.C.).

[30] [1997] R.P.C. 279, Apptd Person.

[31] [1998] R.P.C. 240. S. Thorley Q.C. as the apptd person.

[32] [1999] F.S.R. 491, Laddie J. The mark "overwhelmingly performed a descriptive or technical function".

[33] [1999] E.T.M.R. 505 (note). Regy.

[34] O/080/00, Regy, February 16, 2000.

[35] [1999] E.T.M.R. 146, G. Hobbs Q.C. as the appointed person. In terms of *audible* expression, the mark was caught by s.3(1)(c), but in terms of visible expression, it was not because it did not consist *exclusively* of matters caught by that provision. The application was refused under s.3(1)(b) in both audible and visible expression.

[36] [1999] R.P.C. 304, Regy: "highly unlikely" that the public will *without education* recognise variations on, or different arrangements of, established styling features [of toasters] as badges of origin. This reasoning supported s.3(1)(b) but was used for both. The reason why s.3(1)(c) applied was more straightforward: a toaster indicates the intended purpose of the goods.

[37] *Philips v. Remington* [1999] R.P.C. 809, CA.

Not established:

The mark "P.R.E.P.A.R.E." for revision guides was not excluded from registration by this provision because it did not consist exclusively of the word PREPARE.[38]

WEB LINK (in a device) for computer software.[39]

OHIM examples
Established:

BABY-DRY for disposable diapers ". . . the term 'Baby-Dry', read as **7-72** a whole, immediately informs consumers of the intended purpose of the goods."[40]

BROADBAND CODE DIVISION MULTIPLE ACCESS for telecommunications systems, where BROADBAND and CODE DIVISION MULTIPLE ACCESS separately were accepted to be descriptive.[41]

COMFORT PLUS for carpets, floorcoverings.[42]

COMPANYLINE for insurance and financial affairs.[43]

COMPLETE for soaps, cosmetics, etc.[44]

DOUBLEMINT for chewing gums, cosmetics, dentifrices, phar- **7-73** maceutical preparations.[45]

ENAMELIZE for preparations for cleaning and polishing teeth.[46]

FOODSAVER and FRESHSAVER for vacuum packaging or sealing machines.[47]

GLOBAL CHILLER for cooling apparatus.[48]

IDEAL for online computer access services.[49]

---

[38] [1997] R.P.C. 884, appt'd person, although barred under s.3(1)(b).

[39] [1997] E.T.M.R. 500, Regy. The s.3(1)(c) objection was waived because the mark did not consist exclusively of the words WEBLINK. The mark was refused under section 3(1)(b).

[40] *Baby-Dry* [1999] E.C.R. II-40, Court of First Instance. The Board of Appeal was held to have been wrong to refuse to examine the applicant's arguments based on acquired distinctiveness under Art. 7(3).

[41] Case R 50/1998-3, OHIM BoA.

[42] [1999] E.T.M.R. 575, OHIM BoA. The examiner rejected the application on the basis of the equivalent of s 3(1)(b) alone. The BoA rejected it on both (b) and (c).

[43] The OHIM First Board of Appeal found objections under Arts 7(1)(b) and (c). On appeal, the Court of First Instance upheld the objection under Art. 7(1)(b) and felt it unnecessary to decide whether Art. 7(1)(c) also applied: [2000] E.T.M.R. 271.

[44] [1999] E.T.M.R. 664, OHIM Third BoA: ". . . it would be sufficient that any one meaning of the word 'complete' is understood by the average consumer, who is reasonably well-informed and reasonably observant and circumspect (see. . . *Gut Springenheide*) to describe the intended purpose of the appellant's goods . . ."

[45] Case R 216/1998-1, OHIM BoA.

[46] [1998] E.T.M.R. 658, OHIM BoA.

[47] [1999] E.T.M.R. 191 (note), OHIM BoA. Likewise *Freshsaver* [1999] E.T.M.R. 191 (note): "The fact that other words or expressions exist, which are similar in meaning and thus also capable of being used to designate the goods, . . . does not render less descriptive the mark FRESHSAVER. . . Even if the alternative ways of designating the goods suggested by the appellant were more appropriate or more directly descriptive of the goods. . . competitors might still be interested in using a less directly descriptive, but still appropriate term for designating the goods in question or their purpose."

[48] [2000] E.T.M.R. 234, OHIM Third BoA.

[49] [2000] E.T.M.R. 382, OHIM First BoA.

JIVE for audio and video tapes, compact discs, etc.[50]

LANDSCAPE for furniture, office and kitchen fittings and installation services.[51]

PETIT BEBE for clothing, footwear and headgear, as designating the intended purpose of the goods.[52]

POLY PADS (in a device) for "equine back protectors, pads for saddles and harness protectors" held descriptive, at least for the United Kingdom.[53]

PORTFOLIO held descriptive for books and other printed matter but not for magnetic data carriers, CD-ROMs, computer software for planning, etc.[54]

PRIMA for clothing, luggage, etc.[55]

TELEBINGO for games.[56]

WWW.PRIMEBROKER.COM for software tools for information on publicly traded companies.[57]

Not established:

7–74   Kelloggs applied for a mark consisting of a hexagonal outer perimeter enclosing a grid pattern.[58] The examiner thought the mark was a mere graphic description of goods such as cereals, bread, biscuits, pastry, etc., and hence contrary to Article 7(1)(c). The Board of Appeal disagreed, pointing out that the mark was not a simple shape or design of the type which is generally considered to lack distinctiveness.[59]

IMAGESTREAM for computer software.[60]

LIGHT GREEN[61] and YELLOW, both for chewing gum. Whilst both marks were refused registration under the equivalent of section 3(1)(d), the reasons given by the Board of Appeal for not upholding an objection under the equivalent of 3(1)(c) were odd. The examiner thought LIGHT GREEN could be used to indicate flavour such as apple or lime. The Board of Appeal added peppermint and wood

---

[50] Case R 58/1999–1, OHIM BoA. An argument that the dance was no longer fashionable was held irrelevant.

[51] Case R 473/1999–1, OHIM First BoA, March 22, 2000.

[52] Case R 95/1998–3, OHIM BoA: "Such words belong in the public domain and form part of the store of words available to all traders of baby products for positioning or marketing their products for babies." However, the case was remitted for consideration of evidence of use.

[53] [1999] E.T.M.R. 234, OHIM BoA: ". . . the fact that the trade mark is a created name that does not exist in dictionaries does not preclude the trade mark from being descriptive."

[54] Case R71/1998–3, OHIM BoA.

[55] Case R 83/1999–2, OHIM Second BoA.

[56] [1998] E.T.M.R. 569, OHIM BoA.

[57] [2000] E.T.M.R. 245, OHIM Second BoA.

[58] Case R 199/1998–2, OHIM BoA. The mark looked somewhat like a hexagonal "Shreddie".

[59] In the "very persuasive but non-binding Examination Guidelines": para. 8.3.

[60] Case R 55/1999–1, OHIM BoA: suggestive but not directly descriptive of the goods.

[61] [1999] E.T.M.R. 214. OHIM BoA.

ruff. The flavours cited in YELLOW were lemon, lime and banana or quince. But the fact that a variety of flavours might be indicated by the colour was the reason given for rejecting section 3(1)(c). It is suggested that the fact that the colour might have indicated a number of flavours indicates all the more necessity for an objection under section 3(1)(c).

OILGEAR (in slightly stylised form) for hydraulic pumps and motors—"no immediate link with the goods of the application".[62]

7–75

NETMEETING for computer programs for providing real-time . . . communications over computer networks[63]—"a descriptive sign or indication may be registered whenever it is applied to unrelated products, used in a fanciful way, affected by some alteration considered sufficiently distinctive or combined with one or more descriptive signs or indications in such a way as to result in a new single word, as a whole, without a univocal meaning or understandable reference to the specific goods or services"

"SmartOS" for computer software, interfaces between smartcards and personal computers.[64] ". . . the combination of those two elements is sufficiently novel to endow the term 'SmartOS' with a limited degree of distinctiveness."

SWEDISH FORMULA for cosmetics, soaps, shampoo etc. The examiner's objection was annulled because he did not point to any Swedish formula applicable to any of the goods.[65]

---

[62] [1999] E.T.M.R. 291, OHIM BoA: ". . . enterprises have a legitimate interest in using marks that are so-called allusive or suggestive in the sense that they indicate a link or connection with the activities, goods or services of the enterprise. Such a suggestive or allusive mark is intended to arouse interest in and curiosity for the goods or services of the trade mark owner and will not be understood as describing the kind or other characteristics of the goods or services in question. As a rule, suggestive or allusive marks should not be denied protection. They present no obstacle for competitors to promote their own goods or services."

[63] Case R 26/1998–3 OHIM BoA.

[64] Case R 459/1999–3, OHIM Third BoA: "In determining the distinctive character, it is necessary to make a global assessment of the capacity of the mark to identify the goods or services in the application as coming from a particular undertaking, and thus to distinguish those goods and services from those of other undertakings. In making that assessment, account should be taken of all relevant factors and, in particular, of the inherent characteristics of the claimed mark, of the goods or services with which it is to be used, including whether it contains an element descriptive of those goods or services.

An objection to the descriptive character may only be maintained where the descriptive content is immediately, clearly and unmistakably obvious from the application. If a term that could serve to describe the characteristics of goods is merely hinted at or is suggestive, and is recognisable only on the basis of intellectual conclusions, it does not usually impede the registration.

Furthermore, the assessment of whether a trade mark should be refused on absolute grounds necessarily involves taking into account the presumed expectations of the average consumer who is reasonably well informed and reasonably observant and circumspect."

". . . undertakings have a legitimate interest in using suggestive or allusive trade marks as opposed to purely descriptive marks"—see OILGEAR.

[65] [1999] E.T.M.R. 559, OHIM BoA.

Other examples

7–76 Some examples of possible marks which would fall within the various characteristics mentioned in paragraph (c) are as follows:

> *kind*—mere representations of the goods themselves: for example, a picture simply of a plain bed used for beds; "light", for low tar cigarettes; jumbo, mini, personal (for computers); vertical (for blinds);
>
> *quality*—laudatory words or symbols such as "best", "good", 5 stars; "premium";
>
> *quantity*—the usual indications of quantity—pint, litre, gallon, kg, lb, pound, numbers, "lots"; 12 for wine, 200 for cigarettes;—are obviously descriptive and are excluded from registration. There may be other combinations of numbers in respect of which the decision may not be so clear. Take, as an example, the mark "580" which was the subject of a passing-off action in *Hymac v. Priestman* [1978] R.P.C. 495. The mark was derived from the fact that the excavator in question had a capacity of 5/8ths of a cubic yard but that did not render the mark descriptive. It is suggested that the mark "5/8ths" would be excluded, whereas "580" for excavators ought not to be;
>
> *intended purpose*—"Kettle Clean" for descaling preparations; "kitchen" or "bathroom" for cleaning agents; "marine" for paints;
>
> *value*—two for one; "bargain". Under the 1938 Act "Budget"[66] for car hire services was refused registration, despite apparent proof of factual distinctiveness. Under the 1994 Act it is suggested that "Budget" would fall foul of this provision, but would be saved by the proviso;

7–77

> *geographical origin*—"Smithfield" for meat or "Buxton"[67] for spring water (in the absence of any evidence of use which would be considered under the proviso);
>
> *the time of production of goods*—"just-in-time"; a particular year for wine or "fresh each day" for vegetables;
>
> *the time of rendering of services*—"nine to five", "overnight" or "overnite" for delivery services; "24 hour banking"; day by day;
>
> *other characteristics*—this final category is entirely general and includes any characteristic which may not fall within one of the specific categories, but which is nonetheless descriptive in the particular industry concerned. Some suggested examples are as follows:
>
> > — "Ogen" for melons. The mark was expunged under the 1938 Act because Ogen was the name of a variety of melon[68];

---

[66] [1991] R.P.C. 9.

[67] "Buxton" was in fact registered under the 1938 Act for spring water on substantial evidence of use which showed that the mark was in fact distinctive of water from the springs at Buxton, and that the applicant controlled all the springs.

[68] [1977] R.P.C. 529.

— "lead free" for petrol;
— words which simply describe the get-up of goods or labels;
— a characteristic which describes the effect which the goods or services have or are intended to have, *e.g.* "QuickSlim".

Overcoming a section 3(1)(c) objection

Apart from showing that the mark has acquired distinctiveness through **7–78** use, it may be possible to overcome the objection by restricting the specification of goods or services, particularly if the objection is taken in respect of only part of the specification. This is one of the respects in which it is permissible to amend an application under section 39 of the 1994 Act. It is no longer possible to amend the actual trade mark itself other than in cases of obvious mistake (see section 39(2), *post*).

Section 3(1)(d)/Article 3(1)(d), Article 7(1)(d) CTMR: generic marks

"s.3(1) The following shall not be registered—   **7–79**

(d) trade marks which consist exclusively of signs or indications which have become customary in the current language or in the bona fide and established practices of the trade."

Derivation

The wording of this sub-paragraph is identical to Article 3(1)(d) of the **7–80** TM Directive and Article 7(1)(d) of the CTM Regulation. These provisions are directed at preventing registration of those signs or indications which honest traders customarily use in trade—signs which are generic.

Scope

There is clearly a significant degree of overlap between this provision **7–81** and section 3(1)(c) of the 1994 Act. However, section 3(1)(d) has a role in excluding from registration signs or indications where the descriptive element is not readily apparent, yet they are signs or indications which a number of traders actually use.

Some obvious examples of signs or indications which would be precluded from registration by section 3(1)(d) are marks which consisted of stars for hotel services, stars for brandy, a bunch of grapes for wine, a representation of a chef for food or for restaurant services[69] or of a mechanic or spanner for car repair services. TREAT for dessert sauces and syrups[70] was declared invalid under this ground. However, due to

---

[69] These examples appear in the Registy Work Manual.
[70] *British Sugar Plc v. James Robertson & Sons Ltd* [1996] R.P.C. 281, Jacob J.

the word "exclusively" a mark would not be caught by this ground simply because it included such customary matter, provided the mark contained other distinctive elements.

7–82   The policy underlying this ground is a familiar one. Hence it is appropriate to apply well-known observations even though they were expressed under the 1938 Act. For example, in the United Kingdom Registry:

> "The descriptive nature of the term spelled out above means that it is apt for use by other traders. As Mr Hugh Laddie, as he then was, acting for the Secretary of State said in *PROFITMAKER* [1994] RPC 613 and by reference to *TORQ-SET* [1959] RPC 344:
>
> > 'The honest trader should not need to consult the register to ensure that common or descriptive laudatory words, or not unusual combinations of them, have been monopolised by others.'
>
> That was a case decided under the Trade Marks Act 1938 (as amended) but the comment is apt for application to cases to be determined under the Trade Marks Act 1994, particularly in relation to section 3(1)(d)."[71]

OHIM

7–83 Apart from its most obvious applications, this provision has been interpreted as broadly as possible by the Boards of Appeal at OHIM. For example:

(1) In SUPREME,[72] the Board of Appeal interpreted "the trade" as meaning any part of the trade, indicating there was no need to show the term was in fact used in the trade concerned with the goods for which application was made, relying on the fact that the provision did not refer to products or services. They held that SUPREME was a laudatory term used throughout trade.

(2) In LIGHT GREEN[73] and YELLOW,[74] the Board of Appeal said that the equivalent provision in Article 7(1)(d) applied to "elements commonly used in advertising which provide not so much a special descriptive statement but serve principally to attract customers". They drew the distinction between special descriptive statements (falling within Article 7(1)(c)) and a wider class of signs or indications which are customarily used

---

[71] *Minilite* [2000] E.T.M.R. 256, Regy.
[72] Case R44/1998–3, para. 21, OHIM Third BoA.
[73] *Light Green* [1999] E.T.M.R. 214, OHIM Third BoA (light green for chewing gum).
[74] Case R169/1998–3, OHIM Third BoA (yellow for chewing gum), a decision in identical terms *mutatis mutandis* to *Light Green*.

in trade.[75] Although the applicant argued that both colours were unique and unusual, the Board of Appeal held they were commonly and effectively used in advertising and in trade as a basic colour.

Evidence

The evidence necessary to establish this ground may depend upon the **7–84** tribunal. Certainly OHIM examiners and the United Kingdom Registry will look for evidence from dictionaries and the like to show a mark is customary in the current language of the trade or for evidence of trade usage to show that the mark is customary in the practices of the trade. In *MINI CLAW*,[76] a single entry from an edition of a dictionary published 30 years ago, which did not appear in subsequent editions or in other dictionaries, was insufficient to establish that the word CLAW was current in the language of the gardening trade. Equally, one reference in trade literature (of the opponent) was insufficient to show the term was customary in established practices in the trade.

In OHIM, the evidential requirements appear to be less strict, at least **7–85** at the ex parte stage. In *LIGHT GREEN* and *YELLOW*, this ground was held established apparently on the basis of the general knowledge and experience of the members of the Board of Appeal.[77]

In most cases, if the evidence is insufficient to establish this ground, it may well establish a section 3(1)(c) of the 1994 Act objection.

4. Assessment of distinctive character

In this section we consider the assessment of (1) inherent distinctive **7–86** character and (2) distinctive character acquired through use. In the latter part, we first set out the guidance from the ECJ in *Windsurfing/Chiemsee* and then discuss particular issues concerning secondary meaning, the monopoly problem and primary and secondary marks. We then deal with evidence of distinctiveness and three particular problem areas: mere evidence of use; evidence of association or recognition; evidence in standard form. Finally we deal with a problem which is largely confined to CTMs: the geographical extent to which acquired distinctiveness must be proved under Article 7(3) CTM Regulation.

---

[75] This is reflected in the Examination Guidelines, para. 8.5: "There is some overlap with the previous paragraph [Art. 7(1)(c)] but here account has to be taken of further elements such as words, designs or motifs which do not designate kind etc. but which are in common use in the relevant trade. Thus words such as NET and NETWORK for computers; the letter "L" for driving schools; and bunches of grapes or vine leaves for wine are commonplace in those particular trades. The assessment always has to be made by the examiner in the context of the particular trade in question."

[76] [1999] E.T.M.R. 505 (note), Regy.

[77] For a comment on this decision (and on the decisions of the Swiss Supreme Court in "White/Green Tablets", October 14, 1999 and German Supreme Court and Federal Patent Court in "Yellow/Black", December 10, 1998 and October 25, 1999, respectively), see Johannes/Zurkinden, *Gelb/schwarz* MarkenR 5/2000 at 153–159.

7-87 We start by stating the obvious propositions that:

    (1) whether a sign possesses distinctive character, inherent or acquired, is a question of fact[78];

    (2) whatever the sign or type of sign, the same amount of distinctive character should be required before the sign is properly registered as a trade mark, whether the distinctive character is inherent or whether it has been acquired through use;

    (3) the assessment of inherent distinctive character depends upon the mark itself. This does not mean that the sign or mark is assessed in a vacuum: the trade of the goods or services in question provides the context;

    (4) the assessment of distinctive character acquired through use requires an overall assessment of the way in which the mark has been used to ascertain whether the mark has become distinctive.

7-88 In theory, the same amount of distinctive character should justify registration, whether the distinctiveness is inherent or acquired. In practice, it may appear that considerably more distinctiveness is required of some marks than others. Compare:

    (1) the unused word mark NETMEETING was registered for "computer programs for providing real-time . . . communications over computer networks",[79] a specification which could be shortened to "Net meetings".

    (2) In *British Sugar* the judge would have required evidence that more than 60 per cent of the relevant public took the word mark TREAT for dessert sauces and syrups as a trade mark, for the registration to have remained valid.

The apparent difference is explained by the fact that TREAT had an established descriptive meaning (a negative quality) which has to be displaced by a new secondary distinctive meaning (a positive quality) before the mark could be properly registered. The more descriptive the mark, the more difficult it will be to prove acquired distinctiveness. By contrast, NETMEETING was an unused mark with just enough distinctive character to satisfy the OHIM Board of Appeal.

Inherent distinctive character

7-89 In each of the grounds concerned with distinctiveness, there is a word which sets the standard: section 3(1)(b)—devoid; section 3(1)(c) and (d) and 3(2)—exclusively. To avoid[80] these grounds, the mark must possess

---

[78] Note that the first question referred to the ECJ by the Court of Appeal in *Philips v. Remington* [1999] R.P.C. 809 effectively asks whether there is a category of signs (which are not "capable of distinguishing") which are excluded from registration even if acquired distinctiveness is proved—effectively a question about distinctiveness *in law; cf. York* [1984] R.P.C. 231, HL, under the 1938 Act.

[79] Case R 26/1998–3, OHIM BoA.

[80] Rather than overcome the grounds in s.3(1)(b), (c) and (d), under the proviso.

a minimum degree of distinctive character. An important practical issue arises in the operation of each ground: what is required to surpass the standard? For example, if application is made for a trade mark which contains a descriptive term, what else must the mark contain so that it successfully avoids being *exclusively* a sign or indication included in section 3(1)(c)? One answer is easy enough to state: the mark must contain something else, a surplus[81] or a sufficient capricious addition,[82] some other matter which gives it sufficient distinctive character to justify registration. The quantum of this other matter must depend on the mark, the trade and all relevant circumstances. Various expressions have been used to describe this minimum level. Whilst expressions of this type should not be elevated into statutory requirements, they are nonetheless useful for giving a flavour of what is required. Although the terminology in the 1994 Act has changed, the same techniques as have been used for years can be used to assess whether or not a mark has an inherent distinctive character:

A collection of various expressions was cited by Lloyd J. in *Dualit*: **7–90**

> ". . . a mark has distinctive character if it communicates the fact that the goods with reference to which it is used recurrently are those of one and the same undertaking. Is it taken by the public as a badge of origin: see *British Sugar plc v. James Robertson & Co. Ltd* [1996] R.P.C. 281 at 286? Put differently, does it have a meaning denoting the origin of the goods: *Philips Electronics NV v. Remington Consumer Products Ltd*, Aldous L.J. at section D (ii)? As Jacob J. also observed in *British Sugar plc v. James Robertson & Co. Ltd*, at page 302, quoting earlier authority, to be distinctive a sign must be incapable of fair and honest application to the goods of anyone else."[83]

By contrast, a mere spark of distinctiveness was held not enough.[84]

Examples of concepts used by the OHIM Boards of Appeal are as follows[85]: **7–91**

> A combination of words which did not suggest a direct correlation with the specific goods of interest to the applicant was held to have a minimum distinctive character which enabled it to be eligible for registration: NETMEETING.[86]
>
> "When confronted with the word, the relevant consumer will have no precise idea about the kind of goods nor of the characteristics of the goods in question." "As a rule, suggestive or allusive marks should not be denied protection.": *OILGEAR*.[87]

---

[81] The term used in the United Kingdom Registry Work Manual, Chap. 6, Part 3.2, adopted from the decision of the German court in *Color Collection*.

[82] The term used by Aldous L.J. in *Philips v. Remington* [1999] R.P.C. 809, *e.g.* at 817.

[83] [1999] R.P.C. 890 at para. 28.

[84] By S. Thorley Q.C. sitting as the appointed person in *SHOP!* O/051/00, January 10, 2000.

[85] See also various quotations listed above, under section 3(1)(b) and (c). See paras 7–39 and 7–60 above.

[86] Case R 26/1998–3, OHIM BoA.

[87] [1999] E.T.M.R. 291, OHIM BoA.

If a mental effort is required from consumers in order to transform a suggestive or emotional message into a rational evaluation, that is usually sufficient: *LASER TRACER*.[88]

Evidence

7–92 Often, whether a sign has inherent distinctive character is assessed without explicit reference to any evidence, but in fact the assessment is being made against some knowledge of the relevant trade and of the marks which are used in it. In certain cases, the tribunal must inform itself from evidence of the characteristics of the relevant trade.

Distinctive character acquired through use—the proviso to section 3(1), Article 3(3), Article 7(3) CTM Regulation

7–93 The issue of whether a mark has acquired a distinctive character through the use which has been made of it arises only if the mark is subject to an objection under one or more of section 3(1)(b), (c) or (d). It is now clear that this issue requires an overall assessment of the ability of the mark to distinguish in fact. The overall assessment is made taking into account the presumed expectations of the average consumer of the category of products concerned "[who] is deemed to be reasonably well-informed and reasonably observant and circumspect".[89] The "average consumer" test allows a variety of sources of evidence to be taken into account but discourages repetitious evidence.

Windsurfing Chiemsee

7–94 In *Windsurfing Chiemsee*,[90] the European Court was asked what was required in order for a mark to have acquired distinctive character through use. The mark in question was *Chiemsee*, the name of the largest lake in Bavaria. Although this guidance was given in the context of a mark of geographical significance, it is plain that it is of general application:

"44. The first point to note is that Article 3(3) of the Directive provides that a sign may, through use, acquire a distinctive charac-

---

[88] Case RG2/1998–3, OHIM BoA.

[89] The quote is from *Lloyd Schuhfabrik Meyer & Co GmbH v. Klijsen Handel BV* [1999] F.S.R. 627, ECJ, but the words originate in para. 37 of *Gut Springenheide GmbH & Tusky v. Oberkreisdirektor des Krieses Steinfurt—Amt fur Lebensmitteluberwachung* [1998] E.C.R. I–4657, a case about whether a statement on a pack of eggs was liable to mislead, contrary to an E.C. Regulation on marketing standards for eggs. The concept is not unique to European jurisprudence. When considering the analogous question of whether the defendant's use of "Treat" would be seen as a trade mark or as descriptive use, Jacob J. considered what "the average consumer" would think: see *British Sugar* [1996] R.P.C. 281 at 300.

[90] *Windsurfing Chiemsee Produktions- und Vertriebs GmbH v. Boots- und Segelzubehor Walter Huber & Franz Attenberger* [1999] E.T.M.R. 585, ECJ.

ter which it initially lacked and thus be registered as a trade mark. It is therefore through the use made of it that the sign acquires the distinctive character which is a prerequisite for its registration.

7–95

45. Article 3(3) therefore constitutes a major exception to the rule laid down in Articles 3(1)(b), (c) and (d), whereby registration is to be refused in relation to trade marks which are devoid of any distinctive character, descriptive marks, and marks which consist exclusively of indications which have become customary in the current language or in the bona fide and established practices of the trade.

46. Secondly, just as distinctive character is one of the general conditions for registering a trade mark under Article 3(1)(b), distinctive character acquired through use means that the mark must serve to identify the product in respect of which registration is applied for as originating from a particular undertaking, and thus to distinguish that product from goods of other undertakings.

47. It follows that a geographical name may be registered as a **7–96** trade mark if, following the use which has been made of it, it has come to identify the product in respect of which registration is applied for as originating from a particular undertaking and thus to distinguish that product from goods of other undertakings. Where that is the case, the geographical designation has gained a new significance and its connotation, no longer purely descriptive, justifies its registration as a trade mark.

48. Windsurfing Chiemsee and the Commission are therefore right to assert that Article 3(3) does not permit any differentiation as regards distinctiveness by reference to the perceived importance of keeping the geographical name available for use by other undertakings.

49. In determining whether a mark has acquired distinctive **7–97** character following the use made of it, the competent authority must make an overall assessment of the evidence that the mark has come to identify the product concerned as originating from a particular undertaking, and thus to distinguish that product from goods of other undertakings.

50. In that connection, regard must be had in particular to the specific nature of the geographical name in question. Indeed, where a geographical name is very well known, it can acquire distinctive character under Article 3(3) of the Directive only if there has been long-standing and intensive use of the mark by the undertaking applying for registration. A fortiori, where a name is already familiar as an indication of geographical origin in relation to a certain category of goods, an undertaking applying for registration of the name in respect of goods in that category must show that the use of the mark—both long-standing and intensive—is particularly well established.

177

7–98   51. In assessing the distinctive character of a mark in respect of which registration has been applied for, the following may also be taken into account: the market share held by the mark; how intensive, geographically widespread and long-standing use of the mark has been; the amount invested by the undertaking in promoting the mark; the proportion of the relevant class of persons who, because of the mark, identify goods as originating from a particular undertaking; and statements from chambers of commerce and industry or other trade and professional associations.

7–99   52. If, on the basis of those factors, the competent authority finds that the relevant class of persons, or at least a significant proportion thereof, identify goods as originating from a particular undertaking because of the trade mark, it must hold that the requirement for registering the mark laid down in Article 3(3) of the Directive is satisfied. However, the circumstances in which that requirement may be regarded as satisfied cannot be shown to exist solely by reference to general, abstract data such as predetermined percentages.

53. As regards the method to be used to assess the distinctive character of a mark in respect of which registration is applied for, Community law does not preclude the competent authority, where it has particular difficulty in that connection, from having recourse, under the conditions laid down by its own national law, to an opinion poll as guidance for its judgment (see, to that effect, Case C–210/96 *Gut Springenheide and Tusky* [1998] ECR I-4657, paragraph 37)."

7–100 The true significance of this rather oblique reference to *Gut Springenheide* emerged in *Lloyd*,[91] where the ECJ was concerned with the effect of the distinctive character of a mark upon the global assessment required by *SABEL v. Puma* and *Canon* in determining whether there was a likelihood of confusion for the purposes of infringement under the equivalent of section 10(2). In that context "the perception of marks" in the mind of the average consumer of the category of goods or services in question plays a decisive role. This average consumer was conferred with the characteristics described in *Gut Springenheide*, namely "reasonably well-informed and reasonably observant and circumspect".

7–101 The final stage of development, where this "average consumer" is pressed into service in the determination of distinctive character, is a short step to take and one taken by the Court of Appeal in *Bach Flower Remedies*.[92] The reference to "a relevant class of persons or at least a significant proportion thereof" in paragraph 52 of *Windsurfing* means average consumers with the *Gut Springenheide* characteristics. Hence, Chadwick L.J. stated (at page 534):

[91] *op cit.*
[92] [2000] R.P.C. 513.

"What is required, in the context of the proviso, is that persons in that class, or at least a significant proportion of persons in that class, identify the words or word in question as distinctive of the origin of the goods."

". . . in seeking to apply the test, the court is unlikely to be assisted by repetitious evidence from individual consumers, put forward by each party as the embodiment of the average consumer. The task for the court is to inform itself, by evidence, of the matters of which a reasonably well-informed and reasonably observant and circumspect consumer of the products would know; and then, treating itself as competent to evaluate the effect which those matters would have on the mind of such a person with that knowledge, ask this question: would he say that the words or word identify, for him, the goods as originating from a particular undertaking."

Secondary meaning

In *Windsurfing* the ECJ indicated that the corollary of a mark having **7–102** acquired a distinctive character through use was that the mark "has gained a new significance and its connotation, no longer purely descriptive, justifies its registration as a trade mark."[93] The issue which remains is whether the secondary meaning or new significance must displace the primary non-distinctive meaning, and, to what extent.

These are difficult issues, yet familiar. The same type of issue arises in **7–103** the law of passing off and arose under the old Act. However, the extent to which a descriptive sign must acquire a secondary[94] distinctive meaning in order to satisfy the proviso ought to be different to that required in the law of passing off and is not necessarily the same as was required under the old Act. Of course, it is a question of fact (and therefore of degree) whether a particular sign has acquired sufficient distinctive character to justify registration under the proviso. But stating that principle does not give much guidance as to what "sufficient distinctive character" really means. Already under the 1994 Act there have been a number of cases which mention this issue and unless they are properly understood, they can be misinterpreted. Therefore, in this section we aim to provide some guidance on this issue. The guidance can be stated in these propositions:

(1) It is not necessary for the secondary distinctive meaning to displace entirely the primary descriptive meaning of a sign. However, when the sign is used in relation to the goods or

---

[93] Para. 47, cited above.
[94] In this context, the terms "primary" and "secondary" indicate the sequence in which the meanings were acquired, although they also indicate that the primary descriptive meaning is the default.

services in question, the average consumer should understand
the sign to denote origin.

(2) The extent to which the secondary distinctive meaning must
displace the primary descriptive meaning to justify registration
as a trade mark should be greater than the minimum required
to sustain an action in passing off.

(3) The extent to which the secondary distinctive meaning must
displace the primary descriptive meaning to justify registration
as a trade mark is a question of degree which will depend upon
the degree of descriptiveness of the sign. The more descriptive
the sign, the greater the extent to which the primary descriptive
meaning must be displaced. The more descriptive a sign is, the
greater are the negative (descriptive) qualities of the sign which
must be displaced and overcome by positive distinctive
qualities. Ultimately, when making this judgment the tribunal is
likely to be influenced by considerations which were familiar
under the old Act. To what extent would registration interfere
with the rights of honest traders? To what extent does this sign
really operate as a trade mark? To what extent is it thought
necessary to keep this sign free for others to use[95]?

We take these propositions in turn, discussing the relevant cases.

7–104   First, in *Bach Flower Remedies*, some observations made by Chadwick
L.J. (at page 535) when applying the test of the average consumer, could
be interpreted to mean that the secondary distinctive meaning must
displace the primary descriptive meaning either completely or to a very
substantial extent:

> ". . . a reasonably well informed and reasonably observant and
> circumspect consumer would know, if it be the case, that the word
> or words are widely used in a generic or descriptive sense—even if
> he is, himself, aware that they are also used in a distinctive sense.
> With that knowledge, it seems to me to be impossible for him to say
> that the words identify for him, the goods as originating from a
> particular undertaking. Knowing as he does, that the use of the
> words may be intended as descriptive, he cannot assert that he
> understands them as necessarily distinctive."

7–105 In the particular circumstances before the Court of Appeal, those
observations were correct. The sign "Bach Flower Remedies" had been
allowed to become generic of the type of remedies, even though some
people still regarded the sign as indicating trade origin. However, those
observations could be misapplied in different circumstances where, for

---

[95] Compare the various submissions made in *Windsurfing* and the fact that the ECJ sensibly
avoided any attempt at evaluating the need to which a sign should be kept free for
others.

example, the average consumer was aware that if the sign was used in a particular style or context it indicated trade origin whereas use in a different context might clearly indicate descriptive use. If the average consumer is left in doubt as to the message being conveyed by the sign, that indicates the sign does not have sufficient distinctive character to be registered. On the other hand, registration is justified if the context makes the message clear, one way or the other.

Of course, the context is always defined by the relevant goods or **7–106** services in question. In an entirely different context, the sign may only bear its descriptive meaning, but this does not matter. Laddie J. pointed out in *Jeryl Lynn*[96] that the signs Penguin, Ford and Golf have acquired distinctive character in relation to certain goods, whereas in other contexts, they have retained entirely their descriptive meaning.

Even in the context of the relevant goods or services, it has long been **7–107** the case that a trade mark may be both distinctive and also convey something by way of a description of the goods or services. One need only take the example of a mark which contains a skilful and covert allusion to some characteristic of the goods (for example the purpose or their quality). These are often regarded as being the most valuable trade marks, being distinctive yet also having an element of descriptive character in them. The point goes further, as Jacob J. explained in *Philips*[97]:

> "Now it is of course the case that a mark (particularly a word mark) may be both distinctive of a particular manufacturer and yet also convey something by way of a description of the goods—Mr Pumfrey gave "Weldmesh" for welded mesh as an example. The word denotes the welded mesh of a particular manufacturer (See *WELDMESH Trade Mark* [1966] R.P.C. 220) But you can take this argument too far. There are words which are so descriptive that they cannot be trade marks—"soap" for "soap". The difference is one of degree, but important nonetheless. There are degrees of descriptiveness ranging from the skilful but covert allusion to the common word for the goods. On the scale of distinctiveness you come to a point where a word is so descriptive that it is incapable of distinguishing properly, even if it does so partially."

As for the second proposition, the reason for the suggested distinction **7–108** on the subject of secondary meaning between the law of passing off and registration of a trade mark is as follows. The principles developed in passing off cases allow a flexible approach to the facts of a particular case. If the case involves a sign with a primary descriptive meaning, the court can effectively alter the extent to which it requires the plaintiff to

---

[96] [1999] F.S.R. 491.
[97] In *Philips v. Remington* [1998] R.P.C. 283 at 301, having cited the well-known passage from the judgment of Fletcher Moulton L.J. in *Joseph Crosfield's Application (Perfection Trade Mark)* (1909) 26 R.P.C. 837 at 857.

demonstrate a secondary meaning by balancing the interests of the parties and the public. For example, the plaintiff may have to endure some confusion and small differences may suffice, and a different result may obtain if the court considers that people really are being misled. By contrast, registration of a trade mark confers an exclusive right—a monopoly right. The defences in section 11 only allow a balancing of interests to a very limited extent, and even then the law appears to be reasonably settled that "honest men should not have to look for a defence". In order to justify the exclusive right which covers the wide range of situations which fall within the infringement provisions, it is suggested that the applicant must demonstrate that a secondary distinctive meaning has displaced the primary descriptive meaning to a greater extent than may be required for success in passing off. An applicant who fails to make the grade is then left to prove his case in passing off.

7–109   On the third proposition, consider the relevant dicta from *British Sugar*, where the sign was the laudatory term "Treat" for dessert sauces and syrups:

> "A word or words to be really distinctive of a person's goods must generally be incapable of application to the goods of anyone else".[98]
>
> "It is precisely because a common laudatory word is naturally capable of application to the goods of any trader that one must be careful before concluding that merely its use, however substantial, has displaced its common meaning and has come to denote the mark of a particular trader."[99]
>
> "Is my finding that to some but not most people "Treat" has some trade mark significance enough? This depends on what is meant by a *distinctive character*. Neither the Directive nor the Act throw any light on this. . . . Take a very descriptive or laudatory word. Suppose the proprietor can educate 10% of the public into recognising the word as his trade mark. Can that really be enough to to say it has acquired a *distinctive character* and so enough to let the proprietor lay claim to the word as a trade mark altogether? The character at this stage is partly distinctive but mainly not. I do not think it would be fair to regard the character of the word as *distinctive* in that state of affairs. But if the matter were the other way round, so that to 90% of people it was taken as a trade mark, then I think it would be fair so to regard it. This all suggests that the question of factual *distinctive character* is one of degree. The proviso really means 'has the mark acquired a sufficiently distinctive character that the mark has really become a trade mark'. In the case of common or apt descriptive or laudatory words compelling evidence is needed to establish this . . . it must be shown in a case

---

[98] At 302, citing from the judgment of Lord Russell in *The Shredded Wheat Co.Ltd v. Kelloggs* (1940) 57 R.P.C. 137 at 145.
[99] At 302.

of this sort that the mark has really become accepted by a substantial majority of persons as a trade mark—is or is almost a household word."[1]

Jacob J. suggested that even recognition by 60 per cent of the public as a **7–110** trade mark would not satisfy the proviso for such a common laudatory term, although we suspect that elsewhere in Europe such a figure would be considered sufficient. His approach is consistent with the general guidance provided by the ECJ in *Windsurfing*, where the court indicated that the proviso would be satisfied by a mark which was "no longer *purely* descriptive" (emphasis added). In a case decided after *Windsurfing* (*Messiah from Scratch, op. cit.* at page 51), the appointed person (S. Thorley, Q.C.) correctly observed:

> ". . . it is not necessary that the secondary meaning should have displaced the primary meaning, it is however necessary that it has gained a sufficient new significance as indicating origin to justify registration so as to leave third parties who wish to use the designation in its descriptive sense to rely upon the defence provided by section 11 of the Act."

Thus, we return to the issue of what is sufficient. No mathematical **7–111** answer can be given, it is a question of feel. Compare:

> A sign whose meaning in the absence of use is primarily but not completely descriptive—the type of sign which could only be registered upon evidence of acquired distinctiveness, for example, Weldmesh.
> A sign which has inherent distinctive character, yet which also contains a skilful but covert allusion to the purpose or some other characteristic of the goods.

The latter example should never fall to be considered under the proviso, but it serves to confirm that it cannot be necessary for the descriptive meaning to be entirely displaced. Likewise the former example. Registration of a sign like Weldmesh is only justified when it has been used sufficiently so that the tribunal concludes that an honest trader would not adopt that sign, but if a trader used the description Welded Mesh, he would have a defence.

If the sign in question has very limited "surplus" or "capricious **7–112** addition" over the purely descriptive term, then very extensive use of the sign will be required and in a distinctive sense, so that the primary descriptive meaning of the sign is substantially displaced by the secondary distinctive meaning. Ultimately, these considerations lead back to the various tests which were gathered by Lloyd J. in *Dualit* and cited above.[2]

---

[1] At 306.
[2] See para. 7–90 above.

The monopoly problem

7–113 The monopoly problem is one which is often faced by manufacturers who devise a new product. As Jacob J. put it in *British Sugar*:

> "a manufacturer may coin a new word for a new product and be able to show massive use by him and him alone of that word for the product. Nonetheless the word is apt to be the name of the product, not a trade mark. Examples from old well-known cases of this sort of thing abound. The *Shredded Wheat* saga is a good example:"

7–114 The problem is not confined to the names of products nor to proprietors who enjoy statutory monopolies. The same problem is also faced by manufacturers who enjoy *de facto* monopolies and/or who devise new features of known products: such as stripes in toothpaste. As Hoffmann J. said in *Unilever (Striped Toothpaste No. 2)*[3]:

> "There are many cases which speak of the extreme difficulty which faces a trader who produces a new article to which he attaches a descriptive name in proving that the name has acquired a secondary meaning denoting an article made by him. As Lord Davey said in *The Cellular Clothing Company Ltd v. Maxton & Murray* [1899] A.C. 326 at 344:
>
> > '. . . the evidence of persons who come forward and say that the name in question suggests to their minds and is associated by them with the plaintiff's goods alone is of a very slender character, for the simple reason that the plaintiff was the only maker of the goods during the time that his monopoly lasted, and therefore there was nothing to compare with it . . .'
>
> There is in my view a similar obstacle in the path of a trader who has enjoyed a *de facto* monopoly of a product with a relatively simple feature chosen not as a badge of origin but on the ground that it was likely to appeal to the public. The fact that members of the public now associate that feature with its product tells one nothing about what they would think if a product with a similar feature came upon the market."

7–115 As Laddie J. pointed out in *Jeryl Lynn*, this problem is familiar in the pharmaceutical industry. There, the problem is avoided at the outset by the proprietor of a new drug deploying two names. One is for the generic active ingredient, the other is the trade mark used to identify the particular source. If, however, a trader introduces a new product or service to the market, secures a monopoly in that product or service, and proceeds to use only one name for the product or service, the name is likely to be taken as an indication of type and not origin.

---

[3] [1987] R.P.C. 13 at 19.

The problem is even more acute for visual features of novel products, **7–116** principally because the product will almost certainly bear another distinctive trade mark, which the public will see as a/the badge of origin.[4] In that context the visual feature, such as stripes in toothpaste, is unlikely to be taken as another badge of origin unless steps are taken to educate the public that it is. This is an example of a different, yet allied problem—trying to establish a secondary mark as a badge of origin when it is used in conjunction with a primary and distinctive mark.

Primary and secondary marks

Potentially, this is a problem which faces any trader who claims that **7–117** there is more than one badge of origin for his product or service. The trader has a primary mark which the public see as a badge of origin. However, the trader wishes to establish a secondary mark as an additional badge of origin. Whether he succeeds obviously depends on the facts. The potential problem is avoided if, for example, the second-ary mark has an inherent distinctive character of its own,[5] particularly if such a mark joins a group of other secondary marks on a range of products all sold under a recognised house mark. However, the problem faces any trader who adopts as his secondary mark a descriptive or laudatory word, some feature of the goods or their get-up which is seen as decorative or, worse, functional. The problem inherent in the mark itself is then compounded by being used in conjunction with a distinc-tive mark.

Here, the trader faces a dilemma. He does not want to remove his **7–118** primary distinctive mark from the product altogether, for fear that the public would then be unable to identify the origin of the product. On the other hand, he must reduce the public's reliance on the primary mark and attempt to increase recognition and hence reliance on the secondary mark or feature of the product. This exercise is very difficult to do on the product itself, but is much easier to achieve in advertising where a campaign emphasises the secondary mark to the public. In time, the

---

[4] cf. *Philips v. Remington* [1999] R.P.C. 809, where the picture of the three-headed shaver was invariably seen with the primary marks PHILIPS and PHILISHAVE. Note that Jacob J. thought the evidence showed recognition of the sign and association with Philips, but that the sign did not act as an indicator of origin. The primary message was functional: "here is a three-headed shaver". In the Court of Appeal, Aldous L.J. seems to have accepted that the evidence did show that the sign denoted the goods of Philips, but did not distinguish. The third question referred to the ECJ by the Court of Appeal asks: "Where a trader has been the only supplier of particular goods to the market, is extensive use of a sign, which consists of the shape (or part of the shape) of those goods and which does not include any capricious addition, sufficient to give the sign a distinctive character for the purposes of Article 3(3) in circumstances where as a result of that use a substantial proportion of the relevant trade and public (i) associate the shape with that trader and no other undertaking; (ii) believe that goods of that shape come from that trader absent a statement to the contrary?"

[5] An example is the combination of the ICI and DULUX marks. The example quoted by Jacob J. in *Philips v. Remington* was FORD and FIESTA.

advertising may even drop the primary mark, indicating a degree of confidence on the part of the trader in the ability of his secondary mark to distinguish.[6]

7–119   Examples where the secondary mark was held not to be registrable are as follows:

    (1) The primary mark was "Silver Spoon" in a device. The secondary mark was "Treat", registered on evidence of use. Jacob J. said: "Mere evidence of use of a highly descriptive or laudatory word will not suffice, without more, to prove that it is distinctive of one particular trader—is taken by the public as a badge of origin. This is all the more so when the use has been accompanied by what is undoubtedly a distinctive and well-recognised trade mark." (British Sugar, *op. cit.*)

    (2) The primary marks were "Philips" and "Philishave". The secondary mark was a picture of a three-headed rotary shaver, but was treated as covering the three-dimensional shape as well. The secondary mark was described as "limping" by Jacob J. and as "supporting" by Aldous L.J. The registration of the secondary mark was held invalid, principally because the primary message the mark conveyed was "here is a three headed rotary shaver".[7]

    (3) The primary mark was "Dualit". The secondary mark was essentially the shape of the toaster. Registration of the secondary mark was refused, the applicant failing to show that the secondary mark had acquired a distinctive character of its own, through use—perhaps a hard case.[8]

    (4) In "7", the OHIM Third Board of Appeal stated that ".. where a claimed mark appears together with the name of the supplier for specific products, there is a prima facie presumption that that mark functions as a mere identifier sign." ". . . a mere identifier sign will not function as a trade mark, but rather as a means of distinguishing the appellant's various products from one another."[9]

Evidence of distinctiveness

7–120   Gathering a worthwhile body of evidence which proves that a mark is distinctive is not easy. Marks which are distinctive hardly require evidence, and evidence is usually required where there is a perceived problem with distinctiveness. Generally, a combination of evidence is called for and there is a familiar range of options.[10] The greater the

---

[6] Certain cigarette manufacturers are adept at this type of advertising.
[7] *Philips v. Remington* [1999] R.P.C. 809; [1999] E.T.M.R. 816. CA.
[8] *Dualit* [1999] R.P.C. 890, Lloyd J.
[9] [2000] E.T.M.R. 14, paras 23 and 22.
[10] The U.K. Registry Work Manual provides guidance on evidence of use—see Chap. 6, Parts 7.1–7.4. Likewise OHIM has issued a practice note on Evidence of Use.

perceived difficulty in proving distinctiveness, the further one must explore the range of evidential options.

The starting point is usually financial evidence of turnover and **7–121** advertising and promotional expenditure for the goods or services in question, accompanied by examples of how the mark is used in practice. Evidence from third party trade sources can be powerful, but the weight of such evidence often depends upon its perceived independence. Evidence from suppliers or distributors is generally given less weight than evidence from independent trade associations, consumer organisations and competitors. Evidence from trade buyers sheds little light on whether the relevant class of consumers identify the goods or service in question as originating from a particular undertaking because of the trade mark. As Lloyd J. pointed out in *Dualit*, it is the business of trade buyers to know the products of the different manufacturers in the market.[11]

The ultimate source of evidence is the body of consumers for the **7–122** goods or services in question. Well-conducted opinion polls can be persuasive,[12] but require much thought and care and are often very expensive. The problems which have been experienced in the United Kingdom with the reliability of opinion polls over the years have prompted many to use them solely or primarily as a witness gathering exercise, but the courts are increasingly reluctant to permit repetitious evidence from selected members of the public.[13] Often the most powerful evidence of distinctiveness comes from the successful prosecution of cases in passing off. Even if a passing-off case settles before full trial, evidence of true instances of deception will also prove the distinctiveness of the mark.

Gathering worthwhile evidence requires the practitioner to consider **7–123** the circumstances carefully, to utilise the client's knowledge of the trade and, whilst working within budget, to avoid the most common problems which are seen with evidence of distinctiveness. These problems occur for a variety of reasons: due to lack of communication, lack of knowledge/diligence, budgetary constraints and because the mark is not, in fact, sufficiently distinctive. Sometimes attempts are made to disguise perceived weaknesses in the evidence by shrouding them in obscurity, but this is usually counterproductive because then the tribunal loses confidence in the reliability of such evidence of distinctiveness as exists.

---

[11] *Dualit* [1999] R.P.C. 890 at 898.

[12] The *Philips* case provides an example of differing attitudes to surveys in different Member States. In Sweden, market research appeared to have been accepted uncritically as establishing the picture of the three-headed shaver as distinctive; whereas Jacob J. said ". . . experience of detailed examination of opinion polls (including questioning of interviewees) conducted for the purpose of litigation in the English courts has shown that such polls may not be reliable. They certainly require detailed scrutiny. For instance, leading and non-leading questions often produce quite different answers. And sometimes it turns out that the public were just guessing at matters which had never, in their ordinary shopping, bothered them at all.": [1998] R.P.C. 283 at 303.

[13] See Morritt and Chadwick L.JJ. in *Bach Flower Remedies* [2000] R.P.C. 513 at 526, para. 35 and at 535.

Here, we discuss three particular problems which have been the subject of comment in recent cases. They concern: *"mere* evidence of use"; "evidence of association or recognition"; "evidence in standard form".

Mere evidence of use

7–124 There has been a tendency for applicants seeking to demonstrate distinctiveness acquired through use, to rely on financial evidence of turnover and advertising expenditure.[14] This type of financial evidence is a necessary part of any attempt to prove acquired distinctiveness, but it cannot do the job by itself. As Jacob J. has said:

> "Mere evidence of use of a highly descriptive or laudatory word will not suffice, without more, to prove that it is distinctive of one particular trader—is taken by the public as a badge of origin. This is all the more so when the use has been accompanied by what is undoubtedly a distinctive and well-recognised trade mark."[15]

and, later in the same judgment:

> "I have already described the evidence used to support the original registration. It was really no more than evidence of use. Now it is all too easy to be beguiled by such evidence. There is an unspoken and illogical assumption that "use equals distinctiveness". The illogicality can be seen from an example: no matter how much use a manufacturer made of the word "Soap" as a purported trade mark for soap the word would not be distinctive of his goods."[16]

7–125 To similar effect, Morritt L.J. in *Bach Flower Remedies*:

> "First, use of a mark does not prove that the mark is distinctive. Increased use, of itself, does not do so either. The use and increased use must be in a distinctive sense to have any materiality."[17]

This is the point. It is necessary to combine evidence of the scale of use provided by financial information with evidence that the use has been so as to distinguish—on the product, in relation to the service, in advertising or promotion. Sometimes the way in which the mark is presented to the public indicates whether the owner really trusts the mark to function as a trade mark.

---

[14] This tendency may have been encouraged by the standard form of evidence of use which has been part of the Registry Work Manual for some years. The apparent concentration on turnover and advertising expenditure may obscure the fact that what is required is evidence of distinctiveness and not evidence of use.

[15] *British Sugar* [1996] R.P.C. 281 at 286.

[16] At 302.

[17] [2000] R.P.C. 513 at 530.

Evidence of recognition or association

This type of evidence comes from third parties. It can be convincing if **7–126** either the context or other evidence shows that the recognition is of the sign acting as a trade mark—as a badge of origin. Likewise, with evidence of association. More often, the context or other evidence is missing. As Jacob J. observed in *British Sugar*:

> "recognition [of the word] does not necessarily mean recognition as a trade mark." and ". . . recognition is not the same thing as perception as a trade mark—as not only recognising the word but as regarding it, in itself, as denoting the goods of one particular trader."[18]

Also, the Registrar's hearing officer in *Dualit* said[19]: **7–127**

> "As Jacob J. noted in the *Philips* case, the word 'associates' can have a number of meanings. The word could be used by those that mean 'first come to mind', 'best known one' 'only one I can think of—but there may be others'. None of those meanings amount to recognition of the sign as a trade mark. On the other hand the witness may mean 'that shape tells me it's a Dualit—I'd definitely expect it to be a Dualit and be confused if it wasn't'. That sort of recognition is more likely to support the claim that the sign(s) is regarded as a trade mark."

These are subtle, but important distinctions.

Evidence in standard form

This vice often features with inadequate evidence of association. Thus, **7–128** statements are made in essentially standard form by a number of distributors of the applicant's products containing phrases along the lines of: "I associate [the sign in question] with the products of [the applicant]" (the word "exclusively" may be an optional extra) or "I recognise [the sign in question] as being the trade mark of [the applicant]". Although this type of evidence is put in to help, its effect may be worse than neutral for a number of reasons. First, the basic rule that statements should be written in the witnesses' own words has been infringed with the result that it looks as if the words have been put into the mouth of the witness, and they probably have. Secondly, it is quite unclear what the witness means to say, even if he or she did understand the significance of the words put into their statement. Thirdly, even if it is assumed the witness did understand the significance of the words

---

[18] At 304.
[19] *Dualit Ltd's (Toaster Shapes) Trade Mark Applications* [1999] R.P.C. 304 at 317, Mr Allan James. On appeal, Lloyd J. upheld the decision on somewhat different grounds, but was even more sceptical of the evidence.

used, the tribunal will assume that the witness could not say anything more favourable.

Again, as the Registrar's hearing officer observed in *Dualit*[20]:

"Given that this type of application gives rise to relatively subtle questions of perception, it appears to me to be important for the witnesses' evidence to consist of their own words."

The geographical extent of acquired distinctiveness required for Article 7(3) CTM Regulation

7–129 Article 7(1) of the CTM Regulation sets out the absolute grounds for refusal of an application for a Community trade mark. Article 7(2) provides that Article 7(1) ("The following shall not be registered:") shall apply notwithstanding that the grounds of non-registrability obtain in only part of the Community. Then Article 7(3) provides for the major exception: Article 7(1)(b)(c) and (d) "shall not apply if the trade mark has become distinctive in relation to the goods or services for which registration is requested in consequence of the use which has been made of it."

7–130 Following *Windsurfing*, the OHIM Boards of Appeal have stated that two conditions need to be satisfied for a claim of acquired distinctiveness:

"(1) the trade mark must be used in the Community as a whole or, at least, in a substantial part thereof, in such a way that (2) a sufficiently large part of the relevant class of persons recognises the sign as a distinctive trade mark at the time the application is filed (see. . .*Windsurfing*. . . para. 46)."[21]

Even before *Windsurfing*, applicants argued that Article 7(3) was satisfied if they proved acquired distinctiveness in a substantial part of the Community. However, the Court of First Instance has taken a harder line, ruling in *OPTIONS* that a sign must possess a distinctive character throughout the Community:

". . . in order to be accepted for registration, a sign must possess a distinctive character throughout the Community. That requirement, enabling consumers to distinguish the goods or services of one undertaking from those of other undertakings in accordance with Article 4 [CTMR], is essential for that sign to be able to exercise the function of a Community trade mark in economic life.

7–131 The principle of the unitary character of the Community trade mark is expressly applied in Article 7(2) . . . Article 7(3) . . . must be

---

[20] *ibid.*
[21] see *e.g. Ty Nant* [1999] E.T.M.R. 974, para. 15, OHIM Third Board of Appeal.

read in the light of that principle. On that basis, in order to have the registration of a trade mark accepted under Article 7(3) . . ., the distinctive character acquired through the use of that trade mark must be demonstrated in the substantial part of the Community where it was devoid of any such character under Article 7(1)(b), (c) and (d)."[22]

It appears from that passage that the required distinctive character may **7–132** be inherent, acquired or a combination of the two. For example, if a sign has a descriptive meaning in a particular language, but not in other languages, it will be sufficient for the applicant to prove acquired distinctiveness in those countries where the former language is commonly used, and to rely on inherent distinctiveness in other countries in the Community. What is clear is that distinctive character is required throughout the Community.[23]

It is not necessary to prove use in every Member State of the Community. Advertising and sale of goods in major Member States may well spill over into other countries, particularly in continental Europe, sufficiently to render the sign distinctive in those other countries even though sales there may be small or non-existent.

5. Shapes—section 3(2)

"s. 3(2): A sign shall not be registered as a trade mark if it consists **7–133** exclusively of—

(a) the shape which results from the nature of the goods themselves,
(b) the shape of goods which is necessary to obtain a technical result, or
(c) the shape which gives substantial value to the goods."

Derivation

The wording of paragraphs (a) to (c) of section 3(2) of the 1994 Act is **7–134** identical to the wording in Article 3(1)(e) of the TM Directive and Article 7(1)(e) of the CTM Regulation. Differently worded provisions, which were similar to provisions in Benelux law, were contained in the earliest drafts of the Directive, but their applicability at that stage depended upon whether shapes could constitute trade marks under the law of the particular Member State. The reference to "sign" was retained, as in Article 3(1)(a) of the TM Directive.

---

[22] *Options* Case T–91/99, Court of First Instance, March 30, 2000, paras 24–27.
[23] This is obviously correct, particularly in view of the observations about the role of Art. 7(3)CTM Regulation/Article 3(3) of the TM Directive in *Windsurfing* (see above at para. 7–95).

General

7–135 Section 1(1) of the 1994 Act confirms that a trade mark may consist of the shape of goods or their packaging. Before these shapes can achieve registration as trade marks, they must not only satisfy the representation and distinctiveness requirements of section 3(1), they must overcome these three prohibitions in section 3(2). Each subsection is concerned with a different (but not necessarily distinct) aspect of shape. Section 3(2) is designed to prevent these shapes being registered trade marks for goods.

Relevance of distinctiveness or lack of it

7–136 Distinctiveness or lack of it has no direct relevance to these grounds. They cannot be overcome by proving that the mark has acquired distinctiveness through use. However, the types of shape prohibited under section 3(2) are, by their nature, very likely to have difficulties in satisfying the distinctiveness requirements of section 3(1), so distinctiveness or lack of it is very likely to be in issue.[24] The Court of First Instance has held that these shape objections are not to be equated with lack of distinctiveness under section 3(1)(b)/Article 7(1)(b) CTM Regulation.[25] However, it is suggested that if a shape can be shown to be distinctive in fact, it is an indication that the shape does not consist exclusively of one of the forbidden shapes.

Approach to these grounds

7–137 Once it has been confirmed that the sign in question does consist of a "shape", there are two issues:

(1) does the shape in question fall into one (or more) of the prohibited categories?
(2) does the sign consist *exclusively* of that shape?

Sign and shape

7–138 At the outset it is necessary to clarify what sort of signs constitute shapes within these provisions. In the context of goods, "shape" suggests a three-dimensional form. Consistent with that is the definition of "trade mark" in section 1(1) of the 1994 Act, where it expressly

---

[24] In *BP's Application* [1999] E.T.M.R. 282 (oil containers) the OHIM Second Board of Appeal indicated that even if a shape mark consisting of an ordinary container escapes these shape grounds, it will still require a very high degree of distinctiveness in order to be registrable.

[25] Case T–122/99, "*Soap (device)*", Court of First Instance, February 16, 2000.

includes "the shape of goods or their packaging". Confusion may arise at the stage where the sign is represented graphically. The graphic representation of the sign is in two-dimensions. But is the sign a three-dimensional shape or a two-dimensional drawing or picture of the shape? The answer to this question ought to be clear from the description of the mark on the application form. Even if it is not, it should make no difference to the application of these provisions, and this was the approach taken in *Philips v. Remington*.[26]

For the most part, the "shapes" considered against these provisions **7–139** will be three-dimensional shapes and two-dimensional representations of them, but not exclusively so. It is possible to conceive of two-dimensional shapes (such as silhouettes), and there are certain types of laminar goods which can be argued to be essentially two-dimensional (such as novelty greetings cards), even though they are in fact three-dimensional. The real distinction is between external or exterior features (*i.e.* three-dimensional shapes and two-dimensional representations of them, including silhouettes) and patterns or designs applied to the surface or interior of goods.[27] Fortunately, it is likely to be evident when a sign comprises the shape of goods or their packaging, as opposed to being a two-dimensional design or pattern.

What is the true scope of these provisions?

At first sight, the wording of each provision gives some idea of its **7–140** subject-matter and purpose. Beyond that, it is very difficult to discern the true scope of these provisions. Purposive construction does not help much, because the true purpose of these provisions is as obscure as their scope, and there is very little material, other than the words used, to act as a guide.[28] In *Philips v. Remington*, where the sign was a picture of the head of a three-headed shaver, the scope of each of these provisions was discussed, but the Court of Appeal only referred questions concerning section 3(2)(b) of the 1994 Act—technical result—to the European Court. Ultimately, the authoritative interpretation of these provisions will depend upon what the European Court decides is the purpose of each of them, as and when the Court has the opportunity to consider them.

Policy considerations

As a matter of policy, it is suggested that objections to the registration of **7–141** shapes arise for a number of reasons. First, if a mark consists exclusively of a shape falling within section 3(2) (a) or (b) of the 1994 Act, it is likely

---

[26] See the comments of Jacob J. [1998] R.P.C. 283 at 290.

[27] Under similar but not identical provisions in Benelux law, the Benelux Court of Justice held that shapes only cover three-dimensional designs and not two-dimensional patterns such as the Burberry check: *Burberrys* (December 16, 1991).

[28] By way of general observation, Aldous L.J. in *Philips v. Remington* [1999] R.P.C. 809 at 816 said that (b) and (c) appear "to contain words seeking to exclude from registration certain shapes which are protectable under patents, registered designs, copyright and other intellectual property rights".

to be the type of shape which ought to be available for any trader to use—in other words, the shape is either common or, if not common, it is nonetheless considered non-distinctive and/or should be kept available for all traders to use. Secondly, it may be thought that if any protection for a shape falling within (c) is to be conferred, it should be left to the law of registered designs and unregistered design right. Likewise a shape within (b) should be protectable, if at all, through a patent or design right. These other intellectual property rights are conferred for limited periods of time and traders should not be able to use trade mark registrations to extend the periods of protection indefinitely. Unfortunately, these considerations provide little more than general background.

7–142   It is suggested that two other considerations need to be borne in mind. The first is concerned with the nature of shapes. There is an almost infinite variety of distinct signs which comprise words or logo designs, which can be fashioned from the available materials. By contrast, the stock of distinct shapes available for traders to use for their goods and packaging is much more limited, not least because of manufacturing limitations.[29] The second is the possibility that these provisions could exclude from registration signs which are distinctive and do indicate origin. A purposive approach to construction would seek to minimise the extent to which this could occur. Such an approach should not be difficult, because, as a practical matter, these provisions appear to cover shapes which are unlikely to indicate origin.

Exclusively

7–143   These grounds only apply if the sign consists *exclusively* of one of the prohibited types of shape. This requirement raises two related issues. First, there is the general issue of what degree of "surplus" or "capricious addition" is required to avoid any one of the grounds in section 3(1)(c),(d) and (b) or 3(2) (see para. 7–8 *et seq*; above). Secondly, there are particular considerations applicable to each ground in section 3(2), and these are discussed below.

Shapes resulting from the nature of the goods themselves

7–144   This ground prevents the registration of shapes *resulting from* the nature of the goods. It is not concerned to prevent registration of marks consisting of the shape of the goods themselves. Indeed, there would be no reason to do so since the shape of distinctively shaped goods can function as a trade mark. So this ground requires consideration of what

---

[29] As the White Paper explained (para. 2.17): "The Mathys Committee considered that allowing the registration of the shapes of goods or containers would lead to an unacceptable restriction on the choice of shapes available to other traders, given that in practical terms the choice must be limited by manufacturing techniques."

is meant by "the nature of the goods themselves" and "the shape which results" therefrom.

The nature of the goods themselves

The *nature* of the goods refers to their essential qualities or innate **7–145** characteristics—this is what Aldous L.J. was referring to in *Philips v. Remington* when he said it is difficult to envisage such shapes, except those that are produced in nature, such as bananas.[30] Thus, a sign consisting of the shape of a banana for bananas would be a shape which results from the nature of the goods themselves. So too, would a sign consisting of a bunch of bananas for bananas, the shape of an American football for American footballs or the shape of a lemon for lemons.

Thus, when considering the question as to whether a sign is *exclusively* **7–146** a shape which results from the nature of the goods, careful considera- tion needs to be given to the goods in order to determine their nature, and the sign. Consider the following:

(1) A picture of a lemon as a proposed trade mark for lemons would not be registered because the sign would consist exclusively of a shape which results from the nature of the goods themselves—lemons. Likewise a picture of lemons on the branch, or a silhouette of a lemon.

(2) If the goods were lemon juice, then it is suggested that a picture of a lemon should not fall foul of this particular provision, although other objections would be likely under section 3(1)(b) and (c), subject to proof of distinctive character under the proviso. Likewise if the proposed mark was a yellow plastic container in the shape of a lemon.

What are "the goods"?

Thus far, the analysis is overly simple, because of the specification of **7–147** goods chosen. Applicants are most unlikely to make life so simple. In *Philips v. Remington*, Jacob J. raised the question of how does one define what "the goods" are? He pointed out that if one takes the specification of goods, the result will be partly adventitious. What about the shape of an American football for "balls" and not just American footballs? He considered that one could not go simply by the specification of goods. He suggested that the answer was partly one of degree—one must ask what the goods are as a practical business matter. In the Court of

---

[30] [1999] R.P.C. 809 at 820. An OHIM Board of Appeal held that a 3-D mark of a bar of soap with longitudinal curved indents in the sides was a shape which resulted from the nature of the goods themselves. This was obviously wrong, as was accepted on appeal to the Court of First Instance: Case T–122/99 *"Soap (device)"*, Court of First Instance, February 16, 2000.

Appeal, Aldous L.J. said that "the goods" refer to any of the goods in respect of which the mark is registered or sought to be registered. Thus, he said, a picture of a banana for fruit would be just as objectionable as for bananas.[31]

7–148   In practice, this "American football" problem will always arise and there are two possible solutions to it. One is to say that (subject to the other provisions in section 3 of the 1994 Act) the applicant can have a registration consisting of the shape of an American football provided the specification expressly excludes American footballs. This solution produces an unsatisfactory and anomalous situation when one considers the position of the honest trader who uses the shape of an American football to promote his American footballs. Potentially he is driven to section 11 to find a defence, because American footballs will undoubtedly be similar to other balls used in sport. The result of this analysis strongly supports what Aldous L.J. decided. It is enough if the shape results from the nature of any of the goods for which registration is sought, subject only to usual *de minimis* considerations.

7–149   Thus this particular provision has a limited scope. It may be summarised as "You cannot register the natural shape of the goods". The natural shape of goods is descriptive of them. These are shapes which traders may legitimately want to use.

If this analysis is correct, if the goods have been the subject of substantial design input, then there can be no shape which results from the nature of the goods themselves. This explains why *Philips'* three headed shaver mark did not fall foul of this provision. In *Philips v. Remington*, the mark consisted of a picture of a three-headed rotary electric shaver and was registered for "electric shavers". At first instance, Jacob J. held the mark invalid, *inter alia*, as contrary to section 3(2)(b), but not (a) or (c).[32] The Court of Appeal agreed, but for different reasons.[33]

7–150   In view of the overlap between this ground and section 3(1)(c) (and 3(1)(b) and (d) for that matter), one might ask why the proviso to section 3(1) does not apply to section 3(2)—if a trader can overcome a section 3(1)(c) objection by proving acquired distinctiveness, why not a section 3(2)(a) ground? The answer probably lies in the fact that the natural shapes of goods are so descriptive—comparable to "lemon" for lemons, that there is no practical possibility that a trader would be able to educate the public to see such a shape as a badge of origin.

Shape necessary to obtain a technical result

7–151 If this objection is to be raised at all, the technical result will normally be evident. The issues concern (1) whether the shape is *necessary* to obtain a technical result and (2) whether the sign consists *exclusively* of such a shape.

[31] [1998] R.P.C. 283 at 304, and [1999] R.P.C. 809 at 820.
[32] [1998] R.P.C. 283.
[33] [1999] R.P.C. 809.

Necessary

In *Philips v. Remington*, the three shaving heads were arranged as an **7–152** equilateral triangle. *Philips* proved that other arrangements of three heads produced the same technical result and argued that their shape was not therefore *necessary* to obtain the technical result. Aldous L.J. explained why this argument failed:

> "The subsection must be construed so that its ambit coincides with its purpose. That purpose is to exclude from registration shapes which are merely functional in the sense that they are motivated by and are the result of technical considerations." and
>
> "In my judgment the restriction upon registration imposed by the words 'which is necessary to obtain a technical result' is not overcome by establishing that there are other shapes which can obtain the same technical result. All that has to be shown is that the essential features of the shape are attributable only to the technical result."
>
> He also found: "the trade mark does not contain any feature having trade mark significance. It is a combination of technical features produced to achieve a good practical design." (See pages 821–822).

It is suggested that this reasoning is correct.[34] Essentially one looks at the matter through the eyes of the notional designer of the shape. The shape is unregistrable if it is merely functional in the sense it was motivated by, and the result of, technical considerations.

The argument that a shape is not excluded by this provision if the **7–153** same or a similar technical result can be achieved by other shapes is looking at the problem the wrong way round. The focus of this provision is not on the technical result, but on the shape in question and the technical effect of it. If the shape in question does nothing (in substance) but produce a technical result, then the shape is unregistrable. There may be a variety of shapes which produce the same technical result, but all of them are unregistrable, because honest traders should be able to use all such functional shapes in their products. Take the technical result obtained by a corkscrew. The guts of a corkscrew can employ various designs of helical screw. All of them are necessary to achieve the technical result. A sign comprising just the shape of any one of those designs of helical screw should not be registered. However,

---

[34] Although the following questions have been referred to the ECJ: "(i) Can the restriction imposed by the words 'if it consists exclusively of the shape of goods which is necessary to achieve a technical result' appearing in Article 3(1)(e)(ii) be overcome by establishing that there are other shapes which can obtain the same technical result or (ii) is the shape unregistrable by virtue thereof if it is shown that the essential features of the shape are attributable only to the technical result or (iii) is some other and if so, what test appropriate for determining whether the restriction applies?" These points do not seem particularly difficult to answer.

there is plenty of scope for the designer to make his corkscrew look different to those of other manufacturers, so a sign consisting of the shape of the whole of the corkscrew would not consist exclusively of the prohibited shape. Whether the shape of the whole of the corkscrew was seen as a badge of origin is another matter.

7–154   The sub-text is: if the use of such shapes is to be restricted, it is through the law of designs and patents, but not trade marks. The technical result need not be novel or inventive. Indeed, the more commonplace the technical result, the greater the need to prevent registration of the shape or shapes which are necessary to achieve that result.

Again, a shape which is necessary to obtain a technical result is likely also to indicate the intended purpose of the goods, may be customary and/or non-distinctive in any event (*cf.* section 3(1)(c), (d) and (b)).

Exclusively

7–155 The comments under the previous heading indicate what is required. If most of the aspects of shape are necessary to obtain a technical result, but there is sufficient design freedom to allow parts of the shape to be capricious, not contributing to the technical result, then the issue is whether the "surplus" or the "capricious additions" confer sufficient distinctive character on the sign to justify registration. In the context of shapes, the "surplus" must have a substantial effect on the visual appearance of the sign. As Jacob J. said in *Philips*: "I do not believe that shapes with trivial embellishments or variants are outside the exclusion from registrability."[35]

7–156   Other examples of the application of this provision demonstrate some of the difficulties:

(1) The representation of the mark was this description: "a chewy sweet on a stick". Registration was rightly refused under sections 1(1) and 3(1)(a) of the 1994 Act because the sign was not capable of being represented graphically. However, an objection under section 3(2)(b) was also upheld, on the basis that a stick was an entirely functional characteristic of the goods. This reasoning was wrong because the stick was not exclusively the shape sought to be registered.[36]

(2) Application was made to OHIM and the United Kingdom Registry to register the shape of a bar of soap which had indentations on the longitudinal sides. The applications were refused under section 3(1)(b) and its equivalent mainly because the sign just looked like a bar of soap. The OHIM Board of Appeal also upheld an objection under the equivalent of section 3(2)(b) saying: "the indentation on the longitudinal part func-

---

[35] [1998] R.P.C. 283 at 308.
[36] *Swizzels Matlow Ltd's Appln* [1998] R.P.C. 244, Regy.

tions to allow a better grip of the product. Since it could not conceivably be achieved in any other way, the Board considers that the claimed shape consists of a shape which is necessary to obtain a technical result . . ."[37] Although the decision of the Board of Appeal was overturned by the Court of First Instance on various procedural grounds,[38] the conclusion appears correct, but the reasoning is wrong since one could conceive of other shapes of indentation which would achieve the same technical result. The United Kingdom Registry did not take a section 3(2)(b) objection.[39]

Signs which consist exclusively of the shape which gives substantial value to the goods

Of the three provisions, the purpose and scope of this one is the most **7–157** obscure. As Jacob J. observed in *Philips*[40]: "Good trade marks add value to goods—that is one of the things they are for. So one must not take this exclusion too literally." The difficulty is in deciding what degree of value contributed by the shape should trigger this provision.

Jacob J. went on to say: "I think what is meant is an exclusion of shapes which exclusively add some sort of value (design or functional appearance or perhaps something else though I cannot think of anything) to the goods *disregarding* any value attributable to a trade mark (*i.e.* source identification) function. A question of degree is obviously involved. For instance the Rolls Royce grille adds value to a Rolls Royce. But it does so primarily because it signifies Rolls Royce and not because of its inherent shape." Jacob J. concluded that the shape of the three-headed shaver was recognised as having an engineering function, and for that reason it added substantial value to the goods.

The Court of Appeal disagreed with the approach of Jacob J., saying **7–158** that the purpose of this provision was to exclude "aesthetic-type shapes", *i.e.* shapes which have eye appeal.[41] The decision whether the value is substantial requires: "a comparison . . . between the shape sought to be registered and shapes of equivalent articles. It is only if the shape has, in relative terms, substantial value that it will· be excluded from registration." This approach seems to be correct. However, the application of this provision in practice is likely to remain difficult, as is

---

[37] Case 74/1998–3, OHIM BoA, March 15, 1999, see para. 27.
[38] "*Soap (device)*", Court of First Instance, February 16, 2000.
[39] *Procter & Gamble's Trade Mark Application* [1998] R.P.C. 710, Regy. The headnote is incorrect in saying that a s.3(2)(b) objection "was not made out". The objection was not taken, although perhaps it should have been.
[40] [1998] R.P.C. 283 at 309. With the subsequent approval of the CA, [1999] R.P.C. 809 at 822.
[41] At p. 822. This does not mean, necessarily, that the shape must be registrable as a design.

shown by the United Kingdom Registry decision concerning the shape of Dualit toasters.[42]

> In *Dualit*, the signs were the shape of two models of Dualit toaster. In the Registry, the hearing officer decided, after much analysis (which itself indicates the difficulties in applying this provision), that the eye appeal of the signs did give substantial value to the goods. He seems to have reached this view largely because the Dualit toaster was hailed as a "design classic" but also on the evidence of pricing. The price of the Dualit toasters was about seven times the price of most domestic toasters. However, the Dualit toasters were of catering quality, and the price was comparable with other catering toasters of similar quality. Apparently, the competitors in this new niche market created by Dualit priced their offerings midway between Dualit and the ordinary domestic toasters. The robustness and longevity of the Dualit toasters contributed to their high cost, and some value had to be attributed to the Dualit mark which appeared on the toasters. There was therefore, evidence of some price premium. The hearing officer decided that price was an important factor but not the sole factor to be taken into account.

7–159 Some people are prepared to pay extra for good design. The problem is that "good design" can often involve (1) more expensive design input, (2) better quality materials, (3) a more exclusive product (*i.e.* not mass-produced, possibly with some control over retail distribution). The existence of some or all of these factors is likely to lead to a higher price being charged for the product, compared with products which do the same job. This provision appears to require concentration simply on the shape in question, leaving aside the value attributable to the quality of materials or matters of technical or functional design. This is what the hearing officer in *Dualit* was doing.

7–160 Having stripped out factors irrelevant to this provision, one is left with the aspects of design of shape where the designer has room for manoeuvre: does his or her design input to the shape give substantial value to the goods. This issue is to be answered by comparing the shape sought to be registered with shapes of equivalent articles.[43] If the designer has an established reputation,[44] then it is very likely that

---

[42] *Dualit Limited's (Toaster Shapes) Trade Mark Applications* [1999] R.P.C. 304. Regy. On appeal, Lloyd J. rejected the application under s.3(1)(b) and considered he did not need to deal with the "different and difficult issues" which arose under s.3(2)(c). If it had proved necessary to deal with it, the judge said he would almost certainly have referred the matter to the ECJ for a preliminary ruling.

[43] Bearing in mind that eye appeal may be a requirement for any article in the relevant market.

[44] For example, it is suggested that a sign which consisted exclusively of the shape of a table or chair by Eileen Grey or Philippe Starck for furniture would not be registrable under this provision. Such a sign could be registrable for services, but the consent of the designer or his or her estate might well be required.

substantial value would be found. But even if the designer is unknown, "good design" may well be taken to have added substantial value to goods.

6. Public policy, deceptive marks—section 3(3)

Section 3(3)

"s.3(3): A trade mark shall not be registered if it is   **7–161**

   (a) contrary to public policy or to accepted principles of morality, or

   (b) of such a nature as to deceive the public (for instance as to the nature, quality or geographical origin of the goods or service)."

Section 3(3) implements two separate grounds of refusal in Articles 3.1.f and g of the TM Directive. The wording of paragraphs (a) and (b) is identical to the wording used in the TM Directive and in the CTM Regulation.

Public policy, accepted principles of morality

In section 3(3)(a) of the 1994 Act, there is a good deal of overlap between **7–162** "contrary to public policy" and "contrary to accepted principles of morality". Both phrases are deliberately broad. It is suggested that they are designed to prevent registration of marks which would cause offence to a section of the public.[45] Offence may be caused on matters of race, sex, religious beliefs or general matters of taste and decency. Offence may be used by words and/or images. It should be remembered that there is a dividing line between offensive marks and trade marks which might be considered by some to be in poor taste—the latter should not fall foul of this provision.

   Some useful guidance is given in the Work Manual. It suggests that **7–163** marks which encouraged or promoted drugs,[46] counterfeiting,[47] pornography,[48] criminal activity,[49] and the like would be refused under this provision as being contrary to public policy, whereas fairly mild bad language,[50] fairly,[51] or relatively[52] inoffensive expressions and fairly mild

---

[45] OHIM appears to be using this ground to refuse applications for the names of particularly famous people: applications refused under Art. 7(1)(f) for: BILL CLINTON, FIDEL CASTRO, and JOHANNES PAUL II.
[46] e.g. WHITE DOVE (apparently a type of drug) or YOU DON'T NEED WINGS TO FLY.
[47] e.g. COPYCAT PERFUMES.
[48] e.g. SNUFF MOVIES.
[49] See n. 48.
[50] e.g. RAATZ PIZS for beer; KRAP in a device mark. Both accepted. On the other side of the line, BOLOX would be considered contrary to accepted principles of morality in view of bad language. BOLLOX has been refused as a CTM under the equivalent provision of Art. 7(1)(f) of the CTM Regulation. Likewise, at OHIM: FUCK of the YEAR.
[51] BREWERS DROOP, accepted.
[52] OLD FARTS; BAD ASS BOYS. Both accepted.

slang[53] expressions would not be considered to be contrary to accepted principles of morality.

At first instance in *Philips v. Remington*, Jacob J. invoked the continental concept of *ordre publique*. He expressed the view that this was not aimed at preventing the trade mark system being used to obtain automatic and indefinite extension of the monopoly conferred by a patent, design or copyright.[54]

Deceptive marks

7–164 Section 3(3)(b) of the 1994 Act prevents the registration of deceptive marks, a notion familiar from section 11 of the 1938 Act. The paragraph itself cites some non-exhaustive examples: trade marks which are of such a nature as to deceive the public as to nature, quality or geographical origin of the goods or services. In general, if a mark gives rise to an expectation which will not be fulfilled, then registration will be refused. The expectation (and hence the objection) must be a real one, as opposed to something obscure or fanciful, arising from the mark itself.

7–165 There are two features of this provision to note. First, it is an absolute and not a relative ground for refusal. It is concerned with deceptiveness which is inherent in the mark itself, as opposed to deception caused by the similarity of the mark to another.[55] The latter type of objection arises under the relative grounds in section 5. Likewise, an objection that use of a mark would result in passing off arises under section 5(4)(a) and not under section 3(3)(b). Secondly, the paragraph refers expressly to deception caused by the nature of the mark itself. This does not mean that the mark has to be considered in a vacuum. It must be considered against the goods or services applied for and in the general context of the relevant trade.

Practice

7–166 The practice of the Registry under the 1938 Act was to consider notional use of the mark across the entire specification of goods or services. If there was any possibility of deception, then an objection was raised under section 11. The practice resulted in a large number of objections and consequent limitations on the specifications of goods. This was so, even where there was no realistic possibility of deception but the specification was too wide.[56] The Registry has indicated a change in

---

[53] BONK in a device. Accepted.
[54] [1998] R.P.C. 283 at 309. This point was not considered on appeal.
[55] Relying on *Jardex* [1946] R.P.C. 63, an opponent tried to use s.3(3)(b) against GALAXY for "Preparations for killing weeds and destroying vermin", citing public policy in the risk to children accustomed to eating the chocolate so named. This ground failed, because the mark in itself would not deceive the public. The opposition succeeded under s.5(3): GALAXY, May 19, 2000, Regy.
[56] An example is HARTLEY'S STRAWBERRY JAM for jams or fruit preserves, which previously would have been limited to strawberry jam or fruit preserves consisting primarily of strawberries.

practice, so that under the 1994 Act an objection will only be raised where, in the examiner's view, there is any real possibility of deception of the public. The thinking is that traders will use marks responsibly: if they do use marks deceptively, they will lose the registration under section 47, they will fall foul of trading standards and will lose customers. By contrast, the Examination Guidelines[57] issued by OHIM indicate a more rigorous approach, closer to the practice operated under the 1938 Act. In either case, the examiner has to consider the nature of the trade and its customers: does the mark give rise to a real (as opposed to a fanciful) expectation that the goods are made from a particular material, have a particular quality or come from a particular locality? An examiner's initial concerns may be allayed through discussions with the applicant.

Some examples

(1) nature of goods: composition: ORLWOOLA[58] for suits: descriptive if all wool; deceptive if not;   **7–167**

(2) quality of goods: CHINA-THERM[59] for insulated cups made of plastic;

(3) geographical origin of goods: a mark containing the words "Norwegian Sardines"—when there were no such things[60];

(4) geographical origin of services: a mark comprising a shamrock, but not for services from Ireland[61].

(5) EU CHAMPIONSHIP IN BUSINESS MANAGEMENT refused at OHIM under Article 7.1(g);

(6) FILET-O-FISH, also refused under Article 7.1(c) and (g), presumably because descriptive if the goods were a filet of fish, deceptive if not. Likewise ONLYGLASS.

(7) LEM BRUSCO, refused under Article 7(1)(g), presumably because would cause deception as regards Lambrusco.

Examples of other types of deception which could fall within this provision are: marks which imply official approbation[62] or where a substantial change takes place in the form of trade connection between the user and the goods, so as to render the mark deceptive.[63]

---

[57] Examination Guidelines, para. 8.8.
[59] [1910] 1 Ch. 130.
[59] [1980] F.S.R. 21.
[60] *Concord Canning* (1932) 49 R.P.C. 323.
[61] *cf. McGlennon* (1908) 25 R.P.C. 797 and *Grundig* [1968] R.P.C. 89.
[62] *e.g.* ROYAL WORCESTER was refused under the 1938 Act, s.11, not only for possibly suggesting royal patronage, but also because it failed to make it clear that the Worcester being referred to was in the United States:
[63] The 1994 Act contains no equivalent of s.62 of the 1938 Act, but licensing is now much more common, so the change in trade connection would have to be substantial to render a mark deceptive. *cf.* s.46(1)(d).

Overcoming a section 3(3)(b) objection

7–168 In certain circumstances, an objection under section 3(3)(b) may be overcome: it may be possible to file evidence to show that the mark is not deceptive[64]; the applicant may be able to rely on a previous registration for the same goods or services[65]; or, most frequently, the applicant agrees to limit the specification of goods or services, so as to excise those goods or services for which the mark would be deceptive. There were other methods of overcoming deceptiveness objections under section 11 of the 1938 Act which cannot be employed under the 1994 Act, such as conditions of registration (which no longer exist[66]), amendment of the mark itself[67] or variation clauses.

7–169 Often a mark which is more or less descriptive of some goods or services would be deceptive if used in relation to different goods or services. Thus, an application may face objections under sections 3(1)(c) and 3(3)(b) of the 1994 Act from the outset. Alternatively, the objections may arise at different stages. If the principal objection is under section 3(1)(c), the applicant might suggest limiting the goods or services to avoid the descriptiveness objection, with the result that the mark is deceptive in relation to the remaining goods, attracting a section 3(3)(b) objection. In previous editions of this work, it was suggested (under the 1938 Act) that if the objection fails under one head, it will probably fail under both. Whilst that may be true for much of the time, the rule of thumb is probably less applicable under the new provisions. A mark may avoid section 3(1)(c) of the 1994 Act because it is not *exclusively* an indication designating the kind or quality of the goods, yet have a specification which is wide enough to cause the mark to deceive if used in relation to some goods or services.

7. Illegal marks—section 3(4)

Section 3(4)

7–170 "s.3(4): A trade mark shall not be registered if or to the extent that its use is prohibited in the United Kingdom by any enactment or rule of law or by any provision of Community law."

Influence of the TM Directive

7–171 Article 3(2)(a) of the TM Directive is an optional ground for refusal. It provides that a trade mark shall not be registered, etc., where and to the extent that the use of that trade mark may be prohibited pursuant to the

---

[64] For example, METALBOX for boxes other than metal might be considered deceptive. Evidence would show the mark to have acquired a secondary, distinctive and non-deceptive meaning.

[65] The Work Manual suggests that reliance on a previous registration for the same goods or services is conclusive, but one should consider the possibility that the previous registration was accepted in error.

[66] See Sched. 3 to the Act, para. 3(1).

[67] See s.39(2), which only allows corrections which do not substantially affect the identity of the mark.

provisions of law *other than trade mark law* of the Member State concerned or of Community law. By not using the unchanged words of the Directive, potential confusion has been created over what section 3(4) of the 1994 Act covers. Nonetheless, the effect ought to be the same. When section 3(4) is construed in the light of the TM Directive, it is clear that it can only be referring to matters outside the 1994 Act.

Requirements

This is an absolute ground for refusal and, as indicated above, is **7–172** concerned with the trade mark itself. An objection that use of the mark would cause passing off arises under section 5(4)(a) of the 1994 Act and not under this subsection.

For an objection to arise, it is necessary to identify a specific provision in an Act of Parliament or Statutory Instrument or in Community legislation or a specific rule of law. Examples are as follows:

(1) use of the Red Cross and other emblems, contrary to section 6 of the Geneva Conventions Act 1957;

(2) use of the Royal Arms, if the use would be contrary to section 92(2) of the Patents Act 1977;

(3) use of the word "Anzac", contrary to the "Anzac" (Restriction on Trade Use of Word) Act 1916.

So far as Community legislation is concerned, increasingly the E.U. has **7–173** legislated to protect particular designations of origin or characteristics of goods,[68] and one can expect further legislation in the future. Examples are "Champagne", "Cognac", etc. Only persons producing in the appropriate region and/or according to the right method are entitled to use these terms. At the moment, these two designations are protected by Regulation 823/87 of March 16, 1987, which has been amended several times. This Regulation was enforced to prevent the use of "Champagne" in "Elderflower Champagne": see *Taittinger v. Allbev Ltd* [1993] F.S.R. 641. Under section 3(4) of the 1994 Act, Allbev would be prevented from registering a mark such as "Thorncroft Elderflower Champagne".

8. Specially protected emblems—sections 3(5), 4, 57 and 58

Section 3(5)

"s.3(5): A trade mark shall not be registered in the cases specified, **7–174** or referred to, in section 4 of the 1994 Act (specially protected emblems)."

[68] See Chap. 10.

Purpose

7–175 Section 4 of the 1994 Act provides differing measures of protection for emblems in the following six classes: first, matters Royal; secondly, the flags of the United Kingdom; thirdly, national emblems of signatories to the Paris Convention; fourthly, emblems of certain international organisations; fifthly, coats of arms; and sixthly, Olympic symbols. The first, second and fifth classes are concerned with domestic protection for the types of emblem originating in a Convention country outside the United Kingdom which may qualify for protection under the Paris Convention.

7–176 Protection for these classes of emblems originates from four sources. First, Article 6ter of the Paris Convention. Secondly, the optional provisions of Article 3(2) of the TM Directive allow protection to extend beyond Article 6*ter*, citing signs of "high symbolic value, in particular a religious symbol" and "badges, emblems and escutcheons[69]" of public interest.[70] Thirdly, the choices made by the United Kingdom when implementing the optional provisions of the TM Directive.[71] Fourthly, the Olympic Symbol etc. (Protection) Act 1995 which added subsection (5) to section 4.

Although the extent of protection varies between the classes, the basic object is to prevent trade marks being registered which misrepresent themselves as being "official".

Matters Royal

7–177 In essence, signs which are likely to lead persons to think that Royal patronage or authorisation has been conferred shall not be registered without consent. In fact, the protection is somewhat broader than that, since registration of a mark is prohibited without the consent of Her Majesty or the relevant member of the Royal Family if it contains or consists of any of the following:

(1) any of the Royal arms or any of the principal armorial bearings of the Royal arms or any insignia so nearly resembling them as to be likely to be mistaken for any of them;

(2) a representation of the Royal crown or any of the Royal flags;

(3) a representation of Her Majesty or any member of the Royal family or any colourable imitation thereof; or

(4) words letters or devices likely to lead persons to think that the applicant has or recently has had Royal patronage or authorisation.

7–178 The Trade Mark Registry has been provided with a list of those considered by the Queen to be members of the Royal Family.[72] Repres-

---

[69] An escutcheon is a shield displaying a coat of arms.
[70] See Arts 3(2)(b) and (c) of the TM Directive.
[71] No religious symbols have been included, so far as the U.K. is concerned.
[72] Currently numbering 38.

entations of the Royal Arms and the Royal crowns may be found in Registry Work Manual. Persons wishing to apply for consent should contact the Lord Chamberlain at Buckingham Palace.

The position under the 1938 Act

Under the 1938 Act, certain of these matters were dealt with in section 7–179 61, and certain other matters were left to the Rules, and in particular rule 16. Paragraphs (a) to (d) of section 4(1) are clearly based upon the same paragraphs of Rule 16. Rule 16 obliged the Registrar to consider whether to refuse to accept an application for a mark which included such matters. Now section 4(1) of the 1994 Act forbids registration unless a relevant consent has been given.

Under the 1938 Act, application was made for the mark "Queen 7–180 Diana" [1991] R.P.C. 395. The Registrar refused the application, purporting to apply rule 16. The relevant words of rule 16 were substantially identical to those in section 4(1)(d) of the 1994 Act, namely "the use of any words, letters or devices in such a manner as to be likely to lead persons to think that the applicant either has or recently had had Royal patronage or authorisation".

The Board of Trade allowed an appeal and directed that the mark 7–181 proceed to registration. It was held that rule 16 did not apply since there was no Queen Diana and the mark was not likely to indicate Royal patronage. Due to the similarity in the wording of the provisions, it would appear that an application under the 1994 Act for, say, a "King William IV" mark would not fail by reason of section 4(1), even if no consent was obtained. Section 4(1)(d) only militates against a representation without consent of Royal patronage or authorisation which is either current or dates from the recent past. The paragraph avoids any consideration of what may happen in the future, however likely the future events may seem.

Whilst registration may be obtained of "King Charles III" or "King 7–182 William IV" marks without the appropriate consent from members of the Royal Family and prior to any succession in the monarchy, upon the relevant succession taking place such marks ought to be removed from the Register. Whether the result should be revocation of the mark or a declaration of invalidity and whether any such result may be achieved are matters discussed in Chapter 9.

Flags

Section 4(2) of the 1994 Act provides a measure of protection for the 7–183 Union Jack and the flags of England, Scotland, Wales, Northern Ireland and the Isle of Man. Registration of a trade mark which contains or consists of a representation of any of those flags is prohibited if, in the opinion of the Registrar, use of the trade mark would be misleading or grossly offensive. In addition to this specific prohibition, objections might also arise under section 3(3) and 3(5). Thus, a trade mark which incorporates a representation of the Union Jack could be misleading if it suggests that goods are manufactured in the United Kingdom when they are not.

Article 6ter of the Paris Convention

7–184 Section 4(3) prohibits the registration of a trade mark which falls within the cases mentioned in sections 57 and 58 of the 1994 Act. Those sections implement Article 6ter of the Paris Convention, which is concerned with protection for national or state emblems of Convention countries and with emblems of certain international organisations. Registration of trade marks which consist of or contain the protected emblems is prevented in certain circumstances. In this context, a "Convention country" means a country, other than the United Kingdom, which is a party to the Paris Convention.[73]

7–185 Flags of Convention countries receive automatic protection. All other emblems only receive protection if they have been notified in accordance with the procedure specified in section 59. Briefly, the country concerned notifies the United Kingdom that it desires to protect the emblem in question. In the absence of an objection from the United Kingdom, two months after the notification the emblem is regarded as protected under the Paris Convention. The Registrar keeps a list of the protected emblems, which is open to public inspection.[74]

Section 57: national emblems, etc., of Convention countries

7–186 The emblems concerned are flags and, subject to notification, armorial bearings or other state emblems and official signs or hallmarks which indicate control or warranty in relation to goods or services.

Section 57 provides three levels of protection:

(1) marks containing or consisting of the flag of a Convention country cannot be registered without authorisation of the competent authorities unless it appears to the Registrar that use of the flag in the manner proposed is permitted without such authorisation;

(2) for armorial bearings or any other state emblem protected under the Convention, registration must be refused without authorisation of the competent authorities;

(3) official signs or hallmarks cannot be registered without authorisation of the competent authorities in relation to the same or similar goods or services as those in relation to which they indicate control or warranty.

---

[73] See s.55(1)(b). For a list of the signatories to the Paris Convention, see the WIPO website at www.wipo.org.
[74] Pursuant to s.59(4).

In each case the protection is extended to anything which, from a heraldic point of view imitates the flag, other state emblem, sign or hallmark.

Section 58: emblems of international organisations

Subject to the notification procedure, the emblems concerned are **7–187** armorial bearings, flags or other emblems and abbreviations and names of international intergovernmental organisations of which one or more Convention countries are members. This class of emblems cannot be registered without the authorisation of the organisation concerned unless it appears to the Registrar that the use of the emblem in question does not indicate a connection with the organisation and is not likely to mislead the public as to the existence of a connection. The class is extended to cover anything which, from a heraldic point of view, imitates any such emblem. There is a saving for the rights of any person whose bona fide use of their trade mark began before the relevant provisions of the Convention entered into force for the United Kingdom, on January 4, 1962.

Coats of arms

The combination of section 4(4) of the 1994 Act and rule 9 of the Trade **7–188** Mark Rules 2000 prohibits the registration without consent of a trade mark which consists of or contains any arms to which a person is entitled by virtue of a grant of arms by the Crown or any insignia so nearly resembling such arms as to be likely to be mistaken for them. Consent must be given by or on behalf of the person entitled to the arms. Registration of such a mark does not authorise use of the arms contrary to the laws of arms.

The Registrar of Trade Marks has indicated that he calls upon expert **7–189** assistance from the Garter King of Arms in the operation of this provision. If a mark is considered to nearly resemble armorial bearings, the relevant bearings have to be identified and a copy sent to the applicant. The unresolved question is from whose point of view the nearly resembling test should be applied, particularly since insignia considered to be very similar to the expert heraldic eye might look rather different to a member of the general public.

Bearing in mind that sections 57 and 58 of the 1994 Act do not offer **7–190** any protection for arms originating in the United Kingdom, it might be thought that this subsection was supposed to provide equivalent protection. However, this subsection may be contrasted with the provisions of sections 57(4) and 58(3) which extend their protection to any emblem which "from a heraldic point of view" imitates an emblem protected under the Paris Convention. If the intention was to provide the same degree of protection here as United Kingdom arms receive in Convention countries abroad, the intention may not have been fulfilled. In the absence of express provision indicating a specialist test, the "nearly resembling" test here probably ought to be interpreted from the point of view of the general public.

Olympic symbols

7–191 The Olympic Symbol etc (Protection) Act 1995 caused the addition of section 4(5) to the 1994 Act.[75] This prevents the registration of a trade mark which consists of or contains a "controlled representation" unless the application is made by the proprietor of the Olympics Association Right or with his consent. Currently, the British Olympic Association is the proprietor of that Right and it has indicated that it will not normally grant consent.

7–192 "Controlled representation" includes the Olympic Symbol, the Olympic Motto (Citius, Altius, Fortius), the words Olympic(s), Olympian(s) and Olympiad(s) and a representation of something so similar to the Olympic Symbol or the Olympic Motto as to be likely to create in the public mind an association with those items.

An application filed in 1998 for the word OLYMPIC alone and with the device of an Olympic torch for cooking oils was refused registration under section 3(5) even though the applicant had been using the marks on a significant scale since 1990.[76]

9. Bad faith—section 3(6)

Section 3(6)

7–193 s.3(6): "A trade mark shall not be registered if or to the extent that the application is made in bad faith."

Introduction

7–194 The 1994 Act does not define the term bad faith. The concept is not unknown in United Kingdom law but continental lawyers are likely to be more familiar with it, since consequences flow from acts done *contra bones mores* or in bad faith in many civilian systems of law. The provision in section 3(6) derives from the optional[77] Article 3(2)(d) of the TM Directive. Both provisions contemplate bad faith extending to the

---

[75] In force from September 21, 1995.
[76] Olympic (SRIS O/081/00), Regy.
[77] This provision may be optional because not all countries have trade mark registries which are equipped to examine applications with the rigour of the U.K. Registry. Bad faith is not an absolute ground for refusal of a CTM *application* (see Art. 7), although the relative grounds prevent a registration in the name of an agent of the proprietor of the mark without consent (Art. 8.3). Bad faith is a ground upon which a CTM registration may be declared invalid (Art. 51.1(b)).

whole or only part of the application.[78] If the whole of an application is made in bad faith, it indicates (though not exclusively) that the applicant has no entitlement to the mark or, in words used under the 1938 Act, the applicant is not the proprietor of the mark. It is worth noting that this is the only ground of refusal under which issues of proprietorship can be raised.[79] If the bad faith extends to only part of an application, that indicates (again not exclusively) that the scope of the application is too broad, the prime example being that the specification of goods or services sought is too wide. Those may be the main situations which arise. However, this provision is of the broadest scope. The making of any false statement or representation, even implicit, in connection with an application for a trade mark may be sufficient to fulfil this ground.[80]

When may the issue arise?

Although section 3(6) of the 1994 Act is concerned with the state of **7–195** affairs which existed as at the date of application, the issue of whether the application was made in bad faith can arise in four different ways for a United Kingdom registered trade mark. First, in sufficiently obvious cases, the ground may be raised by the Registry at the examination stage.[81] Secondly, at the opposition stage. Thirdly, in proceedings for a declaration of complete or partial invalidity of a registration under section 47. Fourthly, under section 48(1) (effect of acquiescence). For a CTM, bad faith is not a ground for refusal of a CTM application and the issue can only be raised in proceedings for invalidity under Article 51.1.(b) and to defeat an allegation of acquiescence under Article 53.[82]

Under sections 47 and 48, the allegation that an application was made **7–196** in bad faith can be raised in relation to any registered trade mark, whether the application for it was examined under the 1994 Act or under previous legislation. Although not necessarily determinative, the statements made by the applicant to the Registry at the time of application and during the application stage are likely to be relevant to the issue of bad faith. Hence it is necessary to examine what statements

---

[78] Not as explicitly as Art. 13 of the TM Directive—see G. Hobbs Q.C. as the appointed person in *Demon Ale* [2000] R.P.C. 345 at 355.

[79] An Italian Judge has observed that the purpose of the bad faith provision is there to provide "advanced protection to any party which, even if it has planned to register a trade mark it uses, has not actually done so yet." and also to those situations where the proprietor is still preparing to use his mark, where he has a "legitimate expectation" of protection. See *Benckiser v. Henkel* [1999] E.T.M.R. 614 at 637, Court of Naples.

[80] Although, as G. Hobbs, Q.C. (as the appointed person) put it in "*Demon Ale*" [2000] R.P.C. 345 at 356, "I do not think that section 3(6) requires applicants to submit to an open-ended assessment of their commercial morality". The ground is restricted to *the application* made in bad faith.

[81] See the Registry's Practice Amendment Circular PAC 10/00 concerning "Examination of wide specifications and objections under section 3(6) of the Act".

[82] The first OHIM decisions on bad faith have emerged. They indicate that OHIM is taking a restrictive view of bad faith. See further paras 7–228 *et seq.*, below.

and representations had and have to be made by applicants for trade marks.

An applicant under the 1938 Act

7–197 Section 17(1) of the 1938 Act provided that "Any person claiming to be the proprietor of a trade mark" could apply in the prescribed manner. In *Al-Bassam*[83] the Court of Appeal were concerned with the operation of sections 17 and 18 of the 1938 Act. It was held that the provision in section 17(1) was satisfied if a bona fide claim was made. If, later, an opposition was commenced under section 18 in which the applicant's claim to proprietorship was challenged, then the question of proprietorship had to be decided as a matter of legal right, whether or not the rival claimant was the opponent. Under the 1938 Act, at that latter stage, an inquiry as to whether the claim was made bona fide was of little, if any, relevance.

An applicant under the 1994 Act

7–198 Every application for registration of a trade mark made under the 1994 Act requires a statement by or on behalf of the applicant that: "The Trade Mark is being used by the applicant or with his or her consent, in relation to the goods or services stated, or there is a bona fide intention that it will be so used." This statement on Form TM3 derives from section 32(3) of the Act.[84] As well as the express statement concerning use or a bona fide intention to use the trade mark in relation to the goods or services stated in the application, it is suggested that the applicant also makes an implicit representation through the assertion of use or intention to use that he or she is the person entitled to use the trade mark. Although the issue is whether the application was made in bad faith, even under the 1994 Act the question of proprietorship, as a matter of legal right, is likely to be essential background against which the issue of bad faith is decided.

Pleading and practice

7–199 Before the United Kingdom Registry began to exercise case management, adopting and adapting the principles of the Civil Procedure Rules, bad faith was frequently pleaded[85] only to be abandoned at the hearing, by which time it was clear that there was no evidence to support the

---

[83] [1995] R.P.C. 511, CA.
[84] This section has been pleaded, in conjunction with s.3(6), as a ground of opposition. Section 32(3) provides no separate ground of refusal and should not be pleaded.
[85] Almost as a catch-all, just in case something turned up. There was little adverse consequence.

allegation. There was a lack of appreciation that an allegation of bad faith is a serious one and, like an allegation of fraud, ought to be properly substantiated in a pleading and pleaded only where there exists prima facie evidence justifying the allegation.[86] The introduction of case management in early 2000[87] has meant that unparticularised allegations of bad faith are now unlikely to pass the Registry's initial review of the statement of grounds.

One might have expected allegations of bad faith to have resulted in a **7–200** greater recourse to discovery or disclosure of documents and/or cross-examination. However, in practice, where triable issues of bad faith have arisen in oppositions, the vast majority have been decided without any cross-examination.[88] In at least some cases, it is apparent that the need for cross-examination was avoided by the applicant simply failing to respond at all in his evidence to issues of bad faith raised in the opponent's evidence which called for a response. The absence of cross-examination seems to have caused no difficulty in most cases, since the outcome is normally apparent. However, in more complex or finely balanced situations, an allegation of bad faith may fail unless precise allegations have been pleaded in the statement of grounds, spelt out in the written evidence or are put to the applicant in cross examination.

In the absence of guidance from higher authority, it has been the **7–201** practice[89] of the Registry hearing officers to acknowledge that the Act contains no definition of the term bad faith, leaving it to the tribunal or court to determine whether an application was made in bad faith based upon the circumstances of a particular case (thus far, an entirely correct practice), and to refer to three examples of where bad faith *might* be found. The three examples are taken from some Notes on Sections, published by the Patent Office, and based upon the Notes on Clauses provided to Parliament during the passage of the Trade Marks Bill in relation to section 3(6). The three examples are:

(1) "where the applicant had no bona fide intention to use the mark, or intended to use it, but not for the whole range of goods and services listed in the application."

(2) "where the applicant was aware that someone else intends to use and/or register the mark, particularly where the applicant has a relationship, for example as employee or agent, with that

---

[86] See, in a different context, the comments of Lightman J. in *Melton Medes Ltd v. S.I.B.* [1995] 2 W.L.R. 247 at 256.

[87] See the changes made in the Trade Mark Rules 2000, in force February 17, 2000 and the two "Tribunal Practice Notices" TPN 1/2000 and 2/2000, the first concerned with case management and the second with the bases upon which costs are awarded. With these powers, the Registry is now able to take a tougher line.

[88] Of course, where allegations of bad faith arise in proceedings in the High Court, disclosure and cross-examination are the norm: *e.g. Gromax Plasticulture Ltd v. Don & Low Nonwovens Ltd* [1999] R.P.C. 367, Lindsay J., where the allegation failed. See further below.

[89] See, *e.g. Give Me Five* (SRIS O/133/99), *Kundry SA's Application* [1998] E.T.M.R. 178 , and *Mickey Dees (Nightclub) TM* [1998] R.P.C. 359, all Regy.

other person, or where the applicant has copied a mark being used abroad with the intention of pre-empting the proprietor who intends to trade in the United Kingdom."

(3) "where the mark incorporates the name or image of a well-known person without his agreement. (This should not be taken as meaning that this provision is legislating for the protection of a personal name or reputation—these remain unprotected under English law, but the nexus between unregistrability and the name of a well-known person is that of bad faith in which the application is made.)"

The significance of these notes is capable of being misconstrued[90] and the last example could easily be misunderstood.[91] Now that a body of decisions involving the provision has been established, it is safer to refer to decided cases by way of guidance.[92] The Registry now cite and follow the remarks of Lindsay J. in *Gromax* (see below).[93]

Examples

7–202 Decisions made under section 3(6) of the 1994 Act fall into one of three broad categories: ownership of the mark, intention to use and width of specification. Examples in each of these categories will be discussed in turn, since they raise somewhat different, although sometimes overlapping issues.

Ownership of the Mark

Bad faith established

7–203   (1) Some two years after use of the mark commenced in the United Kingdom, the sole distributor registered a slightly different form of the mark in his own name. The mark had been coined in the USA three years before being used in the United Kingdom. The true owner of the mark succeeded in having his name substituted as proprietor (under section 60). But for that provision, a declaration of invalidity would have been made, it being held that the application was made in bad faith.[94]

---

[90] The first two were referred to by one hearing officer as "examples of where Parliament intended that the bad faith provision should apply". The first two examples may well constitute bad faith, but Parliament made no expression of its intention in that regard in the 1994 Act.

[91] See the judgments in *Elvis Presley* [1999] R.P.C. 567 CA, and [1997] R.P.C. 543, Laddie J. See further, below.

[92] Although it should be remembered that factual analogies are of limited use. It is the principles which matter, *cf.* the use of passing-off cases as authorities.

[93] Although his remarks that: ". . . bad faith includes dishonesty and . . . also some dealings which fall short of the standards of acceptable commercial behaviour observed by reasonable and experienced men in the particular area being examined." are being treated as a definition—which is precisely what Lindsay J. wanted to avoid.

[94] *Travelpro* [1997] R.P.C. 864, Regy. The registered proprietor made no response to the allegations.

(2) A Spanish applicant applied to register JARVARD for items of clothing. In the United Kingdom, the mark was held to be not confusingly similar to HARVARD. In proceedings between the same parties in Spain, the applicant had opposed the opponent's application for HARVARD on the grounds that it was confusingly similar to JARVARD. The applicant had previously applied to register HARVARD for itself in Spain, despite being aware of the opponent's college and of its concern about the possibility of confusion. Bad faith was held to be established, apparently on the basis of "making use of another's reputation" and because the applicant offered no response to the allegations.[95]

(3) The mark applied for showed a "striking similarity" to marks **7–204** which had been long used by the opponent. The applicant did not deny an allegation that he had clearly copied the mark. Application refused.[96]

(4) The opponent acquired a business owned by the applicant. Whilst still employed as a manager by the opponent, the applicant applied for two different marks. Oppositions succeeded under section 3(6).[97]

(5) The opponent, an Australian company, appointed a United **7–205** Kingdom distributor who utilised the services of the applicant to warehouse and distribute the product. The applicant also ordered the product direct from the opponent. Bad faith was held established, the applicant being "fully aware" of the opponent's intention to use the mark in the United Kingdom. The applicant failed to offer any response to the prima facie case.[98]

(6) The opponent had an established business in the U.S. under the mark and had begun to trade in the United Kingdom. The applicant was a United Kingdom customer and had proposed a licence arrangement. The applicant adopted the U.S. mark. When challenged, he sought to register the mark in combination with his own name. The combined mark was confusingly similar to the U.S. mark. Bad faith was established: "It is difficult to see how a person who applies to register a mark in his own name which he has previously recognised as the property of a potential overseas principal can be said to be acting in accordance with acceptable standards of commercial behaviour."[99]

---

[95] *Kundry SA's Application* [1998] E.T.M.R. 178, Regy. Some of the allegations appeared to have little to do with bad faith so far as the U.K. application was concerned.
[96] *Team Lotus* [1999] E.T.M.R. 669, Regy.
[97] *Customer Care* (SRIS O/039/99) and *Profinish* (SRIS O/043/99) both Regy.
[98] *Be Natural* (SRIS O/106/99), Regy.
[99] *New Century* (SRIS O/018/00), Regy.

7-306   (7) An independent producer was hired on a freelance basis to produce a radio programme using the broadcaster's resources. Even though the producer instigated the name BLACK MIX, clearly felt he was the prime mover in persuading the broadcaster to make the programme and had a significant role as producer, his role did not carry with it proprietorial rights over the name. The hearing officer decided the issue of proprietorship, as a matter of legal right, against the applicant and held, in consequence, that the application was made in bad faith despite the finding also that he had "a genuine and strongly held belief . . . that he was entitled to the mark and could apply for registration."[1]

Bad faith not established

7-207   (1) In the early days of a joint venture, one of the participants, the defendant, registered the mark adopted for the products to be sold by the venture. The defendant later ceased to be the manufacturer, but still maintained some measure of quality control over the products. The plaintiff, originally the distributor in the venture, alleged the application had been made in bad faith. It was held that, at the date of application, the defendant honestly regarded itself as *a*, indeed, *the* person launching the product and entitled to apply for registration.[2]

(2) The opponent alleged that the applicant had copied its mark on a visit to a trade show in the USA. The applicant gave an explanation of the derivation of its mark and disputed the opponent's version of a telephone conversation said to be material. Neither party wished to attend a hearing. The allegation of bad faith failed, it being held that the applicant's version of events was more likely.[3]

7-208   (3) A racing driver applied to register his nickname "JOS THE BOSS". The allegation of bad faith from the opponent, Hugo Boss Ltd, was that the applicant had deliberately sought to register a trade mark to which he was not entitled. The opponent wholly failed to discharge the onus on it.[4]

(4) The application was for an "A in a star" device mark. The opponent made an overstated claim to a "worldwide reputation" in their mark, which was held to be very similar. The evidence from both sides was said to be "very thin". The

---

[1] *Black Mix* (SRIS O/048/00), Regy. A case where, subjectively, the applicant really believed the mark was his whereas, objectively, it was held that he could not walk off with the mark. The objective view prevailed.

[2] *Gromax Plasticulture Ltd v. Don & Low Nonwovens Ltd* [1999] R.P.C. 367, Lindsay J., who declined to attempt a definition of bad faith, for fear of the tendency of others later to construe the paraphrase rather than the words of the 1994 Act itself.

[3] *Wackers* [1999] R.P.C. 453, Regy.

[4] *Jo's the Boss* (SRIS O/170/99), Regy.

allegation of bad faith failed since the opponent failed to discharge the onus on it to establish that their mark was well known to the point that the applicant must have known it belonged to them, or would have known through some other circumstance, such as a trade connection.[5]

(5) An allegation that the applicant "should have been aware" of the opponent's mark was held, not surprisingly, to be not sufficient to sustain this ground of bad faith.[6]

No bona fide intention to use the mark

Bad faith established

(1) An apparently dormant company, which offered various ser- **7–209** vices of dubious legality and was operated by "a trade mark broker", registered a mark in the United Kingdom and various other European countries in various classes. The applicant for invalidity had used the mark extensively in the USA. Whilst the Americans must have suspected their mark had been hijacked, the issue was whether the registered proprietor had had a bona fide intention to use the mark. This allegation of bad faith succeeded, the proprietor of the mark failing to respond to the "strong prima facie case" established in all the circumstances.[7]

(2) The applicant, an antique dealer, applied for a mark for "beer; mineral waters". There was some evidence of telephone conversations with the applicant in which he was alleged to have admitted that he made the application to prevent the mark being used on "alcopops", that he had nothing to do with brewing and did not at any stage intend to use the mark in connection with beer. In his counterstatement, the applicant said he was thinking of a mineral water not a beer, but filed no evidence. Since the applicant had no trade in beer and no bona fide intention to trade in beer, the statement to the contrary on his application form was held to have been made in bad faith, leading to the whole of the application being refused.[8] The decision was confirmed on appeal.[9]

Bad faith not established

(1) The opponent alleged the applicant had no bona fide intention **7–210** to use the mark applied for in respect of "telephonic and broadcast communication services via cable, satellite and televi-

---

[5] "*A*" (SRIS O/081/99), Regy.
[6] "*Give Me Five*" (SRIS O/133/99), Regy and "*7 Heaven*" (SRIS O/023/99), Regy, are just two examples where the allegation of bad faith should never have been made. Unless there is a clear intent to ride on the back of an established reputation, the adoption of a mark which is merely similar is unlikely to warrant an allegation of bad faith.
[7] *Oxyfresh* (SRIS O/095/99), Regy.
[8] *Demon Ale* (SRIS O/072/99), Regy.
[9] Appt'd person (G. Hobbs, Q.C.) September 28, 1999. When the basis of the objection was explained to the applicant, he was not disposed to dispute it. Neither the pleadings nor the evidence had made the point clearly.

sion" because the applicant had no licence from the ITC to provide a television broadcasting service. In response, the applicant filed evidence stating it intended to apply for appropriate licences and to commence use once registration of the mark was achieved. Since the application could be one in a sequence of commercial steps, the ground of opposition was dismissed.[10]

(2) A few days after an independent producer and a broadcaster parted company, the producer applied to register BLACK MIX, the name of a radio programme produced by him on a freelance basis for the broadcaster. It was said he had no bona fide intention to use; alternatively that his intention was contingent. A lengthy explanation of the producer's steps to develop a community radio station defeated the attack. Bad faith was established on the issue of proprietorship (see paragraph 7–206, illustration (7), above).[11]

Width of specification

Bad faith established

7–211   (1) A singer, known professionally as Mickey Dee, was employed as manager and joint licensee of a nightclub, which was relaunched shortly after his recruitment as Mickey Dees. He secured registration of MICKEY DEES (NIGHTCLUB) in respect of "provision of nightclub services; presentation of live music performances". The owner of the nightclub applied for a declaration of invalidity, alleging bad faith. The claim succeeded so far as the provision of nightclub services were concerned, because the proprietor of the mark could not claim to be able to provide the full range of services and because he knew the mark was being used by his employer. It was held that the proprietor of the mark was not entitled to claim ownership of the mark in respect of all the services claimed, but was given the opportunity to restrict his registration to "the provision of singing and musician services by an entertainer".[12]

(2) The application was filed in respect of "on-line services including video on-line magazine service". The opponent claimed that the mark was not being used and the applicant had no intention to use. The hearing officer referred to the Registry's current practice which was that the term "on-line services" was too vague and required clarification. The applicant had ceased trading and offered no evidence to support such a wide-ranging specification of services. It was held the application was filed in bad faith.[13]

---

[10] *YTV* (SRIS O/042/99), Regy.
[11] *Black Mix* (SRIS O/048/00), Regy.
[12] *Mickey Dees (Nightclub) TM* [1998] R.P.C. 359, Regy.
[13] *Neon* (SRIS O/020/99), Regy.

(3) In earlier proceedings[14] the opponent applied for revocation for **7-212**
non-use of two marks acquired by the applicant some five years
previously. Immediately prior to the revocation proceedings,
the opponent had given notice of its interest in adopting the
mark, and mentioned that its investigations showed no use of
the marks. This correspondence led to the fresh application for
the same mark. The applicant gave no instructions about the
specification of goods, so its agent, erring on the side of caution,
copied the specifications from the earlier registrations. The
applicant filed evidence saying they had a particular lollipop
product in mind for the mark and indicating the mark would
not be applied to other products in their range. It was held that
the application was filed in bad faith, for two reasons: the
applicant was aware that the opponent wished to use the mark,
the application being filed to present another defence and to
frustrate the intentions of the opponents; secondly, because it
was clear that the applicant had no intention of using the mark
on anything other than a lollipop, whereas the application was
for a wide range of goods: confectionery, chocolate, biscuits,
cakes, etc.[15]

Bad faith not established

Bad faith was alleged on the basis that there was no intention to use the **7-213**
mark in relation to all or any of the goods applied for. The hearing
officer commented that the range of goods applied for was "not overly
wide" and the evidence of use since the application showed the
intentions had been put into practice. The allegation failed.[16]

What is the test?

It has been observed that there is no material to indicate the legislative **7-214**
intent behind the concept of bad faith.[17] However, it is suggested that
the appropriate test, to be applied in all the circumstances, is tolerably
clear. Lindsay J. has said:

> "I shall not attempt to define bad faith in this context [*sc.* of section
> 3(6)]. Plainly it includes dishonesty and, as I would hold, includes
> also some dealings which fall short of the standards of acceptable
> commercial behaviour observed by reasonable and experienced

---

[14] *Magic Ball* (No. 1) SRIS O/084/99, Regy, which succeeded in part.
[15] *Magic Ball* (No. 2) SRIS O/123/99, Regy. On new evidence being admitted on appeal,
the finding of bad faith was reversed: S. Thorley, Q.C. as the appointed person, August 1,
2000.
[16] *Delice* (SRIS O/162/99), Regy.
[17] By Robert Walker J. in ROADRUNNER, *Road Tech Computer Systems Ltd v. Unison
Software (UK) Ltd* [1996] F.S.R. 805 at 817, 818.

men in the particular area being examined. Parliament has wisely not attempted to explain in detail what is or is not bad faith in this context; how far a dealing must so fall-short in order to amount to bad faith is a matter best left to be adjudged not by some paraphrase by the courts (which leads to the danger of the courts then construing not the Act but the paraphrase) but by reference to the words of the Act and upon a regard to all material surrounding circumstances."[18]

Having referred to those observations, G. Hobbs Q.C. (as the appointed person) said (in *Demon Ale* [2000] R.P.C. 345 at 356):

"These observations recognised that the expression 'bad faith' has moral overtones which appear to make it possible for an application for registration to be rendered invalid under section 3(6) by behaviour which otherwise involves no breach of any duty, obliga- tion, prohibition or requirement that is legally binding on the applicant. Quite how far the concept of bad faith can or should be taken consistently with its Community origins in Article 3(2)(d) of the Directive is a matter upon which the guidance of the European Court of Justice seems likely to be required; *Road Tech Computer Systems Ltd v. Unison Software (UK) Ltd* [1996] F.S.R. 805 at 817, 818, *per* Robert Walker J."

Earlier in the decision, (also at p. 356) he said:

". . . the observations of Lord Nicholls on the subject of dishonesty in *Royal Brunei Airlines Sdn. Bhd. v. Philip Tan* [1995] 2 A.C. 378 (PC) at p389 do seem to me to provide strong support for the view that a finding of bad faith may be fully justified even in a case where the applicant sees nothing wrong in his own behaviour."

7–215 Clearly the test is not subjective: if this ground depended wholly upon what the applicant said his state of mind was at the relevant date, it would do little to promote a reliable system of registered trade marks, let alone harmonisation. At the other extreme, it is unlikely that the test is wholly objective, since no account would then be taken of the state of mind of the applicant, which must have some relevance. Therefore, it is suggested that the appropriate test is principally objective with a limited subjective element so that evidence from the applicant as to his state of mind at the time may be taken into account.[19] What an applicant says

---

[18] *Gromax, op cit.*, at 379.
[19] This has the advantage of having the type of flexibility employed in continental systems when consideration is given to acts allegedly done *contra bones mores*. It is also required to take account of the (rare) possibility that there may be evidence from a person (most likely an ex-employee or possibly an assignor) who gives evidence which demonstrates bad faith, *e.g.* that the specification of goods was deliberately extremely broad.

about his state of mind at the relevant time cannot be determinative. Particularly once the allegation of bad faith has been made, an applicant may honestly convince himself that he was in the right, even though an objective observer, applying the standards of a reasonable businessman would view the applicant as being in the wrong. However, in cases which are evenly balanced or near the line and particularly in view of the seriousness of the allegation, evidence from the applicant as to his state of mind and intentions, unless seriously undermined, may defeat an allegation of bad faith.

Perhaps the issue will be most difficult in a case where an applicant **7–216** says (and is believed) that when he made his application he believed he was entitled to make it, thus making a bona fide claim, yet from an objective viewpoint he was not entitled to claim ownership of the mark. Even in this type of situation, the test suggested above allows the issue of bad faith to be decided according to who is entitled, as a matter of legal right, to ownership of the mark, which ought to be the factor of greatest importance.[20]

Other situations

In the light of the above, it is suggested that bad faith would be **7–217** established in the following situations which have not yet arisen for decision. Comment is offered in relation to some of these examples:

Attempts to hijack a mark or spoil a competitor's plans

(1) The applicant has no bona fide intention to use the trade mark **7–218** at all, but wishes to prevent a competitor from using the, or a similar, mark;

(2) The applicant has no present or fixed intention to use the mark, but wishes to stockpile the mark for use at some indeterminate time in the future;

(3) The applicant becomes aware that someone else plans to use the mark, and files a pre-emptive application with a view to selling it.[21]

The specification of goods or services is too broad

(1) The applicant has used the mark on a limited range of goods for **7–219** some years. He has no current plans to expand his use beyond the existing range of goods but the specification of goods for which he applies is much wider.

(2) The applicant has used the mark on a limited range of goods for some years. He has no current plans to expand his use beyond

---

[20] This is basically what happened in *Black Mix* (SRIS O/048/00), Regy.

[21] *cf. British Telecommunications & others v. One in a Million* [1999] 1 W.L.R. 903, CA., where Internet domain names comprising the names of well-known companies were held to be "instruments of fraud" in the hands of traders in domain names.

the existing range of goods but he is advised to apply for a specification of goods of much wider scope, in order to secure the widest infringement rights. He follows the advice.

In this latter example, the applicant might think, having acted on advice from his specialist advisers, that he was safe from an allegation of bad faith. In fact, his position ought to be worse or no better than the applicant in the first example. If such advice were given, the dangers of following the advice should be spelt out. If they are not, then the applicant may ultimately have a claim against his adviser.

(3) The proprietor of the mark secured his registration well before the 1994 Act. When applying, the specification of services was drafted in accordance with the general practice then prevailing so as to cover the services for which the mark was used/ intended to be used plus a wide range of services which were possibly of the same description to ensure the broadest possible rights of infringement.

(4) A mark used by a software house for a specialist accounting software package secured a registration for "computer hardware and software".

7–220 Some discussion of these two examples is required. Where there is a clear discrepancy between actual use/intended use and the specification applied for, bad faith can be found with relative ease. Often the discrepancy will not be so obvious—the Registry have indicated[22] that they can only raise a section 3(6) objection in extreme cases or where vague or wide terminology is used. The difficulty is in deciding the appropriate level of generality in a specification which gives adequate protection to the trader concerned. Often, the appropriate level of generality can only be decided with knowledge of the trade concerned.

7–221 It is likely that a very large number of registrations were made under previous Acts which have specifications of goods or services which are "too broad" according to the new order of the TM Directive and 1994 Act. With the broader infringement provisions of the 1994 Act, it is suggested that registrations should be confined to specifications of those goods or services in respect of which the mark is actually used. There is now no need or place for a registration to provide any additional penumbra of protection around the actual scope of use/intended use. In many cases, the width of the specification is unlikely to make any practical difference. However, in appropriate cases of conflict between the actual business of one party and a wide registration of another, the solution is likely to be an attempt to restrict the width of the specifica-

---

[22] Work Manual, Chap. 6, section 9.11.1, but note rule 57 which allows the Registrar to call for such information or documents as he may require—if necessary to justify a wide specification.

tion with the two-pronged attack of non-use and bad faith. Token use to avoid the charge of non-use may support the allegation of bad faith. If there are difficulties with non-use, then difficult questions may have to be tackled in the allegation of bad faith. The proprietor would argue that he could not possibly be held to have made his application in bad faith because he followed the established practices of the time. This argument could not be met by transposing back in time practices or considerations under the 1994 Act. Ultimately, it may be the case that the degree of harmonisation intended in the Directive was not sufficient to cope with all the problems which might arise in the process of changing from the 1938 Act regime to the new regime.

Marks incorporating the name or image of a well-known person, without their agreement

This is the third example put forward by the Registry as a situation **7–222** where bad faith might be found. Since it can hardly have been the intent of the legislature for this bad faith provision to incorporate a new and distinct right of personality, the wide range of situations covered by this example need careful consideration. It has been indicated that the example was intended only to apply to living persons,[23] but consideration of the possible positions of both living and deceased well-known persons will serve to highlight the difficulties in finding bad faith within this example.

Some people become well known to the public because they are the **7–223** source of products which are sold on an extensive scale and are popular—pop musicians are a prime example. Others, such as sports personalities or entertainers, become famous because of what they do—but what they do does not normally involve the provision of any product or service, other than to the very limited extent of providing entertainment. Generally, therefore, only a relatively small proportion of "famous people" have become so because their name or image indicated the trade origin of products or services. For those that have, one would expect appropriate trade marks to have been registered in the normal way. Where trade mark protection is lacking, such persons may be vulnerable to their trade marks being "hi-jacked" but that is not a problem which is confined to well-known persons and bad faith may be established on the normal principles discussed above.

In certain disciplines, fame brings opportunities to endorse the **7–224** products of particular manufacturers. Endorsement of related products by a well-known sports personality is simply a method of promoting the products in question. The name or image of the well-known person does not and is not intended to indicate trade origin. Far from it. The name or image of the personality is used in conjunction with the trade mark applied to the product. The name or image simply identifies the person.

---

[23] By the Registry's hearing officer in *Jane Austen* SRIS O/198/99, July 12, 1999.

In certain circumstances, personalities may move beyond endorsement to use their own name or image as the trade mark of products related to what they do. Provided that the public are educated to perceive the name or image as indicating trade origin,[24] then such persons have joined the ranks of trade mark owners. Bad faith may arise on the normal principles discussed above, if a third party hijacks the mark.

7–225 Thus far, we have identified some examples where the name or image of well-known persons may indicate trade origin, but no special bad faith rule is required and the normal principles apply. Such persons are the exception rather than the rule. We turn to consider the position of well-known people whose name or image do not, prima facie, indicate trade origin.

In this latter situation, the argument presumably is that bad faith arises because the applicant seeks to exploit the name or image without permission, even though the person in question would not be entitled to register his or her own trade mark. That this argument should succeed is by no means clear since it is difficult to see why "taking advantage of someone else's reputation" without permission should constitute bad faith unless the reputation is one of trade origin. If this type of bad faith argument succeeds, it is limited to the right to stop an exploitative registration, but it is beginning to establish some right of personality. The Court of Appeal in *Elvis Presley* were quite clear that there was no free standing general right to character exploitation enjoyable exclusively by a celebrity. A celebrity could only enjoy rights under the 1938 Act if the critical issue of distinctiveness was established. As to establishing distinctiveness, Simon Brown L.J. said ([1999] R.P.C. 567 at 598):

> "In addressing the critical issue of distinctiveness there should be no *a priori* assumption that only a celebrity or his successors may ever market (or licence the marketing of) his own character. Monopolies should not be so readily created."

It is suggested that the 1994 Act requires the same approach.

7–226 Thus far, we have been considering the position of celebrities either living or recently deceased: persons whose fame may have endured into the period of modern merchandising and/or generated a demand for memorabilia. The use of the name or image of a personality on items of memorabilia is unlikely to be taken as anything other than an indication of the content or character of the goods. Thus, an application for a mark would fail under section 3(1)(c) and/or (b) of the 1994 Act, but not, it is suggested, for bad faith.

---

[24] This may be difficult to achieve. As Laddie J. pointed out at first instance in *Elvis Presley* [1997] R.P.C. 543, people can become so well known that their names then possess very little inherent distinctiveness.

The position may be different as regards items of merchandise which feature the name or image of a well-known living person or group. It largely depends on whether the relevant public have been educated to perceive marks used on merchandise as really indicating trade origin. Use on merchandise of the name in a stylised script which is the form of the trade mark on the principal product may be taken as an indication of trade origin, leaving others to manufacture similar items of merchandise which do not use the "official" script.

As regards famous individuals from history, again it is unlikely that **7–227** the use of their name or image on items of memorabilia or commercial consumer items would be taken as indicating trade origin, without significant education of the public through exclusive use. If the name has come to indicate trade origin, there seems to be no reason why registration should be prevented on the ground of bad faith. The trustees of the Jane Austen Memorial Trust failed to establish bad faith in relation to an application to register the name of the author for soaps and similar items. The allegation was framed largely in terms of some general disentitlement on the applicant's part arising from Jane Austen's fame and literary heritage, but it was held that registration would have no detrimental effect on her literary heritage. Bad faith was not established although the application failed under section 3(1)(b).[25]

Interpretation of "bad faith" at OHIM

As mentioned above, issues of "bad faith" concerning an application for **7–228** a CTM can only be considered in invalidity proceedings or to defeat an allegation of acquiescence. In the first decision of the Cancellation Division,[26] a much narrower view of "bad faith" was applied than in the United Kingdom:

> "Bad faith is a narrow legal concept in the CTMR system. Bad faith is the opposite of good faith, generally implying or involving, but not limited to, actual or constructive fraud, or a design to mislead or deceive another, or any other sinister motive. Conceptually, bad faith can be understood as a 'dishonest intention'. This means that bad faith may be interpreted as unfair practices involving lack of any honest intention on the part of the applicant of the CTM at the time of filing."

The decision concerned a CTM registration for "computer software; **7–229** communications software".[27] The application was said to have been made in bad faith in so far as it extended beyond "telecommunications

[25] *Jane Austen* (SRIS O/198/99), Regy. Although bad faith was not in issue, an application to register "*Diana, Princess of Wales*" for a wide range of goods and services likewise failed under s.3(1)(b): SRIS O/261/OO Regy, July 31, 2000.
[26] Case C000053447/1, *Trillium*, Decision of the First Cancellation Division, March 28, 2000.
[27] *cf. Mercury* [1995] F.S.R. 850 at 864, Laddie J.

switching software". The claim for invalidity failed. In the United Kingdom, it is suggested that the claim would have succeeded. The First Cancellation Division stated categorically that there is no "intention to use" requirement for a CTM application:

> ". . . under European trade mark law, there is no 'intention to use' requirement, and thus the United Kingdom and CTM systems are different. . . . In comparison with the CTM system, the UK 1994 Act differs completely because the use in commerce is not a prerequisite for a CTM registration. In general, and as a matter of principle, it is entirely left to the applicant to file a list of goods and services as long as he sees fit, i.e. a list exceeding his actual scope of business activity, and try later to expand his activities in order to be able to show genuine use of his CTM or face revocation under Article 50(1)(a) CTMR and other sanctions, respectively. It is exactly this 'liberal' concept which underlies Articles 15 and 50 CTMR because otherwise a grace period of five years would make little sense, if any.
>
> There may be cases where an applicant files a list of goods and services where all or part of it does not have the slightest connection with his actual economic activity, and where it might even appear unimaginable that said applicant would ever be able to expand. If in such case the holder of the CTM immediately took action, based on 'remote' goods or services, against third parties, it might be worth considering Article 51(1)(b) CTMR. But this can be left undecided because it is not the case in the present proceedings before us. The CTM is registered, in class 9, for computer software, and the actual activities of the proprietor relate to software."

7–230 With respect, this reasoning appears bizarre for a number of reasons. First, it is contrary to the spirit of both the TM Directive (where the recitals say: "it is essential to require that registered trade marks are actually used.") and the CTM Regulation (where the recitals include: "Whereas there is no justification for protecting Community trade marks . . . except where the trade marks are actually used"). When taken with the provisions concerning non-use, those recitals contemplate use and a limited period of five years within which marks must be put into use, *i.e.* an intention to use existing at the date of application. It is suggested that they do not contemplate "no intention to use" at the date of application with only an assertion that use might take place within five years. Secondly, there appears to be a fundamental misunderstanding of the purpose of the five-year period, after registration, within which a mark must be used. The five-year period is the maximum period which the proprietor has to put his mark into use. It is not a "grace" period which should protect a proprietor whose registration is obviously too broad. Thirdly, underpinning the extracts set out above was the notion[28] that

---

[28] Relying on r. 2(4) of the Implementing Regulation which provides: "The classification of goods and services shall serve exclusively administrative purposes".

"the purpose of a list of classification of products or services under the Nice Agreement has administrative effects only", the suggestion being that even if the registration extended across many classes, it would not affect the reasoning set out above. Fourthly, the illustration given where bad faith might apply fails to take into account the damage which an over-wide registration can cause even if it is not asserted directly against competitors.

It is suggested that OHIM should recognise that there is an implicit **7–231** requirement that the applicant is either using or intends to use the mark for which he has applied. If not, there will be a marked disparity between the protection afforded by a CTM and a United Kingdom registration. The law concerning use and non-use was an integral part of the first stage of harmonisation in the TM Directive, which itself paved the way for the introduction of the CTM. Either the United Kingdom or OHIM is out of step with the harmonised law of trade marks in the E.U. It is suggested that the United Kingdom approach better serves a rational trade mark system, striking a proper balance between competing commercial interests.

CHAPTER 8

RELATIVE GROUNDS FOR REFUSAL OF REGISTRATION

1. Introduction

8–01 This chapter is concerned with the grounds for refusal of registration of a mark which arise from conflicts with earlier marks. These grounds are accordingly referred to as the relative grounds for refusal of registration. They must be contrasted with and are additional to the absolute grounds for refusal of registration which are provided by sections 1 and 3 of the Trade Marks Act 1994 and which relate to the nature of the mark itself, its distinctiveness and other public policy considerations.

8–02 The relative grounds for refusal of registration are essentially provided by sections 5 and 6 of the 1994 Act and these sections implement the mandatory provisions and most of the optional provisions of Article 4 of the Trade Marks Directive.[1]

8–03 The objections fall into essentially two categories, those based on "earlier trade marks" and those based upon "earlier rights". Each of these is defined and the subject of discussion below. The former are primarily concerned with earlier registrations and applications, but are not limited to national trade marks. They include Community trade marks, international marks designating the United Kingdom and marks entitled to protection under the Paris Convention or the WTO Agreement, of which the Agreement on Trade Related Aspects of Intellectual Property Rights (TRIPS) is an integral part. Earlier rights, on the other hand, are concerned with other private rights, such as passing off and copyright which render the use of the mark liable to be prevented. Special protection is also afforded against the unauthorised acts of agents. At the outset it is therefore apparent that the scope of the objections is, in many respects, wider than it was under the Trade Marks Act 1938. In any proceedings they must be addressed separately.

8–04 In this chapter we consider these topics in turn and then the notion of honest concurrent use which, despite having no foundation in the TM Directive, is introduced into the United Kingdom Act and which may be raised before the Registrar, essentially at the examination stage only. It falls away once a mark is the subject of opposition by the proprietor of the earlier trade mark or earlier right.

---

[1] Directive 89/104.

We also address the relative grounds for refusal of registration which **8-05** arise under the Community trade mark system. The Community Trade Mark Regulation[2] allows a trade mark having effect throughout the Community to be obtained on the basis of an application to the Office for Harmonisation in the Internal Market (OHIM). The CTM Regulation broadly follows the same scheme as the TM Directive with regard to the prohibition of the registration of marks which conflict with earlier trade marks or rights. But there are some important differences. In each section of this chapter we explain where the two schemes diverge.

Finally we should say a word about international registrations under **8-06** the Madrid Protocol.[3] International registrations may designate the United Kingdom. Such registrations are entitled to protection in the United Kingdom where, if the particulars were comprised in an application for registration under the 1994 Act, such an application would satisfy the requirements for registration. Accordingly, at examination and opposition, they are subject to the requirements of the relative grounds for refusal of registration of section 5 of the Act. International registrations may also originate in the United Kingdom on the basis of national application or registration. Any such application must also satisfy the requirements of the Act in the usual way.

2. Conflict with earlier trade marks

A. The Objections in Outline

The Act provides that a mark shall not be registered if it conflicts with **8-07** an earlier trade mark in essentially three categories of cases. Each of them has its own requirements which are dealt with separately below. But for convenience they may be broadly summarised as follows: first, where the marks and goods or services are identical; secondly, where because there is a similarity of marks or of goods or services there exists a likelihood of confusion of the public; thirdly, where an earlier mark has a reputation and use of the later mark would take unfair advantage of or be detrimental to the distinctive character or repute of the earlier mark.

It will be noted that in all essential respects these provisions are mirrored in the infringement provisions of section 10 of the 1994 Act. For this reason decisions on each topic are relevant to the other.

B. Section 5(1): Where the marks and the goods or services are identical

General

Section 5(1) of the 1994 Act implements the mandatory provisions of **8-08** Article 4(1)(a) of the TM Directive and provides that a trade mark shall not be registered if it is identical with an earlier trade mark, and the

[2] Council Regulation 40/94, as amended by Regulation 3288/94(2).
[3] Madrid Protocol concerning the International registration of Marks adopted at Madrid on June 27, 1989; given effect to in the U.K. by the Trade Marks (International Registration) Order 1996.

goods or services for which the trade mark is applied for are identical with the goods or services for which the earlier trade mark is protected. For an objection to arise a number of requirements must be satisfied.

8-09   First, there must be an earlier trade mark. This is defined in section 6 of the Act and is considered in paragraph 8–90 *et seq.* below.[4] Secondly, the earlier trade mark must be identical to the mark the subject of the application. It is suggested that this must mean identical for all practical purposes and ignoring trivial differences.

8-10   Thirdly, the goods or services the subject of the application must be the same as those the subject of the earlier trade mark. Although not explicit, it would seem that this provision can only sensibly be interpreted as prohibiting registration where there is an overlap of goods or services.[5] The proprietor of the earlier trade mark and the applicant may use their marks on any of the goods or services in respect of which they have secured or applied for registration. If the marks are identical, and any of the goods or services are identical then the provision must apply. This requirement of two-fold identity will rule out the objection in most cases.

Position under the Community Trade Mark Regulation

8–11   Article 8(1)(a) of the CTM Regulation provides an objection in the same terms, save that it may only be taken upon opposition and by the proprietor of the earlier trade mark or by a licensee authorised by him.[6]

Goods or services for which the earlier trade mark is protected

8–12   The 1994 Act and the corresponding provision of the TM Directive use the word "protected" rather that "registered" in referring to the goods or services the subject of the earlier trade mark.[7] In one sense the goods or services for which such a mark is "protected" extend beyond those in respect of which it is "registered" because of the provisions offering protection in respect of the use of the mark on similar goods or services where there is a likelihood of confusion.

8-13   It is suggested, however, that the words "protected" and "registered" should, at least in the context of earlier *registered* marks, be regarded as synonymous for the reason that any other interpretation would import into the objection a consideration of the likelihood of confusion and that is something which it is evidently specifically designed to avoid.[8]

---

[4] As is the equivalent provision in the CTM Regulation, Art. 8(2).

[5] In accordance with the TM Directive, Art. 13.

[6] CTM Regulation, Art. 42(1)(a).

[7] TM Directive, Art. 4(1)(a). In Art. 4(1)(b), which is implemented by s.5(2), the words are "the goods or services *covered* by the trade marks". The 1994 Act, s.5(2), however, again uses the word "protected" in referring to the goods or services the subject of the earlier trade mark. The CTM Regulation uses the word "protected" in both Art. 8(1)(a) and (b). In the CTM Regulation, Art. 8(5), the word "registered" is used, and this may have implications on the scope of the provision, as discussed in para. 8–68, below.

[8] See Recital 10 of the TM Directive and Recital 7 of the CTM Regulation.

But earlier trade marks also include marks protected under the Paris **8–14** Convention and the TRIPS Agreement as well-known trade marks, and such marks may well not be registered at all. Here it is suggested that the protected goods or services the subject of the earlier mark must, by analogy, be those in respect of which the mark is well known in the United Kingdom.[9]

C. Section 5(2): Where the marks and the goods or services are identical or similar and there is a likelihood of confusion

General

Section 5(2) of the 1994 Act provides: **8–15**

"A trade mark shall not be registered if because—

(a) it is identical with an earlier trade mark and is to be registered for goods or services similar to those for which the earlier trade mark is protected, or

(b) it is similar to an earlier trade mark and is to be registered for goods or services identical with or similar to those for which the earlier trade mark is protected,

there exists a likelihood of confusion on the part of the public, which includes the likelihood of association with the earlier trade mark."

This provision implements the mandatory provisions of Article 4(1)(b) **8–16** of the TM Directive. For all practical purposes its wording is identical to the infringement provision of section 10(2) of the 1994 Act. It prohibits the registration of a trade mark which would be likely to cause confusion of the public as a result of its being identical with or similar to an earlier trade mark and because it is to be registered in respect of goods or services the same as or similar to those the subject of the earlier trade mark. As to the use of the word "protected" in this context, reference is invited to the discussion in paragraphs 8–12 and 8–13 above.

It is apparent from the words of section 10(2) and of Article 4(1)(b), **8–17** that the likelihood of confusion is fundamental to the objection. The objection can only apply where there is a likelihood of confusion on the part of the public. This has also been confirmed by the ECJ in *Sabel v. Puma*[10] where the court stated, at paragraph 18, that:

"In that connection, it is to be remembered that Article 4(1)(b) of the Directive is designed to apply only if, by reason of the identity or similarity both of the marks and of the goods or services which they

---

[9] See 1994 Act, s.56.
[10] [1997] E.C.R. I–6191; [1998] R.P.C. 199. See also *Canon v. MGM* [1998] E.C.R. I–5507; [1997] R.P.C. 117; *Lloyd Schufabrik Meyer v. Klijsen Handel* [1999] E.T.M.R. 690.

designate, 'there exists a likelihood of confusion on the part of the public, which includes the likelihood of association with the earlier trade mark'. It follows from that wording that the concept of the likelihood of association is not an alternative to that of likelihood of confusion, but serves to define its scope. The terms of the provision itself exclude its application where there is no likelihood of confusion on the part of the public."

8-18 In the following sections we consider important issues in relation to this provision and, in particular, how the likelihood of confusion is to be assessed and the factors to be taken into account; whether or not there is a threshold requirement that the goods or services be "similar"; the factors to be taken into account in assessing similarity; and finally, the nature of the relevant confusion. We consider these matters in turn below.

Position under the Community Trade Mark Regulation

8–19 Article 8(1)(b) of the CTM Regulation is in similar terms, save that the objection can only be taken on opposition and by the proprietor of the earlier trade mark or a licensee authorised by him[11] and the likelihood of confusion on the part of the public must be "in the territory in which the earlier trade mark is protected".

Assessment of the likelihood of confusion

8–20 The words of Article 4 of the TM Directive and section 5(2) of the 1994 Act do appear to require that the likelihood of confusion is caused by the identity or similarity of the marks and the goods or services.[12] It is not enough that the likelihood of confusion is caused by some other factors external to the marks, such as associated advertising materials or packaging. In addition these provisions require a likelihood of confusion as to origin, a matter discussed further below.

   The existence of a likelihood of confusion must be found on the evidence.[13]

(a) A global assessment taking into account all relevant factors

8–21 Nevertheless, the likelihood of confusion is to be assessed globally, taking into account all factors relevant to the marks and goods and services in issue, and this will include any reputation attaching to the earlier trade mark. This has been made clear by the ECJ in *Sabel v. Puma*[14]:

   ". . . Article 4(1)(b) does not apply where there is no likelihood of confusion on the part of the public. In that respect it is clear from

---

[11] CTM Regulation, Art. 42(1)(a).
[12] So also in the case of the CTM Regulation, Art. 8(1).
[13] *Marca Mode v. Adidas*, a decision of the ECJ of June 22, 2000.
[14] *Supra*, at paras 22–24. See also *Lloyd Schuhfabrik Meyer (supra)*, at para. 18.

the tenth recital in the preamble to the Directive that the appreciation of the likelihood of confusion 'depends on numerous elements
and, in particular, on the recognition of the trade mark on the
market, of the association which can be made with the used or
registered sign, of the degree of similarity between the trade mark
and the sign and between the goods or services identified'. The
likelihood of confusion must therefore be appreciated globally,
taking into account all factors relevant to the circumstances of the
case.

That global appreciation of the visual, oral or conceptual similarity of the marks in question, must be based on the overall
impression given by the marks, bearing in mind, in particular, their
distinctive and dominant components. The wording of Article
4(1)(b) of the Directive—'. . . there exists a likelihood of confusion
on the part of the public . . .'—shows that the perception of marks
in the mind of the average consumer of the type of goods or
services in question plays a decisive role in the global appreciation
of the likelihood of confusion. The average consumer normally
perceives a mark as a whole and does not proceed to analyse its
various details.

In that perspective, the more distinctive the earlier mark, the
greater will be the likelihood of confusion. It is therefore not
impossible that the conceptual similarity resulting from the fact that
two marks use images with analogous semantic content may give
rise to a likelihood of confusion where the earlier mark has a
particularly distinctive character, either per se or because of the
reputation it enjoys with the public."

(b) The factors to be considered

A global assessment of the likelihood of confusion accordingly requires **8–22**
a consideration of the degree of similarity between the relevant marks,
the degree of similarity between the relevant goods or services, the
likely perception of the marks in the mind of the average consumer of
the goods or services in question and the degree of distinctiveness of the
earlier mark. That distinctiveness may be the result of the inherent
character of the mark or the reputation attaching to it through use.

(c) Similarity of the marks as a relevant factor

In cases where the marks are not identical then clearly a most important **8–23**
part of the assessment of the likelihood of confusion must involve a
consideration of the degree of similarity between them.

In the case of marks which have not been used, the approach to the
issue of confusing similarity is similar to that established under the old
law. It was set out by Jacob J. in *Origins Natural Resources v. Origin
Clothing*[15] in considering the question of infringement under section 10
of the 1994 Act:

---

[15] [1995] F.S.R. 280.

"section 10 of the Trade Marks Act presupposes that the plaintiff's mark is in use or will come into use. It requires the court to assume the mark of the plaintiff is used in a normal and fair manner in relation to the goods for which it is registered and then to assess the likelihood of confusion in relation to the way the defendant uses its mark, discounting external added matter or circumstances. The comparison is mark for [sign]."[16]

8-24 This has since been followed in a number of cases,[17] if not expressly. But where the earlier mark has been used and has acquired a more distinctive nature it seems, following *Sabel v. Puma*, that this is a matter which must be taken into account as a factor likely to increase the risk of confusion.[18] The test set out in *Origins* cannot be taken to be a complete statement of the law.

8-25 It is suggested that the correct approach is to consider a normal and fair use of the mark the subject of the application and, where the earlier mark is a registered mark which has not been used, a normal and fair use of that mark too.[19] Where the earlier mark *has* been used, it is still appropriate to consider a normal and fair use of it and, in the absence of argument or evidence to the contrary, the way in which the proprietor has used it can be said, at the very least prima facie, to be the paradigm case of its use in a normal and fair manner.[20]

8-26 In determining the distinctive character of an earlier registered mark the national court must make an overall assessment of the greater or lesser capacity of the mark to identify the goods or services for which it has been registered as coming from a particular undertaking, and thus to distinguish those goods or services from those of other undertakings.[21]

8-27 In making that assessment, account should be taken, in particular, of the inherent characteristics of the mark, including the fact that it does or does not contain an element descriptive of the goods or services for which it has been registered; the market share held by the mark; how

---

[16] As corrected by Jacob J. himself in *British Sugar v. James Robertson* [1996] R.P.C. 281.

[17] *Wagamama v. City Centre Restaurants* [1995] F.S.R. 713; *British Sugar v. James Robertson, supra; The European v. The Economist* [1988] F.S.R. 283, CA.

[18] Under the old law it was sometimes argued that once a mark becomes a household word it is too well known to be confused with others; see, *e.g. Smith Hayden* ("*Ovax*") (1946) 63 R.P.C. 97 at 102; *Ana Laboratories* (1951) 69 R.P.C. 146. This approach seems virtually untenable in the light of *Sabel v. Puma* and *Canon v. MGM, supra*. But logically it is hard to see why this should be so. The likelihood of confusion is to be determined as a matter of fact (see *Adidas, supra*). Similar marks may more readily be distinguished when one of them is very well known. By contrast, when a mark is very well known the use of the *same mark* on very different goods may be likely to cause confusion.

[19] *Smith Hayden* ("*Ovax*") (1946) 63 R.P.C. 97 at 101; *Berlei v. Bali* ("*Bali*") [1969] R.P.C. 472 HL; these tests have been adopted under the 1994 Act as appropriate in these circumstances: "*Balmoral*" [1999] R.P.C. 297; "*Ener-Cap*" [1999] R.P.C. 362; "*React*" [1999] R.P.C. 529 (Regy.); and [2000] R.P.C. 285 on appeal to the appointed person.

[20] *Premier Brands v. Typhoon*, a decision of Neuberger J., January 21, 2000; *Open Country* [2000] R.P.C. 477, CA.

[21] *Windsurfing Chiemsee v. Huber and Attenberger* [1999] E.C.R. I–2779, para. 49; *Lloyd Schuhfabrik Meyer v. Klijsen Handel* [1999] E.T.M.R. 690, at para. 22.

intensive, geographically widespread and long standing use of the mark has been; the amount invested by the undertaking in promoting the mark; the proportion of the relevant section of the public which, because of the mark, identifies the goods or services as originating from a particular undertaking; and statements from chambers of commerce and industry or other trade and professional associations.[22]

If the reputation attaching to the registered trade mark is relevant in **8-28** determining the likelihood of confusion, in particular as a factor likely to increase the risk of confusion, then it may be anticipated that an applicant for registration will contend that the reputation attaching to his mark is a factor likely to reduce any risk of confusion.[23]

If in fact it is known what use an applicant intends to make of his **8-29** mark, then that use cannot be excluded. Evidence that an intended use is particularly likely to be confusing is helpful to an opponent, to prevent such use being dismissed as unfair or fanciful.[24]

The issue of deceptive resemblance, and the factors to be taken into **8-30** account in assessing it, has received much attention over the years and it is anticipated the approach developed under the old law will be helpful in considering the issue under the 1994 Act. Reference is invited to Chapter 16, where the topic is addressed in detail. For many cases it may be enough to follow the guidance given in *Sabel v. Puma* that account should be taken of the visual, oral and conceptual similarity of the marks in question, including the overall impression given by the marks, and bearing in mind, in particular, their respective distinctive and dominant components.[25]

(d) Similarity of goods and services as a relevant factor

As has been seen, the degree of similarity between the respective goods **8-31** or services is also a relevant matter to take into account in assessing the likelihood of confusion. This requires a consideration of the factors which should be taken into account in assessing that degree of similarity.

It is now clear from decisions of the ECJ and the English courts that it **8-32** is appropriate to take into account all objective factors relating to the goods or services themselves. So far the approach is entirely consistent with that developed under the 1938 Act and relatively straightforward. But it also appears that the TM Directive is more flexible in allowing the degree of recognition of the earlier mark to be taken into account too.

---

[22] *Windsurfing Chiemsee, supra,* at para. 51; *Lloyd Schuhfabrik Meyer, supra,* at para. 23.
[23] It may be argued such an approach is consistent with the TM Directive, Art. 3(3), which makes special provision with regard to the absolute grounds for refusal of Art. 3(1)(b),(c) or (d), where the mark has acquired a distinctive character.
[24] *"Grundig"* [1968] R.P.C. 89; *"Players"* [1965] R.P.C. 363; *"Woodies"* [1965] R.P.C. 366.
[25] See paras 22–24 of the judgment, cited in para. 8–21, of the text, *supra;* applied in *Premier Brands v. Typhoon, supra.* In England under the old law the famous test for word marks was articulated in *Pianotist* (1906) 23 R.P.C. 774 at 777; see also *Smith Hayden ("Ovax")* (1946) 63 R.P.C. 97.

This is certainly the case so far as assessment of the likelihood of confusion is concerned, but it appears that it may also be relevant in determining whether the goods or services are similar at all.[26]

(e) Interdependence of the relevant factors

8–33 Furthermore, a global assessment of the likelihood of confusion implies an interdependence between the various relevant factors. So, a lesser degree of similarity between the goods or services may be offset by a greater similarity between the marks, and vice versa. So also registration of a mark may have to be refused, despite a lesser degree of similarity between the goods or services covered, where the marks are very similar and the earlier mark, in particular its reputation, is highly distinctive.[27]

8–34 In order to assess the degree of similarity between the marks concerned, the national court must determine the degree of visual, aural or conceptual similarity between them and, where appropriate, evaluate the importance to be attached to those different elements taking account of the category of goods or services in question and the circumstances in which they are marketed.[28]

(f) Overall impression is to be considered

8–35 The global appreciation of the likelihood of confusion must, as regards the visual, aural or conceptual similarity of the marks in question, be based upon the overall impression created by them, bearing in mind, in particular, their distinctive and dominant components. The perception of marks in the mind of the average consumer of the category of goods or services in question plays a decisive role in the global appreciation of the likelihood of confusion. The average consumer normally perceives a mark as a whole and does not proceed to analyse its various details.[29]

(g) Imperfect recollection

8–36 Account is to be taken of the fact that the average consumer only rarely has the chance to make a direct comparison between the different marks but must place his trust in the imperfect recollection of them he has kept in his mind. It should also be borne in mind that the average consumer's level of attention is likely to vary according to the category of goods or service in question.[30]

(h) The public

8–37 The 1994 Act and the TM Directive refer to a likelihood of confusion on the part of the public. This would seem to include the trade likely to deal in the relevant goods or services.[31] As to the sort of person to be

---

[26] Reference is invited to the discussion of these issues in paras 8–41 to 8–50, below.
[27] *Sabel v. Puma (supra)*, in particular at paras 22–24; *Canon v. MGM* (ECJ) [1998] E.C.R. I-5507; [1999] R.P.C. 117, in particular at paras 18–28.
[28] *Lloyd Schuhfabrik Meyer, supra*, at para. 27.
[29] *Sabel v. Puma, supra*, at para. 23; *Lloyd Schuhfabrik Meyer, supra*, at para. 25.
[30] *Lloyd Schuhfabrik Meyer, supra*, at para. 26.
[31] Indeed, some marks may only be used in the trade.

considered, the ECJ in *Sabel v. Puma*, in the passage cited in paragraph 8–21, above, considered the position of "the average consumer".[32]

(i) The standard to be applied

There is little by way of guidance at present as to how the test is to be applied. It has been said that the risk of confusion must be "genuine and properly substantiated".[33] This approach is akin to that under the 1938 Act, where the issue was whether there was no reasonable likelihood of confusion amongst a substantial number of persons, although that was a gloss which had to be properly and sensibly applied.[34] **8–38**

For the purposes of the global appreciation, the average consumer of the category of products concerned is deemed to be reasonably well informed and reasonably observant and circumspect.[35]

(j) Point of confusion

As under the old law, it is likely that confusion which occurs after the point of sale can be taken into account, provided it arises from the use of the offending trade mark.[36] A trade mark continues to identify origin even after sale. **8–39**

(k) Date of assessment

The likelihood of confusion must be assessed as at the date of the application for the mark in issue. It is suggested that subsequent experience may nevertheless be relevant as providing an indication of a tendency to confuse.[37] **8–40**

Similar goods or services—a threshold requirement?

It is now established that the degree of similarity between the relevant goods and services is an important matter which must be taken into account in considering the likelihood of confusion[38]: but further and important issues remain. **8–41**

---

[32] See also *Bach Flower Remedies v. Healing Herbs* [2000] R.P.C. 513, CA.

[33] See Opinion of Advocate General Jacobs in *Sabel v. Puma* (*supra*), at paras 52 and 55.

[34] *Smith Hayden ("Ovax")* (1946) 63 R.P.C. 97 at 101; *Berlei v. Bali ("Bali")* [1969] R.P.C. 472 at 496, HL, *per* Lord Upjohn. Similarly, and by analogy with the position under the 1938 Act, there may be confusion within the meaning of the TM Directive even though the purchaser is not, in the end, confused. Under the 1938 Act it was established that if persons were likely to wonder whether the goods were made or services provided by an opponent, then the mark applied for was one which was likely to cause confusion because people's minds would be put into a state of doubt or uncertainty: *Hack* (1940) 58 R.P.C. 91 at 102–103.

[35] *Lloyd Schuhfabrik Meyer, supra*, at para. 26; *Gut Springenheide and Tusky* [1998] E.C.R. I–4657, at para. 31. This test is consistent with earlier U.K. law. So, in considering passing off, the courts have rejected confusion by a "moron in a hurry" in favour of ordinary sensible members of the public: *Morning Star v. Express Newspapers* [1979] F.S.R. 113; *cf. Newsweek v. British Broadcasting Corporation* [1979] R.P.C. 441, CA.

[36] *Levi Strauss v. Kimbyr Investments* [1994] F.S.R. 335 (High Court of New Zealand); *Levi Strauss v. Shah* [1985] R.P.C. 371.

[37] *Helena Rubinstein* [1960] R.P.C. 229.

[38] See paras 8–21 and 8–31, *supra*.

8-42   First, there is the question of whether or not there is a *threshold* requirement that the goods and services are identical or similar before a mark may be refused under section 5(2) of the 1994 Act, corresponding to Article 4(1)(b) of the TM Directive. If there is not a threshold then the question to be addressed is simply whether or not there is a likelihood of confusion taking into account the similarity of the goods or services and all other relevant matters. If there is a threshold, then there can be no application of section 5(2) if the goods or services are not sufficiently alike as to be "similar" within the meaning of the provision, irrespective of the likelihood of confusion. Secondly, and if there is a threshold, then the question arises as to how it is to be assessed.

8-43   As will be seen below, there is much to be said for simply regarding the question of similarity of goods or services as part of a larger and composite question as to whether there is a likelihood of confusion.[39] But hitherto this has not been the approach of the English court, nor, it would seem, of the European Court of Justice; and it is hard to reconcile it with the words of the Act.

8-44   The English court considered these questions in the *British Sugar* case (*supra*) in relation to the infringement provisions of section 10(2) of the 1994 Act. Jacob J. expressly rejected the contention that there was a single composite question. He considered that the issue of whether or not the relevant goods or services were similar was a separate question which had to be answered. If the respective goods or services were not similar, then there could be no infringement under section 10(2) of the Act. Such is clear from his judgment, at page 294:

> "The questions arising under section 10(2)(a) are:
>
> (1) Is the mark used in the course of trade?
> (2) Are the goods for which it is used similar to those covered by the registration?
> (3) Is there a likelihood of confusion because of that similarity?
>
> The first of these questions causes no difficulty here. The problems arise under the second and third questions. British Sugar seek to elide the questions of confusion and similarity. Their skeleton argument contends that there is 'use in relation to a product so similar to a dessert sauce that there exists a likelihood of confusion because the product may or will be used for identical purposes.' I do not think it is legitimate to elide the questions in this way. The sub-section does not merely ask 'will there be confusion?': it asks 'is there similarity of goods?', if so, 'is there a likelihood of confusion?' The point is important. For if one elides the two questions then a strong mark would get protection for a greater range of goods that a weak mark. For instance 'Kodak' for socks or bicycles might well

---

[39] The appointed person has taken this line: see *"Balmoral"* [1999] R.P.C. 297; *"Naturelle"* [1999] R.P.C. 326.

cause confusion, yet these goods are plainly dissimilar from films or cameras. I think that the question of similarity of goods is wholly independent of the particular mark the subject of registration or the defendant's sign."

By parity of reasoning an objection to registration cannot arise under **8-45** section 5(2) unless the goods or services the subject of the earlier trade mark are similar to those the subject of the application. And this is a question that Jacob J. considered should be answered independently of the particular marks in issue.[40] If the goods or services are not similar then there cannot be an objection under section 5(2).[41]

These questions have also been addressed, although not entirely **8-46** clearly, by the European Court of Justice in *Canon v. MGM* [1999] R.P.C. 117. The case concerned an application by MGM to register the mark CANNON in respect of, *inter alia*, films recorded on video tape cassettes (video tape cassettes) and the opposition to it by Canon on the grounds of its earlier trade mark CANON in respect of, *inter alia*, recording and production devices for video tapes (video recorders). The Bundespatentgericht (Federal Patent Court) considered that the goods were not so similar that the average purchaser might form the opinion that they were made by the same enterprise and that accordingly Article 4(1)(b) was not satisfied. On appeal, the Bundesgerichtshof considered that the provision might be satisfied if account could be taken of the reputation attaching to the earlier mark CANON and accordingly referred the following question for a preliminary ruling[42]:

> "May account be taken, when assessing the similarity of the goods or services covered by the two marks, of the distinctive character, in particular the reputation, of the mark with earlier priority . . . so that, in particular, likelihood of confusion within the meaning of Article 4(1)(b) of Directive 89/104 must be taken to exist even if the public attributes the goods and/or services to different places of origin?"

At the hearing argument was directed to the issue of whether the test **8-47** for assessing the similarity of goods or services was objective (*i.e.* unrelated to the nature of the marks in question), as contended for by MGM and the United Kingdom Government, or whether it was permissible to consider goods or services to be similar in relation to particularly distinctive marks when such goods or services would not be considered similar in relation to other less distinctive marks.[43]

---

[40] An approach apparently followed by the Registry, at least initially: see, *e.g.* "*Zippo*" [1999] R.P.C. 173; "*QS by S. Oliver*" [1999] R.P.C. 520.
[41] This approach was also apparently adopted in *Premier Brands v. Typhoon, supra*, an infringement case.
[42] Para. 11 of the judgment.
[43] See paras 31–51 of the opinion of the Advocate General.

8-48   The court held (at paragraph 24) the distinctive character of a trade mark, and in particular its reputation, must be taken into account when determining whether the similarity between the goods or services covered by the two marks is sufficient to give rise to the likelihood of confusion. In so finding the court was clearly following the decision in *Sabel* that the likelihood of confusion must be assessed globally taking into account all relevant matters.

8-49   This finding does not, however, directly address the issue of whether or not there is a threshold test. But in reaching its conclusion the court appears to have considered that there is a threshold and that the question of similarity must itself be assessed globally. In particular it appears to have rejected the contention advanced by MGM in finding, at paragraphs 22 and 23:

> "It is, however, important to stress that, for the purpose of applying Article 4(1)(b), even where a mark is identical to another with a highly distinctive character, it is still necessary to adduce evidence of similarity between the goods or services covered. In contrast to Article 4(4)(a), which expressly refers to the situation in which the goods or services are not similar, Article 4(1)(b) provides that the likelihood of confusion presupposes that the goods or services are identical or similar.
>
> In assessing the similarity of the goods or services concerned, as the French and United Kingdom Governments and the Commission have pointed out, all the relevant factors relating to those goods or services themselves should be taken into account. Those factors include, *inter alia*, their nature, their end users and their method of use and whether they are in competition with each other or are complementary."

8-50 This conclusion is also consistent with the Opinion of the Advocate General. He similarly considered that the degree of recognition of the earlier mark is relevant in deciding whether there is sufficient similarity to give rise to a likelihood of confusion, an approach entirely consistent with *Sabel*. But he also appears to have considered that there is a threshold and that the degree of recognition of the earlier mark may also be taken into account in considering whether the goods or services are similar. Such is apparent from paragraphs 46 to 50 of his Opinion, which include the following passage:

> "I accept that a flexible test of the similarity of goods or services might lead to different interpretations of such similarity in different Member States, a new mark might not be caught by Article 4(1)(b) of the Directive in one Member State simply because it is considered in that State that, despite the reputation of the earlier mark and a likelihood of confusion, the goods or services are not sufficiently similar. In such a case, however, the fact that the earlier trade mark has a reputation may well mean that in that Member State Article

4(4)(a) or Article 5(2) of the Directive (concerning the protection of a mark in relation to dissimilar goods or services) would apply instead."

Similar goods or services—the factors to be considered

(a) The general approach

It appears therefore that, in contrast to the approach of the English court **8–51** in *British Sugar*, the court in *Canon v. MGM* was of the view that in considering the similarity of goods or services it is appropriate to take into account both objective considerations and the degree of distinctiveness of the earlier mark, including in particular its reputation.[44] So it may be permissible to consider goods or services to be similar in relation to particularly distinctive marks when such goods or services would not be considered to be similar in relation to other less distinctive marks.

This makes the task of determining the issue of similarity an **8–52** extremely difficult one. On the one hand the test is not wholly objective and independent of the reputation of the earlier mark. On the other hand it is not to be determined by asking whether the goods or services are sufficiently similar to give rise to a risk of confusion either. Hence it is possible to contemplate an earlier mark with a significant reputation and an application for a mark in relation to other goods or services such that there is a likelihood that confusion will result. Yet the goods or services may still not be similar. It is far from clear how the line is to be drawn in such a case. Moreover, since the fame of marks can and does vary over time, on the basis of *Canon v. MGM* what goods are similar will likewise vary.

(b) Objective considerations

As has been seen, there is a consensus that it is appropriate to consider, **8–53** at least, all factors relating to the goods or services themselves.

Hence the following types of factors may be of assistance:

(1) the uses of the respective goods or services;
(2) the users of the respective goods or services;
(3) the physical nature of the goods or acts of service;
(4) the trade channels through which the goods or services reach the market;
(5) in the case of self-serve consumer items, where in practice they are respectively found or likely to be found in supermarkets and in particular whether they are, or are likely to be, found on the same or different shelves;
(6) the extent to which the respective goods and services are in competition with each other: that inquiry may take into account

---

[44] And this appears to be the approach now followed by the Registry: *Team Lotus Ventures* [1999] E.T.M.R. 669.

how those in trade classify goods, for instance whether market research companies, who of course act for industry, put the goods or services in the same or different sectors.[45]

Resolution of the issue may require evidence directed to the position as at the date of the application.[46]

(c) Some illustrations

8–54 Some decisions concerning the question of similar goods or services under the TM Directive or the CTM Regulation are set out below. These should be regarded as no more than a guide because circumstances may change and vary from territory to territory.[47]

8–55 *Similar goods or services* "Organic fertilisers" similar goods to "chemicals used in horticulture and forestry" since they have a similar function and are likely to be sold in the same shops.[48]

"Wines" similar to "whisky" and "bar services", since people would think that the supplier of one was engaged in the supply of the other.[49]

"Coffee, tea and cocoa" similar to "coffee substitutes" as they are intended for the same use.[50]

8-56 "Skin care, sun care and hair care preparations; perfumery, essential oils, soaps" similar to "perfumes; cosmetics; non-medicated toilet preparations; soaps; shampoos; preparations for the hair; dentifrices; antiperspirants; deodorants for personal use".[51]

"Leather goods, leather bags, other leather goods not specifically made for the things they contain, containers and purses" similar to "clothing".[52]

"Services offered by beauty salons; solarium services" similar to "business assistance with beauty preparations, sales" and "beauty preparations, perfumery, cosmetics dietetic substances" since the goods and services of the conflicting marks could be offered together and be intended for the same public.[53]

8-57 "Consultancy on the organisation and management of commercial and industrial businesses" similar to "assistance to industrial and

---

[45] *British Sugar v. James Robertson* [1996] R.P.C. 281 at 294–297, elaborating the old judicial test of goods of the same description articulated by Romer J. in *Jellinek* (1946) 63 R.P.C. 59 at 70, approved by the House of Lords in *Daiquiri Rum* [1969] R.P.C. 600 at 620. The same list was cited in the Opinion of Advocate General Jacobs in *Canon v. MGM*, (*supra*), at para. 45. In so far as *British Sugar* suggests the question of similarity is to be determined wholly objectively, it must now be regarded as wrong. For further decisions on the test applied under the 1938 Act, reference is invited to the 12th edition of this work, and supplement, at paras 10–11 to 10–15.

[46] See, *e.g.* "Zippo" [1999] R.P.C. 173.

[47] It will be noted that in the case of the CTM Regulation the likelihood of confusion is to be assessed "in the territory where the earlier trade mark is protected": Art. 8(1)(b).

[48] *Humic* [1999] E.T.M.R. 26 (OHIM).

[49] "Balmoral" [1999] R.P.C. 297.

[50] *Lutz Quasdorf v. Les Sirenes* [1999] E.T.M.R. 152 (OHIM).

[51] "Naturelle" [1999] R.P.C. 326.

[52] "QS by S. Oliver" [1999] R.P.C. 520.

[53] *Beauty Shop* [1999] E.T.M.R. 20 (OHIM).

commercial businesses; consultancy information, research, inquiries or business management" in that they both have the same objective of the provision of specific industrial and commercial knowledge to commercial entities in the determination of their choice of business.[54]

"Buttons, press studs, buckles (clothing accessories), buckles for footwear and garments, eyelets and buttonholes for footwear and garments, patches and rivets for garments" in class 26 similar to "outer and inner wear, knitwear including boots, shoes and slippers; clothing articles including boots, shoes and slippers; outer and inner garments of fabric and knitwear, including boots shoes and slippers; clothing articles, shoes and hats".[55]

Goods or services which are not similar "Bags, cases and pocket wallets **8–58** made of leather; umbrellas and parasols" not similar to "cigarette lighters and lighter fuel".[56]

"Sports bags, shopping bags, toilet bags, key bags" not similar to "clothing".[57]

"Electronic devices for attracting and killing insects" not similar to "aromatherapy diffusing apparatus".[58]

Confusion as to origin

The sort of confusion required to satisfy this provision is confusion as to **8–59** origin. It is not enough that on seeing the mark the subject of the application, the earlier mark is "called to mind" if there is no possibility of the customer being under any misapprehension as to the origin of the goods or services. The mere association which the public might make between two trade marks as a result of their analogous semantic content is not in itself a sufficient ground for concluding that there is a likelihood of confusion within the meaning of the provision.[59]

However, confusion as to origin extends beyond simply mistaking the **8-60** one mark for the other. It also includes cases where the public wrongly believe that the goods or services have their origin in the same enterprise or otherwise make a connection between the proprietors of the sign applied for and those of the earlier mark and confuses them.[60]

---

[54] *Mars* [1999] E.T.M.R. 402 (OHIM).
[55] *Zanella SNC's Application* [2000] E.T.M.R. 69 (OHIM).
[56] *"Zippo"* [1999] R.P.C. 173.
[57] *"QS by S.Oliver"* [1999] R.P.C. 520.
[58] *"Lifesystems"* [2000] R.P.C. 851.
[59] *Wagamama v. City Centre Restaurants* [1995] F.S.R. 713; *Sabel v. Puma* [1997] E.C.R. I–6191; [1998] R.P.C. 199. The ECJ declined to interpret the TM Directive so as to include non-origin association as forbidden by Benelux law and explained in *Henri Jullien BV v. Verschuere Norbert (Union, Union Soleure)*, Jurisprudence of Benelux Court of Justice, 1983, p.36; see also *Lucas Bols v. Colgate Palmolive (Claeryn and Klarein)* (1976) 7 I.I.C. 420; Jurisprudence of Benelux Court of Justice 1975, p. 472. The position must be the same under the CTM Regulation.
[60] The ECJ in *Sabel v. Puma* (*supra*), at para. 16, referred to the submission that "the likelihood of association may arise in three sets of circumstances: (1) where the public confuses the sign and the mark in question (likelihood of direct confusion); (2) where the

This connection must be in the nature of an economic link.[61] So if the public believe that the goods or services are under the control and licence of the proprietors of the earlier mark, that would seem to be enough.[62]

D. Section 5(3): Where the use of the mark without due cause would take unfair advantage of or be detrimental to the distinctive character or repute of the earlier mark

General

8–61 Section 5(3) of the 1994 Act provides:

"A trade mark which:

(a) is identical with or similar to an earlier trade mark, and
(b) is to be registered for goods or services which are not similar to those for which the earlier trade mark is protected,

shall not be registered if, or to the extent that, the earlier trade mark has a reputation in the United Kingdom (or in the case of a Community trade mark in the European Community) and the use of the later mark would, without due cause, take unfair advantage of, or be detrimental to, the distinctive character or repute of the earlier trade mark."

---

public makes a connection between the proprietors of the sign and those of the mark and confuses them (likelihood of indirect confusion or association); (3) where the public considers the sign to be similar to the mark and perception of the sign calls to mind the memory of the mark, although the two are not confused (likelihood of association in the strict sense)."

The court considered, at para. 18, it was therefore necessary to determine whether the TM Directive, Art. 4(1)(b), could apply where there was no likelihood of direct or indirect confusion, but only a likelihood of association in the strict sense. It held: "The terms of the provision itself exclude its application where there is no likelihood of confusion on the part of the public".

[61] *Canon v. MGM (supra)*, at para. 30 of the judgment: ". . . there may be a likelihood of confusion within the meaning of Article 4(1)(b) of the Directive even where the public perception is that the goods or services have different places of production. By contrast there can be no such likelihood where it does not appear that the public could believe that the goods or services come from the same undertaking or, as the case may be, from economically linked undertakings". For an illustration of the application of this principle, see *Hij Mannenmode v. Nienhaus & Lotz*, a decision of the District Court of Utrecht [1999] E.T.M.R. 730.

[62] This would of course be entirely within the recognised subject-matter of a trade mark, namely as an indication that the goods or services have originated under the control of a single undertaking which is responsible for their quality. It may also be sufficient if the public believe that the goods or services are simply licensed by the proprietor of the earlier trade mark. After all, that is consistent with the Directive, which provides, in Art. 10(3), that use of the trade mark with the consent of the proprietor shall be deemed to constitute use by the proprietor.

Section 5(3) implements the mandatory provisions of Article 4(3) and the **8-62** optional provisions of Article 4(4)(a)[63] of the TM Directive. For all practical purposes its wording is identical to that of the infringement provision of section 10(3) of the 1994 Act.

This subsection provides a new ground of prohibition in cases where the **8-63** trade mark sought to be registered is identical to or similar to an earlier trade mark and where the goods or services in respect of which registration is sought are not similar to those the subject of the earlier trade mark. In such a case registration is prohibited if or to the extent that the earlier trade mark has a reputation and the use of the later mark without due cause would take unfair advantage of, or be detrimental to, the distinctive character or repute of the earlier trade mark. It is clear from Recital 9 to the TM Directive that this provision reflects the option of Member States to provide extensive protection to those trade marks which have a reputation.

It has been considered that because this provision (or at least its **8-64** infringement counterpart) represents a significant extension to the protection hitherto afforded to proprietors of registered trade marks in this country and because it does not involve such a significant change to the domestic law of at least some of the other Member States of the Community, significant assistance may be available from the jurisprudence developed elsewhere within the European Community.[64] In particular, regard may usefully be had to the law of unfair competition in Germany and the Benelux law of infringement.[65]

---

[63] Although it appears that the Act goes a little further in that Art. 4(4)(a) only refers to earlier trade marks which are *registered* for goods or services which are not similar to those the subject of the application. The Act, on the other hand, refers to the goods or services for which the earlier trade mark is *protected* and so includes, presumably, well known marks under the Paris Convention—such marks falling within the definition of "earlier trade marks" in s.6.

[64] *Premier Brands v. Typhoon, supra.*

[65] In *Premier Brands* the Judge expressly drew assistance from two authorities of the German Federal Supreme Court. As to the case where the use of a sign takes unfair advantage of a mark with an established goodwill he referred to *Dimple* [1985] G.R.U.R. 550, where the German Federal Supreme Court said:

"The courts have repeatedly held that it constitutes an act of unfair competition to associate the quality of one's goods or services with that of prestigious competitive products for the purpose of exploiting the good reputation of a competitor's goods or services in order to enhance one's promotional efforts".

As to the case where the use of the sign is detrimental to a well established mark he referred to *Quick* [1959] G.R.U.R. 182 where the German Federal Supreme Court said:

"[T]he owner of . . . a distinctive mark has a legitimate interest in continuing to maintain the position of exclusivity he acquired through large expenditures of time and money and that everything which could impair the originality and distinctive character of his distinctive mark, as well as the advertising effectiveness derived from its uniqueness, is to be avoided . . . Its basic purpose is not to prevent any form of confusion but to protect an acquired asset against impairment".

He also considered that "dilution" was a useful concept to have in mind when considering the application of s.10(3) to a particular set of facts, a view fortified by the fact that Art. 5(2) is based upon Benelux law; and that this has been said to occur normally in one of two ways, namely by "blurring" or by "tarnishing". Blurring is explained in *Taittinger v. Allbev* [1993] F.S.R. 641 at 678, and an important example of tarnishing is that found in *Lucas Bols v. Colgate Palmolive (Claeryn/Klarein)* (1976) 7 I.I.C. 420; Jurisprudence of Netherlands Court of Justice 1975, at 472. For further discussion see *"Famous and well known Trade Marks"* by Mostert, 1997.

8-65   It is to be noted that the provision does not expressly require any confusion, whether as to origin or otherwise. This is a matter discussed further below. In this respect the provision is drawn in very different terms to the prohibition provided by section 5(2). Accordingly it is necessary in this section to consider each of the requirements of the prohibition.

8-66   Nevertheless in one respect at least it appears that the prohibition is drawn so that its boundaries meet those of section 5(2). This subsection only has application where the goods or services the subject of the application are *not* the same or similar to those the subject of the earlier trade mark.[66] By contrast it seems that in the case of section 5(2) there is a threshold requirement that the respective goods or services *are* similar.[67] Frequently these objections are pleaded in the alternative. In a suitable case a mark could give rise to objections under both provisions, each in respect of separate goods or services.

The relevant date as of which the requirements of the prohibition are to be considered must be the date of application for the mark in issue.[68]

Position under the Community Trade Mark Regulation

8-67   Article 8(5) of the CTM Regulation is in similar terms to section 5(3) of the 1994 Act: But it applies only upon opposition by the proprietor of an earlier trade mark or a licensee authorised by him.[69] Where the earlier trade mark is a Community trade mark it must have a reputation in the Community. Where the earlier trade mark is a national trade mark it must have a reputation in the Member State concerned. In either case the use without due cause of the mark applied for must take advantage of or be detrimental to the distinctive character or repute of the earlier trade mark.

8-68   There is a basis for contending that this provision of the CTM Regulation only applies in the case of earlier *registered* marks. In contrast to the provisions of Article 8(1) which refer to the goods or services for which the earlier mark is *protected*, Article 8(5) refers to the goods or services for which the earlier mark is *registered*.

Goods and services which are not similar

8-69   As discussed above the prohibition can only apply where the respective goods or services are *not* similar. It is suggested that determination of this question involves the same inquiry as is necessary to whether the goods or services *are* similar, in that goods or services must either be similar or not. In that regard reference is invited to paragraphs 8–51 to

---

[66] *Cf. Premier Brands, supra*, where the Judge doubted this was so and *Sabel v. Puma, supra*, at 223.
[67] That is the law in England, until the ECJ indicate to the contrary: *British Sugar v. James Robertson* [1996] R.P.C. 281, and see further the discussion in para. 8–41 *et seq., above*.
[68] And this is the approach taken by the appointed person: see *Corgi* [1999] R.P.C. 549.
[69] CTM Regulation, Art. 42(1)(a).

8–58, above. Where the earlier trade mark has not been used, then the issue is likely to be relatively straightforward and akin to the test under the old law as to whether or not the goods or services are of the same description.[70] Where the earlier trade mark has been used or is otherwise particularly distinctive, then the question may be more complex in the light of *Canon v. MGM*.[71] In particular it seems that in the case of a particularly distinctive mark, goods or services may be regarded as similar when they would not be so regarded in the case of a less distinctive mark.

Goods or services for which the earlier trade mark is protected

The provision only applies in cases where the goods or services the **8–70** subject of the application, are not similar to those *protected* by the earlier trade mark.[72] Accordingly it is important to determine the scope of protection of the earlier trade mark. Reference is invited to paragraph 8–12, above.

Similar trade marks

The mark the subject of the application and the earlier trade mark must **8–71** be identical or similar. This is a subject discussed in relation to the objection under section 5(2) of the 1994 Act and reference is invited to paragraph 8–23 *et seq.*, above.

The earlier trade mark must have a reputation

This is a particular requirement of this prohibition and in that regard is **8–72** to be contrasted with the prohibition under section 5(2) of the 1994 Act. There the objection can apply irrespective of whether the earlier trade mark has any reputation.

The reputation must exist in the United Kingdom or, in the case of a Community trade mark, in the European Community. Reputation is a concept well understood by our courts and may exist independently of goodwill.[73] Accordingly, in the case of earlier national trade marks, it would seem that protection could be afforded under this prohibition where the earlier trade mark has a reputation but no goodwill established by actual use in the United Kingdom.

As to the extent of reputation necessary to support the objection, it **8–73** appears that the degree of knowledge required must be considered to be reached when the earlier mark is known by a significant part of the public concerned by the products or goods covered by the trade mark.[74]

---

[70] See Jacob J. in *British Sugar, supra*, at 297.
[71] See para. 8–51, above.
[72] Or in the case of the CTM Regulation, Art. 8(5), the goods or services for which the earlier mark is registered.
[73] See, for a general discussion of these issues, Chap. 14.
[74] *General Motors v. Yplon* [1999] All E.R. (EC) 865; [1999] E.T.M.R. 950, at para. 24, ECJ. This also seems to be the approach adopted by the Registry: see *Ruefach Marketing* [1999] E.T.M.R. 412.

It should also be noted that the material requirements of the objection discussed below must also be satisfied and this is unlikely to be the case unless the reputation of the earlier trade mark is significant. It also follows that the stronger the distinctive character and reputation of the earlier mark, the easier it is to establish detriment to it.[75] It is not required that the reputation extends throughout the United Kingdom, although it must exist in a substantial part of it.[76]

It is suggested that the relevant date for consideration of this and the other aspects of the objection is the date of the application in issue. The reputation must exist at that date.

Without due cause would take unfair advantage of or be detrimental to the distinctive character or repute of the earlier trade mark

8–74 These are the most crucial words of the prohibition. They appear to contemplate four alternatives, each of which is sufficient for the prohibition to apply. In particular it is sufficient if the use of the later mark in relation to any of the goods or services for which it is to be registered would, without due cause:

(1) take unfair advantage of the distinctive character *or* repute of the earlier trade mark; *or*
(2) be detrimental to the distinctive character *or* repute of the earlier trade mark.

8-75 It is to be noted that these requirements mean that the provision and its infringement counterpart do not have the sweeping effect of preventing the registration or use of a sign which is the same as, or similar to, a registered trade mark with a reputation; nor are they intended to enable the proprietor of a well-known registered trade mark to object as a matter of course to the registration or use of a sign which may remind people of his mark.[77]

(a) Is confusion as to origin necessary?

8–76 It has been held in the case of the equivalent provision dealing with infringement (section 10(3) of the 1994 Act) that confusion as to origin is an implicit, albeit not explicit, requirement of the prohibition.[78] The reasoning behind this approach is, in substance, as follows: under section 10(2) protection is given in relation to similar goods or services where, because of the similarity, there exists a likelihood of confusion on

---

[75] *Premier Brands v. Typhoon, supra; General Motors, supra* at paras 23–27.
[76] *General Motors, supra,* at paras 28–29. So, *e.g.* a reputation in a substantial part of England would appear sufficient.
[77] *Premier Brands v. Typhoon, supra;* and see the discussion of the requirements of the provision below.
[78] *Baywatch v. Home Video Channel* [1997] F.S.R. 22. See also *BASF v. CEP*, an unreported decision of Knox J. of October 26, 1995.

the part of the public. It is illogical for section 10(3) to give greater protection in relation to non similar goods or services (by dispensing with the ingredient of confusion as to origin) than that afforded in relation to similar goods under section 10(2).

It is, however, now becoming clear that the correct interpretation of **8-77** the prohibition is that a likelihood of confusion as to origin is not an essential requirement, although, as will be seen in the discussion below, it may be that in the majority of cases where the prohibition applies it will in fact be present.[79] In particular, it is suggested that it is wrong to write into the provision a requirement which was apparently deliberately left out. It is notable in this regard that the words which the subsection implements appear in the Directive in a number of places, namely Articles 4(3), 4(4)(a) and 5(2) and 5(5). In the case of Article 5(5) the words are also used in a context which strongly suggests that they are apposite to describe a situation where the offending use is not use in a trade mark sense and where it is therefore difficult to see how it could give rise to confusion as to origin.

It is also important to have in mind that the provision applies only **8-78** where the earlier trade mark has a reputation and the other specific requirements are present. These provide a test appropriate to the specific purpose of the provision, which is to protect marks with a reputation. As the European Court of Justice observed in *Sabel v. Puma*,[80] at paragraphs 20 and 21:

> "Furthermore . . . Article 4(3) and (4)(a) and Article 5(2) of the Directive . . . permit the proprietor of a trade mark which has a reputation to prohibit the use without due cause of signs identical with or similar to his mark and do not require proof of confusion, even where there is no similarity between the goods in question.
>
> In that respect, it is sufficient to note that, unlike Article 4(1)(b), those provisions apply exclusively to marks which have a reputation and on condition that use of the third party's mark without due cause takes unfair advantage of, or is detrimental to, the distinctive character or repute of the trade mark."

This has been taken to resolve the issue by Advocate General Jacobs in *General Motors*.[81]

For essentially these reasons the High Court has recently taken the **8-79** position that origin association is not a requirement of the prohibition[82] and this is also the approach taken in the Registry.[83] So also the Court of

---

[79] *Premier Brands v. Typhoon, supra*, makes it clear the provision should not be treated as being subject to any such rule of thumb.
[80] [1997] E.C.R. I–6191; [1998] R.P.C. 199. It is also of note that the Advocate General in his Opinion, at para. 48, expressly rejected the argument that found favour in *Baywatch v. Home Video Channel* and identified the purpose of the provision as being to protect marks with a reputation.
[81] [1999] All E.R. (E.C.) 865 at 870.
[82] *Premier Brands v. Typhoon, supra*.
[83] See: *Oasis Stores* [1998] R.P.C. 649; *"Audi-Med"* [1998] R.P.C. 863; *"Corgi"* [1999] R.P.C. 549, a decision of the appointed person.

Appeal has indicated it is not satisfied that these provisions require the use to be confusing use.[84]

8-80   Further support for this conclusion may be derived from *Barclays Bank v. Advanta* [1996] R.P.C. 307, where Laddie J. (at page 316) considered the meaning of these words in the context of the proviso to section 10(6) of the 1994 Act:

> "At the most these words emphasise that the use of the mark must take unfair advantage of it or be detrimental to it. In other words the use must either give some advantage to the defendant or inflict some harm on the character or repute of the registered mark which is above the level of de minimis."

(b) Without due cause

8–81 There is no guidance in the TM Directive as to the limitation introduced by these words. They have, however, been carefully considered in the *Premier Brands*[85] case. First, it was emphasised that regard must be had to the purpose of the provision, namely to protect the value and goodwill of trade marks, particularly in cases where they are well known, from being unfairly taken advantage of or unfairly harmed. Secondly, the words "being without due cause" have to be read as not merely governing the words "the use of the sign", but also as governing the words "takes unfair advantage of, or is detrimental to". Thirdly, this approach is consistent with the view of the Benelux Court in *Lucas Bols*[86] where, when discussing the meaning of "without justifiable reason" which appeared in a similar context in the Uniform Benelux Trade Mark Act as "without due cause" in section 10(3) of the 1994 Act, the Court said:

> "What this rule requires, as a rule, is that the user (of the mark) is under such a compulsion to use this very mark that he cannot honestly be asked to refrain from doing so regardless of the damages the owner of the mark would suffer from such use, or that the user is entitled to the use of the mark in his own right and does not have to yield this right to that of the owner of the mark . . .".

8-82 In the same case, the Benelux Court suggested that a "justifiable reason" may be "if the user can assert an older right than that of the [registered proprietor]" but went on that whether the alleged infringer could establish a "justifiable reason" must be "resolved by the trial judge according to the particular facts of each case".

(c) Unfair advantage

8–83 This specifically contemplates a benefit accruing to the applicant through the use of the mark applied for. In cases where the public are confused into thinking that there is a commercial connection between

---

[84] *B.T. v. One in a Million* [1999] F.S.R. 1 at 25, CA.
[85] See n. 20, *supra*.
[86] (1976) 7 I.I.C. 420 at 425.

the suppliers of the goods or services supplied under the earlier trade mark and the mark the subject of the application, then it is to be anticipated that the prohibition will apply. Such confusion as to origin (origin association) is likely to take unfair advantage of and be damaging to the distinctive nature or reputation of the earlier trade mark.

The more difficult case is where the earlier trade mark is likely to be **8-84** brought to mind by the use of the mark the subject of the application, but where members of the public are unlikely to believe there is any economic link between the suppliers (non-origin association). Simply being reminded of a similar trade mark with a reputation for dissimilar goods does not necessarily amount to taking unfair advantage of the repute of the mark. So the use of dictionary words which allude to the nature of the goods and cause non origin association is unlikely to be regarded as sufficient in itself to result in the application of the prohibition.[87] It is suggested that the position would be different if the applicant has adopted a highly distinctive earlier trade mark and the use of the mark will inevitably result in an advantage accruing to the applicant and where there is no justification for that use.[88]

(d) Detrimental to the distinctive character or repute of the earlier trade mark

These words encompass two alternatives. It is enough if the use of the **8–85** mark would, without due cause, be detrimental to the distinctive character or repute of the earlier trade mark. Repute is clear enough, it being a requirement that the earlier trade mark has a reputation. What is not so clear is the meaning of distinctiveness in this context. It could be referring to the inherent distinctiveness of the mark or its distinctiveness arising from both its inherent distinctiveness and its distinctiveness in fact. It is suggested that the latter is the preferable interpretation for otherwise there would be no *nexus* between the requirement that the earlier trade mark has a reputation and the requirement that the use of the later mark would take unfair advantage of, or be detrimental to, the distinctive character of the earlier mark.

As before where there is in fact confusion as to origin, it is suggested **8-86** that the prohibition must apply.[89] But for the reasons discussed above in paragraph 8–76 *et seq.*, it is suggested that it is not limited to such cases and that the provision recognises that the use of a famous mark by a party other than the proprietor may cause damage through erosion of distinctiveness or association, even in cases where there is no likelihood of origin confusion. This was recognised by the European Court of Justice and the Advocate General in *Sabel v. Puma*.[90] So also in *British*

---

[87] See, *e.g. Oasis Stores* [1998] R.P.C. 631.
[88] See *Dimple* [1985] G.R.U.R. 550 and the discussion in *Premier Brands, supra* at nn. 20 and 65.
[89] see, *e.g. Sheimer* [2000] R.P.C. 484; [1999] E.T.M.R. 519, use of the mark VISA on condoms bound to have a detrimental effect on the mark VISA used for credit card services. *cf. Oasis Stores* [1998] R.P.C. 631, use of EVEREADY on condoms unlikely to be confused with EVEREADY for batteries.
[90] See para. 8–78 and n. 80, *supra*.

Sugar v. James Robertson Jacob J. said of the corresponding words in section 10(3) of the 1994 Act[91]:

"I only note it might cater for the case where the goods were vastly different but the marks the same or similar and the proprietor could show that the repute of his mark was likely to be affected. The sort of circumstances of the Dutch *Claeryn/Klarein* case (mark for gin infringed by identical sounding mark for detergent, damage to the gin mark image) may fall within this kind of infringement, even though they do not fall within section 10(2) because there is no likelihood of confusion as to trade origin."

8-87 *Premier Brands*[92] establishes there are at least two ways in which detriment may be caused despite an absence of confusion as to origin. First, the use of the later mark may erode the distinctiveness of the earlier mark. Erosion of distinctiveness can be damaging, as observed by Sir Thomas Bingham M.R. in *Taittinger v. Allbev*[93]:

"The first plaintiff's reputation and goodwill in the description Champagne derive not only from the quality of their wine and its glamorous associations, but also from the very singularity and exclusiveness of the description, the absence of qualifying epithets and imitative descriptions. Any product which is not Champagne but which is allowed to describe itself as such must inevitably, in my view, erode the singularity and exclusivity of the description Champagne and so cause the first plaintiffs damage of an insidious but serious kind".

8-88 Secondly, there may be tarnishing, as in *Lucas Bols* where the mark *Claeryn* for gin was held to be infringed by the use of the sign *Klarein* for detergent and the court explained[94]:

"It is . . . possible . . . that the goods to which [the use of] a similar mark relates, appealed to the sensations of the public in such a way that the attraction and the 'capacity of the mark to stimulate the desire to buy' the kind of goods for which it is registered, are impaired."

---

[91] [1996] R.P.C. 281 at 295. The *Claeryn/Klarein* judgment is reported at (1976) 7 I.I.C. 420: see n. 65, *supra*.

[92] See n. 20, *supra*.

[93] [1993] F.S.R. 641 at 678, cited in *Premier Brands*. See also *Parfums Givenchy v. Designer Alternatives* [1994] R.P.C. 243, CA; *cf. Harrods v. Harrodian School* [1996] R.P.C. 697, CA, where some criticism was made of this approach, but in the context of a claim for passing off which requires damage resulting from a misrepresentation.

[94] (1976) 7 I.I.C. 420, and cited in *Premier Brands*. The court in *Premier Brands* also referred to *Sheimer*, *supra*, *American Express v. Libra Approved Laboratories*, 10 US PQ 2d 2006, a decision of the New York District Court, and *Mars* (1995) 26 I.I.C. 282, a decision of the German Federal Supreme Court.

Before the Registrar the following matters are considered relevant in **8-89** considering whether the requirements of the prohibition are satisfied[95]:

(1) the inherent distinctiveness of the earlier trade mark;
(2) the extent of the reputation that the earlier mark enjoys;
(3) the range of goods or services for which the earlier trade mark enjoys a reputation;
(4) the uniqueness or otherwise of the mark in the market place;
(5) whether the respective goods/services, although dissimilar, are in some way related or likely to be sold through the same outlets;
(6) whether the earlier trade mark will be any less distinctive for the goods/services for which it has a reputation than it was before;
(7) whether the reputation of the earlier trade mark is likely to be damaged or tarnished in some significant or material way.

E. Meaning of an earlier trade mark

All of the prohibitions provided by section 5(1), (2) and (3) of the 1994 **8-90** Act are concerned with earlier trade marks. These are defined in section 6 of the Act.

Section 6(1) of the Act identifies the various types of trade mark in relation to which a conflict may arise. In summary they are earlier United Kingdom national registrations, registrations entitled to protection in the United Kingdom under the Madrid Protocol, Community trade marks and marks entitled to protection in the United Kingdom under the Paris Convention or the WTO Agreement (TRIPS)[96] as well-known trade marks. As will be seen, account is to be taken of appropriate priorities and specific provision is made in respect of applications and trade marks which have recently expired.

Registered trade marks, the Madrid Protocol and Community trade marks

In the case of national registered trade marks, international registrations **8-91** designating the United Kingdom and Community trade marks, earlier trade marks are those with a date of application for registration earlier than that of the trade mark in question, taking account (where appropriate) of any priority claimed.[97] Presumably, "where appropriate" means that it is relevant and properly claimed.

---

[95] See *Oasis Stores* [1998] R.P.C. 631; *"Audi-Med"* [1998] R.P.C. 863. OHIM takes a similar line: see, *e.g. Campomar's Application* [2000] E.T.M.R. 50.
[96] The Patents and Trade Marks (World Trade Organisation) Regulations 1999, S.I. 1999 No. 1899.
[97] 1994 Act. s.6(1)(a). And an International trade mark (UK) and Community trade mark may be converted into a national application, without loss of priority.

8-92   In the case of all these types of trade marks, priority may be claimed under the Paris Convention for a period of six months from the date of filing of the first application for that trade mark in a Convention country.[98] So also priority may be claimed from a first filing in one of the countries with whom the United Kingdom has an agreement for the reciprocal protection of trade marks.[99] It is to be noted that the priority period runs from the first application. It is not possible to prolong the period by making applications in different countries and claiming priority from the later one. Priority rights are assignable.[1]

8-93   The Registrar must therefore consider the mark the subject of the application, taking into account its priority claim and, in the light of that, whether there is an earlier relevant trade mark, taking into account its priority claim. It must also be borne in mind that it is possible for an application in respect of different goods or services to have different priority dates or for some of the goods or services to have a priority date earlier than the date of filing and for others to have the priority date of the date of filing.

Where two applications are filed on the same day or claim the same priority date and are otherwise each acceptable, then the Registrar will allow both marks to proceed to registration.

8-99   In the case of Community trade marks, two other matters are notable. First, a Community trade mark application is, in Member States, to be treated as equivalent to a national filing under Article 32 of the CTM Regulation. Secondly, under the Community trade mark regime the proprietor of an earlier trade mark registered in the United Kingdom who applies for, or has secured registration of, an equivalent Community trade mark may surrender the later trade mark or allow it to lapse but retain seniority, that is to say he is deemed to continue to have the same rights as he would have had if the earlier trade mark had continued to be registered. The position of such a proprietor is preserved under the 1994 Act.[2] The seniority of a Community trade mark is to be considered.

Applications for registration

8–95   Earlier trade marks include applications for registration under the domestic regime, the Madrid Protocol and the Community trade mark system, which when registered would be "earlier trade marks".[3] The provision only operates subject to such an earlier application being registered. So the Registrar may suspend an application pending the

---

[98] See 1994 Act, ss.35 and 55, in the case of national registrations; Trade Marks (International Registration) Order 1996, art. 8, in the case of international registrations designating the U.K.; Community Trade Mark Regulation, Art. 29, in the case of Community trade marks.
[99] Under the 1994 Act, s.36.
[1] s.35(6).
[2] s.6(1)(b).
[3] s.6(2).

resolution of any issues concerning the registrability of an earlier application.

Account to be taken of marks for a period of one year after expiry

The 1994 Act provides that a registration which has expired shall **8–96** nevertheless continue to be taken into account in determining the registrability of a later mark for a period of one year after the expiry unless the Registrar is satisfied that there was no bona fide use of the mark during the two years immediately preceding the expiry.[4] The use of the term "expiry" suggests that it does not apply to marks which have been revoked or declared invalid, but is rather concerned with marks which have not been renewed by the due date. Where such a mark is cited then it may be possible to overcome the objection by suspending the application until the year has elapsed or seeking the consent of the original proprietor.

Marks entitled to protection as well known marks

Earlier trade marks include marks which have not been registered or **8–97** even used in this country where they are entitled to protection as well-known marks under the Paris Convention or the WTO Agreement (TRIPS).[5] The scope of protection afforded to such marks must also be considered and, in particular, the "protected" goods or services identified. This is discussed in paragraph 8–14, above.

Position under the Community Trade Mark Regulation

Under the CTM system earlier trade marks are defined to comprise[6]:   **8–98**

(1) Community trade marks, national trade marks registered in any Member State, or, in the case of Belgium, the Netherlands or Luxembourg, at the Benelux Trade Mark Office and any trade marks registered under the Madrid system which have effect in any Member State by designation;
(2) any applications for any such trade marks, subject to their registration;
(3) and any trade marks protected in any Member State as well-known trade marks under the Paris Convention.

As under the TM Directive, account is to be taken, where appropriate, of claimed priorities.

[4] s.6(3).
[5] s.56, as amended by S.I. 1999 No. 1899 defines, for the purposes of the Act, trade marks which are entitled to protection under the Paris Convention or the WTO Agreement. For a discussion of the requirements for qualification, see Chapter 13, para. 13–169, below.
[6] CTM Regulation, Art. 8(2).

8-99   This provision has not been expressly amended to take account of the WTO Agreement (TRIPS).[7] Nevertheless under Article 2 of the WTO Agreement, Members are obliged to comply with Article 6 of the Paris Convention and Article 16(2) of the WTO Agreement provides that Article 6*bis* of the Paris Convention shall apply, *mutatis mutandis*, to services.[8] Accordingly, it is suggested, it is likely the provision would be interpreted so as to include trade marks protected under the WTO Agreement.

F. Acts of agents or representatives

8–100 The Act provides special protection against the unauthorised acts of agents or representatives in seeking to register marks. If an application for registration of a trade mark is made by a person who is an agent or representative of a person who is the proprietor of the mark in a Paris Convention country then, if the proprietor opposes the application, registration shall be refused unless the agent or representative justifies his action.[9]

The Community trade mark system offers similar protection.[10]

3. Conflict with earlier rights

General

8–101 Section 5 of the 1994 Act also prohibits registration where or to the extent that the use of the mark in the United Kingdom is liable to be prevented by what the Act describes as "earlier rights". These are defined by reference to two categories, namely, where the use of the trade mark is liable to be prevented:

(1) by virtue of any rule of law (in particular, the law of passing off) protecting an unregistered trade mark or other sign used in the course of trade; or

(2) by virtue of an earlier right other than those referred to in section 5(1) to (3) (earlier trade marks) or paragraph (a) above, in particular by virtue of the law of copyright, design right or registered designs.[11]

8-102 This provision implements the optional provisions of Article 4(4) of the TM Directive. Depending upon the circumstances it may apply in

---

[7] This was not one of the provisions expressly amended by Regulation 3288/94.

[8] See also Chapter 13, para. 13–168.

[9] 1994 Act, s.60(1),(2) and (5), implementing Article 6 *septies* of the Paris Convention. Section 60(4) also provides that the proprietor may apply for an injunction to restrain the use of the trade mark in the U.K.

[10] CTM Regulation, Art. 8(3). And see also Art. 11 for a right equivalent to that provided by the 1994 Act, s.60(4).

[11] s.5(4).

respect of all or only some of the goods or services the subject of the application.[12] Although not in terms so limited, for practical purposes the objections likely to be considered are those based upon the identified rights in passing off, copyright, design rights and registered designs.

The 1994 Act further specifies that the proprietor of the earlier right is **8–103** the person so entitled to prevent the use of the trade mark, although it is to be noted that the Act does not require that the objection be taken by the proprietor of the earlier right. Nevertheless, identification of the proprietor may be important in two respects. First, if the objection is to be overcome by obtaining a consent under section 5(5), then the consent must be given by the proprietor of the earlier right. Secondly, if honest concurrent use is properly relied upon then, in opposition proceedings, the Registrar shall not refuse the application unless objection on that ground is raised by the proprietor of the earlier right.[13]

The protection of an unregistered trade mark—passing off and related rights

This limb of the prohibition protects a goodwill established in a business **8–104** conducted under an unregistered mark and imports into the relative grounds of objection a consideration of the requirements of the cause of action in passing off.[14] These are considered in detail in Chapter 14.[15] The Registry accordingly looks for evidence of use sufficient to attract a relevant goodwill.[16]

The particular formulation of the provision suggests that the correct **8–105** approach is to consider a normal and fair use of the mark the subject of the application in respect of all the goods or services the subject of the application and whether or not this would result in passing off.[17] In this sense the test is different from that involved in a claim in passing off which would normally require a consideration of all of the circumstances of the defendant's trade.

---

[12] So implementing the TM Directive, Art. 13.

[13] 1994 Act, s.7(2).

[14] The prohibition has similarities to that provided by the 1938 Act, s.11, but important differences too. First, under the old law it was not necessary for the opponent to establish a reputation or goodwill. The question was determined having regard to the "user" of the earlier trade mark: *Berlei v. Bali* ("*Bali*") [1969] R.P.C. 472. Secondly, it was not necessary to show deception in the sense required by passing off. It was enough if peoples' minds were put into a state of doubt or uncertainty: *Hack* (1940) 58 R.P.C. 91. Finally, it was not necessary to establish a likelihood of damage, let alone damage caused by the deception, which is a requirement of the cause of action in passing off.

[15] The basic principles were again explained by the House of Lords in terms of the "classical trinity" in *Reckitt v. Coleman v. Borden* ("*Jif*") [1990] R.P.C. 341. See, particularly, Lord Oliver at 406 and Lord Jauncey at 416. See also the Court of Appeal in *Consorzio del Prosciutto di Parma v. Marks & Spencer* ("*Parma Ham*") [1991] R.P.C. 351 at 368, CA.

[16] "*Wackers*" [1999] R.P.C. 453.

[17] As under the 1938 Act: *Smith Hayden* ("*Ovax*") (1946) 63 R.P.C. 97 at 101; *Berlei v. Bali* ("*Bali*") [1969] R.P.C. 472. This appears to be the approach adopted under the 1994 Act by the appointed person and the Registry: "*Wild Child*" [1998] R.P.C. 455; "*Corgi*" [1999] R.P.C. 549, both decisions of the appointed person; *Oasis Stores* [1998] R.P.C. 631 (Regy.).

8-106   It is suggested that the issue must be determined as at the date of the application for the mark in issue. The question is whether or not use of the mark applied for is liable to be prevented as at that date. If, however, the mark the subject of the application is already in use then this may require consideration of the position at an earlier time too. The relevant date for proving reputation and goodwill in a claim for passing off is the date of commencement of the activities complained of.[18]

8-107   There are other relevant rules of law of a like nature. In particular under section 56 of the 1994 Act a proprietor of a trade mark which is entitled to protection under the Paris Convention or the WTO Agreement (TRIPS) as a well-known trade mark is entitled to restrain by injunction the use of that mark in the United Kingdom. Similarly, under section 60 of the Act the proprietor of a trade mark in a Paris Convention country may apply for an injunction to restrain the unauthorised use of that mark by an agent or representative.

Copyright, design right and registered designs

8–108   This limb of the prohibition deals with any mark, the use of which would result in the infringement of any other earlier right, in particular any copyright, design right or registered design.[19] This range of objections reflects the wide range of marks which may be registered under Act, including sounds, designs and the shapes of goods and their packaging:[20] but it had a parallel under the 1938 Act in the words of section 11.[21]

Position under the Community trade mark regulation

8–109   Although there is a similar prohibition under the CTM system, it is cast in rather different terms. Article 8(4) of the CTM Directive provides:

> "Upon opposition by the proprietor of a non-registered trade mark or of another sign used in the course of trade of more than mere local significance, the trade mark applied for shall not be registered where and to the extent that, pursuant to the law of the Member State governing that sign,
>
> (a) rights to that sign were acquired prior to the date of application for registration of the Community trade mark, or the

---

[18] *"Pub Squash"* [1981] R.P.C. 429 at 494, (PC, NSW).

[19] A consideration of the requirements of a cause of action to protect each of these rights is beyond the scope of this work and the reader is referred to a specialist text, such as *The Modern Law of Copyright* (2nd ed., 1995), *Copinger and Skone James on Copyright* (14th ed., 1999, *Russell-Clarke* (6th ed., 1999).

[20] See, *e.g. Team Lotus Ventures* [1999] E.T.M.R. 669.

[21] "It shall not be lawful to register as a trade mark or part of a trade mark any matter the use of which would . . . be disentitled to protection in a court of justice, or would be contrary to law . . ."; and see also: *"Karo Step"* [1977] R.P.C. 255; *"Oscar"* [1979] R.P.C. 173.

date of the priority claimed for the application for registration of the Community trade mark;

(b) that sign confers on its proprietor the right to prohibit the use of a subsequent trade mark."

As in the case of the other relative objections, it may only be taken on **8-110** opposition. The objection may be taken by the proprietor of the relevant earlier mark or sign or by any person authorised under national law to exercise those rights.[22]

There is also a requirement that the mark or sign has been used and is of more than mere local significance. This appears to require that the use has been such as to generate a reputation and that the reputation must be more than local.

Quite what is meant by local is not explained but it appears to be a **8-111** deliberate inclusion which is designed to cut out of consideration marks which have a reputation of only limited geographical extent within any particular country.[23] This seems the only sensible interpretation of the provision as a whole which is concerned with the protection of unregistered marks *within* a Member State but which are *not* of mere local significance. It may fairly be expected that determination of the scope of the provision will be controversial.

There appears to be no express objection based upon rights outside those generated by use. So, for example, no mention is made of copyright or industrial property rights.[24]

4. Honest concurrent use

Section 7 of the 1994 Act preserves the notion of honest concurrent use **8-112** in limited circumstances. It has no basis in the TM Directive. The section did not appear in the original Bill but in Committee an amendment was moved which would have had the effect that a mark was not to be refused registration where honest concurrent use had been made of it, notwithstanding that it conflicted with an earlier trade mark. It was considered that this amendment would have had the effect of preserving the effect of section 12(2) of the 1938 Act. The amendment was resisted by the Government on the basis that it was doubtful that it could be reconciled with the mandatory provisions of Article 4 of the

---

[22] CTM Regulation, Art. 43(1)(c).
[23] There is, however, a measure of protection for owners of such geographically limited rights in the CTM Regulation, Art. 107. This provides that the proprietor of such a right may oppose the use of the Community trade mark in the territory where his right is protected in so far as the law of the Member State so permits, subject to acquiescence over a period of five years. So under the law of England a person with a goodwill of limited geographical extent could prevent the use of a Community trade mark in so far as it would result in passing off.
[24] Contrast the TM Directive, Art. 4(4)(b). Instead the Regulation provides in Art. 52(2) that these matters may be raised in proceedings for a declaration of invalidity or on the basis of a counterclaim in infringement proceedings.

Directive. This would seem to be correct. Article 4(1) and (2) do not permit such an exception.[25] The current section was a compromise moved on the third reading of the Bill.[26]

There is no equivalent under the Community trade mark system.

The circumstances in which honest concurrent use may be raised

8–113 Section 7 of the 1994 Act provides:

> (1) This section applies where on an application for the registration of a trade mark it appears to the registrar—
>
>   (a) that there is an earlier trade mark in relation to which the conditions set out in section 5(1), (2) or (3) obtain, or
>   (b) that there is an earlier right in relation to which the condition set out in section 5(4) is satisfied,
>
>   but the applicant shows to the satisfaction of the registrar that there has been honest concurrent use of the trade mark for which registration is sought.
> (2) In that case the registrar shall not refuse the application by reason of the earlier trade mark or other earlier right unless objection on that ground is raised in opposition proceedings by the proprietor of that earlier trade mark or earlier right.

8-114 The Act therefore permits an applicant to rely upon honest concurrent use during the course of examination to defeat an objection raised on the basis of an earlier trade mark or earlier right. If the Registrar is satisfied that there has been honest concurrent use, as to which see below, then he must allow the application to proceed to advertisement and, if there is no opposition, to registration. If the proprietor of the earlier trade mark or earlier right opposes the application and the Registrar concludes that the opposition is properly founded and the ground of objection is a valid one, then he must refuse the application. He cannot at that stage rely upon honest concurrent use to dismiss the opposition.[27] Nevertheless it may be appropriate in evaluating the opposition to take into account any period of any side by side use.

8-115 Curiously section 7(2) refers only to an opposition by the *proprietor* of the earlier trade mark or other earlier right. On the words of the section it appears that if an opposition is entered by a party other than the proprietor of the earlier trade mark or other earlier right and such a party relies upon that earlier trade mark or other earlier right, as he is entitled to, then the Registrar must take into account honest concurrent use and, in an appropriate case, allow the mark to proceed to registra-

---

[25] *cf.* Art. 4(5) and (6).
[26] *Hansard*, H.L. Vol. 553, col. 71.
[27] *Road Tech Computer Systems v. Unison Software* [1996] F.S.R. 805.

tion. That party would then have to bring an application for a declaration under section 47 following registration. It is hard to reconcile this with the mandatory words of Article 4 of the TM Directive.

General principles

The 1994 Act defines honest concurrent use for the purposes of the **8–116** section as such use in the United Kingdom, by the applicant or with his consent, as would formerly have amounted to honest concurrent use for the purposes of section 12(2) of the Trade Marks Act 1938. The effect of this section is therefore to introduce the old law of honest concurrent use into the new Act.

This is not a very satisfactory formula. Whilst it may be workable in **8-117** the case of objections raised under section 5(1) or (2) of the 1994 Act it is hard to see how it can be applied in the case of an objection under section 5(3) which deals with the case of the use of the same or similar marks on goods or services which are not similar and where the objection does not call for a likelihood of confusion. There was no equivalent objection under the 1938 Act and circumstances which would have amounted to honest concurrent use for the purposes of section 12(2) are in large part concerned with the likelihood of confusion or evidence of actual confusion.[28] Much the same difficulties arise in the case of an application objectionable under section 5(4) of the 1994 Act.

Main matters to be considered

The main matters which the tribunal should take into account were laid **8-118** down by Lord Tomlin in *Pirie*.[29] Briefly these matters are:

(1) The extent of use in time and quantity and the area of the trade;
(2) the degree of confusion likely to ensue from the resemblance of the marks which is to a large extent indicative of the measure of public inconvenience;
(3) the honesty of the concurrent use;
(4) whether any instances of confusion have in fact been proved; and
(5) the relative inconvenience which would be caused if the mark were registered.

The discretion of the tribunal is unfettered and concurrent registration may be allowed even where the possibility of confusion is considerable. Each case has to be determined on its own merits.[30]

---

[28] See para. 8–11, below.
[29] (1933) 50 R.P.C. 147 at 159, HL. Applied in *Electrix* [1957] R.P.C. 369 at 379. On appeal the questions which arose under the 1938 Act, s.12(2) had no application. See also *Fitton* (1949) 66 R.P.C. 110 at 112; *Peddie* (1944) 61 R.P.C. 31; *Spillers* (1952) 69 R.P.C. 327 at 330. For more recent illustrations see *"Star"* [1990] R.P.C. 522 (Regy.) and *"Budweiser"* [1998] R.P.C. 669; upheld by the CA, February 7, 2000.
[30] A passage cited with approval by the CA in *"Budweiser"*, February 7, 2000 which emphasised that there are dangers in seeking to apply the five reasons found determinative in *Pirie* in every case.

Honesty of concurrent use

8–119 The concurrent use must be "honest".

> "Knowledge of the registration of the opponent's mark may be an important factor where the honesty of the user of the mark sought to be registered is impugned, but where once that honesty of the user has been established, the fact of knowledge loses much of its significance, though it may be a matter not to be wholly overlooked in balancing the considerations for and against registration."[31]

Use in the genuine belief that the mark is not such as to cause confusion is "honest" use.[32]

Public interest

8–120 The tribunal should always consider the public interest. This has long been a matter taken into account in determining whether there is honest concurrent use.[33] Accordingly the Registrar should always consider whether the public are adequately protected. The tribunal will consider whether it is just to register, even if there is some confusion.[34]

Period of use

8–121 No fixed rule can be laid down as to the minimum period of honest concurrent use necessary to lead to registration. The Registrar looks for a reasonable period of use, usually about five years prior to the application date: but this is only a guideline. In *Peddie*,[35] the Registrar stated that he knew of "no reported case in which a period of concurrent use so short as two and a quarter years has been treated as sufficient to bring an application within the advantages of section 12(2) or the previous corresponding section 21 of the repealed Trade Marks Acts 1905 to 1919. But the circumstances here are exceptional" and registration was allowed.

Or other special circumstances

8–122 The 1994 Act does not permit other special circumstances to be taken into account.[36]

---

[31] *Per* Lord Tomlin in *Pirie, supra,* at 159, quoted in *Peddie* (1944) 61 R.P.C. 31 at 36 (Regy.).
[32] *"Bali" (No. 2)* [1978] F.S.R. 193 at 220–221, but the applicant's knowledge of the opponent's mark was relevant on the question of discretion—no longer a material matter under the 1994 Act—and registration was refused.
[33] See *Ehrman* [1897] 2 Ch. 495; 14 R.P.C. 665; *Rosedale* [1968] F.S.R. 93.
[34] *"Buler"* [1975] R.P.C. 275; *"Star", supra; "Budweiser", supra.*
[35] (1944) 61 R.P.C. 31 at 36. See also *Smith Hayden* (1946) 33 R.P.C. 97 at 98 ("Ovax"), nine months not a long enough period; three and a half years use, on a larger scale than opponent, registration allowed, *"Buler"* [1975] R.P.C. 275; two years and 10 months use on a very large scale, registration allowed, *"Granada"* [1979] R.P.C. 303; four years use, starting small, not long and extensive enough to show likelihood of confusion, registration refused, *"Margaret Rose"* [1978] R.P.C. 84.
[36] In contrast to the position under the 1938 Act: see, *e.g. Peddie* (1944) 61 R.P.C. 31; *"Bud"* [1988] R.P.C. 535; *"Budweiser", supra.*

5. General matters

When the objection may be taken

Any of the relative grounds of objection may be taken by the Registrar **8–123** upon examination of the application under section 37 of the 1994 Act or by a third party upon an opposition under section 38(1) of the 1994 Act. Moreover, they may be the subject of third-party observations in writing to the Registrar under section 38(2). Following registration these grounds may be raised upon an application for a declaration of invalidity under section 47.

Position under the Community trade mark regulation

The position under the Community trade mark system is different. The **8–124** relative grounds of objection may only be raised on opposition[37] or under Article 52.[38]

Onus of proof

There is no overall onus on the applicant either before the Registrar or in **8–125** opposition proceedings. And so when an opponent raises objections under section 5 of the 1994 Act he must make them out.[39]

Overcoming the objection—consent of the proprietor of the earlier trade mark or right

No objection can be taken under section 5 of the 1994 Act where the **8–126** proprietor of the earlier trade mark or other earlier right consents to the registration.[40] The Registrar has no discretion to refuse registration in a case where consent has been given but where he considers that confusion may result. The matter is left to the commercial judgment of the proprietor.

Other ways to overcome an objection include filing evidence of use, **8–127** restricting the goods or services the subject of the application, offering a disclaimer or limitation and removal or limitation of the earlier trade mark and division of the application. These are discussed in Chapter 5.

---

[37] See para. 8–111, above.
[38] Declaration of invalidity on application to OHIM or on the basis of a counterclaim in infringement proceedings.
[39] "Audi-Med" [1998] R.P.C. 859; Oasis Stores [1998] R.P.C. 631.
[40] s.5(5).

CHAPTER 9

VALIDITY AND REMOVAL OF TRADE MARKS FROM THE REGISTER

1. Preliminary matters

9–01 This chapter is concerned with ways in which a United Kingdom trade mark may be removed from the register, and, in consequence, with the status of a registered trade mark. A mark may cease to be a registered trade mark in one of four ways. These are logically considered in the following order:

(1) Invalidity: a declaration of invalidity is made by the court or Registrar, upon application under section 47 of the Trade Marks Act 1994. The declaration may concern the whole or part of the registration.

(2) Revocation: the registration is revoked by the court or Registrar, upon application under section 46. Again, revocation may concern the whole or part of the registration.

(3) Surrender: the registration may be surrendered by the proprietor, pursuant to section 45. Again, the whole or part of the registration may be surrendered;

(4) Expiry: the registration is removed because it has expired and has not been renewed.

9-02 Invalidity and revocation are different. The essence of an invalidity attack is that the mark should never have been registered—hence the cross-reference in section 47 to the absolute and relative grounds for refusal contained in sections 3 and 5. It is however possible to defeat an attack based on section 3(1)(b) to (d) grounds by showing that, since registration, the mark has in fact acquired distinctive character. By contrast, revocation is effectively dealing with the consequences of events over the period since registration: since registration, there has been five years non-use, or the mark has become generic or misleading.

9–03 Each of the four ways outlined above produces a different temporal effect:

(a) A declaration of invalidity is the most serious. The consequence of such a declaration is that the registration is deemed never to have been made.[1]

---

[1] 1994 Act, s.47(6), subject to the proviso that "this shall not affect transactions past and closed". See below.

(b) An order for revocation has effect from the date of the application for revocation, unless the Court or Registrar decide that the grounds for revocation existed at some earlier date.

(c) A surrender would appear to take effect from the date when the Registrar publishes the amended entry in the Register, *i.e.* after the Registrar has approved the application to surrender.

(d) If a registration expires it enters a state of limbo for six months before the registration is removed from the Register. If, within that six month period, an application to renew is filed with the appropriate fees, then the registration is renewed. Even after a registration has been removed, it may be restored upon application made within six months of removal, provided it is just to do so.

The structure of this chapter is as follows. In this first section, we **9–04** consider two preliminary topics. First, we consider the status of a registered trade mark and the onus of proof when an invalidity or revocation attack is made. Second, there is the question as to whether sections 46 and 47 contain a residual discretion (in the word "may") not to revoke or invalidate a registration, despite the fact that one or more grounds for revocation or invalidity, as the case may be, have been proved. The subsequent sections are:

2. Invalidity
3. Revocation for Non-use
4. Other grounds for revocation
5. Procedure
6. Surrender
7. Expiry

Status of a registered trade mark and its registered proprietor

Section 2(1) of the 1994 Act provides: **9–05**

"A registered trade mark is a property right obtained by the registration of the trade mark under this Act and the proprietor of a registered trade mark has the rights and remedies provided by this Act."

Section 72 provides: **9–06**

"In all legal proceedings relating to a registered trade mark (including proceedings for rectification of the register) the registration of a person as proprietor of a trade mark shall be prima facie evidence of the validity of the original registration and of any subsequent assignment or other transmission of it."

9–07 Section 72 is a slightly curious provision, but adopts the time-honoured wording which can be traced back to the 1905 Act. It provides that the registration of a person now as the proprietor of a trade mark is prima facie validity of the registration when originally made. The effect of sections 72 and 2(1) appears to mean that as long as a trade mark remains registered it can be enforced, giving the rights and remedies provided by the Act.[2] The fact of registration is prima facie evidence of the validity of the registration. Therefore, in the absence of any attack on a registered trade mark, it is assumed to be valid. Equally, unless attacked, any assignment or transmission of the mark (which has been entered on the Register) which has occurred since the mark was originally registered is assumed to be valid.

Onus of proof

9–08 With one notable exception, if an application is made for a declaration of invalidity or for revocation, the onus lies on the person making the attack to prove the grounds of invalidity and/or revocation relied upon to the normal civil standard of the balance of probabilities. If one or more grounds are proved, this will automatically overcome the prima facie position provided for by section 72 of the 1994 Act. The rights and remedies, if any, which are then available in respect of the registered mark are subject to the temporal effects of the grounds relied upon.

9–09 The exception concerns applications to revoke for non-use. If any question arises as to the use to which a registered trade mark has been put, it is for the proprietor to show what use has been made of the mark.[3] Therefore, an application to revoke for non-use places the onus of proof on the proprietor to prove the use which has been made of the mark. Equally, if the proprietor is not able to show genuine use, the onus rests on him to show that there were proper reasons for the non-use.

9–10 In addition, if an application for invalidity is based on any one of section 3(1)(b) to (d), the onus of proving the ground relied upon rests on the applicant for invalidity. If the proprietor then wishes to overcome the ground for invalidity by proving that since registration the mark has acquired a distinctive character, then the onus of proving that obviously lies on the proprietor.

Evidential burden of proof

9–11 The onus of proof, as explained above, does not change as proceedings progress. By contrast, the evidential burden of proof may well move back and forth as the parties move through the stages of the proceed-

---

[2] Note that this is not quite what the TM Directive provides. See the discussion regarding Article 11 in para. 9–32, below.
[3] 1994 Act, s.100.

ings. Section 72 of the 1994 Act indicates where the evidential burden lies at the outset of any legal proceedings. At that point, the registration itself is prima facie evidence of its validity and of the registration of the proprietor as proprietor. Any person wishing to attack the registration or the status of the proprietor must first present grounds which overcome the prima facie evidence of the registration. If such grounds are supported by evidence,[4] then the evidential burden shifts to the proprietor to produce evidence to the contrary. Ultimately, the validity of the registration is determined according to the normal civil standard of proof.

Discretion?

Both subsections (1) and (2) of s.47 of the 1994 Act provide that: "The **9–12** registration of a trade mark *may* be declared invalid. . .". Equally, section 46(1) provides "The registration of a trade mark *may* be revoked on any of the following grounds. . .". The use of the word "may" in section 46(1) has given rise to debate over whether that word provides a residual discretion not to revoke even though one of the grounds of invalidity or revocation has been made out.

The debate has arisen particularly in cases of non-use, probably **9–13** because the equivalent non-use provisions in the 1938 Act did contain a residual discretion. In the Registry, different hearing officers have reached different conclusions. In *Invermont*[5] the hearing officer reached the conclusion that there was no discretion in section 47, but could not see any reason to infer that the same should apply to revocation in section 46. In *Zippo*,[6] the hearing officer decided there was no residual discretion, largely due to the presence of section 46(5) (partial revocation—"revocation shall relate to those goods or services only"), being independently derived from Article 13 of the TM Directive (which provides for similar treatment in cases of partial revocation and invalidity).

The hang-over from the 1938 Act has unduly influenced this issue in **9–14** the United Kingdom. The equivalent provisions in Articles 3, 4 and 12 of the LTM Directive use the expressions "shall be liable to be declared

---

[4] Again, allegations of non-use are the exception. In the normal way, an application for revocation for non-use must have some substance to it, otherwise it would be frivolous, vexatious and/or an abuse. Penalties are likely to be visited on frivolous applications or applications based on allegations which are untrue. Of course, the way in which the proprietor shows that an application is frivolous is by putting in evidence of (1) his use and (2) that the applicant knew of his use.

[5] [1997] R.P.C. 125. The hearing officer did not have the benefit of argument on the point. There was at least one decision in which the purported exercise of a residual discretion saved the mark from revocation: *Route 66* SRIS O/026/98, February 11, 1998, (Regy). Upon the request of the Registrar, the appointed person referred the appeal to the court, as raising a point of general legal importance as to whether a discretion existed: *A.J. and M.A. Levy's Trade Mark (No.2)* [1999] R.P.C. 358, although the case was settled before any appeal was heard.

[6] [1999] R.P.C. 173.

invalid" and "shall be liable to revocation", which do not clarify the point, as Neuberger J. pointed out in *Premier Brands v. Typhoon* (January 21, 2000):

> "I do not find it surprising that two members of the Trade Marks Registry come to different conclusions on this difficult point. With diffidence, I have reached the conclusion that the view expressed in *ZIPPO* [1999] RPC 173, namely that there is no discretion, is to be preferred. For reasons I have given, I do not find any of the reasons supporting either view particularly strong. However, it does seem to me somewhat odd if the legislature has specifically provided for no revocation in the event of there being good reason for the non-use, but nonetheless has left the Court with a residual discretion, particularly without giving any indication as to what factors should be taken into account when exercising that discretion. Further, consideration of the combined effect of Section 46(1)(c) and (d) suggest to me that it is more likely that the legislature intended that those two paragraphs were to represent mandatory, rather than discretionary, grounds for revocation. Section 46(5) and Article 13 tend to point in favour of the conclusion I have reached. The words 'may' in Section 46(1) and 'liable' in Article 12 are perfectly consistent with the concept of revocation being mandatory but only occurring in the event of an application being made. I also bear in mind that it is not only a privilege for a person to be the proprietor of a registered trade mark, but it represents a monopoly: the Court should not be too ready to perpetuate a monopoly in favour of a person who has not done anything to promote or enjoy it for a period of five years. Decisions of the ECJ to which I have referred show that a major purpose of the trade mark legislation is to protect those who have expended time, effort, ingenuity and money in disseminating a trade mark and building up goodwill in relation to it. It seems to me that the obverse of this approach is that a person who does not use a trade mark for five years or more should lose it."

9–15 This reasoning is correct and perhaps the judge would have been less diffident if argument had been directed to the bigger picture, involving both revocation and invalidity. The issue is clearer in the case of invalidity. If it is found that a mark was registered in breach of an absolute ground for refusal from section 3(1), and the registration cannot be saved by having subsequently acquired a distinctive character, there can be no reason to allow the mark to remain registered.[7] In those circumstances, it must be declared invalid. This demonstrates that "may" in section 47 and "shall be liable to" in Articles 3 and 4 reflect the fact that invalidity and revocation are mandatory but only occur in the event of an application being made.

---

[7] And none are indicated anywhere in the TM Directive or Act.

Although the Hearing Office in *Invermont* could not see any reason to **9–16** infer that the same construction should apply in the case of revocation, it must apply because there is no reason why it should not. In addition, similar reasoning applies in the case of section 46. If a mark is found to have become the common name for the goods in question or if a mark is found to mislead the public, there can be no reason why the registration should not be revoked. In addition, the terms of Article 13 of the TM Directive confirm that there is no residual discretion under either section 46 or 47.

Whatever doubts might remain in the United Kingdom, it is incon- **9–17** ceivable that the European Court of Justice would find that there was a residual discretion not to revoke or invalidate, no doubt for one or more of the reasons set out above. The Court might also be influenced by the provisions of the CTM Regulation which provide "The rights of the proprietor of the Community trade mark shall be declared to be revoked on application. . ." and "A Community trade mark shall be declared invalid on application . . .".[8] Although a Regulation passed in 1994 can hardly be a legitimate aid to construction of a Directive passed in 1988, the Court would no doubt have it well in mind that the purpose of the first stage of harmonisation dictated by the Directive was to pave the way for the Community trade mark system. This purpose would not be fully achieved if the Directive provided for a residual discretion in these important provisions which are the only means to ensure that all trade marks, whenever registered, conform to the same requirements for continued registrability.

2. Invalidity

Section 47 of the 1994 Act sets out the grounds for invalidity of a **9–18** registration. Subject to one exception, if the trade mark is found to have been registered in breach of any of the absolute or relative grounds for refusal contained in sections 3 and 5, then the registration is declared invalid. Attention is therefore directed primarily at the position at the date of application for the mark.

Absolute grounds for invalidity

If a trade mark was registered in breach of section 3 of the 1994 Act or **9–19** any of the provisions referred to in that section,[9] it shall be declared invalid, subject only to one exception. The Act uses the expression "may be declared invalid", but the Directive says "shall be liable to be declared invalid". It is clear that "may" must be construed as "must" or

---

[8] Arts 50, 51 and 52.
[9] This form of wording is appropriate since s.3 incorporates the provisions in s.4, which in turn incorporates parts of ss.57 and 58.

269

"shall". There is no room nor any purpose for a residual discretion not to declare the mark invalid.[10]

9–20   The one exception is provided in section 47(1). If the ground for invalidity is one or more of subsections (1)(b),(c) or (d) of section 3 (no distinctive character, descriptive or generic), then the mark shall not be declared invalid if, in consequence of the use made of it, it has after registration acquired a distinctive character in relation to the goods or services for which it is registered. The wording is the same as that used in the proviso to section 3(1). Whereas the proviso operates to overcome these grounds if the mark has acquired a distinctive character before the date of application, this part of section 47(1) operates in the same way provided the mark has acquired a distinctive character "after registration". The wording appears to permit use prior to application and use prior to the date when the mark was actually put on the Register to contribute to the necessary distinctive character, which reflects reality in any case.

Section 47(1) raises the same issues as are raised under section 3(1). Reference is invited to the relevant part of Chapter 7.

Relative grounds for invalidity

9–21   Section 47(2) of the 1994 Act applies, by way of cross-reference, the relative grounds contained in subsections (1),(2) and (3) of section 5 (conflict with earlier trade marks) and section 5(4) (conflict with earlier rights, including passing off). These grounds for invalidity are not available if the proprietor of the earlier trade mark or other earlier right has consented to the registration. This reflects the fact that these grounds may be raised by any person, whether they are entitled to an earlier trade mark or earlier right or not.

Section 47(2) raises the same issues as are raised under section 5. Reference is invited to the relevant parts of Chapter 8.

When may an application for invalidity be made

9–22   Generally, an application for a declaration of invalidity of a registered trade mark may be made at any time after the mark has been registered. The general position is subject to two areas of qualification. First, the transitional provisions of the 1994 Act and secondly, the effects of acquiescence under section 48(1). These are dealt with in turn.

Transitional provisions

9–23   The 1994 Act defined a trade mark registered under the 1938 Act as an "existing registered mark". At any time after the 1994 Act came into force, an application could be made to invalidate an existing registered

---

[10] See the discussion in the preceding section.

mark under section 47. The transitional provisions provide that for the purposes of such an application, the provisions of the 1994 Act, with one exception, are deemed to have been in force at all material times. The exception is section 5(3) (identical or similar mark, goods or services not similar). In other words, the rules concerning distinctiveness and public policy contained in section 3 and the rules governing conflicts between registered marks and other rights in section 5, all of which had a rough equivalent in one form or another in the old Act are deemed to have applied at all times. Section 5(3) is excluded because there was nothing equivalent in the old Act.

The effect of the transitional provisions creates the potential for a **9–24** mark, whenever it was put on the United Kingdom Register, to face a challenge against the provisions of section 3. The potential for such a challenge under section 5(1),(2) or (4) is much less significant, due to the acquiescence restriction contained in section 48(1)(a), to which we now turn.

Acquiescence

For a person who is entitled to an earlier trade mark or earlier right, **9–25** there is a restriction on his ability to raise grounds for invalidity based on his earlier trade mark or earlier right but not, it seems, any other grounds for invalidity. If such a person has acquiesced in the use of a registered trade mark in the United Kingdom for a continuous period of five years, during which time he was aware of such use, then he ceases to be entitled to apply for a declaration of invalidity of the registered mark based on any earlier trade mark or earlier right to which he is entitled.[11] It is suggested that this acquiescence restriction should apply even where there has been an assignment of the earlier trade mark or earlier right, provided that throughout the requisite five year period both assignor and assignee were aware of and acquiesced in the use of the relevant registered trade mark. Thus, it certainly should not be possible to extend the period of acquiescence required by means of a sham assignment. Equally, any assignee of an earlier trade mark or earlier right must take the assignment subject to any accrued acquiescence right already established prior to the assignment.

Partial invalidity

If the grounds of invalidity exist in respect of only some of the goods or **9–26** services for which the trade mark is registered, the trade mark is declared invalid as regards those goods or services only.[12] The remainder of the registration remains valid and enforceable. It is

---

[11] 1994 Act, s.48(1)(a).
[12] s.47(5).

possible that issues might arise as to how the specification of goods or services should be divided in the event of partial invalidity. This type of issue is much more likely to arise in the case of partial revocation, and is discussed in detail below.

9–27   Neither the TM Directive nor the 1994 Act appear to contemplate partial geographical validity. This could arise in the following circumstances. The applicant for invalidity had and has a goodwill and reputation in a limited geographical area of the United Kingdom. Use of the registered mark in that limited area, but not outside it, would give rise to passing off and would have done so at the date of application for the mark. Although neither Article 13 nor section 47 contemplate this situation, it is suggested it should create no difficulty. In so far as the mark is invalid as covering the geographical area in question, it is declared invalid. Otherwise the validity of the registration is maintained, with a suitable geographical limitation being entered on the Register.

Who may apply

9–28 Section 47(3) of the 1994 Act provides that any person can apply for a declaration of invalidity. This represents a change over the old law, where the applicant had to be a "person aggrieved". In practice this old requirement precluded intermeddlers but did little else except give rise to pointless argument over whether an applicant had *locus standi*. All that has been swept away.

Effect of a declaration of invalidity

9–29 If or to the extent that a trade mark is declared invalid, the registration is deemed never to have been made. The principal consequence of this provision is likely to be that potential liability for infringement disappears with the invalid registration. This deeming provision does not affect transactions past and closed. Thus a past assignment of the registration would not be affected, unless made on the strength of a representation that the mark was valid, which would give rise to a claim for damages/rescission. Equally, an agreement settling a claim for infringement could not be undone and would continue to be enforceable, unless the continued enforcement of an obligation depended upon the mark remaining on the Register. Any injunction previously granted to prevent further infringement of the registration in question would fall away as lacking foundation. If, however, the injunction was in absolute form, preventing any use of the mark XXXX, then the position is less clear. If there were dual claims for infringement of the registered trade mark and for passing off, then the injunction might continue to be supported by the claim for passing off and the continuing threat of damage to goodwill. If not, the injunction might be unenforceable as being in unreasonable restraint of trade. In cases where the point mattered, it would be possible to apply to the court to determine whether the injunction should be varied or discharged.

Influence of the TM Directive

Section 47 of the 1994 Act is the second part of the implementation of **9–30** Articles 3 and 4 of the TM Directive and cross-refers back to sections 3 and 5, which constitute the first part. A question remains whether these two parts amount to full implementation of the Directive. The Directive uses the words "The following shall not be registered or if registered shall be liable to be declared invalid:" before setting out the absolute and relative grounds for both refusal and invalidity. That form of words suggests that if any of the grounds exist as at the date of application, then the application must be refused *and* that (subject to the acquiescence provisions) if any of the grounds exists at any later date, then the registration must be declared invalid. The United Kingdom has implemented the former but not the latter, since section 47 directs attention back to the date of application. It can be argued that the Directive should not be interpreted in this way since Article 12 (grounds for revocation) deals with the consequences of events which have occurred since the mark was put on the Register. There is some overlap between the grounds for revocation and the absolute grounds—(the mark has become the common name for the product or service—compare Article 12.2(a) and section 46(1)(c) with Article 3(1)(d) and section 3(1)(c), and the mark is liable to mislead the public—compare Article 12.2.(b) and section 46(1)(d) with Article 3.1(g) and section 3(3)(b))—which may indicate that it is not necessary to apply the absolute or relative grounds at any date other than the original date of application. However, there are other notable areas of overlap in the Directive which means that the existence of overlap in these provisions is not a reliable aid to construction, one way or the other.

Section 47 also implements provisions of the Directive which support **9–31** Articles 3 and 4, notably Article 13—if the grounds exist in respect of only some of the goods or services for which the mark is registered, then the invalidity extends only to those goods or services.

It appears that the United Kingdom has not expressly implemented **9–32** the mandatory provisions in Article 11.1 and 11.4 of the Directive, whether in section 47 or elsewhere. These provide, in essence, that if or to the extent that a registered trade mark does not fulfil the requirements for use, it cannot be used as an earlier conflicting trade mark upon which to base a relative ground for invalidity. These provisions appear to have effect whether or not an application is brought to revoke for non-use, although in practice it seems unlikely that use would be challenged other than in the context of an application to revoke. If such an application is made, it will be made for the purpose of clearing away the apparently conflicting earlier mark which is being used in the application for a declaration of invalidity. The problem is that, even if the application for invalidity was stayed to await the outcome of the application to revoke for non-use, the conflicting earlier mark would still have effect at the date when the application for invalidity was commenced, unless the applicant for revocation managed to prove that the grounds for revocation existed at a date earlier than the commencement of the application to invalidate. In those circumstances, the court or Registry can, under section 46(6)(b), order that the revocation takes effect from the earlier date. If this occurs, it means that the consequences of not implementing Article 11.1 and 11.4 are avoided. It might have been thought that these circumstances would always occur, with the result that there was no need to make specific provision to implement Articles 11.1 and 11.4. However, the applicant for revocation may or may not be able to prove that grounds for revocation existed at a date earlier than the date when the application to invalidate was commenced. Hence there is a lacuna in the United Kingdom implementation.

9–33   The problem is also alleviated to a very limited extent by the way in which "earlier trade mark" is defined in section 6. Section 6(3) provides that if registrations for United Kingdom or Community trade marks have expired, they shall continue to be taken into account as earlier trade marks for one year following expiry unless the Registrar is satisfied there has been no bona fide use of the mark during the two years immediately preceding the expiry.[13] Apart from this, the rigidity of the definition in section 6 appears to preclude interpretation of the Act in a manner which is consistent with Articles 11.1 and 11.4 of the Directive. If suitable facts arise, the only redress for the disappointed applicant may be to seek compensation from the United Kingdom government for its failure to implement mandatory provisions of the Directive.[14]

The approach at OHIM[15]

9–34 We comment elsewhere on the respects in which the approach at OHIM differs on the application of the absolute and relative grounds for refusal.[16] Here there is one point to be made about how the OHIM Cancellation Divisions approach an invalidity attack, particularly when based on absolute grounds. Instead of deciding an invalidity attack on its merits and on the basis of the evidence put before it, the Cancellation Division has indicated that it treats the original decision of the Examination Division as involving an exercise of discretion which the Cancellation Division cannot upset unless the Examination Division overlooked "substantial criteria" or was made on an insufficient basis. Thus:

"The assessment of whether or not a mark applied for is eligible for registration pursuant to Article 7(1)(b), (c) or (d) CTMR comprises,

---

[13] This is the U.K.'s implementation of the optional provision in the TM Directive, Art. 4.4(f). Even so, it is curious that reference was not made to "genuine" use.
[14] See *Francovich v. Italy* [1991] I E.C.R. 5357; [1993] 2 C.M.L.R. 66, ECJ, and more specialist works.
[15] At the time of writing, the Cancellation Divisions at OHIM had only recently begun issuing decisions.
[16] See generally, Chaps 7 and 8.

to a substantial extent, subjective criteria. In other words: when examining an application along the lines of the said provisions the examiner enjoys a certain degree of discretion. The Office has accepted the challenged Community trade mark for registration. The Cancellation Division form part of the Office at the same level, i.e. we are not 'superior' as regards the Examination Division. With respect to absolute grounds for refusal, cancellation proceedings provide a means of rectification of clear mistakes, they do not provide means of execution of the same scope of discretion with a different result, i.e. they do not provide the possibility of having a decision replaced by another, different one within the same scope of discretion."[17]

The approach taken in this case is deeply flawed, for a number of reasons: **9-35**

(1) A decision whether one of the absolute grounds for refusal exists does not involve an exercise of discretion. It calls for a judgment to be made, if appropriate on the available evidence, as to whether the ground is established or not. The fact that the judgment may be difficult and that it is possible that different examiners might reach differing conclusions does not render the decision as one involving an exercise of discretion.

(2) It fails to take account of the reality, which is that the examiner may have limited information available to him, particularly on the type of issues raised by section 3(1)(c) or (d) grounds (descriptive, generic). A cancellation action based on these grounds is almost invariably brought by someone who is affected by the registration and operates in the same trade. They frequently can supply a wealth of information, particularly about signs in common use in the trade, which was not available to the examiner.

(3) The cancellation action for invalidity ought to be decided on the evidence which is adduced. On that evidence, the issue is: was this mark registered in breach of Article 7(1)(d) (section 3(1)(d))?

(4) The Cancellation Division referred to Article 74(1) of the Community Trade Marks Regulation, as requiring the Division to examine the facts *ex officio*. This had two effects. First, the Division found a German article written in 1998 which expressed the view that nowadays pharmacists used a flat mortar and pestle, rather than the round mortar and pestle, a stylised picture of which constituted the mark in question. The fact that the Division specifically referred to this article in their decision seems to indicate they were unduly influenced by it.

---

[17] *Mortar & Pestle* CTM 172734, OHIM First Cancellation Division, January 31, 2000.

One article does not negate other evidence of common use. The second effect of their application of Article 74(1) was that the Cancellation Division felt the need to discuss the evidence before it with those who had been responsible for this mark in the Examination Division, who expressed the view that their decision would have been the same.

9–36   Whether this or a later decision is appealed, it is to be hoped that the Boards of Appeal take the opportunity to lay down clear guidelines as to the approach which the Cancellation Division should take.

3. Revocation for non-use

9–37 The 1994 Act contains four grounds upon which the registration of a trade mark may be revoked. The first two concern non-use which, in brief outline, are:

> (1) the mark has not been put into genuine use within five years of the date when the mark was put on the Register, and there are no proper reasons for the lack of use;
> (2) there has been an uninterrupted period of five years in which no genuine use of the mark has occurred, and there are no proper reasons for the lack of use.

The effect of revocation is that the life of the registration comes to an end. Unlike the effect of a declaration of invalidity under section 47, the registration continues to have effect whilst it was still "alive", *i.e.* prior to the date of revocation.

9–38   Clearly the two non-use grounds raise a number of common issues. In fact the only difference between the two grounds is in how the requisite five-year period is fixed. In this section, policy and general approach to interpretation are considered first, followed by issues concerning timing; what can constitute use; use of variants of the mark; what constitutes genuine use; proper reasons for non-use; and finally, partial revocation for non-use.

Policy

9–39 One of the recitals to the TM Directive touches upon the subject of non-use: "Whereas in order to reduce the total number of trade marks registered and protected in the Community and, consequently, the number of conflicts which arise between them, it is essential to require that registered trade marks must actually be used or, if not used, be subject to revocation;". In view of the volume and character of applications being filed at Alicante and in national trade mark registries in the E.U., there is scant chance that the aim of reducing the total number of trade marks registered in the Community will be fulfilled. Despite that, it is clear that a registered trade mark is a privilege which should be withdrawn if the mark is not used. For reasons of legal certainty, the five-year period of non-use which will give rise to revocation has to be the same for all proprietors of registered trade marks, although the size and resources available to the proprietor may be taken into account when or if the tribunal has to consider whether there are "proper reasons" for non-use.

General approach to interpretation

The provisions in section 46(1)(a) and (b) of the 1994 Act are very similar **9–40** in their effects to equivalent provisions in the 1938 Act. Similar concepts are expressed using different words. It is a mistake, however, to construe expressions used in section 46 by reference to case law decided on the basis of different expressions used in the 1938 Act, however similar the concepts may be, because it is clear that these provisions do not derive from the 1938 Act, but from the TM Directive. The same point applies (with the exception of the expression "honest concurrent use" in section 7(3), for which specific provision has been made to indicate that it means the same as under the 1938 Act) throughout the 1994 Act, as Aldous L.J. explained (in *Philips v. Remington* [1999] R.P.C. 809 at 815) in the context of section 3:

> "The 1994 Act was passed to implement the Directive which swept away old law and introduced a new law of trade marks for Member States of the European Union. That new law, drafted with input from representatives of the Member States, should not be assumed to be the same as the old UK law nor to be different from it. The law must be determined from the Act construed in the light of the Directive. Cases decided under the old law are no longer authoritative. However, knowledge of the reasoning in such cases can provide awareness of the types of problems that arise during use of trade marks and a general feel for them."

Having cited that passage, Park J. in *Magic Ball* ([2000] R.P.C. 439 at **9–41** 441/2) addressed the particular point before him as to the proper construction of the expression "proper reasons":

> "In the context of this case the important point, as it seems to me, is that it is a mistake to approach the interpretation and application of the key words in section 46(1)—'proper reasons'—by comparing them with the nearest equivalent in the 1938 Act. Section 26 of that Act provided that, notwithstanding non-use for five years, a mark would not be revoked if the non-use was due to 'special circumstances in the trade'. That concept has now been replaced by 'proper reasons'. If this change had merely been a change in the wording of the domestic statute there would be scope for the type

of argument, familiar in cases of construction of United Kingdom statutes, to the effect that the draftsman must have had a deliberate purpose in changing from one form of words—'special circumstances in the trade'—to another—'proper reasons'. A court might then seek to identify the reasons for the change, and, in the light of them, to adopt a construction of the new wording. In my view, however, it would be misguided to adopt that approach in this case. The reason why the 1994 Act uses the expression 'proper reasons' is not because the draftsman decided that the earlier expression 'special circumstances in the trade', should be replaced by a different one, but because he was required to implement the EC Directive, and the words used in the Directive were 'proper reasons'".

Adopting the approach of Aldous L.J., reference is made later in this section to some cases decided under the 1938 Act, in which the reasoning will, it is suggested, provide a general feel for the issues which arise under this part of the 1994 Act.

Timing

9-42 The prospective applicant for revocation wants to choose, within the constraints imposed by the 1994 Act and by the facts in question, the five-year period(s) which will maximise the chances of a successful challenge. Apart from the obvious constraint that a five-year period is required, the constraints imposed by the Act on the choice of a particular five-year period are as follows.

9-43   For a section 46(1)(a) type case (not put into genuine use within five years), the major constraint is the date when the registration formalities were completed for the mark in question. Essentially, section 46(1)(a) gives the proprietor a period of five years from the date when the mark is actually put on the Register to put his mark into genuine use. The relevant date can be found in the Register entry relating to the mark. The application for revocation can be brought as soon as five years has elapsed. In fact, if an application under section 46(1)(a) is contemplated it is normally prudent to commence the application as soon as possible after the five-year period has elapsed, for reasons connected with other constraints imposed by the Act.

9-44   The second constraint is contained in section 46(3). If genuine use is commenced or resumed after the five-year period of non-use but before the application for revocation is made, then the application for revocation will fail. The general effect of this is that it is risky to delay commencing the application for revocation or to choose a five-year period which ended some time before the application was commenced, because the proprietor might be able to show genuine use in the interim period which will defeat the application.

9-45   This second constraint is subject to the qualification in the proviso to section 46(3). Essentially, it provides a three-month grace period after the end of the five-year period in question. Commencement or resumption of genuine use within that three-month period is disregarded unless preparations for the commencement or resumption began before the proprietor became aware that the application for revocation might be made. This creates something of a dilemma for the applicant for revocation. If he notifies the proprietor of his intention to bring an application at too early a stage, he might give the proprietor the chance to put his mark into use before the five-year period in contemplation had elapsed. The applicant then has to deal with the issue of whether the use was genuine or not, which it is better to avoid. If the notification comes too late, then the proprietor might have begun preparations for commencement or resumption of use before he was aware an application might be made, giving rise to the risk that the application would be defeated by commencement or resumption of use within the three-month grace period. Perhaps the best, but not necessarily perfect solution to the dilemma is to notify the proprietor as the five-year period expires. The applicant takes the risk that preparations for use have begun. If, however, it is clear that the preparations began precisely because the proprietor was aware that his five-year period was about to elapse, there would be a strong argument that he was not preparing for genuine use, but to use the mark for the purpose of defeating an application for revocation.

Of course, whether any of the constraints imposed by the Act actually **9–46** operate depends on the facts of the particular situation. Generally, there are two types of situation. The first is where the applicant for revocation suspects that there has been no use of the mark in relation to any of the goods or services for which it is registered. In that type of situation, the applicant wants to choose a five-year period which will ensure success, and not trigger any use which might complicate the situation. The second type of situation is where the mark has been used in relation to particular goods or services, but the applicant for revocation is interested in cutting down the specification of goods or services to remove or reduce the risk of conflict. Again, the applicant wishes to choose a five-year period which will ensure success. In this second type of situation, there is less risk that the proprietor will be able to extend his use so as to cover the whole specification of goods or services. In this sense, the choice of five-year period is less constrained.

The facts are dictated by the actions or inaction of the proprietor of **9–47** the mark. Although the applicant for revocation may well have some information about the lack of use of the mark, he may be able to obtain useful further information from the proprietor's response to an initial challenge of lack of use. However, the proprietor's response is likely to be cagey, so the applicant does not get to know the full facts until after his application has been commenced. Once the proprietor has filed his evidence of use and/or identified any alleged "proper reasons" for non-use, the applicant for revocation should consider whether a different five-year period of non-use can be identified which (1) avoids what appears to be genuine use by the proprietor and/or (2) avoids any periods of time which may be excused by the alleged "proper reasons" and/or (3) will not be defeated by genuine use commenced or resumed after the end of the five year period. Although these matters should be considered, it is frequently the case that there is no room for manoeuvre and the application must be fought on the original basis or settled/ withdrawn.

Use

9–48　The requirement is for "genuine use". For the purposes of analysis however, it is convenient to examine the following aspects in turn: first, what types of use should be taken into account, including the issue of use on promotional items; secondly, use of variants of the mark; thirdly, the goods or services in respect of which the use has occurred; fourthly, whether the use demonstrated is "genuine use".

Types of use

9–49　The 1994 Act does not specify any restrictions on the types of use which can be taken into account. However, bearing in mind section 46(1)(a) and (b) require "genuine use", it is suggested that the use must be as a trade mark, *i.e.* so as to indicate origin.[18] This point should not give rise to detailed debate over whether a trade mark reliably indicates origin. Alleged use should only be excluded if the "mark" is being used in a purely descriptive or decorative way. It should be fairly obvious whether or not such use has occurred.

9–50　Furthermore, it is suggested that, to constitute genuine use, the use relied upon must be use in the course of a trade. In this context, the proviso to section 46(3) draws a clear distinction between use and preparations for use. That is a powerful indicator that preparations for use do not constitute use,[19] although it may be quite difficult to fix the line between the two. It is suggested that a trade in the goods or services in question must have commenced. Test marketing ought to be suffi-cient. Orders placed on component suppliers using the mark were held bona fide use[20] under the 1938 Act, but that is probably too thin to constitute "genuine use" under the 1994 Act. Equally, purely internal deliberations about use of the mark should not be sufficient. In all cases, the decision is whether genuine use has been established.

9–51　The 1994 Act does provide some guidance as to what "use" encom-passes. First, section 103(2) of the 1994 Act provides:

---

[18] This argument failed on the facts in *Esquire* SRIS O/189/00, June 13, 2000 (Regy).
[19] It has been observed that "preparations merely serve to establish an honest basis for actual use that takes place within the three-month period referred to" [in section 46(3)] *"Mer"* SRIS O/007/00, January 18, 2000 (Regy).
[20] *c.f. Hermes* [1982] R.P.C. 425, under the 1938 Act, where there had been no actual sales of goods. Orders placed on a supplier were found to be sufficient to establish bona fide use. Merely putting the mark in a trade directory of marks did not constitute use in the course of trade in relation to goods.

"References in this Act to use (or any particular description of use) of a trade mark . . . include use (or that description of use) otherwise than by means of a graphic representation."

The principal effect of this provision is that oral use of a mark now counts as "use".

Secondly, section 46(2) of the Act specifically includes use made on **9–52** goods for export where, but for this provision, there might have been doubt as to whether such use counted:

". . .use in the United Kingdom includes affixing the trade mark to goods or to the packaging of goods in the United Kingdom solely for export purposes."

Thirdly, account may also be taken of section 10(4):　　　　　　　　　　**9–53**

"For the purposes of this section a person uses a sign if, in particular, he—
(a) affixes it to goods or the packaging thereof;
(b) offers or exposes goods for sale, puts them on the market or stocks them for those purposes under the sign, or offers or supplies services under the sign;
(c) imports or exports goods under the sign;
(d) uses the sign on business papers or in advertising."

Despite the fact that section 10(4) is expressed to apply for the purposes **9–54** of section 10 (only), the types of use set out are the principal ways in which a trade mark is used. These types of use are equally applicable when considering the ways in which a trade mark is alleged to have been used for the purposes of section 46.

Generally, it is suggested that "use" in section 46 should be construed **9–55** broadly and encompasses any use of the trade mark for the purposes of trade.[21] To put the matter another way, if the alleged use for section 46(1)(a) or (b) had been made without the consent of the proprietor, constituted use as a trade mark and constituted section 10(1) infringement, it is suggested that use ought to be taken into account under section 46.

Use on promotional items

Household consumer goods frequently feature "on-pack" promotions, **9–56** where promotional items which have some link to the main product are offered either at a reduced price or given away in exchange for a stated

---

[21] One of the Registry's hearing officers has stated "When evidence is provided by a proprietor in defence of their registration, the Registrar would normally expect to see for example, figures detailing financial turnover or profit from sales of goods or services under the mark, details of exactly what goods or services have been offered under the mark, expenditure on advertising the mark with details of where and when the mark was advertised, exhibits demonstrating how the mark is promoted in advertising and how the mark was placed on goods in the marketplace." *Adrenalin* SRIS O/336/99,

number of vouchers. The promotional items feature the mark applied to the main product.[22] Their purpose is to advertise the main product. The issue is whether the mark on the promotional item is being used in relation to that item or whether, in reality, it is being used in relation to the main product. Under the 1938 Act, there was authority to the effect that use on promotional items was not use as a trade mark in relation to those goods, but constituted use in relation to the principal product.[23] This type of use is often intermittent and infrequent, but a well-informed proprietor will take steps to ensure that suitable promotional items appear at least every five years.

9–57   The proprietor would no doubt argue that he is using his mark in relation to the promotional product, because he has to select the quality of those products and put his reputation behind them. The fact that the mark is also advertising the main product does not prevent it performing a dual function on the promotional item. Overall, it is difficult to see a court finding that this type of use was not genuine use in relation to the promotional items. In addition it would be harsh to deprive the proprietor of the protection afforded to him by his registrations which covered promotional items, particularly if the same or closely similar mark was used in a different trade which might also be supported by use on similar promotional items.

Use of variants of the registered mark

9–58 The first part of section 46(2) of the 1994 Act provides that "use of a trade mark includes use in a form differing in elements which do not alter the distinctive character of the mark in the form in which it was registered. . .". Therefore, if the proprietor relies on use of a variant of the registered mark, the variant must be compared with the registered mark to see whether the differences are such as to alter the distinctive character of the mark. The process of comparison is a matter of impression.[24] The distinctive elements of the mark in the form in which it was registered should be identified. Likewise with the variant. Are the differences significant enough to alter the distinctive character of the mark? If the variant passes the test, then the use of the variant must be taken into account.[25]

---

[22] If the promotional item does not bear the mark, but is supplied in some way under the auspices of the mark, it is unlikely to constitute use of the mark in relation to the promotional items. See, *e.g. Elle T.M.* [1997] F.S.R. 529, Lloyd J., where the registered proprietor tried to rely on the endorsement in its ELLE magazine of cosmetic products marketed under other brands. This was held not use of the ELLE mark in relation to the cosmetics.

[23] *e.g.* Kodak on T-shirts was used in relation to the film, and not the T-shirts: *Kodak* [1990] F.S.R. 49.

[24] For examples, see *Elle T.M.* [1997] F.S.R. 529, Lloyd J. and the *Club Soda* decision, SRIS O/230/98, November 17, 1998 (Regy).

[25] Under the 1938 Act, s.30(1) gave the Registrar a discretion to take account of use of marks not differing in their distinctive elements. There is no such discretion under the 1994 Act.

Relevant goods or services

The use must be in relation to goods or services falling within the **9–59** specification.[26] Use on any other goods or services is irrelevant. If an issue arises as to whether particular goods or services do or do not fall within the specification, it may be necessary to construe what the words used in the specification actually mean. The general approach to construction has been described thus:

> "When it comes to construing a word used in a trade mark specification, one is concerned with how the product is, as a practical matter, regarded for the purposes of trade. After all, a trade mark specification is concerned with use in trade."[27]

The words in the specification must be construed as at the date of application for the mark in question.

Genuine use

The question whether use is genuine must be examined against all the **9–60** circumstances of the case. However, it is possible to identify various factors which indicate whether the use is genuine or not[28]:

(1) If the use was made for the purpose of defeating a non-use attack, then it is not genuine use.[29] The corollary is that once use has been proved and it was made for the purposes of trade and not for the purpose of defeating a possible non-use attack, then it is almost certainly genuine.

(2) The substantiality of the use is a factor to be taken into account[30] but there is no fixed requirement that the use must be substantial as judged by commercial standards. Once it is established that the mark has been used, and the genuineness of

---

[26] Under the 1938 Act, the proprietor could rely on use on goods of the same description, under s.26(1). The only use which can be taken into account under the 1994 Act is use on goods or services for which the mark is registered.

[27] Jacob J. in *British Sugar Plc v. James Robertson & Sons Ltd* [1996] R.P.C. 281 at 288.

[28] This issue is one where it is permissible to take account of observations made in cases decided under the 1938 Act, for two reasons: first, because the requirement for bona fide use was interpreted as genuine use and second, because the observations are common-sense in any event.

[29] The proposition hardly requires support from authority, but examples from the 1938 Act are: *Nerit* [1982] F.S.R. 72, CA; *Concord* [1987] F.S.R. 209; *Huggars* [1979] F.S.R. 79; *Second Sight* [1995] R.P.C. 423; *Trooper* [1994] R.P.C. 26; *Electrolux* (1954) 71 R.P.C. 23. Intermittent or temporary use is usually an indicator of non-genuine use, even though wealthy traders may be able to afford temporary use on a reasonably substantial scale. By contrast, steady use or use backed by an intention to establish a market indicates genuine use.

[30] *Bon Matin Trade Mark* [1989] R.P.C. 537 at 543, as applied in *Zippo* [1999] R.P.C. 173 at 185.

the use is not in question, detailed consideration of the substantiality of the use serves no purpose.

(3) The size of and the resources available to the proprietor may be relevant factors. In the case of a very large company, infrequent or insubstantial use may lead to a different conclusion than in the case of a sole trader.

(4) In a suitable case, a single isolated act of use may constitute genuine use. However, "the fewer the acts relied on the more solidly ought they to be established . . ."[31] Likewise, the tribunal is likely to take a sceptical view if the only use has been on brochures or in advertising.[32]

(5) Even if the use relied upon is not a single isolated act, the quality of the evidence by which the use is sought to be proved may have an effect on the decision as to whether genuine use has been shown.[33]

9–61 Some examples from decided cases are as follows:

(a) Very small numbers of products were given away with purchases of other products only a week or so before the application for revocation was launched and when the proprietor knew the registration was coming under attack. The evidence was not sufficiently clear to indicate whether this was a test marketing exercise or not. The hearing officer was not persuaded there had been any genuine use.[34] Partial revocation was ordered.

(b) Over the relevant five year-period, a representative of the "UK distributor" visited the Spanish proprietor each April, apparently ordering and collecting a small quantity of shoes each time. There was no evidence of what happened to the shoes thereafter, whether the shoes were offered for sale in the United Kingdom or the extent to which actual sales took place. The proprietor failed to discharge the onus on him under section 100.[35]

Proper reasons for non-use

9–62 Whether there are proper reasons for non-use is something to be decided in all the circumstances of the case. One factor which must always be taken into account is the legislative purpose of the non-use

---

[31] Wilberforce J. in *Nodoz* [1962] R.P.C. 1, observations which are equally applicable under the 1994 Act and which have been applied in the Registry: *e.g. Evian*, SRIS O/190/00, June 12, 2000, and *Martinelli*, SRIS O/011/00, January 27, 2000 (both Regy).

[32] *c.f. Elle*, n. 24, above.

[33] See, *e.g. Martinelli*, SRIS O/011/00, January 27, 2000 (Regy).

[34] *Mer* SRIS O/007/00, January 18, 2000 (Regy).

[35] *Martinelli*, SRIS O/011/00, January 27, 2000 (Regy).

provisions (see above), which has been described as the requirement to use a trade mark or lose it. In *Invermont*,[36] the hearing officer gave some guidance, which has been applied subsequently:

> ". . . bearing in mind the need to judge these things in a business sense, and also bearing in mind the emphasis which is, and has always been placed on the requirement to use a trade mark or lose it, I think the word proper, in the context of section 46 means: apt, acceptable, reasonable, justifiable in all the circumstances.
>
> I do not think that the term "proper" was intended to cover normal situations or routine difficulties. I think it much more likely that it is intended to cover abnormal situations in the industry or the market, or even perhaps some temporary but serious disruption affecting the registered proprietor's business. Normal delays caused by some unavoidable regulatory requirement, such as the approval of a medicine, might be acceptable but not, I think, the normal delays found in the marketing function. These are matters within the businessman's own control and I think he should plan accordingly."

As to the first paragraph, Park J. has commented that, whilst the **9–63** adjectives set out there were well chosen, it must not be forgotten that the statutory word which must be applied is "proper" and not any of the near-synonyms suggested.[37] Some examples from decided cases are as follows:

(1) Apart from one period of a month, non-use attacks had been extant against the trade marks for over five years. Throughout that period, negotiations for licensing of the trade marks had been continuing, but the uncertainty created by the existence of the non-use attacks had meant that no licensing agreement could be concluded. It was held these were proper reasons for the non-use.[38]

(2) The proprietor intended to apply the mark to a new type of lollipop which required the development of a new manufacturing technique. The development process started in 1989, was brought in-house in 1991 and had not been completed in 1997, a year after the application to revoke was brought. The problems which had been encountered in the development process were described in evidence and apparently a team of three or four technical personnel had been working almost exclusively and almost continuously on the project. Commercial production was predicted for 2000. It was held there were proper reasons for

---

[36] [1997] R.P.C. 125.
[37] *Magic Ball* [2000] R.P.C. 439 at 442.
[38] *Worth* [1998] R.P.C. 875 (Regy).

the non-use. Arguments that (a) all the reasons for the non-use were within the proprietor's control; (b) that the proprietor should have put out some lollipops produced on unsatisfactory machinery; and (c) that the development process was a "normal situation or a routine difficulty" were rejected.[39]

(3) The sole proprietor of a business cited family considerations and recession in his industry as proper reasons for non-use. The family considerations failed on the facts. As for economic considerations, the hearing officer stated, correctly, that economic downturns, the cyclical nature of some industries, exchange rate movements, interest rate variations and the like have to be taken as part of the normal range of risks that must be accepted as part and parcel of running a business. No proper reasons.[40]

(4) The reason given for the non-use was characterised as a routine difficulty in business in generating funds for investment. No proper reasons.[41]

(4) It was claimed that the existence of a U.S. trade embargo on goods from Cuba had prevented use of the mark and constituted proper reasons for non-use. The embargo had effect because the word HABANA formed part of the mark, and it would have been deceptive to use the mark on goods other than those emanating from Cuba. However, there was no evidence that the mark had ever been used, despite being registered for 26 years before the embargo came into effect in 1962, some 33 years before the date of application for revocation. No proper reasons.[42]

What period of time must be covered by "proper reasons"?

9-64 In the examples given above, where proper reasons were found, they happened to have extended over the entire five-year period of non-use. The issue which has, apparently, not yet arisen for decision is whether the "proper reasons" must excuse the entire five-year period of non-use or whether it is sufficient for the proper reasons to cover a period of, say, a few months so that the period of non-use for which there are no proper reasons amounts to less than five years. It is not easy to predict whether any alleged "proper reasons" must be viewed against the entire five-year period (the "entire period approach") or whether they can be used to deduct from the period of non-use the period for which the proper reasons apply (the "mathematical approach"). If the mathematical approach is correct, can the applicant for revocation nonetheless

---

[39] *Magic Ball Trade Mark* [2000] R.P.C. 439, Park J.
[40] *Anglian Mode*, SRIS O/181/00, May 19, 2000 (Regy).
[41] *Questo*, SRIS O/127/99, May 5, 1999 (Regy).
[42] *Cabanas Habana*, SRIS O/085/99, March 17, 1999 (Regy).

succeed if he manages to prove a total of five years non-use, once the "proper reasons" period has been deducted?

If the period covered by the "proper reasons" falls at the end of the **9–65** five-year period, then the applicant for revocation may be able to move his time frame back in time to avoid that period. If, however, the period falls in the middle or at the beginning of the relevant five-year period, the issue may not be so easily avoided.

The "mathematical approach" is probably not open because of the **9–66** wording of section 46(1)(a) and (b) of the 1994 Act, which direct consideration to "the period of five years following the date of registration" and "an uninterrupted period of five years". This means that any alleged proper reasons must be viewed against the entire five years of non-use. It is however, possible to envisage circumstances where the proper reasons would appear inadequate when viewed against the entire period of non-use, yet the result might appear harsh. Take an example where there has been five years non-use since the mark was put on the register which includes one period of, say, a few months in the middle of the five years where proper reasons for that period of non-use can be shown, for example, because the sole proprietor of the business was ill and unable to work. In those circumstances, the proprietor would argue that he is given a five-year period in which to put his mark into genuine use and that he has not yet had his five years because no account should be taken of his period of illness. Of course, consideration of all the circumstances gives a certain room for manoeuvre even though there is no discretion involved and the tribunal must decide one way or another. In cases of real doubt, the tribunal may refuse the application for revocation, knowing that it is always open for a fresh application for revocation to be brought in a year or two and that use or lack of it in the interim will usually determine the matter. Against that, it should be borne in mind that five years is a generous period within which to require use, particularly in modern commerce.

Partial Revocation

Section 46(5) provides: **9–67**

> "Where grounds for revocation exist in respect of only some of the goods or services for which the trade mark is registered, revocation shall relate to those goods or services only."

In some cases, the application of this provision is straightforward. Some words from the specification of goods or services should obviously be discarded, it being equally obvious which words should remain. However, cases are likely to arise which involve significant issues over the extent to which the specification of goods or services should be cut down. Such issues are part of the wider issue of how specifications of goods and services should be worded under the 1994 Act.

9–68   In *Premier Brands*[43] Neuberger J. suggested, without having had the benefit of argument on the point, that one must take the specification as it stands, so that if use had been proved on some goods which fell within the words used in the specification, that was sufficient. This would mean, for example, that use on one particular type of computer software would support a specification for "computer software". With respect to the judge, this approach is obviously wrong as Jacob J. pointed out shortly afterwards,[44] as well as being inconsistent with the observations made by Laddie J. in *Mercury*.[45]

9–69   It is suggested that the 1994 Act requires a different approach to the drafting of specifications of goods and services to that which was prevalent under the 1938 Act, as amended. It will be recalled that infringement under the 1938 Act required use on or in relation to goods or services which fell within the specification of goods. For this reason, it was natural to apply for and obtain a wide specification of goods. Sometimes, specifications were absurdly wide but in the later years of the operation of the 1938 Act, the United Kingdom Registry did require very wide specifications to be justified.

9–70   Under the 1994 Act, infringement can occur by use on identical, similar and even dissimilar goods or services. Infringement by use on identical goods or services for which the mark is registered does not even require a likelihood of confusion to be demonstrated. It is difficult to see why that absolute protection should extend beyond the goods or services on which the mark is actually used by the proprietor. The trade mark proprietor no longer needs nor can he justify a specification of goods or services which extends beyond the actual use which he makes of his mark. Those proprietors who obtained wide specifications under previous Acts should expect to have such specifications cut down.

9–71   It is suggested that these considerations require a fairly rigorous approach to the drafting of specifications of goods and services— perhaps more rigorous than most practitioners contemplate because they are so accustomed to the practice which was prevalent under the 1938 Act.

9–72   In the light of these considerations, it is suggested that the correct approach under the 1994 Act should be as follows:

(1) If the court or Registry decides that there has been genuine use but only on a particular item or in relation to a particular service, the first question is whether the specification extends unduly beyond the item or service? If so, the inquiry is this: how would the notional reasonable man describe that item? Naturally, the answer depends on all the circumstances, but the answer provides the wording appropriate for that item in the specification of goods.[46]

---

[43] *Premier Brands UK Limited v. Typhoon Europe Ltd*, Neuberger J., January 21, 2000.
[44] *Minerva*, [2000] F.S.R. 734, Jacob J.
[45] *Mercury Communications Ltd v. Mercury Interactive (UK) Ltd* [1995] F.S.R. 850 at 863–865.
[46] This test should avoid the "red tea caddy" problem, posed by Neuberger J. in *Premier Brands, op.cit.* at n. 43. The description of the goods should be accurate but not overly detailed.

(2) If the mark has been used on many different items of a similar nature, there may come a stage where the notional reasonable man would say: "well, all those items are properly described by the collective term, X". It is then appropriate for that collective term to be used in the specification of goods.

(3) The words used in the Nice Classification act as a guide as to which items properly fall within which class, but it is not necessarily appropriate to populate one's specification of goods with terms used in the Nice Classification, unless those terms are prompted by the tests set out in paragraphs 1 and 2 above.

It can be argued that such an approach could give rise to a proliferation **9–73** of revocation applications seeking to cut down specifications of goods or services which were obtained under the old law. This would be unlikely to occur because that type of application for revocation is caused by a perceived conflict or restriction on the applicant's trading. Only the wealthiest of traders could afford to seek to restrict their competitor's specifications out of spite, and they would be well aware that the same action could probably be taken against their own registrations. Even if there were a number of applications of this nature, there is nothing wrong or to be feared by necessary adjustments to take account of the new law of trade marks. It would be far worse to allow one's approach to the new law to be influenced by wording in specifications of goods which happens to have lain undisturbed on the Register for years, unless that wording is examined and decided to be appropriate under the new law.

The only other objection which might be voiced against the approach **9–74** advocated above, is that it could lead to a proliferation of evidence and argument about what the reasonable man would call a particular item. Any such fears would be groundless because:

(a) the court and the Registry are quite capable of controlling unnecessary evidence and argument, and imposing appropriate sanctions;

(b) the proper description of the goods or services in question will often be found in the registrant's own commercial literature. For example, if he calls it a chopping board, that is the answer to the question above. It would be unreasonable of him to argue that the appropriate description was, say, a kitchen utensil in the absence of a range of items which would support the collective term;

(c) evidence would only be received where it concerned a particular and specialised practice in the trade, for example the distinction between diesel engines of particular horsepower.

4. Other grounds for revocation

The other two grounds for revocation are concerned with marks which, **9–75** since registration, have become "generic" or "misleading".

Section 46(1)(c)

9-76 Section 46(1)(c) provides:

> "The registration of a trade mark may be revoked on any of the following grounds:
>
> . . .
>
> (c) that, in consequence of the acts or inactivity of the proprietor, it has become the common name in the trade for a product or service for which it is registered;"

Derivation[47]

9-77 The wording within sub-section (c) of section 46 of the 1994 Act is virtually identical to Article 12(2)(b) of the TM Directive. The introductory words are different: the Directive provides "A trade mark shall also be liable to revocation if, after the date on which it was registered, . . ." which serves to make it clear that the ground is concerned with what has happened to the meaning conveyed by the mark since it was put on the Register. Section 46(1)(c) must be interpreted in that way.

9-78 Note that these introductory words from the Directive do not mean that consideration must be restricted to events (including, in particular, the acts or inactivity of the proprietor) after the date when the mark was put on the Register. The process by which the mark becomes the common name may have started long before that. This provision is concerned with whether the result specified has been achieved.

Scope of this provision and relationship with section 3(1)(d)

9-79 Although it is convenient to describe this ground using the shorthand "generic", the ground is more restricted than that and certainly more restricted than the "generic" absolute ground for refusal contained in section 3(1)(d) of the 1994 Act. Unlike section 3(1)(d), the word "exclusively" is not used, although the requirement that it, the registered mark, has become the common name, etc., means that the result is much the same as if the word exclusively had been included.

Types of marks affected

9-80 The requirement that the mark has become the common name in the trade seems to confine the operation of this provision to word marks. It might possibly extend to other marks which can only be referred to, or which have come to be referred to, using words which are the common name in the trade for a product or service for which the mark is registered.

---

[47] The 1938 Act, s.15, covered, *inter alia*, similar ground. It was invoked in very few cases. The 1994 Act, s.46(1)(c) was not derived in any way from s.15, but exclusively from the TM Directive.

A question of fact

Whether a mark has become the common name in the trade for a **9–81** product or service is a question of fact to be decided in the circumstances. This ground depends on the evidence put forward in support of it. A tribunal would expect to see substantial independent evidence from the trade, either from persons of standing within the trade or from trade organisations and the like, showing the mark in use as the common name in the trade for a relevant product or service. It is suggested that the mark need not be the only name in the trade for the product or service in question, but it must be "the common name", *i.e.* at least the principal common name. Equally, it need not be a name used by everybody in the trade. It is suggested the tribunal should decide the question of fact looking through the eyes of the average person in the trade who is reasonably well-informed.[48] The adoption of a test of this type would help to avoid unnecessary argument about precisely how far it is necessary to prove the extent of use of the mark as the common name, and prevent overly repetitive evidence.

Cause and causation

Note that the cause must be "the acts or inactivity of the proprietor". **9–82** These words reflect the fact that the proprietor bears the responsibility for ensuring that his mark does not become generic. Although the application of this provision is likely to be rare, experience shows that marks become generic in one of the following ways:

First, the mark applied to a novel product can become the name of the **9–83** product, particularly if it enjoys a period of monopoly protection. Shredded Wheat is an example.[49] The pharmaceutical industry is adept at avoiding this problem by coining a generic name for a newly invented drug as well as a trade mark. They can then place emphasis on their trade mark as identifying their drug, and the generic name is there to be used for all substitutes as and when they come on the market. This is one example of the need to police any reference by third parties to a trade mark to ensure that it is not used in a generic sense.[50]

Secondly, and more generally, it is necessary for any proprietor to **9–84** police his mark to prevent others using his mark in a generic manner, although it generally requires many years of neglect before a once-distinctive mark becomes the common name in the trade for the goods. Modern methods of communication, particularly involving the Internet, may speed up the process. Again, a measure of vigilance is required on the part of proprietors.

---

[48] An adaptation of the "average consumer" test. See further, paras 7–100 to 7–101, 8–38, 13–52.

[49] *The Shredded Wheat Co. Ltd v. Kellogg Co. of Great Britain Ltd* (1940) 57 R.P.C. 137.

[50] The CTM Regulation Art. 10, is a specific provision allowing the proprietor of a CTM to take steps to prevent or cure references in dictionaries and the like which use a CTM in a generic sense. There is no corresponding provision in the TM Directive or the 1994 Act.

9–85   Thirdly, the proprietor may use his own mark in the wrong way—as indicating the type of goods, rather than the fact that they originate from him.

The problems and risks in the last two categories are exacerbated for a mark which is more or less descriptive when it achieves registration, perhaps wrongly. If the term is in wide use, this type of mark may well face a dual-pronged attack—invalidity under section 47(1) and sections 3(1)(d) or (c) and revocation under section 46(1)(c) of the 1994 Act.[51]

9–86   It is possible to conceive of circumstances where a mark might become the common name for a product or service because of action by the state or some arm of government, which the proprietor attempted but failed to stop.[52] It would be harsh, in such circumstances, for the proprietor to lose his mark even though he did all that was economically possible to prevent the occurrence. Perhaps the overriding consideration has to be that marks which constitute the common name for the goods should not remain registered as trade marks,[53] that if the proprietor fails to prevent this occurring it should be attributable to his "inactivity", whatever the reason, and he is left to pursue whatever remedy he has against the entity responsible.

Examples:

9–87   First, take the facts of *Daiquiri Rum*: the mark was registered in 1922 for rum. The cocktail (light rum, lime or lemon juice, sugar and ice) originated in Daiquiri in Cuba in about 1919, and became fashionable in the United Kingdom in the 1920s. Plainly "a Daiquiri" was a descriptive term for the cocktail. The mark was held to be an entry wrongly remaining on the Register under section 15 of the 1938 Act, because rum and a rum cocktail were goods of the same description. An application under section 46(1)(c) of the 1994 Act ought to fail because "Daiquiri" would not have become the common name for rum, however common its use as the name of a rum cocktail.

9–88   Secondly, to alter the facts of *Jeryl Lynn*[54]: assume the mark *Jeryl Lynn* was registered when the vaccine was first developed in 1963. An invalidity attack in 1998 would fail, because the mark would not have been registered in breach of section 3 of the 1938 Act. However, a revocation action under section 46(1)(c) of the 1994 would succeed, because the mark had become the common name for the mumps vaccine.

---

[51] The mark VOICE PERSONALS faced the dual attack, which succeeded under s.47(1) and s.3(1)(d): SRIS O/388/99, November 3, 1999 (Regy). The mark TCS (the standard abbreviation for Terne Coated Steel) was found invalid under s.47(1) and s.3(1)(b) and (c): SRIS O/351/99, October 8, 1999 (Regy).

[52] An example of this was the adoption by the E.U. of the symbol for the Euro. It happened to be remarkably similar to a registered trade mark for goods and services in the financial field.

[53] Although s.46(1)(c) does not go that far.

[54] [1999] F.S.R. 491, Laddie J.

Section 46(1)(d) of the 1994 Act

"The registration of a trade mark may be revoked on any of the **9–89** following grounds—

. . .

(d) that in consequence of the use made of it by the proprietor or with his consent in relation to the goods or services for which it is registered, it is liable to mislead the public, particularly as to the nature, quality or geographical origin of those goods or services."

Derivation

The wording within subsection (d) of section 46 of the 1994 Act is **9–90** virtually identical to Article 12(2)(b) of the TM Directive. The introductory words in the Directive read "if, after the date on which it was registered, in consequence . . .". Accordingly, section 46(1)(d) should be interpreted in that sense.

Comparison with section 3(3)(b) of the 1994 Act/Article 3(1)(g) of the TM Directive

Section 3(3)(b) forbids the registration of a mark "if it is of such a nature **9–91** as to deceive the public (for instance as to the nature, quality or geographical origin of the goods or service)." Thus, the same examples are used, yet slightly different expressions define the heart of the provision: liable to mislead the public/of such a nature as to deceive the public. There appears to be no particular reason why different expressions have been used. They appear to mean the same thing.

There are two differences of significance between section 3(3)(b) and **9–92** 46(1)(d). The first relates to the date at which the position is assessed. As an absolute ground for refusal (and invalidity), section 3(3)(b) requires the position to be assessed at the date of application for the mark. Section 46(1)(d) requires the position to be assessed as at the date of application for revocation. The second concerns the cause of the deceptiveness. Under section 3(3)(b), the cause does not matter: a deceptive mark shall not be registered. Section 46(1)(d) only operates if the deceptiveness has been caused by the use which has been made of the mark by the proprietor or with his consent. In other words it is deceptiveness for which the proprietor is responsible, although there is no requirement to prove "blameworthy conduct" as under the 1938 Act.[55] In these respects, section 46(1)(d) has a narrower ambit than section 3(3)(b) and a wider ambit than section 11 of the 1938 Act.

It is suggested that, like section 3(3)(b), section 46(1)(d) looks to the **9–93** mark itself and whether the mark itself is liable to mislead the public. However, unlike section 3(3)(b) (an absolute ground for refusal or

---

[55] *GE* [1973] R.P.C. 297, HL. See at 334, *per* Lord Diplock.

invalidity), the liability to mislead must arise from the use made of the mark. Section 46(1)(a) does not encompass passing-off type deceptiveness. It is in the nature of an absolute objection and not a relative objection (in the sense of sections 3 and 5 respectively).

Application

9–94 The application of this provision is likely to be rare, although one can conceive of circumstances where it becomes applicable:

(1) As originally registered and used, the mark contained a correct allusion to the nature of the goods or services. There is a change in use, so that the mark is then used on goods or services which do not possess the quality to which the mark alludes. The mark is then liable to mislead the public.

(2) The same would apply for a mark which alluded to the quality or geographical origin of the goods or services. Such a change of use can take place at any time, but is more likely to occur following assignment.

(3) If the mark is assigned without goodwill,[56] so that the mark and goodwill are separated, it is likely to deceive the public as to origin. Although that type of deception is not specifically referred to in section 46(1)(d) of the 1994 Act, its presence ought to fulfil this ground.

9–95 Two individuals (BH and GH) originally owned the Scandinavian parent company SIAB which became one of the largest art poster companies in the world. The individuals fell out, with the result that BH took responsibility for continental Europe through a subsidiary ST and GH for North America, the United Kingdom, Eire and Scandinavia through the subsidiary SM. The United Kingdom subsidiary, S Ltd, originally registered the mark SCAN-DECOR in its own name in 1971, but assigned the mark in 1979 to the parent SIAB. GH sold his interest in SIAB to BH, but GH's company, SM, remained the exclusive distributor of SIAB's products in its territory. SM also developed its own products. Termination of the distribution agreement eventually led to litigation by the successor to SIAB against SM and S Ltd for passing off and trade mark infringement. The key issue was who owned the goodwill in the SCANDECOR mark in the United Kingdom. *Held* (by the Court of Appeal) that the local goodwill in Scandecor was owned by S Ltd from 1971 to 1979. When S Ltd assigned the mark to SIAB, the goodwill was expressly excluded. The goodwill established by S Ltd remained exclusively associated with S Ltd. It did not cease to belong to S Ltd because it was licensed by SIAB to use the registered trade mark. SIAB had no pre-existing goodwill in the

---

[56] See Chap. 12.

United Kingdom which it could licence to S Ltd. In addition SIAB had no business in the United Kingdom and did not exercise control over any relevant business activities in the United Kingdom to which its goodwill could attach. The claimants had conceded that if S Ltd owned the goodwill, then their mark was liable to mislead the public and it was revoked under section 46(1)(d). *Scandecor Development AB v. Scandecor Marketing AB & Scandecor Ltd.*[57] The assignment without goodwill appears to have been crucial, not least in its influence on ownership of goodwill generated thereafter.[58]

(4) Equally, if the mark and goodwill become separated for some **9–96** reason other than by an assignment without goodwill, the mark will then be liable to mislead the public.

Take the *GE* case: the American company registered its GE monogram in a roundel in 1907 but made no use of the mark. Meanwhile the English General Electric Company used its device mark comprising GEC in a particular script. When the Americans started to use their mark in the United Kingdom, there was a likelihood of deception. Under the 1938 Act, the Americans were guilty of no "blameworthy" conduct, so the mark remained registered. Under section 46(1)(d), the mark would probably be revoked. *GE*.[59]

(5) Separation of goodwill from the mark can occur through a sustained period of uncontrolled licensing in conjunction with the public coming to identify the licensee as the origin of the goods.

In theory, some confusion may be caused by any assignment or new **9–97** licensing of a mark. A period of temporary but not wide-scale confusion whilst the public adjust to the new state of affairs should not trigger this ground of revocation. Likewise, a period of uncontrolled licensing is unlikely to be sufficient unless, as indicated above, the period is sustained and is accompanied by the additional element of the public identifying the licensee as the source so that, as a matter of fact, the licensee can be said to be the owner of the goodwill in the mark.

A question of fact

Again, this ground of revocation raises a question of fact: is the mark **9–98** liable to mislead the public in consequence of the use made of it? It is suggested that the tribunal must answer this question looking through

---

[57] [1999] F.S.R. 26.

[58] The case appears to have been finely balanced. A slightly different view of the facts could easily have resulted in victory for the claimants.

[59] [1973] R.P.C. 297, HL. The problem with the application of s.46(1)(d) to those facts is this: the GE mark became liable to mislead the public not in consequence of the use made of it, but rather the lack of use. The GE mark became deceptive because GEC had established a goodwill in its mark. However, if use of a mark causes passing off, a court is likely to view it as a mark which should be revoked. Even if that cannot be achieved under s.46(1)(d), an injunction followed by five-years non-use would achieve the same result under s.46(1)(b).

the eyes of the average consumer of the products who is reasonably well informed and reasonably observant and circumspect.[60] As *Scandecor* illustrates, the issue of fact under section 46(1)(d) may depend on a proper understanding of a complicated underlying situation.

5. Procedure

Where to apply

9–99 If the trade mark in question is the subject of any proceedings in court, then any application for a declaration of invalidity or for revocation must be made to the court.[61] If the trade mark in question is not the subject of any proceedings in court,[62] then the applicant for invalidity or revocation has a free choice whether to make his application to the Registrar or to the court.[63] The Registrar does have power to refer any application for invalidity or revocation to the court.[64] This is likely to occur only in special circumstances.

9–100 Section 47(4) of the 1994 Act is a narrow provision which gives the registrar specific power to apply to the court for a declaration of invalidity "in the case of bad faith in the registration of a trade mark". This is presumably to cater for the situation where, after registration, it comes to the attention of the Registrar that the application was made in bad faith. The Registrar can then apply to the court, as a third party tribunal, rather than have to raise and decide the issue within the Registry.

Applications to the court where there are existing proceedings

9–101 If the applicant is a party to existing proceedings in court concerning the trade mark, then an application for a declaration of invalidity or revocation must be brought by way of counterclaim or other CPR Part 20 claim.[65] Often such claims are made in response to a claim for infringement. If, however, the applicant is not a party to existing proceedings concerning the trade mark, he must still bring his application before the court by issuing a CPR Part 8 claim form.[66] It is then

---

[60] At the time of writing there is no authority to this effect, but it is clear that the average consumer test is of general application on all questions concerning confusion, distinctiveness and, here, whether a mark is liable to mislead the public. See Chaps 7–100 *et seq.*, 8–38, 13–52.

[61] 1994 Act, ss.47(3)(a) and 46(4)(a).

[62] A search of the entry on the Register relating to the trade mark in question should reveal whether there are any proceedings on foot. Sometimes there is a slight delay between the commencement of proceedings and an entry appearing in the Register. A potential applicant can always ask the proprietor.

[63] s.47(3).

[64] ss.47(3)(b) and 46(4)(b).

[65] Practice Direction, Patents; etc., para. 24.1.

[66] Practice Direction, Patents; etc., para. 23.5.

open to the court, or any of the parties to the proceedings, to consider whether all matters relating to the trade mark should be determined at the same time. Whatever the method of initiating the application in court, the applicant must serve with his pleading, particulars of the objections to the validity of the registration or of any grounds of revocation on which he relies.[67] A copy of the claim together with a copy of the particulars of objections or grounds of revocation must be served on the Registrar. The Registrar is entitled to take such part in the proceedings as she may think fit, but need not serve a defence or other statement of case unless ordered to do so by the court.[68] Thereafter, the application for invalidity or revocation is dealt with as part and parcel of the action. If the case involves non-use, the registered proprietor is not generally required to put in his evidence of use until the normal exchange of witness statements, and this is one of the principal differences between proceeding in the Registry and court in such cases.

Applications to the court where there are no existing proceedings

If there are no existing proceedings in court, an application for invalidity **9–102** or revocation is initiated by issuing a claim form under CPR Part 8.[69] Part 8 is an adaptation of the old originating summons procedure. One of the unexpected results is that, subject to the parties agreeing different time limits under rule 2.11, the claimant's evidence must be served with the claim form and the defendant's evidence must be served with the acknowledgement of service within 14 days, with 14 days for evidence in reply. This is rather different to what used to happen when this type of application was launched by way of originating motion, when directions would be fixed by the court, if not agreed, at the first hearing of the motion for pleadings if necessary, and service of evidence. There is now more of an onus on the applicant to agree appropriate directions or seek them from the court.

Applications in the Registry

The procedure is specified in the Trade Marks Rules 2000,[70] which reflect **9–103** the latest improvements in practice and procedure in the Registry over the 1938 Act.[71] The procedure applicable for applications for invalidity and revocation on grounds other than non-use is the same, but different from that applicable for an application for revocation on non-use

---

[67] Practice Direction, Patents; etc., para. 24.2.
[68] Practice Direction, Patents; etc., para. 24.3. Frequently, the Registrar plays no part in the proceedings, simply requesting to be kept informed of the outcome.
[69] Practice Direction; Patents; etc., para. 23.5.
[70] S.I. 2000 No. 136, in App. 3, *post*.
[71] The era of uninformative pleadings and repeated extensions of time for evidence has passed. Effectively, pleadings should emulate those in the High Court. See Tribunal Practice Note 1/2000. The Registry also has case management powers (see r. 36).

grounds. The difference is largely explained by the onus placed by section 100 of the 1994 Act on the registered proprietor to prove use.

Non-use

9–104 Applications for non-use are governed by rule 31 of the Trade Marks Rules 2000. The following is a summary. An application for revocation for non-use is initiated on Form TM 26(N)[72] together with a statement of grounds. Within three months the registered proprietor may file his counter-statement with Form TM8 and either two copies of his evidence of use or reasons for non-use. If those are not served, then the Registrar may treat his opposition to the application as having been withdrawn. If they are served, then the applicant has three months to serve his evidence, with a further three months for evidence "strictly in reply" from the registered proprietor. If the applicant serves no evidence then the application is deemed to have been withdrawn.

No further evidence may be filed without leave. The Registry sends the statements of case received from one party to the other, but evidence must be sent directly to the other party at the time of filing and copied to the Registry. All time periods commence on the date of sending, not date of receipt. If any party requests a hearing, then one is appointed. Otherwise, a decision is made and the Registrar sends written notice of the decision, stating the reasons for it. For the purposes of any appeal, the decision dates from when notice of it is sent.

Revocation other than non-use and invalidity

9–105 The procedure on applications for revocation on grounds other than non-use and for invalidity is set out in rules 32 and 33 respectively of the 2000 Rules, which are virtually identical. The following is a summary. Applications are begun on Forms TM26(O) and TM26(I) respectively, in each case accompanied by a statement of grounds.[73] Thereafter, the registered proprietor has six weeks to file his counter-statement, in conjunction with a TM8. If these are not filed, the Registrar has a discretion whether to treat opposition to the application as having been withdrawn. If they are filed, then the applicant has six weeks to file his evidence in support, with six weeks for evidence in support of the reasons stated in the counter-statement, and six weeks for evidence "strictly in reply". Again, time periods commence on the date of sending, not the date of receipt. If the applicant files no evidence in support, then the application is deemed to have been withdrawn. The remainder of the procedure is as set out at the end of the previous paragraph.

---

[72] The "N" evidently stands for "Non-use". Likewise, TM 26(O) for applications on grounds "Other than Non-use", and TM 26(I) for applications for invalidity.
[73] See n. 72.

Appeals

The decision of the Registrar in invalidity or revocation proceedings **9–106** may be appealed either to the appointed person or to the court.[74] The practice and procedure is dealt with in Chapter 5 (para. 5–125 *et seq.*)

Interveners

A person, other than the registered proprietor, with an interest in any **9–107** application to invalidate or revoke can apply under rule 35 of the 2000 Rules for leave to intervene in the proceedings. The Registrar has a general discretion to grant leave upon such terms and conditions as are appropriate. Once leave has been given, the intervener is treated as a party to the proceedings for the purposes of the applicable rules, subject to any terms upon which leave was given.

6. Surrender

Section 45 of the 1994 Act allows the proprietor to surrender his **9–108** registered trade mark in respect of some or all of the goods or services for which it is registered. There was a similar provision in the 1938 Act. What is new in the 1994 Act is the provision, in section 45(2)(b) for rules for protecting the interests of other persons having a right in the registered trade mark. This provision is consistent with the greatly extended powers of licensing of trade marks which are available under the 1994 Act.[75] The relevant rule is rule 26 of the Trade Mark Rules 2000.

The Process of surrender

The process of surrender is initiated by the proprietor sending a notice **9–109** in the prescribed form to the Registrar. Form TM22 is to be used for total surrender. For partial surrender the proprietor must specify on Form TM23 the goods or services in respect of which the registration is to be surrendered. The notice shall have no effect unless the proprietor gives the name and address of any person having a registered interest in the mark and certifies that any such person: (1) has been sent not less than three month's notice of the proprietor's intention to surrender the mark; or (2) is not affected; or (3) if affected, has consented.

Once a notice in proper form has been served, the Registrar makes the **9–110** appropriate entry in the Register and publishes it. Although rule 26(2) of the 2000 Rules provides that the notice has no effect unless the prescribed conditions are satisfied, if it is later discovered that the notice was wrong it is difficult to see how the situation can be rectified once the surrender has taken effect.

---

[74] 1994 Act, s.76.
[75] See ss.29 to 31, dealt with in Chap. 12.

"Registered interest"

9–111 Neither the 1994 Act nor the 2000 Rules contain any definition of "registered interest", although section 25 of the Act shows the ambit of this expression. Section 25(1) refers to persons claiming to have an interest in or under a registered trade mark by virtue of a registrable transaction or claiming to be affected by such a transaction. Section 25(2) defines the different types of registrable transaction—assignments, grants of licences, grants of security interests, the making by personal representatives of an assent or orders for transfer of the court or other competent authority—all of which apply to the registered trade mark in question or any right in or under it. Rule 40 prescribes the information about a registrable transaction which must be entered on the Register. That information includes the identity of persons referred to in section 25(1) and other persons who have an interest in the transaction. Assuming that all registrable transactions have been properly registered, it should be possible to determine from the Register those persons who have a "registered interest" in the trade mark in question.

7. Expiry, renewal, removal and restoration

Expiry and Renewal

9–112 Under the 1994 Act, marks are registered and renewed for periods of 10 years.[76] The process of renewal begins with the Registry sending a notice to the proprietor informing him of the date of expiry and the manner in which the registration may be renewed. At any time within the six months prior to the date of expiry, the proprietor effects renewal of his registration by filing Form TM11 together with the appropriate fee. Renewal takes effect from the date of expiry of the previous registration.

9–113 If the renewal fee is not paid by the date of expiry, the mark is not immediately removed from the Register. First, the fact of non-payment of the renewal fee is published. The proprietor has a period of six months from the date of expiry within which to file a request for renewal together with the renewal fee and an additional renewal fee. Pending the filing of such a request, the registration is in limbo. It has expired but has not been removed from the Register.

Removal

9–114 If no request for renewal (with the necessary fees) is filed within the six months after expiry, then the mark is removed from the Register and the removal is published.

---

[76] See, generally, the 1994 Act, ss.42, 43, and the Trade Mark Rules 2000, rr. 27–30.

Restoration

The proprietor then has a further period of six months from the date of **9–115**
removal of the mark in which to file a request, on Form TM13
accompanied by the appropriate renewal fee and appropriate restoration
fee, to restore the mark to the Register and renew the registration. The
mark will only be restored and renewed if the Registrar is satisfied,
having regard to the circumstances of the failure to renew, that it is just
to do so. The fact of restoration is published, together with the date of
restoration. Presumably the renewal takes effect from the date of expiry,
as before. The status of the mark between the date of expiry and the
date of restoration is unclear. It appears that if the mark is restored to
the Register, the continuity of the registration is also restored. However,
any claim for damages for infringement in the period between expiry
and restoration would appear to have little merit.

CHAPTER 10

GEOGRAPHICAL INDICATIONS AND APPELLATIONS OF ORIGIN

1. Introduction

10–01 The use by traders of marks with geographical significance is both normal and problematic: it is normal to wish to indicate a connection with a particular geographic location, especially if that location gives to the product a cachet or characteristic it would not otherwise have; it is problematic if, in so doing, the trader seeks to fence off part of the commons which should be free to any other trader who does not mislead by using the geographical name.

10–02 The Trade Marks Act, 1938 excluded from registrability a mark which was, according to its ordinary signification, a geographical name[1] and the well-known *"York"* judgment of the House of Lords[2] indicated clearly the disquiet felt by the courts about the possibility that geographical names which others may legitimately wish to use could become the property of trade mark proprietors.[3] Of course, there are many geographical indications which are not (or are no longer) considered by the public to be indications of the geographical source of the goods in respect of which they are used (for example "Mont Blanc" for pens) and these may be registered with little difficulty.

10–03 In the field of passing off[4] in appropriate cases the courts have shown themselves willing to protect groups of traders in a particular geographical location against misleading use of a geographical indication, for example "Champagne",[5] "Advocaat",[6] "Scotch whisky",[7]

---

[1] See the 12th edition of this work, at paras 8–52 *et seq.* Such a mark could, however, be registered as a certification mark under section 37 of the 1938 Act; for an example, see *Stilton* [1967] R.P.C. 173; also see Chap. 11.

[2] [1984] R.P.C. 231, HL; *cf. Waterford T.M.* [1984] F.S.R. 390 (Irish Supreme Court).

[3] For one in the series of cases raising the issue of whether it is trade mark infringement to take whisky from a named distillery, to bottle and sell it as a product of that distillery, see *Allied Domecq v. Murray McDavid* [1997] F.S.R. 864.

[4] See generally Chap. 14.

[5] [1993] F.S.R. 141. See also Regulation 823/87, as amended, which provides protection for the appellations of origin "Champagne" and "Cognac".

[6] [1980] R.P.C. 31, HL.

[7] [1970] R.P.C. 489.

"Swiss".[8] Also, it has been recently reaffirmed that a remedy in passing off may be available to protect a geographical name for a beer, which name may indicate either: (1) that it is brewed in a particular place; or (2) that it is of a particular type associated with that place and so likely to appeal to a particular taste; or (3) that it is the product of one particular brewery at that place.[9] However, unlike elsewhere, there has been in English law no specific protection for "indications of source" or "appellations of origin", both of which are included in "industrial property" in Article 1 of the Paris Convention 1883.[10]

The Trade Marks Act 1994 now provides in section 3(1)(c) that trade **10–04** marks which consist exclusively of signs or designations which serve to indicate geographical origin should not be registered[11] and the *Windsurfing Chiemsee* judgment of the ECJ[12] has interpreted that provision to mean that "geographical names which are liable to be used by undertakings must remain available to such undertakings as indications of the geographical origin of the category of goods concerned".[13] Also, the 1994 Act provides in sections 49 and 50 for the registration of geographical names as certification and collective marks.[14] But, for agricultural products and foodstuffs a new Community system has come into force for the protection through registration of geographical indications and designations of origin.[15]

2. Regulation 2081/92 on the Protection of Geographical Indications and Designations of Origin for Agricultural Products and Foodstuffs

Introduction

Under Regulation 208/92[16] ("the Regulation"), as amended by Regu- **10–05** lation 535/97,[17] protection can be obtained for designations of origin and for geographical indications for agricultural products and foodstuffs.

---

[8] [1999] R.P.C. 826, C.A. It is interesting to compare this decision with that in Germany in which it was held not to be sufficient evidence of confusion for a finding of unfair competition where 10–15 per cent of consumers assumed that chocolate bearing the words "Alpine Milk Chocolate" originated in Switzerland: *Suchard-Milka* 1987 G.R.U.R. 374 (Cologne Court of Appeals).

[9] *Per* Robert Walker J. in *Barnsley Brewery v. RBNB* [1997] F.S.R. 462, citing *Montgomery v. Thompson* ("Stone Ale") [1851] A.C. 217.

[10] Art. 22(2) of TRIPs provides that States must allow for remedies to prevent the public being misled as to the geographical origin of goods or use which constitutes unfair competition within Art. 10*bis* of the Paris Convention. In order to comply with its obligations under TRIPs, Malaysia has passed recently, *inter alia*, the Geographical Indications Act 2000.

[11] See Chap. 7, para. 7–58 *et seq.*

[12] [1999] E.T.M.R. 585.

[13] *ibid.*, at para. 30. See T.M.J. No. 6308 (22/12/99) for the consequential special notice changing Registry practice on the registration of geographical names; also, see Chap. 7.

[14] See Chap. 11.

[15] In addition, Regulation 2082/92 provides for Certificates of Specific Character (CSC), which relate to specific features which distinguish agricultural products or foodstuffs but not where, *inter alia*, they are due to geographical origin. These are beyond the scope of this work.

[16] [1992] O.J. L208/1. The Regulation came into force on July 25, 1993.

[17] [1997] O.J. L083/3.

Wine products or spirit drinks are covered by other legislation.[18] Protection can be obtained by following the application procedure in the Member State in which the geographical area is located. Once registered, the protection can be used to prevent commercial use of the particular designation or indication on products "comparable" to those for which it is registered.

10–06 The legislation was passed to protect indications regarding the origin of agricultural products and foodstuffs products and to harmonise equivalent national "registered designation of origin" systems which existed in most civil law Member States but were particularly important in Mediterranean economies such as Italy, France and Spain.[19]

10–07 The Regulation does not preclude national systems for the protection of geographical indications where there is no link between the indication and quality,[20] as in paragraphs 126 to 128 of the German *Markengesetz*,[21] as long as the protection is only given when there is a sufficiently serious risk of misleading consumers and that, in assessing the level of risk, the relevant criterion is the presumed expectations of an average consumer who is reasonably well-informed and reasonably observant and circumspect.[22] On the other hand, Advocate-General Jacobs considered it unclear whether the Regulation does preclude the co-existence of national systems within the scope of the Regulation,[23] if it does this would affect the validity of geographical indications registered in the United Kingdom as certification or collective marks pursuant to section 49 or 50 of the 1994 Act.

Designations for which protection is available

10–08 Two new forms of protection are provided by the Regulation, namely a protected designation of origin ("PDO") and a protected geographical indication ("PGI"). Both the PDO and PGI refer to the "name of a

---

[18] Geographical designations of origin for wines: Regulation 2392/89; and geographical designations for spirits: Regulation 1576/89. The latter reserves, *inter alia*, the designations "Ouzo" and "Grappa" to Greek and Italian producers, respectively.

[19] For the background to the Regulation, see Kolia *Monopolising Names: EEC Proposals on the Protection of Trade Descriptions of Foodstuffs* [1992] E.I.P.R. 233.

[20] See the Opinion of Advocate General Jacobs (at para. 35) in *Warsteiner*, May 25, 2000 (as yet unreported). This type of geographical indication has been described as "simple" or "quality-neutral": see Beier & Knaak *Geographical Indications of Source in the E.C.* (1994) 25 I.I.C. 1 at 2.

[21] For an explanation of these provisions, see Knaak, *Der Schutz geographischer Herkunftsangaben nach dem neuen Markenrecht* [1995] G.R.U.R. 98.

[22] *ibid.*, at para. 59, citing *Gut Springenheide* [1998] E.C.R. I–4657, paras 30–32. See also *Verbraucherschutzverein E.V. v. Sektkellerei Kessler* [1999] E.T.M.R. 269, for a dispute concerning a German trade mark registered for almost 50 years and a description protected by E.C. Wine Regulation 2392/89: the ECJ found that it was "necessary to establish that the brand name is in fact likely to mislead the consumers concerned and thus affect their economic behaviour", at 281.

[23] *ibid.*, at para. 41. It was stated by Commission official Bertold Schwab in *The Protection of Geographical Indications in the E.C.* [1995] E.I.P.R. 242, that the stance of the Commission was clear: "Nationally protected names not communicated within the six month period [provided by Article 17] as also those which, although communicated, are subject to a decision of non-registration, will cease to be protected": at 245.

region, a specific place or, in exceptional cases, a country, used to describe an agricultural product or a foodstuff" originating in that area[24] with a further requirement depending on whether it is a PDO or PGI. The requirements for a PDO are the more onerous, namely that the quality or characteristics of the agricultural product or foodstuff are "essentially or exclusively due to a particular geographical environment"[25] *and* the production, processing and preparation must take place in that area (with some exceptions).[26] By contrast the PGI merely requires the agricultural product or foodstuff possess "a specific quality, reputation or other characteristics attributable" to the area and just one of the production, processing or preparation elements of the product needs to take place in that area.[27] Thus, all PDOs could fall within the definition of PGI but many PGIs would not be a PDO.

Names that have become generic may not be registered[28] nor those **10–09** which are likely to be confused with a plant variety or animal breed.[29] However, under Article 2.3 "certain traditional geographical or *non-geographical* names" (emphasis added) may be registered as PDOs if other conditions are satisfied: it is under this provision that "Feta" was registered for cheese, even though it is not a geographical name but rather derived from the Italian word for "slice" the registration was subsequently annulled—see para. 10–20).

The application process

Article 5 of the Regulation provides that only a group (or in limited **10–10** circumstances a natural or legal person[30]) is entitled to apply for registration. "Group" is defined as any association of producers and/or processors working with the same agricultural product. Applications are to be sent to the relevant authority in the Member State in which the geographical area is located. In the United Kingdom applications are processed for England, Wales and Northern Ireland by the Ministry of Agriculture, Fisheries and Food,[31] and for Scotland by the Scottish Office of Agriculture, Environment and Fisheries Department.

Product types

The product types for which a PDO or PGI may be registered are beer; **10–11** bread, confectionery, pastry, cakes and other baker's wares; cheese; ciders; essential oils; fresh fish, molluscs and crustaceans and products

---

[24] The words "exclusively or essentially" form part of the similar definition of "appellation of origin" in Art. 2 of the 1958 Lisbon Agreement for the Protection of Appellations of Origin and their International Registration. The U.K. is not a party to this specialised Agreement under the Paris Convention.

[25] Art. 2.

[26] Art. 2(a).

[27] Art. 2(b).

[28] Art. 3.1. The provision defines a "name that has become generic" as one which has become "the common name of an agricultural product or a foodstuff" although it may relate to a place where it was originally produced or marketed. See discussion of "feta", below at para. 10–20.

[29] Art. 3.2.

[30] See Regulation 2037/93 ([1993] O.J. L185/05, Art. 1, for the circumstances.

[31] On Form PFN 1, which also relates to CSCs and is available on the MAFF website.

derived from them; fresh meat and offal; fruit, vegetables and cereals; meat based products; natural gums and resins; natural mineral waters and spring waters; oils and fats; olive oils; other agricultural products; other products of animal origin, for example eggs, honey, etc.

Product specification

10–12 The application must include a product specification[32] to include, at least:

(1) the name of the agricultural product or foodstuff, including the designation of origin or the geographical indication;

(2) a description of the agricultural product or foodstuff including the raw materials, if appropriate, and principal physical, chemical, microbiological and/or organoleptic characteristics of the product or the foodstuff;

(3) the definition of the geographical area;

(4) evidence that the agricultural product or the foodstuff originates in the geographical area for the PDO or PGI, as appropriate;

(5) a description of the method of obtaining the agricultural product or foodstuff and, if appropriate, the authentic and unvarying local methods;

(6) the details bearing out the link with the geographical environment or the geographical origin for the PDO or PGI, as appropriate;

(7) details of the inspection structures to be put in place;

(8) the specific labelling details relating to the indication PDO or PGI, whichever is applicable, or the equivalent traditional national indications;

(9) any requirements laid down by Community and/or national provisions.

Examination

10–13 The Member State vets the application before forwarding it to the European Commission if it considers that it satisfies the requirements of the Regulation. The Commission must examine the application within six months to verify that it complies with Article 4 and if so publish the application in the Official Journal of the European Communities for objections. The Commission is assisted by a committee composed of representatives of each Member State.[33]

Objections

10–14 Objections may be made by Member States within six months of publication in the Official Journal. Any "legitimately concerned natural or legal person"[34] with an objection must channel it through the

---

[32] Art. 4.
[33] Art. 15.
[34] Art. 7.3.

appropriate authority in the Member State in which he resides or is established,[35] although it is not clear what discretion the relevant Member State has in deciding whether and if so in what form to forward the objection to the Commission. It should be noted that trade mark owners themselves do not have any right to object directly to the European Commission but must submit their objections to the relevant national authority. The objection will only be admissible if:

(1) it shows that the application does not comply with the conditions for a PDO or PGI;
(2) it shows that the proposed name would jeopardise the existence of an identical or partly identical name or of a mark or the existence of products which have legally been on the market for at least five years prior to the publication of the application; or
(3) it indicates the name applied for is generic.[36]

If an objection is admissible, the Commission then asks the Member States to reach agreement amongst themselves within three months. If agreement is reached to allow the application, it will be re-published if it has changed or be referred to the committee set up in accordance with Article 15.[37]

If no objections are received, there is no requirement imposed on the **10–15** Commission to check for possible obstacles to registration, so it is important that trade mark owners keep themselves informed about applications and raise in good time any objections with the relevant authority of its Member State. In this context, it is important to note that a PDO or PGI will not be registered where, in the light of a trade mark's reputation and renown and the length of time it has been used, registration is liable to mislead the consumer as to the true identity of the product.[38]

The Ministry of Agriculture, Fisheries and Food maintains a complete list of PDOs and PGIs, which is also available at its web site: *http://www.maff.gov.uk*.

Names from third countries

Names from non-Member States of the Community may be registered **10–16** under Article 12, providing:

(1) the non-E.C. country must be able to give guarantees identical or equivalent to the specification requirement in Article 4 (see above);

---

[35] It would seem sensible for objections by a non-E.U. person to be addressed to the appropriate authority in any Member State in which he is domiciled or has a permanent place of establishment.
[36] Art. 7.4, as amended by Regulation 535/97 ([1997] O.J. L083/0003). The onus of proof is clearly on the national authority objecting.
[37] Art. 7.5.
[38] Art. 14.3.

(2) there must be inspection arrangements in the third country equivalent to those laid down in Article 10 (see below at para. 10–26); and

(3) the third country must provide equivalent reciprocal protection for Community names.

Article 17

10–17 Article 17 provided for a six month period following entry into force of the Regulation for Member States to notify the Commission of names which either were already protected by national laws or were established by usage. These names were not subject to the opposition procedure set out in Article 7.[39]

The first group of PDOs and PGIs were approved under this "grandfather" provision on June 12, 1996[40] which gave Community-wide protection to names (listed in the Annex to the Regulation)[41] which previously had only national protection.

Use

10–18 Only products that meet the requirements of the registered specification can bear the protected name and may be labelled with the indication PDO or PGI.[42] Producers who are not part of the original applicant group may, nevertheless, use the registered name if they can show that their product conforms fully with the registered specification.

Generic names

10–19 Although the requirements for product specifications under Article 4 may be satisfied, a name may not be registered if it has become generic under Article 3. To establish whether or not a name has become generic, account shall be taken of all factors, particularly the following[43]:

(1) the existing situation in the Member States in which the name originates and in areas of consumption;

(2) the existing situation in other Member States;

(3) the relevant national or Community law.

10–20 The ECJ judgment in *"Feta"*[44] was concerned with whether the Commission had acted properly in registering "Feta" as a PDO under

---

[39] For an example of the problems this caused, see *Gorgonzola*, below at paras 10–35 *et seq.*
[40] Regulation 1107/96 [1996] O.J. L148/1.
[41] See n. 63, below for a list of the U.K. registrations. In *Chiciak and Fol* [1998] E.C.R. I–3315 a case involving the registered designation "Epoisses de Bourgogne", the ECJ found that after the entry into force of the Regulation, it is no longer open to Member States to legislate to give different protection to designations of origin for which it has requested registration at Community level.
[42] Art. 8.
[43] Art. 3.1.
[44] [1999] E.T.M.R. 478.

the simplified procedure in Article 17.[45] The Commission did not include the name "Feta" on the list of generic names[46] despite the majority of Member States asking it to do so. The applicant Governments[47] sought to challenge the registration, contending that the name "Feta" did not meet the conditions for registration as a PDO in Article 17.1[48] and also that it constitutes a generic name within the second and third indents of Article 3.1. The applicants noted that Feta had been lawfully produced in several Member States over a significant period.

The Commission contended that strict compliance with the conditions **10–21** laid down in Article 3 was undertaken, but having regard to *Esportur v. LOR SA and Confiserie du Tech SA*,[49] it was appropriate to pay particular attention to the situation in the Member State of origin. The European Court of Justice found that by following this judgment and relying on a survey result the Commission had minimised the importance attached to the second and third requirements of Article 3.1.[50] The Commission had also made a distinction between generic names[51] and the names of products lawfully marketed. This distinction should not mean that a product legally marketed under a name in certain Member States cannot be taken into account when considering whether it has become generic within Article 3.1. Thus, the Court found that the Commission had failed to take properly into account the fact that the name had been used for a considerable period in Member States other than Greece.[52] The Court of Justice upheld the applicants' plea alleging non-compliance with Article 17.2 and the contested Regulation was annulled to the extent that "Feta" was removed from the register as a PDO.

Protection granted

Registered names are protected against: **10–22**

(1) any direct or indirect use of a registered name for products not covered by the specification in so far as those products are comparable to the products registered or using the name exploits the reputation of the protected name;

---

[45] Under Art. 235 E.C. the applicant Member States sought annulment of the Commission's action.

[46] This was the first list published during 1996 pursuant to Regulation 2081/92, Art. 3, and consisted only of six cheeses; Cheddar, Gouda, Edam, Brie, Camembert and Emmenthal.

[47] French, German and Danish Governments.

[48] Art. 17 established a registration procedure known as the "simplified procedure" applicable to names already existing. Art. 17.2 requires compliance with Arts 2 and 4.

[49] [1992] E.C.R. I–5529,a case involving an action by a Spanish association of exporters of nougat called "Turron de Alicante" and "Turron de Jijona" against two French manufacturers of nougat with the same name.

[50] These requirements are the existing situation in other Member States and relevant national and E.C. law.

[51] Art. 3.

[52] Art. 3.1, second indent. All factors in Art. 3.1 must be taken into account.

(2) any misuse, imitation or evocation, even if the true origin of the product is indicated[53] or the name translated or accompanied by an expression such as "style", "type", "method", "as produced in", "imitation", or similar;

(3) any other false or misleading indication on packaging or advertising as to the provenance, origin or essential qualities of the product that may convey a false impression as to its origin[54]; and

(4) any other practice liable to mislead the public as to the true origin of the product.[55]

10–23   The scope of protection accorded to names registered under the Regulation was analysed in *Consorzio del Prosciutto di Parma v. Asda Stores Limited*[56] where the claimant consortium of producers owned a PDO for Parma ham. The defendant sliced, packaged and sold in sliced form, all in the United Kingdom, genuine Parma ham purchased in Italy from a member of the consortium and the consortium sought to stop this activity. However, the High Court held that the Regulation should be interpreted as relating to agricultural activities and not post-production industrial activities such as slicing and packaging. This finding was upheld by the Court of Appeal.[57]

Enforcement

10–24 Once names are registered, they are enforced in the United Kingdom by the Trading Standards (Environmental Health) Department of the various local authorities. However, to date no Statutory Instrument has been passed to implement the Regulation and so it is not clear how there can be enforcement without any detailed legislative provisions dealing, for example, with penalties or remedies. It is submitted that these would sensibly follow those provided for by trade descriptions legislation but at present there is a vacuum.

10–25   Despite this, in the United Kingdom it has been held that the Regulation is not directly effective (enforceable by an individual) but

---

[53] In the *Gorgonzola/Cambozola* decision, *supra*, Jacobs A.-G. noted the presence of these words in concluding that it was irrelevant that the Cambozola wrapping stated that it was a German soft cheese (at para. 39). However, in earlier proceedings (June 1997) the Frankfurt *Oberlandesgericht* found that "Cambozola" did not damage "Gorgonzola" within the meaning of the Regulation, Art. 13.1.b: [1999] E.T.M.R. 135.

[54] In the Control of Misleading Advertisements (Amendment) Regulations 2000 (S.I. 2000, No. 914), which implement the Comparative Advertising Directive 97/55 ([1997] O.J. L290/17), products to which the Regulation applies are defined as "products with designations of origin", Art. 3(1).

[55] Art. 13.1.

[56] [1999] F.S.R. 563. The Consorzio had earlier been unsuccessful in an action for passing off against Marks & Spencer because both the first instance judge (Morritt J.) and the Court of Appeal (Balcombe, Nourse & Leggatt L.JJ.) considered the description "sliced Parma ham" to be true and therefore no misrepresentation: [1991] R.P.C. 351.

[57] Application has been made to the House of Lords for leave to appeal.

rather is directly applicable (enforceable only by organs of the State). The Court of Appeal in the *Parma Ham* case[58] found that it did not have direct effect because it was not sufficiently clear and precise,[59] nor did it provide a source of information to enable the relevant class of persons to be simply and cheaply informed of their rights.[60] On the other hand, in Germany the association of Gorgonzola cheese producers were permitted to bring proceedings (albeit unsuccessfully) under the Regulation against the producer of Cambozola cheese.[61]

All products registered are subject to inspection to ensure that the **10–26** requirements of the specification are met.[62] Applicants nominate an inspection body and these bodies are required to comply with European Standard EN 45011. In some cases, government organisations perform this task whilst in others the trade associations themselves are responsible, for example, the Scottish Quality Beef and Lamb Association and the Stilton Cheese Makers' Association.

Transition period

As noted above, within six months of the entry into force of the **10–27** Regulation, Article 17 of the Regulation allowed Member States to apply for registration, as a PDO or PGI, of marks legally protected in that Member State or, where there was no protection system, those names established by usage. Accepted applications were granted on June 12, 1996 under Regulation 1107/96.[63]

Under Article 13.1 of the Regulation, Member States are permitted to **10–28** maintain national systems that permit the use of names given a PDO or PGI under Article 17 which may breach paragraph 1(a) or (b) of Article 13 (see "Protection Granted", above at para. 10–22) for a period of up to five years from registration.

Further, Article 13.4 allows for the provision of a transitional period where an application has validly been objected to on the grounds that it

---

[58] *Op. cit.; cf. Matthew Gloag & Son Ltd v. Welsh Distillers Ltd* [1998] E.T.M.R. 504, in which Laddie J. refused to strike out the plaintiff's statement of claim alleging breach of Regulation 1576/89 on descriptions of spirits.

[59] Relying on the ECJ judgment in *Fratelli Costanzo Spa v. Comune di Milano* [1989] E.C.R. 1939.

[60] Relying on the Opinion of A.-G. Slynn in *Commission v. Federal Republic of Germany* [1985] E.C.R. 1661 at 1665. Also, see judgment of Laddie J. in *Antonio Munoz s.d. v. Frumar Ltd* [1999] F.S.R. 872, in which an attempt to enforce private rights allegedly arising under the E.U. Grape Regulations was rejected.

[61] [1999] E.T.M.R. 135.

[62] Art. 10. The costs of inspection must be borne by the producers using the protected name (Art. 10.7).

[63] [1996] O.J. L148/01. For the U.K., these were Orkney beef (PDO), Orkney lamb (PDO), Scottish beef (PGI), Scottish lamb (PGI), Shetland lamb (PDO); White Stilton and Blue Stilton cheese (PDO), West Country farmhouse Cheddar cheese (PDO), Beacon Fell traditional Lancashire cheese (PDO), Swaledale cheese and ewes' cheese (PDO), Bonchester cheese (PDO), Buxton blue (PDO), Dovedale cheese (PDO) and Single Gloucester (PDO); Herefordshire cider/perry (PGI), Worcestershire cider/perry (PGI), Gloucestershire cider/perry (PGI); Jersey Royal potatoes (PDO); Newcastle brown ale (PGI), Kentish ale and Kentish strong ale (PGI), Rutland bitter (PGI).

jeopardises a pre-existing name or products on the market for at least five years. It appears that the Commission will allow the non-complying name to continue for up to five years before being phased out.[64]

Conflict with trade marks

10–29 In certain circumstances the existence of a trade mark may hinder or prevent the registration of a PDO or PGI: one of the grounds for objection is that "registration of the name proposed would jeopardize the existence of an entirely or partly identical name or of a mark, or the existence of products which have been legally on the market for at least five years preceding the date of the publication" of the application.[65]

10–30 Article 14.1 of the Regulation sets out the consequence of a PDO or PGI on a subsequent trade mark application relating to the "same type of product": it is submitted that this should be assessed in the same way as "similar goods" under section 5(2) of the 1994 Act. If the application for a trade mark was made after the date of publication of the application for the PDO or PGI, the trade mark application should be refused provided it impinges upon the protection granted to the PDO or PGI under Article 13.[66] If registered despite the existence of an earlier PDO or PGI which it impinges upon, the trade mark shall be declared invalid, including trade marks applied for before publication (in the *Official Journal*) but registered after the publication.[67] Presumably, section 3(4) of the Act would be relied upon for such refusal or invalidity, although it is not clear by whom it should be declared invalid as there is no mechanism in the Act for *ex officio* removal.

10–31 However, Article 14.2 provides that a trade mark registered in good faith before publication of the application for a PDO or PGI may continue in force where there are no grounds for invalidity or revocation of the trade mark under Article 3(1)(c) and (g)[68] or Article 12(2)(b),[69] respectively, of the Trade Mark Directive[70] (sections 3(1)(c) and 3(3)(b) or section 46(1)(d) in the 1994 Act). This provision does not seem to cover

---

[64] Thus, Regulation 2139/98 ([1998] O.J. L270/07) adding "Jambon de Bayon" as a PGI permits various named Danish companies to continue marketing their products under the name for a period of three years from the publication of the Regulation, provided the label showed clearly the true origin of the Danish product.

[65] See Art. 7.4, as amended by Regulation 535/97. Prior to amendment the provision referred to "trade mark" rather than "mark": presumably, the latter is broader and would cover unregistered marks protectable in the U.K. under the law of passing off.

[66] It is understood that the U.K. Registry does not have a set practice of referring to the Register of PDOs and PGIs, although if an application is made in any of Classes 29, 30, 31, 32 or 33 the examiner would consult MAFF reference works and the MAFF website.

[67] Art. 14.1.

[68] A trade mark should not be registered if it is of such a nature as to deceive the public, for instance as to the nature, quality or geographic origin of the goods.

[69] A trade mark may be revoked if "in consequence of the use made of it by the proprietor or with his consent in respect of the goods or services for which it is registered, it is liable to mislead the public, particularly as to the nature, quality or geographical origin" of the goods.

[70] 89/104. See "*Gorgonzola*", below at para. 10–34.

the situation where the prior right is an unregistered mark capable of being protected under the law of passing off, so that use in good faith of such a mark may be stopped.[71] Also, it does not deal with the impact of the proviso to section 3(1) (Article 3(3)), which provides for the possibility of distinctive character acquired through use prior to the date of application for registration.

In addition, it is a ground for refusal of a PDO or PGI if, because of a **10–32** trade mark's reputation and renown, registration would "be liable to mislead the consumer as to the true identity of the product."[72] It is not clear whether this provision relates only to *registered* trade marks but it is submitted that it is so limited as elsewhere in the Regulation references to trade marks are always in the context of the TM Directive (as seems to have been recognised in the 1997 amendment[73] to Article 7.4, which replaced "trade mark" with "mark").

Owners of an unregistered mark comprising or including a geo- **10–33** graphic name should consider registering it in order to avail themselves of this provision in case a future PDO or PGI conflicts with their mark. It is not clear how this may be affected by Article 13.4 of the Regulation (see "Transition Period", above at para. 10–27).

The *Gorgonzola* case

The European Court of Justice case of *Consorzio per la Tutela del* **10–34** *Formaggio Gorgonzola v. Käserei Champignon Hofmeister GmbH & Co. KG*[74] was an Article 234 (ex Article 177) reference from the Commercial Court of Vienna on the conflict between a PDO owned since 1996 by the claimant for a soft white cheese marbled with blue mould, "Gorgonzola", and a registered trade mark owned since 1983 by the defendant in Austria used for a similar soft blue cheese, "Cambozola".[75]

The Court found that use of the mark "Cambozola" "evoked" the **10–35** term "Gorgonzola" since "Cambozola": "ends in the same two syllables and contains the same number of syllables, with the result that the phonetic and visual similarity between the two terms is obvious".[76] It further found that:

"'evocation', as referred to in Article 13(1)(b) of Regulation No. 2081/92, covers a situation where the term used to designate a

---

[71] This would appear to be contrary to Article 24(5) of TRIPs. It is noteworthy in this context that, by Regulation 123/97 (O.J. L022, 24/1/1997), "Whitstable Oysters" is registered as a PGI: cf. *Free Fishers of Whitstable v. Elliott* 4 T.L.R. 273 and *Whitstable Oyster Fisheries v. Hayling* (1900) 17 R.P.C.; 18 R.P.C. 434, for passing off actions involving the name "Whitstable" in relation to oysters.

[72] Art. 14.3.

[73] By Regulation 535/97 ([1997] O.J. L083/03).

[74] [1999] E.T.M.R. 454.

[75] The conflict also concerned the 1951 Stresa Convention on the Use of Appellations of Origin and Designations of Cheese, to which both Italy and Austria were party.

[76] *Op. cit.*, at para. 27.

product incorporates part of a protected designation, so that when the consumer is confronted with the name of the product, the image triggered in his mind is that of the product whose designation is protected. . . .

[It] is possible, . . . for a protected designation to be evoked where there is no likelihood of confusion between the products concerned and even where no Community protection extends to the parts of that designation which are echoed in the term or terms at issue."[77]

10–36   However, by Article 14.2 of the Regulation, for the trade mark to be rendered invalid or revoked in such circumstances, then, provided it was applied for in good faith,[78] there must be shown to be grounds for invalidity or revocation under Article 3.1.(c) and (g) and Article 12.2.(b) of the Trade Mark Directive. The Court found that it was for the national court to decide whether, on the facts, the conditions laid down in Article 14.2 of the Regulation would allow further use of the trade mark.

Concurrent protection

10–37 It is not stated in the Regulation whether the same designation of origin or geographical indication could be registered under the Regulation and as a trade mark and this will depend on the particular national law in the Member State concerned.

Although in most cases in the United Kingdom sections 3(1)(c) and 3(3) of the 1994 Act are likely to prove insuperable obstacles to registration of PDOs or PGIs as trade marks, there appears no reason why, for example, the ducal crown used on Parma ham should not be registered and in appropriate circumstances benefit from the broad scope of protection given by section 10(3).

10–38   Another unclear area is the status of existing trade mark registrations for geographical names which have now been registered by the proprietors as PDOs or PGIs. It is submitted that such trade marks should not be permitted to remain on the Register as the two protection systems are contradictory and if the status of PDO or PGI has been granted, the trade mark should be subject to revocation under section 46(1)(c).[79]

10–39   On the other hand, it is stated expressly in paragraph 3(1) of Schedule 1 of the 1994 Act that "a collective mark may be registered which

---

[77] At paras 25 and 26.

[78] This will depend on whether the national court decides that the applicant "took all reasonable steps at the time of registration to satisfy himself that use of the mark was compatible with the national law (including any applicable international provisions) then in force": at para. 51 of the Advocate-General's Opinion.

[79] In this context it is interesting to note that "Newcastle Brown Ale" was registered as a trade mark in 1993 and also was one of the PGIs registered under the Article 17 fast-track procedure in 1996 (the applicant group was Scottish and Newcastle PLC, the proprietor of the trade mark). Also, "Rutland Bitter", another fast-track PGI, was registered as a trade mark in 1994 by the Grolsch-Ruddles Brewing Company Ltd.

consists of signs or indications which may serve, in trade, to designate the geographical origin of the goods or services" provided that the proprietor may not prohibit the use of the mark by one entitled to use it "in accordance with honest practices" (para. 3(2)). Thus, a PDO or PGI and a United Kingdom collective mark may co-exist. The same applies to certification marks granted in accordance with section 50 and Schedule 2.

CHAPTER 11

COLLECTIVE AND CERTIFICATION MARKS

1. Generally

11–01 The grant and treatment of collective and certification marks is governed by sections 49 and 50 of the Trade Marks Act 1994, together with Schedules 1 and 2. Although "certification marks" have been a feature of the law of registered trade marks in the United Kingdom since the Trade Marks Act 1905 (when they were called "standardisation marks"), it was not possible previously to obtain registration of a so-called "collective mark". Where a mark has been used by a number of traders,[1] the principal civil remedy against misleading use has been in passing off: the *"Swiss chocolate"* type of case involves essentially the protection of a certification mark (which may also but need not be a collective mark).[2] However, the limitations of the action in passing off can be seen in the *"Parma Ham"* case,[3] in which it was found that the Italian association set up to protect the "Prosciutto di Parma" designation of origin was not permitted under procedural rules to bring a representative action on behalf of its members,[4] and in the *"Food Ireland"*[5] case, in which a passing-off claim brought by the plaintiff statutory body established to promote the export of Irish foods failed because it was unable to show that its logo was known in connection with any business in which it was engaged.[6]

2. The Trade Marks Directive

11–02 Article 7*bis* of the Paris Convention requires countries of the Union "to accept for filing and to protect collective marks belonging to associations the existence of which is not contrary to the law of the country of origin,

---

[1] Generally, see Firth, *Collectivity, Control and Joint Adventure—Observations on Marks in Multiple Use* in "Perspectives on Intellectual Property: Trade Marks Retrospective", vol. 7 (Sweet & Maxwell, 2000), pp. 171–178.

[2] See Chap. 14, paras 14–132, *et seq.*, esp. 14–135.

[3] See Chap. 14, at paras 14–135. See also 14–39.

[4] [1991] R.P.C. 351 at 368, *per* Nourse L.J., following Morritt J. at first instance (at 357).

[5] *An Bord Trachtala v. Waterford Foods* [1994] F.S.R. 316 (HC, Ireland).

[6] "[P]rovided the logo achieves, or helps to achieve, its object of identifying Irish food products abroad with a pure and pollution-free environment, it is hardly a major consideration that the name and reputation of the sponsoring body is not known to the prospective customers in Birmingham or Glasgow. It is "Food Ireland" that the logo seeks to promote, not [the plaintiff]": *per* Keane J., at 323.

THE TRADE MARKS DIRECTIVE

even if such associations do not possess an industrial or commercial establishment". Thus, Article 15 of the Trade Marks Directive recognises the right of Member States to permit registration of collective marks and of guarantee or certification marks. It provides that Member States may introduce or maintain in effect provisions governing the registration of such marks which may be additional to those set out in Article 3 and 12 (on absolute grounds for refusal or invalidity and revocation, respectively).

In addition, Article 15(2) permits Member States to derogate from **11–03** Article 3(1)(c) (section 3(1)(c) of the 1994 Act) on the non-registrability of signs or indications of geographical origin where the signs or indications in question may constitute collective, guarantee or certification marks. However, it is specifically provided that such a mark may "not entitle the proprietor to prohibit a third party from using in the course of trade such signs or indications, provided he uses them in accordance with honest practices in industrial or commercial matters; in particular, such a mark may not be invoked against a third party who is entitled to use a geographical name".

3. Collective marks

Definition

Section 49 of the 1994 Act introduces into the United Kingdom regis- **11–04** tered trade mark law the "collective mark", which is defined as "a mark distinguishing the goods or services of members of the association which is the proprietor of the mark from those of other undertakings". The provisions applying to such marks are set out in Schedule 1 to the Act.

Who may own a collective mark

There is no definition of "association" in the 1994 Act, although the **11–05** CTM Regulation does contain one in Article 64(1): "Associations of manufacturers, producers, suppliers of services, or traders which, under the terms of the law governing them, have the capacity in their own name to have rights and obligations of all kinds, to make contracts or accomplish other legal acts and sue and be sued as well as legal persons governed by public law."

Examples of applicants for collective marks are professional bodies or **11–06** trade associations, where certain professional levels or quality require-ments are specified for membership. Frequently the applicant will be a company limited, for example, by guarantee, such as The Institute of Trade Mark Attorneys, and this poses no difficulties. However, where the applicant for registration of a collective mark is an unincorporated association, there must be serious concern that if granted in the name of the unincorporated association the mark will be invalid. It is understood from inquiries of the Registry that it will accept applications in the name of an unincorporated association, either with or without a list of members (although it suggests that a list not be filed as any change of membership would be viewed as an assignment and require appropriate notification and payment of fee). This must be wrong: an unincorporated association cannot sue or be sued[7] as it has no legal capacity to enter into obligations or have rights in its own name. Thus, although section 49 provides that an "association" should be the proprietor of a collective mark, this presupposes that the association is a legal body[8] because otherwise the mark cannot be licensed or enforced by its proprietor. Also, by its wording section 49 would seem to rule out the possibility of the members of an unincorporated association applying for the mark because it would then not be the "association" which is the proprietor and the mark could not perform its function. The position is even clearer where the application is for a Community Trade Mark as Article 64(1) of the CTM Regulation makes it clear that legal personality is a pre-requisite.

The Function of collective marks

11–07 Signs which may be a collective mark are those which distinguish the goods or services of members of the association which is proprietor from those of other undertakings, and section 1(1) of the 1994 Act is to be construed accordingly.[9] The proprietor of a collective mark, which will be the association[10] (if a legal entity), may also use the mark, unlike a certification mark which may not be used by its proprietor.

Indications of geographic origin

11–08 As permitted by Article 15(2) of the TM Directive, paragraph 3 of Schedule 1 provides for the registration of indications of geographical origin, which may otherwise be unregistrable under section 3(1)(c) of the

---

[7] See, e.g. Artistic Upholstery Ltd v. Art Forma (Furniture) Ltd [1999] 4 All E.R. 277. As noted by Shrivastava in a case comment ([2000] I.P.Q. 112): "The implications of this case seem to be, that the goodwill accruing to an unincorporated association is held by its members on trust for each other": such an analysis would not assist the unincorporated association which purports to be the proprietor of a registered collective mark as the definition of collective mark in the 1994 Act, s.49 requires the proprietor to be the association.

[8] "An unincorporated association is not, of course, a legal person" per Lawrence Collins Q.C. in Artistic Upholstery, op. cit., at 284. Cf. Manual of Patent Practice, UK Patent Office (4th ed. 1999), which sets out at para. 7 those "persons" who may apply for a patent, which does not include "a firm, partnership or body which is unincorporate, although in such cases application may be made by individual partners jointly". Whilst the joint application route may be appropriate for partnerships, it is not clear that it is so for unincorporated associations.

[9] Sched. 1, para. 2.

[10] In the Trade Marks Registry Work Manual, Chap. 13 on Collective Marks states that "Collective marks have multiple proprietors", p. 16: this is not correct.

1994 Act. However, such a collective mark may not be used to prohibit the use of the sign in accordance with honest practices in industrial or commercial matters, particularly by a person entitled to use a geographical name.[11]

Misleading marks

However, paragraph 4 of Schedule 1 of the 1994 Act excludes a mark **11–09** from registrability as a collective mark "if the public is liable to be misled as regards the character or significance of the mark, in particular if it is likely to be taken to be something other than a collective mark". It is therefore open to the Registrar to require that a mark includes some indication that it is a collective mark.[12] In this context, it is worth mentioning the decision of Jacob J. in *Association of Certified Public Accountants v. Trade Secretary*[13] where the learned judge confirmed a direction of the Secretary of State under section 32 of the Companies Act 1985 requiring the plaintiff to change its name within six weeks on the ground that using the word "certified" was misleading and likely to cause harm to the public. He found that the word "indicates, or is likely to indicate, to a substantial number of persons, that there is something objectively significant about the members' qualifications, training and experience".[14] It is interesting to speculate whether the Association would have succeeded in an application for a collective mark.

Regulations

An applicant for a collective mark must file with the Registrar within **11–10** nine months of the date of application[15] a copy of the regulations governing the use of the mark, on Form TM35.[16] The regulations must specify who is authorised to use the mark, the conditions for membership of the association and, if there are any, conditions of use, including any sanctions.[17] Once the regulations have been examined and approved by the Registrar (who must be satisfied that they are not "[c]ontrary to public policy or to accepted principles of morality",[18]) the application is published for opposition purposes as any "ordinary" mark would be but noting that the regulations are available for public inspection.

---

[11] Sched. 1, para. 3(2). It is unclear why there is need for this provision in view of s.11(2)(b).
[12] Such an amendment would not fall within s.39(2): see Sched. 2, para. 4, proviso 2.
[13] [1998] 1 W.L.R. 164.
[14] *ibid.*, at 173.
[15] Trade Marks Rules 2000, S.I. 2000 No. 136, r. 22. This is made on Form TM3 with Part 9 filled in to indicate that the application is for a collective mark.
[16] 1994 Act, Sched. 1, para. 5(1).
[17] *ibid.*, Sched. 1, para. 5(2).
[18] *ibid.*, Sched. 1, para. 6(1).

Registration

11–11 Once the application has been advertised and the opposition period expired, the mark proceeds to registration as any other mark would. Any amendments to the regulations must be approved by the Registrar.[19]

Rights of members of the association

11–12 Authorised users of registered collective marks are given the same rights as a licensee under sections 10(5), 19(2) and 89 of the 1994 Act,[20] and the same rights as are given by section 30 in relation to infringement are accorded to authorised users by paragraph 12 of Schedule 1.

Assignment

11–13 It appears that a collective mark may be assigned without the consent of the Registrar (unlike certification marks: see below), although obviously the effect of the assignment ought not to be that any subsequent use is misleading.

Revocation

11–14 In addition to the grounds of revocation set out in section 46 of the 1994 Act for "ordinary" marks, the registration of a collective mark may be revoked on the ground (1) that the manner in which it has been used by the proprietor has caused it to become liable to mislead as regards its character or significance, (2) that the regulations have not been observed or enforced by the proprietor, or (3) that an inappropriate amendment has been made to the regulations.[21] Also, in addition to the usual grounds set out in section 47, a collective mark may be declared invalid on the ground that it was registered in breach of paragraph 4(1)—it was misleading—or paragraph 6(1)—the regulations should not have been approved.[22]

Other respects

11–15 In all other respects, the collective mark is treated as any other registered trade mark.

---

[19] An application to amend should be made on Form TM36 and the Trade Mark Rules 2000 (S.I. 2000 No. 136), r. 23, sets out the procedure for dealing with such an application.
[20] Sched. 1, para. 11(a), (b) and (c).
[21] Sched. 1, para. 13.
[22] Sched. 1, para. 14.

4. Certification marks

Definition

The registration of certification marks is dealt with by section 50 of the **11–16**
1994 Act.[23] The section defines such marks in relation to both goods and
services, whereas under the 1938 Act they were available only for goods.
The mark should indicate "that the goods or services in connection with
which it is used are certified by [its] proprietor . . . in respect of origin,
material, mode of manufacture of goods or performance of services,
quality, accuracy or other characteristics".

Granting authority

Unlike under the Trade Marks Acts 1905, 1919 and 1938, where certain **11–17**
powers were reserved to the Board of Trade (for example, under section
62 of the 1905 Act the Board was required to decide whether it was "to
the public advantage" to grant such a mark), the Registrar is the person
responsible for considering applications for certification marks under
the 1994 Act. Indeed, the whole emphasis of the certification mark as a
special mark has changed and most provisions of the Act apply, along
with the additions set out in Schedule 2.

Registrable trade mark

A trade mark applied for under section 50 of the 1994 Act must be a **11–18**
registrable trade mark, in the sense of sections 1 and 3. Thus, in the
application by the Legal Aid Board for registration of "Legal Aid" the
Registrar concluded that the applicant had failed to provide evidence
that the public recognised the sign "Legal Aid" as a mark which certifies
some aspect of the performance of legal services or conciliation services.
Whilst the Registrar acknowledged that the public recognised "Legal
Aid" as the State Assisted Financial Aid Scheme, this was an entirely
different matter from recognition as the Legal Aid Board's certification
mark. It was therefore found that the sign did not qualify for registration under the proviso to section 3(1). On appeal, Sir Andrew Morrit V.-
C., held that as the mark had acquired a distinctive character through
use, and there was no reason not to infer that the public understood the
nature of the scheme operated by the Board, the mark was capable of
registration as a certification mark.[24]

Proprietor may not use

The effect of section 50 of the 1994 Act is generally to allow associations **11–19**
and traders to register trade marks to be applied to goods and services
certified by them, provided that they do not carry on a business

---

[23] In the 1938 Act it was dealt with in s.37, replacing the 1905 Act, s.62.
[24] SRIS 0/056/00 (Regy) and *Re Legal Aid Board's Trade Mark Application,* October 3, 2000,
    unreported.

involving the supply of goods or services of the kind certified.[25] About a dozen applications to register such marks were made each year under the 1938 Act and it is unlikely that there will be significantly higher numbers under the 1994 Act, especially in view of the introduction of collective marks.

The regime

11–20 Section 50, Schedule 2 and paragraph 19 of Schedule 3 of the 1994 Act (which deals with marks already registered under section 37 of the 1938 Act) set out the provisions specific to marks of this character; Schedule 2 of the 1994 Act and rule 22 of the 2000 Rules deal with the procedure on application to register, and rule 23 with amendment of the deposited regulations; as noted above, all other sections of the 1994 Act apply to certification marks.[26]

Assignment, etc.

11–21 Under Schedule 2, paragraph 12 of the 1994 Act, assignment and other transmission require the consent of the Registrar before they are effective.

Proceedings concerning certification marks

11–22 There has been little litigation concerning certification trade marks. The only two cases under the 1938 Act were concerned with the regis-trability of the mark "Stilton" for cheese[27] (which turned on the ordinary question of distinctiveness of the mark rather than upon any point peculiar to certification trade marks[28]), and an application to expunge the mark "Sea Island Cotton".[29]

---

[25] Counsel for Marks & Spencer in the *Parma Ham* case [1991] R.P.C. 351, suggested that the *Consorzio* could have applied for registration of *Parma Ham* as a certification mark under section 37 of the 1938 Act, but Nourse L.J. declined to comment on this possibility, whilst noting that the action brought was in passing off: "there may be some disappointment amongst the consortium and its members at what they regard as the shortcomings of English law. While the court can fully understand such feelings, they cannot be allowed to affect its decision on the questions before it": at 367.

[26] The 1938 Act adopted the different route of providing a separate code for certification marks (in ss.37, 68 and the First Schedule), with many remaining sections of the Act not applying, *e.g.* s.4 on infringement.

[27] *"Stilton"* [1967] R.P.C. 173. *Union Nationale* (1922) 39 R.P.C. 346, CA was the decision under the 1905 Act, s.62 embodying many of the principles which were then expressly set forth in the 1938 Act, s.37.

[28] Although, in the nature of a certification mark, the kind of distinctiveness required was rather different from that needed for an ordinary mark, *i.e.* merely that the name should denote a cheese having particular properties and also one where a particular method of manufacture in a particular region had been used. A possible s.11 objection was overcome on the ground that all persons who were permitted to use the mark were bound under the regulations to observe the conditions as to process and district.

[29] [1989] R.P.C. 87. The application was made on three main grounds: (1) the proprietors

Regulations

As with collective marks, an applicant for registration of a certification **11–23** mark must file draft regulations governing use of the mark[30] within nine months of the date of the application for registration.[31]

The following basic requirements must be covered in the regulations: (1) who is authorised to use the mark; (2) the characteristics to be certified by the mark; (3) how the certifying body is to test those characteristics and supervise the use of the mark; (4) the fees (if any) to be paid in connection with the operation of the mark; and (5) the procedures for resolving disputes.[32]

It is a ground of refusal by the Registrar that the regulations are **11–24** unsatisfactory,[33] and a ground for revocation that the regulations are not observed.[34] Registration of a certification mark will be refused unless the applicant is competent to certify the goods or services for which the mark is to be registered.[35]

Registration process

Provided the requirements for the regulations set out in Schedule 2, **11–25** paragraph 7(1) of the 1994 Act are met, the mark proceeds to publication, opposition and registration as any "ordinary" mark, although observations may be made on whether the regulations comply with the requirements.[36] The regulations are open to public inspection.

5. Differences between collective and certification marks

Certain marks may be registered either as a collective or a certification **11–26** mark (or as both although it is difficult to envisage circumstances where this might be done). However, only the certification mark is available where the applicant is connected with those who wish to use the mark

---

were no longer competent to certify; (2) there had been failures to observe the provisions of the regulations; and (3) the registration of the marks was no longer to the public advantage. The Board of Trade found that, whilst the proprietor had not been competent to certify for certain periods and there had been breaches which were not to the public advantage, it had not been shown that any member of the public had suffered and the marks were not expunged.

[30] 1994 Act, Sched. 2, para. 6(1). For an example of part of such regulations, see "*Stilton*" *supra*.

[31] On Form TM35: 2000 Rules, r. 22.

[32] 1994 Act, Sched. 2, para. 6(2).

[33] In *Legal Aid Certification Mark Application*, SRIS O/056/00, the hearing officer referred to the deficiencies of greatest concern to be the actual characteristics to be certified, the tests necessary to ensure compliance, and the measures for supervision and control by the proprietors of the mark.

[34] 1994 Act, Sched. 2, para. 15(c).

[35] 1994 Act, Sched. 2, para. 7(1)(b). This was one of the issues raised in the "*Sea Island Cotton*" case, see n. 29, above.

[36] Sched. 2, para. 9.

only through the certification process[37]; whereas, the members of an association may use, or not, the collective mark to indicate membership (and indirectly compliance with the conditions for that membership).[38] The certification mark is more akin to a consumer protection measure than is the collective mark: this is highlighted by the definition of the former as a sign capable of "distinguishing goods or services *which are certified from those which are not*". By comparison, the function of a collective mark is to indicate a trade connection between the goods or services of members of the association and to distinguish them from those of other undertakings.

11–27   A certification mark may not be registered as an "ordinary" trade mark: its purpose is different. On the other hand, a registered collective mark can also be registered as a trade mark: an example is the logo of The Chartered Institute of Patent Agents.

---

[37] Examples include the "Woolmark", owned by I.W.S. Nominee Services Ltd (presumably a company connected with the International Wool Secretariat), and the "Kite" mark, owned by the British Standards Institution.

[38] For example, "Chartered Patent Agent" has been registered as a collective mark by The Chartered Institute of Patent Agents, as has the Chartered Institute's logo (which, as noted in the text, is also registered as a trade mark). Also, "Fellow of ITMA" and "Member of ITMA" have been registered as collective marks by The Institute of Trade Mark Attorneys.

CHAPTER 12

ASSIGNMENTS, TRADE MARKS AS PROPERTY, CO-OWNERSHIP AND LICENCES

1. Outline

Scope of chapter

This chapter concerns the types of assignments permitted in respect of **12–01** registered and unregistered trade marks, and the manner in which they may be implemented. It also covers the nature of trade marks as items of personal property, and the statutory provisions governing co-ownership. Finally, it deals with licensing of registered trade marks, including addressing the rights of licensees to bring proceedings. In relation to the procedural aspects of registering licences and assignments, and of the bringing of infringement proceedings by licensees, fuller details are given in Chapters 3 and 18, although this chapter deals with the consequences of non-registration of assignments and licences.

A common consideration underlying most of the above matters is the **12–02** extent to which a proprietor may deal with his mark without rendering it deceptive. This is not an issue which is new to the Trade Marks Act 1994, or even to the 1938 Act. Indeed, it is an issue which is inherent in the nature of trade marks: given that their function, or at least a major part of their function, is to indicate the origin of goods or services, it will always be open to debate as to how direct or how tenuous the connection between the proprietor and the goods or services may be without the mark becoming more misleading than informative. To understand these issues, and to follow the scheme of the 1994 Act and the problems likely to be involved in its application to dealings with trade marks, it is necessary to begin with a look at the position under the old Acts.

Introduction—the old law and policy

The assignment of registered marks is governed by rules contained in **12–03** the 1994 Act. These do not apply to unregistered marks.[1] They are radically different from the provisions of the Trade Marks Act 1938, being much more permissive.

---

[1] s.24(6).

12–04   Before 1938, the rules governing assignment of registered and unregistered trade marks were much the same. The theory underlying the rules during that period was that the public regarded a trade mark as indicating that the goods bearing the mark emanated from a particular business exclusively, and that, if the link between the mark and the business was broken, it would be contrary to public policy to recognise the continuance of any exclusive right to the mark. Thus, under the Acts before 1938 and at common law, a trade mark and the goodwill of the business concerned had to be assigned together.

12–05   The 1938 Act relaxed that strict position. It was, however, still a major feature of the policy of the 1938 Act to control the manner in which trade marks could be assigned. In particular, although it was possible under the 1938 Act to assign a registered trade mark without goodwill,[2] such transactions were closely policed by the Registrar.[3]

12–06   There were further complications where common law trade marks were assigned at the same time as registered marks; the 1938 Act purported to allow an assignment of a common law trade mark without goodwill in those circumstances,[4] but it was never clear how in fact the assignee could acquire useful rights if he did not obtain the goodwill associated with the mark.[5]

12–07   The 1938 Act also contained detailed provisions controlling the manner in which related marks for similar goods might be assigned, to seek to avoid the danger of deception of the public.[6] Provided that the assignor of a mark complied with the various provisions of the 1938 Act, he would obtain a degree of comfort from the Registrar that the assignment made would be valid.[7]

12–08   The 1938 Act also contained detailed and complex provisions concerning registered user agreements, whose purpose was to regulate situations in which a registered mark was held by its proprietor but used by some other party pursuant to contractual relations between them.[8]

Change in policy

12–09 The 1994 Act contains no express restrictive provisions as to assignment of the kind referred to above. The proprietor's rights of assignment in relation to registered marks are broad and general and expressly extend

---

[2] And, in some situations, an unregistered trade mark: see below.
[3] Trade Marks Act 1938, s.22(7).
[4] Under the 1938 Act, s.22(3).
[5] There is a fuller discussion of these issues in Chapter 13 of the previous edition of this work.
[6] Trade Marks Act 1938, s.22(4)–(6).
[7] See *e.g.* Trade Marks Act 1938, s.22(5).
[8] 1938 Act, s.28, which operated in doctrinal terms by deeming use by a registered user to be used by the proprietor himself. The Act did not contain a general power to grant licences, and the 1905 Act had not permitted licences at all; if a registered mark were used on goods which did not emanate from the proprietor then the mark would be deceptive, while if the goods did emanate from him, no licence would be necessary in the first place.

to assignments without goodwill.[9] However, there is no provision guaranteeing that a trade mark assigned in that way will remain valid, or that the assignment will be valid, and there is also no mechanism to reassure an assignor of one of a number of related marks that they will all remain valid following assignment. There is no method for seeking the Registrar's views as to the effect of an assignment. The power to grant licences is broad and general.

Since the 1994 Act contains general provisions providing for the **12–10** revocation of marks which become deceptive by reason of the manner of their use,[10] it seems clear that its overall scheme is to leave trade mark owners, within broad limits, to organise their own affairs, including by assignments and licences, so as to protect and increase their value, but with the sanction against dealings which lead to deception of the public being the potential revocation of the marks. This overall approach was reflected in the White Paper leading to the 1994 Act,[11] and in the permissive terms of Article 8 of the Directive. The interaction of the assignment and revocation provisions of the 1994 Act is considered in more detail below.

2. Assignments

The new law of assignment, and trade marks as property

The provision of the 1994 Act dealing with assignment generally is **12–11** section 24(1), which provides:

"A registered trade mark is transmissible by assignment, testamentary disposition or operation of law in the same way as other personal or moveable property.

It is so transmissible either in connection with the goodwill of a business or independently."

Section 24 must be read in conjunction with section 22, which provides **12–12** that:

---

[9] 1994 Act, s.24(1).
[10] s.46(1)(d). See Chap. 9 at para. 9–89 et seq.
[11] At para. 4.36 the White Paper stated that: "Whatever may have been the position in 1938, the public is now accustomed to goods and services being supplied under licence from the trade mark owner. For example there has been the growth of franchising operations. The potential for deception is therefore less. Moreover the strongest guarantee that a proprietor will maintain control over the way in which his trade mark is used is that it is in his own interest to do so. A trade mark is a valuable piece of property, in terms both of its power to attract customers and of the royalties which can be demanded from licensees. Its value is however ultimately dependent upon its reputation with the public. If the proprietor tolerates uncontrolled use of his trade mark the value of his property will be diminished. In an extreme case the registration of the mark may become liable to be revoked if it has become deceptive or generic through such use. It is however the responsibility of the proprietor, not the Registrar, to prevent the devaluation of his own property."

"A registered trade mark is personal property (in Scotland, incorporeal moveable property)."

12–13 By section 27 of the 1994 Act, an application for a registered trade mark is subject to the same provisions, and may be assigned in the same way.

These provisions do not arise out of the TM Directive, which does not deal expressly with assignment of registered trade marks.

Types of assignment

Assignment of the whole mark, or partial assignment

12–14 The simplest kind of assignment is one of the whole of a trade mark and all interests in it, but it is not the only possibility. The 1994 Act allows for partial assignments as well, which may be limited so as to apply to only some of the goods or services for which the mark is registered, or so as to apply to use of the mark in a particular manner or in a particular locality.[12]

12–15 These latter two possibilities—assignments which are partial as to manner of use or as to locality—are not easy to understand. In particular, it is difficult to see how they could be implemented without rendering the mark concerned deceptive. For example, if a trade mark owner assigned to another trader the rights in his registration, but only south of Watford, how could members of the public, travelling around the country, realistically be expected to identify the source of goods bearing the mark? And when the goods concerned were transported between the territories of the two traders, the same problem would arise. It is suggested that unless a mark had only a strong local following to begin with, or unless the two traders concerned took care to use other, different, trade marks in addition to the partially assigned mark, deception would be highly likely, if not inevitable.

12–16 Similar difficulties arise in connection with assignments which are partial as to the manner of use of a trade mark (bearing in mind that "manner" of use must mean something different from use in relation to a particular type of goods). For example, suppose an assignment is made of a trade mark but only in relation to the right to import goods bearing the mark, with the original owner retaining the rights of advertisement, sale and so forth: how could the mark continue to function as an indication of the origin of the goods, without deception?

Assignments by way of security; charges

12–17 A registered trade mark may be assigned by way of security in the same manner as for assignments generally.[13] It may also be charged in the same way as any other moveable property.[14] Where an assignment by

---

[12] s.24(2).
[13] s.24(4).
[14] s.24(5).

way of security is made, there is frequently a licence back to the assignor, although in such cases it is not uncommon for the issue of control of the (new) licensee's use by the (new) proprietor to be overlooked.

Formal requirements and procedure for assignments

Assignment to be in writing and signed

By section 24(3) of the 1994 Act, an assignment of a registered trade **12–18** mark is not effective unless it is in writing signed by or on behalf of the assignor or, if applicable, a personal representative.

3. Registration of assignments and other transactions

Registration of assignments

By section 25 of the 1994 Act, assignments and licences of registered **12–19** trade marks are registrable transactions, and details of them may be entered in the Register on application by the proprietor, any other person claiming to have an interest in the mark, or anyone affected by the transaction concerned.[15]

Registration is not compulsory and the validity of a transaction **12–20** between the parties to it is not *per se* affected by non-registration. However, there are two important reasons to register.[16] First, registration protects a person acquiring an interest in a trade mark from another person acquiring a conflicting interest. Secondly, registration is necessary for a licensee or assignee to be able to sue and obtain full relief for infringement.

Effect of non-registration

The effects of a failure to register a registrable transaction are set out in **12–21** section 25(3) and (4) of the 1994 Act.

Subsections (3) and (4) each provide for consequences which flow in the absence of an *application* for registration of a registrable transaction. Once the person seeking to register his interest has made an application, it therefore seems that his interest is protected. If there is a short gap thereafter before his interest or application to register appears on the Register, the risk appears to fall on any others who may be affected. A person who intends to acquire an interest in a trade mark may wish to search the Register more than once to try to avoid the danger this presents.

[15] See s.25(1) and (2). Full details of the procedure for registering such a transaction, and the matters to be registered are given Chap. 3.
[16] A more minor reason is to give protection against the surrender by the proprietor of the mark.

Failure to register and conflicting interests

12–22 Section 25(3)(a) of the 1994 Act is a general provision relating to all registrable transactions and provides that until an application for registration has been made, "the transaction is ineffective as against a person acquiring a conflicting interest in or under the registered trade mark in ignorance of it". It is clear from the context, and as a matter of common sense, that the "it" of which the person acquiring the conflicting interest is required to be ignorant is the transaction, not the registered trade mark in question.

12–23 It is to be noted that the effect of section 25(3)(a) is to render the first transaction ineffective as against the later acquirer of an interest. It does not render the transaction ineffective generally. Further, it is only against a person later acquiring a conflicting interest that the earlier transaction is ineffective, and this may leave room for uncertainty.

12–24 Some later transactions will plainly confer a "conflicting" interest on the person concerned. If A assigns his mark to B, who fails to register, and then purports also to assign it to C, who is ignorant of the assignment to B, then the interest of C plainly conflicts with that of B.[17] Similarly, one would expect that if in the same situation C were granted an exclusive licence, that interest would conflict with B's, since B would not be able to use the trade mark himself were C's rights valid; presumably the consequence would be that as against C, B could not assert his title to the registered trade mark.[18]

12–25 However, what if merely a non-exclusive licence were granted to C? It is unclear whether that would be an interest conflicting with the interest of B, since it would not prevent B from exercising any of his rights under the registration. If it were not a conflicting interest, then B would seem to be able to assert his assignment from A, and thereby avoid the licence to C. Since this would be an unjust result for C, who may well have given valuable consideration to A, and since the situation would be the fault of B because of his failure to register, it is suggested that even a non-exclusive licence should be regarded as a potentially conflicting interest, on the basis that at the very least it deprives B of the ability to sue C under his registration.

12–26 Section 25(3) does not appear to be limited to the case where the person acquiring the potentially conflicting interest has given value for it. It is to be presumed that this omission was deliberate, and it would therefore seem that the section applies in cases where an interest has

---

[17] What would follow thereafter is unclear; one view is that since the assignment to B is ineffective as against C, C obtains title to the registered mark. However, this is not spelt out in the section as explicitly as one might expect were it to be the correct analysis, and it seems surprising that A can execute a good assignment to C at all, since he has lost anything to assign by virtue of his transaction with B. Nonetheless, it is suggested that the better view is that C becomes owner.

[18] How this would work in practice is very unclear, however, since as between A and B, B would be the owner of the mark, and could obtain registration (albeit subject to C's interest), although there would be no privity of contract between B and C so as to regulate the exclusive licence.

been granted by way of gift, or because a third party has provided value to procure its grant. It is also not an express requirement of section 25(3) that the person acquiring the potentially conflicting interest has acted in good faith, although it seems rather unlikely that such a person would act in bad faith *vis-à-vis* the person seeking to acquire an interest under an earlier unregistered transaction yet not (as the section does require) have knowledge of the earlier transaction.

Non-registration of transactions conferring a licence

Licences under registered trade marks are dealt with in more detail **12–27** below, but it is convenient to deal here with the effect of a failure to register them.

Section 25(3)(b) of the 1994 Act is a provision dealing specifically with the effect of a failure to register a transaction conferring a licence. The person claiming to have become a licensee (whether exclusive or non-exclusive) does not obtain the rights relating to infringement provided by section 30 or 31 (as the case may be)[19] until an application is made to register the transaction in question. This may affect relations between that person and the proprietor, as well as the rights of that person against infringers, since a licensee may frequently have the right to call upon the proprietor to bring infringement proceedings.[20]

Effect of non-registration on right to financial relief

As is explained in Chapter 18, both a licensee and a proprietor of a **12–28** registered mark may obtain damages or an account of profits if successful in an infringement action. But as a result of section 25(4) of the 1994 Act the right to obtain financial relief generally depends on an application having been made to register the assignment or agreement whereby such a party obtained his interest.

In general, section 25(4) has the effect that a failure to register that **12–29** transaction will deprive the party concerned of the right to financial relief in respect of acts of infringement committed before the registration of the transaction (and if the transaction has not been registered at all, then no financial relief at all will be available). There are, however, two exceptions.

First, there is a six month grace period. Provided an application for **12–30** the registration of the transaction is made within that period from its date, full financial relief will be available under section 25(4)(a). Further, the grace period is extended by section 25(4)(b) if it was not practicable to apply for registration before the end of it, and provided that an application was made as soon as practicable.

---

[19] The rights provided by ss.30 and 31 are set out in more detail below at paras 12–68 *et seq.*
[20] Under s.30(2).

12–31   Section 25(4) is very similar in its structure and expression to section 68 of the Patents Act 1977, and it is suggested that authorities in relation to that provision will be relevant to the application of section 25(4).

Trusts and equities

12–32 By section 26(1) of the 1994 Act, no notice of any trust is to be entered on the Register, and the Registrar is not affected by trusts, even if notified of them. This does not prevent a trust being created and, as between the parties to it, enforced, but only their legal interests will be entered on the Register.

Applications as objects of property

12–33 By section 27 of the 1994 Act, the provisions of sections 22 to 26 are applicable (with the necessary modifications set out in sections 27(2) and (3)) to applications for registration in the same way as to registered trade marks. As a result, applications for registration are also to be regarded as objects of property, and dealings in them should be registered in the same way as dealings in registered trade marks.

4. Assignments without goodwill

Meaning of goodwill

12–34 The meaning of goodwill is dealt with in detail in Chapter 14. However, it is necessary to consider it to some extent here, since it is important to an understanding of the difficulties attendant on an assignment of a registered trade mark without goodwill.

12–35   However, before embarking on a consideration of whether and how trade marks may be assigned without goodwill, it is worth appreciating that the vast majority of trade mark assignments include the transfer of goodwill. There is usually a specific reason if goodwill is omitted: frequently taxation, or price. Sometimes goodwill is separated from the connected trade mark by their being held by different companies within a group, causing no difficulty while they are in the same ultimate ownership, but giving rise to problems if they later become split.[21] The point to be appreciated in such situations is that even if there is a specific reason for not assigning the goodwill, it needs to be weighed against the possibly considerable risk that the mark in question will be rendered void or unenforceable as a result. Furthermore, if the goodwill is simply left to atrophy in the hands of the assignor of the trade mark, the assignee is likely, in practical terms, to gain the benefit of it. If that is so, it is likely to be preferable to assign it in a formal sense as well.

---

[21] As, *e.g.* happened in *Scandecor Development v. Scandecor Marketing* [1998] F.S.R. 500 and [1999] F.S.R. 26 CA.

The nature of goodwill has been many times stated but has not been **12–36** categorically defined. Its definition is complicated by the fact that to different people in different contexts it means different things. An accountant valuing a company's assets, for example, has a different view of goodwill than a trade mark lawyer. To the former, goodwill includes more or less anything intangible which brings in business, whether it arises from a distinctive trade mark, get-up, etc., or otherwise. To the latter, it is a much narrower notion. Goodwill also falls to be considered in the law of landlord and tenant, and of taxation.[22]

In the context of trade mark law, goodwill has been stated to **12–37** represent, in connection with a business or business product, the value of the attraction to customers which the name and reputation possesses.[23] The matter was considered in *IRC v. Muller's Margarine*,[24] where Lord Macnaghten said:

"It [goodwill] is a thing very easy to describe, very difficult to define. It is the benefit and advantage of the good name, reputation and connection of a business. It is the attractive force which brings in custom. It is the one thing which distinguishes an old-established business from a new business at its first start. The goodwill of a business must emanate from a particular centre or source. However widely extended or diffused its influence may be, goodwill is worth nothing unless it has power of attraction sufficient to bring customers home to the source from which it emanates. Goodwill is composed of a variety of elements. It differs in its composition in different trades and in different businesses in the same trade. One element may preponderate here and another element there . . . For my part, I think that if there is one element common to all cases of goodwill it is the attribute of locality. For goodwill has no independent existence. It cannot subsist by itself. It must be attached to a business. Destroy the business and the goodwill perishes with it, though elements remain which may perhaps be gathered up and revived again. No doubt, where the reputation of a business is very widely spread, or where it is the article produced rather than the producer of the article that has won popular favour, it may be difficult to localise the goodwill. But here, I think there is no difficulty . . . Moreover, under the Stamp Act 1891, we are not required to define the local situation of the goodwill. We have only to determine whether it is or is not situate out of the United Kingdom."

---

[22] See *e.g. Whiteman Smith Motor Company v. Chaplin* [1934] 2 K.B. 35, *IRC v. Muller's Margarine* [1901] A.C. 217. In the former case, the Court of Appeal considered a number of types of customers, including "cats", who continue to frequent a business after a change of ownership because of their attachment to the premises and relative indifference to the identity of the proprietor, and "dogs", who will continue to patronise the former proprietor elsewhere. The former are not the concern of the law of passing off, while the latter are. The law of landlord and tenant has regard to both.

[23] *Reuter v. Muhlens* (1953) 70 R.P.C. 235 at 254.

[24] [1901] A.C. 217 at 223.

12–38 Lord Lindley said:

> "Goodwill regarded as property has no meaning except in connection with some trade, business or calling. In that connection I understand the word to include whatever adds value to a business by reason of situation, name and reputation, connection, introduction to old customers, and agreed absence from competition, or any of these things, and there may be others which do not occur to me. In this wide sense, goodwill is inseparable from the business to which it adds value, and, in my opinion, exists where the business is carried on. Such business may be carried on in one place or country or in several, and if in several there may be several businesses, each having a goodwill of its own."[25]

12–39 However difficult to identify, English goodwill appears to be a species of English personal property capable of being sold or charged or of being bequeathed by will.[26]

12–40 The proprietor of a mark may have a goodwill in England without having a place of business in England, but there must be a business in England.[27]

A vendor who sells the goodwill of his business may not afterwards destroy the goodwill which he has sold by soliciting his former customers.[28]

Assignments without goodwill are permitted

12–41 As is noted above,[29] assignments of registered trade marks, with or without goodwill, are permitted expressly by section 24 of the 1994 Act, and no special formalities are required to achieve them.[30] The important question, however, is whether and to what extent they can be achieved without rendering the mark in question liable to revocation under section 46.

Relationship of section 24 to section 46: Marks which become deceptive

12–42 Section 46(1)(d) of the 1994 Act provides that the registration of a trade mark may be revoked on the ground that:

---

[25] This passage was quoted by Byrne J. in *Rickerby v. Reay* (1903) 20 R.P.C. 380 and by Romer L.J. in *Reuter v. Muhlens* (1953) 70 R.P.C. 235 at 237, who found that goodwill had locality.

[26] *Reuter v. Muhlens* (1953) 70 R.P.C. 235 at 254 *per* Evershed M.R.; *Adrema-Werke v. Custodian of Enemy Property* [1957] R.P.C. 49 at 54.

[27] See *Star Industrial v. Yap Kwee Kor* [1976] F.S.R. 256 (PC, Singapore); *"Advocaat"* [1980] R.P.C. 31 at 105, HL, *per* Lord Fraser. As to the question of foreign businesses with a reputation in the U.K. but no goodwill, Chap. 14, *post*.

[28] *Trego v. Hunt* [1896] A.C. 7 and cases cited by Danckwerts J. in *Reuter v. Muhlens* (1953) 70 R.P.C. 102 at 121, and approved in CA.

[29] See para. 12–11, above.

[30] Moreover, the 1994 Act does not contain the express provision against "trafficking"—*i.e.* dealing in the right to use a registered mark as a commodity in itself without its connoting a true connection in the course of trade—which was found in the 1938 Act, s.28(6), as to which see *"Holly Hobbie"* [1984] F.S.R. 199, HL.

"in consequence of the use made of it by the proprietor or with his consent in relation to the goods or services for which it is registered, it is liable to mislead the public, particularly as to the nature, quality or geographical origin of those goods or services."

The section focuses on the nature of use by or with the consent of the proprietor; on its face it would not seem that a danger of misleading the public which arises from some other factor would leave a mark liable to be revoked.

The important question which requires an answer is how far the **12–43** permissive nature of section 24 can be pressed before the tension with section 46 becomes unbearable. Take an extreme example:

> Trader A has a business which he conducts under a registered trade mark. By reason of his use, he has acquired a goodwill in relation to the business conducted under the mark. A sells his registered mark to B. The agreement between A and B requires that A ceases to use the mark, which he does, but it leaves the goodwill with A and permits him to carry on business as before, selling the same goods to the same customers, which he also does. B begins to use the mark in the course of a new business, on goods covered by the registration, but which are different in quality to the goods of A, and which have no connection with A in any way.

What makes this an extreme example is A's continuing trade under a **12–44** different mark while retaining the goodwill of the old, and the lack of connection of B's new business with A. However, one cannot avoid the conclusion that the public are liable to be misled; they are likely to get the mistaken impression that B's goods are the same as those formerly acquired from A, or are at least from the same trade source. Yet not only are the goods not the same, or from the same trade source, but they are actually still available from A. It is difficult to resist the conclusion that the registration of the mark is liable to be revoked. Yet the transaction between A and B which caused the problem does not on its face in any way offend the provisions of the 1994 Act concerning assignment. It was merely an assignment of a registered trade mark without goodwill, a thing expressly permitted.

Other examples may be much less difficult. If A has never used the **12–45** mark, or only barely used it, so that it has no, or only negligible, goodwill, then an assignment may be much less likely to cause the public to be misled. Similarly, the problems may be much less acute or enduring if A ceases his former trade upon assignment to B. But dwelling on cases where the assignor has no goodwill does not really help to understand the relationship between sections 24 and 46. The basic problem arises not because the assignee does not acquire any goodwill in connection with the mark, but rather because the assignor keeps such goodwill.

12–46   At one level, all transmissions of a trade mark, even with goodwill, are liable to mislead customers, at least for a while. If the founder of a family business retires, leaving it to his children, who already work in it, there may be some customers who will continue to patronise the business under the mistaken impression that the founder is still involved. However, this kind of false impression has never been an objection to an action in passing off[31] or to the registration of a trade mark. It is inevitable, and not regarded as damaging or contrary to the interests of the public or the policy of the law. Any difficulty which it presents is much outweighed by the desirability that a valuable asset such as goodwill be alienable in the right circumstances, and by the fact that the continuing use of a mark in such circumstances conveys far more accurate information (that the goods are from essentially the same source) than inaccurate information.

12–47   Moreover, it must be recognised that the conditions of modern commerce are far different from those prevailing when the earlier trade mark Acts (even the 1938 Act) were implemented.[32] Businesses are much larger, and the mobility of labour is much greater. Well-known trade marks rarely connote the involvement of a particular individual in the production of the goods concerned (no one imagines that there is a Mr Levi Strauss making jeans, for example), and there is a much greater public awareness that trade marks pass with the sale of businesses and are widely licensed.

12–48   The result, it is suggested, is that the courts will have to strike a balance in seeking to reconcile section 24 and 46 of the 1994 Act. If *any* element of public deception leads to a mark becoming vulnerable to revocation, then section 24 will be deprived of meaning, while a reading of section 24 to the effect that any assignment of a mark is permitted without goodwill whatever the effect would be to promote unnecessary deception of the public, which it is the policy of the Act and the TM Directive to avoid. It is further suggested that transitory public confusion in the period immediately after the assignment of a mark ought to be accepted as inevitable, and merely part of the price for allowing assignment at all.

12–49   A similar difficulty had to be grappled with under the 1938 Act, in connection with registered user agreements, licences, and the use of foreign proprietors' marks by domestic distributors in the absence of control generally. The cases were never entirely consistent, and it was hard to discern hard and fast rules as to the connection in the course of trade which was required between the proprietor of a mark and the goods of his licensee in order to avoid the mark becoming deceptive.[33]

---

[31] On the contrary, it may well be passing off for a vendor of a business falsely to represent that he continues to have an involvement in it (see Chap. 14), although to advertise his former connection is generally lawful (see *e.g. Harrods v. Schwartz-Sackin* [1986] F.S.R. 490).

[32] As the White Paper recognised in the passage quoted in para. 12–10, n. 11, above.

[33] Contrast *Bowden Wire v. Bowden Brake* (1913) 30 R.P.C. 45 HL, on the one hand with *"Manus"* (1949) 66 R.P.C. 71, CA, and *"Bostitch"* [1963] R.P.C. 183 on the other.

Certain assignments probably result in invalidity

Nonetheless, it appears highly likely that certain commercial arrange- **12–50** ments must result in a registration becoming liable to revocation. One case decided under the 1994 Act may serve as an illustration, although it was not specifically concerned with section 24.

In *Scandecor Development v. Scandecor Marketing* [1998] F.S.R. 500 and **12–51** [1999] F.S.R. 26, two Scandinavian partners began a successful business in posters, which operated throughout Europe and elsewhere through local subsidiaries, including one in the United Kingdom. The partners fell out and divided areas of the business among themselves. For a period of time the United Kingdom subsidiary controlled distribution in the United Kingdom, being an exclusive distributor of the parent company's products, and selling its own range of calendars, prints and frames. The mark in question, "Scandecor", was known to the trade, but not to the public.

In due course relations between the parties broke down altogether, and the parent company, which owned the relevant registrations, sued for infringement, and for passing off. The United Kingdom subsidiary, now no longer under the ownership of the parent, counterclaimed to revoke the marks and for passing off.

At first instance, the court held that although the parent company did **12–52** not control the products of its former subsidiary, there was "a fairly general recognition" that the products emanated from Scandinavia. It also held that the parent owned the goodwill in relation to posters, and that the goodwill in relation to calendars and the like, generated by the trade of the United Kingdom subsidiary, was shared between it and the parent because of a misconception on the part of customers that they came from the same source as the posters. Although there was confusion about the source of the goods, which could be relevant deception for the purposes of section 46, "indication of origin" in that section was not limited to an indication that the proprietor produced the goods. The relationship between the parent and the subsidiary constituted a sufficient connection.

The Court of Appeal overturned the decision, holding that the judge **12–53** had erred in finding that the parent could have a share in the goodwill as a result of an assumed and incorrect connection between the goods and the parent. It found that the subsidiary owned the relevant goodwill by reason of its having conducted the actual trade in the United Kingdom. The parent's counsel had conceded[34] that on that basis, the registered marks concerned had to be revoked under section 46, by reason of their being no longer distinctive. This concession appears to have been accepted without demur by the Court of Appeal; if it is correct then the consequences in terms of assignments which leave a registered trade mark in different hands from the goodwill associated

---

[34] Recorded at 45.

337

with it are potentially very far-reaching. The Court of Appeal stated "As . . . the mark is not distinctive of [the parent] in the United Kingdom, we order that the registration of the marks be revoked." Put in that broad way, it is hard to see how an assignment of a registered mark without goodwill can ever leave it valid. However, the Court of Appeal did not hear full argument on the point and were not, it seems, directed to section 24. Probably the best view of *Scandecor* is that while it is not in any sense a binding authority as to what may or may not be done under section 24 without rendering a registration invalid, it is an indication that great caution will be necessary in executing assignments of registered trade marks without goodwill, and that a tenuous continuing involvement of the proprietor in the goods sold under the mark is unlikely to save a marginal situation.

5. Unregistered trade marks

Assignments of unregistered trade marks

12–54 Title to a trade mark could not at common law be assigned, and nor could it devolve in gross[35]; but unless the mark connoted a personal connection between its original owner and the goods in connection with which it was used, it could be assigned and transmitted, together with the goodwill of the business in such goods.

12–55 Until it was established that there could be property in a trade mark there could, of course, be no question of the assignment of trade mark rights,[36] although the successors of the original founders of a business no doubt took over and continued to use the old trade marks employed in it, and were protected when other traders sought to pass-off their goods as the goods of the lawful users of the marks.[37] But as soon as trade marks were recognised as the subjects of property, it followed that they were alienable, subject always to this, that the property was lost if the marks became deceptive.

Transfer by implication with goodwill

12–56 Conversely, it was held that the sale and transfer of the goodwill of a business assigned the trade marks used in the business to the purchaser and transferee by implication, and without any express grant being

---

[35] See, *e.g. Pinto v. Badman* (1891) 8 R.P.C. 181; *Thorneloe v. Hill* [1894] 1 Ch. 569; *Ullman v. Leuba* (1908) 25 R.P.C. 673.
[36] See *per* Fry L.J. in *Pinto v. Badman* (1891) 8 R.P.C. 181 at 194, quoting from *Leather Cloth v. American Leather Cloth* (1863) 4 De. G.J.&S. 137.
[37] See, for instance, *Webster v. Webster* (1791) 3 Swan 490, *per* Thurlow LC, and *Motley v. Downman* (1837) 3 My. & Cr. 1; 6 L.J. Ch. (NS) 308.

needed.[38] This is still the law.[39] It is a question of interpretation, to be gathered from the assignment as a whole, whether the trade marks do or do not pass, and an intention not to assign them may appear, notwithstanding the use of the word "goodwill" in the assignment.[40]

A difficult question of fact may arise, whether in particular circumstances a person has purchased the right to represent that he is the successor in business of another.[41]

Assignment of part of business

There is no clear authority as to how far, at common law, a business **12–58** might be split up and parts assigned separately with the relevant trade marks. The history of the *"Sunbeam"* trade mark[42] is an example of such a division having taken place, and the propriety of the transaction was not the subject of any criticism by the courts. Doubts have been expressed whether the rule in regard to assignments is as restrictive as a literal construction of the words of Fry L.J. in *Pinto v. Badman*[43] might suggest. In *Sinclair*,[44] both Maugham J. (at 129) and Lawrence L.J. (at 139) were careful to avoid expressing an opinion that an assignment of part of a business with the relevant trade mark could not be valid at common law.

6. Co-ownership

Nature of co-ownership; co-proprietors' rights *inter se*

Co-ownership of registered trade marks is governed by section 23 of the **12–59** 1994 Act, which is modelled on section 36 of the Patents Act 1977. Section 23(1) provides that where a mark is granted to two or more

---

[38] *Shipwright v. Clements* (1871) 19 W.R. 599; referred to in *Sinclair* (1932) 49 R.P.C. 123. See also *Currie v. Currie* (1898) 15 R.P.C. 339, below, where goodwill was held to pass and therefore the trade marks.
[39] "He who sells the cow doubtless may reserve for himself the contractual right to sup the milk; but in the absence of any such agreement I should be slow indeed to hold that a foreign company was free to use a trade mark in competition in this country with the subsidiary company which it itself had created and then sold to the purchaser": *per* Megarry J. in *"Weston"* [1968] R.P.C. 167 at 183.
[40] *Roger* (1895) 12 R.P.C. 149.
[41] See *Rickersby v. Reay* (1903) 20 R.P.C. 380. See also *Currie v. Currie* (1898) 15 R.P.C. 339, where on dissolution of a partnership without any deed or formal agreement, one partner bought the share of the other partner in the assets, and these were held to include the goodwill and therefore the trade marks. In *Wood v. Hall* (1916) 33 R.P.C. 16, it was contended that an assignment of particular brands and goodwill on the construction of the agreement comprised only the goodwill in the trade under the brands, but this contention failed.
[42] (1916) 33 R.P.C. 389.
[43] (1891) 8 R.P.C. 181 at 194–195: "The brand is an indication of origin . . . . It can be assigned . . . . when the origin is assigned with it. It cannot be assigned when it is divorced from its place of origin, or when, in the hands of the transferee, it would indicate something different to what it indicated in the hands of the transferor."
[44] (1932) 49 R.P.C. 123.

persons jointly, each is entitled to an equal undivided share in it, although they may modify that arrangement by agreement. There does not appear to be any limit to the number of co-proprietors permitted.

12–60   Co-proprietors are entitled to use the trade mark for their own benefit, and they may do so without the permission of the other co-proprietor(s) and without accounting to them (section 23(3)). This extremely liberal provision may not be without its perils, however. Co-proprietors who each independently use the same mark on different goods without reference to one another must be at risk of rendering the mark deceptive and liable to revocation under section 46, for reasons similar to those discussed above in relation to assignments.

12–61   Co-proprietors may not grant a licence under the trade mark, or assign or charge their share in it, without permission of the other co-proprietor(s).[45] This may in practical terms make it unlikely that ownership of a registered mark will pass into the hands of different parties who later use it without reference to one another, since an assignment or licence made in circumstances in which the formal consent of a number of parties is required is likely to be accompanied by contractual provisions as to the later use of the mark.

12–62   Any co-proprietor may bring infringement proceedings, but all the co-proprietors must be joined as parties, by being added either as a claimant or defendant[46] (the purpose of their joinder being, of course, to ensure that they are bound by the decision and thus to prevent the defendant being sued more than once). A co-proprietor joined as defendant in those circumstances is not liable for costs. Interim relief can be sought by a single co-proprietor without joining the others at that stage.[47]

Transitional arrangements as to co-ownership

12–63   The 1938 Act had a different scheme for shared ownership of registered trade marks, which was governed by the rather obscure section 63. That section did have the major advantage, however, that registration as joint proprietors was only permitted where the relations between the parties (presumably usually by contract or partnership) was such that each could only use the mark on behalf of all of them, in relation to goods with which they were all connected in the course of trade. Thus, the danger of deceptive use was greatly limited.

12–64   Schedule 3 paragraph 7 of the 1994 Act governs the transition from section 63 of the 1938 Act to the new section 23. Paragraph 7 provides that so long as the arrangements between the parties remain of the kind described in section 63 of the 1938 Act (use by one on behalf of all, use only on goods with which all are connected), then the provisions of

---

[45] 1994 Act, s.23(4).
[46] s.23(5).
[47] ibid.

section 23(1) and (3), providing for ownership in undivided shares and permitting independent use, will not bite. Otherwise, section 23 takes effect as from the commencement of the 1994 Act in relation to all existing registered trade marks in respect of which multiple proprietors were entered in the Register immediately before commencement.

What paragraph 7 therefore means, in practical terms, is that the **12–65** liberal provisions of section 23(1) and (3) will come into effect either when existing co-proprietors agree that they should and alter the arrangements between themselves to achieve that result, or when the arrangements between them are unilaterally changed by one or more of them without the agreement of the others, should that be possible.

7. Licensing of registered trade marks

Outline of the law

Unlike the sections of the 1994 Act concerning assignments, its pro- **12–66** visions concerning licences arise directly from Article 8 of the TM Directive.

Article 8(1) provides specifically that licences may be exclusive or non-exclusive, may relate to some or all of the goods or services for which the mark concerned is registered, and may be for all or part of the Member State to which the registration relates. These provisions are closely echoed in sections 28 to 30 of the 1994 Act, which also permit licences to be partial as to the manner of use of the mark.[48-49]

Article 8(2) provides that the registered proprietor may sue for **12–67** infringement a licensee who contravenes provisions of his licence as to duration, form in which the mark is used, the goods or services licensed, territory, or quality. No equivalent express provision is to be found in the 1994 Act, and it is most unclear how or whether its infringement provisions achieve the result intended by Article 8(2).

Types of licence, and their incidents

There are thus two main types of licence: exclusive and non-exclusive. **12–68** In addition, either kind may be partial, covering only part of the scope of the registration.

These types of licence are provided for by section 28(1) of the 1994 Act. Section 28 also provides for the formalities of granting a licence (it is required to be in writing signed by or on behalf of the grantor— section 28(2)) and for sub-licences (which may be granted if the licence so provides: section 28(4)).

The additional significance of an exclusive licence is provided for in **12–69** section 29. The section defines an exclusive licence as being one which authorises the licensee to use the mark, as permitted by the exclusive

---

[48-49] By s.28(1)(a).

licence, to the exclusion of all other persons, including the person granting the licence. Because of the reference to "the person granting the licence" and the provisions of section 28(4) as to sub-licences, it is clear that an exclusive licensee can grant an exclusive sub-licence (provided that his licence allows sub-licensing). Section 29(1) also makes it clear that an exclusive licence may be partial in just the same manner(s) as a non-exclusive licence.

12–70   In addition to the exclusive nature of his interest, and no doubt as a reflection of it, an exclusive licensee generally has greater rights in relation to infringers than does a non-exclusive licensee. This is discussed below.

12–71   The nature of a licence under the 1994 Act was held in *Northern Shell v. Conde Nast* [1995] R.P.C. 117 to be a bare permission to use the mark, not conferring on the licensee any proprietary right. By reason of that finding and by reason of the manner in which sections 9 and 10 of the 1994 Act are phrased, it was further held that a licensee cannot sue a person who has the consent of the proprietor for their use of the trade mark. The remedy of a licensee in that situation lies, if at all, in contract. It should be noted, however, that the decision in that case was based on the construction of section 30 of the 1994 Act and the transitional provisions relating to it; the court did not refer expressly to section 31 (and its decision on the 1994 Act was in any event *obiter*, since it had held that the defendant's acts were not an infringement under the 1938 Act, which continued to apply because of the transitional provisions of the 1994 Act concerning continuing acts begun before commencement). Section 31(1) of the 1994 Act provides that in relation to an exclusive licence, the parties may provide that the licensee is to have "the same rights and remedies . . . as if the licence had been an assignment". Although the second part of that subsection makes it clear that the proprietor still cannot be sued for infringement by the exclusive licensee, and although subsection (2) stipulates that the rights and remedies enjoyed are concurrent with those of the proprietor, the subsection still seems to leave open the argument that the nature of the interest enjoyed by an exclusive licensee is more than a bare permission.[50]

Binding on successors (subject to section 25)

12–72   Under section 28(3) of the 1984 Act, licences are binding on a successor to the grantor's interest (and references to the consent of the proprietor elsewhere in the Act must be construed accordingly, *i.e.* to refer to the consent of the proprietor or, in the case of a licence, the predecessor who granted the licence).

---

[50] It might be said that s.31(1) merely confers rights and remedies on the exclusive licensee in order to found his ability to bring proceedings in his own name, but it is hard to see why s.31(1) need have been in the form adopted for it merely in order to achieve that result.

At first sight, section 28(3) might be thought inconsistent with section **12–73** 25, which, as is explained above, provides that licences, being registrable transactions, do not bind unknowing parties to later inconsistent dealings unless an application for registration has been made.[51] In fact, there is no inconsistency. Section 28 states the general rule that successors are bound. It is necessary that there should be such a provision, because there is of course usually no privity of contract between the grantee of the licence and the grantor's successor. However, section 25 has the effect that section 28 will only bite when an application for registration of the licence has been made (or when the successor has knowledge of the licence). Purchasers of the grantor's interest without knowledge of the licence will not be bound in the absence of an application for registration.[52]

By section 29(2), an exclusive licensee has "the same rights against a **12–74** successor in title who is bound by the licence as he has against the person granting the licence". It is most unclear what this adds to section 28(3), or indeed what the "rights" referred to are, since the licensee's statutory rights appear to be transferred by section 28(3) in any event, and the words used do not seem apt to describe contractual rights. Nor, in general can the "rights" referred to be rights to bring infringement proceedings against a successor, since even where an exclusive licensee has a right to sue for infringement in his own name under section 31, he cannot sue the proprietor. It may be that the effect of section 29(2) is to allow an exclusive licensee to sue a successor to a grantor of an exclusive licence which grantor was not himself the proprietor but only an exclusive licensee himself, but why this should be so, and why section 29(2) should be drafted as it is to achieve such a result is equally unclear.

Registration of licences

Licences are registrable transactions. The matters which are required to **12–75** be registered are considered in Chapter 3. The consequences of failure to register are dealt with above.[53]

Rights of licensees as to infringement proceedings

The procedural details concerning the manner in which licensees may **12–76** bring infringement proceedings, or cause them to be brought, are dealt with in Chapter 18. This and the following section are concerned only with the question of what right a licensee has to bring proceedings, or to call on the proprietor to bring them.

---

[51] See para. 12–27, above.
[52] Depending on the meaning of "inconsistent transaction" in s.25(3), which is considered in para. 12–26, above.
[53] See para. 12–27, above.

12-77   The rights of licensees in case of infringement are dealt with in sections 30 and 31 of the 1994 Act. The general scheme is as follows.

12-78   By section 31, an exclusive licensee may, by contract with the proprietor of the mark, be given the same rights and remedies as if the licence had been an assignment, including the right to bring proceedings in his own name.[54] Such a right of action, if granted, is concurrent with that of the proprietor.[55] However, it is in no way compulsory for an exclusive licensee to be given such a right, as is clear from the permissive words of section 31(1), and indeed it is fairly clear from the wording of the section that if the agreement granting the licence is silent, then the exclusive licensee will not have his own right of action.

Section 30 deals with the rights of licensees generally, including, as the second part of section 30(1) makes clear, exclusive licensees not given their own right of action under section 31. Section 30 does not apply to exclusive licensees given their own right of action under section 31.

12-79   The general rule under section 30 is that a licensee is entitled to call on the proprietor (or, by section 30(7), an exclusive licensee having his own right of action from whom a non-exclusive sub-licence has been obtained) to bring infringement proceedings in relation to "any matter which affects his interests".[56] If the proprietor refuses to bring proceedings, or fails to do so within two months, then the licensee may sue himself as if he were the proprietor/exclusive licensee. In contrast with section 31(1), the rights given under section 30 arise automatically unless the licence agreement(s) through which the licensee derives his rights excludes them.[57]

12-80   Both section 30 and section 31 have unusual provisions entitling the court to award damages against an infringer to reflect loss to a licensee, even if the licensee is not a party to the proceedings. In such cases, the court may give directions requiring the claimant to hold such damages for the licensee.[58]

12-81   A licensee cannot successfully bring infringement proceedings against a person operating with the proprietor's consent, although he may have a claim for damages in contract against the proprietor.[59]

---

[54] s.31(1).

[55] s.31(2).

[56] Presumably this includes at least any infringement within the field of use, geographical area, and specification of goods and services covered by the licence, as well as any infringement causing loss and damage to the licensee. The general words used suggest a broad test, and one would also expect them to catch use on goods not identical to those for which the licensee is licensed, but only similar, provided that his commercial interests are affected. Whether a s.10(3) infringement would be caught may be more doubtful, since that kind of infringement is more directed at the integrity of the mark itself, more naturally the area of interest of the proprietor.

[57] s.30(2).

[58] ss.30(6) and 31(6). These provisions are covered in more detail in Chap. 18.

[59] *Northern Shell v. Conde Nast* [1995] R.P.C. 115, but see the discussion in para. 12–71, above, as to whether there may be some doubt over the position of an exclusive licensee under s.31.

Licences rendering a Registered Mark Deceptive

Under the 1938 Act, a difficult problem, never satisfactorily resolved, **12–82** was the degree of control which a trade mark proprietor had to exercise over the activities of those using his mark with his permission, in order to prevent it from becoming deceptive.[60] Although the more marginal cases dealt with under the 1938 Act are hard to reconcile one with another, it was fairly clear that a bare licence of a trade mark under which the licensor/proprietor has no control over the activities of the licensee would render the mark deceptive.[61] As with the tension between the provisions of the 1994 Act concerning assignments without goodwill and revocation in cases of deceptiveness, considered above, there is no express guidance in the Act as to what a proprietor can and cannot do by means of a licence. Even accounting for the broad and apparently liberal provisions of sections 20 to 30 of the 1994 Act, it must surely be the case, particularly where a proprietor ceases to use the mark himself and instead permits licensees to do so without control, that registered marks can in principle be rendered invalid by inappropriate licensing. As a practical matter, trade mark proprietors would be well advised to insert quality control provisions into their licences, requiring goods or services to meet objective, specified standards, at the very least. More so than before, the responsibility of ensuring that a trade mark is used properly rests with the proprietor.

Transitional provisions

The transitional provisions of the 1994 Act relating to licences are to be **12–83** found in Schedule 3 paragraph 9. That paragraph provides that sections 28 and 29(2) (which concern licences generally and the rights of an exclusive licensee against a successor to the licensor) apply only to licences granted after commencement.[62] In relation to licences granted earlier, the 1938 Act continues to apply as to those matters.

Registered user agreements entered on the Register under the 1938 **12–84** Act are to be transferred on commencement to the new Register and there take effect as if registered under section 25 of the 1994 Act.[63]

Applications for registration of registered user agreements not finally **12–85** determined at commencement are either to be treated as being applications under section 25 of the 1994 Act, or under the old law, depending on whether they were still pending before the Registrar at commencement, or had been dealt with by him but not finally disposed of.[64]

---

[60] This has been touched on above: see para. 12–49 and n. 33.
[61] And there was also the provision of the 1938 Act, s.28(6), dealing with trafficking. See *Holly Hobbie* [1984] F.S.R. 199, *supra*.
[62] Sched. 3, para. 9(1).
[63] Sched. 3, para. 9(2).
[64] Sched. 3, para. 9(3), (4).

8. Stamp duty

Abolition in relation to intellectual property

12–86 By section 129 of the Finance Act 2000, stamp duty was abolished on dispositions of, *inter alia*, "any trade marks". This appears to include both registered and unregistered marks (given that no indication to the contrary was given, and in the light of section 1 of the 1994 Act). It also extends to licences or any other right in respect of a trade mark.

Assuming that both registered and unregistered trade marks were meant by the expression, it ought to be the case that stamp duty is not payable on goodwill associated with trade marks, either. The reason is that, as is discussed above, an assignment of a common law trade mark without goodwill is contrary to public policy and void; the section cannot have been intended to promote or encourage such conduct. If goodwill in relation to unregistered marks is not stampable, then it would be illogical if goodwill in relation to registered marks were.

CHAPTER 13

THE DEFINITION OF INFRINGEMENT

1. Preliminary

In this chapter we consider the definition of infringement. It concerns **13–01** national trade marks, international trade marks designating the United Kingdom under the Madrid Protocol and Community trade marks under the Community Trade Marks Regulation. There is a substantial consistency between the approaches adopted in relation to each. This is to be expected because the provisions of the 1994 Act are, in large measure, an implementation of the provisions of the Trade Marks Directive. But in important respects there are differences too. These are in part the inevitable result of the difference in nature between a national trade mark system applying only in one country and a Community system seeking to provide marks which have a unitary character and equal effect throughout the Community. They are also the result of the way the United Kingdom has chosen to implement particular provisions of the TM Directive and to add some home grown provisions of its own. In this chapter we also have regard to the marks of a somewhat different nature provided for under each system, namely collective and certification marks under the 1994 Act and collective marks under the CTM Regulation. These have slightly different provisions to those relating to other trade marks and to each other.

It is a notable feature of the 1994 Act that, in addition to the **13–02** provisions relating to infringement of registered trade marks, protection is conferred on the proprietors of well known trade marks under the Paris Convention and under the WTO Agreement. This protection is dependent neither upon registration nor upon the proprietor establishing that he has any business in the United Kingdom.

The scheme of this chapter is to consider first, infringement in **13–03** relation to national trade marks and the limitations, exceptions and defences thereto, secondly the further rights conferred by the 1994 Act and finally the position under the Community trade mark system and, in particular, where and how it differs from that pertaining to national trade marks.

2. National registered trade marks

A. General

Introduction

13–04 The rights conferred by a national registered trade mark (and an international registration designating the United Kingdom under the Madrid Protocol) are set out in sections 9 and 10 of the 1994 Act. They essentially implement Article 5 of the TM Directive. In construing these new provisions it is therefore generally not appropriate to look back at the Trade Marks Act, 1938, the White Paper or *Hansard*.[1] The old law has been swept away.

13–05 Each of the provisions contained in these sections is considered in detail below. But some points are worthy of general note. First, the 1994 Act affords a substantial enlargement of the rights of a proprietor over those afforded by the 1938 Act. Use is now defined as including use otherwise than by means of a graphical representation.[2] Oral use of a mark can therefore amount to infringement. This is in contrast to the position under the 1938 Act where use was narrowly defined. It was restricted to use of a printed or other visual representation of a mark and use of a mark in relation to goods was defined as referring to the use of the mark upon or in physical or other relation to, the goods.[3]

13–06 Secondly, under the 1938 Act there was a difference in scope between the provisions dealing with restrictions on registration arising from conflicts with earlier marks and the infringement provisions. In particular the proprietor of an earlier registration could block the registration of a mark the subject of a later application in respect of goods of the same description as the goods the subject of the earlier registration.[4] Yet when it came to infringement it was necessary to show the use of the offending mark in relation to goods falling precisely within the scope of the registration.[5] Under the 1994 Act the position has been rationalised. The provisions of section 5 in relation to registration and section 10 in relation to infringement are in very similar terms. In the case of infringement they introduce a right in respect of the use of the registered mark or a mark which is similar to it in relation to goods or services which are similar to those the subject of the registration.

13–07 Thirdly, the new law extends the protection afforded to registered trade marks which have acquired a reputation. Rights are conferred in respect of the use of the registered mark or a mark which is similar to it in relation to goods or services which are not similar to those the subject of the registration, where the use is without due cause and takes unfair advantage of or is detrimental to the distinctive character or the repute of the trade mark.

---

[1] See, *e.g. British Sugar v. James Robertson* [1996] R.P.C. 281 at 292; and *Philips v. Remington* [1999] R.P.C. 809, CA. Although there are exceptions, notably 1994 Act, s.10(6).
[2] 1994 Act, s.103(1).
[3] Trade Marks Act 1938, s.68(2).
[4] 1938 Act, s.12.
[5] 1938 Act, s.4.

Finally, section 10(4) follows the permissive provisions of Article 5(3) **13–08** of the TM Directive in identifying various activities which constitute use of a sign for the purposes of infringement. It specifies that a person uses a sign if, in particular, he:

(1) affixes it to goods or the packaging thereof;

(2) offers or exposes goods for sale, puts them on the market or stocks them for those purposes under the sign, or offers or supplies services under the sign;

(3) imports or exports goods under the sign; or

(4) uses the sign on business papers or in advertising.

It is notable that the definition is not exhaustive. Nevertheless it introduces a degree of clarity absent from the uncertain definition of use in section 68 of the 1938 Act and, as discussed below, it is already clear that, despite the relatively wide language of the provision, the courts will be concerned to construe "use" consistently with the purpose of a trade mark.

In the following sections of this chapter we consider the various **13–09** elements necessary to establish infringement under the provisions of sections 9 and 10 of the Act. It is important to have in mind that principles established in relation to the relative grounds of objection under section 5 are generally applicable to considerations of infringement under section 10, save that in the case of section 5 the comparison is between the earlier trade mark and the mark in respect of which registration is sought and under section 10 the comparison is between the registered mark and the alleged infringement. Accordingly, when we address the assessment of the likelihood of confusion under section 10(2), and the use of a sign in relation to goods or services which are not similar to those in respect of which the mark is registered under section 10(3), we refer back extensively to the consideration of these matters in Chapter 8.

In the course of trade

All of the provisions in section 10 of the 1994 Act relating to infringe- **13–10** ment are qualified by the expression "uses in the course of trade a sign".[6] To constitute an infringement the sign[7] in issue must therefore be used in the course of trade.

"Trade" is defined in section 103(1) of the 1994 Act as including any **13–11** business or profession and, as under the 1938 Act, will include leasing, hire purchase and the like.[8] But now, and in contrast to the position under the 1938 Act, the trade does not necessarily have to be in the goods or services the subject of the registration.[9]

---

[6] Implementing the same words of TM Directive, Art. 5(1) and (2).
[7] The term "sign" is used throughout the 1994 Act, s.10 to describe the mark used by the infringer.
[8] *Aristoc v. Rysta* (1945) 62 R.P.C. 65 at 83, HL.
[9] See para. 13–46 *et seq.*, below.

Activities in the course of trade include communications, for example by way of orders and invoices, with suppliers and trade customers.[10]

13–12 As under the 1938 Act, it should be no answer to an allegation of infringement that the purpose of the mark is to show a business connection with a foreign manufacturer entitled to use the mark in his own country, and not with the British owner of the mark.[11]

Whether rights limited to trade mark or service mark use

13–13 The question arises as to whether the offending use in the course of trade of a sign must be use of that sign as a "trade mark" or "service mark", that is to say as an indication of origin, in order to infringe.[12] The answer to this question under the 1994 Act lies in the proper construction of sections 9 and 10 of the Act.[13] In some cases (particularly where the sign is identical to the registered mark and is used in relation to goods or services the subject of the registration) this question may be of some importance.[14]

13–14 A number of matters suggest that the use must indeed be use in a trade mark or service mark sense. First, the function of a trade mark as expressed in the tenth recital to the TM Directive is, in particular, to guarantee the trade mark as an indication of origin.[15] This is entirely consistent with the approach taken by the European Court of Justice, both before and after the TM Directive, that the guarantee of the identity of the origin of the trade marked product is the "essential function" of a trade mark.[16]

[10] *Beautimatic v. Mitchell* [2000] F.S.R. 267.

[11] See, *e.g.* "4711" (1953) 70 R.P.C. 235; "*Everglide*" [1964] R.P.C. 37 at 42.

[12] This was the position under the 1938 Act. As Dillon L.J. said in *Mothercare UK v. Penguin Books* [1988] R.P.C. 113, at 118:

"Indeed it stands to reason that a Trade Marks Act would only be concerned to restrict the use of a mark as a trade mark or in a trade mark sense, and should be construed accordingly. If descriptive words are legitimately registered in Part A of the register, there is still no reason why other people should not be free to use the words in a descriptive sense, and not in any trade mark sense".

Although not a legitimate aid to construction, it is interesting to note that the domestic view emerged also at the report stage of the Bill. Lord Peston moved an amendment to what is now section 9 of the Act seeking to add a sentence that the use of the mark must be in the course of business and "to indicate a commercial connection" with the goods or services for which the mark is registered, that is to say that the use of the mark must be trade mark use. On behalf of the Government, Lord Strathclyde, Minister of State, Department of Trade and Industry, resisted the amendment, stating:

"As a matter of general trade mark law it is implicit that the use of a registered trade mark must be trade mark use in order that the rights given by the Bill may be enforced" (*Hansard*, H.L., Vol. 552, col. 733).

[13] And, importantly, of the TM Directive, Art. 5.

[14] See, *e.g. Mars v. Cadbury* [1987] R.P.C. 387: ("Treat Size" not used as a trade mark in relation to confectionery); *Mothercare v. Penguin* [1988] R.P.C. 113: ("Mothercare" used as the title of a book not use as a trade mark); *cf. Games Workshop v. Transword Publishers* [1993] F.S.R. 705 (seriously arguable that the title on a series of books was used as a trade mark); *Unidoor v. Marks & Spencer* [1988] R.P.C. 275 (at the interlocutory stage extreme doubt was expressed as to whether the defendants were using the slogan "Coast to Coast" as a trade mark on the front of shirts).

[15] It states: "The protection afforded by the registered trade mark, the function of which is in particular to guarantee the trade mark as an indication of origin. . ."

[16] See, *e.g. Hoffman La Roche v. Centrafarm* [1978] E.C.R. 1139; *Hag II* [1990] E.C.R. I–3711; *I.H.T. v. Ideal Standard* ("*Ideal Standard*") [1994] E.C.R. I–2789.

Secondly, section 9 provides that the proprietor of a registered mark **13-15** has exclusive rights in the trade mark which are infringed by the use of the trade mark without his consent. This appears to be based upon the first sentence of Article 5(1) of the TM Directive[17] and suggests that registration gives exclusivity to the registered proprietor in respect of the use of his mark as a trade mark or in a trade mark sense.[18]

Thirdly, in *Sabel v. Puma*[19] the European Court of Justice found that a **13-16** likelihood of confusion as to origin is a requirement in the case of infringement under s.10(2).[20] It is hard to see how there can be confusion as to origin unless the offending use is use "as a trade mark".

Finally, it may be argued that the whole purpose of Article 5(5) is to **13-17** deal with the case where the mark is used other than in a trade mark sense and that Article 5(1) and (2) should accordingly be construed as limited to cases where the mark is used as a trade mark or in a trade mark sense.[21]

Conversely, it is notable that the words of section 10 do not expressly **13-18** require the infringing use to be trade mark use. The section requires the use in the course of trade of a "sign" in relation to the goods or services. This is consistent with the words of Article 5(1) of the TM Directive which follow the opening sentence.[22]

Furthermore, although section 9(1) uses the words *"are infringed by the* **13-19** *use of the trade mark"*, the definition of trade mark in section 1 of the Act calls for no more than a sign which is capable of being represented graphically and which is *capable* of distinguishing goods and services.[23]

For the moment the courts have concluded that trade mark use is *not* **13-20** necessary, on the basis that this requirement is not in the TM Directive. But at the same time it has been emphasised that the use must be *in relation* to the goods or services.[24] One judge appears to have found that there is a two fold requirement, namely there must be both "use" and "use in relation to" the goods or services.[25] The requirement that the use

---

[17] "The registered trade mark shall confer on the proprietor exclusive rights therein. The proprietor shall be entitled to prevent all third parties not having his consent from using in the course of trade: (a) any sign. . .".

[18] Further, the TM Directive, Art. 5(5), rather suggests that the preceding paragraphs, which relate to the prohibited infringing acts, are concerned with trade mark use.

[19] [1997] E.C.R. 1-6191; [1998] R.P.C. 199; and see the discussion in para. 13-50, below.

[20] But this leaves open the position in relation to s.10(1) and (3).

[21] See *BMW v. Deenik* [1999] E.C.R. I-905; [1999] E.T.M.R. 339, where it was stated by the ECJ at para. 38: "In that connection, it is true that the scope of application of Article 5(1) and (2) of the directive, on the one hand, and Article 5(5) on the other, depends on whether the trade mark is used for the purpose of distinguishing the goods or services in question as originating from a particular undertaking, that is to say, as a trade mark as such, or whether it is used for other purposes."

[22] See n. 17, *supra*.

[23] Implementing the TM Directive, Art. 2. See also Chap. 2.

[24] *British Sugar v. James Robertson* [1996] R.P.C. 281, a decision of Jacob J.; the court declined to follow the decision in "Wet Wet Wet", *Bravado Merchandising v. Mainstream Publishing* [1996] F.S.R. 205, where the matter proceeded on a concession by counsel; *Philips v. Remington* [1998] R.P.C. 283 at 311–312; [1999] R.P.C. 809, CA. This question, together with others, has been referred to the ECJ by the Court of Appeal which expressed a provisional view in agreement with that of Jacob J., the trial judge.

[25] *Trebor Bassett Ltd v. The Football Association* [1997] F.S.R. 211.

must be in relation to goods or services is discussed below and may, in many cases, amount to much the same thing.

13–21   On the assumption that trade mark use is not a necessary requirement of infringement, then any use in the course of trade in relation to the relevant goods or services which satisfies the other provisions of section 10 will, prima facie, infringe. The defendant must look to section 11 or one of the other defences.[26]

It seems therefore that the use by a company of its name will not now escape infringement on the ground that the use is not trade mark use.[27]

Use in relation to goods or services

13–22   To constitute infringement under any head of section 10 of the 1994 Act, the mark must be *used in relation to* goods or services which, depending upon the particular subsection in issue, are the same as, similar to or dissimilar to goods or services the subject of the registration.

(1) The defendant publishes a directory of trade marks which wrongly attributes the plaintiff's registered mark to another company. It is suggested this would not be use in relation to directories or, indeed, any goods.[28]

(2) The petitioner was the registered proprietor of the trade mark "Wet Wet Wet", the name of a pop group, registered in respect of, *inter alia*, books. The respondent published a book, about the group, bearing the title "A Sweet Little Mystery—Wet Wet Wet—The Inside Story". Lord McCluskey concluded the use of "Wet Wet Wet" was use in a trade mark sense of a sign identical to the registered trade mark on goods identical to those for which it was registered. But he found for the respondent under s.11(2): *Bravado Merchandising Services v. Mainstream Publishing* [1996] R.P.C. 205, Ct of Sess. The matter proceeded on a concession by counsel that trade mark use was essential and this, it has been suggested, led to a muddle. The learned judge ought to have found that the use in the title was not *use in relation to* the registered goods.[29]

---

[26] As Aldous L.J. noted in *Philips v. Remington, supra,* many uses which are not trade mark uses may be expected to fall under the protection of that section. And see also para. 13–22, below, as to what is necessary to meet the requirement of "use in relation to goods or services".

[27] In contrast to the position under the 1938 Act, where the matter was at least arguable. See, *Pompadour v. Frazer* [1966] R.P.C. 7; *Duracell v. Ever Ready* [1989] F.S.R. 71. And subject, of course, to any defence available under s.11.

[28] See, under the 1938 Act, *Ravok v. National Trade Press* (1955) 72 R.P.C. 110.

[29] *British Sugar v. James Robertson* [1996] R.P.C. 281 at 293. Jacob J. evidently felt strongly about this, stating: "I have no doubt that the learned Judge reached the right result. It would be fantastic if the new trade mark legislation had the effect of enabling quasi censorship of books about people or companies just because those people or companies had registered their names as trade marks for books". Although agreeing with the result, presumably Jacob J. would have disagreed with the learned judge's conclusion that the use was "trade mark use"; but this would not have advanced the matter, he also being of the view that trade mark use is not a requirement of infringement.

(3) A manufacturer of confectionery sold candy sticks in packets containing a card bearing a photograph and description of a famous footballer. In some cases the player was wearing a playing strip bearing the well known England team logo, showing three lions. The Football Association objected that this constituted an infringement of its registration of that logo as a trade mark in respect of cards. The learned judge held that the manufacturer was not even arguably using the logo, as such, in any real sense of the word "uses" and was certainly not using it as a sign in respect of its cards.[30]

(4) The use of "Kodak" on T-shirts was not use as a trade mark in relation to those goods; rather it was use in relation to films and plates.[31]

(5) An internet service provider used the trade mark Avnet in relation to a service which involved giving to customers an e-mail address and a Web page. In this way it provided a facility for each customer to advertise on the customer's own Web page. Held, this did not constitute use of the mark in relation to "advertising and promotional services".[32]

It seems likely that the important question will be how the trade and **13–23** public understand the sign to be used. No doubt if it is plain that the intention of the defendant is that the sign should be understood to denote the origin of the goods or services in the manner suggested by the claimant, then this will be likely to determine the issue. But often the defendant may reasonably contend that the use of the sign is not intended to be so understood and here, it is suggested, the defendant's intention cannot be determinative. The following examples, decided under the old law, illustrate the point; but now it must be remembered that use in relation to goods or services outside the scope of the registration can amount to infringement if the additional requirements of section 10(2) or 10(3) of the 1994 Act are satisfied.

(a) The plaintiffs owned the trade mark "John Bull" for beer; the defendants owned it for "beer kits" to make beer at home. The defendants advertised their kits so as to call the beer to be made with them, as well as the kits themselves, "John Bull". Held, that this was an infringement under the 1938 Act even though there could never be any trade in beer made from the defendants' kits and even though the home made beer would never be "goods".[33]

---

[30] *Trebor Bassett Ltd v. The Football Association* [1997] F.S.R. 211. Rattee J. felt it was quite unreal to say that the manufacturer was affixing the sign comprising the England logo to its cards, and therefore to goods within the meaning of the 1994 Act, s.10(4)(a), or that it was putting the cards on the market under the sign comprising the England logo within s.10(4)(b).

[31] *"Kodiak"* [1990] F.S.R. 49.

[32] *Avnet v. Isoact* [1998] F.S.R. 16.

[33] *Ind Coope v. Paine* [1983] R.P.C. 326 at 327. A similar case is *Rolls Royce v. Dodd* [1981] F.S.R. 517.

(b) The plaintiffs were the registered proprietors of the device of a cow and the word "cow" in respect of matches. The defendants sold matches in boxes having on them a device of a cow and the words "cow brand" to advertise their condensed milk. This was held to be an infringement under the 1905 Act and, it is suggested, the position would be the same under the 1994 Act.[34]

Activities which constitute use of a sign

13–24 It has never been the law that the spurious mark should be actually affixed to the goods, provided it was so used in relation to them as to be calculated to lead to the belief that the goods were designated by the mark. This position is maintained under the 1994 Act which, in section 10(4) and (5), follows the permissive provisions of Article 5(3) of the TM Directive in identifying the various activities which constitute use of a sign for the purposes of the infringement provisions.

13–25   The definition is not exclusive. It should be read with the definition of use in section 103(2) of the 1994 Act which specifically includes use otherwise than by means of a graphic re-presentation. In this section certain practical aspects of the definition are discussed.

Mere possession

13–26 It would appear that mere possession of goods bearing an offending sign is not an infringement, unless there is an intention to deal in them.[35] This mirrors the position under the 1938 Act.

Point of sale

13–27 A question arises as to whether the offending sign needs to be visible at the point of sale. It is submitted that this is not a requirement, provided that when the sign does become apparent it is understood to be a sign used in the course of trade in relation to the relevant goods.[36] This follows from the wide definition of "use" in section 103(2) of the 1994 Act[37] and the express provision that use of a sign includes use of the sign on business papers, presumably including such items as receipts.

---

[34] *Nitedals v. Lehmann* (1908) 25 R.P.C. 793.

[35] *See Waterford Wedgwood v. David Nagli* [1998] F.S.R. 92 at 105.

[36] This was generally accepted to be the position under the old law. See, *e.g. Esquire v. Roopanand* [1991] R.P.C. 425 (Sup Ct of S.A.); *Cheetah Trade Mark* [1993] F.S.R. 263. It was also the intention of the Government, albeit that this is not a legitimate aid to interpretation; see, *Hansard*, H.L., Vol. 552, col. 740, Lord Strathclyde, Minister for State, Department of Trade and Industry: "The proposed new [s.103(2)] therefore covers not only audible use, but any use of a trade mark which is other than by graphic representation. This would, *e.g.* apply where a trade mark is encoded electronically in a video cassette. It is not visible at the time of sale, and only becomes so when the purchaser plays it. Another instance which has been mentioned is where goods, *e.g.* jewellery, are actually made in the shape of a protected trade mark. All those would be caught by the new provision." But *cf. Unilever (Striped Toothpaste)* [1980] F.S.R. 280.

[37] Contrast the position under the Trade Marks Act 1938, s.68(2), which provided (in relation to goods) that references to the use of a mark should be construed as references to the use of a printed or other visual representation of the mark, and that references to the use of a mark in relation to goods should be construed as references to the use thereof upon, or in physical or other relation to, goods.

Affixes the sign to goods or the packaging

A person who affixes an offending sign to the goods or to the packaging **13–28**
thereof is an infringer,[38] provided he does so in the course of trade. If the
work is carried out by a sub-contractor then it appears that he also
infringes. This will be so even if the goods are being manufactured here
for export.

As to packaging, this provision must be reconciled with section 10(5) **13–29**
which deals with the application of a registered trade mark to material
intended to be used for labelling or packaging. This is simply done if this
provision is limited to packaging actually enclosing the goods rather
than intended to be used in that way in the future.[39]

Offers or exposes goods for sale or offers or supplies services under the sign

A person uses a sign if he offers or exposes goods for sale, puts them on **13–30**
the market or stocks them for those purposes under the sign, or offers or
supplies services under the sign.[40] This is much as under the 1938 Act
but appears to extend a little further. In particular it is now expressly
provided that the stocking of goods for sale under a sign is an
infringement. This would seem to include the case of a trader using the
trade mark as the name of a business dealing in the goods, for example
as the name of a shop through which the goods are sold.[41]

Imports or exports goods under the sign

A person uses a sign if he imports or exports goods under the sign.[42] **13–31**
Importation consists of bringing goods into the territorial jurisdiction;
exportation consists of their removal from the territorial jurisdiction.[43] In
the case of goods to be exported, there is no need to show that the goods
in question have been placed before the consumer or end user in the
United Kingdom.[44]

It may be necessary to determine precisely who is responsible for the **13–32**
alleged importation or export. This may be the owner of the property or
there may be other principals for whom the shippers are acting. In any
case it is no answer that the goods were only inadvertently brought into

---

[38] 1994 Act, s.10(4)(a).
[39] *Beautimatic v. Mitchell* [2000] F.S.R. 267. See also para. 13–35 *et seq.*, below.
[40] 1994 Act, s.10(4)(b).
[41] This would reflect the intention expressed in the White Paper, *Reform of Trade Marks Law*, September 1990, para. 3.27:
    "The new law will make it clear that offering goods, or putting them on the market, or stocking them for these purposes, under a sign which resembles someone else's trade mark is an infringement. This will prevent a trader from using such a sign as the name of a business dealing in goods or services similar to those for which the trade mark is registered."
    This may be contrasted with the position under the 1938 Act illustrated by, *e.g.* "*Autodrome*" [1969] R.P.C. 564.
[42] 1994 Act, s.10(4)(c).
[43] *L.A Gear v. Hi-Tec Sports* [1992] F.S.R. 121 at 129 to 130.
[44] *Beautimatic v. Mitchell, supra.*

the jurisdiction, nor that the goods are only temporarily here while in transit.[45]

Use of the sign on business papers or in advertising

13–33 It is an infringement to use an offending sign on business papers or in advertising: this has always been the law.[46] But with the wider definition of use including oral use of a trade mark it will now be an infringement to advertise using an offending mark by, for example, radio or through oral use of the mark by salesmen.

13–34   Where the mark is used on business papers, such as invoices, it may, however, be important to determine in relation to which goods it is being used:

> Allegedly infringing invoices bearing the registered mark referred to labels. Held, in the particular circumstances of the case, the wording on the invoices was directed towards the labels to be manufactured, and to what was written on those labels, and not to the goods to which they might subsequently be affixed.[47]

Advertisement in the United Kingdom of goods situated abroad may also be an infringement, even if the person who places the advert has no intention to bring them into the jurisdiction. Many publications have circulations in a number of different territories. If a person places an advert containing an offending trade mark in such a publication, knowing it will reach the United Kingdom, then it appears he may well infringe.[48]

Special difficulties arise in the case of comparative advertising and this is addressed as a separate topic.[49]

Materials intended to be used for labelling, packaging, as business papers or for advertising

13–35 The 1994 Act provides that a person who applies a registered trade mark to material intended to be used for labelling or packaging goods, as business papers, or for advertising goods or services, shall be treated as a party to any use of the material which infringes the registered trade mark if, when he applied the mark, he knew or had reason to believe that the application of the mark was not duly authorised by the proprietor or a licensee.[50]

---

[45] *Waterford Wedgwood v. David Nagli* [1988] F.S.R. 92.
[46] As to business papers, see, *e.g.* "*Cheetah*" [1993] F.S.R. 263: use of a mark on delivery notes and on invoices delivered long after sale constituted use of the mark in the course of trade and in relation to the goods.
[47] *Beautimatic v. Mitchell, supra.*
[48] For an example under the old law, see *Reuters v. Muhlens* (1953) 70 R.P.C. 235 at 250, CA. The Internet raises special difficulties, see Chap. 21.
[49] See para. 13–70 *et seq.*, below.
[50] s.10(5).

This provision is new and extends the ambit of infringement beyond **13–36** that provided by section 10(4)(a) and (d). Thus manufacturers of labels, bottles and other materials and others, such as printers, who apply a registered trade mark to material which is ultimately used to infringe will be party to, and liable for, that infringement if they knew or had reason to believe the application was not authorised. Accordingly, if the labelling or packaging is to be taken abroad and only to be applied to the goods outside the United Kingdom then there can be no infringement.[51]

As to the requirement of knowledge, the test to be applied is that laid **13–37** down in *LA Gear v. Hi-Tec Sports*.[52] In relation to "reason to believe", it must be considered whether the defendant knew of facts from which a reasonable man would have arrived at the belief that the application of the mark was not duly authorised by the proprietor or a licensee. Moreover the phrase allows for a period of time to enable the reasonable man to evaluate the facts so as to convert the facts into a reasonable belief.[53]

In contrast to the words of section 10(4), this provision is framed in **13–38** terms of "a person who applies a registered trade mark . . .". Accordingly, it may be argued to be limited such that it only applies if the registered trade mark itself is applied, not a mark which is so similar as to be likely to cause confusion.[54]

B. The categories of infringement

Introduction: Identical marks, resembling marks and the likelihood of confusion, comparative advertising

Section 10 of the 1994 Act defines three different potential categories of **13–39** infringement in implementing Article 5 of the TM Directive. The first involves the use of a sign which is identical to the registered trade mark in relation to goods or services which are identical with those for which the mark is registered. The second involves the use of a sign which is identical or similar to the registered trade mark and in relation to goods or services which are identical or similar to those for which the mark is registered. The third involves the use of a sign which is identical or similar to the registered trade mark and in relation to goods or services which are not similar to those for which the mark is registered. Each category has its own requirements which, in view of the complexity of the topic, are addressed in separate sections below.

In addition to these three principal categories of infringement, the Act **13–40** introduces a fourth category of infringement in section 10(6). This is a curious provision which has no clear foundation in the TM Directive

---

[51] *Beautimatic v. Mitchell*, supra.
[52] [1992] F.S.R. 121 at 129 and at 138, CA. The same test was applied in *Beautimatic v. Mitchell*, supra.
[53] *Cf. Monsoon v. India Imports* [1993] F.S.R. 486.
[54] And possibly therefore primarily directed to counterfeiting.

and has no counterpart in the CTM Regulation. It contains, first of all, a saving in respect of the use by a person of a trade mark for the purpose of identifying goods or services as those of the proprietor or a licensee. But then it continues to create a further category of infringement by providing that any such use, other than in accordance with honest practices in industrial or commercial matters, shall be treated as infringing the registered trade mark if the use, without due cause, takes unfair advantage of, or is detrimental to, the distinctive character or repute of the trade mark. These two aspects of the provision appear to be provided so as to render some, but only some, comparative advertisements an infringement and it has been so construed, as we explain below.

The scope of the registration

13–41 Each of the three categories of infringement referred to above requires the identification of the goods or services the subject of the registered trade mark.[55] All goods and services are divided into a series of classes in accordance with the Nice Classification,[56] and the decision of the Registrar as to the class into which any particular goods or services fall is final.[57] Not only do all goods and services fall within one of the classes, sometimes, under the 1938 Act, the applicant sought or the Registrar required the goods or services of an application to be defined by reference to the class. Under the 1994 Act the application must identify the classes in respect of which registration is sought if it is to proceed to examination.[58]

13–42 In many cases the specification of goods or services of a registered trade mark is clear; but sometimes it is not, either because of the limitation to the goods or services of a class or because the description of goods or services is general or vague. In the former case, and in other cases where it is necessary to determine into which class any particular goods or services fall, it is necessary to look at the Registrar's practice at the date of the application.[59] In the latter case, a particular problem with services, it is necessary to interpret or construe the words used. Here one is concerned with how a product is, as a practical matter, regarded for the purposes of trade[60] or the meaning of the words of the specification as a matter of ordinary language.[61] In keeping with this approach, the test of whether particular goods fall within a specification

---

[55] This was a matter of particular importance under the 1938 Act where infringement required use of the offending mark in relation to goods or services within the scope of the registration. It is of less importance under the 1994 Act because of the wider protection afforded by s.10(2) and (3).

[56] As discussed in Chap. 4.

[57] 1994 Act, s.34(2).

[58] If the applicant does not do this then the Registrar will suggest appropriate classes.

[59] GE Trade Mark [1969] R.P.C. 418 at 458; Avnet v. Isoact [1998] F.S.R. 16; British Sugar v. James Robertson [1996] R.P.C. 281.

[60] British Sugar v. James Robertson, supra.

[61] Beautimatic v. Mitchell, supra.

of goods has been said to be a question for the consumer and not a matter to be determined by expert scientific evidence.[62]

Section 10(1): Where the marks and the goods or services are identical

Section 10(1) of the 1994 Act provides that a person infringes a **13–43** registered trade mark if he uses in the course of trade a sign which is identical with the trade mark in relation to goods or services which are identical with those for which it is registered. This provision implements Article 5(1) of the TM Directive.

This is the simple case. It requires identification of the sign used by **13–44** the defendant and a determination of the goods or services (if any) in relation to which he is using it.[63] They must be the same as those the subject of the registration, subject to *de minimis* exceptions.[64] If he uses the mark as a sign and in the course of trade in relation to any of the goods or services the subject of the registration then there is, prima facie, infringement.

The statutory protection is absolute in the sense that the user cannot **13–45** escape by showing that by something outside the actual mark itself he has distinguished his goods or services from those of the registered proprietor.[65] The comparison is "mark for sign" and requires the identification of the defendant's sign for the purposes of the comparison:

"In most cases there will be no difficulty. It is either there or not. However it is possible for the sign to be hidden or swamped. No one but a crossword fanatic, for instance, would say that 'treat' is present in 'theatre atmosphere'. There is no question of that sort here, however. 'Treat' is there on the Robertson products for all to see."[66]

Section 10(2): Where the marks and the goods or services are identical or similar

Section 10(2) of the Act provides: **13–46**

"A person infringes a registered trade mark if he uses in the course of trade a sign where because—

---

[62] *Unilever v. Johnson Wax* [1989] F.S.R. 145, where a thick liquid lavatory cleaner was held not to fall within "common soap and detergents"; *Beautimatic v. Mitchell, supra*: held, as a matter of ordinary language, skin lightening cream and dry skin lotion were cosmetics; see also *Portakabin v. Powerblast* [1990] R.P.C. 471.

[63] See paras 13–13 *et seq.*, and 13–22 *et seq., supra*, for a discussion of how these matters are determined and whether it is necessary to show the defendant is using the sign as a trade mark. See also the discussion of the equivalent relative ground of objection provided by s.5(1), in Chap. 8, paras 8–08 *et seq.*

[64] In *Origins Natural Resources v. Origin Clothing* [1995] F.S.R. 280, one letter changing singular to plural was apparently sufficient to take the matter out of s.10(1) and into s.10(2).

[65] *Origins, supra; British Sugar v. James Robertson* [1996] R.P.C. 281; *Volvo v. Heritage* [2000] F.S.R. 253; *Saville Perfumery v. June Perfect* (1941) 58 R.P.C. 147 at 161.

[66] On the label marked "ROBERTSON'S Toffee TREAT": *British Sugar, supra*, at 293 to 294.

    (a) the sign is identical with the trade mark and is used in relation to goods or services similar to those for which the trade mark is registered, or

    (b) the sign is similar to the trade mark and is used in relation to goods or services identical with or similar to those for which the trade mark is registered,

there exists a likelihood of confusion on the part of the public which includes the likelihood of association with the trade mark."

13–47 This provision implements Article 5(1)(b) of the TM Directive. It extends the ambit of infringement in particular circumstances where neither the marks nor goods or services need be identical to those the subject of the registration. If the marks are identical or similar and the goods or services are identical or similar to those the subject of the registration and because of that similarity there exists a likelihood of confusion on the part of the public then there is infringement.

13–48 As in the case of identity (*supra*), the provision requires identification of the sign used by the defendant and a determination of the goods or services (if any) in relation to which he is using it.[67] Again the statutory protection is absolute in the sense that the user cannot escape by showing that by something outside the actual mark itself he has distinguished his goods or services from those of the registered proprietor.[68]

13–49 The words of the provision and of the Directive are mirrored in the words of section 5(2) of the 1994 Act and Article 4(1)(b) of the TM Directive which provide a corresponding relative ground of objection to the registration of a trade mark which conflicts with an earlier trade mark. Accordingly the approach to the construction and application of this infringement provision must be the same, save that now the comparison is between the registered trade mark and the allegedly offending sign. In this section of this chapter we identify the issues and indicate where they are discussed or where particular points relevant to infringement arise.

There exists a likelihood of confusion

13–50 There can only be infringement where there exists a likelihood of confusion. This requirement is fundamental to the provision.[69] The risk that the public might believe that the goods or services in question come from the same undertaking or, as the case may be, economically linked undertakings, constitutes a likelihood of confusion within the meaning of Article 5(1)(b) of the Directive.[70]

---

[67] See paras 13–13 *et seq.*, and 13–22 *et seq.*, *supra*, for a discussion of how these matters are determined and whether it is necessary to show the defendant is using the sign as a trade mark.

[68] *British Sugar v. James Robertson* [1996] R.P.C. 281; *Volvo v. Heritage* [2000] F.S.R. 253; *Saville Perfumery v. June Perfect* (1941) 58 R.P.C. 147 at 161.

[69] *Sabel v. Puma* [1997] E.C.R. 1–6191; [1998] R.P.C. 199; and see the discussion in Chap. 8, paras 8–15 to 8–18.

[70] *Lloyd Schufabrik Meyer v. Kliysen Handel* [1999] E.T.M.R. 690 at para. 17; *Canon v. MGM* [1998] E.C.R. I–5507, [1999] R.P.C. 117, para. 29. See the discussion of this issue in Chap. 8, paras 8–59 and 8–60.

Assessment of the likelihood of confusion

As in the case of section 5(2) of the 1994 Act, the words of section 10(2) **13–51** and of Article 5(2)(b) of the TM Directive require that the likelihood of confusion is caused by the identity or similarity of the marks and the goods or services. That likelihood is to be assessed globally taking into account all relevant factors, including the degree of similarity between the relevant marks, the degree of similarity between the relevant goods or services, the likely perception of the marks in the minds of the average consumer of the goods or services in question and the degree of distinctiveness of the earlier mark. That distinctiveness may be the result of the inherent character of the mark or the reputation attaching to it through use. The discussion of these matters in relation to section 5 is relevant in relation to section 10 too.[71]

In brief summary, for the purposes of the global assessment and **13–52** appreciation, the average consumer of the category of products concerned is deemed to be reasonably well informed and reasonably observant and circumspect. However, account is to be taken of the fact that the average consumer only rarely has the chance to make a direct comparison between the different marks but must place his trust in the imperfect picture of them he has kept in his mind. It is also to be borne in mind that the average consumer's level of attention is likely to vary according to the category of goods or services in question.[72]

The date of assessment

As explained, it is now clear that the degree of distinctiveness of the **13–53** registered mark, including that acquired through use, is likely to increase the risk of confusion. It is suggested the likelihood of confusion must exist, at the latest, at the date of commencement of the proceedings. But if relief is to be sought in respect of activities before that date then it would seem that the likelihood of confusion (and so also the distinctiveness of the registered mark) must have existed throughout the time that the activities complained of were conducted.

However this approach could create difficulties, particularly in the **13–54** light of the "global assessment of the likelihood of confusion". So, for example, the reputation of the claimant and the activities of a defendant might not have been sufficient to create a likelihood of confusion at the date of the commencement of those activities. Subsequently, the reputation of the claimant might have increased such that there is a likelihood of confusion, but through no fault or act of the defendant. Accordingly, it might be argued, the relevant date for consideration of the issue should be the date of the commencement of the activities complained of or, in a *quia timet* action, the date of the threat.[73]

---

[71] See Chap. 8, paras 8–20 *et seq.*, where the approach to the assessment of the likelihood of confusion is considered in detail.

[72] *Lloyd Schufabrik Meyer v. Klijsen Handel (supra)* at para. 26; *Gut Springenheide and Tusky* [1968] E.C.R. I–4657 at para. 31.

[73] *cf.* the position in relation to passing off, as to which see Chap. 14.

Similar goods or services

13–55 The goods or services the subject of the registered mark and those the subject of any infringing use must be similar. It appears this is not only a relevant matter to take into account in assessing the likelihood of confusion but is also a threshold requirement before infringement can be found under this provision.[74] The matters to be taken into account in assessing the degree of similarity are discussed in relation to section 5(2) of the 1994 Act.[75]

> The claimant was the proprietor of the mark Viagra, registered in class 5 in respect of veterinary preparations and pharmaceutical substances. The defendant proposed to market a beverage to be used as a mixer under the mark Viagrene. It became apparent that the defendant proposed to market its product as a drink capable of stimulating the libido of men and women by incorporating a natural herb which was thought to act directly on the reproductive organs. Held, once considered in the light of the defendants intention, the similarity between the goods became more pronounced and that infringement under section 10(2) was established.[76]

Confusion as to origin

13–56 The sort of confusion required to satisfy this provision is confusion as to origin. This subject is discussed in relation to section 5(2) of the 1994 Act[77] and the same considerations apply in considering infringement.

Section 10(3): Where the use of the sign without due cause takes unfair advantage of, or is detrimental to, the distinctive character or the repute of the trade mark

13–57 Section 10(3) of the 1994 Act provides:

> "A person infringes a registered trade mark if he uses in the course of trade a sign which,
>
> (a) is identical with or similar to the trade mark, and
> (b) is used in relation to goods or services which are not similar to those for which the trade mark is registered,
>
> where the trade mark has a reputation in the United Kingdom and the use of the sign, being without due cause, takes unfair advantage of, or is detrimental to, the distinctive character or repute of the trade mark."

13–58 This subsection implements the optional provision of Article 5(2) of the TM Directive. It provides a new and important ground of infringement

---

[74] See Chap. 8, paras 8–41 *et seq.*
[75] See Chap. 8, paras 8–51 *et seq.*
[76] *Pfizer v. Eurofood Link*, a decision of S. Thorley Q.C., December 10, 1999.
[77] See Chap. 8, paras 8–59 and 8–60 and para. 13–50, *supra.*.

in cases where a sign is used which is identical or similar to a registered trade mark which has a reputation in the United Kingdom and where the goods or services in relation to which it is used are *not* similar to those for which the trade mark is registered. In such a case, use in the course of trade infringes if, being without due cause, it takes unfair advantage of, or is detrimental to, the distinctive character or repute of the registered trade mark. The words of the subsection mirror those of section 5(3) and accordingly the discussion of that provision in Chapter 8 is equally applicable here, save as indicated below.

Goods or services which are not similar

The words of the provision suggest it can only apply if the alleged **13–59** infringer is using his mark in relation to goods or services which are not similar to those the subject of the registered trade mark.[78] There is accordingly no overlap between the application of this provision and section 10(2) of the 1994 Act.[79]

It must first be determined whether the goods and services are similar **13–60** or not. This is apparently not a question to be determined independently of the marks in issue. In particular, it may depend upon the extent of the reputation attaching to the registered mark,[80] making it a particularly difficult issue to resolve.

Similar trade marks

The registered mark and the sign alleged to infringe must be identical or **13–61** similar. This is a subject discussed in relation to section 5 of the 1994 Act.[81]

The registered mark must have a reputation

The registered trade mark must have a reputation in the United **13–62** Kingdom.[82] Presumably the reputation must exist at the date of the alleged infringement. There is no requirement that the reputation must extend over the whole of the United Kingdom (or the Community, in the case of a Community trade mark). But it appears that it must exist in a substantial part of it.[83] There is no express requirement as to the extent of the reputation necessary, although the degree of required recognition must be considered to be reached when the mark is known by a significant part of the public concerned by the products or service

---

[78] *cf. Premier Brands v. Typhoon*, a decision of Neuberger J., January 21, 2000, and the discussion in Chap. 8, paras 8–66 and 8–69.
[79] Although, of course, the same mark might be registered for different goods or services with the result that the activities of the defendant offend the provisions of both s.10(2) and (3).
[80] See Chap. 8, paras 8–51 *et seq.*
[81] See Chap. 8, paras 8–23 *et seq.*
[82] Or, in the case of a Community trade mark, a reputation in the Community: TM Directive, Art. 4(3).
[83] *General Motors v. Yplon* [1999] All E.R. (E.C.) 865; [1999] E.T.M.R. 950, at para. 28.

covered by the trade mark.[84] Any genuine commercial use of a trade mark will generate at least some reputation, but it must now be doubted whether such a measurable but small reputation would be sufficient.[85]

Without due cause, taking unfair advantage

13–63 These are the most important words of the provision. The use must be without due cause and must take unfair advantage of or be detrimental to the distinctive character or the repute of the trade mark. These words are discussed in the context of objections to registration arising under section 5 of the 1994 Act.[86] But certain aspects of the requirement as it relates to infringement are discussed here.

13–64 In circumstances where the use is such as to cause confusion as to the origin of the goods or services, then it would seem almost inevitable that the effect of that confusion will be to affect detrimentally the distinctive character and the reputation of the registered trade mark. It may also provide an unfair advantage to the alleged infringer. In such circumstances, and absent a specific defence, one can see a court readily finding infringement.[87]

13–65 The provision is not, however, limited to use which is likely to cause confusion as to origin. One deputy judge has found that this must be an inherent requirement of the provision.[88] But for the reasons elaborated in the discussion of these words in relation to section 5, it is suggested that the better interpretation is that it is not.[89]

13–66 It may well be that in most cases and absent a finding of likelihood of confusion, a court would be reluctant to find that the requirements of section 10(3) are satisfied.[90] But the wording of the provision allows for that possibility.[91] It appears that the proprietor may therefore be afforded rights in relation to dissimilar goods which he is not afforded in relation to similar goods.[92] A curious but inevitable result of the wording of the TM Directive.

The stronger the registered mark's distinctive character and reputation the easier it will be to accept that detriment has been caused to it.[93]

---

[84] *General Motors, supra*, at para. 26. English law draws a distinction between reputation and goodwill. The former does not require any trade in this country; the latter requires at least some business here. See, *e.g. Star Industrial v. Yap Kwee Kor* [1976] F.S.R. 256 (PC, Singapore) and Chap. 14.

[85] In the light of *General Motors, supra*. In contrast, in the field of passing off, a small trader with a limited clientele is as much entitled to protect his trade mark as a large concern.

[86] See Chap. 8, paras 8–74 *et seq.*

[87] See, *e.g. B.T. v. One in a Million* [1998] F.S.R. 265; [1999] F.S.R. 1, CA.

[88] *Baywatch v. The Home Video Channel* [1997] F.S.R. 22.

[89] See Chap. 8, paras 8–76 to 8–80. See also *Pfizer v. Eurofood Link, supra*. The deputy judge expressed the view, albeit *obiter*, that confusion was not a requirement of s.10(3).

[90] For an illustration of this, see *BASF v. CEP*, Knox J., October 26, 1995, unreported.

[91] See the discussion of this topic in Chap. 8, paras 8–81 to 8–89. and the authorities there referred to.

[92] One way of ameliorating this problem is to adopt the approach of the Supreme Court of Sweden in *Galliano/Gaetano* [1998] I.I.C. 812, in requiring a higher degree of similarity between the marks than in cases where the goods or services are the same similar.

[93] *General Motors, supra*, at para. 30.

Possible applications of the provision might include, for example, the **13–67** use of a famous trade mark on t-shirts or other merchandise, being goods which are not similar to any goods sold by the registered proprietor. Such use might not even be trade mark use, let alone use which is calculated to cause confusion as to the origin of the goods.[94] But it could result in the traders in such goods benefiting from the reputation of the registered proprietor.[95]

In considering the application of this provision it seems that the whole **13–68** manner of the alleged infringer's trade may be open to scrutiny and to comparison with the manner of trade of the registered proprietor. A "mark for sign" test is likely to be inadequate to determine whether the use complained of has taken advantage of, or been detrimental to, the distinctive character or repute of the registered trade mark.[96]

Date of the assessment

It is suggested that the same considerations apply here as in relation to **13–69** section 10(2).[97]

Comparative advertising

The 1994 Act has a provision specifically drawn to address the issue of **13–70** comparative advertising. It is contained in section 10(6) of the Act and it provides some, but limited, protection against comparative advertising. It does so by creating what, on one view, is a further category of infringement in particular cases involving the use by a third party of a registered trade mark in a comparative advertisement and where, in so doing, the third party uses the trade mark in relation to the goods or services of that proprietor. As will be seen, legislation in the United Kingdom curtailed the use of registered trade marks in comparative advertisements from 1938.[98] The present subsection reflects something of a sea change and the contemporary view, at least in this country, is that

---

[94] See, *e.g. Unidoor v. Marks & Spencer* [1988] R.P.C. 275; *"Kodiak"* [1990] F.S.R. 49; and for the titles of books, see *Mothercare UK v. Penguin Books* [1988] R.P.C. 113; *Games Workshop v. Transworld Publishers* [1993] F.S.R. 705.

[95] Although not a legitimate aid to interpretation it is interesting that this was recognised at the Committee stage of the Bill (see, H.L. Official Report, Public Bill Committee, Trade Marks Bill, Second Sitting, January 18, 1994, cols. 35 and 36). Similarly in the White paper, *Reform of Trade Marks Law*, September 1990, it was noted at para. 3.17:
   "A trade mark may acquire such a wide reputation in relation to particular goods that its use in relation to quite different goods is likely to lead the public into thinking that there is a trade connection. This is probably more so today, when consumers have grown accustomed to supermarkets selling a wide range of goods, or to manufacturers of unrelated goods who are part of the same economic group, than it was when the present law was passed in 1938. Moreover there has grown up the practice of using familiar trade marks to decorate such goods as T-shirts. If the owner of such a mark has no redress then other traders are able to benefit unjustly from his reputation. He may also be denied the opportunity to diversify the exploitation of his mark."

[96] As opposed to the position under the 1994 Act, s.10(1) and (2).

[97] See paras 13–53 and 13–54 above.

[98] In the case of marks registered in Part A of the Register.

comparative advertisements which are fair and accurate do no harm and accordingly should not be prohibited by the use of registered trade marks.

Historical

13–71 Restrictions on the use of a trade mark in comparative advertising were first introduced into the Trade Marks Act 1938. Broadly, section 4(1)(b) of that Act prohibited the use of a mark likely to be taken as "importing a reference" to the registered proprietor or a registered user or to the goods of either of them.[99] The Mathys Report (*British Trade Mark Law and Practice* (Cmnd. 5601), May 1974, paras 80 to 88) recommended that such restrictions should remain but there is no specific provision to this effect in the TM Directive. The White Paper, *Reform of Trade Marks Law*, September 1990, noted at para. 3.28, that comparative advertising was regarded as more acceptable than it used to be but it was still generally felt that an advertiser should not be free to ride on the back of a competitor's trade mark. Accordingly it was proposed that section 4(1)(b) of the 1938 Act would be replaced by a provision allowing a trade mark owner to restrain use in advertising which was contrary to honest practices in industrial or commercial matters and would take unfair advantage of or be detrimental to the distinctive character or repute of the trade mark. This is reflected too in the statement of Lord Strathclyde, Minister of State, Department of Trade and Industry, on behalf of the Government:

> "The government have been persuaded that there is no harm in comparative advertising . . . provided that it makes fair use of a registered trade mark for the purpose of informing the public. As foreshadowed in the White Paper, the Bill seeks to chart a middle course: allowing comparative advertising but providing safeguards for the owner of a registered trade mark."[1]

13–72 In substance this proposal is now embodied in section 10(6) of the 1994 Act. It is a hybrid derived originally from the Paris Convention (Article 10 *bis*(2)): "honest practices in industrial and commercial matters" (and now in Article 6 of the TM Directive) and words found in Articles 4 and 5 of the Directive: "where use of the sign without due cause takes advantage of, or is detrimental to, the distinctive character or repute of the trade mark". As will be seen the courts have taken the view that the purpose of this provision is positively to permit comparative advertisements.

[99] s.4(1)(b), was introduced to overrule the case of *Irving's Yeast Vite v. Horesenail* (1934) 51 R.P.C. 110, HL ("Yeast tablets. A substitute for Yeast-Vite" not an infringement of "Yeast-Vite"). It was applied most famously in *Bismag v. Amblins* [1940] Ch. 667; 57 R.P.C. 209—see illustration in the text.
[1] Parliamentary Debates, HL Official Report, Public Bill Committee, Trade Marks Bill, Second Sitting, January 18, 1994, col. 42.

The provision

Section 10(6) of the 1994 Act is as follows: **13–73**

> "Nothing in the preceding provisions of this section shall be
> construed as preventing the use of a registered trade mark by any
> person for the purpose of identifying goods or services as those of
> the proprietor or a licensee.
>
> But any such use other than in accordance with honest practices
> in industrial or commercial matters shall be treated as infringing the
> registered trade mark if the use without due cause takes advantage
> of, or is detrimental to, the distinctive character or repute of the
> trade mark."

It has no counterpart in the CTM Regulation and no direct foundation in **13–74**
the TM Directive. It is divided into two parts. The first part is a saving
where a registered trade mark is used in relation to the genuine goods.
The second part qualifies the saving by providing that such use which is
not in accordance with honest practices shall be treated as an infringement if it is use which, without due cause, takes advantage, of or is
detrimental to, the distinctive character or repute of the trade mark.

Although, as noted above, the subsection was specifically introduced **13–75**
to address the issue of comparative advertising, it is not in fact so
limited, for it also covers any other use of a trade mark for the purpose
of identifying the genuine goods or services of the proprietor. The two
sorts of use are not quite the same. In the case of a comparative
advertisement, the mark is primarily being used in relation to the
genuine goods or services of the proprietor and those are not goods or
services in which the advertiser is actually dealing.

It is of some importance to consider the nature of this provision and **13–76**
the basis for it because it may have implications in considering the
proper interpretation of the CTM Regulation and indeed the extent of
protection properly afforded under the TM Directive and the CTM
Regulation to the use of a trade mark in relation to the genuine goods or
services of the proprietor.

On one approach it may be argued that since the saving part of **13–77**
section 10(6) has no clear foundation in the TM Directive it must be
concluded that the legislature considered that use of a trade mark in a
comparative advertisement does not fall within the rights conferred by a
registered trade mark under Article 5(1) or (2) in the first place.[2] Were it
otherwise the 1994 Act would have provided a defence or saving not
sanctioned by the Directive. This is a matter developed in relation to the
CTM Regulation in paragraphs 13–197 to 13–205, below. As will be seen,
if this is the correct interpretation of the Directive and the Act, then it
would appear to have the consequence that comparative advertising
using a Community trade mark is not an infringement under the CTM
Regulation.

---

[2] Although, of course, the Directive cannot be construed by reference to the Act.

13–78   On the same approach the second half of the subsection may then be viewed as permitted under the optional provisions of Article 5(5) of the TM Directive which states that paragraphs 1 to 4 of Article 5 shall not affect provisions in any Member State relating to the protection against the use of a sign other than for the purpose of distinguishing goods or services, where use of that sign without due cause takes unfair advantage of, or is detrimental to, the distinctive character or the repute of the trade mark.

13–79   Another approach is to regard comparative advertising as something which, prima facie, falls within Article 5(1) of the Directive and, accordingly, section 10(1) of the Act.[3] After all, on a traditional analysis, such an advertisement does in one sense involve the use of the trade mark in relation to the goods or services of the proprietor[4] and for which, on this assumption, it is registered.

13–80   On this approach all such use is, prima facie, an infringement unless it is taken out of the scope of the prohibited field by section 10(6) which is then properly regarded as a qualified saving only. This is all very well in considering national registrations although, as already indicated, it is not a saving sanctioned by the TM Directive and it must be questioned whether it is therefore properly part of the law at all.[5] But it has important consequences in considering Community trade marks because, as also indicated, there is no equivalent provision in the CTM Directive. Any saving of a comparative advertisement from infringement in the case of Community trade marks must therefore be found elsewhere and, in particular, in notions of consent, exhaustion or under Article 12 of the CTM Regulation.[6]

Construction and application of section 10(6)

13–81   In a comparative advertisement the trade mark is being used to identify the goods or services of the proprietor or licensee. Accordingly such use will fall within the first paragraph of the provision which sets out the freedom to use a trade mark to denote the goods or services of the proprietor or licensee in one's own advertisements. But the freedom is qualified by the second paragraph of the provision. Any use in a comparative advertisement which contravenes the second part of the provision will amount to an infringement.

---

[3] It now seems clear that the use by a person of a trade mark in relation to the genuine goods of the proprietor in which he is dealing *does* fall in Art. 5(1): *BMW v. Deenik* [1999] E.C.R. I–905; [1999] E.T.M.R. 339. But, for the reasons indicated, this use is not quite the same as the use of a trade mark in a comparative advertisement.

[4] *Bismag v. Amblins, supra;* it will also be remembered that the CA considered that the use of the mark was used both in relation to the goods of the proprietor and of the advertiser. See also the discussion in relation to Community trade marks in paras 13–197 *et seq.,* below.

[5] Save in so far as it merely constitutes a repetition of savings or defences to be found elsewhere in the Directive and the Act.

[6] Corresponding to the TM Directive, Art. 6, implemented in the 1994 Act, s.11. See further in the discussion of the position in relation to Community trade marks in paras 13–197 *et seq.,* below.

The meaning of the second paragraph has now been considered in a **13–82** number of cases: *Barclays Bank v. Advanta*[7]; *Vodafone Group v. Orange*[8]; *BT v. AT & T* (a decision of Mr Crystal Q.C., sitting as a deputy judge)[9]; *Cable & Wireless v. BT*.[10] In the latter case (at 389) Jacob J. quoted with approval the summary of the findings of Mr Crystal Q.C., with one qualification:

"(1) The primary objective of section 10 (6) of the 1996 Act is to permit comparative advertising (see *Advanta* at pages 312–313 and 315, and *Vodafone* at page [39[11]]);

(2) As long as the use of a competitor's mark is honest, there is nothing wrong in telling the public of the relative merits of competing goods or services and in using registered marks to identify them (see *Advanta* page 315, *Vodafone* at page [39]);

(3) The onus is on the registered proprietor to show that the factors indicated in the proviso to section 10(6) exist (see *Advanta* at page 315, *Vodafone* at page [39]);

(4) There will be no trade mark infringement unless the use of the registered mark is not in accordance with honest practices (see *Advanta* at page 315);

(5) The test is objective: would a reasonable reader be likely to say, upon being given the full facts, that the advertisement is not honest?[12] (see *Advanta* at page 315, *Vodafone* at page [39]);

(6) Statutory or industry agreed codes of conduct are not a helpful guide as to whether an advertisement is honest for the purposes of section 10(6). Honesty has to be gauged against what is reasonably to be expected by the relevant public of advertisements for the goods or services in issue (see *Advanta* at page 316);

(7) It should be borne in mind that the general public are used to the ways of advertisers and expect hyperbole (see *Advanta* at page 315; *cf. Vodafone* at pages [38 to 39]);

(8) The 1994 Act does not impose on the courts an obligation to try and enforce through the back door of trade mark legislation a more puritanical standard than the public would expect from advertising copy (see *Advanta* at page 315; *Vodafone* at page [39]);

(9) An advertisement which is significantly misleading is not honest for the purposes of section 10(6) (see *Advanta* at page 316, *Vodafone* at pages [39 to 40];

I venture with diffidence to make a number of additional observations.

[7] [1996] R.P.C. 307.
[8] [1997] F.S.R. 34.
[9] December 18, 1996.
[10] [1998] F.S.R. 383. Now followed most recently in *Electrolux v. Dyson* [1999] E.T.M.R. 903. See also *Macmillan Magazines v. RCN Publishing* [1998] F.S.R. 9.
[11] We have inserted the page references of the report of *Vodafone* in [1997] F.S.R. 34.
[12] In trade marks, there is no "one meaning" rule. If a comparison is significantly misleading on an objective basis to a substantial proportion of the reasonable audience, it is not an honest practice within the section: *Vodafone* at 39.

(10) The advertisement must be considered as a whole (*cf. Advanta* at pages 316–318);

(11) As a purpose of the 1994 Act is positively to permit comparative advertising, the court should not hold words in the advertisement to be seriously misleading for interlocutory purposes unless on a fair reading of them in their context and against the background of the advertisement as a whole they can really be said to justify that description;

(12) A minute textual examination is not something upon which the reasonable reader of a advertisement would embark;

(13) The court should therefore not encourage a microscopic approach to the construction of a comparative advertisement on a motion for interlocutory relief."

13–83 The qualification related to "honesty" and the nature of the objective test. Jacob J. considered that the test was objective in this sense: that one should ask whether a reasonable trader could honestly have made the statements he made based upon the information that he had (at 391). It is suggested this qualification must be applied with care. It is possible to imagine circumstances where the advertiser has not made reasonable inquiries and accordingly has honestly made statements based upon the information he had, but where that information was, on any reasonable, objective view, inadequate. Perhaps a better formulation would be to qualify point (5) by the addition after the words "*upon being given the full facts*" of the words "*ascertainable upon reasonable enquiry*".[13]

13–84 Certainly the approach taken by the courts hitherto indicates that they are minded to take a liberal view of what is permissible; this is revealed by the suggestion that the purpose of the legislation is positively to permit comparative advertising[14] and the reference to a need for the advertising to be *significantly* misleading before it will be characterised as offensive. There has been no suggestion that the use of trade marks, even if not necessary, and denigrations of competitors goods are not permissible, provided that they are not significantly misleading. In these respects it may be contended that section 10(6), as interpreted by the courts, has been taken beyond any defence contemplated by the TM Directive or now reflected in the Comparative Advertising Directive.[15]

13–85 (1) The plaintiff, the bank Barclays, ran the Barclaycard credit business and was the proprietor of the registered trade mark BARCLAYCARD. The defendant, RBS Advanta, a joint venture owned by the Royal Bank of Scotland and Advanta Corporation, intended to offer a credit card under the name RBS

---

[13] Otherwise the courts will find themselves back in precisely the position one assumes they were seeking to avoid and leading to absurdities of the kind identified in *Provident Financial v. Halifax Buildings Society* [1994] F.S.R. 81; *cf. Baume v. Moore* [1958] Ch. 907, CA.

[14] *cf.* the legislative history, para. 13–71, *supra*.

[15] See paras 13–89 and 13–90, below.

Advanta VISA card. It issued advertising material identifying fifteen ways the card was a better credit card than its competitors and a comparative table referring expressly to, *inter alia*, BARCLAYCARD. The plaintiff complained that the advertisement was misleading in that it made no mention of other ancillary benefits which the plaintiff offered and which the defendant did not have and that at least six of the fifteen points identified were common to BARCLAYCARD as well. Held, refusing an interlocutory injunction, it was most unlikely any reasonable reader would take the view the advertisement was dishonest; the advertisements conveyed the message that the package, taken as a whole, offered the customer a better deal.[16]

(2) Vodafone and Orange operated rival cellular telephone net- **13–86** works. Orange adopted, for an advertising campaign, the slogan "On average, Orange users save £20 every month", a saving expressly stated to be in comparison with Vodafone's equivalent tariff. It was thereupon sued by Vodafone for malicious falsehood and trade mark infringement. Vodafone contended that the advertisement carried the message that on average Vodafone users would save £20 every month if they had instead been on Orange and in any event the notion of an average was inherently deceptive because the user profile was skewed with most users making relatively little usage of their phones. Held, the claim failed. The ordinary person would understand the advertisement to mean that, on average, if Orange users had been on Vodafone, they would have had to pay £20 more a month. Vodafone users would simply recognise that it might be cheaper to use Orange. It was not established that the advertisement was misleading.[17]

(3) British Telecom issued a brochure to small- and medium-sized **13–87** customers containing the sentence: "Most customers who are using the best Cable & Wireless indirect price package will make savings by using the best package from BT". The brochure continued with an analysis of the costs of calling with BT and Cable & Wireless and a price comparison. The brochure was based upon an analysis carried out by Deloitte & Touche, a leading firm of chartered accountants. Cable & Wireless thereupon launched proceedings for trade mark infringement and sought an injunction pending trial. Held, refusing the injunction, much of the dispute turned on statistical models; it could not be said that honest traders, having the information which BT had, would not be prepared to make the statements which BT had made.[18]

---

[16] *Barclays Bank v. Advanta* [1996] R.P.C. 307.
[17] *Vodafone v. Orange* [1997] F.S.R. 34.
[18] *Cable & Wireless v. British Telecommunications* [1998] F.S.R. 383.

13–88   (4) The plaintiffs were the registered proprietors of the trade mark "Bisurated" for medicines. The defendants were selling in addition to their own medicines proprietary medicines of other manufacturers, including those of the plaintiffs. The defendants issued a pamphlet in which, after a preliminary statement as to the prices of patent medicines, there were set out two columns; in one, headed "List of advertised patent medicines sold by us", prescriptions including *inter alia* "Bisurated Magnesia Tablets" with an analysis and price; in the other, headed "Amblins Medicine (Brand) Prescriptions" (and opposite to the "Bisurated Magnesia Tablets"), the words "Bismuthated Magnesia Tablets", also with an analysis and price which was much lower than the other. The majority of the Court of Appeal held that the mark "Bisurated" was used in relation to both sorts of goods, the defendants' "Bismuthated" tablets as well as the plaintiffs'. Accordingly, under the Trade Marks Act 1938 there was infringement. There seems no doubt that under the 1994 Act the claim would have failed.[19]

The Comparative Advertising Directive

13–89 It is interesting to note that the approach of the courts to comparative advertising and trade mark infringement is not fully consistent with Directive 97/55 of October 6, 1997 amending Directive 84/450 concerning comparative advertising.[20] The earlier Directive requires the prohibition of advertising which is misleading. The later Directive has a specific purpose of laying down the conditions under which comparative advertising is permitted.[21] For the purposes of the later Directive comparative advertising means any advertising which explicitly or by implication identifies a competitor or goods or services offered by a competitor. Article 3a provides that comparative advertising shall, as far as the comparison is concerned, be permitted only when the specified conditions are met. Those conditions are as follows:

(1) it is not misleading according to Articles 2(2), 3 and 7(1)[22];
(2) it compares goods or services meeting the same needs or intended for the same purpose;

[19] *Bismag v. Amblins* [1940] Ch. 667; 57 R.P.C. 209, CA. There were many cases under the 1938 Act, see the 12th edition of Kerly, paras 14–26 and 14–27 and supplement. For a more recent case, objectionable under the old law and which, it is suggested, would have been equally objectionable under the new, see *Compaq v. Dell* [1992] F.S.R. 93.
[20] Directive 97/55, Art. 3, allowed Member States up to 30 months to bring into force laws, regulations and administrative provisions necessary to comply with it.
[21] Directive 97/55, Art. 1(2). The preamble to the Directive rather suggests (in Recitals 13–15) that comparative advertising that does not comply with Directive 97/55 would fall within the exclusive rights conferred by Directive 89/104 (the TM Directive).
[22] These provisions are set out in App. 16. Misleading advertising is broadly defined as any advertisisng which in any way, including its presentation, deceives or is likely to deceive the persons to whom it is addressed or whom it reaches and which, by reason of its deceptive nature, is likely to affect their economic behaviour or which, for those reasons, injures or is likely to injure a competitor.

(3) it objectively compares one or more material, relevant, verifiable and representative features of those goods and services, which may include price;

(4) it does not create confusion in the market place between the advertiser's trade marks, trade names, other distinguishing marks, goods or services and those of a competitor;

(5) it does not discredit or denigrate the trade marks, trade names, other distinguishing marks, goods, services, activities or circumstances of a competitor;

(6) for products with designation of origin, it relates in each case to products with the same designation;

(7) it does not take unfair advantage of the reputation of a trade mark, trade name or other distinguishing marks of a competitor or of the designation of origin of competing products;

(8) it does not present goods or services as imitations or replicas of goods or services bearing a protected trade mark or trade name.

The provision also includes specific restrictions relating to special offers.

The Directive has been implemented in the United Kingdom by the **13–90** Control of Misleading Advertisements) (Comparative Advertisements) (Amendment) Regulations 2000 which came into force in April 2000.[23] These Regulations amend the Control of Misleading Advertisements Regulations 1988[24] by adding comparative advertisements to the regime governing misleading advertisements there set out. The responsibility for enforcement lies with the Director General of Fair Trading. It certainly appears that these Regulations are more restrictive than section 10(6) of the 1994 Act and that an advertisement may offend the Regulations even if it does not amount to an infringement of registered trade mark, at least on the approach to infringement adopted by the courts hitherto. It remains to be seen whether that approach will develop in the light of Directive 97/55.

C. Ancillary matters
Joint liability

Section 10(5) of the 1994 Act makes specific provision for the case where **13–91** a person applies a registered trade mark to material intended to be used for labelling or packaging goods, as business papers or for advertising goods or services. The scope of this provision is discussed in paragraph 13–35 *et seq.*, above. In addition a person who becomes involved in counterfeiting or other infringement may be liable for directing, procuring or combining with others to infringe.[25]

---

[23] S.I. 2000 No. 914.
[24] S.I. 1988 No. 915.
[25] For an exposition of the relevant principles, see *CBS v. Amstrad Consumer Electronics* [1988] 1 A.C. 1013. An example of their application is *White Horse Distillers v. Gregson Associates* [1984] R.P.C. 84. This topic is discussed further in Chap. 18.

Limitation as to validity

13–92 The rights given by a registered trade mark are not subject to an express limitation that the registration must be valid.[26] Nevertheless, under section 46 of the 1994 Act, a mark may be revoked with effect from the date of the application for revocation or, if the Registrar or court is satisfied that the grounds of revocation existed at an earlier date, that date. Furthermore, where the registration of a mark is declared invalid to any extent under section 47, then, to that extent, the registration is deemed never to have been made. Validity is considered elsewhere.[27] As before, an action for infringement is likely to be met by the defence that the mark is invalid and liable to be revoked and a counterclaim for a declaration of invalidity and for an order that the registration be removed from the Register.

Date from which rights are conferred

13–93 The rights of the proprietor have effect from the date of filing of the application for registration. But no infringement proceedings may be begun before the date on which the trade mark is in fact registered.[28] In this respect the position is the same as under the old law.[29]

Locality of infringement

13–94 Trade mark rights are territorial. An infringing act committed outside the United Kingdom cannot be sued upon as an infringement of a United Kingdom registered trade mark.[30] This may be a point of particular relevance in relation to web-sites. The mere fact that websites can be accessed anywhere in the world does not mean that, for trade mark purposes, the law should regard them as being used everywhere in the world. It all depends upon the circumstances, particularly the intention of the website owner and what the reader will understand if he accesses the site.[31]

Burden of proof

13–95 In cases of infringement the burden of proof lies upon the claimant, usually the proprietor of the mark, although in particular circumstances exclusive or even non-exclusive licensees can bring proceedings, joining the proprietor as co-claimant or defendant.[32] The burden of proof lies on the defendant to establish invalidity.

---

[26] This position may be contrasted with that under the 1938 Act where, by s.4, it was specified that a registration gave exclusive rights, if valid.

[27] See Chap. 9.

[28] 1994 Act, s.9(3) and s.40(3).

[29] As to offences and criminal proceedings, see Chap. 19.

[30] But as for bringing proceedings here in respect of infringements of foreign trade marks and vice versa, see Chap. 18.

[31] *1–800 Flowers v. Phonenames* [2000] E.T.M.R. 369; *Euromarket Design Inc. v. Peters*, a decision of Jacob J. of July 25, 2000, as yet unreported. See further, Chap. 21.

[32] See Chap. 18.

D. Savings and exceptions

Limitations entered onto the Register

Section 13 of the 1994 Act provides that where the registration of a trade **13–96** mark is subject to a disclaimer or a limitation, then the rights conferred by section 9 are restricted accordingly. Similarities attributable to nothing more than that which is disclaimed can not support an action for infringement.[33]

Use on the genuine goods or services of the proprietor

It was recognised before the Trade Marks Act of 1938 that a proprietor **13–97** should not have the right to stop the use of a trade mark in connection with what were usually described as "the genuine goods".[34] The reasoning for this limitation was that such use could not cause deception, which was the test of infringement. The Trade Marks Act 1938 incorporated a specific provision to deal with the issue,[35] a provision necessary because there were now cases deemed to be infringements within section 4(1)(b) of that Act, where the use of the mark did not need to involve any likelihood of deception.[36]

The matter is dealt with expressly under the 1994 Act by section 10(6) **13–98** which provides that, in these circumstances, and subject to the proviso, it is not an infringement to use the registered mark for the purpose of identifying goods or services as those of the proprietor or licensee.[37]

In the straightforward case where the trader is doing no more than **13–99** using the trade mark in relation to the genuine goods in which he is dealing, then there will plainly be no difficulty. But in other cases the matter will not be so clear. So for, example, the goods may have deteriorated or been altered or adulterated so as to affect their quality. In other cases bulk goods may simply have been broken down. In such cases, it is suggested, it must be considered whether the original condition of the product has been altered so as to affect the specific subject matter of the trade mark. In short, the principles of exhaustion applicable in the case of parallel imports should be equally applicable here too.[38]

> The defendant, in business as a repairer of automatic transmissions of cars, built himself a car and got it up to look like one of the

---

[33] *The European v. The Economist* [1998] F.S.R. 283, CA.
[34] *Champagne Heidsieck v. Buxton* [1930] 1 Ch. 330; 47 R.P.C. 28; *cf. Farina v. Silverlock* (1885) 1 K. & J. 509; 24 L.J.Ch. 632; 6 De G.M. & G. 214; 24 L.J. Ch. 11, a case prior to the earliest Registration Act.
[35] Trade Marks Act 1938, s.4(3)(a).
[36] *Bismag v. Amblins* [1940] Ch. 667; 57 R.P.C. 209.
[37] See the discussion of this issue in paras 13–73 *et seq., supra*. Because of the dubious origin of this provision, it is suggested that the best approach is to follow the principles set out in the next paragraph.
[38] TM Directive, Art. 7, discussed briefly in para. 13–100, *infra* and in Chap. 15. The issue was considered most recently by the High Court in *Glaxo and Ors. v. Dowelhurst*, an interim decision of Laddie J., February 28, 2000, now referred to the ECJ. There must be legitimate reasons for opposing the use of the mark: *BMW v. Deenik* [1999] E.T.M.R. 339.

plaintiff's. The radiator was a Rolls Royce part bearing their trade mark. On an application for an interlocutory injunction, it was held there was an arguable case of infringement of trade mark notwithstanding that the only use of the mark was on the genuine part and the car.[39]

Parallel imports

13–100 The position in respect of goods put on the market in the EEA is governed by section 12 of the 1994 Act.[40] It provides that a registered trade mark is not infringed by the use of the trade mark in relation to goods which have been put on the market in the EEA under that trade mark by the proprietor or with his consent, unless there are legitimate reasons for the proprietor to oppose further dealings in the goods. This is a complex topic and it is considered in detail in Chapter 15.

13–101 If the goods were first put on the market outside the EEA then it now seems that there may be no exhaustion of trade mark rights unless consent has been given for the importation of those goods into the EEA.[41]

13–102 This is a dramatic change in the law, introduced by the implementation of the TM Directive. Hitherto it had seemed clear that the courts would not permit the use of United Kingdom registered trade marks to prevent the importation of goods, bearing a particular trade mark, where the goods were originally marketed by some branch of the enterprise of which the United Kingdom registered proprietor (or registered user under the 1938 Act) formed part. In effect the courts regarded the mark as applying to the genuine goods, the use having the consent of the registered proprietor.[42] Again this matter is addressed in detail in Chapter 15.

E. Defences to an action for infringement of a registered trade mark

Defences

13–103 The defences discussed in this section must be considered together with the elements which a claimant is required to prove to make out a case of infringement. These are considered above. The most commonly cited defences are set out below:

> (1) the activities complained of were performed with the consent of the proprietor;

---

[39] *Rolls-Royce v. Dodd* [1988] F.S.R. 517, a decision under the 1938 Act but, it is suggested, the result under the 1994 Act would be the same.

[40] Implementing the TM Directive, Art. 7.

[41] *Silhouette International v. Hartlauer* [1999] F.S.R. 729; *Sebago v. Unic* [2000] R.P.C. 63; *cf. Zino Davidoff v. A & G Imports* [1999] R.P.C. 631.

[42] *Revlon* [1980] F.S.R. 80, CA; *cf.* if there was an express denial of a United Kingdom trade mark licence: *Castrol v. Automotive* [1983] R.P.C. 315; or if the quality of the goods sold in each territory was different: *Colgate Palmolive v. Markwell Finance* [1989] R.P.C. 497, CA.

(2) the use complained of is use in relation to the genuine goods or services[43];

(3) the registration is invalid or liable to be revoked;

(4) the defendant has an independent right to use the mark arising from his own registration;

(5) the defendant is using his own name and address;

(6) the defendant is using indications concerning the characteristics of his goods or services;

(7) the defendant is indicating the intended purpose of a product or service;

(8) the defendant has his own right to use the mark arising from an earlier right;

(9) miscellaneous and general defences.

(1) Consent

Section 9 of the 1994 Act makes it clear that the exclusive rights in a **13–103A** trade mark are infringed by the use of the trade mark in the United Kingdom without the consent of the proprietor. As such this is truly a requirement of the cause of action, rather than a defence. If the defendant relies upon a specific licence, then the evidential burden may shift onto him. Licences to use a registered trade mark may be general or limited and are discussed in detail in Chapter 12.

(3) Attack on the validity of the registration

A registration can be attacked in two ways. An application can be made **13–104** for the revocation of the registration and an application can be made for a declaration that the registration of the trade mark is invalid.[44]

A registered trade mark can be revoked on any of the grounds set **13–105** forth in section 46 of the 1994 Act. The grounds of revocation are discussed in detail in Chapter 9. It should be noted that if the grounds of revocation exist in respect of only some of the goods or services for which the mark is registered, then the revocation will relate to those goods or services only. Where a mark is revoked to any extent, then the rights of the proprietor are deemed to have ceased to that extent as from the date of revocation, or if the court or Registrar is satisfied that the grounds of revocation existed at an earlier date, then as from that date.[45]

An application can be made for a declaration that the registration is **13–106** invalid on any of the grounds set forth in section 47 of the 1994 Act. These grounds are discussed in detail in Chapter 9. As in the case of revocation, if the grounds exist in relation to only some of the goods or service for which the mark is registered, then the declaration will be made in respect those goods or services only. The grounds of invalidity relate to the original registration and accordingly, where a declaration of

---

[43] This is discussed above at paras 13–97 to 13–99.
[44] The procedures involved are discussed in Chaps 9 and 18.
[45] s.46(6).

invalidity is made to any extent, the registration is to that extent deemed never to have existed; provided that this does not affect transactions past and closed.[46]

(4) Use of a registered trade mark

13–107 A registered trade mark is not infringed by the use of another registered trade mark in relation to goods or services for which it is registered.[47] This defence was introduced at the Report stage of the Bill and provides equivalent protection under the new law to that previously afforded by section 4(4) of the Trade Marks Act 1938. The defence is not derived from the TM Directive and it has no parallel in the CTM Regulation.[48]

13–108 For the defence to operate the defendant must be using the mark in the form in which it is registered and in relation to the particular goods or services for which it is registered. A court is likely to consider carefully whether or not these requirements are satisfied, as it did under the old law.[49]

    (1) The plaintiffs had the mark "Gor-Ray" registered for, *inter alia*, skirts; the defendants had the mark "Gilray" registered for dresses. The plaintiffs sued for infringement in respect of the use of "Gilray" on separate skirts. There was evidence that in the trade the term "dress" could cover a two-piece suit, including coat and skirt. Harman J. held that since the sale of a dress necessarily included the sale of the skirt of the dress, section 4(4) of the 1938 Act applied. The Court of Appeal took the opposite view. Evershed M.R. observed that "skirts are not, when treated separately, dresses"; and that "the right to use a trade mark for dresses . . . does not involve the right to use that mark in respect of parts of dresses": *Gor-Ray v. Gilray* (1952) 69 R.P.C. 99 at 106; 69 R.P.C. 199 at 205, 206, CA.

    (2) The defendants had a registration of ECONCIL-VK, the plaintiff one of V-CIL-K. The defendant was restrained from using econoCIL-VK (the former letters being about four times smaller than the latter), the court holding that it is a question of fact whether a defendant is using his registered mark and that question is not to be answered by asking whether the mark used would be an infringement of the registered mark: *Lilly (Eli) v. Chelsea Drug* [1966] R.P.C. 14.

Defendant not registered

13–109 The defence applies only to cases where the defendant is actually validly registered. If a defendant is threatened or sued and has not yet registered his mark, although it is capable of registration, then he ought

---

[46] s.47(6).
[47] s.11(1).
[48] See para. 13–213, below.
[49] See, in addition to the illustrations below, *Spillers* (1952) 69 R.P.C. 327; (1953) 70 R.P.C. 51, CA and (1954) 71 R.P.C. 234, HL; *Cluett, Peabody v. McIntyre, Hogg* [1958] R.P.C. 335 at 355.

immediately to apply for registration. In a proper case the court may stay proceedings in an action for infringement until an application for registration has been decided.

In various cases brought under the Trade Marks Act 1938 and earlier **13–110** legislation, such applications were made and it is reasonable to suppose that under the 1994 Act the courts will adopt a similar approach; some illustrations are set out below.[50]

Examples of applications to stay infringement actions

(1) In *Electrolux v. Electrix*[51] it was held that the mark was valid and **13–111** infringed but that in view of the defendant's long concurrent use, relief should be suspended to give the defendants an opportunity to apply for registration. They did so, but failed.[52]

(2) In *Colibri v. Markt*[53] the defendants, who were importers of **13–112** products manufactured by a German firm, failed in their application for a stay of infringement proceedings pending the conclusion of opposition proceedings by the plaintiffs to the German firm's application for a trade mark containing the word "Colibri" as used in Germany and claimed in the action to have been used for 30 years; no particulars of such use had been supplied.

(3) In *Berlei v. Bali*,[54] the defendants had been the registered **13–113** proprietors of the mark "Bali" but this was expunged by the House of Lords on the grounds that it offended section 11 of the Trade Marks Act 1938. The defendants thereupon sought to register the mark under the provisions of section 12(2) of the 1938 Act and at the same time the plaintiffs pressed their action for infringement which had been commenced earlier. Megarry J. refused a stay, observing that a stay should only be granted where the interests of justice (taking into account the claims of both parties) required it. If an injunction were obtained in the action and the defendants subsequently were registered and thus obtained the protection of section 4(4) of the 1938 Act, the injunction could be qualified *ab initio* or varied when registration was effected.[55]

Effect of belated registration

If a defendant secures a registration of his mark, then the registration **13–114** takes effect as of the date of filing of the application for registration. Activities before that date must therefore remain potential infringements, subject to any other defences available.

---

[50] Other older cases are noted in the 12th edition of this book.
[51] (1953) 70 R.P.C. 127; (1954) 71 R.P.C. 23, CA.
[52] *"Electrix"* [1959] R.P.C. 283.
[53] [1959] R.P.C. 8.
[54] [1970] R.P.C. 469.
[55] For the form of order, see [1970] R.P.C. 469.

13–115   If the defendant secures his registration before the commencement of proceedings against him, then the position is straightforward. If he secures his registration in the period between the commencement of proceedings and trial, then no injunction would be granted against him but damages could be awarded in respect of his activities prior to the application for registration. The most difficult cases will be those where the defendant hopes to secure a registration but is unlikely to do so before the trial. Here he would be well advised to consider applying for a stay of the infringement action pending a final decision in respect of the application.[56] If such a stay is not ordered then, it is suggested, he should seek to have the grant of any relief stayed until the application has been decided or that he be given liberty to apply to have any injunction varied and that ancillary relief only be granted subject to a cross-undertaking and the giving of any necessary security.

Validity of defendant's registration

13–116   A complete defence will only be available if the defendant's mark is validly registered. It should be noted that where the registration of a mark is declared invalid pursuant to an application made under section 47 of the 1994 Act, then it is deemed never to have been made. Where a registration is revoked to any extent under section 46, then the rights of the proprietor are deemed to have ceased to that extent as from the date of the application for revocation, or, if the Registrar or court is satisfied that the grounds for revocation existed at an earlier date, then that date. In both cases there will be no protection for the future.

13–117   Any claimant who is met with a defence that the mark complained of is registered should therefore consider whether he has grounds to seek revocation of that registration or a declaration of invalidity in respect of it. It is to be noted however that the opportunity to apply for a declaration that the registration of a later trade mark is invalid is restricted by section 48. This important provision is discussed below.

Effect of acquiescence

13–118   Section 48(1) of the 1994 Act provides that where the proprietor of an earlier trade mark or other earlier right has acquiesced for a continuous period of five years in the use of a registered trade mark in the United Kingdom, being aware of that use, there shall cease to be any entitlement on the basis of that earlier trade mark or other right—

   (1) to apply for a declaration that the registration of the later trade mark is invalid, or
   (2) to oppose the use of the later trade mark in relation to the goods or services in relation to which it has been so used,

unless the registration of the later trade mark was applied for in bad faith.

---

[56] See para. 13–109, *supra*.

This section implements Article 9 of the TM Directive but, at least in **13–119** part, is swamped by the defence provided by section 11(1) which has no foundation in the Directive and is discussed in paragraphs 13–107 to 13–117, above. Nevertheless this provision is important because it restricts the extent to which a declaration of invalidity may be sought in respect of a registered mark, and so also the opportunity for a claimant to attack the registered trade mark of the defendant and behind which it is sheltering.[57] Where the proprietor of the earlier registered mark has acquiesced as called for by the provision, then he may no longer apply for a declaration of invalidity or oppose the use of the later trade mark in relation to the goods or services in relation to which it has been so used, unless the registration of the later trade mark was applied for in bad faith.

It is suggested that the requirement of acquiescence appears to require **13–120** no more or less than inaction with actual knowledge of the use. As in the case of the equivalent provision under the CTM Regulation, there seems to be little scope for importing into the provision English notions of acquiescence or estoppel[58] in the light of the express words relating to time and knowledge. Secondly, if bad faith is shown then it seems the limitation is not applicable in terms either of preventing the attack on the later registration or opposing its use.[59]

Where the provisions of section 48(1) apply, then the proprietor of the **13–121** later mark is not entitled to oppose the use of the earlier trade mark or, as the case may be, the exploitation of the earlier right either. The use of the word oppose must be intended to include any attempt to prevent use by infringement proceedings.

(5) Use by a person of his own name or address, etc.

A registered trade mark is not infringed by the use by a person of his **13–122** own name or address, provided the use is in accordance with honest practices in industrial or commercial matters.[60] This defence implements Article 6(1)(a) of the TM Directive.

Where the defence applies, then the defendant can use the name as a trade mark and a rival trader must sue, if at all, for passing off.[61]

---

[57] Although it seems that in an appropriate case the registration might be attacked on other grounds under s.46 and it will be noted that under s.46(2) the rights of the proprietor may be deemed to have ceased as of an earlier date if the Registrar or court is satisfied that the grounds for revocation existed at an earlier date.

[58] As in *Wilmot v. Barber* (1880) 15 Ch. D. 96 at 105, *per* Fry J., (1881) 17 Ch.D. 772, CA; *Electrolux v. Electrix* (1954) 71 R.P.C. 23 at 32 *et seq.*; *Bulmer v. Bollinger* [1978] R.P.C. 78; *Habib Bank v. Habib Bank* [1982] R.P.C. 1; [1981] 1 W.L.R. 1255, CA.

[59] As to the meaning of bad faith, reference is invited to the discussion in Chap. 7.

[60] 1994 Act, s.11(2)(a).

[61] *Scandecor Development v. Scandecor Marketing* [1998] F.S.R. 500; on appeal this issue was not addressed by the court, see [1999] F.S.R. 26. In this case it seems to have been assumed that the defence covered use of the name as a trade mark. The position was the same under the Trade Marks Act 1938, s.8: *Baume v. Moore* [1957] R.P.C. 459 at 461 to 464; [1958] R.P.C. 226 at 235, CA.

"Name" of the defendant

13–123 It is plain that the defence applies to a natural person. There seems to be no sensible reason why it should not also apply to a company or firm, provided that the other requirements of the defence are met.[62] Nothing in the TM Directive suggests that any distinction is to be drawn between natural persons, firms and companies. But if a corporate or firm name was adopted for the purpose of trading off any reputation attaching to a registered trade mark or for passing off, then it would not satisfy the requirement of being in accordance with honest practices.

13–124 The name of a person is the name by which he is known or called. So in the case of a natural person it will include the name by which he is christened and the name by which he is usually known.[63] In the case of a company it will include its full corporate name and the name by which it is known to its customers; that is to say omitting such words at the end of the name as "Limited", "Corporation", "Incorporated" or other words or letters indicating corporate status.[64] By parity of reasoning, the defence will apply to business names of persons, firms and companies too, provided they are the names by which those persons, firms and companies are known.[65]

Use in accordance with honest practices

13–125 The defence will only apply if the defendant shows that his use is in accordance with honest practices in industrial and commercial matters. These words, derived from the TM Directive, also appear in section 10(6) of the 1994 Act. The Directive gives no assistance as to their interpretation.

13–126 It now seems clear that the test is an objective one.[66] In this context the test has been formulated essentially as follows: would reasonable

---

[62] And it has been so decided for the moment by an English judge in relation to company names: *Scandecor Development AB v. Scandecor Marketing AB, supra;* see also *Euromarket Designs Inc. v. Peters,* a decision of Jacob J. of July 25, 2000, as yet unreported; *cf. NAD Electronics Inc v. NAD Computer Systems Ltd* [1997] F.S.R. 380, where Ferris J. questioned whether the defence applied to the use of the corporate name of an artificial person such as a company. It should also be noted that a statement was entered into the minutes of the Council meeting at which the TM Directive was adopted, that the Council and Commission considered that the terms "his own name" applied only in respect of natural persons. Such minutes are not a legitimate aid to interpretation: *Antonissen* [1991] E.C.R. I–745; *Bautiaa and Societe Francaise Maritime* [1996] E.C.R. I–505; but they do indicate that it is possible that the ECJ might take a different view.

Under Trade Marks Act 1938, s.8, protection extended to the use by a company of its registered name: *Baume v. A.H. Moore* [1957] R.P.C. 459; [1958] R.P.C. 226, CA; *Ballantine v. Ballantyne, Stewart* [1959] R.P.C. 47 at 49; [1959] R.P.C. 273; *Parker-Knoll v. Knoll International* [1961] R.P.C. 346, CA; [1962] R.P.C. 265, HL, and probably to a firm or business name.

[63] *Mercury Communications v. Mercury Interactive* [1995] F.S.R. 850.

[64] *Baume (supra)* [1957] R.P.C. at 461; *Parker-Knoll (supra)* [1962] R.P.C. at 275. It would appear that it is enough, for this element of the defence, if it is the name by which a foreign corporation is known in its own country.

[65] *Mercury (supra)* at 860–863.

[66] See, in the context of s.10(6) the discussion at *supra* paras 13–81 *et seq.,* above and, *Barclays Bank v. Advanta* [1996] R.P.C. 307; *Vodafone Group v. Orange* [1997] F.S.R. 34; *Cable & Wireless v. BT* [1998] F.S.R. 383.

members of the trade concerned say, upon knowing all the relevant facts that the defendant knew, that the use complained of is honest?[67]

In many cases no doubt the answer will be relatively straightforward. **13–127** So, for example, if a person uses his own name, as a brand name, with knowledge of the plaintiff's mark, in a form tending to identify his goods with the plaintiff, then there could be little doubt such use would not be regarded as honest.

But other cases may not be so easy. For example, a person may use a **13–128** contraction of his name as a brand name in relation to goods such that confusion with the plaintiff is likely and where use of his full name would not have that result. It is suggested here that the plaintiff would again succeed. The defendant could avoid confusion and, it may be supposed, an honest person would seek to do just that. But there may be cases where use of even the full name, honestly adopted as a brand name, is likely to cause confusion. This is perhaps the most difficult case of all. It would require a court to consider whether the proviso means, in substance, that the use must be such as not to cause confusion in practice. At least this has the merit of being a relatively concrete test and broadly in line with the own name exception to passing off.[68]

(6) The use of indications concerning the characteristics of the goods, such as kind and quality

Section 11(2)(b) of the 1994 Act provides that a registered trade mark is **13–129** not infringed by the use of indications concerning the kind, quality, quantity, intended purpose, value, geographical origin, the time of production of goods or rendering of services, or other characteristics of goods or services. Again, the use must be in accordance with honest practices in industrial or commercial matters. This provision implements Article 6(1)(b) of the TM Directive.

General

The provision requires a consideration of two issues. First, it must be **13–130** considered whether the use complained about is an indication concerning one of the specified or other characteristics of the goods or services, and secondly, whether the use is in accordance with honest practices in industrial or commercial matters. It is to be noted that the word "necessary" does not appear as a requirement in the provision.[69]

Use in a trade mark sense

An important question arises as to whether the use must be purely **13–131** descriptive to fall within the exception or whether use by the defendant of the description in a trade mark sense, that is to say as an indication of origin, is also excepted.

---

[67] *Volvo v. Heritage* [2000] F.S.R. 253.
[68] See Chap. 14.
[69] *Philips v. Remington* [1999] R.P.C. 809 at 824, CA.

13–132   It seems that various different sorts of trade mark use must be considered. First, there is the use of the indication in relation to the defendant's goods or services, but in such a way that the trade and public will think that the indication is being used by the defendant to denote the origin of the goods or services. An illustration of this under the old law is provided by the case of *Mars v. Cadbury*[70] which involved the use by the defendants of the words "treat size" in relation to their confectionery, but with such size and prominence that the words had acquired a degree of distinctiveness.

13–133   Secondly, there is the use by the defendant of the claimant's mark in a comparative sense. One manufacturer may, for example, wish to claim that his goods are of the same quality, kind and have the same purpose as goods sold under a particular trade mark. In all these cases the registered trade mark is being used in a trade mark sense in relation to the goods of the proprietor: but it is also being used by way of description in relation to the goods of the defendant.[71]

13–134   Thirdly, there is the use by the defendant of the claimant's mark so as to indicate some characteristic of the defendant's goods or services. So, for example, the yarn of one producer might be used by another for the purpose of making clothes, goods may be impregnated with some chemical for the purpose of improving their qualities, instruments may be made of a particular alloy. In all these cases the original materials may have been sold under a particular trade mark which the producer of the finished goods wishes to refer to for the purpose of indicating the quality of his own goods.

13–135   As to the first category of uses, that is to say the use of the sign for the defendant's goods as a descriptor, it has been held that one must first look at the whole context of the use to determine whether the use is descriptive or not. If the mark is being used as a trade mark for the defendant's goods, then it is not being used as a description: *British Sugar v. James Robertson*.[72] The case also deals with the difficult case where an essentially descriptive name has acquired an element of distinctiveness. As Jacob J. said:

> "If a mark is used as a trade mark for the defendant's goods, then it is not used as a description. This conclusion may have important implications where a semi-descriptive mark is validly registered. In particular if the defendant's mark is descriptive to some but has

---

[70] [1987] R.P.C. 387.

[71] Or at least it would be so understood by someone familiar with English trade mark law: *Bismag v. Amblins (Chemists)* [1940] Ch. 667; 57 R.P.C. 209.

[72] [1996] R.P.C. 281 at 297–300; see also *Philips Electronics v. Remington* [1998] R.P.C. 283 at 313; [1999] R.P.C. 809, CA; *The European v. The Economist Newspaper* [1998] F.S.R. 283 at 291, CA—*obiter*. For an illustration of how difficult the question can be, see *Allied Domecq Spirits and Wine v. Murray McDavid* [1997] F.S.R. 864, Ct of Sess: the pursuers were the owners of the trade mark "Laphroaig" and used it in relation to whisky distilled and matured at their Laphroaig distillery on Islay; the defenders obtained surplus stock of the pursuers' whisky from blenders and sold it as coming from "Laphroaig Distillery". The court found, at the interlocutory stage, that the defence was arguable.

trade mark significance to others, he will not be within the section."[73]

13–136 As to the second category of uses, Jacob J. considered this too in *British Sugar*. He considered that one must look at the whole context of the use, and then, provided the use was fair, he concluded that it does fall within the defence:

> "I see no reason why the provision does not permit a fair com-parison between a trade mark owner's goods and those of the defendant. The comparison would have to be honest, but provided it was and was part of a genuine indication of, for instance, quality or price, I think it would be within the provision. Such honest comparative use might well upset the mark's proprietor (proprie-tors particularly do not like price comparisons, even if they are true) but would in no way affect his mark as an indication of trade origin. Indeed the defendant would be using the proprietor's mark precisely for its proper purpose, namely to refer to his goods. I can see nothing in the stated purpose of the Directive indicating that a trade mark monopoly should extend to the point of enabling a proprietor to suppress competition by use of his trade mark in this way."[74]

13–137 There is, as yet, no authority in relation to the third category of cases. But it may be supposed that an English court would take much the same view as it has done in relation to comparative advertising in the *British Sugar* case. After all, this sort of use, provided it is fair and honest, is hardly more offensive than comparative advertising.

13–138 This reveals difficult issues in relation to both the second and third categories of cases. First, the approach taken by the court presupposes that the TM Directive was intended to permit comparative advertising, something that is far from clear.[75] Secondly, there is a distinct difference in the wording of sections 11(2)(b) and (c) of the 1994 Act. The latter specifies that a trade mark is not infringed by *the use of the trade mark* where it is *necessary* to indicate the intended purpose of a product or service. It must be assumed that the words emphasised have a meaning, for otherwise intended purpose is already covered by the former provision. Hence it appears that the Directive contemplates that it is permissible to use the trade mark only where it is *necessary* to indicate *the intended purpose of a product or service*, but not otherwise. And yet on the approach of the English court it appears to be enough that the use is fair and honest.

---

[73] *Supra*, at 299.
[74] *Supra*, at 298.
[75] See para. 13–70 *et seq.*, above, and the discussion of the Comparative Advertising Directive 97/55.

Use in accordance with honest practices

13–139 This requirement is discussed above in relation to the defence of use of own name. In this context certain additional points are worthy of note. Again the test must be objective, and it seems likely that one of the primary considerations will be whether or not the use is likely to cause confusion in practice.[76] If the use is such as to cause confusion, then it is hard to imagine a court determining that the use is honest. Where there is a valid intellectual property right, copying may be a commercial practice which is not honest. But copying *per se* is not a dishonest practice.[77]

(7) Intended purpose of a product or service

13–140 A registered trade mark is not infringed by the use of the trade mark where it is necessary to indicate the intended purpose of a product or service (in particular, as accessories or spare parts), provided the use is in accordance with honest practices in industrial or commercial matters.[78]

13–141 The provision is primarily concerned with accessories and spare parts and provides protection similar to that afforded by section 4(3)(b) of the Trade Marks Act 1938. Here, and in contrast to the other provisions of section 11(2) of the 1994 Act, the provision expressly permits the use of the trade mark of the proprietor, provided the other specified conditions are satisfied.

Use is necessary and in accordance with honest practices

13–142 The TM Directive provides no guidance as to how use which is necessary may be distinguished from that which is not necessary and, as under the old law, it may be presumed there is room for much dispute. At the very least those who wish to use such trade marks would be well advised to ensure that their use is not capable of misinterpretation and that no unnecessary prominence is given to the registered mark.[79] It has been emphasised that the purpose of the provision is not to allow use of valid trade marks except where "necessary" to indicate the purpose.[80]

---

[76] See *The European v. The Economist Newspapers* [1996] F.S.R. 431 at 446; [1998] F.S.R. 283, CA; *Philips v. Remington, supra.*

[77] *Philips v. Remington, supra.*

[78] 1994 Act, s.11(2)(c).

[79] Cases under the old Acts provide some indication of possible pitfalls. See, *e.g. Kodak v. London Stereoscopic* (1903) 20 R.P.C. 337. The case related to expressions such as "Kodak film," and the defence was that such expressions were used by the public as meaning "a film of whatever make for a Kodak camera". The defence failed on the facts. Such use would be unlikely to fare any better today. For other illustrations, see *Neostyle v. Ellam's* (1904) 21 R.P.C. 185, 569; *Yost v. Typewriter Exchange* (1902) 19 R.P.C. 422; *Gledhill v. British Perforated* (1911) 28 R.P.C. 429 at 714; *Minimax v. Moffatt* (1935) 52 R.P.C. 340; *British Northrop v. Texteam* [1974] R.P.C. 57.

[80] *Philips v. Remington, supra.* The Court of Appeal stated (at [1999] R.P.C. 824): "The purpose of this subsection is to allow such use as "This film is suitable for a Kodak camera". The purpose is not to allow use of valid trade marks except where "necessary" to indicate the purpose. The shape of a three headed rotary shaver does indicate the purpose of the product, but the particular shape is not necessary to make that indication"; see also the illustrations in the text.

Until the scope of the defence is further clarified cautious traders should also avoid the use of trade marks where the purpose of their goods could equally well be specified in some other way as, for example, by the use of a generic name or part numbers.

(1) BMW complained about a garage business which issued adver- **13–143** tisements such as "Repairs and maintenance of BMW's" and used the descriptions "BMW specialist" and "Specialised in BMW's". Held, by the European Court of Justice, where an independent trader carried out the maintenance and repair of BMW cars or was a specialist in that field, that fact could not in practice be communicated to customers without the use of the BMW mark.[81]

(2) The defendant was an approved Volvo dealer but after the **13–144** cessation of its authorised dealership began to use the word "Volvo" together with the words "Independent" and "Special- ist", but in much smaller lettering. Held, the manner of use was calculated to cause confusion and accordingly did not satisfy the requirements of the defence under section 11(2)(c) of the 1994 Act.[82]

As in the case of the previous exceptions, it is difficult to imagine any **13–145** case where the use of the trade mark results in confusion, satisfying the requirements of necessary use and being in accordance with honest practices in industrial and commercial matters. As to the latter reference is invited to paragraphs 13–125 *et seq.*, and 13–139, above.

(8) Earlier right

Section 11(3) of the 1994 Act limits the right of a proprietor to take **13–146** action against use of an earlier right. Section 11(3) provides:

> "A registered trade mark is not infringed by the use in the course of trade in a particular locality of an earlier right which applies only in that locality.
>
> For this purpose an "earlier right" means an unregistered trade mark or other sign continuously used in relation to goods or services by a person or a predecessor in title of his from a date anterior to whichever is the earlier of—
>
> (a) the use of the first-mentioned trade mark in relation to those goods or services by the proprietor or a predecessor in title of his, or
>
> (b) the registration of the first-mentioned trade mark in respect of those goods or services in the name of the proprietor or a predecessor in title of his;

---

[81] *BMW v. Deenik* [1999] E.T.M.R. 339.
[82] *Volvo v. Heritage* [2000] F.S.R. 253.

and an earlier right shall be regarded as applying in a particular locality if, or to the extent that, its use in that locality is protected by virtue of any rule of law (in particular, the law of passing off)."

13–147 This provision implements Article 6(2) of the Directive. It provides a defence in particular circumstances where the mark complained of has been used continuously from a date anterior to the earlier of the date of registration or the date of first use of the mark sued upon.[83] It has a number of elements which require consideration.

Earlier rights

13–148 Earlier rights are concerned with unregistered trade marks and signs. To qualify for protection the use of the defendant's trade mark or sign must first have been continuous in relation to the relevant goods or services. Secondly, it must have been by a person or a predecessor in title. Each of these requirements is discussed below. Thirdly, the defendant's trade mark or sign must have been used in relation to goods or services from a date prior to whichever is the earlier of the use of the claimant's trade mark in relation to those goods or services or the registration of that trade mark in respect of those goods or services, in each case by the proprietor or a predecessor in title of his. This aspect of the provision is all very well if the goods or services of the defendant are the same as those the subject of the registration or the use by the claimant or his predecessor. Under the old law this was necessarily the case. But the new law has extended the rights of proprietors over similar and even dissimilar goods and services to those the subject of the registration. In such cases it is very difficult to see how the provision can sensibly be applied, as shown by the following illustration:

> X is proprietor of the mark "Revue" registered in respect of sunglasses as of 1994 and has used the mark on a limited scale in respect of sunglasses since 1996. Y began to use the mark "Revue" for spectacle frames in 1996 and rapidly acquired a reputation and goodwill in the locality of his business. The similarity between the goods and the identity of the marks is such that there is a likelihood of confusion. X commences proceedings and Y claims to have a defence under section 11(3) of the 1994 Act. Y has used the mark in relation to spectacle frames from a date prior to the use by X of the mark in relation to spectacle frames or the registration by X of the mark in respect of spectacle frames. It is certainly arguable Y could sue a third party to prevent them from commencing business in his locality and trading off his reputation and goodwill.

Applying in a particular locality

13–149 The words of the provision appear to make it clear that it is concerned with the protection of persons who have made use of unregistered trade marks in localised areas only. The words "use in the course of trade in a

---

[83] As such it has a number of similarities to the Trade Marks Act 1938, s.7.

particular locality of an earlier right which applies only in that locality" are drawn from Article 6(2) of the TM Directive which uses the words "an earlier right which only applies in a particular locality". Such persons may not have taken the steps necessary to oppose the registration asserted against them under the relative ground of objection provided by section 5(4) of the 1994 Act. Persons who have larger businesses must take steps either to oppose any registration which might interfere with that business or seek a declaration of invalidity under section 47 of the Act. The Act and the Directive give no guidance as to what constitutes a particular locality, but it is suggested that protection would be available where the defendant is able to point to any significant geographical limitation to its business in any country in the United Kingdom.

An earlier right applies in a locality if, or to the extent that, its use in **13–150** that locality is protected by virtue of any rule of law (in particular the law of passing off). So the use by the defendant must be protected. But use is not something which can be protected of itself. A goodwill is required. Accordingly it seems that the court will require that at least some goodwill has been generated in the locality in issue. The question then arises as to the date by which that goodwill must have been established. Although no date is specified, it seems from the provision as a whole that the goodwill must have been established at the earlier of the registration or the first use by the proprietor or a predecessor in title of his.

Continuously used

No exceptions are provided, as they are under section 46 of the 1994 **13–151** Act, where there are proper reasons for non-use. Nevertheless, it is suggested that the phrase "used continuously" must be given a reasonable business interpretation, as it was under the earlier legislation. So, even if the proprietor is not at any particular time actually supplying goods himself, there must be goods in the distribution chain, or on the market. It has been said: "A man who has a trade mark may properly have regard to the state of the market and the demand for the goods; it would be absurd to suppose that he lost his trade mark by not putting more goods on the market when it was glutted."[84] There must be more than occasional use of the mark, though not necessarily "every week or even every month."[85]

It is also suggested that the use must be genuine commercial use and not use effected purely for the purpose of securing a defence under this provision or its predecessor.[86]

---

[84] *Per* Chitty J. in *Mouson v. Boehm* (1884) 26 Ch.D. 398.
[85] *Smith Bartlett v. British Pure Oil* (1934) 51 R.P.C. 157 at 163.
[86] See, *Electrux* (1954) 71 R.P.C. 23, CA; *Nerit* [1982] F.S.R. 82, CA; *cf. Concord* [1987] F.S.R. 209.

Predecessor in title

13–152 These words appear to have been carried forward from section 7 of the 1938 Act. As such it may be concluded they presuppose a valid transfer of the mark from the previous user. Assignments of unregistered trade marks are addressed in Chapter 12.

(9) Miscellaneous and general defences

Personal estoppel

13–153 With the exception of the several matters which are considered below, there is nothing peculiar to the law of trade marks to determine what agreements, or what circumstances constituting a personal estoppel, will prevent a claimant from suing a particular defendant for infringement (or in passing off).

Uncandid conduct

13–154 In *Maxwell v. Hogg*[87] the defendants had received and published for reward from the claimants, advertisements of an intended new magazine, bearing the title of a magazine which they were themselves preparing to publish, without warning the claimants of their own intention; and this uncandid conduct was held to be sufficient ground for dismissing the cross-suit of the defendants for an injunction to prevent the claimants using the name; *cf. Electrolux v. Electrix* (1954) 71 R.P.C. at pages 29–30, CA, where the claimants deliberately delayed replying to a letter asking them to agree to cancellation of their mark until they had used it for long enough to prevent its removal from the Register for non-use; the claimants nevertheless won.

Use outside registration

13–155 It is no ground of estoppel that the claimant extends the use of his mark to goods in respect of which it is not registered.[88]

Acquiescence and laches

13–156 The law on this subject used to be both rather technical and rather obscure, as is illustrated for example, by the "five probanda" referred to in *Willmott v. Barber*.[89] It is now clear, however, that the relevant test is now the much broader one appearing in *Habib Bank v. Habib Bank* [1982] R.P.C. 1, which is whether in all the circumstances it would be unconscionable to allow the claimant to maintain his claim. It is, however, clear that the matters which fall to be considered include the factors identified in the old cases: whether the proprietor induced or

---

[87] (1867) L.R. 2 Ch. 307.
[88] *Jay v. Ladler* (1888) 40 Ch.D. 649; 6 R.P.C. 136 at 139.
[89] (1880) 15 Ch.D. 97.

encouraged the defendant's behaviour, or represented to him that he was entitled so to act, the passage of time, reliance by and detriment to the defendant and so on.

Mere failure to sue, however, without some positive act of encourage- **13–157** ment, is not in general enough to give a defence.[90] A defendant who infringes knowing of the claimants mark can hardly complain if he is later sued upon it,[91] nor is a defendant who starts to infringe without searching the Register of Trade Marks in any better position than if he had searched and so learned of the claimant's mark.[92] Acts of the proprietor done in ignorance of the infringement,[93] or even done without his own registration in mind,[94] will not amount to acquiescence. A defence of estoppel by acquiescence is to be distinguished from a defence that by delay the mark has become *publici juris*.[95]

Delay does not bar the right of action

In general mere delay after knowledge of infringement does not deprive **13–158** the registered proprietor of a trade mark of his statutory rights or of the appropriate remedy for the enforcement of these rights.[96] But inordinate delay can exceptionally provide a defence,[97] and can also form a major ingredient in a case of acquiescence.[98]

1. The claimants used the expression "British Sherry" (and like expressions) for over 100 years before the defendants (representing the producers of "real" sherry, i.e. a wine from the Jerez district of Spain) complained. The claimants were granted a declaration that they were entitled to continue such use, despite the finding that the name "sherry" was not apt to describe the claimants' products. Cross J. held that it would be "altogether unjust to allow the

---

[90] See below, "delay."
[91] *Electrolux v. Electrix, supra,* 71 R.P.C. 23 at 40, *per* Jenkins L.J.
[92] *ibid.*
[93] *ibid.,* and see generally *De Bussche v. Alt* (1878) 8 Ch.D. 286; *Willmott v. Barber* (1881) 17 Ch.D. 772. *Habib, supra,* can hardly be authority for the contrary proposition.
[94] *Electrolux v. Electrix, supra, per* Jenkins L.J. at 41.
[95] *Bollinger v. Goldwell* [1971] R.P.C. 412 (a defence that a mark has become *publici juris* is open to any defendant; a defence of acquiescence depends upon the facts relating to each defendant.).
[96] *per* Jenkins L.J. in *Electrolux v. Electrix* (1954) 71 R.P.C. 23 at 41. As to delay of two years, see *Fullwood v. Fullwood* (1878) 9 Ch.D. 176 at 178, approved by Harman J. in *Manus* (1948) 65 R.P.C. 329; and see *L.C. & D. Ry. v. Bull* (1882) 47 L.T. 413; *Leibig's v. Chemists' Co-operative* (1896) 13 R.P.C. 635, 736, a trade name and passing-off case; *Poiret v. Jules Poiret* (1920) 37 R.P.C. 177 (a trade name case). See also *Vidal Dyes v. Levinstein* (1912) 29 R.P.C. 245, where it is clearly stated that in the case of a patent, mere delay in enforcing rights did not affect the legal position.
[97] *Vine Products v. Mackenzie* [1969] R.P.C. 1.
[98] *Cluett, Peabody v. McIntyre Hogg* ("Arrow" shirts) [1958] R.P.C. 335 at 354. There had been nearly thirty years' delay; and it would seem that Upjohn J. was neither willing to allow the proprietors to use after all that time, nor happy to rest his judgment on delay alone.

defendants to rely on the ignorance of their lawyers, excusable though it was, as to the law on the point in question before the decision in the Spanish Champagne case." *Vine Products v. Mackenzie* [1969] R.P.C. 1 at p. 26.

2. The defendants traded for some twelve years (about half of which were interrupted by the war) under their trade mark before the claimants sued. Held, that in the absence of some positive representation from the claimants there was no defence of delay or acquiescence: *Eletrolux v. Electrix* (1954) 71 R.P.C. 23.

Delay may modify the relief granted

13–159 Unexplained delay that offers no absolute defence may effect the nature of the relief granted. It may cause the court to refuse an interim injunction, however.[99] There would appear to be no instance of refusal of a final injunction for mere delay, and in princple, such refusal would seem inappropriate. A short stay may be appropriate, though:

> Where there had been over a year's delay in bringing the action, the injunction was stayed for six weeks to allow the defendant time to make the arrangements necessary for the alterations of his trade name required by it: *Grant v. Levitt* ("Globe Furnishing Co.") (1901) 18 R.P.C. 361, C.A. It may, of course, be possible for the claimant to show that the delay was reasonable.[1]

Deceptive trade mark and fraudulent trade

13–160 The court may refuse to interfere to protect the use of a deceptive trade mark or to assist a trader who is using his mark for the purposes of a fraudulent trade. This principle was well established in the Court of Chancery, and the maximum *ex turpi causa non oritur actio* is a rule of law. There is, however, a little modern authority on this matter, and the older cases are not very clearly related to the present law of registered marks. The following points, however, would seem sustainable.

13–161 It is of course a defence to an action for infringement, that the mark sued upon is invalid; and one ground of invalidity is that the mark is liable to mislead under section 46.[2] In practical terms, this may deal with nearly all situations likely to arise. The other branch of this proposition, concerned with claimants suing to protect a fraudulent trade, is discussed in para. 13–166, below. In so far as the claimant seeks equitable relief, an injunction in particular, this is always in some degree discretionary.

---

[99] See Chap. 18.

[1] As random intances of explanations of delay, that the courts would seem to have accepted, see *Daniel & Arter v. Whitehouse* [1898] 1 Ch. 685; 15 R.P.C. 134 (claimants thought infringement had ceased); *Rowlands. Mitchell* (1896) 13 R.P.C. 457; (1897) 14 R.P.C. 37, but not reported on this point: infringer not worth suing; *Young v. Holt* (1948) 65 R.P.C. 25 (some four months' delay whilst claimants made certain of the facts; account of profits granted, and not limited to the period after the claimants first complained to the defendants).

[2] See Chap. 7.

Collateral misrepresentation

1. Where the false description was collateral and did not appear in the **13–162** mark in question, and the claimant's trade was not shown to be fraudulent, the court decided that the claimant's legal right of action in respect of the defendant's infringement was not barred, and that he was consequently entitled to an injunction and costs: *Ford v. Foster* (1872) L.R. 7 Ch. 611 ("Eureka Shirts").

2. The following are some miscellaneous examples of case where objections to the claimant's case on the ground of collateral misrepresentation failed: title of a magazine protected, although the magazine purported to be written by someone othere than the author[3]; similar cases with regard to songs[4]; "Holloway's pills and ointment" protected, although the claimant called himself Professor Holloway without warrant, and published exaggerated commendations of his pills[5]; an objection on the ground that the claimants retained a brass plate on the door of their business premises, bearing their predecessor's name , overruled[6]; the claimants alleged that after registration of the mark "Kit" for coffee, fraudulent misrepresentions had been made, by the defendant's predecessors in title, that "Kit" coffee essence was the same as the claimants' "Camp" coffee essence[7]; held that, even if the misrepresentations should be proved, being extraneous to the mark, the use of the mark by the defendants was not necessarily deceptive.

False assertion of registration

Under section 95 it is a penal offence to describe a trade mark as **13–163** registered when it is not. Such a misrepresentation has been sufficient to deprive the proprietor of a mark of an interlocutory injunction in a passing off action.[8] It has been submitted that relief should also be refused at trial, but there is no statutory provision to this effect.[9]

"Trade mark"

The description of an unregistered trade mark as a "trade mark" is no **13–164** offence within section 95, and if the mark is, in fact, as it may be, a trade mark acquired by user, such description is not by itself a misrepresentation.

---

[3] *Hogg v. Kirby* (1803) 8 Ves. 215; 7 R.R. 30.
[4] *Chappell v. Sheard* (1855) 2 K. & J. 117; *Chappell v. Davidson* (1855) 2 K. & J. 123; 8 De G.M. & G. 1.
[5] *Holloway v. Holloway* (1850) 13 Beav. 209.
[6] *Hudson v. Osborne* (1869) 39 LJ.Ch. 79.
[7] *Paterson v. Kit Coffee* (1910) 27 R.P.C. 594.
[8] *Johnson v. Puffer* (1930) 47 R.P.C. 95.
[9] In *Sen Sen v. Britten* [1899] 1 Ch. 692; 16 R.P.C. 137, Stirling J. said, "Of course, if the plaintiffs are brought within the terms of that section they must be denied relief." See also 6th ed. for earlier cases.

Misrepresentation abandoned before, or commencing after, action brought

13–165 A misrepresentation which has been corrected and abandoned before the action is no bar.[10] The same rule is said to apply to one adopted after the commencment of the action.[11] It is submitted that it can make no differnce that the frauds commenced after the action was begun. The objection is that claimant and his business are, when the court takes cognisance of the matter, unworthy of its protection or assistance.

Fraudulent trade

13–166 Where the claimant uses the trade mark in aid of a fraudulent trade, the rule which bars his action is clear but even so, it may be proper to grant in injunction whose purpose is to put an end to the fraud.[12]

13–167 A plea that the claimant made a practice of selling by short weight failed because it was not supported by the evidence.[13] A pianoforte tutor, described as "600th edition, specially revised by Hemy," although the musician referred to had not revised the work for ten years, was held not to be misleading, evidence being given that in the trade an issued of 250 was called an edition.[14] A trade in German cigars sold in boxes bearing a label with the words La Pureza (an old Havana brand), Habana, Ramon, Romedo and additional labels with other words and a sham address in Spanish was held to be fraudulent, the whole get-up being described by Bowen L.J. as "an elaborate concatenation of pictorial lies" intended to pass off the cigars as made in Havana, although evidence was given that the name "Havana" in the cigar trade indicates the shape of the cigar only.[15] The sale of English cigars under a label bearing the word Habana, in boxes marked "British Manufacture," was held not to be fraudulent in the absence of evidence that the claimants represented that their cigars were made in Havana.[16] The application of the name "California Syrup of Figs" to an aperient drug in which fig syrup was used as a flavouring only was held not to be a misrepresentation.[17] In another case[18] the claimants advertisement falsely

---

[10] *Benedictus v. Sullivan* (1895) 12 R.P.C. 25.

[11] See *Siegert v. Findlater* (1878) 7 Ch.D. 801 ("Angostura Bitters"); *Ford v. Foster* (1872) L.R. 7 Ch. 611; *Faulder v. Rushton* (1903) 20 R.P.C. 477 at 489.

[12] This would seem to be the implication of *Coles v. Need* [1934] A.C. 84 at 89–90 (P.C., Australia). Note the further implication that the bar to the action in these cases is not absolute but discretionary. This, a passing-off case, seems to be the most modern authority on the point.

[13] *Guinea Coal (Lee) v. (Haley)* (1869) L.R. 5 Ch. 155.

[14] *Metzler v. Wood* (1878) 8 Ch.D. 606.

[15] *Newman v. Pinto* (1887) 4 R.P.C. 508; *cf. Fuente* [1891] 2 Ch. 166; 8 R.P.C. 214 and *Dexter* [1893] 2 Ch. 262; 10 R.P.C. 269.

[16] *Hargreaves v. Freeman* [1891] 3 Ch. 39; (1891) 8 R.P.C. 237; *cf. Benedictus v. Sullivan*, above, where a Spanish look about the box, and the words "Fabrica de Tobaccos de la Vuetia Abago," was held not to be a representation of foreign manufacture in the face of the words "Regalia Britannica," "Londini"; and see *R. v. Butcher* (1909) 99 L.T. 622; 24 T.L.R. 797 and *Van der Leeuw* [1912] 1 Ch. 40; 28 R.P.C. 708.

[17] *California Fig Syrup v. Taylor's* (1897) 14 R.P.C. 341, Kekewich J.; reversed on appeal on another point, 14 R.P.C. 564.

[18] *Bile Bean v. Davidson* (1905) 22 R.P.C. 553; 23 R.P.C. 725.

stated that the basis of their Bile Beans was an Australian herb discovered by an eminent scientist, whose name was given. There was no such person, and the story of the discovery given in the advertisement was an invention. It was held that the misrepresentation was not a collateral one but affected the very essence of the article offered for sale.

F. Collective and certification marks

The provisions of the 1994 Act relating to infringement apply to **13–168** collective and certification marks too, subject to the limitations and provisions of Schedules 1 and 2 of the Act which apply to collective and certification marks respectively. These Schedules contain particular provisions which reflect the special nature of these marks. In this section we consider those provisions which relate to infringement.

Limitations on infringement provisions—indications of geographical origin

A proprietor of a collective or certification mark is not entitled to **13–169** prevent a third party from using a sign or indication which may serve in trade to designate the geographical origin of the goods or services where the use is in accordance with honest practices in industrial or commercial matters.[19] This limitation reflects the opportunity to register such marks which might otherwise offend section 3(1)(c) of the 1994 Act.[20] The requirement that the use be in accordance with honest practices recurs throughout the infringement provisions, and it is to be expected that it will be interpreted consistently. Accordingly reference is invited to the discussion in paragraphs, 13–125 *et seq.*, 13–139 and 13–142 *et seq.* above.

Infringement: rights of authorised users

There are particular provisions extending the rights given by collective **13–170** and certification marks to authorised users.[21] Some are common to collective and certification marks. Others apply only to collective marks.

The common provisions apply to authorised users certain sections of **13–171** the 1994 Act, just as they apply to a licensee of a trade mark. The sections so applied are section 10(5) (the authorised application of the mark to certain material), section 19(2) (order as to disposal of infringing goods, material or articles) and section 89 (request to Commissioners of Customs and Excise for the prohibition of importation of infringing goods, material or articles).[22] In addition it is provided that in infringement proceedings brought by the proprietor any loss suffered or likely to be suffered by authorised users is to be taken into account and the

---

[19] Scheds 1 and 2, para. 3(2).
[20] Scheds 1 and 2, para. 3(1).
[21] These are the persons specified in the regulations governing the use of the marks.
[22] Sched. 1, para. 11; Sched. 2, para. 13.

court may give appropriate directions as to the extent to which the claimant is to hold any proceeds on behalf of such users.[23]

13–172   In the case of collective marks, but not in the case of certification marks, and subject to any agreement to the contrary, an authorised user may call upon the proprietor to take action in respect of any matter which affects his interests and if he fails to do so, may take action himself, just as in the case of licensees.[24]

G. Transitional provisions

13–173 Existing registrations (whether registered in Part A or B of the register kept under the 1938 Act) were transferred on commencement of the 1994 Act to the Register kept under the Act and have effect for the purposes of infringement as if registered under the Act.[25]

13–174   In general, the scheme provided by the transitional provisions was that the old law continued to apply to infringements committed prior to commencement and the new law applies in relation to acts committed after commencement.[26] Hence sections 9 to 12 of the Act (effects of registration) applies as from the date of commencement and section 14 (action for infringement) applies in relation to acts committed after commencement subject to the saving referred to below.

13–175   The saving provides that it is not an infringement of:

(1) an existing registered mark, or
(2) a registered trade mark of which the distinctive elements are the same or substantially the same as an existing registered mark and which is registered for the same goods or services,

to continue after commencement any use which did not amount to infringement of the existing registered trade mark under the old law.

13–176   It will be noted that the saving is limited in a number of respects. First, the registered mark alleged to be infringed must be an existing registered trade mark or a registered trade mark the distinctive elements of which are the same or substantially the same as an existing registered mark which is registered for the same goods or services. This will protect a defendant against a claimant who applies to register the same mark again and alleges infringement of the second registration. But it will not protect a defendant against a claimant who was using the mark before the Act came into force but did not secure any registration until after it came into force.

13–177   Secondly, the use must have been continuous. This was a concept familiar under the 1938 Act.[27] It is suggested that the courts will give this

[23] Sched. 2, para. 12(6); Sched. 3, para. 14.
[24] Sched. 1, para. 12(1)–(5).
[25] Sched. 3, para. 2.
[26] Sched. 3, para. 4.
[27] *e.g.* the 1938 Act, s.7.

requirement a reasonable business interpretation. So if, for example, the defendant supplies customers periodically to meet their requirements, then the use would nevertheless be continuous.[28]

Thirdly, it seems at least arguable that the continuous use must be by **13–178** the defendant, not, for example, by a licensee or a predecessor in title, of the same mark and not variations of it and in relation to the same goods or services. All of these could be said to be inherent in the requirement "to continue after commencement any use".

Finally an interesting question may arise in relation to old Part B **13–179** marks. Section 5(2) of the 1938 Act provided that in particular circumstances no injunction or other relief should be granted to a plaintiff if the defendant established, to the satisfaction of the court, that the use, of which the plaintiff complained, was not likely to deceive or cause confusion or to be taken as indicating a connection in the course of trade between the goods and some person having the right as proprietor or registered user to use the trade mark. A similar provision applied to services. It seems at least arguable that in such a case the use would nevertheless have amounted to an infringement, the Act merely providing a bar to the grant of relief, and that accordingly the transitional saving provision would not apply. It is submitted, however, that a court would be reluctant to reach such a conclusion.

3. Further rights conferred by the 1994 Act

The Paris Convention and TRIPS

The 1994 Act introduced into the law for the first time important **13–180** provisions based upon the provisions of the Paris Convention.[29] More recently the Act has been amended and modified in pursuance of the United Kingdom's obligations under the WTO Agreement and the Agreement on Trade Related Aspects of Intellectual Property Rights (TRIPS) which is an integral part of the WTO Agreement. Specifically for the purposes of this section it is to be noted that the provisions of sections 55 to 60 of the Act which are discussed below have been amended to extend their scope to include the WTO Agreement.[30] TRIPS provides, so far as material, that members shall comply with Article 6 of the Paris Convention and that nothing in the Agreement shall derogate from existing obligations that members may have to each other under the Paris Convention.

Protection of well known marks under Article 6bis of the Paris Convention and TRIPS

The 1994 Act confers a separate right to protection on the owners of **13–181** well-known trade marks under the Paris Convention and TRIPS. Section 56 of the Act gives effect to Article 6 bis of the Paris Convention and to

---

[28] See, *e.g. Mouson v. Boehm* (1884) 26 Ch.D. 398 and *Smith Bartlett v. British Pure Oil* (1934) 51 R.P.C. 163.
[29] The Paris Convention is set out in App. 21.
[30] S.I. 1999 No. 1899. The relevant provisions of TRIPS are set out in App. 22.

Article 16 of TRIPS so far as it refers to the protection of well-known trade marks.[31] A number of matters call for consideration; first, the necessary qualification for the right and secondly, the right and remedy provided and defences to it.

Qualification for the right

13–182   The protection is provided to the proprietor of a trade mark which is entitled to protection under the Paris Convention or TRIPS as a well-known trade mark.[32] Such a mark is defined as a mark which is well-known in the United Kingdom as being the mark of a person who is a national of a Convention country,[33] or who is domiciled in, or has a real and effective industrial or commercial establishment in, a Convention country, whether or not that person carries on any business, or has any goodwill in the United Kingdom.[34]

13–183   The latter words are of considerable significance and make this provision an important one. It is not a requirement that the proprietor has any goodwill or business in the United Kingdom. Accordingly, he need have no customers here. This is in contrast to the cause of action in passing off which calls for goodwill as a fundamental requirement.[35] All that is required is that the mark is "well-known" in the United Kingdom. No guidance is given in the Paris Convention as to what this means. TRIPS, on the other hand, provides that in determining whether a trade mark is well-known, members shall take account of the knowledge of the trade mark in the relevant sector of the public, including knowledge in the member concerned, which has been obtained as a result of the promotion of the trade mark. It is to be expected that, with this limited guidance, the provision will be construed as a matter of ordinary language so to require that the mark is well established amongst, and familiar to, the interested public and so, in short, that the mark is famous. The original wording of the Paris Convention contemplates the use of the mark by the proprietor and by the other party in relation to "goods".[36] TRIPS provides that Article 6*bis* of the Paris Convention shall apply, *mutatis mutandis*, to services. In any event the 1994 Act is not so limited, providing as it does its own definition of a well-known trade mark and the extent of the right in respect of *goods or services* where the use is likely to cause confusion[37]

---

[31] Art. 6*bis* is set out in full in App. 21. It will be seen that there are other aspects of the provision, such as the prohibitions on registration, which are effectively implemented elsewhere in the Act. The relevant provisions of TRIPS are set out in annex . . .

[32] 1994 Act, s.56(2).

[33] s.56 defines the Paris Convention for the purposes of the Act as the 1883 Convention and any revisions or amendments to it. A Convention country is also defined as any party to the Convention other than the U.K. All Members of TRIPS are now included.

[34] s.56(1).

[35] See the full discussion in Chap. 14.

[36] It uses the words: "a mark . . . used for identical or similar goods".

[37] s.56(2), and see below.

There are a number or ways by which the proprietor may achieve **13–184** qualifying status. In the case of an individual he may be a national of or domiciled in a Convention or member territory.[38] In the case of a body corporate or other legal entity, it may be established under the laws of that territory. Alternatively, in either case, it is sufficient if he has a real and effective industrial or commercial base in a Convention or member country.

Extent of the right and remedy

The proprietor of such a well-known trade mark is entitled to restrain **13–185** by injunction the use in the United Kingdom of a trade mark which, or the essential part of which, is identical or similar to his mark, in relation to identical or similar goods or services, where the use is likely to cause confusion.[39] As in the case of the infringement provisions of section 10(2) of the 1994 Act, the provision calls for a consideration of the extent of the similarity of the goods or services in issue and of the likelihood of confusion. The traditional approach in England would have called for a consideration of these matters separately so that the first step would have been to consider whether the goods or services in issue were similar or not. But it is suggested that consistency with the now established approach under section 10 and the TM Directive will demand that the likelihood of confusion be assessed globally taking into account all relevant factors, including the degree of similarity of the marks in issue, the degree of similarity between the relevant goods or services, the likely perception of the marks in the minds of the average consumer of the goods or services and the degree of distinctiveness of the well-known mark.[40] Nevertheless similarity between the goods or services does still seem to be a threshold requirement, as in the case of infringement.[41]

There appears to be no requirement that the use of the mark **13–186** complained of has damaged or is likely to cause damage to the proprietor of the well-known mark. In this respect the right is again different from passing off, which not only requires the claimant to establish damage or, in the case of a *quia timet* action, the likelihood of damage, but also that the damage is the result of the misrepresentation and confusion. Correspondingly the right provided under section 57 is

---

[38] "National" and "domicile" are not defined and it seems may depend upon the law of that territory. So, for example, British nationality is used to refer to the various forms of British national status and comprises, *inter alia*, the terms British citizen and British subject: see, for a full discussion, Halsbury's Laws, Vol. 4(2); a person is, in general, domiciled in the country in which he is considered by English law to have his permanent home (although a person may sometimes be domiciled in a country although he does not have his permanent home in it); see Dicey & Morris, *Conflict of Laws* (13th ed. Sweet & Maxwell, 2000), Chap. 6.
[39] 1994 Act, s.56(2).
[40] See paras 13–51 and 13–52, *supra*.
[41] See para. 13–55, *supra*.

to an injunction only[42] and there appears to be no right to claim damages or an account of profits.

13–187   The right is expressly subject to the provisions of section 48. This makes provision in the case where the proprietor of an earlier trade mark or right has acquiesced for a continuous period of five years in the use of a registered trade mark in the United Kingdom, being aware of that use. Reference is invited to paragraph 13–118 *et seq.* above for a consideration of that provision. In this context, it is to be noted that it is not clear if the defence applies only in circumstances where the mark complained of by the proprietor of the well-known mark has actually been registered. It is suggested, however, that this is not the intention behind section 56 and that such is made reasonably clear by the way section 48 is imported by reference and the use of the words "effect of acquiescence by proprietor of earlier trade mark". On this basis the defence would be made out where the proprietor of the well-known mark has taken no action for a continuous period of five years in the use of that mark in the United Kingdom when he was aware of that use.

13–188   Section 56(3) provides a saving in respect of the continuation of bona fide[43] use of a trade mark begun before the commencement of the section.[44]

National emblems and emblems of international organisations

13–189   Sections 57 and 58 of the 1994 Act provide protection in respect of flags, armorial bearings, state emblems, official signs and hallmarks of Paris Convention or TRIPS member countries and emblems, names and abbreviations of international intergovernmental organisations. Such signs must be notified under the provisions of section 59 and then may not be registered without the authorisation of the competent authority of the Convention or member country or the international organisation in question. These matters are considered in detail in Chapter 7. For the purposes of this chapter it is important to note that where the authorisation of the competent authority of the Convention or member country or international organisation would be required for registration of a trade mark, then that authority or organisation is entitled to restrain by injunction any use of that mark in the United Kingdom without its authorisation.[45] In the latter case, no rights are afforded against a person whose bona fide use of the trade mark began before January 4, 1962.[46]

---

[42] And, presumably, and at the discretion of the court, an order for delivery up or destruction to support the injunction.
[43] For the meaning of this term, see *Baume v. Moore* [1957] R.P.C. 459; [1958] R.P.C. 226, CA; and the 12th ed. of this book, para. 15–33.
[44] October 31, 1994.
[45] ss.57(6) and 58(4) respectively.
[46] s.58(5).

Acts of an agent or representative

An agent or representative of any person who is a proprietor of a mark **13–190**
in any Convention or member country[47] may restrain any use of the
mark in the United Kingdom which is not authorised by him[48] and
unless the agent or representative justifies his action.[49] This is an
important provision and it is designed to restrain an agent or representative from hi-jacking the mark of a foreign principal. It forms part of
a set of provisions which also prohibit the registration of such a mark
which is not authorised by the proprietor.[50] No injunction shall be
granted in respect of a use in which the overseas proprietor has
acquiesced for a continuous period of three or more years.[51]

Unauthorised use of Royal arms

Section 99 of the 1994 Act prohibits the use, in connection with any **13–191**
business of the Royal arms or any arms closely resembling them,
without the authority of Her Majesty and in such a way as to be likely to
lead to the belief that the use is duly authorised. So also no one, without
the authority of Her Majesty or a member of the Royal family, may use
in connection with any business any device, emblem or title in such a
manner as to be calculated to lead to the belief that he is employed by,
or supplies goods or services to, Her Majesty or that member of the
Royal family.[52] This is a provision which prevents unauthorised use of
Royal warrants. An action may be taken to restrain the offending use by
any person who is in fact authorised to use the arms, device, emblem or
title in question or by the Lord Chamberlain or any person authorised
by him.[53]

---

[47] Defined by the 1994 Act, s.55, as any country, other than the U.K., which is a party to the
Paris Convention and any revision or amendment to it and any member of TRIPS. It
appears that it is not a requirement that the mark is registered in the Convention or
member country of origin, although it seems that it must be in use and properly so by
the person claiming to be the proprietor if he is to be so regarded. Although s.60 is not
specifically referred to in S.I. 1999 No. 1899, s.60 refers to "Convention country" as
defined in s.55(1)(b) and that has been amended by S.I. 1999 No. 1899 to refer to the
WTO Agreement as well as the Paris Convention.
[48] s.60(4).
[49] s.60(5).
[50] s.60(2) and (3).
[51] s.60(6). No mention is made here of knowledge of the use, in contrast to the similar
provisions in respect of acquiescence in s.48. It seems that the difference is probably
attributable to the different origins of the provisions. Section 48 implements the TM
Directive, Art. 9, which expressly refers to knowledge. Section 60(6), on the other hand,
implements Art. 6*septies* of the Paris Convention which provides that "Domestic
legislation may provide an equitable time limit within which the proprietor of the trade
mark must exercise the rights provided for in this Article". Accordingly it is suggested
that a court would require knowledge of the offending use despite the absence of any
express mention of it.
[52] s.99(1) and (2).
[53] s.99(4).

4. Community trade marks

A. Introduction

13–192 This section deals with the issues arising in respect of the infringement of Community trade marks registered pursuant to Council Regulation 40/94 of December 20, 1993 (the CTM Regulation).[54] Such marks have a unitary character and equal effect throughout the Community. The use of a Community trade mark may not be prohibited, nor may it be revoked or declared invalid save in respect of the whole Community. Accordingly the effective working of the Community trade mark system will require a measure of harmonisation of the approaches of the courts of different countries on a scale not seen before.

13–193 The fundamental provisions concerning infringement are contained in Section 2 of Title 2 of the CTM Regulation which makes provision in respect of the "Effects of Community Trade Marks". Article 14 provides that these effects are governed solely by the CTM Regulation but that in other respects, infringement of a Community trade mark is to be governed by the provisions of national law relating to infringement of national trade marks and in accordance with the provisions of Title X of the CTM Regulation. We discuss these further below and, in particular, the respects in which they differ from the infringement provisions relating to national registrations.

13–194 Matters of jurisdiction and procedure in legal actions relating to Community trade marks are dealt with in Articles 90 to 104 of the CTM Regulation. Importantly these make provision in respect of the application of the Brussels Convention[55] and for the designation by Member States of national courts and tribunals of first and second instance as Community trade mark courts.[56] Such courts have exclusive jurisdiction for all infringement actions, for actions for declarations of non-infringement and for actions for revocation and for declarations of invalidity.[57] In England and Wales and Northern Ireland the High Court has been so designated and in Scotland the Court of Session.[58] The Court of Appeal has been designated the court of second instance.

13–195 As explained further in chapter 18, in most circumstances where a Community trade mark court has jurisdiction it extends to acts of infringement committed or threatened within the territory of any of the Member States.[59] This makes a Community trade mark especially valuable.

In the final part of this section we address the infringement aspects of Community Collective marks.

---

[54] See App. 9.
[55] Arts 90, 93 and 94. There are also specific provisions in Art. 105 dealing with cases involving Community and national trade marks. The application of these provisions and of the Brussels Convention is discussed further in Chap. 18, relating to proceedings.
[56] Art. 91.
[57] Art. 92.
[58] Reg. 6 of the CTM Regulations 1996, reproduced in App. 14.
[59] Art. 94.

B. Rights conferred by a Community trade mark

The general rights conferred by a Community trade mark in respect of **13–196** the use of a sign which is the same as or similar to the trade mark are set out in Article 9(1) of the CTM Regulation. This mirrors the provisions of section 10 of the 1994 Act and Article 5(1) and (2) of the TM Directive in relation to national trade marks. So also Article 9(2) of the CTM Regulation identifies specific activities involving the use of the mark which may be prevented and which correspond to those identified in Article 5(2) of the TM Directive. Article 12 of the Regulation limits the effects of a Community trade mark in like manner to Article 6 of the TM Directive. Accordingly, it is to be expected that in the general case the discussion in section 2, above of the various categories of infringement and their different requirements is equally applicable to Community trade marks. There are, however, potentially important differences too and these we discuss in the following sections.

Comparative advertising

The CTM Regulation contains no provision expressly dealing with the **13–197** use of a Community trade mark in a comparative advertisement. In particular it has no provision corresponding to section 10(6) of the 1994 Act which regulates the position in the United Kingdom in relation to national trade marks and expressly permits the use of a national trade mark in a comparative advertisement unless the use is otherwise than in accordance with honest practices and would, without due cause, take unfair advantage of, or be detrimental to, the distinctive character or repute of the trade mark. Accordingly, it seems the position in relation to a Community trade mark must be considered as a matter of principle and of the proper construction of Article 9(1) of the Regulation.

When a trade mark of a competitor is used in an honest comparative **13–198** advertisement which does not mislead, it is almost invariably used in a form which is identical to that the subject of the registration and, at least in one sense, in relation to the goods or services of the competitor which are identical to those in respect of which it is registered.[60] This is the consequence of comparing the goods or services being advertised to those the subject of the registered trade mark. The issue which must be determined is whether this activity offends against Article 9(1) of the Directive.

Article 9(1)(a) confers on the proprietor exclusive rights therein and, **13–199** in particular, the right to prevent third parties, not having his consent, from using in the course of trade any sign identical with the Community trade mark in relation to goods or services in respect of which it is registered. On the face of it that is exactly what the comparative advertiser is doing and so rendering it at least arguable that there is infringement.

---

[60] See the discussion of comparative advertising in relation to national registrations in paras 13–73 et seq., supra.

13–200   Nevertheless this may be considered a most unattractive result. After all the advertiser has done no more than use the mark of the competitor in relation to the competitor's own goods or services and for the purpose of indicating the origin of those goods or services in the competitor, that is to say in a manner which is entirely consistent with the essential function of the trade mark. A number of arguments may be deployed to avoid a finding of infringement in such a case. These are discussed below. It is suggested that the first or second is the most attractive for the reasons we elaborate.

13–201   First, it may be contended that the use of a competitor's trade mark in a comparative advertisement simply does not fall within the scope of Article 9 at all, upon its proper construction. Article 9(1) is concerned with the use by a person of a trade mark in relation to goods or services which he himself is dealing with in the course of trade. As such he is using the mark for the purposes of distinguishing his own goods or services. This interpretation is consistent with the provisions of Article 9(2) which, so far as subparagraphs (a) to (c) are concerned, is clearly only concerned with goods or services in which that person is himself dealing. Subparagraph (d), namely the use of the sign on business papers and in advertising, should, it may be argued, be construed in a like manner. A person who uses a trade mark of a rival in a comparative advertisement is not using the mark for the purposes of distinguishing any goods or services in which he himself is dealing.[61]

13–202   Secondly, and on the assumption that the use of the trade mark *does* fall within the scope of Article 9 then, it may be contended, use in accordance with honest practices is protected by the provisions of Article 12(b).[62]

13–203   Thirdly, it may be argued that the competitor must be taken to have *consented* to the use of his mark in relation to his own goods and services and which he has marketed under the mark. As a matter of English law it is well established that, absent an agreement to the contrary, a person who purchases an article is free to do with it what he will and that includes the freedom to market it and sell it on to others under the mark.[63] Accordingly, it may be argued, he has consented to the use of

---

[61] This argument has the added benefit of introducing a measure of consistency with Art. 5 of the TM Directive and s.10(6) of the U.K. Act. The provisions of the Directive, Art. 5(1) and (2), are in like terms to the CTM Regulation, Art. 9(1). Art. 5(5) of the Directive provides that the earlier paragraphs shall not affect provisions in Member States relating to the protection against the use of a sign other than for the purposes of distinguishing goods or services, where use of that sign without due cause takes unfair advantage of, or is detrimental to, the distinctive character or repute of the trade mark. This provision appears to be the foundation of the 1994 Act, s.10(6) and it has no counterpart in the CTM Regulation.

[62] Corresponding to the TM Directive, Art. 6(1)(d) and implemented by the 1994 Act, s.11(2)(b). In *British Sugar*, Jacob J. considered that the provision was apt for this purpose, see the discussion in para. 13–136, *supra*.

[63] *Betts v. Wilmott* (1871) 6 Ch. App. 239; *National Phonographic Co. of Australia v. Walter T Menck* [1911] A.C. 337; *Zino Davidoff v. A&G Imports* [1999] R.P.C. 631, an interim decision on the issue of international exhaustion and now the subject of a reference to the ECJ.

his mark in relation to his own goods or services and in any way which is not misleading.[64]

Fourthly, in cases involving *goods* marketed under a trade mark in the **13–204** Community, the rights of the proprietor in the United Kingdom are curtailed by Article 13 of the Regulation, which provides that a Community trade mark shall not entitle the proprietor to prohibit its use in relation to goods which have been put on the market in the Community under that trade mark by him or with his consent.[65] Accordingly, it may be argued, it cannot be an infringement to use such a registered mark in relation to such goods in a comparative advertisement.

Neither the third nor the fourth argument is wholly satisfactory. The **13–205** former relies upon a general inference of consent and might be avoided by express words in the agreement of sale to the contrary. The latter relies upon a provision which only deals expressly with the position in relation to goods and, moreover, the provision is obviously primarily directed against attempts to prevent subsequent dealings in and commercialisation of such goods.

Joint liability

There is no express provision in the CTM Regulation addressing the **13–206** issue of joint liability for infringement. This position is to be contrasted with section 10(5) of the 1994 Act which makes provision in respect of materials intended to be used for labelling, packaging as business papers or for advertising.[66] As in the case of national trade marks, a person who becomes involved in counterfeiting or other infringement may nevertheless be liable for directing, procuring or combining with others to infringe.[67]

Reproduction of Community trade marks in dictionaries

One of the important limitations in the prohibition of the use of national **13–207** trade marks arises from the requirements that the offending sign be used in the course of trade and in relation to particular goods or services.[68] While not expressly importing a requirement that the offending sign be used in a trade mark sense, these requirements may nevertheless amount to much the same thing in many cases. The CTM Directive addresses this issue at least in part by including a remedy against the generic use of a Community trade mark in a dictionary or the like. Such use can be very damaging in reducing the distinctiveness

---

[64] As in *Revlon* [1980] F.S.R. 80, CA; *cf. Colgate Palmolive v. Markwell Finance* [1989] R.P.C. 497, CA.

[65] Subject to the provisions of Art. 13(2) which do not bear on this issue.

[66] See the discussion at paras 13–35 *et seq., supra.*

[67] For an exposition of the relevant principles, see *CBS v. Amstrad Consumer Electronics* [1988] 1 A.C. 1013.

[68] See the TM Directive, Art. 5(1) and (2) and the discussion in paras 13–10 *et seq., supra.* The same words appear in the CTM Regulation, Art. 9(1).

of a trade mark. Accordingly, Article 10 of the CTM Regulation provides that if the reproduction of a Community trade mark in a dictionary, encyclopaedia or similar reference work gives the impression that it constitutes the generic name of the goods or services for which the trade mark is registered, the publisher of the work shall, at the request of the proprietor of the Community trade mark, ensure that the reproduction of the trade mark at the latest in the next edition of the publication is accompanied by an indication that it is a registered trade mark.[69] It would seem that this right is enforceable by injunction.

Prohibition on the use of a Community trade mark registered in the name of an agent or representative

13–208   Articles 11 and 18 of the CTM Regulation make provision for the protection of a proprietor where an agent or representative registers and uses the mark without his authorisation. In such a case the proprietor is entitled to oppose the use of the mark and to demand an assignment in his favour of the registration unless the agent or representative justifies his action. It would therefore seem that a number of requirements must be satisfied for the remedies (presumably by injunction) to be available. First, the mark must have been registered by the agent or representative. Secondly, the claimant must be the true proprietor of that registration.[70] Thirdly, the proprietor must show that the registration was secured and that the agent or representative is using the mark or threatening to use it without his authorisation.

C. Savings, exceptions and defences

Introduction

13–209   Just as for the rights conferred by Community trade marks, the CTM Regulation contains much the same savings, exceptions and defences as does the TM Directive for national registered trade marks. So, Article 12 of the Regulation provides for limitations of the effects of Community trade marks in like form to Article 6(1) of the TM Directive where a third party is using his own name and address, or indications concerning the characteristics of the goods or services or a trade mark where it is necessary to indicate the intended purpose of a product or service, in particular as accessories or spare parts.[71] Similarly, Article 13 of the Regulation provides for the exhaustion of the rights conferred by a Community trade mark where goods have been put on the market in the Community under that trade mark by the proprietor or with his consent. This corresponds to Article 7 of the TM Directive.[72]

---

[69] There is no equivalent provision in the TM Directive.
[70] And here satisfy the conditions of Art. 5.
[71] For a discussion of these limitations reference is invited to paras 13–122 *et seq.* and 13–129 *et seq., supra.*
[72] For a discussion of this provision and the other aspects of exhaustion, reference is invited to Chap. 15.

Infringement proceedings may also be defended by an attack on the **13–210** registration which may be brought by counterclaim. So, Article 50 of the Regulation provides for revocation in the event of non-use; if the mark has become the common name in the trade for a product or service in respect of which it is registered; if it has become deceptive; or if the proprietor is no longer properly qualified under Article 5.[73] It may also be declared invalid if it was registered contrary to any of the absolute or relative grounds of objection,[74] and subject to the limitations, in the event of acquiescence, provided by Article 53. Where the grounds for revocation or for a declaration of invalidity exist in respect of only some of the goods or services in respect of which the mark is registered, then it may be revoked or declared invalid in respect of those goods or services only. All these matters may also be raised by way of defence to an action for infringement.[75]

In the following parts of this section we therefore discuss particular **13–211** aspects in which it appears that the savings and defences in respect of Community trade marks may differ from those pertaining to national registrations under the 1994 Act and the TM Directive.

Use in relation to genuine goods or services

There is no specific provision in the CTM Regulation affording a defence **13–212** in respect of the use of the mark in relation to the goods or services of the proprietor. This position is to be contrasted with the position under the 1994 Act in relation to national registrations. Here a specific defence is provided under section 10(6), subject to the proviso that it must be in accordance with honest practices. Nevertheless, it would seem highly unlikely that any court would be prepared to find infringement where the activity in issue related only to the use of the mark in relation to goods or services marketed in the Community under the mark by or with the consent of the proprietor. There are two ways in which this can be achieved. First, it might reasonably be concluded that such use must be deemed to be with the consent of the proprietor, at least in relation to goods or services offered in the Community. Secondly, the exhaustion provisions of Article 13 could be invoked, at least in the case of goods.[76] Accordingly it seems likely that the only areas where there may be an issue are first, comparative advertising,[77] and secondly, international exhaustion.[78] We would only note here that it would seem extraordinary that a different result should be arrived at depending on whether the mark in issue is a Community or a national registration. Indeed it seems such a result would be prohibited because section 10(6) is not expressly

---

[73] Art. 50, discussed in Chap. 6.
[74] Arts 51 and 52, discussed in Chap. 15. The absolute and relative grounds of objection are discussed in Chaps 7 and 8 respectively.
[75] Art. 95(3).
[76] See generally the discussion of these issues in relation to national registrations in paras 13–97 et seq., supra.
[77] See paras 13–70 et seq., supra.
[78] See paras 13–100 et seq., and Chap. 15.

sanctioned as a defence in the TM Directive, so effectively barring any attempt to construe it as affording a broader measure of protection.

Use of a registered Community trade mark

13–213 There is no provision under the CTM Regulation providing an absolute defence to infringement of a registered Community trade mark where the alleged infringer is using a registered Community trade mark in relation to goods or services in respect of which it is registered.[79] This is so whether the mark complained of is registered as a national trade mark under the 1994 Act or is a Community trade mark registered under the CTM Regulation. Instead, the CTM Regulation provides for a measure of protection where the proprietor of an earlier trade mark has acquiesced in the use of the later Community trade mark.

13–214 The owner of an earlier Community trade mark may take action against the user of a later Community trade mark in relation to goods or services in respect of which it is registered save as prohibited by Article 53(1). This provides that where the proprietor of the earlier mark has acquiesced for a period of five years in the use of the later mark in the Community, while being aware of such use, then he shall no longer be entitled on the basis of the earlier mark either to apply for a declaration that the later trade mark is invalid or to oppose the use of the later mark in respect of the goods or services for which the later mark has been used, unless registration of the later trade mark was applied for in bad faith.[80] Correspondingly, in these circumstances, the proprietor of the later Community trade mark is not then entitled to oppose the use of the earlier right either.[81]

13–215 A number of points in this limitation require consideration. First, in the context of this provision acquiescence appears to require no more or less than inaction with actual knowledge of the use. Secondly, if bad faith is shown then it seems the limitation is not applicable in terms either of preventing an attack on the later registration or opposing its use.[82]

Use of an earlier right

13–216 As will be seen from the next section, where the proprietor of an earlier right has acquiesced in the use of a later Community trade mark in a Member State, then his opportunity to oppose the use of the later trade mark is restricted. In these circumstances the proprietor of the later Community trade mark is not entitled to oppose the use of the earlier right.[83] There is also a provision restricting the opportunity of the

---

[79] In contrast to the position under the 1994 Act, s.11(1) in respect of national registrations and the defence there provided in the case of the use of another national registration in relation to goods or services in respect of which it is registered.
[80] Art. 53(1).
[81] Art. 53(3).
[82] As to the meaning of bad faith, reference is invited to the discussion in Chap. 7.
[83] Art. 53. See paras 13–217 to 13–222, below.

proprietor of a Community trade mark to take action against the user of an earlier right which applies only in a particular locality.[84]

D. National laws prohibiting the use of Community trade marks

The Community trade mark system provides a measure of protection **13–217** against the use of a Community trade mark in any particular Member State, including the United Kingdom. These measures fall into two categories, earlier rights of a general nature and earlier rights which apply only in a particular locality. Each is dealt with below.

Earlier rights

Article 106 of the CTM Regulation makes it clear that, save unless **13–218** otherwise provided for, the Regulation does not affect any earlier rights which may exist under the laws of any Member State, to take action against the use of a later Community trade mark in that Member State. Particular provision is made in respect of earlier national trade marks, international marks under the Madrid Protocol designating the United Kingdom, well-known marks under Article 6 *bis* of the Paris Convention or the WTO Agreement (TRIPS) and other non-registered trade marks or other signs used in the course of trade of more than mere local significance which may be protected by an action for passing off in the United Kingdom.[85]

The owner of any of the above rights may take action in the United **13–219** Kingdom in respect of the use in the United Kingdom of a Community trade mark unless he has acquiesced, for a period of five successive years, in the use of the Community trade mark in the United Kingdom while being aware of such use. In those circumstances he is no longer entitled to apply for a declaration that the later Community trade mark is invalid or to oppose its use, unless registration of the Community trade mark was applied for in bad faith.[86] Nor is the proprietor of the later Community trade mark entitled to oppose the use of the earlier right.[87] This provision raises the same issues of interpretation discussed above in relation to earlier Community marks. The points there considered are equally applicable in this context.

Another category provided for is the case where the use of a **13–220** Community trade mark in the United Kingdom would offend against a right to a name, a right of personal portrayal, a copyright or other industrial property right.[88] Here it is clear that in so far as any such

---

[84] Art. 107. This reflects the inability of the user of such a mark to oppose the registration of the Community mark under Art. 8(4). This provision and the meaning of "in a particular locality" are discussed in Chap. 8, paras 8–110 and 8–111. See also, para. 13–222 below.
[85] And set out in Art. 8(2) and (4).
[86] Arts 106 and 53(2).
[87] Art. 53(3).
[88] As provided for in Art. 52(2).

rights may exist in the United Kingdom they may be enforced against the use of the Community trade mark in the United Kingdom.[89]

13-221 In a final catch all, the Regulation provides that it shall, unless otherwise provided for, not affect the right to bring proceedings under the civil, administrative or criminal law of a Member State or under the provisions of Community law for the purpose of prohibiting the use of a Community trade mark, to the extent that the use of a national trade mark may be prohibited under the law of that Member State or under Community law.[90]

Use and protection of an earlier right in a particular locality

13-222 The Community trade mark system affords protection to the proprietor of an earlier right which exists only in a particular locality through the provisions of Article 107 of the CTM Regulation.[91] This provides that the proprietor of such an earlier right may oppose the use of the Community mark in the territory where his right is recognised and protected in so far as the local law so permits. So, in the United Kingdom, where local goodwill is indeed protectable by an action for passing off, it seems the proprietor of the earlier right may apply for an injunction to restrain the use of the Community trade mark and other relief in so far as the use of the Community trade mark will result or has resulted in passing off.[92] This right ceases to apply if the proprietor of the earlier right has acquiesced in the use of the Community trade mark in the United Kingdom for a period of five successive years, he being aware of such use, unless the Community trade mark was applied for in bad faith.[93] Importantly, the proprietor of the Community trade mark may not oppose the use of the earlier right, even though that right may no longer be invoked against the Community trade mark, through acquiescence.

E. Community collective marks

13-223 Community collective marks are generally treated in the same way as ordinary Community trade marks by the CTM Regulation for the purposes of infringement but with two particular modifications which are necessary to take account of their special nature.

Limitations on infringement provisions—indications of geographical origin

13-224 A Community collective mark does not entitle the proprietor to prohibit a third party from using in the course of trade a sign or indication which may serve in trade to designate the geographical origin, provided such

---

[89] Art. 106(1).
[90] Art. 106(2). *e.g.* under E.C. Regulation 2081/92 on the Protection of Geographical Indications and Designations of Origin, Art. 13.
[91] See also para. 13–216, above and Chap. 8, paras 8–110 and 8–111.
[92] Art. 107(1).
[93] Art. 107(2). By acquiescence it would seem the Regulation requires no more than inactivity knowing of the use of the Community trade mark. See para. 13–215, *supra*; as to the meaning of bad faith, reference is invited to the discussion in Chap. 7.

use is in accordance with honest practices in industrial or commercial matters.[94] This limitation is also found in the provisions relating to national collective and certification marks and similarly reflects the ability to register Community collective marks which designate the geographical origin of the goods or services.[95]

Persons who are entitled to bring an action for infringement

Proceedings for infringement of the collective mark may be brought by **13–225** the proprietor and anyone who has the authority to use it.[96] The proprietor is entitled to claim compensation on behalf of persons who have authority to use the collective mark where they have sustained damage through its unauthorised use.[97]

---

[94] Art. 64(2).
[95] The provisions relating to national collective and certification marks also require the use to be in accordance with honest practices; see para. 13–169, above.
[96] Art. 70(1), applying the provisions of Art. 22(3) and (4).
[97] Art. 70(2).

411

THE ACTION FOR PASSING OFF

Structure of this chapter

14–01 This chapter attempts to set out the substantive law of passing off, as well as points of practice peculiar to passing off actions. Other points of practice and the relief available in an action for passing off are dealt with in Chapter 18. As in previous editions, this very long chapter is broken up into sections, principally according to the type of misrepresentation involved:

1. Foundation and Nature of the Action;
2. Goodwill;
3. The Limits of Passing Off;
4. Direct Misrepresentation as to Business or Goods;
5. Imitations of Trade or Service Marks;
6. Trading Names;
7. Imitation of Get-up;
8. Proof of Likelihood of Deception;
9. Defences.

14–02
Inevitably, the same questions tend to arise whatever the type of misrepresentation, leading to some repetition on the one hand and cross-referencing to avoid repetition on the other. Some of the more important common points are dealt with at the beginning of this chapter, where we have also attempted to point out some of the limits of the law of passing off and certain situations which fall outside its scope.

In reading this chapter, the age of a cited case should be borne in mind. Whilst the principles of law have not changed in recent times, there has been a distinct tendency for judicial opinion to become less robust in character and more careful of those who complain of deception. Thus cases which are still good law might well be decided differently today.[1]

---

[1] The case of *Ainsworth v. Walmsley* (1886) L.R. 1 Eq. 518, may serve as an instance. Undoubtedly there was passing off; the defendant expressly asserted that his goods were the claimant's, which was untrue (although the defendant may not have known it). But the court declared that anyone believing the assertion "would have had only their own folly to complain of", for they ought to have known that the goods were probably "doctored", and refused relief. It is hard to imagine such a judgment today.

1. Foundation and nature of the action

Introduction

Passing off is a single common law cause of action which can apply in a **14-03** very wide range of factual situations. The breadth of the tort is such that, despite some views to the contrary, it now appears to be generally accepted that it is permissible to define two forms of the tort: the classic form, defined by the "classical trinity", and the "extended form", typified by the *Champagne,*[2] *Sherry*[3] and *Advocaat*[4] cases. These two forms are not different torts, it is simply more convenient for the purposes of analysis of a particular case to define passing off by reference to one or other of these forms. This highlights a common problem in passing off cases: however authoritative the source used for a definition of the elements of the tort, it is frequently the case that further authority is required to emphasise particular features of the tort as they apply to the facts of the case.[5] Even the "classical trinity" of reputation, misrepresentation and damage to goodwill can be misunderstood without further explanation. Accordingly, in attempting to "define" the cause of action in passing off, it is necessary to look at several different dicta, although the starting point must be *Jif.*[6]

The classical trinity, restated in *Jif*

The *"Jif Lemon"* case is important in at least two respects. First, the **14-04** House of Lords confirmed that each passing off case depended on its own facts.[7] Secondly, their Lordships reverted to the "classical trinity" for their definition of the elements of the cause of action. Lord Oliver put the matters a successful claimant must prove as follows:

"First, he must establish a goodwill or reputation attached to the goods or services which he supplies in the mind of the purchasing public by association with the identifying 'get-up' (whether it consists simply of a brand name or a trade description, or the individual features of labelling or packaging) under which his particular goods or services are offered to the public, such that the get-up is recognised by the public as distinctive specifically of the plaintiff's goods or services.

---

[2] *Bollinger v. Costa Brava Wine* [1960] R.P.C. 16.
[3] *Vine Products v. Mackenzie* [1969] R.P.C. 1
[4] *Warnink v. Townend* [1980] R.P.C. 31, HL.
[5] Gummow J. has remarked ". . . it is to be observed that the law of passing off contains sufficient nooks and crannies to make it difficult to formulate any satisfactory definition in short form.": *Conagra Inc v. McCain Foods (Australia) Pty Ltd* (1992) 106 A.L.R. 465 at 518.
[6] *Reckitt & Colman Products Ltd v. Borden* [1990] R.P.C. 341, HL.
[7] See further below, paras 14–15 *et seq.*

14–05   Secondly, he must demonstrate a misrepresentation by the defendant to the public (whether or not intentional) leading or likely to lead the public to belief that the goods or services offered by him are the goods or services of the plaintiff.

Thirdly, he must demonstrate that he suffers or, in a quia timet action, that he is likely to suffer damage by reason of the erroneous belief engendered by the defendant's misrepresentation that the source of the defendant's goods or services is the same as the source of those offered by the plaintiff."[8]

14–06   Lord Jauncey stated the principles thus[9]:

> "[quoting Lord Langdale] 'a man is not to sell his own goods under the pretence that they are the goods of another man . . .' Accordingly a misrepresentation achieving such a result is actionable because it constitutes an invasion of proprietary rights vested in the plaintiff. However, it is a prerequisite of any successful passing off action that the plaintiff's goods have acquired a reputation in the market and are known by some distinguishing feature. It is also a prerequisite that the misrepresentation has deceived or is likely to deceive and that the plaintiff is likely to suffer damage by such deception. Mere confusion which does not lead to a sale is not sufficient."
>
> "It is not essential . . . that the defendant should misrepresent his goods as those of the plaintiff. It is sufficient that he misrepresents his goods in such a way that it is a reasonably foreseeable consequence of the misrepresentation that the plaintiff's business or goodwill will be damaged."

14–07   These and other statements cited below reflect the fact that, within the action for passing off, "there are accommodated and adjusted *inter se* three sets of interests. There is the plaintiff's interest in protecting his skill, effort and investment, the interest of the defendant in freedom to attract purchasers for his goods and services, and the interest of consumers in having available a range of competitive goods and services for selection by consumers without the practice upon them of misrepresentations."[10]

---

[8] 406.

[9] At 416–7.

[10] , *per* Gummow J. (as he then was, in the Federal Court of Australia) in *Hogan v. Pacific Dunlop Ltd* (1988) 83 A.L.R. 403. His observations were expressed in relation to the action for passing off "as presently understood in Australia". The law in Australia has diverged somewhat from the law in the U.K., notably in territorial considerations, but this general comment holds good. He repeated these notions in *ConAgra Inc v. McCain Foods (Aus) Pty Ltd* (1992) 106 A.L.R. 465 at 517.

The extended form

The reversion to the classical trinity in *Jif* followed the attempt by Lords **14–08**
Diplock and Fraser in *Advocaat* to formulate general propositions of the
law of passing off to take account of its "extended form". Lord
Diplock's formulation was as follows[11]:

> "My Lords, *Spalding v. Gamage* and the later cases make it possible
> to identify five characteristics which must be present in order to
> create a valid cause of action for passing off: (1) a misrepresentation
> (2) made by a trader in the course of trade, (3) to prospective
> customers of his or ultimate consumers of goods or services
> supplied by him, (4) which is calculated to injure the business or
> goodwill of another (in the sense that this is a reasonably foresee-
> able consequence) and (5) which causes actual damage to a business
> or goodwill of a trader by whom the action is brought (or in a *quia
> timet* action) will probably do so."[12]

Lord Fraser in the same case also advanced a five characteristic **14–09**
formulation:

> "It is essential for the plaintiff in a passing-off action to show at
> least the following facts:
>
> (1) That his business consists of, or includes, selling in England a
> class of goods to which the particular trade name applies;
> (2) That the class of goods is clearly defined, and that in the minds
> of the public, or a section of the public, in England, the trade
> name distinguishes that class from other similar goods;
> (3) That because of the reputation of the goods, there is goodwill
> attached to the name;
> (4) That he, the plaintiff, as a member of the class of those who sell
> the goods, is the owner of goodwill in England which is of
> substantial value;
> (5) That he has suffered or is *really likely*[13] to suffer, substantial
> damage to his property in the goodwill by reason of the
> defendants selling goods which are falsely described by the
> trade name to which the goodwill is attached."[14]

---

[11] Accompanied by this warning: "In seeking to formulate general propositions of English
law, however, one must be particularly careful to beware of the logical fallacy of the
undistributed middle. It does not follow that because all passing-off actions can be
shown to present these characteristics, all factual situations which present these
characteristics give rise to a cause of action for passing off."

[12] [1980] R.P.C. 31 at 93.

[13] These italics in the original judgment appear in the report at [1980] R.P.C. 31 at 106, but
not in the report at [1979] A.C. 731 at 756. The advantage of these words is that they
emphasise the element of proportionality: is the damage sufficiently serious? *cf.* Lloyd J.
in *HFC Bank Plc v. Midland Bank Plc* [2000] F.S.R. 176 (settled on appeal).

[14] At 105–106 of the R.P.C. report.

14-10 It is evident that the two formulations are different, yet they should be regarded as complementary.[15] Note particularly Lord Fraser's emphasis on the need to prove that the plaintiff "has suffered, or is *really likely* to suffer substantial damage to his property in the goodwill." The goodwill must be in the country concerned.[16]

Classical trinity vs extended form

14-11 In *Advocaat* (at pages 94–5), Lord Diplock identified the features which distinguished the "extended form" of the tort from the classic form:

> "The features which distinguish it from all previous cases were (a) that the element in the goodwill of each of the individual plaintiffs that was represented by his ability to use without deception (in addition to his individual house mark) the word 'Champagne' to distinguish his wines from sparkling wines not made by the champenois process from grapes produced in the Champagne district of France, was not exclusive to himself but was shared with every other shipper of sparkling wine to England whose wines could satisfy the same condition and (b) that the class of traders entitled to a proprietary right in 'the attractive force which brings in custom' represented by the ability without deception to call one's wines 'Champagne' was capable of continuing expansion, since it might be joined by any future shipper of wine who was able to satisfy that condition."

These distinguishing features were cited with approval by Chadwick L.J. in *Chocosuisse*.[17]

Summary of the current approach

14-12 The present position may be summarised as follows:

(1) for passing off in its classic form, the classical trinity, as expounded in *Jif* and other cases, should normally be applicable and be applied;

(2) for passing off in its extended form, one can apply either the classical trinity or the *Advocaat* tests. Judicial preference seems to vary. In *Parma Ham*,[18] the Court of Appeal welcomed the reversion in *Jif* to the classical trinity. Subsequently, the Court of Appeal has been content to utilise the *Advocaat* tests in *Elderflower Champagne*[19] and *Chocosuisse*;

---

[15] See *Anheuser Busch* [1984] F.S.R. 413 at 463, CA.

[16] See *per* Lord Fraser where he speaks of "goodwill in England" and *Star Industrial v. Yap Kwee Kor* [1976] F.S.R 256 (PC, Singapore).

[17] [1999] R.P.C. 826, CA.

[18] [1991] R.P.C. 351 at 369.

[19] [1993] F.S.R. 641.

(3) there is nothing inherently wrong in applying the *Advocaat* tests **14–13**
to cases of passing off in its classic form,[20] but doing so might
raise the suspicion that the case falls into Lord Diplock's
"undistributed middle". The modern trend is to use the classical
trinity. See, for example, the view of Nourse L.J. in *Parma Ham*:

> "Although those speeches [of Lord Diplock and Lord Fraser]
> are of the highest authority, it has been my experience, and it is
> now my respectful opinion, that they do not give the same
> degree of assistance in analysis and decision as the classical
> trinity of (1) a reputation (or goodwill) acquired by the plaintiff
> in his goods, name, mark etc., (2) a misrepresentation by the
> defendant leading to confusion (or deception), causing (3)
> damage to the plaintiff."[21]

See also similar views expressed by Millett L.J. in *Harrods Ltd v.
Harrodian School Ltd*.[22]

The advantage of the classical trinity, as restated in *Jif*, is that attention is **14–14**
properly drawn to the essential relationships between the three ele-
ments. In a true case of passing off, all three elements are intertwined. It
is the exclusive reputation which provides the necessary foundation for
misrepresentation; the misrepresentation must be one which causes or is
likely to cause damage to goodwill (in other words, the misrepresentation must be "operative" in the transaction and causative of the damage
claimed); and damage to goodwill is at the heart of the cause of action.
Goodwill itself is generated by trading activity, which is usually the
source of reputation. But the existence of a reputation does not automatically establish goodwill. A claimant may be able to demonstrate a
reputation in the United Kingdom giving rise to people being misled by
the defendant's activities, but if he has no goodwill here, his claim will
fail.[23] All these concepts are explained in further detail below.

A question of fact

It has always been the law that every case in which passing off is alleged **14–15**
turns on its own facts. The question whether the use of particular indicia
results in passing off the goods or services of the defendant as those of
the claimant is often one of difficulty, but it is in substance a question of
fact:

---

[20] In *Bristol Conservatories Ltd v. Conservatories Custom Built Ltd* [1989] R.P.C. 455 at 466,
Ralph Gibson L.J. observed that the probanda formulated by Lords Diplock and Fraser
would not, *e.g.* allow for cases of so-called "reverse" passing off (see below at para. 14–
109).
[21] At 568.
[22] [1996] R.P.C. 697 at 711.
[23] See, *e.g. Budweiser*, which should properly be regarded as an instance of the collision of
independent rights in the name Budweiser, giving rise to no liability on either side:
[1984] F.S.R. 413.

"The principle of law may be very plainly stated, that nobody has any right to represent his goods as the goods of somebody else. How far the use of particular words, signs, or pictures, does or does not come up to the proposition enunciated in each particular case must always be a question of evidence, and the more simple the phraseology, the more like it is to a mere description of the article sold, the greater becomes the difficulty of proof, but if the proof establishes the fact, the legal consequence appears to follow."[24]

14–16 So, each of the elements of the claim requires the necessary facts to be established. Often the presence of a misrepresentation has to be inferred from the circumstances:

"The basis of a passing-off action being a false representation by the defendant, it must be proved in each case as a fact that the false representation was made. It may, of course, have been made in express words, but cases of express misrepresentation of this sort are rare. The more common case is where the representation is implied in the use or imitation of a mark, trade name or get-up with which the goods of another are associated in the minds of the public, or of a particular class of the public. In such cases the point to be decided is whether, having regard to all the circumstances of the case, the use by the defendant in connection with the goods of the mark, name or get-up in question impliedly represents such goods to be the goods of the plaintiff, or the goods of the plaintiff of a particular class or quality, or, as it is sometimes put, whether the defendant's use of such mark, name or get-up is calculated to deceive. It would, however, be impossible to enumerate or classify all the possible ways in which a man may make the false representation relied on."[25]

14–17 For those analysing or applying the law, two important consequences follow:

First, each case depends on the evidence, but it is not always easy to predict what the evidence will prove. In straightforward cases, personal expectations or predictions as to the effect of the insignia complained of coincide with what happens in reality. The cases which present the greatest difficulty are those in which the evidence establishes an unusual

---

[24] *per* Halsbury L.C. in *"Camel Hair Belting"* (*Reddaway v. Banham*) [1896] A.C. 199 at 204; 13 R.P.C. 218 at 224. For the case of "business" rather than "goods", see *per* Lord Simonds in *Office Cleaning v. Westminster* (1946) 63 R.P.C. 39 at 42. See *per* Lord Parker in *Spalding v. Gamage* (1915) 32 R.P.C. 000 at 283, 284, 285, quoted below. See generally Kay and Lindley L.JJ. in *"Yorkshire Relish"* [1896] 2 Ch. 54; 13 R.P.C. 235, and Lord Davey in *Cellular Clothing v. Maxton* [1899] A.C. 326 at 343; 16 R.P.C. 397 at 408. See also Buckley L.J. in *Brinsmead v. Brinsmead* (1913) 30 R.P.C. 493 at 506, 507; *Baume v. Moore* [1958] R.P.C. 226 at 229, *per* Romer L.J.; Danckwerts J. in *Adrema v. Adrema GmbH* [1958] R.P.C. 323.
[25] *per* Lord Parker in *Spalding v. Gamage* (1915) 32 R.P.C. 273 at 284.

result. Difficult cases are won and lost on the evidence.[26] Jacob J. has observed:

> "And even if one's own opinion is that deception is unlikely though possible, convincing evidence of deception will carry the day. The *Jif* lemon case . . . is a recent example where overwhelming evidence of deception had that effect. It was certainly my experience in practice that my own view as to the likelihood of deception was not always reliable. As I grew more experienced, I said more and more 'it depends on the evidence'."[27]

Secondly, the use of previous decisions as authorities requires care. There is a fine line between the citation of previous passing off cases to demonstrate principles of law and reliance on cases by way of factual analogy. Often it is necessary to understand the underlying facts to put particular dicta into their proper context, but sometimes the unspoken suggestion is that a factual analogy may also be drawn. Unless the facts are virtually identical, this simply creates unnecessary work.

Reputation

It is essential to the success of any claim in respect of passing off, based **14–18** on the use of a given mark, get-up or other indication of origin, for the claimant to show that this had (at the relevant date) become by user in this country distinctive, to some section of the public, if not of the claimant's goods or business alone, at least of a defined class of goods or business to which those of the claimant belong.

> "It is, of course, essential to the success of any claim in respect of passing-off based on the use of a given mark or get-up that the plaintiff should be able to show that the disputed mark or get-up has become by user in this country distinctive of the plaintiff's goods so that the use in relation to any goods of the kind dealt in by the plaintiff or that mark or get-up will be understood by the trade and the public in this country as meaning that the goods are the plaintiff's goods. The gist of the action is that the plaintiff, by using and making known the mark or get-up in relation to his goods, and thus causing it to be associated or identified with those goods, has acquired a quasi-proprietary right to the exclusive use of the mark or get-up in relation to goods of that kind, which right is invaded by any person who, by using the same or some deceptively similar mark or get-up in relation to goods not of the plaintiff's manufacture, induces customers to buy from him goods not of the plaintiff's

---

[26] *cf. Jif* where all the arguments raised by the defendants on appeal were defeated by the findings of fact.

[27] *Neutrogena Corporation v. Golden Ltd* [1996] R.P.C. 473 at 482 (upheld on appeal).

manufacture as goods of the plaintiff's manufacture, thereby diverting to himself orders intended for and rightfully belonging to the plaintiff."[28]

The mark or other indication concerned need not be universally known. A small trader with limited clientele is as much entitled to protect his brands and business name as any large concern.[29] The overriding consideration, in judging extent of reputation, is whether the claimant has built up a goodwill to the point where substantial damage will be caused to it by the acts he complains of.

The relevant date, when it comes to proving reputation is the date when the defendant commenced the acts complained of.[30]

14–19   It is rare for a passing-off action to be begun unless the goods concerned have some sort of reputation, so that reported cases in which the claimant failed because the name, mark or get-up relied upon simply was not well enough known are rare; though cases in which the badge concerned is associated with the defendant rather than the claimant are sometimes found.[31] In general, however, where a claimant loses through failure to prove his reputation (as distinct from failure to show a deceptive resemblance of the defendant's badge to his) his difficulty is the subtler one that the badge relied on, however well known, does not indicate a common trade origin for his and the defendant's goods.

(1) In an action concerning "Old Innishowen" whiskey, it was established that the name "Old Innishowen" had once been generally known as meaning illicit pot-still whiskey or "poteen", with the result that its use on the claimants' and defendant's whiskeys was less a representation as to trade origin than a representation that the whiskey resembled poteen: *"Old Innishowen" (Watt v. O'Banlon)* (1886) 4 R.P.C. 1.

(2) An action by the manufacturers of the "Rolls" razor against the manufacturers of a "Rolls" cigarette lighter failed. The court was clearly inclined to the view that where two dissimilar products were both called "Rolls" the public would consider that they both claimed to be in the "Rolls Royce" class rather than that they had a common trade origin: *Rolls Razor v. Rolls Lighters* (1949) 66 R.P.C. 137 at 142.

14–20   (3) In an action in which the passing off alleged was the mere sale of copies of the claimants' trinkets, a motion for interlocutory injunction failed in the absence of evidence that any degree of

---

[28] *per* Jenkins L.J. in *"Turmix" (Oertli v. Bowman)* [1957] R.P.C. 388 at 397. *cf.* with *"Manus"* (1948) 65 R.P.C. 329 at 339. See also *post*, paras 14–123 *et seq.* As to the need to show user in this country, see *post*, para. 14–54.

[29] *Chelsea Man* [1985] F.S.R. 567 at 574, upheld on appeal [1987] R.P.C. 189.

[30] *"Pub Squash"* [1981] R.P.C. 429 at 494 (PC, N.S.W.); *J. C. Penney v. Penneys* [1975] F.S.R. 367 at 374 and 381, CA.

[31] *"Turmix," supra,* is one such.

resemblance between the goods would be taken as indicating a
common trade origin: *British American Glass v. Winton* [1962]
R.P.C. 230.

(4) Where the claimants' carpet-shampooing device was sold as the
"Countess Shampoomatic," and the defendants marketed an
"Addis Shampoomatic", an interlocutory injunction was
refused in the absence of evidence of actual confusion: *"Shampoomatic" (Countess Housewares v. Addis)* [1964] R.P.C. 251.

(5) The claimants had a reputation in the United Kingdom as **14–21**
importers of foreign racing bicycling accessories, under the
trade mark "Evian". One item imported by them was a cyclist's
plastic water-bottle, marked "Evian", devised by the proprietors of the well-known "Evian" natural mineral water to
advertise their water. An action for passing off against the sale
of similar bottles not imported by the claimants failed because
(*inter alia*) they did not prove that the "Evian" bottles were in
this country distinctive of them and not of the proprietors of the
water: *Evian v. Bowles* [1965] R.P.C. 327.

(6) Similarly where a defendant (truthfully) described his goods as **14–22**
"Guy Laroche designed for Marcel Fenez" the claimants, as
exclusive English agents for the Paris couturier Guy Laroche,
failed because they had no reputation in that name: *Poister v.
Fenez* [1965] R.P.C. 187.

(7) Where the claimant had done nothing to indicate its connection
with the mark "Coast to Coast", instead using it mainly as a
slogan on T-shirts, Whitford J. expressed the view at the
interlocutory stage that the claimant would have difficulty in
establishing reputation: *Unidoor v. Marks & Spencer* [1988] R.P.C.
275.

Time needed to acquire reputation

It is easier to establish a reputation where a mark has been used for a **14–23**
substantial period of time, but no length of time during which the
claimant or his predecessors must have used the marks in question can
be laid down.[32] In each case the question must be, has the claimant
acquired a sufficient reputation?

(1) The "Fletcher" and "Challenge" companies, both well-known
New Zealand companies, announced a merger under the name

---

[32] Cases where comparatively short times have been sufficient: *Stannard v. Reay* [1967]
R.P.C. 589 (three weeks sufficient for "Mr. Chippy"); *McAndrew v. Bassett ("Anatolia
Liquorice")* (1864) 4 De. G.J. & S. 380 (one and one-half months sufficient); *Allen v. Brown
Watson* [1965] R.P.C. 191 (heavy pre-publication advertising sufficient); *cf. Compatibility
Research v. Computer Psyche* [1967] R.P.C. 201, illus. 5, para. 14–130 (one month
insufficient for descriptive device). See also *BBC v. Talbot* [1981] F.S.R. 228; *Elida Gibbs v.
Colgate-Palmolive* [1983] F.S.R. 95; *My Kinda Bones v. Dr Pepper's Store* [1984] F.S.R. 289;
Marcus Publishing v. Hutton-Wild [1990] R.P.C. 576.

"Fletcher Challenge". Within a few hours of this being announced in Australia, the defendants reserved the name "Fletcher Challenge Pty." at an Australian companies registry. A passing-off injunction was granted by the New South Wales court: *Fletcher Challenge v. Fletcher Challenge Pty.* [1982] F.S.R. 1.[33]

14–24   (2) A period of six months was insufficient to establish a reputation in the name "The Gold AM" for a radio programme comprising "Golden Oldies": *County Sound v. Ocean Sound* [1991] F.S.R. 367. This is an indication of the difficulty in establishing a descriptive name as distinctive.

(3) Where the defendant advertises his goods and workmanship by showing photographs of the claimant's goods and workmanship, the defendant may, simultaneously, be contributing to the goodwill and reputation of the claimant and making a misrepresentation sufficient to found a passing off action: see *Bristol Conservatories v. Conservatories Custom Built Ltd* [1989] R.P.C. 455.

Misrepresentation

14–25 The passages cited above demonstrate that misrepresentation lies at the heart of an action for passing off. They also demonstrate that a successful claimant must prove not only the fact of misrepresentation but also that the misrepresentation was operative or material,[34] in the sense that the allegedly misleading indicia was at least *a* cause[35] of deception or its likelihood amongst the relevant class of consumers and hence damaging to the claimant's goodwill. The existence and effect of misrepresentation in any case is a matter for the court to decide.[36]

14–26 As Lord Parker observed in *Spalding v. Gamage*,[37] it would be impossible to enumerate or classify all the possible ways in which a man might make the false representation relied on. Later sections in this chapter set out the variety of possible misrepresentations which have given rise to liability. Not all representations made in commerce as to a connection between the claimant and the goods or services of the defendant will suffice. As Goff L.J. observed in *Bulmer v. Bollinger*[38]:

"Not every kind of connection claimed will amount to passing off; for example, if one says that one's goods are very suitable to be used in connection with the plaintiff's. On the other hand in my

---

[33] Similarly, but without the foreign element: *Glaxo Plc v. Glaxowellcome Ltd* [1996] F.S.R. 388, Lightman J.
[34] See especially Lord Oliver's third requirement, and Lord Jauncey, *supra*, at paras 14–05 and 14–06, respectively.
[35] *My Kinda Town v. Soll* [1983] R.P.C. 407, CA.
[36] See below, paras 14–257 *et seq*.
[37] (1915) 32 R.P.C. 273 at 284, cited above at para. 14–16.
[38] [1978] R.P.C. 79 at 117.

view there can be a passing off of goods without representing that they are actually the well known goods which the plaintiff produces or a new line which he is supposed to have started. It is sufficient in my view if what is done represents the defendant's goods to be connected with the plaintiff's in such a way as would lead people to accept them on the faith of the plaintiff's reputation. Thus for example it would be sufficient if they were taken to be made under licence, or under some trading arrangement which would give the plaintiff some control over them. . . ."

Millett L.J. was prepared to go slightly further in *Harrods v. Harrodian* **14–27**
School. Having quoted the passage above, he stated[39]:

"It is not in my opinion sufficient to demonstrate that there must be a connection of some kind between the defendant and the plaintiff, if it is not a connection which would lead the public to suppose that the plaintiff has made himself responsible for the quality of the defendant's goods or services."

Proof of fraudulent intention is not essential

Passing-off cases are often cases of deliberate and intentional misrepre- **14–28**
sentation, but it is well settled that fraud is not a necessary element of the right of action,[40] and the absence of an intention to deceive is not a defence.[41] Moreover, literal truth is not necessarily innocent of misrepresentation.

"If a man makes a statement which is true, but which carried with it a false representation and induces the belief that his goods are the plaintiff's goods, he will be restrained by injunction. He cannot rely on the fact that his statement is literally and accurately true if, notwithstanding the truth, it carries with it a false representation."[42]

Proof of fraudulent intention may, however, materially assist a claimant in establishing probability of deception.[43]

[39] [1996] R.P.C. 697 at 713, relying also on Farwell J. in *British Legion v. British Legion Club (Street) Ltd* (1931) 48 R.P.C. 555, where the judge considered that the public would take the defendant club to be "connected in some way" with the plaintiff. But he explained this by saying that some persons would think that it was "either a branch of the plaintiff or a club in some way amalgamated with or under the supervision of the plaintiff and for which the plaintiff had in some way made itself responsible."
[40] *Reddaway v. Bentham* [1892] 2 Q.B. 639; 9 R.P.C. 503 at 507, CA; Halsbury L.C. in *Cellular Clothing v. Maxton* [1899] A.C. 326 at 334; 16 R.P.C. 397 at 404. But *cf.* the cases on enabling others to pass-off, para. 14–267.
[41] *Baume v. Moore* [1958] R.P.C. 226 at 228.
[42] Per Buckley L.J. in *Brinsmead v. Brinsmead* (1913) 30 R P.C. 493 at 506.
[43] See *post*, para. 14–265, and *O.T. v. Cumming* (1915) 32 R.P.C. 69. For if the defendant set out to deceive, the court will readily infer that he succeeded. Fraudulent intent may be implied where the defendant continues to use deceptive marks after complaints have been made to him: *Johnston v. Orr Ewing* (1882) 7 App.Cas. 219 at 229; *Weingarten v. Bayer* (1906) 22 R.P.C. 341 at 357, HL.

14-29   It should be remembered that deliberate imitation of another's goods, get-up, method of trading or trading style does not necessarily involve fraud; a trader is entitled to sail close to the wind, so long as he steers clear of actual misrepresentation.[44] It is, in particular, lawful for a trader to suggest to purchasers that his goods are equivalent to, or a substitute for, those of another,[45] and to choose marks and styles appropriate to that. Furthermore, the cases would seem to imply that it is lawful to adopt a mark so close to another's that customers (whilst aware that there are two marks) will not bother to distinguish between them[46]; something that can cause very great damage as well as great resentment.

Damage

14-30   Proof of damage is not in every case essential to enable the claimant to maintain his action,[47] it depends on the circumstances. If the claimant shows that the defendant is acting so as to pass-off goods as those of the claimant which are not the claimant's it will generally be assumed that the claimant is thereby prevented from selling as many of the goods as he otherwise would; while even if there is no direct loss of sales (as where claimant and defendant are not in direct competition) the confusion between the two suppliers puts the claimant's goodwill at risk. There is indeed some authority for the proposition, that any unauthorised appropriation of or profit from another's business goodwill or professional reputation[48] or business goodwill,[49] inasmuch as it deprives the claimant of the opportunity to exploit his goodwill himself if nothing else. But this doctrine is by no means firmly established, and where the claimant is not a trading business especially, he may well be required to establish a likelihood of actual financial loss from the

---

[44] So Roxburgh J. frequently observed, *arguendo*. He appears never to have put the observation into a judgment, but *Day v. Kennedy* (1952) 70 R.P.C. 19 at 21, 22 comes close to it; *cf. per* Greene M.R. in *Wright Layman & Umney v. Wright* (1949) 66 R.P.C. 149 at 152: "Honest men do not sail near to the wind." But that referred to a man who had passed off. See also, para. 14–68, below.

[45] *cf. post*, para. 14–85 and *King v. Gillard* (1905) 22 R.P.C. 327, CA (a "get-up" case).

[46] *cf. Goya v. Gala* (1952) 69 R.P.C. 188; there are similar cases, but the point seems never to have been expressly decided.

[47] *Procea v. Evans* (1951) 68 R.P.C. 210, and see *Associated Newspapers v. Insert Media* [1991] F.S.R. 380, CA, where the misrepresentation was that the claimants must have authorised and taken responsibility for the defendant's activities, the parties were appealing to the same customers and it was held the defendant intended to exploit the claimant's goodwill (distinguishing *Stringfellows* [1984] R.P.C. 501, CA, a case where little, if any, overlap existed and there was no attempt to trade on the claimant's goodwill).

[48] *Henderson v. Radio Corp.* [1969] R.P.C. 218 (High Ct, Aust.).

[49] *Lego v. Lego M. Lemelstrich* [1983] F.S.R. 155; but *cf. "Judge Dredd," post*, para. 22–62 n. 13. See also *Blazer v. Yardley* [1992] F.S.R. 501, where there was no overlap in trade, but it was accepted there was a serious issue to be tried that the defendant's products might be associated with the claimant. Although an interlocutory injunction was refused on the balance of the risk of injustice, Aldous J. stated that use of the claimant's goodwill by definition causes injury to the claimant and lays open that goodwill to damage by the actions of the defendant.

defendant's actions.[50] Thus it has been held that the assumption of a name,[51] or an address,[52] similar to the name or address of the claimant, without malicious intent, although it may cause annoyance and inconvenience to him—for instance, by delaying his letters—is not actionable unless it is shown to be calculated to injure him in his business. No action lies at the suit of any private person for deception practised upon the public, unless it incidentally causes, or is calculated to cause, damage to him as an individual; if this is not the case, the wrongdoer can only be punished through the criminal law, or in a civil action on information brought in the name of the Attorney-General.[53] In a passing-off action the court is not concerned with the truth or falsity of statements in the defendant's advertisements except so far as they tend to induce the belief that the defendant's goods or business are the claimant's.[54]

Inferiority of the spurious goods need not be shown

It is immaterial to the existence of the claimant's right of action that the **14–31** goods passed off as his are as good as or better than his own[55]; or that the defendant does not undersell him.[56] When it comes to assessment of damages, all such matters are material.[57]

Comparison with the action for the infringement of a trade mark

As a matter of legal history, it may be said that the actions for **14–32** infringement of trade mark and for passing-off have a common origin— the latter is a generalisation of the old action for infringement— but they are now distinct. With the new law of trade marks, the two causes of action have converged somewhat, in the sense that a wider variety of indicia may now be eligible for registration, and reputation can (under section 10(2) of the 1994 Act) and must (under section 10(3)) be relevant. Nonetheless it remains the case that the cause of action in passing off is wider and more flexible, giving protection to all the means by which the claimant's trade or goods may be identified with him, and not just those

---

[50] *Morecombe v. Mecca* [1966] R.P.C. 423 (beauty contests)
[51] *Borthwick v. Evening Post* (1888) 37 Ch.D. 449; *Du Boulay v. Du Boulay* (1869) L.R. 2 P.C. 430.
[52] *Day v. Brownrigg* (1878) 10 Ch.D. 294; *Street v. Bank of Spain and England* (1885) 30 Ch.D. 156 (adoption by the defendants (bankers) of the same cypher telegraphic address as that of the claimant).
[53] *Per* Cotton L.J. in *Native Guano v. Sewage Manure* (1891) 8 R.P.C. 125, at 128; the proposition seems correct, notwithstanding the criticism of this case in *"Advocaat"*, *supra*; see also *Clark v. Freeman* and *Williams v. Hodge*, cited below.
[54] *Bowden Wire v. Bowden Brake* (1913) 30 R.P.C. 580 at 618.
[55] *Blofeld v. Payne* (1833) 4 B. & Ad. 410; *Edelsten v. Edelsten* (1863) 1 De G.J. & S. 185, Westbury L.C.; *per* Lord Blackburn in *Singer v. Loog* (1882) 8 App.Cas. 15 at 29.
[56] *Per* Joyce J. in *Spicer v. Spalding & Hodge* (1915) 32 R.P.C. 52 at 59.
[57] See *post*, paras 18–139 *et seq.*

which he has managed to get registered. It is also more onerous, in the sense that the claimant must prove his reputation and that the defendant's activities involve a false representation damaging to the claimant's goodwill.

14–33   The main consequence of this need to prove in each case that a false representation has been made is less that an action for passing off differs from an action for infringement of trade mark—they do not in general differ greatly—than that a registered trade or service mark is a species of property, and may be regarded as such, to an extent that the right to sue for passing off cannot. Whilst there is no doubt that goodwill may be a saleable asset, and it is goodwill, or reputation, that founds most passing-off actions, it must be remembered that transactions in goodwill do not necessarily give rights against third persons: the "purchaser" of the "right" to use a certain name or badge acquires no right of action, unless he can show that the use of it by others will amount to false representation.

Where trade mark action fails, passing-off action may succeed on the same evidence

14–34   A claimant may fail to make out a case of infringement of a trade mark for various reasons and may yet show that by imitating the mark claimed as a trade mark, or otherwise, the defendant has done what is calculated to pass off his goods as those of the claimant. A claim in "passing off" has generally been added as a second string to actions for infringement, and has on occasion succeeded where the claim for infringement has failed.[58]

The Trade Marks Act affords no bar to a passing-off action

14–35   Subject to possibly one qualification,[59] nothing in the Trade Marks Act 1994 affects a trader's right against another in an action for passing off.[60] It is, therefore, no bar to an action for passing off that the trade name, get-up or any other of the badges identified with the claimant's business, which are alleged to have been copies or imitated by the defendant, might have been, but are not registered as, trade marks, even

---

[58] *Hart v. Colley* (1890) 44 Ch.D. 193; 7 R.P.C. 93. *Jay v. Ladler* (1888) 40 Ch.D. 649; 6 R.P.C. 136; *Montgomery v. Thompson*, 41 Ch.D. 35; 6 R.P.C. 404; [1891] A.C. 217; 8 R.P.C. 361 (CA and HL); *"Yorkshire Relish"* [1897] A.C. 710; 14 R.P.C. 720; *Barber v. Manico* (1893) 10 R.P.C. 93.

[59] See s.48 (effect of acquiescence) (especially s.48(1)(b)) which relates to unregistered as well as registered trade marks, and consequently, though its provision so far as common law rights are concerned are probably only declaratory, must be regarded as qualifying the general provisions of s.2. S.22(3), dealing with assignments, also affects common law rights.

[60] This is expressly declared by s.2(2), but the law was the same under the earlier Acts which, prior to the 1905 Act, contained no such express provision.

though the evidence is wholly addressed to what may be a mark capable of registration. Again, it is no defence to passing off that the defendant's mark is registered.[61] The Act offers advantages to those who register their trade marks, but imposes no penalty upon those who do not. It is equally no bar to an action for passing off that the false representation relied upon is an imitation of a trade mark that is incapable of registration.[62] A passing-off action can even lie against a registered proprietor of the mark sued upon.[63] Such unregistered marks are frequently referred to as "common law trade marks".

New case of fraud or of passing off raised at the trial

If a charge of fraud is to be made at the trial, it is essential that it should **14–36** be put forward clearly and prominently on the pleadings.[64] But the fact that the claimants have not pleaded fraud does not exclude the court from considering whether fraud in fact existed.[65] A claimant who has raised no issue upon his pleadings except in regard to the infringement of his trade mark has been refused leave to amend his claim at the trial so as to start a fresh case of "passing off" in order to save his action.[66]

2. Goodwill

Since the purpose of a claim in passing off is to protect goodwill, and **14–37** essential ingredients in the tort are the existence of goodwill and actual or threatened damage to it, it is as well to identify, as best we can, what goodwill is and the goodwill which is relevant to a claim in passing off. In many situations, the existence and ownership of goodwill are readily

---

[61] See para. 14–276.
[62] "*Camel Hair Belting*" (*Reddaway v. Banham*), quoted *ante*, para. 14–15, was such a mark; it was hopelessly descriptive.
[63] *e.g. Thorne v. Pimms* (1907) 26 R.P.C. 221; see also para. 14–52.
[64] *Leahy, Kelly v. Glover* (1893) 10 R.P.C. 141, HL; *Claudius Ash v. Invicta* (1911) 28 R.P.C. 252 and 597; 29 R.P.C. 465; *cf. United Kingdom Tobacco v. Malayan Tobacco* (1933) 51 R.P.C. 11, PC (fraud neither pleaded nor suggested in cross-examination; finding of fraud unjustified); *Bulmer v. Bollinger* [1978] R.P.C. 79; and see now, CPR 16PD–009. 2(1).
[65] *John Walker v. Ost* [1970] R.P.C. 489 (fraud was found but not pleaded); *Midland Counties Dairy v. Midland Dairies* (1948) 65 R.P.C. 429; *Bulmer v. Bollinger, supra.*
[66] *Native Guano v. Sewage Manure* (1887) 4 R.P.C. 478; 8 R.P.C. 125 (CA and HL); but the whole case was a mess, see *per* Lord Diplock in "*Advocaat*" at [1980] R.P.C. 96. Leave was granted, the defendants not objecting, in *Jay v. Ladler* (1888) 40 Ch.D. 649; 6 R.P.C. 136, and also in *Barber v. Manico* (1893) 10 R.P.C. 93, where the defendants raised the objection. But see *Andrew v. Kuehnrich* (1913) 30 R.P.C. 93, where at the trial the claimants were given leave to amend so as to claim clearly for infringement as well as passing off. *cf. Cellular Clothing v. White* (1953) 70 R.P.C. 9, where the claimants, having included in their writ claims both in infringement and in passing off, limited their statement of claim to passing off, then sought at the trial to add a claim for relief for infringement; Harman J. refused leave, saying that claim had been abandoned. But where claimants had claimed for passing off in their writ, but not in their statement of claim, and had, on an application in chambers stated that they claimed only for infringement of trade mark, they were, nevertheless, allowed to amend by adding a claim for passing off, shortly before the trial: *Rossell v. Hodges* (1918) 35 R.P.C. 285.

apparent or not worth disputing. However, the resolution of disputes over the ownership of goodwill and issues concerning the territoriality of goodwill sometimes require a more precise identification of what is required to found a passing-off action.

What constitutes goodwill

14–38 The nature of goodwill has been stated many times, but has not been defined. It is probably not capable of precise definition. In the context of passing off, it has been stated to represent, in connection with any business or business product, the value of the attraction to customers which the name and reputation possesses.[67] It is often described as "the attractive force which brings in custom", an extract from the classic statements[68] concerning goodwill in *IRC v. Muller's Margarine*[69] by Lords Macnaghten and Lindley. The particular issue in that case was whether the goodwill of a business was located in Germany or in England, for the purposes of the Stamp Acts. That context has undoubtedly contributed to the current view, in English law, that goodwill is "local in character and divisible",[70] a view not shared in Australia, in particular.[71]

Note that the goodwill required to sustain a passing off action is not necessarily the same as goodwill referred to in other contexts.[72]

---

[67] *Reuter v. Muhlens* (1953) 70 R.P.C. 235 at 254.
[68] The relevant passages are cited in Chap. 12, at paras 12–37 and 12–38.
[69] [1901] A.C. 217 at 223.
[70] Lord Diplock, giving the opinion of the Privy Council in *Star Industrial v. Yap Kwee Kor* [1976] F.S.R 256 (PC, Singapore).
[71] See further, below at paras 14–54 *et seq*.
[72] For example, an accountant's notion and valuation of the goodwill of a company, would include "passing off" goodwill, but probably much else besides. The various elements of goodwill (for the purposes of landlord and tenant law) were colourfully described by Scrutton L.J. in *Whiteman Smith Motor Company v. Chaplin* [1934] 2 K.B. 35 at 42, as follows:

"A division of the elements of goodwill was referred to during argument and appears in Mr Merlin's book [on the Landlord and Tenant Act] as 'cat, rat and dog' basis. The cat prefers the old home though the person who has kept the house leaves. The cat represents that part of the customers who continue to go to the old shop, though the old shopkeeper has gone; the probability of their custom may be regarded as an additional value given to the premises by the tenant's trading. The dog represents that part of the customers who follow the person rather than the place; these the tenant may take away with him if he does not go too far. There remains a class of customer who may neither follow the place nor the person, but drift away elsewhere. They are neither a benefit to the landlord nor to the tenant, and have been called 'the rat' for no particular reason expect to keep the epigram to the animal kingdom. I believe my brother Maugham has introduced the rabbit, but I will leave him to explain the position of the rabbit. It is obvious that the division of customers into 'cat, rat and dog' must vary enormously in different cases and different circumstances."

Not all these animals would be relevant in passing off. The dog is really the one who counts—for it is he who wants to deal with a particular enterprise. The cat is really only relevant to the situation where a business is continued in the same location under a new proprietor.

Who may bring an action

There are really only two requirements: first, the claimant must own or **14–39**
have a sufficient property interest[73] in the requisite goodwill; secondly,
the goodwill so owned must be the goodwill which is *really likely* to be
damaged by the alleged misrepresentation.

The first requirement is satisfied by virtually all types of legal person
which carry on commercial activity: individuals, partnerships, corpora-
tions: but probably not by unincorporated associations,[74] who must
bring their action in a different guise. Any dispute over precisely which
of a group of companies owns the requisite goodwill is normally
avoided by having sufficient of the companies as claimants and/or
brushed aside.[75] Some illustrations of the limits of "commercial activity"
are discussed below. The second requirement poses no problem in the
typical passing off case, but trade associations in particular fall foul of it:

(1) Chocosuisse was a trade association representing the interests
of Swiss chocolate manufacturers. Chadwick L.J. was "unable to
identify any business interest or goodwill which the trade
association Chocosuisse is entitled to protect in an action in
England for passing off against a trader. Chocosuisse does not
manufacture or sell Swiss chocolate.": *Chocosuisse*.[76] It would be
otherwise if a trader was misrepresenting himself to be a
member of the association, (see below).
(2) The claimant's logo promoted Irish food and not the claimant
nor any business in which it was engaged: *An Bord Trachtala v.
Waterford Foods*.[77]

The need for some form of commercial activity

It seems clear that the claimant in an action for passing off must show, if **14–40**
not that he has some sort of business which is threatened by the
defendant's activities, at least that his interest is something akin to that
of the owner of a business.[78]

"It should never be forgotten that in these cases the sole right to
restrain anybody from using any name he likes in the course of any

---

[73] *cf.* the *Champagne* type case.
[74] *cf. Workman v. Johns* [1960] R.P.C. 265 at 269 ("Dog Defence") with *British Legion v.
British Legion Club* (1931) 48 R.P.C. 555 at 562, and consider also precisely how the
unincorporated association is supposed to own goodwill. See the illustrations below.
[75] As in *Dawnay, Day & Co. Ltd v. Cantor Fitzgerald International* [2000] R.P.C. 669.
[76] "Chocosuisse" [1999] R.P.C. 826, CA. The same point could have been made in *Parma
Ham* but it was not disputed there. In *Scotch Whisky Association v. J.D. Vintners Ltd*
(March 6, 1996) [1997] Eur. L.R. 446, Sir Richard Scott V.-C. said it was rightly accepted
that the association had no cause of action in passing off.
[77] [1994] F.S.R. 316 (Keane J., HC, Eire).
[78] *Kean v. McGiven* [1982] F.S.R. 119, CA; (name of political party, injunction refused).

business he chooses to carry on is a right in the nature of a trade mark, that is to say, a man has a right to say, 'You must not use a name, whether fictitious or real—you must not use a description, whether true or not, which is to represent, or calculated to represent, to the world that your business is my business, and so, by a fraudulent misstatement, deprive me of the profits of the business which would otherwise come to me.' An individual plaintiff can only proceed on the ground that having established a business reputation under a particular name, he has a right to restrain anyone else from injuring his business by using that name.'"[79]

The business concerned certainly need not be a trading business in any ordinary sense.[80]

14–41   Many instances will be found later in this chapter. Actions about business names as distinct from trade marks are often concerned with service industries rather than trading: see in particular the illustrations to paragraphs 14–194 *et seq*. There are a number of instances of actions for the passing-off of books, plays, films: see the illustrations in paragraphs 14–223 *et seq*. Other instances include disputes between rival beauty contests: *Morecambe v. Mecca* [1962] R.P.C. 145 (no real risk of damage and names not close enough); *Miss World v. James St.* [1981] F.S.R. 309, CA (beauty contest and "ugly contest" film: activities too different); business of looking after children: *Deane v. Schofield* [1962] R.P.C. 179; clubs of one sort or another: *Annabel's v. Schock* [1972] R.P.C. 847, CA (club and escort agency sufficiently "related" for injunction to be granted); *Ad-Lib Club v. Granville, infra*; almost anything fairly called a business will do, but the further one gets from trade the harder, it would seem, to persuade a court to take the complaint seriously.

Further, a business need no longer be in existence at all, provided there remains a residual goodwill which the claimant might wish to sell or use in a reopened business.[81] If once the business is definitely abandoned, however, so that the claimant no longer owns goodwill, there can be no passing off.[82]

---

[79] *Levy v. Walker* (1879) 10 Ch.D. 436 at 447, *per* James L.J.
[80] See above at 14–35.
[81] *Ad-Lib Club v. Granville* [1970] 2 All E.R. 300; [1972] R.P.C. 673 (reputation proved four years after business closed. No intention to abandon goodwill); *cf. Kark v. Odhams* [1962] R.P.C. 163 (illus. 5, para. H-14–226); *Levey v. Henderson-Kenton* [1974] R.P.C. 617; *Thermawear v. Vedonis Thermawarm* [1982] R.P.C. 44 (mark little used for five years before writ).
[82] *Star Industrial v. Yap Kwee Kor* [1976] F.S.R. 256 (PC, Singapore: business in Singapore closed down and goodwill disposed of).

Professional associations and other institutions and organisations

It is clear that a professional association of sufficient standing may sue **14–42** to prevent others imitating either its name or the initials by which qualified persons indicate their membership of it. Similarly, with charitable institutions and perhaps even religious organisations[83]:

(1) In *Society of Accountants and Auditors v. Goodway*,[84] the claimant society sued to restrain non-members from using a name which was calculated to represent them as being members of it, and it was held that it suffered a legal injury thereby, inasmuch that it was of pecuniary value to the society to have as many members as possible, and that the acts complained of, by reducing its status, might affect the number of its members.

(2) In *Society of Incorporated Accountants v. Vincent*[85] the plaintiff society was granted an injunction to restrain the use of the letters "F.S.A.A." or of any other letters or designation likely to induce the belief that the defendant was a fellow of the society.

(3) In *Australian Society of Accountants v. Federation of Australian* **14–43** *Accountants Inc*[86] the defendant was restrained from offering professional accounting qualifications which were solely offered by the claimant, for a price—this was sufficient to constitute trade.

(4) The British Legion (an ex-servicemen's organisation formed after the 1914–18 war) sued to prevent the use of the words "British Legion" in the name of a local club. It was contended that, even allowing a possibility of confusion, there could be no damage to the claimants. It was held that if the defendant club got into trouble, this must inevitably reflect discredit on the claimants, and an injunction was granted: *British Legion v. British Legion Club*.[87]

---

[83] See the Australian case of *A.-G. v. Holy Apostolic & Catholic Church of the East* (1991) 98 A.L.R. 327, Supreme Court of NSW—Young J., but note that English law is stricter on the requirement for goodwill.

[84] [1907] 1 Ch. 489; 24 R.P.C. 159. A similar decision was given in Scotland in *Society of Accountants in Edinburgh v. Corporation of Accountants* (1903) 20 R. 750. See also *Tones and Moore v. Merchant Service Guild* (1908) 25 R.P.C. 474; *British Legion v. British Legion Club* (1931) 48 R.P.C. 555; *Clock v. Clock House* (1936) 53 R.P.C. 269; *Walter v. Ashton* [1902] 2 Ch. 282. There have been in addition a number of unreported cases in which professional associations have secured interlocutory injunctions to protect their names or initials, whilst proposed company names which would obviously be objectionable in this sort of way are known to have been rejected or refused by the Registrar of Companies; for instance (it is believed), certain names of the form "Institution of . . . Engineers.

[85] (1954) 71 R.P.C. 325; *cf. Att.-Gen. and General Council of Medical Education v. Barrett Proprietaries* (1933) 50 R.P.C. 45; an action to restrain the use by the defendants of the letters B.P., being the initial letters of British Pharmacopeia, failed; no evidence of fraud.

[86] (1988) 9 I.P.R. 282.

[87] (1931) 48 R.P.C. 555. The point had arisen before, and it was proved that in all other instances, clubs adopting a title including the words "British Legion" had agreed to accept supervision by the plaintiffs.

14-44   (5) The defendants were restrained from using an accident helpline number which was very similar to the claimant's: *The Law Society of England & Wales v. Griffith.*[88]

(6) The scope of the action in passing off was held wide enough to include deception of the public by one charity such that the goodwill of another was appropriated: *The British Diabetic Association v. The Diabetic Society.*[89]

(7) No interlocutory injunction was granted on the balance of the risk of injustice, and the evidence of reputation was scanty, but the claimant charitable institution was entitled to bring an action: *British Association of Aesthetic Plastic Surgeons v. Cambright Ltd.*[90]

Individual traders and personalities

14-45 The position of an individual trader carrying on business presents no difficulty. The old case of *Clark v. Freeman* would be decided differently today.[91] Sir J. Clarke, an eminent physician, failed to restrain the defendant from selling a quack medicine as "Sir J. Clarke's Consumption Pills", on the basis that he carried on no business of pill-making.

Certainly in English law, passing off does not extend so as to provide a "right of personality", whereas other jurisdictions have gone further[92]:

(1) The claimant was a well-known broadcaster on the Children's Hour programme of the BBC under the name "Uncle Mac". The defendants began selling a cereal under the name "Uncle Mac". It was held that as the claimant was not engaged in any degree in producing or marketing cereals, there could not be passing off by the defendants of any goods or business of the claimant: *McCullock v. May* (1947) 65 R.P.C. 58.[93]

14-46   (2) In *Kaye v. Robertson* [1991] F.S.R. 62 CA, the claimant was held not to be in the position of a trader in relation to the interest in the story regarding the celebrity's accident and recovery.

---

[88] [1995] R.P.C. 16, Aldous J.
[89] [1996] F.S.R. 1, Robert Walker J.
[90] [1987] R.P.C. 459, Scott J. and see *Guide Dog Owners & Friends Association Inc v. Guide Dog Association of NSW & ACT* (1999) 43 I.P.R. 531, FCA.
[91] Lord Selborne said the case had seldom been cited except to be disapproved: *Riviere* (1884) 26 Ch. D. 48. See also *Maxwell v. Hogg* (1867) L.R. 2 Ch. 307; *Springhead v. Riley* (1868) L.R. 6 Eq. 551; *British Medical Association v. Marsh* (1931) 48 R.P.C. 565 at 574, where Maugham J. reviewed the authorities since *Clark v. Freeman.* See also *"Albert Hall"* (1934) 51 R.P.C. 398. *cf.* the case of the name of a private house, para. 14–30; and *cf. Tolley v. Fry* [1931] A.C. 333.
[92] See also the character merchandising cases, discussed below and chap. 22 at paras 22–42 et seq.
[93] The Australian High Court held "Uncle Mac" wrongly decided: but the definition of passing off there propounded is not that of our House of Lords, and the Australian case itself (*Henderson v. Radio Corp.* [1969] R.P.C. 218, professional ballroom dancers suing to prevent representation that defendants' dance-music records were connected with them) could well have been decided the same way by an English court.

(3) In *Hogan v. Pacific Dunlop*[94] the actor who played Crocodile Dundee in the film of that name succeeded in an action for passing off against the defendant who had produced a television commercial which was easily recognisable as a parody of a scene from the film known as the "knife scene". The Crocodile Dundee character was an extension or exaggeration of the claimant's own personality, as projected in various television advertisements in which he had appeared.

Ownership of goodwill

Identification of the person who benefits from and therefore owns the **14–47** attractive force which brings in custom is straightforward in the old-fashioned case of a shop selling its own produce. As commerce has grown in complexity and particularly with the advent of the Internet, there are myriad ways in which goods reach the ultimate consumer and a number of traders are likely to be involved in that process. In these circumstances, issues can arise as to who is the owner of the relevant goodwill. So far as the provision of services is concerned, there tends, necessarily, to be a somewhat more direct relationship between the provider of the service and the consumer. Even here, modern commercial methods, franchising for example, tend to increase the divide between the owner of the goodwill and the consumer. Likewise with the provision of information over the Internet.

Similar issues arise when two parties originally connected with goods **14–48** or services become estranged: who is entitled to the goodwill? The resolution of these issues is not always easy.[95] Ultimately, the issue as to who owns the goodwill is a question of fact, to be determined in all the circumstances. Normally, the issue is decided by the answer to this question[96]: of whom is the indicia (whether it be a name, mark or get-up) distinctive?

There have been a number of cases which have taken the form of **14–49** passing off actions but can also be regarded as disputes over the ownership of goodwill. There are other cases where goodwill has been divided lawfully or shared. In such cases it is now clear that those entitled to the goodwill cannot interfere with each other, but all have a right against third parties. The issue arises most often across territorial boundaries, discussed next. There are a number of further examples in various parts of this chapter.[97]

---

[94] (1988) 83 A.L.R. 403, Gummow J. and (1989) 87 A.L.R. 14 (Sheppard, Beaumont and Burchett JJ.) See also *10th Cantanae Pty Ltd v. Shoshana Pty Ltd* (1987) 79 A.L.R. 299 (Wilcox, Pincus and Gummow JJ.) (failed to establish misrepresentation).

[95] See, *e.g. Scandecor Development v. Scandecor Marketing* [1999] F.S.R. 26, CA.

[96] Note that the views of persons in the trade (who generally know with whom they are dealing) may not indicate the "right" answer to this question.

[97] See paras 14–90 to 14–99, 14–141 to 14–144, 14–294, 14–295.

Foreign manufacturers

14–50 A foreign manufacturer, who does not trade in this country but whose goods are sold in this country, may well acquire a protectable goodwill in his trade name or trade marks.[98] There will then be what in principle is a pure question of fact, whether the goodwill is that of the foreign manufacturer or the importer.[99] This is the sort of question of fact on which a court's finding is easily influenced by its feelings as to the merits of the case; the objection that an importer has no independent goodwill, so often successful when raised on behalf of the manufacturer or of a trader dealing in the manufacturer's own goods,[1] is likely to be brushed aside as a mere technicality when made by a defendant having no connection with the "genuine" goods.

14–51 (1) The claimants were American manufacturers of arc-lamps. An English syndicate had lamps made to their order by the claimants and sold them in England under the mark "Stewart". Later, the syndicate's business passed to the defendants, who took to getting lamps from an English manufacturer, and the American claimants set up a sales agency over here. Both parties claimed the exclusive right to call their lamps "Stewart". It was held that the goodwill in the mark had belonged to the syndicate and so had passed to the defendants; so the defendants got the injunction: *Defries v. Electric Accessories* (1906) 23 R.P.C. 341.

14–52 (2) The firm of Köpke, wine merchants, had previously imported wine from the Quinta de Roriz vineyard in Portugal. At a later stage, they registered a trade mark for wine, "Köpke Roriz", and took to selling under it wine, much of which did not come from the Quinta de Roriz. There was evidence of representations to the public that there was a connection with the Quinta de Roriz. The owners of the vineyard were granted an injunction against Köpke restraining them from selling any other wine under the name "Roriz", the fact that the mark was registered being irrelevant: *Van Zeller v. Mason, Cattley* (1907) 25 R.P.C. 37.

14–53 Even though the claimant is a foreign manufacturer, and the defendant's goods come from the same foreign country, it may be proper to try in this country an action about passing off here, and to allow service of the

---

[98] See, *e.g.* "Panhard," illus. (1), above at para. 14–61.

[99] *cf. Reuter v. Muhlens* (1953) 70 R.P.C. 102; [1954] Ch. 50; 70 R.P.C. 235, CA ("4711") and *Adrema v. Adrema-Werke* [1958] R.P.C. 323 (both enemy-property cases) with *"Manus"* (1948) 65 R.P.C. 329; (1949) 66 R.P.C. 71.

[1] See *Imperial Tobacco v. Bonnan*; illus. (2) para. 14–143; *Dental Mfg v. de Trey* [1912] 3 K B. 76; 29 R.P.C. 617; *"Manus" supra*; *Roberts Numbering Machine v. Davis* (1936) 53 R.P.C. 79. *Cf. Sturtevant Engineering v. Sturtevant Mill* (1936) 53 R.P.C. 430 and *Suhner v. Suhner* [1967] R.P.C. 336.

writ upon the foreign supplier of the defendant's goods for that purpose.[2]

It is not necessary that the association of the claimant's mark with his goods should be known all over the country, or to every person in the area where it is known best.[3]

The territorial nature of goodwill

The claimant in an action founded on passing off in the United Kingdom **14–54** must of course prove that the acts complained of amount to a misrepresentation: which will normally involve proof that he has a reputation in this country—that the disputed badge, trade mark or trade name, is in this country distinctive of his goods or business.[4] But he must do more: since an essential ingredient of passing off is damage (or prospective damage) to goodwill, he must show that he had, at the date when the defendants started up,[5] in this country not merely a reputation but also a goodwill capable of being damaged. Goodwill, however, is local[6]: it is situated where the business is. Thus a foreign claimant may have a reputation in this country—from travellers or periodicals of international circulation or, increasingly, from exposure on the Internet—yet still fail in an action for passing off because he has here no business and so no goodwill. Such cases have been not uncommon in recent years, and have caused considerable difficulty. Where there is a substantial reputation here, our courts will often accept minimal evidence that a business exists here[7]; but there has to be some.

The decisions on this point are not easy to reconcile and in some the **14–55** reasoning is artificial. The more difficult cases raise fundamental questions about whether goodwill must be treated as local or whether it is time to recognise the existence of international goodwill.[8] If goodwill has to be treated as local, then the debate turns to what is required to establish a goodwill in this country: is it sufficient merely to have customers here, in circumstances where no business is being carried on

---

[2] *"Harris Tweed"* (*Macaulay v. Hepworths*) [1961] R.P.C. 184. In the end, however, the dispute was tried in Scotland: [1964] R.P.C. 477. As to jurisdiction over defendants from EEC countries, see Civil Jurisdiction and Judgments Act 1982, Sched. 1, art. 5(3).

[3] *Faulder v. Rushton* (1903) 20 R.P.C. 477, CA ("Silverpan Jam"); and below, para. 14–159, (area), and paras 14–150 *et seq.*, (secondary distinctive meaning).

[4] *Oertli v. Bowman* [1957] R.P.C. 388 at 397, CA; [1959] R.P.C. 1, HL (*"Turmix"*). See also *Goodfellow v. Prince* (1887) 35 Ch.D. 9, CA.

[5] *Anheuser-Busch v. Budejovicky Budvar* [1984] F.S.R. 413 at 462, CA.

[6] *Star Industrial v. Yap Kwee Kor* [1976] F.S.R 256 (PC, Singapore).

[7] See *Poiret*, illus. 2, at para. 14–61; *Penney v. Punjabi Nick* [1979] F.S.R. 26 (Hong Kong: presence of retail trader's purchasing subsidiary in the then Colony enough to support passing-off action against another retailer); *Globelegance v. Sarkissian* [1974] R.P.C. 603; *Esanda v. Esanda Finance* [1984] F.S.R. 96 (N.Z.; Australian company suing in N.Z.); *Nishika v. Goodchild* [1990] F.S.R. 371, Knox J., where the way in which the defendant misrepresented his connection with the claimant's foreign business actually established a sufficiently protectible goodwill here. *cf. Bristol Conservatories* [1989] R.P.C. 455, CA.

[8] See *"The Hit Factory"*, *Pete Waterman Ltd v. CBS United Kingdom Ltd* (1990) 20 I.P.R. 185, Browne-Wilkinson V.-C.

in the United Kingdom?[9] If goodwill does not have to be treated as local,[10] then the focus of the action shifts effectively (as it has done in Canada,[11] Australia[12], New Zealand[13] and elsewhere[14]) to the existence of an international reputation and damage to it.[15]

14–56 Some versions of this type of case present no real difficulty. The first is, where the claimant has no significant reputation here: the name or mark was in origin his, and he may hope to exploit it here someday, but it is not yet here associated in the public mind with any business or any goods. Clearly, his action must fail.[16] This category overlaps the "merchandising" cases discussed below, where the defendant adopts the name of (say) a film or television character before the promoter's "merchandising" operations are under way.[17] The second is, where the claimant simply cannot show damage: it is annoying to him to have his name or mark copied in a foreign country, but he has no business there

---

[9] The positive answer to this question given in *"The Hit Factory"* (*op cit.*), requires distinct modification of the traditional notions of goodwill.

[10] The cases which underpin this approach in English law could have been decided on other grounds: notably: *Crazy Horse* (lack of sufficient reputation, a case dismissing an application for an interlocutory injunction); *Star Industrial* (lack of sufficient reputation in Singapore, the slight trading relied on having ceased three years previously); *Budweiser* (collision of independent rights. Whitford J. at first instance drew the analogy with honest concurrent user from the 1938 Act). The notion that goodwill must be local stems from *IRC v. Muller* (a case about the Stamp Act). The fact that the notion of local goodwill was consistent with most trading arrangements then does not mean that it is necessary to adhere to it now. Obviously, this is a House of Lords point.

[11] *Orkin Exterminating Co. Inc v. Pest Co. of Canada Ltd* (1985) 19 D.L.R. (4th) 90. (Ontario CA; claimant providing services to real property in the United States with customers in Canada who owned United States property but with no Canadian business, held to have a protectable goodwill in Canada).

[12] See *ConAgra, op cit.* at n. 10, para. 14–07, at and the discussion of the Australian and other cases there. Note in particular, the role of fraud in the pre-*Crazy Horse* cases: see Gummow J. at 519–523, citing in particular, Farwell J. in *Panhard Levassor, arguendo*: the defendants either meant "to steal the plaintiffs' business or to prevent them having any in England": "they are wrong on either alternative".

[13] *Dominion Rent A Car v. Budget Rent A Car System* (1987) 9 I.P.R. 367, although there has been disagreement from Casey J. in particular, who dissented in *Dominion* and followed the English approach in *Esanda Ltd v. Esanda Finance Ltd* [1984] F.S.R. 96 at 100.

[14] *e.g.* in Hong Kong see *Tan-Ichi v. Jancar* [1990] F.S.R. 151 (H.K., H Ct); in India *Apple Computer Inc. v. Apple Leasing Industries Ltd* (1992) 22 I.P.R. 257 (HC, Delhi); *Calvin Klein Inc. v. International Apparel Syndicate* [1995] F.S.R. 515 (HC, Calcutta); *Yahoo! Inc. v. Akash Arora* [1999] F.S.R. 931 (HC, Delhi).

[15] *cf.* Learned Hand J. in *Yale Electric Corp. v. Robertson* 26 F. 2d 972 (1928) at 974: "If another uses [the claimant's mark], he borrows the owner's reputation, whose quality no longer lies within his own control. This is an injury, even though the borrower does not tarnish it, or divert any sales by its use; for a reputation, like a face, is the symbol of its possessor and creator, and another can use it only as a mask. And so it has come to be recognised that, unless the borrower's use is so foreign to the owner's as to insure against any identification of the two, it is unlawful."

[16] *Elida Gibbs v. Colgate-Palmolive* [1983] F.S.R. 95, where the defendants, knowing of the claimants' intended launch, got their advertisements in the day before, and the claimants got an interlocutory injunction, may be considered the exception that proves the rule.

[17] See *post*, para. 14–77 and the footnotes thereto; *cf. Taverner Rutledge v. Trexapalm* [1977] R.P.C. 275 ("*Kojak*"): the defendants, not the claimants, had a "licence" from the owners of the television series, but the claimants had the reputation and goodwill and an interim injunction was granted.

and his profits are in no way diminished thereby.[18] More difficult is the case where he has a substantial reputation, which he hopes or even positively intends to exploit by business activities here.[19] The court will then no doubt accept very small indications that exploitation has actually started as justifying intervention.[20] There remain, however, cases where there is a reputation, where there is damage—there may be customers here, even though no business is carried on here and no goods are sold nor services provided here[21]—but the goodwill is situate elsewhere. As will be seen, this type of case is not new, but the problem has become more acute with the increase in international travel, the growth of multinational businesses and the increasing influence of the Internet. Clarification of the law on this point may be some time coming for three reasons: first, a claimant may be able to avoid tackling this issue by proving that the conduct complained of is actionable under the law of a foreign country and the defendant should be restrained here (see below); secondly, if the claimant can show that he is "well-known" in the United Kingdom, he can rely on section 56 of the Trade Marks Act 1994 and any accompanying passing-off claim may not need to be decided; thirdly, special facts are required, the more so because of the previous two points.

(1) The claimants were proprietors of an establishment in Paris **14–57** called "Crazy Horse Saloon". The defendants set up an establishment in London (in some respects similar), advertising it as

---

[18] *Lyngstad v. Anabas* [1977] F.S.R. 62 (foreign pop-group with no merchandising here); *Wienerwald v. Kwan* [1979] F.S.R.381 (Hong Kong: "international" reputation only).

[19] *Athlete's Foot v. Cobra* [1980] R.P.C. 343 (intention to merchandise here, but nobody here yet in trading relation with claimant: no passing off rights); *Amway v. Eurway* [1972] F.S.R. 213 (U.S. company about to trade here which has publicised that: no claim in passing-off); *Home Box Office v. Channel 5 Home Box Office* [1982] F.S.R. 449 (U.S. cable TV company with only slight business links here—held to have sufficient activity to create arguably a goodwill here); *B.B.C. v. Talbot* [1980] F.S.R. 228 (said that preparations for an operation may create protectible goodwill; but no foreign element); *Baskin-Robbins v. Gutman* [1976] F.S.R. 545 (the claimant hoped or intended to merchandise here; the defendant offered an undertaking: the judge refusing to follow *Star Industrial*). In another case the same judge, Graham J., refused to follow "*Crazy Horse*" as inconsistent with the Rome Treaty: *Maxim's v. Dye* [1977] F.S.R. 364. See also "*Rib Shack," My Kinda Bones v. Dr. Pepper's Stove* [1984] R.P.C. 289, where the cases are reviewed: substantial preparations for trade here and substantial reputation but no actual trade: statement of claim not struck out. An extreme case was *Fletcher Challenge v. Fletcher Challenge Pty.* [1982] F.S.R. (NSW; a few hours' reputation only; the court refused to follow "*Crazy Horse*.") This is, of course, just the sort of situation where anticipatory registration of a service mark is called for.

[20] As in *B.B.C. v. Talbot, supra.*

[21] As in *Pete Waterman Ltd v. CBS United Kingdom Ltd* (1990) 20 I.P.R. 185, "*The Hit Factory*" where Sir Nicholas Browne-Wilkinson V.-C., clearly favouring the Australian approach, observed: "In my view, the law will fail if it does not try to meet the challenge thrown up by trading patterns which cross national and jurisdictional boundaries due to a change in technical achievement. The problem is particularly acute with service industries. . . . As a matter of legal principle, I can see no reason why the courts of this country should not protect the trading relationship between a foreign trader and his United Kingdom customers by restraining anyone in this country from passing himself off as the foreign trader."

"Crazy Horse Saloon comes to London". There was evidence of deception and confusion amongst the public in this country. The claimants had circulated publicity material in English through travel agencies in this country but they had no office in this country and took no bookings here. Held, distinguishing the "*Sheraton*" case (at para. 14–62), that the claimants had failed to show a reputation acquired by user[22] in this country on which an action in passing off could be based: *Bernadin v. Pavilion Properties* [1967] R.P.C. 581.

14–58   (2) The claimants, American brewers of "Budweiser" beer, sued for passing off by sales of Czech "Budweiser". At the date when the Czech brewery entered the United Kingdom market, the claimants had some reputation in this country but no customers here, so no local goodwill: their beer had been on sale in American bases here, but that belonged to their U.S. goodwill: *Anheuser-Busch v. Budejovicky Budvar* [1984] F.S.R. 413, CA, approving "*Athlete's Foot*", *supra*, with the warning that "customers" for this purpose include ultimate retail customers, not merely people buying direct from the claimant (at 465).

14–59   (3) The claimants had a shop in Belfast. They advertised throughout Ireland and had customers in Eire. It was held that they had a protectable goodwill in Eire. "*Crazy Horse*" was not followed, the Irish court approving a comment in the tenth edition of this work to the effect that the decision in "*Crazy Horse*" was unreasonable: "*C. & A.*" [1978] F.S.R. 126.

Suppose that the claimant in "*Crazy Horse*" had been established not in Paris, but in Berwick-on-Tweed, with customers both sides of the border between England and Scotland, and suppose an imitation over the border. Obviously, an action for passing off would have succeeded: yet strictly speaking, the goodwill would be in Berwick alone.[23]

14–60   It is, of course, open to the Australian,[24] Irish and other[25] courts simply to say that English law is wrong. Most business men certainly, and probably most lawyers, would agree that the very technical rules as to localisation of goodwill have no relevance here, and that in any real sense a business has goodwill, that the court should protect, throughout

---

[22] There is, of course, good authority for the phrase "reputation acquired by user", but it is submitted that the real point is that the reputation in such cases is unaccompanied by goodwill.

[23] Note the emphasis on "England" in Lord Fraser's propositions, cited *ante*, para. 14–09. This "Berwick" example (and the Irish one, below) do not quite comply even with the later customers in this country test of *Athlete's Foot* and "*Budweiser*" (illus. (2), above), since there are no sales actually in the country; even "*Sheraton*," illus. (3) below, admittedly a borderline case, comes a little closer.

[24] See *ConAgra Inc. v. McCain Foods (Aust) Pty. Ltd* (1992) 106 A.L.R. 465, and particularly the exhaustive analyses of the cases by Lockhart J. at 473–490 (English cases), 490–501 (cases from other jurisdictions) and by Gummow J at 529–536.

[25] see nn. 11–15, above.

its catchment area and not merely where the business is carried on.[26] But if we accept that, in English law, C. & A.'s Irish goodwill was localised in Northern Ireland, does it follow that their action should have failed? If the name "C. & A." had been used by an Eire business, not in Eire but in Northern Ireland, the Irish court would, under the usual rules about foreign torts, have had jurisdiction to intervene.[27] It can hardly prevent the court's having jurisdiction over a tort, that it was partly committed at home and not abroad. Perhaps what was wrong in *"Crazy Horse"* was that the action was framed as an English passing off and not as "concurrence déloyale"?

(1) The claimants, French car manufacturers, had no place of business in England, but a number of English people had purchased their cars and brought them back to this country. They were held to have a reputation and a market in England which the court would protect: *Panhard et Levassor v. Panhard Levassor Motor Co.* (1901) 18 R.P.C. 405. **14–61**

(2) The claimant, a Paris couturier, had customers but no place of business here. It is not clear that any sales took place here, but he occasionally visited England; in particular, a show of his dresses had been held at 10 Downing Street, London. His action for passing off by the use of "Poiret" here succeeded: *Poiret v. Poiret* (1920) 37 R.P.C. 177.

(3) The claimants owned a chain of hotels in the United States and other foreign countries, the principal hotels being called "Sheraton Hotels". There was some evidence of advertising reaching this country and bookings being taken at an office kept by the claimants here. The defendant company, "Sheraton Motels Ltd.", proposed to set up an hotel in this country. An interlocutory injunction was granted, the court observing that there could be only one reason for the defendants' choice of "Sheraton" as part of their name: *"Sheraton"* [1964] R.P.C. 202; following *Poiret v. Poiret*, above. **14–62**

(4) The defendant asserted a concurrent right to use "The Hit Factory" for a recording studio in London, based on its long established and bona fide use of that term in America as part of its business operating recording studios which had an international clientele and reputation. In answer, the claimant asserted the defendant had no protectable goodwill in England, as it had no place of business nor rendered any services here. Browne-Wilkinson V.-C. held (a) the existence of a severable English goodwill attached to a place of business in this country is not the basis of a right in passing off. All that was necessary **14–63**

---

[26] A Canadian appellate court has explicitly taken this view, preferring the Irish approach to the English and saying that the definition of "goodwill" used in the English cases was not necessarily appropriate to passing off: *Orkin v. Pestco* (1985) 19 D.L.R. 90.

[27] See *post*, para. 18–43.

was a trade connection here, which will normally consist of customers forming part of the goodwill, wherever it is situate, which goodwill is being invaded by the acts of the defendant in this country, but that (b) that approach was not open, as being contrary to the decision of the Court of Appeal in *Budweiser* and therefore (c) the presence of customers in this country is sufficient to constitute the carrying on of a business here, whether or not there is a place of business or whether services are provided here. Once it is found there are customers, it is open to find that there is a business here to which the local goodwill is attached; and (d) to the extent that the *Crazy Horse* decision was authority to the contrary, he preferred not to follow it: *"The Hit Factory"*, *Pete Waterman Ltd v. CBS United Kingdom Ltd*.[28]

3. The limits of passing off

What is and what is not passing off

14–64 It may aid understanding to examine briefly some examples of situations which lie outside or around the limits of the law of passing off. Some activities which would constitute unfair competition in continental countries clearly lie outside the scope of the tort. This type of case often lacks one of the essential elements of passing off. We discuss these types of cases first. The cases which are most difficult are those where, at first sight, each of the three elements appears to be present yet closer analysis reveals that, for example, apparent deception is being caused by something other than the alleged misrepresentation, or the damage complained of is dilution of distinctiveness which may not be caused by any deception at all. These cases require a clear understanding of the concepts involved and we discuss some of the common points below. These are also illustrated, of course, throughout this entire chapter.

Passing off is not a general tort of unfair competition

14–65 Article 10*bis* of the Paris Convention stipulates that the Convention countries are bound to assure to persons entitled to the benefits of the Convention an effective protection against unfair competition. Any act of competition contrary to honest practices in industrial or commercial matters constitutes an act of unfair competition. The term "unfair competition" is used in the broad sense adopted by countries such as France, Germany and Switzerland.

---

[28] (1990) 20 I.P.R. 185 at 208/209. His desire to find a way round the obstacles highlights the artificiality of the requirement of goodwill in difficult cases such as the one before him.

Under Article 10*ter*, Convention countries are bound to provide nationals of other Convention countries with appropriate legal remedies to repress effectively the acts referred to in Articles 9 (seizure on importation of goods unlawfully bearing a mark or trade name), 10 (seizure on importation of goods unlawfully bearing false indications as to their source or identity of the producer) and 10*bis*.

English law purports to (but does not fully) comply with the United **14–66** Kingdom's obligations as a member of the Paris Convention through the mixture of passing off, malicious falsehood and a variety of criminal statutory provisions to which must be added an ever increasing amount of legislation emanating from the E.U. Most continental European countries provide a generalised cause of action in "unfair competition". It is clear that English law does not. However, it will be found that acts of "unfair competition" likely to cause any real damage to other traders are with few, if any, exceptions within the concept of passing off, as now understood, or more rarely within malicious falsehood, whilst acts of unfair competition likely to cause real damage to the consuming public are within the criminal law, especially that relating to false trade descriptions. There is no doubt that a broad concept of "unfair competition" would benefit some claimants who lie outside the limits of passing off, particularly those who have trouble establishing the necessary goodwill to found the action.

It is not a tort of misrepresentation which injures another trader

The limits of the law of passing off are essentially defined by the classic **14–67** and extended forms of the tort explained above, even though it has been acknowledged that there may be cases which meet the criteria of the extended form yet still do not amount to passing off—the so-called undistributed middle. However, even what is now characterised as the classic form of passing off has often been treated as only a special instance of a more general rule that any misrepresentation calculated to give one trader the benefit of another's goodwill is actionable; or even more generally that any "misrepresentation . . . calculated to injure another in his trade or business" is to be regarded as passing off.[29] The principle has been even more broadly stated[30]:

> "In the interests of fair trading and in the interest of all who may wish to buy or sell goods the law recognises that certain limitations upon freedom of action are necessary and desirable. In some situations the law has had to resolve what might at first appear to be conflicts between competing rights. In solving the problems which have arisen there has been no need to resort to any abstruse principles but rather . . . to the straightforward principle that

---

[29] *per* Parker J. in *Burberry v. Cording* (1909) 26 R.P.C. 693 at 701.
[30] *per* Lord Morris in *Parker-Knoll v. Knoll International* [1962] R.P.C. 265 at 278.

trading must not only be honest but must not even unintentionally be unfair."

14–68 More recent attempts to invoke a tort of unfair competition or to expand passing off to cover such acts have been rebuffed:

(1) In *Insert Media*, at the interim stage, the claimant argued (in addition to passing off) a separate and distinct cause of action to the effect that the law would prevent deliberate acts calculated to cause damage to the claimant's goodwill, based on *Emperor of Austria v. Day*[31] and *Kingdom of Spain v. Christie*.[32] This claim was rejected, even without the benefit of full argument.[33]

(2) Similarly in *Hodgkinson & Corby v. Wards*: "I turn to consider the law and begin by identifying what is not the law. There is no tort of copying. There is no tort of taking a man's market or customers. Neither the market nor the customers are the plaintiff's to own. There is no tort of making use of another's goodwill as such. There is no tort of competition. I say this because at times the plaintiffs seemed close to relying on such torts", *per* Jacob J.[34]

At common law there is no proprietary right in a name or get-up

14–69 It is well settled that (unless registered as a trade mark) no one has a monopoly in his brand name or get up, however familiar these may be. Passing off is a wrongful invasion of a right of property vested in the claimant; but the property which is protected by an action for passing off is not the claimant's proprietary right in the name or get-up which the defendant has misappropriated, but the goodwill and reputation of his business which is likely to be harmed by the defendant's misrepresentation.[35]

The distinction between confusion and deception

14–70 In many authorities the terms "confusion" and "deception" are used to mean the same thing.[36] However, it is necessary to distinguish between "mere confusion" on the one hand and deception or its likelihood on

---

[31] (1861) 3 De. G.F.& J. 217.
[32] [1986] 1 W.L.R. 1120.
[33] *Mail Newspapers v. Insert Media* [1987] R.P.C. 521. The claimant succeeded at full trial in its claim in passing off. See *Associated Newspapers v. Insert Media* [1991] F.S.R. 380, CA.
[34] *op cit.*
[35] See Millett L.J. in *Harrods Ltd v. Harrodian School Ltd* [1996] R.P.C. 697 at 711.
[36] The prevalence of the use of "confusion" rather than "deception" may be caused by a certain squeamishness on the part of claimants and judges to brand defendants as responsible for deception when there is no deliberate intent to deceive. "Deception" should not be seen as a term of opprobrium, except in cases of fraud.

the other. Mere confusion does not indicate or establish passing off. See the following:

(1) "Then it is said—and again there is no disagreement as to this—that the mere fact that the produce of the appellants and that of the respondents may be confused by members of the public is not of itself sufficient."[37]

(2) "It is also a prerequisite that the misrepresentation has deceived or is likely to deceive and that the plaintiff is likely to suffer damage by such deception. Mere confusion which does not lead to a sale is not sufficient. Thus, if a customer asks for a tin of black shoe polish without specifying any brand and is offered the product of A which he mistakenly believes to be that of B, he may be confused as to what he has got but he has not been deceived into getting it. Misrepresentation has played no part in his purchase."[38]

(3) "No one is entitled to be protected against confusion as such. **14–71** Confusion may result from the collision of two independent rights or liberties and where that is the case neither party can complain; they must put up with the results of the confusion as one of the misfortunes which occur in life. The protection to which a man is entitled is protection against passing off, which is a quite different thing from mere confusion.".[39]

(4) "At the heart of passing off lies deception or its likelihood . . . Never has the tort shown even a slight tendency to stray beyond cases of deception."[40]

The position is complicated somewhat by the fact that the dividing line **14–72** between confusion (no passing off) and deception (resulting in passing off) may seem to vary according to the facts of particular cases. This can lead to circular reasoning: an event was an instance of deception because the court found passing off and vice versa. However, the real distinction between mere confusion and deception lies in their causative effects. Mere confusion has no causative effect (other than to confuse lawyers and their clients), whereas if, in answer to the question: "what moves the public to buy?", the insignia complained of is identified, then it is a case of deception. The distinction is blurred somewhat by cases where instances of what would appear to be deception were proved, yet those instances were treated as being "mere confusion" for which the defendant was not held responsible:

(1) Confusion caused by descriptive names: The parties trade **14–73** under names which are purely descriptive (for example Office Cleaning) and some members of the public mistakenly suppose

---

[37] *per* Lord Oliver in *Jif* [1990] R.P.C. 341 at 412.
[38] *per* Lord Jauncey in *Jif* [1990] R.P.C. 341 at 417.
[39] See *Marengo v. Daily Sketch* [1992] F.S.R. 1 at 2, CA *per* Lord Greene M.R.
[40] *Hodgkinson & Corby v. Wards* [1994] 1 W.L.R. 1564, Jacob J. at 1570.

the defendant's product or service is that of the claimant: for example *Office Cleaning Services v. Westminster Office Cleaning Association* 63 R.P.C. 39 at 43, *per* Lord Simonds; *Jif* [1990] R.P.C. 341 at 412, *per* Lord Oliver.

(2) Confusion caused by cessation of a *de facto* monopoly: the claimant has enjoyed a *de facto* monopoly in a particular product; the defendant breaks the monopoly and some members of the public continue to assume, for a time, that the defendant's product is the claimant's: for example *My Kinda Town v. Soll* [1983] R.P.C. 407, CA; and see *Jif* [1990] R.P.C. 341 at 412, *per* Lord Oliver.

14–74

(3) Confusion caused by lack of source motivation: some members of the public purchase the defendant's product whilst under the impression that it is the claimant's product, but they do not care either way: for example *Hodgkinson & Corby v. Wards* [1994] 1 W.L.R. 1564 at 1574G–1575A, 1576G–1577B.

(4) Confusion caused by features common to the trade: some members of the public are under the impression that the defendant's product emanates from the claimant because of his use of features common to both which are also common to the trade as a whole: for example *Payton v. Snelling* 17 R.P.C. 48 at 57, CA; *Williams v. Bronnley* (1909) 26 R.P.C. 765; *Jif* [1990] R.P.C. 341 at 412, *per* Lord Oliver.

Common field of activity

14–75 There is no rule that the defendant must operate in the same field of activity as the claimant. However, this does not mean an examination of their respective fields of activity is irrelevant. The more remote the activities of the parties, the stronger the evidence needed to establish misrepresentation and the real likelihood of damage that are prerequisites of a right of action in passing off. Although this is a question of fact to be determined in the circumstances of the particular case, instances of decisions may be helpful and are given below.

14–76 It may be said generally that establishing passing off by goods in which the claimant does not trade calls for special evidence to establish that the defendant's actions will induce the belief, if not that his goods are those of the claimant[41] at least that his business is an extension of[42] or

---

[41] As in *"Treasure Cot"*, where the judge (Harman J.) granted a declaration against use on dolls' cots of a mark established for babies' cots: (1950) 67 R.P.C. 89—almost the only case in which he found for a plaintiff in passing off in the absence of fraud—having previously doubted whether a manufacturer could ever monopolise a mark outside his own line of business, in *Rolls Razor v. Rolls (Lighters)* (1949) 66 R.P.C. 137 at 142 (an appeal failed, see at 299); and see the old case of *Warwick v. New Motor* (1910) 27 R.P.C. 161 (cycle tyres and motor tyres); *cf.* from the same period, *Lucas v. Fabry* (1906) 23 R.P.C. 33 (cycle accessories and cycle tyres), relief refused. The real point in such cases will ordinarily be the need to show damage to the claimant's goodwill.

[42] *Eastman v. Griffiths* (1898) 15 R.P.C. 105 ("Kodak" for bicycles: the judge found that there was an "intimate connection" between the photographic and cycle trades, so much so that Kodak would probably take to making bicycles).

somehow connected with[43] that of the claimant, or his goods somehow approved or authorised by the claimant.[44] Where the fields of activity of the parties are different, the burden of proving that the defendant causes real likelihood of damage to the claimant is a very heavy one.[45] There is some authority for saying that goodwill may extend to natural future extensions of a business, so that a plaintiff may be entitled to prevent use of his name or marks on goods he expects to sell in the future[46]; but the Court of Appeal in *"Stringfellows"* doubted that loss of a possible field for "merchandising" of the mark concerned was a permissible head of damage in passing off.[47]

"Character merchandising" presents problems here. Unless the public **14–77** can be shown to be well aware of merchandising in the particular field,[48] there will, in general, be no obvious link between the production of television programmes or films (let alone, a pure "merchandising" operation) and the manufacture of toys, clothes, sweets or anything else with which characters' names may be profitably used. Once merchandising is well under way, someone will have a goodwill, but before then, any goodwill is likely to belong to the defendant who is using the name without a licence rather than to the producer of the programme or film or his licensee.[49] Commercially speaking, however, the defendant may be appropriating an asset of considerable value.

Relief granted

Sunglasses and smoking goods: *Dunhill v. Sunoptic* [1979] F.S.R. 337, CA **14–78** (special evidence that reputation extended that far: at 362); scent packaged with genuine "foambath": *Morny v. Ball & Rogers* [1978] F.S.R.

---

[43] *Manchester Brewery v. North Cheshire* [1899] A.C. 83, HL, and see *Bulmer v. Bollinger* and *Harrods v. Harrodian,* cited above.

[44] As in *Morny v. Ball & Rogers,* listed below at para. 14–78.

[45] *"Stringfellows"* [1984] R.P.C. 501 at 546, 547, CA.

[46] *Eno v. Dunn* (1890) 15 App. Cas. 252 at 258, HL; *"Morning Mail"* (1885) 54 L.J.Ch. 1059 (*per* Cotton, L.J.); *Dunlop v. Dunlop Lubricant* (1899) 16 R.P.C. 12; and *cf.* the cases on foreign companies hoping to trade here, *ante* para. 14–56.

[47] *Supra* at 547. Of course, any adoption of a name by others reduces the potentialities for merchandising: whether that reduction is connected with the suggestion that the name as so used denotes a connection with the claimant is another matter. Merchandising in remote fields could be the more affected, if it became known that the name concerned did not necessarily relate to the claimant. Nevertheless, this was accepted as a head of damage in the earlier case of *"Lego"* [1983] F.S.R. 155 at 194–195.

[48] As in *Mirage Studios v. Counter-Feat Clothing Co Ltd* [1991] F.S.R. 145 (Browne-Wilkinson V.-C.)—Ninja Turtles. The defendant's name did not help. *cf. BBC Worldwide v. Pally Screen Printing* [1998] F.S.R. 665, Laddie J. "Teletubbies", where the claimant failed to secure summary judgment against a producer of T-shirts bearing pictures of the Teletubbies. See generally, Chap. 22, paras 22–42 *et seq.*

[49] *"Kojak"* (*Taverner Rutledge v. Trexapalm*) [1977] R.P.C. 275: the defendants, not the plaintiffs, had a licence from the owners of the T.V. series, but the plaintiffs had the reputation and goodwill and were granted an interlocutory injunction. Likewise in *Nice and Safe Attitude Ltd v. Piers Flook* [1997] F.S.R. 14 (on evidence that the defendant had a licence from NASA and claimant did not, defendant's attempt to modify undertakings failed because claimant had built up (somewhat parasitically) sufficient goodwill for clothing); *"Dallas"* (*Lorimar v. Sterling*) [1982] R.P.C. 395 (South Africa; reviewing the English cases); *"Wombles"* [1977] R.P.C. 99 (hiring out of rubbish skips: no common field of activity).

91 ("strongly arguable case"); cigarettes and whisky: *John Walker v. Rothmans* [1978] F.S.R. 357 (both "Red Label" and some similarity of get up: "serious question," although not sufficient likelihood of damage for injunction pending trial); T-shirts and motor cars: *"Golden Jet"* [1979] R.P.C. 19 (some evidence car manufacturer's emblem had been used on T-shirts); spare car parts service and traffic information system using special car radios: *B.B.C. v. Talbot* [1980] F.S.R. 228; "escort agency" and club: *Annabel's v. Schock* [1972] R.P.C. 838, CA; toilet paper and plastic gloves or babies' pants: *L.R.C. v. Lilla Edets* [1973] R.P.C. 560 (both "Mangold"); electronic check-out system and electronic equipment such as computer-aided design system: *"Computervision"* [1975] R.P.C. 171; protective clothing and pollution control: *Ames Crosta v. Pionex* [1977] F.S.R. 46; children's plastic toys and plastic irrigation equipment: *"Lego"* [1983] F.S.R. 155—a decision which shows how far the courts can go when the name is both highly distinctive and very famous[50]; advertising material inserted into newspapers: *Associated Newspapers v. Insert Media* [1991] F.S.R. 380, CA; building society and estate agency: *Nationwide Building Society v. Nationwide Estate Agents Ltd* [1987] F.S.R. 579 (although interlocutory relief refused on other grounds); hi-fi equipment and computer systems (fields which were converging): *NAD Electronics Inc v. NAD Computer Systems Ltd* [1997] F.S.R. 380.

Relief refused

14-79 "Ugly contest" film and beauty contest: *"Miss Alternative World"* [1981] F.S.R. 309, CA; cars and cinemas: *Granada v. Ford* [1973] R.P.C. 49; builders' sub-contracting, in particular plastering and building materials: *Unitex v. Union Texturing* [1973] R.P.C. 119, CA; pop star and pictures of him: *Merchandising Corpn. of America v. Harpbond* [1983] F.S.R. 32, CA; cable television and television programmes (in U.S.A.) and video hire business: *Home Box Office v. Channel 5 Home Box Office* [1982] F.S.R. 449; night club and frozen chips: *Stringfellows* [1984] R.P.C. 501, CA; clothing and shipping and container leasing: *Ocean Pacific Sunwear v. Ocean Pacific Enterprises* (1990) 17 I.P.R. 405; clothing and toiletries: *Blazer v. Yardley* [1992] F.S.R. 501; high quality food retailing in the United Kingdom and lower quality food wholesaling, mainly abroad: *Fortnum & Mason v. Fortnam Ltd* [1994] F.S.R. 438; amusement parks and hotels: *Walt Disney Productions v. Fantasy Hotel Inc.* (1995) 31 I.P.R. 233; fungicide and directory: *BASF v. CEP(UK)* (1996) 35 I.P.R. 241 (Knox J.); department store and preparatory school: *Harrods Ltd v. Harrodian School* [1996] R.P.C. 697, CA.

Distinguishing between reputation and goodwill

14-80 The concepts of reputation and goodwill are very closely related, not least because they are generated in the vast majority of cases by the same trading activity. However, it will aid understanding of difficult

---

[50] Note that on similar facts the plaintiff lost in Australia even though the action was based on the Trade Practices Acts 1974 which provides a remedy at least as wide as passing off: *Lego Australia v. Paul's* (1982) 42 A.L.R. 344.

cases to have clearly in mind the difference between reputation and goodwill, since they are not synonymous. As "the attractive force which brings in custom", goodwill is a form of legal property, representing the connection between business and customer. Reputation is a matter of fact: to what extent is the indicium in question known in the public mind? The existence of reputation does not require there to be a business in this country, whereas there must be some business or market in this country for goodwill to exist.

The cases concerning the territoriality of goodwill (discussed above) **14–81** demonstrate the distinction between goodwill and reputation. If goods bearing the relevant indicia are in or about to be[51] in circulation in this country, then both reputation and goodwill exist here. If the goods are not in circulation and not about to be in circulation, there is no business and no goodwill here, even if the goods are known here (reputation) and the public would buy the goods if they were available here.[52] The provision of services creates different problems. If the services are in fact provided abroad, the presence of customers here would appear to establish reputation but not goodwill unless some business was actually transacted here.[53]

Dilution of distinctiveness as a head of damage

Dilution or erosion of distinctiveness is usually (but not always) raised **14–82** as a head of damage by a claimant who has difficulty in demonstrating any other way in which his goodwill is being damaged by the alleged misrepresentation.[54] In other words, a claim which depends upon dilution as the sole head of damage normally needs to be treated with some caution. Millett L.J. has explained why:

> "Erosion of the distinctiveness of a brand name has been recognised
> as a form of damage to the goodwill of the business with which the
> name is connected in a number of cases, particularly in Australia
> and New Zealand; but unless care is taken this could mark an
> unacceptable extension to the tort of passing off. To date the law
> has not sought to protect the value of a brand name as such, but the

---

[51] Pre-launch publicity establishes a connection between business and customer, the desire to purchase being fulfilled when the goods become available.

[52] As in *Budweiser, op cit.*

[53] In *Sheraton*, there was some business transacted here: in *Crazy Horse*, there was not. In *The Hit Factory*, no business was conducted here, but the judge held that the mere presence of customers here for services provided in the U.S. was sufficient use in this country to establish a goodwill here.

[54] In the U.K., claims of damage by dilution became familiar since they were often raised by claimants seeking to bolster their irreparable damage in order to secure an interlocutory injunction. In that context, the claims were questioned rarely, if at all, not least because other heads of damage were invariably relied upon. Note that "dilution" is accepted in the U.S. as relevant damage, but only in the context of various statutory provisions. U.S. common law has never recognised "dilution" as a head of damage.

value of the goodwill which it generates; and it insists on proof of confusion[55] to justify its intervention. But the erosion of the distinctiveness of a brand name which occurs by reason of its degeneration into common use as a generic term is not necessarily dependent upon confusion at all. . . . I have an intellectual difficulty in accepting the concept that the law insists on the presence of both confusion and damage and yet recognises as sufficient a head of damage which does not depend on confusion."[56]

14–83 Dilution or erosion of distinctiveness has been accepted as a legitimate head of damage by the Court of Appeal in two cases: *BT v. One in a Million*[57] ("Internet domain names") and *Taittinger v. Allbev*[58] ("Elderflower Champagne"). These cases appear to show that the claimant either has to prove fraud or requires something akin to a monopoly interest in the name or indicia so that there is real damage to the exclusivity in the name. In the former case, the trade name "Marks and Spencer" was unusual and famous, so that its inclusion in an Internet domain name rendered the domain name itself an instrument of deception. Erosion of distinctiveness was *a* but not the only head of (threatened) damage. In the latter case it was. The Champagne houses effectively claimed a monopoly in the term, at least in the drinks field. However, whether the claimant is entitled to exclusivity or a monopoly in a particular name or trading indicia begs the question as to whether passing off is established or not. As Millett L.J. indicated, one should concentrate on whether the essential requirements for passing off have been proved. If relevant deception has been proved, it will rarely, if ever, be necessary for a claimant to rely upon dilution. If the tort moves from its current basis, requiring deception and damage to goodwill, then dilution may become more relevant.[59]

4. Direct misrepresentation as to business or goods

Representation as to goods or services

14–84 Where there is a direct misrepresentation by the defendant that the goods he sells or services he offers are the goods or services of the claimant, the case presents no difficulty, though in earlier days the principle was not clearly understood, and innocence was sometimes

---

[55] In this passage it is evident that Millett L.J. is using "confusion" as meaning "deception".
[56] *Per* Millett L.J. in *Harrods Ltd v. Harrodian School Ltd* [1996] R.P.C. 697 at 715–716.
[57] [1999] F.S.R. 1, CA.
[58] [1993] F.S.R. 641, CA.
[59] For those interested in further detail on dilution, see the article by Hazel Carty (1996) 112 L.Q.R. 632.

accepted as a defence.[60] The fact that a company may have used its own name in making a misrepresentation is irrelevant.[61]

Representation as to nature of goods or services

In general, no action lies for passing-off goods as "similar to"[62] or better **14–85** than[63] or a substitute for[64] those of another, even though that other offers to show that the statements are untrue and are injurious to him.[65] However, as noted by Aldous J. in *Ciba-Geigy v. Parke Davis*,[66] "care must be taken in applying in 1993 general statements of the law made in 1898". Goodwill may lie in a reputation for selling particular goods, and if so a false representation by another that his goods are those goods will be actionable.[67] On the other hand, it is not sufficient that the defendant makes a false representation, it must be a false representation related to the claimant's product or goodwill.[68]

The defendant carried on a business of designing and building **14–86** exhibition stands under the name "Tabasco Design", on the basis that one of the designers used by the defendant was "hot". The makers of the well-known "Tabasco" sauce failed in its application for interim relief: *McIlhenny v. Blue Yonder*, (1998) 39 I.P.R. 187.

"I accept—it is not in controversy—that [the defendant], in adopting the name Tabasco, sought to take advantage of a well-known

---

[60] See *Ainsworth v. Walmsley* (1866) L.R. 1 Eq. 518. Upon the facts proved, nowadays the claimant would probably succeed. The court treated the representation as equivalent to a warranty to the purchaser and no more. *cf.* the defence of "acting innocently" under the Merchandise Marks Act 1887, s.2(2)(c): *Christie v. Cooper* [1900] 2 Q.B. 522.

[61] *NAD Electronics v. NAD Computer Systems* [1997] F.S.R. 380 at 392, *per* Ferris J. and see paras 14–280 *et seq.*

[62] *Magnolia Metal v. Tandem Smelting Syndicate* (1900) 15 R.P.C. 701; 17 R.P.C. 477, HL; *Broad v. Graham Building Supplies (No. 1)* [1969] R.P.C. 285 ("as"); *Broad v. Cast Iron Drainage* [1970] F.S.R. 363 ("similar to").

[63] *White v. Mellin* [1895] A.C. 154.

[64] *"Yeast-Vite"* (1934) 51 R.P.C. 110, HL.

[65] *Hubbuck v. Wilkinson* [1899] 1 Q.B. 86; and see cases last cited. This is a matter of public policy, which has developed over the years, so that the courts may well now intervene where a century ago they would not have: see *per* Lord Diplock in *"Advocaat"* [1980] R.P.C. 31, especially at 94. For example, in *Ciba-Geigy, supra*, the judge noted that "the common law could apply different standards to statements about pharmaceuticals to those made about flour", at 21.

[66] [1994] F.S.R. 8 at 20.

[67] *"Angustura Bitters"* (1878) 7 Ch.D. 801; *"Yorkshire Relish"* [1897] A.C. 710, 14 R.P.C. 720, HL; *Masson, Seeley v. Embossotype* (1924) 41 R.P.C. 160, illus. para. 14–113; *Combe v. Scholl* [1980] R.P.C. 1; and the *"Champagne"* line of cases cited below.

[68] *Schulke & Mayr U.K. v. Alkapharm U.K.* [1999] F.S.R. 161. In *Dr Martens v. Figgins* (1999) 44 I.P.R. 281, it was held that use of the words "The Original" on the defendant's look-alike footwear was sufficient to find passing off, even though the product bore the words "Made in Australia" on the instep: "a potential purchaser or consumer cannot be expected to undertake a reasoned analytical exercise when confronted with [the defendant's product]", *per* Goldberg J. at 389 (although passing off was not found in relation to another defendant who used a distinctive mark on "look-alike" products, at 329).

characteristic of the [claimant's] product. But there is an appropriation only if some property or right is taken and the appropriation, if there is one, is wrongful only if a rule or principle of law forbids it. . . . Authority binding on this court requires me to hold that there is no passing off in the absence of a representation of connection between the [defendant] or its services on the one hand and the [claimant] or its product on the other", *per* Lehane J. at 201.

14–87   In particular, a descriptive term—geographical or otherwise—may denote the goods of a particular trader or a definable class of traders, so that the reputation of goods so described is part of those traders' goodwill: in *"Chocosuisse"* [1999] R.P.C. 826, CA, it was held that the words "Swiss chocolate" were taken by a significant section of the public in England to mean (and to mean only) chocolate made in Switzerland, *per* Chadwick L.J. at 836. Where this is so, a false use of that description for goods not entitled to it will be actionable.[69] But the term must be precise enough to define with reasonable precision the type of product that has acquired the reputation.[70]

Representation as to business

14–88 Cases in which the defendant directly represents that his business is the claimant's business, or a branch of it, or connected with it,[71] are equally clear as soon as the false representation is made out.

In *Law Society of England and Wales v. Griffiths* [1995] R.P.C. 16, the defendants had adopted a telephone number 0800 192939 extremely close to that used for the claimant's "Accident Line" under which the public could telephone 0500 192 939 for advice on personal injuries and referral to a panel solicitor. It was held, in granting an interlocutory injunction, that "[a] person who takes steps which will lead a person who acts in a particular way to conclude that his business is that of another is guilty of passing off just as much as a person who states that his business is that of another".[72]

---

[69] *"Advocaat"* [1980] R.P.C. 31, HL, approving (at 95, 105); *"Spanish Champagne"* [1960] R.P.C. 16 at 31. Any member of the class suffering substantial damage may sue; or some may sue on behalf of the class in a representative action: *post*, para. 14–132.

[70] *"Advocaat"*, *supra*, at [1980] R.P.C. 98 at 104–105, HL. In *"Chocosuisse"*, *op cit.*, the definition of the type of product in which the reputation subsisted was amended in the Court of Appeal to include the absence of added vegetable fat, upon application by the Swiss chocolate manufacturers: at 840.

[71] *Walter v. Ashton* [1902] 2 Ch. 282. The CA said that this case was decided on too narrow a ground: *Harrods v. R. Harrod* (1924) 41 R.P.C. 74. *Pompadour v. Frazer* [1966] R.P.C. 7, where interlocutory relief was refused upon a false representation that the defendant (a former manufacturer of the claimant's goods) was still manufacturing for them, on the ground that this was not passing off, should not be taken as deciding that; it appears rather that the wrong form of injunction was asked for. The court seems in fact to have regarded the case as analogous to that of a representation of the sort of "business connection" discussed in the following paragraph: see at p. 10.

[72] *Per* Aldous J, at 21.

Where in Malaysia the defendant had chosen as its name a French **14–89**
name used by the claimant, it was held that, French hardly ever being
used in Malaysia, this constituted passing off even without any evidence
being adduced by the defendant as to what business activity it was
engaged in: *Compagnie Generale des Eaux v. Compagnie General des Eaux
Sdn Bhd* [1997] F.S.R. 610 (HC Malaysia).

However, in relation to services, very substantial differences between
the get-up of the claimant's restaurants and of the defendant's hotel
were sufficient to defeat a claim of passing off, even though the court
accepted that the defendant had been opportunistic in its adoption of
the name and saw the possibility of extracting "greenmail": *TGI Friday's
Aust v. TGI Friday's* (1999) 45 I.P.R. 43 (Fed Ct of Australia), *per* the Full
Court.[73]

Past members of business

A partner or employee who has left a well-known firm and set up a **14–90**
similar business of his own is entitled to advertise his former connections,[74] unless restrained from doing so by contract with his late partners
or employers,[75] but he must take care to do it so as not to suggest that
the connection is still existing between them and him,[76] or that they have
ceased to carry on business and he is their successor.[77] It would seem
that this principle extends to other types of business connection, such as
that of a supplier of the goods sold by a business.[78]

The same rule holds good of a trader who,[79] or whose trustee in
bankruptcy,[80] has sold the goodwill of his business. It is important to
specify clearly in the sale agreement the future use of names used in the
business.[81]

---

[73] Citing with approval the statement of Lockhart J. in *ConAgra Inc v. McCain Foods (Aust)*
(1992) 33 F.C.R. 302, that "... deliberate copying of the plaintiff's goods does not always
evidence an intention to deceive; it may indicate nothing more than realisation that the
plaintiff has a useful idea which the defendant can turn to his own advantage, though
not intending to pass off his goods as those of the plaintiff": at 345.

[74] *Clark v. Leach* (1862) 32 Beav. 14, Romilly M.R. and Westbury L.C.

[75] As in *Wolmershausen v. O'Connor* (1877) 36 L.T.(N.S.) 921 and *Selby v. Anchor Tube* [1877]
W.N. 191, where the style and goodwill passed, under the articles, to one partner on a
dissolution. An employee must not use information acquired in his employment to
enable him to solicit his employer's customers to deal with him after he has left the
employment: *Robb v. Green* [1895] 2 Q.B. 1 at 315. See also *Pullman v. Pullman* (1919) 36
R.P.C. 240 and *Harrods v. Schwartz-Sackin* [1991] F.S.R. 209, CA, in which the contractual
restriction was held to come to an end with the termination of the concession agreement.
As to sales of goodwill, see Chap. 12.

[76] *Burgess v. Burgess* (1853) 3 De G.M. & G. 896; illus. (1), below; *Van Oppen v. Van Oppen*
(1903) 20 R.P.C. 617. Also, see *Hookham v. Pottage* (1872) L.R. 8 Ch. App 91, followed in
Harrods v. Schwartz-Sackin [1986] F.S.R. 490 at 494.

[77] See the cases next cited and *Labouchere v. Dawson* (1872) L.R. 13 Eq. 322.

[78] *Pompadour v. Frazer* [1996] R.P.C. 7 at 10.

[79] *Churton v. Douglas* (1859) Johns. 174; *Fullwood v. Fullwood* [1873] W.N. 93 and 185.

[80] *Hudson v. Osborne* (1869) 39 L.J.Ch. 79. See below.

[81] See *Greg Cotton Motors v. Neil & Ross Neilson* (1983–84) 2 I.P.R. 214, for an example of the
consequences of not including such a provision.

14–91   Particularly difficult problems may arise upon the severance of business relations between, say, a manufacturer and the distributor of his goods. Where the distributor (claimant) had been selling for a number of years under the mark "Gro-Shield" products manufactured by the supplier (defendant) and had been co-operating with the supplier, upon termination of the commercial relationship (and therefore the trade mark licence) it was held that the goodwill in the mark was owned jointly.[82]

14–92   Where the goodwill of the common business has been attached to the manufacturer's name or mark, it is tempting for the distributor to act improperly in trying to sell his new, competing lines to customers for the old.[83] Where the goodwill has belonged to the distributor, it is tempting for the manufacturer to approach customers and explain that the goods were really his. Whilst the cruder forms of passing off, which may well be unintentional—sales of the "new" lines in response to orders for the old, and the like—can easily enough be stopped in most cases, experience suggests that there are subtler ways of filching goodwill that the courts are at best moderately competent to stop.[84]

14–93   (1) The son of the claimant left his father's employment, and described himself as "late of 107, Strand": *Burgess v. Burgess* (1853) 3 De G.M. & G. 896. An injunction was granted to restrain him from continuing to do so.

(2) A doorplate, bearing the words "Scott and Nixon, late Robert and Walter Scott", was held to be a representation that Walter Scott had retired and that Scott and Nixon were carrying on the business of his old firm: *Scott v. Scott* (1866) 16 L.T.(N.S.) 143.

---

[82] *Gromax Plasticuleure v. Don & Law Nonwovens* [1999] R.P.C. 367: "Gromax, having had the benefit of the distributorship agreement, must now bear that as its burden", *per* Lindsay J. at 389. *Cf. Watson v. Dolmark Industries* (1991–92) 23 I.P.R. 363, in which Gault J. refused to extend the right to licence unregistered marks beyond where there has been a clear connection in the course of trade between the licensed marks and the goods involved and clear marking of the goods informing purchasers of the true position: at 372.

[83] In *C-Shirt v. Barnett* (1997) 37 I.P.R. 315, Lehane J. rejected an argument by the claimant that its former distributor owed it a fiduciary duty not to compete with similar products.

[84] Disputes in circumstances akin to those discussed in the text are reported in *Hilti v. Ucan* [1963] R.P.C. 160; [1964] R.P.C. 206 and in *Bostitch v. McGarry & Cole* [1964] R.P.C. 173. The subtler cases tend never to come to trial. That where the goodwill belongs to the factor, the manufacturer may neither use the factor's marks nor prevent the factor finding another manufacturer is clear from *Defries v. Electric & Ordnance* (1906) 23 R.P.C. 341; *cf. Van Zeller v. Mason, Cattley* (1908) 25 R.P.C. 37 (where the mark was the name of a vineyard, and the merchant was held not entitled to use it for other wines). *cf.* also *"Diehl"* [1970] R.P.C. 435 at 446, where the importer of goods was held entitled as against their manufacturer to retain ownership of the registration of the mark the goods were sold under, but nevertheless it was suggested as possible that use of this mark upon goods of another manufacturer might be deceptive. An instance where the mark was the (foreign) manufacturer's and the (British) merchant was restrained from using it is *"Manus"* (1949) 66 R.P.C. 71. See also paras 14–54 to 14–63.

(3) In a case where no connection had existed between the defen- **14–94** dants and the claimants, but the defendants, having obtained a lease of clay mines formerly leased to the claimants, described themselves in advertisements (referring not only to the mines, but also to certain works where they had carried on a trade similar to that of the claimants) as "E. and J. Pearson (late Harpers and Moore)", the description was held to be a representation calculated to lead the public to believe that the claimants had retired from business: *Harper v. Pearson* (1860) 3 L.T.(N.S.) 547.

(4) The defendant had formerly been the managing director of the **14–95** claimant company but had severed his connection with them, and set up his own competing business. He had in his possession a book of vouchers issued by the claimants and bearing the defendant's name as their managing director, and had used one of these vouchers in the course of his own business. It was held that this was a representation that the business carried on by the defendant was connected with, or was that carried on by, the claimant company. An injunction was granted restraining the defendant from continuing such representation: *Fairest v. Fairest* (1949) 66 R.P.C. 275. In a more recent decision in Singapore, the defendant left on shelves readily accessible to students study notes belonging to her former franchisor and an injunction was granted restraining her from passing them off as her own: *John Robert Powers School Inc. v. Tessensohn* [1995] F.S.R. 947 (CA, Sing.).[85]

(5) Where the claimant and defendant were carrying on business as **14–96** rival dentists in the same street, and, on the expiration of his tenancy, the claimant was compelled to remove, and the defendant put up a board describing himself as the "old-established dentist", this was held to be a representation that the claimant had removed to the defendant's place of business: *Mallan v. Davies* (1887) 3 T.L.R. 221.

(6) Samuel Allen sold his business; it passed to a company, Samuel **14–97** Allen & Sons Ltd, and thence to D. Samuel Allen later formed a new company (in the same trade) which advertised its goods as those of "Original Samuel Allen". This inconvenienced D., who in retaliation formed a new company under the name "Original Samuel Allen & Sons Ltd" (it was refused registration as "Samuel Allen & Sons Ltd," the old name, by reason of another of Samuel Allen's companies). Samuel Allen sued D.'s new company to restrain the use of that name. It was held that "Original Samuel Allen & Sons Ltd." could mean the business that originally was Samuel Allen & Sons Ltd.; and that to

---

[85] The court referred to the *British Conservatories* case, *supra*, as one concerning "inverse" passing off: at 954.

succeed, Samuel Allen would have to show that "Original Samuel Allen" had acquired the secondary meaning of his own new business: *Allen v. Original Samuel Allen* (1915) 32 R.P.C. 33. All in all, it is perhaps surprising that Samuel Allen was claimant and not defendant.

14–98   (7) The claimant acquired the business of a former competitor Yencken Sandy Glass but the purchase agreement stated specifically "the goodwill of the business shall not pass to the purchaser" (apparently for accounting reasons). The claimant then ceased to use the name Yencken Sandy Glass and the defendant started to do so. The claimant succeeded in its application for injunctive relief on the grounds *inter alia* of passing off, as it was still well known in the trade and amongst certain member of the public that the claimant had acquired the business known as "Yencken Sandy Glass": *ACI v. Glamour Glaze* (1987—88) 11 I.P.R. 269.[86]

14–99   Where companies had a common origin, both being subsidiaries of a common parent, it did not constitute passing off for a United Kingdom branch of a foreign corporation to state its ownership on its headed paper and employees' business cards: *Anderson & Lemke Ltd v. Anderson & Lemke Inc* [1989] R.P.C. 124. Although the judge (Hoffmann J.) considered that the casual reader might wonder what, if any, connection there was between the United Kingdom and U.S. companies: "this puzzle is caused by the lawful existence of the two companies with similar names and not by any representation by the defendants." It is important to note that the defendant had adopted the trading style "Business Advertising Europe" and the judge also took comfort from the relative sophistication of the market in which the parties operated.

Pretence of agency

14–100   Another category of false representation of a business connection which has sometimes come before the courts is where the defendant has pretended to be agent for the sale of the claimant's goods.[87]

A retailer of electronic equipment, selling "grey" imports, modified by it for United Kingdom use, held itself out as an authorised dealer of the manufacturer and purported to sell with the manufacturer's guarantee, which such goods did not have. It was ordered, on motion, not to

---

[86] Citing *Ad-Lib Club v. Granville* [1972] R.P.C. 673, see para. 14–41.
[87] *e.g.* "*The Linden Singers.*" *Galer v. Walls*, The Times, August 6, 1964 (injunction sought to restrain the defendant from, *inter alia*, "using notepaper that purported to be the notepaper of [the group of singers, 19 of whose members were claimants], or otherwise representing that he had any authority to act for or on behalf of the group"; an undertaking was given).

deal in the claimant's goods without labelling them to say it was not an authorised dealer and there was no manufacturer's guarantee and to say if the goods had been modified: *Sony v. Saray* [1983] F.S.R. 302, CA. This was an extreme case: the defendant already had a bad trading reputation.[88]

Direct false statement

There may of course be a direct statement by the defendant that he is selling the claimant's goods when he is not, as in those cases where the defendant sells counterfeit goods.[89] But the cases of direct false statements found in the reports are mostly more complex than that: sales of inferior goods of the claimant's own merchandise, for instance[90]: others include placing a deceptive name or title on the facia of a shop,[91] or opening and replying to letters addressed to or intended for the claimant and executing the orders contained therein,[92] or supplying the defendant's goods in pursuance of an order for the claimant's goods, without informing the customer of substitution,[93] or inserting advertising material between the pages of national newspapers without the publishers' consent.[94] It may be assumed that more common in practice are false statements made orally, in meetings with customers or over the telephone. The difficulty of proof where such representations are made orally probably accounts for the small number of reported cases of this type.[95] The right to sue is not dependent on the false representation being made in any special way.[96]

14–101

---

[88] The Canadian Supreme Court has recognised that an action for passing off may be a disguised way of preventing parallel imports and refused any relief on somewhat similar facts, *Consumers Distributing v. Seiko*, (1985) 1 C.P.R. (3d) 12. For E.C. problems relating to the use of passing off to prevent parallel imports, see Chap. 15, and particularly paras 15–37 *et seq.*

[89] For a recent example, see *Gillette UK v. Edenwest* [1994] R.P.C. 279, in which Blackburne J. found that dishonesty on the defendant's part is not necessary before an award of meaningful damages for passing off: at 291.

[90] As in *Spalding v. Gamage* (1915) 32 R.P.C. 273, HL (advertising obsolete model as the new one); *Gillette v. Franks* (1924) 41 R.P.C. 499 (second-hand razor-blades sold as new); and *cf. Masson, Seeley v. Embossotype* (1924) 41 R.P.C. 160 (illus. at para. 14–113).

[91] *e.g, Hookham v. Pottage* (1872) L.R. 8 Ch. 91. As to the purchase of a building with the vendor's name built into it, see *Boussod, Valadon v. Marchant* (1908) 25 R.P.C. 42, CA. As to names of places of business, see para. 14–216.

[92] *Edgington v. Edgington* (1864) 11 L.T.(N.S.) 299 (a single instance proved, injunction refused).

[93] *British Leather Cloth v. Dickens & Cooper* (1914) 31 R.P.C. 337.

[94] *Associated Newspapers v. Insert Media* [1991] F.S.R. 380.

[95] *e.g. Law Society v. Griffiths* [1995] R.P.C. 16.

[96] See, *e.g. Illustrated Newspapers v. Publicity Services* (1938) 55 R.P.C. 172 (binding in of a "supplement" to copies of claimants' publications); *Morny v. Ball & Rogers* [1978] F.S.R. 91 (selling scent packaged together with genuine "Morny" "Foambath"); *Insert Media, op cit.* at n. 94.

False claims to the prizes, medals, patents, copyright or praise due to another

14–102 False claims to the prizes, medals, recommendations or other forms of praise which, in fact, have been gained by the claimant,[97] or to patents under which the claimant and not the defendant is working,[98] require special consideration. If such claims enable the maker to pass his goods or business off as those of the person really entitled to the medals, prizes or patents, the matter is clear. If they do not, then there is old authority for saying that no case can be made.[99] The tendency of the courts in recent years, however, has been to treat all such misrepresentations as actionable if a real probability of damage to the claimant is shown. Merely to reproduce on a label representations of gold medals won by other traders could hardly so influence customers—in these days, at least—as to be a substantial ingredient in passing off; at most it could be evidence of bad faith.

14–103   (1) The claimant's goods were the subject of a television demonstration in which the claimant's identity was not disclosed. The defendants then falsely advertised their similar goods as being "as shown on television". It was held that this was a proper case for an interim injunction but that an undertaking should be accepted in lieu: *Copydex v. Noso* (1952) 69 R.P.C. 38.

14–104   (2) The proprietors of a pipe band well known as "The Dagenham Girl Pipers", failed to obtain interim relief against the proprietor of a newly established band billed as the "The Famous London Girl Pipers", although the costumes used and the performances of the two bands were similar and the use of the term "famous" was ground for suspicion as to the defendants' intentions: *Dagenham Girl Pipers v. Vishnu Pather* (1952) 69 R.P.C. 1.

14–105   (3) The English goodwill of a German manufacturer of eau-de-Cologne was expropriated during the war, and was in due course transferred to an English company. The English com-

---

[97] *National Starch v. Munn's* [1894] A.C. 275 at 281; 11 R.P.C. 294, PC (reference to claimant's medals held a mere disreputable advertising trick). In *King v. Gilliard* (1905) 22 R.P.C. 327, CA, the defendants' representations as to medals, etc., were held at the trial to be untrue, and they were for that reason deprived of costs; reversed in the CA, as any false claims to awards were irrelevant to the particular issue of passing off, and so not proper to be considered in awarding costs. See also *Reuter v. Muhlens* (1953) 70 R.P.C. 102 at 108, 121, illus. (3) below.

[98] *Lawrie v. Baker* (1885) 2 R.P.C. 213; cf. *Pneumatic Rubber Stamp v. Linder* (1898) 15 R.P.C. 525. It was argued in *Hospital for Sick Children v. Walt Disney* [1966] R.P.C. 246 that there could be passing-off by misrepresenting that a film was made under licence from the copyright owner-the action failed on the facts, no comment being made as to whether the cause of action lay.

[99] *Tallerman v. Dowsing* [1900] 1 Ch. 1 (interlocutory injunction refused); though these days a court might well find passing off on such facts—the case is rather similar to *Masson, Seeley v. Embossotype* (1924) 41 R.P.C. 160 (illus. para. 14–113) where the claimant won. In *Testro Bros v. Tennant* (1983–84) 2 I.P.R. 469, the Supreme Court of N.S.W. declined to follow *Tallerman v. Dowsing*, stating that the case was not "of much, if any, authority": *per* Holland J. at 474.

pany sold its eau-de-Cologne (which was not made to the original German formula) under labels copied from those of the German company, the labels including representations of medals won by the German company. This was held legitimate, the goodwill being vested in the English company; the medals were treated as simply part of the get-up: *Reuter v. Muhlens* (1953) 70 R.P.C. 102 at 121.

(4) An action for passing off, alleging that a book was one **14–106** prescribed for an examination whereas it was the claimant's book that was prescribed, failed on the ground that any such representation was only as to quality and that there had been no passing off: *Cambridge University Press v. University Tutorial Press* (1928) 45 R.P.C. 335. It is submitted that such facts would be decided differently today and passing off found.[1]

(5) The defendant was selling goods, not manufactured by or **14–107** under licence from the claimants, bearing the words "manufactured under Ormond Patent No. 273,392". It was held that, assuming these words meant that the defendant had been licensed by the claimants and were untrue, there was no evidence that the claimants were making or selling goods of the kind in question; and accordingly no cause of action had been established: *Ormond v. Knopf* (1932) 49 R.P.C. 634.

(6) It has been said that imitations of the descriptive and commen- **14–108** datory inscriptions and of the directions for use printed on the covers of patent medicines and proprietary articles were once common: *Franks v. Weaver* (1847) 10 Beav. 297, Langdale M.R., and *Massam v. Thorley's* (1880) 14 Ch.D. 748, CA are instances. However, it is unlikely that a court would now tolerate them.

"Reverse" passing off

As discussed above,[2] the classic case of passing off is where the **14–109** defendant misrepresents his goods as those of the claimant, although as Lord Jauncey stated in *Jif Lemon*[3]: "It is not essential ... that the defendant should misrepresent his goods as those of the plaintiff. It is sufficient that he misrepresents his goods in such a way that it is a reasonably foreseeable consequence of the misrepresentation that the plaintiff's business or goodwill will be damaged."[4]

In *Bristol Conservatories v. Conservatories Custom Build* [1989] R.P.C. **14–110** 455, the defendant's salesman showed prospective customers an album of photographs of conservatories, some of which were of conservatories

---

[1] See discussion below of "reverse" passing off.
[2] At para. 14–15 *inter alia*.
[3] *Op. cit.*, at 417.
[4] His Lordship also referred to the classic statement of Lord Langdale in *Perry v. Truefitt* (1842) 6 Beav. 66 at 73: "A man is not to sell his own goods under the pretence that they are the goods of another man."

designed and built by the claimant. Although there was no allegation that anyone looking at the photographs would associate any with the claimant, the Court of Appeal found that there was a reasonable claim for passing off,[5] because if a customer ordered a conservatory from the defendant in response to the photographs he would be supplied with a conservatory not of the stated commercial source but of the defendant's manufacture. The court specifically declined to decide whether there is a form of tort known as "reverse passing off", preferring to find the facts alleged as within the tort of passing off.[6]

14-111   Counsel for the claimant had contended that as a result of the defendant's use of the photographs customers were misled into believing (1) that the defendant was the company which produced the conservatory, (2) that its designs were the same as in the album, and (3) that the defendant had a well-established business. It is submitted that the only misrepresentation on its own actionable in passing off was (1) and that falls squarely within the wrong envisaged by Lord Jauncey and it is unnecessary to rely on any extension of classic principles. Although it was open to the defendant to use photographs of the claimant's product to indicate that it could make products like it,[7] it went further and made an actionable misrepresentation which could have caused damage to the claimant in the form of lost sales (in the sense that all the defendant's potential customers could have been customers of the claimant had not the misrepresentation been made).

14-112   Notwithstanding *Bristol Conservatories*, passing off is not a tort providing a remedy in all cases of deception: it is submitted that Laddie J. went too far in *Matthew Gloag v. Welsh Distillers*[8] when he refused the defendant's application to strike out the claimant's claim for passing off. The defendant sold as "Welsh whisky" a product which was, in reality, Scotch whisky purchased by them in bulk, bottled and then sold. The claimant claimed that this constituted "reverse passing-off" and relied on *Bristol Conservatories*. The judge found that this was arguable. This cannot be right: passing off does not extend to misstatements in the abstract, it is not a tort covering all misdescriptions of products: there must be an actionable misrepresentation which harms the claimant's goodwill in a name or get-up,[9] mere appropriation is not sufficient. Although the defendant's actions may have contravened trade descrip-

---

[5] Applying *Samuelson v. Producers Distributing* (1931) 48 R.P.C. 580, CA and *Plomein Fuel Economiser v. National School of Salesmanship* (1943) 60 R.P.C. 209, CA: the judgment in the former case appears to have been based on the principle, as expressed by Romer L.J. (at 593) "that the court will always interfere by injunction to restrain irreparable injury being done to the plaintiff's property" (in that case, the plaintiff's copyright). The Scottish case of *John Henderson v. A. Munro* (1905) 7 F. 636 (Ct of Sess) was also referred to with approval.

[6] *per* Ralph Gibson L.J., at 464.

[7] *e.g. Broad v. Cast Iron Drainage* [1970] F.S.R. 363.

[8] [1998] F.S.R. 718.

[9] See *"Pub Squash"*, *op. cit.* See *Snyman v. Cooper* (1991) 19 I.P.R. 471 for an example of a case in which the judge had no difficulty in finding that the defendant's misleading reference in advertising to a location in which only the claimant had a shop constituted passing off.

tions legislation or E.U. regulations, there was no representation connecting the "Welsh whisky" product with anyone other than the defendant.[10] This can be contrasted with *Bristol Conservatories* where the photographs were equivalent to such a representation.[11]

System of advertising

The mere adoption by one person of a system of advertising similar to that used by a rival trader will not support a passing-off action[12] nor will the mere adoption of a similar system of window-dressing or decoration of a shop.[13] **14–113**

The claimants were suppliers of type for use in a particular sort of printing machine. The defendants supplied type of an inferior sort for the same machine. The defendants circulated price lists which were practically copies of the claimants', and used samples of work done with the claimants' type for showing to prospective customers. It was found that the defendants were deliberately attempting to find a market for their goods by suggesting (contrary to the fact) that they were the same as the claimants. The claimants were granted an injunction: *Masson, Seeley v. Embossotype* (1924) 41 R.P.C. 160.[14]

Such untrue statements, in a defendant's advertisements, as "the only genuine Bowden Control wires"[15] are only material in so far as they tend to induce the belief that the defendant's goods are the claimant's.[16] **14–114**

Where the defendant used in a comparative advertisement for its generic equivalent pharmaceutical an image (an apple) which the claimant had used for some years in its advertising and promotion of its formerly patented drug, it was held to be unarguable that this constituted passing off.[17]

---

[10] See the analysis of the case law by Fisher J. in *"Tot Toys"*, *supra*, in which the judge concludes: "Source motivation is and always has been an essential ingredient of diversion passing off" (at 365).

[11] For an earlier case on the same lines, see *Masson, Seeley*, at para. 14–113.

[12] *Wertheimer v. Stewart, Cooper* (1906) 23 R.P.C. 481. *Elida Gibbs v. Colgate-Palmolive* [1983] F.S.R. 95 *contra*—but there the parties were agreed that if they both used the same "motif" (analogy between teeth and trees), confusion would result: see at 97. Also, *"Pub Squash"* [1981] R.P.C. 429 (PC, N.S.W.)

[13] *Plotzker v. Lucas* (1907) 24 R.P.C. 551; *Bravingtons v. Barrington Tennant* [1957] R.P.C. 183.

[14] *cf. Ciba-Geigy v. Parke Davis, op. cit.*

[15] *Bowden Wire v. Bowden Brake* (1913) 30 R.P.C. 609, Warrington J.

[16] As to the continuing effect of a misleading advertisement, see *per* Lord Parker in *Spalding v. Gamage* (1915) 32 R.P.C. 273 at 288.

[17] *Ciba-Geigy v. Parke Davis, op. cit.* On the claimant's submission that the advertisements were "knocking advertisements" which wrongfully appropriated the claimant's goodwill, Aldous J. stated: "I believe the advertisements are examples of comparative advertising. Such advertisements are perfectly proper unless registered trade marks are used [the case was prior to the 1994 Act]. They are not knocking advertisements in that they do not suggest that the plaintiff's product is a bad product; they only seek to suggest that the defendant's product is as good a product. Such statements are not actionable according to common law" (at 22–23).

Passing off one quality of goods for another

14–115 It is in general a defence to an action for passing-off goods as those of the claimant that the goods were the claimant's. This defence will not succeed, however, where the goods have been altered or mutilated,[18] or allowed to deteriorate so as not to be the same goods.[19] Furthermore, the court will intervene where one quality of manufacturer's goods is passed off as another quality,[20] as, for example, the sale by the defendants of Continental quality of the claimants' champagne as claimants' English quality.[21] But in order to establish such a case, there must be a definite superior class of article for which the goods of the other class are passed off.[22] The existence of two classes must be established[23]: in *Parma Ham v. Marks & Spencer*,[24] Morritt L.J. commented: "[t]he reason for this requirement. . . is that the court is one of law and not gastronomy and does not adjudicate on the relative merits of particular products".[25] Furthermore, there cannot in general be passing off where the claimant's goods are sold unaltered and with unaltered labels, even though they are goods he does not himself sell in the country.[26]

14–116 The sale of second-hand goods as new is actionable, by the trader whose name or mark they bear, provided always he can show that he is likely to suffer damage thereby.[27] The sale of second-hand goods bearing the claimant's mark without any indication whether or not they are new goods may or may not be deceptive according to the circumstances of the sale. The character of the shop, the price and the appearance of the goods may affect the mind of the customer.[28]

[18] *Westinghouse v. Varsity Eliminator* (1935) 52 R.P.C. 295. Also, see *IBM v. Phoenix* [1994] R.P.C. 251, in which the claimants claimed that the use of "IBM manufactured" on memory cards reworked by the defendant constituted passing off and the court refused to strike out the defence that there was no misrepresentation.

[19] See *Wilts United Dairies v. Robinson* (illus. below) [1958] R.P.C. 94 at 102, CA.

[20] *Spalding v. Gamage* (1915) 32 R.P.C. 273 at 284, *per* Lord Parker. See also *Teacher v. Levy* (1906) 23 R.P.C. 117. As to damages in *Spalding v. Gamage*, see (1918) 35 R.P.C. 101, CA.

[21] *Champagne Heidsieck v. Scotto and Bishop* (1926) 43 R.P.C. 101. Contrast *Champagne Heidsieck v. Buxton* (1929) 47 R.P.C. 28. In *Re "Grand Marnier" Liqueur* [1994] F.S.R. 61 the *Oberlandesgericht* in Frankfurt found that it would be contrary to Art. 30 (now 28) of the E.C. Treaty for national unfair competition law to be used to prohibit use of confusing get-up on an inferior quality product produced alongside a better quality product in a similar get-up in another E.C. Member State.

[22] *Hunt, Roope, Teage v. Ehrmann* [1910] 2 Ch. 198; 27 R.P.C. 512.

[23] *Harris v. Warren* (1918) 35 R.P.C. 217. And see illustration para. 14–117.

[24] [1991] R.P.C. 351, CA.

[25] *Ibid.*, at 363.

[26] *Revlon v. Cripps & Lee* [1980] F.S.R. 85, CA: this is quite apart from the E.U. law objections to restraints on parallel imports from other E.U. countries: *cf.* Chap. 15. But there is no absolute rule excluding passing off in such cases: *cf. Wilkinson Sword v. Cripps & Lee* [1982] F.S.R. 16, where passing off was alleged by sale in the U.K. of blades of export (*i.e.* inferior) quality; the court refused to strike the claim out; *Colgate Palmolive v. Markwell Finance* [1989] R.P.C. 497, CA, in which passing off was found by reason of the inferior quality of the genuine "Colgate" toothpaste imported from Brazil.

[27] See, *e.g.* cases on selling second-hand cars as new: (*Morris Motors v. Lilley* [1959] 1 W.L.R. 1184; *Morris Motors v. Phelan* [1960] 1 W.L.R. 352, 566, illus. (2), below); and razor blades: (*Gillete v. Franks* (1924) 41 R.P.C. 499; *Gillette v. Diamond Edge* (1926) 43 R.P.C. 310 (interim injunction granted)).

[28] *General Electric v. Pryce's* (1933) 50 R.P.C. 232.

(1) The defendants were wholesale grocers. They sold old stock (at **14–117** least 20 months old) of the claimants' condensed milk to grocers at reduced prices, with a recommendation that it be resold at the price ruling before an increase made less than two months before, but without any warning as to its age. Condensed milk begins to deteriorate after six months. The tins were not distinguishable from new stock except by opening them. Held, that the defendants were representing that this was fresh stock: *Wilts United Dairies v. Thomas Robinson* [1958] R.P.C. 94, CA. In *Parma Ham v. Marks & Spencer*, Leggatt L.J. contrasted this case from that before him: "a purchaser of pre-sliced Parma ham cannot be said to have been supplied with something other than what it is described as being, and what he can see it is, assuming that it was from a Parma ham that the slices came", (at 382).

(2) Injunctions will be granted to restrain the selling of second- **14–118** hand motor-cars as "new": and for this purpose a car ceases to be "new" as soon as it has been sold retail, registered and driven away by the purchaser: after that the manufacturer's obligations (in respect of defects and of servicing) are no longer those belonging to a new car: *Morris Motors v. Lilley* [1959] 1 W.L.R. 1184. But if that is so, an injunction against selling cars as "new" is not in proper form, since (with "new" bearing a special meaning) it may act as a trap: *Morris Motors v. Phelan* [1960] R.P.C. 209; *cf. Vanden Plas v. Cars & Caravans* [1965] F.S.R. 93. Furthermore, to describe a car as "brand new" may well not imply that it is "new" in that special sense: *Standard Motor v. Grantchester Garage* [1960] R.P.C. 211.

(3) Where the defendant sold unfinished rejects from the claimant's **14–119** manufacture under the claimant's mark, without explanation, an injunction was granted to restrain the defendant from passing-off goods "not of the plaintiff's finished manufacture or merchandise as and for", the plaintiff's goods: *Britains v. Morris* [1961] R.P.C. 217 ("*Swoppets*").

(4) The claimant published an unexpurgated edition of a salacious **14–120** book previously only published in expurgated form. The claimant used for his edition an altered title. The defendant republished the expurgated edition, giving it the claimant's altered title and was restrained by interlocutory injunction from so doing: *Allen v. Brown Watson* [1965] R.P.C. 191.

(5) The defendants sold second-hand denim garments including **14–121** jeans labelled "Levi's" which had been imported from the USA. The defendants altered such jeans in a number of ways, for example by patching, colouring or cutting off part of the legs, and supplied them to retailers with an additional label bearing the mark "Revise". It was held that this constituted passing off because *inter alia* both the claimant's new products (including new second-hand look jeans) and the defendant's altered prod-

461

ucts were sold alongside each other in shops which sold new goods to the same range of consumers, as well as the fact that the "Revise" label was usually in close proximity to a number of the trade marks of Levi Strauss and the mark "Revise" had been chosen so as to suggest Levi's: *per* Sheppard J., at 209 in *Wingate Marketing v. Levi-Strauss* (1993–94) 28 I.P.R. 193 (Fed Ct of Australia, Full Court).

14–122   (6) Where the defendant sold lenses "to suit" the claimant's helmets, it was held arguable that this constituted passing off where the claimant's helmets fitted with the defendant's lenses would not comply with health and safety regulations: *Hodge Clemco v. Airblast* [1995] F.S.R. 806. The case was described by the judge, Jacob J., as at "the outer limits of the tort of passing off", at 809.[29]

5. Imitations of trade or service mark

The mark or name (or get-up, see below) must be associated with the goods or business of the claimant

14–123 Actions based upon direct misrepresentation are comparatively rare. The claimant's case more commonly is that the defendant has copied or imitated the trading name, the trade mark, the get-up or some other badge or description by which the claimant's business or goods are known to be his. The cases concerned with trading names, and the cases concerned with get-up, are specially considered in later sections of this chapter.[30] The present section is accordingly concerned generally with matters common to all cases of misrepresentation by the use of badges of trade, and with misrepresentation by the use of trade and service marks in particular.

14–124   Where the charge is one of indirect misrepresentation of this sort, the case is usually based on the allegations that (a) a mark, get-up, etc., is distinctive of the claimant's goods exclusively and that (b) the defendant has used the mark or get-up or an imitation so close as to be likely to deceive. It may be fallacious to treat the two allegations as propositions which must be established separately. What has to be proved is one proposition, namely that the defendant's conduct is likely to lead to passing off.[31] Nevertheless, the claimant must establish on the one hand that the badge of trade concerned has been used for goods or a business that are not his—or at least that have no right to the badge[32]—so as to be

---

[29] See also *SDS Biotech v. Power Agrichemicals* [1995] F.S.R. 797 (whether unauthorised use on fungicide of MAFF number gave rise to a cause of action in passing off for authorised traders on the basis of *"Advocaat"*, *op. cit.*; summary judgment was refused by Aldous J.)

[30] See *post*, paras 14–190 *et seq.*; paras 14–237 *et seq.*

[31] *Magnolia Metal v. Tandem Smelting* (1900) 17 R.P.C. 477 at 486, *per* Lord Halsbury; *Office Cleaning v. Westminster* (1946) 63 R.P.C. 39 at 42, *per* Lord Simonds (a trading name case), is to the same effect.

[32] *e.g.* when one quality of goods is passed off for another, all of the same manufacture: para. 14–115.

recommended by it.[33] On the other hand, if the claimant cannot prove the association, in this country, of the mark or get-up concerned with goods that in fact are his (or, in the case of a trading name, associated with his business) the action fails *in limine*.[34] The foundation of an ordinary[35] passing-off case:

> "is that the party alleging it should prove, in the first instance, that any name which he claims as his trade name has been so extensively used in connection with his manufacture or with the goods which he sells that his goods have come to be known in the market by that name; that anyone using that name would intend to refer to his goods, and that anyone to whom the name was used would understand that his goods were referred to."[36]

Furthermore, in order to establish passing off in this way, it must be shown that what the defendant has taken is in itself sufficiently distinctive of the claimant,[37] and further that the confusion or deception relied upon as causing damage to the claimant is caused by the taking of that distinctive matter.[38]   **14–125**

(1) The publishers and owners of the British Pharmacopoeia failed   **14–126**
in an action against Barrett Proprietaries, makers and vendors of medical preparations, to restrain them from using the letters B.P. in connection with such goods, there being no evidence what the public would understand by those letters: *Att.-Gen. and the General Medical Council v. Barrett* (1933) 50 R.P.C. 45.

(2) Three days' use of the name of a new weekly newspaper (of   **14–127**
which 15 copies had been sold before the defendants' publication began) was held insufficient to give the owners any right to stop use of the name for a rival paper. The larger sale of the claimants' paper after the defendants started publication was immaterial: *Licensed Victuallers v. Bingham* (1888) 38 Ch.D. 139; *cf. Maxwell v. Hogg* (1867) L.R. 2 Ch. 307.

(3) The claimants were manufacturers of tobacco-pipes. They had   **14–128**
for many years marked their pipes with an inlaid white spot on the stem. The defendants started selling pipes with a spot on the stem, but larger and coloured. It was held that if spots on

---

[33] Note that the badge, even if a trade mark, need not be placed upon the goods, nor even necessarily used in a way that would infringe a registered mark: it is a pure question of fact whether the use made of the badge is deceptive or not. An injunction will be granted against the particular mischief that has occurred: see the injunctions in *Hendriks v. Montagu* (1881) 17 Ch.D. 638; *Massam v. Thorley* (1880) 14 Ch.D. 748.

[34] *"Turmix"* (*Oertli v. Bowman*) [1957] R.P.C. 388 at 397, CA; approved [1959] R.P.C. 1, HL.

[35] There are of course other sorts of case: where the claimant is not a trader or goods are not involved; or of *"Advocaat"* type, see para. 14–132, below.

[36] *Leahy, Kelly v. Glover* (1893) 10 R.P.C. 141 at 155.

[37] *Imperial v. Phillip Morris* [1984] R.P.C. 293, citing *Payton v. Snelling* (1900) 17 R.P.C. 48, CA (get-up, of which part common).

[38] *My Kinda Town v. Soll* [1983] R.P.C. 407, CA, illus. (4), para. 14–170.

pipe stems were distinctive of the claimants at all, this was so of small white spots only, and the action failed: *Dunhill v. Bartlett* (1922) 39 R.P.C. 426.

14–129 (4) The claimants had a mark for sarongs showing a native cap with the words "Chop Topi Achai". The defendants sold sarongs bearing a label incorporating a markedly different native cap. The claimants alleged that their goods were known as "Chop Topi" ("Cap Brand") sarongs, so that use by others of a sarong mark including any sort of topi (or cap) would be deceptive: but it was held that no such distinctiveness of "Chop Topi" was established: *Mohamed Noordin v. Abdul Kareem* (1931) 48 R.P.C. 491. If the fact of distinctiveness had been proved, it would seem that the action would have succeeded; *cf.* the cases on "essential features" of a trade mark, paras 16-37 *et seq.*

14–130 (5) The claimants in October commenced a new kind of business in the United Kingdom—that of arranging introductions between members of the opposite sex by means of a computer. They used in connection with their business a symbol consisting of a heart combined with the standard biological symbols for male and female. The defendants commenced a similar business in November, using a similar symbol. Stamp J. held that the evidence did not show that the symbol had, in the short time of use, become exclusively associated with the claimants, particularly because of its descriptive nature. "A trader who sets up a new trade has no monopoly of that trade or of the manner of carrying it on, and he cannot prevent a rival trader copying his ideas, notwithstanding that confusion may be caused": *Compatibility Research v. Computer Psyche* [1967] R.P.C. 201; *cf. Stannard v. Reay* [1967] R.P.C. 589, where the claimants commenced their business in the Isle of Wight using a mobile fish and chip van under the name "Mr. Chippy" only three weeks before the defendants did the same thing, but were able to show a considerable drop in earnings and other facts showing a likelihood that the name had achieved at least a degree of distinctiveness in the short period of time involved so that an interlocutory injunction was granted.

14–131 (6) An interlocutory injunction was granted restraining use for the defendant's mechanical excavators of "580", the claimant's type number: *Hymac v. Priestman* [1978] R.P.C. 495.

(7) A service mark case: the claimants were the suppliers of the materials used in a particular permanent-waving process, known as a "Jamal wave". The defendant, asked by customers for a "Jamal wave", used other materials. On evidence suggesting that people asking a hairdresser for a "Jamal wave" wanted to be waved by the claimant's process, held that this was a sort of passing off: *Sales Affiliates v. Le Jean* (1947) 64 R.P.C. 103. The court seemed remarkably doubtful whether this was passing off at all; but no new principle seems to have been involved.

Shared reputation

The claimant in a passing-off action need not show that the badge the **14–132** defendant has taken denotes his goods or business exclusively if the defendant has no right to use it at all[39]: it is enough for him to show that he is one of a definite and ascertainable class[40] of those who are entitled to use it and who consequently suffers damage from its misuse. But if the badge is independently properly used by others than himself, the difficulty of showing that its use by the defendant is calculated to injure his goodwill may be greatly increased.[41] It is accordingly desirable, where the right to use a badge is shared, that as many as practicable of those entitled to use it should join in an action to protect it.[42]

(1) Two firms were separately carrying on business as watch- **14–133** makers under the name Dent. Held, that either might sue a third who had set up a similar business under the same name: *Dent v. Turpin* (1861) 2 J. & H. 139.[43]

(2) The defendants sold Spanish sparkling wine as "Spanish Champagne." The larger producers of Champagne joined together to sue for passing off. Held, that any one producer could have sued: *Bollinger v. Costa Brava* [1960] R.P.C. 16; [1961] R.P.C. 116 at 120; approved HL in *"Advocaat," supra.* See also *Comité Interprofessionnel du Vin de Champagne v. Wineworths Group* [1991] 2 N.Z.L.R. 432.

(3) An oil company and a lamp maker jointly set up a trade in **14–134** lamp oil, which was supplied by the oil company under the trade mark used by the lamp maker for its lamps. When inferior oil was passed off for theirs, they sued successfully as joint claimants: *Shell-Mex and Aladdin v. Holmes* (1937) 54 R.P.C. 287.

(4) One of a set of estate agents, operating in different towns, all known as "Parkers", sued one J.T. Parker to restrain him from doing the same. On a motion for interlocutory injunction (which was granted) the court declined to consider the relevance of the

---

[39] *Bollinger v. Costa Brava* [1960] R.P.C. 16 at 25; *Vine Products v. Mackenzie* [1969] R.P.C. 1 ("*British Sherry*"); *John Walker v. Ost* [1970] R.P.C. 489 ("*Scotch Whisky*"). It may be noted that *Dent v. Turpin*, illus. (1), below, was a case of "concurrent" rights of the Dents in the mark; the "*Aladdin*" case, illus. 3, one of "joint" ownership; whereas *Bollinger v. Costa Brava, supra*, illus. (2), below, is something between the two, with no true trade mark analogy. As in trade mark cases, there is no express authority that the proposition in the text applies to cases of joint ownership, but on general principles it should.

[40] "*Advocaat*" [1980] R.P.C. 31 at 104–105, HL.

[41] See *Jamieson v. Jamieson* (1898) 15 R.P.C. 169 at 193; note that the action failed because the defendants had not used anything identified with the claimant, at 182, not because there were other Jamiesons in the trade in Aberdeen. See also *Whitstable Oyster v. Hayling Fisheries* (1901) 17 R.P.C. 461; 18 R.P.C. 434 and *Mappin and Webb v. Leapman* (1905) 22 R.P.C. 398.

[42] Alternatively, since there is a common interest, common grievance and remedy beneficial to all, it may be appropriate for some to sue in a representative action on behalf of all: *Bollinger v. Goldwell* [1971] R.P.C. 412.

[43] Expressly approved by Lord Diplock in "*Advocaat*", *op. cit.*, at 742.

other companies, "for the purpose of this motion, where the claimants are not claiming any exclusive right to the use of the word 'Parkers' but are claiming merely to restrain the defendant from representing his business as being the business of the plaintiffs": *Parker v. Parker* [1965] R.P.C. 323 at 325.

14–135   (5) The *Consorzio del Prosciutto di Parma* was a body corporate established under the law of Italy, whose members were producers of Parma ham and whose objects were to protect and promote the reputation of Parma ham. Although entitled to sue in passing off on its own behalf, the *Consorzio* could not sue on behalf of its member producers as their interests were not the same. The judge gave leave to amend to join representative producers of Parma ham as additional claimants: [1991] R.P.C. 351 at 357, *per* Morritt J, upheld by the Court of Appeal.[44]

The product names concerned in such cases as "*Spanish Champagne*" and "*Advocaat*" (*supra*) are, of course, not trade marks in the ordinary sense at all; rather, they are analogous to the "certification marks" discussed at chapter 11. But where passing off is concerned, there is no real dividing line between such cases and cases such as "*Dent*" (illus. (1) above) where an ordinary trade mark is shared.

14–136   Where a number of companies within a group all trade under a common name, the courts will usually accept that the goodwill is shared: in "*Dawnay, Day*",[45] the Court of Appeal found it unnecessary to analyse the ownership of the trading name to decide whether it belonged to the holding company or was shared, holding that each company in the group had a legitimate interest for passing off purposes, *per* Sir Richard Scott V.-C.

The claimant himself may be unknown to customers

14–137 It is not necessary to show that the customers who knew the goods of the claimant's firm by a particular name or get-up knew anything whatever about the claimant.[46] It is immaterial that they did not even know his name,[47] for it is sufficient to prove that purchasers of his goods recognised, by the use of the marks in question in connection with them,

---

[44] In *Scotch Whisky Association v. J.D. Vintners*, [1997] Eur. L.R. 446, Sir Richard Scott V.-C. stated that he could see no basis "on which a trade association could maintain a passing off action based on conduct which constitutes a passing off by the defendant of its products for those of the members of the trade association". In "*Chocosuisse*" Chadwick L.J. adopted this reasoning (rather than that of *Parma Ham*) in stating that there was no business interest or goodwill which Chocosuisse, the trade association, was entitled to protect in a passing-off action. Whilst he noted that it would be "convenient" to permit such a representative action, Chadwick L.J. considered that the correct route lay in an alteration of the Rules of Court, at 843–844.
[45] *Post*, para. 14–212.
[46] *United Biscuits v. Asda* [1997] R.P.C. 513.
[47] *Lever v. Goodwin* (1887) 36 Ch.D. 1; 4 R.P.C. 492, CA ("Sunlight Self-Washer Soap"); see "*Yorkshire Relish*" illus. below; "*Jif*", *op cit.*, at 406, *per* Lord Oliver.

that they were goods of a particular class, and to show that such class is, in fact, constituted by his goods.[48]

(1) Thus in *"Yorkshire Relish"*, the claimant's sauce was made **14–138** according to a secret recipe, and was always bought and sold by the name alone. The defendants made a sauce described as a "wonderful match" of the claimant's, and their contention was that the public knew and cared nothing about the actual manufacturer, but wanted only the sauce known as "Yorkshire Relish". The contention failed. Lord Herschell said:

"I think that the fallacy of the appellants' arguments rests on this: that it is assumed that one trader cannot be passing-off his goods as the manufacture of another unless it be shown that the persons purchasing the goods know of the manufacturer by name, and have in their mind when they purchase the goods that they are made by a particular individual. It seems to me that one man may quite well pass off his goods as the goods of another, if he passes them off to people who will accept them as the manufacture of another, though they do not know that other by name at all. In the present case it seems to me that 'Yorkshire Relish' meant the manufacture of a particular person": *Powell v. Birmingham Brewery* [1897] A.C. 710 at 715.

(2) The claimants were manufacturers of washing-blue. Their blue **14–139** did not bear their name, but was sold in bags distinguished by a protruding stick, or "dolly". It was shown that the purchasers of the claimants' blue included many persons of the poorer classes, to whom their name was unknown, and who distinguished their goods by the presence of the dolly, not infrequently asking for it as "dolly blue". The defendants marketed a blue in bags with a dolly and bearing their name. Held, that there was passing off, the defendants' name in the circumstances being inadequate to distinguish their goods: *Edge v. Niccolls* [1911] A.C. 693; 28 R.P.C. 582.

(3) The claimants sold their drug in green and black capsules. The **14–140** defendants proposed to sell the same drug in similar capsules, arguing that the medical profession would not be deceived and that patients were only concerned with getting the same drug as they had had before. Held that the "same again" included not only the drug, but the drug manufactured by the same manufacturer. "Now I myself never received from the defendants a satisfactory answer to the plain question: why do they

---

[48] Paragraph (which has been in this work since at least 1910) quoted by Jenkins L.J. in *Oertli v. Bowman* [1957] R.P.C. 388 at 397. It was also approved by Harman and Russell L.JJ. in *Hoffmann-La Roche v. D.D.S.A.* [1969] F.S.R. 410 at 416, 421.

wish to market their goods in green and black? I can only answer that they wish so to do in order to attract to themselves some part of the claimants' goodwill and trade on their reputation and in fact to represent to the public that their goods are the goods of the claimants. That . . . is exactly the classic case of passing-off,": per Harman L.J. in *Hoffmann-La Roche v. D.D.S.A.* [1969] F.S.R. 410 at 419.

Assignment and devolution of trading name, etc.

14–141 The right to protect the goodwill of a business against the use of deceptive imitations will pass to an assignee of the goodwill. Under section 22(3) of the Trade Marks Act, 1938, unregistered trade marks could in some cases be assigned without the goodwill of the business in which they were used, and it must be presumed that in such cases[49] Parliament intended to give the assignee of the mark without goodwill the right to sue for passing off. However, there is no corresponding provision in the 1994 Act and the general rule as to right to sue in passing off must be taken to now apply generally: only the owner of goodwill can sue to protect it.[50] Thus, in general, if the things which the defendant has copied denote a connection, not with the claimant, but with someone else, the claimant can have no claim to sue in respect of any deception which their use may cause.[51]

14–142 (1) A jury found that the defendant had both infringed the claimant's trade mark and had passed off his goods as those of the claimant. On appeal it appeared that the label and brand copied by the defendant had, not long before the commencement of the action, been assigned, without the business with which they were connected, by certain third parties to the claimant. Upon this ground the Court of Appeal set aside the verdict and entered judgment for the defendants, notwithstanding the finding as to passing off. The case, so far as regards passing off, was not expressly referred to in the judgments, but the principles stated were as applicable to that as to the case for infringement: *Pinto v. Badman* (1891) 8 R.P.C. 181.

14–143 (2) A manufacturing company in England, with a world-wide business in "Gold Flake" cigarettes, had sold to the claimant

---

[49] And it would seem, only in such cases: see *per* Lord Diplock in *Star Industrial v. Yap Kwee Kor* [1976] F.S.R. 256 at 272 (PC, Singapore).

[50] *Thorneloe v. Hill* [1894] 1 Ch. 569; 11 R.P.C. 61 ("*John Forrest*"). Nor can goodwill be licensed to another: *Star Industrial, supra.*

[51] Where goodwill is shared between a number of traders, all of whom are entitled to use the particular badge, any one of them may sue a trader using it with no right to do so at all: see discussion of *Bollinger v. Costa Brava* [1960] R.P.C. 16, *ante* paras 14–132 *et seq.*

company, who were importers in India, the goodwill in India together with trade marks and other rights and assets in India. After the transfer the manufacture was carried on in England by the transferor company for the claimants. The defendants purchased a large quantity of the same brand of cigarettes from the British Army Canteen authorities, which had been originally purchased from the manufacturing company. It was held that the claimant company had acquired no independent reputation as importers, the reputation in India of the brand of "Gold Flake" cigarettes being that of the maker and not of the claimant's company as importers; and that the defendants were in no way passing off the cigarettes sold by them as the claimant company's goods: *Imperial Tobacco of India v. Bonnan* (1924) 4 R.P.C. 441. It would seem to follow from the decision in *"Bostitch"* [1963] R.P.C. 183 that even if the claimant company had itself undertaken manufacture of its cigarettes the reputation in the mark might well have remained that of the transferor: *cf. Diehl* [1970] R.P.C. 435 (where the mark was the importer's and not the manufacturer's).

(3) The claimant claimed only as the mortgagee of a business and **14–144** its name, and had never used, and did not intend to use, the name. The defendant had bought the business, subject to the mortgage, and the claimant sued to prevent him trading under the old name without paying off the mortgage. The action was dismissed: *Beazley v. Soares* (1882) 22 Ch.D. 660.

Use of the name or description of the goods

In an action for passing off[52] by the use of a supposed trade mark, it is **14–145** ordinarily enough for the defendant to show that the mark is a mere name for the goods, regardless of trade origin, and that he has used it accurately—whether the supposed mark be an expression that once was or might have been a trade mark like "Liebig's Extract,"[53] "Chlorodyne",[54] "Linoleum",[55] "Wellington Boots", "Gladstone Bag" and "Hansom Cab"; or is a mere description of the goods, denoting only

---

[52] *cf.* the case where the mark is registered: paras 000, 000. Other cases are *Gamage v. Randall* (1899) 16 R.P.C. 185 ("Shortland" shoes); illus. (1), *post*, para. 14–161; the "Hommel's Haematogen" cases: *Hommel v. Bauer* (1905) 22 R.P.C. 43 and *Hommel's v. Hommel* (1912) 29 R.P.C. 378—all instructive without perhaps being sound. *cf.* also the cases on descriptive trading names, *post*, para 14–150 *et seq.*

[53] *Liebig's v. Hanbury* (1867) 17 L.T.(N.S.) 298; *Liebig v. Anderson* (1886) 55 L.T. 206; and *cf. Same v. Chemists' Co-operative* (1896) 13 R.P.C. 736.

[54] *Browne v. Freeman (No. 1)* (1864) 12 W.R. 305; *(No. 2)* [1873] W.N. 178.

[55] *Linoleum v. Nairn* (1878) 7 Ch.D. 834. *cf. Chesebrough* (1901) 18 R.P.C. 191; 19 R.P.C. 342 ("Vaseline" not descriptive).

their pattern,[56] mode of manufacture,[57] or sale,[58] type,[59] ingredients,[60] quality,[61] or place of origin.[62] But as the cases just cited show, such a defence has often failed, the claimant showing that the expression concerned is distinctive of his goods or business; and a claimant alleging this will in most instances be able to show enough of an arguable case to support a claim for an interlocutory injunction.

14–146   The claimant was the owner of the trade mark "Aertex", for under-wear, etc. The action was based on trap orders, the claimant alleging that goods not of its manufacture had been supplied to persons asking for "Aertex". In the course of the argument, counsel for the claimant conceded that some members of the public used the word "Aertex" as

[56] *Burberrys v. Cording* (1909) 26 R.P.C. 693; *Winser v. Armstrong* (1899) 16 R.P.C. 167 ("Winser Interceptors"). In *Cordes v. Addis* (1923) 40 R.P.C. 133, held that in this country the word "Prophylactic" was descriptive of a particular shape and make of toothbrush. But a word may be shown by evidence to indicate a particular pattern of goods when made by a particular manufacturer, and thus to be distinctive: *Whitfield* [1909] 2 Ch. 373; 26 R.P.C. 657 ("Lawson Tait Bedsteads"; a registration case).

[57] *Singer v. Wilson* (1875) 2 Ch.D. 434; 3 App.Cas. 376; *Same v. Loog* (1877) 18 Ch.D. 395; 8 App.Cas. 15; *Same v. Spence* (1893) 10 R.P.C. 297; *Same v. British Empire* (1903) 20 R.P.C. 313 ("Singer System," "Singer Sewing Machine"). In the last two cases and in *Daimler v. London Daimler* (1907) 24 R.P.C. 379 ("Daimler"), the claimants, after failing in previous actions, established that the name had become distinctive. See also *Bowden Wire v. Bowden Brake (No. 2)* (1913) 30 R.P.C. 609 ("Bowden Control" held to be descriptive). In *Bechstein v. Barker* (1910) 27 R.P.C. 484, the claimants obtained an injunction against passing off by the use of the word "Bechstein", the defendants having sold pianos not of the claimants' manufacture as "Bechstein Model Pianos".

[58] *Symington v. Footman* (1885) 56 L.T. 696 ("Guaranteed Corset").

[59] In *Armstrong Oiler v. Patent Axlebox* (1910) 27 R.P.C. 362, the claimants, who were makers of oilers for the axles of railway carriages claimed that "Armstrong Oilers" meant their oilers, and failed to restrain the defendants from supplying their own goods as "Armstrong Type Oilers". In *Universal Winding v. Hattersley* (1915) 32 R.P.C. 479, held that the defendants were entitled to make and advertise for sale universal machinery by the names "Universal Wind" or "Universal Machine" or "Universal Winding Machinery"; *cf.* the interlocutory injunction granted in *A. V. Roe v. Aircraft Disposal* (1920) 37 R.P.C. 249 restraining the defendants from selling or offering for sale aeroplanes not being of the claimant's manufacture as "Avro" goods, with the addition assented to by the claimants that that was not to prevent the defendants from selling aeroplanes made according to the design "Avro 504 K" as aeroplanes "Avro type" or "type Avro". "Edison" was held to be distinctive: *Edison Storage Batteries v. Britannia* (1931) 48 R.P.C. 350. *cf.* "Blue Orchid", distinctive but not descriptive, in *Delavelle v. Stanley*; "Crystal" (for a ball-point pen, transparent and made from moulding powder such as the trade called "crystal" powders) protected by interlocutory injunction: *Biro-Swan v. Tallon* [1961] R.P.C. 326.

[60] In *Boake, Roberts v. Wayland* (1909) 26 R.P.C. 251, the claimants established that K.M.S. (the initial letters of Kalium Meta Sulphite) meant their goods; *cf. White, Tomkins v. United Confectionery* (1914) 31 R.P.C. 430 (picture indicating flavour of jelly preparation) and *Woodward v. Boulton Macro* (1915) 32 R.P.C. 173 (Gripe Water). See also *Horlick's v. Summerskill* (1916) 34 R.P.C. 63, HL; *Newton Chambers v. Neptune* (1935) 52 R.P.C. 399 ("Medicated with "Izal"; but "medicated" and "with" too small, so that the effect was use of "Izal" as a trade mark).

[61] Where "Vacuum Oil" meant the claimants' oil, the defendants, who described their oil as "Vacuum Motor Oil A Quality", were restrained: *Vacuum Oil v. Gooch* (1909) 27 R.P.C. 76; *Sharpe v. Solomon* (1915) 32 R.P.C. 15 ("Classic" as applied to artistic goods).

[62] *"Rugby Portland Cement"* (1892) 9 R.P.C. 46, CA; *"Whitstable Oysters"* (1901) 18 R.P.C. 434, CA. But the defence failed in *Seixo v. Provezende* (1885) L.R. 1 Ch. 192 ("Seixo Wine"); *Wotherspoon v. Currie* (1872) L.R. 5 H.L. 508 ("Glenfield Starch"); see also "Reading Biscuit" (*Huntley and Palmer v. Reading Biscuit*) (1893) 10 R.P.C. 277; *Bewlay v. Hughes* (1898) 15 R.P.C. 290 ("Dindigul Cigars"); and *"London Candles"*, below, n. 69.

the description of a type of cellular fabric. The judge observed that this admission was fatal to the case, unless it was made clear to the shop assistant that this "customer" was not using the word "Aertex" descriptively: "If customers do use the word descriptively, 50 trap orders will not help you": *Cellular Clothing v. White & Co.* (1953) 70 R.P.C. 9 at 11, *per* Harman J., *arguendo*. But *cf.* the "*Corona*" case, illustration (1), paragraph 14–150.

If, however, the description is used inaccurately, its use may amount **14–147** to passing off, actionable by those whose are able properly to use it.[63]

Thus in particular cases the facts may justify the contention that in relation to accessories for use with a proprietary article, use of the brand name of the article means only that it is such an accessory.[64]

(1) In an action for passing-off of photographic film, the defendants **14–148** alleged that, when applied to films, names such as "Kodak" and "Brownie" merely meant to the general public films for "Kodak" or "Brownie" cameras. The defence failed on the facts, the judge finding that these names meant only Kodak Ltd's films for those cameras: *Kodak v. London Stereoscopic* (1903) 20 R.P.C. 337.

(2) The claimants, manufacturers of "Gledhill" cash tills, sued a **14–149** defendant who produced paper rolls for those tills and sold them as "Gledhill rolls" (or "Gledhill coils") and in boxes stamped "Gledhill". The evidence was that this had been going on for some years, with various makes of till; that the defendants' customers (who were traders) habitually ordered what they knew were the defendants' goods as "Gledhill rolls" (or "coils"), and (from the defendants' customers) that this was normal practice in the trade and never gave rise to complaints. The claimants weakened their case by objecting to the defendants' price list, which (arranged in columns headed "make of till", "dimensions", "price") struck the Court of Appeal as eminently fair. Held that such terms as "Gledhill rolls" had acquired the secondary meaning of "rolls to fit Gledhill tills", and the action failed: *Gledhill v. British Perforated* (1911) 28 R.P.C. 429 (Eve J.), 714, CA.

Descriptive names may be distinctive to some

A word may be distinctive of the claimants' goods to the majority of **14–150** people, but to some people the same word may indicate a characteristic of the goods, for instance, size and shape.

---

[63] See *ante*, para. 14–132, on "Shared reputation" and *cf. post* para. 14–165.

[64] *cf.* the case where the mark is registered: *ante*, para. 000. This is not a contention likely to meet much favour from the court, since the defendant in such cases could easily avoid any possible ambiguity; but see the examples below; *cf. Neostyle v. Ellams* (1904) 21 R.P.C. 185, 569, where it was held on the facts that, although "Neostyle" in England denoted the name of the claimants' duplicating machine, the claimants had no exclusive right to it for accessories. See also *Yost v. Typewriter Exchange* (1902) 19 R.P.C. 422 (Yost pads for a Yost typewriter).

(1) The word "Corona", a name distinctive of the claimants' brand of cigars, had also acquired a meaning descriptive of size and shape, irrespective of brand, so that a request for "a Corona cigar" was ambiguous. The defendant was held to have set up a claim to do that which would, in the majority of cases, be passing off goods, and Russell J. granted an injunction restraining the sale or supply in response to any order for "some cigars, Coronas", or "Corona cigars", or a "Corona cigar", or "Coronas", or a "Corona", cigars or a cigar not of the Corona brand, unless it be first clearly ascertained that the customer who gives the order does not require cigars or a cigar of the Corona brand and no other brand. On appeal the Court of Appeal affirmed the order of Russell J. with the addition of the words "or unless it was made clear to him by word of mouth or otherwise that the cigar supplied was of a brand other than the claimants' brand": *Havana v. Oddenino* [1923] 2 Ch. 243; 40 R.P.C. 229; [1924] 1 Ch. 179; 41 R.P.C. 47.

14–151   (2) The claimants claimed that "Staunton" as applied to chessmen indicated their manufacture exclusively, whilst the defendant's case was that the name was merely descriptive of chessmen made according to designs produced by the famous chess player. There was evidence that the claimants' claim was generally recognised in the trade, other makers' goods being advertised as "Staunton pattern" and the like. It was held that the public generally regarded the name as descriptive; an injunction was granted in the court of first instance restraining the use of the words "genuine Staunton". This was discharged by the Court of Appeal on the ground that if the name was descriptive, the addition of the word "genuine" could make no difference: *Jacques v. Chess* (1940) 57 R.P.C. 77. It is interesting here to compare the observation of Lord Hunter, a quarter of a century later, that "the word 'genuine' has almost begun to acquire a connotation as sinister as the word 'type'": "*Harris Tweed*" [1964] R.P.C. 477 at 550; *cf.* at 510.[65]

14–152   (3) The claimants, Purefoy Engineering, were suppliers of standard engineering components, which were identified in their trade by code numbers given in their catalogue. The defendants took to supplying a similar range of components. The claimants sent a series of "trap orders" to the defendants, for components described as "Purefoy", followed by the claimants' code number. There was evidence that to many people in engineering concerns, such a designation was merely descriptive of the component and did not mean a component made by "Purefoy". The Court of Appeal held that the defendants ought not to

[65] *Cf. Cocks v. Chandler* (1871) L.R. 11 Eq. 446 and *Allen v. Original Samuel Allen* (1915) 32 R.P.C. 33 (illus. (6), *ante*, para. 14–97) where the added word was "original".

supply their own products upon such orders without inquiry whether the claimants' goods were intended or merely an equivalent, and granted an injunction in "*Corona*" form: *Purefoy v. Sykes Boxall* (1954) 71 R.P.C. 227; (1955) 72 R.P.C. 89 at 93, CA. There was extraneous evidence that the defendants were not unwilling to pass off if they could. This case was followed in *Bostitch v. McGarry & Cole* [1964] R.P.C. 173 (where the defendants, formerly sole suppliers of "Bostitch" goods, continued after severance of relations with the claimants to supply their own equivalent goods "without first making it perfectly clear to the inquirer that they cannot supply him with the article he wants, and leaving him an interval to decide what he is going to do,") but it must not be taken as deciding that "if a plaintiff establishes in any given case that A has ordered particular goods under a mark which is established as B's mark and is then supplied with some other goods passing-off must necessarily be established": *per* Whitford J. in *Broad v. Cast Iron Drainage* [1970] F.S.R. 363 at 371.

(4) The defendant adopted the word "Gloss" for its range of **14–153** cosmetics. The claimants were the makers of a successful television soap opera "Gloss" and a company licensed to use the name "Gloss" on a range of toiletries and cosmetics (although it had not yet started doing so). In granting an interlocutory injunction, the judge concluded that the word was almost meaningless in descriptive terms when used on its own. (Counsel for the defendant had conceded the existence of a "merchandising" right): *TVNZ v. Gloss Cosmetic Suppliers* (1991) 19 I.P.R. 663 (HC, N.Z.).

It is not uncommonly found that marks which many members of the **14–154** public use descriptively are, nevertheless, fully distinctive to those in the trade.[66] Such marks are of exceptional value. Whilst they are not easy to protect merely by proceedings for passing off, if they are registered they can without undue difficulty be protected by proceedings for infringement.[67]

Words and terms which prima facie are merely descriptive in the sense just explained may, by use and reputation, acquire a secondary distinctive meaning,[68] so that they may be practically monopolised for

---

[66] *e.g. "Gramophone"* [1910] 2 Ch. 423; followed in *Antec International v. South Western Chicks* [1998] F.S.R. 738, at 744 (finding "Farm Fluid" sufficiently distinctive to justify grant of an interlocutory injunction).

[67] Although such marks are unregistrable, a registration already in existence may well be valid, see *ante*, paras 9–30, 9–79, 9–91.

[68] *Ante*, para. 102.

use in connection with certain classes of goods by a particular trader, since their employment by anyone else would be calculated to deceive.[69]

14–155   The claimant had a trade-mark "Apollo" (for chicken essence) which (as is usual in Chinese speaking countries like Singapore) was habitually used in the form of Chinese characters with rough phonetic resemblance to "Apollo" and with an alternative meaning thought to be attractive (here, "beneficial for restoring strength"). The defendant used as a trade mark similar Chinese characters with a similar punning meaning. In an action for passing off, held, that the claimant must show that his Chinese mark had acquired a secondary meaning denoting his goods, and this he failed to do: *McAlister v. Pasuma* [1975] R.P.C. 601 (HC, Singapore). This would seem to be the wrong test: the question should surely have been, whether the parties' marks were recognised by the public as being trade marks (which they probably were) and if so, whether they were confusingly similar.

Judgment of Parker J. in *Burberrys v. Cording*

14–156   In a case in which the claimants were claiming that the words "Slip-On" were distinctive of their goods,[70] Parker J. summarised the principles of law applicable to the case in the following passage:

> "The principles of law applicable to a case of this sort are well known. On the one hand, apart from the law as to trade marks, no one can claim monopoly rights in the use of a word or name. On the other hand, no one is entitled by the use of any word or name, or indeed in any other way, to represent his goods as being the goods of another to that other's injury. If an injunction be granted restraining the use of a word or name it is no doubt granted to protect property, but the property, to protect which it is granted, is not property in the word or name, but property in the trade or goodwill which will be injured by its use. If the use of a word or name be restrained, it can only be on the ground that such use involves a misrepresentation, and that such misrepresentation has injured, or is calculated to injure, another in his trade or business. If no case of deception by means of such misrepresentation can be proved it is sufficient to prove the probability of such deception, and the court will readily infer such probability if it be shown that the word or name has been adopted with any intention to deceive.

---

[69] See the cases cited in n. 62, and *Montgomery v. Thompson* [1891] A.C. 217; 8 R.P.C. 361 ("Stone Ales" HL). In *Price's Patent Candle v. Ogston and Tennant* (1909) 26 R.P.C. 797 (Scotland) it was found that in Morocco "London Candles" meant the claimants' candles. See further *Reddaway v. Banham* [1896] A.C. 199 at 210; 13 R.P.C. 218, HL; the judgment of Kennedy L.J. in *Daimler v. London Daimler* (1907) 24 R.P.C. 379; and the judgment of Parker J. in *British Vacuum Cleaner v. New Vacuum Cleaner* (1907) 24 R.P.C. 641; cf. *Treasure Cot v. Hamleys* (1950) 67 R.P.C. 89 ("Treasure" when applied to a cot held to be a fancy word).

[70] *Burberrys v. Cording* (1909) 26 R.P.C. 693 at 701.

In the absence of such intention, the degree of readiness with which the court will infer the probability of deception must depend on the circumstances of each particular case, including the nature of the word or name, the use of which is sought to be restrained. It is important for this purpose to consider whether the word or name is prima facie in the nature of a fancy word or name, or whether it is prima facie descriptive of the article in respect of which it is used. It is also important for the same purpose to consider its history, the nature of its use by the person who seeks the injunction, and the extent to which it is or has been used by others. If the word or name is prima facie descriptive or be in general use, the difficulty of establishing the probability of deception is greatly increased. Again, if the person who seeks the injunction has not used the word or name simply for the purpose of distinguishing his own goods from the goods of others, but primarily for the purpose of denoting or describing the particular kind of article to which he has applied it, and only secondarily, if at all, for the purposes of distinguishing his own goods, it will be more difficult for him to establish the probability of deception. But whatever be the nature or history of the word or name, in whatever way it has been used, either by the person seeking the injunction or by others, it is necessary where there has been no actual deception, to establish at least a reasonable[71] probability of deception."

Marks more-or-less descriptive

There is, of course, no sharp division between marks that are descriptive **14–157** and marks that are not: descriptiveness is a matter of degree.[72] As with trade names,[73] to the extent that a trader chooses a descriptive mark, he must expect others to use similarly descriptive marks so that confusion may be inevitable. The courts have sometimes (but not always) had regard to this, and accepted relatively small differences between descriptive marks as sufficient to avoid passing off.[74]

Word formerly common to trade

A word which has, at one time, been in common use in a trade with a **14–158** mere descriptive meaning may subsequently come to have special reference to the goods of a particular trader, who will then be entitled to prevent others using it without sufficiently distinguishing their goods.[75]

---

[71] See as to "reasonable", here, *Delavelle v. Stanley* (1946) 63 R.P.C. 103 at 105.
[72] See the discussion of descriptive marks in Chap. 7.
[73] "*Office Cleaning*," *post*, para. 14–194.
[74] See here the lists in App. 35, noting that there is here a distinction to be drawn between passing off and trade mark infringement (see paras 16–03 to 16–05); and see *McCain v. Country Fair* [1981] R.P.C. 69, CA (only the descriptive part of the claimants' mark taken, no passing off); *Fisons v. Godwin* [1976] R.P.C. 653 is similar; but *cf. Carlsberg v. Tennent* [1972] R.P.C. 847 (OH, Sc.), where an interim interdict was granted to protect the mark "Special brew" for beer; there was some similarity of get-up and the goods were intended to be directly competitive.
[75] *Daimler Motor v. London Daimler* (1906) 23 R.P.C. 718; 24 R.P.C. 379.

A word which has denoted the goods of two or three separate firms may come to denote the goods of one only: *Worcester Royal Porcelain v. Locke* (1902) 19 R.P.C. 479, where the claimants were the successors of all the three firms who had previously used the term "Worcester" to denote their goods.

Area

14–159 Where a word which is prima facie descriptive is claimed as his trade mark by the claimant, he must show that it has acquired a distinctive meaning "amongst those who are purchasers of the goods" in question[76] within a definite area. Such area must extend to a large part of England and Wales, and include the district in which the defendant trades or proposes to trade.[77] If the word still continues to be used and understood with its original descriptive meaning by any considerable section of such persons, it cannot be monopolised.[78] The more appropriate the words claimed are as a description of the goods or of some characteristic of the goods, the greater is the burden of proof required from the claimant.[79]

The question of fact

14–160 The question of fact which has to be answered in the cases under consideration has, accordingly, a negative as well as an affirmative part: Does the word in dispute mean the claimant's goods and not goods (by whomsoever made) of a particular pattern or description?[80] The first part of the question alone is not enough:

---

[76] This was Lord Herschell's phrase in *Reddaway v. Banham* [1896] A.C. 199 at 208; 13 R.P.C. 218 at 227.

[77] *Chivers v. Chivers* (1900) 17 R.P.C. 420 at 429; *Faulder v. Rushton* (1903) 20 R.P.C. 477, CA and the judgment of Moulton L.J. in *Star Cycle v. Frankenburgs* (1907) 24 R.P.C. 405 at 414—small local bona fide users, which had been proved, did not affect his mind much with regard to the issue, the general reputation of the claimants under the name "Star Cycle". See also the judgment of Lord Shand in *Cellular Clothing* below (nn. 78 and 85) at 408. In *Thorne v. Sandow* (1912) 29 R.P.C. 440 at 453 evidence did not suffice to prove that throughout the country "Health Cocoa" had acquired a secondary meaning. See also cases as to registration, in which distinctiveness can only be established in particular districts, above, paras 7–94, 7–179.

[78] *Parsons v. Gillespie* [1898] A.C. 239; 15 R.P.C. 57, PC ("Flaked Oatmeal"); *Cellular Clothing v. Maxton* [1899] A.C. 326; 16 R.P.C. 397 at 403, HL. Where the only evidence that the word "Chequerboard" for fencing was distinctive of the claimants' fencing was that of persons in a special position to know of the origin of the goods, the action failed: *T. & C. v. Victoria* (1931) 48 R.P.C. 148.

[79] *Randall v. Bradley* (1907) 24 R.P.C. 657; affirmed at 773. The action of the claimants (The American Shoe Co.) to restrain the defendants trading as The Anglo-American Shoe Co. was dismissed. *Hommel v. Bauer* (1905) 22 R.P.C. 43: "Haematogen" for a medicine held not to be distinctive. "The '*Camel Hair Belting*' case may be an example of what, under ordinary circumstances, it would be very difficult to establish": *per* Halsbury L.C. in *Cellular Clothing* [1899] A.C. 326 at 336; 16 R.P.C. 397 at 405. See also the judgment of Parker J. in *Burberrys v. Cording* (1909) 26 R.P.C. 693 at 701, 704 and 709 ("Slip-On" coats), cited *ante* at para. 14–156.

[80] *Gamage v. Randall* (1899) 16 R.P.C. 185 at 196; *Reddaway v. Banham* [1896] A.C. 199; 13 R.P.C. 218 ("Camel Hair Belting").

"Where a word is prima facie the name or description of an article, evidence that it is also generally associated with the name of a particular maker is by no means conclusive that it has become a distinctive work which cannot be used of the same article when made by others without risk of deception".[81]

(1) In a dispute about the appellation "Shorland" for cycling **14–161** shoes—a Mr Shorland, a well-known cyclist, having lent his name to the shoe—the defence was that the term was descriptive of the particular pattern of shoe. There was evidence that a number of makers used the name, apart from its use by Gamage's, the claimants; and some evidence that without Gamage's name a "Shorland" shoe would not be taken as made by Gamages. The jury found for the defendants and the Court of Appeal upheld the judgment: *Gamage v. Randall* (1899) 16 R.P.C. 185. No doubt it would inevitably have told against the claimants that they had persistently associated their own name with "Shorland" when advertising the shoe. But the question actually put to the jury made a verdict for the defendants a foregone conclusion:

"If a man goes into a shop which is not Gamages . . . and says **14–162** 'Give me a pair of Shorland shoes' and shoes of this type were produced with no stamp of Gamages' name upon it, do you think that that man understands or believes that he is getting a shoe that comes from Gamages' shop?": see at 196.

If that be a fair question, no retailer can have a valid trade mark. In these days also, the idea that Gamages could, by securing Mr Shorland's permission for use of his name, get some sort of prima facie right to it would have been more familiar to the jury and even the judge: *cf.* paras 14–77, 22–42 *et seq.*

(2) In *"Camel Hair Belting"* the following questions were put to the **14–163** jury—with the approval, it is clear, of the House of Lords: (a) Does "Camel Hair Belting" mean belting made by the plaintiffs as distinct from belting made by other manufacturers? (b) Does it mean belting of a particular kind, without reference to any particular maker? (c) Do the defendants so describe their belting as to be likely to mislead purchasers, and to lead them to buy the defendants' belting as and for the plaintiffs' belting? (d) Did the defendants endeavour to pass off their goods as and for the plaintiffs' goods, so as to be likely to deceive purchasers? The jury said "Yes" to (a), (c) and (d), and "No" to (b); judgment for the plaintiffs.

---

[81] *Per* Parker J., *Burberrys v. Cording* (1909) 26 R.P.C. 693 at 704 (cited *ante*, para. 14–156).

14-164   (3) Where the claimant had been selling, for less than a year, beers under the name "Newquay Real Steam Beer", the court found there to be a serious issue to be tried as to whether the word "Steam" was entitled to protection. The judge did not consider that the adoption of the name by the claimant with the intention of conveying an aura of purity, strength and old-fashioned character put it into the category of descriptive marks described in *Burberry v. Cording* by Parker J.: *Island Trading v. Anchor Brewing* [1989] R.P.C. 287a.[82]

Literally true description may mislead

14-165   "Even a description of goods which is literally true may be so framed as to deceive"[83]; "a statement that is literally true, but which is intended to convey a false impression . . . is not sterling coin.[84]"

Where an ingredient, oxide of iron, was used in making medicinal tablets merely to justify the use of the name "Compound Iron Oxide Tablets", and the name was chosen because it would lead to confusion with the claimants' "Iron-Ox Tablets", and not because it could be said correctly to describe the article, an injunction was granted against the use of the term "iron oxide" without "better distinguishing" the defendants' goods from those of the claimants. The claimants' goods did not contain oxide of iron, which was practically useless as a drug, and the name "Iron-Ox Tablets" was held to indicate their tablets and was not associated by the public with any particular drug: *Iron-Ox v. Co-operative Wholesale Society* (1907) 24 R.P.C. 425. That other traders had adopted (sporadically and locally) the same strategem was not treated as affecting the issue: *cf. post*, paragraph 14–175.

Secondary meaning not acquired while no competition

14-166 If the claimant has had a monopoly in fact of the goods, his difficulty in showing that the name he called them by is distinctive of his goods is increased.[85] In particular, reputation in get-up sufficient to found an action for passing off is not established merely by proof of large sales of a unique product[86]: "if any confusion has taken place it can only be the

---

[82] The judge granted an interlocutory injunction in relation to keg beer but not bottled beer, because there was a greater chance of confusion with the former: at 306.

[83] *per* Lord Davey in *Grand Hotel v. Wilson* (1904) 21 R.P.C. 117 at 134, PC; *Reddaway v. Banham* [1896] A.C. 199 at 212; 13 R.P.C. 218 at 233.

[84] *per* Lord Macnaghten.

[85] *British Vacuum Cleaner v. New Vaccuum Cleaner* (1907) 24 R.P.C. 641 at 652, citing Lord Davey in *"Cellular Clothing"* at 16 R.P.C. 309. "To succeed in such a case [the claimant] must demonstrate more than simply the sole use of the description term. He must demonstrate that it has become so closely associated with his goods as to acquire the secondary meaning not simply of goods of that description but specifically of goods of which he and he alone is the source"; *per* Lord Oliver in *"Jif"*, *op cit.*, at 413.

[86] *Jarman & Platt v. Barget* [1977] F.S.R. 260, CA; *cf. Reckitt & Colman Products v. Borden*, *op cit.*

type of confusion which inevitably occurs when the first competitors appear on the scene to break—and to break quite legitimately—the monopoly previously enjoyed in the use of a new product", *per* Sir Allan Huggins V.P. in *Interlego v. Tyco*.[87] However, in order to succeed in a defence based on what was described in *"Jif"* as "the monopoly assumption" it must be shown that the claimant's mark (or get-up) is "either so ordinary or in such common use that it would be unreasonable that he should claim it as applicable solely to his goods": *per* Lord Oliver, at 413.

(1) A number of grocers proved that when asked by their cus- **14–167** tomers for "Flaked Oatmeal" they supplied the claimant's goods; but there was no evidence of actual deception or confusion, and the value of the evidence first mentioned was discounted by the fact that it wholly or chiefly referred to a period when there were no other goods of the kind in question in the market besides the claimant's goods. The claimant failed: *Parsons v. Gillespie* [1898] A.C. 239 at 254; 15 R.P.C. 57 at 62.

(2) The claimants' evidence consisted of: (a) their own advertise- **14–168** ments, in which they used the word "cellular" to describe their cloth, but did not suggest that its use distinguished their cloth from cloth of a similar description made by others[88]; (b) statements of witnesses who said they understood "cellular goods" to mean the goods of the claimants, but who did not say that they knew of any other manufacturers making similar classes of goods; and (c) consent orders for injunctions obtained against other persons who had used the name. The claimants failed: *Cellular Clothing v. Maxton* [1899] A.C. 326 at 345; 16 R.P.C. at 410.

(3) The name "Shredded Wheat" had been used for many years as **14–169** the name of a breakfast food, originally a patented article. The name was appropriate as a description of the article, as was emphasised by the use of such advertising slogans as "It's all in the shreds"; and even after expiry of the patent, the users of the name were the only makers of that type of breakfast food. The mark "Shredded Wheat" was held invalidly registered, both in England and in Canada: *Canadian Shredded Wheat v. Kellogg* (1938) 55 R.P.C. 125; *"Shredded Wheat"* (1938) 55 R.P.C. 55, 271; (1940) 57 R.P.C. 137, HL.

(4) The claimants had a restaurant called "Chicago Pizza Pie **14–170** Factory", whose main business was selling what they called a "Chicago Pizza". The defendants opened a very similar restaur-

---

[87] *Supra*, at 422.
[88] It is not sufficient to show extensive advertising apart from the effect of the advertisement. "To make an advertisement relevant you must show that it had an effect": *per* Vaughan Williams L.J. in *Christy v. Tipper* (1904) 21 R.P.C. 97 at 101. See also *Chivers v. Chivers* (1900) 17 R.P.C. 420 at 431.

ant called "L.S. Grunts Chicago Pizza Company". There was evidence of substantial confusion between the two; but it was held that since the claimants had given the name "Chicago Pizza" to this dish, they were not entitled to rely as passing off on confusion resulting from the defendants calling it that too: *My Kinda Town v. Soll* [1983] R.P.C. 407, CA.

14–171 (5) For many years the claimant had sold cigarette papers in three weights, each indicated by a colour on the packaging: red, blue and yellow. The defendant launched its own three weights of cigarette papers, whose packaging was readily distinguishable from the claimant's although they also used red, blue and yellow to indicate the three weights. Passing off was alleged on the basis that: (a) the claimant's papers were never on display, being kept under the counter; and (b) that people would ask for a packet of "reds" and be supplied with the defendant's papers. The judge thought that it was by no means clear that a request for "reds" meant the claimant's goods as opposed to papers of that weight. He also thought that any confusion could be avoided by the claimant's ensuring that their goods were put on display; interlocutory relief was refused: *Rizla v. Bryant & May* [1986] R.P.C. 389.

14–172 It was stated by Slade L.J. in the Court of Appeal in *"Jif"*, *op. cit.*, that the so-called monopoly assumption point, *i.e.* if a claimant has had a monopoly his difficulty in showing that the name (or get-up) is distinctive is increased, makes more difficult the defendant's case once the claimant has established a proprietary right in the name or get-up.

> "If a trader enters the market with a class of goods, which have already for many years been sold under a particular get-up by another trader and have by reason of such get-up become identified in the minds of the public as the products of that trader, it is in my judgment ordinarily necessary, if he is to avoid the risk of misrepresentation, for him to take *all the greater* pains to ensure that there are sufficient distinguishing features between the get-up of his goods and those of the other trader. Potential competitors in this class of case may thus be well advised to enter the field quickly, if at all, before a reputation has been established." (at 392).[89]

In the House of Lords, Lord Oliver emphasised the need for the new entrant "to see that the goods can be really distinguished" (citing Romer L.J. in *Payton v. Snelling*), at 414.

Where claimants have other, special names for goods

14–173 The fact that the claimant has for some of his goods a special name does not necessarily negative his right to a more general name.[90]

---

[89] See also *United Biscuits v. Asda* [1997] R.P.C. 513 at 524 (Robert Walker J.) The judge considered that the court was not bound to disregard the fact that the defendant had taken a conscious decision to live dangerously: at 531.

[90] *Ford v. Foster* (1872) L.R. 7 Ch. 611 at 628.

In *"Worcester China"* the claimants had used the terms "Royal Worcester" and "Grainger's Worcester China" for some of their goods, and it was contended that by their conduct they had abandoned or lost their rights in "Worcester China" *simpliciter*, but this defence failed: (1902) 19 R.P.C. 479.

But the use of such special names is a matter to be considered.[91]

Name of introducer or patentee

The name of the inventor or first introducer of goods which are new to **14–174** the market, or the name which he gives to those he manufactures or sells, is very readily adopted as the name of goods by whomsoever they are made; and in the case of goods made under a patent, the court is careful not to extend the patentee's monopoly by forbidding other manufacturers, after the patent has expired, to sell goods lawfully made by them according to its specification under the only name by which they are known.[92]

The name of the first maker or inventor is often understood to imply the good quality of work or materials which has brought the new goods into favour rather than the mode of manufacture or the nature of the ingredients employed.[93] Where this is the case, the use of the name by traders who have no connection with him must almost always be calculated to deceive.

Names may become *publici juris*

Names which once carried a distinctive reference to a particular trader **14–175** may, in consequence of successful piracies, or of their use by the trader himself for goods which are the goods of others, or are put forward as such,[94] or for other reasons,[95] lose it and fall into common use and become *publici juris*, in the same way as trade marks may be lost or abandoned.[96] The proper test whether an exclusive right has become *publici juris* is whether the use of the trade mark by other persons has ceased to deceive the public as to the maker of the article.[97] Accordingly, evidence is admissible to show that a word which was once distinctive

---

[91] *Fels v. Thomas* ("Naphtha Soap") (1903) 21 R.P.C. 85 at 88, CA. The idea that goods habitually carry two trade marks—one the maker's "house mark", the other denoting the particular product, the thing to be called by—was not always recognised in the earlier cases; but it seems to be well understood now.

[92] *"British Vacuum Cleaner"* (1907) 24 R.P.C. 641 at 652, and cases there cited.

[93] See *Massam v. Thorley's, supra*. And *cf.* the cases on designers' names, etc., *post*, paras 14–214, 14–215.

[94] *Wolff v. Nopitsch* (1900) 17 R.P.C. 321 at 330; on appeal (1901) 18 R.P.C. 27, CA.

[95] See *"Gledhill Coils"*, para. 14–149, illus. (2), *ante*.

[96] Chap. 9.

[97] *Ford v. Foster* (1872) L.R. 7 Ch. 611 at 628 ("Eureka" shirts); followed in *Treasure Cot v. Hamleys* (1950) 67 R.P.C. 89 at 90 ("Treasure" for dolls' cots not *publici juris*). Test approved as a basis of a defence: *Bollinger v. Coldwell* [1971] F.S.R. 405.

of a particular trader's goods has become common in the trade. But, where the distinctive meaning alleged is proved to hold generally for the trade and public, cases of small local use for the goods of other traders will not have much effect to displace the evidence.[98] So also, piracy which exceeds in volume the genuine goods may fail to destroy the reputation of a mark, if it remains surreptitious, so that the ultimate consumer never appreciates the true position.

14–176 (1) The mark "Harris Tweed" acquired a widespread reputation as denoting tweed, made in the island of Harris or a neighbouring island, which was essentially the product of a cottage industry. At times after the 1914–18 War, much if not most of what was sold as "Harris Tweed" consisted of machine-made imitations. But these remained surreptitious, with the result that the reputation of the mark was never destroyed, though it became modified in the course of time: *"Harris Tweed"* [1964] R.P.C. 477 at 506, 509, 513–570; *cf. "Maizena"* [1894] A.C. 275; 11 R.P.C. 281 at 293, where substantially the same test was applied but the case went the other way (PC, Australia).

14–177 (2) Where it was proved that the supposed proprietor of an unregistered trade mark had licensed its use by another manufacturer (with whom he was not connected, and over whom he had no control), an action to prevent its use by a third manufacturer was dismissed: for the use under licence must either have been a fraud on the public or else have destroyed any goodwill the licensor may have had: *"John Forrest"* (*Thorneloe v. Hill*) (1894) 11 R.P.C. 61 at 71. Compare *"Bostitch"* [1963] R.P.C. 183, in which the question of validity of a registered mark, whose proprietor had allowed manufacture to be carried on by another company was tested in a very similar way.

Name may become associated with another trader

14–178 The question is, what is the meaning of the name for the time being? It is possible, therefore, for a word which has at one time been the trade mark of one trader to become so identified with the goods of a rival trader as afterwards to become the trade mark of the latter, who may thereby acquire an exclusive right to its use,[99] or, if its association with the original owner has continued, a right concurrent with his right.[1] But

---

[98] *Star Cycle v. Frankenburgs* (1907) 24 R.P.C. 405, Moulton L.J.; and *cf.* "Area", above, para. 14–159; *cf.* the *"Iron-Ox"* case, *ante*, para. 14–165, illus.; and *Goddard v. Watford Co-operative Soc.* (1924) 41 R.P.C. 218 at 231–232.

[99] *Daniel and Arter v. Whitehouse* [1898] 1 Ch. 685; 15 R.P.C. 134 at 140 ("Brazilian Silver"); *Jaeger v. Jaeger Co.* (1927) 44 R.P.C. 437 at 448, CA. This was also the contention of the former marketing company for the overseas supplier in *Essex Electric v. IPC Computer (U.K.)* [1991] F.S.R. 690, where the claimant succeeded in its application for an interlocutory injunction to restrain threats of passing off.

[1] *Edge v. Gallon* (1899) 16 R.P.C. 509 ("Dolly Blue").

in some circumstances—it is none too clear which—a party may be held debarred from setting up such a case, on the ground that his use was wrongful, and he may not rely on his own wrong.

The claimants were Swedish, the defendants their British agents. **14–179** When supplies from Sweden were cut off during the Second World War, the defendants replaced them by British goods, using the same trade mark. It was agreed that they should use the claimant's designs and should use the mark so as to maintain the claimant's goodwill. After the war, the defendants sought to show that the goodwill was now theirs, but were held disentitled by their breach of the agreement from doing so: *"Manus"* (1949) 66 R.P.C. 71 at 76, CA.

Disclaimed word

That a claimant has applied, in order to secure registration of a mark, to **14–180** disclaim some word, device or other thing found in it, should not prevent his establishing if he can that its use by others is deceptive, so as to found an action for passing off,[2] although he may be obliged to prove why he decided to disclaim and how the situation has changed since he did so. In the case of a word or mark which has been expunged from the Register, even though it was expunged without the claimant's assent, the removal of the mark does not and never did prevent the claimant from showing that the mark is, nevertheless, distinctive of his goods.[3] The court may, however, infer that other traders have refrained from using the word, not because they knew it to mean the claimant's goods, but merely because of the registration.[4] A trade mark which has never been registered, or which has been removed from the Register, may be the basis of a passing-off case,[5] for instance, a descriptive word, to which the claimant has a right that is not exclusive.[6]

Geographical names

Most geographical names are prima facie descriptive, of goods originat- **14–181** ing or a business carried on in the place concerned; they may by use come to distinguish a particular manufacturer or a particular undertaking, but can never entirely lose their primary significance.[7] Accordingly:

---

[2] 1994 Act, s.13.
[3] See " *Yorkshire Relish*" (para. 14–139, illus. (1)), and *"Stone Ales"* (below, para. 14–189).
[4] *Hommel v. Bauer* (1904) 21 R.P.C. 576 at 587; (1905) 22 R.P.C. 43, CA, approving the judgment below. *Sed quaere*: if in trade the mark concerned does denote the claimant's goods exclusively, why should it matter how that happened?
[5] *Parker-Knoll v. Knoll International* [1962] R.P.C. 265, HL; (mark "Knoll" not validly registrable, but use by defendants passing off); *cf.* para. 14–34.
[6] See para. 14–132, *ante*.
[7] *cf.* the discussion of distinctiveness of geographical trade marks, *ante*, para. 000. Also, see Chap. 10, on geographical indications.

"In the case of trade names which are prima facie geographically descriptive, a special order has sometimes been made in order to avoid any interference with the honest and proper use of them by persons other than the owner of the trade name."[8] However, reputation may attach to a geographical name that remains purely descriptive of a place or area, so that the right to attach it to goods or business may form part of the goodwill of those who are duly associated with that place or area: in which case, wrongful or dishonest use of that name will be actionable.[9]

14-182   (1) The claimant, being owner of all the collieries in Radstock, except a very small one, traded as the "Radstock Coal Co.", and the defendants began to sell coal under the same name, and also as "The Radstock Colliery Proprietors". An injunction was granted "to restrain the defendants, unless and until they shall acquire a colliery or coal mine within the parish of Radstock, from trading under, or using the name or style of 'The Radstock Colliery Proprietors', or any other name or style signifying that the defendants or either of them are proprietors of any colliery or collieries at Radstock": *Braham v. Beachim* (1878) 7 Ch.D. 848. Subsequently the defendants acquired a colliery, but not in Radstock, and began to trade as "The Radstock Coal and Waggon Co., Colliery Proprietors, Radstock, Somerset", and a motion to commit for breach of the injunction was refused on the ground that the terms used by them did no more than imply that they were proprietors of collieries, and that their place of business was at Radstock, and this was true: (1878) Seb.Dig. at 633, Fry J.

14-183   (2) On a finding that the name "Whitstable Native Oysters" meant the claimants' oysters, and could not be fairly used of French oysters relaid and brought to maturity at Whitstable, the court granted an interlocutory injunction to restrain the use of "Native"; no order as to "Whitstable": *Free Fishers of Whitstable v. Elliott*, 4 T.L.R. 273; [1888] W.N. 27. In the later case of *Whitstable Oyster Fisheries v. Hayling* (1900) 17 R.P.C. 461; 18 R.P.C. 434, it was decided that "Whitstable", as applied to oysters, was descriptive of the place where the oysters reach maturity.

---

[8] These words appeared in the 9th edition of this work and were quoted by Plowman J. in *Bach & Jackson v. Cowan* [1969] R.P.C. 156. In that case the defendant who had recently commenced his hotel business near the claimants' hotel under the name "Pembridge Hotel" was restrained from so doing upon evidence that the claimants' hotel was known as "the Pembridge" even though its full name was the "Pembridge Gardens Hotel". Both hotels were in an area of London where the names of many roads were prefaced by the word "Pembridge".

[9] *Ante*, para. 14-132; "*Spanish Champagne*" and "*Sherry*" cases, below; *John Walker v. Henry Ost* [1970] R.P.C. 489 (a "Scotch whisky" case); but *cf. Lang v. Goldwell* [1977] F.S.R. 353 (OH, Sc). (marketing a drink containing whisky so as to suggest a greater connection with Scotland than it does have, held not passing off).

(3) The claimant owned the only quarry in Brereton (in Chester) **14–184** producing foundry sand. The defendant sold foundry sand as "Brereton sand". There was another Brereton in Staffordshire. An interlocutory injunction was granted restraining the defendant from selling foundry sand as "Brereton", "except sand quarried in the parish of Brereton in the county of Chester or any other parish bearing the name of Brereton"—with a general prohibition of passing off also: *Smith v. Fieldhouse* [1961] R.P.C. 110.

(4) In the *"Spanish Champagne"* case, where a number of cham- **14–185** pagne producers sued in respect of the sale of Spanish sparkling wine as "Spanish Champagne", an injunction was granted restraining the defendants from passing off "as and for wine produced in the district of France known as the Champagne District wine not so produced by advertising, offering for sale or selling the same as Spanish Champagne or under any other name or description that includes the name Champagne": [1961] R.P.C. 116 at 127; [1960] R.P.C. 16 at 17. Any one of them, with substantial English goodwill in the name "Champagne", could have sued: see *"Advocaat"* [1980] R.P.C. 31, HL; *Bulmer v. Bollinger* [1978] R.P.C. 79, CA; (where, however, the description "Champagne perry" for perry made sparkling otherwise than by the champagne process and sold in bottles very different from champagne bottles, was held not deceptive).

(5) The injunction granted in the *"Sherry"* case restrained the **14–186** claimants (who had been sued on a counterclaim) "from using in the course of trade the word 'sherry' in connection with any wine not being wine coming from the Jerez district of Spain otherwise than as part of one or more of the phrases 'British Sherry', 'English Sherry', 'South African Sherry', 'Cyprus Sherry', 'Australian Sherry' and 'Empire Sherry'". The excepted phrases would not have been permitted if there had not been acquiescence: [1969] R.P.C. 1 at 32. Both the *"Champagne"* and *"Sherry"* cases were followed in the *"Whisky"* case, *John Walker v. Ost* [1970] R.P.C. 489.

(6) The defendants were marketing a non-alcoholic drink under the **14–187** name "Elderflower Champagne" in a bottle made up to look like a champagne bottle. In a representative capacity, the champagne house Taittinger sued for passing off. The Court of Appeal found there to have been a misrepresentation that the product was champagne or in some way associated with it and many members of the public would be deceived: *Taittinger v. Allbev* [1993] F.S.R. 641, CA. The court also granted an injunction restraining the use under E.C. Regulation 823/87 protecting the term "Champagne", at 673.

(7) Where the name "Banbury" was distinctive of the claimants, **14–188** the following qualification was added to the defendant's under

taking not to trade under that name, "Provided that nothing in the aforementioned undertaking shall prevent the defendant from making bona fide use of the word 'Banbury' as part of the address on any business for the time being bona fide carried on by it in the Borough of Banbury": *Banbury Buildings v. Sectional Concrete* [1970] R.P.C. 463. An injunction restraining the use of "Banbury" *simpliciter* would have prevented the defendant from carrying on its trade in Banbury altogether, since it could not have used its address.

14–189 "Thus cases of this sort fall into two categories: those where the question is whether the defendant has made a misleading use of a geographical appellation; and those where the allegation is that, although as a geographical appellation the expression complained of may have been accurately used, its use is calculated to represent that the goods are the claimant's".[10] To succeed under the former head, it is enough for the claimant to prove "(1) that he produces the substance in a given place; (2) that no one else produces the substance in that place; (3) that the defendant is selling the substance with the name of that place as a description; and (4) that there is likely to be deception of the public"[11]; although, as "Spanish Champagne" cited above shows, there are other ways of making out a case. It has been said that to succeed under the second head, the claimant must prove that the appellation in dispute has ceased to have a purely descriptive meaning as in "*Stone Ales*,"[12] where, although the right of the appellant to state that his beer was brewed at Stone was recognised, it was held to be subject to an obligation not to do so in any manner calculated to cause the appellant's beer to be passed off as that of the respondents, which was commonly known as "Stone Ale."[13] If, as required by the rule laid down in the authorities, cited above, the claimant proves that an apparently descriptive word which he claims to appropriate has ceased to have a purely descriptive

---

[10] These words (from the 9th edition) were also approved by Plowman J. in *Bach & Jackson v. Cowan, supra.*

[11] "*Brereton sand*" case [1961] R.P.C. 110 at 114, illus. (3), at para. 14–184.

[12] *Worcester Royal v. Locke* (1902) 19 R.P.C. 479. See also "*Yorkshire Relish*" (para. 14–138); and cf. also in *Hopton Wood v. Gething* (1910) 27 R.P.C. 605 at 623–624; held that "Hopton" or "Hopton Wood" in connection with stone did not connote stone from the claimants' quarries only or from a particular seam. In *Grand Hotel v. Wilson* [1904] A.C. 103; 21 R.P.C. 117, held that the defendants were entitled to indicate that their mineral waters came from springs at Caledonia; cf. *Rey v. Lecouturier* [1908] 2 Ch. 715; [1910] A.C. 262; 25 R.P.C. 275; 27 R.P.C. 268 at 278, HL ("Chartreuse"). In *Price's Patent Candle v. Ogston and Tennant* (1909) 26 R.P.C. 797 at 813, (para. 14–154, n. 69), the defendants were restrained from selling their candles as "London candles" without distinguishing. In *Brock v. Pain* (1911) 28 R.P.C. 697, the claimants established that "Crystal Palace" fireworks meant their fireworks, notwithstanding their contract to give displays at the Crystal Palace had ended.

[13] In *Barnsley Brewery v. RBNB* [1997] F.S.R. 462, Robert Walker J. referred to the "*Stone Ales*" case [1891] A.C. 217 in finding that the claimant did not have a strong case for asserting exclusive entitlement to the mark "Barnsley Bitter". He noted that the claimants in "*Stone Ales*" had been brewing in Stone for over 100 years and were the only significant brewery in the town: at 468.

meaning, it may be difficult to imagine how the defendant can be truthfully using the word with that meaning unless the context makes this clear. However, that rule is not easily reconciled with the decision in *"Office Cleaning"*[14]: a business (or trading) name rather than a trade mark case, but there is no line to be drawn between passing-off of goods and of a business.[15] Thus, in *Provident Financial v. Halifax Building Society*,[16] where the claimant was one of the leading motor insurance underwriters and had traded under the name "Halifax Insurance" for more than 25 years, an interlocutory injunction was granted to restrain the defendant from selling motor insurance under the name "Halifax".

6. Trading names[17]

Introductory

The name under which a business trades will almost always be a trade **14–190** mark[18] (or if the business provides services, a service mark, or both). Independently of questions of trade or service mark, however, the name of a business (a trading business or any other[19]) will normally have attached to it a goodwill that the courts will protect. An action for passing off will then lie wherever the defendant company's name, or its intended name, is calculated to deceive, and so to divert business from the claimant, or to occasion a confusion between the two businesses. If this is not made out there is no case.[20] The ground is not to be limited to the date of the proceedings; the court will have regard to the way in which the business may be carried on in the future, and to its not being carried on precisely as carried on at the date of the proceedings.[21] Where there is a probability of confusion in business, an injunction will be

---

[14] See *post*, para. 14–194.

[15] *Bulmer v. Bollinger* [1978] R.P.C. 79, CA.

[16] [1994] F.S.R. 81.

[17] In previous editions of this work, this section was entitled "Business Names", which because of the expansion of the subject-matter has become slightly misleading.

[18] It is very difficult to avoid using the name of a trading business as a trade mark: see *Reuter v. Muhlens* (1953) 70 R.P.C. 235 ("4711"; note the summary way in which the issue of infringement was disposed of); *Wright, Layman & Umney v. Wright* (1949) 66 R.P.C. 149.

[19] See *post*, paras 14–230 *et seq.*, as to actions for passing off by claimants who have no business in the ordinary sense; as to service trades, *cf. Harrod* and n. 20.

[20] See *Electromobile v. British Electromobile* (1908) 25 R.P.C. 149; *British Vacuum Cleaner v. New Vacuum Cleaner* [1907] 2 Ch. 312; 24 R.P.C. 641. It is essential that there should be tangible probability of injury to the property of the claimants; but under the word "property" may well be included the trade reputation of the claimants: *per* Sargant L.J. in *Harrods v. Harrod* (1924) 41 R.P.C. 74 at 86, commenting on *Walter v. Ashton* [1902] 2 Ch. 282. In *Harrod*, the claimants' business comprised a banking department, and the defendant company was registered with the object of carrying on a moneylender's business and it was held that its name was chosen fraudulently.

[21] *Ouvah Ceylon Estate v. Uva Ceylon Rubber Estates* (1910) 27 R.P.C. 753 at 756, CA; *cf. Scottish Union and National Insurance v. Scottish National Insurance* (1909); 26 R.P.C. 105 (defendant company did not intend to carry on any other business than marine insurance, whereas the claimants were a fire and life insurance company).

granted even though the defendants adopted the name innocently[22] and even though the claimant has decided no longer to use the name.[23]

Descriptive names

14–191 Where the claimant's name is descriptive of its business (or is geographically descriptive,[24]) the mere fact that the defendant adopts a name containing the same descriptive words will not establish any sort of case of passing off; a trader cannot monopolise a mere description.[25] The claimant must (as in any other passing-off case) establish that the use by the defendants of their trading style is calculated to lead to the belief that their business is the business of the claimant.[26] To do so, it must, in the ordinary way, establish its reputation: that is, that a substantial number of persons associate the words concerned with its business and its alone; as in any ordinary passing-off action. But the claimant need not establish that the words concerned have ceased to be descriptive or have acquired a secondary meaning[27] if it can prove its case without.[28] The special character of such cases lies in this: that where a business adopts a name containing words in common use, some risk of confusion may be inevitable, and that risk must be run unless the first such business is allowed an unfair monopoly in those words.[29] In such cases the court will accordingly accept comparatively small differences as

---

[22] See e.g. Ouvah Ceylon Estates v. Uva Ceylon Rubber Estates (1910) 27 R.P.C. 753, CA (innocence of defendants assumed, but injunction granted); the point is too well established for other instances to call for notice.

[23] In WMC v. Westgold (1998) 39 I.P.R. 319 (Fed Ct of Aust.) the evidence showed that the claimants were still well-known by the name "Western Mining" even though they had decided a year previously to cease use of it. The judge granted a permanent injunction. This can be contrasted with Elders IXL v. Australian Estates (1986–88) 10 I.P.R. 575 (Fed Ct of Aust.) in which an action for passing off failed because neither of the claimants had used the name "Australian Estates" since acquiring three years earlier the business previously well-known under that name.

[24] Bristol-Myers v. Bristol Pharmaceutical [1968] R.P.C. 259, see para. 14–181, and compare the "geographical" cases, Chap. 10.

[25] See Equity Access v. Westpac (1989) 16 I.P.R. 431, in which Hill J. noted: "Just as the distinction between descriptive and fancy names is not a distinction in law so too it is wrong to see the distinction in black and white terms. The reality is that there is a continuum with at the extremes purely descriptive names at the one end, completely invented names at the other and in between names that contain ordinary English words that are in some way or other at least partly descriptive. The further along the continuum towards the fancy name one goes, the easier it will be for a plaintiff to establish that the words used are descriptive of the plaintiff's business. The closer along the continuum one moves towards a merely descriptive name the more a plaintiff will need to show that the name has obtained a secondary meaning, equating it with the products of the plaintiff (if the name admits of this, a purely descriptive name probably will not) and the easier it will be to see a small difference in names as adequate to avoid confusion": at 448.

[26] Office Cleaning v. Westminster (1946) 63 R.P.C. 39 at 42, HL.

[27] Ibid. at 41.

[28] See comment by Roxburgh J. on the "Office Cleaning" case in General Radio v. General Radio (Westminster) [1957] R.P.C. 471 at 479–480.

[29] Such a monopoly "might even deter others from pursuing the occupation which the words described" per Stephen J. in Hornsby Building Information Centre v. Sydney Building Information Centre (1978) 140 C.L.R. 216.

sufficient to distinguish,[30] unless the facts nevertheless show serious passing-off.[31]

As stated by Templeman L.J. in *McCain International v. Country Fair* **14–192** [1981] R.P.C. 69: "if the plaintiffs introduce a novel product with novel words, but they take the risk of choosing descriptive words, then they run the risk that the defendants cannot be prevented from using those same descriptive words so long as they make it clear that their brands of the product are not the same as the brand of the plaintiffs" (at 81).[32]

There may, of course, be strong commercial reasons for choosing a **14–193** descriptive business name (just as, for short-lived products for example, there may be strong commercial reasons for choosing a descriptive trade mark); and those reasons are likely to be particularly cogent just in the sort of case where a very strong reputation is difficult to establish: so that an action for passing off will be unlikely to succeed in view of the descriptiveness of the name, whilst on the other hand competition from a concern of somewhat similar name can be particularly damaging. Thus the action may be least likely to succeed just where its success could be commercially most valuable. But such actions seldom go beyond the stage of an application for an interim injunction[33]; and here the current practice, under which a claimant need show only an arguable case,[34] means that relief will now be granted in many more instances than the old precedents might suggest.

(1) In the case of two companies doing business as office cleaners **14–194** in the same area, it was held that the difference between "Office Cleaning Services" and "Office Cleaning Association" was sufficient: notwithstanding that "Office Cleaning Association" was not the defendant's corporate title: *Office Cleaning v. Westminster*, above.

(2) See *"General Radio,"* illustration (3), *post*, paragraph 14–287.

(3) Where the claimant had had fruitless discussions with the **14–195** defendant for the "anglicisation" of its U.S. software product "BizPlan Builder" and the defendant later launched its own

---

[30] *Office Cleaning v. Westminster* (1946) 63 R.P.C. 39, HL. More recently, see *Morgan Banks v. Select Personnel* (1991) 20 I.P.R. 289 (CA (N.S.W.)): "Select Personnel" / "Select Appointments".

[31] *e.g. Legal and General v. Daniel* [1968] R.P.C. 253 (claimants known as "Legal and General", defendants using the business name "Legal & General Enquiry Bureau", but putting the emphasis on "Legal & General", interlocutory injunction granted, CA); *Effluent Disposal v. Midlands Effluent Disposal* [1970] R.P.C. 238 (addition of "Midlands" "no distinction at all" because both businesses carried on in the Midlands, interlocutory injunction granted); *Berkeley Hotel v. Berkeley International* [1971] F.S.R. 300 (addition of "International" to "Berkeley Hotel" no distinction. *cf.* the *"Hotel International"* case, *supra*).

[32] Referred to by Burchett J. in *Film Investment Corp. v. Golden Editions* (1994) 28 I.P.R. 1 at 19 (Fed Ct of Aust), rejecting a claim of passing off by the use of the words "animated classics".

[33] In refusing to grant an interlocutory injunction (but ordering a speedy trial) in *Stacey v. 20/20 Communications* [1991] F.S.R. 49, Millett J. noted that the scale of the claimant's business was small and the name at issue (20/20 Telecom) had been adopted by a number of companies in the communications industry: at 53.

[34] See *ante*, paras 18–89 *et seq.*

similar product under the name "BusinessPlan Builder", an interlocutory injunction was granted. The judge (Knox J.) referred, on the issue as to whether "BizPlan Builder" was purely descriptive, to the fact that the defendant had registered its version "BusinessPlan Builder" as a service mark: "they may have been wrong in their implicit assertion that the mark is capable of being distinctive, but it is difficult for them at this stage to contend that they were not arguably right", at 939. *Jian Tools for Sales v. Roderick Manhattan Group* [1995] F.S.R. 924.

14–196   (4) The name "Fantasyland" had been used for more than 35 years by the claimants, Walt Disney Productions, for theme parks, which had been advertised extensively. The court rejected a contention that the name was descriptive (although recognising that it is formed by combining two ordinary words) and granted an injunction restraining use by the defendant of the name on an amusement area described in advertising literature as "an indoor Disneyland": *Triple Five Corp. v. Walt Disney Productions* (1995) 29 I.P.R. 639 (CA of Alberta).

14–197   (5) The claimant had sold for many years a product called "Bar's Bugs", used for cleaning car windscreens. The defendant launched a similar product called "Bug Off". In granting an interlocutory injunction, the judge said, of the name: "When one takes an unusual word like "bug", even though it is a word commonly in use now in this country, and uses it to describe a product, if that word has been used by another party where the word would not normally be used, there is an obligation on the person coming into the market to ensure his product is not confused"; *Bars Products v. Holt Lloyd* (1991) 20 I.P.R. 87 at 92 (HC (N.Z.)).

14–198   (6) Further instances: "Music Corporation" was held not descriptive in the above sense: *Music Corp. of America v. Music Corp. (Great Britain)* (1947) 64 R.P.C. 48; so was "Computervision" for electronic equipment: *Computervision v. Computer Vision* [1975] R.P.C. 171. So was "Midland Dairies" for an ice-cream business: *Midland Counties v. Midland* (1948) 65 R.P.C. 429. "Cool Foods" was held too close to "Chill Foods," although one was whole-sale and the other retail: [1977] R.P.C. 522, (O.H., Sc.). But injunctions have been refused on *"Self Drive"* (*Drive Yourself v. Parish* [1957] R.P.C. 307); *"Credit Management"* ([1961] R.P.C. 157) and *"Tape Recorder Centre"* (*Sylpha v. Tape Recorders* [1961]) R.P.C. 27, one wholesale and the other retail); and injunctions were refused in *Salaried Persons Postal Loans v. Postal and Salaried Loans of Glasgow* ([1966] R.P.C. 24, Sc.) and in *Premier Motor Co. v. Premier Driving School* ([1962] R.P.C. 222). In *Technical Productions v. Contemporary Exhibitions* [1961] R.P.C. 242, the court refused an interlocutory injunction to restrain the defendants holding an exhibition with a title including "refrigeration" at about the same time as and at a near-by hall to the plaintiffs'.

An interlocutory injunction was refused in *Coral Index v. Regent Index* [1970] R.P.C. 147 because the only similarity between the parties' names was the word "Index" which was descriptive of their businesses of accepting wagers on the Financial Times Share Index; a final injunction was refused in *Industrial Furnaces v. Reaves* [1970] R.P.C. 605 at 625 (addition of "Reaves" to the descriptive words "Industrial Furnaces" a "sufficient difference to avert confusion"); an interlocutory injunction was refused in *Pet Library v. Ellson* [1968] F.S.R. 359 ("Ellson's Pet Library", a "plain case"); an interlocutory injunction was refused in *Park Court Hotel v. Trans-World* [1970] F.S.R. 89 ("Hotel International" and "London International Hotel"); an interlocutory injunction was refused in *Country Sound v. Ocean Sound* [1991] F.S.R. 367 ("The Gold A.M." too descriptive, not long enough use), referring to *McCain International v. Country Fair* [1981] R.P.C. 69 ("Oven Chips"). It is of course helpful to a defendant if there are differences in field of activity and if the customers are businesses likely to be clear who they are dealing with, as in *"Credit Management"*, above.

Taking an existing name as a whole

If a new company takes the whole name of a subsisting company, even **14–199** though that name is of a descriptive character, there is a high probability of deception.

(1) The Manchester Brewery Co. Ltd had a brewery and a large business at Manchester. A new company which had acquired a brewery at Macclesfield with a business extending to Manchester, as well as other towns attached to it, was restrained from trading as the "North Cheshire and Manchester Brewery Co. Ltd" on the ground that the use of the name would amount to a representation that the new company was an amalgamation comprising the business of the complainants: *Manchester Brewery v. North Cheshire*.[35]

(2) An injunction was refused against a defendant trading under a **14–200** name whose initials were the claimant's name: but it appears that the court would have intervened if the defendant had traded under its initials: *I.D.W. v. Duncan Harris* [1975] R.P.C. 178. *cf.* an older case, *A.G.S. v. Aeroplane General Sundries*, where the defendants in effect tried to persuade customers that the initials "A.G.S." meant them; held passing-off, notwithstanding that the initials "A.G.S." were in general use to describe the "sundries" in which both companies dealt: (1918) 35 R.P.C. 127, CA.

---

[35] [1899] A.C. 83.

But there is no rule of law that the use of a descriptive word in the name of a new company is deceptive and, therefore, unlawful if it forms part or even the whole of the name of a previously existing company engaged in a similar trade.[36]

Name suggesting a branch or agency

14–201 If the name of the defendant company is one which is calculated to lead to the belief that it is an agency, branch or department of the claimant company, an injunction will be granted,[37] unless, of course, what is suggested is true.[38] In *Harrods v. Harrodian School* [1996] R.P.C. 697, Millett L.J. considered that it was "the gist of the matter" whether people would think that the defendant was "either a branch of the plaintiff or a client in some way amalgamated with or under the supervision of the plaintiff and *for which the plaintiff had in some way made itself responsible"* (emphasis added by the judge).[39]

Name comprising claimant's trade mark

14–202 Injunctions have been granted, in a number of cases, to restrain a defendant from trading under a name resembling or including the claimant's trade mark, as distinct from the claimant's trading name. An injunction against use of the claimant's trade mark as a trade mark, and an injunction against use of it in a trading style, do not necessarily go together, for the types of confusion they are intended to prevent are different. If, however (as must often be the case), use of the claimant's mark in the defendant's trading style leads to its application by others to the defendant's goods, the claimant is entitled to an injunction against such use.[40] It would furthermore seem obvious that if the trade mark is a

---

[36] In *Aerators v. Tollit* (1902) 19 R.P.C. 418, a claim to stop "Automatic Aerator Patents Ltd" failed; *British Vacuum Cleaner v. New Vacuum* [1907] 2 Ch. 312; 24 R.P.C. 641; *Randall v. Bradley* (1907) 24 R.P.C. 657 at 773 ("Anglo-American Shoe Co."); *Electromobile v. British Electromobile* (1907) 24 R.P.C. 688; 25 R.P.C. 149.

[37] *Lloyd's v. Lloyd's (Southampton)* (1912) 29 R.P.C. 433. However it may not be possible to obtain an interlocutory injunction since there may not be an immediate danger of irreparable damage to the claimant, see *Marathon Oil v. Marathon Shipping* [1968] R.P.C. 443. See also paras 14–75 *et seq.*, as to the relevance of a common field of activity. Also, on domain names suggesting a similar connection, see the *"Yahoo!"* case, *post* at para. 14–206, illustration (4).

[38] As in *Habib Bank v. Habib Bank Zurich* [1982] R.P.C. 1: use by defendants of "Habib" was a representation only of some sort of connection with the claimants, and the defendants had in fact originally been set up by the claimants. But note that the claimants had not only set the defendants up in Zurich, but helped to establish them over here: a former associate, coming newly over here where only the claimant was known, could expect little encouragement from the courts. See also *Scandecor Development v. Scandecor Marketing* [1999] F.S.R. 26, CA.

[39] At 712–713, citing Farwell J. in *British Legion v. British Legion Club* (1931) 48 R.P.C. 555. For a similar analysis, see *Triple Five v. Walt Disney* (1995) 29 I.P.R. 639 (CA, Alberta).

[40] See examples below, but *cf.* "*Amami*," *Prichard and Constance v. Amata* (1925) 42 R.P.C. 63; where a business name injunction was refused. Note the part played in these cases by disputes as to the form of injunction.

really inherently distinctive one (as in the "*Kodak*" case, below) most customers will assume that any company with that mark in its name is either an offshoot of the owner of the mark or that owner having changed its name.

(1) The claimants, proprietors of "Wright's Coal Tar Soap", sold, **14–203** *inter alia*, baby powder under their mark "Wright's". The defendant, W.F.T. Wright, trading as "Wright's Chemical Company", also sold baby powder. At the trial, it was found that the defendant had passed his baby powder off as "Wright's" (and he was enjoined from marking his goods "Wright's"), but in spite of a finding that his use of the name "Wright's Chemical Company" had caused dealers in baby powder to call his goods "Wright's" the trial judge refused an injunction against trading under the name "Wright", since it was his own name. The Court of Appeal considered this illogical, and enjoined him from trading under a name of which "Wright" or "Wright's" formed part without clearly distinguishing his business from that of the claimants: *Wright, Layman & Umney v. Wright* (1949) 66 R.P.C. 149.

(2) The claimant owned a trade mark, "Kodak", well known for **14–204** cameras and films. The court enjoined the "Kodak Cycle Co. Ltd.", and another company which had promoted it, from carrying on business under any name comprising the word "Kodak". There was some suggestion that the trades in cameras and in bicycles went together: *Eastman v. Griffiths* (1898) 15 R.P.C. 105.

(3) The claimants had a trade mark of which the essential feature **14–205** was the word "June". The defendants, June Perfect Limited, trading in the same sorts of goods, marked their goods "June". The defendants sold only to Woolworths (who did not confuse them with the claimants) and retail purchasers were not necessarily aware of the defendants' trading style. The House of Lords, whilst dismissing appeals against injunctions granted by the Court of Appeal to restrain infringement and passing off by the use of the word "June", varied the order by omitting a third injunction which had been granted restraining the defendants from carrying on business (in the goods concerned) under any name comprising the word "June" and calculated to deceive the public into the belief that they were the same company as, or connected with, the claimants. The reason for refusing this injunction was that, in the view of the House of Lords, the first defendants could by taking proper precautions sell and deal with the three articles concerned in connection with their name June Perfect Ltd, while clearly distinguishing those goods from the goods of the claimants: *Saville Perfumery v. June Perfect* (1941) 58 R.P.C. 147, HL, speech of Lord Maugham at 176.

14–206   (4) The claimant owned many trade mark registrations around the world for the mark "Yahoo!" and had made an application for registration of it in India. The defendant used the trading name "Netline Internet Solutions" but registered the domain name *yahooindia. com*. In finding that Internet users would likely be deceived into believing a common source or a connection and that domain names performed the same function as trade marks, the court granted an interlocutory injunction: *Yahoo! Inc v. Akash Arora* [1999] F.S.R. 931 (HC, Delhi).

Name need not be the claimant's "real" name

14–207 The name sued upon need not be the personal or corporate name of the claimant.[41] It need not even be that of a predecessor in business, for a business may lawfully adopt and operate under any name which is unappropriated for businesses of the same kind, and when the name has become its by repute, it is as well entitled to protection for that name as for its own.[42]

(1) Where the claimants made and sold a sauce which they called by the name of one of their servants, "Holbrook's Worcester Sauce", and the servant left them and joined the defendants, who advertised that they had acquired the right to make "Holbrook's Worcester Sauce", it was shown that the sauce sold by the claimants was well known as theirs by the name. It was held that they had a right to the name in question, and that Holbrook could not sell it to the defendants, and an interlocutory injunction was granted: *Birmingham Vinegar Brewery v. Liverpool Vinegar* [1888] W.N. 139. In that case the sauce was identified by the name with the claimants, and not with Holbrook; an opposite result would have been reached if the name had been understood to indicate that the latter person was the actual maker of the goods, and that they were his goods of which the claimants happened to be vendors: see next illustration.

14–208   (2) The claimant had organised a series of concerts, conducted by one Herr Richter and known as "Richter Concerts", for many years, when Herr Richter made arrangements to conduct the

---

[41] An assumed name may be part of the goodwill of a business, and the right to use it sold as part of the goodwill, as in *Pomeroy v. Scale* (1907) 24 R.P.C. 177 and cases cited below.
[42] *Isaacson v. Thompson* (1871) 41 L.J.Ch. 101 ("Mme Elise"). The names may be the colloquial name of the claimants: *Heels v. Stafford Heels* (1927) 44 R.P.C. 299, the claimants being known as Heels of Stafford; *Dickinson v. Apsley Press* (1937) 54 R.P.C. 219, the claimants carrying on business at Apsley Mills and being known as "Apsley". In *British Diabetic Assoc. v. Diabetic Society* [1996] F.S.R. 1, Robert Walker J., in referring to the "*Heels*" case, noted "the fact that members of the public make mistakes about a person's name—even that such mistakes are, in absolute terms, numerous—cannot by itself lead to the conclusion that every mistaken variant of a business name is entitled to the same protection as the correct name": at 14–15.

rival concerts of the defendants. It was held that the defendants might rightly advertise their series under the name, since it was understood to mean, not concerts got up by the claimant, but anybody's concerts conducted by Richter: *Franke v. Chappell* (1887) 57 L.T. (N.S.) 141.

Assignment of trading name to or by a limited company

A limited company, by the purchase of a business, often becomes **14–209** entitled to a name which is different from its registered name, and so becomes entitled, if it does not abandon the name, to prevent others so using it as to represent that they are carrying on the business formerly carried on under it: moreover, the company could sell the name with the goodwill.[43] If a limited company sells its goodwill, a third person will not be permitted after the dissolution of that company to adopt its name, so as to lead to the belief that his business is that formerly carried on by the company and so to injure the purchaser.[44]

Licensing of trade name: "franchising"

An Australian company, J.H. Coles Pty. Ltd, authorised a shopkeeper to **14–210** call his shop "J.H. Coles 3d., 6d. and 1s. Stores", the arrangement being that the goods sold in the shop would come from the J.H. Coles company. (There seems to have been a chain of such shops.) The Privy Council (deciding in favour of the company a dispute as to the shopkeeper's right to go on using the name after the authority was determined) appears to have considered this a proper way of working, so long as a connection in the course of trade was maintained between the J.H. Coles company and the goods sold in the shop: *Coles v. Need* (1933) 50 R.P.C. 379. This sort of "franchising" operation has of course since become common; it would probably now be held that not only the franchisor but also any franchisee substantially affected could sue to protect the right to the name. In a different context (a restrictive covenant case), Neuberger J. noted of a franchise relationship: "the franchisor . . . and the franchisee . . . each have a business. They are symbiotic businesses, and the goodwill provision . . . indicates that the franchisee . . . has the benefit of the goodwill as long as he is franchisee": *Dyna-Rod v. Reeve* [1999] F.S.R. 148 at 153.

A new company may continue an established name

A limited company formed to take over a business may adopt and use a **14–211** name embodying a name under which the business has already been lawfully and properly carried on.[45]

---

[43] *Macmillan v. Ehrmann* (1904) 21 R.P.C. 357, 647; *Pearks, Gunston v. Thompson, Talmey* (1901) 18 R.P.C. 185.

[44] *Montreal Lithographing v. Sabiston* [1899] A.C. 610 (JC); *Townsend v. Jarman* (1900) 17 R.P.C. 649.

[45] So that cases where the defendant has done this are treated by the court as "ordinary use of own name" cases, as in *Chivers v. Chivers* (1900) 17 R.P.C. 420, Farwell J. at 426. This was fully recognised in *Tussaud v. Tussaud* (1890) 44 Ch.D. 678, where, however, the condition did not obtain.

However, the purchase of the goodwill of a business (together with the right for the acquirer to represent itself as continuing the former business) does not imply a right to use the trading name formerly used in that business.

14–212   In *Dawnay, Day v. Cantor Fitzgerald* [2000] R.P.C. 669, CA, the court-appointed administrator of a deadlocked company (50 per cent owned by the claimant) had sold to the defendant the assets of the business carried on under the name "Dawnay, Day Securities" ("DDS"). The sale agreement also gave the defendant the right to use the name DDS "so far as it is lawfully able to do so". The Court of Appeal upheld the judgment of Lloyd J. finding passing off. Although the joint venture agreement setting up DDS was silent as to the name under which the new company would trade, one of its provisions permitted the parties "to make it known that the Company is part of the Dawnay, Day Group". The Vice-Chancellor, Sir Richard Scott, found that it was implicit that such use would stop when it was no longer true and, referring to *Coles v. Need*,[46] that the defendant could not show that the use of the name by the joint venture had had "the effect that the style has ceased to be distinctive of the licensor", *i.e.* the claimant. The case highlights the importance of regulating expressly by contract the use of trading names by third parties, including joint venture companies.

Right to use a name not attached to any goodwill cannot be sold

14–213   A vendor who has no business goodwill to sell cannot convey any right to the use of a business or trading name: and in particular, a man cannot give to another the right that he himself may have[47] to trade under his own name.

The claimants, Kingston, Miller & Co. Ltd, were caterers. Thomas Kingston, one of their managers and well known to customers, left them to become managing director of a new catering company, Thomas Kingston & Co. Ltd. It was contended that he had something in the nature of goodwill attached to his name of which he could give the benefit to the defendant company, namely, qualifications such as personal skill and experience in the business. But it was held that he had nothing in the nature of goodwill to transfer, and that, although he could make use of his personal qualifications, the name was not incident to that qualification in the sense that it could be transferred to a third person and give to that third person the right to use it regardless of the fact that it might mislead the public: *Kingston, Miller v. Kingston* [1912] 1 Ch. 575; 29 R.P.C. 289.[48]

14–214   Where a person bearing the surname in dispute is associated with the business in the capacity of designer, or something of that sort, it may be

---

[46] *Op. cit.*
[47] See *post*, paras 14–280 *et seq.*
[48] *Fine Cotton Spinners v. Harwood Cash* [1907] 2 Ch. 184 at 190; 24 R.P.C. 533 at 538.

proper to say so; but only the purchase of an existing goodwill, associated with a particular trading style, can give any special right to the use of that style.[49] An existing goodwill in a rather different trade may suffice to prevent passing off; but an attempt to justify adoption of a questionable name by purchase of a goodwill associated with different goods may well be viewed with suspicion by the court.[50]

Henry Meadows Ltd, manufacturers of internal combustion engines, **14–215** called an engine designed by one Dorman a "Meadows-Dorman" engine. In an action for passing off brought by W.H. Dorman & Co., Meadows contended that they were entitled to use the name "Dorman" to indicate the designer. A qualified injunction only was granted as to use of the name "Dorman", but an absolute injunction restraining use of the term "Meadows-Dorman" for the engines: *Dorman v. Meadows* [1922] 2 Ch. 332; *cf.*, as to the goodwill in the name of a designer, *Bentley v. Lagonda* (1947) 64 R.P.C. 33 at 38–40; and *Birmingham Vinegar Brewery v. Liverpool Vinegar Co.* [1888] W.N. 139; illustration (1), *ante*, paragraph 14–207.

Name of business house or factory

The name of a shop[51] or factory[52] may in effect be a trading name or **14–216** trade mark, to which goodwill attaches, and entitled accordingly to protection against use of similar names so as to pass off. Furthermore, the use of a similar address may be an ingredient in passing-off, particularly where businesses have similar names.[53] There is no right to

---

[49] *cf.* the previous paragraph and *Tussaud v. Tussaud* (1890) 44 Ch.D. 678.

[50] *Holloway v. Clent* (1903) 20 R.P.C. 525; *Rodgers v. Hearnshaw* (1906) 23 R.P.C. 349.

[51] *Boussod, Valadon v. Marchant* (1907) 24 R.P.C. 665; 25 R.P.C. 42 ("Goupil Gallery"); *Bodega v. Owens* (1890) 7 R.P.C. 31; 23 L.R.Ir. 371 ("Bodega Wine Shop"). In *Clock v. Clock House* (1936) 53 R.P.C. 269, an injunction was granted restraining the defendants from carrying on business under certain names of which Clock formed part, but limited to particular premises about five miles distant from the claimants' premises, as well as an injunction in more general terms. See also *Maderia House v. Madeira House (London)* (1930) 47 R.P.C. 481 (interlocutory injunction granted). In *J. Lyons v. G. & K. Restaurants* (1955) 72 R.P.C. 259 (rival restaurants both styled "Egg and Bacon") the court indicated that even had the defendants not offered undertakings they would not have been ordered to change the words on facia of shop. The defendants in fact undertook to change to "Eggs and Bacon". In *Cooper and M'Leod v. Maclachlan* (1902) 18 R.P.C. 380, 19 R.P.C. 27, the defendant was held entitled to use "Castle Brewery", which the claimants also used, there being no probability of deception. As to assignment of marks having a local connotation, see Chap. 12.

[52] *Braham v. Beachim* (1878) 7 Ch.D. 848, Fry J. ("Radstock Colliery"); *Montgomery v. Thompson* [1891] A.C. 217; 8 R.P.C. 361 ("Stone Brewery"). In *Dickinson v. Apsley Press* (1937) 54 R.P.C. 219, the successful claimants carried on business as papermakers and printers at Apsley Mills and were known to their customers as "Apsley".

[53] *Pullman v. Pullman* (1919) 36 R.P.C. 240. *cf. Nicholson v. Buchanan* (1900) 19 R.P.C. 321 ("Black Swan Distillery"), where the business names and businesses were distinct and relief was refused. In *General Equity v. General Corp.* (1995) 32 I.P.R. 481 (Fed Ct of Aust.) the fact that the defendant was trading from next door to premises widely known as the claimant's was viewed unfavourably when coupled with the defendant's adoption of the name "Central" and a similar logo to that of the claimant; notwithstanding these misrepresentations the claim of passing off was dismissed as in two and one-half years there was no evidence of confusion.

the exclusive use of the name of a mere private house,[54] and no cause of action arises where, although the defendant has adopted, for business purposes, an address likely to be confused with that of the claimant,[55] yet the businesses of the parties are so different that only inconvenience can result and no damage to the claimant's goodwill.[56]. Thus, in *Harrods v. Harrodian School*[57] Millett L.J. considered that "[c]ustomers of the plaintiff . . . would . . . be incredulous if they were told that Harrods had opened a preparatory school".

14–217   Cases in which a business has been moved from the shop or factory whose name is associated with it, and the new owner of the building wants to continue to use the old name, may present a little difficulty. On the one hand, it would seem clear that the new owner is not entitled to use the old name as a means of passing off his business as that of the original owner.[58] On the other hand, the disputed name may be known as that of the building rather than of the business carried on there[59]; and furthermore there would seem to be a presumption that the sale of premises, known by a name, carries with it (in the absence of covenants to the contrary) the right to keep that name for them.[60] The issue of covenants should always be borne in mind by the vendors of property bearing a particular name: it would presumably have been open to the vendor of "the Harrodian Club site" to have secured a covenant not to use the name "Harrodian" or anything confusingly similar in connection with a business carried on from the site.

Author's or artist's name or *nom-de-plume*

14–218   An author can restrain the publication under his name of books which are not written by him, on the same principles as a trader can obtain an injunction to protect his trade name or that of his goods[61]:

[54] *Day v. Brownrigg* (1878) 10 Ch.D. 294.

[55] *Cf. Law Society of England & Wales v. Griffiths, op. cit.,* in which a very similar telephone number was the reason for the successful application for an interlocutory injunction.

[56] *Street v. Union Bank* (1885) 30 Ch.D. 156; the claimants were advertising agents; the defendant bank adopted (and registered with the GPO) a cable address that the claimants had used for many years. Confusion occurred but an injunction was refused. A claim by the owners of the Royal Albert Hall to restrain Albert Edward Hall from calling his orchestra "Albert Hall Orchestra" was refused as not being liable to cause confusion; the claimants let the hall for entertainments but did not employ any orchestra: *Corporation of Hall of Arts and Sciences v. Hall,* 51 R.P.C. 398.

[57] *Op. cit.,* at 717.

[58] *Rickerby v. Reay* (1903) 20 R.P.C. 380 (owner entitled to keep name, but advised by court not to use it, as making distinction from former occupier's business harder); *Berkeley v. Berkeley International* [1971] F.S.R. 300 (hotel on old site of claimant's: interlocutory injunction granted). The latter case was referred to in *Pontiac v. CDL Hotels* [1998] F.S.R. 839 at 869–870 in which the court granted an injunction restraining the defendant from using the name "Millennium" for hotel services because of the strong likelihood of a deception that they were associated with the claimant's Millenia property complex, which included the "Ritz Carlton, Millenia Singapore" hotel.

[59] As in *Rickerby v. Reay, supra; Nicholson v. Buchanan, supra. Mason v. Queen* (1886) 23 S.L.R. 641 would seem, if not decided on wrong principles, to be to the same effect—not all the old cases show a full recognition of the law of passing off.

[60] *"Goupil Gallery," supra,* at (1908) 25 R.P.C. 53, CA, *per* Fletcher Moulton, L.J.

[61] *Lord Byron v. Johnson* (1816) 2 Mer. 29; *cf. Barnard v. Pillow* [1868] W.N. 94 (music) and *Martin v. Wright* (1833) 6 Sim. 297 (copy of work of diorama painter).

In *Clark v. Associated Newspapers* [1998] R.P.C. 261 the defendant newspaper *The Evening Standard* published a spoof diary under the title "Alan Clark's Secret Political Diary". The claimant, a well-known politician and diarist, successfully sued for passing off and false attribution (see below). The judge (Lightman J.) found that the layout of the diary in the newspaper "succeeded too well in making the articles look real" and the "contrary representations" (for example the use of the word "Secret" in the title and the content-in part "obvious fantasy, incredible and wild exaggeration") did not sufficiently correct the deception of a substantial number of readers. The judge emphasised that despite his findings the judgment should be no bar to parodies.

A cartoonist may sue upon the use by a rival cartoonist of a **14–219** confusingly similar signature,[62] or an actor to protect his stage name.[63] A *nom-de-plume* prima facie belongs to the author and is considered to be his stock-in trade.[64] Disputes as to the ownership of a *nom-de-plume*, however, normally arise as between author and publisher; and such disputes have in practice been treated as pure questions of contractual right as between the parties, without regard to the considerations peculiar to disputes over a trade mark.[65] Further, it has been held that the writer of a work can maintain an action against the owner of the copyright for the damage occasioned to his reputation by the publication of a new edition of the book, purporting to be prepared by him, but in fact not so prepared.[66]

The author's right to prevent the work of another being passed off as **14–220** his is quite distinct from the moral right which he may have in his own work; a right contained in section 84 of the Copyright, Designs and Patents Act 1988, under which an author has the right not to have any "literary, dramatic, musical or artistic work" falsely attributed to him.[67] But in the case of a serial publication, the right to use the name of the original author or editor may be part of the goodwill of the business of

---

[62] *Marengo v. Daily Sketch* (1948) 65 R.P.C. 242 ("Kem" and "Kim"), HL.

[63] *Hines v. Winnick* [1947] Ch. 708; 64 R.P.C. 113 ("Dr. Crock and his Crackpots"). Although pleaded as a case of passing off one musical sketch for another, the case was decided as one in which to the public the claimant himself was "Dr. Crock".

[64] *Landa v. Greenberg* (1908) 24 T.L.R. 441 ("Aunt Naomi"); referred to in *Modern Fiction v. Fawsett* (1949) 66 R.P.C. 230 at 248 ("Ben Sarto"); *Forbes v. Kemsley Newspapers* (1951) 68 R.P.C. 183 ("Mary Delane").

[65] There is always a tendency for disputes as to the ownership of a mark or of goodwill to be decided purely in terms of rights *inter partes*: see, *e.g. Manus v. Fullwood & Bland* (1949) 66 R.P.C. 71, CA (dispute between manufacturer and agent); "*Oranje*" *v. Kuys* [1973] 1 W.L.R. 1126 (PC, N.Z.: Ownership of newspaper title). But the decisions on *noms-de-plume* seem to show no recognition that the subject of the dispute is of the nature of a trade mark at all.

[66] *Archbold v. Sweet* (1832) 1 M. & R. 162; 5 C. & P. 219. In *Lee v. Gibbings* (1892) 66 L.T. 263, the question was one of libel; interim injunction refused.

[67] See *Clark v. Associated Newspapers* [1998] R.P.C. 261 and, on the predecessor s.43 of the Copyright Act 1956, *Moore v. News of the World* [1972] 1 Q.B. 441.

conducting it, so as to pass on a sale of the goodwill[68]: the original author's name, indeed, becomes a trade mark[69] in the same way as the name of the author of a text-book running into several editions becomes a trade mark.[70]

Upon the principle already stated,[71] the right here under consideration will not enable an author to stop the republication under his name of his own, non-copyright work.[72]

14–221 Where the defendants had acquired the English copyright in an old song which the composer, who had a great reputation and a large sale, considered to be without merit, it was held that the composer's rights against the defendants were qualified and restricted by the defendants' right to state that the song was by the composer. The claimant asked for an injunction to restrain the defendants from representing that the song was a new song of the composer, but it was held that the claimant had not alleged and proved what must be proved in an action for passing-off goods of one class or quality for the claimants' goods of another class or quality, namely, the existence of the two classes of goods: *Harris v. Warren & Phillips* (1918) 35 R.P.C. 217.

Title of newspaper, other periodical, book, film

14–222 Titles of books, newspapers or other publications also are in principle protected in the same way as business names: no cause of action arises, therefore, unless it is shown that the title is known to indicate the claimant's book or paper, so that its use by the defendant would be calculated to lead to deception; and that the circumstances are such as to permit of such deception.[73] There is usually no copyright in such titles.[74]

14–223 The cases show, however, that it is rarely possible these days to persuade a court that the use of similar or even closely similar names for rival newspapers or periodical publications will result in passing off; of course, most periodical titles in particular are largely descriptive; even in

---

[68] *Ward v. Beeton* (1874) L.R. 19 Eq. 207 ("Beeton's Christmas Annual"). Presumably, on such a sale, the court would imply the necessary licence for the use of an author's name, to exclude s.84 of the Copyright, Designs and Patents Act 1988. It appears from the cases on this point to have been customary to refer to the goodwill in the business of conducting a serial publication as the "copyright" in the publication.

[69] *cf. Condy v. Mitchell* (1877) 37 L.T.(N.S.) 766 ("Condy's Fluid").

[70] "Kerly" is clearly a trade mark.

[71] See *ante*, para. 14–218.

[72] *Clemens v. Belford* (1883) 14 Fed.Rep. 728, U.S. ("Mark Twain").

[73] *Mathieson v. Pitman* (1930) 47 R.P.C. 541 (How to Appeal against Your Rates was held not to have acquired a secondary or special meaning).

[74] *ibid.*, at 549.

comparison with the cases on descriptive trading names generally,[75] it is rare for actions on titles of publications to achieve any success.

(1) An interlocutory injunction was granted to the proprietors of a periodical publication for children called Eagle against the use of the word "Eagle" in the name of a children's holiday camp: *Hulton v. White Eagle* (1951) 68 R.P.C. 126.

(2) The proprietors of two weekly newspapers, the London Weekly **14–224** Advertiser and the National Advertiser, sued to restrain the use by a similar periodical of the title National Weekly. No order was made on the motion on the defendants giving an undertaking in the *"Teofani"* or *"Corona"*[76] form: *Brittain v. Trade & Commercial Press* [1957] R.P.C. 134.

(3) The proprietors of a London daily newspaper, The Morning Post, sought to restrain the publishers of a new evening newspaper from calling their paper The Evening Post. The Court of Appeal, holding, as an inference of fact, that there was no probability of the defendants' paper being taken for the claimants', or being taken to have any connection with it so as to cause damage to the claimants, dismissed the action: *Borthwick v. Evening Post* (1888) 37 Ch.D. 449, CA.

(4) The owners of the Evening Times published in Glasgow were **14–225** held not entitled to restrain the publication of a paper of the same name published in London, there being no competition and no resemblance between the papers: *Outram v. London Evening Newspapers* (1911) 28 R.P.C. 308. Similarly the American proprietors of a shilling monthly magazine called Everybody's Magazine failed to obtain an injunction against the proprietors of a penny weekly paper known as Everybody's Weekly, there being no competition and no resemblance except in the word "Everybody's": *Ridgeway v. Amalgamated Press* (1912) 29 R.P.C. 130.

(5) In an action to restrain use of the periodical name "Today", by **14–226** claimants who had published a periodical under that name in the past, but nine years ago had "incorporated" it in another periodical, retaining a mere mention of "Today" on the inside frontispiece, it was held that the claimants no longer had a sufficient reputation to maintain the action: the right to the name of a periodical is not like a trade mark, which, once registered, remains effective until abandoned: *Kark v. Odhams* [1962] R.P.C. 163.

(6) Other instances: Amongst older cases, injunctions were granted **14–227** in "Morning Mail" (*Walter v. Emmott, supra*); "The Grocer" (*Reed v. O'Meara* (1904) 21 L.R.Ir. 216); and on the ground of

---

[75] See *ante*, para. 14–171.
[76] See *Teofani v. Teofani* (1913) 30 R.P.C. 446; *Havana Cigar v. Oddenino* (1924) 41 R.P.C. 47.

gross fraud in "Bradshaw" (*Blacklock v. Bradshaw's* (1926) 43 R.P.C. 27); refused in "Magazine of Fiction" (*Stevens v. Cassell* (1913) 30 R.P.C. 199), "How to Appeal Against Your Rates" (*Mathieson v. Pitman*) (1930) 47 R.P.C. 541); and to "Adventure" against "Hutchinson's Adventure Story Magazine" (*Ridgeway v. Hutchinson* (1923) 40 R.P.C. 335). Amongst newer cases, injunctions were refused to "Rubber & Plastic Age" against "Rubber & Plastics Weekly" (*Rubber & Press v. Maclaren* [1961] R.P.C. 264); to "Maidenhead Advertiser" (known locally as "The Advertiser") against "New Advertiser" (distributed free; *Bayliss v. Darlenko* [1974] F.S.R. 284); to "Morning Star" against "The Star" (no arguable case: *Morning Star v. Express* [1979] F.S.R. 113); to "Athletics Weekly" against "Athletics Monthly" (with a different get-up: *World Athletics v. Webb* [1981] F.S.R. 27, CA); to "Sunday Post" (with small Kent circulation) against "South East Sunday Post" (*Thompson v. Kent Messenger* [1975] R.P.C. 191); to a periodical "Newsweek" against a BBC feature of the same name (in spite of possibility of ambiguous quotations, etc.: *Newsweek v. B.B.C.* [1979] R.P.C. 441, CA). See further *Allen v. Brown Watson* [1965] R.P.C. 191, illustration 4, paragraph 14–120.

14–228   (7) For other cases where an injunction was refused, see: *Advance Magazine Published v. Redwood Publishing* [1993] F.S.R. 449. There was no arguable case that a magazine entitled *BBC Gourmet Good Food* would be confused with the title *Gourmet*. *County Sound v. Ocean Sound* [1991] F.S.R. 367, *ante*, paragraph 14–118, a case involving the name of a radio programme ("The Gold A.M."). *Management Publications v. Blenheim Exhibitions Group* [1991] F.S.R. 348 and 550, CA: the claimants argued that the public would think that the two publications *Management Today* and *Security Management Today* were connected. Held, arguable case in passing off; injunction refused on the balance of convenience. *Marcus Publishing v. Hutton-Wild* [1990] R.P.C. 576, CA, *ante*, paragraph 14–23. *Tamworth Herald v. Thomson Free Newspapers* [1991] F.S.R. 337: the claimant published the *Tamworth Herald* and a free sheet, the *Tamworth Herald Extra*. The defendants proposed to rename *Tamworth Trader* the *Tamworth Herald and Post*. The mastheads looked different and would make it clear that the paper had been renamed. Held, no arguable case.

14–229   For a case where an injunction was granted, see *Morgan Grampian v. Training Personnel* [1992] F.S.R. 267. The claimants published a series of titles including the expression "What's New In . . .". The defendants had used the title "Training Personnel", but changed it to "What's New In Training". An injunction was granted on the balance of convenience.

Plays, films, etc.

An author of a play or musical sketch has similarly the right to prevent **14–230** another person from passing off as a film version of the play or sketch something which is not such a version.[77]

(1) The authors and owners of the copyright in a play called "Sealed Orders" sought to restrain the defendants from using and advertising a film under that name. The action was settled by the defendants agreeing to change the name of their film play to "Orders under Seal", and paying the costs: *Raleigh v. Kinematograph Trading* (1914) 31 R.P.C. 143.

(2) An Australian court granted relief to the owners of a television series against a series with similar title, characters and leading actor: *Hexagon v. A.B.C.* [1976] R.P.C. 628.

Voice of actor

An application for an interlocutory injunction to restrain the broadcast **14–231** of an alleged imitation of the claimant's voice in advertisements on commercial television on the grounds of libel, malicious falsehood and passing off was refused in view of the established practice not to grant interlocutory relief on the ground of libel and that if a claim for passing off was maintainable it would involve the same issues as in libel: *Alastair Sim v. Heinz* [1959] R.P.C. 75.

Company names

Most recent authorities on trading names concern the names of limited **14–232** companies rather than of individuals or of partnerships. The relief claimed in such cases may well include an injunction that will require the defendant to take steps to change its name.[78]

Where an injunction is granted against a limited company carrying on **14–233** business under its registered name, the injunction is usually suspended for a short time to allow the company to change its name.[79]

---

[77] *Samuelson v. Producers* (1931) 48 R.P.C. 447 and 580 (theatrical sketch The New Car and cinematograph film His First Car). *Hines v. Winnick* (1947) 64 R.P.C. 113 ("Dr. Crock and his Crackpots"), sometimes considered as a "stage name" case, was pleaded as passing-off one "musical sketch" for another. In an earlier case, *Houghton v. Film Booking* (1931) 48 R.P.C. 329, the evidence did not establish that the title "The Younger Generation" used in connection with a film meant in the mind of the film-going public a film based on the play of that name by the claimant. In *Loews v. Littler* (1955) 72 R.P.C. 166, held that claimants had not established that the title "Merry Widow" denoted the musical version they owned. See also the form of undertaking agreed in *20th Century-Fox v. Gala Film* [1957] R.P.C. 105, in respect of use as title for films of "Anastasia".

[78] See under "Relief," *post*, para. 18–86, and, *e.g. Manchester Brewery v. North Cheshire* [1899] A.C. 83. See *Hendriks v. Montagu* (1881) 17 Ch.D. 638 for one form of injunction. Non-profit making companies stand in the same position as trading companies in this respect: *Lagos Chamber of Commerce v. Registrar of Companies* (1955) 72 R.P.C. 263, PC.

[79] See, for instance, *Lloyd's v. Lloyd's (Southampton)* (1912) 29 R.P.C. 433; *Midland Counties Dairy v. Midland Dairies* (1948) 65 R.P.C. 429; *Letters v. Letters (Craigton)* [1967] R.P.C. 209 (Scots).

14–234 Where individuals or companies have tried to make a business out of setting up numbers of limited companies with well-known names, which they then try to sell to the owners of those well-known names, the courts have in recent years been robust in their treatment of such behaviour. In *Direct Line Group v. Direct Line Estate Agency Ltd* [1997] F.S.R. 374, Laddie J., granted an interlocutory injunction in a passing-off case brought against three companies with "Direct Line" in their name, noting that the two individual defendants had been behind the registration of a large number of other famous company name registrations. Indicative of the displeasure with which the court viewed such activities, a lump sum order for costs was made with payment to be made within 14 days. Similarly, in *Glaxo v. Glaxowellcome* [1996] F.S.R. 388, Lightman J. granted a mandatory injunction requiring the defendant company and the defendant subscribers to take all steps as lay within their power to change the name of the company. The judge found the defendants to be engaged in a dishonest scheme to appropriate the goodwill of the claimants.

14–235 In *Ben & Jerry's Homemade v. Ben & Jerry's Ice Cream Limited*, unreported judgment of Ferris J., January 19, 1995, an interlocutory injunction was refused as there was no evidence that the defendant had traded and assertions that it had no intention of doing so. This must be wrong as otherwise why incorporate a company under such a distinctive name. Thus, in *Fletcher Challenge v. Fletcher Challenge Pty Ltd* [1982] F.S.R. 1 (S.C., N.S.W.), an injunction was granted in almost identical circumstances to those in *Ben & Jerry's*. The *Fletcher Challenge* case was referred to with approval by Aldous L.J. in the domain name case, *BT v. One in a Million* [1999] F.S.R. 1.[80] In that judgment, Aldous L.J. reviewed the history of passing off cases in which the defendant had equipped himself with means of identification similar to the claimant. He concluded that "there can be discerned from the cases a jurisdiction to grant injunctive relief where a defendant is equipped with or is intending to equip another with an instrument of fraud. . . A name which will, by reason of its similarity to the name of another, inherently lead to passing off is such an instrument": at 18.

Injunction against signatories of memorandum of association

14–236 In *Panhard et Lavassor v. Panhard-Levassor*[81] the injunction was granted against the defendant company and also against the seven signatories of the memorandum of association forbidding them to use the names Panhard and Levassor, and also forbidding the signatories to allow the

---

[80] On domain names generally, see Chap. 21.
[81] [1901] 2 Ch. 513; 18 R.P.C. 405, followed in *Suhner A.G. v. Suhner Ltd.* [1967] R.P.C. 336, in which the *Allen* case (below) was not cited.

company to remain registered under its then present name. But when in *Allen v. Original Samuel Allen* (1915) 32 R.P.C. 33 the claimant sued two solicitors' clerks who had signed the defendant company's memorandum of association, the claim against them was simply rejected as "founded on some misapprehension of the effects of the *'Panhard'* case."

7. Imitation of get-up

It is usually true in some degree that a trader's goods are recognised as **14–237** his by their general appearance, or "get-up". Accordingly, resemblance of get-up is not uncommonly an ingredient in passing off, and it is possible for imitation of get-up alone to amount to passing off. Such cases are rare, since few traders rely on get-up alone to distinguish their goods, so that trade names and word trade marks are ordinarily present too, and in these days, in this country,[82] a difference in names is enough to warn the public that they are getting one trader's goods and not the other's.[83] Accordingly, there can hardly be passing off by get-up alone (in the usual sense of substitution of one make of a product for another) unless the resemblance between the goods is extremely close, so close that it can hardly occur except by deliberate imitation; and even that may not be enough.[84] But there are forms of passing off in which a difference of name is not important: for example, where the goods themselves are distinct enough from the claimant's for a different product name to be expected.[85]

The relative importance to be attributed to names and word marks on the one hand, and to get-up on the other, is a matter upon which different people have different views; with the result that the outcome of disputes about get-up is exceptionally hard to predict.[86]

---

[82] *cf. White, Hudson v. Asian* [1965] R.P.C. 45 (PC, Singapore): Asian customers may be unable to read rival names in roman letters. However, nowadays illiteracy is "an evaporating consideration" in get-up cases: *per* CA Sing. in *Tong Guan Food Products v. Hoe Huat Hng Foodstuffs* [1991] 2 M.L.J. 361 at 367.

[83] *Saper v. Specters* (1953) 70 R.P.C. 173 at 178; and see below.

[84] Compare *Saper v. Specters, supra,* with *Tavener Rutledge v. Specters* [1959] R.P.C. 83 at 84; 355 (CA); note the indication in both cases of deliberate copying of the claimant's get-up, and note that even in the later case an interlocutory injunction was refused: [1957] R.P.C. 498 at 501–502.

[85] And *cf.* the *"Carvino"* case, where the defendant altered the name (only) and printed "new name" on the label: (1912) 29 R.P.C. 81: or so the judge below found; but the Court of Appeal, in the absence of serious evidence of confusion, found this get-up not deceptive.

[86] *Cf. New Way v. Lucking* [1960] R.P.C. 147 with the two *Specters* cases cited above. Differences in the weight allowed to evidence of conscious imitation, and in willingness to infer a fraudulent intention, play their part here too; *cf.* also the majority and minority views in the Irish case of *Adidas v. O'Neill* [1983] F.S.R. 76 (SC, Ir.).

14–238   What is compendiously called the "get-up" of goods—the dress in which they are presented to the buyer[87]—comprises, in particular, the size and shape of the packages,[88] where the goods have no definite outline, or none which is shown to the buyer, the material, colour[89] and decoration of their wrappers, and the lettering and arrangement of their labels.[90] Where what the buyer sees are the goods themselves, not the packaging, get-up may consist in some capricious or fanciful addition to the goods themselves: paintwork, for instance,[91] or colouring[92] or fanciful shaping[93] of the goods. Possibly, even purely functional features may give a distinctive get-up that will support an action for passing off[94]: in *Kemtron*, it was found that an utilitarian feature may constitute get-up provided it is distinctive and open to argument that a combination of utilitarian features may be protected, again as long as distinctive[95]; whereas in *Interlego v. Tyco*,[96] Sir Allan Huggins V.P. rejected this. The better position is that adopted by Fisher J. in *Tot Toys v. Mitchell*[97]: that the copying of a functional feature may support a passing off action but only where the get-up in question comprises the capricious way in which an essentially utilitarian objective has been expressed.[98] In addi-

---

[87] "The get-up of an article means a capricious addition to the article itself, the colour, or shape, it may be, of the wrapper, or anything of that kind; but I strongly object to look at anything that has a value in use as part of the get-up of the article": *per* Fletcher Moulton L.J. in *Williams v. Bronnley* (1909) 26 R.P.C. 765 at 773; a case described by Walton J. in *"Jif"*, *op. cit.*, as "Quite ridiculous": at 355. In *"Roho"*, Jacob J. considered that this passage is not consistent with *Edge v. Niccols, op. cit.*, and stated: "Even if one adopts the notion 'capricious feature' rather than 'capricious addition' (so as to get out of the way the concept of the article on the one hand and a mark or the like being added to it), one ends up with arguments about the necessity of a particular shape: the plaintiff says 'well you could have made it work the same way but made it look different' and the defendant says 'no I couldn't because of such and such technical reason—the shape of my goods is dictated by utility'. The law of registered designs shows what a horrendous road that is, and I cannot think it has any place in a passing off action where the public are being deceived": at 177.

[88] In *Jones v. Hallworth* (1897) 14 R.P.C. 225, the colours, patterns, shape and sizes of the claimant's "Selvyt" dusters were imitated; *cf. Jones v. Anglo-American Optical* (1912) 29 R.P.C. 1 and 361, the action failed. In *Elliott v. Hodgson* (1902) 19 R.P.C. 518, Buckley J., flat-ended cigars were imitated.

[89] As in *White, Hudson, supra*, n. 82.

[90] In *Parker and Smith v. Satchwell* (1900) 17 R.P.C. 713 the show-cards on which the defendant's goods were sold closely resembled those used by the claimants.

[91] See *Terrapin v. Ariston* [1964] F.S.R. 218 at 224, *per* Denning M.R.

[92] As in *Hoffmann-La Roche v. D.D.S.A., ante,* para. 14–140, illus. (3) (colouring of pharmaceutical capsule): *cf. Roche v. Berk* [1973] R.P.C. 473, where the goods were "typical pills" and relief was refused.

[93] *e.g.* the *"Toofies"* case, below, illus. (1), para. 14–248. See also *Adcock-Ingram v. Beecham* [1978] R.P.C. 232 (South Africa: Domed top on an aerosol can held distinctive, but as usual there were differences preventing imitation of that causing passing off).

[94] *Kemtron v. Jimmy's* [1979] F.S.R. 86 (Hong Kong). In noting that despite both parties' products bearing their respective trade marks there did not appear to be any "source motivation" evidence referred to in the judgment, Jacob J. did not consider *Kemtron* "a helpful case", in *"Roho"* [1995] F.S.R. 169 at 179.

[95] *Ibid.*, at 93–94.

[96] (1985–87) 7 I.P.R. 417 (CA,-H.K.).

[97] (1993) 25 I.P.R. 337 at 350 (HC (N.Z.)).

[98] "[I]f there are no obvious alternatives to the way in which an original or unusual idea has been expressed, the very originality or unusualness may help rather than hinder the

tion, such a passing off action would be likely to succeed only in those unusual cases, such as *Edge v. Niccolls* and *"Jif"*, where the shape has become distinctive on its own, rather than in conjunction with a word mark, *and* the defendant has not clearly distinguished his goods.[99]

But cases involving the shape of goods—and today most get-up **14–239** disputes involve the shape of the goods—do present special difficulties. In the absence of deception or confusion, and in the absence of some patent or design monopoly, enforceable copyright, or now registered trade mark,[1] it is not unlawful to copy another's goods,[2] and the courts have shown themselves astute to reject attempts to prevent copying of goods under the guise of passing-off actions.[3] Indeed, there is authority for saying that, regardless of any other considerations, the mere copying of goods as distinct from the copying of something capriciously added to the goods can never amount to passing off.[4] This is hardly a satisfactory approach: it is not easy to see why misleading of the public by close imitation of goods should be treated any differently from misleading of the public in any other way, whilst the distinction between the goods in themselves and features added capriciously to them belongs, perhaps, more to the realms of metaphysics than of commercial design.[5] Certainly there has been a tendency to adopt this

---

defendants" (at 355); *cf*, the judgments of Jacob J. and Aldous L.J. in *Philips v. Remington, op. cit.*, on the meaning of s.3(2)(b) of the 1994 Act: according to Aldous L.J. its purpose was to exclude from registration shapes dictated by technical considerations: at 821.

[99] See below, at 14–243 *et seq.*

[1] As to which, see Chap. 7.

[2] It was decided by Lehane J. in *Philips v. Remington* (1998) 39 I.P.R. 283 that "unless Philips is entitled to a monopoly in that configuration [of its razor head] by virtue of particular intellectual property rights (*e.g.* registered trade marks or registered designs) then another trader may copy it provided that it is clearly indicated that the copied product is not a Philips but a product of the other trader": at 294. The learned judge considered it unnecessary to add "this machine is not a Philips".

[3] See, *e.g. Interlego v. Croner* (1991) 21 I.P.R. 373 (Fed Ct of Aust.) at 47, where mere copying of the claimant's plastic bricks was found not to constitute passing off (although passing off was found for other reasons): "The matters I have to be careful about are that confusion itself is not enough and that one must guard against cases in which customers or potential customers have been misled not by anything done by a defendant but rather by their own misconceptions or misunderstandings": *per* Sheppard J.

[4] *Terrapin v. Ariston, supra,* comes very close to deciding just that, quoting Fletcher Moulton L.J. in *Williams v. Bronnley, supra* n. 21, as authority. See also *Benchairs v. Chair Centre* [1974] R.P.C. 429 (mere copying of goods not a representation as to trade origin); *Hawkins v. Fludes* [1957] R.P.C. 8; and see also the warning in *Jarman & Platt v. Barget* [1977] F.S.R. 260, CA, that large sales of a unique product do not prove that its get-up has a reputation that will support a passing-off action—other evidence of reputation may be hard to get. A case that went the other way is *Plix v. Winstone* [1986] F.S.R. 63 (HC, N.Z.: "Pocket packs" for Kiwi fruit).

[5] It has been accepted for many years, by some designers, that fanciful features are only permissible if they do appear to be integral parts of the design. It is, indeed, interesting to compare this question with the corresponding question arising in the law of registered industrial design itself. It was contended many years ago that to qualify for protection by registration an industrial design must involve some purely ornamental feature added to the article. The House of Lords in due course rejected the contention (*Hecla Foundry v. Walker, Hunter* (1889) 6 R.P.C. 554 at 558–559). It was later held that a design might come too close to being merely the bare bones of an article to be

approach to deal with such cases according to the ordinary principles governing passing off—whilst scrutinising the claimant's evidence of reputation with care, to make sure that any preference shown by the public for his goods results from their associating the particular design or style concerned with the claimant, not merely from a preference for that particular style or design.[6]

14–240   At the same time as the courts have shown a certain tendency to reject out of hand allegations of passing off based merely on copying of the design of the goods,[7] they have shown a complementary tendency to treat as inherently unlawful the copying of fanciful characteristics of goods or packaging.[8] This, too, however, involves a departure from the principles laid down in the earlier authorities. "Apart from monopolies conferred by patents, and apart from protection afforded by registration, it is open to anyone to adopt the ideas or devices of his neighbours and apply them to his own goods provided he clearly distinguishes his goods from those of his neighbour": a proposition which, stated with reference to a fanciful feature of the goods (a white inlaid spot in the wood of a tobacco-pipe near the join to the mouthpiece),[9] would seem to be equally applicable to novelties of packaging. To the same effect more recently: "Some think that copying is unethical; others do not. Often the copyist of today becomes the innovator of tomorrow. Copying is said by some to be the lifeblood of competition, the means of breaking *de facto* market monopolies and keeping down the price of articles not protected by special monopolies such as patents or registered designs. Others say that copyists are parasites on innovators. None of this matters. Certainly it is not the law that copying as such is unlawful: the common law . . . leans against monopolies", *per* Jacob J. in *"Roho"*.[10]

14–241   (1) The claimants sold bags of laundry blue, each bag holding a stick or "dolly" of a particular form. The evidence showed that

registrable (*Tecalemit v. Ewarts (No 2)* (1927) 44 R.P.C. 503 at 507–508); but even that proposition may well go too far—*cf. Cow v. Cannon* [1959] R.P.C. 347 at 353, CA. It is by no means clear that the proposition discussed in the text has any greater merit than the propositions rejected in the design cases, or that the proposition that there can be no action for passing off merely for copying what could have been registered as a design has any greater merit than the proposition (equally rejected by the courts) that nothing protectable by a patent could be a registrable design.

[6] *British American Glass v. Winton* [1962] R.P.C. 230 (copying of ornamental dogs sold without packaging); *Hawkins & Tipson v. Fludes* [1957] R.P.C. 8 at 11; and *Gordon Fraser v. Tatt* [1966] R.P.C. 505 (copying of style of claimants' greeting cards) would seem to illustrate this approach to such matters. It has been argued that the law has gone too far in protecting products by passing-off actions: see Evans *"Passing-Off: The Problem of Product Simulation"* [1968] M.L.R. 642.

[7] On the obstacles facing the registrability of shapes as trade marks, see paras 7–133 to 7–160, above.

[8] It is difficult to account otherwise for the decision in *New Way v. Lucking* [1960] R.P.C. 147.

[9] *"White Spot Pipe"* case (*Dunhill v. Bartlett & Bickley*) (1922) 39 R.P.C. 426 at 438. Note the completely literal way in which (it would seem) the judge concerned used the word "distinguish": a large red spot and a small white spot do not look alike, and that is the whole of the case.

[10] [1995] F.S.R. 169 at 173.

customers bought entirely by the appearance of the goods, relying in particular on the "dolly". The defendants adopted a similar dolly, and the presence on their goods of their name was in these circumstances held an insufficient distinction: *Edge v. Niccolls* [1911] A.C. 693; 28 R.P.C. 582. *Cf. Coca-Cola v. Barr* [1961] R.P.C. 387, where the use of bottles shaped like the claimants, and unlabelled, was considered deceptive: but an interim interdict was refused in respect of drinks of a different colour from the claimants.

(2) The claimants sold their soap in packets wrapped up in a **14–242** peculiar parchment paper, with "Sunlight Self-Washer" printed in spaced type upon the wrapper; the defendants began to use similar packets and paper, with the words "Goodwin's Self-washing Soap" printed upon it in similar type. It was treated as an obvious case of fraud: *Lever v. Goodwin* (1887) 36 Ch.D. 1; 4 R.P.C. 492. *Cf. Lever v. Bedingfield* (1899) 16 R.P.C. 3.

The "Jif" case

In the "Jif" case,[11] Reckett & Colman established that the "Jif" lemon- **14–243** shaped plastic container had acquired a secondary significance. The question then came down to whether Borden, in adopting containers having the most striking feature of the "Jif" get-up, had taken sufficient steps to distinguish their products. It was found that they had not; this despite the fact that the Borden lemons did have labels which were marked "Realemon". The case can be understood in the light of the particular findings of fact; namely that for customers a crucial point of reference was the lemon shape and that virtually no attention was paid to the label. Shoppers had no reason to read the label or pay any attention to it in order to obtain the goods they required.

Borden deployed a number of arguments. First, they contended that a **14–244** distinction must be drawn between a manufactured article itself, and the special trade insignia (such as get-up) used to designate its trade origin. The article itself could not constitute the special insignia of its own origin. Lord Oliver dealt with the argument by rejecting the suggestion that the container was an object in itself rather than part of the get-up. Lord Jauncey, who gave the other principal speech, adopted the more robust position that the shape and configuration of the article could be protected against deception and confusion. He concluded (at 426):

> "this principle [that no man may sell his goods under the pretence that they are the goods of another] applies as well to the goods themselves as to their get-up. A. markets a ratchet screwdriver with a distinctively shaped handle. The screwdriver has acquired a reputation for reliability and utility and is generally recognised by

---

[11] *Op. cit.*

the public as being the produce of A. because of the handle. A. would be entitled to protection against B. if the latter sought to market a ratchet screwdriver with a similarly shaped handle without taking sufficient steps to see that the public was not misled into thinking that his product was that of A."

The critical point here is that the defendant had not taken sufficient steps to avoid deception.[12]

14–245   Borden also contended that mere confusion was not sufficient to found the cause of action; they argued that all that they had done was to adopt a descriptive device and that Reckitt & Colman were not entitled to relief simply because they had used the same device as descriptive of their own goods and had been the only people previously to adopt that description. This, of course, was not a novel proposition. It is well established that where a descriptive term is used, a claimant must show more than simply the sole use of it. He must show that it has acquired secondary meaning not simply of the goods of that description, but also of goods of which he, and he alone, is the source. The difficulty facing Borden was that the trial judge had found as a fact that the "Jif" lemon container was so distinctive.[13]

14–246   Reckitt & Colman, for their part, accepted that they had to establish deception and confusion and argued that the crucial question is "What moves the public to buy?", a question taken from the judgment of Judge Learned Hand in *Crescent Tool Co. v. Kilborn & Bishop* (1917) 147 F. 299 (a case about a copy of an adjustable wrench sold under the trade mark "Crescent").[14] Although not expressly referred to in the speeches, it appears (particularly from the passage cited above from the speech of Lord Jauncey) that this was accepted. What a claimant has to do is to prove that it is deception which moves the public to buy the defendant's goods. If successful, the claimant has proved both the fact of misrepresentation and that the misrepresentation was operative. Lord Oliver rejected Borden's contention that there was sufficient differentiation to avoid confusion: "it can be no answer, in a case where it is demonstrable that the public has been or will be deceived, that they would not have been if they had been more careful, more literate or more perspicacious. Customers have to be taken as they are found": at 415.[15]

---

[12] See also the statement of Glidewell L.J. in the CA: "I wish only to emphasise . . . that if a trader has in fact obtained a monopoly in selling goods in a particular get-up, the longer the monopoly subsists the greater becomes the obligation on another trader who wishes to sell similar goods in competition to ensure that the get-up of his goods is sufficiently distinguished from those already on the market": at 396.

[13] Lord Oliver expressed surprise at the findings at trial of confusion but stated: "it has to be borne in mind that . . . the primary retail outlets for these products are supermarkets . . . and the purchasing member of the public is reliant on his own perception or recollection, unassisted by the opportunity of side-by-side comparison": at 407.

[14] Also referred to by Jacob J. in "*Roho*", *op. cit.*, at 178, as a question which "exactly encapsulates what must be shown" by a claimant. In *Kimberley-Clark v. Fort Sterling* [1997] F.S.R. 877, Laddie J., considered that Jacob J. did not intend to suggest that the claimant must show that sales will be diverted but rather was addressing the question of whether the goodwill and misrepresentation requirements were satisfied: at 889–890.

[15] See also *Clark v. Associated Newspapers* [1998] R.P.C. 261.

Claimant must prove reputation

As in any other passing-off case, a claimant relying upon get-up must **14–247**
prove his reputation: he must prove, that is, that the get-up concerned
indicates his goods and no one else's.[16] In particular, he must show that
distinctiveness lies in the get-up and not (for instance) in his name or
trade marks, if those appear on the goods.[17] Thus, if a claimant by his
cautions and advertisements shows that he relies wholly or mainly on
his trade mark or business name, he makes his case on general get-up,
apart from trade mark or business name, more difficult to establish.[18] A
trader who introduces a new feature into the get-up of his goods does
not thereby acquire any proprietary interest in it, so as to be able to
prevent its use by competitors, until it has become so identified with his
goods that its use by others is calculated to deceive.[19] No case can be
made merely[20] by showing an imitation of the parts of the get-up of
goods which are common to the trade.[21] But very little evidence of user
may be sufficient to establish distinctiveness where the get-up is not

---

[16] See *ante*, para. 14–18; and *Jones v. Anglo-American* (1912) 29 R.P.C. 361; *Saper v. Specters*
(1953) 70 R.P.C. 173 at 174. "If reputation is not established, the question of confusion
does not arise", *per* Megaw L.J. in *Jarman & Platt v. Barget* [1977] F.S.R. 260 at 270. Also,
"*Jif*", *op. cit., per* Lord Oliver, at 406.

[17] See *Schweppes v. Gibbens* (1905) 22 R.P.C. 113, 601 (HL); *King v. Gillard* (1905) 22 R.P.C.
327, CA; and the cases cited in footnotes 18 and 21, especially *Payton v. Snelling*. See *Tot
Toys v. Mitchell, op. cit.* : "The capricious get-up must be a *sine qua non* for customer
recognition even though it may not be its sole cause" (*per* Fisher J. at 355).

[18] *Imperial Tobacco v. Purnell* (1904) 21 R.P.C. 368, 598; and see *Coleman v. Smith* (1912) 29
R.P.C. 81; *Hennessy v. Keating* (1908) 25 R.P.C. 125 and 361 (HL).

[19] Thus, in *Klissers Farmhouse Bakeries v. Harvest Bakeries* [1989] R.P.C. 27, Casey J. rejected
the claimant's claim of distinctiveness in the use on bread packaging of check or
gingham patterns, whilst noting the importance of the fact that the defendant's
packaging had a label showing clearly the maker's name and mark: at 37. Bisson J.
found that checks were a common feature of the trade: at 44.

[20] But where the colouring of the claimants' label was common to the trade, and the goods
were sold under different names, yet the defendants' label contained features liable to
be confused with those of the claimants' label and seemed to have been designed with
that object, the claimants were held to be entitled to succeed both on infringement and
passing off: *Bryant & May v. United Match* (1933) 50 R.P.C. 12.

[21] In *Payton v. Snelling* [1901] A.C. 308; 17 R.P.C. 628, the claimants had been the first to put
coffee in tins enamelled in bright colours; held that the claimants had no monopoly in
such tins; and in *Williams v. Bronnley* (1909) 26 R.P.C. 481, 765, the claimants had been
the first and, for years, the only persons to put on the market shaving-sticks in tin-lined
boxes with maroon covers, but at the date of the action these features were held to be
common. See also *Hubbuck v. Brown* (1900) 17 R.P.C. 148 at 154 (upheld CA, at 638) as to
the fashion of the market. In *White, Tomkins v. United Confectionery* (1914) 31 R.P.C. 430, it
was held that, although the claimants were the only persons who had used a picture of a
particular fruit to denote the flavour of their jelly crystals, they had not shown that the
particular device was identified with their goods. In *Hawkins & Tipson v. Fludes* [1957]
R.P.C. 8, action dismissed as claimants had not discharged onus upon them of showing
patterns woven into their matting to be distinctive of themselves. In *Politechnika I. Pari v.
Dallas Print* [1982] F.S.R. 529, the makers of "Rubik" cubes failed to establish that the
appearance of the cube denoted their goods. On the other hand, in *EMAP v. Security
Publications* [1997] F.S.R. 891, the particular combination of features used on the cover of
the claimant's classic car magazine was found sufficiently distinctive to justify granting
an interlocutory injunction; and in "*Jif*", *op. cit*, Lord Oliver commented of the *Williams
v. Bronnley* line of cases: "[they] established no fresh principle of law, and are really of
very little assistance": at 412.

only novel but striking,[22] even though it consists of a combination of commonly used parts. The case is then analogous to that of a "fancy word": in *United Biscuits v. Asda* [1997] R.P.C. 513, Robert Walker J. considered that the words "Penguin" and "Puffin" were "fancy" in the sense that "an unpalatable bird has no obvious connection with a chocolate-coated sandwich biscuit", at 532. Where the goods themselves are unique, however, merely showing large sales does not prove that their get-up enjoys a reputation.[23]

14–248   (1) The claimants had for some months sold bubble gum in the shape of a set of false teeth, and labelled "Toofy's Bubble Gum". The defendants marketed a similar article, labelled "Margo's Toofies Bubble Gum". On a motion for an interlocutory injunction, the defendants offered an undertaking not to use the word "Toofy's" or "Toofies", and an injunction was refused: Harman J. observing that the claimants "have not shown that any member of the public, seeing bubble-gum in the shape of false teeth, will associate it with any particular manufacturer at all"; and that the claimants had to prove "that bubble gum cannot be made in that shape without representing to the trade and to the public that those goods are the goods of the plaintiffs": *Blundell v. Margolis* (1951) 68 R.P.C. 71.

14–249   (2) The petitioners had for a long period sold whisky in bottles of a special shape which had become known as "Dimple" bottles, the whisky being known as "Dimple" Whisky. Interim relief was first granted, and later a perpetual interdict, against use by the defendants of similar bottles: *Haig v. Forth Blending* (1952) 69 R.P.C. 323 and (1953) 70 R.P.C. 259.[24]

14–250   (3) The claimant had for many years sold a chocolate-coated confectionery product called "Pineapple Lumps", for the previous four years in three sizes of bag with a particular design. The defendant acquired from the receiver a confectionery business which had been marketing *inter alia* a product called "Pineapple Chunks" for many years. The defendant redesigned the packaging and relaunched the product in bags of three sizes the same as those of the claimant (which were an industry norm). An interlocutory injunction was granted, the judge noting the prevalence of impulse purchasing of the particular products: *Griffin v. Regina* (1991) 19 I.P.R. 425 (HC (N.Z.)).

---

[22] *Weingarten v. Bayer* (1905) 22 R.P.C. 341, HL ("Erect Form" with "corsets" written in a flourish of the "E").

[23] *Jarman & Platt v. Bargett* [1977] F.S.R. 260, CA; but large sales of goods under a unique get-up "must go some way" to such proof: *Sodastream v. Thorn Cascade* [1982] R.P.C. 459 at 469, CA (CO_2 in grey cylinders).

[24] But in *Haig v. Brooks* (1955) 72 R.P.C. 247, interim injunction refused as claimants had not shown that there was any likelihood of the public being deceived by the shape of the defendants' bottles.

"Look-alikes"

In a "look-alike" case, the defendant supermarket chain sold a **14–251** chocolate-coated sandwich biscuit under the name "Puffin" and the predominantly red packaging included a cartoon depiction of a puffin. The claimant, who had sold successfully for a number of years a similar biscuit called "Penguin" in predominantly red packaging, sued for passing off (and trade mark infringement). In finding passing off, Robert Walker J. found that a substantial number of consumers would think the two products came from the same manufacturer: *United Biscuits v. Asda* [1997] R.P.C. 513 at 538. The case highlights the practice in recent years of supermarkets marketing their own-brand "look-alike" products to compete with well-known brand leaders and makes clear that where the "look-alike" comes too close to the product it is designed to compete with, there will be passing off. On the other hand where there is clear differentiation, although the "look-alike" has been inspired by the original product, there will be neither misrepresentation nor deception.

In *"Roho"* Jacob J. found the claimant had failed to establish that the **14–252** shape of their cushion, which the defendant had copied was the "crucial point of reference" for those who wanted specifically a Roho cushion made by the claimant. Despite the evidence that almost all those who saw the defendant's product (or a photograph of it) reacted by saying "that is a Roho", this did not prove the customers wanting a Roho cushion would be deceived into buying the defendant's.[25]

Imitation of part of get-up

It is not necessary for passing off that every part of the get-up should be **14–253** imitated, for, though no exclusive right to the use of any single feature of it which is not a registered trade mark is recognised, yet a part of the get-up—a picture, for instance, which is used on the label or wrapper—may be shown to be so identified with the claimant's goods that its use for similar goods is calculated to pass them off as his. The picture, in effect, may become a "common law trade mark".[26]

The claimant used the device of a lady and a bear, in his trade as a **14–254** furrier, by attaching it to the wrappers and boxes in which he sent out his goods, but he had registered it only as a trade mark for sealskin mantles and coats. The defendant began to issue a circular, bearing a similar mark, in connection with his trade which was also that of a furrier. Two injunctions were granted, one restricted to the mantles and coats, to restrain infringement of the trade mark, the other, not so

[25] *Op. cit.*, at 179–181.
[26] See above at para. 14–241, and *Weingarten v. Bayer, supra.*

restricted, to restrain the defendant from using the device so as to deceive the public: *Jay v. Ladler* (1888) 40 Ch.D. 649; 6 R.P.C. 136.

14–255 On the other hand, the imitation of a number of things, each of which is in itself not distinctive of the claimant's goods, may make a strong case on account of the cumulative effect of the detailed resemblances.[27] The taking by the defendant of a word or words, which though not distinctive, form a prominent part of the claimant's label, may strongly contribute to the passing off.[28]

Only things which are put prominently forward so as to be likely to catch the eye of a purchaser and remain in his memory need generally be considered. Thus, the printing on the back or sides of a box may usually be disregarded in considering whether the get-up of goods is likely to deceive.[29]

Get-up of a business

14–256 Passing off by get-up is not confined to goods; thus there have been actions relating to passing off by the get-up of a shop[30] and of an omnibus.[31] In *Taylor Bros v. Taylor Group* (1991) 19 I.P.R. 615 (CA (N.Z.)), the court found it a breach of an earlier injunction, which prohibited the defendant from trading under or by reference to the name "Taylors", for the get-up of the shop to be used in such a way as to suggest continuity, even though the trading name had been changed to "Laytons": "[t]he signs at the premises and on the vans and the stationery used . . . corresponds exactly with the get-up previously used by the [defendant]", at 619–620, *per* Cooke P.

---

[27] *Lever v. Goodwin*, below, at 4 R.P.C. 505–506, CA, and compare with *Lever v. Bedingfield* (1899) 16 R.P.C. 3. See also *Williams v. Bromley* (1909) 26 R.P.C. 481 at 486: "I am not prepared to say that there may not be cases in which a trader may acquire by user an exclusive right of monopoly in respect of a combination of two or more matters, which by themselves are absolutely common to the trade," *per* Neville J. See also *Christiansen's T.M.* (1886) 3 R.P.C. 54, CA.

[28] As the words "Self Washer" in *Lever v. Goodwin* (1887) 36 Ch.D. 1; 4 R.P.C. 492. See also *Knott v. Morgan*, below at n. 31.

[29] *Per* Kekewich J. in *Lever v. Bedingfield* (1898) 15 R.P.C. 453 at 462 (a box of tablets of soap). Also, *Smith's Potato Crisps v. Paige's Potato Crips* (1928) 45 R.P.C. 132: "there is a distinguishing feature in the Defendants' [product] which ought not to be overlooked by any observer with his wits reasonably about him", *per* Lord Hanworth M.R. at 146.

[30] *Laraine Day v. Kennedy* (1953) 70 R.P.C. 19; the action failed, but on the facts. In *My Kinda Town v. Soll* [1983] R.P.C. 407, it was sought to argue that the get-up of the defendant's restaurant caused deception but the Court of Appeal found that the pleadings did not disclose such an assertion: *per* Oliver L.J. at 419.

[31] *Knott v. Morgan* (1836) 2 Keen 213; the fraud consisted in the imitation of the painting of the claimants' omnibuses, the uniforms of their servants and the use of their descriptive title—The London Conveyance Co.: *London General Omnibus v. Felton*, 12 T.L.R. 213; and *London Road Car v. Era Omnibus*, The Times, June 23, 1898; The Times, April 28, 1899, similar.

8. Proof of likelihood of deception

Generally[32]

In the common case the court must be satisfied that the defendant's **14–257** conduct is calculated[33] to pass off other goods as those of the claimant, or, at least, to produce such confusion in the minds of probable customers or purchasers or other persons with whom the claimant has business relations[34] as would be likely to lead to the other goods being bought and sold for his.[35] This is the foundation of the action. Similarly with any other sort of passing off. The claimant has to prove that it is deception which moves the public to buy the defendant's goods.

"... is it, on a balance of probabilities, likely that.. a substantial number of [the relevant class[36]] will be misled into purchasing the defendant's [product] in the belief that it is the respondent's [product].": *per* Lord Oliver in *Jif*.[37]

Mere confusion is not enough.[38] No one is entitled to be protected against confusion as such.[39] At the heart of passing off lies deception or its likelihood. Never has the tort shown even a slight tendency to stray beyond cases of deception. Were it to do so it would enter the field of honest competition, declared unlawful for some reason other than deceptiveness.[40]

The onus of proving deception or its likelihood is upon the claimant.

The question of likelihood of deception is for the court (not the **14–258** witnesses) to decide "looking at the documents and evidence before him."[41] Evidence may be called on the point, but is not essential except

---

[32] As to the tests to be applied in comparing marks, see Chap. 16 on "Deceptive Resemblance." In particular, as to evidence on deceptiveness of resemblance see *post*, paras 16–89 *et seq.*

[33] "calculated" in the sense of being the reasonably foreseeable consequence. Fraud is not required.

[34] As in *Pullman v. Pullman* (1919) 36 R.P.C. 240.

[35] *Schweppes v. Gibbens*, *ante*, para. 14–247.

[36] In that case, the relevant class of persons were members of the public. In general the relevant class are "purchasers or probable purchasers of goods of the kind in question": Viscount Maugham, *Saville Perfumery v. June Perfect* (1941) 58 R.P.C. 147 at 176.

[37] [1990] R.P.C. 341 at 407. This passage indicates that post-sale confusion can really only be relevant in passing off if the confusion persists through and results in a second/ subsequent purchase. The contrary reasoning in *Levi's v. Kimbeyr Investments* [1994] F.S.R. 335, High Ct. N.Z., is not convincing. See also para. 14–06 above.

[38] *Marcus Publishing Plc v. Hutton-Wild Communications Ltd* [1990] R.P.C. 576 C.A. *per* Dillon L.J. at 580; *County Sound Plc v. Ocean Sound Ltd* [1991] F.S.R. 367 CA, *per* Nourse L.J. at 376; quoting Lord Greene M.R. in *Marengo v. Daily Sketch and Sunday Graphic Ltd* (May 17, 1946) now reported at [1992] F.S.R. 1.

[39] Lord Greene M.R. in *Marengo*, *ibid*. The passage in question was not questioned when the decision of the CA was reversed on the facts by the House of Lords: (1948) 65 R.P.C. 242.

[40] Jacob J. in *Hodgkinson & Corby Ltd v. Wards Mobility Ltd* ("Roho") [1994] 1 W.L.R. 1564.

[41] *Spalding v. Gamage* (1915) 32 R.P.C. 273 at 286, HL, *per* Lord Parker of Waddington; it is clear in the context (see the next proposition) that he was contemplating deciding upon the documents alone—as in trade mark cases.

in cases of doubt,[42] and the assistance it gives to the court will be of a limited nature unless it includes evidence of actual deception[43] apart from cases turning on the circumstances and practices of the particular trade.[44] The judge is entitled to give effect to his own opinion as to the likelihood of deception and, in doing so, is not confined to the evidence of the witnesses called at trial.[45] The issue is whether a substantial[46] or large[47] number of relevant trade or public have been misled or are likely to be misled. The deception must be more than momentary and inconsequential.[48]

14–259   (1) An advertisement intended as "comparative advertising" was held to involve passing off on evidence showing that many people took it as an advertisement for the claimants' goods, asserting that they were obtainable from the defendants' outlets: *McDonald's v. Burgerking* [1986] F.S.R. 45.

(2) The claimant had sold lemon juice in yellow, lemon-sized squeezy packs for many years. The defendant introduced their similarly packaged lemon juice, with a prominent neck label.[49] As the trial judge found, "[t]here would be no difficulty in a careful shopper coming to the conclusion that [none of the defendant's products] was a Jif lemon—it would merely be a question of her . . . reading the label." However, on evidence from members of the public who had taken part in a realistic survey, the trial judge found as facts that "The crucial point of

---

[42] *ibid.*

[43] *Parker-Knoll v. Knoll International* [1962] R.P.C. 265 at 285, *per* Lord Hodson, citing *Spalding v. Gamage, supra.* Jacob J. in *Neutrogena Corporation v. Golden Ltd* [1996] R.P.C. 473 (upheld on appeal) made various observations concerning the provision of evidence of deception: (at 483): "The principal advantage [of members of the public giving their evidence in chief by direct oral examination rather than by confirmation of their witness statements] was that they were able to give their account of events directly to me in their own words without any leading.". Generally, market surveys, with statistical analysis of the results, are (at 485–486) "unnecessarily elaborate in a passing off action. The court in a passing off case is not concerned with statistical precision. What it wants to know is whether or not there is a substantial degree of deception or confusion. Moreover pure questionnaire evidence is seldom helpful . . . But unless one can have some real evidence, tested in cross-examination, one cannot really be sure of what was passing through people's minds. Those cases where surveys have proved to be useful have all involved some of the 'pollees' coming to court". In practice, surveys are used now to find witnesses who were allegedly deceived.

[44] *The European Ltd v. The Economist Newspaper Ltd* [1998] F.S.R. 283 at 291, CA; and *Alan Clark v. Associated Newspapers Ltd* [1998] R.P.C. 261, Lightman J. at 271, para 3.

[45] Lord Diplock in *GE Trade* Mark [1973] R.P.C. 297 at 321, cited by Morritt L.J. in *Neutrogena, op. cit.* at 495.

[46] It is not necessary to or to be able to extrapolate from the evidence so as to arrive at any quantitative or qualitative measure of the deception caused by the defendant. See Morritt L.J. in *Neutrogena, op cit.*, at 505. In cases which are near the borderline (and *Neutrogena* was such a case), the Court has to take account of the fact that ". . . there are always some people who are confused and even when products and names are well-differentiated, mistakes do occur". see Jacob J. in *Neutrogena*, at 482.

[47] *Saville Perfumery Ltd v. June Perfect Ltd* (1941) 58 R.P.C. 147 at 175–176, HL.

[48] *Cadbury-Schweppes Pty Ltd v. The Pub Squash Co.* [1981] 1 W.L.R. 193 at 205B, PC.

[49] Photographs of the products are at [1990] R.P.C. 341 at 343.

reference for a shopper who wishes to purchase a Jif squeezy lemon is the lemon shape itself. Virtually no, if any, attention is paid to the label." The lemon shape had acquired a secondary meaning: *Jif* [1990] R.P.C. 341.

(3) A weekly column in the Evening Standard newspaper was **14–260** entitled "Alan Clark's Secret Political Diary". The articles were parodies of the well-known diaries of Alan Clark. On evidence showing that a number of "rational men" and women believed the articles to have been written by the claimant, passing off was held established. Since the issue was one of authorship, it did not matter that some had not read the articles and merely skim read the newspaper: *Alan Clark v. Associated Newspapers Ltd.* [1998] R.P.C. 261.

It is not a defence to prove that there are persons who purchase the goods of a defendant who are not misled, if it is established that there are a large number of persons who are.[50]

The standard required

"The essence of the action for passing off is a deceit practised on the **14–261** public and it can be no answer, in a case where it is demonstrable that the public has been or will be deceived, that they would not have been if they had been more careful, more literate or more perspicacious. Customers have to be taken as they are found." *per* Lord Oliver and *per* Lord Jauncey: "There is ample authority for the view that you must take customers as you find them including the imprudent and the unwary: *R. Johnston & Co. v. Archibald Orr-Ewing & Co* (1882) 7 App. Cas. 219, Lord Selborne L.C. at page 225, Lord Blackburn at page 229; *Powell v. Birmingham Vinegar Brewery Co.* [1896] 2 Ch. 54, Lindley L.J., at page 68.": *Jif.*[51]

Despite the consistency in this approach for well over a century, the **14–262** issue arises as to whether the influence of judgments of the European Court of Justice will lead to or require the adoption of the "average

---

[50] *per* Viscount Maugham, *Saville Perfumery v. June Perfect* (1941) 58 R.P.C. 147 at 175. *cf. Marengo v. Daily Sketch* (1948) 65 R.P.C. 242 at 252, HL (defendant's mark ambiguous). ". . . where it appears to the eye of the court that there is likely to be deception, and there is evidence of rational men that they have been deceived there is little value in the evidence of witnesses who say they have not been deceived.": *per* Lord Simonds at 250. And see *Neutrogena Corporation v. Golden Ltd* [1996] R.P.C. 473 at 491: "There is passing off even if most of the people are not fooled most of the time but enough are for enough of the time. By 'enough' I mean a substantial number of the plaintiff's customers or potential customers deceived for there to be a real effect on the plaintiff's trade or goodwill.": Morritt L.J. quoting Jacob J. at first instance.

[51] [1990] R.P.C. 341 at 415 and 423, respectively. This does not mean, as Lord Jauncey pointed out, that customers who through a lack of interest or idleness have deliberately disregarded distinct labelling of different brands of goods. See also Lightman J. in *Alan Clark (op. cit.)* at 271: "no claim lies if they are indifferent or careless as to [the indicia in dispute]—in that case "who is the author".

consumer" test. This test was developed[52] by the Court in a series of cases in which it had to weigh the risk of consumers being misled against the requirement of the free movement of goods. Essentially, whenever a national court has to determine whether something would mislead the public: "it is necessary to take into account the presumed expectations of an average consumer who is reasonably well informed and reasonably observant and circumspect." The test, based on the principle of proportionality, has a number of advantages. First, it is a uniform test applicable throughout the EEA.[53] Secondly, the test is obviously one for the court to decide. Thirdly, it encourages economy of evidence.[54]

14–263   Although the average consumer test was first advocated by the ECJ in a case involving inter-state trade, it has rapidly pervaded the purely national context[55] to ensure a uniform approach to the issue of likelihood of confusion in the law of registered trade marks under sections 5(2) and 10(2)/Articles 4(1)(b) and 5(1)(b), and possibly to the issue of distinctiveness also, if, as seems likely, the ECJ follow the lead of the Court of Appeal in *Bach Flower Remedies. (ibid.)* Strictly, the ECJ can only influence the law of passing off to the extent that it has effects on the free movement of goods which cannot be objectively justified,[56] and this is unlikely to occur. Even so, the pressure for the uniform adoption of the average consumer test is likely to increase, both at European and national level.[57]

14–264   At first sight, there seems to be no appreciable difference between the traditional approach in passing off cases and the "average consumer" test. If there is any difference, the "average consumer" appears to be more careful and therefore less likely to be misled than the imprudent or

---

[52] The development is described by A.-G. Fennelly in Case C–220/98 *Estee Lauder Cosmetics GmbH v. Lancaster Group GmbH* September 16, 1999. It was first properly formulated in *Gut Springenheide and Tusky v. Oberkreisdirektor Steinfurt* [1998] E.C.R. I–4657.

[53] This does not mean that the test will give the same result in every country. The European Court has recognised that social, cultural or linguistic factors may justify a different conclusion in one Member State to others.

[54] The Court of Appeal in *Bach and Bach Flower Remedies Trade Marks* [2000] R.P.C. 513, not only extended the average consumer test to distinctiveness, but also took the opportunity to use it to discourage repetitive evidence. See *per* Morritt L.J. at 526 and Chadwick L.J. at 534.

[55] One of the recent cases before the Court was a claim brought under German legislation by a German trade association against a German company in the context of a beer brewed in Germany. At least A.-G. Jacobs considered that Art. 30 (now 28) of the Treaty was applicable on the basis of the potential effects of the national legislation on intra-Community trade. A.-G. Jacobs was of the opinion that the average consumer test applied: Case C 312/98 *Schutzverband gegen Unwesen in der Wirtschaft e.V. v. Warsteiner Brauerei Haus Cramer GmbH & Co. KG.* Opinion of A.-G. Jacobs, May 25, 2000.

[56] See further, Chap. 15.

[57] Even if this test is uniformly adopted, and leaving aside social, cultural and linguistic differences between countries, it does not mean that the same standard is being applied everywhere. The average consumer test is one part of the story, the other part being the rigour with which the court scrutinises purported evidence of deception. The English approach is one of the most rigorous (witness the general lack of faith placed in market surveys), whereas courts in other jurisdictions appear to place great faith in precise statistics drawn from market surveys which would be treated very differently by an English judge.

the unwary, which an English court would be entitled to take into account. Bearing in mind the scrutiny which is applied in English courts to evidence of alleged deception, once an English court has decided a likelihood of deception exists, it is very difficult to see that the judge would conclude that he had not also just applied the average consumer test. Otherwise, and if the tests were different, the application of the average consumer test might entail a risk of the public being deceived.

Fraudulent intention

If it is shown to have been intended by the defendant to deceive the **14–265** burden of proof is much lighter[58] and the court will not generally push the inquiry further.[59]

But the intention is only evidence of the actual deception or probability of deception which may be inferred from it.[60] If the court does not believe that there is any probability of deception, the action must fail.[61] The law does not take notice of a fraudulent intention in a man's mind if he does nothing to carry out the fraud.[62]

> "When once you establish the intent to deceive, it is only a short step to proving that the intent has been successful, but still it is a step, even though it be a short step."[63]

The existence of unexpected and unexplained similarities[64] between the **14–266** goods of the defendant and those of the claimant or of similarities which have been modified by colourable differences[65] or by differences and distinctions so arranged as to escape notice[66]; the use by the defendant of descriptions, which, as applied to himself or his own trade, are inaccurate, and by reason of their inaccuracy approach more nearly to the proper description of the claimant,[67] and the gradual approximation

---

[58] *Taylor v. Taylor* (1854) 2 Eq.Rep. 290; 23 L.J.Ch. 255.
[59] *Rolls Razors v. Rolls (Lighters)* (1949) 66 R.P.C. 299 at 303, CA.
[60] "Why should we be astute to say that (the defendant) cannot succeed in doing what he is straining every nerve to do?" Lindley L.J. asked in *Slazenger v. Feltham* (1889) 6 R.P.C. 531 at 538. *Cf. per* Lord Macclesfield in *Mitchell v. Reynolds*, 1 Sm.L.C. (10th ed.) at 391. "He only can suffer by his knavery, and surely Courts of Justice are not concerned lest a man should pay too dear for being a knave." "If you find a defendant who is a knave, you may presume he is not a fool": *per* Cozens-Hardy M.R. in *Claudius Ash v. Invicta* (1912) 28 R.P.C. 597 at 603: but note (below) that the HL took a different view of the case.
[61] *cf. ante*, para. 14–258.
[62] *Lever v. Bedingfield* (1899) 16 R.P.C. 3, CA, overruling 15 R.P.C. 453, Kekewich J. See *Claudius Ash v. Invicta* (1912) 29 R.P.C. 465, HL; *"Pub Squash"* [1981] R.P.C. 429 at 493–4 (PC, N.S.W.).
[63] *Per* Lord Esher M.R. in *Reddaway v. Banham* (1895) 12 R.P.C. 83 at 89.
[64] *Per* Earl Loreburn in *Claudius Ash v. Invicta* (1912) 29 R.P.C. 465 at 475; neither fraud nor probability of deception was proved.
[65] *Slazenger v. Feltham* (1889) 6 R.P.C. 531, CA ("Demon", "Demotic").
[66] *e.g.* "late of", etc. in small letters, para. 14–93.
[67] *Holloway v. Holloway* (1850) 13 Beav. 209. And see *Middlemas v. Molivar* (1921) 38 R.P.C. 97 (mark used by defendant not quite his original name, let alone the name he usually used); also see paras 14–85 *et seq., ante*, and cases there cited.

of the defendant's names, get-up or description to those of the claim-ant,[68] are all obvious badges of fraudulent intention frequently recurring in the cases which come before the court.[69]

Enabling passing off by others

14–267 Deception by the deliberate fraud of a third party, for example a retailer,[70] where the defendant's mark when fairly used is not calculated to deceive, is not imputable to the defendants.[71] On the other hand, it is a common cause of complaint against defendants who are manufac-turers that they are putting an instrument of fraud in the hands of retailers; and the complaint is sound in law. Indeed, the rule goes further. "No man is permitted to use any mark, sign or symbol, device or other name, whereby, without making a direct false representation himself to a purchaser who purchases from him, he enables such purchaser to tell a lie or to make a false representation to somebody else who is the ultimate customer."[72] Nor is it permissible so to mark or describe goods that (even though the defendant may be careful to avoid himself marking the goods with, or advertising them under, a mark that would deceive) subsequent purchasers are induced so to mark them.[73]

14–268   It used to be thought[74] that the tort of passing off is complete only when deceptive goods are sold to a middleman. However, it was held in *BT v. One in a Million* that the tort is committed where a defendant has equipped himself or intends to equip another with an instrument of fraud, even though such cases are probably mere *quia timet* actions.[75]

The defendants were so-called cybersquatters who registered Inter-net domain names such as marksandspencer.com, comprising the

---

[68] *Boulnois v. Peake* (1868) 13 Ch.D. 521n., "Carriage Repository" changed to "New Carriage Bazaar"; *Apollinaris v. Herrfeldt* (1887) 4 R.P.C. 478, CA ("Apollinis"); *Sanitas v. Condy* (1886) 4 R.P.C. 195, 530: 56 L.T. 621 ("Condi-Sanitas"). Lord Macnaghten in the "Camel Hair Belting" case (1896) 13 R.P.C. 218 at 233. See also *Colman v. Farrow* (1898) 15 R.P.C. 198.

[69] See further paras 14–289, 14–290.

[70] As in *Bovril v. Bodega* (1916) 33 R.P.C. 153, where the defendants supplied Oxo-and-Soda when Bovril-and-Soda was asked for.

[71] *Payton v. Snelling* [1901] A.C. 308, 17 R.P.C. 628 at 635, HL; *Schweppes v. Gibbens* (1905) 22 R.P.C. 113 at 120, 121 (CA) 601; *Hennessy v. Keating* (1908) 25 R.P.C. 361 at 367, HL. See *Paterson v. Kit Coffee* (1910) 27 R.P.C. 594 (fraud of predecessors).

[72] *Singer v. Loog* (1880) 18 Ch.D. 395 at 412, cited with approval by Lord Macnaghten in "Camel Hair Belting" [1896] A.C. 199 at 215–216. Hence the established practice of granting injunctions in the form "so as to pass-off or enable others to pass-off"; note that the word is "enable", not "cause", assuming fraud on the part of the "others". See further, *Draper v. Trist* (1939) 56 R.P.C. 429 at 435, 439, CA (citing *Lever v. Goodwin* (1887) 36 Ch.D. 1 at 7). *Trist* was a case on damages: which means that the precise extent of the defendants' wrongful acts was of real importance.

[73] See "Harris Tweed" [1964] R.P.C. 477 at 542 *et seq.*, and at 509, where this is called a "typical passing-off situation".

[74] Based on *My Kinda Town v. Soll* [1983] R.P.C. 15 at 49, where the judge cited, a number of cases in particular *Edelsten v. Edelsten* (1863) 1 De G, J. & S. 185. (My Kinda Town, the "Chicago Pizza" case, was overruled by the CA, but on another point: [1983] R.P.C. 407.)

[75] *BT v. One in a Million* [1999] 1 W.L.R. 903 at 920, CA *per* Aldous L.J. See also at 915–920 for his analysis of the cases.

names of well-known companies. The Internet domain names themselves were held by the Court of Appeal to be instruments of fraud: *BT v. One in a Million*.[76]

The supply of (or even the mere authorisation to use) instruments of deception which the defendant knows are going to be used for passing off (even abroad) is itself a form of passing off which is actionable and takes place when the supply or authorisation occurs.[77] **14–269**

(1) The defendant supplied from England to purchasers in Ecuador single malt whisky together with labels ("Scottish Archer") and empty bottles. The defendant further authorised his Ecuadorian purchaser to use other labels ("White Abbey") which bore his address and which he had registered as a trade mark in Ecuador. The purchaser, to the defendant's knowledge, mixed the whisky with local cane spirit and used the labels on the bottles. The labels were calculated to lead to the belief that the contents were genuine blended Scotch whisky. The defendant was restrained, by Foster J. "from supplying . . . any Scotch Whisky or bottles or labels or other things or documents and from permitting and/or licensing the use of any trade marks or label for the purpose of enabling and/or which are calculated to enable spirits that consist of or include spirits that [are] not [Scotch Whisky] to be passed off in any country as and for Scotch Whisky": *John Walker v. Ost* [1970] R.P.C. 489 at 513. Note that a proviso to the injunction, permitting honest supply of goods which could be used as instruments of deception, was added. *John Walker v. McGibbon* [1975] R.P.C. 506 (OH, Sc.) was a similar case, where the actual sales complained of took place in Scotland.

(2) In a somewhat similar case, an exporter of whisky for foreign admixture who had given the foreign purchaser inadequate advice for avoiding passing off was held liable; the court observing that such an exporter is himself liable only if he "takes part in the passing off": *White Horse v. Gregson* [1984] R.P.C. 84 at 88–9. **14–270**

---

[76] *Op cit.* "Whether any name is an instrument of fraud will depend upon all the circumstances. A name which will, by reason of its similarity to the name of another, inherently lead to passing off, is such an instrument. If a name would not inherently lead to passing off, it does not follow that it is not an instrument of fraud. The court should consider the similarity of the names, the intention of the defendant, the type of trade and all the surrounding circumstances. If it be the intention of the defendant to appropriate the goodwill of another or enable others to do so, I can see no reason why the court should not infer that it will happen, even if there is a possibility that such an appropriation would not take place.": Aldous L.J. at 920.

[77] *John Walker v. Ost* [1970] R.P.C. 489 (illus. below). See also *Saper v. Specters* (1953) 70 R.P.C. 173 at 178–179. Note (at 175) that the box-maker showed the claimants' box to the defendants and solicited orders for an imitation.

Proof of actual deception

14–271 Instances of actual deception need not be proved if the court is otherwise satisfied of the probability of deception[78]; although in the absence of cases of actual deception the evidence adduced must be "of the most cogent sort".[79] On the other hand, cases of actual deception are not necessarily conclusive: for example, where their number is comparatively insignificant[80]; or where the defendant has done nothing but what he was entitled to do, as where he has only used marks common to the trade. Furthermore, people who allow themselves to be deceived seldom make good witnesses, with the result that their evidence can usually be brushed aside by a judge who is not otherwise convinced.[81]

All the circumstances to be considered

14–272 All the circumstances of the case must be considered. Thus where the mark in question is not attached to the goods themselves so as to reach the ultimate purchasers, it may be clear that the trade purchasers to whom the defendant's business is confined are not in danger of being deceived.[82]

Where the alleged passing off is in response to oral orders, the evidence should be clear, and "trap orders" in particular—orders given by agents of the claimant, with the possibility of passing off in mind—must be both clear and fair.[83] This is of particular importance where the claimant's mark resembles a word which is descriptive.[84]

> Where assistants on being asked for "Glacier Mints" supplied other mints of a similar kind which were known locally as "glassy mints," the claimants were held not to have made out their case, there being ample possibility of there having been the misunderstanding which was said to have occurred: *Fox's v. Jobbings* (1932) 49 R.P.C. 352.

---

[78] See para. 14–258, and Parker J. in *Iron-Ox v. Co-operative Wholesale Society* (1907) 24 R.P.C. 425 at 430; *Delavelle v. Stanley* (1943) 60 R.P.C. 103 (*quia timet* action) ("Blue Orchid").

[79] Per Harman J. in *Gor-Ray v. Gilray* (1952) 69 R.P.C. 99 at 105–106; on appeal, 69 R.P.C. 199. Cf. per Roxburgh J. in *Tavener Rutledge v. Specters* [1957] R.P.C. 498 at 502.

[80] *Rutter v. Smith* (1901) 18 R.P.C. 49; and above, para. 14–258; and *Neutrogena, op cit.*

[81] See below, Defences. In *King v. Gillard* (1905) 22 R.P.C. 327, the defendant copied some common elements from the claimant's box.

[82] *Star Cycle v. Frankenburgs* (1907) 24 R.P.C. 46, 405 (use only in trade price lists, etc.); *Fairbank v. Cocos Butter* (1904) 21 R.P.C. 23.

[83] See as to the requirements for a trap order, *Procea v. Evans* (1951) 68 R.P.C. 210; *Stillitz v. Jones & Higgins* (1943) 60 R.P.C. 15; *Cellular Clothing v. White* (1953) 70 R.P.C. 9 at 14. See also Chadwick J. in *Marie Claire v. Hartstone Hosiery Ltd* [1993] F.S.R. 692.

[84] See *Procea v. Evans, supra* ("process" bread); *Cellular Clothing v. White, supra*, 70 R.P.C. 9 at 11.

Where the defendant in response to an order for the claimants' goods by **14–273** their trade name supplies his own goods, it is no defence to say that the persons giving the orders could have discovered, by examination, that the goods supplied did not in fact bear the name.[85]

Obvious differences between the goods themselves are very material to the question of probability of deception.[86]

9. Defences

Table of defences

The defences, other than a simple denial of the acts alleged, which are **14–274** commonly set up, may be tabulated as follows: that—

(1) The name or other badge, which the claimant charges the defendant with having imitated, carried no distinctive reference to the claimant's goods or business.

(2) The defendant has an independent or a concurrent right to use it.[87]

(3) The name or other badge which the defendant is using is not such, or is not so used, as to be calculated to pass off any goods for those of the claimant.[88]

(4) The claimant is debarred from suing the defendant for all or part of the relief he seeks by (a) an agreement, or some personal estoppel[89] (other than those next alluded to); (b) acquiescence[90]; (c) delay[91]; (d) deceptive use of the name or badges he relies on, or because his trade is fraudulent[92]; or (e) E.U. law.[93]

---

[85] *Pearson v. Valentine* (1917) 34 R.P.C. 267 ("Matamac") followed in *French v. Rhind* [1958] R.P.C. 82. See also *Purefoy Engineering v. Sykes, Boxall* (1955) 72 R.P.C. 89 at 93–94, CA; *Procea v. Evans* (1951) 68 R.P.C. 210 at 212. *Broad v. Cast Iron Drainage* [1970] F.S.R. 363, which might appear authority for a different view, depends on the defendant's making it clear what was being supplied before delivery of the goods: see at 368.

[86] *Coleman v. Brown* (1899) 16 R.P.C. 619 ("Wincarnis, Vincalis"); *Reddaway v. Irwell* (1907) 23 R.P.C. 621; 24 R.P.C. 203 ("Lancashire" for hair belting, "Lanco" for balata belting); *Nugget v. Harboro'* (1912) 29 R.P.C. 133 (boot polish and rubber heels). See also *Wilson's v. Meynell* (1929) 46 R.P.C. 80. See further *ante*, para. 14–75, "Common field of activity".

[87] See, as to the right to trade under one's own name, below and para. 14–297; and as to the right to describe honestly the place or origin, etc., of his goods, at para. 14–81, and further, Chap. 13, "Infringement".

[88] Above para. 14–257; and Chap. 18. As to cases where the claimant is not a trader, so that there are no goods, see *ante* para. 14–40 *et seq.*

[89] At paras 13–153 *et seq.*

[90] At paras 13–156 and 13–118 *et seq.*

[91] At paras. 13–158.

[92] At paras 13–160 *et seq.*

[93] See Chap. 15.

(5) There is no likelihood of appreciable damage.

(6) The claimant has no goodwill in this country.[94]

(1) Denial of reputation

14–275 This is a traverse of part of the claimant's case. It may take the form of an allegation that the name or other badge is merely descriptive or has become common.[95] If so, the defence falls under the second head also; and such a positive case must be pleaded. Where the defendant's case is that the claimant has used the badge for too short a time, or in the wrong way, for it to have become distinctive, those points should be pleaded.

(2) Concurrent right

14–276 This defence is discussed below. The most important question here is the right of a man, apart from restriction by contract, to trade honestly under his own name. The statutory right of use given by registration of a mark does not provide a defence to proceedings for passing off by the use of the mark[96]; although it is normally expedient for the claimant in such cases to apply to revoke the registration.

(3) Denial of deception

14–277 This defence also is a mere traverse. It has been considered already.[97]

(4) Estoppel

14–278 The defences collected under the fourth head are precisely analogous to those discussed in Chapter 13[98]; they depend on the same considerations and are governed by the same rules.

(5) Likelihood of damage

14–279 This defence is mainly applicable where the claimant is not a trader[99]; in business name cases where the businesses are not in effective competition[1]; or in cases where the parties deal in different goods.[2] But it may

---

[94] See *ante*, paras 4–54 *et seq.*

[95] Above para. 14–175.

[96] 1994 Act, s.2(2): "... nothing in this Act affects the law relating to passing off". *Van Zeller v. Mason, Cattley* (1907) 25 R.P.C. 37; *Lyle & Kinahan* (1907) 24 R.P.C. 249 at 262; *Eli Lilly v. Chelsea Drug* [1966] R.P.C. 14 at 18. *cf.* in this connection the limited scope of s.11(1) with the width of the final provision of s.2. Registration gives the sort of prima facie case of right to the mark that may affect interlocutory decisions, for instance, provided the mark is not vulnerable for non-use.

[97] See paras 14–257 *et seq.*

[98] See paras 13–153 *et seq.*

[99] See *ante*, paras 14–218 *et seq.*

[1] *e.g.* the newspaper-title cases, *ante*, 14–222.

[2] Since (*ante* para. 14–30) actual damage is not necessary to this cause of action, the claimant who does succeed at the trial in establishing passing off in spite of differences in goods or business will normally have his injunction, although he may be well advised not to take an inquiry as to damages. In interlocutory proceedings, where the case cannot be fully gone into, and where the test is rather whether irreparable damage will result if matters continue as they are until the trial, such matters as differences between the goods are of greater weight. See, *e.g. Lyons Maid v. Trebor* [1967] R.P.C. 222 at 226.

serve in other cases where the matters complained of are too trivial to call for intervention of the court, and may in particular serve to answer a claim for interlocutory relief.

Use of one's own name[3]

Once the claimant has proved the elements necessary for passing off, **14-280** and in particular deception of the public or its likelihood, the concept that the defendant escapes liability because he is making "bona fide" use of his own name, is a difficult one.[4]

The precise nature and extent of this "defence" are none too clear, the rather numerous authorities on the point being difficult to reconcile.[5] The defence is certainly of limited scope, but as yet no superior court has gone so far as to say the defence does not exist. In modern trading conditions, any individual (or company) can adjust their trading style, if they so wish, so as to eliminate deception on the part of the public. In such circumstances, it is difficult to see the justification for upholding any absolute right to trade under one's own name when balanced against the deception of the public or the likelihood of such deception.

The origins of the "defence" lie in certain dicta of Romer J. Certainly, **14-281** the defence does not extend to allowing use of the trader's own name in relation to goods so as to pass off:

"To the proposition of law that no man is entitled so to describe his goods as to represent that the goods are the goods of another, there is no exception."[6]

The difficulty arises on the other half of Romer J.'s proposition:

---

[3] This "defence" is different to that provided in the Trade Marks Act 1994, s.11()(a).
[4] Most, if not all of the cases can be explained on normal principles of passing off (as now understood), without the need for any specific defence but probably only the House of Lords is in a position to explain away all the authorities on this basis. Part of the problem lies in the failure to distinguish clearly between deception and mere confusion. If what we would call "mere confusion" was thought to give rise to liability for passing off, then one can see room for this defence. On the contrary, if passing off is properly limited to cases involving deception or its likelihood. McGechan J. in *Taylors Bros Ltd v. Taylors Group Ltd* [1988] 2 N.Z.L.R. 1 at 23, having stated correctly that (a) the "defence" does not apply if there is actual deception, (b) the "defence" is not required if there is "mere confusion", because there is no passing off, appears to suggest, therefore (c) the "defence" only runs where the court has found only a likelihood of deception. This is a valiant attempt to reconcile the authorities, but it is very difficult to justify such distinctions as a matter of principle—the defence would depend on whether instances of deception came to the claimant's attention. Whether they do or not depends on the circumstances, but it is easy for a court to accept that most do not.
[5] See the analysis of the cases in *Boswell Circus* (*Boswell Wilkie Circus v. Brian Boswell Circus* [1985] F.S.R. 434 (SC, S.A., Natal)), on appeal [1986] F.S.R. 479. See also the analysis of Somers J. in *New Zealand Farmer's Co-operative Association of Canterbury Ltd v. Farmers Trading Co Ltd* (1979) 1 N.Z.I.P.R. 212, summarised by McGechan J. (upheld on appeal) in *Taylor Bros Ltd v. Taylors Group Ltd* [1988] 2 N.Z.L.R. 1. See further, below.
[6] *Rodgers v. Rodgers* (1924) 41 R.P.C. 277 at 291, *per* Romer J., approved in *Parker-Knoll v. Knoll International* [1962] R.P.C. 265, at 279 (Lord Morris) and 284 (Lord Hodson), Lord Guest (at 287) concurring, HL.

"To the proposition of law that no man is entitled to carry on his business in such a way as to represent that it is the business of another, or is in any way connected with the business of another, there is an exception, that a man is entitled to carry on his business in his own name so long as he does not do anything more than that to cause confusion with the business of another, and so long as he does it honestly."[7]

14-282 This proposition, which seems to have originated with Romer J.[8] was doubted by most of the House in *Knoll*.[9] The question is how far it extends. Given that there is no defence, if passing off results from use of the name on goods,[10] or if goods are sold under it,[11] and given that the same must surely be true in relation to services, what is there left that the owner of the name can do? Arguably, the matter turns on the word "confusion." Whenever two people or two companies have the same or similar names, some other people will be uncertain whether they are really the same, or somehow related; that sort of confusion does not in itself involve any misrepresentation by either, so that there will be no passing off.[12] But if that is all this "exception" amounts to, the rule is no different from that governing other sorts of descriptive marks; nor any different from that for marks used on goods[13]:

"It is a question of fact, to be decided on the evidence, whether it is proved that a name or mark has acquired a secondary meaning so that it denotes or has come to mean goods made by a particular person and not goods made by any other person, even though such other person may have the same name. If it is proved on behalf of a claimant that a name or mark has acquired such a secondary meaning, then it is a question for the court whether a defendant,

---

[7] *Rodgers v. Rodgers, supra.*
[8] *Boswell Circus, supra,* at 462 but see *Saunders v. Sun Life* [1894] 1 Ch. 537.
[9] Lord Guest at 287; and two dissentients: Lord Denning at 277 and Lord Devlin at 291.
[10] *Wright, Layman & Umney v. Wright* (1949) 66 R.P.C. 149 at 150–151, CA, illus. below, unaffected, on this point, by the doubts expressed in *Knoll, supra.* The distinction is between using his name as a name and using it as a trade mark; *cf.* using a defendant's address, *Banbury Bldgs. v. Sectional* [1970] R.P.C. 463.
[11] *Parker-Knoll v. Knoll International, supra,* note that the word "Knoll" in question, was held not to be distinctive of the claimants. *Baume v. Moore* [1958] R.P.C. 226 at 236, CA.
[12] Or there may be some historical connection, as in *Habib Bank* [1982] R.P.C. 1 at 31–32, CA.
[13] This is effectively the conclusion reached in New Zealand. When summarising the analysis of Somers J. in the *Farmers* case (at n. 5 above) , McGechan J., in *Taylor Bros Ltd v. Taylors Group Ltd* [1988] 2 N.Z.L.R. 1, acknowledged three limitations on the ostensible scope of this "defence":
"The name used, to come within the exception, must be the actual name of the defendant."
"The exception does not extend to the use of the name "if it will deceive as distinct from merely causing confusion'"
"The exception extends to companies 'with an established business' but 'not to new companies'."
It would seem to follow from this last point that any exception would not extend to companies extending into new areas, either geographical or fields of business.

whatever may be his intention, is so describing his goods that there is a likelihood that a substantial section of the purchasing public will be misled into believing that his goods are the goods of the claimant."[14]

Any exception does not extend to use of abbreviations of the name, **14–283** where the abbreviation increases the risk of confusion.[15]

The claimants, whose principal product was "Wrights' Coal Tar Soap", also used the style "Wrights" on other goods including talcum powder. The defendant, William Frederick Thomas Wright, had commenced to sell toilet preparations about 1934 under the name W. F. T. Wright and about 1943 he changed his trading style to "Wrights' Chemical Company". The claimants at first instance were granted an injunction to restrain the defendant from "passing-off as and for the goods of the claimants pharmaceutical and toilet goods not of the claimants' manufacture or merchandise by the use upon or in connection therewith of the name 'Wright' or 'Wright's' without clearly distinguishing such goods from those of the claimants"—as Greene M.R. said, a common form injunction, according to his recollection and experience. But the claimants were held by the judge not to be entitled to restrain the defendant from carrying on business under a name of which "Wright" or "Wrights" formed part: the real risk of confusion, he said, was in regard to goods sold to the public and not between the respective trading styles by which they were known to the trade. Upon appeal it was held that the second injunction should be granted. The first would give no protection against, for instance, supply of the wrong goods by wholesalers as a result of treating both sorts of goods as "Wrights". The Master of the Rolls stated: "If a man uses his own name and uses it honestly and fairly, and is doing nothing more, he cannot be restrained if confusion results. Once he oversteps the line and confusion results or is calculated to result, the fact that he is using something approaching his own name is no justification"[16]: *Wright, Layman & Umney v. Wright* (1949) 66 R.P.C. 149 at 153, 154. See also where John Thomas Parker formerly connected with a company carrying on business as estate agents under the name "Parkers", set up in business on his own in the same area also as "Parkers", an interlocutory injunction was granted to restrain him from doing so; the judge remarking: "The question is not simply

---

[14] *Per* Lord Morris, *Parker-Knoll v. Knoll International* [1962] R.P.C. 265 at 279.

[15] *Wright, Layman & Umney v. Wright* (1949) 66 R.P.C. 149 at 150 (*arguendo*), 156; *General Radio v. General Radio (Westminster)* [1957] R.P.C. 471; *cf. Aubanel & Alabaster v. Aubanel,* (1949) 66 R.P.C. 343.

[16] This observation would not seem to be affected by the criticism of other remarks of Greene M.R. in this case made in *Knoll, supra,* at [1962] R.P.C. 279 and 284, provided— see above—it is understood as limited to use of the name as a trading style, and not as extending to use of the name as a trade mark for the goods.

whether the defendant can be prevented from using his own name but whether the defendant can be prevented from garnishing that name . . . in such a way that it looks as if the name were being used not by him but by the claimants": *Parker v. Parker* [1965] R.P.C. 323.

Company names

14–284 If the defence exists (see above), it appears to extend to a company with an established business[17] or to a company formed to carry on an established business[18] but the exception does not extend to a company with an established business adopting a new name[19] or to the name of a new company conducting a new business, notwithstanding that the name in dispute may be the personal name of a promoter or other person connected with the company.[20]

14–285   "A new company with a title of which the name 'A', for instance, forms part has none of the natural rights that an individual born with the name 'A' would have."[21]

(1) A German company, which manufactured "Adrema" addressing machines, had, before the war, formed an English company "Adrema Ltd" for the purpose of its trade in the United Kingdom, and allowed the English subsidiary to acquire the entire United Kingdom goodwill in the mark "Adrema". As a result of the war, the two companies ceased to be connected. After the war, the German company (now called "Adrema-Werke GmbH") sought to use its name in trading in its machines in the United Kingdom. When sued by the English company for passing off it offered to submit to a qualified injunction; but Danckwerts J. followed the rather similar "*Sturtevant*" case and granted an absolute injunction (see *post*, paragraph 18–70). The bona fides of the German company were in doubt, but the decision did not rest upon that; whilst in the "*Sturtevant*" case the defendant was an English company newly formed by a foreign parent, but that made no difference—the result (see *per* Danckwerts J. at [1958] R.P.C. 332) would have

---

[17] This follows from *Parker-Knoll v. Knoll International* [1962] R.P.C. 265, notwithstanding Harman L.J. *arguendo* in later proceedings in the same case at [1962] R.P.C. 255; *cf.* at 258. It should be noted, however, that the cases on foreign companies are not altogether easy to reconcile: see the "*Adrema*" and "*Sturtevant*" cases, illus. (1), below.

[18] Since the right to use the name is assignable to the company as part of the goodwill of the business: *ante*, para. 14–141.

[19] For a recent example, see *HFC Bank Plc v. Midland Bank Plc* [2000] F.S.R. 176 at 201–202, Lloyd J. (The case settled on appeal, but any appeal was not going to turn on this point).

[20] *Kingston, Miller v. Kingston* [1912] 1 Ch. 575, 29 R.P.C. 289, illus. *ante*, para. 14–213; *Fine Cotton Spinners v. Cash* [1907] 2 Ch. 184; 24 R.P.C. 533. *cf. Boswell Circus* [1985] F.S.R. 434 at 445, where the South African judge treated the defendant company and "the man behind it" as "for all practical purposes, indistinguishable".

[21] *Per* Joyce J., *Fine Corton Spinners v. Cash, supra*, at 24 R.P.C. 538.

been the same if the parent itself had begun to trade here: *Adrema v. Adrema-Werke* [1958] R.P.C. 323; *Sturtevant Engineering v. Sturtevant Mill* (1936) 53 R.P.C. 430. The distinction from *"Knoll"*, *supra* where the right of the American Knoll company to trade under its own name in this country (by itself or by a British subsidiary) was recognised in spite of passing off, is to be found (it would seem) in the circumstance that in the *"Adrema"* and *"Sturtevant"* cases the British goodwill of the foreign company's business had passed to the claimant, leaving the foreign company somewhat in the position of a vendor of goodwill seeking to go on using the marks in which that goodwill is embodied: *cf. post*, paragraph 14-297. In the *"Knoll"* cases, the parties had never been connected.

(2) The claimant, E. V. Hawtin Ltd, was an importer of gloves, of **14–286** considerable reputation, and alleged that it was known as "Hawtin" or "Hawtins". Its gloves came from Hong Kong. Two merchants, one of them John F. Hawtin, formed a company John F. Hawtin & Co. Ltd, which soon began to import gloves from Hong Kong. Both companies dealt only with the trade, and there was no indication of fraud. Roxburgh J. observed that whilst the defendant could not rely on any exception to any rule (its name could not be treated as that of John F. Hawtin, carrying on business alone or with partners), it had on the facts "a fairly strong moral case". He found the evidence of actual confusion inadequate, and refused an interlocutory injunction: *Hawtin v. Hawtin* [1960] R.P.C. 95. It is always open to the court, where a defendant has a moral case but is in difficulties over the law, to prove hard to satisfy on questions of fact.

(3) The claimant, General Radio Co., was an American company **14–287** but also well known in this country. The defendant, General Radio Co. (Westminster) Ltd was a newly formed British company. The defendant, under the name "General Radio Co.", advertised American radio equipment for sale. In spite of an undertaking by the defendant not to put further advertisements in the press, Roxburgh J. granted an *ex parte* interim injunction to the claimant, restraining the defendant from carrying on business under any name containing the words "General Radio Co." except their own name "General Radio Co. (Westminster) Ltd". But he refused to grant, *ex parte,* an injunction against trading under their full name: *General Radio v. General Radio (Westminster)* [1957] R.P.C. 471. On the full hearing of the motion, an injunction until trial was granted restraining the defendant "from trading in electrical or electronic apparatus under any name containing the words 'General Radio Co.' without clearly distinguishing their goods from those of the claimant: but this order is not to prevent the defendant from trading in their corporate name, provided that equal prominence is given to the words 'Westminster' and 'Limited' as the words of 'General Radio Co'." (at [1957] R.P.C. 496).

14-288   (4) "It is a very strong thing, in the absence of fraud . . ., to grant an injunction which would force the defendant company to change its name before the trial, and really, for practical purposes, decide the issues between the parties before the trial,": *per* Cross J. in *Mansfield v. Gaygirl* [1968] F.S.R. 144. An injunction against issuing advertisements to the public under the company name was granted.

Relevance of fraud

14-289   In the light of the authorities cited above, it would seem clear that in cases of passing off of goods[22] and in cases involving new companies[23] the relevance of the presence or absence of fraudulent intent in "own name" cases is precisely the same as in any other passing-off case.[24] But in cases of confusion of businesses (as distinct from goods), where the defendant is trading under his own name, the claimant must at least prove not merely that some confusion has occurred or is probable but also that the defendant's trading is, if not dishonest, at least unintentionally deceptive. In satisfying a court of this, a strong suspicion of fraudulent intention is naturally of great assistance.

Proximity may be a badge of fraud

14-290   The proximity of the place where the defendant sets up his business to that where a well-known firm is already trading may be evidence to show that, although trading under his own name, the defendant is seeking to take fraudulent advantage of its similarity to the claimant's name. The case of somebody finding a man named Bass and setting up a brewery at Burton as Bass & Co.,[25] and the case of a man starting business as a banker in the Strand under the name of Coutts,[26] have been cited as instances in which it is scarcely conceivable that the use of the name could be honest.

Assumed name or pen name

14-291   Whether or not the same considerations of law as regards a man carrying on a business under his own name apply in the case of a man carrying on a business under an assumed name has not been decided.[27] It has been held that there is no special right to trade under one's nickname.[28]

---

[22] *Parker-Knoll v. Knoll International* [1962] R.P.C. 265 at 284, *per* Lord Hodson.
[23] *Fine Cotton Spinners v. Cash* [1907] 2 Ch. 184 at 190; 24 R.P.C. 533 at 538.
[24] *Parker-Knoll v. Knoll International, supra* [1962] R.P.C. 265 at 285; see also *ante*, para. 14-257.
[25] James L.J. in *Massam v. Thorley* (1880) 14 Ch.D. 748 at 757.
[26] Chitty J. in *Melachrino v. Melachrino Co.* (1887) 4 R.P.C. 215 at 221.
[27] The HL in *Marengo v. Daily Sketch* (1948) 65 R.P.C. 242 ("Kem" and "Kim"), left the point open.
[28] *BIBA Group v. BIBA Boutique* [1980] R.P.C. 413. The defendant prejudiced his case by displaying one of the claimants' advertisements whilst saying he had never heard of them. See also *NAD Electronics Inc v. NAD Computer Systems Ltd* [1997] F.S.R. 380. The man behind the defendant had the nickname Nad, but the judge was not entirely satisfied as to his bona fides.

(1) Jay's Ltd, a London concern, sued to restrain a small Brighton shop from trading as "Jays". There was some evidence of confusion. The defendants, two partners, said that one of them was called Jay; and to evidence from the claimants that her real name was Jacobi replied that she had, when employed by a larger Brighton shop, become known to people in Brighton as "Miss Jay". Eve J. found for the defendants, saying: "The defendant, therefore, as the owner by reputation of the surname 'Jay', has the right to trade under that name": *Jay's v. Jacobi* (1933) 50 R.P.C. 132. But when this case was cited in the *"Wrights"* case, Greene M.R. said of it: "It is perfectly true that the name in which the defendant was carrying on her business at Hove was not her own name in the strict sense; but the judge found that in carrying on that business in that name, which was not her own name, there was no probability of confusion with the well-known business of Jay's in London. Once he had found that, she could carry on her business in the name she was using, since there was no probability of confusion. The reasoning in that case was that there was no probability of confusion. Had Eve J. found on the facts that there was a probability of confusion, I cannot doubt that in the circumstances he would have granted an injunction." The rest of the Court of Appeal concurred: *Wright, Layman & Umney v. Wright* (1949) 66 R.P.C. 149 at 153.

(2) In *Richfield v. Speedy Cables* the claimants' complaint was that **14–292** the defendants had sent out a number of business letters signed "Thomas Richfield". There was a Thomas Richfield prominently associated with the claimants. There were Richfields who were directors of the defendant company but none of them were called Thomas. The signatory of the letter was the stepson of one of them, whose name was not originally Richfield at all but who had called himself "Thomas Richfield" for some years; he was not a director or officer of the defendant company, although he performed "most of the functions of either a director or a secretary". Harman J. granted an interlocutory injunction restraining the defendants from using in connection with their business the name "Thomas Richfield" at all, or using "Richfield" without clearly distinguishing their business from the claimants'—this last, so that the actual Richfield directors could sign letters in their own names: [1957] R.P.C. 47. The action never came to trial.

(3) A company formed to take over a business run by traders **14–293** named Israel and Seabrook was named "Rael-Brook Limited", and two directors, a Mr Seabrook and a Mr Israel, changed their names respectively to Harry Rael-Brook and Graham Rael-Brook. Graham Rael-Brook left the company to become managing director of a company with an entirely different name, trading in similar goods. An *ex parte* application to stop him

531

using his name in advertisements of his company failed.[29] It seems clear that the court regarded this as an "own name" case. It was conceded that Graham Rael-Brook should not use "Rael-Brook" without the Graham.

Other cases of concurrent right

14–294 There are other cases best considered as cases where the defendant has as good a title to use the mark or name complained of as the claimant has to use the mark or name with which (as he alleges) it is likely to be confused: as, for instance, where the defendant has been using his mark or name for nearly as long as the claimant has his[30]; or where both parties are equally unmeritorious.[31] Since, however, there is really no such thing as a right to use a mark or name,[32] such cases require more careful analysis for the purpose of pleading a defence. They may be classified as cases where the mark or name whose use is complained of is distinctive of the defendant, not of the claimant; cases where each party has established an independent reputation and goodwill in particular geographical areas, the dispute arising because one or both have expanded into the area of the other; cases where it is common to the trade, or otherwise not distinctive of either party[33]; cases where in the circumstances the defendant has sufficiently distinguished his goods from those of the claimant[34]; cases where there is no real likelihood of damage[35]; cases where as between claimant and defendant the right to the goodwill the claimant seeks to protect is vested in the defendant, or in neither, or is shared between them[36]; cases where the claimant has no goodwill.[37]

Certain cases of transfer of dissolution of a business here call for more detailed discussion.

---

[29] *Rael-Brook v. Head Shirts* [1963] R.P.C. 6.
[30] *cf.* the limited defence under s.11(3) to actions for infringement, *ante*, para. 13–146 *et seq.*
[31] *cf. Rolls Razor v. Rolls (Lighters)* (1949) 66 R.P.C. 137 at 143; 299 at 301, CA: name "Rolls" adopted by both parties to suggest the quality of a "Rolls-Royce" car.
[32] As distinct from a right to prevent others using it. Note that even the limited right of use given by s.11(1) of the Trade Marks Act gives no defence against proceedings for passing off.
[33] As to marks common to the trade, see *ante*, para. 14–171; as to "otherwise", *cf.* the *Rolls* case, *supra*: or the case of a get-up newly adopted by both parties, or of a descriptive mark.
[34] *e.g.* the "small differences" that suffice to distinguish two names that are equally descriptive: *Office Cleaning v. Westminster* (1946) 63 R.P.C. 39 at 43—or two names or marks that have long been used side-by-side.
[35] *e.g.* cases where no trade is involved (*ante*, paras 14–40 *et seq.*); cases where marks have long been used side-by-side without appreciable confusion.
[36] *cf.* the discussion *ante*, para. 14-218 of disputes over *noms-de-plume*; and *Technical Waxes v. Whitehead* (1953) 70 R.P.C. 230 at 232–233 (defendants alleged right by agreement to use marks concurrently with claimants; but interlocutory injunction granted for protection of public).
[37] *e.g. Anheuser-Busch Inc. v. Budejovicky Budvar Narodni Podnik* [1984] F.S.R. 413, CA.

Purchaser of goodwill

The purchaser of the goodwill of a business (or a partner succeeding to **14–295** it under agreement upon dissolution of partnership) will normally[38] have the right to use the trade name and trade marks under which the business was conducted,[39] even though they comprise the personal name of a late partner,[40] or of any other late owner of the goodwill, but not so as to cast any risk of liability upon the late partner or owner[41] by using his personal name in such manner as to represent that he is still a member of the firm, or carrying on the business.[42]

Partners after dissolution

On the dissolution of a partnership, the goodwill is normally sold; in **14–296** which case, in the absence of special agreement, the right to use the partnership name belongs to the purchaser.[43] But the partners may agree to divide up the goodwill, and if they do, they will each be entitled to make use of the name, in a business similar to that of the partnership, so long as they do not do so deceptively and in particular, do not represent that the others are still their partners.[44]

---

[38] Obviously it depends upon the circumstances and terms of the agreement of sale and purchase. See, *e.g. Dawnay, Day & Co. Ltd v. Cantor Fitzgerald International* [2000] R.P.C. 669.

[39] *Levy v. Walker* (1879) 10 Ch.D. 436, CA; *Currie v. Currie* (1898) 15 R.P.C. 339, Ct of Sess ("Prince Charlie"); *Rickerby v. Reay* (1903) 20 R.P.C. 380 at 388. For cases of colourable purchase of a goodwill, see above paras 14–141 *et seq.*

[40] *Condy v. Mitchell* (1877) 37 L.T. (N.S.) 268, 766. ("Condy's Fluid Co."); *Chappell v. Griffith* (1885) 53 L.T. (N.S.) 459.

[41] *Chatteris v. Isaacson* (1887) 57 L.T. (N.S.) 177. The vendor of the business of "Mme. Elise" agreed that the purchaser should have the exclusive right to use the name "Mme. Elise & Co.". Mme. Elise was his wife's name. Held, the purchaser might use the name only with the addition "& Co." In *Burchell v. Wilde* [1900] 1 Ch. 551, it was held that, upon the division of a solicitor's business between the partners on dissolution, the partner whose name was Burchell would run no risk by reason of the use by the other of the old name, "Burchell & Co". Notice of the change had been given to all the clients. The defendants, in fact, undertook to carry on in business under a different name, namely, Burchell, Wilde & Co. In *Townsend v. Jarman* [1900] 2 Ch. 698; 17 R.P.C. 649, the claimant bought the business of Jarman & Co. Ltd, seedsmen, from a company to whom he and the defendant had, on the dissolution of their partnership, transferred it. He carried on business as "Jarman & Co.", and it was held that the defendant could not complain of this. The defendant had sold the business premises, on which his name "E. J. Jarman" was cut, to the company, who had transferred them to the claimant. It was held that the defendant could not compel the claimant to remove the name.

[42] *Thynne v. Shove* (1890) 45 Ch.D. 577, CA. These partnership cases are not easy to understand. It is difficult to see how continuation of a business under its own name could render former partners liable for its activities; and the cases seem to distinguish here—or some of them do—between cases where the goodwill is actually assigned to the new owners and cases where they merely acquire the business with no explicit assignment of goodwill. It would seem, accordingly, that such cases cannot be considered merely as cases involving passing off, and reference to specialist works on partnership may here be desirable.

[43] It is part of the partnership assets: *Re David and Matthews* [1899] 1 Ch. 378.

[44] *Burchell v. Wilde* [1900] 1 Ch. 551 (Burchell & Co.).

Trader may use his name after the sale of his business, where no contrary agreement

14–297 Where the goodwill of an unincorporated business is sold, or is taken over on the dissolution of a partnership by agreement, without any restrictive condition being imposed upon the late owner or the retiring partner which restrains him from exercising his ordinary right, he is at liberty to start in the same trade again at once under his own name, even though it be the same as, or be similar to, the name under which the old business was, and continues to be, carried on[45]: provided that he does so honestly and without representing to customers that his new business continues or is connected with the business that he has sold.[46] An agreement for the sale of a business carried on under the proprietor's personal name should, accordingly, normally contain appropriate restrictions on his using the name again. The sale of a business conducted by a limited company involving transfer of ownership of the company, raises different considerations, since there can hardly be any justification for giving a similar name to any other company.[47] Even so restrictions on individuals concerned with the old management may be desirable.

Even in the absence of express restrictions the vendor or retiring partner could not trade under the old name if it differed from his own personal name.[48]

Forced sale of goodwill

14–298 A trustee in bankruptcy has no power to contract on behalf of the bankrupt, and the bankrupt is not a grantor so as to be bound by the rule applied in *Trego v. Hunt*.[49] The sale of the goodwill of his business in the bankruptcy, accordingly, throws no obligation upon the bankrupt trader, other than the obligation of the general law, not to represent that

---

[45] *Labouchere v. Dawson* (1872) L.R. 13 Eq. 322.

[46] See below. The cases on this point are old ones, and share the characteristic vagueness of the older "own name" cases. It would seem from the judgment of Parker J., in *Pomeroy v. Scalé* (1907) 24 R.P.C. 177 at 187, that if mere use of his name without proper explanation must necessarily make such a representation, he may not use the name without making the explanation, to each customer if necessary. Buckley J. at 181, put the law slightly differently, but it is submitted that Parker J. would probably be followed today. Probably the vendor may use his own name again, notwithstanding that he thereby reminds customers that he used to be connected with the business sold (provided he does no more), but only on condition that it is absolutely clear that the two businesses are distinct. In *Aubanel & Alabaster v. Aubanel* (1949) 66 R.P.C. 343, the case was treated as on all fours with any ordinary "own name" case: but then, the sale had been some 15 years before, and an injunction was nevertheless granted.

[47] See the discussion, *ante*, para. 14–285, illus. (1), of the *"Adrema"* and *"Sturtevant"* cases. There is indeed some difficulty in reconciling the various lines of authority, and the case cited in n. 45 might well not be followed today.

[48] The grant would then pass the exclusive right to the name: *Pomeroy v. Scale* (1901) 24 R.P.C. 177, but see as to this case, *supra*. See also cases cited in the last three footnotes.

[49] [1896] A.C. 7; see next note.

the business is still carried on by him.[50] The purchaser can accordingly restrain the bankrupt from using a firm name, but not from using his own name.[51]

(1) The claimant had had a cigar factory at Manila, which, owing to **14–299** events consequent on the 1914–18 War, passed into other hands. The claimant retained a factory in Hong Kong and had sold cigars in Shanghai from that factory under similar names and marks to those on the Manila cigars. It was held that the defendant company, assignees of the Manila business, who sold cigars in Shanghai made in the Manila factory, were entitled to do so under similar marks so long as they did not represent their goods to be those of the claimant: *Ingenohl v. Wing On* (1927) 44 R.P.C. 343, PC.

(2) A group of companies traded in the financial sector under the **14–300** name "Dawney, Day". One company in the group was a joint venture, the management of which became deadlocked. An administration order was made with directions for the sale of the business. The administrator sold the business and its goodwill to the defendants, with the right to use the business name "Dawnay, Day Securities" "so far as it is lawfully able to do so. . .". Companies representing the Dawnay, Day group succeeded in preventing the defendants from continuing to use the "Dawnay, Day" name: *Dawnay, Day & Co. Ltd v. Cantor Fitzgerald International.*[52]

The vendor must not represent that his business is the old business, or its successor

The vendor of a business must do nothing, after the sale, which is **14–301** calculated to suggest that he is still carrying on the old business.[53]

A partner, who, after he had sold his share in the business of "John Douglas & Co." to his co-partners, continued to trade as "Churton, Bankart and Hirst, late John Douglas and Co.", was restrained from

---

[50] *Walker v. Mottram* (1881) 19 Ch.D. 355, CA. In *Trego v. Hunt* [1896] A.C. 7. Lord Macnaghten said: "There is all the difference in the world between the case of a man who sells what belongs to himself and receives the consideration, and the man whose property is sold without his consent by his trustee in bankruptcy, and who comes under no obligation, express or implied, to the purchaser from the trustee." See also *Greener v. Morris* [1914] 1 Ch.D. 562 at 566; and as to the effect of a vesting order under Enemy Property legislation, *Reuter v. Muhlens* (1953) 70 R.P.C. 235.

[51] *Wood v. Hall* (1916) 33 R.P.C. 16, Younger J. (sale of goodwill by trustee of deed of arrangement for creditors).

[52] [2000] R.P.C. 669. The Court of Appeal held that the licence to the joint venture company to use the Dawnay, Day name must have been subject to the implied condition that the company would continue to be part of the group.

[53] See *May v. May* (1914) 31 R.P.C. 324. As to subsequent use by the vendor of his own name, see above.

trading as "John Douglas & Co.," or representing that his new business was a continuation of the old business: *Churton v. Douglas* (1859) L.J.Ch. 841.

14–302 The question whether the late owner of a business which has passed into other hands is representing that he is still carrying it on or that a new business of his is its successor, or is only fairly working and advertising the latter business as his own, may be one of difficulty.

The partnership between the parties having expired by effluxion of time, and the goodwill passing under the partnership articles to the claimant, but without any restrictive covenant binding the defendant not to use the firm name or any similar name, the defendant was restrained from issuing a circular to the old customers stating the fact of dissolution and that he had joined a new firm, and asking the customers for a "continuance" of their custom. This was held to be a suggestion, that he was about to carry on, not merely a similar business, as he lawfully might, but the identical business which had passed to the claimant: *Mogford v. Courtenay* (1881) 45 L.T. (N.S.) 303. There is some later authority[54] that he ought to have been restrained from privately soliciting the old customers to deal with him in any terms whatsoever.

---

[54] *Re David and Matthews* [1899] 1 Ch. 378; but the matter is more complex than that: see works on confidential information.

CHAPTER 15

LIMITATIONS ON ENFORCEMENT AND EXPLOITATION

1. Introduction

This chapter is concerned with certain limitations on enforcement of **15–01** registered trade marks, over and above the standard defences to an action for infringement. The limitations discussed in this chapter are essentially derived from law developed at Community and now European Union level. They divide into two principal topics[1]: the first is principally concerned with what has become known as "exhaustion of rights" and the second is concerned with the application of the competition laws of the European Union and the United Kingdom to the exploitation and enforcement of registered trade marks.

The function of this chapter is to examine in detail these limitations on **15–02** the exploitation and enforcement of trade marks. It is beyond the scope of this work to examine wider questions of E.U. law, of Commission practice or general United Kingdom competition law and practice. For these the reader is referred to more general works.[2]

Structure of this chapter

The two principal topics identified above—relating to "exhaustion" **15–03** and "competition" respectively—are dealt with in turn. However, the first topic is conveniently divided under a number of headings. First, it is necessary to explain how the rule of "exhaustion of rights" applies at the level of individual Member States. Section 12 of the Trade Marks Act 1994, derived from Article 7 of the Trade Marks Directive, is one manifestation of the rule. Neither section 12 nor Article 7 contain the whole story. Both carry with them the accumulated case law of the ECJ concerning the application of Articles 28 and 30 (formerly Articles 30

---

[1] Of course, these are not the only aspects of E.U. law which are now relevant to the U.K. law of registered trade marks. The on-going process of harmonisation of the laws of Member States relating to trade marks is dealt with subject by subject in other chapters.
[2] See, *e.g.* Bellamy and Child, *Common Market Law of Competition* (4th ed., 1993 and Supplement 1996, Sweet & Maxwell). A full examination of Community law is contained in the *Encyclopaedia of European Community Law.* A particularly helpful work on Commission practice and procedure is Kerse, *EEC Antitrust Procedure* (4th ed., 1998, Sweet & Maxwell).

and 36) in the field of trade marks and will fall to be interpreted in accordance with any new case law in this area. Accordingly, interpretation of section 12/Article 7 requires a thorough understanding of the existing case law relating to exhaustion of trade mark rights and how it has developed. The development has been somewhat haphazard. In particular, it will be seen that misconceptions about the proper level of trade mark protection[3] underlie some of the more problematic decisions of the European Court in this field.[4]

15–04   The application of the rule of exhaustion in straightforward situations involving intra-E.U. trade calls for little comment. However, the precise limits of the rule, as developed by the European Court, are still being explored, particularly in the repackaging cases. Further current issues are whether the rule applies at all to parallel imports into the EEA, and the position as regards goods which do not originate in the EEA but which are first put on the market in one of the EEA countries which is not also an E.U. State. An issue which has yet to arise, but was foreshadowed in *Dior* concerns whether section 12(2)/Article 7(2) creates a new right. The resolution of these and other undecided issues is greatly assisted by a clear understanding of the principles of E.U. law involved and how they interact. The foregoing gives some explanation as to the structure of this Chapter, which is as follows:

2. Section 12/Article 7 in the Hierarchy of E.U. Law
3. The Development and Application of "Exhaustion of Rights"
4. Repackaging, Relabelling and Rebranding
5. Parallel Imports into the EEA
6. The *Dior* Problem
7. Competition Laws of the E.U. and the United Kingdom
8. Articles 81 and 82
9. Competition Act 1998
10. Trade Marks and Restraint of Trade

2. Section 12/Article 7 in the hierarchy of E.U. law

Interpretation of section 12/Article 7

15–05   Section 12 of the 1994 Act provides as follows:

"Exhaustion of rights conferred by registered trade mark

12(1)—A registered trade mark is not infringed by the use of the trade mark in relation to goods which have been put on the market

---

[3] The context requires a precise evaluation of the function of trade marks, something which is not required in the context of inherent registrability of a mark. There, a mark need only satisfy the minimum requirement of having a distinctive character, and no further investigation of function is required.
[4] Although it should be said that the European Court has had admirable guidance from Advocate General Jacobs in most of the important trade mark cases of the 1990s, from *Hag II* onwards.

in the European Economic Area under that trade mark by the proprietor or with his consent.

(2) Subsection (1) does not apply where there exist legitimate reasons for the proprietor to oppose further dealings in the goods (in particular, where the condition of the goods has been changed or impaired after they have been put on the market)."

Section 12 is derived from Article 7 of the TM Directive. The reference in section 12 to the EEA, as opposed to the reference in the original version of Article 7 to "the Community", is the result of the EEA Agreement.[5] The other slight differences in wording appear immaterial.[6] Since section 12 must be interpreted consistently with Article 7, unless that is impossible,[7] and since consistent interpretation appears possible, in the remainder of this discussion section 12 and Article 7 are treated as being identical.

At the basic level, section 12 poses few problems. Once goods have **15–06** been put on the market by the proprietor or with his consent, his registered trade mark rights cannot be used to prevent further dealings in the goods. The registered trade mark right is said to have been "exhausted" by the first marketing of the goods bearing the trade mark. The limitation contained in section 12(1) has particular relevance in the context of free movement of goods throughout the EEA. Once goods have been placed on the market anywhere in the EEA, national trade mark rights cannot be used to prevent their movement anywhere in the EEA.

One (perhaps unintentional) effect of section 12(1) is that it applies whether or not any inter-state trade is involved. It lays down the rule for domestic exhaustion of rights of trade marks as well as the rule for inter-EEA trade.

The limitation contained in section 12(1) is not absolute. The trade **15–07** mark proprietor may use his registered trade mark rights to oppose further dealings in the goods where there exist legitimate reasons to do so. Section 12(2) gives some non-exhaustive examples of what may constitute legitimate reasons—where the condition of the goods is changed or impaired after they have been put on the market. Other examples of "legitimate reasons" are contained in the case law of the ECJ, particularly under Article 30 (ex 36).[8]

An independent garage in the Netherlands specialised in the sale of second-hand BMW cars and in repairing and maintaining BMWs.

---

[5] Effective from January 1, 1994. The original Art. 7(1) in the Directive was replaced by a version set out in Annex XVII to the EEA Agreement. Essentially, "in the Community" was replaced with "in a Contracting Party".

[6] Art. 7(2) uses the expression "further commercialization of the goods", whereas s.12(2) refers to "further dealings in the goods". In *Paranova* and *Dior*, A.-G. Jacobs commented that "commercialization" in the English version of the Directive appears to be a literal translation of the French word "commercialisation", whereas it would be more normal in English to speak of "further marketing of the goods".

[7] *Marleasing* [1990] E.C.R. I–4135; and *Webb v. EMO Air Cargo* [1993] 1 W.L.R. 49.

[8] See sections 3, 4 and 6 of this chapter, below.

Complaint was made of the use of the BMW mark in advertisements for these goods and services: "BMW Specialist"; "Specialised in BMWs"; "Repairs and maintenance of BMWs". The ECJ held:

(1) In relation to the advertisements for second-hand BMWs, if the trade mark was used in a reseller's advertising in such a way as to give rise to the impression that there is a commercial connection between the reseller and the proprietor, that might give a legitimate reason within Article 7(2). Whether the advertising created that impression is a matter for the national court. On the other hand, if there is no risk that the public will be led to believe there is a commercial connection, the mere fact that the reseller derives an advantage from using the mark in advertisements, provided they are honest and fair, in that they lend an aura of quality to his business does not constitute a "legitimate reason".

(2) In relation to the advertisements for services, Article 7 had no application, but Article 6 had to be interpreted in the same way, as seeking "to reconcile the fundamental interests of trade mark protection with those of the free movement of goods and freedom to provide services in the common market". The same reasoning applied. *BMW v. Deenik.*[9]

15–08 As soon as one moves beyond the basic level, problems begin to appear which cannot be satisfactorily resolved simply from the wording used in section 12/Article 7. For example:

what is the precise scope of the expression "under that trade mark by the proprietor or with his consent"?

how should "consent" be interpreted?

what can constitute a "legitimate reason"?

is "exhaustion" the correct concept?

and, at a deeper level, does the wording of section 12(1) faithfully reflect the state of affairs presented by the EEA Agreement?

The first point is answered below. The second point lies at the heart of the issue concerned with parallel imports into the EEA.[10] The third point lies at the heart of the repackaging cases.[11] The fourth point lies at the heart of a problem which the European Court has created for itself in *Dior* and which it will have to tackle at some point in the future.[12] This problem relates to the scope of protection afforded to, and the true function of, a registered trade mark. The final point gives a further twist to the issue of parallel imports into the EEA.

---

[9] [1999] E.C.R.–I 905; [1999] E.T.M.R. 339.
[10] See section 5, below at paras 15–60 *et seq.*
[11] See section 4, below at paras 15–43 *et seq.*
[12] See section 6, below at paras 15–85 *et seq.*

"Under that trade mark"

Article 7 of the TM Directive is virtually identical to Article 13 of the **15–09** Community Trade Marks Regulation. Despite the fact that the CTM Regulation was passed some six years after the Directive, the *travaux preparatoires* make it clear that the two provisions were drafted at the same time.[13] Both provisions apply to goods put on the market in the EEA *under that trade mark.* That expression is apt for a CTM, but is rather clumsy when transposed into the TM Directive. In the context of the Directive, it must be interpreted as referring not only to the particular national registered trade mark but also all trade marks which: (1) are owned by the same proprietor or by another entity which is economically linked[14]; (2) are identical or virtually identical[15]; and (3) either registered or unregistered[16] which are used by the proprietor or with his consent for putting goods on the market in any state of the EEA. The alternative interpretation is untenable, that it refers only to the particular national trade mark. This is but one example which demonstrates that the proper interpretation of section 12/Article 7 requires knowledge of the accumulated case law of the ECJ on Articles 28 and 30 (formerly Articles 30 and 36) in the field of trade marks.

In two repackaging cases, the European Court has explained the **15–10** proper approach to the interpretation of Article 7. In *Paranova*,[17] the Court held that:

(a) Article 7 comprehensively regulates the question of exhaustion of trade mark rights for products traded in the Community [now EEA];

(b) the Directive must be interpreted in the light of the Treaty rules on free movement of goods;

(c) Article 7(1) reiterates the case law of the Court based on Articles [28 and 30] (ex 30 and 36); and

(d) Article 7(2) must be interpreted in the same way as Article [30] (ex 36).

---

[13] The *travaux preparatoires* also show that the original proposals for the CTM Regulation and TM Directive incorporated a rule of international exhaustion (COM (80) 635 final: [1980] O.J. C351/1). In 1983, the European Parliament proposed the deletion of the rule of international exhaustion and substitution of a rule of Community-wide exhaustion ([1983] O.J. C307/46), a proposal which was adopted by the Commission (COM (84) 470 final—for the Regulation; COM (85) 793 final for the Directive). As for the exceptions to exhaustion early attempts to codify the existing case law of the European Court were abandoned, giving rise to the expression "legitimate reasons", which is wide enough to catch all relevant existing and future case law of the ECJ.

[14] See, *e.g. IHT Internationale Heiztechnik v. Ideal Standard* [1994] E.C.R. I–2789 at 2847, para. 34; [1994] 3 C.M.L.R. 857; [1995] F.S.R. 59.

[15] The case law of the ECJ brushes aside slight differences in marks used in different Member States, *e.g.* Cotonelle/Cottonelle and goes further in the repackaging cases, allowing rebranding, provided it is objectively necessary (*e.g.* Dalacine/Dalacin C/Dalacin) where different marks are used in different Member States. See further below.

[16] *cf. Merck v. Stephar* [1981] E.C.R. 2063; [1981] 3 C.M.L.R. 463. See further below.

[17] *Bristol Myers Squibb v. Paranova* [1996] E.C.R. I–3457; [1996] F.S.R. 225 (AG); and [1997] F.S.R. 102 (ECJ). See further below.

These principles were confirmed in *Loendersloot*.[18] The reason why Article 7 must be interpreted in the same way as Article 30 of the Treaty[19] is because, in the context of trade marks, both provisions are intended to reconcile the fundamental interest in protecting trade mark rights with the fundamental interest in the free movement of goods within the Common Market. In order to resolve the finer points of the repackaging cases and the issue over parallel imports into the EEA, it helps to have a precise understanding of how this process of reconciliation works. A comprehensive interpretation of Article 7 requires us to start from first principles.

The conflict between national trade mark rights and the free movement of goods

15–11 One of the principal objectives of the Treaty of Rome was and remains to establish a single or internal market comprising the territories of all the Member States "characterised by the abolition, as between Member States, of obstacles to the free movement of goods, persons, services and capital".[20] It has long been recognised that a conflict exists between the aim of a single market and the presence of national intellectual property rights, which are particularly suited to dividing up the market along national boundaries.

15–12 In order to resolve the conflict in the field of trade marks, the European Court has had to balance the competing interests: the fundamental aim of the single market and the free movement of goods in the Community against the fundamental interest in the protection of trade mark rights. The way in which the balance is achieved depends upon the relative status of the interests or principles involved.

The principles enshrined in the Treaty

15–13 At the highest level are the principles set out in the E.C. Treaty (originally the Treaty of Rome).[21]

> Article 2: "The Community shall have as its task, by establishing a common market and an economic and monetary union and by implementing common policies or activities referred to in Articles 3

---

[18] [1997] E.C.R. I–6227, para. 18.

[19] Note that it is not permissible to interpret s.12 directly in relation to Art. 30 (ex 36). As a national measure implementing a provision of the Directive, s.12 must be interpreted consistently with Art. 7. Art. 7 may then be interpreted in the light of Art. 30 and applicable case law, even though the result may be exactly the same: see *Paranova* [1996] E.C.R. I–3457, paras 25, 26; [1997] F.S.R. 102.

[20] E.C. Treaty, Art. 3(a).

[21] The E.C. Treaty has been amended by the Single European Act 1986, the Treaty on European Union (the E.U. Treaty) in 1992 and the Treaty of Amsterdam 1997. Art. 12(1) caused renumbering of some of the most familiar Articles. Hence the familiar old Arts 30 and 36 are 28 and 30, and the old Arts 85 and 86 are now 81 and 82.

and 4, to promote throughout the Community a harmonious, balanced and sustainable development of economic activities, . . .".

Article 3: "For the purposes set out in Article 2, the activities of the Community shall include, as provided in this Treaty and in accordance with the timetable set out therein:

(a) the prohibition as between Member States, of customs duties and quantitative restrictions on the import and export of goods, and of all other measures having equivalent effect, . . .

(b) an internal market characterised by the abolition, as between Member States, of obstacles to the free movement of goods, persons, services and capital;

   . . .

(g) a system ensuring that competition in the internal market is not distorted; . . ."

Article 28 (ex 30): "Quantitative restrictions on imports and all measures having equivalent effect shall be prohibited between Member States."

Article 30 (ex 36): "The provisions of [Article 28] shall not preclude prohibitions or restrictions on imports, exports or goods in transit justified on the grounds of . . . the protection of industrial and commercial property. Such prohibitions or restrictions shall not, however, constitute a means of arbitrary discrimination or a disguised restriction on trade between Member States."

Article 295 (ex 222): "This Treaty shall in no way prejudice the rules in Member States governing the system of property ownership."

Community legislation

At the second level, for our purposes, are provisions of Community **15–14** legislation made pursuant to the powers conferred in the E.C. Treaty. The relevant legislation comprises the CTM Regulation and the Trade Marks Directive.

United Kingdom legislation

First, it is necessary to have regard to section 2(1) of the European **15–15** Communities Act 1972, which expressly provides for the supremacy of the Community Treaties, although the key Treaty referred to in the Act is the Treaty establishing the European Community—the "E.C. Treaty"[22]:

---

[22] Other treaties are also within the scope of the Act, but they have no relevance to trade mark law. The E.C. Treaty was previously known as the Rome Treaty. The E.C. Treaty has been amended by the Single European Act 1986, the Treaty on European Union (the E.U. Treaty) signed at Maastricht in 1992 and the Treaty of Amsterdam 1997.

"all such rights, powers, liabilities, obligations and restrictions from time to time created or arising by or under the Treaties, and all such remedies and procedures from time to time provided for by or under the Treaties, as in accordance with the Treaties are without further enactment to be given legal effect or used in the United Kingdom shall be recognised and available in law, and be enforced, allowed and followed accordingly."

In the context of the Trade Marks Act 1994, that provision serves to reinforce what is already obvious: that the relevant provisions of the 1994 Act implement and are derived from the Trade Marks Directive. However, section 12/Article 7 represent just one manifestation of the more general rule known as "exhaustion of rights", and in order to explain how the hierarchy of interests is reconciled, it is necessary to track something of the development of the "exhaustion of rights" rule.

3. The development and application of "exhaustion of rights"

Introduction

15–16 The "exhaustion of rights" principle was developed by the European Court in a series of cases in the 1970s. Seeking to prevent the use of industrial property rights to divide the Common Market, the Court initially sought to achieve its purpose via the use of Article 81 (ex 85). This had a number of difficulties so, once the route via Articles 28 and 30 (ex 30 to 36) was seen, Article 85 ceased to play a significant role in the development. This switch is an indication of the rather haphazard development of the principle.

Principle of exhaustion of rights

15–17   "The proprietor of an industrial or commercial property right protected by the law of a Member State cannot rely on that law to prevent the importation of a product which has lawfully been marketed in another Member State by the proprietor himself or with his consent."[23]

This principle does not depend upon whether the first marketing is in a Member State where there is an industrial property right. It is enough that the goods are put into free circulation by or with the consent of the holder of the right.

Merck could not obtain a patent in Italy although they patented the drug concerned in every other Member State. The defendants

---

[23] *Terrapin v. Terranova* [1976] E.C.R. 1039 at 1061, para. 6; [1976] 2 C.M.L.R. 482 at 505–506; *Merck v. Stephar* [1981] E.C.R. 2063; [1981] 3 C.M.L.R. 463.

imported Merck's product marketed by Merck in Italy. *Held*: The free movement rules of the Treaty prevented Merck from asserting their Dutch patent to prevent sales in Holland: *Merck v. Stephar*.[24]

It follows that the expression "exhaustion of rights" is not wholly apt; **15–18** there need be no right exhausted in the Member State of first marketing, nor does the rule apply where the holder of the right has received a royalty under his right from a compulsory licensee.[25] Nonetheless, the expression is now firmly established.[26]

Evolution of "exhaustion of rights"

The first step was the creation of the distinction between the *existence* of **15–19** the property right and its *exercise*. This step was necessary to overcome Article 222 (now 295): "This Treaty shall in no way prejudice the rules in Member States governing the system of property ownership."

1. Grundig, of Germany, appointed Consten their "sole representative" in France. Consten registered GINT (Grundig INTernational) in France subject to a declaration that it was intended to be placed solely on Grundig's goods. Additionally, Consten undertook to transfer the mark to Grundig (or abandon it altogether) if they ceased to be sole distributors. Grundig used the GINT mark on all their goods, including their German goods. Consten sought to use the GINT trade mark to prevent parallel imports from Germany of Grundig goods. A complaint to the Commission that Grundig and Consten had infringed Article 85 (now 81) was upheld by the Court. The Court recognised the French registration but went on to say "the fact nevertheless remains that it was by virtue of an agreement with Grundig that it was able to effect registration." "Articles 36, 222 and 234 of the Treaty . . . do not exclude any influence whatever of Community law on the exercise of national industrial property rights."[27] Consten was restrained from using its national trade mark rights to prevent parallel imports.

Following *Grundig*, this dichotomy between *existence* and *exercise* of industrial property rights became well established.[28]

---

[24] See n. 16, *supra*.
[25] Case 19/84 *Hoescht v. Pharmon* [1985] 3 C.M.L.R. 775, ECJ (no right of free circulation for drugs sold by compulsory licensee). The compulsory licence is regarded as a state measure, not a permission from the holder of the right.
[26] In the previous edition of this work, the rule was called the free circulation rule. We continue to consider the notion of "free circulation" as more accurate, but "exhaustion of rights" is very firmly established (*e.g.* in s.12/Art. 7) despite being something of a misnomer, as explained in the text.
[27] *Consten and Grundig v. Commission* [1966] E.C.R. 299 at 345; [1966] C.M.L.R. 418 at 476.
[28] See, *e.g. Merck* [1981] E.C.R. 2063 at 2082, para. 11, by the date of which the dichotomy is taken for granted.

15-20   The second step involved the shift from emphasis on Article 85 (now 81) to Article 30 (now 28). The crucial piece of evolution was the decision to treat the reference in Article 30 to "measures having equivalent effect" as including all industrial property rights. This led, eventually, to the implementation of the three stage test which was inherent in what was Articles 30 to 36. First, Article 30 contained the overriding rule "without prejudice to the following provisions" that quantitative restrictions on imports and all measures having equivalent effect between Member States were prohibited. Secondly, of the following provisions, only Article 36 provided a possible justification for the enforcement of an industrial property right so as to prohibit such imports. But the enforcement must be "justified on grounds of . . . the protection of industrial and commercial property." And, thirdly, there is no justification if such enforcement constitutes "a means of arbitrary discrimination or disguised restriction upon trade between Member States."

15-21   The shift to Article 30 took place in the early 1970s. In *Grundig* there had been some almost passing reference to Article 36, but the reference was a little muddled and seems to have been on the basis that Article 36 operated, by way of analogy, as an exception to Article 85. The cases following first indicated the difficulty of the Article 85 approach and then its virtual abandonment.

> 2. Sirena in Italy had acquired the trade marks "Prep" and "Good Morning" by a series of transactions in the 1930s and 1940s. In part there was an assignment from a United States corporation, Mark Allen, and in part (as part of the arrangements with Mark Allen, however) an original registration in the name of Sirena. Novimpex imported goods bearing the marks into Italy from a German licensee of Mark Allen. The European Court reasoned that the original arrangements between Mark Allen and Sirena fell within Article 85 because, although they were apparently over, as active trading arrangements, "it is both necessary and sufficient that they continue to produce their effects after [the Treaty entered into force]": *Sirena v. Eda.*[29]

This reasoning was clearly particularly artificial. The transactions had occurred years before the Treaty. Moreover there were considerable difficulties about the status of the assignment. It seemed to follow that the original assignment to Sirena was invalid—which was a patently absurd result.[30]

15-22   Neither in *Sirena* nor in the next case *Deutsche Grammophon*, was there an express reference to Article 30 itself. But *Deutsche Grammophon* saw a

---

[29] [1971] E.C.R. 69 at 83, para. 12; [1971] C.M.L.R. 260 at 274. Note that the translation in C.M.L.R. is not exactly the same as that in E.C.R.. The latter is the authoritative text. The Italian court's final ruling against Sirena, following the Art. 177 reference, is reported at [1975] 1 C.M.L.R. 409.

[30] And one which the Italian court refused to find in the subsequent proceedings by resorting to a fairly artificial process of reasoning—see [1975] 1 C.M.L.R. 409.

much greater emphasis on the rules for the free movement of goods. The Article 85 reasoning of the earlier cases could hardly be applied because there was no agreement or the like involved. The case represents the first stage in the shift from Article 85 to Article 30.

    3. DG sued Metro in Germany for copyright (strictly "distribution right") infringement in respect of the latter's importation and sale of DG made records from France. The action failed.

The Court noted that even if the exercise of the right did not fall within **15–23** Article 85, the free movement rules should be considered. It stated that the effect of Article 36 "only admits derogations from [the free movement principle] to the extent to which they are justified for the purpose of safeguarding rights which constitute the specific subject-matter of such property". And it went on to state that the use of industrial property rights on the sole ground that initial distribution did not take place on the national territory concerned would be repugnant to the Treaty if it thereby isolated national markets. It concluded by its first formulation of the free movement rule in the following terms:

> "It would be in conflict with the provisions prescribing the free movement of products within the common market for a manufacturer of sound recordings to exercise the exclusive right to distribute the protected articles, conferred upon him by the legislation of a Member State, in such a way as to prohibit the sale in that State of products placed on the market by him or with his consent in another Member State solely because such distribution did not occur within the territory of the first Member State": *Deutsche Grammophon v. Metro*[31]

A number of cases following *Deutsche Grammophon* saw a natural **15–24** expansion of the rule first stated in its narrow form as above. Thus it was applied to trade marks and patents. It reached its most general form, as applying to all forms of industrial property and whether or not a particular national right was exhausted, in *Merck*. And, through successive cases, the Court clarified the legal basis of the rule by particular reference to Article 30.

"Essential function" and "specific subject-matter" of trade marks

Concepts of particular importance which were developed along with the **15–25** rule as to goods in free circulation were the notions of the "essential function" and "specific subject-matter" of an industrial property right. When inter-state trade may be affected by the enforcement of such a right, such enforcement must be justified on the grounds of protection of

---

[31] [1971] E.C.R. 487 at 499–500; [1971] C.M.L.R. 631 at 656–658, para. 13.

the right. In deciding what is or is not justified, regard must be had to what is the essential purpose or function of the right. Initially, the Court was prepared to be bold in declaring the essential purpose—the specific subject-matter—narrowly so that interferences to inter-state trade were kept to a minimum. This was probably the result of the early perception that trade marks were somehow less worthy of protection than other industrial property rights.[32] The balance did not begin to be restored until *HAG II.*

15–26   The first reference to "specific subject-matter" arose in *Deutsche Grammophon*.[33] Since then the concept has widened. In relation to patents the Court has said "the substance of a patent right lies essentially in according the inventor an exclusive right of first placing the product on the market."[34] The Court's definition of the specific subject-matter of trade mark rights was first given in *Centrafarm v. Winthrop*,[35] and was as follows:

> "In relation to trade marks, the specific subject-matter of the industrial property is the guarantee that the owner of the trade mark has the exclusive right to use that trade mark, for the purpose of putting products protected by the trade mark into circulation for the first time, and is therefore intended to protect him against competitors wishing to take advantage of the status and reputation of the trade mark by selling products illegally bearing that trade mark."

15–27   In *HAG I*,[36] the Court referred to the "basic function" of a trade mark as being "to guarantee to consumers that the product has the same origin" and in *Pfizer* it was stated:

> "The main function of a trade mark is to give the consumer or final buyer a guarantee of the identity of origin of the marked product,

---

[32] The marks at issue in *Sirena v. Eda*, "Prep" and "Good Morning" no doubt contributed to this perception: "The exercise of a trade-mark right is particularly apt to lead to a partitioning of markets, and thus to impair the free movement of goods between States which is essential to the Common Market. Moreover, a trade-mark right is distinguishable in this context from other rights of industrial and commercial property, inasmuch as the interests protected by the latter are usually more important, and merit a higher degree of protection, than the interests protected by an ordinary trade mark.": [1971] E.C.R. 69 at 82, para. 7; [1971] C.M.L.R. 260 at 273.

[33] [1971] E.C.R. 487 at 500, para. 11; [1971] C.M.L.R. 631 at 657: "Article 36 only admits derogations from that freedom [*i.e.* of inter-State trade] to the extent to which they are justified for the purpose of safeguarding rights which constitute the specific subject-matter of such property."

[34] *Merck* [1981] E.C.R. 2063 at 2081, para. 9; [1981] C.M.L.R. 463 at 481, para. 9. And see also *Centrafarm v. Sterling Drug*, [1974] E.C.R. 1147; [1974] 2 C.R.L.R. 480, at para. 9: "In relation to patents, the specific subject-matter of the industrial property is the guarantee that to the patentee, to reward the creative effort of the inventor, has the exclusive right to use an invention with a view to manufacturing industrial products and putting them into circulation for the first time, either directly or by the grant of licences to third parties, as well as the right to oppose infringements."

[35] [1974] E.C.R. 1183 at 1194, para. 8; [1974] 2 C.M.L.R. 480 at 508. Note: the unofficial C.M.L.R. translation of this paragraph is significantly different.

[36] [1976] E.C.R. 1039 at 1061, para. 6; [1976] 2 C.M.L.R. 482 at 506.

by enabling him to distinguish this product, with no risk of confusion, from products of a different origin."

The decision in *HAG I* was eventually reversed by the European Court **15–28** in *HAG II*[37] (see below). In *HAG II*, the Court clearly recognised the essential value of trade marks. They enable enterprises to gain customers by the quality of their goods and services, and for that purpose a trade mark must constitute a guarantee that all products bearing it have been manufactured under the supervision of a single enterprise. The Court restated that the specific subject-matter of a trade mark is:

"to grant the owner the right to use the mark for the first marketing of a product and, in this way to protect him against competitors who would like to abuse the position and reputation of the mark by selling products to which the mark has been improperly affixed."

And the essential function of a trade mark was stated to be:

"to give the consumer or final user a guarantee of the identity of the origin of the marked product by enabling him to distinguish, without any possible confusion, that product from others of a different provenance."

It will be seen below that, although these concepts of essential function and specific subject-matter have retained a core consistency, they are used flexibly to adapt to particular situations which come before the European Court. This is readily apparent in the repackaging cases, which are discussed in detail in the next section of this chapter.

Goods of different quality in different states

Situations of this type fall to be decided under section 12 of the 1994 Act **15–29** and Article 7 of the TM Directive. Bearing in mind that Article 7 must be interpreted in the same way as Article 30 (ex 36) of the E.C. Treaty, one can predict the outcome of the two typical situations which might arise.

The first is where the trade mark owner markets goods of different **15–30** quality under the same mark in different Member States. He cannot use his trade mark rights to prevent the free movement of both types of goods throughout the EEA. The most that local law can require is that the public are warned of the different quality of the imported goods.

Imerco, in Denmark, ordered from Broadhurst in the United Kingdom, china services having a particular decoration. Strict quality standards were set, with the result that some 1,000 sub-standard services were rejected. Imerco agreed with Broadhurst that the

---

[37] [1990] I E.C.R. 3711; [1990] 3 C.M.L.R. 571; [1991] F.S.R. 99.

latter could sell the rejects but not in Scandinavia. Broadhurst sold some of the rejects to United Kingdom wholesalers with a prohibition on resale to Denmark. Dansk Supermarket purchased some of the rejects and put them on sale in Denmark. Imerco sued in Denmark for trade mark and copyright infringement. The European Court held that the enforcement of those rights was prevented by Article 30 (now 28), although that did not preclude the possibility of action under consumer protection laws if the conditions of actual sale to the public infringed those laws. *Dansk Supermarket v. Imerco*.[38]

15–31 The second situation is where the proprietor markets goods of one quality under one mark in some Member States and goods of another quality under a different mark in different Member States. Free circulation of both types of goods could not be prevented. On the other hand, a parallel trader could not substitute one mark for the other just because the first mark was better known in a particular Member State.

Marks of common origin

15–32 "Marks of common origin" is a shorthand for the situation which sometimes arises where marks, originally in common ownership, become divided between separate undertakings. This situation raises particular problems in deciding how to balance the free movement of goods in the EEA against the enforcement of trade mark rights. Initially, the European Court did not get the balance quite right, probably because at the time it perceived trade mark rights to be less worthy of protection than other industrial property rights.

1. Originally the HAG trade mark was owned in Germany and Benelux by HAG Germany. In 1935 the Belgian and Luxembourg trade mark registrations were transferred to a subsidiary, HAG Belgium. HAG Belgium was confiscated during the war as being enemy property. As a result, the HAG trade marks in Germany on the one hand and Belgium and Luxembourg on the other were vested in entirely separate enterprises. By the date of the action, the Benelux rights had become vested in Van Zuylen Freres. HAG Germany, through an agent, sought to sell its HAG coffee in Luxembourg whereupon VZF sued for infringement. *Held* (on a reference to the European Court) that "one cannot allow the holder of a trade mark to rely on the exclusiveness of a trade mark right—which may be the consequence of the territorial limitation of national legislation—with a view to prohibiting the marketing in a Member State of goods legally produced in another Member State under an identical trade mark having the same origin": *HAG I*.[39]

---

[38] [1981] E.C.R. 181; [1981] 3 C.M.L.R. 590.
[39] *HAG I* [1974] E.C.R. 731 at 734, para. 12; [1974] 2 C.M.L.R. 127 at 143. The language of the C.M.L.R. report is different but not, in this instance, materially so.

This so-called "common origin" rule went further than the doctrine of **15–33** exhaustion of rights. In particular it did not depend on any exercise of the right of first marketing. Each of the owners of a divided mark was entitled to sell throughout the Community under the mark, whether by himself or through others. The opportunity to reconsider this rule arose in *HAG II.*

2. After the decision in *HAG I,* the VZF firm was purchased by a Swiss company which disposed of most of VZF's coffee business apart from the HAG trade marks. The firm was transformed into a subsidiary of its new owner, trading under the name SA CNL-SUCAL NV ("HAG Belgium"). HAG Belgium then began to supply HAG coffee to the German market, whereupon HAG Germany sued in Germany for infringement. *Held* (on a reference to the European Court) Articles 30 and 36 do not preclude the exercise by a party of trade mark rights to oppose the importation of similar goods marked with the same or confusingly similar trade mark "even though the mark under which the disputed products are imported originally belonged to a subsidiary of the enterprise which opposes the importation and was acquired by a third enterprise as a result of the expropriation of that subsidiary." "Free movement of the goods would undermine the essential function of the trade mark": *HAG II.*[40]

HAG II involved a recognition by the European Court of the essential **15–34** value of trade marks in enabling enterprises to gain customers by the quality of their goods or services. For that purpose a trade mark must constitute a guarantee that all products bearing it have been manufactured under the supervision of a single enterprise.[41] The severity of the "common origin" rule was relaxed, although the judgment in *HAG II* left a number of issues unresolved.

3. The mark "Tayto" was devised by a trader in the Republic of Ireland. An agreement in 1956 gave the use of the "Tayto" name together with selling and production rights in Northern Ireland to the claimant and in due course the claimant obtained a registration for the mark in the United Kingdom. Both traders flourished and competed in each other's territories but kept to their respective territories in their use of the Tayto mark. By the time the United Kingdom and Ireland joined the E.C., the restrictive aspects of the 1956 agreement had ceased to be operative. The defendant imported crisps into Northern Ireland from the Republic and was sued for passing-off and trade mark

---

[40] *HAG II* [1990] I E.C.R. 3711; [1990] 3 C.M.L.R. 571; [1991] F.S.R. 99.
[41] Perhaps the surprising aspect of *HAG II* is the emphasis on the fact that national trade marks are territorial and the function of a trade mark must also be seen as territorial.

infringement. *Held* (before *HAG II* was decided) that on the facts, the common origin doctrine from *HAG I* did not apply because the marks had never been in common *ownership*; nor were they the result of a subdivision of trade mark rights by agreement. *Tayto (Northern Ireland) Ltd v. McKee.*[42]

15–35 One of the issues left unresolved in *HAG II* was whether the common origin doctrine applies if a mark is divided voluntarily but not as part of a deliberate market sharing arrangement? This issue arose in *Ideal Standard*.

4. Registrations of the mark "Ideal Standard" for heating installations and sanitary ware in France and Germany were originally held by national subsidiaries (SA and GmbH, respectively) in the same group. Economic difficulties in about 1976 led to the group ceasing its activities in heating installations, GmbH trading in sanitary ware only, and eventually to the assignment by SA of its business interests in heating installations together with the French trade mark for heating installations to CICH. SA retained the trade mark for sanitary ware. IHT, the German subsidiary of CICH, began to sell heating installations in Germany under the Ideal Standard mark. GmbH sued for infringement of its registration relating to sanitary ware. The European Court held that the considerations in *HAG II* applied whether the splitting of the trade mark was compulsory or by voluntary assignment: *Ideal Standard.*[43]

Essentially, cases involving marks of common origin will be decided on mainstream principles developed under Articles 28 and 30 (ex 30 and 36), there being no special or separate doctrine relating to marks of common origin.[44]

15–36 There is one further aspect of *Ideal Standard* which is worthy of note. It was argued that the assignment of the mark carried with it an implied consent to the assignee putting goods bearing the mark into circulation. This was rejected, on the basis that the consent implicit in an assignment is not the consent required for application of the doctrine of exhaustion of rights.

---

[42] [1991] 3 C.M.L.R. 269 (High Court, Northern Ireland). For another pre-*HAG II* decision, see *Re "Klint"* [1988] 1 C.M.L.R. 340, a decision of the German Federal Supreme Court.

[43] *IHT Internationale Heiztechnik v. Ideal Standard GmbH* [1994] E.C.R. I–2789.

[44] Even before *HAG II*, it had been decided that the common origin doctrine did not apply where the trade mark rights were divided between the Community and elsewhere: *EMI v. CBS* [1976] E.C.R. 811; [1975] 2 C.M.L.R. 235 (the trade mark "Columbia" in the hands of EMI throughout the EEC and in the hands of CBS in the USA as a result of past and now-spent agreements, mergers and de-mergers. EMI held entitled to prevent sale of CBS "Columbia" records unless the word "Columbia" was obliterated).

Free movement of goods, consumer protection and unfair competition/passing off

Most, if not all, Member States have national provisions which can be **15–37** described generally as preventing unfair competition. Increasingly, areas previously covered by general unfair competition provisions are being supplanted by E.U. legislation—there are, for example, a number of Directives which are concerned with consumer protection.[45] Since all these measures can interfere with the free movement of goods, the question arises as to how the conflict is resolved.

Initially, the Court appeared to accept that the need to protect **15–38** producers against unfair competition and consumers against deception regarding the origin of products could constitute justification on grounds of public policy under Article 36 (now 30). Subsequent case law has made it clear that, since Article 36 (now 30) derogates from a fundamental rule of the Treaty enshrined in Article 30 (now 28), it must be interpreted strictly and cannot be extended to objectives—such as protection against unfair competition and consumer protection—which are not expressly referred to in Article 36.[46] The justification for the restriction on the free movement of goods must be found elsewhere.[47]

In *Cassis de Dijon*[48] the Court first articulated a formula whereby the **15–39** restriction on free movement of goods caused by national unfair competition legislation could be justified in order to satisfy overriding or mandatory requirements, which include protection against unfair competition and the defence of the consumer, provided that the legislation is proportionate to its objective. The objective must not be capable of being achieved by measures which are less restrictive of intra-Community trade.[49] In the application of this formula, the risk of misleading consumers cannot override the requirements of the free movement of goods unless the risk is sufficiently serious.[50] In assessing the level of risk, the relevant criterion is the presumed expectations of an average consumer who is reasonably well-informed and reasonably observant and circumspect.[51]

---

[45] *e.g.* Directive 79/112 on the labelling, presentation and advertising of foodstuffs; Directive 84/450 on misleading advertising.

[46] See, *e.g. Commission v. Ireland* [1981] E.C.R. 1625, paras 7–8; *Kohl v. Ringelhan & Rennett* [1984] E.C.R. 3651, para. 14.

[47] See the Opinion of A.-G. Jacobs in Case C–312/98, *Schutzverband gegen Unwesen in der Wirtschaft e.V. v. Warsteiner Brauerei Haus Cramer GmbH & Co. KG*, of May 25, 2000, paras 55–56.

[48] [1979] E.C.R. 649; [1979] 3 C.M.L.R. 494.

[49] "*Cassis de Dijon*" [1979] E.C.R. 649, para. 8; *Pall v. Dahlausen* [1990] E.C.R. I–4827, para. 12; [1990] E.C.R. I–4827, para. 12; *Yves Rocher* [1993] E.C.R. I–2361, para. 12; and *Mars* [1995] E.C.R. I–1923, para. 15.

[50] *Graffione* [1996] E.C.R. I–6039, para. 24, and see below.

[51] *Gut Springenheide and Tusky v. Oberkreisdirektor Steinfurt* [1998] E.C.R. I–4657, paras 30–32. Those interested in the development of the "average consumer" test should consult paras 23–29 of the Opinion of A.-G. Fennelly in Case C–220/98, *Estee Lauder Cosmetics v. Lancaster Group*, September 16, 1999. Of course, the test has now been deployed in the field of registered trade marks, in *Lloyd Schuhfabrik Meyer v. Klijsen Handel* [1999] E.C.R. I–3819, para. 26, to the global assessment required for infringement under the 1994 Act, s.10(2), and by the Court of Appeal in *Bach and Bach Flower Remedies Trade Marks* [2000] R.P.C. 513, to the test for distinctiveness.

In Italy, the registration of "Cotonelle" for toilet paper was declared invalid as being liable to mislead the public into thinking the goods contained cotton, when they did not. In addition, the proprietor was ordered to cease use of the mark, under unfair competition laws. Use of the mark "Cottonelle" continued in France and Spain, where the registrations survived. Fransa parallel imported French goods into Italy. Graffione, a former wholesaler of the products in Italy, objected on the grounds of unfair competition. It was not clear whether the prohibition on use of the mark in Italy applied only to the (former) proprietor or to all. If the former, then unfair competition law could not be used to prevent Fransa parallel importing because Graffione had the ability to do the same. If the prohibition applied to all use of the mark in Italy, then the prohibition had to be necessary to ensure consumer protection, proportionate to that objective and incapable of being achieved by measures which are less restrictive of intra-Community trade. "The national court must, in particular, examine whether the risk of misleading consumers is sufficiently serious to be able to override the requirements for the free movement of goods": *Fratelli Graffione SNC v. Ditta Fransa*.[52]

15–40   In the United Kingdom context, cases of this type are rare, probably because the argument that the free movement of goods requires deception of the public in the United Kingdom is a difficult one. There is greater scope for conflict with more general laws of unfair competition, which do not necessarily depend on proof of deception or its likelihood. It is possible to conceive of a claim in passing off where the Court would have to balance the risk of deception against the requirement for the free movement of goods, particularly if the case was near the borderline, where the risk was slight and only applied to a limited class of people.[53] The wider issue of whether the "average consumer" test should be adopted generally in the law of passing off is dealt with in Chapter 14.

"Arbitrary discrimination or a disguised restriction"

15–41 The last sentence of Article 30 (ex 36) must be seen as a potent reserve weapon available against any attempt to use industrial property rights artificially to divide the EEA, supposing that any such attempt has otherwise overcome the free circulation rules.[54]

Application to service marks

15–42 The considerations discussed above are not directly applicable to trade marks used in relation to services. However, the European Court would no doubt regard as equally objectionable any use of a mark registered in

---

[52] [1996] E.C.R. I–6039; [1997] F.S.R. 538.
[53] Equally, on suitable facts, an order of the "without sufficiently distinguishing" type could be too restrictive of inter-state trade.
[54] *Dowelhurst* is an example, in the event that the views expressed by Laddie J. on necessity and notice are held to be incorrect. See paras 15–53 *et seq.*, below.

respect of services to interfere with the free circulation of goods or services within the EEA, should suitable facts arise.

4. Repackaging, relabelling and rebranding[55]

In the previous edition of this work, it was stated, somewhat **15–43** optimistically, that the limitation of trade mark rights in repackaging cases was now settled—trade mark rights (if enforceable by national law[56]) cannot be enforced to prevent parallel imports from elsewhere in the EEA where the importer has re-packaged the goods fairly. The position can continue to be summarised in that way, although further detail is required. Again, it seems sensible to summarise the evolution of the law in this area to explain its current state.

Originally, different principles were thought to apply to cases of **15–44** repackaging (where the same mark was used in the relevant Member States) as opposed to the rebranding or re-affixing cases (where the trade mark owner used different marks in different Member States and the parallel importer affixed the mark used in the country of importation). However, by the time of *Pharmacia*,[57] it was realised that repackaging, relabelling and rebranding shade into one another, raising very similar issues. It was in *Pharmacia* that the European Court held that the same principles apply.

The commercial significance of repackaging by parallel importers, **15–45** particularly but not exclusively in the field of pharmaceuticals, has required further definition of how the balance is to be struck between the basic interests in free movement of goods and in trade mark rights. In seeking to strike this balance, the decisions of the European Court have again displayed a tendency to be influenced by the particular facts of the case, which have produced some unfortunate consequences— particularly the requirement that the repackager must give notice to the proprietor. Again, the notions of "specific subject-matter" and "essential function" are used to explain how the balance is to be achieved.

Specific subject-matter

Part of the specific subject-matter is the right to prevent use of the trade **15–46** mark which is liable to impair the guarantee of origin, as stated in *Hoffmann-La Roche*:

"In relation to trade marks, the specific subject-matter of the industrial property is the guarantee that the owner of the trade

---

[55] "Re-affixing" is the term used by the European Court to describe the situation where the mark on the goods is replaced by the mark used in the country of import— "rebranding" would seem to be a more accurate term.
[56] See the 1994 Act, s.10(6).
[57] *Pharmacia & Upjohn v. Paranova*, October 12, 1999. See further below.

mark has the exclusive right to use that trade mark, for the purpose of putting products protected by the trade mark into circulation for the first time, and is therefore intended to protect him against competitors wishing to take advantage of the status and reputation of the trade mark by selling products illegally bearing that trade mark. In order to answer the question whether that exclusive right involves the right to prevent the trade-mark being affixed by a third person after the product has been repackaged, regard must be had to the essential function of the trade-mark, which is to guarantee the identity of the origin of the trade-marked product to the consumer or ultimate user, by enabling him without any possibility of confusion to distinguish that product from products which have another origin. This guarantee of origin means that the consumer or ultimate user can be certain that a trade-marked product which is sold to him has not been subject at a previous stage of marketing to interference by a third person, without the authorisation of the proprietor of the trade-mark, such as to affect the original condition of the product. The right attributed to the proprietor of preventing any use of the trade-mark which is likely to impair the guarantee of origin so understood is therefore part of the specific subject-matter of the trade-mark right."[58]

15–47   Eurim-Pharm imported an antibiotic sold under the trade mark Vibramycin. They re-packaged the goods to comply with German rules but in such a way that the trade mark was clearly visible. The re-packaging made it clear that the goods were imported and that Eurim-Pharm was responsible for the re-packaging. The European Court held that the German trade mark was unenforceable because the "consumer or final buyer cannot be misled as to their origin": *Pfizer v. Eurim-Pharm*[59]

The *Paranova* guidelines

15–48   In *Paranova*,[60] the Court summarised and elaborated on the previous re-packaging cases as follows:

> "Save in the circumstances defined in Article 7(2), Article 7(1) of [the Directive] precludes the owner of a trade mark from relying on his rights as owner to prevent an importer from marketing a product which was put on the market in another Member State by the owner or with his consent, even if that importer repackaged the product and reaffixed the trade mark to it without the owner's authorisation.

---

[58] *Hoffmann-La Roche v. Centrafarm* [1978] E.C.R. 1139 at 1164, para. 7; [1978] 3 C.M.L.R. 217, para. 14.
[59] [1981] E.C.R. 2913; [1982] 1 C.M.L.R. 406, applying the criteria in *Hoffmann-La Roche, ibid.*, at para. 14. Photographs of the goods both before and after re-packaging appear at [1982] E.I.P.R. 84.
[60] *Bristol-Myers Squibb v. Paranova A/S* [1996] E.C.R. I–3457; [1996] E.T.M.R. 1.

Article 7(2) of [the Directive] must be interpreted as meaning that the trade mark owner may legitimately oppose the further marketing of a pharmaceutical product where the importer has repackaged the product and re-affixed the trade mark unless:

(1) it is established that reliance on trade-mark rights by the owner in order to oppose the marketing of repackaged products under that trade mark would contribute to the artificial partitioning of the markets between Member States; such is the case, in particular, where the owner has put an identical pharmaceutical product on the market in several Member States in various forms of packaging, and the repackaging carried out by the importer is necessary in order to market the product in the Member State of importation, and also carried out in such conditions that the original condition of the product cannot be affected by it; that condition does not, however, imply that it must be established that the trade-mark owner deliberately sought to partition the markets between Member States; [the "market partitioning condition"]

(2) it is shown that the repackaging cannot affect the original condition of the product inside the packaging; such is the case, in particular, where the importer has merely carried out operations involving no risk of the product being affected, such as, for example, the removal of blister packs, flasks, ampoules or inhalers from their original external packaging and their replacement in new external packaging, the fixing of self-stick labels on the inner packaging of the product, the addition to the packaging of new user instructions or information, or the insertion of an extra article; it is for the national court to verify that the original condition of the product inside the packaging is not indirectly affected, for example, by the fact that the new external or inner packaging of the repackaged product or new user instructions or information omits certain important information or gives inaccurate information, or the fact that an extra article inserted in the packaging by the importer and designed for the ingestion and dosage of the product does not comply with the method of use and the doses envisaged by the manufacturer;

(3) the new packaging clearly states who repackaged the product and the name of the manufacturer in print such that a person with normal eye-sight, exercising a normal degree of attentiveness, would be in a position to understand; similarly, the origin of an extra article from a source other than the trade mark owner must be indicated in such a way as to dispel any impression that the trade mark owner is responsible for it; however, it is not necessary to indicate that the repackaging was carried out without the authorisation of the trade mark owner;

(4) the presentation of the repackaged product is not such as to be liable to damage the reputation of the trade mark and of its owner; thus, the packaging must not be defective, of poor quality, or untidy; and

(5) the importer gives notice to the trade mark owner before the repackaged product is put on sale, and, on demand, supplies him with a specimen of the repackaged product."[61]

15-49 The propositions concerning Article 7(1) of the TM Directive were stated in terms which apply to all goods, whereas the specific guidelines on Article 7(2) (the so-called *Paranova* guidelines) were stated in terms which applied only to pharmaceutical products. In *Loendersloot*,[62] the Court treated the Paranova guidelines as applicable to all goods, with only minor variations. One particular variation from *Loendersloot* (a relabelling case) should be noted:

"The person carrying out the re-labelling must, however, use the means which make parallel trade feasible while causing as little prejudice as possible to the specific subject matter of the trade mark right. Thus, if the statements on the original labels comply with the rules on labelling in force in the Member State of destination, but those rules require additional information to be given, it is not necessary to remove and reaffix or replace the original labels, since the mere application to the bottles in question of a sticker with the additional information may suffice."[63]

15-50 The principles stated in *Hoffmann-La Roche* were extended in *Dior*:

"According to the case law of the Court concerning the repackaging of trade-marked goods, the owner of a trade mark has a legitimate interest, related to the specific subject-matter of the trade mark right, in being able to oppose the commercialisation of those goods if the presentation of the repackaged goods is liable to damage the reputation of the trade mark."[64]

Pharmacia

15-51 Pharmacia marketed an antibiotic, clindamycin, under a variety of marks. It used the trade mark "Dalacin" in Denmark, Germany and Spain, the trade mark "Dalacine" in France and the trade mark

---

[61] [1996] E.C.R. I–3457 at 3543–3545; *cf.* [1996] E.T.M.R. 1 at 21. Note that the E.T.M.R. report does not include the Court's answers to the questions referred. The passages quoted are answers 2 and 3.

[62] *Frits Loendersloot v. George Ballantine & Son Ltd* [1997] E.C.R.–I 6227, where the parallel traders removed the original labels to strip off identification codes and replaced them with original labels or copies.

[63] [1997] E.C.R.–I 6227 at 6260, para. 46.

[64] *Parfums Christian Dior v. Evora* [1998] 1 C.M.L.R. 737 at 766, para. 43.

"Dalacin C" in the other Member States. The existence of the different marks was explained by an agreement with American Home Products in 1968 pursuant to which AHP assisted Pharmacia in obtaining suitable trade mark protection. The parallel importer, Paranova, had two sources of the drug: it purchased capsules in France (Dalacine) and injection phials in Greece (Dalacin C). After repackaging, the drugs were marketed in Denmark under the mark Dalacin. The Court affirmed and elaborated on the test of necessity: *Pharmacia*.[65]

The Court clarified, in *Pharmacia*, what was meant by the first *Paranova* **15–52** condition relating to market partitioning. It held that this meant the replacement of the trade mark must be objectively necessary if the proprietor is to be precluded from opposing it and added (at paras 43–49):

"It follows that it is for the national courts to examine whether the circumstances prevailing at the time of marketing made it objectively necessary to replace the original trade mark by that of the importing Member State in order that the product in question could be placed on the market in that State by the parallel importer. This condition of necessity is satisfied if, in a specific case, the prohibition imposed on the importer against replacing the trade mark hinders *effective access to the markets* of the importing Member State. That would be the case if the rules or practices in the importing Member State prevent the product in question from being marketed in that State under its trade mark in the exporting Member State. This is so where a rule for the protection of consumers prohibits the use, in the importing Member State, of the trade mark used in the exporting Member State on the ground that it is liable to mislead consumers.

In contrast, the condition of necessity will not be satisfied if replacement of the trade mark is explicable solely by the parallel importer's attempt to secure a *commercial advantage*." (emphasis added).

Quite how the national courts are supposed to decide the postulated antithesis between "effective access to the market" and "commercial advantage" was not explained. Naturally that issue arose shortly afterwards, in *Dowelhurst*.

Dowelhurst[66]

Four drug companies brought proceedings against parallel **15–53** importers who engaged in various forms of repackaging. The drug companies focused in particular on (a) whether the repackaging

[65] Case C–379/97, *Pharmacia & Upjohn v. Paranova*, October 12, 1999, [1999] All E.R. (E.C.) 880; [2000] F.S.R. 621, cited passages at 631.
[66] *Glaxo & others v. Dowelhurst & Swingward* [2000] E.T.M.R. 415; [2000] F.S.R. 529.

was "necessary" and (b) the lack of notice given by the parallel importers. As Laddie J. commented, these issues were only manifestations of a fundamental difference of view between the parties as to how domestic trade mark law and the principle of the free movement of goods and exhaustion of rights under the Treaty were to be reconciled.

The drug companies appeared to treat the *Paranova/Pharmacia* guidelines as establishing virtually a stand-alone test with which the parallel traders had to prove compliance in order to avoid infringement. They also took the view that virtually any type of repackaging, overlabelling and advertising carried out by the parallel importers was not "necessary",[67] contending that "necessary" meant essential and not commercially desirable. Even if the repackaging was necessary, the drug companies initially contended that no notice had been given, but later accepted that they had received notice once the repackaged product appeared on the market.

15–54 In a detailed judgment, Laddie J. set about putting the *Paranova/ Pharmacia* guidelines into their proper context, *i.e.* as a part of the balancing exercise between the free movement of goods and enforcement of trade mark rights. He summarised the position in this way:

"(A) Subject to further clarification from the ECJ and the points made below, the core principles underlying Articles 28 and 30 of the Treaty of Rome as applied to intellectual property right cases are as follows. Free movement of goods is fundamental to the creation, operation and development of the Common Market. Derogations from it are only possible where justified under Community law. One such justification exists where the principle of free movement of goods would give protection to activities which undermine an intellectual property right by harming that right's specific subject matter or function. The derogation extends no further than the justification for it. As a consequence, activities which do not harm the specific subject matter of the rights do not fall outside, but are protected by, the principle of free movement of goods. Even where derogation appears to be justified in accordance with the preceding concepts, if it is shown that the proprietor of the rights, deliberately or otherwise, placed his intellectual property rights in the way of free movement of goods for reasons which are not objectively justifiable or is using them to interfere with free movement of goods in a way which is not objectively justifiable, the derogation will not be allowed to prevail and the principles of free movement of goods continue to apply."[68]

---

[67] See, *e.g.* para. 94–95 of the judgment [2000] E.T.M.R. 415 at 453; [2000] F.S.R. 529 at 564.
[68] [2000] E.T.M.R. 415 at 493–494, para. 193(A). [2000] F.S.R. 529 at 600. Note how this passage summarises the hierarchy of principles involved. The last sentence reflects the second part of Article 30: such a derogation would "constitute a means of arbitrary discrimination or a disguised restriction on trade between Member States". In the body of one judgment, these core principles are discussed at para. 34.

Necessity

In context, there was no "stand-alone" requirement of necessity. If there **15–55** was, Laddie J. was of the view that "necessity is proved when it is shown that the use is reasonably required to overcome actual or potential hindrance to further commercialisation of the products. That would be so even if the means adopted is only one of a number of alternative, equally effective, means of achieving that goal". (para. 193(G)).

Notice

So far as the notice requirement was concerned, the judge traced its **15–56** progress from *Hoffmann-La Roche* through the later cases, citing an observation of Advocate-General Jacobs from *Paranova*[69]:

"The precise justification for a requirement that the trade mark owner must receive prior notice of the repackaging is not clear from the judgment in *Hoffmann La-Roche v. Centrafarm*, and there may be circumstances in which such notice would be superfluous."

Laddie J. nonetheless felt compelled by the case law to find that:

"Absent clarification and reconsideration by the ECJ, it appears to be the law, and subject to indications in *Dior* to the contrary effect, that a proprietor can complain about repackaged goods which have had the mark reapplied to the packaging if no prior notice has been given by the importer. His right to do so appears to be unqualified and, in particular, it is not dependent on showing that the activities of the importer will cause the proprietor or his marks any harm."

The judgment of Laddie J. in *Dowelhurst* is a powerful and detailed **15–57** analysis of the case law of the ECJ in this area. A number of questions have been referred to the European Court.[70] The Court should agree with the analysis of Laddie J. and should dispense with the requirement of notice altogether. Due to the detail, the Court is likely to be especially reliant on the assistance of the Advocate-General.

"Disguised restriction"

Oxazepam was sold in the United Kingdom under the mark **15–58** Serenid D and in the Netherlands under the mark Seresta by two different companies within the same group. The parallel importer

---

[69] [1996] E.C.R. I–3457 at 3496, para. 86. In *Dowelhurst*, see paras 135, 193(I).
[70] To catch up with a reference made in November 1999 by the Vienna Regional Court of Appeals for further clarification in relation to the *Paranova* guidelines.

claimed that it was entitled to import Serenid D from the United Kingdom into Holland to sell it there under the Seresta mark. The European Court ruled that the mark owner was justified (within the meaning of Article 36) in preventing the application of his mark to the goods even though he had marketed those goods under a different mark elsewhere in the Community. However, it went on to hold that the exercise of the right *may* constitute a disguised restriction on trade within the meaning of Article 36. It indicated that such would be the case if the mark proprietor had pursued a policy of using different marks in different Member States in order to partition the Common Market: *Centrafarm v. American Home Products.*[71]

15–59 It has yet to be decided what constitutes a practice which gives rise to a "disguised restriction". It should be enough to show that partitioning of the market was an obvious consequence of the policy (the "objective" test), the alternative being a subjective test that partitioning must have been the purpose behind the policy. The European Court is likely to prefer the former view, on the basis that a man must be taken to intend the foreseeable consequences of his own acts.[72] The Court is also likely to take the view that the bigger pharmaceutical companies are well aware of the consequences of adopting different marks in different territories. The decision of the ECJ in *Dowelhurst* and similar cases may shed light on this topic.

5. Parallel imports into the EEA

Summary

15–60 In theory, parallel imports into the EEA could be dealt with according to one of three possible regimes:

1. International exhaustion—with the result that trade mark rights cannot be used to prevent imports into the EEA of goods placed on the market anywhere in the world under the trade mark (subject to Article 7(2) of the TM Directive considerations);
2. Community or EEA-wide exhaustion—with the result that EEA trade mark rights can be used to prevent, without consent (which, in practice, will have to be virtually express consent), imports into the EEA of goods placed on the market elsewhere in the world bearing the trade mark;
3. Some intermediate possibility, decided on a case-by-case basis.

15–61 The European Court has already ruled out option 1, in *Silhouette* and *Sebago*. For reasons which are explained in detail below, it is suggested

---

[71] [1978] E.C.R. 1823; [1979] 1 C.M.L.R. 326.
[72] The German Supreme Court has, however, preferred the subjective view: *Hoffmann-La Roche v. Centrafarm* [1984] 2 C.M.L.R. 561 (replacement not allowed because difference in packs between different states not intended to partition market artificially).

that the European Court will, expressly or by implication, rule out option 3 and rule that option 2 applies, unless or until the E.U. decides, as a matter of economic policy, to change its position.

A related issue concerns the status of parallel imports into EEA countries which are not also E.U. Member States. This is dealt with at the end of this section.

The applicable principles

As explained above, the decisions of the European Court in this area of **15–62** the law can be analysed according to the hierarchy of principles. For present purposes, the overriding principles concern the single market and the free movement of goods within that market of the EEA— Articles 2, 3 and 28. Industrial property rights are accommodated according to the terms of Article 30. The corollary is that if the enforcement of an industrial property right does not interfere with those principles (nor the competition principles) then it is left unaffected.

Silhouette and *Sebago*

The case law of the European Court has demonstrated that the **15–63** principles referred to in the preceding paragraph do have a role to play in cases where products are parallel imported into the EEA. If one Member State were to implement a rule of international exhaustion of trade mark rights, then genuine products placed on the market any- where in the world under a particular trade mark could be imported into that Member State, and a national trade mark could not be enforced to prevent such imports.[73] Those products would then be on the market within the EEA. Either they would be permitted to circulate freely within the EEA or, possibly, Member States which did not agree with international exhaustion might seek to restrict their circulation as goods which were not legitimately put on the market in the EEA. The consequence would be either that a rule of international exhaustion would have been imposed on the EEA by one country or there would be considerable interference in the operation of the single market. It was therefore inevitable that the European Court would rule, as in *Silhouette* and *Sebago*, that no Member State may impose a rule of international exhaustion.[74]

---

[73] Presumably the national court would refuse to enforce a CTM, for the same reasons.
[74] Before *Silhouette* was decided, the EFTA Court issued an Advisory Opinion to a court in Norway (an EEA country, but not a member of the E.U.) on Art. 7(1) of the TM Directive. The EFTA Court concluded that Art. 7(1) left it open to EFTA states to decide whether they wish to introduce or maintain the principle of international exhaustion with regard to goods originating from outside the EEA. This conclusion was reached on the basis that the purpose of the EEA is different to the E.C./E.U., and that the principle of free movement of goods in the EEA applies only to goods *originating* in the EEA, whereas for the E.C. the principle applies to any goods which are put on the market in the Community. Therefore the EEA principle of free movement of goods did not apply to the Maglite torches which originated and were parallel imported from the USA: *Mag Instrument Inc. v. California Trading Co.* [1998] E.T.M.R. 85. See paras 15–81 to 15–84, below.

(1) Some 21,000 pairs of out-of-fashion sunglasses bearing the mark Silhouette were sold by a representative of the Austrian trade mark proprietor to Bulgaria, apparently on condition that they should be sold in Bulgaria or in the former states of the USSR and not exported to other countries. This condition was not proved so the reference to the European Court proceeded on the *assumption* that no consent had been given that the sunglasses could be put on the market in Austria. In those circumstances, the parallel importer argued that Article 7 of the Directive left it open to Member States to provide for international exhaustion. This was rejected, the European Court holding that Article 7 could not be interpreted as leaving it open to the Member States to provide in their domestic law for exhaustion of the rights conferred by a trade mark in respect of products put on the market in non-member countries. Essentially, if one Member State imposed a rule of international exhaustion, this would either mean international exhaustion applied throughout the EEA or it would give rise to barriers within the EEA to the free movement of goods. On the facts before the Court, there was no issue concerning consent within Article 7(1): *Silhouette*.[75]

(2) Sebago sold shoes under the trade marks "Docksides" and "Sebago". Genuine shoes were obtained from El Salvador and sold in Belgium by GB-Unic. Before the Belgian courts, GB-Unic ran two arguments: the first was that Sebago had not prohibited export from El Salvador and accordingly should be deemed to have given implied consent to the marketing of the goods in the Community. This argument was dismissed on the facts. The second argument, which was the only one referred to the European Court, was to the effect that, to prove consent, it was sufficient to show that the same type of goods bearing the marks had been lawfully marketed in the EEA with the consent of the proprietor. This argument was dismissed, because it would, for practical purposes, impose a rule of international exhaustion for all parallel imports: *Sebago*.[76]

The outcome of these cases was not at all surprising bearing in mind that during the drafting of the CTM Regulation and the TM Directive,

[75] [1998] F.S.R. 729. ECJ. *cf. Javico* below.
[76] [2000] R.P.C. 63, A.-G. and ECJ. Although the *Sebago* (the so-called "all or none") argument was dismissed as not relevant in *Davidoff* by Laddie J., there was a sound basis for it. The argument was based on the essential function of a trade mark, *i.e.* to guarantee to the consumer the identity of the product's origin, the object being to enable him to distinguish that product without any risk of confusion from those of different origin. GB-Unic were arguing that the mark on the genuine goods sold by them continued to perform this essential function (see, in particular, para. 16 of the judgment). To put this argument in another way, the sale of the genuine goods by GB-Unic caused no damage to the specific subject matter of the trade mark. The fact that this reasoning was rejected is a further indication that the issue of parallel imports from outside the EEA has nothing to do with the function of trade marks and depends upon economic policy. See further, below.

the decision was taken not to introduce a rule of international exhaustion. The only other alternative was Community or EEA-wide exhaustion, which is what Article 13 of the CTM Regulation and Article 7 of the Directive provide.

The next stage

The next stage is, effectively, a refinement of the reasoning underlying **15–64** *Silhouette* and *Sebago*. If no Member State is permitted to impose a rule of international exhaustion, it must follow that no Member State may implement a rule having equivalent effect. This would occur if one Member State adopted an approach to Article 7 of the TM Directive, and particularly to the issue of consent within Article 7(1) which was radically different to the approach adopted in other Member States. The corollary of this is that, given the same facts, the courts in all Member States ought to reach the same decision on whether or not consent had been given to the products being put on the market in the EEA.

The *Davidoff* decisions

(3) Aftershave bearing the mark "COOL WATER" was manufac- **15–65** tured in France for distribution worldwide. The parallel imports were obtained from Singapore, where the distributor had undertaken not to sell outside his Territory and to oblige his customers to refrain from such sales. No other contractual restrictions were imposed. The product codes on the goods had been partly obliterated, to impede tracing of the source of the parallel goods. The parallel importers argued that the trade mark proprietor had impliedly consented to the goods being imported into the EEA: *Davidoff.*

These same facts came before the English High Court and the equivalent **15–66** court in Scotland. In England, Laddie J. dismissed an application for summary judgment and referred certain questions to the European Court, at the same time making his view plain that "*Silhouette* has bestowed on a trade mark owner a parasitic right to interfere with the distribution of goods which bears little or no relationship to the proper function of the trade mark right". By contrast, in Scotland, on apparently identical facts, Lord Kingarth effectively struck out the defence of implied consent.

Summary of the differences in approach

Underlying the approach of Laddie J. was the (correct) belief that the **15–67** importation of these products, marketed in identical form throughout the world, would cause no damage whatsoever to the specific subject matter of a trade mark. The trade mark on the goods would tell the truth concerning the origin and quality of the goods. To that starting point, one adds the principle of English law, drawn from cases such as *Betts v. Willmott* and *National Phonograph Co. of Australia v. Menck*, that there is a rebuttable presumption that, in the absence of full and explicit restrictions being imposed on purchasers at the time of purchase, the proprietor is treated as consenting to the goods being imported and sold in the EEA. Against that background, the issue of consent is much more likely to be decided in a manner which reflects the essential function of a trade mark.

15–68   By contrast, Lord Kingarth focused directly on the issue of consent. There was no allegation of express consent. Therefore, were the circumstances such as to give rise to an arguable case of implied consent? On the facts, the judge decided not, leaving aside considerations as to whether these parallel imports would cause any damage to the specific subject matter of the trade mark. Lord Kingarth expressly recognised that the action had been brought for commercial purposes, to protect the price differential which existed between Singapore and the United Kingdom.

The different approaches are now analysed in more detail.

Davidoff in England

15–69   Under Article 7(1) of the TM Directive, Laddie J. summarised the principles as follows[77]:

(1) "Within the EEA, the principle of exhaustion of rights applies to trade marks, as to other intellectual property rights. The result is that where goods bearing a trade mark are put on the market within the EEA by the proprietor of the mark or with his consent, his ability to use his trade mark rights to prevent or interfere with further distribution of his goods within the Community is removed (subject to Article 7(2)).

(2) This exhaustion of rights is indefeasible. It is not dependent on the proprietor's consent, deemed or otherwise, to further exploitation of the trade marks. It is an automatic and unavoidable legal consequence of his having put the goods on the market in the EEA or having agreed to them being put on the market in the first place. In other words, once he has consented to the marketing of the *goods*, he cannot use his trade marks to prevent the goods being distributed throughout the Community.

(3) Where goods bearing a trade mark are put on the market outside the EEA by the proprietor of the mark or with his consent ('authorised external goods'), his ability to use his trade

---

[77] [1999] R.P.C. 631, at 644–645, para. 38.

mark rights to prevent or interfere with further distribution of them within the Community is not removed. That is to say there is no principle of indefeasible international exhaustion.

(4) It is not open to a Member State under its own domestic law to deem the proprietor to have agreed irreversibly to allow unfettered movement and sale of authorised external goods within the EEA by reason only of the fact that he put them on the market outside the EEA. That would be to introduce international exhaustion by the back door.

(5) As a corollary of this, the proprietor of the mark used on authorised external goods may chose to retain his ability to object to importation into, circulation within and sale within the EEA, or he may choose to permit such importation, circulation and sale.

(6) Subject to the provisions of Article 7(2), the proprietor of a registered trade mark cannot use it to prevent authorised external goods from entering the EEA if he has agreed, expressly or otherwise, to such entry or he has, directly or otherwise, placed the goods in the hands of a third party under conditions which give the third party a right to distribute and onward sell them without restriction.

(7) In deciding whether the third party has a right to distribute and onward sell them without restriction regard must be had to all the relevant circumstances including the nature of the goods, the circumstances under which they were put on the market, the terms of any contracts for sale and the provisions of any applicable law.

(8) In particular the rights of the third party can be determined by the law of the contract of supply to that customer or the law of the non-EEA country in which the sale to the third party takes place. Where that law includes a rebuttable presumption that, in the absence of full and explicit restrictions being imposed on purchasers at the time of purchase, the proprietor is treated as consenting to the goods being freely imported into and sold in the EEA, courts within the EEA are free to recognise the effect of that law and to allow importation of the authorised external goods accordingly."

In addition to the comments made above, three particular points arise **15–70** from this summary:

(a) The rebuttable presumption which is at the heart of proposition (8) appears to be peculiar to English law. Due to its effects, as explained above, it is most unlikely that the European Court will agree with this proposition.

(b) The particular matters referred to in proposition (7) foreshadow proposition (8). The European Court would be likely to view the "relevant circumstances" rather differently—more in keeping with the approach of the Scots judge (see below).

(c) These propositions draw together two different situations—parallel imports within and into the EEA—in order to advocate that both should depend on the same principles. The notion underlying the whole judgment is that a trade mark should not give the proprietor "the parasitic right to interfere with the distribution of goods which bears little or no relationship to the proper function of the trade mark right."[78] This notion employs concepts developed by the European Court in order to balance the fundamental interest in free movement of goods against the fundamental interest in protecting trade mark rights. However, the European Court is likely to take the view that it is inappropriate to employ these concepts out of that context, not least because the overriding principles of the single market in the EEA and free movement of goods within that market actually require the opposite conclusion.[79] In other words, from the Community law point of view, there is no reason to restrict the rights conferred by the trade mark to prevent parallel imports from outside the EEA. In fact, there is a positive reason not to restrict those rights, because to do so would interfere with the single market and the free movement of goods within that market.

15-71 There is one further problem with the approach to the issue of consent taken by Laddie J. It comes extremely close to imposing consent, particularly in circumstances where the activities complained of evidently cause no damage to the essential function or specific subject-matter of the trade mark. If this was the correct approach to consent in section 12/Article 7, why should the same approach not apply in section 9/Article 5? One could argue that an act of infringement should interfere with or damage the essential function or specific subject-matter of a trade mark. In the vast majority of cases it will, but there is no evidence that Articles 5, 6 and 7 of the TM Directive must be interpreted as being subject to that overriding requirement, and it ought to be impossible to read in such a requirement now. It would create great uncertainty, not least because the concepts of essential function and specific subject-matter are adaptable, as the case requires, even though they both have a core consistency.

Davidoff in Scotland[80]

15-72 In the Scottish case, the parallel importer raised two arguments. The first was despatched by the decision in *Sebago*. The second was similar to the argument which found favour in England—the trade mark proprietor

---

[78] *Davidoff* [1999] R.P.C. 631 at 644, para. 36.
[79] *Silhouette* and *Sebago*. See para. 15–63, *supra*.
[80] *Zino Davidoff v. M&S Toiletries Ltd*, Ct of Sess., Lord Kingarth, [2000] E.T.M.R. 622. The same judgment was given in an associated action: *JOOP! GmbH v. M&S Toiletries Ltd*.

had placed the goods on the market without imposing sufficient restriction on their further marketing so as to prevent all those in the chain of distribution from importing the goods into the EEA. In those circumstances, it was argued that implied consent had been given to the goods being placed on the market in the EEA.

In Scotland, the judge decided that this argument was bound to fail, **15–73** for several reasons:

(1) he came to a clear view that the relevant contractual provisions in the Distributorship Agreement disclosed a clear intention that the goods should be the subject of retail sales within the territory and not beyond. He concluded that the trade mark owner had done all it reasonably could to limit sales to the territory;

(2) he drew attention to a provision in the Agreement which he considered plainly reserved the trade mark owner's rights;

(3) it was significant that this argument could not, under Scots law, be supported by the rebuttable presumption that in the absence of full and explicit restrictions being imposed on purchasers at the time of purchase, the vendor was to be treated as consenting to the goods being used as the purchaser wished—the proposition based, *inter alia*, on *National Phonograph Co. of Australia Ltd v. Menck* [1911] A.C. 336;

(4) the defenders accepted that German law applied to the Distributorship Agreement. Accordingly the burden was on them to plead and prove some effect of German law which might support an arguable case on consent; this they had failed to do.

The judge decided the application on those rather narrow grounds, but **15–74** he clearly favoured four more general considerations:

The first concerned the general approach to construction of "consent" in Article 7(1) of the TM Directive. Article 7(1) is a derogation from the rights conferred on the trade mark owner by Article 5(1). "In general, derogations should not be construed broadly" (para. 34 of the Opinion of the Advocate-General in *Silhouette*[81]). "Against that background before a trade mark proprietor could properly be said to have consented to the putting on the market of particular goods by a third party a reasonable construction would suggest that he must at least have had knowledge of the third party's actings or intended actings in relation to the goods." Such was the approach adopted by the Benelux and German courts in similar circumstances. As the judge pointed out, this approach was manifestly inconsistent with the parallel trader's argument "which sought to construe 'consent' in a very wide way—indeed in a way which appeared to equiparate consent with failure to take steps to prevent."

---

[81] Note that Laddie J. expressed almost precisely the opposite view: "There are compelling reasons why the Courts should not strain to give Article 7(1) and the *Silhouette* decision any wider effect than absolutely necessary" (para. 36 of his judgment).

15–75   The second concerned the practical reality of the parallel trader's approach. Unless a proprietor successfully blocked every avenue of possible later importation into the EEA, he was at risk of being held to have consented to such importation. This argument ran the risk of allowing for international exhaustion by the back door.

15–76   The third concerned the practical effect of leaving the issue of consent to be decided under national laws. This tended to offend against the essential purpose of harmonisation behind the Directive, one of the specific aims of which was to ensure, with certain limited exceptions that trade marks "enjoy the same protection under the legal systems of all the Member States" (Ninth Recital to the TM Directive). This aim would suggest that on the same facts the decision as to whether relevant consent had or had not been given should be the same, irrespective of the nationality of the deciding court or any specialty of the law which governed the contract.

15–77   Finally, it was said that the parallel trader's approach would lead to uncertainty in application. Often a chain of contracts would be involved. It would be difficult to ascertain what would or would not, in a particular case be regarded as sufficient or effective steps to impose restrictions.

Davidoff in the European Court

15–78   Although the judge in Scotland made no reference to the European Court, it is suggested that his approach and reasoning will find favour with the Court. It involves a straightforward approach to the issue of consent. That necessarily means a rejection of the approach taken by Laddie J., despite the fact that it represents a genuine attempt to decide between the parties on the basis of whether the activity complained of damages the specific subject matter of a trade mark.

15–79   In short, the issue raised by parallel imports into the EEA has nothing to do with the essential function of a trade mark or whether a trade mark should confer the ability to interfere with this type of activity. It is purely a matter of economic policy of the E.U. and EEA. (This is the reason why the advent of the Human Rights Act is unlikely to affect the outcome. See paras 22–39 *et seq.* below). The practical result will be that parallel imports into the EEA will result in infringement unless the trade mark proprietor has given consent. Cases of implied consent are likely to be very rare. In practice, unless express consent has been given, parallel imports into the EEA are most likely to result in infringement.

Future policy

15–80   Any change in this area is dependent upon economic policy. The whole question of international exhaustion proved so contentious that it was not possible to agree on a position at the Uruguay Round of GATT which resulted in TRIPS.[82] The perception is that unilateral adoption of international exhaustion by the EEA would almost certainly cause significant damage to the economies of countries within the EEA. The only feasible options appear to be bilateral treaties between the EEA and major trading partners such as the U.S. and Japan.[83] It is very difficult to predict when such developments might occur.

Parallel imports into EEA Member States which are not E.U. Member States

There is a possible breach in the "fortress Europe" established by the **15-81** adoption of EEA-wide exhaustion. The *Mag Instrument*[84] case highlights an imbalance resulting from the EEA Agreement. Essentially, the E.U. states[85] operate the principle of free movement for any goods *put on the market* in the EEA whereas EEA states which are not E.U. States (namely Norway, Iceland and Liechtenstein) only operate the principle of free movement for goods *originating* in the EEA.[86] Part of the EEA Agreement effectively extended Article 7(1) of the TM Directive so that it applied to goods put on the market in the EEA.[87] In return, it appears that the EFTA states were or are supposed to adjust their intellectual property laws to give at least the level of protection for intellectual property prevailing in the Community when the EEA Agreement was

---

[82] See TRIPS, Art. 6.

[83] In its Explanatory Memorandum proposing Community-wide exhaustion for the CTM Regulation (and hence the TM Directive), the Commission stated "On the question of international exhaustion of the rights conferred by the Community trade mark, the Commission has formed the view that the Community legislator should refrain from introducing this principle and make do with the rule of Community-wide exhaustion. The Community must, however, be empowered to conclude, at some future time with important trading partners, bilateral or multilateral agreements whereby international exhaustion is introduced by the contracting parties. The restriction to Community-wide exhaustion, however, does not prevent national courts from extending this principle, in cases of a special nature, in particular where, even in the absence of a formal agreement, reciprocity is guaranteed." COM (84) 470 final, July 31, 1984.

[84] *Mag Instrument Inc. v. California Trading Co.* [1998] E.T.M.R. 85. The EFTA Court concluded that Art. 7(1) left it open to EFTA states to decide whether they wish to introduce or maintain the principle of international exhaustion with regard to goods originating from outside the EEA.

[85] At the time of the EEA Agreement, the Member States of the E.C. were Belgium, Denmark, Germany, Greece, Spain, France, Ireland, Italy, Luxembourg, Netherlands, Portugal and the U.K. Of the EFTA states who signed the EEA Agreement, Austria, Finland and Sweden joined the E.U. as from January 1, 1995.

[86] EEA Agreement, Art. 8(2), applying in the field of IP rights via Arts 11 and 13 EEA (corresponding to Arts 28 and 30 E.C.).

[87] EEA Agreement, Annex XVII, para. 4(c), replaced the original Art. 7(1) with the following: "The trade mark shall not entitle the proprietor to prohibit its use in relation to goods which have been put on the market in a Contracting Party under that trade mark by the proprietor or with his consent." [1994] O.J. L1/483. Effectively, "Contracting Party" means any state of the EEA.

signed[88]—and part of this protection is the EEA-wide exhaustion provided for in Article 7(1) of the TM Directive. This does not seem to have occurred and will not occur unless Norway, Iceland and Liechtenstein either join the E.U. or provide for the same degree of exhaustion as E.U. states, namely EEA-wide and no broader.

15–82   Due to the different principles in the EEA Agreement, the EFTA Court in *Mag Instrument* was able to advise the Norwegian court that it is for EFTA states to decide whether they wish to introduce or maintain the principle of international exhaustion of rights conferred by a trade mark with regard to goods originating outside the EEA. The EFTA Court noted that it was established Norwegian law that international exhaustion applies for trade marks. If Iceland and Liechtenstein also apply international exhaustion, any one of those three countries appear to provide an entry point into the EEA for parallel imports of goods which originate outside the EEA. Once those goods are placed on the market[89] in Norway, Iceland or Liechtenstein, the only issue remaining under Article 7(1) (as amended) of the TM Directive is whether the goods were put on the market (in the EEA) with the consent of the proprietor of the mark. It would seem that this consent issue must be decided according to the law of the state concerned, not least because applying the law of any other Member State would be entirely arbitrary. Presumably, under Norwegian law, the application of international exhaustion also means that the proprietor is deemed to have consented to the goods being placed on the market in Norway. Even though the proprietor of the mark would say he had given no consent at all, giving him the ability to withhold consent would negate the rule of international exhaustion. Equally, allowing the law of any other Member State to determine the issue of consent (in accordance with guidance from the ECJ) would negate the ability of Norway to maintain a rule of international exhaustion.

[88] Protocol 28 on Intellectual Property ([1994] O.J. L1/194) contains the following provisions:

Article 1(2): "Without prejudice to the provisions of this Protocol and of Annex XVII, the Contracting Parties shall upon the entry into force of the Agreement adjust their legislation on intellectual property so as to make it compatible with the principles of the free circulation of goods and services and with the level of protection of intellectual property attained in Community law, including the level of enforcement of those rights.

Article 1(3): "Subject to the procedural provisions of the Agreement and without prejudice to the provisions of this Protocol and of Annex XVII, the EFTA States will adjust, upon request and after consultation between the Contracting Parties, their legislation on intellectual property in order to reach at least the level of protection of intellectual property prevailing in the Community upon signature of this Agreement.".

Article 2 *Exhaustion of Rights* "(1) To the extent that exhaustion is dealt with in Community measures or jurisprudence, the Contracting States shall provide for such exhaustion of intellectual property rights as laid down in Community law. Without prejudice to the future developments of case-law, this provision shall be interpreted in accordance with the meaning established in the relevant rulings of the Court of Justice of the European Communities given prior to the signature of this Agreement."

[89] This would require payment of customs tariffs—see A.-G. Warner in *EMI v. CBS* [1976] E.C.R. 811 at 860. Mere trans-shipment through Norway would mean the goods were not put on the market there.

If this analysis of the consent issue is correct, then Article 7(1) as **15–83** amended has the consequence that no national trade mark right in the EEA can be used to prevent the free movement of those goods throughout the EEA. It would require tortuous reasoning to hold that the imbalance between E.U. and EFTA states constituted "legitimate reasons" for opposing importation into the E.U.

The final point to note is the position of a CTM. Unlike Article 7(1) of **15–84** the TM Directive, the EEA Agreement effected no extension of the exhaustion provision for CTMs in Article 13(1) from "the Community" to "the EEA". For a CTM the territorial effect of the exhaustion provision coincides with the territorial effect of the CTM.[90] Therefore, unless or until Norway, Iceland and Liechtenstein join the CTM system, a CTM is not exhausted by goods under that mark[91] being placed on the market in any of those countries. It follows that Article 13(1) of the CTM Regulation would not prohibit the use of the CTM to prevent importation of those goods into the E.U. By analogy with Article 7 of the TM Directive and the *Paranova* judgment,[92] one would expect the ECJ to hold that Article 13 of the CTM Regulation comprehensively regulates the question of exhaustion of CTM rights. Indeed, there would be no reason to override Article 13 of the CTM Regulation because the EEA principle of the free movement of goods applies only to goods originating in the EEA. Articles 11 and 13 EEA would not apply. By analogy with *Silhouette*, the principle of free movement of goods in the E.U. would require that Article 13 of the CTM Regulation was not overridden.

6. The *Dior* problem

What is the problem?

The problem is whether section 12(2)/Article 7(2) creates a new right **15–85** enforceable by the proprietor of a registered trade mark, over and above the infringement rights conferred by sections 9 and 10/Article 5, as limited by sections 11 and 12(1)/Articles 6 and 7. This problem manifested itself in *Dowelhurst* in a slightly different guise. There the claimants asserted a new or "stand-alone" right conferred by the case law of the ECJ on repackaging.[93] It has been suggested above that the claim in *Dowelhurst* can and should be defeated simply by putting the principles drawn from the case law into their proper context. The claim in *Dior* was linked more directly to Article 7(2). Although the claim in

---

[90] A CTM covers the 15 countries of the E.U.

[91] Note that the interpretation of these words in the CTM context is very different to the interpretation appropriate in the national context. The different interpretation is permissible and is indeed required by the purpose of the respective provisions. See para. 15–09, *supra*.

[92] See para. 15–10, above.

[93] The *Dowelhurst* claim could equally well have been formulated directly under s.12(2)/Art. 7(2), since the ECJ has already held (in *Paranova*), that Art. 7 must be interpreted in the same way as Art. 30 (ex 36).

Dior was rejected, the reasoning has merely postponed the problem. As in *Dowelhurst*, the answer to this problem lies in placing it in its proper context.

Dior

15–86 In *Dior*, the goods were genuine, obtained by means of parallel imports. Dior complained that the advertising for sale of the parallel imports did not correspond to the luxurious and prestigious image of the Dior marks. The European Court held that a trade mark proprietor cannot rely on Article 7(2) of the TM Directive to oppose the use of the trade mark by a reseller who habitually markets articles of the same kind, but not necessarily of the same quality, as the trade-marked goods, in ways customary in the reseller's sector of trade, for the purpose of bringing to the public's attention the further commercialisation of the goods, unless it is established that, given the specific circumstances of the case, the use of the trade mark for this purpose seriously damages the reputation of the trade mark.

15–87   This conclusion was the result of two factors. The first was the readiness of the Court to treat the fourth *Paranova* guideline[94] as capable of establishing a "legitimate reason" by itself. The second was the readiness to extend that guideline so that it applied not only to changes to the *physical* condition of the goods, but also to the *mental* condition of the goods. The Court had re-phrased the key question for its consideration in effect in the following way:

Do the following constitute legitimate reasons within Article 7(2):

"—where the advertising function of the trade mark is endangered by the fact that, as a result of the manner in which the reseller uses the trade mark in order to attract public attention, he damages the luxurious and prestigious image of the trade mark, and

—where, as a result of the way in which the reseller advertises the goods, their 'mental' condition, that is to say the allure, prestigious image and aura of luxury which they have as a result of the manner in which the trademark owner has chosen to present and advertise the goods using his trade mark rights, is changed or impaired."[95]

15–88 Phrasing the question in this way entails the unquestioning acceptance that a registered trade mark with a luxurious and prestigious image has an advertising function which should be protected. Advocate-General Jacobs correctly concluded that any advertising function of a trade mark

---

[94] See para. 15–48, above.
[95] See para. 39 of the judgment. *Parfums Christian Dior S.A. v. Evora B.V.* [1997] E.C.R. I–6013 at 6047; [1998] R.P.C. 166 at 194.

is merely a derivative of the origin function. Despite giving a warning that "the circumstances in which a trade mark owner can invoke his trade mark rights in order to protect his reputation should not be construed too widely", even he seems to have accepted the principle that the trade mark should be protected from damage which is solely caused to the advertising function.[96] All of this discussion about the extent to which a trade mark must be protected took place in the context of striking the balance between free movement of goods and trade mark rights, and quite independently of and without apparent reference to the infringement provisions.

The natural conclusion from *Dior*

Both *Dowelhurst* and *Dior* contained the element of inter-state trade. **15–89** Section 12/Article 7 are not limited to situations which involve inter-state trade. They apply equally in a purely national context. Therefore, it can be argued that *Dior* establishes that section 12(2)/Article 7(2) gives the proprietor a right to interfere in reselling of genuine goods, even in a purely national context, provided the activity of the reseller "seriously damages the reputation of the trade mark".

Support from the notion of "exhaustion"

The argument that section 12(2)/Article 7(2) creates a new right is **15–90** supported by the concept of "exhaustion of rights" which those provisions are meant to embody. By nature, any "legitimate reason" within section 12(2)/Article 7(2) must arise or manifest itself after the first marketing of the goods. If the trade mark right is truly "exhausted" by first marketing, the existence of legitimate reasons under section 12(2) of the 1994 Act must either revive the exhausted right or create a new right. Since the former is a contradiction in terms, the notion of "exhaustion" tends to suggest that section 12(2) creates a new right, whereas the alternative notion (that the rule is one of free circulation) does not.

The answer to the problem

It is suggested that the correct answer to the problem is that section **15–91** 12(2)/Article 7(2) does not create any new right for the proprietor of a trade mark. There is one principal reason why this should be the correct answer. It should be obvious from the TM Directive that, in so far as the advertising function of a trade mark is protected, the protection is conferred directly by section 10/Article 5 (and not via the back door of section 12(2)/Article 7(2)). The corollary is that if this is not the correct

---

[96] See his Opinion, para. 42. [1997] E.C.R. I–6013 at 6027; [1998] R.P.C. 166 at 180/1.

answer, then via the back door route of section 12(2)/Article 7(2), the case law of the ECJ has created a new right for the proprietor of a trade mark. There was no such right available in the United Kingdom under the Trade Marks Act 1938. Since many E.U. countries applied a rule of international exhaustion before the TM Directive was implemented, it seems most unlikely that any other E.U. country previously conferred such a right. It cannot have been intended that the developing case law of the ECJ could create such a right.

15–92   One consequence of this reasoning is that, when the European Court is seeking to strike the appropriate balance between the fundamental interest in the free movement of goods and the fundamental interest in trade mark (or other industrial property) rights (whether under Article 7(2) or Article 30 of the Treaty), it should have regard to the degree of protection afforded to the trade mark by the infringement provisions and not examine in the abstract the protection which the trade mark appears to deserve on the facts of the particular case.[97] In other words, it is necessary to achieve consistency between the protection available in the national context and the protection available in a context which involves inter-state trade. The latter protection may be less than the former, due to the overriding principle of free movement of goods, but it should never be greater.

15–93   If it is thought that the advertising function of a trade mark deserves protection over and above that conferred in section 10/Article 5, then that is a matter for Community legislation and not otherwise.

7. Competition laws of the E.U. and the United Kingdom

15–94 The competition laws of the European Community[98] and the United Kingdom both impose important limitations on the exploitation and enforcement of trade marks. Community competition law applies by virtue of section 2(1) of the European Communities Act 1972.

15–95   The Competition Act 1998[99] introduced into United Kingdom law a domestic competition regime which is modelled on the relevant provisions of the Treaty of Rome, and it is likely that the exploitation and enforcement of trade marks within the United Kingdom will now be subject to more limitations than was previously the case.

---

[97] Without the anchor of the infringement provisions, it is difficult to resist providing some protection against damage which can be seen to be real. Hence unsuccessful claimants in cases like *Paranova* and *Dior* manage to extract a concession from the European Court in, *e.g.* the requirement for notice and the exception for serious damage to reputation, when the right answer is that trade mark proprietors should do without, and lump it.

[98] From January 1, 1994 these were extended by the European Economic Area Agreement (the EEA Agreement) to Iceland, Norway and Liechtenstein, member states of the European Free Trade Area (EFTA). Switzerland, although a member of EFTA, did not accede to the EEA Agreement. The EEA Agreement, Arts 53 and 54, reproduce the E.C. Treaty, Arts 81 and 82.

[99] The Act came into force on March 1, 2000.

8. Articles 81 and 82[1]

The nature of Articles 81 and 82

The basic purpose of Articles 81 and 82 of the E.C. Treaty[2] is to control **15–96** certain types of agreements (Article 81—ex Article 85) and certain types of monopolistic behaviour (Article 82—ex Article 86). Neither provision is directed particularly at trade marks or even intellectual property rights at all (and indeed the E.C. Treaty states in Article 295 (ex Article 222) "this Treaty shall in no way prejudice the rules in Member States governing the system of property ownership"). However, the manner in which such rights are exercised (whether by direct enforcement in the courts or by way of agreements) can fall within the general ambit of the provisions. Primary jurisdiction concerning breaches of either Article is given to the European Commission by virtue of Regulation 17/62, which is the basic implementing Regulation for the Treaty provisions on competition. Appeal against a Commission decision lies to the European Court of First Instance ("CFI"), which has jurisdiction to determine at first instance actions against the Commission relating to the enforcement of E.C. competition rules.[3] The Commission has power to order undertakings to cease their violations and to fine parties for such violations.[4]

In addition, in some cases breaches of either Article may directly **15–97** affect the enforceability of intellectual property rights—so that the breach may be pleaded by way of defence to an infringement action[5]— and also of an agreement exploiting intellectual property rights, which by Article 81(2) is void if contrary to Article 81(1) and not exempt pursuant to Article 81(3). A breach may also give rise to a claim by a party injured.[6]

Breach as a defence

Before turning to the manner in which Articles 81 and 82 affect **15–98** exploitation of trade mark rights, otherwise than by affecting enforcement, it is convenient to consider the extent to which breach of the Articles can constitute a defence to infringement. It has already been noted that the development of the free movement rules under Articles 28 and 30[7] has affected considerably the enforcement of trade marks within the Community.[8]

---

[1] Ex Arts 85 and 86: the renumbering results from the Treaty of Amsterdam 1997, Art. 12(1).
[2] App. 8.
[3] By virtue of Arts 229, 230 and 232 (ex Arts 172, 173 and 175) of the E.C. Treaty and Art. 17/62 of Regulation 17. Appeal from a judgment of the CFI lies to the European Court of Justice.
[4] See Regulation 17/62, Art. 15. See *Kerse, op. cit.*, Chap. 7.
[5] See below.
[6] See below.
[7] Formerly Arts 30 and 36, respectively.
[8] See paras 15–16 *et seq.*

15–99   This use of Articles 28 and 30 has been so significant that all cases where a so-called "Eurodefence" has been successful before the English courts can now be explained as applications of those rules. Thus cases of attempts to divide the geographic territory of the European Community by way of partial assignments or licences for limited parts only of the Community are usually dealt with by application of the doctrine of "first marketing".[9] It is difficult therefore to see any significant need for an independent defence of breach of Articles 81 or 82 where the free circulation rules are invoked. However, the jurisdiction to recognise the defence clearly exists (and in the United Kingdom is likely to become far more important as a result of the coming into force of the Competition Act 1998). Thus in *Sirena*[10] the ECJ said:

> "A trade-mark right, as a legal entity, does not in itself possess those elements of contract or concerted practice referred to in Article 85(1) [now 81(1)]. Nevertheless, the exercise of that right might fall within the ambit of the prohibitions contained in the Treaty each time it manifests itself as the subject, the means or the result of a restrictive practice."[11]

15–100   In *Sirena* itself the ECJ went on to hold that the assignments in the past amounted to a "restrictive practice" and that accordingly the assigned mark could not be enforced to prevent what were effectively parallel imports. The Court also indicated that the exercise of a trade mark right might be prohibited under Article 86 [now 82] of the Treaty.[12]

15–101   The ECJ has also said:

> "The proprietor of an exclusive right may not rely on his right if the prohibition on importation or marketing of which he wishes to avail himself could be connected with an agreement or practice in restraint of competition within the Community contrary to the provisions of the Treaty, in particular those of Art. 85(1) [now 81(1)]": *Keurkoop v. Nancy Kean*.[13]

What type of breach gives rise to a defence?

15–102   However, although the defence of breach of Article 81 or Article 82 is established in general terms, it is rare for it to be used successfully beyond the area covered by the free circulation rules. It cannot be the case that any party in breach of either Article simply is unable to enforce his trade mark or other rights as some sort of outlaw.[14] There has to be

---

[9] See *IHT v. Ideal Standard* [1994] F.S.R. 59; and *CNL-Sucal v. Hag ("Hag II")* [1990] 3 C.M.L.R. 571 (which effectively overruled *Hag I, op. cit.*).
[10] [1971] E.C.R. 69 at 84, para. 9.
[11] See paras 12–06 *et seq.*, below
[12] *Supra* at 85, paras 14–16.
[13] [1982] E.C.R. 2855; [1983] 2 C.M.L.R. 47, para. 26.
[14] See *ICI v. Berk* [1981] 2 C.M.L.R. 91; [1981] F.S.R. 1 at 6, *per* Megarry V.-C.

some close nexus[15] between the proposed exercise of trade mark rights and the breach.[16] There was a tendency for defendants to put forward "Euro-defences" based on Articles 81 and 82 liberally,[17] but the courts have generally adopted a robust attitude and, save in genuine free circulation cases, they have not succeeded.[18] The general attitude now to such defences was summarised by Neuberger J. in *Sandvik AB v. KR Pfiffner (United Kingdom) Ltd*:

> "On the one hand, the court should not make it too easy for a defendant to raise what turns out to be a baseless allegation of Article 86 [ex 82] infringement against a plaintiff, with a view to frightening off the plaintiff or at least increasing the cost and delay to the plaintiff, in establishing his right. On the other hand, it would be wrong to make it too difficult for a defendant with a valid case of Article 86 [now 82] infringement to put his case before the court".[19]

The courts have tended to ignore the fact that in any actual case of **15–103** breach of Articles 81 or 82 the defendant has the additional remedy of a complaint to the European Commission under Regulation 17/62.[20] This can be effective, and the Commission has power to take action by way of interim measures[21] (it should be noted, however, that the Commission has no power to award damages).

---

[15] *Per* Peter Gibson J. in *Holleran v. Daniel Thwaites plc* [1989] 2 C.M.L.R. 917.

[16] Some of the difficulties of any more general rule were pointed out by Megarry V.-C. in *ICI v. Berk, supra*, where a plea of abuse of dominant position (by imposing unfair prices) was struck out because there was no nexus between the abuse and the plaintiffs' cause of action. A case of a close nexus appears to be *L'Oreal* [1980] E.C.R. 3775. In *Nancy Kean*, above, the ECJ said "it is for the national court to ascertain in each case whether the exercise of the exclusive right in question leads to one of the situations which fall under the prohibitions contained in Art. 85 [now 81] and which may, in the context of the exercise of exclusive rights to designs take very different forms, such as, for example, the situation where persons simultaneously or successively file the same design in various member-States in order to divide up the markets within the Community among themselves" (para. 28). The same would obviously apply to trade marks used in this way.

[17] See, *e.g. British Leyland v. T.I. Silencers* [1981] F.S.R. 213; [1981] 2 C.M.L.R. 75, C.A.; *ICI v. Berk, supra.; Hoover v. Hulme* [1982] F.S.R. 565; *WHO v. Stage One* [1980] F.S.R. 268; *Applications des Gaz v. Falks Veritas* [1975] R.P.C. 421.

[18] Although in one case the English Court of Appeal (CA) was persuaded that a Euro-defence to the effect that by reason of the EEC-Portugal trading agreement the free circulation rules applied to EEC–Portuguese trade was so strong as to make the plaintiffs' case unarguable: *Polydor v. Harlequin* [1980] F.S.R. 362; [1980] 2 C.M.L.R. 413. This decision was reversed by the ECJ on the reference made by that Court of Appeal: [1982] 1 C.M.L.R. 677.

[19] [2000] F.S.R. 17 at 68.

[20] Although, in a decision shortly after U.K. accession, Graham J. in *Aero Zipp Fasteners Limited v. YKK Fasteners (UK) Limited* [1973] C.M.L.R. 819, refused to strike out an unparticularised defence founded on Arts 85 and 86 (now 81 and 82) on the ground that the European Commission had already initiated proceedings, which the judge considered would only have occurred if the Commission was "satisfied that there is at least a prima facie case".

[21] *Hasselblad ("Camera Care")* [1982] 1 E.C.R. 1555; [1980] 1 C.M.L.R. 334, ECJ, indicates the criteria for such measures, namely, that the case should be urgent in order to avoid a situation likely to cause serious and irreparable damage to the applicant or which is intolerable to the public interest. The measures taken should be of a temporary and conservatory nature and restricted to what is required in the given situation. See Kerse, *op. cit.,* paras 6–02—6–11.

However, it has been held that where the Commission has not yet made a final decision on a complaint, it is open to (and indeed incumbent upon) an English court to find a just way of regulating the position between the parties in English proceedings.[22] Where the Commission had issued a Statement of Objections, it was held by the Court of Appeal that the national court was not obliged to stay proceedings pending a decision, provided that the case was not clearly in favour of either the plaintiff or the defendant.[23] What should be avoided by national courts is taking decisions which may conflict with those of the Commission.[24] Once a decision has been issued by the Commission, it is legally binding on national courts and such courts may not allow a party whose position was rejected by the Commission to re-litigate the question. Similarly, if proceedings are already afoot but suspended, the national court should decide the case in the same way as the Commission.[25]

Breach giving rise to a claim

15–104 It is clear that any party directly affected by a breach of either Article 81 or Article 82 can not only complain to the European Commission,[26] but can also sue in the national courts for an injunction to restrain continued breach[27] and for damages.[28] So far as trade marks are concerned

---

[22] *Fyffes v. Chiquita Brands International* [1993] F.S.R. 83 at 100.

[23] "The Court's concern is to avoid inconsistent decisions. There is no ground for seeking to prohibit the preparation of an action for trial so long as it does not lead to a decision in advance of a decision by the Commission": *per* Sir Thomas Bingham M.R. in *MTV Europe v. BMG Records (UK) Ltd* [1997] Eu.L.R. 100 at 108, upholding the decision of the trial judge (Evans-Lombe J.) to allow the action to proceed to setting down.

[24] See *Stergios Delimitis v. Henninger Bräu* [1991] E.C.R. I–935. In its 1993 *Notice on co-operation between national courts and the Commission in applying Articles 85 and 86 of the EEC Treaty* the Commission advises: "The national courts may ask the Directorate-General for Competition . . . for information of a procedural nature to enable them to discover whether a certain case is pending before the Commission, whether a case has been the subject of a notification, whether the Commission has officially initiated a procedure or whether it has already taken a position through an official decision or through a comfort letter. If necessary, national courts may also ask the Commission to give an opinion as to how much time is likely to be required for granting or refusing individual exemption for notified agreements or practices, so as to be able to determine the conditions for any decision to suspend proceedings or whether interim measures need to be adopted. The Commission, for its part, will endeavour to give priority to cases which are the subject of national proceedings suspended in this way".

[25] See *Iberian v. BPB and British Gypsum* [1997] I.C.R. 164, and the commentary on it by the judge, Mr Justice Laddie, in *Community Competition Law in English Courts* in Andenas and Jacobs (eds), *European Community Law in the English Courts* (1998, Clarendon Press), pp. 177–178.

[26] Under Reg. 17/62.

[27] *Cutsforth v. Mansfield Inns* [1986] 1 All E.R. 577.

[28] *Garden Cottage v. Milk Marketing Board* [1984] A.C. 130; [1983] 3 C.M.L.R 43; [1984] F.S.R. 23, HL; *Irish Dairy Board v. Milk Marketing Board* [1984] 1 C.M.L.R. 519. The HL in *Garden Cottage* regarded the duty imposed by Art. 86 [now 82] as a statutory duty imposed not only for the general economic prosperity of the Common Market but also for the benefit of private individuals. Thus breach of Art. 86 [now 82] is not within those cases (*e.g.* *Lonrho v. Shell (No. 1)* [1981] A.C. 173; *RCA v. Pollard* [1982] 1 W.L.R. 179) where an individual tries to claim in respect of a breach of the general law. See also *Bourgoin v.*

however, it is difficult to envisage circumstances where this rule may apply.[29] Perhaps a parallel importer whose supplies of the trade-marked goods were withheld as a result of collusion between the manufacturer and his distributors could sue.[30] But he would have to prove that his inability to obtain the goods was indeed the result of a deliberate attempt to partition the Community.

"May affect trade between Member States"

No question under Article 81 or Article 82 can arise unless the conduct **15–105** concerned "may affect trade between Member States",[31] although obviously in the United Kingdom a question may then arise under the Competition Act 1998.[32] This is thus a jurisdictional requirement dividing the competences of the Community and national competition authorities.[33] The ECJ has established (not surprisingly) a *de minimis* principle.[34] What is required is some appreciable effect on trade between Member States.[35] Indeed merely a possibility of such an effect will suffice.[36] The Commission has in the past taken a rather liberal view of the requirement,[37] but recently there has been a marked change in this attitude and a willingness on the part of the Commission to cede

Ministry of Agriculture [1986] 2 C.M.L.R. 627, CA (action against Government for breach of Art. 30 [now 28] actionable as breach of statutory duty where there is an abuse of power). For earlier cases, see *Application des Gaz v. Falks Veritas* [1975] R.P.C. 421, CA; *SABAM* [1974] E.C.R. 51, 333 (ECJ).

[29] See *Glaxo Group Ltd v. Dowelhurst Ltd* [2000] F.S.R. 371, in which the defendants sought to amend their defences and have permission to make counterclaims based on Art. 81(1): in allowing the amendments, even though he considered the evidence of a concerted practice to be "thin", the judge noted "Issues arising under Article 81(1) are likely to add significantly to the costs and duration of a trial and care must be taken to distinguish between an honestly held persecution complex and evidence of collaboration": at 384.

[30] However, it should be borne in mind that unilateral conduct does not fall within Art. 81: in *ADALAT* [1996] O.J. L201/1 the Commission found Bayer to be acting contrary to Art. 81(1) by refusing to supply pharmaceutical wholesalers who were involved in parallel trading. The CFI suspended the Commission's decision requiring Bayer to resume supply, on the ground that it raised "the particularly delicate question as to the circumstances in which a refusal to sell is capable, when it occurs in the context of continuing commercial relations, of constituting one of the aspects of an agreement containing an export prohibition" and that it did not appear on the evidence that there was sufficient consent by the other wholesalers to Bayer's refusal to supply to create an agreement falling within Art. 85(1): [1996] E.C.R. II–383, at paras 41–52.

[31] These words appear in each Article.

[32] See paras 15–126 *et seq.*

[33] On the relationship between Community and national competition laws, see *Kerse*, Chap. 10.

[34] See also the Commission's Notice on Minor Agreements: [1997] O.J. C372/15.

[35] See *Völk* [1969] E.C.R. 295; [1969] C.M.L.R. 273; *Béguelin I* [1971] E.C.R. 949; [1972] C.M.L.R. 81; *La Technique Miniére (LTM)* [1966] E.C.R. 235; [1966] C.M.L.R. 357; *Hugin* [1979] E.C.R. 1969; [1979] 3 C.M.L.R. 345; *European Night Services* [1998] 5 C.M.L.R. 718.

[36] *Michelin* [1983] E.C.R. 3461, para. 104.

[37] See, *e.g. Michelin* [1982] 1 C.M.L.R. 643 at 663; *Advocaat Zwarte Kip* [1974] 2 C.M.L.R. D79 at D85; *AOIP/Beyrard* [1976] 1 C.M.L.R. D14; *SABA* [1976] 1 C.M.L.R. D61, *cf.* SAFCO [1972] C.M.L.R. D83.

responsibility to national authorities.[38] The United Kingdom courts have been reluctant to find an effect on inter-state trade on too speculative a basis and evidence must be shown of a definite effect on past trade or a real likelihood of future trade being affected.[39]

Scope of Article 82

15–106 In order to establish a breach it is of course first necessary to establish that a party is in a dominant position within the Community. There is now a substantial body of authority on what amounts to a "dominant position."[40] As a preliminary step, it is necessary to establish the "relevant market" (for example the class of goods or services concerned) and then determine whether the party concerned is dominant in that market, for example, is in a position to prevent effective competition or otherwise to act without regard to its competitors. So far as industrial property rights are concerned, the ECJ has clearly established that their mere existence does not constitute a "dominant position". Thus in *Sirena* the Court said[41]: "the proprietor of a trademark does not enjoy a 'dominant position' within the meaning of Article 86[now 82] merely because he is in a position to prevent third parties from putting into circulation, on the territory of a Member State, products bearing the same trademark."[42]

15–107 What more is needed to establish a "dominant position"? In *Sirena* the Court suggested that "the proprietor should have the power to impede the maintenance of effective competition over a considerable part of the relevant market, having regard in particular to the existence and position of any producers or distributors who may be marketing similar goods or goods which may be substituted for them".[43] It is possible therefore that a particularly well-known trade mark might have such a powerful goodwill that others could not effectively compete. In such a case the marked product might constitute a relevant market in its own

---

[38] See the Commission Notice on co-operation between national competition authorities and the Commission in handling cases falling within the scope of Arts 85 and 86 (now 81 and 82) of the E.C. Treaty: ([1997] O.J. C–313 3).

[39] In *Chiron v. Murex (No. 2)* [1994] 1 C.M.L.R. 410, CA, the court struck out a pleading of abuse contrary to Art. 86 [82] as there was no effect on trade between Member States; see also *Duracell v. Ever Ready* [1989] R.P.C. 731 and *Sport International B.V. v. Hi-Tec Sports Ltd* [1990] F.S.R. 312 at 318, per Hirst J.

[40] See, *e.g. United Brands* [1978] E.C.R. 207; [1978] 3 C.M.L.R. 83; *Hugin* [1979] E.C.R. 1969; [1979] 3 C.M.L.R. 345; *Commercial Solvents* [1974] E.C.R. 223; [1974] C.M.L.R. 309; *Hoffmann-La Roche* [1979] E.C.R. 46; [1979] 3 C.M.L.R. 211; *Volvo v. Veng* [1988] E.C.R. 6211; *AKZO Chemie* [1991] E.C.R. I–3359; and, generally, Bellamy & Child, *Common Market Law of Competition* (4th ed.), Chap. 7.

[41] [1971] E.C.R. 69 at 83, para. 16; [1971] C.M.L.R. 260 at 275 (there is a slight difference in language in this unofficial report).

[42] See also *EMI v. CBS* [1976] E.C.R. 811 at 849, para. 36; [1976] 2 C.M.L.R. 235; *Parke Davis* [1968] E.C.R. 55; [1968] C.M.L.R. 47 (patents); *DG v. Metro* [1971] E.C.R. 487; [1971] C.M.L.R. 631 (copyright).

[43] *Sirena, loc. cit.,* para. 16. See also *Parke Davis, loc. cit.; Volvo v. Veng* [1988] E.C.R. 6211; *CICRA v. Renault* [1988] E.C.R. 6039.

right and the proprietor of the mark may be in a dominant position.[44] It would by no means follow, however, that the enforcement of rights in such a mark would be forbidden absolutely. That would depend upon whether or not the type of enforcement concerned could be held an "abuse" of the dominant position.[45]

So far as "abuse" of a dominant position arising from monopoly **15–108** rights is concerned, the Court has clearly contemplated that overpricing may constitute an abuse.[46] But it is difficult to see why, given such overpricing, the trade mark right should be wholly unenforceable.[47]

The Commission has held it to be an abuse of a dominant position for a party in such a position to register in one part of the Community a mark it knows or ought to know is used by a competitor elsewhere in the Community.[48]

Scope of Article 81

There is now a considerable amount of authority both of the ECJ and of **15–109** the European Commission concerning the ambit of Article 81(1) and the circumstances in which, even though an agreement might fall within Article 81(1), it might be "exempted" by the Commission under Article 81(3),[49] or fall within the various "block exemptions".[50] They cannot be discussed fully here: we confine ourselves to agreements relating to trade marks and allied matters.[51] Speaking generally, however, any

---

[44] In *United Brands* [1978] E.C.R. 207; [1978] 1 C.M.L.R. 429, the ECJ included in the factors which were important in finding dominance, the quality control imposed in relation to its well-known trade mark Chiquita.

[45] In *Tierce Ladbroke v. Commission* [1997] 5 C.M.L.R. 309, the Court of First Instance held (at para. 131) that for a refusal to licence copyright to amount to an abuse, it had to be related to either a product or a service which was essential for the exercise of the activity in question, in that there was no real or potential substitute. It is difficult to envisage this test being satisfied in relation to a refusal to licence a trade mark. Also, see *Biotrading & Financing v. Biohit Ltd* [1998] F.S.R. 109, in which Aldous L.J. reiterated that enforcement of copyright cannot by itself be an abuse: at 133.

[46] *Sirena, loc. cit.*, para. 17.

[47] See *I.C.I. v. Berk, op. cit.* Similarly, it is difficult to envisage circumstances in which the "essential facilities" notion developed by the ECJ in *Volvo v. Veng* [1988] E.C.R. 6211; [1989] 4 C.M.L.R. 122; and *RTE and ITP* [1995] E.C.R. I–743; [1995] 4 C.M.L.R. 718; would be applied to trade marks as the specific subject-matter does not lend itself to the market-foreclosing behaviour resulting from a refusal to license patents or copyright.

[48] *Osram/Airam Settlement* [1982] 3 C.M.L.R. 614; [1983] F.S.R. 108.

[49] Art. 9(1) of Regulation 17, *op. cit.*, gives the Commission the exclusive power to grant exemptions. By Art. 4(2)(iii) of Regulation 17, trade mark (and other industrial property) assignments or licences to which not more than two undertakings are party need not be notified as long as they only impose restrictions on the exercise of the rights by the assignee or licensee. However, this exception does not apply where the restrictions go beyond the specific subject-matter of the trade mark: in *Windsurfing International Inc. v. Commission* [1986] E.C.R. 611; [1986] 3 C.M.L.R. 489, the ECJ held that the exception did not apply where the restrictions covered goods not covered by the patent and there was a no-challenge clause affecting both patents and trade marks; also the trade mark delimitation agreement in *BAT "Toltecs", supra*, fell outside the exception.

[50] Also, the Commission has developed the practice of issuing so-called comfort letters by which it closes its file on a particular agreement without granting either a negative clearance or individual exemption: see *Kerse, op. cit.*, para. 6–54.

[51] See generally the article by the late Judge Joliet (of the ECJ) *Trademark Licensing Agreements under the EEC Law of Competition* (1983–84) 5 Northwestern Journal of International Law & Business 755.

---

arrangement intended for (or which has the effect of) partitioning the E.C. or restricting competition is almost certainly offensive, provided that trade between Member States is or may be affected.[52]

(1) Assignments of trade marks

15-110 The ECJ has made it clear that any assignment of a trade mark for part of the Community only should not in itself be viewed as having the effect of partitioning the market.[53] Nevertheless, an assignment of a mark (or an agreement to assign) for part of the market alone may fall within Article 81(1) in certain circumstances. As a practical matter, however, it cannot vest in the assignee absolute protection for the countries for which he has taken an assignment: he may be exposed to parallel imports from the remainder of the Community. If, however, the parties go further than a mere assignment, and actively (either by terms of the agreement or by their conduct) seek to partition the Community then there will be a breach of Article 81(1).[54] Indeed an attempt to enforce a trade mark to prevent parallel imports with knowledge of the competition rules may increase the gravity of the breach.

(2) Exclusive licences

15-111 United Kingdom law recognises in section 31(1) of the Trade Marks Act 1994 that trade marks may be licensed exclusively, provided the requirements of section 28(2)[55] are complied with.[56] At one time the Commission took the view that all exclusive licences of industrial property rights fell within Article 85(1) (now 81(1)) and, if they were to be justified at all, needed exemption under Article 85(3) (now 81(3)).[57] As a result of the *Maize Seed* case[58] that view was modified: the European Court drew a distinction between "open" and "closed"

---

[52] Note the comment of Judge Bellamy of the ECJ: "an effects-based system in its pure form is frankly unmanageable. It is totally impractical. If you adopt a wide-ranging test like that adopted by the Court of Justice in *Consten and Grundig*, in the mid 1960s, you immediately find that to make it workable you have to adopt a whole series of exemptions and exceptions, in order to give back to business the legal certainty that it needs and to reduce the administration burden on the authority to within manageable limits" in *The Europeanisation of United Kingdom Competition Law* (eds. Green & Robertson), 1999.

[53] *IHT Internationale Heiztechnik v. Ideal-Standard* [1994] E.C.R. I–2789.

[54] *Ibid.*, "Before a trade mark assignment can be treated as giving effect to an agreement prohibited under Article 85 [now 81], it is necessary to analyse the context, the commitments underlying the assignment, the intention of the parties and the consideration for the assignment": at para. 59. Also, see *Tepea* [1978] E.C.R. 1391; [1978] 3 C.M.L.R. 392.

[55] "A licence is not effective unless it is in writing signed by or on behalf of the grantor."

[56] See Chap. 12.

[57] The argument was that the grant of such a licence was restrictive of trade because it prevented the licensor from granting licences to others, see, *e.g.* *Burroughs* [1972] C.M.L.R. D67; *Kabelmetal* [1975] 2 C.M.L.R. D40; *AOIP/Beyrard* [1976] 1 C.M.L.R. D14. It followed from this that if there were to be exclusive licences within the Community at all, they would need exemption under Art. 85(3) (now 81(3)). In *Campari* the exclusivity was exempted: (1978) 22 C.M.L.R. 397.

[58] *Nungessor* [1982] E.C.R. 2015; [1983] 1 C.M.L.R. 278.

exclusive licences. An "open" exclusive licence is one whereby the owner of the right merely undertakes not to grant other licences in the territory concerned and not himself to compete with his licensee in that territory. Such a licence will not normally fall within Article 81(1), although the particular facts will have to be examined to discover whether the licence has the effect of preventing or distorting competition within the E.C.[59] But if the parties go further, and by their agreement seek to confer absolute territorial protection on the licensee, so that parallel importers or licensees from other territories are excluded, then the licence will be "closed" and fall foul of Article 81(1).[60] The difference can perhaps be put in this way: that exclusive licences may be granted, provided they do not go so far as to attempt to circumvent the free movement rules.

In *Moosehead/Whitbread*[61] the Commission found that an exclusive **15–112** trade mark licence to brew and market beer in the United Kingdom under the "Moosehead" mark fell within Article 81(1). The Commission considered that the exclusivity, coupled with a prohibition on active sales outside the United Kingdom and a ban on marketing competing brands, could affect trade between Member States. However, an individual exemption was granted in view of the competitive state of the United Kingdom beer market.

(3) Block exemptions

So far as patents and know-how are concerned, the Commission has **15–113** issued a block exemption covering certain types of technology licence (including exclusive licences).[62] In the context of technology licences, this contains certain provisions as to what can and cannot be done by way of ancillary clauses concerned with trade marks.[63] There is also a recent block exemption covering vertical agreements and concerted practices[64]

---

[59] Thus the Commission held a 10-year exclusive trade mark licence for the whole E.C. granted on the occasion of the grantor's transfer of its European business to the grantee as constituting protection against competition for an unreasonable length of time: *Tyler* [1982] 3 C.M.L.R. 613; [1973] F.S.R. 109. On the other hand, a three-year non-compete clause included in a sale of a business with goodwill was held not to fall within Art. 85(1) (now 81(1)); *Mecaniver/PPG* [1985] O.J. L35/54; [1985] C.M.L.R. 359. In *Nutricia* [1984] 2 C.M.L.R. 165, the Commission indicated the principles under which an allowable period for a non-compete clause on the sale of a business may be set (four years for a low technology business of sauces and pickles). The benefits of the vertical restraints block exemption, *supra*, are not available where the agreement includes a non-compete obligation the duration of which is either indefinite or exceeds five years: Art. 5(1).

[60] *Supra.*

[61] [1990] O.J. L100/32.

[62] Reg. 240/96: [1996] O.J. L31, which applies to pure patent and know-how licences and to mixed patent and know-how licences.

[63] Namely Art. 1.1(7) accepts "an obligation on the licensee to use only the licensor's trade mark or get-up to distinguish the licensed product during the term of the agreement, provided that the licensee is not prevented from identifying himself as the manufacturer of the licensed products"; and Art. 2.1(11) "obligation on the licensee to mark the licensed product with an indication of the licensor's name or of licensed patent."

[64] Reg. 2790/99: [1999] O.J. 336/21, applied from June 1, 2000: until that date, there applied the previous block exemptions on exclusive distribution and exclusive purchasing (Regs 1983/83 and 1984/83 respectively: [1983] O.J. L.173) and on franchising (Reg. 4087/88: [1988] O.J. L359/46).

which contains an important provision on intellectual property rights: "The exemption provided for in paragraph 1 shall apply to vertical agreements containing provisions which relate to the assignment to the buyer or use by the buyer of intellectual property rights, provided that those provisions do not constitute the primary object of such agreements and are directly related to the use, sale or resale of goods or services by the buyer or its customers."[65] Thus the exemption depends on whether the trade mark licence is or is not the "primary object" of the agreement, where distribution of goods or services and a licence of trade marks are included in the same agreement. These clauses are a good guide as to some types of clause which may be acceptable in other forms of licence.[66]

(4) Licences generally

15–114 It is of course essential in relation to a trade mark licence that there be a right of quality control by the licensor.[67] So to that extent the licensee is put under a requirement which might be suggested is restrictive of competition within the Community and so theoretically caught by Article 81(1). Such a suggestion is clearly wrong. Unless the licence contains other terms (for example a requirement forcing the licensee to use the mark) the licensee is merely given a permission to use the mark where he complies with the quality control provisions.[68] It is noteworthy that the Commission has never considered quality control provisions in a patent licence as restrictive where they were "indispensable for the technically perfect exploitation" of the patent.[69] Since quality control is

---

[65] Art. 2(3).
[66] Note that these block exemptions have no direct application outside the specified agreements. It follows that unless an agreement falls clearly within the provisions of a block exemption, care should be taken to consider whether it may fall within Art. 81(1). If the matter is not clear, negative clearance or an exemption should be sought. However, it should be noted that in June 1999 the Commission broadened the scope of Art. 4(2) of Regulation 17 to exempt all vertical agreements from prior notification requirements: Council Reg. 1216/1999 of June 10, 1999. The practical effect is that companies will no longer have to notify vertical agreements which they believe qualify for an exemption. If an agreement is subsequently subject to litigation and found not to fall within the block exemption, the parties can notify it to the Commission and request an individual exemption under Art. 81(3). Provided the conditions of Art. 81(3) are satisfied, the Commission can grant an exemption retrospectively to the date of the agreement (*cf.* the Competition Act 1998, s.4(5), which gives a similar power to the Director General of Fair Trading).
[67] See Chap. 12.
[68] *e.g. Campari, op. cit.*, in which the Commission found that Art. 85(1) [now 81(1)] does not catch production standards or the licensor's right to inspect and sample: at 408.
[69] See Notice of December 24, 1962 ("the Christmas Message"); *Burroughs* [1972] C.M.L.R. D67; *Raymond/Nagoya* [1972] C.M.L.R. D45. Under Reg. 240/96 an obligation on the licensee to accept quality specifications which are not necessary for a technically satisfactory exploitation of the licensed technology, and to allow the licensor to carry out related checks, is a grey clause which is acceptable (Art. 4(2)(a)) as long as the agreement is notified and the Commission does not oppose an exemption within four months (Art. 4(1)).

of the essence of a valid trade mark licence the same reasoning must apply to such licences.[70]

(5) "No challenge" clauses

It seems clear that clauses in agreements forbidding the licensee to challenge the validity of the licensed right usually fall *within* Article 81(1).[71] However, where it is necessary in order to establish a trade mark in an already crowded market, such a clause may be permitted.[72] A clause permitting the licensor to terminate the licence if such a challenge is made is likely to be permitted.[73] This rule can pose special difficulties in the way of the settlement of litigation. In particular where the validity of the plaintiff's right is contested, the plaintiff will normally desire to see that right recognised in any settlement. Even so, and despite the general desirability of encouraging settlement of litigation, the Commission takes the view that parties may not "reinforce" by contract industrial property rights.[74] In some cases it may be possible to persuade the Commission to regard a particular "no challenge" clause as outside Article 81(1)[75] or to exempt a "no challenge" clause under Article 81(3). It is submitted that in general terms the Commission ought to grant a negative clearance in any case where there is a bona fide dispute being settled. Of course it is equally clear that a "no challenge" clause in respect of a virtually bogus industrial property right could in practice

15–115

---

[70] Thus in *Carlsberg* [1984] O.J. C27/4; [1984] 1 C.M.L.R. 305, the Commission clearly accepted quality control clauses in a much wider commercial agreement, also *Moosehead/Whitbread, supra.* Of course where quality control conditions are imposed on more than one licensee there may be a breach of Art. 81(1) if different standards are applied to equivalent licensees, see: *Carlsberg* [1985] C.M.L.R. 735 at 734.

[71] *BAT "Toltecs"* [1985] 2 C.M.L.R. 470; [1985] F.S.R. 533, at paras 34–5 (ECJ); *Davidson* [1972] C.M.L.R. D52; *Raymond/Nagoya* [1972] C.M.L.R. D45; *Kabelmetal* [1975] 2 C.M.L.R. D40; *AOIP* [1976] 1 C.M.L.R. D15; *Goodyear* [1975] 1 C.M.L.R. D31. The common law rule (based upon the analogy with the law of landlord and tenant) that even in the absence of an express no challenge clause the licensee cannot challenge the title of the right licensed is clearly abrogated so far as agreements affecting trade between Member States are concerned and in domestic situations presumably, may now contravene the Competition Act 1998 (see paras 15–126 *et seq.,* below).

[72] See *Moosehead/Whitbread, supra,* in which the Commission found that such an obligation did not restrict competition within the meaning of Art. 81(1).

[73] See Art. 2.1(15) of the Technology Transfer Block Exemption 240/96, which accepts "a reservation by the licensor of the right to terminate the agreement if the licensee contests the secret or substantial nature of the licensed know-how or challenges the validity of licensed patents within the common market belonging to the licensor or undertakings connected with him". On the other hand, Art. 4(2)(b) includes in the grey list a no-challenge clause in relation to the know-how or patents: the grey clauses are generally restrictive of competition but are accepted provided the Commission does not oppose an exemption within four months of notification (Art. 4(1)).

[74] There is no distinction to be made between agreements putting an end to litigation and other agreements: *Bayer v. Sullhofer* [1990] 4 C.M.L.R. 182; *cf.* the suggestion by Neill L.J. in *Apple Corps Ltd v. Apple Computer Inc, supra,* that such a distinction may be relevant in restraint of trade.

[75] *Penneys* [1978] 2 C.M.L.R. 100 (settlement of major trade mark and passing-off litigation. "No-challenge" for five years accepted as not restrictive, this being the normal period after which a mark is vulnerable for non-use, settlement related solely to trade marks).

amount to no more than a market-sharing agreement and no doubt the Commission would guard against such cases.[76]

15–116 It should be borne in mind by those drafting trade mark delimitation agreements that, where the agreement is for an indefinite period, the validity of a "no challenge" clause may depend on whether the trade mark in question remains in use, or at least is used sufficiently to maintain a trade mark registration.[77]

(6) Agreement to minimise confusion

15–117 It seems clear that an agreement (for example between holders of a mark of "common origin") merely designed to avoid confusion but not to partition the Community is outside Article 81(1).[78] However, a trade mark delimitation agreement would fall within Article 81(1) where it is not evident that the holder of an earlier trade mark could have recourse to national law to prevent the holder of a later mark from using it in one or more Member States.[79]

(7) Obligation on patent licensee to use licensor's mark

15–118 This clause has been held unobjectionable where the licensee is permitted also to use his own mark.[80] It is not clear what attitude the Commission would take where the licensee under a patent was com-

---

[76] *Sirdar/Phildar* [1975] 1 C.M.L.R. D83, appears to be such a case. The marks were fairly obviously not confusable (and were held so on motion: [1975] 1 C.M.L.R. 378; [1975] F.S.R. 309). BAT *"Toltecs"* is another such case: see Commission decision [1982] O.J. L379/19; [1983] 1 C.M.L.R. 412, at paras 43–44. The decision itself was upheld by the ECJ ([1985] 2 C.M.L.R. 470; [1985] F.S.R. 533), although the Court refrained from commenting on this point (para. 35). But the suggestion in the decision of the Commission that the agreement would be caught even if the marks were confusingly similar appears to go too far. Taken logically it would mean that parties could not settle infringement and passing-off cases at all. The only way the holder of the right could prevent imports would be by success in a fought action.

[77] In *Apple Corps Ltd v. Apple Computer Inc, supra*, Neill L.J. stated: "It is plain that to enforce . . . the 'no-challenge' restrictions in the 1981 Agreement it will be necessary for Apple to prove that they have used the marks at the relevant times in the course of their businesses. The actual use of the marks by Apple will be one of the central issues for the court to determine": at para. 80. See also, *Sports International Bussum v. Hi-Tec Sports* [1990] F.S.R. 312, in which a mandatory injunction was granted to restrain an opposition contrary to the terms of a settlement agreement; rejecting an argument that this was equivalent to a no-challenge clause and therefore contrary to Art. 85 [now 81].

[78] *Persil* [1978] 1 C.M.L.R. 395; *Velcro/Aplix* [1989] 4 C.M.L.R. 157. Clearly there is a difference between such an agreement between persons who have concurrent rights to use a mark throughout the E.C. and an agreement where there are no such rights (*e.g.* in a *Terrapin*-like case). In the latter, more restrictive conditions ought to be acceptable, but the Commission might well not agree: see *Sirdar/Phildar, ante.*

[79] *The Community v. Syntex Corp* [1990] 4 C.M.L.R. 343; [1990] F.S.R. 529: the Commission closed its file when the parties amended the agreement to provide for co-existence in all Member States.

[80] *Burroughs* [1972] C.M.L.R. D67. The Technology Transfer Block Exemption (Reg. 240/96) includes in the clauses generally not restrictive of competition, an obligation on the licensee to use only the licensor's trade mark or get up provided the licensee is permitted to identify itself as the manufacturer (Art. 1(7) and an obligation on the licensee to mark the licensed product with an indication of the licensor's name (Art. 2.1(11)).

pelled to use the licensor's mark only, with the result that on expiry of the licence and patent the licensee would find it difficult to continue the business formerly conducted by it. On one view the licensee would be in no worse position than any third party entering the market after expiry of the patent and so the clause is not restrictive. But in practice the clause could have a devastating effect on the licensee's continued ability to conduct his business and the Commission might hold the clause in substance restrictive.

(8) Settlements of actions

Even some settlements of actions can be invalidated under Article 81(1). **15–119**
BAT owned the dormant mark "Dorcet" in Germany and sued a relatively small defendant using the mark "Toltecs Special". Although the "Dorcet" registration was open to cancellation, BAT secured a settlement which was heavily disadvantageous to the defendant. The ECJ held that the agreement was invalid: in substance it served no purpose other than for BAT to control and in the end prevent distribution of the defendant's tobacco in Germany.[81]

This decision is of particular significance: large companies frequently **15–120** own considerable portfolios of registered marks which are either wholly unused or have only token use. If they use such marks to oppress other, genuine, traders they may well be acting in breach of Article 82 and any settlement achieved may fall foul of Article 81(1).

It is important to bear in mind that a settlement agreement which did **15–121** not fall within Article 81(1) at the time it was entered into, may do so subsequently if circumstances change and the agreement is no longer not restrictive of competition, for example because marks have become susceptible to attack on the grounds of non-use or have been abandoned.[82] Also, where a global or E.U.-wide trade mark delimitation (or settlement) agreement is entered into for an indefinite period, it is essential that the parties try to anticipate business developments which may later make the field of use unacceptable to one of the parties.[83]

(9) Selective distribution

It is of course common for manufacturers to distribute their wares **15–122** through a network of dealers. The agreements with such dealers may, if restrictive of inter-state trade, fall within Article 81(1).[84] Any attempt to use passing-off rights to prevent parallel imports where the alleged misrepresentation relates to the nature of a dealer (or the giving of a

---

[81] *BAT "Toltecs"* [1985] 2 C.M.L.R. 470; [1985] F.S.R. 533.

[82] For an example, see *Apple Corps Ltd v. Apple Computer Inc.* [1991] 3 C.M.L.R. 49, particularly Nicholls L.J. at para. 113.

[83] In *Apple, ibid.*, the computer industry developed in ways unforeseen at the date of the agreement and by the time of the dispute six years later the "music" and "computer" markets "were no longer different, separate or distinct": *per* Neill L.J., para. 23.

[84] See, *e.g. Hasselblad v. Commission* [1984] E.C.R. 883; [1984] 1 C.M.L.R. 559; [1984] F.S.R. 321, ECJ; *AEG-Telefunken* [1983] E.C.R. 3151, ECJ.

guarantee), may fail if there was a related breach of Article 81(1).[85] In *Javico v. Yves St Laurent*[86] the ECJ held that a selective distribution system outside the Community may fall foul of Article 81(1) if the agreement contains a provision restricting sales into the Community.[87]

(10) "Franchise agreements"

15–123 These present enormous diversity. The ECJ has noted three types particularly:

> "service franchise agreements, by which the franchisee offers services under the sign and trade name, or indeed the trade mark, of the franchisor and complies with the franchisor's directives; production franchise agreements by which the franchisee himself manufactures, according to the instructions of the franchisor, products which he sells under the franchisor's trade mark; and finally, distribution franchise agreements by which the franchisee restricts himself to the sale of certain products in a shop carrying the mark of the franchisor."[88]

In relation to the third type of agreement there will not normally be a breach of Article 81(1) by a clause protecting the franchisor's know-how. Nor will there be a breach by a clause which enables the franchisor to take appropriate measures to preserve the identity and reputation of the network which is symbolised by the mark, at least where such clauses are indispensable for this purpose.[89]

Procedural questions

15–124 Questions of Community law may arise in essentially two different contexts, namely in proceedings before a national court, or as a result of some direct action involving the European Commission. Where a point arises in proceedings before a national court it may, under Article 234 (formerly 177), be referred to the ECJ.[90] Whenever an agreement is thought potentially to fall within Article 81 an application may be made to the Commission for "negative clearance" or exemption.[91] Only the

---

[85] Thus the decision in *Sony v. Saray* [1983] F.S.R. 302, CA (see para. 14–100) might well have gone the other way if the defendants had not actually had to modify the parallel-imported television sets and they had been imported from an E.C. Member State.

[86] [1998] 5 C.M.L.R. 172.

[87] As long as the effects within the Community are appreciable: *ibid.*, para. 26.

[88] *Pronuptia* [1986] 1 C.M.L.R. 414, para. 13.

[89] *ibid.*, para. 17. This ruling provides a fairly strong indication that a normal trade mark licence agreement with quality control provisions would equally not fall within Art. 81(1).

[90] See the Civil Procedure Rules, RSC, Ord. 114 (contained in Sched. 1 and re-enacted by Part 50, CPR) as to the principles under which references are made. The main purpose of such a reference is to ensure that Community law is applied uniformly by national courts: *Foto-Frost* [1987] E.C.R. 4199.

[91] Parties may accept a so-called comfort letter in lieu of a formal decision and this is the more usual Commission practice. See Kerse, *EEC Antitrust Procedure*, and Bellamy and Child, *Common Market Law of Competition* (4th ed.) for the procedure.

Commission has power to grant an exemption (with review by the Court of First Instance).[92]

Effect of Community law on registrability or validity as such

It seems clear on general principles that no registration can be made of a **15–125** mark whose use is, under the E.C. Treaty or regulations, directly contrary to law.[93] But are there cases where registration can be refused because it would in some way infringe Articles 81 or 82? In principle there seems no reason why not. It would be necessary to prove that the registration formed part of some abusive conduct (for example part of a deliberate market dividing campaign). But given such proof and a sufficiently close nexus between the proposed registration and the abuse, it seems to follow that the use of the mark concerned would, in any event, be contrary to public policy and therefore forbidden under section 3(3)(a) of the Trade Marks Act 1994.

9. Competition Act 1998

The Competition Act 1998, which came into force on March 1, 2000,[94] **15–126** introduced a new regime to deal with restrictive agreements (Chapter I) and abuses of market power (Chapter II), respectively modelled on Articles 81 and 82 of the E.C. Treaty. It is stated expressly that the provisions must be interpreted and applied consistently with judgments of the ECJ and have regard to statements and decisions of the European Commission.[95] The Act repeals the Restrictive Trade Practices Act 1976, the Resale Prices Act 1976 and the provisions of the Competition Act 1980 dealing with anti-competitive practices.

Agreements which do not have an "appreciable effect on competi- **15–127** tion" will not be caught by the Chapter I prohibition. In general, an agreement is unlikely to have an appreciable effect where the combined market shares of the parties involved does not exceed 25 per cent.[96] So-

---

[92] *L'Oréal* [1981] 2 C.M.L.R. 235. The Commission's interpretation of Art. 81 diverges not infrequently from that of the Court of Justice: see, *e.g. Schöller* [1995] E.C.R. II–1611 and *Langnese-Iglo v. Commission* [1995] E.C.R. II–1533. It should be noted that the Commission proposes to decentralise the application of the competition rules and to make the exemption rule in Art. 81(3) directly applicable by Member States' competition authorities: see White Paper on Modernisation of the Rules Implementing Articles 85 and 86 of the E.C. Treaty, Commission Programme No 99/027 of April 28, 1999.

[93] *e.g*, contrary to E.C. wine regulations, as was suggested (without success on the facts) in *Domgarden* [1982] R.P.C. 155.

[94] A transitional period of one year generally applies to any agreement made before the Act came into force: Sched. 13, para. 19(1).

[95] s.60. "Different treatment for intellectual property rights under the Competition Act regime and the European regime seems neither necessary nor desirable and is likely to increase the burden on business of compliance", in "Exclusion of Vertical Agreements: Consultation on a draft Order" (Doc URN 88/1030), para. 22. This ignores the question as to whether judgments of the ECJ which are based expressly or implicitly on the overriding aim of creating a Common Market should be followed with reference to the U.K. Act in respect of which such an aim is irrelevant.

[96] Director-General of Fair Trading's guidelines on The Chapter I Prohibition, March 1999 (OFT 401), paras 2–18 to 2–22.

called "small agreements" which are not price-fixing agreements are given limited immunity:[97] the Chapter I prohibition does not apply to agreements between undertakings the combined turnover of which does not exceed £20 million in the year before the infringement occurred,[98] and the Chapter II prohibition does not apply to conduct of any undertaking whose turnover does not exceed £50 million.[99]

15–128   Most vertical agreements are excluded from the Chapter I prohibition[1]: a "vertical agreement" is defined as

> "an agreement between undertakings, each of which operates, for the purposes of the agreement, at a different level of the production or distribution chain, and relating to the conditions under which the parties may purchase, sell or resell certain goods or services and *includes provisions contained in such agreements which relate to the assignment to the buyer or use by the buyer of intellectual property rights, provided that those provisions do not constitute the primary object of the agreement and are directly related to the use, sale or resale of goods or services by the buyer or its customers.*" (emphasis added)[2]

Thus, where a vertical agreement contains trade mark provisions ancillary to the main purpose, for example a distribution agreement, it will be excluded.

15–129   An agreement which falls within the Chapter I prohibition may be exempted in three ways: (1) by being granted, on application, an individual exemption[3]; (2) by falling within a block exemption[4]; or (3) by benefiting from a parallel exemption where it is covered by an E.C. individual or block exemption,[5] or would be so covered if it had an effect on trade between Member States of the E.C. The exemption criteria[6] to be applied by the Office of Fair Trading (OFT) are very similar to Article 81(3).

15–130   The Chapter II prohibition covers the abuse of a dominant position in the market.[7] Unlike Article 82, which requires a dominant position in the whole or a substantial part of the Community, the provision does not limit its impact in this way: therefore, local dominance would still fall foul of the prohibition.[8]

---

[97] s.39. The immunity does not go to substance, may be withdrawn and does not affect third parties.
[98] Competition Act 1998 (Small Agreements and Conduct of Minor Significance) Regulations 2000, S.I. 2000 No. 262, Art. 3.
[99] *ibid.*, Art. 4.
[1] s.50 and the Competition Act 1998 (Land and Vertical Agreement Exclusion) Order 2000, S.I. 2000 No. 310.
[2] *ibid.*, Art. 2. *Cf.* the Vertical Restraints Block Exemption 2790/99, Art. 2(3) which is in identical terms.
[3] ss.4 and 5.
[4] ss.6–8.
[5] s.10(1).
[6] s.9. They include, in s.9(a)(ii), "promoting technical or economic progress", which may be relevant for intellectual property licences: *cf. Campari, op. cit.*
[7] s.18.
[8] DGFT Guidelines "Market definitions", Part 4.

10. Trade marks and restraint of trade

In a settlement agreement governing the use by the parties of their **15–131** respective trade marks in many countries around the world, the English court did not consider relevant whether particular provisions (in particular the field of use and no challenge clauses) contravened foreign laws, where the parties had chosen English law in the choice of law clause: *Apple Corps Ltd v. Apple Computer Inc.*[9] In order to establish that the agreement was enforceable under the law of restraint of trade, it was necessary for the party relying on it to prove (1) that the restraints contained in it were imposed for the purpose of protecting legitimate interests; and (2) that the restraints were no more than were necessary to protect those interests.[10] It should be noted that the broadened scope of infringement in the Trade Marks Act 1994, especially sections 10(3) and 56, makes the question as to whether a particular registered mark has been used less clearly relevant to the analysis of what are the legitimate interests and the reasonableness of the restraints. Also, it is difficult to envisage circumstances in which the common law of restraint of trade would now be applicable rather than the Competition Act 1998.[11]

[9] [1992] F.S.R. 431. "There must be cases in modern commercial life where world-wide restrictions will be necessary and proper. What the parties to commercial agreements require is certainty and it is natural, and generally desirable, that they should seek to identify a single system of law to govern their relationship": *per* Ferris J. at 456.

[10] [1991] 3 C.M.L.R. 49, CA. In this context, Nicholls L.J. considered that "the essence of Article 85 is not substantially different from the common law principles concerning unreasonable restraints of trade": para. 109.

[11] If the Competition Act 1998 were to be applied today to the facts in the *Apple* case, it is submitted that the analysis would be likely to be more favourable to the defendant's contention that market conditions had altered sufficiently since the parties entered into the delimitation agreement that it had become anti-competitive.

CHAPTER 16

ASSESSING THE DEGREE OF RESEMBLANCE OR SIMILARITY BETWEEN MARKS OR GET-UP

1. Outline, the tests, and onus

Introductory

16–01 Ever since the seventh edition of this work, published in 1951, there has been a chapter entitled "deceptive resemblance", whose function was to consider the degree and nature of resemblance between the parties' respective marks (or get-ups) for an action in passing off or trade mark infringement, or for an opposition to registration, to succeed.

16–02 Until now, "deceptive resemblance" was a pithy and fairly accurate title; it reflected the test for actionability in passing off,[1] as well as the test for near resemblance of marks under the Trade Marks Act 1938.[2] For this edition, however, we have felt that it is time to change the title of the chapter, mainly to reflect the changes brought by the Trade Marks Act 1994.

16–03 There have already been a number of key decisions of the domestic courts[3] and of the ECJ[4] in relation to the 1994 Act and the Trade Marks Directive but, nonetheless, the law of registered trade marks in this area is plainly still developing rapidly, and has already moved from the position under the 1938 Act very considerably. Perhaps one of the most fundamental changes is that in assessing whether there is a likelihood of confusion between two marks,[5] the court now has to consider the degree and nature of use of the claimant's registered mark.[6] In that sense, the

---

[1] Where it is often said that mere confusion is not enough, but a misrepresentation must be shown. See Chap. 14.

[2] Which was defined in s.68 of the 1938 Act as "a resemblance so near as to be likely to deceive or cause confusion".

[3] *e.g. Origins Natural Resources v. Origin Clothing* [1995] F.S.R. 280; *British Sugar v. Robertson* [1996] F.S.R. 281; *Wagamama v. City Centre Restaurants* [1995] F.S.R. 713.

[4] Most notably *Sabel v. Puma* [1997] E.C.R. I–6191, *Canon v. MGM* [1998] E.C.R. I–5507; *Lloyd Schufabrik Meyer v. Klijsen Handel* [1999] E.T.M.R. 690

[5] Strictly, in the context of infringement one should refer to the resemblance between the registered *mark* and the alleged infringing *sign*: see Jacob J. in *British Sugar v. Robertson* [1996] R.P.C. 281, correcting what he had said in *Origins Natural Resources v. Origin Clothing* [1995] F.S.R. 280. For present purposes, however, we will refer to comparison between marks, for simplicity.

[6] *Sabel* and *Canon, supra.*

594

tests for actionability in passing off and in registered trade mark infringement may be converging, but in relation to the degree of confusion/deception needed, the type of confusion or deception necessary, and the notional characteristics of the persons who must be confused or deceived, it seems more likely that the tests are starting to diverge.[7]

It may therefore be that by the time of the next edition of this work it **16–04** will be necessary or desirable to devote separate chapters to this topic in relation to passing off and registered trade marks respectively. For the moment, however, they continue to be considered together. One practical reason for this is that many of the old authorities concern both causes of action, and many modern cases still do so. Another is that the methods of proof available to a litigant are basically the same whatever the cause of action.

In the introduction to the chapter on "deceptive resemblance" in **16–05** previous editions of this work, there was always a warning to the effect that care should be taken in applying the rules set out, because of their different manner of application to passing off and to registered trade marks. Now, the warning must be that in reading the rules and authorities set out below, one must have regard to whether the 1938 Act, the 1994 Act or passing off (or more than one of them) is under consideration.

Scope of chapter

This chapter first identifies the contexts in which the resemblance of **16–06** marks falls to be considered for the purposes of this work. Thereafter it covers the level of confusion or deception required and the persons who must be confused or deceived. Then the numerous rules of comparison are discussed, with particular reference to the way in which they will be affected by the 1994 Act.

Finally, this chapter deals with evidence of confusion or deception **16–07** and the manner in which it may be gathered and presented to the court. This section covers "survey" evidence and evidence from the public generally. In considering survey evidence, consideration is also given to the increasing role of such evidence in showing what significance marks have to the public, in addition to its use to show confusion or deception.

This chapter should be read in conjunction with Appendix 35 which **16–08** contains a list of cases in which contentions of likely confusion or deception have succeeded or failed. As ever, the reader is warned that the cases mentioned there all turned on their own facts, and many were decided under the Acts of 1938 and before.

---

[7] Compare the tests under the 1994 Act, ss.5, 10 (see Chaps 8, 13), with the law on passing off as explained in Chap. 14.

Proceedings to which this chapter relates, and onus

16–09 The main different types of proceedings in which the question of deception or confusion arises are summarised in the paragraphs which follow, and some observations relevant to the proceedings in question are added.

(1) On an application to register, the Registrar or an opponent may object that the trade mark is not registrable by reason of section 5[8] of the 1994 Act. There is no overall onus one way or the other when the Registrar considers the application,[9] but on an opposition, the onus is on the opponent to make out any grounds on which he relies.[10] These matters are considered in more detail in Chapter 5.

16–10 (2) On an application to invalidate a registration under section 47 (by reference back to section 5),[11] the onus is on the applicant for invalidity, by reason of the presumption of validity contained in section 72.

(3) In an action for infringement (see Chapter 13),[12] the onus is on the claimant.

16–11 (4) In an action for "passing-off"[13] (see Chapter 14), the onus is on the claimant.

(5) In both infringement and passing off, in applications for interim injunctions. Here, although the onus is on the claimant, he need show only an arguable case (see Chapter 18).

Likelihood of confusion and other similar tests in the 1994 Act

16–12 In addition to the above situations, which are certainly the main ones, the following sections of the 1994 Act require consideration of the degree of resemblance between marks[14]:

(1) Under sections 16 to 19 (delivery up), remedies are available in relation to signs "identical or similar to" a registered trade mark.[15]

---

[8] And note that s.5(4) includes passing off against an earlier mark as a ground for refusing registration.

[9] "*Eurolamb*" [1997] R.P.C. 279; *Procter & Gamble (soap tablet shape)* [1998] R.P.C. 710; *Procter & Gamble (bottle shape)* [1999] R.P.C. 673, CA.

[10] "*Audi-Med*" [1998] R.P.C. 859; *Oasis Stores* [1998] R.P.C. 631. If, however, the evidence led in order to have the application accepted is rejected on opposition, then there is no overall onus: *Dualit* [1999] R.P.C. 304.

[11] The onus is the same whether the application is made as a counterclaim in infringement proceedings, or on its own by originating process.

[12] If brought under s.10(2) or 10(3); there is no requirement of confusion under s.10(1), that is to say if the alleged infringing sign is identical to the registered mark and is used on goods identical to those the subject of the registration. The same applies, *mutatis mutandis*, to infringement of CTMs.

[13] Including where passing off is invoked as an "earlier right" under s.5(4).

[14] Or between marks and signs: see n. 5, above.

[15] And in addition it is required that the application of the sign should infringe the registration: see Chap. 18.

(2) Under section 46(2), use by the proprietor of a mark "differing **16–13**
    in elements which do not alter the distinctive character of the
    mark" as registered counts as use for the purposes of meeting
    an allegation of invalidity through non-use.[16]

(3) Under section 56(2), the proprietor of a well-known mark
    within the meaning of the Paris Convention may obtain an
    injunction to restrain the use of "a trade mark which, or the
    essential part of which, is identical or similar to the [well-
    known] mark, in relation to identical or similar goods or
    services, where the use is likely to cause confusion."

(4) Under sections 57 and 58, national emblems and emblems of **16–14**
    certain international organisations are protected against
    unauthorised registration of marks consisting of or comprising
    those emblems or "anything which from a heraldic point of
    view imitates any such flag or other emblem . . .". Section 57
    also invokes the test of whether the emblem sought to be
    registered suggests a connection with the international organ-
    isation concerned or is likely to mislead as to the existence of
    such a connection.

(5) Under section 92 (criminal sanctions) and section 97 (forfeiture **16–15**
    in connection with criminal proceedings), the test of whether a
    sign is identical to "or likely to be mistaken for" the registered
    mark is employed.[17]

(6) Under the provisions relating to the powers of the Commis- **16–16**
    sioners of Customs and Excise under Community legislation
    (which do not arise directly from the 1994 Act, but are closely
    related to it).[18] The powers of the Commissioners under domes-
    tic legislation operate by reference to the definition of "infring-
    ing goods" in section 17, which is mentioned above.[19]

(7) Under section 99, use of the Royal or arms "so closely resem- **16–17**
    bling the Royal arms as to be calculated to deceive" in "such
    manner as to be calculated to lead to the belief that" the
    defendant is "duly authorised to use" them, is prohibited. This
    appears to be a passing-off kind of test.

Basic test under the 1994 Act

Before proceeding any further, it is worth setting out the main elements **16–18**
of the basic test which will be applied under the 1994 Act, as explained
by the ECJ in *Sabel v. Puma* and *Lloyd Schuhfabrik v. Meyer*.[20]

(1) It is a global test taking account of all factors relevant to the
    parties' marks and the goods or services in issue.

[16] See Chap. 9.
[17] See Chap. 19.
[18] See Chap. 20.
[19] See s.89.
[20] *Supra.* And see Chap. 8.

16-19   (2) The relevant factors include the degree and nature of use of the claimant's registered mark, its inherent and acquired distinctiveness.

(3) The similarity of the goods/services as well as of the marks themselves is a part of the consideration.

(4) The visual, oral and conceptual[21] similarity of the marks must be considered.

(5) Particular regard is to be had to the dominant and distinctive elements of the marks.[22]

2. Persons to be considered

Whom the mark must be calculated to deceive

16-20 This is an area where some care is needed, for under previous Trade Mark Acts, the test did not materially differ from the test in passing off. It is no longer clear that this is the case.

16-21   In relation to registered trade marks, the relevant standard is to be found in *Lloyd Schuhfabrik v. Meyer*,[23] which was considered and adopted by the Court of Appeal in *Bach Flower Remedies v. Healing Herbs*[24] (in the context of distinctiveness). The relevant person, according to *Lloyd*,[25] is the average consumer, who is considered to be "reasonably well informed and reasonably observant and circumspect", although taking account of the fact that such a person will rarely have the opportunity to make a direct comparison, but rather has to rely on "the imperfect picture of them that he has kept in his mind". It is also relevant that the average consumer's level of attention is likely to vary according to the category of goods or services in question.[26]

16-22   In passing off, the persons to be considered in estimating whether the resemblance between the marks in question is likely to deceive are all of those who are likely to become purchasers[27] of the goods upon which the marks are used, provided that such persons use ordinary care[28] and intelligence.

---

[21] *Sabel v. Puma* also refers to "analogous semantic content".

[22] See, *e.g. The European v. The Economist* [1996] F.S.R. 411, [1998] F.S.R. 283, where the common element between the parties' marks was not distinctive, and the action failed. The case is also interesting because the Court of Appeal endorsed the judge's decision to treat the case as one of passing off, even though trade mark infringement was alleged.

[23] *supra.*

[24] [2000] R.P.C. 513.

[25] In particular, para. 27 of the judgment.

[26] *ibid.*

[27] See, *e.g.* in "G.E." [1973] R.P.C. 297 at 321–322 HL, the distinction drawn between goods sold in a specialised market and goods sold to the general public for consumption or domestic use.

[28] *Christiansen* (1886) 3 R.P.C. 54 at 62, CA; *Coombe v. Mendit* (1913) 30 R.P.C. 709 at 717. The older cases regarding the standard of attention or carefulness to be expected of the ordinary member of the purchasing public are reviewed by the Assistant Registrar in *Angus* (1943) 60 R.P.C. 29 at 31. See also Chap. 14, and the cases below concerning differing levels of care in relation to different kinds of goods and services.

It may be, and time will tell, that these tests are not the same, and that **16–23** the reference in *Lloyd* to a "reasonably well informed and reasonably observant and circumspect" average consumer will have the effect that a likelihood of confusion for the purposes of the 1994 Act will be harder to show than a likelihood of deception for the purposes of passing off, owing to the different notional persons to be considered. This would be unfortunate, and may seem unlikely given that the two areas in many other ways recognise similar considerations, for example, the doctrine of imperfect recollection, and the notion of the "idea" of the mark.[29] For the moment, however, it is a possibility which must be borne in mind.[30]

The ultimate purchasers

It is clearly not enough to show that retailers buying goods for resale **16–24** would not be deceived, since they might themselves fraudulently or carelessly make use of the ambiguous character of the trade mark to deceive their customers, the ultimate purchasers[31]—or more likely, in these days of self-service, allow customers to deceive themselves. Dealers who buy from the manufacturers in order to sell by retail may be aware of attempted infringements and be parties to the fraud.[32]

Some marks are only used in the trade,[33] and in such cases it is **16–25** submitted that it is traders, rather than members of the public, who are to be considered.[34] It may, consequently, be hard to prove a likelihood of confusion or deception in such cases because they are likely to have a clear idea from whom they buy.

Standard of care to be expected

As is noted above in relation to *Lloyd*, and as common experience shows, **16–26** consumers' attention will vary depending on the kind of goods which they are buying, and not all classes of consumers will exercise the same level of care in choosing products.

Many older cases have considered this general issue, including cases going back to times when many consumers were illiterate (likely to be

---

[29] See below.
[30] If the difference does exist, it may even (in theory, at least) have implications for the free movement of goods where an action in passing off lies in the U.K. but an action for trade mark infringement would fail here and in Europe.
[31] *Wilkinson v. Griffith* (1891) 8 R.P.C. 370 at 374. See Mellish L.J. in *Ford v. Foster* (1872) L.R. 7 Ch. 611 at 616; and Lord Selborne in *Singer v. Loog* (1882) 8 App.Cas. 15; and *Powell v. Birmingham Vinegar* in the CA; 13 R.P.C. 235 at 250; and *Edge v. Niccolls* [1911] A.C. 693; 28 R.P.C. 582 at 593.
[32] *Lever v. Goodwin* (1887) 36 Ch.D. 1; 4 R.P.C. 492 at 498.
[33] *e.g.* as in *Scandecor v. Scandecor* [1998] F.S.R. 500 and [1999] F.S.R. 26.
[34] And this appears to be consistent with the exhortation in *Sabel* and *Lloyd* that all the relevant circumstances are to be considered.

relevant now only in relation to goods for export, or aimed at children[35]).

16–27   In considering all of the authorities below, it must be borne in mind that they were decided in relation to passing off or under older Trade Mark Acts, and may be overtaken by the standard under the 1994 Act, should that turn out to be different. With that said, the general principles are as follows:

16–28   (1) It must not be assumed that a very careful or intelligent examination of the mark will be made[36];

   (2) But, on the other hand, it can hardly be significant that unusually stupid people,[37] "fools or idiots"[38], or a "moron in a hurry"[39] may be deceived.

   (3) If the goods are expensive or important to the purchasers and not of a kind usually selected without deliberation,[40] and the customers generally educated persons, these are all matters to be considered.[41]

   (4) If some parts of the mark are common, one must consider whether people who know the distinguishing characteristics of the opponents' mark would be deceived.[42]

---

[35] Note that this point certainly is in keeping with *Lloyd* and the position under the 1994 Act, as considered above. See, for older cases, *Lever v. Goodwin* (1887) 36 Ch.D. 1; 4 R.P.C. 492. *Per* Lord Gorell in *Edge v. Niccolls* (1911) 28 R.P.C. 593. In one case in which the goods (lemonade powders) were largely bought by children, and it was suggested that they would be more easily deceived than adults, Byrne J. stated that, having regard to the nature of the goods which they would be likely to purchase for themselves, they would be less likely to be deceived than grown-up people: *Clark v. Sharp* (1898) 15 R.P.C. 141 at 149, settled on appeal (1898) 15 R.P.C. 268.

[36] *Wotherspoon v. Currie* (1872) L.R. 5 H.L. 508 at 519; "Ordinary purchasers purchasing with ordinary caution": *Seixo v. Provezende* (1865) L.R. 1 Ch. 192; "Ordinary" or "incautious" purchasers: *Powell v. Birmingham Vinegar* (1896) 13 R.P.C. at 258; not "persons of an ideal character who either are particularly innocent or too easily deceived": *Payton v. Snelling* (1900) 17 R.P.C. 48 at 57; 17 R.P.C. 628; and see Kekewich J. in *Marshall v. Sidebotham* (1901) 18 R.P.C. 43 at 49 and *Alaska Packers v. Crooks* (1901) 18 R.P.C. 129 at 137: "The unwary customer is extremely difficult to find"; but *cf. Currie* (1896) 13 R.P.C. 681, where the same judge had twice referred in the case to the "ordinary or unwary purchaser". in contrast to "intelligent persons".

[37] *Payton v. Titus Ward* (1900) 17 R.P.C. 58 at 67; *Scottish Union and National Insurance v. Scottish National Insurance* (1909) 26 R.P.C. 105 at 112; *Crook* (1914) 31 R.P.C. 79 at 85.

[38] Jessel M.R. in *Singer v. Wilson* (1876) 2 Ch.D. 434 at 447; *Smith* (1913) 30 R.P.C. 363 at 366.

[39] *Morning Star v. Express Newspapers* [1979] F.S.R. 113.

[40] Thus far, this principle is in keeping with *Lloyd*.

[41] See *HFC v. Midland* [2000] F.S.R. 176 at 184, and the contrast with "Jif", *Reckitt & Colman v. Borden* [1990] R.P.C. 341. *Pianotist* (1906) 23 R.P.C. 774 ("Neola," "Pianola"); and see *Claudius Ash v. Invicta* (1911) 28 R.P.C. 597; 29 R.P.C. 465, CA and HL where the customers were dentists and their assistants. *Rysta* (1943) 60 R.P.C. 87 at 106, *per* Greene M.R.

[42] See Romer L.J. in *Payton v. Snelling* (1900) 17 R.P.C. 48 at 57 (on appeal, 17 R.P.C. 628, HL; and *Same v. Titus Ward* (1900) 17 R.P.C. 58 at 67 (passing-off cases); also *Alaska Packers v. Crooks*, and *Marshall v. Sidebotham*, above.

New types of mark

A novel feature of the 1994 Act is the possibility of registering new types **16–29** of marks such as smells, sounds, and three-dimensional shapes. Their inherent registrability is considered in Chapter 7. Although their practical significance has yet to be assessed, it is now possible that one will have to inquire whether a smell mark is infringed by a graphical representation, or a sound mark by a smell, or a three-dimensional mark by a two-dimensional representation of it.

It is tentatively suggested that in determining cases of this kind, the **16–30** rules of comparison used for traditional marks will still fall to be applied in general, with the caveat that some of them will be of no, or only very limited, relevance to certain kinds of comparisons. For example, the importance of the first syllable would be of no relevance in relation to marks consisting of a smell (although by close analogy it might be relevant to marks consisting of a musical phrase). It is also suggested that the rule of comparison which will be of the greatest importance in relation to such marks is that which requires attention to the "idea of the mark". Thus, for example, by the application of that rule one would expect a mark consisting of the smell of roses probably to be infringed by a picture of a rose.[43]

3. Rules of comparison

What amount of resemblance is likely to confuse or deceive; proportion of public required to be deceived

Two important, and related, questions which arise are: what degree of **16–31** resemblance must be shown to demonstrate a likelihood of confusion or deception? And, what proportion of the public must be confused or deceived for the test to be satisfied?

The first question must be answered with regard to the principle that similarity *per se* is acceptable, so long as it does not lead to confusion.[44]

It is not, however, possible to discover from the decided cases any **16–32** absolute standard as to the amount of resemblance which may suffice to deceive or cause confusion. As Lord Cranworth said in *Seixo v. Provezende*[45]: "What degree of resemblance is necessary . . . is from the nature of things incapable of definition *a priori*." Nor is the standard always the same: thus in the case of pharmaceutical products, in the absence of restrictions upon their distribution, it is more important that

---

[43] For some new marks, this test may, however, have to modified in order to limit the proprietor to a fair degree of protection. For example, where a colour is registered, the "idea" of the mark may simply be, say, orange. To confer a monopoly in the use of orange for a whole category of goods on that basis would, it is suggested, be excessive.
[44] *e.g. The European v. Economist Newspapers* [1996] F.S.R. 431 and [1998] F.S.R. 283.
[45] (1895) L.R. 1 Ch. 192, cited by Luxmoore L.J. in *Rysta* (1943) 60 R.P.C. 87 at 108.

the public should be protected from the consequences of deception and confusion.[46] It follows that, except in so far as they lay down any general principle, the decided cases are of little assistance in the determination of new questions of fact raised upon other materials.

16–33   In all cases, as stated above, it should be borne in mind that a decision on the question whether a mark so nearly resembles another as to be likely to deceive or cause confusion is not an exercise of discretion by a tribunal but a finding of fact.[47]

16–34   As to the number of persons required to be confused or deceived before an action will succeed, the test is whether, on the balance of probabilities, a substantial number of persons would be.[48] The test has sometimes been phrased as "more than de minimis" or "above a trivial level", but these expressions were disapproved in *Neutrogena v. Golden*,[49] in particular on the basis that they do not necessarily connote the opposite of substantial. In that case, the claimant succeeded although the percentage of persons shown to be confused was really quite small, on the basis that although it was not possible to arrive at any quantitative or qualitative measure of the confusion, it was substantial.

16–35   With the exception of *The European*,[50] the authorities referred to above were decided in the context of passing off and/or the 1938 Act. *The European* was a fairly clear cut case for other reasons, and so it is fair to say that the questions set out above have not been fully considered in connection with the 1994 Act, albeit that there is no indication that they will be approached in a radically different way.

The tribunal can form its opinion

16–36   It has long been established that evidence of the likelihood of confusion or deception led at trial is not necessary, or, when it is led, decisive. The judge is not confined to such evidence, and is entitled to form his own view: *"GE" Trade Mark*,[51] *Re Christiansen's Trade Mark*,[52] *Spalding v. Gamage*,[53] *Neutrogena v. Golden*.[54]

---

[46] *Harker Stagg* (1953) 70 R.P.C. 205. See also *Vitamins* [1956] R.P.C. 1 at 13. The position is otherwise where restrictions upon distribution do exist (see, *e.g. Geigy v. Chelsea Drug* [1966] R.P.C. 64) unless it can be shown that the public will be deceived despite such restrictions (*Hoffman-La Roche v. D.D.S.A.* [1969] F.S.R. 410). Furthermore, where there is a possible doubt, a pharmacist will normally check: *Glaxo v. Pharmax* [1976] F.S.R. 278. Even so, the special risk to patients may make even minimal confusion unacceptable: *Sterwin v. Brocades* ("Danol", "De-Nol") [1979] R.P.C. 81.

[47] *Rysta* (1943) 60 R.P.C. 87 at 105, *per* Greene M.R.

[48] See *Neutrogena v. Golden* [1996] R.P.C. 473, *Reckitt & Colman v. Borden* [1990] R.P.C. 341, *Saville Perfumery v. June Perfect* (1941) 58 R.P.C. 147, and *Re Smith Hayden's Application* (1946) 63 R.P.C. 97.

[49] *Supra.*

[50] *Supra.*

[51] [1973] R.P.C. 297.

[52] (1886) 3 R.P.C. 54.

[53] (1913) 32 R.P.C. 273.

[54] *Supra.*

Idea of the mark

Two marks, when placed side by side, may exhibit many and various **16–37** differences, yet the main idea left on the mind by both may be the same. A person acquainted with one mark, and not having the two side by side for comparison, might well be deceived, seeing the second mark on other goods, into a belief that he was dealing with goods which bore the same mark as that with which he was acquainted. Thus, for example, a mark may represent a game of football; another mark may show players in a different dress, and in very different positions, and yet the idea conveyed by each might be simply a game of football.[55] It would be too much to expect that persons dealing with trade-marked goods, and relying, as they frequently do, upon marks, should be able to remember the exact details of the marks upon the goods with which they are in the habit of dealing. Marks are remembered rather by general impressions or by some significant detail than by any photographic recollection of the whole.[56] Moreover, variations in details might well be supposed by customers to have been made by the owners of the trade mark they are already acquainted with for reasons of their own.[57]

When the question arises whether a mark so resembles another mark **16–38** as to be likely to deceive or cause confusion, it should be determined by considering what is the leading characteristic of each. The one might contain many, even most, of the same elements as the other, and yet the leading, or it may be the only, impression left on the mind might be very different. On the other hand, a critical comparison of two marks might disclose numerous points of difference, and yet the idea which would remain with any person seeing them apart at different times might be the same. Thus it is clear that a mark is infringed if the essential features, or essential particulars of it, are taken.[58] In cases of device marks, especially, it is helpful before comparing the marks to consider what are the essentials of the claimant's device[59]; with word marks, the court is apt to be more impressed by the dangers of giving the claimant what amounts to a monopoly in a large class of words.[60]

---

[55] cf. *Barker* (1885) 53 L.T. 23 ("Huntsman" or "Sportman's" cherry brandy); *Reynolds v. Laffeaty's* [1957] R.P.C. 311, CA; [1958] R.P.C. 387 ("Watermatic" an infringement of "Aquamatic" for water-pistols).

[56] *De Cordova v. Vick* (1951) 68 R.P.C. 103 at 106, PC.

[57] *Johnston v. Orr-Ewing* (1882) 7 App.Cas. 219 (illus. (1), below); *Ravenhead Brick v. Ruabon* (1937) 54 R.P.C. 341 at 349 ("Rus" and "Sanrus"). *Yahoo! v. Akash Arora* [1999] F.S.R. 931 (HC Delhi).

[58] *De Cordova v. Vick* (1951) 68 R.P.C. 103 at 106; *Taw v. Notek* (1951) 68 R.P.C. 271; *Murphy* (1890) 7 R.P.C. 163. See also *Bale & Church v. Sutton Parsons* (1934) 51 R.P.C. 129, *per* Romer L.J. It is less usual for decisions upon applications to register to refer to "essential features": partly, perhaps, because device marks are rarely concerned (cf. below), partly because the sort of evidence used in such cases seldom lends itself to such an approach.

[59] *De Cordova v. Vick, supra; Jaw v. Notek, supra; Saville Perfumery v. June Perfect* (1941) 58 R.P.C. 147 were all cases where the plaintiff's mark was a device mark.

[60] See *London Lubricant* (1925) 42 R.P.C. 264 at 278 ("Tripcastroid"). See also *De Cordova v. Vick*, above; *Hassan El-Madi* (1954) 71 R.P.C. 281 at 289. There are exceptions, however, like the *"Parker-Knoll"* case [1962] R.P.C. 265, where "Knoll" was treated as an essential feature of the mark "Parker-Knoll"; and see the *G.E.C.* cases (illus. (12) and (13) below as to initial marks.

16–39   A similar question may arise where the defendant has added a prefix or suffix to a word mark of the claimant. Such cases have sometimes been disposed of merely by saying that the defendant is necessarily using the claimant's mark; but the sounder approach is to treat the defendant's mark as a combination having "one individual thing which is a monopoly of the plaintiff".[61] It is then necessary to consider how important that thing is to the whole. So also, where the defendant's mark is part of the claimant's. Where a suffix is merely descriptive or simply makes the mark more specific, it will not avoid infringement,[62] and so too where it is apt to suggest an addition to a range of goods.[63]

16–40   To refer in this context to "essential particulars" (which was the expression used in section 9 of the 1938 Act and hence should be regarded with a little caution if authorities based on it are sought to be used in the context of the 1994 Act) suggests that it may be convenient to put the question in the form, whether the defendant has taken those features which give the claimant's mark that distinctiveness needed to support the registration?[64] Such an approach is sometimes convenient; but it does not follow that there can be no infringement unless what the defendant has taken is a registrable mark.[65] A more contemporary way of expressing this idea, put the other way around, is that the central idea of the claimant's mark is of great importance in the comparison, but only if it is distinctive in nature; this was the way it was put by the Court of Appeal in *The European v. The Economist*.[66]

16–41   The importance of having regard to the idea of the mark is such that it may well result in a finding that there is no likelihood of confusion even though in other ways the marks are very similar. For example, registration of LANCER was allowed despite the presence on the Register of LANCIA because, despite the considerable similarity to the ear, the ideas conveyed were very different.[67]

16–42   (1) Both the plaintiff's and the defendant's marks consisted of tickets bearing pictures of two elephants with a banner between them, the figures being differently arranged. Lord Selborne

---

[61] *Sanitas v. Condy* (1886) 4 R.P.C. 580. *cf. Ravenhead Brick v. Ruabon* (1937) 54 R.P.C. 341, where "Rus" was held to be infringed by "Sanrus".

[62] See *Yahoo! v. Akash Arora, supra*.

[63] As in *Portakabin v. Powerblast* [1990] R.P.C. 471: "Porta" infringed by "Portablast".

[64] And this kind of reasoning was adopted and even decisive in *The European v. The Economist* [1996] F.S.R. 431, [1998] F.S.R. 283, where the claimant's mark's main feature was the word "*European*", but that word had been disclaimed from the registration.

[65] Such a contention was expressly rejected in "*Electrix*" [1959] R.P.C. 283 ("Electrix" held unregistrable, as phonetic equivalent of "electrics", for electrical equipment, notwithstanding that it had been held to infringe "Electrux"). But *cf.*, for instance, *Jeyes v. Aliamaid* (1955) 72 R.P.C. 277, where the contention that "J" infringed "Jeyes" might well have been better received if "J" had not so obviously been a mark no trader might monopolise.

[66] *Supra.* And see also *United Biscuits v. Asda* [1997] R.P.C. 513, ("Penguin" v. "Puffin"), where the passing-off claim succeeded, but a trade mark infringement claim based on a "Penguin" mark failed, because there was no pictorial element to the registered mark.

[67] *LANCER Trade Mark* [1987] R.P.C. 303.

said[68]: "Although the mere appearance of these two tickets could not lead anyone to mistake one of them for the other, it might easily happen that they might both be taken by natives of Aden or of India, unable to read and understand the English language, as equally symbolical of the plaintiff's goods.": *Johnston v. Orr-Ewing* (1882) 1 App.Cas. 219.[69]

(2) The registered mark included the words "The Cock o' the North" with a picture of a cock. The applicant's mark consisting of a similar cock was refused, both marks being for Scotch whisky: *Curries* (1896) 13 R.P.C. 681. See however *Fromex SA's Application* [1999] E.T.M.R. 989, OHIM. **16–43**

(3) In *Danish Bacon*[70] Luxmoore J. upheld the decision of the Registrar refusing to register the applicants' device marks consisting of representations of pigs on the grounds that the marks would conflict with the opponents' trade marks one being a picture of three pigs, but quite different from the applicants' picture of three pigs, and the other consisting of the words "Three Pigs Brand". **16–44**

(4) In the *Cat and Barrel* cases,[71] it was found that the plaintiffs' trade mark had come to be known as the "Cat and Barrel Brand", and the marks held to be infringements included combinations of a cat and barrel differing to a considerable extent from that which appeared in the plaintiffs' mark. **16–45**

(5) On the other hand, an application for a mark consisting of the head of a Red Indian was allowed to proceed to advertisement notwithstanding the presence on the Register of a mark consisting of a Red Indian on horseback and the words "Red Indian", which were disclaimed, but this was on the ground that there had been substantial user of the applicant's mark: *Carborundum* (1909) 26 R.P.C. 504. **16–46**

(6) In a case where the plaintiffs were suing to restrain the infringement of their registered trade mark "999" by the use of "99" and the words "double nine", and they had several other triple numbers also registered, it was suggested that the idea of their mark was the repetition of a digit. It was held that the idea of the mark was at the most triplication, and that there was no infringement, and a claim for passing off also failed: *Ardath Tobacco v. Sandorides* (1925) 42 R.P.C. 50. **16–47**

[68] At 225. See also *Baschiera* (1889) 33 S.J. 469; 5 T.L.R. 480; the ground of rejection was that "the dominating portion of each mark was a lion, and the goods were designated by the prevailing feature according to the custom of the trade"; and *Christiansen* (1886) 3 R.P.C. 54, the "*Taendstikker*" case (matchbox labels).
[69] See also *Hollins v. Cotella* (1937) 54 R.P.C. 81.
[70] (1934) 51 R.P.C. 148.
[71] *Boord v. Huddart* (1904) 21 R.P.C. 149; *Same v. Thom* (1907) 24 R.P.C. 697, IH, Scotland. The "*Eastern Dye Works*" case, *Greisheim Electron* (1910) 27 R.P.C. 201 is another illustration of the principle.

16–48 (7) Both the plaintiffs and the defendants used as their trade mark for motor lamps devices in which a pair of motor-car head-lamps were represented as the eyes of a cat, seen full-face. The devices were otherwise very different: the one, essentially a distorted line drawing of an old-fashioned motor-car (with the word "Taw", although that was disclaimed); the other a detailed representation of the head of a cat, with the word "Notek". But it was held that the idea of the marks was the same, and that there was infringement: *Taw v. Notek* (1951) 68 R.P.C. 271.

16–49 (8) Where the opponents were owners of a very well-known mark, consisting of a dog looking into a gramophone with the words "His Master's Voice", an application to register "Pup" for similar goods was allowed, since it did not appear that the opponents' mark was regarded by the public as a "puppy" mark: *Kolster Brandes* (1933) 50 R.P.C. 198.

16–50 (9) Where the opponents had for many years used "Ace" as a mark (without registering it), an application to register a device of aces with the word "Ace" was refused notwithstanding an offer to disclaim the word "Ace"; since regardless of any disclaimer, goods so marked would be referred to as "Ace" goods: *Mellor* (1948) 65 R.P.C. 238; but "ACEC" was allowed in the face of "Ace", one being a word, the other merely a set of initials: *ACEC* [1965] R.P.C. 369.

(10) A mark containing prominently the representation of half an apple was refused registration on account of the words "Apple Brand" in two registered marks: *Pomril* (1901) 18 R.P.C. 181.[72]

16–51 (11) Where on an application to register a mark consisting of four pictures in separate panels, one of which represented a ship, and the application was opposed by the owners of a mark consisting of a ship whose goods had become known as "Ship Brand", it was held that the picture of a ship in the mark applied for, if it stood alone, would lead to confusion and that the four pictures were not combined in such a way as to take from the picture of a ship its individual significance and that therefore there was a probability of deception: *Huxley* (1924) 41 R.P.C. 423.[73]

16–52 (12) On an interlocutory motion to restrain infringement of a mark "GEC" by the use of the mark "CEC", the court said that "The resemblance could hardly be closer, short of actual identity, and might well confuse anyone not having special knowledge." A contention that the defendants' goods were of a highly spe-cialised character, such that customers for them would not be

---

[72] See also *Forth & Clyde v. Sugg* (1928) 45 R.P.C. 382, where "Red Knight" was held to be infringement of "Silent Knight" (gas fires; there was evidence of actual confusion).
[73] See also *Connor* (1924) 41 R.P.C. 458: two very different devices, both with word "Sterling".

confused, failed on the ground that the plaintiffs' goods covered a very wide range and the matter must be considered "over the whole range of potential customers for goods protected by the plaintiff company's marks": *General Electric v. Consolidated Electrodynamics* [1963] R.P.C. 1 at 3, 4. However "MEM" was allowed against opposition by "GEM" (for razor blades), M and G being visually distinct and the ideas of the two words being different: *MEM* [1965] R.P.C. 347.

(13) The (British) General Electric Company had a mark consisting **16–53** of the initials "G.E.C." in script lettering. The (American) General Electric company used the initials "G.E." in script lettering in a "rondel". The two were held confusingly similar, even though they could confuse only by suggesting the confusingly similar company names: "*G.E*" [1973] R.P.C. 297 (HL at 317, 322).

(14) Where an opponent had used "Liebling" for Rhine wines, registration of "Rheinliebling" for such wines was refused: "*Rheinliebling*" [1966] R.P.C. 68.

(15) The plaintiff's mark comprised an oval border, which enclosed **16–54** "Laura Ashley", and a botanical sprig. The defendant's mark comprised a similar oval border, enclosing "Coloroll", and a different sprig. The plaintiff contended that the essential feature of the mark was the oval border. Whitford J. disagreed. His initial view was that the essential feature was "Laura Ashley" and the evidence did not persuade him from that view: *Laura Ashley v. Coloroll* [1987] R.P.C. 1.

(16) The claimant had a registration for "European" with other **16–55** elements, which it used as a banner for a newspaper. The defendant also used a banner with "European" in it, also with other elements which differed from the claimant's. The claim failed because "European" was disclaimed from the registration, so although the central idea of the marks was very close, that was not relevant: *The European v. The Economist* [1996] F.S.R. 431, [1998] F.S.R. 283.

(17) "Zinc" was infringed by "Zn", the chemical symbol for zinc: *Conran v. Mean Fiddler* [1997] F.S.R. 856.

Where the goods are known by a name suggested by the mark

Cases in which the goods of a particular trader have become known by **16–56** a name derived from his trade mark may be considered as carrying a stage further the concept of the "idea of a mark". In these special cases,[74]

---

[74] Note that what is said here assumes that it is proved that the goods have become so known: mere surmise that they may have become so known amounts to little more than argument as to what the idea of the mark is. *cf. Holbrooks* (1909) 26 R.P.C. 791, where the

any other mark which would be likely to suggest the use of the same name for the goods on which it is used, so resembles the former as to be likely to deceive. With the present-day predominance of "word" as distinct from "label" marks, this sort of case is now very rare; though similar considerations could arise in disputes over rival logos. The matter is discussed at length in all earlier editions of this work.

16–57   (1) Where the trade mark of the plaintiff was a crown and the word "Seixo", and his goods had in consequence come to be known in the market as "Crown-Seixo" wine, the defendants were restrained from using marks which led their wine to be described by the same name, although evidence was given that "Seixo" was a common word in Portuguese: *Seixo v. Provezende* (1865) L.R. 1 Ch. 192.[75]

16–58   (2) "L'AMY" was refused under section 12 of the 1938 Act for a mark consisting of a device with a small "LAMY"; notwithstanding that "LAMY" (a foreign surname) was disclaimed: there was no other way of "naming" the goods carrying the LAMY mark: *L'AMY* [1983] R.P.C. 137 at 143 (Regy).

opponents' goods were sold under a name other than that suggested by the applicant's mark. And see *Angus Watson* (1911) 28 R.P.C. 313, Parker J., where the applicants were the registered owners of the trade mark "Skipper" for sardines, and the opponents owned the same word for all other goods in the same class, including tinned salmon. The applicants sought to register for such goods a label with the word "Sailor" prominently appearing under a picture of a sailor, and the opponents alleged that goods sold under that label would by reason of the applicants' own use of the word "Skipper" for sardines become known as "Skipper" salmon, etc.; on appeal to the court the opposition was disallowed, the applicants consenting to amend by altering the word "Sailor" to "Sailor Brand".

[75] Other cases are: *Orr-Ewing v. Johnston* (1880) 13 Ch.D. 434; 7 App.Cas. 219 ("*Two Elephant Yarns*"); *Speer* (1887) 4 R.P.C. 521 ("*Dog, Tower, and Harp Linen*"); *Verreries de l'Etoile* [1894] 1 Ch. 61; 10 R.P.C. 436; [1894] 2 Ch. 26; 11 R.P.C. 142 ("*Red Star Glass*"); *Wilkinson v. Griffith* (1891) 8 R.P.C. 370 ("*Red Medal Polish*"); *Dewhurst* [1896] 2 Ch. 137; 13 R.P.C. 288 ("*Golden Fan Cotton*"); *Currie* (1896) 13 R.P.C. 681 ("*Cock o' the North Whisky*"); the *Cat and Barrel* cases, and *Eastern Dye Works* cited above. In *Cowie v. Herbert* (1897) 14 R.P.C. 436, Ct of Sess, such a case was set up by the plaintiffs, but failed ("*El-Musjid*"), as also did the plaintiffs in *Lever v. Bedingfield* (1899) 16 R.P.C. 3, where the plaintiffs had a small picture of a laundry-maid on the label, and the defendant had the words "Red Maid", and the plaintiffs relied (*inter alia*) on that. See also *Dubonnet* (1915) 31 R.P.C. 453; 32 R.P.C. 241. In *Tatem v. Gaumont* (1917) 34 R.P.C. 181 CA, the plaintiffs, who alleged that their mark had caused their goods to be known as "Black Cat Films", failed in an infringement action to restrain the use of a quite different mark in which a black cat appeared. See also "*Ship Brand*", *Prices' v. Jeyes'* (1902) 19 R.P.C. 17 compromised on the plaintiff's appeal; *cf.* also *Pomril* (1901) 18 R.P.C. 181 ("*Apple Brand*" cider). A somewhat similar point arose in a case in which the applicants and opponents were both companies whose names included the surname "Cording"; it was held that, in the circumstances, the mark "Gnidroc", being the name "Cording" reversed, was calculated to deceive, and registration was refused; but, the opponents not objecting, the application was allowed to proceed in the form "Nidroc": *Cording* (1916) 33 R.P.C. 83 and 325 HL.

The mark as a whole: common elements

The trade mark is the whole thing—the whole picture in relation to each **16–59** of the marks being compared has to be considered. There may be differences in the parts of each mark, but it is important to consider the mode in which the parts are put together and to judge whether the dissimilarity of the part or parts is enough to make the whole dissimilar.

In the case of the application to register "Erectiko",[76] Farwell J. said: "I **16–60** do not think it is right to take a part of the word and compare it with a part of the other word; one word must be considered as a whole and compared with the other word as a whole . . . I think it is a dangerous method to adopt to divide the word up and seek to distinguish a portion of it from a portion of the other word."

Both the applicant and the opponent were mustard merchants, and **16–61** both used square boxes covered with yellow labels printed in black and red; these boxes were common to the trade. The applicant placed upon his labels a picture of a charging buffalo, and the opponent a picture of a bull's head; both pictures were contained within silver rings, and these rings were also common to the trade. Stirling J. said that the buffalo and the bull's head, as printed in the Trade Marks Journal, were very different, but when they were placed upon the coloured labels, the applicant's label too closely resembled that of the opponent to be admitted to the Register: *Farrow*.[77]

It has been said that if the only resemblances between the two marks **16–62** are in parts which are common, so that the owner of the one has taken nothing which is peculiar to the other, then there is at all events no infringement,[78] at any rate unless the claimant has a distinctive arrangement of the common elements. But this approach is hardly suited to a comparison of word marks; and even in relation to label marks or other features of get-up, it would seem more appropriate to consider the case as a whole, with due regard to the background provided by any other marks shown to be in use.

Elements in common use: some dicta

In *Broadhead*,[79] Evershed M.R., following the observations of Lord **16–63** Russell in *Coca Cola Canada v. Pepsi Cola Canada*,[80] stated: "Where you get a common denominator, you must in looking at the competing formulae

---

[76] *Bailey* (1935) 52 R.P.C. 136 at 151, opposed by the proprietors of the trade mark "Erector". Registration refused. See *Broadhead* (1950) 67 R.P.C. 113 at 119. See *per* Evershed M.R. in *Electrolux v. Electrix* (1954) 71 R.P.C. 23 at 31.

[77] (1890) 7 R.P.C. 260; 63 L.T. 233.

[78] *The European v. The Economist* [1996] F.S.R. 431, [1998] F.S.R. 83; *Jamieson v. Jamieson* (1898) 15 R.P.C. 169; *Payton v. Snelling* (1900) 17 R.P.C. 48, especially at 56 (affirmed by HL, 17 R.P.C. 628); *Payton v. Titus Ward* (1900) 17 R.P.C. 58 at 63, all passing-off cases; *Marshall v. Sidebotham* and *Alaska Packers v. Crooks*, above (trade mark and passing off).

[79] (1950) 67 R.P.C. 209 at 215, where a dispute arose as to an admission as to what was fair use of marks "Alka-vescent" and "Alka-Seltzer".

[80] (1942) 59 R.P.C. 127; "Pepsi-Cola" held not an infringement of "Coca-Cola," "Cola" being common to the trade; applied also in *Demuth* (1948) 65 R.P.C. 342 ("Seda Seltzer" not too close to "Alka Seltzer", "Seltzer" being common to the trade).

pay much more regard to the parts of the formulae which are not common—although it does not flow from that that you must treat the words as though the common part was not there at all." Where common parts are included in the trade marks to be compared, or in one of them, the proper course is to look at the marks as wholes, and not to disregard the parts which are common.[81]

16–64   In the *"Kleenoff"* case,[82] Maugham L.J. said: "In the present case my view is that the test of infringement where the trade mark has a descriptive element is the same as the test where it has no descriptive element, except so far as the descriptive element is itself common to the trade."

16–65   In *Harrods*,[83] the Registrar stated: "It is a well-recognised principle that has to be taken into account in considering the possibility of confusion arising between any two trade marks, that, where those two marks contain a common element which is also contained in a number of other marks in use in the same market, such a common occurrence in the market tends to cause purchasers to pay more attention to the other features of the respective marks and to distinguish between them by those features. This principle clearly requires that the marks comprising the common element shall be in fairly extensive use and, as I have mentioned, in use in the markets in which the marks under consideration are being or will be used."

16–66   "It is not right to pull the words to pieces, ACCU- for one part and -IST and -LARM for the other part, next to argue that ACCU reminds you of 'accurate', no matter what the suffix, and to conclude that the upshot will be a monopoly in the natural word": *per* Harman L.J. in *Accutron*.[84]

16–67   In *The European v. The Economist*,[85] Millett L.J. said: ". . . 'European' is the most prominent feature of the plaintiff's mark, but . . . it is not a made-up or invented word but an ordinary word in common use, capable of being used most naturally in a descriptive manner, and in the case of the defendant's newspaper used to describe its character and contents. . . . Where descriptive words are included in a registered trade mark, the courts have always and rightly been exceedingly wary of granting a monopoly in their use."

---

[81] See above and also *Christiansen* (1886) 3 R.P.C. 54 at 61, CA. The fact that a part of the mark is common must be taken into consideration, and if the common feature appears in an unusual way that is an element to be considered: *Orr-Ewing v. Registrar* (1879) 4 App.Cas. 479.

[82] *Bale & Church v. Sutton* (1934) 51 R.P.C. 129 at 144, CA ("Kleenup" held to infringe "Kleenoff," on domestic cleaning material). Typical cases of this sort are *"Accutron"*, below, n. 84, and *"Rheinliebling"* [1966] R.P.C. 68; for cases where the descriptive element was common to the trade, see above.

[83] (1935) 52 R.P.C. 65 at 70. "Hyde Park" for cigarettes opposed by proprietors of marks containing the words "Park" or "Park Drive". Application allowed subject to limitation.

[84] [1966] R.P.C. 152 at 158. Subsequently *"Bulova Accutron"* was also refused, the grounds being that the mark would be taken to be two trade marks, namely, a "house name" together with the trade mark "Accutron": *"Bulova Accutron"* [1969] R.P.C. 102.

[85] [1998] F.S.R. 283 at 289–290.

In *The European*, it so happened that the common element was **16–68** disclaimed from the registration. Disclaimers may no longer be imposed under the 1994 Act, and if registrations are granted containing common elements without a disclaimer, it is suggested that the approach of identifying and allowing for common matter will increase in practical importance very considerably.

Importance of first syllable

It has been accepted in several reported cases that the first syllable of a **16–69** word mark is generally the most important. It has been observed in many cases that there is a "tendency of persons using the English language to slur the terminations of words".[86]

Groups of related marks

Where there are a "series" of marks, registered or unregistered, but in **16–70** use, having a common feature or a common syllable and where all the marks in such a series belong to an opponent, these are generally circumstances adverse to an applicant for a mark containing the common feature, since the public might think that such a mark indicated goods coming from the same source[87]; the strength of this "series" objection depending on how distinctive the common feature is.[88] If the marks in the series are owned by different persons, this tends to negative any proprietorial signification of the common feature and so may assist the applicant,[89] unless the common feature is descriptive of a

---

[86] *London Lubricants* (1925) 42 R.P.C. 264 at 279, CA; "Tripcastroid"), *per* Sargant L.J.; *Enoch* (1947) 64 R.P.C. 119, "Vivicyllin" allowed notwithstanding "Cyllin", at 122; *Bayer* (1947) 64 R.P.C. 125 at 128, "Diasil" allowed notwithstanding "Alasil"; *Demuth* (1948) 65 R.P.C. 342 at 346; "Seda Seltzer" allowed notwithstanding "Alka Seltzer"; *Fitchetts v. Loubet* (1919) 36 R.P.C. 296, "Rito" allowed notwithstanding "Lito" and "Yto"; *Fox* (1920) 37 R.P.C. 37, "Motrate" allowed notwithstanding "Filtrate"; "Cal-U-Test" allowed notwithstanding 12 other "Test" marks with different prefixes, *Cal-U-Test* [1967] F.S.R.. 39; *Capsuloid* (1906) 23 R.P.C. 782, "Tablones" too near "Tabloids"; *Accutron* [1966] R.P.C. 152, "Accutron" too near "Accurist" for watches; and *Buler* [1966] R.P.C. 141, "Buler" too near "Bulova" for watches, are instances of paired marks with common first parts; note that in the first case, where the common part is descriptive, the Registrar refused registration; in the second, where the common part has no separate meaning, he would have allowed registration but the court did not; *cf.* the quotation, *supra*, from the "*Kleenoff*" case. But *cf. Aristoc v. Rysta* 62 R.P.C. 65; *Reynolds v. Lafferty* [1957] R.P.C. 311, CA (interim proceedings), [1958] R.P.C. 387 (final proceedings); "Watermatic" too near "Aquamatic" for water-pistols; *Geigy v. Chelsea Drug* [1966] R.P.C. 64 ("butazolidin" not infringed by "butazone"). "Bensyl" too close to "Bentasil" and "Benvil": *BENSYL Trade Mark* [1992] R.P.C. 529. "Neutralia" confusingly similar to "Neutrogena": *Neutrogena v. Golden* [1996] R.P.C. 473.
[87] *e.g. Accutron* [1966] R.P.C. 152 (opposition by proprietor of "Accurist" and "Accularm"); *Flowstacka* [1968] R.P.C. 66.
[88] "*Frigiking*" [1973] R.P.C. 739 ("King" not distinctive enough for a "series" objection to have much weight).
[89] *Beck, Koller* (1947) 64 R.P.C. 76: "Plyophen" refused in view of many other marks commencing with "Plio"; *British Lead Mills* [1958] R.P.C. 425. ("Welloy" refused: opponents owned many marks beginning with "Wel").

class of goods narrower or different from the goods in respect of which registration is sought. If the marks in a series are merely on the Register, but are not shown to be in use and so known to the public, the above considerations do not apply, and such marks must be considered individually only.[90]

Ear as well as eye must be considered

16–71 The importance of aural similarity is expressly recognised in the jurisprudence of the ECJ: see paragraphs 16-01 *et seq.*, above. This is especially important now that infringement can be committed by oral use of a mark.[91]

The resemblance between two marks must be considered with reference to the ear as well as to the eye.[92] Whether confusion will arise in the course of telephone conversations must also be considered.[93]

16–72 Examination of reported cases shows that where the marks are meaningless words, or words of essentially similar character, the courts give as much weight to phonetic as to visual resemblance.[94] But for a mere accidental phonetic resemblance (in the sense that the idea of the marks, once properly grasped, is quite different) to convince the court of deceptive resemblance calls for something special: for a convincing demonstration that some context likely to occur in actual commerce would convert the accidental resemblance into something approaching identity of sound.[95] However, careless pronunciation and the fact that the actual purchaser may be buying for someone else are both relevant.[96]

---

[90] *"Semigres"* [1979] R.P.C. 330 (Regy; refused for a series of "Sem-" marks); citing *Beck, Koller* (1947) 64 R.P.C. 76.

[91] See Chap. 13.

[92] *County Chemical Appn.* (1937) 54 R.P.C. 182 at 185 ("Arlette"). *"June Perfect"* (1941) 58 R.P.C. 147 at 161. A good example of the possibility of oral confusion being decisive is *Philips* [1969] R.P.C. 78. The two marks were visually entirely different, but because the applicants' mark contained the word "Philips" there was a distinct possibility of oral confusion with the defendants' signature mark which ended with the surname "Phillips".

[93] *Magdalena Securities* (1931) 48 R.P.C. 477 at 487 ("Ucolite" held by court to be too near "Coalite" for registration); *Bayer* (1947) 64 R.P.C. 125 at 133; *Rheinliebling* [1966] R.P.C. 68 at 74 (not apparent over telephone whether mark was one word or two); *Morcream v. Heatherfresh* [1972] R.P.C. 799 (trade name case; too close to "Everfresh", on telephone only; injunction granted specifically against business on telephone).

[94] Thus in *Ouvah Ceylon v. Uva Ceylon* (1910) 27 R.P.C. 645 at 753, the plaintiffs obtained an injunction against the defendants' use of their name, the first word in each being a different spelling of the name of the same district. See also the cases establishing that a mark is unregistrable if it is a phonetic equivalent of an unregistrable mark; *e.g.* "Dex" for bolts ("Deck bolts"), *National Machinery* (1941) 58 R.P.C. 128; "Pirle" (because of "pearl"), *Ripley* (1895) 15 R.P.C. 151; "Electrix" ("electrics" admitted unregistrable), *"Electrix"* [1959] R.P.C. 283; and "Orlwoola", ("all wool"), *Orlwoola* [1910] 1 Ch. 130; 26 R.P.C. 683, 850.

[95] *cf.* "Kidax" [1960] R.P.C. 117 ("Kidax" registered notwithstanding "Daks", for clothing: court not convinced anyone would ask for "Kiddies' Daks"); *Jeyes v. Aliamaid* (1955) 72 R.P.C. 277 (court not convinced anyone would ask just for "3 Jeyes'" (or "J's'"), and possible confusion between "3 bottles of 'J'" and "3 bottles of 'Jeyes'" not sufficient to justify a monopoly of the letter "J"); *Broadhead* (1950) 67 R.P.C. 209 (real possibility of

Since all the circumstances of the trade are to be considered, it is **16–73** relevant to inquire whether and to what extent the customer has to call for goods by name in order to buy them. In public houses, drinks will be offered and ordered orally by name and the likelihood of confusion owing to similarity in the sound of the marks may be high. On the other hand, in supermarkets these days the customer normally takes goods off the shelf without asking for assistance, and the goods bear trade marks prominently where they are easy to see. In such circumstances, Whitford J. observed in *Mars v. Cadbury*[97] (the "Treat Size" case), the importance of the sound of a mark may be diminishing.

Imperfect recollection

This aspect of the comparison between marks has also been adopted by **16–74** the ECJ in relation to the ordinary consumer test: see paragraphs 16–01 *et seq.*, above.

It is clear as a matter of commonsense that the tribunal ought not **16–75** merely to look at the marks as they stand side by side; it is most unlikely in most cases that the customer will have an opportunity for such a comparison. He can only rely on his recollection of the mark he is used to seeing on the goods he is seeking to buy, and allowance must be made for this in estimating the probability of deception. Any other rule would be of no practical use.[98] It has to be borne in mind that the ordinary purchaser has only "an ordinary memory".[99]

> "The question is not whether if a person is looking at two trade marks side by side there would be a possibility of confusion; the question is whether the person who sees the proposed trade mark in the absence of the other trade mark, and in view only of his general recollection of what the nature of the other trade mark was, would be liable to be deceived and to think that the trade mark before him is the same as the other, of which he has a general recollection."[1]

---

confusion between "Alka-Seltzer' Effervescent Tablets" and " "Alka-Vescent' Seltzer Tablets"; registration of "Alka-Vescent" refused). *"Nerit"* [1982] F.S.R. 72, CA, probably goes too far, holding (at 79) that since "Nerit" was too close to "Merit" only phonetically and the idea was different, "Nerit" was registrable as a new mark; but the point is the same. *cf. "Kwik Copy"* [1982] R.P.C. 102: mark visually distinctive but phonetically just "Quick Copy" so unregistrable.
[96] *"Inadine"* [1992] R.P.C. 421.
[97] [1987] R.P.C. 387.
[98] *Seixo v. Provezende* (1865) L.R. 1 Ch. 192; *Wilkinson v. Griffith* (1891) 8 R.P.C. 370; *Hubbuck v. Brown* (1900) 17 R.P.C. 638 at 645. *Ravenhead Brick v. Ruabon* (1937) 54 R.P.C. 341 at 349, *per* Simonds J.: "Sanrus" held to be an infringement of "Rus". *"Coca Cola"* (1942) 59 R.P.C. 127 at 133; *"Ovax"* (1946) 63 R.P.C. 97.
[99] *per* Romer L.J., *"Kleenoff'* (1934) 51 R.P.C. 129 at 141.
[1] *Sandow* (1914) 31 R.P.C. 196 at 205, *per* Sargant J.

16–76 "Whether there has been trade mark infringement is more a matter of feel than science. I have borne in mind all of the arguments advanced by the defendant. However in this case it is significant that the marks are being used in relation to comparatively inexpensive restaurant services. This is an area where imperfect recollection is likely to play an important role. Furthermore the fact that the plaintiff's mark is quite meaningless means that imperfect recollection is more likely.": Laddie J. in *Wagamama v. City Centre Restaurants*[2]; Wagamama infringed by Rajamama (and also passing off). See also *De Cordova v. Vick*,[3] from which Laddie J. quoted thereafter.

16–77 That one of two words was in English and the other in a foreign language would, in general, diminish the probability of confusion through "imperfect recollection".[4]

Marks to be compared as seen in actual use

16–78 This consideration is inherent to the test in passing off; the question is to what extent registered marks are to be considered strictly as they appear on the Register. As is explained below, under the 1938 Act, the appearance of the mark in normal and fair use fell to be considered. It is suggested that this approach ought to be applied under the 1994 Act, and that to do so is in keeping with the approach of the ECJ discussed above,[5] under the rubric that all the circumstances of the trade are to be considered.

16–79 Thus, under the 1938 Act the position was that in comparing marks regard must be had not only to their form as they appear on the Register,[6] but also to the appearance they would present in actual use when fairly and honestly used[7]; to the nature of the goods upon which they are to be employed; to the character and size of the marks themselves; and to the probabilities of their becoming partially or wholly blurred or modified as ordinarily stamped or printed, or by ordinary wear and tear.[8] A mark which is used for hardware goods, and is stamped upon them with a die, is not likely to appear so definitely or to be so readily distinguishable from a similar mark as one which is engraved or printed upon a paper label and so attached to the goods.[9]

16–80 Some marks continue to indicate origin well after the point of sale, and it is suggested that that also is a circumstance which ought to be

---

[2] [1995] F.S.R. 713 at 733.
[3] (1951) 68 R.P.C. 103 at 106.
[4] *"Solibrisa" (Balè)* (1948) 65 R.P.C. 17 at 22.
[5] See paras 16–01 *et seq.*, above.
[6] Jessel M.R. held, in several cases, that the Register only should be looked at: *Re Jelley* (1878) 51 L.J.Ch. 639n.; *Robinson* (1880) 29 W.R. 31; *Mitchell v. Henry* (1880) 15 Ch.D. 181; but in the latter case the CA dissented from his opinion and overruled his decision; *Christiansen* (1886) 3 R.P.C. 54; *Lyle and Kinahan* (1907) 24 R.P.C. 37 and 249.
[7] *"June"* (1941) 58 R.P.C. 147 at 161; *"Ovax"* (1946) 63 R.P.C. 97.
[8] *Lyndon* (1886) 32 Ch.D. 109; 3 R.P.C. 102, CA; *Haines, Batchelor* (1888) 5 R.P.C. 669.
[9] *Haines, Batchelor* (1888) 5 R.P.C. 669 (dog and pig stamps: the objection failed).

taken into account. In *Levi Strauss v. Kimbyr Investments*,[10] the plaintiff's "tab" mark was held infringed because after sale, when the customer was wearing the jeans and all point of sale material had been removed, the "tab" still functioned as an indication of origin.

Colour

Where marks are used in colour, it may undoubtedly affect the **16–81** likelihood of confusion that the colours are or are not the same. Whilst, however, this is often a circumstance of great importance in relation to passing off, it is (except in the rare cases where a mark is registered in particular colours only) ordinarily of less importance in considering infringement: for the owner of a registered mark may use it in any colour. Even so, however, colour should seldom be entirely ignored.

(1) Since the registered proprietor of the device of a star could use **16–82** it in any colour, the words "Red Star" would be as objectionable as the word star by itself: *Verreries de l'Etoile* [1894] 1 Ch. 61; 10 R.P.C. 436; [1894] 2 Ch. 26; 11 R.P.C. 142 ("*Red Star Brand*").

(2) The words "The Golden Fan Brand" were refused registration **16–83** as an essential particular of a mark, on account of the presence on the Register of a fan which was in fact coloured gold in use: *Dewhurst* [1896] 2 Ch. 137; 13 R.P.C. 288.

(3) A triangular frame with the picture of a church inside was **16–84** rejected on the ground that it would, if the whole were coloured red, too nearly resemble Bass's well-known solid red triangle: *Worthington's Case* (1880) 14 Ch.D. 8 (these days it might well be held that a monopoly over triangles generally on this possibly rather speculative basis would be too broad); and see *Hanson* (1887) 37 Ch.D. 112 (red, white & blue coffee label not distinctive without colours).

(4) In an action for infringement of several marks, of which the **16–85** essential feature was the initials "B.P.", the defendants had used the initials "E.P.", always displayed in black on a yellow ground, whereas the plaintiffs' mark was displayed in yellow on green. The possibilities of confusion alleged by the plaintiffs essentially concerned use of the marks by such displays at filling stations. Held that the difference in colour was irrelevant to the question of infringement: *British Petroleum v. European Petroleum* [1968] R.P.C. 54 at 64. Doubtless the position would have been otherwise if the mark had been registered in respect of a particular colour.

---

[10] [1994] F.S.R. 335 (N.Z.). But see Chap. 14, in relation to the value of this authority.

Size

16–86 Size is not in itself a material factor in the comparison: a registered proprietor may use his mark in any size.[11] Where, however, the small size of the mark is such as to render it indistinct, this is material on the basis of the principle already stated. Whether there can be infringement by a mark so small as to be entirely invisible to the naked eye, *quaere*.[12]

All the circumstances of the trade to be considered

16–87 Further, the court must have regard to all the circumstances of the trade[13] in which the marks in question are employed, or are to be employed, and in particular (1) to the nature of the market, whether a home or a foreign one; (2) to the number of other trade marks similar to the contrasted marks already circulating in connection with the same description of goods; (3) to the common marks which are or may be combined with the contrasted marks or either of them; and, generally (4) to the customs and usages of the trade. As with the considerations identified in the foregoing sections, the relevance of all the circumstances of the trade has been endorsed by the ECJ.[14]

16–88   In passing-off actions, also, the circumstances of the trade may be highly material to the question of confusion.[15] In *Portakabin v. Powerblast*,[16] relevant circumstances included the fact that the range of the plaintiff's potential customers for its portable buildings was wide enough to include customers for the defendant's shot-blasting units.

It may also be relevant that goods are sometimes bought for others, and that the customer may not know the purpose for which the goods are acquired: *"Inadine"*.[17]

4. Evidence—general considerations

The role of evidence on the question of resemblance

16–89 The question of whether two marks are deceptively or confusingly similar to one another is for the judge to decide, and as is noted above, he is entitled to make a decision based on his own experience even in

---

[11] *Speer* (1887) 4 R.P.C. 521; 55 L.T. 880. But he may not use part of the mark one size and part another size if the mark is thereby rendered deceptive: *Lilly (Eli) v. Chelsea Drug* [1966] R.P.C. 14.

[12] *"Everglide"* [1964] R.P.C. 37 (mark just visible).

[13] *Cochrane v. McNish* [1896] A.C. 225; 13 R.P.C. 100 ("Club Soda"); Coats (1936) 53 R.P.C. 355 ("Sheen"). See also the cases on pharmaceutical marks cited n. 46, *ante*.

[14] See paras 16–01 *et seq.*, above.

[15] See, *e.g.* *Hayter v. R.B.H.S.* [1977] F.S.R. 285, CA ("B.J.S. Motor Syndicate" not too close as a business name to "J.S.B. Policies", in view of practices at Lloyd's); *Berkeley Hotel v. Berkeley International* [1972] R.P.C. 237 at 244 (relevant to the risk of confusion, that defendants' hotel was to be on plaintiffs' old site).

[16] [1990] R.P.C. 471.

[17] [1992] R.P.C. 421.

the absence of evidence.[18] Thus it has been said that the question of whether the resemblance is too close is one for the tribunal and not the witness.[19]

It has also been said that: **16–90**

"The question of infringement, the question whether one mark is likely to cause confusion with another, is a matter upon which the judge must make up his mind and which, he and he alone, must decide. He cannot abdicate the decision in that matter to witnesses before him. On the other hand, it is equally true that he must be guided in all these matters by the evidence before him and where the evidence is that there has been no confusion that is a material matter which the judge must take into account."[20]

Expert and trade evidence—admissibility

Leaving aside for the moment "survey" evidence, which is a separate **16–91** matter considered below,[21] the admissibility of expert evidence depends on the purpose of adducing the evidence, and the nature of the trade in question.

Thus evidence of the circumstances of the trade, the manner in which **16–92** goods are sold and so on is always admissible[22] (although if the trade is one with which the judge may be expected to have experience of his own, it may be of limited value). Thus, evidence may be given, by retailers,[23] as to the phrases used by customers in asking for goods,[24] and

---

[18] See *Spalding v. Gamage* and *Neutrogena*, nn. 48 and 53, above.

[19] This statement in the previous edition of this work was expressly approved by Dillon L.J. in *Mothercare v. Penguin Books* [1988] R.P.C. 113, and referred to by Knox J. in *Island Trading v. Anchor Brewing* [1989] R.P.C. 287a also. Also, *Harker Stagg* (1954) 71 R.P.C. 136 at 140; *Payton v. Snelling* (1900) 17 R.P.C. 628 (alleged passing off by get-up) at 635. See also *London General Omnibus Co. v. Lavell* [1901] 1 Ch. 135; 18 R.P.C. 74; *North Cheshire Brewery v. Manchester Brewery* [1899] A.C. 83.

[20] *Electrolux v. Electrix* (1954) 71 R.P.C. 23 at 31, *per* Evershed M.R. ("Electrux" and "Electrix"). See also *Cowie v. Herbert* (1897) 14 R.P.C. 436 ("Town Hall") no proof of confusion; "*Kidax*" [1960] R.P.C. 117 at 122, CA. See further as to evidence that there has been no confusion in practice, and/or a lack of positive evidence of confusion, para. 16–100, *post*.

[21] See paras 16–103 *et seq.*, below.

[22] This kind of evidence has long been regarded as being of informative value for the court, as was confirmed in *Dalgety Spillers v. Food Brokers* [1994] F.S.R. 504. Other cases include *George Ballantine v. Ballantyne Stewart* [1959] R.P.C. 47, 186; *Sodastream v. Thorne Cascade* [1982] R.P.C. 459; *Guccio Gucci v. Paolo Gucci* [1991] F.S.R. 89; and *Taittinger v. Allbev* [1993] F.S.R., 641; *Nad Electronics v. Nad Computer Systems* [1997] F.S.R. 380. For older cases, see *e.g. Electrolux v. Electrix (No. 2)* (1953) 70 R.P.C. 127 at 131; following Warrington J. in *Schweppes v. Gibbens* (1905) 22 R.P.C. 113 at 119; Lord Parker in *Spalding v. Gamage* (1915) 32 R.P.C. 273 at 286. See also "*Diasil*" *(Bayer)* (1947) 64 R.P.C. 125, where conditions of sale and purchase of the goods were considered at length, and weight given to the fact that they could be supplied on prescription only, and the other pharmaceutical cases cited para. 46, *ante*; *Players* (1965) R.P.C. 363 (relevant that chocolate cigarettes and real cigarettes are sold in the same shops) and *Picot v. Goya* (1967) R.P.C. 573 (oral confusion not so important because the goods, perfumes, always purchased over the counter and not by telephone).

[23] Evidence from others closely connected with the retail trade may be easier to secure and equally admissible: *e.g.* from the claimant's own sales representatives, from their own observations whilst in customers' shops.

[24] *Elliott Optical* (1952) 69 R.P.C. 169 at 173.

as to the proper inference to be drawn from the wording of the requests.[25] Similarly, a wholesaler may give evidence as to the likely effect on his system of handling orders of concurrent use of the two marks.[26]

16–93   However, the admissibility of direct evidence of an "expert" to the effect that there is likely to be confusion depends on the trade. Evidence concerning a specialist field is much more likely to be admitted than evidence concerning mundane, everyday purchases such as groceries.[27] There does not, however, seem to be a clear dividing line between what is permitted and what is not.

16–94   Thus evidence of this kind was admitted in *Guccio Gucci v. Paolo Gucci*[28] (designer clothes), but rejected in *The European v. The Economist*[29] (newspapers), admitted in *Antec v. South-Western Chicks* (agricultural disinfectant), and in *Nad Electronics v. Nad Computer Systems*[30] (hi-fi and computers). In *United Biscuits v. Asda*,[31] (chocolate biscuits), the evidence was not rejected entirely, but firmly given second place after the judge's own impression.

16–95   The contrast between what is admissible and what is not is well illustrated by *Island Trading v. Anchor Brewing*,[32] where the judge admitted evidence that the public identified the plaintiff's product as "Steam beer",[33] and ordered it as such, but rejected evidence from the trade that the public might be confused.

16–96   The overall position in relation to the 1994 Act was stated in *Bach Flower Remedies v. Healing Herbs*[34] (a case concerned with distinctiveness under section 3 of the 1994 Act rather than infringement under section 10 or relative grounds for refusal under section 5, but relevant nonetheless), as follows:

> "The task for the court is to inform itself, by evidence, of the matters of which a reasonably well informed and reasonably observant and circumspect consumer of the products would know; and then, treating itself as competent to evaluate the effect which those matters would have on the minds of such a person with that knowledge, ask the question."[35]

---

[25] *Sales Affiliates v. Le Jean* (1947) 64 R.P.C. 103 at 110; *"Glastonburys"* (1938) 55 R.P.C. 253 at 262; *Ballantine v. Ballantyne, Stewart* [1959] R.P.C. 273 at 280.

[26] See the defendants' evidence in *"Sunniwite"* (n. 37 below), at 95–96.

[27] Contrast *"GE"* [1973] R.P.C. 297 at 321–322 with *Dalgety Spillers v. Food Brokers* [1994] F.S.R. 504.

[28] *Supra.*

[29] [1996] F.S.R. 431; [1998] F.S.R. 283. The statement by Millett L.J. at 291 that the trade evidence was inadmissible must, it is suggested, be understood in context and not as a general rule that such evidence of likelihood of confusion is always inadmissible.

[30] *Supra.*

[31] [1997] R.P.C. 513 at 538.

[32] [1989] R.P.C. 287a.

[33] And also evidence about publicans' policy in the light of likely customer reaction.

[34] [2000] R.P.C. 513.

[35] *per* Chadwick L.J. at 535.

In some cases it may not be entirely easy to distinguish between direct **16–97** evidence that there is a likelihood of confusion, and evidence about the circumstances of the trade or whether there has been confusion. In *Neutrogena v. Golden,*[36] shopkeepers gave evidence that they were content to stock both parties' products, and had not themselves experienced any signs of confusion. This was held relevant and admissible, although the judge declined to rely on it for other reasons.[37]

Evidence as to other related marks or names in use in the trade is of **16–98** value; but mere evidence of entries on the Register of Trade Marks, without evidence of whether and to what extent the marks or names concerned are used, is of little or no value. Further, regard must be had to the number of different owners of the marks. Evidence that marks were accepted onto the Register without objection is at most evidence of the opinion of the Registrar, and is completely irrelevant in the absence of evidence as to his reasons.[38]

The court may properly refer to dictionaries in order to ascertain not **16–99** only the meaning of a word but also the use to which the thing (if it be a thing) denoted by the word is commonly put.[39] But statements in year books, etc., as to words being trade marks have been held inadmissible.[40]

Presence or absence of evidence of actual confusion or deception

Proof of actual deception, if the mark is in the opinion of the tribunal **16–100** likely to deceive, is unnecessary.[41] Nevertheless, if one or more cases of actual deception are made out to the satisfaction of the court, this will, of course, afford very strong evidence that the resemblance between the marks in question is so close as to be likely to deceive.[42] However, the deception proved must be of the kind relevant to infringement or

---

[36] [1996] R.P.C. 473 at 501–502.

[37] Similar evidence was led in *Lever Bros v. Sunniwite* (1949) 66 R.P.C. 84 at 92 *et seq.*, 97–98 (Romer J.; "Sunlight" and "Sunniwite"). Those of the defendants' witnesses who said in cross-examination that they would, or did, stock "Sunniwite" as well as "Sunlight" were then asked whether they would say the same if it were not "Sunniwite" but "Sunwhite"; a question admitting of no satisfactory answer.

[38] *Neutrogena v. Golden* [1996] R.P.C. 473 at 502–503, referring to *Goya v. Gala of London* (1952) 69 R.P.C. 188. Entry is not evidence of use: *Willesden Varnish v. Young* (1922) 39 R.P.C. 285 at 288, 292; "*Daisil*" (1947) 64 R.P.C. 125 at 128; the point was not raised on appeal. As to the old Business Names Register, see *General Radio v. General Radio (Westminster)* [1957] R.P.C. 471 at 491; note the greater weight given to the telephone directory.

[39] *Coca-Cola of Canada v. Pepsi Cola of Canada* (1942) 59 R.P.C. 127 at 153.

[40] *Havana Cigar v. Oddenino* (1923) 40 R.P.C. 229 at 241; *Jaques v. Chess* (1939) 56 R.P.C. 415; *Delavelle Stanley* (1946) 63 R.P.C. 103 at 109; *Sales Affiliates v. Le Jean* (1947) 64 R.P.C. 103 at 110.

[41] See para. 16–36, above (judge can make his own decision).

[42] See, *e.g Saville Perfumery v. June Perfect* (1941) 58 R.P.C. 147 at 174, *per* Viscount Maugham, HL.

passing off; mere "administrative" confusion such as misdirected post and the like will not assist.[43]

16–101   The absence of evidence of actual deception is a circumstance which varies greatly in weight according to the nature of the case. Even where the proper inference to be drawn is that there has been no confusion,[44] this cannot be conclusive by itself[45]: the decision is for the court, which cannot abdicate it in favour of the witnesses.[46] Nevertheless, where the marks have been circulating side by side in the market[47] where deception is alleged to be probable, the fact that no one appears to have been misled is very material,[48] unless satisfactorily explained. On the other hand, if one or both of the marks is new or nearly new, there can have been no opportunity or little opportunity, for deception to occur.[49] Where the defendants in a passing-off action had issued deceptive literature, it was quite open to the court to draw an inference that some people were deceived.[50]

16–102   The owner of a trade mark is not bound to wait before taking action to see whether his customers will in fact be deceived, for "the very life of a trade mark depends upon the promptitude with which it is vindicated."[51] If he does wait, and fails nevertheless to secure evidence of actual confusion, this will suggest that the risk to his business is small, and incline a court to refuse interim relief at least.[52]

---

[43] See e.g. The European v. The Economist [1996] F.S.R. 431, [1998] F.S.R. 283; HFC v. Midland [2000] F.S.R. 176, CA.

[44] This does not always follow: evidence of actual deception is notoriously difficult to secure. Besides, "the more complete the deception, the less likely its detection" ("Electrux" (1953) 70 R.P.C. 127 at 132, per Lloyd-Jacob J.). It seems clear, in fact, that commercially the real harm arising from the use of confusingly similar marks may often be that the public, whilst aware that there are two brands of goods, cease to care which is which—in which case convincing evidence of confusion could hardly be obtainable. In Neutrogena v. Golden [1996] R.P.C. 473, the trial judge rejected the evidence of retailers that they had not noticed any confusion on the basis that, inherently, it would not become apparent in the shop, but only afterwards.

[45] Edelsten v. Edelsten (1863) 1 De G.J. & S. 185; Campania Général de Tobacos v. Rehder (1887) 5 R.P.C. 61; Paine v. Daniell [1893] 2 Ch. 567, 10 R.P.C. 217.

[46] See para. 16–36, above.

[47] If the marks have been used at different ends of the market in the goods concerned, this will explain absence of confusion: "Bali" [1969] R.P.C. 472, HL; "Da Vinci" [1980] R.P.C. 237 (Regy; too close to "Vincci"). Geographical separation of businesses may equally explain absence of confusion.

[48] For recent examples of this kind of reasoning, see Laura Ashley v. Coloroll [[1987] R.P.C. 1; Elvis Presley Trade Mark [1997] R.P.C. 473; [1999] R.P.C. 567, CA. Older cases include Lambert (1888) 6 R.P.C. 344; 61 L.T. 138, CA; and Baker v. Rawson (1889) 45 Ch.D. 519; 8 R.P.C. 89 at 107. "Kidax" [1959] R.P.C. 295 at 308; Cowie v. Herbert (1897) 14 R.P.C. 436 at 448 (IH). See also "Solavoid" [1977] R.P.C. 1 at 29, PC (N.Z., citing the corresponding passage to this from the 10th edition of this work).

[49] See, e.g. Kimberley Clark v. Fort Sterling [1997] R.P.C. 877. A fortiori in a quia timet action such as "Jif" [1990] R.P.C. 341.

[50] Plomien Fuel Economiser v. National School of Salesmanship (1943) 60 R.P.C. 219.

[51] Johnston v. Orr-Ewing (1880) 13 Ch.D. 434 at 464.

[52] Whilst the absence of actual confusion can often be explained (see above), most likely explanations (except in particular that confusion is taking place undetected) equally imply that little confusion is likely in the immediate future, so tilting the balance of convenience against the claimant, e.g. geographical separation: Evans v. Eradicure [1972] R.P.C. 808.

5. "Survey" evidence and other evidence from consumers

Introduction

It is common in actions for passing off and trade mark infringement for **16–103** evidence to be adduced which concerns the reactions of members of the public to the marks or get-ups the subject of the proceedings, in circumstances where the party to the litigation has gone out to find or create such evidence (as opposed to passively receiving spontaneous evidence of confusion). Probably such evidence is most commonly led by the claimant in order to seek to demonstrate that the defendant's mark or get up is confusingly similar to, or deceptively resembles, his own. Although that is the main purpose of this kind of evidence, it is also sometimes adduced to show what the public understands by the parties' marks, or whether they are distinctive, or understood to indicate origin.[53]

This kind of evidence is often generically referred to as "survey **16–104** evidence", but this term is misleading if used indiscriminately, and in fact evidence of this general kind takes a number of forms, apart from surveys in the strict sense.

When one refers to a "survey" in the strict sense, what is meant is an **16–105** exercise in which a substantial number of persons are asked a series of questions according to explicit detailed instructions. Thereafter, the totality of their responses are collated and presented in the form of statistics, such as: "53% of those asked thought that the defendant's product was a new line from the claimant." This kind of exercise is similar in many ways to market research surveys, and is often designed and/or supervised and/or carried out by persons who have gained their experience in market research organisations such as MORI or Gallup.

However, the term "survey evidence" is also used more loosely to **16–106** refer to any organised exercise whose objective is to seek and obtain evidence from a number of members of the public. A better and more accurate general term for this sort of activity, often used by practitioners these days, is "witness collection programme" or "witness gathering exercise".[54] One reason why the terms have tended to be blurred together is that, as practitioners are well aware, it can often happen that although the court is not taken with a survey *qua* survey, it is nonetheless swayed by the oral evidence of some of the subjects.[55]

---

[53] *e.g. Bach Flower Remedies v. Healing Herbs* [2000] R.P.C. 513. For reasons explained at the end of this section, "survey" evidence to demonstrate that a mark is or is not understood as denoting a source of origin may well become more common in future under the 1994 Act.

[54] *e.g.* in *Bach* at para. 49.

[55] In *Bach* the evidence was rejected under either rubric, but the court plainly accepted that a survey could be deployed as a witness gathering exercise.

16–107   Since their introduction in English litigation in the late 1960s and early 1970s[56] surveys have not, it has to be said, achieved great impact, although there have been instances where they have been given considerable weight. The complexities involved in their preparation, the frequency with which leading or other inappropriate questions are asked, and the general approach that in relation to ordinary consumer goods the court can make its own decision, have all led to a rather hostile attitude. In *Neutrogena v. Golden*,[57] Jacob J. said:

> "[P]ure questionnaire evidence is seldom helpful—there are almost inevitable faults with the questions or the recordal of the answers as well as in later stages of the processing. Of course the court needs to know what evidence was collected, and needs to have the full picture, including particularly what failed surveys, if any there were. But unless one can have some real evidence, tested in cross-examination, one cannot really be sure of what was passing through people's minds. Those cases where surveys have proved to be useful have all involved some of the 'pollees' coming to court."

16–108   The ECJ has now given surveys a similarly lukewarm reception in *Gut Springenheide*,[58] where it held that in general it and the national courts could be expected to make decisions as to the likely state of mind of the "average consumer" without assistance, but that surveys were not ruled out by Community law in difficult cases.

Surveys—rules

16–109   The basic rules for the conduct of a survey, in order for it to be probative, were set out by Whitford J. in *Imperial v. Philip Morris* [1984] R.P.C. 293 at 302–303. The requirements are:

(1) All surveys conducted, their methodology and results must be disclosed.
(2) The totality of all answers must be disclosed.
(3) The questions asked must not be leading.
(4) The questions asked must not lead the interviewee into a field of speculation upon which he would not otherwise have embarked.
(5) Exact answers and not abbreviations must be provided.
(6) Coding must be accurately carried out,[59] and the coding methods disclosed.

---

[56] Early cases included *Coca Cola v. Struthers* [1968] R.P.C. 231, and "*GE*" [1969] R.P.C. 418 (at first instance; the Court of Appeal accepted it, but the House of Lords gave it little weight: [1970] R.P.C. 339 and [1973] R.P.C. 297).
[57] [1996] R.P.C. 473 at 486.
[58] [1998] E.C.R. I–4657.
[59] But preferably not on the spot by the interviewer: *Scott v. Nice Pak*, below.

(7) The instructions given to the interviewers must be disclosed.

An example of leading questions and of questions based on a false **16–110** premise may be found in *Scott v. Nice-Pak*,[60] where, despite the fact that it was not on the market, the consumers were asked if they had bought the defendant's product. The survey was also criticised for providing only "yes" and "no" options in answer to certain questions where the respondents might not know the answer or might be doubtful.

The net effect of these rules, necessary as they are, is that it is very **16–111** difficult to design a survey which will pass muster in court, and their design has become a very specialised art. One technique which improves the chances of useful evidence being obtained is to begin with a very open question, such as "what can you tell me about this product?", and to move on to ones which are gradually more specific, such as "can you tell me who makes this product?". The evidence of respondents who give useful answers to the very broad question is then untainted, while leaving an opportunity still to get evidence from persons who misunderstand what the interest of the interviewer is: very broad questions are apt to receive an answer quite unrelated to the get up or mark of interest. For example, it is not uncommon for respondents to say "it looks expensive" or something of that kind, which may be of tangential relevance, and does not mean that the respondent has nothing to say about the principal question. When they are directed a little more, for example by asking about the origin of the goods, they may then give relevant evidence, although there is of course the risk of an accusation of leading.

Successful and unsuccessful surveys

Lego v. Lego Lemelstrich [1983] F.S.R. 155—evidence accepted. **16–112**
  Imperial Group v. Philip Morris (supra)—rejected.
  Unilever v. Johnson Wax [1989] F.S.R. 145, survey as part of an omnibus survey[61] rejected.
  "Jif" [1990] R.P.C. 341—accepted to varying degrees by the judge, the Court of Appeal and the House of Lords, but strongly supported by "live" evidence.
  United Biscuits v. Burtons [1992] F.S.R. 14—rejected.[62] **16–113**
  The European v. The Economist [1996] F.S.R. 431 and [1998] F.S.R. 283—rejected by the judge and the Court of Appeal (question on a false basis—persons who had never seen the defendant's product presented with the top half of the front page only).

---

[60] [1988] F.S.R. 125, [1989] F.S.R. 100, CA.
[61] An omnibus survey is a long set of questions on a wide range of topics sent to consumers on a regular basis. Interested parties pay for questions to be included.
[62] Evidence obtained with a "tachistoscope" was also rejected in this case, as well as in *Laura Ashley v. Coloroll* [1987] R.P.C. 1.

16-114 *Neutrogena v. Golden* [1996] R.P.C. 473—the plaintiff produced the questionnaires used, but did not rely on them, only on oral evidence from some of the persons interviewed, which was accepted. The defendant's internal market research (not for the purposes of litigation) was relied on as showing confusion.

Pontiac Marina v. CDL Hotels [1997] F.S.R. 725 (High Court of Singapore)—short and uncomplicated survey accepted.

16-115 *Kimberley Clark v. Fort Sterling* [1997] F.S.R. 877—surveys held of limited quantitative value but of some qualitative value as an indication of the attractiveness of the claimant's mark and of whether it overwhelmed the disclaiming material.

Admissibility

16-116 Under the Rules of the Supreme Court and the Civil Evidence Act 1968, there were considerable complications as to the admissibility of survey evidence. A particular problem was that factual proof of what took place during the interviews was necessary, but that if a Civil Evidence Act Notice were served in relation to the interviewee's responses, the opposing party could generally require their attendance.[63] There was also a particular difficulty in the treatment of the evidence of the market researcher who reported on the surveys, since in strict terms his evidence could be said to contain or refer to second or third hand hearsay.[64] Moreover, it was suggested that such an expert could not give evidence on the ultimate matter to be decided by the court (whether or not there was a likelihood of deception).

16-117 These difficulties led to a number of rather unsatisfactory decisions. For example, in the course of *"Jif"*, a decision was given[65] that the person giving evidence as to the surveys was not an expert at all, on the basis that he was merely reporting the results. This analysis, it is suggested, cannot be supported, at least where, as in most cases, evidence is given about general and desirable practice in market research.

16-118 In practice, the Civil Evidence Act requirements were honoured more in the breach than in the observance. In some cases the parties agreed to waive them. Happily these formal difficulties, such as they were, have been removed by the combined effects of the Civil Evidence Act 1995, and Part 8 of the Civil Procedure Rules, which now permit the admission of most hearsay evidence subject to the court's ability to give

---

[63] Unless they were beyond the seas, ill or untraceable. Most of them tended to be ordinary members of the public in the U.K. and therefore available to give evidence if required.

[64] See *"GE"* [1970] R.P.C. 339, CA; *Customglass v. Salthouse* [1976] R.P.C. 589; *Lego v. Lego Lemelstrich* [1983] F.S.R. 155. In the last case, the conclusion was reached that the evidence went to prove public opinion, an external fact, and was therefore not subject to the hearsay rules. The admission of survey-type evidence on interim applications was easier because hearsay was expressly permitted on such occasions under the rules.

[65] [1987] F.S.R. 407.

it such weight as it thinks fit, without the necessity of the witness being brought to court, even if not beyond the seas, etc.

Case management of survey evidence

Surveys, even as witness collection exercises, are apt to throw up a large **16–119** number of respondents. This does not mean that the party relying on the survey is entitled as of right to lead oral evidence from every single one which supports his case. The court has general power under the CPR to restrict the number of "live" witnesses to be called, having regard to the overriding objective in Part 1 of the CPR. Thus in *HFC v. Midland*,[66] in advance of trial, the judge limited the claimant to its 20 (later increased to 27) best witnesses. Subsequently, the claimant was permitted to serve Civil Evidence Act Notices in relation to all respondents, not in order to use their evidence to show confusion, but in order to show that the 27 who were to give oral evidence were representative.[67]

This practice was mentioned and expressly approved in *Bach Flower Remedies v. Healing Herbs*.[68]

Surveys to prove meaning to the public

In addition to demonstrating the likelihood of confusion or deception, **16–120** surveys may be used to show that a party's mark is known to the public, and what it means to them. This is of relevance not only in the context of civil proceedings for passing-off or trade mark infringement, but also in relation to applications to register, and oppositions under section 3 of the 1994 Act. It is clear from cases such as *Windsurfing Chiemsee Produktions v. Huber*[69] (ECJ) that in such cases, evidence will be required more than ever. *Windsurfing* was adopted and applied in *Bach Flower Remedies v. Healing Herbs*.[70]

Surveys for such purposes will require different planning from those **16–121** intended to produce evidence of deception or confusion. They may, in particular, require a different approach to sample selection. In *Dualit's Application*,[71] the survey was rejected because the sample was limited to the class of persons likely to buy the applicant's products, and by eliminating those who said that design was not important to them as a function. Whether such criticisms would lie against a survey intended to show confusion in a relevant section of the public is doubtful.

---

[66] Unreported, Laddie J., May 18, 1999.
[67] Also unreported, Laddie J.
[68] [2000] RPC 513 at para. 35, *per* Morritt L.J.
[69] [1999] E.T.M.R. 585.
[70] *Supra.*
[71] [1999] R.P.C. 890.

CHAPTER 17

TRADE LIBEL AND THREATS

1. Outline of chapter

Introduction

17–01 This chapter is concerned with the tort known as trade libel, and with the statutory action for threats of proceedings for trade mark infringement, which is new to the 1994 Act, although similar provisions have been in force in relation to patents and designs for some time.[1]

17–02 In addition, there are a number of references in this chapter to infringement of registered trade marks under section 10(6) of the Trade Marks Act 1994, the provision mainly concerned with comparative advertising. Section 10(6) is dealt with in full in Chapter 13, but it is necessary and desirable to refer to it in the context of trade libel, partly because many of the most relevant cases have involved both causes of action, partly because the kinds of behaviour they are meant to address are very similar, and partly because many of the same policy considerations underlie them.

Terms used

17–03 This chapter is entitled "trade libel", but there are a number of names for the same tort, including slander of goods, malicious falsehood and injurious falsehood. These terms are used interchangeably in the authorities and in this chapter, although the more modern judgments seem to use the name "malicious falsehood" more than any other. That expression may well be the most apt in any event because it emphasises the crucial importance of malice, while the terms "slander of goods" and "trade libel" give too narrow an impression of the scope of the tort, since it protects financial interests generally and not just commercial ones.[2] Those terms also give perhaps too much of an impression of

---

[1] Patents Act 1977, s.70, and the Copyright, Designs and Patents Act 1988, s.253.

[2] See, *e.g. Shepherd v. Wakeman* (1662) 1 Sid 79, where the plaintiff lost her prospects of marriage owing to a false and malicious claim that she was already married to the defendant; and *Joyce v. Sengupta* [1993] 1 W.L.R. 337, where the plaintiff's claim was that she would be hindered in finding further employment involving positions of trust owing to a false assertion that she had stolen her employer's confidential papers. Her interest was not as a trader, but the falsehood affected her financial position.

proximity to the torts of slander and libel, which are related to malicious falsehood in many respects, but are also very different in others.[3]

17–04

It is worth noting that the Defamation Act 1952[4] recognises that these various terms denote forms of the same general tort, by the use in section 3(1) of the expression "slander of title, slander of goods, and other malicious falsehood".

Policy

The following are the main policy considerations underlying the law of malicious falsehood. They are worth setting out at this stage because they form an obvious and major part of the courts' reasoning in dealing with this cause of action. The policy considerations come particularly to the fore in the kind of cases with which this work and this chapter are concerned, namely disputes between rival traders as to statements made by one about the goods or business of another.

17–05

The first main policy objective is the protection of economic interests. This is the *raison d'etre* of the tort as a whole.

The second main policy consideration is the promotion of competition. The courts recognise that an important vehicle for competition is the ability of one trader to seek to inform the public that his goods are available to be bought and that they have, or may have, advantages over the goods of another trader. This objective is so important that the courts may even permit a trader knowingly to make false statements about his goods in comparison with another trader's. See for example, the speech of Lord Diplock in the *Advocaat* case[5] (in the context of passing off, but with general application on this issue):

17–06

> ". . . in an economic system which has relied on competition to keep down prices and to improve products there may be practical reasons why it should have been the policy of the common law not to run the risk of hampering competition by providing civil remedies to everyone competing in the market who has suffered damage to his business or goodwill in consequence of inaccurate statements of whatever kind that may be made by rival traders about their own wares. The market in which the action for passing

---

[3] The principle differences are that in libel and slander the claimant's reputation is protected, and hence the statement complained of must be defamatory before a claim can succeed, whereas in malicious falsehood any false statement is actionable provided that it is calculated to cause financial damage, and is made maliciously. In malicious falsehood the claimant must prove malice and bears the burden of proving falsity, whereas in defamation falsity is presumed and the defendant must prove the statement to be true.

[4] See para. 17–33, below.

[5] [1979] A.C. 731 at 742, quoted by Aldous J. in *Ciba Geigy v. Parke Davis* [1994] F.S.R. 8 at 20–21, a case about malicious falsehood. The circumstances in which this kind of statement is allowed are considered in more detail below.

off originated was no place for the mealy mouthed; advertisements are not on affidavit; exaggerated claims by a trader about the quality of his wares, assertions that they are better than those of his rivals even though he knows this to be untrue, have been permitted by the common law as venial 'puffing' which gives no cause of action to a competitor even though he can show that he has suffered actual damage in his business as a result."

17–07 This policy consideration is also reflected in the requirement of this tort that malice must be proved. This can be a major difficulty in the path of a claimant suing for malicious falsehood, and the practical result is that a trader who honestly believes what he is saying cannot successfully be sued,[6] at least until the aggrieved rival puts him on notice by demonstrating the falsity of the statement to a sufficient degree of certainty. Moreover, although in the tort of malicious falsehood generally malice can arise in making a false statement for improper motives, the law recognises that the desire of a trader to earn custom at the expense of his rivals is perfectly proper.[7]

17–08 The third main policy consideration is the protection of free speech. This overlaps with the previous consideration, but is of broader application. Its most important practical consequence is the rule, applicable in and arising from the law of defamation, that interim[8] relief is not available to restrain an alleged falsehood if the defendant has an arguable case that the statement in question is true. The law is in a somewhat unclear and unsatisfactory state as to whether and to what extent this rule applies where another cause of action based on the same facts is pleaded as well as or in place of malicious falsehood. At the very least it is clear that in such cases preservation of freedom of speech is an important factor in assessing the balance of convenience.

17–09 The fourth policy consideration is that the courts are not the appropriate forum for resolving differences of opinion between traders as to which party's goods or services are better. The reluctance to deal with this kind of case was made clear over a hundred years ago, and seems to be based both on the courts' unsuitability to determine such issues, and the concern that a large number of time-consuming actions would fall to be tried, and so take up the courts' resources, which could be better used. For example, in *White v. Mellin* [1895] AC 154, Lord Herschell L.C. said (at 165):

"If an action will not lie because a man says that his goods are better than his neighbour's, it seems to me impossible to say that it

---

[6] Even if his belief is not based on reasonable grounds, so long as he is not reckless as to the truth of what he says. Malice is considered in more detail in paras 17–60 to 17–71, below.

[7] See the section on malice, below.

[8] The expression "interim" relief (or injunction) is used herein in preference to the term "interlocutory" as used before the introduction of the Civil Procedure Rules in 1999.

will lie because he says that they are better in this or that or the other respect. Just consider what a door would be opened if this were permitted. That this sort of puffing advertisement is in use is notorious; and we see rival cures advertised for particular ailments. The Court would then be bound to inquire, in an action brought, whether this ointment or this pill better cured the disease which it was alleged to cure—whether a particular article of food was in this respect or that better than another. Indeed, the Courts of law would be turned into a machinery for advertising rival productions by obtaining a judicial determination which of the two was better."

And as a result the courts have preferred to leave determination of **17–10** which trader's goods are better, and statements about which are better, to be determined by the market and the advertising authorities. The courts' scepticism has remained, and has been reinforced to some extent by cases involving malicious falsehood and section 10(6) trade mark infringement brought in the years since the introduction of the 1994 Act. A number of them seem to have been brought against a background of ferocious competition between the parties in the marketplace and personal feelings on the part of their managements, as much to prove a point as to obtain compensation for an injury suffered. In at least one case the trial judge has made strong and explicit statements to such effect in giving judgment: see *Emaco Ltd. v. Dyson Appliances Ltd.*[9] refusing to award either side any costs:

> "[E]ach side is (as I said earlier when delivering judgment on the question of relief) intent on using these proceedings . . . as weapons in a continuing and, it appears, increasingly bitter advertising war. . . . A party who approaches litigation in that way must expect (at the very least) to do so at his own expense.
>
> In all the circumstances, the right course to take in relation to costs, in my judgment, is to leave the costs where they lie: In other words, each party should pay its own costs. If (as I would hope) that serves to discourage other parties from using the courts as a forum for a continuing advertising war, that can only be in the interest of the public, and in particular of other litigants waiting to have their cases heard."

Statement may be a personal libel; relationship with libel

A disparaging statement with regard to a trader's goods may be an **17–11** ordinary libel upon the trader personally and, accordingly, be actionable. Such, for instance, would be the case if the goods were described as worthless[10] or spurious.[11] To write of a trader that he sells such goods

---

[9] The case is reported at [1999] E.T.M.R. 903; the judge made the above observations at a later unreported hearing.

[10] *British Empire v. Linotype* (1898) 79 L.T. 8.

[11] *Liebig's Extract of Meat Co. v. Anderson* (1886) 55 L.T. 206.

may well be defamatory, and all the more so if it is suggested that he does so knowingly. Ordinary libel is a matter beyond the scope of this book, and specialist works on defamation should be consulted.

17–12   It is, however, worth noting at this stage an important practical advantage of the action for malicious falsehood, which is that legal aid is not available to bring a claim in respect of defamation, but may be in respect of malicious falsehood. Where a claim could potentially be pleaded either way, there is nothing wrong in pleading it in malicious falsehood, even if that is done in order to obtain legal aid. It is not an abuse of process to do so, even if the amount of damages which may be obtained in malicious falsehood is small in comparison with what might be obtained if the same action were based in defamation: *Joyce v. Sengupta*.[12] A side effect is that the right to a jury trial will not apply if the claim is brought in malicious falsehood.

Relationship of trade libel with the action for threats

17–13 The action for threats is considered in detail below, but a few useful comparisons can be drawn at this stage.

As will be explained below, the action for threats provided for by the 1994 Act is new and little litigated so far, but is very similar to long-standing provisions concerning threats of actions for patent infringement.

17–14   Malicious falsehood and statutory actions for threats have a number of things in common. The purpose of each is to restrain the making of false and damaging statements about a trader's goods or business. In each case, it is open to the person making the damaging statement to do so if the statement is true.

17–15   However, the statutory actions for threats exist in recognition of the fact that allegations that a trader's goods infringe the intellectual property rights of one of his rivals call for particularly firm treatment. There are a number of reasons for this.

17–16   First of all, threats are inherently likely to be taken seriously. Rarely if ever can they be "puffs". Moreover, threats are particularly pernicious in their effect on the potential customers of the trader whose goods are said to infringe. A potential customer who reads "knocking copy" directed at one of his suppliers only has to be concerned about the quality of the goods he is buying, and is likely to feel able to assess that for himself. But a threat of an infringement action is different; even if the threat is directed to the supplier and not the customer, the customer will fear that he will be unable to obtain supplies at all from that source, or that if he does, he will be in difficulty selling them on, and may even himself be sued.

17–17   There is also the consideration that intellectual property rights are potent tools in business, and that if a trader is granted such a monopoly he should be required to vindicate it directly and properly by showing

---

[12] [1993] 1 W.L.R. 337, CA.

infringement of a valid right, rather than driving off other traders by the use of threats.

These issues are reflected in the different law and procedure appli- **17–18** cable to the common law action for malicious falsehood and the statutory one for threats. In malicious falsehood, the claimant must prove that the statement is false and made maliciously; in threats the onus lies on the owner of the right to prove that there has been infringement if he wishes to justify the threat, and there is no requirement of any mental element.

Procedurally, the difference between the actions of most importance is **17–19** the potential availability of interim relief to restrain threats even if the defendant right holder has an arguable case that the threat was justifiable. Interim relief is made available in recognition of the damage which threats can do and of the speed with which they can do it.

Relationship with section 10(6) infringement

Within the scope of this work, the main significance of the action for **17–20** malicious falsehood and the provisions of section 10(6) are in the field of comparative advertising. Since the 1994 Act came into force, there have been a number of cases where both causes of action were pleaded in respect of the same advertisement or series of advertisements.[13]

In this field, the two causes of action are directed at similar kinds of **17–21** behaviour, although they are aimed at protecting rather different interests. The action for trade mark infringement protects the claimant's interest in the registered mark (and hence the requirement that the use complained of must take unfair advantage, or be detrimental to, the distinctive character of the mark[14]), while the action for malicious falsehood protects the claimant's economic interests generally, whether or not his trade mark is used.

That said, in cases where the defendant has used the claimant's **17–22** registered trade mark in the advertisement complained of, an action for infringement is more favourable to the claimant than an action for malicious falsehood in two very significant respects.

The first main advantage is that malice need not be proven, there **17–23** being no subjective mental element under section 10(6).[15] The second is that that the advertisement will offend under the Act if it is misleading to a substantial proportion of the public, so that the claimant can succeed if the advertisement has two plausible meanings, one of which is false. In malicious falsehood, by contrast, the statement complained of must be given a single meaning, which is either true or false.[16]

[13] See, e.g. Vodafone v. Orange [1997] F.S.R. 34; Macmillan v. RCN Publishing [1998] F.S.R. 9; Cable & Wireless v. BT [1998] F.S.R. 383; Emaco v. Dyson Appliances [1999] E.T.M.R. 903.
[14] The proviso to s.10(6); and see Chap. 13, above.
[15] The test for "honest practices" under s.10(6) is probably whether, objectively assessed, an honest trader possessed of the information which could be obtained by reasonable inquiries, could reasonably make the statement concerned. See Chap. 13, for more details.
[16] See para. 17–57, below.

17–24   Given these advantages, why would one allege malicious falsehood if a claim for infringement of a registered mark were available? One possible reason would be if there were a threat to the validity of the registration in question, although in most of the reported cases to date there has not been a counterclaim for revocation, probably because the actions have tended to be brought by established claimants with established marks.

17–25   Another reason which has been suggested by practitioners is the availability of potentially more extensive disclosure in connection with the issue of malice, such as documents revealing the thinking and planning behind the advertisement complained of. This reasoning is probably mistaken; although the test for "honest practices" under section 10(6) is basically an objective one,[17] documents showing what inquiries and checks the defendant made, planning undertaken, research into how it was expected that consumers would see the advertisement and so on are surely relevant to it.[18] So disclosure ought to be essentially the same in respect of the two causes of action, although its precise scope will of course depend on the pleadings.

17–26   One instance where it might genuinely be worth continuing with both causes of action is if there is good reason to believe that the defendant, even if found to infringe the claimant's trade mark, might continue with a modified advertisement making essentially the same statement but without use of the claimant's trade mark.

17–27   The courts have shown an awareness that a claim for malicious falsehood may be an unnecessary and burdensome addition to an action for trade mark infringement. In *Cable & Wireless v. BT* [1998] F.S.R. 383 at 386, Jacob J. persuaded the claimant to limit its claim to trade mark infringement for that very reason. Although in that case (decided before the Civil Procedure Rules came into force) the claimant voluntarily dropped its claim for malicious falsehood, it would certainly be very much within the spirit of the Rules for the court to use its case management powers to remove an unnecessary claim for malicious falsehood from an action even if the claimant did not agree, on the basis that the cost and effort involved was not proportionate. Of course, it would not be appropriate to do so if there were a serious counterclaim to revoke the registration concerned.

2. Trade libel generally

Elements of the tort

17–28 The essential elements of the tort are: (1) that the defendant has published about the claimant words which are false; (2) that they were published maliciously; and (3) that special damage has followed as the

---

[17] See above and Chap. 13.
[18] Just as in passing off, where intention to deceive is not a necessary element of the tort, but may be most relevant if shown. See Chap. 14.

direct and natural result of their publication. A statement of the essential elements in a modern authority may be found in *Kaye v. Robertson* [1991] F.S.R. 62 at 67, *per* Glidewell L.J.

The third requirement, special damage, was relaxed by the Defamation Act 1952: see below. **17–29**

(a) Traders were restrained from advertising, or representing, or suggesting in their advertisements or circulars, that they or the proprietors of their testator's business, were alone possessed of the secret recipe for cattle food and from representing or suggesting, or doing anything calculated to represent or suggest, that the cattle food manufactured by the plaintiffs[19] was spurious or not genuine: *Thorley's v. Massam* (1880) 14 Ch.D. 763. Subsequently, the executors succeeded in a trade name and passing off action against the company.

(b) Circulars suggested that the goods of the plaintiff were not **17–30** genuine, but were imitations of goods sold by the defendants; their publication was restrained: *Thomas v. Williams* (1880) 14 Ch. D. 864.

(c) The defendant had written that the plaintiffs were proposing to make use of a patented invention of the defendant which he had himself abandoned, leading to a construction that was "inadequate". It was held that this was actionable as a false and malicious statement: *London Ferro-Concrete v. Justicz* (1951) 68 R.P.C. 65 at 261.

(d) The plaintiff's landlord, by maliciously asserting that he was no **17–31** longer a tenant or available, got him struck off his suppliers' register: injunction granted: *Joyce v. Motor Surveys* [1948] Ch. 252.

(e) The sale of old tinned milk manufactured by the plaintiffs as and for the plaintiffs' current stock was held to be passing off *and* a malicious falsehood calculated to injure the plaintiffs' reputation: *Wilts United Dairies v. Robinson* [1957] R.P.C. 220 and [1958] R.P.C. 94.

(f) An allegation in a medical publication that a dentist used an unsatisfactory technique was held capable of bearing a defamatory meaning and it was unnecessary to plead malice as the action was for libel: *Drummond-Jackson v. British Medical Association* [1970] 1 W.L.R. 688.

---

[19] Parties are referred to as the "plaintiff" herein in relation to cases which were decided before the introduction of the Civil Procedure Rules in 1999. In relation to cases taking place since then, and in relation to hypothetical examples, the expression "claimant" is used.

Proof of damage

17-32 In an action for trade libel it used to be held that special damage was the gist of the action, though it was sufficient for grant of an injunction to prove likelihood of actual damage.[20]

If the injury is proved trifling and no threat to repeat the publication is proved, the action may be dismissed.[21]

The interruption of an illegal trade cannot be legal damage.[22]

Defamation Act 1952

17-33 The general rule as to proof of damage was modified by section 3(1) of the Defamation Act 1952 which provides:

> "In an action for slander of title, slander of goods or other malicious falsehood, it shall not be necessary to allege or prove special damage—
>
> (a) if the words upon which the action is founded are calculated to cause pecuniary damage to the plaintiff and are published in writing or other permanent form[23]; or
>
> (b) if the said words are calculated to cause pecuniary damage to the plaintiff in respect of any office, profession, calling, trade or business held or carried on by him at the time of publication."

3. "Puffery" not actionable; rival traders

General

17-34 It is often said that "mere puffs" of the defendant's own goods, or statements that the defendant's goods are better than the claimant's, are not actionable, even if untrue and the cause of damage. In some authorities it is also remarked that such statements are not actionable even if the defendant knows them to be false.[24] It is not easy to reconcile all of these statements unless they are read carefully, and many of the broader ones were made *obiter*.

17-35 The two leading cases are *White v. Mellin*,[25] and *Hubbuck v. Wilkinson*.[26] A clear and useful modern analysis of these and other cases is to be

---

[20] *Thomas v. Williams* (1880) 14 Ch.D. 864; *Reuter v. Muhlens* (1953) R.P.C. 102 at 116 (in the CA at 70 R.P.C. 245, the point was not argued).

[21] *Dicks v. Brooks* (1880) 15 Ch.D. 22.

[22] *Royal Baking Powder* (1901) 18 R.P.C. 95, *per* Lord Davey, Lord Robertson.

[23] Under the 1952 Act, s.5(2), the broadcasting of words is to be treated as being in permanent form.

[24] See the reference to the speech of Lord Diplock in *Advocaat*, para. 17–06, above.

[25] [1894] 3 Ch. 276.

[26] [1899] 1 Q.B. 86.

found in *De Beers Abrasive Products v. International General Electric Co.*[27] *White v. Mellin* and *Hubbuck v. Wilkinson* were both decided before the Defamation Act 1952, at a time when it was always a requirement to plead and prove special damage in order to succeed in a claim for malicious falsehood. This requirement is important to the reasoning in both decisions, and this must be borne in mind in reading them.

In *White v. Mellin*, the defendant bought baby food from the plaintiff **17–36** and sold it on to the public. He attached to the packaging of the plaintiff's food a label which stated that the defendant's own brand of baby food, called "Dr Vance's", was "more nutritious and healthful than any other yet offered". The action failed on appeal to the House of Lords. Lord Herschell L.C. found that the label was sufficiently directed at the plaintiff by reason of being attached to his goods (at 158), and while he doubted whether the label had been shown falsely to disparage the plaintiff's goods, he went on to consider the position on the assumption that it had (at 159). On that basis, he considered that the action should fail because the label was a common kind of puff which the public would not seriously take to mean that the plaintiff's goods were not good, or were less good than anyone else's (at 160). While he also held that there was no malice, there being no evidence of intention to injure the defendant or of a lack of belief by the defendant that what he had said was true (at 161), the primary reason for his decision was the general nature of the statement. That appears from the following passages (at 164):

> "I entertain very grave doubts whether any action could be maintained for an alleged disparagement of another's goods, merely on the allegation that the goods sold by the party who is alleged to have disparaged his competitor's goods are better either generally or in this or that particular respect than his competitors' are. . . . I am dealing with the class of cases which is now before us, where the only disparagement consists in vaunting the superiority of the defendant's own goods."

He rejected a suggestion that a claim that the defendant's goods were **17–37** more nutritious and healthful was not merely a matter of opinion but one of fact (at 165), and he held that there would be no cause of action whether the defendant claimed that his goods were better generally, or in one or more particular respects (also at 165).

Lords Watson and Shand both held that a statement that the defendant's goods are better than the plaintiff's is "a disparagement of which the law takes no cognizance" (at 167 and 171).

However, none of the speeches appears to have been on the basis that **17–38** the truth or falsity of the statement made was not capable of being determined. Lord Morris, for example, stated that "A party does not lay

---

[27] [1975] F.S.R. 323.

himself open to action who bona fide praises his goods as better than another's, and it cannot give a cause of action because on the trial of those competing articles the defendant's article may be ascertained not to be better than the plaintiff's" (at 170). The decision seems primarily to be based on the assumption that the public do not see mere praise of one trader's goods as seriously denigrating those of the trader with whom the comparison is made, and on the policy ground that the courts should not try such disputes between rival traders.[28]

17–39   In *Hubbuck v. Wilkinson*, the defendant published a circular which purported to give details of trials comparing the parties' respective zinc paints, the conclusion being that the defendant's had a slight advantage, but that for all practical purposes the paints were equal. The defendant's paint was much cheaper. The plaintiff alleged that the results reported in the circular were not true.

17–40   Following *White v. Mellin* the Court of Appeal struck out the plaintiff's claim, on the basis that a statement that the defendant's product was as good as or better than the plaintiff's was not actionable, even if false, the cause of loss, and made maliciously (at 91).

17–41   In *De Beers*, the defendant had again published the purported results of a series of comparative tests on the parties' products, which in this case were diamond abrasives (the plaintiff's being natural and the defendant's synthetic). The results given were specific and quantitative, and gave the impression that the plaintiff's abrasives wore unacceptably quickly when used on granite (and the judge considered that that would imply a more general problem with cutting power—at 329).

17–42   The defendant applied unsuccessfully to strike out the claim. In the course of a detailed review of the cases, Walton J. identified two different kinds of extreme case: in the first, a defendant asserts that his goods are the best in the world. That is only a more dramatic way of saying that his goods are better than the claimant's, and is not actionable. In the second kind of case, the defendant asserts that his goods are better than the claimant's by reason of the claimant's goods being "rubbish" (at 329). That, he considered, would be actionable on the basis of the speech of Lord Shand in *White v. Mellin*.

17–43   Walton J. went on to assess how to decide cases falling between those extremes. He considered two tests. The first was whether a reasonable man would consider the defendant's claim to be a serious one. The second was whether the defendant had pointed to a specific deficit in the claimant's goods (at 329). He preferred the first test because it would inherently cope with situations where the defendant's claim would not be taken seriously because, for example, it had been expressed in a light-hearted way. However, both tests were consistent with the authorities and would give the same result in the instant case.

17–44   *Hubbuck v. Wilkinson*, despite its superficial similarities, was distinguished on the basis that a statement that the parties' products were

---

[28] See paras 17–09 and 17-10, above.

equal was not likely to be taken seriously, and because there was no real disparagement of the plaintiff's paint. The statement by the defendant about the parties' abrasives was to be taken seriously because it was presented as a proper scientific test, and could be actionable if it contained disparaging statements (at 332).

It is suggested that three related points of principle can be discerned **17–45** from these cases. They are (1) the statement complained of must specifically denigrate the claimant in order for it to be actionable; (2) the statement will not be actionable unless it is likely to be taken seriously; and (3) general praise of the defendant's goods is not actionable.

Statement must specifically denigrate the claimant

This proposition follows from *White v. Mellin* and *Hubbuck v. Wilkinson.* **17–46** It was recently confirmed *in Schulke & Mayr v. Alkapharm,*[29] where the advertisement complained of contained statements about the defendant's goods which were alleged to be untrue, but did not refer to the plaintiff's or its goods at all. The claim was struck out.

It is also clear from those cases that the denigration must be specific; **17–47** although a statement that the defendant's goods "are the best" implies that the claimant's are not as good, it does not denigrate them. It also offends the third principle, below.

Statement must be intended to be taken seriously

This also follows from the nineteenth century cases, and was made more **17–48** explicit in *De Beers*. Note that in none of those cases was any evidence led as to whether the statements were likely to be taken seriously; the court reached its own conclusions.

The matters which will determine whether a statement is likely to be **17–49** taken seriously will include its level of generality (detailed data with specific conclusions as presented in *De Beers* is more likely to be taken seriously than wide statements about comparative quality of the kind found in *Hubbuck v. Wilkinson*), and its tone. A humorous advertisement may well not be taken seriously: an example was given in *De Beers* of a maker of amphibious cars alleging that his goods were better than a Rolls Royce, because the latter would sink. It was also suggested in that case that a statement may be so vituperative that it would not be taken seriously (at 329).

This principle would appear to be obvious in any event from the basic **17–50** elements of the tort, since a statement which is not likely to be taken seriously can rarely, if ever, be damaging or calculated to cause damage.

Mere general praise of the defendant's goods is not actionable

General praise of the defendant's goods will usually not be actionable **17–51** for one of the two foregoing reasons in any event: it will not denigrate the claimant's goods, and is unlikely to be taken seriously. However, it

[29] [1999] F.S.R. 161.

is clear from the nineteenth century cases, in particular from *Hubbuck v. Wilkinson* (at 91), that this is an independent principle. General praise is not actionable even if false, damaging and made maliciously.

Specific false comparisons which do not denigrate the claimant

17-52 The recent malicious falsehood cases concerned with comparative advertising[30] have mostly concerned price comparisons, in which the defendant has claimed to be cheaper by some specific percentage or amount of money per month. The claimant's allegations have been that the defendant's statement is false, or calculated on a wrong basis, or an inappropriate comparison.

17-53 It is open to question how these cases fit in with the general principles above, which require that the claimant's goods be specifically denigrated. It may be that a price comparison for specific goods asserts that the claimant is more expensive than the defendant, but unless there is an implicit statement that the claimant's goods are unjustifiably expensive, does that really denigrate him or his goods? If, as seems to be the case, it does not, can it be actionable?

17-54 This point was not argued in any of the recent cases referred to above or, it seems, in any of the authorities considered by Walton J. in *De Beers*. In principle, it seems that such statements ought to be actionable. They are by their nature intended and likely to be taken seriously, their prevention would not interfere with the defendant's ability to praise his own goods generally and in broad terms, they are directed specifically at the claimant, and they are intended and likely to draw business directly from the claimant to the defendant, to the claimant's detriment. It can perhaps be said that statements of this kind are so specifically aimed at the claimant, and are so directly in comparison with the defendant, that a slightly wider meaning of "denigrate" or "disparage" is appropriate.

4. Construing the statement, and falsity

General standard, evidence

17-55 The meaning of the statements complained of is determined by the court itself, and (unless circumstances are proved tending to show that their actual meaning, in the particular case, is different from the natural meaning), evidence cannot be adduced to prove that they were not understood according to it.[31]

---

[30] See n. 13, above.
[31] *Royal Baking Powder* (1901) 18 R.P.C. 95 at 101, HL. In *McDonald's v. Burgerking* [1986] F.S.R. 45, the judge appears to have had regard to evidence from members of the public as to how they had in fact understood the advertisement concerned, but there was also a claim for passing off, to which that evidence was primarily directed. It is suggested that normally in a trade libel case, the general rule is that evidence about the meaning of the statements in issue is not admissible. This is related to the "one meaning" rule, as to which see below.

The court will take a practical approach in its reading of the **17–56** statements complained of, with regard to the fact that the public expect a degree of hyperbole in advertising. In *De Beers Abrasive Products v. International General Electric Co.*,[32] Walton J. said (at 328): "in the kind of situation where one expects, as a matter of ordinary common experience, a person to use a certain amount of hyperbole in the description of goods, property or services, the courts will do what any reasonable man would do, namely, take it with a large pinch of salt." See also *McDonald's Hamburgers v. Burgerking*[33]: "Advertisements of this kind are not to be read as if they were some testamentary provision in a will or a clause in some agreement with every word being carefully considered and the words as a whole being compared."

The onus is on the claimant to prove falsity, since it is an essential element of the tort.

"One meaning" rule

In defamation, there is a rule that a statement which is alleged to be **17–57** defamatory has only one true meaning,[34] and that is so even if in fact some members of the public would understand it to mean one thing and others another. A claimant cannot succeed by showing that a reasonable proportion of the public would understand the statement in a defamatory sense. This is a principle of long standing, with its origins and rationale probably lying in the fact that defamation actions are usually tried with juries. It was recently confirmed in *Charleston v. News Group Newspapers*.[35]

It appears that the same rule applies to malicious falsehood, although **17–58** some doubts have been expressed about whether that is so. In *Vodafone v. Orange* [1997] F.S.R. 34, Jacob J. accepted on the authority of *Charleston* that the "one meaning" rule applied to malicious falsehood, the contrary not having been argued. He pointed out, though, that the jury-trial basis for the rule in defamation might not apply to the same extent in malicious falsehood. First, because there is no general right of jury trial in the latter case, and second, because a single meaning needs to be determined in defamation actions so as to assess *quantum* for damage to the claimant's reputation. In malicious falsehood, by contrast, damages are awarded to compensate for pecuniary loss. So long as the words complained of caused the loss in question, it may be that their precise meaning does not matter.

In addition, the "one meaning" rule for malicious falsehood appears **17–59** strange when, as frequently happens, it falls to be applied in the same action as passing off or infringement under section 10(6) of the 1994 Act.

---

[32] [1975] F.S.R. 323.
[33] [1986] F.S.R. 45 at 58.
[34] Leaving aside cases where by reason of circumstances extrinsic to the statement, a legal innuendo is alleged.
[35] [1995] 2 All E.R. 313.

In the latter two torts, it is sufficient if a proportion of the public would be misled by the statement concerned.[36] It seems odd that a claimant may succeed in those causes of action but fail, on the same facts, in a claim for malicious falsehood (assuming malice and likelihood of damage can be shown). That would happen if the statement concerned would be likely to be, and has been, understood by a significant number of persons in a false and damaging sense, but not in its "one meaning". It is hard to see why, in justice, a claimant should fail in a claim for malicious falsehood in such a situation.

5. Malice

Meaning

17–60 The definitions of malice given in the authorities are complex and somewhat unsatisfactory. For example, in *Balden v. Shorter*,[37] Maugham J. approved the following statement:

> ". . . it is now apparently settled that malice in the law of slander of title and other forms of injurious falsehood means some dishonest or otherwise improper motive. A bona fide assertion of title, however mistaken, if made for the protection of one's own interest or for some other proper purpose, is not malicious."

17–61 In the same case, Maugham J. also said that malice "in the sense of a wrongful intention to injure the plaintiffs" was required. This is, or may be, a somewhat different requirement. Sometimes, an intention to injure "without just cause" is stated to be a requirement of the tort, and again, this is not, on the face of it, quite the same as "improper motive".

17–62 Despite these apparent inconsistencies, certain key principles are clear enough. First of all, malice involves a subjective state of mind on the part of the defendant. Even if the defendant had no positive justification for making the statement complained of, it is still necessary to show that he had the necessary mental element of ill-will, intention to injure or the like. Secondly, the reason for the defendant's statement is relevant. If he was seeking to defend his own lawful interest, then the fact that he knew that the claimant would be damaged does not constitute malice. In this connection, it is recognised that a trader's desire to promote his business at the expense of his rivals is a proper one: see *White v. Mellin*

---

[36] See Chaps 13 and 14. The proportion of the public which need be misled for an action in passing off to succeed may simply be more than *de minimis*.

[37] [1933] Ch. 427 at 430, referring to the 7th edition of *Salmond on Torts*. Followed in *Loudon v. Ryder (No. 2)* [1953] Ch. 423, in *London Ferro-Concrete v. Justicz* (1951) 68 R.P.C. 65 at 261 and in *Eothen Films v. Industrial and Commercial Education* [1966] F.S.R. 356, CA. That good faith excludes malice was confirmed by the House of Lords in *Spring v. Guardian Assurance* [1994] 3 W.L.R. 354, *e.g.* at 379, *per* Lord Slynn.

and *Hubbuck v. Wilkinson*.[38] Thirdly, knowledge of the falsity of the statement made amounts to malice.

It was held by the Court of Appeal in *Spring v. Guardian Assurance*[39] **17–63** that the meaning of malice is the same in this tort as in defamation, so authorities from that field may be considered for assistance.

Knowledge of falsity or recklessness

Since the promotion of one trader at the expense of his rivals is regarded **17–64** as a proper objective for the purposes of this tort, the most important kind of malice in the context of this work is knowledge on the part of the defendant that the statement he has made is false (or recklessness as to its truth).[40]

Knowledge of falsity amounts to malice without any more having to be proven. Such a state of mind obviously excludes any suggestion of bona fides on the part of the defendant.

"Recklessness" in this context is a subjective concept. It means that **17–65** the defendant made the false statement without considering or caring whether or not it was true.[41] It is not the same as carelessness.[42] Recklessness is excluded by a belief on the part of the defendant that the statement was true, even if that belief was irrational.[43]

What if the defendant did not believe himself to be making the **17–66** statement alleged by the claimant (or did not turn his mind to it), but a different statement, which he believed to be true? In principle, it would seem that such a state of mind does not amount to malice. There is some support for this view in *McDonald's v. Burgerking* [1986] F.S.R. 45 at 60. It was alleged that the advertisement complained of had falsely stated (by implication, rather than expressly) that McDonald's Big Macs were not 100 per cent pure beef. The judge rejected McDonald's case on malice on the basis that the relevant employees of Burgerking never intended to suggest that McDonald's products were not 100 per cent beef.

Genuine but irrational belief in truth

A genuine belief in the truth of the statement made negates malice, in **17–67** the absence of some other improper motive.[44]

[38] [1895] A.C. 154 at 160–161; [1899] 1 Q.B. 86 at 94.
[39] [1993] 2 All E.R. 273. Note that the Court of Appeal's decision was overturned by the House of Lords (see note above), although not on this point.
[40] It was confirmed that this state of mind amounts to malice in *Kaye v. Robertson* [1991] F.S.R. 62 at 67. Glidewell L.J. also stated that for malice to be shown it was necessary that the words concerned were calculated to cause damage. It is suggested that this simply meant that the words must be likely to damage the plaintiff, thereby preventing the making of false but apparently innocuous statements from being malicious. It does not add the requirement of intention to injure. In practical terms it will rarely make any difference, since either special damage or words calculated to cause pecuniary damage are requirements of the tort in any event.
[41] See *Horrocks v. Lowe* [1975] A.C. 135, *per* Lord Diplock.
[42] *Balden v. Shorter* and *Loudon v. Ryder (No. 2)*, both *supra*.
[43] See *Horrocks v. Lowe*, *supra*.
[44] See *Horrocks v. Lowe*, *supra*.

Effect of notice of falsity

17–68 It not infrequently happens that although the claimant has difficulty in proving that the defendant acted with malice in making the initial publication, events during the proceedings themselves make it clear that the statement was false. In those circumstances, the claimant may be able to obtain relief despite his difficulties in showing that the initial publication was tortious, particularly if the defendant evinces an intention to repeat the statement.

17–69 For example, in *Kaye v. Robertson*,[45] the statement complained of was to the effect that the plaintiff had consented to an interview following a car accident in which he suffered head injuries. In fact, he had not consented, and the question arose of whether the defendant had known of his lack of consent. The Court of Appeal held on the evidence that the defendant's staff realised that the plaintiff was unable to consent from his condition during the interview. It also said that even if that had not been so, the affidavit sworn on the claimant's behalf would have put the defendant on notice of the statement's falsity so that "any subsequent publication of the falsehood would inevitably be malicious". An interim injunction was granted.

Improper purpose

17–70 As is pointed out above, in the world of commerce it will be rare that malice consists purely in making a statement with an improper purpose. The maker of the statement will usually be seeking to promote his own sales, which is not improper. However, it is not at all impossible.

Improper purposes include sheer spite, revenge and the like.

Delay in suing not evidence of malice

17–71 Upon an application for an interim injunction to restrain the publication of threats[46] by the defendant, it is not sufficient proof, if it is any evidence at all, of want of good faith, to show that he has commenced an action for infringement of trade mark, or for passing-off goods against the claimant, but has neglected to apply in it for an interim injunction[47]; nor to show even a long delay in bringing an action for infringement, if the delay is properly explained.[48]

Libel on inventor

17–72 In an action brought for falsely and maliciously publishing passages in a book depriving the plaintiff of the credit for being the first inventor of a machine, the statement of claim was struck out on the ground that the

---

[45] [1991] F.S.R. 62 at 68. See also *Loudon v. Ryder (No. 2)* [1953] Ch. 423, where malice was not proven but declaratory relief was granted; and by way of contrast, *Reuter v. Muhlens* (1953) 70 R.P.C. 102 at 235, CA, where a declaration was refused.

[46] In respect of threats of trade mark infringement proceedings, there is now a statutory right of action which does not depend on absence of good faith (as to which, see *infra*) but for some other kinds of threats the action for malicious falsehood is still appropriate.

[47] *Anderson v. Liebig's* (1881) 45 L.T. (N.S.) 757.

[48] *Incandescent Gas Light v. Sunlight* (1897) 14 R.P.C. 180.

passages complained of were not libellous. But Vaughan Williams L.J. said that he must not be supposed in any way to be affirming such a proposition as that you cannot libel anyone by denying his title to a reputation which he may have obtained as an inventor or as a man of science. *Wilde v. Thompson*.[49]

6. Proceedings

Solicitor or other agent

There is old authority to the effect that a solicitor who has made a **17–73** publication merely as agent for the real defendants should not normally be joined as a defendant.[50] Frequently in such instances it will be hard to prove or even plead that the solicitor acted with malice in the initial publication, since in most cases he will have acted bona fide in accordance with his instructions. There is plainly no rule of law that a solicitor in such situations may not be sued though, and there are a number of instances where they have been.[51] In particular, it may be necessary or desirable to sue the solicitors to the "real" defendants if the latter would not be able to pay any damages which might be awarded.

Publication of an apology

The publication of an apology actually made by the plaintiffs to the **17–74** defendants is justifiable, though it may have been extracted from the plaintiffs under duress of civil or criminal proceedings in respect of the false marking of their goods.[52]

No interim injunction where justification arguable

It has long been the position in the law of defamation that an interim **17–75** injunction will not be granted to restrain the publication of an alleged defamatory statement if the defendant states an intention to justify the statement, and the statement is such that a reasonable jury could find it to be true.[53]

---

[49] (1903) 20 R.P.C. 361 at 775.
[50] *Incandescent v. Sunlight* (1897) 14 R.P.C. 180 at 186, 190.
[51] See *Mentmore v. Fomento* (1955) 72 R.P.C. 157, where the solicitor was made a party and an undertaking given on his behalf; *CHC v. Hopkins and Woods* [1993] F.S.R. 241 (the action subsequently failed); and *Brain v. Ingledew Brown Bennison & Garrett* [1996] F.S.R. 341 (this was a threats case under the Patents Act 1977. Threats of trade mark proceedings are dealt with in more detail below, but note that that tort does not have a mental element, and therefore does not present the difficulty of proving malice on the part of a professional adviser).
[52] *Fisher v. Apollinaris* (1875) L.R. 10 Ch. 297.
[53] *Bonnard v. Perryman* [1891] 2 Ch. 269.

17–76   This rule also applies to claims for malicious falsehood by virtue of the decision of the Court of Appeal in *Bestobell Paints v. Bigg*,[54] and is an exception to the principles of *American Cyanamid*.[55]

17–77   The modern rationale for the rule is the protection of freedom of speech,[56] although historically its origins were connected with the respective functions of the judge and jury in defamation actions.

Interim injunction in other cases

17–78   Although the general rule in *Bestobell Paints v. Bigg* will usually prevent a successful application for an interim injunction to restrain an alleged malicious falsehood, there are exceptions.

First, an interim injunction may be granted (and provided that there is a likelihood of damage, presumably usually will be) where the statement is so unarguably false that only an unreasonable jury could accept it as true.[57]

17–79   Secondly, an interim injunction may be granted where the dispute between the parties is over the meaning of the statement in question, it being clear that the statement is false if it bears the meaning for which the claimant contends. For example, in *Compaq v. Dell*,[58] the defendant had published a number of advertisements comparing the parties' prices for various personal computers. The plaintiff's computers shown in the advertisements differed materially from the defendant's (the judge holding that no reasonable jury could find otherwise), but the plaintiff alleged that the advertisement suggested that they were essentially the same. The defendant denied that such a suggestion was made. In those circumstances, Aldous J held that the principles from *American Cyanamid* should be applied, but that potential interference with the defendant's freedom of speech was a relevant factor to take into account in assessing the balance of convenience. On that basis, he granted an interim injunction.

17–80   Thirdly, there are circumstances where an interim injunction may be granted when a cause of action other than malicious falsehood is relied on, even though malicious falsehood is or could be pleaded as well. This principle has been considered in a number of cases, and the resulting position is not clear or satisfactory.

17–81   In *Microdata v. Rivendale*,[59] the defendant had alleged that the plaintiff had no right to deal in certain computer software which it was seeking to sell to its customers. The plaintiff framed its case in interference with contractual relations rather than malicious falsehood, and the Court of Appeal held that in those circumstances the *Bestobell* rule did not apply,

---

[54] [1975] F.S.R. 421.
[55] *Herbage v. Times Newspapers, The Times*, May 1, 1981.
[56] See, *e.g. Microdata v. Rivendale* [1991] F.S.R. 681.
[57] *Kaye v. Robertson* [1991] F.S.R. 62.
[58] [1992] F.S.R. 93.
[59] [1991] F.S.R. 681.

and "ought not to be applied any further than is necessary to preserve the fundamental right of free speech".[60] It is notable that the facts of the case reeked of bad faith on the part of the defendant, and this may well have had an effect on the result.

A similar situation arose in *Western Front v. Vestron*[61] (although the **17–82** defendant's conduct was not so obviously blameworthy). Counsel for the defendant sought to criticise the reasoning of the court in *Microdata v. Rivendale*, but the judge held himself to be bound by it, despite considerable reservations and with the hope that it would be reconsidered. The same happened in *Consorzio del Prosciutto di Parma v. Marks & Spencer*,[62] a passing-off case, where Morritt J. held that *American Cyanamid* should be applied, but with the importance of freedom of speech being considered as part of the balance of convenience.

The whole line of authority was considered by Ferris J. in *Essex* **17–83** *Electric v. IPC Computers*.[63] There, the plaintiff sued for malicious falsehood and interference with contractual relations. While it accepted that the *Bestobell* rule applied to the former claim, it relied on *Microdata v. Rivendale* to seek an interim injunction in respect of the latter, and it succeeded. Ferris J. took the same course as Morritt J. had.

An interim injunction was also granted in *Gulf Oil v. Page*[64] where, in an action for libel, conspiracy was also pleaded.

The state of affairs arrived at in this line of cases is, it is suggested, **17–84** unsatisfactory and rather arbitrary. If the reason for the *Bestobell Paints v. Bigg* rule is a policy decision that restraining arguably truthful statements prior to trial is unacceptable because of its impact on freedom of speech, then one would not expect its scope to be limited to a particular cause of action. There is no persuasive reason in the cases why interference with contractual relations, say, should be treated any differently from malicious falsehood. The reason given in *Microdata v. Rivendale*, that a different interest may be protected by the former tort,[65] is not convincing, it is suggested. In each case the commercial interest protected is the ability of the claimant to do business with his customers, without interference by damaging statements from the defendant, and that is so regardless of the cause of action pleaded. It having been decided that that interest should yield to the defendant's interest in being able to exercise free speech (at least until trial and provided that the statement is at least arguably true), that decision ought in principle to apply whatever the cause of action. Moreover, the addition of a cause of action other than malicious falsehood may be either specifically designed to obtain an interim injunction by avoiding the *Bestobell Paints*

---

[60] *per* May L.J. at 686.
[61] [1987] F.S.R. 66.
[62] [1990] F.S.R. 530.
[63] [1991] F.S.R. 690.
[64] [1987] Ch. 327.
[65] As is suggested in the section of the judgement of Griffiths L.J. quoted in *Essex Electric* at 702, and also in the judgment of May L.J. quoted there.

v. Bigg rule (as may have been the case in *Essex Electric v. IPC*, where the real gist of the complaint was the defendant's statements and not the plaintiff's specific contracts with its customers), or available only fortuitously (in *Gulf Oil v. Page* an interim injunction based on a claim in conspiracy was granted since the defendant had assistance in publishing the statement. Presumably if he had acted alone then the only claim would have been for defamation or malicious falsehood and no interim injunction would have been available. This is not a rational distinction.)

17–85   In addition, there are other authorities which go the other way, and so suggest that the rule against interim injunctions where the statement is capable of justification applies more broadly than where the only claim is for malicious falsehood. See, for example, *Sim v. H.J. Heinz* [1959] R.P.C. 75, CA and *Lord Brabourne v. Hough* [1981] F.S.R. 79. In the latter case, the defendant intended to publish a biography of Lord Louis Mountbatten and to claim that it was authorised. The plaintiff alleged that it was not, and sued in passing off (and for interference with contractual relations, but not for defamation or malicious falsehood). An interim injunction was refused by analogy to the rule in defamation and malicious falsehood. In the former case, the well-known actor Alastair Sim complained that his voice had been imitated by an actor. He sued for libel, malicious falsehood and passing off, but an interim injunction was refused by reference to the rule applicable in libel cases.

17–86   It is suggested that a proper analysis of all these cases is assisted by bearing in mind once again the analysis behind the decision in *Compaq v. Dell*. Where there is no doubt that the statement complained of has been made, but the issue is whether it is true or false, then in principle the rule in *Bestobell Paints v. Bigg* ought to apply regardless of the precise cause of action. Where the statement complained of is not express and is said to have been made by implication or innuendo or get-up (as in *Compaq v. Dell* itself, and in most passing-off cases, certainly including the *Parma Ham* case), but it is plainly false if it has been made, then *American Cyanamid* ought to be applied, with the issue of free speech falling to be considered as an element of the balance of convenience. On this basis, *Lord Brabourne v. Hough* was rightly decided (since, unusually for a passing-off case, it was clear that the statement was made but not whether it was true), but *Sim v. H.J. Heinz* may be regarded as a doubtful application of the *Bestobell Paints v. Bigg* rule, since if the advertisement did in fact suggest that Alastair Sim had done the voiceover, it was unarguably false (the result might still have been the same, of course).

Action survives to executors

17–87 Because the cause of action in malicious falsehood protects financial interests, rather than the claimant's reputation, a claim survives the death of the claimant.[66]

---

[66] *Hatchard v. Mege* (1887) 18 Q.B.D. 771, Law Reform Act 1934, s.1(1).

Limitation

The limitation period in relation to trade libel is one year, by virtue of **17–88** section 4A of the Limitation Act 1980, as amended by section 5(2) of the Defamation Act 1996.

Relief and refusal of relief

The relief available to a successful claimant in malicious falsehood is **17–89** damages (or an inquiry as to damages) and an injunction to restrain repetition of the statement concerned. The injunction ought only to restrain the repetition of the statement complained of or an equivalent statement, *i.e.* statements which have been found to be false.

Relief (and particularly costs) may be refused where one or both **17–90** parties are conducting the proceedings for the purposes of publicity rather than in pursuit of genuine grievances: *Emaco v. Dyson Appliances.*[67]

Disclosure of addressees of falsehoods

The court has power in an appropriate case to order, before trial, **17–91** disclosure of the names and addresses of those persons to whom allegedly malicious false statements have been made, so that the claimant can seek to mitigate its loss by disabusing them of any false impression: *CHC Software v. Hopkins & Woods* [1993] F.S.R. 241.

7. Misleading reports of proceedings

May be malicious falsehood

A false statement about proceedings may be a malicious falsehood **17–92** provided that it satisfies the usual elements of the tort. So, for example, falsely to state that a person is a party to an action when he in fact is not, or to state that proceedings have been brought to a successful conclusion when they have not, would plainly be actionable (given malice and likelihood of damage). However, to state correctly that proceedings are underway, if true, is not actionable, and nor, probably, is it capable of being a malicious falsehood to state that a party is confident, or even very confident, about the outcome of proceedings.[68] Such statements are unlikely to be taken seriously in any event.

May be contempt also

Statements about pending proceedings may also amount to a contempt **17–93** of court, if they are likely to prejudice the conduct or fair trial of the proceedings, and this may be so even if the statements are true. Again,

---

[67] [1999] E.T.M.R. 903.
[68] See *Goulard v. Lindsay* (1887) 4 R.P.C. 189.

however, confident statements about the likely outcome will usually not be wrongful; they are unlikely to affect the outcome, especially since most civil cases are not now heard by juries, and this kind of statement is not likely to affect potential witnesses.[69]

Contempt of court generally is outside the scope of this work; the reader should refer to specialist works.

8. Threats

Background to the provisions

17–94 It has been recognised for many years, in the context of patents that threats of proceedings may be extremely pernicious. Some of the reasons for this are considered above.[70] As a result, a statutory action for threats of patent infringement was introduced. It is now enacted by section 70 of the Patents Act 1977. There are parallel provisions in respect of registered and unregistered designs: section 26 of the Registered Designs Act 1948 and section 253 of the Copyright, Designs and Patents Act 1988.

The 1994 Act has for the first time introduced a provision making threats of trade mark infringement proceedings actionable. The relevant provision is section 21.

Analogy to provisions about threats under the Patents Act

17–95 Section 21 of the 1994 Act was not introduced to give effect to any provision of the Trade Marks Directive. It is a domestic provision passed in order to extend the threats action available in relation to patent infringement to the field of trade marks, as its close similarity to section 70 of the Patents Act 1977 makes clear. It therefore is to be construed in that context rather than in the context of the Directive. The approach of construing section 21 by reference to section 70 of the Patents Act 1977 was followed in *Prince plc v. Prince Sports Group Inc.*[71] Although there are differences in wording between the sections, in most cases it may be expected that the authorities in relation to section 70 will be applied to section 21.

May be malicious falsehood

17–96 In principle, an allegation that the goods of one trader infringe the registered trade mark of another may be a malicious falsehood. However, proving malice and falsity, particularly at an interim stage,

---

[69] See, *e.g. Carl-Zeiss Stiftung v. Rayner & Keeler* [1961] R.P.C. 1; *Easipower v. Gordon Moore* [1963] R.P.C. 8.
[70] See paras 17–16 to 17–19.
[71] [1998] F.S.R. 21.

will be difficult. If the person making the threat has a bona fide belief in its truth, then a claim for malicious falsehood should fail. It is therefore hard to think of any reason to bring an action for malicious falsehood if a claim under the 1994 Act is available.

The action for threats

Section 21 provides: **17–97**

(1) Where a person threatens another with proceedings for infringement other than—

(a) the application of the mark to goods or their packaging,

(b) the importation of goods to which, or to the packaging of which, the mark has been applied, or

(c) the supply of services under the mark,

any person aggrieved may bring proceedings for relief under this section.

(2) The relief which may be applied for is any of the following— **17–98**

(a) a declaration that the threats are unjustifiable,

(b) an injunction against the continuance of the threats,

(c) damages in respect of any loss he has sustained by reason of the threats;

and the plaintiff is entitled to such relief unless the defendant shows that the acts in respect of which proceedings were threatened constitute (or if done would constitute) an infringement of the registered trade mark concerned.

(3) If that is shown by the defendant, the plaintiff is nevertheless **17–99** entitled to relief if he shows that the registration of the trade mark is invalid or liable to be revoked in a relevant respect.

(4) The mere notification that a trade mark is registered, or that **17–100** an application for a trade mark has been made, does not constitute a threat of proceedings for the purposes of this section.

Hence, the pattern of the section is as follows (the individual issues are considered in more detail below).

First, the claimant must show that a threat has been made, which **17–101** threat is not in relation to one of the matters listed in subsection (1)(a) to (c). The matters excepted by subsection (1)(a) to (c) may be referred to as "primary" infringements. So, broadly speaking, the claimant has to prove that the threat was made in respect of secondary infringement, which generally means dealing in infringing goods other than by importation or manufacture.

Secondly, the claimant must show that he is a "person aggrieved". **17–102**

If the claimant proves those matters, then he is entitled to succeed unless the defendant, the person who has made the threat, proves that there has in fact been an infringement (or, that there would be an infringement if the claimant carries out the acts in question in future).

17–103   If the person making the threat proves that there has been or would be an infringement, then the claimant may yet succeed if he proves that the registration concerned is invalid or liable to be revoked "in a relevant respect[72]".

17–104   The section thus makes it clear that the claimant bears the onus of proving that there has been a threat, that he is aggrieved, and, if infringement is proven, that the registration concerned is invalid. The person making the threat bears the onus of proving infringement.

17–105   Note that there is no requirement in the section that the person aggrieved must be the same as the person against whom it is threatened that proceedings will be brought. They may be different persons, and in fact the most important cases where threats proceedings are brought are instances where they are different persons, as where a trader sues in relation to threats made to his customers or his suppliers.

What threats are actionable—primary infringers, services

17–106 Under section 70(4) of the Patents Act 1977, threats in relation to importation and manufacture are exempted from being actionable. Section 21 of the 1994 Act is in similar terms, although primary acts of infringement are excluded from the definition of the tort itself rather than being the subject of a separate exception as in section 70(4).

17–107   The rationale for the distinction is to strike a balance between the legitimate interest of the patentee or trade mark owner in warning infringers, and the right of others not to be vexed by threats without actually being sued. A direct warning to the source (in the United Kingdom) of infringing goods is therefore allowed, but threats to his customers may be actionable, because of the danger that they will stop patronising him whether or not the allegation of infringement is a good one.

17–108   However, section 70 of the Patents Act 1977 has caused some difficulties, because the exception from actionability is expressed by reference to the alleged infringing act, and not by reference to the person threatened. Hence, if a manufacturer is threatened in relation to his subsequent dealings in the products which he has made (secondary infringements) as well as in relation to the manufacture itself (primary infringement), then section 70(4) will not apply, and the threat is actionable.[73] It seems likely that the same result would be achieved in

---

[72] Presumably, this means that the claimant will succeed if the threat is at least in part in relation to goods or services for which the registration is invalid, rather than only if the threat is wholly in relation to goods or services for which it is invalid. In other words, the claimant is entitled to succeed if, by reason of the partial validity of the registration, the threat is partly, but not entirely, justifiable. This is consistent with the words used ("a relevant respect", rather than "all relevant respects"), and with the policy of the section.

[73] See *Cavity Trays v. RMC Panel Products* [1996] R.P.C. 361; *Therm-A-Stor v. Weatherseal Windows* [1981] F.S.R. 579; *Johnson Electric v. Mabuchi Motors* [1986] F.S.R. 280 at 288; and *Bowden v. Acco* [1990] R.P.C. 427.

relation to section 21 of the 1994 Act.[74] Although this position is in keeping with the words of both Acts, it gives rise to a curious result, because a threat to a manufacturer which relates exclusively to manufacture is not actionable (even though the manufacturer will almost certainly infer that he would also be sued in respect of sale of the same product), while a threat which mentions sale of the same goods, which would be understood to have exactly the same impact, is.

The upshot is that a primary infringer may be threatened with **17–109** impunity, provided that the threat is carefully expressed to relate to primary infringement alone. Accordingly, letters of threat need to be drafted with great care. Logically, it could follow that a threat expressed to be purely in relation to primary infringement but which is sent to a person who only carries on activities capable of being secondary infringements would not be actionable. However, such a threat might well be construed to be an implicit threat in relation to secondary infringement as well, especially if its sender was aware that the recipient did not carry on acts capable of being a primary infringement, and/or if the expression of the letter appeared to be a device to avoid the statutory threats provisions.[75]

Section 21 recognises a category of primary infringer which is not **17–110** relevant under the Patents Act 1977, namely suppliers of services. By their nature, of course, services cannot be passed down a chain of supply, and customers in receipt of services will not usually infringe a trade mark under which those services are supplied. The result is that threats in relation to services do not present the same danger of damage as threats in relation to goods, and accordingly they are excluded from the ambit of section 21.

In *Prince plc v. Prince Sports Groups Inc.*,[76] the plaintiff only provided **17–111** services, having, on the evidence before the court, no trade in goods. The threat complained of merely asserted the defendant's various trade marks, without stating whether it was intended to sue the plaintiff in relation to goods or services. Because the plaintiff only supplied services, the defendant argued that the threat should be construed as extending only to services, and hence outside section 21. Neuberger J. held[77] that because section 21 is concerned to prevent threats being made casually or recklessly, it is incumbent on a person who wishes to take advantage of one of the excepting paragraphs of subsection (1) to indicate so in terms. It is suggested, however, that there is nothing in the words of section 21 to require such a person to express his reliance on

---

[74] Such was accepted by the judge in *Prince plc v. Prince Sports Group Inc.* [1998] F.S.R. 21 at 33, although the contrary was not argued.
[75] See, e.g. *L'Oréal v. Johnson & Johnson*, unreported, Lightman J., March 7, 2000, where the judge held that a letter which expressly asserted that the trade mark owner had not decided whether to sue was an implicit threat. Important factors included the deliberate obscurity of the letter and the fact that proceedings in Ireland were already on foot and were referred to in the letter.
[76] [1998] F.S.R. 21.
[77] At 33.

any of the exceptions in terms, and in *Brain v. Ingledew Brown Bennison & Garrett*,[78] the Court of Appeal rejected the argument that a general threat should usually be regarded as a threat in respect of all potentially infringing acts. Rather, it is a question of construction in the particular circumstances which prevail. Aldous L.J. said (at 352):

> "Even if it be assumed that the letter contained a threat in general terms it does not follow that the recipient would read it as making a threat of proceedings in respect of all potentially infringing acts. A letter such as [the one in question], when written to a person who only operated a process, could be understood as being a threat of infringement by carrying out the process; whereas a letter written in general terms to a person who not only carried out the process but sold the products of that process, could be understood in a different way."

Threats in relation to applications for a trade mark

17-112 Under section 70 of the Patents Act 1977, it is actionable to make a threat of infringement in relation to an application for a patent which has not been granted: *Brain v. Ingledew Brown Bennison & Garrett*.[79] The decision in that case depended on the construction of section 69 of the Patents Act 1977 (giving various rights in relation to applications for patents which can be asserted retrospectively once the patent is granted). That section has no exact parallel in the 1994 Act, but it seems likely that the same result would be achieved, and a threat made in relation to an application for a trade mark is actionable.[80] In any event, such a threat will normally be understood to be a threat to bring proceedings once registration is achieved, and will therefore be actionable on that basis.[81]

17-113 In addition, section 21(4) of the 1994 Act, which exempts from actionability a mere notification of a registration, also exempts notification that an application has been made, and such a provision would not have been necessary unless it were contemplated that a threat in relation to an application could be actionable.

17-114 The fact that a threat may be made in relation to an ungranted application may cause difficulties if the application remains ungranted by the time of trial. In *Brain v. Ingledew Brown Bennison & Garrett* (No. 2),[82] Laddie J. held that the court would not allow a trial on hypothetical patent claims which might not be granted, but rather that a person making threats in respect of an application for a patent took the risk that

---

[78] [1996] F.S.R. 341.
[79] [1996] F.S.R. 341.
[80] Since it is recognised that an actionable threat can be made by someone who has no patent at all, this result is obviously right: see *Brain* at 347, approving a statement by the judge at first instance to that effect.
[81] See *per* Aldous L.J. in *Brain* at 347–348.
[82] [1997] F.S.R. 271.

it would not be granted by trial, and he struck out the defence of justification. The same reasoning would presumably apply in relation to the 1994 Act. Although it is probably less common for the specification of goods for a trade mark to change during prosecution than for the claims of a patent to be amended, there obviously remains the possibility that a trade mark application will not be granted at all.

Person Aggrieved

The requirement that the claimant be a person aggrieved by the threat in **17–115** question is not a difficult one to satisfy. Save perhaps in very exceptional circumstances, the person threatened is always aggrieved, and so is anyone else who can show that his commercial interests are or are likely to be adversely affected in a real as opposed to a fanciful or minimal way.[83] Clearly, a person whose customers or suppliers are threatened will be a person aggrieved, and that is so even if he manages to assuage their fears so that no recoverable loss is suffered.[84]

A person involved in the management of a company may be a person **17–116** aggrieved if he has sufficient personal interest in the effect of the threats, for example if the company threatened is simply a vehicle for the commercial interests of the principal shareholder and executive.[85]

Construing the alleged threat

Construing an alleged threat is a practical matter, to be decided on the **17–117** basis of the effect it would have on an ordinary reader, and should not be an exercise in unrealistic forensic analysis.[86] It is a jury-type question to be decided against the appropriate matrix of fact. A letter which is innocuous on its face may be a threat when placed in context (and the reverse is possible, though less likely).[87] For these reasons, the question of whether a threat has been made will usually require a trial, although not always.[88]

A series of letters should be looked at as a whole to determine **17–118** whether they contain a threat.[89] However, if an earlier letter in a series makes a threat, the threat is not negated by a later explanation, although the relief to be granted could be affected.[90]

---

[83] See *Prince plc. v. Prince Sports Group Inc.* [1998] F.S.R. 21 at 33 to 34, referring to *Brain v. Ingledew Brown Bennison & Garrett* [1996] F.S.R. 341.
[84] *Brain v. Ingledew Brown Bennison & Garrett (No. 3)* [1997] F.S.R. 511.
[85] *ibid.*
[86] *Brain v. Ingledew Brown Bennison & Garrett (No. 3)* [1997] F.S.R. 511; *L'Oreal v. Johnson & Johnson, supra.*
[87] *Brain v. Ingledew Brown Bennison & Garrett* [1996] F.S.R. 341 at 349.
[88] *ibid.*, although summary judgment was given in *Prince plc. v. Prince Sports Group Inc.* [1998] F.S.R. 21.
[89] *Brain v. Ingledew Brown Bennison & Garrett (No. 3)* [1997] F.S.R. 511 at 521.
[90] *Prince plc. v. Prince Sports Group Inc.* [1998] F.S.R. 21 at 27–28.

Availability of interim relief

17–119 An interim injunction is available to restrain the making of threats, notwithstanding the rule in *Bestobell Paints v. Bigg*[91] in relation to malicious falsehood. The reason is that threats cause severe damage quickly, and the statutory provisions against them would be of little use if the remedy of an interim injunction were not available. See *Johnson Electric v. Mabuchi Motors*.[92]

Defences

17–120 Justification, *i.e.* proof that the acts the subject of the threat are or would be an infringement, is a defence by virtue of section 21(2) of the 1994 Act. Where the person threatened has not yet done the acts concerned, it may be more difficult to show that they would infringe (certainly if the infringement in question would be under section 10(2), where surrounding circumstances would be relevant), but given the policy of section 21 and the courts' attitude to threats, it is highly likely that that would be held to be a risk taken by the person making the threat.

17–121 Mere notification that a trade mark is registered, or that an application has been made, is not actionable by virtue of section 21(4). However, persons seeking to take advantage of that provision should be very careful not to go even a fraction further than what is permitted, lest a threat be inferred.[93] Probably the most cautious and only truly safe approach is to say "In accordance with section 21(4) of the Trade Marks Act 1994 I hereby notify you that the mark XYZ is a registered trade mark appearing on the Register of Trade Marks as number 123,456.", and absolutely nothing more.

Effect of issuing proceedings before making threat

17–122 It is not actionable as a threat to report the mere existence of proceedings, subject to the comments above about the risk of malicious falsehood and contempt of court.[94]

Relief

17–123 The relief available under section 21 is set out in subsection (2): a declaration that the threats are unjustifiable, an injunction, and damages. Although the subsection is phrased in terms which suggest that the

---

[91] [1975] F.S.R. 421.
[92] [1986] F.S.R. 281.
[93] For an example of how not to proceed, see *L'Oréal v. Johnson & Johnson, supra.*
[94] See, *e.g. Carl-Zeiss Stiftung v. Rayner & Keeler* [1961] R.P.C. 1; *Easipower v. Gordon Moore* [1963] R.P.C. 8.

grant of that relief is mandatory once the claimant proves his case, it is clear that the court retains its general discretionary jurisdiction.[95] Hence, although an injunction and an inquiry will usually be granted, it is not automatic. In particular, an inquiry may not be granted if there is no evidence of loss.[96]

Except in unusual circumstances, relief going beyond that specified in section 21 will not be granted. The legislature has decided what relief is appropriate.[97]

Community Trade Marks

The provisions of section 21 apply to Community Trade Marks pursuant **17–124** to paragraph 4 of the Community Trade Mark Regulations 1996.[98]

Threats made "without prejudice"

It is an abuse of process to plead that a threat was made at a "without **17–125** prejudice" meeting, and an action based on such a plea will be struck out.[99]

[95] *Prince plc. v. Prince Sports Group Inc.* [1998] F.S.R. 21; *Brain v. Ingledew Brown Bennison & Garrett (No. 3)* [1997] F.S.R. 511 at 526, relying on *Allied Maples v. Simmons & Simmons* [1995] 1 W.L.R. 1602.

[96] *Prince plc. v. Prince Sports Group Inc.* [1998] F.S.R. 21 at 36–37, where an inquiry was refused initially with leave to the plaintiff to lead evidence of damage, which it later did. See also *Brain v. Ingledew Brown Bennison & Garrett (No. 3)* [1997] F.S.R. 511 at 525–528, where Laddie J held that usually an inquiry will follow from a finding of an actionable threat, and ordered an inquiry with considerable misgivings, on the basis that the evidence of damage was slight but not such as to be rejected altogether. That was a legal aid case; the inquiry is normally of course at the claimant's risk as to costs: *McDonald's v. Burgerking* [1987] F.S.R. 112.

[97] *Prince plc. v. Prince Sports Group Inc.* [1998] F.S.R. 21 at 41–42.

[98] See App. 14, *post.*

[99] *Unilever v. Procter & Gamble* [2000] F.S.R. 344.

CHAPTER 18

CIVIL PROCEEDINGS FOR TRADE MARK INFRINGEMENT AND PASSING OFF

1. Scope of chapter

18-01 The substantive law of registered trade marks and passing off has largely already been considered. The present chapter is concerned essentially with matters of practice and procedure. The matters covered include the requirements to be satisfied before an action may be brought, jurisdictional matters as to the proper forum for such disputes, both domestic and international remedies, both interim and final, costs, and appeals. Many of the issues covered are common to passing off as much as to trade mark infringement, although a number of formal matters are applicable only to the latter.

Certain aspects of civil litigation concerned specifically with Community Trade Marks are not dealt with here, but rather in Chapter 6.

2. Statutory action for infringement

Infringement of mark contrasted with passing-off

18-02 Although many of the principles applicable are common to both forms of action (and the two are frequently combined in a single action), it is important to bear in mind the differences between actions which are brought to prevent or to recover damages for the infringement of trade mark, and those which are compendiously described as "passing-off actions." In an action of the first kind the claimant complains that the defendant has infringed his mark by using an identical or similar mark, and he relies on his statutory title to the exclusive use of the mark in question for the goods or services specified in his registration, or goods or services similar thereto[1]; in an action of the second kind the claimant's case is less specialised, for he complains that the defendant is using means which are calculated to pass-off, or to cause to be passed-off, the goods or business of the defendant as and for those of the claimant, and the means may or may not comprise or consist of the taking of a mark, either registered or not.

---

[1] Or even, under the 1994 Act, s.10(3), dissimilar goods.

An action for infringement is necessarily an action upon a registered **18–03**
mark, by reason of section 2(2) of the 1994 Act which provides as
follows:

> "No proceedings lie to prevent or recover damages for the infringe-
> ment of an unregistered trade mark as such; but nothing in this Act
> affects the law relating to passing off."

Effects of section 2(2)

Any attempt to ascertain the practical effect of this prohibition is **18–04**
attended by some difficulty. It is questionable whether there ever was
any right of action for infringement of an unregistered trade mark, other
than an action for passing-off by the use of the mark.[2]

The express words in the second part of section 2(2), preserving the **18–05**
law of passing-off from being altered by the 1994 Act, imply that it will
be no defence to an action for passing off that the defendant is
registered as proprietor of the mark which he is using; but, where this is
the case it is usual for the claimant at the same time to apply to have the
registration revoked.[3]

Under the 1938 Act, the provision equivalent to section 2(2)[4] was held **18–06**
not to affect the right of the owner of an unregistered trade mark to
oppose a potentially conflicting registration,[5] and no doubt the same
would apply in relation to the 1994 Act.

Right to sue for infringement of a registered trade mark

The claimant in an action for infringement of a registered mark must **18–07**
generally establish his title to sue either as proprietor or as an exclusive
licensee, although in certain instances a licensee with no general right of
action may be entitled to sue if the proprietor fails to do so when called
upon.[6] He must then prove that the defendant has acted or threatens to
act in such a way as to infringe the right conferred by registration as
defined by the 1994 Act.

These subjects, the relief which may be obtained, and the procedure to
be followed will now be examined.

3. The claimant's title—infringement of registered marks

Title conferred by registration

The claimant's title as proprietor under the 1994 Act depends on the **18–08**
existence of a valid registration.[7] The fact that a person is registered as
proprietor of a mark is prima facie evidence of the validity of the

---

[2] The reason for insertion of this or similar provisions in successive Trade Marks Acts is
discussed further in the earlier editions of this work.
[3] *e.g. Rey v. Lecouturier* [1910] A.C. 262; 27 R.P.C. 268.
[4] s.2.
[5] *Mellor* (1948) 65 R.P.C. 238 (Regy).
[6] See Chap. 12.
[7] 1994 Act, s.9.

original registration and of any subsequent assignment or transmission thereof.[8]

18–09 The action may not be commenced until the mark is on the Register, notwithstanding that a registration once applied for will (if in due course achieved) date back to the application.[9] Under previous Acts, an assignee could commence an action for infringement of a mark on the Register without registration of the assignment,[10] and it would seem that that should still be the position, in particular because sections 9, 10 and 14 of the 1994 Act refer to "the proprietor" rather than "the registered proprietor", and because section 25, dealing with the consequences of non-registration, provides for an inability to obtain damages in certain circumstances, but not an inability to bring or maintain an action altogether. It should be noted that in relation to copyright infringement proceedings, an equitable owner may bring an action before obtaining legal title, provided that he either perfects his title before judgement or joins the legal owner,[11] so as to remove the risk that the defendant may be sued again. Assuming that an action may be brought by a trade mark proprietor whose interest is not on the Register, one would expect similar procedural safeguards to be required.

Exclusive licensee as claimant in his own right

18–10 Unless their licence provides otherwise, licensees under a registered trade mark may bring proceedings to restrain infringements which affect them, should the proprietor fail to do so: this is dealt with in the next section. The present section is concerned with the interest of an exclusive licensee who is positively given, by his licence agreement, the right to sue in his own name. The nature of the interest which the exclusive licensee obtains in such a situation is dealt with in Chapter 12. Here, we deal with procedural matters concerning an exclusive licensee in such a situation.

18–11 As will appear below, the fact that an exclusive licensee has a right to sue in his own name affects not only the manner in which he may bring proceedings, but also, in certain circumstances, the manner in which the proprietor may do so.

18–12 The rights of action which an exclusive licensee obtains under section 31 of the 1994 Act are concurrent with those of the proprietor,[12] and the

---

[8] s.72.

[9] ss.9(3) and 40(3).

[10] *Ihlee v. Henshaw* (1886) 31 Ch.D. 323; 3 R.P.C. 15. This case was decided on the 1883 Act, but the position would seem to be unchanged.

[11] See *e.g. Orwin v. Attorney-General* [1998] F.S.R. 415, and generally *Copinger and Skone James on Copyright* (14th Ed.) at 5–182.

[12] s.31(2). Of course, the exclusive licensee's rights to use the registered mark and to sue for infringements of it need not extend across the whole scope of the registration; the licence may be partial, limited to certain goods, or areas, or manners of use, as is explained in Chap. 12. Where the licence is partial, the rights of the exclusive licensee and the proprietor will only be concurrent in relation to those parts of the registration over which the licensee has rights; in relation to the remainder, the proprietor alone will have rights: such is clear from the wording of ss.28 and 31, particularly s.31(4).

defendant may avail himself of any defence which would have been available to him had the proprietor brought the action[13] (and it appears that this includes personal defences such as licence or acquiescence).

By section 31(4): **18–13**

> "Where proceedings for infringement of a registered trade mark brought by the proprietor or an exclusive licensee relate wholly or partly to an infringement in respect of which they have concurrent rights of action, the proprietor, or, as the case may be, the exclusive licensee may not, without the leave of the court, proceed with the action unless the other is joined as a plaintiff or added as a defendant."

Thus, for example, if an exclusive licence relates to some but not all of the types of goods the subject of a registration, and gives the licensee a right to sue in his own name, and an infringer uses the mark on those types of goods, or on those types of goods and other goods covered by the registration but not by the licence, then the proprietor and the licensee can both sue, but both must be made parties.

Joinder of the additional party is not required in order to obtain **18–14** interim relief.[14]

Where a proprietor or licensee is joined to proceedings under section 31(4) but takes no part, then he shall not be made liable for any costs.[15]

Somewhat peculiarly, section 31(8) appears to allow the proprietor **18–15** and exclusive licensee to contract out of the provisions of section 31(4) and (5). While one can understand the possibility that they might wish to make a contractual agreement as to the costs of proceedings brought by the one without the involvement of the other (since the other may yet derive a benefit from them), it seems surprising that the parties should be able to vary the requirement of section 31(4) that both should be joined if their rights are concurrent, since such provisions are usually made in order to protect a defendant from being sued twice for the same infringement. By contrast, section 30, considered below, does not allow the parties to modify the provisions equivalent to section 31(4) and (5) by agreement between themselves.

The relationship between proprietor and licensee may also affect the **18–16** relief which each can obtain (particularly as to damages and delivery up) in an action for infringement where their rights are concurrent. The 1994 Act deals with these issues in the broad and flexible provisions of section 31(6) and (7).

---

[13] s.31(3).
[14] s.31(4), last sentence.
[15] s.31(5).

18–17   Section 31(6) provides that, where there are concurrent rights of action, the court is to take the terms of the licence into account in assessing damages, as well as any award of damages already made.[16] It is clear that the purpose of requiring reference to the terms of the licence is not simply to avoid the proprietor or licensee being awarded a sum which exceeds the actual damage to him, allowing for the licence, since the section provides that the court may, if they are not both parties,[17] direct that the one is to hold relevant proceeds on behalf of the other. In other words, the section expressly envisages that one of them may recover damages to reflect loss to the other, even though that other is not a party. This is an unusual approach; it is even possible to imagine a party being awarded damages from infringement proceedings of which he is not aware, and it certainly could happen that a proprietor or licensee recovers damages which have been assessed in a manner over which he had no control. It appears that in general it would be much more desirable that both holders of concurrent rights should generally be made parties, which makes it all the more strange that the parties are apparently able to contract out of section 31(4), and, indeed, section 31(6).[18]

18–18   The court may not award an account of profits if an award of damages has been made or an account already directed in favour of the other party with a concurrent right.[19] If an account is ordered, the court is to apportion the proceeds in a manner which it considers just, having regard to the licence agreement.[20] These provisions apply whether or not both of the concurrent right holders are parties to the action.

18–19   As to delivery up, section 31(7) provides that the proprietor must notify an exclusive licensee with a concurrent right of action of any application for an order under section 16,[21] and empowers the court to make an order under section 16 upon the application of an exclusive licensee, having regard to the terms of the licence.[22] Of course, if both are parties to the action then the licensee will presumably know of the application anyway, but there could be a problem if, as is possible, the

---

[16] s.31(6)(a).
[17] As may happen if the court gives permission for one to be omitted under s.31(4), or, apparently, if the licence agreement permits one to proceed without the other.
[18] By s.31(8), referred to above.
[19] s.31(6)(b).
[20] s.31(6)(c).
[21] The provisions of s.16 are considered below in paras 18–122 et seq.
[22] It is not altogether clear on the wording of s.31(7) whether the licensee's right to apply under s.16 is contingent on, and to be exercised only in the context of, an application by the proprietor, or whether it is wholly independent. Since s.31(1) provides that the parties may by agreement confer on the licensee all the same rights *and remedies* as if the licence had been an assignment (albeit subject to the following provisions of s.31), and since if the right to apply under s.16 were contingent then there could be cases where no claimant could apply for delivery up (if the licensee were the only claimant), it appears that the right must be independent. However, the existence of the curious requirement that the proprietor must notify the licensee of an application under s.16 without a corresponding requirement that the licensee notify the proprietor may tend to suggest the contrary.

licensee is a party while the proprietor is not. For some reason the section does not expressly require the licensee to give the proprietor notice of an application by him.

In no circumstances can the exclusive licensee sue the proprietor: his remedy against the proprietor lies, if anywhere, in contract. See *Northern Shell v. Conde Nast*.[23] **18–20**

Licensees without their own right of action

Section 30 of the 1994 Act confers a more limited right of action than does section 31. It confers such a right on non-exclusive licensees and on exclusive licensees whose agreement with the proprietor takes them outside section 31. The provisions of sections 30 and 31 are mutually exclusive, since section 30(1) excludes from the provisions of that section exclusive licensees having a right of action under section 31. **18–21**

Unless the right is excluded by the agreement(s) from which he derives his licence, a licensee may, under section 31(2) call upon the proprietor to take infringement proceedings in respect of any matter "which affects his interests".[24] If the proprietor refuses to bring proceedings, or fails to do so within two months after being called upon, then the licensee may bring proceedings in his own name as if he were the proprietor.[25] As with section 31(4) and (5), section 30(4) and (5) provide that the proprietor must be joined as a party unless the court permits otherwise, but that that requirement is not to affect the granting of interim relief, and that the proprietor is not liable for costs if he does not take part in the proceedings. **18–22**

Section 30 is unclear as to the remedies which a licensee may obtain if successful in an action brought under section 30, and a particular question appears to arise over his right to recover damages. On the one hand, the section provides for the licensee to sue "as if he were the proprietor",[26] and this coupled with section 14(2), which provides that all relief is available to the proprietor in an infringement action as would be available in respect of the infringement of any other property right, would suggest that damages ought to be available. However, section 30 lacks the provision of section 31 giving an exclusive licensee "the same rights and remedies" as if the mark had been assigned to him, and section 30(6) provides that in infringement proceedings brought by the proprietor loss suffered by a licensee is to be taken into account, without stipulating what is to be done if the licensee is the claimant. This is to be contrasted with section 31(6), where it is plainly envisaged that both the proprietor and the exclusive licensee may recover damages. **18–23**

---

[23] [1995] R.P.C. 117, considered further in Chap. 12.
[24] The scope of this term is considered in Chap. 12.
[25] s.31(3).
[26] s.30(3).

18-24   Since it is plainly envisaged that damages may be recovered by the proprietor to reflect loss to a non-exclusive licensee (as a result of section 30(6)), and since it is envisaged that sums recovered as a result should be held for and pass to the licensee, it is clear that there is no intention in section 30 to exclude such persons from recovering financial relief altogether. Hence the better view probably is that a non-exclusive licensee can recover damages under section 30. It is unsatisfactory, however, that this does not explain the differences between sections 30 and 31 referred to above. A further possibility is that a non-exclusive licensee may recover damages as a result of section 30, but only through the medium of the proprietor (who will usually also be a party under section 30(4)).

18-25   There is no provision under section 30 entitling a non-exclusive licensee to take advantage of the statutory provisions relating to delivery up. This is an unfortunate omission, but it may be that the non-exclusive licensee could obtain delivery up by relying on the common law rights of a property owner as preserved by section 14 of the 1994 Act.

18-26   Although it is not expressly stated, it seems that, whatever the position in relation to damages, a non-exclusive licensee must at the very minimum have the right to obtain an injunction to restrain further infringements through proceedings under section 30; without it, the ability to bring an action at all would be worthless. Obtaining an interim injunction is plainly contemplated by section 30(4). Assuming that an injunction to restrain infringement is available in proceedings brought under section 30, this would provide another basis for the remedy of delivery up, which the common law has traditionally treated as a head of mandatory relief which may be awarded to ensure compliance with a prohibitory injunction.

Co-proprietors

18-27   Each co-proprietor may sue for infringement in his own right, and the permission of the other co-proprietors is not required to do so.[27] However, all the other co-proprietors must be joined as a claimant or a defendant before the action can proceed, unless the court gives permission for their omission.[28] There are the usual provisos that interim relief can be obtained without the joinder of all the co-proprietors, and that those joined as parties but who do not take part are not liable for costs.[29]

Concurrent registrations

18-28   Where, as distinguished from a registration owned by co-proprietors, there are concurrent registrations of resembling marks, the use of a mark by a stranger may be an infringement of the right of more than

---

[27] This is clear from the structure of s. 23(4) and (5).
[28] s.32(5).
[29] *ibid.*

one proprietor. In such cases any of the registered proprietors can sue by himself and obtain an injunction.[30] The assessment of damages may present some difficulty; and unless the proprietors of all the marks were parties, an account of profits could presumably not be ordered.

Death of a proprietor

Infringement of a registered mark being an interference with a right of property[31] injuring the estate of the proprietor, proceedings may be begun or continued by the executors of a deceased proprietor.[32] Benefici- aries under a will or intestacy who become entitled to the mark can secure registration and sue as proprietors.[33] The authorities for these propositions were decided under previous Acts, but the position ought to be the same, since the fundamental nature of the proprietor's right, as one of property, has not changed.   **18–29**

4. Commencement of passing off or infringement action

In what court an infringement or passing off action should be commenced

Actions for infringement of a registered trade mark are now to be commenced in the Chancery Division of the High Court.[34] If such an action were commenced in any other Division, it would be transferred to the Chancery Division, and indeed it would be a breach of counsel's duty to allow proceedings to be started in another Division.[35] The Court of Appeal has emphasised that even a passing-off action (which will involve, generally, less technical questions) should be brought in that Division.[36] The position is therefore a *fortiori* in the case of infringement actions, quite apart from the statutory provisions.   **18–30**

No jurisdiction in the County Court?

It is unclear whether the county court has jurisdiction to hear proceed- ings concerning infringement of registered trade marks. The difficulty is that many of the important powers which fall to be exercised in   **18–31**

---

[30] This follows from ss.9 and 10 of the Act.
[31] s.14.
[32] *Oakey v. Dalton* (1887) 35 Ch.D. 700: 4 R.P.C. 313.
[33] *Massam v. Thorley's* (1880) 14 Ch.D. 748 at 754 (C.A.).
[34] Supreme Court Act 1981, s.61 and Sched. 1, together with CPR, Part 49 and Intellectual Property Practice Direction, CPR Practice Direction, para. 22.1.
[35] *Apac Rowena v. Norpol Packaging* [1991] F.S.R. 272.
[36] *McCain v. Country Fair* [1981] R.P.C. 69.

connection with such proceedings, including in particular the power to revoke or invalidate a mark,[37] and the power to order erasure or delivery up[38] can only be exercised by "the court",[39] which is defined in section 75 of the 1994 Act as being the High Court (unless the context requires otherwise; but there does not seem anything in the context of the provisions just referred to which might require any other meaning). However, there is some confusion over these provisions: see, for example, rule 49.18B, of the County Court Rules which purports to apply the CPR Intellectual Property Practice Direction[40] to applications to the county court under section 19 of the 1994 Act.[41]

18–32   There is old authority that the county court does not have jurisdiction to try actions for infringement of a registered trade mark,[42] at least if an injunction is claimed. The case turned on the power of the county court to try "personal actions", which was held to exclude trade mark infringement. However, the term now used in the equivalent provision, section 15 of the County Courts Act 1984 is "any action founded in . . . tort", which would seem to include trade mark infringement, being an action for interference with a statutory property right. Hence the result might be different now.

18–33   Even if the county court has jurisdiction to try infringement actions, it is plainly undesirable that it should do so if validity of the claimant's registration is in issue,[43] and it is suggested that if validity is sought to be put in issue, such proceedings should automatically be transferred to the High Court, even leaving aside strict questions of jurisdiction. Further, given the doubts over its power to order delivery up under the statutory powers of the 1994 Act, the county court is not an attractive venue in any event.

18–34   As to passing off, which is entirely a creature of the common law of torts, there appears to be no reason in principle why an action could not be brought in the county court, and no statutory obstacle to doing so. Whether it would be appropriate is of course another matter. In *Ideal General v. Edelson* [1957] R.P.C. 252, the county court judge apparently decided that he had no jurisdiction to entertain a claim in passing off, but no reasoning is set out, and it appears that he declined jurisdiction mainly because there was also a claim for slander, which by statute was clearly outside the court's jurisdiction.

---

[37] 1994 Act, ss.46(4) and 47(3).
[38] ss.15(1), 16(1), 19(1).
[39] Revocation and invalidity may be dealt with by the Registry as well, of course, but that is not relevant to the point under consideration.
[40] CPR Practice Direction 2D relating to specialist proceedings.
[41] But without an explanation of the county court's own jurisdiction over such an application. To add to the confusion the Intellectual Property Practice Direction contains no particular provisions relating to s.19.
[42] *Bow v. Hart* [1905] 1 K.B. 592; 22 R.P.C. 222, CA.
[43] Because, if it continues to conduct the case, the defendant will be forced to sue for revocation in the High Court, and there will inevitably be a multiplicity of proceedings.

5. Service out of the jurisdiction

Service out of the jurisdiction without permission

Service out of the jurisdiction is now dealt with in Part 6 of the CPR. **18–35**
There are two different schemes relevant to this work: service without
leave in cases provided for by the Brussels and Lugano Conventions, as
implemented by the Civil Jurisdiction and Judgment Acts 1982 and
1991,[44] which is dealt with by rule 6.19(1),[45] and service where leave is
required, in all other cases, which is dealt with in rule 6.20 of the CPR.

The scheme in relation to service without permission of the court **18–36**
under rule 6.19(1) is that it is permitted so long as (1) the defendant is
domiciled in a Convention territory[46] (including the United Kingdom),
(2) the same cause of action is not being litigated between the same
parties in any of those countries, and (3) the claim is one which the
United Kingdom court has power to determine under the 1982 Act.

The basic rule of the 1982 Act is that defendants should be sued in the **18–37**
courts where they are domiciled.[47] However, in cases concerning tort, a
defendant may also be sued, if desired, in the courts of the state where
the harmful act occurred.[48] Hence in the case of infringements committed in this jurisdiction, proceedings may be served without leave on
a defendant domiciled in a state to which rule 6.19(1) applies.

Service out with the permission of the court

Service out with the permission of the court under rule 6.20 of the CPR **18–38**
follows a somewhat similar pattern; a defendant domiciled in this
jurisdiction may be served abroad under rule 6.20(1), and in the case of
claims in tort, a defendant domiciled abroad may be served with
proceedings under rule 6.20(8) if damage was sustained, or if the act
leading to damage was committed, here. In addition, service out may be
allowed if a claim is made for an injunction to restrain a defendant from
doing, or order him to do, an act in the jurisdiction, under rule 6.20(2).
The procedure to be followed in making an application for service out
under rule 6.20 is set out in rule 6.21. Such an application is by no means
a formality; the claimant must satisfy the court that its claim raises a

---

[44] Referred to below together as "the 1982 Act", since the latter amended the former.
[45] r. 6.19(2) contains provisions in relation to other enactments
[46] This is a definition used by the CPR in place of the 1982 Act's expression "Contracting
State", which is defined in ss.1(3) and 1(1). Essentially it means any E.C. or EFTA
Member State, although there are exceptions.
[47] Brussels Convention, Art. 2, which forms Sched. 1 to the 1982 Act.
[48] Sched. 1, art 5(3). This has been interpreted by the ECJ to allow a defendant to be sued
either where the tortious act was committed or where the damage which it caused was
suffered: *Handelskwerkerij v. Mines de Potasses d'Alsace* [1976] E.C.R. 1735.

serious issue to be tried,[49] and that the High Court is the appropriate forum.[50]

6. Jurisdiction over foreign trade marks

Courts trying infringement of foreign trade marks

18–39 Difficult problems may arise where the courts of one state attempt to try the infringement of a trade mark registered in another state, even if that other state is a signatory to the Brussels or Lugano Conventions. The problems are particularly acute if the validity of the registration is attacked or likely to be attacked.

18–40 It will be observed that in principle under the Brussels or Lugano Convention a court in, say, England may try a claim against a person domiciled here in which the allegation is that that person infringed, say, a French trade mark. Indeed, the general rule under article 2 of Schedule 1 to the 1982 Act is that such a person should be sued in the place of domicile. There would also be the option, in that example, of suing such a person in France, the place of the tort,[51] under article 5(3). That an action for infringement of a foreign intellectual property right may be tried in the United Kingdom was confirmed in *Pearce v. Ove Arup* [1999] F.S.R. 525, CA, where it was held that the High Court had jurisdiction to try an action in which infringement of Dutch copyright by the construction of a building in the Netherlands was alleged (the reason for the action being brought in the United Kingdom was the availability of legal aid here). That case also established that the old double actionability rule[52] did not apply to cases concerning territorial intellectual property rights.[53] The case is unclear as to what the position is in

---

[49] *Seaconsar v. Bank Markazi* [1991] A.C. 43.
[50] This is a matter of weighing a number of factors, the basic principles being set out in *Spiliada Maritime v. Cansulex* [1987] A.C. 460. In relation to trade mark infringement and passing off, if the acts complained of took place in the U.K. then it is highly likely that the High Court will be the *forum conveniens* because of the need for evidence from the trade and public, and because of the desirability of having a tribunal familiar with commerce in the U.K.
[51] Registered trade marks are territorial, and so can only be infringed in their country of registration: see the 1994 Act, s.9, which makes it clear that the proprietor has the exclusive rights to the mark in the U.K., and *LA Gear v. Whelan* [1991] F.S.R. 670, followed in *Waterford v. David Nagli* [1998] F.S.R. 92.
[52] See rule 203 in the 12th Edition of Dicey & Morris, *Conflict of Laws*, 1993, now superseded, as explained in Chap. 35 of the 13th Edition.
[53] It had previously been suggested, *e.g.* in *Def Lepp Music v. Stuart-Brown* [1986] R.P.C. 273, that because the law of the U.K. as to copyright is territorial, so that an act would only be an infringement if committed in the U.K., the requirement of the double actionability rule that the act complained of be tortious under the *lex fori* could not be met. The Court of Appeal rejected the argument in *Pearce v. Ove Arup* (at 559–561), but it had in any event been overtaken by the passage of the Private International Law (Miscellaneous Provisions Act) 1995, ss.10–12.

relation to trying in the United Kingdom alleged infringements of trade marks registered in states which are not covered by the 1982 Act.[54]

However, the ability in principle to sue in the United Kingdom for **18–41** infringement of foreign intellectual property rights is considerably complicated in the context of trade marks by the fact that they are registered rights, and Article 16 of the Brussels Convention[55] provides that in the case of "proceedings concerned with the registration or validity of patents, trade marks, designs, or other similar rights required to be deposited or registered", the courts of the state in which registration has taken place are to have exclusive jurisdiction, regardless of domicile and overriding the provisions of Article 5. In the context of patents, there have been numerous attempts, most frequently and most successfully in the courts of the Netherlands, to sue for infringement of rights registered abroad. The attraction of doing so is not so much the ability to sue in the Netherlands rather than elsewhere in respect of infringements taking place in a single European jurisdiction, but rather to seek to obtain a "pan-European" injunction, covering numerous jurisdictions, from a single set of proceedings.[56] There has been considerable debate about whether such an approach is permitted under the Conventions, because although proceedings for patent infringement do not *per se* necessarily involve questions of validity, it is of course extremely common for a defendant in a patent action to defend himself by alleging the invalidity of the patent in suit; and it is quite clear that that question can only be tried in the state where the patent is registered. At least in the United Kingdom view of patent litigation, an infringement action concerns validity to the extent that the scope of the claims bears on both, particularly where there is a "squeeze", although in continental jurisdictions the connection is not seen as being so close. The question of whether such pan-European proceedings in respect of patent infringement may be brought in a single European jurisdiction have been considered on a number of occasions by the United Kingdom courts, and indeed reference to the ECJ has been made, although the proceedings concerned ended before the ECJ could rule.[57] The position of the United Kingdom courts, subject to any future reference to the ECJ,

---

[54] In *Tyburn Productions v. Doyle*, Vinelott J., held on the basis of *British South Africa Company v. Companhia de Mocambique* [1893] A.C. 602 that a claim in respect of U.S. copyright was not justiciable in the U.K. The *Mocambique* case was considered in detail by the Court of Appeal in *Pearce*, and while it was clearly decided that its effect had been abrogated by the 1982 Act for those states covered by it, there is no clear decision as to the rest of the world, and the *Tyburn* case was neither expressly approved nor disapproved. It is, however, not easy to see how the 1982 Act would affect the position as to the rest of the world.

[55] Sched. 1, art. 16, to the 1982 Act. See App. 33.

[56] This approach is assisted by Art. 6(1), which permits the joinder of additional defendants in proceedings instituted in a given jurisdiction against one defendant.

[57] See, *e.g. Fort Dodge Animal Health* [1998] F.S.R. 222, CA. For a view from another European jurisdiction, see *Expandable Grafts v. Boston Scientific* [1999] F.S.R. 352, Court of Appeal of the Hague, which seems to be converging with the U.K. position, and moving towards an acceptance that Article 16 prevents multi-jurisdictional decisions on the substantive merits, although not interim or accelerated hearings.

appears to be that at least where validity is genuinely in issue, infringement can only be tried in the state where the patent in question is registered.

18–42   This does not mean, however, that the position will be the same in relation to registered trade marks, for two reasons. First, in many more trade mark cases than patent cases, there is no serious attack on the validity of the claimant's registration. In such cases, Article 16 probably ought to have no effect; the only issue is infringement, and that is triable outside the state where the right is registered, under Article 5(3) as interpreted in *Pearce*. Secondly, where the validity of a trade mark registration is attacked in infringement proceedings, it is usually much less connected with the infringement issues than is the case in patent infringement proceedings, so that it may be harder to say that the infringement proceedings "concern" validity.

Passing off abroad

18–43   Passing off is a tort, and passing off which has taken place abroad may be sued for in England, subject to the defendant being a person over whom the English court can and will exercise jurisdiction. Formerly, it was necessary to satisfy the double actionability rule,[58] but that has been changed by sections 10 to 12 of the Private International Law (Miscellaneous Provisions) Act 1995. In general now, only the law of the country where the passing off has been committed will be relevant. It will be necessary to lead evidence of that law rather than merely relying on the presumption that it is the same as the law of England: *Alfred Dunhill v. Sunoptic*,[59] *Waterford v. David Nagli*.[60]

18–44   The difficulties of jurisdiction posed by Article 16 of the Brussels Convention in relation to registered trade marks[61] do not apply to passing off, which does not depend on the existence of a registered right, or other statutory monopoly, and is justiciable here under the general principles of conflict of laws and/or under Articles 2 and 5 of the Convention.

Lis alibi pendens: Articles 21 and 22 and *forum conveniens*

18–45   Because more than one court may have jurisdiction over the same claim under the Brussels Convention (most commonly, for example, the court of the defendant's domicile under Article 2 and the court of the place of

---

[58] *i.e.* that the acts complained of would be passing off if committed in the U.K. and would be actionable in the country where they were committed. See, *e.g. Walker v. Ost* [1970] R.P.C. 489 at 509 *et. seq.* See also para. 18–41 and nn. 54 and 55, above.

[59] [1979] F.S.R. 337.

[60] [1998] F.S.R. 92.

[61] Nor does the *Tyburn Productions/Mocambique* point concerning copyright, referred to above, arise.

the tort under Article 5), it is necessary that there should be rules to determine which court should proceed if the same or related claims are sought to be brought in more than one court. Article 21 provides that where the same claim between the same parties is brought in more than one court, the court second seised must decline jurisdiction.[62] Article 22 provides that if related claims are brought in different courts ("related" meaning that they need not be identical as to parties or claims, but must present the risk of giving rise to irreconcilable decisions), the court second seised may decline jurisdiction; it has a discretion whether or not to do so. For an application of these principles, see for example *Mecklermedia v. DC Congress* [1997] F.S.R. 627.

Similar problems may arise outside the ambit of the Brussels Conven-   **18–46** tion and the 1982 Act, either in the context of an application to serve out of the jurisdiction with permission (or an application to set aside leave), or in the context of an application to restrain proceedings abroad. In any such case the question for the court is which jurisdiction is the *forum conveniens* for the dispute. Although the evidential onus may vary depending on the nature of the application, the main relevant matters are set out in *Spiliada Maritime v. Cansulex* [1987] A.C. 460.

7. Vicarious and joint liability

For the general principles applicable in relation to joint liability based on   **18–47** procurement or common design, see *CBS v. Amstrad*, and *Credit Lyonnais v. ECGD*.[63]

Employer responsible for servant's acts

An employer will be held responsible for the wrongful acts of infringe-   **18–48** ment or passing-off on the part of his servant done in the course of the employer's business and within the scope of the employment, notwithstanding that the acts were done without the employer's knowledge,[64] or even contrary to his express orders.[65] But it does not follow that an injunction will be granted in every case where this is established.[66]

Agents and partners of infringer

The action is one of tort, and, consequently, every infringer is liable to   **18–49** be sued, whether he acted on his own behalf or as agent for a principal. But a mere servant (as distinct from an employee who has direction of

---

[62] This does not preclude an application for interim relief, however, under Art. 24.
[63] [1988] R.P.C. 567; [1998] 1 Lloyd's Rep. 19.
[64] *Cusenier v. Gaiety Bars* (1902) 19 R.P.C. 357; and *Havana Cigar Factories v. Tiffin* (1909) 26 R.P.C. 473, where the Court of Appeal held the defendant company liable for the acts of the persons entrusted by it with the selling of the particular goods.
[65] *Grierson, Oldham v. Birmingham Hotel* (1901) 18 R.P.C. 158 ("Big Tree Brand") where an hotel company was held responsible for passing off by waiters contrary to orders; *Monro v. Hunter* (1904) 21 R.P.C. 296. *cf.* a Scottish case, *Montgomerie v. Young* (1904) 20 R.P.C. 781; 21 R.P.C. 285, I.H. reversing the Lord Ordinary.
[66] *Lever Bros v. Masbro* (1912) 29 R.P.C. 34, and 225 CA.

the infringer's affairs[67]) should not, without some special reason, be added as a defendant.[68]

Directors and promoters

18-50 Directors of a limited company which infringes are not liable merely because they are directors, but only for infringing acts that they personally have committed or directed.[69] Accordingly, in cases where it is desirable to join directors as defendants—as it well may be,[70] especially in view of the modern practice of forming companies without available assets to carry on any doubtful activity—specific infringements should be alleged against them. Persons directly responsible for the promotion of a company for the purpose of doing a wrongful act may be liable[71]: this would seem to extend to a holding company forming a subsidiary for purposes of infringement. Where personal defendants are joined in such cases, particulars of the acts relied on will be ordered where necessary.[72] The numerous authorities in this area were recently helpfully summarised in *MCA Records v. Charly Records* (unreported, Rimer J., March 22, 2000).

Parent and group companies

18-51 Similarly, it is frequently sought to join as a defendant the parent of the company actually carrying on the allegedly infringing acts, either in order to be able effectively to enforce any award for damages, or for disclosure. In such cases, it is not enough to show that the parent company knew and approved of the acts concerned,[73] or even that it knowingly assisted the conduct in question.[74] It must be shown either that it procured or induced or conspired in the commission of the conduct, or was involved in its commission.[75]

---

[67] *Adrema v. Adrema-Werke* (1954) 71 R.P.C. 345.

[68] *cf. Daniel and Arter v. Whitehouse* (1898) 16 R.P.C. 71 (a motion to commit).

[69] See the discussion of earlier cases in *Evans v. Spritebrand* [1985] F.S.R. 267, CA. Note in particular that *White Horse v. Gregson* [1984] R.P.C. 61 at 91 (an unusual case, of failure to prevent passing off abroad rather than positively committing it) goes too far in holding that "before a director can be held personally liable for a tort committed by his company he must not only commit or direct the tortious act or conduct but he must do so deliberately or recklessly and so as to make it his own, as distinct from the act or conduct of the company."

[70] *cf. Adrema, supra*, 71 R.P.C. 345 at 347: "Right and proper" to join directors as defendants.

[71] *Panhard et Levassor v. Panhard Levassor Motor Co.* [1901] 2 Ch. 513; 18 R.P.C. 405. Contrast *Pritchard & Constance v. Amata* (1925) 42 R.P.C. 63 at 73.

[72] *British Thomson-Houston v. Irradiant* (1924) 41 R.P.C. 338.

[73] As in, *e.g. Mead v. Riverwood* [1997] F.S.R. 484

[74] *Credit Lyonnais v. ECGD* [1998] 1 Lloyd's Rep. 19.

[75] *Credit Lyonnais, supra.; Unilever v. Chefaro* [1994] F.S.R. 135. A list of most of the numerous authorities on this topic may be found in *Sepracor v. Hoechst Marion Roussel* [1999] F.S.R. 746.

8. The relief granted

Outline of the types of relief available

In general, the relief available to a successful claimant is much the same **18–52** whether he succeeds for registered trade mark infringement, for passing off, or both. However, as will appear below, the 1994 Act has introduced a new statutory regime relating to erasure and delivery up[76] which applies to actions for infringement and not to passing off. In certain areas, this may give a registered owner broader protection than the common law remedies previously available.

By section 14 of the 1994 Act, all relief is available in an action for **18–53** infringement of a registered trade mark as is available in respect of any other property right. The section does not appear to suggest that the statutory remedies provided by section 15 to 19 replace the remedies available at common law and in equity for invasions of property rights, so it appears that they are concurrent. This is unlikely to be of great practical significance unless there is some formal or procedural difficulty with proceeding by the statutory route, in which case a claimant may wish to rely on his common law and equitable rights.[77]

In general, a successful claimant may obtain an order for (1) an **18–54** injunction restraining further infringements of his rights; (2) the delivery up for the destruction of, or for the erasure of the marks from, any goods already marked with the spurious mark and in the possession or under the control of the defendant, as well as of deceptive labels, advertising material, etc.; (3) and an inquiry as to damages in respect of the past infringement, or in lieu, an account of the profits made by the defendant by the sale of the spuriously marked goods.

In addition to the relief obtainable by an action for infringement, the Act provides machinery for causing infringing goods to be treated as prohibited imports.[78]

Submission of order to registrar

Under the Intellectual Property Practice Direction[79] the successful party **18–55** in any matter decided under the 1938 Act or the 1994 Act is required to serve a copy of the order made on the Registrar.

---

[76] ss.15–19.

[77] 1994 Act, s.2(1), states that "the proprietor of a registered trade mark has the rights and remedies provided by this Act", and it has been suggested that this means that the only remedies available to a proprietor are, as a result, those given by the Act. However, it seems that this cannot be right, if for no other reason than that there is no statutory provision for the grant of an injunction. Moreover , the words of s. 2(1) do not suggest that the proprietor has no other rights or remedies.

[78] See Chap. 20.

[79] CPR, Practice Direction 2D.

9. Final injunctions

General considerations

18–56 In general, a claimant whose rights have been invaded will obtain an injunction to restrain further wrongs from being committed against him, but his entitlement is not absolute. The exceptions to the general rule are much the same for passing off as for trade mark infringement, and they are considered together below.

18–57 The form of injunction granted may, by contrast, differ substantially depending on the cause of action, for passing off does not give an absolute exclusive right to use a mark, so that the injunction granted may be framed to allow the defendant to continue to use the offending mark provided that he does not cause deception. This is often phrased as a positive obligation on him sufficiently to distinguish his goods from the claimant's. These matters are considered below, separately for passing off and for infringement of registered marks.

Further infringement must be threatened or be likely to occur

18–58 The grant of an injunction in trade mark and passing off cases is governed by the general rules applicable where other rights are concerned. There must be some threat or probability that the infringement will be commenced, continued, or repeated, or the court will not interfere.[80] If an actual infringement is shown to have occurred, that is usually sufficient and the claimant is not bound to wait until it has been frequently repeated, or until warning has been given and been disregarded,[81] for "the life of a trade mark depends upon the promptitude with which it is vindicated."[82]

18–59   (1) In *Steiner v. Stevens* it was held that the plaintiffs were entitled to an injunction and costs though the evidence showed that the sale was due to a mistake, but the defendant had refused to make any apology or offer any undertaking.[83]

18–60   (2) In *Myers v. Field*[84] infringement was by mistake and there was no apparent probability of the defendants repeating it. No injunction was granted but (the defendants having denied the

---

[80] An act having a continuing effect, *e.g.* the issue of a large number of circulars, is not sufficiently met by the offer of an undertaking not to repeat it, without anything to neutralise the effect of what has been done: *Yeatman v. Homberger* (1912)29 R.P.C. 561 and 645; *Hindhaugh v. Inch* (1923) 40 R.P.C. 368; *Spalding v. Gamage* (1915) 32 R.P.C. 273 at 289, 290, HL. The court will presume that a trader will use his mark so as not to be deceptive, if it is capable of being used without the probability of being deceptive, unless some reason to the contrary is shown: *Kutnow* (1893) 10 R.P.C. 401.

[81] See *Upmann v. Forester* (1883) 24 Ch.D. 231.

[82] *Johnston v. Orr-Ewing* (1882) 7 App.Cas. 219 at 229, 230.

[83] [1957] R.P.C. 439.

[84] (1954) 71 R.P.C. 435.

infringement) the plaintiffs were granted a declaration: the order reciting that in the opinion of the court the acts complained of were inadvertent.

If the action is commenced before any undertaking has been given, a **18-61** subsequent offer or even an undertaking out of court will not usually be sufficient unless an undertaking is offered in the defence,[85] although in some instances, the undertaking of an innocent infringer has been accepted by the court.[86] If an offer is made on an application for an interim injunction, the fact that the offer was made should be recited in the order on the motion,[87] and if the defendant wishes to adhere to the offer, it should be repeated in the defence. Where the defendant makes an offer in the defence to give an undertaking or submit to an injunction, the claimant is entitled to apply for an order embodying the offer, and to the costs even if the costs are not offered, and even if the relief offered is much less than claimed.[88] It is not necessary that any actual infringement should have occurred if it is proved that the defendant contemplates committing or has threatened to commit one,[89] and it is sufficient evidence of this that he is in possession of a considerable quantity of spuriously marked goods, even though it is only as a forwarding agent.[90]

Enforcing agreed terms

Where, as is not uncommon, an action is settled and a "Tomlin" order **18-62** made staying proceedings, on terms scheduled to the order, except for the purpose of enforcing the terms, the court (in case the terms are not observed) can grant an injunction and order an inquiry as to damages on application in the original action[91] by the aggrieved party.[92] The court will not enforce such terms if they are too vague.[93]

Form of injunction—infringement of a registered trade mark

The usual form of injunction simply restrains infringement of the mark **18-63** concerned, referring to it by number. This kind of order, expressed by reference simply to the right infringed, is the usual one in intellectual

---

[85] *Fram v. Morton* (1922) 40 R.P.C. 33, CA.
[86] *Rose v. Loftus* (1878) 47 L.J.Ch. 576.
[87] *Stillitz v. Jones & Higgins* (1943) 60 R.P.C. 15.
[88] *Clark v. Clark's Shoe Service* (1935) 52 R.P.C. 254, following *Winkle v. Gent* (1914) 31 R.P.C. 473.
[89] *Emperor of Austria v. Day and Kossuth* (1861) 3 De G.F. & J. 217 at 240, 247–249.
[90] *Upmann v. Elkan* (1871) L.R. 12 Eq. 140; L.R. 7 Ch. 130; or a commission agent: *Catterson v. Anglo-Foreign* (1911) 28 R.P.C. 74.
[91] See *Phillips v. Clarke* [1970] Ch. 322.
[92] *Hyatt v. Pollard* (1935) 52 R.P.C. 115. See also *Green v. Rozen* [1955] 2 All E.R. 797.
[93] *Wilson & Whitworth v. Express & Independent Newspapers* [1969] R.P.C. 165.

property cases.[94] Frequently, the particular infringement of which the defendant has been proved to have been guilty is expressly referred to in the order, a general restraint being added.

18–64 However, although the usual order is in terms of the right infringed, the court retains a discretion to craft the injunction to the circumstances of the case (or, as mentioned above, to grant no injunction). In particular, where an infringement is such that an injunction of some kind is appropriate, but a general restraint against infringement would be an unfair imposition on the defendant because it would force him to steer a wide course so as to avoid it, and the infringement was inadvertent or innocent, a narrowly drawn injunction directed only at the specific acts found to infringe may be granted.[95]

18–65 The court will not usually in anticipation lay down a course of conduct for the defendant.[96] It is not the practice of the court to say in advance what is or is not sufficient to distinguish between marks.[97]

As it is not usually an infringement to use the claimant's mark upon his own goods, that is, goods which possess the attribute connoted by the mark,[98] the injunction can be expressed so as to prevent this being a breach of its terms.[99]

18–66 Where mere use of the defendant's own name would be prima facie a breach of the injunction, it is possible to include in the order an express reference to section 11 of the 1994 Act.[1]

A special order may be appropriate where the defendant is applying to register his infringing mark.[2]

Form of injunction—passing-off action

18–67 The form of the injunction granted varies considerably, according to the nature of the deceptive representation which the defendant is shown to have made use of, or threatened to make use of.

A declaration may be granted and not an injunction, in the absence of a threat by the defendants to continue the acts complained of.[3]

---

[94] See, *e.g. Spectravest v. Aperknit* [1988] F.S.R. 161 at 170.
[95] *Coflexip v. Stolt Comex* [1999] F.S.R. 473; *Microsoft v. Plato,* unreported, July 15, 1999, CA.
[96] *Kerfoot v. Cooper* (1908) 25 R.P.C. 508 (*"Sweet Lips Cachous"*).
[97] *Brittain v. Trade & Commercial Press* [1957] R.P.C. 134.
[98] See, *e.g. Condy v. Taylor* (1887) 56 L.T. 891. Use of the mark on the claimant's "own" goods may be an infringement in some cases concerned with parallel imports, or with repackaging under the 1994 Act, s.12. The matter is discussed in more detail in Chaps 13, 15.
[99] *cf.* the "passing-off" case *Braham v. Beachim* (1878) 7 Ch.D. 848. But see n. 1, below.
[1] The CA did so in *Parker-Knoll v. Knoll International* [1961] R.P.C. 346—a case decided under the 1938 Act, where section 8 was the relevant provision; see the order, printed at 373. The House of Lords showed no disapproval ([1962] R.P.C. 265 at 278, 283, 287, 288, 292); but Harman L.J. disapproved strongly, describing the order as made as a contradiction in terms: [1962] R.P.C. 243 at 256.
[2] See *Berlei v. Bali* [1972] R.P.C. 568.
[3] *Treasure Cot v. Hamleys* (1950) 67 R.P.C. 89. Liberty to apply for an injunction was granted.

Where a defendant has imitated or adopted the claimant's distinctive **18–68** trade mark or business name, the order may be an absolute injunction that he shall not use or carry on business under that name.[4] In a case before 1938[5] the court refused to grant an absolute injunction against selling goods under an unregistered mark, saying that the defendant would be entitled if he wished to sell under the mark with an explanation that the goods were not those of the plaintiff. This has not been the practice, and it is not thought that the argument would appeal to a modern court as applicable in every case.

(1) There are circumstances—for instance, in the bars of busy **18–69** public houses—where it is virtually impossible for managers to prevent supply of any available brand of a commodity, regardless of what is asked for. The court may then, passing off having been proved, be asked to limit the injunction granted to what is practicable whilst continuing to sell goods other than the claimant's. In some cases it will[6]; in others it will not.[7]

(2) In a dispute between a British company and its former German **18–70** parent, as to the right to use the mark "Adrema" which formed the main part of each party's name, it was held that the goodwill connected with that mark in the United Kingdom belonged to the British company, the plaintiff, exclusively. An injunction was granted restraining the defendant from selling, advertising or offering for sale in the United Kingdom any addressing or costing machines or equipment therefore under any name or mark comprising the name or mark "Adrema" or any other name or mark so closely resembling the name or mark "Adrema" as to be calculated to pass-off or enable others to pass-off such machines or equipment as and for the plaintiffs' machines or equipment: *Adrema v. Adrema- Werke* [1958] R.P.C. 323 at 332, following *Sturtevant Eng. v. Sturtevant Mill* (1936) 53 R.P.C. 430. But Upjohn L.J. has said: "Perhaps that can be justified on the facts of that case but the general practice is to grant an injunction in the qualified form where the defendant is only using his own name": *Parker-Knoll v. Knoll International* [1961] R.P.C. 346 at 362.

---

[4] As in *Hendriks v. Montagu* 17 Ch.D. 638. See *Manus v. Fullwood & Bland* (1949) 66 R.P.C. 71 at 77; the order is quoted at (1949) 66 R.P.C. 285 at 286, *per* Roxburgh J. *cf. Aubanel & Alabaster v. Aubanel* (1949) 66 R.P.C. 343 at 347, where the injunction was qualified.

[5] *Lissen v. Harley* (1929) 46 R.P.C. 11; *cf. La Radiotechnique v. Weinbaum* [1928] Ch. 1; 44 R.P.C. 361, where it was suggested that a claim for an absolute injunction might make the action not an action for passing off but one for infringement of an unregistered trade mark and so unsustainable.

[6] If rival brands are established on the market, a defendant in such cases cannot comply with an absolute injunction by switching to one claimant's goods without laying himself open to attack by the rival suppliers.

[7] *Showerings v. Entam* [1975] F.S.R. 45.

Qualified injunctions

18–71 In a case where it may be possible for the defendant to use the mark or name in question without passing off, the injunction is granted in qualified form.[8]

Where the mark or name is one in which the claimant cannot claim an exclusive right, but which to many people indicates his goods or business, it is proper to qualify the injunction against using it by such words as "without clearly" (or "sufficiently") distinguishing his goods from the claimant's.[9] In cases where use of the mark or name without qualification need not be deceptive, an even weaker form may be employed: the prohibition being qualified by the addition "so as to represent" or "so as to lead to the belief" that the defendant's goods or business are the claimant's.[10] In the special case of a word that is used by some as a description of the goods, although to some it is a trade mark of the claimant, what is known as the "Havana" or "Corona" form may be adopted,[11] the prohibition being qualified by such words as "without making it clear to the customer that it is not of the goods of the claimant".

18–72   (1) The *Pinet* cases illustrate the different cases to which the absolute and the limited forms of injunctions are respectively applicable. In the first case it was supposed that the assignor to the defendant company had traded under his own name, "Pinet", and a limited injunction was granted. Subsequently it

---

[8] See, *e.g. Massam v. Thorley's* (1880) 14 Ch.D. 748 at 762, CA. For a form of injunction in a business name case in which the plaintiffs had not an exclusive but only a qualified right in a particular word, *see Daimler (1904) v. London Daimler* (1907) 24 R.P.C. 379. As to "own name" cases generally, see *Parker-Knoll v. Knoll International, supra.*

[9] See the *"Stone Ales"* case, *per* Lord Watson and Lord Macnaghten: *Montgomery v. Thompson* [1891] A.C. 217; 8 R.P.C. 361; see also *Thompson v. Bent's Brewery* (1891) 8 R.P.C. 479. In *Magnolia Metal v. Atlas Metal* (1897) 14 R.P.C. 389, Collins J. granted an injunction in this form, and the plaintiffs unsuccessfully appealed asking for an absolute prohibition, *cf.* the form in *Short's v. Short* (1914) 31 R.P.C. 294 at 300. Injunctions were granted in this form, for instance, in the following cases: *Seixo v. Provezende* (1865) L.R. 1 Ch.192; *Johnston v. Orr-Ewing* (1882) 13 Ch.D. 434; 7 App.Cas. 219 at 234n; *Powell v. Birmingham Brewery* ("*Yorkshire Relish*") [1897] A.C. 710; *Bewlay v. Hughes* (1898) 15 R.P.C. 290 ("*Dindigul Cigars*"); *Grezier v. Autran* (1896) 13 R.P.C. 1, and *Rey v. Lecouturier* (1908) 25 R.P.C. 265; [1910] A.C. 262; 27 R.P.C. 268, HL (both "*Chartreuse*"). See also Lord Macnaghten in *Reddaway v. Banham* [1896] A.C. 199 at 221; 13 R.P.C. 218 at 234.

[10] *e.g. Slazenger v. Feltham* (1889) 6 R.P.C. 531 (injunction against stamping "Demotic" on lawn-tennis racquets qualified by CA by adding "so as to represent that [they] are manufactured by the plaintiffs, or in any other way from passing-off, etc."). In *Redwing v. Redwing Forest* (1947) 64 R.P.C. 67, it was disputed how much of the order the qualifying words governed.

[11] From the "*Corona*" case, *Havana Cigar v. Oddenino* [1923] 2 Ch. 243; 40 R.P.C. 229. A declaration in this form was granted (in similar circumstances) in *Treasure Cot v. Hamleys* (1950) 67 R.P.C. 89 at 94: "A declaration that the defendants are not entitled to sell as 'Treasure Cots' any toy cots not supplied by or through the plaintiffs without making it clear to the customer that they are not connected with the plaintiffs." Another example is *Purefoy v. Sykes Boxall* (1955) 72 R.P.C. 89 CA. As to what does "make it clear", *cf. Bostitch v. McGarry & Cole* [1963] R.P.C. 183.

was discovered that this was not his own name, but a name adopted for the purpose of fraud, and thereupon an absolute injunction was decreed: *Pinet v. Maison Pinet* (1897) 14 R.P.C. 933; *Pinet v. Maison Louis Pinet* (1898) 15 R.P.C. 65.

(2) In "Stone Ales" *supra*, "Stone" being the name of the town **18–73** where the plaintiff's ales were made, the qualified form of injunction—"without clearly distinguishing"—would normally have been appropriate. Nevertheless, an injunction to restrain the defendant (inter alia) from selling beer not of the plaintiff's manufacture, under the term "Stone Ales" or "Stone Ale", or in any way so as to induce the belief that such ale was of the plaintiff's manufacture, was maintained, the court holding that the ordinary qualified form of injunction would be more stringent, as it would in effect prevent the defendant using the term "Stone Ale" at all.

(3) The plaintiff had trade marks, registered for perfumery and **18–74** toilet articles, of which the word "June" was the essential feature. The defendants, June Perfect Ltd, sold hair lotions, shampoos and lipsticks, bearing their name, to Messrs. Woolworths, who put them on retail sale, thereby passing them off as the plaintiff's. The Court of Appeal granted injunctions against infringement of trade mark; against passing-off by use of the word "June"; and against continuing to trade in those articles under the name "June Perfect Ltd." (see 68 R.P.C. at 166, 167, 168); but limited the passing-off injunction to the three specific articles mentioned, and qualified it by the words "without clearly distinguishing, etc." (see 68 R.P.C. at 167). The House of Lords discharged the injunction against trading under the defendants' existing name, since they traded only with retailers, who need not be misled. The House observed that the other two injunctions should give adequate protection; whilst the form adopted for the passing-off injunction supported the view that the defendants might "be able by proper precautions to sell the three articles in connection with their name of June Perfect Ltd. while clearly distinguishing those goods from the [plaintiffs'] goods": *Saville Perfumery v. June Perfect* (1941) 58 R.P.C. 147 at 176.

(4) The term "Goddard's Plate Powder," orginally meaning the **18–75** powder of a Mr Goddard, had come to mean the goods of the plaintiff only, except to a small number of people who accepted powder made by Goddard's daughter. The defendants, when asked for "Goddard's Plate Powder," supplied Miss Goddard's plate powder without explanation or inquiry. An injunction was granted in the "Havana" form: *Goddard v. Watford Co-op* (1924) 41 R.P.C. 218.

(5) The plaintiffs were credit-check traders (that is, provided the **18–76** money for credit sales by retail traders), working by the issue of documents known in the area concerned as "Ideal Checks". The

defendants were retail traders. The plaintiffs having refused to supply their "Ideal Checks" to the defendants, the defendants obtained credit checks from another company and (with fraudulent intent) advertised them as "Ideal Checks". The use of the defendants' name "The Ideal Clothing Co." was not calculated to deceive. An injunction was granted "restraining the defendants. . . from using any form of words in newspaper advertisements or otherwise calculated to deceive persons into the belief that the defendants' said business is carried on by the plaintiffs or is in any way connected with the plaintiffs' business as credit check traders or that the defendants are authorised to issue or accept Ideal Checks": *Ideal General v. Ideal Clothing* [1957] R.P.C. 252 at 259.

18–77 The qualification "without clearly distinguishing" is precise enough, and the order should not go into further detail. "It has been said many times that it is no part of the function of this court to examine imaginary cases of what the defendant could or could not do under this form of injunction. The best guide, if he is an honest man, is his own conscience; and it is certainly not the business of this court to give him instructions or hints as to how near the wind he can sail."[12]

Temporary or contingent prohibition

18–78 The defendant has, in some instances been restrained from using a word or words which could not be used by him at all, except deceptively, so long as this should continue to be the case; for instance, from calling his bitters "Angostura Bitters" until he should find out how to make the real "Angostura Bitters"[13]; or from using the name "Radstock Colliery Proprietors" until he should be able to sell coal from Radstock.[14]

No rule as to what distinction is sufficient

18–79 No general rule can be laid down as to what additions to the objectionable matter will be sufficient to effect the requisite distinction.[15]

It must depend upon the circumstances of each case.[16] It is no answer to say that the custom of the trade is not to distinguish.[17]

---

[12] *Per* Greene M.R., *Wright, Layman & Umney v. Wright* (1949) 66 R.P.C. 149 at 152. See also *Letters v. Letters (Craigton)* [1967] R.P.C. 209, SC; *Sterling Winthrop v. Bayer* [1967] R.P.C. 326 and *Bach & Jackson v. Cowan* [1969] R.P.C. 156 at 164 for examples of courts' refusals to tell a defendant how far he can go.

[13] *Siegert v. Findlater* (1878) 7 Ch.D. 801.

[14] *Braham v. Beachim* (1878) 7 Ch. D 848.

[15] "No court has ever said how the distinction is to be made": *per* Sterling J. in *Powell v. Birmingham Vinegar* [1896] 2 Ch. 54 at 64. Also *Kerfoot v. Cooper* (1908) 25 R.P.C. 508. See also *Clark v. Associated Newspapers* [1998] R.P.C. 281.

[16] See *Warsop v. Warsop* (1904) 21 R.P.C. 481, where "A. Warsop" was held to be sufficiently distinguished from "B. Warsop & Sons Ltd".

[17] *Reddaway v. Ahlers*, illus. 1, below.

(1) Since the decision in *Reddaway v. Banham*, there have been three **18–80** reported cases as to "camel-hair" belting in which the question has arisen whether the defendant sufficiently distinguished, namely, *Reddaway v. Ahlers* (1902) 19 R.P.C. 12; *Reddaway v. Frictionless Engine Packing* (1902) 19 R.P.C. 505; and *Reddaway v. Stevenson* (1903) 20 R.P.C. 276. In the second of these cases it was held that the prefixing of the defendant's name was sufficient, although they were not manufacturers, but the result was different in the last case, where it was pointed out that each case must rest on its own facts.

(2) The plaintiffs being the owners of natural springs at Caledonia, **18–81** Ontario, sold the water as "Caledonia Water" or "Caledonia Springs Water". They had, however, no exclusive right to the word "Caledonia", and the defendants, who owned springs in the same neighbourhood and sold "Natural Saline water from the New Springs at Caledonia", were held to have sufficiently distinguished: *Grand Hotel v. Wilson* [1904] A.C. 103; 21 R.P.C. 117, PC.

(3) In an action of Parker-Knoll Ltd. against an American company. **18–82** Knoll International Ltd, the use by the defendants of the mark "Knoll" or "Knoll International" was held to be deceptive, and an injunction granted against doing so without clearly distinguishing their goods. It was later held that both use of the mark "Knoll International of U.S.A." and use as a mark of stylised initials "K.I." (with an indication whose initials they were) were breaches of the injunction: *Parker-Knoll v. Knoll International* [1962] R.P.C. 243 (Wilberforce J. and CA). But a later motion for contempt based on the use of "Knoll International", failed so far as passing-off went, the plaintiffs having failed—as in National Advertiser, below—to prove that the distinction was inadequate: *Parker Knoll v. Knoll Overseas* [1985] F.S.R. 349 at 363–364.

(4) Where the plaintiffs had two weekly papers, the London **18–83** Weekly Advertiser and (much less well known) the National Advertiser almost identical in content, and the defendants adopted the title "National Weekly", it was held that in this exceptional case printing "No connection with any other paper whatsoever" might be a sufficient distinction: for those likely to be confused could be people who knew the National Advertiser only as a subsidiary of the London Weekly Advertiser: *Brittain v. Trade & Commercial Press (No. 2)* [1957] R.P.C. 271.

Where the order is in respect of a word which has, in fact become the **18–84** claimant's trade mark, used as the name of the claimant's goods, the most careful differentiation of the get-up of the goods,[18] and the greatest

---

[18] In *Powell v. Birmingham Vinegar* the bottles and labels on the defendants' "Yorkshire Relish" were totally different from those of the plaintiffs. They are shown in (1896) 13 R.P.C. at 237, 238 and 240.

possible prominence of the defendant's own name[19] upon his labels may not be enough. In such cases the limitation of the order is more likely to mislead the defendant than to protect him in his assumed right to use the word.

Injunction directed to future consignments of goods only

18–85 In a case where the plaintiffs refrained from taking proceedings on learning that the defendants had received a small quantity of the infringing goods, but waited until they had got a larger consignment, Malins V.-C. ordered the injunction to be directed to stop the sale of future consignments only.[20] It is submitted, however, that the calculated conduct of the plaintiffs was not a sufficient reason for allowing the goods already received to be sold under the deceptive labels. It has certainly been held that acquiescence, not sufficient to bar the claimant's right, may, in some classes of action, cause the court to refuse relief by injunction, and to grant the claimant damages only,[21] but the case last referred to did not involve any continuing fraud or deception.[22]

Mandatory injunctions; orders to change name

18–86 The court has power to make mandatory as well as prohibitory injunctions. Procedurally, mandatory injunctions may be more difficult, because they require to be policed, but this is simply a factor to be considered (and in relation to interim injunctions it is a matter going to the balance of convenience, since it may be more prone to cause injustice than an order preserving the status quo[23]).

18–87 Mandatory relief in a passing-off action may include an order to compel the defendants to state that they are not connected with the claimant, where they are selling the claimant's goods but also falsely giving the impression that they are authorised agents.[24]

18–88 A defendant whose company name is inherently deceptive may be ordered to change its name. Such an order may even be made at an

---

[19] In *Daniel and Arter v. Whitehouse* (1898) 16 R.P.C. 71, "F. Whitehouse's Brazilian Silver" was held to be an infringement of an order not to use "Brazilian Silver" without distinguishing, etc.

[20] *Angle-Swiss v. Swiss* [1871] W.N. 163.

[21] *Sayers v. Collyer* (1884) 28 Ch.D. 103, *per* Fry L.J. A case relating to a restrictive covenant in regard to buildings. In a passing-off action a delay of three and a half years was under the circumstances of the case held not to disentitle the plaintiffs to an injunction: *Reddaway v. Stevenson* (1903) 20 R.P.C. 276 (injunction but no damages).

[22] The action for infringement may wholly fail, because the defendant has used the plaintiff's mark so long that there is no longer any deception, as in *Londonderry v. Russell* (1886) 2 T.L.R. 843; 3 T.L.R. 360.

[23] *Nottingham Building Society v. Eurodynamics* [1993] F.S.R. 468. [1995] F.S.R. 605, CA.

[24] *Sony v. Saray* [1983] F.S.R. 302, where it was held that undertakings from the defendants were worthless, and they were ordered to put disclaiming stickers on goods of the claimants sold by them.

interim stage: *Glaxo v. Glaxowellcome*.[25] Likewise, a company registering a website with a name which is so inherently deceptive as to amount to an instrument of fraud may be ordered to change the name of the site or to transfer it to the claimant: *Marks and Spencer v. One-in-a-million*[26] (the order there being made following a successful application for summary judgment).

10. Interim injunctions

Outline

The claimant in an infringement or passing off action may apply for an **18–89** interim injunction to restrain the defendant, until the hearing of the action or further order, from continuing or committing the infringement or deceptive conduct of which he complains. Quite apart from the advantages of stopping the infringement without delay, experience shows that a successful application for an interim injunction frequently puts an end to the litigation and the infringement, with a great saving in expense compared with a full trial.

However, in recent years there has been a growing trend for appli- **18–90** cations for interim injunctions, when made, to be refused or adjourned to trial, with an order for a speedy trial. In some cases, trials have taken place within two or three months from the issuing of proceedings, which used to be the kind of period taken for a full scale application for an interim injunction to come on for hearing in the 1980s and early 1990s. This kind of order has much more frequently been made in cases where there is a legitimate dispute between the parties as to the defendant's right to use the name or mark concerned; it is not really of application in counterfeiting cases.

Applications without notice

Where an application for relief is made without notice, especially, there **18–91** is an obligation upon the applicant to make full disclosure to the court of all facts material to the application. An order made upon evidence not making full disclosure will usually be discharged, or not continued; but this does not prevent a further application once full disclosure has been made,[27] and there remains a discretion not to discharge the order if justice requires that some relief be continued.[28]

Appeal from the grant or refusal of interim relief

In present practice, the decision upon an application for an interim **18–92** injunction is essentially an exercise of judicial discretion, with which the Court of Appeal will interfere only where the decision below is wrong in principle.[29]

---

[25] [1996] F.S.R. 388.
[26] [1998] F.S.R. 265, [1999] F.S.R. 1.
[27] *Yardley v. Higson* [1984] R.P.C. 304, CA.
[28] *Brink's Mat v. Elcombe* [1988] 1 W.L.R. 1350.
[29] *Elan Digital v. Elan Computer* [1984] F.S.R. 373 at 384, 386, CA.

The general test for the grant of an interim injunction

18-93 In general, applications for interim relief are decided on the *American Cyanamid* principles: in outline, this means that a claimant must show an arguable case against the defendant, and that (if he is right) continuance of the defendant's activities until the trial is likely to cause substantial damage to him that is irreparable in the sense that it will not be compensated by an order for damages at the trial.[30] Damages may be an inadequate remedy either because the defendant is or will be unable to pay, or because the nature of the damage being sustained by the claimant is such that it cannot be assessed in money terms or repaired by the expenditure of money after success at trial. The potential damage to the claimant which must be considered is limited to damages which he could recover at trial if successful: damages which would be suffered but which would be too remote to recover are irrelevant: *Peaudouce v. Kimberley Clark.*[31]

18-94 In trade-mark infringement cases irreparable damage, in this sense, is relatively easily shown, since infringement may easily destroy the value of a mark or at least nullify expensive advertising in a way that is hard to quantify for the purposes of an inquiry into damages.[32] This has more recently come to be referred to, in cases where the defendant's conduct is not directly damaging but merely reduces the distinctive character of the claimant's mark, as "dilution". It is, however, an important and recognised head of recoverable damage which has been successfully invoked by claimants on a number of occasions.[33]

18-95 Where all that can be shown, however, is that some damage is likely and ought not to be allowed to go on for too long, an order for a speedy trial may be more appropriate than an injunction, as has been mentioned above.

18-96 The defendant may meet the application by showing that he genuinely intends to defend[34] and that he also would (if an injunction were granted and were shown at the trial to have been unjustified) suffer damage not reparable by an order for damages under the cross-undertaking that accompanies any interim injunction. If the defendant is able so to do,[35] the matter then depends on the "balance of conve-

---

[30] *American Cyanamid v. Ethicon* [1975] A.C. 396; [1975] R.P.C. 513, HL (a patent infringement case). This marked a major change in the practice on such applications, so that previous authorities are now of little or no value. Furthermore, the balance of convenience is so much a matter of personal judgment of the special facts of the particular case, that later decisions are rarely of much help either.

[31] [1996] F.S.R. 680.

[32] *Elan Digital v. Elan Computers* [1984] F.S.R. 373 at 385, CA; defendants' proposed operations, though in a different field from the plaintiffs, would "swamp" the plaintiffs' goodwill; grant of injunction upheld. See below for further authorities in relation to the "swamping" argument.

[33] See the discussion on dilution in Chap. 14.

[34] *Smith & Nephew v. 3M* [1982] R.P.C. 92, CA: (patent case).

[35] But to do so he must be specific, and give details. If he leaves the court in doubt as to the size of the problems which an interim injunction would occasion, he risks the court finding against him: *Antec v. South Western Chicks* [1997] F.S.R. 278.

nience"[36]: that is, on the relative extent of the damage to one or other party if the injunction is or is not granted. The ability of the parties to meet an order for damages on the scale contemplated will be relevant.[37] In general, the likelihood that one or other party will succeed at the trial is not a relevant consideration: but the likely extent of confusion or deception clearly may be[38]; whilst in cases where the interim proceedings are likely to determine the dispute finally, one way or the other, the probabilities of success are clearly relevant.[39]

Application of *American Cyanamid* principles to trade mark cases

While it has been confirmed that *American Cyanamid* principles apply in **18–97** general to applications for interim relief in trade mark and passing-off cases,[40] there are certain important considerations, specific to such actions, which need to be borne in mind. In particular, although it is usually neither necessary nor appropriate to assess the degree of probability of success which the claimant's action has (provided that it is arguable, and subject to the principle of *American Cyanamid* that the merits may be resorted to as a "tie-breaker" if the balance of convenience is very even,[41]) in trade mark and passing off cases, it is very hard to avoid doing so, since the better the claimant's case on the likelihood of deception (frequently the major issue) the greater the harm which he is likely to suffer. Accordingly, in appropriate cases, where the state of the evidence permits it, the court may seek to weigh up the merits in deciding whether to grant interim relief. This was confirmed in, for example, *Financial Times v. Evening Standard*,[42] and more recently in *Antec v. South Western Chicks*.[43] However, such an approach is not always necessary, since factors other than the relative merits may be determinative of the application, and where the facts are sufficiently complex, carrying out a "not-so-mini" trial to assess the merits will not be appropriate: *Blazer v.Yardley*.[44]

Additionally, there are cases where it is clear that the outcome of an **18–98** application for interim relief will decide the whole action, in particular where the application is made before or soon after the defendant has started to use the mark alleged to infringe, and in circumstances where

---

[36] *American Cyanamid, supra.*
[37] For an example of a case where the defendant's inability to pay was a significant factor in the grant of an interim injunction, see *The Law Society v. Society of Lawyers* [1996] F.S.R. 739. See also *Antec v. South Western Chicks* [1997] F.S.R. 278, where ability to pay was a factor.
[38] See below.
[39] See below.
[40] See, *e.g. County Sound v. Ocean Sound* [1991] F.S.R. 367, CA.
[41] This principle was applied in, *e.g. Mirage Studios v. Counter-Feat Clothing* [1991] F.S.R. 145.
[42] [1991] F.S.R. 7 at 10–11
[43] [1997] F.S.R. 278, citing *Series 5 Software v. Clarke* [1996] F.S.R. 273.
[44] [1992] F.S.R. 501 at 506–507.

it is clear that he will have to abandon it permanently for another if an injunction is granted. In such cases, the court may have to do the best it can to assess the merits and grant or refuse an injunction based on its conclusion.[45]

18–99   There has also been a tendency on the part of the courts to be willing to assess the merits at the interim stage, and to decide the application on that basis, where it is clear that the arguments of one side or the other on the issue of likelihood of confusion are hopeless or close to hopeless. Examples of such cases include *Furnitureland v. Harris*,[46] *Financial Times v. Evening Standard*,[47] *Tamworth Herald v. Thomson*,[48] *United Biscuits v. Burton Biscuits*[49] (part of case held unarguably bad, part held arguable), *Advance Magazines v. Redwood*,[50] *Rizla v. Bryant and May*.[51] This is in no way a departure from the *American Cyanamid* principles, which require the court first of all to decide whether there is a triable issue; it is rather a result of the fact that in passing off and trade marks cases, the court is able to assess the factual issue of likelihood of confusion on the basis of its own impression and experience.

Status quo

18–100 Where convenience is evenly balanced, the court should incline towards preserving the "status quo"[52]: that is to say, the *status quo ante bellum,* so that the Court should here look for the *casus belli* with a view to intervening against it.[53] In general, the status quo is the state of affairs existing immediately before the issue of the proceedings, or, if there has been unreasonable delay between the issue of the proceedings and the application for an injunction, immediately before the application: *Garden Cottage Foods v. Milk Marketing Board*.[54]

18–101   However, care is needed in this analysis, and it may not be so simple as to say that the status quo, in the case of a newly launched product

---

[45] See *Cayne v. Global Natural Resources* [1984] 1 All E.R. 225 generally in relation to the principle of assessing the merits where an interim decision is likely to decide the dispute finally. For authorities in the field of passing-off and trade mark infringement specifically, see *Boots v. Approved Prescription Services* [1988] F.S.R. 45; *Post Office v. Interlink* [1989] F.S.R. 369; *Stacey v. 2020 Communications* [1991] F.S.R. 49; *Gala of London v. Chandler* [1991] F.S.R. 294; *Management Publications v. Blenheim Exhibitions* [1991] F.S.R. 348 and 550, CA; *Blazer v. Yardley* [1992] F.S.R. 501; *B.B.C. v. Talbot* [1980] F.S.R. 228; *Parnass/Pelly v. Hodges* [1982] F.S.R. 329; *Elan Digital v. Elan Computers* [1984] F.S.R. 373 at 386, CA. In *Entec v. Abacus* [1992] F.S.R. 332, CA, a copyright case, the defendant successfully defeated an application for an interim injunction by arguing that the grant of one would cause its bankruptcy and hence there would never be a trial. The argument succeeded on the basis of the *Cayne* principle.
[46] [1989] F.S.R. 536.
[47] [1991] F.S.R. 7.
[48] [1991] F.S.R. 337.
[49] [1992] F.S.R. 14.
[50] [1993] F.S.R. 449.
[51] [1986] R.P.C. 389.
[52] *American Cyanamid, supra.*
[53] *Metric Resources v. Leasemetrix* [1979] F.S.R. 571 (passing-off case). See also, as to "status quo", *Dunhill v. Sunoptic* [1979] F.S.R. 337 at 376, CA (passing-off case).
[54] [1984] A.C. 130.

which is alleged to infringe, is that the product is not on the market. In *Blazer v. Yardley*,[55] where the defendant had recently launched a product which the plaintiff alleged amounted to passing off, it was held that granting an injunction would not preserve the status quo. The status quo was not limited to the presence or absence of the defendant from the market, but also included the state of the market, which would be changed by the grant of an injunction. Moreover, since an injunction would effectively prevent the defendant from returning to the disputed name for all time, that would also be a change to the status quo, in which the use of the name by the defendant was a possibility. By contrast, in *Morgan Grampian v. Training Personnel*,[56] the defendant changed the name of an existing publication to one alleged to constitute passing off, and the court held that the status quo would be preserved by the grant of an injunction. In *Reckitt & Colman v. Borden*[57] (the "Jif" case), it was held that the grant of an interim injunction would preserve the status quo, the defendant's product not having been launched.

A related issue is the question of defendants who act with "eyes **18–102** open", in the sense of knowing that the claimant may object to their conduct, it sometimes being argued that such persons are undeserving of sympathy. There is something a little illogical about the argument, since it would seem wrong to count against such a defendant the fact that he has considered his proposed conduct and concluded that it would be lawful, particularly when there is a good chance that his conclusion is correct. However, it has been taken into account in favour of claimants in a number of cases, and in particular it has been held that where a defendant presses on boldly with a high risk strategy knowing of a likely objection from the claimant, doing so should not improve his position in relation to the assessment of the status quo or the balance of convenience: *Peaudouce v. Kimberley Clark*.[58]

Other factors relevant to the balance of convenience

It is probably impossible to list all of the matters which may be relevant **18–103** in relation to the balance of convenience, but in addition to the matters referred to above, the following have been recognised as being of weight.

The defendant's freedom of speech is a relevant factor. This issue is considered in detail in Chapter 17 in connection with malicious false-hood, where it is more relevant, but even in a "pure" passing off case, it has been held that freedom of speech is a relevant factor: *Consorzio del Prosciutto di Parma v. Marks & Spencer*.[59]

---

[55] [1992] F.S.R. 501.
[56] [1992] F.S.R. 267.
[57] [1987] F.S.R. 228.
[58] [1996] F.S.R. 681, and see also *Jian Tools v. Roderick* [1995] F.S.R. 924, *Morgan Grampian v. Training Personnel* [1992] F.S.R. 267, where a lack of prudence by the defendant in not checking whether the name objected to was already in use was held against it on the balance of convenience.
[59] [1990] F.S.R. 530.

18–104   Another factor of importance in certain cases is "swamping", which is to say that where the defendant is a much bigger concern than the claimant, it may be that his use will be so extensive that by trial the claimant's reputation will have been overwhelmed. This is of course a rather unusual situation, but it can be a very significant point, as for example in *Provident Financial v. Halifax Building Society*.[60]

Compromise of interim application; variation of interim order

18–105   It often happens that the interim application is settled by the defendant offering, and the claimant accepting, a compromise in the form of an undertaking or injunction giving part of what was sought. Where this is done, however, the parties will be bound by it: a claimant who finds confusion worse than he supposed cannot come back to ask for more,[61] nor can a defendant whose offer was based on a wrong view of the law ask to be released.[62] Where the court has already made an order giving directions, upon undertakings by the defendant, it will not normally entertain an application for summary judgment, because to do so is to some extent inconsistent with the giving of directions for disclosure and pleadings, although it has jurisdiction to do so, and may do so if there has been a change of circumstances since the order for directions.[63]

18–106   It is also possible to apply to vary an interim order. The court will not, however, do so unless there has been a significant change in circumstances: *Gordino Ltd. v. Burgess*.[64]

Interim injunction refused on account of delay

18–107   Any significant, unnecessary delay in applying for interim relief is likely to tilt the balance of convenience against the claimant.[65] That does not mean that proceedings should be started without warning; delay due to failure of the defendants to answer letters may be excused.[66] Also, a degree of hesitation owing to a desire to avoid litigation is understandable and not normally a bar to relief.[67] A confidential notification by a defendant to a claimant of an intended course of action is nonetheless a notification, and delay thereafter is relevant: *Silicon Graphics v. Indigo Graphic*.[68]

---

[60] [1994] F.S.R. 81.
[61] *G.C.T. v. Lawie Marsh* [1973] R.P.C. 432 (passing-off case).
[62] *Chanel v. Woolworth* [1981] F.S.R. 196, CA.
[63] *Fabre v. Ronco* [1984] F.S.R. 148.
[64] [1988] 1 W.L.R. 890, CA.
[65] The older cases, indicating that avoidable delay is an absolute bar to interim relief, are in general not now followed; but it remains true that all reasonable speed in making the application is desirable.
[66] *"Under Six Club"* (*Deane v. Schofield*) [1962] R.P.C. 179: penalty in costs, where a letter would have sufficed to stop the acts complained of.
[67] *"Oxford Marmalade"*, *CPC v. Keenan* [1986] F.S.R. 527.
[68] [1994] F.S.R. 403.

Interim injunction limited as closely as possible

The interim injunction, being intended only to preserve the claimant's **18–108** right from serious detriment until the hearing, is, at any rate in cases which appear to be doubtful or honestly disputed, limited as closely as possible to what is sufficient to attain that end.[69] The claimant must give a cross-undertaking to abide by any order of the court as to damages for the loss (if any) occasioned by it to the defendant, should it turn out at the trial that it ought not to have been granted. If an undertaking to the court is given in lieu of an interim injunction there is similarly inserted in the order a cross-undertaking in damages. Where the claimant is a foreign corporation it and its British subsidiary may give the cross-undertaking.[70]

11. Enforcement and breaches of injunctions

Enforcement of the injunction

Breaches of an injunction or undertaking are contempts of court, which **18–109** may be punished by the committal of the guilty person, or by ordering him to pay a fine or costs. Before the court will punish a breach of an injunction or undertaking, it must be clear that a breach has been committed.[71] Accordingly, where an injunction is granted in general terms, and the defendant is not doing the specific thing on which the judgment was founded; or the injunction having been obtained by default, no specific thing has been admitted or found to be an infringement; the claimant may, when moving for contempt, be in some difficulty[72]: for it is inconvenient to try an action upon such a motion.

Where the defendant under an injunction or an undertaking wishes to **18–110** be relieved therefrom in respect of particular acts he may apply to the court, but must make out a case in favour of that relief.[73]

Unintentional breach of the injunction

It may be assumed that, if the court is satisfied that the defendant has **18–111** honestly tried to comply with its order, it will be unwilling to send him to prison because he has failed in his endeavour. But the court has

[69] *Biro-Swan v. Tallon* [1961] R.P.C. 326; *Bowater-Scott v. Modo* [1969] F.S.R. 330 (passing-off injunction refused where registered trade mark injunction sufficient).
[70] *Hobart v. Cannon* [1959] R.P.C. 269; *Ferragamo v. Lotus* (1950) 67 R.P.C. 175.
[71] See, *e.g. Redwing v. Redwing Forest* (1947) 64 R.P.C. 67 (passing-off case; undertaking broken only on one of two possible constructions; no order on motion for sequestration).
[72] *Ripley v. Arthur* (1902) 19 R.P.C. 443, a passing-off case; *Multiform v. Whitmarley* [1957] R.P.C. 260 at 262, HL. Accordingly, the claimant in such a case will normally do better to start a fresh action, although where the defendant is doing the specific thing forbidden by the earlier injunction, contempt proceedings are the only proper remedy; *Sterling-Winthrop v. Bayer* [1966] R.P.C. 477. Often an injunction is not of much value against a wrongdoer who is both astute and determined. Fortunately, few wrongdoers are either, let alone both.
[73] *Sterling-Winthrop v. Bayer* [1967] R.P.C. 326. The court will seldom relieve from an undertaking or an injunction made by consent, by way of compromise with the claimant's demands: see *Chanel v. Woolworth, supra.*

jurisdiction to commit for disobedience to an order which is not shown to have been wilful.[74] If the defendant is in the wrong, even though by mistake or misfortune, he may be ordered to pay the costs of the application.[75] In recent years, a more forgiving attitude has been taken by the courts, and in one case, where the defendant was striving honestly to obey an order made without notice in the absence of the supervising solicitor, who had gone away to serve another defendant, the claimant was ordered to pay the costs of the application to commit, even though technically a breach had been committed: *Adam Phones v. Goldschmidt*.[76] The same attitude may be taken by the court where an employee has committed a breach and so put his employer in technical contempt despite that employer's best efforts to avoid such a situation arising.[77]

Choice of a new mark by the defendant

18–112 The court will not compel an honest trader to alter his mark more than is necessary to protect the claimant's rights. But the court will not usually assist a defendant by indicating how far he may safely go.[78]

Delay in application to commit

18–113 If the claimant delays taking steps to enforce the injunction for a considerable time after he knows of the fresh infringement, the delay may cause the court to refuse to commit.[79]

12. Erasure, destruction, delivery up

Statutory remedies for infringement of registered marks

18–114 In addition to the common law and equitable remedies available in respect of passing-off and trade mark infringement by virtue of their being actions in tort, there is now a statutory regime providing for erasure of infringing marks, and destruction or delivery up of offending goods. These remedies are to be found in sections 15 to 19 of the 1994

---

[74] *Hewitt v. Mansell*, 29 S.J. 66. In *Parker v. Cooper* (1901) 18 R.P.C. 319, Cozens-Hardy J. refused to commit the defendant for an isolated instance of passing-off by the defendant's son without the defendant's knowledge.

[75] *Daniel and Arter v. Whitehouse* (1898) 16 R.P.C. 71; *Vine Products v. Mackenzie* [1968] F.S.R. 625. *cf. Frenkel v. Orru* [1968] R.P.C. 49 (special circumstances, no order for costs).

[76] [2000] F.S.R. 163. See also *Bhimji v. Chatwani* [1991] 1 W.L.R. 989, *BT v. Nextcall* (unreported) Jacob J., January 25, 2000.

[77] See *BT v. Nextcall, supra*; *Showerings v. Entam* [1975] F.S.R. 45.

[78] *cf. Kerfoot v. Cooper* (1908) 25 R.P.C. 508; and see the passing-off cases, *supra* paras 18–67 to 18–77.

[79] See Turner L.J. in *Rodgers v. Nowill* (1847) 3 De G.M. & G. 614; 22 L.J.Ch. 404. But delay is not a defence, *Chanel v. F.G.M. Cosmetics* [1981] F.S.R. 471.

Act. These remedies apply only to actions for infringement of a registered mark, not to passing off claims, in respect of which only the former common law remedies are available.

To what articles the statutory remedies apply

The statutory remedies apply to "infringing goods", "infringing material", and "infringing articles". These terms are defined in section 17(2), (4) and (5) respectively of the 1994 Act. **18–115**

In broad terms, goods are "infringing goods" if, first, they bear (or their packaging bears) the registered mark in question, or a mark similar to it, and, secondly, the application of the mark to them was, or, had it been done in the United Kingdom, would have been, an infringement of the registration. Section 17(2)(c) broadens the definition to a rather unclear extent by including goods in relation to which "the sign has otherwise been used . . . in such a way as to infringe the registered trade mark."

Section 17(2) of the 1994 Act is silent as to the notional circumstances in which it is to be assumed that the offending mark was applied to the goods outside the United Kingdom for the purposes of the test under section 17(2)(b). Decisions under related provisions of copyright law suggest that what should be considered is application by the persons who did in fact mark the goods (see, for example, *CBS v. Charmdale*[80]). In most situations, particularly where the goods are counterfeit, this nuance will not matter. But where the goods have been marked by a person in some way connected with the claimant, perhaps by virtue of being a company in common ownership, or holding some kind of licence, it could be of great importance. This is particularly so having regard to the English courts' reluctance to permit trade marks to be used to prevent the importation of goods put on the market by a company related to the United Kingdom trade mark owner, as in *Revlon v. Cripps & Lee*.[81] **18–116**

Goods are not capable of being "infringing goods" if by virtue of an enforceable Community right, they may lawfully be imported into the United Kingdom.[82]

"Infringing materials" are defined by section 17(4), and are materials such as labels, wrappers, business papers or advertising materials which, first, bear the registered mark or a mark similar to it, and, secondly, are used, or intended to be used, in a manner which would infringe. It is plain from the words of section 17(4) that the intention required is merely intention to use. There is no requirement that the person concerned should know or intend that such use would amount to an infringement. **18–117**

---

[80] [1981] Ch. 91.
[81] [1980] F.S.R. 85. And see Chap. 15, generally.
[82] 1994 Act, s.17(3).

18–118 "Infringing articles" are defined by section 17(5). They must satisfy a two-stage test. First, they must be specifically designed or adapted for making copies of a sign identical or similar to the registered mark in question. Secondly, the person possessing them must know or have reason to believe that they have been used or are to be used to make infringing goods or materials. The section is, regrettably, unclear as to what this involves, since the reference back to infringing materials itself involves incorporation of the mental element of section 17(4). As a minimum, it is suggested that the person in possession of the allegedly infringing article must know that it will be used to make materials and what the manner of use of those materials will be (even if he may be ignorant as to whether that use would infringe).

Statutory order for erasure, removal or obliteration

18–119 By section 15 of the 1994 Act, the court may order a person who has been found to infringe a registered trade mark to cause the offending sign to be erased, removed or obliterated from any infringing goods, materials or articles in his possession, custody or control. If it is not reasonably practicable for the sign to be erased, the person may be ordered to destroy the goods, materials or articles in question.

18–120 Of course, many unsuccessful defendants in trade mark actions, particularly of the kind involving counterfeiting, may not be trustworthy, and to put the erasure of the offending mark or destruction of the offending goods in their hands would just be a recipe for them to be spirited away only to appear somewhere else. For this reason, section 15(2) permits the court, where an order under section 15(1) has not been complied with, or seems unlikely to be complied with, to direct that the goods, materials or articles be delivered up to some other person for erasure or destruction. It is to be assumed that frequently the person to whom they are so delivered up will be the claimant.

18–121 It is important to note, by contrast with section 16 (which is considered below), that for the court to exercise its powers under this provision, a finding of infringement must have been made against the person in possession of the goods, materials or articles concerned.

Statutory order for delivery up

18–122 Section 16 of the 1994 Act permits a trade mark proprietor to apply to the court for an order for the delivery up (to himself or to someone else directed by the court) of infringing goods, materials or articles in the possession, custody or control of another person in the course of a business.

18–123 An order under section 16 may not be made after the period provided for by section 18 (which is considered in more detail below, but is basically six years from the date of application of the mark), and may not be made unless the court also makes, or it appears that there are grounds for making, an order under section 19 (which is considered below and relates to disposal of infringing goods, materials or articles).

It is important to note that while section 16 requires that the goods, **18–124** materials or articles in question must be "infringing", it does not require that the person against whom the order is sought must have infringed within the meaning of section 10, or intend to do so. An order under the section may therefore be made against a person who is merely the keeper of infringing goods, etc.

This raises the question of the level of proof required under the **18–125** section. Of course, if the person against whom delivery up is sought has lost an infringement action against the proprietor of the mark there should be no difficulty. Likewise, if the proprietor has succeeded in relation to certain kinds of goods at a trial there should be little difficulty in satisfying the court under section 16 even if the application is made against someone other than the unsuccessful defendant. But what if an application is made under section 16 against an innocent person who does not know whether the goods in question are infringing, in circumstances where the proprietor has not previously vindicated his rights? It is suggested that the right answer is that in such cases the applicant must show on the balance of probabilities that the goods are in fact infringing, not merely that they might be or are arguably so. In the context of the very similar provisions of the Copyright, Designs and Patents Act 1998, sections 99 and 114, it has been suggested that the lower standard of proof is correct,[83] but that seems wrong in principle.[84]

The person to whom delivery up is made must keep the infringing **18–126** goods, materials or articles pending the making of an order under section 19 of the 1994 Act.[85]

Application for order for disposal

At the same time as, or after, an application for delivery up under **18–127** section 16 of the 1994 Act has been made, a further application may be made for an order dealing with the disposal of the goods, materials or articles concerned. The possible outcomes are an order for destruction, an order for forfeiture, or no order. Unfortunately, there is no apparent jurisdiction under section 19 to order removal or erasure of the mark, as there is under section 15.

In deciding what order, if any, to make, the court must consider the **18–128** other remedies available to the trade mark owner in an infringement action, and whether they would be adequate to compensate the proprietor and any licensee, and protect their interests. This rather complicates

---

[83] *Lagenes v. It's At* [1991] F.S.R. 492.
[84] For a cogent criticism of the decision and an explanation as to why the proper view is that the goods must be shown actually to be infringing, see *Laddie Prescott & Vitoria, Modern Law of Copyright*, (2nd ed.) paras 24.35–6.
[85] s.16(3).

matters, since one remedy available in infringement proceedings (but not under section 19) is removal or erasure of the mark. It therefore seems open to the court to decide that removal would be sufficient protection, but not open to it to order it, unless and until infringement proceedings are successfully brought. This is illogical, and it is suggested that the court would only decline to order forfeiture or destruction on that basis if infringement proceedings could be brought relatively easily and swiftly. If the bringing of infringement proceedings would be difficult or lengthy (perhaps because identifying the infringer would be a problem—recalling that the infringer may not himself be a party to proceedings under section 19), it is suggested that the court will be inclined to order destruction or forfeiture.

18–129 Section 19(1) contemplates that an order for forfeiture in favour of the proprietor may be made, and presumably would be seriously considered in a case where his financial remedies appeared inadequate because of the impecuniosity of the defendant.

If the court decides that no order is appropriate, then the goods are to be returned to the person from whom they were delivered up.[86]

18–130 Any person having an interest in the goods is entitled to appear in proceedings under section 19. A "person having an interest" is not defined in the section, save that section 19(6) states that it includes any person in whose favour an order under the equivalent provisions of the Copyright, Designs and Patents Act 1988 could be made. It is suggested that the term should be understood broadly so as to include anyone whose financial interests could be affected by the forfeiture or destruction of the goods, and any person responsible for their safekeeping. Thus their owner, their bailee, any person having a security interest in them, any person who has sought to buy or sell them, and any person having the benefit of a court order relating to them should all be included. It is certainly clear that more than one person may have an interest in the same goods, and where that is so, the court must make such order as it thinks just.[87] This will involve identifying those parties whose interests would be served by the permanent removal of the goods from circulation (such as the proprietor of the registered mark in question), and those parties who would lose financially as a result (such as an owner of the goods who is innocent of any infringement), and balancing their needs. This may be particularly difficult if, as is suggested above, an order for erasure or obliteration is not available under section 19 of the 1994 Act.

18–131 A person having an interest in infringing goods may also appeal against any order made under section 19, even if he did not appear at the hearing.[88] The order is not to be carried into effect until the time for appeal has expired and any appeal made has been finally determined.[89]

---

[86] s.19(5).
[87] s.19(4).
[88] s.19(3)(b).
[89] s.19(3).

Although section 19 provides that rules of court may be made as to **18–132** the service of notice on persons having an interest in infringing goods, materials or articles, none have been made. It is therefore suggested that the ordinary forms of application for interim or final relief be used. A person having an interest in such goods is entitled to appear whether served with a notice or not.[90]

Period after which statutory delivery up is not available

By section 18 of the 1994 Act, delivery up is not available after the **18–133** expiry of six years from the application of the infringing mark to infringing goods or their packaging, or to infringing materials, or from the making of infringing articles. If the proprietor of the trade mark was under a disability during that period or was prevented by fraud or concealment from finding out the facts entitling him to apply for delivery up, the period of six years runs from the time when his disability ends or when he could with reasonable diligence have found out the facts entitling him to apply.

Remedies available under the court's general powers

We now consider the relief available other than under the 1994 Act.   **18–134**

Erasure of the spurious marks

The court not only forbids further infringement by its injunction, but, **18–135** where the defendant is proved to have spuriously marked articles in his possession or under his control, it usually orders the erasure of the marks,[91] or the delivery up of the marked articles for that purpose, or, if erasure is impracticable, for destruction.

Thus, in *Slazenger v. Feltham*,[92] where the word "Demotic", an **18–136** infringement of the plaintiffs' mark "Demon", was stamped upon the defendants' tennis racquets, it was ordered that the defendants should make an affidavit verifying the number of the racquets and that they should either deliver up the racquets to the plaintiffs to be destroyed, or satisfactorily erase from them the name "Demotic" in the presence of the plaintiffs or their agent.

In the same way, the court usually orders obliteration of the mark **18–137** from labels, wrappings, advertising "literature", etc., in the defendant's possession, with delivery up as an alternative.

The order for delivery up or obliteration may be stayed pending an appeal.

---

[90] s.19(3)(a).
[91] *Dent v. Turpin* (1861) 2 J. & H. 139; 30 L.J.Ch. 495; *Upmann v. Elkan* (1871) L.R. 7 Ch. 130.
[92] (1889) 6 R.P.C. 531; 5 T.L.R. 365.

Delay

18–138 A claimant may fail to get an order for delivery up if he unduly delays the commencement of his action.[93]

13. Financial remedies—damages and accounts of profits

No distinction between infringement and passing off

18–139 So far as concerns the relief by way of damages or an account of profits there appears to be no reason to distinguish between actions for infringement and actions for passing off. However in passing off actions where the claimant is not a trader in the ordinary sense, a claim for damages may present difficulties: see Chapter 14.

Nominal damages

18–140 It was long ago decided at common law that the mere proof of an infringement entitles the claimant to damages.[94] Consequently, no allegation of special damage is a necessary part of his case.[95] The natural consequence of an infringement, even though it be made in complete ignorance of the claimant's rights, is that the infringer must pay at least nominal damages, and the costs of action: so that, if he acted under the direction of a third person, he may reasonably compound with the proprietor of the mark on these terms, and claim an indemnity from his principal.[96]

Onus of showing substantial damage lies on the claimant

18–141 In order to obtain an order for an account of profits or an inquiry as to damages, the claimant need in general only show that he may be able to recover substantial damages. This is not a high hurdle at all, and in general the attitude of the court is that the defendant can be protected against the costs of an inquiry or account which results in no, or only a very small award, by making a payment into court and thus letting the claimant bear the risk of the costs of the proceeding. Hence an inquiry should be ordered even if the court feels serious doubt about the claimant's ability to recover any substantial amount.[97] However, this

---

[93] *County Chemical v. Frankenburg* (1904) 21 R.P.C. 722: five months' delay before complaint; the boxes complained of being capable of being used in ways not a breach of the injunction.

[94] *Blofeld v. Payne* (1833) 4 B. & Ad. 410. The jury gave him a farthing.

[95] *Rodgers v. Nowill* (1847) 5 C.B. 109. See also *Reddaway v. Bentham* [1892] 2 Q.B. 639; 9 R.P.C. 503.

[96] *Dixon v. Fawcus* (1861) 3 E. & E. 537. As to third party procedure for claiming an indemnity, see *Hennessy v. Dompé* (1902) 19 R.P.C. 333.

[97] If the claimant is successful on an application for summary judgment but has not led evidence of loss and damage, the court may allow him a further opportunity to submit evidence in support of an order for an inquiry or account. See *Prince plc v. Prince Sports Group Inc.* [1998] F.S.R. 21; *Beautimatic v. Mitchell* [2000] F.S.R. 267.

attitude is taken even where the claimant is legally aided so that the defendant cannot obtain substantial protection by way of a payment in.[98]

However, where the claimant fails to clear this low threshold, the **18–142** court may award nominal damages or fix a sum without ordering an account or an inquiry as to damages. In exceptional circumstances, that course may be followed if the evidence of damage is not sufficient to justify the costs of an inquiry.[99]

If the claimant pursues an inquiry or account, the onus of showing **18–143** what loss he has actually sustained by reason of the defendant's conduct lies upon him. It cannot be presumed, in the absence of evidence, that the amount of goods sold by the defendant under an infringing trade mark would, but for the defendant's unlawful use of the claimant's mark, have been sold by the claimant.[1] The proper form of an order for an inquiry as to damages occasioned by the infringement of a mark is, therefore, what damage (if any) has the claimant sustained by reason of the acts, repetition of which is restrained by the judgment.[2]

Basic principles for assessing damages

The basic principles for the assessment of damages in a patent case were **18–144** considered by Jacob J. in *Gerber v. Lectra*.[3] The following principles are applicable to trade mark infringement:

(1) Damages are compensatory only, to put the claimant in the same position he would have been in had the wrong not been sustained.[4]

(2) The burden of proof lies on the claimant, but damages are to be assessed liberally.[5]

(3) Where the claimant has licensed his right, the damages are the lost royalty.[6]

(4) It is irrelevant that the defendant could have competed lawfully.[7]

---

[98] See, *e.g. Brain v. Ingledew Brown Bennison & Garrett (No. 3)* [1997] F.S.R. 511 at 525–8, *McDonald's v. Burgerking* [1987] F.S.R. 112.

[99] *cf.* the passing-off cases, such as *Rose v. Loftus* (1878) 47 L.J.Ch. 576; *Samuelson v. Producers* (1931) 48 R.P.C. 580 at 590.

[1] *Leather Cloth v. Hirschfeld* (1865) L.R. 1 Eq. 299; *Magnolia Metal v. Atlas Metal* (1879) 14 R.P.C. 389, CA; *Alexander v. Henry* (1895) 12 R.P.C. 360, illus. 2, below. In the first two of these cases, the plaintiffs were given nominal damages only; but this would in general seem to be inappropriate (except in a *quia timet* action): a finding of passing off almost necessarily implies that some damage will have been caused, and in recent times courts have customarily so assumed—as in the later cases cited below.

[2] *Spalding v. Gamage* (1915) 32 R.P.C. 273, HL; (1918) 35 R.P.C. 101, CA.

[3] [1995] R.P.C. 383.

[4] *General Tire v. Firestone* [1976] R.P.C. 197.

[5] *ibid.*

[6] *ibid.* Jacob J. held in *Gerber* that this follows from the first proposition. It is less likely to be of application in trade mark cases than in patent cases because the prevalence of exploitation by licensing is less.

[7] *United Horse-Shoe v. Stewart* (1888) 5 R.P.C. 260.

(5) Where the claimant has exploited his right by his own sales, he can claim lost profit on sales by the defendant he would have made otherwise, and lost profit on his own sales to the extent that he was forced by the infringement to reduce his own price.

18–145   Jacob J. also held as part of principle (5) that a claimant who obtains damages for sales by the defendant which he has proved would have been made by him in the absence of the infringement, will be entitled to damages on the basis of a reasonable royalty for all the other infringements, but it has been doubted whether this particular principle applies to trade mark cases.[8]

18–146   It is important to note that in assessing damages for lost sales on a compensatory basis, it will be necessary for the court to determine what proportion of the defendant's customers have been confused. The claimant is not entitled to damages for sales to persons who have not been misled, since he has suffered no loss in respect of them, and, arguably, no actionable wrong has been committed in respect of sales to them.[9] If he were to recover damages in relation to such persons, he would be over-compensated. This principle distinguishes passing-off and trade mark infringement from other intellectual property proceedings such as those for patent infringement, where all the defendant's activities of a given kind infringe.

Other heads of damage

18–147   In general, the only injury which is done by an infringement is that the defendant's goods or services are sold instead of those of the claimant, and the sale of the latter is, in some degree, diminished in consequence. But it may appear that further damage has been done, for instance, where spurious goods are so inferior to the genuine as to injure the trade reputation of the claimant,[10] or where the stress of the competition compels the claimant to lower his prices and thus suffer loss.

18–148   The cost of advertisements to counteract the effect of the defendant's conduct may be taken into account.[11] Further, the legal costs of putting on notice foreign manufacturers of infringing materials have been held recoverable.[12]

18–149   In the area of damages for patent infringement it has been held that, provided causation is shown, and subject to the normal rules as to

---

[8] *Dormeuil v. Feraglow* [1990] R.P.C. 449. The case did not decide that damages assessed as a royalty were not available; it merely held that their availability or otherwise should not be decided on an application for an interim payment, and that there was no binding authority that they were available. In support of the argument that damages assessed on the "user" principle are available, see *Stoke on Trent City Council v. W&J Wass* [1988] 1 W.L.R. 1406; *Meters v. Metropolitan Gas Meters* (1911) 29 R.P.C. 157.

[9] See *Spalding v. Gamage, supra*, and *Draper v. Trist* (1939) 56 R.P.C. 429.

[10] As in *Alexander v. Henry*, illus. 2 below.

[11] *Spalding v. Gamage* (1918) 35 R.P.C. 101, CA.

[12] *Dormeuil v. Feraglow* [1990] R.P.C. 449.

remoteness of damage, it is possible to recover damages for items sold as a result of an infringing sale, even if such ancillary items do not themselves infringe.[13] There appears no reason why this principle should not apply to trade mark infringement in appropriate circumstances.

Damage caused to subsidiary

In principle, a claimant may recover damages suffered by a subsidiary **18–150** company, provided that he himself has a cause of action, and the damage to the subsidiary causes damage to him. But in such cases, the claimant must prove the quantum of his loss properly; it is not to be assumed that the loss of a pound by the subsidiary will necessarily result in the same loss to the parent.[14]

Date to which damages are reckoned

If the infringement is a continuing one, the damages ought to be **18–151** assessed down to the time of the assessment.

Examples: **18–152**

(1) In a case where the plaintiffs were foreign manufacturers, and the defendants, former British agents for the plaintiffs, claimed that the mark in suit now belonged to them, it was held (a) that the acts of the defendants had delayed the plaintiffs' resumption of trade in this country by many years; (b) that damages were recoverable for this although the plaintiffs might have disregarded the defendants' claim and resumed trade at an earlier date; (c) judgment for infringement of trade mark and passing-off had not restored the plaintiffs' goodwill in its entirety; and (d) that the profits made by the defendants were not the measure of the damage suffered by the plaintiffs: *Manus v. Fullwood* (1954) 71 R.P.C. 243 (£10,000 damages awarded).

(2) Where by a persistent course of fraudulent imitation of the plaintiffs' mark the defendants succeeded in so damaging the plaintiff's goodwill in Mexico as to destroy their control of the Mexican market for their goods, with the result that thereafter the defendants could compete effectively with the plaintiffs in Mexico without further infringement, the damage done to the plaintiffs by the subsequent lawful competition—loss of business, and loss of profit through forced reduction of prices—was held attributable to the infringement: *Alexander v. Henry* (1895) 12 R.P.C. 360.

---

[13] *Gerber v. Lectra* [1995] R.P.C. 383; [1997] R.P.C. 443, CA.
[14] See *Gerber v. Lectra, supra.*

Innocence no defence to damages

18–153 A defendant cannot avoid an order for an inquiry by showing that he infringed innocently. The claimant has a right to damages regardless of the defendant's state of mind, and that is so regardless of whether the cause of action is infringement of a registered mark, or passing off.[15]

Order for account

18–154 The ordinary form of the order for an account directs an account of the profits made by the defendant in selling or otherwise disposing of the goods bearing the spurious mark or marks, to be taken by the master, with liberty to apply.

18–155 The account should not be limited to sales made to persons who bought the goods as and for the goods of the claimant, by reason of the use of the infringing mark upon them.[16] The mischief done by the spurious marking of the goods is not merely that it is calculated to deceive immediate purchasers from the infringers, but that it puts "a weapon calculated to be fraudulently used by the middlemen"[17] into their hands, by which they may intentionally, or not, deceive the ultimate purchasers. The account should be of such profits as ought to be treated as having been improperly made by the defendant.[18]

Basic principles applicable to an account

18–156 Accounts of profits in trade mark cases have been rare in the United Kingdom, but the following are probably sound basic principles:

(1) An account is confined to profits actually made, its purpose being to deprive the defendant of unjust enrichment rather than to punish him.[19]

(2) An account is addressed to identifying profits caused, in the legal sense, by the infringement.[20]

(3) The fact that the defendant's profits could have been made in a non-infringing fashion is irrelevant.[21]

(4) The claimant must take the defendant as he finds him, and may not argue that the defendant could have made greater profits by trading in a different fashion.[22]

---

[15] *Gillette v. Edenwest* [1994] R.P.C. 279; *Spalding v. Gamage* (1915) 32 R.P.C. 273 at 283, HL; *Henry Heath v. Gorringe* (1924) 41 R.P.C. 457.

[16] *Lever v. Goodwin* (1887) 36 Ch.D. 1; 4 R.P.C. 492.

[17] *Price's Patent Candle v. Ogston and Tennant* (1909) 26 R.P.C. 797 at 814. See also *Saxlehner v. Apollinaris* [1897] 1 Ch. 893; 14 R.P.C. 645.

[18] *My Kinda Town v. Soll* [1982] F.S.R. 147.

[19] *My Kinda Town v. Soll, supra; Celanese v. BP* [1999] R.P.C. 203.

[20] *Celanese v. BP, supra.*

[21] *Celanese v. BP, supra.*

[22] *Celanese v. BP, supra; Dart v. Decor* [1994] F.S.R. 567.

(5) Where only parts of the defendant's activities infringed, profits attributable to the non-infringing parts are not caused by the infringement, and the overall profits must be apportioned.[23]

(6) Overheads should be dealt with so as to arrive as closely as possible at the true profit.[24]

(7) The defendant cannot generally deduct opportunity cost.[25]

(8) General overheads may be apportioned to the infringing activity, subject to the above principles.[26]

Election between damages and profits

Damages are a matter of right; the account of profits is an equitable **18–157** remedy and the court has a discretion whether or not to grant it. Accordingly, a successful claimant in an infringement action is entitled to an inquiry as to damages (at his own risk as to costs) in any case where there is a prospect that the inquiry would reach a positive result[27]; whilst only in certain cases will the court grant an account of profits. In these cases, the claimant has an option (exercisable at the conclusion of the hearing of the case) to claim either damages or profits: he cannot have both.[28] Accordingly, it is usual in particulars of claim to ask for the two in the alternative. The principle upon which the court grants an account of profits is that where one party owes a duty to another, the person to whom the duty is owed is entitled to recover from the other party every benefit which that other party has received by virtue of his fiduciary position if in fact he has obtained it without the knowledge or consent of the party to whom he owed the duty.[29] An account is generally refused if the defendant had no knowledge of the claimant's mark and, when ordered, is limited to the period during which such knowledge had existed; whilst knowledge or absence of knowledge does not affect the right to damages.[30]

A claimant who has been successful in an action for trade mark **18–158** infringement or passing off may not have sufficient knowledge of the defendant's activities to make an informed decision as to whether he should seek an inquiry as to damages or an account of profits. In such a case he may seek disclosure before making his election: *Island Records v. Tring*.[31] Disclosure given in such circumstances should be limited to that which is necessary for the claimant to make an informed decision within a reasonable time; he is not entitled to all the disclosure which would be

---

[23] *Celanese v. BP, supra.*
[24] *Dart v. Decor, supra.*
[25] *ibid.*
[26] *ibid.*
[27] See references to *McDonalds v. Burgerking* etc., *supra.*
[28] *Neilson v. Belts* (1871) L.R. 5 H.L. 1; followed in *De Vitre v. Betts* (1868) L.R. 6 H.L. 319. See *per* Cotton L.J. in *Lever v. Goodwin* (1887) 36 Ch.D. 1; 4 R.P.C. 492.
[29] *Electrix* (1953) 70 R.P.C. 158.
[30] See above.
[31] [1995] F.S.R. 560.

given in the inquiry, and in appropriate circumstances an audited schedule of infringing dealings may be a substitute for documentary disclosure.[32]

Refusal because of delay or acquiescence

18–159 The court may refuse to order an account of profits,[33] or order it to be taken only from the date of the letter before action,[34] where the claimant has neglected to take proceedings after becoming aware of the infringement. There have been passing-off cases in which damages were refused to the claimant on the ground of delay verging on acquiescence[35]; but it is not easy to see on what principle, nor how this could be right in actions for infringement.

18–160 In a case where there had been some delay, and some amount of misrepresentation in his business on the plaintiff's part, and the defendant's proper trade was larger than that of the plaintiffs, the account was limited to profits earned since the commencement of the suit: *Ford v. Foster* (1872) L.R. 7 Ch. 611 at 633.

Profits or damages only go back for six years

18–161 Damages can only be recovered, and the profits to be included in the account can only be reckoned, in respect of infringements occurring less than six years before the issue of the proceedings,[36] subject to the exception in the case of concealed fraud which is part of the general law.

Costs of inquiry or account

18–162 The costs of the inquiry as to damages or the account of profits should generally be reserved until the result of the inquiry or account is known,[37] at any rate. If no damages or profits are found to have been incurred or made,[38] or if the proceedings subsequent to the judgment are oppressively conducted by the claimant, or if the defendant has made a sufficient offer,[39] the claimant ought to pay the costs. But where the

---

[32] *ibid.*
[33] *Harrison v. Taylor* (1865) 11 Jur.(N.S.) 408; 12 L.T. (N.S.) 339; *Beard v. Turner* (1866) 13 L.T. (N.S.) 746. Or, perhaps, only down to the date when the claimants learnt of the infringement: *Electrolux v. Electrix* (1954) 70 R.P.C. 158. See also *Crossley v. Derby* (1834) 1 Webster's P.C. 119, a patent case.
[34] *Lever v. Sunniwite* (1949) 66 R.P.C. 84; *cf. Young v. Holt* (1948) 65 R.P.C. 25 ("Mendoza").
[35] *Reddaway v. Stevenson* (1903) 20 R.P.C. 276, three years' delay before action; *Gledhill v. British Perforated* (1911) 28 R.P.C. 429, delay of over two years.
[36] *per* Mellish L.J. in *Ford v. Foster* (1872) L.R. 7 Ch. 611 at 633; Limitation Act 1980, s.2. See also *Electrolux v. Electrix* (1954) 70 R.P.C. 158.
[37] *per* Fry J. in *Slack v. Midland Ry.* (1880) 16 Ch.D. 81, a case of nuisance.
[38] *Tonge v. Ward* (1869) 21 L.T. (N.S.) 480.
[39] *Fettes v. Williams* (1908) 25 R.P.C. 511, a design case, in which the damages were assessed at less than the amount of the offer, and the plaintiffs were ordered to pay the costs of the inquiry and of the further consideration. See also *Draper v. Trist* (1939) 56 R.P.C. 225.

defendant had filed a false affidavit greatly understating the number of goods sold, although the account showed that he had made no profit, Chitty J. said it was a case for investigation, and allowed the plaintiff costs.[40]

14. Costs

Costs in the discretion of the judge

Subject to the provision in section 73 of the 1994 Act as to the effect of a **18–163** "certificate of contested validity", as to which see below, the costs of and incident to an action for the infringement of a trade mark, as the costs in any other action, are in the discretion of the court, and the court has full power to determine by whom and to what extent such costs shall be paid.

Unsuccessful party usually ordered to pay costs

The court or judge in general follows the ordinary rule that the **18–164** unsuccessful party shall pay the costs of the litigation. This principle is now expressly incorporated in the rules under rule 44.3(2) of the CPR. Most of the authorities referred to below are from before the introduction of the CPR, and should therefore be approached with a little care, but in general the principles have not changed so much as to render them inapplicable. They remain useful guides.

Where each party is successful on part of the case, it is usual to give **18–165** whichever party succeeds on the dispute as a whole the costs, save so far as these are increased by the issues upon which he has failed[41]; unless there was only one main issue.[42] More rarely, the costs of the different issues are ordered to be separately assessed, and given to the party succeeding on them, but the CPR now deprecates this practice, and in so far as it is practicable, the court ought instead to award the winning party either a proportion of his costs, or his costs from a certain date.[43]

In carrying out this assessment, the court is to consider all the **18–166** circumstances, including the parties' conduct before and after proceedings began, and whether and to what extent a party has been successful.[44]

---

[40] *Dicks v. Jackson*, March 31, 1884, cited *Sebastian* (5th ed.), p. 251.
[41] *Saxlehner v. Apollinaris* [1897] 1 Ch. 893; 14 R.P.C. 645; *Lever v. Bedingfield* (1898) 15 R.P.C. 453; *Hipkins v. Plant* (1898) 15 R.P.C. 294.
[42] The court has often made some rough apportionment of costs, without giving detailed reasons for it: as in *Bourne v. Swan & Edgar* (1903) 20 R.P.C. 105.
[43] CPR, r. 44.3(7).
[44] CPR, r. 44.4(4) and (5).

In some cases of isolated instances of infringement or passing off, the claimant has been refused relief at the trial, and been ordered to pay the costs of the action.[45]

Offer by defendant, or by claimant

18-167 The procedure relating to offers and payments into court is now codified by Part 36 of the CPR.

An unsuccessful defendant must usually pay costs, although he has only defended a mark which he honestly adopted without being aware of its too great resemblance to the claimant's mark,[46] and though he has acted without fraud and in ignorance of the claimant's rights.[47] But by offering the claimant all that he is entitled to,[48] that is, in the case of the innocent holder[49] of spuriously marked goods, an undertaking[50] not to part with them until the spurious marks have been removed,[51] and all requisite information to enable the claimant to stop the infringement,[52] and the payment of the assessed costs (if any) already incurred by him in the action, if an action has been commenced—the defendant may escape liability for subsequent costs.[53] If the claimant, after such an offer has been made, commences or continues proceedings against the

[45] *Leahy v. Glover* (1893) 10 R.P.C. 141 HL, and *Rutter v. Smith* (1901) 18 R.P.C. 49, where only a single act of passing off by a servant, since discharged, was proved, and costs were given against the plaintiffs; and see the other similar cases cited below in relation to trap orders, see paras 18–212. In *Burberry v. Watkinson* (1906) 23 R.P.C. 141, Warrington J., in a case where the defendant had been misled by his supplier, refused to order any injunction and made no order for costs. But cases differ: *cf. Bass, Ratcliff and Gretton v. Laidlaw* (1909) 26 R.P.C. 211; *Kodak v. Grenville* (1908) 25 R.P.C. 416; and *Myers v. Fields* (1954) 71 R.P.C. 435.
[26] *Blair v. Stock* (1884) 52 L.T. 123; *cf.* the registration case, *Hyde* (1878) 7 Ch.D. 724.
[47] *Edelsten v. Edelsten* (1863) 1 De G.J. & S. 185.
[48] But where the defendants altered their mark after action, but declined to give an undertaking and pay the costs of the action, an injunction was granted and they were ordered to pay costs: *Spicer v. Spalding & Hodge* (1915) 32 R.P.C. 52; and see *Steiner v. Stevens* [1957] R.P.C. 439.
[49] In a case of fraud, the claimant may, notwithstanding that the defendant has made a full offer to submit, be allowed the whole costs although he proceeds to trial: *Jameson v. Clarke* (1902) 19 R.P.C. 255.
[50] The claimant is not bound to accept an undertaking in the case of an infringer with notice, or where there is reasonable risk that it will be necessary to take steps to enforce it. In such a case the claimant will usually be allowed the costs of a motion for judgment: *Gandy Belt v. Fleming, Birkby* (1901) 18 R.P.C. 276; but at all events the defendant must pay the costs of the claimant obtaining an injunction by consent: *Slazenger v. Pigott* (1895) 12 R.P.C. 439. *cf. Jenkins v. Hope* [1896] 1 Ch. 278; 13 R.P.C. 57 (a patent case, where the plaintiff ought to have accepted an undertaking, the infringement being very small).
[51] Except, perhaps, by returning them to the consignor: see *Upmann v. Elkan* (1871) L.R. 7 Ch. 130.
[52] The claimant is not entitled to the publication of an apology: *British Blue Spot v. Keene* (1931) 48 R.P.C. 375, though it may be reasonable to ask for an apology and undertaking in lieu of an injunction in open court, and to apply for an injunction if this is refused: *Kodak v. Illingworth* (1925) 43 R.P.C. 33; or to receive a list of the defendant's customers, if not entitled to an inquiry or account: *Hipkins v. Plant* (1898) 15 R.P.C. 294.
[53] But the defendant must not ask for a term to which he is not legally entitled, as, for instance, that the claimant should not advertise the undertaking: *Hipkins v. Plant* (1898) 15 R.P.C. 297; *Clay v. Godfrey Phillips* (1910) 27 R.P.C. 508.

defendant making it, he will usually be ordered to pay him his costs subsequently incurred.[54] A letter offering too little too late will not assist a defendant.[55]

Under Part 36 of the CPR, a claimant may now make an offer to settle **18–168** proceedings. He may offer to accept less than is sought by his statement of case, with the sanction against the defendant that if he in fact obtains more than that offered, his recovery in costs, and in interest on costs, may be increased.[56]

Notice of action is unnecessary

Formally, no notice need be given to the alleged infringer before the **18–169** action is brought.[57] But even before the CPR it was considered bad practice to sue without warning, in the absence of some special reason for doing so.[58] Moreover, there may be a risk when an action is commenced without warning, especially against a mere retailer, that the defendant may satisfy the court that the infringement was inadvertent and that there was no reason for apprehending any repetition.[59] Further, the court may not award the claimant his costs if the defendant would have been willing to concede the claimant's demand if notice had been given.[60]

With the introduction of the CPR, these considerations have even **18–170** more force. It is a principal focus of the CPR to encourage parties to enter into a dialogue, and to exchange information, before proceedings are begun. The object is to promote settlements by avoiding the entrenchment which can result from proceedings being begun. In many fields of litigation there are formal pre-action protocols as a result.[61] There are none yet in intellectual property matters,[62] but it still is likely

---

[54] CPR, r. 36.20. *Slazenger v. Spalding* (1910) 27 R.P.C. 20; *Rippingille's v. Clarke's* (1917) 34 R.P.C. 365. In *Catterson v. Anglo Foreign* (1911) 28 R.P.C. 74, the defendants, who were commission agents and alleged that they were innocent importers from abroad, were held not to have met the plaintiff's complaint in a proper manner, and an injunction was granted with costs.

[55] *Colgate Palmolive v. Markwell Finance* [1990] R.P.C. 197.

[56] CPR, r. 36.21.

[57] The very life of a trade mark depends upon the promptitude with which it is vindicated: *Johnston v. Orr-Ewing* (1882) 7 App.Cas. 219. And see *Customagic v. Headquarter & General* [1968] F.S.R. 150 (two successful trap orders justified immediate proceedings without warning).

[58] *e.g.* because an application for an *Anton Piller* order is to be made, or in counterfeiting cases generally.

[59] *e.g. Leahy v. Glover* (1893) 10 R.P.C. 141; *Bass v. Laidlaw* (1909) 26. R.P.C. 211. Contrast *Bovril v. Bodega* (1916) 33 R.P.C. 153 at 155 and *Sterner v. Stevens* [1957] R.P.C. 439.

[60] See *e.g. Ucan v. Hilti* [1968] F.S.R. 248 (motion launched without notice and defendants gave undertaking before hearing, defendants' costs in cause).

[61] And CPR, r. 26.4 allows the stay of proceedings at an early stage in order to allow negotiations to take place.

[62] Partly because the statutory threats provisions make it difficult to enter into a dialogue with a secondary infringer without the potential claimant being at risk of committing an actionable threat.

that the precipitate bringing of proceedings will result in the claimants being punished in costs.

Instances of claimants deprived of costs

18-171 Again, it should be borne in mind that the following cases were decided before the introduction of the CPR.

(1) Where the plaintiff was entitled to an injunction only, and his right to this was admitted on the second day of the trial, he was given costs up to that time, and was ordered to pay the subsequent costs: *Magnolia Metal v. Atlas Metal* (1897) 14 R.P.C. 389 at 400 (passing off).

18-172 (2) In a passing-off case, in which the defendants offered any undertaking at an early stage of the trial, and the plaintiffs refused the offer, and pressed for an injunction and it was held that there had been no fraud, and that, if any wrongful acts had been done, they had been done accidentally or by inadvertence, and an injunction was refused, no order was made as to costs; and an appeal by the plaintiffs was dismissed with costs: *Lever v. Masbro' Equitable* (1912) 29 R.P.C. 33 and 225.

18-173 (3) Where an action was brought for infringement and passing off by the use of a label, and the defendants offered to submit to an injunction as regards the trade mark, but not as regards passing off by use of the mark, the plaintiffs were held entitled to go on and seek an injunction against passing off: *Hat Manufacturers v. Tomlin* (1906) 23 R.P.C. 413; but plaintiffs who in such a case accepted the offer, but afterwards continued the action as regards passing off, were ordered to pay the costs from the date of the offer: *Vernon v. Buchanan's* (1906) 23 R.P.C. 17.

18-174 (4) Where wharfingers with whom the spuriously marked goods had been warehoused in the ordinary course of trade, and who were entitled to a lien for their charges, were added as defendants, and the plaintiffs proceeded to trial against them, the Court of Appeal, reversing Fry J., ordered that their costs of action should be paid by the plaintiffs: *Moet v. Pickering* (1878) 8 Ch.D. 372.

18-175 (5) In a trivial case, where an action had been commenced without notice against the innocent purchaser of an inconsiderable quantity of spuriously marked goods, and he at once submitted to do as the court directed, costs were refused: *American Tobacco v. Guest* [1892] 1 Ch. 630; 9 R.P.C. 218.[63]

---

[63] *cf. Rose v. Loftus* (1878) 47 L.J.Ch. 576.

Other instances

Costs have been refused to a successful claimant because he claimed an **18–176** injunction too wide in its terms.[64] Where the plaintiffs set up claims to a copyright in a music tutor, as well as an exclusive right to its title, and failed as to the copyright, they were allowed only half their taxed costs of action.[65] On similar grounds, claimants have been ordered to pay,[66] or have been deprived of,[67] the costs occasioned by allegations which they have failed to prove, although they have succeeded and obtained the general costs of their actions. But where the plaintiff, in an action for infringing his trade mark and also for passing off, failed as regards the infringement in respect of some of the goods for which he used, but had not registered, the trade mark, and succeeded as to the rest of the action, and the defendant was held to have been guilty of deliberate infringement in breach of an undertaking previously given by him, the plaintiff was not deprived of his costs.[68] If the claimant's case had been overlaid with unnecessary evidence, he may be deprived of the costs of such evidence.[69] Where a claimant, acting reasonably, launches a motion for an interim injunction, but the position changes before the hearing, so that he no longer seeks relief, the appropriate course may be to adjourn the application to the trial of the action with the costs of both parties being costs in the case.[70]

Defendant deprived of costs

(1) Successful defendants have been deprived of their costs where **18–177** the evidence made it clear that they had acted, or intended to act, dishonestly.[71] Thus, where features of the defendants' wrapper had been taken from the plaintiffs', but not so as to infringe the plaintiffs' rights, the Court of Appeal, whilst dismissing the action and giving the defendants the costs of their successful appeal, refused to give them costs of the action: *Lever v. Bedingfield* (1899) 16 R.P.C. 3.

(2) In cases in which the claimant fails because he is carrying on a fraudulent trade, and the defendant stands in *pari delictu*, the practice has been to dismiss the action without costs.[72]

---

[64] In *Rodgers v. Rodgers* (1924) 41 R.P.C. 277, where the court was of the opinion that the case might never have been contested if the plaintiffs' claim had not been too wide, no costs were awarded.
[65] *Metzler v. Wood* (1878) 8 Ch.D. 606.
[66] *Saxlehner v. Apollinaris* [1897] 1 Ch. 893; 14 R.P.C. 645.
[67] *Montgomerie v. Young* (1903) 20 R.P.C. 781. On appeal the defendants wholly succeeded: (1904) 21 R.P.C. 285. In *O.T. v. Gumming* (1915) 32 R.P.C. 69 (Scot.) the plaintiffs, having failed in personal charges of fraud against the defendants, were given, although successful in the action, three-fourths only of their costs.
[68] *Jay v. Ladler* (1888) 40 Ch.D. 649; 6 R.P.C. 136, *Hodgson v. Kynoch* (1898) 15 R.P.C. 465.
[69] *Daimler v. London Daimler* (1907) 24 R.P.C. 379, plaintiffs given one-half costs of evidence.
[70] *Leng v. Gold Star* [1967] F.S.R. 75.
[71] As in *Claudius Ash v. Invicta* (1912) 29 R.P.C. 465, HL; (see at 470, 476) and *Lambert & Butler v. Goodbody* (1902) 19 R.P.C. 377 at 383. But there are limits to the discretion to deprive a successful defendant of its costs: *King v. Gillard* (1905) 22 R.P.C. 327 at 332 *et seq.* CA.
[72] *Newman v. Pinto* (1887) 4 R.P.C. 508; 57 L.T. 31, CA; *Thorneloe v. Hill* (1894) 11 R.P.C. 61.

18-178

(3) A successful defendant has been deprived of costs because he has made an unfounded charge of fraud.[73]

(4) Where defendants in a passing-off action, represented by the same solicitors, severed in defence, and the taxing master disallowed some of the costs of separate defences and the briefs at the trial on the ground that the companies and their defences were practically identical, it was held that this was a matter which the court had power to review, that the defences were not practically identical, and that the items should not have been altogether struck out: *Spalding v. Gamage* [1914] 2 Ch. 405; 31 R.P.C. 431.

Immediate payment of costs

18-179 There are two methods under the CPR by which immediate payment of costs by a successful party may be achieved. In relation to hearings of less than a day, the judge or master hearing the application ought usually to assess the costs himself and order payment.[74] Where an order for costs is made in a party's favour but detailed assessment is ordered, the court may make an order for an amount to be paid on account.[75]

Certificate of contested validity

18-180 Section 73 of the 1994 Act (section 60 of the 1938 Act was to the same effect) provides that in any proceedings before the court in which the validity of the registration of a registered trade mark is contested and is decided in favour of the proprietor of the trade mark, the court may certify to that effect. In any subsequent proceeding in which the validity of the registration comes into question the proprietor of the trade mark on obtaining a final order or judgment in his favour is entitled to have his full costs "as between solicitor and client", unless the court directs that he ought not to have them.[76]

18-181 As the CPR now stands, however, whilst it is hardly open to the rules to override the Act, there would seem to be no machinery for giving effect to the specific provision as to costs "as between solicitor and client": the court may order costs to be assessed either on the standard or on the indemnity basis: CPR, rule 44.4. It therefore seems that in practice the only order which can be made is for assessment on the indemnity basis which does, in practice, give the successful party an appreciably higher level of return.

---

[73] *Hargreaves v. Freeman* [1891] 3 Ch. 39; 8 R.P.C. 237, but *cf. King v. Gillard* [1905] 2 Ch. 7; 21 R.P.C. 589; 22 R.P.C. 327.

[74] CPR, Part 44PD, paras 4.3 and 4.4.

[75] CPR, r. 44.3(8), and see *Mars v. Teknowledge* [2000] F.S.R. 138.

[76] Instances of grant of a certificate were *Imperial Tobacco v. De Pasquali* (1918) 35 R.P.C. 185, CA; *Bentley v. Lagonda* (1947) 64 R.P.C. 33; *Pan Press* (1948) 65 R.P.C. 193; *Manus v. Fullwood & Bland* (1948) 65 R.P.C. 329.

The validity of a trade mark may be affected by events occurring at any time, so that although validity may have been established in one case, there may subsequently arise further grounds for questioning validity, and this may be a reason for certifying in later proceedings that solicitor and client costs should not be ordered. **18–182**

Under the 1938 Act, a certificate was granted where the question of validity was argued, although there was no application to revoke or rectify.[77] The grant is a matter of discretion and has been refused where an application to rectify was abandoned without argument.[78] An application to rectify the Register under section 26 of the 1938 Act on the grounds of non-use was held not to attack validity, so that on its failure a certificate was not given.[79] **18–183**

The order granting a certificate was held not to be appealable under earlier Acts.[80]

15. Appeal

Stay pending appeal

Where a claimant is successful at trial he is usually entitled to an injunction pending appeal, and the onus is on the defendant to apply for a stay. The application for a stay is dealt with on much the same principles as an application for an interim injunction, in the sense that the court must do the best it can to secure justice in the long term, having regard to the fact that its decision may be overturned in the Court of Appeal.[81] However, the fact that the claimant has been successful is the most material factor to bear in mind, and it should be appreciated that a stay deprives the successful claimant, at least for a while, of the fruits of success. A claimant who successfully resists a stay must normally give a cross undertaking in damages.[82] In some cases, the defendant will be required to secure moneys for the payment of damages as a term of the stay.[83] **18–184**

A stay of an order for delivery up is more readily granted, for obvious practical reasons, providing that satisfactory steps can be taken to **18–185**

[77] *Major v. Franklin* (1908) 25 R.P.C. 406.
[78] Certificate refused in *Bourne v. Swan and Edgar* (1903) 20 R.P.C. 105.
[79] *Lever v. Sunniwite* (1949) 66 R.P.C. 84. See also *Parkington* (1946) 63 R.P.C. 171, where an application was made to limit the area of use of the registered mark under the 1938 Act, s.26(2), and it was held that the applicant's use had not been honest concurrent use within the meaning of s.12(2) of that Act. A certificate of validity was refused.
[80] *Haslam v. Hall* (1888) 5 R.P.C. 144 (a patent case where the court had found the patent partially invalid). The point there taken by the CA, that their jurisdiction is limited to appeals from judgments and orders (which a certificate is not) would seem equally relevant to the current Supreme Court Act 1981.
[81] See *Minnesota Mining and Manufacturing v. Johnson & Johnson* [1976] R.P.C. 671, CA; *Minnesota Mining and Manufacturing v. Rennicks* [1992] R.P.C. 331.
[82] *ibid.*
[83] As in *"Oxford Marmalade", CPC v. Keenan* [1986] F.S.R. 527, where the defendant undertook to pay 10 per cent of receipts into a joint account.

prevent the goods in question from entering circulation in the meantime.[84]

18–186   An inquiry as to damages or an account of profits is not usually stayed pending appeal, and a claimant who wishes to press ahead with one is normally entitled to do so at his own risk as to costs should the decision in his favour be overturned on appeal. The same applies to an assessment of costs.[85]

18–187   A stay of the injunction pending an appeal from the Court of Appeal to the House of Lords, the defendants undertaking to keep an account, was granted in a patent case on the ground of difference of opinion in the court, coupled with the fact that there was no possible doubt as to the plaintiffs getting their damages if an appeal failed: *Consolidated Pneumatic v. Dark*.[86]

Interim injunction continued over appeal

18–188   In a case where the plaintiffs were disputing the right of the defendant to certain marks registered in his name, but failed both at the trial and in the Court of Appeal, the judge of first instance suspended over the appeal the discharge of an interim injunction against dealing with the marks; the Court of Appeal, whilst granting leave to appeal to the House of Lords, refused to continue the injunction, the defendants having offered undertakings: *Adrema-Werke v. Custodian of Enemy Property*.[87]

Appeal expedited

18–189   In a case where the defendant desired to appeal against an injunction which the plaintiff had obtained, the court on his application, and on the ground that the continuance of the injunction would do irreparable damage to his business, advanced the case to the head of the list.[88]

Stay of order for new trial

18–190   An application to stay a new trial ordered to take place by the Court of Appeal, pending an appeal against the order to the House of Lords, was refused in *Edge v. Johnson*.[89]

---

[84] *e.g.* granted in *Parker and Smith v. Satchwell* (1901) 18 R.P.C. 299, where the delivery up was stayed, although a stay of the injunction was refused. Also *Presto v. Orme, Evans* (1900) 17 R.P.C. 218 at 227; and *Gillette v. Anglo-American* (1912) 29 R.P.C. 341.
[85] *Minnesota Mining & Manufacturing v. Rennicks, supra; Lucas v. Gaedor* [1978] R.P.C. 389.
[86] (1907) 24 R.P.C. 593 at 640.
[87] [1956] R.P.C. 301 at 306; [1957] R.P.C. 49 at 60, CA.
[88] *Lazenby v. White* (1870) L.R. 6 Ch. 89, CA. But the main argument in the case, that if the defendant succeeded on the appeal he would not be compensated for the stopping of his business, is not in these days necessarily so cogent: the CA will, in a proper case, require the claimant to give a cross-undertaking in damages pending appeal.
[89] (1892) 9 R.P.C. 134.

Appeal in case of fraud

Where the judge of first instance has found, or has refused to find, **18–191** fraud, the Court of Appeal is usually very unwilling to reverse his finding; but there are some cases in which this has been done.

(1) In a trade name case a finding of fraud was reversed, the court **18–192** being able to act without relying on the evidence of the defendant, which the judge below had not believed: *Jamieson v. Jamieson* (1898) 15 R.P.C. 169.

(2) In a case in which the judge below found that the get-up of the defendants' goods was calculated to deceive, and expressed his dissatisfaction with the defendants' principal witness, and said that he could not exonerate the defendants from intention to deceive, the Court of Appeal held that these reflections were unjustified, and that the get-up was in fact not calculated to deceive: *Coleman v. Smith* [1911] 2 Ch 572; 28 R.P.C. 645; 29 R.P.C. 81.[90]

(3) In *Jif*,[91] the Court of Appeal held that the evidence before the **18–193** trial judge was not sufficient to support his findings of fraudulent intention by the defendants.

Costs of appeal

The costs of an appeal are normally given to the party succeeding in the **18–194** appeal, notwithstanding that there may have been good reason for depriving him of his costs below.[92]

16. Practice and evidence

Pleading

There is no reason to think that the CPR changes the principles set out **18–195** below, which are as much a matter of common sense and fairness as anything else, although it may be that pleadings will be fuller under the CPR than previously.

The ordinary rules as to pleadings apply to actions for the infringe- **18–196** ment of trade marks. If fraud is alleged it must be clearly pleaded.[93] Material facts only should be pleaded. Thus, for example, where a party alleges a continuing course of the exercise of quality control (so as to show a "connection in the course of trade") he need not give particulars of the vast number of details involved.[94]

---

[90] See also *Claudius Ash v. Invicta* (1911) 28 R.P.C. 252 and 597; (1912) 29 R.P.C. 465; *Williams v. Bronnley* (1909) 26 R.P.C. 481 and 765.
[91] [1990] R.P.C. 341.
[92] *Newman v. Pinto* (1887) 57 L.T. 31; 3 T.L.R. 685; 4 R.P.C. 508.
[93] See *e.g. Claudius Ash v. Invicta* (1912) 29 R.P.C. 465, HL.
[94] *General Electric v. Simplex-G.E.* [1971] R.P.C. 351; [1971] F.S.R. 106.

18–197   If the claimant alleges that actual deception has occurred, he will be ordered to give particulars of the person deceived.[95] So also if he relies upon trap orders. If the defendant pleads that the claimant's registration is invalid, he must give particulars of the invalidity alleged.[96]

18–198   Where a defendant alleges common use of the mark in question, he is likely to be ordered to give particulars of such use.[97] If reliance is placed by the defendant on use by other traders of marks with features similar to those of the claimant's mark, so as to support a contention that the claimant's right is limited to certain features, particulars of such use should be given.[98] Where a defendant alleges use by himself he may be ordered to give particulars of the user alleged.[99]

18–199   Where a defendant pleaded that the acts complained of were done by an employee outside his authority and contrary to express instructions given by the defendant, he was ordered to give particulars of the instructions.[1]

18–200   Where a defendant pleads that the words complained of are a bona fide description of the character or quality of his goods, he may be ordered to give particulars of the character or quality which the words describe.[2]

18–201   In a passing-off case in which the plaintiffs alleged that their cigars had come to be known by a name consequent on the use of red bands, they were ordered to give particulars of the date when the cigars first became so known.[3]

Disclosure of documents

18–202 The ordinary rules governing disclosure, set out in Part 31 of the CPR, also apply to trade mark actions. But a process which enables a rival trader to extract from his opponent information concerning his cus-

---

[95] *Humphries v. Taylor* (1888) 39 Ch.D. 693; 5 R.P.C. 687; *Whitstable Oyster Fishery v. Hayling* (1900) 17 R.P.C. 461; (1901) 18 R.P.C. 434; and where a claimant at the trial desires to give evidence of such a case which has not been pleaded, the defendant will generally be entitled to ask for an adjournment, as in *Lines Brothers v. Farris* (1925) 43 R.P.C. 64 at 68.

[96] Intellectual Property Proceedings Practice Direction, CPR Specialist Proceedings Practice Direction 2D, para. 24.2.

[97] *Aquascutum v. Moore* (1903) 20 R.P.C. 640; *Schweppes v. Gibbens* (1905) 22 R.P.C. 113 at 116. But if a defendant pleads that the article in question is generally known by the name which the claimant alleges is distinctive, and does not rely on particular users, he will not be ordered to give particulars of the general knowledge: *Boake Roberts v. Wayland* (1909) 26 R.P.C. 249. Formerly, in a passing-off case, a bare denial by the defendant of the claimant's allegation that a mark is distinctive of his goods will not entitle the claimant to ask for particulars of use by other traders (*La Radiotechnique v. Weinbaum* (1927) 44 R.P.C. 361), but this is likely to be changed under the CPR, certainly if the plea is not simply to found a case that the claimant's use has not been sufficiently extensive to make the mark distinctive, but is on the footing of a positive allegation that use by others is such that distinctiveness is lacking.

[98] *Willesden Varnish v. Young & Marten* (1922) 39 R.P.C. 285 at 289.

[99] *Beindorff v. Chambers* (1928) 45 R.P.C. 122.

[1] *Boston Marine v. Wheeler & Thomson* (1954) 71 R.P.C. 432 (passing-off case).

[2] *Coca Cola v. Duckworth* (1928) 45 R.P.C. 225.

[3] *Imperial Tobacco v. Purnell* (1903) 20 R.P.C. 719.

tomers, his trade, and his mode of doing business is extremely likely to be abused; whilst in cases where a large business is affected, even the ordinary order for disclosure of documents may be very oppressive.[4] The court, therefore, will, upon a proper case being shown, modify the common orders so that they shall occasion no more inconvenience to the party to whom they are directed than is necessary to ascertain the rights of his opponent.[5] These principles are now expressly reflected in the CPR, which limits the extent of standard disclosure,[6] and requires a search for documents which is no more than is reasonable in the circumstances, having regard to the number of documents involved, the nature and complexity of the proceedings, the ease and expense of retrieving the documents concerned, and the significance of documents likely to be found[7]. A party must make it clear what documents he has not felt it reasonable to search for.[8]

Documents given on disclosure may not be used for any purposes **18–203** other than the proceedings in which they are disclosed,[9] unless read or referred to in open court, or the court or the disclosing party (and the person to whom the document belongs, if different) gives permission. Under the old Rules of Court, permission to use disclosed documents for other purposes would only be given in exceptional circumstances,[10] and it seems that this standard is likely to be maintained, since the purpose of the rule is to encourage frank disclosure by giving proper protection to the disclosing party. An exception exists in relation to *"Anton Piller"* search orders, which may more readily, with permission, be used to commence proceedings against third parties shown by the seized material to be involved in infringing the claimant's rights.[11]

Disclosure of sales

Disclosure in regard to the sales effected by the defendant under the **18–204** disputed mark is not, in general, where the infringement is denied, material, until the fact that the mark is an infringement of the claimant's rights has been decided.[12] After an account of profits or an inquiry as to damages has been directed, full disclosure will generally be ordered, although in some cases, audited schedules of sales may be ordered instead, or by agreement.[13]

---

[4] *Wills* [1892] 3 Ch. 201; 9 R.P.C. 346, CA.
[5] *Andrew v. Kuehnrich* (1912) 29 R.P.C. 698, CA.
[6] r. 31.6.
[7] r. 31.7.
[8] r. 31.7(3).
[9] CPR, r. 31.22.
[10] *Crest Homes v. Marks* [1987] A.C. 289.
[11] See *Sony v. Anand; Seiko Time v. Domicrest* [1981] F.S.R. 398. By contrast see *Cobra v. Rata* [1997] F.S.R. 317, where leave to use documents obtained on an *Anton Piller* raid in support of contempt proceedings was refused.
[12] See *e.g. Benbow v. Low* (1880) 16 Ch.D. 93.
[13] *Leather Cloth v. Hirschfeld* (1865) 1 H. & M. 295; *Powell v. Birmingham Brewery* (1897) 14 R.P.C. 1; *Saccharin v. Chemicals and Drugs* [1900] 2 Ch. 556; 17 R.P.C. 612; *"Manus"* (1949) 66 R.P.C. 285.

18–205   Disclosure of the identity of suppliers or customers is not infrequently sought at an interim stage by a claimant seeking to trace the source and destination of goods which have passed through a defendant's hands. There is certainly jurisdiction to grant such an order,[14] but it will be exercised with care, and in particular it is usually easier to get disclosure of suppliers' names than customers, because that relief is more helpful to the claimant and less potentially damaging to the defendant.[15] Fear of violence by the person whose identity is ordered to be disclosed is not an answer to such an application except in extraordinary circumstances: *Coca Cola v. Gilbey.*[16]

"Anton Piller," "Mareva" and similar orders

18–206 During the 1970s the courts evolved a number of remedies of particular value in cases of serious or deliberate violations of industrial property rights. In particular it is now possible in strong cases to obtain orders, without notice being given to the defendant, requiring the defendant to permit the claimant's solicitors to search premises for infringing goods or documents relating thereto[17] and to require the defendant forthwith to disclose his source of supply of such goods[18]. Similarly there is power to "freeze" a defendant's assets where there is evidence of a risk that such assets will be dissipated before a money judgment can be enforced.[19]

18–207   These orders are now, under the CPR, referred to as "search orders" and "freezing orders", respectively, and are provided for by rule 25(1)(f) and (g) of the CPR. A considerable body of authority in relation to them has grown up since their invention, and the reader is referred to specialised works on the topic.[20]

Disclosure against a third party

18–208 There is power to order disclosure of the identity of the true tortfeasor against an innocent third party who gets "mixed up" in transactions relating to infringing goods.[21] This includes the jurisdiction to order disclosure so as to enable the claimant to effect service when he already knows the identity of the intended defendant.[22]

---

[14] *Lagenes v. It's At* [1991] F.S.R. 492.
[15] *Jade v. Antiference* [1996] F.S.R. 461; *Sega v. Alca* [1982] F.S.R. 516; *Charles of the Ritz v. Jory* [1986] F.S.R. 14.
[16] [1996] F.S.R. 23.
[17] *Anton Piller v. Manufacturing Processes* [1976] Ch. 55; [1976] R.P.C. 71.
[18] *EMI v. Sarwar* [1976] F.S.R. 146.
[19] The *"Mareva"* injunction, the power to grant which was specifically confirmed by the Supreme Court Act 1981, s.37(3).
[20] See *e.g. Gee on Mareva and Anton Piller Orders,* (4th ed).
[21] *Norwich Pharmacal v. Customs & Excise* [1974] A.C. 133; [1974] R.P.C. 101, HL. And see now CPR, rr. 31.17 and 18.
[22] *Coca Cola v. BT* [1999] F.S.R. 518: disclosure in relation to mobile telephone customer ordered so as to effect service.

Interim injunction against innocent third party

There is also power to obtain an interim injunction against a third party, **18–209** for example a carrier, who happens to have custody or control of goods which infringe a claimant's rights.[23] Reference should also be made to the section above dealing with applications for delivery up under section 19 of the 1994 Act.[24]

Documents referred to in the pleadings, etc.

Production and inspection of copies of documents which are referred to **18–210** in any statement of case, witness statement, witness summary or affidavit may be ordered.[25]

Evidence of title

Registration is prima facie evidence of the validity of the original **18–211** registration and of all assignments and transmissions of the mark (section 72 of the 1994 Act).

Trap orders

In general, proof of a single act of infringement by the defendant is **18–212** sufficient to justify the claimant in bringing his action, and the evidence relied on is frequently the sale by the defendant of the spurious goods to the claimant or his agent, who has bought them merely for the purpose of procuring evidence. Though orders of this sort, generally referred to as "trap orders", have not infrequently been the subject of unfavourable comment, they are often the only means by which evidence can be obtained, and, if they are fairly given, there is no impropriety in adopting this procedure.[26] The object is to show what the defendant is doing or what is likely to be the result of some ambiguous advertisement or marking, and the orders must, therefore, be fairly given, and of a character which is not unlikely to occur in ordinary practice.[27] Orders

---

[23] *Norwich Pharmacal v. Customs & Excise* in the CA at [1974] A.C. 133 at 146; [1972] R.P.C. 743. The decision in the HL does not affect this point. See also *Washburn v. Cunard* (1889) 6 R.P.C. 398 and *Smith, Kline & French v. Harbottle* [1980] R.P.C. 363.

[24] See paras 18–122 *et seq.*, above.

[25] CPR, r. 31.14.

[26] *Wakefield v. Purser* (1934) 51 R.P.C. 167 at 171; *Walt Disney Productions v. Gurvitz* [1982] F.S.R. 446 (a contempt case). In *Marie Claire v. Hartstone* [1993] F.S.R. 692, the defendant argued that the plaintiff's solicitors had practised a deception during their involvement in a trap purchase. Chadwick J held that there was nothing, from the perspective of the court, wrong in the solicitors' involvement, since the plaintiff itself would have been entitled to make the trap order, and if nothing else the solicitor's presence ensured an accurate record. He pointed out, however, that the deceptive nature of the trap order might be a matter for the Law Society. See Chap. 22, in relation to the potential impact of human rights issues on the use of trap orders.

[27] *Californian Fig Syrup v. Taylor's* (1897) 14 R.P.C. 564, CA; *Carr v. Crisp* (1902) 19 R.P.C. 497, Byrne J.

in writing, where they are practicable, are to be preferred; but in a class of business where orders are nearly always oral, a written order may inevitably arouse suspicion and, therefore, be of no practical use. In all cases the defendant should be promptly informed as to what is alleged to have occurred so that he may have the opportunity of investigating the incidents while the recollection of those concerned is fresh.[28] All the circumstances surrounding trap orders have to be scrutinised with great care.[29] The courts will not necessarily grant relief in respect of isolated instances which may not be sufficient to prove any apprehension that passing-off is likely to occur, and the needs of the case may sometimes be met by a special order as to costs.[30]

Stay of other proceedings

18–213 Where High Court proceedings involve the same or very similar issues to those raised in proceedings in an inferior tribunal such as the Registry, an injunction may be granted restraining a party from pursuing those other proceedings, as happened in *Sears v. Sears Roebuck*.[31]

---

[28] e.g. *Fox's Glacier Mints v. Jobbings* (1932) 49 R.P.C. 352; *Hampshire v. General Kaputine* (1930) 47 R.P.C. 437 at 444; *Broad v. Cast Iron Drainage* [1970] F.S.R. 363.

[29] *Stillitz v. Jones and Higgins* (1943) 60 R.P.C. 15 at 17.

[30] *Hennessy v. Kennett* (1877) Seb.Dig. at 331, Malins V.-C.; *cf. Leahy, Kelly v. Glover* (1893) 10 R.P.C. 141, HL, where a single instance of the sale of goods by the defendant's shopwoman, not shown to have been with his authority, was considered insufficient to support a case of passing off; *Rutter v. Smith* (1901) 18 R.P.C. 49; and *Knight v. Crisp* (1904) 21 R.P.C. 671 similar cases; *Burberry v. Watkinson* (1906) 23 R.P.C. 141, an isolated instance of mistake; and *Armstrong Oiler v. Patent Axlebox* (1910) 27 R.P.C. 362, an isolated instance of a mistake by a workman, and the plaintiffs, who failed on the rest of the case, were ordered to pay the costs, except so far as they had, down to the giving of an undertaking, been increased by this complaint. See also *Carr v. Crisp* (1902) 19 R.P.C. 497, where Byrne J. said that if one instance only had been proved he would have followed *Leahy v. Glover*; and *Kodak v. Grenville* (1908) 25 R.P.C. 416, where the only question was as to costs; *cf. Hennessy v. Neary* (1902) 19 R.P.C. 36 (Ireland). In *French v. Rhind* [1958] R.P.C. 82 (a passing-off case) it was contended that the manner of conducting the oral trap order was unsatisfactory; but unsuccessfully, following *Pearson v. Valentine* (1917) 34 R.P.C. 267, where it was held that it was not sufficient for a person who receives an order for a particular brand to send another brand and leave it to the customer to find out himself that it is a different brand. See further *L'Oreal v. Coiffeur Supplies* [1961] R.P.C. 219 (interim injunctions granted on a single written trap order); *Cellular Clothing v. White* (1953) 70 R.P.C. 9 (*arguendo*, observations on possible ambiguities in trap orders; need to give notice at once); and contrast *Bostitch v. McGarry & Cole* [1964] R.P.C. 173 at 177 with *Hilti v. Ucan* [1963] R.P.C. 160; [1964] R.P.C. 206 (both cases of defendants who had ceased to sell goods bearing the plaintiffs' mark; in "Bostitch", there was delivery of the defendants' goods on written trap orders for the plaintiffs', interim injunction granted; in "Hilti", such an injunction was refused on a single trap order—in writing, but handed over, not sent by post—and again on a verbal trap order, there being a conflict of evidence). See also *Showerings v. Blackpool Tower* [1975] F.S.R. 40.

[31] [1993] R.P.C. 385, since upheld in the Court of Appeal (where the Registry had refused a stay) and see generally Chap. 5, for the circumstances in which the Registry will itself order a stay.

CHAPTER 19

CRIMINAL PROCEEDINGS

1. Outline

The Trade Marks Act 1994 creates two main categories of offences. The **19–01** first, which is likely to be of far greater practical importance of the two, concerns "unauthorised" use of a trade mark (sections 92 and 93). It is primarily aimed at counterfeiting, but as will be suggested below, it seems that the definitions of the offences created are so broad that many other kinds of behaviour will or may also amount to a criminal offence. Similar offences—but of more restricted scope—were previously provided for by the Copyright, Designs and Patents Act 1988,[1] which was added by amendment as sections 58A to 58D into the Trade Marks Act 1938.

The second category of offence concerns making false statements **19–02** about the registered status of a mark, either by falsifying the Register or entries in it (section 94 of the 1994 Act), or by representing that a mark is registered when in fact it is not (section 95). Similar provisions were contained in the 1938 Act.[2]

In addition, it is an offence to make unauthorised use of the Royal **19–03** arms (section 99 of the 1994 Act).

This chapter also covers forfeiture of counterfeit goods (sections 97 and 98).

2. Offences involving unauthorised use

Unauthorised use—general scheme of section 92

Subsections (1) to (3) of section 92 of the 1994 Act, each create separate **19–04** offences. In outline,[3] subsection (1) concerns applying an offending mark to goods or dealing in or keeping goods carrying such a mark; subsection (2) concerns the making use or keeping of packaging or documents bearing an offending mark, and subsection (3) concerns making or keeping articles designed for reproducing an offending mark.

---

[1] s.300.
[2] ss.59 and 60.
[3] The acts to which each of the subsections relate are considered in more detail in paras 19–20 et seq.

19–05   The offences created by the section all require that the defendant's use be in relation to goods. It is not an offence to misuse a mark in relation to services, or in the creation of advertising or other materials for services.[4]

19–06   It is an important feature of the subsections that the elements of the offences do not include a requirement of infringement of the mark in question within the meaning of Part I of the Act. Subsection (5), which is discussed below, provides a defence only if the defendant believed on reasonable grounds that his acts were not infringements. It does not create a general defence of non-infringement.

19–07   This is to be contrasted with the provisions of the 1938 Act introduced by the Copyright, Designs and Patents Act 1988. Section 58A, subsections (1) and (2) each required that the defendant not be entitled to use the mark on the goods in question, *i.e.* that his use must infringe. In addition, it was independently a defence for him to show that he had believed on reasonable grounds that he was entitled to use the mark, even if his belief was wrong.[5]

19–08   It does not seem to be an element of any of the offences under section 92 of the 1994 Act, that the defendant mislead or intend to mislead his customers into thinking that the goods in which he is dealing or intending or preparing to deal, are genuine. The offences will be committed even if the defendant's customers are well aware that the goods are counterfeit. This will avoid the problems which have arisen in some cases under the Trade Descriptions Act where defendants have avoided liability by selling counterfeit goods at stalls bearing a warning that the goods are fake.[6]

19–09   For the purposes of section 92, "registered trade mark" includes both Community trade marks and protected international trade marks (UK).[7]

Mens rea

19–10   There is no requirement of dishonest conduct in the definitions of these offences. Save in respect of section 92(2) and (3) of the 1994 Act, the only *mens rea* required is that the defendant act with a view to gain for himself or with intent to cause loss to another.[8] It appears that the first

---

[4] In principle, it seems it would be possible to commit an offence by using on goods a mark identical to one registered in respect only of services, provided that the mark was a famous one, since s.92(4)(b), discussed below, contains no limitation to marks registered in respect of goods.

[5] s.58A(3).

[6] See *Kent County Council v. Price* [1993] 9 E.I.P.R. D–224, a Trade Descriptions Act case, and contrast *Akhtar v. Grout* (1998) 10 I.P.R. 714, a prosecution under s.92, where the defendant, who was convicted, described his counterfeit goods to persons making a trap purchase by saying that "They are not real, but they are good." See, below, however, as to the situation where the marks are not identical. See also *Torbay Council v. Satnam Singh* [2000] F.S.R. 158 at 161, for a statement concerning the policy of these provisions which is in keeping with the above approach.

[7] Community Trade Mark Regulations 1996 reg. 7 (S.I. 1996 No. 1908), Trade Marks (International Registration) Order 1996, art. 17 (S.I. 1996 No. 714).

[8] s.92(1) also requires that keeping material marked with an offending sign in the course of a business be "with a view" to dealing in the goods. This is probably an objective test and is unlikely to be of much practical significance.

716

limb of this test will virtually always be satisfied if the defendant's acts are done for any kind of commercial purpose, including selling or advertising goods bearing an offending mark, or keeping them with a view to selling them.

Section 92(2) requires, in addition, that the materials to which the **19–11** mark is applied be intended to be used for labelling or packaging goods, or as a "business paper",[9] or for advertising goods. This is very likely to be evident from the materials themselves.

Section 92(3) requires, in addition to having a view to gain or **19–12** intention to cause loss, that the defendant knows or had reason to believe that the article specifically designed or adapted to copy the offending mark has been used or is intended to be used to produce goods or material for labelling or packaging goods, or as a business paper in relation to goods, or for advertising goods.[10] There is no requirement that the defendant knows that the use of materials made with the article in question would be wrongful.

The overall result is that in many, and perhaps most, practical cases, **19–13** the *mens rea* of these offences will follow almost automatically from the commission of the offending act, and a defendant who believed that his acts did not infringe will bear the onus of proving that that was the case, under section 92(5). In addition, he will have to prove that he had reasonable grounds for such a belief. What those grounds might be is considered below.[11] A defendant who gives no thought to whether his acts would infringe, but had no reason to believe that they did, will be in danger of committing an offence without any ill motive at all. For this reason alone, it appears that section 92 goes well beyond counterfeiting.[12]

Marks need not be identical

In addition to the readily satisfied requirements of the *mens rea* of these **19–14** offences, it should be noted that the offending mark does not have to be identical to the registered mark in question: it may be merely "likely to be mistaken" for it. This expression is not the same as that used in the section of the 1994 Act dealing with infringement by use of a similar

---

[9] This rather clumsy term presumably covers documents such as invoices, delivery notes, catalogues and the like.

[10] The subsection is unclear as to whether the defendant must know or have reason to believe that the mark will be used on goods for which the relevant registered trade mark is in fact registered (use on goods for which it is not registered will not normally be an offence, because of the operation of subsection (4)), or merely for goods generally. It is suggested that the former is the better view, since it would be strange if a person committed an offence by creating material for copying a mark whose use in due course could not itself be an offence. Of course, in many instances it will be perfectly clear from the surrounding circumstances that the mark was intended to be used on goods for which the relevant registered mark was registered.

[11] Para. 19–31, below.

[12] This appears to be the view of the courts: see *Torbay Council v. Satnam Singh* [2000] F.S.R. 158.

mark.[13] Presumably the test applied will be similar in practical terms to that used in infringement actions, although if anything the language used in section 92 suggests a somewhat narrower test, focusing solely on whether the marks are similar enough to be mistaken one for another. This was the intention of the legislature.[14]

19–15 The fact that the marks need not be identical and may be merely similar is another reason why section 92 extends well beyond counterfeiting. A requirement that the marks be absolutely identical would allow the section to be avoided too easily by counterfeiters, merely by a trivial change to the mark. However, the test used by the section means that a criminal offence may be committed by a person using a mark which the court finds is too similar to a registered mark, even if there were real differences between the marks, and there had been no conscious or dishonest copying of the registered mark in question.

19–16 Whether two non-identical marks are sufficiently close to one another for there to be a likelihood of confusion between them is frequently difficult to judge, and reasonable minds can honestly differ. Many infringement actions have taken place where a defendant has created his own mark with every honest intention, in ignorance of the registered mark in question, and the court has later found that the similarity is sufficient for there to be infringement.

19–17 It is unsatisfactory that the section is so likely to impose criminal liability on the defendant in such a situation, who very probably will not be able to prove that he believed on reasonable grounds that he would not be infringing, since he will not have considered the matter at all and will have had no grounds to think that he did not infringe. A defendant may be able to argue that it is not clear beyond a reasonable doubt that the offending sign is likely to be mistaken for the registered mark, but that is plainly an uncertain course, and it may perfectly well be that the sign in question is likely to be so mistaken, even though independently designed. However, the courts' approach seems to be set against accepting excuses from defendants which would be unduly difficult to refute, on the basis that it would deprive the provisions of their effectiveness in dealing with counterfeiters and the like.[15]

---

[13] s.10(2). See Chap. 13.

[14] H.L. Public Bill Committee, Fourth Sitting, January 20, 1994, col. 96. It is to be hoped that the question of whether the offending sign is likely to be mistaken for the registered mark in question is to be determined by reference to the sign and mark alone, though. If the surrounding circumstances are to be taken into account, then it might be that the problems associated with the Trade Descriptions Act 1968, where the defendant describes the offending goods as "brand copies", or otherwise makes it clear that they are not genuine, will recur: see the reference to *R v. Kent County Council, ex p. Price, supra*. It is also hard to see how the likely circumstances surrounding the ultimate sale to the public can be assessed in relation to a defendant who is prosecuted for applying the mark to the goods, or for keeping goods bearing an offending sign.

[15] See *Torbay Council v. Satnam Singh* [2000] F.S.R. 158 at 161.

Requirement that the proprietor did not consent

Subsections (1) to (3), of section 92 of the 1994 Act, each stipulate that **19–18** the defendant must have acted without the consent of the proprietor of the registered trade mark in question. The drafting of the subsections make it clear that this is a positive element of the offence for the prosecution to prove, rather than a defence on which the defendant bears the onus.

This may be of some significance in cases where a defendant is **19–19** dealing in goods which are very similar to the proprietor's genuine goods, or where he is dealing in "grey" goods. In such situations it can be quite difficult, even in civil proceedings, to prove whether the goods are genuine or fake, or whether their sale in the United Kingdom was consented to by the proprietor, explicitly or impliedly. Proving these matters to the criminal standard will of course be much more difficult still.

Acts constituting offences under section 92

Subsection 92(1) of the 1994 Act makes it an offence to: **19–20**

(a) apply to goods or their packaging a sign identical to, or likely to be mistaken for, a registered trade mark, or

(b) sell or let for hire, offer or expose for sale or hire or distribute, goods which bear, or the packaging of which bears, such a sign, or

(c) have in the defendant's possession, custody or control in the course of a business any such goods with a view to the doing of anything, by himself or another, which would be an offence under (b).

As one would expect, the offence is committed whether the offending **19–21** sign is on the goods themselves or on their packaging. But it does not appear that the offence is committed by selling unlabelled goods in connection with documents such as invoices which describe the goods by reference to the offending sign. That situation would be covered by subsection (2).

Keeping unauthorised goods under subsection (1)(c) is only an offence **19–22** if done in the course of a business. This limitation is necessary to prevent consumers who buy counterfeit goods from committing an offence in keeping the goods at their homes. By necessary implication, though, it means that consumers who privately sell on counterfeit goods which they have bought (even a single item), even if they did not know that the goods were counterfeit, may be committing an offence.

Subsection (1)(c) also only makes it an offence to keep goods or their **19–23** packaging bearing an offending sign if it is with a view to dealing in them by way of sale, hire or the like under subsection (1)(b). This means that some limited categories of business may be entitled lawfully to keep infringing materials, for example for the purposes of scrapping or recycling them.

19–24 Subsection (2) makes it an offence to:

(a) apply a sign identical to, or likely to be mistaken for, a registered trade mark to material intended to be used—

    (i) for labelling or packaging goods,
    (ii) as a business paper in relation to goods, or
    (iii) for advertising goods, or

(b) use in the course of business material bearing such a sign in relation to goods, or for advertising goods, or

(c) have in the defendant's possession, custody or control in the course of a business any such material with a view to the doing of anything, by himself or another, which would be an offence under (b).

19–25 As has been mentioned above, "business paper" is a curious term. It is not further defined in the 1994 Act. It appears that the term was probably used with the intention of covering all kinds of documents which might bear a trade mark and be used in connection with goods, so as to cover invoices, price lists and so on. There is nothing, however, in the subsection to require that the "business paper" be of a kind likely to be seen by a customer, although such papers are plainly covered. So, for example, the internal papers of a business such as inventory lists, which no customer would ever be likely to see, would seem to fall within the definition.

19–26 Subsection (3) makes it an offence to:

(a) make an article specifically designed or adapted for making copies of a sign identical to, or likely to be mistaken for, a registered trade mark, or

(b) have such an article in the defendant's possession, custody or control in the course of a business.

The defendant must also know that the article has been, or is to be used to produce goods, or material for labelling or packaging goods, as a business paper in relation to goods, or for advertising goods.

The goods in question; well-known marks

19–27 By section 92(4), no offence is committed under section 92 unless the goods in question are those for which the trade mark concerned is registered, or the trade mark "has a reputation in the United Kingdom and the use of the sign takes or would take unfair advantage of, or is or would be detrimental to, the distinctive character or the repute of the trade mark". The degree of repute required to satisfy this test is considered in Chapters 8 and 13.

The second limb of section 92(4) echoes the words of section 10(3).[16] **19–28** Its effect will be that an offence may be committed by the use of well-known marks on goods for which they are not registered, and this is likely to be of particular importance in connection with the sale of counterfeit souvenir items of small value which are not the kind of goods produced by the registered proprietor.

Proof that the use of a mark in such circumstances takes unfair **19–29** advantage of it will often follow from the fact that the defendant is using the presence of the mark to sell his goods and turn a profit. Alternatively, use of a prestigious mark on cheap counterfeits may well be detrimental to its repute. These are not matters which are likely to cause any great practical problems of proof.

However, proving the existence of a reputation in the context of a **19–30** criminal prosecution and to the criminal standard of proof may be difficult in practice.[17] Much of the evidence relied upon in civil proceedings to prove reputation would not be admissible in criminal proceedings, in particular because of the hearsay rules.

Defence of reasonable belief of non-infringement

Section 92(5) provides that: **19–31**

> "It is a defence for a person charged with an offence under this section to show that he believed on reasonable grounds that the use of the sign in the manner in which it was used, or was to be used, was not an infringement of the registered trade mark."

The onus of proof is plainly on the person charged. It appears at first reading that the test is two-fold. First, the defendant must have in fact believed that his acts did not or would not infringe. That appears to be a subjective test. Secondly, the defendant must have had reasonable grounds for that belief.

The subsection does not say that the defence is made out if the **19–32** defendant merely proves that there was in fact no infringement. It appears that if a person "takes a chance" on whether the goods infringe, he can be guilty of an offence even if he would have a defence to civil proceedings brought by the proprietor.

A potentially difficult question arises in relation to a person dealing in **19–33** goods who never turns his mind to the issue of whether they infringe or not. There is nothing in the subsection to indicate that the defence extends to such a person, even if there were reasonable grounds

---

[16] See Chap. 13.
[17] Unless the court can be persuaded to take judicial notice of the reputation of extremely well-known marks such as Coca-Cola and the like.

available to him for believing that the goods did not infringe had he inquired.

19–34 However, it should be appreciated that the subsection surely does not require a trader to give his mind to the law of registered trade marks in conducting his business. He must be entitled to some extent to form a lay view of the situation, particularly if the issue is whether the goods are genuine or not, and the purchaser has no reason to think that they are not. So a trader who buys full price goods bearing a registered mark from a reputable source, perhaps one of the trade mark proprietor's own distributors, should be entitled to say "I did not think about the law specifically, but I thought that these were 'genuine' goods because of where they came from". Of course, the situation would be different if the goods were bought at an unusually low price or from a "grey" importer.

19–35 On the other hand, what of a defendant who obtains legal advice that his dealings in goods bearing a trade mark do not infringe, or reaches that conclusion himself on considering the law? This will have little significance in relation to outright counterfeiting cases, but as is observed above, the offences under section 92 cover many other kinds of behaviour.

19–36 Assuming that the defendant properly instructed his lawyers about the facts[18] (or that his own deliberations were reasonably competent), it may well be that the defence under section 92(5) would be available.

19–37 Although ignorance of the *criminal* law is not a defence, a mistake about the *civil* law can negative *mens rea*.[19]

A belief that the trade mark in question is not registered does not provide a defence under this provision: see *Torbay Council v. Satnam Singh* [2000] F.S.R. 158.

Evidence

19–38 Expert evidence is admissible both in relation to whether the goods concerned are genuine and, apparently, as to whether they would infringe the trade mark concerned: *Akhtar v. Grout* (1998) 10 I.P.R. 714 at 717–718. The second proposition is rather puzzling, and the case is probably best understood as being to the effect that expert evidence is

---

[18] Legal advice based on erroneous instructions would surely not provide "reasonable" grounds for a belief that the acts would not infringe, especially if the instructions given were deliberately wrong or incomplete.

[19] See, *e.g. R. v. Smith (David Raymond)* [1974] Q.B. 354, where a mistaken belief as to the ownership of property was a defence to a charge of criminal damage. And see generally Archbold, 1999 edition, section 17–22 at page 1503. It is suggested that the position under s.92 is different from that under the civil provisions of the Copyright, Designs and Patents Act 1988 (and previously the Copyright Act 1956). There, what is required is knowledge of the facts, not an appreciation of the legal conclusion which would follow from them: see, *e.g. Sillitoe v. McGraw Hill* [1983] F.S.R. 545. However, s.92 draws a distinction between the reasonable grounds and the objective belief of the defendant; they are separate matters. In addition, being a criminal provision it should be construed more narrowly.

admissible on the question of whether the public is likely to mistake the offending signs for the registered marks. For some reason the justices did not make a finding as to whether the offending signs and the registered marks were identical (at 716D-E), and therefore received evidence on the issue of whether the signs were likely to be mistaken for the marks. To decide that issue, the court held that they were entitled to hear evidence as to whether the signs infringed the marks.

3. Offences of unauthorised use—procedure

Who can prosecute; relationship with civil proceedings

Under section 6(1) of the Prosecution of Offences Act 1985, any person[20] **19–39** can bring a prosecution under section 92 of the 1994 Act.[21]

As a result, the trade mark proprietor may himself bring a private prosecution. In counterfeiting cases, there is nothing wrong with this, but because of the wide scope of section 92 there is a risk that trade mark owners will bring private prosecutions against other traders where there has been no dishonesty, and the question of whether there is infringement is genuinely debatable, perhaps because of differences between the two marks in question. A trade mark owner might opt for a prosecution instead of or as well as a civil proceedings in such circumstances for a number of reasons. One might be cost, but another less palatable reason would be to put pressure on the defendant.

There has been a recent trend for copyright owners to bring private **19–40** prosecutions in cases which would more normally be the subject of civil proceedings.

In *Thames & Hudson v. DACS* [1995] FSR 153, the defendant to **19–41** criminal proceedings, a well-known art publisher, reacted by seeking a declaration of non-infringement in the High Court, and an injunction restraining DACS from continuing with the prosecution. DACS had prosecuted all the directors of the company in the criminal proceedings, and it was said that that was done without inquiry as to who was actually responsible, and was an indication of a desire to pressurise the company. The court refused to stay the proceedings, on the basis that Parliament had elected to make certain kinds of copyright infringement a crime, and had not limited the statutory provisions to "pirates". However, the judgment also indicated that the High Court was a more suitable forum for determining such disputes, and that the magistrates might wish to adjourn the criminal proceedings pending the resolution of the High Court action.

---

[20] There is conflicting authority as to whether a corporation is a "person" for the purposes of being able to bring a prosecution. An unincorporated association clearly is not, though. See *R. v. Ealing Justices, ex p. Dixon* [1990] 2 Q.B. 91. This issue is mainly a formal one, though, since if a corporate trade mark owner wishes to bring a prosecution it can always do so by an employee.
[21] Although under the 1985 Act, s.6(2), the DPP can take over the conduct of any prosecution, and under s.23 he may thereafter decide not to proceed with it.

19–42 A similar approach may be expected under section 92, but there is an additional complication to be considered where there is an issue over the validity of the trade mark in question. Under section 92, the offence is only committed by the use of a "registered" mark. At least in relation to a declaration of invalidity under section 47 of the 1994 Act, and in many practical situations in relation to revocation under section 46, once a mark is revoked or declared invalid, its registration is treated as never having taken place.[22]

19–43 It would therefore appear that, in principle, revocation of the trade mark in question or a declaration of invalidity under section 46 or 47 would date back, and prevent the commission of an offence under section 92. However, it seems that the mark would actually have to be revoked or declared invalid, and only the Registrar or the court can do that.[23] "The court" is defined by section 75 as being, in England and Wales, the High Court.[24] A criminal court cannot therefore deal with revocation or a declaration of invalidity (and in any event its procedures are not suitable for doing so).

19–44 It would therefore seem that if a defendant wishes to challenge the validity of a trade mark as a defence under section 92,[25] there would have to be a stay of the criminal proceedings to allow an opportunity for that to be done in the High Court or the Registry.

Obligation on local weights and measures authority to enforce

19–45 Under section 93(1) of the 1994 Act, the local weights and measures authority in England and Wales is charged with enforcing within their areas the provisions of section 92. In Northern Ireland, the duty is on the Department of Economic Development.[26]

19–46 For the purposes of enforcing the provisions of section 92, they are given the same powers which they have under the Trade Descriptions Act 1968, sections 27, 28, 29 and 33. In addition, any enactment which

---

[22] s.46 actually provides that the "rights of the proprietor shall be deemed to have ceased" as from the date of the application to revoke, or any earlier date on which the Registrar or court is satisfied the grounds for revocation existed. This may leave open the possibility that a prosecution could be brought on a mark which is liable to be revoked, on the basis that the *registration* is not deemed never to have existed but only the proprietor's rights under it, although the distinction is at best a very fine one. Unless an application to revoke has been brought before a prosecution begins, a defendant relying on s.46 would have to show that the grounds for revocation existed at the time of the alleged offence. This situation seems to be potentially inconsistent with the Trade Marks Directive, Art. 11, which provides that a non-used mark liable to revocation for non-use should not have effect in infringement proceedings or in relation to relative grounds for refusal of registration.

[23] ss.46(4) and 47(3).

[24] Unless the context otherwise requires, and there is nothing in the context of ss.46 or 47 to change the meaning of "court". On the contrary, they obviously mean the High Court.

[25] Once registration was proved, validity would be presumed under s.72 of the Act, and the onus would be on the defendant to prove that the mark was liable to be revoked or was invalid.

[26] s.93(3).

authorises the disclosure of information for the purposes of enforcement of the Trade Descriptions Act 1968 also applies in relation to section 92 of the 1994 Act.[27]

Penalties and procedure under section 92

Offences under section 92 of the 1994 Act are triable either way.   **19–47**

On summary conviction, a defendant is liable to up to six months in prison, or a fine not exceeding the statutory maximum.[28]

On conviction on indictment, a defendant is liable to up to 10 years in **19–48** prison or an unlimited fine.[29] While 10 years in prison may seem like a severe sentence, there is authority in relation to copyright offences that they are serious offences of dishonesty akin to theft,[30] and counterfeiting may involve very large sums.

4. Falsifying the register

Falsification of register

By section 94(1) of the 1994 Act it is an offence to make, or cause to be **19–49** made, a false entry in the Register, knowing or having reason to believe it to be false. This refers to actually meddling with the Register itself, and it is not likely that this provision will be of much practical importance.

By section 94(2) it is an offence to make, or cause to be made, **19–50** anything which falsely purports to be a copy of an entry in the Register, or to tender, or cause to be tendered, in evidence such a thing, knowing or believing that the thing is false. This subsection would cover, for example, making a forged certificate of registration.

Penalties and procedure under section 94

Offences under section 94 of the 1994 Act are triable either way, and the **19–51** penalties are the same as under section 92, except that the maximum period of imprisonment following conviction on indictment is only two years.[31]

5. Falsely representing a mark as registered

Falsely representing mark as registered

Under section 95(1) of the 1994 Act, it is an offence falsely to represent a **19–52** mark as being registered when it is not, or to make a false representation as to the goods or services for which a mark is registered, knowing or having reason to believe that the representation is false.

---

[27] s.93(4).
[28] s.92(6)(a). The statutory maximum is presently £5,000: Criminal Justice Act 1982, s.37(2) as amended by the Criminal Justice Act 1991, s.17(2).
[29] 1994 Act, s.92(6)(b).
[30] *R. v. Carter* [1993] F.S.R. 303.
[31] s.94(3).

19–53   There is a presumption that the word "registered" or any other word or symbol importing a reference to registration (an example would be the R in a circle) is a representation as to registration. Since goods may find their way into the United Kingdom bearing marks which are registered abroad but not here, the presumption can be rebutted by showing that the reference is to registration abroad, and that there, in fact, is a foreign registration for the goods or services in question.[32]

19–54   It should also be noted that falsely representing that a mark is registered might affect a claim for passing off based on the mark in question.[33]

Penalties and procedure under section 95

19–55   Offences under section 95 of the 1994 Act are only triable summarily, and on conviction the maximum penalty is a fine at level 3 on the standard scale.[34]

CTMs and protected international trade marks (UK)

19–56   Virtually identical provisions apply to making misrepresentations about Community trade marks and protected international trade marks (UK).[35] The penalties are the same as under section 95 of the 1994 Act.

6. Forfeiture of counterfeit goods and the like

Forfeiture of counterfeit goods, etc.: overview

19–57   Sections 97 and 98 of the 1994 Act[36] give the criminal courts powers to order the forfeiture of goods, packaging materials, labelling materials or business papers bearing a mark the same as a registered trade mark[37] or likely to be mistaken for it. Articles designed for making copies of such a mark may also be forfeit.

19–58   The general scheme of the forfeiture powers is that goods, which come into the hands of a person in connection with the investigation or

---

[32] s.95(2).

[33] Interlocutory relief was refused on this basis in *Johnson v. Puffer* (1930) 47 R.P.C. 95. There is however no case where relief has been refused at trial on this basis, and it is doubtful whether this approach is in keeping with modern practice. See also *Jamieson v. Jamieson* (1898) 15 R.P.C. 169 at 191, *per* Vaughan Williams L.J.

[34] Presently £1,000: Criminal Justice Act 1982, s.37(2) as amended by the Criminal Justice Act 1991, s.17(2).

[35] Community Trade Mark Regulations 1996, reg. 8 (S.I. 1996 No. 1908), Trade Marks (International Registration) Order 1996 art. 18 (S.I. 1996 No. 714), Apps 14 and 20.

[36] s.97 sets out the powers of forfeiture for England, Wales and Northern Ireland, which are considered in more detail below. s.98 creates similar powers applicable in Scotland.

[37] "Registered trade mark" includes for these purposes a Community trade mark or a protected international trade mark (UK): Community Trade Mark Regulations 1996 reg. 7 (S.I. 1996 No. 1908), Trade Marks (International Registration) Order 1996 (as amended) art. 17 (S.I. 1996 No. 714), Apps 14 and 20.

prosecution of counterfeiting-type offences, can be forfeited by an order of the relevant court. The order can be made in the course of a prosecution, but it is not necessary that there should be a prosecution so long as it appears that an offence of the relevant kind has been committed in relation to the goods.[38]

Persons aggrieved by a forfeiture order are entitled to appeal against **19–59** it.[39]

Goods which are ordered to be forfeited are normally to be destroyed, but it is possible that instead the offending mark may merely be obliterated from them.

Circumstances in which a section 97 application can be made

An application under section 97 of the 1994 Act may be made whenever **19–60** any person comes into possession of goods of the kind described above in connection with the investigation or prosecution of a "relevant offence". "Relevant offence" includes any offence under section 92, or under the Trade Descriptions Act 1968, or any offence involving dishonesty or deception.[40]

It is not a requirement of section 97 of the 1994 Act that the goods in **19–61** question actually be counterfeit, so long as a relevant offence has been committed in relation to them.[41] Since theft is a relevant offence, for example, the section could extend to stolen goods even if it were unknown, or could not be proved, whether or not they were counterfeit.

It is also not a requirement that the goods in question should be in the **19–62** possession of the police or the prosecution. They could be in the possession of the trade mark owner, or of trading standards officers, or anyone else, so long as they came into the possession of that person in connection with the investigation or prosecution of a relevant offence.[42]

Presumably, though, no forfeiture order can be made until the goods **19–63** in question are taken away from the counterfeiter or thief by some means, first because he will not have obtained possession in connection with the investigation or prosecution, and secondly because the right to apply for forfeiture resides with the person in possession.

Where the application should be made

If proceedings for a relevant offence relating to the goods concerned **19–64** have been brought, then the application under section 97 of the 1994 Act may be made to the court dealing with those proceedings.[43] That will be a magistrates' court or the Crown Court, depending on whether the

---

[38] s.97(2)(b).
[39] s.97(3).
[40] s.97(8).
[41] s.97(3).
[42] s.97(1).
[43] s.97(2)(a).

offences are being tried summarily or not. If no application has been made to a court trying the relevant offence, then the application may be made to a magistrates' court.[44] It appears from the permissive words of the section that an application to a magistrates' court can be made either if there is no prosecution at all, or if there is a prosecution but no application for forfeiture is made in the course of it.

A relevant offence must have been committed

19–65 Forfeiture can only be ordered if the court is satisfied that a relevant offence has been committed in relation to the goods concerned. This may well be obvious as a result of a conviction being achieved. In addition, the court can infer the commission of a relevant offence in relation to one set of goods if it is satisfied that a relevant offence has been committed in relation to other goods which are representative of them.[45]

Appeal from order for forfeiture or refusal

19–66 A person aggrieved[46] by the making or refusal of a forfeiture order may appeal to the crown court (in England and Wales) or the county court (in Northern Ireland).[47]

19–67 Regrettably, this leaves it most unclear how, if at all, an appeal can be made against the decision of a Crown Court, trying a relevant offence on indictment, in relation to the making or refusal of a forfeiture order.

Disposal of forfeited goods

19–68 Generally, as mentioned above, goods the subject of a forfeiture order are to be destroyed in accordance with the court's directions.[48] Alternatively, there is power to release the goods to a person specified by the court on condition that that person removes the offending mark, and complies with any order to pay costs made against him in the forfeiture proceedings.[49] The language of this provision suggests that it is principally directed to letting a defendant keep counterfeit goods if it is expected that the mark can and will satisfactorily be removed, but it is not so limited. It could extend, for example, to allowing the return to their owner of stolen counterfeit goods.

---

[44] s.97(2)(b).
[45] 1994 Act, s.97(4).
[46] This will include, presumably, at least, the investigating and prosecuting agencies, the defendant, the owner of the goods, and the owner of the trade mark in question.
[47] s.97(5).
[48] s.97(6).
[49] s.97(7).

7. Misuse of Royal arms, devices, emblems and titles

Unlawful use of Royal arms

Use of the Royal arms (or arms so closely resembling the Royal arms as **19–69** to be calculated to deceive), without the permission of the Queen, in a manner calculated to lead to the belief that the user is duly authorised to use them, is an offence. It is triable summarily only and may be punished by a fine not exceeding level 2 on the standard scale.[50]

In addition, it is forbidden, without the authority of the Queen or **19–70** other member of the Royal family, to use any device, emblem or title in a manner calculated to lead to the belief that the person so using it is employed by, or supplies goods or services to the Queen or that member of the Royal family.[51] It is not an offence to do so, but such acts (and acts amounting to an offence under section 99(1) of the 1994 Act) may be restrained by an injunction in proceedings brought by a person who is authorised to use the device, emblem or title in question, or by any person authorised by the Lord Chamberlain to take such proceedings.[52]

These provisions do not affect the right of the owner of a trade mark **19–71** which includes such arms, devices, emblems or titles to use that trade mark.[53]

8. Offences by partnerships and bodies corporate

General provisions about offences by partnerships

By section 101(1) of the 1994 Act, proceedings for offences alleged to **19–72** have been committed by a partnership must be brought against the partnership in the name of the firm and not of the partners.

However, section 101(1) does not affect the liability of individual **19–73** partners. By section 101(4), where a partnership commits an offence under the 1994 Act, all the partners are guilty and liable to be punished unless they are proved to have been ignorant of the offence or to have attempted to prevent it.

Section 101(2) provides that a partnership is to be treated as a body **19–74** corporate for the purposes of proceedings for an offence under the 1994 Act in relation to (a) any rules of court relating to the service of documents, and (b) certain procedural provisions of the Magistrates' Courts Act 1980.[54]

---

[50] ss.99(1) and (3). Level 2 on the standard scale is presently set at £500: Criminal Justice Act 1982, s.37(2), as amended by the Criminal Justice Act 1991, s.17(2).
[51] 1994 Art, s.99(2).
[52] s.99(4).
[53] s.99(5).
[54] Specified in s.101(2)(b).

If a partnership is fined for an offence under the 1994 Act, the fine must be paid out of partnership assets.[55]

Provisions concerning offences by bodies corporate

19–75 Where a body corporate has committed an offence under the 1994 Act, and it is proved that it did so with the consent or connivance of a director, manager, secretary or other similar officer, or a person purporting to act in such a capacity, that person is also guilty of the offence and liable to be punished.[56]

19–76 This provision concerns the circumstances in which an officer of the company is himself liable for the company's crime. It does not address the separate question of when the company is liable for acts of its officers, which will fall to be determined under the general criminal law, and is outside the scope of this book.

---

[55] s.101(3).
[56] s.101(5).

CHAPTER 20

CUSTOMS POWERS AND PROCEDURES

1. Scope of chapter

In addition to civil and criminal remedies for trade mark infringement, **20–01**
the Trade Marks Act 1994 provides for trade mark owners to invoke the
powers of the Commissioners of Customs and Excise to seize infringing
goods on their entry into the United Kingdom. Moreover, European
legislation has been introduced which seeks to restrict the circulation of
"counterfeit" goods within the E.U. This legislation extends to, among
other things, certain categories of goods and articles which infringe
registered trade mark rights, whether those rights arise under national
legislation or under the Community Trade Marks Regulations. These
two regimes are referred to in this chapter as "the domestic regime" and
"the European regime".

It is not the goal of this chapter to explore the full scope of Customs' **20–02**
powers in relation to goods bearing trade marks, or of all the procedural
complications involved. To do so would involve a consideration of
many aspects of the Customs and Excise Management Act 1979
("CEMA 1979") and the Community Customs Code. The result would
be excessively lengthy, and although Customs' powers are important,
they are on the fringes of the main concerns of this work.

Rather, this chapter is intended to indicate the broad scheme of **20–03**
Customs' powers in relation to goods bearing registered trade marks, to
point to the United Kingdom and European legislation which enacts
those powers, to indicate how the domestic regime and the European
regime interrelate, and to explain in outline the procedure involved in
forfeiture proceedings.

2. Legislation making up the domestic regime

The domestic regime begins with section 89(1) of the 1994 Act, which **20–04**
provides that the proprietor of a registered trade mark[1] may give a
notice to the Commissioners of Customs and Excise ("the Commissioners") asking that infringing goods, materials or articles[2] expected to
arrive in the United Kingdom be treated as prohibited goods.

---

[1] *i.e.* a mark registered under the 1994 Act, excluding a CTM.
[2] These terms import the definitions from s.17, which is explored in more detail in Chap.
19.

By section 89(2), where such a notice is in force, the importation of those goods is prohibited.[3]

20–05   Section 90 gives the Commissioners power to make rules specifying the form in which a notice under section 89 is to be given, and requiring the person giving notice to furnish evidence and to comply with other conditions specified in the regulations.

The result of the importation of such goods being prohibited is that they fall under the provisions of the Customs and Excise Management Act 1979.[4]

20–06   Rules under section 90 have been made: the Trade Marks (Customs) Regulations 1994.[5] Their general effect is to specify the form of notice to be used,[6] to stipulate a fee,[7] to require the giving of such security as the Commissioners require (failing which the notice is ineffective),[8] to indemnify the Commissioners against liability for detaining the goods or for anything happening during their detention,[9] and to require the applicant to provide the Commissioners with the certificate of registration of the mark concerned, together with evidence of renewal.[10]

3. Legislation making up the community regime

20–07   The relevant European legislation consists of Council Regulation 3295/94 (as amended by Regulation 241/99), referred to below as the "Counterfeit and Pirated Goods Regulation",[11] and Commission Regulation 1367/95, which contains implementing measures. The provisions of those Regulations are enacted in the United Kingdom by the Goods Infringing Intellectual Property Rights (Customs) Regulations 1999, and the Goods Infringing Intellectual Property Rights (Consequential Provisions) Regulations 1999.[12]

20–08   The former of those U.K. Regulations tracks the provisions of the 1994 Regulations of the domestic regime fairly closely, providing for the form of notice to be used,[13] security to be provided,[14] and an indemnity to be given[15] in much the same way. Fees are also provided for.[16] In addition, they empower the Commissioners to require the trade mark proprietor

---

[3] There is an exception for goods imported for private and domestic use.
[4] CEMA 1979, s.49, renders goods whose importation is prohibited under any enactment liable to forfeiture; s.139 gives the power to seize goods liable to forfeiture; and Sched. 3 contains the procedure relating to proceedings to condemn goods so seized. See App. 30, *post*.
[5] S.I. 1994 No. 2625, App. 31, *post*.
[6] Reg. 2 and the Sched.
[7] Reg. 3.
[8] Reg. 4.
[9] Reg. 5.
[10] Reg. 6.
[11] App. 2, *post*.
[12] S.I. 1999 No. 1601 and S.I. 1999 No. 1618 respectively, Apps 28, 29, *post*.
[13] Reg. 3.
[14] Reg. 4.
[15] Reg. 5.
[16] Reg. 6.

to provide information allowing the Commissioners to decide whether suspect goods are in fact counterfeit[17]; if the proprietor fails to provide the information (or fails to comply with any other requirement of the Regulations), a decision under them ceases to have any further effect.[18]

The principal effect of the latter of the U.K. Regulations is to apply the **20–09** provisions of the CEMA 1979 referred to above[19] to counterfeit goods as defined by the Counterfeit and Pirated Goods Regulation (which include goods offending against national registrations and CTMs).

4. Interaction of the two regimes

It should first be appreciated that by virtue of section 89(3) of the 1994 **20–10** Act, the domestic regime is excluded wherever the European regime applies. With that said, the general pattern is as follows:

(1) The domestic regime applies to goods, materials or articles which are expected to arrive in the United Kingdom from outside the EEA, or from within the EEA but which have not been in free circulation there[20];

(2) The domestic regime only applies to United Kingdom registered trade marks[21];

(3) The European regime, so far as it relates to registered trade marks, applies to "counterfeit goods".[22] This term is explained in more detail below, but it should be noted at this stage that it is not as extensive as "infringing goods" under the 1994 Act;

(4) The European regime applies to materials offending against United Kingdom registered trade marks and CTMs[23];

(5) The European regime comes into operation where goods suspected of being counterfeit are entered for free circulation, export or re-export, or are found in the course of checks on goods under customs supervision.[24]

5. "Counterfeit goods"

"Counterfeit goods" are defined in Article 1.2. of the Counterfeit and **20–11** Pirated Goods Regulation, as:

"goods, including the packaging thereof, bearing without authorisation a trade mark which is identical to the trade mark validly

---

[17] Reg. 7.
[18] Reg. 8.
[19] s.139 and Sched. 3.
[20] 1994 Act, s.89(1)(b).
[21] See above.
[22] Counterfeit and Pirated Goods Regulation, Art. 1.2(a).
[23] *ibid.*
[24] Counterfeit and Pirated Goods Regulation, Art. 1.1.

registered in respect of the same type of goods, or which cannot be distinguished in its essential aspects from such trade mark, and which thereby infringes the rights of the holder of the trade mark in question under Community law or the law of the Member State where the application for action by the customs authorities is made."

20–12 This makes it clear that infringement under the 1994 Act or the CTM Regulation is necessary but not sufficient for goods sought to be seized under the European regime to be "counterfeit". In addition, the goods must bear the alleged infringing mark without authorisation, that mark must be identical to the registered mark or such that it "cannot be distinguished in its essential aspects" therefrom (plainly a stricter test than that of section 10(2) of the 1994 Act or the equivalent provisions of the CTM Regulation), and it must be used on goods "of the same type" as those for which the complainant's mark is registered (again, plainly a stricter test).

Moreover, Article 1(4) provides that the Counterfeit and Pirated Goods Regulation does not apply to goods which hear a trade mark with the consent of its holder.

20–13 As a result, "counterfeit goods" as defined in the Counterfeit and Pirated Goods Regulation are likely to exclude most parallel imports, and many goods in respect of which infringement is merely strongly arguable. It will only clearly catch goods which are counterfeit in the sense that the man in the street would use that expression: outright forgeries.

6. Procedure in relation to goods seized by Customs

20–14 Once goods have been seized as liable to forfeiture, either under the domestic or the European regime, the governing provision is Schedule 3 of the CEMA 1979.

20–15 The Commissioners are first required to serve notice of seizure on the owner(s) of the item(s) seized.[25] A period of one month is then allowed for any person who alleges that the goods were not in fact liable to forfeiture to give notice to the Commissioners to that effect.[26] The notice must give the name and address of a solicitor in the United Kingdom authorised to accept service, and various other details such as the applicant's name and address.[27] If no notice under paragraph 3 is given, or if the requirements to provide information under paragraph 4 are not met, then the disputed items are deemed to have been forfeited.[28]

Assuming, however, that a proper notice is served in time, the onus falls on the Commissioners to begin proceedings for condemnation by the court.[29] These are called condemnation proceedings.

[25] Sched. 3, para 1(1). There are a few exceptions, which are listed in para. 1(2).
[26] Sched. 3, para. 3.
[27] Sched. 3, para. 4.
[28] Sched. 3, para. 5.
[29] Sched. 3, para. 6.

7. Condemnation proceedings

Condemnation proceedings are civil proceedings, and may be begun in **20–16** either a magistrates' court[30] or in the High Court. Although the proceedings are begun by the Commissioners, as is explained above, and somewhat confusingly in the light of the Woolf reforms and the CPR, the person alleging that the goods concerned are not liable to forfeiture is called the "claimant".[31]

In any condemnation proceedings, whether begun in the High Court **20–17** or the magistrates' court, the claimant or his solicitor must swear that the claimant owned the disputed goods at the time of the seizure.[32] In High Court proceedings, the claimant must give security for the Commissioners' costs as ordered by the court.[33] Default of either of those procedural steps results in the court giving judgment for the Commissioners.[34]

An appeal lies from the magistrates' court to the Crown Court.[35] An appeal in the High Court falls under the normal rules for appeals under the CPR.

Where a thing is in due course condemned as forfeited, then forfeiture, has effect from the date when the liability to forfeiture arose.[36]

8. Prospective powers under the European regime

A feature of the European regime not found in the domestic regime is **20–18** that if goods are found in the course of searches or investigations by Customs which are believed to be counterfeit goods within the meaning of the European regime, Customs may inform the owner of the trade mark concerned, and may suspend release of the goods concerned for three working days to enable the owner to make an application for the seizure of the goods.[37] Thereafter a further period of 10 days is allowed, during which release of the goods is suspended, for the taking of interim measures by Customs,or for the institution of civil proceedings to determine whether the goods are counterfeit.[38] These proceedings may be brought by the Commissioners themselves or by the trade mark owner: *Pointing v. Customs & Excise Commissioners.*[39]

---

[30] By Sched. 3, para. 9, a magistrates' court has jurisdiction if the place of the offence (if any) leading to seizure, or the place of seizure, or the claimant's residence falls within its geographical jurisdiction.
[31] s.1.
[32] Sched. 3, para. 10(1).
[33] Sched. 3, para. 10(2).
[34] Sched. 3, para. 10(3).
[35] Sched. 3, para. 11(1).
[36] Sched. 3, para. 7.
[37] Counterfeit and Pirated Goods Regulation, Art. 4; Goods Infringing Intellectual Property Rights (Consequential Provisions) Regulations 1999, reg. 4.
[38] Counterfeit and Pirated Goods Regulation, Arts. 5–7, Goods Infringing Intellectual Property Rights (Consequential Provisions) Regulations 1999, regs 5–7.
[39] [1999] F.S.R. 394.

20–19   Article 6 of the Counterfeit and Pirated Goods Regulation requires the customs authorities to inform the trade mark owner, on request, of the name and address of the shipper and (if known) the consignee of the goods so as to allow him to institute proceedings. There does not, however, seem to be any specific authorisation for Customs to do so in the statutory instruments implementing the European Regulations, notwithstanding that in the absence of such information the trade mark owner may be unable to bring proceedings, as was recognised by the European Court of Justice in *Re Adidas*.[40] There, it was held that national law would be in contravention of the Regulation if it prohibited provision of such information to the trade mark owner. It is therefore to be presumed that the Commissioners have such power.

9. Power of the Commissioners to disclose information

20–20 By the very nature of their functions, the Commissioners frequently learn, in policing the entry into the United Kingdom of potentially infringing goods, of activities which amount to breaches of the criminal law. By section 91 of the 1994 Act, the Commissioners are specifically empowered to authorise the disclosure to any person who has a function in connection with the investigation or prosecution of offences under section 92 of the 1994 Act, or under the Trade Descriptions Act 1968, of information relating to infringing goods, materials or articles. It is suggested that this section must be construed to mean *potentially* infringing goods, materials or articles, since otherwise the provision would be deprived of much or all of its utility.

[40] [2000] F.S.R. 227.

CHAPTER 21

THE INTERNET

Introduction

Some characterise the Internet as spawning a series of wholly new **21–01**
problems for the law, particularly in the field of registered trade marks
and passing off. In fact, the Internet has done no more than to throw up
existing, sometimes familiar, issues in a different guise. There are three
areas for discussion: registration of domain names, jurisdiction/
infringement and metatags. All three areas require some knowledge of
how the Internet works and the terminology used. These subjects are
dealt with in the next section.

1. Mechanics

The Internet is a large network of linked computers. It is, in effect, a **21–02**
high-speed electronic postal system. The principal reason why it
"works" at a practical level is due to the speed of communication and
the method by which individual computers are identified. For the most
part, we need only concern ourselves with the end points of communication. At one end is the user accessing the Internet from, usually, a PC.
At the other end is a server, on which is stored in electronic form, the
website which the user wishes to access. The user gains access to the
Internet at a gateway, either via an internet service provider (ISP) or via
a smaller, usually internal, network called an Intranet.[1] In the middle is a
highly sophisticated network comprising router and other computers
linked together.

Computers connected to the Internet have unique numerical **21–03**
addresses (for example, 1.256.123.123) so that electronic information is
delivered to the right place. To make these identification numbers more
user friendly, they can be associated with identifiers consisting of
alphanumeric characters. These identifiers are Internet domain names.
Because they are made up from alphanumeric characters, it is possible
for the sequence of characters to spell out words and hence trade marks
or other signs used by businesses.

---

[1] Intranets frequently have a permanent telephone connection to the Internet.

Anatomy of a domain name

21–04 A typical domain name might appear as follows: **www.squiffo.com**. The **www.** element of the name is an abbreviation of "world wide web" and merely indicates that the expression is a domain name accessible via the Internet.[2] Most people are now familiar with the suffix **.com**, which identifies one of the generic Top Level Domains, or gTLDs. In our example, **squiffo** is the second part of the domain name and is called a Second Level Domain (or SLD). This is a sequence of characters which is unique within the set of **.com** domain names and therefore operates as a unique identifier.

21–05　Other gTLDs are **.org**, **.net**, **.gov**.[3] The other category of TLDs are the two letter country code or ccTLDs such as **.uk**, **.fr**, **.de** and **.tm**[4]. Within the **.uk** and other ccTLDs, by convention a series of generic Second Level Domains are used such as **.co**, **.org**, **.net** and **.gov**, etc. Thus, in the domain name **www.squiffo.co.uk**, the Third Level Domain is **squiffo** and is a unique alphanumeric sequence within the **.co.uk** subset and therefore provides this domain name with a means of unique identification.

21–06　There is no central authority regulating the Internet, which is almost entirely governed by convention. The convention, for an American user of the Internet, is that a **.com** domain name generally indicates an American commercial entity, likewise with **.org**—an American organisation and **.gov**—an arm of the U.S. government, for example. For a user of the Internet outside the U.S., a **.com** domain name may indicate an American commercial entity or an international commercial entity (with or without a business in the U.S.). A **.co.uk** suffix generally indicates a United Kingdom commercial entity and a **.net.de** generally indicates a German network, for example. Normally one would expect a website with an address ending in the suffix **.co.uk** to be situate in the United Kingdom. However, all these indications may or may not be true. A **.com** website may well not be operated by an international commercial entity and the server upon which the website is stored may well not be situate in the USA, though frequently they are. Likewise with a **.co.uk** website. The domain name **www.squiffo.co.uk** may do nothing more than link directly to the website identified by **www.squiffo.com** or it may identify a website which is wholly unrelated to that found at the **.com** address.

---

[2] When accessing the website at www.squiffo.com, one often sees "http://www.squiffo.com/index.htm" or ". . .index.html". The letters "http" and "htm" or "html" indicate the language of the communication: HyperText Transfer Protocol and HyperText Markup Language.

[3] There are plans to increase the number of gTLDs which are naturally complemented by plans to increase the generic Second Level Domains used with country code TLDs. Possible candidates are **.store**, **.shop**,

[4] Identifying the U.K., France, Germany and Turkmenistan, respectively. The .tm domain has been suspended, a victim of its own success.

Registration of internet domain names

Registration of domain names is handled by a number of organisations. **21–07** Generally there is one organisation which oversees registration in each country, but there may be several organisations acting as registrars, particularly in those countries where Internet use is well established. The generic TLDs (**.com**, **.org**, **.net**) are currently administered by Network Solutions Inc. in the USA[5]. Domain names with the **.uk** suffix are administered by Nominet UK Limited,[6] and similarly in other countries.

To date, registration of domain names has been conducted by the **21–08** various registrar organisations on a first-come, first-served basis. Some national registries do impose nationality restrictions on the applicant, for example the French authority requires the owner of a **.fr** registration to be a French national or domiciled in France. Such restrictions are not imposed for other domains.

To select a domain name, it must be, therefore, decided which Top **21–09** Level Domain is required. Usually, the applicant will choose the most logical country so that a United Kingdom–based entity might choose the **.uk** Top Level Domain. However, the U.S. domains, **.com, .org,** and **.net**, are perceived as having a certain cachet connoting an international business profile.

Having selected the Top Level Domain, the applicant should then **21–10** select an appropriate Second Level Domain according to the nature of the applicant entity (with the U.S. domains, the Top Level Domain will signify this and the choice of the Top Level Domain name will be influenced by the applicant's nature). Having selected the appropriate Top (and if applicable, Second) Level domain, the applicant should then select a unique alphanumeric Third Level (Second Level in the case of U.S. domains). This should comprise no fewer than two and, for some registration authorities, no more than 26 standard ASCII characters, none of which must be a space break[7] or a forward slash. Some registration authorities have differing rules on the number of characters.

Once the name has been chosen, it is advisable to check that the name **21–11** is available. The whole combination of Levels in the name must be unique in order correctly to identify the user. As far as the registration authorities are initially concerned, the domain name required merely has to be unique. A simple check can be conducted on the Internet. Many registration authorities provide a search engine on their websites to allow one to check on the availability of a chosen domain name or to check details of the owner of a domain name already registered. These

---

[5] The other gTLDs are **.edu, .gov, .int** and **.mil.**
[6] In fact Nominet administer the following SLDs: **.co.uk, .org.uk, .plc.uk, .ltd.uk, .net.uk, .sch.uk**, but not **.ac.uk, .gov.uk, .nhs.uk, .police.uk**, or **.mod.uk.** At the time of writing, proposals for new SLDs are being considered by Nominet, in line with new TLDs by ICANN.
[7] The convention is that spaces in a trade mark or trade name are either left out or indicated by hyphens, *e.g.* **marksandspencer.com** or **marks-and-spencer.com.**

searches are known as "whois" searches. To locate the website for the appropriate country registration authority, simply use the domain name formula, **www.nic.** + country Top Level Domain. For example the TLD for the United Kingdom authority is **.uk** and the website can be located at **www.nic.uk**. Other examples are **www.nic.fr** for France or **www.nic.de** for Germany (Deutschland and hence "**.de**"). The U.S. Registry may be found at **www.networksolutions.com**.

21–12   Clearly, the most desirable part of a domain name is the unique Second/Third Level domain within the Top/Second Level Domain. If this is not available within the chosen Top/Second Level, then it should be remembered that it may be available in an alternative Top Level: the Third Level Domain is only unique to its Top/Second Level. For example, if **squiffo.com** were taken, the applicant might try for **squiffo.org** or **squiffo.co.uk** or even **squiffo1.com**. It is feasible and permissible that all these domains with the same **squiffo** Third/Second Level element could be owned by different entities because they are in different Top/Second Level Domains.

21–13   The application is made via electronic mail to the appropriate registration authority for the chosen Top Level Domain using an application template which can be downloaded from that authority's website. The ability to file domain names is given to members of the domain name authority. Membership can be obtained by anyone; however, most applications are made via a domain name registration company or Internet service provider (ISP) who will make an application on behalf of its client.

21–14   The information required to file a domain name application is straightforward: the name and address of the applicant (including e-mail address), the name and address of the owner's systems administrator, the name and address of the owner's technical contact, the name and address of a billing contact, and finally the identity code of the computer server owned by the applicant to which the domain name will direct web communications. Very often the Internet service provider will provide details of its technical and administrative contacts and server identity on behalf its client because the website to which the domain name will eventually point is inactive or "parked".

21–15   A fee is payable on application. The domain names are allocated on a "first come, first served" basis. A registration lasts for two years and can be renewed upon payment of a fee. If the name is not renewed it will become available again for another owner to acquire.

Transactions involving domain names

21–16   It is possible to transfer the ownership of an Internet domain name. Upon the grant of registration for a domain name, following a successful application and payment of the registration fee, a certificate is issued. The certificate contains a transfer document which can be detached and returned to the registration authority stating the new owner's details. The transfer document is also available on the Internet.

The link between trade marks and domain names

A domain name registration as such is not an intellectual property right: **21–17** it is a contract with the registration authority controlling the Top Level Domain concerned allowing communications to reach the domain name owner's computer via Internet links channelled through the registration authority's server. It does not create a monopoly or any other form of exclusive right. It is in many ways akin to a company name registration which is a unique identifier of a certain company but of itself confers no intellectual property right.

However, there are important intellectual property implications aris- **21–18** ing out of the use of a verbal expression (which a domain name ostensibly is) in the course of trade. The Top and Second Level Domain elements for national registrations and the Top Level Domain for U.S. domain names are generic and do not generate any form of allied IP rights. The rest of a domain name is user defined and may well spell out a trade mark or other sign used in trade leading to trade mark infringement issues and possible passing off.

Use of domain names

Once registered, a domain name may be used in various ways. Gener- **21–19** ally, a domain name forms part of a website address (technically known as an URL—Unique Resource Locator). It may also be used as part of an e-mail address, for example **info@squiffo.com**. Domain names are often used in advertising to point people to information about an organisation: increasingly, they identify a company or organisation. It is also, of course, possible to register a domain name and do nothing with it except keep the registration.

Accessing a website

From a technical point of view, the following is a rather crude **21–20** simplification of what happens when a user accesses a website. However, we believe it to be accurate enough for the purpose of analysis.

The user at his or her PC connects to the Internet, either via an ISP or **21–21** via an intranet. The user identifies the website which he or she desires to visit. This is done either by typing in the domain name or by selecting the website from a search listing or a hyperlink. The last command from the user—either pressing the return key or clicking on the domain name shown on screen—sends an electronic message equivalent to: "please send the web page identified by the domain name". The message is routed through to the web server on which the website is stored. The web server receives the message and responds by sending an electronic message containing the web page back to the PC of the user. The web page is received by the PC and displayed on the user's screen.

Frequently, the first web page received will direct the user to other web pages which form part of the whole website. The user selects a second web page by clicking on the hyperlink. Thus, the user sends a second message "please send me the web page" identified and so the process continues. In between sending and receiving messages, the user's computer is sitting there waiting. Likewise, once the web server has received, processed and responded to the user's request, it is either waiting for another request or dealing with a request from a different user.

The closest analogy is a mail order catalogue which is sent out page by page, upon specific request, the whole process taking seconds rather than the days which would be required to conduct the process by post.

21–22 So far we have only been considering web pages which provide information. If it is possible to make purchases at the website, then the same process applies. The product in question is identified on a particular web page which is being viewed by the user. The web page will have some means by which the user can indicate that he or she wishes to purchase the product. Thus an electronic message is sent "I wish to purchase" in conjunction with the message "please send the next page", which may indicate stock levels and/or contain a request as to how the user is going to pay. So the exchange of messages continues until the transaction is completed. In the absence of any indication to the contrary, the normal rules of offer and acceptance will indicate when and where the contract of purchase was made. Frequently, the terms and conditions on a website will specify when and where a contract is made and the law which governs the contract or, if it does not, those matters will have to be deduced from the circumstances.

Again, the closest analogy to a purchase made over the Internet is a purchase made by post from a mail order catalogue.

Other analogies

21–23 Other analogies have been suggested, largely to suit the argument being presented. Thus a defendant, seeking to argue that his use of a mark on his website only occurs abroad, has argued that someone accessing his website from the United Kingdom should be likened to the use of a "super-telescope", the eye-piece of which is at the user's PC, focused on the website situate at the web server. Even though this "super-telescope" analogy has been accepted as apt on the facts of one case,[8] the explanation above shows that it is inaccurate. It also begs the question.

Metatags

21–24 The pages which make up a website are stored and transmitted electronically. A web page typically comprises a mixture of text and pictures. The creator of a web page uses one of a number of specialist

---

[8] *Euromarket Designs Inc. v. Peters*, Jacob J., July 25, 2000 (unreported).

software languages to give each piece of text and each picture its location on the page. In this way, a web page is built up electronically to produce the effect seen on screen. Underlying what is seen on the user's screen is a mass of hidden software commands.

Most people are aware of the use of search engines to locate particular **21–25** items of interest on the Internet. The ability of a particular search engine to locate what you are looking for depends on whether that search engine has digested the contents of the web page you are looking for. Search engines can digest different levels of information provided by a web page, but generally, search engines work on more than the user sees on his screen. As the Internet has grown, so the number of "hits" produced by any particular search have increased. Techniques have been developed to ensure that your website comes at or near the top of the list of "hits". One of these techniques uses metatags. As the name suggests, these are hidden tags, included in the software which makes up a web page, read by the search engines but not generally visible on the user's screen.[9] Thus, for example, a retailer of sports clothing might put the name of a famous footballer in a metatag to attract search engines to his website. The system is obviously open to abuse. Typical modes of abuse are (1) the use of a competitor's name or trade mark as metatags which can either attract users direct to the website or place the website address in close juxtaposition to that of the competitor in a search listing and (2) the use of the names of famous people or of famous trade marks as metatags.

2. Disputes over domain name registrations

Disputes over domain name registrations fall into one of two categories: **21–26**

(1) there are some domain names which so obviously refer to and identify a particular business or entity, that their registration by a third party amounts to illegitimate hijacking of the name;

(2) there are far more domain names which could be legitimately registered and used by more than one person or business. A particular domain name is secured by the first to register and, in the vast majority of cases, all the others who might like that particular domain name cannot challenge the registration. An example of this type of case is *Pitman Training Ltd v. Nominet UK*,[10] where there were two independent businesses entitled to trade under the name Pitman. The registration of **pitman.co.uk** by one could not be disturbed by the other.

---

[9] Unless he selects View and Source.
[10] [1997] F.S.R. 797, Sir Richard Scott V.-C. A case which establishes that in the U.K., no liability attaches to the Registrar of the domain name for having registered it. The same position applies in the U.S.

21–27 Both situations arise because, hitherto, the Internet has been governed by convention. It has taken some time to find ways to deal with the illegitimate hijacking of domain names, but in general terms, there are three routes by which a dispute may be resolved:

(a) A claimant can bring proceedings for passing off and/or infringement of registered trade mark. The basis for such claims over Internet domain names was clearly established by the Court of Appeal in *One in a Million*.

(b) Most domain name Registrars operate a so-called "Dispute Resolution Service". These schemes are designed to assist the resolution of disputes by agreement between the parties. Such schemes are rarely of any use when a domain name has been hi-jacked, although in appropriate circumstances Registrars will suspend use of a domain name pending the outcome of a dispute.

(c) In late 1999, a new dispute resolution policy was launched by ICANN[11] relating to **.com**, **.net** and **.org** TLDs. The policy is operated at the WIPO[12] Arbitration and Mediation Center and by various other bodies. For the first time, it provides a mechanism for actually deciding disputes over domain name registrations outside formal litigation.

Each of these three methods of challenge are now examined.

One in a Million[13]

21–28 The defendants were dealers in domain names who had registered a number of names which incorporated the names of well-known English companies, such as **marksandspencer.com**, **marksandspencer.co.uk**, **sainsbury.com**, **virgin.org**, **bt.org**, **britishtelecom.com**, **ladbrokes.com**. Although the judge at first instance granted summary judgment for passing off and section 10(3) of the Trade Marks Act 1994 infringement, he did not accept that the mere registration of the domain names constituted passing off. Giving the judgment of the Court of Appeal, Aldous L.J. held that a mere registration could give rise to liability for passing off on two bases. The first was a traditional analysis of reputation, misrepresentation and damage:

> "The placing on a register of a distinctive name such as "marksandspencer" makes a representation to persons who consult the

---

[11] The Uniform Domain Name Dispute Resolution Policy adopted by ICANN—Internet Corporation for Assigned Names and Numbers—August 26, 1999. The policy has also been adopted by certain managers of ccTLDs such as **.nu**, **.tv** and **.ws**—from Niue, Tuvalu and Samoa.

[12] The World Intellectual Property Organisation, based in Geneva. For further details see the website at **www.wipo.org**.

[13] *British Telecommunications Plc & others v. One in a Million Ltd* [1999] 1 W.L.R. 903; [1999] F.S.R. 1, CA.

register that the registrant is connected or associated with the name registered and thus the owner of the goodwill in the name. Such persons would not know of One in a Million and would believe they were connected or associated with the owner of the goodwill in the domain name they had registered. Further, registration of the domain name including the words "Marks & Spencer" is an erosion of the exclusive goodwill in the name which damages or is likely to damage Marks & Spencer Plc."[14]

For the second basis, Aldous L.J. analysed the passing off case law **21–29** concerned with "instruments of deception" and concluded that, in appropriate circumstances, the registration of a domain name can itself constitute an instrument of deception or fraud, leading to liability for passing off.

> "It follows that a court will intervene by way of injunction in passing off cases in three types of case. First, where there is passing off established or it is threatened. Second, where the defendant is a joint tortfeasor with another in passing off, actual or threatened. Third, where the defendant has equipped himself with or intends to equip another with an instrument of fraud. This third type of case is probably a mere quia timet action".[15]

Whether a registration constitutes an instrument of fraud depends on **21–30** all the circumstances. There are essentially two types of case. Some names are so distinctive, denoting one trader and nobody else, that the conclusion may be drawn from the domain name itself. Thus:

> "I also believe that domain names comprising the name "Marks & Spencer" are instruments of fraud. Any realistic use of them as domain names would result in passing off. . ."[16]

The second type of case was illustrated by the other domain names in **21–31** issue, since Aldous L.J. accepted that there are people called Sainsbury and Ladbroke and companies, other than Virgin and BT, who could legitimately use the other domain names in issue. Despite that, the circumstances of the defendant's conduct in that case required the same conclusion as for the domain names incorporating **marksandspencer**.[17]

---

[14] [1999] 1 W.L.R. 903 at 924 F-H; [1999] F.S.R. 1 at 23.
[15] [1999] 1 W.L.R. 903 at 920 F-G; [1999] F.S.R. 1 at 18.
[16] [1999] 1 W.L.R. 903 at 925A; [1999] F.S.R. 1 at 23.
[17] The claimant's case is always assisted if the defendant registers the name and then offers to sell it to the claimant. Alternatively, the defendant may advertise the domain name for sale at a price which reflects how well known the claimant is. More difficult are the cases where the defendant registers the name and is then careful not to make overt offers to sell. Those defendants then wait for the claimant to make them an offer. However, such a blocking registration may deprive the claimant of the ability to exploit his goodwill as he would like, and Aldous L.J.'s analysis means that, in appropriate circumstances, a blocking registration gives rise to liability.

Finally, the finding of a section 10(3) of the 1994 Act infringement was upheld, on the basis of sufficient threat to infringe.

Application of the decision in *One in a Million*

21–32 Naturally, the reasoning of the Court of Appeal in *One in a Million* is not restricted to domain names. The reasoning was based, in part, on cases concerning the registration of company names.[18] It is obviously applicable to cases concerning the registration of company names and, indeed to any system of registration[19] which is publicly accessible, where the thing registered may spell out a trade mark and is liable to be used in trade.

Jurisdiction

21–33 For this type of claim, jurisdiction depends on the domicile of the registrant of the domain name and not upon the country where the domain name Registrar is based. Thus, it is appropriate to deal with an English hijacker in England, whether he has registered a **.com** name or a domain name indicating some other country. If the claimant does not have registered or common law rights in the domicile of the hijacker, he may be able to bring a claim under section 56 (well-known marks) of the 1994 Act. Failing that, he will have to persuade a court in his own country to exercise extra-territorial jurisdiction over the defendant and generally this requires some substantial link between that country and the defendant.

The Nominet UK Dispute Resolution Service

21–34 Some domain name registrars operate their own dispute resolution services with regard to the Top Level Domains they control. Nominet UK Limited in the United Kingdom is a good example. A structured, informal means of settlement has been set out by Nominet, which offers a three tier system for resolving disputes over the rightful ownership of a domain name.

The first solution offered is an "investigation". The dispute is analysed by a senior member of the executive staff of Nominet UK Limited who will offer an impartial decision.

21–35 The second approach offered is termed "Formal Action Under the Rules". Under the rules relating to **.uk** domain name registration, to which all applicants for registration submit as part of the registration process, the registration of a domain name may be suspended by

---

[18] *Glaxo v. Glaxowellcome* [1996] F.S.R. 388; *Direct Line Group v. Direct Line Estate Agency Ltd* [1997] F.S.R. 374.
[19] *e.g.* alphanumeric telephone numbers: *cf. 800-FLOWERS* [2000] E.T.M.R. 369.

Nominet UK Limited. Nominet will make an initial decision with regard to a suspension and should this decision prove unacceptable, the matter is referred to an independent expert from a panel, consulted on a rota basis. The expert is sent all papers, correspondence and evidence relating to the dispute. The expert will ask the parties to enter one written submission within 14 days of receipt of the papers. The expert may invite the parties to appear before him/her, but there will be no hearing at which witnesses can be called. Within one month of receipt of the papers, the expert will offer a recommendation. Nominet will then take into account the recommendation and decide whether or not to suspend the registration. If any party is dissatisfied, the dispute can be referred to the third means of resolution.

The third method is "The Nominet Alternative Dispute Resolution **21–36** Service". The dispute is heard before a neutral third party mediator under the CEDR (Centre for Dispute Resolution) Rules. Nominet has procured special rates for the conduct of such mediations. The idea of the mediation is to assist the parties in arriving at a settlement which may form a contract and be enforceable under the law of contract through the courts.

ICANN

In October 1999, the Internet Corporation for Assigned Names and **21–37** Numbers (ICANN) launched a Domain Name Dispute Resolution Policy that is now exercised by the World Intellectual Property Organisation and certain other organisations. The Policy currently applies only to names in the **.com**, **.net**, and **.org** Top Level Domains and certain country code domain names. If the system proves successful, it may well be adopted by other registries in the future.

When applying for registration of a domain name in a Top Level **21–38** Domain operated by a registration authority subscribing to the ICANN Policy, the applicant agrees that:

(1) all statements made in the application are true and accurate; and
(2) to the applicant's knowledge, the registration of the domain name will not infringe the rights of a third party; and
(3) it will not knowingly use the domain name in violation of any applicable laws or regulations.

The registration authority will cancel, transfer or otherwise change a **21–39** domain name if the registrant so instructs it, if a competent court orders it, or upon a decision of an administrative panel (such as WIPO, Disputes.org/eResolution.ca Consortium, or the National Arbitration Forum) employing the ICANN Policy. The matter is decided by either an individual expert or, at the election of the complainant, a panel of three experts.

Substantive rules[20]

21–40 In disputes to which the ICANN Policy pertains and pursuant to paragraph 4(a) of the Policy the claimant must assert and prove that:

(1) the disputed domain name is identical or confusingly similar to a trade mark in which the complaining party has rights; *and*

(2) the registered party has no rights or legitimate interests in respect of the domain name; *and*

(3) the registered party is using the domain name in bad faith.

21–41 For the purposes of the Policy, "bad faith" is defined as:

(a) where the circumstances surrounding the registration of the domain name indicate that it was primarily acquired for the purpose of selling, renting or otherwise transferring the domain name registration to the complainant owning the trade mark rights to the name, or to a competitor of the claimant, for valuable consideration in excess of documented out-of-pocket expenses relating directly to the domain name acquisition; or

(b) where the domain name has been registered to prevent the owner of trade mark rights in the name from reflecting the mark in a corresponding domain name where the registrant has engaged in a pattern of such conduct; or

(c) where the domain name has been registered primarily for the purpose of disrupting the business of a competitor; or

(d) where by using the domain name the registrant has attempted to attract commercial gain by luring Internet users to its website by creating a likelihood of confusion with the complainant's mark as to the source, sponsorship, affiliation or endorsement of its website or of a product on the website.

21–42 In response to a claim under the Policy, the defending registrant must be prepared to show that:

(i) before notification of the dispute, its use (or demonstrable preparations for use) of the domain name or a name corresponding to it, was in connection with the bona fide offering of goods or services; or

(ii) it has been commonly known by the domain name even if no trade mark rights have been acquired; or

(iii) it is making legitimate non-commercial or fair use of the domain name without an intent to reap financial gain, to mislead consumers, or to tarnish the trade mark in issue.

Procedure

21–43 The complaint should be filed with the organisation operating the Policy (such as WIPO) in both hard copy and by e-mail. The complaint must contain full contact details of the complainant and his agent; an

---

[20] The ICANN Policy, Rules and Supplemental Rules, together with guidelines for complainant and respondent can all be found on the WIPO website at **www.wipo.org**.

indication of the preferred means of communication; an indication of whether the matter is to be heard by one expert or a panel of three; the name and address of the respondent; details of the trade mark on the basis which the complaint is made (including details of the goods and services concerned); and a description of the grounds for complaint.

If the complaint is in order, it is sent to the registrant/respondent **21–44** within three days of receipt. The respondent has 20 days to submit a response to the complaint. A written decision is produced within 14 days of receipt of the papers by the expert(s). Within three days of the decision, it is communicated to the registration authority, the parties, ICANN and the organisation through which the complaint was channelled. A majority decision by a panel of three experts is final.

The ICANN policy in practice

The ICANN Policy, as operated by WIPO, is proving to be very **21–45** popular.[21] The procedure is quicker and cheaper than normal litigation. The jurisdiction is international in nature. There is a relatively high success rate for complainants.[22] In certain circumstances, the ICANN Policy produces an outcome for a claimant which he or she would not achieve under the law of passing off or infringement of registered trade mark. This is particularly true for celebrities, who have difficulties in passing off (see Chapter 22 on Merchandising).

(1) The domain names **jeanettewinterson.com**, **jeanettewinter-** **21–46** **son.org** and **jeanettewinterson.net** were required to be transferred to the well-known author. Having referred to *One in a Million*, the panel observed that "In this case, the issue is not whether the Respondent has committed passing-off by registering the three domain names in issue, it is merely whether under English common law unauthorised use of a mark can be restrained other than by an action for infringement of a trade mark." and "The case for decision here does not concern whether or not passing-off has occurred but whether the Complainant has rights in her name sufficient to constitute a trade mark for the purposes of para 4a of the Policy."[23]

(2) **juliaroberts.com** was required to be transferred to the well- **21–47** known actress. In her case, an American panel referred to the *Jeanette Winterson* decision and observed: "The Policy does not require that the Complainant should have rights in a registered trade mark or service mark. It is sufficient that the Complainant should satisfy the Administrative Panel that she has rights in a

---

[21] 716 cases had been filed by the end of June 2000.
[22] To the end of June 2000, 64 per cent of cases had been decided in favour of the complainant, 13 per cent in favour of the respondent and 23 per cent of cases had been withdrawn.
[23] Case No.D2000-0235: *Jeanette Winterson v. Mark Hogarth*.

common law trademark or sufficient rights to ground an action for passing off."[24] This decision confirms a literal interpretation of paragraph 4(a) of the Policy. The complainant need not have sufficient rights to succeed in law against this respondent, but he or she must have some "rights" in the name. It may be sufficient to show that "rights" exist in one country which the Panel thinks is significant.

21–48   (3) Gordon Sumner, professionally known as "Sting", failed in his attempt to have the domain name **sting.com** transferred or cancelled. The Panel thought that the ICANN Policy had not intended to create or enforce personality rights, and distinguished the *Jeanette Winterson* and *Julia Roberts* decisions on the facts, accepting that there were a number of legitimate uses for **sting.com**. In spite of the fact that the respondent had offered to sell the domain name to the complainant for reportedly $25,000, this did not mean that the domain name had been registered in bad faith some five years previously. This approach is similar to that required in *One in a Million*: examine all the circumstances. This, and other decisions where the complainant has failed, shows that the Policy only works in favour of the complainant in cases which are reasonably clear cut.[25]

21–49 Most disputes are decided by one expert, drawn from the country in question.[26] This has the distinct advantage that the expert has the necessary knowledge of the local law and can also take into account generally accepted local practices and customs.

21–50   However, it is not all plain sailing. There are still some quite wide differences in the approach taken by experts from different countries. Thus one panel decided that mere registration of a domain name could not constitute bad faith, whereas other panels have decided the exact opposite. The desire to maintain a simple and cheap procedure can result in procedural unfairness: the complainant has no automatic right to respond to the contentions made by the respondent, and it is impossible for the complainant to anticipate every manoeuvre which a respondent may make. There is little opportunity to dispute assertions which are put forward as facts, or statements of intention put forward by registrants. Already, the status of a panel decision is under attack in the courts,[27] although it remains to be seen whether such challenges

---

[24] *Julia Fiona Roberts v. Russell Boyd*, Case No. D2000-0210. The respondent has mounted a challenge to the decision in the U.S. courts.

[25] see, *e.g.* **fuji.com** (respondent had been trading under the Fuji name since 1992); **sampdoria.com** (complainant failed to prove bad faith, the respondent claimed that he would use the domain name to develop a sport and football fan related website)

[26] There appears to be a reasonably high correlation between domicile of complainant and domicile of respondent.

[27] The decision involving **juliaroberts.com** is being challenged in the U.S. courts: Case No. D2000-0210.

have any merit. It would be a shame if the ICANN Policy is beset with legal challenges. Relatively speaking, it provides a cheaper and quicker solution than litigation, but it has its limitations.

3. Jurisdiction and infringement

The type of problem raised by use of marks on the Internet is best **21–51** illustrated with an example. Take the situation where the same trade mark is owned and used by independent companies in the U.S. and the United Kingdom. Each company has a website (**squiffo.com** and **squiffo.co.uk** respectively) which provides information about the company and its products and which features prominent use of the mark. Obviously, both websites can be accessed by an Internet user from anywhere in the world, raising the possibility that someone in the United Kingdom who is familiar with the United Kingdom company will encounter the website of the U.S. company, and vice-versa.[28] The further stage in the example is where one or both companies offers goods or services for sale on their respective websites.

Does the use of the trade mark by the U.S. company on its U.S. **21–52** website constitute infringement of the United Kingdom registered trade mark, and vice-versa? Claimants in this type of situation have argued that use of the trade mark on a website constitutes use of the trade mark throughout the world because the website can be accessed throughout the world.[29] This argument must be wrong and was rejected by Jacob J. in *800–FLOWERS*.[30] Equally, the analogy that the website owner automatically "puts a tentacle onto the user's screen" was also rejected in the same case. At the other extreme, defendants argue that the trade mark is only being used in the country where the web server is situate. This argument may or may not be right, it depends on the circumstances. Defendants also argue that a person in the United Kingdom who accesses a U.S. website is "visiting" the U.S. or using a "supertelescope"[31] to view something in the U.S. from the United Kingdom. This analogy is factually incorrect, as explained above at paras 21–20 to 21–23.

---

[28] This problem is no different from that raised by the two companies advertising in national magazines which happen to spill over in small quantities to the other territory.
[29] An example of the unfairness which can occur if this argument is accepted is provided by the decision of the Nanterre Court of Appeals in France in *SG2 v. Brokat Informationssysteme GmbH*, October 13, 1996. The French claimant had registered "payline" in France for an Internet payment system. The German defendant had registered the same mark in Germany and sold its Internet payment system "Brokat-payline" on the Internet at its site at **www.brokat.de**. The defendant had not sold its system in France and did not intend to do so, because it would infringe French national cryptography regulations. Despite that, the French court granted an injunction preventing the defendant using "payline" in France in any form which extended to the use on the Internet. The court reasoned that the defendant's website could be accessed worldwide and this meant that an infringement had taken place in France.
[30] *1–800 FLOWERS Inc. v. Phonenames Ltd* [2000] E.T.M.R. 369.
[31] An analogy accepted on the facts in *Euromarket Designs v. Peters*, July 25, 2000, Jacob J.

21–53   What is obvious from this example is that a measure of reciprocity is required from the courts of the respective countries, but where is the dividing line? Although this type of conflict is perhaps most likely to arise between the U.S.[32] and the United Kingdom, one can certainly envisage the same conflict arising between two E.U. countries where the law should be exactly the same.

21–54   The dividing line is indicated by normal principles. Infringement in the United Kingdom requires use of the sign in the course of trade in relation to goods or services in the United Kingdom. So the use on the U.S. or any foreign website must constitute use in the course of trade in the United Kingdom before it can amount to infringement of a United Kingdom registered trade mark or, for that matter, passing off in the United Kingdom. This is a question of fact to be decided in all the circumstances:

> ". . .the mere fact that websites can be accessed anywhere in the world does not mean, for trade mark purposes, that the law should regard them as being used everywhere in the world. It all depends on the circumstances, particularly the intention of the website owner and what the reader will understand if he accesses the site."[33]

21–55 This passage from *800–FLOWERS* can be misinterpreted. The issue does not depend on what the website owner says in evidence about his intentions. The inquiry must be objective: what would the reasonable user understand looking at this website? Thus, Jacob J. in *Euromarket Designs* said: ". . .there must be an inquiry as to what the purpose and effect of the advertisement in question is."[34] and "One needs to ask whether the defendant has any trade here, customers buying goods or services for consumption here." Of course, infringement does not require the defendant to have an established trade in the United Kingdom, the only requirement is for use in the course of trade. However, the extent of the defendant's trade with customers in the United Kingdom will be an important factor in the inquiry whether there is use in the course of trade in the United Kingdom.

21–56   When making this type of inquiry, Jacob J. has very sensibly suggested that Internet users are reasonably robust when selecting what to

---

[32] The U.S. courts have also rejected the concept that use on a website is use worldwide. For example, in *Playboy Enterprises v. Chuckleberry Publishing Inc.* (1996) 39 U.S.P.Q. 2d 1746 (District Court of the Southern District of New York), the claimant tried to enforce a 1981 injunction preventing the defendant distributing and selling its Italian "Playmen" men's magazine in the U.S., against the defendant's Italian website which offered access to various photos at two levels—"Playmen-Lite", which was free, and "Playmen-Pro", which required payment. The claimant argued that the defendant should improve its password system so as to eliminate users from the U.S. The court held that the use of "Playmen" was simply on the home page in respect of Italian services. The fact that the website was accessible from the U.S. did not result in breach of the U.S. injunction.

[33] *800-FLOWERS*, at 378.

[34] There being no difference in this context between an advertisement on a website and one in a magazine with international circulation. See Jacob J. in *Euromarket Designs*, para. 15.

look at or investigate further, and use a lot more common sense than most claimants would like. His views may be explained in the following propositions:

(1) The reasonable person,[35] using the Internet expects a search to produce a lot of irrelevant sites, and expects many to be foreign.[36] It follows that the mere fact that a search reveals a reference to a trade mark on a foreign website does not begin to establish use of the sign in the course of trade in the United Kingdom for the purposes of infringement.

(2) Even if it is not immediately obvious from the search results that a site is irrelevant and the user decides to visit an identified site, that does not establish use in the United Kingdom. The user will be able to see fairly quickly that the site is irrelevant, "he will simply say 'this is not for me' and move on".[37]

On the basis of those propositions, and the tests suggested by Jacob J., **21–57** one can suggest the following further propositions:

(a) The expectation that many sites will be foreign means that the user takes at least some notice of the information provided to him about the nationality of the website. That information may be part of the domain name[38] or part of the content of the site.

(b) The appearance of a mark on a foreign website will constitute use of the mark in the course of trade in the United Kingdom if, objectively speaking, the website is aimed at or intended for consumers in the United Kingdom, even if the United Kingdom is only one of the intended markets.

(c) If a significant number of customers in the United Kingdom have purchased goods bearing a mark through a foreign website, then use in the course of trade in the United Kingdom will have been established.

(d) If the only evidence of purchases being made from the United Kingdom is trap purchases conducted on behalf of the claimant, then there is probably no use in the United Kingdom, unless the operation has only just commenced.

It is relatively easy for website owners to make it clear on their website **21–58** whether they wish to and therefore do conduct trade with consumers in foreign countries. A prominent disclaimer may be shown on the home page; alternatively, the terms and conditions of sale may stipulate that products are not for sale to foreign countries; alternatively, the payment methods may themselves prevent sales to foreign countries[39]; alter-

---

[35] Perhaps even "the average consumer".
[36] *Euromarket Designs, op cit.*, para. 23. Also *Avnet Inc. v. Isoact Ltd* [1998] F.S.R. 16, Jacob J.
[37] *800-FLOWERS* [2000] E.T.M.R. 369 at 378.
[38] *e.g.* **crateand barrel-ie.com** or **crateandbarrel.ie**, as in *Euromarket Designs, op cit.*
[39] Leaving aside the possibility that, *e.g.* an American in London may be able to buy from a U.S. website because he uses his U.S. credit card.

natively, the screen on which the user enters the shipping address may not accept a foreign address.[40] In most cases, these types of indications should be determinative, although there will always be the rare case where they are used to conceal the true position.

4. Metatags[41]

21-59 As mentioned above, trade marks or names belonging to others can be used in metatags and, generally, three situations arise. The first is where a trade mark or name of a competitor is used in a metatag; the second is where a famous trade mark is used, but generally the goods or services are different; the third is where the name of a famous person is used.

21-60 Common to all situations where the allegedly infringing mark is contained in a metatag is the issue of whether use in a metatag constitutes use of the mark for the purposes of infringement of registered trade mark and/or passing off. Under the 1994 Act, it is clear that use of a mark in a metatag does constitute use of the sign for the purposes of infringement.[42] The fact that the metatag is normally not seen does not make any difference, due to section 103(2) which specifically includes use "otherwise than by means of a graphic representation". Likewise, for passing off: the fact that the user may not see the metatag does not remove the misrepresentation. In fact, it is likely to increase the occurrence and persistence of deception.

21-61 Apart from that common issue, the three situations fall to be determined on normal principles. In the first situation, use of a competitor's mark is likely to be used in relation to identical goods—hence a section 10(1) infringement—or at least similar goods—section 10(2) infringement. In the second situation, use of a famous mark may constitute a section 10(3) infringement[43] or may be restrained under section 56 of the 1994 Act. Both the first and second situations are likely to result in passing off.

21-62 The third situation presents the usual problems for celebrities where their names are used by unconnected traders. It will only be in rare cases that the celebrity has a valid trade mark registration which is infringed. Likewise, the English law of passing off does not presently extend as far as providing something akin to a right of personality (see

---

[40] *e.g.* a U.S. website may require the prospective purchaser to select a U.S. state for his shipping address.

[41] Reference is invited to the short explanation about metatags at para. 21–24, above.

[42] Accepted in *Road Tech Computer Systems Limited v. Mandata (Management and Data Services) Limited*, May 25, 2000, unreported, a decision of Master Bowman essentially concerning quantum of damages. The defendant had admitted trade mark infringement but not passing off. Summary judgment was granted for both. There are a number of U.S. decisions in which infringement has been found: *Niton Corp. v. Radiation Monitoring Devices Inc.; Playboy Enterprises Inc. v. Calvin Designer Label;* and *Brookfield v. West Coast Entertainment*.

[43] *cf. BT v. One in a Million* [1999] 1 W.L.R. 903, CA.

Chapter 22 on Merchandising generally). The ICANN Dispute Resolution Policy is confined to domain name registrations and there is little or no prospect of those services being extended so as to provide a general jurisdiction over the Internet.[44]

---

[44] Even though the WIPO standing committee on trade marks is examining a draft proposal concerning the protection of trade marks on the Internet.

755

CHAPTER 22

MISCELLANEOUS

1. Trade mark agents

22–01 In general, any act in connection with the registration of a trade mark or any procedure related to a registered trade mark that can be done by or to a person under the Trade Marks Act 1994 can equally be carried out by or done to that person's agent.[1] This general rule is expressly subject to any contrary provision in the Trade Mark Rules.[2] Such an agent can be authorised either orally or in writing, and need not be a registered trade mark agent. However, trade mark agents clearly have particular expertise in dealings with the Patent Office and their conduct is regulated by the Institute of Trade Mark Attorneys and the Secretary of State. This section addresses the powers and duties of registered trade mark agents under the 1994 Act, dealing in turn with the control of the Register of Trade Mark Agents, the powers of the Registrar to refuse to recognise registered agents, privilege as between registered trade mark agents and their clients and the rights of audience of registered trade mark agents.

The Register of Trade Mark Agents

22–02 Section 83 of the 1994 Act empowers the Secretary of State to make rules governing the keeping of a Register of Trade Mark Agents. This provision is identical to those formerly contained in sections 282(1), (2) and (3) of the Copyright, Designs and Patents Act 1988, and the rules made under those subsections, The Register of Trade Mark Agents Rules 1990[3] ("the 1990 Rules"), continue in force unchanged save that references to the "Institute of Trade Mark Agents" were replaced by "Institute of Trade Mark Attorneys" under S.I. 1999 No. 983.

22–03 The Register of Trade Mark Agents ("the Register") was established by rule 3 of the 1990 Rules, and is maintained by the Institute of Trade Mark Attorneys ("the Institute") under control of the Comptroller-

---

[1] 1994 Act, s.82.
[2] Trade Mark Rules 2000, r. 53, and the 1994 Act, s.88, allow the Registrar to refuse to recognise a registered or unregistered trade mark agent in certain circumstances: see para. 22–12, below.
[3] S.I. 1990 No. 1458.

General of Patents, Designs and Trade marks ("the Comptroller"). A "special record" is also maintained[4] of those whose names have been erased from the Register following misconduct, failure to pay fees or by way of correction. Only the details of those who have been erased from the Register are kept on the special record. The details of an agent who would otherwise be entitled to be registered but who is refused registration by reason of misconduct[5] are not entered into the special record. Both the Register and the special record are open to public inspection.

Qualification for registration

The Institute, under the approval of the Comptroller, has the power to **22–04** make rules governing the conduct and general content of examinations for registration as a trade mark agent[6] and has done so. The Regulations for the Examinations for the Registration of Patent Agents and Trade Mark Agents 1991 provide the rules which govern the exams by which a candidate qualifies as a registered trade mark agent. A person who has passed such exams and has either:

(1) completed two years full time practice in the field of intellectual property, with substantial experience in trade mark agency work, under the supervision either of a registered trade mark agent or of a solicitor or barrister (or in Scotland, an advocate) experienced in trade mark agency work in the United Kingdom, or

(2) completed four years of such practice, unsupervised

qualifies for registration.[7] In the four years following commencement of the 1990 Rules various other agents were entitled to qualify for registration on a historical basis, but such provisions have no effect on new registrations. On payment of the required registration fee, those who qualify will be entered on the Register, unless the Secretary of State finds them guilty of misconduct and directs that they should not be registered.[8]

Maintenance of Register

Entries on the Register may be removed on grounds of misconduct[9] or **22–05** non-payment of fees.[10] Errors in the Register can be corrected or erased by the Registrar on request.[11] The Registrar will notify all parties

---

[4] 1990 Rules r. 4.
[5] Pursuant to r. 10(3).
[6] 1990 Rules, r. 8.
[7] 1990 Rules, r. 9.
[8] See para. 22–06, below.
[9] r. 14.
[10] r. 12.
[11] rr. 11 and 13.

affected by the correction of such errors and give them the opportunity to make written representations concerning any such correction or deletion.

Regulation of conduct

22–06 The Secretary of State regulates the conduct of trade mark agents and has the power to investigate allegations of misconduct reported to him. If satisfied, following "due inquiry", that a registered trade mark agent is guilty of misconduct, he may direct that the trade mark agent be removed from the Register on a temporary or permanent basis.[12] On removal, the agent's name is entered into the special record. The procedure for "due inquiry" by the Secretary of State is set out in rules 15 to 19 of the 1990 Rules.

22–07 On commencing such an inquiry the Secretary of State serves a notice on the agent in question informing him of the case against him, setting out the substance of the alleged misconduct, and inviting him to submit written representations concerning the allegations within 21 days. If the agent wishes to make oral representations he must give notice to the Secretary of State at this stage.[13] Copies of the notice and any written representations are served on the Institute.

22–08 At the oral hearing of misconduct proceedings the agent may be represented by any third party or call on any other person to make oral submissions on his behalf (in addition to him) or to give oral or written evidence on his behalf. Rule 16(1) provides that the Secretary of State "shall" permit such evidence and representations at the request of the person affected. The rules of evidence governing such hearings are more lax than in court proceedings. The Secretary of State is not entitled to refuse to admit evidence solely on the grounds that it would not be admissible in a court of law.[14] Indeed, the Rules do not stipulate the basis on which the admission of evidence can be refused by the Secretary of State; presumably wholly irrelevant or scurrilous evidence can be refused as a matter of discretion, although how this tallies with the mandatory admission of evidence under rule 16(1) is not clear.

22–09 The Secretary of State must give written notice of his decision in such proceedings to all parties concerned, but reasons need only be given if the Secretary of State decides to direct that the agent under investigation be removed or suspended from the Register.[15] There is no express provision for appeal from the decision of the Secretary of State. An agent who has been removed from the Register may apply to the Registrar to be reinstated.

22–10 The Secretary of State has similar powers in respect of misconduct by a qualified trade mark agent who has not yet been registered. Following

---

[12] 1990 Rules, r. 14.
[13] 1990 Rules, r. 15(1).
[14] r. 16(3).
[15] r. 17.

an inquiry under the same procedure as for a registered trade mark agent, the Secretary of State may direct that the agent not be registered, although he would otherwise be so entitled.[16]

Section 84 of the 1994 Act makes it a criminal offence for an individual **22–11** falsely to describe themselves as a registered trade mark agent. It is similarly an offence for partnerships and bodies corporate to hold themselves out as a body of registered trade mark agents unless at least one quarter of the partners (or directors as the case may be) are trade mark agents and all those directors or partners who are not registered trade mark agents are registered patent agents.[17]

Registrar may refuse to deal with certain agents

The Registrar of Trade Marks may refuse to recognise a registered (or **22–12** unregistered) trade mark agent in respect of any business under the 1994 Act, if they have[18]:

(1) been convicted of an offence under section 84 of the 1994 Act (see above);
(2) been erased from (and not restored to) the Register of Trade Mark agents on grounds of misconduct; or
(3) been found guilty by the Secretary of State of conduct that would have led to them being removed from the Register if they had in fact been registered.

The Registrar is also entitled to refuse to recognise a partnership or body **22–13** corporate if one of its partners or directors falls within any of the above classes. Of course, the Registrar is not entitled to refuse to recognise a trade mark agent acting on his own behalf, whatever misconduct or offence he has been found guilty of. Agents whom the Registrar refuses to recognise are only prevented from acting as agents on behalf of third parties.

Trade mark agents and privilege

Under the common law no privilege attaches to communications **22–14** between a trade mark agent and his client, whether relating to trade mark matters or otherwise.[19] However, section 284 of the Copyright, Designs and Patents Act 1988 ("CDPA") introduced privilege in respect of communications between clients and their registered trade mark agents[20] concerning the "protection" of designs or trade marks, service

---

[16] 1990 Rules, r. 10(3).
[17] Registered Trade Mark Agents (Mixed Partnerships and Bodies Corporate) Rules 1994, S.I. 1994 No. 363.
[18] 1994 Act, s. 88, Trade Mark Rules 2000, r. 53.
[19] *Dormeuil Trade Mark.* [1983] R.P.C. 131.
[20] And communications between a person and any third party for the purpose of obtaining, or in response to a request for, information which a person is seeking for the purpose of instructing his trade mark agent.

marks or any matter concerning passing off. Such privilege belongs to the client, rather than the trade mark agent. Section 280 of the CDPA bestowed privilege on similar communications between clients and their patent agents. Section 284 of the CDPA was repealed by the 1994 Act, but section 87 of the 1994 Act maintained the same privilege for communications with registered trade mark agents.

22–15   Section 87 of the 1994 Act (and section 284 of the CDPA before it) defined the scope of the privilege granted to communications between clients and their registered trade mark agents (and clients and third parties for the purpose of obtaining, or in response to a request for, information which the client is seeking for the purpose of instructing his trade mark agent) as being equivalent in scope to that afforded to a client in respect of equivalent communications with his solicitor (or for the purposes of instructing his solicitor). Discussions of the scope and nature of the privilege that can be claimed by the client in such circumstances can be found in the commentaries on the Civil Procedure Rules[21] and specialist legal texts. It is not proposed to be dealt with further here.

22–16   It is worthy of note that although the scope of the privilege granted by section 87 of the 1994 Act is defined by reference to that between a client and his solicitor, the section uses different wording in relation to design and trade mark matters on the one hand, and passing off on the other. Privilege is bestowed in respect of "any matter relating to passing off" without limitation, but only in respect of "any matter relating to the *protection* of any design or trade mark".[22] The scope of the phrase "any matter relating to the protection" is clearly narrower than that of the phrase "any matters". If no limitation on the scope of privilege in respect of trade mark or design matters was intended, it is hard to imagine why the words "any matters" were not used throughout the section. It is submitted that correspondence between trade mark agent and client containing advice on purely commercial provisions in a licence (for example) does not relate to the protection of a trade mark and so would not be privileged. However such commercial advice might yet attract privilege if wrapped up or associated with advice relating to the protection of a mark. The test to be applied is presumably to look at the communication in question as a whole and to assess whether or not, on the particular facts and in context, it relates to the protection of a mark.

Rights of audience

22–17 Trade mark agents (whether registered or not) have the right to appear on behalf of their clients in Registry hearings and appeals to the appointed person. Trade mark agents do not have rights of audience

---

[21] CPR, r. 31.3.
[22] Emphasis added.

before the courts, but such rights could be granted by a duly authorised body.[23] The Chartered Institute of Patent Agents ("CIPA") was designated an authorised body for the purposes of granting rights of audience to its members in 1999.[24] The Institute is presently awaiting the outcome of its application to be designated an authorised body. There is no reason to consider that the Institute's application should be refused while that of CIPA was accepted.

2. Company and business names

Company names

A spurious argument used frequently by potential defendants in passing **22–18** off or trade mark infringement actions is that they have registered the name in question as a company name and therefore must be entitled to use it. This is not so.[25]

The choice of company names is regulated by sections 26 to 34 of the **22–19** Companies Act 1985, together with the Company and Business Names Act 1999. Certain names (for example, those suggesting a connection with the Government or a local authority, or implying national or international renown) require the consent of the Secretary of State (in practice through the Registrar of Companies) before they may be included in a company name placed on the Companies Register.[26] Also, it is not permitted to register as a company name a name which is "the same as" one already on the Companies Register.[27]

Once a company has registered its name, the Secretary of State may **22–20** require it to change its name if it is the same as or too like another name on the Companies Register.[28] The procedure is cumbersome and in recent times the passing off action has been used far more to secure the change of name of the later registrant.[29]

Additionally, under section 32 of the Companies Act 1985, the **22–21** Secretary of State has power to require a company to change its name at any time if harm to the public is likely to be caused by its name being misleading.[30]

Business names

Save in relation to companies incorporated outside Great Britain (see **22–22** below at para. 22–24), there is no longer any obligation to register a business name where a person or company is carrying on business

[23] Courts and Legal Services Act 1990, ss. 27, 28.
[24] S.I. 1999 No. 3137. In the six months following its designation as an authorised body, CIPA granted 10 practising certificates
[25] See generally Chap. 14.
[26] 1985 Act, s.26(2)(a).
[27] s.26(1)(c).
[28] s.28(2).
[29] See Chap. 14, paras 14–234 *et seq.*, and especially the decision in *Glaxo plc v. Glaxowellcome Ltd, op.cit.*
[30] See *Association of Certified Public Accountants v. Secretary of State for Trade & Industry* [1998] 1 W.L.R. 164.

under a name different from his or its true name. However, under the provisions of the Business Names Act 1985, if another name is used, all normal business documents are required to state the true name of the persons or company using the business name and an address for service.[31] Also, at any premises where the business is carried on and to which customers or suppliers have access, a notice specifying this information must be displayed in a prominent position.[32] There are minor penalties for non-compliance. Also, a firm or company in breach of the disclosure provisions may lose contractual rights in an action against a party who can show that the breach has caused him financial loss or an inability to bring a claim against the plaintiff.[33]

22–23   Section 3 of the Business Names Act 1985 provides the power for the Secretary of State to issue regulations specifying words and expressions which may not be used as part of a business name without his approval.[34]

Oversea companies

22–24 Under Schedule 21A[35] of the Companies Act 1985 an oversea company[36] which has a branch in Great Britain must inform the Registrar of Companies, amongst other matters, if the name of the company is different from the name under which the business in Great Britain is carried on by the branch.[37] The Registrar of Companies keeps an index of the names of the branches registered under Schedule 21A.[38]

There is no corresponding obligation in section 691 where an oversea company establishes a place of business in Great Britain (but not a branch).[39]

22–25   Within 12 months of the provision of the information required by either section 691 or Schedule 21A as appropriate, section 694 provides that the Secretary of State may object if the name would not be permitted as the name of a domestic company or if it is too like a name

---

[31] s.4. There is an exception for partnerships of more than 20 persons, which must maintain at its principal place of business a list of the names of all the partners provided that: (1) none of the names of the partners appear in the document in question otherwise than in the text or as a signatory; and (2) the document states in legible characters the address of the partnership's principal place of business and a list of the partners' names is open to inspection at that place.

[32] See s.4(1)(b). It should be noted that the so-called "Certificate of Registration" issued by a company in Birmingham, Business Names Registration Plc, is of no greater legal significance than a plain piece of paper with the required information on it.

[33] s.5.

[34] The Company and Business Names Regulations 1981, S.I. 1981 No. 1685, have effect now as if made under s.3.

[35] Given effect by s.690A(2), implementing the Eleventh Company Law Directive 89/666.

[36] As defined in s.744.

[37] Sched. 21A, para. 3(d). The information specified in para. 3 must be notified within one month of the company having opened a branch in Great Britain: para. 1(1).

[38] Companies Act 1985, s.714(1)(aa).

[39] The documents to be delivered to the Registrar are set out in s.691 but do not include an equivalent to Sched. 21A, para. 3(d).

already on the Register,[40] and two months thereafter the oversea company must cease to carry on business under that name.[41]

3. Human rights and trade marks

The Human Rights Act 1998 ("the Act") gives further effect to the rights **22–26** and freedoms protected by the European Convention on Human Rights[42] ("the Convention"). The commencement date of the Act is October 2, 2000. From that date, primary and subordinate legislation must be read and given effect by the courts in a way which is compatible with the Convention[43] and takes into account the decisions and opinions of the European Court of Human Rights.[44]

The Act is not directly justiciable by individuals *per se*, but rather aims **22–27** at the protection of the human rights of individuals against the abuse of power by the State.[45] Under the provisions of the Act, it would be unlawful for a public authority to act in a manner which is incompatible with the Convention.[46] For these purposes, the Act makes it clear that "public authority" includes a court or tribunal.[47] A "person", which includes a corporate entity, may only contend that a public authority has acted (or proposes to act) in a way which is unlawful under the Act if that individual is (or would be) the victim of the unlawful act. On the other hand, the European Court of Human Rights has held that the State has a positive obligation to prevent one person's rights being breached by another private person.[48] In view of this, a court ought at all times to bear in mind and apply the Convention in any proceedings before it, and not merely in actions against a public body allegedly acting contrary to the Convention.

Under the Act the court has wide discretionary powers and may grant **22–28** such relief as it considers just and appropriate,[49] and therefore will have the power to grant injunctions and award damages where in all the circumstances such an award is necessary.[50]

With these wide powers and obligations being given to and imposed **22–29** upon the courts, it is likely that human rights arguments will be raised in many types of legal proceedings, including those concerning the enforcement of intellectual property rights. However, in *Daniels v.*

---

[40] s.694(1) and (2).
[41] s.694(6).
[42] Convention for the Protection of Human Rights and Fundamental Freedoms (Rome, November 4, 1950; TS 71 (1953); Cmnd 8969).
[43] s.3 of the Act.
[44] s.2.
[45] *Per* Lord Irvine, H.L. Report, 29.1.98, col. 422.
[46] s.6(1).
[47] s.6(3) states "In this section 'public authority' includes—(a) a court or tribunal, and (b) any person certain of his functions are functions of a public nature."
[48] *X and Y v. Netherlands* [1985] E.H.R.R. 235.
[49] s.8(1).
[50] s.8(3).

Walker[51] Lord Woolf made it quite clear that at least the higher courts would not be sympathetic to such arguments being raised speculatively: "When the Act of 1998 becomes law, counsel will need to show self-restraint if it is not to be discredited".[52] The principle of most relevance to trade mark infringement and passing off or trade libel actions is the right to freedom of expression set out in Article 10 of the Convention. This states that:

> "1. Everyone has the right to freedom of expression. This right shall include freedom to hold opinions and to receive and impart information and ideas without interference by public authority and regardless of frontiers. . .
>
> (2) The exercise of these freedoms, since it carries with it duties and responsibilities, may be subject to such formalities, conditions, restrictions or penalties as are prescribed by law and are necessary . . . for the protection of the reputation or rights of others, for preventing the disclosure of information received in confidence . . ."

22–30 Section 12 of the Act places an obligation on the court, where it is considering whether to grant any relief in a case, to consider whether such relief may adversely affect the Convention right to freedom of expression.[53] Accordingly, it will be possible for an individual or company (with its own rights to corporate free speech) to request in the context of a trade mark infringement action that the court protects its right to freedom of expression. In strict terms, the award by the court of any injunctive relief preventing a defendant from using (and infringing) a registered trade mark would constitute a fetter on that defendant's freedom of expression. However, the provisions of Article 10(2) of the Convention clearly contemplate this and recognise that the court may grant such injunctions (and other relief) as the right to freedom of expression is subject to such restrictions as are prescribed by law and are necessary for the protection of the rights of others.

22–31 Notwithstanding this, there are clearly limits to the extent to which such a restriction is permissible and it may be that a defendant can raise a freedom of expression defence in cases involving use of the mark on genuine goods, for example. Where such a defence is raised, under section 12(3) the court must be satisfied that the applicant for relief is "likely to establish" its case. This seems to suggest that in such circumstances the *American Cyanamid* principles[54] do not apply but rather a higher standard.

---

[51] [2000] 1 W.L.R. 1382. As the Civil Procedure Rules have as their overriding objective "enabling the court to deal with cases justly" (rule 1.1), the Master of the Rolls considered that the Human Rights Act point did not add anything: at 1386–1387.

[52] At 1387.

[53] s.12(1).

[54] [1975] A.C. 396. See *Series 5* [1996] F.S.R. 273 for a detailed analysis of what that case decided.

In order to assess the courts' likely reaction to the possible conflict **22–32** between trade mark rights and the Convention rights, reference can be made to passing off and defamation actions where the issue of commercial free speech has been raised, particularly as an argument against the grant of an interim injunction.

In defamation actions (including trade libel[55]), the courts have been **22–33** reluctant to restrict the right to free speech unless absolutely necessary. At the interim stage, the courts will generally not grant an injunction to prevent alleged libels if a defendant has pleaded justification and has reasonable grounds for so doing. This practice has been extended in cases such as *Sim v. Heinz*[56] and *Lord Brabourne v. Hough*[57] where the alleged misrepresentation was pleaded in passing off; in the first case, concerning an actor imitated in an advertisement, and the second, an alleged unauthorised biography of Lord Mountbatten. In both cases the injunction was refused as the defendant stated that he intended to justify his claim.

In *Consorzio del Prosciutto di Parma v. Marks & Spencer*[58] the court **22–34** considered the question of commercial free speech in deciding to refuse the plaintiff's application for an interlocutory injunction. Here, Marks & Spencer submitted that they should not be prevented from truthfully informing the public what type of ham they were selling. In assessing the balance of convenience, the court at first instance stated that it did not consider the plaintiff's case "warrants the interference with free speech which the grant of injunctions would involve". Thus, given these cases and the broad provisions of the Convention, the defendant's right to freedom of expression is likely to be an issue raised in trade mark infringement actions, passing off and trade libel, particularly in motions for interim relief. However, *Daniels v. Walker*[59] suggests that the courts will need to be persuaded that Article 10 adds anything to the role which considerations of free speech already play in judicial reasoning and decision-making.

The court's comments in *Ciba-Geigy v. Parke Davis*,[60] a comparative **22–35** advertising case, also should be borne in mind. In this passing off action, Aldous J. stated that the fact that the alleged misrepresentation could be pleaded in both passing-off and in trade libel did not mean that an injunction to restrain the alleged misrepresentation must be refused. In addition, and perhaps more importantly, he added that if he had come to a conclusion that there was a serious issue to be tried, it would have been both appropriate and possible to formulate an injunction to

[55] See Chap. 17.
[56] [1959] R.P.C. 75.
[57] [1981] F.S.R. 421.
[58] [1991] R.P.C. 351, CA.
[59] *Op. cit.*, n. 51.
[60] [1994] F.S.R. 8.

restrain the alleged misrepresentation without substantially infringing upon the defendant's right to free speech. The issue for the court now would be whether the injunction, and its form, is *necessary* for the protection of the rights of others. In this context, arguments may be raised as to whether the specific subject-matter of a trade mark right is being protected.[61]

22–36   The two other Convention rights which may be of relevance in litigation concerning trade marks are the right to respect for private and family life in Article 8 of the Convention ("Everyone has the right to respect for his private and family life, his home and his correspondence") and the right to property contained in Article 1 of Protocol No. 1 to the Convention. Both are subject to "public interest" type exceptions.

22–37   The former is likely to be raised in relation to evidence of wrongdoing obtained by questionable means, for example by trap orders or surveillance, although in *R. v. Broadcasting Standards Commission, ex parte British Broadcasting Corporation*[62] it was left open by the Court of Appeal whether a company has a right to respect for its private life under Article 8.

22–38   The so-called right to property ("Everyone has the right to peaceful enjoyment of his possessions. No one shall be deprived of his possessions except in the public interest") may be relied upon if the Tobacco Advertising Directive[63] is implemented in the United Kingdom and the use of tobacco brands in the advertising and promotion of non-tobacco goods and services is prohibited. It is also a right which could be relied upon in parallel import cases, raising the kind of issues addressed by Laddie J. in *Davidoff*.[64] On the other hand, prima facie a rejection of a trade mark application by the Registry would not seem to be susceptible to challenge under the Article: in *British American Tobacco v. The Netherlands*,[65] a case involving a challenge to a refusal to grant a patent, the European Commission on Human Rights concluded that Article 1 of Protocol No. 1 applied only to existing possessions and did not guarantee any right to acquire property.[66]

---

[61] *Cf.* Chap. 15.

[62] [2000] E.M.L.R. 587.

[63] Directive 98/43 relating to the advertising and sponsorship of Tobacco Products. On June 15, 2000, Advocate-General Fennelly issued an Opinion on the validity of the Directive, concluding that as the Directive cannot be said to advance the interests of the internal market, the Community was not competent to enact it on the basis of the Treaty provisions relied upon: Joined Cases C–376/98 and C–74/99, *Federal Republic of Germany v. European Parliament & Council of the E.U.* and *R. v. Secretary of State for Health, ex p. Imperial Tobacco Ltd and Others*.

[64] See Chap. 15, paras 15–65 *et seq.*, and see further paras 22–39 *et seq.*, below.

[65] (1996) 21 E.H.R.R. 409.

[66] Citing *Van der Mussele* (1984) 6 E.H.R.R. 163, para. 48.

Human rights and parallel imports

It is already well established that commercial speech is protected by **22–39**
Article 10[67], and that all legal entities, irrespective of their corporate
status or the fact that they pursue commercial objectives, benefit from
the protection of Article 10[68]. In these circumstances, a parallel importer
might well invoke Article 10, contending that:

1. an injunction to restrain the importation of genuine goods from
   outside the EEA, even without the consent of the trade mark
   proprietor was in breach;
2. he should be allowed to impart information by the continuing
   presence of the trade mark on the goods without interference
   by public authority and regardless of frontiers;
3. the information imparted by the trade mark was accurate, in
   that it continued correctly to signify source and responsibility
   for quality.[69]

Particularly in the situation where identical goods were marketed **22–40**
througout the world, these circumstances would appear to give rise to a
prima facie interference with the right to freedom of expression. The
issue then arises as to whether such interference is justified under
Article 10(2). The European Commission and Parliament would be likely
to take the view that the adoption of Community-wide exhaustion or
rights and not international exhaustion was a restriction prescribed by
law and necessary in a democratic society. However, this type of
measure of economic policy does not fall comfortably into any of the
interests mentioned in Article 10(2). Possibly, it is necessary in order to
preserve the integrity of the European Economic Area.

It has been observed[70] that the European Court of Humam Rights **22–41**
"has generally deferred to national authorities on the question of the
necessity of interferences with commercial and artistic speech by contrast to political speech". The economic considerations which lie behind
the whole topic of of parellel imports into the EEA can be extremely
complicated. The complexity and the corresponding uncertainty (in
particular the lack of any "right" answer) suggests that the European
Court of Human Rights would decline to interfere in the economic
policy of the EFA.

---

[67] *Markt Intern Verlag v. Federal Republic of Germany* (1989) E.H.R.R. 161, E Ct HR; *Casado Coca v. Spain* (1994) 18 E.H.R.R. 1, E Ct HR; *Jacubowski v. Germany* (1994) 19 E.H.R.R. 64, E Ct HR and *Hertel v. Switzerland* (August 25, 1998) E Ct HR, where the Court held that an injunction restraining a scientist from disseminating views that microwave ovens were dangerous was disproportionate to the legitimate aim of protecting the rights of others, in particular the rights of manufacturers and suppliers of microwave overns to be protected from acts of unfair competition.
[68] *Autronic AG v. Switzerland* (1990) 12 E.H.R.R. 485, E Ct HR.
[69] the expression coined by Laddie J. in *Glaxo Group Ltd v. Dowelhurst* [2000] E.T.M.R. 415.
[70] See Lester & Pannick, *Human Rights Law and Practice* (Butterworths, 1999), para. 4.10.2.

4. Merchandising

Generally

22–42 Over recent years, the business of so-called merchandising using the names and images of celebrities and fictional characters has grown exponentially and is "probably a multi-billion dollar industry in the Western world".[71] The business can be divided into three categories: (1) the exploitation of fictional characters; (2) the exploitation during his or her lifetime of the fame of a celebrity; and (3) the exploitation after her or his death of the enduring fame of a celebrity. Whilst there are many aspects in common in the way the law treats the three categories, there are important differences.

22–43 The exploitation in question will usually involve the licensing of the name at issue together with either one or a number of images: in the first category, an example would be the various Disney characters such as Mickey Mouse; current examples of the second category would be Tiger Woods and Madonna; and the third category would include Elvis Presley and Diana, Princess of Wales. Of course, it could be that a figure in the third category, such as Robin Hood, may transfer to the first category as a result of a film, for example.

22–44 Under English law, there is no right of personality as such,[72] nor indeed a right of privacy.[73] But, as pointed out by Laddie J.: "To stop the use of the whole or part of [a person's] name by another [that person] must show that as a result of such use, the other person is invading some legally recognised right".[74] Recent cases have illustrated the difficulties with protecting such names or likenesses under passing off and trade mark law. In important respects in this area, the law in England has diverged from that elsewhere in the Commonwealth, such as Australia[75] and Canada,[76] where more expansive protection has been accorded.[77]

---

[71] *Per* Anderson J. in *Tony Blain v. Splain* [1994] F.S.R. 497 at 498 (HC (NZ)): a case involving the merchandising of the musical group Metallica and Paul McCartney.

[72] See, generally, Frazer, *Appropriation of Personality—A New Tort?* (1983) 99 L.Q.R. 281, which proposes a statutory tort of appropriation of personality.

[73] See *Kaye v. Robertson* [1991] F.S.R. 62, CA: "This right has so long been disregarded here that it can be recognised now only by the legislature": *per* Leggatt L.J. at 71, noting that a so-called "right of publicity" has been developed in certain jurisdictions in the United States, to protect the commercial interest of celebrities in their identities.

[74] *"Elvis Presley"* [1997] R.P.C. 543 at 547.

[75] See, *e.g.*, the judgments in *Hogan v. Pacific Dunlop*, 12 I.P.R. 225 (Gummow J.) and, on appeal, *Pacific Dunlop Ltd v. Hogan*, 14 I.P.R. 398 (Sheppard, Beaumont and Burchett JJ, Fed. Ct of Australia): a case about a television advertisement for shoes which was an obvious parody of a scene featuring the Crocodile Dundee character played by Paul Hogan from the film "Crocodile Dundee". The parody had not been authorised by or on behalf of Paul Hogan. Gummow J. at first instance and the Full Court on appeal (Sheppard J. dissenting) found passing off.

[76] See, *e.g. Krouse v. Chrysler* (1973) 40 D.L.R. (3d) 15 and *Paramount Pictures v. Howley*, 39 C.P.R. 3d. 419, *per* Van Camp J. (another case involving "Crocodile Dundee").

[77] *Cf.* the South African case of *Lorimar v. Sterling* [1982] R.P.C. 395, involving names from

As mentioned above, merchandising commonly will involve the **22–45** licensing[78] of the name or names in question, frequently together with copyright works, for use on or in relation to particular goods or services. The licences will usually specify quality standards to be complied with by the licensee. The detail and exercise of quality control varies enormously: in *"Holly Hobbie"*[79] the quality control exercisable was described by Lord Brightman as "slight", whereas in other agreements very detailed standards are specified and policed.[80]

As well as copyright, both registered trade marks and the law of **22–46** passing off have been relied upon by licensors and licensees to prevent the sale of unauthorised products, in many cases unsuccessfully on the facts. However, in appropriate circumstances the use of either or both should be considered.

<h3 style="text-align:center">Registered trade marks</h3>

Registration

Historically, in the United Kingdom it has been difficult to register as **22–47** trade marks the names or images on which a merchandising programme is based: under the Trade Marks Act 1938, for example, the mark "Tarzan" was refused registration for films and tapes, and "games, toys and playthings" on the ground that it had a direct reference to the character and quality of the goods.[81] In the words of Salmon L.J.:

> "there is nothing at all in the word TARZAN which would suggest to the public or to the trade that a film or magnetic tape recording had anything to do with the applicant or with anyone else. The word TARZAN when used in connection with a film suggests—and suggests only—that the film has something to do with the well-known fictional person, Tarzan, a man of great strength and agility."[82]

the television series "Dallas".The court found passing off not established on the basis that character merchandising was not so well-known in the country that without proper evidence it could be assumed that the man in the street had any knowledge of it, *per* Van Dijkhorst at 418: "the fact that the names are used in fields totally unrelated to that in which Lorimar does business in South Africa, is of extreme importance. Without any inclination of Lorimar to enter these fields, the public would not expect this American television producer to start manufacturing clothes in South Africa or cater for our culinary tastes, or become interested in those businesses".

[78] All relevant "rights" will often be vested in a merchandising agent, either by way of assignment or licence, and thence licensed or sub-licensed, as the case may be, for particular territories and products.

[79] *Re American Greetings Corp.* [1984] 1 W.L.R. 189 at 197.

[80] *e.g.* the case of *Children's Television Workshop v. Woolworths* [1981] R.P.C. 187, involved the licensing of the Muppets characters under agreements containing rigorous quality standards which were enforced strictly.

[81] *"Tarzan Trade Mark"* [1970] R.P.C. 450, CA. As noted by Edmund-Davies L.J., at 459, the decision on games, toys and the like was not so straightforward as that on films and tapes and turned on the applicant's evidence that such products were "centred on" the Tarzan character, at 457 and 459).

[82] *ibid.*, at 456.

22–48   More recently, the Court of Appeal upheld a judgment of Laddie J.[83] allowing an opponent's appeal against the Registrar's decision to allow registration of "Elvis", "Elvis Presley" and "signature 'Elvis A. Presley'" for goods in Class 3.[84] The applications were made by Elvis Presley Enterprises Inc., which carried on the merchandising activities previously engaged in by or on behalf of the singer when he was alive. Robert Walker L.J. agreed with the conclusion of Laddie J. that the "Elvis" mark had very little distinctiveness, noting:

> "That conclusion was reached by a number of intermediate steps, one of which was the judge's finding that members of the public purchase Elvis Presley merchandise not because it comes from a particular source, but because it carries the name or image of Elvis Presley".[85]

22–49   The court (Simon Brown, Morritt and Robert Walker L.JJ.) therefore agreed with the judge that the "Elvis" mark lacked the distinctiveness required by section 9 of the 1938 Trade Marks Act, and that it was not a word having no direct reference to the character or quality of the goods as required by section 9(1)(b). Morritt L.J. noted in this context that "it is necessary in applying (b) to keep in mind that part of the definition of trade mark which requires that the mark is capable of indicating a connection in the course of trade between the goods and [the applicant]".[86] It was critical to the judgments in this case that the goods for which registration was being sought were what Laddie J characterised as "memorabilia or momentoes" of Elvis Presley, thus making almost inevitable the conclusion that the marks being applied for were neither distinctive nor to be used as trade marks.[87] It is suggested below that an application under the 1994 Act for a similar type of mark which it was intended to merchandise would not necessarily be decided the same way: the *"Elvis"* case was unusual and highlighted well the problems in this area, but should not be taken as authority for the proposition that the names of celebrities (whether living or dead) may not be registered as trade marks.

22–50   In addition to problems with distinctiveness, the owner of a name or mark which it is intended to merchandise has had to overcome the fact that the whole area of licensing of trade marks was one with which the legislature[88] and to a certain extent the courts[89] were uncomfortable.

---

[83] [1997] R.P.C. 543.

[84] [1999] R.P.C. 567.

[85] At 585.

[86] At 592.

[87] As defined in the 1938 Act, s.68(1).

[88] As can be seen from the fiction in the 1938 Act whereby use by a licensee (or registered user) was deemed to be use by the proprietor.

[89] See, *e.g.* *"Pussy Galore" Trade Mark* [1967] R.P.C. 265, in which a company associated with Ian Fleming failed in its application to register "Pussy Galore", the name of a character in the book "Diamonds are Forever". The Board of Trade held that there was no sufficient intention to use (a decision which in earlier editions of this work is characterised as "irreconcilable with the line of cases beginning with 'Bostitch'": see 11th edition at para. 2–04).

Thus, in *"Holly Hobbie"*[90] the House of Lords upheld the Registrar's refusal to register the name of the character in respect of 12 different classes of goods to be made exclusively by the applicant's licensees. The court held that this would constitute "trafficking in the mark"[91] contrary to section 28(6) of the 1938 Act. Lord Bridge (who concurred in the judgment with reluctance) expressed the opinion that section 28(6) "has become a complete anachronism and that the sooner it is repealed the better".[92] The 1994 Act does not contain an equivalent provision and indeed the underlying tenor of that Act is that trade marks may be dealt with as commodities in their own right.

As explained elsewhere,[93] under section 1(1) of the 1994 Act, in order to **22–51** be registered a sign must be capable of distinguishing the goods or services of the proprietor from those of other undertakings and also must not be excluded from registrability by the absolute grounds for refusal set out in section 3. Thus, the sign "David Beckham" may be refused for certain goods on the ground that, as a relatively common name, it is devoid of any distinctive character contrary to section 3(1)(b)[94] (unless it falls within the proviso because, as a result of the use made of it, it has in fact acquired a distinctive character in relation to the relevant goods or services, for example football boots). Where the application is for goods which the average consumer would obviously associate with the celebrity and expect that his or her name on products would be by way of endorsement, for example golfing equipment by Tiger Woods, there should be no difficulty with the application, but when the application relates to goods or services far from the field of activity of the celebrity it should be subject to further inquiry.[95]

The Registry Work Manual notes that where an application is for the **22–52** name of a famous person this raises "complex issues"[96] (referring to the *"Elvis"* case) and states that "there is a greater requirement to consider whether the name is likely to be taken as a badge of origin for the goods/services". However, what must be recognised is that the regime for registration of trade marks under the 1994 Act (and the First Approximation Directive) is more permissive than that of the 1938 Act (under which *Elvis Presley* was decided). Where there is a doubt whether

---

[90] *Re American Greetings Corp's Application* [1984] 1 W.L.R. 189
[91] "Trafficking" means, in the words of Lord Brightman (expressly agreed to by Lord Bridge, at 191), "dealing in a trade mark primarily as a commodity in its own right and not primarily for the purpose of identifying or promoting merchandise in which the proprietor of the mark is interested": at 198.
[92] At 192.
[93] See Chap. 2, generally.
[94] As to the meaning of s.3(1)(b), see above at Chap. 7 generally, and particularly Jacob J., at 306, in the *Treat* case, [1996] R.P.C. 281 and Chadwick L.J. in *Bach* [2000] R.P.C. 513 at 533–535. In order to satisfy the Registry that the mark has distinctive character, it would be necessary to adduce evidence as to how it would be viewed by the average consumer described by the ECJ in *Gut Springenheide* [1998] E.C.R. I–4567 (at para. 31) and *Lloyd Schuhfabrik* [1999] E.T.M.R. 690 (at para. 26).
[95] The Registry may require additional information from the applicant under the Trade Mark Rules 2000, r. 57 (formerly r. 51).
[96] See para. 3.12.9.

the name in question is capable of distinguishing in a trade mark sense, the applicant should be given the benefit of that doubt.[97]

22–53 Whilst it may be that the name of a celebrity such as Bjorn Borg has been used on a variety of products over the years, usually to indicate an endorsement, there seems no reason under the 1994 Act why a company set up by Mr Borg to exploit his renown through merchandising should not make a successful application for registration in relation to, for example, clothing or chinaware. Under the Act it should not be the function of the Registrar to refuse applications for marks which are capable of distinguishing merely because they may be used other than as a trade mark, for example as decoration on a plate or mug. If after registration they are in fact not used as a trade mark, they may be removed by reason of such non-use or use on an application under section 46(1)(a) or (c), respectively. Of course, if it is clear from the circumstances (or as a result of evidence provided under rule 57) that the mark will be used only for the purpose of decoration, the application should be refused.

22–54 On the other hand, there are certain names, especially of deceased celebrities such as Diana, Princess of Wales or Elvis Presley, which as a result of the way in which they have been used may be of such a nature that registration should be refused on the basis that if used on goods the public would be deceived as to their significance, contrary to section 3(3)(b). Also, because they are no longer "capable of distinguishing" origin as required by section 1(1).[98]

Infringement

22–55 In *"British Sugar"*[99] Jacob J. rejected the argument that for there to be infringement the defendant's use must be as a trade mark.[1] However, as regards infringement under section 10(1) and (2) it is arguable that implicit in the need for a likelihood of origin confusion is that the defendant's use of his sign should be as a trade mark, whereas under section 10(3) the detriment may be occasioned by derogatory non-trade mark use.[2] Considering the judgment of Lord McCluskey in *Bravado*

---

[97] Para. 3.12.10 of the Work Manual deals with pictures of famous persons and suggests correctly that such a picture is unlikely to be regarded as indicating the origin of souvenirs or memorabilia relating to that person. However, the possibility of it being so regarded is acknowledged: "In some cases the question . . . may only be capable of being resolved with the benefit of evidence".

[98] See *Bach, op. cit.*

[99] [1996] R.P.C. 281.

[1] See also, Aldous L.J. in *One in a Million, op. cit.*

[2] *Cf.,* the critical analysis of this area by Jaffey *Merchandising and the Law of Trade Marks* [1998] I.P.Q. 240, in which he comments on this point: "the provision could reasonably be understood instead to have the purpose of extending protection beyond origin deceptiveness not in order to secure the merchandising value of the mark to the owner (although this may be the incidental effect), but in order to bolster the protection of the origin function by allowing the trade mark owner to prevent use of his mark that is capable of being deceptive but cannot easily be proved to be": at 262. He concludes: "section 10(3) appears to be designed to give additional protection beyond origin deceptiveness, although this is not how the English courts have interpreted it [relying at the time of the article on the decisions in *Baywatch* and *"Opus"*]": at 263.

Merchandising[3] Jacob J. expressed the view that where "Wet Wet Wet", the name of a pop group, was used in the title of an unauthorised biographical book it did not infringe the group's registration in respect of books,[4] it merely referred to the pop group. He did not consider it necessary for the defendant to have to rely on the defence in section 11(2)(b), as there was not even use falling within section 10.[5]

It seems, therefore, that whether a registered trade mark comprising **22–56** the name of a celebrity or of a fictional character is infringed by use on china, posters, T-shirts and the like will depend on the circumstances, both of the use by the proprietor and the type of use by the alleged infringer.[6] If the public has been educated that the mark is a badge of origin (in the wider sense including approval, selection and endorsement), perhaps by the use of words such as "licensed by" or "official", there will be infringement. However, if the purchaser of a mug with the name (and/or photograph) of their hero or heroine decorating it is indifferent as to who makes it or is responsible for the name being on it, this should not constitute infringement of the registered mark.

What is clear is that the earlier the name is registered as a trade mark **22–57** and the more diligent the owner is in educating the public as to the selection and endorsement functions it performs, the greater the scope of protection the mark will be accorded. The corollary of this is that the more famous a person is when considering registering his or her name as a mark, the more difficult it will be to protect it, both by registration and if registered in infringement proceedings.

Where an application for registration of the name of a celebrity is **22–58** made by, or has been registered by, an unconnected party, it should be refused or declared invalid, as the case may be, on the basis of its being likely to mislead the public (section 3(3)(b)) or as being made in bad faith (section 3(6)).[7]

Criminal proceedings

Where a "merchandising mark" has been registered the proprietor may **22–59** be able to rely on the criminal provisions in section 92 and following of the Trade Marks Act 1994.[8] The importance of this can be seen in *Torbay Council v. Satnam Singh,*[9] a case involving the sale of children's garments bearing the sign "Teletubbies" which unbeknownst to the defendant was registered. It was found by Auld L.J. that the offence is made out if the prosecution prove (1) the fact of registration of a trade mark to

[3] *Op. cit.*
[4] This was surely an example of a mark which should not have been allowed on the Register without evidence that it could function as a badge of origin.
[5] See also, *Trebor Bassett v. The Football Association* [1997] F.S.R. 211.
[6] Similar issues arise with retail marks; see the recent judgment of Jacob J. in *Euromarket Designs Inc. v. Peters* ("*Crate & Barrel*"), July 25, 2000 (as yet unreported).
[7] On bad faith generally, see Chap. 7, paras 7–193 *et seq.*
[8] As to which generally, see Chap. 19.
[9] [2000] F.S.R. 158 (QBD).

which the sign used by the defendant on goods is identical or for which it might be mistaken, (2) that the defendant offers such goods with a view to profit or with intent to cause loss to another, and (3) without the consent of the proprietor. In such circumstances, a registered trade mark, perhaps of dubious validity, is of great value to its proprietor.

Passing off

22–60 Where the name or character which is the subject-matter of a merchandising programme has not been registered as a trade mark, either because this step has not been taken or it has been refused, the "owner" of the name or character may seek to prevent unauthorised use through the medium of a passing-off action. Again, there are difficulties due to the nature of the right protected by such cause of action.[10]

22–61 The classic trinity of reputation/goodwill, misrepresentation and damage has proved troublesome for claimants seeking to prevent the unauthorised use of a name or character on souvenirs or memorabilia. Where the name or character has not been used in the United Kingdom in connection with the particular products in respect of which relief is being sought, the territorial nature of goodwill has posed a problem.

> A local English company, seeing the success of the television series "Kojak" in which the main character sucked lollipops, adopted the name "Kojakpops" for its lollipops. On the basis of its use it brought an action for passing off against the company which had been granted a licence to sell lollipops under the "Kojak" name by the U.S. makers of the television series. In granting an interim injunction, Walton J. described the licence as "writ on water": *Tavener Rutledge v. Trexapalm* [1977] R.P.C. 275.[11]

22–62 Similarly, the "common field of activity" question[12] has proved problematic in passing off cases involving merchandising activity and even though it is now clear that this is not a requirement, it still imposes a significant evidential burden on the claimant in such cases, who must

---

[10] As to which generally, see Chap. 14. Hobbs has commented that "In England . . .the law has tended to part company with commerce in the case of a licence to use unregistered marks and insignia, or material which is not the subject of copyright in the hands of the licensor" in *Passing Off and the Licensing of Merchandising Rights* [1980] E.I.P.R. 47.

[11] And see generally paras 14–54 *et seq.*, esp. 14–56.

[12] See generally paras 14–75 to 14–79 and the cases there cited.

prove both misrepresentation and a real likelihood of damage.[13] In this context it is important for the claimant to adduce evidence of licensing activities or at least an intention to engage in them.[14]

An express misrepresentation as to approval or endorsement, for **22–63** example by stating that products are "official" when they are not, clearly constitutes passing off. On the other hand, in *Harrison and Starkey v. Polydor*[15] George Harrison and Ringo Starr failed in a passing-off action to prevent the issue of a record album of taped interviews with a journalist. The album sleeve was to have printed prominently on the front cover the words "The Beatles" and "from the David Wigg Interviews", together with a number of photographs of The Beatles. An interim injunction was refused by Walton J. as there was no real prospect of the plaintiffs succeeding at trial. There had been no misrepresentation either express or implied.

Evidence must be adduced by the claimant to establish the presence **22–64** of a misrepresentation and in *Mirage Studios v. Counter-Feat*[16] the claimant succeeded in showing that "a substantial number of the buying public now expect and know that where a famous cartoon or television character is reproduced on goods, that reproduction is the result of a licence granted by the owner of the copyright or owner of other rights in the character".[17] The Vice-Chancellor distinguished the *Wombles*, *Kojak* and *Abba* cases[18] on the ground that these had been concerned only with the licensing of names as opposed to the licensing of copyright mater-

---

[13] See, *e.g. Lyngstad v. Anabas* [1977] F.S.R. 62 (a case involving the unauthorised use of photographs of the pop group Abba on badges, T-shirts and pillowslips), in which Oliver J. stated: "I am entirely unsatisfied that there is any real possibility of confusion. I do not think that anyone . . . receiving the goods. . .could reasonably imagine that all the pop stars . . . were giving their approval to the goods offered or that the defendants were doing anything more than catering for a popular demand among teenagers for effigies of their idols": at 68. Also see, in relation to the fictional characters, the Wombles, *Wombles v. Womble Skip Hire* [1975] F.S.R. 488, *cf. IPC Magazines v. Black & White Music* ("Judge Dredd") [1983] F.S.R. 348, where Goulding J. found that a substantial number of people would assume that the plaintiff, owners of the copyright in the comic strip "Judge Dredd", had endorsed the defendant's record containing a song called "Judge Dredd". Despite this, he refused an interim injunction as he could see no likelihood of damage.

[14] See *Stringfellow v. McCain Foods* [1984] R.P.C. 501, CA, in which Slade L.J. noted that the claimant had never contemplated exploitation of his name through merchandising, at 545. In his article cited above at n. 6, Hobbs comments: "In an era of systematic commercialisation, it ought to be possible to establish that injury to a licensing programme is the natural and foreseeable consequence of the pre-emptive marketing of unlicensed merchandise. From there it is a very short step to the full protection of merchandising rights in England" (at 51).

[15] [1977] F.S.R. 1.

[16] [1991] F.S.R. 145

[17] *Per* Sir Nicolas Browne-Wilkinson, V.-C. See also another case involving the "Teenage Mutant Ninja Turtles" characters, *Surge Licensing v. Pearson* 21 I.P.R. 228 (Fed Ct of Australia), in which Einfield J. found that no evidence was required of consumers being actually misled or deceived: it is submitted that the position is different in England and any claimant would be well advised to adduce such evidence.

[18] *Op. cit.*

ial.[19] In *Elvis Presley*[20] Robert Walker L.J. commented that he found the Vice-Chancellor's judgment "very clear and convincing".[21]

22–65   Notwithstanding these developments, for a passing off action to succeed it remains critical to prove that there has been a relevant misrepresentation, *i.e.* one which damages (or is likely to damage) goodwill. Thus, in *BBC Worldwide v. Pally Screen Printing*,[22] a case involving unauthorised use of pictures of the "Teletubbies" characters on T-shirts, Laddie J. refused an application for summary judgment on the issues of copyright infringement and passing off. Of the latter, he considered that

> "it inevitably must be a question of fact whether or not members of the public seeing the T-shirts at issue will be deceived. . .the plaintiffs will need to show that members of the public would look at this type of artwork and consider it to represent the plaintiffs or products made with the plaintiffs' approval. It seems to me that it is quite possible that members of the public will look at T-shirts bearing this artwork and think no more than it is artwork bearing illustrations of well-known television characters without having any regard whatsoever to the source of supply and without having any regard as to whether or not these T-shirts were put out with the sanction of or under the aegis of the plaintiffs."[23]

In other words, the claimant should not rely on the court assuming the misrepresentation required to found the cause of action.

Domain names

22–66 Problems arising from the unauthorised registration of celebrity or character names as domain names are dealt with in Chapter 21.

---

[19] At 158, suggesting also that they may require reconsideration at some point if the evidence before the court as to the public awareness of character merchandising is more favourable.
[20] [1999] R.P.C. 567.
[21] At 582.
[22] [1998] F.S.R. 665.
[23] At 674.

APPENDICES

APPENDICES

PART I

KEY STATUTES

APPENDIX 1

Trade Marks Act 1994

CHAPTER 26

781

782

An Act to make new provision for registered trade marks, implementing Council Directive No. 89/104/EEC of 21st December 1988 to approximate the laws of the Member States relating to trade marks; to make provision in connection with Council Regulation (EC) No. 40/94 of 20th December 1993 on the Community trade mark; to give effect to the Madrid Protocol Relating to the International Registration of Marks of 27th June 1989, and to certain provisions of the Paris

Convention for the Protection of Industrial Property of 20th March 1883, as revised and amended; and for connected purposes.

[21ST JULY 1994]

PART I

REGISTERED TRADE MARKS

Introductory

Trade marks

1.—(1) In this Act a "trade mark" means any sign capable of being repres- **A1–02**
ented graphically which is capable of distinguishing goods or services of one undertaking from those of other undertakings.

A trade mark may, in particular, consist of words (including personal names), designs, letters, numerals or the shape of goods or their packaging.

(2) References in this Act to a trade mark include, unless the context otherwise requires, references to a collective mark (see section 49) or certification mark (see section 50).

Registered trade marks

2.—(1) A registered trade mark is a property right obtained by the registration **A1–03**
of the trade mark under this Act and the proprietor of a registered trade mark has the rights and remedies provided by this Act.

(2) No proceedings lie to prevent or recover damages for the infringement of an unregistered trade mark as such; but nothing in this Act affects the law relating to passing off.

Grounds for refusal of registration

Absolute grounds for refusal of registration

3.—(1) The following shall not be registered— **A1–04**

  (a) signs which do not satisfy the requirements of section 1(1),
  (b) trade marks which are devoid of any distinctive character,
  (c) trade marks which consist exclusively of signs or indications which may serve, in trade, to designate the kind, quality, quantity, intended purpose, value, geographical origin, the time of production of goods or of rendering of services, or other characteristics of goods or services,
  (d) trade marks which consist exclusively of signs or indications which have become customary in the current language or in the *bona fide* and established practices of the trade:

Provided that, a trade mark shall not be refused registration by virtue of paragraph (b), (c) or (d) above if, before the date of application for registration, it has in fact acquired a distinctive character as a result of the use made of it.

(2) A sign shall not be registered as a trade mark if it consists exclusively of—

  (a) the shape which results from the nature of the goods themselves,
  (b) the shape of goods which is necessary to obtain a technical result, or

(c) the shape which gives substantial value to the goods.

(3) A trade mark shall not be registered if it is—

    (a) contrary to public policy or to accepted principles of morality, or

    (b) of such a nature as to deceive the public (for instance as to the nature, quality or geographical origin of the goods or service).

(4) A trade mark shall not be registered if or to the extent that its use is prohibited in the United Kingdom by any enactment or rule of law or by any provision of Community law.

(5) A trade mark shall not be registered in the cases specified, or referred to, in section 4 (specially protected emblems).

(6) A trade mark shall not be registered if or to the extent that the application is made in bad faith.

Specially protected emblems

A1–05   **4.**—(1) A trade mark which consists of or contains—

    (a) the Royal arms, or any of the principal armorial bearings of the Royal arms, or any insignia or device so nearly resembling the Royal arms or any such armorial bearing as to be likely to be mistaken for them or it,

    (b) a representation of the Royal crown or any of the Royal flags,

    (c) a representation of Her Majesty or any member of the Royal family, or any colourable imitation thereof, or

    (d) words, letters or devices likely to lead persons to think that the applicant either has or recently has had Royal patronage or authorisation,

shall not be registered unless it appears to the registrar that consent has been given by or on behalf of Her Majesty or, as the case may be, the relevant member of the Royal family.

(2) A trade mark which consists of or contains a representation of—

    (a) the national flag of the United Kingdom (commonly known as the Union Jack), or

    (b) the flag of England, Wales, Scotland, Northern Ireland or the Isle of Man,

shall not be registered if it appears to the registrar that the use of the trade mark would be misleading or grossly offensive.

Provision may be made by rules identifying the flags to which paragraph (b) applies.

(3) A trade mark shall not be registered in the cases specified in—

    section 57 (national emblems, &c. of Convention countries), or

    section 58 (emblems, &c. of certain international organisations).

(4) Provision may be made by rules prohibiting in such cases as may be prescribed the registration of a trade mark which consists of or contains—

    (a) arms to which a person is entitled by virtue of a grant of arms by the Crown, or

    (b) insignia so nearly resembling such arms as to be likely to be mistaken for them,

unless it appears to the registrar that consent has been given by or on behalf of that person.

Where such a mark is registered, nothing in this Act shall be construed as authorising its use in any way contrary to the laws of arms.

(5) A trade mark which consists of or contains a controlled representation within the meaning of the Olympic Symbol etc. (Protection) Act 1995 shall not be registered unless it appears to the registrar—

(a) that the application is made by the person for the time being appointed under section 1(2) of the Olympic Symbol etc. (Protection) Act 1995 (power of Secretary of State to appoint a person as the proprietor of the Olympics association right), or

(b) that consent has been given by or on behalf of the person mentioned in paragraph (a) above.

Subs. (5) was added by the Olympic Symbol etc. (Protection) Act 1995, s. 13.

Relative grounds for refusal of registration

5.—(1) A trade mark shall not be registered if it is identical with an earlier **A1–06** trade mark and the goods or services for which the trade mark is applied for are identical with the goods or services for which the earlier trade mark is protected.

(2) A trade mark shall not be registered if because—

(a) it is identical with an earlier trade mark and is to be registered for goods or services similar to those for which the earlier trade mark is protected, or

(b) it is similar to an earlier trade mark and is to be registered for goods or services identical with or similar to those for which the earlier trade mark is protected,

there exists a likelihood of confusion on the part of the public, which includes the likelihood of association with the earlier trade mark.

(3) A trade mark which—

(a) is identical with or similar to an earlier trade mark, and

(b) is to be registered for goods or services which are not similar to those for which the earlier trade mark is protected,

shall not be registered if, or to the extent that, the earlier trade mark has a reputation in the United Kingdom (or, in the case of a Community trade mark, in the European Community) and the use of the later mark without due cause would take unfair advantage of, or be detrimental to, the distinctive character or the repute of the earlier trade mark.

(4) A trade mark shall not be registered if, or to the extent that, its use in the United Kingdom is liable to be prevented—

(a) by virtue of any rule of law (in particular, the law of passing off) protecting an unregistered trade mark or other sign used in the course of trade, or

(b) by virtue of an earlier right other than those referred to in subsections (1) to (3) or paragraph (a) above, in particular by virtue of the law of copyright, design right or registered designs.

A person thus entitled to prevent the use of a trade mark is referred to in this Act as the proprietor of an "earlier right" in relation to the trade mark.

(5) Nothing in this section prevents the registration of a trade mark where the proprietor of the earlier trade mark or other earlier right consents to the registration.

Meaning of "earlier trade mark"

6.—(1) In this Act an "earlier trade mark" means—   **A1–07**

(a) a registered trade mark, international trade mark (UK) or Community trade mark which has a date of application for registration earlier than that of the trade mark in question, taking account (where appropriate) of the priorities claimed in respect of the trade marks,

(b) a Community trade mark which has a valid claim to seniority from an earlier registered trade mark or international trade mark (UK), or

(c) a trade mark which, at the date of application for registration of the trade mark in question or (where appropriate) of the priority, claimed in respect of the application, was entitled to protection under the Paris Convention **or the WTO agreement** as a well known trade mark.

(2) References in this Act to an earlier trade mark include a trade mark in respect of which an application for registration has been made and which, if registered, would be an earlier trade mark by virtue of subsection (1)(a) or (b), subject to its being so registered.

(3) A trade mark within subsection (1)(a) or (b) whose registration expires shall continue to be taken into account in determining the registrability of a later mark for a period of one year after the expiry unless the registrar is satisfied that there was no *bona fide* use of the mark during the two years immediately preceding the expiry.

The reference to the WTO Agreement was added by the Patents and Trade Marks (World Trade Organisation) Regulations 1999, S.I. 1999 No. 1899, reg. 13.

Raising of relative grounds in case of honest concurrent use.

A1–08   7.—(1) This section applies where on an application for the registration of a trade mark it appears to the registrar—

(a) that there is an earlier trade mark in relation to which the conditions set out in section 5(1), (2) or (3) obtain, or

(b) that there is an earlier right in relation to which the condition set out in section 5(4) is satisfied,

but the applicant shows to the satisfaction of the registrar that there has been honest concurrent use of the trade mark for which registration is sought.

(2) In that case the registrar shall not refuse the application by reason of the earlier trade mark or other earlier right unless objection on that ground is raised in opposition proceedings by the proprietor of that earlier trade mark or other earlier right.

(3) For the purposes of this section "honest concurrent use" means such use in the United Kingdom, by the applicant or with his consent, as would formerly have amounted to honest concurrent use for the purposes of section 12(2) of the Trade Marks Act 1938.

(4) Nothing in this section affects—

(a) the refusal of registration on the grounds mentioned in section 3 (absolute grounds for refusal), or

(b) the making of an application for a declaration of invalidity under section 47(2) (application on relative grounds where no consent to registration).

(5) This section does not apply when there is an order in force under section 8 below.

Power to require that relative grounds be raised in opposition proceedings

A1–09   8.—(1) The Secretary of State may by order provide that in any case a trade mark shall not be refused registration on a ground mentioned in section 5 (relative grounds for refusal) unless objection on that ground is raised in opposition proceedings by the proprietor of the earlier trade mark or other earlier right.

(2) The order may make such consequential provision as appears to the Secretary of State appropriate—

(a) with respect to the carrying out by the registrar of searches of earlier trade marks, and

(b) as to the persons by whom an application for a declaration of invalidity may be made on the grounds specified in section 47(2) (relative grounds).

(3) An order making such provision as is mentioned in subsection (2)(a) may direct that so much of section 37 (examination of application) as requires a search to be carried out shall cease to have effect.

(4) An order making such provision as is mentioned in subsection (2)(b) may provide that so much of section 47(3) as provides that any person may make an application for a declaration of invalidity shall have effect subject to the provisions of the order.

(5) An order under this section shall be made by statutory instrument, and no order shall be made unless a draft of it has been laid before and approved by a resolution of each House of Parliament.

No such draft of an order making such provision as is mentioned in subsection (1) shall be laid before Parliament until after the end of the period of ten years beginning with the day on which applications for Community trade marks may first be filed in pursuance of the Community Trade Mark Regulation.

(6) An order under this section may contain such transitional provisions as appear to the Secretary of State to be appropriate.

Effects of registered trade mark

Rights conferred by registered trade mark

9.—(1) The proprietor of a registered trade mark has exclusive rights in the **A1–10** trade mark which are infringed by use of the trade mark in the United Kingdom without his consent.

The acts amounting to infringement, if done without the consent of the proprietor, are specified in section 10.

(2) References in this Act to the infringement of a registered trade mark are to any such infringement of the rights of the proprietor.

(3) The rights of the proprietor have effect from the date of registration (which in accordance with section 40(3) is the date of filing of the application for registration):

Provided that—

    (a) no infringement proceedings may be begun before the date on which the trade mark is in fact registered; and

    (b) no offence under section 92 (unauthorised use of trade mark, &c. in relation to goods) is committed by anything done before the date of publication of the registration.

Infringement of registered trade mark

10.—(1) A person infringes a registered trade mark if he uses in the course of **A1–11** trade a sign which is identical with the trade mark in relation to goods or services which are identical with those for which it is registered.

(2) A person infringes a registered trade mark if he uses in the course of trade a sign where because—

    (a) the sign is identical with the trade mark and is used in relation to goods or services similar to those for which the trade mark is registered, or

    (b) the sign is similar to the trade mark and is used in relation to goods or services identical with or similar to those for which the trade mark is registered,

there exists a likelihood of confusion on the part of the public, which includes the likelihood of association with the trade mark.

(3) A person infringes a registered trade mark if he uses in the course of trade a sign which—

(a) is identical with or similar to the trade mark, and

(b) is used in relation to goods or services which are not similar to those for which the trade mark is registered,

where the trade mark has a reputation in the United Kingdom and the use of the sign, being without due cause, takes unfair advantage of, or is detrimental to, the distinctive character or the repute of the trade mark.

(4) For the purposes of this section a person uses a sign if, in particular, he—

(a) affixes it to goods or the packaging thereof;

(b) offers or exposes goods for sale, puts them on the market or stocks them for those purposes under the sign, or offers or supplies services under the sign;

(c) imports or exports goods under the sign; or

(d) uses the sign on business papers or in advertising.

(5) A person who applies a registered trade mark to material intended to be used for labelling or packaging goods, as a business paper, or for advertising goods or services, shall be treated as a party to any use of the material which infringes the registered trade mark if when he applied the mark he knew or had reason to believe that the application of the mark was not duly authorised by the proprietor or a licensee.

(6) Nothing in the preceding provisions of this section shall be construed as preventing the use of a registered trade mark by any person for the purpose of identifying goods or services as those of the proprietor or a licensee.

But any such use otherwise than in accordance with honest practices in industrial or commercial matters shall be treated as infringing the registered trade mark if the use without due cause takes unfair advantage of, or is detrimental to, the distinctive character or repute of the trade mark.

Limits on effect of registered trade mark

A1–12   **11.**—(1) A registered trade mark is not infringed by the use of another registered trade mark in relation to goods or services for which the latter is registered (but see section 47(6) (effect of declaration of invalidity of registration)).

(2) A registered trade mark is not infringed by—

(a) the use by a person of his own name or address,

(b) the use of indications concerning the kind, quality, quantity, intended purpose, value, geographical origin, the time of production of goods or of rendering of services, or other characteristics of goods or services, or

(c) the use of the trade mark where it is necessary to indicate the intended purpose of a product or service (in particular, as accessories or spare parts),

provided the use is in accordance with honest practices in industrial or commercial matters.

(3) A registered trade mark is not infringed by the use in the course of trade in a particular locality of an earlier right which applies only in that locality.

For this purpose an "earlier right" means an unregistered trade mark or other sign continuously used in relation to goods or services by a person or a predecessor in title of his from a date prior to whichever is the earlier of—

(a) the use of the first-mentioned trade mark in relation to those goods or services by the proprietor or a predecessor in title of his, or

(b) the registration of the first-mentioned trade mark in respect of those goods or services in the name of the proprietor or a predecessor in title of his;

and an earlier right shall be regarded as applying in a locality if, or to the extent that, its use in that locality is protected by virtue of any rule of law (in particular, the law of passing off).

Exhaustion of rights conferred by registered trade mark

12.—(1) A registered trade mark is not infringed by the use of the trade mark **A1–13** in relation to goods which have been put on the market in the European Economic Area under that trade mark by the proprietor or with his consent.

(2) Subsection (1) does not apply where there exist legitimate reasons for the proprietor to oppose further dealings in the goods (in particular, where the condition of the goods has been changed or impaired after they have been put on the market).

Registration subject to disclaimer or limitation

13.—(1) An applicant for registration of a trade mark, or the proprietor of a **A1–14** registered trade mark, may—

(a) disclaim any right to the exclusive use of any specified element of the trade mark, or

(b) agree that the rights conferred by the registration shall be subject to a specified territorial or other limitation;

and where the registration of a trade mark is subject to a disclaimer or limitation, the rights conferred by section 9 (rights conferred by registered trade mark) are restricted accordingly.

(2) Provision shall be made by rules as to the publication and entry in the register of a disclaimer or limitation.

Infringement proceedings

Action for infringement

14.—(1) An infringement of a registered trade mark is actionable by the **A1–15** proprietor of the trade mark.

(2) In an action for infringement all such relief by way of damages, injunctions, accounts or otherwise is available to him as is available in respect of the infringement of any other property right.

Order for erasure &c. of offending sign

15.—(1) Where a person is found to have infringed a registered trade mark, **A1–16** the court may make an order requiring him—

(a) to cause the offending sign to be erased, removed or obliterated from any infringing goods, material or articles in his possession, custody or control, or

(b) if it is not reasonably practicable for the offending sign to be erased, removed or obliterated, to secure the destruction of the infringing goods, material or articles in question.

(2) If an order under subsection (1) is not complied with, or it appears to the court likely that such an order would not be complied with, the court may order that the infringing goods, material or articles be delivered to such person as the court may direct for erasure, removal or obliteration of the sign, or for destruction, as the case may be.

Order for delivery up of infringing goods, material or articles

16.—(1) The proprietor of a registered trade mark may apply to the court for **A1–17** an order for the delivery up to him, or such other person as the court may direct, of any infringing goods, material or articles which a person has in his possession, custody or control in the course of a business.

(2) An application shall not be made after the end of the period specified in section 18 (period after which remedy of delivery up not available); and no order shall be made unless the court also makes, or it appears to the court that there are grounds for making, an order under section 19 (order as to disposal of infringing goods, &c.).

(3) A person to whom any infringing goods, material or articles are delivered up in pursuance of an order under this section shall, if an order under section 19 is not made, retain them pending the making of an order, or the decision not to make an order, under that section.

(4) Nothing in this section affects any other power of the court.

Meaning of "infringing goods, material or articles"

A1–18   **17.**—(1) In this Act the expressions "infringing goods", "infringing material" and "infringing articles" shall be construed as follows.

(2) Goods are "infringing goods", in relation to a registered trade mark, if they or their packaging bear a sign identical or similar to that mark and—

    (a) the application of the sign to the goods or their packaging was an infringement of the registered trade mark, or

    (b) the goods are proposed to be imported into the United Kingdom and the application of the sign in the United Kingdom to them or their packaging would be an infringement of the registered trade mark, or

    (c) the sign has otherwise been used in relation to the goods in such a way as to infringe the registered trade mark.

(3) Nothing in subsection (2) shall be construed as affecting the importation of goods which may lawfully be imported into the United Kingdom by virtue of an enforceable Community right.

(4) Material is "infringing material", in relation to a registered trade mark if it bears a sign identical or similar to that mark and either—

    (a) it is used for labelling or packaging goods, as a business paper, or for advertising goods or services, in such a way as to infringe the registered trade mark, or

    (b) it is intended to be so used and such use would infringe the registered trade mark.

(5) "Infringing articles", in relation to a registered trade mark, means articles—

    (a) which are specifically designed or adapted for making copies of a sign identical or similar to that mark, and

    (b) which a person has in his possession, custody or control, knowing or having reason to believe that they have been or are to be used to produce infringing goods or material.

Period after which remedy of delivery up not available

A1–19   **18.**—(1) An application for an order under section 16 (order for delivery up of infringing goods, material or articles) may not be made after the end of the period of six years from—

    (a) in the case of infringing goods, the date on which the trade mark was applied to the goods or their packaging,

    (b) in the case of infringing material, the date on which the trade mark was applied to the material, or

    (c) in the case of infringing articles, the date on which they were made,

except as mentioned in the following provisions.

(2) If during the whole or part of that period the proprietor of the registered trade mark—

(a) is under a disability, or
(b) is prevented by fraud or concealment from discovering the facts entitling him to apply for an order,

an application may be made at any time before the end of the period of six years from the date on which he ceased to be under a disability or, as the case may be, could with reasonable diligence have discovered those facts.

(3) In subsection (2) "disability"—

(a) in England and Wales, has the same meaning as in the Limitation Act 1980;
(b) in Scotland, means legal disability within the meaning of the Prescription and Limitation (Scotland) Act 1973;
(c) in Northern Ireland, has the same meaning as in the Limitation (Northern Ireland) Order 1989.

Order as to disposal of infringing goods, material or articles

19.—(1) Where infringing goods, material or articles have been delivered up in **A1–20** pursuance of an order under section 16, an application may be made to the court—

(a) for an order that they be destroyed or forfeited to such person as the court may think fit, or
(b) for a decision that no such order should be made.

(2) In considering what order (if any) should be made, the court shall consider whether other remedies available in an action for infringement of the registered trade mark would be adequate to compensate the proprietor and any licensee and protect their interests.

(3) Provision shall be made by rules of court as to the service of notice on persons having an interest in the goods, material or articles, and any such person is entitled—

(a) to appear in proceedings for an order under this section, whether or not he was served with notice, and
(b) to appeal against any order made, whether or not he appeared;

and an order shall not take effect until the end of the period within which notice of an appeal may be given or, if before the end of that period notice of appeal is duly given, until the final determination or abandonment of the proceedings on the appeal.

(4) Where there is more than one person interested in the goods, material or articles, the court shall make such order as it thinks just.

(5) If the court decides that no order should be made under this section, the person in whose possession, custody or control the goods, material or articles were before being delivered up is entitled to their return.

(6) References in this section to a person having an interest in goods, material or articles include any person in whose favour an order could be made under this section or under section 114, 204 or 231 of the Copyright, Designs and Patents Act 1988 (which make similar provision in relation to infringement of copyright, rights in performances and design right).

Jurisdiction of sheriff court or county court in Northern Ireland

20. Proceedings for an order under section 16 (order for delivery up of **A1–21** infringing goods, material or articles) or section 19 (order as to disposal of infringing goods, &c.) may be brought—

793

    (a) in the sheriff court in Scotland, or

    (b) in a county court in Northern Ireland.

This does not affect the jurisdiction of the Court of Session or the High Court in Northern Ireland.

Remedy for groundless threats of infringement proceedings

A1–22   **21.**—(1) Where a person threatens another with proceedings for infringement of a registered trade mark other than—

    (a) the application of the mark to goods or their packaging,

    (b) the importation of goods to which, or to the packaging of which, the mark has been applied, or

    (c) the supply of services under the mark,

any person aggrieved may bring proceedings for relief under this section.

(2) The relief which may be applied for is any of the following—

    (a) a declaration that the threats are unjustifiable,

    (b) an injunction against the continuance of the threats,

    (c) damages in respect of any loss he has sustained by the threats;

and the plaintiff is entitled to such relief unless the defendant shows that the acts in respect of which proceedings were threatened constitute (or if done would constitute) an infringement of the registered trade mark concerned.

(3) If that is shown by the defendant, the plaintiff is nevertheless entitled to relief if he shows that the registration of the trade mark is invalid or liable to be revoked in a relevant respect.

(4) The mere notification that a trade mark is registered, or that an application for registration has been made, does not constitute a threat of proceedings for the purposes of this section.

Registered trade mark as object of property

Nature of registered trade mark

A1–23   **22.** A registered trade mark is personal property (in Scotland, incorporeal moveable property).

Co-ownership of registered trade mark

A1–24   **23.**—(1) Where a registered trade mark is granted to two or more persons jointly, each of them is entitled, subject to any agreement to the contrary, to an equal undivided share in the registered trade mark.

(2) The following provisions apply where two or more persons are co-proprietors of a registered trade mark, by virtue of subsection (1) or otherwise.

(3) Subject to any agreement to the contrary, each co-proprietor is entitled, by himself or his agents, to do for his own benefit and without the consent of or the need to account to the other or others, any act which would otherwise amount to an infringement of the registered trade mark.

(4) One co-proprietor may not without the consent of the other or others—

    (a) grant a licence to use the registered trade mark, or

    (b) assign or charge his share in the registered trade mark (or, in Scotland, cause or permit security to be granted over it).

(5) Infringement proceedings may be brought by any co-proprietor, but he may not, without the leave of the court, proceed with the action unless the other, or each of the others, is either joined as a plaintiff or added as a defendant.

A co-proprietor who is thus added as a defendant shall not be made liable for any costs in the action unless he takes part in the proceedings.

Nothing in this subsection affects the granting of interlocutory relief on the application of a single co-proprietor.

(6) Nothing in this section affects the mutual rights and obligations of trustees or personal representatives, or their rights and obligations as such.

Assignment, &c. of registered trade mark

24.—(1) A registered trade mark is transmissible by assignment, testamentary **A1–25** disposition or operation of law in the same way as other personal or moveable property.

It is so transmissible either in connection with the goodwill of a business or independently.

(2) An assignment or other transmission of a registered trade mark may be partial, that is, limited so as to apply—

(a) in relation to some but not all of the goods or services for which the trade mark is registered, or

(b) in relation to use of the trade mark in a particular manner or a particular locality.

(3) An assignment of a registered trade mark, or an assent relating to a registered trade mark, is not effective unless it is in writing signed by or on behalf of the assignor or, as the case may be, a personal representative.

Except in Scotland, this requirement may be satisfied in a case where the assignor or personal representative is a body corporate by the affixing of its seal.

(4) The above provisions apply to assignment by way of security as in relation to any other assignment.

(5) A registered trade mark may be the subject of a charge (in Scotland, security) in the same way as other personal or moveable property.

(6) Nothing in this Act shall be construed as affecting the assignment or other transmission of an unregistered trade mark as part of the goodwill of a business.

Registration of transactions affecting registered trade mark

25.—(1) On application being made to the registrar by— **A1–26**

(a) a person claiming to be entitled to an interest in or under a registered trade mark by virtue of a registrable transaction, or

(b) any other person claiming to be affected by such a transaction,

the prescribed particulars of the transaction shall be entered in the register.

(2) The following are registrable transactions—

(a) an assignment of a registered trade mark or any right in it;

(b) the grant of a licence under a registered trade mark;

(c) the granting of any security interest (whether fixed or floating) over a registered trade mark or any right in or under it;

(d) the making by personal representatives of an assent in relation to a registered trade mark or any right in or under it;

(e) an order of a court or other competent authority transferring a registered trade mark or any right in or under it.

(3) Until an application has been made for registration of the prescribed particulars of a registrable transaction—

(a) the transaction is ineffective as against a person acquiring a conflicting interest in or under the registered trade mark in ignorance of it, and

(b) a person claiming to be a licensee by virtue of the transaction does not have the protection of section 30 or 31 (rights and remedies of licensee in relation to infringement).

(4) Where a person becomes the proprietor or a licensee of a registered trade mark by virtue of a registrable transaction, then unless—

    (a) an application for registration of the prescribed particulars of the transaction is made before the end of the period of six months beginning with its date, or

    (b) the court is satisfied that it was not practicable for such an application to be made before the end of that period and that an application was made as soon as practicable thereafter,

he is not entitled to damages or an account of profits in respect of any infringement of the registered trade mark occurring after the date of the transaction and before the prescribed particulars of the transaction are registered.

(5) Provision may be made by rules as to—

    (a) the amendment of registered particulars relating to a licence so as to reflect any alteration of the terms of the licence, and

    (b) the removal of such particulars from the register—

        (i) where it appears from the registered particulars that the licence was granted for a fixed period and that period has expired, or

        (ii) where no such period is indicated and, after such period as may be prescribed, the registrar has notified the parties of his intention to remove the particulars from the register.

(6) Provision may also be made by rules as to the amendment or removal from the register of particulars relating to a security interest on the application of, or with the consent of, the person entitled to the benefit of that interest.

Trusts and equities

A1–27   **26.**—(1) No notice of any trust (express, implied or constructive) shall be entered in the register; and the registrar shall not be affected by any such notice.

(2) Subject to the provisions of this Act, equities (in Scotland, rights) in respect of a registered trade mark may be enforced in like manner as in respect of other personal or moveable property.

Application for registration of trade mark as an object of property

A1–28   **27.**—(1) The provisions of sections 22 to 26 (which relate to a registered trade mark as an object of property) apply, with the necessary modifications, in relation to an application for the registration of a trade mark as in relation to a registered trade mark.

(2) In section 23 (co-ownership of registered trade mark) as it applies in relation to an application for registration the reference in subsection (1) to the granting of the registration shall be construed as a reference to the making of the application.

(3) In section 25 (registration of transactions affecting registered trade marks) as it applies in relation to a transaction affecting an application for the registration of a trade mark, the references to the entry of particulars in the register, and to the making of an application to register particulars, shall be construed as references to the giving of notice to the registrar of those particulars.

Licensing

Licensing of registered trade mark

A1–29   **28.**—(1) A licence to use a registered trade mark may be general or limited.

A limited licence may, in particular, apply—

(a) in relation to some but not all of the goods or services for which the trade mark is registered, or

(b) in relation to use of the trade mark in a particular manner or a particular locality.

(2) A licence is not effective unless it is in writing signed by or on behalf of the grantor.

Except in Scotland, this requirement may be satisfied in a case where the grantor is a body corporate by the affixing of its seal.

(3) Unless the licence provides otherwise, it is binding on a successor in title to the grantor's interest.

References in this Act to doing anything with, or without, the consent of the proprietor of a registered trade mark shall be construed accordingly.

(4) Where the licence so provides, a sub-licence may be granted by the licensee; and references in this Act to a licence or licensee include a sub-licence or sub-licensee.

Exclusive licences

29.—(1) In this Act an "exclusive licence" means a licence (whether general or **A1–30** limited) authorising the licensee to the exclusion of all other persons, including the person granting the licence, to use a registered trade mark in the manner authorised by the licence.

The expression "exclusive licensee" shall be construed accordingly.

(2) An exclusive licensee has the same rights against a successor in title who is bound by the licence as he has against the person granting the licence.

General provisions as to rights of licensees in case of infringement

30.—(1) This section has effect with respect to the rights of a licensee in **A1–31** relation to infringement of a registered trade mark.

The provisions of this section do not apply where or to the extent that, by virtue of section 31(1) below (exclusive licensee having rights and remedies of assignee), the licensee has a right to bring proceedings in his own name.

(2) A licensee is entitled, unless his licence, or any licence through which his interest is derived, provides otherwise, to call on the proprietor of the registered trade mark to take infringement proceedings in respect of any matter which affects his interests.

(3) If the proprietor—

(a) refuses to do so, or

(b) fails to do so within two months after being called upon,

the licensee may bring the proceedings in his own name as if he were the proprietor.

(4) Where infringement proceedings are brought by a licensee by virtue of this section, the licensee may not, without the leave of the court, proceed with the action unless the proprietor is either joined as a plaintiff or added as a defendant.

This does not affect the granting of interlocutory relief on an application by a licensee alone.

(5) A proprietor who is added as a defendant as mentioned in subsection (4) shall not be made liable for any costs in the action unless he takes part in the proceedings.

(6) In infringement proceedings brought by the proprietor of a registered trade mark any loss suffered or likely to be suffered by licensees shall be taken into account; and the court may give such directions as it thinks fit as to the extent to which the plaintiff is to hold the proceeds of any pecuniary remedy on behalf of licensees.

(7) The provisions of this section apply in relation to an exclusive licensee if or to the extent that he has, by virtue of section 31(1), the rights and remedies of an assignee as if he were the proprietor of the registered trade mark.

Exclusive licensee having rights and remedies of assignee

A1–32   31.—(1) An exclusive licence may provide that the licensee shall have, to such extent as may be provided by the licence, the same rights and remedies in respect of matters occurring after the grant of the licence as if the licence had been an assignment.

Where or to the extent that such provision is made, the licensee is entitled, subject to the provisions of the licence and to the following provisions of this section, to bring infringement proceedings, against any person other than the proprietor, in his own name.

(2) Any such rights and remedies of an exclusive licensee are concurrent with those of the proprietor of the registered trade mark; and references to the proprietor of a registered trade mark in the provisions of this Act relating to infringement shall be construed accordingly.

(3) In an action brought by an exclusive licensee by virtue of this section a defendant may avail himself of any defence which would have been available to him if the action had been brought by the proprietor of the registered trade mark.

(4) Where proceedings for infringement of a registered trade mark brought by the proprietor or an exclusive licensee relate wholly or partly to an infringement in respect of which they have concurrent rights of action, the proprietor or, as the case may be, the exclusive licensee may not, without the leave of the court, proceed with the action unless the other is either joined as a plaintiff or added as a defendant.

This does not affect the granting of interlocutory relief on an application by a proprietor or exclusive licensee alone.

(5) A person who is added as a defendant as mentioned in subsection (4) shall not be made liable for any costs in the action unless he takes part in the proceedings.

(6) Where an action for infringement of a registered trade mark is brought which relates wholly or partly to an infringement in respect of which the proprietor and an exclusive licensee have or had concurrent rights of action—

    (a) the court shall in assessing damages take into account—
         (i) the terms of the licence, and
        (ii) any pecuniary remedy already awarded or available to either of them in respect of the infringement;
    (b) no account of profits shall be directed if an award of damages has been made, or an account of profits has been directed, in favour of the other of them in respect of the infringement; and
    (c) the court shall if an account of profits is directed apportion the profits between them as the court considers just, subject to any agreement between them.

The provisions of this subsection apply whether or not the proprietor and the exclusive licensee are both parties to the action; and if they are not both parties the court may give such directions as it thinks fit as to the extent to which the party to the proceedings is to hold the proceeds of any pecuniary remedy on behalf of the other.

(7) The proprietor of a registered trade mark shall notify any exclusive licensee who has a concurrent right of action before applying for an order under section 16 (order for delivery up); and the court may on the application of the licensee make such order under that section as it thinks fit having regard to the terms of the licence.

(8) The provisions of subsections (4) to (7) above have effect subject to any agreement to the contrary between the exclusive licensee and the proprietor.

Application for registered trade mark

Application for registration

32.—(1) An application for registration of a trade mark shall be made to the **A1–33** registrar.

(2) The application shall contain—

    (a) a request for registration of a trade mark,

    (b) the name and address of the applicant,

    (c) a statement of the goods or services in relation to which it is sought to register the trade mark, and

    (d) a representation of the trade mark.

(3) The application shall state that the trade mark is being used, by the applicant or with his consent, in relation to those goods or services, or that he has a *bona fide* intention that it should be so used.

(4) The application shall be subject to the payment of the application fee and such class fees as may be appropriate.

Date of filing

33.—(1) The date of filing of an application for registration of a trade mark is **A1–34** the date on which documents containing everything required by section 32(2) are furnished to the registrar by the applicant.

If the documents are furnished on different days, the date of filing is the last of those days.

(2) References in this Act to the date of application for registration are to the date of filing of the application.

Classification of trade marks

34.—(1) Goods and services shall be classified for the purposes of the **A1–35** registration of trade marks according to a prescribed system of classification.

(2) Any question arising as to the class within which any goods or services fall shall be determined by the registrar, whose decision shall be final.

Priority

Claim to priority of Convention application

35.—(1) A person who has duly filed an application for protection of a trade **A1–36** mark in a Convention country (a "Convention application"), or his successor in title, has a right to priority, for the purposes of registering the same trade mark under this Act for some or all of the same goods or services, for a period of six months from the date of filing of the first such application.

(2) If the application for registration under this Act is made within that six-month period—

    (a) the relevant date for the purposes of establishing which rights take precedence shall be the date of filing of the first Convention application, and

    (b) the registrability of the trade mark shall not be affected by any use of the mark in the United Kingdom in the period between that date and the date of the application under this Act.

(3) Any filing which in a Convention country is equivalent to a regular national filing, under its domestic legislation or an international agreement, shall be treated as giving rise to the right of priority.

A "regular national filing" means a filing which is adequate to establish the date on which the application was filed in that country, whatever may be the subsequent fate of the application.

(4) A subsequent application concerning the same subject as the first Convention application, filed in the same Convention country, shall be considered the first Convention application (of which the filing date is the starting date of the period of priority), if at the time of the subsequent application—

> (a) the previous application has been withdrawn, abandoned or refused, without having been laid open to public inspection and without leaving any rights outstanding, and
> (b) it has not yet served as a basis for claiming a right of priority.

The previous application may not thereafter serve as a basis for claiming a right of priority.

(5) Provision may be made by rules as to the manner of claiming a right to priority on the basis of a Convention application.

(6) A right to priority arising as a result of a Convention application may be assigned or otherwise transmitted, either with the application or independently.

The reference in subsection (1) to the applicant's "successor in title" shall be construed accordingly.

Claim to priority from other relevant overseas application

A1–37   **36.**—(1) Her Majesty may by Order in Council make provision for conferring on a person who has duly filed an application for protection of a trade mark in—

> (a) any of the Channel Islands or a colony, or
> (b) a country or territory in relation to which Her Majesty's Government in the United Kingdom have entered into a treaty, convention, arrangement or engagement for the reciprocal protection of trade marks,

a right to priority, for the purpose of registering the same trade mark under this Act for some or all of the same goods or services, for a specified period from the date of filing of that application.

(2) An Order in Council under this section may make provision corresponding to that made by section 35 in relation to Convention countries or such other provision as appears to Her Majesty to be appropriate.

(3) A statutory instrument containing an Order in Council under this section shall be subject to annulment in pursuance of a resolution of either House of Parliament.

Registration procedure

Examination of application

A1–38   **37.**—(1) The registrar shall examine whether an application for registration of a trade mark satisfies the requirements of this Act (including any requirements imposed by rules).

(2) For that purpose he shall carry out a search, to such extent as he considers necessary, of earlier trade marks.

(3) If it appears to the registrar that the requirements for registration are not met, he shall inform the applicant and give him an opportunity, within such period as the registrar may specify, to make representations or to amend the application.

(4) If the applicant fails to satisfy the registrar that those requirements are met, or to amend the application so as to meet them, or fails to respond before the end of the specified period, the registrar shall refuse to accept the application.

(5) If it appears to the registrar that the requirements for registration are met, he shall accept the application.

Publication, opposition proceedings and observations

38.—(1) When an application for registration has been accepted, the registrar **A1–39** shall cause the application to be published in the prescribed manner.

(2) Any person may, within the prescribed time from the date of the publication of the application, give notice to the registrar of opposition to the registration.

The notice shall be given in writing in the prescribed manner, and shall include a statement of the grounds of opposition.

(3) Where an application has been published, any person may, at any time before the registration of the trade mark, make observations in writing to the registrar as to whether the trade mark should be registered; and the registrar shall inform the applicant of any such observations.

A person who makes observations does not thereby become a party to the proceedings on the application.

Withdrawal, restriction or amendment of application

39.—(1) The applicant may at any time withdraw his application or restrict the **A1–40** goods or services covered by the application.

If the application has been published, the withdrawal or restriction shall also be published.

(2) In other respects, an application may be amended, at the request of the applicant, only by correcting—

(a) the name or address of the applicant,
(b) errors of wording or of copying, or
(c) obvious mistakes,

and then only where the correction does not substantially affect the identity of the trade mark or extend the goods or services covered by the application.

(3) Provision shall be made by rules for the publication of any amendment which affects the representation of the trade mark, or the goods or services covered by the application, and for the making of objections by any person claiming to be affected by it.

Registration

40.—(1) Where an application has been accepted and—   **A1–41**

(a) no notice of opposition is given within the period referred to in section 38(2), or
(b) all opposition proceedings are withdrawn or decided in favour of the applicant,

the registrar shall register the trade mark, unless it appears to him having regard to matters coming to his notice since he accepted the application that it was accepted in error.

(2) A trade mark shall not be registered unless any fee prescribed for the registration is paid within the prescribed period.

If the fee is not paid within that period, the application shall be deemed to be withdrawn.

(3) A trade mark when registered shall be registered as of the date of filing of the application for registration; and that date shall be deemed for the purposes of this Act to be the date of registration.

(4) On the registration of a trade mark the registrar shall publish the registration in the prescribed manner and issue to the applicant a certificate of registration.

Registration: supplementary provisions

A1–42   **41.**—(1) Provision may be made by rules as to—

(a) the division of an application for the registration of a trade mark into several applications;
(b) the merging of separate applications or registrations;
(c) the registration of a series of trade marks.

(2) A series of trade marks means a number of trade marks which resemble each other as to their material particulars and differ only as to matters of a non-distinctive character not substantially affecting the identity of the trade mark.
(3) Rules under this section may include provision as to—

(a) the circumstances in which, and conditions subject to which, division, merger or registration of a series is permitted, and
(b) the purposes for which an application to which the rules apply is to be treated as a single application and those for which it is to be treated as a number of separate applications.

Duration, renewal and alteration of registered trade mark

Duration of registration

A1–43   **42.**—(1) A trade mark shall be registered for a period of ten years from the date of registration.
(2) Registration may be renewed in accordance with section 43 for further periods of ten years.

Renewal of registration

A1–44   **43.**—(1) The registration of a trade mark may be renewed at the request of the proprietor, subject to payment of a renewal fee.
(2) Provision shall be made by rules for the registrar to inform the proprietor of a registered trade mark, before the expiry of the registration, of the date of expiry and the manner in which the registration may be renewed.
(3) A request for renewal must be made, and the renewal fee paid, before the expiry of the registration.
Failing this, the request may be made and the fee paid within such further period (of not less than six months) as may be prescribed, in which case an additional renewal fee must also be paid within that period.
(4) Renewal shall take effect from the expiry of the previous registration.
(5) If the registration is not renewed in accordance with the above provisions, the registrar shall remove the trade mark from the register.
Provision may be made by rules for the restoration of the registration of a trade mark which has been removed from the register, subject to such conditions (if any) as may be prescribed.
(6) The renewal or restoration of the registration of a trade mark shall be published in the prescribed manner.

Alteration of registered trade mark

A1–45   **44.**—(1) A registered trade mark shall not be altered in the register, during the period of registration or on renewal.

(2) Nevertheless, the registrar may, at the request of the proprietor, allow the alteration of a registered trade mark where the mark includes the proprietor's name or address and the alteration is limited to alteration of that name or address and does not substantially affect the identity of the mark.

(3) Provision shall be made by rules for the publication of any such alteration and the making of objections by any person claiming to be affected by it.

Surrender, revocation and invalidity

Surrender of registered trade mark

45.—(1) A registered trade mark may be surrendered by the proprietor in **A1–46** respect of some or all of the goods or services for which it is registered.

(2) Provision may be made by rules—

(a) as to the manner and effect of a surrender, and
(b) for protecting the interests of other persons having a right in the registered trade mark.

Revocation of registration

46.—(1) The registration of a trade mark may be revoked on any of the **A1–47** following grounds—

(a) that within the period of five years following the date of completion of the registration procedure it has not been put to genuine use in the United Kingdom, by the proprietor or with his consent, in relation to the goods or services for which it is registered, and there are no proper reasons for non-use;
(b) that such use has been suspended for an uninterrupted period of five years, and there are no proper reasons for non-use;
(c) that, in consequence of acts or inactivity of the proprietor, it has become the common name in the trade for a product or service for which it is registered;
(d) that in consequence of the use made of it by the proprietor or with his consent in relation to the goods or services for which it is registered, it is liable to mislead the public, particularly as to the nature, quality or geographical origin of those goods or services.

(2) For the purposes of subsection (1) use of a trade mark includes use in a form differing in elements which do not alter the distinctive character of the mark in the form in which it was registered, and use in the United Kingdom includes affixing the trade mark to goods or to the packaging of goods in the United Kingdom solely for export purposes.

(3) The registration of a trade mark shall not be revoked on the ground mentioned in subsection (1)(a) or (b) if such use as is referred to in that paragraph is commenced or resumed after the expiry of the five year period and before the application for revocation is made:

Provided that, any such commencement or resumption of use after the expiry of the five year period but within the period of three months before the making of the application shall be disregarded unless preparations for the commencement or resumption began before the proprietor became aware that the application might be made.

(4) An application for revocation may be made by any person, and may be made either to the registrar or to the court, except that—

(a) if proceedings concerning the trade mark in question are pending in the court, the application must be made to the court; and

(b) if in any other case the application is made to the registrar, he may at any stage of the proceedings refer the application to the court.

(5) Where grounds for revocation exist in respect of only some of the goods or services for which the trade mark is registered, revocation shall relate to those goods or services only.

(6) Where the registration of a trade mark is revoked to any extent, the rights of the proprietor shall be deemed to have ceased to that extent as from—

(a) the date of the application for revocation, or
(b) if the registrar or court is satisfied that the grounds for revocation existed at an earlier date, that date.

Grounds for invalidity of registration

A1–48   **47.**—(1) The registration of a trade mark may be declared invalid on the ground that the trade mark was registered in breach of section 3 or any of the provisions referred to in that section (absolute grounds for refusal of registration).

Where the trade mark was registered in breach of subsection (1)(b), (c) or (d) of that section, it shall not be declared invalid if, in consequence of the use which has been made of it, it has after registration acquired a distinctive character in relation to the goods or services for which it is registered.

(2) The registration of a trade mark may be declared invalid on the ground—

(a) that there is an earlier trade mark in relation to which the conditions set out in section 5(1), (2) or (3) obtain, or
(b) that there is an earlier right in relation to which the condition set out in section 5(4) is satisfied,

unless the proprietor of that earlier trade mark or other earlier right has consented to the registration.

(3) An application for a declaration of invalidity may be made by any person, and may be made either to the registrar or to the court, except that—

(a) if proceedings concerning the trade mark in question are pending in the court, the application must be made to the court; and
(b) if in any other case the application is made to the registrar, he may at any stage of the proceedings refer the application to the court.

(4) In the case of bad faith in the registration of a trade mark, the registrar himself may apply to the court for a declaration of the invalidity of the registration.

(5) Where the grounds of invalidity exist in respect of only some of the goods or services for which the trade mark is registered, the trade mark shall be declared invalid as regards those goods or services only.

(6) Where the registration of a trade mark is declared invalid to any extent, the registration shall to that extent be deemed never to have been made:

Provided that this shall not affect transactions past and closed.

Effect of acquiescence

A1–49   **48.**—(1) Where the proprietor of an earlier trade mark or other earlier right has acquiesced for a continuous period of five years in the use of a registered trade mark in the United Kingdom, being aware of that use, there shall cease to be any entitlement on the basis of that earlier trade mark or other right—

(a) to apply for a declaration that the registration of the later trade mark is invalid, or
(b) to oppose the use of the later trade mark in relation to the goods or services in relation to which it has been so used,

unless the registration of the later trade mark was applied for in bad faith.

(2) Where subsection (1) applies, the proprietor of the later trade mark is not entitled to oppose the use of the earlier trade mark or, as the case may be, the exploitation of the earlier right, notwithstanding that the earlier trade mark or right may no longer be invoked against his later trade mark.

Collective marks

Collective marks

49.—(1) A collective mark is a mark distinguishing the goods or services of **A1–50** members of the association which is the proprietor of the mark from those of other undertakings.

(2) The provisions of this Act apply to collective marks subject to the provisions of Schedule 1.

Certification marks

Certification marks

50.—(1) A certification mark is a mark indicating that the goods or services in **A1–51** connection with which it is used are certified by the proprietor of the mark in respect of origin, material, mode of manufacture of goods or performance of services, quality, accuracy or other characteristics.

(2) The provisions of this Act apply to certification marks subject to the provisions of Schedule 2.

PART II

COMMUNITY TRADE MARKS AND INTERNATIONAL MATTERS

Community trade marks

Meaning of "Community trade mark"

51. In this Act—   **A1–52**

"Community trade mark" has the meaning given by Article 1(1) of the Community Trade Mark Regulation; and

"the Community Trade Mark Regulation" means Council Regulation (EC) No. 40/94 of 20th December 1993 on the Community trade mark.

Power to make provision in connection with Community Trade Mark Regulation

52.—(1) The Secretary of State may by regulations make such provision as he **A1–53** considers appropriate in connection with the operation of the Community Trade Mark Regulation.

(2) Provision may, in particular, be made with respect to—

(a) the making of applications for Community trade marks by way of the Patent Office;

(b) the procedures for determining *a posteriori* the invalidity, or liability to revocation, of the registration of a trade mark from which a Community trade mark claims seniority;

(c) the conversion of a Community trade mark, or an application for a Community trade mark, into an application for registration under this Act;

(d) the designation of courts in the United Kingdom having jurisdiction over proceedings arising out of the Community Trade Mark Regulation.

(3) Without prejudice to the generality of subsection (1), provision may be made by regulations under this section—

(a) applying in relation to a Community trade mark the provisions of—
  (i) section 21 (remedy for groundless threats of infringement proceedings);
  (ii) sections 89 to 91 (importation of infringing goods, material or articles); and
  (iii) sections 92, 93, 95 and 96 (offences); and

(b) making in relation to the list of professional representatives maintained in pursuance of Article 89 of the Community Trade Mark Regulation, and persons on that list, provision corresponding to that made by, or capable of being made under, sections 84 to 88 in relation to the register of trade mark agents and registered trade mark agents.

(4) Regulations under this section shall be made by statutory instrument which shall be subject to annulment in pursuance of a resolution of either House of Parliament.

The Madrid Protocol: international registration

The Madrid Protocol

A1–54 53. In this Act—

"the Madrid Protocol" means the Protocol relating to the Madrid Agreement concerning the International Registration of Marks, adopted at Madrid on 27th June 1989;

"the International Bureau" has the meaning given by Article 2(1) of that Protocol; and

"international trade mark (UK)" means a trade mark which is entitled to protection in the United Kingdom under that Protocol.

Power to make provision giving effect to Madrid Protocol

A1–55 54.—(1) The Secretary of State may by order make such provision as he thinks fit for giving effect in the United Kingdom to the provisions of the Madrid Protocol.

(2) Provision may, in particular, be made with respect to—

(a) the making of applications for international registrations by way of the Patent Office as office of origin;

(b) the procedures to be followed where the basic United Kingdom application or registration fails or ceases to be in force;

(c) the procedures to be followed where the Patent Office receives from the International Bureau a request for extension of protection to the United Kingdom;

(d) the effects of a successful request for extension of protection to the United Kingdom;

(e) the transformation of an application for an international registration, or an international registration, into a national application for registration;

(f) the communication of information to the International Bureau;

(g) the payment of fees and amounts prescribed in respect of applications for international registrations, extensions of protection and renewals.

(3) Without prejudice to the generality of subsection (1), provision may be made by regulations under this section applying in relation to an international trade mark (UK) the provisions of—

(a) section 21 (remedy for groundless threats of infringement proceedings);

(b) sections 89 to 91 (importation of infringing goods, material or articles); and

(c) sections 92, 93, 95 and 96 (offences).

(4) An order under this section shall be made by statutory instrument which shall be subject to annulment in pursuance of a resolution of either House of Parliament.

The Paris Convention: supplementary provisions

The Paris Convention

55.—(1) In this Act—   **A1–56**

(a) "the Paris Convention" means the Paris Convention for the Protection of Industrial Property of March 20th 1883, as revised or amended from time to time,

(aa) "the WTO agreement" means the Agreement establishing the World Trade Organisation signed at Marrakesh on 15th April 1994, and

(b) a "Convention country" means a country, other than the United Kingdom, which is a party to that Convention.

(2) The Secretary of State may by order make such amendments of this Act, and rules made under this Act, as appear to him appropriate in consequence of any revision or amendment of the Paris Convention **or the WTO agreement** after the passing of this Act.

(3) Any such order shall be made by statutory instrument which shall be subject to annulment in pursuance of a resolution of either House of Parliament. The references to the WTO Agreement was added by the Patents and Trade Marks (World Trade Organisation) Regulations 1999, S.I. 1999 No. 1899.

Protection of well-known trade marks: Article 6bis

56.—(1) References in this Act to a trade mark which is entitled to protection **A1–57** under the Paris Convention **or the WTO agreement** as a well known trade mark are to a mark which is well-known in the United Kingdom as being the mark of a person who—

(a) is a national of a Convention country, or

(b) is domiciled in, or has a real and effective industrial or commercial establishment in, a Convention country,

whether or not that person carries on business, or has any goodwill, in the United Kingdom.

References to the proprietor of such a mark shall be construed accordingly.

(2) The proprietor of a trade mark which is entitled to protection under the Paris Convention **or the WTO agreement** as a well known trade mark is entitled to restrain by injunction the use in the United Kingdom of a trade mark which,

or the essential part of which, is identical or similar to his mark, in relation to identical or similar goods or services, where the use is likely to cause confusion.

This right is subject to section 48 (effect of acquiescence by proprietor of earlier trade mark).

(3) Nothing in subsection (2) affects the continuation of any *bona fide* use of a trade mark begun before the commencement of this section.

The references to the WTO Agreement was added by the Patents and Trade Marks (World Trade Organisation) Regulations 1999, S.I. 1999 No. 1899.

National emblems, &c. of Convention countries: Article 6*ter*

A1–58   57.—(1) A trade mark which consists of or contains the flag of a Convention country shall not be registered without the authorisation of the competent authorities of that country, unless it appears to the registrar that use of the flag in the manner proposed is permitted without such authorisation.

(2) A trade mark which consists of or contains the armorial bearings or any other state emblem of a Convention country which is protected under the Paris Convention **or the WTO agreement** shall not be registered without the authorisation of the competent authorities of that country.

(3) A trade mark which consists of or contains an official sign or hallmark adopted by a Convention country and indicating control and warranty shall not, where the sign or hallmark is protected under the Paris Convention **or the WTO agreement**, be registered in relation to goods or services of the same, or a similar kind, as those in relation to which it indicates control and warranty, without the authorisation of the competent authorities of the country concerned.

(4) The provisions of this section as to national flags and other state emblems, and official signs or hallmarks, apply equally to anything which from a heraldic point of view imitates any such flag or other emblem, or sign or hallmark.

(5) Nothing in this section prevents the registration of a trade mark on the application of a national of a country who is authorised to make use of a state emblem, or official sign or hallmark, of that country, notwithstanding that it is similar to that of another country.

(6) Where by virtue of this section the authorisation of the competent authorities of a Convention country is or would be required for the registration of a trade mark, those authorities are entitled to restrain by injunction any use of the mark in the United Kingdom without their authorisation.

The references to the WTO Agreement was added by the Patents and Trade Marks (World Trade Organisation) Regulations 1999, S.I. 1999 No. 1899.

Emblems, &c. of certain international organisations: Article 6*ter*

A1–59   58.—(1) This section applies to—

(a) the armorial bearings, flags or other emblems, and
(b) the abbreviations and names,

of international intergovernmental organisations of which one or more Convention countries are members.

(2) A trade mark which consists of or contains any such emblem, abbreviation or name which is protected under the Paris Convention **or the WTO agreement** shall not be registered without the authorisation of the international organisation concerned, unless it appears to the registrar that the use of the emblem, abbreviation or name in the manner proposed—

(a) is not such as to suggest to the public that a connection exists between the organisation and the trade mark, or
(b) is not likely to mislead the public as to the existence of a connection between the user and the organisation.

(3) The provisions of this section as to emblems of an international organisation apply equally to anything which from a heraldic point of view imitates any such emblem.

(4) Where by virtue of this section the authorisation of an international organisation is or would be required for the registration of a trade mark, that organisation is entitled to restrain by injunction any use of the mark in the United Kingdom without its authorisation.

(5) Nothing in this section affects the rights of a person whose *bona fide* use of the trade mark in question began before 4th January 1962 (when the relevant provisions of the Paris Convention entered into force in relation to the United Kingdom).

The references to the WTO Agreement was added by the Patents and Trade Marks (World Trade Organisation) Regulations 1999, S.I. 1999 No. 1899.

Notification under Article 6*ter* of the Convention

59.—(1) For the purposes of section 57 state emblems of a Convention country **A1–60** (other than the national flag), and official signs or hallmarks, shall be regarded as protected under the Paris Convention only if, or to the extent that—

    (a) the country in question has notified the United Kingdom in accordance with Article 6*ter*(3) of the Convention that it desires to protect that emblem, sign or hallmark,

    (b) the notification remains in force, and

    (c) the United Kingdom has not objected to it in accordance with Article 6*ter*(4) or any such objection has been withdrawn.

(2) For the purposes of section 58 the emblems, abbreviations and names of an international organisation shall be regarded as protected under the Paris Convention only if, or to the extent that—

    (a) the organisation in question has notified the United Kingdom in accordance with Article 6*ter*(3) of the Convention that it desires to protect that emblem, abbreviation or name,

    (b) the notification remains in force, and

    (c) the United Kingdom has not objected to it in accordance with Article 6*ter*(4) or any such objection has been withdrawn.

(3) Notification under Article 6*ter*(3) of the Paris Convention shall have effect only in relation to applications for registration made more than two months after the receipt of the notification.

(4) The registrar shall keep and make available for public inspection by any person, at all reasonable hours and free of charge, a list of—

    (a) the state emblems and official signs or hallmarks, and

    (b) the emblems, abbreviations and names of international organisations,

which are for the time being protected under the Paris Convention by virtue of notification under Article 6*ter*(3).

(5) Any reference in this section to Article 6*ter* of the Paris Convention shall be construed as including a reference to that Article as applied by the WTO agreement.

The reference to the WTO Agreement was added by the Patents and Trade Marks (World Trade Organisation) Regulations 1999, S.I. 1999 No. 1899.

Acts of agent or representative: Article 6*septies*

60.—(1) The following provisions apply where an application for registration **A1–61** of a trade mark is made by a person who is an agent or representative of a person who is the proprietor of the mark in a Convention country.

(2) If the proprietor opposes the application, registration shall be refused.

(3) If the application (not being so opposed) is granted, the proprietor may—

    (a) apply for a declaration of the invalidity of the registration, or

(b) apply for the rectification of the register so as to substitute his name as the proprietor of the registered trade mark.

(4) The proprietor may (notwithstanding the rights conferred by this Act in relation to a registered trade mark) by injunction restrain any use of the trade mark in the United Kingdom which is not authorised by him.

(5) Subsections (2), (3) and (4) do not apply if, or to the extent that, the agent or representative justifies his action.

(6) An application under subsection (3)(a) or (b) must be made within three years of the proprietor becoming aware of the registration; and no injunction shall be granted under subsection (4) in respect of a use in which the proprietor has acquiesced for a continuous period of three years or more.

Miscellaneous

Stamp duty

A1–62   61. Stamp duty shall not be chargeable on an instrument relating to a Community trade mark or an international trade mark (UK), or an application for any such mark, by reason only of the fact that such a mark has legal effect in the United Kingdom.

PART III

ADMINISTRATIVE AND OTHER SUPPLEMENTARY PROVISIONS

The registrar

The registrar

A1–63   62. In this Act "the registrar" means the Comptroller-General of Patents, Designs and Trade Marks.

The register

The register

A1–64   63.—(1) The registrar shall maintain a register of trade marks.

References in this Act to "the register" are to that register; and references to registration (in particular, in the expression "registered trade mark") are, unless the context otherwise requires, to registration in that register.

(2) There shall be entered in the register in accordance with this Act—

(a) registered trade marks,

(b) such particulars as may be prescribed of registrable transactions affecting a registered trade mark, and

(c) such other matters relating to registered trade marks as may be prescribed.

(3) The register shall be kept in such manner as may be prescribed, and provision shall in particular be made for—

(a) public inspection of the register, and

(b) the supply of certified or uncertified copies, or extracts, of entries in the register.

Rectification or correction of the register

64.—(1) Any person having a sufficient interest may apply for the rectification **A1–65** of an error or omission in the register:

Provided that an application for rectification may not be made in respect of a matter affecting the validity of the registration of a trade mark.

(2) An application for rectification may be made either to the registrar or to the court, except that—

(a) if proceedings concerning the trade mark in question are pending in the court, the application must be made to the court; and

(b) if in any other case the application is made to the registrar, he may at any stage of the proceedings refer the application to the court.

(3) Except where the registrar or the court directs otherwise, the effect of rectification of the register is that the error or omission in question shall be deemed never to have been made.

(4) The registrar may, on request made in the prescribed manner by the proprietor of a registered trade mark, or a licensee, enter any change in his name or address as recorded in the register.

(5) The registrar may remove from the register matter appearing to him to have ceased to have effect.

Adaptation of entries to new classification

65.—(1) Provision may be made by rules empowering the registrar to do such **A1–66** things as he considers necessary to implement any amended or substituted classification of goods or services for the purposes of the registration of trade marks.

(2) Provision may in particular be made for the amendment of existing entries on the register so as to accord with the new classification.

(3) Any such power of amendment shall not be exercised so as to extend the rights conferred by the registration, except where it appears to the registrar that compliance with this requirement would involve undue complexity and that any extension would not be substantial and would not adversely affect the rights of any person.

(4) The rules may empower the registrar—

(a) to require the proprietor of a registered trade mark, within such time as may be prescribed, to file a proposal for amendment of the register, and

(b) to cancel or refuse to renew the registration of the trade mark in the event of his failing to do so.

(5) Any such proposal shall be advertised, and may be opposed, in such manner as may be prescribed.

Powers and duties of the registrar

Power to require use of forms

66.—(1) The registrar may require the use of such forms as he may direct for **A1–67** any purpose relating to the registration of a trade mark or any other proceeding before him under this Act.

(2) The forms, and any directions of the registrar with respect to their use, shall be published in the prescribed manner.

Information about applications and registered trade marks

A1–68   67.—(1) After publication of an application for registration of a trade mark, the registrar shall on request provide a person with such information and permit him to inspect such documents relating to the application, or to any registered trade mark resulting from it, as may be specified in the request, subject, however, to any prescribed restrictions.

Any request must be made in the prescribed manner and be accompanied by the appropriate fee (if any).

(2) Before publication of an application for registration of a trade mark, documents or information constituting or relating to the application shall not be published by the registrar or communicated by him to any person except—

(a) in such cases and to such extent as may be prescribed, or
(b) with the consent of the applicant;

but subject as follows.

(3) Where a person has been notified that an application for registration of a trade mark has been made, and that the applicant will if the application is granted bring proceedings against him in respect of acts done after publication of the application, he may make a request under subsection (1) notwithstanding that the application has not been published and that subsection shall apply accordingly.

Costs and security for costs

A1–69   68.—(1) Provision may be made by rules empowering the registrar, in any proceedings before him under this Act—

(a) to award any party such costs as he may consider reasonable, and
(b) to direct how and by what parties they are to be paid.

(2) Any such order of the registrar may be enforced—

(a) in England and Wales or Northern Ireland, in the same way as an order of the High Court;
(b) in Scotland, in the same way as a decree for expenses granted by the Court of Session.

(3) Provision may be made by rules empowering the registrar, in such cases as may be prescribed, to require a party to proceedings before him to give security for costs, in relation to those proceedings or to proceedings on appeal, and as to the consequences if security is not given.

Evidence before registrar

A1–70   69. Provision may be made by rules—

(a) as to the giving of evidence in proceedings before the registrar under this Act by affidavit or statutory declaration;
(b) conferring on the registrar the powers of an official referee of the Supreme Court as regards the examination of witnesses on oath and the discovery and production of documents; and
(c) applying in relation to the attendance of witnesses in proceedings before the registrar the rules applicable to the attendance of witnesses before such a referee.

Exclusion of liability in respect of official acts

A1–71   70.—(1) The registrar shall not be taken to warrant the validity of the registration of a trade mark under this Act or under any treaty, convention, arrangement or engagement to which the United Kingdom is a party.

(2) The registrar is not subject to any liability by reason of, or in connection with, any examination required or authorised by this Act, or any such treaty, convention, arrangement or engagement, or any report or other proceedings consequent on such examination.

(3) No proceedings lie against an officer of the registrar in respect of any matter for which, by virtue of this section, the registrar is not liable.

Registrar's annual report

71.—(1) The Comptroller-General of Patents, Designs and Trade Marks shall in **A1–72** his annual report under section 121 of the Patents Act 1977, include a report on the execution of this Act, including the discharge of his functions under the Madrid Protocol.

(2) The report shall include an account of all money received and paid by him under or by virtue of this Act.

Legal proceedings and appeals

Registration to be *prima facie* evidence of validity

72. In all legal proceedings relating to a registered trade mark (including **A1–73** proceedings for rectification of the register) the registration of a person as proprietor of a trade mark shall be prima facie evidence of the validity of the original registration and of any subsequent assignment or other transmission of it.

Certificate of validity of contested registration

73.—(1) If in proceedings before the court the validity of the registration of a **A1–74** trade mark is contested and it is found by the court that the trade mark is validly registered, the court may give a certificate to that effect.

(2) If the court gives such a certificate and in subsequent proceedings—

(a) the validity of the registration is again questioned, and
(b) the proprietor obtains a final order or judgment in his favour,

he is entitled to his costs as between solicitor and client unless the court directs otherwise.

This subsection does not extend to the costs of an appeal in any such proceedings.

Registrar's appearance in proceedings involving the register

74.—(1) In proceedings before the court involving an application for—   **A1–75**

(a) the revocation of the registration of a trade mark,
(b) a declaration of the invalidity of the registration of a trade mark, or
(c) the rectification of the register,

the registrar is entitled to appear and be heard, and shall appear if so directed by the court.

(2) Unless otherwise directed by the court, the registrar may instead of appearing submit to the court a statement in writing signed by him, giving particulars of—

(a) any proceedings before him in relation to the matter in issue,
(b) the grounds of any decision given by him affecting it,
(c) the practice of the Patent Office in like cases, or
(d) such matters relevant to the issues and within his knowledge as registrar as he thinks fit;

and the statement shall be deemed to form part of the evidence in the proceedings.

(3) Anything which the registrar is or may be authorised or required to do under this section may be done on his behalf by a duly authorised officer.

The court

A1–76   75. In this Act, unless the context otherwise requires, "the court" means—

(a) in England and Wales and Northern Ireland, the High Court, and
(b) in Scotland, the Court of Session.

Appeals from the registrar

A1–77   76.—(1) An appeal lies from any decision of the registrar under this Act, except as otherwise expressly provided by rules.

For this purpose "decision" includes any act of the registrar in exercise of a discretion vested in him by or under this Act.

(2) Any such appeal may be brought either to an appointed person or to the court.

(3) Where an appeal is made to an appointed person, he may refer the appeal to the court if—

(a) it appears to him that a point of general legal importance is involved,
(b) the registrar requests that it be so referred, or
(c) such a request is made by any party to the proceedings before the registrar in which the decision appealed against was made.

Before doing so the appointed person shall give the appellant and any other party to the appeal an opportunity to make representations as to whether the appeal should be referred to the court.

(4) Where an appeal is made to an appointed person and he does not refer it to the court, he shall hear and determine the appeal and his decision shall be final.

(5) The provisions of sections 68 and 69 (costs and security for costs; evidence) apply in relation to proceedings before an appointed person as in relation to proceedings before the registrar.

Persons appointed to hear and determine appeals

A1–78   77.—(1) For the purposes of section 76 an "appointed person" means a person appointed by the Lord Chancellor to hear and decide appeals under this Act.

(2) A person is not eligible for such appointment unless—

(a) he has a 7 year general qualification, within the meaning of section 71 of the Courts and Legal Services Act 1990;
(b) he is an advocate or solicitor in Scotland of at least 7 years' standing;
(c) he is a member of the Bar of Northern Ireland or solicitor of the Supreme Court of Northern Ireland of at least 7 years' standing; or
(d) he has held judicial office.

(3) An appointed person shall hold and vacate office in accordance with his terms of appointment, subject to the following provisions—

(a) there shall be paid to him such remuneration (whether by way of salary or fees), and such allowances, as the Secretary of State with the approval of the Treasury may determine;
(b) he may resign his office by notice in writing to the Lord Chancellor;
(c) the Lord Chancellor may by notice in writing remove him from office if—

(i) he has become bankrupt or made an arrangement with his creditors or, in Scotland, his estate has been sequestrated or he has executed a trust deed for his creditors or entered into a composition contract, or

(ii) he is incapacitated by physical or mental illness,

or if he is in the opinion of the Lord Chancellor otherwise unable or unfit to perform his duties as an appointed person.

(4) The Lord Chancellor shall consult the Lord Advocate before exercising his powers under this section.

By S.I. 1999 No. 17, art. 3, Sched. 1, para. 17, the Secretary of State's functions under s. 77(4) are to be treated for the purposes of the Scotland Act 1998, s. 63, as being exercisable in or as regards Scotland. By S.I. 1999 No. 678, art. 2(1), the functions of the Lord Advocate under this section are transferred to the Secretary of State.

Rules, fees, hours of business, &c.

Power of Secretary of State to make rules

78.—(1) The Secretary of State may make rules—   **A1–79**

(a) for the purposes of any provision of this Act authorising the making of rules with respect to any matter, and

(b) for prescribing anything authorised or required by any provision of this Act to be prescribed,

and generally for regulating practice and procedure under this Act.

(2) Provision may, in particular, be made—

(a) as to the manner of filing of applications and other documents;

(b) requiring and regulating the translation of documents and the filing and authentication of any translation;

(c) as to the service of documents;

(d) authorising the rectification of irregularities of procedure;

(e) prescribing time limits for anything required to be done in connection with any proceeding under this Act;

(f) providing for the extension of any time limit so prescribed, or specified by the registrar, whether or not it has already expired.

(3) Rules under this Act shall be made by statutory instrument which shall be subject to annulment in pursuance of a resolution of either House of Parliament.

Fees

79.—(1) There shall be paid in respect of applications and registration and **A1–80** other matters under this Act such fees as may be prescribed.

(2) Provision may be made by rules as to—

(a) the payment of a single fee in respect of two or more matters, and

(b) the circumstances (if any) in which a fee may be repaid or remitted.

Hours of business and business days

80.—(1) The registrar may give directions specifying the hours of business of **A1–81** the Patent Office for the purpose of the transaction by the public of business under this Act, and the days which are business days for that purpose.

(2) Business done on any day after the specified hours of business, or on a day which is not a business day, shall be deemed to have been done on the next business day; and where the time for doing anything under this Act expires on a day which is not a business day, that time shall be extended to the next business day.

(3) Directions under this section may make different provision for different classes of business and shall be published in the prescribed manner.

The trade marks journal

A1–82   81. Provision shall be made by rules for the publication by the registrar of a journal containing particulars of any application for the registration of a trade mark (including a representation of the mark) and such other information relating to trade marks as the registrar thinks fit.

Trade mark agents

Recognition of agents

A1–83   82. Except as otherwise provided by rules, any act required or authorised by this Act to be done by or to a person in connection with the registration of a trade mark, or any procedure relating to a registered trade mark, may be done by or to an agent authorised by that person orally or in writing.

The register of trade mark agents

A1–84   83.—(1) The Secretary of State may make rules requiring the keeping of a register of persons who act as agent for others for the purpose of applying for or obtaining the registration of trade marks; and in this Act a "registered trade mark agent" means a person whose name is entered in the register kept under this section.

(2) The rules may contain such provision as the Secretary of State thinks fit regulating the registration of persons, and may in particular—

    (a) require the payment of such fees as may be prescribed, and
    (b) authorise in prescribed cases the erasure from the register of the name of any person registered in it, or the suspension of a person's registration.

(3) The rules may delegate the keeping of the register to another person, and may confer on that person—

    (a) power to make regulations—
        (i) with respect to the payment of fees, in the cases and subject to the limits prescribed by the rules, and
        (ii) with respect to any other matter which could be regulated by the rules, and
    (b) such other functions, including disciplinary functions, as may be prescribed by the rules.

Unregistered persons not to be described as registered trade mark agents

A1–85   84.—(1) An individual who is not a registered trade mark agent shall not—

    (a) carry on a business (otherwise than in partnership) under any name or other description which contains the words "registered trade mark agent"; or
    (b) in the course of a business otherwise describe or hold himself out, or permit himself to be described or held out, as a registered trade mark agent.

(2) A partnership shall not—

    (a) carry on a business under any name or other description which contains the words "registered trade mark agent"; or

816

(b) in the course of a business otherwise describe or hold itself out, or permit itself to be described or held out, as a firm of registered trade mark agents,

unless all the partners are registered trade mark agents or the partnership satisfies such conditions as may be prescribed for the purposes of this section.

(3) A body corporate shall not—

(a) carry on a business (otherwise than in partnership) under any name or other description which contains the words "registered trade mark agent"; or

(b) in the course of a business otherwise describe or hold itself out, or permit itself to be described or held out, as a registered trade mark agent,

unless all the directors of the body corporate are registered trade mark agents or the body satisfies such conditions as may be prescribed for the purposes of this section.

(4) A person who contravenes this section commits an offence and is liable on summary conviction to a fine not exceeding level 5 on the standard scale; and proceedings for such an offence may be begun at any time within a year from the date of the offence.

Power to prescribe conditions, &c. for mixed partnerships and bodies corporate

85.—(1) The Secretary of State may make rules prescribing the conditions to be **A1–86** satisfied for the purposes of section 84 (persons entitled to be described as registered trade mark agents)—

(a) in relation to a partnership where not all the partners are qualified persons, or

(b) in relation to a body corporate where not all the directors are qualified persons,

and imposing requirements to be complied with by such partnerships or bodies corporate.

(2) The rules may, in particular—

(a) prescribe conditions as to the number or proportion of partners or directors who must be qualified persons;

(b) impose requirements as to—

(i) the identification of qualified and unqualified persons in professional advertisements, circulars or letters issued by or with the consent of the partnership or body corporate and which relate to its business, and

(ii) the manner in which a partnership or body corporate is to organise its affairs so as to secure that qualified persons exercise a sufficient degree of control over the activities of unqualified persons.

(3) Contravention of a requirement imposed by the rules is an offence for which a person is liable on summary conviction to a fine not exceeding level 5 on the standard scale.

(4) In this section "qualified person" means a registered trade mark agent.

Use of the term "trade mark attorney"

86.—(1) No offence is committed under the enactments restricting the use of **A1–87** certain expressions in reference to persons not qualified to act as solicitors by the use of the term "trade mark attorney" in reference to a registered trade mark agent.

(2) The enactments referred to in subsection (1) are section 21 of the Solicitors Act 1974, section 31 of the Solicitors (Scotland) Act 1980 and Article 22 of the Solicitors (Northern Ireland) Order 1976.

Privilege for communications with registered trade mark agents

A1–88   87.—(1) This section applies to communications as to any matter relating to the protection of any design or trade mark, or as to any matter involving passing off.
(2) Any such communication—

    (a) between a person and his trade mark agent, or
    (b) for the purpose of obtaining, or in response to a request for, informa-tion which a person is seeking for the purpose of instructing his trade mark agent,

is privileged from, or in Scotland protected against, disclosure in legal proceed-ings in the same way as a communication between a person and his solicitor or, as the case may be, a communication for the purpose of obtaining, or in response to a request for, information which a person is seeking for the purpose of instructing his solicitor.
(3) In subsection (2) "trade mark agent" means—

    (a) a registered trade mark agent, or
    (b) a partnership entitled to describe itself as a firm of registered trade mark agents, or
    (c) a body corporate entitled to describe itself as a registered trade mark agent.

Power of registrar to refuse to deal with certain agents

A1–89   88.—(1) The Secretary of State may make rules authorising the registrar to refuse to recognise as agent in respect of any business under this Act—

    (a) a person who has been convicted of an offence under section 84 (unregistered persons describing themselves as registered trade mark agents);
    (b) an individual whose name has been erased from and not restored to, or who is suspended from, the register of trade mark agents on the ground of misconduct;
    (c) a person who is found by the Secretary of State to have been guilty of such conduct as would, in the case of an individual registered in the register of trade mark agents, render him liable to have his name erased from the register on the ground of misconduct;
    (d) a partnership or body corporate of which one of the partners or directors is a person whom the registrar could refuse to recognise under paragraph (a), (b) or (c) above.

(2) The rules may contain such incidental and supplementary provisions as appear to the Secretary of State to be appropriate and may, in particular, prescribe circumstances in which a person is or is not to be taken to have been guilty of misconduct.

Importation of infringing goods, material or articles

Infringing goods, material or articles may be treated as prohibited goods

A1–90   89.—(1) The proprietor of a registered trade mark, or a licensee, may give notice in writing to the Commissioners of Customs and Excise—

    (a) that he is the proprietor or, as the case may be, a licensee of the registered trade mark,

(b) that, at a time and place specified in the notice, goods which are, in relation to that registered trade mark, infringing goods, material or articles are expected to arrive in the United Kingdom—
    (i) from outside the European Economic Area, or
    (ii) from within that Area but not having been entered for free circulation, and
(c) that he requests the Commissioners to treat them as prohibited goods.

(2) When a notice is in force under this section the importation of the goods to which the notice relates, otherwise than by a person for his private and domestic use, is prohibited; but a person is not by reason of the prohibition liable to any penalty other than forfeiture of the goods.

(3) This section does not apply to goods entered, or expected to be entered, for free circulation in respect of which the proprietor of the registered trade mark, or a licensee, is entitled to lodge an application under Article 3(1) of Council Regulation (EEC) No. 3842/86 laying down measures to prohibit the release for free circulation of counterfeit goods.

(3) This section does not apply to goods entered, or expected to be entered, for free circulation, export, re-export or for a suspensive procedure in respect of which an application may be made under Article 3(1) of Council Regulation (EC) No. 3295/94 laying down measures to prohibit the release for free circulation, export, re-export or entry for a suspensive procedure of counterfeit and pirated goods.

Subs. (3) substituted by the Trade Marks (EC Measures Relating to Counterfeit Goods) Regulations 1995, S.I. 1995 No. 1444.

Power of Commissioners of Customs and Excise to make regulations

90.—(1) The Commissioners of Customs and Excise may make regulations **A1–91** prescribing the form in which notice is to be given under section 89 and requiring a person giving notice—

(a) to furnish the Commissioners with such evidence as may be specified in the regulations, either on giving notice or when the goods are imported, or at both those times, and
(b) to comply with such other conditions as may be specified in the regulations.

(2) The regulations may, in particular, require a person giving such a notice—

(a) to pay such fees in respect of the notice as may be specified by the regulations;
(b) to give such security as may be so specified in respect of any liability or expense which the Commissioners may incur in consequence of the notice by reason of the detention of any goods or anything done to goods detained;
(c) to indemnify the Commissioners against any such liability or expense, whether security has been given or not.

(3) The regulations may make different provision as respects different classes of case to which they apply and may include such incidental and supplementary provisions as the Commissioners consider expedient.

(4) Regulations under this section shall be made by statutory instrument which shall be subject to annulment in pursuance of a resolution of either House of Parliament.

(5) Section 17 of the Customs and Excise Management Act 1979 (general provisions as to Commissioners' receipts) applies to fees paid in pursuance of regulations under this section as to receipts under the enactments relating to customs and excise.

Power of Commissioners of Customs and Excise to disclose information

91. Where information relating to infringing goods, material or articles has **A1–92** been obtained by the Commissioners of Customs and Excise for the purposes of, or in connection with, the exercise of their functions in relation to imported goods, the Commissioners may authorise the disclosure of that information for the purpose of facilitating the exercise by any person of any function in connection with the investigation or prosecution of an offence under section 92 below (unauthorised use of trade mark, &c. in relation to goods) or under the Trade Descriptions Act 1968.

Offences

Unauthorised use of trade mark, &c. in relation to goods

A1–93 **92.**—(1) A person commits an offence who with a view to gain for himself or another, or with intent to cause loss to another, and without the consent of the proprietor—

(a) applies to goods or their packaging a sign identical to, or likely to be mistaken for, a registered trade mark, or
(b) sells or lets for hire, offers or exposes for sale or hire or distributes goods which bear, or the packaging of which bears, such a sign, or
(c) has in his possession, custody or control in the course of a business any such goods with a view to the doing of anything, by himself or another, which would be an offence under paragraph (b).

(2) A person commits an offence who with a view to gain for himself or another, or with intent to cause loss to another, and without the consent of the proprietor—

(a) applies a sign identical to, or likely to be mistaken for, a registered trade mark to material intended to be used—
   (i) for labelling or packaging goods,
   (ii) as a business paper in relation to goods, or
   (iii) for advertising goods, or
(b) uses in the course of a business material bearing such a sign for labelling or packaging goods, as a business paper in relation to goods, or for advertising goods, or
(c) has in his possession, custody or control in the course of a business any such material with a view to the doing of anything, by himself or another, which would be an offence under paragraph (b).

(3) A person commits an offence who with a view to gain for himself or another, or with intent to cause loss to another, and without the consent of the proprietor—

(a) makes an article specifically designed or adapted for making copies of a sign identical to, or likely to be mistaken for, a registered trade mark, or
(b) has such an article in his possession, custody or control in the course of a business,

knowing or having reason to believe that it has been, or is to be, used to produce goods, or material for labelling or packaging goods, as a business paper in relation to goods, or for advertising goods.

(4) A person does not commit an offence under this section unless—

(a) the goods are goods in respect of which the trade mark is registered, or
(b) the trade mark has a reputation in the United Kingdom and the use of the sign takes or would take unfair advantage of, or is or would be detrimental to, the distinctive character or the repute of the trade mark.

(5) It is a defence for a person charged with an offence under this section to show that he believed on reasonable grounds that the use of the sign in the

manner in which it was used, or was to be used, was not an infringement of the registered trade mark.

(6) A person guilty of an offence under this section is liable—

    (a) on summary conviction to imprisonment for a term not exceeding six months or a fine not exceeding the statutory maximum, or both;

    (b) on conviction on indictment to a fine or imprisonment for a term not exceeding ten years, or both.

Enforcement function of local weights and measures authority

93.—(1) It is the duty of every local weights and measures authority to enforce **A1–94** within their area the provisions of section 92 (unauthorised use of trade mark, &c. in relation to goods).

(2) The following provisions of the Trade Descriptions Act 1968 apply in relation to the enforcement of that section as in relation to the enforcement of that Act—

    section 27 (power to make test purchases),

    section 28 (power to enter premises and inspect and seize goods and documents),

    section 29 (obstruction of authorised officers), and

    section 33 (compensation for loss, &c. of goods seized).

(3) Subsection (1) above does not apply in relation to the enforcement of section 92 in Northern Ireland, but it is the duty of the Department of Economic Development to enforce that section in Northern Ireland.

For that purpose the provisions of the Trade Descriptions Act 1968 specified in subsection (2) apply as if for the references to a local weights and measures authority and any officer of such an authority there were substituted references to that Department and any of its officers.

(4) Any enactment which authorises the disclosure of information for the purpose of facilitating the enforcement of the Trade Descriptions Act 1968 shall apply as if section 92 above were contained in that Act and as if the functions of any person in relation to the enforcement of that section were functions under that Act.

(5) Nothing in this section shall be construed as authorising a local weights and measures authority to bring proceedings in Scotland for an offence.

Falsification of register, &c.

94.—(1) It is an offence for a person to make, or cause to be made, a false entry **A1–95** in the register of trade marks, knowing or having reason to believe that it is false.

(2) It is an offence for a person—

    (a) to make or cause to be made anything falsely purporting to be a copy of an entry in the register, or

    (b) to produce or tender or cause to be produced or tendered in evidence any such thing,

knowing or having reason to believe that it is false.

(3) A person guilty of an offence under this section is liable—

    (a) on conviction on indictment, to imprisonment for a term not exceeding two years or a fine, or both;

    (b) on summary conviction, to imprisonment for a term not exceeding six months or a fine not exceeding the statutory maximum, or both.

Falsely representing trade mark as registered

95.—(1) It is an offence for a person—   **A1–96**

(a) falsely to represent that a mark is a registered trade mark, or
(b) to make a false representation as to the goods or services for which a trade mark is registered

knowing or having reason to believe that the representation is false.

(2) For the purposes of this section, the use in the United Kingdom in relation to a trade mark—

(a) of the word "registered", or
(b) of any other word or symbol importing a reference (express or implied) to registration,

shall be deemed to be a representation as to registration under this Act unless it is shown that the reference is to registration elsewhere than in the United Kingdom and that the trade mark is in fact so registered for the goods or services in question.

(3) A person guilty of an offence under this section is liable on summary conviction to a fine not exceeding level 3 on the standard scale.

Supplementary provisions as to summary proceedings in Scotland

A1–97 96.—(1) Notwithstanding anything in section 331 of the Criminal Procedure (Scotland) Act 1975, summary proceedings in Scotland for an offence under this Act may be begun at any time within six months after the date on which evidence sufficient in the Lord Advocate's opinion to justify the proceedings came to his knowledge.

For this purpose a certificate of the Lord Advocate as to the date on which such evidence came to his knowledge is conclusive evidence.

(2) For the purposes of subsection (1) and of any other provision of this Act as to the time within which summary proceedings for an offence may be brought, proceedings in Scotland shall be deemed to be begun on the date on which a warrant to apprehend or to cite the accused is granted, if such warrant is executed without undue delay.

Forfeiture of counterfeit goods, &c.

Forfeiture: England and Wales or Northern Ireland

A1–98 97.—(1) In England and Wales or Northern Ireland where there has come into the possession of any person in connection with the investigation or prosecution of a relevant offence—

(a) goods which, or the packaging of which, bears a sign identical to or likely to be mistaken for a registered trade mark,
(b) material bearing such a sign and intended to be used for labelling or packaging goods, as a business paper in relation to goods, or for advertising goods, or
(c) articles specifically designed or adapted for making copies of such a sign,

that person may apply under this section for an order for the forfeiture of the goods, material or articles.

(2) An application under this section may be made—

(a) where proceedings have been brought in any court for a relevant offence relating to some or all of the goods, material or articles, to that court;
(b) where no application for the forfeiture of the goods, material or articles has been made under paragraph (a), by way of complaint to a magistrates' court.

(3) On an application under this section the court shall make an order for the forfeiture of any goods, material or articles only if it is satisfied that a relevant offence has been committed in relation to the goods, material or articles.

(4) A court may infer for the purposes of this section that such an offence has been committed in relation to any goods, material or articles if it is satisfied that such an offence has been committed in relation to goods, material or articles which are representative of them (whether by reason of being of the same design or part of the same consignment or batch or otherwise).

(5) Any person aggrieved by an order made under this section by a magistrates' court, or by a decision of such a court not to make such an order, may appeal against that order or decision—

(a) in England and Wales, to the Crown Court;
(b) in Northern Ireland, to the county court;

and an order so made may contain such provision as appears to the court to be appropriate for delaying the coming into force of the order pending the making and determination of any appeal (including any application under section 111 of the Magistrates' Courts Act 1980 or Article 146 of the Magistrates' Courts (Northern Ireland) Order 1981 (statement of case)).

(6) Subject to subsection (7), where any goods, material or articles are forfeited under this section they shall be destroyed in accordance with such directions as the court may give.

(7) On making an order under this section the court may, if it considers it appropriate to do so, direct that the goods, material or articles to which the order relates shall (instead of being destroyed) be released, to such person as the court may specify, on condition that that person—

(a) causes the offending sign to be erased, removed or obliterated; and
(b) complies with any order to pay costs which has been made against him in the proceedings for the order for forfeiture.

(8) For the purposes of this section a "relevant offence" means an offence under section 92 above (unauthorised use of trade mark, &c. in relation to goods) or under the Trade Descriptions Act 1968 or any offence involving dishonesty or deception.

A modified form of this section applies under the Olympic Symbol etc. (Protection) Act 1995, s.11

Forfeiture: Scotland

98.—(1) In Scotland the court may make an order for the forfeiture of any— **A1–99**

(a) goods which bear, or the packaging of which bears, a sign identical to or likely to be mistaken for a registered trade mark,
(b) material bearing such a sign and intended to be used for labelling or packaging goods, as a business paper in relation to goods, or for advertising goods, or
(c) articles specifically designed or adapted for making copies of such a sign.

(2) An order under this section may be made—

(a) on an application by the procurator-fiscal made in the manner specified in **Section 134 of the Criminal Procedure (Scotland) Act 1995,** or
(b) where a person is convicted of a relevant offence, in addition to any other penalty which the court may impose.

(3) On an application under subsection (2)(a), the court shall make an order for the forfeiture of any goods, material or articles only if it is satisfied that a relevant offence has been committed in relation to the goods, material or articles.

(4) The court may infer for the purposes of this section that such an offence has been committed in relation to any goods, material or articles if it is satisfied that such an offence has been committed in relation to goods, material or articles which are representative of them (whether by reason of being of the same design or part of the same consignment or batch or otherwise).

(5) The procurator-fiscal making the application under subsection (2)(a) shall serve on any person appearing to him to be the owner of, or otherwise to have an interest in, the goods, material or articles to which the application relates a copy of the application, together with a notice giving him the opportunity to appear at the hearing of the application to show cause why the goods, material or articles should not be forfeited.

(6) Service under subsection (5) shall be carried out, and such service may be proved, in the manner specified for citation of an accused in summary proceedings under the **Criminal Procedure (Scotland) Act 1995.**

(7) Any person upon whom notice is served under subsection (5) and any other person claiming to be the owner of, or otherwise to have an interest in, goods, material or articles to which an application under this section relates shall be entitled to appear at the hearing of the application to show cause why the goods, material or articles should not be forfeited.

(8) The court shall not make an order following an application under subsection (2)(a)—

(a) if any person on whom notice is served under subsection (5) does not appear, unless service of the notice on that person is proved; or

(b) if no notice under subsection (5) has been served, unless the court is satisfied that in the circumstances it was reasonable not to serve such notice.

(9) Where an order for the forfeiture of any goods, material or articles is made following an application under subsection (2)(a), any person who appeared, or was entitled to appear, to show cause why goods, material or articles should not be forfeited may, within 21 days of the making of the order, appeal to the High Court by Bill of Suspension; and **Section 182(5)(a) to (e) of the Criminal Procedure (Scotland) Act 1995** shall apply to an appeal under this subsection as it applies to a stated case under Part II of that Act.

(10) An order following an application under subsection (2)(a) shall not take effect—

(a) until the end of the period of 21 days beginning with the day after the day on which the order is made; or

(b) if an appeal is made under subsection (9) above within that period, until the appeal is determined or abandoned.

(11) An order under subsection (2)(b) shall not take effect—

(a) until the end of the period within which an appeal against the order could be brought under the **Criminal Procedure (Scotland) Act 1995**; or

(b) if an appeal is made within that period, until the appeal is determined or abandoned.

(12) Subject to subsection (13), goods, material or articles forfeited under this section shall be destroyed in accordance with such directions as the court may give.

(13) On making an order under this section the court may if it considers it appropriate to do so, direct that the goods, material or articles to which the order relates shall (instead of being destroyed) be released, to such person as the court may specify, on condition that that person causes the offending sign to be erased, removed or obliterated.

(14) For the purposes of this section—

"relevant offence" means an offence under section 92 (unauthorised use of trade mark, &c. in relation to goods) or under the Trade Descriptions Act 1968 or any offence involving dishonesty or deception, "the court" means—

    (a) in relation to an order made on an application under subsection (2)(a), the sheriff, and

    (b) in relation to an order made under subsection (2)(b), the court which imposed the penalty.

A modified form of this section applies under the Olympic Symbol etc. (Protection) Act 1995, s. 12. The amendments shown above were effected by the Criminal Procedure (Consequential Provisions) (Scotland) Act 1995.

PART IV

MISCELLANEOUS AND GENERAL PROVISIONS

Miscellaneous

Unauthorised use of Royal arms, &c.

99.—(1) A person shall not without the authority of Her Majesty use in **A1–100** connection with any business the Royal arms (or arms so closely resembling the Royal arms as to be calculated to deceive) in such manner as to be calculated to lead to the belief that he is duly authorised to use the Royal arms.

(2) A person shall not without the authority of Her Majesty or of a member of the Royal family use in connection with any business any device, emblem or title in such a manner as to be calculated to lead to the belief that he is employed by, or supplies goods or services to, Her Majesty or that member of the Royal family.

(3) A person who contravenes subsection (1) commits an offence and is liable on summary conviction to a fine not exceeding level 2 on the standard scale.

(4) Contravention of subsection (1) or (2) may be restrained by injunction in proceedings brought by—

    (a) any person who is authorised to use the arms, device, emblem or title in question, or

    (b) any person authorised by the Lord Chamberlain to take such proceedings.

(5) Nothing in this section affects any right of the proprietor of a trade mark containing any such arms, device, emblem or title to use that trade mark.

Burden of proving use of trade mark

100. If in any civil proceedings under this Act a question arises as to the use to **A1–101** which a registered trade mark has been put, it is for the proprietor to show what use has been made of it.

Offences committed by partnerships and bodies corporate

101.—(1) Proceedings for an offence under this Act alleged to have been **A1–102** committed by a partnership shall be brought against the partnership in the name of the firm and not in that of the partners; but without prejudice to any liability of the partners under subsection (4) below.

(2) The following provisions apply for the purposes of such proceedings as in relation to a body corporate—

    (a) any rules of court relating to the service of documents;

(b) in England and Wales or Northern Ireland, Schedule 3 to the Magistrates' Courts Act 1980 or Schedule 4 to the Magistrates' Courts (Northern Ireland) Order 1981 (procedure on charge of offence).

(3) A fine imposed on a partnership on its conviction in such proceedings shall be paid out of the partnership assets.

(4) Where a partnership is guilty of an offence under this Act, every partner, other than a partner who is proved to have been ignorant of or to have attempted to prevent the commission of the offence, is also guilty of the offence and liable to be proceeded against and punished accordingly.

(5) Where an offence under this Act committed by a body corporate is proved to have been committed with the consent or connivance of a director, manager, secretary or other similar officer of the body, or a person purporting to act in any such capacity, he as well as the body corporate is guilty of the offence and liable to be proceeded against and punished accordingly.

Interpretation

Adaptation of expressions for Scotland

A1–103   102. In the application of this Act to Scotland—

"account of profits" means accounting and payment of profits;
"accounts" means count, reckoning and payment;
"assignment" means assignation;
"costs" means expenses;
"declaration" means declarator;
"defendant" means defender;
"delivery up" means delivery;
"injunction" means interdict;
"interlocutory relief" means interim remedy; and
"plaintiff" means pursuer.

Minor definitions

A1–104   103.—(1) In this Act—

"business" includes a trade or profession;
"director", in relation to a body corporate whose affairs are managed by its members, means any member of the body;
"infringement proceedings", in relation to a registered trade mark, includes proceedings under section 16 (order for delivery up of infringing goods, &c.);
"publish" means make available to the public, and references to publication—
(a) in relation to an application for registration, are to publication under section 38(1), and
(b) in relation to registration, are to publication under section 40(4);
"statutory provisions" includes provisions of subordinate legislation within the meaning of the Interpretation Act 1978;
"trade" includes any business or profession.

(2) References in this Act to use (or any particular description of use) of a trade mark, or of a sign identical with, similar to, or likely to be mistaken for a trade mark, include use (or that description of use) otherwise than by means of a graphic representation.

(3) References in this Act to a Community instrument include references to any instrument amending or replacing that instrument.

Index of defined expressions

104. In this Act the expressions listed below are defined by or otherwise fall to **A1–105** be construed in accordance with the provisions indicated—

account of profits and accounts (in Scotland)	section 102
appointed person (for purposes of section 76)	section 77
assignment (in Scotland)	section 102
business	section 103(1)
certification mark	section 50(1)
collective mark	section 49(1)
commencement (of this Act)	section 109(2)
Community trade mark	section 51
Community Trade Mark Regulation	section 51
Convention country	section 55(1)(b)
costs (in Scotland)	section 102
the court	section 75
date of application	section 33(2)
date of filing	section 33(1)
date of registration	section 40(3)
defendant (in Scotland)	section 102
delivery up (in Scotland)	section 102
director	section 103(1)
earlier right	section 5(4)
earlier trade mark	section 6
exclusive licence and licensee	section 29(1)
infringement (of registered trade mark)	section 9(1) and (2) and 10
infringement proceedings	section 103(1)
infringing articles	section 17
infringing goods	section 17
infringing material	section 17
injunction (in Scotland)	section 102
interlocutory relief (in Scotland)	section 102
the International Bureau	section 53
international trade mark (UK)	section 53
Madrid Protocol	section 53
Paris Convention	section 55(1)(a)
plaintiff (in Scotland)	section 102
prescribed	section 78(1)(b)
protected under the Paris Convention	
—well-known trade marks	section 56(1)
—state emblems and official signs or hallmarks	section 57(1)
—emblems, &c. of international organisations	section 58(2)
publish and references to publication	section 103(1)
register, registered (and related expressions)	section 63(1)
registered trade mark agent	section 83(1)
registrable transaction	section 25(2)
the registrar	section 62

rules	section 78
statutory provisions	section 103(1)
trade	section 103(1)
trade mark	
—generally	section 1(1)
—includes collective mark or cer- tification mark	section 1(2)
United Kingdom (references include Isle of Man)	section 108(2)
use (of trade mark or sign)	section 103(2)
well-known trade mark (under Paris Convention)	section 56(1)

Other general provisions

Transitional provisions

A1–106   105. The provisions of Schedule 3 have effect with respect to transitional matters, including the treatment of marks registered under the Trade Marks Act 1938, and applications for registration and other proceedings pending under that Act, on the commencement of this Act.

Consequential amendments and repeals

A1–107   106.—(1) The enactments specified in Schedule 4 are amended in accordance with that Schedule, the amendments being consequential on the provisions of this Act.

(2) The enactments specified in Schedule 5 are repealed to the extent specified.

Territorial waters and the continental shelf

A1–108   107.—(1) For the purposes of this Act the territorial waters of the United Kingdom shall be treated as part of the United Kingdom.

(2) This Act applies to things done in the United Kingdom sector of the continental shelf on a structure or vessel which is present there for purposes directly connected with the exploration of the sea bed or subsoil or the exploitation of their natural resources as it applies to things done in the United Kingdom.

(3) The United Kingdom sector of the continental shelf means the areas designated by order under section 1(7) of the Continental Shelf Act 1964.

Extent

A1–109   108.—(1) This Act extends to England and Wales, Scotland and Northern Ireland.

(2) This Act also extends to the Isle of Man, subject to such exceptions and modifications as Her Majesty may specify by Order in Council; and subject to any such Order references in this Act to the United Kingdom shall be construed as including the Isle of Man.

Commencement

A1–110   109.—(1) The provisions of this Act come into force on such day as the Secretary of State may appoint by order made by statutory instrument.

Different days may be appointed for different provisions and different purposes.

(2) The references to the commencement of this Act in Schedules 3 and 4 (transitional provisions and consequential amendments) are to the commence-

ment of the main substantive provisions of Parts I and III of this Act and the consequential repeal of the Trade Marks Act 1938.

Provision may be made by order under this section identifying the date of that commencement.

Short title

110. This Act may be cited as the Trade Marks Act 1994.   **A1–111**

SCHEDULES

SCHEDULE 1   **Section 49.**

Collective Marks

General

1. The provisions of this Act apply to collective marks subject to the following **A1–112** provisions.

Signs of which a collective mark may consist

2. In relation to a collective mark the reference in section 1(1) (signs of which a trade **A1–113** mark may consist) to distinguishing goods or services of one undertaking from those of other undertakings shall be construed as a reference to distinguishing goods or services of members of the association which is the proprietor of the mark from those of other undertakings.

Indication of geographical origin

3.—(1) Notwithstanding section 3(1)(c), a collective mark may be registered which **A1–114** consists of signs or indications which may serve, in trade, to designate the geographical origin of the goods or services.

(2) However, the proprietor of such a mark is not entitled to prohibit the use of the signs or indications in accordance with honest practices in industrial or commercial matters (in particular, by a person who is entitled to use a geographical name).

Mark not to be misleading as to character or significance

4.—(1) A collective mark shall not be registered if the public is liable to be misled as **A1–115** regards the character or significance of the mark, in particular if it is likely to be taken to be something other than a collective mark.

(2) The registrar may accordingly require that a mark in respect of which application is made for registration include some indication that it is a collective mark.

Notwithstanding section 39(2), an application may be amended so as to comply with any such requirement.

Regulations governing use of collective mark

5.—(1) An applicant for registration of a collective mark must file with the registrar **A1–116** regulations governing the use of the mark.

(2) The regulations must specify the persons authorised to use the mark, the conditions of membership of the association and, where they exist, the conditions of use of the mark, including any sanctions against misuse.

Further requirements with which the regulations have to comply may be imposed by rules.

Approval of regulations by registrar

6.—(1) A collective mark shall not be registered unless the regulations governing the use **A1–117** of the mark—

(a) comply with paragraph 5(2) and any further requirements imposed by rules, and

(b) are not contrary to public policy or to accepted principles of morality.

(2) Before the end of the prescribed period after the date of the application for registration of a collective mark, the applicant must file the regulations with the registrar and pay the prescribed fee.

If he does not do so, the application shall be deemed to be withdrawn.

7.—(1) The registrar shall consider whether the requirements mentioned in paragraph 6(1) are met.

(2) If it appears to the registrar that those requirements are not met, he shall inform the applicant and give him an opportunity, within such period as the registrar may specify, to make representations or to file amended regulations.

(3) If the applicant fails to satisfy the registrar that those requirements are met, or to file regulations amended so as to meet them, or fails to respond before the end of the specified period, the registrar shall refuse the application.

(4) If it appears to the registrar that those requirements, and the other requirements for registration, are met, he shall accept the application and shall proceed in accordance with section 38 (publication, opposition proceedings and observations).

8. The regulations shall be published and notice of opposition may be given, and observations may be made, relating to the matters mentioned in paragraph 6(1).

This is in addition to any other grounds on which the application may be opposed or observations made.

Regulations to be open to inspection

A1–118 9. The regulations governing the use of a registered collective mark shall be open to public inspection in the same way as the register.

Amendment of regulations

A1–119 10.—(1) An amendment of the regulations governing the use of a registered collective mark is not effective unless and until the amended regulations are filed with the registrar and accepted by him.

(2) Before accepting any amended regulations the registrar may in any case where it appears to him expedient to do so cause them to be published.

(3) If he does so, notice of opposition may be given, and observations may be made, relating to the matters mentioned in paragraph 6(1).

Infringement: rights of authorised users

A1–120 11. The following provisions apply in relation to an authorised user of a registered collective mark as in relation to a licensee of a trade mark—

(a) section 10(5) (definition of infringement: unauthorised application of mark to certain material);

(b) section 19(2) (order as to disposal of infringing goods, material or articles: adequacy of other remedies);

(c) section 89 (prohibition of importation of infringing goods, material or articles: request to Commissioners of Customs and Excise).

12.—(1) The following provisions (which correspond to the provisions of section 30 (general provisions as to rights of licensees in case of infringement)) have effect as regards the rights of an authorised user in relation to infringement of a registered collective mark.

(2) An authorised user is entitled, subject to any agreement to the contrary between him and the proprietor, to call on the proprietor to take infringement proceedings in respect of any matter which affects his interests.

(3) If the proprietor—

(a) refuses to do so, or

(b) fails to do so within two months after being called upon,

the authorised user may bring the proceedings in his own name as if he were the proprietor.

(4) Where infringement proceedings are brought by virtue of this paragraph, the authorised user may not, without the leave of the court, proceed with the action unless the proprietor is either joined as a plaintiff or added as a defendant.

This does not affect the granting of interlocutory relief on an application by an authorised user alone.

(5) A proprietor who is added as a defendant as mentioned in sub-paragraph (4) shall not be made liable for any costs in the action unless he takes part in the proceedings.

(6) In infringement proceedings brought by the proprietor of a registered collective mark any loss suffered or likely to be suffered by authorised users shall be taken into account; and the court may give such directions as it thinks fit as to the extent to which the plaintiff is to hold the proceeds of any pecuniary remedy on behalf of such users.

Grounds for revocation of registration

13. Apart from the grounds of revocation provided for in section 46, the registration of a **A1–121** collective mark may be revoked on the ground—

    (a) that the manner in which the mark has been used by the proprietor has caused it to become liable to mislead the public in the manner referred to in paragraph 4(1), or

    (b) that the proprietor has failed to observe, or to secure the observance of, the regulations governing the use of the mark, or

    (c) that an amendment of the regulations has been made so that the regulations—

        (i) no longer comply with paragraph 5(2) and any further conditions imposed by rules, or

        (ii) are contrary to public policy or to accepted principles of morality.

Grounds for invalidity of registration

14. Apart from the grounds of invalidity provided for in section 47, the registration of a **A1–122** collective mark may be declared invalid on the ground that the mark was registered in breach of the provisions of paragraph 4(1) or 6(1).

SCHEDULE 2   Section 50.

CERTIFICATION MARKS

General

1. The provisions of this Act apply to certification marks subject to the following **A1–123** provisions.

Signs of which a certification mark may consist

2. In relation to a certification mark the reference in section 1(1) (signs of which a trade **A1–124** mark may consist) to distinguishing goods or services of one undertaking from those of other undertakings shall be construed as a reference to distinguishing goods or services which are certified from those which are not.

Indication of geographical origin

3.—(1) Notwithstanding section 3(1)(c), a certification mark may be registered which **A1–125** consists of signs or indications which may serve, in trade, to designate the geographical origin of the goods or services.

(2) However, the proprietor of such a mark is not entitled to prohibit the use of the signs or indications in accordance with honest practices in industrial or commercial matters (in particular, by a person who is entitled to use a geographical name).

Nature of proprietor's business

4. A certification mark shall not be registered if the proprietor carries on a business **A1–126** involving the supply of goods or services of the kind certified.

Mark not to be misleading as to character or significance

5.—(1) A certification mark shall not be registered if the public is liable to be misled as **A1–127** regards the character or significance of the mark, in particular if it is likely to be taken to be something other than a certification mark.

(2) The registrar may accordingly require that a mark in respect of which application is made for registration include some indication that it is a certification mark.

Notwithstanding section 39(2), an application may be amended so as to comply with any such requirement.

Regulations governing use of certification mark

A1–128   6.—(1) An applicant for registration of a certification mark must file with the registrar regulations governing the use of the mark.

(2) The regulations must indicate who is authorised to use the mark, the characteristics to be certified by the mark, how the certifying body is to test those characteristics and to supervise the use of the mark, the fees (if any) to be paid in connection with the operation of the mark and the procedures for resolving disputes.

Further requirements with which the regulations have to comply may be imposed by rules.

Approval of regulations, &c.

A1–129   7.—(1) A certification mark shall not be registered unless—

    (a) the regulations governing the use of the mark—

        (i) comply with paragraph 6(2) and any further requirements imposed by rules, and

        (ii) are not contrary to public policy or to accepted principles of morality, and

    (b) the applicant is competent to certify the goods or services for which the mark is to be registered.

(2) Before the end of the prescribed period after the date of the application for registration of a certification mark, the applicant must file the regulations with the registrar and pay the prescribed fee.

If he does not do so, the application shall be deemed to be withdrawn.

8.—(1) The registrar shall consider whether the requirements mentioned in paragraph 7(1) are met.

(2) If it appears to the registrar that those requirements are not met, he shall inform the applicant and give him an opportunity, within such period as the registrar may specify, to make representations or to file amended regulations.

(3) If the applicant fails to satisfy the registrar that those requirements are met, or to file regulations amended so as to meet them, or fails to respond before the end of the specified period, the registrar shall refuse the application.

(4) If it appears to the registrar that those requirements, and the other requirements for registration, are met, he shall accept the application and shall proceed in accordance with section 38 (publication, opposition proceedings and observations).

9. The regulations shall be published and notice of opposition may be given, and observations may be made, relating to the matters mentioned in paragraph 7(1).

This is in addition to any other grounds on which the application may be opposed or observations made.

Regulations to be open to inspection

A1–130   10. The regulations governing the use of a registered certification mark shall be open to public inspection in the same way as the register.

Amendment of regulations

A1–131   11.—(1) An amendment of the regulations governing the use of a registered certification mark is not effective unless and until the amended regulations are filed with the registrar and accepted by him.

(2) Before accepting any amended regulations the registrar may in any case where it appears to him expedient to do so cause them to be published.

(3) If he does so, notice of opposition may be given, and observations may be made, relating to the matters mentioned in paragraph 7(1).

Consent to assignment of registered certification mark

A1–132   12. The assignment or other transmission of a registered certification mark is not effective without the consent of the registrar.

Infringement: rights of authorised users

A1–133   13. The following provisions apply in relation to an authorised user of a registered certification mark as in relation to a licensee of a trade mark—

    (a) section 10(5) (definition of infringement: unauthorised application of mark to certain material);

    (b) section 19(2) (order as to disposal of infringing goods, material or articles: adequacy of other remedies);

    (c) section 89 (prohibition of importation of infringing goods, material or articles: request to Commissioners of Customs and Excise).

14. In infringement proceedings brought by the proprietor of a registered certification mark any loss suffered or likely to be suffered by authorised users shall be taken into account; and the court may give such directions as it thinks fit as to the extent to which the plaintiff is to hold the proceeds of any pecuniary remedy on behalf of such users.

Grounds for revocation of registration

15. Apart from the grounds of revocation provided for in section 46, the registration of a   **A1–134** certification mark may be revoked on the ground—

    (a) that the proprietor has begun to carry on such a business as is mentioned in paragraph 4,

    (b) that the manner in which the mark has been used by the proprietor has caused it to become liable to mislead the public in the manner referred to in paragraph 5(1),

    (c) that the proprietor has failed to observe, or to secure the observance of, the regulations governing the use of the mark,

    (d) that an amendment of the regulations has been made so that the regulations—

        (i) no longer comply with paragraph 6(2) and any further conditions imposed by rules, or

        (ii) are contrary to public policy or to accepted principles of morality, or

    (e) that the proprietor is no longer competent to certify the goods or services for which the mark is registered.

Grounds for invalidity of registration

16. Apart from the grounds of invalidity provided for in section 47, the registration of a   **A1–135** certification mark may be declared invalid on the ground that the mark was registered in breach of the provisions of paragraph 4, 5(1) or 7(1).

SCHEDULE 3   **Section 105.**

TRANSITIONAL PROVISIONS

Introductory

1.—(1) In this Schedule—   **A1–136**

    "existing registered mark" means a trade mark, certification trade mark or service mark registered under the 1938 Act immediately before the commencement of this Act;

    "the 1938 Act" means the Trade Marks Act 1938; and

    "the old law" means that Act and any other enactment or rule of law applying to existing registered marks immediately before the commencement of this Act.

(2) For the purposes of this Schedule—

    (a) an application shall be treated as pending on the commencement of this Act if it was made but not finally determined before commencement, and

    (b) the date on which it was made shall be taken to be the date of filing under the 1938 Act.

Existing registered marks

2.—(1) Existing registered marks (whether registered in Part A or B of the register kept   **A1–137** under the 1938 Act) shall be transferred on the commencement of this Act to the register kept under this Act and have effect, subject to the provisions of this Schedule, as if registered under this Act.

(2) Existing registered marks registered as a series under section 21(2) of the 1938 Act shall be similarly registered in the new register.

Provision may be made by rules for putting such entries in the same form as is required for entries under this Act.

(3) In any other case notes indicating that existing registered marks are associated with other marks shall cease to have effect on the commencement of this Act.

3.—(1) A condition entered on the former register in relation to an existing registered mark immediately before the commencement of this Act shall cease to have effect on commencement.

Proceedings under section 33 of the 1938 Act (application to expunge or vary registration for breach of condition) which are pending on the commencement of this Act shall be dealt with under the old law and any necessary alteration made to the new register.

(2) A disclaimer or limitation entered on the former register in relation to an existing registered mark immediately before the commencement of this Act shall be transferred to the new register and have effect as if entered on the register in pursuance of section 13 of this Act.

Effects of registration: infringement

A1–138   4.—(1) Sections 9 to 12 of this Act (effects of registration) apply in relation to an existing registered mark as from the commencement of this Act and section 14 of this Act (action for infringement) applies in relation to infringement of an existing registered mark committed after the commencement of this Act, subject to sub-paragraph (2) below.

The old law continues to apply in relation to infringements committed before commencement.

(2) It is not an infringement of—
    (a) an existing registered mark, or
    (b) a registered trade mark of which the distinctive elements are the same or substantially the same as those of an existing registered mark and which is registered for the same goods or services,
to continue after commencement any use which did not amount to infringement of the existing registered mark under the old law.

Infringing goods, material or articles

A1–139   5. Section 16 of this Act (order for delivery up of infringing goods, material or articles) applies to infringing goods, material or articles whether made before or after the commencement of this Act.

Rights and remedies of licensee or authorised user

A1–140   6.—(1) Section 30 (general provisions as to rights of licensees in case of infringement) of this Act applies to licences granted before the commencement of this Act, but only in relation to infringements committed after commencement.

(2) Paragraph 14 of Schedule 2 of this Act (court to take into account loss suffered by authorised users, &c.) applies only in relation to infringements committed after commencement.

Co-ownership of registered mark

A1–141   7. The provisions of section 23 of this Act (co-ownership of registered mark) apply as from the commencement of this Act to an existing registered mark of which two or more persons were immediately before commencement registered as joint proprietors.

But so long as the relations between the joint proprietors remain such as are described in section 63 of the 1938 Act (joint ownership) there shall be taken to be an agreement to exclude the operation of subsections (1) and (3) of section 23 of this Act (ownership in undivided shares and right of co-proprietor to make separate use of the mark).

Assignment, &c. of registered mark

A1–142   8.—(1) Section 24 of this Act (assignment or other transmission of registered mark) applies to transactions and events occurring after the commencement of this Act in relation to an existing registered mark; and the old law continues to apply in relation to transactions and events occurring before commencement.

(2) Existing entries under section 25 of the 1938 Act (registration of assignments and transmissions) shall be transferred on the commencement of this Act to the register kept under this Act and have effect as if made under section 25 of this Act.

Provision may be made by rules for putting such entries in the same form as is required for entries made under this Act.

(3) An application for registration under section 25 of the 1938 Act which is pending before the registrar on the commencement of this Act shall be treated as an application for registration under section 25 of this Act and shall proceed accordingly.

The registrar may require the applicant to amend his application so as to conform with the requirements of this Act.

(4) An application for registration under section 25 of the 1938 Act which has been determined by the registrar but not finally determined before the commencement of this Act shall be dealt with under the old law; and sub-paragraph (2) above shall apply in relation to any resulting entry in the register.

(5) Where before the commencement of this Act a person has become entitled by assignment or transmission to an existing registered mark but has not registered his title, any application for registration after commencement shall be made under section 25 of this Act.

(6) In cases to which sub-paragraph (3) or (5) applies section 25(3) of the 1938 Act continues to apply (and section 25(3) and (4) of this Act do not apply) as regards the consequences of failing to register.

Licensing of registered mark

9.—(1) Sections 28 and 29(2) of this Act (licensing of registered trade mark; rights of **A1–143** exclusive licensee against grantor's successor in title) apply only in relation to licences granted after the commencement of this Act; and the old law continues to apply in relation to licences granted before commencement.

(2) Existing entries under section 28 of the 1938 Act (registered users) shall be transferred on the commencement of this Act to the register kept under this Act and have effect as if made under section 25 of this Act.

Provision may be made by rules for putting such entries in the same form as is required for entries made under this Act.

(3) An application for registration as a registered user which is pending before the registrar on the commencement of this Act shall be treated as an application for registration of a licence under section 25(1) of this Act and shall proceed accordingly.

The registrar may require the applicant to amend his application so as to conform with the requirements of this Act.

(4) An application for registration as a registered user which has been determined by the registrar but not finally determined before the commencement of this Act shall be dealt with under the old law; and sub-paragraph (2) above shall apply in relation to any resulting entry in the register.

(5) Any proceedings pending on the commencement of this Act under section 28(8) or (10) of the 1938 Act (variation or cancellation of registration of registered user) shall be dealt with under the old law and any necessary alteration made to the new register.

Pending applications for registration

10.—(1) An application for registration of a mark under the 1938 Act which is pending **A1–144** on the commencement of this Act shall be dealt with under the old law, subject as mentioned below, and if registered the mark shall be treated for the purposes of this Schedule as an existing registered mark.

(2) The power of the Secretary of State under section 78 of this Act to make rules regulating practice and procedure, and as to the matters mentioned in subsection (2) of that section, is exercisable in relation to such an application; and different provision may be made for such applications from that made for other applications.

(3) Section 23 of the 1938 Act (provisions as to associated trade marks) shall be disregarded in dealing after the commencement of this Act with an application for registration.

Conversion of pending application

11.—(1) In the case of a pending application for registration which has not been **A1–145** advertised under section 18 of the 1938 Act before the commencement of this Act, the applicant may give notice to the registrar claiming to have the registrability of the mark determined in accordance with the provisions of this Act.

(2) The notice must be in the prescribed form, be accompanied by the appropriate fee and be given no later than six months after the commencement of this Act.

(3) Notice duly given is irrevocable and has the effect that the application shall be treated as if made immediately after the commencement of this Act.

Trade marks registered according to old classification

A1–146   12. The registrar may exercise the powers conferred by rules under section 65 of this Act (adaptation of entries to new classification) to secure that any existing registered marks which do not conform to the system of classification prescribed under section 34 of this Act are brought into conformity with that system.

This applies, in particular, to existing registered marks classified according to the pre-1938 classification set out in Schedule 3 to the Trade Marks Rules 1986.

Claim to priority from overseas application

A1–147   13. Section 35 of this Act (claim to priority of Convention application) applies to an application for registration under this Act made after the commencement of this Act notwithstanding that the Convention application was made before commencement.

14.—(1) Where before the commencement of this Act a person has duly filed an application for protection of a trade mark in a relevant country within the meaning of section 39A of the 1938 Act which is not a Convention country ("a relevant overseas application"), he, or his successor in title, has a right to priority, for the purposes of registering the same trade mark under this Act for some or all of the same goods or services, for a period of six months from the date of filing of the relevant overseas application.

(2) If the application for registration under this Act is made within that six-month period—

  (a) the relevant date for the purposes of establishing which rights take precedence shall be the date of filing of the relevant overseas application, and

  (b) the registrability of the trade mark shall not be affected by any use of the mark in the United Kingdom in the period between that date and the date of the application under this Act.

(3) Any filing which in a relevant country is equivalent to a regular national filing, under its domestic legislation or an international agreement, shall be treated as giving rise to the right of priority.

A "regular national filing" means a filing which is adequate to establish the date on which the application was filed in that country, whatever may be the subsequent fate of the application.

(4) A subsequent application concerning the same subject as the relevant overseas application, filed in the same country, shall be considered the relevant overseas application (of which the filing date is the starting date of the period of priority), if at the time of the subsequent application—

  (a) the previous application has been withdrawn, abandoned or refused, without having been laid open to public inspection and without leaving any rights outstanding, and

  (b) it has not yet served as a basis for claiming a right of priority.

The previous application may not thereafter serve as a basis for claiming a right of priority.

(5) Provision may be made by rules as to the manner of claiming a right to priority on the basis of a relevant overseas application.

(6) A right to priority arising as a result of a relevant overseas application may be assigned or otherwise transmitted, either with the application or independently.

The reference in sub-paragraph (1) to the applicant's "successor in title" shall be construed accordingly.

(7) Nothing in this paragraph affects proceedings on an application for registration under the 1938 Act made before the commencement of this Act (see paragraph 10 above).

Duration and renewal of registration

A1–148   15.—(1) Section 42(1) of this Act (duration of original period of registration) applies in relation to the registration of a mark in pursuance of an application made after the commencement of this Act; and the old law applies in any other case.

(2) Sections 42(2) and 43 of this Act (renewal) apply where the renewal falls due on or after the commencement of this Act; and the old law continues to apply in any other case.

(3) In either case it is immaterial when the fee is paid.

Pending application for alteration of registered mark

16. An application under section 35 of the 1938 Act (alteration of registered trade mark) **A1–149**
which is pending on the commencement of this Act shall be dealt with under the old law
and any necessary alteration made to the new register.

Revocation for non-use

17.—(1) An application under section 26 of the 1938 Act (removal from register or **A1–150**
imposition of limitation on ground of non-use) which is pending on the commencement of
this Act shall be dealt with under the old law and any necessary alteration made to the
new register.

(2) An application under section 46(1)(a) or (b) of this Act (revocation for non-use) may
be made in relation to an existing registered mark at any time after the commencement of
this Act.

Provided that no such application for the revocation of the registration of an existing
registered mark registered by virtue of section 27 of the 1938 Act (defensive registration of
well-known trade marks) may be made until more than five years after the commencement of this Act.

Application for rectification, &c.

18.—(1) An application under section 32 or 34 of the 1938 Act (rectification or correction **A1–151**
of the register) which is pending on the commencement of this Act shall be dealt with
under the old law and any necessary alteration made to the new register.

(2) For the purposes of proceedings under section 47 of this Act (grounds for invalidity
of registration) as it applies in relation to an existing registered mark, the provisions of this
Act shall be deemed to have been in force at all material times.

Provided that no objection to the validity of the registration of an existing registered
mark may be taken on the ground specified in subsection (3) of section 5 of this Act
(relative grounds for refusal of registration: conflict with earlier mark registered for
different goods or services).

Regulations as to use of certification mark

19.—(1) Regulations governing the use of an existing registered certification mark **A1–152**
deposited at the Patent Office in pursuance of section 37 of the 1938 Act shall be treated
after the commencement of this Act as if filed under paragraph 6 of Schedule 2 to this Act.

(2) Any request for amendment of the regulations which was pending on the
commencement of this Act shall be dealt with under the old law.

Sheffield marks

20.—(1) For the purposes of this Schedule the Sheffield register kept under Schedule 2 to **A1–153**
the 1938 Act shall be treated as part of the register of trade marks kept under that Act.

(2) Applications made to the Cutlers' Company in accordance with that Schedule which
are pending on the commencement of this Act shall proceed after commencement as if
they had been made to the registrar.

Certificate of validity of contested registration

21. A certificate given before the commencement of this Act under section 47 of the 1938 **A1–154**
Act (certificate of validity of contested registration) shall have effect as if given under
section 73(1) of this Act.

Trade mark agents

22.—(1) Rules in force immediately before the commencement of this Act under section **A1–155**
282 or 283 of the Copyright, Designs and Patents Act 1988 (register of trade mark agents;
persons entitled to described themselves as registered) shall continue in force and have
effect as if made under section 83 or 85 of this Act.

(2) Rules in force immediately before the commencement of this Act under section 40 of
the 1938 Act as to the persons whom the registrar may refuse to recognise as agents for the
purposes of business under that Act shall continue in force and have effect as if made
under section 88 of this Act.

(3) Rules continued in force under this paragraph may be varied or revoked by further rules made under the relevant provisions of this Act.

SCHEDULE 4   **Section 106(1).**

CONSEQUENTIAL AMENDMENTS

General adaptation of existing references

A1–156   1.—(1) References in statutory provisions passed or made before the commencement of this Act to trade marks or registered trade marks within the meaning of the Trade Marks Act 1938 shall, unless the context otherwise requires, be construed after the commencement of this Act as references to trade marks or registered trade marks within the meaning of this Act.

(2) Sub-paragraph (1) applies, in particular, to the references in the following provisions—

Industrial Organisation and Development Act 1947	Schedule 1, paragraph 7
Crown Proceedings Act 1947	section 3(1)(b)
Horticulture Act 1960	section 15(1)(b)
Printer's Imprint Act 1961	section 1(1)(b)
Patents Act 1977	section 19(2)
	section 27(4)
	section 123(7)
Unfair Contract Terms Act 1977	Schedule 1, paragraph 1(c)
Judicature (Northern Ireland) Act 1978	section 94A(5)
State Immunity Act 1978	section 7(a) and (b)
Supreme Court Act 1981	section 72(5) Schedule 1, paragraph 1(i)
Civil Jurisdiction and Judgments Act 1982	Schedule 5, paragraph 2
	Schedule 8, paragraph 2(14) and 4(2)
Value Added Tax Act 1983	Schedule 3, paragraph 1
Companies Act 1985	section 396(3A)(a) or (as substituted by the Companies Act 1989) section 396(2)(d)(i)
	section 410(4)(c)(v)
	Schedule 4, Part I, Balance Sheet Formats 1 and 2 and Note (2)
	Schedule 9, Part I, paragraphs 5(2)(d) and 10(2)
Law Reform (Miscellaneous Provisions) (Scotland) Act 1985	section 15(5)
Atomic Energy Authority Act 1986	section 8(2)
Companies (Northern Ireland) Order 1986	article 403(3A)(a) or (as substituted by the Companies (No.2) (Northern Ireland) Order 1990) article 403(2)(d)(i)
	Schedule 4, Part I, Balance Sheet Formats 1 and 2 and Note (2)
	Schedule 9, Part I, paragraphs 5(2)(d) and 10(2)
Consumer Protection Act 1987	section 2(2)(b)
Consumer Protection (Northern Ireland) Order 1987	article 5(2)(b)

838

Income and Corporation Taxes Act 1988	section 83(a)
Taxation of Chargeable Gains Act 1992	section 275(h)
Tribunals and Inquiries Act 1992	Schedule 1, paragraph 34.

References to the Plant Varieties and Seeds Act 1964, s. 5A(4), and the Northern Ireland Constitution Act 1973, Sched. 3, para. 17, were repealed by the Plant Varieties Act 1997 and the Northern Ireland Act 1998 respectively.

2.—(1) The Patents and Designs Act 1907 is amended as follows. **A1–157**

(2) In section 62 (the Patent Office)—

    (a) in subsection (1) for "this Act and the Trade Marks Act 1905" substitute "the Patents Act 1977, the Registered Designs Act 1949 and the Trade Marks Act 1994"; and

    (b) in subsections (2) and (3) for "the Board of Trade" substitute "the Secretary of State".

(3) In section 63 (officers and clerks of the Patent Office)—

    (a) for "the Board of Trade" in each place where it occurs substitute "the Secretary of State"; and

    (b) in subsection (2) omit the words from "and those salaries" to the end.

(4) The repeal by the Patents Act 1949 and the Registered Designs Act 1949 of the whole of the 1907 Act, except certain provisions, shall be deemed not to have extended to the long title, date of enactment or enacting words or to so much of section 99 as provides the Act with its short title.

Patents, Designs, Copyright and Trade Marks (Emergency) Act 1939 (c.107)

3.—(1) The Patents, Designs, Copyright and Trade Marks (Emergency) Act 1939 is **A1–158** amended as follows.

(2) For section 3 (power of comptroller to suspend rights of enemy or enemy subject) substitute—

Power of comptroller to suspend trade mark rights of enemy or enemy subject

    3.—(1) Where on application made by a person proposing to supply goods or services of any description it is made to appear to the comptroller—

        (a) that it is difficult or impracticable to describe or refer to the goods or services without the use of a registered trade mark, and

        (b) that the proprietor of the registered trade mark (whether alone or jointly with another) is an enemy or an enemy subject,

    the comptroller may make an order suspending the rights given by the registered trade mark.

    (2) An order under this section shall suspend those rights as regards the use of the trade mark—

        (a) by the applicant, and

        (b) by any person authorised by the applicant to do, for the purposes of or in connection with the supply by the applicant of the goods or services, things which would otherwise infringe the registered trade mark,

    to such extent and for such period as the comptroller considers necessary to enable the applicant to render well-known and established some other means of describing or referring to the goods or services in question which does not involve the use of the trade mark.

    (3) Where an order has been made under this section, no action for passing off lies on the part of any person interested in the registered trade mark in respect of any use of it which by virtue of the order is not an infringement of the right conferred by it.

    (4) An order under this section may be varied or revoked by a subsequent order made by the comptroller."

(3) In each of the following provisions—

    (a) section 4(1)(c) (effect of war on registration of trade marks),

    (b) section 6(1) (power of comptroller to extend time limits),

    (c) section 7(1)(a) (evidence as to nationality, &c.), and

    (d) the definition of "the comptroller" in section 10(1) (interpretation),

for "the Trade Marks Act 1938" substitute "the Trade Marks Act 1994".

Trade Descriptions Act 1968 (c.29)

4.—(1) In the Trade Descriptions Act 1968, in section 34 (exemption of trade description **A1–159** contained in pre-1968 trade mark)—

(a) in the opening words, omit "within the meaning of the Trade Marks Act 1938"; and

(b) in paragraph (c), for "a person registered under section 28 of the Trade Marks Act 1938 as a registered user of the trade mark" substitute," in the case of a registered trade mark, a person licensed to use it".

Solicitors Act 1974 (c.47)

A1–160   **5.**—(1) Section 22 of the Solicitors Act 1974 (preparation of instruments by unqualified persons) is amended as follows.

(2) In subsection (2)(aa) and (ab) (instruments which may be prepared by registered trade mark agent or registered patent agent) for," trade mark or service mark" substitute "or trade mark".

(3) In subsection (3A) (interpretation)—

(a) in the definition of "registered trade mark agent" for "section 282(1) of the Copyright, Designs and Patents Act 1988" substitute "the Trade Marks Act 1994"; and

(b) in the definition of "registered patent agent" for "of that Act" substitute "of the Copyright, Designs and Patents Act 1988".

House of Commons Disqualification Act 1975 (c.24)

A1–161   **6.**—(1) In Part III of Schedule 1 to the House of Commons Disqualification Act 1975 (other disqualifying offices), for the entry relating to persons appointed to hear and determine appeals under the Trade Marks Act 1938 substitute—

"Person appointed to hear and determine appeals under the Trade Marks Act 1994.".

Restrictive Trade Practices Act 1976 (c.34)

A1–162   **7.**—(1) In Schedule 3 to the Restrictive Trade Practices Act 1976 (excepted agreements), for paragraph 4 (agreements relating to trade marks) substitute—

"**4.**—(1) This Act does not apply to an agreement authorising the use of a registered trade mark (other than a collective mark or certification mark) if no such restrictions as are described in section 6(1) or 11(2) above are accepted, and no such information provisions as are described in section 7(1) or 12(2) above are made, except in respect of—

(a) the descriptions of goods bearing the mark which are to be produced or supplied, or the processes of manufacture to be applied to such goods or to goods to which the mark is to be applied, or

(b) the kinds of services in relation to which the mark is to be used which are to be made available or supplied, or the form or manner in which such services are to be made available or supplied, or

(c) the descriptions of goods which are to be produced or supplied in connection with the supply of services in relation to which the mark is to be used, or the process of manufacture to be applied to such goods.

(2) This Act does not apply to an agreement authorising the use of a registered collective mark or certification mark if—

(a) the agreement is made in accordance with regulations approved by the registrar under Schedule 1 or 2 to the Trade Marks Act 1994, and

(b) no such restrictions as are described in section 6(1) or 11(2) above are accepted, and no such information provisions as are described in section 7(1) or 12(2) above are made, except as permitted by those regulations.".

Copyright, Designs and Patents Act 1988 (c.48)

A1–163   **8.**—(1) The Copyright, Designs and Patents Act 1988 is amended as follows.

(2) In sections 114(6), 204(6) and 231(6) (persons regarded as having an interest in infringing copies, &c.), for "section 58C of the Trade Marks Act 1938" substitute "section 19 of the Trade Marks Act 1994".

(3) In section 280(1) (privilege for communications with patent agents), for "trade mark or service mark" substitute "or trade mark".

Tribunals and Inquiries Act 1992 (c.53)

A1–164   **9.** In Part I of Schedule 1 to the Tribunals and Inquiries Act 1992 (tribunals under direct supervision of Council on Tribunals), for "Patents, designs, trade marks and service marks" substitute "Patents, designs and trade marks".

SCHEDULE 5   Section 106(2).

REPEALS AND REVOCATIONS

A1–165

Chapter or number	Short title	Extent of repeal or revocation
1891 c. 50	Commissioners for Oaths Act 1891.	In section 1, the words "or the Patents, Designs and Trade Marks Acts, 1883 to 1888,".
1907 c. 29.	Patents and Designs Act 1907.	In section 63(2), the words from "and those salaries" to the end.
1938 c. 22.	Trade Marks Act 1938.	The whole Act.
1947 c. 44.	Crown Proceedings Act 1947.	In section 3(1)(b), the words "or registered service mark".
1949 c. 87.	Patents Act 1949.	Section 92(2).
1964 c. 14.	Plant Varieties and Seeds Act 1964.	In section 5A(4), the words "under the Trade Marks Act 1938".
1967 c. 80.	Criminal Justice Act 1967.	In Schedule 3, in Parts I and IV, the entries relating to the Trade Marks Act 1938.
1978 c. 23.	Judicature (Northern Ireland) Act 1978.	In Schedule 5, in Part II, the paragraphs amending the Trade Marks Act 1938.
1984 c. 19.	Trade Marks (Amendment) Act 1984.	The whole Act.
1985 c. 6.	Companies Act 1985.	In section 396— (a) in subsection (3A)(a), and (b) in subsection (2)(d)(i) as inserted by the Companies Act 1989, the words "service mark,".
1986 c. 12.	Statute Law (Repeals) Act 1986.	In Schedule 2, paragraph 2.
1986 c. 39.	Patents, Designs and Marks Act 1986.	Section 2. Section 4(4). In Schedule 1, paragraphs 1 and 2. Schedule 2.
S.I. 1986/1032 (N.I. 6).	Companies (Northern Ireland) Order 1986.	In article 403— (a) in paragraph (3A)(a), and (b) in paragraph (2)(d)(i) as inserted by the Companies (No.2) (Northern Ireland) Order 1990, the words "service mark,".
1987 c. 43.	Consumer Protection Act 1987.	In section 45— (a) in subsection (1), the definition of "mark" and "trade mark"; (b) subsection (4).
S.I. 1987/2049.	Consumer Protection (Northern Ireland) Order 1987.	In article 2— (a) in paragraph (2), the definitions of "mark" and "trade mark"; (b) paragraph (3).
1988 c. 1.	Income and Corporation Taxes Act 1988.	In section 83, the words from "References in this section" to the end.

841

Chapter or number	Short title	Extent of repeal or revocation
1988 c. 48.	Copyright, Designs and Patents Act 1988.	Sections 282 to 284. In section 286, the definition of "registered trade mark agent". Section 300.
1992 c. 12.	Taxation of Chargeable Gains Act 1992.	In section 275(h), the words "service marks" and "service mark".

APPENDIX 2

Trade Marks Act 1938

(1 & 2 GEO. 6, C. 22)

ARRANGEMENT OF SECTIONS

843

An Act to consolidate the Trade Marks Act 1905, the Trade Marks Act 1919 and the Trade Marks (Amendment) Act 1937.

[APRIL 13, 1938.]

REGISTRATION, INFRINGEMENT AND OTHER SUBSTANTIVE PROVISIONS

The register

Register of trade marks etc.

1.—(1) *There shall continue to be kept at the Patent Office for the purposes of this Act* **A2–02** *the record called the register of trade marks, wherein shall be entered all registered trade marks with the names, addresses and descriptions of their proprietors, notifications of assignments and transmissions, the names, addresses and descriptions of all registered users, disclaimers, conditions, limitations, and such other matters relating to registered trade marks as may be prescribed.*

(2) *The register shall continue to be divided into two parts called respectively Part A and Part B.*

(3) *The register shall at all convenient times be open to the inspection of the public, subject to such regulations as may be prescribed.*

(4) *The register shall be kept under the control and management of the Comptroller-General of Patents, Designs and Trade Marks, who is in this Act referred to as "the Registrar."*

1.—(1) **The Comptroller-General of Patents, Designs and Trade Marks (in A2–03 this Act referred to as "the Registrar") shall maintain the register of trade marks, in which shall be entered—**

    (a) **all registered trade marks with the names and addresses of their proprietors;**

(b) notifications of assignments and transmissions;
(c) the names and addresses of all registered users;
(d) disclaimers, conditions and limitations; and
(e) such other matters relating to registered trade marks as may be prescribed.

(2) The register shall continue to be divided into two parts called respectively Part A and Part B.

(3) The register need not be kept in documentary form.

(4) Subject to any rules under this Act, the public shall have a right to inspect the register at the Patent Office at all convenient times.

(5) Any person who applies for a certified copy of an entry in the register or a certified extract from the register shall be entitled to obtain such a copy or extract on payment of a fee prescribed in relation to certified copies and extracts; and the rules may provide that any person who applies for an uncertified copy or extract shall be entitled to such a copy or extract on payment of a fee prescribed in relation to uncertified copies and extracts.

(6) Applications under subsection (5) above or rules made by virtue of that subsection shall be made in such manner as may be prescribed.

(7) In relation to any portion of the register kept otherwise than in documentary form—

(a) the right of inspection conferred by subsection (4) above is a right to inspect the material on the register; and
(b) the right to a copy or extract conferred by subsection (5) above or the rules is a right to a copy or extract in a form in which it can be taken away and in which it is visible and legible.

(8) A certificate purporting to be signed by the Registrar and certifying that any entry which he is authorised by this Act or rules to make has or has not been made, or that any other thing which he is so authorised to do has or has not been done, shall be prima facie evidence, and in Scotland shall be sufficient evidence, of the matters so certified.

(9) A copy of an entry in the register or an extract from the register which is supplied under subsection (5) above and purports to be a certified copy of certified extract shall, subject to subsection (10) below, be admitted in evidence without further proof and without production of any original; and in Scotland such evidence shall be sufficient evidence.

(10) In the application of this section to England and Wales nothing in it shall be taken as detracting from section 69 or 70 of the Police and Criminal Evidence Act 1984 or any provision made by virtue of either of them.

(11) In this section "certified copy" and "certified extract" mean a copy and extract certified by the Registrar and sealed with the seal of the Patent Office.".

Section replaced by 1986 Act, Sched. 1.

Effect of registration and the action for infringement

No action for infringement of unregistered trade mark

A2–04   2. No person shall be entitled to institute any proceedings to prevent, or to recover damages for, the infringement of an unregistered trade mark, but nothing in this Act shall be deemed to affect rights of action against any person for passing-off *goods as the goods of another person* or the remedies in respect thereof.

Amended by 1984 Act, s.1(5)(a).

See s.1 of the 1875 Act, s.1 of the 1877 Act, s.77 of the 1883 Act, and s.42 of the 1905 Act.

Registration to be in respect of particular goods

3. A trade mark must be registered in respect of particular goods or classes of **A2–05** goods, and any question arising as to the class within which any goods fall shall be determined by the Registrar, whose decision shall be final.

See s.2 of the 1875 Act, s.65 of the 1883 Act and s.8 of the 1905 Act.

Right given by registration in Part A, and infringement thereof

4.—(1) Subject to the provisions of this section, and of sections seven and eight **A2–06** of this Act, the registration (whether before or after the commencement of this Act) of a person in Part A of the register as proprietor of a trade mark (other than a certification trade mark) in respect of any goods shall, if valid, give or be deemed to have given to that person the exclusive right to the use of the trade mark in relation to those goods and, without prejudice to the generality of the foregoing words, that right shall be deemed to be infringed by any person who, not being the proprietor of the trade mark or a registered user thereof using by way of the permitted use, uses *a mark identical with it or so nearly resembling it as to be likely to deceive or cause confusion*, in the course of trade **a mark identical with or nearly resembling it**, in relation to any goods in respect of which it is registered, and in such manner as to render the use of the mark likely to be taken either—

(a) as being used as a trade mark; or
(b) in a case in which the use is use upon goods or in physical relation thereto or in an advertising circular or other advertisement issued to the public, as importing a reference to some person having the right either as proprietor or as registered user to use the trade mark or to goods with which such a person as aforesaid is connected in the course of trade.

(2) The right to the use of a trade mark given by registration as aforesaid shall be subject to any conditions or limitations entered on the register, and shall not be deemed to be infringed by the use of any such mark as aforesaid in any mode, in relation to goods to be sold or otherwise traded in any place, in relation to goods to be exported to any market, or in any other circumstances, to which, having regard to any such limitations, the registration does not extend.

(3) The right to the use of a trade mark given by registration as aforesaid shall not be deemed to be infringed by the use of any such mark as aforesaid by any person—

(a) in relation to goods connected in the course of trade with the proprietor or a registered user of the trade mark if, as to those goods or a bulk of which they form part, the proprietor or the registered user conforming to the permitted use had applied the trade mark and has not subsequently removed or obliterated it, or has at any time expressly or impliedly consented to the use of the trade mark; or
(b) in relation to goods adapted to form part of, or to be accessory to, other goods in relation to which the trade mark has been used without infringement of the right given as aforesaid or might for the time being be so used, if the use of the mark is reasonably necessary in order to indicate that the goods are so adapted and neither the purpose nor the effect of the use of the mark is to indicate otherwise than in accordance with the fact a connection in the course of trade between any person and the goods.

(4) The use of a registered trade mark, being one of two or more registered trade marks that are identical or nearly resemble each other, in exercise of the

right to the use of that trade mark given by registration as aforesaid, shall not be deemed to be an infringement of the right so given to the use of any other of those trade marks.

Amended by 1984 Act, Sched. 2, para. 1.
Subs. (1). See s.3 of the 1875 Act, s.76 of the 1883 Act and s.39 of the 1905 Act.
Subs. (2). See s.39 of the 1905 Act.
Subs. (3). New. Necessitated by new definition of infringement.
Subs. (4). See s.39 of the 1905 Act.

Right given by registration in Part B, and infringement thereof

A2–07 5.—(1) Except as provided by subsection (2) of this section, the registration (whether before or after the commencement of this Act) of a person in Part B of the register as proprietor of a trade mark in respect of any goods shall, if valid, give or be deemed to have given to that person the like right in relation to those goods as if the registration had been in Part A of the register, and the provisions of the last foregoing section shall have effect in like manner in relation to a trade mark registered in Part B of the register as they have effect in relation to a trade mark registered in Part A of the register.

(2) In any action for infringement of the right to the use of a trade mark given by registration as aforesaid in Part B of the register, otherwise than by an act that is deemed to be an infringement by virtue of the next succeeding section, no injunction or other relief shall be granted to the plaintiff if the defendant establishes to the satisfaction of the court that the use of which the plaintiff complains is not likely to deceive or cause confusion or to be taken as indicating a connection in the course of trade between the goods and some person having the right either as proprietor or as registered user to use the trade mark.

See s.4 of the 1919 Act.

Infringement by breach of certain restrictions

A2–08 6.—(1) Where, by a contract in writing made with the proprietor or a registered user of a registered trade mark, a purchaser or owner of goods enters into an obligation to the effect that he will not do, in relation to the goods, an act to which this section applies, any person who, being the owner for the time being of the goods and having notice of the obligation, does that act, or authorises it to be done, in relation to the goods, in the course of trade or with a view to any dealing therewith in the course of trade shall be deemed thereby to infringe the right to the use of the trade mark given by the registration thereof, unless that person became the owner of the goods by purchase for money or money's worth in good faith before receiving notice of the obligation or by virtue of a title derived through another who so became the owner thereof.

(2) The acts to which this section applies are—

    (a) the application of the trade mark upon the goods after they have suffered alteration in any manner specified in the contract as respects their state or condition, get-up or packing;

    (b) in a case in which the trade mark is upon the goods, the alteration, part removal or part obliteration thereof;

    (c) in a case in which the trade mark is upon the goods, and there is also thereon other matter, being matter indicating a connection in the course of trade between the proprietor or registered user and the goods, the removal or obliteration, whether wholly or partly, of the trade mark unless that other matter is wholly removed or obliterated;

    (d) in a case in which the trade mark is upon the goods, the application of any other trade mark to the goods;

    (e) in a case in which the trade mark is upon the goods, the addition to the goods of any other matter in writing that is likely to injure the reputation of the trade mark.

(3) In this section references in relation to any goods to the proprietor, to a registered user, and to the registration, of a trade mark shall be construed, respectively, as references to the proprietor in whose name the trade mark is registered, to a registered user who is registered, and to the registration of the trade mark, in respect of those goods, and the expression "upon" includes in relation to any goods a reference to physical relation thereto.

Saving for vested rights

7. Nothing in this Act shall entitle the proprietor or a registered user of a **A2–09** registered trade mark to interfere with or restrain the use by any person of a trade mark identical with or nearly resembling it in relation to goods in relation to which that person or a predecessor in title of his has continuously used that trade mark from a date anterior—

  (a) to the use of the first-mentioned trade mark in relation to those goods by the proprietor or a predecessor in title of his; or
  (b) to the registration of the first-mentioned trade mark in respect of those goods in the name of the proprietor or a predecessor in title of his;

whichever is the earlier, or to object (on such use being proved) to that person being put on the register for that identical or nearly resembling trade mark in respect of those goods under subsection (2) of section twelve of this Act.

See s.41 of the 1905 Act.

Saving for use of name, address, or description of goods

8. No registration of a trade mark shall interfere with—   **A2–10**

  (a) any bona fide use by a person of his own name or of the name of his place of business, or of the name, or of the name of the place of business, of any of his predecessors in business; or
  (b) the use by any person of any bona fide description of the character or quality of his goods, not being a description that would be likely to be taken as importing any such reference as is mentioned in paragraph (b) of subsection (1) of section four, or in paragraph (b) of subsection (3) of section thirty-seven, of this Act.

See s.64(3)(*l*) of the 1883 Act as amended and s.44 of the 1905 Act.

Registrability and validity of registration

Distinctiveness requisite for registration in Part A

9.—(1) In order for a trade mark (other than a certification trade mark) to be **A2–11** registrable in Part A of the register, it must contain or consist of at least one of the following essential particulars:

  (a) the name of a company, individual, or firm, represented in a special or particular manner;
  (b) the signature of the applicant for registration or some predecessor in his business;
  (c) an invented word or invented words;
  (d) a word or words having no direct reference to the character or quality of the goods, and not being according to its ordinary signification a geographical name or a surname;
  (e) any other distinctive mark, but a name, signature, or word or words, other than such as fall within the descriptions in the foregoing

849

paragraphs (a), (b), (c) and (d), shall not be registrable under the provisions of this paragraph except upon evidence of its distinctiveness.

(2) For the purposes of this section "distinctive" means adapted, in relation to the goods in respect of which a trade mark is registered or proposed to be registered, to distinguish goods with which the proprietor of the trade mark is or may be connected in the course of trade from goods in the case of which no such connection subsists, either generally or, where the trade mark is registered or proposed to be registered subject to limitations, in relation to use within the extent of the registration.

(3) In determining whether a trade mark is adapted to distinguish as aforesaid the tribunal may have regard to the extent to which—

(a) the trade mark is inherently adapted to distinguish as aforesaid; and
(b) by reason of the use of the trade mark or of any other circumstances, the trade mark is in fact adapted to distinguish as aforesaid.

See s.10 of the 1875 Act, s.64 of the 1883 Act (amended in 1888) and s.9 of the 1905 Act.

Capability of distinguishing requisite for registration in Part B

A2–12   10.—(1) In order for a trade mark to be registrable in Part B of the register it must be capable, in relation to the goods in respect of which it is registered or proposed to be registered, of distinguishing goods with which the proprietor of the trade mark is or may be connected in the course of trade from goods in the case of which no such connection subsists, either generally or, where the trade mark is registered or proposed to be registered subject to limitations, in relation to use within the extent of the registration.

(2) In determining whether a trade mark is capable of distinguishing as aforesaid the tribunal may have regard to the extent to which—

(a) the trade mark is inherently capable of distinguishing as aforesaid; and
(b) by reason of the use of the trade mark or of any other circumstances, the trade mark is in fact capable of distinguishing as aforesaid.

(3) A trade mark may be registered in Part B notwithstanding any registration in Part A in the name of the same proprietor of the same trade mark or any part or parts thereof.

See s.2 of the 1919 Act.

Prohibition of registration of deceptive, etc., matter

A2–13   11. It shall not be lawful to register as a trade mark or part of a trade mark any matter the use of which would, by reason of its being likely to deceive or cause confusion or otherwise, be disentitled to protection in a court of justice, or would be contrary to law or morality, or any scandalous design.

See s.6 of the 1875 Act, s.73 of the 1883 Act, and s.11 of the 1905 Act.

Prohibition of registration of identical and resembling trade marks

A2–14   12.—(1) Subject to the provisions of subsection (2) of this section, no trade mark shall be registered in respect of any goods or description of goods that is identical with *a trade mark belonging to a different proprietor and already in the register in respect of the same goods or description of goods, or that so nearly resembles such a trade mark as to be likely to deceive or cause confusion* **or nearly resembles a mark belonging to a different proprietor and already on the register in respect of—**

(a) **the same goods,**

   (b) **the same description of goods, or**

   (c) **services or a description of services which are associated with those goods or goods of that description.**

(2) In case of honest concurrent use, or of other special circumstances which in the opinion of the Court or the Registrar make it proper so to do, the Court or the Registrar may permit the registration *of trade marks that are identical or nearly resemble each other in respect of the same goods or descriptions of goods* **by more than one proprietor in respect of—**

   (a) **the same goods,**

   (b) **the same description of goods or**

   (c) **goods and services or descriptions of goods and services which are associated with each other,**
     of marks that are identical or nearly resemble each other,

subject to such conditions and limitations, if any, as the Court or Registrar, as the case may be, may think it right to impose.

(3) Where separate applications are made by different persons to be registered as proprietors respectively of *trade marks that are identical or nearly resemble each other, in respect of the same goods or description of goods* **marks that are identical or nearly resemble each other, in respect of—**

   (a) **the same goods,**

   (a) **the same description of goods, or**

   (c) **goods and services or descriptions of goods and services which are associated with each other,**

the Registrar may refuse to register any of them until their rights have been determined by the Court, or have been settled by agreement in a manner approved by him or on an appeal (which may be brought either to the Board of Trade or to the Court at the option of the appellant) by the Board or the Court, as the case may be.

Amended by 1984 Act, Sched. 2, para. 2.
Subs. (1). See s.6 of the 1875 Act, s.72 of the 1883 Act and s.19 of the 1905 Act.
Subs. (2). See s.21 of the 1905 Act.
Subs. (3). See s.5 of the 1875 Act, s.72 of the 1883 Act and s.20 of the 1905 Act.

Registration in Part A to be conclusive as to validity after seven years

   13.—(1) In all legal proceedings relating to a trade mark registered in Part A of **A2–15** the register (including applications under section thirty-two of this Act) the original registration in Part A of the register of the trade mark shall, after the expiration of seven years from the date of that registration, be taken to be valid in all respects, unless—

   (a) that registration was obtained by fraud, or

   (b) the trade mark offends against the provisions of section eleven of this Act.

(2) Nothing in subsection (1) of section five of this Act shall be construed as making applicable to a trade mark, as being a trade mark registered in Part B of the register, the foregoing provisions of this section relating to a trade mark registered in Part A of the register.

Subs. (1). See s.41 of the 1905 Act.
Subs. (2). See s.3 and Sched. I to the 1919 Act.

Registration subject to disclaimer

   14. If a trade mark—   **A2–16**

(a) contains any part not separately registered by the proprietor as a trade mark; or

(b) contains matter common to the trade or otherwise of a non-distinctive character;

the Registrar or the Board of Trade or the Court, in deciding whether the trade mark shall be entered or shall remain on the register, may require, as a condition of its being on the register,—

(i) that the proprietor shall disclaim any right to the exclusive use of any part of the trade mark, or to the exclusive use of all or any portion of any such matter as aforesaid, to the exclusive use of which the tribunal holds him not to be entitled; or

(ii) that the proprietor shall make such other disclaimer as the tribunal may consider necessary for the purpose of defining his rights under the registration:

Provided that no disclaimer on the register shall affect any rights of the proprietor of a trade mark except such as arise out of the registration of the trade mark in respect of which the disclaimer is made.

See s.15 of the 1905 Act. Prior to that section an applicant had to make in his application disclaimers to all except the essential particulars of his mark, see s.64(2) of the 1883 Act as amended.

Words used as name or description of an article or substance

A2–17   15.—(1) The registration of a trade mark shall not be deemed to have become invalid by reason only of any use, after the date of registration, of a word or words which the trade mark contains, or of which it consists, as the name or description of an article or substance:
Provided that, if it is proved either—

(a) that there is a well-known and established use of the word or words as the name or description of the article or substance by a person or persons carrying on a trade therein, not being use in relation to goods connected in the course of trade with the proprietor or a registered user of the trade mark or (in the case of a certification trade mark) goods certified by the proprietor; or

(b) that the article or substance was formerly manufactured under a patent (being a patent in force on, or granted after, the twenty-third day of December nineteen hundred and nineteen), that a period of two years or more after the cesser of the patent has elapsed, and that the word or words is or are the only practicable name or description of the article or substance;

the provisions of the next succeeding subsection shall have effect.
    (2) Where the facts mentioned in paragraph (a) or (b) of the proviso to the foregoing subsection are proved with respect to any word or words, then—

(a) if the trade mark consists solely of that word or those words, the registration of the trade mark, so far as regards registration in respect of the article or substance in question or of any goods of the same description, shall be deemed for the purposes of section thirty-two of this Act to be an entry wrongly remaining on the register;

(b) if the trade mark contains that word or those words and other matter, the Court or the Registrar, in deciding whether the trade mark shall remain on the register, so far as regards registration in respect of the article or substance in question and of any goods of the same description, may in case of a decision in favour of its remaining on the register require as a condition thereof that the proprietor shall disclaim any right to the exclusive use in relation to that article or substance and any goods of the same description of that word or those words, so, however, that no disclaimer on the register shall affect any rights of the proprietor of a trade mark except such as arise out of the registration of the trade mark in respect of which the disclaimer is made; and

(c) for the purposes of any other legal proceedings relating to the trade mark,—

    (i) if the trade mark consists solely of that word or those words, all rights of the proprietor, whether under the common law or by registration, to the exclusive use of the trade mark in relation to the article or substance in question or to any goods of the same description, or

    (ii) if the trade mark contains that word or those words and other matter, all such rights of the proprietor to the exclusive use of that word or those words in such relation as aforesaid, shall be deemed to have ceased on the date at which the use mentioned in paragraph (a) of the proviso to the foregoing subsection first became well known and established, or at the expiration of the period of two years mentioned in paragraph (b) of that proviso.

(3) No word which is the commonly used and accepted name of any single chemical element or single chemical compound, as distinguished from a mixture, shall be registered as a trade mark in respect of a chemical substance or preparation, and any such registration in force at the commencement of this Act or thereafter shall, notwithstanding anything in section thirteen of this Act, be deemed for the purposes of section thirty-two of this Act to be an entry made in the register without sufficient cause, or an entry wrongly remaining on the register, as the circumstances may require:

Provided that the foregoing provisions of this subsection shall not have effect in relation to a word which is used to denote only a brand or make of the element or compound as made by the proprietor or a registered user of the trade mark, as distinguished from the element or compound as made by others, and in association with a suitable name or description open to the public use.

See s.6 of the 1919 Act.

Effect of limitation as to colour, and of absence thereof

16. A trade mark may be limited in whole or in part to one or more specified **A2–18** colours, and in any such case the fact that it is so limited shall be taken into consideration by any tribunal having to decide on the distinctive character of the trade mark.

If and so far as a trade mark is registered without limitation of colour, it shall be deemed to be registered for all colours.

See s.10 of the 1905 Act.

Procedure for, and duration of, registration

Application for registration

17.—(1) Any person claiming to be the proprietor of a trade mark used or **A2–19** proposed to be used by him who is desirous of registering it must apply in writing to the Registrar in the prescribed manner for registration either in Part A or in Part B of the register.

(2) Subject to the provisions of this Act, the Registrar may refuse the application, or may accept it absolutely or subject to such amendments, conditions or limitations, if any, as he may think right.

(3) In the case of an application for registration of a trade mark (other than a certification trade mark) in Part A of the register, the Registrar may, if the applicant is willing, instead of refusing the application, treat it as an application for registration in Part B and deal with the application accordingly.

(4) In the case of a refusal or conditional acceptance, the Registrar shall, if required by the applicant, state in writing the grounds of his decision and the materials used by him in arriving thereat, and the decision shall be subject to appeal to the Board of Trade or to the Court at the option of the applicant.

(5) An appeal under this section shall be made in the prescribed manner, and on the appeal the tribunal shall, if required, hear the applicant and the Registrar, and shall make an order determining whether, and subject to what amendments, modifications, conditions or limitations, if any, the application is to be accepted.

(6) Appeals under this section shall be heard on the materials stated as aforesaid by the Registrar, and no further grounds of objection to the acceptance of the application shall be allowed to be taken by the Registrar, other than those so stated as aforesaid by him, except by leave of the tribunal hearing the appeal. Where any further grounds of objection are taken, the applicant shall be entitled to withdraw his application without payment of costs on giving notice as prescribed.

(7) The Registrar or the Board of Trade or the Court, as the case may be, may at any time, whether before or after acceptance, correct any error in or in connection with the application, or may permit the applicant to amend his application upon such terms as the Registrar or the Board of Trade or the Court, as the case may be, may think fit.

See s.62(1) of the 1883 Act and s.12 of the 1905 Act.
Subs. (2) is derived from s.5 of the 1919 Act.

Opposition to registration

A2–20   **18.**—(1) When an application for registration of a trade mark has been accepted, whether absolutely or subject to conditions or limitations, the Registrar shall, as soon as may be after acceptance, cause the application as accepted to be advertised in the prescribed manner, and the advertisement shall set forth all conditions and limitations subject to which the application has been accepted:

Provided that the Registrar may cause an application to be advertised before acceptance if it is made under paragraph (e) of subsection (1) of section nine of this Act, or in any other case where it appears to him that it is expedient by reason of any exceptional circumstances so to do, and where an application has been so advertised the Registrar may, if he thinks fit, advertise it again when it has been accepted but shall not be bound so to do.

(2) Any person may, within the prescribed time from the date of the advertisement of an application, give notice to the Registrar of opposition to the registration.

(3) The notice shall be given in writing in the prescribed manner, and shall include a statement of the grounds of opposition.

(4) The Registrar shall send a copy of the notice to the applicant, and within the prescribed time after receipt thereof the applicant shall send to the Registrar, in the prescribed manner, a counter-statement of the grounds on which he relies for his application, and, if he does not do so, he shall be deemed to have abandoned his application.

(5) If the applicant sends such a counter-statement as aforesaid, the Registrar shall furnish a copy thereof to the persons giving notice of opposition, and shall, after hearing the parties, if so required, and considering the evidence, decide whether, and subject to what conditions or limitations, if any, registration is to be permitted.

(6) The decision of the Registrar shall be subject to appeal to the Court.

(7) An appeal under this section shall be made in the prescribed manner, and on the appeal the Court shall, if required, hear the parties and the Registrar, and

shall make an order determining whether, and subject to what conditions or limitations, if any, registration is to be permitted.

(8) On the hearing of an appeal under this section any party may, either in the manner prescribed or by special leave of the Court, bring forward further material for the consideration of the Court.

(9) On an appeal under this section no further grounds of objection to the registration of a trade mark shall be allowed to be taken by the opponent or the Registrar, other than those so stated as aforesaid by the opponent, except by leave of the Court. Where any further grounds of objection are taken, the applicant shall be entitled to withdraw his application without payment of the costs of the opponent on giving notice as prescribed.

(10) On an appeal under this section the Court may, after hearing the Registrar, permit the trade mark proposed to be registered to be modified in any manner not substantially affecting the identity thereof, but in any such case the trade mark as so modified shall be advertised in the prescribed manner before being registered.

(11) If a person giving notice of opposition or an applicant sending a counter-statement after receipt of a copy of such a notice, or an appellant neither resides nor carries on business in the United Kingdom, the tribunal may require him to give security for costs of the proceedings before the tribunal relative to the opposition or to the appeal, as the case may be, and in default of such security being duly given may treat the opposition or application, or the appeal, as the case may be, as abandoned.

Subss. (7) and (8) have been amended slightly in their application to proceedings in Northern Ireland, Judicature (Northern Ireland) Act 1977, s.122(1) and Sched. 5.
Subs. (1). See s.68 of the 1883 Act and s.13 of the 1905 Act.
Subss. (2)–(11). See s.69 of the 1883 Act and s.14 of the 1905 Act.

Registration

19.—(1) When an application for registration of a trade mark in Part A or in **A2–21** Part B of the register has been accepted and either—

(a) the application has not been opposed and the time for notice of opposition has expired, or

(b) the application has been opposed and the opposition has been decided in favour of the applicant,

the Registrar shall, unless the application has been accepted in error or unless the Board of Trade otherwise direct, register the trade mark in Part A or Part B, as the case may be, and the trade mark when registered shall be registered **subject to section 39A(2) below** as of the date of the application for registration, and that date shall be deemed for the purposes of this Act to be the date of registration:

Provided that the foregoing provisions of this subsection, relating to the date as of which a trade mark shall be registered and to the date to be deemed to be the date of registration, shall, as respects a trade mark registered under this Act with the benefit of any enactment relating to international or inter-imperial arrangements, have effect subject to the provisions of that enactment.

(2) On the registration of a trade mark the Registrar shall issue to the applicant a certificate in the prescribed form of the registration thereof sealed with the seal of the Patent Office.

(3) Where registration of a trade mark is not completed within twelve months from the date of the application by reason of default on the part of the applicant, the Registrar may, after giving notice of the non-completion to the applicant in writing in the prescribed manner, treat the application as abandoned unless it is completed within the time specified in that behalf in the notice.

Subs. (1). See s.16 of the 1905 Act. Amended by 1986 Act.

Subs. (2). See s.17 of the 1905 Act.
Subs. (3). See s.63 of the 1883 Act and s.18 of the 1905 Act.

Duration and renewal of registration

A2–22   **20.**—(1) The registration of a trade mark shall be for a period of seven years, but may be renewed from time to time in accordance with the provisions of this section:

Provided that, in relation to a registration as of a date before the appointed day, this subsection shall have effect with the substitution of a period of fourteen years for the said period of seven years.

(2) The Registrar shall, on application made by the registered proprietor of a trade mark in the prescribed manner and within the prescribed period, renew the registration of the trade mark for a period of fourteen years from the date of expiration of the original registration or of the last renewal of registration, as the case may be, which date is in this section referred to as "the expiration of the last registration."

(3) At the prescribed time before the expiration of the last registration of a trade mark, the Registrar shall send notice in the prescribed manner to the registered proprietor of the date of expiration and the conditions as to payment of fees and otherwise upon which a renewal of registration may be obtained, and, if at the expiration of the time prescribed in that behalf those conditions have not been duly complied with, the Registrar may remove the trade mark from the register, subject to such conditions, if any, as to its restoration to the register as may be prescribed.

(4) Where a trade mark has been removed from the register for non-payment of the fee for renewal, it shall, nevertheless, for the purpose of any application for the registration of a trade mark during one year next after the date of the removal, be deemed to be a trade mark that is already on the register:

Provided that the foregoing provisions of this subsection shall not have effect where the tribunal is satisfied either—

    (a) that there has been no bona fide trade use of the trade mark that has been removed during the two years immediately preceding its removal; or

    (b) that no deception or confusion would be likely to arise from the use of the trade mark that is the subject of the application for registration by reason of any previous use of the trade mark that has been removed.

Subs. (1). See s.79(1) of the 1883 Act and s.28 of the 1905 Act.
Subs. (2). See s.79(1) of the 1883 Act and s.29 of the 1905 Act.
Subs. (3). See s.79 of the 1883 Act and s.30 of the 1905 Act.
Subs. (4). See s.79(5) of the 1883 Act and s.31 of the 1905 Act.

Registration of parts of trade marks and of trade marks as a series

A2–23   **21.**—(1) Where the proprietor of a trade mark claims to be entitled to the exclusive use of any part thereof separately, he may apply to register the whole and any such part as separate trade marks.

Each such separate trade mark must satisfy all the conditions of an independent trade mark and shall, subject to the provisions of subsection (3) of section twenty-three and subsection (2) of section thirty of this Act, have all the incidents of an independent trade mark.

(2) Where a person claiming to be the proprietor of several trade marks, in respect of the same goods or description of goods, which, while resembling each other in the material particulars thereof, yet differ in respect of—

    (a) statements of the goods in relation to which they are respectively used or proposed to be used; or

(b) statements of number, price, quality or names of places; or
(c) other matter of a non-distinctive character which does not substantially affect the identity of the trade mark; or
(d) colour;

seeks to register those trade marks, they may be registered as a series in one registration.

Subs. (1). See s.25 of the 1905 Act.
Subs. (2). See s.66 of the 1883 Act and s.26 of the 1905 Act.

Assignment and transmission

Powers of, and restrictions on, assignment and transmission

22.—(1) Notwithstanding any rule of law or equity to the contrary, a **A2–24** registered trade mark shall be, and shall be deemed always to have been, assignable and transmissible either in connection with the goodwill of a business or not.

(2) A registered trade mark shall be, and shall be deemed always to have been, assignable and transmissible in respect either of all the goods in respect of which it is registered, or was registered, as the case may be, or of some (but not all) of those goods.

(3) The provisions of the two foregoing subsections shall have effect in the case of an unregistered trade mark used in relation to any goods as they have effect in the case of a registered trade mark registered in respect of any goods, if at the time of the assignment or transmission of the unregistered trade mark it is or was used in the same business as a registered trade mark, and if it is or was assigned or transmitted at the same time and to the same person as that registered trade mark and in respect of goods all of which are goods in relation to which the unregistered trade mark is or was used in that business and in respect of which that registered trade mark is or was assigned or transmitted.

(4) Notwithstanding anything in the foregoing subsections, a trade mark shall not be, or be deemed to have been, assignable or transmissible in a case in which as a result of an assignment or transmission there would in the circumstances subsist, or have subsisted, whether under the common law or by registration, exclusive rights in more than one of the persons concerned to the use in relation to *the same goods or description of goods,*

(a) **the same goods,**
(b) **the same description of goods, or**
(c) **goods and services or descriptions of goods and services which are associated with each other,**

of trade marks nearly resembling each other or of identical trade marks, if, having regard to the similarity of the goods *and of the trade marks* **or the association of the goods and services or description of goods and services and to the similarity of the trade marks,** the use of trade marks in exercise of those rights would be, or have been, likely to deceive or cause confusion:

Provided that, where a trade mark is, or has been, assigned or transmitted in such a case as aforesaid, the assignment or transmission shall not be deemed to be, or to have been, invalid under this subsection if the exclusive rights subsisting as a result thereof in the persons concerned respectively are, or were, having regard to limitations imposed thereon, such as not to be exercisable by two or more of those persons in relation to goods to be sold, or otherwise traded in, within the United Kingdom (otherwise than for export therefrom) or in relation to goods to be exported to the same market outside the United Kingdom.

(5) The proprietor of a registered trade mark who proposes to assign it in respect of any goods in respect of which it is registered may submit to the Registrar in the prescribed manner a statement of case setting out the circumstances, and the Registrar may issue to him a certificate stating whether, having regard to the similarity of the goods *and* **or the association of the goods and services or descriptions of goods and services and to the similarity** of the trade marks referred to in the case, the proposed assignment of the first-mentioned trade mark would or would not be invalid under the last foregoing subsection, and a certificate so issued shall, subject to the provisions of this section as to appeal and unless it is shown that the certificate was obtained by fraud or misrepresentation, be conclusive as to the validity or invalidity under the last foregoing subsection of the assignment in so far as such validity or invalidity depends upon the facts set out in the case, but, as regards a certificate in favour of validity, only, if application for registration under section twenty-five of this Act of the title of the person becoming entitled is made within six months from the date on which the certificate is issued.

(6) Notwithstanding anything in subsection (1) to (3) of this section, a trade mark shall not, on or after the appointed day, be assignable or transmissible in a case in which as a result of an assignment or transmission thereof there would in the circumstances subsist, whether under the common law or by registration *an exclusive right in one of the persons concerned to the use of the trade mark limited to use in relation to goods to be sold, or otherwise traded in, in a place or places in the United Kingdom, and an exclusive right in another of those persons to the use of a trade mark nearly resembling the first-mentioned trade mark or of an identical trade mark in relation to the same goods or description of goods limited to use in relation to goods to be sold, or otherwise traded in, in another place or other places in the United Kingdom:*

(a) an exclusive right in one of the persons concerned to the use of the mark limited to use in relation to goods to be sold, or otherwise traded in, in a place or places in the United Kingdom; and

(b) an exclusive right in another of the persons concerned to the use of a mark identical with or nearly resembling the mark referred to in paragraph (a) above in relation to—

(i) the same goods,

(ii) the same description of goods, or

(iii) services which are associated with those goods or goods of that description

limited to use in relation to goods to be sold, or otherwise traded in, or services for use, or available for acceptance, in another place or places in the United Kingdom:

Provided that, on application in the prescribed manner by the proprietor of a trade mark who proposes to assign it, or of a person who claims that a trade mark has been transmitted to him or to a predecessor in title of his on or after the appointed day, in any such case, the Registrar, if he is satisfied that in all the circumstances the use of the trade marks in exercise of the said rights would not be contrary to the public interest, may approve the assignment or transmission and an assignment or transmission so approved shall not be deemed to be, or to have been, invalid under this subsection or under subsection (4) of this section, so, however, that in the case of a registered trade mark this provision shall not have effect unless application for the registration under section twenty-five of this Act of the title of the person becoming entitled is made within six months from the date on which the approval is given or, in the case of a transmission, was made before that date.

(7) Where an assignment in respect of any goods of a trade mark that is at the time of the assignment used in a business in those goods is made, on or after the appointed day, otherwise than in connection with the goodwill of that business, the assignment shall not take effect until the following requirements have been

satisfied, that is to say, the assignee must, not later than the expiration of six months from the date on which the assignment is made or within such extended period, if any, as the Registrar may allow, apply to him for directions with respect to the advertisement of the assignment, and must advertise it in such form and manner and within such period as the Registrar may direct.

(8) Any decision of the Registrar under this section shall be subject to appeal to the Court.

Amended by 1984 Act, Sched. 2, para. 3.
See s.2 of the 1875 Act, s.70 of the 1883 Act, and s.22 of the 1905 Act.

Certain trade marks to be associated so as to be assignable and transmissible as a whole only

23.—(1) Trade marks that are registered as, or that are deemed by virtue of **A2–25** this Act to be, associated trade marks shall be assignable and transmissible only as a whole and not separately, but they shall for all other purposes be deemed to have been registered as separate trade marks.

(2) Where a trade mark that is registered, or is the subject of an application for registration, in respect of any goods is identical with another trade mark, that is registered, or is the subject of an application for registration, in the name of the same proprietor in respect of the same goods or description of goods, or so nearly resembles it as to be likely to deceive or cause confusion if used by a person other than the proprietor, the Registrar may at any time require that the trade marks shall be entered on the register as associated trade marks.

Any decision of the Registrar under this subsection shall be subject to appeal to the Board of Trade, or to the Court, at the option of the appellant.

(2A) **Where there is an identicality or near resemblance of marks that are registered, or are the subject of applications for registration in the name of the same proprietor in respect of goods and in respect of services which are associated with these goods or goods of that description, subsection (2) applies as it applies where there is an identicality or near resemblance of marks that are registered, or are the subject of applications for registration, in the name of the same proprietor in respect of the same goods or description of goods.**

(3) Where a trade mark and any part or parts thereof are, by virtue of subsection (1) of section twenty-one of this Act, registered as separate trade marks in the name of the same proprietor, they shall be deemed to be, and shall be registered as, associated trade marks.

(4) All trade marks that are, by virtue of subsection (2) of section twenty-one of this Act, registered as a series in one registration shall be deemed to be, and shall be registered as, associated trade marks.

(5) On application made in the prescribed manner by the registered proprietor of two or more trade marks registered as associated trade marks, the Registrar may dissolve the association as respects any of them if he is satisfied that there would be no likelihood of deception or confusion being caused if that trade mark were used by another person in relation to any of the goods in respect of which it is registered, and may amend the register accordingly.

Any decision of the Registrar under this subsection shall be subject to appeal to the Board of Trade, or to the Court, at the option of the appellant.

Subs. (1). See s.66 of the 1883 Act and s.27 of the 1905 Act.
Subs. (2). See s.24 of the 1905 Act.
Subs. (2A) was added by 1984 Act, Sched. 2, para. 4.
Subs. (3). See s.66 of the 1883 Act and s.25 of the 1905 Act.
Subs. (4). See s.26 of the 1905 Act.
Subs. (5). New.

Power of registered proprietor to assign and give receipts

24. Subject to the provisions of this Act, the person for the time being entered **A2–26** in the register as proprietor of a trade mark shall, subject to any rights appearing from the register to be vested in any other person, have power to assign the trade mark, and to give effectual receipts for any consideration for an assignment thereof.

See s.87 of the 1883 Act and s.38 of the 1905 Act.

Registration of assignments and transmissions

A2–27   **25.**—(1) Where a person becomes entitled by assignment or transmission to a registered trade mark, he shall make application to the Registrar to register his title, and the Registrar shall, on receipt of the application and on proof of title to his satisfaction, register him as the proprietor of the trade mark in respect of the goods in respect of which the assignment or transmission has effect, and shall cause particulars of the assignment or transmission to be entered on the register.

(2) Any decision of the Registrar under this section shall be subject to appeal to the Court.

(3) Except for the purposes of an appeal under this section or of an application under section thirty-two of this Act, a document or instrument in respect of which no entry has been made in the register in accordance with the provisions of subsection (1) of this section shall not be admitted in evidence in any court in proof of the title to a trade mark unless the court otherwise directs.

See s.87 of the 1883 Act and s.33 of the 1905 Act.

Use and non-use

Removal from register and imposition of limitations on ground of non-use

A2–28   **26.**—(1) Subject to the provisions of the next succeeding section, a registered trade mark may be taken off the register in respect of any of the goods in respect of which it is registered on application by any person aggrieved to the Court or, at the option of the applicant and subject to the provisions of section fifty-four of this Act, to the Registrar, on the ground either—

(a) that the trade mark was registered without any bona fide intention on the part of the applicant for registration that it should be used in relation to those goods by him, and that there has in fact been no bona fide use of the trade mark in relation to those goods by any proprietor thereof for the time being up to the date one month before the date of the application; or

(b) that up to the date one month before the date of the application a continuous period of five years or longer elapsed during which the trade mark was a registered trade mark and during which there was no bona fide use thereof in relation to those goods by any proprietor thereof for the time being:

Provided that (except where the applicant has been permitted under subsection (2) of section twelve of this Act to register an identical or nearly resembling trade mark in respect of the goods in question or where the tribunal is of opinion that he might properly be permitted so to register such a trade mark) the tribunal may refuse an application made under paragraph (a) or (b) of this subsection in relation to any goods, if it is shown that there has been before the relevant date or during the relevant period, as the case may be, bona fide use of the [*trade*] mark by [*any*] the proprietor thereof for the time being in relation to [*goods of the same description*]—

(i) goods of the same description, or

(ii) services associated with those goods or goods of that description, being goods **or, as the case may be, services** in respect of which the mark is registered.

(2) Where in relation to any goods in respect of which a trade mark is registered—

  (a) the matters referred to in paragraph (b) of the foregoing subsection are shown so far as regards non-use of the trade mark in relation to goods to be sold, or otherwise traded in, in a particular place in the United Kingdom (otherwise than for export from the United Kingdom), or in relation to goods to be exported to a particular market outside the United Kingdom; and

  (b) a person has been permitted under subsection (2) of section twelve of this Act to register an identical or nearly resembling trade mark in respect of those goods under a registration extending to use in relation to goods to be sold, or otherwise traded in, in that place (otherwise than for export from the United Kingdom), or in relation to goods to be exported to that market, or the tribunal is of opinion that he might properly be permitted so to register such a trade mark;

on application by that person to the Court or, at the option of the applicant and subject to the provisions of section fifty-four of this Act, to the Registrar, the tribunal may impose on the registration of the first-mentioned trade mark such limitations as the tribunal thinks proper for securing that the registration shall cease to extend to such use as last aforesaid.

(3) An applicant shall not be entitled to rely for the purposes of paragraph (b) of subsection (1), or for the purposes of subsection (2), of this section on any non-use of a trade mark that is shown to have been due to special circumstances in the trade and not to any intention not to use or abandon the trade mark in relation to the goods to which the application relates.

See s.37 of the 1905 Act.
Amended by 1986 Act, Sched. 2, §3A.

Defensive registration of well-known trade marks

27.—(1) Where a trade mark consisting of an invented word or invented **A2–29** words has become so well known as respects any goods in respect of which it is registered and in relation to which it has been used that the use thereof in relation to other goods would be likely to be taken as indicating a connection in the course of trade between those goods and a person entitled to use the trade mark in relation to the first-mentioned goods, then, notwithstanding that the proprietor registered in respect of the first-mentioned goods does not use or propose to use the trade mark in relation to those other goods and notwithstanding anything in the last foregoing section, the trade mark may, on the application in the prescribed manner of the proprietor registered in respect of the first-mentioned goods, be registered in his name in respect of those other goods as a defensive trade mark and, while so registered, shall not be liable to be taken off the register in respect of those goods under the last foregoing section.

(2) The registered proprietor of a trade mark may apply for the registration thereof in respect of any goods as a defensive trade mark notwithstanding that it is already registered in his name in respect of those goods otherwise than as a defensive trade mark, or may apply for the registration thereof in respect of any goods otherwise than as a defensive trade mark notwithstanding that it is already registered in his name in respect of those goods as a defensive trade mark, in lieu in each case of the existing registration.

(3) A trade mark registered as a defensive trade mark and that trade mark as otherwise registered in the name of the same proprietor shall, notwithstanding that the respective registrations are in respect of different goods, be deemed to be, and shall be registered as, associated trade marks.

(4) On application by any person aggrieved to the Court or, at the option of the applicant and subject to the provisions of section fifty-four of this Act, to the

Registrar, the registration of a trade mark as a defensive trade mark may be cancelled on the ground that the requirements of subsection (1) of this section are no longer satisfied in respect of any goods in respect of which the trade mark is registered in the name of the same proprietor otherwise than as a defensive trade mark, or may be cancelled as respects any goods in respect of which it is registered as a defensive trade mark on the ground that there is no longer any likelihood that the use of the trade mark in relation to those goods would be taken as giving the indication mentioned in subsection (1) of this section.

(5) The Registrar may at any time cancel the registration as a defensive trade mark of a trade mark of which there is no longer any registration in the name of the same proprietor otherwise than as a defensive trade mark.

(6) Except as otherwise expressly provided in this section, the provisions of this Act shall apply in respect of the registration of trade marks as defensive trade marks and of trade marks so registered as they apply in other cases.

Registered users

A2–30   28.—(1) Subject to the provisions of this section, a person other than the proprietor of a trade mark may be registered as a registered user thereof in respect of all or any of the goods in respect of which it is registered (otherwise than as a defensive trade mark) and either with or without conditions or restrictions.

The use of a trade mark by a registered user thereof in relation to goods with which he is connected in the course of trade and in respect of which for the time being the trade mark remains registered and he is registered as a registered user, being use such as to comply with any conditions or restrictions to which his registration is subject, is in this Act referred to as the "permitted use" thereof.

(2) The permitted use of a trade mark shall be deemed to be use by the proprietor thereof, and shall be deemed not to be use by a person other than the proprietor, for the purposes of section twenty-six of this Act and for any other purpose for which such use is material under this Act or at common law.

(3) Subject to any agreement subsisting between the parties, a registered user of a trade mark shall be entitled to call upon the proprietor thereof to take proceedings to prevent infringement thereof, and, if the proprietor refuses or neglects to do so within two months after being so called upon, the registered user may institute proceedings for infringement in his own name as if he were the proprietor, making the proprietor a defendant.

A proprietor so added as defendant shall not be liable for any costs unless he enters an appearance and takes part in the proceedings.

(4) Where it is proposed that a person should be registered as a registered user of a trade mark, the proprietor and the proposed registered user must apply in writing to the Registrar in the prescribed manner and must furnish him with a statutory declaration made by the proprietor, or by some person authorised to act on his behalf and approved by the Registrar—

(a) giving particulars of the relationship, existing or proposed, between the proprietor and the proposed registered user, including particulars showing the degree of control by the proprietor over the permitted use which their relationship will confer and whether it is a term of their relationship that the proposed registered user shall be the sole registered user or that there shall be any other restriction as to persons for whose registration as registered users application may be made;

(b) stating the goods in respect of which registration is proposed;

(c) stating any conditions or restrictions proposed with respect to the characteristics of the goods, to the mode or place of permitted use, or to any other matter; and

(d) stating whether the permitted use is to be for a period or without limit of period, and, if for a period, the duration thereof;

and with such further documents, information or evidence as may be required under the rules or by the Registrar.

(5) When the requirements of the last foregoing subsection have been complied with, if the Registrar, after considering the information furnished to him under that subsection, is satisfied that in all the circumstances the use of the trade mark in relation to the proposed goods or any of them by the proposed registered user subject to any conditions or restrictions which the Registrar thinks proper would not be contrary to the public interest, the Registrar may register the proposed registered user as a registered user in respect of the goods as to which he is so satisfied subject as aforesaid.

(6) The Registrar shall refuse an application under the foregoing provisions of this section if it appears to him that the grant thereof would tend to facilitate trafficking in a trade mark.

(7) The Registrar shall, if so required by an applicant, take steps for securing that information given for the purposes of an application under the foregoing provisions of this section (other than matter entered in the register) is not disclosed to rivals in trade.

(8) Without prejudice to the provisions of section thirty-two of this Act, the registration of a person as a registered user—

(a) may be varied by the Registrar as regards the goods in respect of which, or any conditions or restrictions subject to which, it has effect, on the application in writing in the prescribed manner of the registered proprietor of the trade mark to which the registration relates;

(b) may be cancelled by the Registrar on the application in writing in the prescribed manner of the registered proprietor or of the registered user or of any other registered user of the trade mark; or

(c) may be cancelled by the Registrar on the application in writing in the prescribed manner of any person on any of the following grounds, that is to say—

    (i) that the registered user has used the trade mark otherwise than by way of the permitted use, or in such a way as to cause, or to be likely to cause, deception or confusion;

    (ii) that the proprietor or the registered user misrepresented, or failed to disclose, some fact material to the application for the registration, or that the circumstances have materially changed since the date of the registration;

    (iii) that the registration ought not to have been effected having regard to rights vested in the applicant by virtue of a contract in the performance of which he is interested.

(9) Provision shall be made by the rules for the notification of the registration of a person as a registered user to any other registered user of the trade mark, and for the notification of an application under the last foregoing subsection to the registered proprietor and each registered user (not being the applicant) of the trade mark, and for giving to the applicant on such an application, and to all persons to whom such an application is notified and who intervene in the proceedings in accordance with the rules, an opportunity of being heard.

(10) The Registrar may at any time cancel the registration of a person as a registered user of a trade mark in respect of any goods in respect of which the trade mark is no longer registered.

(11) Any decision of the Registrar under the foregoing provisions of this section shall be subject to appeal to the Court.

(12) Nothing in this section shall confer on a registered user of a trade mark any assignable or transmissible right to the use thereof.

Proposed use of trade mark by corporation to be constituted, etc.

29.—1) No application for the registration of a trade mark in respect of any **A2–31** goods shall be refused, nor shall permission for such registration be withheld, on the ground only that it appears that the applicant does not use or propose to use the trade mark,—

(a) if the tribunal is satisfied that a body corporate is about to be constituted, and that the applicant intends to assign the trade mark to the corporation with a view to the use thereof in relation to those goods by the corporation; or

(b) if the application is accompanied by an application for the registration of a person as a registered user of the trade mark, and the tribunal is satisfied that the proprietor intends it to be used by that person in relation to those goods and the tribunal is also satisfied that that person will be registered as a registered user thereof immediately after the registration of the trade mark.

(2) The provisions of section twenty-six of this Act shall have effect, in relation to a trade mark registered under the power conferred by the foregoing subsection, as if for the reference, in paragraph (a) of subsection (1) of that section, to intention on the part of an applicant for registration that a trade mark should be used by him there were substituted a reference to intention on his part that it should be used by the corporation or registered user concerned.

(3) The tribunal may, as a condition of the exercise of the power conferred by subsection (1) of this section in favour of an applicant who relies on intention to assign to a corporation as aforesaid, require him to give security for the costs of any proceedings before the tribunal relative to any opposition or appeal, and in default of such security being duly given may treat the application as abandoned.

(4) Where a trade mark is registered in respect of any goods under the power conferred by subsection (1) of this section in the name of an applicant who relies on intention to assign to a corporation as aforesaid, then, unless within such period as may be prescribed, or within such further period not exceeding six months as the Registrar may on application being made to him in the prescribed manner allow, the corporation has been registered as the proprietor of the trade mark in respect of those goods, the registration shall cease to have effect in respect thereof at the expiration of that period, and the Registrar shall amend the register accordingly.

Use of one of associated or substantially identical trade marks equivalent to use of another

A2–32   30.—(1) Where under the provisions of this Act use of a registered trade mark is required to be proved for any purpose, the tribunal may, if and so far as the tribunal thinks right, accept use of an associated registered trade mark, or of the trade mark with additions or alterations not substantially affecting its identity, as an equivalent for the use required to be proved.

(2) The use of the whole of a registered trade mark shall for the purposes of this Act be deemed to be also a use of any registered trade mark, being a part thereof, registered in the name of the same proprietor by virtue of subsection (1) of section twenty-one of this Act.

Subs. (1). See s.27 of the 1905 Act.
Subs. (2). See s.25 of the 1905 Act.

Use of trade mark for export trade

A2–33   31. The application in the United Kingdom of a trade mark to goods to be exported from the United Kingdom, and any other act done in the United Kingdom in relation to goods to be so exported which, if done in relation to goods to be sold or otherwise traded in within the United Kingdom, would constitute use of a trade mark therein, shall be deemed to constitute the use of the trade mark in relation to those goods for any purpose for which such use is material under this Act or at common law.

Rectification and correction of the register

General power to rectify entries in register

32.—(1) Any person aggrieved by the non-insertion in or omission from the **A2–34** register of any entry, or by any entry made in the register without sufficient cause, or by any entry wrongly remaining on the register, or by any error or defect in any entry in the register, may apply in the prescribed manner to the Court or, at the option of the applicant and subject to the provisions of section fifty-four of this Act, to the Registrar, and the tribunal may make such order for making, expunging or varying the entry as the tribunal may think fit.

(2) The tribunal may in any proceeding under this section decide any question that it may be necessary or expedient to decide in connection with the rectification of the register.

(3) In case of fraud in the registration, assignment or transmission of a registered trade mark, the Registrar may himself apply to the Court under the provisions of this section.

(4) Any order of the Court rectifying the register shall direct that notice of the rectification shall be served in the prescribed manner on the Registrar, and the Registrar shall on receipt of the notice rectify the register accordingly.

(5) The power to rectify the register conferred by this section shall include power to remove a registration in Part A of the register to Part B.

Subs. (1) has been amended slightly in its application to proceedings in Northern Ireland, Judicature (Northern Ireland) Act 1978, s.122 and Sched. 5.
Subss. (1)–(4). See s.5 of the 1875 Act, s.90 of the 1883 Act and s.35 of the 1905 Act.
Subs. (5). See s.9(3) of the 1919 Act.

Power to expunge or vary registration for breach of condition

33. On application by any person aggrieved to the Court, or, at the option of **A2–35** the applicant and subject to the provisions of section fifty-four of this Act, to the Registrar, or on application by the Registrar to the Court, the tribunal may make such order as the tribunal may think fit for expunging or varying the registration of a trade mark on the ground of any contravention of, or failure to observe, a condition entered on the register in relation thereto.

Correction of register

34.—(1) The Registrar may, on request made in the prescribed manner by the **A2–36** registered proprietor,—

(a) correct any error in the name **and** address of the registered proprietor of a trade mark;
(b) enter any change in the name **and** address of the person who is registered as proprietor of a trade mark;
(c) cancel the entry of a trade mark on the register;
(d) strike out any goods or classes of goods from those in respect of which a trade mark is registered; or
(e) enter a disclaimer or memorandum relating to a trade mark which does not in any way extend the rights given by the existing registration of the trade mark.

(2) The Registrar may, on request made in the prescribed manner by a registered user of a trade mark, correct any error, or enter any change, in the name **and** address of the registered user.

(3) Any decision of the Registrar under this section shall be subject to appeal to the Board of Trade, or to the Court, at the option of the appellant.

Subss. (1) and (3). See s.91 of the 1883 Act and s.32 of the 1905 Act.

Amendments, Patents, &c., Act 1986, Sched. 2.

Alteration of registered trade mark

A2–37   **35.**—(1) The registered proprietor of a trade mark may apply in the prescribed manner to the Registrar for leave to add to or alter the trade mark in any manner not substantially affecting the identity thereof, and the Registrar may refuse leave or may grant it on such terms and subject to such limitations as he may think fit.

(2) The Registrar may cause an application under this section to be advertised in the prescribed manner in any case where it appears to him that it is expedient so to do, and where he does so, if within the prescribed time from the date of the advertisement any person gives notice to the Registrar in the prescribed manner of opposition to the application, the Registrar shall, after hearing the parties if so required, decide the matter.

(3) Any decision of the Registrar under this section shall be subject to appeal to the Board of Trade, or to the Court, at the option of the appellant.

(4) Where leave as aforesaid is granted, the trade mark as altered shall be advertised in the prescribed manner, unless it has already been advertised, in the form to which it has been altered, in an advertisement under subsection (2) of this section.

See s.92 of the 1883 Act and s.34 of the 1905 Act.

Adaptation of entries in register to amended or substituted classification of goods

A2–38   **36.**—(1) The Board of Trade may from time to time make such rules, prescribe such forms and generally do such things as they think expedient, for empowering the Registrar to amend the register, whether by making or expunging or varying entries therein, so far as may be requisite for the purpose of adapting the designation therein of the goods or classes of goods in respect of which trade marks are registered to any amended or substituted classification that may be prescribed.

(2) The Registrar shall not, in exercise of any power conferred on him for the purpose aforesaid, make any amendment of the register that would have the effect of adding any goods or classes of goods to those in respect of which a trade mark is registered (whether in one or more classes) immediately before the amendment is to be made, or of antedating the registration of a trade mark in respect of any goods:

Provided that this subsection shall not have effect in relation to goods as to which the Registrar is satisfied that compliance with this subsection in relation thereto would involve undue complexity and that the addition or antedating, as the case may be, would not affect any substantial quantity of goods and would not substantially prejudice the rights of any person.

(3) A proposal for the amendment of the register for the purpose aforesaid shall be notified to the registered proprietor of the trade mark affected, shall be subject to appeal by the registered proprietor to the Board of Trade, or at his option to the Court, shall be advertised with any modifications, and may be opposed before the Registrar by any person aggrieved on the ground that the proposed amendment contravenes the provisions of the last foregoing subsection, and the decision of the Registrar on any such opposition shall be subject to appeal to the Court.

Certification trade marks

Certification trade marks

A2–39   **37.**—(1) A mark adapted in relation to any goods to distinguish in the course of trade goods certified by any person in respect of origin, material, mode of manufacture, quality, accuracy or other characteristic, from goods not so certified shall be registrable as a certification trade mark in Part A of the register in respect of those goods in the name, as proprietor thereof, of that person:

Provided that a mark shall not be so registrable in the name of a person who carries on a trade in goods of the kind certified.

(2) In determining whether a mark is adapted to distinguish as aforesaid, the tribunal may have regard to the extent to which—

(a) the mark is inherently adapted to distinguish as aforesaid in relation to the goods in question; and

(b) by reason of the use of the mark or of any other circumstances, the mark is in fact adapted to distinguish as aforesaid in relation to the goods in question.

(3) Subject to the provisions of subsections (4) to (6) of this section, and of sections seven and eight of this Act, the registration of a person as proprietor of a certification trade mark in respect of any goods shall, if valid, give to that person the exclusive right to the use of the trade mark in relation to those goods, and, without prejudice to the generality of the foregoing words, that right shall be deemed to be infringed by any person who, not being the proprietor of the trade mark or a person authorised by him under the regulations in that behalf using it in accordance therewith, uses a mark identical with it or so nearly resembling it as to be likely to deceive or cause confusion, in the course of trade, in relation to any goods in respect of which it is registered, and in such manner as to render the use of the mark likely to be taken either—

(a) as being use as a trade mark; or

(b) in a case in which the use is upon the goods or in physical relation thereto or in an advertising circular or other advertisement issued to the public, as importing a reference to some person having the right either as proprietor or by his authorisation under the relevant regulations to use the trade mark or to goods certified by the proprietor.

(4) The right to the use of a certification trade mark given by registration as aforesaid shall be subject to any conditions or limitations entered on the register, and shall not be deemed to be infringed by the use of any such mark as aforesaid in any mode, in relation to goods to be sold or otherwise traded in any place, in relation to goods to be exported to any market, or in any other circumstances, to which, having regard to any such limitations, the registration does not extend.

(5) The right to the use of a certification trade mark given by registration as aforesaid shall not be deemed to be infringed by the use of any such mark as aforesaid by any person—

(a) in relation to goods certified by the proprietor of the trade mark if, as to those goods or a bulk of which they form part, the proprietor or another in accordance with his authorisation under the relevant regulations has applied the trade mark and has not subsequently removed or obliterated it, or the proprietor has at any time expressly or impliedly consented to the use of the trade mark; or

(b) in relation to goods adapted to form part of, or to be accessory to, other goods in relation to which the trade mark has been used without infringement of the right given as aforesaid or might for the time being be so used, if the use of the mark is reasonably necessary in order to indicate that the goods are so adapted and neither the purpose nor the effect of the use of the mark is to indicate otherwise than in accordance with the fact that the goods are certified by the proprietor:

Provided that paragraph (a) of this subsection shall not have effect in the case of use consisting of the application of any such mark as aforesaid to any goods, notwithstanding that they are such goods as are mentioned in that paragraph, if such application is contrary to the relevant regulations.

(6) Where a certification trade mark is one of two or more registered trade marks that are identical or nearly resemble each other, the use of any of those trade marks in exercise of the right to the use of that trade mark given by registration shall not be deemed to be an infringement of the right so given to the use of any other of those trade marks.

(7) There shall be deposited at the Patent Office in respect of every trade mark registered under this section regulations approved by the Board of Trade for governing the use thereof, which shall include provisions as to the cases in which the proprietor is to certify goods and authorise the use of the trade mark, and may contain any other provisions that the Board of Trade may require or permit to be inserted therein (including provisions conferring a right to appeal to the Registrar against any refusal of the proprietor to certify goods or to authorise the use of the trade mark in accordance with the regulations). Regulations so deposited shall be open to inspection in like manner as the register.

(8) A certification trade mark shall not be assignable or transmissible otherwise than with the consent of the Board of Trade.

(9) The provisions of the First Schedule to this Act shall have effect with respect to the registration of a mark under this section and to marks so registered.

See s.62 of the 1905 Act.

Sheffield marks

Sheffield marks

A2–40   **38.** The provisions of the Second Schedule to this Act shall have effect with respect to the master, wardens, searchers, assistants, and commonalty of the Company of Cutlers in Hallamshire, in the county of York (in this Act called "the Cutlers' Company"), and the marks or devices assigned or registered by the master, wardens, searchers and assistants of that Company.

See s.9 of the 1875 Act, s.81 of the 1883 Act and s.63 of the 1905 Act.

Manchester Branch

Trade marks for textile goods

A2–41   **39.**—(1) The Manchester Branch of the Trade Marks Registry of the Patent Office (in this section referred to as "the Manchester Branch") shall be continued under a chief officer, who shall be styled "the Keeper of the Manchester Branch" and shall act under the direction of the Registrar.

(2) The rules shall specify certain of the classes for the time being established for the purposes of the registration of trade marks (being such of those classes as consist of, or appear to the Board of Trade to relate materially to, any of the following goods, that is to say, goods included immediately before the appointed day in any of the classes numbered twenty-three to thirty-five and thirty-eight respectively and similar goods made from artificial silk or from other artificial fibres) as being classes to which this section applies.

In this section the expression "textile goods" means goods of any of the classes for the time being so specified other than goods of a kind as to which it may be provided by the rules that this section is not to apply thereto.

(3) The rules for prescribing the manner in which applications for the registration of trade marks are to be made shall make provision for the sending of an application for the registration of a trade mark in respect of textile goods to

the Registrar either at the Patent Office or at the Manchester Branch, at the option of the applicant.

(4) The Keeper of the Manchester Branch shall furnish the Registrar with a report on every application for the registration of a trade mark sent to the Manchester Branch, and before deciding under subsection (2) of section seventeen of this Act on any such application, the Registrar shall consider the report.

(5) In respect of textile goods being piece goods—

    (a) no mark consisting of a line heading alone shall be registrable as a trade mark;

    (b) a line heading shall not be deemed to be adapted to distinguish or capable of distinguishing;

    (c) the registration of a trade mark shall not give any exclusive right to the use of a line heading.

(6) There shall be kept at the Manchester Branch for the purposes of this Act a record called the Manchester Record wherein shall be entered copies of all entries in the register relating to trade marks registered in respect of textile goods on or after the appointed day and, as soon as may be, copies of all entries relating to trade marks so registered before the appointed day and for the time being subsisting, and the Manchester Record shall at all convenient times be open to the inspection of the public, subject to such regulations as may be prescribed.

(7) The right of inspection conferred by the last foregoing subsection shall extend to and include the right to inspect all applications whatsoever for registration that were made to the Manchester Branch, between the passing of the Trade Marks Registration Act 1875, and the appointed day, in respect of cotton goods, whether registered, refused, lapsed, expired, withdrawn, abandoned, cancelled or pending.

(8) Refused marks which, immediately before the appointed day, were included in the collection of refused marks kept under rules one hundred and twelve to one hundred and sixteen of the Trade Marks Rules 1920, and are at the time of the application for the registration of a trade mark included in that collection under the rules shall be treated for the purposes of subsections (1) and (2) of section twelve of this Act, but for no other purpose, as if they had been registered trade marks.

(9) Before making any rule, or prescribing any form, that is to deal specially with trade marks registered or proposed to be registered in respect of textile goods other than clothing, the Board of Trade shall send a draft thereof to the Trade and Merchandise Marks Committee of the Manchester Chamber of Commerce, and shall, if the said committee so request, give them an opportunity of being heard.

(10) The Registrar, or the Keeper of the Manchester Branch, may consult the said committee where it appears to him to be expedient so to do with respect to any circumstances peculiar to the cotton trade arising on an application to register a trade mark in respect of textile goods other than clothing.

(11) A certificate purporting to be under the hand of the Keeper of the Manchester Branch as to any copy entered in the Manchester Record of an entry in the register shall be *prima facie* evidence of the entry having been made in the register and of the contents thereof.

(12) The Court of Chancery of the County Palatine of Lancaster shall, with respect to any action or other proceeding in relation to a trade mark registered or proposed to be registered pursuant to an application sent to the Manchester Branch, where the registered proprietor or the proposed registered proprietor is within, or submits to, the jurisdiction of that Court, have the like jurisdiction under this Act as His Majesty's High Court of Justice in England, and the expression "the Court" in this Act shall be construed and have effect accordingly:

Provided that every decision of the Court of Chancery of the County Palatine of Lancaster in pursuance of this subsection shall be subject to the like appeal as decisions of that Court in other cases.

Subs. (12) repealed, Courts Act 1971, s.56 applying Sched. 11.
See s.64 of the 1905 Act. Prior to that section special provision was made in the Rules as to marks for textile goods.
Section inserted by 1986 Act, Sched. 2, para. 4.

Registration of trade mark following overseas application

A2–42   **39A.**—(1) Any person who has applied for protection for any trade mark in a relevant country or his legal representative or assignee shall be entitled on an application for registration made within six months of the application for protection in the relevant country to registration of his mark under this Act in priority to other applicants.

(2) A mark registered on an application made under this section shall be registered as of the date of the application in the relevant country and that date shall be deemed for the purposes of this Act to be the date of registration.

(3) Nothing in this Act shall entitle the proprietor of the mark to recover damages for infringements happening prior to the date of the application for registration under this Act.

(4) The registration of a mark shall not be invalidated by reason only of the use of the mark in the United Kingdom during the period specified in this section as that within which the application may be made.

(5) The application for the registration of a mark under this section must be made in the same manner as an ordinary application under this Act.

(6) Where a person has applied for protection for any mark by an application which—

  (a) in accordance with the terms of a treaty subsisting between any two or more relevant countries is equivalent to an application duly made in any one of those countries; or

  (b) in accordance with the law of any relevant country, is equivalent to an application duly made in that country,

he shall be deemed for the purposes of this section to have applied in that country.

(7) Subject to subsection (7) below, Her Majesty may by Order in Council direct that this section shall apply to a country specified in the Order.

(8) If a country is not a dependent territory, an Order in Council under this section may only be made in relation to it with a view to the fulfilment of a treaty, convention, arrangement or engagement.

(9) An Order in Council under this section shall be subject to annulment in pursuance of a resolution of either House of Parliament and may be varied or revoked by a subsequent Order.

(10) In this section—

  "country" includes any territory;
  "dependent territory" means any of the Channel Islands or a colony;
  "relevant country" means a country which was specified in an Order in Council under this section at the time of the application under this section or such other time as may be specified in the Order in Council."

GENERAL AND MISCELLANEOUS

Rules and fees

Power of Board of Trade to make rules

A2–43   **40.**—(1) The Board of Trade may from time to time make such rules, prescribe such forms and generally do such things as they think expedient—

(a) for regulating the practice under this Act, including the service of documents;

(b) for classifying goods for the purposes of registration of trade marks;

(c) for making or requiring duplicates of trade marks and other documents;

(d) for securing and regulating the publishing and selling or distributing, in such manner as the Board of Trade think fit, of copies of trade marks and other documents;

(e) generally, for regulating the business of the Patent Office in relation to trade marks and all things by this Act placed under the direction or control of the Registrar or of the Board of Trade.

(3) Before making any rules under this Act, the Board of Trade shall publish notice of their intention to make the rules and of the place where copies of the draft rules may be obtained, in such manner as the Board consider most expedient so as to enable persons affected to make representations to the Board before the rules are finally settled.

(4) Any rules so made shall be forthwith advertised twice in the Trade Marks Journal, and shall be laid before both Houses of Parliament, *if Parliament be in session at the time of the making thereof, or, if not, as soon as practicable after the beginning of the then next session of Parliament.*

(5) If either House of Parliament, within the next forty days after any rules have been so laid before it, resolves that the rules or any of them ought to be annulled, the rule or rules shall thenceforth be of no effect, but without prejudice to the validity of anything previously done thereunder or to the making of any new rule or rules.

See s.7 of the 1875 Act, s.101 of the 1883 Act and s.60 of the 1905 Act. Words in italics repealed, S.L.(R.) Act, 1986.

Hours of business and excluded days

40A.—(1) Rules made by the Board of Trade under this Act may specify the hour at which the Patent Office shall be deemed to be closed on any day for purposes of the transaction by the public of business under this Act or of any class of such business, and may specify days as excluded days for any such purposes. A2–44

(2) Any business done under this Act on any day after the hour specified as aforesaid in relation to business of that class, or on a day which is an excluded day in relation to business of that class, shall be deemed to have been done on the next following day not being an excluded day; and where the time for doing anything under this Act expires on an excluded day, that time shall be extended to the next following day not being an excluded day.

Section inserted, Statute Law Repeals Act 1986.

Fees

41. There shall be paid in respect of applications and registration and other matters under this Act such fees as may be, with the sanction of the Treasury, prescribed by the Board of Trade. A2–45

See s.7 of the 1875 Act, s.80 of the 1883 Act and s.61 of the 1905 Act.

Powers and duties of Registrar

Preliminary advice by Registrar as to distinctiveness

42.—(1) The power to give to a person who proposes to apply for the registration of a trade mark in Part A or Part B of the register advice as to whether the trade mark appears to the Registrar *prima facie* to be inherently A2–46 adapted to distinguish, or capable of distinguishing, as the case may be, shall be a function of the Registrar under this Act.

(2) Any such person who is desirous of obtaining such advice must make application to the Registrar therefor in the prescribed manner.

(3) If on an application for the registration of a trade mark as to which the Registrar has given advice as aforesaid in the affirmative, made within three months after the advice is given, the Registrar, after further investigation or consideration, gives notice to the applicant of objection on the ground that the trade mark is not adapted to distinguish, or capable of distinguishing, as the case may be, the applicant shall be entitled, on giving notice of withdrawal of the application within the prescribed period, to have repaid to him any fee paid on the filing of the application.

Hearing before exercise of Registrar's discretion

A2–47   **43.** Where any discretionary or other power is given to the Registrar by this Act or the rules, he shall not exercise that power adversely to the applicant for registration or the registered proprietor of the trade mark in question without (if duly required so to do within the prescribed time) giving to the applicant or registered proprietor an opportunity of being heard.

See s.94 of the 1883 Act and s.53 of the 1905 Act.

Power of Registrar to award costs

A2–48   **44.** In all proceedings before the Registrar under this Act, the Registrar shall have power to award to any party such costs as he may consider reasonable, and to direct how and by what parties they are to be paid, and any such order may, by leave of the Court or a judge thereof, be enforced in the same manner as a judgment or order of the Court to the same effect.

See s.10 of the 1919 Act.

Reports of Registrar

A2–49   **45.** The Comptroller-General of Patents, Designs and Trade Marks shall, in his annual report on the execution by or under him of the Patents and Designs Act 1907, and Acts amending that Act, include a report respecting the execution by or under him of this Act as if it formed a part of or was included in those Acts.

See s.102 of the 1883 Act and s.57 of the 1905 Act.

Legal proceedings and appeals

Registration to be prima facie evidence of validity

A2–50   **46.** In all legal proceedings relating to a registered trade mark (including applications under section thirty-two of this Act) the fact that a person is registered as proprietor of the trade mark shall be *prima facie* evidence of the validity of the original registration of the trade mark and of all subsequent assignments and transmissions thereof.

See s.76 of the 1883 Act and s.40 of the 1905 Act.

Certificate of validity

A2–51   **47.** In any legal proceeding in which the validity of the registration of a registered trade mark comes into question and is decided in favour of the proprietor of the trade mark, the Court may certify to that effect, and if it so certifies then in any subsequent legal proceeding in which the validity of the registration comes into question the proprietor of the trade mark on obtaining a final order or judgment in his favour shall have his full costs, charges and expenses as between solicitor and client, unless in the subsequent proceeding the Court certifies that he ought not to have them.

See s.77 (a) of the 1883 Act and s.46 of the 1905 Act.

Costs of Registrar in proceedings before Court, and payment of costs by Registrar

48.—(1) In all proceedings before the Court under this Act the costs of the **A2–52** Registrar shall be in the discretion of the Court, but, in any proceedings in England or Northern Ireland, the Registrar shall not, except in accordance with the provisions of subsection (2) of this section in a case in which he has appeared in the proceedings, be ordered to pay the costs of any other of the parties.

(2) Where the Registrar appears in any proceedings before the Court in England or Northern Ireland under this Act, section seven of the Administration of Justice (Miscellaneous Provisions) Act 1933 or any corresponding enactment which may be passed by the Parliament of Northern Ireland, as the case may be, shall have effect as it has effect in relation to other proceedings to which the Crown is a party in a court having power to award costs in cases between subjects.

Subs. (1). See s.48 of the 1905 Act.

Trade usage, etc., to be considered

49. In any action or proceeding relating to a trade mark or trade name, the **A2–53** tribunal shall admit evidence of the usages of the trade concerned and of any relevant trade mark or trade name or get-up legitimately used by other persons.

See s.43 of the 1905 Act.

Registrar's appearance in proceedings involving rectification

50.—(1) In any legal proceeding in which the relief sought includes alteration **A2–54** or rectification of the register, the Registrar shall have the right to appear and be heard, and shall appear if so directed by the Court.

(2) Unless otherwise directed by the Court, the Registrar in lieu of appearing and being heard may submit to the Court a statement in writing signed by him, giving particulars of the proceedings before him in relation to the matter in issue or of the grounds of any decision given by him affecting it or of the practice of the Patent Office in like cases or of such other matters relevant to the issues, and within his knowledge as Registrar, as he thinks fit, and the statement shall be deemed to form part of the evidence in the proceeding.

See s.47 of the 1905 Act embodying the previous practice.

Court's power to review Registrar's decision

51. The Court, in dealing with any question of the rectification of the register **A2–55** (including all applications under the provisions of section thirty-two of this Act), shall have power to review any decision of the Registrar relating to the entry in question or the correction sought to be made.

See ss.62(5) and 69(4) of the 1883 Act and s.54 of the 1905 Act.

Discretion of Court in appeals

52. In any appeal from a decision of the Registrar to the Court under this Act, **A2–56** the Court shall have and exercise the same discretionary powers as under this Act are conferred upon the Registrar.

See s.8(2) of the 1919 Act.

Procedure on appeal to Board of Trade

A2–57   **53.** Where under this Act an appeal is made to the Board of Trade, the Board of Trade may, if they think fit, refer the appeal to the Court in lieu of hearing and deciding it themselves, but, unless the Board so refer the appeal, it shall be heard and decided by the Board, and the decision of the Board shall be final.

See ss.62(5) and 69(4) of the 1883 Act and s.59 of the 1905 Act.

Procedure in cases of option to apply to Court or Registrar

A2–58   **54.** Where under any of the foregoing provisions of this Act an applicant has an option to make an application either to the Court or to the Registrar—

    (a) if an action concerning the trade mark in question is pending, the application must be made to the Court;

    (b) if in any other case the application is made to the Registrar, he may, at any stage of the proceedings, refer the application to the Court, or he may, after hearing the parties, determine the question between them, subject to appeal to the Court.

See s.9 of the 1919 Act.

Evidence

Mode of giving evidence

A2–59   **55.** In any proceeding under this Act before the Board of Trade or the Registrar, the evidence shall be given by statutory declaration in the absence of directions to the contrary, but, in any case in which the tribunal thinks it right so to do, the tribunal may take evidence *viva voce* in lieu of or in addition to evidence by declaration. Any such statutory declaration may in the case of appeal be used before the Court in lieu of evidence by affidavit, but if so used shall have all the incidents and consequences of evidence by affidavit.

    In case any part of the evidence is taken *viva voce*, the Board of Trade or the Registrar shall, in respect of requiring the attendance of witnesses and taking evidence on oath, be in the same position in all respects as an official referee of the Supreme Court.

See s.49 of the 1905 Act.

Evidence of orders, etc., of Board of Trade

A2–60   **56.**—(1) All documents purporting to be orders made by the Board of Trade and to be sealed with the seal of the Board, or to be signed by a secretary or an under-secretary or an assistant secretary of the Board, or by any person authorised in that behalf by the President of the Board, shall be received in evidence, and shall be deemed to be such orders without further proof, unless the contrary is shown.

    (2) A certificate, signed by the President of the Board of Trade, that any order made or act done is the order or act of the Board shall be conclusive evidence of the fact so certified.

See s.102(*a*) of the 1883 Act and s.52 of the 1905 Act.

Evidence of entries in register

A2–61   **57.**—*(1) A printed or written copy of any entry in the register, purporting to be certified by the Registrar and sealed with the seal of the Patent Office, shall be admitted in evidence in all courts, and in all proceedings, without further proof or production of the original.*

(2) Any person requiring such a certified copy as aforesaid shall be entitled to obtain it on payment of the prescribed fee.

Section repealed, 1986 Act, Sched. 3, para. 1.
Subs. (1). See s.89 of the 1883 Act and s.50 of the 1905 Act.
Subs. (2). See s.88 of the 1883 Act. No equivalent provision was made in the 1905 Act, but the fee was payable under the Rules.

Evidence of things done by Registrar

58.—*(1) A certificate purporting to be under the hand of the Registrar as to any* **A2–62** *entry, matter or thing that he is authorised by this Act or the rules to make or do shall be prima facie evidence of the entry having been made, and of the contents thereof, and of the matter or thing having been done or not done.*

Section repealed, 1986 Act, Sched. 3, para. 1.
See s.96 of the 1883 Act and s.51 of the 1905 Act.

Fraudulent application or use of trade mark an offence

58A.—**(1) It is an offence, subject to subsection (3) below, for a person—** **A2–63**

    (a) to apply a mark identical to or nearly resembling a registered trade mark to goods, or to material used or intended to be used for labelling, packaging or advertising goods, or

    (b) to sell, let for hire, or offer or expose for sale or hire, or distribute—
        (i) goods bearing such a mark, or
        (ii) material bearing such a mark which is used or intended to be used for labelling, packaging or advertising goods, or

    (c) to use material bearing such a mark in the course of a business for labelling, packaging or advertising goods, or

    (d) to possess in the course of a business goods or material bearing such a mark with a view to doing any of the things mentioned in paragraphs (a) to (c),

when he is not entitled to use the mark in relation to the goods in question and the goods are not connected in the course of trade with a person who is so entitled.

(2) It is also an offence, subject to subsection (3) below, for a person to possess in the course of a business goods or material bearing a mark identical to or nearly resembling a registered trade mark with a view to enabling or assisting another person to do any of the things mentioned in subsection (1)(a) to (c), knowing or having reason to believe that the other person is not entitled to use the mark in relation to the goods in question and that the goods are not connected in the course of trade with a person who is so entitled.

(3) A person commits an offence under subsection (1) or (2) only if—

    (a) he acts with a view to gain for himself or another, or with intent to cause loss to another, and

    (b) he intends that the goods in question should be accepted as connected in the course of trade with a person entitled to use the mark in question;

and it is a defence for a person charged with an offence under subsection (1) to show that he believed on reasonable grounds that he was entitled to use the mark in relation to the goods in question.

(4) A person guilty of an offence under this section is liable—

    (a) on summary conviction to imprisonment for a term not exceeding six months or a fine not exceeding the statutory maximum, or both;

(b) on conviction on indictment to a fine or imprisonment for a term not exceeding ten years, or both.

(5) Where an offence under this section committed by a body corporate is proved to have been committed with the consent or connivance of a director, manager, secretary or other similar officer of the body, or a person purporting to act in any such capacity, he as well as the body corporate is guilty of the offence and liable to be proceeded against and punished accordingly.

In relation to a body corporate whose affairs are managed by its members 'director' means a member of the body corporate.

(6) In this section 'business' includes a trade or profession."

Delivery up of offending goods and material

A2–64   58B.—(1) The court by which a person is convicted of an offence under section 58A may, if satisfied that at the time of his arrest or charge he had in his possession, custody or control—

(a) goods or material in respect of which the offence was committed, or
(b) goods of the same description as those in respect of which the offence was committed, or material similar to that in respect of which the offence was committed, bearing a mark identical to or nearly resembling that in relation to which the offence was committed,

order that the goods or material be delivered up to such person as the court may direct.

(2) For this purpose a person shall be treated as charged with an offence—

(a) in England, Wales and Northern Ireland, when he is orally charged or is served with a summons or indictment;
(b) in Scotland, when he is cautioned, charged or served with a complaint or indictment.

(3) An order may be made by the court of its own motion or on the application of the prosecutor (or, in Scotland, the Lord Advocate or procurator-fiscal), but shall not be made if it appears to the court unlikely that any order will be made under section 58C (order as to disposal of offending goods or material).

(4) An appeal lies from an order made under this section by a magistrates' court—

(a) in England and Wales, to the Crown Court, and
(b) in Northern Ireland, to the county court;

and in Scotland, where an order has been made under this section, the person from whose possession, custody or control the goods or material have been removed may, without prejudice to any other form of appeal under any rule of law, appeal against that order in the same manner as against sentence.

(5) A person to whom goods or material are delivered up in pursuance of an order under this section shall retain it pending the making of an order under section 58C.

(6) Nothing in this section affects the powers of the court under section 43 of the Powers of Criminal Courts Act 1973, *section 223 or 436 of the Criminal Procedure (Scotland) Act 1975* Part II of the Proceeds of Crime (Scotland) Act 1993 or Article 7 of the Criminal Justice (Northern Ireland) Order 1980 (general provisions as to forfeiture in criminal proceedings).

Amended by the Criminal Procedure (consequential provisions) Scotland Act 1993.

Order as to disposal of offending goods or material

A2–65   58C.—(1) Where goods or material have been delivered up in pursuance of an order under section 58B, an application may be made to the court for an order that they be destroyed or forfeited to such person as the court may think fit.

(2) Provision shall be made by rules of court as to the service of notice on persons having an interest in the goods or material, and any such person is entitled—

(a) to appear in proceedings for an order under this section, whether or not he was served with notice, and

(b) to appeal against any order made, whether or not he appeared;

and an order shall not take effect until the end of the period within which notice of an appeal may be given or, if before the end of that period notice of appeal is duly given, until the final determination or abandonment of the proceedings on the appeal.

(3) Where there is more than one person interested in goods or material, the court shall make such order as it thinks just.

(4) References in this section to a person having an interest in goods or material include any person in whose favour an order could be made under this section or under sections 114, 204 or 231 of the Copyright, Designs and Patents Act 1988 (which make similar provision in relation to infringement of copyright, rights in performances and design right).

(5) Proceedings for an order under this section may be brought—

(a) in a county court in England, Wales and Northern Ireland, provided the value of the goods or material in question does not exceed the county court limit for actions in tort, and

(b) in a sheriff court in Scotland;

but this shall not be construed as affecting the jurisdiction of the High Court or, in Scotland, the Court of Session.

Enforcement of section 58A

58D.—The functions of a local weights and measures authority include the **A2–66** enforcement in their area of section 58A.

(2) The following provisions of the Trade Descriptions Act 1968 apply in relation to the enforcement of that section as in relation to the enforcement of that Act—

section 27 (power to make test purchases),
section 28 (power to enter premises and inspect and seize goods and documents),
section 29 (obstruction of authorised officers), and
section 33 (compensation for loss, &c. of goods seized under s.28).

(3) Subsection (1) above does not apply in relation to the enforcement of section 58A in Northern Ireland, but the functions of the Department of Economic Development include the enforcement of that section in Northern Ireland.

For that purpose the provisions of the Trade Descriptions Act 1968 specified in subsection (2) apply as if for the references to a local weights and measures authority and any officer of such an authority there were substituted references to that Department and any of its officers.

(4) Any enactment which authorises the disclosure of information for the purpose of facilitating the enforcement of the Trade Descriptions Act 1968 shall apply as if section 58A above were contained in that Act and as if the functions of any person in relation to the enforcement of that section were functions under that Act.

Sections 58A–58D were added by the Copyright, Designs and Patents Act 1988.

Offences and restraint of use of Royal Arms

Falsification of entries in register a misdemeanour

59.—(1) If any person makes or causes to be made a false entry in the register, **A2–67** or a writing falsely purporting to be a copy of an entry in the register, or produces or tenders or causes to be produced or tendered in evidence any such writing, knowing the entry or writing to be false, he shall be guilty of a misdemeanour.

(2) In the Isle of Man the punishment for an offence under this section shall be imprisonment for any term not exceeding two years, with or without hard labour and with or without a fine not exceeding one hundred pounds, at the discretion of the court.

See s.93 of the 1883 Act and s.66 of the 1905 Act.

Fine for falsely representing a trade mark as registered

A2–68   60.—(1) Any person who makes a representation—

(a) with respect to a mark not being a registered trade mark, to the effect that it is a registered trade mark; or

(b) with respect to a part of a registered trade mark not being a part separately registered as a trade mark, to the effect that it is so registered; or

(c) to the effect that a registered trade mark is registered in respect of any goods in respect of which it is not registered; or

(d) to the effect that the registration of a trade mark gives an exclusive right to the use thereof in any circumstances in which, having regard to limitations entered on the register, the registration does not give that right;

shall be liable on summary conviction to a fine not exceeding *five* [fifty] pounds.

(2) For the purposes of this section, the use in the United Kingdom in relation to a trade mark of the word "registered," or of any other word referring whether expressly or impliedly to registration, shall be deemed to import a reference to registration in the register, except—

(a) where that word is used in physical association with other words delineated in characters at least as large as those in which that word is delineated and indicating that the reference is to registration as a trade mark under the law of a country outside the United Kingdom, being a country under the law of which the registration referred to is in fact in force;

(b) where that word (being a word other than the word "registered") is of itself such as to indicate that the reference is to such registration as last aforesaid; or

(c) where that word is used in relation to a mark registered as a trade mark under the law of a country outside the United Kingdom and in relation to goods to be exported to that country.

(3) An offence under this section committed in the Isle of Man may be prosecuted, and any fine in respect thereof recovered, at the instance of any person aggrieved, in the manner in which offences punishable on summary conviction may for the time being be prosecuted.

The maximum fine was increased by the Criminal Justice Act 1967, Sched. 3.
See s.103 of the 1883 Act and s.67 of the 1905 Act.
Subs. (3). See s.112 of the 1883 Act and s.70 of the 1905 Act.

Restraint of use of Royal Arms, etc.

A2–69   61. If any person, without the authority of Her Majesty, uses, in connection with any trade, business, calling or profession, the Royal Arms (or arms so closely resembling the same as to be calculated to deceive) in such manner as to be calculated to lead to the belief that he is duly authorised so to use the Royal Arms, or if any person, without the authority of Her Majesty or of a member of the Royal Family, uses, in connection with any trade, business, calling or profession, any device, emblem or title in such manner as to be calculated to lead to the belief that he is employed by, or supplies goods to, **or provides services for** His Majesty or such member of the Royal Family, he may, at the suit of any person who is authorised to use such arms or such device, emblem or title, or is authorised by the Lord Chamberlain to take proceedings in that behalf, be restrained by injunction from continuing so to use the same:

Provided that nothing in this section shall be construed as affecting the right, if any, of the proprietor of a trade mark containing any such arms, device, emblem or title to continue to use such trade mark.

See s.68 of the 1905 Act. Amended, 1986 Act, Sched. 2, para. 4.

Miscellaneous

Change of form of trade connection not to be deemed to cause deception

62. The use of a registered trade mark in relation to goods between which and **A2–70** the person using it any form of connection in the course of trade subsists shall not be deemed to be likely to cause deception or confusion on the ground only that the trade mark has been, or is, used in relation to goods between which and that person or a predecessor in title of his a different form of connection in the course of trade subsisted or subsists.

Jointly owned trade marks

63. Where the relations between two or more persons interested in a trade **A2–71** mark are such that no one of them is entitled as between himself and the other or others of them to use it except—

    (a) on behalf of both or all of them, or
    (b) in relation to an article with which both or all of them are connected in the course of trade,

those persons may be registered as joint proprietors of the trade mark, and this Act shall have effect in relation to any rights to the use of the trade mark vested in those persons as if those rights had been vested in a single person.

Subject as aforesaid, nothing in this Act shall authorise the registration of two or more persons who use a trade mark independently, or propose so to use it, as joint proprietors thereof.

Trusts and equities

64.—(1) There shall not be entered in the register any notice of any trust **A2–72** express, implied or constructive, nor shall any such notice be receivable by the Registrar.

(2) Subject to the provisions of this Act, equities in respect of a trade mark may be enforced in like manner as in respect of any other personal property.

Subs. (1). See s.85 of the 1883 Act and s.5 of the 1905 Act.
Subs. (2). See s.87 of the 1883 Act. No express provision to this effect was contained in the 1905 Act.

Restrictions on importation of goods bearing infringing trade marks

64A.—(1) The person who is registered as the proprietor or registered user A2–73 of a trade mark in respect of any goods may give notice in writing to the Commissioners of Customs and Excise (in this section referred to as the Commissioners)—

(a) that he is the proprietor or registered user of that trade mark, and

(b) that such goods bearing the trade mark are expected to arrive in the United Kingdom at a time and place and by a consignment specified in the notice, and

(c) that the use within the United Kingdom of the trade mark in relation to the goods would infringe the proprietor's exclusive right to that use, and

(d) that he requests the Commissioners to treat the goods as prohibited goods.

(2) Where a notice has been given under this section in respect of any goods bearing a trade mark and has not been withdrawn and the requirements of any regulations made under this section are complied with, then, subject to the following provisions of this section, the importation into the United Kingdom of the goods shall, if the condition of paragraph (c) of the preceding subsection is satisfied, be deemed to be prohibited unless the importation is for the private and domestic use of the person importing the goods.

(3) The Commissioners may make regulations prescribing the form in which notices are to be given under this section, and requiring a person giving such a notice, either at the time of giving the notice or at the time when the goods in question are imported, or at both those times, to furnish the Commissioners with such evidence, and to comply with such other conditions (if any), as may be specified in the regulations, and any such regulations may include such incidental and supplementary provisions as the Commissioners consider expedient for the purposes of this section.

(4) Without prejudice to the generality of the preceding subsection, regulations made under that subsection may include provision for requiring a person who has given a notice under subsection (1) of this section, or a notice purporting to be a notice under that subsection,—

(a) to pay such fees in respect of the notice as may be prescribed by the regulations;

(b) to give to the Commissioners such security as may be so prescribed, in respect of any liability or expense which they may incur in consequence of the detention of any goods to which the notice relates, or in consequence of anything done in relation to goods so detained;

(c) whether any such security is given or not, to keep the Commissioners indemnified against any such liability or expense as is mentioned in the preceding paragraph.

(5) For the purposes of section 17 of the Customs and Excise Management Act 1979 (which relates to the disposal of duties) any fees paid in pursuance of regulations made under this section shall be treated as money collected on account of duties (whether of customs or excise) charged on imported goods.

(6) Regulations under subsection (3) of this section shall be made by statutory instrument, which shall be subject to annulment in pursuance of a resolution of either House of Parliament.

Added by s.17 of the Trade Descriptions Act 1968. Subs. (5) amended by Sched. 4 of the Customs and Excise Management Act 1979. S.16 of the Merchandise Marks Act 1887 contained a similar, but more general, provision.

Recognition of agents

A2–74   65. Where by this Act any act has to be done by or to any person in connection with a trade mark or proposed trade mark or any procedure relating thereto, the Act may under and in accordance with the rules, or in particular cases by special leave of the Board of Trade, be done by or to an agent of that person duly authorised in the prescribed manner.

See. s.55 of the 1905 Act.

Saving for jurisdiction of courts in Scotland, Northern Ireland and Isle of Man

66.—(1) The provisions of this Act conferring a special jurisdiction on the **A2–75** Court as defined by this Act shall not, except so far as the jurisdiction extends, affect the jurisdiction of any court in Scotland or Northern Ireland in any proceedings relating to trade marks; and with reference to any such proceedings in Scotland the expression "the Court" means the Court of Session; and with reference to any such proceedings in Northern Ireland the expression "the Court" means the High Court of Justice in Northern Ireland.

(2) Nothing in this Act shall affect the jurisdiction of the courts in the Isle of Man in proceedings for infringement or in any action or proceedings respecting a trade mark competent to those courts.

Subs. (1). See s.111 of the 1883 Act and s.69 of the 1905 Act.
Subs. (2). See s.112 of the 1883 Act and s.70 of the 1905 Act.

Exercise of powers of Board of Trade

67. *All things required or authorised under this Act to be done by, to or before the* **A2–76** *Board of Trade may be done by, to or before the President or a secretary or an under-secretary or an assistant secretary of the Board or any person authorised in that behalf by the President of the Board.*

Repealed by Sched. 4 of the Industrial Expansion Act 1968. S. 14 of that Act contains an equivalent general provision.
See s.102*a*(1) of the 1883 Act, as amended, and s.58 of the 1905 Act.

Supplemental

Interpretation

68.—(1) In this Act, unless the context otherwise requires, the following **A2–77** expressions have the meanings hereby assigned to them respectively, that is to say—

"the appointed day" has the meaning assigned to it by section seventy-one of this Act;

"assignment" means assignment by act of the parties concerned;

"the Court" means (subject to provisions relating to Scotland, Northern Ireland or the Isle of Man) Her Majesty's High Court of Justice in England;

"limitations" means any limitations of the exclusive right to the use of a trade mark given by the registration of a person as proprietor thereof, including limitations of that right as to mode of use, as to use in relation to goods to be sold, or otherwise traded in, in any place within the United Kingdom, or as to use in relation to goods to be exported to any market outside the United Kingdom;

"mark" includes a device, brand, heading, label, ticket, name, signature, word, letter, numeral, or any combination thereof;

"permitted use" has the meaning assigned to it by subsection (1) of section twenty-eight of this Act;

"prescribed" means [subject to provisions relating to Northern Ireland] in relation to proceedings before the Court, prescribed by rules of court, and, in other cases, prescribed by this Act or the rules;

"the register" means the register of trade marks kept under this Act;

"registered trade mark" means a trade mark that is actually on the register;

"registered user" means a person who is for the time being registered as such under section twenty-eight of this Act;

"the Registrar" means the Comptroller-General of Patents, Designs and Trade Marks;

"the rules" means rules made by the Board of Trade under section thirty-six or section forty of this Act;

"trade mark" means, except in relation to a certification trade mark, a mark used or proposed to be used in relation to goods for the purpose of indicating, or so as to indicate, a connection in the course of trade between the goods and some person having the right either as proprietor or as registered user to use the mark, whether with or without any indication of the identity of that person, and means, in relation to a certification trade mark, a mark registered or deemed to have been registered under section thirty-seven of this Act;

"transmission" means transmission by operation of law, devolution on the personal representative of a deceased person, and any other mode of transfer not being assignment;

"United Kingdom" includes the Isle of Man.

(2) References in this Act to the use of a mark shall be construed as references to the use of a printed or other visual representation of the mark, and references therein to the use of a mark in relation to goods shall be construed as references to the use thereof upon, or in physical or other relation to, goods.

(2A) For the purposes of this Act goods and services are associated with each other if it is likely that those goods might be sold or otherwise traded in and those services might be provided by the same business, and so with descriptions of goods and descriptions of services.

(2B) Reference in this Act to a near resemblance of marks are references to a resemblance so near as to be likely to deceive or cause confusion.

(3) In the application of this Act to Scotland, the expressions "injunction," "plaintiff" and "defendant" mean respectively "interdict," "pursuer" and "defender."

Amended by Sched. 5 to the Judicature (Northern Ireland) Act 1978.
Subs. (1). S.117 of the 1883 Act and s.3 of the 1905 Act were the earlier definition sections.
Subs. (2A) and (2B) added by 1984 Act, s.1(5)(*b*).

Transitional provisions

A2–78   69. The transitional provisions set out in the Third Schedule to this Act shall have effect with respect to the matters therein mentioned respectively.

Repeal and savings

A2–79   70.—(1) *The enactments set out in the Fourth Schedule to this Act are hereby repealed to the extent specified in the third column of that Schedule.*

(2) Nothing in this Act shall affect any order, rule, regulation or requirement made, table of fees or certificate issued, notice, decision, determination, direction or approval given, application made, or thing done, under any enactment repealed by this Act; and every such order, rule, regulation, requirement, table of fees, certificate, notice, decision, determination, direction, approval, application or thing shall, if in force at the commencement of this Act, continue in force and shall, so far as it could have been made, issued, given or done under this Act, have effect as if made, issued given or done under the corresponding enactment of this Act.

(3) Any document referring to any enactment repealed by this Act shall be construed as referring to the corresponding enactment of this Act.

(4) Nothing in this section shall be taken to prejudice the provisions of section thirty-eight of the Interpretation Act 1889.

Subs. (1) repealed but not so as to revive the repealed provisions by Statute Law Revision Act 1950, Sched. I.

Section 38 of the Interpretation Act has been replaced by s.16 of the Interpretation Act 1978.

Short title, commencement and extent

71.—(1) This Act may be cited as the Trade Marks Act 1938.   **A2–80**

(2) *This Act shall come into operation on the date fixed by order made under subsection (5) of section thirty-three of the Trade Marks (Amendment) Act 1937, for the coming into operation of that Act (in this Act referred to as "the appointed day"), immediately after the coming into operation of that Act.*

(3) It is hereby declared that this Act extends to Northern Ireland.

(4) This Act shall extend to the Isle of Man.

Subs. (2) repealed but the Act to continue in force, Statute Law Revision Act 1950, Sched. I.

SCHEDULES

FIRST SCHEDULE   Section 37

CERTIFICATION TRADE MARKS

1.—(1) An application for the registration of a mark under section thirty-seven of this **A2–81** Act must be made to the Registrar in writing in the prescribed manner by the person proposed to be registered as the proprietor thereof.

(2) The provisions of subsection (2) and of subsections (4) to (7) of section seventeen of this Act shall have effect in relation to an application under the said section thirty-seven as they have effect in relation to an application under subsection (1) of the said section seventeen, except that for references therein to acceptance of an application there shall be substituted references to authorisation to proceed with the application.

(3) In dealing under the said provisions with an application under the said section thirty-seven the tribunal shall have regard to the like considerations, so far as relevant, as if the application were an application under section seventeen of this Act and to any other considerations (not being matters within the competence of the Board of Trade under subparagraph (5) of this paragraph) relevant to applications under the said section thirty-seven, including the desirability of securing that a certification trade mark shall comprise some indication that it is such a trade mark.

(4) An applicant for the registration of a mark under the said section thirty-seven shall transmit to the Registrar draft regulations for governing the use thereof at such time before the decision of the Registrar on the application as he may require in order to enable him to consider the draft, and the Registrar shall report thereon to the Board of Trade.

(5) When authorisation to proceed with an application has been given, the Board of Trade shall consider the application with regard to the following matters, that is to say:

(a) whether the applicant is competent to certify the goods in respect of which the mark is to be registered;

(b) whether the draft regulations are satisfactory; and

(c) whether in all the circumstances the registration applied for would be to the public advantage;

and may either—

(i) direct that the application shall not be accepted; or

(ii) direct the Registrar to accept the application, and approve the regulations, either without modification and unconditionally or subject to any conditions or limitations, or to any amendments or modifications of the application or of the regulations, which they think requisite having regard to any of the matters aforesaid;

but, except in the case of a direction for acceptance and approval without modification and unconditionally, the Board shall not decide the matter without giving the applicant an opportunity of being heard:

Provided that the Board may, at the request of the applicant made with the concurrence of the Registrar, consider the application with regard to any of the matters aforesaid before authorisation to proceed with the application has been given, so however that the Board shall be at liberty to reconsider any matter on which they have given a decision under this proviso if any amendment or modification is thereafter made in the application or in the draft regulations.

2.—(1) When an application has been accepted, the Registrar shall, as soon as may be after such acceptance, cause the application as accepted to be advertised in the prescribed manner, and the provisions of subsections (2) to (11) of section eighteen of this Act shall have effect in relation to the registration of the mark as if the application had been an application under section seventeen of this Act:

Provided that, in deciding under the said provisions, the tribunal shall have regard only to the considerations referred to in subparagraph (3) of the last foregoing paragraph, and a decision under the said provisions in favour of the applicant shall be conditional on the determination in his favour by the Board of Trade under subparagraph (2) of this paragraph of any opposition relating to any of the matters referred to in subparagraph (5) of the last foregoing paragraph.

(2) When notice of opposition is given relating to any of the matters referred to in subparagraph (5) of the last foregoing paragraph, the Board of Trade shall, after hearing the parties, if so required, and considering any evidence, decide whether, and subject to what conditions or limitations, or amendments or modifications of the application or of the regulations, if any, registration is, having regard to those matters, to be permitted.

3.—(1) The regulations deposited in respect of a certification trade mark may, on the application of the registered proprietor, be altered by the Registrar, with the consent of the Board of Trade.

(2) The Board of Trade may cause an application for their consent to be advertised in any case where it appears to the Board that it is expedient to so do, and, where the Board cause an application to be advertised, if within the prescribed time from the date of the advertisement any person gives notice to the Board of opposition to the application, the Board shall not decide the matter without giving the parties an opportunity of being heard.

4.—(1) The Board of Trade may, on the application in the prescribed manner of any person aggrieved, or on the application of the Registrar, make such order as they think fit for expunging or varying any entry in the register relating to a certification trade mark, or for varying the deposited regulations, on the ground—

    (a) that the proprietor is no longer competent, in the case of any of the goods in respect of which the trade mark is registered, to certify those goods;

    (b) that the proprietor has failed to observe a provision of the deposited regulations to be observed on his part;

    (c) that it is no longer to the public advantage that the trade mark should be registered; or

    (d) that it is requisite for the public advantage that, if the trade mark remains registered, the regulations should be varied;

and neither the Court nor the Registrar shall have any jurisdiction to make an order under section thirty-two of this Act on any of those grounds.

(2) The Registrar shall rectify the register and the deposited regulations in such manner as may be requisite for giving effect to an order made under the foregoing subparagraph.

5. Notwithstanding anything in section forty-four of this Act, the Registrar shall not have any jurisdiction to award costs to or against any party on an appeal to him against a refusal of the proprietor of a certification trade mark to certify goods or to authorise the use of the trade mark.

6. The following provisions of this Act shall not have effect in relation to a certification trade mark, that is to say, section four, section six, section nine, sections seventeen and eighteen (except as expressly applied by this Schedule), subsections (4) to (8) of section twenty-two, sections twenty-six to twenty-nine, section sixty-two, and any provisions the operation of which is limited by the terms thereof to registration in Part B of the Register.

SECOND SCHEDULE   Section 38

SHEFFIELD MARKS

A2–82   1. The Cutlers' Company shall continue to keep at Sheffield the register of trade marks (in this Schedule called "the Sheffield register") kept by them immediately before the appointed day, and, save as otherwise provided by this Schedule, the Sheffield register shall for all purposes form part of the register.

2. An application by a person carrying on business in Hallamshire, or within six miles thereof, for the registration of a trade mark in respect of metal goods may be made either to the Registrar, or to the Cutlers' Company, at the option of the applicant.

3. An application for the registration of a trade mark made to the Cutlers' Company shall be notified to the Registrar in the prescribed manner, and the Cutlers' Company shall not proceed with such an application until authorised so to do by the Registrar.

4. The Registrar shall consider an application notified to him as aforesaid and shall either authorise the Cutlers' Company to proceed therewith or, if it appears to him that there is any objection to the application, shall give notice of his objection to the Cutlers' Company, who shall communicate it to the applicant.

5. Within the prescribed time after receipt of a notice of objection under the last foregoing paragraph, the applicant may submit to the Cutlers' Company either orally or in writing arguments against, or proposals for meeting, the objection, and the Cutlers' Company shall notify to the Registrar any arguments or proposals so submitted to them together with any observations that they may desire to make thereon.

6. The Registrar shall consider any arguments, proposals or observations notified to him as aforesaid and shall, if so required by an applicant who has submitted arguments or proposals as aforesaid, give the applicant an opportunity of being heard by him, and may refuse authorisation to proceed with the application or may authorise the Cutlers' Company to proceed therewith either without modification and unconditionally or subject to such conditions, amendments or modifications, or to such limitations, if any, as he may think right.

7. Where the Registrar refuses authorisation to proceed with an application, or authorises the Cutlers' Company to proceed therewith subject as aforesaid, the provisions of subsections (4) to (6) of section seventeen of this Act shall have effect in relation to the refusal or conditional authorisation as they have effect in relation to a refusal to accept, or a conditional acceptance of, an application, except that for references therein to acceptance of the application there shall be substituted references to authorisation to the Cutlers' Company to proceed with the application.

8. Upon the registration of a trade mark in the Sheffield register, the Cutlers' Company shall give notice thereof to the Registrar, who shall thereupon enter the trade mark in the register, and such registration shall bear date as of the day of the application to the Cutlers' Company and have the same effect as if the application had been made to the Registrar on that day.

9. The provisions of this Act and of the rules with respect to the registration of trade marks, and all matters relating thereto, shall, subject to the provisions of this Schedule (and notwithstanding anything in any Act relating to the Cutlers' Company), apply to the registration of trade marks in respect of metal goods by the Cutlers' Company and to all matters relating thereto, and this Act and the rules shall, so far as applicable, be construed accordingly with the substitution of the Cutlers' Company, the office of the Cutlers' Company, and the Sheffield register, for the Registrar, the Patent Office, and the register respectively, and notice of every entry, cancellation, or correction made in the Sheffield register shall be given to the Registrar by the Cutlers' Company:

Provided that anything that by virtue of this Schedule is required or authorised to be done by, before or in relation to the Cutlers' Company or at their office may, with the consent of the party or parties concerned, be done by, before or in relation to the Registrar or at the Patent Office, as the case may be.

10. When the Registrar receives an application for the registration of a trade mark in respect of metal goods, he shall in the prescribed manner notify the application and proceedings thereon to the Cutlers' Company.

11. Any person aggrieved by a decision of the Cutlers' Company in respect of anything done or omitted under this Act may, in the prescribed manner, appeal to the Court or, in a case in which the decision had been a decision of the Registrar, the person aggrieved would have had an option under this Act of appealing to the Board of Trade, to the Court or the Board at the option of the appellant.

12.—(1) For the purposes of this Schedule the expression "metal goods" means all metals, whether wrought, unwrought, or partly wrought, and all goods which are comprised in any of such classes as may be prescribed as being classes which refer predominantly to metal goods, and are goods composed wholly or principally of any metal; and for the purpose of determining whether any goods are goods principally of any metal regard shall be had to the importance and nature of the metal part or parts of the goods having regard to the purposes for which the goods are adapted.

(2) Any question arising in connection with an application made to the Cutlers' Company for the registration of a trade mark as to whether the goods in respect of which

the trade mark is proposed to be registered are metal goods, shall be referred to and determined by the Registrar, whose decision shall be final.

(3) The validity of the registration by the Cutlers' Company of a trade mark shall not be questioned on the ground only that the goods in respect of which it is so registered are not metal goods.

13. A certificate purporting to be under the hand of the master of the Cutlers' Company as to any entry, matter or thing that the Cutlers' Company are authorised by this Schedule or the rules to make or do shall be prima facie evidence of the entry having been made and of the contents thereof and of the matter or thing having been done or not done.

THIRD SCHEDULE   Section 69

TRANSITIONAL PROVISIONS

Validity of registrations under previous Acts

A2–83
1.—(1) Subject to the provisions of this paragraph and of section thirteen of this Act, the validity of the original entry of a trade mark on the register of trade marks existing at the commencement of the Trade Marks Act 1905, or on any of the registers of trade marks kept under previous Acts that were deemed part of the same record as the last-mentioned register, shall be determined in accordance with the Acts in force at the date of such entry, and any such trade mark shall retain its original date, but for all other purposes it shall be deemed to have been registered under the Trade Marks Act 1905.

(2) No trade mark which was on the register at the commencement of the Trade Marks Act 1905, and which under that Act was then a registrable trade mark, shall be removed from the register on the ground that it was not registrable under the Acts in force at the date of its registration.

(3) No trade mark which was on the register at the commencement of the Trade Marks (Amendment) Act 1937, and which, having regard to any amendment by that Act of the Trade Marks Act 1905, or of the Trade Marks Act 1919, whether as respects limitations that might be imposed on registration or as respects any other matter, was then a registrable trade mark under the Trade Marks Acts 1905 to 1937, shall be removed from the register on the ground that it was not registrable under the Acts in force at the date of its registration.

(4) Nothing in the Trade Marks (Amendment) Act 1937, shall be taken to have invalidated the original registration of a trade mark that immediately before the commencement of that Act was validly on the register.

(5) Nothing in section thirty-six of the Trade Marks Act 1905, or in the Trade Marks (Amendment) Act 1937, shall be construed as having subjected any person to any liability in respect of any act or thing done before the commencement of those Acts respectively to which he would not have been subject under the Acts then in force.

Assignments and transmissions (before appointed day) giving exclusive rights in different places in the United Kingdom

A2–84
2.—(1) The validity of an assignment or transmission of a trade mark effected or claimed to have been effected before the appointed day, in any such case as is mentioned in subsection (6) of section twenty-two of this Act, shall be determined as if the provisions contained in subsections (1) to (5) of that section had not been enacted:

Provided that, on application made in the prescribed manner within two years from the commencement of this Act, by a person who claims that an assignment or transmission of a registered trade mark to him or to a predecessor in title of his has so been effected, the Registrar shall have the like jurisdiction as under the proviso to subsection (6) of section twenty-two of this Act, and an assignment or transmission approved by him shall not be deemed to have been invalid on the ground of the subsistence of such rights as are mentioned in the said subsection (6) or on the ground that the assignment or transmission was effected otherwise than in connection with the goodwill of a business or was effected in respect of some (but not all) of the goods in respect of which the trade mark was registered, if application for the registration under section twenty-five of this Act of the title of the person becoming entitled is made within six months from the date on which the approval is given, or was made before that date.

(2) Any decision of the Registrar under this paragraph shall be subject to appeal to the Court.

Saving as to retrospective provisions relating to assignments and transmissions

A2–85
3. The retrospective provisions contained in section twenty-two of this Act, and in the last foregoing paragraph, shall have effect without prejudice to any determination of a competent tribunal that was made before the appointed day, or to the determination of

any appeal from a determination so made, or to any title acquired for valuable consideration before the appointed day.

Association of Trade Marks assignable or transmissible as a whole only under the Trade Marks Act 1919
4. Where immediately before the appointed day a trade mark was registered in Part B of **A2–86** the register subject to a condition rendering it assignable or transmissible only as a whole with another trade mark registered in the name of the same proprietor or with two or more other trade marks so registered, and not separately, the trade marks shall be deemed to be associated trade marks, and the entries in the register relating thereto may be amended accordingly.

Previous use of a trade mark by person becoming registered user on application made within one year of appointed day
5. Where a person is registered as a registered user of a trade mark on an application **A2–87** made within one year from the commencement of this Act, subsection (2) of section twenty-eight of this Act shall have effect in relation to any previous use (whether before or after the commencement of this Act) of the trade mark by that person, being use in relation to the goods in respect of which he is registered and, where he is registered subject to conditions or restrictions, being use such as to comply substantially therewith, as if such previous use had been permitted use.

Use of trade mark for export trade before appointed day
6. Section thirty-one of this Act shall be deemed to have had effect in relation to an act **A2–88** done before the appointed day as it has effect in relation to an act done after the commencement of this Act, without prejudice, however, to any determination of a competent tribunal which was made before the appointed day, or to the determination of any appeal from a determination so made.

Trade marks registered under section sixty-two of the Trade Marks Act 1905, to be deemed to have been registered under section thirty-seven of this Act
7. Section thirty-seven of this Act shall have effect, in relation to a trade mark that **A2–89** immediately before the appointed day was on the register by virtue of section sixty-two of the Trade Marks Act 1905, as if the said section thirty-seven had been in force at the date of the registration of the trade mark and it had been registered under that section, subject however to the following modifications, that is to say:
   (a) the proviso to subsection (1) of the said section thirty-seven shall not apply;
   (b) in a case in which regulations for governing the use of the trade mark are deposited at the Patent Office at the commencement of this Act, those regulations shall be deemed to have been deposited under the said section thirty-seven;
   (c) in a case in which no such regulations are deposited at the commencement of this Act, the proprietor shall be at liberty, or may be required by the Board of Trade as a condition of the continuance of the registration, to deposit at any time thereafter such regulations as the Board may permit or require; and
   (d) in a case in which no such regulations are for the time being deposited, the said section thirty-seven shall have effect as if references therein, and in the First Schedule to this Act, to the regulations had been omitted.

Cotton marks registered before appointed day
8. No registration as of a date before the appointed day of a cotton mark as defined in **A2–90** section sixty-four of the Trade Marks Act 1905, in respect of cotton piece goods or cotton yarn shall give any exclusive right to the use of any letter, numeral, line heading, or any combination thereof.

FOURTH SCHEDULE

ENACTMENTS REPEALED

A2–91

Session and Chapter	Short Title	Extent of Repeal
5 Edw. 7, c. 15	The Trade Marks Act 1905	The whole Act, so far as not already repealed
9 & 10 Geo. 5, c. 79	The Trade Marks Act 1919	The whole Act, so far as not already repealed
1 Edw. 8 & 1 Geo. 6, c. 49	The Trade Marks (Amendment) Act 1937	The whole Act

This Schedule was repealed but not so far as to revive the Acts repealed by it, Statute Law Revision Act 1950.

Part II

REGISTRY MATERIALS

APPENDIX 3

The Trade Marks Rules 2000

S.I. 2000 No. 136

ARRANGEMENT OF RULES

A3–01

Preliminary

APPENDIX 3

Renewal and restoration

Revocation, invalidation and rectification

Case Management and pre-hearing review

The register

Change of classification

Request for information, inspection of documents and confidentiality

Agents

Decision of registrar, evidence and costs

Appeals

The Secretary of State, in exercise of the powers conferred upon him by sections 4(4), 13(2), 25(1), (5) and (6), 34(1), 35(5), 38(1) and (2), 39(3), 40(4), 41(1) and (3), 43(2), (3), (5) and (6), 44(3), 45(2), 63(2) and (3), 64(4), 65, 66 (2), 67(1) and (2), 68(1) and (3), 69, 76(1), 78, 80(3), 81, 82 and 88 of, paragraph 6(2) of Schedule 1 to, paragraph 7(2) of Schedule 2 to, and paragraphs 10(2), 12 and 14(5) of Schedule 3 to, the Trade Marks Act 1994, after consultation with the Council on Tribunals pursuant to section 8(1) of the Tribunals and Inquiries Act 1992, hereby makes the following Rules:-

Preliminary

Citation and commencement

1. These Rules may be cited as the Trade Marks Rules 2000 and shall come **A3–02** into force on 17th February 2000.

Interpretation

2.—(1) In these Rules, unless the context otherwise requires— **A3–03**
"the Act" means the Trade Marks Act 1994;
"the Journal" means the Trade Marks Journal published in accordance with rule 71 below;
"the Office" means the Patent Office;
"old law" means the Trade Marks Act 1938 (as amended) and any rules made thereunder existing immediately before the commencement of the Act;
"proprietor" means the person registered as the proprietor of the trade mark;
"publish" means publish in the Journal;
"send" includes give;
"specification" means the statement of goods or services in respect of which a trade mark is registered or proposed to be registered;
"United Kingdom" includes the Isle of Man.
(2) In these Rules, except where otherwise indicated, a reference to a section is a reference to that section in the Act, a reference to a rule is a reference to that

rule in these Rules, a reference to a Schedule is a reference to that Schedule to these Rules and a reference to a form is a reference to that form as published by the registrar under rule 3 below.

(3) In these Rules references to the filing of any application, notice or other document, unless the contrary intention appears, are to be construed as references to its being delivered to the registrar at the Office.

Forms and directions of the registrar under s. 66

A3–04 3.—(1) Any forms required by the registrar to be used for the purpose of registration of a trade mark or any other proceedings before her under the Act pursuant to section 66 and any directions with respect to their use shall be published and any amendment or modification of a form or of the directions with respect to its use shall be published.

(2) A requirement under this rule to use a form as published is satisfied by the use either of a replica of that form or of a form which is acceptable to the registrar and contains the information required by the form as published and complies with any directions as to the use of such a form.

Requirement as to fees

A3–05 4.—(1) The fees to be paid in respect of any application, registration or any other matter under the Act and these Rules shall be those (if any) prescribed in relation to such matter by rules under section 79 (fees).

(2) Any form required to be filed with the registrar in respect of any specified matter shall be subject to the payment of the fee (if any) prescribed in respect of that matter by those rules.

Application for registration

Applications for registration; s. 32 (Form TM3)

A3–06 5.—(1) An application for the registration of a trade mark shall be filed on Form TM3 and shall be subject to the payment of the application fee and such class fees as may be appropriate.

(2) An application for registration of a three-dimensional mark shall not be treated as such unless the application contains a statement to that effect.

(3) Where colour is claimed as an element of the trade mark, it shall not be treated as such unless the application contains a statement to that effect and specifies the colour.

(4) An application to register a trade mark which is or includes a word shall be treated as an application to register that word in the graphical form shown in the application, unless the applicant includes a statement that the application is for registration of the word without regard to its graphical form.

Claim to priority; ss. 35 & 36

A3–07 6.—(1) Where a right to priority is claimed by reason of an application for protection of a trade mark duly filed in a Convention country under section 35 or in another country or territory in respect of which provision corresponding to that made by section 35 is made under section 36, particulars of that claim shall be included in the application for registration under rule 5 above and, where no certificate as is referred to in paragraph (2) below is filed with the application, such particulars shall include the country or countries and the date or dates of filing.

(2) Unless it has been filed at the time of the filing of the application for registration, there shall be filed, within three months of the filing of the

application under rule 5, a certificate by the registering or other competent authority of that country certifying, or verifying to the satisfaction of the registrar, the date of the filing of the application, the country or registering or competent authority, the representation of the mark, and the goods or services covered by the application.

Classification of goods and services; s. 34

7.—(1) For the purposes of trade mark registrations in respect of goods dated **A3–08** before 27th July 1938, goods are classified in accordance with Schedule 2 to these Rules, except where a specification has been converted, whether under the old law or under rule 46 below, to Schedule 3.

(2) For the purposes of trade mark registrations in respect of goods dated on or after 27th July 1938 and for the purposes of any registrations dated before that date in respect of which the specifications were converted under the old law, and for the purposes of trade mark registrations in respect of services, goods and services are classified in accordance with Schedule 3, which sets out the current version of the classes of the International Classification of Goods and Services.

Application may relate to more than one class and shall specify the class (Form TM3A)

8.—(1) An application may be made in more than one class of Schedule 3.   **A3–09**

(2) Every application shall specify the class in Schedule 3 to which it relates and shall list the goods or services appropriate to that class.

(3) If the application relates to more than one class in Schedule 3 the specification contained in it shall set out the classes in consecutive numerical order.

(4) If the specification contained in the application lists items by reference to a class in Schedule 3 in which they do not fall, the applicant may request, by filing Form TM3A, that his application be amended to include the appropriate class for those items, and upon the payment of such class fee as may be appropriate the registrar shall amend his application accordingly.

Prohibition on registration of mark consisting of arms; s. 4

9. Where a representation of any arms or insignia as is referred to in section **A3–10** 4(4) appears in a mark, the registrar shall refuse to accept an application for the registration of the mark unless satisfied that the consent of the person entitled to the arms has been obtained.

Address for service (Form TM33)

10.—(1) For the purposes of any proceedings before the registrar under these **A3–11** Rules or any appeal from a decision of the registrar under the Act or these Rules, an address for service in the United Kingdom shall be filed by—

(a) every applicant for the registration of a trade mark;
(b) every person opposing an application for registration of a trade mark;
(c) every applicant applying to the registrar under section 46 for the revocation of the registration of a trade mark, under section 47 for the invalidation of the registration of a trade mark, or under section 64 for the rectification of the register;
(d) every person granted leave to intervene under rule 35 (the intervener); and
(e) every proprietor of a registered trade mark which is the subject of an application to the registrar for the revocation, invalidation or rectification of the registration of the mark.

(2) The address for service of an applicant for registration of a trade mark shall upon registration of the mark be deemed to be the address for service of the

registered proprietor, subject to any filing to the contrary under paragraph (1) above or rule 44(2) below.

(3) In any case in which an address for service is filed at the same time as the filing of a form required by the registrar under rule 3 which requires the furnishing of an address for service, the address shall be filed on that form and in any other case it shall be filed on Form TM33.

(4) Anything sent to any applicant, opponent, intervener or registered proprietor at his address for service shall be deemed to be properly sent; and the registrar may, where no address for service is filed, treat as the address for service of the person concerned his trade or business address in the United Kingdom, if any.

(5) An address for service in the United Kingdom may be filed at any time by the proprietor of a registered trade mark and by any person having an interest in or charge on a registered trade mark which has been registered under rule 40.

(6) Where an address for service is not filed as required by paragraph (1) above, the registrar shall send the person concerned notice to file an address for service within two months of the date of the notice and if that person fails to do so—

    (a) in the case of an applicant as is referred to in sub-paragraph (a) or (c), the application shall be treated as abandoned;

    (b) in the case of a person as is referred to in sub-paragraph (b) or (d), he shall be deemed to have withdrawn from the proceedings; and

    (c) in the case of the proprietor referred to in sub-paragraph (e), he shall not be permitted to take part in any proceedings.

Deficiencies in application; s. 32

A3–12   **11.** Where an application for registration of a trade mark does not satisfy the requirements of section 32(2), (3) or (4) or rule 5(1) or 8(2), the registrar shall send notice thereof to the applicant to remedy the deficiencies or, in the case of section 32(4), the default of payment and if within two months of the date of the notice the applicant—

    (a) fails to remedy any deficiency notified to him in respect of section 32 (2), the application shall be deemed never to have been made; or

    (b) fails to remedy any deficiency notified to him in respect of section 32 (3) or rule 5(1) or 8(2) or fails to make payment as required by section 32 (4) the application shall be treated as abandoned.

Publication, observations, oppositions and registration

Publication of application for registration; s. 38(1)

A3–13   **12.** An application which has been accepted for registration shall be published.

Opposition proceedings; s. 38(2) (Forms TM7, TM8 & TM9c)

A3–14   **13.**—(1) Notice of opposition to the registration of a trade mark shall be filed on Form TM7 within three months of the date on which the application was published under rule 12, and shall include a statement of the grounds of opposition; the registrar shall send a copy of the notice and the statement to the applicant.

(2) Where the opposition is based on an earlier trade mark there shall be included in the notice:

    (a) a representation of that mark; and

    (b) if registered, the classes in respect of which that mark is registered; and

    (c) the goods and services in respect of which that mark is registered, or if not registered, used; and

    (d) where the earlier mark is defined in section 6(1)(a) and (b),

        (i) the application and/or registration number(s) of that mark, and

        (ii) except in the case of a mark the subject of an application not yet published, the number of the publication in which it was published.

(3) Subject to paragraphs (4) and (5) below, within three months of the date on which a copy of the notice and statement is sent by the registrar to the applicant, the applicant may file a counter-statement, in conjunction with notice of the same on Form TM8; where such a notice and counter-statement are filed within the prescribed period, the registrar shall send a copy of the Form TM8 and the counter-statement to the person opposing the application.

(4) Subject to paragraph (5), at any time before the expiry of the period prescribed in paragraph (3) above for filing of Form TM8 by the applicant the registrar may, on request, grant an extension of three months to that period where such request is filed on Form TM9c and with the agreement of both the applicant and the opposing party (the "cooling off period"); the registrar may, on request, extend the cooling off period for a further three months where such request is filed on Form TM9c and with the agreement of both the applicant and the opposing party.

(5) Within one month after the expiry of the cooling off period the applicant may file a counter-statement, in conjunction with notice of the same on Form TM8; where such a notice and counter-statement are filed within that one month period, the registrar shall send a copy of the Form TM8 and the counter-statement to the person opposing the application.

(6) Where a notice and counter-statement are not filed by the applicant within the period prescribed by paragraph (3) or paragraph (5) as appropriate, he shall be deemed to have withdrawn his application for registration.

(7) Within three months of the date upon which a copy of the counter-statement is sent by the registrar to the person opposing the registration, that person may file such evidence as he may consider necessary to adduce in support of his grounds of opposition and shall send a copy thereof to the applicant.

(8) If the person opposing the registration files no evidence under paragraph (7) above in support of his grounds of opposition, he shall, unless the registrar otherwise directs, be deemed to have withdrawn his opposition.

(9) If the person opposing the registration files evidence under paragraph (7) above or the registrar otherwise directs under paragraph (8) above, the applicant who has filed a notice and counter-statement under paragraph (3) or paragraph (5) as appropriate above may, within three months of the date on which either a copy of the evidence or a copy of the direction is sent to him, file such evidence as he may consider necessary to adduce in support of his application for registration and shall send a copy thereof to the person opposing the application.

(10) Within three months of the date upon which a copy of the applicant's evidence is sent to him under paragraph (9) above, the person opposing the application may file evidence in reply which shall be confined to matters strictly in reply to the applicant's evidence, and shall send a copy thereof to the applicant.

(11) No further evidence may be filed, except that, in relation to any proceedings before her, the registrar may at any time if she thinks fit give leave to either party to file such evidence upon such terms as she may think fit.

(12) Upon completion of the evidence the registrar shall request the parties to state by notice to her in writing whether they wish to be heard; if any party requests to be heard the registrar shall send to the parties notice of a date for the hearing.

Decision of registrar in opposition proceedings

A3–15   **14.**—(1) When the registrar has made a decision on the acceptability of an application for registration following the procedure under rule 13, she shall send the applicant and the person opposing the application written notice of it, stating the reasons for her decision.

(2) For the purpose of any appeal against the registrar's decision the date of the decision shall be the date when notice of the decision is sent under paragraph (1) above.

Observations on application to be sent to applicant; s. 38(3)

A3–16   **15.** The registrar shall send to the applicant a copy of any documents containing observations made under section 38(3).

Publication of registration; s. 40

A3–17   **16.** On the registration of the trade mark the registrar shall publish the registration, specifying the date upon which the trade mark was entered in the register.

Amendment of application

Amendment of application; s. 39 (Form TM21)

A3–18   **17.** A request for an amendment of an application to correct an error or to change the name or address of the applicant or in respect of any amendment requested after publication of the application shall be made on Form TM21.

Amendment of application after publication; s. 39 (Form TM7)

A3–19   **18.**—(1) Where, pursuant to section 39, a request is made for amendment of an application which has been published and the amendment affects the representation of the trade mark or the goods or services covered by the application, the amendment or a statement of the effect of the amendment shall also be published.

(2) Notice of opposition to the amendment shall be filed on Form TM7 within one month of the date on which the application as amended was published under paragraph (1) above, and shall include a statement of the grounds of objection and, in particular, how the amendments would be contrary to section 39(2).

(3) The provisions of rule 13 shall apply to proceedings relating to the opposition to the amendment of the application as they apply to proceedings relating to opposition to the registration of a trade mark.

Division, merger and series of marks

Division of application; s. 41 (Form TM12)

A3–20   **19.**—(1) At any time before registration an applicant may send to the registrar a request on Form TM12 for a division of his application for registration (the original application) into two or more separate applications (divisional applications), indicating for each division the specification of goods or services; each divisional application shall be treated as a separate application for registration with the same filing date as the original application.

(2) Where the request to divide an application is sent after publication of the application, any objections in respect of, or opposition to, the original application

shall be taken to apply to each divisional application and shall be proceeded with accordingly.

(3) Upon division of an original application in respect of which notice has been given to the registrar of particulars relating to the grant of a licence, or a security interest or any right in or under it, the notice and the particulars shall be deemed to apply in relation to each of the applications into which the original application has been divided.

Merger of separate applications or registrations; s. 41 (Form TM17)

20.—(1) An applicant who has made separate applications for registration of a **A3–21** mark may, at any time before preparations for the publication of any of the applications have been completed by the Office, request the registrar on Form TM17 to merge the separate applications into a single application.

(2) The registrar shall, if satisfied that all the applications which are the subject of the request for merger—

    (a) are in respect of the same trade mark,
    (b) bear the same date of application, and
    (c) are, at the time of the request, in the name of the same person, merge them into a single application.

(3) The proprietor of two or more registrations of a trade mark may request the registrar on Form TM17 to merge them into a single registration; and the registrar shall, if satisfied that the registrations are in respect of the same trade mark, merge them into a single registration.

(4) Where any registration of a trade mark to be merged under paragraph (3) above is subject to a disclaimer or limitation, the merged registration shall also be restricted accordingly.

(5) Where any registration of a trade mark to be merged under paragraph (3) above has had registered in relation to it particulars relating to the grant of a licence or a security interest or any right in or under it, or of any memorandum or statement of the effect of a memorandum, the registrar shall enter in the register the same particulars in relation to the merged registration.

(6) The date of registration of the merged registration shall, where the separate registrations bear different dates of registration, be the latest of those dates.

Registration of a series of trade marks; s. 41 (Form TM12)

21.—(1) The proprietor of a series of trade marks may apply to the registrar on **A3–22** Form TM3 for their registration as a series in a single registration and there shall be included in such application a representation of each mark claimed to be in the series; and the registrar shall, if satisfied that the marks constitute a series, accept the application.

(2) At any time before preparations of publication of the application have been completed by the Office, the applicant under paragraph (1) above may request on Form TM12 the division of the application into separate applications in respect of one or more marks in that series and the registrar shall, if she is satisfied that the division requested conforms with section 41(2), divide the application accordingly.

(3) At any time the applicant for registration of a series of trade marks or the proprietor of a registered series of trade marks may request the deletion of a mark in that series, and the registrar shall delete the mark accordingly.

(4) The division of an application into one or more applications under paragraph (2) above shall be subject to the payment of a divisional fee and such application and class fees as are appropriate.

Collective and certification marks

Filing of regulations for collective and certification marks; Schs. 1 & 2 (Form TM35)

A3–23   22. Within nine months of the date of the application for the registration of a collective or certification mark, the applicant shall file Form TM35 accompanied by a copy of the regulations governing the use of the mark.

Amendment of regulations of collective and certification marks; Sch. 1 para. 10 and Sch. 2 para. 11 (Forms TM36 & TM7)

A3–24   23.—(1) An application for the amendment of the regulations governing the use of a registered collective or certification mark shall be filed on Form TM36.

(2) Where it appears expedient to the registrar that the amended regulations should be made available to the public she shall publish a notice indicating where copies of the amended regulations may be inspected.

(3) Any person may, within three months of the date of publication of the notice under paragraph (2) above, make observations to the registrar on the amendments relating to the matters referred to in paragraph 6(1) of Schedule 1 in relation to a collective mark, or paragraph 7(1) of Schedule 2 in relation to a certification mark; the registrar shall send a copy thereof to the proprietor.

(4) Any person may, within three months of the date of publication of the notice, file notice on Form TM7 to the registrar of opposition to the amendment, accompanied by a statement of the grounds of opposition, indicating why the amended regulations do not comply with the requirements of paragraph 6(1) of Schedule 1 or, as the case may be, paragraph 7(1) of Schedule 2.

(5) The registrar shall send a copy of the notice and the statement to the proprietor and thereafter the procedure in paragraphs (3) and (6)–(12) of rule 13 shall apply to the proceedings as they apply to proceedings relating to opposition to an application for registration.

Disclaimers, limitations and alteration or surrender of registered trade mark

Registration subject to disclaimer or limitation; s. 13

A3–25   24. Where the applicant for registration of a trade mark or the proprietor by notice in writing sent to the registrar—

(a) disclaims any right to the exclusive use of any specified element of the trade mark, or
(b) agrees that the rights conferred by the registration shall be subject to a specified territorial or other limitation,

the registrar shall make the appropriate entry in the register and publish such disclaimer or limitation.

Alteration of registered trade mark; s. 44 (Forms TM25 & TM7)

A3–26   25.—(1) The proprietor may request the registrar on Form TM25 for such alteration of his registered mark as is permitted under section 44; and the registrar may require such evidence by statutory declaration or otherwise as to the circumstances in which the application is made.

(2) Where, upon the request of the proprietor, the registrar proposes to allow such alteration, she shall publish the mark as altered.

(3) Any person claiming to be affected by the alteration may within three months of the date of publication of the alteration under paragraph (2) send a

notice on Form TM7 to the registrar of opposition to the alteration and shall include a statement of the grounds of opposition; the registrar shall send a copy of the notice and the statement to the proprietor and thereafter the procedure in paragraphs (3) and (6)–(12) of rule 13 shall apply to the proceedings as they apply to proceedings relating to opposition to an application for registration.

Surrender of registered trade mark; s. 45 (Forms TM22 & TM23)

26. (1) Subject to paragraph (2) below, the proprietor may surrender a **A3–27** registered trade mark, by sending notice to the registrar—

> (a) on Form TM22 in respect of all the goods or services for which it is registered; or
> (b) on Form TM23, in respect only of those goods or services specified by him in the notice.

(2) A notice under paragraph (1) above shall be of no effect unless the proprietor in that notice—

> (a) gives the name and address of any person having a registered interest in the mark, and
> (b) certifies that any such person —
>> (i) has been sent not less than three months' notice of the proprietor's intention to surrender the mark, or
>> (ii) is not affected or if affected consents thereto.

(3) The registrar shall, upon the surrender taking effect, make the appropriate entry in the register and publish the same.

Renewal and restoration

Reminder of renewal of registration; s. 43

27.—(1) Subject to paragraph (2) below, at any time not earlier than six months **A3–28** nor later than one month before the expiration of the last registration of a trade mark, the registrar shall (except where renewal has already been effected under rule 28 below) send to the registered proprietor notice of the approaching expiration and inform him at the same time that the registration may be renewed in the manner described in rule 28 below.

(2) If it appears to the registrar that a trade mark may be registered under section 40 at any time within six months before or at any time after the date on which renewal would be due (by reference to the date of application for registration), the registrar shall be taken to have complied with paragraph (1) if she sends to the applicant notice thereof within one month following the date of actual registration.

Renewal of registration; s. 43 (Form TM11)

28. Renewal of registration shall be effected by filing a request for renewal on **A3–29** Form TM11 at any time within the period of six months ending on the date of the expiration of the registration.

Delayed renewal and removal of registration; s. 43 (Form TM11)

29.—(1) If on the expiration of the last registration of a trade mark, the renewal **A3–30** fee has not been paid, the registrar shall publish that fact; and if, within six months from the date of the expiration of the last registration, the request for renewal is filed on Form TM11 accompanied by the appropriate renewal fee and additional renewal fee, the registrar shall renew the registration without removing the mark from the register.

(2) Where no request for renewal is filed as aforesaid, the registrar shall, subject to rule 30 below, remove the mark from the register.

(3) Where a mark is due to be registered after the date on which it is due for renewal (by reference to the date of application for registration), the request for renewal shall be filed together with the renewal fee and additional renewal fee within six months after the date of actual registration.

(4) The removal of the registration of a trade mark shall be published.

Restoration of registration; s. 43 (Form TM13)

A3–31   30.—(1) Where the registrar has removed the mark from the register for failure to renew its registration in accordance with rule 29 above, she may, upon a request filed on Form TM13 within six months of the date of the removal of the mark accompanied by the appropriate renewal fee and appropriate restoration fee, restore the mark to the register and renew its registration if, having regard to the circumstances of the failure to renew, she is satisfied that it is just to do so.

(2) The restoration of the registration shall be published, with the date of restoration shown.

Revocation, invalidation and rectification

Procedure on application for revocation (on the grounds of non-use); s. 46(1) (a) and (b) (Forms TM8 & TM26(N))

A3–32   31.—(1) An application to the registrar for revocation under section 46(1)(a) or (b) of the registration of a trade mark shall be made on Form TM26(N) together with a statement of the grounds on which the application is made; the registrar shall send a copy of the application and the statement to the proprietor.

(2) Within three months of the date on which a copy of the notice and statement is sent by the registrar to the proprietor, the proprietor may file a counter-statement, in conjunction with notice of the same on Form TM8 and either:

(a) two copies of evidence of use made of the mark; or
(b) reasons for non-use of the mark.

Where such a notice and counter-statement, and evidence of use of the mark or reasons for non-use of the mark, are filed within the prescribed period, the registrar shall send a copy of the Form TM8 and the counter-statement, and the evidence of use of the mark or the reasons for non-use of the mark, to the applicant.

(3) Where a counter-statement, in conjunction with a notice of the same, on Form TM8, and evidence of use of the mark or reasons for non-use of the mark, are not filed by the proprietor within the period prescribed by paragraph (2), the registrar may treat his opposition to the application as having been withdrawn.

(4) Within three months of the date upon which a copy of the Form TM8 and counter-statement is sent by the registrar to the applicant, the applicant may file such evidence as he may consider necessary to adduce in support of the grounds stated in his application and shall send a copy thereof to the proprietor.

(5) If the applicant files no evidence under paragraph (4) above in support of his application, he shall, unless the registrar otherwise directs, be deemed to have withdrawn his application.

(6) If the applicant files evidence under paragraph (4) above or the registrar otherwise directs under paragraph (5) above, the proprietor who has filed a notice and counter-statement under paragraph (2) above may, within three months of the date on which either a copy of the evidence or a copy of the direction is sent to him, file such further evidence as he may consider necessary

in support of the reasons stated in the counter-statement and shall send a copy thereof to the applicant.

(7) Within three months of the date upon which a copy of the proprietor's evidence is sent to him under paragraph (6) above, the applicant may file evidence in reply which shall be confined to matters strictly in reply to the proprietor's evidence, and shall send a copy thereof to the proprietor.

(8) No further evidence may be filed, except that, in relation to any proceedings before her, the registrar may at any time if she thinks fit give leave to either party to file such evidence upon such terms as she may think fit.

(9) Upon completion of the evidence the registrar shall request the parties to state by notice to her in writing whether they wish to be heard; if any party requests to be heard the registrar shall send to the parties notice of a date for the hearing.

(10) When the registrar has made a decision on the application she shall send the parties to the proceedings written notice of it, stating the reasons for her decision; and for the purposes of any appeal against the registrar's decision the date when the notice of the decision is sent shall be taken to be the date of the decision.

Procedure on application for revocation (on grounds other than non-use); s.46(1)(c) or (d) (Forms TM8 & TM26(0))

32.—(1) An application to the registrar for revocation under section 46(1) (c) or **A3–33** (d) of the registration of a trade mark shall be made on Form TM26(0) together with a statement of the grounds on which the application is made; the registrar shall send a copy of the application and the statement to the proprietor.

(2) Within six weeks of the date on which a copy of the application and statement is sent by the registrar to the proprietor, the proprietor may file a counter-statement, in conjunction with notice of the same on Form TM8; where such a notice and counter-statement are filed within the prescribed period, the registrar shall send a copy of the Form TM8 and the counter-statement to the applicant.

(3) Where a notice and counter-statement are not filed by the proprietor within the period prescribed by paragraph (2), the registrar may treat his opposition to the application as having been withdrawn.

(4) Within six weeks of the date upon which a copy of the counter-statement is sent by the registrar to the applicant, the applicant may file such evidence as he may consider necessary to adduce in support of the grounds stated in his application and shall send a copy thereof to the proprietor.

(5) If the applicant files no evidence under paragraph (4) above in support of his application, he shall, unless the registrar otherwise directs, be deemed to have withdrawn his application.

(6) If the applicant files evidence under paragraph (4) above or the registrar otherwise directs under paragraph (5) above, the proprietor who has filed a notice and counter-statement under paragraph (2) above may, within six weeks of the date on which either a copy of the evidence or a copy of the direction is sent to him, file such evidence as he may consider necessary in support of the reasons stated in the counter-statement and shall send a copy thereof to the applicant.

(7) Within six weeks of the date upon which a copy of the proprietor's evidence is sent to him under paragraph (6) above, the applicant may file evidence in reply which shall be confined to matters strictly in reply to the proprietor's evidence, and shall send a copy thereof to the proprietor.

(8) No further evidence may be filed, except that, in relation to any proceedings before her, the registrar may at any time if she thinks fit give leave to either party to file such evidence upon such terms as she may think fit.

(9) Upon completion of the evidence the registrar shall request the parties to state by notice to her in writing whether they wish to be heard; if any party

requests to be heard the registrar shall send to the parties notice of a date for the hearing.

(10) When the registrar has made a decision on the application she shall send the parties to the proceedings written notice of it, stating the reasons for her decision; and for the purposes of any appeal against the registrar's decision the date when the notice of the decision is sent shall be taken to be the date of the decision.

Procedure on application for invalidation; s.47 (Forms TM8 & TM26(1))

A3–34   **33.**—(1) An application to the registrar for a declaration of invalidity under section 47(1) or (2) of the registration of a trade mark shall be made on Form TM26(1) together with a statement of the grounds on which the application is made; the registrar shall send a copy of the application and the statement to the proprietor.

(2) Within six weeks of the date on which a copy of the application and statement is sent by the registrar to the proprietor, the proprietor may file a counter-statement, in conjunction with notice of the same on Form TM8; where such a notice and counter-statement are filed within the prescribed period, the registrar shall send a copy of the Form TM8 and the counter-statement to the applicant.

(3) Where a notice and counter-statement are not filed by the proprietor within the period prescribed by paragraph (2), the registrar may treat his opposition to the application as having been withdrawn.

(4) Within six weeks of the date upon which a copy of the counter-statement is sent by the registrar to the applicant, the applicant may file such evidence as he may consider necessary to adduce in support of the grounds stated in his application and shall send a copy thereof to the proprietor.

(5) If the applicant files no evidence under paragraph (4) above in support of his application, he shall, unless the registrar otherwise directs, be deemed to have withdrawn his application.

(6) If the applicant files evidence under paragraph (4) above or the registrar otherwise directs under paragraph (5) above, the proprietor who has filed a notice and counter-statement under paragraph (2) above may, within six weeks of the date on which either a copy of the evidence or a copy of the direction is sent to him, file such evidence as he may consider necessary to adduce in support of the reasons stated in the counter-statement and shall send a copy thereof to the applicant.

(7) Within six weeks of the date upon which a copy of the proprietor's evidence is sent to him under paragraph (6) above, the applicant may file evidence in reply which shall be confined to matters strictly in reply to the proprietor's evidence, and shall send a copy thereof to the proprietor.

(8) No further evidence may be filed, except that, in relation to any proceedings before her, the registrar may at any time if she thinks fit give leave to either party to file such evidence upon such terms as she may think fit.

(9) Upon completion of the evidence the registrar shall request the parties to state by notice to her in writing whether they wish to be heard; if any party requests to be heard the registrar shall send to the parties notice of a date for the hearing.

(10) When the registrar has made a decision on the application she shall send the parties to the proceedings written notice of it, stating the reasons for her decision; and for the purposes of any appeal against the registrar's decision the date when the notice of the decision is sent shall be taken to be the date of the decision.

Procedure on application for rectification; s.64 (Form TM26(R))

A3–35   **34.**—(1) An application for rectification of an error or omission in the register under section 64(1) shall be made on Form TM26(R) together with:

    (a) a statement of the grounds on which the application is made; and

    (b) any evidence to support those grounds.

(2) Where any application is made under paragraph (1) by a person other than the proprietor of the registered trade mark the registrar—

    (a) shall send a copy of the application and the statement, together with any evidence filed, to the proprietor; and

    (b) may give such direction as she thinks fit with regard to the filing of subsequent evidence upon such terms as she may think fit.

(3) Upon completion of the evidence the registrar shall request the parties to state by notice to her in writing whether they wish to be heard; if any party requests to be heard the registrar shall send to the parties notice of a date for the hearing.

(4) When the registrar has made a decision on the application she shall send the parties to the proceedings written notice of it, stating the reasons for her decision; and for the purposes of any appeal against the registrar's decision the date when the notice of the decision is sent shall be taken to be the date of the decision.

Procedure for intervention

35.—(1) Any person, other than the registered proprietor, claiming to have an **A3–36** interest in proceedings on an application under rule 31, rule 32, rule 33 or rule 34 may file an application to the registrar on Form TM27 for leave to intervene, stating the nature of his interest and the registrar may, after hearing the parties concerned if so required, refuse such leave or grant leave upon such terms and conditions (including any undertaking as to costs) as she thinks fit.

(2) Any person granted leave to intervene (the intervener) shall, subject to any terms and conditions imposed in respect of the intervention, be treated as a party to the proceedings for the purposes of the application of the provisions of rule 31, rule 32, rule 33 or rule 34 (as appropriate).

Case Management Conference and Pre-Hearing Review

Case Management Conference; s.78

36. At any stage of any proceedings before her, the registrar may direct that **A3–37** the parties to the proceedings attend a case management conference where they shall have an opportunity to be heard with regard to the future conduct of the proceedings, and in particular with regard to the proposed exercise of any of the registrar's powers. The registrar shall give the parties at least fourteen days notice of the date of the case management conference.

Pre-hearing review; s.78

37. Before hearing any party that desires to be heard in any proceedings **A3–38** before her, the registrar may direct that the parties to the proceedings attend a pre-hearing review at which she may give such directions as to the conduct of the hearing as she may think fit. The registrar shall give the parties at least fourteen days notice of the date of the pre-hearing review.

The register

Form of register; s.63(1)

38. The register required to be maintained by the registrar under section 63 (1) **A3–39** need not be kept in documentary form.

Entry in register of particulars of registered trade marks; s.63(2) (Form TM24)

A3–40   39. In addition to the entries in the register of registered trade marks required to be made by section 63(2)(a), there shall be entered in the register in respect of each trade mark registered therein the following particulars—

(a) the date of registration as determined in accordance with section 40 (3) (that is to say, the date of the filing of the application for registration);

(b) the actual date of registration (that is to say, the date of the entry in the register);

(c) the priority date (if any) to be accorded pursuant to a claim to a right to priority made under section 35 or 36;

(d) the name and address of the proprietor;

(e) the address for service (if any) as furnished pursuant to rule 10 above;

(f) any disclaimer or limitation of rights under section 13(1)(a) or (b);

(g) any memorandum or statement of the effect of any memorandum relating to a trade mark of which the registrar has been notified on Form TM24;

(h) the goods or services in respect of which the mark is registered;

(i) where the mark is a collective or certification mark, that fact;

(j) where the mark is registered pursuant to section 5(5) with the consent of the proprietor of an earlier trade mark or other earlier right, that fact;

(k) where the mark is registered pursuant to a transformation application,

(a) the number of the international registration, and

(b) either:

(i) the date accorded to the international registration under Article 3(4), or

(ii) the date of recordal of the request for extension to the United Kingdom of the international registration under Article 3ter, as the case may be, of the Madrid Protocol;

(l) where the mark arises from the conversion of a Community trade mark or an application for a Community trade mark, the number of any other registered trade mark from which the Community trade mark or the application for a Community trade mark claimed seniority and the earliest seniority date.

Entry in register of particulars of registrable transactions; s. 25

A3–41   40. Upon application made to the registrar by such person as is mentioned in section 25(1)(a) or (b) there shall be entered in the register the following particulars of registrable transactions, that is to say—

(a) in the case of an assignment of a registered trade mark or any right in it—

(i) the name and address of the assignee,

(ii) the date of the assignment, and

(iii) where the assignment is in respect of any right in the mark, a description of the right assigned;

(b) in the case of the grant of a licence under a registered trade mark—

(i) the name and address of the licensee,

(ii) where the licence is an exclusive licence, that fact,

(iii) where the licence is limited, a description of the limitation, and

(iv) the duration of the licence if the same is or is ascertainable as a definite period;

(c) in the case of the grant of any security interest over a registered trade mark or any right in or under it—

(i) the name and address of the grantee,

(ii) the nature of the interest (whether fixed or floating), and

(iii) the extent of the security and the right in or under the mark secured;

(d) in the case of the making by personal representatives of an assent in relation to a registered trade mark or any right in or under it—

    (i) the name and address of the person in whom the mark or any right in or under it vests by virtue of the assent, and

    (ii) the date of the assent; and

(e) in the case of a court or other competent authority transferring a registered trade mark or any right in or under it—

    (i) the name and address of the transferee,

    (ii) the date of the order, and

    (iii) where the transfer is in respect of a right in the mark, a description of the right transferred;

and, in each case, there shall be entered the date on which the entry is made.

Application to register or give notice of transaction; ss. 25 & 27(3) (Forms TM16, TM24, TM50 & TM51)

41.—(1) An application to register particulars of a transaction to which section **A3–42** 25 applies or to give notice to the registrar of particulars of a transaction to which section 27(3) applies shall be made, subject to paragraph (2) below,

(a) relating to an assignment or transaction other than a transaction referred to in sub-paragraphs (b) to (d) below, on form TM16;

(b) relating to a grant of a licence, on form TM50;

(c) relating to an amendment to, or termination of a licence, on form TM51;

(d) relating to the grant, amendment or termination of any security interest, on form TM24; and

(e) relating to the making by personal representatives of an assent or to an order of a court or other competent authority, on form TM24.

(2) An application under paragraph (1) above shall—

(a) where the transaction is an assignment, be signed by or on behalf of the parties to the assignment;

(b) where the transaction falls within sub-paragraphs (b), (c) or (d) of paragraph (1) above, be signed by or on behalf of the grantor of the licence or security interest;

or be accompanied by such documentary evidence as suffices to establish the transaction.

(3) Where the transaction is effected by an instrument chargeable with duty, the application shall be subject to the registrar being satisfied that the instrument has been duly stamped.

(4) Where an application to give notice to the registrar has been made of particulars relating to an application for registration of a trade mark, upon registration of the trade mark, the registrar shall enter those particulars in the register.

Public inspection of register; s. 63(3)

42.—(1) The register shall be open for public inspection at the Office during **A3–43** the hours of business of the Office as published in accordance with rule 70 below.

(2) Where any portion of the register is kept otherwise than in documentary form, the right of inspection is a right to inspect the material on the register.

Supply of certified copies etc; s. 63(3) (Form TM31R)

43. The registrar shall supply a certified copy or extract or uncertified copy or **A3–44** extract, as requested on Form TM31R, of any entry in the register.

Request for change of name or address in register; s. 64(4) (Forms TM21 & TM33)

A3–45   44.—(1) The registrar shall, on a request made on Form TM21 by the proprietor of a registered trade mark or a licensee or any person having an interest in or charge on a registered trade mark which has been registered under rule 40, enter any change in his name or address as recorded in the register.

(2) The registrar may at any time, on a request made on Form TM33 by any person who has furnished an address for service under rule 10 above, if the address is recorded in the register, change it.

Removal of matter from register; s. 64(5) (Form TM7)

A3–45   45.—(1) Where it appears to the registrar that any matter in the register has ceased to have effect, before removing it from the register—

(a) she may, where she considers it appropriate, publish her intention to remove that matter, and

(b) where any person appears to her to be affected by the removal, she shall send notice of her intention to that person.

(2) Within three months of the date on which her intention to remove the matter is published, or notice of her intention is sent, as the case may be—

(a) any person may file notice of opposition to the removal on form TM7; and

(b) the person to whom a notice is sent under paragraph (1)(b) above may file, in writing—

(i) his objections, if any, to the removal, or

(ii) a request to have his objections heard orally;

and where such opposition or objections are made, rule 54 shall apply.

(3) If the registrar is satisfied after considering any objections or opposition to the removal that the matter has not ceased to have effect, she shall not remove it.

(4) Where there has been no response to the registrar's notice she may remove the matter; where representations objecting to the removal of the entry have been made (whether in writing or orally) the registrar may, if she is of the view after considering the objections that the entry or any part thereof has ceased to have effect, remove it or, as appropriate, the part thereof.

Change of classification

Change of classification; ss. 65(2) & 76(1)

A3–47   46.—(1) Subject to section 65(3), the registrar may—

(a) in order to reclassify the specification of a registered trade mark founded on Schedule 2 to one founded on Schedule 3, or

(b) consequent upon an amendment of the International Classification of Goods and Services referred to in rule 7(2) above,

make such amendments to entries on the register as she considers necessary for the purposes of reclassifying the specification of the registered trade mark.

(2) Before making any amendment to the register under paragraph (1) above the registrar shall give the proprietor of the mark written notice of her proposals for amendments and shall at the same time advise him that—

(a) he may make written objections to the proposals, within three months of the date of the notice, stating the grounds of his objections, and

(b) if no written objections are received within the period specified the registrar will publish the proposals and he will not be entitled to make any objections thereto upon such publication.

(3) If the proprietor makes no written objections within the period specified in paragraph (2)(a) above or at any time before the expiration of that period gives the registrar written notice of his intention not to make any objections, the registrar shall as soon as practicable after the expiration of that period or upon receipt of the notice publish the proposals.

(4) Where the proprietor makes written objections within the period specified in paragraph (2)(a) above, the registrar shall, as soon as practicable after she has considered the objections, publish the proposals or, where she has amended the proposals, publish the proposals as amended; and her decision shall be final and not subject to appeal.

Opposition to proposals; ss. 65(3) & 76(1) (Form TM7)

47.—(1) Notice of any opposition shall be filed on Form TM7 within three **A3–48** months of the date of publication of the proposals under rule 46 above and there shall be stated in the notice the grounds of opposition and, in particular, how the proposed amendments would be contrary to section 65(3).

(2) The registrar may require or admit evidence directed to the questions in issue and if so requested by any person opposing the proposal give that person the opportunity to be heard thereon before deciding the matter.

(3) If no notice of opposition under paragraph (1) above is filed within the time specified, or where any opposition has been determined, the registrar shall make the amendments as proposed and shall enter in the register the date when they were made; and her decision shall be final and not subject to appeal.

Request for information, inspection of documents and confidentiality

Request for information; s. 67(1) (Form TM31C)

48. A request for information relating to an application for registration or to a **A3–49** registered trade mark shall be made on Form TM31C.

Information available before publication; section 67(2)

49.—(1) Before publication of an application for registration the registrar shall **A3–50** make available for inspection by the public the application and any amendments made to it and any particulars contained in a notice given to the registrar under rule 41.

(2) Nothing in section 67(2) relating to publication of information shall be construed as preventing the publication of decisions on cases relating to trade marks decided by the registrar.

Inspection of documents; ss. 67 & 76(1)

50.—(1) Subject to paragraphs (2) and (3) below, the registrar shall permit all **A3–51** documents filed or kept at the Office in relation to a registered mark or, where an application for the registration of a trade mark has been published, in relation to that application, to be inspected.

(2) The registrar shall not be obliged to permit the inspection of any such document as is mentioned in paragraph (1) above until she has completed any procedure, or the stage in the procedure which is relevant to the document in question, which she is required or permitted to carry out under the Act or these Rules.

(3) The right of inspection under paragraph (1) above does not apply to—

(a) any document until fourteen days after it has been filed at the Office;
(b) any document prepared in the Office solely for use therein;
(c) any document sent to the Office, whether at its request or otherwise, for inspection and subsequent return to the sender;
(d) any request for information under rule 48 above;
(e) any document issued by the Office which the registrar considers should be treated as confidential;
(f) any document in respect of which the registrar issues directions under rule 51 below that it be treated as confidential.

(4) Nothing in paragraph (1) shall be construed as imposing on the registrar any duty of making available for public inspection—

(a) any document or part of a document which in her opinion disparages any person in a way likely to damage him; or
(b) any document or information filed at or sent to or by the Office before 31st October 1994, or
(c) any document or information filed at or sent to or by the Office after 31st October 1994 relating to an application for registration of a trade mark under the Trade Marks Act 1938.

(5) No appeal shall lie from a decision of the registrar under paragraph (4) above not to make any document or part of a document available for public inspection.

Confidential documents

A3–52   51.—(1) Where a document other than a form required by the registrar and published in accordance with rule 3 above is filed at the Office and the person filing it requests, at the time of filing or within fourteen days of the filing, that it or a specified part of it be treated as confidential, giving his reasons, the registrar may direct that it or part of it, as the case may be, be treated as confidential, and the document shall not be open to public inspection while the matter is being determined by the registrar.

(2) Where such direction has been given and not withdrawn, nothing in this rule shall be taken to authorise or require any person to be allowed to inspect the document or part of it to which the direction relates except by leave of the registrar.

(3) The registrar shall not withdraw any direction given under this rule without prior consultation with the person at whose request the direction was given, unless the registrar is satisfied that such prior consultation is not reasonably practical.

(4) The registrar may where she considers that any document issued by the Office should be treated as confidential so direct, and upon such direction that document shall not be open to public inspection except by leave of the registrar.

(5) Where a direction is given under this rule for a document to be treated as confidential a record of the fact shall be filed with the document.

Agents

Proof of authorisation of agent may be required; s. 82 (Form TM33)

A3–53   52.—(1) Where an agent has been authorised under section 82, the registrar may in any particular case require the personal signature or presence of the agent or the person authorising him to act as agent.

(2) Where after a person has become a party to proceedings before the registrar, he appoints an agent for the first time or appoints one agent in

substitution for another, the newly appointed agent shall file Form TM33, and any act required or authorised by the Act in connection with the registration of a trade mark or any procedure relating to a trade mark may not be done by or to the newly appointed agent until on or after the date on which he files that form.

(3) The registrar may by notice in writing sent to an agent require him to produce evidence of his authority.

Registrar may refuse to deal with certain agents; s. 88

53. The registrar may refuse to recognise as agent in respect of any business **A3–54** under the Act—

(a) a person who has been convicted of an offence under section 84;

(b) an individual whose name has been erased from and not restored to, or who is suspended from, the register of trade mark agents on the ground of misconduct;

(c) a person who is found by the Secretary of State to have been guilty of such conduct as would, in the case of an individual registered in that register, render him liable to have his name erased from it on the ground of misconduct;

(d) a partnership or body corporate of which one of the partners or directors is a person whom the registrar could refuse to recognise under paragraph (a), (b) or (c) above.

Decision of registrar, evidence and costs

Decisions of registrar to be taken after hearing

54.—(1) Without prejudice to any provisions of the Act or these Rules **A3–55** requiring the registrar to hear any party to proceedings under the Act or these Rules, or to give such party an opportunity to be heard, the registrar shall, before taking any decision on any matter under the Act or these Rules which is or may be adverse to any party to any proceedings before her, give that party an opportunity to be heard.

(2) The registrar shall give that party at least fourteen days' notice of the time when he may be heard unless that party consents to shorter notice.

Evidence in proceedings before the registrar; s.69

55.—(1) Where under these Rules evidence may be admitted by the registrar **A3–56** in any proceedings before her, it shall be by the filing of a statutory declaration or affidavit.

(2) The registrar may in any particular case take oral evidence in lieu of or in addition to such evidence and shall, unless she otherwise directs, allow any witness to be cross-examined on his statutory declaration, affidavit or oral evidence.

(3) Where these Rules provide for the use of an affidavit or statutory declaration, a witness statement verified by a statement of truth may be used as an alternative; the Registrar may give a direction as she thinks fit in any particular case that evidence must be given by affidavit or statutory declaration instead of or in addition to a witness statement verified by a statement of truth.

(4) The practice and procedure of the High Court with regard to witness statements and statements of truth, their form and contents and the procedure governing their use are to apply as appropriate to all proceedings under these Rules.

(5) Where in proceedings before the registrar, a party adduces evidence of a statement made by a person otherwise than while giving oral evidence in the proceedings and does not call that person as a witness, the registrar may, if she

thinks fit, permit any other party to the proceedings to call that person as a witness and cross-examine him on the statement as if he had been called by the first-mentioned party and as if the statement were his evidence in chief.

Making and subscription of statutory declaration or affidavit

A3–57 56.—(1) Any statutory declaration or affidavit filed under the Act or these Rules shall be made and subscribed as follows –

    (a) in the United Kingdom, before any justice of the peace or any commissioner or other officer authorised by law in any part of the United Kingdom to administer an oath for the purpose of any legal proceedings;

    (b) in any other part of Her Majesty's dominions or in the Republic of Ireland, before any court, judge, justice of the peace or any officer authorised by law to administer an oath there for the purpose of any legal proceedings; and

    (c) elsewhere, before a commissioner for oaths, notary public, judge or magistrate.

(2) Any document purporting to have affixed, impressed or subscribed thereto or thereon the seal or signature of any person authorised by paragraph (1) above to take a declaration may be admitted by the registrar without proof of the genuineness of the seal or signature, or of the official character of the person or his authority to take the declaration.

Registrar's power to require documents, information or evidence

A3–58 57. At any stage of any proceedings before the registrar, she may direct that such documents, information or evidence as she may reasonably require shall be filed within such period as she may specify.

Registrar to have power of an official referee; s. 69

A3–59 58.—(1) The registrar shall in relation to the examination of witnesses on oath and the disclosure and production of documents have all the powers of an official referee of the Supreme Court.

(2) The rules applicable to the attendance of witnesses before such a referee shall apply in relation to the attendance of witnesses in proceedings before the registrar.

Hearings before registrar to be in public

A3–60 59.—(1) The hearing before the registrar of any dispute between two or more parties relating to any matter in connection with an application for the registration of a mark or a registered mark shall be in public unless the registrar, after consultation with those parties who appear in person or are represented at the hearing, otherwise directs.

(2) Nothing in this rule shall prevent a member of the Council on Tribunals or of its Scottish Committee from attending a hearing in his capacity as such.

Costs of proceedings; s. 68

A3–61 60. The registrar may, in any proceedings before her under the Act or these Rules, by order award to any party such costs as she may consider reasonable, and direct how and by what parties they are to be paid.

Security for costs; s. 68

A3–62 61.—(1) The registrar may require any person who is a party in any proceedings before her under the Act or these Rules to give security for costs in relation to those proceedings; and she may require security for the costs of any appeal from her decision.

(2) In default of such security being given, the registrar, in the case of the proceedings before her, or, in the case of an appeal, the person appointed under section 76 may treat the party in default as having withdrawn his application, opposition, objection or intervention, as the case may be.

Decision of registrar (Form TM5)

62.—(1) When, in any proceedings before her, the registrar has made a A3–63 decision, she shall send to each party to the proceedings written notice of it, and for the purposes of any appeal against that decision, subject to paragraph (2) below, the date on which the notice is sent shall be taken to be the date of the decision.

(2) Where a statement of the reasons for the decision is not included in the notice sent under paragraph (1) above, any party may, within one month of the date on which the notice was sent to him, request the registrar on form TM5 to send him a statement of the reasons for the decision and upon such request the registrar shall send such a statement; and the date on which that statement is sent shall be deemed to be the date of the registrar's decision for the purpose of any appeal against it.

Appeals

Appeal to person appointed; s. 76

63.—(1) Notice of appeal to the person appointed under section 76 shall be A3–64 sent to the registrar within 28 days of the date of the registrar's decision which is the subject of the appeal accompanied by a statement in writing of the appellant's grounds of appeal and of his case in support of the appeal.

(2) The registrar shall send the notice and the statement to the person appointed.

(3) Where any person other than the appellant was a party to the proceedings before the registrar in which the decision appealed against was made, the registrar shall send to that person a copy of the notice and the statement.

Determination whether appeal should be referred to court; s. 76(3)

64.—(1) Within 28 days of the date on which the notice of appeal is sent by the A3–65 registrar under rule 63(3) above;

    (a) the registrar, or

    (b) any person who was a party to the proceedings in which the decision appealed against was made,

may request that the person appointed refer the appeal to the court.

(2) Where the registrar requests that the appeal be referred to the court, she shall send a copy of the request to each party to the proceedings.

(3) A request under paragraph (1)(b) above shall be sent to the registrar; the registrar shall send it to the person appointed and shall send a copy of the request to any other party to the proceedings.

(4) Within 28 days of the date on which a copy of a request is sent by the registrar under paragraph (2) or (3) above, the person to whom it is sent may make representations as to whether the appeal should be referred to the court.

(5) In any case where it appears to the person appointed that a point of general legal importance is involved in the appeal, he shall send to the registrar and to every party to the proceedings in which the decision appealed against was made, notice thereof.

(6) Within 28 days of the date on which a notice is sent under paragraph (5) above, the person to whom it was sent may make representations as to whether the appeal should be referred to the court.

Hearing of appeal; s. 76(4)

A3–66 65.—(1) Where the person appointed does not refer the appeal to the court, he shall send notice of the time and place appointed for the hearing of the appeal—

(a) where no person other than the appellant was a party to the proceedings in which the decision appealed against was made, to the registrar and to the appellant, and

(b) in any other case, to the registrar and to each person who was a party to those proceedings.

(2) The provisions of rule 54(2) and rules 55 to 61 shall apply to the person appointed and to proceedings before the person appointed as they apply to the registrar and to proceedings before the registrar.

(3) The person appointed shall send a copy of his decision, with a statement of his reasons therefor, to the registrar and to each person who was a party to the proceedings before him.

Correction of irregularities, calculation and extension of time

Correction of irregularities of procedure

A3–67 66. Subject to rule 68 below, any irregularity in procedure in or before the Office or the registrar, may be rectified on such terms as the registrar may direct.

Calculation of times and periods

A3–68 67.—(1) Where, on any day, there is—

(a) a general interruption or subsequent dislocation in the postal services of the United Kingdom, or

(b) an event or circumstances causing an interruption in the normal operation of the Office,

the registrar may certify the day as being one on which there is an "interruption" and, where any period of time specified in the Act or these Rules for the giving, making or filing of any notice, application or other document expires on a day so certified the period shall be extended to the first day next following (not being an excluded day) which is not so certified.

(2) Any certificate of the registrar given pursuant to this rule shall be posted in the Office.

(3) If in any particular case the registrar is satisfied that the failure to give, make or file any notice, application or other document within any period of time specified in the Act or these Rules for such giving, making or filing was wholly or mainly attributable to a failure or undue delay in the postal services in the United Kingdom, the registrar may, if she thinks fit, extend the period so that it ends on the day of the receipt by the addressee of the notice, application or other document (or, if the day of such receipt is an excluded day, on the first following day which is not an excluded day), upon such notice to other parties and upon such terms as she may direct.

(4) In this rule "excluded day" means a day which is not a business day of the Office under the registrar's direction pursuant to section 80, as published in accordance with rule 70 below.

Alteration of time limits (Form TM9)

A3–69 68.—(1) The time or periods—

(a) prescribed by these Rules, other than the times or periods prescribed by the rules mentioned in paragraph (3) below, or

(b) specified by the registrar for doing any act or taking any proceedings,

subject to paragraph (2) below, may, at the written request of the person or party concerned, or on the initiative of the registrar, be extended by the registrar as she thinks fit and upon such terms as she may direct.

(2) Where a request for the extension of a time or periods prescribed by these Rules—

(a) is sought in respect of a time or periods prescribed by rules 13, 18, 23, 25, 31, 32, 33 or 34, the party seeking the extension shall send a copy of the request to each person party to the proceedings;

(b) is filed after the application has been published under rule 12 above the request shall be on Form TM9 and shall in any other case be on that form if the registrar so directs.

(3) The rules excepted from paragraph (1) above are rule 10(6) (failure to file address for service), rule 11 (deficiencies in application), rule 13(1) (time for filing opposition), rules 13(3) and 13(5) (time for filing counter-statement), rule 13(4) (cooling off period) save as provided for in that rule, rule 23(4) (time for filing opposition), rule 25(3) (time for filing opposition), rule 29 (delayed renewal), rule 30 (restoration of registration), rule 31(2) (time for filing counter-statement), rule 32(2) (time for filing counter-statement), rule 33(2) (time for filing counter-statement), and rule 47 (time for filing opposition).

(4) Subject to paragraph (5) below, a request for extension under paragraph (1) above shall be made before the time or period in question has expired.

(5) Where the request for extension is made after the time or period has expired, the registrar may, at her discretion, extend the period or time if she is satisfied with the explanation for the delay in requesting the extension and it appears to her to be just and equitable to do so.

(6) Where the period within which any party to any proceedings before the registrar may file evidence under these Rules is to begin upon the expiry of any period in which any other party may file evidence and that other party notifies the registrar that he does not wish to file any, or any further, evidence the registrar may direct that the period within which the first mentioned party may file evidence shall begin on such date as may be specified in the direction and shall notify all parties to the dispute of that date.

(7) without prejudice to the above, in the case of any irregularity or prospective irregularity in or before the Office or the registrar which—

(a) consists of a failure to comply with any limitation as to times or periods specified in the Act or these Rules or the old law as that law continues to apply and which has occurred or appears to the registrar as likely to occur in the absence of a direction under this rule, and

(b) is attributable wholly or in part to an error, default or omission on the part of the Office or the registrar and which it appears to her should be rectified,

she may direct that the time or period in question shall be altered in such manner as she may specify upon such terms as she may direct.

Filing of documents, hours of business, Trade Marks Journal and translations

Filing of documents by electronic means

69. The registrar may, at her discretion, permit as an alternative to the sending **A3–70** by post or delivery of the application, notice or other document in legible form the filing of the application, notice or other document by electronic means subject to such terms or conditions as she may specify either generally by published notice or in any particular case by written notice to the person desiring to file any such documents by such means.

Directions on hours of business; s. 80

A3–71   70. Any directions given by the registrar under section 80 specifying the hours of business of the Office and business days of the Office shall be published and posted in the Office.

Trade Marks Journal; s. 81

A3–72   71. The registrar shall publish a journal, entitled "The Trade Marks Journal", containing particulars of any application for the registration of a trade mark (including a representation of the mark), such information as is required to be published under these Rules and such other information as the registrar thinks fit.

Translations

A3–73   72.—(1) Where any document or part thereof which is in a language other than English is filed or sent to the registrar in pursuance of the Act or these Rules, the registrar may require that there be furnished a translation into English of the document or that part, verified to the satisfaction of the registrar as corresponding to the original text.

(2) The registrar may refuse to accept any translation which is in her opinion inaccurate and thereupon another translation of the document in question verified as aforesaid shall be furnished.

Transitional provisions and revocations

Pending applications for registration; Sch. 3, para. 10(2)

A3–74   73. Where an application for registration of a mark made under the old law is advertised on or after 31st October 1994, the period within which notice of opposition may be filed shall be three months from the date of advertisement, and such period shall not be extendible.

Revocation of previous Rules

A3–75   74.—(1) The Rules specified in Schedule 1 are hereby revoked.
(2) Except as provided by rule 73 above, where—

> (a) immediately before these Rules come into force, any time or period prescribed by the Rules hereby revoked has effect in relation to any act or proceeding and has not expired, and
> (b) the corresponding time or period prescribed by these Rules would have expired or would expire earlier,

the time or period prescribed by those Rules and not by these Rules shall apply to that act or proceeding.

(3) Any proceeding commenced before the registrar before the entry into force of these Rules shall proceed under the Trade Mark Rules 1994 as amended or old law as appropriate; but where a new step is to be taken on or after 26th April 2000 in relation to any proceedings commenced under the Trade Mark Rules 1994 these Rules shall apply to such proceedings from that date.

SCHEDULE 1   **Rule 74**

REVOCATIONS

A3–76

Rules revoked	Reference
The Trade Marks Rules 1994	S.I. 1994/2583
The Trade Marks (Amendment) Rules 1998	S.I. 1998/925

SCHEDULE 2   **Rule 7(1)**

CLASSIFICATION OF GOODS (PRE-1938)

Class 1 Chemical substances used in manufactures, photography, or philosophical **A3–77** research, and anti-corrosives.
Class 2 Chemical substances used for agricultural, horticultural, veterinary and sanitary purposes.
Class 3 Chemical substances prepared for use in medicine and pharmacy.
Class 4 Raw, or partly prepared, vegetable, animal, and mineral substances used in manufactures, not included in other Classes.
Class 5 Unwrought and partly wrought metals used in manufacture.
Class 6 Machinery of all kinds, and parts of machinery, except agricultural and horticultural machines and their parts included in Class 7.
Class 7 Agricultural and horticultural machinery, and parts of such machinery.
Class 8 Philosophical instruments, scientific instruments, and apparatus for useful purposes; instruments and apparatus for teaching.
Class 9 Musical instruments.
Class 10 Horological instruments.
Class 11 Instruments, apparatus, and contrivances, not medicated, for surgical or curative purposes, or in relation to the health of men or animals.
Class 12 Cutlery and edge tools.
Class 13 Metal goods, not included in other Classes.
Class 14 Goods of precious metals and jewellery, and imitations of such goods and jewellery.
Class 15 Glass.
Class 16 Porcelain and earthenware.
Class 17 Manufactures from mineral and other substances for building or decoration.
Class 18 Engineering, architectural, and building contrivances.
Class 19 Arms, ammunition, and stores, not included in Class 20.
Class 20 Explosive substances.
Class 21 Naval architectural contrivances and naval equipments not included in other Classes.
Class 22 Carriages.
Class 23 (a) Cotton yarn; (b) Sewing cotton.
Class 24 Cotton piece goods.
Class 25 Cotton goods not included in other Classes.
Class 26 Linen and hemp yarn and thread.
Class 27 Linen and hemp piece goods.
Class 28 Linen and hemp goods not included in other Classes.
Class 29 Jute yarns and tissues, and other articles made of jute, not included in other Classes.
Class 30 Silk, spun, thrown, or sewing.
Class 31 Silk piece goods.
Class 32 Silk goods not included in other Classes.
Class 33 Yarns of wool, worsted, or hair.
Class 34 Cloths and stuffs of wool, worsted, or hair.
Class 35 Woollen and worsted and hair goods, not included in other Classes.
Class 36 Carpets, floor-cloth, and oil-cloth.
Class 37 Leather, skins unwrought and wrought, and articles made of leather not included in other Classes.

Class 38 Articles of clothing.

Class 39 Paper (except paper hangings), stationery, and bookbinding.

Class 40 Goods manufactured from india-rubber and gutta-percha not included in other Classes.

Class 41 Furniture and upholstery.

Class 42 Substances used as food or as ingredients in food.

Class 43 Fermented liquors and spirits.

Class 44 Mineral and aerated waters, natural and artificial, including ginger beer.

Class 45 Tobacco, whether manufactured or unmanufactured.

Class 46 Seeds for agricultural and horticultural purposes.

Class 47 Candles, common soap, detergents; illuminating, heating, or lubricating oils; matches; and starch, blue, and other preparations for laundry purposes.

Class 48 Perfumery (including toilet articles, preparations for the teeth and hair, and perfumed soap).

Class 49 Games of all kinds and sporting articles not included in other Classes.

Class 50 Miscellaneous:—

   (1) Goods manufactured from ivory, bone or wood, not included in other Classes.

   (2) Goods manufactured from straw or grass, not included in other Classes.

   (3) Goods manufactured from animal and vegetable substances, not included in other Classes.

   (4) Tobacco pipes.

   (5) Umbrellas, walking sticks, brushes and combs for the hair.

   (6) Furniture cream, plate powder.

   (7) Tarpaulins, tents, rick-cloths, rope (jute or hemp), twine.

   (8) Buttons of all kinds other than of precious metal or imitations thereof.

   (9) Packing and hose.

  (10) Other goods not included in the foregoing Classes.

SCHEDULE 3   Rule 7(2)

CLASSIFICATION OF GOODS AND SERVICES

Goods

A3–78 Class 1 Chemicals used in industry, science and photography, as well as in agriculture, horticulture and forestry; unprocessed artificial resins, unprocessed plastics; manures; fire extinguishing compositions; tempering and soldering preparations; chemical substances for preserving foodstuffs; tanning substances; adhesives used in industry.

Class 2 Paints, varnishes, lacquers; preservatives against rust and against deterioration of wood; colorants; mordants; raw natural resins; metals in foil and powder form for painters, decorators, printers and artists.

Class 3 Bleaching preparations and other substances for laundry use; cleaning, polishing, scouring and abrasive preparations; soaps; perfumery, essential oils, cosmetics, hair lotions; dentifrices.

Class 4 Industrial oils and greases; lubricants; dust absorbing, wetting and binding compositions; fuels (including motor spirit) and illuminants; candles, wicks.

Class 5 Pharmaceutical, veterinary and sanitary preparations; dietetic substances adapted for medical use, food for babies; plasters, materials for dressings; material for stopping teeth, dental wax; disinfectants; preparations for destroying vermin; fungicides, herbicides.

Class 6 Common metals and their alloys; metal building materials; transportable buildings of metal; materials of metal for railway tracks; non-electric cables and wires of common metal; ironmongery, small items of metal hardware; pipes and tubes of metal; safes; goods of common metal not included in other classes; ores.

Class 7 Machines and machine tools; motors and engines (except for land vehicles); machine coupling and transmission components (except for land vehicles); agricultural implements (other than hand operated); incubators for eggs.

Class 8 Hand tools and implements (hand operated); cutlery; side arms; razors.

Class 9 Scientific, nautical, surveying, electric, photographic, cinematographic, optical, weighing, measuring, signalling, checking (supervision), life-saving and teaching apparatus and instruments; apparatus for recording, transmission or reproduction of sound or images; magnetic data carriers, recording discs; automatic vending machines and mechanisms for coin-operated apparatus; cash registers, calculating machines, data processing equipment and computers; fire-extinguishing apparatus.

Class 10 Surgical, medical, dental and veterinary apparatus and instruments, artificial limbs, eyes and teeth; orthopaedic articles; suture materials.

Class 11 Apparatus for lighting, heating, steam generating, cooking, refrigerating, drying, ventilating, water supply and sanitary purposes.

Class 12 Vehicles; apparatus for locomotion by land, air or water.

Class 13 Firearms; ammunition and projectiles; explosives; fireworks.

Class 14 Precious metals and their alloys and goods in precious metals or coated therewith, not included in other classes; jewellery, precious stones; horological and chronometric instruments.

Class 15 Musical instruments.

Class 16 Paper, cardboard and goods made from these materials, not included in other classes; printed matter; bookbinding material; photographs; stationery; adhesives for stationery or household purposes; artists' materials; paint brushes; typewriters and office requisites (except furniture); instructional and teaching material (except apparatus); plastic materials for packaging (not included in other classes); playing cards; printers' type; printing blocks.

Class 17 Rubber, gutta-percha, gum, asbestos, mica and goods made from these materials and not included in other classes; plastics in extruded form for use in manufacture; packing, stopping and insulating materials; flexible pipes, not of metal.

Class 18 Leather and imitations of leather, and goods made of these materials and not included in other classes; animal skins, hides; trunks and travelling bags; umbrellas, parasols and walking sticks; whips, harness and saddlery.

Class 19 Building materials (non-metallic); non-metallic rigid pipes for building; asphalt, pitch and bitumen; non-metallic transportable buildings; monuments, not of metal.

Class 20 Furniture, mirrors, picture frames; goods (not included in other classes) of wood, cork, reed, cane, wicker, horn, bone, ivory, whalebone, shell, amber, mother-of-pearl, meerschaum and substitutes for all these materials, or of plastics.

Class 21 Household or kitchen utensils and containers (not of precious metal or coated therewith); combs and sponges; brushes (except paint brushes); brush-making materials; articles for cleaning purposes; steelwool; unworked or semi-worked glass (except glass used in building); glassware, porcelain and earthenware not included in other classes.

Class 22 Ropes, string, nets, tents, awnings, tarpaulins, sails, sacks and bags (not included in other classes); padding and stuffing materials (except of rubber or plastics); raw fibrous textile materials.

Class 23 Yarns and threads, for textile use.

Class 24 Textiles and textile goods, not included in other classes; bed and table covers.

Class 25 Clothing, footwear, headgear.

Class 26 Lace and embroidery, ribbons and braid; buttons, hooks and eyes, pins and needles; artificial flowers.

Class 27 Carpets, rugs, mats and matting, linoleum and other materials for covering existing floors; wall hangings (non-textile).

Class 28 Games and playthings; gymnastic and sporting articles not included in other classes; decorations for Christmas trees.

Class 29 Meat, fish, poultry and game; meat extracts; preserved, dried and cooked fruits and vegetables; jellies, jams, fruit sauces; eggs, milk and milk products; edible oils and fats.

Class 30 Coffee, tea, cocoa, sugar, rice, tapioca, sago, artificial coffee; flour and preparations made from cereals, bread, pastry and confectionery, ices; honey, treacle; yeast, baking-powder; salt, mustard; vinegar, sauces (condiments); spices; ice.

Class 31 Agricultural, horticultural and forestry products and grains not included in other classes; live animals; fresh fruits and vegetables; seeds, natural plants and flowers; foodstuffs for animals, malt.

Class 32 Beers; mineral and aerated waters and other non-alcoholic drinks; fruit drinks and fruit juices; syrups and other preparations for making beverages.

Class 33 Alcoholic beverages (except beers).
Class 34 Tobacco; smokers' articles; matches.

Services

A3–79 Class 35 Advertising; business management; business administration; office functions.
Class 36 Insurance; financial affairs; monetary affairs; real estate affairs.
Class 37 Building construction; repair; installation services.
Class 38 Telecommunications.
Class 39 Transport; packaging and storage of goods; travel arrangement.
Class 40 Treatment of materials.
Class 41 Education; providing of training; entertainment; sporting and cultural activities.
Class 42 Providing of food and drink; temporary accommodation; medical, hygienic and beauty care; veterinary and agricultural services; legal services; scientific and industrial research; computer programming; services that cannot be placed in other classes.

APPENDIX 4

The Trade Marks (Fees) Rules 2000

S.I. 2000 No. 137

The Secretary of State, in exercise of the powers conferred by sections 54 and **A4–01** 79 of the Trade Marks Act 1994 ("the Act"), of the power conferred on him by the Department of Trade and Industry (Fees) Order 1988, and of all other powers enabling him in that behalf, hereby makes the following Rules:—

1. These Rules may be cited as the Trade Marks (Fees) Rules 2000 and shall **A4–02** come into force on 17th February 2000.

2. These Rules shall be construed as one with the Trade Marks Rules 2000 and **A4–03** the Trade Marks (International Registration) Order 1996.

3. The fees to be paid in respect of any matters arising under the Act, the **A4–04** Trade Marks Rules 2000 and the Trade Marks (International Registration) Order 1996 shall be those specified in the Schedule to these Rules; and in any case where a form specified in the Schedule as the corresponding form in relation to any matter is specified in the Trade Marks Rules 2000 or the Trade Marks (International Registration) Order 1996 that form shall be accompanied by the fee, if any, specified in respect of that matter (unless the Rules or the Order otherwise provide).

4. Where a fee has been paid in error, the registrar shall repay the same; and **A4–05** where a fee is paid in excess of the amount specified hereunder, the registrar shall remit the amount paid in excess.

5. The Trade Mark (Fees) Rules 1998 are hereby revoked. **A4–06**

SCHEDULE   **Rule 3**

FEES PAYABLE

(In this section references to a rule are references to that rule in the Trade Marks Rules **A4–07** 2000 and references to an article are references to that article in the Trade Marks (International Registration) Order 1996)

Number of corresponding form	Item	Amount £
TM3	Application for registration of a trade mark (rule 5) or a series of trade marks (rule 21)	200
	Class fee (rule 5), for each class over one	50
	Transformation application (articles 19–20)	—
TM3A	Application for additional classes following examination of a mark (rule 8(3)), for each additional class	50
TM5	Request to the registrar for a statement of the reasons for his decision (rule 62(2))	100
TM7	Notice of opposition to the registration of a mark (rule 13(1)), to the amendment of an application (rule 18(2)), or to the amendment of the regulations relating to a certification or collective trade mark (rule 23(4)), to the alteration of a registered trade mark (rule 25(3)), to the removal of matter from the register (rule 45(2)(a)), to the reclassification of a mark from Schedule 2 to Schedule 3 (rule 47(1))	200

	Notice of opposition on the conferring of protection to the international registration (article 10)	200
TM9	Request for extension of time (rule 68(2))	50
TM9c	Request for extension to cooling off period (rule 13(4))	—
TM11	Renewal of registration (rule 28)	200
	Class fee for each class over one	50
	Delayed renewal of registration (rule 29(1)	50
TM12	Request for division of an application (rule 19(1))	100
TM13	Request for the restoration and renewal of a registration removed from the register for failure to renew (rule 30(1))	100
TM16	Request to enter details of an assignment (rule 41(1)(a))	50
TM17	Request to merge either applications or registrations (rule 20(1))	—
TM23	Request by the registered proprietor for the partial surrender of a registered trade mark (rule 26(1)(b))	—
TM24	Application to record or cancel a registrable transaction other than an assignment or licence (rule 41(I)(d))	—
	Application to record or cancel a notifiable transaction (article 6)	—
TM26 (N)	Request for the revocation of a registration (on grounds of non-use) (rule 31)	200
	Request for the revocation of a protected international trade mark (UK) (on grounds of non-use) (article 13)	200
TM26(O)	Request for the revocation of a registration (on grounds other than non-use) (rule 32)	200
	Request for the revocation of a protected international trade mark (UK) (on grounds other than non-use) (article 13)	200
TM26 (I)	Request for the invalidation of a registration (rule 33)	200
	Request for the invalidation of a protected international trade mark (UK) (article 13)	200
TM26 (R)	Request for the rectification of a registration (rule 34)	—
	Request for the rectification of the supplementary register (article 15)	—
TM28	Recordal of concurrent registration (article 21)	—
TM31C	Request for information about applications and registered trade marks (rule 48)	20
TM31M	Request for information in relation to an international trade mark (UK) (article 25)	20
TM31R	Request for certified copy of an entry on the register (rule 43), per certificate	20

TM35	Filing of regulations governing the use of a certification or collective mark (rule 22)	200
TM36	Request to amend regulations governing the use of a certification or collective mark (rule 23(1))	100
TM50	Application for the registration of a licence under registered trade mark (rule 41(1)(b))	—
	Submission fee for an application for international registration to the International Bureau by the Patent Office (article 22)	40
	Handling fee for the transmission by the Patent Office of monies payable to the International Bureau for renewal of an international registration (article 31)	20

APPENDIX 5

Trade Mark Registry Forms

Form TM3

Official fee due

The
Patent
Office

A5–01

Application to register a trade mark

The Patent Office
Trade Marks Registry
Cardiff Road, Newport
South Wales NP9 1RH

Please refer to notes for guidance on completing this form

1. Your reference

2. Representation of the mark

3. State "Yes" here if the mark is a word or words without any particular form of presentation

4. If the mark is not a word or a picture, indicate here *(for example 3-dimensional)*

5. If the application is for a series of marks, indicate how many marks in the series

6. If this application claims priority, indicate the priority date *(s)* claimed, the country, and the number

Date	Country	Number

7. If this is a transformation application under the Madrid Protocol, state the transformation date and the international registration number

Date	Registration number

(REV/2) W

Form TM3

Form TM3

8. Specification of goods/services.

If the space provided for the specification of goods/services is insufficient then please continue on separate sheets. List the classes in consecutive numerical order and list alongside each class the goods or services appropriate to that class.

Class number	List of goods/services
Class number	

(REV/2) W

Form TM3

Form TM3

List the classes in consecutive numerical order and list alongside each class the goods or services appropriate to that class.

Class number	List of goods/services

Class number	

(REV/2) W

Form TM3

9. Indicate if this application is for :
    a) a trade mark
    b) a certification mark
  or c) a collective mark	

10. If colour is claimed, indicate here and state the colour *(s)*	
11. Indicate any limitations or disclaimers	
12. Full name, address and postcode of the applicant Trade Marks ADP number *(if you know it)* *If the applicant is a corporate body, give country and, if applicable, state of incorporation*	
13. Name of agent *(if appropriate)* Address for service in the United Kingdom to which all correspondence should be sent *(including postcode)* *[see note m]* Trade Marks ADP number *(if you know it)*	
The trade mark is being used by the applicant or with his or her consent, in relation to the goods or services stated, or there is a bona fide intention that it will be so used. Signature	
Name *(block capitals)*	
Date	
Name and daytime telephone number of person to contact	
State number of sheets attached to this form	

(REV/2) W

How to fill in Form TM3 - Application to register a trade mark

Important :

- *You cannot amend your mark after you have sent us your application form.*
- *The fee is not refundable if your mark turns out not to be registrable for any reason.*

We therefore urge you to read these notes carefully in conjunction with our booklet "Registering a Trade Mark" before making your application. You should also read our "Search and Advisory Service" booklet before sending your application to us.

If there is not enough space for any of your answers on the form, especially section 8, use separate sheets. Number each one and state in the box at the bottom of the last page how many extra sheets you have used. A sample of a completed Form TM3 is enclosed.

What to put in each section of the form

Section	What is needed
1.	Your reference. You don't have to provide one, but if you do we will use it whenever we contact you.
2.	Provide a representation of your mark, which may be a word and/or a picture, **inside** the box at section 2. A trade mark can also be something other than a word and/or a picture, but it must be capable of being represented graphically. We can accept applications if the mark is larger than the box. In this case you can send us the mark on a separate sheet which must then be no larger than A4 size. However, if you want to make an International Application at a later date, then the mark must be no larger than the 8cm by 8cm box on this form.
3.	If you state "Yes", we will consider the word(s) in the mark to be in plain type. You may find it helpful to insert "Yes", for example, if you fill in the form by hand, but intend to use the mark in a printed form. If you leave this section blank, we will consider the style in which the word(s) is shown to be a feature of the mark.
4.	If the mark which you insert in the box at section 2 is not a word and/or a picture, please tell us exactly what it is, for example, it could be a 3-dimensional shape.
5.	A "series" is a number of marks which resemble each other in their important features and differ only in minor features which do not substantially affect the identity of the mark.
6.	If you are claiming priority from an earlier application made in a country which is party to the Paris Convention (for the Protection of Industrial Property) for any of the goods and/or services in your application, provide full details in this section.
7.	You only need to fill in this section if you are transforming a UK designation under an International Registration into a UK application.
8.	List **all** the goods/services you trade in, or intend to trade in, using the mark applied for. If your application covers goods/services in more than one class, please group them together by class. There is a list of goods/services by class at Appendix I of the booklet "Registering a Trade Mark" (goods are in Classes 1-34, and services in Classes 35-42). If you cannot find your goods/services in this list, please contact us. Please note that you cannot add goods/services to your application once you have sent your application form to us.

9. State which type of mark you are applying for, normally this will be a) a trade mark. If you are applying for a certification or collective mark, state this here. Note that you must file the regulations for such marks within nine months of making this application.

10. If you want to claim that any colour(s) in your mark is a feature of the mark, state this here, and also state what colour(s) you are claiming.

11. If you want to disclaim the right to the exclusive use of any specified part of the mark, or limit use of the mark, state this here.

12. Please provide as much detail as possible. If you have previously applied for a trade mark, you will find the "Trade Marks ADP number" (which is our reference number for your name and address) on your previous filing receipt(s).

13. If you appoint someone (for example, a Trade Marks agent) to deal with your application for you, give details here. You do not have to appoint an agent, but you can still specify a UK address, other than that given in section 12, to which we will send correspondence (we call this an "address for service"). If you leave this section blank, we will write to you at the address given in section 12 - as long as it is in the UK. You can change or appoint an agent or address for service at any time after application by sending us a Form TM33 which is available from us.

Declaration: You must sign and date the form.

It will also help us to sort out any possible queries if you can provide the name and daytime telephone number of someone we can contact.

Fees
It costs £200 to apply to register a mark in one class of goods/services, and £50 for each additional class. Please remember that this fee is not refundable if the mark turns out not to be registrable for any reason - it covers the cost of examination of the application. Please make cheques payable to "The Patent Office".

Returning the form to us
When you have completed the form, please return it **with the appropriate fee** to:
The Patent Office, Trade Marks Registry, Cardiff Road, NEWPORT, South Wales, NP10 8QQ.

Then what happens?
We will send you a receipt for your application confirming:
(1) all the details you have given us, and
(2) the date when we received it - this will be your filing date.

Provided you have paid the correct fee, we will examine your application within two months of receipt, and either confirm that your application is acceptable, or send you a written Examination Report which will list all the objections against it.

Help   If you need any more help with the form, or have any other queries before making your application, please:

*   *call us on 0645 500505 (charged at local rate)*
*   *e-mail us on Enquiries@patent.gov.uk*

Form TM3

Official fee due

The Patent Office

A5–02

Application to register a trade mark

Please refer to notes for guidance on completing this form

The Patent Office
Trade Marks Registry
Cardiff Road, Newport
South Wales NP9 1RH

1. Your reference	BLG/JS

2. Representation of the mark

Blogwidge

3. State "Yes" here if the mark is a word or words without any particular form of presentation	Yes
4. If the mark is not a word or a picture, indicate here *(for example 3-dimensional)*	
5. If the application is for a series of marks, indicate how many marks in the series	

6. If this application claims priority, indicate the priority date(s) claimed, the country, and the number

Date	Country	Number

7. If this is a transformation application under the Madrid Protocol, state the transformation date and the international registration number

Date	Registration number

(REV/2)

Form TM3

Form TM3

---

8. Specification of goods/services.

If the space provided for the specification of goods/services is insufficient then please continue on separate sheets. List the classes in consecutive numerical order and list alongside each class the goods or services appropriate to that class.

Class number	List of goods/services
9	Computers, computer hardware, modems, data processing apparatus, computer software for database management, sound recordings, tapes, cassettes, compact discs, films, video recordings.

Class number	
42	Computer advisory, consultancy and design services, leasing, rental and hire of computer software, computer programming.

(REV/2)

Form TM3

Form TM3

List the classes in consecutive numerical order and list alongside each class the goods or services appropriate to that class.

Class number	List of goods/services

Class number

(REV/2)

Form TM3

933

Form TM3

9. Indicate if this application is for :
   a) a trade mark
   b) a certification mark
or c) a collective mark
	a

10. If colour is claimed, indicate here and state the colour *(s)*	
11. Indicate any limitations or disclaimers	

12. Full name, address and postcode
   of the applicant
 	
   Trade Marks ADP number
   (if you know it)
 	
   *If the applicant is a corporate body, give
   country and, if applicable, state of
   incorporation*
	Bloggins plc
	49 Acacia Avenue
	London
	W32 1XY

13. Name of agent *(if appropriate)*
 	
   Address for service in the United Kingdom
   to which all correspondence should be sent
   (including postcode)
   [see note m]
 	
   Trade Marks ADP number
   (if you know it)	

The trade mark is being used by the applicant or with his or her consent, in relation to the goods or services stated, or there is a bona fide intention that it will be so used. Signature	*J Smith*
Name *(block capitals)*	JOHN SMITH
Date	1 February 1999
Name and daytime telephone number of person to contact	0171 293 4819
State number of sheets attached to this form	

(REV/2)   Form TM3

Form TM3 A

Official fee due

**The
Patent
Office**

A5–03

Application for additional classes

Please refer to notes for guidance on completing this form

The Patent Office
Trade Marks Registry
Cardiff Road, Newport
South Wales NP9 1RH

1. Application to which this request relates	Number	*(Lowest)* Class

2. Classes to be added to the original application	

3. Specification of goods/services for the additional classes

List the classes in consecutive numerical order and list alongside each class the goods or services appropriate to that class.

Class number	List of goods/services

(REV/1)

Form TM3 A

Form TM3 A

4. Full name, address and postcode of the applicant	
Trade Marks ADP number *(if you know it)*	
5. Name of agent *(if appropriate)*	
'Address for service' in the United Kingdom to which all correspondence should be sent *(including postcode)* *[see note d]*	
Trade Marks ADP number *(if you know it)*	
Your reference	
Signature	
Name *(block capitals)*	
Date	
Name and daytime telephone number of person to contact	
State number of sheets attached to this form	

General notes

a) Complete this form in capital letters or type it.

b) If there is not enough space for your answer to any section of this form, use separate sheets. Number each one and write on the form how many extra sheets you have used.

c) Once you have completed this form you must remember to sign and date it.

d) If your address for service is different from your agent, then please give us full details of both.

e) If you need help or have any questions, please contact the Trade Marks Registry on 0645 500505.

Form TM3 A

Official fee due

The
Patent
Office

Form TM5   **A5–04**

Request to the Registrar for a statement of grounds of decision

The Patent Office
Trade Marks Registry
Cardiff Road, Newport
South Wales NP9 1RH

Please refer to notes for guidance on completing this form

1. Give details of the application or registration	Number	*(Lowest)* Class
or		
the designation under the Madrid Protocol to which this request relates	Number	*(Lowest)* Class
2. Date of Registrar's decision		
3. Full name and address of applicant or agent making the request *(including postcode)*		
Trade Marks ADP number *(if you know it)*		
Your reference		
Signature		
Name *(block capitals)*		
Date		
Name and daytime telephone number of person to contact		
State number of sheets attached to this form		

(REV/1)

Form TM5

Form TM5

Specific notes

a) If your application for a trade mark is refused or protection of an international trade mark (UK) is refused you can ask the Registrar for a statement of grounds of the decision. This must be requested within one month of the date on which the decision was sent to you.

General notes

b) Complete the form in capital letters or type it.

c) If there is not enough space for your answer to any section of this form, use separate sheets. Number each one and write on the form how many extra sheets you have used.

d) Once you have completed the form you must remember to sign and date it.

e) If your address for service is different from your agent, then please give us full details of both.

f) If you need help or have any questions, please contact the Trade Marks Registry on 0645 500505.

Form TM5

Form TM7

Official fee due

A5–05

Notice of opposition

Please refer to notes for guidance on completing this form

The Patent Office
Trade Marks Registry
Cardiff Road, Newport
South Wales NP10 8QQ

	Number	*(lowest)* Class	Journal
1. Give details of the application or registration *or* the designation under the Madrid Protocol to which this opposition relates			

2. Full name of the applicant or registered proprietor	
3. Full name, address and postcode of opponent	
Trade Marks ADP number *(if you know it)*	
4. Name of agent *(if appropriate)*	
'Address for service' in the United Kingdom to which all correspondence should be sent *(including postcode)* *[see note i]*	
Trade Marks ADP number *(if you know it)*	
Your reference	

Signature	**Declaration** *I confirm the accuracy and truth of the matter contained in the accompanying statement of case*
Name *(block capitals)*	
Date	
Name and daytime telephone number of person to contact	
State the number of sheets attached to this form	

(REV/3)

Form TM7

Specific notes

a) *This form is used to notify the Registrar that you want to oppose any of the following:*

    1) an application
    2) an international trade mark (UK)
    3) re-classification from schedule 3 to 4
    4) an amendment of an application
    5) an amendment to a registered trade mark
    6) an amendment to the regulations relating to collective or certification marks

b) *This form must be filed within the period allowed for such action. For (1, 2, 3, 5 & 6) above, this period is three months from the date of publication in the Trade Marks Journal, for (4) the period is one month.*

c) *Please indicate each class you wish to oppose.*

d) *This form must be accompanied by a statement of case in support of your opposition. You are required to declare the truth and accuracy of the matter contained in the accompanying statement of case.*

e) *Guidance notes on opposition procedures are available on request from the Law Section of the Trade Marks Registry.*

General notes

f) *Complete this form in capital letters or type it.*

g) *If there is not enough space for your answer to any section of this form, use separate sheets. Number each one and write on the form how many extra sheets you have used.*

h) *Once you have completed the form you must remember to sign and date it.*

i) *If your address for service is different from your agent, then please give us full details of both.*

j) *If you need help or have any questions, please contact the Trade Marks Registry on 0645 500505.*

Form TM7

Form TM8

No official fee due

A5–06

Form for counterstatement

The Patent Office
Trade Marks Registry
Cardiff Road, Newport
South Wales NP10 8QQ

Please refer to the notes for guidance on completing this form

	Number	*(Lowest)* Class
1. Give details of the application or registration *or* the designation under the Madrid Protocol to which this counterstatement relates		
2. Full name of applicant or registered proprietor		
3. Opposition or revocation number		
4. Name of agent *(if appropriate)*		
'Address for service' in the United Kingdom to which all correspondence should be sent *(including postcode)* *[see note g]*		
Trade Marks ADP number *(if you know it)*		
Your reference		

	Declaration
	I confirm the accuracy and truth of the matter contained in the accompanying counter statement.
Signature	
Name *(block capitals)*	
Date	
Name and daytime telephone number of person to contact	
State the number of sheets attached to this form	

(REV/2)

Form TM8

Specific notes

a) This form is used if you want to defend your application or international trade mark (UK) against a third party who has lodged **either** an opposition against your application **or** an application to revoke, rectify or invalidate your registration or protected international trade mark (UK). (Rules 13, 31, 32, 33 and 34 of the Trade Marks Rules 2000 and Article 10 and 13 of the Trade Marks (International Registration) Order 1996 (as amended) refer).

b) You must send us details of the grounds for this counterstatement on a separate sheet of paper. You are required to declare the accuracy and truth of the matter contained in the attached counter statement.

c) Guidance notes on opposition and on revocation/rectification/invalidity procedures are available on request from the Law Section of the Trade Marks Registry.

General notes

d) Complete this form in capital letters or type it.

e) If there is not enough space for your answer to any section of this form, use separate sheets. Number each one and write on the form how many extra sheets you have used.

f) Once you have completed the form you must remember to sign and date it.

g) If your address for service is different from your agent, then please give us full details of both.

h) If you need help or have any questions, please contact the Trade Marks Registry on 0645 500505.

A5–07

Form TM9

Official fee due

Request for an extension of time on an application

Please refer to notes for guidance on completing this form

The Patent Office
Trade Marks Registry
Cardiff Road, Newport
South Wales NP9 1RH

1. Give details of the application	Number	*(Lowest)* Class
or		
the designation under the Madrid Protocol to which this request refers	Number	*(Lowest)* Class
2. Give the period of further time required in months		
3. Give the reasons for this request		
4. Full name of requestor		
5. Name of agent *(if appropriate)*		
'Address for service' in the United Kingdom to which all correspondence should be sent *(including postcode)* *[see note e]*		
Trade Marks ADP number *(if you know it)*		
Your reference		
Registry reference		
Signature		
Name *(block capitals)*		
Date		
Name and daytime telephone number of person to contact		
State number of sheets attached to this form		

FOR OFFICIAL USE ONLY
Dear Sir/Madam
Your request for an extension of time as detailed above has been granted.

Yours faithfully

(REV/1)

Form TM9

Specific notes

a) You should use this form if you want an extension of time in the following instances:

- Any extension under Rule 13 (the filing of evidence); or
- Any extension under Rule 62 on an ex-parte hearing case which exceeds an initial three month period.
- Where this form is being used to request an extension of time in opposition, revocation, invalidity or rectification proceedings a copy of the request should be sent to every other person who at the time is a party to those proceedings.

General notes

b) Complete the form in capital letters or type it

c) If there is not enough space for your answer to any section of this form, use separate sheets. Number each one and write on the form how many extra sheets you have used.

d) Once you have completed the form you must remember to sign and date it.

e) If your address for service is different from your agent, then please give us full details of both.

f) If you need help or have any questions, please contact the Trade Marks Registry on 0645 500505.

Form TM9c

A5–08

Request for a cooling off period
or for an extension of such a period

Please refer to notes for guidance on completing this form

The Patent Office
Trade Marks Registry
Cardiff Road, Newport
South Wales NP10 8QQ

1. Give details of the application Please provide the following information	
Application/designation No:	
Opposition No:	
Lowest Class:	
2. Full name of requestor	
3. Name of agent *(if appropriate)*	
'Address for service' in the United Kingdom to which all correspondence should be sent *(including postcode)* *[see note e]*	
Trade Marks ADP number *(if you know it)*	
Your reference	
Registry reference	
4.	**Declaration** *I confirm that the other party to these proceedings has agreed to this request to enter/extend the cooling off period.*
Signature	
Name *(block capitals)*	
Date	
Name and daytime telephone number of person to contact	
State the number of sheets attached to this form	

(REV/2)

Form TM9c

Specific notes

a) You should use this form if you want to request to enter the cooling off period or the extension to the cooling off period.

- In order for the registrar to grant this request, you should obtain the agreement of the other party (or their representative), to the request before signing the declaration in box 4. You may also attach their written agreement to the request to this form if you wish.

- please note, only one extension of the cooling off period is permitted.

General notes

b) Complete the form in capital letters or type it

c) If there is not enough space for your answer to any section of this form, use separate sheets. Number each one and write on the form how many extra sheets you have used.

d) Once you have completed the form you must remember to sign and date it.

e) If your address for service is different from your agent, then please give us full details of both.

f) If you need help or have any questions, please contact the Trade Marks Registry on 0645 500505.

Form TM9c

The
**Patent
Office**

Form TM11

A5–09

Official fee due

Renewal of trade mark registration

Your trade mark renewal is due on the date shown below

The Patent Office
Trade Marks Registry
Cardiff Road, Newport
South Wales NP9 1RH

Please refer to notes for guidance on completing this form

1. Registration number	
2. Classes	
3. Full name and address of registered proprietor Trade Marks ADP number *(if you know it)*	
4. Give the following details of the registration to be renewed Due date of renewal Specify which classes are to be renewed *(if you are not renewing all of them)* Amount of renewal fee Amount of additional renewal fee *(if appropriate)* Total amount paid	
5. Full name, address and postcode of the person to whom the certificate should be sent Trade Marks ADP number *(if you know it)* Your reference	
Signature	
Name *(block capitals)*	
Date	
Name and daytime telephone number of person to contact	

PLEASE DISREGARD THIS NOTICE IF YOU HAVE ALREADY SUBMITTED A TM11 AND RENEWAL FEE

An additional renewal fee of £50.00 will be incurred if your mark is renewed up to 6 months after the due date of renewal; thereafter the mark will be removed from the register.

(REV/1)

Form TM11

APPENDIX 5

Specific notes

a) Please sign and return the TM11 with appropriate fee for renewal of your trade mark.

b) If you want to renew a multiclass registration you must send a fee for each class of goods or services. You may choose to renew only those classes which you retain an interest in.

c) The request for renewal must be made and the renewal fee paid before the expiry of the registration. Failing this if the request is made and the fee paid within 6 months then the mark may be renewed but an additional renewal fee will be payable. (Section 43 of the Trade Marks Act 1994 refers).

d) If you have not renewed the registration within the six month period immediately after expiry (see c above) you have a further six months in which to request the restoration of the registration on form TM13 and pay the appropriate fee. Applications for restoration will not be accepted if they are received by the Patent Office more than twelve months after the date of expiry. (Rule 30 of the Trade Marks Rules 1994 refers).

e) You must send a separate form for each trade mark number.

General notes

f) Complete the form in capital letters or type it.

g) If there is not enough space for your answer to any section of this form, use separate sheets. Number each one and write on the form how many extra sheets you have used.

h) Once you have completed the form you must remember to sign and date it.

i) If you need help or have any questions, please contact the Trade Marks Registry on 0645 500505.

Form TM11

948

Form TM12

Official fee due

The
Patent
Office

A5–10

Request to divide an application

The Patent Office
Trade Marks Registry
Cardiff Road, Newport
South Wales NP9 1RH

Please refer to notes for guidance on completing this form

	Number	*(Lowest)* Class
1. Give details of the application to be divided		

2. Is this request to:
    a) divide the specification of goods or services?
    or
    b) divide a series of marks?
    (indicate a) or b) as appropriate)
    [see note b]		

3. If this request is to divide an application into more than two parts, write how many parts you want it divided into		
4. Full name, address and postcode of applicant Trade Marks ADP number *(if you know it)*		
5. Name of agent *(if appropriate)* 'Address for service' in the United Kingdom to which all correspondence should be sent *(including postcode)* *[see note h]* Trade Marks ADP number *(if you know it)* Your reference		
Signature		
Name *(block capitals)*		
Date		
Name and daytime telephone number of person to contact		
State number of sheets attached to this form		

Reminder:
List on a separate sheet (a) the goods or services (by class number) to be removed to a divisional application, or (b) representations of the marks to be divided.

(REV/1)

Form TM12

Form TM12

Specific notes

a) You may use this form to divide a specification of goods or services, or on the basis of a geographical limitation or both, or to divide a series of marks. You cannot divide both a specification of goods or services and a series of marks on the same form.

b) Section 41 of the Trade Marks Act 1994 allows for the division of an application (Rule 19 also refers). This may apply, for example, where a multiclass application may not proceed because of objections arising against some of the goods or services covered by the application. In this case, the application could be divided, with part of the application proceeding to registration in respect of those goods or services which do not face objections, whilst the other part is held up until the objections are settled.

c) You cannot divide a registered trade mark.

d) If you are dividing a specification of goods or services then the only fee payable is the division fee.
If you are dividing a series of marks then the following fees are payable:
- one divisional fee;
- a fresh application fee for each extra application created; and
- any class fee if appropriate (see Rule 21(4)).

General notes

e) Complete the form in capital letters or type it.

f) If there is not enough space for your answer to any section of this form, use separate sheets. Number each one and write on the form how many extra sheets you have used.

g) Once you have completed the form you must remember to sign and date it.

h) If your address for service is different from your agent, then please give us full details of both.

i) If you need help or have any questions, please contact the Trade Marks Registry on 0645 500505.

Form TM12

Form TM13

Official fee due

A5–11

Request for the restoration and renewal of a registration removed from the Register because of non-payment of the renewal fee

Please refer to notes for guidance on completing this form

The Patent Office
Trade Marks Registry
Cardiff Road, Newport
South Wales NP9 1RH

1. Registration number	
2. Classes *(if you are not renewing all of them)* *[see note b]*	
3. Full name, address and postcode of the registered proprietor Trade Marks ADP number *(if you know it)*	
4. Full name, address and postcode of applicant for restoration and renewal *(if different from 3 above)*	
5. Name of agent *(if appropriate)* 'Address for service' in the United Kingdom to which all correspondence should be sent *(including postcode)* *[see note f]* Trade Marks ADP number *(if you know it)* Your reference	
Signature	
Name *(block capitals)*	
Date	
Name and daytime telephone number of person to contact	
State number of sheets attached to this form	

Reminder:
You can only apply to restore a registration on this form after 6 months of the mark having expired but no later than 12 months.

(REV/1)

Form TM13

Specific notes

a) If you have not renewed the registration within the six month period after the date of expiry, you have another six months to request the restoration of the registration by filling in form TM11 along with this one and sending us the fees. We will not accept applications to restore the registration after twelve months from the date of expiry. (Section 43 of the Trade Marks Act 1994 and Rule 30 of the Trade Marks Rules 1994 refer).

b) If you want to renew a multiclass registration you must send a fee for each class of goods or services. You may choose to renew only those classes which you retain an interest in.

General notes

c) Complete the form in capital letters or type it.

d) If there is not enough space for your answer to any section of this form, use separate sheets. Number each one and write on the form how many extra sheets you have used.

e) Once you have completed the form you must remember to sign and date it.

f) If your address for service is different from your agent, then please give us full details of both.

g) If you need help or have any questions, please contact the Trade Marks Registry on 0645 500505.

Form TM16

Official fee due

The
**Patent
Office**

A5–12

Application to register a change of proprietor

Please refer to notes for guidance on completing this form

The Patent Office
Trade Marks Registry
Cardiff Road, Newport
South Wales NP9 1RH

	Number(s)	*(Lowest)* Class
1. Give details of the applications or registrations for which a change in ownership is to be recorded		
2. Full name of current applicant/registered proprietor		
3. Full name, address and postcode of new proprietor Trade Marks ADP number *(if you know it)*		
4. If the new proprietor is a corporate body give country and if applicable State of Incorporation *If the name of the new proprietor is the same as the old proprietor, then provide both the new and old company registration numbers:* old number new number		
5. Date new proprietor took over ownership		
6. If only part of the ownership has been transferred give the rights or goods or services transferred		

(REV/1)

Form TM16

Form TM16

7. Indicate whether you wish to be:- a) Address for service b) Agent c) Both *for* d) This transaction only e) All transactions *(indicate a) to e) as appropriate)* *[see note b]* If you have indicated d) please note that original Agent and Address for Service will be re-entered into our records as soon as this transaction has been completed If you have completed this section please provide details and ADP Number Your reference	
8. Please sign and confirm that Stamp Duty *has been paid/is not payable *(delete as appropriate) *[see note c]* Signature	
9. Provide below an authorisation to change the record or send separate documentary evidence *[see note a]* Signature of the registered proprietor *(or his or her representative)*	
Status of Signatory	
Name *(block capitals)*	
Date	
Signature of the new proprietor *(or his or her representative)*	
Status of Signatory	
Name *(block capitals)*	
Date	
Name, signature and daytime telephone number *(of person completing these forms)*	
State number of sheets attached to this form	

Form TM16

Form TM16

Specific notes

a) This form is used to record the details of the transfer of ownership of a Trade Mark (Section 25 of the Trade Marks Act 1994 refers). The form must be signed by the assignor and the assignee (or his or her representative). It is acceptable for this to be signed in the name of the firm or company. If you cannot do this, you may send us documentary evidence to support this transaction. Any documentary evidence submitted with this form will be open to public inspection.

b) If no address for service is shown in Box 7, or, if the address for service is for this transaction only, the existing address for service (if any) will be re-entered on the register.

c) The declaration, relating to Stamp Duty, at Box 8 must be completed or proof of payment of the duty must be shown to the Registrar (Rule 35 of the Trade Marks Rules 1994 refers).

d) In order to claim the date the transaction took effect this form must be filed at the Trade Mark Registry within six months of that date (Section 25(4) of the Trade Mark Act 1994 refers). If the transaction is not registered within the six month period, the effective date will be recorded as the actual date of filing the form.

General notes

e) Complete the form in capital letters or type it.

f) If there is not enough space for your answer to any section of this form, use separate sheets. Number each one and write on the form how many extra sheets you have used.

g) Once you have completed the form you must remember to sign and date it.

h) If your address for service is different from your agent, please give us full details of both.

i) If you need help or have any questions, please contact the Trade Marks Registry on 0645 500505.

Form TM16

A5–13   Form TM17

No official fee due

Request to merge either applications or registrations

The Patent Office
Trade Marks Registry
Cardiff Road, Newport
South Wales NP9 1RH

Please refer to notes for guidance on completing this form

	Number(s)	*(Lowest)* Class
1. Give details of the applications or registrations to which this request relates		
2. Full name, address and postcode of the applicant or registered proprietor		
3. Give details of the merged specifications *[see note e]*		
4. Indicate whether you wish to be:- a) Address for service b) Agent c) Both *for* d) This transaction only e) All transactions *(indicate a) to e) as appropriate)* *[see note i]* If you have completed this section please provide details and ADP number *(if you know it)* Your reference		
Signature		
Name *(block capitals)*		
Date		
Name and daytime telephone number of person to contact		
State number of sheets attached to this form		

(REV/1)   Form TM17

Specific notes

a) Section 41 of the Trade Marks Act 1994 allows the merging of separate applications or registrations into a single application or registration (Rule 20 also refers). Applications cannot be merged with registrations.

b) Applications can be merged at any time before they are accepted for advertisement and must:
  - have the same <u>application date</u> (this is the date of filing, Section 40(3) of the Trade Marks Act 1994);
  - be for the same marks; and
  - be in the same ownership.

c) Registrations to be merged must:
  - be for the same marks; and
  - be in the same ownership.

Registered marks can be merged even if the <u>registration dates</u> (this is the date of entry onto the register) are different, but the new merged registration will be given the latest filing date.
The renewal date for the merged registration will be the one with the latest filing date. Renewal fees for all the classes covered by the merged registration will be due on this date.

d) You may want to use this procedure, for example, if an application has been divided or part of a registration was transferred legally to someone else but now returned to a single ownership.

e) You may wish to suggest an amended specification for all the merged applications or registrations. The Registry will consider the acceptability of the edited specification.

General notes

f) Complete the form in capital letters or type it.

g) If there is not enough space for your answer to any section of this form, use separate sheets. Number each one and write on the form how many extra sheets you have used.

h) Once you have completed the form you must remember to sign and date it.

i) If your address for service is different from your agent, then please give us full details of both.

j) If you need help or have any questions, please contact the Trade Marks Registry on 0645 500505.

Form TM17

A5–14

Form TM21

No official fee due

The
Patent
Office

Request to change the details of an application or a registration

Request to change the details of a designation under the Madrid Protocol

Please refer to notes for guidance on completing this form

The Patent Office
Trade Marks Registry
Cardiff Road, Newport
South Wales NP9 1RH

	Number(s)	*(Lowest)* Class	Licensee numbers *(if applicable)*
1. Give details of the applications or registrations			
or			
the designations under the Madrid Protocol this will affect:	Number(s)	*(Lowest)* Class	Licensee numbers *(if applicable)*
Do you wish to change:			
a) All of the trade marks belonging to this proprietor			
or			
b) Only those listed			
(indicate a) or b) as appropriate)			
2. Full name, address and postcode of the proprietor or the licensee on the record			
Trade Marks ADP number *(if you know it)*			
3. Do you wish to record a change of:			
a) name of the proprietor *[for designations under the Madrid Protocol see note a]*			
b) name of the licensee *(s)*			
c) name of person having an interest in the mark			
d) address of the proprietor *(s)* *[for designations under the Madrid Protocol see note a]*			
e) address of the licensee *(s)*			
f) address of the person having an interest in the mark			
(indicate a) to f) as appropriate)			
For other changes please see Section 5			
4. New name or address and postcode to be entered on the Register or Supplementary Register			

(REV/1)

Form TM21

Form TM21

5. Other amendments a) give details of the changes *(including, if appropriate, specifications)*	
b) give details if the change is because of a clerical error	
6. Name of agent *(if appropriate)*	
'Address for service' in the United Kingdon to which all correspondence should be sent *(including postcode)* *[see note j]*	
Trade Marks ADP number *(if you know it)* Your reference	
	Declaration *I declare that there has been no change in the actual proprietorship of the application(s) or registration(s).*
Signature	
Name *(block capitals)*	
Date	
Name and daytime telephone number of person to contact	
State number of sheets attached to this form	

(REV/1)

Form TM21

A5–15

Form TM22

No official fee due

The
Patent
Office

Notice to surrender a registration

The Patent Office
Trade Marks Registry
Cardiff Road, Newport
South Wales NP9 1RH

Please refer to notes for guidance on completing this form

1. Give details of the registration to be surrendered	Registration Number *(Lowest)* Class
2. Full name, address and postcode of the registered proprietor	
3. Indicate whether you wish to be:- a) Address for Service b) Agent c) Both *(indicate a) to c) as appropriate)* If you have completed this section please provide details and ADP number *(if you know it)* Your reference	
4. Are there any licensees or does any one else have a registered interest in the registration? *(if yes write the details on a separate sheet)*	
5.	Declaration *I confirm that there are no parties having a registered interest in the mark* or *I confirm that those with a registered interest in the mark (see attached sheet), have been notified three months prior to this form being filed, or that they consent to the surrender.*
Signature	
Name *(block capitals)*	
Date	
Name and daytime telephone number of person to contact	
State number of sheets attached to this form	

(REV/1)

Form TM22

Form TM22

Specific notes

a) *The proprietor of a registered trade mark can surrender their legal rights to all or part of the goods or services for which it is registered. (Section 45 of the Trade Marks Act 1994 refers).*

b) *This form is used if you are giving up your legal rights to the whole trade mark registration, and you should use a separate form for each trade mark affected.*

c) *Do not use this form if you are giving up your legal rights to only some of the goods or services. Please use form TM23 instead.*

d) *A separate form is required for each registration to be surrendered.*

e) *You must tell the people that have an interest in your mark that you are going to give up your rights in the mark 3 months beforehand, or they should consent to this. You also need to attach a list of all the interested parties to this form. (Section 45 of the Trade Marks Act 1994 and Rule 26 of the Trade Marks Rules 1994 refer).*

General notes

f) *Complete the form in capital letters or type it.*

g) *If there is not enough space for your answer to any section of this form, use separate sheets. Number each one and write on the form how many extra sheets you have used.*

h) *Once you have completed the form you must remember to sign and date it.*

i) *If you need help or have any questions, please contact the Trade Marks Registry on 0645 500505.*

Form TM22

A5–16

No official fee due

The
Patent
Office

Notice of a partial surrender of the specification of goods or services for which the mark is registered

Please refer to notes for guidance on completing this form

The Patent Office
Trade Marks Registry
Cardiff Road, Newport
South Wales NP9 1RH

	Registration number	*(Lowest)* Class
1. Give details of the registration this applies to		
2. Full name, address and postcode of the registered proprietor		
3. Indicate whether you wish to be:- a) Address for Service b) Agent c) Both for d) This transaction only e) All transactions *(indicate a) to e) as appropriate)* *[see note j]* If you have completed this section please provide details and ADP Number *(if you know it)* Your reference		
4. Goods or services to be surrendered *[see note f]*		
5. Are there any licensees or does any one else have a registered interest in the registration? *(if yes write the details on an attached sheet)*		
Signature	Declaration *I confirm that there are no parties having a registered interest in the mark* *or* *I confirm that those with a registered interest in the mark (see attached sheet), have been notified three months prior to this form being filed, or that they consent to the surrender.*	

(REV/1)

Form TM23

Form TM23

Name *(block capitals)*	
Date	
Name and daytime telephone number of person to contact	
State number of sheets attached to this form	

Specific notes

a) The proprietor of a registered trade mark can surrender their legal rights to all or part of the goods or services for which is registered. (Section 45 of the Trade Marks Act 1994 refers).

b) This form is used if you are giving up your legal rights to only some of the goods or services, and you should use an attached form for each trade mark affected.

c) Do not use this form if you are giving up your legal rights to the whole of the registration. Please use form TM22 instead.

d) Only one registration number is allowed on each form.

e) You must inform all of the people who have an interest in your mark that you are going to give up some of your rights in the mark 3 months beforehand, or they should consent to this. You also need to attach a list of all the interested parties to this form. (Section 45 of the Trade Marks Act 1994 and Rule 26 of the Trade Marks Rules 1994 refer).

f) If the goods or services to be surrendered fall in more than one class the they should be listed by class.

General notes

g) Complete the form in capital letters or type it.

h) If there is not enough space for your answer to any section of this form, use separate sheets. Number each one and write on the form how many extra sheets you have used.

i) Once you have completed the form you must remember to sign and date it.

j) If your address for service is different from your agent, then please give us full details of both.

k) If you need help or you have any questions, please contact the Trade Marks Registry on 0645 500505.

Form TM23

A5–17

The Patent Office

Form TM24

Application to record or cancel a registrable transaction other than an assignment or licence

Application to record or cancel a notifiable transaction for a designation under the Madrid Protocol

Please refer to notes for guidance on completing this form

The Patent Office
Trade Marks Registry
Cardiff Road, Newport
South Wales NP9 1RH

1. Give details of the registrations this will affect	Number(s)	*(Lowest)* Class
or		
the designations under the Madrid Protocol this will affect	Number(s)	*(Lowest)* Class
2. Full name, address and postcode of the grantor		
Trade Marks ADP number *(if you know it)*		
3. FOR DOMESTIC TRADE MARKS:		
Full name, address and postcode of the person recorded, or to be recorded, as having an interest in the registered trade marks shown above		
FOR DESIGNATIONS UNDER THE MADRID PROTOCOL:		
Full name, address and postcode of the licensee or person recorded, or to be recorded, as having an interest in the designations under the Madrid Protocol shown above		
4. Indicate whether you wish to be:-		
a) Address for service b) Agent c) Both		
for		
d) This transaction only e) All transactions *(indicate a) to e) as appropriate)* *[See note n]*		
If you have completed this section, please provide details and ADP number *(if you know it)*		
Your reference:-		

(REV/1)

Form TM24

5. **FOR DOMESTIC TRADE MARKS:**

Details of the registrable transaction to be
recorded or cancelled including:
(where appropriate)

a) the nature of the interest
   (whether fixed or floating)
b) the extent of the security and the right
   in or under the mark secured

**FOR DESIGNATIONS UNDER THE
MADRID PROTOCOL:**

Details of the notifiable transaction to be
recorded or cancelled as follows:-

Where granting of any security interests:

a) the nature of the interest
   (whether fixed or floating)
b) the extent of the security and the right
   in or under the mark

Where granting a licence:

c) date licence starts
d) date licence ends (if any)
e) is the licence to be exclusive?
f) is the licensee to be recorded for all the
   goods and services for which the
   international trade mark (UK) is protected?

If not, state specific goods or services the
licensee is to be recorded against in each case

6. Signature of the grantor *(or his or her representative)*

Signature

Name *(block capitals)*

Date

7. Signature of the person shown at section 3
   (or his or her representative)

Signature

Name *(block capitals)*

Date

Name and daytime telephone number
(of person completing this form)

State number of sheets attached
to this form

(REV/1)   Form TM24

Specific notes

This form can be used for both domestic trade marks and for designations under the Madrid Protocol for the following transactions:

DOMESTIC TRADE MARKS

a) *Section 25 of the Trade Marks Act 1994 and Rule 35 of the Trade Marks Rules 1994 allow for a person who claims to have an interest in, (or under) a registered trade mark to apply to have the details of that claim entered onto the Register. This claim may stem from:*

 - *the person being granted the trade mark as a security interest, or any right in or under it;*

 - *the making by personal representatives of an assent for the trade mark, or any right in or under it;*

 - *a court or other competent authority transferring the trade mark, or any right in or under it.*

b) *Such a right may also be removed.*

c) *For changes in name and address of the person having an interest in the trade mark, please use Form TM21.*

d) *In the case of transferring your legal rights to someone else, please use Form TM16.*

e) *To record a licence, please use Form TM50.*

FOR DESIGNATIONS UNDER THE MADRID PROTOCOL

f) *Article 6 of the Trade Marks (International Registration) Order 1996, allows for a person claiming to have an interest in (or under) an international trade mark (UK) to apply to have the details of a notifiable transaction entered in the supplementary register. The following are notifiable transactions:*

 - *the grant of a licence under a protected international trade mark (UK); or*

 - *the granting of any security interest (whether fixed or floating) over an international trade mark (UK) or any right in or under it.*

g) *Such a right may also be removed.*

h) *To amend the recordal of a licence, please use Form TM51.*

i) *For changes in name and address of the person having an interest in the trade mark, please use Form TM21.*

j) *This form must be signed by the grantor (or his or her representative). It is acceptable for this to be signed in the name of the firm or company. If you cannot do this, you may send us documentary evidence to support this transaction. Any documentary evidence submitted with this form will be open to public inspection.*

General notes

k) *Complete the form in capital letters or type it.*

l) *If there is not enough space for your answer to any section of this form, use separate sheets. Number each one and write on the form how many extra sheets you have used.*

m) *Once you have completed the form you must remember to sign and date it.*

n) *If your address for service is different from your agent, then please give us full details of both.*

o) *If you need help or have any questions, please contact the Trade Marks Registry on 0645 500505.*

(REV/1)   **Form TM24**

A5–18

Form TM25

No official fee due

**The
Patent
Office**

Request for alteration of a registered mark

Please refer to notes for guidance on completing this form

The Patent Office
Trade Marks Registry
Cardiff Road, Newport
South Wales NP9 1RH

1. Give details of the registrations this will affect	Number	*(Lowest)* Class

2. Full name, address and postcode of the registered proprietor

3. Details of the change to the mark

If the mark is pictorial then please attach a copy of the amended mark here

FOOTNOTE

The Trade Marks Act 1994, Section 44 states the Registrar may, at the request of the proprietor, allow the alteration of a registered trade mark where the mark includes the proprietor's name or address and the alteration is limited to alteration of that name or address and does not substantially affect the identity of the mark.

(REV/1)

Form TM25

Form TM25

4. Indicate whether you wish to be:- a) Address for Service b) Agent c) Both *for* d) This transaction only e) All transactions *(indicate a) to e) as appropriate)* *[see note d]* If you have completed this section please provide details and ADP number *(if you know it)* Your reference	
Signature	
Name *(block capitals)*	
Date	
Name and daytime telephone number of person to contact	
State number of sheets attached to this form	

General notes

a) *Complete the form in capital letters or type it.*

b) *If there is not enough space for your answer to any section of this form, use separate sheets. Number each one and write on the form how many extra sheets you have used.*

c) *Once you have completed the form you must remember to sign and date it.*

d) *If your address for service is different from your agent, then please give us full details of both.*

e) *If you need help or have any questions, please contact the Trade Marks Registry on 0645 500505.*

Form TM25

Form TM26(I)

Official fee due

A5–19

Application for a declaration that a registration be declared invalid

Application for the invalidation of a protected international trade mark (UK);

Please refer to notes for guidance on completing this form

The Patent Office
Trade Marks Registry
Cardiff Road, Newport
South Wales NP10 8QQ

1. Give details of the registration *or* the designation under the Madrid Protocol for which invalidity is sought	Number	Class/es
2. Full name of registered proprietor		
3. Full name, address and postcode of applicant for declaration of invalidity		
4. Name of agent *(if appropriate)* 'Address for service' in the United Kingdom to which all correspondence should be sent *(including postcode)* *[see note j]* Trade Marks ADP number *(if you know it)* Your reference		
5. Signature	**Declaration** *I declare that to the best of my knowledge there is no action concerning the registration pending in the courts. I confirm the accuracy and truth of the matter contained in the accompanying statement of case.*
Name *(block capitals)*	
Date	
Name and daytime telephone number of person to contact	
State the number of sheets attached to this form	

(REV/2)

Form TM26(I)

Form TM26(I)

Specific notes

a) *This form is used to request the invalidation of a registered trade mark,*

or

b) *the invalidation of a protected international trade mark (UK);*

c) *If proceedings concerning the trade mark are waiting to be dealt with in court, you must apply to the court.*

d) *The Registrar may refer an application for declaration of invalidity to the court at any stage.*

e) *This form must be accompanied by a statement of case in support of your application. You are required to declare the accuracy and truth of the matter contained in the accompanying statement of case.*

f) *Guidance notes on invalidity procedures are available on request from the Law Section of the Trade Marks Registry.*

General notes

g) *Complete the form in capital letters or type it.*

h) *If there is not enough space for your answer to any section of this form, use separate sheets. Number each one and write on the form how many extra sheets you have used.*

i) *Once you have completed the form you must remember to sign and date it.*

j) *If your address for service is different from your agent, then please give us full details of both.*

k) *If you need help or have any questions, please contact the Trade Marks Registry on 0645 500505.*

(REV/2)

Form TM26(I)

Form TM26(N)

Official fee due

A5–20

Application for the revocation of a registration on the grounds of non-use

Application for the revocation of a protected international trade mark (UK); on the grounds of non-use

Please refer to notes for guidance on completing this form

The Patent Office
Trade Marks Registry
Cardiff Road, Newport
South Wales NP10 8QQ

1. Give details of the registration *or* the designation under the Madrid Protocol for which revocation is sought	Number	Class/es
2. Full name of registered proprietor		
3. Full name, address and postcode of applicant for revocation		
4. Name of agent *(if appropriate)* 'Address for service' in the United Kingdom to which all correspondence should be sent *(including postcode)* *[see note j]* Trade Marks ADP number *(if you know it)* Your reference		

5.	Declaration
	I declare that to the best of my knowledge there is no action concerning the registration pending in the courts. I confirm the truth and accuracy of the matter contained in the accompanying statement of case.
Signature	
Name *(block capitals)*	
Date	
Name and daytime telephone number of person to contact	
State the number of sheets attached to this form	

(REV/2)

Form TM26(N)

Form TM26(N)

Specific notes

a) *This form is used to request the revocation of a registered trade mark, under Section 46(1)(a) or (b)*

   or

b) *the revocation of a protected international trade mark (UK); under Section 46(1)(a) or (b)*

c) *If proceedings concerning the trade mark are waiting to be dealt with in court, you must apply to the court.*

d) *The Registrar may refer an application for revocation, to the court at any stage.*

e) *This form must be accompanied by a statement of case in support of your application. You are required to declare the truth and accuracy of the matter contained in the accompanying statement of case.*

f) *Guidance notes on revocation procedures are available on request from the Law Section of the Trade Marks Registry.*

General notes

g) *Complete the form in capital letters or type it.*

h) *If there is not enough space for your answer to any section of this form, use separate sheets. Number each one and write on the form how many extra sheets you have used.*

i) *Once you have completed the form you must remember to sign and date it.*

j) *If your address for service is different from your agent, then please give us full details of both.*

k) *If you need help or have any questions, please contact the Trade Marks Registry on 0645 500505.*

(REV/2)

Form TM26(N)

Form TM26(O)

Official fee due

A5–21

Application for the revocation of a registration on grounds other than non-use

Application for the revocation of a protected international trade mark (UK) on grounds other than non-use

Please refer to notes for guidance on completing this form

The Patent Office
Trade Marks Registry
Cardiff Road, Newport
South Wales NP10 8QQ

1. Give details of the registration *or* the designation under the Madrid Protocol for which revocation invalidity is sought	Number	Class/es
2. Full name of registered proprietor		
3. Full name, address and postcode of applicant for revocation		
4. Name of agent *(if appropriate)* 'Address for service' in the United Kingdom to which all correspondence should be sent *(including postcode)* *[see note J]* Trade Marks ADP number *(if you know it)* Your reference		

5.		Declaration *I declare that to the best of my knowledge there is no action concerning the registration pending in the courts. I confirm the truth and accuracy of the matter contained in the accompanying statement of case.*
	Signature	
	Name *(block capitals)*	
	Date	
	Name and daytime telephone number of person to contact	
	State the number of sheets attached to this form	

(REV/2)

Form TM26(O)

Form TM26(O)

Specific notes

a) *This form is used to request the revocation of a registered trade mark, under Section 46(1)(c) or (d) of the Act.*

    or

b) *the revocation of a protected international trade mark (UK)*

c) *If proceedings concerning the trade mark are waiting to be dealt with in court, you must apply to the court.*

d) *The Registrar may refer an application for revocation to the court at any stage.*

e) *This form must be accompanied by a statement of case in support of your application. You are required to declare the accuracy and truth of the matter contained in the accompanying statement of case.*

f) *Guidance notes on revocation procedures are available on request from the Law Section of the Trade Marks Registry.*

General notes

g) *Complete the form in capital letters or type it.*

h) *If there is not enough space for your answer to any section of this form, use separate sheets. Number each one and write on the form how many extra sheets you have used.*

i) *Once you have completed the form you must remember to sign and date it.*

j) *If your address for service is different from your agent, then please give us full details of both.*

k) *If you need help or have any questions, please contact the Trade Marks Registry on 0645 500505.*

(REV/2)

Form TM26(O)

Form TM26(R)

A5–22

Application for the rectification of a registration

Application for the rectification of the supplementary register

Please refer to notes for guidance on completing this form

The Patent Office
Trade Marks Registry
Cardiff Road, Newport
South Wales NP10 8QQ

	Number(s)	Class/es
1. Give details of the registration(s) *or* the designation(s) under the Madrid Protocol for which rectification is sought		
2. Full name of registered proprietor		
3. Full name, address and postcode of applicant for rectification		
4. Name of agent *(if appropriate)* 'Address for service' in the United Kingdom to which all correspondence should be sent *(including postcode)* *[see note j]* Trade Marks ADP number *(if you know it)* Your reference		

5.	Declaration
	I declare that to the best of my knowledge there is no action concerning the registration pending in the courts. I confirm the truth and accuracy of the matter contained in the accompanying statement of case.
Signature	
Name *(block capitals)*	
Date	
Name and daytime telephone number of person to contact	
State the number of sheets attached to this form	

(REV/2)

Form TM26(R)

975

A5–23

Form TM26(R)

Application for the rectification of a registration

Application for the rectification of the supplementary register

Please refer to notes for guidance on completing this form

The Patent Office
Trade Marks Registry
Cardiff Road, Newport
South Wales NP10 8QQ

	Number(s)	Class/es
1. Give details of the registration(s) *or* the designation(s) under the Madrid Protocol for which rectification is sought		
2. Full name of registered proprietor		
3. Full name, address and postcode of applicant for rectification		
4. Name of agent *(if appropriate)* 'Address for service' in the United Kingdom to which all correspondence should be sent *(including postcode)* *[see note j]* Trade Marks ADP number *(if you know it)* Your reference		

5.

Signature

Declaration
I declare that to the best of my knowledge there is no action concerning the registration pending in the courts. I confirm the truth and accuracy of the matter contained in the accompanying statement of case.

Name *(block capitals)*

Date

Name and daytime telephone number of person to contact

State the number of sheets attached to this form

(REV/2)

Form TM26(R)

Form TM27

No official fee due

**The
Patent
Office**

A5–24

Application to intervene in proceedings for the revocation, invalidation or rectification of a registration

Application to intervene in proceedings for the revocation or invalidation of a protected international trade mark (UK) or rectification of the supplementary register

Please refer to notes for guidance on completing this form

The Patent Office
Trade Marks Registry
Cardiff Road, Newport
South Wales NP9 1RH

	Number	*(Lowest)* Class	Revocation/invalidation number
1. Give details of the registration this will affect			
or			
the designation under the Madrid Protocol to which this request relates	Number	*(Lowest)* Class	Revocation/invalidation number
2. Full name and address of registered proprietor			
3. Full name, address and postcode of applicant for intervention			
4. Name of agent *(if appropriate)*			
'Address for service' in the United Kingdom to which all correspondence should be sent for the intervenor *(including postcode) [see note g]*			
Trade Marks ADP number *(if you know it)*			
Your reference			

REMINDER
Have you attached the grounds of your application to intervene?
(REV/1)

Form TM27

Signature	
Name *(block capitals)*	
Date	
Name and daytime telephone number of person to contact	
State the number of sheets attached to this form	

Specific notes

a) *This form is used if you wish to intervene in proceedings for the revocation, rectification or declaration of invalidity of the registration of a trade mark,*

or

b) *to intervene in proceedings for the revocation or invalidation of a protected international trade mark (UK) or rectification of the supplementary register.*

c) *This form must be accompanied by a statement of the grounds of your application.*

General notes

d) *Complete the form in capital letters or type it.*

e) *If there is not enough space for your answer to any section of this form, use separate sheets. Number each one and write on the form how many extra sheets you have used.*

f) *Once you have completed the form you must remember to sign and date it.*

g) *If your address for service is different from your agent, then please give us full details of both.*

h) *If you need help or have any questions, please contact the Trade Marks Registry on 0645 500505.*

Form TM28

No official fee due

The
Patent
Office

A5–25

Request for Recordal of concurrent registration

Please refer to notes for guidance on completing this form

The Patent Office
Trade Marks Registry
Cardiff Road, Newport
South Wales NP9 1RH

	Number(s)	*(Lowest)* Class
1. Give details of the domestic registration(s) this will affect		
Give details of the designation(s) under the Madrid Protocol to which this request relates	Number(s)	*(Lowest)* Class
2. Full name, address of the holder of the protected international trade mark (UK)		
3. Name of agent *(if appropriate)* Address for service in the United Kingdom to which correspondence should be sent *[see note e]*		
Your Reference		
Signature		
Name *(block capitals)*		
Date		
Name and daytime telephone number of person to contact		
State the number of sheets attached to this form		

(REV/1)

Form TM28

Specific notes

a) This form is used to request that the protected international registration (UK) is noted in the register against the registered trade mark.

b) The provisions of Article 21 apply only where:

- the registered trade mark is also a protected international trade mark (UK)
- the proprietor of the registered trade mark is the holder of the international trade mark (UK)
- all the goods or services in respect of which the trade mark is registered are protected under the protected international trade mark (UK)
- the date of registration of the registered trade mark is earlier than the date specified in relation to the international trade mark (UK).

General notes

c) Complete the form in capital letters or type it.

d) If there is not enough space for your answer to any section of this form, use separate sheets. Number each one and write on the form how many extra sheets you have used.

e) If your address for service is different from your agent, then please give us full details of both.

f) Once you have completed the form you must remember to sign and date it.

g) If you need help or have any questions please contact the Trade Marks Registry on 0645 500505.

Form TM31C

A5–26

Official fee due

The
Patent
Office

Request for information about applications and registered marks

The Patent Office
Trade Marks Registry
Cardiff Road, Newport
South Wales NP9 1RH

Please refer to notes for guidance on completing this form

1. Give details of the application or registration to which this request relates	Number	*(Lowest)* Class
2. Indicate for which category or categories of events you require notification *(A to H as detailed below)* *(A separate fee is payable for each category indicated)*		

Category	You will be notified of:
A	application published or withdrawn, refused or deemed abandoned before publication
B	current or future formal opposition filed against a new trade mark application
C	application registered or withdrawn, refused or abandoned after publication
D	unpaid renewal (registration in additional renewal fee period)
E	registration renewed or expired
F	full surrender or successful revocation resulting in the removal of a mark from the register
G	assignment application received
H	assignment in full or partial assignment

(REV/1)

Form TM31C

Form TM31C

3. If your request is for an event not listed in 2, give details here	
4. Full name, address and postcode to which notifications should be sent Trade Marks ADP number *(if you know it)* Your reference	
Signature	
Name *(block capitals)*	
Date	
Name and daytime telephone number of person to contact	
State number of sheets attached to this form	

Reminder

A fee is required for each category you have indicated.

Specific notes

a) *Since the Trade Marks Register is a public record, anyone can ask to be told about any action on any application or registration. The form lists the categories which you can be notified about. This form is not open to public inspection and information is disclosed only to the person filing the form.*

b) *A separate form should be used for each trade mark number.*

c) *A separate fee is payable for each category you want to be notified of.*

General notes

d) *Complete the form in capital letters or type it.*

e) *If there is not enough space for your answer to any section of this form, use separate sheets. Number each one and write on the form how many extra sheets you have used.*

f) *Once you have completed the form you must remember to sign and date it.*

g) *If you need help or have any questions, please contact the Trade Marks Registry on 0645 500505.*

Form TM31C

form TM31M

Official fee due

The
Patent
Office

A5–27

Request for information in relation to an international trade mark (UK)

Please refer to notes for guidance on completing this form

The Patent Office
Trade Marks Registry
Cardiff Road, Newport
South Wales NP9 1RH

1. Give details of the international trade mark (UK) to which this request relates	Number	*(Lowest)* Class
2. Indicate for which category or categories of events you require notification *(A to F as detailed below)* *(A separate fee is payable for each category indicated)*		

Category	You will be notified of:
A	publication of an international trade mark (UK) in the UK Trade Marks Journal or total/partial refusal before publication
B	formal opposition filed against an international trade mark (UK)
C	international trade mark (UK) protected or withdrawn, refused or abandoned after publication
D	renewal of the protected international trade mark (UK)
E	successful revocation or declaration of invalidity of a protected international trade mark (UK)
F	change of ownership of an international trade mark (UK)

(REV/1)

Form TM31M

3. Full name, address and postcode to which notifications should be sent	
Trade Marks ADP number *(if you know it)*	
Your reference	
Signature	
Name *(block capitals)*	
Date	
Name and daytime telephone number of person to contact	
State the number of sheets attached to this form	

Reminder: *A fee is required for each category you have indicated*

Specific notes

a) This form is used to request information relating to an international trade mark registration designating the United Kingdom under the Madrid Protocol (Article 25 of the Trade Marks (International Registration) Order 1996).
The form lists the categories you can be informed about.

b) A separate form should be used for each international trade mark (UK) number.

c) A separate fee is payable for each category you want to be notified of.

General notes

d) Complete the form in capital letters or type it.

e) If there is not enough space for your answer to any section of this form, use separate sheets. Number each one and write on the form how many extra sheets you have used.

f) Once you have completed the form you must remember to sign and date it.

g) If you need help or have any questions, please contact the Trade Marks Registry on 0645 500505.

(REV/1)

Form TM31M

Form TM31R

Official fee due

A5–28

Request for a Certified Copy

The Patent Office
Trade Marks Registry
Cardiff Road, Newport
South Wales NP9 1RH

Please refer to notes for guidance on completing this form

1. Give details of the applications or registrations which the certificates are for	Number(s)	*(Lowest)* Class
or		
designation(s) under the Madrid Protocol for which a certificate is required	Number(s)	*(Lowest)* Class
2. State the number of certified copies required		
3. If certificates are for obtaining registration abroad list the countries		
4. State any special requirements needed: a) representation of the mark in colour *[see note c]* b) details as filed *[see note c]* c) for use in legal proceedings d) anything else, please specify *(indicate a) to d) as appropriate)*		
5. Full name, address and postcode to which the certificates should be sent		
Your Reference		
Signature		
Name *(block capitals)*		
Date		
Name and daytime telephone number of person to contact		
State the number of sheets attached to this form		

REMINDER   *A fee is required for each certificate requested*

(REV/1)

Form TM31R

Form TM31R

Specific notes

a) This form is used to request a certificate from the Registrar concerning the details of a trade mark or a protected international trade mark (UK). You might need a certificate to prove you have made an application, or have a registration in the United Kingdom, or a protected international trade mark (UK), or in legal proceedings (Rule 37 of the Trade Marks Rules 1994 refers).

b) If you are going to use the certificate for obtaining registration abroad you must list the country or countries, so that the certificate is prepared in the correct way.

c) For domestic applications please provide a copy of the Form TM3 as originally filed if you require a certificate showing:

   (i) trade mark in colour; or

   (ii) TM3 as filed if the form TM3 has subsequently been amended during the course of the examination.

General notes

d) Complete the form in capital letters or type it.

e) If there is not enough space for your answer to any section of this form, use separate sheets. Number each one and write on the form how many extra sheets you have used.

f) Once you have completed the form you must remember to sign and date it.

g) If you need help or have any questions please contact the Trade Marks Registry on 0645 500505.

(REV/1)

Form TM31R

Form TM33

No official fee due

A5–29

Request to appoint or change an agent or to enter or change an address for service

Please refer to notes for guidance on completing this form

The Patent Office
Trade Marks Registry
Cardiff Road, Newport
South Wales NP9 1RH

1. Give details of the applications or registrations this will affect	Number(s)	*(Lowest)* Class	Licensee Numbers
or			
the designation under the Madrid Protocol to which this request relates	Number(s)	*(Lowest)* Class	Licensee Numbers
2. Full name of (a) proprietor (b) opponent (c) licensee *(indicate a) to c) as appropriate)*			
3. On behalf of the proprietor, grantor, licensee or opponent we notify you that we are the authorised: a) agent and address for service *or* b) address for service *or* c) agent *(indicate a) to c) as appropriate)*			
4. Is the agent or address for service authorised for: a) all transactions *or* b) this transaction only *(indicate a) or b) and if b) provide details of transaction)*			
5. New address for service or agent's details to be recorded			
Trade Marks ADP number *(if you know it)*			
Your reference			
Signature			
Name *(block capitals)*			
Date			
Name and daytime telephone number of person to contact			
State number of sheets attached to this form			

(REV/1)

Form TM33

987

Specific notes

a) *This form is used if you want to appoint an agent either for the first time or to replace an existing agent recorded against a trade mark application or registration or international trade mark (UK) or protected international trade mark (UK). You may also use it to enter or change an address for service. (Rules 10 and 38 of the Trade Marks Rules 1994 refer).*

b) *This form can be used for as many cases as you need. You should indicate at Section 1 the registration or application numbers of all the cases affected by these changes.*

General notes

c) *Complete the form in capital letters or type it.*

d) *If there is not enough space for your answer to any section of this form, use separate sheets. Number each one and write on the form how many extra sheets you have used.*

e) *Once you have completed the form you must remember to sign and date it.*

f) *If you need help or have any questions, please contact the Trade Marks Registry on 0645 500505.*

Form TM33

Form TM35

Official fee due

The
Patent
Office

A5–30

Filing of regulations governing the use of certification or collective marks

Please refer to notes for guidance on completing this form

The Patent Office
Trade Marks Registry
Cardiff Road, Newport
South Wales NP9 1RH

1. Give details of the applications to which the regulations relate	Number(s)	*(Lowest)* Class
or		
the designation under the Madrid Protocol to which this request relates	Number(s)	*(Lowest)* Class
2. Does this request relate to: a) certification marks *or* b) collective marks *(indicate a) or b) as appropriate)*		
3. Full name of applicant		
4. Name of agent *(if appropriate)* 'Address for service' in the United Kingdom to which all correspondence should be sent *(including postcode)* *[see note f]* Trade Marks ADP number *(if you know it)* Your reference		
Signature		
Name *(block capitals)*		
Date		
Name and daytime telephone number of person to contact		
State number of sheets attached to this form		

(REV/1)

Form TM35

989

Specific notes

a) This form is used to file the regulations for a certification or collective mark within nine months from the date of application (Schedule 2 Paragraph 6, and Schedule 1 Paragraph 5, of the Trade Marks Act 1994 refer).

b) You should say in Section 2 of the form if the regulations apply to certification or collective marks. The regulations can refer to a number of marks, but they cannot apply to a mixture of both certification and collective marks.

General notes

c) Complete the form in capital letters or type it.

d) If there is not enough space for your answer to any section of this form, use separate sheets. Number each one and write on the form how many extra sheets you have used.

e) Once you have completed the form you must remember to sign and date it.

f) If your address for service is different from your agent, then please give give us full details of both.

g) If you need help or have any questions, please contact the Trade Marks Registry on 0645 500505.

Form TM36

A5–31

The
Patent
Office

Official fee due

Application to amend the regulations governing the use of a certification or collective mark

The Patent Office
Trade Marks Registry
Cardiff Road, Newport
South Wales NP9 1RH

Please refer to notes for guidance on completing this form

1. Give details of the applications or registrations	Number(s)	*(Lowest)* Class
or		
designation under the Madrid Protocol to which this request relates	Number(s)	*(Lowest)* Class
2. Does this request relate to: a) certification marks or b) collective marks *(indicate a) or b) as appropriate)*		
3. Does this request relate to: a) applications or b) marks already registered *(indicate a) or b) as appropriate)*		
4. Full name of applicant		
5. Name of agent *(if appropriate)* 'Address for service' in the United Kingdom to which all correspondence should be sent *(including postcode)* *[see note g]* Trade Marks ADP number *(if you know it)* Your reference		
Signature		
Name *(block capitals)*		
Date		
Name and daytime telephone number of person to contact		
State number of sheets attached to this form		

(REV/1)

Form TM36

Form TM36

Specific notes

a) This form is used when you want to amend any regulations that have already been filed. (Schedule 2 Paragraph 11, and Schedule 1 Paragraph 10, of the Trade Marks Act 1994 refer).

b) You should say in Section 2 of the form if the regulations apply to certification or collective marks. The regulations can refer to a number of marks, but they cannot apply to a mixture of both certification and collective marks.

c) You should say in Section 3 of the form whether these amended regulations apply to applications/international trade marks (UK) or registered marks/protected international trade marks (UK). These amendments to the regulations can refer to a number of marks, but they cannot apply to a mixture of both applications and registered marks.

General notes

d) Complete the form in capital letters or type it.

e) If there is not enough space for your answer to any section of this form, use separate sheets. Number each one and write on the form how many extra sheets you have used.

f) Once you have completed the form you must remember to sign and date it.

g) If your address for service is different from your agent, then please give us full details of both.

h) If you need help or have any questions, please contact the Trade Marks Registry on 0645 500505.

Form TM36

Form TM50

No official fee due

A5–32

Application to Register a Licensee

Please refer to notes for guidance on completing this form

The Patent Office
Trade Marks Registry
Cardiff Road, Newport
South Wales NP9 1RH

1. Give details of the trade marks you want a licensee recorded against	Number(s)	*(Lowest)* Class
2. Full name, address and postcode of the proprietor		
3. Full name, address and postcode of the licensee		

4. a) Date licence starts
 	
  b) Date licence ends
    (if any)		

5. Is the licence to be exclusive		
6. Is the licensee to be recorded for all goods or services for which the mark is registered/ application applied for? If not, state which specific goods or services or limited geographical area the licensee is to be recorded against in each case		

(REV/1)

Form TM50

Form TM50

7. Name of agent *(if appropriate)*	
'Address for service' in the United Kingdom to which all correspondence should be sent *(including postcode)* *(see note l)*	
Trade Marks ADP number *(if you know it)*	
Your reference	
8. Signature of the registered proprietor or grantor *(or his or her representative)*	
Signature	
Name *(block capitals)*	
Date	
9. Signature of the new licensee *(or his or her representative)*	
Signature	
Name *(block capitals)*	
Date	
Name and daytime telephone number *(of person to contact)*	
State number of sheets attached to this form	

(REV/1)

Form TM50

994

Form TM50

Specific notes

a) This form is used to record details of a licence granted by the proprietor of a trade mark (Sections 25, 28 and 29 of the Trade Marks Act 1994 refers). If you wish to record details of granting a licence under a protected international trade mark (UK) please use form TM24.

b) You should give the start date of the licence and the end date if appropriate.

c) If the licence is for part of the goods/services only, please give a description of the goods or services to which the licence will apply.

d) If multi class please list all the classes you wish to have a licensee recorded against.

e) This form must be signed by the grantor of the licence (or his or her representative). It is acceptable for this to be signed in the name of the firm or company. If you cannot do this, you may send us documentary evidence to support this transaction. Any documentary evidence submitted with this form will be open to public inspection.

General notes

f) Complete the form in capital letters or type it.

g) If there is not enough space for your answer to any section of this form, use separate sheets. Number each one and write on the form how many extra sheets you have used.

h) Once you have completed the form you must remember to sign and date it.

i) If your address for service is different from your agent, then please give us full details of both.

j) If you need help or have any questions please contact the Trade Marks Registry on 0645 500505.

(REV/1)

Form TM50

A5–33

Form TM51

No official fee due

The
Patent
Office

Application to remove or amend the recordal of a licence

Please refer to notes for guidance on completing this form

The Patent Office
Trade Marks Registry
Cardiff Road, Newport
South Wales NP9 1RH

	Number(s)	*(Lowest)* Class	Licensee numbers
1. Give details of the trade marks affected			
or			
the designations under the Madrid Protocol this will affect	Number(s)	*(Lowest)* Class	Licensee numbers

2. Full name of the proprietor of the trade marks or designations under the Madrid Protocol shown above

3. Full name of the licensee whose licence will be removed or amended

4. Please indicate whether this request is for:

    a) removal

    b) amendment

    (if b) please give details)

5. Name of agent *(if appropriate)*

Address for service in the United Kingdom to which all correspondence should be sent *(including postcode)* *[see note g]*

Your reference

(REV/1)

Form TM51

Form TM51

6. Signature of grantor of licence *(or his or her representative)*	
Name *(block capitals)*	
Date	
Name and daytime telephone number of person to contact	
7. Name of person completing this form *(if different from 6 above)*	
State number of sheets attached to this form	

Specific notes

a) *This form is used if an existing record of a licence is to be removed or amended (Section 25 of the Trade Marks Act 1994 refers and Article 6 of the Trade Marks (International Registration) Order 1996).*

b) *If you are the licensee you must get either the registered proprietor or the grantor (or their representative) of either the domestic trade mark or protected international trade mark (UK) to sign the form .*

c) *This form must be signed by the grantor of the licence (or his or her representative). It is acceptable for this to be signed in the name of the firm or company. If you cannot do this, you may send us documentary evidence to support this transaction. Any documentary evidence submitted with this form will be open to public inspection.*

General notes

d) *Complete the form in capital letters or type it.*

e) *If there is not enough space for your answer to any section of this form, use separate sheets. Number each one and write on the form how many extra sheets you have used.*

f) *Once you have completed the form you must remember to sign and date it.*

g) *If your address for service is different from your agent, then please give us full details of both.*

g) *If you need help or have any questions please contact the Trade Marks Registry on 0645 500505.*

(REV/1)

Form TM51

A5–34

Form TM/EOT

No official fee due

> The Patent Office
> Trade Marks Registry
> Cardiff Road
> NEWPORT
> South Wales
> NP9 1RH

REQUEST FOR AN EXTENSION OF TIME ON TRADE MARK APPLICATION

Application No: **in Class(es):**
Registry Ref: **Agent's Ref:**

We request an extension of time of   months from   to   in order to deal with outstanding matters on this application. The reasons for the request are as follows:

Yours faithfully

· ---

Application No: **in Class(es):**   **The Patent Office**
Agent's Ref: **Trade Marks Registry**
                                           Cardiff Road
                                           Newport NP9 1RH

GRANT OF REQUEST FOR AN EXTENSION OF TIME

Agent's name and address:-   Dear Sirs

Your request has been granted for an extension of time until:

Yours faithfully

TRADE MARKS EXAMINATION SECTION

Notes

You should use this form if you want an extension of time on an application which has been examined, and to which objections have been raised, but has not had an *ex parte* hearing held on it.

Please complete both the top and bottom parts of the form, especially the box for the return address.

We will sign and date the tear-off slip and return it to the address given if we grant the request.

Practice Notes

Tribunal Practice Notice

(TPN 1/2000)

<small>PRACTICE IN PROCEEDINGS BEFORE THE COMPTROLLER</small>

A6–01   1. This Practice Notice advises Patent Office customers of changes in practice in the way the Office operates as a tribunal hearing "with notice" (also known as *inter partes*) and "without notice" (also known as *ex parte*) proceedings, as well as reaffirming the continuation of certain existing practices. The changes, which are effective for all such proceedings from 26 April 2000, are among a number of measures that are being introduced following the Patent Office's review of its proceedings following Lord Woolf's report *Access to Justice*, which recommended major changes to the administration of civil justice in the courts of England and Wales. Those recommendations have since been implemented in the Civil Procedure Rules 1998. In line with the general principles set down by Lord Woolf, the Office's measures are intended to simplify and improve the speed of such proceedings before the Comptroller and thereby reduce the cost to Patent Office customers. The Standing Advisory Committee on Industrial Property and other interested parties, including the Council on Tribunals, were consulted about the proposals that emerged from the review and their views were taken into account in settling the final package of changes.

2. Some of the changes required amendment to the statutory rules. In the case of patents, registered designs and design right proceedings, these changes were respectively introduced by the Patents (Amendment) (No 2) Rules 1999, the Registered Designs (Amendment) Rules 1999, and the Design Right (Proceedings Before Comptroller) (Amendment) Rules 1999, all of which statutory instruments came into force on 22 December 1999. (Notices in the Patents & Designs Journal, Trade Marks Journal and Designs in View of 15 December 1999 gave more information about these SIs.) Changes to the trade marks rules were introduced as part of a general consolidation forming the Trade Marks Rules 2000 which came into force on 17 February 2000.

3. Many other of the changes arising from the review can, however, be introduced by altering established formal practice. This Practice Notice sets out how those changes are being made, as well as explaining how certain of the rule changes already implemented are being operated. Except as otherwise stated, this Practice Notice covers the full range of tribunal proceedings before the Comptroller, that is patents, trade marks, registered designs and design right, and references to "the rules" should accordingly be read generically.

4. The general practice with regard to the award of costs is set out in a separate notice *TPN 2/2000* entitled "Costs in Proceedings before the Comptroller".

The Overriding Objective

5. In its role as a tribunal, the Office adheres to the same overriding objective **A6–02** as the court for dealing with cases justly, as set out in rule 1.1 of the Civil Procedure Rules 1998. This includes, so far as is practicable:

(a) ensuring that the parties are on an equal footing;
(b) saving expense;
(c) dealing with the case in ways which are proportionate—
    (i) to the amount of money involved;
    (ii) to the importance of the case;
    (iii) to the complexity of the issues; and
    (iv) to the financial position of each party;
(d) ensuring that it is dealt with expeditiously and fairly; and
(e) allotting to it an appropriate share of the court's resources, while taking into account the need to allot resources to other cases.

Summary

6. The following main matters are addressed in this Practice Notice: **A6–03**

- The Office and parties should endeavour to complete *with notice* proceedings within 18 months. (paragraph 7)
- The periods for filing a counterstatement and evidence in patents, registered designs and design right proceedings has been shortened from two months to six weeks except when lodging an opposition, *e.g.* opposition to amend a patent specification under rule 40(2). (paragraph 8)
- The periods for filing a counterstatement and evidence in trade marks revocation (on grounds other than non-use), invalidation and rectification proceedings has been shortened to six weeks. However, the period will remain at three months in opposition and revocation on grounds of non-use proceedings, though an additional "cooling-off" period of three months at the start opposition proceedings will be granted when sought by both parties. (paragraph 9)
- Hearing Officers will have discretion to shorten prescribed periods, (paragraph 10)
- The Office will set a period within which a preliminary (interlocutory) hearing should take place and give parties 14 days to agree a date in that period. The Office will fix a date if after 14 days the parties do not agree a date within this period, although Hearing Officers may override the 14 days if there are genuine difficulties. (paragraph 13)
- At the commencement of the final evidence round, the Office will aim to fix a date for a substantive hearing for approximately four months later. (paragraph 14)
- The party commencing action should provide a statement of case which properly sets out the grounds on which the case against the other side is to be based. If a party fails to provide sufficient information, the Patent Office may challenge the statement. Until the statement of case is in order the proceedings will not be progressed. (paragraphs 15 to 19)
- The Office has provided broad guidelines on how to set out a statement of case. (paragraphs 20 to 25)
- A declaration of the truth of the information in claims and defences is required for trade marks proceedings and encouraged in other proceedings. (paragraph 27)
- The Office will accept a witness statement in evidence although Hearing Officers are authorised to require the filing of an affidavit or statutory declaration if they consider it necessary. (paragraph 30)

- Exceptionally the Office is prepared to accept unsigned witness statements or unsworn statutory declarations or affidavits as meeting time deadlines provided a proper version of the evidence is filed within a specified period. The Hearing Officer may impose a cost penalty if, in the event, the formal evidence is different from that originally filed. (paragraph 31)
- Where a party adduces evidence of a statement made by another person and does not call that person as a witness, the Hearing Officer may permit the other party to call that person and cross examine them. (paragraph 32)
- In deciding whether to grant specific disclosure, Hearing Officers will generally follow principles which mirror those applied by the courts. (paragraphs 33 to 37)
- The Office intends issuing questionnaires on a selective basis prior to evidence rounds. (paragraph 38)
- Hearing Officers will adopt the selective use of "case management conferences" taking into account the circumstances of the case, *e.g.* the need to clarify issues, the degree of complexity, any related actions and any wider public interest issues. (paragraphs 39 and 40)
- Hearing Officers are also empowered to call a "pre-hearing review" prior to a hearing which will give them the opportunity to clarify matters and issue directions on the conduct of the hearing. (paragraph 41)
- The Office will routinely ask parties if they have considered Alternative Dispute Resolution (ADR) and Hearing Officers will be prepared to stay proceedings where ADR is being used or seriously considered. They may also take into account a party's unreasonable refusal to consider ADR when awarding costs. (paragraph 42)
- In patents revocation hearings the applicant will be invited to open proceedings while in trade marks opposition hearings the opponent will be invited to open. (paragraph 43)
- Hearing Officers will retain discretion to deal with excessively long speeches and cross examination. (paragraph 44)
- Parties will generally be expected to supply skeleton arguments and authorities at least two days before a hearing. (paragraph 45)
- Adducing new evidence during a hearing will be discouraged and will only be allowed after the other party has had sufficient time to digest it. As a rule, documents will only be allowed to be introduced in cross examination which are designed to test the honesty and reliability of a witness. (paragraph 46)
- The Office will encourage parties to hold hearings, case management conferences and pre-hearing reviews using telephone conferencing arrangements and video links in suitable cases. (paragraph 47)
- Hearing Officers will offer parties the opportunity for proceedings to be decided without the need for a hearing. (paragraph 48)

Time Related Issues

Timescale for *with notice* proceedings

A6–04   7. It has been a central aim of the Patent Office's response to the Woolf Report that proceedings before the Comptroller should be conducted expeditiously within a reasonable overall time frame whilst still ensuring that parties have a full opportunity to present their case. The Office and parties should aim to complete *with notice* proceedings within 18 months of commencement, that is to say from the date when proceedings are formally joined by the filing of a counterstatement. Faster handling will be appropriate where a matter of particular public interest arises or when the parties themselves jointly request and work towards this end.

8. A number of rule changes bear on the period for filing pleadings and evidence, and harmonise practice where possible across the range of actions handled by the Office. Hence, the relevant patents, registered designs and design right rules have been amended so that the period for filing counterstatements and evidence has been shortened from two months to six weeks except when lodging an opposition, *e.g.* opposition to amend a patent specification under rule 40(2) of the Patents Rules (as amended).

9. The Trade Marks Rules 2000 provide for the six-week period to apply to revocation (on grounds other than non-use), invalidation and rectification proceedings. The corresponding time period for opposition and revocation on grounds of non-use will remain at three months. In addition, there will be provision for a cooling off period of three months at the start of opposition proceedings which will be granted when sought by both parties. This will be extendable (again at the request of both parties) by three months.

10. The rules will continue to provide discretion to extend statutory periods in certain circumstances. However, the rules are amended to afford Hearing Officers discretion to shorten many prescribed periods where appropriate. Such circumstances might be expected to arise where both parties to an action seek accelerated processing, or where external factors demand a decision in a shorter time frame than the standard period would permit.

11. Replies to the questionnaire that the Office proposes issuing on a selected basis prior to the evidence round (see paragraph 33 below) should help Hearing Officers decide whether the circumstances in a particular case warrant extending the period for filing evidence.

12. The anticipated benefits of speedier case handling will not be achieved if parties, their professional advisers and the Office do not work within the overall 18-month objective for the completion of *with notice* proceedings.

Fixing dates for preliminary hearings

13. In the case of preliminary hearings the Office will discontinue its practice **A6–05** in patents, design right and registered designs proceedings of allowing the parties an open-ended window within which to agree a hearing date. Instead, the Office will set a window within which a preliminary hearing should take place and will give the parties 14 days (if possible) within which to notify the Office of their agreed date. Failing such notification, the Office will itself *set* a date within the window. The Office will, however, endeavour to give minimum periods of notice and Hearing Officers will have discretion to override the 14 days in those cases where a party has a genuine difficulty in agreeing a hearing date. On the other hand, the 14-day period may be abbreviated in exceptional circumstances demanding a very urgent hearing. It is the intention of the Trade Marks Directorate to adopt a similar approach in the fullness of time but in the meantime, because of the backlog of preliminary hearings involving trade mark cases, the Directorate will continue its present practice of fixing dates for such hearings.

Fixing dates for main or substantive hearings

14. At the commencement of the final evidence round, the Office will aim to **A6–06** arrange a date for main or substantive hearings for approximately four months later. The Hearing Officer will, however, have discretion to direct that an earlier date, or exceptionally a later date, be fixed. Parties will be able to offer an alternative agreed date which is no later than that fixed by the Office. In the short term, because of the backlog of substantive hearings involving trade marks cases, the Trade Marks Directorate will continue its present policy of fixing dates.

Statements of Case

Pertinent and adequate statements of case

A6–07   15. In all proceedings before the Patent Office claimants are required to set out a statement of case on which the action is proceeding. The other party, for example the applicant for registration or the proprietor of the patent or trade mark, is then required to submit a counterstatement setting out the basis of the defence. Over the years a practice has built up, particularly in trade mark proceedings, whereby the statement of case has to a large extent been a recitation of the particular sections of the legislation under which the action is to proceed, with no particularisation of the case. In LIFESAVERS [1997] RPC page 567 the Hearing Officer said that in his view, "the substantive issues in this case and therefore the areas of contention between the parties have not yet been clearly defined. This is not surprising because it is only in the evidence rounds that the nature and areas of conflict are clarified." In recent judgements, the Vice-Chancellor has criticised that approach and in DEMON ALE [2000] RPC 345 Mr Geoffrey Hobbs QC acting as the Appointed Person has stated:

> "Considerations of justice, fairness, efficiency and economy combined to make it necessary for the pleadings of the parties in Registry proceedings to provide a focussed statement of the grounds upon which they intend to maintain that the Tribunal should or should not do what it has been asked to do."

16. It will be necessary, therefore, in all proceedings before the Comptroller for the party commencing the action to provide (in association with the appropriate form, *e.g.* TM7 Notice of Opposition) a statement of case upon which the case against the other side is to be based. This must include all of the grounds which the party intends to pursue and which are to be supported by evidence (where appropriate).

17. In future, the mere recitation of the section of the Act (or the provisions of a Rule) will not be sufficient to mount an action. There must be a sufficient degree of particularisation for the other side (and the Patent Office) to have a clear view of the nature of the dispute and have sufficient detail of, for example, the earlier trade marks or earlier rights and their use, on which the litigant intends to proceed.

18. As Mr Hobbs stated in the DEMON ALE decision:

> "The statement should not be prolix. It should however, be full in the sense indicated by Mr Simon Thorley QC in COFFEE MIXJ [1998] RPC 717 at 722; it must be full in the sense that it must outline each of the grounds ..... relied upon and state the case relied upon in support of those grounds. It should be as succinct as possible but it must be complete."

19. If a party fails to provide sufficient information in the statement of case as to the nature or extent of the grounds upon which the proceedings rely, the Patent Office may challenge the statement and seek to have it put in proper order. In those cases where there may be only some of the grounds of the action fully pleaded, the party or their representative will be asked to provide such further information as may be reasonably required to complete the statement, or to delete the deficient grounds. Until the statement of case is in order, the proceedings will not be progressed and the subsequent delay may be a factor which will be taken into account at the point at which costs are determined.

Presentation of statement of case

A6–08   20. With a view to fostering greater uniformity of court practice, Lord Woolf's report set out basic requirements for presenting a statement of case. Although proceedings before the Office usually commence with the lodging of an official form, there is considerable variation of practice in framing supporting statements, particularly where private litigants are involved. The Office believes that it would be of assistance to litigants if they were given broad guidelines on how to set out their statements. This should in turn help the Office in identifying the type of action that is being launched.

21. In general the claimant (*i.e.* the person initiating the proceedings) should set out in their statement:

- the matter in issue
- the facts to be relied on, and
- the relief sought.

22. Whilst sometimes the **matter in issue** is implicit in the nature of the proceedings, generally it needs to be set out in detail. For example, the grounds on which revocation of a patent or invalidation of a trade mark is sought must be set out fully. The **facts to be relied on** (as distinct from the evidence that will later be adduced to prove those facts) should also be set out concisely but fully. Whilst in the past statements filed in proceedings before the Comptroller have sometimes been lacking in real detail as to the facts, statements must now be reasonably detailed. The **relief sought** should be clearly stated. Costs need be not specifically claimed in a statement, though they usually are.

23. In their counter-statement, the defendant must state:

- which of the allegations in the statement they deny and why (and if they intend to put forward an alternative version of events, what that version is);
- which of the allegations in the statement they are unable to admit or deny but require the claimant to prove;
- which of the allegations in the statement they admit.

24. The purpose of the counter-statement is to narrow down the field of dispute, because the claimant will not need to prove any allegations which the defendant admits. Whilst in the past counter-statements have sometimes been very sketchy, that is no longer acceptable. If a counter-statement leaves uncertainty about what is and is not in dispute, it is inadequate. Thus, the counter-statement must deal specifically with every allegation in the statement. (Indeed, any allegation not dealt with is generally deemed to be admitted by the defendant.) Again, costs need not be specifically claimed, though they usually are.

25. If the presentation of a statement or counter-statement is clearly inadequate, the Comptroller will refuse to serve it. Of course, even when a statement or counter-statement is served that does not mean the Comptroller has decided it is satisfactory, and the recipient is still entitled to object to its adequacy.

Supply of Documents with statements of case

26. The Office considered removing from the patents rules the requirement to **A6–09** supply documents with the statement of case, bearing in mind that the documents would have to be re-filed later as part of the evidence. However, patent practitioners did not consider it unduly burdensome to file such documents twice and to the contrary felt that it was important for the other party in proceedings to have sight of any documents referred to in the statement of case at the earliest opportunity so that they were fully aware of the case against them. It has therefore been decided to maintain present provisions in the rules that requires that copies of any documents referred to in statements of case should be supplied with the statements themselves.

Confirming accuracy and truth of a statement of case

27. The Office has decided to adopt Lord Woolf's recommendation that claims **A6–10** and defences should contain a declaration on behalf of the parties confirming the accuracy and truth of the matter contained in them. Such a declaration is

required for trade marks proceedings and encouraged in other proceedings. It should be noted that such a declaration is necessary if a party wanted, in any subsequent appeal to the High Court, a statement of case to be taken into account as evidence.

28. Examples of a declaration that would be acceptable are:

"I/we confirm that the information contained in this statement of case is true to the best of my/our knowledge and belief."
or
"I/we believe the information contained in this statement of case to be true."

29. If, in the event, a statement or counter-statement proves to be inaccurate or untrue then, in the absence of any clear and justified explanation for the breach, the Hearing Officer will take this into account when making an award for costs.

Evidence

Witness Statements

A6–11   30. The rules have been amended to permit as an alternative to sworn evidence the filing of evidence in the form of a "witness statement" verified by a statement of truth. Hearing Officers are also authorised to require the filing of an affidavit or statutory declaration instead of a witness statement if they consider such a sworn statement to be more appropriate in a particular case. A witness statement must be in writing and signed and dated and should contain the evidence which the person signing it would be allowed to give orally. It should also contain a statement by the witness that he believes the facts in it are true.

Filing evidence not in proper form

A6–12   31. The Office intends continuing with its existing practice of requiring receipt of formally correct affidavits, statutory declarations or witness statements to trigger subsequent evidence stages. The Office will not normally accept the receipt of unsigned witness statements or unsworn affidavits or statutory declarations as meeting time deadlines, but exceptionally the Hearing Officer will be prepared to do so provided a proper version of the evidence is filed within a period the Office may specify. If, in the event, the formal evidence was shown to be inconsistent with the previously filed informal evidence, the Hearing Officer may impose a cost penalty on the party concerned when deciding on the award of costs. Parties should take care to ensure that evidence filed by facsimile transmission is received by the Office in its entirety and is legible.

Witness evidence

A6–13   32. The rules have also been amended so that where a party adduces evidence of a statement made by a person otherwise than while giving oral evidence in proceedings and does not call that person as a witness, the Hearing Officer may permit any other party to call that person as a witness and cross-examine them on their statement.

Disclosure

A6–14   33. Disclosure is not common in proceedings before the Comptroller and the Office does not expect that to change. However, parties do seek it from time to time, and the principles the Office will apply in deciding whether to grant it will mirror those applied by the courts.

34. The principles the Office has traditionally applied reflected Order 24 of the old Rules of the Supreme Court, and this approach was endorsed by Aldous J. in

Merrell Dow Pharmaceuticals Inc's (Terfenadine) Patent [1991] RPC 221. Thus the questions the Office has considered are whether the documents concerned relate to the matters in question in the proceedings and whether their disclosure is necessary to dispose fairly of the proceedings or to reduce costs. As in the courts, even if these tests were satisfied there was always discretion to refuse to order specific disclosure, for example if the value of the material to the applicant was outweighed by the burden it would impose on the opponent, as discussed in *Molyncke AB v Proctor and Gamble Ltd (No 3)* [1990] RPC 498, or if the categories of documents were in such general terms as to amount to a "fishing discovery", as discussed in *British Leyland Motor Corporation v Wyatt Interpart Co Ltd* [1979] FSR 39.

35. Under the Civil Procedure Rules 1998 the courts can order either "standard" disclosure (*i.e.* all relevant documents in a party's control) or "specific" disclosure (usually, an order to disclose specific documents or classes of documents). It is unlikely a Hearing Officer would ever order standard disclosure, but he or she may order specific disclosure. The court's Practice Direction on specific disclosure says that:

> "the court will take into account all the circumstances of the case and, in particular, the overriding objective described in Part 1."

36. The Office will follow these principles when considering requests for disclosure in the future. It takes the view that this does not involve discarding the old tests because they are still a sensible part of considering all the circumstances of the case. However, the Office will now additionally put greater emphasis on the principle of proportionality and on the need to ensure proceedings are dealt with expeditiously.

37. A party applying for specific discovery must explain its reasons in full and must identify the documents or classes of documents it seeks as clearly as is reasonably possible. Vague or excessively broad requests are unlikely to be granted.

Case Management

Questionnaires

38. The Office intends issuing questionnaires on a selective basis, prior to the **A6–15** evidence rounds, which should help parties and Hearing Officers gain a clearer appreciation of the issues.

Case Management Conferences

39. The Office has decided to adopt the selective use of case management **A6–16** conferences. A decision on whether or not to hold such a conference will rest with the Hearing Officer taking into account the circumstances of the case including, for instance, the need to clarify the issues, the degree of complexity, any related actions between the parties and any wider public interest issues. The rules have been amended to give the Office the necessary powers.

40. The legal and technical nature of intellectual property disputes means that they are usually conducted by professional representatives. Case management conferences should be attended by these representatives. The parties themselves will not be expected to attend but should be invited to do so if they so wish.

Pre-Hearing Reviews

41. The rules have been amended to give Hearing Officers power to call a **A6–17** "pre-hearing review" prior to a hearing if they consider it appropriate. Such reviews will provide Hearing Officers with an opportunity to clarify issues,

1007

particularly in complex cases, and issue directions on the conduct of hearings. This should help the parties focus on matters of most relevance.

Alternative Disputes Resolution (ADR)

A6–18   42. The Patent Office cannot itself provide ADR services as it would be placed in a difficult if not impossible position then to rule on the dispute if it were to return for determination by a Hearing Officer. However, except in the case of revocation action where there may be a public interest, the Office will routinely ask parties whether they have considered ADR and, where appropriate, will provide them with information about ADR. The Office will be prepared to stay proceedings in those cases where ADR is being used or seriously considered. Such stays will be closely controlled and subject to review by the Hearing Officer. Hearing Officers may also take into account a party's unreasonable refusal to consider ADR when awarding costs.

Conduct of Hearing, Issuing of Decisions

Order for presenting case

A6–19   43. The normal practice in *with notice* hearings is that the right to open is vested in the party who bears the initial burden of proof, *e.g.* the referrer in patent entitlement proceedings. The exception has been in applications to revoke a patent where the opponent to the application is invited to open. The Office has decided that henceforth the applicant will be invited to open proceedings at revocation hearings. Also, in trade mark opposition hearings, the opponent will now be invited to open the proceedings.

Time spent on hearing and cross examination

A6–20   44. The Patent Office does not, as a rule, intend imposing time limits on the length of hearings and the time spent on cross-examination. However, Hearing Officers will retain discretion to deal with excessively long speeches and cross-examinations.

Supply of skeleton arguments prior to hearing

A6–21   45. The Office is keen to encourage the use of skeleton arguments at hearings as they can be of considerable benefit in organising submissions and making efficient use of hearing time. Moreover, they help focus the mind and enable the Hearing Officer and the parties and their representatives to gain a better appreciation of the issues and arguments. Therefore, Hearing Officers will generally **expect** parties, particularly those that are represented by professional practitioners, to supply skeleton arguments, together with authorities, at least two days before the date of a hearing.

Presentation of new evidence at a hearing

A6–22   46. The practice of adducing new evidence during a hearing is to be discouraged as it can spring surprises. Even if a Hearing Officer decides to admit such evidence it will generally be allowed only after the Hearing Officer and the other party have had sufficient time to read and digest it. Hearing Officers will however, as a rule, allow documents to be introduced in cross-examination which are designed to test the honesty or reliability of a witness.

Use of telephone and video conferencing for hearings

A6–23   47. The Patent Office recognises that the use of telephone and video conferencing facilities is likely to have little application for substantive hearings. However, the scope of their use in procedural hearings can be significant by saving costs and making better use of time for both the parties and the Hearing Officer. The Office accepts that such facilities must be used with care so as not to disadvantage either party. In this respect, the Office has taken account of the firm line taken by the Patents Court on the use of telephone summonses (*e.g. Robert Hewitt v P McCann Ltd*, 30 March 1998, in which Laddie J gave the clear reminder that telephone summonses exist to save costs, that their availability must not be ignored, and that doing so could be reflected in cost orders). In view of this, and bearing this in mind Lord Woolf's encouragement of greater use of IT in legal proceedings, the Office intends encouraging parties to hold suitable hearings, case management conferences and pre-hearing reviews using telephone conferencing arrangements and video links.

Deciding cases without a hearing

48. The Office will adopt a proactive stance towards settling dispute cases **A6–24** without the need for hearings whilst retaining the fundamental right of parties to be heard. Parties will at least be offered the opportunity of a decision in this way.

49. Enquiries about this notice should be addressed to:

Mike Wright	Ann Corbett
The Patent Office	The Patent Office
Patents and Designs Directorate	Trade Marks Directorate
Room 3.Y54	Room 2.005
Concept House	Government Buildings
Cardiff Road	Cardiff Road
Newport	Newport
South Wales	South Wales
NP10 8QQ	NP10 8QQ
Tel 01633 814576	Tel 01633 811029
Fax 01633 814347	Fax 01633 811175
E-mail	E-mail
mike.wright@patent.gov.uk	*ann.corbett@patent.gov.uk*

Tribunal Practice Notice

(TPN 2/2000)

Costs in Proceedings before the Comptroller

1. As part of its response to Lord Woolf's report *Access to Justice*, the Patent **A6–25** Office has, in consultation with its users, reviewed the awarding of costs in proceedings before the Comptroller. This Practice Notice sets out the Comptroller's practice on costs following that review.

Summary

2. The following are the main points addressed in this Practice Notice: **A6–26**

- The present policy of costs awards being informed by a scale set by the Office in consultation with its users, and reviewed from time to time, will continue. (paragraph 8)
- The scale of costs has been revised: the revised scale shown in *annex A* will apply to proceedings commenced on or after 22 May 2000, while

the unrevised scale shown at *annex B* will continue to apply to proceedings commenced before that date. (paragraph 11)

- Hearing Officers will be prepared to exceed the scale when circumstances warrant it, in particular but not exclusively to deal proportionately with breaches of rules, delaying tactics and other unreasonable behaviour. (paragraphs 8 and 9)
- Hearing Officers will actively consider making an award at preliminary hearings and not merely carry all costs over to the final decision. (paragraphs 12 and 13)
- A deadline for payment will be attached to a costs award. (paragraph 14)
- Security for costs will be determined on application for an amount appropriate in the case. (paragraph 16)
- In appeals to the High Court or the Registered Designs Appeal Tribunal against her without-notice decisions, the Comptroller will generally seek her costs, while being willing not to do so, for example in cases where the party is likely to suffer some form of hardship if a costs award were made against them. (paragraph 19)

The Comptroller's Power and Discretion

A6–27   3. The Comptroller and hence Hearing Officers acting for her have a wide discretion to award costs under section 107 of the Patents Act 1977, section 30 of the Registered Designs Act 1949, section 68 of the Trade Marks Act 1994, section 44 of the Trade Marks Act 1938 and section 250 of the Copyright, Designs and Patents Act 1988. Factors influencing the exercise of the Comptroller's discretion in relation to the award of costs have been considered by Hearing Officers from time to time in their decisions. The leading case, however, is *Rizla Ltd's Application* [1993] RPC 365, a patents case in which judgement was given by Anthony Watson QC sitting as a Deputy Judge of the High Court.

4. On page 374 of *Rizla*, the Deputy Judge held that:

> "The wording of section 107 could not in my view be clearer and confers on the Comptroller a very wide discretion with no fetter other than the overriding one that he must act judicially. I see no reason why the previously adopted practice could not be altered by the Comptroller in the same way as from time to time an important decision leads the courts to adopt a different attitude to what had previously been accepted practice. Thus, if the Comptroller felt it was appropriate, a form of compensatory costs could become the norm."

He went on to say:

> "As a matter of jurisdiction, I entertain no doubt that if the Comptroller were of the view that a case had been brought without any *bona fide* belief that it was soundly based or if in any other way he were satisfied that his jurisdiction was being used other than for the purpose of resolving genuine disputes, he has the power to order compensatory costs."

On page 377, towards the end of his judgement he said:

> "Counsel was unable to refer me to any reported case where such a strong order for costs had been made by the Comptroller and therefore there is no established yardstick to measure what might be regarded as exceptional. I believe a case such as the present can only be regarded as exceptional if it can be shown that the losing party has abused the process of the Comptroller by commencing or maintaining a case without a genuine belief that there is an issue to be tried. In my view, this is not shown to be such a case."

Significantly, the Deputy Judge added:

> "There are of course a large number of other circumstances such as deliberate delay, unnecessary adjournments *etc.* where the Comptroller will be entitled to award compensatory costs, but it is unnecessary to define what is clearly a wide discretion."

5. In the light of *Rizla*, the Office considers that the existing legislation provides the power to operate a nominal cost regime or a full cost recovery regime—or anything in between—and that no legislative change is necessary to put in hand any revision of that sort.

The use of a scale

6. It is the long-established practice that costs in proceedings before the **A6–28** Comptroller are awarded after consideration of guidance given by a standard published scale and are not intended to compensate parties for the expense to which they may have been put. Rather, an award of costs is intended to represent only a contribution to that expense.

7. In comments received from users, this existing practice was defended by some, partly on the grounds of maintaining the tribunal as a low cost one, and partly because the scale provides some certainty for businesses in budgeting for the costs they might incur. Others felt that the Office's powers in relation to costs should be significantly increased. It was also suggested that the level of costs should reflect the Office's disapproval of any breaches of the rules or unreasonable delay or complication caused by a party.

8. Users' comments taken as a whole supported the general thrust of the present policy based upon fixed reasonable costs, provided that there is the flexibility to award costs off the scale where the circumstances warrant it. The Office also believes this is the way to proceed, since it provides a low cost tribunal for all litigants, but especially unrepresented ones and SMEs, and builds in a degree of predictability as to how much proceedings before the Comptroller, if conscientiously handled by the party, may cost them. The present policy of generally awarding costs informed by guidance drawn from a scale will therefore be retained. However, the Office envisages the necessary flexibility as going beyond the criterion of "without a genuine belief that there is an issue to be tried" developed in the *Rizla* case. It is vital that the Comptroller has the ability to award costs off the scale, approaching full compensation, to deal proportionately with wider breaches of rules, delaying tactics or other unreasonable behaviour. The fact that this flexibility and the Comptroller's willingness to exercise it in suitable cases has been the subject of consultation and publicity means that there will have been "an established yardstick" underpinning a change in the previous practice.

9. It would be impossible to indicate all of the circumstances in which a Hearing Officer could or should depart from the scale of costs; indeed it would be wrong to attempt to fetter his or her discretion is such a way. The overriding factor is to act judicially in all the facts of a case. That said, it is possible to conceive of examples. A party seeking an amendment to its statement of case which, if granted, would cause the other side to have to amend its statement or would lead to the filing of further evidence, might expect to incur a costs penalty if the amendment had clearly been avoidable. In another example, the costs associated with evidence filed in respect of grounds which are in the event not pursued at the main or substantive hearing might lead to award which departs from the scale. Costs may also be affected if a losing party unreasonably rejected efforts to settle a dispute before an action was launched or a hearing held, or unreasonably declined the opportunity of an appropriate form of Alternative Dispute Resolution (ADR). A party's unnotified failure to attend a hearing would also be a relevant factor.

The numbers on the scale

A6–29   10. The views of users, and the feeling of the Office itself, is that the amounts set out in the current scale, last revised in a notice published on 1 June 1994, should be adjusted to take better account of the real cost involved in litigation before the Comptroller.

11. With the implementation of the Trade Marks Act 1994 and the need for parties to take into account decisions of OHIM and the ECJ, and decisions on Directive issues handed down by courts in other jurisdictions, the costs of litigation before the Registrar are becoming somewhat higher than in the recent past. Similar factors are also arising in patents cases. In addition, the nature of preliminary hearings is becoming more significant and time-consuming. It is therefore not unreasonable to uprate the present scale of costs to reflect more appropriately the actual costs of litigation, while still maintaining the underlying contribution-not-compensation approach. A survey of recent substantive decisions indicates that the average award of costs by Hearing Officers in patents and trade marks cases is around £700. This is an insignificant sum, even as a contribution, in the current climate. The Office has proposed, and users have not disagreed, that an average closer to £2,000 would be more suitable: this would not represent full cost recovery but would be a realistic contribution. A revised scale which should deliver an average award of that order is set out at annex A. The new scale at annex A will be applicable in respect of an award of costs in proceedings commenced on or after 22 May 2000. The scale published in the Office's journals on 1 June 1994, and reproduced at *annex B*, will continue to apply in proceedings commenced before that date.

Timing of costs awards and their payment

A6–30   12. Users have remarked that the Office should be encouraged to award costs at any stage of proceedings and to order that an identified sum be paid immediately or within a limited and defined number of days. The Office agrees that in the current post-Woolf climate a regime which associates costs more closely with their cause is desirable. It is too easy when costs are, as now, generally rolled over into the final decision, for the reason they were awarded to be lost sight of, for example when an award is made to penalise the taking of a purely technical point to a preliminary hearing.

13. The Office therefore intends, far more frequently than in the past, to make costs orders as the cause of them arises. Examples of situations in which such an award might be made are:

(a) where "blame" can be attached to one or the other party, *e.g.* a missed deadline;

(b) where amendment to the statements of case is being sought (particularly when evidence has already been filed by the other side), although that could be tempered if the statements are being amended to remove a ground and make them more focussed.

14. A deadline for payment will be attached to the award, that deadline being 7 days after the expiry of the appeal period, unless an appeal is lodged in which case payment of the costs awarded would be suspended pending the appeal. So, for example, in the case of a costs award made following a patents hearing on a procedural point, if the decision was not appealed the costs would be payable within 7 days after expiry of the 14-day appeal period, and failure to make payment would have implications for the continuation of the case.

Licence of right cases

A6–31   15. It has been customary in licence of right cases for the Comptroller not to make an award of costs unless one side pursues unreasonable terms or the circumstances of the particular case are sufficiently unusual to warrant a departure from that practice. It is not intended to alter that approach, except to the extent that the flexibility to address procedural difficulties may bite.

Security for costs

16. It has been the normal practice in patent proceedings for the Office **A6–32** automatically to require a party that is not based in a Brussels Convention state to provide security for a fixed sum of £900. This contrasts with the practice followed in trade mark proceedings and the courts where security for costs is only ordered on application and following consideration by the Hearing Officer or the judge. As there is no good reason why the practice in patents proceedings should be different, the Office has decided to bring it into line with that followed elsewhere and to consider awarding such security only on application and not on the Office's own initiative. Moreover, instead of an award of a standard amount such as £900, the award should be determined, after consideration of argument and, if necessary evidence, wholly on a case by case basis proportionate to the estimated costs likely to be awarded at its conclusion.

"Without notice" (also known as *ex parte*) proceedings

17. The Office has decided not to change its practice of not awarding costs in **A6–33** "without notice" proceedings before the Comptroller.

18. In trade mark cases appealed to the Appointed Person, it is regarded as in keeping with the low cost of that appeal route for each side to bear its own costs. The Comptroller will continue with that approach.

19. As for appeals to the High Court (or Court of Session in Scotland) or the Registered Designs Appeal Tribunal (RDAT), the practice has varied as between the patents, designs and some trade mark appeals which follow that route. Should the Comptroller lose on appeal, she would expect costs to be awarded against her; there is therefore an argument that the public purse should be recompensed by a similar award should the decision go in the other direction. On the other hand, it might be argued that litigants in person should be given special treatment and that the Comptroller should not seek costs in such cases. Having reviewed the situation in consultation with users, it has been decided that on balance the Comptroller should seek costs in the full range of the without-notice appeals which she defends in the High Court or RDAT, while being willing not to do so in cases where the party is likely to suffer some form of hardship if a costs award is made against them, or where a significant point of general legal interest is involved.

20. Enquiries about this notice should be addressed to:

Mike Wright	Ann Corbett
The Patent Office	The Patent Office
Patents and Designs Directorate	Trade Marks Directorate
Room 3.Y54	Room 2.005
Concept House	Government Buildings
Cardiff Road	Cardiff Road
Newport	Newport
South Wales	South Wales
NP10 8QQ	NP10 8QQ
Tel 01633 814576	Tel 01633 811029
Fax 01633 814347	Fax 01633 811175
E-mail	E-mail
mike.wright@patent.gov.uk	*ann.corbett@patent.gov.uk*

Scale of Costs Applicable in Proceedings Commenced on or after 22 May 2000

A6–34 (1) Application or Notice of Opposition and accompanying statement — £300 plus statutory fee (if any)

(2) Considering statement of case in reply — £200

or

(1) Considering Application or Notice of Opposition and accompanying statement

(2) Statement of case in reply — £300

(3) Preparing and filing evidence — Up to £1,500

(4) Considering evidence — One half of Item 3

(5) Preparation for and attendance at Hearing — Up to £1,500

(6) Where a party appears in person or where attendance of a party's witnesses is required by the opposite party, allowance will be made for general expenses and travelling, but the allowance for general expenses will not normally exceed £250 per person per day, nor an overall maximum per party of £750 per day.

Scale of costs applicable in proceedings commenced before 22 May 2000

A6–35 (This scale was first published in a notice in the Office's journals on 1 June 1994.)

(1) Application or Notice of Opposition and accompanying Statement — £100 plus statutory fee (if any)

(2) Perusing Counter-statement — £35

or

(1) Perusing Application or Notice of Opposition and accompanying statement — £35

(2) Counter-statement — £100

(3) Preparing and filing evidence — £200–£400

(4) Perusing evidence — one half of Item 3

(5) Preparation for and attendance at Hearing — £200–£900

(6) Where the Applicant or Opponent appears in person and where attendance of witnesses is required by the opposite party, allowance will be made for general expenses and travelling, but the allowance for general expenses will not normally exceed £25 per day.

PART III

GENERAL EUROPEAN MATERIALS

APPENDIX 7

First Council Directive 89/104 of December 21, 1988

To approximate the laws of the Member States relating to trade marks

([1989] O.J. L40/1)

THE COUNCIL OF THE EUROPEAN COMMUNITIES,   **A7–01**

Having regard to the Treaty establishing the European Economic Community, and in particular Article 100a thereof,

Having regard to the proposal from the Commission,

In cooperation with the European Parliament,

Having regard to the opinion of the Economic and Social Committee,

Whereas the trade mark laws at present applicable in the Member States contain disparities which may impede the free movement of goods and freedom to provide services and may distort competition within the common market; whereas it is therefore necessary, in view of the establishment and functioning of the internal market, to approximate the laws of Member States;

Whereas it is important not to disregard the solutions and advantages which the Community trade mark system may afford to undertakings wishing to acquire trade marks;

Whereas it does not appear to be necessary at present to undertake full-scale approximation of the trade mark laws of the Member States and it will be sufficient if approximation is limited to those national provisions of law which most directly affect the functioning of the internal market;

Whereas the Directive does not deprive the Member States of the right to continue to protect trade marks acquired through use but takes them into account only in regard to the relationship between them and trade marks acquired by registration;

Whereas Member States also remain free to fix the provisions of procedure concerning the registration, the revocation and the invalidity of trade marks acquired by registration; whereas they can, for example, determine the form of trade mark registration and invalidity procedures, decide whether earlier rights should be invoked either in the registration procedure or in the invalidity procedure or in both and, if they allow earlier rights to be invoked in the registration procedure, have an opposition procedure or an *ex officio* examination procedure or both; whereas Member States remain free to determine the effects—of revocation or invalidity of trade marks;

Whereas this Directive does not exclude the application to trade marks of provisions of law of the Member States other than trade mark law, such as the provisions relating to unfair competition, civil liability or consumer protection;

Whereas attainment of the objectives at which this approximation of laws is aiming requires that the conditions for obtaining and continuing to hold a registered trade mark are, in general, identical in all Member States; whereas, to this end, it is necessary to list examples of signs which may constitute a trade mark, provided that such signs are capable of distinguishing the goods or services of one undertaking from those of other undertakings; whereas the grounds for refusal or invalidity concerning the trade mark itself, for example, the absence of any distinctive character, or concerning conflicts between the trade mark and earlier rights, are to be listed in an exhaustive manner, even if some of these grounds are listed as an option for the Member States which will therefore be able to maintain or introduce those grounds in their legislation; whereas Member States will be able to maintain or introduce into their legislation grounds of refusal or invalidity linked to conditions for obtaining and continuing to hold a trade mark for which there is no provision of approximation, concerning, for example, the eligibility for the grant of a trade mark, the renewal of the trade mark or rules on fees, or related to the non-compliance with procedural rules;

Whereas in order to reduce the total number of trade marks registered and protected in the Community and, consequently, the number of conflicts which arise between them, it is essential to require that registered trade marks must actually be used or, if not used, be subject to revocation; whereas it is necessary to provide that a trade mark cannot be invalidated on the basis of the existence of a non-used earlier trade mark, while the Member States remain free to apply the same principle in respect of the registration of a trade mark or to provide that a trade mark may not be successfully invoked in infringement proceedings if it is established as a result of a plea that the trade mark could be revoked; whereas in all these cases it is up to the Member States to establish the applicable rules of procedure;

Whereas it is fundamental, in order to facilitate the free circulation of goods and services, to ensure that henceforth registered trade marks enjoy the same protection under the legal systems of all the Member States; whereas this should however not prevent the Member States from granting at their option extensive protection to those trade marks which have a reputation;

Whereas the protection afforded by the registered trade mark, the function of which is in particular to guarantee the trade mark as an indication of origin, is absolute in the case of identity between the mark and the sign and goods or services; whereas the protection applies also in case of similarity between the mark and the sign and the goods or services; whereas it is indispensable to give an interpretation of the concept of similarity in relation to the likelihood of confusion; whereas the likelihood of confusion, the appreciation of which depends on numerous elements and, in particular, on the recognition of the trade mark on the market, of the association which can be made with the used or registered sign, of the degree of similarity between the trade mark and the sign and between the goods or services identified, constitutes the specific condition for such protection; whereas the ways in which likelihood of confusion may be established, and in particular the onus of proof, are a matter for national procedural rules which are not prejudiced by the Directive;

Whereas it is important, for reasons of legal certainty and without inequitably prejudicing the interests of a proprietor of an earlier trade mark, to provide that the latter may no longer request a declaration of invalidity nor may he oppose the use of a trade mark subsequent to his own of which he has knowingly tolerated the use for a substantial length of time, unless the application for the subsequent trade mark was made in bad faith;

Whereas all Member States of the Community are bound by the Paris Convention for the Protection of Industrial Property; whereas it is necessary that the provisions of this Directive are entirely consistent with those of the Paris Convention; whereas the obligations of the Member States resulting from this Convention are not affected by this Directive; whereas, where appropriate, the second subparagraph of Article 234 of the Treaty is applicable,

HAS ADOPTED THIS DIRECTIVE:

Article 1

Scope

This Directive shall apply to every trade mark in respect of goods or services **A7–02** which is the subject of registration or of an application in a Member State for registration as an individual trade mark, a collective mark or a guarantee or certification mark, or which is the subject of a registration or an application for registration in the Benelux Trade Mark Office or of an international registration having effect in a Member State.

Article 2

Signs of which a trade mark may consist

A trade mark may consist of any sign capable of being represented graph- **A7–03** ically, particularly words, including personal names, designs, letters, numerals, the shape of goods or of their packaging, provided that such signs are capable of distinguishing the goods or services of one undertaking from those of other undertakings.

Article 3

Grounds for refusal or invalidity

1. The following shall not be registered or if registered shall be liable to be **A7–04** declared invalid:

   (a) signs which cannot constitute a trade mark;
   (b) trade marks which are devoid of any distinctive character;
   (c) trade marks which consist exclusively of signs or indications which may serve, in trade, to designate the kind, quality, quantity, intended purpose, value, geographical origin, or the time of production of the goods or of rendering of the service, or other characteristics of the goods or service;
   (d) trade marks which consist exclusively of signs or indications which have become customary in the current language or in the *bona fide* and established practices of the trade;
   (e) signs which consist exclusively of:
       — the shape which results from the nature of the goods themselves, or
       — the shape of goods which is necessary to obtain a technical result, or
       — the shape which gives substantial value to the goods;
   (f) trade marks which are contrary to public policy or to accepted principles of morality;
   (g) trade marks which are of such a nature as to deceive the public, for instance as to the nature, quality or geographical origin of the goods or service;
   (h) trade marks which have not been authorized by the competent author- ities and are to be refused or invalidated pursuant to Article 6 *ter* of the Paris Convention for the Protection of Industrial Property, hereinafter referred to as the "Paris Convention".

2. Any Member State may provide that a trade mark shall not be registered or, if registered, shall be liable to be declared invalid where and to the extent that:

1019

(a) the use of that trade mark may be prohibited pursuant to provisions of law other than trade mark law of the Member State concerned or of the Community;

(b) the trade mark covers a sign of high symbolic value, in particular a religious symbol;

(c) the trade mark includes badges, emblems and escutcheons other than those covered by Article 6 *ter* of the Paris Convention and which are of public interest, unless the consent of the appropriate authorities to its registration has been given in conformity with the legislation of the Member State;

(d) the application for registration of the trade mark was made in bad faith by the applicant.

3. A trade mark shall not be refused registration or be declared invalid in accordance with paragraph 1 (b),(c) or (d) if, before the date of application for registration and following the use which has been made of it, it has acquired a distinctive character. Any Member State may in addition provide that this provision shall also apply where the distinctive character was acquired after the date of application for registration or after the date of registration.

4. Any Member State may provide that, by derogation from the preceding paragraphs, the grounds of refusal of registration or invalidity in force in that State prior to the date on which the provisions necessary to comply with this Directive enter into force, shall apply to trade marks for which application has been made prior to that date.

Article 4

Further grounds for refusal or invalidity concerning conflicts with earlier rights

A7–05   1. A trade mark shall not be registered or, if registered, shall be liable to be declared invalid:

(a) if it is identical with an earlier trade mark, and the goods or services for which the trade mark is applied for or is registered are identical with the goods or services for which the earlier trade mark is protected;

(b) if because of its identity with, or similarity to, the earlier trade mark and the identity or similarity of the goods or services covered by the trade marks, there exists a likelihood of confusion on the part of the public, which includes the likelihood of association with the earlier trade mark.

2. "Earlier trade marks" within the meaning of paragraph 1 means:

(a) trade marks of the following kinds with a date of application for registration which is earlier than the date of application for registration of the trade mark, taking account, where appropriate, of the priorities claimed in respect of those trade marks:
   (i) Community trade marks;
   (ii) trade marks registered in the Member State or, in the case of Belgium, Luxembourg or the Netherlands, at the Benelux Trade Mark Office;
   (iii) trade marks registered under international arrangements which have effect in the Member State;

(b) Community trade marks which validly claim seniority, in accordance with the Regulation on the Community trade mark, from a trade mark referred to in (a) (ii) and (iii), even when the latter trade mark has been surrendered or allowed to lapse;

(c) applications for the trade marks referred to in (a) and (b), subject to their registration;

(d) trade marks which, on the date of application for registration of the trade mark, or, where appropriate, of the priority claimed in respect of the application for registration of the trade mark, are well known in a Member State, in the sense in which the words "well known" are used in Article 6 *bis* of the Paris Convention;

3. A trade mark shall furthermore not be registered or, if registered, shall be liable to be declared invalid if it is identical with, or similar to, an earlier Community trade mark within the meaning of paragraph 2 and is to be, or has been, registered for goods or services which are not similar to those for which the earlier Community trade mark is registered, where the earlier Community trade mark has a reputation in the Community and where the use of the later trade mark without due cause would take unfair advantage of, or be detrimental to, the distinctive character or the repute of the earlier Community trade mark.

4. Any Member State may furthermore provide that a trade mark shall not be registered or, if registered, shall be liable to be declared invalid where, and to the extent that:

(a) the trade mark is identical with, or similar to, an earlier national trade mark within the meaning of paragraph 2 and is to be, or has been, registered for goods or services which are not similar to those for which the earlier trade mark is registered, where the earlier trade mark has a reputation in the Member State concerned and where the use of the later trade mark without due cause would take unfair advantage of, or be detrimental to, the distinctive character or the repute of the earlier trade mark;

(b) rights to a non-registered trade mark or to another sign used in the course of trade were acquired prior to the date of application for registration of the subsequent trade mark, or the date of the priority claimed for the application for registration of the subsequent trade mark and that non-registered trade mark or other sign confers on its proprietor the right to prohibit the use of a subsequent trade mark;

(c) the use of the trade mark may be prohibited by virtue of an earlier right other than the rights referred to in paragraphs 2 and 4 (b) and in particular:
  (i) a right to a name;
  (ii) a right of personal portrayal;
  (iii) a copyright;
  (iv) an industrial property right;

(d) the trade mark is identical with, or similar to, an earlier collective trade mark conferring a right which expired within a period of a maximum of three years preceding application;

(e) the trade mark is identical with, or similar to, an earlier guarantee or certification mark conferring a right which expired within a period preceding application the length of which is fixed by the Member State;

(f) the trade mark is identical with, or similar to, an earlier trade mark which was registered for identical or similar goods or services and conferred on them a right which has expired for failure to renew within a period of a maximum of two years preceding application, unless the proprietor of the earlier trade mark gave his agreement for the registration of the later mark or did not use his trade mark;

(g) the trade mark is liable to be confused with a mark which was in use abroad on the filing date of the application and which is still in use there, provided that at the date of the application the applicant was acting in bad faith.

5. The Member States may permit that in appropriate circumstances registration need not be refused or the trade mark need not be declared invalid where

the proprietor of the earlier trade mark or other earlier right consents to the registration of the later trade mark.

6. Any Member State may provide that, by derogation from paragraphs 1 to 5, the grounds for refusal of registration or invalidity in force in that State prior to the date on which the provisions necessary to comply with this Directive enter into force, shall apply to trade marks for which application has been made prior to that date.

Article 5

Rights conferred by a trade mark

A7–06   1. The registered trade mark shall confer on the proprietor exclusive rights therein. The proprietor shall be entitled to prevent all third parties not having his consent from using in the course of trade:

    (a) any sign which is identical with the trade mark in relation to goods or services which are identical with those for which the trade mark is registered;

    (b) any sign where, because of its identity with, or similarity to, the trade mark and the identity or similarity of the goods or services covered by the trade mark and the sign, there exists a likelihood of confusion on the part of the public, which includes the likelihood of association between the sign and the trade mark.

2. Any Member State may also provide that the proprietor shall be entitled to prevent all third parties not having his consent from using in the course of trade any sign which is identical with, or similar to, the trade mark in relation to goods or services which are not similar to those for which the trade mark is registered, where the latter has a reputation in the Member State and where use of that sign without due cause takes unfair advantage of, or is detrimental to, the distinctive character of the repute of the trade mark.

3. The following, *inter alia*, may be prohibited under paragraphs 1 and 2:

    (a) affixing the sign to the goods or to the packaging thereof;

    (b) offering the goods, or putting them on the market or stocking them for these purposes under that sign, or offering or supplying services thereunder;

    (c) importing or exporting the goods under the sign;

    (d) using the sign on business papers and in advertising.

4. Where, under the law of the Member State, the use of a sign under the conditions referred to in 1 (b) or 2 could not be prohibited before the date on which the provisions necessary to comply with this Directive entered into force in the Member State concerned, the rights conferred by the trade mark may not be relied on to prevent the continued use of the sign.

5. Paragraphs 1 to 4 shall not affect provisions in any Member State relating to the protection against the use of a sign other than for the purposes of distinguishing goods or services, where use of that sign without due cause takes unfair advantage of, or is detrimental to, the distinctive character or the repute of the trade mark.

Article 6

Limitation of the effects of a trade mark

A7–07   1. The trade mark shall not entitle the proprietor to prohibit a third party from using, in the course of trade,

(a) his own name or address;
(b) indications concerning the kind, quality, quantity, intended purpose, value, geographical origin, the time of production of goods or of rendering of the service, or other characteristics of goods or services;
(c) the trade mark where it is necessary to indicate the intended purpose of a product or service, in particular as accessories or spare parts;

provided he uses them in accordance with honest practices in industrial or commercial matters.

2. The trade mark shall not entitle the proprietor to prohibit a third party from using, in the course of trade, an earlier right which only applies in a particular locality if that right is recognized by the laws of the Member State in question and within the limits of the territory in which it is recognized.

Article 7

Exhaustion of the rights conferred by a trade mark

1. The trade mark shall not entitle the proprietor to prohibit its use in relation **A7–08** to goods which have been put on the market in the Community under that trade mark by the proprietor or with his consent.

2. Paragraph 1 shall not apply where there exist legitimate reasons for the proprietor to oppose further commercialization of the goods, especially where the condition of the goods is changed or impaired after they have been put on the market.

Article 8

Licensing

1. A trade mark may be licensed for some or all of the goods or services for **A7–09** which it is registered and for the whole or part of the Member State concerned. A licence may be exclusive or non-exclusive.

2. The proprietor of a trade mark may invoke the rights conferred by that trade mark against a licensee who contravenes any provision in his licensing contract with regard to its duration, the form covered by the registration in which the trade mark may be used, the scope of the goods or services for which the licence is granted, the territory in which the trade mark may be affixed, or the quality of the goods manufactured or of the services provided by the licensee.

Article 9

Limitation in consequence of acquiescence

1. Where, in a Member State, the proprietor of an earlier trade mark as **A7–10** referred to in Article 4 (2) has acquiesced, for a period of five successive years, in the use of a later trade mark registered in that Member State while being aware of such use, he shall no longer be entitled on the basis of the earlier trade mark either to apply for a declaration that the later trade mark is invalid or to oppose the use of the later trade mark in respect of the goods or services for which the later trade mark has been used, unless registration of the later trade mark was applied for in bad faith.

2. Any Member State may provide that paragraph 1 shall apply *mutatis mutandis* to the proprietor of an earlier trade mark referred to in Article 4 (4) (a) or an other earlier right referred to in Article 4 (4) (b) or (c).

3. In the cases referred to in paragraphs 1 and 2, the proprietor of a later registered trade mark shall not be entitled to oppose the use of the earlier right, even though that right may no longer be invoked against the later trade mark.

Article 10

Use of trade marks

A7–11   1. If, within a period of five years following the date of the completion of the registration procedure, the proprietor has not put the trade mark to genuine use in the Member State in connection with the goods or services in respect of which it is registered, or if such use has been suspended during an uninterrupted period of five years, the trade mark shall be subject to the sanctions provided for in this Directive, unless there are proper reasons for non-use.

2. The following shall also constitute use within the meaning of paragraph 1:

  (a) use of the trade mark in a form differing in elements which do not alter the distinctive character of the mark in the form in which it was registered;
  (b) affixing of the trade mark to goods or to the packaging thereof in the Member State concerned solely for export purposes.

3. Use of the trade mark with the consent of the proprietor or by any person who has authority to use a collective mark or a guarantee or certification mark shall be deemed to constitute use by the proprietor.

4. In relation to trade marks registered before the date on which the provisions necessary to comply with this Directive enter into force in the Member State concerned:

  (a) where a provision in force prior to that date attaches sanctions to non-use of a trade mark during an uninterrupted period, the relevant period of five years mentioned in paragraph 1 shall be deemed to have begun to run at the same time as any period of non-use which is already running at that date;
  (b) where there is no use provision in force prior to that date, the periods of five years mentioned in paragraph 1 shall be deemed to run from that date at the earliest.

Article 11

Sanctions for non-use of a trade mark in legal or administrative proceedings

A7–12   1. A trade mark may not be declared invalid on the ground that there is an earlier conflicting trade mark if the latter does not fulfil the requirements of use set out in Article 10(1), (2) and (3) or in Article 10(4), as the case may be.

2. Any Member State may provide that registration of a trade mark may not be refused on the ground that there is an earlier conflicting trade mark if the latter does not fulfil the requirements of use set out in Article 10(1), (2) and (3) or in Article 10 (4), as the case may be.

3. Without prejudice to the application of Article 12, where a counter-claim for revocation is made, any Member State may provide that a trade mark may not be successfully invoked in infringement proceedings if it is established as a result of a plea that the trade mark could be revoked pursuant to Article 12 (1).

4. If the earlier trade mark has been used in relation to part only of the goods or services for which it is registered, it shall, for purposes of applying paragraphs 1, 2 and 3, be deemed to be registered in respect only of that part of the goods or services.

Article 12

Grounds for revocation

1. A trade mark shall be liable to revocation if, within a continuous period of **A7–13** five years, it has not been put to genuine use in the Member State in connection with the goods or services in respect of which it is registered, and there are no proper reasons for non-use; however, no person may claim that the proprietor's rights in a trade mark should be revoked where, during the interval between expiry of the five-year period and filing of the application for revocation, genuine use of the trade mark has been started or resumed; the commencement or resumption of use within a period of three months preceding the filing of the application for revocation which began at the earliest on expiry of the continuous period of five years of non-use, shall, however, be disregarded where preparations for the commencement or resumption occur only after the proprietor becomes aware that the application for revocation may be filed.

2. A trade mark shall also be liable to revocation if, after the date on which it was registered,

    (a) in consequence of acts or inactivity of the proprietor, it has become the common name in the trade for a product or service in respect of which it is registered;

    (b) in consequence of the use made of it by the proprietor of the trade mark or with his consent in respect of the goods or services for which it is registered, it is liable to mislead the public, particularly as to the nature, quality or geographical origin of those goods or services.

Article 13

Grounds for refusal or revocation or invalidity relating to only some of the goods or services

Where grounds for refusal of registration or for revocation or invalidity of a **A7–14** trade mark exist in respect of only some of the goods or services for which that trade mark has been applied for or registered, refusal of registration or revocation or invalidity shall cover those goods or services only.

Article 14

Establishment *a posteriori* **of invalidity or revocation of a trade mark**

Where the seniority of an earlier trade mark which has been surrendered or **A7–15** allowed to lapse, is claimed for a Community trade mark, the invalidity or revocation of the earlier trade mark may be established *a posteriori*.

Article 15

Special provisions in respect of collective marks, guarantee marks and certification marks

1. Without prejudice to Article 4, Member States whose laws authorize the **A7–16** registration of collective marks or of guarantee or certification marks may provide that such marks shall not be registered, or shall be revoked or declared

1025

invalid, on grounds additional to those specified in Articles 3 and 12 where the function of those marks so requires.

2. By way of derogation from Article 3 (1) (c), Member States may provide that signs or indications which may serve, in trade, to designate the geographical origin of the goods or services may constitute collective, guarantee or certification marks. Such a mark does not entitle the proprietor to prohibit a third party from using in the course of trade such signs or indications, provided he uses them in accordance with honest practices in industrial or commercial matters; in particular, such a mark may not be invoked against a third party who is entitled to use a geographical name.

Article 16

National provisions to be adopted pursuant to this Directive

A7–17   1. The Member States shall bring into force the laws, regulations and administrative provisions necessary to comply with this Directive not later than 28 December 1991. They shall immediately inform the Commission thereof.

2. Acting on a proposal from the Commission, the Council, acting by qualified majority, may defer the date referred to in paragraph 1 until 31 December 1992 at the latest.

3. Member States shall communicate to the Commission the text of the main provisions of national law which they adopt in the field governed by this Directive.

Article 17

Addressees

A7–18   This Directive is addressed to the Member States.
Done at Brussels, December 21, 1988.

APPENDIX 8

E. C. Treaty Extracts

Article 28 {EEC 30}

Quantitative restrictions on imports and all measures having equivalent effect **A8–01** shall be prohibited between Member States.

Article 30 {EEC 36}

The provisions of Articles 28 and 29 shall not preclude prohibitions or **A8–02** restrictions on imports, exports or goods in transit justified on grounds of public morality, public policy or public security; the protection of health and life of humans, animals or plants; the protection of national treasures possessing artistic, historic or archaeological value; or the protection of industrial and commercial property. Such prohibitions or restrictions shall not, however, constitute a means of arbitrary discrimination or a disguised restriction on trade between Member States.

Article 81 {EEC 85}

1. The following shall be prohibited as incompatible with the common market: **A8–03** all agreements between undertakings, decisions by associations of undertakings and concerted practices which may affect trade between Member States and which have as their object or effect the prevention, restriction or distortion of competition within the common market, and in particular those which:
   - (a) directly or indirectly fix purchase or selling prices or any other trading conditions;
   - (b) limit or control production, markets, technical development, or investment;
   - (c) share markets or sources of supply;
   - (d) apply dissimilar conditions to equivalent transactions with other trading parties, thereby placing them at a competitive disadvantage;
   - (e) make the conclusion of contracts subject to acceptance by the other parties of supplementary obligations which, by their nature or according to commercial usage, have no connection with the subject of such contracts.

2. Any agreements or decisions prohibited pursuant to this Article shall be automatically void.

3. The provisions of paragraph 1 may, however, be declared inapplicable in the case of:
   - — any agreement or category of agreements between undertakings;

   - — any decision or category of decisions by associations of undertakings;
   - — any concerted practice or category of concerted practices;

which contributes to improving the production or distribution of goods or to promoting technical or economic progress, while allowing consumers a fair share of the resulting benefit, and which does not:

1027

    (a) impose on the undertakings concerned restrictions which are not indispensable to the attainment of these objectives;

    (b) afford such undertakings the possibility of eliminating competition in respect of a substantial part of the products in question.

Article 82 {EEC 86}

A8–04   Any abuse by one or more undertakings of a dominant position within the common market or in a substantial part of it shall be prohibited as incompatible with the common market in so far as it may affect trade between Member States. Such abuse may, in particular, consist in:

    (a) directly or indirectly imposing unfair purchase or selling prices or other unfair trading conditions;

    (b) limiting production, markets or technical development to the prejudice of consumers;

    (c) applying dissimilar conditions to equivalent transactions with other trading parties, thereby placing them at a competitive disadvantage;

    (d) making the conclusion of contracts subject to acceptance by the other parties of supplementary obligations which, by their nature or according to commercial usage, have no connection with the subject of such contracts.

PART IV

CTM MATERIALS

APPENDIX 9

Council Regulation 40/94 of December 20, 1993

On the Community trade mark

THE COUNCIL OF THE EUROPEAN UNION,   **A9–01**

Having regard to the Treaty establishing the European Community, and in particular Article 235 thereof,

Having regard to the proposal from the Commission,

Having regard to the opinion of the European Parliament,

Having regard to the opinion of the Economic and Social Committee,

Whereas it is desirable to promote throughout the Community a harmonious development of economic activities and a continuous and balanced expansion by completing an internal market which functions properly and offers conditions which are similar to those obtaining in a national market; whereas in order to create a market of this kind and make it increasingly a single market, not only must be barriers to free movement of goods and services be removed and arrangements be instituted which ensure that competition is not distorted, but, in addition, legal conditions must be created which enable undertakings to adapt their activities to the scale of the Community, whether in manufacturing and distributing goods or in providing services; whereas for those purposes, trade marks enabling the products and services of undertakings to be distinguished by identical means throughout the entire Community, regardless of frontiers, should feature amongst the legal instruments which undertakings have at their disposal;

Whereas action by the Community would appear to be necessary for the purpose of attaining the Community's said objectives; whereas such action involves the creation of Community arrangements for trade marks whereby undertakings can by means of one procedural system obtain Community trade marks to which uniform protection is given and which produce their effects throughout the entire area of the Community; whereas the principle of the unitary character of the Community trade mark thus stated will apply unless otherwise provided for in this Regulation;

Whereas the barrier of territoriality of the rights conferred on proprietors of trade marks by the laws of the Member States cannot be removed by approximation of laws; whereas in order to open up unrestricted economic activity in the whole of the common market for the benefit of undertakings, trade marks need to be created which are governed by a uniform Community law directly applicable in all Member States;

Whereas since the Treaty has not provided the specific powers to establish such a legal instrument, Article 235 of the Treaty should be applied;

Whereas the Community law relating to trade marks nevertheless does not replace the laws of the Member States on trade marks; whereas it would not in fact appear to be justified to require undertakings to apply for registration of their trade marks as Community trade marks; whereas national trade marks continue to be necessary for those undertakings which do not want protection of their trade marks at Community level;

Whereas the rights in a Community trade mark may not be obtained otherwise than by registration, and registration is to be refused in particular if the trade mark is not distinctive, if it is unlawful or if it conflicts with earlier rights;

Whereas the protection afforded by a Community trade mark, the function of which is in particular to guarantee the trade mark as an indication of origin, is absolute in the case of identity between the mark and the sign and the goods or services; whereas the protection applies also in cases of similarity between the mark and the sign and the goods or services; whereas an interpretation should be given of the concept of similarity in relation to the likelihood of confusion; whereas the likelihood of confusion, the appreciation of which depends on numerous elements and, in particular, on the recognition of the trade mark on the market, the association which can be made with the used or registered sign, the degree of similarity between the trade mark and the sign and between the goods or services identified, constitutes the specific condition for such protection;

Whereas it follows from the principle of free flow of goods that the proprietor of a Community trade mark must not be entitled to prohibit its use by a third party in relation to goods which have been put into circulation in the Community, under the trade mark, by him or with his consent, save where there exist legitimate reasons for the proprietor to oppose further commercialization of the goods;

Whereas there is no justification for protecting Community trade marks or, as against them, any trade mark which has been registered before them, except where the trade marks are actually used;

Whereas a Community trade mark is to be regarded as an object of property which exists separately from the undertakings whose goods or services are designated by it; whereas accordingly, it must be capable of being transferred, subject to the overriding need to prevent the public being misled as a result of the transfer. It must also be capable of being charged as security in favour of a third party and of being the subject matter of licences;

Whereas administrative measures are necessary at Community level for implementing in relation to every trade mark the trade mark law created by this Regulation; whereas it is therefore essential, while retaining the Community's existing institutional structure and balance of powers, to establish an Office for Harmonization in the Internal Market (trade marks and designs) which is independent in relation to technical matters and has legal, administrative and financial autonomy; whereas to this end it is necessary and appropriate that it should be a body of the Community having legal personality and exercising the implementing powers which are conferred on it by this Regulation, and that it should operate within the framework of Community law without detracting from the competencies exercised by the Community institutions;

Whereas it is necessary to ensure that parties who are affected by decisions made by the Office are protected by the law in a manner which is suited to the special character of trade mark law; whereas to that end provision is made for an appeal to lie from decisions of the examiners and of the various divisions of the Office; whereas if the department whose decision is contested does not rectify its decision it is to remit the appeal to a Board of Appeal of the Office, which is to decide on it; Whereas decisions of the Boards of Appeal are, in turn, amenable to actions before the Court of Justice of the European Communities, which has jurisdiction to annul or to alter the contested decision;

Whereas under Council Decision 88/591/ECSC, EEC, Euratom of 24 October 1988 establishing a Court of First Instance of the European Communities, as amended by Decision 93/350/Euratom, ECSC, EEC of 8 June 1993, that Court shall exercise at the first instance the jurisdiction conferred on the Court of Justice by the Treaties establishing the Communities—with particular regard to appeals lodged under the second subparagraph of Article 173 of the EC Treaty—and by the acts adopted in implementation thereof, save as otherwise provided in an act setting up a body governed by Community law; whereas the jurisdiction which this Regulation confers on the Court of Justice to cancel and reform decisions of the appeal courts shall accordingly be exercised at the first instance by the Court in accordance with the above Decision;

Whereas in order to strengthen the protection of Community trade marks the Member States should designate, having regard to their own national system, as limited a number as possible of national courts of first and second instance having jurisdiction in matters of infringement and validity of Community trade marks;

Whereas decisions regarding the validity and infringement of Community trade marks must have effect and cover the entire area of the Community, as this is the only way of preventing inconsistent decisions on the part of the courts and the Office and of ensuring that the unitary character of Community trade marks is not undermined; whereas the rules contained in the Brussels Convention of Jurisdiction and the Enforcement of Judgments in Civil and Commercial Matters will apply to all actions at law relating to Community trade marks, save where this Regulation derogates from those rules;

Whereas contradictory judgments should be avoided in actions which involve the same acts and the same parties and which are brought on the basis of a Community trade mark and parallel national trade marks; whereas for this purpose, when the actions are brought in the same Member State, the way in which this is to be achieved is a matter for national procedural rules, which are not prejudiced by this Regulation, whilst when the actions are brought in different Member States, provisions modelled on the rules on *lis pendens* and related actions of the abovementioned Brussels Convention appear appropriate;

Whereas in order to guarantee the full autonomy and independence of the Office, it is considered necessary to grant it an autonomous budget whose revenue comes principally from fees paid by the users of the system; whereas however, the Community budgetary procedure remains applicable as far as any subsidies chargeable to general budget of the European Communities are concerned; whereas moreover, the auditing of accounts should be undertaken by the Court of Auditors;

Whereas implementing measures are required for the Regulation's application, particularly as regards the adoption and amendment of fees regulations and an Implementing Regulation; Whereas such measures should be adopted by the Commission, assisted by a Committee composed of representatives of the Member States, in accordance with the procedural rules laid down in Article 2, procedure III(b), of Council Decisions 87/373/EEC of 13 July 1987 laying down the procedures for the exercise of implementing powers conferred on the Commission,

HAS ADOPTED THIS REGULATION:

TITLE I

GENERAL PROVISIONS

Article 1

COMMUNITY TRADE MARK

1. A trade mark for goods or services which is registered in accordance with **A9–02** the conditions contained in this Regulation and in the manner herein provided is hereinafter referred to as a 'Community trade mark'.

2. A Community trade mark shall have a unitary character. It shall have equal effect throughout the Community: it shall not be registered, transferred or surrendered or be the subject of a decision revoking the rights of the proprietor

or declaring it invalid, nor shall its use be prohibited, save in respect of the whole Community. This principle shall apply unless otherwise provided in this Regulation.

Article 2

OFFICE

A9–03   An Office for Harmonization in the Internal Market (trade marks and designs), hereinafter referred to as "the Office", is hereby established.

Article 3

CAPACITY TO ACT

A9–04   For the purpose of implementing this Regulation, companies or firms and other legal bodies shall be regarded as legal persons if, under the terms of the law governing them, they have the capacity in their own name to have rights and obligations of all kinds, to make contracts or accomplish other legal acts and to sue and be sued.

TITLE II

THE LAW RELATING TO TRADE MARKS

SECTION 1

DEFINITION OF A COMMUNITY TRADE MARK OBTAINING A COMMUNITY TRADE MARK

Article 4

SIGNS OF WHICH A COMMUNITY TRADE MARK MAY CONSIST

A9–05   A Community trade mark may consist of any signs capable of being represented graphically, particularly words, including personal names, designs, letters, numerals, the shape of goods or of their packaging, provided that such signs are capable of distinguishing the goods or services of one undertaking from those of other undertakings.

Article 5

PERSONS WHO CAN BE PROPRIETORS OF COMMUNITY TRADE MARKS

A9–06   1. The following natural or legal persons, including authorities established under public law, may be proprietors of Community trade marks:

  (a) nationals of the Member States; or

   (b) *nationals of other States which are parties to the Paris Convention for the protection of industrial property, hereinafter referred to as "the Paris Convention"; or*

  (b) nationals of other States which are parties to the Paris Convention for the protection of industrial property, hereinafter referred to as "the Paris Convention", or to the Agreement establishing the World Trade Organization; or

   (c) nationals of States which are not parties to the Paris Convention who are domiciled or have their seat or who have real and effective industrial or commercial establishments within the territory of the Community or of a State which is party to the Paris Convention; or

   (d) *nationals, other than those referred to under subparagraph (c), of any State which is not party to the Paris Convention and which, according to published findings, accords to nationals of all the Member States the same protection for trade marks as it accords to its own nationals and, if nationals of the Member States are required to prove registration in the country of origin, recognizes the registration of Community trade marks as such proof.*

  (d) nationals, other than those referred to under subparagraph (c), of any State which is not party to the Paris Convention or to the Agreement establishing the World Trade Organization and which, according to published findings, accords to nationals of all the Member States the same protection for trade marks as it accords to its own nationals and, if nationals of the Member States are required to prove registration in the country of origin, recognizes the registration of Community trade marks as such proof.

2. With respect to the application of paragraph 1, stateless persons as defined by Article 1 of the Convention relating to the Status of Stateless Persons signed at New York on 28 September 1954, and refugees as defined by Article 1 of the Convention relating to the Status of Refugees signed at Geneva on 28 July 1951 and modified by the Protocol relating to the Status of Refugees signed at New York on 31 January 1967, shall be regarded as nationals of the country in which they have their habitual residence.

3. Persons who are nationals of a State covered by paragraph 1 (d) must prove that the trade mark for which an application for a Community trade mark has been submitted is registered in the State of origin, unless, according to published findings, the trade marks of nationals of the Member States are registered in the State of origin in question without proof of prior registration as a Community trade mark or as a national trade mark in a Member State.

The words in bold replaced the words in italics as a result of Regulation 3288/94, amending the CTM Regulation to take account of the effect of the Uruguay Round.

Article 6

MEANS WHEREBY A COMMUNITY TRADE MARK IS OBTAINED

A Community trade mark shall be obtained by registration.   **A9–07**

Article 7

ABSOLUTE GROUNDS FOR REFUSAL

1. The following shall not be registered: **A9–08**

   (a) signs which do not conform to the requirements of Article 4;

(b) trade marks which are devoid of any distinctive character;
(c) trade marks which consist exclusively of signs or indications which may serve, in trade, to designate the kind, quality, quantity, intended purpose, value, geographical origin or the time of production of the goods or of rendering of the service, or other characteristics of the goods or service;
(d) trade marks which consist exclusively of signs or indications which have become customary in the current language or in the bona fide and established practices of the trade;
(e) signs which consist exclusively of:
   (i) the shape which results from the nature of the goods themselves; or
   (ii) the shape of goods which is necessary to obtain a technical result; or
   (iii) the shape which gives substantial value to the goods;
(f) trade marks which are contrary to public policy or to accepted principles of morality;
(g) trade marks which are of such a nature as to deceive the public, for instance as to the nature, quality or geographical origin of the goods or service;
(h) trade marks which have not been authorized by the competent authorities and are to be refused pursuant to Article 6ter of the Paris Convention;
(i) trade marks which include badges, emblems or escutcheons other than those covered by Article 6ter of the Paris Convention and which are of particular public interest, unless the consent of the appropriate authorities to their registration has been given.
(j) **trade marks for wines which contain or consist of a geographical indication identifying wines or for spirits which contain or consist of a geographical indication identifying spirits with respect to such wines or spirits not having that origin.**

2. Paragraph 1 shall apply notwithstanding that the grounds of non-registrability obtain in only part of the Community.
3. Paragraph 1 (b), (c) and (d) shall not apply if the trade mark has become distinctive in relation to the goods or services for which registration is requested in consequence of the use which has been made of it.

The words in bold were inserted by Regulation 3288/94, amending the CTM Regulation to take account of the effect of the Uruguay Round.

Article 8

RELATIVE GROUNDS FOR REFUSAL

A9–09 1. Upon opposition by the proprietor of an earlier trade mark, the trade mark applied for shall not be registered:

(a) if it is identical with the earlier trade mark and the goods or services for which registration is applied for are identical with the goods or services for which the earlier trade mark is protected;
(b) if because of its identity with or similarity to the earlier trade mark and the identity or similarity of the goods or services covered by the trade marks there exists a likelihood of confusion on the part of the public in the territory in which the earlier trade mark is protected; the likelihood of confusion includes the likelihood of association with the earlier trade mark.

2. for the purposes of paragraph 1, 'Earlier trade marks' means:

(a) trade marks of the following kinds with a date of application for registration which is earlier than the date of application for registration of the Community trade mark, taking account, where appropriate, of the priorities claimed in respect of those trade marks:

   (i) Community trade marks;

   (ii) trade marks registered in a Member State, or, in the case of Belgium, the Netherlands or Luxembourg, at the Benelux Trade Mark Office;

   (iii) trade marks registered under international arrangements which have effect in a Member State;

(b) applications for the trade marks referred to in subparagraph (a), subject to their registration;

(c) trade marks which, on the date of application for registration of the Community trade mark, or, where appropriate, of the priority claimed in respect of the application for registration of the Community trade mark, are well known in a Member State, in the sense in which the words "well known" are used in Article 6 bis of the Paris Convention.

3. Upon opposition by the proprietor of the trade mark, a trade mark shall not be registered where an agent or representative of the proprietor of the trade mark applies for registration thereof in his own name without the proprietor's consent, unless the agent or representative justifies his action.

4. Upon opposition by the proprietor of a non-registered trade mark or of another sign used in the course of trade of more than mere local significance, the trade mark applied for shall not be registered where and to the extent that, pursuant to the law of the Member State governing that sign,

(a) rights to that sign were acquired prior to the date of application for registration of the Community trade mark, or the date of the priority claimed for the application for registration of the Community trade mark;

(b) that sign confers on its proprietor the right to prohibit the use of a subsequent trade mark.

5. Furthermore, upon opposition by the proprietor of an earlier trade mark within the meaning of paragraph 2, the trade mark applied for shall not be registered where it is identical with or similar to the earlier trade mark and is to be registered for goods or services which are not similar to those for which the earlier trade mark is registered, where in the case of an earlier Community trade mark the trade mark has a reputation in the Community and, in the case of an earlier national trade mark, the trade mark has a reputation in the Member State concerned and where the use without due cause of the trade mark applied for would take unfair advantage of, or be detrimental to, the distinctive character or the repute of the earlier trade mark.

SECTION 2

EFFECTS OF COMMUNITY TRADE MARKS

Article 9

RIGHTS CONFERRED BY A COMMUNITY TRADE MARK

1. A Community trade mark shall confer on the proprietor exclusive rights **A9–10** therein. The proprietor shall be entitled to prevent all third parties not having his consent from using in the course of trade:

1037

(a) any sign which is identical with the Community trade mark in relation to goods or services which are identical with those for which the Community trade mark is registered;

(b) any sign where, because of its identity with or similarity to the Community trade mark and the identity or similarity of the goods or services covered by the Community trade mark and the sign, there exists a likelihood of confusion on the part of the public; the likelihood of confusion includes the likelihood of association between the sign and the trade mark;

(c) any sign which is identical with or similar to the Community trade mark in relation to goods or services which are not similar to those for which the Community trade mark is registered, where the latter has a reputation in the Community and where use of that sign without due cause takes unfair advantage of, or is detrimental to, the distinctive character or the repute of the Community trade mark.

2. The following, *inter alia*, may be prohibited under paragraph 1:

(a) affixing the sign to the goods or to the packaging thereof;

(b) offering the goods, putting them on the market or stocking them for these purposes under that sign, or offering or supplying services thereunder;

(c) importing or exporting the goods under that sign;

(d) using the sign on business papers and in advertising.

3. The rights conferred by a Community trade mark shall prevail against third parties from the date of publication of registration of the trade mark. Reasonable compensation may, however, be claimed in respect of matters arising after the date of publication of a Community trade mark application, which matters would, after publication of the registration of the trade mark, be prohibited by virtue of that publication. The court seized of the case may not decide upon the merits of the case until the registration has been published.

Article 10

REPRODUCTION OF COMMUNITY TRADE MARKS IN DICTIONARIES

A9–11 If the reproduction of a Community trade mark in a dictionary, encyclopaedia or similar reference work gives the impression that it constitutes the generic name of the goods or services for which the trade mark is registered, the publisher of the work shall, at the request of the proprietor of the Community trade mark, ensure that the reproduction of the trade mark at the latest in the next edition of the publication is accompanied by an indication that it is a registered trade mark.

Article 11

PROHIBITION ON THE USE OF A COMMUNITY TRADE MARK REGISTERED IN THE NAME OF AN AGENT OR REPRESENTATIVE

A9–12 Where a Community trade mark is registered in the name of the agent or representative of a person who is the proprietor of that trade mark, without the proprietor's authorization, the latter shall be entitled to oppose the use of his mark by his agent or representative if he has not authorized such use, unless the agent or representative justifies his action.

Article 12

LIMITATION OF THE EFFECTS OF A COMMUNITY TRADE MARK

A Community trade mark shall not entitle the proprietor to prohibit a third **A9–13** party from using in the course of trade:

(a) his own name or address;

(b) indications concerning the kind, quality, quantity, intended purpose, value, geographical origin, the time of production of the goods or of rendering of the service, or other characteristics of the goods or service;

(c) the trade mark where it is necessary to indicate the intended purpose of a product or service, in particular as accessories or spare parts, provided he uses them in accordance with honest practices in industrial or commercial matters.

Article 13

EXHAUSTION OF THE RIGHTS CONFERRED BY A COMMUNITY TRADE MARK

1. A Community trade mark shall not entitle the proprietor to prohibit its use **A9–14** in relation to goods which have been put on the market in the Community under that trade mark by the proprietor or with his consent.

2. Paragraph 1 shall not apply where there exist legitimate reasons for the proprietor to oppose further commercialization of the goods, especially where the condition of the goods is changed or impaired after they have been put on the market.

Article 14

COMPLEMENTARY APPLICATION OF NATIONAL LAW RELATING TO INFRINGEMENT

1. The effects of Community trade marks shall be governed solely by the **A9–15** provisions of this Regulation. In other respects, infringement of a Community trade mark shall be governed by the national law relating to infringement of a national trade mark in accordance with the provisions of Title X.

2. This Regulation shall not prevent actions concerning a Community trade mark being brought under the law of Member States relating in particular to civil liability and unfair competition.

3. The rules of procedure to be applied shall be determined in accordance with the provisions of Title X.

SECTION 3

USE OF COMMUNITY TRADE MARKS

Article 15

USE OF COMMUNITY TRADE MARKS

1. If, within a period of five years following registration, the proprietor has not **A9–16** put the Community trade mark to genuine use in the Community in connection with the goods or services in respect of which it is registered, or if such use has

1039

been suspended during an uninterrupted period of five years, the Community trade mark shall be subject to the sanctions provided for in this Regulation, unless there are proper reasons for non-use.

2. The following shall also constitute use within the meaning of paragraph 1:

(a) use of the Community trade mark in a form differing in elements which do not alter the distinctive character of the mark in the form in which it was registered;

(b) affixing of the Community trade mark to goods or to the packaging thereof in the Community solely for export purposes.

3. Use of the Community trade mark with the consent of the proprietor shall be deemed to constitute use by the proprietor.

SECTION 4

COMMUNITY TRADE MARKS AS OBJECTS OF PROPERTY

Article 16

DEALING WITH COMMUNITY TRADE MARKS AS NATIONAL TRADE MARKS

A9–17 1. Unless Articles 17 to 24 provide otherwise, a Community trade mark as an object of property shall be dealt with in its entirety, and for the whole area of the Community, as a national trade mark registered in the Member State in which, according to the Register of Community trade marks,

(a) the proprietor has his seat or his domicile on the relevant date; or

(b) where subparagraph (a) does not apply, the proprietor has an establishment on the relevant date.

2. In cases which are not provided for by paragraph 1, the Member State referred to in that paragraph shall be the Member State in which the seat of the Office is situated.

3. If two or more persons are mentioned in the Register of Community trade marks as joint proprietors, paragraph 1 shall apply to the joint proprietor first mentioned; failing this, it shall apply to the subsequent joint proprietors in the order in which they are mentioned. Where paragraph 1 does not apply to any of the joint proprietors, paragraph 2 shall apply.

Article 17

TRANSFER

A9–18 1. A Community trade mark may be transferred, separately from any transfer of the undertaking, in respect of some or all of the goods or services for which it is registered.

2. A transfer of the whole of the undertaking shall include the transfer of the Community trade mark except where, in accordance with the law governing the transfer, there is agreement to the contrary or circumstances clearly dictate otherwise. This provision shall apply to the contractual obligation to transfer the undertaking.

3. Without prejudice to paragraph 2, an assignment of the Community trade mark shall be made in writing and shall require the signature of the parties to the contract, except when it is a result of a judgment; otherwise it shall be void.

4. Where it is clear from the transfer documents that because of the transfer the Community trade mark is likely to mislead the public concerning the nature, quality or geographical origin of the goods or services in respect of which it is registered, the Office shall not register the transfer unless the successor agrees to limit registration of the Community trade mark to goods or services in respect of which it is not likely to mislead.

5. On request of one of the parties a transfer shall be entered in the Register and published.

6. As long as the transfer has not been entered in the Register, the successor in title may not invoke the rights arising from the registration of the Community trade mark.

7. Where there are time limits to be observed *vis-à-vis* the Office, the successor in title may make the corresponding statements to the Office once the request for registration of the transfer has been received by the Office.

8. All documents which require notification to the proprietor of the Community trade mark in accordance with Article 77 shall be addressed to the person registered as proprietor.

Article 18

TRANSFER OF A TRADE MARK REGISTERED IN THE NAME OF AN AGENT

Where a Community trade mark is registered in the name of the agent or **A9–19** representative of a person who is the proprietor of that trade mark, without the proprietor's authorization, the latter shall be entitled to demand the assignment in his favour of the said registration, unless such agent or representative justifies his action.

Article 19

RIGHTS IN REM

1. A Community trade mark may, independently of the undertaking, be given **A9–20** as security or be the subject of rights in rem.

2. On request of one of the parties, rights mentioned in paragraph 1 shall be entered in the Register and published.

Article 20

LEVY OF EXECUTION

1. A Community trade mark may be levied in execution. **A9–21**

2. As regards the procedure for levy of execution in respect of a Community trade mark, the courts and authorities of the Member States determined in accordance with Article 16 shall have exclusive jurisdiction.

3. On request of one the parties, levy of execution shall be entered in the Register and published.

Article 21

BANKRUPTCY OR LIKE PROCEEDINGS

A9–22   1. Until such time as common rules for the Member States in this field enter into force, the only Member State in which a Community trade mark may be involved in bankruptcy or like proceedings shall be that in which such proceedings are first brought within the meaning of national law or of conventions applicable in this field.

2. Where a Community trade mark is involved in bankruptcy or like proceedings, on request of the competent national authority an entry to this effect shall be made in the Register and published.

Article 22

LICENSING

A9–23   1. A Community trade mark may be licensed for some or all of the goods or services for which it is registered and for the whole or part of the Community. A licence may be exclusive or non-exclusive.

2. The proprietor of a Community trade mark may invoke the rights conferred by that trade mark against a licensee who contravenes any provision in his licensing contract with regard to its duration, the form covered by the registration in which the trade mark may be used, the scope of the goods or services for which the licence is granted, the territory in which the trade mark may be affixed, or the quality of the goods manufactured or of the services provided by the licensee.

3. Without prejudice to the provisions of the licensing contract, the licensee may bring proceedings for infringement of a Community trade mark only if its proprietor consents thereto. However, the holder of an exclusive licence may bring such proceedings if the proprietor of the trade mark, after formal notice, does not himself bring infringement proceedings within an appropriate period.

4. A licensee shall, for the purpose of obtaining compensation for damage suffered by him, be entitled to intervene in infringement proceedings brought by the proprietor of the Community trade mark.

5. On request of one of the parties the grant or transfer of a licence in respect of a Community trade mark shall be entered in the Register and published.

Article 23

EFFECTS VIS-À-VIS THIRD PARTIES

A9–24   1. Legal acts referred to in Article 17, 19 and 22 concerning a Community trade mark shall only have effects *vis-à-vis* third parties in all the Member States after entry in the Register. Nevertheless, such an act, before it is so entered, shall have effect *vis-à-vis* third parties who have acquired rights in the trade mark after the date of that act but who knew of the act at the date on which the rights were acquired.

2. Paragraph 1 shall not apply in the case of a person who acquires the Community trade mark or a right concerning the Community trade mark by way of transfer of the whole of the undertaking or by any other universal succession.

3. The effects *vis-à-vis* third parties of the legal acts referred to in Article 20 shall be governed by the law of the Member State determined in accordance with Article 16.

4. Until such time as common rules for the Member States in the field of bankruptcy enter into force, the effects *vis-à-vis* third parties of bankruptcy or like proceedings shall be governed by the law of the Member State in which such proceedings are first brought within the meaning of national law or of conventions applicable in this field.

Article 24

THE APPLICATION FOR A COMMUNITY TRADE MARK AS AN OBJECT OF PROPERTY

Articles 16 to 23 shall apply to applications for Community trade marks. **A9–25**

TITLE III

APPLICATION FOR COMMUNITY TRADE MARKS

SECTION 1

FILING OF APPLICATIONS AND THE CONDITIONS WHICH GOVERN THEM

Article 25

FILING OF APPLICATIONS

1. An application for a Community trade mark shall be filed, at the choice of **A9–26** the applicant,

   (a) at the Office; or
   (b) at the central industrial property office of a Member State or at the Benelux Trade Mark Office. An application filed in this way shall have the same effect as if it had been filed on the same date at the Office.

2. Where the application is filed at the central industrial property office of a Member State or at the Benelux Trade Mark Office, that office shall take all steps to forward the application to the Office within two weeks after filing. It may charge the applicant a fee which shall not exceed the administrative costs of receiving and forwarding the application.

3. Applications referred to in paragraph 2 which reach the Office more than one month after filing shall be deemed withdrawn.

4. Ten years after the entry into force of this Regulation, the Commission shall draw up a report on the operation of the system of filing applications for Community trade marks, together with any proposals for modifying this system.

Article 26

CONDITIONS WITH WHICH APPLICATIONS MUST COMPLY

1. An application for a Community trade mark shall contain: **A9–27**

(a) a request for the registration of a Community trade mark;
(b) information identifying the applicant;
(c) a list of the goods or services in respect of which the registration is requested;
(d) a representation of the trade mark.

2. The application for a Community trade mark shall be subject to the payment of the application fee and, when appropriate, of one or more class fees.

3. An application for a Community trade mark must comply with the conditions laid down in the implementing Regulation referred to in Article 140.

Article 27

DATE OF FILING

A9–28   The date of filing of a Community trade mark application shall be the date on which documents containing the information specified in Article 26 (1) are filed with the Office by the applicant or, if the application has been filed with the central office of a Member State or with the Benelux Trade Mark Office, with that office, subject to payment of the application fee within a period of one month of filing the abovementioned documents.

Article 28

CLASSIFICATION

A9–29   Goods and services in respect of which Community trade marks are applied for shall be classified in conformity with the system of classification specified in the Implementing Regulation.

SECTION 2

PRIORITY

Article 29

RIGHT OF PRIORITY

A9–30   *1. A person who has duly filed an application for a trade mark in or for any State party to the Paris Convention, or his successors in title, shall enjoy, for the purpose of filing a Community trade mark application for the same trade mark in respect of goods or services which are identical with or contained within those for which the application has been filed, a right of priority during a period of six months from the date of filing of the first application.*

1. A person who has duly filed an application for a trade mark in or for any State party to the Paris Convention or to the Agreement establishing the World Trade Organization, or his successors in title, shall enjoy, for the purpose of filing a Community trade mark application for the same trade mark in respect of goods or services which are identical with or contained within those for which the application has been filed, a right or priority during a period of six months from the date of filing of the first application.

2. Every filing that is equivalent to a regular national filing under the national law of the State where it was made or under bilateral or multilateral agreements shall be recognized as giving rise to a right of priority.

3. By a regular national filing is meant any filing that is sufficient to establish the date on which the application was filed, whatever may be the outcome of the application.

4. A subsequent application for a trade mark which was the subject of a previous first application in respect of the same goods or services, and which is filed in or in respect of the same State shall be considered as the first application for the purposes of determining priority, provided that, at the date of filing of the subsequent application, the previous application has been withdrawn, abandoned or refused, without being open to public inspection and without leaving any rights outstanding, and has not served as a basis for claiming a right of priority. The previous application may not thereafter serve as a basis for claiming a right of priority.

5. *If the first filing has been made in a State which is not a party to the Paris Convention, paragraphs 1 to 4 shall apply only in so far as that State, according to published findings, grants, on the basis of a first filing made at the Office and subject to conditions equivalent to those laid down in this Regulation, a right of priority having equivalent effect.*

5. If the first filing has been made in a State which is not a party to the Paris Convention or to the Agreement establishing the World Trade Organization, paragraphs 1 to 4 shall apply only in so far as that State, according to published findings, grants, on the basis of the first filing made at the Office and subject to conditions equivalent to those laid down in this Regulation, a right of priority having equivalent effect.

The words in bold replaced the words in italics as a result of Regulation 3288/94, amending the CTM Regulation to take account of the effect of the Uruguay Round.

Article 30

CLAIMING PRIORITY

An applicant desiring to take advantage of the priority of a previous **A9–31** application shall file a declaration of priority and a copy of the previous application. If the language of the latter is not one of the languages of the Office, the applicant shall file a translation of the previous application in one of those languages.

Article 31

EFFECT OF PRIORITY RIGHT

The right of priority shall have the effect that the date of priority shall count as **A9–32** the date of filing of the Community trade mark application for the purposes of establishing which rights take precedence.

Article 32

EQUIVALENCE OF COMMUNITY FILING WITH NATIONAL FILING

A Community trade mark application which has been accorded a date of filing **A9–33** shall, in the Member States, be equivalent to a regular national filing, where appropriate with the priority claimed for the Community trade mark application.

SECTION 3

EXHIBITION PRIORITY

Article 33

EXHIBITION PRIORITY

A9–34 1. If an applicant for a Community trade mark has displayed goods or services under the mark applied for, at an official or officially recognized international exhibition falling within the terms of the Convention on International Exhibitions signed at Paris on 22 November 1928 and last revised on 30 November 1972, he may, if he files the application within a period of six months from the date of the first display of the goods or services under the mark applied for, claim a right of priority from that date within the meaning of Article 31.

2. An applicant who wishes to claim priority pursuant to paragraph 1 must file evidence of the display of goods or services under the mark applied for under the conditions laid down in the Implementing Regulation.

3. An exhibition priority granted in a Member State or in a third country does not extend the period of priority laid down in Article 29.

SECTION 4

CLAIMING THE SENIORITY OF A NATIONAL TRADE MARK

Article 34

CLAIMING THE SENIORITY OF A NATIONAL TRADE MARK

A9–35 1. The proprietor of an earlier trade mark registered in a Member State, including a trade mark registered in the Benelux countries, or registered under international arrangements having effect in a Member State, who applies for an identical trade mark for registration as a Community trade mark for goods or services which are identical with or contained within those for which the earlier trade mark has been registered, may claim for the Community trade mark the seniority of the earlier trade mark in respect of the Member State in or for which it is registered.

2. Seniority shall have the sole effect under this Regulation that, where the proprietor of the Community trade mark surrenders the earlier trade mark or allows it to lapse, he shall be deemed to continue to have the same rights as he would have had if the earlier trade mark had continued to be registered.

3. The seniority claimed for the Community trade mark shall lapse if the earlier trade mark the seniority of which is claimed is declared to have been revoked or to be invalid or if it is surrendered prior to the registration of the Community trade mark.

Article 35

CLAIMING SENIORITY AFTER REGISTRATION OF THE COMMUNITY TRADE MARK

A9–36 1. The proprietor of a Community trade mark who is the proprietor of an earlier identical trade mark registered in a Member State, including a trade mark registered in the Benelux countries, or of a trade mark registered under

1046

international arrangements having effect in a Member State, for identical goods or services, may claim the seniority of the earlier trade mark in respect of the Member State in or for which it is registered.

2. Article 34 (2) and (3) shall apply.

TITLE IV

REGISTRATION PROCEDURE

SECTION 1

EXAMINATION OF APPLICATIONS

Article 36

EXAMINATION OF THE CONDITIONS OF FILING

1. The Office shall examine whether: **A9–37**

  (a) the Community trade mark application satisfies the requirements for the accordance of a date of filing in accordance with Article 27;
  (b) the Community trade mark application complies with the conditions laid down in the Implementing Regulation;
  (c) where appropriate, the class fees have been paid within the prescribed period.

2. Where the Community trade mark application does not satisfy the requirements referred to in paragraph 1, the Office shall request the applicant to remedy the deficiencies or the default on payment within the prescribed period.

3. If the deficiencies or the default on payment established pursuant to paragraph 1 (a) are not remedied within this period, the application shall not be dealt with as a Community trade mark application. If the applicant complies with the Office's request, the Office shall accord as the date of filing of the application the date on which the deficiencies or the default on payment established are remedied.

4. If the deficiencies established pursuant to paragraph 1 (b) are not remedied within the prescribed period, the Office shall refuse the application.

5. If the default on payment established pursuant to paragraph 1 (c) is not remedied within the prescribed period, the application shall be deemed to be withdrawn unless it is clear which categories of goods or services the amount paid is intended to cover.

6. Failure to satisfy the requirements concerning the claim to priority shall result in loss of the right of priority for the application.

7. Failure to satisfy the requirements concerning the claiming of seniority of a national trade mark shall result in loss of that right for the application.

Article 37

EXAMINATION OF THE CONDITIONS RELATING TO THE ENTITLEMENT OF THE PROPRIETOR

1. Where, pursuant to Article 5, the applicant may not be the proprietor of a   **A9–38**
Community trade mark, the application shall be refused.

2. The application may not be refused before the applicant has been given the opportunity to withdraw his application or submit his observations.

Article 38

EXAMINATION AS TO ABSOLUTE GROUNDS FOR REFUSAL

A9–39 1. Where, under Article 7, a trade mark is ineligible for registration in respect of some or all of the goods or services covered by the Community trade mark application, the application shall be refused as regards those goods or services.

2. Where the trade mark contains an element which is not distinctive, and where the inclusion of said element in the trade mark could give rise to doubts as to the scope of protection of the trade mark, the Office may request, as a condition for registration of said trade mark, that the applicant state that he disclaims any exclusive right to such element. Any disclaimer shall be published together with the application or the registration of the Community trade mark, as the case may be.

3. The application shall not be refused before the applicant has been allowed the opportunity of withdrawing or amending the application or of submitting his observations.

SECTION 2

SEARCH

Article 39

SEARCH

A9–40 1. Once the Office has accorded a date of filing to a Community trade mark application and has established that the applicant satisfies the conditions referred to in Article 5, it shall draw up a Community search report citing those earlier Community trade marks or Community trade mark applications discovered which may be invoked under Article 8 against the registration of the Community trade mark applied for.

2. As soon as a Community trade mark application has been accorded a date of filing, the Office shall transmit a copy thereof to the central industrial property office of each Member State which has informed the Office of its decision to operate a search in its own register of trade marks in respect of Community trade mark applications.

3. Each of the central industrial property offices referred to in paragraph 2 shall communicate to the Office within three months as from the date on which it received the Community trade mark application a search report which shall either cite those earlier national trade marks or trade mark applications discovered which may be invoked under Article 8 against the registration of the Community trade mark applied for, or state that the search has revealed no such rights.

4. An amount shall be paid by the Office to each central industrial property office for each search report provided by that office in accordance with paragraph 3. The amount, which shall be the same for each office, shall be fixed by the Budget Committee by means of a decision adopted by a majority of three-quarters of the representatives of the Member States.

5. The Office shall transmit without delay to the applicant for the Community trade mark the Community search report and the national search reports received within the time limit laid down in paragraph 3.

6. Upon publication of the Community trade mark application, which may not take place before the expiry of a period of one month as from the date on which the Office transmits the search reports to the applicant, the Office shall inform the proprietors of any earlier Community trade marks or Community trade mark applications cited in the Community search report of the publication of the Community trade mark application.

7. The Commission shall, five years after the opening of the Office for the filing of applications, submit to the Council a report on the operation of the system of searching resulting from this Article, including the payments made to Member States under paragraph 4, and, if necessary, appropriate proposals for amending this Regulation with a view to adapting the system of searching on the basis of the experience gained and bearing in mind developments in searching techniques.

SECTION 3

PUBLICATION OF THE APPLICATION

Article 40

PUBLICATION OF THE APPLICATION

1. If the conditions which the application for a Community trade mark must **A9–41** satisfy have been fulfilled and if the period referred to in Article 39 (6) has expired, the application shall be published to the extent that it has not been refused pursuant to Articles 37 and 38.

2. Where, after publication, the application is refused under Articles 37 and 38, the decision that it has been refused shall be published upon becoming final.

SECTION 4

OBSERVATIONS BY THIRD PARTIES AND OPPOSITION

Article 41

OBSERVATIONS BY THIRD PARTIES

1. Following the publication of the Community trade mark application, any **A9–42** natural or legal person and any group or body representing manufacturers, producers, suppliers of services, traders or consumers may submit to the Office written observations, explaining on which grounds under Article 7, in particular, the trade mark shall not be registered ex officio. They shall not be parties to the proceedings before the Office.

2. The observations referred to in paragraph 1 shall be communicated to the applicant who may comment on them.

Article 42

OPPOSITION

1. Within a period of three months following the publication of a Community **A9–43** trade mark application, notice of opposition to registration of the trade mark may be given on the grounds that it may not be registered under Article 8:

(a) by the proprietors of earlier trade marks referred to in Article 8 (2) as well as licensees authorized by the proprietors of those trade marks, in respect of Article 8 (1) and (5);

(b) by the proprietors of trade marks referred to in Article 8 (3);

(c) by the proprietors of earlier marks or signs referred to in Article 8 (4) and by persons authorized under the relevant national law to exercise these rights.

2. Notice of opposition to registration of the trade mark may also be given, subject to the conditions laid down in paragraph 1, in the event of the publication of an amended application in accordance with the second sentence of Article 44 (2).

3. Opposition must be expressed in writing and must specify the grounds on which it is made. It shall not be treated as duly entered until the opposition fee has been paid. Within a period fixed by the Office, the opponent may submit in support of his case facts, evidence and arguments.

Article 43
EXAMINATION OF OPPOSITION

A9–44 1. In the examination of the opposition the Office shall invite the parties, as often as necessary, to file observations, within a period set them by the Office, on communications from the other parties or issued by itself.

2. If the applicant so requests, the proprietor of an earlier Community trade mark who has given notice of opposition shall furnish proof that, during the period of five years preceding the date of publication of the Community trade mark application, the earlier Community trade mark has been put to genuine use in the Community in connection with the goods or services in respect of which it is registered and which he cites as justification for his opposition, or that there are proper reasons for non-use, provided the earlier Community trade mark has at that date been registered for not less than five years. In the absence of proof to this effect, the opposition shall be rejected. If the earlier Community trade mark has been used in relation to part only of the goods or services for which it is registered it shall, for the purposes of the examination of the opposition, be deemed to be registered in respect only of that part of the goods or services.

3. Paragraph 2 shall apply to earlier national trade marks referred to in Article 8 (2) (a), by substituting use in the Member State in which the earlier national trade mark is protected for use in the Community.

4. The Office may, if it thinks fit, invite the parties to make a friendly settlement.

5. If examination of the opposition reveals that the trade mark may not be registered in respect of some or all of the goods or services for which the Community trade mark application has been made, the application shall be refused in respect of those goods or services. Otherwise the opposition shall be rejected.

6. The decision refusing the application shall be published upon becoming final.

SECTION 5

WITHDRAWAL, RESTRICTION AND AMENDMENT OF THE APPLICATION

Article 44
WITHDRAWAL, RESTRICTION AND AMENDMENT OF THE APPLICATION

A9–45 1. The applicant may at any time withdraw his Community trade mark application or restrict the list of goods or services contained therein. Where the application has already been published, the withdrawal or restriction shall also be published.

2. In other respects, a Community trade mark application may be amended, upon request of the applicant, only by correcting the name and address of the applicant, errors of wording or of copying, or obvious mistakes, provided that such correction does not substantially change the trade mark or extend the list of goods or services. Where the amendments affect the representation of the trade mark or the list of goods or services and are made after publication of the application, the trade mark application shall be published as amended.

SECTION 6

REGISTRATION

Article 45

REGISTRATION

Where an application meets the requirements of this Regulation and where no **A9–46** notice of opposition has been given within the period referred to in Article 42 (1) or where opposition has been rejected by a definitive decision, the trade mark shall be registered as a Community trade mark, provided that the registration fee has been paid within the period prescribed. If the fee is not paid within this period the application shall be deemed to be withdrawn.

TITLE V

DURATION, RENEWAL AND ALTERATION OF COMMUNITY TRADE MARKS

Article 46

DURATION OF REGISTRATION

Community trade marks shall be registered for a period of ten years from the **A9–47** date of filing of the application. Registration may be renewed in accordance with Article 47 for further periods of ten years.

Article 47

RENEWAL

1. Registration of the Community trade mark shall be renewed at the request **A9–48** of the proprietor of the trade mark or any person expressly authorized by him, provided that the fees have been paid.

2. The Office shall inform the proprietor of the Community trade mark, and any person having a registered right in respect of the Community trade mark, of the expiry of the registration in good time before the said expiry. Failure to give such information shall not involve the responsibility of the Office.

3. The request for renewal shall be submitted within a period of six months ending on the last day of the month in which protection ends. The fees shall also

be paid within this period. Failing this, the request may be submitted and the fees paid within a further period of six months following the day referred to in the first sentence, provided that an additional fee is paid within this further period.

4. Where the request is submitted or the fees paid in respect of only some of the goods or services for which the Community trade mark is registered, registration shall be renewed for those goods or services only.

5. Renewal shall take effect from the day following the date on which the existing registration expires. The renewal shall be registered.

Article 48

ALTERATION

A9–49   1. The Community trade mark shall not be altered in the register during the period of registration or on renewal thereof.

2. Nevertheless, where the Community trade mark includes the name and address of the proprietor, any alteration thereof not substantially affecting the identity of the trade mark as originally registered may be registered at the request of the proprietor.

3. The publication of the registration of the alteration shall contain a representation of the Community trade mark as altered. Third parties whose rights may be affected by the alteration may challenge the registration thereof within a period of three months following publication.

TITLE VI

SURRENDER, REVOCATION AND INVALIDITY

SECTION 1

SURRENDER

Article 49

SURRENDER

A9–50   1. A Community trade mark may be surrendered in respect of some or all of the goods or services for which it is registered.

2. The surrender shall be declared to the Office in writing by the proprietor of the trade mark. It shall not have effect until it has been entered in the Register.

3. Surrender shall be entered only with the agreement of the proprietor of a right entered in the Register. If a licence has been registered, surrender shall only be entered in the Register if the proprietor of the trade mark proves that he has informed the licensee of his intention to surrender; this entry shall be made on expiry of the period prescribed by the Implementing Regulation.

SECTION 2

GROUNDS FOR REVOCATION

Article 50

GROUNDS FOR REVOCATION

A9–51   1. The rights of the proprietor of the Community trade mark shall be declared to be revoked on application to the Office or on the basis of a counterclaim in infringement proceedings:

(a) if, within a continuous period of five years, the trade mark has not been put to genuine use in the Community in connection with the goods or services in respect of which it is registered, and there are no proper reasons for non-use; however, no person may claim that the proprietor's rights in a Community trade mark should be revoked where, during the interval between expiry of the five-year period and filing of the application or counterclaim, genuine use of the trade mark has been started or resumed; the commencement or resumption of use within a period of three months preceding the filing of the application or counterclaim which began at the earliest on expiry of the continuous period of five years of non-use shall, however, be disregarded where preparations for the commencement or resumption occur only after the proprietor becomes aware that the application or counterclaim may be filed;

(b) if, in consequence of acts or inactivity of the proprietor, the trade mark has become the common name in the trade for a product or service in respect of which it is registered;

(c) if, in consequence of the use made of it by the proprietor of the trade mark or with his consent in respect of the goods or services for which it is registered, the trade mark is liable to mislead the public, particularly as to the nature, quality or geographical origin of those goods or services;

(d) if the proprietor of the trade mark no longer satisfies the conditions laid down by Article 5.

2. Where the grounds for revocation of rights exist in respect of only some of the goods or services for which the Community trade mark is registered, the rights of the proprietor shall be declared to be revoked in respect of those goods or services only.

SECTION 3

GROUNDS FOR INVALIDITY

Article 51

ABSOLUTE GROUNDS FOR INVALIDITY

1. A Community trade mark shall be declared invalid on application to the **A9–52** Office or on the basis of a counterclaim in infringement proceedings,

(a) where the Community trade mark has been registered in breach of the provisions of Article 5 or of Article 7;

(b) where the applicant was acting in bad faith when he filed the application for the trade mark.

2. Where the Community trade mark has been registered in breach of the provisions of Article 7 (1) (b), (c) or (d), it may nevertheless not be declared invalid if, in consequence of the use which has been made of it, it has after registration acquired a distinctive character in relation to the goods or services for which it is registered.

3. Where the ground for invalidity exists in respect of only some of the goods or services for which the Community trade mark is registered, the trade mark shall be declared invalid as regards those goods or services only.

Article 52

RELATIVE GROUNDS FOR INVALIDITY

A9–53 1. A Community trade mark shall be declared invalid on application to the Office or on the basis of a counterclaim in infringement proceedings:

(a) where there is an earlier trade mark as referred to in Article 8 (2) and the conditions set out in paragraph 1 or paragraph 5 of that Article are fulfilled;

(b) where there is a trade mark as referred to in Article 8 (3) and the conditions set out in that paragraph are fulfilled;

(c) where there is an earlier right as referred to in Article 8 (4) and the conditions set out in that paragraph are fulfilled.

2. A Community trade mark shall also be declared invalid on application to the Office or on the basis of a counterclaim in infringement proceedings where the use of such trade mark may be prohibited pursuant to the national law governing the protection of any other earlier right an in particular:

(a) a right to a name;

(b) a right of personal portrayal;

(c) a copyright;

(d) an industrial property right.

3. A Community trade mark may not be declared invalid where the proprietor of a right referred to in paragraphs 1 or 2 consents expressly to the registration of the Community trade mark before submission of the application for a declaration of invalidity or the counterclaim.

4. Where the proprietor of one of the rights referred to in paragraphs 1 or 2 has previously applied for a declaration that a Community trade mark is invalid or made a counterclaim in infringement proceedings, he may not submit a new application for a declaration of invalidity or lodge a counterclaim on the basis of another of the said rights which he could have invoked in support of his first application or counterclaim.

5. Article 51 (3) shall apply.

Article 53

LIMITATION IN CONSEQUENCE OF ACQUIESCENCE

A9–54 1. Where the proprietor of a Community trade mark has acquiesced, for a period of five successive years, in the use of a later Community trade mark in the Community while being aware of such use, he shall no longer be entitled on the basis of the earlier trade mark either to apply for a declaration that the later trade mark is invalid or to oppose the use of the later trade mark in respect of the goods or services for which the later trade mark has been used, unless registration of the later Community trade mark was applied for in bad faith.

2. Where the proprietor of an earlier national trade mark as referred to in Article 8 (2) or of another earlier sign referred to in Article 8 (4) has acquiesced, for a period of five successive years, in the use of a later Community trade mark in the Member State in which the earlier trade mark or the other earlier sign is protected while being aware of such use, he shall no longer be entitled on the basis of the earlier trade mark or of the other earlier sign either to apply for a declaration that the later trade mark is invalid or to oppose the use of the later trade mark in respect of the goods or services for which the later trade mark has

been used, unless registration of the later Community trade mark was applied for in bad faith.

3. In the cases referred to in paragraphs 1 and 2, the proprietor of a later Community trade mark shall not be entitled to oppose the use of the earlier right, even though that right may no longer be invoked against the later Community trade mark.

SECTION 4

CONSEQUENCES OF REVOCATION AND INVALIDITY

Article 54

CONSEQUENCES OF REVOCATION AND INVALIDITY

1. The Community trade mark shall be deemed not to have had, as from the **A9–55** date of the application for revocation or of the counterclaim, the effects specified in this Regulation, to the extent that the rights of the proprietor have been revoked. An earlier date, on which one of the grounds for revocation occurred, may be fixed in the decision at the request of one of the parties.

2. The Community trade mark shall be deemed not to have had, as from the outset, the effects specified in this Regulation, to the extent that the trade mark has been declared invalid.

3. Subject to the national provisions relating either to claims for compensation for damage caused by negligence or lack of good faith on the part of the proprietor of the trade mark, or to unjust enrichment, the retroactive effect of revocation or invalidity of the trade mark shall not affect:

    (a) any decision on infringement which has acquired the authority of a final decision and been enforced prior to the revocation or invalidity decision;

    (b) any contract concluded prior to the revocation or invalidity decision, in so far as it has been performed before that decision; however, repayment, to an extent justified by the circumstances, of sums paid under the relevant contract, may be claimed on grounds of equity.

SECTION 5

PROCEEDINGS IN THE OFFICE IN RELATION TO REVOCATION OR INVALIDITY

Article 55

APPLICATION FOR REVOCATION OR FOR A DECLARATION OF INVALIDITY

1. An application for revocation of the rights of the proprietor of a Community **A9–56** trade mark or for a declaration that the trade mark is invalid may be submitted to the Office:

    (a) where Articles 50 and 51 apply, by any natural or legal person and any group or body set up for the purpose of representing the interests of

1055

manufacturers, producers, suppliers of services, traders or consumers, which under the terms of the law governing it has the capacity in its own name to sue and be sued;

(b) where Article 52 (1) applies, by the persons referred to in Article 42 (1);

(c) where Article 52 (2) applies, by the owners of the earlier rights referred to in that provision or by the persons who are entitled under the law of the Member State concerned to exercise the rights in question.

2. The application shall be filed in a written reasoned statement. It shall not be deemed to have been filed until the fee has been paid.

3. An application for revocation or for a declaration of invalidity shall be inadmissible if an application relating to the same subject matter and cause of action, and involving the same parties, has been adjudicated on by a court in a Member State and has acquired the authority of a final decision.

Article 56

EXAMINATION OF THE APPLICATION

A9–57   1. In the examination of the application for revocation of rights or for a declaration of invalidity, the Office shall invite the parties, as often as necessary, to file observations, within a period to be fixed by the Office, on communications from the other parties or issued by itself.

2. If the proprietor of the Community trade mark so requests, the proprietor of an earlier Community trade mark, being a party to the invalidity proceedings, shall furnish proof that, during the period of five years preceding the date of the application for a declaration of invalidity, the earlier Community trade mark has been put to genuine use in the Community in connection with the goods or services in respect of which it is registered and which he cites as justification for his application, or that there are proper reasons for non-use, provided the earlier Community trade mark has at that date been registered for non-use, provided the earlier Community trade mark has at that date been registered for not less than five years. If, at the date on which the Community trade mark application was published, the earlier Community trade mark had been registered for not less than five years, the proprietor of the earlier Community trade mark shall furnish proof that, in addition, the conditions contained in Article 43 (2) were satisfied at that date. In the absence of proof to this effect the application for a declaration of invalidity shall be rejected. If the earlier Community trade mark has been used in relation to part only of the goods or services for which it is registered it shall, for the purpose of the examination of the application for a declaration of invalidity, be deemed to be registered in respect only of that part of the goods or services.

3. Paragraph 2 shall apply to earlier national trade marks referred to in Article 8 (2) (a), by substituting use in the Member State in which the earlier national trade mark is protected for use in the Community.

4. The Office may, if it thinks fit, invite the parties to make a friendly settlement.

5. If the examination of the application for revocation of rights or for a declaration of invalidity reveals that the trade mark should not have been registered in respect of some or all of the goods or services for which it is registered, the rights of the proprietor of the Community trade mark shall be revoked or it shall be declared invalid in respect of those goods or services. Otherwise the application for revocation of rights or for a declaration of invalidity shall be rejected.

6. The decision revoking the rights of the proprietor of the Community trade mark or declaring it invalid shall be entered in the Register upon becoming final.

Title VII

Appeals

Article 57

DECISIONS SUBJECT TO APPEAL

1. An appeal shall lie from decisions of the examiners, Opposition Divisions, **A9–58** Administration of Trade Marks and Legal Divisions and Cancellation Divisions. It shall have suspensive effect.

2. A decision which does not terminate proceedings as regards one of the parties can only be appealed together with the final decision, unless the decision allows separate appeal.

Article 58

PERSONS ENTITLED TO APPEAL AND TO BE PARTIES TO APPEAL PROCEEDINGS

Any party to proceedings adversely affected by a decision may appeal. Any **A9–59** other parties to the proceedings shall be parties to the appeal proceedings as of right.

Article 59

TIME LIMIT AND FORM OF APPEAL

Notice of appeal must be filed in writing at the Office within two months after **A9–60** the date of notification of the decision appealed from. The notice shall be deemed to have been filed only when the fee for appeal has been paid. Within four months after the date of notification of the decision, a written statement setting out the grounds of appeal must be filed.

Article 60

INTERLOCUTORY REVISION

1. If the department whose decision is contested considers the appeal to be **A9–61** admissible and well founded, it shall rectify its decision. This shall not apply where the appellant is opposed by another party to the proceedings.

2. If the decision is not rectified within one month after receipt of the statement of grounds, the appeal shall be remitted to the Board of Appeal without delay, and without comment as to its merit.

Article 61

EXAMINATION OF APPEALS

1. If the appeal is admissible, the Board of Appeal shall examine whether the **A9–62** appeal is allowable.

2. In the examination of the appeal, the Board of Appeal shall invite the parties, as often as necessary, to file observations, within a period to be fixed by the Board of Appeal, on communications from the other parties or issued by itself.

Article 62

DECISIONS IN RESPECT OF APPEALS

A9–63   1. Following the examination as to the allowability of the appeal, the Board of Appeal shall decide on the appeal. The Board of Appeal may either exercise any power within the competence of the department which was responsible for the decision appealed or remit the case to that department for further prosecution.

2. If the Board of Appeal remits the case for further prosecution to the department whose decision was appealed, that department shall be bound by the *ratio decidendi* of the Board of Appeal, in so far as the facts are the same.

3. The decisions of the Boards of Appeal shall take effect only as from the date of expiration of the period referred to in Article 63 (5) or, if an action has been brought before the Court of Justice within that period, as from the date of rejection of such action.

Article 63

ACTIONS BEFORE THE COURT OF JUSTICE

A9–64   1. Actions may be brought before the Court of Justice against decisions of the Boards of Appeal on appeals.

2. The action may be brought on grounds of lack of competence, infringement of an essential procedural requirement, infringement of the Treaty, of this Regulation or of any rule of law relating to their application or misuse of power.

3. The Court of Justice has jurisdiction to annul or to alter the contested decision.

4. The action shall be open to any party to proceedings before the Board of Appeal adversely affected by its decision.

5. The action shall be brought before the Court of Justice within two months of the date of notification of the decision of the Board of Appeal.

6. The Office shall be required to take the necessary measures to comply with the judgment of the Court of Justice.

TITLE VIII

COMMUNITY COLLECTIVE MARKS

Article 64

COMMUNITY COLLECTIVE MARKS

A9–65   1. A Community collective mark shall be a Community trade mark which is described as such when the mark is applied for and is capable of distinguishing the goods or services of the members of the association which is the proprietor

1058

of the mark from those of other undertakings. Associations of manufacturers, producers, suppliers of services, or traders which, under the terms of the law governing them, have the capacity in their own name to have rights and obligations of all kinds, to make contracts or accomplish other legal acts and to sue and be sued, as well as legal persons governed by public law, may apply for Community collective marks.

2. In derogation from Article 7 (1) (c), signs or indications which may serve, in trade, to designate the geographical origin of the goods or services may constitute Community collective marks within the meaning of paragraph 1. A collective mark shall not entitle the proprietor to prohibit a third party from using in the course of trade such signs or indications, provided he uses them in accordance with honest practices in industrial or commercial matters; in particular, such a mark may not be invoked against a third party who is entitled to use a geographical name.

3. The provisions of this Regulation shall apply to Community collective marks, unless Articles 65 to 72 provide otherwise.

Article 65

REGULATIONS GOVERNING USE OF THE MARK

1. An applicant for a Community collective mark must submit regulations **A9–66** governing its use within the period prescribed.

2. The regulations governing use shall specify the persons authorized to use the mark, the conditions of membership of the association and, where they exist, the conditions of use of the mark including sanctions. The regulations governing use of a mark referred to in Article 64 (2) must authorize any person whose goods or services originate in the geographical area concerned to become a member of the association which is the proprietor of the mark.

Article 66

REFUSAL OF THE APPLICATION

1. In addition to the grounds for refusal of a Community trade mark **A9–67** application provided for in Articles 36 and 38, an application for a Community collective mark shall be refused where the provisions of Article 64 or 65 are not satisfied, or where the regulations governing use are contrary to public policy or to accepted principles of morality.

2. An application for a Community collective mark shall also be refused if the public is liable to be misled as regards the character or the significance of the mark, in particular if it is likely to be taken to be something other than a collective mark.

3. An application shall not be refused if the applicant, as a result of amendment of the regulations governing use, meets the requirements of paragraphs 1 and 2.

Article 67

OBSERVATIONS BY THIRD PARTIES

Apart from the cases mentioned in Article 41, any person, group or body **A9–68** referred to in that Article may submit to the Office written observations based on the particular grounds on which the application for a Community collective mark should be refused under the terms of Article 66.

Article 68

USE OF MARKS

A9–69   Use of a Community collective mark by any person who has authority to use it shall satisfy the requirements of this Regulation, provided that the other conditions which this Regulation imposes with regard to the use of Community trade marks are fulfilled.

Article 69

AMENDMENT OF THE REGULATIONS GOVERNING USE OF THE MARK

A9–70   1. The proprietor of a Community collective mark must submit to the Office any amended regulations governing use.
2. The amendment shall not be mentioned in the Register if the amended regulations do not satisfy the requirements of Article 65 or involve one of the grounds for refusal referred to in Article 66.
3. Article 67 shall apply to amended regulations governing use.
4. For the purposes of applying this Regulation, amendments to the regulations governing use shall take effect only from the date of entry of the mention of the amendment in the Register.

Article 70

PERSONS WHO ARE ENTITLED TO BRING AN ACTION FOR INFRINGEMENT

A9–71   1. The provisions of Article 22 (3) and (4) concerning the rights of licensees shall apply to every person who has authority to use a Community collective mark.
2. The proprietor of a Community collective mark shall be entitled to claim compensation on behalf of persons who have authority to use the mark where they have sustained damage in consequence of unauthorized use of the mark.

Article 71

GROUNDS FOR REVOCATION

A9–72   Apart from the grounds for revocation provided for in Article 50, the rights of the proprietor of a Community collective mark shall be revoked on application to the Office or on the basis of a counterclaim in infringement proceedings, if:

(a) the proprietor does not take reasonable steps to prevent the mark being used in a manner incompatible with the conditions of use, where these exist, laid down in the regulations governing use, amendments to which have, where appropriate, been mentioned in the Register;
(b) the manner in which the mark has been used by the proprietor has caused it to become liable to mislead the public in the manner referred to in Article 66 (2);
(c) an amendment to the regulations governing use of the mark has been mentioned in the Register in breach of the provisions of Article 69 (2),

unless the proprietor of the mark, by further amending the regulations governing use, complies with the requirements of those provisions.

Article 72

GROUNDS FOR INVALIDITY

Apart from the grounds for invalidity provided for in Articles 51 and 52, a **A9–73** Community collective mark which is registered in breach of the provisions of Article 66 shall be declared invalid on application to the Office or on the basis of a counterclaim in infringement proceedings, unless the proprietor of the mark, by amending the regulations governing use, complies with the requirements of those provisions.

TITLE IX

PROCEDURE

SECTION 1

GENERAL PROVISIONS

Article 73

STATEMENT OF REASONS ON WHICH DECISIONS ARE BASED

Decisions of the Office shall state the reasons on which they are based. They **A9–74** shall be based only on reasons or evidence on which the parties concerned have had on opportunity to present their comments.

Article 74

EXAMINATION OF THE FACTS BY THE OFFICE OF ITS OWN MOTION

1. In proceedings before it the Office shall examine the facts of its own motion; **A9–75** however, in proceedings relating to relative grounds for refusal of registration, the Office shall be restricted in this examination to the facts, evidence and arguments provided by the parties and the relief sought.
2. The Office may disregard facts or evidence which are not submitted in due time by the parties concerned.

Article 75

ORAL PROCEEDINGS

1. If the Office considers that oral proceedings would be expedient they shall **A9–76** be held either at the instance of the Office or at the request of any party to the proceedings.

2. Oral proceedings before the examiners, the Opposition Division and the Administration of Trade Marks and Legal Division shall not be public.

3. Oral proceedings, including delivery of the decision, shall be public before the Cancellation Division and the Boards of Appeal, in so far as the department before which the proceedings are taking place does not decide otherwise in cases where admission of the public could have serious and unjustified disadvantages, in particular for a party to the proceedings.

Article 76

TAKING OF EVIDENCE

A9–77 1. In any proceedings before the Office, the means of giving or obtaining evidence shall include the following:

- (a) hearing the parties;
- (b) requests for information;
- (c) the production of documents and items of evidence;
- (d) hearing witnesses;
- (e) opinions by experts;
- (f) statements in writing sworn or affirmed or having a similar effect under the law of the State in which the statement is drawn up.

2. The relevant department may commission one of its members to examine the evidence adduced.

3. If the Office considers it necessary for a party, witness or expert to give evidence orally, it shall issue a summons to the person concerned to appear before it.

4. The parties shall be informed of the hearing of a witness or expert before the Office. They shall have the right to be present and to put questions to the witness or expert.

Article 77

NOTIFICATION

A9–78 The Office shall, as a matter of course, notify those concerned of decisions and summonses and of any notice or other communication from which a time limit is reckoned, or of which those concerned must be notified under other provisions of this Regulation or of the Implementing Regulation, or of which notification has been ordered by the President of the Office.

Article 78

RESTITUTIO IN INTEGRUM

A9–79 1. The applicant for or proprietor of a Community trade mark or any other party to proceedings before the Office who, in spite of all due care required by the circumstances having been taken, was unable to observe a time limit *vis-à-vis* the Office shall, upon application, have his rights re-established if the non-observance in question has the direct consequence, by virtue of the provisions of this Regulation, of causing the loss of any right or means of redress.

2. The application must be filed in writing within two months from the removal of the cause of non-compliance with the time limit. The omitted act must be completed within this period. The application shall only be admissible within the year immediately following the expiry of the unobserved time limit. In the case of non-submission of the request for renewal of registration or of non-payment of a renewal fee, the further period of six months provided in Article 47 (3), third sentence, shall be deducted from the period of one year.

3. The application must state the grounds on which it is based and must set out the facts on which it relies. It shall not be deemed to be filed until the fee for re-establishment of rights has been paid.

4. The department competent to decide on the omitted act shall decide upon the application.

5. The provisions of this Article shall not be applicable to the time limits referred to in paragraph 2 of this Article, Articles 29 (1) and 42 (1).

6. Where the applicant for or proprietor of a Community trade mark has his rights re-established, he may not invoke his rights vis-à-vis a third party who, in good faith, has put goods on the market or supplied services under a sign which is identical with or similar to the Community trade mark in the course of the period between the loss of rights in the application or in the Community trade mark and publication of the mention of re-establishment of those rights.

7. A third party who may avail himself of the provisions of paragraph 6 may bring third party proceedings against the decision re-establishing the rights of the applicant for or proprietor of a Community trade mark within a period of two months as from the date of publication of the mention of re-establishment of those rights.

8. Nothing in this Article shall limit the right of a Member State to grant *restitutio in integrum* in respect of time limits provided for in this Regulation and to be observed *vis-à-vis* the authorities of such State.

Article 79

REFERENCE TO GENERAL PRINCIPLES

In the absence of procedural provisions in this Regulation, the Implementing **A9–80** Regulation, the fees regulations or the rules of procedure of the Boards of Appeal, the Office shall take into account the principles of procedural law generally recognized in the Member States.

Article 80

TERMINATION OF FINANCIAL OBLIGATIONS

1. Rights of the Office to the payment of a fee shall be extinguished after four **A9–81** years from the end of the calendar year in which the fee fell due.

2. Rights against the Office for the refunding of fees or sums of money paid in excess of a fee shall be extinguished after four years from the end of the calendar year in which the right arose.

3. The period laid down in paragraphs 1 and 2 shall be interrupted in the case covered by paragraph 1 by a request for payment of the fee and in the case covered by paragraph 2 by a reasoned claim in writing. On interruption it shall begin again immediately and shall end at the latest six years after the end of the year in which it originally began, unless, in the meantime, judicial proceedings

to enforce the right have begun; in this case the period shall end at the earliest one year after the judgement has acquired the authority of a final decision.

SECTION 2

COSTS

Article 81

COSTS

A9–82   1. The losing party in opposition proceedings, proceedings for revocation, proceedings for a declaration of invalidity or appeal proceedings shall bear the fees incurred by the other party as well as all costs, without prejudice to Article 115 (6), incurred by him essential to the proceedings, including travel and subsistence and the remuneration of an agent, adviser or advocate, within the limits of the scales set for each category of costs under the conditions laid down in the Implementing Regulation.

2. However, where each party succeeds on some and fails on other heads, or if reasons of equity so dictate, the Opposition Division, Cancellation Division or Board of Appeal shall decide a different apportionment of costs.

3. The party who terminates the proceedings by withdrawing the Community trade mark application, the opposition, the application for revocation of rights, the application for a declaration of invalidity or the appeal, or by not renewing registration of the Community trade mark or by surrendering the Community trade mark, shall bear the fees and the costs incurred by the other party as stipulated in paragraphs 1 and 2.

4. Where a case does not proceed to judgment the costs shall be at the discretion of the Opposition Division, Cancellation Division or Board of Appeal.

5. Where the parties conclude before the Opposition Division, Cancellation Division or Board of Appeal a settlement of costs differing from that provided for in the preceding paragraphs, the department concerned shall take note of that agreement.

6. On request the registry of the Opposition Division or Cancellation Division or Board of Appeal shall fix the amount of the costs to be paid pursuant to the preceding paragraphs. The amount so determined may be reviewed by a decision of the Opposition Division or Cancellation Division or Board of Appeal on a request filed within the prescribed period.

Article 82

ENFORCEMENT OF DECISIONS FIXING THE AMOUNT OF COSTS

A9–83   1. Any final decision of the Office fixing the amount of costs shall be enforceable.

2. Enforcement shall be governed by the rules of civil procedure in force in the State in the territory of which it is carried out. The order for its enforcement shall be appended to the decision, without other formality than verification of the authenticity of the decision, by the national authority which the Government of each Member State shall designate for this purpose and shall make known to the Office and to the Court of Justice.

3. When these formalities have been completed on application by the party concerned, the latter may proceed to enforcement in accordance with the national law, by bringing the matter directly before the competent authority.

4. Enforcement may be suspended only by a decision of the Court of Justice. However, the courts of the country concerned shall have jurisdiction over complaints that enforcement is being carried out in an irregular manner.

SECTION 3

INFORMATION OF THE PUBLIC AND OF THE OFFICIAL AUTHORITIES OF THE MEMBER STATES

Article 83

REGISTER OF COMMUNITY TRADE MARKS

The Office shall keep a register to be known as the Register of Community **A9–84** trade marks, which shall contain those particulars the registration or inclusion of which is provided for by this Regulation or by the Implementing Regulation. The Register shall be open to public inspection.

Article 84

INSPECTION OF FILES

1. The files relating to Community trade mark applications which have not yet **A9–85** been published shall not be made available for inspection without the consent of the applicant.

2. Any person who can prove that the applicant for a Community trade mark has stated that after the trade mark has been registered he will invoke the rights under it against him may obtain inspection of the files prior to the publication of that application and without the consent of the applicant.

3. Subsequent to the publication of the Community trade mark application, the files relating to such application and the resulting trade mark may be inspected on request.

4. However, where the files are inspected pursuant to paragraphs 2 or 3, certain documents in the file may be withheld from inspection in accordance with the provisions of the Implementing Regulation.

Article 85

PERIODICAL PUBLICATIONS

A9–86

The Office shall periodically publish:

(a) a Community Trade Marks Bulletin containing entries made in the Register of Community trade marks as well as other particulars the publication of which is prescribed by this Regulation or by the Implementing Regulation;

(b) an Official Journal containing notices and information of a general character issued by the President of the Office, as well as any other information relevant to this Regulation or its implementation.

Article 86

ADMINISTRATIVE COOPERATION

A9–87   Unless otherwise provided in this Regulation or in national laws, the Office and the courts or authorities of the Member States shall on request give assistance to each other by communicating information or opening files for inspection. Where the Office lays files open to inspection by courts, Public Prosecutors' Offices or central industrial property offices, the inspection shall not be subject to the restrictions laid down in Article 84.

Article 87

EXCHANGE OF PUBLICATIONS

A9–88   1. The Office and the central industrial property offices of the Member States shall despatch to each other on request and for their own use one or more copies of their respective publications free of charge.

2. The Office may conclude agreements relating to the exchange or supply of publications.

SECTION 4

REPRESENTATION

Article 88

GENERAL PRINCIPLES OF REPRESENTATION

A9–89   1. Subject to the provisions of paragraph 2, no person shall be compelled to be represented before the Office.

2. Without prejudice to paragraph 3, second sentence, natural or legal persons not having either their domicile or their principal place of business or a real and effective industrial or commercial establishment in the Community must be represented before the Office in accordance with Article 89 (1) in all proceedings established by this Regulation, other than in filing an application for a Community trade mark; the Implementing Regulation may permit other exceptions.

3. Natural or legal persons having their domicile or principal place of business or a real and effective industrial or commercial establishment in the Community may be represented before the Office by an employee, who must file with it a signed authorization for insertion on the files, the details of which are set out in the Implementing Regulation. An employee of a legal person to which this paragraph applies may also represent other legal persons which have economic connections with the first legal person, even if those other legal persons have neither their domicile nor their principal place of business nor a real and effective industrial or commercial establishment within the Community.

Article 89

PROFESSIONAL REPRESENTATIVES

A9–90   1. Representation of natural or legal persons before the Office may only be undertaken by;

(a) any legal practitioner qualified in one of the Member States and having his place of business within the Community, to the extent that he is entitled, within the said State, to act as a representative in trade mark matters; or

(b) professional representatives whose names appear on the list maintained for this purpose by the Office.

Representatives acting before the Office must file with it a signed authorization for insertion on the files, the details of which are set out in the Implementing Regulation.

2. Any natural person who fulfils the following conditions may be entered on the list of professional representatives:

(a) he must be a national of one of the Member States;

(b) he must have his place of business or employment in the Community;

(c) he must be entitled to represent natural or legal persons in trade mark matters before the central industrial property office of the Member State in which he has his place of business or employment. Where, in that State, the entitlement is not conditional upon the requirement of special professional qualifications, persons applying to be entered on the list who act in trade mark matters before the central industrial property office of the said State must have habitually so acted for at least five years. However, persons whose professional qualification to represent natural or legal persons in trade mark matters before the central industrial property office of one of the Member States is officially recognized in accordance with the regulations laid down by such State shall not be subject to the condition of having exercised the profession.

3. Entry shall be effected upon request, accompanied by a certificate furnished by the central industrial property office of the Member State concerned, which must indicate that the conditions laid down in paragraph 2 are fulfilled.

4. The President of the Office may grant exemption from:

(a) the requirement of paragraph 2 (c), second sentence, if the applicant furnishes proof that he has acquired the requisite qualification in another way;

(b) the requirement of paragraph 2 (a) in special circumstances.

5. The conditions under which a person may be removed from the list of professional representatives shall be laid down in the Implementing Regulation.

TITLE X

JURISDICTION AND PROCEDURE IN LEGAL ACTIONS RELATING TO COMMUNITY TRADE MARKS

SECTION 1

APPLICATION OF THE CONVENTION ON JURISDICTION AND ENFORCEMENT

Article 90

APPLICATION OF THE CONVENTION ON JURISDICTION AND ENFORCEMENT

1. Unless otherwise specified in this Regulation, the Convention on Jurisdic- **A9–91** tion and the Enforcement of Judgments in Civil and Commercial Matters, signed in Brussels on 27 September 1968, as amended by the Conventions on the

Accession to that Convention of the States acceding to the European Communities, the whole of which Convention and of which Conventions of Accession are hereinafter referred to as the 'Convention on Jurisdiction and Enforcement', shall apply to proceedings relating to Community trade marks and applications for Community trade marks, as well as to proceedings relating to simultaneous and successive actions on the basis of Community trade marks and national trade marks.

2. In the case of proceedings in respect of the actions and claims referred to in Article 92:

    (a) Articles 2, 4, 5 (1), (3), (4) and (5) and Article 24 of the Convention on Jurisdiction and Enforcement shall not apply;

    (b) Articles 17 and 18 of that Convention shall apply subject to the limitations in Article 93 (4) of this Regulation;

    (c) the provisions of Title II of that Convention which are applicable to persons domiciled in a Member State shall also be applicable to persons who do not have a domicile in any Member State but have an establishment therein.

SECTION 2

DISPUTES CONCERNING THE INFRINGEMENT AND VALIDITY OF COMMUNITY TRADE MARKS

Article 91

COMMUNITY TRADE MARK COURTS

A9–92   1. The Member States shall designate in their territories as limited a number as possible of national courts and tribunals of first and second instance, hereinafter referred to as 'Community trade mark courts', which shall perform the functions assigned to them by this Regulation.

2. Each Member State shall communicate to the Commission within three years of the entry into force of this Regulation a list of Community trade mark courts indicating their names and their territorial jurisdiction.

3. Any change made after communication of the list referred to in paragraph 2 in the number, names or territorial jurisdiction of the courts shall be notified without delay by the Member State concerned to the Commission.

4. The information referred to in paragraphs 2 and 3 shall be notified by the Commission to the Member States and published in the Official Journal of the European Communities.

5. As long as a Member State has not communicated the list as stipulated in paragraph 2, jurisdiction for any proceedings resulting from an action or application covered by Article 92, and for which the courts of that State have jurisdiction under Article 93, shall lie with that court of the State in question which would have jurisdiction *ratione loci* and *ratione materiae* in the case of proceedings relating to a national trade mark registered in that State.

Article 92

JURISDICTION OVER INFRINGEMENT AND VALIDITY

A9–93   The Community trade mark courts shall have exclusive jurisdiction:

(a) for all infringement actions and—if they are permitted under national law—actions in respect of threatened infringement relating to Community trade marks;

(b) for actions for declaration of non-infringement, if they are permitted under national law;

(c) for all actions brought as a result of acts referred to in Article 9 (3), second sentence;

(d) for counterclaims for revocation or for a declaration of invalidity of the Community trade mark pursuant to Article 96.

Article 93

INTERNATIONAL JURISDICTION

1. Subject to the provisions of this Regulation as well as to any provisions of **A9–94** the Convention on Jurisdiction and Enforcement applicable by virtue of Article 90, proceedings in respect of the actions and claims referred to in Article 92 shall be brought in the courts of the Member State in which the defendant is domiciled or, if he is not domiciled in any of the Member States, in which he has an establishment.

2. If the defendant is neither domiciled nor has an establishment in any of the Member States, such proceedings shall be brought in the courts of the Member State in which the plaintiff is domiciled or, if he is not domiciled in any of the Member States, in which he has an establishment.

3. If neither the defendant nor the plaintiff is so domiciled or has such an establishment, such proceedings shall be brought in the courts of the Member State where the Office has its seat.

4. Notwithstanding the provisions of paragraphs 1, 2 and 3:

(a) Article 17 of the Convention on Jurisdiction and Enforcement shall apply if the parties agree that a different Community trade mark court shall have jurisdiction;

(b) Article 18 of that Convention shall apply if the defendant enters an appearance before a different Community trade mark court.

5. Proceedings in respect of the actions and claims referred to in Article 92, with the exception of actions for a declaration of non-infringement of a Community trade mark, may also be brought in the courts of the Member State in which the act of infringement has been committed or threatened, or in which an act within the meaning of Article 9 (3), second sentence, has been committed.

Article 94

EXTENT OF JURISDICTION

1. A Community trade mark court whose jurisdiction is based on Article 93 (1) **A9–95** to (4) shall have jurisdiction in respect of:

— acts of infringement committed or threatened within the territory of any of the Member States,

— acts within the meaning of Article 9 (3), second sentence, committed within the territory of any of the Member States.

2. A Community trade mark court whose jurisdiction is based on Article 93 (5) shall have jurisdiction only in respect of acts committed or threatened within the territory of the Member State in which that court is situated.

Article 95

PRESUMPTION OF VALIDITY—DEFENCE AS TO THE MERITS

A9–96   1. The Community trade mark courts shall treat the Community trade mark as valid unless its validity is put in issue by the defendant with a counterclaim for revocation or for a declaration of invalidity.

2. The validity of a Community trade mark may not be put in issue in an action for a declaration of non-infringement.

3. In the actions referred to in Article 92 (a) and (c) a plea relating to revocation or invalidity of the Community trade mark submitted otherwise than by way of a counterclaim shall be admissible in so far as the defendant claims that the rights of the proprietor of the Community trade mark could be revoked for lack of use or that Community trade mark could be declared invalid on account of an earlier right of the defendant.

Article 96

COUNTERCLAIMS

A9–97   1. A counterclaim for revocation or for a declaration of invalidity may only be based on the grounds for revocation or invalidity mentioned in this Regulation.

2. A Community trade mark court shall reject a counterclaim for revocation or for a declaration of invalidity if a decision taken by the Office relating to the same subject matter and cause of action and involving the same parties has already become final.

3. If the counterclaim is brought in a legal action to which the proprietor of the trade mark is not already a party, he shall be informed thereof and may be joined as a party to the action in accordance with the conditions set out in national law.

4. The Community trade mark court with which a counterclaim for revocation or for a declaration of invalidity of the Community trade mark has been filed shall inform the Office of the date on which the counterclaim was filed. The latter shall record this fact in the Register of Community trade marks.

5. Article 56 (3), (4), (5) and (6) shall apply.

6. Where a Community trade mark court has given a judgment which has become final on a counterclaim for revocation or for invalidity of a Community trade mark, a copy of the judgment shall be sent to the Office. Any party may request information about such transmission. The Office shall mention the judgment in the Register of Community trade marks in accordance with the provisions of the Implementing Regulation.

7. The Community trade mark court hearing a counterclaim for revocation or for a declaration of invalidity may stay the proceedings on application by the proprietor of the Community trade mark and after hearing the other parties and may request the defendant to submit an application for revocation or for a declaration of invalidity to the Office within a time limit which it shall determine. If the application is not made within the time limit, the proceedings shall continue; the counterclaim shall be deemed withdrawn. Article 100 (3) shall apply.

Article 97

APPLICABLE LAW

A9–98   1. The Community trade mark courts shall apply the provisions of this Regulation.

2. On all matters not covered by this Regulation a Community trade mark court shall apply its national law, including its private international law.

3. Unless otherwise provided in this Regulation, a Community trade mark court shall apply the rules of procedure governing the same type of action relating to a national trade mark in the Member State where it has its seat.

Article 98

SANCTIONS

1. Where a Community trade mark court finds that the defendant has **A9–99** infringed or threatened to infringe a Community trade mark, it shall, unless there are special reasons for not doing so, issue an order prohibiting the defendant from proceeding with the acts which infringed or would infringe the Community trade mark. It shall also take such measures in accordance with its national law as are aimed at ensuring that this prohibition is complied with.

2. In all other respects the Community trade mark court shall apply the law of the Member State to which the acts of infringement or threatened infringement were committed, including the private international law.

Article 99

PROVISIONAL AND PROTECTIVE MEASURES

1. Application may be made to the courts of a Member State, including **A9–100** Community trade mark courts, for such provisional, including protective, measures in respect of a Community trade mark or Community trade mark application as may be available under the law of that State in respect of a national trade mark, even if, under this Regulation, a Community trade mark court of another Member State has jurisdiction as to the substance of the matter.

2. A Community trade mark court whose jurisdiction is based on Article 93 (1), (2), (3) or (4) shall have jurisdiction to grant provisional and protective measures which, subject to any necessary procedure for recognition and enforcement pursuant to Title III of the Convention on Jurisdiction and Enforcement, are applicable in the territory of any Member State. No other court shall have such jurisdiction.

Article 100

SPECIFIC RULES ON RELATED ACTIONS

1. A Community trade mark court hearing an action referred to in Article 92, **A9–101** other than an action for a declaration of non-infringement shall, unless there are special grounds for continuing the hearing, of its own motion after hearing the parties or at the request of one of the parties and after hearing the other parties, stay the proceedings where the validity of the Community trade mark is already in issue before another Community trade mark court on account of a counterclaim or where an application for revocation or for a declaration of invalidity has already been filed at the Office.

2. The Office, when hearing an application for revocation or for a declaration of invalidity shall, unless there are special grounds for continuing the hearing, of

its own motion after hearing the parties or at the request of one of the parties and after hearing the other parties, stay the proceedings where the validity of the Community trade mark is already in issue on account of a counterclaim before a Community trade mark court. However, if one of the parties to the proceedings before the Community trade mark court so requests, the court may, after hearing the other parties to these proceedings, stay the proceedings. The Office shall in this instance continue the proceedings pending before it.

3. Where the Community trade mark court stays the proceedings it may order provisional and protective measures for the duration of the stay.

Article 101

JURISDICTION OF COMMUNITY TRADE MARK COURTS OF SECOND INSTANCE—FURTHER APPEAL

A9–102 1. An appeal to the Community trade mark courts of second instance shall lie from judgments of the Community trade mark courts of first instance in respect of proceedings arising from the actions and claims referred to in Article 92.

2. The conditions under which an appeal may be lodged with a Community trade mark court of second instance shall be determined by the national law of the Member State in which that court is located.

3. The national rules concerning further appeal shall be applicable in respect of judgments of Community trade mark courts of second instance.

SECTION 3

OTHER DISPUTES CONCERNING COMMUNITY TRADE MARKS

Article 102

SUPPLEMENTARY PROVISIONS ON THE JURISDICTION OF NATIONAL COURTS OTHER THAN COMMUNITY TRADE MARK COURTS

A9–103 1. Within the Member State whose courts have jurisdiction under Article 90 (1) those courts shall have jurisdiction for actions other than those referred to in Article 92, which would have jurisdiction *ratione loci* and *ratione materiae* in the case of actions relating to a national trade mark registered in that State.

2. Actions relating to a Community trade mark, other than those referred to in Article 92, for which no court has jurisdiction under Article 90 (1) and paragraph 1 of this Article may be heard before the courts of the Member State in which the Office has its seat.

Article 103

OBLIGATION OF THE NATIONAL COURT

A9–104 A national court which is dealing with an action relating to a Community trade mark, other than the action referred to in Article 92, shall treat the trade mark as valid.

SECTION 4

TRANSITIONAL PROVISION

Article 104

TRANSITIONAL PROVISION RELATING TO THE APPLICATION OF THE
CONVENTION ON JURISDICTION AND ENFORCEMENT

The provisions of the Convention on Jurisdiction and Enforcement which are **A9–105**
rendered applicable by the preceding Articles shall have effect in respect of any
Member State solely in the text of the Convention which is in force in respect of
that State at any given time.

TITLE XI

EFFECTS ON THE LAWS OF THE MEMBER STATES

SECTION 1

CIVIL ACTIONS ON THE BASIS OF MORE THAN ONE TRADE MARK

Article 105

SIMULTANEOUS AND SUCCESSIVE CIVIL ACTIONS ON THE BASIS OF
COMMUNITY TRADE MARKS AND NATIONAL TRADE MARKS

1. Where actions for infringement involving the same cause of action and **A9–106**
between the same parties are brought in the courts of different Member States,
one seized on the basis of a Community trade mark and the other seized on the
basis of a national trade mark:

(a) the court other than the court first seized shall of its own motion
decline jurisdiction in favour of that court where the trade marks
concerned are identical and valid for identical goods or services. The
court which would be required to decline jurisdiction may stay its
proceedings if the jurisdiction of the other court is contested;

(b) the court other than the court first seized may stay its proceedings
where the trade marks concerned are identical and valid for similar
goods or services and where the trade marks concerned are similar and
valid for identical or similar goods or services.

2. The court hearing an action for infringement on the basis of a Community
trade mark shall reject the action if a final judgment on the merits has been given
on the same cause of action and between the same parties on the basis of an
identical national trade mark valid for identical goods or services.

3. The court hearing an action for infringement on the basis of a national trade
mark shall reject the action if a final judgment on the merits has been given on
the same cause of action and between the same parties on the basis of an
identical Community trade mark valid for identical goods or services.

4. Paragraphs 1, 2 and 3 shall not apply in respect of provisional, including protective, measures.

SECTION 2

APPLICATION OF NATIONAL LAWS FOR THE PURPOSE OF PROHIBITING THE USE OF COMMUNITY TRADE MARKS

Article 106

PROHIBITION OF USE OF COMMUNITY TRADE MARKS

A9–107 1. This Regulation shall, unless otherwise provided for, not affect the right existing under the laws of the Member States to invoke claims for infringement of earlier rights within the meaning of Article 8 or Article 52 (2) in relation to the use of a later Community trade mark. Claims for infringement of earlier rights within the meaning of Article 8 (2) and (4) may, however, no longer be invoked if the proprietor of the earlier right may no longer apply for a declaration that the Community trade mark is invalid in accordance with Article 53 (2).

2. This Regulation shall, unless otherwise provided for, not affect the right to bring proceedings under the civil, administrative or criminal law of a Member Sate or under provisions of Community law for the purpose of prohibiting the use of a Community trade mark to the extent that the use of a national trade mark may be prohibited under the law of that Member State or under Community law.

Article 107

PRIOR RIGHTS APPLICABLE TO PARTICULAR LOCALITIES

A9–108 1. The proprietor of an earlier right which only applies to a particular locality may oppose the use of the Community trade mark in the territory where his right is protected in so far as the law of the Member State concerned so permits.

2. Paragraph 1 shall cease to apply if the proprietor of the earlier right has acquiesced in the use of the Community trade mark in the territory where his right is protected for a period of five successive years, being aware of such use, unless the Community trade mark was applied for in bad faith.

3. The proprietor of the Community trade mark shall not be entitled to oppose use of the right referred to in paragraph 1 even though that right may no longer be invoked against the Community trade mark.

SECTION 3

CONVERSION INTO A NATIONAL TRADE MARK APPLICATION

Article 108

REQUEST FOR THE APPLICATION OF NATIONAL PROCEDURE

A9–109 1. The applicant for or proprietor of a Community trade mark may request the conversion of his Community trade mark application or Community trade mark into a national trade mark application:

1074

(a) to the extent that the Community trade mark application is refused, withdrawn, or deemed to be withdrawn;

(b) to the extent that the Community trade mark ceases to have effect.

2. Conversion shall not take place:

(a) where the rights of the proprietor of the Community trade mark have been revoked on the grounds of non-use, unless in the Member State for which conversion is requested the Community trade mark has been put to use which would be considered to be genuine use under the laws of that Member State;

(b) for the purpose of protection in a Member State in which, in accordance with the decision of the Office or of the national court, grounds for refusal of registration or grounds for revocation or invalidity apply to the Community trade mark application or Community trade mark.

3. The national trade mark application resulting from the conversion of a Community trade mark application or a Community trade mark shall enjoy in respect of the Member State concerned the date of filing or the date of priority of that application or trade mark and, where appropriate, the seniority of a trade mark of that State claimed under Article 34 or 35.

4. Where:

— the Community trade mark application is deemed to be withdrawn or is refused by a decision of the Office which has become final,

— the Community trade mark ceases to have effect as a result of a decision of the Office which has become final or as a result of registration of surrender of the Community trade mark,

the Office shall notify to the applicant or proprietor a communication fixing a period of three months from the date of that communication in which a request for conversion may be filed.

5. Where the Community trade mark application is withdrawn or the Community trade mark ceases to have effect as a result of failure to renew the registration, the request for conversion shall be filed within three months after the date on which the Community trade mark application is withdrawn or on which the registration of the Community trade mark expires.

6. Where the Community trade mark ceases to have effect as a result of a decision of a national court, the request for conversion shall be filed within three months after the date on which that decision acquired the authority of a final decision.

7. The effect referred to in Article 32 shall lapse if the request is not filed in due time.

Article 109

SUBMISSION, PUBLICATION AND TRANSMISSION OF THE REQUEST FOR CONVERSION

1. A request for conversion shall be filed with the Office and shall specify the **A9–110** Member States in which application of the procedure for registration of a national trade mark is desired. The request shall not be deemed to be filed until the conversion fee has been paid.

2. If the Community trade mark application has been published, receipt of any such request shall be recorded in the Register of Community trade marks and the request for conversion shall be published.

3. The Office shall check whether conversion may be requested in accordance with Article 108 (1), whether the request has been filed within the period laid

down in Article 108 (4), (5) or (6), as the case may be, and whether the conversion fee has been paid. If these conditions are fulfilled, the Office shall transmit the request to the central industrial property offices of the States specified therein. At the request of the central industrial property office of a State concerned, the Office shall give it any information enabling that office to decide as to the admissibility of the request.

Article 110

FORMAL REQUIREMENTS FOR CONVERSION

A9–111   1. Any central industrial property office to which the request is transmitted shall decide as to its admissibility,

2. A Community trade mark application or a Community trade mark transmitted in accordance with Article 109 shall not be subjected to formal requirements of national law which are different from or additional to those provided for in this Regulation or in the Implementing Regulation.

3. Any central industrial property office to which the request is transmitted may require that the applicant shall, within not less than two months:

(a) pay the national application fee;
(b) file a translation in one of the official languages of the State in question of the request and of the documents accompanying it;
(c) indicate an address for service in the State in question;
(d) supply a representation of the trade mark in the number of copies specified by the State in question.

TITLE XII

THE OFFICE

SECTION 1

GENERAL PROVISIONS

Article 111

LEGAL STATUS

A9–112   1. The Office shall be a body of the Community. It shall have legal personality.

2. In each of the Member States the Office shall enjoy the most extensive legal capacity accorded to legal persons under their laws; it may, in particular, acquire or dispose of movable and immovable property and may be a party to legal proceedings.

3. The Office shall be represented by its President.

Article 112

STAFF

A9–113   1. The Staff Regulations of officials of the European Communities, the Conditions of Employment of other servants of the European Communities, and the rules adopted by agreement between the Institutions of the European

Communities for giving effect to those Staff Regulations and Conditions of Employment shall apply to the staff of the Office, without prejudice to the application of Article 131 to the members of the Boards of Appeal.

2. Without prejudice to Article 120, the powers conferred on each Institution by the Staff Regulations and by the Conditions of Employment of other servants shall be exercised by the Office in respect of its staff.

Article 113

PRIVILEGES AND IMMUNITIES

The Protocol on the Privileges and Immunities of the European Communities **A9–114** shall apply to the Office.

Article 114

LIABILITY

1. The contractual liability of the Office shall be governed by the law **A9–115** applicable to the contract in question.

2. The Court of Justice shall be competent to give judgment pursuant to any arbitration clause contained in a contract concluded by the Office.

3. In the case of non-contractual liability, the Office shall, in accordance with the general principles common to the laws of the Member States, make good any damage caused by its departments or by its servants in the performance of their duties.

4. The Court of Justice shall have jurisdiction in disputes relating to compensation for the damage referred to in paragraph 3.

5. The personal liability of its servants towards the Office shall be governed by the provisions laid down in their Staff Regulations or in the Conditions of Employment applicable to them.

Article 115

LANGUAGES

1. The application for a Community trade mark shall be filed in one of the **A9–116** official languages of the European Community.

2. The languages of the Office shall be English, French, German, Italian and Spanish.

3. The applicant must indicate a second language which shall be a language of the Office the use of which he accepts as a possible language of proceedings for opposition, revocation or invalidity proceedings.

If the application was filed in a language which is not one of the languages of the Office, the Office shall arrange to have the application, as described in Article 26 (1), translated into the language indicated by the applicant.

4. Where the applicant for a Community trade mark is the sole party to proceedings before the Office, the language of proceedings shall be the language used for filing the application for a Community trade mark. If the application was made in a language other than the languages of the Office, the Office may send written communications to the applicant in the second language indicated by the applicant in his application.

5. The notice of opposition and an application for revocation or invalidity shall be filed in one of the languages of the Office.

6. If the language chosen, in accordance with paragraph 5, for the notice of opposition or the application for revocation or invalidity is the language of the application for a trade mark or the second language indicated when the application was filed, that language shall be the language of the proceedings.

If the language chosen, in accordance with paragraph 5, for the notice of opposition or the application for revocation or invalidity is neither the language of the application for a trade mark nor the second language indicated when the application was filed, the opposing party or the party seeking revocation or invalidity shall be required to produce, at his own expense, a translation of his application either into the language of the application for a trade mark, provided that it is a language of the Office, or into the second language indicated when the application was filed. The translation shall be produced within the period prescribed in the implementing regulation. The language into which the application has been translated shall then become the language of the proceedings.

7. Parties to opposition, revocation, invalidity or appeal proceedings may agree that a different official language of the European Community is to be the language of the proceedings.

Article 116

PUBLICATION; ENTRIES IN THE REGISTER

A9–117 1. An application for a Community trade mark, as described in Article 26 (1), and all other information the publication of which is prescribed by this Regulation or the implementing regulation, shall be published in all the official languages of the European Community.

2. All entries in the Register of Community trade marks shall be made in all the official languages of the European Community.

3. In cases of doubt, the text in the language of the Office in which the application for the Community trade mark was filed shall be authentic. If the application was filed in an official language of the European Community other than one of the languages of the Office, the text in the second language indicated by the applicant shall be authentic.

Article 117

A9–118 The translation services required for the functioning of the office shall be provided by the translation centre of the bodies of the union once this begins operation.

Article 118

CONTROL OF LEGALITY

A9–119 1. The Commission shall check the legality of those acts of the President of the Office in respect of which Community law does not provide for any check on legality by another body and of acts of the Budget Committee attached to the Office pursuant to Article 133.

2. It shall require that any unlawful acts as referred to in paragraph 1 be altered or annulled.

3. Member States and any person directly and personally involved may refer to the Commission any act as referred to in paragraph 1, whether express or implied, for the Commission to examine the legality of that act. Referral shall be made to the Commission within 15 days of the day on which the party concerned first became aware of the act in question. The Commission shall take a decision within one month. If no decision has been taken within this period, the case shall be deemed to have been dismissed.

SECTION 2

MANAGEMENT OF THE OFFICE

Article 119

POWERS OF THE PRESIDENT

1. The Office shall be managed by the President. **A9–120**
2. To this end the President shall have in particular the following functions and powers:

(a) he shall take all necessary steps, including the adoption of internal administrative instructions and the publication of notices, to ensure the functioning of the Office;

(b) he may place before the Commission any proposal to amend this Regulation, the Implementing Regulation, the rules of procedure of the Boards of Appeal, the fees regulations and any other rules applying to Community trade marks after consulting the Administrative Board and, in the case of the fees regulations and the budgetary provisions of this Regulation, the Budget Committee;

(c) he shall draw up the estimates of the revenue and expenditure of the Office and shall implement the budget;

(d) he shall submit a management report to the Commission, the European Parliament and the Administrative Board each year;

(e) he shall exercise in respect of the staff the powers laid down in Article 112 (2);

(f) he may delegate his powers.

3. The President shall be assisted by one or more Vice-Presidents. If the President is absent or indisposed, the Vice-President or one of the Vice-Presidents shall take his place in accordance with the procedure laid down by the Administrative Board.

Article 120

APPOINTMENT OF SENIOR OFFICIALS

1. The President of the Office shall be appointed by the Council from a list of **A9–121** at most three candidates, which shall be prepared by the Administrative Board. Power to dismiss the President shall lie with the Council, acting on a proposal from the Administrative Board.
2. The term of office of the President shall not exceed five years. This term of office shall be renewable.

3. The Vice-President or Vice-Presidents of the Office shall be appointed or dismissed as in paragraph 1, after consultation of the President.

4. The Council shall exercise disciplinary authority over the officials referred to in paragraphs 1 and 3 of this Article.

SECTION 3

ADMINISTRATIVE BOARD

Article 121

CREATION AND POWERS

A9–122   1. An Administrative Board is hereby set up, attached to the Office. Without prejudice to the powers attributed to the Budget Committee in Section 5—budget and financial control—the Administrative Board shall have the powers defined below.

2. The Administrative Board shall draw up the lists of candidates provided for in Article 120.

3. It shall fix the date for the first filing of Community trade mark applications, pursuant to Article 143 (3).

4. It shall advise the President on matters for which the Office is responsible.

5. It shall be consulted before adoption of the guidelines for examination in the Office and in the other cases provided for in this Regulation.

6. It may deliver opinions and requests for information to the President and to the Commission where it considers that this is necessary.

Article 122

COMPOSITION

A9–123   1. The Administrative Board shall be composed of one representative of each Member State and one representative of the Commission and their alternates.

2. The members of the Administrative Board may, subject to the provisions of its rules of procedure, be assisted by advisers or experts.

Article 123

CHAIRMANSHIP

A9–124   1. The Administrative Board shall elect a chairman and a deputy chairman from among its members. The deputy chairman shall *ex officio* replace the chairman in the event of his being prevented from attending to his duties.

2. The duration of the terms of office of the chairman and the deputy chairman shall be three years. The terms of office shall be renewable.

Article 124

MEETINGS

A9–125   1. Meetings of the Administrative Board shall be convened by its chairman.

2. The President of the Office shall take part in the deliberations, unless the Administrative Board decides otherwise.

3. The Administrative Board shall hold an ordinary meeting once a year; in addition, it shall meet on the initiative of its chairman or at the request of the Commission or of one-third of the Member States.

4. The Administrative Board shall adopt rules of procedure.

5. The Administrative Board shall take its decisions by a simple majority of the representatives of the Member States. However, a majority of three-quarters of the representatives of the Member States shall be required for the decisions which the Administrative Board is empowered to take under Article 120 (1) and (3). In both cases each Member State shall have one vote.

6. The Administrative Board may invite observers to attend its meetings.

7. The Secretariat for the Administrative Board shall be provided by the Office.

SECTION 4

IMPLEMENTATION OF PROCEDURES

Article 125

COMPETENCE

For taking decisions in connection with the procedures laid down in this **A9–126** Regulation, the following shall be competent:

(a) Examiners;
(b) Opposition Divisions;
(c) an Administration of Trade Marks and Legal Division;
(d) Cancellation Divisions;
(e) Boards of Appeal.

Article 126

EXAMINERS

An examiner shall be responsible for taking decisions on behalf of the Office in **A9–127** relation to an application for registration of a Community trade mark, including the matters referred to in Articles 36, 37, 38 and 66, except in so far as an Opposition Division is responsible.

Article 127

OPPOSITION DIVISIONS

1. An Opposition Division shall be responsible for taking decisions on an **A9–128** opposition to an application to register a Community trade mark.

2. An Opposition Division shall consist of three members. At least one of the members must be legally qualified.

Article 128

ADMINISTRATION OF TRADE MARKS AND LEGAL DIVISION

1. The Administration of Trade Marks and Legal Division shall be responsible **A9–129** for those decisions required by this Regulation which do not fall within the competence of an examiner, an Opposition Division or a Cancellation Division. It

shall in particular be responsible for decisions in respect of entries in the Register of Community trade marks.

2. It shall also be responsible for keeping the list of professional representatives which is referred to in Article 89.

3. A decision of the Division shall be taken by one member.

Article 129

CANCELLATION DIVISIONS

A9–130 1. A Cancellation Division shall be responsible for taking decisions in relation to an application for the revocation or declaration of invalidity of a Community trade mark.

2. A Cancellation Division shall consist of three members. At least one of the members must be legally qualified.

Article 130

BOARDS OF APPEAL

A9–131 1. The Boards of Appeal shall be responsible for deciding on appeals from decisions of the examiners, Opposition Divisions, Administration of Trade Marks and Legal Division and Cancellation Divisions.

2. A Board of Appeal shall consist of three members. At least two of the members must be legally qualified.

Article 131

INDEPENDENCE OF THE MEMBERS OF THE BOARDS OF APPEAL

A9–132 1. The members, including the chairmen, of the Boards of Appeal shall be appointed, in accordance with the procedure laid down in Article 120, for the appointment of the President of the Office, for a term of five years. They may not be removed from office during this term, unless there are serious grounds for such removal and the Court of Justice, on application by the body which appointed them, takes a decision to this effect. Their term of office shall be renewable.

2. The members of the Boards of Appeal shall be independent. In their decisions they shall not be bound by any instructions.

3. The members of the Boards of Appeal may not be examiners or members of the Opposition Divisions, Administration of Trade Marks and Legal Division or Cancellation Divisions.

Article 132

EXCLUSION AND OBJECTION

A9–133 1. Examiners and members of the Divisions set up within the Office or of the Boards of Appeal may not take part in any proceedings if they have any personal interest therein, or if they have previously been involved as representatives of one of the parties. Two of the three members of an Opposition Division shall not have taken part in examining the application. Members of the Cancellation Divisions may not take part in any proceedings if they have participated in the final decision on the case in the proceedings for registration or opposition proceedings. Members of the Boards of Appeal may not take part in appeal proceedings if they participated in the decision under appeal.

2. If, for one of the reasons mentioned in paragraph 1 or for any other reason, a member of a Division or of a Board of Appeal considers that he should not take part in any proceedings, he shall inform the Division or Board accordingly.

3. Examiners and members of the Divisions or of a Board of Appeal may be objected to by any party for one of the reasons mentioned in paragraph 1, or if suspected of partiality. An objection shall not be admissible if, while being aware of a reason for objection, the party has taken a procedural step. No objection may be based upon the nationality of examiners or members.

4. The Divisions and the Boards of Appeal shall decide as to the action to be taken in the cases specified in paragraphs 2 and 3 without the participation of the member concerned. For the purposes of taking this decision the member who withdraws or has been objected to shall be replaced in the Division or Board of Appeal by his alternate.

SECTION 5

BUDGET AND FINANCIAL CONTROL

Article 133

BUDGET COMMITTEE

1. A Budget Committee is hereby set up, attached to the Office. The Budget **A9–134** Committee shall have the powers assigned to it in this Section and in Article 39 (4).

2. Articles 121 (6), 122, 123 and 124 (1) to (4), (6) and (7) shall apply to the Budget Committee *mutatis mutandis*.

3. The Budget Committee shall take its decisions by a simple majority of the representatives of the Member States. However, a majority of three-quarters of the representatives of the Member States shall be required for the decisions which the Budget Committee is empowered to take under Articles 39 (4), 135 (3) and 138. In both cases each Member State shall have one vote.

Article 134

BUDGET

1. Estimates of all the Office's revenue and expenditure shall be prepared for **A9–135** each financial year and shall be shown in the Office's budget, and each financial year shall correspond with the calendar year.

2. The revenue and expenditure shown in the budget shall be in balance.

3. Revenue shall comprise, without prejudice to other types of income, total fees payable under the fees regulations, and, to the extent necessary, a subsidy entered against a specific heading of the general budget of the European Communities, Commission Section.

Article 135

PREPARATION OF THE BUDGET

A9–136   1. The President shall draw up each year an estimate of the Office's revenue and expenditure for the following year and shall send it to the Budget Committee not later than 31 March in each year, together with a list of posts.

2. Should the budget estimates provide for a Community subsidy, the Budget Committee shall immediately forward the estimate to the Commission, which shall forward it to the budget authority of the Communities. The Commission may attach an opinion on the estimate along with an alternative estimate.

3. The Budget Committee shall adopt the budget, which shall include the Office's list of posts. Should the budget estimates contain a subsidy from the general budget of the Communities, the Office's budget shall, if necessary, be adjusted.

Article 136

FINANCIAL CONTROL

A9–137   Control of commitment and payment of all expenditure and control of the existence and recovery of all revenue of the Office shall be carried out by the Financial Controller appointed by the Budget Committee.

Article 137

AUDITING OF ACCOUNTS

A9–138   1. Not later than 31 March in each year the President shall transmit to the Commission, the European Parliament, the Budget Committee and the Court of Auditors accounts of the Office's total revenue and expenditure for the preceding financial year. The Court of Auditors shall examine them in accordance with Article 188c of the Treaty.

2. The Budget Committee shall give a discharge to the President of the Office in respect of the implementation of the budget.

Article 138

FINANCIAL PROVISIONS

A9–139   The Budget Committee shall, after consulting the Court of Auditors of the European Communities and the Commission, adopt internal financial provisions specifying, in particular, the procedure for establishing and implementing the Office's budget. As far as is compatible with the particular nature of the Office, the financial provisions shall be based on the financial regulations adopted for other bodies set up by the Community.

Article 139

FEES REGULATIONS

A9–140   1. The fees regulations shall determine in particular the amounts of the fees and the ways in which they are to be paid.

1084

2. The amounts of the fees shall be fixed at such a level as to ensure that the revenue in respect thereof is in principle sufficient for the budget of the Office to be balanced.

3. The fees regulations shall be adopted and amended in accordance with the procedure laid down in Article 141.

TITLE XIII

FINAL PROVISIONS

Article 140

COMMUNITY IMPLEMENTING PROVISIONS

1. The rules implementing this Regulation shall be adopted in an Implement- **A9–141** ing Regulation.

2. In addition to the fees provided for in the preceding Articles, fees shall be charged, in accordance with the detailed rules of application laid down in the Implementing Regulation, in the cases listed below:

1. alteration of the representation of a Community trade mark;
2. late payment of the registration fee;
3. issue of a copy of the certificate of registration;
4. registration of the transfer of a Community trade mark;
5. registration of a licence or another right in respect of a Community trade mark;
6. registration of a licence or another right in respect of an application for a Community trade mark;
7. cancellation of the registration of a licence or another right;
8. alteration of a registered Community trade mark;
9. issue of an extract from the Register;
10. inspection of the files;
11. issue of copies of file documents;
12. issue of certified copies of the application;
13. communication of information in a file;
14. review of the determination of the procedural costs to be refunded.

3. The Implementing Regulation and the rules of procedure of the Boards of Appeal shall be adopted and amended in accordance with the procedure laid down in Article 141.

Article 141

ESTABLISHMENT OF A COMMITTEE AND PROCEDURE FOR THE ADOP-TION OF IMPLEMENTING REGULATIONS

1. The Commission shall be assisted by a Committee on Fees, Implementation **A9–142** Rules and the Procedure of the Boards of Appeal of the Office for Harmoniza-tion in the Internal Market (trade marks and designs), which shall be composed of representatives of the Member States and chaired by a representative of the Commission.

2. The representative of the Commission shall submit to the Committee a draft of the measures to be taken. The Committee shall deliver its opinion on the draft

within a time limit which the chairman may lay down according to the urgency of the matter. The opinion shall be delivered by the majority laid down in Article 148 (2) of the Treaty in the case of decisions which the Council is required to adopt on a proposal from the Commission. The votes of the representatives of the Member States within the Committee shall be weighted in the manner set out in that Article. The chairman shall not vote.

The Commission shall adopt the measures envisaged if they are in accordance with the opinion of the Committee.

If the measures envisaged are not in accordance with the opinion of the Committee, or if no opinion is delivered, the Commission shall, without delay, submit to the Council a proposal relating to the measures to be taken. The Council shall act by a qualified majority.

If, on the expiry of a period of three months from the date of referral to the Council, the Council has not acted, the proposed measures shall be adopted by the Commission, save where the Council has decided against the measures by a simple majority.

Article 142

COMPATIBILITY WITH OTHER COMMUNITY LEGAL PROVISIONS

A9–143   This Regulation shall not affect Council Regulation (EEC) No 2081/92 on the protection of geographical indications and designations of origin for agricultural products and foodstuffs of 14 July 1992, and in particular Article 14 thereof.

Article 143

ENTRY INTO FORCE

A9–144   1. This Regulation shall enter into force on the 60th day following that of its publication in the Official Journal of the European Communities.

2. The Member States shall within three years following entry into force of this Regulation take the necessary measures for the purpose of implementing Articles 91 and 110 hereof and shall forthwith inform the Commission of those measures.

3. Applications for Community trade marks may be filed at the Office from the date fixed by the Administrative Board on the recommendation of the President of the Office.

4. Applications for Community trade marks filed within three months before the date referred to in paragraph 3 shall be deemed to have been filed on that date.

This Regulation shall be binding in its entirety and directly applicable in all Member States.

Done at Brussels, December 20, 1993.

Appendix 10

Council Regulation 3288/94 of December 22, 1994

Amending Regulation 40/94 on the Community trade mark for the implementation of the agreements concluded in the framework of the Uruguay Round
[1994] O.J. L349/83)

THE COUNCIL OF THE EUROPEAN UNION,   **A10–01**

Having regard to the Treaty establishing the European Community, and in particular Article 235 thereof,

Having regard to the proposal from the Commission,

Having regard to the opinion of the European Parliament (1),

Whereas the Agreement establishing the World Trade Organization (hereinafter, the 'WTO Agreement') was signed on behalf of the Community; whereas the Agreement on Trade-Related Aspects of Intellectual Property Rights (hereinafter, the 'TRIPs Agreement'), annexed to the WTO Agreement, contains detailed provisions on the protection of intellectual property rights whose purpose is the establishment of international disciplines in this area in order to promote international trade and prevent trade distortions and friction due to the lack of adequate and effective intellectual property protection;

Whereas in order to ensure that all relevant Community legislation is in full compliance with the TRIPs Agreement, the Community must take certain measures in relation to current Community acts on the protection of intellectual property rights; whereas these measures entail in some respects the amendment or modification of Community acts; whereas these measures also entail complementing current Community acts;

Whereas Regulation (EC) No 40/94 creates the Community trade mark (2); whereas Article 5 of Regulation (EC) No 40/94 defines the 'Persons who can be proprietors of Community trade marks' by referring notably to the Paris Convention for the protection of industrial property and requires reciprocal national treatment from countries which are not parties to the Paris Convention; whereas Article 29 of Regulation (EC) No 40/94, concerning the right of priority, also needs to be amended in this respect; whereas in order to comply with the national treatment obligation in Article 3 of the TRIPs Agreement, these provisions should be modified to ensure that nationals of all WTO Members, even if the Member in question is not a party to the Paris Convention, receive a treatment no less favourable than that accorded to nationals of Community Member States;

Whereas Article 23 (2) of the TRIPs Agreement provides for the refusal or invalidation of trade marks which contain or consist of false geographical indications for wines and spirits without the condition that they are of such a nature as to deceive the public, a new subparagraph (j) has to be added to Article 7 (1) of Regulation (EC) No 40/94,

HAS ADOPTED THIS REGULATION:

Article 1 Regulation (EC) No 40/94 is amended as follows:

1. Article 5 (1) (b) shall be replaced by the following: **A10–02**

'(b) nationals of other States which are parties to the Paris Convention for the protection of industrial property, hereinafter referred to as 'the Paris Convention', or to the Agreement establishing the World Trade Organization;

2. Article 5 (1) (d) shall be replaced by the following:

'(d) nationals, other than those referred to under subparagraph (c), of any State which is not party to the Paris Convention or to the Agreement establishing the World Trade Organization and which, according to published findings, accords to nationals of all the Member States the same protection for trade marks as it accords to its own nationals and, if nationals of the Member States are required to prove registration in the country of origin, recognizes the registration of Community trade marks as such proof.'

3. In Article 7 (1) after subparagraph (i) the following shall be added:

'(j) trade marks for wines which contain or consist of a geographical indication identifying wines or for spirits which contain or consist of a geographical indication identifying spirits with respect to such wines or spirits not having that origin.'

4. Article 29 (1) shall be replaced by the following:

'1. A person who has duly filed an application for a trade mark in or for any State party to the Paris Convention or to the Agreement establishing the World Trade Organization, or his successors in title, shall enjoy, for the purpose of filing a Community trade mark application for the same trade mark in respect of goods or services which are identical with or contained within those for which the application has been filed, a right or priority during a period of six months from the date of filing of the first application.'

5. Article 29 (5) shall be replaced by the following:

'5. If the first filing has been made in a State which is not a party to the Paris Convention or to the Agreement establishing the World Trade Organization, paragraphs 1 to 4 shall apply only in so far as that State, according to published findings, grants, on the basis of the first filing made at the Office and subject to conditions equivalent to those laid down in this Regulation, a right of priority having equivalent effect.'

Article 2

A10–03   This Regulation shall enter into force on January 1, 1995.
It shall be applicable as of January 1, 1996.

This Regulation shall be binding in its entirety and directly applicable in all Member States.
Done at Brussels, December 22, 1994.

APPENDIX 11

Commission Regulation 2868/95 of December 13, 1995

Implementing Council Regulation (EC) No 40/94 on the Community trade mark

([1995] O.J. L303/1)

THE COMMISSION OF THE EUROPEAN COMMUNITIES,   **A11–01**

Having regard to the Treaty establishing the European Community,

Having regard to Council Regulation (EC) No 40/94 of 20 December 1993 on the Community trade mark as amended by Regulation (EC) No 3288/94, and in particular Article 140 thereof,

Whereas Regulation (EC) No 40/94 (hereinafter 'the Regulation') creates a new trade mark system allowing a trade mark having effect throughout the Community to be obtained on the basis of an application to the Office for Harmonization in the Internal Market (trade marks and designs) ('the Office');

Whereas for this purpose, the Regulation contains the necessary provisions for a procedure leading to the registration of a Community trade mark, as well as for the administration of Community trade marks, for appeals against decisions of the Office and for proceedings for the revocation or invalidation of a Community trade mark;

Whereas Article 140 of the Regulation provides that the rules implementing the Regulation shall be adopted in an implementing regulation;

Whereas the implementing regulation is to be adopted in accordance with the procedure laid down in Article 141 of the Regulation;

Whereas this implementing regulation therefore lays down the rules necessary for implementing the provisions of the Regulation on the Community trade mark;

Whereas these rules should ensure the smooth and efficient operating of trade mark proceedings before the Office;

Whereas in accordance with Article 116 (1) of the Regulation, all the elements of the application for a Community trade mark specified in its Article 26 (1) as well as any other information the publication of which is prescribed by this implementing regulation should be published in all the official languages of the Community;

Whereas, however, it is not appropriate for the trade mark itself, names, addresses, dates and any other similar data to be translated and published in all the official languages of the Community;

Whereas the Office should make available standard forms for proceedings before the Office in all official languages of the Community;

Whereas the measures envisaged in this Regulation are in accordance with the opinion of the Committee established under Article 141 of the Regulation,

HAS ADOPTED THIS REGULATION:

Article 1

The rules implementing the Regulation shall be as follows: **A11–02**

TITLE I

APPLICATION PROCEDURE

RULE 1

CONTENT OF THE APPLICATION

A11–03 (1) The application for a Community trade mark shall contain:

(a) a request for registration of the mark as a Community trade mark;

(b) the name, address and nationality of the applicant and the State in which he is domiciled or has his seat or an establishment. Names of natural persons shall be indicated by the person's family name and given name(s). Names of legal entities, as well as bodies falling under Article 3 of the Regulation, shall be indicated by their official designation, which may be abbreviated in a customary manner; furthermore, the law of the State governing them shall be indicated. The telegraphic and teletype address, telephone as well as fax numbers and details of other data communications links may be given. Only one address shall, in principle, be indicated for each applicant; where several addresses are indicated, only the address mentioned first shall be taken into account, except where the applicant designates one of the addresses as an address for service;

(c) a list of the goods and services for which the trade mark is to be registered, in accordance with Rule 2;

(d) a representation of the mark in accordance with Rule 3;

(e) if the applicant has appointed a representative, his name and the address of his place of business in accordance with point (b); if the representative has more than one business address or if there are two or more representatives with different business addresses, the application shall indicate which address shall be used as an address for service; where such an indication is not made, only the first-mentioned address shall be taken into account as an address for service;

(f) where the priority of a previous application is claimed pursuant to Article 30 of the Regulation, a declaration to that effect, stating the date on which and the country in or for which the previous application was filed;

(g) where exhibition priority is claimed pursuant to Article 33 of the Regulation, a declaration to that effect, stating the name of the exhibition and the date of the first display of the goods or services;

(h) where the seniority of one or more earlier trade marks, registered in a Member State, including a trade mark registered in the Benelux countries or registered under international arrangements having effect in a Member State (hereinafter referred to as 'earlier registered trade marks, as referred to in Article 34 of the Regulation') is claimed pursuant to Article 34 of the Regulation, a declaration to that effect, stating the Member State or Member States in or for which the earlier mark is registered, the date from which the relevant registration was effective, the number of the relevant registration, and the goods and services for which the mark is registered;

(i) where applicable, a statement that the application is for registration of a Community collective mark pursuant to Article 64 of the Regulation;

(j) specification of the language in which the application has been filed, and of the second language pursuant to Article 115 (3) of the Regulation;

(k) the signature of the applicant or his representative.

(2) The application for a Community collective mark may include the regulations governing its use.

(3) The application may include a statement by the applicant that he disclaims any exclusive right to an element of the trade mark which is not distinctive, to be specified by the applicant.

(4) If there is more than one applicant, the application may contain the appointment of one applicant or representative as common representative.

RULE 2

LIST OF GOODS AND SERVICES

(1) The common classification referred to in Article 1 of the Nice Agreement **A11–04** Concerning the International Classification of Goods and Services for the Purposes of the Registration of Marks of 15 June 1957, as revised and amended, shall be applied to the classification of the goods and services.

(2) The list of goods and services shall be worded in such a way as to indicate clearly the nature of the goods and services and to allow each item to be classified in only one class of the Nice Classification.

(3) The goods and services shall, in principle, be grouped according to the classes of the Nice classification, each group being preceded by the number of the class of that Classification to which that group of goods or services belongs and presented in the order of the classes under that Classification.

(4) The classification of goods and services shall serve exclusively administrative purposes. Therefore, goods and services may not be regarded as being similar to each other on the ground that they appear in the same class under the Nice Classification, and goods and services may not be regarded as being dissimilar from each other on the ground that they appear in different classes under the Nice Classification.

RULE 3

REPRESENTATION OF THE MARK

(1) If the applicant does not wish to claim any special graphic feature or **A11–05** colour, the mark shall be reproduced in normal script, as for example, by typing the letters, numerals and signs in the application. The use of small letters and capital letters shall be permitted and shall be followed accordingly in publications of the mark and in the registration by the Office.

(2) In cases other than those referred to in paragraph 1, the mark shall be reproduced on a sheet of paper separate from the sheet on which the text of the application appears. The sheet on which the mark is reproduced shall not exceed DIN A4 size (29,7 cm high, 21 cm wide) and the space used for the reproduction (type-area) shall not be larger than 26,2 cm x 17 cm. A margin of at least 2,5 cm shall be left on the left-hand side. Where it is not obvious, the correct position of the mark shall be indicated by adding the word 'top' to each reproduction. The reproduction of the mark shall be of such quality as to enable it to be reduced or enlarged to a size not more than 8 cm wide by 16 cm high for publication in the Community Trade Mark Bulletin. The separate sheet shall also indicate the name and address of the applicant. Four copies of the separate sheet carrying the reproduction shall be filed.

(3) In cases to which paragraph 2 applies, the application shall contain an indication to that effect. The application may contain a description of the mark.

(4) Where registration of a three-dimensional mark is applied for, the application shall contain an indication to that effect. The representation shall consist of a photographic reproduction or a graphic representation of the mark. The representation may contain up to six different perspectives of the mark.

(5) Where registration in colour is applied for, the application shall contain an indication to that effect. The colours making up the mark shall also be indicated. The reproduction under paragraph 2 shall consist of the colour reproduction of the mark.

(6) The President of the Office may determine that, as far as the requirements of paragraph 2 are concerned, the mark may be reproduced in the text of the application itself and not on a separate sheet of paper and that the the number of copies of the reproduction of the mark may be less than four.

RULE 4

FEES FOR THE APPLICATION

A11–06 The fees payable for the application shall be:

    (a) the basic fee;
       and
    (b) a class fee for each class exceeding three to which the goods or services belong according to Rule 2.

RULE 5

FILING OF THE APPLICATION

A11–07 (1) The Office shall mark the documents making up the application with the date of its receipt and the file number of the application. The Office shall issue to the applicant without delay a receipt which shall include at least the file number, a representation, description or other identification of the mark, the nature and the number of the documents and the date of their receipt.

(2) If the application is filed with the central industrial property office of a Member Sate or at the Benelux Trade Mark Office in accordance with Article 25 of the Regulation, the office of filing shall number all the pages of the application with arabic numerals. Before forwarding, the office of filing shall mark the documents making up the application with the date of receipt and the number of pages. The office of filing shall issue to the applicant without delay a receipt which shall include at least the nature and the number of the documents and the date of their receipt.

(3) If the Office receives an application forwarded by the central industrial property office of a Member State or the Benelux Trade Mark Office, it shall mark the application with the date of receipt and the file number and shall issue to the applicant without delay a receipt in accordance with the second sentence of paragraph 1, indicating the date of receipt at the Office.

RULE 6

CLAIMING PRIORITY

A11–08 (1) Where the priority of one or more previous applications pursuant to Article 30 of the Regulation is claimed in the application, the applicant shall indicate the file number of the previous application and file a copy of it within three months from the filing date. The copy shall be certified to be an exact copy of the previous application by the authority which received the previous application, and shall be accompanied by a certificate issued by that authority stating the date of filing of the previous application.

(2) Where the applicant wishes to claim the priority of one or more previous applications pursuant to Article 30 of the Regulation subsequent to the filing of the application, the declaration of priority, stating the date on which and the country in or for which the previous application was made, shall be submitted within a period of two months from the filing date. The indications and evidence required under paragraph 1 shall be submitted to the Office within a period of three months from receipt of the declaration of priority.

(3) If the language of the previous application is not one of the languages of the Office, the Office shall require the applicant to file, within a period specified by the Office, which shall be not less than three months, a translation of the previous application into one of these languages.

(4) The President of the Office may determine that the evidence to be provided by the applicant may consist of less than is required under paragraph 1, provided that the information required is available to the Office from other sources.

RULE 7

EXHIBITION PRIORITY

(1) Where the exhibition priority pursuant to Article 33 of the Regulation has **A11–09** been claimed in the application, the applicant shall, within three months from the filing date, file a certificate issued at the exhibition by the authority responsible for the protection of industrial property at the exhibition. This certificate shall declare that the mark was in fact used for the goods or services, and shall state the opening date of the exhibition and, where the first public use did not coincide with the opening date of the exhibition, the date of such first public use. The certificate must be accompanied by an identification of the actual use of the mark, duly certified by the abovementioned authority.

(2) Where the applicant wishes to claim an exhibition priority subsequently to the filing of the application, the declaration of priority, indicating the name of the exhibition and the date of the first display of the goods or services, shall be submitted within a period of two months from the filing date. The indications and evidence required under paragraph 1 shall be submitted to the Office within a period of three months from receipt of the declaration of priority.

RULE 8

CLAIMING THE SENIORITY OF A NATIONAL TRADE MARK

(1) Where the seniority of one or more earlier registered trade marks, as **A11–10** referred to in Article 34 of the Regulation, has been claimed in the application, the applicant shall, within three months from the filing date, submit a copy of the relevant registration. The copy must be certified by the competent authority to be an exact copy of the relevant registration.

(2) Where the applicant wishes to claim the seniority of one or more earlier registered trade marks as referred to in Article 34 of the Regulation, subsequent to the filing of the application, the declaration of seniority, indicating the Member State or Member States in or for which the mark is registered, the date from which the relevant registration was effective, the number of the relevant registration, and the goods and services for which the mark is registered, shall

be submitted within a period of two months from the filing date. The evidence required under paragraph 1 shall be submitted to the Office within a period of three months from receipt of the declaration of seniority.

(3) The Office shall inform the Benelux Trade Mark Office or the central industrial property office of the Member State concerned of the effective claiming of seniority.

(4) The President of the Office may determine that the evidence to be provided by the applicant may consist of less than is required under paragraph 1, provided that the information required is available to the Office from other sources.

RULE 9

EXAMINATION OF REQUIREMENTS FOR A FILING DATE AND OF FORMAL REQUIREMENTS

A11–11 (1) If the application fails to meet the requirements for according a filing date because:

  (a) the application does not contain:
    (i) a request for registration of the mark as a Community trade mark;
    (ii) information identifying the applicant;
    (iii) a list of the goods and services for which the mark is to be registered;
    (iv) a representation of the trade mark; or
  (b) the basic fee for the application has not been paid within one month of the filing of the application with the Office or, if the application has been filed with the central industrial property office of a Member State or with the Benelux Trade Mark Office, with that office, the Office shall notify the applicant that a date of filing cannot be accorded in view of those deficiencies.

(2) If the deficiencies referred to under paragraph 1 are remedied within two months of receipt of the notification, the date on which all the deficiencies are remedied shall determine the date of filing. If the deficiencies are not remedied before the time limit expires, the application shall not be dealt with as a Community trade mark application. Any fees paid shall be refunded.

(3) Where, although a date of filing has been accorded, the examination reveals that

  (a) the requirements of Rules 1, 2 and 3 or the other formal requirements governing applications laid down in the Regulation or in these Rules are not complied with;
  (b) the full amount of the class fees payable under Rule 4 (b), read in conjunction with Commission Regulation (EC) No 2869/95 (hereinafter 'the Fees Regulation') has not been received by the Office;
  (c) where priority has been claimed pursuant to Rules 6 and 7, either in the application itself or within two months after the date of filing, the other requirements of the said Rules are not complied with; or
  (d) where seniority has been claimed pursuant to Rule 8, either in the application itself or within two months after the date of filing, the other requirements of Rule 8 are not complied with, the Office shall invite the applicant to remedy the deficiencies noted within such period as it may specify.

(4) If the deficiencies referred to in paragraph 3 (a) are not remedied before the time limit expires, the Office shall reject the application.

(5) If the outstanding class fees are not paid before the time limit expires, the application shall be deemed to have been withdrawn, unless it is clear which class or classes the amount paid is intended to cover. In the absence of other criteria to determine which classes are intended to be covered, the Office shall take the classes in the order of the classification. The application shall be deemed to have been withdrawn with regard to those classes for which the class fees have not been paid or have not been paid in full.

(6) If the deficiencies referred to in paragraph 3 concern the claim to priority, the right of priority for the application shall be lost.

(7) If the deficiencies referred to in paragraph 3 concern the claim to seniority, the right of seniority in respect of that application shall be lost.

(8) If the deficiencies referred to in paragraph 3 concern only some of the goods and services, the Office shall refuse the application, or the right of priority or the right of seniority shall be lost, only in so far as those goods and services are concerned.

RULE 10

EXAMINATION OF THE CONDITIONS RELATING TO THE ENTITLEMENT TO BE PROPRIETOR

Where, pursuant to Article 5 of the Regulation, the applicant is not entitled to **A11–12** be the proprietor of a Community trade mark, the Office shall notify the applicant thereof. The Office shall specify a period within which the applicant may withdraw the application or submit his observations. Where the applicant fails to overcome the objections to registration, the Office shall refuse the application.

RULE 11

EXAMINATION AS TO ABSOLUTE GROUNDS FOR REFUSAL

(1) Where, pursuant to Article 7 of the Regulation, the trade mark may not be **A11–13** registered for all or any part of the goods or services applied for, the office shall notify the applicant of the grounds for refusing registration. The Office shall specify a period within which the applicant may withdraw or amend the application or submit his observations.

(2) Where, pursuant to Article 38 (2) of the Regulation, registration of the Community trade mark is subject to the applicant's stating that he disclaims any exclusive right in the non-distinctive elements in the mark, the Office shall notify the applicant thereof, stating the reasons, and shall invite him to submit the relevant statement within such period as it may specify.

(3) Where the applicant fails to overcome the ground for refusing registration or to comply with the condition laid down in paragraph 2 within the time limit, the Office shall refuse the application in whole or in part.

RULE 12

PUBLICATION OF THE APPLICATION

The publication of the application shall contain: **A11–14**

(a) the applicant's name and address;
(b) where applicable, the name and business address of the representative appointed by the applicant other than a representative falling within

the first sentence of Article 88 (3) of the Regulation; if there is more than one representative with the same business address, only the name and business address of the first-named representative shall be published and it shall be followed by the words 'and others'; if there are two or more representatives with different business addresses, only the address for service determined pursuant to Rule 1 (1) (e) shall be published; where an association of representatives is appointed under Rule 76 (9), only the name and business address of the association shall be published;

(c) the reproduction of the mark, together with the indications and descriptions pursuant to Rule 3; where registration in colour is applied for, the publication shall contain the indication 'in colour' and indicate the colour or colours making up the mark;

(d) the list of goods and services, grouped according to the classes of the Nice classification, each group being preceded by the number of the class of that classification to which that group of goods or services belongs, and presented in the order of the classes of that classification;

(e) the date of filing and the file number;

(f) where applicable, particulars of the claim of priority pursuant to Article 30 of the Regulation;

(g) where applicable, particulars of the claim of exhibition priority pursuant to Article 33 of the Regulation;

(h) where applicable, particulars of the claim of seniority pursuant to Article 34 of the Regulation;

(i) where applicable, a statement that the mark has become distinctive in consequence of the use which has been made of it, pursuant to Article 7 (3) of the Regulation;

(j) where applicable, a statement that the application is for a Community collective mark;

(k) where applicable, a statement by the applicant disclaiming any exclusive right to an element of the mark pursuant to Rule 1 (3) or Rule 11 (2);

(l) the language in which the application was filed and the second language which the applicant has indicated pursuant to Article 115 (3) of the Regulation.

RULE 13

AMENDMENT OF THE APPLICATION

A11–15 (1) An application for amendment of the application under Article 44 of the Regulation shall contain:

(a) the file number of the application;

(b) the name and the address of the applicant in accordance with Rule 1 (1) (b);

(c) where the applicant has appointed a representative, the name and the business address of the representative in accordance with Rule 1 (1) (e);

(d) the indication of the element of the application to be corrected or amended, and that element in its corrected or amended version;

(e) where the amendment relates to the representation of the mark, a representation of the mark as amended, in accordance with Rule 3.

(2) Where the application for amendment is subject to the payment of a fee, the application shall not be deemed to have been filed until the required fee has been paid. If the fee has not been paid or has not been paid in full, the Office shall inform the applicant accordingly.

(3) If the requirements governing the amendment of the application are not fulfilled, the Office shall communicate the deficiency to the applicant. If the deficiency is not remedied within a period to be specified by the Office, the Office shall reject the application for amendment.

(4) Where the amendment is published pursuant to Article 44 (2) of the Regulation, Rules 15 to 22 shall apply mutatis mutandis.

(5) A single application for amendment may be made for the amendment of the same element in two or more applications of the same applicant. Where the application for amendment is subject to the payment of a fee, the required fee shall be paid in respect of each application to be amended.

(6) Paragraphs 1 to 5 shall apply mutatis mutandis for applications to correct the name or the business address of a representative appointed by the applicant. Such applications shall not be subject to the payment of a fee.

RULE 14

CORRECTION OF MISTAKES AND ERRORS IN PUBLICATIONS

(1) Where the publication of the application contains a mistake or error **A11–16** attributable to the Office, the Office shall correct the mistake or error acting of its own motion or at the request of the applicant.

(2) Where a request as referred to in paragraph 1 is made by the applicant, Rule 13 shall apply mutatis mutandis. The request shall not be subject to the payment of a fee.

(3) The corrections effected under this Rule shall be published.

(4) Article 42 (2) of the Regulation and Rules 15 to 22 shall apply mutatis mutandis where the correction concerns the list of goods or services or the representation of the mark.

TITLE II

PROCEDURE FOR OPPOSITION AND PROOF OF USE

RULE 15

CONTENTS OF THE NOTICE OF OPPOSITION

(1) Opposition may be entered on the basis of one or more earlier marks **A11–17** within the meaning of Article 8 (2) of the Regulation ('earlier marks') or of one or more other earlier rights within the meaning of Article 8 (4) of the Regulation ('earlier rights').

(2) The notice of opposition shall contain:

(a) as concerns the application against which opposition is entered:
  (i) the file number of the application against which opposition is entered;
  (ii) an indication of the goods and services listed in the Community trade mark application against which opposition is entered;
  (iii) the name of the applicant for the Community trade mark;
(b) as concerns the earlier mark or the earlier right on which the opposition is based:
  (i) where the opposition is based on an earlier mark, a statement to that effect and an indication that the earlier mark is a Community

mark or an indication of the Member State or Member States including, where applicable, the Benelux, where the earlier mark has been registered or applied for, or, where the earlier mark is an internationally registered mark, an indication of the Member State or Member States including, where applicable, the Benelux, to which protection of that earlier mark has been extended;

  (ii) where available, the file number or the registration number and the filing date, including the priority date of the earlier mark;

  (iii) where the opposition is based on an earlier mark which is a well-known mark within the meaning of Article 8 (2) (c) of the Regulation, an indication to that effect and an indication of the Member State or Member States in which the earlier mark is well-known;

  (iv) where the opposition is based on an earlier mark having a reputation within the meaning of Article 8 (5) of the Regulation, an indication to that effect, and an indication of where that earlier mark is registered or applied for in accordance with subparagraph (i);

  (v) where the opposition is based on an earlier right, an indication to that effect, and an indication of the Member State or Member States where that earlier right exists;

  (vi) a representation and, where appropriate, a description of the earlier mark or earlier right;

  (vii) the goods and services in respect of which the earlier mark has been registered or applied for or in respect of which the earlier mark is well-known within the meaning of Article 8 (2) (c) of the Regulation or has a reputation within the meaning of Article 8 (5) of the Regulation; the opposing party shall, when indicating all the goods and services for which the earlier mark is protected, also indicate those goods and services on which the opposition is based;

(c) as concerns the opposing party:

  (i) where the opposition is entered by the proprietor of the earlier mark or of the earlier right, his name and address in accordance with Rule 1 (1) (b) and an indication that he is the proprietor of such mark or right;

  (ii) where opposition is entered by a licensee, the name of the licensee and his address in accordance with Rule 1 (1) (b) and an indication that he has been authorized to enter the opposition;

  (iii) where the opposition is entered by the successor in title to the registered proprietor of a Community trade mark who has not yet been registered as new proprietor, an indication to that effect, the name and address of the opposing party in accordance with Rule 1 (1) (b), and an indication of the date on which the application for registration of the new proprietor was received by the Office or, where this information is not available, was sent to the Office;

  (iv) where opposition is entered on the basis of an earlier right by a person who is not the proprietor of that right, the name of the person and his address in accordance with Rule 1 (1) (b) and an indication that the is entitled under the relevant national law to exercise that right;

  (v) where the opposing party has appointed a representative, the name of the representative and his business in accordance with Rule 1 (1) (e);

(d) a specification of the grounds on which the opposition is based.

(3) Paragraphs 1 and 2 shall apply mutatis mutandis to an opposition entered pursuant to Article 8 (3) of the Regulation.

RULE 16

FACTS, EVIDENCE AND ARGUMENTS PRESENTED IN SUPPORT OF THE OPPOSITION

(1) Every notice of opposition may contain particulars of the facts, evidence **A11–18** and arguments presented in support of the opposition, accompanied by the relevant supporting documents.

(2) If the opposition is based on an earlier mark which is not a Community trade mark, the notice of opposition shall preferably be accompanied by evidence of the registration or filing of that earlier mark, such as a certificate of registration. If the opposition is based on a well-known mark as referred to in Article 8 (2) (c) of the Regulation or on a mark having a reputation as referred to in Article 8 (5) of the Regulation, the notice of opposition shall in principle be accompanied by evidence attesting that it is well-known or that it has a reputation. If the opposition is entered on the basis of any other earlier right, the notice of opposition shall in principle be accompanied by appropriate evidence on the acquisition and scope of protection of that right.

(3) The particulars of the facts, evidence and arguments and other supporting documents as referred to in paragraphs 1, and the evidence referred to in paragraph 2 may, if they are not submitted together with the notice of opposition or subsequent thereto, be submitted within such period after commencement of the opposition proceedings as the Office may specify pursuant to Rule 20 (2).

RULE 17

USE OF LANGUAGES IN OPPOSITION PROCEEDINGS

(1) Where the notice of opposition is not filed in the language of the **A11–19** application for registration of the Community trade mark, if that language is one of the languages of the Office, or in the second language indicated when the application was filed, the opposing party shall file a translation of the notice of opposition in one of those languages within a period of one month from the expiry of the opposition period.

(2) Where the evidence in support of the opposition as provided for in Rule 16 (1) and (2) is not filed in the language of the opposition proceedings, the opposing party shall file a translation of that evidence into that language within a period of one month from the expiry of the opposition period or, where applicable, within the period specified by the Office pursuant to Rule 16 (3).

(3) Where the opposing party or the applicant informs the Office, before the date on which the opposition proceedings shall be deemed to commence pursuant to Rule 19 (1), that the applicant and the opposing party have agreed on a different language for the opposition proceeding pursuant to Article 115 (7) of the Regulation, the opposing party shall, where the notice of opposition has not been filed in that language, file a translation of the notice of opposition in that language within a period of one month from the said date.

RULE 18

REJECTION OF NOTICE OF OPPOSITION AS INADMISSIBLE

(1) If the Office finds that the notice of opposition does not comply with the **A11–20** provisions of Article 42 of the Regulation, or where the notice of opposition does not clearly identify the application against which opposition is entered or the

earlier mark or the earlier right on the basis of which the opposition is being entered, the Office shall reject the notice of opposition as inadmissible unless those deficiencies have been remedied before expiry of the opposition period. If the opposition fee has not been paid within the opposition period, the notice of opposition shall be deemed not to have been entered. If the opposition fee has been paid after the expiry of the opposition period, it shall be refunded to the opposing party.

(2) If the Office finds that the notice of opposition does not comply with other provisions of the Regulation or of these Rules, it shall inform the opposing party accordingly and shall call upon him to remedy the deficiencies noted within a period of two months. If the deficiencies are not remedied before the time limit expires, the Office shall reject the notice of opposition as inadmissible.

(3) Any decision to reject a notice of opposition as inadmissible under paragraphs 1 or 2 shall be communicated to the applicant.

RULE 19

COMMENCEMENT OF OPPOSITION PROCEEDINGS

A11–21 (1) If the Office does not reject the notice of opposition in accordance with Rule 18, it shall communicate the opposition to the applicant and shall invite him to file his observations within such period as it may specify. The Office shall draw the applicant's attention to the fact that the opposition proceedings shall be deemed to commence two months after receipt of the communication, unless the applicant informs the Office, before the expiry of this period, that he withdraws his application or restricts the application to goods and services against which the opposition is not directed.

(2) The Office may, pursuant to Rule 71, grant an extension of the period referred to in the second sentence of paragraph 1 where such request is presented jointly by the applicant and the opposing party.

(3) There the application is withdrawn or restricted within the period specified in the second sentence of paragraph 1 or within any extension of that period granted under paragraph 2, the Office shall inform the opposing party accordingly and shall refund the opposition fee.

RULE 20

EXAMINATION OF OPPOSITION

A11–22 (1) If the application is not withdrawn or restricted pursuant to Rule 19, the applicant shall file his observations within the period specified by the Office in its communication referred to in the first sentence of Rule 19 (1).

(2) Where the notice of opposition does not contain particulars of the facts, evidence and arguments as referred to in Rule 16 (1) and (2), the Office shall call upon the opposing party to submit such particulars within a period specified by the Office. Any submission by the opposing party shall be communicated to the applicant who shall be given an opportunity to reply within a period specified by the Office.

(3) If the applicant files no observations, the Office may give a ruling on the opposition on the basis of the evidence before it.

(4) The observations filed by the applicant shall be communicated to the opposing party who shall be called upon by the Office, if it considers it necessary to do so, to reply within a period specified by the Office.

(5) If, pursuant to Article 44 (1) of the Regulation, the applicant restricts the list of goods and services, the Office shall communicate this to the opposing party

and call upon him, within such period as it may specify, to submit observations stating whether he maintains the opposition and, if so, against which of the remaining goods and services.

(6) The Office may suspend any opposition proceeding where the opposition is based on an application for registration pursuant to Article 8 (2) (b) of the Regulation until a final decision is taken in that proceeding, or where other circumstances are such that such suspension is appropriate.

RULE 21

MULTIPLE OPPOSITIONS

(1) Where a number of oppositions have been entered in respect of the same **A11–23** application for a Community trade mark, the Office may deal with them in one set of proceedings. The Office may subsequently decide to no longer deal with them in this way.

(2) If a preliminary examination of one or more oppositions reveals that the Community trade mark for which an application for registration has been filed is possibly not eligible for registration in respect of some or all of the goods or services for which registration is sought, the Office may suspend the other opposition proceedings. The Office shall inform the remaining opposing parties of any relevant decisions taken during those proceedings which are continued.

(3) Once a decision rejecting the application has become final, the oppositions on which a decision was deferred in accordance with paragraph 2 shall be deemed to have been disposed of and the opposing parties concerned shall be informed accordingly. Such disposition shall be considered to constitute a case which has not proceeded to judgment within the meaning of Article 81 (4) of the Regulation.

(4) The Office shall refund 50% of the opposition fee paid by each opposing party whose opposition is deemed to have been disposed of in accordance with paragraphs 1, 2 and 3.

RULE 22

PROOF OF USE

(1) Where, pursuant to Article 43 (2) or (3) of the Regulation, the opposing **A11–24** party has to furnish proof of use or show that there are proper reasons for non-use, the Office shall invite him to provide the proof required within such period as it shall specify. If the opposing party does not provide such proof before the time limit expires, the Office shall reject the opposition.

(2) The indications and evidence for the furnishing of proof of use shall consist of indications concerning the place, time, extent and nature of use of the opposing trade mark for the goods and services in respect of which it is registered and on which the opposition is based, and evidence in support of these indications in accordance with paragraph 3.

(3) The evidence shall, in principle, be confined to the submission of supporting documents and items such as packages, labels, price lists, catalogues, invoices, photographs, newspaper advertisements, and statements in writing as referred to in Article 76 (1) (f) of the Regulation.

(4) Where the evidence supplied pursuant to paragraphs 1, 2 and 3 is not in the language of the opposition proceedings, the Office may require the opposing party to submit a translation of that evidence in that language, within a period specified by the Office.

TITLE III

REGISTRATION PROCEDURE

RULE 23

REGISTRATION OF THE TRADE MARK

A11–25   (1) The registration fee provided for in Article 45 of the Regulation shall consist of

(a) a basic fee;
   and
(b) a class fee for each class exceeding three in respect of which the mark is to be registered.

(2) Where no opposition has been entered or where any opposition entered has been finally disposed of by withdrawal, rejection or other disposition, the Office shall request the applicant to pay the registration fee within two months of receipt of the request.

(3) If the registration fee is not paid within due time, it may still be validly paid within two months of notification of a communication pointing out the failure to observe the time limit, provided that within this period the additional fee specified in the Fees Regulations is paid.

(4) On receipt of the registration fee the mark applied for and the particulars referred to in Rule 84 (2) shall be recorded in the Register of Community trade marks.

(5) The registration shall be published in the Community Trade Marks Bulletin.

(6) The registration fee shall be refunded if the trade mark applied for is not registered.

RULE 24

CERTIFICATE OF REGISTRATION

A11–26   (1) The Office shall issue to the proprietor of the trade mark a certificate of registration which shall contain the entries in the Register provided for in Rule 84 (2) and a statement to the effect that those entries have been recorded in the Register.

(2) The proprietor of the trade mark may request that certified or uncertified copies of the certificate of registration be supplied to him upon payment of a fee.

RULE 25

ALTERATION OF THE REGISTRATION

A11–27   (1) An application for alteration of the registration pursuant to Article 48 (2) of the Regulation shall contain:

(a) the registration number,
(b) the name and the address of the proprietor of the mark in accordance with Rule 1 (1) (b);

(c) where the proprietor has appointed a representative, the name and the business address of the representative in accordance with Rule 1 (1) (e);

(d) the indication of the element in the representation of the mark to be altered and that element in its altered version;

(e) a representation of the mark as altered, in accordance with Rule 3.

(2) The application shall be deemed not to have been filed until the required fee has been paid. If the fee has not been paid or has not been paid in full, the Office shall inform the applicant accordingly.

(3) If the requirements governing the alteration of the registration are not fulfilled, the Office shall communicate the deficiency to the applicant. If the deficiency is not remedied within a period to be specified by the Office, the Office shall reject the application.

(4) Where the registration of the alteration is challenged pursuant to Article 48 (3) of the Regulation, the provisions on opposition contained in the Regulation and in these Rules shall apply mutatis mutandis.

(5) A single application may be made for the alteration of the same element in two or more registrations of the same proprietor. The required fee shall be paid in respect of each registration to be altered.

RULE 26

CHANGE OF THE NAME OR ADDRESS OF THE PROPRIETOR OF THE COMMUNITY TRADE MARK OR OF HIS REGISTERED REPRESENTATIVE

(1) A change of the name or address of the proprietor of the Community trade **A11–28** mark which is not an alteration of the Community trade mark pursuant to Article 48 (2) of the Regulation and which is not the consequence of a whole or partial transfer of the registered mark shall, at the request of the proprietor, be recorded in the register.

(2) An application for the change of the name or address of the proprietor of the registered mark shall contain:

(a) the registration number of the mark;

(b) the name and the address of the proprietor of the mark as recorded in the register;

(c) the indication of the name and address of the proprietor of the mark, as amended, in accordance with Rule 1 (1) (e).

(d) where the proprietor has appointed a representative, the name and the business address of the representative, in accordance with Rule 1 (1) (e).

(3) The application shall not be subject to payment of a fee.

(4) A single application may be made for the change of the name or address in respect of two or more registrations of the same proprietor.

(5) If the requirements governing the recording of a change are not fulfilled, the Office shall communicate the deficiency to the applicant. If the deficiency is not remedied within a period to be specified by the Office, the Office shall reject the application.

(6) Paragraphs 1 to 5 shall apply mutatis mutandis to a change of the name or address of the registered representative.

(7) Paragraphs 1 to 6 shall apply mutatis mutandis to applications for Community trade marks. The change shall be recorded in the files kept by the Office on the Community trade mark application.

RULE 27

CORRECTION OF MISTAKES AND ERRORS IN THE REGISTER AND IN THE PUBLICATION OF THE REGISTRATION

(1) Where the registration of the mark or the publication of the registration **A11–29** contains a mistake or error attributable to the Office, the Office shall correct the error or mistake of its own motion or at the request of the proprietor.

1103

(2) Where such a request is made by the proprietor, Rule 26 shall apply mutatis mutandis. The request shall not be subject to payment of a fee.

(3) The Office shall publish the corrections made under this Rule.

RULE 28

CLAIMING SENIORITY AFTER REGISTRATION OF THE COMMUNITY TRADE MARK

A11–30 (1) An application pursuant to Article 35 of the Regulation to obtain the seniority of one or more earlier registered trade marks as referred to in Article 34 of the Regulation, shall contain:

(a) the registration number of the Community trade mark;

(b) the name and address of the proprietor of the Community trade mark in accordance with Rule 1 (1) (b);

(c) where the proprietor has appointed a representative, the name and the business address of the representative in accordance with Rule 1 (1) (e);

(d) an indication of the Member State or Member States in or for which the earlier mark is registered, the date from which the relevant registration was effective, the number of the relevant registration, and the goods and services for which the earlier mark is registered;

(e) an indication of the goods and services in respect of which seniority is claimed;

(f) a copy of the relevant registration; the copy must be certified as an exact copy of the relevant registration by the competent authority.

(2) If the requirements governing the claiming of seniority are not fulfilled, the Office shall communicate the deficiency to the applicant. If the deficiency is not remedied within a period specified by the Office, the Office shall reject the application.

(3) The Office shall inform the Benelux Trade Mark Office or the central industrial property office of the Member State concerned of the effective claiming of seniority.

(4) The President of the Office may determine that the material to be provided by the applicant may consist of less than is required under paragraph 1 (f), provided that the information required is available to the Office from other sources.

TITLE IV

RENEWAL

RULE 29

NOTIFICATION OF EXPIRY

A11–31 At least six months before expiry of the registration the Office shall inform the proprietor of the Community trade mark, and any person having a registered right, including a licence, in respect of the Community trade mark, that the registration is approaching expiry. Failure to give such notification shall not affect the expiry of the registration.

RULE 30

RENEWAL OF REGISTRATION

(1) An application for renewal shall contain: **A11–32**

   (a) where the application is filed by the proprietor of the trade mark, his name and address in accordance with Rule 1 (1) (b);

   (b) where the application is filed by a person expressly authorized to do so by the proprietor of the mark, the name and address of that person and evidence that he is authorized to file the application;

   (c) where the applicant has appointed a representative, the name and business address of the representative in accordance with Rule 1 (1) (e);

   (d) the registration number;

   (e) an indication that renewal is requested for all the goods and services covered by the registration or, if the renewal is not requested for all the goods and services for which the mark is registered, an indication of those classes or those goods and services for which renewal is requested or those classes or those goods and services for which renewal is not requested, grouped according to the classes of the Nice classification, each group being preceded by the number of the class of that classification to which that group of goods or services belongs and presented in the order of the classes of that classification.

(2) The fees payable under Article 47 of the Regulation for the renewal of a Community trade mark shall consist of:

   (a) a basic fee;

   (b) a class fee for each class exceeding three in the list of classes in respect of which renewal is applied for as shown in paragraph 1 (e); and

   (c) where applicable, the additional fee for late payment of the renewal fee or late submission of the request for renewal, pursuant to Article 47 (3) of the Regulation, as specified in the Fees Regulation.

(3) Where the application for renewal is filed within the time periods provided for in Article 47 (3) of the Regulation, but the other conditions governing renewal provided for in Article 47 of the Regulation and these Rules are not satisfied, the Office shall inform the applicant of the deficiencies found. If the application is filed by a person whom the proprietor of the trade mark has expressly authorized to do so, the proprietor of the trade mark shall receive a copy of the notification.

(4) Where an application for renewal is not submitted or is submitted after expiry of the period provided for in the third sentence of Article 47 (3) of the Regulation, or if the fees are not paid or are paid only after the period in question has expired, or if the deficiencies are not remedied within that period, the Office shall determine that the registration has expired and shall so notify the proprietor of the Community trade mark and, where appropriate, the applicant and the person recorded in the Register as having rights in the mark. Where the fees paid are insufficient to cover all the classes of goods and services for which renewal is requested, such a determination shall not be made if it is clear which class or classes are to be covered. In the absence of other criteria, the Office shall take the classes into account in the order of classification.

(5) Where the determination made pursuant to paragraph 4 has become final, the Office shall cancel the mark from the register. The cancellation shall take effect from the day following the day on which the existing registration expired.

(6) Where the renewal fees provided for in paragraph 2 have been paid but the registration is not renewed, those fees shall be refunded.

TITLE V

TRANSFER, LICENCES AND OTHER RIGHTS, CHANGES

RULE 31

TRANSFER

A11–33   (1) An application for registration of a transfer under Article 17 of the Regulation shall contain:

    (a) the registration number of the Community trade mark;

    (b) particulars of the new proprietor in accordance with Rule 1 (1) (b);

    (c) where not all the registered goods or services are included in the transfer, particulars of the registered goods or services to which the transfer relates;

    (d) documents duly establishing the transfer in accordance with Article 17 (2) and (3) of the Regulation;

(2) The application may contain, where applicable, the name and business address of the representative of the new proprietor, to be set out in accordance with Rule 1 (1) (e).

(3) Transfers to any natural or legal persons who cannot be proprietors of Community trade marks pursuant to Article 5 of the Regulation shall not be registered.

(4) The application shall not be deemed to have been filed until the required fee has been paid. If the fee is not paid or is not paid in full, the Office shall so notify the applicant.

(5) It shall constitute sufficient proof of transfer under paragraph 1(d):

    (a) that the application for registration of the transfer is signed by the registered proprietor or his representative and by the successor in title or his representative; or,

    (b) that the application, if submitted by the successor in title, is accompanied by a declaration, signed by the registered proprietor or his representative, that he agrees to the registration of the successor in title; or

    (c) that the application is accompanied by a completed transfer form or document, as specified in Rule 83 (1) (d), signed by the registered proprietor or his representative and by the successor in title or his representative.

(6) Where the conditions applicable to the registration of a transfer, as laid down in Article 17 (1) to (4) of the Regulation, in paragraphs 1 to 4 above, and in other applicable Rules are not fulfilled, the Office shall notify the applicant of the deficiencies. If the deficiencies are not remedied within a period specified by the Office, it shall reject the application for registration of the transfer.

(7) A single application for registration of a transfer may be submitted for two or more marks, provided that the registered proprietor and the successor in title are the same in each case.

(8) Paragraphs 1 to 7 shall apply mutatis mutandis to applications for Community trade marks. The transfer shall be recorded in the files kept by the Office concerning the Community trade mark application.

RULE 32

PARTIAL TRANSFERS

A11–34   (1) Where the application for registration of a transfer relates only to some of the goods and services for which the mark is registered, the application shall contain an indication of the goods and services to which the partial transfer relates.

(2) The goods and services in the original registration shall be distributed between the remaining registration and the new registration so that the goods and services in the remaining registration and the new registration shall not overlap.

(3) Rule 31 shall apply mutatis mutandis to applications for registrations of a partial transfer.

(4) The Office shall establish a separate file for the new registration, which shall consist of a complete copy of the file of the original registration and the application for registration of the partial transfer; a copy of that application shall be included in the file of the remaining registration. The Office shall also assign a new registration number to the new registration.

(5) Any application made by the original proprietor pending with regard to the original registration shall be deemed to be pending with regard to the remaining registration and the new registration. Where such application is subject to the payment of fees and these fees have been paid by the original proprietor, the new proprietor shall not be liable to pay any additional fees with regard to such application.

RULE 33

REGISTRATION OF LICENCES AND OTHER RIGHTS

(1) Rule 31 (1) (a) (b) and (c), (2), (4) and (7) shall apply mutatis mutandis to **A11–35** the registration of the grant or transfer of a licence, to registration of the creation or transfer of a right in rem in respect of a Community trade mark, and to registration of enforcement measures. However, where a Community trade mark is involved in bankruptcy or like proceedings, the request of the competent national authority for an entry in the register to this effect shall not be subject to payment of a fee.

(2) Where the Community trade mark is licensed for only part of the goods and services for which the mark is registered, or for only a part of the Community, or for a limited period of time, the application for registration shall indicate the goods and services or the part of the Community or the time period for which the licence is granted.

(3) Where the conditions applicable to registration, as laid down in Articles 19, 20 or 22 of the Regulation, in paragraphs 1 and 2 above, and the other applicable Rules are not fulfilled, the Office shall notify the applicant of the irregularity. If the irregularity is not corrected within a period specified by the Office, it shall reject the application for registration.

(4) Paragraphs 1, 2 and 3 shall apply mutatis mutandis to applications for Community trade marks. Licences, rights in rem and enforcement measures shall be recorded in the files kept by the Office concerning the Community trade mark application.

RULE 34

SPECIAL PROVISIONS FOR THE REGISTRATION OF A LICENCE

(1) A licence in respect of a Community trade mark shall be recorded in the **A11–36** Register as an exclusive licence if the proprietor of the trade mark or the licensee so request.

(2) A licence in respect of a Community trade mark shall be recorded in the Register as a sub-licence where it is granted by a licensee whose licence is recorded in the Register.

(3) A licence in respect of a Community trade mark shall be recorded in the Register as a licence limited as to the goods and services or as a territorially

limited licence if it is granted for only a part of the goods or services for which the mark is registered or if it is granted only for a part of the Community.

(4) A licence in respect of a Community trade mark shall be recorded in the Register as a temporary licence if it is granted for a limited period of time.

RULE 35

CANCELLATION OR MODIFICATION OF THE REGISTRATION OF LICENCES AND OTHER RIGHTS

A11–37 (1) A registration effected under Rule 33 (1) shall be cancelled at the request of one of the persons concerned.

(2) The application shall contain:

    (a) the registration number of the Community trade mark;
       and
    (b) particulars of the right whose registration is to be cancelled.

(3) Application for cancellation of the registration of a licence or another right shall not be deemed to have been filed until the required fee has been paid. If the fee is not paid or is not paid in full, the Office shall so notify the applicant. However, the request of the competent national authority for the cancellation of an entry where a Community trade mark is involved in bankruptcy or like proceedings shall not be subject to payment of a fee.

(4) The application shall be accompanied by documents showing that the registered right no longer exists or by a statement by the licensee or the holder of another right, to the effect that he consents to cancellation of the registration.

(5) Where the requirements for cancellation of the registration are not satisfied, the Office shall notify the applicant of the irregularity. If the irregularity is not corrected within a period specified by the Office, it shall reject the application for cancellation of the registration.

(6) Paragraphs 1, 2, 4 and 5 shall apply mutatis mutandis to a request for the modification of a registration effected under Rule 33 (1).

(7) Paragraphs 1 to 6 shall apply mutatis mutandis to entries made in the files pursuant to Rule 33 (4).

Title VI

Surrender

RULE 36

SURRENDER

A11–38 (1) A declaration of surrender pursuant to Article 49 of the Regulation shall contain:

    (a) the registration number of the Community trade mark;
    (b) the name and address of the proprietor in accordance with Rule 1 (1) (b);
    (c) where a representative has been appointed, the name and business address of the representative in accordance with Rule 1 (1) (e);
    (d) where surrender is declared only for some of the goods and services for which the mark is registered, the goods and services for which the

surrender is declared or the goods and services for which the mark is to remain registered.

(2) Where a right of a third party relating to the Community trade mark is entered in the register, it shall be sufficient proof of his agreement to the surrender that a declaration of consent to the surrender is signed by the proprietor of that right or his representative. Where a licence has been registered, surrender shall be registered three months after the date on which the proprietor of the Community trade mark satisfies the Office that he has informed the licensee of his intention to surrender it. If the proprietor proves to the Office before the expiry of that period that the licensee has given his consent, the surrender shall be registered forthwith.

(3) If the requirements governing surrender are not fulfilled, the Office shall communicate the deficiencies to the declarant. If the deficiencies are not remedied within a period to be specified by the Office, the Office shall reject the entry of the surrender in the Register.

TITLE VII

REVOCATION AND INVALIDITY

RULE 37

APPLICATION FOR REVOCATION OR FOR A DECLARATION OF INVALIDITY

An application to the Office for revocation or for a declaration of invalidity **A11–39** pursuant to Article 55 of the Regulation shall contain:

  (a) as concerns the registration in respect of which revocation or a declaration of invalidity is sought;
    (i) the registration number of the Community trade mark in respect of which revocation or a declaration of invalidity is sought;
    (ii) the name and address of the proprietor of the Community trade mark in respect of which revocation or a declaration of invalidity is sought;
    (iii) a statement of the registered goods and services in respect of which revocation or a declaration of invalidity is sought;
  (b) as regards the grounds on which the application is based,
    (i) in the case of an application pursuant to Article 50 or Article 51 of the Regulation, a statement of the grounds on which the application for revocation or a declaration of invalidity is based;
    (ii) in the case of an application pursuant to Article 52 (1) of the Regulation, particulars of the right on which the application for a declaration of invalidity is based and if necessary particulars showing that the applicant is entitled to adduce the earlier right as grounds for invalidity;
    (iii) in the case of an application pursuant to Article 52 (2) of the Regulation, particulars of the right on which the application for a declaration of invalidity is based and particulars showing that the applicant is the proprietor of an earlier right as referred to in Article 52 (2) of the Regulation or that he is entitled under the national law applicable to lay claim to that right;

1109

       (iv) an indication of the facts, evidence and arguments presented in support of those grounds;
    (c) as concerns the applicant,
       (i) his name and address in accordance with Rule 1 (1) (b);
       (ii) if the applicant has appointed a representative, the name and the business address of the representative, in accordance with Rule 1 (1)(e).

RULE 38

LANGUAGES USED IN REVOCATION OR INVALIDITY PROCEEDINGS

A11–40   (1) Where the application for revocation or for a declaration of invalidity is not filed in the language of the application for the registration of the Community trade mark, if that language is one of the languages of the Office, or in the second language indicated when the application was filed, the applicant for revocation or for a declaration of invalidity shall file a translation of his application in one of those two languages within a period of one month from the filing of his application.

(2) Where the evidence in support of the application is not filed in the language of the revocation or invalidity proceedings, the applicant shall file a translation of that evidence into that language within a period of two months after the filing of such evidence.

(3) Where the applicant for revocation or for a declaration of invalidity or the proprietor of the Community trade mark inform the Office before the expiry of a period of two months from receipt by the Community trade mark proprietor of the communication referred to in Rule 40 (1), that they have agreed on a different language of proceedings pursuant to Article 115 (7) of the Regulation, the applicant shall, where the application was not filed in that language, file a translation of the application in that language within a period of one month from the said date.

RULE 39

REJECTION OF THE APPLICATION FOR REVOCATION OR FOR DECLARATION OF INVALIDITY AS INADMISSIBLE

A11–41   (1) If the Office finds that the application does not comply with Article 55 of the Regulation, Rule 37 or any other provision of the Regulation or these Rules, it shall inform the applicant accordingly and shall call upon him to remedy the deficiencies found within such period as it may specify. If the deficiencies are not remedied before expiry of the time limit, the Office shall reject the application as inadmissible.

(2) Where the Office finds that the required fees have not been paid, it shall inform the applicant accordingly and shall inform him that the application will be deemed not to have been filed if the required fees are not paid within a period specified by the Office. If the required fees are paid after expiry of the period specified by the Office, they shall be refunded to the applicant.

(3) Any decision to reject an application for revocation or for a declaration of invalidity under paragraph 1 shall be communicated to the applicant. Where the application is considered not to have been filed pursuant to paragraph 2, the applicant shall be informed accordingly.

RULE 40

EXAMINATION OF THE APPLICATION FOR REVOCATION OR FOR A DECLARATION OF INVALIDITY

(1) If the Office does not reject the application in accordance with Rule 39, it **A11–42** shall communicate such application to the proprietor of the Community trade mark and shall request him to file his observations within such period as it may specify.

(2) If the proprietor of the Community trade mark files no observations, the Office may decide on the revocation or invalidity on the basis of the evidence before it.

(3) Any observations filed by the proprietor of the Community trade mark shall be communicated to the applicant, who shall be requested by the Office, if it sees fit, to reply within a period specified by the Office.

(4) All communications under Article 56 (1) of the Regulation and all observations filed in this respect shall be sent to the parties concerned.

(5) If the applicant, under Article 56 (2) or (3) of the Regulation, has to furnish proof of use or proof that there are proper reasons for non-use, Rule 22 shall apply mutatis mutandis.

RULE 41

MULTIPLE APPLICATIONS FOR REVOCATION OR FOR A DECLARATION OF INVALIDITY

(1) Where a number of applications for revocation or for a declaration of **A11–43** invalidity have been filed relating to the same Community trade mark, the Office may deal with them in one set of proceedings. The Office may subsequently decide no longer to deal with them in this way.

(2) Rule 21 (2) (3) and (4) shall apply mutatis mutandis.

TITLE VIII

COMMUNITY COLLECTIVE MARKS

RULE 42

APPLICATION OF PROVISIONS

The provisions of these Rules shall apply to Community collective marks, **A11–44** subject to Rule 43.

RULE 43

REGULATION GOVERNING COMMUNITY COLLECTIVE MARKS

(1) Where the application for a Community collective trade mark does not **A11–45** contain the regulations governing its use pursuant to Article 65 of the Regulation, those regulations shall be submitted to the Office within a period of two months after the date of filing.

1111

(2) The regulations governing Community collective marks shall specify:

  (a) the name of the applicant and his office address;
  (b) the object of the association or the object for which the legal person governed by public law is constituted;
  (c) the bodies authorized to represent the association or the said legal person;
  (d) the conditions for membership;
  (e) the persons authorized to use the mark;
  (f) where appropriate, the conditions governing use of the mark, including sanctions;
  (g) where appropriate, the authorization referred to in the second sentence of Article 65 (2) of the Regulation.

TITLE IX

CONVERSION

RULE 44

APPLICATION FOR CONVERSION

A11–46   (1) An application for conversion of a Community trade mark application or a registered Community trade mark into a national trademark application pursuant to Article 108 of the Regulation shall contain:

  (a) the name and the address of the applicant for conversion in accordance with Rule 1 (1) (b);
  (b) where the applicant for conversion has appointed a representative, the name and the business address of the representative in accordance with Rule 1 (1) (e);
  (c) the filing number of the Community trade mark application or the registration number of the Community trade mark;
  (d) the date of filing of the Community trade mark application or the Community trade mark and, where applicable, particulars of the claim to priority for the Community trade mark application or the Community trade mark pursuant to Articles 30 and 33 of the Regulation and particulars of the claim to seniority pursuant to Articles 34 and 35 of the Regulation;
  (e) a representation of the mark as contained in the application or as registered;
  (f) the specification of the Member State or the Member States in respect of which conversion is requested;
  (g) where the request does not relate to all of the goods and services for which the application has been filed or for which the trade mark has been registered, an indication of the goods and services for which conversion is requested, and, where conversion is requested in respect of more than one Member State and the list of goods and services is not the same for all Member States, an indication of the respective goods and services for each Member State;
  (h) where conversion is requested pursuant to Article 108 (4) of the Regulation, an indication to that effect;
  (i) where conversion is requested pursuant to Article 108 (5) of the Regulation following a withdrawal of an application for registration, an

1112

indication to that effect, and the date on which the application for registration was withdrawn;

(j) where conversion is requested pursuant to Article 108 (5) of the Regulation following a failure to renew the registration, an indication to that effect, and the date on which the period of protection has expired, the period of three months provided for in Article 108 (5) of the Regulation shall begin to run on the day following the last day on which the request for renewal can be presented pursuant to Article 47 (3) of the Regulation;

(k) where conversion is requested pursuant to article 108 (6) of the Regulation, an indication to that effect, the date on which the decision of the national court has become final, and a copy of that decision.

(2) Where a copy of a court decision pursuant to paragraph 1 (k) is required, that copy may be submitted in the language in which the decision was given.

RULE 45

EXAMINATION OF APPLICATION FOR CONVERSION

(1) Where the application for conversion does not comply with the require- **A11–47** ments of Article 108 (1) of the Regulation or was not filed within the relevant period of three months, the Office shall reject it.

(2) Where the conversion fee has not been paid within the relevant period of three months, the Office shall inform the applicant that the application for conversion shall be deemed not to have been filed.

(3) Where the other requirements governing conversion as provided for in Rule 44 and in other Rules governing such applications are not fulfilled, the Office shall inform the applicant accordingly and invite him to remedy the deficiency within a period specified by the Office. If the deficiencies are not remedied within that period, the Office shall reject the application for conversion.

RULE 46

PUBLICATION OF APPLICATION FOR CONVERSION

(1) Where the application for conversion relates to a Community trade mark **A11–48** application which has already been published in the Community Trade Mark Bulletin pursuant to Article 40 of the Regulation or where the application for conversion relates to a Community trade mark, the application for conversion shall be published in the Community Trade Marks Bulletin.

(2) The publication of the application for conversion shall contain:

(a) the filing number or the registration number of the trade mark in respect of which conversion is requested;

(b) a reference to the previous publication of the application or the registration in the Community Trade marks Bulletin;

(c) an indication of the Member State or Member States in respect of which conversion has been requested;

(d) where the request does not relate to all of the goods and services for which the application has been filed or for which the trade mark has been registered, an indication of the goods and services for which conversion is requested;

(e) where conversion is requested in respect of more than one Member State and the list of goods and services is not the same for all Member

States, an indication of the respective goods and services for each Member State;

(f) the date of the application for conversion.

RULE 47

TRANSMISSION TO CENTRAL INDUSTRIAL PROPERTY OFFICES OF THE MEMBER STATES

A11–49   Where the application for conversion complies with the requirements of the Regulation and these Rules, the Office shall transmit without delay the application for conversion to the central industrial property offices of the Member States specified therein, including the Benelux Trade Mark Office. The Office shall inform the applicant of the date of transmission.

Title X

Appeals

RULE 48

CONTENT OF THE NOTICE OF APPEAL

A11–50   (1) The notice of appeal shall contain:

(a) the name and address of the appellant in accordance with rule 1 (1) (b);

(b) where the appellant has appointed a representative, the name and the business address of the representative in accordance with Rule 1 (1) (e);

(c) a statement identifying the decision which is contested and the extent to which amendment or cancellation of the decision is requested.

(2) The notice of appeal shall be filed in the language of the proceedings in which the decision subject to the appeal was taken.

RULE 49

REJECTION OF THE APPEAL AS INADMISSIBLE

A11–51   (1) If the appeal does not comply with Articles 57, 58 and 59 of the Regulation and Rule 48 (1) (c) and (2), the Board of Appeal shall reject it as inadmissible, unless each deficiency has been remedied before the relevant time limit laid down in Article 59 of the Regulation has expired.

(2) If the Board of Appeal finds that the appeal does not comply with other provisions of the Regulation or other provisions of these Rules, in particular Rule 48 (1) (a) and (b), it shall inform the appellant accordingly and shall request him to remedy the deficiencies noted within such period as it may specify. If the appeal is not corrected in good time, the Board of Appeal shall reject it as inadmissible.

(3) If the fee for appeal has been paid after expiry of the period for the filing of appeal pursuant to Article 59 of the Regulation, the appeal shall be deemed not to have been filed and the appeal fee shall be refunded to the appellant.

RULE 50

EXAMINATION OF APPEALS

(1) Unless otherwise provided, the provisions relating to proceedings before **A11–52** the department which has made the decision against which the appeal is brought shall be applicable to appeal proceedings mutatis mutandis.

(2) The Board of Appeal's decision shall contain:

    (a) a statement that it is delivered by the Board;

    (b) the date when the decision was taken;

    (c) the names of the Chairman and of the other members of the Board of Appeal taking part;

    (d) the name of the competent employee of the registry;

    (e) the names of the parties and of their representatives;

    (f) a statement of the issues to be decided;

    (g) a summary of the facts;

    (h) the reasons;

    (i) the order of the Board of Appeal, including, where necessary, a decision on costs.

(3) The decision shall be signed by the Chairman and the other members of the Board of Appeal and by the employee of the registry of the Board of Appeal.

RULE 51

REIMBURSEMENT OF APPEAL FEES

The reimbursement of appeal fees shall be ordered in the event of interlocu- **A11–53** tory revision or where the Board of Appeal deems an appeal to be allowable, if such reimbursement is equitable by reason of a substantial procedural violation. In the event of interlocutory revision, reimbursement shall be ordered by the department whose decision has been impugned, and in other cases by the Board of Appeal.

TITLE XI

GENERAL PROVISIONS

Part A

Decisions and communications of the Office

RULE 52

FORM OF DECISIONS

(1) Decisions of the Office shall be in writing and shall state the reasons on **A11–54** which they are based. Where oral proceedings are held before the Office, the decision may be given orally. Subsequently, the decision in writing shall be notified to the parties.

(2) Decisions of the Office which are open to appeal shall be accompanied by a written communication indicating that notice of appeal must be filed in writing at the Office within two months of the date of notification of the decision from which appeal is to be made. The communications shall also draw the attention of the parties to the provisions laid down in Articles 57, 58 and 59 of the Regulation. The parties may not plead any failure to communicate the availability proceedings.

RULE 53

CORRECTION OF ERRORS IN DECISIONS

A11–55 In decisions of the Office, only linguistic errors, errors of transcription and obvious mistakes my be corrected. They shall be corrected by the department which took the decision, acting of its own motion or at the request of an interested party.

RULE 54

NOTING OF LOSS OF RIGHTS

A11–56 (1) If the Office finds that the loss of any rights results from the Regulation or these Rules without any decision having been taken, it shall communicate this to the person concerned in accordance with Article 77 of the Regulation, and shall draw his attention to the substance of paragraph 2 of this Rule.

(2) If the person concerned considers that the finding of the Office is inaccurate, he may, within two months after notification of the communication referred to in paragraph 1, apply for a decision on the matter by the Office. Such decision shall be given only if the Office disagrees with the person requesting it; otherwise the Office shall amend its finding and inform the person requesting the decision.

RULE 55

SIGNATURE, NAME, SEAL

A11–57 (1) Any decision, communication or notice from the Office shall indicate the department or division of the Office as well as the name or the names of the official or officials responsible. They shall be signed by the official or officials, or, instead of a signature, carry a printed or stamped seal of the Office.

(2) The President of the Office may determine that other means of identifying the department or division of the Office and the name of the official or officials responsible or an identification other than a seal may be used where decisions, communications or notices are transmitted by telecopier or any other technical means of communication.

Part B

Oral proceedings and taking of evidence

RULE 56

SUMMONS TO ORAL PROCEEDINGS

A11–58 (1) The parties shall be summoned to oral proceedings provided for in Article 75 of the Regulation and their attention shall be drawn to paragraph 3 of this Rule. At least one month's, notice of the summons shall be given unless the parties agree to a shorter period.

(2) When issuing the summons, the Office shall draw attention to the points which in its opinion need to be discussed in order for the decision to be taken.

(3) If a party who has been duly summoned to oral proceedings before the Office does not appear as summoned, the proceedings may continue without him.

RULE 57

TAKING OF EVIDENCE BY THE OFFICE

(1) Where the Office considers it necessary to hear the oral evidence of parties, **A11–59** of witnesses or of experts or to carry out an inspection, it shall take a decision to that end, stating the means by which it intends to obtain evidence, the relevant facts to be proved and the date, time and place of hearing or inspection. If oral evidence of witnesses and experts is requested by a party, the decision of the Office shall determine the period of time within which the party filing the request must make known to the Office the names and addresses of the witnesses and experts whom the party wishes to be heard.

(2) The period of notice given in the summons of a party, witness or expert to give evidence shall be at least one month, unless they agree to a shorter period. The summons shall contain:

(a) an extract from the decision mentioned in paragraph 1, indicating in particular the date, time and place of the hearing ordered and stating the facts regarding which the parties, witnesses and experts are to be heard;

(b) the names of the parties to proceedings and particulars of the rights which the witnesses or experts may invoke under Rule 59 (2) to (5).

RULE 58

COMMISSIONING OF EXPERTS

(1) The Office shall decide in what form the report made by an expert whom it **A11–60** appoints shall be submitted.

(2) The terms of reference of the expert shall include:

(a) a precise description of his task;

(b) the time limit laid down for the submission of the expert report;

(c) the names of the parties to the proceedings;

(d) particulars of the claims which he may invoke under Rule 59 (2), (3) and (4).

(3) A copy of any written report shall be submitted to the parties.

(4) The parties may object to an expert on grounds of incompetence or on the same grounds as those on which objection may be made to an examiner or to a member of a Division or Board of Appeal pursuant to Article 132 (1) and (3) of the Regulation. The department of the Office concerned shall rule on the objection.

RULE 59

COSTS OF TAKING OF EVIDENCE

(1) The taking of evidence by the Office may be made conditional upon **A11–61** deposit with it, by the party who has requested the evidence to be taken, of a sum which shall be fixed by reference to an estimate of the costs.

(2) Witnesses and experts who are summoned by and appear before the Office shall be entitled to reimbursement of reasonable expenses for travel and subsistence. An advance for these expenses may be granted to them by the Office. The first sentence shall apply also to witnesses and experts who appear before the Office without being summoned by it and are heard as witnesses or experts.

(3) Witnesses entitled to reimbursement under paragraph 2 shall also be entitled to appropriate compensation for loss of earnings, and experts to fees for their work. These payments shall be made to the witnesses and experts after they have fulfilled their duties or tasks, where such witnesses and experts have been summoned by the Office of its own initiative.

(4) The amounts and the advances for expenses to be paid pursuant to paragraphs 1, 2 and 3 shall be determined by the President of the Office and shall be published in the Official Journal of the Office. The amounts shall be calculated on the same basis as the compensation and salaries received by officials in grades A4 to A8 as laid down in the Staff Regulations of Officials of the European Communities and Annex VII thereto.

(5) Final liability for the amounts due or paid pursuant to paragraphs 1 to 4 shall lie with:

(a) the Office where the Office, at its own initiative, considered it necessary to hear the oral evidence of witnesses or experts;
or

(b) the party concerned where that party requested the giving of oral evidence by witnesses or experts, subject to the decision on apportionment and fixing of costs pursuant to Articles 81 and 82 of the Regulation and Rule 94. Such party shall reimburse the Office for any advances duly paid.

RULE 60

MINUTES OF ORAL PROCEEDINGS AND OF EVIDENCE

A11–62   (1) Minutes of oral proceedings or the taking of evidence shall be drawn up, containing the essentials of the oral proceedings or of the taking of evidence, the relevant statements made by the parties, the testimony of the parties, witnesses or experts and the result of any inspection.

(2) The minutes of the testimony of a witness, expert or party shall be read out or submitted to him so that he may examine them. It shall be noted in the minutes that this formality has been carried out and that the person who gave the testimony approved the minutes. Where his approval is not given, his objections shall be noted.

(3) The minutes shall be signed by the employee who drew them up and by the employee who conducted the oral proceedings or taking of evidence.

(4) The parties shall be provided with a copy of the minutes.

(5) Upon request, the Office shall make available to the parties transcripts of recordings of the oral proceedings, in typescript or in any other machine-readable form. The release under the first sentence of the oral proceedings shall be subject to the payment of the costs incurred by the Office in making such transcript. The amount to be charged shall be determined by the President of the Office.

Part C

Notifications

RULE 61

GENERAL PROVISIONS ON NOTIFICATIONS

(1) In proceedings before the Office, any notifications to be made by the Office **A11–63** shall take the form of the original document, of a copy thereof certified by, or bearing the seal of, the Office or of a computer print-out bearing such seal. Copies of documents emanating from the parties themselves shall not require such certification.

(2) Notifications shall be made

    (a) by post in accordance with Rule 62;

    (b) by hand delivery in accordance with Rule 63;

    (c) by deposit in a post box at the Office in accordance with Rule 64;

    (d) by telecopier and other technical means in accordance with Rule 65;

    (e) by public notification in accordance with Rule 66.

RULE 62

NOTIFICATION BY POST

(1) Decisions subject to a time limit for appeal, summonses and other **A11–64** documents as determined by the President of the Office shall be notified by registered letter with advice of delivery. Decisions and communications subject to some other time limit shall be notified by registered letter, unless the President of the Office determines otherwise. All other communications shall be ordinary mail.

(2) Notifications in respect of addresses having neither their domicile nor their principal place of business nor an establishment in the Community and who have not appointed a representative in accordance with Article 88 (2) of the Regulation shall be effected by posting the document requiring notification by ordinary mail to the last address of the addressee known to the Office. Notification shall be deemed to have been effected when the posting has taken place.

(3) Where notification is effected by registered letter, whether or not with advice of delivery, this shall be deemed to be delivered to the addressee on the 10th day following that of its posting, unless the letter has failed to reach the addressee or has reached him at a later date. In the event of any dispute, it shall be for the Office to establish that the letter has reached its destination or to establish the date on which it was delivered to the addressee, as the case may be.

(4) Notification by registered letter, with or without advice of delivery, shall be deemed to have been effected even if the addressee refuses to accept the letter.

(5) To the extent that notification by post is not covered by paragraphs 1 to 4, the law of the State on the territory of which notification is made shall apply.

RULE 63

NOTIFICATION BY HAND DELIVERY

Notification may be effected on the premises of the Office by hand delivery of **A11–65** the document to the addressee, who shall on delivery acknowledge its receipt.

RULE 64

NOTIFICATION BY DEPOSIT IN A POST BOX AT THE OFFICE

A11–66   Notification may also be effected to addressees who have been provided with a post box at the Office, by depositing the document therein. A written notification of deposit shall be inserted in the files. The date of deposit shall be recorded on the document. Notification shall be deemed to have taken place on the fifth day following deposit of the document in the post box at the Office.

RULE 65

NOTIFICATION BY TELECOPIER AND OTHER TECHNICAL MEANS

A11–67   (1) Notification by telecopier shall be effected by transmitting either the original or a copy, as provided for in Rule 61 (1), of the document to be notified. The details of such transmission shall be determined by the President of the Office.

(2) Details of notification by other technical means of communication shall be determined by the President of the Office.

RULE 66

PUBLIC NOTIFICATION

A11–68   (1) If the address of the addressee cannot be established, or if notification in accordance with Rule 62 (1) has proved to be impossible even after a second attempt by the Office, notification shall be effected by public notice. Such notice shall be published at least in the Community Trade Marks Bulletin.

(2) The President of the Office shall determine how the public notice is to be given and shall fix the beginning of the one-month period on the expiry of which the document shall be deemed to have been notified.

RULE 67

NOTIFICATION TO REPRESENTATIVES

A11–69   (1) If a representative has been appointed or where the applicant first named in a common application is considered to be the common representative pursuant to Rule 75 (1), notifications shall be addressed to that appointed or common representative.

(2) If several representatives have been appointed for a single interested party, notification to any one of them shall be sufficient, unless a specific address for service has been indicated in accordance with Rule 1 (1) (e).

(3) If several interested parties have appointed a common representative, notification of a single document to the common representative shall be sufficient.

RULE 68

IRREGULARITIES IN NOTIFICATION

A11–70   Where a document has reached the addressee, if the Office is unable to prove that it has been duly notified, or if provisions relating to its notification have not been observed, the document shall be deemed to have been notified on the date established by the Office as the date of receipt.

RULE 69

NOTIFICATION OF DOCUMENTS IN THE CASE OF SEVERAL PARTIES

Documents emanating from parties which contain substantive proposals, or a **A11–71** declaration of withdrawal of a substantive proposal, shall be notified to the other parties as a matter of course. Notification may be dispensed with where the document contains no new pleadings and the matter is ready for decision.

Part D

Timelimits

RULE 70

CALCULATION OF TIME LIMITS

(1) Periods shall be laid down in terms of full years, months, weeks or days. **A11–72**

(2) Calculation shall start on the day following the day on which the relevant event occurred, the event being either a procedural step or the expiry of another period. Where that procedural step is a notification, the event considered shall be the receipt of the document notified, unless otherwise provided.

(3) Where a period is expressed as one year or a certain number of years, it shall expire in the relevant subsequent year in the month having the same name and on the day having the same number as the month and the day on which the said event occurred. Where the relevant month has no day with the same number the period shall expire on the last day of that month.

(4) Where a period is expressed as one month or a certain number of months, it shall expire in the relevant subsequent month on the day which has the same number as the day on which the said event occurred. Where the day on which the said event occurred was the last day of a month or where the relevant subsequent month has no day with the same number the period shall expire on the last day of that month.

(5) Where a period is expressed as one week or a certain number of weeks, it shall expire in the relevant subsequent week on the day having the same name as the day on which the said event occurred.

RULE 71

DURATION OF TIME LIMITS

(1) Where the Regulation or these Rules provide for a period to be specified by **A11–73** the Office, such period shall, when the party concerned has its domicile or its principal place of business or an establishment within the Community, be not less than one month, or, when those conditions are not fulfilled, not less than two months, and no more than six months. The Office may, when this is appropriate under the circumstances, grant an extension of a period specified if such extension is requested by the party concerned and the request is submitted before the original period expired.

(2) Where there are two or more parties, the Office may extend a period subject to the agreement of the other parties.

RULE 72

EXPIRY OF TIME LIMITS IN SPECIAL CASES

(1) If a time limit expires on a day on which the Office is not open for receipt **A11–74** of documents or on which, for reasons other than those referred to in paragraph 2, ordinary mail is not delivered in the locality in which the Office is located, the

time limit shall extend until the first day thereafter on which the Office is open for receipt of documents and on which ordinary mail is delivered. The days referred to in the first sentence shall be as determined by the President of the Office before the commencement of each calendar year.

(2) If a time limit expires on a day on which there is a general interruption or subsequent dislocation in the delivery of mail in a Member State or between a Member State and the Office, the time limit shall extend until the first day following the end of the period of interruption or dislocation, for parties having their residence or registered office in the State concerned or who have appointed representatives with a place of business in that State. In the event of the Member State concerned being the State in which the Office is located, this provision shall apply to all parties. The duration of the abovementioned period shall be as determined by the President of the Office.

(3) Paragraphs 1 and 2 shall apply mutatis mutandis to the time limits provided for in the Regulation or these Rules in the case of transactions to be carried out with the competent authority within the meaning of Article 25 (1) (b) of the Regulation.

(4) If an exceptional occurrence such as natural disaster or strike interrupts or dislocates the proper functioning of the Office so that any communication from the Office to parties concerning the expiry of a time limit is delayed, acts to be completed within such a time limit may still be validly completed within one month after the notification of the delayed communication. The date of commencement and the end of any such interruption or dislocation shall be as determined by the President of the Office.

Part E

Interruption of proceedings

RULE 73

INTERRUPTION OF PROCEEDINGS

A11–75   (1) Proceedings before the Office shall be interrupted:

(a) in the event of the death or legal incapacity of the applicant for or proprietor of a Community trade mark or of the person authorized by national law to act on his behalf. To the extent that the above events do not affect the authorization of a representative appointed under Article 89 of the Regulation, proceedings shall be interrupted only on application by such representative;

(b) in the event of the applicant for or proprietor of a Community trade mark, as a result of some action taken against his property, being prevented for legal reasons from continuing the proceedings before the Office;

(c) in the event of the death or legal incapacity of the representative of an applicant for or proprietor of a Community trade mark or of his being prevented for legal reasons resulting from action taken against his property from continuing the proceedings before the Office.

(2) When, in the cases referred to in paragraph 1 (a) and (b), the Office has been informed of the identity of the person authorized to continue the proceedings before the Office, the Office shall communicate to such person and to any interested third parties that the proceedings shall be resumed as from a date to be fixed by the Office.

(3) In the case referred to in paragraph 1 (c), the proceedings shall be resumed when the Office has been informed of the appointment of a new representative of the applicant or when the Office has notified to the other parties the communication of the appointment of a new representative of the proprietor of the Community trade mark. If, three months after the beginning of the interruption of the proceedings, the Office has not been informed of the appointment of a new representative, it shall inform the applicant for or proprietor of the Community trade mark:

(a) where Article 88 (2) of the Regulation is applicable, that the Community trade mark application will be deemed to be withdrawn if the information is not submitted within two months after this communication is notified; or

(b) where Article 88 (2) of the Regulation is not applicable, that the proceedings will be resumed with the applicant for or proprietor of the Community trade mark as from the date on which this communication is notified.

(4) The time limits, other than the time limit for paying the renewal fees, in force as regards the applicant for or proprietor of the Community trade mark at the date of interruption of the proceedings, shall begin again as from the day on which the proceedings are resumed.

Part F

Waiving of enforced recovery procedures

RULE 74

WAIVING OF ENFORCED RECOVERY PROCEDURES

The President of the Office may waive action for the enforced recovery of any **A11–76** sum due where the sum to be recovered is minimal or where such recovery is too uncertain.

Part G

Representation

RULE 75

APPOINTMENT OF A COMMON REPRESENTATIVE

(1) If there is more than one applicant and the application for a Community **A11–77** trade mark does not name a common representative, the applicant first named in the application shall be considered to be the common representative. However, if one of the applicants is obliged to appoint a professional representative, such representative shall be considered to be the common representative unless the applicant named first in the application has appointed a professional representative. The same shall apply mutatis mutandis to third parties acting in common in filing notice of opposition or applying for revocation or for a declaration of invalidity, and to joint proprietors of a Community trade mark.

(2) If, during the course of proceedings, transfer is made to more than one person, and such persons have not appointed a common representative, paragraph 1 shall apply. If such application is not possible, the Office shall require such persons to appoint a common representative within two months. If this request is not complied with, the Office shall appoint the common representative.

RULE 76

AUTHORIZATIONS

A11–78 (1) Representatives acting before the Office must file with it a signed authorization for inclusion in the files. The authorization may cover one or more applications or one or more registered trade marks.

(2) A general authorization enabling a representative to act in respect of all trade mark transactions of the party giving the authorization may be filed.

(3) The authorization may be filed in any language of the Office and in the language of the proceedings if that language is not one of the languages of the Office.

(4) Where the appointment of a representative is communicated to the Office, the necessary authorization shall be filed within a period specified by the Office. If the authorization is not filed in due time, proceedings shall be continued with the represented person. Any procedural steps other than the filing of the application taken by the representative shall be deemed not to have been taken if the represented person does not approve them. The application of Article 88 (2) of the Regulation shall remain unaffected.

(5) Paragraphs 1 to 3 shall apply mutatis mutandis to a document withdrawing an authorization.

(6) Any representative who has ceased to be authorized shall continue to be regarded as the representative until the termination of his authorization has been communicated to the Office.

(7) Subject to any provisions to the contrary contained therein, an authorization shall not terminate vis-à-vis the Office upon the death of the person who gave it.

(8) Where several representatives are appointed by the same party, they may, notwithstanding any provisions to the contrary in their authorizations, act either jointly or singly.

(9) The authorization of an association of representatives shall be deemed to be an authorization of any representative who can establish that he practises within that association.

RULE 77

REPRESENTATION

A11–79 Any notification or other communication addressed by the Office to the duly authorized representative shall have the same effect as if it had been addressed to the represented person. Any communication addressed to the Office by the duly authorized representative shall have the same effect as if it originated from the represented person.

RULE 78

AMENDMENT OF THE LIST OF PROFESSIONAL REPRESENTATIVES

A11–80 (1) The entry of a professional representative in the list of professional representatives, as referred to in Article 89 of the Regulation, shall be deleted at his request.

(2) The entry of a professional representative shall be deleted automatically:

    (a) in the event of the death or legal incapacity of the professional representative;

    (b) where the professional representative is no longer a national of a Member State, unless the President of the Office has granted an exemption under Article 89 (4) (b) of the Regulation;

    (c) where the professional representative no longer has his place of business or employment in the Community;

    (d) where the professional representative no longer possesses the entitlement referred to in the first sentence of Article 89 (2) (c) of the Regulation.

(3) The entry of a professional representative shall be suspended of the Office's own motion where his entitlement to represent natural or legal persons before the central industrial property office of the Member State as referred to in the fist sentence of Article 89 (2) (c) has been suspended.

(4) A person whose entry has been deleted shall, upon request pursuant to Article 89 (3) of the Regulation, be reinstated in the list of professional representatives if the conditions for deletion no longer exist.

(5) The Benelux Trade Mark Office and the central industrial property offices of the Member States concerned shall, where they are aware thereof, promptly inform the Office of any relevant events under paragraphs 2 and 3.

(6) The amendments of the list of professional representatives shall be published in the Official Journal of the Office.

Part H

Written communications and forms

RULE 79

COMMUNICATION IN WRITING OR BY OTHER MEANS

Applications for the registration of a Community trade mark as well as any **A11–81** other application provided for in the Regulation and all other communications addressed to the Office shall be submitted as follows:

    (a) by submitting a signed original of the document in question at the Office, such as by post, personal delivery, or by any other means; annexes to documents submitted need not be signed;

    (b) by transmitting a signed original by telecopier in accordance with Rule 80;

    (c) by telex or telegram in accordance with Rule 81;

    (d) by transmitting the contents of the communication by electronic means in accordance with Rule 82.

RULE 80

COMMUNICATION BY TELECOPIER

(1) Where an application for registration of a trade mark is submitted to the **A11–82** Office by telecopier and the application contains a reproduction of the mark pursuant to Rule 3 (2) which does not satisfy the requirements of that Rule, the

required number of original reproductions shall be submitted to the Office in accordance with Rule 79 (a). Where the reproductions are received by the Office within a period of one month from the date of the receipt of the telecopy by the Office, the application shall be deemed to have been received by the Office on the date on which the telecopy was received by the Office. Where the reproductions are received by the Office after the expiry of that period and the reproduction is necessary for the obtaining of a filing date, the application shall be deemed to have been received by the Office on the date on which the reproductions were received by the Office.

(2) Where a communication received by telecopier is incomplete or illegible, or where the Office has reasonable doubts as to the accuracy of the transmission, the Office shall inform the sender accordingly and shall invite him, within a period to be specified by the Office, to retransmit the original by telecopy or to submit the original in accordance with Rule 79 (a). Where this request is complied with within the period specified, the date of the receipt of the retransmission or of the original shall be deemed to be the date of the receipt of the original communication, provided that where the deficiency concerns the granting of a filing date for an application to register a trade mark, the provisions on the filing date shall apply. Where the request is not complied with within the period specified, the communication shall be deemed not to have been received.

(3) Any communication submitted to the Office by telecopier shall be considered to be duly signed if the reproduction of the signature appears on the printout produced by the telecopier.

(4) The President of the Office may determine additional requirements of communication by telecopier, such as the equipment to be used, technical details of communication, and methods of identifying the sender.

RULE 81

COMMUNICATION BY TELEX OR TELEGRAM

A11–83   (1) Where an application for registration of a trade mark is submitted to the Office by telex or by telegram and the application contains a reproduction of the mark pursuant to Rule 3 (2), Rule 80 (1) shall apply mutatis mutandis.

(2) Where a communication is submitted by telex or telegram, Rule 80 (2) shall apply mutatis mutandis.

(3) Where a communication is submitted by telex or telegram, the indication of the name of the sender shall be deemed equivalent to the signature.

RULE 82

COMMUNICATION BY ELECTRONIC MEANS

A11–84   (1) Where an application for registration of a trademark is submitted by electronic means and the application contains a reproduction of the mark pursuant to Rule 3 (2), Rule 80 (1) shall apply mutatis mutandis.

(2) Where a communication is sent by electronic means, Rule 80 (2) shall apply mutatis mutandis.

(3) Where a communication is sent to the Office by electronic means, the indication of the name of the sender shall be deemed to be equivalent to the signature.

(4) The President of the Office shall determine the requirements as to communication by electronic means, such as the equipment to be used, technical details of communication, and methods of identifying the sender.

RULE 83

FORMS

(1) The Office shall make available free of charge forms for the purpose of: **A11–85**

(a) filing an application for a Community trade mark;
(b) entering opposition to registration of a Community trade mark;
(c) applying for an amendment of an application or a registration, for correction of names and addresses and of mistakes and errors;
(d) applying for the registration of a transfer and the transfer form and transfer document provided for in Rule 31 (5);
(e) applying for the registration of a licence;
(f) applying for renewal of the registration of a Community trade mark;
(g) applying for revocation or for a declaration of invalidity of a Community trade mark;
(h) applying for restitutio in integrum;
(i) making an appeal;
(j) authorizing a representative, in the form of an individual authorization and in the form of a general authorization.

(2) The Office may make other forms available free of charge.
(3) The Office shall make available the forms referred to in paragraphs 1 and 2 in all the official languages of the Community.
(4) The Office shall place the forms at the disposal of the Benelux Trade Mark Office and the Member States' central industrial property offices free of charge.
(5) The Office may also make available the forms in machine-readable form.
(6) Parties to proceedings before the Office shall use the forms provided by the Office, or copies of these forms, or forms with the same content and format as these forms, such as forms generated by means of electronic data processing.
(7) Forms shall be completed in such a manner as to permit an automated input of the content into a computer, such as by character recognition or scanning.

Part I

Information of the public

RULE 84

REGISTER OF COMMUNITY TRADE MARKS

(1) The Register of Community Trade Marks may be maintained in the form of   **A11–86**
an electronic database.
(2) The Register of Community Trade Marks shall contain the following entries:

(a) the date of filing the application;
(b) the file number of the application;
(c) the date of the publication of the application;
(d) the name, the address and the nationality of the applicant and the State in which he is domiciled or has his seat or establishment;
(e) the name and business address of the representative, other than a representative falling within the first sentence of Article 88 (3) of the

Regulation; where there is more than one representative, only the name and business address of the first named representative, followed by the words and others, shall be recorded; where an association of representatives is appointed, only the name and address of the association shall be recorded;

(f) the reproduction of the mark, with indications as to its nature, unless it is a mark falling under Rule 3 (1); where the registration of the mark is in colour, the indication 'in colour' with an indication of the colour or colours making up the mark; where applicable, a description of the mark;

(g) an indication of the goods and services by their names, grouped according to the classes of the Nice Classification; each group shall be preceded by the number of the class of that classification to which that group of goods and services belongs and shall be presented in the order of the classes of that classification;

(h) particulars of claims of priority pursuant to Article 30 of the Regulation;

(i) particulars of claims of exhibition priority pursuant to Article 33 of the Regulation;

(j) particulars of claims of seniority of an earlier registered trade mark as referred to in Article 34 of the Regulation;

(k) a statement that the mark has become distinctive in consequence of the use which has been made of it, pursuant to Article 7(3) of the Regulation;

(l) a declaration by the applicant disclaiming any exclusive right to some element of the mark pursuant to Article 38(2) of the Regulation;

(m) an indication that the mark is a collective mark;

(n) the language in which the application was filed and the second language which the applicant has indicated in his application, pursuant to Article 115(3) of the Regulation;

(o) the date of registration of the mark in the Register and the registration number.

(3) The Register of Community Trade Marks shall also contain the following entries, each accompanied by the date of recording of such entry:

(a) changes in the name, the address or the nationality of the proprietor of a Community trade mark or in the State in which he is domiciled or has his seat or establishment;

(b) changes in the name or business address of the representative, other than a representative falling within Article 88 (3), first sentence, of the Regulation;

(c) when a new representative is appointed, the name and business address of that representative;

(d) alterations of the mark pursuant to Article 48 of the Regulation and corrections of mistakes and errors;

(e) notice of amendments to the regulations governing the use of the collective mark pursuant to Article 69 of the Regulation;

(f) particulars of claims of seniority of an earlier registered trade mark as referred to in Article 34 of the Regulation, pursuant to Article 35 of the Regulation;

(g) total or partial transfers pursuant to Article 17 of the Regulation;

(h) the creation or transfer of a right in rem pursuant to Article 19 of the Regulation and the nature of the right in rem;

(i) levy of execution pursuant to Article 20 of the Regulation and bankruptcy or like proceedings pursuant to Article 21 of the regulation;

(j) the grant or transfer of a licence pursuant to Article 22 of the Regulation and, where applicable, the type of licence pursuant to Rule 34;

(k) renewal of the registration pursuant to Article 47 of the Regulation, the date from which it takes effect and any restrictions pursuant to Article 47 (4) of the Regulation;

(l) a record of the determination of the expiry of the registration pursuant to Article 47 of the Regulation;

(m) a declaration of surrender by the proprietor of the mark pursuant to Article 49 of the Regulation;

(n) the date of submission of an application pursuant to Article 55 of the Regulation or of the filing of a counterclaim pursuant to Article 96 (4) of the Regulation for revocation or for a declaration of invalidity;

(o) the date and content of the decision on the application or counterclaim pursuant to Article 56 (6) or the third sentence of Article 96 (6) of the Regulation;

(p) a record of the receipt of a request for conversion pursuant to Article 109 (2) of the Regulation;

(q) the cancellation of the representative recorded pursuant to paragraph 2 (e);

(r) the cancellation of the seniority of a national mark;

(s) the modification or cancellation from the Register of the items referred to in subparagraphs (h), (i) and (j).

(4) The President of the Office may determine that items other than those referred to in paragraphs 2 and 3 shall be entered in the Register.

(5) The proprietor of the trade mark shall be notified of any change in the Register.

(6) The Office shall provide certified or uncertified extracts from the Register on request, on payment of a fee.

Part J

Community Trade Marks Bulletin and Official Journal of the Office

RULE 85

COMMUNITY TRADE MARKS BULLETIN

(1) The Community Trade Marks Bulletin shall be published in periodic **A11–87** editions. The Office may make available to the public editions of the Bulletin on CD-ROM or in any other machine-readable form.

(2) The Community Trade Marks Bulletin shall contain publications of applications and of entries made in the Register as well as other particulars relating to applications or registrations of trade marks whose publication is prescribed by the Regulation or by these Rules.

(3) Where particulars whose publication is prescribed in the Regulation or in these Rules are published in the Community Trade Marks Bulletin, the date of issue shown on the Bulletin shall be taken as the date of publication of the particulars.

(4) To the extent that the entries regarding the registration of a trade mark contain no changes as compared to the publication of the application, the publication of such entries shall be made by way of a reference to the particulars contained in the publication of the application.

(5) The elements of the application for a Community trade mark, as set out in Article 26 (1) of the Regulation as well as any other information the publication of which is prescribed in Rule 12 shall, where appropriate, be published in all the official languages of the Community.

(6) The Office shall take into account any translation submitted by the applicant. If the language of the application is not one of the languages of the

Office, the translation into the second language indicated by the applicant shall be communicated to the applicant. The applicant may propose changes to the translation within a period to be specified by the Office. If the applicant does not respond within this period or if the Office considers the proposed changes to be inappropriate, the translation proposed by the Office shall be published.

RULE 86

OFFICIAL JOURNAL OF THE OFFICE

A11–88 (1) The Official Journal of the Office shall be published in periodic editions. The Office may make available to the public editions of the Official Journal on CD-ROM or in any other machine-readable form.

(2) The Official Journal shall be published in the languages of the Office. The President of the Office may determine that certain items shall be published in all the official languages of the Community.

RULE 87

DATA BANK

A11–89 (1) The Office shall maintain an electronic data bank with the particulars of applications for registration of trade marks and entries in the Register. The Office may also make available the contents of this data bank on CD-ROM or in any other machine-readable form.

(2) The President of the Office shall determine the conditions of access to the data bank and the manner in which the contents of this data bank may be made available in machine-readable form, including the charges for these acts.

Part K

Inspection of files and keeping of files

RULE 88

PARTS OF THE FILE EXCLUDED FROM INSPECTION

A11–90 The parts of the file which shall be excluded from inspection pursuant to Article 84 (4) of the Regulation shall be:

   (a) documents relating to exclusion or objection pursuant to Article 132 of the Regulation;
   (b) draft decisions and opinions, and all other internal documents used for the preparation of decisions and opinions;
   (c) parts of the file which the party concerned showed a special interest in keeping confidential before the application for inspection of the files was made, unless inspection of such part of the file is justified by overriding legitimate interests of the party seeking inspection.

RULE 89

PROCEDURES FOR THE INSPECTION OF FILES

A11–91 (1) Inspection of the files of Community trade mark applications and of registered Community trade marks shall either be of the original document, or of copies thereof, or of technical means of storage if the files are stored in this way.

The means of inspection shall be determined by the President of the Office. The request for inspection of the files shall not be deemed to have been made until the required fee has been paid.

(2) Where inspection of the files of a Community trade mark application is requested, the request shall contain an indication and evidence to the effect that the applicant

(a) has consented to the inspection; or

(b) has stated that after the trade mark has been registered he will invoke the rights under it against the party requesting the inspection.

(3) Inspection of the files shall take place on the premises of the Office.

(4) On request, inspection of the files shall be effected by means of issuing copies of file documents. Such copies shall incur fees.

(5) The office shall issue on request certified or uncertified copies of the application for a Community trade mark or of those file documents of which copies may be issued pursuant to paragraph 4 upon payment of a fee.

RULE 90

COMMUNICATION OF INFORMATION CONTAINED IN THE FILES

Subject to the restrictions provided for in Article 84 of the Regulation and Rule **A11–92** 88, the Office may, upon request, communicate information from any file of a Community trade mark applied for or of a registered Community trade mark, subject to payment of a fee. However, the Office may require the exercise of the option to obtain inspection of the file itself should it deem this to be appropriate in view of the quantity of information to be supplied.

RULE 91

KEEPING OF FILES

(1) The Office shall keep the files relating to Community trade mark appli- **A11–93** cations and registered Community trade marks for at least five years from the end of the year in which:

(a) the application is rejected or withdrawn or is deemed to be withdrawn;

(b) the registration of the Community trade mark expires completely pursuant to Article 47 of the Regulation;

(c) the complete surrender of the Community trade mark is registered pursuant to Article 49 of the Regulation;

(d) the Community trade mark is completely removed from the Register pursuant to Article 56 (6) or Article 96 (6) of the Regulation.

(2) The President of the Office shall determine the form in which the files shall be kept.

Part L

Administrative cooperation

RULE 92

EXCHANGE OF INFORMATION AND COMMUNICATIONS BETWEEN THE OFFICE AND THE AUTHORITIES OF THE MEMBER STATES

(1) The Office and the central industrial property offices of the Member States **A11–94** shall, upon request, communicate to each other relevant information about the filing of applications for Community trade marks or national marks and about

proceedings relating to such applications and the marks registered as a result thereof. Such communications shall not be subject to the restrictions provided for in Article 84 of the Regulation.

(2) Communications between the Office and the courts or authorities of the Member States which arise out of the application of the Regulation or these Rules shall be effected directly between these authorities. Such communication may also be effected through the central industrial property offices of the Member States.

(3) Expenditure in respect of communications under paragraphs 1 and 2 shall be chargeable to the authority making the communications, which shall be exempt from fees.

RULE 93

INSPECTION OF FILES BY OR VIA COURTS OR AUTHORITIES OF THE MEMBER STATES

A11–95   (1) Inspection of files relating to Community trade marks applied for or registered Community trade marks by courts or authorities of the Member States be of the original documents or of copies thereof, otherwise Rule 89 shall not apply.

(2) Courts or Public Prosecutors' Offices of the Member States may, in the course of proceedings before them, open files or copies thereof transmitted by the Office to inspection by third parties. Such inspection shall be subject to Article 84 of the Regulation. The Office shall not charge any fee for such inspection.

(3) The Office shall, at the time of transmission of the files or copies thereof to the courts or Public Prosecutors' Offices of the Member States, indicate the restrictions to which the inspection of files relating to Community trade marks applied for or registered Community trade marks is subject pursuant to Article 84 of the Regulation and Rule 88.

Part M

Costs

RULE 94

APPORTIONMENT AND FIXING OF COSTS

A11–96   (1) Apportionment of costs pursuant to Article 81 (1) and (2) of the Regulation shall be dealt with in the decision on the opposition, the decision on the application for revocation or for a declaration of invalidity of a Community trade mark, or the decision on the appeal.

(2) Apportionment of costs pursuant to Article 81 (3) and (4) of the Regulation shall be dealt with in a decision on costs by the Opposition Division, the Cancellation Division or the Board of Appeal.

(3) A bill of costs, with supporting evidence, shall be attached to the request for the fixing of costs provided for in the first sentence of Article 81 (6) of the Regulation. The request shall be admissible only if the decision in respect of which the fixing of costs is required has become final. Costs may be fixed once their credibility is established.

(4) The request provided for in the second sentence of Article 81 (6) of the Regulation for a review of the decision of the registry on the fixing of costs, stating the reasons on which it is based, must be filed at the Office within one month after the date of notification of the awarding of costs. It shall not be deemed to be filed until the fee for reviewing the amount of the costs has been paid.

(5) The Opposition Division, the Cancellation Division or the Board of Appeal, as the case may be, shall take a decision on the request referred to in paragraph 4 without oral proceedings.

(6) The fees to be borne by the losing party pursuant to Article 81 (1) of the Regulation shall be limited to the fees incurred by the other party for opposition, for an application for revocation or for a declaration of invalidity of the Community trade mark and for appeal.

(7) Cost essential to the proceedings and actually incurred by the successful party shall be borne by the losing party in accordance with Article 81 (1) of the Regulation on the basis of the following maximum rates:

- (a) travel expenses of one party for the outward and return journey between the place of residence or the place of business and the place where oral proceedings are held or where evidence is taken, as follows:
  - (i) the cost of the first-class rail-fare including usual transport supplements where the total distance by rail does not exceed 800 km;
  - (ii) the cost of the tourist-class air-fare where the total distance by rail exceeds 800 km or the route includes a sea-crossing;
- (b) subsistence expenses by one party equal to the daily subsistence allowance for officials in grades A4 to A8 as laid down in Article 13 of Annex VII to the Staff Regulations of Officials of the European Communities;
- (c) travel expenses of representatives within the meaning of Article 89 (1) of the Regulation and of witnesses and of experts, at the rates provided for in subparagraph (a);
- (d) subsistence expenses of representatives within the meaning of Article 89 (1) of the Regulation and of witnesses and experts, at the rates provided for in subparagraph (b);
- (e) costs entailed in the taking of evidence in the form of examination of witnesses, opinions by experts or inspection up to ECU 300 per proceedings;
- (f) cost of representation, within the meaning of Article 89 (1) of the Regulation,
  - (i) of the opposing party in opposition proceedings: up to ECU 250;
  - (ii) of the applicant in opposition proceedings: up to ECU 250;
  - (iii) of the applicant in proceedings relating to revocation or invalidity of a Community trade mark: up to ECU 400;
  - (iv) of the proprietor of the trade mark in proceedings relating to revocation or invalidity of a Community trade mark: up to ECU 400;
  - (v) of the appellant in appeal proceedings: up to ECU 500;
  - (vi) of the defendant in appeal proceedings: up to ECU 500;

Where the taking of evidence in any of the abovementioned proceedings involves the examination of witnesses, opinions by experts or inspection, an additional amount shall be granted for representation costs of up to ECU 600 per proceedings;

- (g) where the successful party is represented by more than one representative within the meaning of Article 89 (1) of the Regulation, the losing party shall bear the costs referred to in subparagraphs (c), (d) and (f) for one such person only;
- (h) the losing party shall not be obliged to reimburse the successful party for any costs, expenses and fees other than those referred to in subparagraphs (a) to (g).

Part N

Languages

RULE 95

APPLICATIONS AND DECLARATIONS

A11–97   Without prejudice to Article 115 (5) of the Regulation,

    (a) any application or declaration relating to a Community trade mark application may be filed in the language used for filing the application for a Community trade mark or in the second language indicated by the applicant in his application;

    (b) any application or declaration relating to a registered Community trade mark may be filed in one of the languages of the Office. However, when the application is filed by using any of the forms provided by the Office pursuant to Rule 83, such forms may be used in any of the official languages of the Community, provided that the form is completed in one of the languages of the Office, as far as textual elements are concerned.

RULE 96

WRITTEN PROCEEDINGS

A11–98   (1) Without prejudice to Article 115 (4) and (7) of the Regulation, and unless otherwise provided for in these Rules, in written proceedings before the Office any party may use any language of the Office. If the language chosen is not the language of the proceedings, the party shall supply a translation into that language within one month from the date of the submission of the original document. Where the applicant for a Community trade mark is the sole party to proceedings before the Office and the language used for the filing of the application for the Community trade mark is not one of the languages of the Office, the translation may also be filed in the second language indicated by the applicant in his application.

(2) Unless otherwise provided for in these Rules, documents to be used in proceedings before the Office may be filed in any official language of the Community. Where the language of such documents is not the language of the proceedings the Office may require that a translation be supplied, within a period specified by it, in that language or, at the choice of the party to the proceeding, in any language of the Office.

RULE 97

ORAL PROCEEDINGS

A11–99   (1) Any party to oral proceedings before the Office may, in place of the language of proceedings, use one of the other official languages of the Community, on condition that he makes provision for interpretation into the language of proceedings. Where the oral proceedings are held in a proceeding concerning the application for registration of a trade mark, the applicant may use either the language of the application or the second language indicated by him.

(2) In oral proceedings concerning the application for registration of a trade mark, the staff of the Office may use either the language of the application or the second language indicated by the applicant. In all other oral proceedings, the staff of the Office may use, in place of the language of the proceedings, one of the other languages of the Office, on condition that the party or parties to the proceedings agree to such use.

(3) In the case of taking of evidence, any party to be heard, witness or expert who is unable to express himself adequately in the language of proceedings, may use any of the official languages of the Community. Should the taking of evidence be decided upon following a request by a party to the proceedings, parties to be heard, witnesses or experts who express themselves in languages other than the language of proceedings may be heard only if the party who made the request makes provision for interpretation into that language. In proceedings concerning the application for registration of a trade mark, in place of the language of the application, the second language indicated by the applicant may be used. In any proceedings with only one party the Office may on request of the party concerned permit derogations from the provisions in this paragraph.

(4) If the parties and Office so agree, any official language of the Community may be used in oral proceedings.

(5) The Office shall, if necessary, make provision at its own expense for interpretation into the language of proceedings, or, where appropriate, into its other languages, unless this interpretation is the responsibility of one of the parties to the proceedings.

(6) Statements by staff of the Office, by parties to the proceedings and by witnesses and experts, made in one of the languages of the Office during oral proceedings shall be entered in the minutes in the language employed. Statements made in any other language shall be entered in the language of proceedings. Amendments to the text of the application for or the registration of a Community trade mark shall be entered in the minutes in the language of proceedings.

RULE 98

CERTIFICATION OF TRANSLATIONS

(1) When a translation of any document is to be filed, the Office may require **A11–100** the filing, within a period to be specified by it, of a certificate that the translation corresponds to the original text. Where the certificate relates to the translation of a previous application pursuant to Article 30 of the Regulation, such period shall not be less than three months after the date of filing of the application. Where the certificate is not filed within that period, the document shall be deemed not to have been received.

(2) The President of the Office may determine the manner in which translations are certified.

RULE 99

LEGAL AUTHENTICITY OF TRANSLATIONS

In the absence of evidence to the contrary, the Office may assume that a **A11–101** translation corresponds to the relevant original text.

1135

Part O

Organization of the Office

RULE 100

ALLOCATION OF DUTIES

A11–102   (1) The President of the Office shall determine the examiners and their number, the members of the Opposition Divisions and Cancellation Divisions, and the members of the Administration of Trade Marks and Legal Division. He shall allocate duties to the examiners and the Divisions.

(2) The President of the Office may provide that examiners may also be members of the Opposition Divisions, Cancellation Divisions, and the Administration of Trade Marks and Legal Division, and that members of these Divisions may also be examiners.

(3) In addition to the responsibilities vested in them under the Regulation, the President of the Office may allocate further duties to the examiners and the members of the Opposition Divisions, Cancellation Divisions and the Administration of Trade Marks and Legal Division.

(4) The President of the Office may entrust to other members of the staff of the Office who are not examiners or members of any of the Divisions mentioned in paragraph 1 the execution of individual duties falling to the examiners, Opposition Divisions, Cancellation Divisions or the Administration of Trade Marks and Legal Division and involving no special difficulties.

TITLE XII

RECIPROCITY

RULE 101

PUBLICATION OF RECIPROCITY

A11–103   (1) If necessary, the President of the Office shall request the Commission to enquire whether a State which is not party to the Paris Convention or to the Agreement establishing the World Trade Organization accords reciprocal treatment within the meaning of Article 5 (1) (d), Article 5 (3) and Article 29 (5) of the Regulation.

(2) If the Commission determines that reciprocal treatment in accordance with paragraph 1 is accorded, it shall publish a communication to this effect in the Official Journal of the European Communities.

(3) Article 5 (1) (d), Article 5 (3) and Article 29 (5) of the Regulation shall take effect for the nationals of the States concerned from the date of publication in the Official Journal of the European Communities of the communication referred to in paragraph 2, unless the communications states an earlier date from which it is applicable. They shall cease to be effective from the date of publication in the Official Journal of the European Communities of a communication of the Commission to the effect that reciprocal treatment is no longer accorded, unless the communication states an earlier date from which it is applicable.

(4) Communications referred to in paragraphs 2 and 3 shall also be published in the Official Journal of the Office.

Article 2

TRANSITIONAL PROVISIONS

(1) Any application for registration of a Community trade mark filed within **A11–104** three months prior to the date determined pursuant to Article 143 (3) of the Regulation shall be marked by the Office with the filing date determined pursuant to that provision and with the actual date of receipt of the application.

(2) With regard to the application, the priority period of six months provided for in Articles 29 and 33 of the Regulation shall be calculated from the date determined pursuant to Article 143 (3) of the Regulation.

(3) The Office may issue a receipt to the applicant prior to the date determined pursuant to Article 143 (3) of the Regulation.

(4) The Office may examine the applications prior to the date determined pursuant to Article 143 (3) of the Regulation and communicate with the applicant with a view to remedying any deficiencies prior to that date. Any decisions with regard to such applications may be taken only after that date.

(5) With regard to the application, the Office shall not carry out any search pursuant to Article 39 (1) of the Regulation, regardless of whether or not a priority was claimed for such application pursuant to Articles 29 or 33 of the Regulation.

(6) Where the date of receipt of an application for the registration of a Community trade mark by the Office, by the central industrial property office of a Member State or by the Benelux Trade Mark Office is before the commencement of the three months period specified in Article 143 (4) of the Regulation the application shall be deemed not to have been filed. The application shall be informed accordingly and the application shall be sent back to him.

Article 3

ENTRY INTO FORCE

This Regulation shall enter into force on the seventh day following that of its **A11–105** publication in the Official Journal of the European Communities.

This Regulation shall be binding in its entirety and directly applicable in all Member States.
Done at Brussels, December 13, 1995.

APPENDIX 12

Commission Regulation 2869/95 of December 13, 1995

On the fees payable to the Office for Harmonization in the Internal Market (Trade Marks and Designs)

([1995] O.J. L303/33)

THE COMMISSION OF THE EUROPEAN COMMUNITIES,

A12–01 Having regard to the Treaty establishing the European Community,

Having regard to Council Regulation (EC) No 40/94 of 20 December 1993 on the Community trade mark, as amended by Regulation (EC) No 3288/94, and in particular Article 139 thereof,

Having regard to Commission Regulation (EC) No 2868/95 of 13 December 1995, implementing Council Regulation (EC) No 40/94 on the Community trade mark (3),

Whereas Article 139 (3) of Regulation (EC) No 40/94 (hereinafter 'the Regulation') provides that the fees regulations shall be adopted in accordance with the procedure laid down in Article 141 of the Regulation;

Whereas Article 139 (1) of the Regulation provides that the fees regulations shall determine in particular the amount of the fees and the ways in which they are to be paid;

Whereas Article 139 (2) of the Regulation provides that the amounts of the fees shall be fixed at such a level as to ensure that the revenue in respect thereof is in principle sufficient for the budget of the Office for Harmonization in the Internal Market (trade marks and designs) ('the Office') to be balanced;

Whereas, however, in the Office's start-up phase, balance can be achieved only if there is a subsidy from the general budget of the European Communities, in accordance with Article 134 (3) of the Regulation;

Whereas the basic fee for the application for a Community trade mark shall include the amount which the Office must pay to each central industrial property office of the Member States for each search report provided by such offices in accordance with Article 39 (4) of the Regulation;

Whereas to ensure the necessary flexibility, the President of the Office ('the President') should be empowered, subject to certain conditions, to lay down the charges which may be payable to the Office in respect of services it may render, the charges for access to the Office's data bank and the making available of the contents of this data bank in machine-readable form, and to set charges for the sale of its publications;

Whereas, in order to facilitate the payment of fees and charges, the President should be empowered to authorize methods of payment which are additional to those explicitly provided for in this Regulation;

Whereas it is appropriate that the fees and charges payable to the Office should be fixed in the same currency unit as is used for the budget of the Office;

Whereas the budget of the Office is fixed in ecus;

Whereas, moreover, the fixing of these amounts in ecus avoids discrepancies that may result from exchange rate variations;

Whereas payments in cash should be made in the currency of the Member State where the Office has its seat;

Whereas the measures envisaged in this Regulation are in accordance with the opinion of the Committee established under Article 141 of the Regulation,

HAS ADOPTED THIS REGULATION:

Article 1

GENERAL

The following shall be levied in accordance with this Regulation:

A12–02

    (a) fees to be paid to the Office as provided for in the Regulation and in Regulation (EC) No 2868/95;

Article 2

FEES PROVIDED FOR IN THE REGULATION AND REGULATION (EC) NO 2868/95

The fees to be paid to the Office under Article 1 (a) shall be as follows:

A12–03

1.	Basic fee for the application for an individual mark (Article 26(2); Rule 4(a))	975 ecu
2.	Fee for each class of goods and services exceeding three for an individual mark (Article 26(2); Rule 4 (b))	200 ecu
3.	Basic fee for the application for a collective mark (Articles 26(2) and 64(3); Rules 4(a) and 42)	1675 ecu
4.	Fee for each class of goods and services exceeding three for a collective mark (Article 26(2) and 64(3); Rules 4(b) and 42)	400 ecu
5.	Opposition fee (Article 42(3); Rule 18(1))	350 ecu
6.	Fee for the alteration of the representation of a trade mark (point 1 of Article 140(2) and Article 44(2); Rule 13(2))	200 ecu
7.	Basic fee for the registration of an individual mark (Article 45; Rule 23(1)(a))	1100 ecu
8.	Fee for each class of goods and services exceeding three for an individual mark (Article 45; Rule 23(1)(b))	200 ecu
9.	Basic fee for the registration of a collective mark (Articles 45 and 64(3); Rules 23(1)(a) and 42)	2200 ecu
10.	Fee for each class of goods and services exceeding three for a collective mark (Articles 45 and 64 (3), Rules 23(1)(b) and 42)	400 ecu
11.	Additional fee for the late payment of the registration fee (point 2 Article 140(2), Rule 23(3))	25% of the belated registration fee, subject to a maximum of 750 ecu
12.	Basic fee for the renewal for an individual mark (Article 47(1), Rule 30(2)(a))	2500 ecu

13. Fee for each class of goods and services exceeding three for an individual mark (Article 47(1), Rule 30(2)(b))	Fee for each class of goods and services exceeding three for an individual mark (Article 47(1), Rule 30(2)(b))
14. Basic fee for the renewal for a collective mark (Articles 47(1) and 64(3), Rules 30(2)(a) and 42)	5000 ecu
15. Fee for each class of goods and services exceeding three for a collective mark (Articles 47(1) and 64(3), Rules 30(2)(b) and 42)	1000 ecu
16. Additional fee for the late payment of the renewal fee or the late submission of the request for renewal (Article 47(3), Rule 30(2)(c))	25% of the belated renewal fee, subject to a maximum of 1500 ecu
17. Fee for the application for revocation or for a declaration of invalidity (Article 55(2), Rule 39(2))	700 ecu
18. Appeal fee (Article 59, Rule 49(1))	800 ecu
19. Fee for *restitutio in intergrum* (Article 78(3))	200 ecu
20. Fee for the conversion of a mark into a national trade mark application (Article 109(1), Rule 45(2))	200 ecu
21. Fee for the recording of the whole or partial transfer of an application for a Community trade mark (Article 24 and point 4 of Article 140(2); Rule 31(4) and (8))	200 ecu per entry, but, where multiple requests are submitted in the same application or at the same time, not to exceed a total of 1000 ecu.
22. Fee for the registration of the whole or partial transfer of a registered Community trade mark (point 4 of Article 140(2); Rule 31(4))	200 ecu per registration, but, where multiple requests are submitted in the same application or at the same time, not to exceed a total of 1000 ecu

23. Fee for the registration of a licence or another right in respect of a registered Community trade mark (point 5 of Article 140(2), Rule 33(1)) or an application for a Community trade mark (point 6 of Article 140(2), Rule 33(4):
   a. grant of a licence
   b. transfer of a licence
   c. creation of a right in rem
   d. transfer of a right in rem
   e. levy of execution
	200 ecu per registration, but, where multiple requests are submitted in the same application or at the same time, not to exceed a total of 1000 ecu

24. Fee for the cancellation of the registration of a licence or other right (point 7 of Article 140(2), Rule 35(3))	200 ecu per cancellation, but, where multiple requests lare submitted in the same application or at the same time, not to exceed a total of 1000 ecu
25. Fee for the alteration of a registered Community trade mark (point 8 of Article 140(2), Rule 25(2))	200 ecu

26. Fee for the issue of a copy of the application for a Community trade mark (point 12 of Article 140(2), Rule 89(5)), a copy of the certificate of registration (point 3 of Article 140(2), Rule 24(2), or an extract from the register (point 9 of Article 140(2), Rule 84 (6))

    (a) uncertified copy or extract   10 ecu

    (b) certified copy or extract   30 ecu

27. Fee for the inspection of the files (point 10 of Article   30 ecu 140 (2) No. 10, Rule 89(1))

28. Fee for the issue of copies of file documents (point 11 of Article 140(2) no 11, Rule 89(5))

    (a) uncertified copy   10 ecu

    (b) certified copy   30 ecu

        plus per page, exceeding 10   1 ecu

29. Fee for the communication of information in a file   10 ecu (point 13 of Article 140(2), Rule 90)

    plus per page, exceeding 10   1 ecu

30. Fee for the review of the determination of the pro-   100 ecu ceral costs to be refunded (point 14 of Article 140(2), Rule 94(4))

Article 3

CHARGES LAID DOWN BY THE PRESIDENT

1. The President shall lay down the amount to be charged for any services **A12–04** rendered by the Office other than those specified in Article 2.

2. The President shall lay down the amount to be charged for the Community Trade Marks Bulletin and the Official Journal of the Office as well as any other publications issued by the Office.

3. The amounts of the charges shall be laid down in ecus.

4. The amounts of the charges laid down by the President in accordance with paragraphs 1 and 2 shall be published in the Official Journal of the Office.

Article 4

DUE DATE FOR FEES AND CHARGES

1. Fees and charges in respect of which the due date is not specified in the **A12–05** Regulation or in Regulation No 2868/95 shall be due on the date of receipt of the request for the service for which the fee or the charge is incurred.

2. The President may decide not to make services mentioned in paragraph 1 dependent upon the advance payment of the corresponding fees or charges.

Article 5

PAYMENT OF FEES AND CHARGES

1. Fees and charges due to the Office shall be paid   **A12–06**

    (a) by payment or transfer to a bank account held by the Office,

(b) by delivery or remittance of cheques made payable to the Office, or

(c) in cash.

2. The President may allow methods of payment other than those set out in paragraph 1, in particular by means of deposits in current accounts held with the Office.

3. Determinations made pursuant to paragraph 2 shall be published in the Official Journal of the Office.

Article 6

CURRENCIES

A12–07 1. Payments or transfers to a bank account referred to in Article 5 (1) (a), by delivery or remittance of cheques referred to in Article 5 (1) (b) or any other method of payment allowed by the President pursuant to Article 5 (2) shall be made in ecus.

2. The payments in cash referred to in Article 5 (1) (c) shall be made in the currency of the Member State where the Office has its seat. The President shall determine the ecus equivalents in that currency on the basis of the exchange rate in force, which are fixed daily by the Commission and published in the Official Journal of the European Communities in accordance with Council Regulation (EC) No 3320/94 (4).

Article 7

PARTICULARS CONCERNING PAYMENT

A12–08 1. Every payment must indicate the name of the person making the payment and must contain the necessary information to enable the Office to establish immediately the purpose of the payment. In particular, the following information shall be provided:

(a) when the application fee is paid, the purpose of the payment, namely 'application fee';

(b) when the registration fee is paid, the file number of the application which is the basis for the registration and the purpose of the payment, namely 'registration fee';

(c) when the opposition fee is paid, the file number of the application and the name of the applicant for the Community trade mark against which opposition is entered, and the purpose of the payment, namely 'opposition fee';

(d) when the revocation fee and the invalidity fee are paid, the registration number and the name of the proprietor of the Community trade mark against which the application is directed, and the purpose of the payment, namely 'revocation fee' or 'invalidity fee'.

2. If the purpose of the payment cannot immediately be established, the Office shall require the person making the payment to notify it in writing of this purpose within such period as it may specify. If the person does not comply with this request in due time, the payment shall be considered not to have been made. The amount which has been paid shall be refunded.

Article 8

DEEMED DATE OF PAYMENT

1. The date on which any payment shall be considered to have been made to **A12–09** the Office shall be as follows:

    (a) in the cases referred to in Article 5 (1) (a), the date on which the amount of the payment or of the transfer is actually entered in a bank account held by the Office;

    (b) in the case referred to in Article 5 (1) (b), the date of the receipt of the cheque at the Office, provided that the cheque is met;

    (c) in the cases referred to in Article 5 (1) (c), the date of receipt of the amount of the cash payment.

2. Where the President allows, in accordance with the provisions of Article 5 (2), other methods of paying fees than those set out in Article 5 (1), he shall also lay down the date on which such payments shall be considered to have been made.

3. Where, under the provisions of paragraphs 1 and 2, payment of a fee is not considered to have been made until after the expiry of the period in which it was due, it shall be considered that this period has been observed if evidence is provided to the Office that the person who made the payment—

    (a) in a Member State, within the period within which the payment should have been made:

        (i) effected the payment through a banking establishment;

        (ii) duly gave an order to a banking establishment to transfer the amount of the payment; or

        (iii) dispatched at a post office or otherwise a letter bearing the address of the Office and containing a cheque within the meaning of Article 5 (1) (b), provided that the cheque is met;
           and—

    (b) paid a surcharge of 10% on the relevant fee or fees, but not exceeding ECU 200; no surcharge is payable if a condition according to sub-paragraph (a) has been fulfilled not later than 10 days before the expiry of the period for payment.

4. The Office may request the person who made the payment to produce evidence as to the date on which a condition according to paragraph 3 (a) was fulfilled and, where required, to pay the surcharge referred to in paragraph 3 (b), within a period to be specified by it. If the person fails to comply with this request or if the evidence is insufficient, or if the required surcharge is not paid in due time, the period for payment shall be considered not to have been observed.

Article 9

INSUFFICIENCY OF THE AMOUNT PAID

1. A time limit for payment shall, in principle, be considered to have been **A12–10** observed only if the full amount of the fee has been paid in due time. If the fee is not paid in full, the amount which has been paid shall be refunded after the period for payment has expired.

2. The Office may, however, in so far as this is possible within the time remaining before the end of the period, give the person making the payment the

opportunity to pay the amount lacking or, where this is considered justified, overlook any small amounts lacking without prejudice to the rights of the person making the payment.

Article 10

REFUND OF INSIGNIFICANT AMOUNTS

A12–11 1. Where an excessive sum is paid to cover a fee or a charge, the excess shall not be refunded if the amount is insignificant and the party concerned has not expressly requested a refund. The President shall determine what constitutes an insignificant amount.

2. Determinations by the President pursuant to paragraph 1 shall be published in the Official Journal of the Office.

Article 11

ENTRY INTO FORCE

A12–12 This Regulation shall enter into force on the seventh day following its publication in the Official Journal of the European Communities.

This Regulation shall be binding in is entirety and directly applicable in all Member States.

Done at Brussels, 13 December 1995.

APPENDIX 13

Commission Regulation 216/96 of February 5, 1996

Laying down the rules of procedure of the Boards of Appeal of the Office for Harmonization in the Internal Market (Trade Marks and Designs)

([1996] O.J. L28/11)

THE COMMISSION OF THE EUROPEAN COMMUNITIES,

Having regard to the Treaty establishing the European Community; **A13–01**

Having regard to Council Regulation (EC) No 40/94 of 20 December 1994 on the Community trade mark, as amended by Regulation (EC) No 3288/94, and in particular Article 140(3) thereof;

Whereas Regulation (EC) No 40/94 (hereinafter 'the Regulation') creates a new trade mark system allowing a trade mark having effect throughout the Community to be obtained on the basis of an application to the Office for Harmonization in the Internal Market (Trade Marks and Designs) ('the Office');

Whereas for this purpose the Regulation contains in particular the necessary provisions for a procedure leading to the registration of a Community trade marks, as well as for the administration of Community trade marks, for appeals against decisions of the Office and for proceedings in relation to revocation or invalidity of a Community trade mark;

Whereas under Article 130 of the Regulation, the Boards of Appeal are to be responsible for deciding on appeals from decisions of the examiners, the Opposition Divisions, the Administration of Trade Marks and Legal Division and the Cancellation Divisions;

Whereas Title VII of the Regulation contains basic principles regarding appeals against decisions of examiners, the Opposition Divisions, the Administration of Trade Marks and Legal Division and the Cancellation Divisions;

Whereas Title X of Commission Regulation (EC) No 2868/95 of 13 December 1995 implementing Council Regulation No 40/94 on the Community Trade Mark (3) contains implementing rules to Title VII of the Regulation;

Whereas this Regulation supplements those other rules, in particular as regards the organization of the Boards and the oral procedure;

Whereas before the beginning of each working year a scheme should be established for the distribution of business between the Boards of Appeal by an Authority established for that purpose; whereas to this end the said Authority should apply objective criteria such as classes of products and services or initial letters of the names of applicants;

Whereas to facilitate the handling and disposal of appeals, a rapporteur should be designated for each case, who should be responsible inter alia for preparing communications with the parties and drafting decisions;

Whereas the parties to proceedings before the Boards of Appeal may not be in a position or may not be willing to bring questions of general relevance to a pending case to the attention of the Boards of Appeal; whereas, therefore, the Boards of Appeal should have the power, of their own motion or pursuant to a request by the President, to invite the President of the Office, to submit comments on questions of general interest in relation to a case pending before the Boards of Appeal;

Whereas the measures provided for in this Regulation are in accordance with the opinion of the Committee established under Article 141 of the Regulation;

HAS ADOPTED THIS REGULATION:

Article 1

ALLOCATION OF DUTIES AND AUTHORITY COMPETENT TO ALLOCATE

A13–02 1. Before the beginning of each working year, duties shall be allocated to the Boards of Appeal according to objective criteria, and the members of each of the Boards and their alternates shall be designated. Any member of a Board of Appeal may be designated for several Boards of Appeal as a member or an alternate. These measures may, where necessary, be amended during the working year in question.

2. The measures referred to in paragraph 1 shall be taken by an Authority composed of the President of the Office as Chairman, the Vice-President of the Office responsible for the Boards of Appeal, the Chairmen of the Boards of Appeal and three other members of the Boards of Appeal elected by the full membership of those Boards, except the Chairmen, for the working year in question. The Authority may validly deliberate only if at least five of its members are present, including the President or the Vice-President of the Office and two Chairmen of Boards of Appeal. Decisions shall be taken by majority vote. In the event of a tie, the vote of the Chairman shall be decisive. The Authority may lay down its internal rules of procedure.

3. The Authority provided for in paragraph 2 shall decide on conflicts regarding the allocation of duties among different Boards of Appeal.

4. Until more than three Boards of Appeal have been set up, the Authority referred to in paragraph 2 shall consist of the President of the Office, who shall act as Chairman, the Vice-President of the Office responsible for the Boards of Appeal, the Chairman or Chairmen of the Boards of Appeal which have already been set up and one other member of the Boards of Appeal elected by their full membership of the Board, except the Chairman or Chairmen, for the working year in question. The Authority may validly deliberate only if at least three of its members are present, including the President or the Vice-President of the Office.

Article 2

REPLACEMENT OF MEMBERS

A13–03 1. Reasons for replacement by alternates shall in particular include leave, sickness, inescapable commitments and the grounds of exclusion set out in Article 132 of the Regulation.

2. Any member asking to be replaced by an alternate shall without delay inform the Chairman of the Board concerned of his unavailability.

Article 3

EXCLUSION AND OBJECTION

A13–04 1. If a Board has knowledge of a possible reason for exclusion or objection under Article 132 (3) of the Regulation which does not originate from a member himself or from any party to the proceedings, the procedure of Article 132 (4) of the Regulation shall be applied.

2. The member concerned shall be invited to present his comments as to whether there is a reason for exclusion or objection.

3. Before a decision is taken on the action to be taken pursuant to Article 132 (4) of the Regulation, there shall be no further proceedings in the case.

Article 4

RAPPORTEURS

1. The Chairman of each Board shall for each appeal designate a member of **A13–05** his Board, or himself, as rapporteur.

2. The rapporteur shall carry out a preliminary study of the appeal. He may prepare communications to the parties subject to the direction of the Chairman of the Board. Communications shall be signed by the rapporteur on behalf of the Board.

3. The rapporteur shall prepare internal meetings of the Board and the oral proceedings.

4. The rapporteur shall draft decisions.

Article 5

REGISTRIES

1. Registries shall be established for the Boards of Appeal. Registrars shall be **A13–06** responsible for the discharge of the functions of the Registries. One of the Registrars may be designated Senior Registrar.

2. The Authority provided for in Article 1 (2) may entrust to the Registrars the performance of functions which involve no legal or technical difficulties, particularly with regard to representation, the submission of translations, inspection of files and notifications.

3. The Registrar shall submit to the Chairman of the Board concerned a report on the admissibility of each newly-filed appeal.

4. Minutes of oral proceedings and of the taking of evidence shall be drawn up by the Registrar or, if the President of the Office has agreed thereto, such other officer of the Office as the Chairman of the Board may designate.

Article 6

CHANGE IN THE COMPOSITION OF A BOARD

1. If the composition of a Board is changed after oral proceedings, the parties **A13–07** to the proceedings shall be informed that, at the request of any party, fresh oral proceedings shall be held before the Board in its new composition. Fresh oral proceedings shall also be held if so requested by the new member and if the other members of the Board have given their agreement.

2. The new member shall be bound to the same extent as the other members by an interim decision which has already been taken.

3. If, when a Board has already reached a final decision, a member is unable to act, he shall not be replaced by an alternate. If the Chairman is unable to act, then the member of the Board concerned having the longer service on the Board, or where members have the same length of service, the older member, shall sign the decision on behalf of the Chairman.

1147

Article 7

JOINDER OF APPEAL PROCEEDINGS

A13–08   1. If several appeals are filed against a decision, those appeals shall be considered in the same proceedings.
2. If appeals are filed against separate decisions and all the appeals are designated to be examined by one Board having the same composition, that Board may deal with those appeals in joined proceedings with the consent of the parties.

Article 8

REMISSION TO THE DEPARTMENT OF FIRST INSTANCE

A13–09   Where the proceedings of the department of first instance whose decision is the subject of an appeal are vitiated by fundamental deficiencies, the Board shall set aside the decision and, unless there are reasons for not doing so, remit the case to that instance or decide the matter itself.

Article 9

ORAL PROCEEDINGS

A13–10   1. If oral proceedings are to take place, the Board shall ensure that the parties have provided all relevant information and documents before the hearing.
2. The Board may, when issuing the summons to attend oral proceedings, add a communication drawing attention to matters which seem to be of special significance, or to the fact that certain questions appear no longer to be contentious, or containing other observations that may help to concentrate on essentials during the oral proceedings.
3. The Board shall ensure that the case is ready for decision at the conclusion of the oral proceedings, unless there are special reasons to the contrary.

Article 10

COMMUNICATIONS TO THE PARTIES

A13–11   If a Board deems it expedient to communicate with the parties regarding a possible appraisal of substantive or legal matters, such communication shall be made in such a way as not to imply that the Board is in any way bound by it.

Article 11

COMMENTS ON QUESTIONS OF GENERAL INTEREST

A13–12   The Board may, on its own initiative or at the written, reasoned request of the President of the Office, invite him to comment in writing or orally on questions of general interest which arise in the course of proceedings pending before it.

The parties shall be entitled to submit their observations on the President's comments.

Article 12

DELIBERATIONS PRECEDING DECISIONS

The rapporteur shall submit to the other members of the Board a draft of the **A13–13** decision to be taken and shall set a reasonable time-limit within which to oppose it or to ask for changes. The Board shall meet to deliberate on the decision to be taken if it appears that the members of a Board are not all of the same opinion. Only members of the Board shall participate in the deliberations; the Chairman of the Board concerned may, however, authorize other officers such as registrars or interpreters to attend. Deliberations shall be secret.

Article 13

ORDER OF VOTING

1. During the deliberations between members of a Board, the opinion of the **A13–14** rapporteur shall be heard first, and, if the rapporteur is not the Chairman, the Chairman last.
2. If voting is necessary, votes shall be taken in the same sequence, save that if the Chairman is also the rapporteur, be shall vote last. Abstentions shall not be permitted.

Article 14

ENTRY INTO FORCE

This Regulation shall enter into force the third day following its publication in **A13–15** the Official Journal of the European Communities.

This Regulation shall be binding in its entirety and directly applicable in all Member States.
Done at Brussels, February 5, 1996.

APPENDIX 14

The Community Trade Mark Regulations 1996

S.I. 1996 No. 1908

A14–01 The Secretary of State, in exercise of powers confected by section 52 of the Trade Marks Act 1994 hereby makes the following Regulations:—

A14–02 **1.**—(1) These Regulations may be cited as the Community Trade Mark Regulations 1996 and come into force on 14th August 1996.

(2) These Regulations extend to England and Wales, Scotland and Northern Ireland.

Interpretation

A14–03 **2.** In these Regulations—

"the Act" means the Trade Marks Act 1994, and references to a section are, unless the context otherwise requires, to sections of that Act;

"the Community Trade Mark Regulation" means Council Regulation (EC) No. 40/94 of 20th December 1993 on the Community trade mark;

"the Rules" means the Trade Marks Rules 1994 and references to a rule shall, unless the context otherwise requires, be construed accordingly.

Determination *a posteriori* of invalidity and liability to revocation

A14–04 **3.**—(1) Where the proprietor of a Community trade mark claims the seniority of a registered trade mark which has been removed from the register under section 43 or has been surrendered under section 45, application may be made to the registrar or to the court by any person for a declaration that, if the registered trade mark had not been so removed or surrendered, it would have been liable to be revoked under section 46 or declared invalid under section 47.

(2) Where a registered trade mark has been surrendered in respect of some only of the goods or services for which it is registered, paragraph (1) above shall apply in relation to those goods or services.

(3) The provisions of section 46 or 47 (as the case may be), sections 72, 74 and 76, with necessary modifications, apply in relation to an application under paragraph (1) above.

(4) The provisions of rule 31, with necessary modifications, apply in relation to the procedure on applications made under paragraph (1) above.

Groundless threats of infringement proceedings

A14–05 **4.** The provisions of section 21 apply in relation to a Community trade mark as in relation to a registered trade mark.

Privilege for communications with professional representatives

A14–06 **5.** The provisions of section 87 (privilege for communications between a person and his registered trade mark agent) apply in relation to persons on the list of professional representatives maintained in pursuance of Article 89 of the Community Trade Mark Regulation ("professional representatives") and for this purpose the definition of "trade mark agent" in subsection (3) of that section includes professional representatives.

Importation of infringing goods, material or articles

6. The provisions of section 89 (infringing goods, material or articles may be **A14–07** treated as prohibited goods) section 90 and section 91 of the Act (power of Commissioners of Customs and Excise to disclose information) apply in relation to goods which are, in relation to a Community trade mark, infringing goods, material or articles, and for the purposes of those provisions—

  (a) references to a registered trade mark shall include a Community trade mark;
  (b) the Trade Marks (Customs) Regulations 1994 shall apply in relation to notices given under the provisions of section 89.

Offences and forfeiture

7. The provisions of section 92 (unauthorised use of trade mark, etc., in **A14–08** relation to goods), section 93 (enforcement function of local weights and measures authority), section 97 (forfeiture: England and Wales) and section 98 (forfeiture: Scotland) apply in relation to a Community trade mark and for the purposes of those provisions—

  (a) references to a registered trade mark shall include a Community trade mark;
  (b) references to goods in respect of which a trade mark is registered shall include goods in respect of which a Community trade mark is registered.

Falsely representing trade mark as a Community trade mark

8.—(1) It is an offence for a person—   **A14–09**

  (a) falsely to represent that a mark is a Community trade mark, or
  (b) to make a false representation as to the goods or services for which a Community trade mark is registered,

knowing or having reason to believe that the representation is false.

(2) A person guilty of an offence under this regulation is liable on summary conviction to a fine not exceeding level 3 on the standard scale.

Designation of Community Trade Mark courts

9. For the purposes of Article 91 of the Community Trade Mark Regulation, **A14–10** the following courts are designated as Community trade mark courts—

  (a) in England and Wales and Northern Ireland, the High Court, and
  (b) in Scotland, the Court of Session.

Conversion

10.—(1) The provisions of this Regulation apply where the applicant for or the **A14–11** proprietor of a Community trade mark requests the conversion of his Community trade mark application or Community trade mark into an application for registration of a trade mark under the Act ("conversion application") pursuant to Article 108 of the Community Trade Mark Regulation.

(2) Where the registrar decides that a request for a conversion application is admissible pursuant to Article 108, it shall be treated as an application for registration of a trade mark under the Act.

(3) A decision of the registrar in relation to a conversion application shall be treated as a decision of the registrar under the Act.

Application of Trade Marks Rules 1994

A14–12   **11.** Except as otherwise provided, or where their application would be inconsistent with the provisions of these Regulations, the Rules shall apply, with the necessary modifications, to these Regulations.

PART V

OTHER EUROPEAN MATERIALS

Council Regulation 2081/92 of July 14, 1992

On the protection of geographical indications and designations of origin for agricultural products and foodstuffs

([1992] O.J. L208/1)

THE COUNCIL OF THE EUROPEAN COMMUNITIES,   **A15–01**

Having regard to the Treaty establishing the European Economic Community, and in particular Article 43,

Having regard to the proposal from the Commission,

Having regard to the opinion of the European Parliament,

Having regard to the opinion of the Economic and Social Committee,

Whereas the production, manufacture and distribution of agricultural products and foodstuffs play an important role in the Community economy;

Whereas, as part of the adjustment of the common agricultural policy the diversification of agricultural production should be encouraged so as to achieve a better balance between supply and demand on the markets; whereas the promotion of products having certain characteristics could be of considerable benefit to the rural economy, in particular to less-favoured or remote areas, by improving the incomes of farmers and by retaining the rural population in these areas;

Whereas, moreover, it has been observed in recent years that consumers are tending to attach greater importance to the quality of foodstuffs rather than to quantity; whereas this quest for specific products generates a growing demand for agricultural products or foodstuffs with an identifiable geographical origin;

Whereas in view of the wide variety of products marketed and of the abundance of information concerning them provided, consumers must, in order to be able to make the best choice, be given clear and succinct information regarding the origin of the product;

Whereas the labelling of agricultural products and foodstuffs is subject to the general rules laid down in Council Directive 79/112/EEC of 18 December 1978 on the approximation of the laws of the Member States relating to the labelling, presentation and advertising of foodstuffs; whereas, in view of their specific nature, additional special provisions should be adopted for agricultural products and foodstuffs from a specified geographical area;

Whereas the desire to protect agricultural products or foodstuffs which have an identifiable geographical origin has led certain Member States to introduce "registered designations of origin"; whereas these have proved successful with producers, who have secured higher incomes in return for a genuine effort to improve quality, and with consumers, who can purchase high quality products with guarantees as to the method of production and origin;

Whereas, however, there is diversity in the national practices for implementing registered designations or origin and geographical indications; whereas a Community approach should be envisaged; whereas a framework of Community rules on protection will permit the development of geographical indications and designations of origin since, by providing a more uniform approach, such a framework will ensure fair competition between the producers of products bearing such indications and enchance the credibility of the products in the consumers' eyes;

Whereas the planned rules should take account of existing Community legislation on wines and spirit drinks, which provide for a higher level of protection;

Whereas the scope of this Regulation is limited to certain agricultural products and foodstuffs for which a link between product or foodstuff characteristics and geographical origin exists; whereas, however, this scope could be enlarged to encompass other products or foodstuffs;

Whereas existing practices make it appropriate to define two different types of geographical description, namely protected geographical indications and protected designations of origin;

Whereas an agricultural product or foodstuff bearing such an indication must meet certain conditions set out in a specification;

Whereas to enjoy protection in every Member State geographical indications and designations of origin must be registered at Community level; whereas entry in a register should also provide information to those involved in trade and to consumers;

Whereas the registration procedure should enable any person individually and directly concerned in a Member State to exercise his rights by notifying the Commission of his opposition;

Whereas there should be procedures to permit amendment of the specification, after registration, in the light of technological progress or withdrawal from the register of the geographical indication or designation of origin of an agricultural product or foodstuff if that product or foodstuff ceases to conform to the specification on the basis of which the geographical indication or designation of origin was granted;

Whereas provision should be made for trade with third countries offering equivalent guarantees for the issue and inspection of geographical indications or designations of origin granted on their territory;

Whereas provision should be made for a procedure establishing close cooperation between the Member States and the Commission through a Regulatory Committee set up for that purpose,

HAS ADOPTED THIS REGULATION:

Article 1

A15–02   1. This Regulation lays down rules on the protection of designations of origin and geographical indications of agricultural products intended for human consumption referred to in Annex II to the Treaty and of the foodstuffs referred to in Annex I to this Regulation and agricultural products listed in Annex II to this Regulation.

However, this Regulation shall not apply to wine products or to spirit drinks.

Annex I may be amended in accordance with the procedure set out in Article 15.

2. This Regulation shall apply without prejudice to other specific Community provisions.

3. Council Directive 83/189/EEC of 28 March 1983 laying down a procedure for the provision of information in the field of technical standards and regulations shall not apply to the designations of origin and geographical indications covered by this Regulation.

Article 2

1. Community protection of designations of origin and of geographical **A15–03**
indications of agricultural products and foodstuffs shall be obtained in accordance with this Regulation.

2. For the purposes of this Regulation:

    (a) designation of origin: means the name of a region, a specific place or, in
        exceptional cases, a country, used to describe an agricultural product or
        a foodstuff:
        — originating in that region, specific place or country, and
        — the quality or characteristics of which are essentially or
          exclusively due to a particular geographical environment with its
          inherent natural and human factors, and the production, process-
          ing and preparation of which take place in the defined geograph-
          ical area;
    (b) geographical indication: means the name of a region, a specific place or,
        in exceptional cases, a country, used to describe an agricultural product
        or a foodstuff:
        — originating in that region, specific place or country, and
        — which possesses a specific quality, reputation or other characteris-
          tics attributable to that geographical origin and the production
          and/or processing and/or preparation of which take place in the
          defined geographical area.

3. Certain traditional geographical or non-geographical names designating an
agricultural product or a foodstuff originating in a region or a specific place,
which fulfil the conditions referred to in the second indent of paragraph 2 (a)
shall also be considered as designations of origin.

4. By way of derogation from Article 2 (a), certain geographical designations
shall be treated as designations of origin where the raw materials of the products
concerned come from a geographical area larger than or different from the
processing area, provided that:
    — the production area of the raw materials is limited,
    — special conditions for the production of the raw materials exist, and
    — there are inspection arrangements to ensure that those conditions are
      adhered to.

5. For the purposes of paragraph 4, only live animals, meat and milk may be
considered as raw materials. Use of other raw materials may be authorized in
accordance with the procedure laid down in Article 15.

6. In order to be eligible for the derogation provided for in paragraph 4, the
designations in question may be or have already been recognized as designations of origin with national protection by the Member State concerned, or, if no
such scheme exists, have a proven, traditional character and an exceptional
reputation and renown.

7. In order to be eligible for the derogation provided for in paragraph 4,
applications for registration must be lodged within two years of the entry into
force of this Regulation.

Article 3

1. Names that have become generic may not be registered. **A15–04**

For the purposes of this Regulation, a "name that has become generic" means
the name of an agricultural product or a foodstuff which, although it relates to
the place or the region where this product or foodstuff was originally produced

or marketed, has become the common name of an agricultural product or a foodstuff.

To establish whether or not a name has become generic, account shall be taken of all factors, in particular:

— the existing situation in the Member State in which the name originates and in areas of consumption,
— the existing situation in other Member States,
— the relevant national or Community laws.

Where, following the procedure laid down in Articles 6 and 7, an application of registration is rejected because a name has become generic, the Commission shall publish that decision in the Official Journal of the European Communities.

2. A name may not be registered as a designation of origin or a geographical indication where it conflicts with the name of a plant variety or an animal breed and as a result is likely to mislead the public as to the true origin of the product.

3. Before the entry into force of this Regulation, the Council, acting by a qualified majority on a proposal from the Commission, shall draw up and publish in the Official Journal of the European Communities a non-exhaustive, indicative list of the names of agricultural products or foodstuffs which are within the scope of this Regulation and are regarded under the terms of paragraph 1 as being generic and thus not able to be registered under this Regulation.

Article 4

A15–05 1. To be eligible to use a protected designation of origin (PDO) or a protected geographical indication (PGI) an agricultural product or foodstuff must comply with a specification.

2. The product specification shall include at least:

(a) the name of the agricultural product or foodstuffs, including the designation of origin or the geographical indication;

(b) a description of the agricultural product or foodstuff including the raw materials, if appropriate, and principal physical, chemical, microbiological and/or organoleptic characteristics of the product or the foodstuff;

(c) the definition of the geographical area and, if appropriate, details indicating compliance with the requirements in Article 2 (4);

(d) evidence that the agricultural product or the foodstuff originates in the geographical area, within the meaning of Article 2 (2) (a) or (b), whichever is applicable;

(e) a description of the method of obtaining the agricultural product or foodstuff and, if appropriate, the authentic and unvarying local methods;

(f) the details bearing out the link with the geographical environment or the geographical origin within the meaning of Article 2 (2) (a) or (b), whichever is applicable;

(g) details of the inspection structures provided for in Article 10;

(h) the specific labelling details relating to the indication PDO or PGI, whichever is applicable, or the equivalent traditional national indications;

(i) any requirements laid down by Community and/or national provisions.

Article 5

A15–06 1. Only a group or, subject to certain conditions to be laid down in accordance with the procedure provided for in Article 15, a natural or legal person, shall be entitled to apply for registration.

For the purposes of this Article, "Group" means any association, irrespective of its legal form or composition, of producers and/or processors working with the same agricultural product or foodstuff. Other interested parties may participate in the group.

2. A group or a natural or legal person may apply for registration only in respect of agricultural products or foodstuffs which it produces or obtains within the meaning of Article 2 (2) (a) or (b).

3. The application for registration shall include the product specification referred to in Article 4.

4. The application shall be sent to the Member State in which the geographical area is located.

5. The Member State shall check that the application is justified and shall forward the application, including the product specification referred to in Article 4 and other documents on which it has based its decision, to the Commission, if it considers that it satisfies the requirements of this Regulation.

If the application concerns a name indicating a geographical area situated in another Member State also, that Member State shall be consulted before any decision is taken.

6. Member States shall introduce the laws, regulations and administrative provisions necessary to comply with this Article.

Article 6

1. Within a period of six months the Commission shall verify, by means of a **A15–07** formal investigation, whether the registration application includes all the particulars provided for in Article 4.

The Commission shall inform the Member State concerned of its findings.

2. If, after taking account of paragraph 1, the Commission concludes that the name qualifies for protection, it shall publish in the Official Journal of the European Communities the name and address of the applicant, the name of the product, the main points of the application, the references to national provisions governing the preparation, production or manufacture of the product and, if necessary, the grounds for its conclusions.

3. If no statement of objections is notified to the Commission in accordance with Article 7, the name shall be entered in a register kept by the Commission entitled "Register of protected designations of origin and protected geographical indications", which shall contain the names of the groups and the inspection bodies concerned.

4. The Commission shall publish in the Official Journal of the European Communities:

— the names entered in the Register,
— amendments to the Register made in accordance with Article 9 and 11.

5. If, in the light of the investigation provided for in paragraph 1, the Commission concludes that the name does not qualify for protection, it shall decide, in accordance with the procedure provided for in Article 15, not to proceed with the publication provided for in paragraph 2 of this Article.

Before publication as provided for in paragraphs 2 and 4 and registration as provided for in paragraph 3, the Commission may request the opinion of the Committee provided for in Article 15.

Article 7

1. Within six months of the date of publication in the Official Journal of the **A15–08** European Communities referred to in Article 6 (2), any Member State may object to the registration.

2. The competent authorities of the Member States shall ensure that all persons who can demonstrate a legitimate economic interest are authorized to consult the application. In addition and in accordance with the existing situation in the Member States, the Member States may provide access to other parties with a legitimate interest.

3. Any legitimately concerned natural or legal person may object to the proposed registration by sending a duly substantiated statement to the competent authority of the Member State in which he resides or is established. The competent authority shall take the necessary measures to consider these comments or objection within the deadlines laid down.

4. A statement of objection shall be admissible only if it:

— either shows non-compliance with the conditions referred to in Article 2,

— or shows that the proposed registration of a name would jeopardize the existence of an entirely or partly identical name or trade mark or the existence of products which are legally on the market at the time of publication of this regulation in the Official Journal of the European Communities,

— or indicates the features which demonstrate that the name whose registration is applied for is generic in nature.

5. Where an objection is admissible within the meaning of paragraph 4, the Commission shall ask the Member States concerned to seek agreement among themselves in accordance with their internal procedures within three months. If:

(a) agreement is reached, the Member States in question shall communicate to the Commission all the factors which made agreement possible together with the applicant's opinion and that of the objector. Where there has been no change to the information received under Article 5, the Commission shall proceed in accordance with Article 6 (4). If there has been a change, it shall again initiate the procedure laid down in Article 7;

(b) no agreement is reached, the Commission shall take a decision in accordance with the procedure laid down in Article 15, having regard to traditional fair practice and of the actual likelihood of confusion. Should it decide to proceed with registration, the Commission shall carry out publication in accordance with Article 6 (4).

Article 8

A15–09   The indications PDO, PGI or equivalent traditional national indications may appear only on agricultural products and foodstuffs that comply with this Regulation.

Article 9

A15–10   The Member State concerned may request the amendment of a specification, in particular to take account of developments in scientific and technical knowledge or to redefine the geographical area.

The Article 6 procedure shall apply *mutatis mutandis*.

The Commission may, however, decide, under the procedure laid down in Article 15, not to apply the Article 6 procedure in the case of a minor amendment.

1160

Article 10

1. Member States shall ensure that not later than six months after the entry **A15–11** into force of this Regulation inspection structures are in place, the function of which shall be to ensure that agricultural products and foodstuffs bearing a protected name meet the requirements laid down in the specifications.

2. An inspection structure may comprise one or more designated inspection authorities and/or private bodies approved for that purpose by the Member State. Member States shall send the Commission lists of the authorities and/or bodies approved and their respective powers. The Commission shall publish those particulars in the Official Journal of the European Communities.

3. Designated inspection authorities and/or approved private bodies must offer adequate guarantees of objectivity and impartiality with regard to all producers or processors subject to their control and have permanently at their disposal the qualified staff and resources necessary to carry out inspection of agricultural products and foodstuffs bearing a protected name.

If an inspection structure uses the services of another body for some inspections, that body must offer the same guarantees. In that event the designated inspection authorities and/or approved private bodies shall, however, continue to be responsible *vis-à-vis* the Member State for all inspections.

As from 1 January 1998, in order to be approved by the Member States for the purpose of this Regulation, private bodies must fulfil the requirements laid down in standard EN 45011 of 26 June 1989.

4. If a designated inspection authority and/or private body in a Member State establishes that an agricultural product or a foodstuff bearing a protected name of origin in that Member State does not meet the criteria of the specification, they shall take the steps necessary to ensure that this Regulation is complied with. They shall inform the Member State of the measures taken in carrying out their inspections. The parties concerned must be notified of all decisions taken.

5. A Member State must withdraw approval from an inspection body where the criteria referred to in paragraphs 2 and 3 are no longer fulfilled. It shall inform the Commission, which shall publish in the Official Journal of the European Communities a revised list of approved bodies.

6. The Member States shall adopt the measures necessary to ensure that a producer who complies with this Regulation has access to the inspection system.

7. The costs of inspections provided for under this Regulation shall be borne by the producers using the protected name.

Article 11

1. Any Member State may submit that a condition laid down in the product **A15–12** specification of an agricultural product or foodstuff covered by a protected name has not been met.

2. The Member State referred to in paragraph 1 shall make its submission to the Member State concerned. The Member State concerned shall examine the complaint and inform the other Member State of its findings and of any measures taken.

3. In the event of repeated irregularities and the failure of the Member States concerned to come to an agreement, a duly substantiated application must be sent to the Commission.

4. The Commission shall examine the application by consulting the Member States concerned. Where appropriate, having consulted the committee referred to in Article 15, the Commission shall take the necessary steps. These may include cancellation of the registration.

Article 12

A15–13   1. Without prejudice to international agreements, this Regulation may apply to an agricultural product or foodstuff from a third country provided that:

— the third country is able to give guarantees identical or equivalent to those referred to in Article 4,
— the third country concerned has inspection arrangements equivalent to those laid down in Article 10,
— the third country concerned is prepared to provide protection equivalent to that available in the Community to corresponding agricultural products for foodstuffs coming from the Community.

2. If a protected name of a third country is identical to a Community protected name, registration shall be granted with due regard for local and traditional usage and the practical risks of confusion.

Use of such names shall be authorized only if the country of origin of the product is clearly and visibly indicated on the label.

Article 13

A15–14   1. Registered names shall be protected against:

(a) any direct or indirect commercial use of a name registered in respect of products not covered by the registration in so far as those products are comparable to the products registered under that name or insofar as using the name exploits the reputation of the protected name;
(b) any misuse, imitation or evocation, even if the true origin of the product is indicated or if the protected name is translated or accompanied by an expression such as "style", "type", "method", "as produced in", "imitation" or similar;
(c) any other false or misleading indication as to the provenance, origin, nature or essential qualities of the product, on the inner or outer packaging, advertising material or documents relating to the product concerned, and the packing of the product in a container liable to convey a false impression as to its origin;
(d) any other practice liable to mislead the public as to the true origin of the product.

Where a registered name contains within it the name of an agricultural product or foodstuff which is considered generic, the use of that generic name on the appropriate agricultural product or foodstuff shall not be considered to be contrary to (a) or (b) in the first subparagraph.

2. However, Member States may maintain national measures authorizing the use of the expressions referred to in paragraph 1 (b) for a period of not more than five years after the date of publication of this Regulation, provided that:

— the products have been marketed legally using such expressions for at least five years before the date of publication of this Regulation,
— the labelling clearly indicates the true origin of the product.

However, this exception may not lead to the marketing of products freely on the territory of a Member State where such expressions are prohibited.

3. Protected names may not become generic.

Article 14

A15–15   1. Where a designation of origin or geographical indication is registered in accordance with this Regulation, the application for registration of a trade mark corresponding to one of the situations referred to in Article 13 and relating to the same type of product shall be refused, provided that the application for registration of the trade mark was submitted after the date of the publication provided for in Article 6 (2).

Trade marks registered in breach of the first subparagraph shall be declared invalid.

This paragraph shall also apply where the application for registration of a trade mark was lodged before the date of publication of the application for registration provided for in Article 6 (2), provided that that publication occured before the trade mark was registered.

2. With due regard for Community law, use of a trade mark corresponding to one of the situations referred to in Article 13 which was registered in good faith before the date on which application for registration of a designation of origin or geographical indication was lodged may continue notwithstanding the registration of a designation of origin or geographical indication, where there are no grounds for invalidity or revocation of the trade mark as provided respectively by Article 3 (1) (c) and (g) and Article 12 (2) (b) of First Council Directive 89/104/EEC of 21 December 1988 to approximate the laws of the Member States relating to trade marks.

3. A designation of origin or geographical indication shall not be registered where, in the light of a trade mark's reputation and renown and the length of time it has been used, registration is liable to mislead the consumer as to the true identity of the product.

Article 15

The Commission shall be assisted by a committee composed of the representa- **A15–16** tives of the Member States and chaired by the representative of the Commission.

The representative of the Commission shall submit to the committee a draft of the measures to be taken. The committee shall deliver its opinion on the draft within a time limit which the chairman may lay down according to the urgency of the matter. The opinion shall be delivered by the majority laid down in Article 148 (2) of the Treaty in the case of decisions which the Council is required to adopt on a proposal from the Commission. The votes of the representatives of the Member States within the committee shall be weighted in the manner set out in that Article. The chairman shall not vote.

The Commission shall adopt the measures envisaged if they are in accordance with the opinion of the committee.

If the measures envisaged are not in accordance with the opinion of the committee, or if no opinion is delivered, the Commission shall, without delay, submit to the Council a proposal relating to the measures to be taken. The Council shall act by a qualified majority.

If, on the expiry of a period of three months from the date of referral to the Council, the Council has not acted, the proposed measures shall be adopted by the Commission.

Article 16

Detailed rules for applying this Regulation shall be adopted in accordance **A15–17** with the procedure laid down in Article 15.

Article 17

1. Within six months of the entry into force of the Regulation, Member States **A15–18** shall inform the Commission which of their legally protected names or, in those Member States where there is no protection system, which of their names established by usage they wish to register pursuant to this Regulation.

2. In accordance with the procedure laid down in Article 15, the Commission shall register the names referred to in paragraph 1 which comply with Articles 2 and 4. Article 7 shall not apply. However, generic names shall not be added.

3. Member States may maintain national protection of the names communicated in accordance with paragraph 1 until such time as a decision on registration has been taken.

Article 18

A15–19   This Regulation shall enter into force twelve months after the date of its publication in the Official Journal of the European Communities.

This Regulation shall be binding in its entirety and directly applicable in all Member States.

Done at Brussels, July 14, 1992.

ANNEX I

Foodstuffs referred to in Article 1 (1)
— Beer,
— Natural mineral waters and spring waters,
— Beverages made from plant extracts,
— Bread, pastry, cakes, confectionery, biscuits and other baker's wares,
— Natural gums and resins.

ANNEX II

Agricultural products referred to in Article 1 (1)
— Hay
— Essential oils.

APPENDIX 16

Council Directive 84/450 of September 10, 1984

Relating to the approximation of the laws, regulations and administrative provisions of the Member States concerning misleading advertising

Concerning misleading and comparative advertising

([1984] O.J. L250/17)

The amendments shown in bold type (insertions) and italics (deletions) were made by the 1997 amending Directive 97/55, to be found in Appendix 17, *post*.

THE COUNCIL OF THE EUROPEAN COMMUNITIES,   A16–01

Having regard to the Treaty establishing the European Economic Community, and in particular Article 100 thereof,

Having regard to the proposal from the Commission,

Having regard to the opinion of the European Parliament,

Having regard to the opinion of the Economic and Social Committee,

Whereas the laws against misleading advertising now in force in the Member States differ widely; whereas, since advertising reaches beyond the frontiers of individual Member States, it has a direct effect on the establishment and the functioning of the common market;

Whereas misleading advertising can lead to distortion of competition within the common market;

Whereas advertising, whether or not it induces a contract, affects the economic welfare of consumers;

Whereas misleading advertising may cause a consumer to take decisions prejudicial to him when acquiring goods or other property, or using services, and the differences between the laws of the Member States not only lead, in many cases, to inadequate levels of consumer protection, but also hinder the execution of advertising campaigns beyond national boundaries and thus affect the free circulation of goods and provision of services;

Whereas the second programme of the European Economic Community for a consumer protection and information policy provides for appropriate action for the protection of consumers against misleading and unfair advertising;

Whereas it is in the interest of the public in general, as well as that of consumers and all those who, in competition with one another, carry on a trade, business, craft or profession, in the common market, to harmonize in the first instance national provisions against misleading advertising and that, at a second stage, unfair advertising and, as far as necessary, comparative advertising should be dealt with, on the basis of appropriate Commission proposals;

Whereas minimum and objective criteria for determining whether advertising is misleading should be established for this purpose;

Whereas the laws to be adopted by Member States against misleading advertising must be adequate and effective;

Whereas persons or organizations regarded under national law as having a legitimate interest in the matter must have facilities for initiating proceedings

1165

against misleading advertising, either before a court or before an administrative authority which is competent to decide upon complaints or to initiate appropriate legal proceedings;

Whereas it should be for each Member State to decide whether to enable the courts or administrative authorities to require prior recourse to other established means of dealing with the complaint;

Whereas the courts or administrative authorities must have powers enabling them to order or obtain the cessation of misleading advertising;

Whereas in certain cases it may be desirable to prohibit misleading advertising even before it is published; whereas, however, this in no way implies that Member States are under an obligation to introduce rules requiring the systematic prior vetting of advertising;

Whereas provision should be made for accelerated procedures under which measures with interim or definitive effect can be taken;

Whereas it may be desirable to order the publication of decisions made by courts or administrative authorities or of corrective statements in order to eliminate any continuing effects of misleading advertising;

Whereas administrative authorities must be impartial and the exercise of their powers must be subject to judicial review;

Whereas the voluntary control exercised by self-regulatory bodies to eliminate misleading advertising may avoid recourse to administrative or judicial action and ought therefore to be encouraged;

Whereas the advertiser should be able to prove, by appropriate means, the material accuracy of the factual claims he makes in his advertising, and may in appropriate cases be required to do so by the court or administrative authority;

Whereas this Directive must not preclude Member States from retaining or adopting provisions with a view to ensuring more extensive protection of consumers, persons carrying on a trade, business, craft or profession, and the general public,

HAS ADOPTED THIS DIRECTIVE:

Article 1

A16–02   *The purpose of this Directive is to protect consumers, persons carrying on a trade or business or practising a craft or profession and the interests of the public in general against misleading advertising and the unfair consequences thereof.*

The purpose of this Directive is to protect consumers, persons carrying on a trade or business or practising a craft or profession and the interests of the public in general against misleading advertising and the unfair consequences thereof and to lay down the conditions under which comparative advertising is permitted;

Article 2

A16–03   For the purposes of this Directive:

1. "advertising" means the making of a representation in any form in connection with a trade, business, craft or profession in order to promote the supply of goods or services, including immovable property, rights and obligations;

2. "misleading advertising" means any advertising which in any way, including its presentation, deceives or is likely to deceive the persons to whom it is addressed or whom it reaches and which, by reason of its deceptive nature, is

likely to affect their economic behaviour or which, for those reasons, injures or is likely to injure a competitor;

2a "comparative advertising" means any advertising which explicitly or by implication identifies a competitor or goods or services offered by a competitor;

3. "person" means any natural or legal person

Article 3

In determining whether advertising is misleading, account shall be taken of all **A16–04** its features, and in particular of any information it contains concerning:

(a) the characteristics of goods or services, such as their availability, nature, execution, composition, method and date of manufacture or provision, fitness for purpose, uses, quantity, specification, geographical or commercial origin or the results to be expected from their use, or the results and material features of tests or checks carried out on the goods or services;

(b) the price or the manner in which the price is calculated, and the conditions on which the goods are supplied or the services provided;

(c) the nature, attributes and rights of the advertiser, such as his identity and assets, his qualifications and ownership of industrial, commercial or intellectual property rights or his awards and distinctions.

Article 3a

1. Comparative advertising shall, as far as the comparison is concerned, be **A16–05** permitted when the following conditions are met:

(a) it is not misleading according to Articles 2 (2), 3 and 7 (1);

(b) it compares goods or services meeting the same needs or intended for the same purpose;

(c) it objectively compares one or more material, relevant, verifiable and representative features of those goods and services, which may include price;

(d) it does not create confusion in the market place between the advertiser and a competitor or between the advertiser's trade marks, trade names, other distinguishing marks, goods or services and those of a competitor;

(e) it does not discredit or denigrate the trade marks, trade names, other distinguishing marks, goods, services, activities, or circumstances of a competitor;

(f) for products with designation of origin, it relates in each case to products with the same designation;

(g) it does not take unfair advantage of the reputation of a trade mark, trade name or other distinguishing marks of a competitor or of the designation of origin of competing products;

(h) it does not present goods or services as imitations or replicas of goods or services bearing a protected trade mark or trade name.

2. Any comparison referring to a special offer shall indicate in a clear and unequivocal way the date on which the offer ends or, where appropriate, that the special offer is subject to the availability of the goods and services, and, where the special offer has not yet begun, the date of the start of the period during which the special price or other specific conditions shall apply.

Article 4

A16–06   1. *Member States shall ensure that adequate and effective means exist for the control of misleading advertising in the interests of consumers as well as competitors and the general public. Such means shall include legal provisions under which persons or organizations regarded under national law as having a legitimate interest in prohibiting misleading advertising may:*

    (a) *take legal action against such advertising; and/or*

    (b) *bring such advertising before an administrative authority competent either to decide on complaints or to initiate appropriate legal proceedings.*

It shall be for each Member State to decide which of these facilities shall be available and whether to enable the courts or administrative authorities to require prior recourse to other established means of dealing with complaints, including those referred to in Article 5.

1. Member States shall ensure that adequate and effective means exist to combat misleading advertising and for the compliance with the provisions on comparative advertising in the interests of consumers as well as competitors and the general public.

Such means shall include legal provisions under which persons or organizations regarded under national law as having a legitimate interest in prohibiting misleading advertising or regulating comparative advertising may:

    (a) take legal action against such advertising; and/or

    (b) bring such advertising before an administrative authority competent either to decide on complaints or to initiate appropriate legal proceedings;

2. Under the legal provisions referred to in paragraph 1, Member States shall confer upon the courts or administrative authorities powers enabling them, in cases where they deem such measures to be necessary taking into account all the interests involved and in particular the public interest:

— *to order the cessation of, or to institute appropriate legal proceedings for an order for the cessation of, misleading advertising, or*

— *if misleading advertising has not yet been published but publication is imminent, to order the prohibition of, or to institute appropriate legal proceedings for an order for the prohibition of, such publication,*

— **to order the cessation of, or to institute appropriate legal proceedings for an order for the cessation of, misleading advertising or unpermitted comparative advertising, or**

— **if the misleading advertising or unpermitted comparative advertising has not yet been published but publication is imminent, to order the prohibition of, or to institute appropriate legal proceedings for an order for the prohibition of, such publication,**

even without proof of actual loss or damage or of intention or negligence on the part of the advertiser.

Member States shall also make provision for the measures referred to in the first subparagraph to be taken under an accelerated procedure:

— either with interim effect, or

— with definitive effect,

on the understanding that it is for each Member State to decide which of the two options to select.

Furthermore, Member States may confer upon the courts or administrative authorities powers enabling them, with a view to eliminating the continuing effects of misleading advertising the cessation of which has been ordered by a final decision:

Furthermore, Member States may confer upon the courts or administrative authorities powers enabling them, with a view to eliminating the continuing effects of misleading advertising or unpermitted comparative advertising, the cessation of which has been ordered by a final decision:

— to require publication of that decision in full or in part and in such form as they deem adequate,
— to require in addition the publication of a corrective statement.

3. The administrative authorities referred to in paragraph 1 must:

(a) be composed so as not to cast doubt on their impartiality;
(b) have adequate powers, where they decide on complaints, to monitor and enforce the observance of their decisions effectively;
(c) normally give reasons for their decisions.

Where the powers referred to in paragraph 2 are exercised exclusively by an administrative authority, reasons for its decisions shall always be given. Furthermore in this case, provision must be made for procedures whereby improper or unreasonable exercise of its powers by the administrative authority or improper or unreasonable failure to exercise the said powers can be the subject of judicial review.

Articles 5

This Directive does not exclude the voluntary control of misleading advertising by **A16–07** *self-regulatory bodies and recourse to such bodies by the persons or organizations referred to in Article 4 if proceedings before such bodies are in addition to the court or administrative proceedings referred to in that Article.*

This Directive does not exclude the voluntary control, which Member States may encourage, of misleading or comparative advertising by self-regulatory bodies and recourse to such bodies by the persons or organisations referred to in Article 4 if proceedings before such bodies are in addition to the court or administrative proceedings referred to in that Article.

Article 6

Member States shall confer upon the courts or administrative authorities **A16–09** powers enabling them in the civil or administrative proceedings provided for in Article 4:

(a) *to require the advertiser to furnish evidence as to the accuracy of factual claims in advertising if, taking into account the legitimate interests of the advertiser and any other party to the proceedings, such a requirement appears appropriate on the basis of the circumstances of the particular case; and*

(a) **to require the advertiser to furnish evidence as to the accuracy of factual claims in advertising if, taking into account the legitimate interest of the advertiser and any other party to the proceedings, such a requirement appears appropriate on the basis of the circumstances of the particular case and in the case of comparative advertising to require the advertiser to furnish such evidence in a short period of time; and**

(b) to consider factual claims as inaccurate if the evidence demanded in accordance with (a) is not furnished or is deemed insufficient by the court or administrative authority.

Article 7

This Directive shall not preclude Member States from retaining or adopting **A16–10** *provisions with a view to ensuring more extensive protection for consumers, persons carrying on a trade, business, craft or profession, and the general public.*

1. This Directive shall not preclude Member States from retaining or adopting provisions with a view to ensuring more extensive protection, with regard to misleading advertising, for consumers, persons carrying on a trade, business, craft or profession, and the general public.

2. Paragraph 1 shall not apply to comparative advertising as far as the comparison is concerned.

3. The provisions of this Directive shall apply without prejudice to Community provisions on advertising for specific products and/or services or to restrictions or prohibitions on advertising in particular media.

4. The provisions of this Directive concerning comparative advertising shall not oblige Member States which, in compliance with the provisions of the Treaty, maintain or introduce advertising bans regarding certain goods or services, whether imposed directly or by a body or organization responsible, under the law of the Member States, for regulating the exercise of a commercial, industrial, craft or professional activity, to permit comparative advertising regarding those goods or services. Where these bans are limited to particular media, the Directive shall apply to the media not covered by these bans.

5. Nothing in this Directive shall prevent Member States from, in compliance with the provisions of the Treaty, maintaining or introducing bans or limitations on the use of comparisons in the advertising of professional services, whether imposed directly or by a body or organization responsible, under the law of the Member States, for regulating the exercise of a professional activity.

Article 8

A16–10 Member States shall bring into force the measures necessary to comply with this Directive by 1 October 1986 at the latest. They shall forthwith inform the Commission thereof.

Member States shall communicate to the Commission the text of all provisions of national law which they adopt in the field covered by this Directive.

Article 9

A16–11 This Directive is addressed to the Member States.

Done at Brussels, September 10, 1984.

APPENDIX 17

Directive 97/55 of European Parliament and of the Council of October 1997

Amending Directive 84/450 concerning misleading advertising so as to include comparative advertising

([1997] O.J. L290/18)

THE EUROPEAN PARLIAMENT AND THE COUNCIL OF THE EUROPEAN **A17–01** UNION,

Having regard to the Treaty establishing the European Community, and in particular Article 100a thereof,

Having regard to the proposal from the Commission,

Having regard to the opinion of the Economic and Social Committee,

Acting in accordance with the procedure laid down in Article 189b of the Treaty, in the light of the joint text approved by the Conciliation Committee on 25 June 1997,

(1) Whereas one of the Community's main aims is to complete the internal market; whereas measures must be adopted to ensure the smooth running of the said market; whereas the internal market comprises an area which has no internal frontiers and in which goods, persons, services and capital can move freely;

(2) Whereas the completion of the internal market will mean an ever wider range of choice; whereas, given that consumers can and must make the best possible use of the internal market, and that advertising is a very important means of creating genuine outlets for all goods and services throughout the Community, the basic provisions governing the form and content of comparative advertising should be uniform and the conditions of the use of comparative advertising in the Member States should be harmonized; whereas if these conditions are met, this will help demonstrate objectively the merits of the various comparable products; whereas comparative advertising can also stimulate competition between suppliers of goods and services to the consumer's advantage;

(3) Whereas the laws, regulations and administrative provisions of the individual Member States concerning comparative advertising differ widely; whereas advertising reaches beyond the frontiers and is received on the territory of other Member States; whereas the acceptance or non-acceptance of comparative advertising according to the various national laws may constitute an obstacle to the free movement of goods and services and create distortions of competition; whereas, in particular, firms may be exposed to forms of advertising developed by competitors to which they cannot reply in equal measure; whereas the freedom to provide services relating to comparative advertising should be assured; whereas the Community is called on to remedy the situation;

(4) Whereas the sixth recital of Council Directive 84/450/EEC of 10 September 1984 relating to the approximation of laws, regulations and

1171

administrative provisions of the Member States concerning misleading advertising states that, after the harmonization of national provisions against misleading advertising, "at a second stage..., as far as necessary, comparative advertising should be dealt with, on the basis of appropriate Commission proposals";

(5) Whereas point 3 (d) of the Annex to the Council Resolution of 14 April 1975 on a preliminary programme of the European Economic Community for a consumer protection and information policy includes the right to information among the basic rights of consumers; whereas this right is confirmed by the Council Resolution of 19 May 1981 on a second programme of the European Economic Community for a consumer protection and information policy, point 40 of the Annex, which deals specifically with consumer information; whereas comparative advertising, when it compares material, relevant, verifiable and representative features and is not misleading, may be a legitimate means of informing consumers of their advantage;

(6) Whereas it is desirable to provide a broad concept of comparative advertising to cover all modes of comparative advertising;

(7) Whereas conditions of permitted comparative advertising, as far as the comparison is concerned, should be established in order to determine which practices relating to comparative advertising may distort competition, be detrimental to competitors and have an adverse effect on consumer choice; whereas such conditions of permitted advertising should include criteria of objective comparison of the features of goods and services;

(8) Whereas the comparison of the price only of goods and services should be possible if this comparison respects certain conditions, in particular that it shall not be misleading;

(9) Whereas, in order to prevent comparative advertising being used in an anti-competitive and unfair manner, only comparisons between competing goods and services meeting the same needs or intended for the same purpose should be permitted;

(10) Whereas the international conventions on copyright as well as the national provisions on contractual and non-contractual liability shall apply when the results of comparative tests carried out by third parties are referred to or reproduced in comparative advertising;

(11) Whereas the conditions of comparative advertising should be cumulative and respected in their entirety; whereas, in accordance with the Treaty, the choice of forms and methods for the implementation of these conditions shall be left to the Member States, insofar as those forms and methods are not already determined by this Directive;

(12) Whereas these conditions should include, in particular, consideration of the provisions resulting from Council Regulation (EEC) No 2081/92 of 14 July 1992 on the protection of geographical indications and designations of origin for agricultural products and foodstuffs, and in particular Article 13 thereof, and of the other Community provisions adopted in the agricultural sphere;

(13) Whereas Article 5 of First Council Directive 89/104/EEC of 21 December 1988 to approximate the laws of the Member States relating to trade marks confers exclusive rights on the proprietor of a registered trade mark, including the right to prevent all third parties from using, in the course of trade, any sign which is identical with, or similar to, the trade mark in relation to identical goods or services or even, where appropriate, other goods;

(14) Whereas it may, however, be indispensable, in order to make comparative advertising effective, to identify the goods or services of a competitor, making reference to a trade mark or trade name of which the latter is the proprietor;

(15) Whereas such use of another's trade mark, trade name or other distinguishing marks does not breach this exclusive right in cases where it complies with the conditions laid down by this Directive, the intended target being solely to distinguish between them and thus to highlight differences objectively;

(16) Whereas provisions should be made for the legal and/or administrative means of redress mentioned in Articles 4 and 5 of Directive 84/450/ EEC to be available to control comparative advertising which fails to meet the conditions laid down by this Directive; whereas according to the 16th recital of the Directive, voluntary control by self-regulatory bodies to eliminate misleading advertising may avoid recourse to administrative or juridical action and ought therefore to be encouraged; whereas Article 6 applies to unpermitted comparative advertising in the same way;

(17) Whereas national self-regulatory bodies may coordinate their work through associations or organizations established at Community level and *inter alia* deal with cross-border complaints;

(18) Whereas Article 7 of Directive 84/450/EEC allowing Member States to retain or adopt provisions with a view to ensuring more extensive protection for consumers, persons carrying on a trade, business, craft or profession, and the general public, should not apply to comparative advertising, given that the objective of amending the said Directive is to establish conditions under which comparative advertising is permitted;

(19) Whereas a comparison which presents goods or services as an imitation or a replica of goods or services bearing a protected trade mark or trade name shall not be considered to fulfil the conditions to be met by permitted comparative advertising;

(20) Whereas this Directive in no way affects Community provisions on advertising for specific products and/or services or restrictions or prohibitions on advertising in particular media;

(21) Whereas, if a Member State, in compliance with the provisions of the Treaty, prohibits advertising regarding certain goods or services, this ban may, whether it is imposed directly or by a body or organization responsible under the law of that Member State for regulating the exercise of a commercial, industrial, craft or professional activity, be extended to comparative advertising;

(22) Whereas Member States shall not be obliged to permit comparative advertising for goods or services on which they, in compliance with the provisions of the Treaty, maintain or introduce bans, including bans as regards marketing methods or advertising which targets vulnerable consumer groups; whereas Member States may, in compliance with the provisions of the Treaty, maintain or introduce bans or limitations on the use of comparisons in the advertising of professional services, whether imposed directly or by a body or organization responsible under the law of the Member States for regulating the exercise of a professional activity;

(23) Whereas regulating comparative advertising is, under the conditions set out in this Directive, necessary for the smooth running of the internal market and whereas action at Community level is therefore required; whereas the adoption of a Directive is the appropriate instrument because it lays down uniform general principles while allowing the Member States to choose the form and appropriate method by which to attain these objectives; whereas it is in accordance with the principle of subsidiarity,

HAVE ADOPTED THIS DIRECTIVE:

Article 1

A17–02   Directive 94/450/EEC is hereby amended as follows:
(1) The title shall be replaced by the following:

"Council Directive of 10 September 1984 concerning misleading and comparative advertising";

(2) Article 1 shall be replaced by the following:

"Article 1

The purpose of this Directive is to protect consumers, persons carrying on a trade or business or practising a craft or profession and the interests of the public in general against misleading advertising and the unfair consequences thereof and to lay down the conditions under which comparative advertising is permitted."

(3) The following point shall be inserted in Article 2:

"2a 'comparative advertising' means any advertising which explicitly or by implication identifies a competitor or goods or services offered by a competitor;"

(4) The following Article shall be added:

"Article 3a

1. Comparative advertising shall, as far as the comparison is concerned, be permitted when the following conditions are met:

(a) it is not misleading according to Articles 2 (2), 3 and 7 (1);
(b) it compares goods or services meeting the same needs or intended for the same purpose;
(c) it objectively compares one or more material, relevant, verifiable and representative features of those goods and services, which may include price;
(d) it does not create confusion in the market place between the advertiser and a competitor or between the advertiser's trade marks, trade names, other distinguishing marks, goods or services and those of a competitor;
(e) it does not discredit or denigrate the trade marks, trade names, other distinguishing marks, goods, services, activities, or circumstances of a competitor;
(f) for products with designation of origin, it relates in each case to products with the same designation;
(g) it does not take unfair advantage of the reputation of a trade mark, trade name or other distinguishing marks of a competitor or of the designation of origin of competing products;
(h) it does not present goods or services as imitations or replicas of goods or services bearing a protected trade mark or trade name.

2. Any comparison referring to a special offer shall indicate in a clear and unequivocal way the date on which the offer ends or, where appropriate, that the special offer is subject to the availability of the goods and services,

and, where the special offer has not yet begun, the date of the start of the period during which the special price or other specific conditions shall apply.";

(5) The first and second subparagraphs of Article 4 (1) shall be replaced by the following:

"1. Member States shall ensure that adequate and effective means exist to combat misleading advertising and for the compliance with the provisions on comparative advertising in the interests of consumers as well as competitors and the general public.

Such means shall include legal provisions under which persons or organizations regarded under national law as having a legitimate interest in prohibiting misleading advertising or regulating comparative advertising may:

(a) take legal action against such advertising; and/or
(b) bring such advertising before an administrative authority competent either to decide on complaints or to initiate appropriate legal proceedings.";

(6) Article 4 (2) is hereby amended as follows:

(a) the indents in the first subparagraph shall be replaced by the following:

"—to order the cessation of, or to institute appropriate legal proceedings for an order for the cessation of, misleading advertising or unpermitted comparative advertising, or
—if the misleading advertising or unpermitted comparative advertising has not yet been published but publication is imminent, to order the prohibition of, or to institute appropriate legal proceedings for an order for the prohibition of, such publication,";

(b) the introductory wording to the third subparagraph shall be replaced by the following:

"Furthermore, Member States may confer upon the courts or administrative authorities powers enabling them, with a view to eliminating the continuing effects of misleading advertising or unpermitted comparative advertising, the cessation of which has been ordered by a final decision:";

(7) Article 5 shall be replaced by the following:

"Article 5

This Directive does not exclude the voluntary control, which Member States may encourage, of misleading or comparative advertising by self-regulatory bodies and recourse to such bodies by the persons or organisations referred to in Article 4 if proceedings before such bodies are in addition to the court or administrative proceedings referred to in that Article."

(8) Article 6 (a) shall be replaced by the following:

"(a) to require the advertiser to furnish evidence as to the accuracy of factual claims in advertising if, taking into account the legitimate interest of the advertiser and any other party to the proceedings, such a requirement appears appropriate on the basis of the circumstances of the particular case and in the case of comparative advertising to require the advertiser to furnish such evidence in a short period of time; and";

(9) Article 7 shall be replaced by the following:

"Article 7

1. This Directive shall not preclude Member States from retaining or adopting provisions with a view to ensuring more extensive protection, with regard to misleading advertising, for consumers, persons carrying on a trade, business, craft or profession, and the general public.

2. Paragraph 1 shall not apply to comparative advertising as far as the comparison is concerned.

3. The provisions of this Directive shall apply without prejudice to Community provisions on advertising for specific products and/or services or to restrictions or prohibitions on advertising in particular media.

4. The provisions of this Directive concerning comparative advertising shall not oblige Member States which, in compliance with the provisions of the Treaty, maintain or introduce advertising bans regarding certain goods or services, whether imposed directly or by a body or organization responsible, under the law of the Member States, for regulating the exercise of a commercial, industrial, craft or professional activity, to permit comparative advertising regarding those goods or services. Where these bans are limited to particular media, the Directive shall apply to the media not covered by these bans.

5. Nothing in this Directive shall prevent Member States from, in compliance with the provisions of the Treaty, maintaining or introducing bans or limitations on the use of comparisons in the advertising of professional services, whether imposed directly or by a body or organization responsible, under the law of the Member States, for regulating the exercise of a professional activity."

Article 2

Complaints systems

A17–03 The Commission shall study the feasibility of establishing effective means to deal with cross-border complaints in respect of comparative advertising. Within two years after the entry into force of this Directive the Commission shall submit a report to the European Parliament and the Council on the results of the studies, accompanied if appropriate by proposals.

Article 3

A17–04 1. Member States shall bring into force the laws, regulations and administrative provisions necessary to comply with this Directive at the latest 30 months after its publication in the Official Journal of the European Communities. They shall forthwith inform the Commission thereof.

2. When Member States adopt these measures, they shall contain a reference to this Directive or shall be accompanied by such reference on the occasion of their official publication. The methods of making such reference shall be laid down by Member States.

3. Member States shall communicate to the Commission the text of the main provisions of domestic law which they adopt in the field governed by this Directive.

Article 4

A17–05 This Directive is addressed to the Member States.

Done at Brussels, October 6, 1997.

C 136, 19. 5. 1994, p. 4.
C 49, 24. 2. 1992, p. 35.

Commission declaration

The Commission declares that it intends to submit the report referred to in Article 2 as far as possible at the same time as the report on complaints systems provided for in Article 17 of Directive 97/7/EC on the protection of consumers in respect of distance contracts.

Appendix 18

The Control of Misleading Advertisements Regulations 1988

S.I. 1988 No. 915

(As amended *inter-alia*, by the Broadcasting Act 1990 and the Control of Misleading Advertisements (Amendment) Regulations 2000)

A18–01 Whereas the Secretary of State is a Minister designated for the purposes of section 2(2) of the European Communities Act 1972 in relation to measures relating to the control of advertising;

And whereas a draft of these Regulations has been approved by a resolution of each House of Parliament pursuant to section 2(2) of and paragraph 2(2) of Schedule 2 to that Act;

Now, therefore, the Secretary of State in exercise of the powers conferred on him by section 2(2) of that Act and of all other powers enabling him in that behalf hereby makes the following Regulations:

Citation and commencement

A18–02 **1.**—(1) These Regulations may be cited as the Control of Misleading Advertisements Regulations 1988 and shall come into force on 20th June 1988.

Interpretation

A18–03 **2.**—(1) In these Regulations—

"advertisement" means any form of representation which is made in connection with a trade, business, craft or profession in order to promote the supply or transfer of goods or services, immovable property, rights or obligations;

"broadcast advertisement" means any advertisement included or proposed to be included in any programme or teletext transmission broadcast by the IBA and includes any advertisement included or proposed to be included in a licensed service by the reception and immediate re-transmission of broadcasts made by the IBA;

"Cable Authority" means the authority mentioned in section 1(1) of the Cable and Broadcasting Act 1984;

"the Commission" means the Independent Television Commission;

"court", in relation to England and Wales and Northern Ireland, means the High Court, and, in relation to Scotland, the Court of Session;

"Director" means the Director General of Fair Trading;

"IBA" means the Independent Broadcasting Authority mentioned in section 1(1) of the Broadcasting Act 1981;

"licensable service" has the meaning given by section 2(2) of the Cable and Broadcasting Act 1984;

"licensed service" means a licensable service in respect of which the Cable Authority has granted a licence pursuant to section 4 of the Cable and Broadcasting Act 1984;

"licensed service" means—
(a) in relation to a complaint made to the Commission, a service in respect of which the Commission have granted a licence under Part I or II of the Broadcasting Act 1990; and
(b) in relation to a complaint made to the Radio Authority, a service in respect of which the Radio Authority have granted a licence under Part III of that Act;
and "licensed local delivery service" means a service in respect of which the Commission have granted a licence under Part II of that Act;

"products with designation of origin" are those products to which Council Regulation (EEC) No. 2081/92 of 14 July 1992 applies;

"publication" in relation to an advertisement means the dissemination of that advertisement whether to an individual person or a number of persons and whether orally or in writing or in any other way whatsoever, and "publish" shall be construed accordingly.

"relevant body" means the Commission or the Radio Authority;

"on S4C" has the same meaning as in Part I of the Broadcasting Act 1990;

"the Welsh Authority" has the same meaning as in that Act;

(2) For the purposes of these Regulations an advertisement is misleading if in any way, including its presentation, it deceives or is likely to deceive the persons to whom it is addressed or whom it reaches and if, by reason of its deceptive nature, it is likely to affect their economic behaviour or, for those reasons, injures or is likely to injure a competitor of the person whose interests the advertisement seeks to promote.

(2A) For the purposes of these Regulations an advertisement is comparative if in any way, either explicitly or by implication, it identifies a competitor or goods or services offered by a competitor.

(3) In the application of these Regulations to Scotland for references to an injunction or an interlocutory injunction there shall be substituted references to an interdict or an interim interdict respectively.

The words in italics were deleted, and the words in bold inserted, by the Broadcasting Act 1990, Sched. 20 or the Control of Misleading Advertisements (Amendment) Regulations 2000.

Application

3.—(1) These Regulations do not apply to— A18–04
(a) the following advertisements issued or caused to be issued by or on behalf of an authorised person or appointed representative, that is to say—
(i) investment advertisements; and
(ii) any other advertisements in respect of investment business, except where any such advertisements relate exclusively to any matter in relation to which the authorised person in question is an exempted person; and
(b) advertisements of a description referred to in section 58(1)9d) of the Financial Services Act 1986, *except where any such advertisements consist of or any part of the matters referred to in section 58(1)(d)(ii) of that Act as being required of permitted to be published by an approved exchange under Part V of that Act.*

(2) In this regulation "appointed representative", *"approved exchange"*, "authorised person", "exempted person", "investment advertisement" and "investment business" have the same meanings as in the Financial Services Act 1986.

The words in italics were removed by the Public Offers of Securities Regulations 1995, S.I. 1995 No. 1537. See also S.I. 1995 No. 3275 and S.I. 1998 No. 3218 for the interpretation of this regulation.

Complaints to the Director

A18–05 4.—(1) Subject to paragraphs (2) and (3) below, it shall be the duty of the Director to consider any complaint made to him that an advertisement is misleading **or is a comparative advertisement and is not permitted under regulation 4A, below,** unless the complaint appears to the Director to be frivolous or vexatious.

(2) The Director shall not consider any complaint which these Regulations require or would require, leaving aside any question as to the frivolous or vexatious nature of the complaint, *the IBA or the Cable Authority,* **the Commission, the Radio Authority or the Welsh Authority** to consider.

(3) Before considering any complaint under paragraph (1) above the Director may require the person making the complaint to satisfy him that—

(a) there have been invoked in relation to the same or substantially the same complaint about the advertisement in question such established means of dealing with such complaints as the Director may consider appropriate, having regard to all the circumstances of the particular case;

(b) a reasonable opportunity has been allowed for those means to deal with the complaint in question; and

(c) those means have not dealt with the complaint adequately.

(4) In exercising the powers conferred on him by these Regulations the Director shall have regard to—

(a) all the interests involved and in particular the public interest; and

(b) the desirability of encouraging the control, by self-regulatory bodies, of advertisements.

The words in italics were deleted, and the words in bold inserted by the Broadcasting Act 1990, Sched. 20 or the Control of Misleading Advertisements (Amendment) Regulations 2000.

Comparative Advertisements

A18–06 4A—(1) A comparative advertisement shall, as far as the comparison is concerned, be permitted only when the following conditions are met:—

(a) it is not misleading;

(b) it compares goods or services meeting the same needs or intended for the same purpose;

(c) it objectively compares one or more material, relevant, verifiable and representative features of those goods and services, which may include price;

(d) it does not create confusion in the market place between the advertiser and a competitor or between the advertiser's trade marks, trade names, other distinguishing marks, goods or services and those of a competitor;

(e) it does not discredit or denigrate the trade marks, trade names, other distinguishing marks, goods, services, activities, or circumstances of a competitor;

(f) for products with designation of origin, it relates in each case to products with the same designation;

(g) it does not take unfair advantage of the reputation of a trade mark, trade name or other distinguishing marks of a competitor or of the designation of origin of competing products;

(h) it does not present goods or services as imitations or replicas of goods or services bearing a protected trade mark or trade name.

(2) In the case of a comparative advertisement referring to a special offer, such an advertisement is not permitted unless it indicates in a clear and

unequivocal way the date on which the offer ends or, where appropriate, that the special offer is subject to the availability of the goods and services, and, where the special offer has not yet begun, the date of the start of the period during which the special price or other specific conditions shall apply.

(3) The provisions of this regulation shall not be construed as—

(a) conferring a right of action in any civil proceedings in respect of any contravention of this regulation (save as provided for in these Regulations); or

(b) derogating from any right of action or other remedy (whether civil or criminal) in proceedings instituted otherwise than by virtue of these Regulations."

This regulation was added by the Control of Misleading Advertisements (Amendment) Regulations 2000.

Applications to the Court by the Director

5.—(1) If, having considered a complaint about an advertisement pursuant to regulation 4(1) above, he considers that the advertisement is misleading **or is a comparative advertisement and is not permitted under regulation 4A**, the Director may, if he thinks it appropriate to do so, bring proceedings for an injunction (in which proceedings he may also apply for an **interim** injunction) against any person appearing to him to be concerned or likely to be concerned with the publication of the advertisement. **A18–07**

(2) The Director shall give reasons for his decision to apply or not to apply, as the case may be, for an injunction in relation to any complaint which these Regulations require him to consider.

The words in bold were added by the Control of Misleading Advertisements (Amendment) Regulations 2000.

Functions of the Court

6.—(1) The court on an application by the Director may grant an injunction on such terms as it may think fit but (except where it grants an **interim** injunction) only if the court is satisfied that the advertisement to which the application relates is misleading **or is a comparative advertisement and is not permitted under regulation 4A**. Before granting an injunction the court shall have regard to all the interests involved and in particular the public interest. **A18–08**

(2) An injunction may relate not only to a particular advertisement but to any advertisement in similar terms or likely to convey a similar impression.

(3) In considering an application for an injunction the court may, whether or not on the application of any party to the proceedings, require any person appearing to the court to be responsible for the publication of the advertisement to which the application relates to furnish the court with evidence of the accuracy of any factual claim made in the advertisement. The court shall not make such a requirement unless it appears to the court to be appropriate in the circumstances of the particular case, having regard to the legitimate interests of the person who would be the subject of or affected by the requirement and of any other person concerned with the advertisement.

(4) If such evidence is not furnished to it following a requirement made by it under paragraph (3) above or if it considers such evidence inadequate, the court may decline to consider the factual claim mentioned in that paragraph accurate.

(5) The court shall not refuse to grant an injunction for lack of evidence that—

(a) the publication of the advertisement in question has given rise to loss or damage to any person; or

(b) the person responsible for the advertisement intended it to be misleading or failed to exercise proper care to prevent its being misleading;

(c) **the person responsible for the comparative advertisement intended to breach the conditions in regulation 4A(1) and (2) or failed to exercise proper care to meet the conditions in regulation 4A(1) and (2).**

(6) An injunction may prohibit the publication or the continued or further publication of an advertisement.
The words in bold were added by the Control of Misleading Advertisements (Amendment) Regulations 2000.

Powers of the Director to obtain and disclose information and disclosure of information generally

A18–09   7.—(1) For the purpose of facilitating the exercise by him of any functions conferred on him by these Regulations, the Director may, by notice in writing signed by him or on his behalf, require any person to furnish to him such information as may be specified or described in the notice or to produce to him any documents so specified or described.

(2) A notice under paragraph (1) above may—

(a) specify the way in which and the time within which it is to be complied with; and

(b) be varied or revoked by a subsequent notice.

(3) Nothing in this regulation compels the production or furnishing by any person of a document or of information which he would in an action in a court be entitled to refuse to produce or furnish on grounds of legal professional privilege or, in Scotland, on the grounds of confidentiality as between client and professional legal adviser.

(4) If a person makes default in complying with a notice under paragraph (1) above the court may, on the application of the Director, make such order as the court thinks fit for requiring the default to be made good, and any such order may provide that all the costs or expenses of and incidental to the application shall be borne by the person in default or by any officers of a company or other association who are responsible for its default.

(5) Subject to any provision to the contrary made by or under any enactment, where the Director considers it appropriate to do so for the purpose of controlling misleading advertisements **or comparative advertisements which do not comply with regulation 4A,** he may refer to any person any complaint (including any related documentation about an advertisement or disclose to any person any information (whether or not obtained by means of the exercise of the power conferred by paragraph (1) above).

(6) For the purpose of enabling information obtained under certain enactments to be used for facilitating the performance of functions under these Regulations, the following amendments shall be made in provisions respecting disclosure of information, that is to say—

(a) in section 133 of the Fair Trading Act 1973 there shall be inserted—
(i) at the end of paragraph (a) of subsection (2) the words "the Control of Misleading Advertisements Regulations 1988 or";
(ii) at the end of subsection (3) the words "or the Control of Misleading Advertisements Regulations 1988";
(b) in section 174 of the Consumer Credit Act 1974 there shall be inserted—
(i) after the words "Consumer Protection Act 1987" in paragraph (a) of subsection (3) the words "or the Control of Misleading Advertisements Regulations 1988";
(ii) after the words "Fair Trading Act 1973" in paragraph (c) of subsection (3) the words "or under the Control of Misleading Advertisements Regulations 1988";
(c) in section 41 of the Restrictive Trade Practices Act 1976 there shall be inserted—

  (i) at the end of paragraph (a) of subsection (1) the words "or the Control of Misleading Advertisements Regulations 1988";

  (ii) after the words "Fair Trading Act 1973" in paragraph (c) of subsection (1) the words "or the Control of Misleading Advertisements Regulations 1988";

 (d) in section 10 of the Estate Agents Act 1979 there shall be inserted—

  (i) after the words "Consumer Protection Act 1987" in paragraph (a) of subsection (3) the words "or the Control of Misleading Advertisments Regulations 1988";

  (ii) after the words "other enactments" in paragraph (c) of subsection (3) the words "or subordinate legislation";

 (e) in section 19 of the Competition Act 1980 there shall be inserted—

  (i) after the words "the enactments" in paragraphs (a) and (c) of subsection (2) the words "or subordinate legislation";

  (ii) after the words "the enactments" in subsection (3) the words "and subordinate legislation" and after the words "Consumer Protection Act 1987" in that subsection the words "(k) the Control of Misleading Advertisements Regulations 1988";

 (f) in section 101 of the Telecommunications Act 1984 there shall be inserted—

  (i) after the words "the enactments" in paragraphs (b) and (d) of subsection (2) the words "or subordinate legislation";

  (ii) after the words "the enactments" in subsection (3) the words "and subordinate legislation" and after the words "Consumer Protection Act 1987" in that subsection the words "(i) the Control of Misleading Advertisments Regulations 1988";

 (g) in section 74 of the Airports Act 1986 there shall be inserted—

  (i) after the words "the enactments" in paragraphs (a) and (c) of subsection (2) the words "or subordinate legislation";

  (ii) after the words "the enactment" in subsection (3) the words "and subordinate legislation" and after the words "Consumer Protection Act 1987" in that subsection the words "(j) the Control of Misleading Advertisements Regulations 1988";

 (h) in section 42 of the Gas Act 1986 there shall be inserted—

  (i) after the words "the enactments" in paragraphs (b) and (e) of subsection (2) he words "or subordinate legislation";

  (ii) after the words "the enactments" in subsection (3) the words "and subordinate legislation" and after the words "Consumer Protection Act 1987" in that subsection the words "(k) the Control of Misleading Advertisements Regulations 1988".

(7) Subject to paragraph (5) above, any person who knowingly discloses, otherwise than for the purposes of any legal proceedings or of a report of such proceedings or the investigation of any criminal offence, any information obtained by means of the exercise of the power conferred by paragraph (1) above without the consent either of the person to whom the information relates, or, if the information relates to a business, the consent of the person for the time being carrying on that business, shall be guilty of an offence and liable on summary conviction to imprisonment for a term not exceeding 3 months or to a fine not exceeding £2,000 or to both.

(8) The Director may arrange for the dissemination in such form and manner as he considers appropriate of such information and advice concerning the operation of these Regulations as may appear to him to be expedient to give to the public and to all persons likely to be affected by these Regulations.

The words in bold were added by the Control of Misleading Advertisements (Amendment) Regulations 2000.

Complaints to the IBA

A18–10   **8.**—*(1) It shall be the duty of the IBA to consider any complaint made to it that a broadcast advertisement is misleading, unless the complaint appears to the IBA to be frivolous or vexatious.*

(2) The IBA shall give reasons for its decisions.

(3) In exercising the powers conferred on it by these Regulations the IBA shall have regard to all the interests involved and in particular the public interest.

Control by the IBA of misleading advertisements

A18–11   **9.**—*(1) If, having considered a complaint about a broadcast advertisement pursuant to regulation 8(1) above, it considers that the advertisement is misleading, the IBA may, if it thinks it appropriate to do so, refuse to broadcast the advertisement.*

(2) The IBA may require any person appearing to it to be responsible for a broadcast advertisement which the IBA believes may be misleading to furnish it with evidence as to the accuracy of any factual claim made in the advertisement. In deciding whether or not to make such a requirement the IBA shall have regard to the legitimate interests of any person who would be the subject of or affected by the requirement.

(3) If such evidence is not furnished to it following a requirement made by it under paragraph (2) above or if it considers such evidence inadequate, the IBA may consider the factual claim inaccurate.

Complaints to the Cable Authority

A18–12   **10.**—*(1) Subject to paragraph (2) below, it shall be the duty of the Cable Authority to consider any complaint made to it that any advertisement included or proposed to be included in a licensed service is misleading, unless the complaint appears to the Authority to be frivolous or vexatious.*

(2) The Cable Authority shall not consider any complaint about an advertisement included or proposed to be included in a licensed service by the reception and immediate re-transmission of broadcasts made by the IBA or the British Broadcasting Corporation.

(3) In exercising the powers conferred on it by these Regulations the Cable Authority shall have regard to all the interests involved and in particular the public interest.

Control by the Cable Authority of misleading advertisements

A18–13   **11.**—*(1) If, having considered a complaint about an advertisement pursuant to regulation 10(1) above, it considers that the advertisement is misleading, the Authority may, if it thinks it appropriate to do so, exercise the power conferred on it by section 15(1) of the Cable and Broadcasting Act 1984 (power to give directions) in relation to the advertisement.*

(2) The Authority shall give reasons for its decision to give or not to give, as the case may be, a direction in accordance with paragraph (1) above in any particular case.

(3) The Authority may require any person appearing to it to be responsible for an advertisement which the Authority believes may be misleading to furnish it with evidence as to the accuracy of any factual claim made in the advertisement. In deciding whether or not to make such a requirement the Authority shall have regard to the legitimate interests of any person who would be the subject of or affected by the requirement.

(4) If such evidence is not furnished to it following a requirement made by it under paragraph (3) above or if it considers such evidence inadequate, the Authority may consider the factual claim inaccurate.

Complaints to the Commission and the Radio Authority

A18–14   **8.**—**(1) Subject to paragraph (2) below, it shall be the duty of a relevant body to consider any complaint made to it that any advertisement included or proposed to be included in a licensed service is misleading or is a comparative advertisement which is not permitted under regulations 4A, unless the complaint appears to the body to be frivolous or vexatious.**

(2) The Commission shall not consider any complaint about an advertisement included or proposed to be included in a licensed local delivery service by the reception and immediate re-transmission of broadcasts made by the British Broadcasting Corporation.

(3) A relevant body shall give reasons for its decisions.

(4) In exercising the powers conferred on it by these Regulations a relevant body shall have regard to all the interests involved and in particular the public interest.

Control by the Commission and the Radio Authority of misleading advertisements and comparative advertisements

9.—(1) If, having considered a complaint about an advertisement pursuant A18–15 to regulation 8(1) above, it considers that the advertisement is misleading or is a comparative advertisement which is not permitted under regulations 4A, a relevant body may, if it thinks it appropriate to do so, exercise in relation to the advertisement the power conferred on it—

(a) where the relevant body is the Commission, by section 9(6) of the Broadcasting Act 1990 (power of Commission to give directions about advertisements), or

(b) where the relevant body is the Radio Authority, by section 93(6) of that Act (power of Radio Authority to give directions about advertisements).

(2) A relevant body may require any person appearing to it to be responsible for an advertisement which the body believes may be misleading or may be a comparative advertisement which is not permitted under regulation 4A to furnish it with evidence as to the accuracy of any factual claim made in the advertisement. In deciding whether or not to make such a requirement the body shall have regard to the legitimate interests of any person who would be the subject of or affected by the requirement.

(3) If such evidence is not furnished to it following a requirement made by it under paragraph (2) above or if it considers such evidence inadequate, a relevant body may consider the factual claim inaccurate.

Complaints to the Welsh Authority

10.—(1) Subject to paragraph (2) below, it shall be the duty of the Welsh A18–16 Authority to consider any complaint made to them that any advertisement broadcast or proposed to be broadcast misleading or may be a comparative advertisement which is not permitted under regulations 4A, unless the complaint appears to the Authority to be frivolous or vexatious.

(2) The Welsh Authority shall not consider any complaint about an advertisement broadcast or proposed to be broadcast on S4C by the reception and immediate re-transmission of broadcasts made by the British Broadcasting Corporation.

(3) The Welsh Authority shall give reasons for their decisions.

(4) In exercising the powers conferred on them by these Regulations the Welsh Authority shall have regard to all the interests involved and in particular the public interest.

Control by the Welsh Authority of misleading advertisements and comparative advertisements

11.—(1) If, having considered a complaint about an advertisement pursuant to regulation 10(1) above, they consider that the advertisement is misleading or is a comparative advertisement which is not permitted under regulations 4A, the Welsh Authority may, if they think it appropriate to do so, refuse to broadcast the advertisement.

(2) The Welsh Authority may require any person appearing to them to be responsible for an advertisement which the Authority believe may be misleading or may be a comparative advertisement which is not permitted under regulation 4A, to furnish them with evidence as to the accuracy of any factual claim made in the advertisement. In deciding whether or not to make such a requirement the Authority shall have regard to the legitimate interests of any person who would be the subject of or affected by the requirement.

(3) If such evidence is not furnished to them following a requirement made by them under paragraph (2) above within a time specified by the Welsh Authority or if they consider such evidence inadequate, the Welsh Authority may consider the factual claim inaccurate.

New regulations 8 to 11 (in bold) were substituted for the previous regulations 8 to 11 (in italics) by the Broadcasting Act 1990, Sched. 20, and were amended by the Control of Misleading Advertisements (Amendment) Regulation 2000.

PART VI

MADRID INTERNATIONAL MATERIALS

APPENDIX 19

PROTOCOL RELATING TO THE MADRID AGREEMENT CONCERNING THE INTERNATIONAL REGISTRATION OF MARKS

(Adopted in Madrid on June 27, 1989)

List of the Articles of the Protocol

A19–01

ARTICLE 1

MEMBERSHIP IN THE MADRID UNION

The States party to this Protocol (hereinafter referred to as "the Contracting A19–02
States"), even where they are not party to the Madrid Agreement Concerning

1189

the International Registration of Marks as revised at Stockholm 1967 and as amended in 1979 (hereinafter referred to as "the Madrid (Stockholm) Agreement"), and the organizations referred to in Article 14(1)(b) which are party to this Protocol (hereinafter referred to as "the Contracting Organizations") shall be members of the same Union of which countries party to the Madrid (Stockholm) Agreement are members. Any reference in this Protocol to "Contracting Parties" shall be construed as a reference to both Contracting States and Contracting Organizations.

ARTICLE 2

SECURING PROTECTION THROUGH INTERNATIONAL REGISTRATION

A19–03 (1) Where an application for the registration of a mark has been filed with the Office of a Contracting Party, or where a mark has been registered in the register of the Office of a Contracting Party, the person in whose name that application (hereinafter referred to as "the basic application") or that registration (hereinafter referred to as "the basic registration") stands may, subject to the provisions of this Protocol, secure protection for his mark in the territory of the Contracting Parties, by obtaining the registration of that mark in the register of the International Bureau of the World Intellectual Property Organization (hereinafter referred to as "the international registration," "the International Register," "the International Bureau" and "the Organization," respectively), provided that,

 (i) where the basic application has been filed with the Office of a Contracting State or where the basic registration has been made by such an Office, the person in whose name that application or registration stands is a national of that Contracting State, or is domiciled, or has a real and effective industrial or commercial establishment, in the said Contracting State,

 (ii) where the basic application has been filed with the Office of a Contracting Organization or where the basic registration has been made by such an Office, the person in whose name that application or registration stands is a national of a State member of that Contracting Organization, or is domiciled, or has a real and effective industrial or commercial establishment, in the territory of the said Contracting Organization.

(2) The application for international registration (hereinafter referred to as "the international application") shall be filed with the International Bureau through the intermediary of the Office with which the basic application was filed or by which the basic registration was made (hereinafter referred to as "the Office of origin"), as the case may be.

(3) Any reference in this Protocol to an "Office" or an "Office of a Contracting Party" shall be construed as a reference to the office that is in charge, on behalf of a Contracting Party, of the registration of marks, and any reference in this Protocol to "marks" shall be construed as a reference to trademarks and service marks.

(4) For the purposes of this Protocol, "territory of a Contracting Party" means, where the Contracting Party is a State, the territory of that State and, where the Contracting Party is an intergovernmental organization, the territory in which the constituting treaty of that intergovernmental organization applies.

ARTICLE 3

INTERNATIONAL APPLICATION

A19–04 (1) Every international application under this Protocol shall be presented on the form prescribed by the Regulations. The Office of origin shall certify that the particulars appearing in the international application correspond to the particu-

1190

lars appearing, at the time of the certification, in the basic application or basic registration, as the case may be. Furthermore, the said Office shall indicate,

(i) in the case of a basic application, the date and number of that application,

(ii) in the case of a basic registration, the date and number of that registration as well as the date and number of the application from which the basic registration resulted.

The Office of origin shall also indicate the date of the international application.

(2) The applicant must indicate the goods and services in respect of which protection of the mark is claimed and also, if possible, the corresponding class or classes according to the classification established by the Nice Agreement Concerning the International Classification of Goods and Services for the Purposes of the Registration of Marks. If the applicant does not give such indication, the International Bureau shall classify the goods and services in the appropriate classes of the said classification. The indication of classes given by the applicant shall be subject to control by the International Bureau, which shall exercise the said control in association with the Office of origin. In the event of disagreement between the said Office and the International Bureau, the opinion of the latter shall prevail.

(3) If the applicant claims colour as a distinctive feature of his mark, he shall be required—

(i) to state the fact, and to file with his international application a notice specifying the colour or the combination of colours claimed;

(ii) to append to his international application copies in colour of the said mark, which shall be attached to the notifications given by the International Bureau; the number of such copies shall be fixed by the Regulations.

(4) The International Bureau shall register immediately the marks filed in accordance with Article 2. The international registration shall bear the date on which the international application was received in the Office of origin, provided that the international application has been received by the International Bureau within a period of two months from that date. If the international application has not been received within that period, the international registration shall bear the date on which the said international application was received by the International Bureau. The International Bureau shall notify the international registration without delay to the Offices concerned. Marks registered in the International Register shall be published in a periodical gazette issued by the International Bureau, on the basis of the particulars contained in the international application.

(5) With a view to the publicity to be given to marks registered in the International Register, each Office shall receive from the International Bureau a number of copies of the said gazette free of charge and a number of copies at a reduced price, under the conditions fixed by the Assembly referred to in Article 10 (hereinafter referred to as "the Assembly"). Such publicity shall be deemed to be sufficient for the purposes of all the Contracting Parties, and no other publicity may be required of the holder of the international registration.

ARTICLE 3ᵇⁱˢ

TERRITORIAL EFFECT

The protection resulting from the international registration shall extend to any **A19–05** Contracting Party only at the request of the person who files the international application or who is the holder of the international registration. However, no such request can be made with respect to the Contracting Party whose Office is the Office of origin.

ARTICLE 3TER

REQUEST FOR "TERRITORIAL EXTENSION"

A19–06   (1) Any request for extension of the protection resulting from the international registration to any Contracting Party shall be specially mentioned in the international application.

(2) A request for territorial extension may also be made subsequently to the international registration. Any such request shall be presented on the form prescribed by the Regulations. It shall be immediately recorded by the International Bureau, which shall notify such recordal without delay to the Office or Offices concerned. Such recordal shall be published in the periodical gazette of the International Bureau. Such territorial extension shall be effective from the date on which it has been recorded in the International Register; it shall cease to be valid on the expiry of the international registration to which it relates.

ARTICLE 4

EFFECTS OF INTERNATIONAL REGISTRATION

A19–07   (1)(a)   From the date of the registration or recordal effected in accordance with the provisions of Articles 3 and 3ter, the protection of the mark in each of the Contracting Parties concerned shall be the same as if the mark had been deposited direct with the Office of that Contracting Party. If no refusal has been notified to the International Bureau in accordance with Article 5(1) and (2) or if a refusal notified in accordance with the said Article has been withdrawn subsequently, the protection of the mark in the Contracting Party concerned shall, as from the said date, be the same as if the mark had been registered by the Office of that Contracting Party.

(b)   The indication of classes of goods and services provided for in Article 3 shall not bind the Contracting Parties with regard to the determination of the scope of the protection of the mark.

(2) Every international registration shall enjoy the right of priority provided for by Article 4 of the Paris Convention for the Protection of Industrial Property, without it being necessary to comply with the formalities prescribed in Section D of that Article.

ARTICLES 4BIS

REPLACEMENT OF A NATIONAL OR REGIONAL REGISTRATION BY AN INTERNATIONAL REGISTRATION

A19–08   (1) Where a mark that is the subject of a national or regional registration in the Office of a Contracting Party is also the subject of an international registration and both registrations stand in the name of the same person, the international registration is deemed to replace the national or regional registration, without prejudice to any rights acquired by virtue of the latter, provided that

   (i) the protection resulting from the international registration extends to the said Contracting Party under Article 3ter (1) or (2),

  (ii) all the goods and services listed in the national or regional registration are also listed in the international registration in respect of the said Contracting Party,

 (iii) such extension takes effect after the date of the national or regional registration.

(2) The Office referred to in paragraph (1) shall, upon request, be required to take note in its register of the international registration.

<h2 style="text-align:center">ARTICLE 5</h2>

REFUSAL AND INVALIDATION OF EFFECTS OF INTERNATIONAL REGIS-
TRATION IN RESPECT OF CERTAIN CONTRACTING PARTIES

(1) Where the applicable legislation so authorizes, any Office of a Contracting **A19–09** Party which has been notified by the International Bureau of an extension to that Contracting Party, under Article 3ter(1) or (2), of the protection resulting from the international registration shall have the right to declare in a notification of refusal that protection cannot be granted in the said Contracting Party to the mark which is the subject of such extension. Any such refusal can be based only on the grounds which would apply, under the Paris Convention for the Protection of Industrial Property, in the case of a mark deposited direct with the Office which notifies the refusal. However, protection may not be refused, even partially, by reason only that the applicable legislation would permit registration only in a limited number of classes or for a limited number of goods or services.

(2)(a) Any Office wishing to exercise such right shall notify its refusal to the International Bureau, together with a statement of all grounds, within the period prescribed by the law applicable to that Office and at the latest, subject to subparagraphs (b) and (c), before the expiry of one year from the date on which the notification of the extension referred to in paragraph (1) has been sent to that Office by the International Bureau.

  (b) Notwithstanding subparagraph (a), any Contracting Party may declare that, for international registrations made under this Protocol, the time limit of one year referred to in subparagraph (a) is replaced by 18 months.

  (c) Such declaration may also specify that, when a refusal of protection may result from an opposition to the granting of protection, such refusal may be notified by the Office of the said Contracting Party to the International Bureau after the expiry of the 18-month time limit. Such an Office may, with respect to any given international registration, notify a refusal of protection after the expiry of the 18-month time limit, but only if—

     (i) it has, before the expiry of the 18-month time limit, informed the International Bureau of the possibility that oppositions may be filed after the expiry of the 18-month time limit, and

    (ii) the notification of the refusal based on an opposition is made within a time limit of not more than seven months from the date on which the opposition period begins; if the opposition period expires before this time limit of seven months, the notification must be made within a time limit of one month from the expiry of the opposition period.

  (d) Any declaration under subparagraphs (b) or (c) may be made in the instruments referred to in Article 14(2), and the effective date of the

1193

declaration shall be the same as the date of entry into force of this Protocol with respect to the State or intergovernmental organization having made the declaration. Any such declaration may also be made later, in which case the declaration shall have effect three months after its receipt by the Director General of the Organization (hereinafter referred to as "the Director General"), or at any later date indicated in the declaration, in respect of any international registration whose date is the same as or is later than the effective date of the declaration.

(e) Upon the expiry of a period of ten years from the entry into force of this Protocol, the Assembly shall examine the operation of the system established by subparagraphs (a) to (d). Thereafter, the provisions of the said subparagraphs may be modified by a unanimous decision of the Assembly.

(3) The International Bureau shall, without delay, transmit one of the copies of the notification of refusal to the holder of the international registration. The said holder shall have the same remedies as if the mark had been deposited by him direct with the Office which has notified its refusal. Where the International Bureau has received information under paragraph (2)(c)(i), it shall, without delay, transmit the said information to the holder of the international registration.

(4) The grounds for refusing a mark shall be communicated by the International Bureau to any interested party who may so request.

(5) Any Office which has not notified, with respect to a given international registration, any provisional or final refusal to the International Bureau in accordance with paragraphs (1) and (2) shall, with respect to that international registration, lose the benefit of the right provided for in paragraph (1).

(6) Invalidation, by the competent authorities of a Contracting Party, of the effects, in the territory of that Contracting Party, of an international registration may not be pronounced without the holder of such international registration having, in good time, been afforded the opportunity of defending his rights. Invalidation shall be notified to the International Bureau.

ARTICLE 5BIS

DOCUMENTARY EVIDENCE OF LEGITIMACY OF USE OF CERTAIN ELEMENTS OF THE MARK

A19–10 Documentary evidence of the legitimacy of the use of certain elements incorporated in a mark, such as armorial bearings, escutcheons, portraits, honorary distinctions, titles, trade names, names of persons other than the name of the applicant, or other like inscriptions, which might be required by the Offices of the Contracting Parties shall be exempt from any legalization as well as from any certification other than that of the Office of origin.

ARTICLE 5TER

COPIES OF ENTRIES IN INTERNATIONAL REGISTER; SEARCHES FOR ANTICIPATIONS; EXTRACTS FROM INTERNATIONAL REGISTER

A19–11 (1) The International Bureau shall issue to any person applying therefor, upon the payment of a fee fixed by the Regulations, a copy of the entries in the International Register concerning a specific mark.

(2) The International Bureau may also, upon payment, undertake searches for anticipations among marks that are the subject of international registrations.

(3) Extracts from the International Register requested with a view to their production in one of the Contracting Parties shall be exempt from any legalization.

ARTICLE 6

PERIOD OF VALIDITY OF INTERNATIONAL REGISTRATION; DEPENDENCE AND INDEPENDENCE OF INTERNATIONAL REGISTRATION

(1) Registration of a mark at the International Bureau is effected for ten years, **A19–12** with the possibility of renewal under the conditions specified in Article 7.

(2) Upon expiry of a period of five years from the date of the international registration, such registration shall become independent of the basic application or the registration resulting therefrom, or of the basic registration, as the case may be, subject to the following provisions.

(3) The protection resulting from the international registration, whether or not it has been the subject of a transfer, may no longer be invoked if, before the expiry of five years from the date of the international registration, the basic application or the registration resulting therefrom, or the basic registration, as the case may be, has been withdrawn, has lapsed, has been renounced or has been the subject of a final decision of rejection, revocation, cancellation or invalidation, in respect of all or some of the goods and services listed in the international registration. The same applies if—

   (i) an appeal against a decision refusing the effects of the basic application,

  (ii) an action requesting the withdrawal of the basic application or the revocation, cancellation or invalidation of the registration resulting from the basic application or of the basic registration, or

 (iii) an opposition to the basic application results, after the expiry of the five-year period, in a final decision of rejection, revocation, cancellation or invalidation, or ordering the withdrawal, of the basic application, or the registration resulting therefrom, or the basic registration, as the case may be, provided that such appeal, action or opposition had begun before the expiry of the said period. The same also applies if the basic application is withdrawn, or the registration resulting from the basic application or the basic registration is renounced, after the expiry of the five-year period, provided that, at the time of the withdrawal or renunciation, the said application or registration was the subject of a proceeding referred to in item (i), (ii) or (iii) and that such proceeding had begun before the expiry of the said period.

(4) The Office of origin shall, as prescribed in the Regulations, notify the International Bureau of the facts and decisions relevant under paragraph (3), and the International Bureau shall, as prescribed in the Regulations, notify the interested parties and effect any publication accordingly. The Office of origin shall, where applicable, request the International Bureau to cancel, to the extent applicable, the international registration, and the International Bureau shall proceed accordingly.

ARTICLE 7

RENEWAL OF INTERNATIONAL REGISTRATION

(1) Any international registration may be renewed for a period of ten years **A19–13** from the expiry of the preceding period, by the mere payment of the basic fee and, subject to Article 8(7), of the supplementary and complementary fees provided for in Article 8(2).

(2) Renewal may not bring about any change in the international registration in its latest form.

(3) Six months before the expiry of the term of protection, the International Bureau shall, by sending an unofficial notice, remind the holder of the international registration and his representative, if any, of the exact date of expiry.

(4) Subject to the payment of a surcharge fixed by the Regulations, a period of grace of six months shall be allowed for renewal of the international registration.

ARTICLE 8

FEES FOR INTERNATIONAL APPLICATION AND REGISTRATION

A19–14   (1) The Office of origin may fix, at its own discretion, and collect, for its own benefit, a fee which it may require from the applicant for international registration or from the holder of the international registration in connection with the filing of the international application or the renewal of the international registration.

(2) Registration of a mark at the International Bureau shall be subject to the advance payment of an international fee which shall, subject to the provisions of paragraph (7)(a), include,

(i) a basic fee;

(ii) a supplementary fee for each class of the International Classification, beyond three, into which the goods or services to which the mark is applied will fall;

(iii) a complementary fee for any request for extension of protection under Article 3ter.

(3) However, the supplementary fee specified in paragraph (2)(ii) may, without prejudice to the date of the international registration, be paid within the period fixed by the Regulations if the number of classes of goods or services has been fixed or disputed by the International Bureau. If, upon expiry of the said period, the supplementary fee has not been paid or the list of goods or services has not been reduced to the required extent by the applicant, the international application shall be deemed to have been abandoned.

(4) The annual product of the various receipts from international registration, with the exception of the receipts derived from the fees mentioned in paragraph (2)(ii) and (iii), shall be divided equally among the Contracing Parties by the International Bureau, after deduction of the expenses and charges necessitated by the implementation of this Protocol.

(5) The amounts derived from the supplementary fees provided for in paragraph (2)(ii) shall be divided, at the expiry of each year, among the interested Contracting Parties in proportion to the number of marks for which protection has been applied for in each of them during that year, this number being multiplied, in the case of Contracting Parties which make an examination, by a coefficient which shall be determined by the Regulations.

(6) The amounts derived from the complementary fees provided for in paragraph (2)(iii) shall be divided according to the same rules as those provided for in paragraph (5).

(7)(a) Any Contracting Party may declare that, in connection with each international registration in which it is mentioned under Article 3ter, and in connection with the renewal of any such international registration, it wants to receive, instead of a share in the revenue produced by the supplementary and complementary fees, a fee (hereinafter referred to as "the individual fee") whose amount shall be indicated in the declaration, and can be changed in further declarations, but may not be higher than the equivalent of the amount which the said Contracting Party's Office would be entitled to receive from an applicant for a ten-year registration, or from the holder of a registration for a ten-year renewal of that registration, of the mark in the register of the said Office, the said amount being diminished by the savings resulting from the international procedure. Where such an individual fee is payable,

    (i) no supplementary fees referred to in paragraph (2)(ii) shall be payable if only Contracting Parties which have made a declaration under this subparagraph are mentioned under Article 3ter, and

    (ii) no complementary fee referred to in paragraph (2)(iii) shall be payable in respect of any Contracting Party which has made a declaration under this subparagraph.

(b) Any declaration under subparagraph (a) may be made in the instruments referred to in Article 14(2), and the effective date of the declaration shall be the same as the date of entry into force of this Protocol with respect to the State or intergovernmental organization having made the declaration. Any such declaration may also be made later, in which case the declaration shall have effect three months after its receipt by the Director General, or at any later date indicated in the declaration, in respect of any international registration whose date is the same as or is later than the effective date of the declaration.

ARTICLE 9

RECORDAL OF CHANGE IN THE OWNERSHIP OF AN INTERNATIONAL REGISTRATION

At the request of the person in whose name the international registration **A19–15** stands, or at the request of an interested Office made *ex officio* or at the request of an interested person, the International Bureau shall record in the International Register any change in the ownership of that registration, in respect of all or some of the Contracting Parties in whose territories the said registration has effect and in respect of all or some of the goods and services listed in the registration, provided that the new holder is a person who, under Article 2(1), is entitled to file international applications.

ARTICLE 9bis

RECORDAL OF CERTAIN MATTERS CONCERNING AN INTERNATIONAL REGISTRATION

The International Bureau shall record in the International Register   **A19–16**

    (i) any change in the name or address of the holder of the international registration,

    (ii) the appointment of a representative of the holder of the international registration and any other relevant fact concerning such representative,

    (iii) any limitation, in respect of all or some of the Contracting Parties, of the goods and services listed in the international registration,

    (iv) any renunciation, cancellation or invalidation of the international registration in respect of all or some of the Contracting Parties,

    (v) any other relevant fact, identified in the Regulations, concerning the rights in a mark that is the subject of an international registration.

ARTICLE 9TER

FEES FOR CERTAIN RECORDALS

A19–17   Any recordal under Article 9 or under Article 9bis may be subject to the payment of a fee.

ARTICLE 9^{QUARTER}

COMMON OFFICE OF SEVERAL CONTRACTING STATES

A19–18   (1) If several Contracting States agree to effect the unification of their domestic legislations on marks, they may notify the Director General—

    (i) that a common Office shall be substituted for the national Office of each of them, and

    (ii) that the whole of their respective territories shall be deemed to be a single State for the purposes of the application of all or part of the provisions preceding this Article as well as the provisions of Articles 9^{quinquies} and 9^{sexies}.

(2) Such notification shall not take effect until three months after the date of the communication thereof by the Director General to the other Contracting Parties.

ARTICLE 9^{QUINQUIES}

TRANSFORMATION OF AN INTERNATIONAL REGISTRATION INTO NATIONAL OR REGIONAL APPLICATIONS

A19–19   Where, in the event that the international registration is cancelled at the request of the Office of origin under Article 6(4), in respect of all or some of the goods and services listed in the said registration, the person who was the holder of the international registration files an application for the registration of the same mark with the Office of any of the Contracting Parties in the territory of which the international registration had effect, that application shall be treated as if it had been filed on the date of the international registration according to Article 3(4) or on the date of recordal of the territorial extension according to Article 3ter(2) and, if the international registration enjoyed priority, shall enjoy the same priority, provided that—

    (i) such application is filed within three months from the date on which the international registration was cancelled,

    (ii) the goods and services listed in the application are in fact covered by the list of goods and services contained in the international registration in respect of the Contracting Party concerned, and

    (iii) such application complies with all the requirements of the applicable law, including the requirements concerning fees.

ARTICLE 9^{SEXIES}

SAFEGUARD OF THE MADRID (STOCKHOLM) AGREEMENT

A19–20   (1) Where, with regard to a given international application or a given international registration, the Office of origin is the Office of a State that is party to both this Protocol and the Madrid (Stockholm) Agreement, the provisions of this Protocol shall have no effect in the territory of any other State that is also party to both this Protocol and the Madrid (Stockholm) Agreement.

(2) The Assembly may, by a three-fourths majority, repeal paragraph (1), or restrict the scope of paragraph (1), after the expiry of a period of ten years from the entry into force of this Protocol, but not before the expiry of a period of five years from the date on which the majority of the countries party to the Madrid (Stockholm) Agreement have become party to this Protocol. In the vote of the Assembly, only those States which are party to both the said Agreement and this Protocol shall have the right to participate.

ARTICLE 10

ASSEMBLY

(1)(a) The Contracting Parties shall be members of the same Assembly as the **A19–21** countries party to the Madrid (Stockholm) Agreement.

  (b) Each Contracting Party shall be represented in that Assembly by one delegate, who may be assisted by alternate delegates, advisors, and experts.

  (c) The expenses of each delegation shall be borne by the Contracting Party which has appointed it, except for the travel expenses and the subsistence allowance of one delegate for each Contracting Party, which shall be paid from the funds of the Union.

(2) The Assembly shall, in addition to the functions which it has under the Madrid (Stockholm) Agreement, also—

  (i) deal with all matters concerning the implementation of this Protocol;

  (ii) give directions to the International Bureau concerning the preparation for conferences of revision of this Protocol, due account being taken of any comments made by those countries of the Union which are not party to this Protocol;

  (iii) adopt and modify the provisions of the Regulations concerning the implementation of this Protocol;

  (iv) perform such other functions as are appropriate under this Protocol.

(3)(a) Each Contracting Party shall have one vote in the Assembly. On matters concerning only countries that are party to the Madrid (Stockholm) Agreement, Contracting Parties are not party to the said Agreement shall not have the right to vote, whereas, on matters concerning only Contracting Parties, only the latter shall have the right to vote.

  (b) One-half of the members of the Assembly which have the right to vote on a given matter shall constitute the quorum for the purposes of the vote on that matter.

  (c) Notwithstanding the provisions of subparagraph (b), if, in any session, the number of the members of the Assembly having the right to vote on a given matter which are represented is less than one-half but equal to or more than one-third of the members of the Assembly having the right to vote on that matter, the Assembly may make decisions but, with the exception of decisions concerning its own procedure, all such decisions shall take effect only if the conditions set forth hereinafter are fulfilled. The International Bureau shall communicate the said decisions to the members of the Assembly having the right to vote on the said matter which were not represented and shall invite them to express in writing their vote or abstention within a period of three months from the date of the communication. If, at the expiry of this period, the

1199

number of such members having thus expressed their vote or abstention attains the number of the members which was lacking for attaining the quorum in the session itself, such decisions shall take effect provided that at the same time the required majority still obtains.

(d) Subject to the provisions of Articles 5(2)(e), 9^sexies (2), 12 and 13(2), the decisions of the Assembly shall require two-thirds of the votes cast.

(e) Abstentions shall not be considered as votes.

(f) A delegate may represent, and vote in the name of, one member of the Assembly only.

(4) In addition to meeting in ordinary sessions and extraordinary sessions as provided for by the Madrid (Stockholm) Agreement, the Assembly shall meet in extraordinary session upon convocation by the Director General, at the request of one-fourth of the members of the Assembly having the right to vote on the matters proposed to be included in the agenda of the session. The agenda of such an extraordinary session shall be prepared by the Director General.

ARTICLE 11

INTERNATIONAL BUREAU

A19–22   (1) International registration and related duties, as well as all other administrative tasks, under or concerning this Protocol, shall be performed by the International Bureau.

(2)(a) The International Bureau shall, in accordance with the directions of the Assembly, make preparations for the conferences of revision of this Protocol.

(b) The International Bureau may consult with intergovernmental and international non-governmental organizations concerning preparations for such conferences of revision.

(c) The Director General and persons designated by him shall take part, without the right to vote, in the discussions at such conferences of revision.

(3) The International Bureau shall carry out any other tasks assigned to it in relation to this Protocol.

ARTICLE 12

FINANCES

A19–23   As far as Contracting Parties are concerned, the finances of the Union shall be governed by the same provisions as those contained in Article 12 of the Madrid (Stockholm) Agreement, provided that any reference to Article 8 of the said Agreement shall be deemed to be a reference to Article 8 of this Protocol. Furthermore, for the purposes of Article 12(6)(b) of the said Agreement, Contracting Organizations shall, subject to a unanimous decision to the contrary by the Assembly, be considered to belong to contribution class I (one) under the Paris Convention for the Protection of Industrial Property.

ARTICLE 13

AMENDMENT OF CERTAIN ARTICLES OF THE PROTOCOL

A19–24   (1) Proposals for the amendment of Articles 10, 11, 12, and the present Article, may be initiated by any Contracting Party, or by the Director General. Such proposals shall be communicated by the Director General to the Contracting Parties at least six months in advance of their consideration by the Assembly.

1200

(2) Amendments to the Articles referred to in paragraph (1) shall be adopted by the Assembly. Adoption shall require three-fourths of the votes cast, provided that any amendment to Article 10, and to the present paragraph, shall require four-fifths of the votes cast.

(3) Any amendment to the Articles referred to in paragraph (1) shall enter into force one month after written notification of acceptance, effected in accordance with their respective constitutional processes, have been received by the Director General from three-fourths of those States and intergovernmental organizations which, at the time the amendment was adopted, were members of the Assembly and had the right to vote on the amendment. Any amendment to the said Articles thus accepted shall bind all the States and intergovernmental organizations which are Contracting Parties at the time the amendment enters into force, or which become Contracting Parties at a subsequent date.

ARTICLE 14

BECOMING PARTY TO THE PROTOCOL; ENTRY INTO FORCE

(1)(a) Any State that is a party to the Paris Convention for the Protection of **A19–25** Industrial Property may become party to this Protocol.

(b) Furthermore, any intergovernmental organization may also become party to this Protocol where the following conditions are fulfilled:

(i) at least one of the member States of that organization is a party to the Paris Convention for the Protection of Industrial Property;

(ii) that organization has a regional Office for the purposes of registering marks with effect in the territory of the organization, provided that such Office is not the subject of a notification under Article 9^{quater}.

(2) Any State or organization referred to in paragraph (1) may sign this Protocol. Any such State or organization may, if it has signed this Protocol, deposit an instrument of ratification, acceptance or approval of this Protocol or, if it has not signed this Protocol, deposit an instrument of accession to this Protocol.

(3) The instruments referred to in paragraph (2) shall be deposited with the Director General.

(4)(a) This Protocol shall enter into force three months after four instruments of ratification, acceptance, approval or accession have been deposited, provided that at least one of those instruments has been deposited by a country party to the Madrid (Stockholm) Agreement and at least one other of those instruments has been deposited by a State not party to the Madrid (Stockholm) Agreement or by any of the organizations referred to in paragraph (1)(b).

(b) with respect to any other State or organization referred to in paragraph (1), this Protocol shall enter into force three months after the date on which its ratification, acceptance, approval or accession has been notified by the Director General.

(5) Any State or organization referred to in paragraph (1) may, when depositing its instrument of ratification, acceptance or approval of, or accession to, this Protocol, declare that the protection resulting from any international registration effected under this Protocol before the date of entry into force of this Protocol with respect to it cannot be extended to it.

ARTICLE 15

DENUNCIATION

(1) This Protocol shall remain in force without limitation as to time. **A19–26**

(2) Any Contracting Party may denounce this Protocol by notification addressed to the Director General.

(3) Denunciation shall take effect one year after the day on which the Director General has received the notification.

(4) The right of denunciation provided for by this Article shall not be exercised by any Contracting Party before the expiry of five years from the date upon which this Protocol entered into force with respect to that Contracting Party.

(5)(a) Where a mark is the subject of an international registration having effect in the denouncing State or intergovernmental organization at the date on which the denunciation becomes effective, the holder of such registration may file an application for the registration of the same mark with the Office of the denouncing State or intergovernmental organization, which shall be treated as if it had been filed on the date of the international registration according to Article 3(4) or on the date of recordal of the territorial extension according to Article 3ter(2) and, if the international registration enjoyed priority, enjoy the same priority, provided that—

    (i) such application is filed within two years from the date on which the denunciation became effective,

    (ii) the goods and services listed in the application are in fact covered by the list of goods and services contained in the international registration in respect of the denouncing State or intergovernmental organization, and

    (iii) such application complies with all the requirements of the applicable law, including the requirements concerning fees.

(b) The provisions of subparagraph (a) shall also apply in respect of any mark that is the subject of an international registration having effect in Contracting Parties other than the denouncing State or intergovernmental organization at the date on which denunciation becomes effective and whose holder, because of the denunciation, is no longer entitled to file international applications under Article 2(1).

ARTICLE 16

SIGNATURE; LANGUAGES; DEPOSITARY FUNCTIONS

A19–27

(1)(a) This Protocol shall be signed in a single copy in the English, French and Spanish languages, and shall be deposited with the Director General when it ceases to be open for signature at Madrid. The texts in the three languages shall be equally authentic.

(b) Official texts of this Protocol shall be established by the Director General, after consultation with the interested governments and organizations, in the Arabic, Chinese, German, Italian, Japanese, Portuguese and Russian languages, and in such other languages as the Assembly may designate.

(2) This Protocol shall remain open for signature at Madrid until December 31 1989.

(3) The Director General shall transmit two copies, certified by the Government of Spain, of the signed texts of this Protocol to all States and intergovernmental organizations that may become party to this Protocol.

(4) The Director General shall register this Protocol with the Secretariat of the United Nations.

(5) The Director General shall notify all States and international organizations that may become or are party to this Protocol of signatures, deposits of

instruments of ratification, acceptance, approval or accession, the entry into force of this Protocol and any amendment thereto, any notification of denunciation and any declaration provided for in this Protocol.

APPENDIX 20

The Trade Marks (International Registration) Order 1996

S.I. 1996 No. 714

(As amended by the Trade Marks (International Registration) (Amendment) Order 2000, S.I. 2000 No.138)

A20–01   ARRANGEMENT OF ARTICLES

Preliminary

The Secretary of State, in exercise of the powers conferred on him by section 54 of the Trade Marks Act 1994 thereby makes the following Order:—

Preliminary

Citation commencement and extent

1.—(1) This Order may be cited as the Trade Marks (International Registra- **A20–02** tion) Order 1996 and comes into force on 1st April 1996.

(2) This Order extends to England and Wales, Scotland, Northern Ireland and the Isle of Man.

Interpretation

2. In this Order— **A20–03**

"the Act" means the Trade Marks Act 1994, and references to a section are, unless the context otherwise requires, to sections of that Act;

"basic application" and "basic registration" have the respective meanings given by article 22;

"Common Regulations" means the regulations adopted under article 10 of the Madrid Protocol with effect from 1 April 1996;

"international application" means an application to the International Bureau for registration of a trade mark in the International Register;

"International Bureau" means the International Bureau of the World Intellectual Property Organisation;

"International Register" means the register of trade marks maintained by the International Bureau for the purposes of the Madrid Protocol;

"international registration" means the registration of a trade mark in the International Register;

"international regislation designating the United Kingdom" means an international registration in relation to which a request has been made (either in the relevant international application or subsequently) for extension of protection to the United Kingdom under Article 3ter (1) or (2) of the Madrid Protocol;

"notifiable transaction" has the meaning given by article 6;

"protected international trade mark (UK)" has the meaning given by article 12, and references to "protection" and "protected" shall be construed accordingly;

"the Rules" means the Trade Marks Rules 1994, and references to a rule shall unless the context otherwise requires, be construed accordingly;

"the Rules" means the Trade Marks Rules 2000 and references to a rule shall, unless the context otherwise requires, be construed accordingly;

"supplementary register" has the meaning given by article 24;

"transformation application" has the meaning given by article 19;

"United Kingdom" includes the Isle of Man.

International Registrations Designating the United Kingdom

Entitlement to protection

3.—(1) An international registration designating the United Kingdom shall be **A20–04** entitled to become protected subject to the provisions of articles 9 to 12 where, if the particulars of the international registration were comprised in an application for registration of a trade mark under the Act, such an application would satisfy the requirements for registration (including any imposed by the Rules).

(2) For that purpose, sections 32 to 34, rules 5 to 8 and rules 10 and 11 shall be disregarded.

Effects of Protected International Trade Mark (UK)

A20–05   4.—(1) The proprietor of a protected international trade mark (UK) has, subject to the provisions of this Order, the same rights and remedies as are given by or under sections 9 to 12 and 14 to 20 to the proprietor of a registered trade mark, subject to the limits on effect and to the provisions relating to exhaustion which are applicable to a registered trade mark by virtue of section 11 and section 12 respectively.

(2) For the purposes of section 9 (rights conferred by registered trade mark)—

(a) the rights of the proprietor shall have effect as of the date on which it is to be treated as registered pursuant to article 12 or article 21;

(b) a protected international trade mark (UK) shall be treated as being in fact registered when it becomes protected pursuant to article 12.

(3) References in sections 10 and 11 to goods or services in respect of which a trade mark is registered are to goods or services in respect of which a protected international trade mark (UK) confers protection in the United Kingdom.

(4) Where the holder of an international registration designating the United Kingdom by notice in writing sent to the registrar—

(a) disclaims any right to the exclusive use of any specified element of the trade mark, or

(b) agrees that the rights conferred in the United Kingdom by the international registration shall be subject to a specified territorial or other limitation.

the registrar shall enter the disclaimer or limitation in the supplementary register and shall publish the disclaimer or limitation.

(5) Where a protected international trade mark (UK) is subject to a disclaimer or limitation, the rights conferred in relation to it by the application of section 9 are restricted accordingly.

(6) The remedy for groundless threats of infringement proceedings given by section 21 applies in relation to a protected international trade mark (UK) as in relation to a registered trade mark; and for this purpose—

(a) the reference in section 21(3) to the registration of the trade mark shall be treated as a reference to protection of a protected international trade mark (UK); and

(b) the reference in section 21(4) to notification that a trade mark is registered, or that an application for registration has been made, shall be treated as a reference to notification that a trade mark is a protected international trade mark (UK) or is the subject of an international application or international registration designating the United Kingdom.

International Trade mark (UK) as an object of property

A20–06   5. The provisions of sections 22, 23, 24 (except subsection (2)(b)) and 26 (which relate to a registered trade mark as an object of property) apply, with the necessary modifications, in relation to an international trade mark (UK) as in relation to a registered trade mark.

Notification of transactions

A20–07   6.—(1) The following are notifiable transactions for the purposes of this article—

   (a) the grant of a licence under a protected international trade mark (UK);

   (b) the granting of any security interest (whether fixed or floating) over an international trade mark (UK) or any right in or under it.

(2) On application being made to the registrar by—

   (a) a person claiming to be entitled to an interest in or under an international trade mark (UK) by virtue of a notifiable transaction, or

   (b) any other person claiming to be affected by such a transaction.

the prescribed particulars of the transaction shall be entered in the supplementary register.

(3) The following are relevant transactions for the purposes of this article—

   (a) a notifiable transaction;

   (b) an assignment of an international trade mark (UK) or any right in it;

   (c) the making by personal representatives of an assent in relation to an international trade mark (UK) or any right in or under it;

   (d) an order of a court or other competent authority transferring an international trade mark (UK) or any right in or under it.

(4) Until (in the case of a notifiable transaction) an application has been made for registration of the prescribed particulars or (in the case of any other relevant transaction) the transaction has been recorded in the International Register—

   (a) the transaction is ineffective as against a person acquiring an interest in or under the international trade mark (UK) in ignorance of it, and

   (b) a person claiming to be a licensee by virtue of the transaction does not have the protection of section 30 or 31 (rights and remedies of licensee in relation to infringement).

(5) Where a person becomes the proprietor or a licensee of an international trade mark (UK) by virtue of a relevant transaction, then unless—

   (a) an application for registration of the transaction (in the case of a notifiable transaction) is made, or (in the case of any other relevant transaction) a request for recordal in the International Register is made, before the end of a period of six months beginning with its date, or

   (b) the court is satisfied that it was not practicable for such an application or request for recordal to be made before the end of that period and that an application or request for recordal (as the case may be) was made as soon as practicable thereafter.

he is not entitled to damages or an account of profits in respect of any infringement of the international trade mark (UK) occurring after the date of the transaction and before (in the case of a notifiable transaction) the prescribed particulars of the transaction are registered or (in the case of any other relevant transaction) the transaction is recorded in the International Register.

(6) "Prescribed particulars" means the particulars prescribed by rule 40.

Licensing

7.—(1) The provisions of sections 28 to 31 apply, with the necessary modifica- **A20–08** tions, in relation to licences to use a protected international trade mark (UK).

(2) The reference in section 28(1) to goods or services for which a trade mark is registered shall be treated as a reference to goods or services in respect of which the trade mark is protected in the United Kingdom.

Priority

8.—(1) The provisions of section 35 (claim to priority of Convention appli- **A20–09** cation) apply, subject as mentioned below, so as to confer a right to priority in relation to protection of an international registration designating the United Kingdom as they apply in relation to registering a trade mark under the Act.

(2) Subsection (5) of that section does not apply and the manner of claiming priority shall be determined in accordance with the Madrid Protocol and the Common Regulations.

Examination

A20–10 9.—(1) Upon receiving from the International Bureau notification of an international registration designating the United Kingdom, the registrar shall examine whether it satisfies the requirements of article 3.

(2) For that purpose, he shall carry out a search, to such extent as he considers necessary, of earlier trade marks.

(3) If it appears to the registrar that the requirements referred to in paragraph (1) above are not met, or are met only in relation to some of the goods or services in respect of which protection in the United Kingdom has been requested, he shall give notice of refusal to the International Bureau.

(4) Notice of refusal shall specify a period within which the holder may make representations.

(5) A holder making representations shall file an address for service in the United Kingdom on Form TM33.

Publication, opposition proceedings and observations

A20–11 10.—(1) Where following examination pursuant to article 9 it appears to the registrar that the requirements of article 3 are met in relation to all or some of the goods or services comprised in the international registration, the registrar shall publish a notice specifying particulars of the international registration and specifying the goods or services for which protection will be conferred.

(2) Any person may, within three months of the date of publication pursuant to paragraph (1) above, give notice to the registrar of opposition to the conferring of protection.

The notice shall be given in writing in the manner prescribed by rule 13, shall include a statement of the grounds of opposition and shall where opposition is based on an earlier trade mark indicate the goods or services on which the opposition is based.

(3) The registrar shall, upon notice of opposition being given, and in any event within four months of publication pursuant to paragraph (1) above, give notice of refusal to the International Bureau stating the matters relating to the opposition referred to in paragraph (2) above.

(4) *Within three months of the date on which notice of refusal based on opposition is given to the International Bureau, the holder may file a counter-statement, in conjunction with notice of the same on Form TM8 and an address for service in the United Kingdom.*

(4) Subject to paragraphs (4A) and (4B) below, within three months of the date on which notice of refusal based on opposition is given to the International Bureau, the holder may file a counter-statement, in conjunction with notice of the same on Form TM8 and an address for service in the United Kingdom.

(4A) Subject to paragraph (4B), at any time before the expiry of the period prescribed by paragraph (4) above for filing of Form TM8 by the holder the registrar may, on request, grant an extension of three months to that period where such request is filed on Form TM9c and with the agreement of both the holder and the opposing party (the "cooling off period"); the registrar may, on request, extend the cooling off period for a further three months where such request is filed on Form TM9c and with the agreement of both the holder and the opposing party.

(4B) Within one month after the expiry of the cooling off period the holder may file a counter-statement, in conjunction with notice of the same on Form TM8 and an address for service in the United Kingdom.

(5) Subject to the provisions of this article, rules 13 and 14 shall apply in relation to opposition proceedings, with the substitution of the holder for the applicant.

(5A) The provisions of rule 36 (case management) and rule 37 (pre-hearing review) shall apply in relation to opposition proceedings.

(6) Where a notice has been published pursuant to paragraph (1) above, any person may, at any time before the trade mark has become protected in accordance with article 12, make observations in writing to the registrar as to whether the trade mark should be protected.

A person who makes observations does not thereby become a party to proceedings in relation to the request for protection.

Notices of refusal

11.—(1) Except where refusal is based on an opposition, notice of refusal shall **A20–12** not be given after the expiry of 18 months from the date on which the notification of the request for extension was sent to the United Kingdom.

(2) The registrar shall inform the International Bureau that oppositions may be filed after the expiry of the period of 18 months referred to in paragraph (1) above unless, at least four months before the expiry of the said period, he has published the notice referred to in article 10(1).

(3) Notices of refusal shall set out the matters required by Article 5 of the Madrid Protocol and Rule 17 of the Common Regulations.

(4) Where—

(a) notice of refusal has been given pursuant to article 9(3), and
   (i) the holder makes representations within the period specified under article 9(4), or
   (ii) the holder makes no representations within the period, or informs the registrar that he does not intend to make any representations, or
(b) notice of refusal based on an opposition has been given pursuant to article 10(3) and
   (i) the holder files a counter-statement within the period specified in article 10(4) or **10(4B)**, or
   (ii) the holder files no counter-statement within that period or informs the registrar that he does not intend to file a counter-statement,

the registrar shall inform the International Bureau of that fact.

(5) Where—

(a) after notice of refusal has been given pursuant to article 9(3), the holder makes representations within the period specified under article 9(4); or
(b) after notice of refusal based on an opposition, the holder files a counter-statement within the period specified in article 10(4) or **10(4B)**.

the registrar shall, upon a final decision being made in relation to the refusal, notify the International Bureau of that decision.

(6) For the purposes of paragraph (5) above, a final decision shall be regarded as being made where—

(a) the registrar, or the appointed person or the court on appeal or further appeal from the registrar, decides whether the refusal shall be upheld, in whole or in relation to some only of the goods or services in relation to which protection in the United Kingdom is requested, and any right of appeal against that decision expires or is exhausted;
(b) the representations or counter-statement are withdrawn; or
(c) the proceedings relating to the refusal are discontinued or abandoned.

Protection

12.—(1) Where—   **A20–13**

(a) following examination and publication pursuant to articles 9 and 10—

    (i) the period of 18 months from the date on which the notification of the request for extension was sent to the United Kingdom has not expired, but the period for giving notice of refusal based on an opposition in accordance with article 10(3) expires without notice of refusal (whether based on opposition or otherwise) having been given.

    (ii) the period of 18 months from the date on which the notification of the request for extension was sent to the United Kingdom has expired, and the period for giving notice of opposition in accordance with article 10(2) expires without notice of opposition having been given,

    (iii) *notice of refusal has been given in respect of some only of the goods or services in respect of which protection in the United Kingdom has been requested and the registrar informs the International Bureau in accordance with article 11(4) that the holder has made no representations within the period specified in article 9(4) or has filed no counter-statement within the period specified in article 10(4) (as the case may be) or that the holder has informed the registrar that he does not intend to make such representations or file such a counter-statement, or*

    (iii) **notice of refusal has been given in respect of some only of the goods or services in respect of which protection in the United Kingdom has been requested and the registrar informs the International Bureau in accordance with article 11(4) that the holder has made no representations within the period specified in article 9(4) or has filed no counter-statement within the period specified in article 10(4) or 10 (4B) (as the case may be) or that the holder has informed the registrar that he does not intend to make such representations or file such a counter-statement, or**

    (iv) notice of refusal has been given in respect of all or some of the goods or services in respect of which protection in the United Kingdom has been requested and the registrar notifies the International Bureau in accordance with article 11(5) that a final decision has been made that the refusal is withdrawn, or is withdrawn in respect of some of the goods or services in respect of which protection in the United Kingdom has been requested; or

(b) the period of 18 months from the date on which the notification of the request for extension was sent to the United Kingdom expires without any notice of refusal having been given and without the International Bureau having been informed that oppositions may be filed after the expiry of that period,

the trade mark which is the subject of the request for protection shall thereupon be protected as a protected international trade mark (UK); and in a case where a refusal subsists in respect of some of the goods or services in respect of which protection in the United Kingdom has been requested, protection shall apply only as regards the remaining goods or services.

(2) For the purposes of application by this Order of provisions of the Act, subject to article 21, a trade mark so protected shall be treated as being registered under the Act as of the following date:—

(a) where the request for extension of protection to the United Kingdom is mentioned in the international application, or is made subsequently, but on or before the date of the international registration, the date of that international registration;

(b) where the request for such extension is made subsequently to the international registration, the date on which the request is recorded in the International Register.

(3) When a trade mark becomes protected pursuant to this article, the registrar shall publish particulars of the international registration specifying the date on which, and the goods or services in respect of which, protection is conferred.

Revocation and Invalidity

13.—(1) The provisions of section 46 (revocation of registration) and section 47 **A20–14** (grounds for invalidity of registration) shall apply, subject to the adaptations set out below, so as to permit the protection of a protected international trade mark (UK) to be revoked, or declared invalid.

(2) The reference in section 46(1) to the date of completion of the registration procedure shall be construed as a reference to the date of the protected international trade mark (UK) becoming protected; the reference in section 46(2) to the form in which a trade mark was registered shall be construed as reference to the form in which it is protected; and the references in section 46(5) and section 47(5) to goods or services for which the trade mark is registered shall be construed as references to those in respect of which it is protected.

(3) The references in section 46 to the registration of a trade mark being revoked and the references in section 47 to the registration of a trade mark being declared invalid shall be construed as references to the protection of a protected international trade mark (UK) being revoked or declared invalid, as the case may be.

(4) The provisions of rule 31, with necessary modifications, apply in relation to the procedure on application for revocation and declaration of invalidity of protection of a protected international trade mark (UK).

(4) The provisions of rules 31, 32 and 33, with necessary modifications, apply respectively in relation to the procedure on application for revocation (on grounds of non-use), revocation (on grounds other than non-use) and declaration of invalidity of protection of a protected international trade mark (UK).

(4A) The provisions of rule 35 (intervention), rule 36 (case management) and rule 37 (pre-hearing review) apply in relation to a procedure on application for revocation (on grounds of non-use), revocation (on grounds other than non-use) and declaration of invalidity of protection of a protected international trade mark (UK).

(5) Where the protection of a protected international trade mark (UK) is revoked or declared invalid to any extent, the registrar shall notify the International Bureau, and

(a) in the case of a revocation, the rights of the proprietor shall be deemed to have ceased to exist to that extent as from the date on which the revocation is recorded in the International Register;

(b) in the case of a declaration of invalidity, the trade mark shall to that extent be deemed never to have been a protected international trade mark (UK):

Provided that this shall not affect transactions past and closed as at the date when the invalidity is recorded in the International Register.

Effect of acquiescence

14. Section 48 (effect of acquiescence) applies where the proprietor of an **A20–15** earlier trade mark has acquiesced for a continuous period of five years in the use of a protected international trade mark (UK); and for that purpose—

(a) the reference to a registered trade mark shall be construed as including a protected international trade mark (UK);

(b) the references to registration shall include references to protection of a protected international trade mark (UK).

Proceedings relating to invalidity and revocation of protection

A20–16   **15.**—(1) The provisions of section 73 (certificate of validity of contested registration) apply, with the necessary modifications, in relation to proceedings before the court in which the validity of the protection of a protected international trade mark (UK) is contested.

(2) The provisions of section 74 (registrar's appearance in proceedings involving the registrar) apply, with the necessary modifications, in relation to proceedings before the court involving an application for—

   (a) the revocation of the protection of a protected international trade mark (UK);

   (b) a declaration of the invalidity of the protection of a protected international trade mark (UK);

   (c) the rectification of the supplementary register.

Importation of infringing goods, materials or articles

A20–17   **16.** The provisions of section 89 (infringing goods, material or articles may be treated as prohibited goods) section 90 and section 91 of the Act (power of Commissioners of Customs and Excise to disclose information) apply in relation to goods which are, in relation to a protected international trade mark (UK), infringing goods, materials or articles, and for the purposes of those provisions—

   (a) references to a registered trade mark shall be to a protected international trade mark (UK);

   (b) the Trade Marks (Customs) Regulations 1994 shall apply in relation to notices given under the provisions of section 89.

Offences and forfeiture

A20–18   **17.**—(1) The provisions of section 92 (unauthorised use of trade mark, etc, in relation to goods), section 93 (enforcement function of local weights and measures authority), section 97 (forfeiture: England and Wales) and section 98 (forfeiture: Scotland) apply in relation to a protected international trade mark (UK).

(2) For the purposes of the provisions referred to in paragraph (1) above—

   (a) references to a registered trade mark shall be treated as references to a protected international trade mark (UK);

   (b) references to goods in respect of which a trade mark is registered shall be treated as references to goods in respect of which a protected international trade mark (UK) confers protection in the United Kingdom.

(3) No offence under section 92 in relation to a protected international trade mark is committed by anything done before the date of publication pursuant to article 12(3).

Falsely representing trade mark as a protected international trade mark (UK)

A20–19   **18.**—(1) It is an offence for a person—

   (a) falsely to represent that a mark is a protected international trade mark (UK), or

   (b) to make a false representation as to the goods or services for which a protected international trade mark (UK) confers protection in the United Kingdom

knowing or having reason to believe that the representation is false.

(2) A person guilty of an offence under this article is liable on summary conviction to a fine not exceeding level 3 on the standard scale.

Transformation of an International Registration into a National Application

Transformation applications

19.—(1) The provisions of this article apply where—   **A20–20**

(a) an international registration designating the United Kingdom is cancelled at the request of the Office of origin under Article 6(4) of the Madrid Protocol in respect of all or some of the goods or services listed in the registration;

(b) an applicant (a "transformation application") is made to the registrar, within three months of the date on which the international registration was cancelled, for registration in the United Kingdom of a trade mark identical to that comprised in the international registration in respect of some or all of the goods or services in respect of which the international registration was cancelled; and

(c) the application is made by the person who was the holder of the international registration immediately before its cancellation.

(2) A transformation application shall be made on Form TM3 and shall state that it is made by way of transformation.

(3) A trade mark registered pursuant to a transformation application shall be treated as if it were registered as of the date of the international registration according to Article 3(4) of the Madrid Protocol or, where the request for extension to the United Kingdom was made subsequently to the international registration, on the date of recordal of that request according to Article 3ter of the Madrid Protocol, and that date shall be deemed for the purposes of the Act to be the date of registration.

Procedure on transformation application

20.—(1) Where the international trade mark (UK) has become protected **A20–21** pursuant to article 12 on or before the actual date on which the transformation application is made ("the transformation date") the trade mark shall be registered under the Act.

(2) Where the international registration designating the United Kingdom has not become protected under article 12 at the transformation date and a notice has been published pursuant to article 10(1) in respect of the trade mark, the registrar shall treat the publication of such notice as being the publication of the transformation application under section 38(1) and shall publish a notice that it is being so treated. Any opposition shall be treated as opposition under section 38(2).

(3) Where a notice has not yet been published pursuant to article 10(1) at the transformation date and the registrar has issued a notice of refusal pursuant to article 9(3), the registrar shall for the purposes of the transformation application treat the notice of refusal as if it had been issued under section 37(3).

The registrar shall in that event inform the applicant of the nature of the response required of him in respect of his transformation application and shall further specify the period within which the applicant must respond to the registrar.

Concurrent Registrations

Effects of international registration where trade mark is also registered under the Act

21.—(1) The provisions of this article apply, without prejudice to the rights **A20–22** and remedies conferred in respect of a trade mark registered under the Act, where—

(a) the registered trade mark is also a protected international trade mark (UK);

(b) the proprietor of the registered trade mark is the holder of the international trade mark (UK);

(c) all the goods or services in respect of which the registered trade mark is registered are protected under the protected international trade mark (UK);

(d) the date of registration of the registered trade mark is earlier than the date specified in article 12(2) in relation to the international trade mark (UK).

(2) For the purposes of application by this Order of the provisions of the Act, the protected international trade mark (UK) shall be treated, notwithstanding the provisions of article 12(2), as being registered under the Act as of the date of registration of the registered trade mark as regards all the goods or services in respect of which the registered trade mark was registered.

(3) For the purpose of determining whether the international trade mark (UK) is an earlier trade mark, it shall be treated as having the date of application of the registered trade mark as regards all the goods or services in respect of which the registered trade mark was registered, taking account (where appropriate) of the priorities claimed in respect of the registered trade mark.

(4) Where the conditions specified in paragraph (1) above are satisfied in relation to a trade mark, the provisions of paragraphs (2) and (3) above shall continue to apply in respect of the relevant international trade mark (UK) notwithstanding that the relevant registered trade mark lapses or is surrendered, but shall cease to apply if it is revoked or declared invalid.

(5) On the application of the holder of the protected international trade mark (UK), the registrar shall note the international registration in the register against the registered trade mark.

(6) For the purposes of paragraph (5) above, the holder of the protected international trade mark (UK) shall make an application to the registrar using Form TM28.

International Applications Originating in the United Kingdom

Applications for international registration

A20–23   22.—(1) An applicant for the registration of a trade mark, or the proprietor of a registered trade mark, may, subject to the provisions of this article, apply through the registrar for the international registration of the trade mark.

(2) An application for international registration may be made only where the applicant for such registration is—

(a) a British citizen, a British dependent territories citizen, a British overseas citizen, a British subject or a British protected person;

(b) a body or a corporation sole incorporated or constituted under the law of any part of the United Kingdom;

(c) a person domiciled in the United Kingdom: or

(d) a person who has a real and effective industrial or commercial establishment in the United Kingdom.

(3) The particulars appearing in the application shall correspond with the particulars appearing at that time in the basic application or basic registration as the case may be.

(4) The applicant for international registration shall provide at the request of the registrar such evidence as may be necessary to satisfy him that the applicant is eligible to make the application in accordance with paragraph (2) above.

(5) If an international application complies with the requirements set out in this article, the registrar shall submit the international application to the International Bureau.

(6) In this Order—

(a) "basic application" means an application for registration of a trade mark in the United Kingdom in respect of which application is made for international registration:

(b) "basic registration" means a trade mark registered in the United Kingdom in respect of which application is made for international registration.

Notification to International Bureau

23.—(1) Where the registrar has submitted an application for international **A20–24** registration, he shall notify the International Bureau of the occurrence of any of the events specified in paragraph (2) below and shall request the International Bureau to cancel the international registration as regards those goods or services covered by the international application in respect of which the basic application or basic registration has ceased to subsist by reason of that event.

(2) The following events are specified for the purposes of paragraph (1) above:

(a) before the expiry of five years from the date of the international registration, the registrar refuses to accept the basic application as regards some or all of the goods or services covered by the international registration or, after accepting the application refuses to register the trade mark as regards some or all of those goods or services, having regard to matters coming to his notice since he accepted the application, and in either case that decision becomes a final decision, whether before or after the expiry of that period of five years;

(b) opposition proceedings begun before the expiry of five years from the date of the international registration result in a final decision not to register the trade mark as regards some or all of the goods or services covered by the international registration;

(c) the basic application is withdrawn, or is restricted as regards goods or services covered by the international registration, as a result of a request by the applicant made before the expiry of five years from the date of the international registration, or made subsequently when the basic application was at the time of the request subject to an appeal against refusal of registration or to opposition proceedings begun in either case before the expiry of that five year period;

(d) the registration resulting from the basic application or the basic registration expires without renewal and is removed from the register before the expiry of five years from the date of the international registration and no request for its restoration is made within the time specified in rule 30 or such a request is made and a final decision is made to refuse the request;

(e) a final decision is made to revoke or declare invalid the registration resulting from the basic application or the basic registration, as a result of proceedings begun before the expiry of five years from the date of the international registration:

(f) the registration resulting from the basic application, or the basic registration, is surrendered as a result of a request by the proprietor made before the expiry of five years from the date of the international registration, or made subsequently where at the time of the request—

(i) the basic application was subject to an appeal against refusal of registration or to opposition proceedings; or

1215

(ii) the registration resulting from the basic application, or the basic registration, was subject to proceedings for revocation or invalidation;

and such appeal or proceedings were begun before the expiry of five years from the date of the international registration.

(3) For the purposes of this article:—

(a) a final decision shall be regarded as made where—
  (i) any right of appeal against the decision expires or is exhausted, or
  (ii) proceedings relating to an application or registration are discontinued or abandoned;

(b) reference to an application being withdrawn includes its being deemed to be withdrawn, or abandoned, or deemed never to have been made.

Miscellaneous and General Provisions

Supplementary Register

A20–25   24.—(1) The registrar shall maintain a register ("the supplementary register") for the purpose of recording, in relation to international trade marks (UK)—

(a) disclaimers and limitations;
(b) notifiable transactions.

(2) The supplementary register need not be kept in documentary form.

(3) Rules **40 to 45** apply, with the necessary modifications, in relation to the supplementary register.

Disclosure of Information

A20–26   25.—(1) Before publication of notice under article 10(1) in relation to an international registration designating the United Kingdom, the registrar shall not publish or communicate to any person documents or information relating to the international registration other than as provided in paragraph (2) below.

(2) In relation to an international registration designating the United Kingdom, the registrar shall on request make available for inspection by the public all information in his possession which is recorded in the International Register concerning that registration, the particulars contained in any application for registration of a notifiable transaction and any entry in the supplementary register resulting from such an application.

(3) Subject to paragraph (5) below, after publication of notice under article 10(1) in relation to an international registration designating the United Kingdom, the registrar shall on request provide a person with such information and permit him to inspect such document, relating to the international registration as may be specified in the request.

(4) A request for information relating to an international registration designating the United Kingdom shall be made on Form TM31M.

(5) Paragraphs (2) to (5) of rule **50**, and rule **51**, apply in relation to the right of inspection conferred by paragraph (3) above.

(6) Where a person has been notified that an international registration designates the United Kingdom and that the proprietor will, if the registration becomes a protected international trade mark (UK), bring proceedings against him in respect of acts done after publication of notice under article 10(1), the registrar shall on request permit inspection under paragraph (3) above notwithstanding that such notice has not been published and that paragraph shall apply accordingly.

Exclusion of Liability

A20–27   26.—(1) The registrar is not subject to any liability by reason of, or in connection with, any examination required or authorised by this Order, or in any report or other proceedings consequent on such examination.

(2) No proceedings lie against an officer of the registrar in respect of any matter for which, by virtue of this article, the registrar is not liable.

Evidence of certain matters relating to an international registration

27.—(1) In all legal proceedings relating to an international trade mark (UK), **A20–28** the registration of a person as holder of an international trade mark (UK) shall be prima facie evidence of the validity of the original international registration and of any subsequent assignment or other transmission of it.

(2) Judicial notice shall be taken of the following—

(a) the Madrid Protocol and the Common Regulations;
(b) copies issued by the International Bureau of entries in the International Register;
(c) copies of the periodical gazette published by the International Bureau.

(3) Any document mentioned in paragraph (2)(b) or (c) above shall be admissible as evidence of any instrument or other act thereby communicated of the International Bureau.

(4) Evidence of any instrument issued by the International Bureau or any entry in or extract from such a document may be given in any legal proceedings by production of a copy; and any document purporting to be such a copy shall be received in evidence.

(5) In any legal proceedings in Scotland, evidence of any matter given in any manner authorised by this article shall be sufficient evidence of it.

(6) In this article, "legal proceedings" includes proceedings before the registrar.

Agents

28. Any act required or authorised by this Order to be done by or to a person **A20–29** in connection with a request for protection of an international registration as a protected international trade mark (UK) or any procedure relating to a protected international trade mark (UK) may be done by or to an agent authorised by that person orally or in writing.

Burden of proving use of international trade mark (UK)

29. If in any civil proceedings pursuant to this Order a question arises as to the **A20–30** use to which an international trade mark (UK) has been put, it is for the holder to show what use has been made of it.

Communication of information to the International Bureau

30. Notwithstanding section 67(2) or any other enactment or rule of law, the **A20–31** registrar may communicate to the International Bureau any information which the United Kingdom is required to communicate by virtue of this Order or pursuant to the Madrid Protocol or the Common Regulations.

Transmission of fees to the International Bureau

31. The registrar may accept for transmission to the International Bureau fees **A20–32** payable to the International Bureau in respect of an application for international registration originating in the United Kingdom or a renewal of such an international registration, subject to such terms and conditions as he may specify, either generally by published notice, or in any particular case by written notice to the applicant desiring to make payment by such means.

Application of Trade Marks Rules 2000

32.—(1) Except as otherwise provided, or where their application would be **A20–33** inconsistent with the provisions of this Order, the Rules shall apply, with the necessary modifications, in relation to an international registration designating the United Kingdom, (including a protected international trade mark (UK)) as in relation to a registered trade mark or application.

(2) In their application to an international registration designating the United Kingdom, the Rules shall be treated in all respects as rules made under the Act and, in particular, rules relating to costs and security for costs and to evidence before the registrar shall be enforceable in relation to proceedings under this Order in the same manner as in relation to proceedings relating to a registered trade mark or application.

PART VII

OTHER INTERNATIONAL MATERIALS

APPENDIX 21

Paris Convention for the Protection of Industrial Property of March 20, 1883,[1] as revised at Brussels on December 14, 1900,[2] at Washington on June 2, 1911,[3] at the Hague on November 6, 1925,[4] at London on June 2, 1934,[5] at Lisbon on October 31, 1958,[6] and at Stockholm on July 14, 1967

ARTICLE 1

[Establishment of the Union; Scope of Industrial Property][*]

(1) The countries to which this Convention applies constitute a Union for the protection of industrial property. **A21–01**

(2) The protection of industrial property has as its object patents, utility models, industrial designs, trademarks, service marks, trade names, indications of source or appellations of origin, and the repression of unfair competition.

(3) Industrial property shall be understood in the broadest sense and shall apply not only to industry and commerce proper, but likewise to agricultural and extractive industries and to all manufactured or natural products, for example, wines, grain, tobacco leaf, fruit, cattle, minerals, mineral waters, beer, flowers, and flour.

(4) Patents shall include the various kinds of industrial patents recognized by the laws of the countries of the Union, such as patents of importation, patents of improvement, patents and certificates of addition, etc.

ARTICLE 2

[National Treatment for Nationals of Countries of the Union]

(1) Nationals of any country of the Union shall, as regards the protection of industrial property, enjoy in all the other countries of the Union the advantages that their respective laws now grant, or may hereafter grant, to nationals; all **A21–02**

[1] Commercial No. 28 (1884), C. 4043.
[2] Treaty Series No. 15 (1902), Cd. 1084.
[3] Treaty Series No. 8 (1913), Cd. 6805.
[4] Treaty Series No. 16 (1928), Cmd. 3167.
[5] Treaty Series No. 55 (1938), Cmd. 5833.
[6] Treaty Series No. 38 (1962), Cmnd. 1715.
[*] Articles have been given titles to facilitate their identification. There are no titles in the signed (French) text.

without prejudice to the rights specially provided for by this Convention. Consequently, they shall have the same protection as the latter, and the same legal remedy against any infringement of their rights, provided that the conditions and formalities imposed upon nationals are complied with.

(2) However, no requirement as to domicile or establishment in the country where protection is claimed may be imposed upon nationals of countries of the Union for the enjoyment of any industrial property rights.

(3) The provisions of the laws of each of the countries of the Union relating to judicial and administrative procedure and to jurisdiction, and to the designation of an address for service or the appointment of an agent, which may be required by the laws on industrial property are expressly reserved.

ARTICLE 3

[Same Treatment for Certain Categories of Persons as for Nationals of Countries of the Union]

A21–03   Nationals of countries outside the Union who are domiciled or who have real and effective industrial or commercial establishments in the territory of one of the countries of the Union shall be treated in the same manner as nationals of the countries of the Union.

ARTICLE 4

[A to I. Patents, Utility Models, Industrial Designs, Marks, Inventors' Certificates: Right of Priority.—G. Patents: Division of the Application]

A21–04   **A.**—(1) Any person who has duly filed an application for a patent, or for the registration of a utility model, or of an industrial design, or of a trademark, in one of the countries of the Union, or his successor in title, shall enjoy, for the purpose of filing in the other countries, a right of priority during the periods hereinafter fixed.

(2) Any filing that is equivalent to a regular national filing under the domestic legislation of any country of the Union or under bilateral or multilateral treaties concluded between countries of the Union shall be recognized as giving rise to the right of priority.

(3) By a regular national filing is meant any filing that is adequate to establish the date on which the application was filed in the country concerned, whatever may be the subsequent fate of the application.

A21–05   **B.**—Consequently, any subsequent filing in any of the other countries of the Union before the expiration of the periods referred to above shall not be invalidated by reason of any acts accomplished in the interval, in particular, another filing, the publication or exploitation of the invention, the putting on sale of copies of the design, or the use of the mark, and such acts cannot give rise to any third-party right or any right of personal possession. Rights acquired by third parties before the date of the first application that serves as the basis for the right of priority are reserved in accordance with the domestic legislation of each country of the Union.

A21–06   **C.**—(1) The periods of priority referred to above shall be twelve months for patents and utility models, and six months for industrial designs and trademarks.

(2) These periods shall start from the date of filing of the first application; the day of filing shall not be included in the period.

(3) If the last day of the period is an official holiday, or a day when the Office is not open for the filing of applications in the country where protection is claimed, the period shall be extended until the first following working day.

(4) A subsequent application concerning the same subject as a previous first application within the meaning of paragraph (2), above, filed in the same country of the Union, shall be considered as the first application, of which the filing date shall be the starting point of the period of priority, if, at the time of filing the subsequent application, the said previous application has been withdrawn, abandoned, or refused, without having been laid open to public inspection and without leaving any rights outstanding, and if it has not yet served as a basis for claiming a right of priority. The previous application may not thereafter serve as a basis for claiming a right of priority.

D.—(1) Any person desiring to take advantage of the priority of a previous **A21–07** filing shall be required to make a declaration indicating the date of such filing and the country in which it was made. Each country shall determine the latest date on which such declaration must be made.

(2) These particulars shall be mentioned in the publications issued by the competent authority, and in particular in the patents and the specifications relating thereto.

(3) The countries of the Union may require any person making a declaration of priority to produce a copy of the application (description, drawings, etc.) previously filed. The copy, certified as correct by the authority which received such application, shall not require any authentication, and may in any case be filed, without fee, at any time within three months of the filing of the subsequent application. They may require it to be accompanied by a certificate from the same authority showing the date of filing, and by a translation.

(4) No other formalities may be required for the declaration of priority at the time of filing the application. Each country of the Union shall determine the consequences of failure to comply with the formalities prescribed by this Article, but such consequences shall in no case go beyond the loss of the right of priority.

(5) Subsequently, further proof may be required.

Any person who avails himself of the priority of a previous application shall be required to specify the number of that application; this number shall be published as provided for by paragraph (2), above.

E.—(1) Where an industrial design is filed in a country by virtue of a right of **A21–08** priority based on the filing of a utility model, the period of priority shall be the same as that fixed for industrial designs.

(2) Furthermore, it is permissible to file a utility model in a country by virtue of a right of priority based on the filing of a patent application, and vice versa.

F.—No country of the Union may refuse a priority or a patent application on **A21–09** the ground that the applicant claims multiple priorities, even if they originate in different countries, or on the ground that an application claiming one or more priorities contains one or more elements that were not included in the application or applications whose priority is claimed, provided that, in both cases, there is unity of invention within the meaning of the law of the country.

With respect to the elements not included in the application or applications whose priority is claimed, the filing of the subsequent application shall give rise to a right of priority under ordinary conditions.

G.—(1) If the examination reveals that an application for a patent contains **A21–10** more than one invention, the applicant may divide the application into a certain number of divisional applications and preserve as the date of each the date of the initial application and the benefit of the right of priority, if any.

(2) The applicant may also, on his own initiative, divide a patent application and preserve as the date of each divisional application the date of the initial application and the benefit of the right of priority, if any. Each country of the Union shall have the right to determine the conditions under which such division shall be authorized.

A21–11 H.—Priority may not be refused on the ground that certain elements of the invention for which priority is claimed do not appear among the claims formulated in the application in the country of origin, provided that the application documents as a whole specifically disclose such elements.

A21–12 I.—(1) Applications for inventors' certificates filed in a country in which applicants have the right to apply at their own option either for a patent or for an inventor's certificate shall give rise to the right of priority provided for by this Article, under the same conditions and with the same effects as applications for patents.

(2) In a country in which applicants have the right to apply at their own option either for a patent or for an inventor's certificate, an applicant for an inventor's certificate shall, in accordance with the provisions of this Article relating to patent applications, enjoy a right of priority based on an application for a patent, a utility model, or an inventor's certificate.

ARTICLE 4ᴮᴵˢ

[Patents: Independence of Patents Obtained for the Same Invention in Different Countries]

A21–13 (1) Patents applied for in the various countries of the Union by nationals of countries of the Union shall be independent of patents obtained for the same invention in other countries, whether members of the Union or not.

(2) The foregoing provision is to be understood in an unrestricted sense, in particular, in the sense that patents applied for during the period of priority are independent, both as regards the grounds for nullity and forfeiture, and as regards their normal duration.

(3) The provision shall apply to all patents existing at the time when it comes into effect.

(4) Similarly, it shall apply, in the case of the accession of new countries, to patents in existence on either side at the time of accession.

(5) Patents obtained with the benefit of priority shall, in the various countries of the Union, have a duration equal to that which they would have, had they been applied for or granted without the benefit of priority.

ARTICLE 4ᵀᴱᴿ

[Patents: Mention of the Inventor in the Patent]

A21–14 The inventor shall have the right to be mentioned as such in the patent.

ARTICLE 4 QUATER

[Patents: Patentability in Case of Restrictions of Sale by Law]

A21–15 The grant of a patent shall not be refused and a patent shall not be invalidated on the ground that the sale of the patented product or of a product obtained by means of a patented process is subject to restrictions or limitations resulting from the domestic law.

ARTICLE 5

[A. Patents: Importation of Articles; Failure to Work or Insufficient Working; Compulsory Licenses.—B. Industrial Designs: Failure to Work; Importation of Articles.—C. Marks: Failure to Use; Different Forms; Use by Co-proprietors.—D. Patents, Utility Models, Marks, Industrial Designs: Marking]

A.—(1) Importation by the patentee into the country where the patent has **A21–16** been granted of articles manufactured in any of the countries of the Union shall not entail forfeiture of the patent.

(2) Each country of the Union shall have the right to take legislative measures providing for the grant of compulsory licenses to prevent the abuses which might result from the exercise of the exclusive rights conferred by the patent, for example, failure to work.

(3) Forfeiture of the patent shall not be provided for except in cases where the grant of compulsory licenses would not have been sufficient to prevent the said abuses. No proceedings for the forfeiture or revocation of a patent may be instituted before the expiration of two years from the grant of the first compulsory license.

(4) A compulsory license may not be applied for on the ground of failure to work or insufficient working before the expiration of a period of four years from the date of filing of the patent application or three years from the date of the grant of the patent, whichever period expires last; it shall be refused if the patentee justifies his inaction by legitimate reasons. Such a compulsory license shall be non-exclusive and shall not be transferable, even in the form of a grant of a sub-license, except with that part of the enterprise or goodwill which exploits such license.

(5) The foregoing provisions shall be applicable, mutatis mutandis, to utility models.

B.—The protection of industrial designs shall not, under any circumstance, be **A21–17** subject to any forfeiture, either by reason of failure to work or by reason of the importation of articles corresponding to those which are protected.

C.—(1) If, in any country, use of the registered mark is compulsory, the **A21–18** registration may be cancelled only after a reasonable period, and then only if the person concerned does not justify his inaction.

(2) Use of a trademark by the proprietor in a form differing in elements which do not alter the distinctive character of the mark in the form in which it was registered in one of the countries of the Union shall not entail invalidation of the registration and shall not diminish the protection granted to the mark.

(3) Concurrent use of the same mark on identical or similar goods by industrial or commercial establishments considered as co-proprietors of the mark according to the provisions of the domestic law of the country where protection is claimed shall not prevent registration or diminish in any way the protection granted to the said mark in any country of the Union, provided that such use does not result in misleading the public and is not contrary to the public interest.

D.—No indication or mention of the patent, of the utility model, of the **A21–19** registration of the trademark, or of the deposit of the industrial design, shall be required upon the goods as a condition of recognition of the right to protection.

ARTICLE 5ᴮᴵˢ

[All Industrial Property Rights: Period of Grace for the Payment of Fees for the Maintenance of Rights; Patents: Restoration]

A21–20 (1) A period of grace of not less than six months shall be allowed for the payment of the fees prescribed for the maintenance of industrial property rights, subject, if the domestic legislation so provides, to the payment of a surcharge.

(2) The countries of the Union shall have the right to provide for the restoration of patents which have lapsed by reason of non-payment of fees.

ARTICLE 5ᵀᴱᴿ

[Patents: Patented Devices Forming Part of Vessels, Aircraft, or Land Vehicles]

A21–21 In any country of the Union the following shall not be considered as infringements of the rights of a patentee:
1. the use on board vessels of other countries of the Union of devices forming the subject of his patent in the body of the vessel, in the machinery, tackle, gear and other accessories, when such vessels temporarily or accidentally enter the waters of the said country, provided that such devices are used there exclusively for the needs of the vessel;
2. the use of devices forming the subject of the patent in the construction or operation of aircraft or land vehicles of other countries of the Union, or of accessories of such aircraft or land vehicles, when those aircraft or land vehicles temporarily or accidentally enter the said country.

ARTICLE 5ᵠᵁᴬᵀᴱᴿ

[Patents: Importation of Products Manufactured by a Process Patented in the Importing Country]

A21–22 When a product is imported into a country of the Union where there exists a patent protecting a process of manufacture of the said product, the patentee shall have all the rights, with regard to the imported product, that are accorded to him by the legislation of the country of importation, on the basis of the process patent, with respect to products manufactured in that country.

ARTICLE 5ᵠᵁᴵᴺᵠᵁᴵᴱˢ

[Industrial Designs]

A21–23 Industrial designs shall be protected in all the countries of the Union.

ARTICLE 6

[Marks: Conditions of Registration; Independence of Protection of Same Mark in Different Countries]

A21–24 (1) The conditions for the filing and registration of trademarks shall be determined in each country of the Union by its domestic legislation.

(2) However, an application for the registration of a mark filed by a national of a country of the Union in any country of the Union may not be refused, nor may a registration be invalidated, on the ground that filing, registration, or renewal, has not been effected in the country of origin.

(3) A mark duly registered in a country of the Union shall be regarded as independent of marks registered in the other countries of the Union, including the country of origin.

ARTICLE 6BIS

[Marks: Well-Known Marks]

(1) The countries of the Union undertake, ex officio if their legislation so **A21–25** permits, or at the request of an interested party, to refuse or to cancel the registration, and to prohibit the use, of a trademark which constitutes a reproduction, an imitation, or a translation, liable to create confusion, of a mark considered by the competent authority of the country of registration or use to be well known in that country as being already the mark of a person entitled to the benefits of this Convention and used for identical or similar goods. These provisions shall also apply when the essential part of the mark constitutes a reproduction of any such well-known mark or an imitation liable to create confusion therewith.

(2) A period of at least five years from the date of registration shall be allowed for requesting the cancellation of such a mark. The countries of the Union may provide for a period within which the prohibition of use must be requested.

(3) No time limit shall be fixed for requesting the cancellation or the prohibition of the use of marks registered or used in bad faith.

ARTICLE 6TER

[Marks: Prohibitions concerning State Emblems, Official Hallmarks, and Emblems of Intergovernmental Organizations]

(1) (a) The countries of the Union agree to refuse or to invalidate the **A21–26** registration, and to prohibit by appropriate measures the use, without authorization by the competent authorities, either as trademarks or as elements of trademarks, of armorial bearings, flags, and other State emblems, of the countries of the Union, official signs and hallmarks indicating control and warranty adopted by them, and any imitation from a heraldic point of view.

(b) The provisions of subparagraph (a), above, shall apply equally to armorial bearings, flags, other emblems, abbreviations, and names, of international intergovernmental organizations of which one or more countries of the Union are members, with the exception of armorial bearings, flags, other emblems, abbreviations, and names, that are already the subject of international agreements in force, intended to ensure their protection.

(c) No country of the Union shall be required to apply the provisions of subparagraph (b), above, to the prejudice of the owners of rights acquired in good faith before the entry into force, in that country, of this Convention. The countries of the Union shall not be required to apply the said provisions when the use or registration referred to in subparagraph (a), above, is not of such a nature as to suggest to the public that a connection exists between the organization concerned and the armorial bearings, flags, emblems, abbreviations, and names, or if such use or registration is probably not of such a nature as to mislead the public as to the existence of a connection between the user and the organization.

(2) Prohibition of the use of official signs and hallmarks indicating control and warranty shall apply solely in cases where the marks in which they are incorporated are intended to be used on goods of the same or a similar kind.

(3) (a) For the application of these provisions, the countries of the Union agree to communicate reciprocally, through the intermediary of the International Bureau, the list of State emblems, and official signs and hallmarks indicating control and warranty, which they desire, or may hereafter desire, to place wholly or within certain limits under the protection of this Article, and all subsequent modifications of such list. Each country of the Union shall in due course make available to the public the lists so communicated.

Nevertheless such communication is not obligatory in respect of flags of States.

(b) The provisions of subparagraph (b) of paragraph (1) of this Article shall apply only to such armorial bearings, flags, other emblems, abbreviations, and names, of international intergovernmental organizations as the latter have communicated to the countries of the Union through the intermediary of the International Bureau.

(4) Any country of the Union may, within a period of twelve months from the receipt of the notification, transmit its objections, if any, through the intermediary of the International Bureau, to the country or international intergovernmental organization concerned.

(5) In the case of State flags, the measures prescribed by paragraph (1), above, shall apply solely to marks registered after November 6, 1925.

(6) In the case of State emblems other than flags, and of official signs and hallmarks of the countries of the Union, and in the case of armorial bearings, flags, other emblems, abbreviations, and names, of international intergovernmental organizations, these provisions shall apply only to marks registered more than two months after receipt of the communication provided for in paragraph (3), above.

(7) In cases of bad faith, the countries shall have the right to cancel even those marks incorporating State emblems, signs, and hallmarks, which were registered before November 6, 1925.

(8) Nationals of any country who are authorized to make use of the State emblems, signs, and hallmarks, of their country may use them even if they are similar to those of another country.

(9) The countries of the Union undertake to prohibit the unauthorized use in trade of the State armorial bearings of the other countries of the Union, when the use is of such a nature as to be misleading as to the origin of the goods.

(10) The above provisions shall not prevent the countries from exercising the right given in paragraph (3) of Article 6^{quinquies}, Section B, to refuse or to invalidate the registration of marks incorporating, without authorization, armorial bearings, flags, other State emblems, or official signs and hallmarks adopted by a country of the Union, as well as the distinctive signs of international intergovernmental organizations referred to in paragraph (1), above.

ARTICLE 6^{QUATER}

[Marks: Assignment of Marks]

A21–27 (1) When, in accordance with the law of a country of the Union, the assignment of a mark is valid only if it takes place at the same time as the transfer of the business or goodwill to which the mark belongs, it shall suffice for the recognition of such validity that the portion of the business or goodwill located in that country be transferred to the assignee, together with the exclusive right to manufacture in the said country, or to sell therein, the goods bearing the mark assigned.

(2) The foregoing provision does not impose upon the countries of the Union any obligation to regard as valid the assignment of any mark the use of which by the assignee would, in fact, be of such a nature as to mislead the public, particularly as regards the origin, nature, or essential qualities, of the goods to which the mark is applied.

ARTICLE 6^{QUINQUIES}

[Marks: Protection of Marks Registered in One Country of the Union in the Other Countries of the Union]

A.—(1) Every trademark duly registered in the country of origin shall be **A21–28** accepted for filing and protected as in the other countries of the Union, subject to the reservations indicated in this Article. Such countries may, before proceeding to final registration, require the production of a certificate of registration in the country of origin, issued by the competent authority. No authentication shall be required for this certificate.

(2) Shall be considered the country of origin the country of the Union where the applicant has a real and effective industrial or commercial establishment, or, if he has no such establishment within the Union, the country of the Union where he has his domicile, or, if he has no domicile within the Union but is a national of a country of the Union, the country of which he is a national.

B.—Trademarks covered by this Article may be neither denied registration nor **A21–29** invalidated except in the following cases:

1. when they are of such a nature as to infringe rights acquired by third parties in the country where protection is claimed;
2. when they are devoid of any distinctive character, or consist exclusively of signs or indications which may serve, in trade, to designate the kind, quality, quantity, intended purpose, value, place of origin, of the goods, or the time of production, or have become customary in the current language or in the bona fide and established practices of the trade of the country where protection is claimed;
3. when they are contrary to morality or public order and, in particular, of such a nature as to deceive the public. It is understood that a mark may not be considered contrary to public order for the sole reason that it does not conform to a provision of the legislation on marks, except if such provision itself relates to public order.

This provision is subject, however, to the application of Article 10bis.

C.—(1) In determining whether a mark is eligible for protection, all the factual **A21–30** circumstances must be taken into consideration, particularly the length of time the mark has been in use.

(2) No trademark shall be refused in the other countries of the Union for the sole reason that it differs from the mark protected in the country of origin only in respect of elements that do not alter its distinctive character and do not affect its identity in the form in which it has been registered in the said country of origin.

A21–31   D.—No person may benefit from the provisions of this Article if the mark for which he claims protection is not registered in the country of origin.

A21–32   E.—However, in no case shall the renewal of the registration of the mark in the country of origin involve an obligation to renew the registration in the other countries of the Union in which the mark has been registered.

A21–33   F.—The benefit of priority shall remain unaffected for applications for the registration of marks filed within the period fixed by Article 4, even if registration in the country of origin is effected after the expiration of such period.

ARTICLE 6^SERIES

[Marks: Service Marks]

A21–34   The countries of the Union undertake to protect service marks. They shall not be required to provide for the registration of such marks.

ARTICLE 6^SEPTIES

[Marks: Registration in the Name of the Agent or Representative of the Proprietor Without the Latter's Authorization]

A21–35   (1) If the agent or representative of the person who is the proprietor of a mark in one of the countries of the Union applies, without such proprietor's authorization, for the registration of the mark in his own name, in one or more countries of the Union, the proprietor shall be entitled to oppose the registration applied for or demand its cancellation or, if the law of the country so allows, the assignment in his favor of the said registration, unless such agent or representative justifies his action.

(2) The proprietor of the mark shall, subject to the provisions of paragraph (1), above, be entitled to oppose the use of his mark by his agent or representative if he has not authorized such use.

(3) Domestic legislation may provide an equitable time limit within which the proprietor of a mark must exercise the rights provided for in this Article.

ARTICLE 7

[Marks: Nature of the Goods to which the Mark is Applied]

A21–36   The nature of the goods to which a trade mark is to be applied shall in no case form an obstacle to the registration of the mark.

ARTICLE 7BIS

[Marks: Collective Marks]

A21–37   (1) The countries of the Union undertake to accept for filing and to protect collective marks belonging to associations the existence of which is not contrary to the law of the country of origin, even if such associations do not possess an industrial or commercial establishment.

(2) Each country shall be the judge of the particular conditions under which a collective mark shall be protected and may refuse protection if the mark is contrary to the public interest.

(3) Nevertheless, the protection of these marks shall not be refused to any association the existence of which is not contrary to the law of the country of origin, on the ground that such association is not established in the country where protection is sought or is not constituted according to the law of the latter country.

ARTICLE 8

[Trade Names]

A trade name shall be protected in all the countries of the Union without the **A21–38** obligation of filing or registration, whether or not it forms part of a trademark.

ARTICLE 9

[Marks, Trade Names: Seizure, on Importation, etc., of Goods Unlawfully Bearing a Mark or Trade Name]

(1) All goods unlawfully bearing a trademark or trade name shall be seized on **A21–39** importation into those countries of the Union where such mark or trade name is entitled to legal protection.

(2) Seizure shall likewise be effected in the country where the unlawful affixation occurred or in the country into which the goods were imported.

(3) Seizure shall take place at the request of the public prosecutor, or any other competent authority, or any interested party, whether a natural person or a legal entity, in conformity with the domestic legislation of each country.

(4) The authorities shall not be bound to effect seizure of goods in transit.

(5) If the legislation of a country does not permit seizure on importation, seizure shall be replaced by prohibition of importation or by seizure inside the country.

(6) If the legislation of a country permits neither seizure on importation nor prohibition of importation nor seizure inside the country, then, until such time as the legislation is modified accordingly, these measures shall be replaced by the actions and remedies available in such cases to nationals under the law of such country.

ARTICLE 10

[False Indications: Seizure, on Importation, etc., of Goods Bearing False Indications as to their Source or the Identity of the Producer]

(1) The provisions of the preceding Article shall apply in cases of direct or **A21–40** indirect use of a false indication of the source of the goods or the identity of the producer, manufacturer, or merchant.

(2) Any producer, manufacturer, or merchant, whether a natural person or a legal entity, engaged in the production or manufacture of or trade in such goods

1231

and established either in the locality falsely indicated as the source, or in the region where such locality is situated, or in the country falsely indicated, or in the country where the false indication of source is used, shall in any case be deemed an interested party.

ARTICLE 10BIS

[Unfair Competition]

A21–41   (1) The countries of the Union are bound to assure to nationals of such countries effective protection against unfair competition.

(2) Any act of competition contrary to honest practices in industrial or commercial matters constitutes an act of unfair competition.

(3) The following in particular shall be prohibited:

1. all acts of such a nature as to create confusion by any means whatever with the establishment, the goods, or the industrial or commercial activities, of a competitor;
2. false allegations in the course of trade of such a nature as to discredit the establishment, the goods, or the industrial or commercial activities, of a competitor;
3. indications or allegations the use of which in the course of trade is liable to mislead the public as to the nature, the manufacturing process, the characteristics, the suitability for their purpose, or the quantity, of the goods.

ARTICLE 10TER

[Marks, Trade Names, False Indications, Unfair Competition: Remedies, Right to Sue]

A21–42   (1) The countries of the Union undertake to assure to nationals of the other countries of the Union appropriate legal remedies effectively to repress all the acts referred to in Articles 9, 10, and 10bis.

(2) They undertake, further, to provide measures to permit federations and associations representing interested industrialists, producers, or merchants, provided that the existence of such federations and associations is not contrary to the laws of their countries, to take action in the courts or before the administrative authorities, with a view to the repression of the acts referred to in Articles 9, 10, and 10bis, in so far as the law of the country in which protection is claimed allows such action by federations and associations of that country.

ARTICLE 11

[Inventions, Utility Models, Industrial Designs, Marks: Temporary Protection at Certain International Exhibitions]

A21–43   (1) The countries of the Union shall, in conformity with their domestic legislation, grant temporary protection to patentable inventions, utility models, industrial designs, and trademarks, in respect of goods exhibited at official or officially recognized international exhibitions held in the territory of any of them.

(2) Such temporary protection shall not extend the periods provided by Article 4. If, later, the right of priority is invoked, the authorities of any country may provide that the period shall start from the date of introduction of the goods into the exhibition.

(3) Each country may require, as proof of the identity of the article exhibited and of the date of its introduction, such documentary evidence as it considers necessary.

ARTICLE 12

[Special National Industrial Property Services]

(1) Each country of the Union undertakes to establish a special industrial **A21–44** property service and a central office for the communication to the public of patents, utility models, industrial designs, and trademarks.

(2) This service shall publish an official periodical journal. It shall publish regularly:

(a) the names of the proprietors of patents granted, with a brief designation of the inventions patented;
(b) the reproductions of registered trademarks.

ARTICLE 13

[Assembly of the Union]

(1) (a) The Union shall have an Assembly consisting of those countries of the **A21–45** Union which are bound by Articles 13 to 17.

(b) The Government of each country shall be represented by one delegate, who may be assisted by alternate delegates, advisors, and experts.

(c) The expenses of each delegation shall be borne by the Government which has appointed it.

(2) (a) The Assembly shall:

(a) deal with all matters concerning the maintenance and development of the Union and the implementation of this Convention;
(ii) give directions concerning the preparation for conferences of revision to the International Bureau of Intellectual Property (hereinafter designated as "the International Bureau") referred to in the Convention establishing the World Intellectual Property Organization[7] (hereinafter designated as "the Organization"), due account being taken of any comments made by those countries of the Union which are not bound by Articles 13 to 17;
(iii) review and approve the reports and activities of the Director-General of the Organization concerning the Union, and give him all necessary instructions concerning matters within the competence of the Union;
(iv) elect the members of the Executive Committee of the Assembly;

[7] Treaty Series No. 52 (1970), Cmnd. 4408.

   (v) review and approve the reports and activities of its Executive Committee, and give instructions to such Committee;

   (vi) determine the program and adopt the triennial budget of the Union, and approve its final accounts;

   (vii) adopt the financial regulations of the Union;

   (viii) establish such committees of experts and working groups as it deems appropriate to achieve the objectives of the Union;

   (ix) determine which countries not members of the Union and which intergovernmental and international nongovernmental organizations shall be admitted to its meetings as observers;

   (x) adopt amendments to Articles 13 to 17;

   (xi) take any other appropriate action designed to further the objectives of the Union;

   (xii) perform such other functions as are appropriate under this Convention;

   (xiii) subject to its acceptance, exercise such rights as are given to it in the Convention establishing the Organization.

(b) With respect to matters which are of interest also to other Unions administered by the Organization, the Assembly shall make its decisions after having heard the advice of the Coordination Committee of the Organization.

(3) (a) Subject to the provisions of subparagraph (b), a delegate may represent one country only.

(b) Countries of the Union grouped under the terms of a special agreement in a common office possessing for each of them the character of a special national service of industrial property as referred to in Article 12 may be jointly represented during discussions by one of their number.

(4) (a) Each country member of the Assembly shall have one vote.

(b) One-half of the countries members of the Assembly shall constitute a quorum.

(c) Notwithstanding the provisions of subparagraph (b), if, in any session, the number of countries represented is less than one-half but equal to or more than one-third of the countries members of the Assembly, the Assembly may make decisions but, with the exception of decisions concerning its own procedure, all such decisions shall take effect only if the conditions set forth hereinafter are fulfilled. The International Bureau shall communicate the said decisions to the countries members of the Assembly which were not represented and shall invite them to express in writing their vote or abstention within a period of three months from the date of the communication. If, at the expiration of this period, the number of countries having thus expressed their vote or abstention attains the number of countries which was lacking for attaining the quorum in the session itself, such decisions shall take effect provided that at the same time the required majority still obtains.

(d) Subject to the provisions of Article 17 (2), the decisions of the Assembly shall require two-thirds of the votes cast.

(e) Abstentions shall not be considered as votes.

(5) (a) Subject to the provisions of subparagraph (b), a delegate may vote in the name of one country only.

(b) The countries of the Union referred to in paragraph (3)(b) shall, as a general rule, endeavor to send their own delegations to the sessions of the Assembly. If, however, for exceptional reasons, any such country cannot send its own delegation, it may give to the delegation of another such country the power to vote in its name, provided that each delegation may vote by proxy for one country only. Such power to vote shall be granted in a document signed by the Head of State or the competent Minister.

(6) Countries of the Union not members of the Assembly shall be admitted to the meetings of the latter as observers.

(7) (a) The Assembly shall meet once in every third calendar year in ordinary session upon convocation by the Director-General and, in the absence of

exceptional circumstances, during the same period and at the same place as the General Assembly of the Organization.

(b) The Assembly shall meet in extraordinary session upon convocation by the Director-General, at the request of the Executive Committee or at the request of one-fourth of the countries members of the Assembly.

(8) The Assembly shall adopt its own rules of procedure.

ARTICLE 14

[Executive Committee]

(1) The Assembly shall have an Executive Committee.   **A21–46**

(2) (a) The Executive Committee shall consist of countries elected by the Assembly from among countries members of the Assembly. Furthermore, the country on whose territory the Organization has its headquarters shall, subject to the provisions of Article 16(7)(b), have an *ex officio* seat on the Committee.

(b) The Government of each country member of the Executive Committee shall be represented by one delegate, who may be assisted by alternate delegates, advisors, and experts.

(c) The expenses of each delegation shall be borne by the Government which has appointed it.

(3) The number of countries members of the Executive Committee shall correspond to one-fourth of the number of countries members of the Assembly. In establishing the number of seats to be filled, remainders after division by four shall be disregarded.

(4) In electing the members of the Executive Committee, the Assembly shall have due regard to an equitable geographical distribution and to the need for countries party to the Special Agreements established in relation with the Union to be among the countries constituting the Executive Committee.

(5) (a) Each member of the Executive Committee shall serve from the close of the session of the Assembly which elected it to the close of the next ordinary session of the Assembly.

(b) Members of the Executive Committee may be re-elected, but only up to a maximum of two-thirds of such members.

(c) The Assembly shall establish the details of the rules governing the election and possible re-election of the members of the Executive Committee.

(6) (a) The Executive Committee shall:

- (a) prepare the draft agenda of the Assembly;
- (ii) submit proposals to the Assembly in respect of the draft program and triennial budget of the Union prepared by the Director-General;
- (iii) approve, within the limits of the program and the triennial budget, the specific yearly budgets and programs prepared by the Director-General;
- (iv) submit, with appropriate comments, to the Assembly the periodical reports of the Director-General and the yearly audit reports on the accounts;
- (v) take all necessary measures to ensure the execution of the program of the Union by the Director-General, in accordance with the decisions of the Assembly and having regard to circumstances arising between two ordinary sessions of the Assembly;
- (vi) perform such other functions as are allocated to it under this Convention.

(b) With respect to matters which are of interest also to other Unions administered by the Organization, the Executive Committee shall make its decisions after having heard the advice of the Coordination Committee of the Organization.

(7) (a) The Executive Committee shall meet once a year in ordinary session upon convocation by the Director-General, preferably during the same period and at the same place as the Coordination Committee of the Organization.

(b) The Executive Committee shall meet in extraordinary session upon convocation by the Director-General, either on his own initiative, or at the request of its Chairman or one-fourth of its members.

(8) (a) Each country member of the Executive Committee shall have one vote.

(b) One-half of the members of the Executive Committee shall constitute a quorum.

(c) Decisions shall be made by a simple majority of the votes cast.

(d) Abstentions shall not be considered as votes.

(e) A delegate may represent, and vote in the name of, one country only.

(9) Countries of the Union not members of the Executive Committee shall be admitted to its meetings as observers.

(10) The Executive Committee shall adopt its own rules of procedure.

ARTICLE 15

[International Bureau]

A21–47   (1) (a) Administrative tasks concerning the Union shall be performed by the International Bureau, which is a continuation of the Bureau of the Union united with the Bureau of the Union established by the International Convention for the Protection of Literary and Artistic Works.[8]

(b) In particular, the International Bureau shall provide the secretariat of the various organs of the Union.

(c) The Director-General of the Organization shall be the chief executive of the Union and shall represent the Union.

(2) The International Bureau shall assemble and publish information concerning the protection of industrial property. Each country of the Union shall promptly communicate to the International Bureau all new laws and official texts concerning the protection of industrial property. Furthermore, it shall furnish the International Bureau with all the publications of its industrial property service of direct concern to the protection of industrial property which the International Bureau may find useful in its work.

(3) The International Bureau shall publish a monthly periodical.

(4) The International Bureau shall, on request, furnish any country of the Union with information on matters concerning the protection of industrial property.

(5) The International Bureau shall conduct studies, and shall provide services, designed to facilitate the protection of industrial property.

(6) The Director-General and any staff member designated by him shall participate, without the right to vote, in all meetings of the Assembly, the Executive Committee, and any other committee of experts or working group. The Director-General, or a staff member designated by him, shall be *ex officio* secretary of these bodies.

(7) (a) The International Bureau shall, in accordance with the directions of the Assembly and in cooperation with the Executive Committee, make the preparations for the conferences of revision of the provisions of the Convention other than Articles 13 to 17.

---

[8] Treaty Series No. 53 (1970), Cmnd. 4412.

(b) The International Bureau may consult with intergovernmental and international non-governmental organizations concerning preparations for conferences of revision.

(c) The Director-General and persons designated by him shall take part, without the right to vote, in the discussions at these conferences.

(8) The International Bureau shall carry out any other tasks assigned to it.

ARTICLE 16

[Finances]

(1) (a) The Union shall have a budget.   **A21–48**

(b) The budget of the Union shall include the income and expenses proper to the Union, its contribution to the budget of expenses common to the Unions, and, where applicable, the sum made available to the budget of the Conference of the Organization.

(c) Expenses not attributable exclusively to the Union but also to one or more other Unions administered by the Organization shall be considered as expenses common to the Unions. The share of the Union in such common expenses shall be in proportion to the interest the Union has in them.

(2) The budget of the Union shall be established with due regard to the requirements of coordination with the budgets of the other Unions administered by the Organization.

(3) The budget of the Union shall be financed from the following sources:

    (a) contributions of the countries of the Union;

    (ii) fees and charges due for services rendered by the International Bureau in relation to the Union;

    (iii) sale of, or royalties on, the publications of the International Bureau concerning the Union;

    (iv) gifts, bequests, and subventions;

    (v) rents, interests, and other miscellaneous income.

(4) (a) For the purpose of establishing its contribution towards the budget each country of the Union shall belong to a class, and shall pay its annual contributions on the basis of a number of units fixed as follows:

Class I	25
Class II	20
Class III	15
Class IV	10
Class V	5
Class VI	3
Class VII	1

(b) Unless it has already done so, each country shall indicate, concurrently with depositing its instrument of ratification or accession, the class to which it wishes to belong. Any country may change class. If it chooses a lower class, the country must announce such change to the Assembly at one of its ordinary sessions. Any such change shall take effect at the beginning of the calendar year following the said session.

(c) The annual contribution of each country shall be an amount in the same proportion to the total sum to be contributed to the budget of the Union by all countries as the number of its units is to the total of the units of all contributing countries.

(d) Contributions shall become due on the first of January of each year.

(e) A country which is in arrears in the payment of its contributions may not exercise its right to vote in any of the organs of the Union of which it is a member if the amount of its arrears equals or exceeds the amount of the contributions due from it for the preceding two full years. However, any organ of the Union may allow such a country to continue to exercise its right to vote in that organ if, and as long as, it is satisfied that the delay in payment is due to exceptional and unavoidable circumstances.

(f) If the budget is not adopted before the beginning of a new financial period, it shall be at the same level as the budget of the previous year, as provided in the financial regulations.

(5) The amount of the fees and charges due for services rendered by the International Bureau in relation to the Union shall be established, and shall be reported to the Assembly and the Executive Committee, by the Director-General.

(6) (a) The Union shall have a working capital fund which shall be constituted by a single payment made by each country of the Union. If the fund becomes insufficient, the Assembly shall decide to increase it.

(b) The amount of the initial payment of each country to the said fund or of its participation in the increase thereof shall be a proportion of the contribution of that country for the year in which the fund is established or the decision to increase it is made.

(c) The proportion and the terms of payment shall be fixed by the Assembly on the proposal of the Director-General and after it has heard the advice of the Coordination Committee of the Organization.

(7) (a) In the headquarters agreement concluded with the country on the territory of which the Organization has its headquarters, it shall be provided that, whenever the working capital fund is insufficient, such country shall grant advances. The amount of these advances and the conditions on which they are granted shall be the subject of separate agreements, in each case, between such country and the Organization. As long as it remains under the obligation to grant advances, such country shall have an *ex officio* seat on the Executive Committee.

(b) The country referred to in subparagraph (a) and the Organization shall each have the right to denounce the obligation to grant advances, by written notification. Denunciation shall take effect three years after the end of the year in which it has been notified.

(8) The auditing of the accounts shall be effected by one or more of the countries of the Union or by external auditors, as provided in the financial regulations. They shall be designated, with their agreement, by the Assembly.

ARTICLE 17

[Amendment of Articles 13 to 17]

A21–49 (1) Proposals for the amendment of Articles 13, 14, 15, 16, and the present Article, may be initiated by any country member of the Assembly, by the Executive Committee, or by the Director-General. Such proposals shall be communicated by the Director-General to the member countries of the Assembly at least six months in advance of their consideration by the Assembly.

(2) Amendments to the Articles referred to in paragraph (1) shall be adopted by the Assembly. Adoption shall require three-fourths of the votes cast, provided that any amendment to Article 13, and to the present paragraph, shall require four-fifths of the votes cast.

(3) Any amendment to the Articles referred to in paragraph (1) shall enter into force one month after written notifications of acceptance, effected in accordance

with their respective constitutional processes, have been received by the Director-General from three-fourths of the countries members of the Assembly at the time it adopted the amendment. Any amendment to the said Articles thus accepted shall bind all the countries which are members of the Assembly at the time the amendment enters into force, or which become members thereof at a subsequent date, provided that any amendment increasing the financial obligations of countries of the Union shall bind only those countries which have notified their acceptance of such amendment.

ARTICLE 18

[Revision of Articles 1 to 12 and 18 to 30]

(1) This Convention shall be submitted to revision with a view to the **A21–50** introduction of amendments designed to improve the system of the Union.

(2) For that purpose, conferences shall be held successively in one of the countries of the Union among the delegates of the said countries.

(3) Amendments to Articles 13 to 17 are governed by the provisions of Article 17.

ARTICLE 19

[Special Agreements]

It is understood that the countries of the Union reserve the right to make **A21–51** separately between themselves special agreements for the protection of industrial property, in so far as these agreements do not contravene the provisions of this Convention.

ARTICLE 20

[Ratification or Accession by Countries of the Union; Entry Into Force]

(1) (a) Any country of the Union which has signed this Act may ratify it, and if **A21–52** it has not signed it, may accede to it. Instruments of ratification and accession shall be deposited with the Director-General.

(b) Any country of the Union may declare in its instrument of ratification or accession that its ratification or accession shall not apply:

(a) to Articles 1 to 12, or
(ii) to Articles 13 to 17.

(c) Any country of the Union which, in accordance with subparagraph (b), has excluded from the effects of its ratification or accession one of the two groups of Articles referred to in that subparagraph may at any later time declare that it extends the effects of its ratification or accession to that group of Articles. Such declaration shall be deposited with the Director-General.

(2) (a) Articles 1 to 12 shall enter into force, with respect to the first ten countries of the Union which have deposited instruments of ratification or

accession without making the declaration permitted under paragraph (1) (b) (i), three months after the deposit of the tenth such instrument of ratification or accession.[9]

(b) Articles 13 to 17 shall enter into force, with respect to the first ten countries of the Union which have deposited instruments of ratification or accession without making the declaration permitted under paragraph (1) (b) (ii), three months after the deposit of the tenth such instrument of ratification or accession.[10]

(c) Subject to the initial entry into force, pursuant to the provisions of subparagraphs (a) and (b), of each of the two groups of Articles referred to in paragraph (1) (b) (i) and (ii), and subject to the provisions of paragraph (1) (b), Articles 1 to 17 shall, with respect to any country of the Union, other than those referred to in subparagraphs (a) and (b), which deposits an instrument of ratification or accession or any country of the Union which deposits a declaration pursuant to paragraph (1) (c), enter into force three months after the date of notification by the Director-General of such deposit, unless a subsequent date has been indicated in the instrument or declaration deposited. In the latter case, this Act shall enter into force with respect to that country on the date thus indicated.

(3) With respect to any country of the Union which deposits an instrument of ratification or accession, Articles 18 to 30 shall enter into force on the earlier of the dates on which any of the groups of Articles referred to in paragraph (1) (b) enters into force with respect to that country pursuant to paragraph (2) (a), (b), or (c).[11]

ARTICLE 21

[Accession by Countries Outside the Union; Entry Into Force]

A21–53   (1) Any country outside the Union may accede to this Act and thereby become a member of the Union. Instruments of accession shall be deposited with the Director-General.

(2) (a) With respect to any country outside the Union which deposits its instrument of accession one month or more before the date of entry into force of any provisions of the present Act, this Act shall enter into force, unless a subsequent date has been indicated in the instrument of accession, on the date upon which provisions first enter into force pursuant to Article 20 (2) (a) or (b); provided that:

    (a) if Articles 1 to 12 do not enter into force on that date, such country shall, during the interim period before the entry into force of such provisions, and in substitution therefor, be bound by Articles 1 to 12 of the Lisbon Act,

    (ii) if Articles 13 to 17 do not enter into force on that date, such country shall, during the interim period before the entry into force of such provisions, and in substitution therefor, be bound by Articles 13 and 14 (3), (4), and (5) of the Lisbon Act.

If a country indicates a subsequent date in its instrument of accession, this Act shall enter into force with respect to that country on the date thus indicated.

[9] Articles 1–12 entered into force on May 19, 1970.
[10] Articles 13–17 entered into force on April 26, 1970.
[11] Articles 18–30 entered into force on April 26, 1970.

(b) With respect to any country outside the Union which deposits its instrument of accession on a date which is subsequent to, or precedes by less than one month, the entry into force of one group of Articles of the present Act, this Act shall, subject to the proviso of subparagraph (a), enter into force three months after the date on which its accession has been notified by the Director-General, unless a subsequent date has been indicated in the instrument of accession. In the latter case, this Act shall enter into force with respect to that country on the date thus indicated.

(3) With respect to any country outside the Union which deposits its instrument of accession after the date of entry into force of the present Act in its entirety, or less than one month before such date, this Act shall enter into force three months after the date on which its accession has been notified by the Director-General, unless a subsequent date has been indicated in the instrument of accession. In the latter case, this Act shall enter into force with respect to that country on the date thus indicated.

ARTICLE 22

[Consequences of Ratification or Accession]

Subject to the possibilities of exceptions provided for in Articles 20 (1) (b) and 28 (2), ratification or accession shall automatically entail acceptance of all the clauses and admission to all the advantages of this Act. **A21–54**

ARTICLE 23

[Accession to Earlier Acts]

After the entry into force of this Act in its entirety, a country may not accede to earlier Acts of this Convention. **A21–55**

ARTICLE 24

[Territories]

(1) Any country may declare in its instrument of ratification or accession, or may inform the Director-General by written notification any time thereafter, that this Convention shall be applicable to all or part of those territories, designated in the declaration or notification, for the external relations of which it is responsible. **A21–56**

(2) Any country which has made such a declaration or given such a notification may, at any time, notify the Director-General that this Convention shall cease to be applicable to all or part of such territories.

(3) (a) Any declaration made under paragraph (1) shall take effect on the same date as the ratification or accession in the instrument of which it was included, and any notification given under such paragraph shall take effect three months after its notification by the Director-General.

(b) Any notification given under paragraph (2) shall take effect twelve months after its receipt by the Director-General.

ARTICLE 25

[Implementation of the Convention on the Domestic Level]

A21–57   (1) Any country party to this Convention undertakes to adopt, in accordance with its constitution, the measures necessary to ensure the application of this Convention.

(2) It is understood that, at the time a country deposits its instrument of ratification or accession, it will be in a position under its domestic law to give effect to the provisions of this Convention.

ARTICLE 26

[Denunciation]

A21–58   (1) This Convention shall remain in force without limitation as to time.   (2) Any country may denounce this Act by notification addressed to the Director-General. Such denunciation shall constitute also denunciation of all earlier Acts and shall affect only the country making it, the Convention remaining in full force and effect as regards the other countries of the Union.

(3) Denunciation shall take effect one year after the day on which the Director-General has received the notification.

(4) The right of denunciation provided by this Article shall not be exercised by any country before the expiration of five years from the date upon which it becomes a member of the Union.

ARTICLE 27

[Application of Earlier Acts]

A21–59   (1) The present Act shall, as regards the relations between the countries to which it applies, and to the extent that it applies, replace the Convention of Paris of March 20, 1883, and the subsequent Acts of revision.

(2) (a) As regards the countries to which the present Act does not apply, or does not apply in its entirety, but to which the Lisbon Act of October 31, 1958, applies, the latter shall remain in force in its entirety or to the extent that the present Act does not replace it by virtue of paragraph (1).

(b) Similarly, as regards the countries to which neither the present Act, nor portions thereof, nor the Lisbon Act applies, the London Act of June 2, 1934, shall remain in force in its entirety or to the extent that the present Act does not replace it by virtue of paragraph (1).

(c) Similarly, as regards the countries to which neither the present Act, nor portions thereof, nor the Lisbon Act, nor the London Act applies, the Hague Act of November 6, 1925, shall remain in force in its entirety or to the extent that the present Act does not replace it by virtue of paragraph (1).

(3) Countries outside the Union which become party to this Act shall apply it with respect to any country of the Union not party to this Act or which, although party to this Act, has made a declaration pursuant to Article 20(1)(b)(i). Such countries recognize that the said country of the Union may apply, in its relations with them, the provisions of the most recent Act to which it is party.

ARTICLE 28

[Disputes]

(1) Any dispute between two or more countries of the Union concerning the **A21–60** interpretation or application of this Convention, not settled by negotiation, may, by any one of the countries concerned, be brought before the International Court of Justice by application in conformity with the Statute of the Court, [12] unless the countries concerned agree on some other method of settlement. The country bringing the dispute before the Court shall inform the International Bureau; the International Bureau shall bring the matter to the attention of the other countries of the Union.

(2) Each country may, at the time it signs this Act or deposits its instrument of ratification or accession, declare that it does not consider itself bound by the provisions of paragraph (1). With regard to any dispute between such country and any other country of the Union, the provisions of paragraph (1) shall not apply.

(3) Any country having made a declaration in accordance with the provisions of paragraph (2) may, at any time, withdraw its declaration by notification addressed to the Director-General.

ARTICLE 29

[Signatures, Languages, Depositary Functions]

(1) (a) This Act shall be signed in a single copy in the French language and **A21–61** shall be deposited with the Government of Sweden.

(b) Official texts shall be established by the Director-General, after consultation with the interested Governments, in the English, German, Italian, Portuguese, Russian and Spanish languages, and such other languages as the Assembly may designate.

(c) In case of differences of opinion on the interpretation of the various texts, the French text shall prevail.

(2) This Act shall remain open for signature at Stockholm until January 13, 1968.

(3) The Director-General shall transmit two copies, certified by the Government of Sweden, of the signed text of this Act to the Governments of all countries of the Union and, on request, to the Government of any other country.

(4) The Director-General shall register this Act with the Secretariat of the United Nations.

(5) The Director-General shall notify the Governments of all countries of the Union of signatures, deposits of instruments of ratification or accession and any declarations included in such instruments or made pursuant to Article 20(1)(c), entry into force of any provisions of this Act, notifications of denunciation, and notifications pursuant to Article 24.

ARTICLE 30

[Transitional Provisions]

(1) Until the first Director-General assumes office, references in this Act to the **A21–62** International Bureau of the Organization or to the Director-General shall be deemed to be references to the Bureau of the Union or its Director, respectively.

[12] Treaty Series No. 67 (1946), Cmd. 7015.

APPENDIX 22

Agreement on Trade-Related Aspects of Intellectual Property Rights

MEMBERS

A22–01 Desiring to reduce distortions and impediments to international trade, and taking into account the need to promote effective and adequate protection of intellectual property rights, and to ensure that measures and procedures to enforce intellectual property rights do not themselves become barriers to legitimate trade;

Recognizing, to this end, the need for new rules and disciplines concerning:

(a) The applicability of the basic principles of GATT 1994 and of relevant international intellectual property agreements or conventions;

(b) the provision of adequate standards and principles concerning the availability, scope and use of trade-related intellectual property rights;

(c) the provision of effective and appropriate means for the enforcement of trade-related intellectual property rights, taking into account differences in national legal systems;

(d) the provision of effective and expeditious procedures for the multilateral prevention and settlement of disputes between governments; and

(e) transitional arrangements aiming at the fullest participation in the results of the negotiations;

Recognizing the need for a multilateral framework of principles, rules and disciplines dealing with international trade in counterfeit goods;

Recognizing that intellectual property rights are private rights;

Recognizing the underlying public policy objectives of national systems for the protection of intellectual property, including developmental and technological objectives;

Recognizing also the special needs of the least-developed country Members in respect of maximum flexibility in the domestic implementation of laws and regulations in order to enable them to create a sound and viable technological base;

Emphasizing the importance of reducing tensions by reaching strengthened commitments to resolve disputes on trade-related intellectual property issues through multilateral procedures;

Desiring to establish a mutually supportive relationship between the WTO and the World Intellectual Property Organization (referred to in this Agreement as "WIPO") as well as other relevant international organizations;

HEREBY AGREE AS FOLLOWS:

Part I. General Provisions and Basic Principles

Article 1

Nature and scope of obligations

1. Members shall give effect to the provisions of this Agreement. Members **A22–02** may, but shall not be obliged to, implement in their law more extensive protection than is required by this Agreement, provided that such protection does not contravene the provisions of this Agreement. Members shall be free to determine the appropriate method of implementing the provisions of this Agreement within their own legal system and practice.

2. For the purposes of this Agreement, the term "intellectual property" refers to all categories of intellectual property that are the subject of Sections 1 through 7 of Part II.

3. Members shall accord the treatment provided for in this Agreement to the nationals of other Members.[1] In respect of the intellectual property right, the nationals of other Members shall be understood as those natural or legal persons that would meet the criteria for eligibility for protection provided for in the Paris Convention (1967), the Berne Convention (1971), the Rome Convention and the Treaty on Intellectual Property in Respect of Integrated Circuits, were all Members of the WTO members of those conventions.[2] Any Member availing itself of the possibilities provided in paragraph 3 of Article 5 or paragraph 2 of Article 6 of the Rome Convention shall make a notification as foreseen in those provisions to the Council for Trade-Related Aspects of Intellectual Property Rights (the "Council for TRIPs")

Article 2

Intellectual property conventions

1. In respect of Parts II, III and IV of this Agreement, Members shall comply **A22–03** with Articles 1 through 12, and Article 19, of the Paris Convention (1967).

2. Nothing in Parts I to IV of this Agreement shall derogate from existing obligations that Members may have to each other under the Paris Convention, the Berne Convention, the Rome Convention and the Treaty on Intellectual Property in Respect of Integrated Circuits.

---

[1] When "nationals" are referred to in this Agreement, they shall be deemed, in the case of a separate customs territory Member of the WTO, to mean persons, natural or legal, who are domiciled or who have a real and effective industrial or commercial establishment in that customs territory.

[2] In this Agreement, "Paris Convention" refers to the Paris Convention for the Projection of Industrial Property; "Paris Convention (1967)" refers to the Stockholm Act of this Convention of 14 July 1967. "Berne Convention" refers to the Berne Convention for the Protection of Literary and Artistic Works; "Berne Convention (1971)" refers to the Paris Act of this Convention of 24 July 1971. "Rome Convention" refers to the International Convention for the Protection of Performers, Producers of Phonograms and Broadcasting Organizations, adopted at Rome on 26 October 1961. "Treaty on Intellectual Property in Respect of Integrated Circuits" (IPIC Treaty) refers to the Treaty on Intellectual Property in Respect of Integrated Circuits, adopted at Washington on 26 May 1989 "WTO Agreement" refers to the Agreement Establishing the WTO.

Article 3

National treatment

A22–04   1. Each Member shall accord to the nationals of other Members treatment no less favourable than that it accords to its own nationals with regard to the protection[3] of intellectual property, subject to the exceptions already provided in, respectively, the Paris Convention (1967), the Berne Convention (1971), the Rome Convention or the Treaty on Intellectual Property in Respect of Integrated Circuits. In respect of performers, producers of phonograms and broadcasting organizations, this obligation only applies in respect of the rights provided under this Agreement. Any Member availing itself of the possibilities provided in Article 6 of the Berne Convention (1971) or paragraph 1(b) of Article 16 of the Rome Convention shall make a notification as foreseen in those provisions to the Council for TRIPs.

2. Members may avail themselves of the exceptions permitted under paragraph 1 in relation to judicial and administrative procedures, including the designation of an address for service or the appointment of an agent within the jurisdiction of a Member, only where such exceptions are necessary to secure compliance with laws and regulations which are not inconsistent with the provisions of this Agreement and where such practices are not applied in a manner which would constitute a disguised restriction on trade.

Article 4

Most-favoured-nation treatment

A22–05   With regard to the protection of intellectual property, any advantage, favour, privilege or immunity granted by a Member to the nationals of any other country shall be accorded immediately and unconditionally to the nationals of all other Members. Exempted from this obligation are any advantage, favour, privilege or immunity accorded by a Member:

(a) deriving from international agreements on judicial assistance or law enforcement of a general nature and not particularly confined to the protection of intellectual property;

(b) granted in accordance with the provisions of the Berne Convention (1971) or the Rome Convention authorizing that the treatment accorded be a function not of national treatment but of the treatment accorded in another country;

(c) in respect of the rights of performers, producers of phonograms and broadcasting organizations not provided under this Agreement;

(d) deriving from international agreements related to the protection of intellectual property which entered into force prior to the entry into force of the WTO Agreement, provided that such agreements are notified to the Council for TRIPs and do not constitute an arbitrary or unjustifiable discrimination against nationals of other Members.

Article 5

Multilateral agreements on acquisition or maintenance of protection

A22–06   The obligations under Articles 3 and 4 do not apply to procedures provided in multilateral agreements concluded under the auspices of WIPO relating to the acquisition or maintenance of intellectual property rights.

---

[3] For the purposes of Article 3 and 4, "protection" shall include matters affecting the availability, acquisition, scope, maintenance and enforcement of intellectual property rights as well as those matters affecting the use of intellectual property rights specifically addressed in this Agreement.

Article 6

Exhaustion

For the purposes of dispute settlement under this Agreement, subject to the **A22–07** provisions of Articles 3 and 4 nothing in this Agreement shall be used to address the issue of the exhaustion of intellectual property rights.

Article 7

Objectives

The protection and enforcement of intellectual property rights should contrib- **A22–08** ute to the promotion of technological innovation and to the transfer and dissemination of technology, to the mutual advantage of producers and users of technological knowledge and in a manner conducive to social and economic welfare, and to a balance of rights and obligations.

Article 8

Principles

Members may, in formulating or amending their laws and regulations, adopt **A22–09** measures necessary to protect public health and nutrition, and to promote the public interest in sectors of vital importance to their socio-economic and technological development, provided that such measures are consistent with the provisions of this Agreement.

2. Appropriate measures, provided that they are consistent with the provisions of this Agreement, may be needed to prevent the abuse of intellectual property rights by right holders or the resort to practices which unreasonably restrain trade or adversely affect the international transfer of technology.

Part II. Standards Concerning the Availability, Scope and Use of Intellectual Property Rights

SECTION 1. COPYRIGHT AND RELATED RIGHTS

Article 9

Relation to the Berne Convention

1. Members shall comply with Articles 1 through 21 of the Berne Convention **A22–10** (1971) and the Appendix thereto. However, Members shall not have rights or obligations under this Agreement in respect of the rights conferred under Article 6*bis* of that Convention or of the rights derived therefrom.

2. Copyright protection shall extend to expressions and not to ideas, pro- cedures, methods of operation or mathematical concepts as such.

Article 10

Computer programs and compilations of data

1. Computer programs, whether in source or object code, shall be protected as **A22–11** literary works under the Berne Convention (1971).

2. Compilations of data or other material, whether in machine readable or other form, which by reason of the selection or arrangement of their contents constitute intellectual creations shall be protected as such. Such protection, which shall not extend to the data or material itself, shall be without prejudice to any copyright subsisting in the data or material itself.

Article 11

Rental rights

A22–12 In respect of at least computer programs and cinematographic works, a Member shall provide authors and their successors in title the right to authorize or to prohibit the commercial rental to the public of originals or copies of their copyright works. A Member shall be excepted from this obligation in respect of cinematographic works unless such rental has led to widespread copying of such works which is materially impairing the exclusive right of reproduction conferred in that Member on authors and their successors in title. In respect of computer programs, this obligation does not apply to rentals where the program itself is not the essential object of the rental.

Article 12

Term of protection

A22–13 Whenever the term of protection of a work, other than a photographic work or a work of applied art, is calculated on a basis other than the life of a natural person, such term shall be no less than 50 years from the end of the calendar year of authorized publication, or, failing such authorized publication within 50 years from the making of the work, 50 years from the end of the calendar year of making.

Article 13

Limitations and exceptions

A22–14 Members shall confine limitations or exceptions to exclusive rights to certain special cases which do not conflict with a normal exploitation of the work and do not unreasonably prejudice the legitimate interests of the right holder.

Article 14

Protection of performers, producers of phonograms (sound recordings) and broadcasting organizations

A22–15 1. In respect of a fixation of their performance on a phonogram, performers shall have the possibility of preventing the following acts when undertaken without their authorization: the fixation of their unfixed performance and the reproduction of such fixation. Performers shall also have the possibility of preventing the following acts when undertaken without their authorization: the broadcasting by wireless means and the communication to the public of their live performance.

2. Producers of phonograms shall enjoy the right to authorize or prohibit the direct or indirect reproduction of their phonograms.

3. Broadcasting organizations shall have the right to prohibit the following acts when undertaken without their authorization: the fixation, the reproduction of fixations, and the rebroadcasting by wireless means of broadcasts, as well as the communication to the public of television broadcasts of the same. Where Members do not grant such rights to broadcasting organizations, they shall provide owners of copyright in the subject matter of broadcasts with the possibility of preventing the above acts, subject to the provisions of the Berne Convention (1971).

4. The provisions of Article 11 in respect of computer programs shall apply *mutatis mutandis* to producers of phonograms and any other right holders in phonograms as determined in a Member's law. If on 15 April 1994 a Member has in force a system of equitable remuneration of right holders in respect of the rental of phonograms, it may maintain such system provided that the commercial rental of phonograms is not giving rise to the material impairment of the exclusive rights of reproduction of right holders.

5. The term of the protection available under this Agreement to performers and producers of phonograms shall last at least until the end of a period of 50 years computed from the end of the calendar year in which the fixation was made or the performance took place. The term of protection granted pursuant to paragraph 3 shall last for at least 20 years from the end of the calendar year in which the broadcast took place.

6. Any Member may, in relation to the rights conferred under paragraphs 1, 2 and 3, provide for conditions, limitations, exceptions and reservations to the extent permitted by the Rome Convention. However, the provisions of Article 18 of the Berne Convention (1971) shall also apply, *mutatis mutandis*, to the rights of performers and producers of phonograms in phonograms.

Section 2. Trademarks

Article 15

Protectable subject matter

1. Any sign, or any combination of signs, capable of distinguishing the goods **A22–16** or services of one undertaking from those of other undertakings, shall be capable of constituting a trademark. Such signs, in particular words including personal names, letters, numerals, figurative elements and combinations of colours as well as any combination of such signs, shall be eligible for registration as trademarks. Where signs are not inherently capable of distinguishing the relevant goods or services, Members may make registrability depend on distinctiveness acquired through use. Members may require, as a condition of registration, that signs be visually perceptible.

2. Paragraph 1 shall not be understood to prevent a Member from denying registration of a trademark on other grounds, provided that they do not derogate from the provisions of the Paris Convention (1967).

3. Members may make registrability depend on use. However, actual use of a trademark shall not be a condition for filing an application for registration. An application shall not be refused solely on the ground that intended use has not taken place before the expiry of a period of three years from the date of application.

4. The nature of the goods or services to which a trademark is to be applied shall in no case form an obstacle to registration of the trademark.

5. Members shall publish each trademark either before it is registered or promptly after it is registered and shall afford a reasonable opportunity for

petitions to cancel the registration. In addition, Members may afford an opportunity for the registration of a trademark to be opposed.

Article 16

Rights conferred

A22–17   1. The owner of a registered trademark shall have the exclusive right to prevent all third parties not having the owner's consent from using in the course of trade identical or similar signs for goods or services which are identical or similar to those in respect of which the trademark is registered where such use would result in a likelihood of confusion. In case of the use of an identical sign for identical goods or services, a likelihood of confusion shall be presumed. The rights described above shall not prejudice any existing prior rights, nor shall they affect the possibility of Members making rights available on the basis of use.

2. Article 6*bis* of the Paris Convention (1967) shall apply, *mutatis mutandis*, to services. In determining whether a trademark is well-known, Members shall take account of the knowledge of the trademark in the relevant sector of the public, including knowledge in the Member concerned which has been obtained as a result of the promotion of the trademark.

3. Article 6*bis* of the Paris Convention (1967) shall apply, *mutatis mutandis*, to goods or services which are not similar to those in respect of which a trademark is registered, provided that use of that trademark in relation to those goods or services would indicate a connection between those goods or services and the owner of the registered trademark and provided that the interests of the owner of the registered trademark are likely to be damaged by such use.

Article 17

Exceptions

A22–18   Members may provide limited exceptions to the rights conferred by a trademark, such as fair use of descriptive terms, provided that such exceptions take account of the legitimate interests of the owner of the trademark and of third parties.

Article 18

Term of protection

A22–19   Initial registration, and each renewal of registration, of a trademark shall be for a term of no less than seven years. The registration of a trademark shall be renewable indefinitely.

Article 19

Requirement of use

A22–20   1. If use is required to maintain a registration, the registration may be cancelled only after an uninterrupted period of at least three years of non-use, unless valid reasons based on the existence of obstacles to such use are shown by the trademark owner. Circumstances arising independently of the will of the owner of the trademark which constitute an obstacle to the use of the trademark, such as import restrictions on or other government requirements for goods or services protected by the trademark, shall be recognized as valid reasons for non-use.

2. When subject to the control of its owner, use of a trademark by another person shall be recognized as use of the trademark for the purpose of maintaining the registration.

Article 20

Other requirements

The use of a trademark in the course of trade shall not be unjustifiably **A22–21** encumbered by special requirements, such as use with another trademark, use in a special form or use in a manner detrimental to its capability to distinguish the goods or services of one undertaking from those of other undertakings. This will not preclude a requirement prescribing the use of the trademark identifying the undertaking producing the goods or services along with, but without linking it to, the trademark distinguishing the specific goods or services in question of that undertaking.

Article 21

Licensing and assignment

Members may determine conditions on the licensing and assignment of **A22–22** trademarks, it being understood that the compulsory licensing of trademarks shall not be permitted and that the owner of a registered trademark shall have the right to assign the trademark with or without the transfer of the business to which the trademark belongs.

SECTION 3. GEOGRAPHICAL INDICATIONS

Article 22

Protection of geographical indications

1. Geographical indications are, for the purposes of this Agreement, indica- **A22–23** tions which identify a good as originating in the territory of a Member, or a region or locality in that territory, where a given quality, reputation or other characteristic of the good is essentially attributable to its geographical origin.

2. In respect of geographical indications, Members shall provide the legal means for interested parties to prevent:

(a) the use of any means in the designation or presentation of a good that indicates or suggests that the good in question originates in a geograph-ical area other than the true place of origin in a manner which misleads the public as to the geographical origin of the good;

(b) any use which constitutes an act of unfair competition within the meaning of Article 10*bis* of the Paris Convention (1967).

3. A Member shall, *ex officio* if its legislation so permits or at the request of an interested party, refuse or invalidate the registration of a trademark which

contains or consists of a geographical indication with respect to goods not originating in the territory indicated, if use of the indication in the trademark for such goods in that Member is of such a nature as to mislead the public as to the true place of origin.

4. The protection under paragraphs 1, 2 and shall be applicable against a geographical indication which, although literally true as to the territory, region or locality in which the goods originate, falsely represents to the public that the goods originate in another territory.

Article 23

Additional protection for geographical indications for wines and spirits

A22–24   1. Each Member shall provide the legal means for interested parties to prevent use of a geographical indication identifying wines for wines not originating in the place indicated by the geographical indication in question or identifying spirits for spirits not originating in the place indicated by the geographical indication in question, even where the true origin of the goods is indicated or the geographical indication is used in translation or accompanied by expressions such as "kind", "type", "style", "imitation" or the like.[4]

2. The registration of a trademark for wines which contains or consists of a geographical indication identifying wines or for spirits which contains or consists of a geographical indication identifying spirits shall be refused or invalidated, *ex officio* if a Member's legislation so permits or at the request of an interested party, with respect to such wines or spirits not having this origin.

3. In the case of homonymous geographical indications for wines, protection shall be accorded to each indication, subject to the provisions of paragraph 4 of Article 22. Each Member shall determine the practical conditions under which the homonymous indications in question will be differentiated from each other, taking into account the need to ensure equitable treatment of the producers concerned and that consumers are not misled.

4. In order to facilitate the protection of geographical indications for wines, negotiations shall be undertaken in the Council for TRIPs concerning the establishment of a multilateral system of notification and registration of geographical indications for wines eligible for protection in those Members participating in the system.

Article 24

International negotiations; exceptions

A22–25   1. Members agree to enter into negotiations aimed at increasing the protection of individual geographical indications under Article 23. The provisions of paragraphs 4 through 8 below shall not be used by a Member to refuse to conduct negotiations or to conclude bilateral or multilateral agreements. In the context of such negotiations, Members shall be willing to consider the continued applicability of these provisions to individual geographical indications whose use was the subject of such negotiations.

2. The Council for TRIPs shall keep under review the application of the provisions of this Section; the first such review shall take place within two years

---

[4] Notwithstanding the first sentence of Article 42, Members may with respect to these obligations, instead provide for enforcement by administrative action.

of the entry into force of the WTO Agreement. Any matter affecting the compliance with the obligations under these provisions may be drawn to the attention of the Council, which, at the request of a Member, shall consult with any Member or Members in respect of such matter in respect of which it has not been possible to find a satisfactory solution through bilateral or plurilateral consultations between the Members concerned. The Council shall take such action as may be agreed to facilitate the operation and further the objectives of this Section.

3. In implementing this Section, a Member shall not diminish the protection of geographical indications that existed in that Member immediately prior to the date of entry into force of the WTO Agreement.

4. Nothing in this Section shall require a Member to prevent continued and similar use of a particular geographical indication of another Member identifying wines or spirits in connection with goods or services by any of its nationals or domiciliaries who have used that geographical indication in a continuous manner with regard to the same or related goods or services in the territory of that Member either (a) for at least 10 years preceding 15 April 1994 or (b) in good faith preceding that date.

5. Where a trademark has been applied for or registered in good faith, or where rights to a trademark have been acquired through use in good faith either:

(a) before the date of application of these provisions in that Member as defined in Part VI; or

(b) before the geographical indication is protected in its country of origin;

measures adopted to implement this Section shall not prejudice eligibility for or the validity of the registration of a trademark, or the right to use a trademark, on the basis that such a trademark is identical with, or similar to, a geographical indication.

6. Nothing in this Section shall require a Member to apply its provisions in respect of a geographical indication of any other Member with respect to goods or services for which the relevant indication is identical with the term customary in common language as the common name for such goods or services in the territory of that Member. Nothing in this Section shall require a Member to apply its provisions in respect of a geographical indication of any other Member with respect to products of the vine for which the relevant indication is identical with the customary name of a grape variety existing in the territory of that Member as of the date of entry into force of the WTO Agreement.

7. A Member may provide that any request made under this Section in connection with the use or registration of a trademark must be presented within five years after the adverse use of the protected indication has become generally known in that Member or after the date of registration of the trademark in that Member provided that the trademark has been published by that date, if such date is earlier than the date on which the adverse use became generally known in that Member, provided that the geographical indication is not used or registered in bad faith.

8. The provisions of this Section shall in no way prejudice the right of any person to use, in the course of trade, that person's name or the name of that person's predecessor in business, except where such name is used in such a manner as to mislead the public.

9. There shall be no obligation under this Agreement to protect geographical indications which are not or cease to be protected in their country of origin, or which have fallen into disuse in that country.

SECTION 4. INDUSTRIAL DESIGNS

Article 25

Requirements for protection

A22–26   1. Members shall provide for the protection of independently created industrial designs that are new or original. Members may provide that designs are not
new or original if they do not significantly differ from known designs or
combinations of known design features. Members may provide that such
protection shall not extend to designs dictated essentially by technical or
functional considerations.

   2. Each Member shall ensure that requirements for securing protection for
textile designs, in particular in regard to any cost, examination or publication, do
not unreasonably impair the opportunity to seek and obtain such protection.
Members shall be free to meet this obligation through industrial design law or
through copyright law.

Article 26

Protection

A22–27   1. The owner of a protected industrial design shall have the right to prevent
third parties not having the owner's consent from making, selling or importing
articles bearing or embodying a design which is a copy, or substantially a copy,
of the protected design, when such acts are undertaken for commercial
purposes.

   2. Members may provide limited exceptions to the protection of industrial
designs, provided that such exceptions do not unreasonably conflict with the
normal exploitation of protected industrial designs and do not unreasonably
prejudice the legitimate interests of the owner of the protected design, taking
account of the legitimate interests of third parties.

   3. The duration of protection available shall amount to at least 10 years.

SECTION 5. PATENTS

Article 27

Patentable subject matter

A22–28   1. Subject to the provisions of paragraphs 2 and 3, patents shall be available
for any inventions, whether products or processes, in all fields of technology,
provided that they are new, involve an inventive step and are capable of
industrial application.[5] Subject to paragraph 4 of Article 65, paragraph 8 of
Article 70 and paragraph 3 of this Article, patents shall be available and patent
rights enjoyable without discrimination as to the place of invention, the field of
technology and whether products are imported or locally produced.

---

[5] For the purposes of this Article, the terms "inventive step" and "capable of industrial
application" may be deemed by a Member to be synonymous with the terms "non-
obvious" and "useful" respectively.

2. Members may exclude from patentability inventions, the prevention within their territory of the commercial exploitation of which is necessary to protect *ordre public* or morality, including to protect human, animal or plant life or health or to avoid serious prejudice to the environment, provided that such exclusion is not made merely because the exploitation is prohibited by their law.

3. Members may also exclude from patentability:

(a) diagnostic, therapeutic and surgical methods for the treatment of humans or animals;

(b) plants and animals other than micro-organisms, and essentially biological processes for the production of plants or animals other than non-biological and microbiological processes. However, Members shall provide for the protection of plant varieties either by patents or by an effective *sui generis* system or by any combination thereof. The provisions of this subparagraph shall be reviewed four years after the date of entry into force of the WTO Agreement.

Article 28

Rights conferred

1. A patent shall confer on its owner the following exclusive rights: A22–29

(a) where the subject matter of a patent is a product, to prevent third parties not having the owner's consent from the acts of: making, using, offering for sale, selling, or importing[6] for these purposes that product;

(b) where the subject matter of a patent is a process, to prevent third parties not having the owner's consent from the act of using the process, and from the acts of: using, offering for sale, selling, or importing for these purposes at least the product obtained directly by that process.

2. Patent owners shall also have the right to assign, or transfer by succession, the patent and to conclude licensing contracts.

Article 29

Conditions on patent applicants

1. Members shall require that an applicant for a patent shall disclose the A22–30 invention in a manner sufficiently clear and complete for the invention to be carried out by a person skilled in the art and may require the applicant to indicate the best mode for carrying out the invention known to the inventor at the filing date or, where priority is claimed, at the priority date of the application.

2. Members may require an applicant for a patent to provide information concerning the applicant's corresponding foreign applications and grants.

Article 30

Exceptions to rights conferred

Members may provide limited exceptions to the exclusive rights conferred by a A22–31 patent, provided that such exceptions do not unreasonably conflict with a normal exploitation of the patent and do not unreasonably prejudice the

---

[6] This right, like all other rights conferred under this Agreement in respect of the use, sale, importation or other distribution of goods, is subject to the provisions of Article 6.

legitimate interests of the patent owner, taking account of the legitimate interests of third parties.

Article 31

Other use without authorization of the right holder

A22–32   Where the law of a Member allows for other use[7] of the subject matter of a patent without the authorization of the right holder, including use by the government or third parties authorized by the government, the following provision shall be respected:

(a)   authorization of such use shall be considered on its individual merits;

(b)   such use may only be permitted if, prior to such use, the proposed user has made efforts to obtain authorization from the right holder on reasonable commercial terms and conditions and that such efforts have not been successful within a reasonable period of time. This requirement may be waived by a Member in the case of a national emergency or other circumstances of extreme urgency or in cases of public non-commercial use. In situations of national emergency or other circumstances of extreme urgency, the right holder shall, nevertheless, be notified as soon as reasonably practicable. In the case of public non-commercial use, where the government or contractor, without making a patent search, knows or has demonstrable grounds to know that a valid patent is or will be used by or for the government, the right holder shall be informed promptly;

(c)   the scope and duration of such use shall be limited to the purpose for which it was authorized, and in the case of semi-conductor technology shall only be for public non-commercial use or to remedy a practice determined after judicial or administrative process to be anti-competitive;

(d)   such use shall be non-exclusive;

(e)   such use shall be non-assignable, except with that part of the enterprise or goodwill which enjoys such use;

(f)   any such use shall be authorized predominantly for the supply of the domestic market of the Member authorizing such use;

(g)   authorization for such use shall be liable, subject to adequate protection of the legitimate interests of the persons so authorized, to be terminated if and when the circumstances which led to it cease to exist and are unlikely to recur. The competent authority shall have the authority to review, upon motivated request, the continued existence of these circumstances;

(h)   the right holder shall be paid adequate remuneration in the circumstances of each case, taking into account the economic value of the authorization;

(i)   the legal validity of any decision relating to the authorization of such use shall be subject to judicial review or other independent review by a distinct higher authority in that Member;

(j)   any decision relating to the remuneration provided in respect of such use shall be subject to judicial review or other independent review by a distinct higher authority in that Member;

(k)   Members are not obliged to apply the conditions set forth in subparagraphs (b) and (f) where such use is permitted to remedy a practice determined after judicial or administrative process to be anti-

[7] "Other use" refers to use other than that allowed under Article 30.

1256

competitive. The need to correct anti-competitive practices may be taken into account in determining the amount of remuneration in such cases. Competent authorities shall have the authority to refuse termination of authorization if and when the conditions which led to such authorization are likely to recur;

(l) where such use is authorized to permit the exploitation of a patent ("the second patent") which cannot be exploited without infringing another patent ("the first patent"), the following additional conditions shall apply:

    (i) the invention claimed in the second patent shall involve an important technical advance of considerable economic significance in relation to the invention claimed in the first patent;

    (ii) the owner of the first patent shall be entitled to a cross-licence on reasonable terms to use the invention claimed in the second patent; and

    (iii) the use authorized in respect of the first patent shall be non-assignable except with the assignment of the second patent.

Article 32

Revocation/forfeiture

An opportunity for judicial review of any decision to revoke or forfeit a patent **A22–33** shall be available.

Article 33

Term of protection

The term of protection available shall not end before the expiration of a period **A22–34** of twenty years counted from the filing date.[8]

Article 34

Process patents: burden of proof

1. For the purposes of civil proceedings in respect of the infringement of the **A22–35** rights of the owner referred to in paragraph 1(b) of Article 28, if the subject matter of a patent is a process for obtaining a product, the judicial authorities shall have the authority to order the defendant to prove that the process to obtain an identical product is different from the patented process. Therefore, Members shall provide, in at least one of the following circumstances, that any identical product when produced without the consent of the patent owner shall, in the absence of proof to the contrary, be deemed to have been obtained by the patented process:

(a) if the product obtained by the patented process is new;

(b) if there is a substantial likelihood that the identical product was made by the process and the owner of the patent has been unable through reasonable efforts to determine the process actually used.

---

[8] It is understood that those Members which do not have a system of original grant may provide that the term of protection shall be computed from the filing date in the system of original grant.

2. Any Member shall be free to provide that the burden of proof indicated in paragraph 1 shall be on the alleged infringer only if the condition referred to in subparagraph (a) is fulfilled or only if the condition referred to in subparagraph (b) is fulfilled.

3. In the adduction of proof to the contrary, the legitimate interests of defendants in protecting their manufacturing and business secrets shall be taken into account.

SECTION 6. LAYOUT-DESIGNS (TOPOGRAPHIES) OF INTEGRATED CIRCUITS

Article 35

Relation to the IPIC Treaty

A22–36   Members agree to provide protection to the layout-designs (topographies) of integrated circuits (referred to int his Agreement as "layout-designs") in accordance with Articles 2 through 7 (other than paragraph 3 of Article 6). Article 12 and paragraph 3 of Article 16 of the Treaty on Intellectual Property in Respect of Integrated Circuits and, in addition, to comply with the following provisions.

Article 36

Scope of the protection

A22–37   Subject to the provisions of paragraph 1 of Article 37, Members shall consider unlawful the following acts if performed without the authorization of the right holder[9]: importing, selling, or otherwise distributing for commercial purposes a protected layout-design, an integrated circuit in which a protected layout-design is incorporated, or an article incorporating such an integrated circuit only in so far as it continues to contain an unlawfully reproduced layout-design.

Article 37

Acts not requiring the authorization of the right holder

A22–38   1. Notwithstanding Article 36, no Member shall consider unlawful the performance of any of the acts referred to in that Article in respect of an integrated circuit incorporating an unlawfully reproduced layout-design or any article incorporating such an integrated circuit where the person performing or ordering such acts did not know and had no reasonable ground to know, when acquiring the integrated circuit or article incorporating such an integrated circuit, that it incorporated an unlawfully reproduced layout-design. Members shall provide that, after the time that such person has received sufficient notice that the layout-design was unlawfully reproduced, that person may perform any of the acts with respect to the stock on hand or ordered before such time, but shall be liable to pay to the right holder a sum equivalent to a reasonable royalty such

---

[9] The term "right holder" in this Section shall be understood as having the same meaning as the term "holder of the right" in the IPIC Treaty.

as would be payable under a freely negotiated licence in respect of such a layout-design.

2. The conditions set out in subparagraphs (a) through (k) of Article 31 shall apply *mutatis mutandis* in the event of any non-voluntary licensing of a layout-design or of its use by or for the government without the authorization of the right holder.

Article 38

Term of protection

1. In Members requiring registration as a condition of protection, the term of **A22–39** protection of layout-designs shall not end before the expiration of a period of 10 years counted from the date of filing an application for registration or from the first commercial exploitation wherever in the world it occurs.

2. In Members not requiring registration as a condition for protection, layout-designs shall be protected for a term of no less than 10 years from the date of the first commercial exploitation wherever in the world it occurs.

3. Notwithstanding paragraphs 1 and 2, a Member may provide that protection shall lapse 15 years after the creation of the layout-design.

SECTION 7. PROTECTION OF UNDISCLOSED INFORMATION

Article 39

1. In the course of ensuring effective protection against unfair competition as **A22–40** provided in Article 10*bis* of the Paris Convention (1967), Members shall protect undisclosed information in accordance with paragraph 2 and data submitted to governments or governmental agencies in accordance with paragraph 3.

2. Natural and legal persons shall have the possibility of preventing information lawfully within their control from being disclosed to, acquired by, or used by others without their consent in a manner contrary to honest commercial practices[10] so long as such information:

(a) is secret in the sense that it is not, as a body or in the precise configuration and assembly of its components, generally known among or readily accessible to persons within the circles that normally deal with the kind of information in question;

(b) has commercial value because it is secret; and

(c) has been subject to reasonable steps under the circumstances, by the person lawfully in control of the information, to keep it secret.

3. Members, when requiring, as a condition of approving the marketing of pharmaceutical or of agricultural chemical products which utilize new chemical entities, the submission of undisclosed test or other data, the origination of which involves a considerable effort, shall protect such data against unfair commercial use. In addition, Members shall protect such data against disclosure, except where necessary to protect the public, or unless steps are taken to ensure that the data are protected against unfair commercial use.

---

[10] For the purpose of this provision, "a manner contrary to honest commercial practices" shall mean at least practices such as breach of contract, breach of confidence and inducement to breach, and includes the acquisition of undisclosed information by third parties who knew, or were grossly negligent in failing to know, that such practices were involved in the acquisition.

SECTION 8. CONTROL OF ANTI-COMPETITIVE PRACTICES IN CONTRACTUAL LICENCES

Article 40

A22–41   1. Members agree that some licensing practices or conditions pertaining to intellectual property rights which restrain competition may have adverse effects on trade and may impede the transfer and dissemination of technology.

2. Nothing in this Agreement shall prevent Members from specifying in their legislation licensing practices or conditions that may in particular cases constitute an abuse of intellectual property rights having an adverse effect on competition in the relevant market. As provided above, a Member may adopt, consistently with the other provisions of this Agreement, appropriate measures to prevent or control such practices, which may include for example exclusive grantback conditions, conditions preventing challenges to validity and coercive package licensing, in the light of the relevant laws and regulations of that Member.

3. Each Member shall enter, upon request, into consultations with any other Member which has cause to believe that an intellectual property right owner that is a national or domiciliary of the Member to which the request for consultations has been addressed is undertaking practices in violation of the requesting Member's laws and regulations on the subject matter of this Section, and which wishes to secure compliance with such legislation, without prejudice to any action under the law and to the full freedom of an ultimate decision of either Member. The Member addressed shall accord full and sympathetic consideration to, and shall afford adequate opportunity for, consultations with the requesting Member, and shall cooperate through supply of publicly available non-confidential information of relevance to the matter in question and of other information available to the Member, subject to domestic law and to the conclusion of mutually satisfactory agreements concerning the safeguarding of its confidentiality by the requesting Member.

4. A Member whose nationals or domiciliaries are subject to proceedings in another Member concerning alleged violation of that other Member's laws and regulations on the subject matter of this Section shall, upon request, be granted an opportunity for consultations by the other Member under the same conditions as those foreseen in paragraph 3.

Part III. Enforcement of Intellectual Property Rights

SECTION 1. GENERAL OBLIGATIONS

Article 41

A22–42   1. Members shall ensure that enforcement procedures as specified in this Part are available under their law so as to permit effective action against any act of infringement of intellectual property rights covered by this Agreement, including expeditious remedies to prevent infringements and remedies which constitute a deterrent to further infringements. These procedures shall be applied in such a manner as to avoid the creation of barriers to legitimate trade and to provide for safeguards against their abuse.

2. Procedures concerning the enforcement of intellectual property rights shall be fair and equitable. They shall not be unnecessarily complicated or costly, or entail unreasonable time-limits or unwarranted delays.

3. Decisions on the merits of a case shall preferably be in writing and reasoned. They shall be made available at least to the parties to the proceeding without undue delay. Decisions on the merits of a case shall be based only on evidence in respect of which parties were offered the opportunity to be heard.

4. Parties to a proceeding shall have an opportunity for review by a judicial authority of final administrative decisions and, subject to jurisdictional provisions in a Member's law concerning the importance of a case, of at least the legal aspects of initial judicial decisions on the merits of a case. However, there shall be no obligation to provide an opportunity for review of acquittals in criminal cases.

5. It is understood that this Part does not create any obligation to put in place a judicial system for the enforcement of intellectual property rights distinct from that for the enforcement of law in general, nor does it affect the capacity of Members to enforce their law in general. Nothing in this Part creates any obligation with respect to the distribution of resources as between enforcement of intellectual property rights and the enforcement of law in general.

SECTION 2. CIVIL AND ADMINISTRATIVE PROCEDURES AND REMEDIES

Article 42

Fair and equitable procedures

Members shall make available to right holders[11] civil judicial procedures **A22–43** concerning the enforcement of any intellectual property right covered by this Agreement. Defendants shall have the right to written notice which is timely and contains sufficient detail, including the basis of the claims. Parties shall be allowed to be represented by independent legal counsel, and procedures shall not impose overly burdensome requirements concerning mandatory personal appearances. All parties to such procedures shall be duly entitled to substantiate their claims and to present all relevant evidence. The procedure shall provide a means to identify and protect confidential information, unless this would be contrary to existing constitutional requirements.

Article 43

Evidence

1. The judicial authorities shall have the authority, where a party has **A22–44** presented reasonably available evidence sufficient to support its claims and has specified evidence relevant to substantiation of its claims which lies in the control of the opposing party, to order that this evidence be produced by the opposing party, subject in appropriate cases to conditions which ensure the protection of confidential information.

2. In cases in which a party to a proceeding voluntarily and without good reason refuses access to, or otherwise does not provide necessary information within a reasonable period, or significantly impedes a procedure relating to an enforcement action, a Member may accord judicial authorities the authority to make preliminary and final determinations, affirmative or negative, on the basis of the information presented to them, including the complaint or the allegation presented by the party adversely affected by the denial of access to information, subject to providing the parties an opportunity to be heard on the allegations or evidence.

---

[11] For the purpose of this Part, the term "right holder" includes federations and associations having legal standing to assert such rights.

Article 44

Injunctions

A22–45 1. The judicial authorities shall have the authority to order a party to desist from an infringement, *inter alia* to prevent the entry into the channels of commerce in their jurisdiction of imported goods that involve the infringement of an intellectual property right, immediately after customs clearance of such goods. Members are not obliged to accord such authority in respect of protected subject matter acquired or ordered by a person prior to knowing or having reasonable grounds to know that dealing in such subject matter would entail the infringement of an intellectual property right.

2. Notwithstanding the other provisions of this Part and provided that the provisions of Part II specifically addressing use by governments, or by third parties authorized by a government, without the authorization of the right holder are complied with, Members may limit the remedies available against such use to payment of remuneration in accordance with subparagraph (h) of Article 31. In other cases, the remedies under this Part shall apply or, where these remedies are inconsistent with a Member's law, declaratory judgments and adequate compensation shall be available.

Article 45

Damages

A22–45 1. The judicial authorities shall have the authority to order the infringer to pay the right holder damages adequate to compensate for the injury the right holder has suffered because of an infringement of that person's intellectual property right by an infringer who knowingly, or with reasonable grounds to know, engaged in infringing activity.

2. The judicial authorities shall also have the authority to order the infringer to pay the right holder expenses, which may include appropriate attorney's fees. In appropriate cases, Members may authorize the judicial authorities to order recovery of profits and/or payment of pre-established damages even where the infringer did not knowingly, or with reasonable grounds to know, engage in infringing activity.

Article 46

Other remedies

A22–47 In order to create an effective deterrent to infringement, the judicial authorities shall have the authority to order that goods that they have found to be infringing be, without compensation of any sort, disposed of outside the channels of commerce in such a manner as to avoid any harm caused to the right holder, or, unless this would be contrary to existing constitutional requirements, destroyed. The judicial authorities shall also have the authority to order that materials and implements the predominant use of which has been in the creation of the infringing goods be, without compensation of any sort, disposed of outside the channels of commerce in such a manner as to minimize the risks of further infringements. In considering such requests, the need for proportionality between the seriousness of the infringement and the remedies ordered as well as the interests of third parties shall be taken into account. In regard to counterfeit trademark goods, the simple removal of the trademark unlawfully affixed shall not be sufficient, other than in exceptional cases, to permit release of the goods into the channels of commerce.

Article 47

Right of information

Members may provide that the judicial authorities shall have the authority, **A22–48** unless this would be out of proportion to the seriousness of the infringement, to order the infringer to inform the right holder of the identity of third persons involved in the production and distribution of the infringing goods or services and of their channels of distribution.

Article 48

Indemnification of the defendant

1. The judicial authorities shall have the authority to order a party at whose **A22–49** request measures were taken and who has abused enforcement procedures to provide to a party wrongfully enjoined or restrained adequate compensation for the injury suffered because of such abuse. The judicial authorities shall also have the authority to order the applicant to pay the defendant expenses, which may include appropriate attorney's fees.

2. In respect of the administration of any law pertaining to the protection or enforcement of intellectual property rights, Members shall only exempt both public authorities and officials from liability to appropriate remedial measures where actions are taken or intended in good faith in the course of the administration of that law.

Article 49

Administrative procedures

To the extent that any civil remedy can be ordered as a result of administra- **A22–50** tive procedures on the merits of a case, such procedures shall conform to principles equivalent in substance to those set forth in this Section.

SECTION 3. PROVISIONAL MEASURES

Article 50

1. The judicial authorities shall have the authority to order prompt and **A22–51** effective provisional measures:

   (a) to prevent an infringement of any intellectual property right from occurring, and in particular to prevent the entry into the channels of commerce in their jurisdiction of goods, including imported goods immediately after customs clearance;

   (b) to preserve relevant evidence in regard to the alleged infringement.

2. The judicial authorities shall have the authority to adopt provisional measures *inaudita altera parte* where appropriate, in particular where any delay is

likely to cause irreparable harm to the right holder, or where there is a demonstrable risk of evidence being destroyed.

3. The judicial authorities shall have the authority to require the applicant to provide any reasonably available evidence in order to satisfy themselves with a sufficient degree of certainty that the applicant is the right holder and that the applicant's right is being infringed or that such infringement is imminent, and to order the applicant to provide a security or equivalent assurance sufficient to protect the defendant and to prevent abuse.

4. Where provisional measures have been adopted *inaudita altera parte*, the parties affected shall be given notice, without delay after the execution of the measures at the latest. A review, including a right to be heard, shall take place upon request of the defendant with a view to deciding, within a reasonable period after the notification of the measures, whether these measures shall be modified, revoked or confirmed.

5. The applicant may be required to supply other information necessary for the identification of the goods concerned by the authority that will execute the provisional measures.

6. Without prejudice to paragraph 4, provisional measures taken on the basis of paragraphs 1 and 2 shall, upon request by the defendant, be revoked or otherwise cease to have effect, if proceedings leading to a decision on the merits of the case are not initiated within a reasonable period, to be determined by the judicial authority ordering the measures where a Member's law so permits or, in the absence of such a determination, not to exceed 20 working days or 31 calendar days, whichever is the longer.

7. Where the provisional measures are revoked or where they lapse due to any act or omission by the applicant, or where it is subsequently found that there has been no infringement or threat of infringement of an intellectual property right, the judicial authorities shall have the authority to order the applicant, upon request of the defendant, to provide the defendant appropriate compensation for any injury caused by these measures.

8. To the extent that any provisional measure can be ordered as a result of administrative procedures, such procedures shall conform to principles equivalent in substance to those set forth in this Section.

SECTION 4. SPECIAL REQUIREMENTS RELATED TO BORDER MEASURES[12]

Article 51

Suspension of release by customs authorities

A22–52   Members shall, in conformity with the provisions set out below, adopt procedures[13] to enable a right holder, who has valid grounds for suspecting that the importation of counterfeit trademark or pirated copyright goods[14] may take

[12] Where a Member has dismantled substantially all controls over movement of goods across its border with another Member with which it forms part of a customs union, it shall not be required to apply the provisions of this Section at that border.

[13] It is understood that there shall be no obligation to apply such procedures to imports of goods put on the market in another country by or with the consent of the right holder, or to goods in transit.

[14] For the purposes of this Agreement:
  (a) "counterfeit trademark goods" shall mean any goods, including packaging, bearing without authorization a trademark which is identical to the trademark validly registered in respect of such goods, or which cannot be distinguished in its essential aspects from such a trademark, and which thereby infringes the rights of the owner of the trademark in question under the law of the country of importation;
  (b) "pirated copyright goods" shall mean any goods which are copies made without the consent of the right holder or person duly authorized by the right holder in the country of production and which are made directly or indirectly from an article where the making of that copy would have constituted an infringement of a copyright or a related right under the law of the country of importation.

place, to lodge an application in writing with competent authorities, administrative or judicial, for the suspension by the customs authorities of the release into free circulation of such goods. Members may enable such an application to be made in respect of goods which involve other infringements of intellectual property rights, provided that the requirements of this Section are met. Members may also provide for corresponding procedures concerning the suspension by the customs authorities of the release of infringing goods destined for exportation from their territories.

Article 52

Application

Any right holder initiating the procedures under Article 51 shall be required **A22–53** to provide adequate evidence to satisfy the competent authorities that, under the laws of the country of importation, there is *prima facie* an infringement of the right holder's intellectual property right and to supply a sufficiently detailed description of the goods to make them readily recognizable by the customs authorities. The competent authorities shall inform the applicant within a reasonable period whether they have accepted the application and, where determined by the competent authorities, the period for which the customs authorities will take action.

Article 53

Security or equivalent assurance

1. The competent authorities shall have the authority to require an applicant to **A22–54** provide a security or equivalent assurance sufficient to protect the defendant and the competent authorities and to prevent abuse. Such security or equivalent assurance shall not unreasonably deter recourse to these procedures.

2. Where pursuant to an application under this Section the release of goods involving industrial designs, patents, layout-designs or undisclosed information into free circulation has been suspended by customs authorities on the basis of a decision other than by a judicial or other independent authority, and the period provided for in Article 55 has expired without the granting of provisional relief by the duly empowered authority, and provided that all other conditions for importation have been complied with, the owner, importer, or consignee of such goods shall be entitled to their release on the posting of a security in an amount sufficient to protect the right holder for any infringement. Payment of such security shall not prejudice any other remedy available to the right holder, it being understood that the security shall be released if the right holder fails to pursue the right of action within a reasonable period of time.

Article 54

Notice of suspension

The importer and the applicant shall be promptly notified of the suspension of **A22–55** the release of goods according to Article 51.

Article 55

Duration of suspension

If, within a period not exceeding 10 working days after the applicant has been **A22–56** served notice of the suspension, the customs authorities have not been informed that proceedings leading to a decision on the merits of the case have been initiated by a party other than the defendant, or that the duly empowered authority has taken provisional measures prolonging the suspension of the release of the goods, the goods shall be released, provided that all other conditions for importation or exportation have been complied with; in appropriate cases, this time-limit may be extended by another 10 working days. If proceedings leading to a decision on the merits of the case have been initiated, a review, including a right to be heard, shall take place upon request of the defendant with a view to deciding, within a reasonable period, whether these measures shall be modified, revoked or confirmed. Notwithstanding the above, where the suspension of the release of goods is carried out or continued in accordance with a provisional judicial measure, the provisions of paragraph 6 of Article 50 shall apply.

Article 56

Indemnification of the importer and of the owner of the goods

A22–57 Relevant authorities shall have the authority to order the applicant to pay the importer, the consignee and the owner of the goods appropriate compensation for any injury caused to them through the wrongful detention of goods or through the detention of goods released pursuant to Article 55.

Article 57

Right of inspection and information

A22–58 Without prejudice to the protection of confidential information, Members shall provide the competent authorities the authority to give the right holder sufficient opportunity to have any goods detained by the customs authorities inspected in order to substantiate the right holder's claims. The competent authorities shall also have authority to give the importer an equivalent opportunity to have any such goods inspected. Where a positive determination has been made on the merits of a case, Members may provide the competent authorities the authority to inform the right holder of the names and addresses of the consignor, the importer and the consignee and of the quantity of the goods in question.

Article 58

Ex officio action

A22–59 Where Members require competent authorities to act upon their own initiative and to suspend the release of goods in respect of which they have acquired *prima facie* evidence that an intellectual property right is being infringed:

(a) the competent authorities may at any time seek from the right holder any information that may assist them to exercise these powers;
(b) the importer and the right holder shall be promptly notified of the suspension. Where the importer has lodged an appeal against the suspension with the competent authorities, the suspension shall be subject to the conditions, *mutatis mutandis*, set out at Article 55;
(c) Members shall only exempt both public authorities and officials from liability to appropriate remedial measures where actions are taken or intended in good faith.

Article 59

Remedies

A22–60 Without prejudice to other rights of action open to the right holder and subject to the right of the defendant to seek review by a judicial authority, competent authorities shall have the authority to order the destruction or disposal of infringing goods in accordance with the principles set out in Article 46. In regard to counterfeit trademark goods, the authorities shall not allow the re-exportation of the infringing goods in an unaltered state or subject them to a different customs procedure, other than in exceptional circumstances.

Article 60

De minimis imports

Members may exclude from the application of the above provisions small **A22–61** quantities of goods of a non-commerical nature contained in travellers' personal luggage or sent in small consignments.

SECTION 5. CRIMINAL PROCEDURES

Article 61

Members shall provide for criminal procedures and penalties to be applied at **A22–62** least in cases of wilful trademark counterfeiting or copyright piracy on a commercial scale. Remedies available shall include imprisonment and/or monetary fines sufficient to provide a deterrent, consistently with the level of penalties applied for crimes of a corresponding gravity. In appropriate cases, remedies available shall also include the seizure, forfeiture and destruction of the infringing goods and of any materials and implements the predominant use of which has been in the commission of the offence. Members may provide for criminal procedures and penalties to be applied in other cases of infringment of intellectual property rights, in particular where they are committed wilfully and on a commercial scale.

Part IV. Acquisition and Maintenance of Intellectual Property Rights and Related Inter-partes Procedures

Article 62

1. Members may require, as a condition of the acquisition or maintenance of **A22–63** the intellectual property rights provided for under Sections 2 through 6 of Part II, compliance with reasonable procedures and formalities. Such procedures and formalities shall be consistent with the provisions of this Agreement.

2. Where the acquisition of an intellectual property right is subject to the right being granted or registered, Members shall ensure that the procedures for grant or registration, subject to compliance with the substantive conditions for acquisition of the right, permit the granting or registration of the right within a reasonable period of time so as to avoid unwarranted curtailment of the period of protection.

3. Article 4 of the Paris Convention (1967) shall apply *mutatis mutandis* to service marks.

4. Procedures concerning the acquisition or maintenance of intellectual property rights and, where a Member's law provides for such procedures, administrative revocation and *inter partes* procedures such as opposition, revocation and cancellation, shall be governed by the general principles set out in paragraphs 2 and 3 of Article 41.

5. Final administrative decisions in any of the procedures referred to under paragraph 4 shall be subject to review by a judicial or quasi-judicial authority. However, there shall be no obligation to provide an opportunity for such review

of decisions in cases of unsuccessful opposition or administrative revocation, provided that the grounds for such procedures can be the subject of invalidation procedures.

Part V. Dispute Prevention and Settlement

Article 63

Transparency

A22–64   1. Laws and regulations, and final judicial decisions and administrative rulings of general application, made effective by a Member pertaining to the subject matter of this Agreement (the availability, scope, acquisition, enforcement and prevention of the abuse of intellectual property rights) shall be published, or where such publication is not practicable made publicly available, in a national language, in such a manner as to enable governments and right holders to become acquainted with them. Agreements concerning the subject matter of this Agreement which are in force between the government or a governmental agency of a Member and the government or a governmental agency of another Member shall also be published.

2. Members shall notify the laws and regulations referred to in paragraph 1 to the Council for TRIPs in order to assist that Council in its review of the operation of the Agreement. The Council shall attempt to minimize the burden on Members in carrying out this obligation and may decide to waive the obligation to notify such laws and regulations directly to the Council if consultations with WIPO on the establishment of a common register containing these laws and regulations are successful. The Council shall also consider in this connection any action required regarding notifications pursuant to the obligations under this Agreement stemming from the provisions of Article 6*ter* of the Paris Convention (1967).

3. Each Member shall be prepared to supply, in response to a written request from another Member, information of the sort referred to in paragraph 1. A Member, having reason to believe that a specific judicial decision or administrative ruling or bilateral agreement in the area of intellectual property rights affects its rights under this Agreement, may also request in writing to be given access to or be informed in sufficient detail of such specific judicial decisions or administrative rulings or bilateral agreements.

4. Nothing in paragraphs 1, 2 and 3 shall require Members to disclose confidential information which would impede law enforcement or otherwise be contrary to the public interest or would prejudice the legitimate commercial interests of particular enterprises, public or private.

Article 64

Dispute settlement

A22–65   1. The provisions of Article XXII and XXIII of GATT 1994 as elaborated and applied by the Dispute Settlement Understanding shall apply to consultations and the settlement of disputes under this Agreement except as otherwise specifically provided herein.

2. Subparagraphs 1(b) and 1(c) of Article XXIII of GATT 1994 shall not apply to the settlement of disputes under this Agreement for a period of five years from the date of entry into force of the WTO Agreement.

3. During the time period referred to in paragraph 2, the Council for TRIPs shall examine the scope and modalities for complaints of the type provided for under subparagraphs 1(b) and 1(c) of Article XXIII of GATT 1994 made pursuant to this Agreement, and submit its recommendations to the Ministerial Conference for approval. Any decision of the Ministerial Conference to approve such recommendations or to extend the period in paragraph 2 shall be made only by consensus, and approved recommendations shall be effective for all Members without further formal acceptance process.

Part VI. Transitional Arrangements

Article 65

Transitional arrangements

1. Subject to the provisions of paragraphs 2, 3 and 4, no Member shall be **A22–66** obliged to apply the provisions of this Agreement before the expiry of a general period of one year following the date of entry into force of the WTO Agreement.
2. A developing country Member is entitled to delay for a further period of four years the date of application, as defined in paragraph 1, of the provisions of this Agreement other than Articles 3, 4 and 5.
3. Any other Member which is in the process of transformation from a centrally-planned into a market, free-enterprise economy and which is undertaking structural reform of its intellectual property system and facing special problems in the preparation and implementation of intellectual property laws and regulations, may also benefit from a period of delay as foreseen in paragraph 2.
4. To the extent that a developing country Member is obliged by this Agreement to extend product patent protection to areas of technology not so protectable in its territory on the general date of application of this Agreement for that Member, as defined in paragraph 2, it may delay the application of the provisions on product patents of Section 5 of Part II to such areas of technology for an additional period of five years.
5. A Member availing itself of a transitional period under paragraphs 1, 2, 3 or 4 shall ensure that any changes in its laws, regulations and practice made during that period do not result in a lesser degree of consistency with the provisions of this Agreement.

Article 66

Least-developed country Members

1. In view of the special needs and requirements of least-developed country **A22–67** Members, their economic, financial and administrative constraints, and their need for flexibility to create a viable technological base, such Members shall not be required to apply the provisions of this Agreement, other than Articles 3, 4 and 5, for a period of 10 years from the date of application as defined under paragraph 1 of Article 65. The Council for TRIPs shall, upon duly motivated request by a least-developed country Member, accord extensions of this period.
2. Developed country Members shall provide incentives to enterprises and institutions in their territories for the purpose of promoting and encouraging technology transfer to least-developed country Members in order to enable them to create a sound and viable technological base.

Article 67

Technical cooperation

In order to facilitate the implementation of this Agreement, developed country **A22–68** Members shall provide, on request and on mutually agreed terms and conditions, technical and financial cooperation in favour of developing and least-developed country Members. Such cooperation shall include assistance in the preparation of laws and regulations on the protection and enforcement of intellectual property rights as well as on the prevention of their abuse, and shall include support regarding the establishment or reinforcement of domestic offices and agencies relevant to these matters, including the training of personnel.

Part VII. Institutional Arrangements: Final Provisions

Article 68

Council for Trade-Related Aspects of Intellectual Property Rights

A22–69   The Council for TRIPs shall monitor the operation of this Agreement and, in particular, Members' compliance with their obligations hereunder, and shall afford Members the opportunity of consulting on matters relating to the trade-related aspects of intellectual property rights. It shall carry out such other responsibilities as assigned to it by the Members, and it shall, in particular, provide any assistance requested by them in the context of dispute settlement procedures. In carrying out its functions, the Council for TRIPs may consult with and seek information from any source it deems appropriate. In consultation with WIPO, the Council shall seek to establish, within one year of its first meeting, appropriate arrangements for cooperation with bodies of that Organization.

Article 69

International cooperation

A22–70   Members agree to cooperate with each other with a view to eliminating international trade in goods infringing intellectual property rights. For this purpose, they shall establish and notify contact points in their administrations and be ready to exchange information on trade in infringing goods. They shall, in particular, promote the exchange of information and cooperation between customs authorities with regard to trade in counterfeit trademark goods and pirated copyright goods.

Article 70

Protection of existing subject matter

A22–71   1. This Agreement does not give rise to obligations in respect of acts which occurred before the date of application of the Agreement for the Member in question.

2. Except as otherwise provided for in this Agreement, this Agreement gives rise to obligations in respect of all subject matter existing at the date of application of this Agreement for the Member in question, and which is protected in that Member on the said date, or which meets or comes subsequently to meet the criteria for protection under the terms of this Agreement. In respect of this paragraph and paragraphs 3 and 4, copyright obligations with respect to existing works shall be solely determined under Article 18 of the Berne Convention (1971), and obligations with respect to the rights of producers of phonograms and performers in existing phonograms shall be determined solely under Article 18 of the Berne Convention (1971) as made applicable under paragraph 6 of Article 14 of this Agreement.

3. There shall be no obligation to restore protection to subject matter which on the date of application of this Agreement for the Member in question has fallen into the public domain.

4. In respect of any acts in respect of specific objects embodying protected subject matter which become infringing under the terms of legislation in conformity with this Agreement, and which were commenced, or in respect of which a significant investment was made, before the date of acceptance of the WTO Agreement by that Member, any Member may provide for a limitation of the remedies available to the right holder as to the continued performance of such acts after the date of application of this Agreement for that Member. In such cases the Member shall, however, at least provide for the payment of equitable remuneration.

5. A Member is not obliged to apply the provisions of Article 11 and of paragraph 4 of Article 14 with respect to originals or copies purchased prior to the date of application of this Agreement for that Member.

6. Members shall not be required to apply Article 31, or the requirement in paragraph 1 of Article 27 that patent rights shall be enjoyable without discrimination as to the field of technology, to use without the authorization of the right holder where authorization for such use was granted by the government before the date this Agreement became known.

7. In the case of intellectual property rights for which protection is conditional upon registration, applications for protection which are pending on the date of application of this Agreement for the Member in question shall be permitted to be amended to claim any enhanced protection provided under the provisions of this Agreement. Such amendments shall not include new matter.

8. Where a Member does not make available as of the date of entry into force of the WTO Agreement patent protection for pharmaceutical and agricultural chemical products commensurate with its obligations under Article 27, that Member shall:

    (a) notwithstanding the provisions of Part VI, provide as from the date of entry into force of the WTO Agreement a means by which applications for patents for such inventions can be filed;

    (b) apply to these applications, as of the date of application of this Agreement, the criteria for patentability as laid down in this Agreement as if those criteria were being applied on the date of filing in that Member or, where priority is available and claimed, the priority date of the application; and

    (c) provide patent protection in accordance with this Agreement as from the grant of the patent and for the remainder of the patent term, counted from the filing date in accordance with Article 33 of this Agreement, for those of these applications that meet the criteria for protection referred to in subparagraph (b).

9. Where a product is the subject of a patent application in a Member in accordance with paragraph 8(a), exclusive marketing rights shall be granted, notwithstanding the provisions of Part VI, for a period of five years after obtaining marketing approval in that Member or until a product patent is granted or rejected in that Member, whichever period is shorter, provided that, subsequent to the entry into force of the WTO Agreement, a patent application has been filed and a patent granted for that product in another Member and marketing approval obtained in such other Member.

Article 71

Review and amendment

1. The Council for TRIPs shall review the implementation of this Agreement **A22–72** after the expiration of the transitional period referred to in paragraph 2 of Article 65. The Council shall, having regard to the experience gained in its implementa-

tion, review it two years after that date, and at identical intervals thereafter. The Council may also undertake reviews in the light of any relevant new developments which might warrant modification or amendment of this Agreement.

2. Amendments merely serving the purpose of adjusting to higher levels of protection of intellectual property rights achieved, and in force, in other multilateral agreements and accepted under those agreements by all Members of the WTO may be referred to the Ministerial Conference for action in accordance with paragraph 6 of Article X of the WTO Agreement of the basis of a consensus proposal from the Council for TRIPs.

Article 72

Reservations

A22–73   Reservations may not be entered in respect of any of the provisions of this Agreement without the consent of the other Members.

Article 73

Security exceptions

A22–74   Nothing in this Agreement shall be construed:

    (a) to require a Member to furnish any information the disclosure of which it considers contrary to its essential security interests; or

    (b) to prevent a Member from taking any action which it considers necessary for the protection of its essential security interests;

        (i) relating to fissionable materials or the materials from which they are derived;

        (ii) relating to the traffic in arms, ammunition and implements of war and to such traffic in other goods and materials as is carried on directly or indirectly for the purpose of supplying a military establishment;

        (iii) taken in time of war or other emergency in international relations; or

    (c) to prevent a Member from taking any action in pursuance of its obligations under the United Nations Charter for the maintenance of international peace and security.

APPENDIX 23

The Trade Marks (Claims to Priority from Relevant Countries) Order 1994

S.I. 1994 No. 2803

Her Majesty, in exercise of the powers conferred upon Her by section 36(1) and (2) of **A23–01** the Trade Marks Act 1994, is pleased, by and with the advice of Her Privy Council, to order, and it is hereby ordered, as follows:—

1. This Order may be cited as the Trade Marks (Claims to Priority from Relevant **A23–02** Countries) Order 1994 and shall come into force on 5th December 1994.

2. In this Order— **A23–03**

"the Act" means the Trade Marks Act 1994;
"duly filed" means a filing which is adequate to establish the date on which the application was filed in the relevant country in question, whatever may be the subsequent fate of the application; and
"relevant country" means any country or territory specified in the Schedule to this Order.

3. A person who has duly filed an application for the protection of a trade mark in a **A23–04** relevant country shall have a right to priority, for the purpose of registering the same trade mark under the Act for some or all of the same goods or services, for a period of six months from the date of filing of the application in that country.

4. Where the application for registration under the Act is made within the aforesaid **A23–05** period of six months—

(a) the relevant date for the purpose of establishing which rights take precedence shall be the date of the filing of the application in the relevant country, and

(b) the registrability of the trade mark shall not be affected by any use of the mark in the United Kingdom in the period between that date and the date of the application under the Act.

5. A subsequent application concerning the same subject as the first appli- **A23–06** cation, duly filed in the same relevant country, shall be considered the first application to be filed in that country (of which the filing date shall be the starting date of the period of priority) if at the time of the subsequent application—

(a) the previous application has been withdrawn, abandoned or refused, without having been laid open to public inspection and without leaving any rights outstanding, and

(b) it has not yet served as a basis for claiming a right of priority.

6. A previous application may not serve as a basis for claiming a right of **A23–07** priority where a subsequent application is considered, in accordance with article 5 above, as the first application to be duly filed.

7. A right to priority conferred by this Order— **A23–08**

(a) shall (unless otherwise stated in the application) vest in the person filing the application or his successor in title; and

(b) may be assigned or otherwise transmitted, either with the application or independently.

A23–09 8.—(1) Where a right to priority is claimed by reason of an application to which this Order relates, particulars of that claim shall be included in the application for registration filed under the Act and, unless a certificate as is referred to in paragraph (2) below is filed with the application, such particulars shall include the relevant country and the date of filing.

(2) There shall be filed within three months of the filing of the application for registration under the Act a certificate by the registering or other competent authority of the relevant country certifying, or verifying to the satisfaction of the registrar—

    (a) the date of the filing of the application,
    (b) the relevant country or registering or competent authority,
    (c) the representation of the mark, and
    (d) the goods or services covered by the application.

A23–09

SCHEDULE   Article 2

RELEVANT COUNTRIES

Ecuador
Hong Kong

APPENDIX 24

S.I. 1995 No. 2997

The Trade Marks (Claims to Priority from Relevant Countries) (Amendment) Order 1995

Her Majesty, in exercise of the powers conferred upon Her by section 36(1) and (2) of **A24–01** the Trade Marks Act 1994, is pleased, by and with the advice of Her Privy Council, to order, and it is hereby ordered, as follows:

1. This Order may be cited as the Trade Marks (Claims to Priority from **A24–02** Relevant Countries) (Amendment) Order 1995 and shall come into force on 1st January 1996.

2. For the Schedule to the Trade Marks (Claims to Priority from Relevant **A24–03** Countries) Order 1994, there shall be substituted the Schedule to this Order.

SCHEDULE   Article 2

RELEVANT COUNTRIES

Antigua and Barbuda   **A24–03**
Bahrain
Belize
Bolivia
Botswana
Brunei Darussalam
Colombia
Djibouti
Dominica
Ecuador
Guatemala
Hong Kong
India
Jamaica
Kuwait
Macau
Maldives
Mozambique
Myanmar
Namibia
Nicaragua
Pakistan
Sierra Leone
Thailand

The Patents and Trade Marks (World Trade Organisation) Regulations 1999

S.I. 1999 No. 1899

A25–01   The Secretary of State, being a Minister designated for the purposes of section 2(2) of the European Communities Act 1972 in relation to measures relating to patents and trade marks, in exercise of powers conferred by section 2 (2) of the said Act of 1972, hereby makes the following Regulations:—

PART I

INTRODUCTORY PROVISIONS

Citation and commencement

A25–02   **1.**—(1) These Regulations may be cited as the Patents and Trade Marks (World Trade Organisation) Regulations 1999.

(2) These Regulations come into force on 29th July 1999.

Interpretation

A25–03   **2.** In these Regulations—

"the 1977 Act" means the Patents Act 1977;
"the 1994 Act" means the Trade Marks Act 1994;
"the 1995 rules" means the Patent Rules 1995.

PART II

AMENDEMENTS OF THE PATENTS ACT 1977

Compulsory licences: general

A25–04   **3.** For section 48 of the 1977 Act substitute—
"**Compulsory licences: general**
48.—(1) At any time after the expiration of three years, or of such other period as may be prescribed, from the date of the grant of a patent, any person may apply to the comptroller on one or more of the relevant grounds—

(a) for a licence under the patent;
(b) for an entry to be made in the register to the effect that licences under the patent are to be available as of right; or

(c) where the applicant is a government department, for the grant to any person specified in the application of a licence under the patent.

(2) Subject to sections 48A and 48B below, if he is satisfied that any of the relevant grounds are established, the comptroller may—

(a) where the application is under subsection (1)(a) above, order the grant of a licence to the applicant on such terms as the comptroller thinks fit;
(b) where the application is under subsection (1)(b) above, make such an entry as is there mentioned;
(c) where the application is under subsection (1)(c) above, order the grant of a licence to the person specified in the application on such terms as the comptroller thinks fit.

(3) An application may be made under this section in respect of a patent even though the applicant is already the holder of a licence under the patent; and no person shall be estopped or barred from alleging any of the matters specified in the relevant grounds by reason of any admission made by him, whether in such a licence or otherwise, or by reason of his having accepted a licence.

(4) In this section "the relevant grounds" means—

(a) in the case of an application made in respect of a patent whose proprietor is a WTO proprietor, the grounds set out in section 48A (1) below;
(b) in any other case, the grounds set out in section 48B(1) below.

(5) A proprietor is a WTO proprietor for the purposes of this section and sections 48A, 48B, 50 and 52 below if—

(a) he is a national of, or is domiciled in, a country which is a member of the World Trade Organisation; or
(b) he has a real and effective industrial or commercial establishment in such a country.

(6) A rule prescribing any such other period under subsection (1) above shall not be made unless a draft of the rule has been laid before, and approved by resolution of, each House of Parliament."

Compulsory licences: WTO proprietors

4. After section 48 of the 1977 Act insert—   A25–05

"Compulsory licences: WTO proprietors.

48A.—(1) In the case of an application made under section 48 above in respect of a patent whose proprietor is a WTO proprietor, the relevant grounds are—

(a) where the patented invention is a product, that a demand in the United Kingdom for that product is not being met on reasonable terms;
(b) that by reason of the refusal of the proprietor of the patent concerned to grant a licence or licences on reasonable terms—
   (i) the exploitation in the United Kingdom of any other patented invention which involves an important technical advance of considerable economic significance in relation to the invention for which the patent concerned was granted is prevented or hindered, or
   (ii) the establishment or development of commercial or industrial activities in the United Kingdom is unfairly prejudiced;
(c) that by reason of conditions imposed by the proprietor of the patent concerned on the grant of licences under the patent, or on the disposal

or use of the patented product or on the use of the patented process, the manufacture, use or disposal of materials not protected by the patent, or the establishment or development of commercial or industrial activities in the United Kingdom, is unfairly prejudiced.

(2) No order or entry shall be made under section 48 above in respect of a patent whose proprietor is a WTO proprietor unless—

 (a) the applicant has made efforts to obtain a licence from the proprietor on reasonable commercial terms and conditions; and
 (b) his efforts have not been successful within a reasonable period.

(3) No order or entry shall be so made if the patented invention is in the field of semi-conductor technology.

(4) No order or entry shall be made under section 48 above in respect of a patent on the ground mentioned in subsection (1)(b)(i) above unless the comptroller is satisfied that the proprietor of the patent for the other invention is able and willing to grant the proprietor of the patent concerned and his licensees a licence under the patent for the other invention on reasonable terms.

(5) A licence granted in pursuance of an order or entry so made shall not be assigned except to a person to whom the patent for the other invention is also assigned.

(6) A licence granted in pursuance of an order or entry made under section 48 above in respect of a patent whose proprietor is a WTO proprietor—

 (a) shall not be exclusive;
 (b) shall not be assigned except to a person to whom there is also assigned the part of the enterprise that enjoys the use of the patented invention, or the part of the goodwill that belongs to that part;
 (c) shall be predominantly for the supply of the market in the United Kingdom;
 (d) shall include conditions entitling the proprietor of the patent concerned to remuneration adequate in the circumstances of the case, taking into account the economic value of the licence; and
 (e) shall be limited in scope and in duration to the purpose for which the licence was granted."

Compulsory licences: other cases

A25–06   5. After section 48A of the 1977 Act insert—

"**Compulsory licences: other cases**
  48B.—(1) In the case of an application made under section 48 above in respect of a patent whose proprietor is not a WTO proprietor, the relevant grounds are—

 (a) where the patented invention is capable of being commercially worked in the United Kingdom, that it is not being so worked or is not being so worked to the fullest extent that is reasonably practicable;
 (b) where the patented invention is a product, that a demand for the product in the United Kingdom—

   (i) is not being met on reasonable terms, or
   (ii) is being met to a substantial extent by importation from a country which is not a member State;

 (c) where the patented invention is capable of being commercially worked in the United Kingdom, that it is being prevented or hindered from being so worked—

     (i) where the invention is a product, by the importation of the product from a country which is not a member State,

    (ii) where the invention is a process, by the importation from such a country of a product obtained directly by means of the process or to which the process has been applied;

(d) that by reason of the refusal of the proprietor of the patent to grant a licence or licences on reasonable terms—

     (i) a market for the export of any patented product made in the United Kingdom is not being supplied, or

    (ii) the working or efficient working in the United Kingdom of any other patented invention which makes a substantial contribution to the art is prevented or hindered, or

   (iii) the establishment or development of commercial or industrial activities in the United Kingdom is unfairly prejudiced;

(e) that by reason of conditions imposed by the proprietor of the patent on the grant of licences under the patent, or on the disposal or use of the patented product or on the use of the patented process, the manufacture, use or disposal of materials not protected by the patent, or the establishment or development of commercial or industrial activities in the United Kingdom, is unfairly prejudiced.

(2) Where—

(a) an application is made on the ground that the patented invention is not being commercially worked in the United Kingdom or is not being so worked to the fullest extent that is reasonably practicable; and

(b) it appears to the comptroller that the time which has elapsed since the publication in the journal of a notice of the grant of the patent has for any reason been insufficient to enable the invention to be so worked, he may by order adjourn the application for such period as will in his opinion give sufficient time for the invention to be so worked.

(3) No order or entry shall be made under section 48 above in respect of a patent on the ground mentioned in subsection (1)(a) above if—

(a) the patented invention is being commercially worked in a country which is a member State; and

(b) demand in the United Kingdom is being met by importation from that country.

(4) No entry shall be made in the register under section 48 above on the ground mentioned in subsection (1)(d)(i) above, and any licence granted under section 48 above on that ground shall contain such provisions as appear to the comptroller to be expedient for restricting the countries in which any product concerned may be disposed of or used by the licensee.

(5) No order or entry shall be made under section 48 above in respect of a patent on the ground mentioned in subsection (1)(d)(ii) above unless the comptroller is satisfied that the proprietor of the patent for the other invention is able and willing to grant to the proprietor of the patent concerned and his licensees a licence under the patent for the other invention on reasonable terms."

Opposition, appeal and arbitration

6. For section 52 of the 1977 Act substitute—   A25–07

"Opposition, appeal and arbitration

52.—(1) The proprietor of the patent concerned or any other person wishing to oppose an application under sections 48 to 51 above may, in accordance with rules, give to the comptroller notice of opposition; and the comptroller shall consider any opposition in deciding whether to grant the application.

(2) Where an order or entry has been made under section 48 above in respect of a patent whose proprietor is a WTO proprietor—

(a) the proprietor or any other person may, in accordance with rules, apply to the comptroller to have the order revoked or the entry cancelled on the grounds that the circumstances which led to the making of the order or entry have ceased to exist and are unlikely to recur;

(b) any person wishing to oppose an application under paragraph (a) above may, in accordance with rules, give to the comptroller notice of opposition; and

(c) the comptroller shall consider any opposition in deciding whether to grant the application.

(3) If it appears to the comptroller on an application under subsection (2)(a) above that the circumstances which led to the making of the order or entry have ceased to exist and are unlikely to recur, he may—

(a) revoke the order or cancel the entry; and

(b) terminate any licence granted to a person in pursuance of the order or entry subject to such terms and conditions as he thinks necessary for the protection of the legitimate interests of that person.

(4) Where an appeal is brought—

(a) from an order made by the comptroller in pursuance of an application under sections 48 to 51 above;

(b) from a decision of his to make an entry in the register in pursuance of such an application;

(c) from a revocation or cancellation made by him under subsection (3) above; or

(d) from a refusal of his to make such an order, entry, revocation or cancellation,

the Attorney General, the appropriate Law Officer within the meaning of section 4A of the Crown Suits (Scotland) Act 1857 or the Attorney General for Northern Ireland, or such other counsel as any of them may appoint, shall be entitled to appear and be heard.

(5) Where an application under sections 48 to 51 above or subsection (2) above is opposed, and either—

(a) the parties consent, or

(b) the proceedings require a prolonged examination of documents or any scientific or local investigation which cannot in the opinion of the comptroller conveniently be made before him,

the comptroller may at any time order the whole proceedings, or any question or issue of fact arising in them, to be referred to an arbitrator or arbiter agreed on by the parties or, in default of agreement, appointed by the comptroller.

(6) Where the whole proceedings are so referred, unless the parties otherwise agree before the award of the arbitrator or arbiter is made, an appeal shall lie from the award to the court.

(7) Where a question or issue of fact is so referred, the arbitrator or arbiter shall report his findings to the comptroller."

Minor amendments of 1977 Act

25–08   7.—(1) After subsection (5) of section 5 of the 1977 Act (priority date) insert—

"(6) References in subsection (5) above to a convention country include references to a country, other than the United Kingdom, which is a member of the World Trade Organisation."

(2) In subsection (1) of section 50 of that Act (exercise of powers on applications), after the words "in respect of a patent" insert the words "whose proprietor is not a WTO proprietor".

(3) In subsection (2) of that section, for the words "such an application" substitute the words "any application under section 48 above".

(4) In subsection (2) of section 54 of that Act (special provisions), after the words "means a country other than a member state" insert the words "or a member of the World Trade Organisation".

(5) In subsection (7) of section 60 of that Act (meaning of infringement), in the definitions of "relevant ship" and "relevant aircraft, hovercraft or vehicle", after the words "1983" insert the words "or which is a member of the World Trade Organisation".

Part II: transitional provisions

8.—(1) A WTO proprietor of a patent in respect of which an order or entry has **25–09** been made under section 48 of the 1977 Act before the relevant date may apply to the comptroller—

(a) to have the order revoked or the entry cancelled on the grounds that the grounds on which the order or entry was made are not set out in subsection (1) of section 48A of that Act; or

(b) to have the conditions subject to which any licence was granted before that date in pursuance of the order or entry modified on the grounds that the licence does not satisfy the requirements set out in subsection (6) of that section.

(2) If it appears to the comptroller on an application under paragraph (1)(a) that the grounds on which the order or entry was made are not set out in section 48A(1) of the 1977 Act, he may—

(a) revoke the order or cancel the entry; or

(b) terminate any licence granted to a person in pursuance of the order or entry subject to such terms and conditions as he thinks necessary for the protection of the legitimate interests of that person.

(3) If it appears to the comptroller on an application under paragraph (1)(b) that the conditions of the licence should be modified, he may modify the conditions accordingly; but in doing so he shall have regard to the need to protect the legitimate interests of the holder of the licence.

(4) Subsections (1), (4) and (5) of section 52 of the 1977 Act shall apply to an application under paragraph (1) as they apply to an application under sections 48 to 51 of that Act, but as if the reference in subsection (1) to the proprietor of the patent or any other person were a reference to any person.

(5) Section 48A(5) of the 1977 Act shall apply to a licence granted on or after the relevant date in pursuance of an entry made before that date in relation to a patent whose proprietor is a WTO proprietor, if the entry was made—

(a) before the commencement date and on the ground mentioned in section 48(3)(d)(ii) of that Act; or

(b) on or after that date and on the ground mentioned in section 48B(1)(d)(ii) of that Act.

(6) Section 48A(6) of the 1977 Act shall apply to a licence granted on or after the relevant date in pursuance of an entry made before that date in relation to a patent whose proprietor is a WTO proprietor.

(7) A proprietor is a WTO proprietor for the purposes of this regulation if—

    (a) he is a national of, or is domiciled in, a country which is a member of the World Trade Organisation; or

    (b) he has a real and effective industrial or commercial establishment in such a country.

(8) In this regulation—

"the commencement date" means the date of the coming into force of these Regulations;

"the relevant date" means the commencement date or, if later, the date on which the proprietor of the patent became a WTO proprietor.

PART III

AMENDMENTS OF THE PATENTS RULES 1995

Application for: compulsory licence under section 48(1), or revocation or cancellation under section 52(2)(a), of the 1977 Act

A25–10   9. For rule 68 of the 1995 rules substitute—

"**68.** An application under section 48(1) or 52(2)(a) shall be made on Patents Form 2/77 and shall be accompanied by a statement in duplicate of the facts upon which the applicant relies and evidence in duplicate verifying the statement.".

Procedure on receipt of application under section 48, 51 or 52 of the 1977 Act

A25–11   10. For rule 70 of the 1995 rules substitute—

"**70.**—(1) If upon consideration of the evidence submitted under rule 68 (application for: compulsory licence under section 48(1) or revocation or cancellation under section 52(2)(a)) or rule 69 (application by Minister under section 51), the comptroller is not satisfied that a prima facie case is made out for—

    (a) the making of an order or an entry, or

    (b) the revocation of an order or cancellation of an entry,

as the case may be, he shall notify the applicant accordingly, and unless, within one month of making such notification, the applicant requests to be heard in the matter, the comptroller shall refuse the application.

(2) Where the applicant requests a hearing within the time allowed, the comptroller, after giving the applicant the opportunity of being heard, shall determine whether the application may proceed or whether it shall be refused.

(3) If upon consideration of the evidence the comptroller is satisfied that a prima facie case has been made out for—

    (a) the making of an order or an entry, or

    (b) the revocation of an order or cancellation of an entry,

as the case may be, or if, after hearing the applicant, he so determines, he shall direct that the application shall be advertised in the Journal, and shall send a copy of the application, the statement and the evidence filed in support thereof—

1282

    (c) where the application is under subparagraph (a), to the proprietor of the patent and to any other person shown on the register as having any right in or under the patent; or

    (d) where the application is under subparagraph (b), to any person shown on the register as having any right in or under the patent.".

Opposition under section 52 of the 1977 Act

11. For paragraph (1) of rule 71 of the 1995 rules substitute—   **A25–12**

  "**71.**—(1) Within two months of the date of the advertisement in the Journal of an application under rule 70(3), any person may give notice to the comptroller of opposition under section 52(1) or 52(2)(b), as the case may be, to the application on Patents Form 15/77.".

Part III: transitional provisions

12. Rules 68, 70 and 71 of the 1995 rules shall apply to an application, or **A25–13** opposition to an application, under regulation 8(1) as they apply to an application or opposition under section 48, or section 52, of the 1977 Act.

PART IV

AMENDMENTS OF THE TRADE MARKS ACT 1994

Amendments of 1994 Act

13.—(1) In subsection (1)(c) of section 6 of the 1994 Act (meaning of "earlier **A25–14** trade mark"), after the words "protection under the Paris Convention" insert the words "or the WTO agreement".

(2) In subsection (1) of section 55 of the 1994 Act (Paris Convention: supplementary provisions), omit the word "and" at the end of paragraph (a) and after that paragraph insert—

  "(aa) 'the WTO agreement' means the Agreement establishing the World Trade Organisation signed at Marrakesh on 15th April 1994, and".

(3) In subsection (2) of that section, after the words "the Paris Convention" there shall be inserted the words "or the WTO agreement".

(4) In subsections (1) and (2) of section 56 of that Act (protection of well-known trade marks), after the words "the Paris Convention" insert the words "or the WTO agreement".

(5) In subsections (2) and (3) of section 57 of that Act (national emblems etc. of Convention countries), after the words "the Paris Convention" insert the words "or the WTO agreement".

(6) In subsection (2) of section 58 of that Act (emblems etc. of certain international organisations), after the words "the Paris Convention" insert the words "or the WTO agreement".

(7) After subsection (4) of section 59 of that Act (notification under Article 6ter of Convention) insert—

  "(5) Any reference in this section to Article 6ter of the Paris Convention shall be construed as including a reference to that Article as applied by the WTO agreement".

Part IV: transitional provisions

14.—(1) The amendment of section 56(2) of the 1994 Act made by regulation **A25–15** 13(4) shall not affect the continuation of any bona fide use of a trade mark begun before the 1st January 1996.

1283

(2) The amendment made by regulation 13(6) shall not affect the rights of a person whose bona fide use of the trade mark in question began before that date.

PART VIII

CUSTOMS MATERIALS

APPENDIX 26

COUNCIL REGULATION (EC) No. 3295/94
of December 22, 1994

laying down measures to prohibit the release for free circulation, export, re-export or entry for a suspensive procedure of counterfeit and pirated goods

([1994] O.J. L341/8)

Note: This Regulation is printed as amended by Regulation 241/1999, with deletions in italics and additions in bold.

THE COUNCIL OF THE EUROPEAN UNION,   A26–01
Having regard to the Treaty establishing the European Community, and in particular Article 113 thereof,
Having regard to the proposal from the Commission,
Having regard to the opinion of the European Parliament,
Having regard to the opinion of the Economic and Social Committee,
Whereas Council Regulation (EEC) No 3842/86 of 1 December 1986 laying down measures to prohibit the release for free circulation of counterfeit goods has been in force since 1 January 1988; whereas conclusions should be drawn from the experience gained during the early years of its implementation with a view to improving the operation of the system it set up;
Whereas the marketing of counterfeit goods and pirated goods causes considerable injury to law-abiding manufacturers and traders and to holders of the copyright or neighbouring rights and misleads consumers; whereas such goods should as far as possible be prevented from being placed on the market and measures should be adopted to that end to deal effectively with this unlawful activity without impeding to freedom of legitimate trade; whereas this objective is also being pursued through efforts being made along the same lines at international level;
Whereas, in so far as counterfeit or pirated goods and similar products are imported from third countries, it is important to prohibit their release for free circulation in the Community or their entry for a suspensive procedure and to set up an appropriate procedure enabling the customs authorities to act to ensure that such a prohibition can be properly enforced;
Whereas action by the customs authorities to prohibit the release for free circulation of counterfeit or pirated goods or their entry for a suspensive procedure should also apply to the export or re-export of such goods from the Community;
Whereas, as regards suspensive procedures and re-export subject to notification, action by the customs authorities will take place only where suspected counterfeit or pirated goods are discovered during a check;
Whereas the Community takes into account the terms of the GATT agreement on trade-related intellectual property issues, including a trade in counterfeit goods, in particular the measures to be taken at the frontier;
Whereas provision should be made that the customs authorities are empowered to take decisions on applications for action to be taken that are submitted to them;

1287

Whereas action by the customs authorities should consist either in suspending the release for free circulation, export or re-export of goods suspected of being counterfeit or pirated or in detaining such goods when they are entered for a suspensive procedure or re-exported subject to notification for as long as is necessary to enable it to be determined whether the goods are actually counterfeit or pirated;

Whereas it is appropriate to authorize the Member States to detain the goods in question for a certain period even before an application by the right holder has been lodged or approved in order to allow him to lodge an application for action by the customs authorities;

Whereas the competent authority should decide cases submitted to it by reference to the criteria which are used to determine whether goods produced in the Member State concerned infringe intellectual property rights; whereas Member States' provisions on the competence of the judicial authorities and procedures are not affected by this Regulation;

Whereas it is necessary to determine the measures to be applied to the goods in question where it is established that they are counterfeit or pirated; whereas those measures should not only deprive those responsible for trading in such goods of the economic benefits of the transaction and penalize them but also constitute an effective deterrent to further transactions of the same kind;

Whereas in order to avoid serious disruption to the clearing of goods contained in travellers' personal luggage, it is necessary to exclude from the scope of this Regulation goods which may be counterfeit or pirated which are imported from third countries within the limits laid down by Community rules in respect of relief from customs duty;

Whereas uniform application of the common rules laid down by this Regulation must be ensured and to that end a Community procedure must be established enabling measures implementing these rules to be adopted within appropriate periods and mutual assistance between the Member States, of the one part, and between the Member States and the Commission, of the other part, to be strengthened so as to ensure greater effectiveness;

Whereas it will be appropriate to consider the possibility of increasing the number of intellectual property rights covered by this Regulation in the light, *inter alia*, of the experience gained in its implementation;

Whereas Regulation (EEC) No 3842/86 should therefore be repealed,

HAS ADOPTED THIS REGULATION:

CHAPTER I

GENERAL

Article 1

A26–02   1. *This Regulation lays down:*

    (a) the conditions under which the customs authorities shall take action where goods suspected of being counterfeit or pirated are:

      — entered for free circulation, export or re-export,

      — found when checks are made on goods placed under a suspensive procedure within the meaning of Article 84 (1) (a) of Council Regulation (EEC) No 2913/92 of 12 October 1992 establishing the Community Customs Code, or re-exported subject to notification; and

    (b) the measures which shall be taken by the competent authorities with regard to those goods where it has been established that they are indeed counterfeit or pirated.

2. *For the purposes of this Regulation:*

    (a) *"counterfeit goods" means:*

        — *goods, including the packaging thereof, being without authorization a trade mark which is identical to the trade mark validly registered in respect of the same type of goods, or which cannot be distinguished in its essential aspects from such trade mark, and which thereby infringes the rights of the holder of the trade mark in question under Community law or the law of the Member State in which the application for action by the customs authorities is made,*

        — *any trade mark symbol (logo, label, sticker, brochure, instructions for use or guarantee document) whether presented separately or not, in the same circumstances as the goods referred to in the first indent,*

        — *packaging materials bearing the trade marks of counterfeit goods, presented separately in the same circumstances as the goods referred to in the first indent;*

    (b) *"pirated goods" means goods which are or embody copies made without the consent of the holder of the copyright or neighbouring rights, or of the holder of a design right, whether registered under national law or not, or of a person duly authorized by the holder in the country of production, where the making of those copies infringes the right in question under Community law or the law of the Member State in which the application for action by the customs authorities is made;*

    (c) *"holder of a right" means the holder of a trade mark, as referred to in (a), and/ or one of the rights referred to in (b), or any other person authorized to use the trade mark and/or rights, or their representative;*

    (d) *"declaration for release for free circulation, for export or for re-export" means declarations made in accordance with Article 61 of Regulation (EEC) No 2913/92.*

3. *Any mould or matrix which is specifically designed or adapted for the manufacture of a counterfeit trade mark or of goods bearing such a trade mark or of pirated goods shall be treated as "counterfeit or pirated goods", as appropriate, provided that the use of such moulds or matrices infringes the rights of the holder of a right under Community law or the law of the Member State in which the application for action by the customs authorities is made.*

4. *This Regulation shall not apply to goods which bear a trade mark with the consent of the holder of that trade mark or which are protected by a copyright or neighbouring right or a design right and which have been manufactured with the consent of the holder of the right but are placed in one of the situations referred to in paragraph 1 without the latter's consent.*

Nor shall it apply to goods referred to in the first subparagraph which have been manufactured or bear a trade mark under conditions other than those agreed with the holders of the rights in question.

Article 1

1. **This Regulation lays down:**   **A26–03**

    (a) the conditions under which the customs authorities shall take action where goods suspected of being goods referred to in paragraph 2(a) are:

        — entered for free circulation, export or re-export, in accordance with Article 61 of Council Regulation (EEC) No 2913/92 of 12 October 1992 establishing the Community Customs Code,

        — found in the course of checks on goods under customs supervision within the meaning of Article 37 of Council Regulation

(EEC) No 2913/92, placed under a suspensive procedure within the meaning of Article 84(1)(a) of that Regulation, re-exported subject to notification or placed in a free zone or free warehouse within the meaning of Article 166 thereof; and

(b) the measures which shall be taken by the competent authorities with regard to those goods where it has been established that they are indeed goods referred to in paragraph 2(a).

2. For the purposes of this Regulation:

(a) "goods infringing an intellectual property right" means
  — "counterfeit goods", namely:
  — goods, including the packaging thereof, bearing without authorization a trade mark which is identical to the trade mark validly registered in respect of the same type of goods, or which cannot be distinguished in its essential aspects from such trade mark, and which thereby infringes the rights of the holder of the trade mark in question under Community law or the law of the Member State where the application for action by the customs authorities is made,
  — any trade mark symbol (logo, label, sticker, brochure, instructions for use, guarantee document) whether presented separately or not, in the same circumstances as the goods referred to in the first indent,
  — packaging materials bearing the trade marks of counterfeit goods, presented separately in the same circumstances as the goods referred to in the first indent;
  — "pirated goods", namely: goods which are or embody copies made without the consent of the holder of the copyright or neighbouring rights, or of the holder of a design right, whether registered under national law or not, or of a person duly authorized by the holder in the country of production, where the making of those copies infringes the right in question under Community law or the law of the Member State in which the application for action by the customs authorities is made;
  — goods infringing, in the Member State in which the application for action by the customs authorities is made, a patent under the law of that Member State or a supplementary protection certificate as provided for by Council Regulation (EEC) No 1768/92 or Regulation (EC) No 1610/96 of the European Parliament and of the Council.

(b) "holder of a right" means the holder of a trade mark, a patent or a certificate and/or one of the rights referred to in (a), or any other person authorized to use that trademark, patent, certificate and/or right, or a representative thereof;

(c) "Community trademark" means the trademark defined in Article 1 of Council Regulation (EC) No 40/94;

(d) "certificate" means the supplementary protection certificate provided for by Regulation (EEC) No 1768/92 or by Regulation (EC) No 1610/96.

3. Any mould or matrix which is specifically designed or adapted for the manufacture of a counterfeit trade mark or of goods bearing such a trade mark, for the manufacture of goods infringing a patent or a certificate or for the manufacture of pirated goods shall be treated as goods referred to in paragraph 2(a), provided that the use of such moulds or matrices infringes the rights of the holder of the right in question under Community law or the law of the Member State in which the application for action by the customs authorities is made.

4. This Regulation shall not apply to goods which bear a trade mark with the consent of the holder of that trade mark or which are protected by a patent or a certificate, by a copyright or neighbouring right or by a design right and which have been manufactured with the consent of the holder of the right but are placed in one of the situations referred to in paragraph 1(a) without the latter's consent.

It shall similarly not apply to goods referred to in the first subparagraph which have been manufactured or bear a trade mark under conditions other than those agreed with the holder of the rights in question.

CHAPTER II

Prohibition of the release for free circulation, export, re-export *or of the placing under a suspensive procedure of counterfeit goods and pirated goods*, placing under a suspensive procedure, or placing in a free zone or warehouse, of goods infringing certain intellectual property rights

Article 2

The release for free circulation, export, re-export or placing under a suspensive A26–04 *procedure of goods founds to be counterfeit or pirated on completion of the procedure provided for in Article 6 shall be prohibited.*

The entry into the Community, release for free circulation, export, re-export, A26–05 placing under a suspensive procedure or placing in a free zone or free warehouse of goods found to be goods referred to in Article 1(2)(a) on completion of the procedure provided for in Article 6 shall be prohibited.

CHAPTER III

APPLICATION FOR ACTION BY THE CUSTOMS AUTHORITIES

Article 3

1. In each Member State, the holder of a right may lodge an application in A26–06 writing with the competent service of the customs authority for action by the customs authorities where the goods are placed in one of the situations referred to in Article 1 (1) (a).

Where the applicant holds a Community trade mark, the application may seek action not only by the customs authorities of the Member State in which the application is lodged but by the customs authorities of one or more other Member States as well.

Where electronic data interchange systems exist, Member States may provide that the application for customs action can be made by using a data processing technique.

2. The application referred to in paragraph 1 shall include:

- a sufficiently detailed description of the goods to enable the customs authorities to recognize them,
- proof that the applicant is the holder of the right for the goods in question.

The holder of the right must also provide all other pertinent information available to him to enable the competent customs service to take a decision in full knowledge of the facts without, however, that information being a condition of admissibility of the application.

By way of indication, in the case of pirated goods, **or of goods infringing patents or certificates** that information shall, wherever possible, include:

- the place where the goods are situated or the intended destination,
- particulars identifying the consignment or packages,
- the scheduled date of arrival or departure of the goods,
- the means of transport used,
- the identity of the importer, exporter or holder.

3. *The application must specify the length of the period during which the customs authorities are requested to take action.*

4. *The applicant may be charged a fee to cover the administrative costs incurred in dealing with the application. The fee shall not be disproportionate to the service provided.*

3. Save where the second subparagraph of paragraph 1 is applied, the application must specify the length of the period during which the customs authorities are requested to take action.

Applications under the second subparagraph of paragraph 1 shall indicate the Member State or States in which the customs authorities are requested to take action.

4. The applicant may be charged a fee to cover the administrative costs incurred in dealing with the application.

The applicant or his representative may also be charged a fee in each of the Member States where the decision granting the application is effective, to cover the costs incurred in implementing the said decision.

Such fees shall not be disproportionate to the service provided.

5. The competent customs service with which an application drawn up pursuant to paragraph 2 has been lodged shall deal with the application and shall forthwith notify the applicant in writing of its decision.

Where that service grants the application, the service shall specify the period during which the customs authorities shall take action. That period may, upon application by the holder of the right, be extended by the service which took the initial decision.

Where an application is submitted under the second subparagraph of paragraph 1 the said period shall be set at one year, but may be extended for a further year, at the right-holder's request, by the service which took the original decision.

Any refusal to grant an application shall give the reasons for refusal and may form the subject of an appeal.

6. Member States may require the holder of a right, where his application has been granted, or where action as referred to in Article 1 (1) (a) has been taken pursuant to Article 6 (1), to provide a security:

- to cover any liability on his part *vis-à-vis* the persons involved in one of the operations referred to in Article 1 (1) (a) where the procedure initiated pursuant to Article 6 (1) is discontinued owing to an act or omission by the holder of the right or where the goods in question are subsequently found not be *counterfeit or pirated,* **goods referred to in Article 1(2)(a)**

— to ensure payment of the costs incurred in accordance with this Regulation, in keeping the goods under customs control pursuant to Article 6.

Where an application is submitted under the second subparagraph of paragraph 1, the security shall be provided in each of the Member States in which it is required and the decision granting the application is effective.

7. *The holder of the right shall be obliged to inform the service referred to in paragraph 1 should the right cease to be validly registered or should it expire.*

7. The holder of the right is required to inform the service referred to in paragraph 1 and, where appropriate, the service or services referred to in the second subparagraph of Article 5(2), if his right should happen no longer to be validly registered or to have expired.

8. Each Member State shall designate the service within the customs authority competent to receive and deal with the applications referred to in this Article.

9. Paragraphs 1 to 8 shall apply mutatis mutandis to the extension of the decision on the original application.

Article 4

Where, in the course of checks made under one of the customs procedures **A26–07** referred to in Article 1 (1) (a) and before an application by the holder of the right has been lodged or approved, it appears evident to the customs office that goods are *counterfeit or pirated*, **goods referred to in Article 1(2)(a)**, the customs authority may, in accordance with the rules in force in the Member States concerned, notify the holder of the right, where known, of a possible infringement thereof. The customs authority shall be authorized to suspend release of the goods or detain them for a period of three working days to enable the holder of the right to lodge an application for action in accordance with Article 3.

Article 5

The decision granting the application by the holder of the right shall be forwarded **A26–08** *immediately to the customs offices of the Member State which are liable to be concerned with the goods alleged in the application to be conterfeit or pirated.*

1. The decision granting the application by the holder of the right shall be **A26–09** forwarded immediately to the customs offices of the Member State which are liable to be concerned with the goods alleged in the application to be goods referred to in Article 1(2)(a).

2. Where an application is submitted under the second subparagraph of Article 3(1), the first indent of Article 250 of Regulation (EEC) No 2913/92 shall apply mutatis mutandis to the decision granting the said application and the decisions extending or repealing it.

When the decision granting the said application has been taken, it shall be up to the applicant to forward that decision together, where appropriate, with any other useful information and any translations to the customs-authority service referred to in the first subparagraph of Article 3(1) in the Member State or States where the applicant has requested that action be taken. However, with the agreement of the applicant, the information and translations may be forwarded directly by the customs-authority service which took the decision. The applicant shall provide additional information as deemed necessary for the execution of the decision, at the request of the customs authorities of the other Member States concerned.

The period referred to in the third subparagraph of Article 3(5) shall run from the date on which the decision granting the application was taken. The said decision shall not enter into force in the Member State or States to which it is addressed until the submission referred to in the second subparagraph has been made and, where appropriate, until the fee referred to in the second subparagraph of Article 3(4) has been paid and the security referred to in Article 3(6) has been provided. However, the period of validity of the said decision may not, in any circumstances, exceed the period of one year from the date of adoption of the decision granting the original application.

The said decision shall then be forwarded immediately to the national customs offices liable to be concerned with the alleged counterfeit goods to which it relates.

This paragraph shall apply mutatis mutandis to any decision to extend the original decision.

CHAPTER IV

CONDITIONS GOVERNING ACTION BY THE CUSTOMS AUTHORITIES AND BY THE AUTHORITY COMPETENT TO TAKE A SUBSTANTIVE DECISION

Article 6

A26–10   1. Where a customs office to which the decision granting an application by the holder of a right has been forwarded pursuant to Article 5 is satisfied, after consulting the applicant where necessary, that goods placed in one of the situations referred to in Article 1(1)(a) correspond to the description of the *counterfeit or pirated goods* **goods referred to in Article 1(2)(a)** contained in that decision, it shall suspend release of the goods or detain them.

The customs office shall immediately inform the service which dealt with the application in accordance with Article 3. That service or the customs office, shall forthwith inform the declarant and the person who applied for action to be taken. In accordance with national provisions on the protection of personal data, commercial and industrial secrecy and professional and administrative confidentiality, the customs office or the service which dealt with the application shall notify the holder of the right, at his request, of the name and address of the declarant and, if known, of those of the consignee so as to enable the holder of the right to ask the competent authorities to take a substantive decision. The customs office shall afford the applicant and the persons involved in any of the operations referred to in Article 1 (1) (a) the opportunity to inspect the goods whose release has been suspended or which have been detained.

When examining the goods the customs office may take samples in order to expedite the procedure.

2. The law in force in the Member State within the territory of which the goods are placed in one of the situations referred to in Article 1 (1) (a) shall apply as regards:

   (a) referral to the authority competent to take a substantive decision and immediate notification of the customs service or office referred to in paragraph 1 of that referral, unless referral is effected by that service or office;
   (b) reaching the decision to be taken by that authority. In the absence of Community rules in this regard, the criteria to be used in reaching that decision shall be the same as those used to determine whether goods

produced in the Member State concerned infringe the rights of the holder. Reasons shall be given for decisions adopted by the competent authority.

Article 7

1. If, within 10 working days of notification of suspension of release or of **A26–11** detention, the customs office referred to in Article 6 (1) has not been informed that the matter has been referred to the authority competent to take a substantive decision on the case in accordance with Article 6 (2) or that the duly empowered authority has adopted interim measures, the goods shall be released, provided that all the customs formalities have been complied with and the detention order has been revoked.

This period may be extended by a maximum of 10 working days, in appropriate cases.

2. *In the case of goods suspected of infringing design rights, the owner, the importer or the consignee of the rights, the owner, the importer or the consignee of the goods shall be able to have the goods in question released or their detention revoked against provision of a security, provided that:*

— *the customs service or office referred to in Article 6(1) has been informed, within the time limit referred to in paragraph 1, that the matter has been referred to the authority competent to take a substantive decision referred to in said paragraph 1,*

— *on expiry of the time limit, the authority empowered for this purpose has not imposed interim measures, and*

— *all the customs formalities have been completed.*

The security must be sufficient to protect the interests of the holder of the right. Payment of the security shall be without prejudice to the other remedies open to the holder of the right. Where the matter has been referred to the authority competent to take a substantive decision other than on the initiative of the holder of the right, the security shall be released if that person does not exercise his right to institute legal proceedings within 20 working days of the date on which he is notified of the suspension of release or detention. Where the second subparagraph of paragraph 1 applies, this period may be extended to a maximum of 30 working days.

2. **In the case of goods suspected of infringing patents, certificates or design rights, the owner, importer or consignee of the goods shall be able to have the goods in question released or their detention revoked against provision of a security, provided that:**

(a) **the customs service or office referred to in Article 6(1) has been informed, within the time limit referred to in paragraph 1 of this Article, that the matter has been referred to the authority competent to take a substantive decision referred to in the aforesaid paragraph 1;**

(b) **on expiry of the time limit, the authority empowered for this purpose has not imposed interim measures; and**

(c) **all the customs formalities have been completed.**

The security must be sufficient to protect the interests of the holder of the right. Provision of the security shall be without prejudice to the other remedies open to the holder of the right. Where the matter has been referred to the authority competent to take a substantive decision other than on the initiative of the holder of the patent, certificate or design right, the security shall be released if that person does not exercise his right to institute legal proceedings within 20 working days of the date on which he is notified of the

suspension of release or detention. Where the second subparagraph of paragraph 1 applies, this period may be extended to a maximum of 30 working days.

3. The conditions governing storage of the goods during the period of suspension of release or detention shall be determined by each Member State.

CHAPTER V

PROVISIONS APPLICABLE TO GOODS FOUND TO BE *COUNTERFEIT OR PIRATED GOODS* **GOODS INFRINGING AN INTELLECTUAL PROPERTY RIGHT**

Article 8

A26–12   1. *Without prejudice to the other rights of action open to the holder of a trade mark which is found to have been counterfeited or the holder of a copyright or neighbouring right or of a design right which is found to have been pirated. Member States shall adopt the measures necessary to allow the competent authorities:*

> (a) *as a general rule, and in accordance with the relevant provisons of national law, to destroy goods found to be counterfeit or pirated, or dispose of them outside commercial channels in such a way as to preclude injury to the holder of the right, without compensation of any sort and at no cost to the exchequer;*
> (b) *to take, in respect of such goods, any other measures which effectively deprive the persons concerned of the economic benefits of the transaction.*

The following in particular shall not be regarded as having such effect:

> — *re-exporting the counterfeit or pirated goods in the unaltered state,*
> — *other than in exceptional cases, simply removing the trade marks which have been affixed to the counterfeit goods without authorization,*
> — *placing the goods under a different customs procedure.*

2. *The counterfeit or pirated goods may be handed over to the exchequer. In that event, paragraph 1 (a) shall apply.*

3. *In addition to the information given pursuant to the second subparagraph of Article 6 (1) and under the conditions laid down therein, the customs office or the competent service shall inform the holder of the right, upon request, of the names and addresses of the consignor, of the importer or exporter and of the manufacturer of the goods found to be counterfeit or pirated and of the quantity of the goods in question.*

A26–13   1. **Without prejudice to the other forms of legal recourse open to the right-holder, Member States shall adopt the measures necessary to allow the competent authorities:**

> (a) **as a general rule, and in accordance with the relevant provisions of national law, to destroy goods found to be goods referred to in Article 1(2)(a), or dispose of them outside the channels of commerce in such a way as to preclude injury to the holder of the right, without compensation of any sort and without cost to the Exchequer;**
> (b) **to take, in respect of such goods, any other measures having the effect of effectively depriving the persons concerned of the economic benefits of the transaction.**

Save in exceptional cases, simply removing the trademarks which have been affixed to the counterfeit goods without authorization shall not be regarded as having such effect.

2. The goods referred to in Article 1(2)(a) may be handed over to the Exchequer. In that case, paragraph 1(a) shall apply.

3. In addition to the information given pursuant to the second subparagraph of Article 6(1) and under the conditions laid down therein, the customs office or the competent service shall inform the holder of the right, upon request, of the names and addresses of the consignor, of the importer or exporter and of the manufacturer of the goods found to be goods referred to in Article 1(2)(a) and of the quantity of the goods in question.

CHAPTER VI

FINAL PROVISIONS

Article 9

1. Save as provided by the law of the Member State in which the application is made, **A26–14** *the acceptance of an application drawn up in accordance with Article 3 (2) shall not entitle the holder of a right to compensation where counterfeit or pirated goods are not detected by a customs office and are released or no action is taken to detain them in accordance with Article 6 (1).*

2. Save as provided by the law of the Member State in which the application is made, exercise by a customs office or by another duly empowered authority of the powers conferred on them in regard to combating counterfeit or pirated goods shall not render them liable to the persons involved in the operations referred to in Article 1 (1) (a) or Article 4, in the event of their suffering loss or damage as a result of their action.

1. Save as provided by the law of the Member State in which an application in accordance with Article 3(2) is lodged or, in the case of an application under the second subparagraph of Article 3(1), by the law of the Member State in which goods referred to in Article 1(2)(a) escape detection by a customs office, the acceptance of an application shall not entitle the holder of a right to compensation where such goods are not detected by a customs office and are released or no action is taken to detain them in accordance with Article 6(1).

2. Save as provided by the law of the Member State in which the application is made or, in the case of an application under the second subparagraph of Article 3(1), by the law of the Member State in which loss or damage is incurred, exercise by a customs office or by another duly empowered authority of the powers conferred on them in regard to taking measures against goods referred to in Article 1(2)(a) shall not render them liable towards the persons involved in the operations referred to in Article 1(1)(a) or Article 4, in the event of their suffering loss or damage as a result of their action.

3. The civil liability of the holder of a right shall be governed by the law of the Member State in which the goods in question were placed in one of the situations referred to in Article 1 (1) (a).

Article 10

This Regulation shall not apply to goods of a non-commercial nature con- **A26–15** tained in travellers' personal luggage within the limits laid down in respect of relief from customs duty.

Article 11

Moreover, each Member State shall introduce penalties to apply in the event **A26–16** of infringements of Article 2. Such penalties *must be sufficiently severe to encourage compliance with the relevant provisions* **shall be effective and proportionate and constitute an effective deterrent.**

Article 12

A26–17   The provisions necessary for the application of this Regulation shall be adopted in accordance with the procedure laid down in Article 13(3) and (4).

Article 13

A26–18   1. The Commission shall be assisted by the Committee set up under Article 247 of Regulation (EEC) No 2913/92.

2. The Committee shall examine any matter concerning implementation of this Regulation which its chairman may raise, either on his own initiative or at the request of the representative of a Member State.

3. The representative of the Commission shall submit to the Committee a draft of the measures to be taken. The Committee shall deliver its opinion on the draft within a time limit which the chairman may lay down according to the urgency of the measures to be taken. The opinion shall be delivered by the majority laid down in Article 148 (2) of the Treaty in the case of decisions which the Council is required to adopt on a proposal from the Commission. The votes of the representatives of the Member States within the Committee shall be weighted in the manner set out in that Article. The chairman shall not vote.

4. The Commission shall adopt measures which shall apply immediately. However, if the measures are not in accordance with the opinion of the Committee, they shall be communicated by the Commission to the Council forthwith. In the event:

— the Commission shall defer application of the measures which it has decided for not more than three months from the date of their communication,

— the Council, acting by a qualified majority, may take a different decision within the time limit provided for in the first indent.

Article 14

A26–19   Member States shall communicate all relevant information on the application of this Regulation to the Commission.

The Commission shall communicate that information to the other Member States.

For the purpose of the application of this Regulation, the provisions of Regulation (EEC) No 1468/81 of 19 May 1981 on mutual assistance between the administrative authorities of the Member States and cooperation between the latter and the Commission to ensure the correct application of the law on customs or agricultuaral matters shall apply *mutatis mutandis*.

The details of the information procedure shall be drawn up in the framework of the implementing provisions in accordance with Article 13(2), (3) and (4).

Article 15

A26–20   Within two years of the entry into force of this Regulation, the Commission shall, on the basis of the information referred to in Article 14, report to the European Parliament and the Council on the operation of the system particularly with regard to the economic and social consequences of counterfeiting and shall propose any amendments or additions required, within a period of two years from the implementation of this Regulation.

Article 16

Regulation (EEC) No 3842/86 shall be repealed as from the date of implemen- **A26–21** tation of this Regulation.

Article 17

This Regulation shall enter into force on the third day following its publication **A26–22** in the *Official Journal of the European Communities.*
It shall apply from 1 July 1995.
This Regulation shall be binding in its entirety and directly applicable in all Member States.
Done at Brussels, December 22, 1994.

APPENDIX 27

Commission Regulation 1367/95 of June 16, 1995

Laying down provisions for the implementation of Council Regulation (EC) No 3295/94 laying down measures to prohibit the release for free circulation, export, re-export or entry for a suspensive procedure of counterfeit and pirated goods

([1995] O.J. L133/2)

A27–01 THE COMMISSION OF THE EUROPEAN COMMUNITIES,

Having regard to the Treaty establishing the European Community,

Having regard to Council Regulation (EC) No 3295/94 of 22 December 1994 laying down measures to prohibit the release for free circulation, export, re-export or entry for a suspensive procedure of counterfeit and pirated goods, and in particular Articles 12, 13 and 14 thereof,

Whereas Regulation (EC) No 3295/94 introduced common rules with a view to prohibiting the release for free circulation, export, re-export or entry for a suspensive procedure of counterfeit and pirated goods and dealing effectively with the illegal marketing of such goods without impeding the freedom of legitimate trade;

Whereas the nature of the proof of ownership of intellectual property required by the second indent of the first subparagraph of Article 3 (2) of Regulation (EC) No 3295/94 should be established;

Whereas Article 14 of Regulation (EC) No 3295/94 provides that Member States are to communicate to the Commission all relevant information for applying that Regulation and that the Commission is to communicate that information to the other Member States; whereas the procedure for exchanging that information should be laid down;

Whereas Commission Regulation (EEC) No 3077/87 should be repealed;

Whereas the measures provided for in this Regulation are in accordance with the opinion of the Customs Code Committee,

HAS ADOPTED THIS REGULATION:

Article 1

A27–02 For the purposes of Article 1 (2) (c) of Regulation (EC) No 3295/94, hereinafter referred to as "the basic Regulation" the holder of a right or any other person authorized to use the right may be represented by a natural or legal person; such a person includes a collecting society which has as its sole or principal purpose the management or administration of copyrights or neighbouring rights.

Article 2

A27–03 The proof that the applicant holds one of the rights referred to in points (a) and (b) of Article 1 (2) of the basic Regulation, which must be submitted when applying for action in accordance with the second indent of the first subparagraph of Article 3 (2) of that Regulation, shall be as follows:

(a) where the holder of the right applies himself:
- in the case of a right that is registered or for which an application has been lodged (trademark or design right): proof of registration with the relevant office or lodging of the application,
- in the case of a copyright, neighbouring rights or design right that is unregistered or for which an application has not been lodged: any proof of authorship or of his status as original holder;

(b) where the application is made by any other person authorized to use one of the rights referred to in points (a) and (b) of Article 1 (2) of the basic Regulation in addition to the proof required under (a) hereof: the document by virtue of which the person is authorized to use the right in question;

(c) where a representative of the holder or of any other person authorized to use one of the rights referred to in points (a) and (b) of Article 1 (2) of the basic Regulation applies: in addition to the proof required under (a) and (b) hereof, proof of authorization to act.

Article 3

The pertinent information referred to in the second subparagraph of Article 3 **A27-04** (2) of the basic Regulation shall include particulars of the goods, notably their value and their packaging, plus any information that could help distinguish them from goods for which there is a protected right, under the terms of the second subparagraph of Article 3 (2), this information should be as detailed as possible to enable the customs authorities, using risk analysis, to identify suspect consignments accurately and without excessive effort.

Article 4

If an application is lodged in accordance with Article 4 of the basic Regulation **A27-05** before expiry of the time-limit of three days, the time-limits referred to in Article 7 of the Regulation shall be counted from the day of receipt of the request for action.

If the customs authority suspends release of the goods or detains them in accordance with Article 4 of the basic Regulation, it shall forthwith inform the declarant.

Article 5

1. Each Member State shall, at the earliest opportunity, send the Commission **A27-06** detailes of:

(a) the laws, regulations or administrative provisions which it adopts in implementation of this Regulation. It shall likewise inform the Commission of any provisions of its national law which preclude informing the holder as provided for in the second subparagraph of Article 6 (1) and in Article 8 (3) of the basic Regulation;

(b) the competent customs department responsible for receiving and handling the holder's written application, referred to in Article 3 (8) of the basic Regulation.

2. To enable the Commission to monitor the effective application of the procedure laid down by the basic Regulation and draw up, in due course, the

report referred to in Article 15 thereof, each Member State shall send the Commission:

(a) at the end of each calendar year, a list of all the written applications under Article 3 (1) of the basic Regulation, together with the name and address of the holder, a brief description of the goods and, where relevant, the trademark, and the action taken in response to the application;

(b) at the end of each quarter, a list of specific cases in which goods have been detained or their release suspended. The information provided on each case must include:

— the name and address of the holder of the right and a brief description of the goods and, where relevant, the trademark, and

— the customs situation, country of consignment or destination, description, quantity and declared value of the goods the release of which has been suspended or which have been detained, and the date of such suspension or detention.

3. The Commission shall, in an appropriate manner, communciate to all Member States such information as it receives pursuant to this Article. Details of cases provided for in point (b) of paragraph 2 shall be sent quarterly to the Member States by the Commission.

4. Details communicated pursuant to paragraphs 1, 2 and 3 may be used only for the purposes established by the basic Regulation.

Article 6

A27–07 Regulation (EEC) No 3077/87 is hereby repealed with effect from 1 July 1995.

Article 7

A27–08 This Regulation shall enter into force on the third day following its publication in the *Official Journal of the European Communities*.
It shall apply from 1 July 1995.

This Regulation shall be binding in its entirety and directly applicable in all Member States.
Done at Brussels, June 16, 1995.

Appendix 28

The Goods Infringing Intellectual Property Rights (Customs) Regulations 1999

S.I. 1999 No. 1601

The Commissioners of Customs and Excise, being a Department designated for the purposes of section 2(2) of the European Communities Act 1972 in relation to measures relating to counterfeit and pirated goods, goods infringing a patent and goods infringing a supplementary protection certificate, in exercise of the powers conferred upon them by the said section 2(2) and of all other powers enabling them in that behalf, hereby make the following Regulations: **A28–01**

1. These Regulations may be cited as the Goods Infringing Intellectual **A28–02** Property Rights (Customs) Regulations 1999 and shall come into force on 1st July 1999.

2. In these Regulations— **A28–03**

"application" means an application under Article 3(1) of the Council Regulation, and "applicant" shall be construed accordingly;

"business day" has the meaning given in section 92 of the Bills of Exchange Act 1882;

"the Commissioners" means the Commissioners of Customs and Excise;

"Community trademark" means a trademark as defined in Council Regulation (EC) No. 40/94;

"the Council Regulation" means Council Regulation (EC) No. 3295/94, as amended by Council Regulation (EC) No. 241/1999, laying down measures concerning the entry into the Community and the export and re-export from the Community of goods infringing certain intellectual property rights;

"decision" means a decision granting an application in accordance with Article 3(5) of the Council Regulation;

"goods infringing an intellectual property right" has the meaning given by Article 1(2)(a) of the Council Regulation (counterfeit goods, pirated goods and goods infringing a patent or supplementary protection certificate), and "intellectual property right" shall be construed accordingly.

3. Except where it specifies a Community trademark which the applicant holds **A28–04** or is authorised to use and seeks action by the customs authorities of another member State, an application made to the Commissioners shall be in the form set out in the Schedule to these Regulations, or a form to the like effect approved by the Commissioners, containing full particulars of the matters specified therein.

4.—(1) The applicant shall give to the Commissioners such security or further **A28–05** security, within such time and in such manner, whether by deposit of a sum of money or guarantee, as the Commissioners may require, against the matters mentioned in paragraph (2) below.

(2) The matters against which security or further security shall be given are all actions, proceedings, claims and demands whatsoever which may be taken or made against, or costs and expenses which may be incurred by, the Commissioners in consequence of the detention of, or anything done in relation to, any goods to which the application or decision relates.

A28–06   5. In every case, whether any security or further security is given or not, the applicant shall keep the Commissioners indemnified against all such liability and expense as is mentioned in regulation 4(2) above and in particular shall repay to them all expense which may be incurred by them in consequence of the detention of, or anything done in relation to, any goods to which the application or decision relates.

A28–07   6.—(1) Where a decision is given, the applicant shall pay the Commissioners a fee of the relevant amount in relation to each of the following—

    (a) the period specified in the decision; and

    (b) any period by which that period is extended.

(2) The fee mentioned in paragraph (1) above shall be payable notwithstanding that the application is not made to the Commissioners but—

    (a) the application specifies a Community trademark which the applicant holds or is authorised to use;

    (b) the application has been made to the customs authorities of another member State;

    (c) the application seeks action by the Commissioners; and

    (d) a decision granting the application has been forwarded to the Commissioners in accordance with Article 5(2) of the Council Regulation.

(3) For the purposes of this regulation the relevant amount is—

    (a) for a period not exceeding one month, £200 plus VAT;

    (b) for a period not exceeding three months, £400 plus VAT;

    (c) for a period not exceeding six months, £700 plus VAT;

    (d) for a period not exceeding twelve months, £1,200 plus VAT; or

    (e) for a period of or exceeding twelve months—

        (i) £1,200 plus VAT for each complete period of twelve months, and

        (ii) an amount calculated in accordance with sub-paragraphs (a) to (d) above for any additional period.

A28–08   7. In the event that the Commissioners require the applicant to examine a sample of detained goods which appear to them both to correspond to the description of goods contained in a decision and to be goods infringing an intellectual property right the applicant shall, within 10 business days from the date of the request by the Commissioners, or within such further time, not exceeding 10 business days, as the Commissioners may allow, provide such information as the Commissioners may require in order to be satisfied that the sample is comprised of goods infringing an intellectual property right.

A28–09   8. A decision shall have no effect or no further effect where—

    (a) the applicant has failed to comply with any of the requirements of these Regulations;

    (b) any change, following the making of the application, which takes place in the ownership or authorised use of the intellectual property right specified in the application, is not communicated in writing to the Commissioners; or

    (c) the intellectual property right specified in the application expires.

A28–10   9. The Counterfeit and Pirated Goods (Customs) Regulations 1995 are hereby revoked.

SCHEDULE

A28–11   Application Form (Notes)
Application Form (Parts 1 to 3)
Application Form (Parts 4 to 7)
Application Form (Parts 8 to 10)

The Goods Infringing Intellectual Property Rights (Consequential Provisions) Regulations 1999

S.I. 1999 No. 1618

The Secretary of State, being designated for the purposes of section 2(2) of the European **A29–01** Communities Act 1972 in relation to measures relating to counterfeit and pirated goods, goods infringing a patent and goods infringing a supplementary protection certificate, in exercise of powers conferred on him by the said section 2(2), and of all other enabling powers, hereby makes the following Regulations:

1. These Regulations may be cited as the Goods Infringing Intellectual **A29–02** Property Rights (Consequential Provisions) Regulations 1999 and shall come into force on 1st July 1999.

2.—(1) In these Regulations: **A29–03**

"the 1979 Act" means the Customs and Excise Management Act 1979;

"application" means an application under Article 3(1) of the Council Regulation;

"business day" has the meaning given by section 92 of the Bills of Exchange Act 1882;

"the Commissioners" means the Commissioners of Customs and Excise;

"the Council Regulation" means Council Regulation (EC) No. 3295/94 as amended by Council Regulation (EC) No. 241/1999, laying down measures concerning the entry into the Community and the export and re-export from the Community of goods infringing certain intellectual property rights;

"counterfeit goods" has the meaning given by Article 1(2)(a) of the Council Regulation;

"decision" means a decision granting an application in accordance with Article 3(5) of the Council Regulation;

"design right" has the meaning given by section 213(1) of Part III of the Copyright, Designs and Patents Act 1988;

"goods infringing an intellectual property right" has the meaning given by Article 1(2)(a) of the Council Regulation (counterfeit goods, pirated goods and goods infringing a patent or supplementary protection certificate), and related expressions shall be construed accordingly;

"goods infringing a patent" has the same meaning as in the Council Regulation;

"goods infringing a supplementary protection certificate" has the same meaning as in the Council Regulation;

"holder of a right" has the meaning given by Article 1(2)(b) of the Council Regulation;

"pirated goods" has the meaning given by Article 1(2)(a) of the Council Regulation;

"registered design" shall be construed in accordance with the Registered Designs Act 1949.

(2) For the purposes of the Council Regulation, any reference in it to "copyright, or neighbouring rights" is to be construed as a reference to "copyright, or rights in performances".

(3) These Regulations shall apply to goods which fall to be treated by virtue of Article 1(3) of the Council Regulation as being goods within paragraph (2)(a) of

that Article as they apply to any goods within that paragraph; but these Regulations shall not apply to any goods in relation to which the Council Regulation does not apply by virtue of Article 1(4) thereof.

A29–04   3. Subject to paragraph (2) of regulation 4 below, goods infringing an intellectual property right which correspond to the description of goods contained in a decision shall be liable to forfeiture if any of the conditions mentioned in Article 1(1)(a) of the Council Regulation applies during the period specified in the decision.

A29–05   4.—(1) If, in the course of checks carried out in relation to goods as regards which any of the conditions mentioned in Article 1(1)(a) of the Council Regulation applies and before an application is made in respect of those goods, or, if made, before a decision is given, it appears to the Commissioners that the goods are goods infringing an intellectual property right, the Commissioners may, in accordance with Article 4 of the Council Regulation—

> (a) notify a holder of a right of the possible infringement of the right;
> (b) suspend the release of, or detain, those goods; and
> (c) if they do so suspend or detain, invite the holder of a right, in the absence of an existing application, to make an application within three business days of the date of suspension or detention.

(2) If at any time during the period of suspension or detention under paragraph (1) above a decision is given in respect of the goods, the condition mentioned in Article 1(1)(a) of the Council Regulation shall be taken to have applied during the period specified in the decision for the purposes of regulation 3 above.

(3) Where no application in respect of the goods is or has been made by any holder of a right within three business days of the date of suspension or detention, the suspension or detention shall cease.

A29–06   5.—(1) Subject to regulation 6 below, section 139 of, and Schedule 3 to, the 1979 Act (provisions as to detention, seizure and condemnation of goods, etc; forfeiture) shall apply in respect of any goods liable to forfeiture by virtue of regulation 3 above as they apply in respect of goods liable to forfeiture under the customs and excise Acts; and, accordingly:—

> (a) section 144 of the 1979 Act (protection of officers, etc in relation to seizure and detention of goods etc) shall apply in respect of seizure or detention effected by virtue of this regulation; and
> (b) sections 145, 146 and 152 to 155 of the 1979 Act (general provisions as to legal proceedings) shall apply in respect of condemnation proceedings brought by virtue of this regulation.

(2) Where in any condemnation proceedings brought by virtue of paragraph (1) above any question arises as to whether or not any goods are or were liable to forfeiture under regulation 3 above, the burden of proof shall lie upon the party alleging that they are not or were not so liable.

A29–07   6.—(1) Regulation 5 above shall not apply in relation to goods as regards which the decision specifies as subsisting in those goods any one or more of the following intellectual property rights (whether or not they also appear to infringe any other intellectual property right):

> (a) a patent;
> (b) a supplementary protection certificate;
> (c) a registered design;
> (d) design right.

(2) A holder of a right may, within 10 business days of his having been notified by the Commissioners of the suspension of release of the goods or of the goods having been detained, give notice in writing to the Commissioners waiving, for the purpose of both the Council Regulation and of these Regu-

lations, any intellectual property right of his in the goods, being a right mentioned in sub-paragraphs (a) to (d) in paragraph (1) above.

(3) Where notice has been given in accordance with paragraph (2) above—

(a) any right so waived shall be disregarded, as regards that holder of a right, in determining whether the goods fall within paragraph (1) above; and

(b) the goods shall accordingly be treated for the purposes of the Council Regulation and these Regulations as if that person did not have the right concerned in those goods.

(4) The following provisions of the 1979 Act shall apply to any goods falling within paragraph (1) above as they apply in respect of goods liable to forfeiture under the customs and excise Acts:

(a) section 139, except subsections (5) and (6) (things seized or detained to be dealt with or disposed of as Commissioners direct; Schedule 3 to have effect);

(b) section 144.

(5) Any thing seized or detained by virtue of this regulation shall be dealt with in such manner as the Commissioners may direct; but this paragraph shall apply subject to section 139(3) and (4) of the 1979 Act (detention or seizure by a constable; things retained in the custody of the police) in the cases there mentioned.

7.—(1) In the case of goods falling within paragraph (1) of regulation 6 above, **A29–08** the commencement of the proceedings described in paragraph (2) below, and only such proceedings, shall constitute a referral to the authority competent to take a substantive decision for the purposes of the Council Regulation.

(2) The proceedings mentioned in paragraph (1) above are proceedings commenced in the relevant court by a holder of a right alleging that the goods infringe an intellectual property right of his and seeking relief which that court has the power to grant after a finding of such infringement.

(3) Without prejudice to any provision of the Council Regulation, if at any time the Commissioners—

(a) are not satisfied, or cease to be satisfied, that the proceedings described in paragraph (2) above have been commenced; or

(b) are satisfied that such proceedings have been withdrawn or otherwise terminated without other such proceedings having been commenced, the suspension of the release of the goods or their detention shall cease.

(4) For the purposes of this regulation proceedings shall not be taken to have been commenced before—

(a) an originating process has been issued or, in the case of the Court of Session, signeted by the relevant court;

(b) that process has been served on the other party or, if more than one, all the other parties to the proceedings, in accordance with the rules of the court concerned.

(5) In paragraph (4) above, the reference to an originating process is a reference to—

(a) in England and Wales, a claim form;

(b) in Scotland, a summons; or

(c) in Northern Ireland, a writ.

(6) For the purposes of this regulation the relevant court is—

(a) in England and Wales, the High Court or any patents county court having jurisdiction by virtue of an order under section 287 of the Copyright, Designs and Patents Act 1988;

(b) in Scotland, the Court of Session; or

(c) in Northern Ireland, the High Court.

A29–09 8. Nothing in these Regulations shall be taken to affect—

(a) any power of the Commissioners conferred otherwise than by any provision of these Regulations to suspend the release of, or detain, any goods; or

(b) the power of any court to grant any relief, including any power to make an order by way of interim relief.

A29–10 9. The Counterfeit and Pirated Goods (Consequential Provisions) Regulations 1995 are hereby revoked.

APPENDIX 30

Customs and Excise Management Act 1979

1979 CHAPTER 2

Interpretation

An Act to consolidate the enactments relating to the collection and management **A30–01** of the revenues of customs and excise and in some cases to other matters in relation to which the Commissioners of Customs and Excise for the time being perform functions, with amendments to give effect to recommendations of the Law Commission and the Scottish Law Commission.

[22ND FEBRUARY 1979]

Be it enacted by the Queen's most Excellent Majesty, by and with the advice and consent of the Lords Spiritual and Temporal, and Commons, in this present Parliament assembled, and by the authority of the same, as follows:—

PART I

PRELIMINARY

Interpretation

1.—(1) In this Act, unless the context otherwise requires—   **A30–02**
. . .
> "armed forces means the Royal Navy, the Royal Marines, the regular army and the regular air force, and any reserve or auxiliary force of any of those services which has been called out on permanent service, or called into actual service, or embodied;
> "assigned matter" means any matter in relation to which the Commissioners are for the time being required in pursuance of any enactment to perform any duties;
. . .
> "boundary" means the land boundary of Northern Ireland;
> "British ship" means a British ship within the meaning of the Merchant Shipping Act 1894, so, however, as not to include a ship registered in any country other than the United Kingdom, the Channel Islands, the Isle of Man or a colony within the meaning of the British Nationality Act 1948;
> "claimant", in relation to proceedings for the condemnation of any thing as being forfeited, means a person claiming that the thing is not liable to forfeiture;
. . .
> "commander", in relation to an aircraft, includes any person having or taking the charge or command of the aircraft;
> "the Commissioners" means the Commissioners of Customs and Excise;
. . .

"container" includes any bundle or package and any box, cask or other receptacle whatsoever;

"the customs and excise Acts" means the Customs and Excise Acts 1979 and any other enactment for the time being in force relating to customs or excise;

"the Customs and Excise Acts 1979" means— this Act, the Customs and Excise Duties (General Reliefs) Act 1979, the Alcoholic Liquor Duties Act 1979, the Hydrocarbon Oil Duties Act 1979, the Matches and Mechanical Lighters Duties Act 1979, and the Tobacco Products Duty Act 1979;

"customs warehouse" means a place of security approved by the Commissioners under subsection (2) (whether or not it is also approved under subsection (1)) of section 92 below;

. . .

"customs and excise station" has the meaning given by "section 26 below;

"excise warehouse" means a place of security approved by the Commissioners under subsection (1) (whether or not it is also approved under subsection (2)) of section 92 below, and, except in that section, also includes a distiller's warehouse;

"exporter", in relation to goods for exportation or for use as stores, includes the shipper of the goods and any person performing in relation to an aircraft functions corresponding with those of a shipper;

"goods" includes stores and baggage;

"holiday", in relation to any part of the United Kingdom, means any day that is a bank holiday in that part of the United Kingdom under the Banking and Financial Dealings Act 1971, Christmas Day, Good Friday and the day appointed for the purposes of customs and excise for the celebration of Her Majesty's birthday;

. . .

"importer", in relation to any goods at any time between their importation and the time when they are delivered out of charge, includes any owner or other person for the time being possessed of or beneficially interested in the goods and, in relation to goods imported by means of a pipe-line, includes the owner of the pipe-line;

"justice" and "justice of the peace" in Scotland includes a sheriff and in Northern Ireland, in relation to any powers and duties which can under any enactment for the time being in force be exercised and performed only by a resident magistrate, means a resident magistrate;

"land" and "landing", in relation to aircraft, include alighting on water;

"law officer of the Crown" means the Attorney General or in Scotland the Lord Advocate or in Northern Ireland the Attorney General for Northern Ireland;

. . .

"master", in relation to a ship, includes any person having or taking the charge or command of the ship;

. . .

"occupier", in relation to any bonded premises, means the person who has given security to the Crown inrespect of those premises;

"officer" means, subject to section 8(2) below, a person commissioned by the Commissioners;

"owner", in relation to an aircraft, includes the operator of the aircraft;

. . .

"prescribed sum", in relation to the penalty provided for an offence, has the meaning given by section 171(2) below;

"prohibited or restricted goods" means goods of a class or description of which the importation, exportation or carriage coastwise is for the time being prohibited or restricted under or by virtue of any enactment;

"proper", in relation to the person by, with or to whom, or the place at which, anything is to be done, means the person or place appointed or authorised in that behalf by the Commissioners;

"proprietor", in relation to any goods, includes any owner, importer, exporter, shipper or other person for the time being possessed of or beneficially interested in those goods;

"Queen's warehouse" means any place provided by the Crown or appointed by the Commissioners for the deposit of goods for security thereof and of the duties chargeable thereon;

. . .

"ship" and "vessel" include any boat or other vessel whatsoever (and, to the extent provided in section 2 below, any hovercraft);

"shipment" includes loading into an aircraft, and "shipped" and cognate expressions shall be construed accordingly;

"stores" means, subject to subsection (4) below, goods for use in a ship or aircraft and includes fuel and spare parts and other articles of equipment, whether or not for immediate fitting;

. . .

"transit or transhipment", in relation to the entry of goods, means transit through the United Kingdom or transhipment with a view to the reexportation of the goods in question;

. . .

"vehicle" includes a railway vehicle;

"warehouse", except in the expressions "Queen's warehouse" and "distiller's warehouse", means a place of security approved by the Commissioners under subsection (1) or (2) or subsections (1) and (2) of section 92 below and, except in that section, also includes a distiller's warehouse; and "warehoused" and cognate expressions shall, subject to subsection (4) of that section, be construed accordingly;

. . .

Forfeiture, offences, etc. in connection with importation

Forfeiture of goods improperly imported

49.—(1) Where—   A30–03

(a) except as provided by or under the Customs and Excise Acts 1979, any imported goods, being goods chargeable on their importation with customs or excise duty, are, without payment of that duty—
  (i) unshipped in any port,
  (ii) unloaded from any aircraft in the United Kingdom,
  (iii) unloaded from any vehicle in, or otherwise brought across the boundary into, Northern Ireland, or
  (iv) removed from their place of importation or from any approved wharf, examination station or transit shed; or

(b) any goods are imported, landed or unloaded contrary to any prohibition or restriction for the time being in force with respect thereto under or by virtue of any enactment; or

(c) any goods, being goods chargeable with any duty or goods the importation of which is for the time being prohibited or restricted by or under any enactment, are found, whether before or after the unloading thereof, to have been concealed in any manner on board any ship or aircraft or, while in Northern Ireland, in any vehicle; or

(d) any goods are imported concealed in a container holding goods of a different description; or

(e) any imported goods are found, whether before or after delivery, not to correspond with the entry made thereof, or

(f) any imported goods are concealed or packed in any manner appearing to be intended to deceive an officer,

those goods shall, subject to subsection (2) below, be liable to forfeiture.

(2) Where any goods, the importation of which is for the time being prohibited or restricted by or under any enactment, are on their importation either—

(a) reported as intended for exportation in the same ship, aircraft or vehicle; or

(b) entered for transit or transhipment; or

(c) entered to be warehoused for exportation or for use as stores,

the Commissioners may, if they see fit, permit the goods to be dealt with accordingly.

. . .

Forfeiture

Provisions as to detention seizure and condemnation of goods, etc.

A30–04   139.—(1) Any thing liable to forfeiture under the customs and excise Acts may be seized or detained by any officer or constable or any member of Her Majesty's armed forces or coastguard.

(2) Where any thing is seized or detained as liable to forfeiture under the customs and excise Acts by a person other than an officer, that person shall, subject to subsection (3) below, either—

(a) deliver that thing to the nearest convenient office of customs and excise; or

(b) if such delivery is not practicable, give to the Commissioners at the nearest convenient office of customs and excise notice in writing of the seizure or detention with full particulars of the thing seized or detained.

(3) Where the person seizing or detaining any thing as liable to forfeiture under the customs and excise Acts is a constable and that thing is or may be required for use in connection with any proceedings to be brought otherwise than under those Acts it may, subject to subsection (4) below, be retained in the custody of the police until either those proceedings are completed or it is decided that no such proceedings shall be brought.

(4) The following provisions apply in relation to things retained in the custody of the police by virtue of subsection (3) above that is to say—

(a) Notice in writing of the seizure or detention and of the intention to retain the thing in question in the custody of the police, together with full particulars as to that thing, shall be given to the Commissioners at the nearest convenient office of customs and excise;

(b) any officer shall be permitted to examine that thing and take account thereof at any time while it remains in the custody of the police;

(c) nothing in the Police (Property) Act 1897 shall apply in relation to that thing.

(5) Subject to subsections (3) and (4) above and to Schedule 3 to this Act, any thing seized or detained under the customs and excise Acts shall, pending the determination as to its forfeiture or disposal, be dealt with, and, if condemned or deemed to have been condemned or forfeited, shall be disposed of in such manner as the Commissioners may direct.

(6) Schedule 3 to this Act shall have effect for the purpose of forfeitures, and of proceedings for the condemnation of any thing as being forfeited, under the customs and excise Acts.

(7) If any person, not being an officer, by whom any thing is seized or detained or who has custody thereof after its seizure or detention, fails to

comply with any requirement of this section or with any direction of the Commissioners given there-under, he shall be liable on summary conviction to a penalty of £50.

(8) Subsections (2) to (7) above shall apply in relation to any dutiable goods seized or detained by any person other than an officer notwithstanding that they were not so seized as liable to forfeiture under the customs and excise Acts.

SCHEDULE 3   Sections 139, 143 and 145

PROVISIONS RELATING TO FORFEITURE

Notice of seizure

1.—(1) The Commissioners shall, except as provided in sub-paragraph (2) below, give notice of the seizure of any thing as liable to forfeiture and of the grounds therefor to any person who to their knowledge was at the time of the seizure the owner or one of the owners thereof.   **A30–05**

(2) Notice need not be given under this paragraph if the seizure was made in the presence of—

(a) the person whose offence or suspected offence occasioned the seizure; or

(b) the owner or any of the owners of the thing seized or any servant or agent of his; or

(c) in the case of any thing seized in any ship or aircraft, the master or commander.

2. Notice under paragraph 1 above shall be given in writing and shall be deemed to have been duly served on the person concerned—

(a) if delivered to him personally; or

(b) if addressed to him and left or forwarded by post to him at his usual or last known place of abode or business or, in the case of a body corporate, at their registered or principal office; or

(c) where he has no address within the United Kingdom, or his address is unknown, by publication of notice of the seizure in the London, Edinburgh or Belfast Gazette.

Notice of claim

3. Any person claiming that any thing seized as liable to forfeiture is not so liable shall, within one month of the date of the notice of seizure or, where no such notice has been served on him within one month of the date of the seizure, give notice of his right in writing to the Commissioners at any office of customs and exercise.   **A30–06**

4.—(1) Any notice under paragraph 3 above shall specify the name and address of the claimant and, in the case of a claimant who is outside the United Kingdom, shall specify the name and address of a solicitor in the United Kingdom who is authorised to accept service of process and to act on behalf of the claimant.

(2) Service of process upon a solicitor so specified shall be deemed to be proper service upon the claimant.

Condemnation

5. If on the expiration of the relevant period under paragraph 3 above for the giving of notice of claim in respect of any thing no such notice has been given to the Commissioners, or if, in the case of any such notice given, any requirement of paragraph 4 above is not complied with, the thing in question shall be deemed to have been duly condemned as forfeited.   **A30–07**

6. Where notice of claim in respect of any thing is duly given in accordance with paragraphs 3 and 4 above, the Commissioners shall take proceedings for the condemnation of that thing by the court, and if the court finds that the thing was at the time of seizure liable to forfeiture the court shall condemn it as forfeited.

7. Where any thing is in accordance with either of paragraphs 5 or 6 above condemned or deemed to have been condemned as forfeited, then, without prejudice to any delivery up or sale of the thing by the Commissioners under paragraph 16 below, the forfeiture shall have effect as from the date when the liability to forfeiture arose.

Proceedings for condemnation by court

8. Proceedings for condemnation shall be civil proceedings and may be instituted—   **A30–08**

(a) in England or Wales either in the High Court or in a magistrates' court;

(b) in Scotland either in the Court of Session or in the sheriff court;

(c) in Northern Ireland either in the High Court or in a court of summary jurisdiction.

9. Proceedings for the condemnation of any thing instituted in a magistrates' court in England or Wales, in the sheriff court in Scotland or in a court of summary jurisdiction in Northern Ireland may be so instituted—

(a) in any such court having jurisdiction in the place where any offence in connection with that thing was committed or where any proceedings for such an offence are instituted; or

(b) in any such court having jurisdiction in the place where the claimant resides or, if the claimant has specified a solicitor under paragraph 4 above, in the place where that solicitor has his office; or

(c) in any such court having jurisdiction in the place where that thing was found, detained or seized or to which it is first brought after being found, detained or seized.

10.—(1) In any proceedings for condemnation instituted in England, Wales or Northern Ireland, the claimant or his solicitor shall make oath that the thing seized was, or was to the best of his knowledge and belief, the property of the claimant at the time of the seizure.

(2) In any such proceedings instituted in the High Court, the claimant shall give such security for the costs of the proceedings as may be determined by the Court.

(3) If any requirement of this paragraph is not complied with, the court shall give judgment for the Commissioners.

11.—(1) In the case of any proceedings for condemnation instituted in a magistrates' court in England or Wales, without prejudice to any right to require the statement of a case for the opinion of the High Court, either party may appeal against the decision of that court to the Crown Court.

(2) In the case of any proceedings for condemnation instituted in a court of summary jurisdiction in Northern Ireland, without prejudice to any right to require the statement of a case for the opinion of the High Court, either party may appeal against the decision of that court to the county court.

12. Where an appeal, including an appeal by way of case stated, has been made against the decision of the court in any proceedings for the condemnation of any thing, that thing shall, pending the final determination of the matter, be left with the Commissioners or at any convenient office of customs and excise.

Provisions as to proof

A30–09   13. In any proceedings arising out of the seizure of any thing, the fact, form and manner of the seizure shall be taken to have been as set forth in the process without any further evidence thereof, unless the contrary is proved.

14. In any proceedings, the condemnation by a court of any thing as forfeited may be proved by the production either of the order or certificate of condemnation or of a certified copy thereof purporting to be signed by an officer of the court by which the order or certificate was made or granted.

Special provisions as to certain claimants

A30–10   15. For the purposes of any claim to, or proceedings for the condemnation of, any thing, where that thing is at the time of seizure the property of a body corporate, of two or more partners or of any number of persons exceeding five, the oath required by paragraph 10 above to be taken and any other thing required by this Schedule or by any rules of the court to be done by, or by any person authorised by, the claimant or owner may be taken or done by, or by any other person authorised by, the following persons respectively that is to say—

(a) where the owner is a body corporate, the secretary or some duly authorised officer of that body;

(b) where the owners are in partnership, any one of those owners;

(c) where the owners are any number of persons exceeding five not being in partnership, any two of those persons on behalf of themselves and their co-owners.

Power to deal with seizures before condemnation, etc.

A30–11   16. Where any thing has been seized as liable to forfeiture the Commissioners may at any time if they see fit and notwithstanding that the thing has not yet been condemned, or is not yet deemed to have been condemned, as forfeited—

   (a) deliver it up to any claimant upon his paying to the Commissioners such sum as they think proper, being a sum not exceeding that which in their opinion represents the value of the thing, including any duty or tax chargeable thereon which has not been paid;

   (b) if the thing seized is a living creature or is in the opinion of the Commissioners of a perishable nature, sell or destroy it.

17.—(1) If, where any thing is delivered up, sold or destroyed under paragraph 16 above, it is held in proceedings taken under this Schedule that the thing was not liable to forfeiture at the time of its seizure, the Commissioners shall, subject to any deduction allowed under sub-paragraph (2) below, on demand by the claimant tender to him—

   (a) an amount equal to any sum paid by him under sub-paragraph (a) of that paragraph; or

   (b) where they have sold the thing, an amount equal to the proceeds of sale; or

   (c) where they have destroyed the thing, an amount equal to the market value of the thing at the time of its seizure.

(2) Where the amount to be tendered under sub-paragraph (1)(a), (b) or (c) above includes any sum on account of any duty or tax chargeable on the thing which had not been paid before its seizure the Commissioners may deduct so much of that amount as represents that duty or tax.

(3) If the claimant accepts any amount tendered to him under sub-paragraph (1) above, he shall not be entitled to maintain any action on account of the seizure, detention, sale or destruction of the thing.

(4) For the purposes of sub-paragraph (1)(c) above, the market value of any thing at the time of its seizure shall be taken to be such amount as the Commissioners and the claimant may agree or, in default of agreement, as may be determined by a referee appointed by the Lord Chancellor (not being an official of any government a department), whose decision shall be final and conclusive; and the procedure on any reference to a referee shall be such as may be determined by the referee.

*   *   *   *   *   *

APPENDIX 31

The Trade Marks (Customs) Regulations 1994

S.I. 1994 No. 2625

A31–01 The Commissioners of Customs and Excise, in exercise of the powers conferred on them by section 90(1), (2) and (3) of the Trade Marks Act 1994 and of all other powers enabling them in that behalf, hereby make the following Regulations:

A31–02 1. These Regulations may be cited as the Trade Marks (Customs) Regulations 1994 and shall come into force on 31st October 1994.

A31–03 2. If notice is given under section 89(1) of The Trade Marks Act 1994 by the proprietor of licensee of a registered trade mark in respect of certain goods it shall be in the form set out in the Schedule to these Regulations or a form to the like effect approved by the Commissioners; and separate notices shall be given in respect of each arrival of such goods.

A31–04 3. A fee of £30 (plus value added tax) in respect of each notice shall be paid to the Commissioners at the time it is given.

A31–05 4. The person giving the notice shall give to the Commissioners such security or further security within such time and in such manner, whether by deposit of a sum of money or guarantee, as the Commissioners may require, in respect of any liability or expense which they may incur in consequence of the notice by reason of the detention of any goods or anything done to goods so detained: and if such security or further security is not given within the time specified by the Commissioners, then (but without prejudice to the operation of regulation 5 below) the notice shall have no effect.

A31–06 5. In every case, whether any security or further security is given or not, the person who has given the notice shall keep the Commissioners indemnified against all such liability and expense as is mentioned in regulation 4 above.

A31–07 6.—(1) The person giving the notice shall, either on giving notice or when the goods are imported, furnish the Commissioners with the certificate of registration (or a copy of it) issued by the Registrar of Trade Marks on the registration of the trade mark specified in the notice, together with evidence that such registration was duly renewed at all such times as it may have expired.

(2) If such a certificate or copy and, where applicable, evidence of renewal is not furnished in accordance with paragraph (1) above then the goods shall not be detained, or, if detained, shall be released, and (but without prejudice to the operation of regulation 5 above) any notice given in respect of them shall have no effect.

A31–08 7. The Trade Marks (Customs) Regulations 1970 are hereby revoked.

A31–09   SCHEDULE

NOTICE UNDER SECTION 89 TRADE MARKS ACT 1994 REQUESTING INFRINGING GOODS, MATERIAL OR ARTICLES TO BE TREATED AS PROHIBITED GOODS

Please read these notes before completing this notice

1. This notice may only be given by the proprietor of a registered trade mark, or a licensee. A separate notice must be given in respect of each consignment.

2. Please note that in Part 3 it is not mandatory to provide details other than the time and place of expected arrival of infringing goods but it will greatly increase the prospect of intercepting the consignment concerned if all the details requested are given.

THE TRADE MARKS (CUSTOMS) REGULATIONS 1994

3. A fee of £30 (plus VAT) is payable for each notice given. Please enclose a cheque for the required amount, made payable to "Commissioners of Customs and Excise".

4. A copy of the certificate of registration for the trade mark, as well as the certificate of renewal (where applicable), is to be enclosed with the notice, **or** submitted when the goods are imported.

5. The person who has given notice shall keep the Commissioners of Customs and Excise indemnified against any liability or expense which they may incur in consequence of the notice by reason of the detention of any goods or anything done to goods detained. The person giving the notice may be required to provide a security to cover this indemnity.

1 Person giving notice

*I/We

. . . .
Full name of signatory in BLOCK LETTERS

give notice to the Commissioners of Customs and Excise that

. . . .
Name and address of proprietor or licensee in BLOCK LETTERS

. . . .

. . . .
is the *proprietor/licensee of a trade mark registered in the United Kingdom and that infringing goods, material or articles are expected to arrive in the United Kingdom, and *I/we request that they be treated as prohibited goods.

*Delete as necessary

2 Details of infringing goods, material or articles

Trade mark . . . .

Infringing goods, material or articles . . . .

Quantity . . . .

Commodity Code(s) . . . .

3 Details of expected importation

Place of importation . . . .

Method of importation . . . .
Please include details of ship, aircraft or vehicle, where known

Expected date of arrival . . . .

Country of origin . . . .

Country of consignment . . . .

Importer's details . . . .
Please include VAT number, if known

Consignor's details . . . .

APPENDIX 31

4 Declaration

I declare that the information given by me in this notice is true.

Signature ....

    (*Sole Proprietor/Partner/Director/Company Secretary/Duly Authorised Person)

Date...

---

5 Submission of notice

Please send the completed notice, fee and copies of relevant certificates to:
HM Customs and Excise
CD3A
New King's Beam House
22 Upper Ground
London SE1 9PJ

1318

PART IX

PROCEDURAL MATERIALS

APPENDIX 32

Civil Procedure Rules Extracts

The Civil Procedure Rules

PART 6

A32–01

SERVICE OF DOCUMENTS

AMENDED BY THE CIVIL PROCEDURE (AMENDENT NO. 2) RULES 2000, THE CIVIL PROCEDURE (AMENDMENT NO. 3) RULES 2000, AND THE CIVIL PROCEDURE (ADMENDMENT NO. 4) RULES 2000

CONTENTS

I. GENERAL RULES ABOUT SERVICE

II. SPECIAL PROVISIONS ABOUT SERVICE OF THE CLAIM FORM

III. SPECIAL PROVISIONS ABOUT SERVICE OUT OF THE JURISDICTION

1321

I. General rules about service

Part 6 Rules about service apply generally

A32–02 6.1 The rules in this Part apply to the service of documents, except where—

(a) any other enactment, a rule in another Part, or a practice direction makes a different provision; or

(b) the court orders otherwise.

Methods of service—general

A32–03 6.2 (1) A document may be served by any of the following methods—

(a) personal service, in accordance with rule 6.4;

(b) first class post;

(c) leaving the document at a place specified in rule 6.5;

(d) through a document exchange in accordance with the relevant practice direction; or

(e) by fax or other means of electronic communication in accordance with the relevant practice direction.

(Rule 6.8 provides for the court to permit service by an alternative method)

(2) A company may be served by any method permitted under this Part as an alternative to the methods of service set out in—

(a) section 725 of the Companies Act 1985 (service by leaving a document at or posting it to an authorised place);

(b) section 695 of that Act (service on overseas companies); and

(c) Section 694A of that Act (service of documents on companies incorporated outside the U.K. and Gibraltar and having a branch in Great Britain).

Who is to serve

A32–04 6.3 (1) The court will serve a document which it has issued or prepared except where—

(a) a rule provides that a party must serve the document in question;

(b) the party on whose behalf the document is to be served notifies the court that he wishes to serve it himself;

(c) a practice direction provides otherwise;

(d) the court orders otherwise; or

(e) the court has failed to serve and has sent a notice of non-service to the party on whose behalf the document is to be served in accordance with rule 6.11.

(2) Where the court is to serve a document, it is for the court to decide which of the methods of service specified in rule 6.2 is to be used.

(3) Where a party prepares a document which is to be served by the court, that party must file a copy for the court, and for each party to be served.

Personal Service

A32–05 6.4 (1) A document to be served may be served personally, except as provided in paragraph (2).

(2) Where a solicitor—

    (a) is authorised to accept service on behalf of a party; and

    (b) has notified the party serving the document in writing that he is so authorised,

a document must be served on the solicitor, unless personal service is required by an enactment, rule, practice direction or court order.

(3) A document is served personally on an individual by leaving it with that individual.

(4) A document is served personally on a company or other corporation by leaving it with a person holding a senior position within the company or corporation.

(The service practice direction sets out the meaning of "senior position")

(5) A document is served personally on a partnership where partners are being sued in the name of their firm by leaving it with—

    (a) a partner; or

    (b) a person who, at the time of service, has the control or management of the partnership business at its principal place of business.

Address for service

6.5 (1) Except as provided by Section III of this Part (service out of the **A32–06** jurisdiction) a document must be served within the jurisdiction.

("Jurisdiction" is defined in rule 2.3)

(2) A party must give an address for service within the jurisdiction.

(3) Where a party—

    (a) does not give the business address of his solicitor as his address for service; and

    (b) resides or carries on business within the jurisdiction,

he must give his residence or place of business as his address for service.

(4) Any document to be served—

    (a) by first class post;

    (b) by leaving it at the place of service;

    (c) through a document exchange; or

    (d) by fax or by other means of electronic communication,

must be sent or transmitted to, or left at, the address for service given by the party to be served.

(5) Where—

    (a) a solicitor is acting for the party to be served; and

    (b) the document to be served is not the claim form;

    (c) the party's address for service is the business address of his solicitor.

(Rule 6.13 specifies when the business address of a defendant's solicitor may be the defendant's for service in relation to the claim form)

(Rule 42.1 provides that if the business address of his solicitor is given, that solicitor will be treated as acting for that party)

(6) Where—

    (a) no solicitor is acting for the party to be served; and

    (b) the party has not given an address for service,

the document must be sent or transmitted to, or left at, the place shown in the following table.

(Rule 6.2(2) sets out the statutory methods of service on a company)

NATURE OF PARTY TO BE SERVED	PLACE OF SERVICE
Individual	Usual or last known residence.
Proprietor of a business	Usual or last known residence; or Place of business or last known place of business.
Individual who is suing or being sued in the name of a firm	Usual or last known residence; or Principal or last known place of business of the firm.
Corporation incorporated in England and Wales other than a company	Principal office of the corporation; or Any place within the jurisdiction where the corporation carries on its activities and which has a real connection with the claim.
Company registered in England and Wales	Principal office of the company; or Any place of business of the company within the jurisdiction which has a real connection with the claim.
Any other company or corporation	Any place within the jurisdiction where the corporation carries on its activities; or Any place of business of the company within the jurisdiction

(7) This rule does not apply where an order made by the court under rule 6.8 (service by an alternative method) specifies where the document in question may be served.

Service of documents on children and patients

A32–07   **6.6** (1) The following table shows the person on whom a document must be served if it is a document which would otherwise be served on a child or a patient—

TYPE OF DOCUMENT	NATURE OF PARTY	PERSON TO BE SERVED
Claim form	Child who is not also a patient	One of the child's parents or guardians; or If there is no parent or guardian or person with whom the child resides or in whose care the child is.
Claim form	Patient	The person authorised under Part VII of the Mental Health Act 10 to conduct the proceedings in the name of the patient or on his behalf or If there is no person so authorised, the person with whom the patient resides or in whose care the patient is.

Application for an order appointing a litigation friend, where a child or patient has no litigation friend	Child or patient	See rule 21.8.
Any other document	Child or patient	The litigation friend who is conducting proceedings on behalf of the child or patient.

(2) The court may make an order permitting a document to be served on the child or patient, some person other than the person specified in the table in this rule.

(3) An application for an order under paragraph (2) may be made without notice.

(4) The court may order that, although a document has been served on someone other than the person specified in the table, the document is to be treated as if it had been properly served.

(5) This rule does not apply where the court has made an order under rule 21.2(3) allowing to conduct proceedings without a litigation friend.

(Part 21 contains rules about the appointment of a litigation friend)

Deemed service

6.7 (1) A document which is served in accordance with these rules or any relevant practice direction shall be deemed to be served on the day shown in the following table (Rule 2.8 excludes Saturday, Sunday, a Bank Holiday, Christmas Day or Good Friday from calculations of periods of 5 days or less)— **A32–08**

METHOD OF SERVICE	DEEMED DAY OF SERVICE
First class post	The second day after it was posted.
Document exchange	The second day after it was left at the document exchange.
Delivering the document to or leaving it at a permitted address	The day after it was delivered to or left at the permitted address.
Fax	If it is transmitted on a business day before 4p.m of that day; or In any other case, on the business day after the day on which it is transmitted.
Other electronic method	The second day after the day on which it is transmitted.

(2) If a document is served personally—
    (a) after 5 p.m., on a business day; or
    (b) at any time on a Saturday, Sunday or a Bank Holiday, it will be treated as being served on next business day.

(3) In this rule—
    'business day' means any day except Saturday, Sunday or a bank holiday; and
    'bank holiday' includes Christmas Day and Good Friday.

Service by an alternative method

6.8 (1) Where it appears to the court that there is a good reason to authorise service by a method not permitted by these Rules, the court may make an order permitting service by an alternative method. **A32–09**

(2) An application for an order permitting service by an alternative method—
    (a) must be supported by evidence; and
    (b) may be made without notice.
(3) An order permitting service by an alternative method must specify—
    (a) the method of service; and
    (b) the date when the document will be deemed to be served.

Power of court to dispense with service

A32–10   **6.9** (1) The court may dispense with service of a document.
(2) An application for an order to dispense with service may be made without notice.

Certificate of service

A32–11   **6.10** Where a rule, practice direction or court order requires a certificate of service, the certificate must state—
    (a) that the document has not been returned undelivered; and
    (b) the details set out in the following table—

METHOD OF SERVICE	DETAILS TO BE CERTIFIED
Post	Date of posting
Personal	Date of personal service
Document exchange	Date of delivery to the document exchange
Delivery of document to or leaving it at a permitted place	Date when the document was delivered to or left at a permitted place
Fax	Date and time of transmission
Other electronic means	Date of transmission and the means used
Alternative method permitted by the court	As required by the court

Notice of non-service

A32–12   **6.11** Where—
    (a) a document is to be served by the court; and
    (b) the court is unable to serve it,
the court must send a notice of non-service stating the method attempted to the party who requested service.

II. Special Provisions about Service of the Claim Form

General rules about service subject to special rules about service of claim form

A32–13   **6.12** The general rules about service are subject to the special rules about service contained in rules 6.13 to 6.16.

Service of claim form by the court—defendant's address for service

A32–14   **6.13** (1) Where a claim form is to be served by the court, the claim form must include the defendant's address for service.
(2) For the purposes of paragraph (1), the defendant's address for service may be the business address of the defendant's solicitor if he is authorised to accept service on the defendant's behalf but not otherwise.

(Rule 6.5 contains general provisions about the address for service)

Certificate of service relating to the claim form

6.14 (1) Where a claim form is served by the court, the court must send the **A32–15**
claimant a notice which include the date when the claim form is deemed to be
served under rule 6.7.

(2) Where the claim form is served by the claimant—
  (a) he must file a certificate of service within 7 days of service of the claim
      form; and
  (b) he may not obtain judgment in default under Part 12 unless he has filed
      the certificate of service.

(Rule 6.10 specifies what a certificate of service must show)

Service of claim form by contractually agreed method

6.15 (1) Where— **A32–16**
  (a) a contract contains a term providing that, in the event of a claim being
      issued in relation to the contract, the claim form may be served by a
      method specified in the contract; and
  (b) a claim form containing only a claim in respect of that contract is
      issued,
the claim forms shall, subject to paragraph (2), be deemed to be served on the
defendant if it is served by a method specified in the contract.

(2) Where the claim form is served out of the jurisdiction in accordance with
the contract, it shall be deemed to be served on the defendant unless—
  (a) permission to serve it out of the jurisdiction has been granted under
      Rule 6.20; or
  (b) it may be served without permission under Rule 6.19.

Service of claim form on agent of principal who is overseas

6.16 (1) Where— **A32–17**
  (a) the defendant is overseas; and
  (b) the conditions specified in paragraph (2) are satisfied
the court may, on an application only, permit a claim form relating to a contract
to be served on the defendant's agent.

(2) The court may not make an order under this rule unless it is satisfied
that—
  (a) the contract to which the claim relates was entered into within the
      jurisdiction with or through the defendant's agent; and
  (b) at the time of the application either the agent's authority has not been
      terminated or he is still in business relations with his principal.

(3) An application under this rule—
  (a) must be supported by evidence; and
  (b) may be made without notice.

(4) An order under this rule must state a period within which the defendant
must respond to particulars of claim.

(Rule 9.2 sets out how a defendant may respond to particulars of claim)

(5) The power conferred by this rule is additional to the power conferred by
rule 6.8 (service by an alternative method).

(6) Where the court makes an order under this rule, the claimant must send to
the defendant copies of—
  (a) the order; and
  (b) the claim form.

(Other rules about service can be found—
  (a) in Schedule 1, in the following RSC—O.10 (certain actions for the
      possession of land (service out of the jurisdiction); O.30 (receivers); O.52
      (application for committal order); (writ of habeas corpus); O.69 (foreign

process); O.77 (service on the Crown); O.97 (Landlord and Tenant Acts); O.106 (Solicitors Act 1974); O.113 (summary proceedings for possession of land);
- (b) in Schedule 2, in the following CCR—O.3 (appeal to the county court); O.7 (recovery and mortgage possession claims); O.24 (summary proceedings for recovery of land and possession orders); O.33 (interpleader); O.42 (service on the Crown); O.43 (Landlord and Tenant Acts); O.45 (application for detailed assessment of returning officer's account); O.45 (application for direction for use of blood tests); O.48B (order for enforcement of parking penalties); O.49 (notice to repair under Chancel Repairs Act 1932; applications under various statutes); and
- (c) in relation to certain enforcement proceedings, in the provisions in the Schedules dealing with those proceedings.)

III. Special Provisions about Service out of the Jurisdiction

Scope of this Section

A32–18   **6.17** This Section contains rules about—
- (a) service out of the jurisdiction;
- (b) how to obtain the permission of the court to serve out of the jurisdiction; and
- (c) the procedure for serving out of the jurisdiction.

(Rule 2.3 defines "jurisdiction")

Definitions

A32–19   **6.18** For the purposes of this Part—
- (a) "the 1982 Act" means the Civil Jurisdiction and Judgments Act 1982;
- (b) "the Hague Convention" means the Convention on the service abroad of judicial and ex judicial documents in civil or commercial matters signed at the Hague on November 15;
- (c) "Contracting State" has the meaning given by section 1(3) of the 1982 Act;
- (d) "Convention territory" means the territory or territories of any Contracting State to which Brussels or Lugano Conventions (as defined in section 1(1) of the 1982 Act) apply;
- (e) "Civil Procedure Convention" means the Brussels and Lugano Conventions and any other Convention entered into by the United Kingdom regarding service outside the jurisdiction.
- (f) "United Kingdom Overseas Territory" means those territories as set out in the relevant direction.
- (g) "domicile" is to be determined in accordance with sections 41 to 46 of the 1982 Act;
- (h) "claim form" includes peitition and application notice; and
- (i) "claim" includes petition and application.

(Rule 6.30 provides that where an application notice is to be served out of the jurisdiction this Part, rules 6.21(4), 6.22 and 6.23 do not apply)

Service out of the jurisdiction where the permission of the court is not required

A32–20   **6.19** (1) A claim form may be served on a defendant out of the jurisdiction where each claim includes the claim form made against the defendant to be served is a claim which the court has determined under the 1982 Act and—
- (a) no proceedings between the parties concerning the same claim are pending in the courts of any part of the United Kingdom or any other Convention territory; and

(b)   (i) the defendant is domiciled in the United Kingdom or in any Convention territory;

    (ii) Article 16 of Schedule 1, 3C or 4 to the 1982 Act refers to the proceedings; or

    (iii) the defendant is a party to an agreement conferring jurisidiction to which Article 17 Schedule 1, 3C or 4 to the 1982 Act refers.

(2) A claim form may be served on a defendant out of the jurisdiction where each claim includes the claim form made against the defendant to be served is a claim which, under any other enactment, the court has power to determine, although—

(a) the person against whom the claim is made is not within the jurisdiction; or

(b) the facts giving rise to the claim did not occur within the jurisdiction.

(3) Where a claim form is to be served out of the jurisdiction under this rule, it must contain the statement of the grounds on which the claimant is entitled to serve it out of the jurisdiction.

Service out of the jurisdiction where the permission of the court is required

6.20 In any proceedings to which rule 6.19 does not apply, a claim form may **A32–21** be served out of the jurisdiction with the permission of the court if—

General grounds

(1) a claim is made for a remedy against a person domiciled within the jurisdiction;

(2) a claim is made for an injunction ordering the defendant to do or refrain from doing a an act within the jurisdiction;

(3) a claim is made against someone on whom the claim form has been or will be served and—

(a) there is between the claimant and that person a real issue which it is reasonable for a court to try; and

(b) the claimant wishes to serve the claim form on another person who is a necessary other party to that claim;

(3A) a claim is a Part 20 claim and the person to be served is a necessary or proper party to a claim against the Part 20 claimant;

Claims for interim remedies

(4) a claim is made for an interim remedy under section 25(1) of the 1882 Act;

Claims in relation to contracts

(5) a claim is made in respect of a contract where the contract—

(a) was made within the jurisdiction;

(b) was made by or through an agent trading or residing within the jurisdiction;

(c) is governed by English law; or

(d) contains a term to the effect that the court shall have jurisdiction to determine any claim in respect of the contract;

(6) a claim is made in respect of a breach of contract committed within the jurisdiction;

(7) a claim is made for a declaration that no contract exists where, if the contract was found it would comply with the conditions set out in paragraph (5);

Claims in tort

(8) a claim is made in tort where—

(a) damage was sustained within the jurisdiction; or
(b) the damage sustained resulted from an act committed within the jurisdiction;

Enforcement

(9) a claim is made to enforce any judgment or arbitral award;

Claims about property within the jurisdiction

(10) the whole subject matter of a claim relates to property located within the jurisdiction;

Claims about trusts etc.

(11) a claim is made for any remedy which might be obtained in proceedings to execute the trusts of a written instrument where—
(a) the trusts ought to be executed according to English law; and
(b) the person on whom the claim form is to be served is a trustee of the trusts;
(12) a claim is made for any remedy which might be obtained in proceedings for the administration of the estate of a person who died domiciled within the jurisdiction;
(13) a claim is made in probate proceedings which includes a claim for the rectification of a will;
(14) a claim is made for a remedy against the defendant as constructive trustee where the defendant's alleged liability arises out of acts committed within the jurisdiction;
(15) a claim is made for restitution where the defendant's alleged liability arises out of acts committed within the jurisdiction;
(Probate proceedings are defined in the Contentious Probate Proceedings practice direction supplementing Part 49)

Claims by the Inland Revenue

(16) a claim is made by the Commissioner of the Inland Revenue relating to duties or taxes against a defendant not domiciled in Scotland or Northern Ireland;

Claim for costs order in favour of or against third parties

(17) a claim is made by a party to proceedings for an order that the court exercise its power under section 51 of the Supreme Court Act 1981 to make a costs order in favour of or against a person who is not a party to those proceedings;
(Rule 48.2 sets out the procedure where the court is considering whether to exercise its discretion to make a costs order in favour of or against a non-party)

Claims under various enactments

(18) a claim made under an enactment specified in the relevant practice direction.

Application for permission to serve claim form out of the jurisdiction

A32–22   **6.21** (1) An application for permission under rule 6.20 must be supported by written evidence stating—
(a) the grounds on which the application is made and the paragraph or paragraphs of rule 6.20 relied on;

(b) that the claimant believes that his claim has a reasonable prospect of success; and

(c) the defendant's address or, if not known, in what place or country the defendant is, or is likely to be found.

(2) Where the application is made in respect of a claim referred to in rule 6.20(3), the written evidence must also state the grounds on which the witness believes that there is between the claimant and the person on whom the claim form has been, or will be served, a real issue which it is reasonable for the court to try.

(2A) The court will not give permission unless satisfied that England and Wales is the proper place in which to bring the claim.

(3) Where—

(a) the application is for permission to serve a claim form in Scotland or Northern Ireland;

(b) it appears to the court that the claimant may also be entitled to a remedy there, the court in deciding whether to give permission, shall—

   (i) compare the cost and convenience of proceeding there or in the jurisdiction; and

   (ii) (where relevant) have regard to the powers and jurisdiction of the Sheriff court in Scotland or the county courts or courts of summary jurisdiction in Northern Ireland.

(4) An order giving permission to serve a claim form out of the jurisdiction must specify the periods within which the defendant may—

(a) file an acknowledgment of service;

(b) file or serve an admission; and

(c) file a defence.

(Part 11 sets out the procedure by which a defendant may dispute the court's jurisdiction)

Period for acknowledging service or admitting the claim where the claim form is served out of the jurisdiction under rule 6.19

6.22 (1) This rule sets out the period for filing an acknowledgment of service **A32–23** or filing or serving an admission where a claim form has been served out of the jurisdiction under rule 6.19.

(Part 10 contains rules about the acknowledgment of service and Part 14 contains rules about admissions)

(2) If the claim form is to be served under rule 6.19(1) in Scotland, Northern Ireland or in the European territory of another Contracting State the period is—

(a) where the defendant is served with a claim form which states that particulars of claim follow, 21 days after the service of the particulars of claim; and

(b) in any other case, 21 days after service of the claim form.

(3) If the claim form is to be served under rule 6.19(1) in any other territory of a Contracting State the period is—

(a) where the defendant is served with a claim form which states that particulars of claim follow, 31 days after the service of the particulars of claim; and

(b) in any other case, 31 days after service of the claim form.

(4) If the claim form is to be served under—

(a) rule 6.19(1) in a country not referred to in paragraphs (2) or (3); or

(b) rule 6.19(2),

the period is set out in the relevant practice direction.

Period for filing a defence where the claim form is served out of the jurisdiction under rule 6.19

6.23 (1) This rule sets out the period for filing a defence where a claim form **A32–24** has been served out of the jurisdiction under rule 6.19.

(Part 15 contains rules about the defence)

(2) If the claim form is to be served under rule 6.19(1) in Scotland, Northern Ireland or in the European territory of another Contracting State the period is—

    (a) 21 days after service of the particulars of claim; or

    (b) if the defendant files an acknowledgment of service, 35 days after service of the particulars of claim.

(3) If the claim form is to be served under rule 6.19(1) in any other territory of a Contracting State the period is—

    (a) 31 days after service of the particulars of claim; or

    (b) if the defendant files an acknowledgment of service, 45 days after service of the particulars of claim.

(4) If the claim form is to be served under—

    (a) rule 6.19(1) in a country not referred to in paragraphs (2) or (3); or

    (b) rule 6.19(2),

the period is set out in the relevant practice direction.

Method of service—general provisions

A32–25   6.24 (1) Where a claim form is to be served out of the jurisdiction, it may be served by any method—

    (a) permitted by the law of the country in which it is to be served;

    (b) provided for by—

        (i) rule 6.25 (service through foreign governments, judicial authorities and British Consular authorities); or

        (ii) rule 6.26 (service on a State); or

    (c) permitted by a Civil Procedure Convention.

(2) Nothing in this rule or in any court order shall authorise or require any person to do anything in the country where the claim form is to be served which is against the law of that country.

Service through foreign governments, judicial authorities and British Consular authorities

A32–26   6.25 (1) Where a claim form is to be served on a defendant in any country which is a party to the Hague Convention, the claim form may be served—

    (a) through the authority designated under the Hague Convention in respect of that country;

    (b) if the law of that country permits—

        (i) through the judicial authorities of that country, or

        (ii) through a British Consular authority in that country.

(2) Where—

    (a) paragraph (4) (service in Scotland etc., other than under the Hague Convention) does apply; and

    (b) a claim form is to be served on a defendant in any country which is a party to a Civil Procedure Convention (other than the Hague Convention) providing for service in that country,

the claim form may be served, if the law of that country permits—

        (i) through the judicial authorities of that country; or

        (ii) through a British Consular authority in that country (subject to any provisions of the applicable convention about the nationality of persons who may be served by such a method).

(3) Where—

    (a) paragraph (4) (service in Scotland etc., other than under the Hague Convention) does apply; and

    (b) a claim form is to be served on a defendant in any country with respect to which there is a Civil Procedure Convention providing for service in that country,

the claim form may be served, if the law of that country so permits—

    (i) through the government of that country, where that government
        is willing to serve it;
    (ii) through a British Consular authority in that country.

(4) Except where a claim form is to be served in accordance with paragraph (1) (service under the Hague Convention), the methods of service permitted by this rule are not available when a claim form is to be served in—

    (a) Scotland, Northern Ireland, the Isle of Man or the Channel Islands;
    (b) any Commonwealth State;
    (c) any United Kingdom Overseas Territory; or
    (d) the Republic of Ireland.

Procedure where service is to be through foreign governments, judicial authorities and British Consular authorities

6.26 (1) This rule applies where the claimant wishes to serve the claim form **A32–27** through—

    (a) the judicial authorities of the country where the claim form is to be served;
    (b) a British Consular authority in that country;
    (c) the authority designated under the Hague Convention in respect of that country; or
    (d) the government of that country.

(2) Where this rule applies, the claimant must file—

    (a) a request for service of the claim form by the method in paragraph (1) that he has chosen;
    (b) a copy of the claim form;
    (c) any translation required under rule 6.28; and
    (d) any other documents, copies of documents or translations required by the relevant practice direction.

(3) When the claimant files the documents specified in paragraph (2), the court officer will—

    (a) seal the copy of the claim form; and
    (b) forward the documents to the Senior Master.

(4) The Senior Master will send documents forwarded under this rule—

    (a) where the claim form is being served through the authority designated under the Hague Convention, to that authority; or
    (b) in any other case, to the Foreign and Commonwealth Office with a request that it arranges the claim to be served by the method indicated in the request for service filed under paragraph (2) or, where that request indicates alternative methods, by the most convenient method.

(5) An official certificate which—

    (a) states that the claim form has been served in accordance with this rule either personally or in accordance with the law of the country in which service was effected;
    (b) specifies the date on which the claim form was served; and
    (c) is made by—
        (i) a British Consular authority in the country where the claim form was served;
        (ii) the government or judicial authorities in that country; or
        (iii) any other authority designated in respect of that country under the Hague Convention,

shall be evidence of the facts stated in the certificate.

(6) A document purporting to be an official certificate under paragraph (5) shall be treated as a certificate, unless it is proved not to be.

Service of claim form on State where court permits service out of the jurisdiction

6.27 (1) This rule applies where a claimant wishes to serve the claim form on a **A32–28** State.

(2) The claimant must file in the Central Office of the Royal Courts of Justice—
    (a) a request for service to be arranged by the Foreign and Commonwealth Office;
    (b) a copy of the claim form; and
    (c) any translation required under rule 6.28.

(3) The Senior Master will send documents filed under this rule to the Foreign and Commonwealth Office with a request that it arranges for the claim form to be served.

(4) An official certificate by the Foreign and Commonwealth Office stating that a claim form has been duly served on a specified date in accordance with a request made under this rule is evidence of that fact.

(5) A document purporting to be such a certificate shall be treated as such a certificate, unless proved not to be.

(6) Where—
    (a) section 12(6) of the State Immunity Act 1978[13] applies; and
    (b) the State has agreed to a method of service other than through the Foreign and Commonwealth Office,
the claim may be served either by the method agreed or in accordance with this rule.

(Section 12(6) of the State Immunity Act 1978 provides that section 12(1) of that Act, which prescribes a method for serving documents on a State, does not prevent the service of any form or other document in a manner to which the State has agreed)

(7) In this rule "State" has the meaning given by section 14 of the State Immunity Act 1978.

Translation of claim form

A32–29   **6.28** (1) Except where paragraph (4) or (5) applies, every copy of the claim form filed under rule 6.27 (service through judicial authorities, foreign governments etc.) or 6.27 (service on State) be accompanied by a translation of the claim form.

(2) The translation must be—
    (a) in the official language of the country in which it is to be served; or
    (b) if there is more than one official language of that country, in any official language which is appropriate to the place in the country where the claim form is to be served.

(3) Every translation filed under this rule must be accompanied by a statement by the person making it that it is a correct translation, and the statement must include—
    (a) the name of the person making the translation;
    (b) his address; and
    (c) his qualifications for making a translation.

(4) The claimant is not required to file a translation of a claim form filed under rule 6.26 (service through judicial authorities, foreign governments etc.) where the claim form is to be served—
    (a) in a country of which English is an official language; or
    (b) on a British subject,
unless a Civil Procedure Convention expressly requires a translation.

(5) The claimant is not required to file a translation of a claim form filed under rule 6.27 (service on State) where English is an official language of the State where the claim form is to be served.

Undertaking to be responsible for expenses of the Foreign and Commonwealth Office

A32–30   **6.29** Every request for service filed under rule 6.26 (service through judicial authorities, or governments etc.) or rule 6.27 (service on State) must contain an undertaking by the person making the request—

    (a) to be responsible for all expenses incurred by the Foreign and Commonwealth Office foreign judicial authority; and

    (b) to pay those expenses to the Foreign and Commonwealth Office or foreign judicial authority on being informed of the amount.

Service of documents other than the claim form

6.30 (1) Where an application notice is to be served out of the jurisdiction **A32–31** under this Section of this Part—

    (a) rules 6.21(4), 6.22 and 6.23 do not apply; and

    (b) where the person on whom the application notice has been served is not a party to proceedings in the jurisdiction in which the application is made, that person may make application to the court under rule 11(1) as if he were a defendant and rule 11(2)does not apply.

(Rule 6.21(4) provides that an order giving permission to serve a claim form out of the jurisdiction must specify the periods within which the defendant may (a) file an acknowledgment of service, (b) file or serve an admission, and (c) file a defence)

(Rule 6.22 provides rules for the period for acknowledging service or admitting the claim where the claim form is served out of the jurisdiction under rule 6.19)

(Rule 6.23 provides rules for the period for filing a defence where the claim form is served out of the the jurisdiction under rule 6.19)

(The practice direction supplementing this Section of this Part provides that where an application notice is to be served out of the jurisdiction in accordance with this Section Part, the court must have regard to the country in which the application notice is to be served setting the date for the hearing of the application and giving any direction about service of the respondent's evidence)

(Rule 11(1) provides that a defendant may make an application to the court to dispute the court's jurisdiction to try the claim or argue that the court should not exercise its jurisdiction. Rule 11(2) provides that a defendant who wishes to make such an application must first file an acknowledgment of service in accordance with Part 10)

(2) Unless paragraph (3) applies, where the permission of the court is required for a claim to be served out of the jurisdiction the permission of the court must also be obtained for service out of the jurisdiction of any other document to be served in the proceedings.

(3) Where—

    (a) the court gives permission for a claim form to be served out of the jurisdiction; and

    (b) the claim form states that particulars of claim are to follow, the permission of the court is required to serve the particulars of claim out of the jurisdiction.

Proof of service

6.31 Where—   **A32–32**

    (a) a hearing is fixed when the claim is issued;

    (b) the claim form is served on a defendant out of the jurisdiction; and

    (c) that defendant does not appear at the hearing,

the claimant may take no further steps against that defendant until the claimant files written evidence showing that the claim form has been duly served.

PRACTICE DIRECTION—SERVICE

This Practice Direction supplements CPR Part 6

Methods of service

1.1 The various methods of service are set out in rule 6.2.   **A32–33**

1.2 The following provisions apply to the specific methods of service referred to.

Service by non-electronic means

Service by Document Exchange

A32–34 **2.1** Service by document exchange (DX) may take place only where:
(1) the party's address for service includes a numbered box at a DX, or
(2) the writing paper of the party who is to be served or of his legal representative sets out the box number, and
(3) the party or his legal representative has not indicated in writing that they are unwilling to accept service by DX.
2.2 Service by DX is effected, unless the contrary is proved, by leaving the document addressed to the numbered box:
(1) at the DX of the party who is to be served, or
(2) at a DX which sends documents to that party's DX every business day.

Service by electronic means

Service by Facsimile

A32–35 **3.1** Subject to the provisions of paragraph 3.2 below, where a document is to be served by facsimile (fax):
(1) the party who is to be served or his legal representative must previously have indicated in writing to the party serving—
    (a) that he is willing to accept service by fax, and
    (b) the fax number to which it should be sent.
(2) if the party on whom the document is to be served is acting by a legal representative, the fax must be sent to the legal representative's business address, and
(3) a fax number—
    (a) provided in writing expressly for the purpose of accepting service where the party to be served is acting in person, or
    (b) set out on the writing paper of the legal representative of the party who is to be served, or
    (c) set out on a statement of case or a response to a claim filed with the court,
shall be taken as sufficient written indication for the purposes of paragraph 3.1(1).
3.2 A legal representative's business address must be within the jurisdiction and is the physical location of his office. Where an electronic address or identification is given in conjuction with the business address, the electronic address will be deemed to be at the business address.
3.3 Service by other electronic means may take place only where:
(1) the party serving the document and the party on whom it is to be served are both acting by legal representative,
(2) the document is served at the legal representative's business address, and
(3) the legal representative who is to be served has previously expressly indicated in writing to the party serving his willingness to accept service by this means and has provided—
    (a) his e-mail address, or
    (b) other electronic identification such as an ISDN or other telephonic link number.
3.4 Where a document is served by fax or other electronic means, the party serving the document is not required in addition to send a copy by post or

document exchange, but if he does not do so and the document is proved not to have been received then the court may, on any application arising out of that non-receipt, take account of the fact that a hard copy was not sent.

Service on certain individuals

Personal service on partners

4.1 Where partners are sued in the name of a partnership, service should be in **A32–36** accordance with rule 6.4(5) and the table set out in rule 6.5(5) where it refers to an "individual who is suing or being sued in the name of a firm".

4.2 A claim form or particulars of claim which are served by leaving them with a person at the principal or last known place of business of the partnership, must at the same time have served with them a notice as to whether that person is being served:

(1) as a partner,

(2) as a person having control or management of the partnership business, or

(3) as both.

Service on Members of H.M. Forces and United States Air Force

Omitted.

A32–37

Service generally

Personal Service on a Company or other corporation

6.1 Personal service on a registered company or corporation in accordance **A32–38** with rule 6.4(4) service effected by leaving a document with "a person holding a senior position".

6.2 Each of the following persons is a person holding a senior position:

(1) in respect of a registered company or corporation, a director, the treasurer, secretary, chief executive, manager or other officer of the company or corporation, and

(2) in respect of a corporation which is not a registered company, in addition to those persons set out in (1), the mayor, chairman, president, town clerk or similar officer of the corporation.

Change of address

7 A party or his legal representative who changes his address for service shall **A32–39** give notice in writing of the change as soon as it has taken place to the court and every other party.

Service by the court

8.1 Where the court effects service of a document in accordance with rule **A32–40** 6.3(1) and (2), the method will normally be by first class post.

8.2 Where a party receives a notice of non-service of a document by the court, he should take steps to effect service of the document himself as the court is under no further duty to effect service.

8.3 Where the court effects service of a claim form, delivers a defence to a claimant or notifies a claimant that the defendant has filed an acknowledgment of service, the court will also serve or deliver a copy of any notice of funding that has been filed provided—

(a) it was filed at the same time as the claim form, defence or acknowledg-ment of service, and

(b) copies were provided for service.

Content of Evidence

The following applications relating to service require evidence in support

A32–41– 46   **9.1** An application for an order for service by an alternative method should be supported by evidence stating:

(1) the reason an order for an alternative method of service is sought, and

(2) what steps have been taken to serve by other permitted means.

9.2 An application for service of a claim form relating to a contract on the agent of a principal who is overseas should be supported by evidence setting out:

(1) full details of the contract and that it was entered into within the jurisdiction with or through an agent who is either an individual residing or carrying on business within the jurisdiction, or a registered company or corporation having a registered office or a place of business within the jurisdiction,

(2) that the principal for whom the agent is acting was, at the time the contract was entered into and is at the time of making the application, neither an individual, registered company or corporation as described in (1) above, and

(3) why service out of the jurisdiction cannot be effected.

PRACTICE DIRECTION 6B

SERVICE OUT OF THE JURISDICTION

This Practice Direction Supplements Section III of Part 6

Service out of the jurisdiction where permission of the Court is not required

A32–47   **1.1** The usual form of words of the statement required by Rule 6.19(3) should be:—

"I state that the High Court of England and Wales has power under the Civil Jurisdiction and Judgments Act 1982 to hear this claim and that no proceedings are pending between the parties in Scotland, Northern Ireland or another Convention territory of any contracting state as defined by section 1 (3) of the Act".

1.2 However, in proceedings to which Rule 6.19(1)(b)(ii) applies, the statement should be:—

"I state that the High Court of England and Wales has power under the Civil Jurisdiction and Judgments Act 1982, the claim having as its object rights in rem in immovable property or tenancies in immovable property (or otherwise in accordance with the provisions of Article 16 of Schedule 1, 3C or 4 to that Act) to which Article 16 of Schedule 1, 3C or 4 to that Act applies, to hear the claim and that no proceedings are pending between the parties in Scotland, Northern Ireland or another Convention territory of any contracting state as defined by Section 1 (3) of the Act".

1.3 And in proceedings to which Rule 6.19(1)(b)(iii) applies, the statement should be:—

1338

"I state that the High Court of England and Wales has power under the Civil Jurisdiction and Judgments Act 1982, the defendant being a party to an agreement conferring jurisdiction to which Article 17 of Schedule 1, 3C or 4 to that Act applies, to hear the claim and that no proceedings are pending between the parties in Scotland, Northern Ireland or another Convention territory of any contracting state as defined by Section 1 (3) of the Act".

1.4 A claim form appearing to be for service on a defendant under the provisions of Rule 6.19 which does not include a statement in the form of 1.1, 1.2 or 1.3 above will be marked on issue "Not for service out of the jurisdiction".

1.5 Where a claim form is served without particulars of claim, it must be accompanied by a copy of Form N1C (notes for defendants).

Service out of the jurisdiction where permission is required

Documents to be filed under Rule 6.26(2)(d)

2.1 A complete set of the following documents must be provided for each **A32–48** party to be served out of the jurisdiction:

(1) A copy of particulars of claim if not already incorporated in or attached to the claim.

(2) A duplicate of the claim form of the particulars of claim and of any documents accompanying the claim and of any translation required by Rule 6.28.

(3) Forms for responding to the claim;

(4) Any translation required under Rule 6.28 and paragraphs 4.1 and 4.2, in duplicate.

2.2 The documents to be served in certain countries require legalisation and the Foreign Process Section (Room E02), Royal Courts of Justice will advise on request. Some countries require legislation and some require a formal letter of request, see Form No. 34 to Table 2 of Practice Direction to Part 4 which must be signed by the Senior Master of the Queen's Bench Division irrespective of the Division of the High Court or any county court in which the order was made.

Service in Scotland, Northern Ireland, the Channel Islands, the Isle of Man, Commonwealth countries, United Kingdom Overseas Territories and the Republic of Ireland

3.1 The requirements of Section III of Part 6, do not apply to the countries **A32–49** listed in Rule 6.25(4) and service should be effected by the claimant or his agent direct except in the case of a Commonwealth State where the judicial authorities have required service to be in accordance with Rule 6.24(1)(b)(i). These are presently Malta and Singapore.

3.2 For the purposes of Rule 6.25(4)(c), the following countries are United Kingdom Overseas Territories:—

(a) Anguilla;
(b) Bermuda;
(c) British Antarctic Territory;
(d) British Indian Ocean Territory;
(e) Cayman Islands;
(f) Falklands Islands and Dependencies;
(g) Gibraltar;
(h) Monserrat;
(i) Pitcairn, Henderson, Ducie and Oeno;
(j) St. Helena and Dependencies;
(k) South Georgia and South Sandwich Islands;

    (l) Sovereign Base Areas of Akrotiri and Dhekalia;
    (m) Turks and Caicos Islands; and
    (n) Virgin Islands.

Translations

A32–50   **4.1** Rule 6.28 applies to particulars of claim not included in a claim form as well as to claim forms.

4.2 Where a translation of a claim form is required under Rule 6.28, the claimant must also file a translation of all the forms that will accompany the claim form.

(It should be noted that English is not an official language in the Province of Quebec).

Service with the permission of the Court under certain Acts

A32–51   **5.1** Rule 6.20(18) provides that a claim form may be served out of the jurisdiction with the Court's permission if the claim is made under an enactment specified in the relevant Practice Direction.

5.2 These enactments are:
    (1) The Nuclear Installations Act 1965,
    (2) The Social Security Contributions and Benefits Act 1992,
    (3) The Directive of the Council of the European Communities dated 15 March 1976 No. 76/308/EEC, where service is to be effected in a member state of the European Union,
    (4) The Drug Trafficking Offences Act 1994,
    (5) The Financial Services Act 1986,
    (6) The Banking Act 1987,
    (7) Part VI of the Criminal Justice Act 1988,
    (8) The Immigration (Carriers' Liability) Act 1987,
    (9) Part II of the Immigration and Asylum Act 1999,
    (10) Schedule 2 to the Immigration Act 1971.

5.3 Under the State Immunity Act 1978, the foreign state being served is allowed an additional two months over the normal period for filing an acknowledgment of service or defence or for filing or serving an admission allowed under paragraphs 7.3 and 7.4.

Service of petitions, application notices and orders

A32–52   **6.1** The provisions of Section III of Part 6 (special provisions about service out of the jurisdiction) apply to service out of the jurisdiction of a petition, application notice or order.

(Rule 6.30(1) contains special provisions relating to application notices).

6.2 Where an application notice is to be served out of the jurisdiction in accordance with Section III of Part 6 the Court must have regard to the country in which the application notice is to be served in setting the date for the hearing of the application and giving any direction about service of the respondent's evidence.

Where the permission of the Court is required for a claim form to be served out of the jurisdiction the permission of the Court, unless rule 6.30(3) applies, must also be obtained for service out of the jurisdiction of any other document to be served in the proceedings and the provisions of this Practice Direction will, so far as applicable to that other document, apply.

When particulars of claim are served out of the jurisdiction any statement as to the period for responding to the claim contained in any of the forms required by Rule 7.8 to accompany the particulars of claim must specify the period prescribed under Rule 6.22 or 6.23 or (as the case may be) by the order permitting service out of the jurisdiction (see Rule 6.21(4)).

Period for responding to a claim form

A32–53   **7.1** Where a claim form has been served out of the jurisdiction without permission under Rule 6.19—

(1) Rule 6.22 sets out the period for filing an acknowledgement of service or filing or serving an admission;

(2) Rule 6.23 sets out the period for filing a defence.

7.2 Where an order grants permission to serve a claim form out of the jurisdiction, the periods within which the defendant may—

(1) file an acknowledgment of service;

(2) file or serve an admission;

(3) file a defence,

will be calculated in accordance with paragraphs 7.3 and 7.4 having regard to the Table below.

(Rule 6.21 (4) requires an order giving permission for a claim form to be served out of the jurisdiction to specify the period within which the defendant may respond to the claim form).

7.3 The period for filing an acknowledgment of service under Part 10 or filing or serving an admission under Part 14 is—

(1) where the defendant is served with a claim form which states that particulars of claim are to follow, the number of days listed in the Table after service of the particulars of claim; and

(2) in any other case, the number of days listed in the Table after service of the claim form.

For example: where a defendant has been served with a claim form (accompanied by particulars of claim) in the Bahamas, the period for acknowledging service or admitting the claim is 22 days after service.

7.4 The period for filing a defence under Part 15 is—

(1) the number of days listed in the Table after service of the particulars of claim, or

(2) where the defendant has filed an acknowledgment of service, the number of days listed in the Table plus an additional 14 days after the service of the particulars of claim.

For example, where a defendant has been served with particulars of claim in Gibraltar and has acknowledged service, the period for filing a defence is 45 days after service of the particulars of claim.

Period for responding to an application notice

8.1 Where an application notice or order needs to be served out of the jurisdiction, the period for responding to service is 7 days less than the number of days listed in the Table. **A32–54**

Civil Jurisdiction and Judgment Act 1982

9.1 The following countries are parties to this Act:— **A32–55**

Austria	Italy
Belgium	Luxembourg
Denmark	Netherlands
France	Norway
Finland	Portugal
Germany	Scotland
Gibraltar	Spain
Greece	Switzerland
Iceland	Sweden
Ireland	

Address for service & further information

10.1 A defendant is required by Rule 6.5(2) to give an address for service within the jurisdiction. **A32–56**

10.2 Further information concerning service out of the jurisdiction can be obtained from the Foreign Process Section, Room E02, Royal Courts of Justice, Strand, London WC2A 2LL (telephone 020 7936 6691).

Table

A32–57

Place or country	number of days
Abu Dhabi	22
Afghanistan	23
Albania	25
Algeria	22
Angola	22
Anguilla	31
Antigua	23
Antilles (Netherlands)	31
Argentina	22
Armenia	21
Ascension	31
Australia	25
Austria	21
Azores	23
Bahamas	22
Bahrain	22
Balearic Islands	21
Bangladesh	23
Barbados	23
Belarus	21
Belgium	21
Belize	23
Benin	25
Bermuda	31
Bhutan	28
Bolivia	23
Bosnia-Herzegovina	21
Botswana	23
Brazil	22
Brunei	25
Bulgaria	23
Burkina Faso	23
Burma	23
Burundi	22
Cameroon	22
Canada	22
Canary Islands	22
Cape Verde Islands	25
Caroline Islands	31
Cayman Islands	31
Central African Republic	25
Chad	25
Chile	22
China	24
Christmas Island	27
Cocos (Keeling) Islands	41
Colombia	22
Comoros	23
Congo (People's Republic)	25
Corsica	21
Costa Rica	23
Croatia	21
Cuba	24
Cyprus	31
Cyrenaica (see Libya)	21

Korea (South)	24
Kuwait	22
Laos	30
Latvia	21
Lebanon	22
Lesotho	23
Liberia	22
Libya	21
Liechtenstein	21
Lithuania	21
Luxembourg	21
Macau	31
Macedonia	21
Madagascar	23
Madeira	31
Malawi	23
Malaya	24
Maldive Islands	26
Mali	25
Malta	21
Mariana Islands	26
Marshall Islands	32
Mauritania	23
Mauritius	22
Mexico	23
Moldova	21
Monaco	21
Montserrat	31
Morocco	22
Mozambique	23
Nauru Island	36
Nepal	23
Netherlands	21
Nevis	24
New Caledonia	31
New Hebrides (now Vanuatu)	29
New Zealand	26
New Zealand Island Territories	50
Nicaragua	24
Niger (Republic of)	25
Nigeria	22
Norfolk Island	31
Norway	21
Oman (Sultanate of)	22
Pakistan	23
Panama (Republic of)	26
Papua New Guinea	26
Paraguay	22
Peru	22
Philippines	23
Pitcairn Island	31
Poland	21
Portugal	21
Portuguese Timor	31
Puerto Rico	23
Qatar	23
Reunion	31

PART 20

COUNTERCLAIMS AND OTHER ADDITIONAL CLAIMS

A32–58 CONTENTS

Purpose of Part 20

A32–59 **20.1** The purpose of Part 20 is to enable Part 20 claims to be managed in the most convenient and effective manner.

Meaning of "Part 20 claim"

A32–60 **20.2** (1) A Part 20 claim is any claim other than a claim by a claimant against a defendant and includes:

(a) a counterclaim by a defendant against the claimant or against the claimant and some other person;

(b) a claim by a defendant against any person (whether or not already a party) for contribution or indemnity or some other remedy; and

(c) where a Part 20 claim has been made against a person who is not already a party, any claim made by that person against any other person (whether or not already a party).

1346

(2) In this Part "Part 20 claimant" means a person who makes a Part 20 claim.

Part 20 claim to be treated as a claim for the purposes of the rules

20.3 (1) A Part 20 claim shall be treated as if it were a claim for the purposes of **A32–61** these Rules, except as provided by this Part.

(2) The following rules do not apply to Part 20 claims—

    (a) rules 7.5 and 7.6 (time within which a claim form may be served);

    (b) rule 16.3(5) (statement of value where claim to be issued in the High Court); and

    (c) Part 26 (case management—preliminary stage).

(3) Part 12 (default judgment) applies to a Part 20 claim only if it is a counterclaim.

(4) With the exception of—

    (a) rules 14.1(1) and 14.1(2) (which provide that a party may admit the truth of another party's case in writing); and

    (b) rule 14.3(1) (admission by notice in writing—application for judgment), which apply to all Part 20 claims, Part 14 (admissions) applies to a Part 20 claim only if it is a counterclaim.

(Rule 12.3.(2) sets out how to obtain judgment in default of defence where the Part 20 claim is a counterclaim against the claimant, and rule 20.11 makes special provision for default judgment some categories of Part 20 claims.)

Defendant's counterclaim against the claimant

20.4 (1) A defendant may make a counterclaim against a claimant by filing **A32–62** particulars of the counterclaim.

(2) A defendant may make a counterclaim against a claimant—

    (a) without the court's permission if he files it with his defence; or

    (b) at any other time with the court's permission.

(Part 15 makes provision for a defence to a claim and applies to a defence to a counterclaim by virtue of rule 20.3)

(3) Part 10 (acknowledgment of service) does not apply to a claimant who wishes to defend a counterclaim.

Counterclaim against a person other than the claimant

20.5 (1) A defendant who wishes to counterclaim against a person other than **A32–63** the claimant must apply to the court for an order that that person be added as defendant to the counterclaim.

(2) An application for an order under paragraph (1) may be made without notice unless the court directs otherwise.

(3) Where the court makes an order under paragraph (1), it will give directions as to the management of the case.

Defendant's claim for contribution or indemnity from co-defendant

20.6 A defendant who has filed an acknowledgment of service or a defence **A32–64** may make a Part 20 claim for contribution or indemnity against another defendant by—

    (a) filing a notice containing a statement of the nature and grounds of his claim; and

    (b) serving that notice on the other defendant.

Procedure for making any other Part 20 claim

20.7 (1) This rule applies to any Part 20 claim except—   **A32–65**

    (a) a counterclaim; and

    (b) a claim for contribution or indemnity made in accordance with rule 20.6.

(2) A Part 20 claim is made when the court issues a Part 20 claim form.

(3) A defendant may make a Part 20 claim—

    (a) without the court's permission if the Part 20 claim is issued before or at the same time as he files his defence;

    (b) at any other time with the court's permission.

(Rule 15.4 sets out the period for filing a defence)

(4) Particulars of a Part 20 claim must be contained in or served with the Part 20 claim.

(5) An application for permission to make a Part 20 claim may be made without notice, unless the court directs otherwise.

Service of a Part 20 claim form

A32–66   **20.8** (1) Where a Part 20 claim may be made without the court's permission, the Part 20 claim form must—

    (a) in the case of a counterclaim, be served on every other party when a copy of the defence is served;

    (b) in the case of any other Part 20 claim, be served on the person against whom it is made within 14 days after the date on which the party making the Part 20 claim files his defence.

(2) Paragraph (1) does not apply to a claim for contribution or indemnity made in accordance with rule 20.6.

(3) Where the court gives permission to make a Part 20 claim it will at the same time give direction as to the service of the Part 20 claim.

Matters relevant to question of whether a Part 20 claim should be separate from main claim

A32–67   **20.9** (1) This rule applies where the court is considering whether to—

    (a) permit a Part 20 claim to be made;

    (b) dismiss a Part 20 claim; or

    (c) require a Part 20 claim to be dealt with separately from the claim by the claimant against the defendant.

(Rule 3.1(2)(e) and (j) deal respectively with the court's power to order that part of proceedings be dealt with as separate proceedings and to decide the order in which issues are to be tried)

(2) The matters to which the court may have regard include—

    (a) the connection between the Part 20 claim and the claim made by the claimant against the defendant;

    (b) whether the Part 20 claimant is seeking substantially the same remedy which some other person is claiming from him; and

    (c) whether the Part 20 claimant wants the court to decide any question connected with the subject-matter of the proceedings—

        (i) not only between existing parties but also between existing parties and a person not already party; or

        (ii) against an existing party not only in a capacity in which he is already a party but also in some further capacity.

Effect of service of a Part 20 claim

A32–68   **20.10** (1) A person on whom a Part 20 claim is served becomes a party to the proceedings if he is not a party already.

(2) When a Part 20 claim is served on an existing party for the purpose of requiring the court to decide a question against that party in a further capacity, that party also becomes a party in the further capacity specified in the Part 20 claim.

Special provisions relating to default judgment on a Part 20 claim other than a counterclaim or a contribution or indemnity notice

A32–69   **20.11** (1) This rule applies if—

    (a) the Part 20 claim is not—
        (i) a counterclaim; or
        (ii) a claim by a defendant for contribution or indemnity against
           another defendant under rule 20.6 and
    (b) the party against whom a Part 20 claim is made fails to file an
        acknowledgment of service or defence in respect of the Part 20 claim.
  (2) The party against whom the Part 20 claim is made—
    (a) is deemed to admit the Part 20 claim, and is bound by any judgment or
        decision in the main proceedings in so far as it is relevant to any matter
        arising in the Part 20 claim;
    (b) subject to paragraph (3), if default judgment under Part 12 is given
        against the Part 20 claimant, the Part 20 claimant may obtain judgment
        in respect of the Part 20 claim by filing a request in the relevant practice
        form.
  (3) A Part 20 claimant may not enter judgment under paragraph (2)(b) without
the court's permission if—
    (a) he has not satisfied the default judgment which has been given against
        him; or
    (b) he wishes to obtain judgment for any remedy other than a contribution
        or indemnity.
  (4) An application for the court's permission under paragraph (3) may be
made without notice unless the court directs otherwise.
  (5) The court may at any time set aside or vary a judgment entered under
paragraph (2)(b).

Procedural steps on service of a Part 20 claim form on a non-party

  20.12 (1) Where a Part 20 claim form is served on a person who is not already **A32–70**
a party it must be accompanied by—
    (a) a form for defending the claim;
    (b) a form for admitting the claim;
    (c) a form for acknowledging service; and
    (d) a copy of—
        (i) every statement of case which has already been served in the
           proceedings; and
        (ii) such other documents as the court may direct.
  (2) A copy of the Part 20 claim form must be served on every existing party.

Case management where there is a defence to a Part 20 claim form

  20.13 (1) Where a defence is filed to a Part 20 claim the court must consider the **A32–71**
future conduct of the proceedings and give appropriate directions.
  (2) In giving directions under paragraph (1) the court must ensure that, so far
as practicable, the Part 20 claim and the main claim are managed together.
  (CCR Order 42, in Schedule 2, makes provision for a Part 20 claim against the
Crown where the Crown is not a party)

PRACTICE DIRECTION—COUNTERCLAIMS AND OTHER PART 20 CLAIMS

This Practice Direction supplements CPR Part 20

A Part 20 claim is any claim other than the claim by the claimant against the
defendant.

Cases where court's permission to make a Part 20 claim is required

  1.1 Rules 20.4(2)(b), 20.5(1) and 20.7(3)(b) set out the circumstances in which **A32–72**
the court's permission will be needed for making a Part 20 claim.

1.2 Where an application is made for permission to make a Part 20 claim the application notice should be filed together with a copy of the proposed Part 20 claim.

Applications for permission to issue a Part 20 claim

A32–73 **2.1** An application for permission to make a Part 20 claim must be supported by evidence stating:

(1) the stage which the action has reached,

(2) the nature of the claim to be made by the Part 20 claimant or details of the question or issue which needs to be decided,

(3) a summary of the facts on which the Part 20 claim is based, and

(4) the name and address of the proposed Part 20 defendant.

(For further information regarding evidence see the practice direction which supplements Part 32).

2.2 Where delay has been a factor contributing to the need to apply for permission to make a Part 20 claim an explanation of the delay should be given in evidence.

2.3 Where possible the applicant should provide a timetable of the action to date.

2.4 Rules 20.5(2) and 20.7(5) allow applications to be made to the court without notice unless the court otherwise directs.

General

A32–74 **3** The Civil Procedure Rules apply generally to Part 20 claims as if they were claims. Parties should be aware that the provisions relating to failure to respond will apply.

Statement of Truth

A32–75 **4.1** The contents of a Part 20 claim should be verified by a statement of truth. Part 22 requires a statement of case to be verified by a statement of truth.

4.2 The form of the statement of truth should be as follows: "[I believe][the [Part 20 claimant]* believes] that the facts stated in this statement of case are true, *(For the purpose of this practice direction the Part 20 claimant means any party making a Part 20 claim.)

4.3 Attention is drawn to rule 32.14 which sets out the consequences of verifying a statement of case containing a false statement without an honest belief in its truth.

(For information regarding statements of truth see Part 22 and the practice direction which supplements it.)

Case management where there is a Part 20 defence

A32–76 **5.1** Where the Part 20 defendant files a defence, other than to a counterclaim, the court will arrange a hearing to consider case management of the Part 20 claim.

5.2 The court will give notice of the hearing to each party likely to be affected by any order made at the the hearing.

5.3 At the hearing the court may:

(1) treat the hearing as a summary judgment hearing,

(2) order that the Part 20 proceedings be dismissed,

(3) give directions about the way any claim, question or issue set out in or arising from the Part 20 claim should be dealt with,

(4) give directions as to the part, if any, the Part 20 defendant will take at the trial of the claim,

(5) give directions about the extent to which the Part 20 defendant is to be bound by any judgment decision to be made in the claim.

5.4 The court may make any of the orders in 5.3(1) to (5) either before or after any judgment in the claim has been entered by the claimant against the defendant.

Form of counterclaim

6.1 Where a defendant to a claim serves a counterclaim under this Part, the **A32–77** defence and counterclaim should normally form one document with the counterclaim following on from the defence.

6.2 Where a claimant serves a reply and a defence to counterclaim, the reply and the defence to the counterclaim should normally form one document with the defence to counterclaim following from the reply.

Titles of proceedings where there are Part 20 claims

7.1 The title of every Part 20 claim should include: **A32–78**
(1) the full name of each party, and
(2) his status in the proceedings (e.g. claimant, defendant, Part 20 claimant, Part 20 defendant, etc. For example: AB Claimant CD Defendant/Part 20 Claimant EF Part 20 Defendant

7.2 Where a defendant makes a counterclaim not only against the claimant but also against a non-party the title should show this as follows: AB Claimant/Part 20 Defendant CD Defendant/Part 20 Claimant and XY Part 20 Defendant

7.3 Where there is more than one Part 20 claim, the parties to the first Part 20 claim should be described as "Part 20 Claimant (1st claim)" and "Part 20 Defendant (1st claim)", the parties to the second Part 20 claim should be described as "Part 20 Claimant (2nd claim)" and "Part 20 Defendant (2nd claim)", and so on. For example: AB Claimant and Part 20 Defendant (2nd claim) CD Defendant and Part 20 Claimant (1st claim) EF Part 20 Defendant (1st claim) and Part 20 Claimant (2nd claim) GH Part 20 Defendant (2nd claim)

7.4 Where the full name of a party is lengthy it must appear in the title but thereafter in the statement of case it may be identified by an abbreviation such as initials or a recognised shortened name.

7.5 Where a party to proceedings has more than one status eg. Claimant and Part 20 Defendant (2nd claim) or Part 20 Defendant (1st claim) and Part 20 Claimant (2nd claim) the combined status must appear in the title but thereafter it may be convenient to refer to the party by name e.g. Mr Smith or, if paragraph 7.4 applies, by initials or a shortened name.

7.6 Paragraph 4 of the practice direction supplementing Part 7 contains further directions regarding the title to proceedings.

PART 25

A32–79

INTERIM REMEDIES AND SECURITY FOR COSTS

CONTENTS

1. INTERIM REMEDIES

II. Security for Costs

I. Interim Remedies

Orders for interim remedies

A32–80   **25.1** (1) The court may grant the following interim remedies—

(a) an interim injunction;

(b) an interim declaration;

(c) an order—

  (i) for the detention, custody or preservation of relevant property;

  (ii) for the inspection of relevant property;

  (iii) for the taking of a sample of relevant property;

  (iv) for the carrying out of an experiment on or with relevant property;

  (v) for the sale of relevant property which is of a perishable nature or which for any other good reason it is desirable to sell quickly; and

  (vi) for the payment of income from relevant property until a claim is decided;

(d) an order authorising a person to enter any land or building in the possession of a party to proceedings for the purposes of carrying out an order under sub-paragraph (c);

(e) an order under section 4 of the Torts (Interference with Goods) Act 1977 to deliver up goods;

(f) an order (referred to as a "freezing injunction")—

  (i) restraining a party from removing from the jurisdiction assets located there; or

  (ii) restraining a party from dealing with any assets whether located within the jurisdiction or not.

(g) an order directing a party to provide information about the location of relevant property or assets or to provide information about relevant property or assets which are or may be the subject of an application for a freezing injunction;

(h) an order (referred to as a "search order") under section 7 of the Civil Procedure Act 1997 (order requiring a party to admit another party to premises for the purpose of preserving evidence etc.);

  (i) an order under section 33 of the Supreme Court Act 1981 or section 52 of the County Courts Act 1984 (order for disclosure of documents or inspection of property before a claim has been made);

(j) an order under section 34 of the Supreme Court Act 1981 or section 53 of the County Courts Act 1984 (order in certain proceedings for disclosure of documents or inspection of property against a non-party);

(k) an order (referred to as an order for interim payment) under rule 25.6 for payment by a defendant on account of any damages, debt or other sum (except costs) which the court may hold the defendant liable to pay;

 (l) an order for a specified fund to be paid into court or otherwise secured, where there is a dispute over a party's right to the fund;

 (m) an order permitting a party seeking to recover personal property to pay money into court pending the outcome of the proceedings and directing that, if he does so, the property shall be given up to him; and

 (n) an order directing a party to prepare and file accounts relating to the dispute.

(Rule 34.2 provides for the court to issue a witness summons requiring a witness to produce documents to the court at the hearing or on such date as the court may direct)

(2) In paragraph (1)(c) and (g), "relevant property" means property (including land) which is the subject of a claim or as to which any question may arise on a claim.

(3) The fact that a particular kind of interim remedy is not listed in paragraph (1) does not affect any power that the court may have to grant that remedy.

(4) The court may grant an interim remedy whether or not there has been a claim for a final remedy of that kind.

Time when an order for an interim remedy may be made

25.2 (1) An order for an interim remedy may be made at any time, including— **A32–81**

 (a) before proceedings are started; and

 (b) after judgment has been given.

(Rule 7.2 provides that proceedings are started when the court issues a claim form)

(2) However—

 (a) paragraph (1) is subject to any rule, practice direction or other enactment which provides otherwise;

 (b) the court may grant an interim remedy before a claim has been made only if—

  (i) the matter is urgent; or

  (ii) it is otherwise desirable to do so in the interests of justice; and

 (c) unless the court otherwise orders, a defendant may not apply for any of the orders listed in rule 25.1(1) before he has filed either an acknowledgement of service or a defence.

(Part 10 provides for filing an acknowledgement of service and Part 15 for filing a defence)

(3) Where the court grants an interim remedy before a claim has been commenced, it may give directions requiring a claim to be commenced.

(4) In particular, the court need not direct that a claim be commenced where the application is made under section 33 of the Supreme Court Act 1981 or section 52 of the County Courts Act 1984 (order for disclosure, inspection etc. before commencement of a claim).

How to apply for an interim remedy

25.3 (1) The court may grant an interim remedy on an application made **A32–82** without notice if it appears to the court that there are good reasons for not giving notice.

(2) An application for an interim remedy must be supported by evidence, unless the court orders otherwise.

(3) If the applicant makes an application without giving notice, the evidence in support of the application must state the reasons why notice has not been given.

(Part 3 lists general powers of the court)

(Part 23 contains general rules about making an application)

Application for an interim remedy where there is no related claim

25.4 (1) This rule applies where a party wishes to apply for an interim remedy **A32–83** but—

(a) the remedy is sought in relation to proceedings which are taking place, or will take place, outside the jurisdiction; or

(b) the application is made under section 33 of the Supreme Court Act 1981 or section 52 of the County Courts Act 1984 (order for disclosure, inspection etc. before commencement) before the claim has been commenced.

(2) An application under this rule must be made in accordance with the general rules about applications contained in Part 23.

(The following provisions are also relevant—

- Rule 25.5 (inspection of property before commencement or against a non-party)
- Rule 31.16 (orders for disclosure of documents before proceedings start)
- Rule 31.17 (orders for disclosure of documents against a person not a party))

Inspection of property before commencement or against a non-party

A32–84   25.5 (1) This rule applies where a person makes an application under—

(a) section 33(1) of the Supreme Court Act 1981 or section 52(1) of the County Courts Act 1984 (inspection etc. of property before commencement);

(b) section 34(3) of the Supreme Court Act 1981 or section 53(3) of the County Courts Act 1984 (inspection etc. of property against a non-party).

(2) The evidence in support of such an application must show, if practicable by reference to any statement of case prepared in relation to the proceedings or anticipated proceedings, that the property—

(a) is or may become the subject matter of such proceedings; or

(b) is relevant to the issues that will arise in relation to such proceedings.

(3) A copy of the application notice and a copy of the evidence in support must be served on—

(a) the person against whom the order is sought; and

(b) in relation to an application under section 34(3) of the Supreme Court Act 1981 or section 53 (3) of the County Courts Act 1984, every party to the proceedings other than the applicant.

Interim payments—general procedure

A32–85   25.6 (1) The claimant may not apply for an order for an interim payment before the end of the period for filing an acknowledgement of service applicable to the defendant against whom the application is made.

(Rule 10.3 sets out the period for filing an acknowledgement of service.)

(Rule 25.1(1)(k) defines an interim payment.)

(2) The claimant may make more than one application for an order for an interim payment.

(3) A copy of an application notice for an order for an interim payment must—

(a) be served at least 14 days before the hearing of the application; and

(b) be supported by evidence.

(4) If the respondent to an application for an order for an interim payment wishes to rely on written evidence at the hearing, he must—

(a) file the written evidence; and

(b) serve copies on every other party to the application, at least 7 days before the hearing of the application.

(5) If the applicant wishes to rely on written evidence in reply, he must—

(a) file the written evidence; and

(b) serve a copy on the respondent, at least 3 days before the hearing of the application.

(6) This rule does not require written evidence—

(a) to be filed if it has already been filed; or

(b) to be served on a party on whom it has already been served.

(7) The court may order an interim payment in one sum or in instalments.

(Part 23 contains general rules about applications)

Interim payments—conditions to be satisfied and matters to be taken into account

25.7 (1) The court may make an order for an interim payment only if—   **A32–86**

(a) the defendant against whom the order is sought has admitted liability to pay damages or some other sum of money to the claimant;

(b) the claimant has obtained judgment against that defendant for damages to be assessed or for a sum of money (other than costs) to be assessed;

(c) except where paragraph (3) applies, it is satisfied that, if the claim went to trial, the claimant would obtain judgment for a substantial amount of money (other than costs) against the defendant from whom he is seeking an order for an interim payment; or

(d) the following conditions are satisfied—

(i) the claimant is seeking an order for possession of land (whether or not any other order is sought); and

(ii) the court is satisfied that, if the case went to trial, the defendant would be held liable (even if the claim for possession fails) to pay the claimant a sum of money for the defendant's occupation and use of the land while the claim for possession was pending.

(2) In addition, in a claim for personal injuries the court may make an order for an interim payment of damages only if—

(a) the defendant is insured in respect of the claim;

(b) the defendant's liability will be met by—

(i) an insurer under section 151 of the Road Traffic Act 1988; or

(ii) an insurer acting under the Motor Insurers Bureau Agreement, or the Motor Insurers Bureau where it is acting itself; or

(c) the defendant is a public body.

(3) In a claim for personal injuries where there are two or more defendants, the court may make order for the interim payment of damages against any defendant if—

(a) it is satisfied that, if the claim went to trial, the claimant would obtain judgment for substantial damages against at least one of the defendants (even if the court has not yet determined which of them is liable); and

(b) paragraph (2) is satisfied in relation to each of the defendants.

(4) The court must not order an interim payment of more than a reasonable proportion of the like amount of the final judgment.

(5) The court must take into account—

(a) contributory negligence; and

(b) any relevant set-off or counterclaim.

Powers of court where it has made an order for interim payment

25.8 (1) Where a defendant has been ordered to make an interim payment, or **A32–87** has in fact made an interim payment (whether voluntarily or under an order), the court may make an order to adjust the interim payment.

(2) The court may in particular—

(a) order all or part of the interim payment to be repaid;

(b) vary or discharge the order for the interim payment;

(c) order a defendant to reimburse, either wholly or partly, another defendant who has made interim payment.

(3) The court may make an order under paragraph (2)(c) only if—

(a) the defendant to be reimbursed made the interim payment in relation to a claim in respect which he has made a claim against the other defendant for a contribution, indemnity or other remedy; and

(b) where the claim or part to which the interim payment relates has not been discontinued or disposed of, the circumstances are such that the court could make an order for interim payment under rule 25.7.

(4) The court may make an order under this rule without an application by any party if it makes the order when it disposes of the claim or any part of it.

(5) Where—

(a) a defendant has made an interim payment; and

(b) the amount of the payment is more than his total liability under the final judgment or order,

the court may award him interest on the overpaid amount from the date when he made the interim payment.

Restriction on disclosure of an interim payment

A32–88   **25.9** The fact that a defendant has made an interim payment, whether voluntarily or by court order, must not be disclosed to the trial judge until all questions of liability and the amount of money to be awarded have been decided unless the defendant agrees.

Interim injunction to cease if claim is stayed

A32–89   **25.10** If—

(a) the court has granted an interim injunction; and

(b) the claim is stayed other than by agreement between the parties,

the interim injunction shall be set aside unless the court orders that it should continue to have effect even though the claim is stayed.

Interim injunction to cease after 14 days if claim struck out

A32–90   **25.11** (1) If—

(a) the court has granted an interim injunction; and

(b) the claim is struck out under rule 3.7 (sanctions for non-payment of certain fees),

the interim injunction shall cease to have effect 14 days after the date that the claim is struck out unless paragraph (2) applies.

(2) If the claimant applies to reinstate the claim before the interim injunction ceases to have effect under paragraph (1), the injunction shall continue until the hearing of the application unless the court orders otherwise.

II. Security for Costs

Security for costs

A32–91   **25.12** (1) A defendant to any claim may apply under this Section of this Part for security for his costs of the proceedings.

(Part 3 provides for the court to order payment of sums into court in other circumstances. Rule 20.3 provides for this Section of this Part to apply to Part 20 claims)

(2) An application for security for costs must be supported by written evidence.

(3) Where the court makes an order for security for costs, it will—

(a) determine the amount of security; and

(b) direct—

(i) the manner in which; and

(ii) the time within which,

the security must be given.

Conditions to be satisfied

A32–92   **25.13** (1) The court may make an order for security for costs under rule 25.12 if—

(a) it is satisfied, having regard to all the circumstances of the case, that it is just to make such an order; and

(b)   (i) one or more of the conditions in paragraph (2) applies, or

   (ii) an enactment permits the court to require security for costs.

(2) The conditions are—

(a) the claimant is an individual—

   (i) who is ordinarily resident out of the jurisdiction; and

   (ii) is not a person against whom a claim can be enforced under the Brussels Convention and the Lugano Convention, as defined by section 1(1) of the Civil Jurisdiction and Judgment Act 1982;

(b) the claimant is a company or other incorporated body—

   (i) which is ordinarily resident out of the jurisdiction; and

   (ii) is not a body against whom a claim can be enforced under the Brussels Conventions and the Lugano Convention;

(c) the claimant is a company or other body (whether incorporated inside or outside Great Britain) and there is reason to believe that it will be unable to pay the defendant's costs if ordered to do so;

(d) the claimant has changed his address since the claim was commenced with a view to evading the consequences of the litigation;

(e) the claimant failed to give his address in the claim form, or gave an incorrect address in that form;

(f) the claimant is acting as a nominal claimant, other than as a representative claimant under Part 19, and there is reason to believe that he will be unable to pay the defendant's costs if ordered to do so;

(g) the claimant has taken steps in relation to his assets that would make it difficult to enforce an order for costs against him.

(Rule 3.4 allows the court to strike out a statement of case and Part 24 for it to give summary judgment)

Security for costs other than from the claimant

25.14 (1) The defendant may seek an order against someone other than the **A32–93** claimant, and the court may make an order for security for costs against that person if—

(a) it is satisfied, having regard to all the circumstances of the case, that it is just to make such an order; and

(b) one or more of the conditions in paragraph (2) applies.

(2) The conditions are that the person—

(a) has assigned the right to the claim to the claimant with a view to avoiding the possibility of a costs order being made against him; or

(b) has contributed or agreed to contribute to the claimant's costs in return for a share of the money or property which the claimant may recover in the proceedings; and

(c) is a person against whom a costs order may be made.

(Rule 48.2 makes provision for costs orders against non-parties)

Security for costs of an appeal

25.15 (1) The court may order security for costs of an appeal against—   **A32–94**

(a) an appellant;

(b) a respondent who also appeals,

on the same grounds as it may order security for costs against a claimant under this Part.

(2) The court may also make an order under paragraph (1) where the appellant, or the respondent who also appeals, is a limited company and there is reason to believe it will be unable to pay the costs of the other parties to the appeal should its appeal be unsuccessful.

PRACTICE DIRECTION—INTERIM PAYMENTS

Amended August 31, 2000

This Practice Direction supplements CPR Part 25

General

A32–95   **1.1** Rule 25.7 sets out the conditions to be satisfied and matters to be taken into account before the courts make an order for an interim payment.

1.2 The permission of the court must be obtained before making a voluntary interim payment in respect of a claim by a child or patient.

Evidence

A32–96   **2.1** An application for an interim payment of damages must be supported by evidence dealing with the following:

(1) the sum of money sought by way of an interim payment,

(2) the items or matters in respect of which the interim payment is sought,

(3) the sum of money for which final judgment is likely to be given,

(4) the reasons for believing that the conditions set out in rule 25.7 are satisfied,

(5) any other relevant matters,

(6) in claims for personal injuries, details of special damages and past and future loss, and

(7) in a claim under the Fatal Accidents Act 1976, details of the person(s) on whose behalf the claim is made and the nature of the claim.

2.2 Any documents in support of the application should be exhibited, including, in personal injuries claims, the medical report(s).

2.3 If a respondent to an application for an interim payment wishes to rely on written evidence at the hearing he must comply with the provisions of rule 25.6(4).

2.4 If the applicant wishes to rely on written evidence in reply he must comply with the provisions of rule 25.6(5).

Interim payment where account to be taken

24.1 This section of this practice direction applies if a party seeks an interim payment under rules 25.7(b) where the court has ordered an account to be taken.

24.2 If the evidence on the application for interim payment shows that the account is bound to result in a payment to the applicant, the court will, before making an order for interim payment, order that the liable party pay to the applicant "the amount shown by the account to be due".

Instalments

A32–97   **3** Where an interim payment is to be paid in instalments the order should set out:

(1) the total amount of the payment,

(2) the amount of each instalment,

(3) the number of instalments and the date on which each is to be paid, and

(4) to whom the payment should be made.

Compensation recovery payments

A32–98   **4.1** Where in a claim for personal injuries there is an application for an interim payment of damages:

(1) which is other than by consent,

(2) which falls under the heads of damage set out in column 1 of Schedule 2 of the Social Security (Recovery of Benefits) Act 1997 in respect of recoverable benefits received by the claimant set out in column 2 of that Schedule, and

(3) where the defendant is liable to pay recoverable benefits to the Secretary of State, the defendant should obtain from the Secretary of State a certificate of recoverable benefits.

4.2 A copy of the certificate should be filed at the hearing of the application for an interim payment.

4.3 The order will set out the amount by which the payment to be made to the claimant has been reduced according to the Act and the Social Security Recovery of Benefits) Regulations 1997.

Adjustment of final judgment figure

5.1 In this paragraph "judgment" means: A32–99
(1) any order to pay a sum of money,
(2) a final award of damages,
(3) an assessment of damages.

5.2 In a final judgment where an interim payment has previously been made which is less than the total amount awarded by the judge, the order should set out in a preamble:
(1) the total amount awarded by the judge, and
(2) the amounts and dates of the interim payment(s).

5.3 The total amount awarded by the judge should then be reduced by the total amount of any interim payments, and an order made for entry of judgment and payment of the balance.

5.4 In a final judgment where an interim payment has previously been made which is more than the total amount awarded by the judge, the order should set out in a preamble:
(1) the total amount awarded by the judge, and
(2) the amounts and dates of the interim payment(s).

5.5 An order should then be made for repayment, reimbursement, variation or discharge under rule 25, and for interest on an overpayment under rule 25.8(5).

5.6 A practice direction supplementing Part 40 provides further information concerning adjustment of the final judgment sum.

PRACTICE DIRECTION—ACCOUNTS AND INQUIRIES

This Practice Direction supplements CPR Part 25

An application for an order for accounts and inquiries may also be made **A32–100**
under Part 24 (summary judgment). Reference should be made to paragraph 6 of the practice direction that supplements that Part.

1. The remedies that the court may grant under Part 25 include orders directing accounts to be taken and inquiries to be made.
2. The court may, on application or on its own initiative, at any stage in the proceedings, whether before or after judgment, make an order directing any necessary accounts to be taken or inquiries to be made.
3. Every direction for an account to be taken or an inquiry to be made shall be numbered in the order so that, as far as possible, each distinct account and inquiry is given its own number.

(This practice direction replaces RSC Order 43, rule 2 and applies to county court proceedings as well as to High Court proceedings.)

(The accounts and inquiries practice direction supplementing Part 40 contains provisions regarding the taking of an account or conduct of an inquiry after the order for the account or inquiry has been made.)

PRACTICE DIRECTION—INTERIM INJUNCTIONS

This Practice Direction supplements CPR Part 25
Jurisdiction

1.1 High Court Judges and any other Judge duly authorised may grant **A32–101**
"search orders" and "freezing injunctions".

1.2 In a case in the High Court, Masters and district judges have the power to grant injunctions:

(1) by consent,

(2) in connection with charging orders and appointments of receivers,

(3) in aid of execution of judgments

1.3 In any other case any judge who has jurisdiction to conduct the trial of the action has the power to grant an injunction in that action.

1.4 A Master or district judge has the power to vary or discharge an injunction granted by any Judge with consent of all the parties.

Making an application

A32–102
2.1 The application notice must state:

(1) the order sought, and

(2) the date, time and place of the hearing.

2.2 The application notice and evidence in support must be served as soon as practicable after issue and in any event not less than 3 days before the court is due to hear the application.

2.3 Where the court is to serve, sufficient copies of the application notice and evidence in support for the court and for each respondent should be filed for issue and service.

2.4 Whenever possible a draft of the order sought should be filed with the application notice and a disk containing the draft should also be available to the court. This will enable the court officer to arrange any amendments to be incorporated and for the speedy preparation and sealing of the order. The current word processing system to be used is WordPerfect 5.1.

Evidence

A32–103
3.1 Applications for search orders and freezing injunctions must be supported by affidavit evidence.

3.2 Applications for other interim injunctions must be supported by evidence set out in either:

(1) a witness statement, or

(2) a statement of case provided that it is verified by a statement of truth, or

(3) the application provided that it is verified by a statement of truth, unless the court, an Act, a rule or a practice direction requires evidence by affidavit.

3.3 The evidence must set out the facts on which the applicant relies for the claim being made against the respondent, including all material facts of which the court should be made aware.

3.4 Where an application is made without notice to the respondent, the evidence must also set out why notice was not given.

(See Part 32 and the practice direction that supplements it for information about evidence.)

Urgent applications and applications without notice

A32–104
4.1 These fall into two categories:

(1) applications where a claim form has already been issued, and

(2) applications where a claim form has not yet been issued, and, in both cases, where notice of application has not been given to the respondent.

4.2 These applications are normally dealt with at a court hearing but cases of extreme urgency may be dealt with by telephone.

4.3 Applications dealt with at a court hearing after issue of a claim form:

(1) the application notice, evidence in support and a draft order (as in 2.4 above) should be filed in the court two hours before the hearing wherever possible,

(2) if an application is made before the application notice has been issued, a draft order (as in 2. above) should be provided at the hearing, and the

application notice and evidence in support should be filed with the court on the same or next working day or as ordered by the court, and

(3) except in cases where secrecy is essential, the applicant should take steps to notify the respondent informally of the application.

4.4 Applications made before the issue of a claim form:

(1) in addition to the provisions set out at 4.3 above, unless the court orders otherwise, either the applicant must undertake to the court to issue a claim form immediately or the court will give directions for the commencement of the claim,

(2) where possible the claim form should be served with the order for the injunction,

(3) an order made before the issue of a claim form should state in the title after the names of the applicant and respondent "the Claimant and Defendant in an Intended Action".

4.5 Applications made by telephone:

(1) where it is not possible to arrange a hearing, application can be made between 10.00 a.m. and 5.00 p.m. weekdays by telephoning the Royal Courts of Justice on 0171 936 6000 and asking to be put in contact with a High Court Judge of the appropriate Division available to deal with a emergency application in a High Court matter. The appropriate district registry may also be contacted by telephone. In county court proceedings, the appropriate county court should be contacted,

(2) where an application is made outside those hours the applicant should either—

(a) telephone the Royal Courts of Justice on 0171 936 6000 where he will be put in contact with the clerk to the appropriate duty judge in the High Court (or the appropriate area Circuit Judge where known), or

(b) the Urgent Court Business Officer of the appropriate Circuit who will contact the local duty judge.

(3) where the facility is available it is likely that the judge will require a draft order to be faxed to him.

(4) the application notice and evidence in support must be filed with the court on the same or next working day or as ordered, together with two copies of the order for sealing,

(5) injunctions will be heard by telephone only where the applicant is acting by counsel or solicitor.

Orders for injunctions

5.1 Any order for an injunction, unless the court orders otherwise, must **A32–105** contain:

(1) an undertaking by the applicant to the court to pay any damages which the respondent(s) (or other party served with or notified of the order) sustain which the court considers the applicant should pay,

(2) if made without notice to any other party, an undertaking by the applicant to the court to serve the respondent the application notice, evidence in support and any order made as soon as practicable,

(3) if made without notice to any other party, a return date for a further hearing at which the other party can be present,

(4) if made before filing the application notice, an undertaking to file and pay the appropriate fee the same or next working day, and

(5) if made before issue of a claim form—

(a) an undertaking to issue and pay the appropriate fee on the same or next working day, or

(b) directions for the commencement of the claim.

5.2 An order for an injunction made in the presence of all parties to be bound by it or made at a hearing of which they have had notice, may state that it is effective until trial or further order.

5.3 Any order for an injunction must set out clearly what the respondent must do or not do.

Freezing injunctions

Orders to restrain disposal of assets worldwide and within England and Wales

A32–106   6 Examples of Freezing Injunctions are annexed to this practice direction.

Search orders

Orders for the preservation of evidence and property

A32–107   **7.1** The following provisions apply to search orders in addition to those listed above.
The Supervising Solicitor:
7.2 The Supervising Solicitor must be experienced in the operation of search orders. A Supervising Solicitor may be contacted either through the Law Society or, for the London area, through the London Solicitor Litigation Association.
   7.3 Evidence:
   (1) the affidavit must state the name, firm and its address, and experience of the Supervising Solicitor, also the address of the premises and whether it is a private or business address, and
   (2) the affidavit must disclose very fully the reason the order is sought, including the probability that relevant material would disappear if the order were not made.
   7.4 Service:
   (1) the order must be served personally by the Supervising Solicitor, unless the court otherwise orders, and must be accompanied by the evidence in support and any documents capable of being copied,
   (2) confidential exhibits need not be served but they must be made available for inspection by the respondent in the presence of the applicant's solicitors while the order is carried out and afterwards be retained by the respondent's solicitors on their undertaking not to permit the respondent—
      (a) to see them or copies of them except in their presence, and
      (b) to make or take away any note or record of them,
   (3) the Supervising Solicitor may be accompanied only by the persons mentioned in the order,
   (4) the Supervising Solicitor must explain the terms and effect of the order to the respondent in every day language and advise him of his right to—
      (a) legal advice, and
      (b) apply to vary or discharge the order,
   (5) where the Supervising Solicitor is a man and the respondent is likely to be an unaccompanied woman, at least one other person named in the order must be a woman and must accompany the Supervising Solicitor, and
   (6) the order may only be served between 9.30 a.m. and 5.30 p.m. Monday to Friday unless the court otherwise orders.
   7.5 Search and custody of materials:
   (1) no material shall be removed unless clearly covered by the terms of the order,
   (2) the premises must not be searched and no items shall be removed from them except in the presence of the respondent or a person who appears to be a responsible employee of the respondent,
   (3) where copies of documents are sought, the documents should be retained for no more than two days before return to the owner,
   (4) where material in dispute is removed pending trial, the applicant's solicitors should place it in the custody of the respondent's solicitors on their undertaking to retain it in safekeeping and to produce it to the court when required,

(5) in appropriate cases the applicant should insure the material retained in the respondent's solicitors' custody,

(6) the Supervising Solicitor must make a list of all material removed from the premises and supply a copy of the list to the respondent,

(7) no material shall be removed from the premises until the respondent has had reasonable time to check the list,

(8) if any of the listed items exists only in computer readable form, the respondent must immediately give the applicant's solicitors effective access to the computers, with all necessary password to enable them to be searched, and cause the listed items to be printed out,

(9) the applicant must take all reasonable steps to ensure that no damage is done to any computer or data,

(10) the applicant and his representatives may not themselves search the respondent's computer unless they have sufficient expertise to do so without damaging the respondent's system,

(11) the Supervising Solicitor shall provide a report on the carrying out of the order to the applicant's solicitors,

(12) as soon as the report is received the applicant's solicitors shall—

(a) serve a copy of it on the respondent, and

(b) file a copy of it with the court, and

(13) where the Supervising Solicitor is satisfied that full compliance with paragraph 7.5(7) and (8) above is impracticable, he may permit the search to proceed and items to be removed without compliance with the impracticable requirements.

General

8.1 The Supervising Solicitor must not be an employee or member of the applicant's firm of solicitors. **A32–108**

8.2 If the court orders that the order need not be served by the Supervising Solicitor, the reason for so ordering must be set out in the order.

8.3 The search order must not be carried out at the same time as a police search warrant.

8.4 There is no privilege against self incrimination in Intellectual Property cases (see the Supreme Court Act 1981, section 72) therefore in those cases, paragraph (4) of the Respondent's Entitlements and any other references to incrimination in the Search Order, should be removed.

8.5 Applications in intellectual property cases should be made in the Chancery Division.

8.6 An example of a Search Order is annexed to this Practice Direction.

Annex

Freezing Injunction IN THE [HIGH COURT OF JUSTICE]
Order to restrain assets in [CHANCERY DIVISION]
England and Wales [Strand, London WC2A 2LL]
Before The Honourable Mr Justice [**]**

A32–109

Claim No.

Dated

Applicant

Seal

Respondent

Name, address and reference of Respondent

PENAL NOTICE
IF YOU THE WITHIN NAMED [] DISOBEY THIS
ORDER YOU MAY BE HELD TO BE IN CONTEMPT OF COURT AND LIABLE TO
IMPRISONMENT OR FINED OR YOUR ASSETS SEIZED
IMPORTANT
NOTICE TO THE RESPONDENT
You should read the terms of the Order and the Guidance Notes very carefully. You are advised to consult a Solicitor as soon as possible.
This Order prohibits you, the Respondent, from dealing with your assets up to the amount stated in the Order, but subject to any exceptions set out at the end of the Order. You have a right to ask the Court to vary or discharge this Order.
If you disobey this Order you may be found guilty of Contempt of Court and may be sent to prison or fined. In the case of a Corporate Respondent, it may be fined, its Directors may be sent to prison or fined or its assets may be seized.

THE ORDER

A32–110 An application was made today [*date*] by [Counsel][Solicitors][or *as may be*] for the Applicant to Mr Justice [[   ] who heard the application. The Judge read the affidavits listed in Schedule A and accepted the undertakings set out in Schedule B at the end of this Order. As a result of the application **IT IS ORDERED** that until [[   ] ("the return date")] [or further Order of the Court]:—

1 The Respondent must not remove from England and Wales or in any way dispose of or deal with or diminish the value of any of his assets which are in England and Wales whether in his own name or not and whether solely or jointly owned up to the value of £

This prohibition includes the following assets in particular:—
(a) the property known as [*title/address*] or the net sale money after payment of any mortgages if it has been sold;
(b) the property and assets of the Respondent's business known as (or carried on at [*address*]) or the sale money if any of them have been sold; and
(c) any money in the account numbered [*a/c number*] at [*title/address*].

2 If the total unincumbered value of the Respondent's assets in England and Wales exceeds £   , the Respondent may remove any of those assets from England and Wales or may dispose of or deal with them so long as the total unincumbered value of his assets still in England and Wales remains above £   .

3 Exceptions to this Order:—
(1) This Order does not prohibit the Respondent from spending
£   a week towards his ordinary living expenses
[and £   a week towards his ordinary and proper business expenses] and also £   a week [*or* a reasonable sum] on legal advice and representation. But before spending any money the Respondent must tell the Applicant's legal representatives where the money is to come from.
[(2) This Order does not prohibit the Respondent from dealing with or disposing of any of his assets in the ordinary and proper course of business.]
(3) The Respondent may agree with the Applicant's legal representatives that the above spending limits should be increased or that this Order should be varied in any other respect, but any agreement must be in writing.
(4) The Respondent may cause this Order to cease to have effect if the Respondent provides security by paying the sum of £   into Court or makes provision for security in that sum by another method agreed with the Applicant's legal representatives.

4 The Respondent must:—
(1) Inform the Applicant in writing at once of all his assets in England and Wales and whether in his own name or not and whether solely or jointly owned, giving the value, location and details of all such assets. [The Respondent may be entitled to refuse to provide some or all of this information on the grounds that it may incriminate him. *This sentence may be inserted in cases not covered by the Theft Act 1968, s.31.*]
(2) Confirm the information in an affidavit which must be served on the Applicant's legal representatives within [   ] days after this Order has been served on the Respondent.
[5 *Where an Order for service by an alternative means or service out of the jurisdiction has been made*—
(1) The Applicant may issue and serve a Claim Form on the Respondent at [*address*] by [*method of service*].

(2) If the Respondent wishes to defend the Claim where the Claim Form states that Particulars of Claim are to follow he must complete and return the Acknowledgement of Service within [ ] days of being served with the Claim Form. Where the Particulars of Claim are served with the Claim Form, and the Respondent wishes to defend part or all of the Claim he must complete and return an Acknowledgement of Service within [ ] days of being served with the Claim Form or a Defence within [ ] days.

GUIDANCE NOTES

EFFECT OF THIS ORDER

(1) A respondent who is an individual who is ordered not to do something must not do **A32–111** it himself or in any other way. He must not do it through others acting on his behalf or on his instructions or with his encouragement.

(2) A respondent which is a corporation and which is ordered not to do something must not do it itself or by its directors, officers, employees or agents or in any other way.

VARIATION OR DISCHARGE OF THIS ORDER

The Respondent (or anyone notified of this Order) may apply to the court at any time to vary or discharge this Order (or so much of it as affects that person), but anyone wishing to do so must first inform the Applicant's legal representatives.

PARTIES OTHER THAN THE APPLICANT AND RESPONDENT

(1) Effect of this Order: **A32–112**
It is a Contempt of Court for any person notified of this Order knowingly to assist in or permit a breach of this Order. Any person doing so may be sent to prison, fined or have his assets seized.

(2) Set off by banks:
This injunction does not prevent any bank from exercising any right of set off it may have in respect of any facility which it gave to the respondent before it was notified of this Order.

(3) Withdrawals by the Respondent:
No bank need enquire as to the application or proposed application of any money withdrawn by the Respondent if the withdrawal appears to be permitted by this Order.

INTERPRETATION OF THIS ORDER

(1) In this Order, where there is more than one Respondent, (unless otherwise stated), **A32–113** references to "the Respondent" means both or all of them.

(2) A requirement to serve on "the Respondent" means on each of them. However, the Order is effective against any Respondent on whom it is served.

(3) An Order requiring "the Respondent" to do or not to do anything applies to all Respondents.

COMMUNICATIONS WITH THE COURT

All communications to the Court about this Order should be sent, where the Order is **A32–114** made in the Chancery Division, to [Room TM 510], Royal Courts of Justice, Strand, London WC2A 2LL quoting the case number. The telephone number is 0171 936 [6827]; and where the order is made in the Queen's Bench Division, to Room W11 (0171 936 6009). The offices are open between 10 a.m. and 4.30 p.m. Monday to Friday.

SCHEDULE A

AFFIDAVITS

The Applicant relied on the following affidavits: **A32–115**

[name]	[number of affidavit]	[date sworn]	[filed on behalf of]
(1)			

SCHEDULE B

(2) UNDERTAKINGS GIVEN TO THE COURT BY THE APPLICANT

(1) If the Court later finds that this Order has caused loss to the Respondent, and **A32–116** decides that the Respondent should be compensated for that loss, the Applicant will comply with any Order the Court may make.

(2) The Applicant will on or before [*date*] cause a written guarantee in the sum of £   to be issued from a bank having a place of business within England or Wales, such guarantee being in respect of any Order the Court may make pursuant to paragraph (1) above. The Applicant will further, forthwith upon issue of the guarantee, cause a copy of it to be served on the Respondent.

(3) As soon as practicable the Applicant will [issue and serve on the Respondent a Claim Form in the form of the draft produced to the Court] [serve on the Respondent the Claim Form] claiming the appropriate relief, together with this Order.

(4) The Applicant will cause an affidavit to be sworn and filed [substantially in the terms of the draft affidavit produced to the Court] [confirming the substance of what was said to the Court by the Applicant's Counsel/Solicitors].

[(5) *Where a return date has been given*—As soon as practicable the Applicant will serve on the Respondent an Application for the return date together with a copy of the affidavits and exhibits containing the evidence relied on by the Applicant.]

(6) Anyone notified of this Order will be given a copy of it by the Applicant's legal representatives.

(7) The Applicant will pay the reasonable costs of anyone other than the Respondent which have been incurred as a result of this Order including the costs of ascertaining whether that person holds any of the Respondent's assets and if the Court later finds that this Order has caused such person loss, and decides that such person should be compensated for that loss, the Applicant will comply with any Order the Court may make.

(8) If for any reason this Order ceases to have effect (including in particular where the Respondent provides security as provided for above or the Applicant does not provide a bank guarantee as provided for above), the Applicant will forthwith take all reasonable steps to inform, in writing, any person or company to whom he has given notice of this Order, or who he has reasonable grounds for supposing may act upon this Order, that it has ceased to have effect.

NAME AND ADDRESS OF APPLICANT'S LEGAL REPRESENTATIVES

The Applicant's Legal Representatives are:–
[Name, address, reference, fax and telephone numbers both in and out of office hours.]

ANNEX

32–117   **Freezing Injunction** IN THE [HIGH COURT OF JUSTICE]
Order to restrain assets worldwide [CHANCERY DIVISION][Strand, London WC2A 2LL]
Before The Honourable Mr Justice [   ]

Claim No.

Dated

Applicant

Seal

Respondent

Name, address and reference of Respondent

PENAL NOTICE
IF YOU THE WITHIN NAMED [] DISOBEY THIS
ORDER YOU MAY BE HELD TO BE IN CONTEMPT OF COURT AND LIABLE TO
IMPRISONMENT OR FINED OR YOUR ASSETS SEIZED

IMPORTANT
NOTICE TO THE RESPONDENT
You should read the terms of the Order and the Guidance Notes very carefully. You are advised to consult a Solicitor as soon as possible.
This Order prohibits you, the Respondent, from dealing with your assets up to the amount stated in the Order, but subject to any exceptions set out at the end of the Order. You have a right to ask the Court to vary or discharge this Order.
If you disobey this Order you may be found guilty of Contempt of Court and may be sent to prison or fined. In the case of a Corporate Respondent, it may be fined, its Directors may be sent to prison or fined or its assets may be seized.

THE ORDER

An application was made today [*date*] by [Counsel] [Solicitors] [*or as may be*] for the **A32–118** Applicant to Mr Justice [   ] who heard the application. The Judge read the affidavits listed in Schedule A and accepted the undertakings set out in Schedule B at the end of this Order. As a result of the application IT IS ORDERED that until [[   ] ("the return date")] [further Order of the Court]:—

1. The Respondent must not:—
(1) remove from England and Wales or in any way dispose of or deal with or diminish the value of any of his assets which are in England and Wales whether in his own name or not and whether solely or jointly owned up to the value of £   , or
(2) in any way dispose of or deal with or diminish the value of any of his assets whether they are in or outside England or Wales whether in his own name or not and whether solely or jointly owned up to the same value. This prohibition includes the following assets in particular:—
   (a) the property known as [*title/address*] or the net sale money after payment of any mortgages if it has been sold;
   (b) the property and assets of the Respondent's business known as (or carried on at [*address*]) or the sale money if any of them have been sold; and
   (c) any money in the account numbered [*a/c number*] at [*title/address*].

2 (1) If the total unincumbered value of the Respondent's assets in England and Wales exceeds £   , the Respondent may remove any of those assets from England and Wales or may dispose of or deal with them so long as the total unincumbered value of his assets still in England and Wales remains above £   .
(2) If the total unincumbered value of the Respondent's assets in England and Wales does not exceed £   , the Respondent must not remove any of those assets from England and Wales and must not dispose of or deal with any of them, but if he has other assets outside England and Wales the Respondent may dispose of or deal with those assets so long as the total unincumbered value of all his assets whether in or outside England and Wales remains above £   .

3 Exceptions to this Order:—
(1) This Order does not prohibit the Respondent from spending
£   a week towards his ordinary living expenses
[and £   a week towards his ordinary and proper business expenses] and also £   a week [*or a reasonable sum*] on legal advice and representation. But before spending any money the Respondent must tell the Applicant's legal representatives where the money is to come from.
[(2) This Order does not prohibit the Respondent from dealing with or disposing of any of his assets in the ordinary and proper course of business.]
(3) The Respondent may agree with the Applicant's legal representatives that the above spending limits should be increased or that this Order should be varied in any other respect, but any agreement must be in writing.
(4) The Respondent may cause this Order to cease to have effect if the Respondent provides security by paying the sum of £   into Court or makes provision for security in that sum by another method agreed with the Applicant's legal representatives.

4 The Respondent must:—
(1) Inform the Applicant in writing at once of all his assets whether in or outside England and Wales and whether in his own name or not and whether solely or jointly owned, giving the value, location and details of all such assets. [The Respondent may be entitled to refuse to provide some or all of this information on the grounds that it may incriminate him. *This sentence may be inserted in cases not covered by the Theft-Act 1968, s.31 .*]
(2) Confirm the information in an affidavit which must be served on the Applicant's legal representatives within [   ] days after this Order has been served on the Respondent.

[**5** *Where an Order for service by an alternative means or service out of the jurisdiction has been made*—
 (1) The Applicant may issue and serve a Claim Form on the Respondent at [*address*] by [*method of service*]
 (2) If the Respondent wishes to defend the Claim he must complete and return the Notice of Intention to Defend within [ ] days of being served with the Claim Form.]

GUIDANCE NOTES

EFFECT OF THIS ORDER

A32–119 (1) A Respondent who is an individual who is ordered not to do something must not do it himself or in any other way. He must not do it through others acting on his behalf or on his instructions or with his encouragement.

 (2) A Respondent which is a corporation and which is ordered not to do something must not do it itself or by its directors, officers, employees or agents or in any other way.

VARIATION OR DISCHARGE OF THIS ORDER

A32–120 The Respondent (or anyone notified of this Order) may apply to the Court at any time to vary or discharge this Order (or so much of it as affects that person), but anyone wishing to do so must first inform the Applicant's legal representatives.

PARTIES OTHER THAN THE APPLICANT AND RESPONDENT

A32–121 (1) Effect of this Order:—
It is a Contempt of Court for any person notified of this Order knowingly to assist in or permit a breach of this Order. Any person doing so may be sent to prison, fined or have his assets seized.
 (2) Effect of this Order outside England and Wales:—
The terms of this Order do not affect or concern anyone outside the jurisdiction of this Court until it is declared enforceable by or is enforced by a Court in the relevant country and then they are to affect him only to the extent they have been declared enforceable or have been enforced **UNLESS** the person is:
  (i) a person to whom this Order is addressed or an officer or an agent appointed by power of attorney of that person; or
  (ii) a person who is subject to the jurisdiction of this Court and (a) has been given written notice of this Order at his residence or place of business within the jurisdiction of this Court and (b) is able to prevent acts or omissions outside the jurisdiction of this Court which constitute or assist in a breach of the terms of this Order.
 (3) Set off by Banks:—
This injunction does not prevent any bank from exercising any right of set off it may have in respect of any facility which it gave to the Respondent before it was notified of this Order.
 (4) Withdrawals by the Respondent:—
No bank need enquire as to the application or proposed application of any money withdrawn by the Respondent if the withdrawal appears to be permitted by this Order.

INTERPRETATION OF THIS ORDER

A32–122 (1) In this Order, where there is more than one Respondent, (unless otherwise stated) references to "the Respondent" means both or all of them.

 (2) A requirement to serve on "the Respondent" means on each of them. However, the Order is effective against any Respondent on whom it is served.

 (3) An Order requiring "the Respondent" to do or not to do anything applies to all Respondents.

COMMUNICATIONS WITH THE COURT

A32–123 All communications to the Court about this Order should be sent, where the Order is made in the Chancery Division, to [Room TM 510], Royal Courts of Justice, Strand, London WC2A 2LL quoting the case number. The telephone number is 0207936 [6827];

and where the order is made in the Queen's Bench Division, to Room W11 (0207936 6009). The offices are open between 10 a.m. and 4.30 p.m. Monday to Friday.

SCHEDULE A

AFFIDAVITS

The Applicant relied on the following affidavits: **A32–124**
[name]   [number of affidavit]   [date sworn]   [filed on behalf of]
   (1)
   (2)

SCHEDULE B

UNDERTAKINGS GIVEN TO THE COURT BY THE APPLICANT

(1) If the Court later finds that this Order has caused loss to the Respondent, and **A32–125** decides that the Respondent should be compensated for that loss, the Applicant will comply with any Order the Court may make.

(2) The Applicant will on or before [*date*] cause a written guarantee in the sum of £ to be issued from a bank having a place of business within England or Wales, such guarantee being in respect of any Order the Court may make pursuant to paragraph (1) above. The Applicant will further, forthwith upon issue of the guarantee, cause a copy of it to be served on the Respondent.

(3) As soon as practicable the Applicant will [issue and serve on the Respondent a Claim Form in the form of the draft produced to the Court] [serve on the Respondent the Claim Form] claiming the appropriate relief, together with this Order.]

(4) The Applicant will cause an affidavit to be sworn and filed [substantially in the terms of the draft affidavit produced to the Court] [confirming the substance of what was said to the Court by the Applicant's Counsel/Solicitors].

(5) Where a return date has been given- As soon as practicable the Applicant will serve on the Respondent an application for the return date together with a copy of the affidavits and exhibits containing the evidence relied on by the Applicant.]

(6) Anyone notified of this Order will be given a copy of it by the Applicant's legal representatives.

(7) The Applicant will pay the reasonable costs of anyone other than the Respondent which have been incurred as a result of this Order including the costs of ascertaining whether that person holds any of the Respondent's assets and if the Court later finds that this Order has caused such person loss, and decides that such person should be compensated for that loss, the Applicant will comply with any Order the Court may make.

(8) If for any reason this Order ceases to have effect (including in particular where the Respondent provides security as provided for above or the Applicant does not provide a bank guarantee as provided for above), the Applicant will forthwith take all reasonable steps to inform, in writing, any person or company to whom he has given notice of this Order, or who he has reasonable grounds for supposing may act upon this Order, that it has ceased to have effect.

[(9) The Applicant will not without the leave of the Court begin proceedings against the Respondent in any other jurisdiction or use information obtained as a result of an Order of the Court in this jurisdiction for the purpose of civil or criminal proceedings in any other jurisdiction.]

[(10) The Applicant will not without the leave of the Court seek to enforce this Order in any country outside England and Wales [or seek an Order of a similar nature including Orders conferring a charge or other security against the Respondent or the Respondent's assets].

NAME AND ADDRESS OF APPLICANT'S LEGAL REPRESENTATIVES

The Applicant's Legal Representatives are:—
[Name, address, reference, fax and telephone numbers both in and out of office hours.]

Annex

A32–126 **Search Order** IN THE [HIGH COURT OF JUSTICE]
Order to preserve evidence [CHANCERY DIVISION]
and property [Strand, London WC2A 2LL]
Before The Honourable Mr Justice [   ]

Claim No.

Dated

Applicant

Seal

Respondent

Name, address and reference of Respondent

PENAL NOTICE
IF YOU THE WITHIN NAMED [] DISOBEY THIS
ORDER YOU MAY BE HELD TO BE IN CONTEMPT OF COURT AND LIABLE TO
IMPRISONMENT OR FINED OR YOUR ASSETS SEIZED
IMPORTANT
NOTICE TO THE RESPONDENT
You should read the terms of the Order and the Guidance Notes very carefully. You are
advised to consult a Solicitor as soon as possible.
This Order orders you, the Respondent, to allow the persons mentioned in the Order to
enter the premises described in the Order and to search for, examine and remove or copy
the articles specified in the Order. The persons so named will have no right to enter the
premises or, having entered, to remain at the premises, unless you give your consent to
their doing so. If, however, you withhold your consent you will be in breach of this Order
and may be held to be in Contempt of Court.
The Order also requires you to hand over any of such articles which are under your
control and to provide information to the Applicant's Solicitors, and prohibits you from
doing certain acts.
If you, the Respondent, disobey this Order you may be found guilty of contempt of
Court and may be sent to prison or fined. In the case of a Corporate Respondent, it may be
fined, its Directors may be sent to prison or fined or its assets may be seized.

THE ORDER

A32–127 AN APPLICATION was made today [*date*] by [Counsel] [Solicitors] for the Applicant to
Mr Justice [   ] who heard the application. The Judge read the affidavits listed in
Schedule F at the end of this Order and accepted the undertakings by the Applicant, the
Applicant's Solicitors and the Supervising Solicitor set forth in the Schedules at the end of
this Order. As a result of the application IT IS ORDERED that until [   ] ("the return
date")] [or further Order of the Court]:—
  1. (1) The Respondent must allow Mr/Mrs/Miss [   ] ("the Supervising
Solicitor"), together with Mr [   ] a Solicitor of the Supreme Court, and a partner
in the firm of [   ] the Applicant's Solicitors and up to [   ] other persons
being [*their capacity*] accompanying them, to enter the premises mentioned in Schedule A
to this Order and any other premises of the Respondent disclosed under paragraph 4(1)
below and any vehicles under the Respondent's control on or around the premises so that
they can search for, inspect, photograph or photocopy, and deliver into the safekeeping of
the Applicant's Solicitors all the documents and articles which are listed in Schedule B to
this Order ("the listed items") or which Mr [   ] believes to be listed items.

(2) The Respondent must allow those persons to remain on the premises until the search is complete, and to re-enter the premises on the same or the following day in order to complete the search.

2. (1) No item may be removed from the premises until a list of the items to be removed has been prepared, and a copy of the list has been supplied to the person served with the Order, and he has been given a reasonable opportunity to check the list.

(2) The premises must not be searched, and items must not be removed from them, except in the presence of the Respondent or a person appearing to be a responsible employee of the Respondent or in control of the premises.

(3) If the Supervising Solicitor is satisfied that full compliance with paragraph 2(1) or (2) above is impracticable, he may permit the search to proceed and items to be removed without compliance with the impracticable requirements.

3. (1) The Respondent must immediately hand over to the Applicant's Solicitors any of the listed items which are in his possession or under his control save for any computer or hard disk integral to any computer.

(2) If any of the listed items exists only in computer readable form, the Respondent must immediately give the Applicant's Solicitors effective access to the computers, with all necessary passwords, to enable them to be searched, and cause the listed items to be printed out. A print-out of the items must be given to the Applicant's Solicitors or displayed on the computer screen so that they can be read and copied. All reasonable steps shall be taken by the Applicant to ensure that no damage is done to any computer or data. The Applicant and his representatives may not themselves search the Respondent's computers unless they have sufficient expertise to do so without damaging the Respondent's system.

4. (1) The Respondent must immediately inform the Applicant's Solicitors:—
    (a) where all the listed items are; and
    (b) so far as he is aware—
        (i) the name and address of everyone who has supplied him, or offered to supply him, with listed items,
       (ii) the name and address of everyone to whom he has supplied, or offered to supply, listed items, and
     (iii) full details of the dates and quantities of every such supply and offer.

(2) Within [ ] days after being served with this Order the Respondent must swear an affidavit setting out the above information.

5. (1) Except for the purpose of obtaining legal advice, the Respondent or anyone else with knowledge of this Order must not directly or indirectly inform anyone of these proceedings or of the contents of this Order, or warn anyone that proceedings have been or may be brought against him by the Applicant until [   ] the return date] [or further Order of the Court].

(2) The Respondent must not destroy, tamper with, cancel or part with possession, power, custody or control of the listed items otherwise than in accordance with the terms of this Order.

(3) [*Insert any negative injunctions.*]

[**6** *Insert any further order.*]

GUIDANCE NOTES

EFFECT OF THIS ORDER

(1) A Respondent who is an individual who is ordered not to do something must not do **A32–128** it himself or in any other way. He must not do it through others acting on his behalf or on his instructions or with his encouragement.

(2) A Respondent which is a corporation and which is ordered not to do something must not do it itself or by its directors officers employees or agents or in any other way.

(3) This Order must be complied with either by the Respondent himself or by an employee of the Respondent or other person appearing to be in control of the premises and having authority to permit the premises to be entered and the search to proceed.

(4) This Order requires the Respondent or his employee or other person appearing to be in control of the premises and having that authority to permit entry to the premises immediately the Order is served upon him, except as stated in paragraph 6 below.

RESPONDENT'S ENTITLEMENTS

A32–129   (1) Before you the Respondent or the person appearing to be in control of the premises allow anybody onto the premises to carry out this Order you are entitled to have the solicitor who serves you with this Order explain to you what it means in everyday language.

(2) You are entitled to insist that there is nobody [or nobody except Mr] present who could gain commercially from anything he might read or see on your premises.

(3) You are entitled to refuse to permit entry before 9:30 a.m. or after 5:30 p.m. or at all on Saturday and Sunday unless the Court has ordered otherwise.

(4) Except in certain cases, you may be entitled to refuse to permit disclosure of any documents which may incriminate you ("incriminating documents") or to answer any questions if to do so may incriminate you. It may be prudent to take advice, because if you so refuse, your refusal may be taken into account by the Court at a later stage.

(5) You are entitled to refuse to permit disclosure of any documents passing between you and your Solicitors or Patent or Trade Mark Agents for the purpose of obtaining advice ("privileged documents").

(6) You are entitled to seek legal advice, and to ask the Court to vary or discharge this Order, provided you do so at once, and provided you do not disturb or move anything in the interim and that meanwhile you permit the Supervising Solicitor (who is a Solicitor acting independently of the Applicant) to enter, but not start to search.

(7) Before permitting entry to the premises by any person other than the Supervising Solicitor, you (or any other person appearing to be in control of the premises) may gather together any documents you believe may be [incriminating or] privileged and hand them to the Supervising Solicitor for the Supervising Solicitor to assess whether they are [incriminating or] privileged as claimed. If the Supervising Solicitor concludes that any of the documents may be [incriminating or] privileged documents or if there is any doubt as to their status the Supervising Solicitor shall exclude them from the search and shall retain the documents of doubtful status in his possession pending further order of the Court. While this is being done, you may refuse entry to the premises by any other person, and may refuse to permit the search to begin, for a short time (not to exceed two hours, unless the Supervising Solicitor agrees to a longer period). If you wish to take legal advice and gather documents as permitted, you must first inform the Supervising Solicitor and keep him informed of the steps being taken.

RESTRICTIONS ON SERVICE

A32–130   Paragraph 1 of the Order is subject to the following restrictions:—

(1) This Order may only be served between 9:30 a.m. and 5:30 p.m. on a weekday unless the Court has ordered otherwise.

(2) This Order may not be carried out at the same time as a police search warrant.

(3) This Order must be served by the Supervising Solicitor, and paragraph 1 of the Order must be carried out in his presence and under his supervision. Where the premises are likely to be occupied by an unaccompanied woman and the Supervising Solicitor is a man, at least one of the persons accompanying him as provided by paragraph 1 of the Order shall be a woman.

(4) This Order does not require the person served with the Order to allow anyone [or anyone except Mr] to enter the premises who in the view of the Supervising Solicitor could gain commercially from anything he might read or see on the premises if the person served with the Order objects.

VARIATION OR DISCHARGE OF THIS ORDER

A32–131   The Respondent (or anyone notified of this Order) may apply to the Court at any time to vary or discharge this Order (or so much of it as affects that person), but anyone wishing to do so must first inform the Applicant's Solicitors.

INTERPRETATION OF THIS ORDER

A32–132   (1) In this Order, where there is more than one Respondent, references to "the Respondent" means both or all of them.

(2) A requirement to serve on "the Respondent" means on each of them. However, the Order is effective against any Respondent on whom it is served.

(3) An Order requiring "the Respondent" to do or not to do anything applies to all Respondents.

(4) Any other requirement that something shall be done to or in the presence of "the Respondent" means to or in the presence of any one of them or in the case of a firm or company a director or a person appearing to the Supervising Solicitor to be a responsible employee.

COMMUNICATIONS WITH THE COURT

All communications to the Court about this Order should be sent, where the Order is **A32–133** made in the Chancery Division, to [Room TM 510], Royal Courts of Justice, Strand, London, WC2A 2LL quoting the case number. The telephone number is 0171 936 [6827]; and where the order is made in the Queen's Bench Division, to Room W11 (0171 936 6009). The offices are open between 10 a.m. and 4.30 p.m. Monday to Friday.

SCHEDULE A

The premises   **A32–134**

SCHEDULE B

The listed items

SCHEDULE C

UNDERTAKINGS GIVEN TO THE COURT BY THE APPLICANT

(1) If the Court later finds that this Order or carrying it out has caused loss to the **A32–135** Respondent, and decides that the Respondent should be compensated for that loss, the Applicant will comply with any Order the Court may make. Further, if the carrying out of this Order has been in breach of the terms of this Order or otherwise in a manner inconsistent with the Applicant's Solicitors' duties as Officers of the Court the Applicant will comply with any order for damages the Court may make.

[(2) As soon as practicable to issue a Claim Form [in the form of the draft produced to the Court] [claiming appropriate relief.]]

[(3) To [swear and file an affidavit] [cause an affidavit to be sworn and filed] [substantially in the terms of the draft produced to the Court] [confirming the substance of what was said to the Court by the Applicant's Counsel/Solicitors].]

(4) To serve on the Respondent at the same time as this Order is served upon him:
- (i) the Claim Form, or if not issued, the draft produced to the Court,
- (ii) an Application for hearing on [*date*],
- (iii) copies of the affidavits [or draft affidavits] and exhibits capable of being copied containing the evidence relied on by the Applicant [Copies of the confidential exhibits need not be served, but they must be made available for inspection by or on behalf of the Respondent in the presence of the Applicant's Solicitors while the Order is carried out. Afterwards they must be provided to a Solicitor representing the Respondent who gives a written undertaking not to permit the Respondent to see them or copies of them except in his presence and not to permit the Respondent to make or take away any note or record of the exhibits.], and
- (iv) a note of any allegation of fact made orally to the Judge where such allegation is not contained in the affidavits or draft affidavits read by the Judge.

(5) To serve on the Respondent a copy of the Supervising Solicitor's report on the carrying out of this Order as soon as it is received.

(6) Not, without the leave of the Court, to use any information or documents obtained as a result of carrying out this Order nor to inform anyone else of these proceedings except for the purposes of these proceedings (including adding further Respondents) or

commencing civil proceedings in relation to the same or related subject matter to these proceedings until after the return date.

[(7) To maintain pending further order the sum of £   in an account controlled by the Applicant's Solicitors.]

[(8) To insure the items removed from the premises.]

SCHEDULE D

UNDERTAKINGS GIVEN BY THE APPLICANT'S SOLICITORS

A32–136   (1) To answer at once to the best of their ability any question whether a particular item is a listed item.

(2) To return the originals of all documents obtained as a result of this Order (except original documents which belong to the Applicant) as soon as possible and in any event within two working days of their removal.

(3) While ownership of any item obtained as a result of this Order is in dispute, to deliver the article into the keeping of Solicitors acting for the Respondent within two working days from receiving a written undertaking by them to retain the article in safe keeping and to produce it to the Court when required.

(4) To retain in their own safe keeping all other items obtained as a result of this Order until the Court directs otherwise.

SCHEDULE E

UNDERTAKINGS GIVEN BY THE SUPERVISING SOLICITOR

A32–137   (1) To offer to explain to the person served with the Order its meaning and effect fairly and in everyday language, and to inform him of his right to seek legal advice (such advice to include an explanation that the Respondent may be entitled to avail himself of [the privilege against self-incrimination or] [legal professional privilege]) and apply to vary or discharge the Order as mentioned in the Respondent's Entitlements above.

(2) To make and provide to the Applicant's Solicitors and to the Judge who made this Order (for the purposes of the Court file) a written report on the carrying out of the Order.

SCHEDULE F

AFFIDAVITS

A32–138   The Applicant relied on the following affidavits:—
[name] [number of affidavit] [date sworn] [filed on behalf of]

NAME AND ADDRESS OF APPLICANT'S SOLICITORS

The Applicant's Solicitors are:—
[Name, address, reference, fax and telephone numbers both in and out of office hours.]

PART 31

A32–139   DISCLOSURE AND INSPECTION OF DOCUMENTS

CONTENTS

Scope of this part

31.1 (1) This Part sets out rules about the disclosure and inspection of **A32–140** documents.

(2) This Part applies to all claims except a claim on the small claims track.

Meaning of disclosure

31.2 A party discloses a document by stating that the document exists or has **A32–141** existed.

Right of inspection of a disclosed document

31.3 (1) A party to whom a document has been disclosed has a right to inspect **A32–142** that document except where—

(a) the document is no longer in the control of the party who disclosed it;

(b) the party disclosing the document has a right or a duty to withhold inspection of it; or

(c) paragraph (2) applies.

(Rule 31.8 sets out when a document is in the control of a party)

(Rule 31.19 sets out the procedure for claiming a right or duty to withhold inspection)

(2) Where a party considers that it would be disproportionate to the issues in the case to permit inspection of documents within a category or class of document disclosed under rule 31.6(b)—

(a) he is not required to permit inspection of documents within that category or class; but

(b) he must state in his disclosure statement that inspection of those documents will not be permitted on the grounds that to do so would be disproportionate.

(Rule 31.6 provides for standard disclosure)

(Rule 31.10 makes provision for a disclosure statement)

(Rule 31.12 provides for a party to apply for an order for specific inspection of documents)

Meaning of document

31.4 In this Part—   **A32–143**

"document" means anything in which information of any description is recorded; and "copy", in relation to a document, means anything onto which information recorded in the document has been copied, by whatever means and whether directly or indirectly.

Disclosure limited to standard disclosure

A32–144   **31.5** (1) An order to give disclosure is an order to give standard disclosure unless the court directs otherwise.

(2) The court may dispense with or limit standard disclosure.

(3) The parties may agree in writing to dispense with or to limit standard disclosure.

(The court may make an order requiring standard disclosure under rule 28.3 which deals with directions in relation to cases on the fast track and under rule 29.2 which deals with case management in relation to cases on the multi-track)

Standard disclosure—what documents are to be disclosed

A32–145   **31.6** Standard disclosure requires a party to disclose only—
- (a) the documents on which he relies; and
- (b) the documents which—
  - (i) adversely affect his own case;
  - (ii) adversely affect another party's case; or
  - (iii) support another party's case; and
- (c) the documents which he is required to disclose by a relevant practice direction.

Duty of search

A32–146   **31.7** (1) When giving standard disclosure, a party is required to make a reasonable search for documents falling within rule 31.6(b) or (c).

(2) The factors relevant in deciding the reasonableness of a search include the following—
- (a) the number of documents involved;
- (b) the nature and complexity of the proceedings;
- (c) the ease and expense of retrieval of any particular document; and
- (d) the significance of any document which is likely to be located during the search.

(3) Where a party has not searched for a category or class of document on the grounds that to do so would be unreasonable, he must state this in his disclosure statement and identify the category or class of document.

(Rule 31.10 makes provision for a disclosure statement)

Duty of disclosure limited to documents which are or have been in a party's control

132–147   **31.8** (1) A party's duty to disclose documents is limited to documents which are or have been in his control.

(2) For this purpose a party has or has had a document in his control if—
- (a) it is or was in his physical possession;
- (b) he has or has had a right to possession of it; or
- (c) he has or has had a right to inspect or take copies of it.

Disclosure of copies

132–148   **31.9** (1) A party need not disclose more than one copy of a document.

(2) A copy of a document that contains a modification, obliteration or other marking or feature—
- (a) on which a party intends to rely; or
- (b) which adversely affects his own case or another party's case or supports another party's case; shall be treated as a separate document.

(Rule 31.4 sets out the meaning of a copy of a document)

Procedure for standard disclosure

31.10 (1) The procedure for standard disclosure is as follows.   **A32–149**

(2) Each party must make and serve on every other party, a list of documents in the relevant practice form.

(3) The list must identify the documents in a convenient order and manner and as concisely as possible.

(4) The list must indicate—

(a) those documents in respect of which the party claims a right or duty to withhold inspection, and

(b) (i) those documents which are no longer in the party's control; and

(ii) what has happened to those documents.

(Rule 31.19 (3) and (4) require a statement in the list of documents relating to any document inspection of which a person claims he has a right or duty to withhold)

(5) The list must include a disclosure statement.

(6) A disclosure statement is a statement made by the party disclosing the documents—

(a) setting out the extent of the search that has been made to locate documents which he is required to disclose;

(b) certifying that he understands the duty to disclose documents; and

(c) certifying that to the best of his knowledge he has carried out that duty.

(7) Where the party making the disclosure statement is a company, firm, association or other organisation, the statement must also—

(a) identify the person making the statement; and

(b) explain why he is considered an appropriate person to make the statement.

(8) The parties may agree in writing—

(a) to disclose documents without making a list; and

(b) to disclose documents without the disclosing party making a disclosure statement.

(9) A disclosure statement may be made by a person who is not a party where this is permitted under a relevant practice direction.

Duty of disclosure continues during proceedings

31.11 (1) Any duty of disclosure continues until the proceedings are **A32–150** concluded.

(2) If documents to which that duty extends come to a party's notice at any time during the proceedings, he must immediately notify every other party.

Specific disclosure or inspection

31.12 (1) The court may make an order for specific disclosure or specific **A32–151** inspection.

(2) An order for specific disclosure is an order that a party must do one or more of the following things—

(a) disclose documents or classes of documents specified in the order;

(b) carry out a search to the extent stated in the order;

(c) disclose any documents located as a result of that search.

(3) An order for specific inspection is an order that a party permit inspection of a document referred to in rule 31.3(2).

(Rule 31.3(2) allows a party to state in his disclosure statement that he will not permit inspection of a document on the grounds that it would be disproportionate to do so)

Disclosure in stages

31.13 The parties may agree in writing, or the court may direct, that disclosure **A32–152** or inspection or both shall take place in stages.

Documents referred to in statements of case etc.

A32–153   **31.14** A party may inspect a document mentioned in—
   (a) a statement of case;
   (b) a witness statement;
   (c) a witness summary;
   (d) an affidavit; or
   (e) subject to rule 35.10(4), an expert's report.
(Rule 35.10(4) makes provision in relation to instructions referred to in an expert's report)

Inspection and copying of documents

A32–154   **31.15** Where a party has a right to inspect a document—
   (a) that party must give the party who disclosed the document written notice of his wish to inspect;
   (b) the party who disclosed the document must permit inspection not more than 7 days after the date on which he received the notice; and
   (c) that party may request a copy of the document and, if he also undertakes to pay reasonable copying costs, the party who disclosed the document must supply him with a copy not more than seven days after the date on which he received the request.
(Rule 31.3 and 31.14 deal with the right of a party to inspect a document)

Disclosure before proceedings start

A32–155   **31.16** (1) This rule applies where an application is made to the court under any Act for disclosure before proceedings have started.
   (2) The application must be supported by evidence.
   (3) The court may make an order under this rule only where—
   (a) the respondent is likely to be a party to subsequent proceedings;
   (b) the applicant is also likely to be a party to those proceedings;
   (c) if proceedings had started, the respondent's duty by way of standard disclosure, set out in rule 31.6, would extend to the documents or classes of documents of which the applicant seeks disclosure; and
   (d) disclosure before proceedings have started is desirable in order to—
      (i) dispose fairly of the anticipated proceedings;
      (ii) assist the dispute to be resolved without proceedings; or
      (iii) save costs.
   (4) An order under this rule must—
   (a) specify the documents or the classes of documents which the respondent must disclose; and
   (b) require him, when making disclosure, to specify any of those documents—
      (i) which are no longer in his control; or
      (ii) in respect of which he claims a right or duty to withhold inspection.
   (5) Such an order may—
   (a) require the respondent to indicate what has happened to any documents which are no longer in his control; and
   (b) specify the time and place for disclosure and inspection.

Orders for disclosure against a person not a party

A32–156   **31.17** (1) This rule applies where an application is made to the court under any Act for disclosure by a person who is not a party to the proceedings.
   (2) The application must be supported by evidence.
   (3) The court may make an order under this rule only where—
   (a) the documents of which disclosure is sought are likely to support the case of the applicant or adversely affect the case of one of the other parties to the proceedings; and

(b) disclosure is necessary in order to dispose fairly of the claim or to save costs.

(4) An order under this rule must—

(a) specify the documents or the classes of documents which the respondent must disclose; and

(b) require the respondent, when making disclosure, to specify any of those documents—

    (i) which are no longer in his control; or

    (ii) in respect of which he claims a right or duty to withhold inspection.

(5) Such an order may—

(a) require the respondent to indicate what has happened to any documents which are no longer in his control; and

(b) specify the time and place for disclosure and inspection.

Rules not to limit other powers of the court to order disclosure

31.18 Rules 31.16 and 31.17 do not limit any other power which the court may have to order— **A32–157**

(a) disclosure before proceedings have started; and

(b) disclosure against a person who is not a party to proceedings.

Claim to withhold inspection or disclosure of a document

31.19 (1) A person may apply, without notice, for an order permitting him to withhold disclosure of a document on the ground that disclosure would damage the public interest. **A32–158**

(2) Unless the court orders otherwise, an order of the court under paragraph (1)—

(a) must not be served on any other person; and

(b) must not be open to inspection by any person.

(3) A person who wishes to claim that he has a right or a duty to withhold inspection of a document, or part of a document, must state in writing—

(a) that he has such a right or duty; and

(b) the grounds on which he claims that right or duty.

(4) The statement referred to in paragraph (3) must be made—

(a) in the list in which the document is disclosed; or

(b) if there is no list, to the person wishing to inspect the document.

(5) A party may apply to the court to decide whether a claim made under paragraph (3) should be upheld.

(6) For the purpose of deciding an application under paragraph (1) (application to withhold disclosure) or paragraph (3) (claim to withhold inspection) the court may—

(a) require the person seeking to withhold disclosure or inspection of a document to produce that document to the court; and

(b) invite any person, whether or not a party, to make representations.

(7) An application under paragraph (1) or paragraph (5) must be supported by evidence.

(8) This Part does not affect any rule of law which permits or requires a document to be withheld from disclosure or inspection on the ground that its disclosure or inspection would damage the public interest.

Restriction on use of a privileged document inspection of which has been inadvertently allowed

31.20 Where a party inadvertently allows a privileged document to be inspected, the party who has inspected the document may use it or its contents only with the permission of the court. **A32–159**

Consequence of failure to disclose documents or permit inspection

31.21 A party may not rely on any document which he fails to disclose or in respect of which he fails to permit inspection unless the court gives permission. **A32–160**

Subsequent use of disclosed documents

A32–161   **31.22** (1) A party to whom a document has been disclosed may use the document only for the purpose of the proceedings in which it is disclosed, except where—

(a) the document has been read to or by the court, or referred to, at a hearing which has been held in public;

(b) the court gives permission; or

(c) the party who disclosed the document and the person to whom the document belongs agree.

(2) The court may make an order restricting or prohibiting the use of a document which has been disclosed, even where the document has been read to or by the court, or referred to, at a hearing which has been held in public.

(3) An application for such an order may be made—

(a) by a party; or

(b) by any person to whom the document belongs.

False disclosure statements

A32–162   **31.23** (1) Proceedings for contempt of court may be brought against a person if he makes, or causes to be made, a false disclosure statement, without an honest belief in its truth.

(2) Proceedings under this rule may be brought only—

(a) by the Attorney General; or

(b) with the permission of the court.

PRACTICE DIRECTION—DISCLOSURE AND INSPECTION

This Practice Direction supplements CPR Part 31

General

A32–163   **1.1** The normal order for disclosure will be an order that the parties give standard disclosure

1.2 In order to give standard disclosure the disclosing party must make a reasonable search for documents falling within the paragraphs of rule 31.6.

1.3 Having made the search the disclosing party must (unless rule 31.10(8) applies) make a list of the documents of whose existence the party is aware that fall within those paragraphs and which are or have been in the party's control (see rule 31.8).

1.4 The obligations imposed by an order for standard disclosure may be dispensed with or limited either by the court or by written agreement between the parties. Any such written agreement should be lodged with the court.

The search

A32–164   **2** The extent of the search which must be made will depend upon the circumstances of the case including, in particular, the factors referred to in rule 31.7(2). The parties should bear in mind the overriding principle of proportionality (see rule 1.1(2)(c)). It may, for example, be reasonable to decide not to search for documents coming into existence before some particular date, or to limit the search for documents in some particular place or places, or to documents falling into particular categories.

The list

A32–165   **3.1** The list should be in Form N265.

3.2 In order to comply with rule 31.10(3) it will normally be necessary to list the documents in date order, to number them consecutively and to give each a concise description (eg. letter, claimant to defendant). Where there is a large number of documents all falling into a particular category the disclosing party may list those documents as a category rather than individually e.g. 50 bank statements relating to account number—at—Bank,—19—to—19—; or, 35 letters passing between—and—between—19—a—19—.

3.3 The obligations imposed by an order for disclosure will continue until the proceedings come to an end. If, after a list of documents has been prepared and served, the existence of further documents to which the order applies comes to the attention of the disclosing party, the party must prepare and serve a supplemental list.

Disclosure statement

4.1 A list of documents must (unless rule 31.10(8)(b) applies) contain a **A32–166** disclosure statement complying with rule 31.10. The form of disclosure statement is set out in the Annex to this practice direction.

4.2 The disclosure statement should:

(1) expressly state that the disclosing party believes the extent of the search to have been reasonable in all the circumstances, and

(2) in setting out the extent of the search (see rule 31.10(6)) draw attention to any particular limitations on the extent of the search which were adopted for proportionality reasons and give the reasons why the limitations were adopted, e.g. the difficulty or expense that a search not subject to those limitations would have entailed or the marginal relevance of categories of documents omitted from the search.

4.3 Where rule 31.10(7) applies, the details given in the disclosure statement about the person making the statement must include his name and address and the office or position he holds in the disclosing party.

4.4 If the disclosing party has a legal representative acting for him, the legal representative must endeavour to ensure that the person making the disclosure statement (whether the disclosing party or, in a case in which rule 31.10(7) applies, some other person) understands the duty of disclosure under rule 31.

4.5 If the disclosing party wishes to claim that he has a right or duty to withhold a document, or part of a document, in his list of documents from inspection (see rule 31.19(3)), he must state in writing:

(1) that he has such a right or duty, and

(2) the grounds on which he claims that right or duty.

4.6 The statement referred to in paragraph 4.5 above should normally be included in the disclosure statement and must indicate the document, or part of a document, to which the claim relates.

4.7 An insurer or the Motor Insurers' Bureau may sign a disclosure statement on behalf of a party where the insurer or the Motor Insurers' Bureau has a financial interest in the result of proceedings brought wholly or partially by or against that party. Rule 31.10(7) and paragraph 4.3 above shall apply to the insurer or the Motor Insurers' Bureau making such a statement.

Specific disclosure

5.1 If a party believes that the disclosure of documents given by a disclosing **A32–167** party is inadequate he may make an application for an order for specific disclosure (see rule 31.12).

5.2 The application notice must specify the order that the applicant intends to ask the court to make and must be supported by evidence (see rule 31.12(2) which describes the orders the court may make).

5.3 The grounds on which the order is sought may be set out in the application notice itself but if not there set out must be set out in the evidence filed in support of the application.

5.4 In deciding whether or not to make an order for specific disclosure the court will take into account all the circumstances of the case and, in particular, the overriding objective described in Part 1. But if the court concludes that the party from whom specific disclosure is sought has failed adequately to comply with the obligations imposed by an order for disclosure (whether by failing to make a sufficient search for the documents or otherwise) the court will usually make such order as is necessary to ensure that those obligations are properly complied with.

Claims to withhold disclosure or inspection of a document

A32–168   **6.1** A claim to withhold inspection of a document, or part of a document, disclosed in a list of documents does not require an application to the court. Where such a claim has been made, a party who wishes to challenge it must apply to the court (see rule 31.19(5)).

6.2 Rule 31.19(1) and (6) provide a procedure enabling a party to apply for an order permitting disclosure of the existence of a document to be withheld.

Inspection of documents mentioned in expert's report (rule 31.14(e))

A32–169   **7** Reference should be made to the practice direction supplementing Part 35 (Experts and Assessors) for provisions dealing with applications to inspect these documents.

Annex

Disclosure statement

A32–170   I, the above named claimant [or defendant] [if party making disclosure is a company, firm or other organisation identify here who the person making the disclosure statement is and why he is the appropriate person to make state that I have carried out a reasonable and proportionate search to locate all the documents which I am required to disclose under the order made by the court on day of. I did not search:
(1) for documents predating . . . .,
(2) for documents located elsewhere than . . . .,
(3) for documents in categories other than . . . .
I certify that I understand the duty of disclosure and to the best of my knowledge I have carried out that duty. I certify that the list above is a complete list of all documents which are or have been in my control and which I am obliged under the said order to disclose.

A32–171

PART 36

OFFERS TO SETTLE AND PAYMENTS INTO COURT

AMENDED BY THE CIVIL PROCEDURE (AMENDMENT NO. 4) RULES 2000

CONTENTS

Scope of this Part

36.1 (1) This Part contains rules about—   **A32–172**
    (a) offers to settle and payments into court; and
    (b) the consequences where an offer to settle or payment into court is made in accordance with this Part.

(2) Nothing in this Part prevents a party making an offer to settle in whatever way he chooses, but if that offer is not made in accordance with this Part, it will only have the consequences specified in this Part if the court so orders.

(Part 36 applies to Part 20 claims by virtue of rule 20.3)

Part 36 offers and Part 36 payments—general provisions

36.2 (1) An offer made in accordance with the requirements of this Part is **A32–173** called—
    (a) if made by way of a payment into court, "a Part 36 payment";
    (b) otherwise "a Part 36 offer".

(Rule 36.3 sets out when an offer has to be made by way of a payment into court)

(2) The party who makes an offer is the "offeror".

(3) The party to whom an offer is made is the "offeree".

(4) A Part 36 offer or a Part 36 payment—
    (a) may be made at any time after proceedings have started; and
    (b) may be made in appeal proceedings.

(5) A Part 36 offer or a Part 36 payment shall not have the consequences set out in this Part while the claim is being dealt with on the small claims track unless the court orders otherwise.

(Part 26 deals with allocation to the small claims track)

(Rule 27.2 provides that Part 36 does not apply to small claims)

A defendant's offer to settle a money claim requires a Part 36 payment

36.3 (1) Subject to rules 36.5(5) and 36.23, an offer by a defendant to settle a **A32–174** money claim will not have the consequences set out in this Part unless it is made by way of a Part 36 payment.

(2) A Part 36 payment may only be made after proceedings have started.

(Rule 36.5(5) permits a Part 36 offer to be made by reference to an interim payment)

(Rule 36.10 makes provision for an offer to settle a money claim before the commencement proceedings)

(Rule 36.23 makes provision for where benefit is recoverable under the Social Security (Recovery of Benefit) Act 1997)

Defendant's offer to settle the whole of a claim which includes both a money claim and a non-money claim

A32–175   **36.4** (1) This rule applies where a defendant to a claim which includes both a money claim and a non-money claim wishes—

(a) to make an offer to settle the whole claim which will have the consequences set out in this Part; and

(b) to make a money offer in respect of the money claim and a non-money offer in respect of a non-money claim.

(2) The defendant must—

(a) make a Part 36 payment in relation to the money claim; and

(b) make a Part 36 offer in relation to the non-money claim.

(3) The Part 36 payment notice must—

(a) identify the document which sets out the terms of the Part 36 offer; and

(b) state that if the claimant gives notice of acceptance of the Part 36 payment he will be treated as also accepting the Part 36 offer.

(Rule 36.6 makes provision for a Part 36 payment notice)

(4) If the claimant gives notice of acceptance of the Part 36 payment, he shall also be taken as giving notice of acceptance of the Part 36 offer in relation to the non-money claim.

Form and content of a Part 36 offer

A32–176   **36.5** (1) A Part 36 offer must be in writing.

(2) A Part 36 offer may relate to the whole claim or to part of it or to any issue that arises in it.

(3) A Part 36 offer must—

(a) state whether it relates to the whole of the claim or to part of it or to an issue that arises in it and if so to which part or issue;

(b) state whether it takes into account any counterclaim; and

(c) if it is expressed not to be inclusive of interest, give the details relating to interest set out in rule 36.22(2).

(4) A defendant may make a Part 36 offer limited to accepting liability up to a specified proportion.

(5) A Part 36 offer may be made by reference to an interim payment.

(Part 25 contains provisions relating to interim payments)

(6) A Part 36 offer made not less than 21 days before the start of the trial must—

(a) be expressed to remain open for acceptance for 21 days from the date it is made; and

(b) provide that after 21 days the offeree may only accept it if—

(i) the parties agree the liability for costs; or

(ii) the court gives permission.

(7) A Part 36 offer made less than 21 days before the start of the trial must state that the offeree may only accept it if—

(a) the parties agree the liability for costs; or

(b) the court gives permission.

(Rule 36.8 makes provision for when a Part 36 offer is treated as being made)

(8) If a Part 36 offer is withdrawn it will not have the consequences set out in this Part.

Notice of a Part 36 payment

A32–177   **36.6** (1) A Part 36 payment may relate to the whole claim or part of it or to an issue that arises in it.

(2) A defendant who makes a Part 36 payment must file with the court a notice ("Part 36 payment notice") which—

(a) states the amount of the payment;

(b) states whether the payment relates to the whole claim or to part of it or to any issue that arises in it and if so to which part or issue;

(c) states whether it takes into account any counterclaim;

(d) if an interim payment has been made, states that the defendant has taken into account the interim payment; and

(e) if it is expressed not to be inclusive of interest, gives the details relating to interest set out in rule 36.22(2).

(Rule 25.6 makes provision for an interim payment)

(Rule 36.4 provides for further information to be included where a defendant wishes to settle the whole of a claim which includes a money claim and a non-money claim)

(Rule 36.23 makes provision for extra information to be included in the payment notice in a case where benefit is recoverable under the Social Security (Recovery of Benefit) Act 1997)

(3) The court will serve the Part 36 payment notice on the offeree unless the offeror informs the court, when the money is paid into court, that the offeror will serve the notice.

(4) Where the offeror serves the Part 36 payment notice he must file a certificate of service.

(Rule 6.10 specifies what must be contained in a certificate of service)

(5) A Part 36 payment may be withdrawn or reduced only with the permission of the court.

Offer to settle a claim for provisional damages

36.7 (1) A defendant may make a Part 36 payment in respect of a claim which **A32–178** includes a claim for provisional damages.

(2) Where he does so, the Part 36 payment notice must specify whether or not the defendant is offering to agree to the making of an award of provisional damages.

(3) Where the defendant is offering to agree to the making of an award of provisional damages the payment notice must also state—

(a) that the sum paid into court is in satisfaction of the claim for damages on the assumption that the injured person will not develop the disease or suffer the type of deterioration specified in the notice;

(b) that the offer is subject to the condition that the claimant must make any claim for further damages within a limited period; and

(c) what that period is.

(4) Where a Part 36 payment is—

(a) made in accordance with paragraph (3); and

(b) accepted within the relevant period in rule 36.11,

the Part 36 payment will have the consequences set out in rule 36.13, unless the court orders otherwise.

(5) If the claimant accepts the Part 36 payment he must, within 7 days of doing so, apply to the court for an order for an award of provisional damages under rule 41.2.

(Rule 41.2 provides for an order for an award of provisional damages)

(6) The money in court may not be paid out until the court has disposed of the application made in accordance with paragraph (5).

Time when a Part 36 offer or a Part 36 payment is made and accepted

36.8 (1) A Part 36 offer is made when received by the offeree. **A32–179**

(2) A Part 36 payment is made when written notice of the payment into court is served on the offeree.

(3) An improvement to a Part 36 offer will be effective when its details are received by the offeree.

(4) An increase in a Part 36 payment will be effective when notice of the increase is served on the offeree.

(5) A Part 36 offer or Part 36 payment is accepted when notice of its acceptance is received by the offeror.

Clarification of a Part 36 offer or a Part 36 payment notice

A32–180 **36.9** (1) The offeree may, within 7 days of a Part 36 offer or payment being made, request the offeror to clarify the offer or payment notice.

(2) If the offeror does not give the clarification requested under paragraph (1) within 7 days of receiving the request, the offeree may, unless the trial has started, apply for an order that he does so.

(3) If the court makes an order under paragraph (2), it must specify the date when the Part 36 offer or Part 36 payment is to be treated as having been made.

Court to take into account offer to settle made before commencement of proceedings

A32–181 **36.10** (1) If a person makes an offer to settle before proceedings are begun which complies with the provisions of this rule, the court will take that offer into account when making any order as to costs.

(2) The offer must—
- (a) be expressed to be open for at least 21 days after the date it was made;
- (b) if made by a person who would be a defendant were proceedings commenced, include the offer to pay the costs of the offeree incurred up to the date 21 days after the date it was made; and
- (c) otherwise comply with this Part.

(3) If the offeror is a defendant to a money claim—
- (a) he must make a Part 36 payment within 14 days of service of the claim form; and
- (b) the amount of the payment must be not less than the sum offered before proceedings began.

(4) An offeree may not, after proceedings have begun, accept—
- (a) an offer made under paragraph (2); or
- (b) a Part 36 payment made under paragraph (3), without the permission of the court.

(5) An offer under this rule is made when it is received by the offeree.

Time for acceptance of a defendant's Part 36 offer or Part 36 payment

A32–182 **36.11** (1) A claimant may accept a Part 36 offer or a Part 36 payment made not less than 21 days before the start of the trial without needing the court's permission if he gives the defendant written notice of acceptance not later than 21 days after the offer or payment was made.

(Rule 36.13 sets out the costs consequences of accepting a defendant's offer or payment without needing the permission of the court)

(2) If—
- (a) a defendant's Part 36 offer or Part 36 payment is made less than 21 days before the start of the trial; or
- (b) the claimant does not accept it within the period specified in paragraph (1)—
  - (i) if the parties agree the liability for costs, the claimant may accept the offer or payment without needing the permission of the court;
  - (ii) if the parties do not agree the liability for costs the claimant may only accept the offer or payment with the permission of the court.

(3) Where the permission of the court is needed under paragraph (2) the court will, if it gives permission, make an order as to costs.

Time for acceptance of a claimant's Part 36 offer

A32–183 **36.12** (1) A defendant may accept a Part 36 offer made not less than 21 days before the start of the trial without needing the court's permission if he gives the claimant written notice of acceptance not later than 21 days after the offer was made.

(Rule 36.14 sets out the costs consequences of accepting a claimant's offer without needing the permission of the court)

(2) If—

    (a) a claimant's Part 36 offer is made less than 21 days before the start of the trial; or

    (b) the defendant does not accept it within the period specified in paragraph (1)—

        (i) if the parties agree the liability for costs, the defendant may accept the offer without needing the permission of the court;

        (ii) if the parties do not agree the liability for costs the defendant may only accept the offer with the permission of the court.

(3) Where the permission of the court is needed under paragraph (2) the court will, if it gives permission, make an order as to costs.

Costs consequences of acceptance of a defendant's Part 36 offer or Part 36 payment

36.13 (1) Where a Part 36 offer or a Part 36 payment is accepted without **A32–184** needing the permission of the court the claimant will be entitled to his costs of the proceedings up to the date of serving notice of acceptance.

(2) Where—

    (a) a Part 36 offer or a Part 36 payment relates to part only of the claim; and

    (b) at the time of serving notice of acceptance the claimant abandons the balance of the claim,

the claimant will be entitled to his costs of the proceedings up to the date of serving notice acceptance, unless the court orders otherwise.

(3) The claimant's costs include any costs attributable to the defendant's counterclaim if the Part 36 offer or the Part 36 payment notice states that it takes into account the counterclaim.

(4) Costs under this rule will be payable on the standard basis if not agreed.

Costs consequences of acceptance of a claimant's Part 36 offer

36.14 Where a claimant's Part 36 offer is accepted without needing the **A32–185** permission of the court the claimant will be entitled to his costs of the proceedings up to the date upon which the defendant serves notice of acceptance.

The effect of acceptance of a Part 36 offer or a Part 36 payment

36.15 (1) If a Part 36 offer or Part 36 payment relates to the whole claim and is **A32–186** accepted, the claim will be stayed.

(2) In the case of acceptance of a Part 36 offer which relates to the whole claim—

    (a) the stay will be upon the terms of the offer; and

    (b) either party may apply to enforce those terms without the need for a new claim.

(3) If a Part 36 offer or a Part 36 payment which relates to part only of the claim is accepted—

    (a) the claim will be stayed as to that part; and

    (b) unless the parties have agreed costs, the liability for costs shall be decided by the court.

(4) If the approval of the court is required before a settlement can be binding, any stay which would otherwise arise on the acceptance of a Part 36 offer or a Part 36 payment will take effect only when that approval has been given.

(5) Any stay arising under this rule will not affect the power of the court—

    (a) to enforce the terms of a Part 36 offer;

    (b) to deal with any question of costs (including interest on costs) relating to the proceedings;

(c) to order payment out of court of any sum paid into court.

(6) Where—

    (a) a Part 36 offer has been accepted; and

    (b) a party alleges that—

        (i) the other party has not honoured the terms of the offer; and

        (ii) he is therefore entitled to a remedy for breach of contract, the party may claim the remedy by applying to the court without the need to start a new claim unless the court orders otherwise.

Payment out of a sum in court on the acceptance of a Part 36 payment

A32–187   **36.16** Where a Part 36 payment is accepted the claimant obtains payment out of the sum in court by making a request for payment in the practice form.

Acceptance of a Part 36 offer or a Part 36 payment made by one or more, but not all, defendants

A32–188   **36.17** (1) This rule applies where the claimant wishes to accept a Part 36 offer or a Part 36 payment made by one or more, but not all, of a number of defendants.

(2) If the defendants are sued jointly or in the alternative, the claimant may accept the offer or payment without needing the permission of the court in accordance with rule 36.11(1) if—

    (a) he discontinues his claim against those defendants who have not made the offer or payment; and

    (b) those defendants give written consent to the acceptance of the offer or payment.

(3) If the claimant alleges that the defendants have a several liability to him the claimant may—

    (a) accept the offer or payment in accordance with rule 36.11(1); and

    (b) continue with his claims against the other defendants if he is entitled to do so.

(4) In all other cases the claimant must apply to the court for—

    (a) an order permitting a payment out to him of any sum in court; and

    (b) such order as to costs as the court considers appropriate.

Other cases where a court order is required to enable acceptance of a Part 36 offer or a Part 36 payment

A32–189   **36.18** (1) Where a Part 36 offer or a Part 36 payment is made in proceedings to which rule 21.10 applies—

    (a) the offer or payment may be accepted only with the permission of the court; and

    (b) no payment out of any sum in court shall be made without a court order.

(Rule 21.10 deals with compromise etc. by or on behalf of a child or patient)

(2) Where the court gives a claimant permission to accept a Part 36 offer or payment after the has started—

    (a) any money in court may be paid out only with a court order; and

    (b) the court must, in the order, deal with the whole costs of the proceedings.

(3) Where a claimant accepts a Part 36 payment after a defence of tender before claim has been put forward by the defendant, the money in court may be paid out only after an order of the court.

(Rule 37.3 requires a defendant who wishes to rely on a defence of tender before claim to make a payment into court)

Restriction on disclosure of a Part 36 offer or a Part 36 payment

A32–190   **36.19** (1) A Part 36 offer will be treated as "without prejudice except as to costs".

(2) The fact that a Part 36 payment has been made shall not be communicated to the trial judge until all questions of liability and the amount of money to be awarded have been decided.

(3) Paragraph (2) does not apply—
- (a) where the defence of tender before claim has been raised;
- (b) where the proceedings have been stayed under rule 36.15 following acceptance of a Part 36 offer or Part 36 payment; or
- (c) where—
    - (i) the issue of liability has been determined before any assessment of the money claimed; and
    - (ii) the fact that there has or has not been a Part 36 payment may be relevant to the question of the costs of the issue of liability.

Costs consequences where claimant fails to do better than a Part 36 offer or a Part 36 payment

36.20 (1) This rule applies where at trial a claimant—   A32–191
- (a) fails to better a Part 36 payment; or
- (b) fails to obtain a judgment which is more advantageous than a defendant's Part 36 offer.

(2) Unless it considers it unjust to do so, the court will order the claimant to pay any costs incurred by the defendant after the latest date on which the payment or offer could have been accepted without needing the permission of the court.

(Rule 36.11 sets out the time for acceptance of a defendant's Part 36 offer or Part 36 payment)

Costs and other consequences where claimant does better than he proposed in his Part 36 offer

36.21 (1) This rule applies where at trial—   A32–192
- (a) a defendant is held liable for more; or
- (b) the judgment against a defendant is more advantageous to the claimant, than the proposals contained in a claimant's Part 36 offer.

(2) The court may order interest on the whole or part of any sum of money (excluding interest) awarded to the claimant at a rate not exceeding 10% above base rate for some or all of the period starting with the latest date on which the defendant could have accepted the offer without needing the permission of the court.

(3) The court may also order that the claimant is entitled to—
- (a) his costs on the indemnity basis from the latest date when the defendant could have accepted the offer without needing the permission of the court; and
- (b) interest on those costs at a rate not exceeding 10% above base rate.

(4) Where this rule applies, the court will make the orders referred to in paragraphs (2) and (3) unless it considers it unjust to do so.

(Rule 36.12 sets out the latest date when the defendant could have accepted the offer)

(5) In considering whether it would be unjust to make the orders referred to in paragraphs (2) and (3) above, the court will take into account all the circumstances of the case including—
- (a) the terms of any Part 36 offer;
- (b) the stage in the proceedings when any Part 36 offer or Part 36 payment was made;
- (c) the information available to the parties at the time when the Part 36 offer or Part 36 payment was made; and
- (d) the conduct of the parties with regard to the giving or refusing to give information for the purposes of enabling the offer or payment into court to be made or evaluated.

(6) Where the court awards interest under this rule and also awards interest on the same sum and for the same period under any other power, the total rate of interest may not exceed 10% above base rate.

Interest

A32–193   **36.22** (1) Unless—
    (a) a claimant's Part 36 offer which offers to accept a sum of money; or
    (b) a Part 36 payment notice, indicates to the contrary, any such offer or payment will be treated as inclusive of all interest until the last date on which it could be accepted without needing the permission of the court.
    (2) Where a claimant's Part 36 offer or Part 36 payment notice is expressed not to be inclusive of interest, the offer or notice must state—
    (a) whether interest is offered; and
    (b) if so, the amount offered, the rate or rates offered and the period or periods for which it is offered.

Deduction of benefits

A32–194   **36.23** (1) This rule applies where a payment to a claimant following acceptance of a Part 36 offer or Part 36 payment into court would be a compensation payment as defined in section 1 of the Social Security (Recovery of Benefits) Act 1997.
    (2) A defendant to a money claim may make an offer to settle the claim which will have the consequences set out in this Part, without making a Part 36 payment if—
    (a) at the time he makes the offer he has applied for, but not received, a certificate of recoverable benefit; and
    (b) he makes a Part 36 payment not more than 7 days after he receives the certificate.
    (Section 1 of the 1997 Act defines "recoverable benefit")
    (3) A Part 36 payment notice must state—
    (a) the amount of gross compensation;
    (b) the name and amount of any benefit by which that gross amount is reduced in accordance with section 8 and Schedule 2 to the 1997 Act; and
    (c) that the sum paid in is the net amount after deduction of the amount of benefit.
    (4) For the purposes of rule 36.20, a claimant fails to better a Part 36 payment if he fails to obtain judgment for more than the gross sum specified in the Part 36 payment notice.
    (5) Where—
    (a) a Part 36 payment has been made; and
    (b) application is made for the money remaining in court to be paid out,
the court may treat the money in court as being reduced by a sum equivalent to any further recoverable benefits paid to the claimant since the date of payment into court and may direct payment out accordingly.

PRACTICE DIRECTION—OFFERS TO SETTLE AND PAYMENTS INTO COURT

This Practice Direction supplements CPR Part 36

Part 36 offers and Part 36 payments

A32–195   **1.1** A written offer to settle a claim or part of a claim or any issue that arises in it made in accordance with the provisions of Part 36 is called:
    (1) if made by way of a payment into court, a Part 36 payment, or

(2) if made otherwise, a Part 36 offer.

1.2 A Part 36 offer or Part 36 payment has the costs and other consequences set out in rules 36.13, 36.14, 36.20 and 36.21.

1.3 An offer to settle which is not made in accordance with Part 36 will only have the consequences specified in that Part if the court so orders and will be given such weight on any issue as to costs as the court thinks appropriate.

Parties and Part 36 offers

2.1 A Part 36 offer, subject to paragraph 3 below, may be made by any party. **A32–196**

2.2 The party making an offer is the "offeror" and the party to whom it is made is the "offeree".

2.3 A Part 36 offer may consist of a proposal to settle for a specified sum or for some other remedy.

2.4 A Part 36 offer is made when received by the offeree.

2.5 An improvement to a Part 36 offer is effective when its details are received by the offeree.

Parties and Part 36 payments

3.1 An offer to settle for a specified sum made by a defendant must, in order **A32–197** to comply with Part 36, be made by way of a Part 36 payment into court.

3.2 A Part 36 payment is made when the Part 36 payment notice is served on the claimant.

3.3 An increase to a Part 36 payment will be effective when notice of the increase is served on the claimant.

(For service of the Part 36 payment notice see rule 36.6(3) and (4).)

3.4 A defendant who wishes to withdraw or reduce a Part 36 payment must obtain the court's permission to do so.

3.5 Permission may be obtained by making an application in accordance with Part 23 stating the reason giving rise to the wish to withdraw or reduce the Part 36 payment.

Making a Part 36 payment

4.1 To make a Part 36 payment the defendant must file the following **A32–198** documents:

(1) where that court is a county court or a district registry—
    (a) the Part 36 payment notice, and
    (b) the payment, usually a cheque made payable to Her Majesty's Paymaster General, with the court, and

(2) where that court is the Royal Courts of Justice—
    (a) the Part 36 payment notice with the court, and
    (b) the payment, usually a cheque made payable to the Accountant General of the Supreme Court, and
    (c) a sealed copy of the Claim Form,
    (d) the Court Funds Office form 100 with the Court Funds Office.

Part 36 offers and part 36 payments—general provisions

5.1 A Part 36 offer or a Part 36 payment notice must: **A32–199**

(1) state that it is a Part 36 offer or that the payment into court is a Part 36 payment, and

(2) be signed by the offeror or his legal representative.

5.2 The contents of a Part 36 offer must also comply with the requirements of rule 36.5(3), (5) and (6).

5.3 The contents of a Part 36 payment notice must comply with rule 36.6(2) and, if rule 36.23 applies, with rule 36.23(3).

5.4 A Part 36 offer or Part 36 payment will be taken to include interest unless it is expressly stated in the offer or the payment notice that interest is not included, in which case the details set out in rule 36.2 must be given.

5.5 Where a Part 36 offer is made by a company or other corporation, a person holding a senior position in the company or corporation may sign the offer on the offeror's behalf, but must state the position he holds.

5.6 Each of the following persons is a person holding a senior position:

(1) in respect of a registered company or corporation, a director, the treasurer, secretary, chief executive, manager or other officer of the company or corporation, and

(2) in respect of a corporation which is not a registered company, in addition to those persons set out in (1), the mayor, chairman, president, town clerk or similar officer of the corporation.

Clarification of Part 36 offer or payment

A32–200   **6.1** An offeree may apply to the court for an order requiring the offeror to clarify the terms of a Part 36 offer or Part 36 payment notice (a clarification order) where the offeror has failed to comply within 7 days to a request for clarification.

6.2 An application for a clarification order should be made in accordance with Part 23.

6.3 The application notice should state the respects in which the terms of the Part 36 offer or Part 36 payment notice, as the case may be, are said to need clarification.

Acceptance of a Part 36 offer or payment

A32–201   **7.1** The times for accepting a Part 36 offer or a Part 36 payment are set out in rules 36.11 and 36.12.

7.2 The general rule is that a Part 36 offer or Part 36 payment made more than 21 days before the start of the trial may be accepted within 21 days after it was made without the permission of the court. The costs consequences set out in rules 36.13 and 36.14 will then come into effect.

7.3 A Part 36 offer or Part 36 payment made less than 21 days before the start of the trial cannot be accepted without the permission of the court unless the parties agree what the costs consequences on acceptance will be.

7.4 The permission of the court may be sought:

(1) Before the start of the trial, by making an application in accordance with Part 23, and

(2) After the start of the trial, by making an application to the trial judge.

7.5 If the court gives permission it will make an order dealing with costs and may order that, in the circumstances, the costs consequences set out in rules 36.13 and 36.14 will apply.

7.6 Where a Part 36 offer or Part 36 payment is accepted in accordance with rule 36.11(1) or rule 36.12 the notice of acceptance must be sent to the offeror and filed with the court.

7.7 The notice of acceptance:

(1) Must set out—

    (a) the claim number, and

    (b) the title of the proceedings,

(2) Must identify the Part 36 offer or Part 36 payment notice to which it relates, and

(3) Must be signed by the offeree or his legal representative (see paragraphs 6.5 and 6.6 above).

7.8 Where:

(1) the court's approval, or

(2) an order for payment of money out of court, or

(3) an order apportioning money in court—

    (a) between the Fatal Accidents Act 1976 and the Law Reform (Miscellaneous Provisions) Act 1934, or

(b) between the persons entitled to it under the Fatal Accidents Act 1976, is required for acceptance of a Part 36 offer or Part 36 payment, application for the approval the order should be made in accordance with Part 23.

7.9 The court will include in any order made under paragraph 7.8 above a direction for;

(1) the payment out of the money in court, and

(2) the payment of interest.

7.10 Unless the parties have agreed otherwise:

(1) Interest accruing up to the date of acceptance will be paid to the offeror, and

(2) Interest accruing as from the date of acceptance until payment out will be paid to the offeree.

7.11 A claimant may not accept a Part 36 payment which is part of a defendant's offer to settle the whole claim consisting of both a money and a non-money claim unless at the same time he accepts the offer to settle the whole of the claim. Therefore:

(1) if a claimant accepts a Part 36 payment which is part of a defendant's offer to settle the whole of the claim, or

(2) if a claimant accepts a Part 36 offer which is part of a defendant's offer to settle the whole of the claim, the claimant will be deemed to have accepted the offer to settle the whole of the claim.

(See paragraph 8 below for the method of obtaining money out of court.)

Payment out of court

8.1 To obtain money out of court following acceptance of a Part 36 payment, **A32–202** the claimant should file a request for payment with the court 16.

8.2 The request for payment should contain the following details:

(1) Where the party receiving the payment—

    (a) is legally represented—

        (i) the name, business address and reference of the legal representative, and

        (ii) the name of the bank and the sort code number, the title of the account and the account number where the payment is to be transmitted, and

(2) Where the party is acting in person—

    (a) his name and address, and

    (b) his bank account details as in (ii) above.

8.3 Where the request for payment is made to the Royal Courts of Justice, the claimant should also complete Court Funds Office form 201 and file it in the Court Funds Office.

8.4 Subject to paragraph 9.5(1) and (2), if a party does not wish the payment to be transmitted into his bank account or if he does not have a bank account, he may send a written request to the Accountant-General for the payment to be made to him by cheque.

8.5 Where a party seeking payment out of court has provided the necessary information, the payment:

(1) Where a party is legally represented, must be made to the legal representative.

(2) if the party is not legally represented but is, or has been, in receipt of legal aid in respect of the proceedings and a notice to that effect has been filed, should be made to the Legal Aid Board by direction of the court,

(3) Where a person entitled to money in court dies without having made a will and the court is satisfied—

    (a) that no grant of administration of his estate has been made, and

    (b) that the assets of his estate, including the money in court, do not exceed in value the amount specified in any order in force under section 6 of the Administration of Estates (Small Payments) Act 1965, payment may be ordered to be made to the person appearing to have the prior right to a grant of administration of the estate of the deceased, e.g. a widower, widow, child, father, mother, brother or sister of the deceased.

Foreign currency

A32–203   **9.1** Money may be paid into court in a foreign currency:

(1) Where it is a Part 36 payment and the claim is in a foreign currency, or

(2) Under a court order.

9.2 The court may direct that the money be placed in an interest bearing account in the currency of the claim or any other currency.

9.3 Where a Part 36 payment is made in a foreign currency and has not been accepted within 21 days, the defendant may apply for an order that the money be placed in an interest bearing account.

9.4 The application should be made in accordance with Part 23 and should state:

(1) That the payment has not been accepted in accordance with rule 36.11, and

(2) The type of currency on which interest is to accrue.

Compensation recovery

A32–204   **10.1** Where a defendant makes a Part 36 payment in respect of a claim for a sum or part of a sum:

(1) which falls under the heads of damage set out in column 1 of Schedule 2 of the Social Security (Recovery of Benefits) Act 1997 in respect of recoverable benefits received by the claimant as set out in column 2 of that Schedule, and

(2) Where the defendant is liable to pay recoverable benefits to the Secretary of State, the defendant should obtain from the Secretary of State a certificate of recoverable benefits and file the certificate with the Part 36 payment notice.

10.2 If a defendant wishes to offer to settle a claim where he has applied for but not yet received a certificate of recoverable benefits, he may, provided that he makes a Part 36 payment not more than 7 days after he has received the certificate, make a Part 36 offer which will have the costs and other consequences set out in rules 36.13 and 36.20.

10.3 The Part 36 payment notice should state in addition to the requirements set out in rule 36.6(2):

(1) the total amount represented by the Part 36 payment (the gross compensation),

(2) that the defendant has reduced this sum by £   , in accordance with section 8 of and Sched. 2 to the Social Security (Recovery of Benefits) Act 1997, which was calculated as follows:

Name of benefit   Amount

and

(3) that the amount paid in, being the sum of £   is the net amount after the deduction of the amount of benefit.

10.4 On acceptance of a Part 36 payment to which this paragraph relates, a claimant will receive the sum in court which will be net of the recoverable benefits.

10.5 In establishing at trial whether a claimant has bettered or obtained a judgment more advantageous than a Part 36 payment to which this paragraph relates, the court will base its decision on the gross sum specified in the Part 36 payment notice.

General

A32–205   **11.1** Where a party on whom a Part 36 offer, a Part 36 payment notice or a notice of acceptance is to be served is legally represented, the Part 36 offer, Part 36 payment notice and notice of acceptance must be served on the legal representative.

11.2 In a claim arising out of an accident involving a motor vehicle on a road or in a public place:

(1) where the damages claimed include a sum for hospital expenses, and

(2) the defendant or his insurer pays that sum to the hospital under section 157 of the Road Traffic Act 1988,

the defendant must give notice of that payment to the court and all the other parties to the proceedings.

11.3 Money paid into court:

(1) as a Part 36 payment which is not accepted by the claimant, or

(2) under a court order,

will be placed after 21 days in a basic account 17 (subject to paragraph 11.4 below) for interest to accrue.

11.4 Where money referred to in paragraph 11.3 above is paid in in respect of a child or patient it will be placed in a special investment account 18 for interest to accrue

(A practice direction supplementing Part 21 contains information about the investment of money in court in respect of a child or patient.)

(Practice directions supplementing Part 40 contain information about adjustment of the judgment sum in respect of recoverable benefits, and about structured settlements.)

(A practice direction supplementing Part 41 contains information about provisional damages awards.)

PART 44

GENERAL RULES ABOUT COSTS

AMENDED BY THE CIVIL PROCEDURE (AMENDMENT No. 3) RULES 2000

CONTENTS

A32–206

Scope of this part

44.1 This Part contains general rules about costs and entitlement to costs.   A32–207
(The definitions contained in Part 43 are relevant to this Part)

Solicitor's duty to notify client

A32–208   44.2 Where—
(a) the court makes a costs order against a legally represented party; and
(b) the party is not present when the order is made, the party's solicitor must notify his client in writing of the costs order no later than 7 days after the solicitor receives notice of the order.

Court's discretion and circumstances to be taken into account when exercising its discretion as to costs

A32–209   44.3 (1) The court has discretion as to—
(a) whether costs are payable by one party to another;
(b) the amount of those costs; and
(c) when they are to be paid.
(2) If the court decides to make an order about costs—
(a) the general rule is that the unsuccessful party will be ordered to pay the costs of the successful party; but
(b) the court may make a different order.
(3) The general rule does not apply to the following proceedings—
(a) proceedings in the Court of Appeal on an application or appeal made in connection with proceedings in the Family Division; or
(b) proceedings in the Court of Appeal from a judgment, direction, decision or order given or made in probate proceedings or family proceedings.
(4) In deciding what order (if any) to make about costs, the court must have regard to all the circumstances, including—
(a) the conduct of all the parties;
(b) whether a party has succeeded on part of his case, even if he has not been wholly successful; and
(c) any payment into court or admissible offer to settle made by a party which is drawn to the court's attention (whether or not made in accordance with Part 36).
(Part 36 contains further provisions about how the court's discretion is to be exercised where payment into court or an offer to settle is made under that Part)
(5) The conduct of the parties includes—
(a) conduct before, as well as during, the proceedings and in particular the extent to which the parties followed any relevant pre-action protocol;
(b) whether it was reasonable for a party to raise, pursue or contest a particular allegation or issue;
(c) the manner in which a party has pursued or defended his case or a particular allegation or issue; and
(d) whether a claimant who has succeeded in his claim, in whole or in part, exaggerated his claim.
(6) The orders which the court may make under this rule include an order that a party must pay—
(a) a proportion of another party's costs;
(b) a stated amount in respect of another party's costs;
(c) costs from or until a certain date only;
(d) costs incurred before proceedings have begun;
(e) costs relating to particular steps taken in the proceedings;
(f) costs relating only to a distinct part of the proceedings; and
(g) interest on costs from or until a certain date, including a date before judgment.
(7) Where the court would otherwise consider making an order under paragraph (6)(f), it must instead, if practicable, make an order under paragraph (6)(a) or (c).
(8) Where the court has ordered a party to pay costs, it may order an amount to be paid on account before the costs are assessed.

(9) Where a party entitled to costs is also liable to pay costs the court may assess the costs which that party is liable to pay and either—

    (a) set off the amount assessed against the amount the party is entitled to be paid and direct him to pay any balance; or

    (b) delay the issue of a certificate for the costs to which the party is entitled until he has paid the amount which he is liable to pay.

Costs orders relating to funding arrangements

44.3A (1) The court will not assess any additional liability until the conclusion **A32–210** of the proceedings, or the part of the proceedings, to which the funding arrangement relates.

("Funding arrangement" and "additional liability" are defined in rule 43.2)

(2) At the conclusion of the proceedings, or the part of the proceedings, to which the funding arrangement relates the court may—

    (a) make a summary assessment of all the costs, including any additional liability;

    (b) make an order for detailed assessment of the additional liability but make a summary assessment of the other costs; or

    (c) make an order for detailed assessment of all the costs.

(Part 47 sets out the procedure for the detailed assessment of costs)

Limits on recovery under funding arrangements

44.3B (1) A party may not recover as an additional liability—   **A32–211**

    (a) any proportion of the percentage increase relating to the cost to the legal representative of the postponement of the payment of his fees and expenses;

    (b) any provision made by a membership organisation which exceeds the likely cost to that party of the premium of an insurance policy against the risk of incurring a liability to pay the costs of other parties to the proceedings;

    (c) any additional liability for any period in the proceedings during which he failed to provide information about a funding arrangement in accordance with a rule, practice direction or court order;

    (d) any percentage increase where a party has failed to comply with—

        (i) a requirement in the costs practice direction; or

        (ii) a court order,

to disclose in any assessment proceedings the reasons for setting the percentage increase at the level stated in the conditional fee agreement. (2) This rule does not apply in an assessment under rule 48.9 (assessment of a solicitor's bill to his client).

(Rule 3.9 sets out the circumstances the court will consider on an application for relief from a sanction for failure to comply with any rule, practice direction or court order)

Basis of assessment

44.4 (1) Where the court is to assess the amount of costs (whether by summary **A32–212** or detailed assessment) it will assess those costs—

    (a) on the standard basis; or

    (b) on the indemnity basis, but the court will not in either case allow costs which have been unreasonably incurred or are unreasonable in amount.

(Rule 48.3 sets out how the court decides the amount of costs payable under a contract)

(2) Where the amount of costs is to be assessed on the standard basis, the court will—

    (a) only allow costs which are proportionate to the matters in issue; and

    (b) resolve any doubt which it may have as to whether costs were reasonably incurred or reasonable and proportionate in amount in favour of the paying party.

(Factors which the court may take into account are set out in rule 44.5)

(3) Where the amount of costs is to be assessed on the indemnity basis, the court will resolve any doubt which it may have as to whether costs were reasonably incurred or were reasonable in amount in favour of the receiving party.

(4) Where—

    (a) the court makes an order about costs without indicating the basis on which the costs are to be assessed; or

    (b) the court makes an order for costs to be assessed on a basis other than the standard basis or the indemnity basis

the costs will be assessed on the standard basis.

(5) This rule and Part 47 (detailed assessment of costs by a costs officer) do not apply to the extent that regulations made under the Legal Aid Act 1988 determine the amount payable.

(6) Where the amount of a solicitor's remuneration in respect of non-contentious business is regulated by any general orders made under the Solicitors Act 1974, the amount of the costs to be allowed in respect of any such business which falls to be assessed by the court will be decided in accordance with those general orders rather than this rule and rule 44.5.

Factors to be taken into account in deciding the amount of costs

A32–213   **44.5** (1) The court is to have regard to all the circumstances in deciding whether costs were—

    (a) if it is assessing costs on the standard basis—

        (i) proportionately and reasonably incurred; or

        (ii) were proportionate and reasonable in amount, or

    (b) if it is assessing costs on the indemnity basis—

        (i) unreasonably incurred; or

        (ii) unreasonable in amount.

(2) In particular the court must give effect to any orders which have already been made.

(3) The court must also have regard to—

    (a) the conduct of all the parties, including in particular—

        (i) conduct before, as well as during, the proceedings; and

        (ii) the efforts made, if any, before and during the proceedings in order to try to resolve the dispute;

    (b) the amount or value of any money or property involved;

    (c) the importance of the matter to all the parties;

    (d) the particular complexity of the matter or the difficulty or novelty of the questions raised;

    (e) the skill, effort, specialised knowledge and responsibility involved;

    (f) the time spent on the case; and

    (g) the place where and the circumstances in which work or any part of it was done.

(Rule 35.4(4) gives the court power to limit the amount that a party may recover with regard to the fees and expenses of an expert)

Fixed costs

A32–214   **44.6** A party may recover the fixed costs specified in Part 45 in accordance with that Part.

Procedure for assessing costs

A32–215   **44.7** Where the court orders a party to pay costs to another party (other than fixed costs) it may either—

    (a) make a summary assessment of the costs; or

    (b) order detailed assessment of the costs by a costs officer, unless any rule, practice direction or other enactment provides otherwise.

(The costs practice direction sets out the factors which will affect the court's decision under this rule)

Time for complying with an order for costs

44.8 A party must comply with an order for the payment of costs within 14 **A32–216** days of—
  (a) the date of the judgment or order if it states the amount of those costs;
  (b) if the amount of those costs (or part of them) is decided later in accordance with Part 47, the date of the certificate which states the amount; or
  (c) in either case, such later date as the court may specify.
(Part 47 sets out the procedure for detailed assessment of costs)

Costs on the small claims track and fast track

44.9 (1) Part 27 (small claims) and Part 46 (fast track trial costs) contain special **A32–217** rules about—
  (a) liability for costs;
  (b) the amount of costs which the court may award; and
  (c) the procedure for assessing costs.
(2) Once a claim is allocated to a particular track, those special rules shall apply to the period before, as well as after, allocation except where the court or a practice direction provides otherwise.

Limitation on amount court may allow where a claim allocated to the fast track settles before trial

44.10 (1) Where the court—   **A32–218**
  (a) assesses costs in relation to a claim which—
        (i) has been allocated to the fast track; and
        (ii) settles before the start of the trial; and
  (b) is considering the amount of costs to be allowed in respect of a party's advocate for preparing for the trial,
it may not allow, in respect of those advocate's costs, an amount that exceeds the amount of fast track trial costs which would have been payable in relation to the claim had the trial taken place.
(2) When deciding the amount to be allowed in respect of the advocate's costs, the court shall have regard to—
  (a) when the claim was settled; and
  (b) when the court was notified that the claim had settled.
(3) In this rule, "advocate" and "fast track trial costs" have the meanings given to them by Part 46.
(Part 46 sets out the amount of fast track trial costs which may be awarded)

Costs following allocation and re-allocation

44.11 (1) Any costs orders made before a claim is allocated will not be affected **32–219** by allocation.
(2) Where—
  (a) a claim is allocated to a track; and
  (b) the court subsequently re-allocates that claim to a different track, then unless the court orders otherwise, any special rules about costs applying—
        (i) to the first track, will apply to the claim up to the date of re-allocation; and
        (ii) to the second track, will apply from the date of re-allocation.
(Part 26 deals with the allocation and re-allocation of claims between tracks)

Cases where costs orders deemed to have been made

44.12 (1) Where a right to costs arises under—   **32–220**

    (a) rule 3.7 (defendant's right to costs where claim struck out for non-payment of fees);

    (b) rule 36.13(1) (claimant's right to costs where he accepts defendant's Part 36 offer or Part 36 payment);

    (c) rule 36.14 (claimant's right to costs where defendant accepts the claimant's Part 36 offer; or

    (d) rule 38.6 (defendant's right to costs where claimant discontinues),

a costs order will be deemed to have been made on the standard basis.

(2) Interest payable pursuant to section 17 of the Judgments Act 1838 or section 74 of the County Courts Act 1984 on the costs deemed to have been ordered under paragraph (1) shall begin to run from the date on which the event which gave rise to the entitlement to costs occurred.

Costs-only proceedings

32–221   **44.12A** (1) This rule sets out a procedure which may be followed where—

    (a) the parties to a dispute have reached an agreement on all issues (including what party is to pay the costs) which is made or confirmed in writing; but

    (b) they have failed to agree the amount of those costs; and

    (c) no proceedings have been started.

(2) Either party to the agreement may start proceedings under this rule by issuing a claim form in accordance with Part 8.

(3) The claim form must contain or be accompanied by the agreement or confirmation.

(4) In proceedings to which this rule applies the court—

    (a) may

        (i) make an order for costs; or

        (ii) dismiss the claim; and

    (b) must dismiss the claim if it is opposed.

(5) Rule 48.3 (amount of costs where costs are payable pursuant to a contract) does not apply to claims started under the procedure in this rule.

(Rule 7.2 provides that proceedings started when the court issues a claim form at the request of the claimant)

(Rule 8.1(6) provides that a practice direction may modify the Part 8 procedure)

Special situations

32–222   **44.13** (1) Where the court makes an order which does not mention costs no party is entitled to costs in relation to that order.

(2) The court hearing an appeal may, unless it dismisses the appeal, make orders about the costs of the proceedings giving rise to the appeal as well as the costs of the appeal.

(3) Where proceedings are transferred from one court to another, the court to which they are transferred may deal with all the costs, including the costs before the transfer.

(4) Paragraph (3) is subject to any order of the court which ordered the transfer.

Court's powers in relation to misconduct

32–223   **44.14** (1) The court may make an order under this rule where—

    (a) a party or his legal representative, in connection with a summary or detailed assessment, fails to comply with a rule, practice direction or court order; or

    (b) it appears to the court that the conduct of a party or his legal representative, before or during the proceedings which gave rise to the assessment proceedings, was unreasonably improper.

(2) Where paragraph (1) applies, the court may—
- (a) disallow all or part of the costs which are being assessed; or
- (b) order the party at fault or his legal representative to pay costs which he has caused a any other party to incur.

(3) Where—
- (a) the court makes an order under paragraph (2) against a legally represented party; and
- (b) the party is not present when the order is made, the party's solicitor must notify his client in writing of the order no later than 7 days after the solicitor receives notice of the order.

(Other rules about costs can be found—
- (a) in Schedule 1, in the following RSC—0.45 (court may order act to be done at the expense of disobedient party); 0.47 (writ of *fieri facias* to enforce payment of costs); and
- (b) in Schedule 2, in the following CCR—0.27 (attachment of earnings— judgment creditor's entitlement to costs); 0.28 (costs on judgment summons); 0.30 (garnishee proceedings—judgment creditor's entitle- ment to costs); 0.49 (costs incurred in making a payment in under section 63 of the Trustee Act 1925 to be assessed by the detailed procedure)).

Providing information about funding arrangements

44.15 (1) A party who seeks to recover an additional liability must provide **32–224** information about the funding arrangement to the court and to other parties as required by a rule, practice direction or court order.

(2) Where the funding arrangement has changed, and the information a party has previously provided in accordance with paragraph (1) is no longer accurate, that party must file notice of the change and serve it on all other parties within 7 days.

(3) Where paragraph (2) applies, and a party has already filed—
- (a) an allocation questionnaire; or
- (b) a listing questionnaire,

he must file and serve a new estimate of costs with the notice.

(The costs practice direction sets out—
- the information to be provided when a party issues or responds to a claim form, file an allocation questionnaire, a listing questionnaire, and a claim for costs;
- the meaning of estimate of costs and the information required in it)

(Rule 44.3B sets out situations where a party will not recover a sum representing any additional liability)

Adjournment where legal representative seeks to challenge disallowance of any amount of percentage increase

44.16 Where— **32–225**
- (a) the court disallows any amount of a legal representative's percentage increase in summary or detailed assessment proceedings; and
- (b) the legal representative applies for an order that the disallowed amount should continue to be payable by his client,

the court may adjourn the hearing to allow the legally represented party to be notified of the order sought.

(Regulation 3(2)(b) of the Conditional Fee Agreements Regulations 2000 provides that a conditional fee agreement which provides for a success fee must state that any amount of a percentage increase disallowed on assessment ceases to be payable unless the court is satisfied that it should continue to be so payable)

APPENDIX 32

Application of costs rules

32–226 **44.17** This Part and Part 45 (fixed costs), Part 46 (fast track trial costs), Part 47 (procedure for detailed assessment of costs and default provisions) and Part 48 (special cases), do not apply to the assessment of costs in proceedings to the extent that—

(a) section 11 of the Access to Justice Act 1999, and provisions made under that Act, or

(b) regulations made under the Legal Aid Act 1988,

make different provision. (The costs practice direction sets out the procedure to be followed where a party was wholly or partially funded by the Legal Services Commission)

DIRECTIONS RELATING TO PART 44—GENERAL RULES ABOUT COSTS

Supplementing Part 44 of The Civil Procedure Rules

Solicitor's Duty to Notify Client: Rule 44.2

A32–227 **7.1** For the purposes of rule 44.2 "client" includes a party for whom a solicitor is acting and any other person (for example, an insurer, a trade union or the LSC) who has instructed the solicitor to act or who is liable to pay his fees.

7.2 Where a solicitor notifies a client of an order under that rule, he must also explain why the order came to be made.

7.3 Although rule 44.2 does not specify any sanction for breach of the rule the court may, either in the order for costs itself or in a subsequent order, require the solicitor to produce to the court evidence showing that he took reasonable steps to comply with the rule.

Court's Discretion and Circumstances to be taken into Account when Exercising its Discretion as to Costs: Rule 44.3

A32–228 **8.1** Attention is drawn to the factors set out in this rule which may lead the court to depart from the general rule stated in rule 44.3(2) and to make a different order about costs.

8.2 In a probate claim where a defendant has in his defence given notice that he requires the will to be proved in solemn form (see paragraph 8.3 of the Contentious Probate Practice Direction Supplementing Part 49), the court will not make an order for costs against the defendant unless it appears that there was no reasonable ground for opposing the will. The term "probate claim" is defined in paragraph 1.2 of the Contentious Probate Practice Direction.

8.3 (1) The court may make an order about costs at any stage in a case.

(2) In particular the court may make an order about costs when it deals with any application, makes any order or holds any hearing and that order about costs may relate to the costs of that application, order or hearing.

(3) Rule 44.3A(1) provides that the court will not assess any additional liability until the conclusion of the proceedings or the part of the proceedings to which the funding arrangement relates. (Paragraphs 2.4 and 2.5 above explain when proceedings are concluded. As to the time when detailed assessment may be carried out see paragraphs 27.1, below.)

8.4 In deciding what order to make about costs the court is required to have regard to all the circumstances including any payment into court or admissible offer to settle made by a party which is drawn to the court's attention (whether or not it is made in accordance with Part 36). Where a claimant has made a Part

1402

36 offer and fails to obtain a judgment which is more advantageous than that offer, that circumstance alone will not lead to a reduction in the costs awarded to the claimant under this rule.

8.5 There are certain costs orders which the court will commonly make in proceedings before trial. The following table sets out the general effect of these orders. The table is not an exhaustive list of the orders which the court may make.

Term	Effect
• Costs • Costs in any event	The party in whose favour the order is made is entitled to the costs in respect of the part of the proceedings to which the order relates, whatever other costs orders are made in the proceedings.
• Costs in the case • Costs in the application	The party in whose favour the court makes an order for costs at the end of the proceedings is entitled to his costs of the part of the proceedings to which the order relates.
• Costs reserved	The decision about costs is deferred to a later occasion, but if no later order is made the costs will be costs in the case.
• Claimant's/ Defendant's costs in the case/ application	If the party in whose favour the costs order is made is awarded costs at the end of the proceedings, that party is entitled to his costs of the part of the proceedings to which the order relates. If any other party is awarded costs at the end of the proceedings, the party in whose favour the final costs order is made is not liable to pay the costs of any other party in respect of the part of the proceedings to which the order relates.
• Costs thrown away	Where, for example, a judgment or order is set aside, the party in whose favour the costs order is made is entitled to the costs which have been incurred as a consequence. This includes the costs of— preparing for and attending any hearing at which the judgment or order which has been set aside was made; preparing for and attending any hearing to set aside the judgment or order in question; preparing for and attending any hearing at which the court orders the proceedings or the part in question to be adjourned; any steps taken to enforce a judgment or order which has subsequently been set aside.

1403

● Costs of and caused by	Where, for example, the court makes this order on an application to amend a statement of case, the party in whose favour the costs order is made is entitled to the costs of preparing for and attending the application and the costs of any consequential amendment to his own statement of case.
● Costs here and below	The party in whose favour the costs order is made is entitled not only to his costs in respect of the proceedings in which the court makes the order but also to his costs of the proceedings in any lower court. In the case of an appeal from a Divisional Court the party is not entitled to any costs incurred in any court below the Divisional Court.
● No order as to costs	Each party is to bear his own costs of the part of the proceedings to which the order relates whatever costs order the court makes at the end of the proceedings.
● Each party to pay his own costs	

8.6 Where, under rule 44.3(8), the court orders an amount to be paid before costs are assessed—

(1) the order will state that amount, and

(2) if no other date for payment is specified in the order rule 44.8 (Time for complying with an order for costs) will apply.

Fees of counsel

A32–229   8.7 (1) This paragraph applies where the court orders the detailed assessment of the costs of a hearing at which one or more counsel appeared for a party.

(2) Where an order for costs states the opinion of the court as to whether or not the hearing was fit for the attendance of one or more counsel, a costs officer conducting a detailed assessment of costs to which that order relates will have regard to the opinion stated.

(3)(a) The court will generally express an opinion only where:

(b) the paying party asks it to do so;

(c) more than one counsel appeared for a party or,

(d) the court wishes to record its opinion that the case was not fit for the attendance of counsel.

Fees payable to Conveyancing Counsel Appointed by the Court to Assist it

A32–230   8.8 (1) Where the court refers any matter to the conveyancing counsel of the court the fees payable to counsel in respect of the work done or to be done will be assessed by the court in accordance with rule 44.3.

(2) An appeal from a decision of the court in respect of the fees of such counsel will be dealt with under the general rules as to appeals set out in Part 52. If the appeal is against the decision of an authorised court officer, it will be dealt with in accordance with rules 47.20 to 47.23.

Costs Orders Relating to Funding Arrangements: Rule 44.3a

A32–231   9.1 Under an order for payment of "costs" the costs payable will include an additional liability incurred under a funding arrangement.

9.2 (1) If before the conclusion of the proceedings the court carries out a summary assessment of the base costs it may identify separately the amount allowed in respect of: solicitors' charges; counsels' fees; other disbursements; and any value added tax (VAT). (Sections 13 and 14 of this Practice Direction deal with summary assessment.)

(2) If an order for the base costs of a previous application or hearing did not identify separately the amounts allowed for solicitor's charges, counsel's fees and other disbursements, a court which later makes an assessment of an additional liability may apportion the base costs previously ordered.

Limits on Recovery Under Funding Arrangements: Rule 44.3b

10.1 In a case to which rule 44.3B(1)(c) or (d) applies the party in default may **A32–232** apply for relief from the sanction. He should do so as quickly as possible after he becomes aware of the default. An application, supported by evidence, should be made under Part 23 to a costs judge or district judge of the court which is dealing with the case. (Attention is drawn to rules 3.8 and 3.9 which deal with sanctions and relief from sanctions).

10.2 Where the amount of any percentage increase recoverable by counsel may be affected by the outcome of the application, the solicitor issuing the application must serve on counsel a copy of the application notice and notice of the hearing as soon as practicable and in any event at least 2 days before the hearing. Counsel may make written submissions or may attend and make oral submissions at the hearing. (Paragraph 1.4 contains definitions of the terms "counsel" and "solicitor".)

Factors to be taken Into Account in Deciding the Amount of Costs: Rule 44.5

11.1 In applying the test of proportionality the court will have regard to rule **A32–233** 1.1(2)(c). The relationship between the total of the costs incurred and the financial value of the claim may not be a reliable guide. A fixed percentage cannot be applied in all cases to the value of the claim in order to ascertain whether or not the costs are proportionate.

11.2 In any proceedings there will be costs which will inevitably be incurred and which are necessary for the successful conduct of the case. Solicitors are not required to conduct litigation at rates which are uneconomic. Thus in a modest claim the proportion of costs is likely to be higher than in a large claim, and may even equal or possibly exceed the amount in dispute.

11.3 Where a trial takes place, the time taken by the court in dealing with a particular issue may not be an accurate guide to the amount of time properly spent by the legal or other representatives in preparation for the trial of that issue.

11.4 Where a party has entered into a funding arrangement the costs claimed may, subject to rule 44.3B include an additional liability.

11.5 In deciding whether the costs claimed are reasonable and (on a standard basis assessment) proportionate, the court will consider the amount of any additional liability separately from the base costs.

11.6 In deciding whether the base costs are reasonable and (if relevant) proportionate the court will consider the factors set out in rule 44.5.

11.7 Subject to paragraph 17.8(2), when the court is considering the factors to be taken into account in assessing an additional liability, it will have regard to the facts and circumstances as they reasonably appeared to the solicitor or counsel when the funding arrangement was entered into and at the time of any variation of the arrangement.

11.8 In deciding whether a percentage increase is reasonable relevant factors to be taken into account may include:—

The risk that the circumstances in which the costs, fees or expenses would be payable might or might not occur;

    (a) the legal representative's liability for any disbursements;

    (b) what other methods of financing the costs were available to the receiving party.

    (c) The court has the power, when considering whether a percentage increase is reasonable, to allow different percentages for different items of costs or for different periods during which costs were incurred.

11.9 A percentage increase will not be reduced simply on the ground that, when added to base costs which are reasonable and (where relevant) proportionate, the total appears disproportionate.

11.10 In deciding whether the cost of insurance cover is reasonable, relevant factors to be taken into account include:

(1) where the insurance cover is not purchased in support of a conditional fee agreement with a success fee, how its cost compares with the likely cost of funding the case with a conditional fee agreement with a success fee and supporting insurance cover;

(2) the level and extent of the cover provided;

(3) the availability of any pre-existing insurance cover;

(4) whether any part of the premium would be rebated in the event of early settlement;

(5) the amount of commission payable to the receiving party or his legal representatives or other agents.

11.11 Where the court is considering a provision made by a membership organisation, rule 44.3B(1) (b) provides that any such provision which exceeds the likely cost to the receiving party of the premium of an insurance policy against the risk of incurring a liability to pay the costs of other parties to the proceedings is not recoverable. In such circumstances the court will, when assessing the additional liability, have regard to the factors set out in paragraph 11.10 above, in addition to the factors set out in rule 44.5.

Procedure for Assessing Costs: Rule 44.7

A32–234   **12.1** Where the court does not order fixed costs (or no fixed costs are provided for) the amount of costs payable will be assessed by the court. This rule allows the court making an order about costs either—

    (a) to make a summary assessment of the amount of the costs, or

    (b) to order the amount to be decided in accordance with Part 47 (a detailed assessment).

12.2 An order for costs will be treated as an order for the amount of costs to be decided by a detailed assessment unless the order otherwise provides.

12.3 Whenever the court awards costs to be assessed by way of detailed assessment it should consider whether to exercise the power in rule 44.3(8) (Courts Discretion as to Costs) to order the paying party to pay such sum of money as it thinks just on account of those costs.

Summary Assessment: General Provisions

A32–235   **13.1** Whenever a court makes an order about costs which does not provide for fixed costs to be paid the court should consider whether to make a summary assessment of costs.

13.2 The general rule is that the court should make a summary assessment of the costs:

(1) at the conclusion of the trial of a case which has been dealt with on the fast track, in which case the order will deal with the costs of the whole claim, and

(2) at the conclusion of any other hearing, which has lasted not more than one day, in which case the order will deal with the costs of the application or matter to which the hearing related. If this hearing disposes of the claim, the order may deal with the costs of the whole claim;

(3) in hearings in the Court of Appeal to which Paragraph 14 of the Practice Direction supplementing Part 52 (Appeals) applies;

unless there is good reason not to do so e.g. where the paying party shows substantial grounds for disputing the sum claimed for costs that cannot be dealt with summarily or there is insufficient time to carry out a summary assessment.

13.3 The general rule in paragraph 13.2 does not apply to a mortgagee's costs incurred in mortgage possession proceedings or other proceedings relating to a mortgage unless the mortgagee asks the court to make an order for his costs to be paid by another party. Paragraphs 49.3 and 49.4 deal in more detail with costs relating to mortgages.

13.4 Where an application has been made and the parties to the application agree an order by consent without any party attending, the parties should agree a figure for costs to be inserted in the consent order or agree that there should be no order for costs. If the parties cannot agree the costs position, attendance on the appointment will be necessary but, unless good reason can be shown for the failure to deal with costs as set out above, no costs will be allowed for that attendance.

13.5 (1) It is the duty of the parties and their legal representatives to assist the judge in making a summary assessment of costs in any case to which paragraph 13.2 above applies, in accordance with the following paragraphs.

(2) Each party who intends to claim costs must prepare a written statement of the costs he intends to claim showing separately in the form of a schedule:

  (a) the number of hours to be claimed,
  (b) the hourly rate to be claimed,
  (c) the grade of fee earner;
  (d) the amount and nature of any disbursement to be claimed, other than counsel's fee for appearing at the hearing,
  (e) the amount of solicitor's costs to be claimed for attending or appearing at the hearing,
  (f) the fees of counsel to be claimed in respect of the hearing, and
  (g) any value added tax (VAT) to be claimed on these amounts.

(3) The statement of costs should follow as closely as possible Form N260 and must be signed by the party or his legal representative. Where a litigant is an assisted person or is a LSC funded client or is represented by a solicitor in the litigant's employment the statement of costs need not include the certificate appended at the end of Form N260.

(4) The statement of costs must be filed at court and copies of it must be served on any party against whom an order for payment of those costs is intended to be sought. The statement of costs should be filed and the copies of it should be served as soon as possible and in any event not less than 24 hours before the date fixed for the hearing.

(5) Where the litigant is or may be entitled to claim an additional liability the statement filed and served need not reveal the amount of that liability.

13.6 The failure by a party, without reasonable excuse, to comply with the foregoing paragraphs will be taken into account by the court in deciding what order to make about the costs of the claim, hearing or application, and about the costs of any further hearing or detailed assessment hearing that may be necessary as a result of that failure.

13.7 If the court makes a summary assessment of costs at the conclusion of proceedings the court will specify separately

(1) the base costs, and if appropriate, the additional liability allowed as solicitor's charges, counsel's fees, other disbursements and any VAT; and

(2) the amount which is awarded under Part 46 (Fast Track Trial Costs).

13.8 The court awarding costs cannot make an order for a summary assessment of costs by a costs officer. If a summary assessment of costs is appropriate but the court awarding costs is unable to do so on the day, the court must give directions as to a further hearing before the same judge.

13.9 The court will not make a summary assessment of the costs of a receiving party who is an assisted person or LSC funded client.

13.10 A summary assessment of costs payable by an assisted person or LSC funded client is not by itself a determination of that person's liability to pay those costs (as to which see rule 44.17 and paragraphs 20.1 to 22.33 of this Practice Direction).

13.11 (1) The court will not make a summary assessment of the costs of a receiving party who is a child or patient within the meaning of Part 21 unless the solicitor acting for the child or patient has waived the right to further costs (see paragraph 51.1 below).

(2) The court may make a summary assessment of costs payable by a child or patient.

13.12 (1) Attention is drawn to rule 44.3A which prevents the court from making a summary assessment of an additional liability before the conclusion of the proceedings or the part of the proceedings to which the funding arrangement relates. Where this applies, the court should nonetheless make a summary assessment of the base costs of the hearing or application unless there is a good reason not to do so.

(2) Where the court makes a summary assessment of the base costs all statements of costs and costs estimates put before the judge will be retained on the court file.

13.13 The court will not give its approval to disproportionate and unreasonable costs. Accordingly:

(a) When the amount of the costs to be paid has been agreed between the parties the order for costs must state that the order is by consent.

(b) If the judge is to make an order which is not by consent, the judge will, so far as possible, ensure that the final figure is not disproportionate and/or unreasonable having regard to Part 1 of the CPR. The judge will retain this responsibility notwithstanding the absence of challenge to individual items in the make-up of the figure sought. The fact that the paying party is not disputing the amount of costs can however be taken as some indication that the amount is proportionate and reasonable. The judge will therefore intervene only if satisfied that the costs are so disproportionate that it is right to do so.

Summary Assessment where Costs Claimed Include an Additional Liability

Orders made before the conclusion of the proceedings

A32–236   **14.1** The existence of a conditional fee agreement or other funding arrangement within the meaning of rule 43.2 is not by itself a sufficient reason for not carrying out a summary assessment.

14.2 Where a legal representative acting for the receiving party has entered into a conditional fee agreement the court may summarily assess all the costs (other than any additional liability).

14.3 Where costs have been summarily assessed an order for payment will not be made unless the court has been satisfied that in respect of the costs claimed, the receiving party is at the time liable to pay to his legal representative an amount equal to or greater than the costs claimed. A statement in the form of the certificate appended at the end of Form N260 may be sufficient proof of liability. The giving of information under rule 44.15 (where that rule applies) is not sufficient.

14.4 The court may direct that any costs, for which the receiving party may not in the event be liable, shall be paid into court to await the outcome of the case, or shall not be enforceable until further order, or it may postpone the receiving party's right to receive payment in some other way.

Orders made at the conclusion of the proceedings

14.5 Where there has been a trial of one or more issues separately from other **A32–237** issues, the court will not normally order detailed assessment of the additional liability until all issues have been tried unless the parties agree.

14.6 Rule 44.3A(2) sets out the ways in which the court may deal with the assessment of the costs where there is a funding arrangement. Where the court makes a summary assessment of the base costs:

(1) The order may state separately the base costs allowed as (a) solicitor's charges, (b) counsel's fees, (c) any other disbursements and (d) any VAT;

(2) the statements of costs upon which the judge based his summary assessment will be retained on the court file.

14.7 Where the court makes a summary assessment of an additional liability at the conclusion of proceedings, that assessment must relate to the whole of the proceedings; this will include any additional liability relating to base costs allowed by the court when making a summary assessment on a previous application or hearing.

14.8 Paragraph 13.13 applies where the parties are agreed about the total amount to be paid by way of costs, or are agreed about the amount of the base costs that will be paid. Where they disagree about the additional liability the court may summarily assess that liability or make an order for a detailed assessment.

14.9 In order to facilitate the court in making a summary assessment of any additional liability at the conclusion of the proceedings the party seeking such costs must prepare and have available for the court a bundle of documents which must include—

(1) a copy of every notice of funding arrangement (Form N251) which has been filed by him;

(2) a copy of every estimate and statement of costs filed by him;

(3) a copy of the risk assessment prepared at the time any relevant funding arrangement was entered into and on the basis of which the amount of the additional liability was fixed.

Costs on the Small Claims Track and Fast Track: Rule 44.9

15.1 (1) Before a claim is allocated to one of those tracks the court is not **A32–238** restricted by any of the special rules that apply to that track.

(2) Where a claim has been allocated to one of those tracks, the special rules which relate to that track will apply to work done before as well as after allocation save to the extent (if any) that an order for costs in respect of that work was made before allocation.

(3)

(i) This paragraph applies where a claim, issued for a sum in excess of the normal financial scope of the small claims track, is allocated to that track only because an admission of part of the claim by the defendant reduces the amount in dispute to a sum within the normal scope of that track.

(See also paragraph 7.4 of the practice direction supplementing CPR Part 26)

    (ii) On entering judgment for the admitted part before allocation of the balance of the claim the court may allow costs in respect of the proceedings down to that date.

Costs following Allocation and Re-Allocation: Rule 44.11

A32–239   **16.1** This paragraph applies where the court is about to make an order to re-allocate a claim from the small claims track to another track.

16.2 Before making the order to re-allocate the claim, the court must decide whether any party is to pay costs to any other party down to the date of the order to re-allocate in accordance with the rules about costs contained in Part 27 (The Small Claims Track).

16.3 If it decides to make such an order about costs, the court will make a summary assessment of those costs in accordance with that Part.

Costs—Only Proceedings: Rule 44.12a

A32–240   **17.1** A claim form under this rule should be issued in the court which would have been the appropriate office in accordance with rule 47.4 had proceedings been brought in relation to the substantive claim. A claim form under this rule should not be issued in the High Court unless the dispute to which the agreement relates was of such a value or type that had proceedings been begun they would have been commenced in the High Court.

17.2 A claim form which is to be issued in the High Court at the Royal Courts of Justice will be issued in the Supreme Court Costs Office.

17.3 Attention is drawn to rule 8.2 (in particular to paragraph (b)(ii)) and to rule 44.12A(3). The claim form must:

    (1) identify the claim or dispute to which the agreement to pay costs relates;

    (2) state the date and terms of the agreement on which the claimant relies;

    (3) set out or have attached to it a draft of the order which the claimant seeks;

    (4) state the amount of the costs claimed; and,

    (5) state whether the costs are claimed on the standard or indemnity basis. If no basis is specified the costs will be treated as being claimed on the standard basis.

17.4 The evidence to be filed and served with the claim form under Rule 8.5 must include copies of the documents on which the claimant relies to prove the defendant's agreement to pay costs.

17.5 A costs judge or a district judge has jurisdiction to hear and decide any issue which may arise in a claim issued under this rule irrespective of the amount of the costs claimed or of the value of the claim to which the agreement to pay costs relates. A court officer may make an order by consent under paragraph 17.7, or an order dismissing a claim under paragraph 17.9 below.

17.6 When the time for filing the defendant's acknowledgement of service has expired, the claimant may by letter request the court to make an order in the terms of his claim, unless the defendant has filed an acknowledgement of service stating that he intends to contest the claim or to seek a different order.

17.7 Rule 40.6 applies where an order is to be made by consent. An order may be made by consent in terms which differ from those set out in the claim form.

17.8 (1) An order for costs made under this rule will be treated as an order for the amount of costs to be decided by a detailed assessment to which Part 47 and the practice directions relating to it apply. Rule 44.4(4) (determination of basis of assessment) also applies to the order.

(2) In cases in which an additional liability is claimed, the costs judge or district judge should have regard to the time when and the extent to which the claim has been settled and to the fact that the claim has been settled without the need to commence proceedings.

17.9 A claim will be treated as opposed for the purposes of rule 44.12A(4)(b) if the defendant files an acknowledgement of service stating that he intends to contest the proceedings or to seek a different remedy. An order dismissing it will be made as soon as such an acknowledgement is filed. The dismissal of a claim under rule 44.12A(4) does not prevent the claimant from issuing another claim form under Part 7 or Part 8 based on the agreement or alleged agreement to which the proceedings under this rule related.

17.10 (1) Rule 8.9 (which provides that claims issued under Part 8 shall be treated as allocated to the multi-track) shall not apply to claims issued under this rule. A claim issued under this rule may be dealt with without being allocated to a track.

(2) Rule 8.1(3) and Part 24 do not apply to proceedings brought under rule 44.12A.

17.11 Nothing in this rule prevents a person from issuing a claim form under Part 7 or Part 8 to sue on an agreement made in settlement of a dispute where that agreement makes provision for costs, nor from claiming in that case an order for costs or a specified sum in respect of costs.

Court's Powers in Relation to Misconduct: Rule 44.14

18.1 Before making an order under rule 44.14 the court must give the party or **A32–241** legal representative in question a reasonable opportunity to attend a hearing to give reasons why it should not make such an order.

18.2 Conduct before or during the proceedings which gave rise to the assessment which is unreasonable or improper includes steps which are calculated to prevent or inhibit the court from furthering the overriding objective.

18.3 Although rule 44.14(3) does not specify any sanction for breach of the obligation imposed by the rule the court may, either in the order under paragraph (2) or in a subsequent order, require the solicitor to produce to the court evidence that he took reasonable steps to comply with the obligation.

Providing Information about Funding Arrangements: Rule 44.15

19.1 (1) A party who wishes to claim an additional liability in respect of a **A32–242** funding arrangement must give any other party information about that claim if he is to recover the additional liability. There is no requirement to specify the amount of the additional liability separately nor to state how it is calculated until it falls to be assessed. That principle is reflected in rules 44.3A and 44.15, in the following paragraphs and in Sections 6, 13, 14 and 31 of this Practice Direction. Section 6 deals with estimates of costs, Sections 13 and 14 deal with summary assessment and Section 31 deals with detailed assessment.

(2) In the following paragraphs a party who has entered into a funding arrangement is treated as a person who intends to recover a sum representing an additional liability by way of costs.

(3) Attention is drawn to paragraph 57.9 of this Practice Direction which sets out time limits for the provision of information where a funding arrangement is entered into between 31 March and 2 July 2000 and proceedings relevant to that arrangement are commenced before 3 July 2000.

Method of giving information

19.2 (1) In this paragraph, "claim form" includes petition and application **A32–243** notice, and the notice of funding to be filed or served is a notice containing the information set out in Form N251.

(2)

    (a) A claimant who has entered into a funding arrangement before starting the proceedings to which it relates must provide information to the court by filing the notice when he issues the claim form.

    (b) He must provide information to every other party by serving the notice. If he serves the claim form himself he must serve the notice with the claim form. If the court is to serve the claim form, the court will also serve the notice if the claimant provides it with sufficient copies for service.

(3) A defendant who has entered into a funding arrangement before filing any document—

    (a) must provide information to the court by filing notice with his first document. A "first document" may be an acknowledgement of service, a defence, or any other document, such as an application to set aside a default judgment.

    (b) must provide information to every party by serving notice. If he serves his first document himself he must serve the notice with that document. If the court is to serve his first document the court will also serve the notice if the defendant provides it with sufficient copies for service.

(4) In all other circumstances a party must file and serve notice within 7 days of entering into the funding arrangement concerned.

(5) There is no requirement in this Practice Direction for the provision of information about funding arrangements before the commencement of proceedings. Such provision is however recommended and may be required by a pre-action protocol.

Notice of change of information

A32–244   **19.3** (1) Rule 44.15 imposes a duty on a party to give notice of change if the information he has previously provided is no longer accurate. To comply he must file and serve notice containing the information set out in Form N251. Rule 44.15(3) may impose other duties in relation to new estimates of costs.

(2) Further notification need not be provided where a party has already given notice—

    (a) that he has entered into a conditional fee agreement with a legal representative and during the currency of that agreement either of them enters into another such agreement with an additional legal representative; or

    (b) of some insurance cover, unless that cover is cancelled or unless new cover is taken out with a different insurer.

(3) Part 6 applies to the service of notices.

(4) The notice must be signed by the party or by his legal representative.

Information which must be provided

A32–245   **19.4** (1) Unless the court otherwise orders, a party who is required to supply information about a funding arrangement must state whether he has—

entered into a conditional fee agreement which provides for a success fee within the meaning of section 58(2) of the Courts and Legal Services Act 1990;

taken out an insurance policy to which section 29 of the Access to Justice Act 1999 applies;

made an arrangement with a body which is prescribed for the purpose of section 30 of that Act;

or more than one of these.

(2) Where the funding arrangement is a conditional fee agreement, the party must state the date of the agreement and identify the claim or claims to which it relates (including Part 20 claims if any).

(3) Where the funding arrangement is an insurance policy the party must state the name of the insurer, the date of the policy and must identify the claim or claims to which it relates (including Part 20 claims if any).

(4) Where the funding arrangement is by way of an arrangement with a relevant body the party must state the name of the body and set out the date and terms of the undertaking it has given and must identify the claim or claims to which it relates (including Part 20 claims if any).

(5) Where a party has entered into more than one funding arrangement in respect of a claim, for example a conditional fee agreement and an insurance policy, a single notice containing the information set out in Form N251 may contain the required information about both or all of them.

19.5 Where the court makes a Group Litigation Order, the court may give directions as to the extent to which individual parties should provide information in accordance with rule 44.15. (Part 19 deals with Group Litigation Orders.)

Procedure where Legal Representative wishes to Recover from His Client an Agreed Percentage Increase which has been Disallowed or Reduced on Assessment: Rule 44.16

20.1 Attention is drawn to Regulation 3(2)(b) of the Conditional Fee Agree- **A32–246** ments Regulations 2000, which provides that any amount of an agreed percentage increase, which is disallowed on assessment, ceases to be payable under that agreement unless the court is satisfied that it should continue to be so payable. Rule 44.16 allows the court to adjourn a hearing at which the legal representative acting for the receiving party applies for an order that a disallowed amount should continue to be payable under the agreement.

20.2 In the following paragraphs "counsel" means counsel who has acted in the case under a conditional fee agreement which provides for a success fee. A reference to counsel includes a reference to any person who appeared as an advocate in the case and who is not a partner or employee of the solicitor or firm which is conducting the claim or defence (as the case may be) on behalf of the receiving party.

Procedure following Summary Assessment

20.3 (1) If the court disallows any amount of a legal representative's percent- **A32–247** age increase, the court will, unless sub-paragraph (2) applies, give directions to enable an application to be made by the legal representative for the disallowed amount to be payable by his client, including, if appropriate, a direction that the application will be determined by a costs judge or district judge of the court dealing with the case.

(2) The court that has made the summary assessment may then and there decide the issue whether the disallowed amount should continue to be payable, if:

(a) the receiving party and all parties to the relevant agreement consent to the court doing so;

(b) the receiving party (or, if corporate, an officer) is present in court; and

(c) the court is satisfied that the issue can be fairly decided then and there.

Procedure following Detailed Assessment

20.4 (1) Where detailed assessment proceedings have been commenced, and **A32–248** the paying party serves points of dispute (as to which see Section 34 of this Practice Direction), which show that he is seeking a reduction in any percentage increase charged by counsel on his fees, the solicitor acting for the receiving party must within 3 days of service deliver to counsel a copy of the relevant points of dispute and the bill of costs or the relevant parts of the bill.

(2) Counsel must within 10 days thereafter inform the solicitor in writing whether or not he will accept the reduction sought or some other reduction. Counsel may state any points he wishes to have made in a reply to the points of dispute, and the solicitor must serve them on the paying party as or as part of a reply.

(3) Counsel who fails to inform the solicitor within the time limits set out above will be taken to accept the reduction unless the court otherwise orders.

20.5 Where the paying party serves points of dispute seeking a reduction in any percentage increase charged by a legal representative acting for the receiving party, and that legal representative intends, if necessary, to apply for an order that any amount of the percentage disallowed as against the paying party shall continue to be payable by his client, the solicitor acting for the receiving party must, within 14 days of service of the points of dispute, give to his client a clear written explanation of the nature of the relevant point of dispute and the effect it will have if it is upheld in whole or in part by the court, and of the client's right to attend any subsequent hearings at court when the matter is raised.

20.6 Where the solicitor acting for a receiving party files a request for a detailed assessment hearing it must if appropriate, be accompanied by a certificate signed by him stating:

(1) that the amount of the percentage increase in respect of counsel's fees or solicitor's charges is disputed;

(2) whether an application will be made for an order that any amount of that increase which is disallowed should continue to be payable by his client;

(3) that he has given his client an explanation in accordance with paragraph 20.5; and,

(4) whether his client wishes to attend court when the amount of any relevant percentage increase may be decided.

20.7 (1) The solicitor acting for the receiving party must within 7 days of receiving from the court notice of the date of the assessment hearing, notify his client, and if appropriate, counsel in writing of the date, time and place of the hearing.

(2) Counsel may attend or be represented at the detailed assessment hearing and may make oral or written submissions.

20.8 (1) At the detailed assessment hearing, the court will deal with the assessment of the costs payable by one party to another, including the amount of the percentage increase, and give a certificate accordingly.

(2) The court may decide the issue whether the disallowed amount should continue to be payable under the relevant conditional fee agreement without an adjournment if:

(a) the receiving party and all parties to the relevant agreement consent to the court deciding the issue without an adjournment,

(b) the receiving party (or, if corporate, an officer or employee who has authority to consent on behalf of the receiving party) is present in court, and

(c) the court is satisfied that the issue can be fairly decided without an adjournment.

(3) In any other case the court will give directions and fix a date for the hearing of the application.

Application of Costs Rules: Rule 44.17

A32–249   **21.1** Rule 44.17(b) excludes the costs rules to the extent that regulations under the Legal Aid Act 1988 make different provision. The primary examples of such regulations are the regulations providing prescribed rates (with or without enhancement).

21.2 Rule 44.17(a) also excludes the procedure for the detailed assessment of costs in cases to which Section 11 of the Access to Justice Act 1999 applies, whether it applies in whole or in part. In these excluded cases the procedure for determination of costs is set out in Section 22 of this Practice Direction.

21.3 Section 11 of the Access to Justice Act 1999 provides special protection against liability for costs for litigants who receive funding by the LSC (Legal Services Commission) as part of the Community Legal Service. Any costs ordered to be paid by a LSC funded client must not exceed the amount which is reasonable for him to pay having regard to all the circumstances including:

(a) the financial resources of all the parties to the proceedings, and

(b) their conduct in connection with the dispute to which the proceedings relate.

21.4 In this Practice Direction

"cost protection" means the limit on costs awarded against a LSC funded client set out in Section 11(1) of the Access to Justice Act 1999.

"partner" has the meaning given by the Community Legal Service (Costs) Regulations 2000.

21.5 Whether or not cost protection applies depends upon the "level of service" for which funding was provided by the LSC in accordance with the Funding Code approved under section 9 of the Access to Justice Act 1999. The levels of service referred to are:

(1) Legal Help—advice and assistance about a legal problem, not including representation or advocacy in proceedings.

(2) Help at Court—advocacy at a specific hearing, where the advocate is not formally representing the client in the proceedings.

(3) Family Mediation.

(4) Legal Representation—representation in actual or contemplated proceedings. Legal Representation can take the form of Investigative Help (limited to investigating the merits of a potential claim) or Full Representation.

(5) Approved Family Help—this can take the form of Help with Mediation (legal advice in support of the family mediation process) or General Family Help (help negotiating a settlement to a family dispute without recourse to adversarial litigation).

(6) Support Funding—partial funding in expensive cases that are primarily being funded privately, under or with a view to a conditional fee agreement. Support Funding can take the form of Investigative Support (equivalent to *Investigative Help*) or Litigation Support (equivalent to *Full Representation*).

21.6 Levels of service (4) (5) and (6) are provided under a certificate (similar to a legal aid certificate). The certificate will state which level of service is covered. Where there are proceedings, a copy of the certificate will be lodged with the court.

21.7 Cost protection does not apply where:

(1) The LSC funded client receives Help at Court;

(2) the LSC funded client receives Litigation Support (but see further, paragraph 21.8);

(3) the LSC funded client receives Investigative Support (except where the proceedings for which Investigative Support was given are not pursued after the certificate is discharged). Investigative Support will not normally cover the issue of proceedings (except for disclosure), but cost protection may be relevant if the defendant seeks an assessment of pre-action costs;

(4) the LSC funded client receives Legal Help only i.e. where the solicitor is advising, but not representing a litigant in person. However, where the LSC funded client receives Legal Help e.g. to write a letter before action, but later receives Legal Representation or Approved Family Help in respect of the same dispute, cost protection does apply to all costs incurred by the receiving party in the funded proceedings or prospective proceedings.

21.8 Where cost protection does not apply, the court may award costs in the normal way. In the case of Litigation Support, costs that are not covered by the

LSC funded client's insurance are usually payable by the LSC rather than the funded client, and the court should order accordingly (see Regulation. 6 of the Community Legal Service (Cost Protection) Regulations 2000).

21.9 Where work is done before the issue of a certificate, cost protection does not apply to those costs, except where:

(1) pre-action Legal Help is given and the LSC funded client subsequently receives Legal Representation or Approved Family Help in the same dispute; or

(2) where urgent work is undertaken immediately before the grant of an emergency certificate when no emergency application could be made as the LSC's offices were closed, provided that the solicitor seeks an emergency certificate at the first available opportunity and the certificate is granted.

21.10 If a LSC funded client's certificate is revoked, costs protection does not apply to work done before or after revocation.

21.11 If a LSC funded client's certificate is discharged, costs protection only applies to costs incurred before the date on which funded services ceased to be provided under the certificate. This may be a date before the date on which the certificate is formally discharged by the LSC (Burridge v Stafford: Khan v Ali [2000] 1 WLR 927, [1999] 4 All ER 660 C.A.).

Assessing a LSC Funded Client's Resources

A32–250   **21.12** The first £100,000 of the value of the LSC funded client's interest in the main or only home is disregarded when assessing his or her financial resources for the purposes of S.11 and cannot be the subject of any enforcement process by the receiving party. The receiving party cannot apply for an order to sell the LSC funded client's home, but could secure the debt against any value exceeding £100,000 by way of a charging order.

21.13 The court may only take into account the value of the LSC funded client's clothes, household furniture, tools and implements of trade to the extent that it considers that having regard to the quantity or value of the items, the circumstances are exceptional.

21.14 The LSC funded client's resources include the resources of his partner, unless the partner has a contrary interest in the dispute in respect of which funded services are provided.

Party acting in a Representative, Fiduciary or Official Capacity

A32–251   **21.15** (1) Where a LSC funded client is acting in a representative, fiduciary or official capacity, the court shall not take the personal resources of the party into account for the purposes of either a Section 11 order or costs against the Commission, but shall have regard to the value of any property or estate or the amount of any fund out of which the party is entitled to be indemnified, and may also have regard to the resources of any persons who are beneficially interested in the property, estate or fund.

(2) The purpose of this provision is to ensure that any liability is determined with reference to the value of the property or fund being used to pay for the litigation, and the financial position of those who may benefit from or rely on it.

Costs against the LSC

A32–252   **21.16** Regulation 5 of the Community Legal Service (Cost Protection) Regulations 2000 governs when costs can be awarded against the LSC. This provision only applies where cost protection applies and the costs ordered to be paid by the LSC funded client do not fully meet the costs that would have been ordered to be paid by him if cost protection did not apply.

21.17 In this Section and the following two Sections of this Practice Direction "non-funded party" means a party to proceedings who has not received LSC funded services in relation to these proceedings under a legal aid certificate or a certificate issued under the LSC Funding Code other than a certificate which has been revoked.

21.18 The following criteria set out in Regulation 5 must be satisfied before the LSC can be ordered to pay the whole or any part of the costs incurred by a non-funded party:

(1) the proceedings are finally decided in favour of a non-funded party;

(2) the non-funded party provides written notice of intention to seek an order against the LSC within three months of the making of the section 11(1) costs order;

(3) the court is satisfied that it is just and equitable in the circumstances that provision for the costs should be made out of public funds; and

(4) where costs are incurred in a court of first instance, the following additional criteria must also be met:

    (i) the proceedings were instituted by the LSC funded client; and

    (ii) the non-funded party will suffer severe financial hardship unless the order is made.

("Section 11(1) costs order" is defined in paragraph 22.1, below).

21.19 In determining whether conditions (3) and (4) are satisfied, the court shall take into account the resources of the non-funded party and his partner, unless the partner has a contrary interest.

Effect of Appeals

21.20 (1) An order for costs can only be made against the LSC when the **A32–253** proceedings (including any appeal) are finally decided. Therefore, where a court of first instance decides in favour of a non-funded party and an appeal lies, any order made against the LSC shall not take effect unless:

(a) where permission to appeal is required, the time limit for permission to appeal expires, without permission being granted;

(b) where permission to appeal is granted or is not required, the time limit for appeal expires without an appeal being brought.

(2) Accordingly, if the LSC funded client appeals, any earlier order against the LSC can never take effect. If the appeal is unsuccessful, an application can be made to the appeal court for a fresh order.

Orders for Costs to which Section 11 of the Access to Justice Act 1999 Applies

22.1 In this Practice Direction: **A32–254**

    "order for costs to be determined" means an order for costs to which Section 11 of the Access to Justice Act 1999 applies under which the amount of costs payable by the LSC funded client is to be determined by a costs judge or district judge under Section 23 of this Practice Direction.

    "order specifying the costs payable" means an order for costs to which Section 11 of the Act applies and which specifies the amount which the LSC funded client is to pay.

    "full costs" means, where an order to which Section 11 of the Act applies is made against a LSC funded client, the amount of costs which that person would, had cost protection not applied, have been ordered to pay.

    "determination proceedings" means proceedings to which paragraphs 22.1 to 22.10 apply.

    "Section 11(1) costs order" means an order for costs to be determined or an order specifying the costs payable other than an order specifying the costs payable which was made in determination proceedings.

    "statement of resources" means

        (1) a statement, verified by a statement of truth, made by a party to proceedings setting out:

(a) his income and capital and financial commitments during the previous year and, if applicable, those of his partner;

(b) his estimated future financial resources and expectations and, if applicable, those of his partner ("partner" is defined in paragraph 21.4, above);

(c) a declaration that he and, if applicable, his partner, has not deliberately foregone or deprived himself of any resources or expectations;

(d) particulars of any application for funding made by him in connection with the proceedings; and,

(e) any other facts relevant to the determination of his resources; or

(2) a statement, verified by a statement of truth, made by a client receiving funded services, setting out the information provided by the client under Regulation 6 of the Community Legal Service (Financial) Regulations 2000, and stating that there has been no significant change in the client's financial circumstances since the date on which the information was provided or, as the case may be, details of any such change.

"Regional Director" means any Regional Director appointed by the LSC and any member of his staff authorised to act on his behalf.

22.2 Regulations 8 to 13 of the Community Legal Service (Costs) Regulations 2000 set out the procedure for seeking costs against a funded client and the LSC. The effect of these Regulations is set out in this section and the next section of this Practice Direction.

22.3 As from 5 June 2000, Regulations 9 to 13 of the Community Legal Service (Costs) Regulations 2000 also apply to certificates issued under the Legal Aid Act 1988 where costs against the assisted person fall to be assessed under Regulation 124 of the Civil Legal Aid (General) Regulations 1989. In this section and the next section of this Practice Direction the expression "LSC funded client" includes an assisted person (defined in rule 43.2).

22.4 Regulation 8 of the Community Legal Service (Costs) Regulations 2000 provides that a party intending to seek an order for costs against a LSC funded client may at any time file and serve on the LSC funded client a statement of resources. If that statement is served 7 or more days before a date fixed for a hearing at which an order for costs may be made, the LSC funded client must also make a statement of resources and produce it at the hearing.

22.5 If the court decides to make an order for costs against a LSC funded client to whom cost protection applies it may either:

(1) make an order for cost to be determined, or

(2) make an order specifying the costs payable.

22.6 If the court makes an order for costs to be determined it may also

(1) state the amount of full costs, or

(2) make findings of facts, e.g., concerning the conduct of all the parties which are to be taken into account by the court in the subsequent determination proceedings.

22.7 The court will not make an order specifying the costs payable unless:

(1) it considers that it has sufficient information before it to decide what amount is a reasonable amount for the LSC funded client to pay in accordance with Section 11 of the Act, and

(2) either—

(a) the order also states the amount of full costs, or

(b) the court considers that it has sufficient information before it to decide what amount is a reasonable amount for the LSC funded client to pay in accordance with Section 11 of the Act and is satisfied that, if it were to determine the full costs at that time, they would exceed the amounts specified in the order.

22.8 Where an order specifying the costs payable is made and the LSC funded client does not have cost protection in respect of all of the costs awarded in that order, the order must identify the sum payable (if any) in respect of which the LSC funded client has cost protection and the sum payable (if any) in respect of which he does not have cost protection.

22.9 The court cannot make an order under Regulations 8 to 13 of the Community Legal Service (Costs) Regulations 2000 except in proceedings to which the next section of this Practice Direction applies.

Determination Proceedings and Similar Proceedings under the Community Legal Service (Costs) Regulations 2000

23.1 This section of this Practice Direction deals with: **A32–255**
(1) proceedings subsequent to the making of an order for costs to be determined,
(2) variations in the amount stated in an order specifying the amount of costs payable and
(3) the late determination of costs under an order for costs to be determined.
23.2 In this section of this Practice Direction "appropriate court office" means:
(1) the district registry or county court in which the case was being dealt with when the Section 11(1) order was made, or to which it has subsequently been transferred; or
(2) in all other cases, the Supreme Court Costs Office.
23.3 (1) A receiving party seeking an order specifying costs payable by an LSC funded client and/or by the LSC may within 3 months of an order for costs to be determined, file in the appropriate court office an application in Form N244 accompanied by:
(a) the receiving party's bill of costs (unless the full costs have already been determined);
(b) the receiving party's statement of resources; and
(c) if the receiving party intends to seek costs against the LSC, written notice to that effect.
(2) If the LSC funded client's liability has already been determined and is less than the full costs, the application will be for costs against the LSC only. If the LSC funded client's liability has not yet been determined, the receiving party must indicate if costs will be sought against the LSC if the funded client's liability is determined as less than the full costs.
(The LSC funded client's certificate will contain the addresses of the LSC funded client, his solicitor, and the relevant Regional Office of the LSC.)
23.4 The receiving party must file the above documents in the appropriate court office and (where relevant) serve copies on the LSC funded client and the Regional Director. Failure to file a request within the 3 months time limit specified in Regulation 10(2) is an absolute bar to the making of a costs order against the LSC.
23.5 On being served with the application, the LSC funded client must respond by filing a statement of resources and serving a copy of it on the receiving party (and the Regional Director where relevant) within 21 days. The LSC funded client may also file and serve written points disputing the bill within the same time limit. (Under rule 3.1 the court may extend or shorten this time limit.)
23.6 If the LSC funded client fails to file a statement of resources without good reason, the court will determine his liability (and the amount of full costs if relevant) and need not hold an oral hearing for such determination.
23.7 When the LSC funded client files a statement or the 21 day period for doing so expires, the court will fix a hearing date and give the relevant parties at

least 14 days notice. The court may fix a hearing without waiting for the expiry of the 21 day period if the application is made only against the LSC.

23.8 Determination proceedings will be listed for hearing before a costs judge or district judge.

23.9 Where the LSC funded client does not have cost protection in respect of all of the costs awarded, the order made by the costs judge or district judge must in addition to specifying the costs payable, identify the full costs in respect of which cost protection applies and the full costs in respect of which cost protection does not apply.

23.10 The Regional Director may appear at any hearing at which a costs order may be made against the LSC. Instead of appearing, he may file a written statement at court and serve a copy on the receiving party. The written statement should be filed and a copy served, not less than 7 days before the hearing.

Variation of an order specifying the costs payable

A32–256   **23.11** (1) This paragraph applies where the amount stated in an order specifying the costs payable plus the amount ordered to be paid by the LSC is less than the full costs to which cost protection applies.

(2) The receiving party may apply to the court for a variation of the amount which the LSC funded client is required to pay on the ground that there has been a significant change in the client's circumstances since the date of the order.

23.12 On an application under paragraph 23.11, where the order specifying the costs payable does not state the full costs:

(1) the receiving party must file with his application the receiving party's statement of resources and bill of costs and copies of these documents should be served with the application.

(2) The LSC funded client must respond to the application by making a statement of resources which must be filed at court and served on the receiving party within 21 days thereafter. The LSC funded client may also file and serve written points disputing the bill within the same time limit.

(3) The court will, when determining the application assess the full costs identifying any part of them to which cost protection does apply and any part of them to which cost protection does not apply.

23.13 On an application under paragraph 23.11 the order specifying the costs payable may be varied as the court thinks fit. That variation must not increase:

(1) the amount of any costs ordered to be paid by the LSC, and

(2) the amount payable by the LSC funded client,

(3) to a sum which is greater than the amount of the full costs plus the costs of the application.

23.14 (1) Where an order for costs to be determined has been made but the receiving party has not applied, within the three month time limit under paragraph 23.2, the receiving party may apply on any of the following grounds for a determination of the amount which the funded client is required to pay:

(a) there has been a significant change in the funded client's circumstances since the date of the order for costs to be determined; or

(b) material additional information about the funded client's financial resources is available which could not with reasonable diligence have been obtained by the receiving party at the relevant time; or

(c) there were other good reasons for the failure by the receiving party to make an application within the time limit.

(2) An application for costs payable by the LSC cannot be made under this paragraph.

23.15 (1) Where the receiving party has received funded services in relation to the proceedings, the LSC may make an application under paragraphs 23.11 and 23.14 above.

(2) In respect of an application under paragraph 23.11 made by the LSC, the LSC must file and serve copies of the documents described in paragraph 23.12(1)

23.16 An application under paragraph 23.11, 23.14 and 23.15 must be commenced before the expiration of 6 years from the date on which the court made the order specifying the costs payable, or (as the case may be) the order for costs to be determined.

23.17 Applications under paragraphs 23.11, 23.14 and 23.15 should be made in the appropriate court office and should be made in Form N244 to be listed for a hearing before a costs judge or district judge.

PART 49

SPECIALIST PROCEEDINGS

A32–257

49 (1) These Rules shall apply to the proceedings listed in paragraph (2) subject to the provisions in the relevant practice direction which applies to those proceedings.

(2) The proceedings referred to in paragraph (1) are—

    (a) admiralty proceedings;

    (b) arbitration proceedings;

    (c) commercial and mercantile actions;

    (d) Patents Court business (as defined by the relevant practice direction) and proceedings under—

        (i) the Copyright, Designs and Patents Act 1988;

        (ii) the Trade Marks Act 1994; and

        (iii) the Olympic Symbol etc Protection Act 1995 and Olympics Association Right (Infringement Proceedings) Regulations 1995;

    (e) Technology and Construction Court Business (as defined by the relevant practice direction);

    (f) proceedings under the Companies Act 1985 and the Companies Act 1989; and

    (g) contentious probate proceedings.

2D INTELLECTUAL PROPERTY PROCEEDINGS

PRACTICE DIRECTION—PATENTS ETC.

This Practice Direction supplements CPR, Part 49 and replaces, with modifications, **A32–258** *RSC, Order 104, Order 100 and Order 93, Rule 24, and CCR, Order 48A and Order 49, Rule 4A*

Editorial Introduction

This Practice Direction—Patents, etc., supplements CPR, Pt 49. It replaces, with modifications, RSC, O.104 (proceedings relating to patents, registered designs and under the Defence Contracts Act 1958), O.100 (trade marks) and O.93 (applications under ss.114, 204 or 231 of the Copyright, Designs and Patents Act 1988) and the equivalent rules for the Patents County Court and CCR, O.48A and O.49A. Most of the changes are designed to ensure that the same terminology applies to these specialist proceedings as apply to all others. Furthermore, some minor changes have to be made to ensure that case management in these areas is consistent with the new system.

As before, all claims made under the Patent Acts, the Registered Design Acts and under the Defence Contracts Act are assigned either to the Patents Court, a part of the Chancery Division of the High Court, or the Patents County Court (2(a)). There is a possibility of transfer from one to the other. Every claim allocated to the Patents Court will be allocated to the multi-track. As a consequence the rules relating to track allocation do not apply

(2(d)). It should be noted that claims and appeals arising under the Trade Marks Acts 1938 and 1994, and the Olympic Symbol, etc., Act 1995 are assigned to the Chancery Division, not the Patents Court (para. 21). In practice, actions for passing off and under the Copyright, etc., Act are also dealt with by the Chancery Division. All these types of cases are treated as any other form of litigation and the track allocation rules apply. With very few exceptions, all applications in patent and registered design matters are made direct to the Patents Court. Paragraph 4 contains detailed provisions relating to applications in the Patents Court for the amendment of patent specifications.

The Practice Direction requires the parties to take various steps to limit the scope of the dispute between them and to reduce the amount of material relied on at the trial. To this end, para. 6 stipulates that the claimant in a patent action must identify not only what the acts of infringement relied on are but also the particular claims which are said to be infringed. Similarly, in those cases where the defendant intends to attack the validity of a patent, para. 7 contains detailed provisions requiring him to specify the nature of the attack and any prior art he intends to rely upon. Similar directions exist for proceedings in which the validity of a trade mark is being put in issue (para. 23). Paragraph 9 limits the scope of disclosure in patent actions, particularly by exempting old documentation from disclosure and providing any claimant who is relying on commercial success to support the validity of his patent with a means of avoiding disclosure of the extensive documentation which might otherwise be relevant to that issue. Any part wishing to rely on experiments has to comply with para. 10 which specifies, amongst other things, the date on which a notice of experiments must be served. In fact, the order for directions made in patent actions frequently includes more detailed provisions for the timing and content of a notice of experiments. A standard form notice of experiments is annexed to the *Patents Court Guide*. (The latest issue of that document can be obtained from the Patents Court website at www.courtservice.gov.uk/highhome.htm.) Paragraph 12 prevents a party from relying on any evidence of which the other party has had inadequate notice.

Paragraph 13 sets a time limit of 28 days within which applications must be made to the Court in cases where the Comptroller General of Patents has either declined to deal with a question or application made to him under the 1977 Act or where he certifies under s.72(7)(b) that it is a matter which would be more properly determined by the Court.

The procedure to be adoped when an employee applies for compensation under s.40 of the 1977 Act is set out in para. 14, while para. 15 sets out the procedure to be adopted for appeals to the Court from decisions of the Comptroller where such an appeal lies.

General

A32–259   **1.1** This practice directions applies to the business of the Patents Court and proceedings under the Copyright, Designs and Patents Act 1988, the Trade Marks Acts 1938 and 1994 and the Olympic Symbol, etc. Protection Act 1995 and Olympic Association Right (Infringement Proceedings) Regulations 1995.

1.2 The Civil Procedure Rules apply to Patents Court business and proceedings under the Copyright, Designs and Patents Act 1988, the Trade Marks Acts 1938 and 1994 and the Olympic Symbol, etc. Protection Act 1995 and Olympic Association Right (Infringement Proceedings) Regulations 1995 subject to the provisions of this and any other Patents Court practice direction.

1.3 Definitions.

In this Practice Direction—

"the 1949 Act" means the Patents Act 1949;

"the 1977 Act" means the Patents Act 1977;

"the Comptroller" means the Comptroller-General of Patents, Designs and Trade Marks;

"the Court" means the Patents Court;

"existing patent" means a patent mentioned in section 127(2) (a) or (c) of the 1977 Act;

"the journal" means the journal published pursuant to rules made under section 123(6) of the 1977 Act;

"1977 Act patent" means a patent under the 1977 Act;

"patent" means an existing patent or a 1977 Act patent and includes any application for a patent, supplementary protection certificate granted pursuant to the Patents (Supplementary Protection Certificates) Rules

1997, the Patents (Supplementary Protection Certificate for Medicinal Products) Regulations 1992 and the Patents (Supplementary Protection Certificate for Plant Protection Products) Regulations 1996.

"Patents Court" includes the Patents Court of the High Court and thePatents County Court.

"Patents Court business" includes:

(a) any claim under the Patents Acts 1949 to 1961 and 1977;

(b) any claim under the Registered Designs Acts 1949 to 1961;

(c) any claim under the Defence Contracts Act 1958, and

(d) all proceedings for the determination of a question or the making of a declaration relating to a patent (or an application for a patent) under the inherent jurisdiction of the High Court.

"the CPR" means the Civil Procedure Rules.

Allocation of patents court business

2.1 Patents Court business may be dealt with either in the High Court or the **A32–260** Patents county court.

2.2 Before the issue of a claim form relating to Patents Court business, the claim form, whether it is to be issued in the High Court or the county court, should be marked in the top right hand corner "Patents Court" and the claim will then be allocated to the Patents Court.

2.3 The Patents Court is a specialist list for the purposes of Part 30 of the CPR but no order for the transfer of proceedings to or from the Patents Court shall be made unless the parties have either:

(a) had an opportunity of being heard on the issue, or

(b) consented to the order.

2.4 Every claim in the Patents Court will be allocated to the multi-track and the CPR relating to allocation questionnaires and track allocation will not apply.

2.5 (1) Where a claim has been allocated to the Patents Court either on issue (*i.e.* in every case in which the claim form has been marked Patents Court) or by transfer to the Patents Court, an application for directions (including an application for a fixed date of hearing) shall be made by the claimant within 14 days of the filing by the defendant of an acknowledgment of service or of a defence (whichever is the earlier) or, as the case may be, within 14 days of the date of the order of transfer.

(2) If the claimant does not make an application in accordance with paragraph 2.5, any other party may do so or may apply for the claim of claimant in default to be struck out or dismissed.

(3) Any application under this paragraph must be made to a judge of the Patents Court unless a judge of the Patents Court otherwise directs.

(4) On the hearing of the application for directions under paragraph 2.5(1) the judge shall give directions for any further directions hearing and direct the time by which the hearing of any further application for directions is to take place.

2.6 Except where inconsistent with the provisions of this Practice Direction, CPR Part 29 and the Multi-track Practice Direction apply to Patents Court business.

2.7 This practice direction shall apply with any necessary modifications to proceedings in respect of Registered Designs.

Service of documents

3.1 This rule applies to the service of any document on a party until such time **A32–261** as that party has provided an address for service in accordance with CPR rule 6.5.

3.2 Subject to sub-paragraph (3) below, for the purposes of any proceedings relating to a patent or a registered design (including proceedings for revocation, declaration as to non-infringement or groundless threats of infringement proceedings or any other proceedings of a kind mentioned in this Practice Direction) where any document is served in the manner authorised by CPR Part 6 at an address for service given in the register kept under section 32 of the 1977 Act or, as the case may be, section 17 of the Registered Designs Act 1949.

(1) service shall be deemed to have been effected on the registered proprietor of the patent or registered design on the date on which the document was served at the said address;

(2) the party on whom service is deemed to have been effected under sub-paragraph (a) shall be treated, for the purposes of any provision of these rules which specifies a time-limit for responding to the document so served (whether by filing or serving an admission, filing a defence, acknowledging service, or otherwise), as having been served on the seventh day after the date on which the document was served at the said address.

3.3 Nothing in paragraph 3.2 shall prevent service being effected on the proprietor in accordance with the provisions of Part 6 of the CPR.

Application in proceedings before the court for permission to amend a patent specification under s.30 of the 1949 act or s.75 of the 1977 act

A32–262   **4.1** A patentee or the proprietor of a patent intending to apply in proceedings before the Court under section 30 of the 1949 Act or under section 75 of the 1977 Act for permission to amend his specification must give notice of his intention to the Comptroller accompanied by a copy of an advertisement—

(1) identifying the proceedings pending before the Court in which it is intended to apply for such permission;

(2) giving particulars of the amendment sought;

(3) stating the applicant's address for service within the United Kingdom;

(4) stating that a Statement of Reasons is available from that address; and

(5) stating that any person intending to oppose the amendment must within 28 days after the appearance of the advertisement give written notice of his intention to the applicant; such notice to be accompanied by a Statement of Opposition;

and the Comptroller shall insert the advertisement once in the journal. A person who gives notice in accordance with the advertisement shall be entitled to be heard on the application subject to any direction of the Court as to costs.

4.2 The applicant must at the same time as giving notice to the Comptroller serve a copy of the Statement of Reasons together with a copy of the patent as proposed to be amended on all parties to the proceedings.

4.3 The Statement of Reasons referred to in paragraph 4.1 (4) shall contain full particulars of the amendment sought, of the reasons therefor and of the reasons why the applicant contends that in the exercise of discretion the amendment should be allowed. In particular the Statement should contain:

(1) A statement whether the amendment is by way of deletion of claims or re-writing of claims.

(2) In so far as it involves re-writing claims, details as to why the proposed amendment is in accordance with the statutory requirements of an amendment.

(3) In so far as the amendment is sought to distinguish (more clearly) over prior art, an indication of the prior art.

4.4 The Statement of Opposition shall contain full particulars of all grounds of opposition to the application to amend.

4.5 As soon as may be after the expiration of 35 days from the appearance of the advertisement the applicant must make his application under the said section 30 or 75, as the case may be, by an application notice in the proceedings before the Court; and the application notice, together with a copy of the specification certified by the Comptroller and showing in coloured ink the amendment sought, must be served on the Comptroller, the parties to the proceedings and any person who has given notice of his intention to oppose the amendment.

4.6 Not less than two days before the date fixed for the hearing of the application, the applicant, the Comptroller, the parties to the proceedings and any other opponent should serve on all other parties and on the Court a Statement of Directions being the directions which that party seeks for the further conduct of the proceedings. Any of the foregoing not serving a Statement of Directions shall take no further part in the proceedings without permission of the Court and shall not be liable for the costs thereof.

4.7 On the hearing of the amendment application the Court shall give such directions for its further conduct as it thinks necessary or expedient and, in particular, directions—

(1) determining whether the application shall be heard forthwith or with the other proceedings relating to the patent in question or separately and, if separately, fixing the date of hearing thereof;

(2) as to whether any evidence is necessary, and, if so, as to the manner in which that evidence shall be given and, if written evidence is to be given, fixing the times within which the affidavits or witness statements must be filed;

(3) as to whether any disclosure is necessary, and, if so, as to the extent of disclosure and the manner and time within which the same is to be given.

4.8 Where the Court allows a specification to be amended, the applicant must forthwith file with the Comptroller an office copy of the order made in the Court and, if so required by the Court or Comptroller, leave at the Patent Office a new specification and drawings as amended, prepared in compliance with the 1949 or 1977 Act, whichever is applicable, and the rules made under those Acts respectively.

4.9 The Comptroller shall cause a copy of the order to be inserted at least once in the journal.

Application for revocation

5.1 An application under section 72 of the 1977 Act for the revocation of a **A32–263** patent shall be commenced by the issue of a claim form. This direction does not apply to an application made in existing proceedings. An application in existing proceedings shall be made by way of a counterclaim or other Part 20 claim (as defined in CPR rule 20.2 (1)).

Claim for infringement

6.1 The claimant in a claim for infringement must serve with his claim form **A32–264** particulars of the infringement relied on, showing which of the claims in the specification of the patent are alleged to be infringed and giving at least one instance of each type of infringement alleged.

6.2 If a defendant in such a claim alleges, as a defence to the claim, that at the time of the infringement there was in force a contract or licence relating to the patent made by or with the consent of the claimant and containing a condition or term void by virtue of section 44 of the 1977 Act, he must serve on the claimant particulars of the date of, and parties to, each such contract or licence and particulars of each such condition or term.

Objections to validity

7.1 A person who presents a claim for the revocation of a patent must serve **A32–265** with his claim form particulars of the objections to the validity of the patent on which he relies.

7.2 A party to a claim concerning a patent who either challenges the validity of the patent or applies by counterclaim or other Part 20 claim for revocation of the patent must, serve his defence, counterclaim or other Part 20 claim (as the case may be), together with particulars of the objections to the validity of the patent on which he relies, within 42 days after service upon him of the claim form.

7.3 Particulars given pursuant to paragraph 7.1 or 7.2 must state every ground on which the validity of the patent is challenged and must include such particulars as will clearly define every issue (including any challenge to any claimed priority date) which it is intended to raise.

7.4 If the grounds stated in the particulars of objections include want of novelty or want of any inventive step, the particulars must state the manner, time and place of every prior publication or user relied upon and, if prior user is alleged, must:

(1) specify the name of every person alleged to have made such user,

(2) state whether such user is alleged to have continued until the priority date of the claim in question or of the invention, as may be appropriate, and, if not, the earliest and latest date on which such user is alleged to have taken place,

(3) contain a description accompanied by drawings, if necessary, sufficient to identify such user, and

(4) if such user relates to machinery or apparatus, state whether the machinery or apparatus is in existence and where it can be inspected.

7.5 If either (a) in the case of an existing patent one of the grounds stated in the particulars of objections is that the invention, so far as claimed in any claim of the complete specification, is not useful, or, (b) in the case of a patent one of the grounds stated in the particulars of objections is that the specification of the patent does not disclose the invention clearly enough and completely enough for the invention to be performed and it is intended, in connection with either of such grounds, to rely on the fact that an example of the invention which is the subject of any claim cannot be made to work, either at all or as described in the specification, the particulars must state that fact and identify each such claim and must include particulars of each such example, specifying the respects in which it is alleged that it does not work or does not work as described.

7.6 In any proceedings relating to a patent in which the validity of the Patent has been put in issue on the ground of obviousness a party who wishes to rely on the commercial success of the patent must state in his pleadings the grounds upon which he so relies.

Admissions

A32–266 **8.1** Where a party desires any other party to admit any facts, he shall, within 21 days after service of a reply or after the expiration of the period fixed for the service thereof, serve on that other party a notice requiring him to admit for the purpose of the claim the facts specified in the notice.

8.2 A party upon whom a notice under paragraph 8.1 is served shall within 21 days after service thereof serve upon the party making the request a notice stating in respect of each fact specified in the notice whether or not he admits it.

Disclosure and inspection

A32–267 **9.1** CPR Part 31 shall apply in a claim for infringement of a patent or a declaration of non-infringement of a patent or any proceedings where the validity of a patent is in issue.

9.2 Standard disclosure does not require the disclosure of documents in the following exempt classes:

(1) documents relating to the infringement of a patent by a product or process if, before serving a list of documents, the party against whom the allegation of infringement is made has served on the other parties full particulars of the product or process alleged to infringe, including if necessary drawings or other illustrations;

(2) documents relating to any ground on which the validity of a patent is put in issue, except documents which came into existence within the period beginning two years before the earliest claimed priority date and ending two years after that date; and

(3) documents relating to the issue of commercial success.

9.3 Where the issue of commercial success arises in any proceedings specified in paragraph 9.1, the patentee shall, within such time limit as the Court may direct, serve a schedule containing the following details—

1426

(1) where the commercial success relates to an article or product—

    (a) an identification of the article or product (for example by product code number) which the patentee asserts has been made in accordance with the claims of the patent;

    (b) a summary by convenient periods of sales of any such article or product;

    (c) a summary for the equivalent periods of sales, if any, of any equivalent prior article or product marketed before the article or product mentioned in sub-paragraph (a); and

    (d) a summary by convenient periods of any expenditure on advertising and promotion which supported the marketing of the articles or products mentioned in sub-paragraph (a) and (c),

(2) where the commercial success relates to the use of a process—

    (a) an identification of the process the patentee asserts has been used in accordance with the claims of the patent;

    (b) a summary by convenient periods of the revenues received from the use of such process;

    (c) a summary for the equivalent periods of the revenues, if any, received from the use of any equivalent prior art process; and

    (d) a summary by convenient periods of any expenditure which supported the use of the process mentioned in sub-paragraphs (a) and (c).

Experiments

10.1 Where a party desires to establish any fact by experimental proof he **A32–268** must, at least 21 days before the service of the application notice for directions under paragraph 10.3 or within such other time as the Court may direct at a hearing for further directions pursuant to paragraph 2.5(4), serve on the other party a notice stating the facts which he desires to establish and giving full particulars of the experiments proposed to establish them.

10.2 A party upon whom a notice under paragraph 10.1 is served shall, within 21 days after service thereof, serve upon the other party a notice stating in respect of each fact whether or not he admits it.

10.3 Where any fact which a party desires to establish by experimental proof is not admitted he shall apply to the Court for directions in respect of such experiments.

Application for further directions

11.1(1) The parties must comply with any directions given by the judge **A32–269** pursuant to paragraph 2.5(4) in respect of any hearing for further directions.

(2) If the claimant does not serve an application notice for further directions in accordance with this paragraph, the defendant may do so.

(3) The application notice must be accompanied by minutes of the order proposed, and such other documents as will be necessary for the hearing of the application.

11.2 At a further directions hearing under this paragraph the judge may give such directions relating to:

(1) the service of further pleadings or of further information pursuant to Part 18 of the CPR;

(2) disclosure and inspection of documents;

(3) requests for or the making of admissions pursuant to paragraphs 8.1 and 8.2 above and Part 14 of the CPR;

(4) the obtaining of written evidence relating to matters requiring expert knowledge, and for the filing of affidavits or witness statements and the service of copies thereof on the other parties,

(5) the holding of a meeting of such experts as the judge may specify, for the purpose of producing a joint report on the state of the relevant art;

(6) the exchanging of experts' reports, in respect of those matters on which they are not agreed;

(7) the making of experiments, tests, inspections or reports;

(8) the determination, as a preliminary issue, of any question that may arise including any questions as to the construction of the specification or other documents);

and otherwise as the judge thinks necessary or expedient for the purpose of giving effect to the overriding objective. Where evidence is directed to be given by affidavit or witness statement, the witnesses must attend at the trial for cross-examination unless, with the concurrence of the Court, the parties otherwise agree.

11.3 On the hearing of an application under this paragraph the judge shall consider, if necessary of his own initiative, whether:

(a) the parties' advisers should be required to meet for the purpose of agreeing which documents will be required at the trial and of paginating such documents;

(b) an independent scientific adviser should be appointed to assist the Court, whether as an assessor under CPR rule 35.15 or otherwise.

Restrictions on admission of evidence

A32–270   **12.1** Except with the permission of the judge hearing any claim or other proceedings relating to a patent, no evidence shall be admissible in proof of any alleged infringement, or of any objection to the validity, of the patent, if the infringement or objection was not raised in the particulars of infringements or objections, as the case may be.

12.2 In any claim or other proceedings relating to a patent, evidence which is not in accordance with a statement contained in particulars of objections to the validity of the patent shall not be admissible in support of such an objection unless the judge hearing the proceeding allows the evidence to be admitted.

12.3 If any machinery or apparatus alleged to have been used before the priority date mentioned in paragraph 7.4(2) is in existence at the date of service of the particulars of objections, no evidence of its user before that date shall be admissible unless it is proved that the party relying on such user offered, where the machinery or apparatus is in his possession, inspection of it to the other parties to the proceedings or, where it is not, used all reasonable endeavours to obtain inspection of it for those parties.

Determination of question or application where comptroller declines to deal with it

A32–271   **13** Where the Comptroller—

(1) declines to deal with a question under section 8(7), 12(2), 37(8) or 61(5) of the 1977 Act;

(2) declines to deal with an application under section 40(5) of that Act, or

(3) certifies under section 72(7)(b) of that Act that the question whether a patent should be revoked is one which would more properly be determined by the court,

any person entitled to do so may, within 28 days after the Comptroller's decision apply to the Court to determine the question or application.

Application by employee for compensation under section 40 of the 1977 Act

A32–272   **14.1** An application by an employee for compensation under section 40(1) or (2) of the 1977 Act shall be begun by the issue of a claim form within the period which begins when the relevant patent is granted and which expires one year after it has ceased to have effect.

Provided that, where a patent has ceased to have effect by reason of a failure to pay any renewal fee within the period prescribed for the payment thereof and an application for restoration is made to the Comptroller under section 28 of the said Act, the said period shall—

(1) if restoration is ordered, continue as if the patent had remained continuously in effect, or

(2) if restoration is refused, be treated as expiring one year after the patent ceased to have effect or six months after the refusal, whichever is the later.

14.2 Either at the hearing of an application for directions under paragraph 2.5(1) or at a hearing of an application for further directions under paragraphs 11.1–11.3, the Court must give directions as to the manner in which the evidence (including any accounts of expenditure and receipts relating to the claim) shall be given at the hearing of the claim and, if written evidence is to be given, specify the period within which witness statements or affidavits must be filed.

14.3 The Court must also give directions as to the provision by the defendant to the claimant, or a person deputed by him for the purpose, of reasonable facilities for inspecting and taking extracts from the books of account by which the defendant proposes to verify the accounts mentioned in paragraph 14.2 or from which those accounts have been derived.

Procedure for the determination of certain disputes

15.1 The following proceedings must be begun by the issue of a claim form, **A32–273** that is to say—

(1) proceedings for the determination of any dispute referred to the court under—

    (a) section 48 of the 1949 Act or section 58 of the 1977 Act;

    (b) paragraph 3 of Schedule 1 to the Registered Designs Act 1949;

    (c) section 4 of the Defence Contracts Act 1958; or

    (d) section 252 of the Copyright, Designs and Patent Act 1988;

(2) any application under section 45(3) of the 1977 Act.

Appeals from the comptroller

16.1 In this paragraph "the Court" means the Patents Court of the High Court. **A32–274**

16.2 An appeal to the Court from a decision of the Comptroller in any case in which a right of appeal is given by the 1949 or 1977 Act must be brought by issuing a Notice of Appeal. The parties are, in this paragraph, referred to as "appellant" and "respondent" respectively.

16.3 The Notice of Appeal shall be issued:

(1) in the case of a decision on a matter of procedure, within 14 days after the date of the decision; and

(2) in any other case, within six weeks after the date of the decision.

16.4 The Comptroller may determine whether any decision is on a matter of procedure and any such determination shall itself be a decision on a matter of procedure.

16.5 Except with permission of the Court, no appeal shall be entertained unless the Notice of Appeal has been issued within the period specified in paragraph 16.3 or within such further time as the Comptroller may allow upon request made to him prior to the expiry of that period.

16.6 The Notice of Appeal may be given in respect of the whole or any specific part of the decision of the Comptroller and must specify the grounds of the appeal and the relief which the appellant seeks.

16.7 Except with the permission of the Court the appellant shall not be entitled on the hearing of the appeal to rely on any ground of appeal or to apply for any relief not specified in the Notice of Appeal.

16.8 The appellant shall, within 21 days of issuing the Notice of Appeal, serve a copy thereof on the Comptroller and any other party to the proceedings before the Comptroller.

16.9 After receiving the Notice of Appeal the Comptroller shall lodge with the Clerk or other person in charge of the Patents Court list all papers relating to the matter which is subject of the appeal.

16.10 A respondent who, not having appealed from the decision of the Comptroller, desires to contend on the appeal that the decision should be varied, either in any event or in the event of the appeal being allowed in whole or in part, must give notice to that effect, specifying the grounds of that contention and the relief which he seeks from the Court.

16.11 A respondent who desires to contend on the appeal that the decision of the Comptroller should be affirmed on grounds other than those set out in the decision must give notice to that effect, specifying the grounds of that contention.

16.12 A respondent's notice shall be served on the Comptroller and on the appellant and every other party to the proceedings before the Comptroller within 4 days after service of the Notice of Appeal by the respondent, or within such further time as the Court may direct.

16.13 A party by whom a respondent's notice is given must within 5 days after service of the notice on the appellant, furnish 2 copies of the notice to the Clerk or other person in charge of the Patents List.

16.14 The Clerk or other person in charge of the Patents list shall give to the Comptroller and to the appellant and every other party to the proceedings before the Comptroller not less than seven days' notice of the date appointed for the hearing of the appeal, unless the Court directs shorter notice to be given.

16.15 An appeal shall be by way of rehearing and the evidence used on appeal shall be the same as that used before the Comptroller and, except with the permission of the Court, no further evidence shall be given.

16.16 Any notice given in proceedings under this rule may be signed by or served on any patent agent, or member of the Bar of England and Wales not in actual practice, who is acting for the person giving the notice or, as the case may be, the person on whom the notice is to be served, as if the patent agent or member of the Bar were a solicitor.

16.17 The Notice of Appeal shall be in the form annexed hereto or in such other form as may be approved by the Court.

Communication of information to the European Patent Office

17.1 The Court may authorise the communication to the European Patent Office or the competent authority of any country which is a party to the European Patent Convention of any such information in the files of the court as the Court thinks fit.

17.2 Before complying with a request for the disclosure of information under paragraph 17.1 the Court shall afford to any party appearing to be affected by the request the opportunity of making representations, in writing or otherwise, on the question whether the information should be disclosed.

Claim for rectification of register of patents or designs

18.1 Where a claim is made for the rectification of the register of patents, the claimant shall at the same time as serving the other party serve a copy of the claim form and the accompanying documents on the Comptroller, who shall be entitled to appear and to be heard on the application.

Other intellectual property matters included in this practice direction

A. Copyright matters

Additional damages under Section 97(2) of the Copyright, Designs and Patents Act 1988

19.1 Where a claimant seeks to recover additional damages under section 97(2) of the Copyright, Designs and Patents Act 1988, he must so state in his claim form and the particulars of claim must set out the grounds relied upon in support.

A32–275

A32–276

A32–277

Applications for delivery up and forfeiture under Sections 99, 114, 195, 204, 230 or 231 of the Copyright Designs and Patents Act 1988

20.1 An application under Sections 99, 114, 195, 204, 230 or 231 of the **A32–278** Copyright, Designs and Patents Act 1988 ("CDPA") shall be made by the issue of a claim form or, if made in existing proceedings, an application notice in those proceedings.

20.2 Where such an application is made the applicant shall serve the claim form or application notice on all persons having an interest in the goods, material or articles within the meaning of sections 114, 204 or 231 of the CDPA in so far as such persons are reasonably ascertainable.

B. Trademark matters

Definitions

21.1 In this section of this practice direction—   **A32–279**
   "the 1938 Act" means the Trade Marks Act 1938 as amended by the Trade
   Marks (Amendment) Act 1984 and the Patents, Designs and Marks
   Act 1986;
   "the 1994 Act" means the Trade Marks Act 1994;
   "the Olympic Symbol Act" means the Olympic Symbol etc. (Protection)
   Act 1995;
   "the Olympic Symbol Regulations" means the Olympic Association Right
   (Infringement Proceedings) Regulations 1995;
   "the Registrar" means the Comptroller-General of Patents, Designs and
   Trade Marks;
   "the register" means the register of trade marks maintained by the
   Registrar pursuant to section 63 of the 1994 Act;
   "appointed person" means a person appointed by the Lord Chancellor to
   hear and decide appeals under the 1994 Act.

Assignment to the Chancery Division

22.1 Proceedings in the High Court under the 1938 Act, the 1994 Act or the **A32–280** Olympic Symbol Act and Regulations shall be dealt with in the Chancery Division.

Appeals and applications under the 1938 Act, the 1994 Act and the Olympic Symbol Act and the Olympic Symbol Regulations

23.1 Every appeal to the High Court under the 1938 Act or the 1994 Act shall **A32–281** be heard and determined by a single judge.

23.2 Such appeals shall be brought by a Notice of Appeal in such form as may be approved by the court.

23.3 The Notice of Appeal must be issued within 28 days of the decision appealed from.

23.4 Within 21 days of issue the Notice of Appeal must be served on the Registrar and any Respondents and lodged with the Clerk or other person in charge of the Chancery List.

23.5 Every other application to the High Court under the said Acts and the Olympic Symbol Regulations must be begun by the issue of a claim form under CPR Part 8 or, if made in existing proceedings, an application notice in those proceedings.

23.6 Notices of Appeal, claim forms or application notices by which any such application is begun must be served on the Registrar.

23.7 Where—

(1) the Registrar refers to the High Court an application made to him under the 1938 Act or the 1994 Act;

(2) the Board of Trade under the 1938 Act or an appointed person under section 76 of the 1994 Act refers to that Court an appeal, then unless within one month after receiving notification of the decision to refer, the applicant or the appellant, as the case may be, makes to that Court the application or appeal referred, he shall be deemed to have abandoned it.

23.8 The period prescribed above in relation to an appeal to which paragraph 23.1 applies or the period prescribed by paragraph 23.7 in relation to an application or appeal to which that paragraph applies, may be extended by the Registrar on the application of any party interested and may be so extended although the application is not made until after the expiration of that period, but the foregoing provision shall not be taken to affect the power of the Court to extend that period.

23.9 Where under subsection (6) of section 17 or subsection (9) of section 18 of the 1938 Act an appellant becomes entitled and intends to withdraw the application which is the subject-matter of the appeal, he must give notice of his intention to the Registrar and to any other party to the appeal within one month after the Court has given permission under the said subsection (6) or the said subsection (9), as the case may be, for further grounds of objection to be taken.

23.10 Where an application is made under section 19 of the 1994 Act or under Regulation 5 of the Olympic Symbol Regulations the applicant shall serve the claim form or application notice on all persons having an interest in the goods, material or articles within the meaning of section 19 of the 1994 Act or Regulation 5 of the Olympic Symbol Regulations as the case may be insofar as such persons are reasonably ascertainable.

Proceedings for infringement of registered trade mark; validity of registration disputed or revocation or rectification sought

A32–282   **24.1** Where in any proceedings a claim is made for relief for infringement of the rights conferred on the proprietor of a registered trade mark by section 9 of the 1994 Act, the party against whom the claim is made may in his defence put in issue the validity of the registration of that trade mark or may apply by counterclaim or other Part 20 claim for an order for revocation of the registration or for a declaration of invalidity of the registration or for rectification of the register, or may do any or all of those things.

24.2 A party to any such proceedings who in his pleading (whether a defence or counterclaim or other Part 20 claim) disputes the validity of the registration of a registered trade mark or seeks a declaration of invalidity or an order for revocation of the registration, or rectification of the register, must serve with his pleading particulars of the objections to the validity of the registration or of any grounds for revocation or rectification, on which he relies.

24.3 A party to any such proceedings who applies for an order for revocation of the registration or for a declaration of invalidity of the registration or for rectification of the register must serve on the Registrar a copy of his counterclaim or other Part 20 claim together with a copy of the particulars mentioned in paragraph 24.2 and the Registrar shall be entitled to take such part in the proceedings as he may think fit but need not serve a defence or other statement of case unless ordered to do so by the Court.

Service of documents

A32–283   **25.1** This rule applies to the service of any document on a party until such time as that party has provided an address for service in accordance CPR rule 6.5.

25.2 Subject to paragraph 25.3 for the purposes of any proceedings relating to a registered trade mark (including proceedings for revocation, declaration of invalidity or non-infringement or groundless threats of infringement proceedings or any other proceedings under the 1938 Act or the 1994 Act), where any document is served in the manner authorised by Part 6 of the CPR at an address for service given in the register kept under section 63 of the 1994 Act—

(1) service shall be deemed to have been effected on the registered proprietor of the trade mark on the date on which the document was served at the said address;

(2) the party on whom service is deemed to have been effected under sub-paragraph (1), shall be treated, for the purposes of any provision which specifies a time-limit for responding to the document so served (whether by acknowledging service, giving notice of intention to defend or otherwise), as having been served on the seventh day after the date on which the document was served at the said address.

25.3 Nothing in paragraph 25.2 shall prevent service being effected on the proprietor in accordance with the provisions of CPR Part 6.

Service of orders on the Registrar

Where an order is made by the Court in any case under the 1938 Act or the 1994 Act, the person in whose favour the order is made (if there is more than one, such one of them as the Court shall direct) shall serve an office copy of the order on the Registrar.

A32–284

In the High Court of Justice Chancery Division Patents Court

NOTICE OF APPEAL

(a) Here insert the nature of the application or proceedings, the name of the Patentee or Applicant, the number of the Patent or Application for Letters Patent followed by the name of the Opponent (if any)

(b) Patent Agent or Applicant in person

(c) Here insert name(s) and full address(es) of Appellant(s)

(d) Here insert "the decision 'or' that part of the decision" as the case may be

(e) Here insert "Comptroller General" or "Officer acting for the Comptroller General" as the case may be

(f) Summarise the decision appealed against

(g) Here set out the grounds of appeal

(h) Here set out the relief which the Appellant seeks

(i) To be signed by the Appellant personally or by his duly authorised representative

(j) To be addressed to the other side and to their authorised representative and to the Comptroller-General at the Patent Office.

IN THe MATTER(a)

(e.g. of an Application by ....
and
an Opposition by ....)

TAKE NOTICE that the HIGH COURT OF JUSTICE, CHANCERY DIVISION, PATENTS COURT, will be moved before a Judge of the Patents Court at a time to be set by the Patents Court not less than twenty-four days after service of this notice, or so soon thereafter as Counsel(b) can be heard by Counsel(b), on behalf of (c)

....
by the way of appeal from(d) ....
of the(e) ....
dated the .... day of .... 19 ....
whereby he(f) ....
....
....
....

The grounds of appeal are as follows:—(g)

I/WE ask the Patents Court to grant the relief set out below:—(h)

DATE ....
SIGNATURE ....(i)
ADDRESS ....
....
....
TO ....(j)
....

NOTE: Two copies of this Notice of Appeal must be sent to the Chancery Chambers (Room 307), Thomas More Building, Royal Courts of Justice, Strand, London WC2A 2LL. They must be accompanied with the remittance for the prescribed fee. The remittance must if sent by post be paid by Bankers Draft or **postal order made payable to H.M. Paymaster General and crossed.** *A copy of the notice must be sent to the Comptroller-General at the Patent Office, Room GR15, Concept House, Cardiff Road, Gwent NP10 1RH and to any party entitled to appear before the Patents Court within the period prescribed by paragraph 16 of* **the Patents Practice Direction**

PART 52   A32–285

APPEALS

This Part came into force on May 2, 2000. The following transitional provisions apply:—
Where a person has filed a notice of appeal or applied for permission to appeal before May 2, 2000—
(a) Part 52 shall not apply to the appeal to which that notice or application relates; and
(b) The rules of court relating to appeals in force immediately before May 2, 2000 shall apply to that appeal as if they had not been revoked.

CONTENTS

I. GENERAL RULES ABOUT APPEALS

II. SPECIAL PROVISIONS APPLYING TO THE COURT OF APPEAL

I. General Rules about Appeals

Scope and interpretation

52.1 (1) The rules in this Part apply to appeals to—   A32–286
    (a) the civil division of the Court of Appeal;
    (b) the High Court; and
    (c) a county court.
(2) This Part does not apply to—
    (a) an appeal against an order under Part 27 (the small claims track); or
    (b) an appeal in detailed assessment proceedings against a decision of an authorised court officer.
(Rules 27.12 and 27.13 deal with appeals against orders under Part 27 (the small claim track))
(Rules 47.21 to 47.26 deal with appeals against a decision of an authorised court officer in detailed assessment proceedings)
(3) In this Part—

(a) "appeal" includes an appeal by way of case stated;
(b) "appeal court" means the court to which an appeal is made;
(c) "lower court" means the court, tribunal or other person or body from whose decision an appeal is brought;
(d) "appellant" means a person who brings or seeks to bring an appeal;
(e) "respondent" means—
 (i) a person other than the appellant who was a party to the proceedings in the lower court who is affected by the appeal; and
 (ii) a person who is permitted by the appeal court to be a party to the appeal; and
(f) "appeal notice" means an appellant's or respondent's notice.
(4) This Part is subject to any rule, enactment or practice direction which sets out special provisions with regard to any particular category of appeal.

Parties to comply with practice direction

A32–287   **52.2** All parties to an appeal must comply with the relevant practice direction.

Permission

A32–288   **52.3** (1) An appellant or respondent requires permission to appeal—
(a) where the appeal is from a decision of a judge in a county court or the High Court, except where the appeal is against—
 (i) a committal order;
 (ii) a refusal to grant habeas corpus; or
 (iii) a secure accommodation order made under section 25 of the Children Act 1989(a);
(b) as provided by the relevant practice direction.
(Other enactments may provide that permission is required for particular appeals)
(2) An application for permission to appeal may be made—
(a) to the lower court at the hearing at which the decision to be appealed was made; or
(b) to the appeal court in an appeal notice.
(Rule 52.4 sets out the time limits for filing an appellant's notice at the appeal court. Rule 52.5 sets out the time limits for filing a respondent's notice at the appeal court. Any application permission to appeal to the appeal court must be made in the appeal notice (see rules 52.4(1) and 52.5(3)).
(Rule 52.13(1) provides that permission is required from the Court of Appeal for all appeals to that court from a decision of a county court or the High Court which was itself made on appeal).
(3) Where the lower court refuses an application for permission to appeal, a further application for permission to appeal may be made to the appeal court.
(4) Where the appeal court, without a hearing, refuses permission to appeal, the person seeking permission may request the decision to be reconsidered at a hearing.
(5) A request under paragraph (4) must be filed within seven days after service of the notice of permission has been refused.
(6) Permission to appeal will only be given where—
(a) the court considers that the appeal would have a real prospect of success; or
(b) there is some other compelling reason why the appeal should be heard.
(7) An order giving permission may—
(a) limit the issues to be heard; and
(b) be made subject to conditions.
(Rule 3.1(3) also provides that the court may make an order subject to conditions)
(Rule 25.15 provides for the court to order security for costs of an appeal)

Appellant's notice

52.4 (1) Where the appellant seeks permission from the appeal court it must be **A32–289** requested in the appellant's notice.

(2) The appellant must file the appellant's notice at the appeal court within—

    (a) such period as may be directed by the lower court; or

    (b) where the court makes no such direction, 14 days after the date of the decision of the court that the appellant wishes to appeal.

(3) Unless the appeal court orders otherwise, an appeal notice must be served on each respondent—

    (a) as soon as practicable; and

    (b) in any event not later than 7 days,

after it is filed.

Respondent's notice

5.25 (1) A respondent may file and serve a respondent's notice.   **A32–290**

(2) A respondent who—

    (a) is seeking permission to appeal from the appeal court; or

    (b) wishes to ask the appeal court to uphold the order of the lower court for reasons different from or additional to those given by the lower court,

must file a respondent's notice.

(3) Where the respondent seeks permission from the appeal court it must be requested in the respondent's notice.

(4) A respondent's notice must be filed within—

    (a) such period as may be directed by the lower court; or

    (b) where the court makes no such direction, 14 days after the date in paragraph (5).

(5) The date referred to in paragraph (4) is—

    (a) the date the respondent is served with the appellant's notice where—

        (i) permission to appeal was given by the lower court; or

        (ii) permission to appeal is not required;

    (b) the date the respondent is served with notification that the appeal court has given the appellant permission to appeal; or

    (c) the date the respondent is served with notification that the application for permission to appeal and the appeal itself are to be heard together.

(6) Unless the appeal court orders otherwise a respondent's notice must be served on the appellant and any other respondent—

    (a) as soon as practicable; and

    (b) in any event not later than 7 days,

after it is filed.

Variation of time

52.6 (1) An application to vary the time limit for filing an appeal notice must **A32–291** be made to the appeal court.

(2) The parties may not agree to extend any date or time limit set by—

    (a) these Rules;

    (b) the relevant practice direction; or

    (c) an order of the appeal court or the lower court.

(Rule 3.1(2)(a) provides that the court may extend or shorten the time for compliance with the rule, practice direction or court order (even if an application for extension is made after the time for compliance has expired))

(Rule 3.1(2)(b) provides that the court may adjourn or bring forward a hearing)

Stay

52.7 Unless—   **A32–292**

(a) the appeal court or the lower court orders otherwise; or

(b) the appeal is from the Immigration Appeal Tribunal,

an appeal shall not operate as a stay of any order or decision of the lower court.

Amendment of appeal notice

A32–293   **52.8** An appeal notice may not be amended without the permission of the appeal court.

Striking out appeal notices and setting aside or imposing conditions on permission to appeal

A32–294   **52.9** (1) The appeal court may—

(a) strike out the whole or part of an appeal notice;

(b) set aside permission to appeal in whole or in part;

(c) impose or vary conditions upon which an appeal may be brought.

(2) The court will only exercise its powers under paragraph (1) where there is a compelling reason for doing so.

(3) Where a party was present at the hearing at which permission was given he may not subsequently apply for an order that the court exercise its powers under sub-paragraph or (1)(c).

Appeal court's powers

A32–295   **52.10** (1) In relation to an appeal the appeal court has all the powers of the lower court.

(Rule 52.1(4) provides that this Part is subject to any enactment that sets out special provisions with regard to any particular category of appeal—where such an enactment gives statutory power to a tribunal, person or other body it may be the case that the appeal court may not exercise that power on an appeal)

(2) The appeal court has power to—

(a) affirm, set aside or vary any order or judgment made or given by the lower court;

(b) refer any claim or issue for determination by the lower court;

(c) order a new trial or hearing;

(d) make orders for the payment of interest;

(e) make a costs order.

(3) In an appeal from a claim tried with a jury the Court of Appeal may, instead of ordering a new trial—

(a) make an order for damages; or

(b) vary an award of damages made by the jury.

(4) The appeal court may exercise its powers in relation to the whole or part of an order of the lower court.

(Part 3 contains general rules about the court's case management powers)

Hearing of appeals

A32–296   **52.11** (1) Every appeal will be limited to a review of the decision of the lower court unless—

(a) a practice direction makes different provision for a particular category of appeal; or

(b) the court considers that in the circumstances of an individual appeal it would be in the interests of justice to hold a re-hearing.

(2) Unless it orders otherwise, the appeal court will not receive—

(a) oral evidence; or

(b) evidence which was not before the lower court.

(3) The appeal court will allow an appeal where the decision of the lower court was—

(a) wrong; or

(b) unjust because of a serious procedural or other irregularity in the proceedings in the court.

(4) The appeal court may draw any inference of fact which it considers justified on the evidence.

(5) At the hearing of the appeal a party may not rely on a matter not contained in his appeal unless the appeal court gives permission.

Non-disclosure of Part 36 offers and payments

(1)**52.12** The fact that a Part 36 offer or Part 36 payment has been made must **A32–297** not be disclosed to the judge of the appeal court who is to hear and finally determine an appeal until all questions (other than costs) have been determined.

(2) Paragraph (1) does not apply if the Part 36 offer or Part 36 payment is relevant to the substance of the appeal.

(3) Paragraph (1) does not prevent disclosure in any application in the appeal proceedings disclosure of the fact that a Part 36 offer or Part 36 payment has been made is properly relevant to the matter to be decided.

II Special provisions applying to the court of appeal

Second appeals to the court

52.13 (1) Permission is required from the Court of Appeal for any appeal to **A32–298** that court from a decision of a county court or the High Court which was itself made on appeal.

(2) The Court of Appeal will not give permission unless it considers that—
  (a) the appeal would raise an important point of principle or practice; or
  (b) there is some other compelling reason for the Court of Appeal to hear it.

Assignment of appeals to the Court of Appeal

52.14 (1) Where the court from or to which an appeal is made or from which **A32–299** permission to appeal is sought ("the relevant court") considers that—
  (a) an appeal which is to be heard by a county court or the High Court would raise an important point of principle or practice; or
  (b) there is some other compelling reason for the Court of Appeal to hear it,
the relevant court may order the appeal to be transferred to the Court of Appeal.

(The Master of the Rolls has the power to direct that an appeal which would be heard by a county court or the High Court should be heard instead by the Court of Appeal—see section 57 of the Access to Justice Act 1999)(a)

(2) The Master of the Rolls or the Court of Appeal may remit an appeal to the court in which the original appeal was or would have been brought.

Judicial review appeals

52.15 (1) Where permission to apply for judicial review has been refused at a **A32–300** hearing in the High Court the person seeking that permission may apply to the Court of Appeal for permission to appeal.

(2) An application in accordance with paragraph (1) must be made within 7 days of the decision of the High Court to refuse to give permission to apply for judicial review.

(3) On an application under paragraph (1), the Court of Appeal may, instead of giving permission to appeal, give permission to apply for judicial review.

(4) Where the Court of Appeal gives permission to apply for judicial review in accordance with paragraph (3), the case will proceed in the High Court unless the Court of Appeal orders otherwise.

Who may exercise the powers of the Court of Appeal

A32–301   52.16 (1) A court officer assigned to the Civil Appeals Office who is—
(a) a barrister; or
(b) a solicitor
may exercise the jurisdiction of the Court of Appeal with regard to the matters set out in paragraph (2) with the consent of the Master of the Rolls.
(2) The matters referred to in paragraph (1) are—
(a) any matter incidental to any proceedings in the Court of Appeal;
(b) any other matter where there is no substantial dispute between the parties; and
(c) the dismissal of an appeal or application where a party has failed to comply with any rule or practice direction.
(3) A court officer may not decide an application for—
(a) permission to appeal;
(b) bail pending an appeal;
(c) an injunction;
(d) a stay of any proceedings, other than a temporary stay of any order or decision of the lower court over a period when the Court of Appeal is not sitting or cannot conveniently be convened.
(4) Decisions of a court officer may be made without a hearing.
(5) A party may request any decision of a court officer to be reviewed by the Court of Appeal.
(6) At the request of a party, a hearing will be held to reconsider a decision of—
(a) a single judge; or
(b) a court officer,
made without a hearing.
(7) A single judge may refer any matter for a decision by a court consisting of two or more judges.
(Section 54(6) of the Supreme Court Act 1981(a) provides that there is no appeal from the decision of a single judge on an application for permission to appeal)
(Section 58(2) of the Supreme Court Act 1981(b) provides that there is no appeal to the House of Lords from decisions of the Court of Appeal that—
(a) are taken by a single judge or any officer or member of staff of that court in proceedings incidental to any cause or matter pending before the civil division of that court; and
(b) do not involve the determination of an appeal or of an application for permission to appeal.
and which may be called into question by rules of court. Rules 52.16(5) and (6) provide the procedure for the calling into question of such decisions)

PRACTICE DIRECTION 52

Appeals

This Practice Direction supplements Part 52

Contents

A32–302   1.1 This practice direction is divided into three sections:
Section I—General provisions about appeals
Section II—General provisions about statutory appeals and appeals by way of case stated
Section III—Provisions about specific appeals

Section I—General Provisions About Appeals

2.1 This practice direction applies to all appeals to which Part 52 applies **A32–303** except where specific provision is made for appeals to the Court of Appeal.

2.2 For the purpose only of appeals to the Court of Appeal from cases in family proceedings this Practice Direction will apply with such modifications as may be required.

Routes of appeal

2A.1 Subject to paragraph 2A.2, the following table sets out to which court or **A32–304** judge an appeal is to be made (subject to obtaining any necessary permission):

Decision of:	Appeal made to:
District judge of a county court	Circuit judge
Master or district judge of the High Court	High Court judge
Circuit judge	High Court judge
High Court judge	Court of Appeal

2A.2 Where the decision to be appealed is a final decision—
  (a) in a claim allocated to the multi-track under rules 12.7, 14.8 or 26.5; or
  (b) made in specialist proceedings (to which rule 49(2) refers) the appeal is to be made to the Court of Appeal (subject to obtaining any necessary permission).

2A.3 A "final decision" is a decision of a court that would finally determine (subject to any possible appeal or detailed assessment of costs) the entire proceedings whichever way the court decided the issues before it.

2A.4 A decision of a court is to be treated as a final decision for routes of appeal purposes where it:
  (a) is made at the conclusion of part of a hearing or trial which has been split into parts and
  (b) would, if it had been made at the conclusion of that hearing or trial, have been a final decision.

2A.5 An order made:
  (a) on a summary or detailed assessment of costs; or
  (b) is not a "final decision" and any appeal from such an order will follow the appeal routes set out in the table in paragraph 2A.1.

Section 16(1) of the Supreme Court Act 1981 (as amended); section 77(1) of the County Courts Act 1984 (as amended); and the Access to Justice Act 1999 (Destination of Appeals) Order 2000 set out the provisions governing routes of appeal)

2A.6 (1) Where the decision to be appealed is a final decision in a Part 8 claim treated as allocated to the multi-track under rule 8.9(c) the court to which the permission application is made should, if permission is given, and unless the appeal would lie to the Court of Appeal in any event, consider whether to order the appeal to be transferred to the Court of Appeal under rule 52.14.

(2) An appeal against a final decision on a point of law in a case which did not involve any substantial dispute of fact would normally be a suitable appeal to be so transferred, (see also paragraph 10.1)

Grounds for appeal

3.1 Rule 52.11(3) (a) and (b) sets out the circumstances in which the appeal **A32–305** court will allow an appeal.

3.2 The grounds of appeal should set out clearly the reasons why rule 52.11(3)(a) or (b) is said to apply.

Permission to appeal

4.1 Rule 52.3 sets out the circumstances when permission to appeal is required. **A32–306**

4.2 The permission of—
    (a) the Court of Appeal; or
    (b) where the lower court's rules allow, the lower court
is required for all appeals to the Court of Appeal except as provided for by statute or rule 52.3.

(The requirement of permission to appeal may be imposed by a practice direction—see rule 52.3(b)).

4.3 Where the lower court is not required to give permission to appeal, it may give an indication of its opinion as to whether permission should be given.

(Rule 52.1(3)(c) defines "lower court")

Appeals from case management decisions

A32–307   **4.4** Case management decisions include decisions made under rule 3.1(2) and decisions about:
    (1) disclosure;
    (2) filing of witness statements or experts reports;
    (3) directions about the timetable of the claim;
    (4) adding a party to a claim;
    (5) security for costs;
    4.5 Where the application is for permission to appeal from a case management decision, the court dealing with the application may take into account whether:
    (1) the issue is of sufficient significance to justify the costs of an appeal;
    (2) the procedural consequences of an appeal (e.g. loss of trial date) outweigh the significance of the case management decision;
    (3) it would be more convenient to determine the issue at or after trial.

Court to which permission to appeal application should be made

A32–308   **4.6** An application for permission should be made orally at the hearing at which the decision to be appealed against is made.
    4.7 Where:
    (1) no application for permission to appeal is made at the hearing; or
    (2) the lower court refuses permission to appeal,
an application for permission to appeal may be made to the appeal court in accordance with rules 52.3(2) and (3).
    4.8 There is no appeal from a decision of the appeal court, made at an oral hearing, to allow or refuse permission to appeal to that court. See section 54(4) of the Access to Justice Act 1999 and rule 52.3(3) and (4).

Second appeals

A32–309   **4.9** An application for permission to appeal from a decision of the High Court or a county court which was itself made on appeal must be made to the Court of Appeal.
    4.10 If permission to appeal is granted the appeal will be heard by the Court of Appeal.

Consideration of Permission without a hearing

A32–310   **4.11** Applications for permission to appeal may be considered by the appeal court without a hearing.
    4.12 If permission is granted without a hearing the parties will be notified of that decision and the procedure in paragraphs 6.1 to 6.7 will then apply.
    4.13 If permission is refused without a hearing the parties will be notified of that decision with the reasons for it. The decision is subject to the appellant's right to have it reconsidered at an oral hearing. This may be before the same judge.

4.14 A request for the decision to be reconsidered at an oral hearing must be filed at the appeal court within 7 days after service of the notice that permission has been refused. A copy of the request must be served by the appellant on the respondent at the same time. If no request is made for the decision to be reconsidered, it will become final after the time limit for making the request has expired.

Permission hearing

4.15 Notice of the hearing need not be given to the respondent unless the court **A32–311** so directs. The appeal court will usually so direct if the appellant is asking for a remedy against the respondent pending the appeal.

4.16 If notice of the hearing is to be given to the respondent, the appellant must supply the respondent with a copy of the bundle (see paragraph 5.6) within 7 days of being notified, or such other period as the court may direct. The costs of providing that bundle shall be borne by the appellant initially, but will form part of the costs of the permission application.

Appellants in receipt of services funded by the Legal Services Commission applying for permission to appeal

4.17 Where the appellant is in receipt of services funded by the Legal Services **A32–312** Commission (or legally aided) and permission to appeal has been refused by the appeal court without a hearing, the appellant must send a copy of the reasons the appeal court gave for refusing permission to the relevant office of the Legal Services Commission as soon as it has been received from the court. The court will require confirmation that this has been done if a hearing is requested to re-consider the question of permission.

Limited permission

4.18 Where a court, under rule 52.3(7) confines its permission to some issues **A32–313** only, it should expressly refuse permission on any remaining issues. Those other issues may only be raised at the hearing of the appeal with the appeal court's permission. The court and the respondent should be informed of any intention to raise such an issue as soon as practicable after notification of the court's order.

4.19 An application to raise a remaining issue will normally be dealt with at the outset of the appeal unless the court otherwise directs.

Appellant's notice

5.1 An appellant's notice (N161) must be filed and served in all cases. Where **A32–314** an application for permission to appeal is made to the appeal court it must be applied for in the appellant's notice.

Extension of time for filing appellant's notice

5.2 If an appellant requires an extension of time for filing his notice the **A32–315** application must be made in the appellant's notice. The notice should state the reason for the delay and the steps taken prior to the application being made.

5.3 Where the appellant's notice includes an application for an extension of time and permission to appeal has been given or is not required the respondent has the right to be heard on that application. He must be served with a copy of the appellant's bundle. However, a respondent who unreasonably opposes an extension of time runs the risk of being ordered to pay the appellant's costs of that application.

5.4 If an extension of time is given following such an application the procedure at paragraphs 6.1 to 6.6 applies.

Applications

A32–316   **5.5** Notice of an application to be made to the appeal court for a remedy incidental to the appeal (e.g. an interim remedy under rule 25.1 or an order for security for costs) may be included in the appeal notice or in a Part 23 application notice.
(Rule 25.15 deals with security for costs of an appeal)
(Paragraph 10 of this practice direction contains other provisions relating to applications)

Documents

A32–317   **5.6** The appellant must lodge the following documents with his appellant's notice in every case except where the appellant's notice relates to a refusal of permission to apply for judicial review (see paragraph 15.3 below):
(1) one additional copy of the appellant's notice for the appeal court; and
(2) one copy of the appellant's notice for each of the respondents;
(3) one copy of any skeleton argument (see paragraph 5.9);
(4) a sealed copy of the order being appealed;
(5) any order giving or refusing permission to appeal, together with a copy of the reasons for that decision;
(6) any witness statements or affidavits in support of any application included in the appellant's notice; and
(7) a bundle of documents in support of the appeal—this should include copies of the documents referred to in paragraphs (1) to (6) and any other documents which the appellant reasonably considers necessary to enable the appeal court to reach its decision on the hearing of the application or appeal. Documents which are extraneous to the issues to be considered should be excluded. The other documents will, subject to paragraph 5.7, include:
(a) any affidavit or witness statement filed in support of the application for permission to appeal or the appeal,
(b) a suitable record of the reasons for judgment of the lower court (see paragraph 5.12);
(c) where permission to appeal has been given or permission is not required; any relevant transcript or note of evidence (see paragraph 5.15 below),
(d) statements of case,
(e) any application notice (or case management documentation) relevant to the subject of the appeal,
(f) in cases where the decision appealed was itself made on appeal, the first order, the reasons given and the appellant's notice of appeal from that order,
(g) in cases where the appeal is from a Tribunal, a copy of the Tribunal's reasons for the decision, a copy of the decision reviewed by the Tribunal and the reasons for the original decision,
(h) in the case of judicial review or a statutory appeal, the original decision which was the subject of the application to the lower court,
(i) relevant affidavits, witness statements, summaries, experts' reports and exhibits;
(j) any skeleton arguments relied on in the lower court; and
(k) such other documents as the court may direct.
5.7 Where it is not possible to file all the above documents, the appellant must indicate which documents have not yet been filed and the reasons why they are not currently available.
5.8 Where bundles comprise more than 150 pages excluding transcripts of judgment and other transcripts of the proceedings in the lower court only those documents which the court may reasonably be expected to pre-read should be

included. A full set of documents should then be brought to the hearing for reference.

Skeleton arguments

5.9 (1) The appellant's notice must, subject to (2) and (3) below, be accom- **A32–318** panied by a skeleton argument. Alternatively the skeleton argument may be included in the appellant's notice. Where the skeleton argument is so included it will not form part of the notice for the purposes of rule 52.8.

(2) Where it is impracticable for the appellant's skeleton argument to accompany the appellant's notice it must be lodged and served on all respondents within 14 days of filing the notice.

(3) An appellant who is not represented need not lodge a skeleton argument but is encouraged to do so since this will be helpful to the court.

Content of skeleton arguments

5.10 Skeleton arguments for the appeal court should contain a numbered list **A32–319** of points stated in no more than a few sentences which should both define and confine the areas of controversy. Each point should be followed by references to any documentation on which the appellant proposes to rely.

5.11 The appellant should consider what other information the appeal court will need. This may include a list of persons who feature in the case or glossaries of technical terms. A chronology of relevant events will be necessary in most appeals. In the case of points of law, authorities relied on should be cited with reference to the particular pages where the principle concerned is set out.

Suitable record of the judgment

5.12 Where the judgment to be appealed has been officially recorded by the **A32–320** court, an approved transcript of that record should accompany the appellant's notice. Photocopies will not be accepted for this purpose. However, where there is no officially recorded judgment, the following documents will be acceptable:

Written judgments

(1) Where the judgment was made in writing a copy of that judgment **A32–321** endorsed with the judge's signature.

Note of judgment

(2) When judgment was not officially recorded or made in writing a note of **A32–322** the judgment (agreed between the appellant's and respondent's advocates) should be submitted for approval to the judge whose decision is being appealed. If the parties cannot agree on a single note of the judgment, both versions should be provided to that judge with an explanatory letter. For the purpose of an application for permission to appeal the note need not be approved by the respondent or the lower court judge.

Advocates' notes of judgments where the appellant is unrepresented

(3) When the appellant was unrepresented in the lower court it is the duty of **A32–323** any advocate for the respondent to make his/her note of judgment promptly available, free of charge to the appellant where there is no officially recorded judgment or if the court so directs. Where the appellant was represented in the lower court it is the duty of his/her own former advocate to make his/her note available in these circumstances. The appellant should submit the note of judgment to the appeal court.

Reasons for Judgment in Tribunal cases

A32–324   (4) A sealed copy of the Tribunal's reasons for the decision.

5.13 An appellant may not be able to obtain an official transcript or other suitable record of the lower court's decision within the time within which the appellant's notice must be filed. In such cases the appellant's notice must still be completed to the best of the appellant's ability on the basis of the documentation available. However it may be amended subsequently with the permission of the appeal court.

Advocates' notes of judgments

A32–325   **5.14** Advocates' brief (or, where appropriate, refresher) fee includes:
(1) remuneration for taking a note of the judgment of the court;
(2) having the note transcribed accurately;
(3) attempting to agree the note with the other side if represented;
(4) submitting the note to the judge for approval where appropriate;
(5) revising it if so requested by the judge,
(6) providing any copies required for the appeal court, instructing solicitors and lay client; and
(7) providing a copy of his note to an unrepresented appellant.

Transcripts or Notes of Evidence

A32–326   **5.15** When the evidence is relevant to the appeal an official transcript of the relevant evidence must be obtained. Transcripts or notes of evidence are generally not needed for the purpose of determining an application for permission to appeal.

Notes of evidence

A32–327   **5.16** If evidence relevant to the appeal was not officially recorded, a typed version of the judge's notes of evidence must be obtained.

Transcripts at public expense

A32–328   **5.17** Where the lower court or the appeal court is satisfied that an unrepresented appellant is in such poor financial circumstances that the cost of a transcript would be an excessive burden the court may certify that the cost of obtaining one official transcript should be borne at public expense.

5.18 In the case of a request for an official transcript of evidence or proceedings to be paid for at public expense, the court must also be satisfied that there are reasonable grounds for appeal. Whenever possible a request for a transcript at public expense should be made to the lower court when asking for permission to appeal.

Filing and service of appellant's notice

A32–329   **5.19** Rule 52.4 sets out the procedure and time limits for filing and serving an appellant's notice. The appellant must file the appellant's notice at the appeal court within such period as may be directed by the lower court which should not normally exceed 28 days or, where the lower court directs no such period, within 14 days of the date of the decision that the appellant wishes to appeal.

5.20 Where the lower court judge announces his decision and reserves the reasons for his judgment or order until a later date, he should, in the exercise of powers under rule 52.4 (2)(a), fix a period for filing the appellant's notice at the appeal court that takes this into account.

5.21 Except where the appeal court orders otherwise, a sealed copy of the appellant's notice, including any skeleton arguments, must be served on all respondents to the appeal in accordance with the timetable prescribed by rule 52.4(3) except where this requirement is modified by paragraph 5.9(2) in which case the skeleton argument should be served as soon as it is lodged.

5.22 Unless the court otherwise directs a respondent need not take any action when served with an appellant's notice until such time as notification is given to him that permission to appeal has been given.

5.23 The court may dispense with the requirement for service of the notice on a respondent. Any application notice seeking an order under rule 6.9 to dispense with service should set out the reasons relied on and be verified by a statement of truth.

5.24 Where the appellant is applying for permission to appeal in his appellant's notice, there is no requirement at this stage for copies of the documents referred to at paragraph 5.6 to be served on the respondents. However, if permission has been given by the lower court or permission is not required, copies of all the documents must be served on the respondents with the appellant's notice.

(Paragraph 5.6 provides for certain documents to be filed with an appellant's notice)

Amendment of Appeal Notice

5.25 An appeal notice may be amended with permission. Such an application **A32–330** to amend and any application in opposition will normally be dealt with at the hearing unless that course would cause unnecessary expense or delay in which case a request should be made for the application to amend to be heard in advance.

Procedure after Permission is Obtained

6.1 This paragraph sets out the procedure where: **A32–331**
(1) permission to appeal is given by the appeal court; or
(2) the appellant's notice is filed in the appeal court and—
  (a) permission was given by the lower court; or
  (b) permission is not required.

6.2 If the appeal court gives permission to appeal, copies of all the documents referred to at paragraph 5.6 must be served on the respondents within 7 days of receiving the order giving permission to appeal.

(Part 6 (service of documents) provides rules on service))

6.3 The appeal court will send the parties—
(1) notification of—
  (a) the date of the hearing or the period of time (the "listing window") during which the appeal is likely to be heard; and
  (b) in the Court of Appeal, the date by which the appeal will be heard (the "hear by date");
(2) where permission is granted by the appeal court a copy of the order giving permission to appeal; and
(3) any other directions given by the court.

Appeal Questionnaire in the Court of Appeal

6.4 The Court of Appeal will send an Appeal Questionnaire to the appellant **A32–332** when it notifies him of the matters referred to in paragraph 6.3.

6.5 The appellant must complete and lodge the Appeal Questionnaire within 14 days of the date of the letter of notification of the matters in paragraph 6.3. The Appeal Questionnaire must contain:
(1) if the appellant is legally represented, the advocate's time estimate for the hearing of the appeal;

(2) where a transcript of evidence is relevant to the appeal; confirmation that a transcript of evidence has been ordered where this is not already in the bundle of documents.

(3) confirmation that copies of the appeal bundle are being prepared and will be held ready for the use of the Court of Appeal and an undertaking that they will be supplied to the court on request. For the purpose of these bundles photocopies of the transcripts will be accepted

(4) confirmation that copies of the Appeal Questionnaire and the appeal bundle have been served on the respondents and the date of that service;

Time estimates

A32–333 **6.6** The time estimate included in an Appeal Questionnaire must be that of the advocate who will argue the appeal. It should exclude the time required by the court to give judgment. If the respondent disagrees with the time estimate, the respondent must inform the court within 7 days of receipt of the Appeal Questionnaire. In the absence of such notification the respondent will be deemed to have accepted the estimate proposed on behalf of the appellant.

Respondent

A32–334 **7.1** A respondent who wishes to ask the appeal court to vary the order of the lower court in any way must appeal and permission will be required on the same basis as for an appellant.

7.2 A respondent who wishes only to request that the appeal court upholds the judgment or order of the lower court whether for the reasons given in the lower court or otherwise does not make an appeal and does not therefore require permission to appeal in accordance with rule 52.3(1).

7.3 A respondent who wishes to appeal or who wishes to ask the appeal court to uphold the order of the lower court for reasons different from or additional to those given by the lower court must file a respondent's notice.

Time limits

A32–335 **7.4** The time limits for filing a respondent's notice are set out in rule 52.5 (4) and (5).

7.5 Where an extension of time is required the extension must be requested in the respondent's notice and the reasons why the respondent failed to act within the specified time must be included.

Respondent's skeleton argument

A32–336 **7.6** The respondent must provide a skeleton argument for the court in all cases where he proposes to address arguments to the court. The respondent's skeleton argument may be included within a respondent's notice. Where a skeleton argument is included within a respondent's notice it will not form part of the notice for the purposes of rule 52.8.

7.7 Where the skeleton argument is not included within a respondent's notice it should be lodged and served no later than 21 days after the respondent receives the appellant's skeleton argument.

(Rule 52.5(4) sets out the period for filing and serving a respondent's notice)

Content of skeleton arguments

A32–337 **7.8** A respondent's skeleton argument must conform to the directions at paragraphs 5.10 and 5.11 above with any necessary modifications. It should, where appropriate, answer the arguments set out in the appellant's skeleton argument.

Applications within respondent's notices

7.9 A respondent may include an application within a respondent's notice in **A32–338** accordance with paragraph 5.5 above.

Filing respondent's notices and skeleton arguments

7.10 The respondent must lodge the following documents with his respond- **A32–339** ent's notice in every case:
(1) two additional copies of the respondent's notice for the appeal court;
(2) one copy each for the appellant and any other respondents; and
(3) two copies of any skeleton arguments.
7.11 If the respondent does not file a respondent's notice, he will not be entitled, except with the permission of the court, to rely on any ground not relied on in the lower court.
7.12 If the respondent wishes to rely on any documents in addition to those filed by the appellant he must prepare a supplemental bundle and lodge it at the appeal court with his respondent's notice. He must serve a copy of the supplemental bundle at the same time as serving the respondent's notice on the persons required to be served in accordance with rule 52.5(6).
7.13 The respondent's notice and any skeleton argument must be served in accordance with the time limits set out in rule 52.5(6) except this requirement is modified by paragraph 7.7.

Appeals to the High Court

8.1 This paragraph applies where the appeal court is the High Court and the **A32–340** lower court is a county court.
8.2 The following table sets out the following venues for each Circuit—
(a) Appeal centres—court centres where appeals to which this paragraph applies may be managed and heard.
(b) Hearing only centres—court centres where appeals to which this paragraph applies may be heard by order made at an appeal centre (see paragraph 8.5)

Circuit	Appeal Centres	Hearing Only Centres
Midland and Oxford Circuit	**Birmingham** **Nottingham**	**Oxford** **Lincoln** **Leicester** **Northampton** **Stafford**
North Eastern Circuit	**Leeds** **Newcastle** **Sheffield**	**Teesside**
Northern Circuit	**Manchester** **Liverpool** **Preston**	**Carlisle**
Wales and Chester Circuit	**Cardiff** **Swansea** **Chester** **Bristol**	

Western Circuit

               Truro

       Winchester   **Plymouth**
       Central London:

       Royal Courts of Justice
       Provincial: **Chelmsford**
       Lewes   **St Albans**

South Eastern Circuit

       Luton   **Maidstone**

       Norwich
       Reading

8.3 The appellant's notice must be filed in the District Registry at an appeal centre on the Circuit in which the lower court is situated. Unless the appeal court otherwise orders the appeal will be managed and heard at that appeal centre.

8.4 The appeal court may transfer an appeal to another appeal centre (whether or not on the same circuit). In deciding whether to do so the court will have regard to the criteria in rule 30.3 (criteria for a transfer order). The appeal court may do so either on application by a party or of its own initiative. Where an appeal is transferred under this paragraph, notice of transfer must be served on every person on whom the appellant's notice has been served. An appeal may not be transferred to an appeal centre on another circuit, either for management or hearing, unless the consent of a Presiding Judge of that circuit has been obtained.

8.5 Directions may be given for—

(1) an appeal to be heard at a hearing only centre; or

(2) an application in an appeal to be heard at any other venue.

instead of at the appeal centre managing the appeal.

8.6 Unless a direction has been made under 8.5, any application in the appeal must be made at the appeal centre where the appeal is being managed.

8.7 A respondent's notice must be filed at the appeal centre where the appellant's notice was filed unless the appeal has been transferred to another appeal centre, in which case it must be filed at that appeal centre.

8.8 The appeal court may adopt all or any part of the procedure set out in paragraphs 6.4 to 6.6

8.9 (1) Appeals and applications for permission to appeal will be heard by a High Court Judge or by a person authorised under paragraphs (1), (2) or (4) of the Table in section 9(1) of the Supreme Court Act 1981 to act as a judge of the High Court;

(2) Other applications in the appeal may be heard and directions in the appeal may be given either by a High Court Judge or by any person authorised under section 9(1) of the Supreme Court Act 1981 to act as a judge of the High Court.

8A.1 The Designated Civil Judge in consultation with his Presiding Judges has responsibility in allocating appeals from decisions of district judges to circuit judges.

Re-hearings

A32–341   **9.1** The hearing of an appeal will not be a re-hearing (as opposed to a review of the decision of the lower court) if the appeal is from the decision of a minister, person or other body and the minister, person or other body—

(1) did not hold a hearing to come to that decision; or

(2) held a hearing to come to that decision, but the procedure adopted did not provide for the consideration of evidence.

Appeals Transferred to the Court of Appeal

A32–342   **10.1** Where an appeal is transferred to the Court of Appeal under rule 52.14 the Court of Appeal may give such additional directions as are considered appropriate.

Applications

11.1 Where a party to an appeal makes an application whether in an appeal **A32–343** notice or by Part 23 application notice, the provisions of Part 23 will apply.

11.2 The applicant must file the following documents with the notice

(1) one additional copy of the application notice for the appeal court and one copy for each of the respondents;

(2) where applicable a sealed copy of the order which is the subject of the main appeal;

(3) A bundle of documents in support which should include:

    (a) the Part 23 application notice,

    (b) any witness statements and affidavits filed in support of the application notice,

    (c) the documents specified in paragraph 5.6 (6) above in so far as they have not already been filed with the appellant's notice.

Disposing of applications or appeals by consent

Dismissal of applications or appeals by consent

12.1 These paragraphs do not apply where any party to the proceedings is a **A32–344** child or patient.

12.2 Where an appellant does not wish to pursue an application or an appeal, he may request the appeal court for an order that his application or appeal be dismissed. Such a request must contain a statement that the appellant is not a child or patient. If such a request is granted it will usually be on the basis that the appellant pays the costs of the application or appeal.

12.3 If the appellant wishes to have the application or appeal dismissed without costs, his request must be accompanied by a consent signed by the respondent or his legal representative stating that the respondent is not a child or patient and consents to the dismissal of the application or appeal without costs.

12.4 Where a settlement has been reached disposing of the application or appeal, the parties may make a joint request to the court stating that none of them is a child or patient, and asking that the application or appeal be dismissed by consent. If the request is granted the application or appeal will be dismissed.

Allowing unopposed appeals or applications on paper

13.1 The appeal court will not make an order allowing an appeal unless **A32–345** satisfied that the decision of the lower court was wrong. Where the appeal court is requested by all parties to allow an application or an appeal the court may consider the request on the papers. The request should state that none of the parties is a child or patient and set out the relevant history of the proceedings and the matters relied on as justifying the proposed order and be accompanied by a copy of the proposed order.

Procedure for Structured settlements and consent orders involving a child or patient

13.2 Settlements relating to appeals and applications where one of the parties **A32–346** is a child or a patient; and structured settlements which are agreed upon at the appeal stage require the court's approval.

Child

13.3 In cases involving a child a copy of the proposed order signed by the **A32–347** parties' solicitors should be sent to the appeal court, together with an opinion from the advocate acting on behalf of the child.

Patient

A32–348   **13.4** Where a party is a patient the same procedure will be adopted, but the documents filed should also include any relevant reports prepared for the Court of Protection and a document evidencing formal approval by that court where required.

Structured settlements

A32–349   **13.5** Where a structured settlement has been negotiated in a case which is under appeal the documents filed should include those which would be required in the case of a structured settlement dealt with at first instance. Details can be found in the Practice Direction which supplements CPR Part 40.

Summary Assessment of Costs

A32–350   **14.1** Costs are likely to be assessed by way of summary assessment at the following hearings:
   (1) Contested directions hearings;
   (2) Applications for permission to appeal at which the respondent is present;
   (3) Dismissal list hearings in the Court of Appeal at which the respondent is present;
   (4) Appeals from case management decisions; and
   (5) Appeals listed for one day or less.
   14.2 Parties attending any of the hearings referred to in paragraph 14.1 should be prepared to deal with the summary assessment.

Other special provisions regarding the court of appeal

Filing of Documents

A32–351   **15.1** (1) The documents relevant to proceedings in the Court of Appeal, Civil Division must be filed in the Civil Appeals Office Registry, Room E307, Royal Courts of Justice, Strand, London, WC2A 2LL.
   (2) The Civil Appeals Office will not serve documents and where service is required by the CPR or this practice direction it must be effected by the parties.

Master in the Court of Appeal, Civil Division

A32–352   **15.2** When the Head of the Civil Appeals Office acts in a judicial capacity pursuant to rule 52.16, he shall be known as Master. Other eligible officers may also be designated by the Master of the Rolls to exercise judicial authority under rule 52.16 and shall then be known as Deputy Masters.

Judicial Review Appeals

A32–353   **15.3** Where the Court of appeal gives permission to apply for judicial review under rule 52.15 (3) the court may, hear the application for judicial review. This will be rare, but may be appropriate where, for example, the High Court is bound by authority or for some other reason, an appeal to the Court of Appeal will be inevitable.
   15.4 Paragraphs 5.6 and 5.19 above do not apply to cases where the appeal notice seeks permission to appeal a refusal to give permission to apply for judicial review. In such cases the following documents must be filed with the appellant's notice:

(1) one additional copy of the appellant's notice for the Court of Appeal;

(2) one copy of the appellant's notice for each of the respondents to be sealed and returned;

(3) the order refusing permission to apply for judicial review;

(4) Form 86A;

(5) a copy of the original decision which is the subject of the application to the High Court;

(6) any witness statements or affidavits in support of any application included in the appellant's notice;

(7) a copy of the bundle of documents used in the High Court;

(8) the skeleton argument relied on in the High Court; and

(9) a transcript of the judgment.

15.5 The time for filing an appellant's notice in these circumstances is set out in rule 52.15(1). The arrangements for service on the respondent in paragraph 5.21 apply.

15.6 Where it is not possible to file all these documents, the appellant must indicate which documents have not yet been filed and the reasons why they are not currently available.

Listing and hear-by dates

15.7 The management of the list will be dealt with by the listing officer under the direction of the Master. **A32–354**

15.8 The Civil Appeals List of the Court of Appeal is divided as follows:

The applications list—applications for permission to appeal and other applications.

The appeals list—appeals where permission to appeal has been given or where an appeal lies without permission being required.

The expedited list—appeals or applications where the Court of Appeal has directed an expedited hearing. The current practice of the Court of Appeal is summarised in *Unilever plc. v. Chefaro Proprietaries Ltd. (Practice Note)* [1995] 1 W.L.R. 24.

The stand-out list—Appeals or application which, for good reason, are not at present ready to proceed and have been stood out by judicial direction.

The fixtures list—where a hearing date for the appeal is fixed in advance.

The second fixtures list—if an appeal is designated as a "second fixture" it means that a hearing date is arranged in advance on the express basis that the list is fully booked for the period in question and therefore the case will be heard only if a suitable gap occurs in the list.

The short-warned list—appeals which the court considers may be prepared for the hearing by an advocate other than the one originally instructed with a half day's notice, or, if the court so directs, 48 hours notice.

15.9 Once an appeal is listed for hearing from the short-warned list it becomes the immediate professional duty of the advocate instructed in the appeal, if he is unable to appear at the hearing, to take all practicable measures to ensure that his lay client is represented at the hearing by an advocate who is fully instructed and able to argue the appeal.

Requests for directions

15.10 To ensure that all requests for directions are centrally monitored and correctly allocated, all requests for directions or rulings (whether relating to listing or any other matters) should be made to the Civil Appeals Office. Those seeking directions or rulings must not approach the supervising Lord Justice either directly, or via his or her clerk. **A32–355**

Lists of authorities

15.11 Once the parties have been notified of the date fixed for hearing the appellant's advocate shall file, after consulting his opponent, for the purpose of pre-reading by the court, one bundle containing photocopies of the principal **A32–356**

authorities upon which each side will rely at the hearing, with the relevant passages marked. There will in general be no need to include authorities for propositions not in dispute. This bundle should be made available 28 days before the hearing, unless the period of notice of the hearing is less than 28 days in which case the bundle should be filed immediately. Such bundles should not normally contain more than 10 authorities. If any party intends, during the hearing to refer to other authorities these may be included in a second agreed bundle to be filed by the parties at the hearing. Alternatively, and in place of the second bundle only, a list of authorities and text may be delivered to the office of the Head Usher of the Court of Appeal no later than 5.30pm on the last working day before the hearing is to commence.

Reserved judgments of the Court of Appeal

A32–357   **15.12** Unless the court orders otherwise, copies of a written judgment will be made available to the parties' legal advisers by 4 p.m. on the second working day before judgment is due to be pronounced on the condition that the contents are not communicated to the parties themselves until one hour before the listed time for pronouncement of judgment.

15.13 The judgment is made available to legal advisers primarily to enable them to consider the judgment and decide what consequential orders they should seek. The condition is imposed to prevent the outcome of the case being publicly reported before judgment is given, since the judgment is confidential until then. Every page of the judgment will be marked "Unapproved judgment: No permission is given to copy or use in court". These words carry the authority of the court.

15.14 Where a party is not legally represented a copy of the judgment will be made available to him at the same time as to legal advisers. It must be treated as confidential until pronouncement of judgment.

Section II—General Provisions about Statutory Appeals and Appeals by way of Case Stated

A32–358   **16.1** This section of this practice direction contains general provisions about statutory appeals (paragraphs 17.1–17.6) and appeals by way of case stated (paragraphs 18.1–18.20).

16.2 Where any of the provisions in this section provide for documents to be filed at the appeal court, these documents are in addition to any documents required under Part 52 or section I of this practice direction.

Statutory appeals

A32–359   **17.1** This part of this section—
    (a) applies where under any enactment an appeal (other than by way of case stated) lies to the court from a Minister of State, government department, tribunal or other person ("statutory appeals"); and
    (b) is subject to any provision about a specific category of appeal in any enactment or Section III of this practice direction.

Part 52

A32–360   **17.2** Part 52 applies to statutory appeals with the following amendments:

Filing of appellant's notice

A32–361   **17.3** The appellant must file the appellant's notice at the appeal court within 28 days after the date of the decision of the lower court he wishes to appeal.

17.4 Where a statement of the reasons for a decision is given later than the notice of that decision, the period for filing the appellant's notice is calculated from the date on which the statement is received by the appellant.

Service of appellant's notice

17.5 In addition to the respondents to the appeal, the appellant must serve the **A32–362** appellant's notice in accordance with rule 52.4(3) on the chairman of the tribunal, Minister of State, government department or other person from whose decision the appeal is brought.

Right of Minister etc. to be heard on the appeal

17.6 Where the appeal is from an order or decision of a Minister of State or **A32–363** government department, the Minister or department, as the case may be, is entitled to attend the hearing and to make representations to the court.

Appeals by way of Case Stated

18.1 This part of this section—   **A32–364**
(1) applies where under any enactment—
    (a) an appeal lies to the court by way of case stated; or
    (b) a question of law may be referred to the court by way of case stated; and
(2) is subject to any provision about to a specific category of appeal in any enactment or Section III of this practice direction.

Part 52

18.2 Part 52 applies to appeals by way of case stated subject to the following **A32–365** amendments.

Case stated by Crown Court or Magistrates' Court

Application to state a case

18.3 The procedure for applying to the Crown Court or a Magistrates' Court to **A32–366** have a case stated for the opinion of the High Court is set out in the Crown Court Rules 1982 and the Magistrates' Courts Rules 1981 respectively.

Filing of appellant's notice

18.4 The appellant must file the appellant's notice at the appeal court within 10 **A32–367** days after he receives the stated case.

Documents to be lodged

18.5 The appellant must lodge the following documents with his appellant's **A32–368** notice:
(1) the stated case;
(2) a copy of the judgment, order or decision in respect of which the case has been stated; and
(3) where the judgment, order or decision in respect of which the case has been stated was itself given or made on appeal, a copy of the judgment, order or decision appealed from.

Service of appellant's notice

18.6 The appellant must serve the appellant's notice and accompanying **A32–369** documents on all respondents within 4 days after they are filed or lodged at the appeal court.

Case stated by Minister, government department, tribunal or other person

Application to state a case

A32–370 **18.7** The procedure for applying to a Minister, government department, tribunal or other person ("Minister or tribunal etc.") to have a case stated for the opinion of the court may be set out in—
(1) the enactment which provides for the right of appeal; or
(2) any rules of procedure relating to the Minister or tribunal etc.

Signing of stated case by Minister or tribunal etc.

A32–371 **18.8** A case stated by a tribunal must be signed by the chairman or president of the tribunal. A case stated by any other person must be signed by that person or by a person authorised to do so.

Service of stated case by Minister or tribunal etc.

A32–372 **18.9** The Minister or tribunal etc. must serve the stated case on—
(1) the party who requests the case to be stated; or
(2) the party as a result of whose application to the court, the case was stated.
18.10 Where an enactment provides that a Minister or tribunal etc. may state a case or refer a question of law to the court by way of case stated without a request being made, the Minister or tribunal etc. must—
(1) serve the stated case on those parties that the Minister or tribunal etc. considers appropriate; and
(2) give notice to every other party to the proceedings that the stated case has been served on the party named and on the date specified in the notice.

Filing and service of appellant's notice

A32–373 **18.11** The party on whom the stated case was served must file the appellant's notice and the stated case at the appeal court and serve copies of the notice and stated case on—
(1) the Minister or tribunal etc. who stated the case; and
(2) every party to the proceedings to which the stated case relates,
within 14 days after the stated case was served on him.
18.12 Where paragraph 18.10 applies the Minister or tribunal etc. must—
(1) file an appellant's notice and the stated case at the appeal court; and
(2) serve copies of those documents on the persons served under paragraph 18.10,
within 14 days after stating the case.
18.13 Where—
(1) a stated case has been served by the Minister or tribunal etc. in accordance with paragraph 18.9; and
(2) the party on whom the stated case was served does not file an appellant's notice in accordance with paragraph 18.11, any other party may file an appellant's notice with the stated case at the appeal court and serve a copy of the notice and the case on the persons listed in paragraph 18.11 within the period of time set out in paragraph 18.14.
18.14 The period of time referred to in paragraph 18.13 is 14 days from the last day on which the party on whom the stated case was served may file an appellant's notice in accordance with paragraph 18.11.

Amendment of stated case

A32–374 **18.15** The court may amend the stated case or order it to be returned to the Minister or tribunal etc. for amendment and may draw inferences of fact from the facts stated in the case.

Right of Minister etc. to be heard on the appeal

18.16 Where the case is stated by a Minister or government department, that A32–375 Minister or department, as the case may be, is entitled to appear on the appeal and to make representations to the court.

Application for order to state a case

18.17 An application to the court for an order requiring a minister or tribunal A32–376 etc. to state a case for the decision of the court, or to refer a question of law to the court by way of case stated must be made to the court which would be the appeal court if the case were stated.

18.18 An application to the court for an order directing a Minister or tribunal etc. to—

(1) state a case for determination by the court; or

(2) refer a question of law to the court by way of case stated, must be made in accordance with CPR Part 23.

18.19 The application notice must contain—

(1) the grounds of the application;

(2) the question of law on which it is sought to have the case stated; and

(3) any reasons given by the minister or tribunal etc. for his or its refusal to state a case.

18.20 The application notice must be filed at the appeal court and served on—

(1) the minister, department, secretary of the tribunal or other person as the case may be; and

(2) every party to the proceedings to which the application relates,

within 14 days after the appellant receives notice of the refusal of his request to state a case.

Extradition

19.1 Paragraphs 18.3 to 18.6 apply to appeals by case stated under—   A32–377

(1) section 7 of the Criminal Justice Act 1988; and

(2) section 7A of the Fugitive Offenders Act 1967,

and references in those paragraphs to appellant and respondent shall be construed as references to the requesting state and the person whose surrender is sought respectively.

19.2 An application for an order under either of the sections mentioned in paragraph 19.1 or under section 2A of the Backing of Warrants (Republic of Ireland) Act 1965 requiring a court to state a case must be made in accordance with paragraphs 18.17 to 18.20 and the references in those paragraphs to a tribunal and the secretary of a tribunal shall be construed as references to the court and the clerk of the court respectively.

Section III—Provisions about Specific Appeals

20.1 This section of this Practice Direction provides special provisions about A32–378 the appeals to which the following table refers. This Section is not exhaustive and does not create, amend or remove any right of appeal.

20.2 Part 52 applies to all appeals to which this section applies subject to any special provisions set out in this section.

Where any of the provisions in this section provide for documents to be filed at the appeal court, these documents are in addition to any documents required under Part 52 or sections I or II of this practice direction.

20.3   Appeals to the Court of Appeal   Paragraph

Appeals to the Court of Appeal

Appeal against order for revocation of patent

A32–379   **21.2** (1) This paragraph applies where an appeal lies to the Court of Appeal from an order for the revocation of a patent.

(2) The appellant must serve the appellant's notice on the Comptroller-General of Patents, Designs and Trade Marks (the "Comptroller") in addition to the persons to be served under rule 52.4(3) and in accordance with that rule.

(3) Where, before the appeal hearing, the respondent decides not to oppose the appeal or not to attend the appeal hearing, he must immediately serve notice of that decision on—

(a) the Comptroller; and

(b) the appellant.

(4) Where the respondent serves a notice in accordance with paragraph (3), he must also serve copies of the following documents on the Comptroller with that notice—

(a) the petition;

(b) any statements of claim;

(c) any written evidence filed in the claim.

(5) Within 14 days after receiving the notice in accordance with paragraph (3), the Comptroller must serve on the appellant a notice stating whether or not he intends to attend the appeal hearing.

(6) The Comptroller may attend the appeal hearing and oppose the appeal—

(a) in any case where he has given notice under paragraph (5) of his intention to attend; and

(b) in any other case (including, in particular, a case where the respondent withdraws his opposition to the appeal during the hearing) if the Court of Appeal so directs or permits.

Appeal from Patents Court on appeal from Comptroller

A32–380   **21.3** Where the appeal is from a decision of the Patents Court which was itself made on an appeal from a decision of the Comptroller-General of Patents, Designs and Trade Marks, the appellant must serve the appellant's notice on the Comptroller in addition to the persons to be served under rule 52.4(3) and in accordance with that rule.

Appeals in cases of contempt of court

A32–381   **21.4** In an appeal under section 13 of the Administration of Justice Act 1960 (appeals in cases of contempt of court), the appellant must serve the appellant's notice on the court from whose order or decision the appeal is brought in addition to the persons to be served under rule 52.4(3) and in accordance with that rule.

APPENDIX 33

Civil Jurisdiction and Judgments Act 1982

(1982, c.27)

GENERAL NOTE

A33–02   This Act incorporates into United Kingdom law the E.C. Convention on Jurisdiction and Enforcement of Judgments in Civil and Commercial Matters of 1968, known as the "Brussels Convention", As stated in s.2(2), "for convenience of reference" the English text of this Convention is set out in Sched. 1 to the Act.

PART I

IMPLEMENTATION OF THE CONVENTIONS

Main implementing provisions

Interpretation of references to the conventions and contracting states

A33–03   1.—(1) In this Act—

"the 1968 Convention" means the Convention on jurisdiction and the enforcement of judgments in civil and commercial matters (including the Protocol annexed to that Convention), signed at Brussels on 27th September 1968;

"the 1971 Protocol" means the Protocol on the interpretation of the 1968 Convention by the European Court, signed at Luxembourg on 3rd June 1971;

"the Accession Convention" means the Convention on the accession to the 1968 Convention and the 1971 Protocol of Denmark, the Republic of Ireland and the United Kingdom, signed at Luxembourg on 9th October 1978;

"the 1982 Accession Convention" means the Convention on the accession of the Hellenic Republic to the 1968 Convention and the 1971 Protocol, with the adjustments made to them by the Accession Convention, signed at Luxembourg on 25th October 1982;

"the 1989 Accession Convention" means the Convention on the accession of the Kingdom of Spain and the Portuguese Republic to the 1968 Convention and the 1971 Protocol, with the adjustments made to them by the Accession Convention and the 1982 Accession Convention, signed at Donostia—San Sebastian on 26th May 1989;

"the Brussels Conventions" means the 1968 Convention, the 1971 Protocol, the Accession Convention, the 1982 Accession Convention and the 1989 Accession Convention;

"the Lugano Convention" means the Convention on jurisdiction and the enforcement of judgments in civil and commercial matters (including the Protocols annexed to that Convention) opened for signature at Lugano on 16th September 1988 and signed by the United Kingdom on 18th September 1989.

(2) In this Act, unless the context otherwise requires—

(a) references to, or to any provision of, the 1968 Convention or the 1971 Protocol are references to the Convention, Protocol or provision as amended by the Accession Convention, the 1982 Accession Convention and the 1989 Accession Convention; and

(b) any reference to a numbered Article without more is a reference—
  (i) to the Article so numbered of the 1968 Convention, in so far as the provision applies in relation to that Convention, and
  (ii) to the Article so numbered of the Lugano Convention, in so far as the provision applies in relation to that Convention,

and any reference to a sub-division of a numbered Article shall be construed accordingly.

(3) In this Act—

"Contracting State", without more in any provision means—
  (a) in the application of the provision in relation to the Brussels Conventions, a Brussels Contracting State; and
  (b) in the application of the provision in relation to the Lugano Convention, a Lugano Contracting State;

"Brussels Contracting State" means—
  (a) one of the original parties to the 1968 Convention (Belgium, the Federal Republic of Germany, France, Italy, Luxembourg and The Netherlands); or
  (b) one of the parties acceding to that Convention under the Accession Convention (Denmark, the Republic of Ireland and the United Kingdom), or under the 1982 Accession Convention (the Hellenic Republic), or under the 1989 Accession Convention (Spain and Portugal);

being a state in respect of which the Accession Convention has entered into force in accordance with Article 39 of that Convention, or being a state in respect of which the 1982 Accession Convention has entered into

1461

force in accordance with Article 15 of that Convention, or being a state in respect of which the 1989 Accession Convention has entered into force in accordance with Article 32 of that Convention, as the case might be;

"Lugano Contracting State" means one of the original parties to the Lugano Convention, that is to say— Austria, Belgium, Denmark, Finland, France, the Federal Republic of Germany, the Hellenic Republic, Iceland, the Republic of Ireland, Italy, Luxembourg, the Netherlands, Norway, Portugal, Spain, Sweden, Switzerland and the United Kingdom, being a State in relation to which that Convention has taken effect in accordance with paragraph 3 or 4 of Article 61.

GENERAL NOTE

A33–04   Amended by the Civil Jurisdiction and Judgments Act 1982 (Amendment) Order 1989 (S.I. 1989 No. 1346); the Civil Jurisdiction and Judgments Act 1982 (Amendment) Order 1990 (S.I. 1990 No. 2591); and the Civil Jurisdiction and Judgments Act 1991, s.2.

The Conventions to have the force of law

A33–05   2.—(1) The Brussels Conventions shall have the force of law in the United Kingdom, and judicial notice shall be taken of them.

(2) For convenience of reference there are set out in Schedules 1, 2, 3, 3A and 3B respectively the English texts of—

(a) the 1968 Convention as amended by Titles II and III of the Accession Convention, by Titles II and III of the 1982 Accession Convention and by Titles II and III of, and Annex I(d) to, the 1989 Accession Convention;

(b) the 1971 Protocol as amended by Title IV of the Accession Convention, by Title IV of the 1982 Accession Convention and by Titles IV of the 1989 Accession Convention;

(c) Titles V and VI of the Accession Convention (transitional and final provisions) as amended by Title V of the 1989 Accession Convention;

(d) Titles V and VI of the 1982 Accession Convention (transitional and final provisions); and

(e) Titles VI and VII of the 1989 Accession Convention (transitional and final provisions),

being texts prepared from the authentic English texts referred to in Articles 37 and 41 of the Accession Convention, in Article 17 of the 1982 Accession Convention and in Article 34 of the 1989 Accession Convention.

GENERAL NOTE

A33–06   Amended by the Civil Jurisdiction and Judgments Act 1982 (Amendment) Order 1989 (S.I. 1989 No.1346); the Civil Jurisdiction and Judgments Act 1982 (Amendment) Order 1990 (S.I.1990 No.2591); and the Civil Jurisdiction and Judgments Act 1991, s.3, Sched. 2, para. 1.

"1968 Convention . . . 1971 Protocol"

This Convention, *i.e.* the Brussels Convention, and the attached 1971 Protocol are set out in respectively, Scheds 1 and 2 of the Act. See paras 33–38 *et seq.*

Interpretation of the Conventions

A33–07   3.—(1) Any question as to the meaning or effect of any provision of the Brussels Convention shall, if not referred to the European Court in accordance with the 1971 Protocol, be determined in accordance with the principles laid down by and any relevant decision of the European Court.

(2) Judicial notice shall be taken of any decision of, or expression of option by, the European Court on any such question.

(3) Without prejudice to the generality of subsection (1), the following reports (which are reproduced in the Official Journal of the Communities), namely—

   (a) the reports by Mr. P. Jenard on the 1968 Convention and the 1971 Protocol; and

   (b) the report by Professor Peter Schlosser on the Accession Convention; and

   (c) the report by Professor Demetrios I. Evrigenis and Professor K. D. Kerameus on the 1982 Accession Convention; and

   (d) the report by Mr. Martino de Almeida Cruz, Mr. Manuel Desantes Real and Mr. P. Jenard on the 1989 Accession Convention,

may be considered in ascertaining the meaning or effect of any provision of the Conventions and shall be given such weight as is appropriate in the circumstances.

GENERAL NOTE

Amended by the Civil Jurisdiction and Judgments Act 1982 (Amendment) Order 1989 **A33–08** (S.I. 1989 No.1346); the Civil Jurisdiction and Judgments Act 1982 (Amendment) Order 1990 (S.I. 1990 No. 2591); and the Civil Jurisdiction and Judgments Act 1991, s.3, Sched. 2, para. 1.

The Lugano Convention to have the force of law

3A.—(1) The Lugano Convention shall have the force of law in the United **A33–09** Kingdom and judicial notice shall be taken of it.

(2) For convenience of reference there is set out in Schedule 3C the English text of the Lugano Convention.

GENERAL NOTE

Added by the Civil Jurisdiction and Judgments Act 1991, s.1(1). **A33–10**

"Lugano Convention"

The text of this Convention is set out in Sched. 3C of the Act as amended. The Lugano Convention is made between the Member States of the E.C. and those of the European Free Trade Association (EFTA). It is very closely modelled on the Brussels Convention. The amendments to the 1982 Act required to accommodate the Lugano Convention were introduced by the Civil Jurisdiction and Judgments Act 1991. See further, para. 33–145 below.

Interpretation of the Lugano Convention

3B.—(1) In determining any question as to the meaning or effect of a provision **A33–11** of the Lugano Convention, a court in the United Kingdom shall, in accordance with Protocol No. 2 to that Convention, take account of any principles laid down in any relevant decision delivered by a court of any other Lugano Contracting State concerning provisions of the Convention.

(2) Without prejudice to any practice of the courts as to the matters which may be considered apart from this section, the report of the Lugano Convention by Mr. P. Jenard and Mr G. Möller (which is reproduced in the Official Journal of the Communities of 28th July 1990) may be considered in ascertaining the meaning or effect of any provision of the Convention and shall be given such weight as is appropriate in the circumstances.

GENERAL NOTE

Added by the Civil Jurisdiction and Judgments Act 1991, s.1(1). For Jenard and Möller **A33–12** report, see O.J. [1990] C189/07.

* * * *

Other Supplementary provisions

Allocation within U.K of jurisdiction with respect to trusts and consumer contracts

A33–13 10.—(1) The provisions of this section have effect for the purpose of allocating within the United Kingdom jurisdiction in certain proceedings in respect of which the 1968 Convention or the Lugano Convention confers jurisdiction on the courts of the United Kingdom generally and to which section 16 does not apply.

(2) Any proceedings which by virtue of Article 5(6) (trusts) are brought in the United Kingdom shall be brought in the courts of the part of the United Kingdom in which the trust is domiciled.

(3) Any proceedings which by virtue of the first paragraph of Article 14 (consumer contracts) are brought in the United Kingdom by a consumer on the ground that he is himself domiciled there shall be brought in the courts of the part of the United Kingdom in which he is domiciled.

GENERAL NOTE

A33–14 Amended by the Civil Jurisdiction and Judgments Act 1991, s.3, Sched. 2.

"To which section 16 does not apply"

Section 16 deals with the allocation within the U.K. of jurisdiction in certain civil proceedings. The provisions set out in Sched. 4 to the Act (which contains a modified version of Title II of the Brussels Convention) have effect for determining, for each part of the U.K., whether the courts of law of that part have jurisdiction.

* * * *

PART IV

MISCELLANEOUS PROVISIONS

Provisions relating to jurisdiction

Interim relief and protective measures in cases of doubtful jurisdiction

A33–15 24.—(1) Any power of a court in England and Wales or Northern Ireland to grant interim relief pending trial or pending the determination of an appeal shall extend to a case where—

(a) the issue to be tried, or which is the subject of the appeal, relates to the jurisdiction of the court to entertain the proceedings; or

(b) the proceedings involve the reference of any matter to the European Court under the 1971 Protocol.

(2) [*Applies to Scotland*]

(3) Subsections (1) and (2) shall not be construed as restricting any power to grant interim relief or protective measures which a court may have apart from this section.

GENERAL NOTE

"The issue to be tried . . . relates to the jurisdiction of the court"

A33–16 For example, where the issue is whether the court, or a court in a Contracting State, has jurisdiction under the Brussels Convention. See also Art. 24 of the Brussels Convention.

Interim relief in England and Wales and Northern Ireland in the absence of substantive proceedings

25.—(1) The High Court in England and Wales or Northern Ireland shall have **A33–17** power to grant interim relief where—

(a) proceedings have been or are to be commenced in a Brussels or Lugano Contracting State other than the United Kingdom or in a part of the United Kingdom other than that in which the High Court in question exercises jurisdiction; and

(b) they are or will be proceedings whose subject-matter is within the scope of the 1968 Convention as determined by Article 1 (whether or not the Convention has effect in relation to the proceedings).

(2) On an application for any interim relief under subsection (1) the court may refuse to grant that relief if, in the opinion of the court, the fact that the court has no jurisdiction apart from this section in relation to the subject-matter of the proceedings in question makes it inexpedient for the court to grant it.

(3) Her Majesty may by Order in Council extend the power to grant interim relief conferred by subsection (1) so as to make it exercisable in relation to proceedings of any of the following descriptions, namely—

(a) proceedings commenced or to be commenced otherwise than in a Brussels or Lugano Contracting State;

(b) proceedings whose subject-matter is not within the scope of the 1968 Convention as determined by Article 1;

(c) [. . .]

(4) An Order in Council under subsection (3)—

(a) may confer power to grant only specified descriptions of interim relief;

(b) may make different provision for different classes of proceedings, for proceedings pending in different countries or courts outside the United Kingdom or in different parts of the United Kingdom, and for other different circumstances; and

(c) may impose conditions or restrictions on the exercise of any power conferred by the order.

(5) [. . .]

(6) Any Order in Council under subsection (3) shall be subject to annulment in pursuance of a resolution of either House of Parliament.

(7) In this section "interim relief", in relation to the High Court in England and Wales or Northern Ireland, means interim relief of any kind which that court has power to grant in proceedings relating to matters within its jurisdiction, other than—

(a) a warrant for the arrest of property; or

(b) provision for obtaining evidence.

GENERAL NOTE

Subss. (1)(a) and (3)(a) amended by the Civil Jurisdiction and Judgments Act 1991, s.3, **A33–18** Sched. 2, para. 12(a); subs.(1)(b) amended by para. 12. Subss. (3)(c) and (5) repealed by the Arbitration Act 1996. The power to grant interim relief under subs. (1) has been extended by the Civil Jurisdiction and Judgments Act 1982 (Interim Relief) Order 1997.

Security in Admiralty proceedings in England and Wales or Northern Ireland in case of stay, etc.

26.—(1) Where in England and Wales or Northern Ireland a court stays or **A33–19** dismisses Admiralty proceedings on the ground that the dispute in question should be submitted to the determination of the courts of another part of the

United Kingdom or of an overseas country, the court may, if in those proceedings property has been arrested or bail or other security has been given to prevent or obtain release from arrest—

    (a) order that the property arrested be retained as security for the satisfaction of any award or judgment which—

        (i) is given in respect of the dispute in the legal proceedings in favour of which those proceedings are stayed or dismissed; and

        (ii) is enforceable in England and Wales or, as the case may be, in Northern Ireland, or

    (b) order that the stay or dismissal of those proceedings be conditional on the provision of equivalent security for the satisfaction of any such award or judgment.

(2) Where the court makes an order under subsection (1), it may attach such conditions to the order as it thinks fit, in particular conditions with respect to the institution or prosecution of the relevant legal proceedings.

(3) Subject to any provision made by rules of court and to any necessary modifications, the same law and practice shall apply in relation to property retained in pursuance of an order made by a court under subsection (1) as would apply if it were held for the purposes of proceedings in that court.

GENERAL NOTE

A33–20 Amended by the Arbitration Act 1996.

* * * *

Domicile

Proceedings in England and Wales or Northern Ireland for torts to immovable property

A33–21 30.—(1) The jurisdiction of any court in England and Wales or Northern Ireland to entertain proceedings for trespass to, or any other tort affecting, immovable property shall extend to cases in which the property in question is situated outside that part of the United Kingdom unless the proceedings are principally concerned with a question of the title, or the right to possession of, that property.

(2) Subsection (1) has effect subject to the 1968 Convention and the Lugano Convention and to the provisions set out in Schedule 4.

GENERAL NOTE

A33–22 Amended by the Civil Jurisdiction and Judgments Act 1991, s.3, Sched. 2, para. 13.

* * * *

PART V

SUPPLEMENTARY AND GENERAL PROVISIONS

GENERAL NOTE

A33–23 Under the Brussels Convention, domicile rather than presence (or nationality), is the key to the allocation of jurisdiction among the courts of the Contracting States, see Arts 2 and 52, paras 33–40 and 33–109, below. Consequently, this Part of the Act, *inter alia*, enacts particular rules governing domicile.

41.—(1) Subject to Article 52 (which contains provisions for determining whether a **A33–24** party is domiciled in a Contracting State), the following provisions of this section determine, for the purposes of the 1968 Convention the Lugano Convention and this Act, whether an individual is domiciled in the United Kingdom or in a particular part of, or place in, the United Kingdom or in a state other than a Contracting State.

(2) An individual is domiciled in the United Kingdom if and only if—

    (a) he is resident in the United Kingdom; and

    (b) the nature and circumstances of his residence indicate that he has a substantial connection with the United Kingdom.

(3) Subject to subsection (5), an individual is domiciled in a particular part of the United Kingdom if and only if—

    (a) he is resident in that part; and

    (b) the nature and circumstances of his residence indicate that he has a substantial connection with that part.

(4) An individual is domiciled in a particular place in the United Kingdom if and only if he—

    (a) is domiciled in the part of the United Kingdom in which that place is situated; and

    (b) is resident in that place.

(5) An individual who is domiciled in the United Kingdom but in whose case the requirements of subsection (3)(b) are not satisfied in relation to any particular part of the United Kingdom shall be treated as domiciled in the part of the United Kingdom in which he is resident.

(6) In the case of an individual who—

    (a) is resident in the United Kingdom, or in a particular part of the United Kingdom; and

    (b) has been so resident for the last three months or more, the requirements of subsection (2)(b) or, as the case may be, subsection (3)(b) shall be presumed to be fulfilled unless the contrary is proved.

(7) An individual is domiciled in a state other than a Contracting State if and only if—

    (a) he is resident in that state; and

    (b) the nature and circumstances of his residence indicate that he has a substantial connection with that state.

GENERAL NOTE

Subs. (1) amended by the Civil Jurisdiction and Judgments Act 1991, s.3, Sched. 2, para. 16. **A33–25**

Domicile and seat of corporation or association

42.—(1) For the purposes of this Act the seat of a corporation or association (as **A33–26** determined by this section) shall be treated as its domicile.

(2) The following provisions of this section determine where a corporation or association has its seat—

    (a) for the purpose of Article 53 (which for the purposes of the 1968 Convention or, as the case may be, the Lugano Convention equates the domicile of such a body with its seat); and

    (b) for the purposes of this Act other than the provisions mentioned in section 43(1)(b) and (c).

(3) A corporation or association has its seat in the United Kingdom if and only if—

(a) it was incorporated or formed under the law of a part of the United Kingdom and has its registered office or some other official address in the United Kingdom; or

(b) its central management and control is exercised in the United Kingdom.

(4) A corporation or association has its seat in a particular part of the United Kingdom if and only if it has its seat in the United Kingdom and—

(a) it has its registered office or some other official address in that part; or
(b) its central management and control is exercised in that part; or
(c) it has a place of business in that part.

(5) A corporation or association has its seat in a particular place in the United Kingdom if and only if it has its seat in the part of the United Kingdom in which that place is situated and—

(a) it has its registered office or some other official address in that place; or
(b) its central management and control is exercised in that place; or
(c) it has a place of business in that place.

(6) Subject to subsection (7), a corporation or association has its seat in a state other than the United Kingdom if and only if—

(a) it was incorporated or formed under the law of that state and has its registered office or some other official address there; or
(b) its central management and control is exercised in that state.

(7) A corporation or association shall not be regarded as having its seat in a Contracting State other than the United Kingdom if it is shown that the courts of that state would not regard it as having its seat there.

(8) In this section—

"business" includes any activity carried on by a corporation or association, and "place of business" shall be construed accordingly;

"official address", in relation to a corporation or association, means an address which it is required by law to register, notify or maintain for the purpose of receiving notices or other communications.

GENERAL NOTE

A33–27 Subs.(2) (a) amended by the Civil Jurisdiction and Judgments Act 1991, s.3, Sched. 2, para. 17.

Seat of corporation or association for purposes of article 16(2) and related provisions

A33–28 43.—(1) The following provisions of this section determine where a corporation or association has its seat for the purposes of—

(a) Article 16(2) of the 1968 Convention or of the Lugano Convention (which confers exclusive jurisdiction over proceedings relating to the formation or dissolution of such bodies, or to the decisions of their organs);
(b) Articles 5A and 16(2) in Schedule 4; and
(c) Rules 2(12) and 4(1) (b) in Schedule 8.

(2) A corporation or association has its seat in the United Kingdom if and only if—

(a) it was incorporated or formed under the law of a part of the United Kingdom; or
(b) its central management and control is exercised in the United Kingdom.

(3) A corporation or association has its seat in a particular part of the United Kingdom if and only if it has its seat in the United Kingdom and—

    (a) subject to subsection (5), it was incorporated or formed under the law of that part; or

    (b) being incorporated or formed under the law of a state other than the United Kingdom, its central management and control is exercised in that part.

(4) A corporation or association has its seat in a particular place in Scotland if and only if it has its seat in Scotland and—

    (a) it has its registered office or some other official address in that place; or

    (b) it has no registered office or other official address in Scotland, but its central management and control is exercised in that place.

(5) A corporation or association incorporated or formed under—

    (a) an enactment forming part of the law of more than one part of the United Kingdom; or

    (b) an instrument having effect in the domestic law of more than one part of the United Kingdom,

shall, if it has a registered office, be taken to have its seat in the part of the United Kingdom in which that office is situated, and not in any other part of the United Kingdom.

(6) Subject to subsection (7), a corporation or association has its seat in a Contracting State other than the United Kingdom if and only if—

    (a) it was incorporated or formed under the law of that state; or

    (b) its central management and control is exercised in that state.

(7) A corporation or association shall not be regarded as having its seat in a Contracting State other than the United Kingdom if—

    (a) it has its seat in the United Kingdom by virtue of subsection 2(a); or

    (b) it is shown that the courts of that other state would not regard it for the purposes of Article 16(2) as having its seat there.

(8) In this section "official address" has the same meaning as in section 42.

GENERAL NOTE

Subs.(1)(a) amended by the Civil Jurisdiction and Judgments Act 1991, s.3, Sched. 2, para. 18.   **A33–29**

Persons deemed to be domiciled in the United Kingdom for certain purposes

    44.—(1) This section applies to—   **A33–30**

    (a) proceedings within Section 3 of Title II of the 1968 Convention or Section 3 of Title II of the Lugano Convention (insurance contracts), and

    (b) proceedings within Section 4 of Title II of either of those Conventions (consumer contracts).

(2) A person who, for the purposes of proceedings to which this section applies arising out of the operations of a branch, agency or other establishment in the United Kingdom, is deemed for the purposes of the 1968 Convention or, as the case may be, of the Lugano Convention to be domiciled in the United Kingdom by virtue of—

    (a) Article 8, second paragraph (insurers); or

    (b) Article 13, second paragraph (suppliers of goods, services or credit to consumers), shall, for the purposes of those proceedings, be treated for the purposes of this Act as so domiciled and as domiciled in the part of the United Kingdom in which the branch, agency or establishment in question is situated.

GENERAL NOTE

A33–31 Subs.(1) amended by the Civil Jurisdiction and Judgments Act 1991, s.3, Sched. 2, para. 19.

Domicile of trusts

A33–32 45.—(1) The following provisions of this section determine, for the purposes of the 1968 Convention the Lugano Convention and this Act, where a trust is domiciled.

(2) A trust is domiciled in the United Kingdom if and only if it is by virtue of subsection (3) domiciled in a part of the United Kingdom.

(3) A trust is domiciled in a part of the United Kingdom if and only if the system of law of that part is the system of law with which the trust has its closest and most real connection.

GENERAL NOTE

A33–33 Subs.(1) amended by the Civil Jurisdiction and Judgments Act 1991, s.3, Sched. 2, para. 20.

Domicile and seat of the crown

A33–34 46.—(1) For the purposes of this Act the seat of the Crown (as determined by this section) shall be treated as its domicile.

(2) The following provisions of this section determine where the Crown has its seat—

(a) for the purposes of the 1968 Convention and the Lugano Convention (in each of which Article 53 equates the domicile of a legal person with its seat); and

(b) for the purposes of this Act.

(3) Subject to the provisions of any Order in Council for the time being in force under subsection (4)—

(a) the Crown in right of Her Majesty's government in the United Kingdom has its seat in every part of, and every place in, the United Kingdom; and

(aa) the Crown in right of the Scottish Administration has its seat in, and in every place in, Scotland; and

(b) the Crown in right of Her Majesty's government in Northern Ireland has its seat in, and in every place in, Northern Ireland.

(4) Her Majesty may by Order in Council provide that, in the case of proceedings of any specified description against the Crown in right of Her Majesty's government in the United Kingdom, the Crown shall be treated for the purposes of the 1968 Convention the Lugano Convention and this Act as having its seat in, and in every place in, a specified part of the United Kingdom and not in any other part of the United Kingdom.

(5) An Order in Council under subsection (4) may frame a description proceedings in any way, and in particular may do so by reference to the government department or officer of the Crown against which or against whom they fall to be instituted.

(6) Any Order in Council made under this section shall be subject to annulment in pursuance of a resolution of either House of Parliament.

(7) Nothing in this section applies to the Crown otherwise than in right of Her Majesty's government in the United Kingdom, the Scottish Administration or Her Majesty's government in Northern Ireland.

GENERAL NOTE

Subss.(2) (a) & (4) amended by the Civil Jurisdiction and Judgments Act 1991, s.3, Sched. **A33–35**
2, para. 21. Subss. (3) and (7) are amended by the Scotland Act 1998 (c.46), s.125, Sched. 8,
para. 18.

Saving for powers to stay, sist, strike out or dismiss proceedings

49. Nothing in this Act shall prevent any court in the United Kingdom from **A33–36**
staying, sisting, striking out or dismissing any proceedings before it, on the
ground of *forum non conveniens* or otherwise, where to do so is not inconsistent
with the 1968 Convention or, as the case may be, the Lugano Convention.

GENERAL NOTE

Amended by the Civil Jurisdiction and Judgments Act 1991, s.3, Sched. 2, para. 24.   **A33–37**

SCHEDULES

Section 2(2)(a)   SCHEDULE 1

TEXT OF 1968 CONVENTION, AS AMENDED

GENERAL NOTE

The text set out below is the version of the 1968 Convention as inserted in Sched. 1 to the **A33–38**
1982 Act by the Civil Jurisdiction and Judgments Act 1982 (Amendment) Order 1990 (S.I.
1990 No. 2591), art. 12(1), Sched. 1, following upon the accession to the European
Community of Spain and Portugal. For the earlier version of the Convention inserted
following the accession of Greece, see the Civil Jurisdiction and Judgments Act 1982
(Amendment) Order 1989 (S.I. 1989 No. 1346), art. 9(1), Sched. 1. Section 3(3) of the 1982
Act, as amended, states that:
    "the reports by Mr. P. Jenard on the 1968 Convention and the 1971 Protocol; and the
        reports by Professor Peter Schlosser, Professor Demetrios I. Evrigenis, Professor
        K.D. Kerameus, Mr. Martinho de Almedia Cruz, Mr. Manuel Desantes Real and
        Mr. P. Jenard on the various Accession Conventions between 1978 and 1989,"

may be considered in ascertaining the meaning or effect of any provision in the
Convention and "shall be given such weight as is appropriate in the circumstances".
These reports were published in the Official Journal of the European Communities. For
more detailed analysis of the Convention see the leading textbooks, *e.g.* Dicey & Morris,
Conflict of Laws (13th ed.), and Briggs & Rees, *Civil Jurisdiction and Judgments* (2nd ed.).

* * * *

TITLE I

SCOPE

Article 1

This Convention shall apply in civil and commercial matters whatever the nature of the **A33–39**
court or tribunal. It shall not extend, in particular, to revenue, customs or administrative
matters.
    The Convention shall not apply to—
    1. The status or legal capacity of natural persons, rights in property arising out of
        a matrimonial relationship, wills and succession.
    2. Bankruptcy, proceedings relating to the winding-up of insolvent companies or
        other legal persons, judicial arrangements, compositions and analogous
        proceedings.
    3. Social security.
    4. Arbitration.

TITLE II

JURISDICTION

SECTION 1

GENERAL PROVISIONS

Article 2

A33–40   Subject to the provisions of this Convention, persons domiciled in a Contracting State shall, whatever their nationality, be sued in the courts of that State.

Persons who are not nationals of the State in which they are domiciled shall be governed by the rules of jurisdiction applicable to nationals of that State.

GENERAL NOTE

"Persons domiciled in a Contracting State"

A33–41   See ss.41–46 of the 1982 Act, paras 33–24 to 33–34, above.

Article 3

A33–42   Persons domiciled in a Contracting State may be sued in the courts of another Contracting State only by virtue of the rules set out in Sections 2 to 6 of this Title.

In particular the following provisions shall not be applicable as against them—

. . .

—in the United Kingdom: the rules which enable jurisdiction to be founded on:

   (a) the document instituting the proceedings having been served on the defendant during his temporary presence in the United Kingdom; or

   (b) the presence within the United Kingdom of property belonging to the defendant; or

   (c) the seizure by the plaintiff of property situated in the United Kingdom.

Article 4

A33–43   If the defendant is not domiciled in a Contracting State, the jurisdiction of the courts of each Contracting State shall, subject to the provisions of Article 16, be determined by the law of that State.

As against such a defendant, any person domiciled in a Contracting State may, whatever his nationality, avail himself in that State of the rules of jurisdiction there in force, and in particular those specified in the second paragraph of Article 3, in the same way as the nationals of that State.

SECTION 2

SPECIAL JURISDICTION

Article 5

A33–44   A person domiciled in a Contracting State may, in another Contracting State, be sued—

   1. In matters relating to a contract, in the courts for the place of performance of the obligation in question; in matters relating to individual contracts of employment, this place is that where the employee habitually carries out his work, or if the employee does not habitually carry out his work in any one country, the employer may also be sued in the courts for the place where the business which engaged the employee was or is now situated.

   2. In matters relating to maintainance, in the courts for the place where the maintenance creditor is domiciled or habitually resident or, if the matter is ancillary to proceedings concerning the status of a person, in the court which, according to its own law, has jurisdiction to entertain those proceedings, unless that jurisdiction is based solely on the nationality of one of the parties.

1472

3. In matters relating to tort, delict or quasi-delict, in the courts for the place where the harmful event occurred.
4. As regards a civil claim for damages or restitution which is based on an act giving rise to criminal proceedings, in the court seised of those proceedings, to the extent that that court has jurisdiction under its own law to entertain civil proceedings.
5. As regards a dispute arising out of the operations of a branch, agency or other establishment, in the courts for the place in which the branch, agency or other establishment is situated.
6. As settlor, trustee or beneficiary of a trust created by the operation of a statute, or by a written instrument, or created orally and evidenced in writing, in the courts of the Contracting State in which the trust is domiciled.
7. As regards a dispute concerning the payment of remuneration claimed in respect of the salvage of a cargo or freight, in the court under the authority of which the cargo or freight in question—
   (a) has been arrested to secure such payment, or
   (b) could have been so arrested, but bail or other security has been given;
   provided that this provision shall apply only if it is claimed that the defendant has an interest in the cargo or freight or had such an interest at the time of salvage.

GENERAL NOTE

"In matters relating to individual contracts of employment"

In Point 1 these words and the text following were added by Civil Jurisdiction and **A33–45** Judgments Act 1982 (Amendment) Order 1990 at the time of the revision of the 1968 Convention upon the accession of Spain and Portugal. The opportunity was taken to make this modification in the light of experience.
The corresponding Point in Art. 5.1 of the Lugano Convention reads:
"A person domiciled in a Contracting State may, in another Contracting State, be sued:
   1. In matters relating to a contract, in the courts for the place of performance of the obligation in question; in matters relating to individual contracts of employments, this place is that where the employee habitually carries out his work, or if the employee does not habitually carry out his work in any one country, this place shall be the place of business through which he was engaged;".

Article 6

A person domiciled in a Contracting State may also be sued— **A33–46**
   1. Where he is one of a number of defendants, in the courts for the place where any one of them is domiciled.
   2. As a third party in an action on a warranty or guarantee or in any other third party proceedings, in the court seised of the original proceedings, unless these were instituted solely with the object of removing him from the jurisdiction of the court which would be competent in his case.
   3. On a counter-claim arising from the same contract or facts on which the original claim was based, in the court in which the original claim is pending.
   4. In matters relating to a contract, if the action may be combined with an action against the same defendant in matters relating to rights in rem in immovable property, in the court of the Contracting State in which the property is situated.

GENERAL NOTE

"In matters relating to a contract"

Point 4 of this Article was added by Civil Jurisdiction and Judgments Act 1982 **A33–47** (Amendment) Order 1990 at the time of the revision of the 1968 Convention upon the accession of Spain and Portugal. The opportunity was taken to make this modification in the light of experience.

Article 6a

A33–48 Where by virtue of this Convention a court of a Contracting State has jurisdiction in actions relating to liability from the use or operation of a ship, that court, or any other court substituted for this purpose by the internal law of that State, shall also have jurisdiction over claims for limitation of such liability.

GENERAL NOTE

"Relating to liability from"

A33–49 The corresponding Article in the Lugano Convention reads "relating to liability arising from".

SECTION 3

JURISDICTION IN MATTERS RELATING TO INSURANCE

Article 7

A33–50 In matters relating to insurance, jurisdiction shall be determined by this Section, without prejudice to the provisions of Articles 4 and 5 point 5.

Article 8

A33–51 An insurer domiciled in a Contracting State may be sued—
    1. in the courts of the State where he is domiciled, or
    2. in another Contracting State, in the courts for the place where the policy-holder is domiciled, or
    3. if he is a co-insurer, in the courts of a Contracting State in which proceedings are brought against the leading insurer.
An insurer who is not domiciled in a Contracting State but has a branch, agency or other establishment in one of the Contracting States shall, in disputes arising out of the operations of the branch, agency or establishment, be deemed to be domiciled in that State.

Article 9

A33–52 In respect of liability insurance or insurance of immovable property, the insurer may in addition be sued in the courts for the place where the harmful event occurred. The same applies if movable and immovable property are covered by the same insurance policy and both are adversely affected by the same contingency.

Article 10

A33–53 In respect of liability insurance, the insurer may also, if the law of the court permits it, be joined in proceedings which the injured party had brought against the insured.
The provisions of Articles 7, 8 and 9 shall apply to actions brought by the injured party directly against the insurer, where such direct actions are permitted.
If the law governing such direct actions provides that the policy-holder or the insured may be joined as a party to the action, the same court shall have jurisdiction over them.

GENERAL NOTE

"Injured party had brought"

A33–54 The corresponding Article in the Lugano Convention reads "injured party has brought".

Article 11

A33–55 Without prejudice to the provisions of the third paragraph of Article 10, an insurer may bring proceedings only in the courts of the Contracting State in which the defendant is domiciled, irrespective of whether he is the policy-holder, the insured or a beneficiary.

The provisions of this Section shall not affect the right to bring a counterclaim in the court in which, in accordance with this Section, the original claim is pending.

Article 12

The provisions of this Section may be departed from only by an agreement on jurisdiction— **A33–56**

1. which is entered into after the dispute has arisen, or
2. which allows the policy-holder, the insured or a beneficiary to bring proceedings in courts other than those indicated in this Section, or
3. which is concluded between a policy-holder and an insurer, both of whom are domiciled in the same Contracting State, and which has the effect of conferring jurisdiction on the courts of that State even if the harmful event were to occur abroad, provided that such an agreement is not contrary to the law of that State, or
4. which is concluded with a policy-holder who is not domiciled in a Contracting State, except in so far as the insurance is compulsory or relates to immovable property in a Contracting State, or
5. which relates to a contract of insurance in so far as it covers one or more of the risks set out in Article 12a.

GENERAL NOTE

"Whom are domiciled in the same Contracting State"

Cf., Art. 15(3). The corresponding Article in the Lugano Convention (and in some earlier **A33–57** versions of the Brussels Convention) reads "whom are at the time of conclusion of the contract domiciled or habitually resident in the same Contracting State".

Article 12a

The following are the risks referred to in point 5 of Article 12— **A33–58**

1. Any loss of or damage to—
   (a) sea-going ships, installations situated offshore or on the high seas, or aircraft, arising from perils which relate to their use for commercial purposes;
   (b) goods in transit other than passengers' baggage where the transit consists of or includes carriage by such ships or aircraft.
2. Any liability, other than for bodily injury to passengers or loss of or damage to their baggage—
   (a) arising out of the use or operation of ships, installations or aircraft as referred to in point 1 (a) above in so far as the law of the Contracting State in which such aircraft are registered does not prohibit agreements on jurisdiction regarding insurance of such risks;
   (b) for loss or damage caused by goods in transit as described in point 1 (b) above.
3. Any financial loss connected with the use or operation of ships, installations or aircraft as referred to in point 1 (a) above, in particular loss of freight or charterhire.
4. Any risk or interest connected with any of those referred to in points 1 to 3 above.

SECTION 4

JURISDICTION OVER CONSUMER CONTRACTS

Article 13

In proceedings concerning a contract concluded by a person for a purpose which can be **A33–59** regarded as being outside his trade or profession, hereinafter called "the consumer", jurisdiction shall be determined by this Section, without prejudice to the provisions of Article 4 and point 5 of Article 5, if it is—

1. a contract for the sale of goods on instalment credit terms, or
2. a contract for a loan repayable by instalments, or for any other form of credit, made to finance the sale of goods, or
3. any other contract for the supply of goods or a contract for the supply of services, and
    (a) in the State of the consumer's domicile the conclusion of the contract was preceded by a specific invitation addressed to him or by advertising; and
    (b) the consumer took in that State the steps necessary for the conclusion of the contract.

Where a consumer enters into a contract with a party who is not domiciled in a Contracting State but has a branch, agency or other establishment in one of the Contracting States, that party shall, in disputes arising out of the operations of the branch, agency or establishment, be deemed to be domiciled in that State.

This Section shall not apply to contracts of transport.

Article 14

A33–60   A consumer may bring proceedings against the other party to a contract either in the courts of the Contracting State in which that party is domiciled or in the courts of the Contracting State in which he is himself domiciled.

Proceedings may be brought against a consumer by the other party to the contract only in the courts of the Contracting State in which the consumer is domiciled.

These provisions shall not affect the right to bring a counter-claim in the court in which, in accordance with this Section, the original claim is pending.

Article 15

A33–61   The provisions of this Section may be departed from only by an agreement—
1. which is entered into after the dispute has arisen, or
2. which allows the consumer to bring proceedings in courts other than those indicated in this Section, or
3. which is entered into by the consumer and the other party to the contract, both of whom are at the time of conclusion of the contract domiciled or habitually resident in the same Contracting State, and which confers jurisdiction on the courts of that State, provided that such an agreement is not contrary to the law of that State.

Section 5

Exclusive Jurisdiction

Article 16

A33–62   The following courts shall have exclusive jurisdiction, regardless of domicile:
1. (a) in proceedings which have as their object rights *in rem* in immovable property or tenancies of immovable property, the courts of the Contracting State in which the property is situated;
    (b) however, in proceedings which have as their object tenancies of immovable property concluded for temporary private use for a maximum period of six consecutive months, the courts of the Contracting State in which the defendant is domiciled shall also have jurisdiction, provided that the landlord and the defendant are natural persons and are domiciled in the same Contracting State.

2. In proceedings which have as their object the validity of the constitution, the nullity or the dissolution of companies or other legal persons or associations of natural or legal persons, or the decisions of their organs, the courts of the Contracting State in which the company, legal person or association has its seat.

3. In proceedings which have as their object the validity of entries in public registers, the courts of the Contracting State in which the register is kept.

4. In proceedings concerned with the registration or validity of patents, trade marks, designs, or other similar rights required to be deposited or registered, the courts of the Contracting State in which the deposit or registration has been applied for, has taken place or is under the terms of an international convention deemed to have taken place.

5. In proceedings concerned with the enforcement of judgments, the courts of the Contracting State in which the judgment has been or is to be enforced.

GENERAL NOTE

"Tenancies of immovable property"

Alterations to the circumstances in which concurrent jurisdiction would be enjoyed by the **A33–63** courts of Contracting States were made by Civil Jurisdiction and Judgments Act 1982 (Amendment) Order 1990 at the time of the revision of the 1968 Convention upon the accession of Spain and Portugal. The opportunity was taken to make this modification in the light of experience.

Article 6.1(b) in the Lugano Convention reads:

"however, in proceedings which have as their object tenancies of immovable property concluded for temporary private use for a maximum period of six consecutive months, the courts of the Contracting State in which the defendant is domiciled shall also have jurisdiction, provided that the tenant is a natural person and neither party is domiciled in the Contracting State in which the property is situated;".

SECTION 6

PROROGATION OF JURISDICTION

Article 17

If the parties, one or more of whom is domiciled in a Contracting State, have agreed that **A33–64** a court or the courts of a Contracting State are to have jurisdiction to settle any disputes which have arisen or which may arise in connection with a particular legal relationship, that court or those courts shall have exclusive jurisdiction. Such an agreement conferring jurisdiction shall be either—

  (a) in writing or evidenced in writing, or

  (b) in a form which accords with practices which the parties have established between themselves, or

  (c) in international trade or commerce, in a form which accords with a usage of which the parties are or ought to have been aware and which in such trade or commerce is widely known to, and regularly observed by, parties to contracts of the type involved in the particular trade or commerce concerned.

Where such an agreement is concluded by parties, none of whom is domiciled in a Contracting State, the courts of other Contracting States shall have no jurisdiction over their disputes unless the court or courts chosen have declined jurisdiction.

The court or courts of a Contracting State on which a trust instrument has conferred jurisdiction shall have exclusive jurisdiction in any proceedings brought against a settlor, trustee or beneficiary, if relations between these persons or their rights or obligations under the trust are involved.

Agreements or provisions of a trust instrument conferring jurisdiction shall have no legal force if they are contrary to the provisions of Articles 12 or 15, or if the courts whose jurisdiction they purport to exclude have exclusive jurisdiction by virtue of Article 16.

If an agreement conferring jurisdiction was concluded for the benefit of only one of the parties, that party shall retain the right to bring proceedings in any other court which has jurisdiction by virtue of this Convention.

In matters relating to individual contracts of employment an agreement conferring jurisdiction shall have legal force only if it is entered into after the dispute has arisen or if the employee invokes it to seise courts other than those for the defendant's domicile or those specified in article 5(1).

GENERAL NOTE

The first paragraph of this Article was substantially amended by the Civil Jurisdiction **A33–65** and Judgments Act 1982 (Amendment) Order 1990 at the time of the revision of the 1968 Convention upon the accession of Spain and Portugal. The opportunity was taken to make this modification in the light of experience. O.10, r.3 (service of writ in pursuance of contract) provides that where a contract contains an agreement conferring jurisdiction to which the 1982 Act applies and the writ is served under O.11, r.1(2) the writ shall be deemed to have been duly served on the defendant.

"Individual contracts of employment"

In the Lugano Convention the points within Art. 17 are numbered and the final point, numbered 5, reads as follows: "In matters relating to individual contracts of employment an agreement conferring jurisdiction shall have legal force only if it is entered into after the dispute has arisen."

Article 18

A33–66   Apart from jurisdiction derived from other provisions of this Convention, a court of a Contracting State before whom a defendant enters an appearance shall have jurisdiction. This rule shall not apply where appearance was entered solely to contest the jurisdiction, or where another court has exclusive jurisdiction by virtue of Article 16.

Section 7

Examination as to Jurisdiction and Admissibility

Article 19

A33–67   Where a court of a Contracting State is seised of a claim which is principally concerned with a matter over which the courts of another Contracting State have exclusive jurisdiction by virtue of Article 16, it shall declare of its own motion that it has no jurisdiction.

Article 20

A33–68   Where a defendant domiciled in one Contracting State is sued in a court of another Contracting State and does not enter an appearance, the court shall declare of its own motion that it has no jurisdiction unless its jurisdiction is derived from the provisions of the Convention.

The court shall stay the proceedings so long as it is not shown that the defendant has been able to receive the document instituting the proceedings or an equivalent document in sufficient time to enable him to arrange for his defence, or that all necessary steps have been taken to this end.

The provisions of the foregoing paragraph shall be replaced by those of Article 15 of the Hague Convention of 15th November 1965 on the service abroad of judicial and extrajudicial documents in civil or commercial matters, if the document instituting the proceedings or notice thereof had to be transmitted abroad in accordance with that Convention.

General Note

"Provisions of the convention"

A33–69   Would seem to mean "this" Convention, *i.e.* the Brussels Convention.

Section 8

Lis Pendens—Related Actions

Article 21

A33–70   Where proceedings involving the same cause of action and between the same parties are brought in the courts of different Contracting States, any court other than the court first seised shall of its own motion stay its proceedings until such time as the jurisdiction of the court first seised is established.

Where the jurisdiction of the court first seised is established, any court other than the court first seised shall decline jurisdiction in favour of that court.

GENERAL NOTE

"Stay its proceedings"

This phrase and the words following it in the first paragraph of this Article were **A33–71** substituted for the words "decline jurisdiction in favour of that court". The substitution was made by the Civil Jurisdiction and Judgments Act 1982 (Amendment) Order 1990 at the time of the revision of the 1968 Convention upon the accession of Spain and Portugal. The opportunity was taken to make this modification in the light of experience.

Article 22

Where related actions are brought in the courts of different Contracting States, any court **A33–72** other than the court first seised may, while the actions are pending at first instance, stay its proceedings.

A court other than the court first seised may also, on the application of one of the parties, decline jurisdiction if the law of that court permits the consolidation of related actions and the court first seised has jurisdiction over both actions.

For the purposes of this Article, actions are deemed to be related where they are so closely connected that it is expedient to hear and determine them together to avoid the risk of irreconcilable judgments resulting from separate proceedings.

Article 23

Where actions come within the exclusive jurisdiction of several courts, any court other **A33–73** than the court first seised shall decline jurisdiction in favour of that court.

SECTION 9

PROVISIONAL, INCLUDING PROTECTIVE, MEASURES

Article 24

Application may be made to the courts of a Contracting State for such provisional, **A33–74** including protective, measures as may be available under the law of that State, even if, under this Convention, the courts of another Contracting State have jurisdiction as to the substance of the matter.

* * * *

TITLE III

RECOGNITION AND ENFORCEMENT

Article 25

For the purposes of this Convention "judgment" means any judgment given by a court **A33–75** or tribunal of a Contracting State, whatever the judgment may be called, including a decree, order, decision or writ of execution, as well as the determination of costs or expenses by an officer of the court.

SECTION 1

RECOGNITION

Article 26

A judgment given in a Contracting State shall be recognised in the other Contracting **A33–76** States without any special procedure being required.

Any interested party who raises the recognition of a judgment as the principal issue in a dispute may, in accordance with the procedures provided for in Sections 2 and 3 of this Title, apply for a decision that the judgment be recognised.

If the outcome of proceedings in a court of a Contracting State depends on the determination of an incidental question of recognition that court shall have jurisdiction over that question.

Article 27

A33–77   A judgment shall not be recognised:

1. if such recognition is contrary to public policy in the State in which recognition is sought;
2. where it was given in default of appearance, if the defendant was not duly served with the document which instituted the proceedings or with an equivalent document in sufficient time to enable him to arrange for his defence;
3. if the judgment is irreconcilable with a judgment given in a dispute between the same parties in the State in which recognition is sought;
4. if the court of the State of origin, in order to arrive at its judgment, has decided a preliminary question concerning the status or legal capacity of natural persons, rights in property arising out of a matrimonial relationship, wills or succession in a way that conflicts with a rule of the private international law of the State in which the recognition is sought, unless the same result would have been reached by the application of the rules of private international law of that State;
5. if the judgment is irreconcilable with an earlier judgment given in a non-contracting State involving the same cause of action and between the same parties, provided that this latter judgment fulfils the conditions necessary for its recognition in the state addressed.

Article 28

A33–78   Moreover, a judgment shall not be recognised if it conflicts with the provisions of Sections 3, 4 or 5 of Title II, or in a case provided for in Article 59.

In its examination of the grounds of jurisdiction referred to in the foregoing paragraph, the court or authority applied to shall be bound by the findings of fact on which the court of the State of origin based its jurisdiction.

Subject to the provisions of the first paragraph, the jurisdiction of the court of the State of origin may not be reviewed; the test of public policy referred to in point 1 of Article 27 may not be applied to the rules relating to jurisdiction.

GENERAL NOTE

Lugano Convention

A33–79   An additional paragraph has been inserted between paras 2 and 3 of this Article:

A judgment may furthermore be refused recognition in any case provided for in Article 54B(3) or 57(4).

Application

The mischief at which this Article is directed is the recognition and enforcement of a judgment of a court which did not have jurisdiction under Section 3, 4 or 5 of Title II to the Convention. It is not concerned with whether the foreign court had jurisdiction on an issue which would subsequently have fallen to be decided by the court of another Contracting State (*Berkeley Administration Inc. v. McClelland (No. 2)* [1995] I.L.Pr. 201).

Article 29

A33–80   Under no circumstances may a foreign judgment be reviewed as to its substance.

Article 30

A33–81   A court of a Contracting State in which recognition is sought of a judgment given in another Contracting State may stay the proceedings if an ordinary appeal against the judgment has been lodged.

A court of a Contracting State in which recognition is sought of a judgment given in Ireland or the United Kingdom may stay the proceedings if enforcement is suspended in the State of origin, by reason of an appeal.

SECTION 2
ENFORCEMENT
Article 31

A33–82   A judgment given in a Contracting State and enforceable in that State shall be enforced in another Contracting State when, on the application of any interested party, it has been declared enforceable there.

However, in the United Kingdom, such a judgment shall be enforced in England and Wales, in Scotland, or in Northern Ireland when, on the application of any interested party, it has been registered for enforcement in that part of the United Kingdom.

Article 32

1. The application shall be submitted: **A33–83**
   — in Belgium, to the tribunal de première instance or rechtbank van eerste aanleg,
   — in Denmark, to the byret,
   — in the Federal Republic of Germany, to the presiding judge of a chamber of the Landgericht,
   — in Greece, to the Μονομελεζ Ποωτοδιχειο,
   — in Spain, to the Juzgado de Primera Instancia,
   — in France, to the presiding judge of the tribunal de grande instance,
   — in Ireland, to the High Court,
   — in Italy, to the corte d'appello,
   — in Luxembourg, to the presiding judge of the tribunal d'arrondissement,
   — in the Netherlands, to the presiding judge of the arrondissementsrechtbank,
   — in Portugal, to the Tribunal Judicial de Circulo,
   — in the United Kingdom:
      1. in England and Wales, to the High Court of Justice, or in the case of maintenance judgment to the Magistrates' Court on transmission by the Secretary of State;
      2. in Scotland, to the Court of Session, or in the case of a maintenance judgment to the Sheriff Court on transmission by the1 Secretary of State;
      3. in Northern Ireland, to the High Court of Justice, or in the case of a maintenance judgment to the Magistrates' Court on transmission by the Secretary of State.

2. The jurisdiction of local courts shall be determined by reference to the place of domicile of the party against whom enforcement is sought. If he is not domiciled in the State in which enforcement is sought, it shall be determined by reference to the place of enforcement.

GENERAL NOTE

Lugano Convention

—the list of courts to which the application is made is supplemented in the Lugano **A33–84** Convention with courts of the additional Contracting States.

Article 33

The procedure for making the application shall be governed by the law of the State in **A33–85** which enforcement is sought.

The applicant must give an address for service of process within the area of jurisdiction of the court applied to. However, if the law of the State in which enforcement is sought does not provide for the furnishing of such an address, the applicant shall appoint a representative *ad litem*.

The documents referred to in Articles 46 and 47 shall be attached to the application.

Article 34

The court applied to shall give its decision without delay; the party against whom **A33–86** enforcement is sought shall not at this stage of the proceedings be entitled to make any submissions on the application.

The application may be refused only for one of the reasons specified in Articles 27 and 28. Under no circumstances may the foreign judgment be reviewed as to its substance.

Article 35

The appropriate officer of the court shall without delay bring the decision given on the **A33–87** application to the notice of the applicant in accordance with the procedure laid down by the law of the State in which enforcement is sought.

Article 36

A33–88   If enforcement is authorised, the party against whom enforcement is sought may appeal against the decision within one month of service thereof.

If that party is domiciled in a Contracting State other than that in which the decision authorising enforcement was given, the time for appealing shall be two months and shall run from the date of service, either on him in person or at his residence. No extension of time may be granted on account of distance.

Article 37

A33–89   1. An appeal against the decision authorising enforcement shall be lodged in accordance with the rules governing procedure in contentious matters:

— in Belgium, with the tribunal de première instance or rechtbank van eerste aanleg,
— in Denmark, with the landsret,
— in the Federal Republic of Germany, with the Oberlandesgericht,
— in Greece, with the Εφετειο,
— in Spain, with the Audiencia Provincial,
— in France, with the cour d'appel,
— in Ireland, with the High Court,
— in Italy, with the corte d'appello,
— in Luxembourg, with the Court supérieure de justice sitting as a court of civil appeal,
— in the Netherlands, with the arrondissementsrechtbank,
— in Portugal, with the Tribunal de Relação,
— in the United Kingdom:
  (a) in England and Wales, with the High Court of Justice, or in the case of a maintenance judgment with the Magistrates' Court;
  (b) in Scotland, with the Court of Session, or in the case of a maintenance judgment with the Sheriff Court;
  (c) in Northern Ireland, with the High Court of Justice, or in the case of a maintenance judgment with the Magistrates' Court.

2. The judgment given on the appeal may be contested only:

— in Belgium, Greece, Spain, France, Italy, Luxembourg and in the Netherlands, by an appeal in cassation,
— in Denmark, by an appeal to the højesteret, with the leave of the Minister of Justice,
— in the Federal Republic of Germany, by a Rechtschwerde,
— in Ireland, by an appeal on a point of law to the Supreme Court,
— in Portugal, by an appeal on a point of law,
— in the United Kingdom, by a single further appeal on a point of law.

GENERAL NOTE

Lugano Convention

A33–90   The list of courts to which the application shall be submitted is supplemented in the Lugano Convention with courts of the additional Contracting States.

Article 38

A33–91   The court with which the appeal under Article 37 (1) is lodged may, on the application of the appellant, stay the proceedings if an ordinary appeal has been lodged against the judgment in the State of origin or if the time for such an appeal has not yet expired; in the latter case, the court may specify the time within such an appeal is to be lodged.

Where the judgment was given in Ireland or the United Kingdom, any form of appeal available in the State of origin shall be treated as an ordinary appeal for the purposes of the first paragraph.

The court may also make enforcement conditional on the provision of such security as it shall determine.

GENERAL NOTE

Lugano Convention

A33–92   The text of the first paragraph of Art. 38 differs and is set out below:

The court with which the appeal under the first paragraph of Art. 37 is lodged may, on the application of the appellant, stay the proceedings if an ordinary appeal has been lodged against the judgment in the State of origin or if the time for such an appeal has not yet expired; in the latter case, the court may specify the time within which such an appeal is to be lodged.

Article 39

During the time specified for an appeal pursuant to Article 36 and until any such appeal **A33–93** has been determined, no measures of enforcement may be taken other than protective measures taken against the property of the party against whom enforcement is sought.

The decision authorising enforcement shall carry with it the power to proceed to any such protective measures.

Article 40

1. If the application for enforcement is refused, the applicant may appeal: **A33–94**
   — in Belgium, to the cour d'appel or hof van beroep,
   — in Denmark, to the landsret,
   — in the Federal Republic of Germany, to the Oberlandesgericht,
   — in Greece, to the Εφετειο,
   — in Spain, to the Audiencia Provincial,
   — in France, to the court d'appel,
   — in Ireland, to the High Court,
   — in Italy, to the corte d'appello,
   — in Luxembourg, to the Cour supérieure de justice sitting as a court of civil appeal,
   — in the Netherlands, to the gerechtshof,
   — in Portugal, to the Tribunal da Relação,
   — in the United Kingdom,
     (a) in England and Wales, to the High Court of Justice, or in the case of a maintenance judgment to the Magistrates' Court;
     (b) in Scotland, to the Court of Session, or in the case of a maintenance judgment to the Sheriff Court,
     (c) in Northern Ireland, to the High Court of Justice, or in the case of a maintenance judgment to the Magistrates' Court.

2. The party against whom enforcement is sought shall be summoned to appear before the appellate court. If he fails to appear, the provisions of the second and third paragraphs of Article 20 shall apply even where he is not domiciled in any of the Contracting States.

GENERAL NOTE

Lugano Convention

The list of courts to which the applicant may appeal is supplemented in the Lugano **A33–95** Convention with courts of the additional Contracting States.

Article 41

A judgment given on an appeal provided for in Article 40 may be contested only: **A33–96**
   — in Belgium, Greece, Spain, France, Italy, Luxembourg and in the Netherlands, by an appeal in cassation,
   — in Denmark, by an appeal to the højesteret, with the leave of the Minister of Justice,
   — in the Federal Republic of Germany, by a Rechtsbeschwerde,
   — in Ireland, by an appeal on a point of law to the Supreme Court,
   — in Portugal, by an appeal on a point of law,
   — in the United Kingdom, by a single further appeal on a point of law.

GENERAL NOTE

Lugano Convention

The list of courts to which a judgment on appeal may be contested is supplemented in the **A33–97** Lugano Convention with courts of the additional Contracting States.

Article 42

A33–98 Where a foreign judgment has been given in respect of several matters and enforcement cannot be authorised for all of them, the court shall authorise the enforcement for one or more of them.

An applicant may request partial enforcement of a judgment.

Article 43

A33–99 A foreign judgment which orders a periodic payment by way of a penalty shall be enforceable in the State in which enforcement is sought only if the amount of the payment has been finally determined by the courts of the State of origin.

Article 44

A33–100 An applicant who, in the State of origin has benefited from complete or partial legal aid or exemption from costs or expenses, shall be entitled, in the procedures provided for in Articles 32 to 35, to benefit from the most favourable legal aid or the most extensive exemption from costs or expenses provided for by the law of the State addressed.

However, an applicant who requests the enforcement of a decision given by an administrative authority in Denmark in respect of a maintenance order may, in the State addressed, claim the benefits referred to in the first paragraph if he presents a statement from the Danish Ministry of Justice to the effect that he fulfils the economic requirements to qualify for the grant of complete or partial legal aid or exemption from costs or expenses.

General Note

Lugano Convention

A33–101 The text of the second paragraph of Art. 44 differs and is set out below:

However, an applicant who requests the enforcement of a decision given by an administrative authority in Denmark or in Iceland in respect of a maintenance order may, in the State addressed, claim the benefits referred to in the first paragraph if he presents a statement from, respectively, the Danish Ministry of Justice or the Icelandic Ministry of Justice to the effect that he fulfils the economic requirements to qualify for the grant of complete or partial legal aid or exemption from costs or expenses.

Article 45

A33–102 No security, bond or deposit, however described, shall be required of a party who in one Contracting State applies for enforcement of a judgment given in another Contracting State on the ground that he is a foreign national or that he is not domiciled or resident in the State in which enforcement is sought.

Section 3

Common Provision

Article 46

A33–103 A party seeking recognition or applying for enforcement of a judgment shall produce:
1. a copy of the judgment which satisfies the conditions necessary to establish its authenticity;
2. in the case of a judgment given in default, the original or a certified true copy of the document which establishes that the party in default was served with the document instituting the proceedings or with an equivalent document.

Article 47

A33–104 A party applying for enforcement shall also produce:
1. documents which establish that, according to the law of the State of origin the judgment is enforceable and has been served;
2. where appropriate, a document showing that the applicant is in receipt of legal aid in the State of origin.

Article 48

If the documents specified in point 2 of Articles 46 and 47 are not produced, the court **A33–105** may specify a time for their production, accept equivalent documents or, if it considers that it has sufficient information before it, dispense with their production.

If the court so requires, a translation of the documents shall be produced; the translation shall be certified by a person qualified to do so in one of the Contracting States.

Article 49

No legalisation or other similar formality shall be required in respect of the documents **A33–106** referred to in Articles 46 or 47 or the second paragraph of Article 48, or in respect of a document appointing a representative *ad litem*.

TITLE IV

AUTHENTIC INSTRUMENTS AND COURT SETTLEMENTS

Article 50

A document which has been formally drawn up or registered as an authentic **A33–107** instrument and is enforceable in one Contracting State shall, in another Contracting State, be declared enforceable there, on application made in accordance with the procedures provided for in Article 31 *et seq.* The application may be refused only if enforcement of the instrument is contrary to public policy in the State addressed.

The instrument produced must satisfy the conditions necessary to establish its authenticity in the State of origin.

The provisions of Section 3 of Title III shall apply as appropriate.

Article 51

A settlement which has been approved by a court in the course of proceedings and is **A33–108** enforceable in the State in which it was concluded shall be enforceable in the State addressed under the same conditions as authentic instruments.

TITLE V

GENERAL PROVISIONS

Article 52

In order to determine whether a party is domiciled in the Contracting State whose **A33–109** courts are seised of a matter, the court shall apply its internal law.

If a party is not domiciled in the State whose courts are seised of the matter, then, in order to determine whether the party is domiciled in another Contracting State, the court shall apply the law of that State.

GENERAL NOTE

A third paragraph in this Article was omitted by the Civil Jurisdiction and Judgments **A33–110** Act 1982 (Amendment) Order 1990 at the time of the revision of the 1968 Convention upon the accession of Spain and Portugal. The opportunity was taken to make this modification in the light of experience.

Article 53

For the purposes of this Convention, the seat of a company or other legal person or **A33–111** association of natural or legal persons shall be treated as its domicile. However, in order to determine that seat, the court shall apply its rules of private international law.

In order to determine whether a trust is domiciled in the Contracting State whose courts are seised of the matter, the court shall apply its rules of private international law.

TITLE VI

TRANSITIONAL PROVISIONS

Article 54

The provisions of the Convention shall apply only to legal proceedings instituted and to **A33–112** documents formally drawn up or registered as authentic instruments after its entry into force in the State of origin and, where recognition or enforcement of a judgment or authentic instruments is sought, in the State addressed.

However, judgments given after the date of entry into force of this Convention between the State of origin and the State addressed in proceedings instituted before that date shall be recognised and enforced in accordance with the provisions of Title III if jurisdiction was founded upon rules which accorded with those provided for either in Title II of this Convention or in a convention concluded between the State of origin and the State addressed which was in force when the proceedings were instituted.

If the parties to a dispute concerning a contract had agreed in writing before 1 June 1988 for Ireland or before 1 January 1987 for the United Kingdom that the contract was to be governed by the law of Ireland or of a part of the United Kingdom, the courts of Ireland or of that part of the United Kingdom shall retain the right to exercise jurisdiction in the dispute.

Article 54a

A33–113   For a period of three years from 1 November 1986 for Denmark and from 1 June 1988 for Ireland, jurisdiction in maritime matters shall be determined in these States not only in accordance with the provisions of Title II, but also in accordance with the provisions of paragraphs 1 to 6 following. However, upon the entry into force of the International Convention relating to the arrest of sea-going ships, signed at Brussels on 10 May 1952, for one of these States, these provisions shall cease to have effect for that State.

1. A person who is domiciled in a Contracting State may be sued in the courts for one of the States mentioned above in respect of a maritime claim if the ship to which the claim relates or any other ship owned by him has been arrested by judicial process within the territory of the latter State to secure the claim, or could have been so arrested there but bail or other security has been given, and either:
   (a) the claimant is domiciled in the latter State; or
   (b) the claim arose in the latter State; or
   (c) the claim concerns the voyage during which the arrest was made or could have been made; or
   (d) the claim arises out of a collision or out of damage caused by a ship to another ship or to goods or persons on board either ship, either by the execution or non-execution of a manoeuvre or by the non-observance of regulations; or
   (e) the claim is for salvage; or
   (f) the claim is in respect of a mortgage or hypothecation of the ship arrested.

2. A claimant may arrest either the particular ship to which the maritime claim relates, or any other ship which is owned by the person who was, at the time when the maritime claim arose, the owner of the particular ship. However, only the particular ship to which the maritime claim relates may be arrested in respect of the maritime claims set out in (5) (o), (p) or (q) of this Article.

3. Ships shall be deemed to be in the same ownership when all the shares therein are owned by the same person or persons.

4. When in the case of a charter by demise of a ship the charterer alone is liable in respect of a maritime claim relating to that ship, the claimant may arrest that ship or any other ship owned by the charterer, but no other ship owned by the owner may be arrested in respect of such claim. The same shall apply to any case in which a person other than the owner of a ship is liable in respect of a maritime claim relating to that ship.

5. The expression "maritime claim" means a claim arising out of one or more of the following:
   (a) damage caused by any ship either in collision or otherwise;
   (b) loss of life or personal injury caused by any ship or occurring in connection with the operation on any ship;
   (c) salvage;
   (d) agreement relating to the use or hire of any ship whether by charterparty or otherwise;
   (e) agreement relating to the carriage of goods in any ship whether by charterparty or otherwise;
   (f) loss of or damage to goods including baggage carried in any ship;
   (g) general average;
   (h) bottomry;
   (i) towage;

   (j) pilotage;
  (k) goods or materials wherever supplied to a ship for her operation or maintenance;
  (l) construction, repair or equipment of any ship or dock charges and dues;
 (m) wages of masters, officers or crew;
  (n) master's disbursements, including disbursements made by shippers, charterers or agents on behalf of a ship or her owner;
  (o) dispute as to the title to or ownership of any ship;
  (p) disputes between co-owners of any ship as to the ownership, possession, employment or earnings of that ship;
  (q) the mortgage of hypothecation of any ship.

6. In Denmark, the expression "arrest" shall be deemed as regards the maritime claims referred to in 5(o) and (p) of this Article, to include a "forbud", where that is the only procedure allowed in respect of such a claim under Articles 646 to 653 of the law on civil procedure (lov om rettens pleje).

TITLE VII

RELATIONSHIP TO OTHER CONVENTIONS

Article 55

Subject to the provisions of the second paragraph of Article 54, the Article 56, this **A33–114** Convention shall, for the States which are parties to it, supersede the following conventions concluded between two or more of them.

— the Convention between Belgium and France on jurisdiction and the validity and enforcement of judgments, arbitration awards and authentic instruments, signed at Paris on 8th July, 1899,

— the Convention between Belgium and the Netherlands on jurisdiction, bankruptcy, and the validity and enforcement of judgments, arbitration awards and authentic instruments, signed at Brussels on 28th March, 1925,

— the Convention between France and Italy on the enforcement of judgments in civil and commercial matters, signed at Rome on 3rd June, 1930,

— the Convention between the United Kingdom and the French Republic providing for the reciprocal enforcement of judgments in civil and commercial matters, with Protocol, signed at Paris on 18th January, 1934,

— the Convention between the United Kingdom and the Kingdom of Belgium, providing for the reciprocal enforcement of judgments in civil and commercial matters, with Protocol, signed at Brussels on 2nd May, 1934,

— the Convention between Germany and Italy on the recognition and enforcement of judgments in civil and commercial matters, signed at Rome on 9th March, 1936,

— the Convention between the Federal Republic of Germany and the Kingdom of Belgium on the mutual recognition and enforcement of judgments, arbitration awards and authentic instruments in civil and commercial matters, signed at Bonn on 30th June, 1958,

— the Convention between the Kingdom of the Netherlands and the Italian Republic on the recognition and enforcement of judgments in civil and commercial matters, signed at Rome on 17th April, 1959,

— the Convention between the United Kingdom and the Federal Republic of Germany for the reciprocal recognition and enforcement of judgments in civil and commercial matters, signed at Bonn on 15th July, 1960,

— the Convention between the Kingdom of Greece and the Federal Republic of Germany for the reciprocal recognition and enforcement of judgments, settlements and authentic instruments in civil and commercial matters, signed in Athens on 4th November, 1961,

— the Convention between the Kingdom of Belgium and the Italian Republic on the recognition and enforcement of judgments and other enforceable instruments in civil and commercial matters, signed at Rome on 6th April, 1962,

— the Convention between the Kingdom of the Netherlands and the Federal Republic of Germany on the mutual recognition and enforcement of judgments and other enforceable instruments in civil and commercial matters, signed at The Hague on 30th August, 1962,

— the Convention between the United Kingdom and the Republic of Italy for the reciprocal recognition and enforcement of judgments in civil and commercial

1487

matters, signed at Rome on 7th February, 1964, with amending Protocol signed at Rome on 14th July, 1970,

— the Convention between the United Kingdom and the Kingdom of the Netherlands providing for the reciprocal recognition and enforcement of judgments in civil matters, signed at The Hague on 17th November, 1967,

— the Convention between Spain and France on the recognition and enforcement of judgment and arbitration awards in civil and commercial matters, signed at Paris on 28th May, 1969,

— the Convention between Spain and Italy regarding legal aid and the recognition and enforcement of judgments in civil and commercial matters, signed at Madrid on 22nd May, 1973,

— the Convention between Spain and the Federal Republic of Germany on the recognition and enforcement of judgments, settlements and enforceable authentic instruments in civil and commercial matters, signed at Bonn on 14th November, 1983.

and, in so far as it is in force:

— the Treaty between Belgium, the Netherlands and Luxembourg on jurisdiction, bankruptcy, and the validity and enforcement of judgments, arbitration awards and authentic instruments, signed at Brussels on 24th November, 1961.

Article 56

A33–115   The Treaty and the conventions referred to in Article 55 shall continue to have effect in relation to matters to which this Convention does not apply.

They shall continue to have effect in respect of judgments given and documents formally drawn up or registered as authentic instruments before the entry into force of this Convention.

Article 57

A33–116   1. This Convention shall not affect any conventions to which the Contracting States are or will be parties and which in relation to particular matters, govern jurisdiction or the recognition or enforcement of judgments.

2. With a view to its uniform interpretation, paragraph 1 shall be applied in the following manner:

(a) this Convention shall not prevent a court of a Contracting State which is a party to a convention on a particular matter from assuming jurisdiction in accordance with that Convention, even where the defendant is domiciled in another Contracting State which is not a party to that Convention. The court hearing the action shall, in any event, apply Article 20 of this Convention;

(b) judgments given in a Contracting State by a court in the exercise of jurisdiction provided for in a convention on a particular matter shall be recognised and enforced in the other Contracting State in accordance with this Convention.

Where a convention on a particular matter to which both the State of origin and the State addressed are parties lays down conditions for the recognition or enforcement of judgments, those conditions shall apply. In any event, the provisions of this Convention which concern the procedure for recognition and enforcement of judgments may be applied.

3. This Convention shall not affect the application of provisions which, in relation to particular matters, govern jurisdiction or the recognition or enforcement of judgments and which are or will be contained in acts of the institutions of the European Communities or in national laws harmonised in implementation of such acts.

GENERAL NOTE

Lis Pendens

A33–117   When a specialised convention contains certain rules of jurisdiction but no provision as to *lis pendens*, Arts 21 and 22 of the Judgments Convention applies. The specialised convention will preclude the application of the Judgments Convention only in relation to questions governed by the specialised convention (*The Tatry* [1995] I.L.Pr. 81, E.C. Case No. 406/92).

Article 58

A33–118   Until such time as the Convention on jurisdiction and the enforcement of judgments in civil and commercial matters, signed at Lugano on 16th September, 1988, takes effect with regard to France and the Swiss Confederation, this Convention shall not affect the rights granted to Swiss nationals by the Convention between France and the Swiss Confederation on jurisdiction and enforcement of judgments in civil matters, signed at Paris on 15th June, 1869.

Article 59

This Convention shall not prevent a Contracting State from assuming, in a convention on the recognition and enforcement of judgments, an obligation towards a third State not to recognise judgments given in other Contracting States against defendants domiciled or habitually resident in the third State where, in cases provided for in Article 4, the judgment could only be founded on a ground of jurisdiction specified in the second paragraph of Article 3. **A33–119**

However, a Contracting State may not assume an obligation towards a third State not to recognise a judgment given in another Contracting State by a court basing its jurisdiction on the presence within that State of property belonging to the defendant, or the seizure by the plaintiff of property situated there:

1. if the action is brought to assert or declare proprietary or possessory rights in that property, seeks to obtain authority to dispose of it, or arises from another issue relating to such property, or,
2. if the property constitutes the security for a debt which is the subject-matter of the action.

Article 60

Deleted. **A33–120**

Articles 61–63

* * * *

Article 64

The Secretary-General of the Council of the European Communities shall notify the signatory State of: **A33–121**

  (a) the deposit of each instrument of ratification;
  (b) the date of entry into force of this Convention;
  (c) ...;
  (d) any declaration received pursuant to Article IV of the Protocol;
  (e) any communication made pursuant to Article VI of the Protocol.

Article 65

The Protocol annexed to this Convention by common accord of the Contracting States shall form an integral part thereof. **A33–122**

Article 66

This Convention is concluded for an unlimited period. **A33–123**

Article 67

Any Contracting State may request the revision of this Convention. In this event, a revision conference shall be convened by the President of the Council of the European Communities. **A33–124**

Article 68

* * * *

Section 2(2)(b)   SCHEDULE 2

TEXT OF 1971 PROTOCOL, AS AMENDED

GENERAL NOTE

The text set out below is the version of the 1971 Protocol inserted in Sched. 2 of the 1982 Act by the Civil Jurisdiction and Judgments Act 1982 (Amendment) Order 1990 (S.I. 1990 No. 2591) Art. 12(2), Sched. 2, following upon the accession to the European Community **A33–125** of Spain and Portugal. It has the force of law in the United Kingdom, see s.3(1) of the 1982 Act. Section 3(3) of the 1982 Act, as amended, states that the report by Mr. P. Jenard on the 1971 Protocol may be considered in ascertaining the meaning or effect of any provision in the 1971 Protocol and "shall be given such weight as is appropriate in the circumstances". This report was published in the *Official Journal of the European Communities* (O.J.) 1979, C.59) and is re-printed in various European law texts.

Article 1

A33–126 The Court of Justice of the European Communities shall have jurisdiction to give rulings on the interpretation of the Convention on jurisdiction and the enforcement of judgments in civil and commercial matters and of the Protocol annexed to that Convention, signed at Brussels on 27th September 1968, and also on the interpretation of the present Protocol...

Article 2

A33–127 The following courts may request the Court of Justice to give preliminary rulings on questions of interpretation—
    1. —... ...
        — in the United Kingdom: the House of Lords and courts to which application has been made under the second paragraph of Article 37 or under Article 41 of the Convention.
    2. The courts of the Contracting States when they are sitting in an appellate capacity.
    3. In the case provided for in Article 37 of the Convention, the courts referred to in that Article.

Articles 3

A33–128 1. Where a question of interpretation of the Convention or of one of the other instruments referred to in Article 1 is raised in a case pending before one of the courts listed in point 1 of Article 2, that court shall, if it considers that a decision on the question is necessary to enable it to give judgment, request the Court of Justice to give a ruling thereon.
    2. Where such a question is raised before any court referred to in point 2 or 3 of Article 2, that court may, under the conditions laid down in paragraph 1, request the Court of Justice to give a ruling thereon.

* * * * *

Section 16   SCHEDULE 4

TITLE II OF 1968 CONVENTION AS MODIFIED FOR ALLOCATION OF JURISDICTION WITHIN U.K.

TITLE II

JURISDICTION

SECTION I

GENERAL PROVISIONS

Article 2

A33–129 Subject to the provisions of this **Title**, persons domiciled in a **part of the United Kingdom** shall ... be sued in the courts of that **part**.

* * * *

Article 3

A33–130 Persons domiciled in a **part of the United Kingdom** may be sued in the courts of another **part of the United Kingdom** only by virtue of the rules set out in Sections **2, 4, 5 and 6** of this Title.

* * * * *

Section 2

Special Jurisdiction

Article 5

A person domiciled **in a part of the United Kingdom** may, in another **part of the** **A33–131** United Kingdom, be sued:

(1) in matters relating to a contract, in the courts for the place of performance of the obligation in question, in matters relating to individual contracts of employment, this place is that where the employee habitually carries out his work, or if the employee does not habitually carry out his work in any one country, the employer may also be sued in the courts for the place where the business which engaged the employee was or is now situated;

(2) in matters relating to maintenance, in the courts for the place where the maintenance creditor is domiciled or habitually resident or, if the matter is ancillary to proceedings concerning the status of a person, in the court which, according to its own law, has jurisdiction to entertain those proceedings, unless that jurisdiction is based solely on the nationality of one of the parties;

(3) in matters relating to tort, delict or quasi-delict, in the courts for the place where the harmful event occurred **or in the case of a threatened wrong is likely to occur;**

(4) as regards a civil claim for damages or restitution which is based on an act giving rise to criminal proceedings, in the court seised of those proceedings, to the extent that that court has jurisdiction under its own law to entertain civil proceedings;

(5) as regards a dispute arising out of the operations of a branch, agency or other establishment, in the courts for the place in which the branch, agency or other establishment is situated;

(6) in his capacity as a settlor, trustee or beneficiary of a trust created by the operation of a statute, or by a written instrument, or created orally and evidenced in writing, in the courts of the **part of the United Kingdom** in which the trust is domiciled;

(7) as regards a dispute concerning the payment of remuneration claimed in respect of the salvage of a cargo or freight, in the court under the authority of which the cargo or freight in question

(a) has been arrested to secure such payment, or

(b) could have been so arrested, but bail or other security has been given; provided that this provision shall apply only if it is claimed that the defendant has an interest in the cargo or freight or had such an interest at the time of salvage;

(8) **in proceedings—**

(a) **concerning a debt secured on immovable property; or**

(b) **which are brought to assert, declare or determine proprietary or possessory rights, or rights of security, in or over movable property, or to obtain authority to dispose of movable property,**

in the courts of the part of the United Kingdom in which the property is situated.

Article 5a

Proceedings which have as their object a decision of an organ of a company or other **A33–132** **legal person or of an association of natural or legal persons may, without prejudice to the other provisions of this Title, be brought in the courts of the part of the United Kingdom in which that company, legal person or association has its seat.**

Article 6

A person domiciled in a **part of the United Kingdom** may, **in another part of the** **A33–133** United Kingdom, also be sued:

(1) where he is one of a number of defendants, in the courts for the place where any one of them is domiciled;

(2) as a third party in an action on a warranty or guarantee or in any other third party proceedings, in the court seised of the original proceedings, unless these were instituted solely with the object of removing him from the jurisdiction of the court which would be competent in his case;

(3) on a counterclaim arising from the same contract or facts on which the original claim was based, in the court in which the original claim is pending.

(4) in matters relating to a contract, if the action may be combined with an action against the same defendant in matters relating to right *in rem*, in immovable property, in the court of the **part of the United Kingdom** in which the property is situated.

Article 6a

A33–134   Where by virtue of this **Title** a court of a **part of the United Kingdom** has jurisdiction in actions relating to liability arising from the use or operation of a ship, that court, or any other court substituted for this purpose by the internal law of that **part**, shall also have jurisdiction over claims for limitation of such liability.

* * * *

Section 4

Jurisdiction over Consumer Contracts

Article 13

A33–135   In proceedings concerning a contract concluded by a person for a purpose which can be regarded as being outside his trade or profession, hereinafter called "the consumer", jurisdiction shall be determined by this Section, without prejudice to the provisions of Articles ... 5(5) **and (8)(b), if it is:**

(1) a contract for the sale of goods on instalment credit terms, or

(2) a contract for a loan repayable by instalments, or for any other form of credit, made to finance the sale of goods, or

(3) any other contract for the supply of goods or a contract for the supply of services and ... the consumer took **in the part of the United Kingdom in which · be is domiciled** the steps necessary for the conclusion of the contract.

* * * *

This Section shall not apply to contracts of transport **or insurance.**

Article 14

A33–136   A consumer may bring proceedings against the other party to a contract either in the courts of the **part of the United Kingdom** in which that party is domiciled or in the courts of the **part of the United Kingdom** in which he is himself domiciled.

Proceedings may be brought against a consumer by the other party to the contract only in the courts of the **part of the United Kingdom** in which the consumer is domiciled.

These provisions shall not affect the right to bring a counterclaim in the court in which, in accordance with this Section, the original claim is pending.

Article 15

A33–137   The provisions of this Section may be departed from only by an agreement:

(1) which is entered into after the dispute has arisen, or

(2) which allows the consumer to bring proceedings in courts other than those indicated in this Section, or

(3) which is entered into by the consumer and the other party to the contract, both of whom are at the time of conclusion of the contract domiciled or habitually resident in the same **part of the United Kingdom,** and which confers jurisdiction on the courts of that **part,** provided that such an agreement is not contrary to the law of that **part.**

Section 5

Exclusive Jurisdiction

Article 16

A33–138   The following courts shall have exclusive jurisdiction, regardless of domicile:

(1)   (a) in proceedings which have as their object rights *in rem* in immovable property or tenancies of immovable property, the courts of the part of the United Kingdom in which the property is situated;

        (b) however, in proceedings which have as their object tenancies of immovable property concluded for temporary private use for a maximum period of six consecutive months, the courts of the part of the United Kingdom in which the defendant is domiciled shall also have jurisdiction, provided that the landlord and the tenant are natural persons and are domiciled in the same part of the United Kingdom;

(2) in proceedings which have as their object the validity of the constitution, the nullity or the dissolution of companies or other legal persons or associations of natural or legal persons . . . the courts of the **part of the United Kingdom** in which the company, legal person or association has its seat;

(3) in proceedings which have as their object the validity of entries in public registers, the courts of the **part of the United Kingdom** in which the register is kept;

* * * *

(5) in proceedings concerned with the enforcement of judgments, the courts of the **part of the United Kingdom** in which the judgment has been or is to be enforced.

SECTION 6

PROROGATION OF JURISDICTION

Article 17

If the parties . . . have agreed that a court or the courts of a **part of the United Kingdom**   **A33–139** are to have jurisdiction to settle any disputes which have arisen or which may arise in connection with a particular legal relationship, **and, apart from this Schedule, the agreement would be effective to confer jurisdiction under the law of that part,** that court or those courts shall have . . . jurisdiction . . .

The court or courts of a **part of the United Kingdom** on which a trust instrument has conferred jurisdiction shall have . . . jurisdiction in any proceedings brought against a settlor, trustee or beneficiary, if relations between these persons or their rights or obligations under the trust are involved.

Agreements or provisions of a trust instrument conferring jurisdiction shall have no legal force if they are contrary to the provisions of Article . . . 15, or if the courts whose jurisdiction they purport to exclude have exclusive jurisdiction by virtue of Article 16.

* * * *

In matters relating to individual contracts of employment an agreement conferring jurisdiction shall have legal force only if it is entered into after the dispute has arisen or if the employee invokes it to seise courts other than those for the defendant's domicile or those specified in Article 5(1).

Article 18

Apart from jurisdiction derived from other provisions of this **Title**, a court of **a part of**   **A33–140** **the United Kingdom** before whom a defendant enters an appearance shall have jurisdiction. This rule shall not apply where appearance was entered solely to contest the jurisdiction, or where another court has exclusive jurisdiction by virtue of Article 16.

SECTION 7

EXAMINATION AS TO JURISDICTION AND ADMISSIBILITY

Article 19

Where a court of a **part of the United Kingdom** is seised of a claim which is principally   **A33–141** concerned with a matter over which the courts of another **part of the United Kingdom** have exclusive jurisdiction by virtue of Article 16, it shall declare of its own motion that it has no jurisdiction.

1493

Article 20

A33–142   Where a defendant domiciled in one **part of the United Kingdom** is sued in a court of another **part of the United Kingdom** and does not enter an appearance, the court shall declare of its own motion that it has no jurisdiction unless its jurisdiction is derived from the provisions of this **Title**.

The court shall stay the proceedings so long as it is not shown that the defendant has been able to receive the document instituting the proceedings or an equivalent document in sufficient time to enable him to arrange for his defence, or that all necessary steps have been taken to this end.

* * * *

SECTION 9

PROVISIONAL, INCLUDING PROTECTIVE, MEASURES

Article 24

A33–143   Application may be made to the courts of a **part of the United Kingdom** for such provisional, including protective, measures as may be available under the law of that Part, even if, under this Title, the courts of another **part of the United Kingdom** have jurisdiction as to the substance of the matter.

GENERAL NOTE

A33–144   Amended by S.I. 1993 No. 603.

Civil Jurisdiction And Judgments Act 1991

(1991 c.12)

An Act to give effect to the Convention on jurisdiction and the enforcement of judgments in civil and commercial matters, including the Protocols annexed thereto, opened for signature at Lugano on 16th September 1988; and for purposes connected therewith.

[9TH MAY 1991]

BE IT ENACTED by the Queen's most Excellent Majesty, by and with the advice and consent of the Lords Spiritual and Temporal, and Commons, in this present Parliament assembled, and by the authority of the same, as follows:—

Implementation and interpretation of the Lugano Convention

A33–145   1.—(1) The Civil Jurisdiction and Judgments Act 1982 (in this Act referred to as "the 1982 Act") shall have effect with the insertion of the following after section 3—

The Lugano Convention to have the force of law

"**3A.**—(1) The Lugano Convention shall have the force of law in the United Kingdom, and judicial notice shall be taken of it.

(2) For convenience of reference there is set out in Schedule 3C the English text of the Lugano Convention.

Interpretation of the Lugano Convention

3B.—(1) In determining any question as to the meaning or effect of a provision of the Lugano Convention, a court in the United Kingdom shall, in accordance with Protocol No. 2 to that Convention, take account of any principles laid down in any relevant decision delivered by a court of any other Lugano Contracting State concerning provisions of the Convention.

1494

(2) Without prejudice to any practice of the courts as to the matters which may be considered apart from this section, the report on the Lugano Convention by Mr P. Jenard and Mr G. Möller (which is reproduced in the Official Journal of the Communities of 28th July 1990) may be considered in ascertaining the meaning or effect of any provision of the Convention and shall be given such weight as is appropriate in the circumstances."

(2) In section 9 of that Act, after subsection (1) (which, as amended, will govern the relationship between other conventions and the 1968 and Lugano Conventions) there shall be inserted—

"(1A) Any question arising as to whether it is the Lugano Convention or any of the Brussels Conventions which applies in the circumstances of a particular case falls to be determined in accordance with the provisions of Article 54B of the Lugano Convention."

(3) After Schedule 3B to that Act there shall be inserted the Schedule 3C set out in Schedule 1 to this Act.

Interpretation of the 1982 Act

2.—(1) Section 1 of the 1982 Act (interpretation of references to the Conventions and Contracting States) shall be amended in accordance with the following provisions of this section. **A33–146**

(2) In subsection (1), in the definition of "the Conventions", for the words "the Conventions" there shall be substituted the words "the Brussels Conventions".

(3) At the end of that subsection there shall be added—

"the Lugano Convention" means the Convention on jurisdiction and the enforcement of judgments in civil and commercial matters (including the Protocols annexed to that Convention) opened for signature at Lugano on 16th September 1988 and signed by the United Kingdom on 18th September 1989."

(4) In subsection (2), for paragraph (b) (citation of Articles) there shall be substituted—

"(b) any reference in any provision to a numbered Article without more is a reference—

(i) to the Article so numbered of the 1968 Convention, in so far as the provision applies in relation to that Convention, and

(ii) to the Article so numbered of the Lugano Convention, in so far as the provision applies in relation to that Convention,

and any reference to a sub-division of a numbered Article shall be construed accordingly."

(5) In subsection (3) (definition of "Contracting State") for the words "In this Act 'Contracting State' means—" there shall be substituted the words—

"In this Act—

'Contracting State', without more, in any provision means—

(a) in the application of the provision in relation to the Brussels Conventions, a Brussels Contracting State; and

(b) in the application of the provision in relation to the Lugano Convention, a Lugano Contracting State;

'Brussels Contracting State' means—".

(6) At the end of that subsection there shall be added—

"'Lugano Contracting State' means one of the original parties to the Lugano Convention, that is to say—Austria, Belgium, Denmark, Finland, France, the Republic of Germany, the Hellenic Republic, Iceland, the Republic of Ireland, Italy, Luxembourg, the Netherlands, Norway, Portugal, Spain, Sweden, Switzerland and the United Kingdom, being a State in relation to which the Convention has taken effect in accordance with paragraph 3 or 4 of Article 61."

Other amendments of the 1982 Act

A33–147   3. The 1982 Act shall have effect with the amendments specified in Schedule 2 to this Act, which are either consequential on the amendments made by sections 1 and 2 above or otherwise for the purpose of implementing the Lugano Convention.

Application to the Crown

A33–148   4. The amendments of the 1982 Act made by this Act bind the Crown in accordance with the provisions of section 51 of that Act.

Short title, interpretation, commencement and extent

A33–149   5.—(1) This Act may be cited as the Civil Jurisdiction and Judgments Act 1991.

(2) In this Act—

"the 1982 Act" means the Civil Juridiction and Judgments Act 1982;

"the Lugano Convention" has the same meaning as it has in the 1982 Act by virtue of section 2(3) above.

(3) This Act shall come into force on such day as the Lord Chancellor and the Lord Advocate may appoint in an order made by statutory instrument.

(4) This Act extends to Northern Ireland.

Section 1(3)   **SCHEDULES**

SCHEDULE 1

Schedule to be inserted as Schedule 3C to the 1982 Act

"SCHEDULE 3C   Section 3A(2)

Text of the Lugano Convention: Convention on Jurisdiction and the enforcement of Judgments in Civil and Commercial Matters

Arrangement of Provisions

1496

TITLE VIII. FINAL PROVISIONS (Articles 60–68)
PROTOCOL NO. 1—ON CERTAIN QUESTIONS OF JURISDICTION, PROCEDURE AND ENFORCEMENT
PROTOCOL NO. 2—ON THE UNIFORM INTERPRETATION OF THE CONVENTION
PROTOCOL NO. 3—ON THE APPLICATION OF ARTICLE 57

PREAMBLE

The High Contracting Parties to this Convention, Anxious to strengthen in their **A33–151** territories the legal protection of persons therein established, Considering that it is necessary for this purpose to determine the international jurisdiction of their courts, to facilitate recognition and to introduce an expeditious procedure for securing the enforcement of judgments, authentic instruments and court settlements, Aware of the links between them, which have been sanctioned in the economic field by the free trade agreements concluded between the European Economic Community and the States members of the European Free Trade Association, Taking into account the Brussels Convention of 27 September 1968 on jurisdiction and the enforcement of judgments in civil and commercial matters, as amended by the Accession Conventions under the successive enlargements of the European Communities, Persuaded that the extension of the principles of that Convention to the States parties to this instrument will strengthen legal and economic co-operation in Europe, Desiring to ensure as uniform an interpretation as possible of this instrument, Have in this spirit decided to conclude this Convention and Have agreed as follows:

TITLE 1

SCOPE

Article 1

This Convention shall apply in civil and commercial matters whatever the nature of the **A33–152** court or tribunal. It shall not extend, in particular, to revenue, customs or administrative matters.
The Convention shall not apply to:
1. the status or legal capacity of natural persons, rights in property arising out of a matrimonial relationship, wills and succession;
2. bankruptcy, proceedings relating to the winding-up of insolvent companies or other legal persons, judicial arrangements, compositions and analogous proceedings;
3. social security;
4. arbitration.

TITLE II

JURISDICTION

SECTION 1

GENERAL PROVISIONS

Article 2

Subject to the provisions of this Convention, persons domiciled in a Contracting State **A33–153** shall, whatever their nationality, be sued in the courts of that State.
Persons who are not nationals of the State in which they are domiciled shall be governed by the rules of jurisdiction applicable to nationals of that State.

Article 3

Persons domiciled in a Contracting State may be sued in the courts of another **A33–154** Contracting State only by virute of the rules set out in Sections 2 to 6 of this Title.
In particular the following provisions shall not be applicable as against them:
— in Belgium: Article 15 of the civil code (Code civil—Burgerlijk Wetboek) and Article 638 of the judicial code (Code judiciaire—Gerechtelijk Wetboek),

1497

— in Denmark: Article 246(2) and (3) of the law on civil procedure (Lov om rettens pleje),
— in the Federal Republic of Germany: Article 23 of the code of civil procedure (Zivilprozeßordnung),
— in Greece: Article 40 of the code of civil procedure (Κωδικαζ πολιτικηζ δικονομιαζ),
— in France: Articles 14 and 15 of the civil code (Code civil),
— in Ireland: the rules which enable jurisdiction to be founded on the document instituting the proceedings having been served on the defendant during his temporary presence in Ireland,
— in Iceland: Article 77 of the Civil Proceedings Act (lög um megðfergð einkamála í héraði),
— in Italy: Articles 2 and 4, Nos 1 and 2 of the code of civil procedure (Codice di procedura civile),
— in Luxembourg: Articles 14 and 15 of the civil code (Code civil),
— in the Netherlands: Articles 126(3) and 127 of the code of civil procedure (Wetboek van Burgerlijke Rechtsvordering),
— in Norway: Section 32 of the Civil Proceedings Act (tvistemålsloven),
— in Austria: Article 99 of the Law on Court Jurisdiction (Jurisdiktionsnorm),
— in Portugal: Articles 65(1)(c), 65(2) and 65A(c) of the code of civil procedure (Código de Processo Civil) and Article 11 of the code of labour procedure (Código de Processo de Trabalho),
— in Switzerland: le for du lieu du séquestre/Gerichtsstand des Arrestortes/foro del luogo del sequestro within the meaning of Article 4 of the loi fédérale sur le droit international privé/Bundesgesetz über das international Privatrecht/legge federale sul diritto internazionale privato,
— in Finland: the second, third and fourth sentences of Section 1 of Chapter 10 of the Code of Judicial Procedure (oikeudenkäymiskaari/rättegångsbalken),
— in Sweden: the first sentence of Section 3 Procedure of Chapter 10 of the Code of Judicial (Rättegångsbalken),
— in the United Kingdom: the rules which enable jurisdiction to be founded on:
  (a) the document instituting the proceedings having been served on the defendant during his temporary presence in the United Kingdom; or
  (b) the presence within the United Kingdom of property belonging to the defendant; or
  (c) the seizure by the plaintiff of property situated in the United Kingdom.

Article 4

A33–155 If the defendant is not domiciled in a Contracting State, the jurisdiction of the courts of each Contracting State shall, subject to the provisions of Article 16, be determined by the law of that State.
As against such a defendant, any person domiciled in a Contracting State may, whatever his nationality, avail himself in that State of the rules of jurisdiction there in force, and in particular those specified in the second paragraph of Article 3, in the same way as the nationals of that State.

SECTION 2

SPECIAL JURISDICTION

Article 5

A33–156 A person domiciled in a Contracting State may, in another Contracting State, be sued:
  1. in matters relating to a contract, in the courts for the place of performance of the obligation in question; in matters relating to individual contracts of employment, this place is that where the employee habitually carries out his work, or if the employee does not habitually carry out his work in any one country, this place shall be the place of business through which he was engaged;
  2. in matters relating to maintenance, in the courts for the place where the maintenance creditor is domiciled or habitually resident or, if the matter is ancillary to proceedings concerning the status of a person, in the court which, according to its own law, has jurisdiction to entertain those proceedings, unless that jurisdiction is based solely on the nationality of one of the parties;

3. in matters relating to tort, delict or quasi-delict, in the courts for the place where the harmful event occurred;
4. as regards a civil claim for damages or restitution which is based on an act giving rise to criminal proceedings, in the court seised of those proceedings, to the extent that that court has jurisdiction under its own law to entertain civil proceedings;
5. as regards a dispute arising out of the operations of a branch, agency or other establishment, in the courts for the place in which the branch, agency or other establishment is situated;
6. in his capacity as settlor, trustee or beneficiary of a trust created by the operation of a statute, or by a written instrument, or created orally and evidenced in writing, in the courts of the Contracting State in which the trust is domiciled;
7. as regards a dispute concerning the payment of remuneration claimed in respect of the salvage of a cargo or freight, in the court under the authority of which the cargo or freight in question:
    (a) has been arrested to secure such payment,
    or
    (b) could have been so arrested, but bail or other security has been given;
    provided that this provision shall apply only if it is claimed that the defendant has an interest in the cargo or freight or had such an interest at the time of salvage.

Article 6

A person domiciled in a Contracting State may also be sued: **A33–157**
1. where he is one of a number of defendants, in the courts for the place where any one of them is domiciled;
2. as a third party in an action on a warranty or guarantee or in any other third party proceedings, in the court seized of the original proceedings, unless these were instituted solely with the object of removing him from the jurisdiction of the court which would be competent in his case;
3. on a counterclaim arising from the same contract or facts on which the original claim was based, in the court in which the original claim is pending;
4. in matters relating to a contract, if the action may be combined with an action against the same defendant in matters relating to rights *in rem* in immovable property, in the court of the Contracting State in which the property is situated.

Article 6A

Where by virtue of this Convention a court of a Contracting State has jurisdiction in **A33–158** actions relating to liability arising from the use or operation of a ship, that court, or any other court substituted for this purpose by the internal law of that State, shall also have jurisdiction over claims for limitation of such liability.

Section 3

Jurisdiction in Matters Relating to Insurance

Article 7

In matters relating to insurance, jurisdiction shall be determined by this Section, without **A33–159** prejudice to the provisions of Article 4 and 5(5).

Article 8

An insurer domiciled in a Contracting State may be sued: **A33–160**
1. in the courts of the State where he is domiciled; or
2. in another Contracting State, in the courts for the place where the policy-holder is domiciled; or
3. if he is a co-insurer, in the courts of a Contracting State in which proceedings are brought against the leading insurer.
An insurer who is not domiciled in a Contracting State but has a branch, agency or other establishment in one of the Contracting States shall, in disputes arising out of the operations of the branch, agency or establishment, be deemed to be domiciled in that State.

Article 9

A33–161   In respect of liability insurance or insurance of immovable property, the insurer may in addition be sued in the courts for the place where the harmful event occurred. The same applies if movable and immovable property are covered by the same insurance policy and both are adversely affected by the same contingency.

Article 10

A33–162   In respect of liability insurance, the insurer may also, if the law of the court permits it, be joined in proceedings which the injured party has brought against the insured.

The provisions of Articles 7, 8 and 9 shall apply to actions brought by the injured party directly against the insurer, where such direct actions are permitted.

If the law governing such direct actions provides that the policy-holder or the insured may be joined as a party to the action, the same court shall have jurisdiction over them.

Article 11

A33–163   Without prejudice to the provisions of the third paragraph of Article 10, an insurer may bring proceedings only in the courts of the Contracting State in which the defendant is domiciled, irrespective of whether he is the policy-holder, the insured or a beneficiary.

The provisions of this Section shall not affect the right to bring a counterclaim in the court in which, in accordance with this Section, the original claim is pending.

Article 12

A33–164   The provisions of this Section may be departed from only by an agreement on jurisdiction:

1. which is entered into after the dispute has arisen; or
2. which allows the policy-holder, the insured or a beneficiary to bring proceedings in courts other than those indicated in this Section; or
3. which is concluded between a policy-holder and an insurer, both of whom are at the time of conclusion of the contract domiciled or habitually resident in the same Contracting State, and which has the effect of conferring jurisdiction on the courts of that State even if the harmful event were to occur abroad, provided that such an agreement is not contrary to the law of the State; or
4. which is concluded with a policy-holder who is not domiciled in a Contracting State, except in so far as the insurance is compulsory or relates to immovable property in a Contracting State; or
5. which relates to a contract of insurance in so far as it covers one or more of the risks set out in Article 12A.

Article 12A

A33–165   The following are the risks referred to in Article 12(5):

1. any loss of or damage to:
   (a) sea-going ships, installations situated offshore or on the high seas, or aircraft arising from periods which relate to their use for commercial purposes;
   (b) goods in transit other than passengers' baggage where the transit consists of or includes carriage by such ships or aircraft;
2. any liability, other than for bodily injury to passengers or loss of or damage to their baggage;
   (a) arising out of the use or operation of ships, installations or aircraft as referred to in (1)(a) above in so far as the law of the Contracting State in which such aircraft are registered does not prohibit agreements on jurisdiction regarding insurance of such risks;
   (b) for loss or damage caused by goods in transit as described in (1)(b) above;
3. any financial loss connected with the use or operation of ships, installations or aircraft as referred to in (1)(a) above, in particular loss of freight or charter-hire;
4. any risk or interest connected with any of those referred to in (1) to (3) above.

SECTION 4
JURISDICTION OVER CONSUMER CONTRACTS
Article 13

A33–166   In proceedings concerning a contract concluded by a person for a purpose which can be regarded as being outside his trade or profession, hereinafter called "the consumer", jurisdiction shall be determined by this Section, without prejudice to the provisions of Articles 4 and 5(5), if it is:

1. a contract for the sale of goods on instalment credit terms; or
2. a contract for a loan repayable by instalments, or for any other form of credit, made to finance the sale of goods; or
3. any other contract for the supply of goods or a contract for the supply of services, and
    (a) in the State of the consumer's domicile the conclusion of the contract was preceded by a specific invitation addressed to him or by advertising, and
    (b) the consumer took in that State the steps necessary for the conclusion of the contract.

Where a consumer enters into a contract with a party who is not domiciled in a Contracting State but has a branch, agency or other establishment in one of the Contracting States, that party shall, in disputes arising out of the operations of the branch, agency or establishment, be deemed to be domiciled in that State.

This section shall not apply to contracts of transport.

Article 14

A consumer may bring proceedings against the other party to a contract either in the courts of the Contracting State in which that party is domiciled or in the courts of the Contracting State in which he is himself domiciled. **A33–167**

Proceedings may be brought against a consumer by the other party to the contract only in the courts of the Contracting State in which the consumer is domiciled.

These provisions shall not affect the right to bring a counterclaim in the court in which, in accordance with this Section, the original claim is pending.

Article 15

The provisions of this Section may be departed from only by an agreement: **A33–168**
    1. which is entered into after the dispute has arisen; or
    2. which allows the consumer to bring proceedings in courts other than those indicated in this Section; or
    3. which is entered into by the consumer and the other party to the contract, both of whom are at the time of conclusion of the contract domiciled or habitually resident in the same Contracting State, and which confers jurisdiction on the courts of that State, provided that such an agreement is not contrary to the law of that State.

Section 5

Exclusive Jurisdiction

Article 16

The following courts shall have exclusive jurisdiction, regardless of domicile: **A33–169**
    1. (a) in proceedings which have as their object rights *in rem* in immovable property or tenancies of immovable property, the courts of the Contracting State in which the property is situated;
       (b) however, in proceedings which have as their object tenancies of immovable property concluded for temporary private use for a maximum period of six consecutive months, the courts of the Contracting State in which the defendant is domiciled shall also have jurisdiction, provided that the tenant is a natural person and neither party is domiciled in the Contracting State in which the property is situated;
    2. in proceedings which have as their object the validity of the constitution, the nullity or the dissolution of companies or other legal persons or associations or natural or legal persons, or the decisions of their organs, the courts of the Contracting State in which the company, legal person or association has its seat;
    3. in proceedings which have as their object the validity of entries in public registers, the courts of the Contracting State in which the register is kept;
    4. in proceedings concerned with the registration or validity of patents, trade marks, designs, or other similar rights required to be deposited or registered, the courts of the Contracting State in which the deposit or registration has been applied for, has taken place or is under the terms of an international convention deemed to have taken place;

5. in proceedings concerned with the enforcement of judgments, the courts of the Contracting State in which the judgment has been or is to be enforced.

SECTION 6

PROROGATION OF JURISDICTION

Article 17

A33–170   1. If the parties, one or more of whom is domiciled in a Contracting State, have agreed that a court or the courts of a Contracting State are to have jurisdiction to settle any disputes which have arisen or which may arise in connection with a particular legal relationship, that court or those courts shall have exclusive jurisdiction. Such an agreement conferring jurisdiction shall be either:

(a) in writing or evidenced in writing, or
(b) in a form which accords with practices which the parties have established between themselves, or
(c) in international trade or commerce, in a form which accords with a usage of which the parties are or ought to have been aware and which in such trade or commerce is widely known to, and regularly observed by, parties to contracts of the type involved in the particular trade or commerce concerned.

Where such an agreement is concluded by parties, none of whom is domiciled in a Contracting State, the courts of other Contracting States shall have no jurisdiction over their disputes unless the court or courts chosen have declined jurisdiction.

2. The court or courts of a Contracting State on which a trust instrument has conferred jurisdiction shall have exclusive jurisdiction in any proceedings brought against a settlor, trustee or beneficiary, if relations between these persons or their rights or obligations under the trust are involved.

3. Agreements or provisions of a trust instrument conferring jurisdiction shall have no legal force if they are contrary to the provisions of Article 12 or 15, or if the courts whose jurisdiction they purport to exclude have exclusive jurisdiction by virtue of Article 16.

4. If an agreement conferring jurisdiction was concluded for the benefit of only one of the parties, that party shall retain the right to bring proceedings in any other court which has jurisdiction by virtue of this Convention.

5. In matters relating to individual contracts of employment an agreement conferring jurisdiction shall have legal force only if it is entered into after the dispute has arisen.

Article 18

A33–171   Apart from jurisdiction derived from other provisions of this Convention, a court of a Contracting State before whom a defendant enters an appearance shall have jurisdiction. This rule shall not apply where appearance was entered solely to contest the jurisdiction, or where another court has exclusive jurisdiction by virtue of Article 16.

SECTION 7

EXAMINATION AS TO JURISDICTION AND ADMISSIBILITY

Article 19

A33–172   Where a court of a Contracting State is seised of a claim which is principally concerned with a matter over which the courts of another Contracting State have exclusive jurisdiction by virtue of Article 16, it shall declare of its own motion that it has no jurisdiction.

Article 20

A33–173   Where a defendant domiciled in one Contracting State is sued in a court of another Contracting State and does not enter an appearance, the court shall declare of its own motion that it has no jurisdiction unless its jurisdiction is derived from the provisions of this Convention.

The court shall stay the proceedings so long as it is not shown that the defendant has been able to receive the document instituting the proceedings or an equivalent document in sufficient time to enable him to arrange for his defence, or that all necessary steps have been taken to this end.

1502

The provisions of the foregoing paragraph shall be replaced by those of Article 15 of the Hague Convention of 15 November 1965 on the service abroad of judicial and extra judicial documents in civil or commercial matters, if the document insituting the proceedings or notice thereof had to be transmitted abroad in accordance with that Convention.

SECTION 8

LIS PENDENS—RELATED ACTIONS

Article 21

Where proceedings involving the same cause of action and between the same parties are brought in the courts of different Contracting States, any court other than the court first seised shall of its own motion stay its proceedings until such time as the jurisdiction of the court first seised is established. **A33–174**

Where the jurisdiction of the court first seised is established, any court other than the court first seised shall decline jurisdiction in favour of that court.

Article 22

Where related actions are brought in the courts of different Contracting States, any court other than the court first seised may, while the actions are pending at first instance, stay its proceedings. **A33–175**

A court other than the court first seised may also, on the application of one of the parties, decline jurisdiction if the law of that court permits the consolidation of related actions and the court first seised has jurisdiction over both actions.

For the purposes of this Article, actions are deemed to be related where they are so closely connected that it is expedient to hear and determine them together to avoid the risk of irreconcilable judgments resulting from separate proceedings.

Article 23

Where actions come within the exclusive jurisdiction of several courts, any court other than the court first seised shall decline jurisdiction in favour of that court. **A33–176**

SECTION 9

PROVISIONAL, INCLUDING PROTECTIVE, MEASURES

Article 24

Application may be made to the courts of a Contracting State for such provisional, including protective, measures as may be available under the law of that State, even if, under this Convention, the courts of another Contracting State have jurisdiction as to the substance of the matter. **A33–177**

TITLE III

RECOGNITION AND ENFORCEMENT

Article 25

For the purposes of this Convention, "judgment" means any judgment given by a court of tribunal of a Contracting State, whatever the judgment may be called, including a decree, order, decision of writ of execution, as well as the determination of costs or expenses by an officer of the court. **A33–178**

SECTION 1

RECOGNITION

Article 26

A judgment given in a Contracting State shall be recognised in the other Contracting States without any special procedure being required. **A33–179**

Any interested party who raises the recognition of a judgment as the principal issue in a dispute may, in accordance with the procedures provided for in Sections 2 and 3 of this Title, apply for a decision that the judgment be recognised.

If the outcome of proceedings in a court of a Contracting State depends on the determination of an incidental question of recognition that court shall have jurisdiction over that question.

Article 27

A33–180   A judgment shall not be recognised:

1. if such recognition is contrary to public policy in the State in which recognition is sought;
2. where it was given in default of appearance, if the defendant was not duly served with the document which instituted the proceedings or with an equivalent document in sufficient time to enable him to arrange for his defence;
3. if the judgment is irreconcilable with a judgment given in a dispute between the same parties in the State in which recognition is sought;
4. if the court of the State of origin, in order to arrive at its judgment, has decided a preliminary question concerning the status or legal capacity of natural persons, rights in property arising out of a matrimonial relationship, wills or succession in a way that conflicts with a rule of the private international law of the State in which the recognition is sought, unless the same result would have been reached by the application of the rules of private international law of that State;
5. if the judgment is irreconcilable with an earlier judgment given in a non-contracting State involving the same cause of action and between the same parties, provided that this latter judgment fulfils the conditions necessary for its recognition in the State addressed.

Article 28

A33–181   Moreover, a judgment shall not be recognised if it conflicts with the provisions of Sections 3, 4 or 5 of Title II or in a case provided for in Article 59.

A judgment may furthermore be refused recognition in any case provided for in Article 54B(3) or 57(4).

In its examination of the grounds of jurisdiction referred to in the foregoing paragraphs, the court or authority applied to shall be bound by the findings of fact on which the court of the State of origin based its jurisdiction.

Subject to the provisions of the first and second paragraphs, the jurisdiction of the court of the State of origin may not be reviewed; the test of public policy referred to in Article 27(1) may not be applied to the rules relating to jurisdiction.

Article 29

A33–182   Under no circumstances may a foreign judgment be reviewed as to its subtance.

Article 30

A33–183   A court of a Contracting State in which recognition is sought of a judgment given in another Contracting State may stay the proceedings if an ordinary appeal against the judgment has been lodged.

A court of a Contracting State in which recognition is sought of a judgment given in Ireland or the United Kingdom may stay the proceedings if enforcement is suspended in the State of origin by reason of an appeal.

Section 2

Enforcement

Article 31

A33–184   A judgment given in a Contracting State and enforceable in that State shall be enforced in another Contracting State when, on the application of any interested party, it has been declared enforceable there.

However, in the United Kingdom, such a judgment shall be enforced in England and Wales, in Scotland, or in Northern Ireland when, on the application of any interested party, it has been registered for enforcement in that part of the United Kingdom.

Article 32

1. The application shall be submitted: **A33–185**
   — in Belgium, to the tribunal de premiére instance or rechtbank van eerste aanleg,
   — in Denmark, to the byret,
   — in the Federal Republic of Germany, to the presiding judge of a chamber of the Landgericht,
   — in Greece, to the μονομελεζ πρωτοδικειο,
   — in Spain, to the Juzgado de Primera Instancia,
   — in France, to the presiding judge of the tribunal de grande instance,
   — in Ireland, to the High Court,
   — in Iceland, to the héraðsdómari,
   — in Italy, to the corte d'appello,
   — in Luxembourg, to the presiding judge of the tribunal d'arrondissement,
   — in the Netherlands, to the presiding judge of the arrondissementsrechtbank,
   — in Norway, to the herredsrett or byrett as namsrett,
   — in Austria, to the Landesgericht or the Kreisgericht,
   — in Portugal, to the Tribunal Judicial de Círculo,
   — in Switzerland:
     (a) in respect of judgments ordering the payment of a sum of money, to the juge de la mainlevée/Rechtsöffnungsrichter/giudice competente a pronunciare sul rigetto dell'opposizione, within the framework of the procedure governed by Articles 80 and 81 of the loi fédérale sur la poursuite pour dettes et la faillite/Bundesgesetz über Schuldbetreibung und Konkurs/legge federale sulla esecuzione e sul fallimento;
     (b) in respect of judgments ordering a performance other than the payment of a sum of money, to the juge cantonal d'exequatur compétent/ zuständiger kantonaler Vollstreckungsrichter/giudice cantonale competente a pronunciare l'exequatur,
   — in Finalnd, to the ulosotonhaltija/överexekutor,
   — in Sweden, to the Svea hovrätt,
   — in the United Kingdom:
     (a) in England and Wales, to the High Court of Justice, or in the case of a maintenance judgment to the Magistrates' Court on transmission by the Secretary of State;
     (b) in Scotland, to the Court of Session, or in the case of a maintenance judgment to the Sheriff Court on transmission by the Secretary of State;
     (c) in Northern Ireland, to the High Court of Justice, or in the case of a maintenance judgment to the Magistrates' Court on transmission by the Secretary of State.
2. The jurisdiction of local courts shall be determined by reference to the place of domicile of the party against whom enforcement is sought. If he is not domiciled in the State in which enforcement is sought, it shall be determined by reference to the place of enforcement.

Article 33

The procedure for making the application shall be governed by the law of the State in **A33–186** which enforcement is sought.

The applicant must give an address for service of process within the area of jurisdiction of the court applied to. However, if the law of the State in which enforcement is sought does not provide for the furnishing of such an address, the applicant shall appoint a representative *ad litem*.

The documents referred to in Articles 46 and 47 shall be attached to the application.

Article 34

The court applied to shall give its decision without delay; the party against whom **A33–187** enforcement is sought shall not at this stage of the proceedings be entitled to make any submissions on the application.

The application may be refused only for one of the reasons specified in Articles 27 and 28. Under no circumstances may the foreign judgment be reviewed as to its substance.

Article 35

The appropriate officer of the court shall without delay bring the decision given on the **A33–188** application to the notice of the applicant in accordance with the procedure laid down by the law of the State in which enforcement is sought.

Article 36

A33–189   If enforcement is authorised, the party against whom enforcement is sought may appeal against the decision within one month of service thereof.

If that party is domiciled in a Contracting State other than that in which the decision authorising enforcement was given, the time for appealing shall be two months and shall run from the date of service, either on him in person or at his residence. No extension of time may be granted on account of distance.

Article 37

A33–190   1. An appeal against the decision authorising enforcement shall be lodged in accordance with the rules governing procedure in contentious matters:
— in Belgium, with the tribunal de première instance or rechtbank van eerste aanleg,
— in Denmark, with the landsret,
— in the Federal Republic of Germany, with the Oberlandesgericht,
— in Greece, with the ἐφετείο,
— in Spain, with the Audiencia Provincial,
— in France, with the cour d'appel,
— in Ireland, with the High Court,
— in Iceland, with the héraðsdómari,
— in Italy, with the corte d'appello,
— in Luxembourg, with the Cour supérieure de justice sitting as a court of civil appeal,
— in the Netherlands, with the arrondissementsrechtbank,
— in Norway, with the lagmannsrett,
— in Austria, with the Landesgericht or the Kreisgericht,
— in Portugal, with the Tribunal da Relação,
— in Switzerland, with the tribunal cantonal/Kantonsgericht/tribunale cantonale,
— in Finland, with the hovioikeus/hovrätt,
— in Sweden, with the Svea hovrätt,
— in the United Kingdom:
    (a) in England and Wales, with the High Court of Justice, or in the case of a maintenance judgment with the Magistrates' Court;
    (b) in Scotland, with the Court of Session, or in the case of a maintenance judgment with the Sheriff Court;
    (c) in Nothern Ireland, with the High Court of Justice, or in the case of a maintenance judgment with the Magistrates' Court;
2. The judgment given on the appeal may be contested only:
— in Belgium, Greece, Spain, France, Italy, Luxembourg and in the Netherlands, by an appeal in cassation,
— in Denmark, by an appeal to the højesteret, with the leave of the Minister of Justice,
— in the Federal Repubic of Germany, by a Rechtsbeschwerde,
— in Ireland, by an appeal on a point of law to the Supreme Court,
— in Iceland, by an appeal to the Hæstiréttur,
— in Norway, by an appeal (kjæremål or anke) to the Hoyesteretts Kjæremålsutvalg or Hoyesterett,
— in Austria, in the case of an appeal, by a Revisionsrekurs and, in the case of opposition proceedings, by a Berufung with the possibility of a Revision,
— in Portugal, by an appeal on a point of law,
— in Switzerland, by a recours de droit public devant le tribunal fédéral/ staatsrechtliche Beschwerde beim Bundesgericht/ricorso di diritto pubblico davanti al tribunale federale,
— in Finland, by an appeal to the korkein oikeus/högsta domstolen,
— in Sweden, by an appeal to the högsta domstolen,
— in the United Kingdom, by a single further appeal on a point of law.

Article 38

A33–191   The court with which the appeal under the first paragraph of Article 37 is lodged may, on the application of the appellant, stay the proceedings if an ordinary appeal has been lodged against the judgment in the State of origin or if the time for such an appeal has not yet expired; in the latter case, the court may specify the time within which such an appeal is to be lodged.

Where the judgment was given in Ireland or the United Kingdom, any form of appeal available in the State of origin shall be treated as an ordinary appeal for the purpose of the first paragraph.

The court may also make enforcement conditional on the provision of such security as it shall determine.

Article 39

During the time specified for an appeal pursuant to Article 36 and until any such appeal **A33–192** has been determined, no measures of enforcement may be taken other than protective measures taken against the property of the party against whom enforcement is sought.

The decision authorising enforcement shall carry with it the power to proceed to any such protective measures.

Article 40

1. If the application for enforcement is refused, the applicant may appeal: **A33–193**
   — in Belgium, to the cour d'appel or hof van beroep,
   — in Denmark, to the landsret,
   — in the Federal Republic of Germany, to the Oberlandesgericht,
   — in Greece, to the εφετείο,
   — in Spain, to the Audiencia Provincial,
   — in France, to the court d'appel,
   — in Ireland, to the High Court,
   — in Iceland, to the héragdßsdómari,
   — in Italy, to the corte d'appello,
   — in Luxembourg, to the Cour supérieure de justice sitting as a court of civil appeal,
   — in the Netherlands, to the gerechtshof,
   — in Norway, to the lagmannsrett,
   — in Austria, to the Landesgericht or the Kreisgericht,
   — in Portugal, to the Tribunal da Relação,
   — in Switzerland, to the tribunal cantonal/Kantonsgericht/tribunale cantonale,
   — in Finland, to the hovioikeus/hovrätt,
   — in Sweden, the Svea hovrätt,
   — in the United Kingdom:
     (a) in England and Wales, to the High Court of Justice, or in the case of a maintenance judgment to the Magistrates' Court;
     (b) in Scotland, to the Court of Session, or in the case of a maintenance judgment to the Sheriff Court;
     (c) in Northern Ireland, to the High Court of Justice, or in the case of a maintenance judgment to the Magistrates' Court.

2. The party against whom enforcement is sought shall be summoned to appear before the appellate court. If he fails to appear, the provisons of the second and third paragraphs of Article 20 shall apply even where he is not domiciled in any of the Contracting States.

Article 41

A judgment given on an appeal provided for in Article 40 may be contested only: **A33–194**
   — in Belgium, Greece, Spain, France, Italy, Luxembourg and in the Netherlands, by an appeal in cassation,
   — in Denmark, by an appeal to the højesteret, with the leave of the Minister of Justice,
   — in the Federal Republic of Germany, by a Rechtsbeschwerde,
   — in Ireland, by an appeal on a point of law to the Supreme Court,
   — in Iceland, by an appeal to the Hæstiréttur,
   — in Norway, by an appeal (kjæremål or anke) to the Hoyesteretts kjæremålsutvalg or Hoyesterett,
   — in Austria, by a Revisionsrekurs,
   — in Portugal, by an appeal on a point of law,
   — in Switzerland, by a recours de droit public devant le tribunal fédéral/ staatsrechtliche Beschwerde beim Bundesgericht/ricorso di diritto pubblico davanti al tribunale federale,

— in Finland, by an appeal to the korkein oikeus/högsta domstolen,
— in Sweden, by an appeal to the högsta domstolen,
— in the United Kingdom, by a single further appeal on a point of law.

Article 42

A33–195   Where a foreign judgment has been given in respect of several matters and enforcement cannot be authorised for all of them, the court shall authorise enforcement for one or more of them.

An applicant may request partial enforcement of a judgment.

Article 43

A33–196   A foreign judgment which orders a periodic payment by way of a penalty shall be enforceable in the State in which enforcement is sought only if the amount of the payment has been finally determined by the courts of the State of origin.

Article 44

A33–197   An applicant who, in the State of origin, has benefited from complete or partial legal aid or exemption from costs or expenses, shall be entitled, in the procedures provided for in Articles 32 to 35, to benefit from the most favourable legal aid or the most extensive exemption from costs or expenses provided for by the law of the State addressed.

However, an applicant who requests the enforcement of a decision given by an administrative authority in Denmark or in Iceland in respect of a maintenance order may, in the State addressed, claim the benefits referred to in the first paragraph if he presents a statement from, respectively, the Danish Ministry of Justice or the Icelandic Ministry of Justice to the effect that he fulfils the economic requirements to qualify for the grant of complete or partial legal aid or exemption from costs or expenses.

Article 45

A33–198   No security, bond or deposit, however described, shall be required of a party who in one Contracting State applies for enforcement of a judgment given in another Contracting State on the ground that he is a foreign national or that he is not domiciled or resident in the State in which enforcement is sought.

Section 3

Common Provisions

Article 46

A33–199   A party seeking recognition or applying for enforcement of a judgment shall produce:
1. a copy of the judgment which satisfies the conditions necessary to establish its authenticity;
2. in the case of a judgment given in default, the original or a certified true copy of the document which establishes that the party in default was served with the document instituting the proceedings or with an equivalent document.

Article 47

A33–200   A party applying for enforcement shall also produce:
1. documents which establish that, according to the law of the State of origin, the judgment is enforceable and has been served;
2. where appropriate, a document showing that the applicant is in receipt of legal aid in the State of origin.

Article 48

A33–201   If the documents specified in Article 46(2) and Article 47(2) are not produced, the court may specify a time for their production, accept equivalent documents or, if it considers that it has sufficient information before it, dispense with their production.

If the court so requires, a translation of the documents shall be produced; the translation shall be certified by a person qualified to do so in one of the Contracting States.

Article 49

A33–202   No legislation or other similar formality shall be required in respect of the documents referred to in Article 46 or 47 or the second paragraph of Article 48, or in respect of a document appointing a representative *ad litem*.

TITLE IV

AUTHENTIC INSTRUMENTS AND COURT SETTLEMENTS

Article 50

A document which has been formally drawn up or registered as an authentic **A33–203** instrument and is enforceable in one Contracting State shall, in another Contracting State, be declared enforceable there, on application made in accordance with the procedures provided for in Articles 31 *et seq.* The application may be refused only if enforcement of the instrument is contrary to public policy in the State addressed.

The instrument produced must satisfy the conditions necessary to establish its authenticity in the State of origin.

The provisions of Section 3 of Title III shall apply as appropriate.

Article 51

A settlement which has been approved by a court in the course of proceeedings and is **A33–204** enforceable in the State in which it was concluded shall be enforceable in the State addressed under the same conditions as authentic instruments.

TITLE V

GENERAL PROVISIONS

Article 52

In order to determine whether a party is domiciled in the Contracting State whose **A33–205** courts are seised of a matter, the court shall apply its internal law.

If a party is not domiciled in the State whose courts are seised of the matter, then in order to determine whether the party is domiciled in another Contracting State, the court shall apply the law of that State.

Article 53

For the purposes of this Convention, the seat of a company or other legal person or **A33–206** association of natural or legal persons shall be treated as its domicile. However, in order to determine that seat, the court shall apply its rules of private international law.

In order to determine whether a trust is domiciled in the Contracting State whose courts are seised of the matter, the court shall apply its rules of private international law.

TITLE VI

TRANSITIONAL PROVISIONS

Article 54

The provisions of this Convention shall apply to legal proceedings instituted and to **A33–207** documents formally drawn up or registered as authentic instruments after its entry into force in the State of origin and, where recognition or enforcement of a judgment or authentic instrument is sought, in the State addressed.

However, judgments given after the date of entry into force of this Convention between the State of origin and the State addressed in proceedings instituted before that date shall be recognised and enforced in accordance with the provisions of Title III if jurisdiction was founded upon rules which accorded with those provided for either in Title II of this Convention or in a convention concluded between the State of origin and the State addressed which was in force when the proceedings were instituted.

If the parties to a dispute concerning a contract had agreed in writing before the entry into force of this Convention that the contract was to be governed by the law of Ireland or of a part of the United Kingdom, the courts of Ireland or of that part of the United Kingdom shall retain the right to exercise jurisdiction in the dispute.

Article 54A

For a period of three years from the entry into force of this Convention for Denmark, **A33–208** Greece, Ireland, Iceland, Norway, Finland and Sweden, respectively, jurisdiction in maritime matters shall be determined in these States not only in accordance with the provisions of Title II, but also in accordance with the provisions of paragraphs 1 to 7 following. However, upon the entry into force of the International Convention relating to the arrest of sea-going ships, signed at Brussels on 10 May 1952, for one of these States, these provisions shall cease to have effect for that State.

1. A person who is domiciled in a Contracting State may be sued in the courts of one of the States mentioned above in respect of a maritime claim if the ship to which the claim relates or any other ship owned by him has been arrested by judicial process within the territory of the latter State to secure the claim, or could have been so arrested there but bail or other security has been given, and either:
   (a) the claimant is domiciled in the latter State; or
   (b) the claim arose in the latter State; or
   (c) the claim concerns the voyage during which the arrest was made or could have been made; or
   (d) the claim arises out of a collision or out of damage caused by a ship to another ship or to goods or persons on board either ship, either by the execution or non-execution of a manoeuvre or by the non-observance of regulations; or
   (e) the claim is for salvage; or
   (f) the claim is in respect of a mortgage or hypothecation of the ship arrested.

2. A claimant may arrest either the particular ship to which the maritime claim relates, or any other ship which is owned by the person who was, at the time when the maritime claim arose, the owner of the particular ship. However, only the particular ship to which the maritime claim relates may be arrested in respect of the maritime claims set out in 5(o), (p) or (q) of this Article.

3. Ships shall be deemed to be in the same ownership when all the shares therein are owned by the same person or persons.

4. When in the case of a charter by demise of a ship the charterer alone is liable in respect of a maritime claim relating to that ship, the claimant may arrest that ship or any other ship owned by the charterer, but no other ship owned by the owner may be arrested in respect of such claim. The same shall apply to any case in which a person other than the owner of a ship is liable in respect of a maritime claim relating to that ship.

5. The expression "maritime claim" means a claim arising out of one or more of the following:
   (a) damage caused by any ship either in collision or otherwise;
   (b) loss of life or personal injury caused by any ship or occurring in connection with the operation of any ship;
   (c) salvage;
   (d) agreement relating to the use or hire of any ship whether by charterparty or otherwise;
   (e) agreement relating to the carriage of goods in any ship whether by charterparty or otherwise;
   (f) loss of or damage to goods including baggage carried in any ship;
   (g) general average;
   (h) bottomry;
   (i) towage;
   (j) pilotage;
   (k) goods or materials wherever supplied to a ship for her operation or maintenance;
   (l) construction, repair or equipment or any ship or dock charges and dues;
   (m) wages of masters, officers or crew;
   (n) master's disbursements, including disbursements made by shippers, charterers or agents on behalf of a ship or her owner;
   (o) dispute as to the title to or ownership of any ship;
   (p) disputes between co-owners of any ship as to the ownership, possession, employment or earnings of that ship;
   (q) the mortgage or hypothecation of any ship.

6. In Demark, the expression "arrest" shall be deemed, as regards the maritime claims referred to in 5.(o) and (p) of this Article, to include a "forbud", where that is the only procedure allowed in respect of such a claim under Articles 646 to 653 of the law on civil procedure (lov om rettens pleje).

7. In Iceland, the expression "arrest" shall be deemed, as regards the maritime claims referred to in 5.(o) and (p) of this Article, to include a "logbann", where that is the only procedure allowed in respect of such a claim under Chapter III of the law on arrest and injunction (lög um kyrrsetningu og lögbann).

TITLE VII

RELATIONSHIP TO THE BRUSSELS CONVENTION AND TO OTHER CONVENTIONS

Article 54B

1. This Convention shall not prejudice the application by the Member States of the **A33–209** European Communities of the Convention on Jurisdiction and the Enforcement of Judgments in Civil and Commercial Matters, signed at Brussels on 27 September 1968 and of the Protocol on interpretation of that Convention by the Court of Justice, signed at Luxembourg on 3 June 1971, as amended by the Conventions of Accession to the said Convention and the said Protocol by the States acceding to the European Communities, all of these Conventions and the Protocol being hereinafter referred to as the "Brussels Convention".

2. However, this Convention shall in any event be applied:
   (a) in matters of jurisdiction, where the defendant is domiciled in the territory of a Contracting State which is not a member of the European Communities, or where Article 16 or 17 of this Convention confers a jurisdiction on the courts of such a Contracting State;
   (b) in relation to a *lis pendens* or to related actions as provided for in Article 21 and 22, when proceedings are instituted in a Contracting State which is not a member of the European Communities and in a Contracting State which is a member of the European Communities;
   (c) in matters of recognition and enforcement, where either the State of origin or the State addressed is not a member of the European Communities.

3. In addition to the grounds provided for in Title III recognition or enforcement may be refused if the ground of jurisdiction on which the judgment has been based differs from that resulting from this Convention and recognition or enforcement is sought against a party who is domiciled in a Contracting State which is not a member of the European Communities, unless the judgment may otherwise be recognised or enforced under any rule of law in the State addressed.

Article 55

Subject to the provisions of the second paragraph of Article 54 and of Article 56, this **A33–210** Convention shall, for the States which are parties to it, supersede the following conventions concluded between two or more of them:
— the Convention between the Swiss Confederation and France on jurisdiction and enforcement of judgments in civil matters, signed at Paris on 15 June 1869,
— the Treaty between the Swiss Confederation and Spain on the mutual enforcement of judgments in civil or commercial matters, signed at Madrid on 19 November 1896,
— the Convention between the Swiss Confederation and the German Reich on the recognition and enforcement of judgments and arbitration awards, signed at Berne on 2 November 1929,
— the Convention between Denmark, Finland, Iceland, Norway and Sweden on the recognition and enforcement of judgments, signed at Copenhagen on 16 March 1932,
— the Convention between the Swiss Confederation and Italy on the recognition and enforcement of judgments, signed at Rome on 3 January 1933,
— the Convention between Sweden and the Swiss Confederation on the recognition and enforcement of judgments and arbitral awards, signed at Stockholm on 15 January 1936,
— the Convention between the Kingdom of Belgium and Austria on the reciprocal recognition and enforcement of judgments and authentic instruments relating to maintenance obligations, signed at Vienna on 25 October 1957,
— the Convention between the Swiss Confederation and Belgium on the recognition and enforcement of judgments and arbitration awards, signed at Berne on 29 April 1959,

1511

- the Convention between the Federal Republic of Germany and Austria on the reciprocal recognition and enforcement of judgments, settlements and authentic instruments in civil and commercial matters, signed at Vienna on 6 June 1959,
- the Convention between the Kingdom of Belgium and Austria on the reciprocal recognition and enforcement of judgments, arbitral awards and authentic instruments in civil and commercial matters, signed at Vienna on 16 June 1959,
- the Convention between Austria and the Swiss Confederation on the recognition and enforcement of judgments, signed at Berne on 16 December 1960,
- the Convention between Norway and the United Kingdom providing for the reciprocal recognition and enforcement of judgments in civil matters, signed at London on 12 June 1961,
- the Convention between the United Kingdom and Austria providing for the reciprocal rcognition and enforcement of judgments in civil and commercial matters, signed at Vienna on 14 July 1961, with amending Protocol signed at London on 6 March 1970,
- the Convention between the Kingdom of the Netherlands and Austria on the reciprocal recognition and enforcement of judgments and authentic instruments in civil and commercial matters, signed at The Hague on 6 February 1963,
- the Convention between France and Austria on the recognition and enforcement of judgments and authentic instruments in civil and commercial matters, signed at Vienna on 15 July 1966,
- the Convention between Luxembourg and Austria on the recognition and enforcement of judgments and authentic instruments in civil and commercial matters, signed at Luxembourg on 29 July 1971,
- the Convention between Italy and Austria on the recognition and enforcement of judgments in civil and commercial matters, of judicial settlements and of authentic instruments, signed at Rome on 16 November 1971,
- the Convention between Norway and the Federal Republic of Germany on the recognition and enforcement of judgments and enforceable documents, in civil and commercial matters, signed at Oslo on 17 June 1977,
- the Convention between Denmark, Finland, Iceland, Norway and Sweden on the recognition and enforcement of judgments in civil matters, signed at Copenhagen on 11 October 1977,
- the Convention between Austria and Sweden on the recognition and enforcement of judgments in civil matters, signed at Stockholm on 16 September 1982,
- the Convention between Austria and Spain on the recognition and enforcement of judgments, settlements and enforceable authentic instruments in civil and commercial matters, signed at Vienna on 17 February 1984,
- the Convention between Norway and Austria on the recognition and enforcement of judgments in civil matters, signed at Vienna on 21 May 1984, and
- the Convention between Finland and Austria on the recognition and enforcement of judgments in civil matters, signed at Vienna on 17 November 1986.

Article 56

A33–211   The Treaty and the conventions referred to in Article 55 shall continue to have effect in relation to matters to which this Convention does not apply.

They shall continue to have effect in respect of judgments given and documents formally drawn up or registered as authentic instruments before the entry into force of this Convention.

Article 57

A33–212   1. This Convention shall not affect any conventions to which the Contracting States are or will be parties and which, in relation to particular matters, govern jurisdiction or the recognition or enforcement of judgments.

2. This Convention shall not prevent a court of a Contracting State which is party to a convention referred to in the first paragraph from assuming jurisdiction in accordance with that convention, even where the defendant is domiciled in a Contracting State which is not a party to that convention. The court hearing the action shall, in any event, apply Article 20 of this Convention.

3. Judgments given in a Contracting State by a court in the exercise of jurisdiction provided for in a convention referred to in the first paragraph shall be recognised and enforced in the other Contracting States in accordance with Title III of this Convention.

4. In addition to the grounds provided for in Title III, recognition or enforcement may be refused if the State addressed is not a contracting party to a convention referred to in the first paragraph and the person against whom recognition or enforcement is sought is domiciled in that State, unless the judgment may otherwise be recognised or enforced under any role of law in the State addressed.

5. Where a convention referred to in the first paragraph to which both the State of origin and the State addressed are parties lays down conditions for the recognition or enforcement of judgments, those conditions shall apply. In any event, the provisions of this Convention which concern the procedures for recognition and enforcement of judgments may be applied.

Article 58

(None)

Article 59

This Convention shall not prevent a Contracting State from assuming, in a convention **A33–213** on the recognition and enforcement of judgments, an obligation towards a third State not to recognise judgments given in other Contracting States against defendants domiciled or habitually resident in the third State where, in cases provided for in Article 4, the judgment could only be founded on a ground of jurisdiction specified in the second paragraph of Article 3.

However, a Contracting State may not assume an obligation towards a third State not to recognise a judgment given in another Contracting State by a court basing its jurisdiction on the presence within that State of property belonging to the defendant, or the seizure by the plaintiff of property situated there:

1. if the action is brought to assert or declare proprietary or possessory rights in that property, seeks to obtain authority to dispose of it, or arises from another issue relating to such property, or
2. if the property constitutes the security for a debt which is the subject-matter of the action.

Title VIII

Final Provisions

Article 60

The following may be parties to this Convention: **A33–214**
- (a) States which, at the time of the opening of this Convention for signature, are members of the European Communities or of the European Free Trade Association;
- (b) States which, after the opening of this Convention for signature, become members of the European Communities or of the European Free Trade Association;
- (c) States invited to accede in accordance with Article 62(1)(b).

Article 61

1. This Convention shall be opened for signature by the States members of the European **A33–215** Communities or of the European Free Trade Association.

2. The Convention shall be submitted for ratification by the signatory States. The instruments of ratification shall be deposited with the Swiss Federal Council.

3. The Convention shall enter into force on the first day of the third month following the date on which two States, of which one is a member of the European Communities and the other a member of the European Free Trade Association, deposit their instruments of ratification.

4. The Convention shall take effect in relation to any other signatory State on the first day of the third month following the deposit of its instrument of ratification.

Article 62

1. After entering into force this Convention shall be open to accession by: **A33–216**
- (a) the States referred to in Article 60(b);

(b) other States which have been invited to accede upon a request made by one of the Contracting States to the depositary State. The depositary State shall invite the State concerned to accede only if, after having communicated the contents of the communications that this State intends to make in accordance with Article 63, it has obtained the unanimous agreement of the signatory States and the Contracting States referred to in Article 60(a) and (b).

2. If an acceding State wishes to furnish details for the purposes of Protocol No. 1, negotiations shall be entered into to that end. A negotiating conference shall be convened by the Swiss Federal Council.

3. In respect of an acceding State, the Convention shall take effect on the first day of the third month following the deposit of its instrument of accession.

4. However, in respect of an acceding State referred to in paragraph 1(a) or (b), the Convention shall take effect only in relations between the acceding State and the Contracting States which have not made any objections to the accession before the first day of the third month following the deposit of the instrument of accession.

Article 63

A33–217   Each acceding State shall, when depositing its instrument of accession, communicate the information required for the application of Articles 3, 32, 37, 40, 41 and 55 of this Convention and furnish, if need be, the details prescribed during the negotiations for the purposes of Protocol No. 1.

Article 64

A33–218   1. This Convention is concluded for an initial period of five years from the date of its entry into force in accordance with Article 61(3), even in the case of States which ratify it or accede to it after that date.

2. At the end of the initial five-year period, the Convention shall be automatically renewed from year to year.

3. Upon the expiry of the initial five-year period, any Contracting State may, at any time, denounce the Convention by sending a notification to the Swiss Federal Council.

4. The denunciation shall take effect at the end of the calendar year following the expiry of a period of six months from the date of receipt by the Swiss Federal Council of the notification of denunciation.

Article 65

A33–219   The following are annexed to this Convention:
— a Protocol No. 1, on certain questions of jurisdiction, procedure and enforcement,
— a Protocol No. 2, on the uniform interpretation of the Convention,
— a Protocol No. 3, on the application of Article 57.
These Protocols shall form an integral part of the Convention.

Article 66

A33–220   Any Contracting State may request the revision of this Convention. To that end, the Swiss Federal Council shall issue invitations to a revision conference within a period of six months from the date of the request for revision.

Article 67

A33–221   The Swiss Federal Council shall notify the States represented at the Diplomatic Conference of Lugano and the States who have later acceded to the Convention of:
(a) the deposit of each instrument of ratification or accession;
(b) the dates of entry into force of this Convention in respect of the Contracting States;
(c) any denunciation received pursuant to Article 64;
(d) any declaration received pursuant to Article Ia of Protocol No. 1;
(e) any declaration received pursuant to Article Ib of Protocol No. 1;
(f) any declaration received pursuant to Article IV of Protocol No. 1;
(g) any communication made pursuant to Article VI of Protocol No. 1.

Article 68

A33–222   This Convention, drawn up in a single original in the Danish, Dutch, English, Finnish, French, German, Greek, Icelandic, Irish, Italian, Norwegian, Portuguese, Spanish and Swedish languages, all fourteen texts being equally authentic, shall be deposited in the archives of the Swiss Federal Council. The Swiss Federal Council shall transmit a certified copy to the Government of each State represented at the Diplomatic Conference of Lugano and to the Government of each acceding State.

PROTOCOL NO. 1

ON CERTAIN QUESTIONS OF JURISDICTION, PROCEDURE AND ENFORCEMENT

The High Contracting Parties have agreed upon the following provisions, which shall be annexed to the Convention: **A33–223**

Article I

Any person domiciled in Luxembourg who is sued in a court of another Contracting State pursuant to Article 5(1) may refuse to submit to the jurisdiction of that court. If the defendant does not enter an appearance the court shall declare of its own motion that it has no jurisdiction. **A33–224**

An agreement conferring jurisdiction, within the meaning of Article 17, shall be valid with respect to a person domiciled in Luxembourg only if that person has expressly and specifically so agreed.

Article Ia

1. Switzerland reserves the right to declare, at the time of depositing its instrument of ratification, that a judgment given in another Contracting State shall be neither recognised nor enforced in Switzerland if the following conditions are met: **A33–225**

  (a) the jurisdiction of the court which has given the judgment is based only on Article 5(1) of this Convention; and
  (b) the defendant was domiciled in Switzerland at the time of the introduction of the proceedings; for the purposes of this Article, a company or other legal person is considered to be domiciled in Switzerland if it has its registered seat and the effective centre of activities in Switzerland; and
  (c) the defendant raises an objection to the recognition or enforcement of the judgment in Switzerland, provided that he has not waived the benefit of the declaration foreseen under this paragraph.

2. This reservation shall not apply to the extent that at the time recognition or enforcement is sought a derogation has been granted from Article 59 of the Swiss Federal Constitution. The Swiss Government shall communicate such derogations to the signatory States and the acceding States.

3. This reservation shall cease to have effect on 31 December 1999. It may be withdrawn at any time.

Article Ib

Any Contracting State may, by declaration made at the time of signing or of deposit of its instrument of ratification or of accession, reserve the right, notwithstanding the provisions of Article 28, not to recognise and enforce judgments given in the other Contracting States if the jurisdiction of the court of the State of origin is based, pursuant to Article 16(1) (b), exclusively on the domicile of the defendant in the State of origin, and the property is situated in the territory of the State which entered the reservation. **A33–226**

Article II

Without prejudice to any more favourable provisions of national laws, persons domiciled in a Contracting State who are being prosecuted in the criminal courts of another Contracting State of which they are not nationals for an offence which was not intentionally committed may be defended by persons qualified to do so, even if they do not appear in person. **A33–227**

However, the court seised of the matter may order appearance in person; in the case of failure to appear, a judgment given in the civil action without the person concerned having had the opportunity to arrange for his defence need not be recognised or enforced in the other Contracting States.

Article III

In proceedings for the issue of an order for enforcement, no charge, duty or fee calculated by reference to the value of the matter in issue may be levied in the State in which enforcement is sought. **A33–228**

Article IV

A33–229   Judicial and extrajudicial documents drawn up in one Contracting State which have to be served on persons in another Contracting State shall be transmitted in accordance with the procedures laid down in the conventions and agreements concluded between the Contracting States.

Unless the State in which service is to take place objects by declaration to the Swiss Federal Council, such documents may also be sent by the appropriate public officers of the State in which the document has been drawn up directly to the appropriate public officers of the State in which the addressee is to be found. In this case the officer of the State of origin shall send a copy of the document to the officer of the State applied to who is competent to forward it to the addressee. The document shall be forwarded in the manner specified by the law of the State applied to. The forwarding shall be recorded by a certificate sent directly to the officer of the State of origin.

Article V

A33–230   The jurisdiction specified in Articles 6(2) and 10 in actions on a warranty or guarantee or in any other third party proceedings may not be resorted to in the Federal Republic of Germany, in Spain, in Austria and in Switzerland. Any person domiciled in another Contracting State may be sued in the courts:

— of the Federal Republic of Germany, pursuant to Articles 68, 72, 73 and 74 of the code of civil procedure (Zivilprozeßordnung) concerning third-party notices,
— of Spain, pursuant to Article 1482 of the civil code,
— of Austria, pursuant to Article 21 of the code of civil procedure (Zivilprozeßordnung) concerning third-party notices,
— of Switzerland, pursuant to the appropriate provisions concerning third-party notices of the cantonal codes of civil procedure.

Judgments given in the other Contracting States by virtue of Article 6(2) or Article 10 shall be recognised and enforced in the Federal Republic of Germany, in Spain, in Austria and in Switzerland in accordance with Title III. Any effects which judgments given in these States may have on third parties by application of the provisions in the preceding paragraph shall also be recognised in the other Contracting States.

Article Va

A33–231   In matters relating to maintenance, the expression "court" includes the Danish, Icelandic and Norwegian administrative authorities.

In civil and commercial matters, the expression "court" includes the Finnish ulosotonhaltija/överexekutor.

Article Vb

A33–232   In proceedings involving a dispute between the master and a member of the crew of a sea-going ship registered in Denmark, in Greece, in Ireland, in Iceland, in Norway, in Portugal or in Sweden concerning remuneration or other conditions of service, a court in a Contracting State shall establish whether the diplomatic or consular officer responsible for the ship has been notified of the dispute. It shall stay the proceedings so long as he has not been notified. It shall of its own motion decline jurisdiction if the officer, having been duly notified, has exercised the powers accorded to him in the matter by a consular convention, or in the absence of such a convention has, within the time allowed, raised any objection to the exercise of such jurisdiction.

Article Vc

(None)

Article Vd

A33–233   Without prejudice to the jurisdiction of the European Patent Office under the Convention on the grant of European patents, signed at Munich on 5 October 1973, the courts of each Contracting State shall have exclusive jurisdiction, regardless of domicile, in proceedings concerned with the registration or validity of any European patent granted for that State which is not a Community patent by virtue of the provision of Article 86 of the Convention for the European patent for the common market, signed at Luxembourg on 15 December 1975.

Article VI

The Contracting States shall communicate to the Swiss Federal Council the text of any **A33–234** provisions of their laws which amend either those provisions of their laws mentioned in the Convention or the lists of courts specified in Section 2 of Title III.

PROTOCOL NO. 2

ON THE UNIFORM INTERPRETATION OF THE CONVENTION

Preamble

The High Contracting Parties, **A33–235**
Having regard to Article 65 of this Convention,
Considering the substantial link between this Convention and the Brussels Convention,
Considering that the Court of Justice of the European Communities by virtue of the Protocol of 3 June 1971 has jurisdiction to give rulings on the interpretation of the provisions of the Brussels Convention,
Being aware of the rulings delivered by the Court of Justice of the European Communities on the interpretation of the Brussels Convention up to the time of signature of this Convention,
Considering that the negotiations which led to the conclusion of the Convention were based on the Brussels Convention in the light of these rulings,
Desiring to prevent, in full deference to the independence of the courts, divergent interpretations and to arrive at as uniform an interpretation as possible of the provisions of the Convention, and of these provisions and those of the Brussels Convention which are substantially reproduced in this Convention,
Have agreed as follows:

Article 1

The courts of each Contracting State shall, when applying and interpreting the **A33–236** provisions of the Convention, pay due account to the principles laid down by any relevant decision delivered by courts of the other Contracting States concerning provisions of this Convention.

Article 2

1. The Contracting Parties agree to set up a system of exchange of information **A33–237** concerning judgments delivered pursuant to this Convention as well as relevant judgments under the Brussels Convention. This system shall comprise:
   — transmission to a central body by the competent authorities of judgments delivered by courts of last instance and the Court of Justice of the European Communities as well as judgments of particular importance which have become final and have been delivered pursuant to this Convention or the Brussels Convention,
   — classification of these judgments by the central body including, as far as necessary,
   — the drawing-up and publication of translations and abstracts,
   — communication by the central body of the relevant documents to the competent national authorities of all signatories and acceding States to the Convention and to the Commission of the European Communities.
2. The central body is the Registrar of the Court of Justice of the European Communities.

Article 3

1. A Standing Committee shall be set up for the purposes of this Protocol. **A33–238**
2. The Committee shall be composed of representatives appointed by each signatory and acceding State.
3. The European Communities (Commission, Court of Justice and General Secretariat of the Council) and the European Free Trade Association may attend the meetings as observers.

Article 4

1. At the request of a Contracting Party, the depositary of the Convention shall convene **A33–239** meetings of the Committee for the purpose of exchanging views on the functioning of the Convention and in particular on:

— the development of the case-law as communicated under the first paragraph first indent of Article 2,
— the application of Article 57 of the Convention.
2. The Committee, in the light of these exchanges, may also examine the appropriateness of starting on particular topics a revision of the Convention and make recommendations.

PROTOCOL No. 3

ON THE APPLICATION OF ARTICLE 57

A33–240   The High Contracting Parties have agreed as follows:
1. For the purposes of the Convention, provisions which, in relation in particular matters, govern jurisdiction or the recognition or enforcement of judgments and which are, or will be, contained in acts of the institutions of the European Communities shall be treated in the same way as the conventions referred to in paragraph 1 of Article 57.
2. If one Contracting State is of the opinion that a provision contained in an act of the institutions of the European Communities is incompatible with the Convention, the Contracting States shall promptly consider amending the Convention pursuant to Article 66, without prejudice to the procedure established by Protocol No. 2.

SCHEDULE 2

OTHER AMENDMENTS OF THE 1982 ACT

Section 3

A33–241   1. The words "Brussels Conventions" shall be substituted for the word "Conventions" wherever occurring in section 2 (the Conventions to have the force of law) and section 3 (interpretation of the Conventions).
2. In section 4(1) (enforcement of judgments other than maintenance orders) and section 5(1) (recognition and enforcement of maintenance orders) after the words "an application under Article 31" there shall be inserted the words "of the 1968 Convention or of the Lugano Convention".
3. In section 6 (appeals under Article 37, second paragraph and Article 41)—
    (a) in subsection (1), after the words "referred to" there shall be inserted the words "in the 1968 Convention and the Lugano Convention"; and
    (b) in subsection (3), after the words "referred to" there shall be inserted the words "in each of those Conventions".
4. In section 9 (provisions supplementary to Title VII of the 1968 Convention) in subsection 1(1)—
    (a) after the words "Title VII of the 1968 Convention" there shall be inserted the words "and, apart from Article 54B, of Title VII of the Lugano Convention"; and
    (b) for the words "that convention" there shall be substituted the words "the Convention in question".
5. In section 10 (allocation within UK of jurisdiction in proceedings with respect to trusts and consumer contracts in respect of which the 1968 Convention confers jurisdiction on UK courts generally), in subsection (1) after the words "the 1968 Convention" there shall be inserted the words "or the Lugano Convention".
6. In section 11 (proof and admissibility of certain judgments and related documents for the purposes of the 1968 Convention) in subsection (1), after the words "For the purposes of the 1968 Convention" there shall be inserted the words "and the Lugano Convention".
7. In section 12 (provisions for issue of copies of, and certificates in connection with, UK judgments for purposes of the 1968 Convention) after the words "the 1968 Convention" there shall be inserted the words "or the Lugano Convention".
8. In section 13 (modifications to cover authentic instruments and court settlements) in subsection (1)—
    (a) after the words "the 1968 Convention" in paragraph (a) there shall be inserted the words "or the Lugano Convention";
    (b) after the words "Title IV of the 1968 Convention" there shall be inserted the words "or, as the case may be, Title IV of the Lugano Convention"; and
    (c) for the words "that Convention" there shall be substituted the words "the Convention in question".
9. In section 14 (modifications consequential on revision of the Conventions)—

(a) for the words "any of the Conventions", wherever occuring in subsections (1) and (3), there shall be substituted the words "the Lugano Convention or any of the Brussels Conventions"; and

(b) in subsection (1), after the words "any revision connected with the accession to" there shall be inserted the words "the Lugano Convention or".

10. In section 15 (interpretation of Part I)—

(a) in subsection (1), in the definition of "maintenance order", after the words "maintenance judgment within the meaning of the 1968 Convention" there shall be inserted the words "or, as the case may be, the Lugano Convention"; and

(b) in subsection (3), after the words "authorised or required by the 1968 Convention" there shall be inserted the words "the Lugano Convention".

11. In section 16 (allocation within UK of jurisdiction in certain civil proceedings)—

(a) in paragraph (a) of subsection (1), for the words "the Convention" there shall be substituted the words "that or any other Convention";

(b) In paragraph (b) of that subsection, after the words "Article 16" there shall be inserted the words "of the 1968 Convention"; and

(c) in subsection (4), after the words "subject to the 1968 Convention" there shall be inserted the words "and the Lugano Convention".

12. The words "Brussels or Lugano Contracting State" shall be substituted for the words "Contracting State" wherever occurring in each of the following provisions, that is to say—

(a) in subsections (1)(a) and (3) (a) of section 25 (interim relief in England and Wales or Northern Ireland in the absence of substantive proceedings);

(b) in subsections (2) (a) and (3) (a) and (d) of section 27 (which makes for Scotland similar provision to that made by section 25 for England and Wales); and

(c) in section 28 (application of section 1 of the Administration of Justice (Scotland) Act 1972);

and, in section 25(1) (b), for the words "the Convention" there shall be substituted the words "that or any other Convention".

13. In section 30 (proceedings in England and Wales or Northern Ireland for torts to immovable property) in subsection (2), after the words "subject to the 1968 Convention" there shall be inserted the words "and the Lugano Convention".

14. In section 32 (overseas judgments given in proceedings brought in breach of agreement for settlement of disputes) in subsection (4) (saving for judgments required to be recognised or enforced in UK under the 1968 Convention etc) in paragraph (a), after the words "under the 1968 Convention" there shall be inserted the words "or the Lugano Convention".

15. In section 33 (certain steps not to amount to submission to the jurisdiction of an overseas court) in subsection (2) (saving for judgments required to be recognised or enforced in England and Wales or Northern Ireland under the 1968 Convention) after the words "under the 1968 Convention" there shall be inserted the words "or the Lugano Convention".

16. In section 41 (determination of domicile of individuals for the purposes of the 1968 Convention etc) in subsection (1), after the words "for the purposes of the 1968 Convention" there shall be inserted the words "the Lugano Convention".

17. In section 42 (domicile and seat of corporation or association) in subsection (2) (a), after the words "for the purposes of the 1968 Convention" there shall be inserted the words "or, as the case may be, the Lugano Convention".

18. In section 43 (seat of corporation or association for purposes of Article 16(2) and related provisions) in subsection (1) (a), after the words "Article 16(2)" there shall be inserted the words "of the 1968 Convention or of the Lugano Convention".

19.—(1) In section 44 (persons deemed to be domiciled in UK for certain purposes) in subsection (I)—

(a) in paragraph (a) (which provides that the section applies to Proceedings within Section 3 of Title II of the 1968 Convention) after the words "the 1968 Convention" there shall be inserted the words "or Section 3 of Title II of the Lugano Convention"; and

(b) in paragraph (b) (proceedings within Section 2 of that Title) for the words "that Title" there shall be substituted the words "Title II of either of those Conventions".

(2) In subsection (2) of that section, after the words "is deemed for the purposes of the 1968 Convention" there shall be inserted the words "or, as the case may be, of the Lugano Convention".

20. In section 45 (domicile of trusts) in subsection (1), after the words "for the purposes of the 1968 Convention" there shall be inserted the words "the Lugano Convention".

21.—(1) In section 46 (domicile and seat of the Crown) in subsection (2) (a), after the words "for the purposes of the 1968 Convention" there shall be inserted the words "and the Lugano Convention" and for the words "(in which" there shall be substituted the words "(in each of which".

(2) In subsection (4) of that section (Order in Council with respect to seat of the Crown) after the words "for the purposes of the 1968 Convention" there shall be inserted the words "the Lugano Convention".

22. In section 47 (modifications occasioned by decisions of the European Court as to meaning or effect of the Conventions) for the word "Conventions", wherever occuring, there shall be substituted the words "Brussels Conventions".

23. In section 48 (matters for which rules of court may provide)—
    (a) in subsection (1), for the words "or the Conventions" there shall be substituted the words "the Lugano Convention or the Brussels Conventions"; and
    (b) in subsection (3), for the words "the Conventions" there shall be substituted the words "the Lugano Convention, the Brussels Conventions".

24. In section 49 (saving for powers to stay, sist, strike out or dismiss proceedings where to do so is not inconsistent with the 1968 Convention) after the words "the 1968 Convention" there shall be inserted the words "or, as the case may be, the Lugano Convention".

25. In section 50 (general interpretation) the following definitions shall be inserted at the appropriate places—
    "'Brussels Contracting State' has the meaning given by section 1 (3)";
    "'the Brussels Conventions' has the meaning given by section 1 (1)";
    "'Lugano Contracting State' has the meaning given by section 1 (3)";
    "'the Lugano Convention' has the meaning given by section 1 (1)";
and the entry relating to "the Conventions" is hereby repealed.

PART X

OTHER

APPENDIX 34

The "Heraldic Convention" for representation
of colours

According to this convention, which is used to enable coloured marks to be **A34–01** represented in the black-and-white of the Trade Marks Journal, colours are represented by shading as follows:

Red (gules): Vertical lines.
Green (vert): diagonal lines descending left to right.
Blue (azure): Horizontal lines.
Purple (purpure): Diagonal lines descending right to left.
Yellow or gold (or): Dotted ground.
Chestnut or deep orange (Tennè): Diagonal lines descending right to left and horizontal lines, crossing.
Black (sable): Horizontal and vertical lines crossing.
White (argent): Plain ground.

This convention should be used when preparing blocks for printing representations of marks. The Registry's explanation of the convention adds: "Intermediate colours should, as far as possible be shown by increasing or diminishing the intensity of the lines."

APPENDIX 35

List of contrasted marks and names

A35–01   "How can observations of judges upon other and quite different facts bear upon the present case, in which the only question is what is the result of the evidence?" Lord Watson asked in *Johnston v. Orr-Ewing*[1]; but the habit of referring to reported cases at the hearing of such questions is invetererate and lists of cases are given below.

1. Trade Marks

(1) CONTRASTED DEVICES

A35–02   A pointer eating out of a pot, too near for registration to a similar dog standing by pail with "Stanch" beneath it.[2] A twisted curved horn with a twig bearing two roses, too near a similar untwisted horn with a cord having two loops in the same place as the roses in the twig.[3] A triangular frame with words upon it and a church inside, too near Bass's solid triangle[4]; so also a white diamond within a red diamond.[5] A half-length figure of a milkmaid, with the word "Dairymaid", too near a full-length figure of a milkmaid carrying two pails.[6] A woman's head wearing as helmet with "Athena" beneath, not too near a man's head with "Way" beneath.[7] A tower in an oval border, with a dog and harp, too near a tower, dog and harp without any border.[8] An oval label containing interlaced triangular frames with a stag's head within them, too near an oval label with three superimposed solid triangles; although the lettering on the marks was conspiciously different.[9] A suspended sheep, with the words "Golden Fleece", too near sheep with the same words.[10] A pig in outline, and H.B. & Co., not too near shaded pointer dog and "Stanch",[11] A tobacco pipe and dart, not too near a tobacco pipe alone.[12] A charging buffalo, too near a bull's head, both silver rings on yellow wrappers.[13] Lion bearing a sheaf, too near a lion with a crown.[14] An elephant in a border, with lettering round it, an

[1] (1882) 7 App.Cas. 219.
[2] *Jelly's Appn.* (1878) 51 L.J.Ch. 639n.
[3] *Rosing's Appn.* (1878) 54 L.J.Ch. 975n.
[4] *Worthington's T.M.* (1880) 14 Ch.D. 8.
[5] *Turney & Sons'. T.M.* (1894) 11 R.P.C. 37.
[6] *Anglo-Swiss Condensed Milk v. Metcalf* (1886) 31 Ch.D. 454; 3 R.P.C. 28.
[7] *Lyndon's T. M.* 32 Ch.D. 109; 3 R.P.C. 102.
[8] *Speer's T. M.* (1887) 4 R.P.C. 521.
[9] *Biegel's T. M.* (1887) 4 R.P.C. 525; 57 L.T. 247.
[10] *Australian Wine Importers* (1889) 41 Ch.D. 278; (1889) 6 R.P.C. 311.
[11] *Haines, Batchelor & Co.'s T. M.* (1888) 5 R.P.C. 669.
[12] *Lambert's T. M.* (1888) 5 R.P.C. 542; (1889) 6 R.P.C. 344; 61 L.T. 138.
[13] *Farrlow's T. M.* (1890) 7 R.P.C. 260; 63 L.T. 233.
[14] *Murphy's T. M.* (1890) R.P.C. 163.

infringement of a somewhat different elephant alone.[15] Winged cross surrounded by two circles, not an infringement of a lighthouse similarly surrounded.[16] Two red medals and a balloon, an infringement of a lable with two red medals only, being used for polish known in India as red metal polish.[17] A cock in the centre, with a piece of plaid with the words "Prince Charlie, King o' the Hieland Hearts", too near a label baring the words "The Cock o' the North" with a cock over a coat of arms, with a Highlander and a horse.[18] Representation of the Royal Exchange, Glasgow, and the words "Royal Exchange Whisky" below, refused registration because it would give the right to restrain a label bearing the same representation with the words "Bodega Special Whisky" below.[19] C.B. & Co. and also C.B.D. held to infringe device of a corset and the letters C.B. within a star, and of C.B. corsets.[20] The device of a red deer's head, not an infringement of a device of a moose's head.[21] The device of the cut of half an apple cut vertically with the word "Pomril" across it, too near a mark containing a representation of an apple and the words "Apple Brand", both marks being for cider.[22] J. B. D. in an oval ring, an infringement of G. B. D. in an oval ring.[23] A showcard with a device having some of the features and lines of a diamond and the word "famous" on it, not an infringement of a plain diamond.[24] A sphinx in combination with Egyptian scenery not an infringement of a sphinx in a different position.[25] A rampant cat on a horizontal barrel, known as the "Cat Brand" or "Cat and Barrel Brand", held to be infringed by a cat's head and fore-quarters out of the top of a barrel on end, with the words "Cat Brand".[26] The same trade mark held to be infringed by a cat sitting on the top of a barrel place on end.[27] A labael with a signature, not infringed by a label similar in structure, but having the defendant's name prominently upon it.[28] An ace of spades with the word "Hub" on it held to be an infringement of an ace of clubs with the word "Club" on it.[29] A shamrock with a stalk twisted so as to form "& Co.", not too near a compound mark of a crown and a shamrock in a different position with the letters M. V.[30] A diamond divided into two triangles, and bearing upon it a device and monogram, refused registration on the ground, *inter alia*, of similarity to other diamond marks.[31] A representation of the head of a Red Indian allowed notwithstanding representation of a Red Indian on horseback with the words "Red Indian" underneath.[32] Mark consisting of a swan within an oval and the words "Swann & Co." not too near the device of a swan with a small boy sitting on its back.[33] View of Blackfriars Bridge with St. Paul's Cathedral in the background, infringed by a view of the bridge with a supposed town containing a similar building in the background, the labels being of similar

[15] *Upper Assam Tea v. Herbert* (1890) 7 R.P.C. 183.
[16] *Baker v. Rawson* (1890) 45 Ch.D. 519; 8 R.P.C. 89.
[17] *Wilkinson v. Griffith* (1891) 8 R.P.C. 370.
[18] *Currie's Appn.* (1896) 13 R.P.C. 681.
[19] *Rogers' T.M.* (1895) 12 R.P.C. 149.
[20] *Bayer v. Connell Bros.* (1899) 16 R.P.C. 157. In Ireland before Porter M.R. See also *Bayer v. Baird* (1898) 15 R.P.C. 615 (S. Ct of Sess).
[21] *Alaska Packers' Association v. Crooks & Co.* (1899) 16 R.P.C. 503; (1901) 18 R.P.C. 129.
[22] *Pomril Ltd's Appn.* (1901) 18 R.P.C. 181.
[23] *Maréchal and Ruchon v. McColgan* (1901) 18 R.P.C. 262 (Ireland).
[24] *Bass, Ratcliffe & Gretton Ltd v. Davenport & Sons' Brewery Ltd* (1902) 19 R.P.C. 129 and 529.
[25] *Lambert & Butler v. Goodbody* (1902) 19 R.P.C. 377.
[26] *Boord & Son v. Huddart* (1904) 21 R.P.C. 149.
[27] *Boord & Son v. Thom & Cameron Ltd* (1907) 24 R.P.C. 697.
[28] *Dawson v. Stewart* (1905) 22 R.P.C. 250.
[29] *Munday v. Carey* (1905) 22 R.P.C. 273.
[30] *Shamrock & Co.'s Appn.* (1907) 24 R.P.C. 569.
[31] *La Union Agricola's T. M.s* (1908) 25 R.P.C. 295.
[32] *Carborundum Co.'s Appn.* (1909) 26 R.P.C. 504.
[33] *Holbrook's Appn.* (1909) 26 R.P.C. 791.

shape and having a device within a circle.[34] Although the plaintiffs' and defendants' names were on their respective labels, an injunction against passing off granted.[35] A representation of Eastern Dye Works held to be too near a different representation of the same subject.[36] Circular cake of dental composition with a raised edge and engine-turned with a band across it with the name. "Stent's", the letter "G" above, and a picture of a plate below the bank, held not to infringe and not liable to be passed off as a circular cake of dental composition with a raised edge and engine-turned in a different pattern with the name "Stents" across it in a panel and an impression plate above and below the panel, the plaintiffs not having a monopoly of the name "Stent", and the defendants' mark having been used for thirteen years, there being evidence that the limited class of purchasers for the goods would not be deceived.[37] Heart-shaped design with the initials "E.A.S.", not infringed by a more conventionally shaped heart with a letter and number, the initials being the characteristic of the plaintiffs' trade mark.[38] Letters A, B and C, and A, B, each within a diamond, held not to be infringed by a mark consisting of the letters A, B, C, in a device representing interlocked pieces of steel, and, although the plaintiffs' steel of particular qualities was known as "A Steel", "B Steel", etc., an injunction restraining the defendant from passing off by describing his steel as "A, B, C Steel" dissolved; also in an application by the plaintiffs to register a mark consisting of the letters A, B, C, in interlocked diamonds, that this mark was too near the defendant's unregistered mark.[39] The get-up of motor cabs consisting of a colouring of the cabs which was common, with the letters W. & G. in a peculiar script form, held to have been imitated by a get-up of similar colouring with the letters M. G.[40] Letter "S" twined round the body of a female, and within a wreath, too near a mark consisting of the letter "S" twined round a bird and within an oval.[41] "White Standard Table Jelly Crystals" ("White Standard" being the registered trade mark), with a single fruit denoting the flavour not a passing off of the defendant's goods as "White's Jelly Crystals" with a represention of the particular fruit, being goods sold by the plaintiffs.[42] Label containing prominently a picture of a cat lying down and a bottle of tonic wine and the words "Dubonnet Wine", not too near (1) a rampant cat on a barrel; or (2) a lable containing a sitting cat between the words "Gato Brand" ("gato" being Spanish and Portuguese for cat) and the words "Port Wine",[43] Five-pointed star in red with the letter "T" in green and "Texco" in black, not too near other star marks on the Register, not used in red, there being no evidence that any of the goods were known as star goods.[44] A label with a cat shown prominently, not to near a cat in a different attitude and in a widely different label, the cat being held to be common for the goods (gin).[45] Trade mark consisting of a skeleton map of Ireland with the proprietor's name across it, held not infringed by advertisements consiting of trays and tablets decorated with the map of Ireland and bearing the defendant's name.[46] Word "Bravo" in English and Russian charac-

[34] *Price's Patent Candle v. Ogston & Tennant* (1909) 26 R.P.C. 797.

[35] *Wright, Crossley & Co. v. Blezard* (1910) 27 R.P.C. 299.

[36] *Greisheim Electron*, 27 R.P.C. 201.

[37] *Claudius Ash v. Invicta* (1911) 28 R.P.C. 252, 597; (1912) 29 R.P.C. 465.

[38] *Schwerdtfeger v. Hart* (1912) 29 R.P.C. 236.

[39] *Andrew v. Kuehnrich* (1913) 30 R.P.C. 677.

[40] *W. & G. Du Cros v. Gold* (1913) 30 R.P.C. 117.

[41] *Sandow's Appn.* (1914) 31 R.P.C. 196.

[42] *White, Tomkins & Courage v. United Confectionery* (1914) 31 R.P.C. 430.

[43] *Dubonnet's Appn.* (1914) 31 R.P.C. 453; (1915) 32 R.P.C. 241.

[44] *Texas Co.'s Appn.* (1914) 31 R.P.C. 53; (1915) 32 R.P.C. 442. Before the Registrar's appeal was heard one of the marks cited was removed from the Register, and by consent no order was made on the appeal.

[45] *Bagots Hutton* (1915) 32 R.P.C. 333; [1916] 2 A.C. 382; (1916) R.P.C. 357.

[46] *Dunan Alerdice v. Burke* (1916) 33 R.P.C. 341.

ters within a triangle on its base not too near the letters "J.A.S." within an inverted triangle, a triangle being common to the trade.[47] Black cat on a globe not infringed by a device of a black cat standing behind a circular device.[48] Lable with the word "Victor" as its most prominent feature too near a trade mark consisting of the word "Victory" and a laurel wreath.[49] Mark consisting of four panels, one of which contained a representation of a ship, too near a trade mark of a warship, the opponents' goods being known as "Ship Brand".[50] Ace of spades with device of superimposed aces (for playing cards) not an infringement of plaintiffs' similar but more artistic device.[51] Device of an oxcart not an infringement being common in the trade and device not used as a trade mark.[52] "99" and words "double nine" not in infringement of "999" or calculated to deceive.[53] Picture of a girl with the words "cabaret girl" too near pictures of dancing girls with the words "carnival" and "columbine".[54] Lighthouse for illuminating oils not infringed by the use of a petrol pump in the form of lighthouse and no passing off.[55] Head and shoulders with the word "Gardener", too near a similar picture of a younger man.[56] Labels having a generally similar appearance.[57] Sow and three little pigs, too near "Three Pigs Brand" and another picture.[58] Sun and moon trade marks not infringed by word "Permacola" with part of sun against the letter P.[59] Labels having figures of elephants.[60] Similarity of "portrait marks."[61] Design of superimposed aces together with the word "Ace" not allowed in view of use of word "Ace" by opponents for over forty years.[62] Word "Arrow" an infringement of 3 intersecting arrows plus words "Arrow Brand."[63] Corkscrew in form of lady's head sold under name "Lulu" not infringed by screw in form of clown's head sold under the name "Clown".[64] Figure of guardsman, with name "Guards", for cigarettes, too close to "Guardsman" for tobacco to be registered; but "Guardsman" for pipes not restrained in view of "Guards" cigarette mark unless with similar figure of guardsman.[65] Symbols used by scientists to indicate sex, conjoined with a heart, descriptive of business of arranging introductions and not distinctive of plaintiffs' (new) business.[66] Shamrock device within a shield surmounted by the word "Grundig" and a crown not confusingly similar to a shamrock device alone for registration.[67] "Philips" in a shield device too close to signature "Chas. H. Phillips" for registration.[68] Two horse-drawn 2-wheeled vehicles not too close.[69] Three-leafed cloverleaf with long stem, confusingly similar to stylised

[47] *Crispin's Appn.* (1917) 34 R.P.C. 249.
[48] *Tatem v. Gaumont* (1918) 34 R.P.C. 181.
[49] *Massachusetts Saw Works* (1918) 35 R.P.C. 137.
[50] *Huxley's Appn.* (1924) 41 R.P.C. 423.
[51] *Goodall v. Waddington* (1924) 41 R.P.C. 465 and 658.
[52] *Young v. Grierson, Oldham* (1924) 41 R.P.C. 548.
[53] *Ardath v. W. Sandorides* (1925) 42 R.P.C. 50.
[54] *Distributing Corporation* (1927) 44 R.P.C. 225.
[55] *Carless, Capel & Leonard v. Pilmore-Bedford* (1928) 45 R.P.C. 205.
[56] *Morris & Jones* (1934) 51 R.P.C. 199.
[57] *Bryant & May v. United Match* (1933) 50 R.P.C. 12.
[58] *Danish Bacon's Appn.* (1934) 51 R.P.C. 148.
[59] *Hollins v. Cotella* (1937) 54 R.P.C. 81.
[60] *Bear v. Prayag Narain* (1941) 58 R.P.C. 25.
[61] *Subbiah Nadar v. Kumaraval Nadar* (1946) 63 R.P.C. 187.
[62] *Mellor's Appn.* (1948) 65 R.P.C. 238.
[63] *Cluett, Peabody v. McIntyre Hogg, Marsh* [1958] R.P.C. 335.
[64] *Universal Agencies v. Swolf* [1959] R.P.C. 247.
[65] *"Guards" T. M.* [1964] R.P.C. 9; *Carreras v. Frankau* [1964] R.P.C. 210.
[66] *Compatibility Research v. Computer Psyche* [1967] R.P.C. 201 (interlocutory injunction refused).
[67] *"Grundig" T. M.* [1968] R.P.C. 89.
[68] *"Phillips" T. M.* [1969] R.P.C. 8.
[69] [1985] R.P.C. 381.

three leafed clover mark.[70] An oval device containing the word "Coloroll" and a botanical sprig, not too near an oval device containing the words "Laura Ashley" and a botanical sprig.[71] The use of pink paper for financial news in the Evening Standard, not confusingly similar to the use of pink paper in the Financial Times.[72] A stylised device of the sun rising over a valley above the words "Waterford Foods", not confusingly similar to a stylised device of the sun rising over a valley leading to the sea above the words "Food Ireland".[73] An apple with about one-quarter bitten out, not likely to be associated with a whole apple device.[74] Coloured tabs on the right rear pocket of denim trousers, confusingly similar to coloured tabs on the left rear pocket of denim trousers.[75] Newspaper banner comprising "The European", not confusingly similar to a banner for "European Voice".[76] A device of two ovals, one contained within the other, the inner oval encompassing the word "Barilla", infringed by a device consisting of two ovals, one contained within the other, the inner one encompassing the word "Danis".[77] A device comprising three concentric "C's", likely to be confused with a device consisting of five concentric "C's".[78] Shape of a champagne bottle engraved with a motif and the words "Demoiselle de Champagne", infringed by a similarly shaped and engraved bottle carrying the words "Belle de Champagne".[79] Trade marked bottle shape infringed.[80] The use of three parallel stripes on sportswear, confusingly similar to a trade mark incorporating three parallel stripes applied to clothing.[81] The cursive signature "Elvis Presley", confusingly similar to "Elvisly Yours" in a similar cursive script.[82] A device consisting of the word "Naturelle" with the verticals of the letter N extended to form an oval enclosing both the word itself and three flowers, too close to the word mark "Natrel".[83] Three headed electric razor, admitted to be too close to a trade marked depiction of a three headed electric razor (but trade mark invalid).[84] Device of the word "Telecom" with red and grey dots between the letters, not infringed in a satirical newspaper article by the word "Teurer" with red and grey dots between the letters.[85] Stylised brush stroke and the word "Masters", too similar to registered stylised brush stroke.[86] A device of crossed arrows, not too similar to a device of crossed arrows and the words "Unidad De Farmacovigilancia Glaxo".[87] A black square containing the word "Booknet" in white, confusingly similar to a black square containing the words "Le Book" in white.[88] Three dimensional mark for a cylindrical device with recessed ends, not infringed by a similar cylindrical device.[89] "Dinokids" not confusingly similar to a device of a young dinosaur above the word

[70] *SHAMROCK Trade Mark* [1986] F.S.R. 271.
[71] *Laura Ashley Ltd v. Coloroll Ltd* [1987] R.P.C. 1.
[72] *The Financial Times Ltd v. Evening Standard Co. Ltd* [1991] F.S.R. 7.
[73] *An Bord Trachtala v. Waterford Foods Plc* [1994] F.S.R. 317.
[74] *Ciba-Geigy Plc v. Parke Davis & Co. Ltd* [1994] F.S.R. 8.
[75] *Levi Strauss v. Kimbyr Investments Ltd* [1994] F.S.R. 335.
[76] *The European Ltd v. The Economist Newspapers Ltd* [1996] F.S.R. 431.
[77] *Barilla Alimentare SPA v. Danis SRL* [1996] E.T.M.R. 43 (Italy) (also [1999] E.T.M.R. 677).
[78] *C (Device Trade Mark)* [1998] R.P.C. 439.
[79] *Vranken SA v. Champagne H. Germain et Fils SA* [1998] E.T.M.R. 390 (France) .
[80] *Kabushiki Kaisha Yakult Honsha v. Danone Nederland BV* [1998] E.T.M.R. 465 (Benelux).
[81] *Adidas A.G. v. N. V. Famco* [1998] E.T.M.R. 616 (Commercial Court, Belgium).
[82] *ELVIS PRESLEY Trade Marks* [1999] R.P.C. 567.
[83] *NATURELLE Trade Mark* [1999] R.P.C. 326.
[84] *Philips Electronics NV v. Remington Consumer Products Ltd* [1999] R.P.C. 809.
[85] *"Alles Wird Teurer"* [1999] E.T.M.R. 49 (Germany).
[86] *Reufach Marketing GmbH's Application* [1999] E.T.M.R. 412.
[87] *Grupo Grifols SA's Application* [1999] E.T.M.R. 507 (OHIM).
[88] *Sarl Le Book Editions v. Ste EPC Edition Presse Communications* [1999] E.T.M.R. 554 (France).
[89] *Mars BV v. Societe Des Produits Nestle SA* [1999] E.T.M.R. 862 (Benelux).

"Dino".[90] A three-dimensional mark for a blue bottle, not infringed by a similarly shaped blue bottle.[91] "Coq D'Or" (and cockerel device), not confusingly similar to "Victoria" (and cockerel device).[92] Circular device enclosing a spanner head shape and the word "React", distinguishable from the word mark "Reactor".[93] An oval device with decorative border containing the words "Nathalies Gobelins", confusingly similar to an oval device with a decorative border containing the words "Gobelins Art".[94] The letter "K" enclosed in a rhombus, not confusingly similar to a letter "V" (or "L") in a circle, surrounded by a square border.[95] Stylised, modern looking, letter "L", not confusingly similar to a differently stylised, old fashioned looking, letter "L".[96] "Nike" in white on a black square, detrimental to the reputation of a prior mark consisting of "Nike" in white italics on a red square.[97] A proposed three-dimensional mark for a bottle in the shape of a football boot with three stripes on the outside upper, took advantage of and was detrimental to a mark for three stripes on the outside upper of footwear.[98]

(2) CONTRASTED WORDS

"White Rose", too near "Rosaline."[99] "Condi-Sanitas", infringements of "San- **A35–03** itas."[1] "Boyd's Universal Harness Composition", in a label with the Arms of the City of Dublin, not an infringement of "Propert's Improved Harness Composition" in a label with a fox's head, the labels being similarly got up.[2] "Apollinis", an infringement of "Apollinaris".[3] "Steinberg", and infringement of "Steinway", used with similar devices.[4] "Emollio", too near "Emolline".[5] "Emolliolorum", not too near "Molliscorium."[6] "Swift's Specific" not calculated to deceive merely because the words were descriptive of the opponent's drug.[7] "Oomoo", not to near "Emu".[8] "Kokoko", too near the common word "Coco".[9] "Demotic", an infringement of "Demon".[10] "Dunn's Fruit Salt Baking Powder", too near "Eno's Fruit Salt";[11] subsequently held to be an infringement.[12] "El Devino", an infringement of "El Destino".[13] Label with "El Destinacion", an infringement of a similar label with "El Destino".[14] Label with "London Pickles", an infringement of a similar label with "London Pickle Co."[15] "Stafford", an infringement

---

[90] *Herbalife International Inc's Application* [1999] E.T.M.R. 882 (OHIM).
[91] *Ty Nant Spring Water Ltd v. Lemon & Co. SRL* [1999] E.T.M.R. 969 (Italy).
[92] *Fromex SA's Application* [1999] E.T.M.R. 989 (OHIM).
[93] *REACT AND DEVICE Trade Mark* [2000] R.P.C. 285.
[94] *Rose's Lace Boutique v. BVBA Parcles* [2000] E.T.M.R. 1 (Benelux).
[95] *Stillwater Designs and Audio Inc's Application* [2000] E.T.M.R. 35 (OHIM).
[96] *Loewe SA's Application* [2000] E.T.M.R. 40 (OHIM).
[97] *Campomar SL's Application* [2000] E.T.M.R. 50 (OHIM).
[98] *Inlima SL's Application* [2000] E.T.M.R. 325.
[99] *White Rose T. M.* (1885) 30 Ch.D. 505.
[1] *Sanitas v. Condy* (1886) 4 R.P.C. 195 and 530; 56 L.T. 621.
[2] *Beddow v. Boyd* (188) 4 R.P.C. 310.
[3] *Apollinaris Co. v. Herfeldt* (1887) 4 R.P.C. 478.
[4] *Steinway v. Henshaw* (1888) 5 R.P.C. 77.
[5] *Grossmith's T. M.* (1889) 6 R.P.C. 180; 60 L.T. 612.
[6] *Talbot's T. M.* (1894) 11 R.P.C. 77.
[7] *Swift's T. M.* (1889) 6 R.P.C. 352.
[8] *Burgoyne's T. M.* (1889) 6 R.P.C. 227; 61 L.T. 39.
[9] *Jackson & Co.'s T. M.* (1889) 6 R.P.C. 80.
[10] *Slazenger v. Feltham* (1889) 6 R.P.C. 531.
[11] *Eno v. Dunn* (1889) 41 Ch.D. 439; (1890) 15 App.Cas. 252; (1890) 7 R.P.C. 311.
[12] (1893) 10 R.P.C. 261.
[13] *Pinto v. Trott* (1891) 8 R.P.C. 173.
[14] *Pinto v. Badman* (1891) 8 R.P.C. 181.
[15] *Hammond v. Malcolm, Brunker* (1892) 9 R.P.C. 301.

of "Trafford"; "Fort" of "Fortress"; "New Mistress"; but not "New Matron", "New Master", of "Master", or "Mistress"; but "South African" not an infringement of a mark consisting of a negro's head and the word "African".[16] "Vincalis", not too near "Wincarnis", the goods being different in appearance and use.[17] "Triticumina", not infringed by "Triticine".[18] Signature "Robert Crawford", not infringement of signature "Daniel Crawford".[19] "Margarita", an infringement of "La Flor de Margaretta".[20] "Savoline", an infringement of "Savonol".[21] "Ivory", for soap, not necessarily calculated to cause the goods to be confused with "Ivy" soap.[22] "Night Cap", not too near "Red Cap" or "Mother Red Cap".[23] "Valtine", too near "Valentine".[24] "S. Griffiths", three stars and I.X.L., not infringed by "E. Griffiths" and three stars, the stars being common marks of quality.[25] "St. Ives" cheese held too similar to "St. Ivel", registered for cheese.[26] "Neostyle", not to near "Cyclostyle".[27] "Securine", an infringement of "Seccotine".[28] "Cocosoline", not an infringement of "Cottolene".[29] Mark including the words "Jock Scott", too near "Scotch Jock".[30] "Tablones", to near "Tabloids".[31] "Neola", not to near "Pianola".[32] "Lanco", not too near "Lancashire".[33] "B.A.S.", too near B.S.A.".[34] "Midland Star", not too near "Star",[35] alleged passing off, there being several names in use in the trade which included the word "star". "Glen Thorne" for whisky, too near "Thorne's" whisky.[36] "Aquatite", not too near "Aquascutum", there being other names in the trade (water-proof garments) also beginning with "Aqua".[37] "Osowoolo", too near "Orlwoola".[38] "Murrilo", too near "Muralo".[39] "Colonial", not an infringement of or liable to be passed off as "Colonel".[40] "Sailor" beneath a picture of a sailor not too near "Skipper", although the picture was associated with the word "Skipper" in respect of other goods.[41] "Murad", too near "Muratti".[42] "Pick Them Out", preceded by work "Bargains", too near device of a pick and the word "Pick".[43] "Carvino", not to neawr "Wincarnis".[44] "Aqua-Repela", too near "Repellus", owing to the probability of abbreviation to

[16] *Smith and Wellstood v. Carron* (1896) 13 R.P.C. 108.
[17] *Colman v. Brown* (1899) 16 R.P.C. 619 (passing off).
[18] *Meaby v. Triticine* (1898) 15 R.P.C. 1.
[19] *Crawford v. Bernard* (1894) 11 R.P.C. 580.
[20] *Benedictus v. Sullivan, Powell* (1895) 12 R.P.C. 25.
[21] *Field v. Wagel* (1900) 17 R.P.C. 266.
[22] *Goodwin v. Ivory Soap* (1901) 18 R.P.C. 389.
[23] *Hedley's T. M.s* (1900) 17 R.P.C. 719.
[24] *Valentine Meat Juice v. Valentine Extract* (1900) 17 R.P.C. 673 (passing off) (and see (1901) 18 R.P.C. 175).
[25] *Marshall v. Sidebotham* (1901) 18 R.P.C. 43.
[26] *Aplin and Barrett v. Richards* (1903) 20 R.P.C. 799.
[27] *Neostyle's T. M.* (1903) 20 R.P.C. 329 and 803.
[28] *McCaw, Stevenson & Orr v. Nickols* (1903) 21 R.P.C. 15.
[29] *Fairbank v. Cocos Butter* (1904) 21 R.P.C. 23.
[30] *Booth's Appn.* (1904) 21 R.P.C. 18.
[31] *Capsuloid's Appn.* (1906) 23 R.P.C. 782.
[32] *Pianotist's Appn.* (1906) 23 R.P.C. 774.
[33] *Reddaway v. Irwell and Eastern* (1906) 23 R.P.C. 621; (1907) 24 R.P.C. 203.
[34] *Birmingham Small Arms v. Webb* (1907) 24 R.P.C. 27, passing off.
[35] *Stay Cycle v. Frankenburgs* (1907) 24 R.P.C. 46 and 405.
[36] *Thorne v. Pimms* (1909) 26 R.P.C. 221, rectification and passing off.
[37] *Aquascutum v. Cohen and Wilks* (1909) 26 R.P.C. 651.
[38] *Brock* (1909) 26 R.P.C. 683.
[39] *Muralo v. Taylor* (1910) 27 R.P.C. 261, passing off.
[40] *St. Mungo v. Viper* (19100 27 R.P.C. 420.
[41] *Angus Watson* (1911) 28 R.P.C. 313.
[42] *Muratti v. Murad* (1911) 28 R.P.C. 497.
[43] *Briggs v. Dunn* (1911) 28 R.P.C. 704, infringement and passing off.
[44] *Coleman v. Smith* [1911] 2 Ch. 572; (1911) 28 R.P.C. 645; (1912) 29 R.P.C. 81.

"Repela".[45] "Schicht" held to be calculated to deceive by reason of the resemblance to "Sunlight".[46] "Stateroom", too near "State Express", the latter often abbreviated to "State".[47] "Limit", not too near "Summit".[48] "Herogen", not too near "Ceregen", the goods being different.[49] "Mendit" not an infringement of "Mendine", the right to the exclusive use of "Mend" being disclaimed.[50] "Onsoria", held on interloctury motion to be an infringment of "Anzora".[51] "Swankie", not too near a mark consisting of the word "Swan" with a picture of a swan.[52] "Lavroma", not an infringement of "Lavona" or "Lavona".[53] "British Dominion Bond", with distinctive lettering and a monogram, too near "British Bond", with similar lettering and a monogram, in a passing off action.[54] "Ca Radium", an infringement of "Radium".[55] "Malagole", for pens, too near a mark bearing the name "J. B. Mallat", "Mallet" pens being well known.[56] "Anchola", not too near "Anchovette", which was registered with a disclaimer of "Anchov".[57] "Gnidroc" too near the name "Cording", which was part of the name of the opponent company, J. C. Cording & Co. Ltd; as well as that of the applicant company.[58] "Oxot", an infringement of "Oxo".[59] "The Regiment", for cigarettes, not an infringement of "Regimental" or "Regimental Cigarettes".[60] "Victor" too near "Victory" and a laurel wreath.[61] "Rito", not an infringement of "Lito" or of a trade mark consisting of "Y-To" and a device.[62] "Motrate" not too near "Filtrate".[63] "Vino" and "Vyno", too near "Harvino".[64] "Molivar" and "La Molivar" too near "Bolivar".[65] "Zykol", too near "Zeekol".[66] "Egall", too near "Egrol".[67] "Pan-pep", not too near "Peps".[68] "Galaxy", with "The Milky Way", too near "Glaxo".[69] "Germocea", too near "Germolene".[70] "Cream of the North", not too near "Royal Northern Cream", in a label quite dissimilar, "Cream" being common in the trade (Whisky).[71] "Sterling" across a coin, too near a word. the symbol of a pound and the world "Lockstitch".[72] "Freia", too near "Fry".[73] "Hemvo", too near "Harvo".[74] "Amata", and infringement of "Amami".[75]

---

[45] *Wilks' Appn.* (1912) 29 R.P.C. 21.
[46] *Schicht's Appn.* (1912) 29 R.P.C. 483.
[47] *United Kingdom Tobacco* (1912) 29 R.P.C. 489.
[48] *Smith's Appn.* (1913 30 R.P.C. 363.
[49] *British Drug Houses* (1913) 30 R.P.C. 74.
[50] *Coombe v. Mendit* (1913) 30 R.P.C. 709.
[51] *Lewis v. Vine* (1914) 31 R.P.C. 12.
[52] *Crook's T. M.* (1914) 31 R.P.C. 79.
[53] *Tokalon v. Davidson* (1914) 31 R.P.C. 74; (1915) 32 R.P.C. 133.
[54] *Spicer v. Spalding & Hodge* (1915) 32 R.P.C. 52.
[55] *Brighten v. Cavendish* (1915) 32 R.P.C. 229.
[56] *Hinks, Wells* (1916) 33 R.P.C. 281.
[57] *Waide's Appn.* (1916) 33 R.P.C. 320.
[58] *Cording's Appn.* (1916) 33 R.P.C. 83 and 325.
[59] *Oxo v. King* (1917) 34 R.P.C. 165.
[60] *Imperial Tobacco v. De Pasquali* (1918) 35 R.P.C. 185.
[61] *Massachusetts Saw Works* (1918) 35 R.P.C. 137.
[62] *Fitchetts v. Loubet* (1919) 36 R.P.C. 296.
[63] *Fox's Appn.* (1920) 37 R.P.C. 37.
[64] *Wheatley, Akeroyd* (1920) 37 R.P.C. 137.
[65] *Middlemas & Wood v. Moliver* (1921) 38 R.P.C. 97.
[66] *J. Brown's Appn.* (1921) 38 R.P.C. 15.
[67] *Egg Products* (1922) 39 R.P.C. 155.
[68] *United Chemists* (1923) 40 R.P.C. 219.
[69] *Smiths' Appn.* (1923) 40 R.P.C. 77.
[70] *Taylor's Appn.* (1923) 40 R.P.C. 193.
[71] *Hutchinson's Appn.* (1924) 41 R.P.C. 538.
[72] *Connor's Appn.* (1924) 41 R.P.C. 458.
[73] *Freia Chocolate* (1924) 41 R.P.C. 653.
[74] *Hemmings's Appn.* (1924) 41 R.P.C. 672.
[75] *Prichard & Constance v. Amata* (1925) 42 R.P.C. 63.

"Tripcastroid", not too near "Castrol".[76] "Muralol", an infringement of "Mirabol".[77] "Faris Cycle", not too near "Fairycycle".[78] "Nuvol", too near "Nujol".[79] "Nuvola", too near "Nujol".[80] "Justikon", an infringement of "Ustikon".[81] "Red Knight", an infringement of "Silent Knight".[82] "Camay", too near "Cameo".[82] "Ernalde",not an infringement of "Nilde".[84] "Sunshine Snow" and picture not an infringement of "Snowfire" and picture.[85] "Ucolite" too near "Coalite".[86] "Brick", too near "Brico".[87] not too near "Lektrik", the goods being different.[88] "Abermill Bond, made in Great Britain", not too near "Hammermill".[89] "Pup", not too near (for gramophones, etc.) to a representation of a dog listening to a gramophone.[90] "Pine-exx", an infringement of "Pinette".[91] "Kleen-up", an infringement of "Kleenoff".[92] "Hyde Park", allowed notwithstanding registered marks including "Park" or "Park Drive", subject to a limitation as to goods.[93] "Erectiko", too near to "Erector".[94] "Maria Lisette", an infringement of "Marie Elizabeth".[95] "Arlette", allowed notwithstanding "Ardenette" subject to limitation as to goods.[96] "Sanrus", in infringement of "Rus".[97] "Pepsi Cola", not an infringement of Coca Cola".[98] "Geoff Ray", an infringement of both "Gor-Ray" and "Kone Ray".[99] "Stayco", not too near "Gayco".[1] "Honomol", too near "Honyol".[2] "Rysta", too near "Aristoc".[3] "Supavite", too near " Supervita".[4] "Morex", allowed notwithstanding "Rex" and "Morrisflex".[5] "Jardex", too near "Jardox".[6] "Ovax", allowed notwithstanding "Hovis" and "Ovi".[7] "Plyopher", not allowed in view of Pliobond". "Pliowax" and 12 other marks commencing with "Plio".[8] "Vivicyllin", allowed notwithstanding "Cyllin".[9] "Diasil", allowed notwithstanding "Alasil", subject to limitation as to goods.[10] "Eastex", allowed notwithstanding "Lastex".[11] "Solibrisa", allowed notwithstanding "Summer

[76] *London Lubricants* (1925) 42 R.P.C. 264.
[77] *Walpamur v. Sanderson* (1926) 43 R.P.C. 385.
[78] *Lines Bros v. Farris* (1925) 43 R.P.C. 64 (a passing-off case).
[79] *McDowell's Appn.* (1927) R.P.C. 335, HL.
[80] *Savage's Appn.* (1927) 44 R.P.C. 1.
[81] *Davis v. Sussex Rubber* (1927) 44 R.P.C. 412.
[82] *Forth and Clyde v. Sugg* 1928 45 R.P.C. 382.
[83] *Proctor and Gamble v. Pugsley Dingman* (1929) 46 R.P.C. (application for registration).
[84] *Soc. Nildé v. Ernaidé* (1929) 46 R.P.C. 453.
[85] *Hampshire v. General Kaputine* (1930) R.P.C. 437.
[86] *Magdalena Securities* (1931) 48 R.P.C. 477.
[87] *Lauritzen's Appn.* (1931) 48 R.P.C. 392.
[88] *Lundberg* (1932) 49 R.P.C. 15.
[89] *Pirie's Appn.* (1932) 49 R.P.C. 195; (1933) 50 R.P.C. 147.
[90] *"Pup"* (1933) 50 R.P.C. 198.
[91] *Dixon v. Taylor and Cowells* (1933) 50 R.P.C. 405.
[92] *Bale and Churhc v. Sutton, Parsons* (1934) 51 R.P.C. 129.
[93] *Harrods Appn.* (1935) 52 R.P.C. 65.
[94] *Bailey* (1935) 52 R.P.C. 136.
[95] *Fialho v. Simond* (1937) 54 R.P.C. 193.
[96] *City Chemical's Appn.* (1937) 54 R.P.C. 182.
[97] *Ravenhead Brick v. Ruabon* (1937) 54 R.P.C. 341.
[98] *Coca Cola of Canada v. Pepsi Cola of Canada* (1942) 59 R.P.C. 127.
[99] *Stillitz v. Jones & Higgins* (1943) 60 R.P.C. 15.
[1] *Angus's Appn.* (1943) 60 R.P.C. 29.
[2] *Marshall's Appn.* (1943) 60 R.P.C. 147.
[3] (1943) 60 R.P.C. 87 and (1945) 62 R.P.C. 65, HL.
[4] (1944) 61 R.P.C. 31.
[5] *Darwin's Appn.* (1946) R.P.C. 1.
[6] *Edward's Appn.* (1946) 63 R.P.C. 19.
[7] *Smith Hayden* (1946) 63 R.P.C. 97.
[8] *Beck, Koller* (1947) 64 R.P.C. 76.
[9] *Enoch's Appn.* (1947) 64 R.P.C. 119.
[10] *Bayer's Appn.* (1947) 64 R.P.C. 125.
[11] *"Eastex"* (1947) 64 R.P.C. 142: case decided under the special rules relating to defensive marks.

Breeze".[12] "Burwear", too near unregistered mark "Bairnswear".[13] "Seda-Seltzer" allowed notwithstanding "Alka-Seltzer".[14] "Sunfleck", too near "Sunflex".[15] "Sunniwite", an infringement of "Sunlight".[16] "Chemico", not allowed in view of "Chemia".[17] "Alka-Vescent", not allowed in view of "Alka-Seltzer".[18] "Karsote Vapour Rub", an infringement of "Vapo Rub".[19] "Gilray", not too near "Gor-Ray".[20] "Gala", not too near "Goya".[21] "Star Dust", too near "Starmist".[22] "Dreamland", not allowed, in view of "Slumberland".[23] "Vanildene", not allowed, in view of "Vaseline".[24] "Micronic", allowed notwithstanding "Microvee".[25] "Sprattykat" might be confused with "Kit-e-Kat", but interlocutory relief refused.[26] "Algelox", allowed notwithstanding "Aludrox".[27] "Electrix" an infringement of "Electrux".[28] "vivos", allowed notwithstanding "Hovis".[29] Dustic", allowed notwithstanding "Bostik".[30] "White Ship", not allowed in view of "Old Ship".[31] "Pretty Kitty", not too near "Kit-e-Kat".[32] "Chamlet", too near "Babycham".[33] "Kokola", too near "Coco Cola".[34] "Pem Books", too near "Pan Books".[35] "Red Shield", etc., not allowed, in view of "Red Seal". etc.[36] "Welloy", refused registration, in view of "Walloy".[37] "Ikf Koyo", not allowed, in view of "S.K.F." and "Skefko".[38] "Watermatic", too near "Aquamatic".[39] "Naturalizet", too near "Naturalizer".[40] "Kidax" allowed notwithstanding "Daks".[41] "Velva-Glo" too close to "Vel-Glo".[42] "Knoll International" too close to "Parker-Knoll".[43] "Palexa" too close to "Plix".[44] "Galvalloy" not too close to "Galvafroid".[45] "Wells Whip" too close to "Walls Whip".[46] "Guards" with figure too close to "Guardsman" for registration but (the goods being different) "Guardsman"

[12] Baléy's Appn. (1948) 65 R.P.C. 17.
[13] Burcombe's Appn. (1948) 65 R.P.C. 179.
[14] Demuth's Appn. (1948) 65 R.P.C. 342.
[15] Crowther's Appn. (1948) 65 R.P.C. 369.
[16] Lever Bros v. Sunniwite (1949) 66 R.P.C. 84.
[17] County Chemical's Appn. (1949) 66 R.P.C. 268.
[18] Broadhead's Appn. (1950) 67 R.P.C. 113, 209.
[19] De Cordova v. Vick (1951) 68 R.P.C. 103, 226, 270.
[20] Gor-Ray v. Gilray (1952) 69 R.P.C. 99, 199.
[21] Goya v. Gala (1952) 69 R.P.C. 188.
[22] Steiner v. Raymond (1951) 69 R.P.C. 40.
[23] Whitling's Appn. (1952) 69 R.P.C. 219.
[24] Ana Laboratories (1951) 69 R.P.C. 146.
[25] Automotive Products (1953) 70 R.P.C. 224.
[26] Chappie v. Spratts (1954) 71 R.P.C. 455.
[27] Harker Stagg's T. M. (1954) 71 R.P.C. 136.
[28] Electrolux v. Electrix (1953) 70 R.P.C. 127, 155; (1954) 71 R.P.C. 23, CA.
[29] Spiller's Appn. (1952) 69 R.P.C. 327; 70 R.P.C. 51; (1954) 71 R.P.C. 234, HL.
[30] Dundas' (R. K.) Appn. (1955) 72 R.P.C. 151.
[31] Mellor's Appn. (1955) 72 R.P.C. 82.
[32] Chappie v. Warrington Canners (1955) 72 R.P.C. 73.
[33] Showerings v. Bulmer [1956] R.P.C. 307.
[34] Coca Cola v. Highlande [1957] R.P.C. 313.
[35] Pan Books v. Word Distributors [1957] R.P.C. 366.
[36] Warwick Upholstery [1958] R.P.C. 488.
[37] British Lead Mills [1958] R.P.C. 425.
[38] Koyo Seiko Kabushiki Kaisha [1957] R.P.C. 297; [1958] R.P.C. 112, CA.
[39] Reynolds v. Laffeaty's [1957] R.P.C. 311; [1958] R.P.C. 387, CA.
[40] Brosn Shoe [1958] R.P.C. 406; [1959] R.P.C. 29 (rectification).
[41] "Kiddax" [1960] R.P.C. 117, CA.
[42] "Velva-Glo" T. M. [1961] R.P.C. 225 (fluorescent paints). Registration refused.
[43] "Parker-Knoll" case [1962] R.P.C. 265; held that "Knoll" was a distinctive feature of "Parker-Knoll" and that "Knoll International" was bound to get shortened to "Knoll". Injunctions granted (HL).
[44] Hair-setting compositions; there were suggestions of dishonesty: L'Oreawl v. Coiffeur Supplies [1961] R.P.C. 219. Interlocutory injunctions granted.
[45] "Galva—" being common: "Galvalloy" [1963] R.P.C. 34. Registration allowed.
[46] Ice Cream: Walls v. Wells Whip [1964] R.P.C. 197. Interlocutory injunction granted.

not necessarily deceptively close to "Guards" unless accompanied by device.[47] "Merrie Jane" a borderline case as against "Mary Jane".[48] "Merrimacs" too close to "Macs".[49] "Accutron" too close to "Accurist".[50] "Buler" too close to "Bulova".[51] "Acec" not too close to "Ace" for registration.[52] "V-CIL-K" infringed by "econoCIL-VK".[53] "Butazolidin" not infringed by "Butazone".[54] "Rheinliebling" too close to "Liebling" for registration.[55] "Transfermatic" too close to "Cross Transfermatic" and "Transfer-matic" (rectification).[56] "Picot" not infringed by "Piquant".[57] "B.P." not infringed by "E.P."[58] "Coca-Cola" not infringed by "Koalo Kola".[59] "Pristacin" infringed by "Bristacyn".[60] "Bulova Accutron" too close to "Accurist" for registration".[61] "Bali" too close to "Berlei" (rectification).[62] "Cal-U-Test" not too close to marks with suffix "Test" (common to trade).[63] "Handy Andies" infringed by "Handi Hanki".[64] "Kennomeat" (for dog food) infringed by "Ken-L" (for cat food).[65] "Pick of the Pops" too close to "Top of the Pops"[66] "Frigiking" allowed in Part B against "Thermo-King".[67] "English Leather" too close to "Imperial Leather".[68] "Skins" too close to "Skinners".[69] "Phildar" not too close to "Sirdar".[70] "Predenema" too close to "Predsol Enema".[71] "Happi-Nappi" not too close to "Napp".[72] "Kojack Lollies" too close to "Kojapops".[73] "Titch" not too close to "Botstitch".[74] "Solavoid"[75] and

[47] "Guards" with figure of guardsman refused registration for cigarettes in face of "Guardsman" for tobacco, "Guards" [1964] R.P.C. 9; interlocutory injunction granted against "Guardsman" with figure of guardsman for pipes, in view of similar figure on plaintiffs' "Guards" cigarettes; but no injunction against "Guardsman" for the pipes in itself: Carreras v. Farnkau & Co. [1964] R.P.C. 210.

[48] Dresses: distinct possibility of confusion but confusion not inevitable, so interlocutory injunction refused on balance of convenience: "Mary Jane" case [1961] R.P.C. 389.

[49] Medicated sweet: Macleans v. Lightbrown (1937) 54 R.P.C. 230. Injunction granted.

[50] "Accutron" T. M. [1966] 152 (watches).

[51] "Buler" T. M. [1966] R.P.C. 141 (watches). There was some evidence of confusion abroad. The marks were treated as pronounced "Booler" and "Boo Lova".

[52] ACEC T. M. [1965] R.P.C. 369.

[53] Lilly (Eli) v. Chelsea Drug [1966] R.P.C. 14. The letters "econo" were four times smaller than the capitals.

[54] Geigy v. Chelsea Drug [1966] R.P.C. 65. Special circumstances of pharmaceutical trade taken into account (interlocutory motion in Vacation Court).

[55] Rheinliebling [1966] R.P.C. 68 (Rhein wines).

[56] "Transfermatic" [1966] R.P.C. 568. (Certain dicta, but not decision, disapproved in "Bali" [1969] R.P.C. 472).

[57] Picot v. Goya [1967] R.P.C. 573 (perfumes).

[58] British Petroleum v. European Petroleum [1968] R.P.C. 54 (petrol).

[59] Coca-Cola v. Struthers [1968] R.P.C. 231 (Scots) (soft drinks).

[60] Bristol-Myers v. Bristol Pharmaceutical [1968] R.P.C. 259 (pharmaceuticals).

[61] "Bulova Accutron" [1969] R.P.C. 102. The Court of Appeal had already held "Accutron" too close, "Accutron" [1966] R.P.C. 152.

[62] "Bali" [1969] R.P.C. 472 (brassières).

[63] "Cal-U-Test" [1967] F.S.R. 39 (Reg.).

[64] Bowater-Scott v. Modo [1969] F.S.R. 330.

[65] Spillers v. Quaker Oats [1969] F.S.R. 510, compromised on appeal, [1970] F.S.R. 11.

[66] Pickwick v. Multiple Sound [1972] R.P.C. 786, CA (passing off).

[67] [1973] R.P.C. 739.

[68] Mem v. Cussons [1974] R.P.C. 7 (Bermuda, where "Imperial Leather" was the only "Leather" mark).

[69] In Things v. Leather Garments [1974] F.S.R. (passing off of jeans).

[70] Sirdar v. Mulliez [1975] F.S.R. 309 (Eire).

[71] Glaxo v. Pharmax [1976] F.S.R. 278 (passing off; prima facie case of likely confusion but no injunction since pharmacists check).

[72] [1976] R.P.C. 611 (Regy).

[73] Taverner Rutledge v. Trexapalm [1977] R.P.C. 275 ("Kojak" a TV character; passing off).

[74] Textron v. Stephens [1977] R.P.C. 283.

[75] [1977] R.P.C. 1, PC(N.Z.).

"Pol Rama"[76] not too close to "Polaroid" (sunglasses). "Zing" too near "Ping".[77] "Rheumaton" not too close to "Rheumanosticon".[78] "Tingate" too near "Colgate" in Trinidad.[79] "Turbogaz" too near "Turbotorch".[80] "Tornado" not too near "Torna".[81] "Fif" not too near "Jif".[82] "Unimax" too near "Univac".[83] "Sorbislo" too near "Sorbitrate".[84] "Country Fair Oven Chips" not too near "McCain Oven Chips".[85] "Merit" not too near "Nerit".[86] "Da Vinci" too close to "Vincci".[87] "Keebler" too near "Keiller".[88] "Vedonis Thermawarm" (sometimes mis-written by customers and dealers as "Vedonis Thermawear") too close to "Thermawear".[89] "Pruriderm" too close to "Prioderm".[90] "Kodiak" not allowed because of "Kodak".[91] "Lancer" allowed despite "Lancia".[92] "Benji" confusingly similar to "Bendy".[93] "Mother Care/Other Care" not confusingly similar to "Mothercare".[94] "Charles of the Ritz" and "Ritz" not confusingly similar to "Ritz".[95] "Chelsea Man" confusingly similar to "Chelsea Girl".[96] "Furniture City" distinguishable from "Furnitureland".[97] "Lifeguard" not an infringement of "Lifebuoy".[98] "Portablast" infringed "Porta".[99] "Star" too close to "Spar".[1] "Terbuline" too close to "Terbolan" and "Terbalin".[2] "Thermos Prima" not confusingly similar to "Primark".[3] "Torre Nova" distinguishable from "Torres".[4] "Security Management Today" not similar to "Management Today", but there was a risk of association.[5] "Tamworth Herald and Post" (and disclaimer) not confusing despite "Tamworth Herald".[6] "Bensyl" confusingly similar to "Bentasil" and "Benvil".[7] "Inadin" too close to "Anadin" and "Anadin Extra".[8] "What's New In Training" magazine confusingly similar to the "What's New In . . ." stable of magazines.[9] "Primasport" allowed notwithstanding "Primark".[10] "Univer" confusingly similar to "Univet".[11] "BBC Gourmet

[76] [1977] R.P.C. 581 (Regy.).
[77] [1978] R.P.C. 47 (Regy.).
[78] [1978] R.P.C. 406 (Regy.).
[79] Colgate v. Pattron [1978] R.P.C. 635, PC (infringement and passing off).
[80] [1978] R.P.C. 206 (Regy.).
[81] [1979] R.P.C. 155 (Regy.).
[82] [1979] R.P.C. 355.
[83] [1979] R.P.C. 469 (Regy.).
[84] Stuart v. Rona [1981]. F.S.R. 20 ("high probability" of confusion).
[85] McCain v. Country Fair [1981] R.P.C. 69, CA (passing off).
[86] "Nerit" [1982] F.S.R. 72, CA. A remarkable decision.
[87] [1908] R.P.C. 237 (Regy.).
[88] [1980] R.P.C. 243 (Regy.).
[89] Thermawear v. Vedonis [1982] R.P.C. 44 (infringement and passing off).
[90] [1985] R.P.C. 187 (Regy.).
[91] KODIAK Trade Mark [1987] R.P.C. 269.
[92] LANCER Trade Mark [1987] R.P.C. 303.
[93] BENJI Trade Mark [1988] R.P.C. 251.
[94] Mothercare U.K. Ltd v. Penguin Books Ltd [1988] R.P.C. 133.
[95] The Ritz Hotel Ltd v. Charles of the Ritz Ltd [1989] R.P.C. 333 (Australia).
[96] CHELSEA MAN Trade Mark [1989] R.P.C. 111.
[97] Furnitureland Ltd v. Harris [1989] 1 F.S.R. 536.
[98] Unilever Plc v. Johnson Wax [1989] 1 F.S.R. 145.
[99] Portakabin Ltd v. Powerblast Ltd [1990] R.P.C. 471.
[1] STAR Trade Mark [1990] R.P.C. 522.
[2] TERBULINE Trade Mark [1990] R.P.C. 21.
[3] THERMOS PRIMA Trade Mark [1991] R.P.C. 120.
[4] TORRE NOVA Trade Mark [1991] R.P.C. 109.
[5] Management Publications Ltd v. Blenheim Exhibitions Group Plc [1991] F.S.R. 348.
[6] Tamworth Herald Co Ltd v. Thomson Free Newspapers Ltd [1991] F.S.R. 337.
[7] BENSYL Trade Mark [1992] R.P.C. 529.
[8] INADIN Trade Mark [1992] R.P.C. 421.
[9] Morgan-Grampian v. Training Personnel Ltd [1992] F.S.R. 267.
[10] PRIMASPORT Trade Mark [1992] F.S.R. 515.
[11] UNIVER Trade Mark [1993] R.P.C. 239.

GoodFood" sufficiently different from "Gourmet".[12] "E. Quadra" too similar to "Quattro".[13] "Waterford Foods" (and device) distinguishable from "Food Ireland" (and device).[14] "Diclomax Retard" (and device) not confusingly similar to "Voltarol Retard" (and device).[15] "Stellacream" too close to "Brylcreem".[16] "Jockey" allowed notwithstanding "Joker".[17] "Eye-Crom" confusingly similar to "Vicrom".[18] "Mini-Lift (serum)" confusingly similar to "Lift Serum" but not with "Crown Lift".[19] "Rose Cardin" refused in the light of "The Rose Garden".[20] "Origin" too similar to "Origins".[21] "Rajamama" confusingly similar to "Wagamama".[22] "International Telesis Group" too close to "Pacific Telesis International".[23] "Harrodian School" not too similar to "Harrods".[24] "Neutralia" confusingly similar to "Neutrogena".[25] "Paton Calvert Cordon Bleu" distinguishable from "Constance Spry Cordon Blue" and from "Le Cordon Bleu, Paris, 1895".[26] "Opus" not infringed by "Farming Opus".[27] "Streetball" allowed despite "Setball".[28] "Eternity" not allowed in the face of "'Eternity' (used in conjunction with 'Calvin Klein')".[29] "Puffin (and get up)" confusingly similar to "Penguin (and get up)".[30] "Babewatch" not confusingly similar to "Baywatch".[31] "Zinc" infringed by "Zn" and "Zincbar", and would be infringed by "ZN", "Sinc" and "Sync".[32] "Green Peace" too close to "Greenpeace".[33] "Vibradox" not confusingly similar to "Vibramycin".[34] "McAllan" confusingly similar to "McDonald's".[35] "Brava" infringed "Bravo".[36] "Stephanskreuz" (St Stephan's cross) allowed notwithstanding "Stephanskrone" (St Stephan's crown).[37] "Queen's Club" too similar to "Queen's Garden".[38] "Izod Lacoste" (and crocodile device) confusingly similar to "Lacoste" (and crocodile device).[39] "Le Lido" not confusingly similar to "Lido".[40] "UK Used" refused in the light of "Used".[41] "Comfort and Joy" not confusingly similar to "Joy".[42] "Audi-Med" allowed notwithstanding "Audi".[43] "Neutritive" likely to be

[12] *Advance Magazine Publishing v. Redwood Publishing Ltd* [1993] F.S.R. 449.
[13] *QUATTRO Trade Mark* [1993] F.S.R. 759 (Germany).
[14] *An Bord Trachtala v. Waterford Foods Plc* [1994] F.S.R. 316.
[15] *Ciba-Geigy Plc v. Parke Davis & Co. Ltd* [1994] F.S.R. 8.
[16] *Beecham Group v. Mohammed Ahmed Banafi* [1994] F.S.R. 685 (Saudi Arabia).
[17] *JOCKEY Trade Mark* [1994] F.S.R. 269.
[18] *Fisons Plc v. Norton Healthcare Ltd* [1994] F.S.R. 745.
[19] *MINI-LIFT Trade Mark* [1995] R.P.C. 128.
[20] *ROSE CARDIN Trade Mark* [1995] R.P.C. 246.
[21] *Origins Natural Resources v. Origin Clothing Ltd* [1995] F.S.R. 280.
[22] *Wagamama Ltd v. City Centre Restaurants Plc* [1995] F.S.R. 713.
[23] *INTERNATIONAL TELESIS GROUP Service Mark* [1996] R.P.C. 45.
[24] *Harrods Ltd v. Harrodian School Ltd* [1996] R.P.C. 697.
[25] *Neutrogena Corporation v. Golden Ltd* [1996] R.P.C. 473.
[26] *PATON CALVERT CORDON BLEU Trade Mark* [1996] R.P.C. 94.
[27] *BASF Plc v. CEP (UK) Plc* [1996] E.T.M.R. 51.
[28] *Adidas AG's Application* [1996] E.T.M.R. 67 (Portugal).
[29] *ETERNITY Trade Mark* [1997] R.P.C. 155.
[30] *United Biscuits v. Asda* [1997] R.P.C. 513.
[31] *Baywatch Production Co Inc v. The Home Video Channel* [1997] F.S.R. 22.
[32] *Sir Terence Orby Conran v. Mean Fiddler Holdings Ltd* [1997] F.S.R. 856.
[33] *Stichting Greenpeace Council v. Income Team Ltd* [1997] F.S.R. 149 (Hong Kong).
[34] *Pfizer International Inc v. Durascan Medical Products A/S* [1997] E.T.M.R. 86 (Netherlands).
[35] *McDonald's Corporation USA v. Allen Bjerrum Pedersen* [1997] E.T.M.R. 151 (Netherlands).
[36] *Bravo Industry of Coffees SA v. Fiat Auto SpA* [1997] E.T.M.R. 167 (Greece).
[37] *STEPHANSKRUEZ Trade Mark Application* [1997] E.T.M.R. 182 (Germany).
[38] *QUEEN'S CLUB Trade Mark Application* [1997] E.T.M.R. 345 (Germany).
[39] *La Chemise Lacoste SA v. Centro Tessile SrL* [1997] E.T.M.R. 520 (Italy).
[40] *Le Lido SA v. Nationale Stichting Tot Exploitatie Van Casinospelen in Nederland* [1997] E.T.M.R. 537 (Netherlands).
[41] *Application of Union Mills SrL* [1997] E.T.M.R. 568.
[42] *Application of Merri Mayers-Head* [1997] E.T.M.R. 577.
[43] *AUDI-MED Trade Mark* [1998] R.P.C. 863.

confused with "Bionutritive a La Germastine".[44] "Eveready" allowed notwithstanding "Ever Ready".[45] "Open Country" distinguishable from "Openair".[46] "SWC Super Farm Fluid" too close to "Antec Farm Fluid S".[47] "Millennium" too close to "Millenia".[48] "The European" not confusingly similar to "European Voice".[49] "Jarvard" not confusingly similar to "Harvard".[50] Use of "Ca m'interesse" in the title of a radio program, confusingly similar to "Ca M'Interesse" registered for magazines.[51] "Visa" not infringed by "Visa Pour Le Muscle".[52] "Balmoral" too close to "Balmoral" and "Balmoral International".[53] "Elvis" and "Elvis Presley" not too close to "Elvisly Yours".[54] "Ener-Cap" registrable despite "EnerRing" and "EnerSeal".[55] "Fountain" confusingly similar to "Font Fountain".[56] "Lifesystems" distinguishable from "Lifestream".[57] "Naturelle" too close to "Natrel".[58] "Polaclip" allowed despite "Polaroid".[59] "QS by S. Oliver" too similar to "QS".[60] "Stopcar" confusingly similar to "Stopcard".[61] "Beauty Free Shop" too close to "Beauty Free".[62] "Humica, S.A." confusingly similar to "Humica".[63] "Horizon" (and device) distinguishable from "Ariston".[64] "La Sirena" registrable despite "Siena".[65] "Joy One Year" an infringement of "Joy".[66] "Jois & Jo" not confusingly similar to "Joy".[67] "Saint John's" not confusingly similar to "Saint-James".[68] "Isenbeck" not too close to "Beck's".[69] "Bill Baker Remembering The Glenn Miller Army Air Force Orchestra" not an infringement of "Glenn Miller".[70] "Pandau" not confusingly similar to "Up and Down".[71] "Andak" too close to "Zantac".[72] "Halloween" infringed by "Haribo-Halloween".[73] "Felix Le Souriceau" confusingly similar to "Felix the Cat".[74] "Sodeco" confusingly similar to "Sodexho".[75] "Technocite" infringed by "Techno Cite", but not confusingly similar to "Cite Des Sciences et De

[44] NEUTRITIVE Trade Mark [1998] R.P.C. 621.
[45] Oasis Stores Ltd's Trade Mark Application [1998] R.P.C. 631.
[46] OPEN COUNTRY Trade Mark [1998] R.P.C. 408.
[47] Antec International Ltd v. South-Western Chicks (Warren) Ltd [1998] F.S.R. 738.
[48] Pontiac Marina Pte Ltd v. CDL Hotels International Ltd [1998] F.S.R. 839 (Singapore).
[49] The European Ltd v. The Economist Newspapers Ltd [1998] F.S.R. 283.
[50] Kundry SA's Application [1998] E.T.M.R. 178.
[51] SNC Prisma Presse v. SA Europe 1 Telecompagne [1998] E.T.M.R. 515 (France).
[52] Visa International (U.S.) v. Editions Jibena [1998] E.T.M.R. 580 (France).
[53] BALMORAL Trade Mark [1999] R.P.C. 297.
[54] ELVIS PRESLEY Trade Marks [1999] R.P.C. 567.
[55] ENER-CAP Trade Mark [1999] R.P.C. 362.
[56] FOUNTAIN Trade Mark [1999] R.P.C. 490.
[57] LIFESYSTEMS Trade Mark [1999] R.P.C. 851.
[58] NATURELLE Trade Mark [1999] R.P.C. 326.
[59] POLACLIP Trade Mark [1999] R.P.C. 282.
[60] QS BY S. OLIVER Trade Mark [1999] R.P.C. 520.
[61] Electro Cad Australia Pty Ltd v. Mejati RCS Sdn Bhd [1999] F.S.R. 291 (Malaysia).
[62] Beauty Shop BVBA's Application [1999] E.T.M.R. 20 (OHIM).
[63] Humic SA's Application [1999] E.T.M.R. 26 (OHIM).
[64] BAT Ltd's Application [1999] E.T.M.R. 32 (OHIM).
[65] Lutz Quasdorf v. Les Sirenes SA [1999] 152 E.T.M.R. (OHIM).
[66] Jean Patou SA v. Ste Zag Zeitschriften Verlag AG [1999] E.T.M.R. 157 (France).
[67] GTR Group's Application [1999] E.T.M.R. 164.
[68] Lyon v. SA Rhums Martiniquais Saint-James [1999] E.T.M.R. 188 (France).
[69] Warsteiner Brauerei Haus GmbH & Co's Application [1999] E.T.M.R. 225 (OHIM) .
[70] Glenn Miller Productions Inc v. Stichting Bill Bakers Big Band Corporation [1999] E.T.M.R. 247 (Netherlands).
[71] Re PANDAU [1999] E.T.M.R. 267 (Spain).
[72] Glaxo Group Ltd v. Knoll Aktiengesellschaft [1999] E.T.M.R. 358 (Denmark).
[73] Optos-Opus (SARL) v. SA Haribo Ricqles Zan. [1999] E.T.M.R. 362 (France).
[74] Ste Felix The Cat Productions Inc v. Ste Polygram [1999] E.T.M.R. 370 (France).
[75] Mars GB's Application [1999] E.T.M.R. 402 (OHIM).

L'Industrie".[76] "Geo Poche" too close to "Geo".[77] "Fashion for You by NL" confusingly similar to "You" and "4 You".[78] "J'M" (incorporating the famous McDonalds arched 'M') not too close to "J'M Bien".[79] "21st Century Film" not confusingly similar to "XXIeme Siecle".[80] "Benecol" distinguishable from "Becel".[81] "First Lady" distinguishable from "Lady".[82] "Coq D'Or" (and cockerel device) not confusingly similar to "Victoria" (and cockerel device).[83] "Stitches" too close to "Broken Stitches".[84] "React" (and device) sufficiently different from "Reactor".[85] "Club Europe" not confusingly similar to "Club World".[86] "Amaze Collection" not confusingly similar to "Ama Zing".[87] "Jack and Danny's Rock Café" confusingly similar to "Hard Rock Café".[88] "Tahtimerkki Kauris" (in English, 'Sign of the Zodiac Capricorn') distinguishable from "Horoscope".[89] "Eudermin" confusingly similar to "Eucerin".[90] "Viagrene" too close to "Viagra".[91] "Nike" (and 'tick' device) deceptive in the light of "Nike" (and statue device).[92] "Dynalink" registrable despite "Dynanet".[93] "Principles" unregistrable in the light of "Principe".[94] "Super Mega" not an infringement of "Super Power" or "Mega Force".[95] "Cool and Slim" not too similar to "Slim".[96]

2. Trade Names

(1) Injunctions Granted

Hoby (carrying on The Grosvenor Library) v. The Grosvenor Library Co.[97]; Hendricks (on behalf of the Universal Life Assurance Society) v. Montagu (promoter of the Universe Life Assurance Association[98]; The Accident Insurance Co. Ltd v. The Accident, Disease and General Insurance Co. Ltd[99]; Madame Tussaud & Son Ltd v. Louis Tussaud Ltd[1]; Wolmershausen v. G. S. Wolmershausen & Co. Ltd[2]; Premier Cycle Co. Ltd v. Premier Tube Co. Ltd[3]; John Brinsmead & Co. v. Thomas Edward Brinsmead & Sons

[76] Sarl Cargo Communication v. La Cite Des Sciences et De L'Industrie [1999] E.T.M.R. 545 (France).
[77] Ste Prisma Presse v. SA Editions Economica [1999] E.T.M.R. 549 (France).
[78] Hij Mannenmode BV v. Nienhaus & Lotz GmbH [1999] E.T.M.R. 730 (Benelux).
[79] Norbert Robert Bertucci v. McDonald's Corporation [1999] E.T.M.R. 742 (France).
[80] Casaubon v. 21st Century Film France [1999] E.T.M.R. 787 (France).
[81] Unilever NV v. Raisio Yhtyma Oy [1999] E.T.M.R. 847 (Benelux).
[82] Sarl Succes De Paris v. SA Parfums Van Cleef et Arpels [1999] E.T.M.R. 869 (France).
[83] Fromex SA's Application [1999] E.T.M.R. 989 (OHIM).
[84] The House of Stitches Pty Ltd's Application [1999] E.T.M.R. 994 (OHIM).
[85] REACT AND DEVICE Trade Mark [2000] R.P.C. 285.
[86] CLUB EUROPE Trade Mark [2000] R.P.C. 329.
[87] AMAZE COLLECTION Trade Mark [2000] R.P.C. 725.
[88] Neil King's Application [2000] E.T.M.R. 22.
[89] Aaro Forsman OY's Application [2000] E.T.M.R. 142 (Finland).
[90] Icart SA's Application [2000] E.T.M.R. 180 (OHIM).
[91] Pfizer Ltd v. Eurofood Link (UK) Ltd [2000] E.T.M.R. 187.
[92] Comercial Iberica de Exclusivas Deportivas v. Nike International Ltd [2000] E.T.M.R. 189 (Spain).
[93] Askey Computer Corporation's Application [2000] E.T.M.R. 214 (Finland).
[94] Principles Retail Ltd's Application [2000] E.T.M.R. 240 (OHIM).
[95] Sarl Mega Press v. Pressimage [2000] E.T.M.R. 403 (France).
[96] Slim International v. Delta Protypos Milk industry [2000] E.T.M.R. 409 (Greece).
[97] 28 W.R. 386.
[98] (1881) 17 Ch.D. 638.
[99] (1884) 54 Ch.D. 104.
[1] (1890) 44 Ch.D. 678.
[2] [1892] W.N. 87.
[3] (1896) 12 T.L.R. 481, interlocutory injunction granted, the defendant company's works had for six years been known as Premier Mills.

Ltd[4]; *Pinet et Cie v. Maison Pinet Ltd*[5]; *Pinet et Cie v. Maison Louis Pinet Ltd.*[6]
Eastman (whose trade name was "Kodak") *v. Griffiths* (promoters of the *Kodak Cycle Co. Ltd)*[7]; *Manchester Brewery Co. Ltd v. North Cheshire and Manchester Brewery Co. Ltd*[8];
Valentine Meat Juice Co. v. Valentine Extract Co. Ltd[9]; *Pearks, Gunston Tee Ltd*
(carrying on business as Talmey & Co.) v. Thompson, Talmey & Co.[10]; *Panhard et Levassor v. Panhard-Levassor Motor Co. Ltd*[11]; *Randall (trading as American Shoe Co.)
v. British and American Shoe Co.*[12]; *Fine Cotton Spinners, and John Cash & Sons Ltd v. Harwood, Cash & Co. Ltd*[13]; *International Plasmon v. Plasmonade Ltd*[14]; *Standard Bank of South Africa Ltd v. Standard Bank Ltd*[15]; *Dunlop Pneumatic Tyre Co. Ltd v. Dunlop Lubricant Co.*[16]; *Ouvah Ceylon Estates Ltd v. Uva Ceylon Rubber Estates Ltd*[17];
Murattie & Sons Ltd v. Murad Ltd[18]; *Kingston, Miller & Co. Ltd v. Thomas Kingston & Co. Ltd*[19]; *Lloyd's v. Lloyd's (Southampton) Ltd*[20]; *Lloyd's Bank v. Lloyd's Investment Trust Co. Ltd*[21]; *Facsimile Letter Printing Co. Ltd v. Facsimile Typewriting Co.*[22];
Daimler Motor Co. (1904) Ltd v. London Daimler Co. Ltd[23]; *Teofani & Company Ltd v. A. Teofani*[24]; *Ewing (trading as the Buttercup Dairy Company) v. Buttercup Magarine Company Ltd*[25]; *Albion Motor Company Ltd v. Albion Carriage and Motor Body Works Ltd*[26]; *R. & J. Pullman Ltd v. Pullman*[27]; *Poiret v. Jules Poiret Ltd and A.S. Nash*[28];
M.P. Guimaraens & Son v. Fonseca and Vasconcellos[29]; *Dutton, Massey & Co. (Liverpool) Ltd v. Dutton, Massey & Co. Ltd*[30]; *Joseph Rodgers & Sons Ltd v. W. N. Rodgers & Co.*[31]; *Harrods Ltd v. R. Harrod Ltd*[32]; *Reliance Rubber Company Ltd v. Reliance Tyre Company Ltd*[33]; *Heels v. Stafford Heels Ltd* (the plaintiffs being commonly

[4] (1896) 12 T.L.R. 631; 13 T.L.R. 3. *cf.* the second *Brinsmead* case (1913) 30 R.P.C. 493, CA.
[5] (1897) 14 R.P.C. 933.
[6] (1898) 15 R.P.C. 65.
[7] (1898) 15 R.P.C. 105.
[8] [1899] A.C. 83.
[9] (1900) 17 R.P.C. 673.
[10] (1901) 18 R.P.C. 185.
[11] [1901] 2 Ch. 513; 18 R.P.C. 405.
[12] (1902) 19 R.P.C. 393.
[13] [1907] 2 Ch. 184; 24 R.P.C. 533.
[14] (1905) 22 R.P.C. 543, interlocutory injunction granted.
[15] (1909) 26 R.P.C. 310.
[16] (1899) 16 R.P.C. 12.
[17] (1910) 27 R.P.C. 753. Ouvah and Uva were alternative spellings of the name of the same province in Ceylon, and both companies were rubber companies.
[18] (1911) 28 R.P.C. 497.
[19] [1912] 1 Ch. 575; 29 R.P.C. 298.
[20] (1912) 29 R.P.C. 433.
[21] (1912) 29 R.P.C. 545.
[22] (1912) 29 R.P.C. 557.
[23] (1907) 24 R.P.C. 379. In *Army and Navy Co-operative Society Ltd v. Army, Navy and Civil Service Co-operative Society of South Africa Ltd* (1902) R.P.C. 574, on appeal from an interlocutory injunction, the defendants agreed to change their name to "Naval, Military and Civil Service Co-operative Society of South Africa Ltd". In *Hopton Wood Stone Firms Ltd v. Gething (trading as Hoptin Stone and Marble Quarrying Co.)* (1910) 27 R.P.C. 605, the defendant undertook to prefix the word "New" to that style.
[24] (1913) 30 R.P.C. 446.
[25] [1917] 2 Ch. 1; 34 R.P.C. 232.
[26] (1917) 34 R.P.C. 257.
[27] (1919) 36 R.P.C. 240. This case was exceptional in its nature because the allegation was that people who *supplied* goods (skins for manufacture into leather) would be deceived, and probability of confusion was held to be established. *Held* that the plaintiff was entitled to a declaration with liberty to apply for an injunction.
[28] (1920) 37 R.P.C. 177.
[29] (1921) 38 R.P.C. 388.
[30] (1922) 40 R.P.C. 413; (1924) 41 R.P.C. 67, CA.
[31] (1924) 41 R.P.C. 277.
[32] (1924) 41 R.P.C. 74.
[33] (1924) 42 R.P.C. 91.

known as Heels of Stafford)[34]; *Heppels Ltd v. Eppels Ltd*[35]; *Edison Accumulator Ltd v. Edison Storage Batteries Ltd*[36]; *Mills v. Chapman*[37]; *F. W. Woolworth & Co. Ltd v. Woolworths (Australasia) Ltd*[38]; *Madeira House Co. Ltd v. Madeira House (London) Ltd*[39]; *British Legion v. British Legion Club (Street) Ltd*[40]; *British Medical Association v. Marsh*[41]; *Crystalate Gramaphone Record Manufacturing Co. Ltd v. British Crystalite Co. Ltd*[42]; *Radio Rentals Ltd v. Rentals Ltd*[43]; *Hesketh Estates (Southport) Ltd v. Droitwich Brine Banks Ltd*[44]; *The Clock Ltd v. The Clock House Hotel*[45]; *Sturtevant Engineering Co. Ltd v. Sturtevant Mill Co. Ltd of U.S.A.*[46]; *John Dickinson Ltd v. Apsley Press Ltd*[47]; *Saville Perfumery Ltd v. June Perfect Ltd and F. W. Woolworth & Co. Ltd*[48]; *Plomien Fuel Economiser v. National School of Salesmanship Ltd*[49]; *Delavelle (G.B.) Ltd v. Harry Stanley*[50]; *Hines v. Winnick*[51]; *Sales Affiliates Ltd v. Le Jean Ltd*[52]; *C.C. Wakefield & Co. Ltd v. Sydney N. Laurence*[53]; *British Bata Shoe Company Ltd v. Czecholsovakia Bata Co. Ltd*[54]; *Music Corporation of America and another v. Music Corporation (Great Britian) Ltd*[55]; *Midland Counties Dairy Ltd v. Midland Dairies Ltd*[56]; *Marengo v. Daily Sketch (Kem & Kim)*[57]; *Wright, Layman & Umney Ltd v. Wright*[58]; *Dr. Barnado's Homes: National Incorporated Association v. Barnado Amalgamated Industries Ltd and Jack Benardout*[59]; *Brestian v. Try* restraining use of "Charles of London*[60]; *Parker Knoll Ltd v. Knoll International Ltd*[61]; *Southern Music Publishing Co. Ltd v. Southern Songs Ltd*[62]; *John Letters & Co. Ltd v. Letters (Craigton) Ltd*[63]; *Suhner & Co. A.G. v. Suhner Ltd*[64]; *Legal & General Assurance Society v. Daniel (trading as Legal & General Enquiry Bureau)*[65]; *Cavendish House (Cheltenham) Ltd v. Cavendish-*

[34] (1927) 44 R.P.C. 299.
[35] (1929) 46 R.P.C. 96.
[36] (1929) 46 R.P.C. 432.
[37] (1930) 47 R.P.C. 115; the plaintiff's circus was known as "London Olympia Circus" and the defendant was restrained from using the words "London Olympia" in connection with a circus.
[38] (1930) 47 R.P.C. 337.
[39] (1930) 47 R.P.C. 481.
[40] (1931) 48 R.P.C. 555. Street was the name of a place in Somerset. The Club had no authority from the British Legion.
[41] (1931) 48 R.P.C. 565, the defendant was restrained from using the initials B.M.A., by which the plaintiffs were known.
[42] (1934) 51 R.P.C. 315.
[43] (1934) 51 R.P.C. 407.
[44] (1935) 52 R.P.C. 39, the plaintiffs being the owners of brine baths at Droitwich and carrying on business as "Brine Baths"; the hotels being only five miles apart.
[45] (1936) 53 R.P.C. 269.
[46] (1936) 53 R.P.C. 430.
[47] (1937) 54 R.P.C. 219, the plaintiffs being known as "Apsley."
[48] (1941) 58 R.P.C. 147.
[49] (1943) 60 R.P.C. 219.
[50] (1946) 63 R.P.C. 103 ("Blue Orchid" for brilliance).
[51] (1947) 64 R.P.C. 113 ("Dr Crock and his Crackpots").
[52] (1947) 64 R.P.C. 103 ("Jamal and Vapet").
[53] (1947) 64 R.P.C. 95.
[54] (1947) 64 R.P.C. 72 (interim injunction).
[55] (1947) 64 R.P.C. 48.
[56] (1948) 65 R.P.C. 429.
[57] (1948) 65 R.P.C. 242.
[58] (1948) 65 R.P.C. 186; 66 R.P.C. 149.
[59] (1949) 66 R.P.C. 103 (interlocutory injunction).
[60] [1957] R.P.C. 443; [1958] R.P.C. 161.
[61] [1958] R.P.C. 317.
[62] [1966] R.P.C. 137 (interlocutory injunction).
[63] [1967] R.P.C. 209 (Scots) (interim interdict).
[64] [1967] R.P.C. 336 (interim injunction to subscribers of defendants' memorandum of association to restrain them from "allowing the defendants to remain registered under its present name").
[65] [1968] R.P.C. 253 (interlocutory injunction).

Woodhouse Ltd[66]; "Pembridge Hotel" too close to "Pembridge Gardens Hotel."[67]; *Effluent Disposal Ltd v. Midlands Effluent Disposal Ltd*[68]; *Laurie Mansfield Ltd (makers of Gay Girl ladies' clothing) v. Gaygirl Ltd*[69]; *Hammond & Champness (known as "H & C" or "H + C") v. H.A.C. Lifts Ltd.*[70]

"Nationwide Estate Agents" likely to be confusingly similar to "Nationwide".[71] "Chelsea Man" confusingly similar to "Chelsea Girl" (but no injunction as prior use established).[72] "2020 Communications" confusingly similar to "20/20 Telecom".[73] "Rajamama" confusingly similar to "Wagamama".[74] "International Telesis Group" too close to "Pacific Telesis International".[75] "Diabetic Society" confusingly similar to "British Diabetic Association".[76] "NAD Computer Systems" confusingly similar to "NAD Electronics".[77] "Compagnie Generale Des Eaux Sdn Bhd" confusingly similar to "Compagnie Generale Des Eaux".[78] "Zinc" infringed by "Zn" and "Zincbar", and would be infringed by "ZN", "Sinc" and "Sync".[79] "McAllan" confusingly similar to "McDonald's".[80] "Millennium Hotels" too close to "Ritz-Carlton, Millenia Singapore".[81] "RWS Translations" too similar to "Translations".[82] "Kilkenny Brewing Company Ltd" confusingly similar to "Kilkenny Irish Beer".[83-84]

(2) Injunctions refused

London and Provincial Law Assurance Society v. London and Provincial **A35–05** *Joint Stock Life Assurance Co.*[85]; Although there was evidence that the former company was usually called the London and Provincial Insurance Co.; *London Assurance v. London and Westminster Assurance Corporation*[86]; *Colonial Life Assurance Co. v. Home and Colonial Assurance Co. Ltd*[87]; *London and County Banking Co. v. Capital and Counties Bank* (cited in the next case); *Merchant Banking Co. of London v. Merchants', Joint Stock Bank*[88]; *The Army and Navy Co-operative Society Ltd v. The Junior Army and Navy Stores Ltd*[89]; *Australian Mortgage Land and Finance Co. v. Australian and New Zealand Mortagage Co.*[90]; *National Cash Register Co. Ltd v.*

---

[66] [1970] R.P.C. 234 (interlocutory injunction granted despite delay of eight months because of very strong prima facie case).
[67] *Bach & Jackson Ltd v. Cowan* [1969] R.P.C. 156. (interlocutory injunction. Name not descriptive despite location of both hotels in "Pembridge" area).
[68] [1970] R.P.C. 238 (interlocutory injunction).
[69] [1968] F.S.R. 144 (interlocutory injunction).
[70] [1975] F.S.R. 125.
[71] *Nationwide Building Society v. Nationwide Estate Agents Ltd* [1987] F.S.R. 579.
[72] *CHELSEA MAN Trade Mark* [1989] R.P.C. 111.
[73] *Stacey v. 2020 Communications Plc* [1991] F.S.R. 49.
[74] *Wagamama Ltd v. City Centre Restaurants Plc* [1995] F.S.R. 713.
[75] *INTERNATIONAL TELESIS GROUP Service Mark* [1996] R.P.C. 45.
[76] *The British Diabetic Association v. The Diabetic Society* [1996] F.S.R. 1.
[77] *NAD Electronics Inc v. NAD Computer Systems Ltd* [1997] F.S.R. 380 .
[78] *Compagnie Generale Des Eaux v. Compagnie Generale Des Eaux Sdn Bhd* [1997] F.S.R. 610.
[79] *Sir Terence Orby Conran v. Mean Fiddler Holdings Ltd* [1997] F.S.R. 856.
[80] *McDonald's Corporation USA v. Allen Bjerrum Pedersen* [1997] E.T.M.R. 151 (Denmark).
[81] *Pontiac Marina Pte Ltd v. CDL Hotels International Ltd* [1998] F.S.R. 839 (Singapore).
[82] *Sarl RWS Translations Ltd v. Getten* [1999] E.T.M.R. 258 (France).
[83-84] *Guinness Ireland Group v. Kilkenny Brewing Company Ltd* [1999] E.T.M.R. 807 (Eire).
[85] (1847) 17 L.J.Ch. 37.
[86] (1863) 32 L.J.Ch. 664.
[87] 33 Beav. 548; 33 L.J.Ch. 741.
[88] (1879) 9 Ch.D. 560.
[89] (1879) Seb.Dig. at 393.
[90] [1880] W.N. 6, CA.

Theeman (who was trading as the *Cash Register Co.)*[91]*; Saunders* (on behalf of the *Sun Life Assurance Society) v. The Sun Life Assurance Co. of Canada*[92]*; Scottish Union and National Insurance Co. v. Scottish National Insurance Co. Ltd*[93]*; Daimler Motor Car Co. Ltd v. British Motor Traction Co. (who were about to register the Daimler Wagon Co. Ltd)*[94]*; Aerators Ltd v. Tolllit* (the defendants being about to register Automatic Aerator Patents Ltd[95]*; Electromobile Co. Ltd v. British Electromobile Co. Ltd*[96]*; British Vacuum Cleaner Co. Ltd v. New Vacuum Cleaner Co. Ltd*[97]*; H. E. Randall Ltd (trading as American Shoe Co.) v. Bradley (trading as Anglo-American Shoe Co.)*[98]*; Dunlop Pneumatic Tyre Co. Ltd v. Dunlop Motor Co. Ltd*[99]*; Meikle (trading as Kelvindale Chemical Co.) v. Williamson (trading as Kelvinside Chemical Co.)*[1]*; Royal Insurance Co. Ltd v. Midland Insurance Co.*[2]*; Elliott (trading as the Trade Extension Co.) v. Expansion of Trade Ltd*[3]*; Standard Ideal Co. v. Standard Sanitary Manufacturing Co.*[4]*; John Brinsmead & Sons Ltd v. Brinsmead*[5]*; Bowden Wire Ltd v. Bowden Brake Co. Ltd*[6]*; Waring and Gillow Ltd. v. Gillow and Gillow Ltd*[7]*; Society of Motor Manufacturers and Traders Ltd v. Motor Manufacturers' and Traders' Mutual Insurance Co. Ltd.*[8] In *Bumstead v. the General Revesionary Co. Ltd,* an interlocutury injunction was refused, because although the defendant company had adopted a name resembling that of the company of which the plaintiff was secretary, the General Reversionary and Investment Co., yet there was no probabililty of deception because the former was a small Liverpool concern, and the latter a very large London one.[9] *Tigon Mining and Finance Corporation Ltd v. South Tigon Mining Co. Ltd*[10]*; Jay's Ltd v. Jacobi and Limburg*[11]*; Rolls Razor Ltd v. Rolls (Lighters) Ltd and Others*[12]*; Natural Chemicals Ltd v. Veno's Drug Co. Ltd and Irving's Yeast-Vite (Consolidated) v. Amblins Chemists Ltd*[13]*; John Jacques and Sons Ltd v. Chess (a firm)*[14]*; Bear (Thomas) and Sons (India) Ltd v. Prayag Narain and Jagernath*[15]*; Stelletz v. Jones and Higgins Ltd*[16]*; V. S. Subbiah Nadar v. E. P. Kumaraval and*

[91] (1907) 24 R.P.C. 211.
[92] [1894] 1 Ch. 537 (injunction against the use of the defendants' full name was refused, but the defendants gave an undertaking substantially not to use the name of "The Sun" or "The Sun Life" without adding the words "of Canada").
[93] (1908) 25 R.P.C. 560 (Scotland). The classes of business were quite distinct.
[94] (1901) 18 R.P.R. 465. cf. *Daimler Motor Car (1904) Ltd v. London Daimler Motor Co. Ltd* (1907) 24 R.P.C. 379.
[95] [1902] 2 Ch. 319; 19 R.P.C. 418.
[96] (1908) 25 R.P.C. 149.
[97] [1907] 2 Ch. 312; 24 R.P.C. 641.
[98] (1907) 24 R.P.C. 657, 773.
[99] [1907] A.C. 430; 24 R.P.C. 572.
[1] (1909) 26 R.P.C. 775, Ct of Sess (Scotland).
[2] (1909) 25 R.P.C. 728; 26 R.P.C. 95. The plaintiffs became successors in business in the year 1892, of the Midland Counties Insurance Co.
[3] (1909) 27 R.P.C. 54.
[4] (1910) 27 R.P.C. 789.
[5] (1913) 30 R.P.C. 493.
[6] (1913) 30 R.P.C. 580.
[7] (1916) 33 R.P.C. 173.
[8] (1925) 42 R.P.C. 307.
[9] (1888) 4 T.L.R. 621.
[10] (1931) 48 R.P.C. 526, the word "Tigon" was held to have acquired a geographical signification, and there was no passing off of any goods.
[11] (1933) 50 R.P.C. 132; the defendants were using the name "Jays", but the first defendant had previously been known in business as "Miss Jay".
[12] (1949) 66 R.P.C. 137 and 299.
[13] (1940) 57 R.P.C. 323.
[14] (1939) 56 R.P.C. 415 and 57 R.P.C. 77, CA, reversing Crossman J. (use of "Staunton" for chessmen).
[15] (1941) 58 R.P.C. 25.
[16] (1943) 60 R.P.C. 15.

Others[17]*; Office Cleaning Services Ltd v. Westminster Window and General Cleaners*[18]*; Harold Lee (Mantles) Ltd v. Harold Harley (Fashions) Ltd*[19]*; Drive Yourself Hire Co. (London) Ltd v. Parish (trading as Self Drive Cars)*[20]*; Dorothy Perkins Ltd v. Polly Perkins of Picadilly Ltd*[21]*; Green Arrow Rentaflower Ltd v. Renta Flower Ltd*[22]*; Salaried Persons Postal Loans Ltd v. Postal & Salaried Loans of Glasgow Ltd*[23]*; Morecombe & Heysham (Promoters of "Miss Great Britain" beauty contest) v. Mecca Ltd (Promoters of "Miss Britain")*[24]*; Bristol-Myers Co. v. Bristol Pharmaceutical Co. Ltd*[25]*; Marathon Oil Co. v. Marathon Shipping Co. Ltd*[26]*; Coral Index Ltd v. Regent Index Ltd*[27]*; The Pet Library (London) Ltd v. Walter Ellson & Son Ltd ("Ellson's Pet Library")*[28]*; Park Court Hotel Ltd ("Hotel International") v. Trans-World Hotels Ltd ("London International Hotel")*[29]*; Industrial Furnaces Ltd v. Reaves Industrial Furnaces Ltd*[30]*; Banbury Buildings Ltd v. Sectional Concrete Buildings Ltd ("Banbury Mail Order")*[31]*; Sterling-Winthrop Inc. v. Farbenfabriken Bayer A.G.*[32] "Furniture City" distiguiushable from "Furnitureland".[33] "Kem" not confusingly similar to "Kim".[34]

[17] (1946) 63 R.P.C. 187 (Photo Mark Beedies).
[18] (1944) 61 R.P.C. 21, 133, CA, (reversing Morton J.); 63 R.P.C. 39, HL.
[19] (1954) 71 R.P.C. 57.
[20] [1957] R.P.C. 307.
[21] [1962] R.P.C. 153; dress shops, the plaintiffs had none in the town where the defendants' was, interlocutory injunction refused on the balance of convenience.
[22] [1966] R.P.C. 19 (Scots). (Interim interdict recalled because delay had prejudiced defendants' position).
[23] [1966] R.P.C. 24 (Scots). (Interim interdict recalled because names were descriptive and balance of covenience was in defendants' favour).
[24] [1962] R.P.C. 145 (interlocutory relief refused); [1966] R.P.C. 423 (final relief refused). The case turned on the limited sorts of confusion held relevant.
[25] [1968] R.P.C. 259 (interlocutory injunction).
[26] [1968] R.P.C. 443 (interlocutory injunction). Case turned on balance of convenience, particularly the fact that the businesses were in different fields.
[27] [1970] R.P.C. 147 (interlocutory injunction). Businesses were gambling on performance of Share Index.
[28] [1968] F.S.R. 359 (interlocutory injunction).
[29] [1970] F.S.R. 89 (interlocutory injunction). Court accepted small differences.
[30] [1970] R.P.C. 605.
[31] [1970] R.P.C. 463.
[32] [1966] R.P.C. 477 ("Bayer" distinctive of plaintiffs, but interlocutory injunction refused against "Bayer, Germany).
[33] *Furnitureland Ltd. v. Harris* [1989] 1 F.S.R. 536.
[34] *Marengo v. Daily Sketch* [1992] F.S.R. 1.

APPENDIX 36

Olympic Symbol etc. (Protection) Act 1995

1995 CHAPTER 32

A36–01 An Act to make provision about the use for commercial purposes of the Olympic symbol and certain words associated with the Olympic games; and for connected purposes.

[19TH JULY 1995]

The Olympics association right

Creation

A36–02 **1.**—(1) There shall be a right, to be known as the Olympics association right.

(2) The right shall carry with it the rights and remedies provided by this Act, which shall be exercisable by such person as the Secretary of State may by order made by statutory instrument appoint for the purposes of this subsection.

(3) An order under subsection (2) above which revokes a previous order under that subsection may contain such supplementary and transitional provision as the Secretary of State thinks fit.

(4) A statutory instrument containing an order under subsection (2) above shall be subject to annulment in pursuance of a resolution of either House of Parliament.

Rights conferred

A36–03 **2.**—(1) The Olympics association right shall confer exclusive rights in relation to the use of the Olympic symbol, the Olympic motto and the protected words.

(2) Subject to sections 4 and 5 below, the rights conferred by subsection (1) above shall be infringed by any act done in the United Kingdom which—

 (a) constitutes infringement under section 3 below, and

 (b) is done without the consent of the person for the time being appointed under section 1 (2) above (in the Act referred to as "the proprietor").

(3) The proprietor may exploit the rights conferred by subsection (1) above for gain, but may not make any disposition of, or of any interest in or over, them.

(4) This section shall not have effect to permit the doing of anything which would otherwise be liable to be prevented by virtue of a right—

 (a) subsisting immediately before the day on which this Act comes into force, or

 (b) created by—

  (i) the registration of a design under the Registered Designs Act 1949 on or after the date on which this Act comes into force, or

  (ii) the registration of a trade mark under the Trade Marks Act 1994 on or after that day.

(5) Consent given for the purposes of subsection (2) (b) above by a person appointed under section 1(2) above shall, subject to its terms, be binding on any person subsequently appointed under that provision; and references in this Act to doing anything with, or without, the consent of the proprietor shall be construed accordingly.

Infringement

3.—(1) A person infringes the Olympics association right if in the course of **A36–04** trade he uses—

(a) a representation of the Olympic symbol, the Olympic motto or a protected word, or

(b) a representation of something so similar to the Olympic symbol or the Olympic motto as to be likely to create in the public mind an association with it,

(in this Act referred to as "a controlled representation").

(2) For the purposes of this section, a person uses a controlled representation if, in particular, he—

(a) affixes it to goods or the packaging thereof,

(b) incorporates it in a flag or banner,

(c) offers or exposes for sale, puts on the market or stocks for those purposes goods which bear it or whose packaging bears it,

(d) imports or exports goods which bear it or whose packaging bears it,

(e) offers or supplies services under a sign which consists of or contains it, or

(f) uses it on business papers or in advertising.

Limits on effect

4.(1) The Olympics association right is not infringed by use of a controlled **A36–05** representation where—

(a) the use consists of use in a work of any of the descriptions mentioned in subsection (3) below, and

(b) the person using the representation does not intend the work to be used in relation to goods or services in circumstances which would involve an infringement of the Olympics association right,

provided the use is in accordance with honest practices in industrial or commercial matters.

(2) The Olympics association right is not infringed by use of a controlled representation where—

(a) the use consists of use of a work of any of the descriptions mentioned in subsection (3) below, and

(b) the use of the work is not in relation to goods or services,

provided the use of the representation is in accordance with honest practices in industrial or commercial matters.

(3) The descriptions of work referred to in subsections (1)(a) and (2)(a) above are a literary work, a dramatic work, a musical work, an artistic work, a sound recording, a film, a broadcast and a cable programme, in each case within the meaning of Part I of the Copyright, Designs and Patents Act 1988.

(4) For the purposes of subsection (2)(b) above, there shall be disregarded any use in relation to a work which—

(a) is of any of the descriptions mentioned in subsection (3) above, and

(b) is to any extent about the Olympic games or the Olympic movement.

(5) For the purposes of subsection (2)(b) above, use of a work in relation to goods shall be disregarded where—

(a) the work is to any extent about the Olympic games or the Olympic movement, and

(b) the person using the work does not do so with a view to gain for himself or another or with the intent to cause loss to another.

(6) In the case of a representation of a protected word, the Olympics association right is not infringed by use which is not such as ordinarily to create an association with—

(a) the Olympic games or the Olympic movement, or

(b) a quality ordinarily associated with the Olympic games or the Olympic movement.

(7) In the case of a representation of a protected word, the Olympics association right is not infringed by use which creates an association between the Olympic games or the Olympic movement and any person or thing where the association fairly represents a connection between the two, provided the use is in accordance with honest practices in industrial or commercial matters.

(8) The Olympics association right is not infringed by use of a controlled representation where—

    (a) the use is in relation to goods which bear, or whose packaging bears, the representation,

    (b) the goods are not infringing goods by virtue of paragraph (a) or (b) of section 7(2) below, and

    (c) the use involves doing any of the things mentioned in section 3(2)(c) or (d) above.

(9) The Olympics association right is not infringed by use of a controlled representation where—

    (a) the use is in relation to goods,

    (b) the goods have been put on the market in the European Economic Area by the proprietor or with his consent, and

    (c) the representation was used in relation to the goods when they were so put on the market.

(10) Subsection (9) above shall not apply where there exist legitimate reasons for the proprietor to oppose further dealings in the goods (in particular, where the condition of the goods has been changed or impaired after they have been put on the market).

(11) The Olympics association right is not infringed by use of a controlled representation where—

    (a) the use is for the purposes of an undertaking, and

    (b) the way in which the representation is used for the purposes of the undertaking is a way in which it has been continuously used for those purposes since a date prior to the commencement of this Act.

(12) In the case of a representation of a protected word, the Olympics association right is not infringed by use as part of—

    (a) the name of a company, being a name which was the company's corporate name immediately before the day on which this Act comes into force, or

    (b) the name under which a business is carried on, being a business which was carried on under that name immediately before the day on which this Act comes into force.

(13) The Olympics association right is not infringed by use of a controlled representation where the use—

    (a) takes place under a right subsisting immediately before the day on which this Act comes into force, or

    (b) is liable to be prevented by virtue of such a right.

(14) The Olympics association right is not infringed by use of a controlled representation where the use—

    (a) takes place under a right created by—

        (i) the registration of a design under the Registered Designs Act 1949 on or after the day on which this Act comes into force, or

        (ii) the registration of a trade mark under the Trade Marks Act 1994 on or after that day, or

    (b) is liable to be prevented by virtue of such a right.

(15) The Olympics association right is not infringed by use of a controlled representation for the purposes of—

    (a) judicial or parliamentary proceedings, or

    (b) a Royal Commission or statutory inquiry.

(16) In subsection (15) above—

"judicial proceedings" includes proceedings before any court, tribunal or person having authority to decide any matter affecting a person's legal rights or liabilities;

"parliamentary proceedings" includes proceedings of the Northern Ireland Assembly or of the European Parliament;

"Royal Commission" includes a Commission appointed for Northern Ireland by the Secretary of State in pursuance of the prerogative powers of Her Majesty delegated to him under section 7(2) of the Northern Ireland Constitution Act 1973; and

"statutory inquiry" means an inquiry held or investigation conducted in pursuance of a duty imposed or power conferred by or under an enactment.

(17) In this section, references to use of a work in relation to goods include use of a work on goods.

Power to prescribe further limits on effect

5.—(1) The Secretary of State may by order made by statutory instrument **A36–06** specify additional cases in which the Olympics association right is not infringed.

(2) Without prejudice to the generality of subsection (1) above, the matters by reference to which a case may be specified under that subsection include—

    (a) the description of controlled representation used, and

    (b) the description of persons by whom a controlled representation is used.

(3) An order under this section may contain such supplementary and transitional provision and savings as the Secretary of State thinks fit.

Remedies in relation to infringement

Action for infringement

6.—(1) An infringement of the Olympics association right shall be actionable **A36–07** by the proprietor.

(2) In an action for infringement, all such relief by way of damages, injunctions, accounts or otherwise shall be available to the proprietor as is available in respect of the infringement of a property right.

Orders in relation to infringing goods material or articles

7.—(1) The Secretary of State may by regulations make, in relation to **A36–08** infringing goods, material and articles, provision corresponding to that made by the following provisions of the Trade Marks Act 1994 in relation to goods, material and articles which are infringing goods, material and articles for the purposes of that Act—

    section 15 (order for erasure etc. of offending sign),

    section 16 (order for delivery up of infringing goods, material or articles),

    section 18 (period after which remedy of delivery up not available),

    section 19 (order as to disposal of infringing goods, material or articles), and

    section 20 (jurisdiction in Scotland and Northern Ireland in relation to proceedings for an order under section 16 or 19).

(2) Goods are "infringing goods" for the purposes of this Act if they or their packaging bear a controlled representation and—

    (a) the application of the representation to the goods or their packaging was an infringement of the Olympics association right,

(b) the goods are proposed to be imported into the United Kingdom and the application of the representation in the United Kingdom to them or their packaging would be an infringement of that right, or

(c) the representation has otherwise been used in relation to the goods in such a way as to infringe that right.

(3) Material is "infringing material" for the purposes of this Act if it bears a controlled representation and either—

(a) it is used for labelling or packaging goods, as a business paper, or for advertising goods or services, in such a way as to infringe the Olympics association right, or

(b) it is intended to be so used and such use would infringe that right.

(4) Articles are "infringing articles" for the purposes of this Act if they are articles—

(a) which are specifically designed or adapted for making copies of a controlled representation, and

(b) which a person has in his possession, custody or control, knowing or having reason to believe that they have been or are to be used to produce infringing goods or material.

(5) The power conferred by subsection (1) above shall be exercisable by statutory instrument which shall be subject to annulment in pursuance of a resolution of either House of Parliament.

(6) Nothing in subsection (2) above shall be construed as affecting the importation of goods which may lawfully be imported into the United Kingdom by virtue of an enforceable Community right.

Criminal sanctions

Offences in relation to goods

A36–09 8.—(1) A person shall be guilty of an offence if with a view to gain for himself or another, or with intent to cause loss to another, and without the consent of the proprietor, he—

(a) applies a controlled representation to goods or their packaging,

(b) sells or lets for hire, offers or exposes for sale or hire or distributes goods which bear, or the packaging of which bears, such a representation, or

(c) has in his possession, custody or control in the course of a business any such goods with a view to the doing of anything, by himself or another, which would be an offence under paragraph (b) above.

(2) A person shall be guilty of an offence if with a view to gain for himself or another, or with intent to cause loss to another, and without the consent of the proprietor, he—

(a) applies a controlled representation to material intended to be used—

  (i) for labelling or packaging goods,

  (ii) as a business paper in relation to goods, or

  (iii) for advertising goods,

(b) uses in the course of a business material bearing such a representation for labelling or packaging goods, as a business paper in relation to goods, or for advertising goods, or

(c) has in his possession, custody or control in the course of a business any such material with a view to the doing of anything, by himself or another, which would be an offence under paragraph (b) above.

(3) A person shall be guilty of an offence if with a view to gain for himself or another, or with intent to cause loss to another, and without the consent of the proprietor, he—

(a) makes an article specifically designed or adapted for making copies of a controlled representation, or

    (b) has such an article in his possession, custody or control in the course of a business,

knowing or having reason to believe that it has been, or is to be, used to produce goods, or material for labelling or packaging goods, as a business paper in relation to goods, or for advertising goods.

(4) It shall be a defence for a person charged with an offence under this section to show that he believed on reasonable grounds that the use of the representation in the manner in which it was used, or was to be used, was not an infringement of the Olympics association right.

(5) A person guilty of an offence under this section shall be liable—

    (a) on summary conviction, to a fine not exceeding the statutory maximum, and

    (b) on conviction on indictment, to a fine.

Supplemental provisions to summary proceedings Scotland

9.—(1) Notwithstanding anything in section 331 of the Criminal Procedure **A36–10** (Scotland) Act 1975, summary proceedings in Scotland for an offence under this Act may be begun at any time within six months after the date on which evidence sufficient in the Lord Advocate's opinion to justify the proceedings came to his knowledge.

(2) For the purposes of subsection (1) above—

    (a) a certificate of the Lord Advocate as to the date mentioned in that subsection shall be conclusive evidence, and

    (b) proceedings in Scotland shall be deemed to be begun on the date on which a warrant to apprehend or to cite the accused is granted, if such warrant is executed without undue delay.

Partnership and bodies corporate

10. Section 101 of the Trade Marks Act 1994 (offences committed by part- **A36–11** nerships and bodies corporate) shall apply in relation to an offence under this Act as it applies in relation to an offence under that Act.

Forfeiture of counterfeit goods, etc.

Forfeiture: England and Wales or Northern Ireland

11.—(1) Section 97 of the Trade Marks Act 1994 (which makes provision about **A36–12** the forfeiture of certain goods, material or articles which come into the possession of any person in connection with the investigation or prosecution of a relevant offence) shall also have effect with the following modifications.

(2) In subsection (1) (which describes the goods, material or articles concerned)—

    (a) in paragraph (a), for "sign identical to or likely to be mistaken for a registered trade mark" there shall be substituted "representation within paragraph (a) or (b) of section 3(1) of the Olympic Symbol etc. (Protection) Act 1995", and

    (b) in paragraphs (b) and (c), for "sign" there shall be substituted "representation".

(3) In subsection (7)(a) (power of court to direct release instead of destruction on condition that offending sign erased etc.) for "sign" there shall be substituted "representation".

(4) In subsection (8) (which defines "relevant offence") for "section 92 above (unauthorised use of trade mark etc. in relation to goods)" there shall be substituted "section 8 of the Olympic Symbol etc. (Protection) Act 1995".

Forfeiture: Scotland

12.—(1) Section 98 of the Trade Marks Act 1994 (which makes provision about **A36–13** the forfeiture of certain goods, material or articles on application by the procurator-fiscal or where a person is convicted of a relevant offence) shall also have effect with the following modifications.

(2) In subsection (1) (which describes the goods, material or articles concerned)—

(a) in paragraph (a), for "sign identical to or likely to be mistaken for a registered trade mark" there shall be substituted "representation within paragraph (a) or (b) of section 3(1) of the Olympic Symbol etc. (Protection) Act 1995", and

(b) in paragraphs (b) and (c), for "sign" there shall be substituted "representation".

(3) In subsection (13) (power of court to direct release instead of destruction on condition that offending sign erased etc.) for "sign" there shall be substituted "representation".

(4) In subsection (14), in the definition of "relevant offence", for "section 92 (unauthorised use of trade mark, &c. in relation to goods)" there shall be substituted "section 8 of the Olympic Symbol etc. (Protection) Act 1995".

Restrictions on acquisition of competing rights

Registration designs and trade marks

A36–14 13.—(1) In section 1 of the Registered Designs Act 1949 (designs registrable under Act) there shall be inserted at the end—

"(6) A design shall not be registered if it consists of or contains a controlled representation within the meaning of the Olympic Symbol etc. (Protection) Act 1995 unless it appears to the registrar—

(a) that the application is made by the person for the time being appointed under section 1(2) of the Olympic Symbol etc. (Protection) Act 1995 (power of Secretary of State to appoint a person as the proprietor of the Olympics association right), or

(b) that consent has been given by or on behalf of the person mentioned in paragraph (a) of this subsection."

(2) In section 4 of the Trade Marks Act 1994 (which specifies cases where a trade mark shall not be registered) there shall be inserted at the end—

"(5) A trade mark which consists of or contains a controlled representation within the meaning of the Olympic Symbol etc. (Protection) Act 1995 shall not be registered unless it appears to the registrar—

(a) that the application is made by the person for the time being appointed under section 1(2) of the Olympic Symbol etc. (Protection) Act 1995 (power of Secretary of State to appoint a person as the proprietor of the Olympics association right), or

(b) that consent has been given by or on behalf of the person mentioned in paragraph (a) above."

(3) This section has effect in relation to applications for registration made on or after the day on which this Act comes into force.

Acquisition of design right

A36–15 14.—(1) In section 213 of the Copyright, Designs and Patents Act 1988 (design right in original designs) after subsection (5) there shall be inserted—

"(5A) Design right does not subsist in a design which consists of or contains a controlled representation within the meaning of the Olympic Symbol etc. (Protection) Act 1995."

(2) Subsection (1) above has effect in relation to designs created on or after the day on which this Act comes into force.

(3) For the purposes of subsection (2) above, a design is created on the first day on which—

(a) it is recorded in a design document, or

(b) an article is made to it.

Miscellaneous

Power to give directions to proprietor

15.—(1) The proprietor shall comply with any directions given by the **A36–16**
Secretary of State with respect to the exercise of the rights conferred by section
2(1) above.

(2) Directions under this section may be of a general or particular character
and may be varied or revoked by subsequent directions.

(3) A transaction between any person and the proprietor in his capacity as
such shall not be void by reason only that the transaction was carried out in
contravention of a direction given under this section; and a person dealing with
the proprietor shall not be concerned to see or enquire whether a direction under
this section has been given or complied with.

Remedy for groundless threats of infringement proceedings

16.—(1) Where the proprietor threatens another with proceedings for infringe- **A36–17**
ment of the Olympics association right other than—
  (a) the application to goods or their packaging of a controlled
      representation,
  (b) the importation of goods to which, or to the packaging of which, such a
      representation has been applied, or
  (c) the supply of services under a sign which consists of or contains such a
      representation,
any person aggrieved may bring proceedings for relief under this section.

(2) The relief which may be applied for is any of the following—
  (a) a declaration that the threats are unjustifiable,
  (b) an injunction against the continuance of the threats, and
  (c) damages in respect of any loss he has sustained by the threats;

(3) A plaintiff under this section shall be entitled to the relief applied for
unless the defendant shows that the acts in respect of which proceedings were
threatened constitute (or if done would constitute) an infringement of the
Olympics association right.

(4) The mere notification of the rights conferred by this Act shall not constitute
a threat of proceedings for the purposes of this section.

Burden of proof

17.—(1) Subject to subsection (2) below, if in any civil proceedings under this **A36–18**
Act a question arises as to the use to which a controlled representation has been
put, it shall be for the proprietor to show what use was made of it.

(2) If in any civil proceedings under this Act a question arises as to the
application of any of subsections (1), (2) and (6) to (15) of section 4 above or any
case specified under section 5 above, it shall be for the person who alleges that
the subsection or case applies to show that it does.

General

Interpretation

18.—(1) In this Act—   **A36–19**
    "business" includes a trade or profession;

"controlled representation" has the meaning given by section 3(1) above;

"infringing articles" has the meaning given by section 7(4) above;

"infringing goods" has the meaning given by section 7(2) above;

"infringing material" has the meaning given by section 7(3) above;

"Olympic motto" means the motto of the International Olympic Committee, "Citius, altius, fortius";

"Olympic symbol" means the symbol of the International Olympic Committee, consisting of five interlocking rings;

"proprietor" has the meaning given by section 2(2) above; and

"trade" includes a business or profession.

(2) For the purposes of this Act each of the following is a protected word, namely, "Olympiad", "Olympiads", "Olympian", "Olympians", "Olympic" and "Olympics".

(3) In this Act, references to the Olympic motto or a protected word include the motto or word in translation into any language.

(4) In the application of this Act to Scotland—

"accounts" means count, reckoning and payment;

"declaration" means declarator;

"defendant" means defender;

"injunction" means interdict; and

"plaintiff" means pursuer.

Short title, commencement and extent

A36–20   19.—(1) This Act may be cited as the Olympic Symbol etc. (Protection) Act 1995.

(2) This Act shall come into force on such day as the Secretary of State may by order made by statutory instrument appoint.

(3) This Act extends to Northern Ireland.

INDEX